The Politics Book

The Politics Book

A lexicon of political facts from
Abu Ghraib to Zippergate

Nicholas Comfort

POLITICO'S

First published in Great Britain 2005 by
Politico's Publishing, an imprint of
Methuen Publishing Limited
11–12 Buckingham Gate
London
SW1E 6LB

10 9 8 7 6 5 4 3 2 1

A CIP catalogue record for this book is available from the British Library.

ISBN 1 84275 138 7

Printed and bound in Great Britain by
St. Edmundsbury Press, Bury St. Edmunds, Suffolk.

Introduction

If a week is a long time in politics, twelve years is an eternity. It is that long since *Brewer's Politics*, the precursor of this volume, first appeared, and in that time the lexicon of politics has changed and grown almost daily. From Abu Ghraib to Zippergate, words, phrases, concepts, movements and people of whom we could have had no conception in 1993 are now part of our heritage. Twelve years ago New Labour had yet to be born, sleaze was rated a purely American phenomenon, no European Commission had ever been removed, a Presidential election decided by the Supreme Court seemed inconceivable, and a chain of terrorist atrocities on the scale of 9/11 even more so. Each of these, and many more, has left its mark on the language of politics, which will no doubt develop just as fast and just as unpredictably over the next dozen years.

This dictionary, then, is a snapshot of where the language of politics has got to. It has always been the richest of languages, because of the vivid way in which many of our politicians express themselves, from the sound-bites with which they woo the voters to the devastating put-downs they use on each other – not to mention the verdicts the media and the public pass on them. Yet this collection goes far beyond slogans and insults; it embraces the broad sweep of the verbal currency in which not only politics but government is conducted, covering party organisation, diplomacy, defence, economics, community action and procedural terms that vary from one legislature to another – plus the memorable sayings, nicknames, scandals and political landmarks that have given political life its texture over the past two centuries.

It can take time for a political phrase to take hold. Several years may elapse after an event or a scandal before memorable words emerge from the mass of verbiage, generally because of repeated use by the media. Conversely, other phrases – and people – wither on the vine. A book of this kind is thus a living organism, permanently in a state of change if the publisher will permit; there always has to be a cut-off point, however, and for this collection it is the outcome of the 2005 UK General Election and France's rejection of the European Constitution, and the London bombings.

I am fortunate that *Politico's* has had the vision to take forward less quirkily but on an even grander scale the project first begun as *Brewer*. As far as I am concerned this is essentially a new book. Some entries may appear the same, but all have been re-examined and most reworked. Many have been moved to a more logical place in the alphabet, others have been left out, and a number of omissions rectified. But the march of history and of language has ensured that a large amount of this book is completely new.

Because politics reflects life, many of the phrases used in its practice are highly emotive and even offensive. I have kept myself to the guidelines I applied in 1993: of showing political life and language 'warts and all'. A few phrases I quote may well offend some readers; one or two offend me, but I stand by their inclusion. I have not attempted to be 'politically correct', but I have tried to avoid giving needless offence to anyone on grounds of their political or religious beliefs, race, gender, disability or sexual orientation. The incompetent, the inarticulate and the dishonest have no such protection.

Having had so long to prepare for this volume, I have had to rely less on others for their help than when I first tried to compile a political dictionary; I have also had this time round the inestimable assistance of the Internet. However, I would like to reiterate my special thanks to the Rt Hon. Gordon Brown MP, the late Donald Dewar and Charles Reiss, latterly political editor of the *Evening Standard*, for their encouragement in those early days. My own experience has also broadened after three decades in journalism with spells as a lobbyist, a policy official in Whitehall and special adviser to a Cabinet minister – the Rt Hon. Helen Liddell whose knowledge is as encyclopaedic as her spirit is generous. Yet I could not have produced this book on my own. Numerous journalistic, political, business and civil service colleagues have assisted me, sometimes unwittingly, by drawing new terminology to my attention. I am indebted once again to Richard A. Lidinsky, Vice-President for Government Affairs of Sea Containers America Inc., and Robert C. Gray, the Hon. & Mrs John C. Kunkel Professor of Government at Franklin and Marshall College, Lancaster, Pennsylvania for keeping me abreast of events and terminology in Washington. Lord (Jeffrey) Archer, Peter Clarke, Greg Rosen and Martin Rosenbaum have all made helpful suggestions, as have several of the politicians mentioned in my previous text, a couple of whom I had been overly churlish to in print. My daughter Caroline contributed some valuable Australian phrases while working in the office of the Premier of New South Wales, and my younger son Alex set up my computer. I must also acknowledge a debt to William Safire's *New Political Dictionary*; I have done everything in my power not to plagiarise this remarkable work, but there have been one or two points from it that I have simply had to take on board.

Finally I must again thank Politico's for having encouraged me to see this project through when other publishers baulked at the prospect. Iain Dale and Sean Magee have been enthusiastic from the outset, and since the company passed to Methuen I have met with equal support and encouragement from Emma Musgrave. They have done their bit; all you, the reader, now have to do is browse.

Nicholas Comfort

London

July, 2005

A

A. A-bomb Shorthand for the ATOMIC BOMB, the original NUCLEAR WEAPON as dropped at HIROSHIMA, and in differentiating it from the later and more powerful hydrogen bomb (H-BOMB). Used principally by participants in the debate over whether such weapons should exist.

à la lanterne! (Fr. to the lamp-post) One of the deadliest cries of the mob during the early days of the FRENCH REVOLUTION and the Reign of TERROR, meaning: 'String them up!' It was directed first against ARISTOCRATS and persons suspected of being so. *See* ÇA IRA.

ABs The sociological and marketing term for the upper, professional and managerial classes, on the scale A, B, C1, C2, D, E. It is used in OPINION POLLS to categorise those questioned and ensure a representative sample. *See* C2s for full explanation.

ABC trial The last prosecution authorised by a Labour government under the unreformed OFFICIAL SECRETS ACT. The 21-month proceedings against Crispin Aubrey, John Berry and Duncan Campbell (their initials provide the name) for actions that allegedly endangered national security ended in 1978 in the withdrawal of the most serious charges, with only Berry receiving a (suspended) prison sentence. Berry was a former corporal in Signals Intelligence; Aubrey and Campbell journalists to whom he passed information.

abdication Renunciation of the THRONE by a reigning monarch. It is generally irrevocable, though in 1990 King Baudoin of Belgium abdicated for one day so as to avoid signing legislation permitting abortion. In Britain's **abdication crisis** of 1936, the as yet uncrowned Edward VIII determined to marry the twice-divorced American Wallis Simpson. This required legislation both by Westminster and the Parliaments of the DOMINIONS; political leaders were opposed, as was the Church of England whose 'SUPREME HEAD' the SOVEREIGN is; but when the story broke on 3 December the public was on the King's side. The confrontation between a determined King and an equally determined ESTABLISHMENT put the British constitution to one of its severest tests and endangered Stanley BALDWIN's government. Edward VIII decided he could not put his throne first; in his abdication broadcast on 11 December he told the nation and Empire:

> 'I have found it impossible to carry the heavy burden of responsibility, and to discharge my duties as King as I would wish to do, without the help and support of the woman I love'

> His mind was made up, and those who know him will know what that means.
>
> STANLEY BALDWIN
> in the House of Commons

ABM Treaty The US-Soviet treaty of 1972 which banned land-based anti-ballistic missile systems, except at one site each. ABMs had been employed by each SUPERPOWER in the 1960s to give them the ability to retaliate even after a FIRST STRIKE by the other. An important breakthrough in ARMS CONTROL, it was largely but not totally complied with by both parties until its repudiation by George W. BUSH in 2001 as his administration attempted to revive the STAR WARS concept.

abolitionist A campaigner for the termination of a practice seen as undesirable, *e.g.* the death penalty. First applied to SLAVERY, the abolitionist movement originated in 1831 when William Lloyd Garrison founded the LIBERATOR.

Abominable no-man *See* ADAMS, SHERMAN.

Aboriginal Rights Amendment An amendment to Australia's constitution, made by REFERENDUM in 1967, to remove discriminatory wording and enable the COMMONWEALTH Parliament to pass laws specifically benefiting Aborigines.

Abraham, Martin and John A tribute in song to three slain giants of American politics – Abraham LINCOLN, Martin Luther KING and John F. KENNEDY – written by Dick Holler the day after Robert F. Kennedy's assassination in June 1968. It created a new career for the former rock singer Dion who, as Dion DiMucci, recorded it, reaching second place in the US charts and selling a miilion copies by the following February. It has been widely recorded since by other artists.

Abscam (short for Arab-scam) The FBI 'sting' operation which all but destroyed the reputation of the US CONGRESS in 1980. During a 23-month undercover operation, a phony Arab sheikh named Kambir Abdul Rahman (actually an ex-convict) set out to buy influence in CONGRESS, with 100 agents in various disguises offering legislators $1 million. The scandal broke that February when the FBI released videotapes showing several Congressmen gleefully taking money. Only one of those chosen as potentially on the take, Sen. Larry Pressler, told the 'sheikh' he was suggesting something illegal. Rep. Richard Kelly stuffed $25,000 into his pockets, asking: 'Does it show?' Rep. John Jenrette boasted: 'I've got larceny in my blood', and Rep. Michael 'Ozzie' Myers rhymed: 'Bullshit walks, money talks.' One Senator resigned as a result of Abscam, Myers became the first Congressman to be expelled, and nineteen people (including six Congressmen) were sentenced to jail.

abseil In mountaineering (originally from the German), letting oneself down a rock face with a double rope. In Britain, adopted as a form of protest by militant lesbians who abseiled into the HOUSE OF LORDS from the public gallery in 1989 to highlight their opposition to what became CLAUSE 28. The word is also used figuratively, as when a fellow Labour MP accused Ken Livingstone (*see* RED KEN) of having 'abseiled across the face of British politics' from his original extreme left-wing position.

absolutism Insistence on total fulfilment of a political creed or platform. Also the state of mind behind absolute MONARCHY. Ernst Friedrich Hubert Munster, Hanoverian AMBASSADOR to Russia 1801–04, characterised the TSARIST political system as '**absolutism tempered by ASSASSINATION**'.

abstain To take a deliberate decision not to vote, out of dislike of the alternatives available. The act of abstaining is **abstention**. The Independent Irish republican MP Frank Maguire described his (rare) attendance but failure to vote in the 1979 VOTE OF CONFIDENCE that brought down James CALLAGHAN's Labour government as a '**positive abstention**'.

abstentionism A policy of refusing to participate in the political process as a protest against the system, practised at times by SINN FEIN (whose members originally refused to participate in elections and still refuse to take their seats at Westminster) and some far-left groups.

Abu Ghraib The fearsome-looking prison in Baghdad which was the scene of great cruelty toward its inmates under Saddam Hussein, and which to the embarrassment of George W. BUSH hosted equally degrading treatment of prisoners by members of the US occupying forces after Saddam's overthrow. The transmission of pictures of detained Iraqis being humiliated by their captors, aired by CBS Television in May 2004, triggered a worldwide wave of revulsion, and earned Defense Secretary Donald Rumsfeld (*see* UNKNOWNS) an unprecedented dressing-down from the President for not having alerted him when the PENTAGON first learned of the abuses. (Similar allegations against UK troops in the south of Iraq led to some convictions, though the authenticity of photographic evidence published by the *Daily Mirror* was discredited). Bush went on Arabic television to apologise for the violations, and Rumsfeld made an abject appearance before committees of the House and Senate on 7 May, saying:

> These events occurred on my watch. As Secretary of Defense, I am accountable for them and I take full responsibility . . . I failed to recognise how important it was to elevate a matter of such gravity to the highest levels, including the President and the members of Congress.

> Was this really the operation I had voted for? Did I really think, when the House of Commons voted to support the American action, that it would be carried out with such boneheaded stupidity? These people seem not only to lack the faintest idea of how to bring peace to Iraq, they also seem not to understand the values which we hoped to bring to that country.
>
> BORIS JOHNSON, *Daily Telegraph*, 6 May 2004

Abu Nidal One of the most militant and deadly Palestinian groups, linked to terrorists around the world prior to the rise of AL QAEDA and named after its founder. Abu Nidal was one of the *noms de guerre* of Sabri Khalil al-Banna (1939–2002), the son of a wealthy Palestinian fruit merchant, who left school at 13 and drifted into a political extremism in which he felt outgunned by intellectuals. His Revolutionary Council of AL FATAH was founded in 1973 as a populist breakaway from AL FATAH, which it regarded until a partial reconciliation in the mid-1980s as traitors under sentence of death; Abu Nidal promoted himself as 'the answer to all Arab suffering and misfortune'.

By 1988 Abu Nidal was blamed by the PLO for over 100 terrorist actions, 56 against Palestinians; he was also claimed by some to have been behind that year's LOCKERBIE bombing. The group first seized the Saudi embassy in Paris to force the release of the BLACK SEPTEMBER leader Abu Daoud. In 1975 it killed the Secretary-General of the Afro-Asian People's Organisation in Cyprus, and in 1978 the PLO representative in Paris and several Iraqi diplomats abroad. On 3 June 1982 the group seriously wounded the Israeli ambassador in London, provoking the Israeli invasion of Lebanon three days later. In 1983 it assassinated Dr Issam Sartawi, a close adviser of Yasser Arafat who advocated reconciliation between Palestinians and Jews, and in 1986 Abu Nidal's 'Che Guevara Brigade' killed the Arab mayor of Nablus in the OCCUPIED TERRITORIES. On 8 November 1987 its guerrillas seized a yacht off the Israeli coast; it was 1990 before the five French and Belgian tourists on board were released.

The group was initially based in Iraq, but from the late 1970s Syrian influence grew. In 1983 al-Banna was expelled from Baghdad to Damascus, but returned the next year for cardiac treatment. On 12 February 1988 an Italian court sentenced him to life imprisonment *in absentia* for a massacre at Rome airport in 1985; the same month the group struck at Vienna. Meanwhile Syria had expelled the group to Libya and dismissed Abu Nidal's close ally General al-Khouli as head of Air Force Intelligence. In 1989 the Libyans, facing SANCTIONS over Abu Nidal's presence, shut down his office in Tripoli and put him under house arrest. Thereafter Abu Nidal lost influence to other Arab and Islamic terrorist groups; he was found dead with gunshot wounds in Baghdad in 2002.

All contact with the Jewish state will be punishable by death.

ABU NIDAL

ACAS Advisory Conciliation and Arbitration Service. The impartial body set up under the auspices of Britain's then Department of Employment by the 1975 Employment Protection Act to help parties in industrial disputes resolve their differences.

acceptance speech The speech delivered by a newly-selected candidate for office, agreeing to take up the challenge and setting supporters' sights on victory. The term is especially used of the speech made by a US Presidential NOMINEE to the party CONVENTION that has nominated him or her.

access The decisive element – according to Hedrick Smith the 'trump card' – in the power battle for the ear of any leader, especially between their staffers. Mike Deaver, after leaving the Reagan White House to work – illegally – as a LOBBYIST, boasted: 'There's no question that I've got as good access as anybody.' Access is highly prized by lobbyists and outside interests generally as essential to gain influence and affect decision-making at the very highest level. *See* CASH FOR ACCESS.

accession (1) The commencement of a MONARCH's reign on the death or ABDICATION of his or her predecessor. (2) The act of a nation in joining a grouping of states. Each country joining the EUROPEAN UNION does so by a Treaty of Accession.

accidental President *See* PRESIDENT.

accountability The requirement that an elected representative should be answerable for his or her actions to the voters, or the EXECUTIVE to the LEGISLATURE.

Achille Lauro The Italian cruise liner hijacked in October 1985 by Palestinian guerrillas who shot dead and threw overboard a wheelchair-bound American Jewish passenger. The terrorists surrendered after the Egyptian government offered to fly them to safety in Tunisia, but US navy jets intercepted their plane and forced them to land in Sicily. The Italian government imprisoned the terrorists, but allowed their leader to escape. America's response to the incident demonstrated an increasingly tough response from President REAGAN to terrorist attacks on Americans. The *Achille Lauro* sank off Somalia in 1994. Abu Abbas, leader of the hijackers, was captured near Baghdad by US forces in April 2003; he died in captivity a year later.

ACLU American Civil Liberties Union. An essentially liberal organisation which defends the civil rights of all, including its opponents.

A criminals' lobby.

Former Attorney-General ED MEESE (1931–)

ACP countries African, Caribbean and Pacific. The EUROPEAN UNION's term for THIRD WORLD states qualifying for aid under the LOMÉ CONVENTION. Nations in Asia and the Indian subcontinent were not mentioned because the countries originally aided – though this has gradually changed – were primarily former French colonies.

acquis communautaire The body of existing EU law, especially the *status quo* a state must accept as a basis for negotiations on its ACCESSION to membership.

Act A legislative measure that has passed through all its stages as a BILL, and has been assented to by the HEAD OF STATE. In the US CONGRESS, a BILL technically becomes an Act when one HOUSE has debated the measure, considered all amendments and had it ENGROSSED before it is passed to the other.

> There is no reference to fun in any Act of Parliament. Sir A. P. HERBERT (1890–1971)

act print In the US SENATE, the reprint of a BILL that has arrived from the HOUSE, been engrossed and has been referred by the PRESIDING OFFICER of the SENATE to the relevant STANDING COMMITTEE.

Act of Union (1) The measure under which the kingdoms of England and Scotland were formally united on 1 May 1707, and a lingering cause for discontent among Scots. A Treaty of Union, guaranteeing Scotland 45 places in the HOUSE OF COMMONS and sixteen in the HOUSE OF LORDS in return for acknowledging that on Queen Anne's death the CROWN would pass to the House of Hanover, was drawn up during 1706 by Commissioners from the two countries. The Scots accepted common taxation, coinage and weights and measures and a common flag (*see* UNION JACK), but retained their own legal system, based on Roman rather than Common law. The Scots Parliament voted itself out of existence by approving the Treaty in January 1707, but only after its members had been heavily bribed by England; it would be July 1999 before a Parliament would sit again in Edinburgh (*see* HOLYROOD, SCOTLAND ACT). At WESTMINSTER the Treaty also had a rough ride, largely through City of London pressure to prevent goods imported into Scotland before the Union being exported duty-free to England after it. Legislation to this effect, which would have severely strained the new Union, was averted only by the Queen PROROGUING Parliament.

> Now there's an end to ane old song.
> Lord SEAFIELD, Scotland's last LORD CHANCELLOR, sealing the Act

(2) The Act passed by both the Westminster and the Irish Parliaments on 28 March 1800 which, from the start of the following year, abolished the Dublin assembly and put Ireland entirely under the control of Westminster. Ireland was granted 100 MPs, four spiritual PEERS and 28 temporal. The Act was repudiated in January 1922 by the Provisional Government of the IRISH FREE STATE under Michael Collins.

action. action, and action now Franklin D. ROOSEVELT's promise – and demand – when he took office to implement the NEW DEAL.

action, not words The slogan on which Edward HEATH's Conservatives fought Britain's 1966 GENERAL ELECTION. Harold WILSON's Labour government was re-elected with a greatly increased majority. Heath's phrasing was not quite original; **actions speak louder than words** had been a favourite dictum of Theodore ROOSEVELT (*see* BULL MOOSE).

Action Directe An extreme left-wing terrorist group active in France during the 1980s.

Action Française An extreme right-wing group in France, most active between the wars and during the German occupation; also the name of its newspaper. Strongly NATIONALIST and ANTI-SEMITIC, it was founded by the poet and political journalist Charles Maurras with the aim of overthrowing the THIRD REPUBLIC and restoring the Monarchy. France's various Pretenders, and the Catholic church, were at times embarrassed by its support, and it lost what credibility it had through its COLLABORATION during the VICHY regime of 1940–44.

action this day Winston CHURCHILL's annotation of documents brought to him during WORLD WAR II to which he gave the highest priority.

day of action The name given to the protests called by the Trades Union Congress (TUC) in the early 1980s against the industrial legislation of the THATCHER government. They could not be termed STRIKES, because political strikes in Britain have always been illegal. The response was patchy to thin, weakening further the unions' already weak bargaining hand after the WINTER OF DISCONTENT.

direct action A general term for various forms of CIVIL DISOBEDIENCE, peaceful and otherwise, in support of political aims. The **direct actionists** were a faction headed by Bill HAYWOOD, leader of the International Workers of the World (*see* WOBBLIES), who were expelled from the US Socialist Party in

1913 for advocating a political strategy based on violence, sabotage and general strikes.

industrial action A collective term for strikes, overtime bans, work-to-rules, sick-outs, etc. – any action by workers designed to gain concessions from their employers.

sympathetic action Such action taken by workers in support of others, against an employer with whom they have no grievance.

> The continuation of negotiations by other means.
> DENIS MCSHANE

active service unit The PROVISIONAL IRA's term for one of its GUERRILLA groups, especially those operating on the British mainland or in Continental Europe.

activist An eager and hard-working member of a political group. The word was first used in 1907 in connection with the philosophical theory of **activism**.

ADA rating The regular assessment by the ultra-liberal Americans for Democratic Action, co-founded by Eleanor Roosevelt (*see* FIRST LADY OF THE WORLD), of how Senators and Congressmen have voted on key items of legislation. Among conservative legislators a low ADA rating is a matter of pride.

Adams. Adams Chronicles The 1970s PBS television series, and accompanying book by Jack Shepherd, telling the true story of four generations of a family at the heart of America's governing elite from the Revolution into the 20th century. Like the KENNEDYS, the Adams dynasty was afflicted by tragedy: manic depression, alcoholism and self-destruction. The suicide of John Quincy Adams' eldest son George in 1829 made a deep impression on the nation. The family's outstanding members were **John** Adams (1735–1826), 2nd President of the United States, his wife **Abigail** (1744–1818) and their eldest son **John Quincy** Adams, 6th President.

John Adams was a Massachusetts delegate to the CONTINENTAL CONGRESS, envoy to France, Holland and Britain and the nation's first Vice President. A FEDERALIST, he defeated JEFFERSON for the Presidency in 1796, but lost to him in 1800. He was the first President to occupy the WHITE HOUSE, and died aged 90 on the same day as Jefferson. Of himself, he said: 'I do not know when I became a politician, for that I never was,' and his most frequent diary entry was 'At home, thinking'. His chosen epitaph was: 'Here lies John Adams, who took upon himself responsibility for peace with France in the year 1800.' Jefferson saw good in John Adams, but also termed him 'vain, irritable and a bad calculator of the force and probable effect of the motives which govern men.' Generally tolerant, John Adams nevertheless shared with many fellow revolutionaries an intense dislike of Thomas Paine:

> Such a mongrel between pig and puppy, begotten by a mongrel boar on a bitch wolf, never before in any age of the world was suffered by the poltroonery of mankind to run through such a career of mischief. Call it then the Age of Paine.

John Quincy Adams was described by Alfred Steinberg as 'a short, stout, bald, brilliant and puritanical twig off a short, stout, bald, brilliant and puritanical tree'. He worked as an aide to his father, followed in his footsteps as a lawyer and DIPLOMAT, served as a US Senator, and as Secretary of State devised the MONROE DOCTRINE. He was elected President in 1824 by the HOUSE despite finishing second to Andrew Jackson (*see* CORRUPT BARGAIN), but Jackson took his revenge after one term. Uniquely, he went back to CONGRESS, serving in the House for eighteen years before dying at his desk. He said of himself: 'I am a man of cold, reserved and forbidding manners', and this view was widely shared, W. H. Lyttleton reminiscing: 'Of all the men whom it was ever my lot to accost and to waste civilities with, he was the most doggedly and systematically repulsive.' John Quincy Adams' wife Louisa had a word for the entire clan:

> As it regards women, the Adams family are one and all particularly harsh and severe in their characters. There seems to exist no sympathy, no tenderness for the weakness of the sex.

The dynasty lasted until the death in 1927 of the historian Brooks Adams, youngest grandson of John Quincy. He had written:

> It is now full four generations since John Adams wrote the constitution of Massachusetts. It is time that we perished. The world is tired of us.

Sherman Adams affair The EISENHOWER ADMINISTRATION's one notable INFLUENCE-PEDDLING scandal, arising from resentment in Washington at the power wielded by Sherman Adams, former Governor of New Hampshire, as assistant to the President. Hard-working and efficient, Adams was known as the **Abominable No-Man** because of his power to kill legislators' pet schemes. (The nickname is a play on 'abominable snowman', the term then used for the mythical Yeti of the Himalayas.) Adams was accused by the HOUSE OF

REPRESENTATIVES of manipulating regulatory agencies in return for a $700 vicuna coat and a $2400 oriental rug from his friend Bernard Goldfine, a Boston industrialist who was under investigation by the government. He was forced to resign in September 1958 despite Eisenhower's insistence that 'I need him'; the scandal was a factor in the Democrats' LANDSLIDE victory in that November's Congressional elections. Unbeknown to the HOUSE, Adams had been receiving $15,000 a month from Goldfine before and during his WHITE HOUSE years. This was revealed to Eisenhower in 1961 by his successor JOHN F. KENNEDY and his brother/Attorney General Robert K. KENNEDY, but was not made public for many years.

> How dreadful it is that cheap politicians can so pillory an honorable man.
>
> DWIGHT D. EISENHOWER, 16 September 1958

additional member A form of PROPORTIONAL REPRESENTATION in which some seats are filled by the FIRST PAST THE POST system and others are then allocated according to the parties' share of the votes cast.

Adlai Stevenson moment *See* STEVENSON.

administration (1) The art or practice of carrying on the business of government and implementing its decisions. (2) In America, the structure and personnel of government installed by a particular President, and the span of time they serve. For example, the FORD administration was the government answerable to Gerald FORD during his period as President.

> While the people retain their virtue and vigilance, no administration, by an extreme of wickedness or folly, can very seriously injure the government in the short space of four years.
>
> ABRAHAM LINCOLN

administrative assistant A staffer who ensures the smooth running of the office of a US SENATOR OR CONGRESSMAN, or of one of the committees of either House. An experienced administrative assistant can exert considerable influence, hopefully on behalf of his or her employer. *Compare* RESEARCH ASSISTANT.

Admiralty House. The building used by British Prime Ministers as offices and even a residence when NUMBER TEN Downing Street is unavailable through rebuilding, and at other times by senior members of the Government; it is also used for hospitality and other purposes by the Ministry of Defence. Built by S. P. Cockrell in 1786–88 as the residence of the First Lord of the Admiralty, it stands a little back from WHITEHALL just above the Horse Guards. Harold MACMILLAN lived there for a considerable time while Number 10 was being completely rebuilt, and John MAJOR used it for everything except CABINET meetings during security work at Downing Street after an almost-successful IRA mortar attack. It is often confused with the **Admiralty Arch** at the entrance to Trafalgar Square from The Mall, which is also occupied by the Government.

adoption meeting In Britain, the meeting at the start of an election campaign at which a prospective CANDIDATE is formally adopted to fight a seat by the local party. Once adopted, any spending on the candidate's behalf has to be within the legal ceiling.

Adullamites A group of right-wing Liberal MPs and peers, led by Robert Lowe, who opposed GLADSTONE's 1866 REFORM BILL and reaffirmed the role of Liberals as enlightened defenders of property. They gained their name from a Biblical reference (1 *Samuel* xxii.1,2) by their critic John Bright, who said of Lowe:

> The Rt Hon. Gentleman is the first of the new Party who has retired into what may be called his political cave of Adullam – and he has called about him everyone that was in distress and everyone that was discontented.

adultery An activity much practised by legislators in most of the world's great capitals, and a staple of political scandals. Gary Hart's Presidential hopes for 1988 were destroyed when Paul Taylor of the *Washington Post* asked him: 'Have you ever committed adultery?' and Hart replied: 'Follow me.' The media took him at his word, and found Miss Donna Rice (*see* MONKEY BUSINESS).

I don't see why we can't get along just as well with a polygamist who doesn't poly as with a monogamist who doesn't monog The attributed comment of Sen. Boies Penrose (1860–1921) in support of seating the first Mormon Senator, Reed Smoot, in 1903. The sentence has also been attributed to Theodore ROOSEVELT in a speech the previous year.

I would rather commit adultery than drink a pint of beer The statement in support of temperance delivered in the 1920s HOUSE OF COMMONS by Nancy, Lady Astor (1879–1964). It produced from the veteran Labour MP Jack Jones the classic intervention: 'Who wouldn't?' It was some time before order was restored.

> I was told as a young man that the two occupational hazards of the House of Commons were alcohol and adultery. The huroosh that follows the intermittent revelations of the sexual goings-on of an unlucky MP has convinced us that the only safe pleasure for a parliamentarian is a bag of sweets.
>
> JULIAN CRITCHLEY, MP (Con.)

advance. Advance Australia Fair The patriotic song written c. 1878 by Peter Dodds McCormick (d. 1916) which was declared the national anthem on 19 April 1984. The original anthem from 1788 was GOD SAVE THE KING (or QUEEN); efforts to replace it produced repeated deadlock between *Advance Australia Fair* and *Waltzing Matilda*. In 1974 Gough WHITLAM announced, after an OPINION POLL and an abortive competition that produced 1400 entries, that *Advance Australia Fair* would be the national tune, but its original words were not adopted as an anthem. In a REFERENDUM in 1977 *Advance Australia Fair* beat *Waltzing Matilda* by 65.2% to 34.8% after *God Save the Queen* and *Song of Australia* were eliminated. With the proclamation of *Advance Australia Fair* as national anthem in 1984, the playing of *God Save the Queen* was limited to occasions when a member of the Royal family was present. An authorised set of words was adopted, the first verse being:

> Australians let us all rejoice, for we are young and free;
> We've golden soil and wealth for toil, our home is girt by sea;
> Our land abounds in nature's gifts of beauty rich and rare;
> In history's page at every stage Advance Australia Fair.
> In joyful strains then let us sing
> Advance Australia Fair.

advance man A staff member who travels ahead of a politician or candidate to make sure that everything necessary for the success of their trip has been arranged, that all facilities are in place and that welcoming crowds and the media will be on hand.

adversarial politics The system of politics, fundamental at WESTMINSTER, which depends on permanent and gladiatorial contest between two main parties who in turn form the government and a loyal OPPOSITION. The opposite of CONSENSUS politics, it is regarded as obsolete and harmful by other parties and many who are alienated from politics.

adversary A political opponent, by inference on an institutionalised basis and thus in the opposite party to oneself. Traditionally, a new MP arriving at the COMMONS pointed to the benches opposite and said: 'I see that is where the enemy sit.' An elderly colleague corrected him: 'Those are your adversaries. Your enemies are behind you.'

> Nothing perplexes an adversary so much as an appeal to his honour. DISRAELI

advice and consent The phrase in the US CONSTITUTION which enshrines the prerogative of the SENATE in the RATIFICATION of treaties (with a two-thirds majority required) and the CONFIRMATION of Presidential appointees. The phrase is traceable back to eighth-century England and is enshrined in the WESTMINSTER legislative process (*see* BE IT ENACTED). As *Advise and Consent*, it became the title of a Pulitzer Prize-winning 1959 novel, and subsequent movie, by Allen Drury about a President's efforts to push through the appointment of a questionably liberal SECRETARY OF STATE. The procedure was thrashed out between George WASHINGTON and the first Senate in the summer of 1789, after initial disagreements. *See* CLARENCE THOMAS CASE.

AFDC. Aid to Families with Dependent Children. A key element of welfare provision in the United States, eviscerated in the mid-1990s by the Republican Congress; in August 1996 President CLINTON reluctantly signed a BILL transferring much responsibility for welfare from the Federal government to the States.

affiliation (Lat. *filius*, son) The process by which an organisation associates itself with a political party, paying a fee and gaining some say in the programme and conduct of that party. In Britain the best example is the affiliation of individual TRADE UNIONS to the LABOUR PARTY. Since the purge of the MILITANT TENDENCY in the mid-1980s Labour has published a list of affiliated organisations, most of them political societies or pressure groups, involvement in which is not incompatible with membership of the party.

affirmation The process by which someone with no religious belief, or strong objections to the taking of OATHS, swears allegiance to the State on taking office or adds weight to his or her testimony.

affirmative action The policy, particularly in America from the mid-1970s, of giving preferential treatment to members of a disadvantaged group in order to make up for under-representation or past DISCRIMINATION. Also known as **reverse discrimination**, it has been used in particular to promote women and members of ethnic minorities even if they do not meet the qualifications previously demanded of all candidates. As such it has provoked a BACKLASH from qualified white males and others who feel they are being unfairly excluded; efforts by President REAGAN to restrict it were thwarted by a 1986 SUPREME COURT ruling, but it has been practised more sparingly since. *See* BAKKE CASE; QUOTA.

Afghan Ron The nickname given to **Ron Brown** (1940–), the left-wing Labour MP for Edinburgh Leith 1979–92, because of his close links with, and visits to, the Soviet-backed Najibullah regime in Afghanistan; he was also a guest in Libya, interceding with Colonel Gaddafi for the release of detained Britons. He was DESELECTED by his party after reputedly frolicking in a COMMONS shower with his female researcher and subsequently appearing in court for allegedly stealing items of underwear from her flat. What offended Leith's Labour activists was not the inference of adultery but the bottle of champagne he opened in front of television cameras on being freed.

AFL-CIO American Federation of Labor-Congress of Industrial Organizations. The **AFL** was founded in 1886 by Samuel Gompers (1850–1924) and rapidly became white male skilled labour's representative body. It split in 1935 when the United Mine Workers' leader John L. Lewis pulled out and formed the **CIO**; Lewis, a strong supporter of industrial unionism which the craft-orientated AFL opposed, made the break dramatically, landing a right cross on the jaw of the Carpenters' president William Hutcheson. In 1937 the AFL expelled the CIO unions, who started recruiting black workers and women on a large scale. The AFL and CIO unions' rival recruitment campaigns initially resulted in violence and death. The CIO as it developed under the United Auto Workers' Walter Reuther was much more liberal than the trenchantly anti-Communist AFL, but did not merit Rep. Clarence Brown's tag 'a conduit of communism'. In 1955 the organisations merged, with 15 million members and George Meany (1894–1979) as president; Meany, who headed the AFL-CIO for 24 years, was a fierce opponent of union rackets – in 1957 the organisation expelled the TEAMSTERS.

> Everything outside the AFL-CIO is Hoboken.
> AFL-CIO President LANE KIRKLAND (1922–99)

Africa. scramble for Africa The rush by the European powers in the closing years of the 19th century to satisfy their IMPERIALIST ambitions by grabbing as yet unclaimed (by the white man) parts of Africa.

> These same powers must be told in a clear, firm and definite voice: 'Scram from Africa'.
> TOM MBOYA, Kenyan nationalist leader, 1958

African American The favoured term since the 1990s for Americans originally of African descent; *Black*, and before that *Negro*, had previously been preferred. In Britain the term **Afro-Caribbean** is favoured, reflecting the migration to the UK since WORLD WAR II of West Indians of predominantly African origin.

African National Congress *See* ANC.

African Union The name under which the former OAU relaunched itself in Durban on 9 July 2002, retaining that organisation's 53 members. In its new guise as a cross between the UNITED NATIONS and EUROPEAN UNION, it has stepped up its interest in economic development and its involvement in PEACEKEEPING. It comprises an Assembly of heads of state, an Executive Council of foreign ministers, a Permanent Representatives Committee of ambassadors, a nine-strong Commission with its own president, specialised technical committees, a Pan-African Parliament, a Court of Justice, an Economic, Social and Cultural Council, the African Central Bank, African Monetary Fund and African Investment Bank, and a Peace and Security Council.

Africanisation (1) The process by which newly independent African countries replace Europeans in official posts by their own nationals. (2) The emotive and hostile term used by President Andrew Johnson and others for radical Republican moves during RECONSTRUCTION to give blacks the right to vote.

Agadir crisis The dispute between France and Germany in the run-up to WORLD WAR I triggered by Germany's despatch of the warship *Panther* in July 1911 to the Moroccan port of Agadir. Germany claimed to be protecting its interests in response to the arrival of French troops in Morocco. Tensions were raised throughout Europe; LLOYD GEORGE in his MANSION HOUSE SPEECH warned both countries that Britain, too, had interests in the region. Berlin responded angrily and there were fears of a

German attack on the Royal Navy. The dispute was settled by a Franco-German agreement signed on 4 November, but hostility between the two nations remained – and the crisis had brought France and Britain closer together.

Age of Reason, The The religio/political treatise published in Paris in 1794–96 by the English radical writer Thomas Paine (1737–1809), which encouraged a wave of intellectual ferment in continental Europe and the new American republic. In it, he set out his beliefs with such frankness that he was called a 'dirty little atheist'; Paine, who had been brought up in a Quaker home, wrote: 'The only idea man can affix to the name of God is that of a 1st. cause of all things'.

> Tom Paine invented the name of the Age of Reason; and he was one of those sincere but curiously simple men who really did think that an age of reason was beginning, at the time when it was really ending. G.K. CHESTERTON

agency An office performing a function of government, subordinate to but not totally controlled by a CABINET department. In Britain the number of such agencies was limited until the 1980s, but they have since proliferated (*see* NEXT STEPS). In America they have long been numerous; the first was the Federal Trade Commission, set up in 1887. President CARTER complained on taking office that there were seventeen agencies with responsibility for migratory birds.

> A Government agency is the nearest thing to eternal life we'll ever see on this earth.
> RONALD REAGAN

alphabet agencies The plethora of bodies set up by President Franklin D. ROOSEVELT to implement the NEW DEAL, which became known by their initials. The most important were the NRA (National Recovery Administration), **RFC** (Reconstruction Finance Corporation), **AAA** (Agricultural Adjustment Administration or 'Triple A') and **WPA** (Works Progress Administration).

agenda (Lat. to be done) The schedule for the conduct of a meeting, setting out in order the issues to be raised.

agenda-setting Co-ordinated NEWS MANAGEMENT (*see* SPIN) by a party to ensure that the issues debated at a particular time, even by other parties, are those it wishes to discuss and on which it believes it will score most heavily.

hidden agenda An undeclared programme which an invididual, party or government conceals behind a more innocuous statement of what it plans to do. In Britain's 1983 election a number of LEAKED documents, notably on family policy, led the CONSERVATIVES' opponents to assert with a degree of corroboration that Margaret THATCHER had such an agenda. Since then it has been a normal campaigning tactic to accuse one's opponents of having such an agenda, whether or not there is evidence.

agent One of the cornerstones of British political life, the person employed by a party at CONSTITUENCY level to develop the local organisation, supervise fund-raising, organise campaigning, see that electoral law is observed and make sure the vote is got out. Most Conservative agents are salaried, most Labour and Liberal Democrat agents are part-timers.

agent-general The quasi-diplomatic representative of one of Canada's provinces in Britain or an Australian state.

Agent Orange The powerful defoliant used by the US military during the VIETNAM WAR to strip away tree cover from areas where large Communist troop concentrations were believed to be hiding. Sprayed from the air, it poisoned many civilians and its use was widely condemned by environmentalists and human rights groups.

agent-provocateur A person who infiltrates a political party or movement in order to disrupt it, or encourage it to take steps that push it into conflict with the authorities, destroy its basis of support or lead to its becoming discredited.

Parliamentary agent At WESTMINSTER, a lawyer who specialises in preparing Private BILLS for submission to Parliament, or in collating and lodging objections to them.

Agincourt speech The title, recalling the stirring eve-of-battle speech in Shakespeare's *Henry V*, bestowed by the media on the address to his men by Lt-Col Tim Collins of the Royal Irish Regiment prior to the US/UK action in Iraq in March/April 2003. Col. Collins' words so encapsulated the coalition's war aims that President George W. BUSH had them hung up in the OVAL OFFICE. Col. Collins ended the war having to refute claims by a US reservist major – dismissed by an official inquiry – that he had brutalised Iraqi civilians, but his words retain their force:

> We go to liberate, not to conquer. We are entering Iraq to free a people and the only flag that will be flown in that ancient land is their own.

Show respect for them.

There are some who are alive at this moment who will not be alive shortly. Wipe them out if that is what they choose. But if you are ferocious in battle, remember to be magnanimous in victory.

Iraq is steeped in history. It is the site of the Garden of Eden, the Great Flood and the birthplace of Abraham. Tread lightly there.

You will have to go a long way to find a more decent, generous and upright people than the Iraqis. You wll be embarrassed by their hospiality even though they have nothing. Their children will be poor. In years to come they will know that the light of liberation in their lives was brought by you.

If there are casualties of war, then remember that when they woke up and got dressed in the morning they did not plan to die this day. Allow them dignity in death.

It is my foremost intention to bring every single one of you out alive. But there may be people among us who will not see the end of this campaign. We will put them in their sleeping bags and send them back. There will be no time for sorrow.

The enemy should be in no doubt that we are his nemesis and that we are bringing about his rightful destruction. As they die they will know their deeds have brought them to this place. Show them no pity. It is a big step to take another human life. It is not to be taken lightly.

agitator (Lat. a stirrer-up) A person who stirs up dissatisfaction, unrest and support for radical action among the public or specific parts of it. The term was in use by the early 19th century, then as now not entirely as a compliment; the Irish patriot Daniel O'Connell (1775–1847) was described as **'the great agitator'**. Shortly before the 1976 Presidential election the pastor of PLAINS Baptist church embarrassed Democratic nominee Jimmy CARTER by announcing that members had voted to ban 'niggers and CIVIL RIGHTS agitators'.

Those who profess to favour freedom, and yet deprecate agitation, are men who want rain without thunder and lightning. They want the ocean without the roar of its waves.

FREDERICK DOUGLASS (c. 1817–95)

agitprop (Russ. *agitatsiya propaganda*, agitation PROPAGANDA) Dramatic, literary, media or artistic activity designed to promote Marxist ideology, within Communist-controlled societies and worldwide. The term was coined by Georgy Plekhanov and elaborated by LENIN in *What Is To Be Done* (1902). 'Agitation' implied the use of political slogans and half-truths to exploit mass grievances and mould public opinion; 'propaganda' in this context meant using rational, scientific and historic arguments to train and INDOCTRINATE Communist Party members. In 1920 the Soviet Party's CENTRAL COMMITTEE established a Department of Agitation and Propaganda, which remained in charge of this activity until the collapse of the party and the Soviet state in 1991.

Agnew resignation The departure from office of Richard NIXON's Vice President, Spiro T. Agnew (1918–), on 10 October 1973, which paved the way for the presidency of the unelected Gerald FORD. Agnew, a hero of HARD-HAT conservatives, pleaded no contest to a charge of evading income tax as Baltimore County executive, Governor of Maryland and Vice President. US attorneys found evidence that Agnew had until recently been receiving bribes and kickbacks from home-state contractors. Two days after Agnew's resignation and barely a week before the SATURDAY NIGHT MASSACRE that brought WATERGATE to a head, Nixon nominated Ford, then House MINORITY LEADER, to succeed him. The outgoing VEEP was sentenced to three years' probation and fined $10,000 – a sentence criticised as light but defended as being in the national interest. Agnew had gained a national reputation for blunt public utterances, some of which, like his comments on the INNER CITIES, were regarded as outright GAFFES. Insisting on his probity, Agnew had told supporters:

I have been accused of putting my foot in my mouth, but I have never put my hand in your pocket.

agonising reappraisal A change in policy stemming from a painful acceptance that the preferred course of action has not worked. The phrase is attributed to the US SECRETARY OF STATE John Foster Dulles, who told the NORTH ATLANTIC COUNCIL in Paris on 14 December 1953:

If EDC (the European Defence Community) should fail, the United States might be compelled to make an agonizing reappraisal of its basic policy.

agrarian parties Political parties which give farmers and the peasantry an organised voice and a coherent programme. They have had the greatest success in Central and Eastern Europe, but have also had some impact in the US Farm Belt (*see* Farmer-LABOR) and in Canada's prairie provinces.

agreement to differ In UK politics, an acceptance that members of a government cannot reach unanimity on a single divisive issue, but that that issue should not be allowed to bring that government down. The first such agreement – though not referred to as such at the time – was the readiness of ASQUITH's government in 1913 to accept that while a majority wanted VOTES FOR WOMEN, the Prime Minister himself remained opposed to female suffrage. The term was first used in respect of the readiness of Liberal FREE TRADERS to serve in the 1931 NATIONAL GOVERNMENT, despite its commitment to maintain tariffs. A further example was the continuance of Harold WILSON's Labour government in 1975, when a minority of the CABINET was actively campaigning for a 'No' vote in the EC REFERENDUM while the majority backed the 'Yes' campaign.

> We agree on everything, including the fact that we don't see eye to eye.
>
> HENRY KISSINGER and GOLDA MEIR

Ahern, Bertie *See* ANORAK MAN; BERTIE BOWL.

air. Air Force One The aircraft currently used on official business by the PRESIDENT of the United States. The title has been bestowed on successive models of Boeing (originally a 707) from the early 1960s; the most celebrated was the 707, know also by its tail number of 27000, which was used by every President from Richard NIXON to George W. BUSH and flew over 1 million miles. It conveyed Nixon to California after his resignation, took Jimmy CARTER to meet the hostages held in Iran when they were released, carried Ronald REAGAN to Berlin to deliver his 'tear down the wall' speech, was used by Bill CLINTON to carry several dozen Democratic donors and was stripped of Presidential linen and crockery by Clinton's staffers as he flew out of Washington for post-Presidential life in New York. No. 27000 was retired to the Reagan Presidential Library in California. George BUSH Sr. traded up to a 747-200B which became the Presidential first choice, and it was this aircraft that inspired a 1997 *Air Force One* movie starring Harrison Ford. It includes VIP office and sleeping accommodation, a secure communications network, and space for staffers and a travelling press pool. Its title reflects the Air Force's prime role in transporting the President. *See also* MARINE ONE.

> I thought Air Force One was going to be a palace. Major disappointment. It's no work of art. It's decorated in California PC decor and earth tones, wheat and gray. It was sterile. The first cabin, with two large side beds, a desk and chairs, TV and VCR, belonged to the President. The next one was the President's doctor's. Air Force One had a full hospital. I don't think any previous Air Force One had surgery facilities. Nancy Reagan built the plane.
>
> MARY MATALIN

The plane that flies the VICE PRESIDENT is known as **Air Force Two.** Asked what he liked about it, Dan QUAYLE said: 'You don't have to have a ticket, and you never lose your luggage.'

air raid shelter A politician who chooses, or is chosen, to share the responsibility of others for some calamity, and thus enable them to hang on. The phrase was first, and famously, used by LLOYD GEORGE on 7 May 1940 in the COMMONS debate that led to the fall of CHAMBERLAIN's government. After CHURCHILL had defended the Government's conduct of the war, the former Liberal premier observed:

> The Right Honourable Gentleman must not allow himself to be converted into an air raid shelter to keep the splinters from hitting his colleagues.

John MAJOR, apparently unaware of its original context, used the phrase in CABINET on 17 September 1992 in the aftermath of BLACK WEDNESDAY. He insisted that CHANCELLOR Norman Lamont, who was under heavy outside pressure to resign, should not be made an 'air raid shelter' for policies agreed by the entire Government.

Al Aqsa Martyrs A radical subgroup of AL FATAH which emerged after the resumption of the INTIFADA in 2001. Comprised of militant members of Yasser Arafat's security services and led by Marwan Barghouti until his arrest by the Israelis during their incursion of April 2002 (*see* JENIN), it was estimated to be responsible for 70 per cent of terrorist attacks against Israel, including suicide bombings. The Al Aqsa mosque in Jerusalem is one of Islam's most sacred sites, and the group's title reflects the conviction of Palestinian Muslims that Jerusalem should be the capital of their state.

Al Fatah (Arab. the victory) The Palestinian guerrilla and political organisation which has dominated the leadership of the PLO since 1969. Founded in Kuwait in 1958 by Yasser Arafat (1929–2004) to fight for the return of Palestine to the Arabs, it carried out its first guerrilla action from Jordan in 1964. Expelled in the BLACK SEPTEMBER of 1970, it withdrew to Lebanon where it carried on the guerrilla campaign until the Israeli invasion of 1982. For a time from 1983 Al Fatah was split between factions in Tripoli, Lebanon and Tunis; but it regrouped, building support in the GAZA STRIP and WEST BANK, to launch the INTIFADA in 1987 and subsequently to provide the muscle behind Arafat's leadership of the PALESTINIAN AUTHORITY.

Al Jazeera (Arab. the peninsula) The independent Arabic satellite television service operated from Qatar which attracted world-wide attention after 9/11 when it carried an exclusive interview with Osama BIN LADEN, and subsequently several statements from him on video. Although these transmissions earned Al Jazeera the nickname 'TALEBAN TV' in the United States, its output is independent, reflecting the wishes of Sheikh Hamad of Qatar who founded Al Jazeera in 1996 after the Saudi government had pulled the plug on a similar venture with the BBC because the broadcasters refused to be censored. Its lively discussion of issues previously taboo in the Arab world has earned it an audience of millions in the region and beyond; every Arab and Middle Eastern government except the Lebanon has complained about its transmissions. During the IRAQ WAR of 2003 Al Jazeera first enraged the British government by showing the bodies of dead UK soldiers, then saw some of its reporters banned by Saddam Hussein's regime.

Al Qaeda (Arab. the base) The fanatically anti-American Islamic terrorist organisation led by Osama BIN LADEN that carried out the attacks on the WORLD TRADE CENTER and the PENTAGON on 11 September 2001 (9/11); these stung President George W. BUSH into launching his WAR AGAINST TERRORISM, the immediate consequence being the ousting of the TALEBAN regime in Afghanistan which had been harbouring Bin Laden. Al Qaeda had its origins in the extreme Islamic fundamentalist groupings in Egypt that had assassinated President Sadat in 1982. It gained impetus from well-financed Saudi fanatics, of whom Bin Laden was a prime example, and from the US-backed campaign to oust the Russians from Afghanistan in the 1980s through the agency of militant MUJAHIDEEN. America's tactic succeeded, only for Bin Laden and others to turn against the US (notably over its stationing of troops in Saudi Arabia, which they regarded as sacrilege) and open camps in Afghanistan and elsewhere to train terrorists against them. Bin Laden proclaimed that Al Qaeda's aim was 'to unite all Muslims and establish a government that follows the rule of the Caliphs', i.e. to overthrow most existing Muslim governments by force. 9/11 was the culmination of a series of atrocities including a previous attempt to bomb the World Trade Center, suicide attacks on US embassies in NAIROBI and Dar es Salaam and the bombing of the USS *Cole* in Aden Harbour, the US reaction to which had been limited and piecemeal. It took the havoc caused in that one day for America and its allies to realise the extent and seriousness of the threat and to organise against it. Despite their defeat by US and allied forces in Afghanistan, Bin Laden and key supporters were able to regroup in the border region of Pakistan and continue to taunt America by video, while planning fresh atrocities such as the BALI, MADRID and LONDON BOMBINGS.

Albany Regency *See* REGENCY.

albatross An individual who becomes an incubus or handicap to a government or political party; the notion stems from Coleridge's poem *The Ancient Mariner*, in which the mariner brings a curse on his ship by shooting the albatross that has flown over it, bringing luck to the crew. The word was put to its most damning use during the SUEZ crisis when Aneurin BEVAN called Selwyn (later Lord Selwyn) Lloyd, Foreign Secretary from 1955–60, 'a putrefying albatross around the neck of this government'.

Albertzheimer's disease. Shorthand among Dublin politicians for the insistence by the Fianna Fail TAOISEACH Albert Reynolds that the DECOMMISSIONING of terrorist weapons had not been implied in the DOWNING STREET DECLARATION, forerunner of the 1998 GOOD FRIDAY AGREEMENT. The agreement came close to foundering on several occasions because of Unionist demands that the IRA decommission, and the Republican movement's extreme reluctance to do so, and in these circumstance Reynolds' powers of recollection came under pressure, hence the comparison with Alzheimer's disease.

alderman In England and Wales, a senior member of a local authority elected by that body and not by the voters; aldermanic seats were abolished in the local government reorganisation of 1974. In America, ward representatives on some city councils are styled aldermen.

Aldermaston marches The four-day anti-nuclear marches between TRAFALGAR SQUARE and the Atomic Weapons Research Establishment at Aldermaston, Berkshire, between 1958 and 1963 which put CND on the map and made the cause of nuclear disarmament respectable to the British public. The first began in London; in subsequent years Trafalgar Square was the destination, and the scene of a mass RALLY attracting up to 100,000 people.

Algérie Française (Fr. Algeria is French) The rallying cry of the opponents of French withdrawal from Algeria who first brought General DE GAULLE to power in 1958, then turned against him when he pressed ahead with independence. At times of protest, Paris echoed with the sound of car horns blaring the slogan as three quick blasts and two slow. *See also* FOUR GENERALS, OAS.

alienation The process by which elements of the public become detached from and hostile to the political process, seeing it as incapable of meeting their needs or simply as irrelevant. In its extreme forms a cause of civil unrest or even REVOLUTION, alienation has been particularly associated with ethnic groups who feel the system is rigged against them or simply ignores them, groups who have chosen to disengage like Britain's New Age Travellers, and the UNDERCLASS as a whole.

Alliance The umbrella under which Britain's LIBERAL PARTY and SDP fought the General Elections of 1983 and 1987, winning 23 seats in the first and 22 in the second but polling a respectable share of the popular vote. It was not a purely electoral machine, the two parties having started to work together – and share out candidacies – within months of the SDP's formation in 1981. The Alliance was always under strain: in 1983 the SDP leader Roy JENKINS began as 'Prime Minister Designate', but the Liberal leader David Steel (*see* BOY DAVID) had his role reduced at the ETTRICK BRIDGE SUMMIT, and in 1987 Steel and Dr David OWEN (*see* OWENITES), who now led the SDP, pursued different strategies; the comedian Rory Bremner christened them 'the quack and the dead'. Immediately after that election Steel demanded a merger of the two parties, thus triggering a split in the SDP that wrecked the Alliance, though eventually producing a united party (*see* LIBERAL DEMOCRATS) under Paddy Ashdown.

> Two cocks in one pen never did agree.
> Derbyshire voter to Alliance candidate, 1983

> They have a new colour. They call it gold. It looks like yellow to me.
> MARGARET THATCHER, 1987

Alliance for Progress A partnership for economic and social improvement between the United States and the countries of Latin America, proposed by President KENNEDY in March 1961 and accepted by all Latin states except Cuba at a conference in Punta del Este, Uruguay, five months later. America agreed to foot most of the bill for a series of projects to improve living standards, and Kennedy became a popular figure in the southern continent. The Alliance eventually ran out of steam, partly because of concern among private investors at the instability of several recipient states.

> An alliance between one millionnaire and many beggars.
> FIDEL CASTRO, 1964

> Where is the Alliance? Where is the progress?
> Sen. EVERETT DIRKSEN, 1967

Peace, commerce and honest friendship with all nations, entangling alliances with none One of the guidelines set for American policy by Thomas JEFFERSON in his first INAUGURAL ADDRESS, on 4 March 1801. **Atlantic Alliance** The antithesis of the principle enunciated above. *See* ATLANTIC. **Triple Alliance** *See* TRIPLE.

Allighan case The expulsion from the HOUSE OF COMMONS on 30 October 1947 of Garry Allighan, Labour MP for Gravesend, for breaching the 'PRIVILEGE and decorum' of the House. Allighan wrote in *World's Press News* that MPs gave confidential information to strangers while drunk, and took money for tip-offs to the Press; he was also held to have 'persistently misled' the investigating committee, thus committing a CONTEMPT OF THE HOUSE. The vote to expel him was 187–75.

Allons, enfants de la patrie (Fr. let's go, children of our country) The opening words of the MARSEILLAISE, written in 1792 by Claude Joseph Rouget de Lisle (1760–1836).

ALP (1) The widely-used abbreviation for the Australian LABOR PARTY. (2) The American Labor Party, a New York State liberal group created in 1936 out of Labor's Non-Partisan League, founded to enable supporters of Franklin D. ROOSEVELT to bypass TAMMANY HALL, with which many trade unionists were feuding. Communists infiltrated the ALP after 1939, and in 1944 non-Communist union leaders effectively killed it by breaking away to found the LIBERAL PARTY.

alternate A person designated to take the place of a DELEGATE if that delegate is unable to carry out his or her duties, notably attendance at meetings.

alternatives The staple diet of politics, despite Margaret THATCHER's claim that none exist (*see* THERE IS NO ALTERNATIVE). The UK CABINET SECRETARY Burke Trend reckoned: 'The acid test of any political question is: "What is the alternative?"', while Henry KISSINGER declared that 'the absence of alternatives clears the mind marvellously'.

alternative vote *See* VOTE.

Alton Bill The Bill to reduce the final date for termination of a pregnancy from 28 weeks to 18, promoted at WESTMINSTER in 1987–88 by the Liberal MP David (now Lord) Alton (1951–). Despite widespread support for some reduction, it ran out of Parliamentary time because Alton and fellow PRO-LIFE campaigners refused to accept any compromise on the time limit.

AM. (1) Assembly Member A member of the WELSH ASSEMBLY. Ministers in the devolved administration based on the Assembly, styled the WELSH ASSEMBLY GOVERNMENT, take the title ASSEMBLY SECRETARY.

(2) The UK CABINET COMMITTE, chaired by the Prime Minister, that deals with asylum and migration issues.

ambassador The highest-ranking diplomatic representative of one country stationed in another; most countries send career diplomats, but America's ambassadors are often wealthy POLITICAL APPOINTEES. Also a representative of the President appointed to conduct international negotiations or act as a roving envoy.

> An honest man sent abroad to lie for the Commonwealth.
>
> Sir HENRY WOTTON (1568–1639)

Amen Corner (1) Supporters of a political party who automatically follow the party line, as if they were saying 'Amen' at the end of a prayer. The original Amen Corner, at the west end of London's Paternoster Row, was where monks finished their *Pater Noster* (Our Father) as they processed to St Paul's Cathedral on Corpus Christi Day. (2) A length of corridor in New York's Fifth Avenue Hotel used by BOSS PLATT to meet members of the Republican MACHINE, to the same effect. (3) More recently, Pat Buchanan's derogatory term for supposedly pro-Israeli elements in the US media.

amendment A change made to a BILL during its passage through a legislature, a MOTION under debate or, most portentously, the US CONSTITUTION since its enactment. Twenty-seven amendments (the first ten of them in the BILL OF RIGHTS) have so far been enacted. An amendment to the Constitution may originate with CONGRESS – as all have so far – or with a National CONVENTION called at the request of two-thirds of the States. Two-thirds of both HOUSES of Congress must support the amendment, and to take effect it must then be RATIFIED by three-quarters of the State legislatures (which means 38 states) or by special constitutional conventions in as many states. A State may not reverse a vote to ratify, but can reconsider a vote not to.

> Amendments to the constitution ought to not be too frequently made; (if) continually tinkered with it would lose all its prestige and dignity, and the old instrument would be lost sight of altogether in a short time.
>
> President ANDREW JOHNSON, 22 February 1866

dilatory amendment An amendment put forward with the intention of delaying debate; in the US CONGRESS, a ruling that an amendment is dilatory will prevent its being debated.

killer amendment In the US CONGRESS, an amendment whose adoption would wreck the purpose of the measure being debated. Known at WESTMINSTER as a **wrecking amendment.**

manuscript amendment At WESTMINSTER, an amendment put forward during debate for acceptance by the CHAIR, as opposed to one appearing on the ORDER PAPER. Such amendments are usually accepted only when it is clear the proposal being debated does not reflect the will of the HOUSE; a rare example was the acceptance of a manuscript amendment from Tony BENN during the debate on the ZIRCON affair when the Labour left-winger remarkably persuaded backbench Tories that the Government was seeking to abridge their rights.

non-germane amendment An amendment not relevant to the purposes of a BILL, specifically when inserted by the US SENATE into a measure originally passed by the HOUSE OF REPRESENTATIVES.

amendment tree A structure of amendments put forward by the promoter of a BILL, which effectively prevents its opponents from destroying the package; perfected in the US SENATE by Bob Dole, it ties supporters to the Bill by giving them a chance to back amendments protecting their pet programmes. *See also* ANTHONY AMENDMENT; BOLAND AMENDMENT; CUNNINGHAM AMENDMENT; ERA; ROOKER-WISE AMENDMENT; STEIGER AMENDMENT; WEATHERILL AMENDMENT and the relevant numbers for amendments to the US CONSTITUTION.

America. America First (1) The ISOLATIONIST campaign to keep America out of WORLD WAR II, drawing its title from a slogan of Woodrow WILSON's; it kept up an onslaught against US involvement between HITLER's invasion of Poland in September 1939 and Japan's attack on PEARL HARBOR. The **America First Committee** embraced pro-Nazis, communists (until Hitler's attack on Russia) and ordinary Americans who felt the war was none of their business. (2) The slogan of the ultra-conservative Pat Buchanan in his campaign against George BUSH Snr in the 1992 Republican PRIMARIES; though it faltered after the first half-dozen contests, Buchanan's charge that Bush had neither ideas nor ideology played its part in the President's ultimate defeat.

America is back The declaration by Arnold Schwarzenegger (*see* GOVERNATOR), Republican governor of California, in support of George W. BUSH's re-election, to the party's New York CONVENTION on 31 August 2004, which delivered much of the party's liberal wing to a highly conservative TICKET. Schwarzenegger capitalised on his movie strong-man image to applaud Bush's tough line over Iraq and against AL QAEDA at a convention themed to portray his Democratic challenger John KERRY as indecisive.

large America The vision of America's IMPERIALISTS, and specifically the supporters of MCKINLEY in the 1900 Presidential election; supporters of William Jennings Bryan (*see* PRAIRIE AVENGER), who opposed the acquisition of overseas territories, were said to favour a 'small America'.

Middle America *See* MIDDLE.

Come home, America The theme of George McGovern's ACCEPTANCE SPEECH at the 1972 Democratic convention in Miami Beach. His aim was to touch a deeper chord with the people than the radical platform devised by convention delegates whom Shirley MacLaine described as 'a couple of high schools, a grape boycott, a BLACK PANTHER rally and four or five politicians who walked in the wrong door'. McGovern appealed for America to rediscover its virtues and values – but interminable floor action meant that he did not deliver it until 3 a.m., thus missing his PRIME TIME audience.

it's morning again in America The confident theme of Ronald Reagan's ACCEPTANCE SPEECH after being nominated for a second term by the Republicans' DALLAS convention in 1984. It was the high point of the FEELGOOD FACTOR; public satisfaction won Reagan a landslide victory over Walter Mondale (*see* NORWEGIAN WOOD), but within months the longest HONEYMOON in US electoral history was over.

the frontier of America is on the Rhine A comment reputedly made by Franklin D. ROOSEVELT to SENATORS at a WHITE HOUSE meeting on 31 January 1939, which enraged America's ISOLATIONISTS. FDR disowned the remark, describing it as a 'deliberate lie', but Americans who were convinced he was leading them into war saw their worst fears confirmed, while the UK and French governments took heart from his apparent commitment to oppose any German advance. However, Neville CHAMBERLAIN observed around this time: 'It is always best and safest to count on nothing from the Americans but words.'

there is nothing wrong with America that cannot be cured by what is right with America The key phrase of the INAUGURAL ADDRESS delivered by Bill CLINTON after being sworn in as 42nd President of the United States on 20 January 1993.

Voice of America (VOA) The overseas radio broadcasting network of the US Information Agency; it was founded in 1942 for PROPAGANDA purposes but now promotes a favourable image of America through a balanced worldwide output of news and entertainment; its European studios are in Prague. VOA broadcasts from Washington in English and 41 other languages, reaching an estimated weekly audience of 120 million. It is often confused with **Radio Free Europe/Radio Liberty**, the Munich-based organisations funded by Congress but run by private US citizens, whose role and purpose since the end of the COLD WAR have been unclear.

American Plan The campaign waged by US business at the height of the RED SCARE after WORLD WAR I, aimed at convincing the public that COLLECTIVE BARGAINING and the CLOSED SHOP were 'un-American'. Its backers included the American Bankers Association and the National Association of Manufacturers. By 1920 there were American Plan Associations in every state of the Union, 46 of them in Illinois. The campaign succeeded in blocking most legislative moves to strengthen union rights, but subsided as the threat of revolution evaporated.

American Revolution The overall term used by politicians and historians for the welling up of communal and political consciousness in Britain's American colonies which culminated in the DECLARATION OF INDEPENDENCE, the war which secured America's freedom and the devising by the FOUNDING FATHERS of the political system which endures to this day. Looking back, John ADAMS reckoned that 'the revolution was in the mind of the people, and this was effected from 1760 to 1775, before a drop of blood was shed at Lexington.' The revolution produced many memorable phrases. When Britain first closed the port of Boston in 1774, Benjamin FRANKLIN wrote: 'You may reduce their cities to ashes, but the flame of liberty in North America shall not be extinguished.' But Dr Samuel Johnson regarded much of the talk of principle as humbug, asking: 'How is it that we hear the loudest yelps for liberty from the drivers of negroes?' When the colonists finally lost patience with what they saw as a string of provocations, Thomas Paine declared: 'The period of debate is closed. Arms as the last resort decide the contest.' The Lutheran pastor Peter Muhlenberg reputedly told his congregation in Woodstock, Virginia: 'There is a time for all things, a time to preach and a time to pray, but those times have passed away. There is a time to fight, and that time has come.' And early in 1777 PITT THE ELDER said portentously: 'If I were an American as I am an Englishman, while a foreign troop was landed in my country, I would never lay down my arms – never, never, never!'

> These are times that try men's souls. The summer soldier and the sunshine patriot will, in this crisis, shrink from the service of their country; but he that stands it now deserves the love and thanks of man and woman.
>
> THOMAS PAINE, December 1776

> Americans of the revolutionary generation proved themselves the most creative statesmen in modern history, perhaps in all history.
>
> HENRY STEELE COMMAGER, 1970

> No other revolution, worthy of the name, ended so happily. HUGH BROGAN

Daughters of the American Revolution *See* DAR.

American System The combination of TARIFFS, a national bank and improved transportation put forward by Henry Clay (1777–1852) as SPEAKER of the HOUSE OF REPRESENTATIVES between 1823 and 1825. The plan, intended to enable farms and factories to exchange goods more easily and ease dependence on European produce and markets, prompted America's first PROTECTIONIST tariff in 1824 but failed to win Clay the Presidency.

Americanism A word brandished by US politicians, largely in the late 19th and early 20th centuries, whose meaning – beyond a general patriotism – was rarely defined. Theodore ROOSEVELT termed it 'the virtues of courage, justice, honour, truth, sincerity and hardihood – the virtues that made America', yet President HARDING confessed: 'I don't know much about Americanism, but it's a damn good word to carry an election'. With MCCARTHYISM, defined by its founder as 'Americanism with its sleeves rolled up', the word gained sinister connotations. Sen. Margaret Chase Smith observed: 'Those who shout the loudest about Americanism in making character assassinations all too frequently ignore some of the basic principles of Americanism: the right to criticise, the right to hold unpopular beliefs, the right to protest, the right to independent thought'. And Malcolm X stated: 'I am not an American. I am one of 22 million black people who are victims of Americanism.'

no one can kill Americans and brag about it. No one Ronald Reagan's truculent justification of America's 1986 LIBYAN BOMBING in retaliation for the alleged involvement of Colonel Gaddafi's agents in the bombing of a disco in Berlin, in which several US service personnel were killed.

My fellow Americans *See* MY.

Ames case The most serious spy scandal to hit America's Central Intelligence Agency (CIA). Aldrich Ames, the CIA's head of Soviet counter-intellingence, was discovered in 1994 to have been spying for the Russians since 1985. During that time Ames and his Colombian-born wife Rosario, who denied recruiting him for Moscow, were paid over $1 million by the Russians for information handed over at drops around WASHINGTON, and at least twelve US agents and informants met their deaths as a result. Ames, who insisted his treachery was not ideologically motivated, pleaded guilty and in April 1994 was jailed for life without parole; his wife also got a stiff sentence. CIA director James Woolsey was forced to resign that December after being criticised for not shaking up the agency following the arrests.

amnesty A general order for the release of

prisoners or the pardoning of as yet unpunished offenders, as an act of clemency to mark some event or a deliberate act of policy. Most controversially, President CARTER ordered a partial amnesty for Vietnam DRAFT-dodgers who had fled to Canada. The PROVISIONAL IRA for many years told its bombers that, if caught, they would serve only a minimum sentence as it would coerce the UK government into granting an amnesty; in the event, many had their imprisonment shortened by the GOOD FRIDAY AGREEMENT.

Amnesty International A pressure group, founded in, and run from, the UK, which monitors the detention of POLITICAL PRISONERS throughout the world, keeps their plight in front of public opinion and campaigns for their release.

General Amnesty Act The Act pushed through the US CONGRESS in 1872 by a coalition of Democrats and Republicans who felt that RECONSTRUCTION was going too far. It restored political privileges to all but 500 former supporters of the CONFEDERACY; by 1876 only three States were still controlled by radical Republicans elected with the support of black voters.

Amsterdam. Treaty of Amsterdam The treaty concluded in 1997 by member states of the EUROPEAN UNION which reduced the scope for member States to veto collective decisions, increased the powers of the EUROPEAN PARLIAMENT and lowered national frontiers.

An Phoblacht (Irish: The Nation) The Dublin-based weekly organ of SINN FEIN, founded in 1925 by Maurice Twomey, and under the control of Gerry Adams since 1977 when he forcibly merged into it the Belfast-based *Republican News*. Essentially a vehicle for the PROVISIONALS' ideology and propaganda, it circulates both among Republicans in Ireland and hard-line Celtic supporters in Scotland.

anarchism The philosophy that asserts that society functions best without organised government, and that no government is legitimate unless its actions are truly consented to by those they affect. The 17th-century thinker Thomas Hobbes anticipated its attraction, writing in LEVIATHAN: 'No man believes that want of government is any new kind of government'. The anarchist pioneer Pierre-Joseph Proudhon wrote in 1850: 'Our idea of anarchism is launched: non-government is developing as non-property did before'. Thirty years later Prince Kropotkin declared: 'Permanent revolt by word of mouth, in writing, by the dagger, by the rifle, dynamite . . . everything is good for us which falls outside legality.' Such comments created the Victorian stereotype of anarchists as East European bombers; they were banned from the US after the American-born Leo Czolgosz assassinated President McKINLEY in 1900, and SACCO AND VANZETTI were almost certainly executed for their beliefs. Yet the US anarchist Emma Goldman wrote: 'Anarchism is the only philosophy which brings to man the consciousness of himself', and despite its Utopian naivety it remains to its adherents a noble aspiration.

> Christ was an anarchist who succeeded.
> ANDRÉ MALRAUX (1901–76)

> I don't bother to vote. I'm an anarchist anyway. I don't think it makes any difference who has his duke in the till.
> ROBERT MITCHUM

anarcho-syndicalists Anarchist workers who advocate seizing control of industries through strikes and violence. The movement (*see* SYNDICALISM), was strong in Republican Spain.

anarchy The total breakdown in order stemming from the absence of an effective government (*see also* FAILED STATE). Not to be confused with anarchism, which in its pure form aims for peace and harmony. Jeremy Bentham (1748–1832) declared that 'tyranny and anarchy are never far asunder', while Napoleon saw opportunistically that 'anarchy is always the stepping-stone to absolute power'.

> Lawlessness is lawlessness. Anarchy is anarchy. Neither race or color nor frustration is an excuse for either lawlessness or anarchy.
> US Solicitor-General THURGOOD MARSHALL, 15 August 1966

ANC African National Congress. The movement that led the struggle against APARTHEID in South Africa, and went on to take power under Nelson MANDELA (since 2001 Thabo Mbeki) after winning the country's first multiracial election in April 1994. It was formed at Bloemfontein in 1912 as the South African National Congress by the Zulu clergyman J. W. Dube 'to protect the interests of all coloured people in South Africa'. Inspired by MAHATMA Gandhi's campaigning in South Africa, it formed a common front in 1926 with the Indian community. From 1948, when the NATIONAL PARTY began to erect the structure of apartheid, the ANC led the non-white resistance, from 1952–67 under the moderate leadership of Chief Albert Luthuli. Together with the more militant PAC, it was banned in 1960 and increasingly turned to violence through its military wing UMKHONTO WE SIZWE, led by Mandela, who was arrested in 1962 and jailed for life for asbotage (*see* RIVONIA TRIAL). Oliver Tambo, supported by South Africa's hard-line Communist Party, led the ANC from exile for a quarter of a century during which it was harrassed by Pretoria's undercover squads, maintaining a political organisation within the country and conducting occasional guerrilla action. When F.W. de Klerk signalled the end of apartheid he opened secret talks with the ANC, and in 1989 Mandela – whose continued imprisonment on ROBBEN ISLAND prompted world-wide protests – was released to a hero's welcome. Despite his age he took over the leadership from the ailing Tambo; he led the ANC first into the CODESA talks on a democratic future for the country and then to victory at the polls, with 252 out of 400 seats. Mandela formed a coalition with his old foe the National Party, which took only 83 seats, and the fractious INKATHA Freedom Party with just 43. Mandela knew he had to change South Africa in a hurry to hold the support of impatient black voters who expected better housing, education, electricity, water and jobs. He also had to cope with his militant and charismatic estranged second wife Winnie, whose powerbase in the ANC offset her scandalous conduct and led him to make her a junior minister until in 1995 she defied him to make a foreign trip. Sacked and divorced, her influence faded after her conviction for fraud. Mandela's government made some progress in delivering voters' expectations while maintaining racial and economic stability, but the challenges for Mbeki were as great, with the additional problem of soaring HIV infection whose link to AIDS Mbeki refused for some time to accept. In 2003, after defections from other parties, the ANC achieved the two-thirds majority necessary to entrench its power by amending the constitution, and the following year it retained power with 70 per cent of the popular vote.

> We are not a political party. We are a government in waiting.
>
> NELSON MANDELA, 1991

Andean Pact The agreement signed at Cartagena, Colombia, in 1969 between Bolivia, Chile, Colombia, Ecuador, Peru and Venezuela to enable them to compete with Latin America's more industrialised economies. Chile withdrew in 1977, but rejoined in 1990; Ecuador temporarily left in the early 1980s over its border dispute with Peru. The *Acuerda de Cartagena* established an Andean Council, a Parliament of five members from each state meeting in turn in each, and a Court of Justice. Progress on economic development has been made since the introduction in 1984 of an Andean peso to reduce dependency on the dollar, wih projects for agriculture, transport, social welfare and education. In 1989 an Andean SUMMIT committed members to closer links and nuclear non-proliferation.

Andizhan massacre The episode on 13 May 2005 that brought to a head resentment at the authoritarian rule of Islam Karimov, post-Soviet president of Uzbekhistan and obliged the West to take notice. Demonstrators gathered in the town square in support of local businessmen alleged to be involved with Islamic militants who had been freed from jail by their relatives; troops opened fire and killed several hundred of them. The spread of the protests was limited by Karimov's control of the media; he announced from Tashken that the demonstrators had attacked the troops and had been trying to overthrow the government. Up to almost this point America had kept silent about abuses of human rights in Uzbekhistan because it had established a base there close to the border with Afghanistan; the year before, the British Ambassador, Craig Murray, had been ordered home after exposing some of the worst abuses, allegedly because he had embarrassed Washington.

Anglo. Anglo-Irish Agreement The accord in November 1985 between Margaret THATCHER's UK government and the FINE GAEL/Labour coalition led by Garret FitzGerald, which gave the Republic its first formal say in the affairs of Northern Ireland on behalf of the Catholic minority. An inter-governmental conference was formed to discuss security, political and legal questions and cross-border co-operation, and a secretariat comprising officials of each government was set up in Belfast. The two Ulster UNIONIST parties condemned the accord as a betrayal, the more so as Mrs Thatcher had always taken a stridently pro-Unionist line. For Enoch POWELL, who had idolised her, it was the final breach; when she defended the Agreement, he remarked: 'There you have it, straight from Jezebel's own mouth.' There were widespread LOYALIST protests and violence the next spring, linked to an ULSTER SAYS NO campaign in which every Official Unionist MP resigned their seat to fight BY-ELECTIONS; all but one were re-elected. The Agreement for a time improved UK-Irish relations, showed that Britain was looking for progress and reduced grassroots support for SINN FEIN. But it left a legacy of Unionist bitterness and did nothing to check the IRA's terrorist campaign for a united Ireland. It took the DOWNING STREET DECLARATION of 1993 and the 1998 GOOD FRIDAY AGREEMENT at last to raise hopes of peace.

Anglo-Saxons The derogatory term used by many French politicians, President DE GAULLE in particular, for the British and Americans and their world-view. The Anglophone world has long been baffled by the resentment shown by the French establishment, combining cultural contempt, nationalist envy and ideological distaste for economic liberalism and manifesting itself in France's determination to frustrate US and British foreign policy, from its refusal fully to engage in NATO, through its efforts in 1992 to sabotage the URUGUAY ROUND of GATT negotiations (*see* BLAIR HOUSE AGREEMENT) to its manoeuvring in 2002–03 to thwart international action to disarm Saddam Hussein and Blair's advancing of ECONOMIC REFORM.

Angry Brigade A radical group with ANARCHIST sympathies which instigated a sporadic campaign of bombings and fire-arms attacks on ESTABLISHMENT targets in the UK in the late 1960s and early 1970s. A relatively ineffective counterpart to the equally middle-class BAADER-MEINHOF GANG, some of its members were imprisoned for a bomb attack on the home of the Employment Secretary Robert Carr (later Lord Carr of Hadley) in 1971.

animal. *Animal Farm* One of the most vicious satires on STALINISM, written in 1945 by the British novelist George Orwell (Eric Blair, 1903–50). It is set on a farm where the animals seize control from the farmer and set up a COMMUNE based on equality, only for a pig named Napoleon to grab absolute power under the slogan **All animals are EQUAL, but some are more equal than others**. Any illusions Orwell, a socialist, may have had about communism where shattered when he fought in the SPANISH CIVIL WAR and saw at first hand the way the communists undermined and destroyed their leftist allies; he wrote *Animal Farm* after watching a wartime cinema newsreel praising Stalin as a loyal ally of Britain. The book enraged the KREMLIN and was banned in most communist countries; it has survived the eclipse of communism as a parable against all forms of exploitative TOTALITARIANISM.

> I do not know this George Orwell. But I tell you one thing: he must have lived in Ghana.
>
> West African journalism student to his tutor, Tom Hopkinson, late 1960s

Animal Liberation Front The militant UK group, acting on behalf of animals but with an entirely human membership, which from the late 1970s has staged numerous acts of violence in protest at cruelty toward captive animals, and animal husbandry in general. Based largely in the West Country but active throughout England, its targets have included shops which have been firebombed for selling furs, and laboratories from which animals have been released or whose staff and shareholders have been harrassed, as in the case of Huntingdon Life Sciences. The term 'Animal Liberation' was coined by Peter Singer (1946–), founder of the International Association of Bioethics and later Professor of Philosophy at Monash University, Melbourne.

> The Provisional RSPCA.
>
> JASPER CARROTT

Animals, the A publicity unit set up by Paul Keating when Labor Prime Minister of Australia to gather and disseminate derogatory information about political opponents. It was shut down by the incoming Liberal government of John Howard.

annexation The forcible incorporation of one nation's territory into another; most notoriously NAZI Germany's takeover of the bulk of Poland in September 1939. In almost the same sense, it had been used nearly a century before of the courtship by the 52-year-old President Tyler (*see* OLD VETO) of the 23-year-old WASHINGTON belle Julia Gardiner, who became his second wife and bore him seven children to add to his previous eight.

Annexation Manifesto The declaration printed by the *Montreal Gazette* in October 1849, signed by more than 300 English-speakers from the city, which called for 'a peaceful and friendly separation from [the] British connexion and a union upon equal terms with the great North American Confederacy of Sovereign States'. This was one of the few occasions on which a demand for the union of Canada with the United States was put forward with enough vigour to be taken seriously in London.

Annexationists The IMPERIALIST advocates of American acquisition of the Republic of Hawaii, which had been declared in 1894, who got their way in 1898 when CONGRESS annexed the islands by joint resolution. They claimed that Hawaii might otherwise fall under foreign (Japanese) control; it would give America a Pacific naval base and offer opportunities for investment. The election of President MCKINLEY, a protest by Japan against annexation and the outbreak of the SPANISH-AMERICAN WAR all hastened the step. Hawaii did not gain STATEHOOD until 1959.

Annie's Bar The bolt-hole in the bowels of the Palace of WESTMINSTER where MPs and LOBBY journalists only can unwind and exchange confidences. The original Annie's, off the Members' Lobby, was destroyed when a German bomb hit the Commons CHAMBER on 10 May 1941. The post-war Labour government, at the urging of its teetotal Chief WHIP William Whiteley who feared Ministers would LEAK information too easily, refused to reopen it. It was 1969 before Annie's reopened below stairs, close to the Parliamentary barber's shop, on the initiative of Robert Maxwell, then chairman of the Commons Catering Committee; Annie, the pre-war barmaid, returned to pull the first ceremonial pint for the Conservative leader Edward HEATH. The new Annie's fulfilled its purpose for almost a quarter of a century, despite a high correlation between the hard core of MPs frequenting it and DESELECTION by constituency parties. Its use declined; in 1992 a firm of American consultants proposed its closure, but instead it was relocated in 1995 to the former staff bar, tucked away 50 yards further from the stairs to the Chamber. Ceremonially reopened by the now Sir Edward Heath, it became in 1996 the subject of a Channel 4 serial produced by Prince Edward's Ardent Productions. Annie's remained thinly used, but was relaunched in March 2002 after further refurbishment by Speaker Michael Martin and Barbara Windsor, landlady of the fictitious 'Queen Vic' in the BBC soap opera *Eastenders*. *See also* BARLOW MEMORIAL AWARD.

> A useful if well-lubricated workshop for MPs and journalists alike.
>
> IAN AITKEN, *Evening Standard*

annuit coeptis (Lat. God has favoured our undertakings) One of the many Latin mottoes with Masonic connections inscribed on the insigina of the United States at its inception, and appearing to this day on the dollar bill. The phrase is taken from Book IX of Vergil's *Aeneid*.

annunciator The system of closed-circuit television in the Palace of WESTMINSTER that informs MPs and peers in other parts of the building of what is taking place in each CHAMBER. When either HOUSE is sitting, the annunciator lists the item of business under discussion, who is speaking and their CONSTITUENCY – though generally not their position in the Government, if they have one – and how long they have been on their feet – against a green background for the Commons and a maroon one for the Lords. Each system also shows when there is a DIVISION in either House or in a STANDING COMMITTEE. The system, upgraded over the years, was first installed in 1968, replacing an earlier, less widespread, system of piano-keys typing out the name of the member speaking on a continuous paper strip; this had been in service since the 1870s.

Anorak Man The nickname of Bertie Ahern (1951–), Ireland's FIANNA FAIL TAOISEACH from 1997– , which reflected on his style of dress and 'man of the people' tastes. Ahern, a keen sports enthusiast, had no problem with the epithet, saying: 'When I was playing football I always wore an anorak. Then when I was out in a suit I found it much more handy to wear an anorak. I didn't like long coats.'

another place An alternative to 'the OTHER PLACE' for members of one HOUSE at WEST-MINSTER wishing to refer to the other.

Anschluss (Ger. union, connection) The takeover of Austria by Germany in 1938, viewed by HITLER and many inhabitants of both countries as a reunification unjustly denied by the Treaty of VERSAILLES after the break-up of the Austro-Hungarian Empire. In 1934 Austrian NAZIS mounted a COUP aimed at unification; it was put down but Germany continued to interfere in Austria's affairs. In February 1938, Hitler summoned Austria's Chancellor Kurt von Schuschnigg to the EAGLE'S LAIR at Berchtesgaden and demanded that he bring Nazis into his Cabinet. Schuschnigg tried to call a PLEBISCITE on Austrian independence, and resigned when he was frustrated. German troops entered Vienna amid scenes of jubilation on 13 March 1938 and the

Anschluss was proclaimed. After Germany's defeat in WORLD WAR II, the victorious Allies abrogated the union in December 1945 by recognising the second Austrian Republic.

Anthony amendment THE NINETEENTH AMENDMENT to the US CONSTITUTION, also known as the WOMEN'S SUFFRAGE AMENDMENT, that guaranteed women the vote when it was RATIFIED on 26 August 1920. Named after the ABOLITIONIST, suffragist and temperance campaigner **Susan B. Anthony** (1820–1906), it was first introduced in 1878 by Sen. Aaron Sargent of California. However, it took the advances made by women in WORLD WAR I to persuade CONGRESS to follow a growing number of states, culminating in New York in 1917 after a campaign by the suffragist CARRIE CATT, and grant them the vote. The HOUSE backed the amendment on 10 January 1918 amid scenes of counterproductive militancy, and the SENATE finally capitulated on 18 August 1920.

anti-. anti-clericalism Opposition to the Roman Catholic church exerting too great an influence over government and public life; a particular force in Republican France.

anti-Communist A COLD WAR campaigner against communism, of whom Sen. Joseph MCCARTHY was an extreme manifestation. Also the profession given by one of the accused in the WATERGATE burglary trial. John Foster Dulles maintained that the world was 'divided into two kinds of people: Christian anti-communists and the others'; Ronald REAGAN declared:

> A Communist reads Marx and Lenin. An anti-Communist understands Marx and Lenin.

Anti-Duhring The book attacking the 'reformist' wing of Germany's Social Democratic Party which Friedrich Engels (1820–95) published in 1878; it was directed against the faction's intellectual leader, Eugen Duhring. The ideas set out in it, including that of the withering away of the STATE, made an important impact on a new generation of socialists.

anti-Federalists (1) The opponents of RATIFICATION of the US CONSTITUTION in 1787–88; they argued that equal representation for each State in the SENATE would disadvantage the most populous States, and that over-large electorates for members of the HOUSE would encourage corruption in Congressional elections. (2) The name chosen by UK opponents of moves toward a more centralised EUROPEAN UNION in which the COMMISSION would exercise greater power; some self-styled anti-Federalists are in fact ANTI-MARKETEERS.

anti-globalisation *See* GLOBALISATION.

Anti-Imperialist League The group formed in 1898 by opponents of US territorial and colonial expansion. It was particularly opposed to the ANNEXATION of the Philippines, but was unable to stop an enterprise that cost more lives than the SPANISH-AMERICAN WAR as Filipinos led by Aguinaldo resisted for three years. One of the League's leaders was the PRAIRIE AVENGER William Jennings Bryan, who argued that America had become a world power 'without the use of a sword or a Gatling gun'. He said:

> Our form of government, our traditions, our present interests and our future welfare all forbid our entering upon a career of conquest.

anti-intellectualism The strand in politics that deplores the influence of academics and other thinkers on shaping policy and responding to events. The WHITE HOUSE aide Jack Valenti said of LBJ:

> He doesn't like cold intellectuals around him. He wants people who will cry when an old lady falls down in the street.

anti-Marketeer An opponent of UK entry to and continued membership of the EUROPEAN COMMUNITY and now the EUROPEAN UNION; after 30 years of membership and with controversy over Europe as sharp as ever, they frequently masquerade as EUROSCEPTICS.

Anti-Nazi League A coalition of ANTI-RACIST groups founded in the late 1970s by the UK SOCIALIST WORKERS' PARTY to challenge organisations like the BRITISH MOVEMENT and NATIONAL FRONT (now BNP) on the streets, and still sporadically active today. Though it claimed to be a mass movement and gained the backing of a few celebrities, it developed into a group of white radicals and Asian militants whose confrontation of racist marchers led to violence, and arrests on both sides. The League revived in the early 1990s after a BNP councillor was elected in Tower Hamlets. Violent demonstrations followed near the BNP headquarters at Bexley, with black police officers saying they had been targeted.

anti-racism Organised opposition to RACISM, either through the formation of political or VIGILANTE groups to counter racist demonstrations or attacks, or through public bodies outlawing and preventing discrimination against ethnic minorities, and ensuring what they see as sensitive – and critics view as provocative – teaching in schools.

anti-Semitism Hatred of and opposition to Jews and all things Jewish, present in all supposedly civilised Western and Islamic societies but raised into an obscene art form by the NAZIs for whom Heinrich Himmler declared:

> Anti-Semitism is exactly the same as de-lousing. Getting rid of lice is not a question of ideology, it is a matter of cleanliness.

The US academic J. M. Cameron wrote in 1982: 'Anti-Semitism circulates in the European bloodstream like a permanent infection'; the 19th-century German writer Treitschke declared: 'Wherever he finds his life sullied by the filth of Judaism the German must turn from it, and learn to speak the truth boldly about it'; and in 1990 a Western journalist in Warsaw was told: 'Why should there not be anti-Semitism in Poland when there are so few Jews left? We have traffic jams, and there are hardly any cars.' Even Ulysses S. GRANT was not immune. In 1862 he issued an infamous order – immediately rescinded by LINCOLN – which read:

> The Jews, as a class violating every regulation of trade established by the Treasury Department and also departmental orders, are hereby expelled from the [War] department within 24 hours from the receipt of this order.

August Bebel called anti-Semitism 'the socialism of fools', while LLOYD GEORGE declared: 'Of all the bigotries that savage the human temper there is none so stupid.' But it has mainly been left to Jews themselves to combat anti-Semitism. When DISRAELI was insulted in the Commons by Daniel O'Connell, he replied:

> Yes, I am a Jew, and when the ancestors of the Right Honourable Gentleman were brutal savages in an unknown island, mine were priests in the Temple of Solomon.

A similar riposte was made to an anti-Semitic US Senator by Sen. Judah Philip Benjamin (1811–84):

> The gentleman will please remember that when his half-civilized ancestors were hunting the wild boar in Silesia, mine were princes of the earth.

Anti-Trust Laws The legislation under which various US ADMINISTRATIONS have sought to break the power of monopolies and trusts and to create a framework for genuine economic competition. It is policed by the Anti-Trust division of the Justice Department. Popular pressure to weaken the trusts, and especially those controlling many of America's railroads, came to a head in 1889 after years when the SENATE, in particular, had been widely perceived to be in their pocket. President Benjamin HARRISON recommended Congressional action and in 1890 the SHERMAN ACT was passed. Few prosecutions followed until Theodore ROOSEVELT became President, and the scope of the law was broadened by the CLAYTON ACT of 1914.

anti-war movement The loose coalition of radical and liberal groups opposed to the VIETNAM WAR. Large and at times unruly rallies were held in New York and California from 1965; and in 1967, as the protests grew in size, Dr Martin Luther KING proposed a merger of the anti-war and CIVIL RIGHTS movements. The movement played a key part in the ending of Lyndon B. JOHNSON's Presidency – and also, unintentionally, in the election of Richard NIXON through the Democrats' choice of the anti-war Sen. George McGovern as their1972 Presidential candidate. In the autumn of 1969 millions demonstrated against the war across America, Vice President AGNEW dismissing them as 'an effete corps of snobs who characterized themselves as INTELLECTUALS'. The most tragic event of the campaign occurred with the KENT STATE shootings in May 1970; the following April, 2000 Vietnam veterans rallied against the war in WASHINGTON, many throwing their medals on to the CAPITOL steps. Protests and CIVIL DISOBEDIENCE tailed off as the withdrawal of US troops began.

Anyone for Denis? The farce based on life at NUMBER TEN Downing Street in the early years of Margaret THATCHER's government, staged at the Whitehall Theatre *c.* 1982 with Angela Thorne as the IRON LADY and John Wells as her husband, Denis; it ran for a considerable time. The title was a play on the old cliché 'Anyone for tennis?'. Mrs Thatcher was portrayed as a forceful master in her own house and her husband as an amiable buffer with a taste for gin who had shrewdly developed his own techniques for survival. The tone of the play owed much to the DEAR BILL column in PRIVATE EYE; Wells was co-author of both.

ANZUS Treaty A mutual defence treaty signed in 1951 by Australia, New Zealand and the US, under which each pledged to defend itself against the common danger (of communist aggression) and declared that an attack on any signatory was a threat to all.

From the mid-1980s it became a dead letter as New Zealand refused to accept any US ships without an undertaking that they carried no nuclear arms, and Australia also went through an anti-nuclear phase.

apartheid (Afrik. apartness) The policy of racial SEGREGATION implemented by the NATIONAL PARTY in South Africa between its coming to power in 1948 and the reforms pushed through by President F. W. de Klerk from 1989. It was denounced by almost every other country in the world, prompting virtual ostracism of South Africa in the fields of sport and culture and widespread, but not consistently enforced, trade SANCTIONS. At home it was bitterly contested both by liberal Whites (*see* BLACK SASH) and both moderate and militant Africans and Coloureds (*see* ANC; BLACK CONSCIOUSNESS; PAC). Such resistance led to the TREASON and RIVONIA trials, the imprisonment of key activists like Nelson MANDELA, and to the SHARPEVILLE massacre and other atrocities. Segregation already existed in 1948, but the National Party extended and codified it, notably through the GROUP AREAS ACT and the population registration act of 1950. Under the latter, everyone in South Africa had to be registered under their assessed racial origin: White, Coloured or Bantu; a category for Asians was added later. Movement of non-Whites was controlled by the notorious PASS LAWS. Other laws banned mixed marriages, established separate education, and prohibited non-White participation in government. The policy also encouraged African tribalism, to keep black South Africans from drifting to the cities and developing a middle class and political organisation, and served as a form of 'divide and rule', which also lay behind the encouragement given the Zulu INKATHA movement as apartheid was dismantled. From 1970 most Africans were held to be citizens of tribal BANTUSTANS or Homelands, which were declared independent and generally given the poorest land. However, millions were by now living in townships from which they poured daily to work in the cities; it was here that the outlawed ANC developed its strength. Apartheid began to wither in the 1980s as the demand for labour outstripped the availability of qualified Whites, and as world pressure and internal resistance began to bite. The ANC was legalised in 1990 and took power at the first multi-racial elections in 1994; despite some extremist sabre-rattling, the Afrikaner establishment yielded up power without a fight.

> We did what God intended us to do.
>
> Prime Minister Dr HENRIK VERWOERD, 1961

> We don't want apartheid liberalised. We want it dismantled. You can't improve something that's intrinsically evil.
>
> Archbishop DESMOND TUTU, 1985

> All oppression is repugnant, but there is an obscenity about oppression based on no more than the colour of a person's skin.
>
> Australian Prime Minister MALCOLM FRASER, 1979

apathy Lack of interest by the ELECTORS, much decried by politicians but useful to them when potentially unpopular policies fail to spark opposition, and consequently a danger if a fanatical minority is in sight of power. Edmund BURKE maintained that 'the only thing necessary for the triumph of evil is for good men to do nothing', and US Treasury secretary Bill Simon that 'bad politicians are sent to Washington by good people who don't want to vote'. After the 1989 European ELECTIONS Ireland's TANAISTE Brian Lenihan observed: 'There was so much apathy that Pat O'Connor only voted once.' O'Connor, Charles HAUGHEY's election agent, was known as Pat Pat O'Connor because he had once been convicted of voting twice.

> I am not prepared to go about the country stirring up apathy.
>
> WILLIAM WHITELAW (*see* WILLIE), *attr*

APEC Asian Pacific Economic Co-Operation. The trade-orientated regional grouping of nations brought together in 1989 by Australia and given formal shape at the 1993 Seattle summit when seventeen states took up membership. Its headquarters are in Singapore. There are now 21 members: Australia, Brunei, Canada, Chile, China, Hong Kong, Indonesia, Japan, South Korea, Malaysia, Mexico, New Zealand, Papua New Guinea, Peru, the Philippines, Russia, Singapore, Taiwan, Thailand, the USA and Vietnam. The slowness of the URUGUAY ROUND of world trade talks provided the impetus for its formation; at Tokyo in 1995 members committed themselves to work for Pacific FREE TRADE by 2020 (2010 between developed members), and there have subsequently been initiatives on economic co-operation, competitiveness and regulatory reform. Psychologically, the formation of APEC and America's commitment to it were also signs of the US's increasing orientation toward Asia.

apologise One of the hardest things for any politician to do, but one that will be required of them if they breach Parliamentary etiquette or are to survive the exposure of personal misjudgement or wrongdoing. Joseph Chamberlain's motto was 'Never apologise, never explain, never retract'; Spiro Agnew's, 'Apologise now. It will save time later'. UK Transport Secretary Paul Channon, son of 'CHIPS', described his post as 'the only job I know where you are expected to apologise to others when they are late for your meetings'. In the CHAMBER an apology to the CHAIR can be a humiliating experience, but a gifted speaker can turn it to advantage. When Barbara Castle, Transport Secretary in the late 1960s, complained that Iain Macleod had accused her of not knowing what she was doing, Macleod's apology was damning:

> It seems that during the previous debate I suggested the Right Honourable Lady did not know what she was doing. I ask the House to consider what they would have thought of me if I had suggested that she did know what she was doing.

apologist A writer, pamphleteer or speaker who concentrates on justifying the actions and policies of a particular regime, party or group.

Apostles The semi-secret and self-perpetuating dining club formed by undergraduates at Trinity College, Cambridge, in the mid-1930s; seen at the time as a harmless exercise in snobbery, it turned out during the BLUNT CASE to have been one of the most fertile recruiting grounds for Soviet spies.

apparatchik An originally Soviet term for a BUREAUCRAT, *apparat* being the Communist Party machine; it has come to imply someone who robotically carries out any task they are instructed to perform. Not surprisingly, it has gained world-wide currency. When Robert H. BORK was asked by Senators during his abortive CONFIRMATION hearings if he would ever resign as a Justice of the SUPREME COURT, he said:

> I don't want to be regarded as an apparatchik, an organization man who does whatever the organization wants.

appeasement The word used by Neville CHAMBERLAIN for his dealings with HITLER (notably at MUNICH) in the late 1930s, which were intended to preserve peace, which has become a byword throughout the world for weakness in the face of bullying. Chamberlain hoped to mollify Hitler and avoid war by conceding enough of other countries' territory to satisfy NAZI ambitions; the justification now advanced is that he bought himself valuable time for Britain to prepare to defend itself when war did break out. Sir Robert Vansittart (1881–1957), permanent secretary at the Foreign Office (*see* FCO), wrote at the close of 1936 when the threat was already forming:

> Time is the very material commodity which the Foreign Office is expected to provide in the same way as other departments provide other war material.

The term was first used as a pejorative by Lord Lothian in a letter to *The Times* in 1934 objecting to 'a limitation of arms by political appeasement'. The policy's leading opponent was CHURCHILL, who cuttingly described an appeaser as 'one who feeds a crocodile, hoping it will eat him last', and observed on Chamberlain's triumphant return from Munich:

> Britain and France had to choose between war and dishonour. They chose dishonour. They will have war.

War did indeed come within the year, and appeasement has had a bad press ever since. During the TRUMAN ADMINISTRATION Sen. William Jenner attacked General George MARSHALL as 'an errand boy, a front man, a stooge, or a conspirator for this administration's crazy assortment of COLLECTIVIST cut-throat crackpots and communist FELLOW-TRAVELLING appeasers'. And as the SUEZ CRISIS approached in 1956, the Conservative MP Sir Godfrey Nicholson told the Commons:

> Appeasement has never won a race yet. It is a bad horse, bred by good intentions out of paralysis of will.

Appomattox Courthouse The crossroads in Virginia, 20 miles north-east of Lynchburg, where America's CIVIL WAR formally ended on 9 April 1865, though some fighting continued elsewhere until July. Robert E. Lee handed his sword to Ulysses S. GRANT and the two generals agreed terms: his 27,800 CONFEDERATE troops to return home, with their horses for the spring ploughing and rations from UNION stores, and a promise that no Confederate soldier, from Lee downwards, would face punishment provided he kept to the terms of his parole. LINCOLN's reaction was that it was 'providential' Congress was not in session; he told his Cabinet on 14 April: 'We should get the Union re-established before

Congress comes together in December'. That evening he was assassinated.

apportionment The allocation of seats in the US HOUSE OF REPRESENTATIVES between the various states, on the basis of the ten-yearly census. The Bureau of the Census works out how many of the 435 Representatives each state is entitled to, and its computation becomes law unless CONGRESS changes the formula.

Apprentice Boys of Derry One of the most important events in the ORANGE calendar in Northern Ireland is the Apprentice Boys' procession at the height of the MARCHING SEASON. Both a gesture of defiance toward the Catholic majority in the city and a reaffirmation of LOYALIST determination, it commemorates the arrival of food supplies on 28 July 1689 to relieve the two-month siege of 30,000 Protestant refugees in Derry by Catholic forces loyal to the ousted King James II. The siege, with the Battle of the BOYNE, occupies a central place in Protestant mythology, its relief seen by Loyalists as decisive to the survival of their community. Derry's military governor, Robert Lundy, advised surrender as the JACOBITE forces – which were not over-strong – closed in, and fled when his advice was rejected; at the end of the commemoration each year he is burned in effigy.

appropriations The allocation by the US CONGRESS of funds for spending on particular projects, a task co-ordinated by committees in the HOUSE and SENATE overseeing a network of sub-committees (thirteen in the House) for each area of expenditure. The system and process provide endless opportunities to alter the ADMINISTRATION's budgetary priorities.

> All were agreed on one point, however. If Congress would make a sufficient appropriation, a colossal benefit would result. MARK TWAIN

approval rating The barometer of public confidence in a political leader provided by OPINION POLLS. Voters are asked whether they are satisfied or dissatisfied with a particular politician's performance, and the approval rating is the positive figure given, e.g. 67% support is converted by SPIN DOCTORS into a 67% approval rating. For a leader in trouble, an approval rating below 30% is not unknown.

après moi le déluge (Fr. after me, the flood) A saying associated with most ABSOLUTE rulers who have considered themselves indispensable, but in fact said after the battle of Rossbach in 1757 by Madame de Pompadour (1721–1764), mistress of King Louis XV of France. It was used a century later by the Austrian STATESMAN Metternich.

April Fool! One of the most unexpected moments in the US HOUSE OF REPRESENTATIVES came early in April 1941, when Rep. Robert Fleming Rich, a grumpy PROHIBITIONIST Republican from Pennsylvania, rose to his feet. Rich so often intervened with bad-tempered cries of 'Where are we going to get the money?' that colleagues would roar the words in unison when he stood up. This time, Rich got his own back: he simply exclaimed: 'April Fool!' and sat down again, to tumultuous applause.

Arab. Arab boycott *See* BOYCOTT.

Arab League An organisation of states, originally 22 in number, founded in 1945 to foster economic, political and cultural co-operation throughout the Arab world. The League has experienced divisions on many issues, notably the status of Israel, the formation of a Palestinian state, the Lebanese civil war (for which it established an Arab deterrent force in 1976) and the crisis precipitated between Arab nations by Iraq's invasion of Kuwait in 1990 and the subsequent GULF WAR.

Aras na Uachtarain The formal title, in Irish, of the official home of Ireland's President in Phoenix Park, Dublin. Formerly the residence of the VICEROY, it dates from 1753. *See* GOING FOR THE PARK.

arbitration The process whereby an inter-governmental, commercial or industrial dispute is referred to a third party who will consider the arguments put by both sides and then propose a decision, which in many cases will be binding. **Pendulum arbitration** is a process increasingly employed by ACAS under which the arbitrator is committed to accept one side's case *in toto*; the purpose is to ensure that each submits realistic demands, instead of inflating them in the hope of gaining more.

Archivist of the United States The federal official who not only supervises the National Archives containing America's most historic documents, but is charged with submitting any AMENDMENT to the CONSTITUTION approved by a two-thirds vote of both HOUSES OF CONGRESS to the States for RATIFICATION.

Ard Fheis (Ir. high summit) The title given

in the Irish Republic to the annual CONFERENCES of most political parties.

are. Are you better off than you were four years ago? Ronald REAGAN's most telling remark in his televised DEBATE with Jimmy CARTER in Cleveland on 28 October 1980; it was reputedly written for him by David Gergen.

Are you now, or have you ever been, a member of the Communist Party? The stock question asked by Rep. J. Parnell Thomas (1895–1970) at sittings of the House UN-AMERICAN ACTIVITIES Committee between 1947 and 1957, which became to critics of the process the trademark of MCCARTHYISM.

Are you thinking what we're thinking? The slogan of Michael HOWARD and the CONSERVATIVE PARTY in the 2005 UK general ELECTION. A number of prominent Tories saw the outcome as demonstrating that they were not.

Arena (Sp. *Alianza Republicana Nacionalista,* National Republican Alliance) The right-wing party in El Salvador whose candidate, Alfredo Cristiani, came to power in the Central American country's 1989 Presidential ELECTION. To the surprise of Western liberals (and the Salvadorean far right) Cristiani not only took tough action against left-wing FMLN guerrillas but cracked down on the DEATH SQUADS linked to the military. His even-handedness was an important contribution to the general success of the CONTADORA peace plan for the region.

Argentinian Firecracker The stage name of the stripper Fanne Foxe (Annabell Battistella) with whom the veteran Arkansas Congressman Wilbur Mills (1910–92) had a highly public dalliance that cost him the chairmanship of WAYS AND MEANS. Mills, who served 38 years in CONGRESS, had wielded awesome power from his chair for seventeen years; when he caught POTOMAC FEVER in 1971, one colleague asked him: 'Wilbur, why do you want to run for President and lose your grip on the country?' Then, at 2 a.m. on 7 October 1974, 38-year-old Ms Foxe jumped out of his car and threw herself into WASHINGTON's Tidal Basin; she was rescued by police patrolmen who had just booked Mills for speeding and driving without lights. Mills was re-elected the following month after warning his constituents against 'drinking champagne with foreigners', but that December he appeared on stage with Ms Foxe at the Boston Burlesque Theater, and admitted that he was an alcoholic – something colleagues had known for years. In May 1975, after several attempts to dry out, he was stripped of his powers; he served out his time in Congress, then took a job as a well-paid tax consultant. Ms Foxe made a low-budget movie that was pulled from a Washington cinema after one night.

Argumenti i Fakti (Russ. Arguments and Facts) The weekly paper that served as the organ of GLASNOST in Soviet Russia as Mikhail GORBACHEV's reforms got under way from 1986. Its circulation rocketed into the millions as readers wrote in with complaints about the way the system was operating, and ideas for making it work better.

aristocracy (Gr. government by the best) (1) A system of government in which the 'best' – those of a superior social class – take the decisions. Aristotle termed it 'that form of government in which education and discipline are qualifications for suffrage and office-holding'; the 19th-century Russian revolutionary Alexander Herzen saw it rather diferently: 'a more or less civilised form of cannibalism'. (2) The privileged social class itself, the **aristocrats**, in Britain being identified with hereditary PEERS and their families. In France, they were abbreviated by their detractors to '*les ariostos*' (*see* A LA LANTERNE). Mirabeau saw them as 'the intermediary between the King and the people, just as the sporting dog is the intermediary between the sportsman and the hare', and Heinrich Heine sneered at aristocrats as 'asses who talk about horses'. Yet the most vitriolic comments were made by LLOYD GEORGE, when the HOUSE OF LORDS was trying to wreck his PEOPLE'S BUDGET. He said:

> An aristocracy is like cheese; the older it gets, the higher it becomes.

and

> A fully-equipped Duke costs as much to keep up as two Dreadnoughts, and Dukes are just as great a terror – and they last longer.

It is wrong to assume that the word 'aristocracy' means nothing in America. Despite the absence of a titled nobility, there has been no shortage of self-important or patrician people eager to fill the vacuum. Ralph Waldo Emerson described each such 'aristocrat' as 'a democrat ripe and gone to seed'.

> An aristocrat in a republic is like a chicken whose head has been cut off. It may run about in a lively

way, but in fact it is dead.

NANCY MITFORD (1904–73), *Noblesse Oblige*

Arlington National Cemetery The 500 acres of Virginia hillside facing across the POTOMAC to WASHINGTON where many of the great of America are buried – together with 163,000 dead from every one of the nation's wars. President TAFT, L'Enfant, the planner of Washington, William Jennings Bryan (*see* PRAIRIE AVENGER), Abraham LINCOLN's son Robert, John F. KENNEDY and Robert F. Kennedy are all buried there. JFK's tomb with its eternal flame lies close to the Custis-Lee Mansion, built in 1802 by George WASHINGTON's adoptive son and later the home of Robert E. Lee, whose memorial the house now is. The cemetery was designated in 1864, an act later held illegal by the SUPREME COURT which ordered the Lee family to be compensated. The first burial, on 13 May 1865, was of a CONFEDERATE prisoner who had died in hospital; the Memorial Amphitheatre to America's dead in WORLD WAR I was dedicated in 1920, and the tomb of the Unknown Soldier in 1932.

Armalite and ballot box The twin strategy of the PROVISIONAL IRA: to force Britain out of NORTHERN IRELAND through a campaign of violence while making electoral gains in Nationalist areas through SINN FEIN, its POLITICAL WING. The phrase was first used by Danny Morrison at Sinn Fein's 1981 ARD FHEIS in Dublin. The Armalite (*compare* KALASHNIKOV) is the US-made rifle which is the Provisionals' basic weapon.

armed conflict The term used by Anthony EDEN to describe the Anglo-French intervention at SUEZ in 1956, which he insisted was not an act of war; it was ridiculed by critics of the action. Eden told the HOUSE OF COMMONS on 4 November 1956:

> We are not at war with Egypt. We are in a state of armed conflict.

armed struggle The PROVISIONAL IRA's characterisation of its campaign of violence to secure British withdrawal from NORTHERN IRELAND, and ideally the overthrow of the Irish Republic. The term has since gained a global currency *see* ZAPATISTAS.

armistice The cessation of hostilities while a formal peace is negotiated. **Armistice Day** was 11 November 1918, the day WORLD WAR I ended; it is commemorated in Britain as **Remembrance Day** on the nearest Sunday. *See also* CENOTAPH.

armoured train The train in which TROTSKY toured the infant Soviet Union to rally the RED ARMY during the CIVIL WAR with the WHITES that followed the BOLSHEVIK revolution. Covered with thick steel plate as protection against artillery fire and plastered with revolutionary slogans, it served as Trotsky's mobile military and political headquarters, and was guarded by troops hand-picked for their loyalty and commitment.

arms. arms control The generic term for the various processes by which the international community, and specific nations, have endeavoured to halt and reverse the ARMS RACE. It has embraced apparently interminable negotiations in Geneva involving the SUPERPOWERS and various combinations of other countries, depending on whether NUCLEAR or CONVENTIONAL WEAPONS are involved and which potential theatres of conflict are concerned, though the end of the COLD WAR and the proliferation of terrorism have reduced the point and value of bilateral agreements between major powers, some of which like the ABM TREATY have in any case been repudiated. The arms control process has nevertheless led over the years to the CFE, INF, SALT and START agreements. In America such negotiations have since 1961 been the province of the **Arms Control and Disarmament Agency** (ACDA), though for much of the REAGAN and George W. BUSH ADMINISTRATIONS the negotiating process has been in the hands of HAWKS rather than disarmers.

arms for hostages The notion behind the IRAN-CONTRA AFFAIR: that by supplying Iran with arms, America could gain enough leverage in Tehran to secure the release of Western HOSTAGES held by Islamic militants in Beirut.

arms race The race between the SUPERPOWERS throughout the COLD WAR to establish a clear lead over each other in NUCLEAR WEAPONRY, both in terms of quantity and effectiveness.

> We have a three to one advantage over the Russians, which I understand means we have the potential to kill all the Russians twice and they have the potential to kill us one and a quarter times. Sen. EUGENE MCCARTHY, 1968

> The Soviets have been quite single-minded. They increased their defense expenditures as we increased ours. And they increased their defense expenditures as we decreased ours.
>
> US Defense Secretary HAROLD BROWN, 1979

> The nuclear arms race has no military purpose.
> Earl MOUNTBATTEN of Burma, 1979

> We have gone on piling weapon upon weapon, missile upon missile, new levels of destructiveness upon old levels . . . Like the victims of some kind of hypnotism, like men in a dream, like lemmings heading for the sea, like the children of Hamelin marching blindly behind their Pied Piper. GEORGE F. KENNAN, 1982

right to keep and bear arms *See* RIGHT.

Army-McCarthy hearings *See* MCCARTHY.

Arnold. Benedict Arnold US shorthand for a turncoat or traitor. Benedict Arnold (1741–1801) was a major-general in the Revolutionary army who, given the command of West Point in 1780, conspired with the British to surrender the garrison. When his intrigue was discovered, he fled to the British and fought for them briefly before taking refuge in England.

Arthur, Chester *See* ELEGANT ARTHUR.

Articles 2 and 3 The provisions of the CONSTITUTION of the Irish Republic which constituted a claim to sovereignty over the SIX COUNTIES of NORTHERN IRELAND, and as such were anathema to Ulster UNIONISTS. They were repealed following a referendum in the wake of the 1998 GOOD FRIDAY AGREEMENT.

Aryanism The basic test imposed on all Germans by the NAZIs in the mid to late 1930s, to establish racial purity and disqualify all those with any element of Jewish descent from participating in the Master Race. A certificate of Aryanism was required for any official post, and lack of it meant exclusion from the professions and eventually from society. HITLER had foreshadowed the drawing of such a distinction in MEIN KAMPF, which stressed the supremacy of the Aryan (originally an Indo-Persian) race.

asbo Anti-Social Behaviour Order. The principal weapon introduced by Tony BLAIR's government to tackle the nuisance of 'neighbours from Hell' and persistent juvenile delinquency. By June 2005 some 5,000 had been granted by the courts, barring those involved from areas where they had caused trouble or ruling out particular behaviours; one woman who had repeatedly tried to commit suicide was barred from all bridges over the Thames. Asbos have made some difference, though the courts have not been consistent in punishing breaches. ASB is the CABINET COMMITTEE, chaired by the Prime Minister, which oversees the tackling of anti-social behaviour.

Ascendancy The ethos of 18th-century Ireland under Anglo-Irish Protestant domination, prior to the NINETY-EIGHT and the UNION with England. The social elite looked back on it as a golden age; the average Irish family as a period of oppression.

ASEAN Association of South East Asian Nations. The grouping of states at the west of the PACIFIC RIM, formed in 1967 to promote collective economic and political stability. Founded by Indonesia, Malaysia, the Philippines, Thailand, Singapore and Brunei, ASEAN has become a steadily stronger voice in the world with the rapid development of its members' economies, and through its greater homogeneity remains a greater force than APEC.

ASIO Australian Security Intelligence Organisation. The agency that seeks to protect Australia and its institutions from internal and external threat. Overseas intelligence gathering is handled by an offshoot, ASIS (Australian Secret Intelligence Service). ASIO was set up in 1949 because of suspected Soviet penetration of the Department of External Affairs in Canberra, and the PETROV CASE was an early success. Until 1968 it was run with an iron hand by Sir Charles Spry, who had lobbied for its creation. Close links were established with the CIA and MI5, and at least one MI5 officer joined it because he believed his own agency was penetrated by Soviet agents. ASIO went through a controversial patch in the 1970s when Labor ministers accused it of keeping them under surveillance – one, Lionel Murphy having his headquarters raided in a vain search for hostile files; there was also an embarrassing incident when agents 'hijacked' a Sydney hotel in a training exercise without the police or hotel management being informed. ASIO has since regained its equilibrium.

ask not what you can do for your country *See* COUNTRY.

Asquith, Herbert Henry (1st Earl of Oxford and Asquith, 1852–1928), Prime Minister (Liberal) from 1908 to 1916 and the last head of a purely Liberal government. A Yorkshire-born barrister, he became MP for East Fife in 1886 and six years later was HOME SECRETARY under GLADSTONE, whose biographer Sir Philip Magnus rated him 'the best Home Secretary of the century'. In opposition he was a LIBERAL IMPERIALIST during the BOER WAR, and on the party's return to power in 1905 took part in the RELUGAS COMPACT which aimed to make Asquith, rather than CAMPBELL-BANNERMAN, effective head of the government; a fellow-member of the Compact, Lord Haldane, wrote: 'From the beginning (he) meant to be Prime Minister'. C-B hung on, yet made Asquith CHANCELLOR; on his death early in 1908 Asquith was the obvious successor. Asquith's CABINET included such vibrant figures as LLOYD GEORGE, and the young CHURCHILL, and kept up a reforming programme including DISESTABLISHMENT of the Welsh church, the foundations of the WELFARE STATE, and the curbing of the powers of the HOUSE OF LORDS when it resisted the PEOPLE'S BUDGET. Asquith was ready to force the creation of hundreds of Liberal PEERS to get the BUDGET through, telling King George V:

> I hold my office not only by favour of the Crown, but by the confidence of the people, and I should be guilty indeed of treason if in this supreme moment of a great struggle I were to betray their trust.

His government was also dogged by agitation for VOTES FOR WOMEN, which Asquith opposed, the slide toward war with Germany (*see* WE WANT EIGHT AND WE WON'T WAIT), growing industrial unrest and steadily-increasing tension in Ireland as HOME RULE legislation was finally enacted. Asquith faced down the CURRAGH MUTINY, but the situation in Ireland was explosive when war broke out in Europe. Asquith was appalled by the implications of war, and disconcerted by the attention it brought him, saying:

> I have never before been a popular character with the man in the street, and in all this dark and dangerous business it gives me scant pleasure.

He was not a great war leader, prosecuting the conflict conscientiously but without imagination; Lady Tree once tellingly asked him at dinner: 'Mr Asquith, do you take an interest in the war?' He also moved slowly to form a wartime COALITION, his biographer Roy JENKINS writing: 'Although he had always been a moderate in politics, he hated the idea of bringing Tories into his Cabinet,' and after two years of stalemate on the battlefield Lloyd George, who had branded him 'a soft-nosed torpedo', conspired with the Conservatives to oust him. His colleague Lord Grey lamented: 'He took no steps to secure his own position or to add to his general reputation'.

Asquith remained leader of the Liberal Party, and his insistence on keeping his position as L.G. flirted with the Tories opened up a damaging and probably fatal split. Episodes such as the MAURICE LETTER and the HONOURS SCANDAL distanced the two men still further, and after the coalition broke up in 1922 each Liberal faction lost heavily at the polls, with Labour moving up to take power. Asquith lost his seat in 1918, returned in 1920 after a spectacular by-election win at Paisley, but was finally unseated in 1923. He did not give up the party leadership until 1926, by when he had taken a peerage.

Asquith was renowned for his mental precision, Churchill writing: 'His mind opened and shut smoothly and exactly, like the breech of a gun', while Lord Robert Cecil reminisced that 'he brought to Cabinet meetings the cold calculation he displayed at the bridge table'. His stamina was renowned, his son Cyril writing: 'He could stand more in the way of late hours and airless meetings than any other public man. It was a matter of indifference to him whether he inhaled cigar smoke or oxygen.' His obsession with detail was also legendary; Lloyd George observed:

> Asquith worries too much about small points. If you were buying a large mansion he would come to you and say: 'Have you thought there is no accommodation for the cat?'

This trait could land him in trouble. Once a HECKLER, referring to an episode when he was Home Secretary, called out: 'Why did you murder the miners at Featherstone in '92?' Instead of rebutting the slander, he replied: 'It was not '92, it was '93.'

Asquith was not an outstanding speaker, W. T. Stead terming him 'a forensic gladiator who never made a heart beat quicker by his words, and who never by any possibility brought a lump into his hearers' throats'. Yet he was well read and articulate, though John Morley found him 'unnecessarily cassant'. He knew that he could seem a plodder, once saying to his second wife, the socialite Margot Tennant:

> Character is better than brains, and loyalty more valuable than either, but I shall have to work with the material that has been given to me.

She said of his public image: 'His modesty amounts to a deformity,' also describing him as 'a cold, unsympathetic man, loved by some, admired by a few'. Asquith became a heavy drinker; Lord Alfred Douglas christened him **Old Squiffy** and the word stuck to describe anyone who had over-indulged. Yet BONAR LAW remarked: 'Asquith, when drunk, could make a better speech than any of us sober.' Roy Jenkins observed that 'there was always in his character a surprising but strong streak of recklessness', and this showed in the stream of mildly compromising notes he wrote to the young Venetia Stanley – even from the government front bench – until her marriage.

> Bland and wicked, and with only a nodding acquaintance with the truth.
> LADY CUNARD

> Arthur Balfour is wicked and moral. Asquith is good and immoral. CHURCHILL

> The inveterate lack of ideals and imagination seems really unredeemed; when one has peeled off the brown paper wrapping of phrases and compromise – just nothing at all.
> LYTTON STRACHEY

> For twenty years he has held a season ticket on the line of least resistance, and gone wherever the train of events has carried him, lucidly justifying his position at whatever point he has happened to find himself.
> LEO AMERY in the House of Commons, 1916

> With him died the best part of the classical tradition in English politics. ROY JENKINS

assassination Political murder, usually of a person in authority, described by George Bernard Shaw as 'the extreme form of censorship'. Its victims over the centuries include Julius Caesar, the British Prime Minister Spencer Perceval, Abraham LINCOLN, Archduke Franz Ferdinand at SARAJEVO, John F. KENNEDY and his brother Robert, Dr Martin Luther KING, MAHATMA Gandhi, Indira and Rajiv GANDHI (*see* NEHRU DYNASTY) and the former Swedish premier Olof Palme. The word derives from the *assassins*, a fanatical Islamic sect founded in the 11th century who terrorised Persia and Syria for over 200 years; those who carried out their missions were rewarded with gifts of hashish, hence the name. Under EXECUTIVE ORDER 12333, signed by President REAGAN in 1981, 'no person employed by or acting on behalf of the US government shall engage in or conspire to engage in assassination' of foreign leaders, no matter how hostile they were to America's interests. An exception has since been made in the case of AL QAEDA.

> A President has to expect these things. The only thing you have to worry about is bad luck. Never have bad luck.
> HARRY S TRUMAN after the BLAIR HOUSE attempt on his life, November 1950.

absolutism tempered by assassination *See* ABSOLUTISM.

character assassination Efforts by a person's political opponents to destroy his or her reputation so that the individual concerned can be removed as a potential threat.

Assisted Places Scheme (1) The scheme devised by Margaret THATCHER's Conservative government to enable bright children from poorer families to be educated at fee-paying schools. It was controversially abolished when Labour returned to power in 1997. (2) The nickname given by male chauvinist Labour MPs to a change in the rules for Parliamentary Labour Party (*see* PLP) elections made in the mid-1990s in an effort, not entirely successful, to get more women into the SHADOW CABINET.

association The term used by Britain's Conservatives and Liberal Democrats to describe their organisation in each CONSTITUENCY; one of their MPs will talk of 'my association'. Labour's equivalent is the CLP.

freedom of association *See* FREEDOM.

Asuncion, Treaty of *See* MERCOSUR.

Aswan High Dam The massive construction project in Egypt whose funding precipitated the SUEZ CRISIS of 1956. The Egyptian leader Colonel Nasser NATIONALISED the Suez Canal Company to finance construction of the dam after America withdrew its offer of funds; the EISENHOWER ADMINISTRATION felt Cairo was establishing over-close ties with Moscow. The $1 billion dam was finally opened in 1971; it created Lake Nasser, the world's largest reservoir controlling the irrigation of over 3 million acres, and the temple of Abu Simbel had to be raised to save it from inundation.

asylum seeker An applicant for POLITICAL ASYLUM in a country far from home, and from the late 1990s colloquially an illegal immigrant (especially to the UK) who on arrival claims asylum in order to avoid deportation. The monitoring and processing of asylum seekers – many but far from all of whose claims are justified – have posed an increasing headache for Conservative and Labour governments as their number has increased. *See also* SANGATTE.

at. at a stroke *See* STROKE.

at-large A US term for the ELECTION of a legislator or official by all the voters of a State or city, instead of by those of a specific

DISTRICT or WARD. At-large elections to the HOUSE OF REPRESENTATIVES – save for those States electing only one member – were abolished in 1967.

ATF (Bureau of) **Alcohol, Tobacco and Firearms** The US Government investigative and law enforcement agency which deals with infractions of federal law in these areas, and whose agents receive a high profile in major outbreaks of gun crime. Peculiarly, it is answerable to the TREASURY. *See also* WACO SIEGE

Atlantic. Atlantic Alliance A commonly-used term for NATO, underlining America's role in the defence of western Europe.

Atlantic Charter The eight-point declaration of principles on which peace was to be based after the defeat of the AXIS powers in WORLD WAR II, agreed by President ROOSEVELT and Winston CHURCHILL on 14 August 1941 at secret meetings on warships off Newfoundland. Conclusion of the Charter, comparable to WILSON'S FOURTEEN POINTS but less ambitious, was cited by Axis leaders as evidence that FDR had already taken America into the war; its commitment to 'final destruction of the NAZI tyranny' was hard to reconcile with US NEUTRALITY. Churchill hoped it would 'make Japan ponder', but four months later PEARL HARBOR was attacked. The Charter also made first mention of the UNITED NATIONS, a term originated by Roosevelt to avoid the impression that he was concluding an alliance without CONGRESSional approval.

Atlanticist A Western European committed to close strategic, diplomatic and cultural co-operation with America; the term is used as a mild pejorative by left-wingers for enthusiastic supporters of NATO and, implicitly, of NUCLEAR WEAPONS.

atomic bomb The bomb, depending on nuclear fission, whose successful detonation in New Mexico on 16 July 1945 confronted humanity with the prospect of being exterminated by its leaders, and which remains a threat to this day. The MANHATTAN PROJECT brought together sufficient quantities of fissile material (a critical mass) to prompt a self-sustaining, uncontrolled chain reaction. When J. Robert Oppenheim (1904–67), the director of the project, saw the awesome power of the first explosion and its MUSHROOM CLOUD, he recalled a quotation from the *Bhagavad Gita*:

> I have become Death, the shatterer of worlds.

A number of senior scientists on the project were so horrified at their creation that they suggested its destructive power be publicly demonstrated to the Japanese. Oppenheimer and key figures in the TRUMAN ADMINISTRATION opposed this, and the bomb was dropped on HIROSHIMA on 6 August. Three days later a second was used against NAGASAKI, after which Japan capitulated. These are the only two occasions on which nuclear weapons have been used in warfare, though the threat was ever-present during the COLD WAR, once the Soviet Union had developed its own bomb in 1949. Britain from 1952, France from 1960, China (1964), India (1974) and Pakistan also have nuclear weapons; Israel, South Africa and possibly Brazil, Algeria and Taiwan have the capability. Iraq was close to achieving it on the outbreak of the GULF WAR; America sees nuclear developments by both Iran and North Korea as a threat to world peace.

> If only I had known, I would have become a watchmaker. ALBERT EINSTEIN, 1945

> The greatest thing in history.
> HARRY S TRUMAN, 1945

See PAPER TIGER.

Atoms for Peace The programme pioneered by the Eisenhower administration to loan US uranium to nations willing to use it for peaceful purposes.

> There is no evil in the atom – only in men's souls.
> ADLAI STEVENSON

Attlee, Clement later Earl Attlee (1883–1967), the man of few words who led Britain's LABOUR PARTY for 20 years, served with distinction as CHURCHILL's wartime deputy, and from 1945 to 1951 led the great reforming government that created the WELFARE STATE. An Oxford-educated lawyer converted to socialism by experience of the East London slums, Attlee returned from WORLD WAR I with the rank of major to become mayor of Stepney. Elected to Parliament in 1922, he held junior posts under Ramsay MACDONALD prior to the GREAT BETRAYAL of 1931; one of relatively few Labour MPs to hold their seats in the subsequent ELECTION, he was elected leader in 1935 'for the remaining weeks of the Parliamentary term' in place of George Lansbury. Hugh Dalton characterised the contest between Attlee and Herbert Morrison as 'a choice between a nonentity and a drunk'. Labour's fortunes recovered a little at the 1935 election, and by the outbreak of war Attlee had done much to restore the party's morale. In 1940 his refusal to take Labour into a COALITION under anyone other than Churchill was decisive; Attlee became a key member of the WAR CABINET, deputising for Churchill whenever he was out of the country. Churchill respected Attlee, but did not like being stood up to, saying: 'He combines a limited outlook with strong qualities of resistance.'

With Germany defeated in May 1945, Attlee withdrew Labour from the coalition and precipitated an election. The party chairman Harold Laski was convinced he would lead it to defeat (*see* THANK YOU FOR YOUR LETTER), but in the event Labour won by a LANDSLIDE. Attlee took office facing formidable problems: a crippled economy, run-down industries, a serious housing shortage, bloated armed forces to demobilise, imperial commitments far beyond Britain's capacity to sustain, the incipient COLD WAR and crisis in the Middle East. He also had to meet the high expectations of voters, especially ex-servicemen who had voted Labour in millions, and to keep the peace between such giants as Morrison, Ernest BEVIN and Aneurin BEVAN. The late 1940s under Attlee's leadership were the heyday of democratic socialism as key industries were NATIONALISED, the National Health Service (NHS) established and India granted its independence. Attlee saw Britain through a crippling FUEL CRISIS in 1947 and serious economic difficulties, exacerbated by America presenting its bill for wartime support, which culminated in DEVALUATION in 1949. He pressed ahead with development of the independent nuclear DETERRENT, backed the establishment of NATO, joined in the KOREAN WAR and acquiesced in the foundation of Israel, to which the party, though not all his ministers, was warmly committed. The 1945 Government had its embarrassments, including the BUDGET LEAK and the GROUNDNUT SCHEME, but never lost a BY-ELECTION and increased its vote in 1950. But it now had only a tiny minority and was running out of steam; Attlee called a further election late in 1951, and lost. He stayed on as leader to fight a further election in 1955, taking the heat from the campaigning of the BEVANITES for more left-wing policies, but retired once he was certain Morrison would not succeed him; Hugh GAITSKELL was elected leader. Attlee went to the HOUSE OF LORDS with an EARLDOM; in later years he spoke strongly against Britain joining the COMMON MARKET.

Attlee is famed for his lack of obvious charisma. His only passion, apart from his family, was cricket. He himself admitted: 'I have none of the qualities which create publicity', and 'I am a diffident man. I find it hard to carry on a conversation.' Once, taking a colleague to a restaurant and finding himself without cash, he observed: 'I could pay by cheque. Trouble is, I'm not known here.' His opponents were scathing. Churchill once reputedly commented: 'An empty taxicab drew up at the HOUSE OF COMMONS and Mr Attlee got out,' and said: 'Mr Attlee is a very modest man. But then, he has much to be modest about.' He denied ever having called him 'a sheep in sheep's clothing', but one anonymous Westminster wit did say:

> The door of 10 Downing Street opened and the cat put out Mr Attlee.

In 1945 Bevan wrote in TRIBUNE: 'He brings to the fierce struggle of politics the tepid enthusiasm of a lazy summer afternoon at a cricket match,' and two years later the *Economist* editorialised: 'Mr Attlee touches nothing that he does not dehydrate.' George Orwell was even more uncomplimentary, writing:

> He reminds me of a dead fish before it has had time to stiffen.

Attlee was economic with words. He would dismiss ministers with the sole comment; 'I'm making some changes. Not up to it.' When his Food Minister John Stratchey wanted to publish a book of poems, Attlee wrote to him: 'Can't publish. Lines don't scan.' When confronted by a hostile meeting of the PLP in 1952 he announced: 'King dead – meeting adjourned.' And when approached in retirement by a young Labour CANVASSER he simply said: 'Already a member.' Almost his longest recorded comment was his advice to young Labour MPs about contact with the PRESS BARON Lord Beaverbrook: 'He is a magnet to all young men, and I warn you that if you talk to him no good will come of it.'

> He would never use one syllable when none would do. Among the longest comments I ever extracted from him was: 'Wouldn't serve any useful purpose.' DOUGLAS JAY

> Feed a grub with royal jelly and it may become a queen. CHURCHILL

> Charisma? He did not recognise the word except as a clue in his beloved *Times* crossword.
> JAMES MARGACH

> Few thought he was even a starter.
> There were many who thought themselves
> smarter.

But he ended PM
CH and OM
An Earl, and a Knight
Of the Garter. ATTLEE

Attorney-General In America, the head of the Justice Department and a senior member of the ADMINISTRATION, the post having become more politicised in the 20th century. In Britain, the government's chief law officer, with both political and legal functions, who attends the CABINET as required and may also lead the prosecution in major trials.

audace. l'audace, l'audace et toujours l'audace (Fr. daring, still more daring, and always daring) This motto of the FRENCH REVOLUTION was first uttered by Danton (1759–94) in a speech to the Legislative Committee of General Defence on 2 September 1792.

Au H_2O One of the symbols of Barry GOLDWATER's 1964 US Presidential campaign, combining the chemical symbols for gold (*Au*) and water (H_2O).

audience The regular weekly meeting at Buckingham Palace (usually on a Tuesday evening) at which the UK Prime Minister briefs the SOVEREIGN on current political events; the term applies to all such meetings, and also to personal consultations between the Sovereign and the Heads of Government of COMMONWEALTH countries which are still monarchies. The term is also used to describe meetings between individuals and the Pope.

Augean stables The ultimate in cleansing of a corrupt political system. The term stems from the labours of Heracles in Greek mythology, one of which involved the cleansing of the stables of King Augeas, which were feet deep in dung deposited over 30 years by 3000 oxen; the hero achieved this by diverting a river through the premises.

Ausgleich (Ger. compromise). The accommodation made by the Habsburg Emperor Franz Josef I in 1867, which technically created the dual monarchy of Austria-Hungary. Under pressure from his Hungarian subjects to accept their separate identity, he accepted the crown of St Stephen and recognised the integrity of Hungary's borders in return for the Budapest Parliament's acknowledging his responsibility for foreign affairs and defence. The *Ausgleich*, which lasted until the collapse of the empire in 1918, was partly designed to prevent Bismarck drawing Hungary into Prussia's ambit.

autarky A political and social system that depends on a rigorous national commitment to economic self-sufficiency.

authoritarianism A system of government depending on the exercise of overweening power by the State.

authority (1) The existence or exercise of legitimate power. Fidel Castro said after the Cuban revolution:

> We hope that in the future few if any men will have the authority, which we, the creators of this revolution, have had, because it is dangerous for men to have so much authority.

(2) An appointed or elected body empowered to exercise certain powers over a community, an area of government or a section of the population, as in the PALESTINIAN AUTHORITY.

autocrat A leader who rules personally without powerful lieutenants or any pretence of a representative government; TSARIST Russia was long regarded as the ultimate **autocracy**, Count Sergei Uvarov (1786–1855) describing the system as 'the main condition of Russia's political existence'.

> I shall be an autocrat, that is my trade. And the Good Lord will forgive me – that is his.
> CATHERINE THE GREAT (1729–86)

Avanti! (Ital. forward!) The newspaper of Italy's socialist party, traditionally produced in Milan, which from 1911 to 1914 was edited by Mussolini (*see* DUCE) until his expulsion from the party for advocating war with Austria.

AWACS Air Warning and Control System. The modified Boeing 747 jumbo jets developed by the US Air Force in the early 1970s to provide a continual airborne radar watch for hostile incoming flights and to guard against NUCLEAR attack. America sold the planes to a number of its NATO allies – though not until the mid-1980s to Britain, which first spent almost £1 billion on developing the rival Nimrod before concluding that its avionics could not be made reliable. In one Nimrod trial, the radar 'detected' a tanker crossing the North Sea at 400 knots and another intruder that turned out to be the bowl of its own lavatory. In 1981 the REAGAN ADMINISTRATION sold several AWACS to Saudi Arabia, overcoming bitter CONGRESSIONAL resistance mounted by AIPAC, the pro-Israel lobbying group. AWACS should not be confused with the jumbo that provides the President with an emergency command post from which he can conduct a nuclear war if the WHITE HOUSE is threatened, or is destroyed after he has managed to escape.

Axis The alliance between NAZI Germany and FASCIST Italy concluded by HITLER and Mussolini in October 1936. It was formed after Italy's invasion of Abyssinia that year had made clear Il DUCE's contempt for the LEAGUE OF NATIONS, and paved the way for both leaders openly to flout the League. Mussolini said:

> This Berlin-Rome connection is not so much a diaphragm as an axis, around which can revolve all those states of Europe with a will towards collaboration and peace.

In 1937 Japan joined the Axis. *See also* PACT OF STEEL.

axis of evil George W. BUSH's description of Iran, Iraq and North Korea in his January 2002 STATE OF THE UNION message, intended to identify these countries as supporters of international terrorism in the wake of the 9/11 attacks. His choice of words – the phrase was originated by his speech-writer David Frum – anticipated the 2003 WAR ON IRAQ, hampered Western efforts to rebuild relations with Iran, which had not been a supporter of AL QAEDA, and destabilised initiatives to restore links between South and North Korea. The next month Cuba, Libya and Syria were added to the list. *Compare* KERNEL OF EVIL.

Ayatollah (Farsi. token of God) The word in Iran for an authoritative holy man, but used throughout the world for Ruhalla Khomeini (1902–89), the militant Shi'ite cleric whose followers brought down the Shah in 1979 and who for the next ten years ruled Iran as a ruthless medieval theocracy. Khomeini was acclaimed an ayatollah in 1950, but was arrested and exiled from the city of Qum for attacking the Shah's westernising policies, especially the emancipation of women. Ejected from Iraq by Saddam Hussein in 1978, he settled in Paris just as the Shah was losing his grip; a month after the Shah's overthrow he was given a hero's reception in Tehran by 3 million people. For a year he ruled alone, imposing strict observance of Islamic law and fomenting the occupation of the Embassy of the United States, which he termed the GREAT SATAN, to start the HOSTAGE CRISIS. From 1980 Iran was nominally in the hands of an elected government, but Khomeini still exerted immense influence, mellowing just enough to accept a ceasefire in the IRAN-IRAQ WAR in 1986, saying: 'I have drunk poison.' The kidnappers of Western hostages in Beirut were loyal to Khomeini, if not acting under his orders, but the Ayatollah was not directly involved in the IRAN-CONTRA AFFAIR. In the last years of his life he sowed the seeds for further strain between Iran and the West by issuing a FATWA ordering all good Muslims to murder the UK-based author Salman Rushdie, whose book *The Satanic Verses* he considered blasphemous.

aye. aye lad, but never forget – Monty had a picture of Rommel in his bloody caravan The crushing retort delivered by an elderly reporter from the *Guardian* to Winston CHURCHILL, grandson of the war leader, fighting his first election campaign at Manchester Gorton in 1967. Churchill, who would win a seat at the next attempt, had told a BY-ELECTION press conference how encouraged he was that skilled workers in a local engineering plant had his picture from his ELECTION ADDRESS over their machines.

as many as are of that opinion say 'Aye' The call made by the SPEAKER of the HOUSE OF COMMONS straight after putting the QUESTION. If the shout of 'Aye' is met by a shout of 'No', the Speaker will call:

> DIVISION – CLEAR THE LOBBIES! **The Ayes to the right, the Noes to the left.**

When the votes are announced at the end of the division, he or she will declare either: **'The Ayes have it'** or 'The Noes have it'. If the first chorus of 'Aye' is not responded to, or only half-heartedly, the Speaker will announce straight away that 'the Ayes have it'.

In the US HOUSE OF REPRESENTATIVES the words used by the Speaker for a VOICE-VOTE are very similar. The Chair says: 'As many as are in favor say Aye. As many as are not in favor say: No.' If the result is not clear-cut, the Chair then says that a division has been demanded and adds: 'As many as are in favor will rise and stand until counted'. As at WESTMINSTER, the result is announced by the TELLERS, then repeated by the Speaker.

Azania An alternative name for South Africa, used in the days of APARTHEID by some nationalists and principally the Pan-Africanist Congress (PAC), whose military wing (*compare* POLITICAL WING) was the **Azanian People's Liberation Army.** It was originally the name of an Iron Age civilisation that occupied the area between 500 and 1500 AD. Evelyn Waugh used the name for an imaginary African kingdom in his novel *Black Mischief* (1932).

B

B. B and K UK headline-writers' tag for the joint Soviet leaders, Prime Minister Marshal Nikolai Alexandrovich Bulganin (1895–1975) and First Secretary Nikita Sergeyevich Khrushchev (1894–1971), on their visit to Britain in 1956. *See* CRABB AFFAIR.

B1 Bob. The nickname of the former USAF pilot Rep. Bob Dornan (1933–), who from 1978 until his defeat in 1996 campaigned energetically for production of the aircraft in his Orange County, California Congressional district. Dornan once swam under the bridge at CHAPPAQUIDDICK to test Sen. Edward KENNEDY's claim that he had been unable to save Mary Jo Kopechne, and in a bid for the 1996 Republican Presidential NOMINATION denounced President CLINTON as 'a sleazeball who can't keep his pants on'. Prior to his final Congressional race, he boasted: 'Every lesbian spear-chucker in America is hoping I get defeated', but it was the Hispanic migrant vote which beat him by just 979 votes – a result he insisted was fraudulent.

B1 bomber The aircraft that symbolised the determination of the CARTER ADMINISTRATION to rein in defence projects it considered poor value, and of the REAGAN administration to push the boat out. Rockwell International sought to ensure the supersonic successor to the B52 would go ahead by allocating work to plants and subcontractors in 48 states and more than 400 of the 435 Congressional districts. When President Carter cancelled the project at prototype stage in 1977, CONGRESS fell just short of an OVERRIDE. The company kept key workers together in the hope of a Republican victory, lobbied hard and was given the order to restart soon after Ronald Reagan entered the WHITE HOUSE. The B1's production run was limited, and defence experts remain divided over whether the aircraft has justified its immense cost. *See also* POLITICAL ENGINEERING.

> I've been getting some flak about ordering the production of the B1. How was I to know it was an airplane? I thought it was vitamins for the troops.
> RONALD REAGAN

B-Specials The armed special constabulary which over half a century earned a reputation for brutalising the Catholic minority in NORTHERN IRELAND. It was formed in 1920 almost entirely of Protestants, including many former members of the ULSTER VOLUNTEER FORCE and other PARAMILITARY bodies. The B-Specials acted as Ulster's Home Guard during WORLD WAR II and performed many non-controversial duties. But with the upsurge of CIVIL RIGHTS activity in 1968 many of the B-Specials, and elements of the Royal Ulster Constabulary (*see* RUC), took the law into their own hands and attacked first the largely peaceful civil rights demonstrators (*see* BURNTOLLET) and then Catholic areas of Belfast. The outcry caused by their activities led the UK government to order their disbandment in 1970 following the highly critical Hunt report on the policing of Ulster.

> Pubescent youths, old men and thugs.
> BRIAN WESLEY, *Sheffield Morning Telegraph.*

Baader-Meinhof gang The popular name for the RED ARMY FACTION, first and most notorious of the urban GUERRILLA groups that plagued West Germany from 1968–69. Founded by Andreas Baader (1943–77), his lover Ulrike Meinhof (1934–76), Horst Mahler and Gudrun Esslin, and consisting mainly of radicalised middle-class former students, it turned to violence against organs of NATO and the West German state, which it termed the 'STRAWBERRY REICH', following the attempted assassination of the leftish former student leader Rudi Dutschke. Its most spectacular coup was the rescue of Baader from prison in Berlin on 14 May 1970. Meinhof was arrested in Hannover in 1972 and hanged herself in prison; in revenge, the gang murdered Attorney-General Siegfried Bruback. Meinhof was described in her funeral eulogy as 'the most significant woman in German politics since Rosa Luxemburg'. Baader too committed suicide after the failure of the Mogadishu aircraft hijack in October 1977, a joint operation with Palestinian extremists which had been designed to free him. Gang members who had kidnapped Hans-Martin Schleyer, head of Daimler-Benz, killed him as a reprisal; after this the gang went into sharp decline, with most of its members dead or in prison and the young eschewing revolution. By the late 1980s it was a spent force.

> Don't argue – destroy.
>
> Slogan of the Red Army Faction

Baath Party (Arab renaissance) The militant party, founded in Damascus in 1943 by Michel Aflaq, which advocates the formation of a single Arab socialist nation. It took power in Syria as 'the leading party in State and society' in 1963, then became the base of Saddam Hussein's grip on power (*see* BUTCHER OF BAGHDAD) – with the Syrian and Iraqi governments becoming mortal enemies until the closing months of Saddam's regime.

deBaathification The process of ridding and excluding from Iraqi public life former henchmen of Saddam Hussein, as carried out from the spring of 2003 by the US/British interim ADMINISTRATION. *Compare* DENAZIFICATION.

back. back me or sack me The definitive challenge by a leader to a rebellious party (*compare* PUT UP OR SHUT UP). In 1977 James CALLAGHAN (*see* SUNNY JIM) told Britain's Labour Party conference: 'Either back us or sack us.'

back to basics The phrase with which John MAJOR tried to relaunch his government at the 1993 CONSERVATIVE PARTY conference, but which backfired. He aimed in his speech to identify the party with traditional values, but right-wing ministers used the event to launch what was seen as a campaign to deprive single mothers of welfare benefits. It also coincided with a wave of 'SLEAZE' allegations, starting with press stories that Steve Norris, a Transport Minister, had been involved with five women as his marriage broke down. Norris kept his job, but early in 1994 Tim Yeo resigned as an Environment Minister when it was revealed he had fathered a child out of wedlock, and the Earl of Caithness (another Transport Minister) quit after his wife shot herself over his relations with other women. More resignations followed over sexual and financial impropriety (*see* CASH FOR QUESTIONS), and Major's government took a serious blow to its credibility. The icing on the cake came in 2002 when it was revealed that Major himself had had a four-year affair with Edwina Currie (*see* CRUELLA DE VILLE) before entering Downing Street.

backbencher A member of a legislature who (at WESTMINSTER) does not hold a Ministerial post or OPPOSITION portfolio or (in the US CONGRESS) is not a party office-holder, committee chairman or RANKING MEMBER. The back benches in the HOUSE OF COMMONS lie below or behind the TREASURY BENCH or the Opposition front bench.

background The basis on which information is given to journalists by political SOURCES, to explain the full picture rather than for direct use, and certainly not for attribution. A briefing conducted on these terms is a **backgrounder**. The most sensitive such information is said to be given on **deep background**. *Compare* LOBBY TERMS.

backing winners The keynote of an INTERVENTIONIST policy in which an agency of the state invests in or directs sectors of industry that it believes can thrive with government support.

backlash A bitter, often violent, reaction by a community or ethnic group against a perceived threat. The word was first used in the late 1950s of action by whites in the southern US and major cities against increased black assertiveness and visibility; it also applies to community pressure for VIGILANTE action against rising crime.

backstabber An 'ally' capable of betrayal. The term dates back at least to this 1906 quote from the *Westminster Gazette*:

> I will tell you my idea of a false friend and backstabber – to sweat the workman for a personal profit and fawn on him for political profit, to promise old-age pensions for votes and having got the votes, to refuse them.

Former WHITE HOUSE CHIEF OF STAFF Donald Regan told Congressmen investigating the IRAN-CONTRA AFFAIR that he was not so worried about 'spears in the breast' from them as 'knives in the back' from ex-colleagues.

backwoodsman A minor political figure with reactionary views, specifically a PEER who seldom attends the HOUSE OF LORDS but will always oppose change if persuaded to travel up to vote. Originally, in America, a backwoodsman was an inhabitant of remote, impenetrable country.

bad for Britain, bad for Europe and bad for the whole free world Harold MACMILLAN's view of DE GAULLE's NON! in January 1963 to his application for Britain to join the COMMON MARKET. In 1950 MACMILLAN had said that when Labour rejected the SCHUMAN PLAN:

> This has been a black week for Britain; for the Empire; for Europe; and for the peace of the world.

Bad Godesberg declaration The statement in which West Germany's SPD finally broke with MARXISM and embraced the MARKET ECONOMY, aiming to end decades of opposition by capturing the middle ground including liberal Catholic voters. The party congress at Bad Godesberg, just outside Bonn, that endorsed it in 1959 paved the way for power, Willy Brandt becoming Chancellor ten years later.

Bad Godesberg meeting The talks between HITLER and Neville CHAMBERLAIN at the resort's Hotel Dreesen on 22–23 September 1938 that paved the way for the MUNICH AGREEMENT. Hitler rejected an Anglo-French plan for Czech concessions on the SUDETEN question; Chamberlain flew home after FOREIGN SECRETARY Halifax warned him opinion was hardening against APPEASEMENT.

badge messenger At WESTMINSTER, one of the uniformed messengers, mostly male and late middle-aged, who preside over the galleries of the HOUSE OF COMMONS and tour the building to locate MPs and give them messages. They take their name from the gilt badges that hang from their necks.

bag and baggage The key phrase of GLADSTONE's attack on Turkey's BULGARIAN ATROCITIES. On 5 May 1877 he told the HOUSE OF COMMONS:

> Let the Turks now carry off their abuses in the only possible manner, namely by carrying off themselves. Their Zaptiehs and their Mindirs, their Bimbishis and their Yuzbachis, their Kaimakams and their Pashas, one and all, bag and baggage, shall, I hope, clear out from the province they have desolated and profaned.

The sentiments were not original. In 1829 Palmerston had written:

> I confess that I should not be sorry some day to see the Turk kicked out of Europe and compelled to go and sit cup-legged, smoke his pipe, chew his opium and cut off heads on the Asiatic side of the Bosphorus.

baggage The ideological impedimenta of belonging to a party or grouping that prevent an individual rejecting outdated or unpopular ideas and embracing new ones.

Baghdad. Baghdad bombing The single greatest atrocity against UNITED NATIONS personnel, the destruction by a suicide truck bomber on 19 August 2003 of the UN's headquarters in the Iraqi capital, with the loss of 23 lives including its special envoy Sergio Vieira de Mello. The attack, presumed to be the work of BAATH PARTY fanatics, impeded the task of restoring normality in Iraq, already hampered by attacks on US troops and oil installations; although it caused outrage at the UN, it did not reduce the resolve of France and other opponents of the war not to get involved.

Baghdad bounce The upsurge in stock market prices and economic activity, and in the political fortunes of Tony BLAIR's Labour government, that were predicted to follow the successful US/British military campaign to overthrow Saddam Hussein in March/April 2003. Some economic upturn followed, but the strains on the LABOUR PARTY caused by Blair's resort to force and the continuing violence fed through to heavy losses in local and Scottish elections the following month, and lost it a seat to the LIBERAL DEMOCRATS in the 2005 general election.

Baghdad Pact A treaty for military and economic co-operation signed by Iraq and Turkey in 1955 and later joined by Iraq, Pakistan and Britain to create a front against Soviet southward ambitions. Its initial purpose was frustrated by the refusal of America (out of deference to pro-Israel sentiment) and Egypt (before SUEZ) to join. In 1959 Iraq withdrew, America became an associate member and the signatory states became **CENTO** (Central Treaty Organisation). By the fall of the Shah of Iran in 1979 the pact was dormant; CENTO was subsequently dissolved.

Butcher of Baghdad The nickname widely applied in the West to Saddam Hussein (1937–), the BAATHIST President of Iraq from 1979 until his overthrow by US and British forces in April 2003. It was bestowed after his invasion of Kuwait in 1990, in respect of his record of atrocities against his own people. A party member since 1957 and a participant as an army officer in the revolution of 1968, Saddam consolidated his power with a series of ruthless PURGES, chemical warfare against rebellious Kurds and civilians in Northern Iraq and systematic brutality against the Shi'ites and Marsh Arabs of the South. Saddam also instigated the IRAN-IRAQ WAR of 1980–88, in which 1.5 million people died; at this stage he was abetted by the West, even shaking hands with Donald Rumsfeld who as US Defense

Secretary would preside over his removal. The belief that he was a bulwark against the Islamic fundamentalism of the AYATOLLAHS died hard in WASHINGTON and in London, where the SUPERGUN and MATRIX-CHURCHILL affairs seriously embarrassed the Conservative government when Kuwait was invaded. By 2003, when America and Britain broke ranks in a bid to prevent Saddam developing WEAPONS OF MASS DESTRUCTION in defiance of the UNITED NATIONS, all such illusions had gone. Saddam deployed Baath Party activists to compel Iraqis to resist the invaders at gunpoint, but vanished early in the conflict leaving COMICAL ALI to rally the nation and predict victory. It was 14 December 2003, after several months of Baathist GUERRILLA action against coalition troops, before he was captured by the Americans, in a hole under farm buildings near his home town of Tikrit. He was arraigned the following June, still insisting he was President of Iraq and claiming President BUSH to be the true criminal.

MP for Baghdad Central The nickname applied to George Galloway (1954–), Labour MP for Glasgow Kelvin, from 1987 to 2005, and subsequent leader of RESPECT, who embraced Arab and Palestinian causes. He was the most outspoken opponent of action to disarm or overthow Saddam Hussein. Galloway praised Saddam as 'indefatigable' when he met him in Baghdad, and denounced Tony BLAIR and George W. Bush as 'wolves' for seeking to overthrow him. In the wake of the conflict, a *Daily Telegraph* reporter found files in Iraq's ruined Foreign Ministry purporting to show that the Iraqis had been paying Galloway at least £375,000 a year from the UN-supervised OIL FOR FOOD programme; Galloway sued for libel and won. In the 2005 general election he stood for Respect against the Blairite Oona King in the strongly Labour but also heavily Muslim seat of Bethnal Green & Bow, and won. (*See* MR BLAIR, THIS IS FOR IRAQ.) Within a month he had also defended himself in flamboyant style before Congressional critics in Washington (*see* LION OF THE BRITISH PARLIAMENT).

bagman A person who carries and distributes cash for bribes and payoffs on behalf of a politician in higher places. The word has – understandably – been ruled libellous by courts in the United States.

Bailie Vass A nickname for SIR ALEC Douglas-Home coined by PRIVATE EYE after the Aberdeen *Evening Express* transposed picture captions of the then Prime Minister and a so-named local official. During the 1964 election the magazine issued car stickers reading:

> Up your ass with Bailie Vass!

Baird nomination The first embarrassment of the CLINTON ADMINISTRATION: the failure of the President's nominee as ATTORNEY-GENERAL, Zoe Baird, to secure CONFIRMATION by the SENATE. On the eve of Clinton's INAUGURATION on 20 January 1993, it emerged that Ms Baird, a law partner of SECRETARY OF STATE Warren Christopher, had hired an ILLEGAL Peruvian immigrant couple to drive and look after her children. Although Ms Baird and her husband had paid $12,000 in back taxes and a $2,900 penalty to the Immigration and Naturalisation Service, Senate critics argued that no one could head the Justice Department who had been caught in such an illegality. To make matters worse, Clinton's second nominee, Judge Kimba Wood, turned out to have used a Trinidadian illegal as a babysitter; her nomination too was withdrawn.

Baker. Bobby Baker affair Baker (1928–) was a notorious WASHINGTON INFLUENCE PEDDLER whom even President Johnson, who told him: 'You're like a son to me', could not save from jail. He arrived with $60 in his pocket from Pickens, South Carolina, aged just 14 to be a Congressional PAGE, and two decades later was making $300,000 a year on a salary of $19,600 as secretary to the SENATE MAJORITY LEADER. Indicted in 1966 for pocketing $80,000 of a $100,000 'campaign contribution' he had solicited, he was convicted of fraud, larceny and tax evasion and sentenced to one to three years. Paroled in 1972, Baker returned to Washington to manage his assets. When sentenced, Baker said:

> Like my bosses and sponsors in the Senate, I was ambitious and eager to feather my personal nest.

But after his release he insisted:

> I made mistakes, and I'm going to admit those mistakes. But I was put in jail for something that didn't happen. If having girlfriends and drinking whisky is immoral, then I'm guilty. But nobody was buying Bobby Baker.

Baker amendments The amendments to the PANAMA CANAL TREATIES required by SENATE MINORITY LEADER Howard Baker as the price for his support. One allowed US military intervention in Panama, the other secured 20 extra US fighter planes for Israel and a Saudi promise not to use its American-built planes against Israel.

Baker v Carr A landmark decision of the US SUPREME COURT, which held in 1962 that town-dwellers in Tennessee were being denied 'equal protection of the laws' through the rurally-dominated state legislature's failure to REAPPORTION itself.

Bakke case The 1978 milestone case in which the US SUPREME COURT set limits to the use of AFFIRMATIVE ACTION. Allan Bakke sued the University of California for denying him a graduate school place when ethnic minority candidates with inferior records were being admitted, and won.

balance. balance of payments The difference between the value of a country's imports and exports, with allowance made for 'invisible earnings' such as insurance or tourism. Deficits in Britain's balance of payments were the cause of repeated STERLING crises during the late 1960s, but far larger deficits are now accepted as a matter of course.

balance of power (1) The theory that war is less likely when potential combatants, or opposing alliances, are of equal strength. The doctrine was first applied to 18th-century Europe, its earliest recorded use being by WALPOLE in the Commons on 13 February 1741. It was responsible for the system of alliances which kept the powers of Europe in rough equilibrium except when disrupted by Napoleon, the Kaiser and Hitler, and was both the reason for the COLD WAR and the reason why it did not lead to nuclear conflict. It always had its critics, John Bright in the mid-19th century denouncing its requirement for vast armies as 'a gigantic system of outdoor relief for the aristocracy', and Clement ATTLEE saying in the 1930s:

> We ought to give up altogether the old traditional doctrine of the Balance of Power – that balance of armed strength we used to support for so many years. That is obsolete now. The way to get peace is not through the Balance of Power but through the LEAGUE OF NATIONS.

Yet President Nixon was stating more than the obvious when he said in 1972:

> The only alternative to a balance of power is an imbalance of power.

(2) The balance between the parties or blocs in any elected body. If two parties are of equal strength and there is one unaligned member, that member holds the balance of power.

balance of terror A nuclear-age variant of the doctrine of the balance of power, based simply upon the assumption that the consequences of nuclear war are too horrifying for either side to risk starting one. Implicit in the phrase was the implication that they just might.

balanced budget The aim of successive US administrations, seldom likely since the GREAT SOCIETY and the VIETNAM WAR pushed Federal spending ahead of resources. FDR promised a balanced budget in 1932 but let spending rip under the NEW DEAL; Ronald REAGAN ridiculed Jimmy CARTER for failing to balance the budget, then presided over a rocketing deficit. In 1992 George BUSH backed a **Balanced Budget Amendment** to the Constitution, but the House of Representatives narrowly rejected it. The idea resurfaced in the CONTRACT WITH AMERICA, but while the Clinton administration achieved a balanced budget in four years out of eight, the budget slipped back into deficit under George W. BUSH.

> The budget should be balanced, the treasury should be refilled, public debt should be reduced, the arrogance of officialdom should be tempered and controlled, assistance to foreign lands should be curtailed lest Rome become bankrupt, the mobs should be forced to work and not depend on government for subsistence.
> CICERO (*attr.*)

Baldwin, Stanley 1st Earl Baldwin of Bewdley (1867–1947). One of 20th-century Britain's most durable leaders, leader of the Conservative Party from 1923 to 1937 and three times Prime Minister (May–December 1923, 1924–29, 1935–37). He started his Ministerial career in LLOYD GEORGE's coalition government, which he was instrumental in terminating, was crucial in advising George V to send for RAMSAY MACDonald after his own defeat at the close of 1923, and served for four years in MacDonald's NATIONAL GOVERNMENT which he came to dominate.

His priorities were at first sight Victorian; he once recalled: 'When the call came to me to form a government, one of my first thoughts was that it should be a government of which Harrow (school) should not be ashamed.' He was consistently underrated; Lord Curzon, who had assumed he and not Baldwin would succeed BONAR LAW, dismissed him as 'a man of no experience, and of the utmost insignificance'. But he was a skilled political operator, saying: 'I would rather be an opportunist and float than go to the bottom with my principles around my neck'. Baldwin's strength was in doggedness rather than flair, Lord Beaverbrook, his greatest critic, declaring: 'His successive attempts to find a policy remind me of the chorus in a third-rate revue. His evasions appear in different scenes and in new dresses, and every time they dance with renewed and despairing vigour. But it is the same old gig.'

CHURCHILL scorned his final government as 'decided only to be undecided, resolved to be irresolute, adamant for drift, solid for fluidity, all-powerful to be impotent'. Of his speaking style, Aneurin BEVAN commented: 'Murmurs of admiration break out as this second-rate orator trails his tawdry wisps of mist over the Parliamentary scene.' But Harold MACMILLAN felt that 'Baldwin was never quite sure that anybody was right, especially himself', and on Baldwin's retirement CHURCHILL observed: 'The candle in that great turnip has gone out.'

Baldwin's final premiership was dominated by his disavowal of the APPEASEMENT-minded HOARE-LAVAL PACT, a belated REARMAMENT programme and his handling of the 1936 ABDICATION crisis, of which he remarked:

> When I was a little boy in Worcestershire reading history books, I never thought that I should have to interfere between a King and his mistress.

But interfere he did, preventing Edward VIII broadcasting an appeal for public support and suppressing evidence that the DOMINIONS were not totally opposed to his marrying Mrs Simpson. Lord Home, an MP at the time, asserted: 'When the history of the century is written Baldwin will top the list in domestic achievement – and his handling of the Abdication crisis will tip the balance, for he saved our Constitutional monarchy.'

Baldwin had an acute nose for avoiding trouble. He once observed:

> The Roman Catholic Church, the Brigade of Guards and the miners – you should never rub your nose up against any of them.

This was both a strength and a weakness; Churchill, and much of public opinion, blamed him for Britain's lack of preparedness for WORLD WAR II (*see* YEARS THAT THE LOCUSTS HAVE EATEN) – though Baldwin did ensure that Britain had a SOVEREIGN minded to resist the NAZIS – and confided when asked to contribute to an 80th birthday gift for Baldwin: 'It would have been better had he never lived.' The Beaverbrook press accused him of refusing to give up his house's iron gates for the war effort, and when the ageing Baldwin heard the crowd jeer him, he asked: 'Why do they hate me so?'

Balfour declaration The promise of a national home for the Jews in Palestine, made in 1917 by the former British Conservative Prime Minister Arthur Balfour (1848–1930), which has dictated the subsequent history of the Middle East. Made in a letter to the ZIONIST leader Lionel Walter (2nd Baron) Rothschild (1868–1937), it was conditional on the rights of existing non-Jewish residents being maintained and the rights of Jewish citizens in other countries also being respected. Dean Inge (1860–1954) commented, probably unfairly,

> When he launched his scheme for peopling Palestine with Jewish immigrants, I am credibly informed that he did not know there were any Arabs in the country.

The declaration was repudiated by the British government in 1939, but Jewish immigration to that point and the flight from Europe during and after the HOLOCAUST turned it into reality. (The term is also used for the statement made at the 1926 Imperial conference on the nature of the emerging COMMONWEALTH – *see* STATUTE OF WESTMINSTER.) Balfour made the declaration of a Jewish state when FOREIGN SECRETARY in LLOYD GEORGE's COALITION.

He had been Prime Minister from 1902 until his defeat in 1905 after splitting the Tory Party on the TARIFF issue, resigning the leadership in 1911 ostensibly on health grounds but in fact because of growing internal criticism. Balfour owed his early advancement to being a nephew of Lord SALISBURY, but when he took office, according to Roy JENKINS, 'he amazed the HOUSE OF COMMONS by the ruthlessness of his policy and the tenacity of his debating. His soubriquet changed from "Pretty Fanny" to "Bloody Balfour"'. GLADSTONE termed him 'Artful Arthur', but he was also an infuriating dilettante; he once opined: 'Nothing matters very much, and very few things matter at all'. Lloyd George described his impact as 'no more than a whiff of scent on a lady's pocket handkerchief'; to J. M. KEYNES, Balfour was 'the most extraordinary *objet d'art* our society has ever produced'. CHURCHILL described him as 'a powerful, graceful cat walking delicately and unsoiled across a rather muddy street'.

Balfour Must Go The watchword of a series of whispering campaigns aimed at

Balfour's removal from the Tory leadership. First used in 1911 by Leo Maxse in the *National Review*, its origin was 'the Saloon Must Go', adopted in 1895 as slogan of America's PROHIBITIONist Anti-Saloon League. Suitably modified, it was used in 1930 against BALDWIN by the PRESS BARONS Beaverbrook and Rothermere; in each case the abbreviation to **B.M.G.** was also used. In the early 1960s **Marples Must Go**, directed against Ernest Marples, then Minister of Transport, was daubed on Britain's first motorway bridges. In a few places it can still be seen.

Mr Balfour's poodle LLOYD GEORGE's dismissive term for the HOUSE OF LORDS, responding in the COMMONS on 26 June 1907 to a claim that the Upper House was acting as the 'watchdog of the nation' in rejecting the ASQUITH government's programme. L.G. said:

> No mastiff, it is the Rt Honourable Gentleman's poodle, it fetches and carries for him, barks and bites anybody he sets it on to.

Bali bombing The car-bombing in the previously idyllic resort of Kuta on 12 October 2002 which sparked a firestorm that killed 202 people – including 88 Australians and 28 Britons – and left at least 250 more injured. The bombing caused a national trauma in Australia, which had never been so badly affected by a terrorist incident. Together with two other blasts, one outside the US CONSULATE on the island, it was blamed by Western governments on Indonesian supporters of AL QAEDA against whom the Jakarta government undertook a belated crackdown. In August 2003 Amrozi Bin Nurhasyim was sentenced to death for his part in the bombing; his gleeful reaction at being awarded martyrdom enraged relatives of the victims.

Balkanisation The fragmentation of a large and relatively stable political unit into ill-assorted and feuding parts. The term derives from the warfare and instability that broke out in the Balkans – continuing to this day – as the decaying Ottoman Empire lost its grip.

ballot The paper used to cast one's VOTE in secret; the process of holding a vote conducted by this method, which generally replaced the SHOW OF HANDS during the 19th century; the right to cast such a vote. Also a process of drawing lots, as in the ballot for Parliamentary time for PRIVATE MEMBERS' BILLS at WESTMINSTER.

the ballot is stronger than the bullet Abraham LINCOLN's poignant declaration of faith in democracy in a speech on 18 May 1858. He also said:

> To give the victory to the right, no bloody bullets, but peaceful ballots only, are necessary.

give us the ballot The theme of one of Dr Martin Luther KING's definitive speeches, in WASHINGTON. He said:

> Give us the ballot, and we will no longer have to worry the Federal government about our basic rights.

ballot box The box, normally made of metal but now increasingly of plastic, in which voting papers are cast, and kept until they are counted; hence the symbol of democracy.

> The ballot box is a most inadequate mechanism of change. SIMONE DE BEAUVOIR

Armalite and ballot box *See* ARMALITE.

ballot-rigging A corrupt practice that occasionally afflicts trade unions, generally when two rival ideological factions are struggling for control. Notorious examples include the communist ballot-rigging within Britain's Electrical Trades Union, exposed in the late 1950s, and in Australia's Federal Iron Workers' Association a decade earlier. In more recent, but unproven, cases staff at a union headquarters were said to be suffering a 'severe outbreak of writer's cramp' just as the ballot closed.

absentee ballot A system under which VOTERS unable to reach the POLLS may vote by post or by PROXY. During America's CIVIL WAR eleven states enabled soldiers in the Union army to vote by mail; the right was first extended to citizens in Vermont in 1896.

Australian ballot An American name for the secret ballot, which 33 states had adopted by 1892. In the UK the secret ballot was introduced by the **Ballot Act**, 1872.

butterfly ballot A ballot paper with boxes to be punched out or marked which are positioned on either side of a central spine. Such ballots when used in PALM BEACH COUNTY, Florida, during the 2000 Presidential ELECTION were claimed to have misled large numbers of Democratic voters into punching the box for the far-right candidate Pat Buchanan instead of Al GORE, whose box was opposite. Confusion of this kind was reckoned by the Democrats to have cost them the state and the election.

down the ballot Someone standing for a relatively minor post in American ELECTIONS where a complete set of office-holders is being chosen and all appear on the same ballot paper in order of importance.

on the ballot Another way of describing a candidate for office; it is an abbreviation of 'on the ballot paper'.

on the —th ballot The point at which a Presidential candidate is finally nominated at a party CONVENTION when no obvious FRONT-RUNNER has emerged in the PRIMARIES.

provisional ballot In some American states, a ballot that a person is permitted to cast when there is doubt over their eligibility to vote or when they have moved house, which will be added to the candidates' tallies later if that eligibility is proven. The casting of 175,000 provisional ballots in Ohio, more than the gap between the candidates of 140,000 but which would have taken at least ten days to verify, left the outcome of the 2004 Presidential ELECTION unresolved for some hours until John KERRY's decision to CONCEDE rather than repeat the exhaustive challenges seen in Florida four years before.

Balmoral The family home in Scotland of the British SOVEREIGN, purchased by Prince Albert for Queen Victoria in 1848. For most of the decade after his death she lived in seclusion in the castle, remotely situated at the top of Deeside, until DISRAELI tempted her back into public life. Every September, the Prime Minister travels to Balmoral to spend a few days with the Royal family.

> Siberia.
>
> Sir HENRY CAMPBELL-BANNERMAN

baloney A favourite American term for nonsense or rubbish, common from the 1920s and popularised by Al Smith, Governor of New York, when he said in a 1936 campaign speech: 'No matter how you slice it, it's still baloney'. Its origin is commonly assumed to be the Bologna sausage – hence the slicing – but this is not proven. On 9 February 1943 Rep. Clare Boothe Luce (1903–87) in her MAIDEN SPEECH, coined the world **globaloney** to describe the internationalist post-war theories of Vice President Henry Wallace.

Bambi and Thumper The nicknames applied to Tony BLAIR and John Prescott (*see* TWO JAGS) during the Labour leadership contest of 1994, when the two men fought each other yet were regarded as an eventual DREAM TICKET. The names came from Walt Disney's *Snow White*, Bambi being the delicate deer and Thumper the combative rabbit. The nicknames were bestowed by Labour's future Agriculture Minister Nick Brown, and first used in print by Jon Craig of the *Daily Express*. Prescott revelled in his name, having a 'Thumper' rabbit on his desk; Blair did not.

Bamboo Curtain The veil of secrecy and suspicion drawn between communist China and its SATELLITE COUNTRIES and the non-communist nations of both the West and the Far East. The term is analogous to the IRON CURTAIN, though the bamboo version was more ideological and cultural than military.

ban. Ban the Bomb! The definitive slogan of CND and other movements opposed to NUCLEAR WEAPONS and NUCLEAR WAR. It originated in the early 1950s with the communist-front WORLD PEACE COUNCIL, but was taken up by CND at the first ALDERMASTON MARCH.

banning order The restriction on political activity imposed on both black and white dissidents in South Africa under the Internal Security Act of 1977. 'Banned' people were prevented from appearing in public or expressing political opinions, and in some cases were required to live in remote areas.

banana. banana republic A derisive term for a poverty-stricken country without a stable civilian government, run by a corrupt dictatorial clique and subservient to outside (e.g. US) commercial interests; it first applied to certain states in Latin America but is now used to describe any country whose political system is a laughing-stock. It had its origin in Minor Keith's United Fruit Company, which in the 1870s built railroads in Costa Rica and grew bananas to generate traffic for them, developing a stranglehold on much of Central America. In 1954 President EISENHOWER permitted the CIA to overthrow Guatemala's government to protect United Fruit's operations.

> Louisiana is a banana republic which should declare bankruptcy, secede from the Union and apply for foreign aid.
>
> Rep. KEVIN REILLY (1928–)

In his MAIDEN SPEECH in the HOUSE OF COMMONS in 1992 Michael Fabricant, Conservative MP for Mid-Staffordshire, noted that his constituency was shaped like a banana – going on to call it his banana republic.

banana skin An unnoticed fact or political issue which suddenly trips up a politician or government. The term became commonplace in early 1980s Britain when Margaret THATCHER's government hit a series of unforeseen difficulties; Deputy Prime Minister WILLIE Whitelaw was deputed to 'watch out for banana skins'.

banana wars The trade sanctions imposed by the US during the 1990s, with the EU threatening to retaliate, as America strove to end European states' reliance for banana imports on their former colonies, notably in West Africa and the Caribbean, rather than from Central American plantations, many of them producing for America's Chiquita brand. US sanctions had Scottish cashmere textiles as a prime target. The dispute was settled in April 1999 after the WTO had ruled in favour of the US.

Bandung Conference The conference of 29 African and Asian states in 1955 at Bandung in West Java, Indonesia at which the policy of NON-ALIGNMENT was agreed. The conference took a strongly ANTI-COLONIALIST line.

bandwagon effect The process by which a party or movement attracts support by virtue of its growing success or popularity; at the point of BREAKTHROUGH, well-known people not previously identified with the movement will **jump on the bandwagon** in order to boost their own prospects or prestige. The bandwagon is the vehicle which pulls or conveys the band in a circus procession.

bank. bank rate *See* MINIMUM LENDING RATE.

bankers' ramp The conspiracy theory offered by LABOUR PARTY loyalists to explain the collapse of Ramsey MACDONALD's second government in 1931 (*see* GREAT BETRAYAL). Britain's banks were supposed to have deliberately pushed the economy into crisis to split the party and bring about the formation of the NATIONAL GOVERNMENT. That September, Hugh Dalton (1887–1962) told a meeting at Bishop Auckland:

> The Labour Party . . . would not stand idly by and see our social services butchered to make a bankers' holiday.

Bantustan A manufactured name for a manufactured entity: South Africa's black 'Homelands' set up to deny the majority full rights in white-controlled urban areas by asserting that their allegiance lay somewhere else. It was derived by the architects of APARTHEID from *Bantu*, one of the peoples in question, and *-stan*, a state (as in Hindustan, Pakistan). The first to be created was Transkei in 1973; it received full 'independence' in 1976.

Bar Homa. The Hebrew name for Jebel Abu Ghneim, the hill abutting Arab East Jerusalem where the Israeli Prime Minister Benjamin Netanyahu promoted a Jewish settlement in early 1997, with deleterious effects for the PEACE PROCESS.

Bar of the House At WESTMINSTER, the point at the far end of the CHAMBER of the HOUSE OF COMMONS from the CHAIR, to which those alleged to have committed CONTEMPT of the House are summoned. A new member must wait at the Bar of the House until summoned to take the OATH. The Bar comprises two rods which can be drawn across from the end of benches opposite the Chair to form a boundary.

> I knew that if I ever lost 500 men without the clearest necessity, I should be brought upon my knees to the bar of the House of Commons.
>
> The DUKE OF WELLINGTON

In the US CAPITOL, the bar is a similar point at the rear of the HOUSE OF REPRESENTATIVES where, in bygone days, members had to present themselves during a QUORUM CALL; they now report direct to the Clerk.

Barber boom The period of apparent runaway prosperity in Britain in 1972–73 under Edward HEATH, whose CHANCELLOR OF THE EXCHEQUER Anthony (later Lord) Barber (1920–) was given credit at the time. He received corresponding blame when the economy went abruptly into reverse as INFLATION took hold; Enoch POWELL blamed Barber for failing to control the MONEY SUPPLY.

Barlow memorial award. The highly unofficial award made each spring in the 1980s by denizens of ANNIE'S BAR in the PALACE OF WESTMINSTER to the teller of the most obscene and tasteless story heard there. It commemorated Sir Frank Barlow (d. 1979), a noted raconteur who worked for Labour leaders from ATTLEE to CALLAGHAN, eventually as secretary of the Parliamentary party. Winners included police officers from the MEMBERS' LOBBY, a senior correspondent from the *Times* and several Conservative MPs. The shortest winner, entered by PC Ken Thomas in 1982, was:

> Q: Why do you bind sellotape round a hamster?
> A: So it doesn't split when you fuck it.

In these more sensitive times, the Barlow award has been superseded by a competition for the most tasteless tie of the year.

Barnett Formula The mathematical formula that determines change in the level of public spending in Scotland, Wales and Northern Ireland by comparison with England. It was devised in 1978 as a temporary fix by Joel (later Lord) Barnett (1923–), Chief Secretary to the TREASURY in James CALLAGHAN's Labour government, but has survived despite efforts by its critics, particular in the North-East of England, to replace it with something that would divert more cash to the areas they represent. Updated each year, the formula determines how much more each devolved administration should spend by comparing its population with that of England; Scotland generally received just over 10% of extra spending than in England, Wales just under 6% and Northern Ireland over 3%.

barnstorming Highly energetic campaigning by a politician, combining a large amount of travel with a crowded programme of rousing speeches. The term has its origin in the travelling theatre, which set up stage in farmers' barns.

Baron (1) In Britain, the formal title of the lowest degree of hereditary LORD and of all male life PEERS. When the veteran Labour MP Bill Blyton told his wife he had been elevated to the Lords and was 'Baron Blyton now', she replied: 'Thou's been barren these forty years!' (2) In the US CONGRESS, the barons were the conservative Democrats who until the early 1970s chaired every committee under the SENIORITY rule, and thus wielded immense power.

barracking Systematic chanting from sections of the audience at a meeting, or from the opposing side of a legislature, to unsettle or shout down the person who is attempting to speak.

barricades A traditional feature of popular uprisings, particularly in Paris, with obstacles dragged into the street to form a barrier against any attempt by riot police or troops to move in and 'restore order'. In Paris the slogan *Aux Barricades!* (To the barricades!) has marked the start of numerous challenges either to an occupying force (notably the Germans in 1944) or to the authority of the state.

Barry, Kevin The 18-year-old Dublin medical student whose execution by the British on 1 November 1920 prompted a BACKLASH in support of Irish independence and gave rise to one of the Republic's most moving patriotic songs. Barry took part in an IRA raid for arms on a military convoy in Church Street in which six soldiers died. Captured at the scene, he was court-martialled and hanged at Mountjoy Prison. His sacrifice and execution aroused deep feeling, and scores of his fellow students immediately joined the IRA. In the HOUSE OF COMMONS the hanging was condemned by Labour's J. H. Thomas. The song written by Terrence Ward of the *Irish Press* to commemorate Barry's death has become part of Irish folklore, for committed Republicans and liberal patriots alike. Its first verse is:

> In Mountjoy jail one Sunday morning
> High upon the gallows tree,
> Kevin Barry gave his young life
> For the cause of liberty.

On 14 October 2001 Kevin Barry's remains were reinterred, receiving a state funeral.

Bartlet, Josiah *See* PRESIDENT BARTLET.

Base rate *See* MINIMUM LENDING RATE.

Basic Law The 'temporary' legal framework set by the BUNDESTAG on 23 May 1949 for the government of the German Federal Republic (WEST GERMANY) formed in the former American, British and French zones. It has survived to be the CONSTITUTION of the reunified German state. Drawing heavily on the lessons of suffering under the NAZIS, it guarantees human freedoms, sexual equality and the right of ASYLUM for any foreigner seeking it. Politically, it established a liberal but ADVERSARIAL democracy, with power-sharing between the centre and the LANDER. Amendments to the basic law may be made by a two-thirds vote of the Bundestag, but most of its fundamentals are ENTRENCHED.

bastards The epithet with which the increasingly frustrated John MAJOR, against his better judgement and to his belief in private, branded EUROSCEPTIC dissidents within his CABINET over dinner on 23 July 1993. Unfortunately for the Prime Minister, the other guests included Michael Brunson, political editor of Independent Television News, and his expression hit the headlines the following day. One of the 'bastards', John Redwood, would two years later stand against Major for the leadership.

In Australian politics the term is more freely and almost affectionately used. In 1974 Gough WHITLAM told a Labor CAUCUS meeting:

> I do not mind the Liberals, still less do I mind the Country Party, calling me a bastard. I am only doing my job if they do. But I hope you will not publicly call me a bastard, as some bastards in the caucus have.

Poor Bastards Bill The BILL introduced by the Democratic CONGRESSMAN Morris Udall in the early 1960s to ensure that the illegitimate children of civil servants qualified for benefits. President KENNEDY signed the Bill and the next weekend Udall, back in his Arizona district, was confronted by a member of the John BIRCH Society who asked him: 'You guys are throwing our money away in Africa, Europe and everywhere else. When are you going to do something for the poor bastards in this country?' Udall replied:

> I'm glad you asked that question. Why, just last week . . .

Bastille The notorious prison fortress in Paris, the storming of which by the mob on 14 July 1789 marked the start of the FRENCH REVOLUTION. Lafayette sent the key to the Bastille to George WASHINGTON, who received it as 'a token gained for liberty'. The freeing of prisoners was an anti-climax; the mob of over 5,000 found only seven: four forgers, two madmen and an Irish lord imprisoned for 30 years for debt. Yet **Bastille Day** became Republican France's great national holiday, and the occasion for an outpouring of patriotic fervour.

> How much the greatest event it is that ever happened in the world! and how much the best.
>
> CHARLES JAMES FOX (1749–1806)

Batasuna (Basque unity) Known initially as **Herri Batasuna**, the Basque separatist political party founded in 1978 which enjoyed considerable support despite (or because of) its closeness to the terrorist group ETA until outlawed by Spain's Supreme Court in March 2003. That summer the organisers of the Tour de France outraged the Spanish government by accepting sponsorship from the French arm of Batasuna.

baton round The name given by security forces in NORTHERN IRELAND to plastic bullets in the late 1970s, after the projectiles had killed a number of rioters and demonstrators. *See also* rubber BULLET.

baton round *See* BULLET.

battle. Battle of Margaret's Shoulder *see* WAR OF JENNIFER'S EAR.

battlebus The self-contained mobile election headquarters used by (Sir) David Steel (*see* BOY DAVID) (1938–), leader of Britain's LIBERAL PARTY, in the 1979 and subsequent General Elections. It included facilities for writing and duplicating speeches and press handouts, telephoning senior party figures, relaxation and servicing the travelling press, some of whom were aboard. The idea caught on with other party leaders when they took to the road to campaign.

battleground states The States where a US Presidential ELECTION is determined, because they hold the decisive votes in the ELECTORAL COLLEGE. Which States they are varies a little from election to election because the appeal of each TICKET differs, but the battleground generally includes the states of the industrial Midwest: Illinois, Michigan and Ohio.

Battling Bob The nickname won by Sen. Robert la Follette (1855–1925) of Wisconsin. A popular hero in the Midwest by the turn of the century, la Follette twice broke with the Republicans to offer a POPULIST alternative to the two established parties. In 1911 he formed the National Progressive Republican League, which formed the base for Theodore ROOSEVELT's BULL MOOSE candidacy the following year. Again, in 1924, he led his followers out of the Republican Party to run for the Presidency as a PROGRESSIVE. He won 5 million votes but carried only his home state, and died the following year.

Bay Street Boys The clique of white merchants who ran the Bahamas like a private club until 1967, when Lynden Pindling and his Progressive Liberal Party broke their power. Sir Lynden, as he became, ruled for 25 years, becoming unaccountably rich as allegations spread of corruption and collusion with drug traffickers. In 1992 he in turn was ousted by Hubert Ingraham's Free National Movement.

Be it enacted . . . The formal statement that a BILL has been passed into law, which appears immediately after the statement of the measure's purpose. An ACT of the US CONGRESS carries the rubric: 'Be it enacted by the SENATE and HOUSE OF REPRESENTATIVES of the United States of America in Congress assembled'; the traditional wording for UK laws, from which it stems, is: 'Be it enacted by the Queen/King's most excellent Majesty, by and with the ADVICE AND CONSENT of the LORDS Spiritual and Temporal, and COMMONS, in this present Parliament assembled, and by the authority of the same . . .'

beam-splitter The almost invisible TELEPROMPTER which enables a politician to pick up the next phrase of a speech, giving an impression of spontaneity and control when in fact the occasion has been carefully rehearsed. Margaret THATCHER and Ronald REAGAN were the first masters of this type of autocue.

bean soup An institution of the HOUSE restaurant in the US CAPITOL for over a century. It was first promoted by Fred T. Dubois, Senator for Idaho from 1891–97 and 1901–07, who in 1900 held a contest for a standardised US bean soup recipe. It has been on the menu every day since 1904 when Speaker Joseph Cannon (*see* FOUL-MOUTHED JOE) found none was on offer. The waiter told him the chef had thought the weather too clammy to serve it, but Cannon told him: 'Hell and thunderation! I had my mouth set for bean soup. Get me the chef.' Cannon castigated the chef, then told him: 'From now on, hot or cold, rain, snow or shine, I want bean soup on the menu every day.' And so it has been, to the delight of many.

Bear, the To Westerners, the menacing image conjured up by a strong Russia, in Tsarist times, under communism and even at times under the democracy that has succeeded it. The image has been in use, especially by cartoonists, since at least the early 19th century.

beard and sandals The deprecatory nickname for the environmentalist and pacifist fringe of Britain's LIBERAL PARTY, which gained a reputation for turning up in strength at the annual party assembly and embarrassing the leadership with its whimsical line. In 1986 this faction was blamed for an anti-NUCLEAR motion that wrecked the joint defence policy of the SDP/Liberal ALLIANCE and was widely blamed by both for the parties' poor showing in the following year's election and the subsequent break-up of the Alliance. Many of this tendency moved to the GREEN PARTY, giving it a firmly idealistic cast but rendering it unelectable in the process. At the Greens' 1991 conference the chairman called the 'the man with the beard in the back row' to speak, and several dozen people came forward.

beast. Beast of Baghdad *See* BAGHDAD.

Beast of Bolsover The nickname revelled in over three decades at WESTMINSTER by **Dennis Skinner** (1932–), the consistently left-wing MP for Bolsover in Derbyshire. Skinner, a miner for 21 years who described himself in *Who's Who* as coming from 'good working-class stock', entered Parliament in 1970 and quickly became known for his fiery pursuit of class warfare and his support for the rebel CLAY CROSS COUNCILLORS, several of whom were his relatives. Skinner's outspokenness and his refusal to compromise led to numerous clashes with the SPEAKER and demands for him to leave the CHAMBER. His sustained interruption of the SDP leaders Roy JENKINS and Dr David OWEN, whom he regarded as traitors to Labour, did much to limit their effectiveness in the COMMONS. A committed Parliamentarian and a forceful member of Labour's National Executive, Skinner earned respect among Tories for his uncorruptibility and his refusal to be diverted or to kow-tow to his own party leadership. Indeed, Margaret THATCHER's most memorable lines in her farewell speech as Prime Minister were based on a Skinner interruption.

Beast of Buffalo The Republicans' nickname in the 1884 Presidential ELECTION for Grover CLEVELAND, reflecting his corpulence, his firmness, his energy and the fact that he had fathered an illegitimate child (*see* MA, MA, WHERE'S MY PA?). Its deployment failed to stop Cleveland defeating James G. Blaine, who was widely perceived as corrupt.

bed. bed blockers The irreverent label pinned by young Parliamentary supporters of Michael HOWARD in the run-up to the 2005 UK ELECTION on veteran Conservative MPs who they claimed were occupying seats without working energetically for the cause. The targets of this criticism retaliated by branding the young Turks the '**Notting Hill Set**'. The original bed-blockers were elderly NHS patients who, although recovered enough to be discharged from hospital, had to stay in because social services could not provide domiciliary or residential care for them.

bed-sit brigade The name bestowed by Harold WILSON on the dedicated left-wingers (from the MILITANT TENDENCY and a range of BENNITE and hard LEFT groups) who in the 1970s and early 1980s moved into constituencies with a moribund local LABOUR PARTY to work for the DESELECTION of the sitting Labour MP. They gained the label because they often rented bed-sitting rooms for the duration of their campaign.

Bedchamber crisis The constitutional crisis that broke in Britain in 1839 when on the fall of Melbourne's WHIG ministry the young Queen Victoria refused to part with her ladies of the bedchamber, many of whom were wives, sisters or daughters of leading Whigs. The Queen's resistance prevented Robert PEEL forming a Tory government, and her confidant and mentor Viscount Melbourne, who still had a narrow majority, was recalled; only after an election did Peel return to power.

I have no doubt that Melbourne is as passionately fond of the Queen as he might be of his daughter if he had one, and the more so because he has the capacity for loving without anyone to love. It is become his province to educate, instruct and inform the most interesting mind and character in the world.

CHARLES GREVILLE, *Memoirs*

Bedtime for Bonzo The 1951 movie in which Ronald REAGAN starred with a chimpanzee, giving rise to numerous jokes, all of them obvious, when he embarked on a political career.

Beeching Report The report produced in 1962 by the senior ICI executive Dr Richard (later Lord) Beeching (1913–85) which caused a furore by advocating the closure of more than half of Britain's railway system. Commissioned by Ernest Marples (*see* BALFOUR MUST GO), Transport Minister in the MACMILLAN government, it was largely implemented after Labour came to power in 1964.

beef. beef mountain *See* MOUNTAIN.

Beef Tribunal The panel set up by the Irish government to inquire into the scandal surrounding the Goodman Group, the Republic's largest beef operator, after the company, which had received £I120 million in Government credits for exports to Iraq, was discovered in 1991 to have engaged in fraud and tax evasion, escaped proper oversight of shipments and illegally reboxed consignments. The tribunal reported in 1994 that there had been widespread irregularities and that the company had exploited its closeness to FIANNA FAIL Ministers. The TAOISEACH Albert Reynolds (*see* ALBERTZHEIMER's DISEASE), who had approved the guarantees as Minister for Industry and Commerce against the advice of officials, was saved from disgrace by the IRA calling a ceasefire on 31 August 1994, just before the crucial debate in the DAIL.

where's the beef? *See* WHERE.

Beehive, the The universal nickname for the Executive Wing of New Zealand's Parliament building in Wellington, designed by Sir Basil Spence in 1964 and completed in 1981. It stems from the shape of the building, which has ten floors above ground and four below and stands 72 metres high. The CABINET meets fortnightly on the top floor, the Prime Minister's office is on the ninth and Cabinet Ministers' on lower floors. New Zealand's CIVIL DEFENCE headquarters is situated in the basement, and a tunnel links the Beehive with an annexe on the other side of Bowen Street.

beer. beer and sandwiches at Number Ten Harold WILSON's practice of inviting trade union leaders to Downing Street to resolve potentially damaging industrial disputes, with a national strike on occasions averted after marathon talks when beer and sandwiches were served. Its adoption in the 1966 seamen's strike (*see* TIGHTLY KNIT GROUP OF POLITICALLY MOTIVATED MEN) and subsequent disputes was scorned by the Conservatives; Edward HEATH (who relented) and Margaret THATCHER (who did not) both insisted they would never indulge in such tactics. *Compare* Coffee and Danish at the WHITE HOUSE.

we have been borne down in a torrent of gin and beer GLADSTONE's lament on the Liberals' heavy defeat in the 1874 general ELECTION; the Conservatives had been heavily backed by the BEERAGE.

Beerage A derogatory collective term for the heads of the brewing industry who from the late 19th century gave unquestioning support to Britain's CONSERVATIVE PARTY, frequently receiving seats in the HOUSE OF LORDS as their reward. The link between the brewers and the Tories, which persists to this day, was forged in part when the LIBERAL PARTY in the 1870s began to represent the NONCONFORMIST CONSCIENCE by taking an increasingly hostile attitude to drink.

Beirut. Beirut airport bombing The devastating attack on the main US barracks in the Lebanon on 23 October 1983 that left 241 marines dead, hastening America's withdrawal the following February from the MULTINATIONAL FORCE endeavouring to keep the peace there. The attack, by an Islamist suicide truck bomber, was followed by one on the French peace-keeping barracks which killed 58 troops. The atrocity, which a special commission blamed partly on lax security, was seized on by opponents of the REAGAN ADMINISTRATION to argue that the Marines should never have been sent in; Reagan kept public anger in check by ordering US troops into GRENADA two days later. He insisted he would not pull the Marines out of Beirut, but signed the order on 1 February 1984 just as his press secretary was denouncing Democrats demanding the pullout as 'unpatriotic'. In April 1983, 63 people died when the US Embassy in Beirut was bombed by ISLAMIC JIHAD; a new embassy was found and in September 1984 that, too, was bombed, with 40 deaths.

Beirut hostages *See* HOSTAGES.

Belgrano affair The most controversial incident of the FALKLANDS WAR, the sinking on 2 May 1982 of the Argentine cruiser *General Belgrano* (the former USS *Phoenix*, a survivor of PEARL HARBOR) by the British submarine *Conqueror*. A long-running political argument ensued in Britain, not because 323 Argentine sailors had died but because, contrary to what Margaret THATCHER and defence ministers told the COMMONS, the *Belgrano* had been steaming away from the Falklands for eight hours when torpedoed. Naval staff officers withheld that intelligence from Ministers and the politicians when they discovered the facts (in Mrs Thatcher's case two years later) felt obliged to defend the service. The inconsistencies that crept into official explanations led the Labour MP Tam Dalyell to launch a campaign to prove that the sinking had been engineered to torpedo the PERUVIAN PEACE PLAN, asking his final question the week before his retirement in 2005. The Prime Minister, in a 1983 election PHONE-IN, was put on the rack over the *Belgrano* by a Bristol housewife, Diana Gould, her hesitant answers raising lasting doubts over their veracity. The gradual emergence of a COVER-UP heartened conspiracy theorists and led to the prosecution and acquittal of the senior MoD civil servant Clive PONTING under the OFFICIAL SECRETS ACT for LEAKing information about the sinking to Dalyell and the *Observer* newspaper. The *Belgrano* campaigners suffered a reverse on the tenth anniversary of the sinking when the ship's commander, Captain Hector Bonzo, told *The Times*:

> The attack on the *Belgrano* did not violate the laws of a military conflict. If I had been a British commander confronted by the enemy ship, I would have done exactly the same.

Belknap scandal The juiciest of the scandals that gave the Grant administration a probably unjustified reputation for corruption (*see* GRANTISM). Secretary for War William W. Belknap resigned abruptly in 1876 to escape IMPEACHMENT, after it was found that he had taken bribes to grant the right to sell supplies to the Indians. The story broke in a Congressional hearing on 29 February when Caleb Marsh, a trader at Fort Sill in the Indian territories, testified to having paid $25,000 over six years to Carrie and Puss Belknap, the attractive, vivacious sisters whom Belknap had married in turn. Belknap resigned amid rumours that he had attempted suicide; although cleared by the SENATE he spent the rest of his life in disgrace, but the stylish Puss Belknap continued to captivate WASHINGTON society and the press.

bell. on the bell *See* ON.

bellwether A political trend-setter, or an electoral area with a record of indicating how the country as a whole will vote. The bellwether was originally the sheep, often with a bell around its neck, whom the rest of the flock would follow.

below the gangway In the HOUSE OF COMMONS, the seats at the end of the CHAMBER away from the CHAIR. On both sides of the House, the gangway runs backward to separate the Front BENCH from the *hoi polloi*; on the Government side the first seat at the front below the gangway was occupied in retirement from 1955–64 by Sir Winston CHURCHILL, and for even longer, from 1979–97, by Sir Edward HEATH. Sir Edward shared the bench with senior Tory backbenchers, some of them right-wingers who were no friends of his, sharing the description of BOVVER BOYS bestowed on the left-wing occupants of Labour's below-gangway front bench.

bench. bench of bishops The bench next to the Government front bench in the HOUSE OF LORDS where the two Anglican archbishops and the 24 bishops with places in the Upper House (the **Lords spiritual**) are seated.

back benches The seats in the HOUSE OF COMMONS occupied by all those MPs who are not members of the Government, or official Opposition SPOKESMEN. A Minister who leaves office is said to be 'returning to the back benches', even if they take their seat on the front bench BELOW THE GANGWAY. *See also* BACKBENCHER.

front bench (1) The seats above the gangway on either side of the HOUSE OF COMMONS, close to the CHAIR and facing the DESPATCH BOX, where members of the CABINET and SHADOW CABINET sit as of right, joined by junior Ministers and spokesmen respectively when the business of the House requires. (2) A collective term for the entire Opposition team of shadow Ministers and spokesmen.

Treasury Bench The official term for the Government front bench in the HOUSE OF COMMONS, reflecting the Prime Minister's formal title as First Lord of the TREASURY and, some would say, the grip that the Treasury exercises over any Government.

Benelux The collective term by which Belgium, the Netherlands and Luxembourg are known. It originated in the customs union the three countries formed in 1948, and remains in use because of the many issues on which the three act as one within the EUROPEAN UNION.

benign neglect The stance toward the problems of black Americans, both economic and in relation to CIVIL RIGHTS, adopted by the NIXON administration; a settled climate in which 'black capitalism' could supposedly thrive was preferred. The phrase was first used in a memorandum to NIXON by Daniel Patrick MOYNIHAN, which was leaked to the press in 1970. Moyhihan advised:

> The time may have come when the issue of race could benefit from a period of benign neglect. The subject has been too much talked about. The forum has been too much taken over by hysterics, paranoids, and boodlers on all sides. We may need a period in which negro progress continues and racial rhetoric fades. The ADMINISTRATION can help bring this about by paying close attention to such progress – as we are doing – while seeking to avoid situations in which extremists of either race are given opportunities for martyrdom, heroics, histrionics or whatever.

Benn. Bennery A derogatory term for the combination of POPULISM, WORKERS' CONTROL and (to its critics) dangerous eccentricity which **Tony** (Anthony Wedgwood) **Benn** (1925–) pursued as UK Industry Secretary in 1974–75 before being moved by Harold WILSON to the less controversial Energy portfolio in his Labour government. Benn championed NATIONALISATION, state involvement in private industry and conversion of loss-making factories into workers' CO-OPERATIVES with a schoolboyish zeal and a patrician manner which led the novelist Malcolm Bradbury to term him 'the Bertie Wooster of Marxism'. His policies earned him bitter enemies in the Tory Party and Fleet Street; Benn himself said: 'If I rescued a child from drowning, the press would no doubt headline the story: "Benn grabs child."' The Liberal Cyril Smith (*see* BIG CYRIL) asserted: 'He did more to British industry in one speech than the combined efforts of the Luftwaffe and the U-boats did in the whole of the last war.' Yet Benn was to earn even greater vituperation from right-wingers in his own party when hard LEFT **Bennites**, campaigning for 'party democracy', provoked the GANG OF FOUR into leaving Labour to start the SDP. He himself came within a whisker in 1981 of ousting Denis HEALEY as deputy leader to capture the party. Healey, when told of Benn's challenge, said: 'Yes, and tomorrow he is parachuting into Scotland to hold peace talks with the Duke of Hamilton.' *See* HESS MISSION.

Benn has been a paradox, combining sudden enthusiasms and U-TURNS as he moved to the left (notably on NUCLEAR policy and Europe) with a strong belief in the rights of Parliament (*see* ZIRCON) and the individual; these inconsistencies, and his own personal charm, shine through his seven acclaimed volumes of diaries. But his greatest legacy (until the HOUSE OF LORDS was reformed) was a change in the law so that heirs to PEERAGES could renounce their titles and remain eligible to sit in the HOUSE OF COMMONS. Elected an MP for Bristol in 1950, Benn succeeded as Viscount Stansgate when his father died in 1960; his seat was declared vacant, he fought a BY-ELECTION, won it, but was barred from the Commons. He instigated legislation to make peerages disclaimable for life, and on its passage was re-elected for his old seat. There was a dramatic sequel: within months Lord Hailsham renounced his peerage in a bid for the Tory leadership; another peer, Lord Home, was chosen and also gave up his title to become SIR ALEC Douglas-Home.

Benn served as Postmaster-General, Minister of Technology and Minister of Power in the 1964–70 Wilson government; Bernard Levin wrote: 'He threw himself into Sixties technology with the enthusiasm (not to say the language) of a newly-enrolled Boy Scout demonstrating knot-tying to indulgent parents.' In opposition Benn moved leftward, championing on the party's National Executive a markedly more socialist PLATFORM adopted in 1973. On Labour's return in 1974, Benn was given first Industry and then Energy, where he oversaw the birth of North Sea oil; he had not yet turned against nuclear power. Once a pro-European, he was a leader of the anti-EC faction in the Wilson-CALLAGHAN CABINET, and secured a REFERENDUM in 1975 on Britain's continued membership. When Labour lost power in 1979, Benn emerged as leader of the left, infuriating first Callaghan and then his successor, Michael FOOT, and pushing through a 1983 election manifesto scorned by party moderates as the LONGEST SUICIDE NOTE IN HISTORY. He posed Neil KINNOCK fewer headaches; he lost his seat in 1983, and by the time he returned as MP for Chesterfield, the trauma of Labour's worst defeat for half a century and the decline of the hard left had weakened his support. He continued in the Commons as an effective, and in many ways respected, BACKBENCHER until 2001 when, as a rebuke to NEW LABOUR, he gave up his seat 'to concentrate on politics'.

> Tomfool issues, barmy ideas, a kind of ageing, perennial youth who immatures with age.
> HAROLD WILSON

> Less of a wide-eyed Trot than a very English phenomenon: a descendant of the Puritans and the Nonconformists and, despite his doubts about the Almighty, 19th-century Christian socialists.
> JOHN MORTIMER

> He has had more conversions on the road to Damascus than a Syrian long-distance truck driver.
> JIMMY REID

Berkeley rules The rules under which the first election for the CONSERVATIVE PARTY leadership was held in 1965, Edward HEATH defeating Reginald Maudling by 150 votes to 133, with other candidates well behind, to succeed SIR ALEC Douglas-Home. They were devised by and named after Humphrey Berkeley (1926–94) who was then Conservative MP for Lancaster; after losing his seat he was first a Labour and then an SDP candidate. Previously the leader had **'emerged'** after consultations within the MAGIC CIRCLE of the party hierarchy, leading to bitterness and CABINET resignations when Sir Alec was unexpectedly preferred to Lord Hailsham and RAB Butler in 1963. The Berkeley rules themselves were felt to be flawed, so Sir Alec devised a more thorough system, whose first use resulted in Margaret THATCHER defeating Heath a decade later.

Berlaymont The BRUSSELS heaquarters of the EUROPEAN COMMISSION; with its three wings curving from a central core, it has come to represent both the power and the bureaucracy of the EU. Within the Berlaymont, an official's status is determined by the number of windows in their office; a COMMISSIONER has up to 32. The building was evacuated, supposedly temporarily, in 1991 when dangerously high asbestos levels were detected. It was supposed to be reoccupied by 1997, but it was 2004 before the Commissioners moved back in; the cost of refurbishment rose from £66 million to £860 million, with every extra day's delay costing EU taxpayers £155,000.

Berlin. Berlin airlift The response of Britain and America to the blockade that STALIN imposed on 24 June 1948 on all road, rail and canal links from the West through the Soviet zone of Germany to West Berlin. He hoped to force the Allies out of Berlin, on which he had already tried to impose the Soviet currency, and incorporate West Berlin into East Germany, but he was foiled by an airlift by over 1000 planes which for 321 days met the needs of more than 2 million West Berliners, bringing in over 2.5 million tons of cargo including fuel, and flying out its exports. Shooting down the planes would have meant war; Stalin was not prepared to go this far and in May 1949 he relented and the links were reopened, in return for four-power talks on the future of Berlin.

Berlin crisis The crisis in the summer of 1961 which culminated in the building of the BERLIN WALL. The Soviet leader Nikita S. Khrushchev challenged the Western powers – Britain, America and France – to sign a German peace treaty by the end of the year or see the USSR conclude a separate treaty with East Germany, not recognising the status of West Berlin. The allies stood firm and both sides built up their forces until the KREMLIN backed down, but then East Germany began building the Wall.

Berlin Wall The barrier which from 13 August 1961 until 9 November 1989 sealed off West Berlin from the communist-controlled territory of East Germany and East Berlin that surrounded it. Erected to prevent East Germans fleeing to the West – 30,000 crossed over the previous month – it consisted in its final form of two walls of concrete two metres high, separated by a no man's land tens of metres wide which could be raked by gunfire from border police in watchtowers. Crossing was possible at a handful of checkpoints for road (*see* CHECKPOINT CHARLIE), rail, canal and metro traffic, but in practice only citizens of the occupying powers (Britain, America, France and the Soviet Union) and handpicked West Berliners who paid for the privilege were allowed through. The building of the wall brought East-West tension over Berlin to a new height; John F. KENNEDY confessed that 'a wall is better than a war', but spoke out strongly against it in his ICH BIN EIN BERLINER speech. The wall was breached amid scenes of jubilation as the East German communist regime collapsed; its leader Erich Honecker was later put on trial for having ordered the shooting of escapers, though freed on health grounds early in 1993. The wall itself, apart from short stretches kept as memorials to the dozens shot trying to escape, was broken up for souvenirs.

Congress of Berlin The international negotiations in June-July 1878 which stabilised the Balkans, where Turkish influence was declining, until the war of 1912–13. Russia gained territory from the Turks after intervening to protect the Christian population of Bulgaria, and Britain took control of Cyprus.

Bermuda agreements The agreements between British and US governments which since 1946 have regulated air traffic between the two countries, governing the number of airlines permitted to fly the routes and the destinations to which they may fly. The agreements are open to renegotiation, but the determination of each side to secure more for its own airlines without reciprocating has produced repeated stalemates. The last successful negotiation produced the **Bermuda 2** agreement in 1977, but even this was only concluded after the US authorities had given orders for UK planes to be turned back at midnight if final concessions were not made.

Berrigans The two radical New England Catholic priests who throughout the 1970s and into the 1980s were leading lights in the militant ANTI-WAR and peace movements. In 1970 Fr Daniel and Fr Philip Berrigan were jailed for burning DRAFT cards in protest at the VIETNAM WAR. Daniel was released in February 1972; Philip, who with Sister Elizabeth McAlister had been caught smuggling letters into prison, was freed that December. The sentences did not deter them from mounting further high-profile protests.

Bertie Bowl The 65,000-seat national stadium mooted for construction at Abbotstown on the outskirts of Dublin to enable the Republic of Ireland to co-host the 2008 European football championships with Scotland. The project was the brainchild of the FIANNA FAIL TAOISEACH Bertie Ahern (*see* ANORAK MAN); his championing of the scheme was a factor in his party's near outright victory in Ireland's 2002 general ELECTION. The project went on hold when the Scottish/Irish bid to stage the championships was rejected by UEFA, and in January 2004 the Government decided instead to upgrade Lansdowne Road rugby ground.

Berufsverbot (Ger. prohibition of vocation) The regulation barring political radicals – suspected communists and extreme leftists – from holding office in the West German civil service and educational system, and their successor services throughout reunified Germany. It was enforced with particular vigour during the 1970s when East German efforts to infiltrate the bureaucracy of the West coincided with the upsurge of terrorism. Liberals saw the prevention of at times harmless individuals from earning a living, particularly as teachers or minor officials, as an affront to civil liberties.

Beslan siege The bloody hostage-taking by Chechen and Arab fighters at a school in North Ossetia, close to Chechnya, on 1–3 September 2004 which exceeded the MOSCOW THEATRE SIEGE both in the number of captives taken – over 1100 – and in the scale of casualties when the siege ended. 338 people were confirmed killed – children, parents, teachers, captors and troops – and 746 taken to hospital with a further 400 unaccounted for. Some 30 mothers and toddlers had been released and negotiations were under way for more to be freed when an explosion – apparently caused by one of the Chechens' own bombs – led Russian troops to move in. 27 hostage-takers were killed – at least ten of them Arabs – and three taken alive; several more were thought to have escaped. The Chechens had evaded border patrols and other security checks to get to the school and booby-trap it during the summer holidays, taking children, teachers and parents captive on the first day back.

best. *Best and the Brightest, The* The 1972 book by the *New York Times* writer David Halberstam which catalogued the destruction of the high hopes of the KENNEDY administration and JOHNSON's GREAT SOCIETY in the morass of the VIETNAM WAR. The title emphasised the way in which some of the finest minds in America, brought together to high purpose by two Democratic Presidents, either created or were unable to prevent the war that tore America apart and destroyed its self-confidence.

why not the best? *See* WHY.

you do your worst, and we will do our best Winston CHURCHILL's challenge to HITLER in a speech on 14 July 1941, immediately after Germany's invasion of Russia.

Betsygate The alleged scandal in the autumn of 2003 which contributed to the overthrow of the UK Conservative leader Iain Duncan Smith (*see* IDS). Critics of his leadership leaked to the media e-mails purporting to show that he had employed his wife Betsy as his CONSTITUENCY secretary at public expense but had not given her any work to do. Supporters and opponents alike saw the allegations as a pretext to increase pressure for his removal, but the response of CENTRAL OFFICE, with potential witnesses pressed to sign statements that they would not incriminate Duncan Smith, weakened his position still further. After his replacement by Michael Howard, the Parliamentary Commissioner for Standards totally exonerated the Duncan Smiths.

better red than dead *See* RED.

Bevan, Aneurin (1897–1960), the Welsh firebrand who galvanised left-wing politics in Britain after WORLD WAR II, polarising the LABOUR PARTY, and who is best remembered as founder of the NHS. One of thirteen children, Bevan followed his father down the pit at 13, but soon showed powers of oratory and leadership and at 29 was one of the South Wales miners' leaders in the GENERAL STRIKE. Elected to Parliament for the ILP in 1929 and Labour in 1931, he soon took over LLOYD GEORGE's mantle as the most brilliant, emotional and fiery orator of his day; his biographer Michael FOOT wrote: 'Bevan would be possessed by Lloyd George's terrible urge to claw down the enemy.' He was a thorn in CHURCHILL's side throughout World War II, though the great man confessed: 'He is one of the few people I would sit still and listen to.' When Labour took power in 1945 Churchill commented: 'He will be just as great a curse to this country in peace as he was a squalid nuisance in time of war.' Yet his most constructive period was as Minister of Health in ATTLEE's CABINET, when he created the NHS in 1948 despite the obstruction of most of the medical profession; in 1951 he resigned, with Harold WILSON and John Freeman, over the imposition of charges for spectacles and false teeth. After Labour lost power that year, the Bevanites tried Attlee to the limit by pressing a radical left-wing agenda and ignoring party discipline, Bevan narrowly escaping expulsion from the party. A furious Attlee told Labour MPs: 'Just when we were beginning to win the match, our outside-left has scored against his own side.' Bevan's ally Richard CROSSMAN said of him: 'NYE wasn't cut out to be a leader; he was cut out to be a prophet,' and he himself said: 'If the Labour Party is not going to be a socialist party, I don't want to lead it.' Yet Bevan was not just an embarrassment to the Labour leadership; he was a devastating critic of the Tories (*see* ALBATROSS; ORGAN GRINDER). Harold MACMILLAN once remarked: 'He keeps prophesying the end of the capitalist system, and is prepared to play any part in its burial except that of mute.' He also had the readiest wit; when Churchill upbraided him for not 'taking the trouble to dress properly' for the Queen's Coronation dinner by wearing formal dress, Bevan replied: 'Prime Minister, your fly buttons are undone!' When Hugh GAITSKELL replaced Attlee as leader, he found Bevan ranged against him; after Labour's defeat in the 1955 election Bevan challenged for the leadership, winning 70 votes to Gaitskell's 157 and 40 for Herbert Morrison, and was elected party treasurer. Bevan did not follow his fellow left-wingers in embracing UNILATERALISM, and after SUEZ he was reconciled with Gaitskell, becoming SHADOW FOREIGN SECRETARY and, a year before his death, deputy Labour leader. His wife Jennie Lee, herself a Labour MP and a future Arts Minister, wrote: 'Nye was born old and died young.'

> The greatest Parliamentary orator since Charles James Fox.
> R. A. BUTLER

See also His own worst ENEMY.

Bevanites The left-wing supporters of Aneurin Bevan who caused serious problems for the leaders of Britain's LABOUR PARTY from March 1952, when 57 Labour MPs broke ranks to vote against the new Conservative government's defence policy. The vote led to the imposition of tight party discipline, with anyone who defied the decisions of the Parliamentary Labour Party (PLP) facing explusion. Led by Bevan, Michael FOOT, Tom Driberg and Richard CROSSMAN, the group had strong support in the CONSTITUENCY parties and several seats on Labour's National Executive, though only Bevan won election to the SHADOW CABINET. In 1954 they broke with the leadership over GERMAN REARMAMENT after a 113–104 party vote to support it; Bevan resigned from the Shadow Cabinet. The next year Bevan had the WHIP withdrawn after 62 MPs ABSTAINed on Labour's official amendment to the Defence White Paper and he interrupted ATTLEE's speech. Right-wingers led by Herbert Morrison wanted Bevan out of the party, but the NEC by one vote accepted a compromise from Attlee under which Bevan stayed in, provided he apologised. However, SUEZ soon united the party against the Tory government, after GAITSKELL's initial support for intervention. The Bevanites never regained their strength as an irritant, and when the party next split, over UNILATERALISM, Bevan, now SHADOW FOREIGN SECRETARY, sided with the leadership.

> An uneasy coalition of well-meaning emotionalists, rejects, frustrates, crackpots and FELLOW-TRAVELLERS, making Fred Karno's army look like a Brigade of Guards.
> HUGH DALTON

Beveridge Report The report produced in 1942 by the UK economist William Henry (later Lord) Beveridge (1879–1963) which paved the way for the post-war WELFARE STATE. Nominally the result of a review set up by the Ministry of Health in 1941, the *Report on Social Insurance and the Allied Services* was almost entirely Beveridge's work. He advocated the reorganisation of social insurance to provide a minimum national income, and depended on three assumptions: a National Health Service (NHS), family allowances and a Government guarantee of FULL EMPLOYMENT. It was recognised even by CHURCHILL as a basis for action, but was adopted most enthusiastically by Labour as a central feature of its post-war programme. Many of its recommendations were implemented after 1945; however, Beveridge's advocacy of WORKFARE was quietly ignored. Beveridge was given full credit by Labour, despite being an active Liberal.

Bevin boys Young men conscripted during WORLD WAR II to work in Britain's coal mines under the Emergency Powers (Defence) Act of 1940. **Ernest Bevin** (1881–1951), Minister of Labour and National Service, directed in 1943 that one in ten men called up between the ages of 18 and 25 should go down the mines; the scheme continued for a time after the war. Bevin, in his own words, was 'a turn-up in a million'. Orphaned at seven, he was a Baptist preacher before becoming a trade union organiser, rising to form the Transport and General Workers' Union from 32 separate bodies, serving at its General Secretary for almost 20 years; he was an influential figure in the 1926 GENERAL STRIKE. He was himself conscripted into CHURCHILL's wartime COALITION, his success in organising the labour market establishing him as one of Labour's ELECTION-winners in 1945; Angus Calder wrote: 'Bevinism in industry was symbolised by the growing understanding of the value of music and entertainment in helping people to work faster.' Bevin as a union leader had always wielded influence in the LABOUR PARTY. At its 1935 conference he destroyed George Lansbury's PACIFIST campaign by accusing him of 'trailing his conscience around from conference to conference asking to be told what to do with it'; when Lansbury's friends complained, he told them: 'He has been going around in saint's clothes for years, waiting for martyrdom; I set fire to the faggots.'

Bevin went on to serve as FOREIGN SECRETARY in ATTLEE's government until forced to resign through ill-health in 1951; he took a firm line with the Russians at the start of the COLD WAR, standing up to STALIN over BERLIN, and NATO was his lasting creation. Kingsley Martin wrote: 'Bevin always treated the Soviet Union as if it were a breakaway faction of the Transport and General Workers' Union'. In the process, as Harold MACMILLAN pointed out, 'he imposed on an unwilling and hesitant party a policy of resistance to Soviet Russia and to Communism'. Bevin was less happy with the birth of Israel, agreeing reluctantly to a Jewish state he was sure would solve none of the region's problems; nor was he keen on a united Europe. Neither was he happy speaking in the COMMONS, once saying: 'I gets up when they nudges me and I sits down when they pulls me coat'. And Michael FOOT recalled: 'A speech from EB on a major occasion had all the horrid fascination of a public execution.' Yet he is rated one of the great Foreign Secretaries; asked once to define his policy, Bevin said: 'My policy is to be able to take a ticket at Victoria Station and go where I damn well please.'

> There was no other position in the Foreign Office, unless it was that of a rather truculent liftman on the verge of retirement . . . which it would have been possible to imagine his filling.
> ROY JENKINS

> Like Churchill he seemed a visitor from the 18th century – of the company of Chatham and Samuel Johnson, men of strong hearts and strong opinions.
> Obituary, *The Times*

> Bevin often bullied in a good cause; he was a bully all the same.
> ALAN BULLOCK

bicameral system A system under which a nation's legislature has two CHAMBERS rather than one (a UNICAMERAL system), providing checks and balances and lessening the risk of ELECTIVE DICTATORSHIP. At the birth of the United States, Benjamin FRANKLIN wrote that 'a plural legislature is as necessary to good government as a single EXECUTIVE'.

Biffo The nickname at WESTMINSTER, originating in the cartoon character Biffo the Bear, both for John Biffen (1930–), a CABINET Minister under Margaret

THATCHER from 1979 to 1987 (*see* SEMI-DETACHED), and for the irrepressible Tory backbencher Geoffrey Dickens (1931–95) (*see* HORSEFACE). For Biffen the sobriquet was a contraction of his name; the Labour MP Joe Ashton also gave it to Dickens, saying that it stood for 'Big Ignorant Fool From Oldham'.

big. Big Ben The popular nickname for the clock tower at the northern end of the Palace of WESTMINSTER, overlooking PARLIAMENT SQUARE and Westminster Bridge. Parties are permitted to climb the steps of the tower, which contains several suites of members' offices that have never been used. The name should correctly refer only to the 13-tonne bell that chimes the hours. Big Ben took its name from Sir Benjamin Hall, Commissioner of Works when the bell was installed in 1859. It was first cast at Stockton in 1856, but on arrival by sea it developed a four-foot crack and was recast at Whitechapel; it cracked again and the Astronomer Royal solved the problem by having a lighter hammer fitted.

Big Bill The popular name for William Hale Thompson (1867–1944), three times Mayor of Chicago, who was noted for his anti-British views. He once threatened to punch King George V on the nose if he ever visited Chicago. *See also* WOBBLIES.

Big Brother An all-pervading authority able to keep all its citizens under continual observation and intrude into their lives in every respect; hence the adoption of the title, at first in Holland, by television programmes depicting a group of people continually monitored in an isolated house. The name comes from one of the most powerful phrases in George Orwell's novel NINETEEN EIGHTY-FOUR, whose central characters are constantly reminded that their deviations from the official line may be being watched. The allusion was implicitly to the Soviet bloc, but it could apply to many other societies and is by opponents of closed-circuit television and identity cards.

> The posters were plastered everywhere . . . BIG BROTHER IS WATCHING YOU the caption said, while the dark eyes looked deep into Winston's own.
>
> *Nineteen Eighty-Four,* p.1

Big Conversation The consultative exercise launched by Tony BLAIR and members of his government in November 2003 to secure public input into Labour's MANIFESTO for the upcoming general ELECTION. The exercise generated controversy because of complaints that the questions asked of the voters were loaded, and because generally sympathetic pressure groups which were asked to submit statements for the consultation's website found that critical comments had been edited out.

Big Cyril The popular nickname for **Sir Cyril Smith** (1928–), Liberal MP for the Lancashire town of Rochdale from 1972 to 1992. A vast man weighing 25 stones, Smith's habit of speaking his mind did not make him a natural party man, but he was an effective campaigner and, as the jovial proprietor of a spring-making company who lived with his old mother, a popular media personality.

Big Four The four Allied leaders – Woodrow WILSON, Georges Clemenceau (*see* the TIGER), Lloyd George (*see* L.G.) and Orlando of Italy – who set punitive peace terms for Germany at VERSAILLES after WORLD WAR I.

big government One of the great targets of US conservatives, a sprawling government machine that becomes the master, not the servant, of the people.

> If the government is big enough to give you all you want, it is big enough to take it all away.
>
> Sen. BARRY GOLDWATER'S ACCEPTANCE SPEECH at the 1964 Republican convention

Big Idea The critical new dimension to a party's policy that can capture the voters' imagination and ensure victory. Much sought by strategists, especially in Britain's LABOUR PARTY prior to its fourth successive defeat in 1992.

Big Mo A US term for the critical momentum that will carry a political campaign through to victory. The phrase was coined in the late 1970s; in 1980 George BUSH Sr claimed to have the 'Big Mo' after beating Ronald REAGAN in the Iowa CAUCUS. Despite appearances, it has nothing to do with the hugely popular British Labour politician Mo Mowlam.

big tent strategy Outreach by a political party to secure the widest range of support by blurring its message. The theory originated with the Republican NOMINEE Bob Dole during the 1996 Presidential campaign, when he argued that with a loose enough PLATFORM it would be possible to accommodate both PRO-LIFE and PRO-CHOICE supporters. Dole's approach was rejected by an anti-abortion majority at the party's San Diego convention and he went down to defeat by Bill CLINTON. The term was later used by Tony BLAIR to categorise a policy under which the supporters of parties other than Labour would be put forward for public appointments. For a time it also characterised his efforts to involve the Liberal Democrats in his government through a joint CABINET COMMITTEE.

Bikini state A reference neither to the swimsuit nor to the atoll where early NUCLEAR tests were conducted, but the level of alertness against terrorist attack displayed in the foyer of UK government establishments. Like the more recent US system, it is colour-coded; at times of special tension it is raised from 'Black' to 'Black Special'.

bilaterals Talks or negotiations involving two heads of govermnent or Ministers, often taking place on the fringe of an international conference of a larger number of leaders. In Britain the term also applies to the haggling over cash between the CHIEF SECRETARY of the TREASURY and individual spending Ministers during COMPREHENSIVE SPENDING REVIEWS.

Bilderberg The international conferences, named after the Bilderberg Hotel at Arnhem where the first was held in 1954, which have brought Western politicians, industrialists and trade unionists together to promote closer transatlantic understanding. They were started by Joseph Retinger, a Pole who settled in Britain after WORLD WAR II, and were chaired by Prince Bernhard of the Netherlands until his disgrace in the LOCKHEED SCANDAL. They have been denounced by CONSPIRACY THEORISTS in America as part of a left-wing plot to rule the world and subvert the United States.

bilingualism A policy of giving more or less equal weight to two languages in a particular jurisdiction, for instance Welsh in Wales or French in various provinces of Canada; the alternative is to enshrine the majority language, as in BILL 101. When Bill Clements, governor of Texas from 1987 to 1991, tried to learn Spanish to promote bilingualism, one state legislator remarked:

> Good. Now he'll be bi-ignorant.

Bill An item of proposed legislation, when presented to a legislature and during its passage, at the end of which it becomes an ACT. Speaker John Nance Garner (*see* CACTUS JACK) used to tell SPONSORS:

> Hell, don't tell me what the Bill says. Just tell me what it does.

Bill of Rights (1) The Bill passed at WESTMINSTER after the GLORIOUS REVOLUTION of 1689 which declared that James II (James VII of Scotland) had ABDICATED, established William III (William of ORANGE) and Mary II as joint monarchs, barred Roman Catholics from ascending the THRONE and remedied a number of James's perceived abuses, for instance by making it illegal to keep a standing army in peacetime. (2) The first ten AMENDMENTS to the US CONSTITUTION, proposed in 1789 and ratified on 15 September 1791. They added several basic safeguards to the Constitution, starting with FREEDOM OF SPEECH and also including the RIGHT TO KEEP AND BEAR ARMS, immunity from search without proper warrant, protection against self-incrimination and a guarantee of due process, the right to a speedy and public trial and a strict construction of the powers of the FEDERAL government. Drafted and campaigned for by James MADISON, the Bill met opposition from Alexander HAMILTON who asked: 'Why declare that things shall not be done which there is no power to do? Why, in short, have a Bill of Rights?' But Thomas Jefferson declared:

> A Bill of Rights is what the people are entitled to against every government on earth, general or particular, and what no just government should refuse or rest on inference.

Bill 101 The law put forward by Quebec's PQ government after its election in 1976 which made French the province's sole official language and imposed severe restraints on the use of English in business, education and many other fields of life. Its enactment caused a number of Anglophones to leave Quebec for the United States or English-speaking provinces, but did not prove the first step to the province's separation from Canada, as its promoters had hoped.

clean Bill In the US HOUSE OF REPRESENTATIVES, a Bill which is reported by the relevant committee without any amendments having been made.

companion Bill A Bill introduced in one HOUSE of the US CONGRESS which is identical to one put forward in the other.

enrolled Bill A Bill as finally approved by both HOUSES of CONGRESS, if necessary after a House-SENATE CONFERENCE, for signature by the President. The wording and punctuation have to be exactly as decided, with all AMENDMENTS adequately reflected. The enrolled Bill is printed on parchment paper, with the Clerk of the House or Secretary of the Senate certifying in which House it originated. It is examined for accuracy by the Committee on House Administration or the Secretary of the

Senate, and is then signed by the SPEAKER of the House and the VICE PRESIDENT or PRESIDENT PRO TEM before transmission by the Committee to the WHITE HOUSE.

Finance Bill The Bill incorporating the detailed taxation and other provisions of each UK BUDGET. Immediate tax changes are made in BUDGET RESOLUTIONS voted on at the close of the Budget debate, but the Finance Bill, which can run into hundreds of pages, is only brought forward once the tech nical work is complete, with debate (including late-night sessions in COMMITTEE) usually concluding four months after the Budget. The Finance Bill does not have to be debated or approved by the HOUSE OF LORDS.

handout Bill A minor and usually non-controversial measure prepared by a UK government department in the hope that an MP who is successful in the BALLOT for PRIVATE MEMBERS' BILLS can be persuaded to introduce it. While relatively few Private Members' Bills reach the statute book, this means of legislating can be attractive to departments which see no prospect of obtaining Parliamentary TIME for enacting such legislation themselves.

Hybrid Bill *See* HYBRID.

non-contentious Bill At WESTMINSTER, a measure over which there is no disagreement and for which only a limited amount of TIME need be allocated.

one-house Bill In the US CONGRESS, legislation promoted by an individual member purely to make a point rather than with any realistic hope of its enactment.

Paving Bill In the UK political system, a Bill preparing the way for a PRIVATISATION or some other event where authority is needed in advance of the definitive legislation; the Paving Bill for the eventual abolition of the GLC was a case in point. Moreover, in November 1992 John MAJOR's government took the unprecedented step of staging a **Paving Debate** before COMMITTEE STAGE of the European Communities (Amendment) Bill incorporating the MAASTRICHT TREATY. It had already been given a SECOND READING by a majority of 244, but after close referenda in Denmark and France and a hard-fought party conference debate, Major wanted clear authority to continue; he got it by a majority of just three.

Private Bill (1) At WESTMINSTER, a Bill brought forward by an individual, a company or a public body. Until the 1994 Transport and Works Act most dealt with the construction of railways and tramways; now they mainly refer to local bye-laws, harbours and markets although occasionally Bills enabling a couple within the probilited degrees to marry (usually a step-parent and stepchild) are promoted in the HOUSE OF LORDS. The procedure for dealing with a Private Bill involves a different committee process from government legislation. (2) In the US CONGRESS, a Bill affecting an individual rather than the public at large, for instance to deal with an individual immigration or naturalisation case or to settle a claim by or against the federal government.

Private Member's Bill A Bill promoted at WESTMINSTER by a BACKBENCH MP; most are minor changes to the law suggested by government departments (*see* HANDOUT BILL) or pressure groups, but the procedure has been used to promote major reforms to the law on abortion and obscenity and to try to introduce FREEDOM OF INFORMATION and ban hunting. Several Fridays each year are set aside for debating such Bills, a BALLOT is held for the top 20 to be debated, and despite formal obstacles (*see* OBJECT!) in an average session over half a dozen such Bills, including some originating in the Lords, reach the statute book.

Public Bill (1) At WESTMINSTER, any piece of legislation put forward by the government. (2) In the US CONGRESS, one that affects the public generally, regardless of who promotes it.

Reported Bill A Bill that has been considered and endorsed by a Committee of either House of CONGRESS, and is placed on the relevant CALENDAR for future debate. It is accompanied by a 'committee report' from one of the committee's members, which describes the scope and purpose of the Bill and the reasons for recommending approval; this is intended for use by the courts and other agencies, if the measure is passed, to ascertain the meaning intended by Congress.

Ten Minute Rule Bill At WESTMINSTER, a measure a BACKBENCH MP can introduce after QUESTION TIME to make a point or obtain the sense of the HOUSE. The sponsor may speak for ten minutes, or allow an opponent half the time; those opposed to the Bill are free to divide the House. In 1978–79 the Conservative OPPOSITION used such votes to demonstrate majority support for each of their proposed industrial relations reforms. Ten Minute Rule Bills, once passed, appear at the bottom of the list of Private Member's Bills for discussion on a Friday, and once every few years such a Bill, if on a matter of pressing need and supported by the Government, does get onto the statute book.

Billygate A considerable embarrassment for President CARTER, arising from a free trip to Libya unwisely accepted by his beer-swilling brother Billy. On his return, Billy founded a Libyan-Arab-Georgia Friendship Society, and hit the headlines in January 1979 by urinating on an airport runway while waiting to greet a Libyan delegation. The Justice Department demanded that he register as a foreign agent, which he at first refused to do, saying of Jewish protesters: 'They can kiss my ass.' The President, aware that key support was compromised, had Billy checked into an alcohol rehabilitation clinic, and a SENATE investigation concluded that Billy had done little for the $200,000 the Libyans had paid him. However, the damage was done, the President admitting to 'bad judgment' in asking his brother to intercede with Libya to press for the release of the Tehran HOSTAGES.

> I got a mamma (*see* MIZ LILLIAN) who joined the PEACE CORPS and went to India when she was 68. I got one sister who's a Holy Roller preacher. I got another sister who wears a helmet and rides a motorcycle. And I got a brother who thinks he's going to be President. So that makes me the only sane person in the family.
>
> BILLY CARTER, 1976

bimbo eruption The memorable phrase, coined during Bill CLINTON's governorship of Arkansas by his chief of staff Betsey Wright, for the repeated stories of improper sexual conduct which dogged his career and culminated in ZIPPERGATE and his near-impeachment. It characterised the way such (highly plausible) allegations would surface in the media whenever Clinton had reached a new and crucial stage in his rise to power, as those from Paula JONES (about sexual harassment) and Gennifer FLOWERS (of a long-running affair) did on the eve of his running for the Presidency.

bin Laden, Osama (1955–) The tall, charismatic and sinister youngest son of a Saudi construction magnate with Yemeni roots who became the driving force of AL QAEDA and the scourge of America (through 9/11 and other outrages) and of all Muslim governments that did not share his ISLAMIST fundamentalism. Born in Jeddah, bin Laden, who had independent wealth, enjoyed a Western-style youth but embraced militant Islam and went to Afghanistan in 1979 to fight the Russians. He financed hospitals, roads and storage depots in Afghanistan for the MUJAHEDDIN, and founded the militant MAK group in Pakistan to raise funds. In 1988 he founded Al Qaeda as a global campaign for his brand of Islam and against the West. He returned to Saudi Arabia in 1989 but was expelled two years later for inciting Saudis to attack US troops who he claimed had violated the holy places of Islam by their presence on Saudi soil. He took up residence in Sudan where he invested much of his fortune, but was expelled in 1996 and returned to Afghanistan, where he co-ordinated Al Qaeda's campaign of terrorism and its training camps under the protection of the TALEBAN. When US-led forces overthrew the Taleban he fled to the Tora Bora mountains in eastern Afghanistan; US efforts to kill or capture him foundered on their preference for paying supposedly sympathetic Afghans to cut off his line of escape rather than send in ground troops. Though a number of his lieutenants had been killed or arrested, bin Laden continued to taunt the West from the frontier region of Pakistan.

Bingham Report (1) The report, concluded in September 1978, of the inquiry into SANCTIONS-BUSTING to supply the Smith regime in Rhodesia, which was headed by Thomas Bingham QC. The inquiry, set up the year before by the Labour Foreign Secretary Dr David OWEN, embarrassed the Government when it was suggested that Harold WILSON had known about the continued supply of Rhodesia by Shell, BP and Total, despite denials at the time. Bingham concluded that some breaches had been committed, but moves to set up a fuller inquiry petered out. (2) The report on the collapse of the Bank of Credit and Commerce International submitted in 1992 by the now Lord Justice Bingham. He largely exonerated the authorities and the Bank of England of charges that prompter action to close a bank being defrauded on a massive scale would have saved thousands of depositors from bankruptcy – not to mention Scotland's tiny Western Isles Council, which lost £23 million.

bipartisanship Co-operation between normally opposed parties in pursuit of a common aim deemed to be non-controversial. The virtual unanimity achieved may not mean that the policy is the right one; the Victorian Liberal MP G. W. Erskine Russell wrote:

> When the government of the day and the opposition of the day take the same side, one can be almost sure that some great wrong is at hand.

Britain's main parties have generally followed a bipartisan policy toward NORTHERN

IRELAND, while the US CONGRESS has at times adopted one on key foreign policy issues, Sen. Arthur H. Vandenberg loftily declaring:

> To me bipartisan means a mutual effort, under our indispensable two-party system, to unite our official voice at the water's edge so that America speaks with the maximum authority . . . It does not involve the remotest surrender of free debate in determining our position.

> I don't intend to be in on the crash-landing unless I can be in on the take-off.
>
> HAROLD STASSEN (*attr.*)

> If you're going to lie down with the dogs, you're going to get fleas. Sen. TRENT LOTT

Birch. John Birch Society An ultra-conservative US secret society founded on 9 December 1958 by Robert H. W. Welch (1899–1985), a retired Boston candy manufacturer, to combat Communism and other potential threats to the American way of life. The society is named in honour of Captain John Birch, a Baptist missionary and US Army intelligence officer killed by Chinese Communists in August 1945. Welch regarded Birch as the first US victim of the Cold War.

> I don't believe I have any moral justification for repudiating them.
>
> RONALD REAGAN

Birmingham campaign The non-violent campaign for racial INTEGRATION and CIVIL RIGHTS mounted by Dr Martin Luther KING and the Southern Christian Leadership Council in the spring of 1963 to break one of the strongest bastions of SEGREGATION. Huge demonstrations were mounted day after day, and television viewers across America saw BULL Connor, the Alabama city's commissioner of public safety, turn dogs and firehoses on the protesters, including children. Hundreds of arrests were made, but new recruits filled the gaps until the city's businessmen capitulated and offered to end segregation in restaurants and discrimination in jobs. Mass demonstrations by black Americans in support of President KENNEDY's Civil Rights Bill, and for its strengthening, spread across America, culminating in the MARCH ON WASHINGTON FOR JOBS AND FREEDOM.

> Now is the time to lift our national policy from the quicksand of racial injustice to the solid rock of human dignity.
>
> MARTIN LUTHER KING, letter from Birmingham city jail, 16 April 1963

Birmingham Six The six Irish residents of Birmingham who were convicted in July 1975 of the bombings of the *Mulberry Bush* and *Tavern In The Town* pubs in the city centre the previous November which killed 21 people and injured almost 200. The bombings prompted the Labour government to rush through the Prevention of TERRORISM Act. The six were Hugh Callaghan, Patrick Hill, Gerrard Hunter, Richard McIlkenny, William Power and John Walker; five of them had been arrested as they boarded the Belfast boat off a train that left Birmingham just before the explosions. Though the trial judge said they had been convicted on the clearest evidence, doubts were raised over the forensic evidence and the conduct of the police in obtaining statements – one of which subsequently appeared to have been forged – and confessions. A campaign gradually got under way on their behalf, and after the Court of Appeal had twice rejected moves to overturn the convictions, they were finally set free on 14 March 1991, having been in custody for over sixteen years. The furore over this and a series of other miscarriages of justice, most of them IRA-related, raised deep concerns about the workings of the legal system and the police, and prompted the establishment of a ROYAL COMMISSION which recommended machinery for reviewing suspect cases.

Bismarck, Prince Otto von *See* IRON CHANCELLOR.

bisque A variant of a PAIR at WESTMINSTER, an arrangement under which an MP is excused from attending the HOUSE by party WHIPS; the term has nothing to do with soup, coming from the game of croquet when a player can agree to miss a turn. The practice was introduced in the 1983–87 Parliament when a Conservative majority of almost 150 left many Tories without a pair; it was little used after 1992 when the majority fell to 21, and was not resorted to by Labour after 1997 despite even larger majorities.

Bitburg affair The furore around President REAGAN's visit to the Kolmeshohe German war cemetery at Bitburg in May 1985. Planned as a gesture of reconciliation, the trip backfired politically when US officials, and then the press, belatedly discovered that the cemetery included graves of 47 men from the *Waffen SS*. Jewish groups, 53 senators, 390 members of the HOUSE and Nancy Reagan herself all urged the President not to go, but he went ahead rather than publicly snub his host, Chancellor Kohl. The President acknowledged that 'some old wounds have been reopened', and with dignity undid much of the damage.

BJP. Bharatiya Janata Party The Hindu nationalist party that grew from the **Jana Sangh** movement, founded after the birth of the Indian state, which profited in turn from the disarray of CONGRESS from the 1970s, from communal friction with Muslims over which faith should have a temple at Ayodhya and from concern in India after 9/11 about Islamic terrorism allegedly fomented by Pakistan and the continuing tension in Kashmir. From 1977 the forerunner of the BJP took part in the JANATA government. The BJP under Atal Bihari Vijpayee briefly formed a minority government in May 1996 until a United Front was formed to keep it out, but returned in March 1998 to take power until its unexpected defeat by Congress in April 2004.

black. Black and Tans The irregulars enlisted by LLOYD GEORGE's government in 1920 to supplement the Royal Irish Constabulary as political disorder in Ireland reached its height; though withdrawn a year later, they left behind a record of indiscriminate brutality against Irish Nationalists. The name came from a pack of hounds in Co. Limerick, and was applied because of their mixed black and tan uniforms, there being a shortage of police uniforms.

Black Caucus *See* CONGRESSIONAL BLACK CAUCUS.

Black Codes The laws to restrict the liberties of freed slaves, introduced by states in America's South in 1865–66 to blunt the edge of RECONSTRUCTION after the CIVIL WAR. Marriages were at last permitted and the right to hold property granted, but conditions of work little short of slavery were laid down, freedmen having to hire themselves out by the year. While the Codes deprived most black people of the vote, they failed to bring back the old plantation system, as in the end the labourers could not be compelled to work as before.

Black Consciousness The moderate ANTI-APARTHEID movement founded in South Africa by Steve Biko (1946–77), who was to die of head injuries in police custody. The film *Cry Freedom* (1987) paid tribute to his life and vision.

> The most potent weapon in the hands of the oppressor is the mind of the oppressed.
>
> STEVE BIKO

Black Hand Gang (1) (Serbo-Croat *Ujedinjenje Ili Smrt*, Unity or Death) The popular name for the Serb secret society responsible for the assassination of Archduke Franz Ferdinand at SARAJEVO on 28 June 1914, which led directly to the outbreak of WORLD WAR I. The Gang, headed by Col. Dragutin Dimitrievic of Serbian military intelligence, aimed to recover lands that had historically belonged to Serbia. (2) A criminal society, once active in New York, and largely made up of Italians.

black is beautiful The BLACK POWER slogan current in America from 1966 and attributed to Stokely Carmichael.

blackleg (1) In industrial disputes, an abusive term used by strikers for a person who has carried on working. (2) The word which, used by Sen. John Randolph of Virginia in 1826, provoked SPEAKER Henry Clay into challenging him to a duel; at that time it meant a dishonest gambler. The duel took place by the POTOMAC upstream from Washington on 8 April; after two exchanges of shots inflicted no injuries, Randolph and Clay shook hands and buried their difference.

blacklist A list of individuals considered unsuitable for employment because of their political views or personal lives. It was used in the days of MCCARTHYISM for people barred from Hollywood's motion picture industry for alleged links with the COMMUNIST Party, and is used by some employers to prevent the employment of militant trade unionists.

Black Monday (1) The US SUPREME COURT's action on 27 May 1935 in declaring the National Recovery Administration (NRA) UNCONSTITUTIONAL, which appeared to strike a deadly blow at Franklin D. ROOSEVELT's NEW DEAL. The President thought so, declaring that the Court had reinstated the 'HORSE AND BUGGY definition of interstate commerce'. Its ruling in what became known as the Sick CHICKEN case was in fact followed by a fresh burst of New Deal activity and the re-enactment of much of the legislation struck down, but it reminded Roosevelt's administration that it had to act within the CONSTITUTION. (2) The plunge in share prices on 19 October 1987, when the Dow Jones average on Wall Street fell by 23% and London and most other markets followed suit. Caused by computerised selling of stock in New York, some of it triggered by a hurricane which closed London markets the previous Friday, it was thought likely to lead to RECESSION, but reflationary measures to avert this, especially in Britain, produced OVERHEATING instead.

Black Muslims The Islamic sect, founded

in 1931, that has flourished in urban America since the mid-1960s. The most famous Black Muslims have been Malcolm X and the boxer Muhammad Ali, who was stripped of his world heavyweight title when he refused to fight in VIETNAM. As well as the mainstream sect itself, a number of splinter groups have also been established, one of the most successful being the disciplinarian **Nation of Islam**.

Black Panthers A US black revolutionary organisation founded in October 1966, which was briefly notorious for demanding the release of all black prisoners from US gaols and for a series of shootouts with the police which killed about 25 of its members. Yet despite their militancy the Black Panthers were also one of the few NEW LEFT groups actually to field candidates for public office. The origin of the name was probably the black panther adopted as an emblem in 1965 by the SNCC, and used by a group of BLACK POWER candidates who contested Alabama elections in 1966. A Black Panther Party emerged in California the following year led by Huey Newton and Eldridge Cleaver, preaching total separation from white society and urging black Americans to take up arms in 'self-defence'. In 1968 Newton was jailed for manslaughter for his part in one of the shootouts, prompting a 'Free Huey' campaign, and in 1970 the Panthers' Chicago leader was shot dead in his bed by police officers; his head of security was a police agent, recruited under J. Edgar Hoover's COINTELPRO programme. The movement lapsed in the 1970s after internal rifts and the arrest, defection or death of leading members. One, H. 'Rap' Brown, was jailed in 2002 for a subsequent murder.

> The panther is a fierce animal, but he will not attack until he is backed into a corner. Then he will strike out.
>
> HUEY NEWTON

Black Power A slogan first used by the US black leader Stokely Carmichael during a confrontation with police at Greenwood, Mississippi on 16 June 1966, subsequently adopted by various black or radical organisations. It implied a rejection of both INTEGRATION as a political goal and the pacifism of the CIVIL RIGHTS movement led by Dr Martin Luther KING, who was deeply suspicious of the word 'power'. As such, it sparked keen debate among black Americans, gradually gaining the initiative from less militant campaigning, and alienated many white liberals. This applied particularly to the clenched-fist Black Power salute, dramatically given by the sprinters Tommie Smith and John Carlos during the US National Anthem at their medal ceremony at the 1968 Mexico Olympics; they were expelled from the games and ordered home.

> To ask Negroes to get in the Democratic Party is like asking Jews to join the NAZI party.
>
> STOKELY CARMICHAEL

> The slogan 'Black Power' and what has been associated with it has set the Civil Rights movement back considerably in the United States over the period of the last several months.
>
> Sen. ROBERT KENNEDY, 8 December 1966

black propaganda. *See* PROPAGANDA.

Black Rod The Royal appointee, generally a former military man, who controls the functioning and security of the HOUSE OF LORDS, his counterpart in the COMMONS being the SERJEANT-AT-ARMS. His most visible function is to convey messages from the Lords to the Commons, and to ask them to attend the State Opening of Parliament and the PROROGATION ceremony; to demonstrate their independence, the Commons shut the door on him and he has to knock for admission. On 13 November 1979 Labour MPs, incensed that Michael HESELTINE had announced council house rent increases in a WRITTEN ANSWER, too late for debate, physically prevented Black Rod entering to bring the session to an end. In 2002 Black Rod became involved in a highly political spat with Downing Street after reputedly leaking to the press an exchange in which Tony BLAIR's staff appeared to be trying to upgrade his involvement in the Queen Mother's funeral. No. 10 lodged a complaint to the Press Complaints Commission, then embarrassingly withdrew it as Black Rod, Sir Michael Willcocks, stood his ground.

Black Sash The organisation of white liberal women in South Africa which, throughout the time of APARTHEID, staged dignified VIGILS against the policy and the RACISM it stood for.

Black Sections The groups set up in various constituency Labour parties, mainly in London, in the mid-1980s by left-wingers determined that ethnic minority members should have separate representation in the party. Their advocates hailed them as essential to the involvement of black and Asian Britons in mainstream politics; their opponents, mainly in the trade unions, denounced them as APARTHEID in reverse. Labour's National Executive (*see* NEC) and party conference refused to endorse the sections, and ultimately the compromise of a political society within the party open to all ethnic minority members was implemented.

Black September A Palestinian terrorist group founded in 1972, the name commemorating the expulsion of the PLO from Jordan in 1970. The MUNICH OLYMPICS MASSACRE of 1972 was staged by the group, as well as several HIJACKINGS and ASSASSINATIONS; one of its activists, Leila Khaled, was arrested in London in the early 1970s and deported lest the group stage attacks in Britain. King Hussein of Jordan was at the top of its assassination list, and Australia's pro-Israeli trade union leader (and later Prime Minister) Bob HAWKE was also believed to be a target.

Blackshirts Mussolini's (*see* DUCE) Italian FASCISTS, named after the distinguishing garment they wore. A similar uniform was adopted by the British Union of Fascists under Sir Oswald MOSLEY. It was also a name for the German SS (*Schutzstaffeln*) led by Heinrich Himmler. *See also* BLUESHIRTS, BROWNSHIRTS.

> Before the organisation of the Blackshirt movement, free speech did not exist in this country.
>
> SIR OSWALD MOSLEY

> The only actions we shall employ will be English ones. We shall rely on the good old English fist.
>
> MOSLEY

Black Thursday The name given to 24 October 1929, the day when the GREAT CRASH on Wall Street began. After some selling the pervious day, a record 12.9 million shares were dumped on the market, ruining thousands of investors and some brokers, even though a consortium led by the Morgan banking house moved in to steady prices. The market steadied on the Friday, but selling began after a statement from President HOOVER, intended to reassure but worded so as to hint that the stock market might be less sound than the economy as a whole. On **Black Tuesday**, 29 October, the bottom fell out of the market. 650,000 shares in US Steel were unloaded in the first three minutes, company after company collapsed and by the end of the day 16.4 million shares had been sold, at a loss of $10 million.

Black Wednesday The day, 17 September 1992, which saw the UK DEVALUE the pound and pull out of the Exchange Rate Mechanism (ERM). With the pound sliding against the mark after tensions between CHANCELLOR Norman Lamont and the BUNDESBANK, the Bank of England raised interest rates from 10% to 12% and then to 15% in a vain attempt to halt the slide. With at least $8 billion of Britain's currency reserves (more than twice the cost of the GULF WAR) spent on this ultimately futile exercise, Lamont pulled sterling out of the ERM and the pound began a 45-pfennig fall against the mark; interest rates reverted to 12% and returned to 10% later in the week. Black Wednesday did serious political damage to John MAJOR's government and brought almost universal calls for Lamont's resignation, but he stayed until the following spring (*see* JE NE REGRETTE RIEN) – partly because Major stressed that the failed policy, supported by the Labour OPPOSITION, had been his. However, the medium-term effect of devaluation was to break away from the savagely deflationary policies of the Bundesbank and pave the way for economic recovery – and by early 1993, with interest rates down to 6% and Britain cut off from moves toward a single European currency, many Conservatives were speaking of **Golden Wednesday**.

> Now we've all been screwed by the CABINET!
>
> THE SUN

Baa, Baa, Black Sheep Press reports in 1987 that Labour-controlled Islington council had banned the rhyme in nursery schools as RACIST marked the high point of controversy over the activities of the 'Loony LEFT' in London. The council denied banning the rhyme, but some nurseries in other boroughs had; where it is still sung 'white' is now often substituted for 'black'.

Blair. Blair House The four-storey yellow brick Georgian mansion across from the WHITE HOUSE, where Robert E. Lee refused the UNION command before the CIVIL WAR. The US Government bought it in WORLD WAR II as a guest house; Presidents stay there the night before their INAUGURATION and during building work at the White House. Harry S TRUMAN was there when on 1 November 1950 two Puerto Ricans burst in and tried to shoot him; Griselio Torrseola was shot by SECRET SERVICE agents, Oscar Collazo was sentenced to death but Truman reprieved him. The **Blair House Agreement** with the EUROPEAN COMMUNITY on oilseeds and farm subsidies, concluded in December 1992 in the teeth of French resistance (*see* ANGLO-SAXONS), removed a last obstacle to the URUGUAY ROUND of world tariff reductions.

Blair, Tony (Anthony Charles Lynton Blair, 1953–) The leader under whom the LABOUR PARTY shed the last trappings of doctrinaire SOCIALISM and, as **New Labour**, won landslide victories in 1997 and 2001, and a third term with a reduced majority in 2005, as a radical force representing Britain's broad majority. In power he presided over a government that delivered economic stability and constitutional change, but struggled to match expectations over public service DELIVERY. The longest serving Labour Prime Minister, he went six years before losing a senior colleague through resignation on a point of principle, when Robin COOK and, belatedly, Clare SHORT quit in protest at the decision to go to war with Iraq without the support of the United Nations. Elected in good measure as a reaction against Tory SLEAZE, Blair promised and largely delivered a more ethical style of government, but came under bitter fire from critics who claimed that his ADMINISTRATION was dominated by SPIN rather than substance. During his second term his close relationship with Gordon BROWN came under strain as supporters of the CHANCELLOR pressed for him to honour the agreement reputedly reached at GRANITA in 1994 and prepare to hand over NO. 10. On the world stage, Blair tried to align Britain more closely with Europe while maintaining very close relations first with Bill CLINTON and then, after 9/11, with George W. BUSH. His readiness to work with the latter irked the left, and on the eve of the IRAQ WAR in March 2003, 139 out of 407 Labour MPs rebelled. Blair kept his nerve, but victory in battle did not end the friction. After the suicide of Dr David KELLY his role in the drawing up of the 'DODGY DOSSIER' on Saddam's WEAPONS OF MASS DESTRUCTION and of the Government's treatment of Dr Kelly over his contacts with the BBC were thoroughly scrutinised by the HUTTON INQUIRY; while Blair was cleared of any wrongdoing, the findings of the inquiry were widely disbelieved.

Distrust over Iraq was a major factor in Labour's loss of ground in the 2005 election.

Blair's origins combined the humble (his father was fostered to a Glasgow shipyard family) and the comfortable (Blair was educated at Edinburgh's prestigious Fettes College). He became an active Christian at Oxford, but did not enter Labour politics until he became a barrister in London, where he met his wife CHERIE, daughter of the actor Tony Booth, a Labour CANDIDATE and successful lawyer. Blair fought his first seat in 1982, became MP for Sedgefield in his home county of Durham the next year, and with Labour's fortunes low, advanced rapidly in partnership with Brown. As Home Affairs spokesman he positioned Labour as 'TOUGH ON CRIME, AND TOUGH ON THE CAUSES OF CRIME'. When John SMITH died in May 1994, Blair was the instant leadership favourite, and a 'DREAM TICKET' with John Prescott (*see* TWO JAGS) for deputy formed (*see* BAMBI AND THUMPER). Blair defeated Prescott and Margaret Beckett for the leadership on 21 July 1994, then acted to remove what he saw as the last obstacle to a Labour government, replacing CLAUSE FOUR with a new statement of values.

> We both use Colgate toothpaste.
>
> GEORGE W. BUSH

> He has achieved great things since 1997 but, paradoxically, he is in danger of destroying his legacy as he becomes increasingly obsessed by his place in history.
>
> CLARE SHORT, resignation speech, 12 May 2003

Blair's babes The dozens of young Labour women MPs first elected in 1997 who were widely regarded as the backbone of Tony Blair's support as Prime Minister. *See also* STEPFORD WIVES.

Mr Blair, this is for Iraq The opening words of George Galloway's trenchant victory speech after the founder of RESPECT had defeated the Blairite Oona King to win Bethnal Green and Bow in the 2005 general election, after one of the most bruising campaigns of recent times, fought on the IRAQ WAR. He continued:

> All the people you have killed and all the loss of life comes back to haunt you and the best thing the Labour Party can do is sack you tomorrow morning.

He went on to call for the resignation of the RETURNING OFFICER for presiding over a 'shambles' of an election, and accuse the 'corrupt' Tower Hamlets council of producing an electoral register full of 'ghost votes'. A week later a US SENATE committee accused Galloway of involvement in the OIL FOR FOOD scandal, a charge he flatly rejected. *See also* MP FOR BAGHDAD CENTRAL, LION OF THE BRITISH PARLIAMENT.

blame game politics The art of ensuring that if a policy misfires, the blame falls on someone else. In WASHINGTON the SEPARATION OF POWERS enables the President to blame the CONGRESS, unless it is more convenient to blame his staff. Ronald REAGAN, up to the IRAN-CONTRA AFFAIR, was reckoned a master of the art. *See also* PREPARE THREE ENVELOPES.

blanket protest The protest staged by

convicted IRA men in the MAZE PRISON from 1980 to gain the POLITICAL STATUS accorded to suspects during INTERNMENT. Men **'on the blanket'** refused prison clothes, wearing only grey blankets. It spawned a DIRTY PROTEST and a HUNGER STRIKE; several prisoners died before limited freedoms were conceded.

Blears the Bike The inadvertently unfortunate phrase used in the House of Commons on 24 April 2001 by the then junior Transport Minister Keith Hill. He was endeavouring to compliment his fellow Labour MP Hazel Blears on her enthusiasm for cycling, but the phrase he used is more often employed to denote promiscuity. A horrified Hill apologised profusely to his colleague, he was demoted to the back benches at the next reshuffle, but later resumed his Ministerial career.

bleeding hearts A derogatory term for political LIBERALS and their tendency to agonise over the human condition, popularised in the 1930s by the COLUMNIST Westwood Pegler (1894–1969). 'Bleeding-heart liberals' were targeted in 1947 by the House Committee on UN-AMERICAN ACTIVITIES, and in 1968 Pierre TRUDEAU, preparing to invoke Canada's WAR MEASURES ACT against Quebec terrorism, said of his critics:

> There are a lot of bleeding hearts around who just don't like to see people with helmets and guns. All I can say is go and bleed – it is more important to keep law and order in society than to be worried about weak-kneed people.

blind trust (1) A legal/financial structure that enables investments to be made on behalf of politicians without them being aware of the details, so as to avoid any suspicion of conflict of interest. In the United States it has long been customary for any politician required to show financial probity and freedom from GRAFT to place their investments in a blind trust administered by a third party. In Britain such trusts became necessary with the NOLAN and other reforms of the 1990s as public opinion reacted against SLEAZE. The purchase of two flats in Bristol with capital from the BLAIRS' blind trust (the proceeds from the sale of their London home) precipitated the CHERIEGATE, though Tony Blair after consulting the CABINET SECRETARY determined that the rules governing blind trusts had not been broken. (2) A device for funding the private offices of Labour politicians through donations from wealthy supporters whose identity was kept from them. Intended to head off accusations of sleaze, the procedure was nevertheless ruled unethical once the party was returned to power in 1997.

blip A sudden downturn (or upturn) in one or more economic indicators which is out of line with the long-term trend. Politicians use the term to gloss over bad figures; when the UK economy in 1989 began to slide into RECESSION, CHANCELLOR Nigel Lawson scorned the first indicators as a blip.

blitz. blitzing A form of CANVASSING in which party workers call on as many voters in a neighbourhood as possible in a short time, urging them to turn out and vote, rather than taking time to ascertain and record which of them can be relied on. It is often used when a senior politician is visiting a key constituency, so that he or she can meet the maximum number of voters.

Blitzkrieg (Ger. lightning war) (1) The devastating motorised advance of German armies through the Low Countries and France in May 1940, which rewrote the war manuals; HITLER repeated the tactics against Russia the following year, with initial success. The German air assault on London and other UK cities after the Battle of Britain, in which the HOUSE OF COMMONS CHAMBER was destroyed on 10 May 1941, was known as the **Blitz**. When Israeli tanks launched a pre-emptive attack on adjoining Arab states to start the SIX DAY WAR, *Time* headlined it **'The Blintzkrieg'**. (2) The crash COLLECTIVISATION programme ordered by East Germany's communist leader Walter Ulbricht in 1959–60.

Bloc Quebecois The federal arm of the PQ (Parti Quebecois) which represents Quebec's SEPARATISTS in Parliament at Ottawa, and which, after the CANADIAN MELTDOWN of October 1993, supplanted the Conservatives for seven years as the official OPPOSITION. Founded earlier in 1993 by Lucien Bouchard, a former Conservative Cabinet Minister, who moved on in 1995 to become PQ Premier of Quebec, it is now led by Gilles Duceppe.

block captain One of the essential cogs in US MACHINE POLITICS, tasked with delivering votes in a city block to a party and watching out for those in need of help or PATRONAGE.

blockade A naval operation to discourage and, if necessary, prevent ships conveying supplies to a nation or community under siege. General Franco's (*see* CAUDILLO) navy staged a blockade of Republican Spain during the SPANISH CIVIL WAR which enterprising captains including **Potato Jones** (Captain D. I. Jones, 1870–1962) attempted to break. A US blockade to prevent Soviet ships carrying nuclear missiles reaching Cuba brought the CUBAN MISSILE CRISIS to a head.

blood. Blood and Iron The phrase that epitomises the MILITARISM that lay behind the rise of Prussia under Bismarck (*see* IRON CHANCELLOR) and Germany's subsequent headlong rush toward WORLD WAR I. Bismarck is credited with being its author; on 30 September 1862 he told the Prussian Chamber:

> The great questions of our day cannot be solved by speeches and majority votes . . . but by iron and blood.

Yet the phrase was not original; the 1st-century Roman orator Quintilian used the words *sanguine et ferrum* – blood and iron.

blood, sweat and tears The slightly-modified public recollection of Winston CHURCHILL's dramatic first speech as Prime Minister to the HOUSE OF COMMONS on 13 May 1940; he was taking office after the fall of Neville CHAMBERLAIN as the German BLITZKRIEG was sweeping toward Paris. His exact words were:

> I would say to the House, as I said to those who have joined this Government: 'I have nothing to offer you but blood, toil, tears and sweat.

Churchill may actually have meant to say 'blood, sweat and tears', which would have been a quotation from Byron. Indeed some radio listeners thought that was what he did say when his speech – re-delivered – was broadcast later.

Bloody Sunday (1) The riot that broke out in London's TRAFALGAR SQUARE on 13 November 1887 during a demonstration by the unemployed, which prompted William Booth, founder of the Salvation Army, and others to campaign for better conditions for the capital's poor. It culminated in Cunningham Grahame, a Scottish laird and radical MP, and the future Liberal CABINET MINISTER John Burns being convicted of unlawful assembly. (2) The murderous attack by TSARIST troops on 22 January 1905 on a deputation of workers and peasants led by Father Gapon as they marched to the Winter Palace in St Petersburg to present a petition to the 'Little Father'. Hundreds of unarmed people were killed. (3) The killing by the IRA on 21 November 1920 of eleven Englishmen thought to be spies. The BLACK AND TANS retaliated by killing twelve spectators at a football match at CROKE PARK, Dublin that afternoon. (4) The greatest single error by British security forces in Northern Ireland during the recent troubles, the fatal shooting by paratroops on 30 January 1972 of fourteen Catholic anti-INTERNMENT marchers in the Bogside area of Londonderry. The demonstration had been banned and the troops had itchy trigger fingers, and disaster ensued. The atrocity provoked riots in Dublin in which the British embassy was burned down, and drove many hitherto law-abiding Nationalists into the arms of the IRA. At WESTMINSTER, wrote the Labour MP Philip Whitehead,

> Bernadette Devlin (*see* FIDEL CASTRO IN A MINISKIRT) bore down on the huge bulk of the HOME SECRETARY [Reginald Maudling] like a pocket battleship, and battered him into something approaching wakefulness.

Bloody Sunday did untold damage to Britain's image throughout the world – especially in America where fund-raising for the Provisionals (*see* NORAID) rocketed. A judicial inquiry set up by the HEATH government exonerated the paras. Three decades later Tony BLAIR's Labour government set up a further exhaustive inquiry under Lord Justice Saville which took evidence over three years from 919 participants including IRA leaders, (anonymous) ex-paratroops and, in January 2003, Sir Edward Heath, who vehemently denied that the government had given any encouragement for the shootings. He said:

> The tragic deaths in Londonderry outraged the Roman Catholic community, increased support for the IRA and destroyed the prospect for a political initiative. It is therefore absurd to suggest that (the Government) intended, or was prepared to risk, the events which occurred.

rivers of blood *See* RIVERS.

there are worse things than bloodshed, and slavery is one of them The stirring words of the Irish nationalist revolutionary Padraic Pearse (1879–1916) in his book *The Coming Revolution* (1913). Three years later Pearse led the EASTER RISING in Dublin, delivering the Proclamation of Independence as head of the 'Provisional Government of the Irish Republic'. He surrendered on 19 April and was executed on 3 May. Pearse wrote:

> We may make mistakes in the beginning and shoot the wrong people, but . . . there are many things worse than bloodshed, and slavery is one of them.

waving the bloody shirt *See* WAVING.

bludger An Australian term for an idler on unemployment pay, the equivalent of 'scrounger' in Britain or the US 'welfare queen'. Gough WHITLAM's Labor ministry was accused by the Liberal opposition of encouraging 'dole bludgers' while increasing tax burdens on the MIDDLE CLASS.

blue (1) The campaign colour of America's DEMOCRATIC PARTY, in contrast to the Republicans' RED. Both parties campaign in patriotic red, white and blue, but use their own colour – as do the media on election nights – in order to make the contrast. (2) The campaign colour (with a couple of regional exceptions) of Britain's CONSERVATIVE PARTY, hence the expression 'true blue' for a committed Tory. (3) The progressive Conservatives who governed Ontario continuously from 1943 to 1984 were known as the **Big Blue Machine**.

Blue and the Gray The rival combatants in America's CIVIL WAR: blue for the UNION and grey for the CONFEDERACY. In 1938, 73 years after the end of hostilities, 1845 survivors from the two armies – 1359 from the North and 486 from the South – gathered at GETTYSBURG, scene in 1863 of one of the war's most hard-fought engagements, for a final reunion, at which President ROOSEVELT unveiled a memorial of Eternal Light. Despite their extreme age, just one veteran died on the final day and six more on the way home; the last lived on until 1949. Astoundingly the last reunion of the widows of Civil War combatants took place on 1 July 1997, two of the three survivors attending.

blue book At WESTMINSTER, the report of a Commons SELECT COMMITTEE or other document issued by the HOUSE; those produced by the LORDS are coloured red.

blue-collar An originally US term for manual, as opposed to clerical (white-collar) workers.

blue dress The semen-stained garment retained by Monica LEWINSKY as a trophy of her encounters with Bill CLINTON in an anteroom to the OVAL OFFICE which became one of the talking-points of the ZIPPERGATE affair. Lewinsky told her PENTAGON confidante Linda Tripp:

> I'll never wash it again.

blue helmets The universal nickname for UNITED NATIONS PEACEKEEPING troops, who wear a blue helmet with the letters *UN* in place of their national uniform headgear.

Blue Laws The Sunday observance laws current in a number of American States, and especially those regulating the Sunday opening of shops and stores.

blue-ribbon panel or **commission** WASHINGTON-speak for a group of eminent Americans appointed by the President or a federal agency to inquire into or resolve a particular issue. The UK equivalent is the GREAT AND THE GOOD.

blue-rinse brigade An uncomplimentary term for the massed ranks of women constituency activists in Britain's CONSERVATIVE PARTY who assemble at its conferences and traditionally demanded tougher policies on law and order; it refers to their coiffure and is only coincidentally of political significance.

blue slip WASHINGTON-speak for the note sent to individual SENATORS by the MAJORITY LEADER seeking support for a Presidential NOMINATION to a particular office; the note states that if no response is received the Senator's approval will be assumed, but in fact failure by enough to return the slip may lead to the nomination being withdrawn.

Blueshirts The FASCIST 'National Guard' founded in Ireland on 20 July 1933 by General Eoin O'Duffy (1892–1944), Commissioner of the Garda (police) until his dismissal that year by de Valera. Outlawed within a month, it had grown out of the Army Comrades' Association founded the year before. O'Duffy became President of FINE GAEL two months after founding the Blueshirts, but resigned the next year and in 1935 founded the National Corporate Party. In the SPANISH CIVIL WAR a Blueshirt battalion led by O'Duffy fought alongside Franco's (*see* CAUDILLO) troops; on his death O'Duffy was accorded a State funeral.

blue skies thinking. A term for long-range policy development much used by Tony BLAIR and his advisers. It gained some discredit when applied within Downing Street to less rigorous studies by Lord Birt, former director-general of the BBC, into crime and the future of the railways.

Blue Streak The missile developed by the UK to deliver its independent DETERRENT, which was cancelled in 1960 when President EISENHOWER agreed to supply Britain with the POLARIS submarine-launched missile and the air-delivered SKYBOLT. Two years later, the KENNEDY administration cancelled Skybolt, embarrassing Harold MACMILLAN, who had negotiated the original deal in BERMUDA.

blue-water navy One of the attributes of a WORLD POWER, a navy able to command the great oceans as well as patrolling home waters. The term has a Victorian ring, but was first used between the World Wars by UK Admiralty officials who favoured building large ships to be deployed in distant parts of the world; in consequence Britain went into WORLD WAR II with no landing craft. The phrase was revived in the 1960s and 1970s by the Soviet Admiral Gorchkov as his fast-expanding navy broadened its horizons.

clear blue water Code used by Michael Portillo and other Conservative right-wingers from 1994 onwards for their push for John MAJOR's Conservative government to swing to the right to open up a distinct ideological difference as Tony BLAIR's NEW LABOUR moved to capture the middle ground. Major resisted this pressure. **clear red water** was the term adopted by Rhodri Morgan as leader of Labour in Wales from 2000 for his strategy of pursuing a more left-wing strategy in the WELSH ASSEMBLY than Tony Blair's government in London; his line was vindicated by a strong showing in the 2003 elections as Labour elsewhere in Britain lost ground.

Blunt case The belated exposure in 1979 of Sir Anthony Blunt (1907–83) as the FOURTH MAN in the BURGESS AND MACLEAN affair. Blunt, a distinguished art historian and former surveyor of the Queen's pictures, had been recruited at Cambridge in the 1930s by Soviet intelligence while a member of the APOSTLES. He was a Soviet agent during the war while working for MI5, and in 1951 arranged Burgess and Maclean's flight to the Soviet Union. In 1964 he confessed his treachery, but was guaranteed immunity from prosecution in return for telling all he knew. When Margaret THATCHER heard this on coming to power she insisted, against the advice of senior civil servants, on making a detailed explanation to the HOUSE OF COMMONS of what many MPs saw as a classic ESTABLISHMENT cover-up; in the ensuing furore, Blunt was stripped of his KNIGHTHOOD. In November 1979 the ATTORNEY-GENERAL, Sir Michael Havers, told MPs that when confronted with his treachery, Blunt

> maintained his denial. He was offered immunity from prosecution. He sat in silence for a while. He got up, looked out of the window, poured himself a drink and after a few minutes he confessed. Later he co-operated, and he continued to co-operate. That is how the immunity was given and how Blunt responded.

Blythe, William Jefferson The original name of Bill CLINTON, who was born on 19 August 1946 three months after his father, William Blythe, was killed in a car crash. When he was 15, the future President took the surname of his stepfather, Roger Clinton. For another President who changed his name, *see* LESLIE KING.

BMG. *See* BALFOUR MUST GO.

B'nai Brith (Heb. Sons of the Covenant) The oldest Jewish organisation in the world, founded in New York in 1843, which exercises considerable political influence through the respect in which it is held by Jewish and Gentile politicians alike. *B'nai Brith* is closely identified with the **Anti-Defamation League**, which it established in 1913 to counter anti-Jewish prejudice.

BND *Bundesnachrichtendienst* (Ger. Federal Information Service) The internal and overseas security and intelligence organisation set up by the West German government in 1956, and now serving the reunited nation; its headquarters is at Pullach. The BND absorbed the covert force created after the war by Reinhold Gehlen, a former section head in Hitler's *Abwehr* who was trusted by the Americans.

BNP The normal term for the **British National Party**, an extreme right-wing and anti-migrant grouping which has largely taken over the mantle of the **National Front** in fomenting racial tension, it was widely blamed for the extent and violence of the riots in Oldham and Bradford in the summer of 2001. Founded by John Tyndall in 1982 after a split in the National Front, and led since 1999 by Nick Griffin, a Cambridge graduate, it won its first council seat in the Isle of Dogs in 1993, but has had its greatest success building resentment in northern cities against Asian (and especially Muslim) communities alleged to have been given preferential treatment by local councils. In the 2003 municipal elections the BNP took sixteen seats, nine of them in Burnley where it became the official opposition. Two years later it polled 16 per cent in the general election at Barking.

> When (people) start voting for the BNP it's time to admit that things have gone badly wrong.
>
> Conservative Party chairman THERESA MAY, party conference speech 7 October 2002

board. Board of Education The informal gatherings of HOUSE Democratic and Republican leaders that took place most afternoons around 5 p.m. in a first-floor CAPITOL hideaway from 1928 until the mid-1960s. A chance meeting between SPEAKER Nicholas LONGWORTH and Minority Leader

John Nance Garner (*see* CACTUS JACK) developed into regular sessions to get round PROHIBITION and keep the wheels of House BUSINESS rolling. Sometimes Longworth played his Stradivarius, on other occasions members would play poker; always they drank bourbon and what Garner called 'branch water'. The name was coined by Rep. Albert McDuffie of Alabama, a regular attender, because the Speaker would take in young Congressmen to 'educate' them into voting his way; Garner, who took over as host as Speaker from 1931, explained:

> We pay the tuition by supplying the liquor.

Sam RAYBURN carried on the tradition from 1940, even inviting Vice President TRUMAN. From one such session on 12 April 1945, Truman was called to the WHITE HOUSE to be told by Eleanor ROOSEVELT that her husband was dead and he was now President. Apart from a hiatus from 1952 to 1954 when the teetotal Republican Joe Martin interrupted his reign, Rayburn stayed in the chair until his death in 1961; it fizzled out under his successor John McCormack, but its spirit lived on in Speakers Carl Albert and 'TIP' O'Neill, both 'Board' members as rising Congressmen.

Board of Trade *See* TRADE.

boat people Refugees or illegal immigrants who have fled from their homeland or some intermediate point by boat in the hope of settling in a safer, more prosperous country across the water. The term originally applied to the flood of refugees from VIETNAM who, following the Communist victory in 1975, crowded onto anything that could float to head for a better life in America, or any other free country that would have them. Many drowned when their overloaded craft sank, others were murdered or raped by pirates, but tens of thousands made it to a mixed welcome in other South-east Asian countries. As conditions in Vietnam improved its neighbours became less welcoming, and in the late 1980s the British authorities in Hong Kong attempted, against US opposition, to REPATRIATE some of the 40,000 boat people in camps in the colony who were ruled to be migrants rather than refugees. The term has since been used for fugitives to the US from Cuba (*see* ELIAN) or Haiti, for Albanians and Kurds targeting Italy and for Afghans and Iraqis trying to reach Australia.

Boatman Jim The nickname of **James Abram Garfield** (1831–81), 20th President of the United States (Republican, Mar-Sep 1881), who had worked as a boy on the Ohio Canal. A CIVIL WAR general, professor and eight-term CONGRESSMAN, Garfield was elected SPEAKER in 1878. President GRANT considered him 'not possessed of the backbone of an angleworm', but after his narrow victory over Winfield Hancock (his ELECTORAL COLLEGE margin was wider) he disproved this. He took on the powerful Sen. Roscoe Conkling, naming William H. Robertson to run the New York Custom House instead of a Conkling nominee and saying:

> This will settle the question of whether the President of the United States is registering clerk of the Senate or the Executive of the United States.

Garfield was shot at a Washington station on 2 July 1881 by Charles Guiteau, a disappointed office-seeker; Garfield observed: 'He must have have been crazy. What would he have wanted to shoot me for?' He died eleven weeks later; he should have been saved but doctors mistakenly tried to recover the bullet.

> How could anyone be so cold-hearted as to want to kill my baby? Garfield's mother

Bobbety The nickname of Lord Cranborne (Robert Cecil), later the 5th Marquess of Salisbury (1893–1972). Appointed a junior Foreign Office (*see* FCO) minister by BALDWIN, he resigned with Anthony EDEN over APPEASEMENT, and ABSTAINED in the vote on the MUNICH AGREEMENT. He served as Leader of the LORDS under CHURCHILL, Eden and MACMILLAN, but moved to the right, threatening to quit over Churchill's overtures to Russia after STALIN's death, and finally resigning in 1957 over the release of Archbishop Makarios from detention (*see* ENOSIS). His role in determining the succession to Eden early in 1957 was crucial. *See* WAB OR HAWOLD?.

Bobby One nickname (another was **Mandy**) for Peter Mandelson, (1953–), the grandson of Herbert Morrison who transformed the image of the LABOUR PARTY under Neil KINNOCK by banishing glum left-wingers to the fringes of the party conference platform and introducing the RED ROSE party emblem. He later proved too hot a potato for Tony BLAIR, twice having to resign from his CABINET despite his administrative skills at the Department of Trade and Industry and in Northern Ireland before leaving the COMMONS in 2004 to become a EUROPEAN COMMISSIONER. His first departure, over the ROBINSON LOAN, was inevitable, but the second, early in 2000 over the affair of the HINDUJA passports, was arguably unnecessary; Mandelson believed he had been forced out by Alastair Campbell, Blair's head of communications, to spare the government from an embarrassment that did not materialise. Mandelson in opposition was a past master of SPIN, running the party's PR machine with consummate skill but earning the enmity of Gordon BROWN and John Prescott (*see* TWO JAGS). Differing explanations for his nickname reflected his perennial desire to appear a confidant of the leadership, and the mistrust in which he was held by some. Mandelson claimed that Blair gave him the codename 'Bobby' (after RFK, he suggested) so that he could deliver confidential telephone advice to the leader without colleagues knowing it was him. Critics around his Hartlepool, north-east England constituency claimed its origin lay in 'Bobby Shaftoe', a local folk song, because he had shafted so many colleagues. In 1999 Mandelson gave the name to his golden retriever puppy.

Bodenstown The burial place, on the Liffey west of Dublin, of Wolfe Tone, the Irish patriot who brought French forces to assist the rebellion of NINETY-EIGHT. Each year it is the scene of the **Bodenstown Parade**, staged by SINN FEIN as a rally for hard-line Republicans.

Body, the The nickname of Jesse Ventura (real name James Janos), the former professional wrestler, US Navy SEAL and radio 'shock jock' who was elected as Independent (REFORM PARTY) Governor of Minnesota in 1998, defeating the Democrat Hubert H. HUMPHREY III. He governed well if controversially, and to the relief of the established parties did not seek a second term.

Boer War The conflict between 1899 and 1902 in which British forces subdued the independent Afrikaner states of what is now South Africa, paving the way for the country's unification under the British flag; it is sometimes known as the Second Boer War, the first having been fought in 1880–81. It saw the humiliation of the British Army by Boer commandos on several occasions, and gave a foretaste of the brutality of 20th-century warfare. British victory was only secured after harsh measures, including the confinement of Boer women and children to CONCENTRATION CAMPS, where 20,000 died. The Liberal opposition leader Henry Campbell-Bannerman (*see* C-B) was moved to say:

> When is a war not a war? When it is carried out by methods of barbarism in South Africa.

The war created a serious split in the LIBERAL PARTY, some LIBERAL UNIONISTS realigning themselves with the Conservatives, and the radicals being denounced as PRO-BOERS. The KHAKI ELECTION, held with victory apparently near, brought a comfortable victory for Lord SALISBURY's ruling Conservative/Unionists.

> A war that has been forced upon this country.
>
> Sir EDWARD GREY

> When you enter a war purely for the purpose of plunder, I know of nothing which is more degrading to the country or more hideous in its effects on the mind and character of the people engaged on it.
>
> LLOYD GEORGE

See also CHURCHILL; DEFEAT; MAFFICKING; VEREENIGING TREATY.

Bofors scandal The scandal that in 1989 brought down the Indian government of Rajiv Gandhi (1944–91), son of Indira Gandhi and grandson of Jahawarlal Nehru (*see* NEHRU DYNASTY). It concerned £30 million in kickbacks allegedly paid to Indian politicians and officials by the Swedish armaments company to secure a £775 million howitzer contract in 1986. One of those implicated in an Indian police report was Gopichand HINDUJA, one of two wealthy Indian brothers resident in the UK, the fast-tracking of whose applications for British citizenship in the late 1990s precipitated Peter Mandelson's (*see* BOBBY) second resignation from Tony BLAIR's CABINET in January 2001. Corruption charges against the Hindujas involving $5.5 million were dismissed by the Indian High Court in May 2005.

bog-standard comprehensives *See* COMPREHENSIVISATION.

Bogside The area outside the walls of Protestant (London) Derry where Catholics first settled in the 17th century. It became a stronghold of REPUBLICANism after the 'Battle of the Bogside' when LOYALISTS, backed by the B-SPECIALS, besieged it on 13 August 1969 at the start of the renewed TROUBLES.

Boiler Room The nerve centre in Little Rock, Arkansas, from which Bill CLINTON's successful 1992 campaign for the US Presidency was orchestrated. It was from here that James Carville (*see* RAGIN' CAJUN) handled the media, getting across key messages (*see* 'It's the ECONOMY, stupid', the reminder Carville pinned up in the Boiler Room) and combating repeated BIMBO

ERUPTIONS, notably the Gennifer FLOWERS affair. Historically the term has also been used for a TELEPHONE BANK, as such operations have frequently been housed in basements and the like.

Boipatong massacre The worst black-on-black atrocity in the run-up to majority rule in South Africa, an attack on African National Congress (ANC) supporters at Boipatong, in the Vaal, on 17 June 1992 which left 39 people dead. It was carried out by hostel-dwelling supporters of INKATHA, but it suited last-ditch white supporters of APARTHEID in ruling circles. A judicial inquiry ruled that although the security forces had not actually instigated the killings, they could have done more to prevent them. The subsequent massacre of 28 ANC supporters at Bishu on 7 September by Ciskei security forces further heightened tensions between the ANC and both Inkatha and the Pretoria government, threatening but not derailing progress to MAJORITY RULE.

Bokassa diamonds The scandal surrounding a gift of diamonds to France's President Valéry Giscard d'Estaing from the self-styled Emperor Bokassa I of the Central African Republic. The transaction was unearthed by the satirical magazine *Le Canard Enchainé*; Giscard at first denied it, then said that the diamonds had only been small ones. His benefactor, Jean-Bedel Bokassa, a French colonial soldier from 1939 to 1960, had overthrown the Republic's first President, David Dacko, in 1966 and after ten years of autocratic rule crowned himself Emperor and commissioned a gigantic palace; its cold stores contained the carcases of opponents on whom he was said to have feasted. In 1979 Giscard, perhaps embarrassed by disclosure of the gift, sent in French paratroops to restore Dacko. Bokassa fled, but returned in 1986; two years later he was jailed for life for crimes including a massacre of 100 schoolchildren, but acquitted of cannibalism. He was released under an amnesty in 1993, and died in 1996.

Boland amendment The CONGRESSional sanction, voted in 1982, against the REAGAN ADMINISTRATION providing training or military supplies to the Nicaraguan CONTRAS. The amendment to the Defense Appropriation Act, named after Rep. Edward Boland of Massachusetts, Chairman of the House Intelligence Committee, was passed unanimously by the House because members feared the CIA was secretly helping the Contras in their war against the SANDINISTA government. The next year Boland pushed through a second amendment setting a ceiling on funding for the Contras and urging the President to negotiate. With the exposure of the IRAN-CONTRA AFFAIR in 1986, both the TOWER COMMISSION and Congressional hearings showed that the Boland amendment had been flagrantly violated.

boll weevils The 50 or so Conservative Southern Democrats whose Conservative Democratic Forum is a cohesive and influential voting bloc, though slightly less so since the Republicans consolidated their post-1970s gains in the South. They took the name from the cotton weevil which bores from within, signifying their intention of making their presence felt in the Democratic CAUCUS as whole – even though many were elected by running against the party's national platform on defence spending and budget deficits. The boll weevils' support was critical to Ronald REAGAN's ability to win CONGRESSional votes early in his presidency. *Compare* GIPSY MOTHS.

Bolsheviks (Russ. the majority) The hard-line Russian advocates of PROLETARIAN revolution who broke with the MENSHEVIKS in 1903 and whose leaders planned and agitated in exile, during which LENIN reputedly said:

> Give us a child for eight years and it will be a Bolshevik for ever.

In 1917 the Bolsheviks, with Mensheviks and liberals, first overthrew the TSARIST system and then, in the OCTOBER REVOLUTION, crushed the domestic opposition to win total power. Despite their name the Bolsheviks were the majority only of the Russian Social-Democratic Labour Party from which they stemmed. Once in power, Lenin and STALIN preferred to call themselves COMMUNISTS, and 'Bolshevik' soon became a term of abuse in the West. In Britain, the word **Bolshie** came to be applied to any bloody-minded and unco-operative individual, especially in the field of trade unionism.

> A Socialist who wants to do something about it.
> GEORGE BERNARD SHAW

> Czarism in overalls.
> GEORGE JEAN NATHAN (1882–1958)

> Nature has no cure for this sort of madness, though I have known a legacy from a rich relative work wonders.
> F. E. SMITH (Lord BIRKENHEAD), 1927

Bolshevism run mad The description accorded to Labour's REFLATIONARY election programme in 1931 by Philip Snowden,

CHANCELLOR in the NATIONAL GOVERNMENT, who had been a leading member of the party until the GREAT BETRAYAL shortly before.

Bomb, the Shorthand throughout the 1950s and into the '60s for the ATOMIC BOMB, and the threat to world peace and survival which it represented, as in CND's simplest slogan BAN THE BOMB.

bomb North Vietnam back into the Stone Age The election pledge delivered in 1968 by George Wallace's RUNNING-MATE, the former Air Force general Curtis Le May (1906–90). While the Wallace ticket won considerable support from HARD-HAT voters for its policies on race and VIETNAM, Le May's comments on the war frightened off many potential supporters and were seized on by opponents to depict him as a war-crazed nut. What Le May in fact said was that the Communist North must stop its infiltration of South Vietnam or 'we're going to bomb them back into the Stone Age'.

Bomber Thorpe The accolade bestowed on the UK LIBERAL PARTY leader Jeremy THORPE in 1966 after he called for the RAF to bomb Rhodesia in order to end the state of UDI declared the previous year by the Smith regime.

the bomber will always get through Stanley BALDWIN's chilling phrase, presaging the miseries of the BLITZ, that encouraged Britons in the 1930s to imagine that there was no defence against aerial bombardment, and thus strengthened the mood against REARMAMENT. On 10 November 1932 Baldwin told the COMMONS:

> I think it is well also for the man in the street to realise that there is no power on earth that can protect him from being bombed. Whatever people may tell him, the bomber will always get through.

bombing halt The pause in the bombing of North Vietnam ordered by Lyndon B. JOHNSON on 31 March 1968 when he announced his decision not to run again for the Presidency. He hoped it would lead to a negotiated end to the VIETNAM WAR, but the conflict was to continue into the NIXON ADMINISTRATION's second term.

Bonar Law, Andrew (1858–1923), Prime Minister (Conservative) October 1922–May 1923 when cancer forced him to resign. Born in Canada, the UNKNOWN PRIME MINISTER made his fortune as an iron merchant in Glasgow, became a UNIONIST MP in 1900 and after the Conservatives' two election defeats in 1910 succeeded BALFOUR the following year as party leader. Pushed forward by Lord Beaverbrook, Bonar Law told him: 'If I am a great man, then a good many of the great men of history are frauds'; indeed Roy JENKINS wrote: 'Simplicity was one of his few engaging characteristics.' A bachelor, his only interest outside politics and business was bridge. Bonar Law was a model of Scots-Canadian dourness. ASQUITH considered that 'he has not the brains of a Glasgow bailie'; Austen Chamberlain termed him 'an amateur who will always remain one', while LLOYD GEORGE reminisced: 'Bonar would never make up his mind on anything, [though] once a question had been decided, he would stick with it and fight it to a finish.' He served in the wartime coalitions under Asquith and Lloyd George as Colonial Secretary, CHANCELLOR OF THE EXCHEQUER, LEADER OF THE HOUSE and LORD PRIVY SEAL before retiring in 1921. When the Conservatives withdrew from the coalition in 1922, forcing Lloyd George's resignation, he was recalled as Prime Minister, but was almost immediately afflicted by illness.

bonding session The much-ridiculed gathering of William HAGUE's SHADOW CABINET and supporting MPs at Eastbourne in October 1997, the highlight of which was the singing of WORLD WAR II songs around the piano by pullover-wearing front-benchers. Intended as a team-building exercise, the occasion conveyed instead the impression that under Hague the CONSERVATIVE Party had fallen under the influence of management consultants, which Hague had once been. Subsequent events had a less artificially informal feel.

Boneless Wonder The nickname for the UK Prime Minister Ramsay MACDONALD, cruelly awarded him by Winston CHURCHILL. In the COMMONS on 28 January 1931, Churchill said:

> I remember when I was a child being taken to the celebrated Barnum's Circus . . . The exhibit which I most desired to see was the one described as 'the Boneless Wonder'. My parents judged that the spectacle would be too revolting for my youthful eyes, and I have waited fifty years to see the Boneless Wonder sitting on the Treasury bench.

bonfire of controls The cull of expendable wartime controls and restrictions on business and the consumer which the young Harold WILSON, President of the Board of Trade in ATTLEE's government, announced early in 1949. Wilson abolished controls which required the issuing of 900,000 licences a year, and over six weeks completely abolished the rationing of clothes. This break with austerity contributed to Labour's narrow re-election in 1950. However, Labour's continued identification with post-war drabness and shortage was a factor in the party's eventual defeat in 1951, after Wilson had resigned from the CABINET.

Bongo-Bongo Land The description of THIRD WORLD countries which landed the devil-may-care Alan CLARK in hot water c. 1987, prompting accusations of racism. The patrician Clark was given to languidly outrageous comments, controversy over which dogged his time as a middle-ranking minister under Margaret THATCHER, to whom he was devoted, and John MAJOR. He once evoked a protest from the Philippine Embassy by voicing regret that the nobility now had their children brought up by Filipinos rather than home-grown help. He was especially unrepentant about this comment, having received an election poster from the African leader of the same name reading: *Gagnez avec Bongo! See also* MATRIX-CHURCHILL AFFAIR.

Bonus Army The mass of unemployed WORLD WAR I ex-servicemen who converged on WASHINGTON in 1932 as a 'Bonus Expeditionary Force' and refused to go home until CONGRESS authorised immediate payment of the 20-year bonus for veterans it had voted in 1924. By mid-June 15,000 were camped on the MALL in tarpaper shacks and packing crate huts; most left in the following month after President HOOVER refused to meet them, but some 2,000 refused to disband. Believing they might resort to violence, Hoover on 28 July sent General Douglas Macarthur with infantry, cavalry and tanks to drive them from the capital, leaving two veterans dead; this action contributed to his defeat by Franklin D. ROOSEVELT later that year. When Bonus Army members returned to press the new administration for help, Eleanor Roosevelt, at FDR's suggestion, took coffee out to them and joined in 'There's a long, long trail'.

> Hoover sent the Army – Roosevelt sent his wife.
> ANON Bonus Army veteran

boom An unsustainable high point in the economic cycle, a time of growth, plenteous money and near-full employment leading, if not checked, to OVERHEATING. Inevitably a boom is followed by an economic slowdown, but if the situation is badly handled it can lead, as occurred in Britain from the late 1980s, to RECESSION – or even depression and slump.

boom and bust The pejorative used by Gordon BROWN to pillory the UK Conservative governments of the 1980s and '90s for allegedly having lurched alternately from periods of runaway growth to deep despair. In office as CHANCELLOR from 1997, Brown undertook to pursue steady growth through POST NEO-CLASSICAL ENDOGENOUS GROWTH THEORY, and largely succeeded. *Compare* STOP-GO.

boondoggle The useless spending of public money on make-work projects, originally with reference to the US government's NEW DEAL expenditure in the 1930s to combat the GREAT DEPRESSION. In his 1987 STATE OF THE UNION address, President REAGAN told CONGRESS:

> We can carve out the boondoggles and PORK.

'Boondoggle' was a Frontier word for time taken up in leatherwork – boondoggles (woggles in the UK) are the plaited lanyards or thongs worn by many US Boy and Girl Scouts. The word's political use derives from a 1935 investigation of public relief in New York City, when a Mr Robert Marshall testified that he taught 'boon doggles':

> Making belts in leather, or maybe belts by weaving ropes, or it might be belts by working in canvas, maybe a tent or a sleeping bag. In other words it is a chamber of horrors where boys perform crafts that are not designed for finess and fine work, but simply for a utility purpose.

Border poll The REFERENDUM in NORTHERN IRELAND called by the HEATH Government in March 1973, in which 58% of the electorate supported the province remaining in the UK. The majority of votes was overwhelming as all but a few thousand opponents of PARTITION abstained.

Bork, to A US term for the undermining of a political opponent by targeting a candidate for public office whom they support. It arose from the SENATE's blocking in 1987 of the appointment of the ultra-conservative Judge Robert H. Bork (1927–) to the SUPREME COURT after an extensive media campaign against him which induced four members of the American Bar Association's vetting panel to declare him 'not qualified'. Bork, a Justice of the US Court of Appeals, had served as acting ATTORNEY-GENERAL after Elliot Richardson's resignation during President Nixon's 1974 'SATURDAY NIGHT MASSACRE'. Fervent objections to his nomination from liberal and other groups led

CONGRESS to question him closely on his consistent opposition to CIVIL RIGHTS legislation and his refusal to accept a 'right to privacy'. In 30 hours of testimony Bork managed to alienate even some conservatives, and the Senate rejected his confirmation by 58 to 42. President REAGAN denounced the hearings as a 'LYNCH mob'. In March 2001 the ABA panel, which had assessed virtually every candidate for judicial office since 1953, was itself 'Borked' by George W. BUSH, to the delight of conservatives in the profession.

borough In the UK a municipal authority, originally a town but now any local authority area which chooses to be described as such. New York City is divided into five boroughs – Manhattan, Brooklyn, the Bronx, Queens and Richmond (Staten Island); in Alaska, however, a borough is the same as a COUNTY.

borough constituency Under a technicality of UK electoral law, predominantly urban seats receive this designation and CANDIDATES standing for ELECTION are allowed to incur slightly higher expenses.

pocket borough In Britain's electoral system, a town so firmly under the control of a patron or family (or now of a party) that it will always return their nominee without question. A common phenomenon before the 1832 REFORM ACT, the term has survived to describe a handful of Conservative seats where the CONSTITUENCY ASSOCIATION still respects a patron's choice of candidate . . . or a Labour seat where a single trade union holds sway.

rotten borough Again in the unreformed House of Commons, a constituency where the electorate was small enough and corrupt enough for a candidate to ensure his election by the payment of lavish bribes – unless his opponent paid even more. It is now used as a pejorative term for Labour-held seats where the selection process is in the hands of a self-perpetuating few.

boss (1) In America, the head of a political MACHINE; also a term of abuse for one powerful CAUCUS by another. The word comes from the Dutch *baas*, meaning master or foreman, and was popularised by servants who, after the AMERICAN REVOLUTION, did not want to address anyone as 'Master'. It was in political use by the 1860s, and remained so for a century. Those given the name included:

Boss (Richard) **Croker** of New York. Asked why he stayed silent when the STAR SPANGLED BANNER was sung, an aide said: 'He doesn't want to commit himself.'

Boss John F. (HONEY FITZ) **Fitzgerald** of Boston, grandfather of President KENNEDY. Fitzgerald was twice elected Mayor through the activities and loyalty of his Irish-descended DEAROS, providing a colourful ADMINISTRATION riddled with GRAFT.

Boss (Sen. Thomas) **Platt (**1833–1910) of New York, who sought to gag the reforming governor, Theodore ROOSEVELT, by getting him elected in 1896 as MCKINLEY's Vice President. His plan backfired when McKinley was shot six months after his inauguration and Roosevelt became President.

Boss Tube A facetious but apt 1980s term for the immense influence of television ('the tube') over US public opinion.

> Television has largely replaced the political parties as the middleman between candidates and voters. Boss Tube has succeeded Boss TWEED OF TAMMANY HALL, Boss Crump of Memphis, and the DALEY MACHINE in Chicago.
>
> HEDRICK SMITH, *The Power Game*

Boss (William March) **Tweed** Perhaps the most notorious of all TAMMANY bosses. Tweed controlled every political appointment in New York during 20 years as Commissioner of Public Works, taking between $100 and $200 million in kickbacks. On one occasion the books were cooked to show that a plasterer had earned $138,137.50 for two days' work. Tweed did not operate alone or pocket all the money himself; he was helped enthusiastically by a corrupt group of Tammany associates known as the **Tweed Ring**. Tweed was toppled in 1870 by his fellow Democrat Samuel Tilden through articles in *Harper's Weekly*, accompanied by Thomas Nast's celebrated cartoons, and investigative reporting in the *New York Times*; after a series of trials he was imprisoned, escaped to Cuba but was recaptured, dying in jail in 1878. Tweed summed up his political philosophy as:

> As long as I count the votes, what are you going to do about it?

(2) **BOSS** APARTHEID South Africa's Bureau of State Security, its principal intelligence organisation which during the 1970s, in particular, waged a ruthless campaign against opponents of the system at home and worldwide. One of its exploits was to frame the UK anti-apartheid campaigner and future CABINET MINISTER Peter Hain for an alleged bank robbery.

(3) **The Boss** A common political nickname used of, among others, the Irish Prime Minister Charles HAUGHEY; Franklin D. ROOSEVELT; Margaret THATCHER; and the FIRST LADY Bess TRUMAN (by her husband).

Boston. Boston massacre The attack by British Redcoats on snowball-throwing Bostonians on 5 March 1770 which left four civilians dead. It sparked radical passions throughout New England which were partly responsible for Lord North's new government in Britain repealing a range of unpopular duties imposed in 1768 – except those on tea.

Boston police strike The stoppage in 1919 by three-quarters of the Boston force over their right, denied by the police commissioner, to affiliate to the American Federation of Labor (*see* AFL-CIO). Governor Calvin COOLIDGE sent in the state militia to prevent a breakdown in law and order; though the situation was already under control, one of SILENT CAL's rare statements won popular approval:

> There is no right to strike against the public safety by anybody, anywhere, anytime.

Boston Tea Party The incident popularly taken as the start of the AMERICAN REVOLUTION, when on 16 December 1773 Bostonians led by Samuel Adams and dressed as Indians dumped the cargo of three tea ships into the harbour in protest at the tax on tea and the East India Company's monopoly over its shipment. Chanting 'Boston harbour a teapot tonight', they boarded the ships by moonlight and tipped 342 chests of tea over the side. When news of the Tea Party reached Britain the next month, a series of Coercive Acts curbing the freedoms of the colonies were quickly passed, together with the QUEBEC ACT. These, in turn, provoked the convening of the CONTINENTAL CONGRESS.

> The boldest stroke which had yet been struck in America.
>
> Mass. Governor THOMAS HUTCHINSON

> The question is whether the destruction of this tea was necessary. I apprehend it was absolutely and indispensably so. . . To let it be landed would be giving up the principle of taxation by Parliamentary authority, against which the Continent has struggled for 10 years.
>
> JOHN ADAMS

Boundary Commission (1) The body set up after the PARTITION of Ireland in 1921 to delineate the border between NORTHERN IRELAND and the Republic. The founders of the Republic expected it to include NATIONALIST areas of the SIX COUNTIES contiguous with the South, but the exercise was rendered void when UNIONIST leaders in the North made it clear they would not accept the Commission's recommendations. (2) The impartial body which determines UK Parliamentary boundaries at each REDISTRIBUTION; there are separate Commissions for England, Wales, Scotland and Northern Ireland.

Bourbons The nickname acquired by the arch-conservative, white supremacist Democratic Party leaders who gained control of America's solid SOUTH at the end of RECONSTRUCTION. A combination of former planters and southern Whites who had done well out of Reconstruction, their determination to turn back the clock by depriving blacks of their limited rights brought a natural comparison with the royal house of France (and several other countries) whose stiff-necked inability to countenance change cost several their heads or their thrones. It was of the original Bourbons that Talleyrand wrote:

> They have learned nothing and forgotten nothing.

bourgeois An originally French term for the middle class; the word entered the English language in the 16th century, but only became derogatory with its adoption by MARX and Engels to represent the class enemy, and those who lacked the imagination to embrace revolutionary theories. In the *Communist Manifesto* (1848) they wrote:

> The essential condition for the existence and sway of the bourgeois class is the formation and augmentation of capital, the condition for wage labour. What the bourgeoisie therefore produces is its own gravediggers. Its fall and the victory of the proletariat are equally inevitable.

And in a maybe less serious vein,

> The bourgeois, not content with having the women and daughters of their wage-slaves at command . . . find it capital amusement to seduce each other's wives.

Since then, *bourgeois* has been the standard Communist term for any idea or behaviour that differs from their own.

> The European bourgeoisie has its reasons to be frightened. The proletariat has its reasons to rejoice.
>
> LENIN on Russia's defeat by Japan at Port Arthur, 1895

> The political art of the British bourgeois consists in shortening the revolutionary beak of the proletariat, thereby not enabling him to pierce the shell of the capitalist state. TROTSKY

> To carry out socialist work in a bourgeois democracy is impossible.
> Spanish Prime Minister FRANCISCO LARGO CABALLERO (1869–1946).

petit-bourgeois An even more dismissive variant of 'bourgeois' used by Marx for the small-minded middle class.

bovver boys' bench At Westminster, originally the front bench BELOW THE GANGWAY on the OPPOSITION side of the HOUSE OF COMMONS which up to 1997 was home to a huddle of left-wingers – notably Dennis Canavan, Bob Cryer and Dennis Skinner (*see* BEAST OF BOLSOVER) who were vocal interrupters but shrewd debaters. The epithet was increasingly transferred to the corresponding bench on the government side, from which boisterous right-wingers assailed John MAJOR's Ministers, principally over Europe. The original 'bovver boys' were aggressive 1970s football hooligans who wore heavy 'bovver (bother) boots'.

Bow Group A group of young liberal Tories formed in the late 1950s which has had a considerable impact on party thinking, though since the 1980s its centre of gravity has moved rightwards. It takes its name from Bow in East London, where the group held its inaugural meeting, addressed by Geoffrey HOWE, in a room over a pub; its magazine, which at times has been equally influential, is *Crossbow*. Several Ministers in the HEATH, THATCHER and MAJOR CABINETS were Bow Groupers early in their careers. *Compare* RIPON SOCIETY.

box. the box The single pew holding six to eight people, next to the Government benches in the HOUSE OF COMMONS and just behind the CHAIR, from which officials monitor and assist the progress of their Minister during debates.

doing the boxes For UK Ministers, the task of going through the red boxes of official papers which they are expected to read, and where necessary sign, each night when they get home.

pick a box The system used in Australia since 1984 for electing members of the SENATE. The BALLOT paper is divided by a thick black line; above it are boxes giving a choice of parties, and below it boxes for candidates. A voter may either place the figure 1 in a square above the line, voting one party's TICKET, or number all candidates' squares in order of preference.

Boxer Rebellion The rising against foreigners in China in 1899–1900, in which the secret society of 'Boxers' took a leading part. Its Chinese name was *I Ho Chuan*, signifying 'righteousness, harmony and fists', implying training in martial arts to build character. The Boxers tore up railway lines, sacked churches, attacked foreign missions and murdered some 300 foreigners before they were suppressed by an international force put together by America and the European colonial powers. The rising created conditions for a grab of what was left of independent China by those powers, but America extended its OPEN DOOR POLICY and bought them off for a time.

boy. Boy David The nickname given to **David** (later Sir David and Lord) **Steel** (1938–), leader of Britain's LIBERAL PARTY 1976–88, by condescending figures in the Conservative and Labour leaderships. The son of a former Moderator of the General Assembly of the Church of Scotland, Steel was the 'baby' of the COMMONS when he won a by-election in 1965, but quickly made a reputation by pushing through a Private Member's Bill to legalise abortion. As party leader, he safely navigated the Liberals through the trauma of the THORPE CASE, negotiated the LIB-LAB PACT with Labour and extricated the party from it, and encouraged the formation of the SDP; but he retained a boyish demeanour. Steel fought two elections in ALLIANCE with the SDP; in the first (1983) he reduced the role of the SDP's ROY JENKINS at the ETTRICK BRIDGE SUMMIT, and in the second (1987) he was handicapped by vicious satire from SPITTING IMAGE making him look like David OWEN's junior partner. Immediately after the election he demanded merger of the two parties, triggering splits in each. Steel stood down as leader when the LIBERAL DEMOCRATS were formed, remaining the new party's foreign affairs spokesman. From 1999 to 2003 he was inaugural PRESIDING OFFICER of the Scottish Parliament.

Boy Orator of the Platte A nickname for the American POPULIST William Jennings Bryan (*see* PRAIRIE AVENGER) in his first (1896) campaign for the Presidency. The tag turned out to be two-edged, Sen. Joseph Foraker pointing out that the Platte river in Nebraska was 'six inches deep, and six miles wide at the mouth'.

Boy Patriots The Parliamentary opponents who harried Robert WALPOLE toward the end of his 21-year ministry; an influential member from 1736 was the prodigy William Pitt (PITT THE ELDER).

The Boys on the Bus *See* BUS.

boycott The organised shunning of an individual, event or business in protest at the politics they represent, or as a protest at the involvement of others who are considered beyond the pale. The term originated in the avoidance of Captain Boycott, a Co. Mayo landowner, by Irish land reformers led by Charles Stewart PARNELL; on 19 September 1880 Parnell told a meeting in Ennis:

> When a man takes a farm from which another has been evicted, you must show him on the roadside when you meet him; you must show him in the streets of the town; you must show him in the fair and the market place; and even in the place of worship, by leaving him severely alone – by putting him into a moral Coventry, by isolating him from his kind as if he were a leper of old. You must show him your detestation of the crimes he has committed.

The boycott became a widely-used weapon, by CIVIL RIGHTS campaigners against the segregated bus line in Montgomery, Alabama; by the Arab states against companies doing business with Israel; by countries opposed to APARTHEID against exports from South Africa and sporting events competed in by all-white teams from South Africa or nations who had continued to send teams there; by US athletes against the 1980 Moscow Olympics in protest at the Soviet invasion of Afghanistan; and by US liberals against fruit produced by non-unionised migrant labour – and for a time against Coors beer.

Boyne, Battle of the The decisive engagement on 1 July 1690 between Protestant forces loyal to William of ORANGE and Catholic supporters of the ousted King James II. The battle, on the banks of the river Boyne three miles west of Drogheda, had wide European implications and involved, as well as Irish fighters on both sides, French, German and Walloon troops for James and English, Germans and Danes for William. SECTARIAN rivalry and tension already existed, especially in ULSTER, yet the Protestant victory set the agenda for centuries of bitterness, provocation and violence which continue to this day. In LOYALIST areas of Belfast, larger-than-life pictures of **King Billy** adorn gable ends of houses, and his victory remains a critical part of the folk memory and of communal pride – as well as a provocation to Catholics.

bracketing A mild form of political dirty tricks, in which a candidate's campaign team minimises the impact of an opponent's visit to a particular town by arranging high-profile events there on the preceding and/or following day.

Bradlaugh case The furore caused by the refusal of Charles Bradlaugh (1833–91), the radical Liberal elected for Northampton in 1880 at the fourth attempt, to take the Parliamentary OATH. Bradlaugh's insistence on being allowed to AFFIRM, as may now be done, caused uproar in the COMMONS; he was refused his seat, and the scenes were repeated again in 1881 and 1882 when the voters re-elected him (*compare* BENN). He was formally excluded from the House in 1884 but the next year won yet another election; this time the SPEAKER, exasperated by the intransigence of all parties, seated Bradlaugh despite bitter protests. His refusal to take the oath was not his only breach of Victorian conventions; to the horror of the Queen he was an advocate of birth control, and he was living in sin with the redoubtable feminist Annie Besant.

Brady Bill The measure for limited GUN CONTROL promoted after Ronald REAGAN's press secretary Jim Brady received serious head wounds in John Hinckley's attempt on the President's life on 30 March 1981. Despite CONGRESSional sympathy and Brady's own pressure, lobbying by the NRA and opposition from Reagan himself blocked the Bill's ban on 'Saturday Night Special' handguns. The surviving provisions – a five-day waiting period and background checks on handgun purchasers – were finally enacted as part of the 1994 CLINTON crime package, only passing the SENATE after two FILIBUSTERS.

brain. Brain(s) Trust The group of unofficial advisers on economic and social reform on whom Franklin D. ROOSEVELT relied in the 1932 election campaign and into the opening years of the NEW DEAL; they also acted as speechwriters. James Kieran of the *New York Times* nicknamed the group the Brains Trust because its members were academics, among them the Columbia University professors Raymond Moley (its organiser), Adolph Berle and Rexford Tugwell. FDR modified the nickname to *Brain Trust* and used it himself.

> This country is being run by a group of college professors. This brain trust is endeavouring to force Socialism on the American people.
>
> Sen. HENRY D. HATFIELD

brainwashing The psychological techniques employed on US officers and men taken prisoner by the Communists during the KOREAN WAR, so that they would spout anti-American propaganda on their release. The phrase acquired a political connotation in 1967 when Governor George Romney of Michigan, the Presidential favourite of liberal Republicans, claimed in a Detroit TV interview that he had been 'brainwashed' by the military on a trip to VIETNAM. He had meant to say that he had been brainwashed by President JOHNSON, not by the generals. Richard NIXON seized on Romney's gaffe, renounced his decision to quit politics just before Romney withdrew from the race in February 1968, and went on to win the Presidency.

> Romney convinced many Americans that he didn't have a brain worth washing.
>
> DAVID WALLECHINSKY and IRVING WALLACE, *The People's Almanac*

Branch Dravidian massacre The term used by its detractors on the far right to describe the bungled Federal operation at Waco, Texas on 19 April 1993 to enter the compound of the self-styled Branch Dravidian Church and the ensuing deaths of 80 of its adherents, 24 of them children. After a 51-day standoff when leaders of the Church refused to accept a warrant requiring them to give up illegally-held firearms, (FBI and ATF) agents stormed their compound as it was set on fire from within; most of the occupants died, some of burns and asphyxiation, others of bullet wounds. An independent investigation by former Senator John Danforth concluded that those with gunshot wounds had been shot by their co-religionists and not by the FBI, but these findings were hotly disputed by relatives of the dead. The episode was a serious embarrassment to the newly-elected CLINTON ADMINISTRATION and especially for ATTORNEY-GENERAL Janet Reno, but she survived to leave office eight years later with her reputation high.

Brandt Commission The international commission convened by the UNITED NATIONS in 1977 under the former West German CHANCELLOR Willy Brandt (1913–92) which raised the alarm over the plight of the THIRD WORLD. Its report, NORTH-SOUTH: *A Programme for Survival 1980*, recommended urgent steps for fairer and greater trade between the rich 'North' and the poor 'South'. World leaders reviewed the report at the CANCUN SUMMIT, but did not act on its recommendations. In 1983 the Commission produced a second report which warned of 'conflict and catastrophe' if the imbalance was not addressed.

Brassard affair The furore and embarrassment occasioned by a fourteen-minute phone call to Queen Elizabeth II by Pierre Brassard, a Montreal disc jockey, on the eve of the October 1995 Quebec referendum. Pretending to be the Canadian Prime Minister Jean Chrétien, Brassard in a broadcast seven-minute extract lured the Queen into conceding the referendum could 'go the wrong way' and agreeing to speak on Canadian TV; 'Chrétien' said the message should be brief enough to fit on a cornflake packet. Brassard had previously got through to the Pope and asked him to fit a propeller on his skullcap.

bread and circuses (Lat. *panis et circenses*) The bribing of the masses with their own money to keep a government in office. The term stems from the practice of Senators and Emperors in ancient Rome of staging lavish public entertainments and providing the public with free food as a means of averting popular discontent.

break. breaking the mould The process which the founders of Britain's SDP hoped to precipitate, with voters abandoning traditional class-based party loyalties when given a new alternative. The dream lasted six years; the SDP/Liberal ALLIANCE collapsed after the 1987 election, and by 1992 the traditional two-PARTY system had almost reasserted itself.

breakthrough Under the FIRST PAST THE POST system, the point at which a party starts converting growing electoral support into seats. In Britain the LIBERAL DEMOCRATS would require around 35% of the vote before each extra percentage point paid a handsome dividend in seats; in Scotland the breakthrough point for the SNP is higher because of the strength of Labour support in the Central Belt.

Bretton Woods The conference at Bretton Woods, New Hampshire attended by the US, Britain and Canada, which led to the establishment of the International Monetary Fund (IMF) and WORLD BANK. The Bretton Woods system, as it became known, involved a world monetary structure pegged to the dollar and governed, in the last resort, by the US TREASURY. The creation of the IMF provided a valuable safety net for STERLING, but at an initially heavy cost to Britain that hindered her post-war recovery. The system collapsed in 1971 when West Germany floated the mark and the NIXON ADMINISTRATION followed suit by floating the dollar.

Brewster case The landmark 1971 WASHINGTON INFLUENCE-PEDDLING case that forced LOBBYISTS to avoid offering money in the same conversation as they asked a legislator for their vote on a particular issue. Former Sen. Daniel Brewster of Maryland was convicted of unlawfully accepting $24,500 in campaign funds in return for his vote on postal-rate legislation.

Brezhnev Doctrine The policy, associated with the Soviet leader Leonid Brezhnev (1906–82), under which the Soviet Union reserved the right to intervene, with its WARSAW PACT allies, in the domestic affairs of SATELLITE states in defence of socialism and its own global interests. The crushing of the PRAGUE SPRING of 1968 was an example of the doctrine in practice; defending it in a speech to the Polish Communist Party congress on 12 November 1968, Brezhnev said:

> When internal and external forces which are hostile to Socialism try to turn the development of any Socialist country towards the restoration of a capitalist regime . . . it becomes a problem not only of the people concerned, but a common problem and concern of all Socialist countries.

The COLD WAR lasted as long as the KREMLIN was ready to impose the doctrine; in 1989 Mikhail GORBACHEV abandoned it and the Communist regimes of eastern Europe were swept from power.

bridge A deliverer of continuity, a preserver of values into a new era or a mediator between communities or nations. The process is known as **bridge-building.**

> I believe in building bridges, but we should only build our end of the bridge.
>
> RICHARD NIXON, speech at Lakeside, California 1967

The term was memorably used by the 1996 Republican nominee Bob Dole (1923–); in his ACCEPTANCE SPEECH in San Diego that August, Dole, capitalising on his mature age, asked Americans to let him be the 'bridge between past and present'. Two weeks later at the Democrats' Chicago convention, Bill CLINTON countered by asking voters to make him 'the bridge to the future'.

Brighton. Brighton bombing The most devastating attack by the IRA on Britain's political leadership, which came within a whisker of ASSASSINATING Margaret THATCHER and her entire CABINET. On the final night (11 October) of the 1984 CONSERVATIVE PARTY conference, a bomb planted weeks before exploded in the Grand Hotel around 3.20 a.m. immediately above the room where Mrs Thatcher and her husband were awake. The Prime Minister and most of her senior colleagues had a miraculous escape, but five people including the Conservative MP Sir Anthony Berry were killed and two Cabinet ministers, Norman Tebbit (*see* CHINGFORD SKINHEAD) and John Wakeham, suffered very serious injuries; Wakeham also lost his wife and Margaret Tebbit was left paralysed. Marks & Spencer opened its Brighton store to clothe survivors who had fled in their pyjamas; the conference continued as scheduled, Mrs Thatcher going ahead with her closing speech that afternoon. Anti-terrorist checks at the conference had been lax because the police were more concerned with possible violent protests by striking miners. Mrs Thatcher showed great coolness amid the rubble, but that weekend at CHEQUERS wept over 'A DAY I WAS MEANT NOT TO SEE'; the IRA commented chillingly: 'WE ONLY HAVE TO BE LUCKY ONCE'.

> What a coup for the Paddys. The whole thing has a whiff of the TET OFFENSIVE.
>
> ALAN CLARK, *Diaries*

like Brighton pier – all right as far as it goes, but inadequate for getting to France Neil KINNOCK's description of the Conservatives' ambivalent policy on Europe, from a HOUSE OF COMMONS speech on 2 February 1981.

brinkmanship The art of going to the verge of war, but no further; specifically America's taking of the toughest line possible short of war against the Soviet Union during the COLD WAR. The word was coined by, and used in criticism of, US SECRETARY OF STATE John Foster Dulles (1888–1959); in 1956 he stated that America had three times gone to the brink with the Soviets, adding: 'If you are scared to go to the brink, you are lost.' Dulles' attitude scared many in the West; Adlai Stevenson scorned it as **the art of positive brinking.**

Britain forward, not back Labour's slogan for the 2005 general election campaign, in which it retained power with a reduced majority. It was supplemented late in the campaign by **'if you value it. vote for it"**, to rally all wavering Labour traditionalists.

Britain. Britain is no longer a world power; all they have got are generals and admirals and bands The verdict of General George Brown, chairman of the US JOINT CHIEFS OF STAFF, in an interview in October 1976. The comment aroused adverse reaction in Britain, but nothing like as strong as that to Dean Acheson's 'lost an EMPIRE and not yet found a role' fourteen years previously.

I'm backing Britain The slogan coined by the publisher, Labour MP and eventual mass fraudster Robert Maxwell in 1968 to encourage the public to buy British-made goods. It inspired frantic activity and self-sacrifice on the part of some workers and a forgettable song from Bruce Forsyth, but had no lasting impact.
See also GREAT BRITAIN.

British. British disease The combination of industrial unrest, low productivity and economic decline which the nations of continental Europe detected in Britain in the 1960s and '70s, and which they held out as a grim warning to their own people. In 1963 Tony BENN defined the British disease as 'galloping obsolescence'.

British Empire *See* EMPIRE.

British Gazette The newspaper produced by the UK government during the 1926 GENERAL STRIKE, belligerently edited by Winston CHURCHILL, then CHANCELLOR OF THE EXCHEQUER. Churchill called the strikers 'the enemy' and called for their 'unconditional surrender'. The TUC countered with its own publication, the *British Worker*. Churchill did not take the exercise entirely seriously; years later in the COMMONS, he taunted Labour MPs:

> If ever you inflict on us another General Strike . . . [INTERRUPTION] . . . I swear that we will inflict on you . . . another *British Gazette*!

British Movement One of the many small but nauseating RACIST and NEO-FASCIST groups which proliferated in less affluent parts of Britain during the 1980s. A splinter from the NATIONAL FRONT, it was most evident in south-east London and parts of central Scotland until upstaged by the British National Party (BNP).

British North America Act The legislation enacted by the Westminster Parliament in 1867 that established Canada as a DOMINION and a CONFEDERATION, initially of Quebec, Ontario, Nova Scotia and New Brunswick. It remained the basis for Canada's CONSTITUTION until its PATRIATION in 1982.

British rebate The compensatory payment conceded by Britain's partners at the 1984 FONTAINEBLEAU SUMMIT after five years of agitation by Margaret THATCHER (*see* Give me my MONEY back) which reduced the UK's substantial net contribution to the European Community (later EU) by two-thirds in recognition that other member states, notably France, did disproportionately well out of the Common Agricultural Policy (CAP). Sporadic efforts by other member states to abolish the rebate came to nothing, but France's President CHIRAC launched a concerted campaign against it in the spring of 2005 after French voters had rejected the EUROPEAN CONSTITUTION, thus critically weakening his position at home. At a bad-tempered EU summit in Brussels that June, Tony BLAIR insisted he would only put the rebate – by now worth £3 billion each year – on the table as part of a wholesale reform of the budget that transferred funding from agriculture to science, development and education.

the British are coming! The warning sent out by night-riders from Boston on 18 April 1775 when General Thomas Gage sent 700 British infantrymen secretly (he hoped) to capture or destroy a military store at Concord, 20 miles away, so as to deny it to rebel farmers. They were met at the village of Lexington by 75 volunteers, or MINUTEMEN; shots were fired (by whom is unknown) and in the ensuing exchanges the Redcoats left eight Americans dead and ten wounded. The British went on to Concord, found the stores has been hidden from them, and on the way back to Boston suffered heavy losses from sharpshooters. Lexington marked the opening of the War of INDEPENDENCE, and the cry 'the British are coming!' entered history.

broad church A party or movement containing highly disparate elements stretching across the political spectrum. The term was used by Tony BENN to justify the right of the MILITANT TENDENCY and other hard LEFT groups to operate within the UK LABOUR PARTY. *Compare* BIG TENT.

broadcast. election broadcast In the UK, a Party Political Broadcast (PPB) transmitted during an ELECTION campaign. Every party fielding more than a certain number of candidates nationally, or in a particular region, is allocated a quota of time on radio and television, paid political advertising on the air being banned. In the period when the leaders of SINN FEIN were barred generally from speaking on the air, these broadcasts were the only times when their voices could be heard; at other times their words were spoken by actors.

Ministerial broadcast A broadcast made by the Prime Minister, CHANCELLOR or occasionally another member of the British CABINET to announce, justify or otherwise comment on some major development. The OPPOSITION has the right to reply in a broadcast of corresponding length and prominence. Apart from the annual BUDGET broadcasts and exceptional events such as the onset of war or the devaluation of the pound, such broadcasts have become a rarity.

party political broadcast *See* PPB.

public service broadcasting The concept of broadcasting as a means of educating, entertaining and informing the nation, free of advertising and the dictates of commercialism. This was the principle behind the formation of the BBC, maintained rigidly by Lord Reith but slightly eroded by governmental pressures and the fads of internal management since the late 1980s.

broccoli The vegetable whose too-frequent presence on the WHITE HOUSE menu provoked a public outburst from George BUSH Senior. The President's comments infuriated America's farmers, and trailer-loads of broccoli were delivered, unsolicited, to the White House. Staffers arranged their distribution to the needy in the Washington/Baltimore area. One of Hillary CLINTON's first actions as FIRST LADY was to restore broccoli to the menu. *Compare* SWEETBREADS.

Broederbond (Afrik. brotherhood) The semi-secret and highly conservative society to which most members of South Africa's Afrikaner ESTABLISHMENT belong, and which was for long a force for cohesion and reaction within the ruling NATIONAL PARTY and a cornerstone of APARTHEID.

broker A state or leader who seeks to resolve differences between others, acting as an impartial MEDIATOR, is said to be brokering a settlement. Leaders in this position sometimes use the term **honest broker** to describe themselves. As the Congress of BERLIN in 1878 Bismarck (*see* IRON CHANCELLOR), declared:

> If we are to negotiate peace, I imagine an essentially modest role, that of honest broker, who really intends to do business.

When Harold WILSON offered his good offices to bring about an end to the VIETNAM WAR, cynics at home said this was because while he might not be honest, Britain couldn't be broker.

power broker A largely US term for the men in SMOKE-FILLED ROOMS who determine who is put forward to govern. Hedrick Smith, in *The Power Game*, wrote:

> The most influential voices in Congress are power brokers back home.

brokered convention In US politics, a CONVENTION where there is deadlock between the delegations representing rival candidates, and the outcome is finally determined by party bosses in that SMOKE-FILLED ROOM.

Brookings Institution One of Washington's most influential THINK TANKS. Based near Dupont Circle, this generally liberal body recruits distinguished Fellows from the worlds of politics and political science, diplomacy, economics and journalism, giving them the opportunity to develop their own ideas. Apart from producing its own assessments of events and policies, Brookings brings together experienced figures from public life to exchange opinions and judgements, both formally and informally.

brother The brotherhood of man has long been an ideal, and in the 20th century developed connotations both of trade union SOLIDARITY and the breaking down of barriers between racial groups.

> We do not want men of another colour for our brothers-in-law, but we do want them for our brothers. BOOKER T. WASHINGTON

Brother, let me take you out of your misery! Neil KINNOCK's caricature of the outdated approach adopted by Britain's trade union leaders to prosperous manual workers, which, delivered at Labour's 1987 conference, was widely seen as a dig at the TGWU leader Ron Todd.

Brothers, we're on our way! The exuberant motto of the deputy Labour leader George BROWN in 1963–4 as the party anticipated its return to power under Harold WILSON, newly united and with the Conservatives in disarray. As it was, Labour only scraped home with a majority of six, and struggled to gain momentum.

Brown. Brown v Topeka Board of Education The landmark US SUPREME COURT ruling on 17 May 1954 that overturned its previous position that SEPARATE BUT EQUAL facilities should be provided for the races, and declared SEGREGATED education to be UNCONSTITUTIONAL. A black child, Linda Brown, had been turned away from an all-white school; the court unanimously struck down a Kansas State law that required segregated classrooms, declaring that 'separate education facilities are inherently unequal', and that such laws in seventeen States were a denial of the FOURTEENTH AMENDMENT. Chief Justice Earl WARREN stated that segregating black children from others solely because of their race 'generates a feeling of inferiority as to their status in a community that may affect their HEARTS AND MINDS in a way unlikely ever to be undone'. In 1955 the Court ordered that DESEGREGATION of public schools should begin 'with all deliberate speed', but it was years before the goal was achieved.

> I don't believe that you can change the hearts of men with laws and decisions.
>
> President EISENHOWER

> The law may not change the heart – but it can restrain the heartless.
>
> Dr MARTIN LUTHER KING

Brown, Gordon (1951–) The 'IRON CHANCELLOR' who was the rock on which Tony BLAIR's Labour government from 1997 was founded, despite increasing tensions after the 2001 ELECTION victory over when (or if) Blair would hand over the leadership to him, as Brown's supporters believed he had been promised. His stewardship of a strong economy through belt-tightening during the government's first term enabled him to inject record sums into the NHS in the second and allowed the economy to ride out the worst of the global economic downturn after 9/11. A son of the manse from Kirkcaldy, Brown enjoyed a precocious academic record at school and Edinburgh University despite the loss of an eye playing rugby. As the university's student rector he saw off an attempt by the Vice-Chancellor, Sir Michael Swann, to remove him for revealing in the student newspaper that the university had lied over its investments in South Africa; through his then girlfriend who was a god-daughter of Prince Philip, Brown mobilised the PRIVY COUNCIL to block Swann's move. Brown went into television, but in 1983 was elected MP for Dunfermline East, sharing an office with Blair who had also bucked Labour's worst election result of the century. The two harried Tory ministers, and in 1987 Brown was elected to the SHADOW CABINET, immediately trouncing Chancellor Nigel Lawson in debate. In 1992 John SMITH made Brown Shadow Chancellor. Initially Blair deferred to Brown, who was his closest political friend, but when Smith died suddenly in 1994 Brown was forced to accept that Blair had the momentum and reluctantly agreed not to oppose him (*see* GRANITA). He worked closely with Blair to secure Labour's 1997 LANDSLIDE, rigidly curbing spending pledges by other Shadow Ministers. In office, he stunned the financial markets by giving the BANK OF ENGLAND the freedom to set interest rates, and kept a tight fiscal stance as employment and prosperity grew, enabling him to ease off and inject spending into the economy as growth slowed from 2001. He was also more cautious than Blair about adopting the EURO, setting FIVE ECONOMIC TESTS for joining and determining in June 2003 that only one of them had been fulfilled. The TREASURY's influence is always powerful, but under Brown, Labour's most successful Chancellor, it reached its apogee with every spending department tied firmly into not just his strategy but his priorities, which were more 'OLD LABOUR' than Blair's. Blair tried to sideline Brown before the 2005 election, installing Alan Milburn to head the campaign, but after a shaky start spent the final stages touring the country with Brown to highlight the strength of Labour's leadership and play down talk of splits.

don't just say Brown, say hopeless! A punning Conservative bumper sticker directed against George (later Lord George) Brown (1914–85), the colourful deputy to Harold WILSON in the Labour government of 1964. The slogan, directed at Brown's stewardship of economic policy as head of the short-lived Department of Economic Affairs and originator of the NATIONAL PLAN as well as at his frequent DRINK-induced GAFFES, was a play on the popular bread advertisement 'Don't just say brown, say Hovis!'

John Brown's Body The rhyme commemorating the ABOLITIONIST hanged in 1859 after leading the raid on HARPER'S FERRY that became the marching song of the North in America's CIVIL WAR and reverberated around the world. Written either by Thomas Bingham Bishop or Charles Sprague Hall, it went:

> John Brown's body lies a-mouldering in the grave (three times),
> His soul is marching on!

The *Battle Hymn of the Republic* (MINE EYES HAVE SEEN THE GLORY OF THE COMING OF THE LORD) was written to the same melody – the hymn tune *Gone to be a soldier in the army of the Lord.*

Brownies A mildly derogatory term for the supporters and nominees of Gordon Brown in Tony BLAIR's 1997 Labour government, reflecting the immense influence of the CHANCELLOR, which stretched far beyond the TREASURY, and the existence of a strong alternative powerbase to the Prime Minister, who initially remained a close personal friend.

Brownshirts HITLER's brown-shirted NAZI *Sturmabteilung* (stormtroopers) or SA, formed in 1921. Under Ernst Rohm the Brownshirts staged street brawls with the Nazis' opponents and became a mass movement whose size and lack of accountability worried the FÜHRER. On 30 June 1934 Rohm and other leaders of the SA were murdered on his orders in the NIGHT OF THE LONG KNIVES, power passing to the SS.

Bruges To the UK EUROSCEPTIC right, the symbol of resistance to a Federal Europe, stemming from Margaret THATCHER's speech in the ancient Belgian town on 20 September 1988 in which she scorned the centralising socialism of Jacques DELORS and defended national SOVEREIGNTY. Mrs Thatcher, in a speech which also applauded the SINGLE MARKET, declared:

> We have not succeeded in rolling back the frontiers of the state in Britain only to see them reimposed at a European level.

Her speech is commemorated in the **Bruges Group** of opponents to closer European union, which was an irritant to John MAJOR during the negotiation of the MAASTRICHT TREATY but was weakened when some of its members stood against Conservative candidates as 'anti-Federalists' in 1992. Some of its adherents moved on to the REFERENDUM PARTY and UKIP.

Brundtland Report The report published in 1988 by the UN World Commission on Environment Development, chaired by Norway's Labour Prime Minister Mrs Gro Harlem Brundtland (1939–). It argued for 'SUSTAINABLE DEVELOPMENT', stressing that only under strict conditions can economic growth be reconciled with the dictates of the environment. It stressed the critical importance for global survival of preserving such a balance in the Amazon Basin, sub-Saharan Africa and other regions.

Brussels The headquarters city of the EUROPEAN UNION, and to EUROSCEPTICS a symbol for excessive BUREAUCRACY and ludicrous DIRECTIVES. The Conservatives sought to capitalise on this in the 1989 EUROPEAN PARLIAMENT elections with the slogan: 'Don't vote and you'll live on a diet of Brussels.' It was intended to imply that Labour gains would leave Britain subject to a regime of Europe-wide regulation; instead many electors took it as an invitation to abstain.

Bryan, William Jennings *See* BOY ORATOR; PRAIRIE AVENGER.

BSE *See* MAD COW DISEASE.

Bubba One of the many nicknames of President Bill CLINTON, reflecting in a patronising way his Southern origins and easy social manner. An abbreviation of 'brother', 'Bubba' was originally used by black Southerners but now has strong REDNECK connotations. Its use as a pejorative did Clinton no harm in the search for votes among conservative Southern white males; when asked about it during the 1992 campaign, he responded:

> There's a little Bubba in both of us [Clinton and Al GORE] – in the sense that we both come from small towns, where people have old-fashioned values and want their country to be the best country in the world – and I don't think that's all that bad.

buck. the buck stops here The hand-lettered sign that President TRUMAN kept on his desk in the OVAL OFFICE. The phrase, meaning that the ultimate responsibility rests with the President, comes from poker.

a bigger bang for a buck President EISENHOWER's aim in pressing for shrewder and more economical defence spending, as opposed to the escalating BUDGET pressed for by the MILITARY-INDUSTRIAL COMPLEX.

buck the market *See* MARKET.

bucking the trend A phrase describing an ELECTION result which runs against the current trend of opinion POLLS, or which, in a particular electoral area, is out of line with the results of other elections held at the same time.

Buckingham Palace *See* PALACE, THE.

Buddy The chocolate Labrador retriever owned by Bill CLINTON during his later years in the WHITE HOUSE. Given to the Clintons at three months old in December 1997 by Tony Harrington, a former Clinton campaign lawyer, Buddy became a national figure. When he was neutered in March 1998 at the height of the ZIPPERGATE affair, several cartoonists suggested that the President, rather than his dog, should have undergone the veterinarian's knife. When Buddy died, Clinton bought another Labrador named **Seamus**.

Budget (1) At WESTMINSTER, the financial and economic statement presented annually by the CHANCELLOR – customarily in March, but from 1993 to 1997 in November – in which he sets out his taxation regime for the year ahead. This is subsequently legislated for in the FINANCE BILL. Prior to 1993 and again since 1998, the public spending programme has been presented separately in the autumn (*see* pre-BUDGET REPORT). Harold MACMILLAN described **Budget Day** as: 'rather like a school speech day – a bit of a bore, but there it is.' Since the early 18th century ritual and mystique have grown up around the Budget: pre-Budget PURDAH; the Chancellor's appearance on the steps of NUMBER ELEVEN Downing Street, holding the BUDGET BOX containing his speech; the glass of water or stronger liquid on the DESPATCH BOX; and his Ministerial BROADCAST that night explaining his plans.

> The immediate judgement on a Budget is almost invariably wrong. IAIN MACLEOD (1913–70)

(2) In WASHINGTON, the ADMINISTRATION's spending plans presented to CONGRESS at the end of each January; TAX-WRITING is undertaken by the Congress, which also makes changes of its own to the Budget. The end product is generally an increased Budget deficit because of the desire for tax breaks for favoured groups and for PORK. Norman Ornstein concluded that: 'historically, Congress was certainly an accomplice in increasing deficits – but Presidents were the masterminds.'

> The accounts of the United States ought to be, and may be made, as simple as those of a common farmer, and capable of being understood by common farmers.
>
> THOMAS JEFFERSON to JAMES MADISON, 1806

> If the definition of a good Budget proposal is to distribute dissatisfaction, ours is a real winner.
>
> RONALD REAGAN

> I didn't know much about Budgets – but I knew more than the rest of them.
>
> DAVID STOCKMAN, President Reagan's first Budget Director

> In government the Budget is the message.
>
> I.F. STONE

(3) The name of Sir Geoffrey HOWE's dog while his master was CHANCELLOR (1979–83). While Sir Geoffrey was FOREIGN SECRETARY, it was succeeded by SUMMIT.

balanced Budget *See* BALANCED.

Budget leak (1) Claims in 1936 that details of the NATIONAL GOVERNMENT's Budget had been leaked to a private individual who had used the information to make money. The report of an official tribunal that investigated the allegations led to the resignation of the Colonial Secretary, J.H. Thomas. (2) The incident that forced the resignation of Hugh Dalton (1887–1962) as CHANCELLOR OF THE EXCHEQUER in ATTLEE's government. On his way through the LOBBY of the COMMONS to present his Budget on 13 November 1947, Dalton told John Carvel of the London evening paper *The Star*:

> No more on tobacco, a penny on beer, something on dogs and [football] pools but not on horses, increase in Purchase Tax, but only on items now taxable, Profits Tax doubled.

An astonished Carvel phoned the scoop to his office, and the paper ran a 'Stop Press' announcement of tax changes before the Chancellor was able to inform the Commons – though no-one there or in the City would have seen it. This grave breach of protocol by the garrulous Dalton left him with no option but to resign. He returned to the CABINET in 1948 as Chancellor of the DUCHY OF LANCASTER, but never regained his influence.

Budget resolutions In the UK HOUSE OF COMMONS, the resolutions put to the vote at the end of the (usually four-day) debate straight after the Budget. They include the basic changes in taxes and EXCISE DUTIES which are to take effect immediately or at the start of the new tax year. The more detailed provisions of the Budget are legislated for in the FINANCE BILL in the subsequent months. In the US CONGRESS, '**concurrent resolutions on the Budget**' are passed each year to co-ordinate the revenue and spending decisions to be taken by the various committees involved in the budgetary process. Action on the resolutions, which set spending levels and direct the committees to achieve them, has to be completed by 15 April.

Budget shutdown The closure of the US Federal government twice during 1995–96 as the Republican Congress led by Speaker NEWT Gingrich (*see* CONTRACT WITH AMERICA) took on President CLINTON over his spending plans in an attempt to weaken him as he sought a second term. The shutdown did the Republicans, and especially Gingrich, serious political damage, though they, as well as Clinton, were re-elected in 1996; it was claimed that Gingrich engineered the shutdown out of pique at being made to sit at the back of AIR FORCE ONE on an official visit. Sen. John McCain lamented that 'pictures of Federal workers and their kids around empty Christmas trees' as a result of the shutdown played straight into Clinton's hands.

Congressional Budget Office (CBO) The office established by the Budget and

IMPOUNDMENT Control Act of 1974 to produce for CONGRESS independent analysis of the economy and of the ADMINISTRATION's Budget proposals. The change ended the situation in which the President and his staff could make assertions about the economy and the implications of their Budget that Congress was unable to challenge. The CBO has made a sizeable impact on the balance of power in WASHINGTON by challenging efforts by administrations of both parties to massage the figures.

Green Budget The consultative document produced by Gordon BROWN in November 1997 looking ahead to his Budget the following spring. It was a forerunner of the pre-BUDGET REPORT.

mini-Budget A package of economic and tax measures presented by a CHANCELLOR at a different time from his formal Budget, usually in response to a sudden worsening in the state of the UK economy. Tory and Labour Chancellors have each brought in mini-Budgets, but there have been few since the 1970s – if only because BLACK WEDNESDAY during Norman Lamont's Chancellorship occurred during a Parliamentary recess.

Office of Management and Budget *See* OMB; TOMB.

People's Budget *See* PEOPLE.

pre-Budget Report The STATEMENT by the CHANCELLOR to the HOUSE OF COMMONS in November which since 1998 has replaced the Autumn Budget, and the Autumn STATEMENT which preceded it. In it he sets out public spending plans for the coming year, and gives an overview of the performance of the economy and the current state of the public finances.

Zero-based budgeting *See* ZERO.

Buenos Aires bombing The destruction on 18 July 1994 by an unidentified terrorist group – now suspected of links to AL QAEDA – of the Argentine offices of the Jewish Mutual Association which left 85 people dead and 200 injured. It followed the bombing of the Israeli embassy in the Argentine capital in March 1992 which killed 30 people and injured more than 200, and was believed to be a reprisal by HEZBOLLAH for Israel's assassination of its leader Sheikh Abbas Musawi. In August 2003 Hade Soleimanpour, Iranian Ambassador to Argentina at the time, was arrested in Co. Durham where he was studying, for extradition on charges of conspiracy to murder, sparking an angry reaction from Tehran before HOME SECRETARY David Blunkett halted the proceedings; an Iranian diplomat in Belgium was also arrested.

bugging The tapping of private telephone conversations by the security and INTELLIGENCE services, and others with less authority and justification. In Britain, tapping is supposed only to happen under a warrant from the HOME SECRETARY; in SPYCATCHER Peter Wright wrote of MI5 in the mid-1970s:

> We bugged and burgled our way across London.

In the mid-1980s hints of further abuses, coupled with a ruling from the EUROPEAN COURT, led to the Interception of Communications Act which codified the arrangements for legitimate tapping.

In America the exposure of the FBI's COINTELPRO campaign and abuses by the CIA and the NIXON administration led eventually to CONGRESSional OVERSIGHT of intelligence matters. In 1966 Justice William O. Douglas had warned:

> We are rapidly entering the age of no privacy, where everybody is open to surveillance, at all times, where there are no secrets from government.

And the next year President Lyndon JOHNSON declared:

> Every man should know that his conversation, his correspondence and his personal life are private. I have urged Congress – except where the national security is at stake – to take action to that end.

Buggins' turn The culture in which the leadership of a political organisation devolves on the next person in line, regardless of ability. A politer US word is SENIORITY.

build-down A proposal for nuclear ARMS CONTROL and disarmament put forward by America in the early 1980s. Pressed strongly by Sen. Sam Nunn of Georgia, it would have involved cutting the size of both US and Soviet arsenals at the same time as they were being 'modernised', older weapons being replaced by fewer, more effective new ones. President REAGAN was tempted by the idea, which won the backing of 45 SENATORS, but it was resisted by the PENTAGON and was not seriously pressed by US arms negotiators in Geneva, where the Russians walked out soon after over the deployment of CRUISE MISSILES in Europe.

Bulgarian atrocities The massacre of Christians in Bulgaria by the Turks in 1876 that gave GLADSTONE an ideal platform for a bout of righteous campaigning. Gladstone did not begin the agitation, but brought it to a head with his pamphlet *The Bulgarian Horrors*, which sold 200,000 copies in its first month. DISRAELI was his target, not because of any suggestion that he condoned the massacre, but because he was determined to prevent Russia moving in to fill any vacuum left by Turkey. Russia attacked Turkey in 1877 and made sweeping gains which Disraeli was able to moderate at the Congress of BERLIN the following year. Gladstone was still able to extract some capital from the issue in his MIDLOTHIAN CAMPAIGN of 1880. *See also* BAG AND BAGGAGE.

Bull. Bull Connor The usual name for Eugene Connor, the REDNECK Commissioner of Public Safety for Birmingham, Alabama, who in the spring of 1963 gained notoriety for setting his police force and fire hoses against CIVIL RIGHTS demonstrators led by Dr Martin Luther KING, and making mass arrests. For five years prior to these protests, Connor had harassed and bugged local civil rights activists led by the Rev. Fred Shuttlesworth, and had threatened to close white-owned stores that agreed to serve blacks. He predicted that blood 'would run in the streets' before Birmingham was integrated.

> At his disposal were a large police force, vicious attack dogs, electric cattle prods, the WHITE CITIZENS' COUNCIL, the KU KLUX KLAN, and the established institutions of Southern white society.
>
> ALDON D. MORRIS, *Origins of the Civil Rights Movement*

bullhorn The portable instrument known to UK politicians and campaigners as a megaphone or loud-hailer, used to make a speaker's voice audible at impromptu outdoor meetings or to marshal DEMONSTRATIONS.

Bull Moose The breakaway POPULIST ticket on which Theodore ROOSEVELT, disillusioned with his successor President TAFT, made a comeback in 1912. After a stirring series of PRIMARY victories, he formed a PROGRESSIVE PARTY and with California governor Hiram Johnson as his running-mate he won 27.5% of the popular vote, splitting the REPUBLICAN PARTY, pushing Taft into third place and handing the election to Woodrow WILSON. Roosevelt had coined the phrase as far back as 1900, when he wrote to Sen. Mark Hanna:

> I am as strong as a bull moose, and you may use me to the limit.

Five minutes after being shot in Milwaukee on 14 October 1912, Roosevelt told his audience: 'Friends, I ask you to be as quiet as possible. I don't know whether you fully understand that I have been shot, but it takes more than that to kill a Bull Moose.'

bullet In WASHINGTON, a bold dot in the margin of the CONGRESSIONAL RECORD denoting items that have been inserted by members and are not transcripts of words uttered in the CHAMBER.

bullet point or **bull point** The key point, or one of them, that a politician is anxious to get across in a speech.

bullet vote In an ELECTION where there are several vacancies to be filled, the determination of a voter to go for one candidate only and ignore the other contests.

bite the bullet To brace oneself and take a difficult decision. President George BUSH Sen. said of Bill CLINTON's attitude to the GULF WAR:

> I bit the bullet, and he bit his nails.

I am simply a bullet fired by the Colne Valley workers against the established order The comment made by Victor Grayson, the charismatic socialist who later disappeared without a trace, on winning the historic 1907 BY-ELECTION for Labour in this Yorkshire stronghold of Liberalism. Grayson also declared: 'If the people have no shrapnel, they have broken bottles.'

rubber bullet A projectile made from hard rubber and fired from a special weapon, used for riot control. The rubber bullet, or BATON ROUND, was developed by UK government scientists for use in NORTHERN IRELAND and was based on the wooden police baton that could be fired at rioters from a gun, as used by the Hong Kong police in the late 1960s. The rubber bullet was supposed to be bounced off the ground and not fired directly into crowds, but it, and its successor the **plastic bullet** or **baton round** (a solid PVC cylinder), have been responsible for the deaths of at least twelve people, six of them children, in Northern Ireland since 1970.

Bullock Report The 1976 report to the UK government by a committee headed by the historian Professor Alan Bullock that recommended a degree of industrial democracy, with representatives of the workforce on company boards. The Labour government was eager for such representation, but trade union leaders insisted that the board members be appointed by them, not elected by the workers as a whole. As a result it was

2003 before another Labour government gave workers even minimal rights to be consulted about corporate decisions.

Bullshot of the Year award Not a mishearing, but the award made for many years by members of Congress playing paddleball – a cross between squash and tennis – in the RAYBURN BUILDING gym to the player who supposedly cheats and argues most; it became a mark of esteem, requiring the holder to chair the gym's annual dinner.

bully pulpit A high-profile public office whose occupants used it to campaign for causes dear to them; specifically the US Presidency as mobilised by Theodore ROOSEVELT and some others since to rally and inspire the nation. 'Bully' was a term of approbation much used by Roosevelt, not an exploitation of a position of strength against the weak.

Bullying-manner The nickname of Sir Reginald Manningham-Buller (later Lord Dilhorne, 1905–80), inverting his surname, which he gained as ATTORNEY-GENERAL between 1954 and 1962. When he led the prosecution against the Eastbourne doctor John Bodkin Adams in 1957 for allegedly murdering an elderly lady patient for her money, Mr Justice (later Lord) Devlin described him and Adams as 'the two most self-righteous men in England'; Adams was acquitted after a seventeen-day trial at the Old Bailey.

Bundesbank Germany's CENTRAL BANK, a key player in the European and world economy until the advent of the EURO, when its powers and those of twelve of its counterparts to set interest rates passed to the EUROPEAN CENTRAL BANK; it retains domestic powers such as banking supervision. Based like its successor at Frankfurt, it was independent of the Federal government and had as its overwhelming priority under statute the control of INFLATION. In 1992 its tough interest rate policy resulting from the cost of German reUNIFICATION and an ensuing rise in prices created strains in the ERM that culminated first in DEVALUATION of the Italian and Spanish currencies, and then in BLACK WEDNESDAY when the UK devalued and withdrew from the mechanism.

Bundesrat The indirectly-elected upper house of the German legislature, comprising representatives of the sixteen LÄNDER. Each Land has four, five or six votes, which must be cast as a block.

Bundestag The more powerful lower house of the German legislature, whose main functions are to pass laws, elect the CHANCELLOR and keep the Federal government in check. Elected every four years, it can only be dissolved prematurely when the Federal President is convinced there are 'exceptional circumstances'. Since reUNIFICATION in 1990 it has had 662 members.

Bundist A NAZI supporter, generally of German origin, in America prior to US entry into WORLD WAR II. The name came from the *Deutschland-Amerika Bund*, the Nazi-backed organisation which campaigned for closer links with Germany, and for staying out of the war.

Bunker, the The LOBBY briefing room, seating around 40 journalists, which was opened in the basement of No. 10 Downing Street in September 1995. The 11a.m. Lobby meeting, previously held in the Press Secretary's tiny office with journalists entering via No. 10's historic front door, was held in the 'bunker', accessed by steps down from the side of the building, until Alastair Campbell threw the event open to all accredited journalists in May 2002, after which a larger room off the premises was needed.

bunker mentality A syndrome in which leaders consider themselves under siege, developing a persecution complex and steadily withdrawing from contact with all but the most trusted aides and advisers. The phrase has its origin in the *Führerbunker* where HITLER spent the final days of his life, ordering phantom divisions into action as the Russians closed on Berlin. It was used appropriately of the NIXON WHITE HOUSE; the mood first appeared soon after Nixon's inauguration in reaction to violent protests against the VIETNAM WAR, but returned in full force as WATERGATE began to threaten the President's survival.

bunkum Irrelevant nonsense advanced as an argument. The word derives from North Carolina's Buncombe County, whose Congressman, Felix Walter (*see* OLD OIL-JUG), made a tedious speech in the HOUSE in 1820 on the MISSOURI COMPROMISE and declared that he was speaking 'for Buncombe'. The name stuck – unfortunately for the Revolutionary War hero Col. Edward Buncombe after whom the county was named. The word has also been contracted to **bunk**.

bunkum and balderdash The trademark expression of Margaret THATCHER's press secretary Bernard Ingham (*see* YORKSHIRE

RASPUTIN), who would use it in LOBBY meetings about any news report or question he considered fanciful. *Compare* GARBAGIC.

Bureau The body which supervises the running and expenditure of the EUROPEAN PARLIAMENT; it comprises the Parliament's President and fourteen Vice-Presidents, all elected by the Parliament every 2½ years. When political decisions are to be made, the chairmen of the party groups also attend. Five **quaestors** (all MEPs) advise the Bureau on administrative and financial matters.

bureaucracy Government by unfeeling paper-shufflers, or the dead hand of OFFICIALDOM itself. The word **bureaucrat** was first used in 1842 when Count Karl von Nesselrode, Minister to Tsar Nicholas I, was described in a letter as 'bureaucrat to the great autocrat'. Bureaucracy has ever since been a target for politicians, who either berate 'faceless bureaucrats' for blocking their decisions or complain that its efficiency makes it over-powerful. Balzac termed it 'the giant power wielded by pigmies', Lord Grimond 'the antithesis of democracy'; J.F. KENNEDY described dealing with bureaucracy as 'like trying to nail jelly to the wall' and Sen. Eugene McCarthy warned that 'an efficient bureaucracy is the greatest threat to liberty'.

> The nearest thing to immortality on earth is a government bureau.
>
> JAMES F. BYRNES, *Speaking Frankly,* 1947

> We declared our independence 200 years ago, and we are not about to lose it now to paper shufflers and computers.
>
> President FORD

> Bureaucrat: a Democrat who holds some office that a Republican wants.
>
> Vice President ALBEN BARKLEY

Burgess and Maclean The two British FOREIGN OFFICE diplomats, Guy Burgess (1911–63) and Donald Maclean (1913–83), who worked undetected as Soviet agents during WORLD WAR II and the COLD WAR that followed, before defecting suddenly to the Soviet Union in 1951. Both came from privileged backgrounds and were members of a group of mainly homosexual young men recruited at Cambridge University in the 1930s (*see* APOSTLES). Burgess, an alcoholic, was a relatively junior official; Maclean, as a member of MI6 with access to classified information who had aroused US suspicions while serving in WASHINGTON, could do more damage. They defected after being warned by another agent, the THIRD MAN Harold (Kim) Philby (1912–88), that the net was closing in on them; their flight was arranged by Anthony BLUNT, unmasked three decades later as the FOURTH MAN. Burgess, Maclean and eventually Philby led a melancholic existence in Moscow, nostalgic for home but insisting that the sacrifice had been worthwhile.

Burke. Burke's address to the electors of Bristol One of the standard texts of Parliamentary democracy, establishing that a member of a legislature is a REPRESENTATIVE elected to exercise his or her own judgement and not a DELEGATE. It was delivered on 3 November 1774 by the radical Edmund Burke (1729–97), who said:

> Your representative owes you, not his industry only, but his judgment; and he betrays, instead of serving, you if he sacrifices it to your opinion.

He was unlikely in any event to have reflected the views of his constituents; he once confided:

> I believe in any body of men in England I should have been in the minority.

Burke, a Dublin-born WHIG, condemned Lord North's handling of the American colonies and lost his Bristol seat in 1780 for supporting a relaxation of the laws against Catholics. He was re-elected the same year for Malton, sitting until 1794. He took an active part in the IMPEACHMENT of Warren Hastings, and ended his career with vitriolic and increasingly desperate attacks on the FRENCH REVOLUTION, by which time he was close to becoming a TORY. Burke left behind him a great reputation as an orator, but his contemporary Sheridan observed:

> When posterity read the speeches of Burke, they will hardly be able to believe that, during his lifetime, he was not considered a first-rate speaker, nor even a second-rate one.

Thomas Paine considered Burke's oratory superficial, saying: 'He pities the plumage, but forgets the dying bird.' Yet Dr Johnson was captivated:

> You could not stand five minutes with that man beneath a shed, while it rained, but you must be convinced you had been standing with the greatest man you had ever seen.

Burke's great rival in later years was Charles James Fox; he said of Fox's passion for Revolutionary France: 'He is like a cat – fond of the house tho' the family be gone.' Fox wrote: 'Burke was a damned wrong-headed fellow, through his whole life jealous and obstinate. He would never support any measure, however convinced in his heart he might be of its utility, if it had first been proposed by another.'

> Though equal to all things, for all things unfit,
> Too nice for a statesman, too proud for a wit.
>
> OLIVER GOLDSMITH

> As he rose like a rocket, he fell like a stick.
>
> THOMAS PAINE

Burke Act *See* DAWES ACT.

burn. burn, baby, burn! One of the most incendiary slogans of US black militants from the mid-1960s. Spiro AGNEW once attacked black community leaders in Baltimore as a 'ready-mix, instantaneous, circuit-riding, Hanoi-visiting, caterwauling, riot-inciting, burn-down-America type of leaders'.

burn everything English but their coal! The slogan coined by the disillusioned Irish cleric Jonathan Swift (1667–1745) which, with its combination of violence and BOYCOTT, greatly appealed to later REPUBLICAN revolutionaries.

burning the house to roast the pig Justice Felix Frankfurter's verdict on the anti-obscenity laws of various States when the US SUPREME COURT declared them UNCONSTITUTIONAL in 1957.

book-burning The ultimate intolerance by a regime or faction devoted to stamping out culture as a whole, or views with which it disagrees. The NAZIS held bonfires of books that conflicted with their 'perverted science'. When in 1948 Rep. John Taber took the Library of CONGRESS to task for publishing a monthly list of new Soviet books, his leftist New York colleague Vito Marcantonio suggested he appropriate 'a reasonable amount of money for the burning of books'.

Burns Report The report on the practicalities of foxhunting commissioned from Lord Burns, former chief economist at the TREASURY, by Tony BLAIR's government in 2000 as it endeavoured to find relief from the overwhelming pressure of backbench Labour MPs to ban the pursuit outright. The report, inevitably, was inconclusive but encouraged Ministers to float the 'middle way' under which hunting would continue under regulation. This had, embarrassingly, to be abandoned in mid-debate in July 2003 when it became plain the majority would only accept an outright ban, which was passed into law the following year.

Burntollet One of the violent incidents that marked the resumption of the TROUBLES in NORTHERN IRELAND and pushed the CIVIL RIGHTS movement into the arms of the waiting IRA. It occurred on 4 January 1969, when a PAISLEYITE mob ambushed a 'People's Democracy' march from Belfast to Derry at Burntollet Bridge, while police stood by.

Burr-Hamilton duel The tragic episode on 11 July 1804 when the brilliant but much detested Alexander HAMILTON was shot dead by JEFFERSON's Vice President, Aaron Burr (1756–1836). New England FEDERALISTS opposed to the LOUISIANA PURCHASE because it would dilute their influence were preparing to SECEDE from the UNION and turned to Burr for help. He agreed to run for Governor of New York and then lead the state into a new Northern confederation. Hamilton heard of the plot and revealed it; Burr already hated him for turning the tied ELECTORAL COLLEGE against him three years before by calling him 'a cold-blooded Catiline . . . a profligate, a voluptuary . . . no doubt insolvent', and challenged him to a duel. The confrontation with pistols took place beside the Hudson at Weehawken, New Jersey. When the command: 'Present!' was given, Burr fired, and Hamilton fired over him as he fell forward, his supporters later claiming he had fired to miss. A grand jury in Bergen, New Jersey, indicted Burr for murder, and he fled to Georgia and South Carolina, journeying 400 miles through swamps by canoe and hatching a plot to separate New Orleans from the Union. Hamilton left seven children and debts of $55,000, and Burr was dogged for the rest of his life by the anonymous rhyme:

> Oh Burr, Oh Burr, what hast thou done,
> Thou hast shooted dead Great Hamilton.
> You hid among a bush of thistle
> And shooted him with a great hoss pistol!

bury. now is a good day to get out anything we want to bury The comment e-mailed to colleagues on 9/11 by Jo Moore, SPECIAL ADVISER to UK Transport Secretary Stephen Byers, which to NEW LABOUR's critics epitomised the worst excesses of SPIN. Ms Moore's suggestion, made before the full implications of the attacks on the twin towers and the PENTAGON were known, was that on a busy news day the department should release pending news items which were political negatives, notably an announcement on the level of councillors' allowances. The LEAKING of these sentiments was a great embarrassment to Tony BLAIR's government and seriously hampered the conduct of business, as the OPPOSITION and the media were able to claim that any announcement of bad news was being delayed until it could be put out surreptitiously, thus forcing all adverse news to be put out with the maximum publicity. The episode heightened tensions within Byers' Department of Transport, Local Government and the Regions, which finally erupted on 15 February 2002 when Martin Sixsmith, head of news at the DTLR, leaked a memo to Jo Moore accusing her of planning to put out further bad news on the day of Princess Margaret's funeral. Moore in fact had no such plans, but both she and Sixsmith were forced to resign, further damaging the reputation of Byers (*see* RAILTRACK) and the DTLR, particularly as Sixsmith held out for several weeks after Byers had told the COMMONS he was ready to go (*see also* FUCKED). Byers eventually resigned on 28 May 2002, stating that his own continued presence in the Government had become a 'distraction' (*see* Those who know me best know that I am not a LIAR). Days later a further row broke over an email sent to the LABOUR PARTY by his other special adviser, Dan Corry, asking whether the highly vocal Paddington Rail Crash Survivors' Group had links with the Conservatives.

bus. a bus driven by the Marx Brothers A Spanish diplomat's description of Italy's PRESIDENCY of the EUROPEAN COMMUNITY in the second half of 1990; officials in Rome were furious, but blamed the British who they mistakenly thought had originated it.

buses for Cuba The export deal that strained UK-US relations c. 1961. It involved the sale of buses built by Leyland to Fidel Castro's Cuba, the subject of a US trade EMBARGO. The tension was eased somewhat when the ship carrying one consignment of buses sank in the Thames estuary.

are those your own buses? The remark reputedly made by Nicholas Ridley (*see* GERMAN RACKET) when, as Transport Secretary, he visited a London bus garage to see how the industry worked. It was during Ridley's tenure of the Department of Transport, 1983–86, that bus services outside the capital were DEREGULATED.

The Boys on the Bus The classic account of how the media covers a US Presidential ELECTION – and indeed how it conducts itself generally – written in 1972 by Timothy Crouse while covering George McGovern's campaign for *Rolling Stone*. It remains both one of the best, and one of the funniest, books ever written about political journalism, even though most of the names and the faces have changed. *See also* ZOO PLANE.

If you see me at the back of the bus One of the most popular songs among the FREEDOM RIDERS who campaigned for the DESEGREGATION of bus services in America's Deep South. Written by Pete Seeger, it originated in the MONTGOMERY BUS BOYCOTT when Mrs Rosa Parkes refused to sit in the seats reserved for blacks at the back of a bus.

man on the Clapham omnibus *See* MAN.

number 11 bus One of the great hypothetical questions at Westminster is who would take over as a party leader 'if they were run over by a number 11 bus', the route between Liverpool Street Station and Fulham Broadway which passes the end of DOWNING STREET. During Margaret THATCHER's first term, a television programme polled Tory BACKBENCHERS on whom they would like to take over should such a mishap occur; for some time afterward, government WHIPS were trying to ascertain who replied: 'The bus driver'. Lord Carrington, Mrs Thatcher's first FOREIGN SECRETARY, had more basic doubts, observing: 'The bus wouldn't dare.'

busing The process under which children are transferred by bus from one part of an American city to another in order to ensure that each school contains an ethnic mix; it reached its height in the early 1970s, and has since declined. Busing, ordered by the courts in some cities to end virtual SEGREGATION of neighbourhood schools, actually heightened racial tension in some places by enraging white parents who objected to their children being bused to predominantly black schools. Working-class parents who had moved to 'better' neighbourhoods because of the local schools now felt they had to give their children a private education to maintain that advantage; in the 1972 Presidential ELECTION both Richard NIXON and (initially) George Wallace attracted votes by attacking busing. *See also* SCHOOLS YOU CAN WALK TO.

Bush, George Herbert Walker (1924–), 41st President of the United States (Republican, 1989–93) and father of President George W. Bush (*see below*). George Bush came to the Presidency after eight years as Ronald REAGAN's Vice President with a glittering resumé: son of a distinguished New England Senator, a DFC as the youngest Navy pilot of WORLD WAR II, successful Texas oilman, two-term CONGRESSMAN, twice-defeated Senatorial candidate, US AMBASSADOR to the UNITED

NATIONS (1971–73), Chairman of the Republican NATIONAL COMMITTEE (1973–74), unofficial ambassador to China (1974–75) and director of the CIA (1976–77). He ran against Reagan for the 1980 Republican nomination (*see* VOODOO ECONOMICS), and eight years later defeated Michael Dukakis to become the first Vice President since Van Buren to win 'promotion' to the executive mansion. Conservatives suspected this patrician New Englander of lacking right-wing convictions, Sen. Robert Dole memorably identifying these doubts with a TV commercial reciting Bush's resumé as the camera panned across a forest path to show NO FOOTPRINTS IN THE SNOW. But Bush doggedly insisted:

> If CARTER can do it with no credentials, I can do it with these fantastic credentials; the fact that nobody else knows it is kind of discouraging.

He went on to conduct a highly negative campaign; he pilloried the wooden Dukakis as a 'liberal', accusing him of favouring FLAG-BURNING and being soft on criminals (*see* WILLIE HORTONISM), and went on to win a convincing victory.

Bush declared in his INAUGURAL address: 'We must hope to give [our children] a sense of what it means to be a loyal friend, a loving parent, a citizen who leaves his home, his neighbourhood and town better than he found it', and his aim was to be remembered as 'the education President.' Yet his main interest, inevitably given his record, was in foreign affairs. He pressed ahead with ARMS CONTROL agreements with the collapsing Soviet Union; sent US troops into PANAMA in May 1989 to overthrow the hated strongman Manuel Noriega who had just rigged a Presidential election, having him arrested on drug-trafficking charges; through SECRETARY OF STATE James Baker he took a tougher line with the Israeli government over its reluctance to co-operate with the PEACE PROCESS; and in August 1990, stiffened by a visiting Margaret THATCHER, he committed US forces to drive the invading Iraqis out of Kuwait. The following February Bush instigated Operation Desert Storm, in which US, British, French and allied Arab forces delivered what appeared to be a knockout blow to SADDAM HUSSEIN (*see* BEAST OF BAGHDAD), then halted on fulfilling objectives set by the UN.

In the summer of 1991 Bush seemed impregnable. However, Saddam survived, having brutally suppressed an uprising by Shi'ites who had expected American support; the US economy was turning down; and the President, a fitness fanatic, was having problems with his health. First mild heart trouble was diagnosed, causing the *National Jewish Post and Opinion* to gloat: 'Bush's heart problem was visited on him by God for his treatment of Israel,' and then, on a visit to Tokyo in early 1992, he vomited over the Japanese Prime Minister at a State banquet (*see* POTUS BARFED). By now it was evident that, apart from Bush's basic dignity – which would enhance his reputation as his successor suffered the indignities of ZIPPERGATE – and his sincerity, his greatest asset was his grandmotherly wife Barbara, who could mix it with the best of them. When Bush sought re-election as Vice President in 1984, she had said of his opponent Geraldine Ferraro:

> My husband and I have no intention of hiding our wealth – not like that four-million-dollar – I can't say it, but it rhymes with 'rich'.

An early PRIMARY challenge by the conservative columnist Pat Buchanan made Bush look vulnerable, and while the Democrats struggled to find a nominee before the emergence of Bill CLINTON, the intervention of H. Ross PEROT to mock him as a failure heightened the impression. Bush now had to justify the domestic achievements of his ADMINISTRATION, but the jibe of former Democratic Sen. Paul Tsongas that he was 'America's foreign minister' struck home, and the more Bush tried to appear tough, the more the voters remembered the WIMP FACTOR. His own comments such as 'just a splash of tea, please', when offered a drink in a workmen's canteen heightened the impression; Texas State Sen. Carl Parker commented:

> Reagan can portray a real macho guy. Bush can't. He comes off looking like Liberace.

When Bush's otherwise loyal predecessor observed from retirement that 'he doesn't seem to stand for anything', he struck another chord. When the Mafia don John Gotti was jailed in New York during the primary campaign, Washington jokers asked the difference between him and Bush, replying: 'At least Gotti has one conviction.' Bush was handicapped by his ability to murder the English language, although his son, and his own Vice President Dan QUAYLE, could outdo him in this respect. Mary McGrory wrote:

> The only speech part that he has mastered completely is the *non sequitur*.

He himself admitted, giving a toast in 1989

to the Pakistani Prime Minister Benazir Bhutto:

> Fluency in English is something that I'm not often accused of.

His howlers were notorious. He said in a 1988 campaign speech in Detroit that: 'America's freedom is the example to which the world expires.' He caused consternation at a Republican rally in Twin Falls, Idaho by declaring: 'For 7½ years I have worked alongside him [Reagan], and I am proud to be his partner. We have had triumphs, we have made mistakes, we have had sex . . .' Of the Alaska pipeline he said: 'The caribou love it. They rub up against it, and they have babies.' He told one startled audience: 'I hope I stand for anti-bigotry, anti-Semitism, anti-racism', and he once declared his intention to 'make sure that everybody who has a job wants a job'.

Bush could be downright tactless. He described his three half-Mexican grandchildren in Houston as 'the little brown ones over there'. But above all he was capable of total gibberish, his finest effort coming when he visited a Union, New Jersey high school and told bewildered students:

> I'm delighted that Barbara Bush is with me today, and I – she got a good, clean bill of health yesterday from Walter Reed Hospital, I might add – and then – But I'm taking another look at our doctor. He told her it's okay to kiss the dog – I mean – no, it's okay to kiss your husband, but don't kiss the dog. So I don't know exactly what that means.

After early reverses in the 1992 campaign, Bush said: 'I've been very kind and gentle. I'll still be kind, and I'm now debating how gentle to be'; but he told David FROST: 'I will do what I have to do to get re-elected.' There followed a campaign even more negative than that of 1988, with NEGATIVE RESEARCH about Clinton's private life put to the fullest use, and Tory strategists imported from England mounting an attack on Clinton's tax plans that embarrassed John MAJOR once the votes were in. The election slipped away from Bush in the final two weeks as the Clinton campaign rebutted all charges against it and Ross PEROT (who had dropped out of the campaign for over two months) won enough Republican waverers to put Clinton into the WHITE HOUSE. Bush in defeat was gracious and dignified, raising the suspicion that he had not been hungry for a second term, and after a genial handover to the Clintons, he and Barbara helicoptered to retirement in Texas. Bush appeared a steadily more substantial figure as Clinton's trysts on the fringe of the OVAL OFFICE became public and then as his son struggled to establish himself. He pursued an active business career, and in 1997 at the age of 72 made a parachute jump in Arizona, the first since he was shot down in 1944.

> He was one of the most decent, honest and patriotic Americans I have ever met. He had great personal courage . . . but he had never had to think through his beliefs and fight for them when they were hopelessly unfashionable as Ronald Reagan and I had had to do.
>
> MARGARET THATCHER, *The Downing Street Years*

> I was smart enough to recognise a bad marriage and get out of it. I'm smart enough to recognise a bad President and get out of that.
>
> CINDY RIOUX-MATTA, Ridgewood, NJ, September 1992

> Bush and his advisers misread the year, the country and his opponent.
>
> ELIZABETH DREW, *New Yorker*

> Bush had two faults. He didn't care for domestic politics, and he didn't care for people.
>
> CHARLES WHEELER, BBC television

(*See also* CONCENTRATION CAMPS; KENNEBUNKPORT; MILLIE; PEARL HARBOR; READ MY LIPS. NO NEW TAXES.)

Bush, George Walker (DUBYA) (1946–), 43rd President of the United States (Republican) and elder son of President George Herbert Bush; the only son of a President to win the presidency himself and secure a second term. George W. Bush was declared by the SUPREME COURT the winner (*see* BUSH V. GORE) of the most closely contested election in US history 37 days after his contest with Al Gore had resulted in a virtual dead heat, with 537 bitterly disputed votes in Florida (where his younger brother Jeb was governor) at issue. Bush had a strong family pedigree, had worked in his father's 1988 Presidential campaign and was for six years (1994–2000) Governor of Texas, the first to be elected for four consecutive terms (*see* SHRUB). Yet his main ambition after graduating from Yale in 1968 and gaining a Harvard MBA had been to become Baseball Commissioner, and he came within sight of his goal as managing general partner of the Texas Rangers, having put together a consortium to purchase the franchise in 1989. He also had a patchy career in business, being less sure than his father in his choice of associates. Bush and his team – of whom Vice President Richard Cheney and Defense Secretary Donald Rumsfeld often appeared the true centres of power – organised confidently for the

Presidency even before being awarded the election. In office they pursued a markedly conservative social and tax-cutting agenda with strong input from NEO-CONSERVATIVES and the religious RIGHT, while pointedly re-establishing the dignity of an office and a WHITE HOUSE they believed had been sullied by Bill CLINTON and ZIPPERGATE. Bush's early years were tarnished by the ENRON scandal, not least because of Cheney's association with the corporation and the access it enjoyed until its crash.

His Presidency was defined by 9/11, the WAR AGAINST TERRORISM and the IRAQ WAR, which he justified through Iraq's membership of his AXIS OF EVIL as well as through the insistence that SADDAM HUSSEIN was ready to use WEAPONS OF MASS DESTRUCTION and had links with AL QAEDA. Bush was visiting a school in Florida on 11 September 2001 when he was told of the suicide attacks on the WORLD TRADE CENTER and the PENTAGON, and for the rest of a panicky day AIR FORCE ONE shuttled him between bases in the South until it was considered safe to return to WASHINGTON and then to visit the destruction at GROUND ZERO. In the meantime Cheney – who had not long before suffered a heart attack – took control from a secure command centre. After a hesitant initial reaction (*see* THOSE FOLKS), Bush declared that 'in our grief and anger we have found our mission and our moment', committing US troops to extirpate Al Qaeda and overthrow the TALEBAN regime in Afghanistan that had been sheltering it. He also established a Department of HOMELAND SECURITY to tighten and co-ordinate the domestic watch against terrorism, which had been seriously ineffective in the run-up to 9/11 as suicide bombers trained at US flying schools and criss-crossed the country under sporadic observation from unco-ordinated security agencies. The US-led coalition ousted the Taleban and drove Osama BIN LADEN into lawless country on the Afghan-Pakistani border, but was unable either to capture and kill Bin Laden or to break up his organisation, which conducted further atrocities, notably the BALI and MADRID BOMBINGS. Taleban and Al Qaeda suspects who were detained in Afghanistan and elsewhere were flown to Guantanamo Bay in Cuba, where they were held in strict detention at CAMP X-RAY pending their trial by military tribunal in the face of protests by HUMAN RIGHTS watchdogs.

Bush's inner circle was determined to complete the job left unfinished by his father and oust Saddam, if necessary without the backing of the UNITED NATIONS which had supported the 1990–91 GULF WAR. Blair, who had given America total support after 9/11, also signed up to action against Iraq and persuaded Bush to give the UN several chances before he and his intimates ran out of patience and sent in the troops in March 2003. The action was swift and decisive and Iraq was liberated within a month, but as with Afghanistan and Al Qaeda, the men at the heart of the regime survived; after 100 days 36 of the 55 key BAATH PARTY leaders and Saddam supporters on a US-distributed pack of cards had been rounded up, but it was July before US troops killed Saddam's sons Uday and Qusay in a shoot-out in Mosul and Saddam remained at large for several months, taunting Bush with audio tapes urging resistance as a GUERRILLA campaign killed more US troops each day. Partly under pressure from Britain, Bush – whose foreign policy agenda was dominated by disagreements between Secretary of State Colin Powell, a DOVE, and the hard-line NATIONAL SECURITY ADVISER Condoleezza Rice (also an African-American) who generally had the backing of Rumsfeld and succeeded Powell in 2005 – followed victory in Iraq with an initiative to resolve the Israeli-Palestinian conflict through a ROAD MAP to peace. However, America's credibility in Iraq and throughout the Middle East was left in tatters by the revelations of barbarous treatment of detainees at ABU GHRAIB, as coalition forces were confronted by INSURGENTS including remnants of Saddam's military and security apparatus, militant Shi'ite militias and foreign fighters with links to Al Qaeda.

Bush's record on domestic policy largely escaped scrutiny until the fall of Baghdad in April 2003, save that the economy was already heading into recession before 9/11 and that its continued flatness as concern over terrorism was matched by the Enron and other scandals impacted on his popularity. However, he did focus strongly and with some success on raising educational standards, notably through his NO CHILD LEFT BEHIND ACT. In his campaign for re-election, Bush concentrated on the threat to America's security and his resolve in standing up to terror, accusing his Democratic challenger John KERRY of weakness and inconsistency, while pro-Bush elements attacked Kerry's war record (*see* SWIFT BOAT VETERANS FOR TRUTH). Yet the result in 2004 was almost as close as four years previously, with the outcome in Ohio (itself close enough for Kerry to ponder, then reject a challenge) holding the key.

Even more than his father, Bush struggled with the English language; indeed he was perceived by many who had dealings with him as being out of his depth intellectually. As a candidate he struggled to name the President of Pakistan, calling him simply GENERAL . . . it was ironic that Al Qaeda should throw him and General Musharraf together just a year later. And the one *froideur* in his close relationship with Blair came when the British Prime Minister could not resist telling colleagues that Bush had complained in a phone call: 'The trouble with the French is that they have no word for entrepreneur.' Other dicta have included: 'Welcome to Mrs Bush, and my fellow astronauts'; 'The vast majority of our imports come from outside the country'; 'It's time for the human race to enter the solar system'; 'It isn't pollution that's harming the environment. It's the impurities in our air and water that are doing it'; 'Nigeria is an important continent'; 'It is white' (when asked by a child what the White House was like); 'I know that human beings and fish can coexist peacefully'; 'It's clearly a budget. It's got a lot of numbers in it'; 'There's no doubt in my mind, not one doubt in my mind, that we will fail'; 'I am mindful not only of preserving executive powers for myself, but for my predecessors as well'; and 'I am here to make an announcement that this Thursday, ticket counters and airplanes will fly out of Reagan Airport.'

Nevertheless the sheer commitment of his senior CABINET members made Bush always a force to be reckoned with on the world or the domestic stage. Yet on some issues, notably global warming and KYOTO, he was out of step even with America's allies.

See also CRAWFORD; DEFLATION; ENEMIES; MAJOR LEAGUE ASSHOLE; PAKIS.

> If you said to me, name 25 million people who would maybe be president of the United States, he wouldn't have been in that category.
>
> Former business associate DAVID RUBENSTEIN

> The most incompetent and dangerous President in living memory.
>
> Mark Latham, 2003, prior to his election as Australian LABOR PARTY leader

> George is normally in bed by now (9p.m.). If he really wants to end tyranny in this world he will have to stay up later.
>
> LAURA BUSH at the White House Correspondents' dinner, 30 April 2005

Bush v Gore The most important SUPREME COURT case in US electoral history, in which the Justices voted 5–4 on 12 December 2000 not to order a wider RECOUNT of Presidential votes cast in Florida, thus dooming Al GORE's attempt to overturn George W. Bush's apparent victory in the state, and consequently the entire ELECTION. Gore reluctantly accepted 'the finality of this outcome' which left him the winner of the popular vote but three votes short of a majority in the ELECTORAL COLLEGE. He conceded the following day 'for the sake of the unity of our people and the strength of our democracy'.

business The term used in many legislatures for the volume of legislation and other items that have to be fitted into the time available. At WESTMINSTER the **business of the House** has a particular importance, as the government feels obliged to get it through, and the OPPOSITION's role is to make selective attempts at delay, the balance being maintained by negotiations through the USUAL CHANNELS.

business as usual The declaration that WORLD WAR I would not be allowed to interfere with Britain's daily life, made by Winston CHURCHILL in a speech at London's GUILDHALL on 9 November 1914, two months into the conflict. The First Lord of the Admiralty said:

> The maxim of the British people is 'Business as Usual'.

business managers The team at WESTMINSTER comprising the government WHIPS and the Leader of each HOUSE who endeavour to ensure that legislation flows smoothly, that the committee system is fully manned and produces no shocks, and that OPPOSITION delaying tactics arising from misunderstandings between the parties are avoided.

business statement At WESTMINSTER, a statement from the LEADER OF THE HOUSE announcing the business for the coming week, or a change in the programme already arranged. The routine business statement each Thursday gives rise to Business QUESTIONS.

a man I can do business with The words with which Margaret THATCHER is supposed to have indicated to fellow Western leaders, notably Ronald REAGAN, that Mikhail GORBACHEV was serious about ending the COLD WAR. What she actually said after meeting him at CHEQUERS at the end of 1985 was: 'I like Mr Gorbachev. We can do business together.' The IRON LADY may not have realised that, in 1961, Earl ATTLEE reminisced of STALIN:

He was clearly a pretty ruthless tyrant, but a man you could do business with.

I never knew a pollytician go wrong until he's been contaminated by contact with a businessman A classic *bon mot* from 'Mr Dooley', the Irish-American cog in a political MACHINE created by the humorist Finley Peter Dunne (1867–1936).

less government in business, and more business in government One of the campaign pledges of Warren HARDING when he won the US Presidency in 1920. The TEAPOT DOME scandal that ensued was probably not what he had in mind.

lose the business The setback suffered by Government BUSINESS MANAGERS at WESTMINSTER when dissidents in the HOUSE OF COMMONS keep one day's sitting going until the following morning, forcing the abandonment of whatever was due to have been discussed that day. On very rare occasions, such tactics on the previous night have wiped out Prime Minister's QUESTION TIME, but successive tightenings of the rules since the early 1990s have greatly reduced the scope for such disruption.

next business A procedural device common to many UK elected bodies and organisations: the opportunity to end a debate which is getting nowhere by moving 'next business' and passing to the following item on the AGENDA.

opposed private business The time allotted in the UK HOUSE OF COMMONS by the Chairman of WAYS AND MEANS for the debate of Private BILLS to which objection has been lodged.

the business of America is business The statement for which President Coolidge (*see* SILENT CAL) is best known, as well as being the longest. It sums up the ethos of 1920s America and explains the Republicans' tenure of the WHITE HOUSE from 1920 until the onset of the GREAT DEPRESSION.

butcher of Baghdad *See* BAGHDAD.

Butler. Butler Education Act The landmark Act passed in 1944 which established the structure of state education in England and Wales for the post-war period, much of it surviving the COMPREHENSIVISATION of the late 1960s and even the Baker Act of 1988 (*see* GERBIL). The brainchild of R.A. (RAB) Butler, President of the Board of Education, it was the most significant piece of legislation for peacetime passed at WESTMINSTER during WORLD WAR II. Butler's greatest achievement was in resolving the argument that had rumbled on for decades over how the Church of England's schools could be incorporated into the State system, and what proportion of the cost of Roman Catholic education the State would meet. The one fly in the ointment was that a combination of YOUNG TURK Tories and Labour MPs inflicted a one-vote defeat on the Government over equal pay for teachers – the CHURCHILL government's first COMMONS defeat in four years.

Butler inquiry The inquiry by the former CABINET SECRETARY Lord Butler and a panel of PRIVY COUNCILLORS into intelligence failures over WEAPONS OF MASS DESTRUCTION in the run-up to the 2003 IRAQ WAR and the inclusion of dubious and over-hyped information in the UK Government's 'DODGY DOSSIER' detailing the threat from Saddam Hussein (*see* Butcher of BAGHDAD). Tony BLAIR and colleagues were widely assumed to have leaned on the intelligence community to agree to weak information being included in the dossier, a claim that gained added currency from the BBC report that triggered the David KELLY AFFAIR, Kelly's suicide and the subsequent HUTTON INQUIRY. Reporting in July 2004, Lord Butler criticised Blair for telling MPs the dossier was authoritative; stated that John Scarlett, director-designate of MI6, had been unduly influenced by DOWNING STREET; concluded that no single individual was to blame; upheld as 'credible' intelligence, disputed by WASHINGTON after being included in the STATE OF THE UNION message, that Saddam had tried to buy uranium in Niger; described as not accurate the dossier's 45-MINUTE CLAIM on Saddam's ability to deploy chemical weapons at short notice; ruled that CABINET GOVERNMENT had been undermined by the informality of decision-making over the dossier; and concluded that available intelligence had been pushed 'to the outer limits but not beyond'. Opponents of the war who had dismissed Hutton as a WHITEWASH were quick to pass the same judgement on Butler, whose criticisms Blair accepted.

I can honestly say I have never had to make a harder judgement.
TONY BLAIR, House of Commons, 14 July 2004

Butskellism The moderate CONSENSUS POLITICS that reigned at WESTMINSTER in the early 1950s, when CHURCHILL's Conservative government undid very little of Labour's NATIONALISATION and left the WELFARE STATE intact. In particular it reflected continuity in economic policy, with the Tory Chancellor R.A. Butler (*see* RAB) picking up where Labour's Hugh GAITSKELL had left off. The word first appeared in the *Economist* of 13 February 1954:

> Mr Butskell is already a well-known figure in dinner table conversations in both Westminster and Whitehall, and the time has come to introduce him to a wider audience.

butter mountain *See* MOUNTAIN.

Buttiglione nomination The crisis that enveloped the EUROPEAN UNION in 2004, coincidentally in the week of the signature in Rome of the EUROPEAN CONSTUTUTION, over the nomination by the incoming PRESIDENT OF THE COMMISSION, José Manuel Barroso, of the Italian ultra-conservative Rocco Buttiglione as Justice and Security Commissioner. Buttigilione's public utterances against homosexuals, single mothers and working women had appalled many, and his confirmation hearing by a committee of MEPs voted to reject him by a majority of one. The Parliament could only reject Buttiglione by voting down the entire new Commission, but the votes were there. On the eve of that vote on 27 October, Barroso withdrew his team for further consideration, Buttiglione standing down two days later with the promise of a Ministerial post from Italy's Prime Minister Silvio Berlusconi. The old Commission headed by Romano Prodi had to remain in office for over three weeks beyond the scheduled date for the changeover.

by-election (1) In the UK political system, an ELECTION held outside the normal cycle or (for a Parliamentary seat) other than during a general election. It is caused by the death or resignation of the INCUMBENT, or by their appointment to a post (e.g. in the judiciary) that bars them from effective office. A Parliamentary by-election is set in motion by the SPEAKER issuing a WRIT for the poll to take place. As by-elections afford the most obvious, and at times the most dramatic, test of a government's popularity and that of the various parties and the readiness of the electors to give them a bloody nose, great media attention is devoted to them and they are thus that more keenly fought, with a close eye kept on the SWING. Eccentrics such as Commander Bill Boaks and Screaming Lord Sutch of the OFFICIAL MONSTER RAVING LOONY PARTY have spent a lifetime contesting by-elections while repeatedly losing their DEPOSIT, though Sutch did kill off the SDP by finishing ahead of it at Bootle in 1990. *See also* EATANSWILL, MINDER, ORPINGTON MAN, OXFORD BY-ELECTION. (2) The MID-TERM Congressional elections held in the United States, in OFF-YEARS when there is no Presidential contest.

C

C The official title of the head of Britain's Secret Intelligence Service or MI6, whose identity was an official secret until 1999 when Sir Richard Dearlove was named as its new director. All correspondence is addressed and copied to him as 'C'; he always responds in green ink. 'M' in the James Bond novels and movies was an amalgam of 'C' and the Director of Naval Intelligence, Admiral Godfrey, under whom Bond's creator Ian Fleming served early in the WORLD WAR II.

CA The Constitutional Affairs committe of the UK CABINET, chaired by the DEPUTY PRIME MINISTER.

C-B The nickname of Britain's Liberal Prime Minister **Sir Henry Campbell-Bannerman** (1836–1908); the only other UK politician to be known by his initials is LLOYD GEORGE, who coincidentally sat in Campbell-Bannerman's CABINET.

CSpan The cable television channel founded by Brian Lamb which carries (frequently live) proceedings of the US CONGRESS and actuality from US ELECTION campaigns, and has brought QUESTION TIME at WESTMINSTER to US viewers. CSpan has carried debates in the HOUSE since 14 March 1979, when Al GORE, then a Tennessee Congressman, made the first televised speech; CSpan2 was added to cover the SENATE. Members of Congress have found CSpan's live coverage when it goes into SPECIAL ORDERS an ideal way of winning publicity; its airing of a 1985 Senate hearing on 'porn-rock' brought a flood of requests for tapes. Some 60 million US homes can now receive it.

> CSpan2's constant televising of the Senate's proceedings has sharply diminished the incidence of public drunkenness, crotch grabbing, page fondling and general tomfoolery that was once the rule among those august officials.
>
> CHRISTOPHER HITCHENS, *Vogue*

> The antithesis of the soundbite.
>
> CSPAN

> CSpan is more real than being there.
>
> Speaker NEWT GINGRICH

C2s In Britain, the critical 29% of the population who are skilled manual workers and their families, and whose votes win and lose ELECTIONS. Margaret THATCHER's success in capturing the C2s from Labour was critical to her victory in 1979 and the Conservatives' re-election in 1983, 1987 and 1992; from 1983 Labour readjusted its policies and campaigning in an effort to win them back, but it was 1997 before Tony BLAIR won over not only the C2s but much of the middle class as well. The classification is one of six indicators of social class devised in 1962 by the Institute of Practitioners in Advertising: A (upper middle class: professional and managerial, 3%); B (middle class: administrative and professional, 14% (*see* ABs)); C1 (lower middle class: supervisory and clerical, 22%); C2; D (working class: semi-skilled and unskilled, 18%); and E (lowest level: pensioners and casual workers, 14% (*see* DEs)).

Ça ira (Fr. That will go its way) Benjamin FRANKLIN's off-the-cuff remark in Paris in 1776–77 on America's War of Independence (*see* AMERICAN REVOLUTION), which was taken in the FRENCH REVOLUTION as the opening line of its most militant song: '*Ça ira* (3 times), *les aristos À LA LANTERNE*!' (string up the aristocrats on the nearest lamp-post!)

cabal A clique, or group of intriguers. The origin is said to be the initials of the Ministry appointed by Charles II in 1670: Clifford, Ashley, Buckingham, Arlington, Lauderdale. But it actually comes from the French *cabale*, an intriguing faction, and Hebrew *cabala*, secret knowledge.

Cabinet (1) The group of senior Ministers or departmental heads in charge of a government through regular, usually weekly, meetings; from the French *cabinet*, a small room. In Britain, an inner core of PRIVY COUNCILLORS on whom the monarch relied for advice in the late 17th century, it became a formal group of MINISTERS two centuries before its existence was recognised by statute in 1937. Macaulay wrote: 'a man in office, and out of the Cabinet, is a mere slave', and Aneurin BEVAN advised:

> There are only two ways of getting into the Cabinet. One is to crawl up the staircase of preferment on your belly; the other way is to kick them in the teeth. But for God's sake don't mix the two methods.

In Britain and principal COMMONWEALTH countries, the Cabinet comprises senior Ministers who are members of the LEGISLATURE. In America, where the term was first used by James MADISON in 1793, it has a less crucial role, has no statutory basis and consists of politically-appointed department heads (*see* SEPARATION OF POWERS). Abraham LINCOLN put his Cabinet in perspective by announcing: 'One aye, seven nays; the ayes have it'. A century later TRB wrote: 'IKE has picked a Cabinet of eight millionaires and a plumber.' Henry KISSINGER reckoned that 'every President since KENNEDY seems to have trusted his WHITE HOUSE aides more than his Cabinet', while Ronald REAGAN said of his Cabinet:

> Ronald Reagan slept here.

(2) In the EUROPEAN COMMISSION and continental Europe, the team of officials and advisers working to a Prime Minister, Minister or European Commissioner. The leader of such a team is the **chef de Cabinet**.

(3) In UK local government, the system used by an increasing number of authorities where a single elected member takes charge of an area of activity, for example highways or cleansing, instead of all decisions having to await the meeting of an all-party committee.

Cabinet committee One of the numerous sub-groups of Ministers covering a field of government activity (the economy, foreign affairs, counter-terrorism), sometimes chaired by the head of government but often, in the UK, by the DEPUTY PRIME MINISTER. Prior to the 2005 General Election there were 61; Tony BLAIR cut this back to 44.

Cabinet government In the UK, the doctrine of governing by ministerial agreement, rather than at the *fiat* of the Prime Minister. To Sir Geoffrey HOWE Cabinet government was 'all about trying to persuade one another from within'; Richard CROSSMAN concluded that 'the post-war epoch has seen the final transformation of Cabinet government into Prime Ministerial government', and Ministers on the losing end of an argument such as Clare SHORT and, by the end of his service under Margaret THATCHER, Sir Geoffrey himself, have volubly agreed. The Australian Prime Minister Malcolm Fraser offered a reason:

> A willingness to consult your senior colleagues indicates a willingness not to proceed with the decision.

cabinet member A term current since the late 1990s in English local government for the senior member of a local authority with responsibility for a particular portfolio, e.g. planning, housing or social services. It reflects a shift from the previous universal system of all matters being decided by committees of elected members; the committees still meet, but the cabinet member has greater freedom of action.

Cabinet Minister In Britain, a Minister who sits by right in the Cabinet. A Minister who attends Cabinet as required but does not receive the full salary is a **Minister of Cabinet Rank.** A member of the US Cabinet is a **Cabinet Officer**.

Cabinet Office In WHITEHALL, the small Government department closely linked to NUMBER TEN which supervises the machinery of government, taking a co-ordinating role in such issues as counter-terrorism, Europe and E-GOVERNMENT.

Cabinet papers The documents circulated prior to and stemming from UK Cabinet meetings; by convention no incoming government may see its predecessor's papers, and former Ministers wishing to refresh their memory have to apply to see their own.

Cabinet Room The location of Cabinet meetings: in NUMBER TEN on the first floor overlooking the garden, in the WHITE HOUSE since 1934 in the WEST WING overlooking the ROSE GARDEN, each chair bearing a brass plaque with its occupant's name.

Cabinet Secretary In WHITEHALL, the very senior official, often the head of the CIVIL SERVICE, who services the Cabinet and keeps its minutes. In WASHINGTON (1) the secretary to the Cabinet, a relatively junior WHITE HOUSE appointment; (2) an individual member of the Cabinet.

Cabinet War Rooms The complex of rooms off Whitehall, beneath the TREASURY, from where CHURCHILL and his staff commanded the British war effort from 1940 until 1945 whenever London came under aerial attack. They are now open to the public.

Blubbering Cabinet GLADSTONE's last Cabinet meeting on 1 March 1894 when several ministers broke into tears at the Grand Old Man's departure. Others stifled them in case he decided to postpone his retirement one more time.

inner Cabinet In Britain, a nucleus of Ministers occasionally formed by the Prime Minister on a semi-permanent basis to tackle particularly sensitive questions, or to reinforce his leadership.

kitchen Cabinet An informal group of friends or advisers on whom a leader relies to an extent resented by others; the term was first applied to the entourage of President Andrew Jackson (*see* OLD HICKORY), and in Britain to Harold WILSON (*see* Lady FORKBENDER).

on/in the margins of Cabinet Minister-speak for business transacted informally between Cabinet members while waiting for the meeting to commence, or after it has finished.

reporting Cabinet A meeting which hears reports from Ministers on events and policy development, rather than taking decisions.

Second Eleven Cabinet A pejorative term for Britain's BONAR LAW administration, which included several forgettable members.

Shadow Cabinet *See* SHADOW.

War Cabinet A small group of senior Ministers charged with prosecution of a war.

Cable Street, battle of The violent disorder in October 1936 stemming from a march through a largely Jewish quarter of London's East End and attacks on Jewish shops by Sir Oswald Mosley's BLACKSHIRTS, who were driven out of the neighbourhood by local residents and their leftist supporters. Public disgust at the episode led to the passing of the PUBLIC ORDER ACT, which banned the wearing of political uniforms.

Cactus Jack Nickname for John Nance Garner (1868–1967), the Texan who was SPEAKER of the HOUSE OF REPRESENTATIVES from 1931 to 1933 and FDR's Vice President in his first two terms (1933–41); Garner had tipped the nomination to Roosevelt at the 1932 Democratic Convention.

cadre An individual or small group providing activist, militant leadership, especially in a Communist or MAOIST movement. From the Latin *quadrum*, square, originally the framework of a regiment.

CAFTA Central American Free Trade Area. The trading bloc comprising the United States, Costa Rica, El Salvador, Guatemala, Honduras and Panama, legislation for which was presented to CONGRESS in April 2004. CAFTA would open up the Central American countries' restricted financial services and telecoms markets to US business, but not the heavily subsidised US agricultural market. The agreement was criticised by some for its failure to enshrine trade union and HUMAN RIGHTS and was fiercely lobbied against by the US sugar industry. *Compare* NAFTA.

Cairns group A group of seventeen nations led by Australia, originally set up to champion freer world trade in farm produce during the URUGUAY ROUND of GATT negotiations. It took its name from the Queensland town where the group first met.

Calendar In the US CONGRESS, the various schedules, printed daily, of BILLS down for debate in either HOUSE. The House of Representatives has five. The **Union Calendar** and the **House Calendar** are the main ones, listing public Bills that have been favourably reported. The **Consent Calendar** contains Bills transferred from those calendars on the initiative of any member wishing to expedite their progress. If no objection is raised for three days running when the Consent Calendar is read, the Bill passes; any objection strikes it from that Calendar. There are also a **Private Calendar** and a **Calendar of Motions to Discharge Bills**, and each committee has its own **Legislative Calendar**.

calendar days Those days on which the HOUSE OF REPRESENTATIVES is in session.

Calendar Wednesday Each Wednesday, unless the House decides otherwise, the STANDING COMMITTEES are called in turn and may call up for consideration any reported Bills pending on the House or Union Calendar. After no more than two hours' debate divided equally between supporters and opponents, a simple majority of members present will pass the measure.

Californi(c)ation The devastation of unspoilt areas of America's West Coast states with unplanned urban sprawl: industrial development, speculative housing, shopping malls and other benefits of the southern Californian way of life. As in the 1970s environmentalist sticker

> Don't Californicate Oregon.

Caligula's horse A politician promoted to an office way above his abilities, and operating as a cipher, from the Roman Emperor Caligula who threatened to make his horse Incitatus consul to spite the Senate. When President John Quincy ADAMS appointed Richard Rush Secretary of the Treasury, Rep. John Randolph commented:

> Never were abilities so much below mediocrity so well rewarded; no, not when Caligula's horse was made consul.

In 1935 Sen. Carter Glass of Virginia was so offended by Sen. Huey (KINGFISH) Long that he accused the voters of Louisiana of going one further and making the posterior of a horse a US Senator.

call. call an election (1) The setting in motion of an ELECTION campaign by the person authorised to dissolve the body in question. (2) In America, to predict the outcome of an election from the first few results declared.

Call Me God, Kindly Call Me God, God Calls Me God WHITEHALL *argot* for the three great CIVIL SERVICE (esp. diplomatic) honours awarded by the Crown: **CMG** (Commander of the Order of St Michael and St George), **KCMG** (Knight Commander) and **GCMG** (Knight Grand Commander). The unofficial titles were cited by Anthony Sampson in his *Anatomy of Britain.*

call-in The US word for PHONE-IN, pioneered in the 1980 election campaign by CSPAN.

Call up In the US HOUSE OF REPRESENTATIVES, the SPEAKER's action in bringing up a BILL for a vote. In Britain, CONSCRIPTION, as practised throughout the 1950s.

Callaghan, (Leonard) James (later Lord, 1912–2005). The Labour politician who held all three great offices of State – CHANCELLOR, HOME SECRETARY and FOREIGN SECRETARY – before serving as Prime Minister from 1976–79. The son of a Naval petty officer, Callaghan left school to join the Inland Revenue and became assistant secretary of the tax officers' trade union before joining the Navy himself in WORLD WAR II (*see* STOKER JIM). He was elected an MP for Cardiff in 1945, serving until 1987 when he took a Life PEERAGE. A junior Minister under ATTLEE, he made his mark in opposition as a tough Centrist with a trade unionist's eye for creating alliances. On Hugh GAITSKELL's death he stood for the leadership, finishing third behind Harold WILSON and George BROWN. When Labour returned to power in 1964 he became Chancellor, a series of STERLING crises (*see* JULY MEASURES) and periods of relative stability (*see* STEADY AS SHE GOES!) alternating until the trauma of DEVALUATION in 1967. Callaghan resigned, but took the Home Office, where he gained a reputation on the left for illiberality for his efforts to tighten the immigration laws (*see* PATRIALITY). However, his most controversial acts in the closing phase of the first Wilson government were his blocking of independently-recommended boundary changes that might have cost Labour seats at the 1970 election – which it lost anyway – and his ruthless torpedoing of the trade union reform proposals IN PLACE OF STRIFE. He became Foreign Secretary in 1974 just as the crisis in Cyprus provoked by the Greek COLONELS came to a head; he was criticised because Britain, as one of Cyprus's three guarantors, failed to prevent the Turkish invasion and the island's subsequent partition.

When Wilson suddenly resigned in 1976, Callaghan beat Michael FOOT to succeed him. As Prime Minister he had to cope almost at once with the economic crisis which led to the IMF being brought in. He also, despite an eroding Parliamentary majority, inherited an ambitious legislative programme, including the NATIONALISATION of aircraft and shipbuilding and DEVOLUTION for Scotland and Wales. In 1977 he bought Labour a year by concluding the LIB-LAB PACT with David Steel (*see* BOY DAVID); the economy began to revive and in 1978 Labour's re-election began to look thinkable, but after ruling out an October election (*see* THERE I WAS, WAITING AT THE CHURCH) the WINTER OF DISCONTENT undermined Callaghan's credibility (*see* CRISIS, WHAT CRISIS?) and after the abortive Scottish REFERENDUM the OPPOSITION parties united in a no-CONFIDENCE vote on 28 March 1979 and brought down the Government amid electrifying scenes by 311 votes to 310. Callaghan did his best in the ensuing election campaign, but the tide was with Margaret THATCHER and Labour went back into opposition to begin the process of tearing itself to pieces which brought the formation of the SDP two years later and kept it out of power until 1997. Callaghan stayed on for 18 months; he had promised Denis HEALEY he would 'take the shine off the ball' for him, but it was Foot – just – who won the vote to succeed him. From the back benches he warned Mrs Thatcher repeatedly that cuts in the Royal Navy were risking conflict over the FALKLANDS . . . and was proved right.

Until he showed himself a competent and fair Prime Minister, Callaghan did not always inspire confidence or admiration. Hugh Dalton branded him 'too stupid by three-quarters'; Michael FOOT 'PC Callaghan' (reflecting his work at Westminster for the Police Federation); Woodrow Wyatt as 'skilful in debate, persuasive in politics and disastrous at his job';

Edward HEATH 'the man of indecision' and John Lennon, playing on words, 'Mr Caravans'. The public and the media saw him as benign (*see* SUNNY JIM), but it was his alleged duplicity that aroused most comment from his colleagues. Richard CROSSMAN complained: 'He talks to me in the friendliest way and fights me ruthlessly behind my back'; Wilson condemned him as 'individually ambitious and inordinately weak – so weak that as Chancellor of the Exchequer he used to weep on my shoulder and then go away and intrigue against me'; Roy JENKINS lamented: 'There is no case I can think of in history where a man combined such a powerful political personality with so little intelligence.' Callaghan's then son-in-law Peter Jay caused amusement when, after his appointment as Ambassador to Washington, he revealed:

> As the Prime Minister put it to me, he saw his role as being Moses leading Britain to the Promised Land.

The Labour MP Austin Mitchell (*see* HADDOCK) responded: 'As Moses, he would have mistimed his arrival at the parting of the waves.' In somewhat the same vein, Callaghan himself confided: 'When I am shaving in the morning I say to myself I would like to emigrate, and then I wonder: "Where would I go?"'

Yet Callaghan ended his career having lived down his reputation as a bruiser who could not always be trusted, and earning plaudits on all sides for his patriotism, his common sense and his use of graceful but basic English (he was the first non-graduate Prime Minister since CHURCHILL). He went on to become Britain's longest-lived Prime Minister, dying the day before his 93rd birthday.

> He suffers most from what you might regard as a fatal defect in a Chancellor. He is always wrong.
> IAIN MACLEOD

> If Hugh Gaitskell's motto was 'FIGHT, FIGHT AND FIGHT AGAIN', Callaghan's is 'manoeuvre, manoeuvre and manoeuvre again'.
> IAN BRADLEY, *The Times*

> Living proof that the short-term schemer and the frustrated bully can be made manifest in one man.
> HUGO YOUNG

> Wrong on devaluation, East of Suez, immigration policy, most libertarian issues at the Home Office, trade union reform and Europe, but sound on the Atlantic alliance, no dogmatic supporter of nationalisation and with a built-in respect for the rule of law.
> ROY JENKINS

> A patriot with the interests of Britain at heart, whose worst tribulations had been inflicted by his own party.
> MARGARET THATCHER

> A lot of people say I'm not clever at all – but I became Prime Minister and they didn't.
> Lord CALLAGHAN, 1992

Cambridge mafia The group of late 1950s and '60s Cambridge graduates who formed a key element in Margaret THATCHER's CABINETS. It included Sir Leon Brittan (*see* WESTLAND AFFAIR), Kenneth Clarke (*see* KEN AND EDDIE SHOW), Sir Norman Fowler, John Selwyn Gummer, Michael HOWARD, David Howell, Norman Lamont (*see* BLACK WEDNESDAY) and Sir John Nott. Former office-holders in CUCA (the University Conservative Association), the Cambridge Union or the BOW GROUP, their outlook was for the most part moderate and pragmatic rather than THATCHERITE.

Camelot (1) The mythical kingdom of the 6th-century English King Arthur as portrayed in the Lerner-Loewe musical of that name, evoked to describe the glittering memory of the brief KENNEDY presidency and the hope and glamour it brought to WASHINGTON. Alan J. Lerner was JFK's classmate at Choate and Harvard. Though the word now has a sceptical tinge, it was coined by Jacqueline Kennedy (JACKIE O) and Theodore H. White took it up in a Jackie-inspired piece in *LIFE* shortly after JFK's assassination. She recited the song:

> Don't let it be forgot
> That there was once a spot, for one brief shining moment
> That was known as Camelot.

And explained:

> Camelot had suddenly become the symbol of those THOUSAND DAYS when people the world over saw a bright new light of hope shining from the WHITE HOUSE. For myself, I have never been able to see a performance of *Camelot* again.

(2) The company entrusted by John MAJOR's government with running the UK's National Lottery from its inception; under Labour it successfully challenged in the courts a move by the lottery's supervisory body to transfer the contract to a consortium headed by Sir Richard Branson.

Camp David The Presidential retreat in Maryland's Catoctin Mountains, 50 miles north-west of Washington. Created by Franklin D. ROOSEVELT in 1942 as *Shangri-La*, EISENHOWER renamed the cluster of cabins, where he could relax and converse with distinguished guests, after his grandson.

Camp David agreement The agreement that ended the 31-year state of war between Israel and Egypt, reached there in 1979 after days of intensive talks between Jimmy CARTER, Menachem Begin and Anwar Sadat. It brought mutual diplomatic RECOGNITION between the two countries and the return of Sinai to Egyptian rule, but did not, as hoped, presage a wider Middle East settlement. Begin termed it 'a great day in the annals of our two nations. It is thanks to our fallen heroes that we have reached this day'. And Sadat prayed: 'Let there be no more war or bloodshed between Arabs and Israelis. Let there be no more suffering or denial of rights. Let there be no more fear or loss of face.' In July 2000 Bill CLINTON hosted similar talks between Israeli Prime Minister Ehud Barak and the PLO President Yasser Arafat; it came close to success, but Arafat rejected proposals from Barak far more generous than any subsequently put on offer.

Camp Delta (originally **Camp X-Ray**) The prison camp established by the US Government on the naval base at Guantánamo Bay in Cuba late in 2001 to house AL QAEDA and TALEBAN suspects captured in Afghanistan during the WAR AGAINST TERRORISM. The site was chosen because it is in legal limbo, not on US soil but with the detainees having no access to the Cuban courts. Eventually 680 suspects from 45 countries (including three children) were housed there pending trial by US military tribunal, their firm treatment arousing complaints of HUMAN RIGHTS abuses from the left and sections of the media. After a few months Camp X-Ray was supplanted by the more permanent Camp Delta, but the regime was little changed, evoking censure from the High Court in London when lawyers for the nine UK Taleban suspects tried unsuccessfully to secure their release; Tony BLAIR subsequently urged President BUSH to let UK citizens stand trial in British courts. However a Chechen detained there pleaded with his mother not to be sent home for trial in Russia.

> It is not horror that crushes your spirits when you enter the cells at Camp Delta. Instead, it is an absolute sense of defeat.
>
> DAVID RENNIE, *Daily Telegraph*, 24 May 2003

Camp Zeist The former US Army barracks in Holland, eight miles from Utrecht, where the two Libyan suspects in the LOCKERBIE bombing, Abdelbaset al Megrahi and Amin Khalifa Fhima, stood trial before a Scottish court after being handed over by Colonel Gaddafi to the United Nations in April 1999. The two men were housed in a hardened nuclear shelter that had been the camp hospital; the trial took place in a former schoolroom. Fhima left after his acquittal in January 2000; Megrahi stayed until his appeal was dismissed in March 2002, when he was transferred to Barlinnie prison, Glasgow, and the camp was handed back to the Dutch authorities.

campaign (1) The gruelling, wounding and often costly contest for a political office, or the duration of the electoral process and an individual CANDIDATE's part in it. President TAFT declared it 'the most uncomfortable four months of my life'. Adlai STEVENSON reckoned: 'The hardest thing about any political campaign is how to win without proving that you are unworthy of winning'; he also said that 'you learn more about yourself while campaigning for just one week than in six months spent with a psychiatrist'. The more ruthless Richard NIXON said: 'You don't win campaigns on a diet of dishwater and milktoast.' Rosalynn Carter felt that 'nothing is more thrilling than the urgency of a campaign', while Governor Mario Cuomo mused:

> You campaign in poetry – you govern in prose.

(2) An organised attempt to rally public opinion for a particular cause, or the body promoting such a campaign.

campaign button The small, round, pale badge supporting a candidate which has been the commonplace of US elections since the early days of the Republic. From George WASHINGTON's second term there were holed coin-like tokens fixed in place by ribbons. Other lapel devices, more like jewellery, came along in the 1850s; buttons in the modern sense date from 1892.

campaign contributions The financial life-blood of US electoral politics, and historically a rich vein for corruption – 'good old-fashioned GRAFT in a very thin disguise' as the reformer Mark Green put it. In the late 19th century Sen. Boies Penrose told businessmen:

> You send us to Congress; we pass laws under which you make money; and out of your profits you further contribute to our campaign funds to send us back again to pass more laws to enable you to make more money.

Theodore ROOSEVELT was convinced 'the need for collecting large campaign funds would vanish if CONGRESS provided an

APPROPRIATION for the proper and legitimate expenses of each of the great national parties'. And as pressure for such support for Presidential campaign funding finally paid off (*see* MATCHING FUNDS), Hubert HUMPHREY said:

> Campaign financing is a curse. It's the most disgusting, demeaning, disenchanting, debilitating experience of a politician's life.

See also SOFT MONEY.

Campaign for Democratic Socialism A GAITSKELLITE group which sought to counter left-wing influences in Britain's LABOUR PARTY in the early 1960s, specifically by supporting NATO and NUCLEAR WEAPONS.

Campaign for Labour Party Democracy The hard LEFT group which broke the hold of Labour MPs over the party, provoked the GANG OF FOUR into leaving it to found the SDP, almost secured in 1981 the election of Tony BENN as deputy Labour leader and contributed to Labour's overwhelming defeat at the 1983 general election.

Campaign for Nuclear Disarmament *See* CND.

Campaign Group The group of hard LEFT Labour MPs which split from the TRIBUNE GROUP in 1982 to form a rival and more uncompromising body. This BENNITE faction began strongly but quickly shrank as a reaction set in to the left-wing policies and splits that had cause Labour's 1983 defeat. It later renamed itself the **Socialist Campaign group**. Andrew Marr, in the *Independent*, described the maverick Labour MP and Scots laird Tam Dalyell (*see* BELGRANO) as 'possibly the only member of the Campaign Group to keep peacocks'.

single-issue campaign *See* ISSUE.

Campbell case The episode in which the Attorney-General in Ramsay MACDONALD's first UK Labour government initiated, then withdrew, a prosecution for incitement to mutiny against John Campbell, acting editor of the Communist *DAILY WORKER*. The former Liberal Prime Minister Herbert ASQUITH's call for a SELECT COMMITTEE inquiry into whether political pressure had been applied was carried by 364–198 in the COMMONS in October 1924, forcing MacDonald to call an ELECTION. The case created the climate for the ZINOVIEV LETTER to do Labour great electoral damage, with the Conservatives deriving all the benefit.

Campbell-Bannerman, Sir Henry (1836–1908), Britain's LIBERAL Prime Minister from 1905 until his death. Born a Campbell in Glasgow, he added 'Bannerman' in 1872 as the price for receiving a family inheritance. Elected an MP in 1868, he became GLADSTONE's Chief Secretary for Ireland in 1884, strongly supporting his HOME RULE policy. As Secretary for War he was the occasion of the fall of ROSEBERY's government; it was defeated in a snap division over C-B's alleged failure to supply sufficient CORDITE for the Army. Rudyard Kipling termed him

> The mildly nefarious
> Wildly barbarious
> Beggar that kept the cordite down.

Joseph Chamberlain said as C-B's career recovered: 'I sometimes think that cordite has entered his soul.' Even before the cordite vote, the *SPECTATOR* was terming him 'the dark horse of the Gladstonian party on whom a great many knowing people are inclined to put their money', And as the Liberal Party tired of the chaos it suffered under Rosebery and Harcourt, it turned in 1899 to C-B as its leader. The *Nation* later editorialised:

> He came to the rescue of the Liberal Party when it was a mere hulk, floating captainless and rudderless.

Immediately he was confronted with the BOER WAR which split the party and led to his being perceived by the Tories and some of his own party as unpatriotic; his former associate Lord Milner dismissed him as 'merely too revolting'. But he held the Liberals together, and when Balfour's government fell in 1905 won a landslide election victory.

Senior and ambitious colleagues wanted him to give them real power (*see* RELUGAS COMPACT); they persuaded Edward VII to offer him a peerage, which he did with the words: 'We are not as young as we were, Sir Henry'. But C-B stood his ground, developed an ascendancy over the Commons (*see* ENOUGH OF THIS FOOLERY!) and for three years, until halted by cancer, led a successful reforming government. He paved the way for the social reforms of the ASQUITH ministry, and for the curbing of the HOUSE OF LORDS, but his greatest achievement was reconciliation between whites in South Africa, with English-speakers and Afrikaners who had been at war just before uniting in self-government under the British flag. Their future leader Jan Smuts saw him as 'almost commonplace to the superficial view, but a real man, shrewd and worldly-wise.'

C-B was widely regarded as stuffy, if

cultured, indolent but unflappable. Queen Victoria reckoned him 'a good, honest Scotchman'; Beatrice Webb dismissed him as 'a quite stupid person for a leader – well suited to a position of wealthy squire or sleeping partner in an inherited business'. *The Times* described him as 'not prone to excess of activity', and he himself wrote: 'I am a great believer in bed, in keeping everything horizontal. The heart and everything else go slower, and the whole system is refreshed.' But the appearance was deceptive, the King's private secretary Arthur Ponsonby recalling: 'He had an acute sense of humour which I should never have expected from the dull colourless figure by which he seemed to be represented publicly.' Margot Asquith hailed him as 'essentially a *bon vivant*, a *boulevardier* and a humorist', though she dismissed his election address as 'quite good, but not as striking as Robespierre's'. Sir Gordon Voules reminisced: 'He had an extraordinarily methodical mind which enabled him to get through the maximum of work with the minimum of labour'. In CABINET he was crisp and to the point, John Morley recalling: 'He always knew his mind, and we were all aware that he knew it.' Yet he was personally modest, Ponsonby writing: 'He was constantly forgetting he was Prime Minister. He would ask why people crowded round when he went out shopping alone.' Though the radical Lord Haldane once termed him 'that dear old Tory', he ruffled enough feathers for the reactionary Lord Lansdowne to write after his death: 'Personally, I hold a very strong view as to the impropriety of erecting a monument to Sir Henry Campbell-Bannerman in Westminster Abbey'.

> The man about whom almost all is forgotten.
>
> NICOLAS BENTLEY

Campobello The Roosevelt family's summer home in New Brunswick where in 1921 FDR contracted the polio that left him paralysed.

can of worms An issue which becomes more complex and damaging the more thoroughly it is investigated. President NIXON used the expression to John Dean on 15 September 1972 about the original WATERGATE indictments.

Canada. Canada Act (1) The WESTMINSTER legislation of 1791 which divided the old province of Quebec into two, effectively creating English-speaking Ontario. (2) The Westminster legislation, passed in 1982, that finally PATRIATED the Canadian constitution and removed the last vestiges of rule from London. It was passed after fierce arguments over whether the necessary degree of unanimity in Canada existed.

Canada First The movement founded in 1868 which during the next decade gained wide support for a policy of national assertiveness based on PROTECTIONISM and 'a voice in the treaties concerning Canada'.

O Canada! Canada's national anthem, approved by Parliament in 1967 to replace GOD SAVE THE QUEEN, and officially adopted on 27 June 1980 under the National Anthem Act. It was written in French by Judge Adolphe-Basil Routhier, to music by Calixa Lavallée, and first performed in QUEBEC City on 24 June 1880. It was not heard in English until 1901, when it was sung in Toronto for the future King George V; the present English translation was written in 1908 by Robert Stanley Weir (1858–1926), with slight amendments after the 1967 debate. The English version begins:

> O Canada! Our home and native land!
> True patriot love in all thy sons command.
> With glowing hearts we see thee rise,
> The True North, strong and free!
> From far and wide, O Canada, we stand on guard for thee.
> God keep our land glorious and free!
> O Canada, we stand on guard for thee.
> O Canada, we stand on guard for thee!

Canadian Alliance The right-wing POPULIST party with its roots in Western Canada which, as successor to the REFORM PARTY, from 2000 formed the official OPPOSITION in Ottawa. Its first leader was Stockwell Day, who was replaced in 2002 by Stephen Harper. In October 2003 its MPs voted 51–1 to merge with the PROGRESSIVE CONSERVATIVES to form a united CONSERVATIVE PARTY to fight the 2004 ELECTION.

Canadian Meltdown The most devastating defeat for a governing political party in the history of Western democracy, the rout of Canada's PROGRESSIVE CONSERVATIVES under Kim Campbell (*see* don't blame me, I got TANKS) in October 1993. From enjoying a majority, the party was reduced overnight to one single MP, and took a decade to re-establish itself. The main cause and beneficiary of the Conservatives' collapse was the newborn REFORM PARTY, but the LIBERALS too gained seats to take power.

Canal Zone The ten-mile-wide US enclave carved out of Panama in 1903 when that state was formed from the northern tip of Colombia (as a result of a revolution with which WASHINGTON connived) to include and protect the Panama Canal. Jurisdiction reverted to Panama in 1979 under the PANAMA CANAL TREATIES, and sovereignty – and the canal – in 2000. At its inception Theodore ROOSEVELT said: 'I took the Canal Zone and let the CONGRESS debate it. And while the debate goes on, the canal does too.' Roosevelt wanted a legal pretext for his actions, but ATTORNEY-GENERAL Philander Chase Knox (1853–1921) told him: 'Mr President, do not let so great an achievement suffer from any taint of legality.' During the 1978 SENATE debates on the Treaty, Sen. Strom Thurmond, echoing Ronald REAGAN, declared:

> We bought it. We paid for it. It is ours.

Canard Enchainé, Le (Fr. The chained duck) France's cutting satirical weekly, which over the decades has destroyed several political careers, reduced many politicians to figures of ridicule and occasionally, as with the BOKASSA DIAMONDS, broken highly significant stories. In 1994 Prime Minister Alain Juppé was so enraged by *Le Canard* that he banned his staff from buying it. *Le Canard* responded by sending him a free subscription.

Cancun summit (1) The NORTH-SOUTH summit of world leaders at the Mexican resort of Cancun in October 1981 to approve the BRANDT COMMISSION's report on the THIRD WORLD. While the report gained general endorsement, there was little positive action.

> Mrs Gandhi, and others, wanted more cheap loans in the future. That was what lay behind the pressure, which I was determined to resist, to place the IMF and the WORLD BANK directly under UNITED NATIONS control . . . I said that there was no way in which I was going to put British deposits into a bank which was totally run by those on overdraft. They saw the point.
>
> MARGARET THATCHER, *The Downing Street Years*

(2) The abortive world trade conference at Cancun in September 2003 which tried and failed to bring the DOHA ROUND to a conclusion, and was marked by ANTI-GLOBALISATION protests, though less violent than at SEATTLE.

candidate Someone who puts themself up for election for a public office. The *New York Times* once declared: 'The best character that can be given any candidate is that he is so rich he does not need to steal'; just as cynically George O. Ludcke rhymed: 'The candidate never wore diapers as a baby way back when/It seems that no one could ever pin him down, even then.' Sen. Eugene McCarthy reckoned: 'It is dangerous for any national candidate to say things that people might remember', and Lyn Nofziger, asked during the 1976 REAGAN campaign what the demeanour of a Presidential candidate should be, replied: 'Demeanour the better.' Most politicians hate being a candidate. Adlai STEVENSON said: 'A presidential candidate has to shave twice a day – and I didn't like that'. Walter Mondale (*see* NORWEGIAN WOOD), hesitating to run in 1984, declared: 'I don't want to spend the next two years in Holiday Inns', but Jimmy CARTER put a better face on it:

> The advantage of being a presidential candidate is that you have a much broader range of issues to be fuzzy about.

Manchurian candidate Someone who has been programmed (e.g. by a foreign power) to obey orders without thinking. The term originated with Richard Condon's 1959 novel of that name, and a 1962 film by John Frankenheimer (since remade), about a US prisoner of war who returns from Korea unaware that he has been BRAINWASHED as an ASSASSIN by the Chinese.

paper candidate One who is put forward purely 'on paper' to give a party's supporters the chance to exercise their vote in a hopeless case and does not fight an active campaign.

prospective candidate A person who has been SELECTED to fight a seat, but has yet to be ADOPTED at the formal start of the campaign.

The Candidate The 1972 film in which Robert Redford plays a candidate created by advertising and PR men, who is elected a Senator for California. In the final scene, the victorious Redford asks:

> What do we do now?

Cannon Building In Washington, the first of the HOUSE office buildings erected to the south of the CAPITOL. Work on the building, named after Rep. Joe Cannon of Illinois, Speaker 1903–11 (FOUL-MOUTHED JOE), began in 1903.

Cannon's precedents *See* PRECEDENTS.

Can't pay – won't pay The slogan used in Britain – especially in London and Scotland – in 1990–92 by militant campaigners against the POLL TAX.

cantonisation The breaking-up of a state into smaller units usually based on ethnic identity, as when Serbs and Croats tried to break away from Bosnia in 1992. A *canton* is one of the units of the Swiss Confederation.

Canuck letter The Republican-engineered cause of Sen. Edmund Muskie's exit from the 1972 Presidential race, in which he had been expected to be a Democratic FRONT-RUNNER. Canuck is an abusive term for a French-Canadian, and was used in a letter to William Loeb, ultra-right publisher of the Manchester, New Hampshire, *Union Leader*. It quoted a Muskie aide as telling a meeting in Florida of his native Maine: 'We don't have blacks but we do have Canucks', and urged the audience to 'Come to New England and see'. The letter had in fact been concocted by the NIXON camp's dirty tricks department as part of its RATFUCKING operation; deputy WHITE HOUSE communications director Ken Clawson privately boasted of being the author, then publicly denied it. Loeb published the letter, together with a front-page editorial headed 'Senator Muskie insults Franco-Americans', two weeks before the NEW HAMPSHIRE PRIMARY in which thousands of former French-Canadians were eligible to vote. Muskie burst into tears attacking Loeb's editorial on the STUMP, and his campaign began to fall apart – as the Republicans had hoped.

canvass, to In America, to scrutinise the ballots cast at an election to ensure the count has been fair.

canvassing The practice of all political parties, mainly at election time, of ACTIVISTS calling on as many voters as possible to locate their support. In Britain canvassing traditionally involved banging on doors, but increasingly the American style of telephone canvassing is now followed. *See also* BLITZING, PHONE BANK, VOTER ID.

CAP The EUROPEAN UNION's **Common Agricultural Policy**, under which around 70% of the EU Budget is devoted to subsidising farmers – large-scale producers, peasants and part-timers – creating the opportunity for massive fraud by agro-business. Based on promoting the over-production of inferior produce, it has long been an irritant to relations with the United States and more liberal world trade agreements. A series of reforms such as the MCSHARRY PLAN have only nibbled at the edges; more sweeping changes mooted in 2003 to accompany the ENLARGEMENT of the EU were largely delayed at the insistence of France, the main beneficiary. After France's rejection of the EUROPEAN CONSTITUTION in 2005 and President CHIRAC's targeting of the BRITISH REBATE, Tony BLAIR made abolition of the rebate conditional on reform of the CAP.

Cap of Maintenance A Papal gift to Henry VIII for upholding the faith, carried in the Royal Procession at the State Opening of Parliament by the Leader of the Lords, and held up on a stick to be displayed to the crowd (Fr. maintenir – to hold in the hand) as a sign of the monarch's compassion. Originally worn under the crown to keep it in place, it became purely symbolic:

> A rat on a stick.
>
> LORD (Fred) PEART

Cap the Knife The nickname earned by Caspar Weinberger (1917–) when serving as cost-cutting and tax-reducing Director of Finance to Governor Ronald REAGAN of California. It was amended to **Cap the Ladle** in a 1981 Herblock cartoon because of the enormous sums Weinberger obtained and disbursed for military projects as Reagan's Secretary of Defense. In December 1992 the outgoing President BUSH gave Weinberger a PARDON for allegedly giving false testimony over the IRAN-CONTRA scandal, amid signs that Bush would also be implicated.

> The first person in history to overdraw a blank check.
>
> Sen. Bob DOLE

Cape to Cairo The driving slogan of late 19th-century British IMPERIALISM, and in particular the expansionist plans of Cecil Rhodes (1853–1902), who dreamed of constructing a railway entirely on British land from South Africa to the Mediterranean.

capital The money and other resources necessary for the ownership of business, and that ownership personified. Karl MARX asserted that capital 'comes into the world dripping from hand to foot, from every pore, with blood and dirt'; Abraham LINCOLN argued less emotively that 'capital is only the fruit of LABOR, and could never have existed if labor had not first existed.'

capitalism The form of economic organisation which predominates in the industrialised West, and which has seen off COMMUNISM, for almost a century its mortal foe. It combines private property, free ENTERPRISE and the vast majority of the workforce in wealth-creating employment. The original theory of capitalism posited an entirely free MARKET in which small entrepreneurs hire individual workers to achieve the maximum output for the lowest price; increasingly that model has been distorted by the growth of monopolies and MULTINATIONALS.

To the left, capitalism is inherently flawed

and dangerous. The French socialist Jean Jaures (1859–1914) asserted that 'capitalism carries within itself war as clouds carry rain'. PANDIT Nehru believed that 'the conflict between capitalism and democracy is inherent and continuous'. Arthur Scargill, Marxist leader of Britain's National Union of Mineworkers, declared: 'Life under capitalism has convinced me that there is no moral or political justification for the continuation of the free enterprise system.' And Neil KINNOCK, long before his dash to make Labour ELECTABLE, wrote in 1975:

> We cannot remove the evils of capitalism without taking its source of power – ownership.

KEYNES reckoned that 'capitalism, wisely managed, can probably be made more efficient for attaining economic ends than any alternative system yet in sight, but that in itself is in many ways extremely objectionable'. And CHURCHILL made this comparison:

> The inherent vice of capitalism is the unequal sharing of blessings; the inherent virtue of communism is the equal sharing of miseries.

popular capitalism The economic regime advocated by Margaret THATCHER in the 1980s. It hinged on the bulk of the population becoming shareholders as State industries were PRIVATISED, and on the growth of small business as opposed to large, unionised concerns.

unacceptable face of capitalism The key phrase of the Lonrho affair, which shook the British ESTABLISHMENT in 1973. The international mining and trading company Lonrho was accused of making large payoffs to business contacts, including the former Tory Cabinet Minister Duncan Sandys, later Lord Duncan-Sandys (1904–87), a non-executive director of the company who accepted £130,000 from it for giving up a consultancy job. The money was to be paid into a tax-free account in the Cayman Islands. The transaction was not illegal, but provided evidence of the exploitation of tax loopholes by top people which was seized on by opponents of Edward HEATH's government. To the surprise of many, Heath made a scornful criticism of his own, saying on 15 May 1973 in reply to a COMMONS question from the Liberal Jo Grimond:

> It is the unpleasant and unacceptable face of capitalism, but one should not suggest that the whole of British industry consists of practices of this kind.

capitalist An owner of capital, and an advocate or an integral part of the capitalist system; a term of abuse widely used by COMMUNISTS and the far left.

> The capitalists are so hungry for profits that they will sell us the rope to hang them with.
>
> LENIN (*attr.*)

> The peace of the world has been preserved not by statesmen but by capitalists.
>
> DISRAELI on the impact of Rothschild loans to Italy and Russia, 1863

capitalist-roader A term of abuse by Chinese Communist leaders for anyone who steps out of line, originally used by the MAOISTS against allegedly BOURGEOIS rivals (often pro-Soviet) whom they accused of wanting elements of a MARKET economy. The tables were turned when the leadership after Mao's death denounced the GANG OF FOUR as capitalist-roaders, and the term became less used in the 1990s as China's leaders gave full rein to capitalism without relaxing their political grip.

Capital Territory The 2400 sq. km. enclave carved from New South Wales in 1911 to contain Australia's federal capital of Canberra; in 1915 land at Jervis Bay on the New South Wales coast was added to provide a port. Canberra was planned by the US architect Burley Griffin, who won an international competition in 1911; its population now exceeds 313,000. Parliament first met there in 1927. In 1988 the Commonwealth Parliament granted it self-government; the following year it elected a Labor government under Rosemary Follett, Australia's first woman chief minister.

Capitol The building dominating Washington that houses the US CONGRESS; also the comparable buildings in each of the 50 state capitals. The Capitol was designed by William Thornton (1759–1828) and subsequently heavily modified – particularly through the construction of a high, rather than a low, dome – and extended. George WASHINGTON laid the cornerstone on 18 September 1793; the first wing was ready for use late in 1800. On 24 August 1814 the still-uncompleted Capitol was burned by the British in reprisal for the burning by US troops of the Parliament House at York (Toronto). Rear-Admiral George Cockburn gave the order, asking:

> Shall this harbour of YANKEE democracy be burned?

The damage was quickly repaired, and the original building completed on 6 December 1819, but construction was still under way during the CIVIL WAR; Abraham LINCOLN justified the work by saying: 'If people see the Capitol going on, it is a sign that we intend the UNION shall go on.' The Capitol, which for 134 years also housed the SUPREME COURT, now stands 287 ft. 5½ in. high, is 350 ft. wide and more than 751 ft. long. It has 540 rooms, and its floor area covers 16½ acres.

> We have built no national temples but the Capitol.
>
> Rep. RUFUS CHOATE (1799–1859)

Capo. I propose you to play the part of Capo The NAZI slur which provoked a diplomatic incident between Germany and Italy when uttered in the EUROPEAN PARLIAMENT by the Italian Prime Minister Silvio Berlusconi on 2 July 2003, the second day of Italy's presidency of the EU. Heckled by a German Social Democrat, Martin Schulz, about his allegedly corrupt activities, Berlusconi responded: 'In Italy, a producer is now shooting a film about the Nazi concentration camps. I propose you to play the role of Capo.' (A Capo was a camp guard selected by the SS from among the detainees.) His words provoked protests from the German government and leaders of the Strasbourg Assembly. Berlusconi first blamed the SIMULTANEOUS TRANSLATION but was claimed by the Germans to have retracted. Things went from bad to worse a week later when Italy's Tourism Minister Stefano Stefani, a member of the xenophobic LIGA NORD, described German tourists as 'hyper-nationalistic, arrogant blonds'. Chancellor Gerhard Schroder cancelled his holiday in Italy; days later Stefani was forced to resign. *Compare* ITALIAN TANKS.

capping The process by which central government imposes limits on the level of taxes a local authority can levy. It was devised by Margaret THATCHER's government in the early 1980s to curb alleged runaway spending by Labour councils which was bringing the RATES into disrepute; when it failed, Mrs Thatcher brought in the POLL TAX. When the COUNCIL TAX replaced it, government retained the capping power and by 2004 the Labour government was threatening to invoke it against councils whose inflation-busting tax rises had triggered a protest movement among pensioners.

Carbonari (Ital. charcoal burners) The radical secret society which agitated in the early 19th century for a republican form of government and served as a spur to Italian unification. It was founded in the Kingdom of Naples, where it was ruthlessly suppressed after disorders in 1813. It spread rapidly throughout Italy, prompting risings against the Bourbons in 1820 and throughout the divided country in the following decade. It faded away before the RISORGIMENTO, but paved the way for it.

card. card-carrying member Technically a paid-up member of any political organisation, but in practice a sinister term from the days of MCCARTHYISM for a member of the US COMMUNIST PARTY. The phrase came to life on 3 October 1950 when McCarthy charged that there were '57 card-carrying members of the Communist Party' in the STATE DEPARTMENT and demanded action against them from President TRUMAN. In the 1988 Presidential campaign, George BUSH resurrected the inference behind the term when he accused his Democratic rival Michael Dukakis of being 'a card-carrying member of the American Civil Liberties Union'.

card vote *See* VOTE.

Cardiff Bay The site of the headquarters being constructed for the WELSH ASSEMBLY. Unlike the SCOTTISH PARLIAMENT, the Assembly took its time in commissioning a building in which to meet, and regards itself as having avoided the cost overruns which made the HOLYROOD project so controversial. Welsh Ministers also claimed to put a cap on costs by sacking the prestigious architect Lord Rogers after estimates for the building had risen from £12 million to £47 million; he was later partially brought back into the project.

careerist A politician dedicated to his or her own advancement at the expense of any commitment to principle or to colleagues. Michael FOOT once self-deprecatingly remarked of Tony BLAIR that 'no-one who joined the Labour Party while I was leader could be accused of careerism'. Blair had, in fact, joined the party some years previously.

caretaker government An interim administration appointed until a government with full authority can be elected or sworn in. In Britain, CHURCHILL formed a caretaker government in May 1945 after Labour withdrew from the wartime COALITION; it resigned two months later after Labour won a general election.

CARICOM The Caribbean Community, formed in 1973 by former British colonies in the region to co-ordinate economic and foreign policy. Its founder members were

Antigua, Barbados, the Bahamas, Belize, Dominica, Grenada, the Grenadines, Guyana, Jamaica, Montserrat, St Kitts and Nevis, St Lucia, St Vincent, Trinidad and Tobago.

caring but daring One of the slogans for the 'new politics' of Britain's SDP adumbrated by Dr David OWEN after he became its leader in 1983. Another was 'tough but tender'. Owen's aim was to demonstrate that the SDP was not a 'soggy' party of BLEEDING-HEART liberals.

Carlos *See* JACKAL.

Carlton Club The club in St James's, London, which is the embodiment of the CONSERVATIVE PARTY's Establishment and the continuity of its traditions.

Carlton Club revolt The decision taken by Conservative backbenchers, meeting at the club on 19 October 1922, to force their leaders to break with LLOYD GEORGE's coalition. The pretext was L.G.'s handling of the CHANAK CRISIS. Lloyd George resigned, and the Conservatives took power under BONAR LAW. The memory of the revolt is perpetrated in the 1922 COMMITTEE.

> The cabin boys have taken over the ship.
> F.E. SMITH (Lord Birkenhead, 1872–1930)

Caroline The aircraft, named after his daughter then aged almost three, from which John F. KENNEDY campaigned for the Presidency in 1960.

carpetbagger Someone who arrives to start a political career in a town where he or she has no roots. It was originally a derogatory term for the Northern whites who headed south after America's CIVIL WAR; some genuinely wanted to establish a fair society, more sought political advancement and riches during RECONSTRUCTION. The newcomers earned the name because of the cheap travelling bags made of carpeting with which many of them, especially bankers, arrived – and frequently vanished.

carrot and stick The combination of incentives and penalties which a government is able to use on recalcitrant groups in society. When the latter are used there are often cries of 'all stick and no carrot'. The term relates to the two methods of getting a donkey to move, the inference being that the group in question is as obstinate as an ass.

carry In a US Presidential election, a candidate carries each State where he or she obtains the most votes, and thus wins its support in the ELECTORAL COLLEGE.

Carswell nomination The furore surrounding President NIXON's nomination in 1970 of federal judge G. Harrold Carswell (1917–) of Florida to the SUPREME COURT. The SENATE, after furious protests by CIVIL RIGHTS groups, rejected Carswell because of his allegedly racist views and actions (he had broadcast a white supremacist speech in 1948), as well as an undistinguished judicial record. In 1976 he was arrested for making advances to an undercover police officer in a Tallahassee mall. Carswell was one of several conservatives Nixon nominated to eliminate the liberal bias of the WARREN COURT; his nomination of Warren E. Burger as CHIEF JUSTICE was approved, but with four vacancies occurring he struggled to find candidates acceptable to the Senate.

> Even if he is mediocre, there are a lot of mediocre judges and people and lawyers. They are entitled to a little representation too, aren't they?
> Sen. ROMAN HRUSKA (1904–99)

Carter, Jimmy James Earl Carter (1924–), 39th President of the United States (Democrat, 1977–81). The first President from America's Deep South since the CIVIL WAR, and a man of high principle whose good intentions came to be perceived as weakness, but who in a lengthy retirement earned high respect for his humanitarian work. A peanut farmer, born-again Southern Baptist, former Naval officer and one-term Governor of Georgia, Carter capitalised on public disillusion with WASHINGTON POST-WATERGATE to come from nowhere to win the 1976 Democratic NOMINATION with his simple slogan 'WHY NOT THE BEST?'. His issues director Stuart Eizenstat reckoned Carter 'the most conservative of the Democratic candidates'. In his ACCEPTANCE speech he declared: 'We have been shaken by a tragic war abroad, and by scandals and broken promises at home. Our people are searching for new voices, new ideas and new leaders.' Carter was one of the most overtly religious Presidents, prior to George W. BUSH, teaching Sunday school and insisting: 'We should live our lives as though Christ was coming this afternoon.' He told the American people: 'I will never lie to you', and at times embarrassingly he did more than most Presidents to keep his word. He was supported throughout his presidency by his wife Rosalynn (*see* STEEL MAGNOLIA) who shared his beliefs and took an active interest in government; her special issue was mental health.

Carter started way ahead of Gerald FORD but a lacklustre campaign punctuated by his LUST IN MY HEART *Playboy* interview and his claim to have seen a UFO, coupled with public doubts about an 'outsider' in the WHITE HOUSE, led to his only scrambling victory. He had problems putting together an ADMINISTRATION and his early weeks in the White House foreshadowed frayed relations with the Democratic Congress. Nelson Pollsby wrote: 'Nothing in his prior experience as a politician, certainly nothing in his experience of the nomination process, led him to the view that he needed to come to terms with the rest of the Democratic Party.' Republican Rep. James Leach said: 'There was something about him that brought out an instinct to do battle', and Hedrick Smith wrote: 'He circled his wagons with young Georgians inexperienced in Washington and suffered the consequences'. Carter himself reminisced:

> I treated the Congress as if they were the Georgia legislature, and they treated me as if I was governor of Georgia.

White House staffer Mark Siegel was more acid: 'Congress was the enemy. The Carter people regarded TIP O'Neill as a horse's ass, and if you call someone a horse's ass in the White House, do you know how fast that gets back to someone?'

Carter frankly and disconcertingly shared his doubts about America's strength, telling a Kentucky town meeting in 1979: 'I thought a lot about our nation and what I should do as President. And Sunday night before last, I made a speech about the two problems of our country – energy and malaise.' But he also had an assertive streak, saying: 'People who meet with me had better know the subject, because I know it.' He did indeed involve himself more than other Presidents in the minutiae of government. Roy JENKINS reckoned that 'his weakness did not lie in his brain, which was quick, orderly and fact-absorbing. His faults, such as they were, were mainly ones of style.' His press secretary Jody Powell wrote: 'He would rather spend the next hour on the ifs, ands or buts of the decision he had to make, than on the selling of the decision.' Hedrick Smith commented: 'He slaved like an indentured servant and the public watched him sink in the morass of detail', and David Broder: 'He finished up less like the captain of a ship than a frantic white-water rafter.'

Congress mauled a first initiative on energy (*see* MORAL EQUIVALENT OF WAR), the Bert LANCE affair blurred his moral image, his praise for the Shah contradicted his forceful stand on HUMAN RIGHTS, and episodes like the KILLER RABBIT gave an impression of weakness. Carter's main successes were in foreign affairs – the CAMP DAVID AGREEMENT and the PANAMA CANAL TREATIES – but INFLATION and the HOSTAGE CRISIS with Iran (*see* OCTOBER SURPRISE) ruined his hopes of re-election in 1980. He was weakened by a challenge from Sen. Edward KENNEDY, then outgunned by Ronald REAGAN; the GREAT COMMUNICATOR scorned his foreign policy as 'like the sorry tapping of Neville CHAMBERLAIN's umbrella on the cobblestones of MUNICH'), but hit even harder on the economy. Carter also earned ridicule by saying in a Presidential debate: 'I had a discussion with my daughter Amy the other day before I came here to ask her what the most important issue was. She said she thought NUCLEAR WEAPONRY and the control of nuclear arms'.

After a heavy defeat, he concentrated on charitable work and troubleshooting, and regained the nation's respect; a Carter administration reunion in 1989 attracted a favourable press. He set up the Carter Center in Atlanta for peaceful resolution of disputes worldwide, defusing tension with North Korea over its nuclear programme, attempting to end the war in Sudan and in 1994 persuading Haiti's military junta to make way for the elected President Aristide. In 2002 he was awarded the Nobel Peace Prize.

> My main concern is propping up the people around me who tend to panic (and who might possibly have a better picture of the situation than I do).
>
> JIMMY CARTER, Diary 31 July 1980

> He had the character of a saint and the personality of an egg-timer.
>
> HAROLD EVANS

> It was impossible not to like him. But he had no large vision of America's future.
>
> MARGARET THATCHER

Carterised To be weakened to the point of ridicule, a word stemming from Carter's presidency which his critics saw as a national humiliation. It was much used in the early REAGAN years when the Carter presidency appeared the nadir of America's fortunes, but has been less heard since.

carthorse The public image for several decades of Britain's Trades Union Congress (TUC), as evoked in the 1930s by the NEW STATESMAN and *Manchester Guardian* cartoonist David Low (1891–1963).

Casa Rosada (Sp. Pink House) The Presidential palace in Buenos Aires from whose balcony successive Argentine leaders – notably Juan PERON and his charismatic wife Eva (*see* EVITA) – have whipped up their supporters. The process was reversed after defeat in the FALKLANDS WAR of 1982 when the military dictator Leopold Galtieri (1926–2003) was booed off the balcony, paving the way for the return of democracy.

Casement diaries The journals of Sir Roger Casement (1864–1916), a senior civil servant, knighted for his work on international human rights, who became a fervent Irish nationalist. After retiring, he attempted on the outbreak of WORLD WAR I to organise a shipment of arms from Germany to equip a rising in Ireland and recruit prisoners of war in Germany to fight the British. He was captured on landing from a German submarine on 21 April 1916, two days before the EASTER RISING, sentenced to death and executed in London on 3 August; his body was eventually returned to Ireland by Harold WILSON for burial with respect. The diaries, leaked when he sought a reprieve, revealed Casement to be an active homosexual and turned opinion against him; they were seen in Ireland as forgeries and a crude attempt to smear him, but when they were published in 1994, experts concluded they were authentic.

cash for questions The WESTMINSTER scandal that first broke in July 1994 when the *Sunday Times* reported that two Conservative MPs had taken £1000 each from a reporter posing as a businessman to table Parliamentary questions. It led to Ministerial resignations and an imprisonment, destroying several political careers as it came to typify the SLEAZE of the THATCHER/MAJOR years. The *Sunday Times* report led in April 1995 to the COMMONS' suspension for two weeks of David Tredinnick, who had eventually returned the money, and Graham Riddick, who did so before the story broke. The Committee on PRIVILEGES rebuked a third Tory, Bill Walker, who suggested the 'businessman' donate his £1000 to charity, and censured the paper for trying to suborn up to 20 MPs (*compare* ABSCAM).

In October 1994 Tim Smith resigned as a NORTHERN IRELAND Minister after the *Guardian* revealed he had taken £2000 a time from Mohamed Al Fayed, the owner of Harrods, for asking Parliamentary questions; he gave up his seat in 1997 after it emerged that he had received £25000 in total. Neil Hamilton, Corporate Affairs Minister, refused to quit over similar disclosures, but was forced to when he was found to have misled the Deputy Prime Minister Michael HESELTINE and the CABINET SECRETARY Sir Robin Butler about his relationship with Al Fayed and the LOBBYIST Ian Greer. Hamilton persuaded Parliament to change the law on PRIVILEGE to enable him to sue the *Guardian* for libel, then withdrew on the eve of the trial in October 1996; the newspaper then published full details of Hamilton's financial links with Greer and of four further MPs who had received payments *via* Greer. After losing his seat to the Independent Martin Bell in 1997, Hamilton sued Al Fayed for libel in a much-publicised trial and lost, but continued to protest his innocence. The affair also caused the resignation of David Willetts (*see* TWO BRAINS) as Paymaster General in December 1996. As a WHIP he had attempted to use the Tory majority on the Privileges Committee to clear Hamilton; the correspondence came to light after Hamilton dropped his libel action against the *Guardian*. The Committee decided that Willetts had 'dissembled' in an attempt to subvert the disciplinary process; he resigned that day, but returned to the front BENCH in opposition.

Sir Robin Butler rejected allegations against Jonathan Aitken over a stay at Al Fayed's Ritz hotel in Paris while a Government Minister, but the *Guardian* secured crucial evidence over the financing of the stay by sending a **'cod fax'** to the Ritz claiming to be from Aitken's office. Aitken resigned as Chief Secretary, and was sentenced to a year in prison for perjury.

'Cash for questions' spawned a number of derivatives. **Cash for access** described the furore in July 1998 over claims – never fully substantiated – by Peter Mandelson's (*see* BOBBY) former assistant Derek Draper, now a lobbyist, that he could gain access for clients to key personnel in DOWNING STREET in return for money. And **cash for wigs** was the media's term for a £200-a-head Labour lawyers' fundraising event at London's Atlantic Bar and Grill to which sympathisers were invited in February 2001 by the LORD CHANCELLOR, Lord Irvine.

cash limits The budgeting principle embraced by Margaret THATCHER's government from the early 1980s. A total was set for each department and programme, and cost rises had to be absorbed.

casual vacancy A vacancy to an elected body that has to be filled at a time when no ELECTIONS are scheduled, as a result of the death, resignation or even expulsion of a member.

casus belli (Lat. the occasion of war) An act or incident justifying a resort to war; the grounds for waging war or pursuing a dispute.

cat. Cat and Mouse Act The popular name for the Prisoners (Temporary Discharge for Ill-Health) Act of 1913, put through by the Liberal HOME SECRETARY Reginald McKenna to prevent imprisoned SUFFRAGETTES from achieving martyrdom by going on hunger STRIKE. Prisoners too weak for further FORCE-FEEDING were released on licence, but were subject to re-arrest.

Cat Bill veto Adlai STEVENSON's refusal in 1949, as Governor of Illinois, to sign a bill promoted by bird lovers to restrain cats. 'The problem of cat versus bird is as old as time,' he wrote to the state legislature. The Bill, he said, was a precedent for intervention in 'the age old problems of dog versus cat, bird versus bird, or even bird versus worm'. The State of Illinois had 'enough to do without trying to control feline delinquency'.

catch-all The pejorative term widely attached to Section 2 of Britain's 1911 OFFICIAL SECRETS ACT, which outlawed unauthorised communication of official information to anybody by a Crown servant, in theory making it an offence for a civil servant even to tell a friend what was on the menu in the office canteen. The section was discredited by a series of injudicious prosecutions (*see* ABC TRIAL, PONTING AFFAIR), and a far less draconian measure replaced it in 1989.

Catherine Place meeting The informal gathering of Ministers late on 20 November 1990, at the home of the deputy chief whip Tristan Garel-Jones, which concluded that Margaret THATCHER would have to step down as Prime Minister. Diehard Thatcherites are convinced the meeting was called to plot against her after her failure to eliminate Michael HESELTINE in the first round of the Tory leadership ballot. Apart from Garel-Jones, who went on to run Douglas Hurd's campaign, those present included Norman Lamont, who would lead John MAJOR's campaign, and four other members of the CABINET. Some felt she would lose in a second ballot, others that she might win but would be fatally weakened. They reported their views to the Chief Whip, and to Mrs Thatcher's staff; the Prime Minister polled individual Cabinet members herself, and within 36 hours she resigned. Alan CLARK, the only right-winger there, wrote in his diary:

> The really sickening thing was the urgent and unanimous abandonment of the Lady. Except for William (Waldegrave)'s little opening tribute, she was never mentioned again.

Cato Street conspiracy A plot by some 50 followers of the socialist radical Thomas Spence (1750–1814) led by Arthur Thistlewood, to assassinate Lord Liverpool's CABINET at a dinner on 22 February 1820 and declare a republic. The group had been penetrated by a government spy, and its members were arrested before they could leave their base in Cato Street off London's Edgware Road; the principal conspirators were tried for TREASON and hanged.

caucus A closed meeting of a party group, usually to agree a line to be adhered to and candidates to be supported; also the organised members of a party in a legislature. The verb **to caucus** means to go into a meeting where party matters will be resolved. The term emerged in early 18th-century Boston with the **Caucus** (or Caucas) **Club**, where the politically-involved gathered to choose CANDIDATES for office before their presentation to the voters; H. L. Mencken traced the word to the Algonquin Indian for 'counsellor'. It was in common use by 1824, when Republican members of CONGRESS attempted to instal William H. Crawford as the party's Presidential candidate. The *Baltimore Morning Chronicle* reported: 'The poor little political bird of ominous note and plumage, denominated a *CAUCUS*, was hatched at Washington on Saturday last.'

> The difference between a caucus and a cactus is that a cactus has all the pricks on the outside.
>
> Rep. MORRIS UDALL (1922–), *attr.*

Iowa caucuses *See* IOWA.

Caudillo (Sp. leader, chief) The title taken by the dictator General **Francisco Franco** (1892–1975) after the victory of his Nationalist forces in the SPANISH CIVIL WAR. As leader of the FALANGE, Franco gave the term a similar meaning to DUCE or FUHRER, the titles chosen by his counterparts Mussolini or Hitler to symbolise the personification of the nation in the leader. The title died with Franco, there being no room for such a figure in the CONSTITUTIONAL MONARCHY that was to replace his fascist state.

cause A goal whose achievement takes on the nature of a struggle or a crusade, and becomes a way of life to the exclusion of everything else. Most worked-for revolutions, and the continuing drive for a united Ireland, have been referred to by their adherents simply as 'the cause'. Thomas Paine wrote of the AMERICAN REVOLUTION: 'It is not a few acres of ground, but a cause, that we are defending, and whether we defeat the enemy in one battle or by degrees, the consequences will be the same'; he also remarked:

> A bad cause will ever be supported by bad means and bad men.

Theodore ROOSEVELT declared that:

> No man is worth his salt who is not ready at all times to risk his well-being, to risk his body, to risk his life in some great cause.

The term implies not only sacrifice, but long struggle, setbacks and even the possibility of the goal being unachievable, Wendell Willkie once saying:

> I would rather lose in a cause I knew some day would triumph, than triumph in a cause that I know some day will fail.

CBI Confederation of British Industry. The body which represents most of Britain's large companies, in the manufacturing, utility and transport sectors, in their dealings with and lobbying of government. Formed in 1965 to succeed the Federation of British Industry (FBI), it has 250,000 members. Unlike the rival, more ideological Institute of Directors it campaigns for direct help for industry from the state, and is in touch with the trades unions and non-Conservative political parties.

CCC The Civil Contingencies Committee of the UK CABINET, dealing with the preparation for and handling of major civil disasters, chaired by the HOME SECRETARY. *See also* COBRA.

CCF Commonwealth Co-Operative Federation. The forerunner of Canada's New Democratic Party (NDP) founded at Regina in 1933 by farm, labour, socialist and intellectual groups and veterans of the PROGRESSIVE movement. With J.S. Woodsworth as leader it became within a year the official opposition in British Columbia and Saskatchewan. Anti-war in the 1930s and a reluctant supporter of Canadian involvement in WORLD WAR II, the CCF benefited from wartime regimentation to become Ontario's second party in 1943 and win power in Saskatchewan under T.C. Douglas the next year – holding it until 1966. By then, in 1961, the CCF had merged with the Canadian Labour Congress to form the NDP.

> No CCF government will rest content until it has eradicated CAPITALISM and put into operation the full programme of socialised planning which will lead to the establishment in Canada of the Co-Operative Commonwealth.
>
> REGINA DECLARATION, 1933

CDU Christian Democratic Union. The right-of-centre party, founded in 1945 by Konrad Adenauer and Catholics and Protestants alike who had stood clear of the NAZIs or resisted them, which became one of the two great parties of West Germany and, since 1990, of the reunified nation. It has generally governed in alliance with Bavaria's CSU. Under Adenauer as CHANCELLOR Germany achieved reconciliation with France, under Ludwig Erhard the ECONOMIC MIRACLE took effect and under Helmut Kohl Germany was reunified after the fall of the BERLIN WALL. From 1966 to 1969 the CDU governed with its great rival, the left-of-centre SPD, in the GRAND COALITION.

ceasefire An agreement between two warring armies to halt hostilities while efforts are made to negotiate a peace settlement. In some cases, as with the KOREAN WAR, a ceasefire or armistice will remain in force for decades without the war being formally ended or a peace agreement reached.

Cecchini report The EUROPEAN COMMISSION's economic justification for the SINGLE MARKET which broadly took effect from 1992, named after Paolo Cecchini, who chaired the team of EC officials who compiled it in 1987–88. Published in sixteen volumes after a two-year study in which 11000 businesses were questioned, it estimated the costs of continuing with an 'uncommon market' at $243 billion a year. It predicted that completion of the single market would 'trigger a SUPPLY-SIDE shock to the Community economy as a whole' and lead to lower prices, greater competition, lower government deficits, reduced inflation and 'very substantial job creation'.

cell A tiny unit of membership in a REVOLUTIONARY or terrorist movement, self-contained so as to maintain secrecy and limit any damage caused by infiltration. The cell was a basis of Communist organisation in hostile environments, and is the most secure unit for a terrorist group; the IRA reorganised on this basis in the late 1970s after being infiltrated by British agents.

Celtic fringe The mountainous and coastal constituencies of the Scottish Highlands and Islands, west Wales and Devon and Cornwall – bastions of Celtic culture and frequently of language – which just kept Liberalism alive at WESTMINSTER from the 1930s to the 1960s, when the party's chance of winning seats in the rest of the country was negligible (*see* TELEPHONE BOX). The radical tradition of these areas patchily resisted the rise of Labour, initially because of the continuing appeal of LLOYD GEORGE, himself the ultimate Celt (*see* WELSH WIZARD).

cemetery vote A technique much (and illegally) used by political BOSSES in America, Ireland and elsewhere, a vote cast on behalf of an ELECTOR who has died in order to rig an ELECTION. The story has been told of several candidates, notably Presidents Rutherford Hayes (*see* OLD 8 TO 7) and Lyndon JOHNSON, of the little boy found sobbing for his father. 'But your father's been dead for ten years,' a concerned adult tells him. The boy replies: 'Last night he came back to vote for LBJ and he never came to see me.' Scrupulous bosses only cast posthumous votes on behalf of known deceased supporters of their candidate.

Cenotaph (Gr. *Kenos*, empty; *taphos*, tomb) The obelisk erected in WHITEHALL to commemorate the dead of WORLD WAR I, before which the leaders of the nation stand in tribute each Remembrance Sunday (the Sunday nearest to Armistice Day, 11 November). Designed by Sir Edwin Lutyens, the Cenotaph was dedicated at the first such ceremony in 1920. The two-minute silence at 11 a.m. is the most solemn moment of the year, recalling the COMMONWEALTH's 'glorious dead' in all the wars since 1914. *See also* DONKEY JACKET.

censure A disciplinary measure taken by a legislature that denotes strong disapproval of a member's statement or action but stops short of suspension or EXCLUSION. One such was the censure of Sen. Thomas Dodd by the US SENATE in June 1967 for using CAMPAIGN CONTRIBUTIONS to settle personal bills; he kept his seat and his SENIORITY. The word 'censure' is not always the one used; Sen. Joseph MCCARTHY was 'condemned' by the SENATE, while erring members of the HOUSE are REPRIMANDED. Members of the UK HOUSE OF COMMONS may also be censured, the POULSON AFFAIR in the mid-1970s being a rare occurrence.

vote of censure A motion put down by the OPPOSITION at WESTMINSTER in order to mount a concerted attack on the Government over a specific issue or set of issues; unlike a vote of No-CONFIDENCE, which covers a Government's entire performance, its success will not necessarily bring about the fall of the Prime Minister or force a general ELECTION.

CENTO *See* BAGHDAD PACT.

central. central banks The national banks of the CAPITALIST world which between them endeavour to control, subject to MARKET forces, the relative levels of currencies and of interest rates – and through them seek to maintain world prosperity and economic stability. America's FED is independent though its chairman is Federally-appointed; the Bank of England, owned by the State since 1946, reaches its decisions in consultation with the TREASURY but from 1997 has been free to set interest rates; the EUROPEAN CENTRAL BANK, which took charge of the EUROZONE in 2001 in succession to a dozen national central banks, has largely inherited the rugged independence of the BUNDESBANK.

> The job of a central banker is not easy at the best of times. It has been said that he must always exude confidence, without actually lying.
>
> DENIS HEALEY

Central Committee The main executive committee of the Soviet COMMUNIST PARTY when in office, elected by the party congress. The main power resided in the POLITBURO and the Secretariat.

Central Council The two-day annual business meeting of Britain's CONSERVATIVE PARTY, held each March until 1998 at Harrogate, when the NATIONAL UNION was wound up and the event was turned into a less bureaucratic **Spring Conference**. As well as carrying out the party's housekeeping, it afforded the Tory leader and senior spokesmen a chance to enthuse constituency ACTIVISTS and make speeches aimed at the ELECTORATE at large, some five weeks before the local elections.

Central Office The headquarters organisation of the CONSERVATIVE PARTY, which moved in April 2004 to 25 Victoria Street, WESTMINSTER after half a century in Smith Square. In the party infighting that marred the leadership of Iain Duncan Smith (*see* IDS), the Smith Square building became known to staff as **Chateau Despair,** and one of Michael HOWARD's first actions as leader was to instigate a move. Headed by the party chairman, Central Office constitutes one of three legs of the movement: the voluntary party in the country, Central Office, and the Parliamentary Party, which once again elects the Tory leader after a brief flirtation with choice by the entire membership.

Central Policy Review Staff *See* THINK TANK.

Central Powers The collective term used during WORLD WAR I for the ultimately-defeated central European alliance of Germany and Austria-Hungary.

centre (1) The MIDDLE GROUND in politics, whose generally moderate adherents all but the most ideologically-based parties have wooed in the hope of winning power.

> Anyone who throws away the centre loses the capacity to govern.
>
> WILLY BRANDT (1913–92)

A **centrist** party is one that occupies the middle ground, frequently needing to form COALITIONs with other parties to gain a share in power and as often wooed by them. **Centre-left** and **centre-right** emerged in the late 1970s as terms for politicians and parties with an obvious political slant, but not driven by an uncompromising ideology.

(2) **The Centre**, the heart of power and government, especially one exuding strong policies and control. The term was especially used in the early years of NEW LABOUR to describe the centre of power close to Tony BLAIR from which policy dictates and choices of personnel emerged, for implementation and acceptance by the wider government and party machines.

Ceres Socialist studies, research and education centre. A radical left-wing GINGER GROUP which for four decades has pressed adventurous policies on France's Socialist Party, notably in offering an alternative to the increasingly moderate course steered by President MITTERRAND. A leading light has been Jean-Pierre Chevènement (1939–), intermittently secretary of CERES since 1965, who resigned as Defence Minister in 1991 in protest at France's involvement in the GULF WAR, and as Minister of the Interior a decade later over plans to give limited self-government to Corsica. *Ceres* was the Roman goddess of creation, and her image, bearing a sheaf of corn, has long been a symbol of the French republic.

CETA Comprehensive Employment and Training Act. The Act passed in 1973 under which US Federal funds are made available to state and local governments to provide jobs and training for the unemployed.

CFE Conventional Forces in Europe. The agreement between 22 NATO and WARSAW PACT countries, signed in Paris on 20 November 1990, which marked the end of COLD WAR tension by dictating huge cuts in the weaponry and forces of the opposing alliances. It was concluded at the CSCE (*see* OSCE) conference in Vienna the previous week after US Secretary of State James Baker and Soviet Foreign Minister Eduard Shevardnadze resolved the final differences between the superpowers. CFE imposed the heaviest cuts in Soviet weaponry – tanks, artillery, armoured vehicles, helicopters and aircraft – and ended the Warsaw Pact's heavy superiority in troop numbers.

> The most substantial and far-reaching agreement for the reduction of armaments which has yet been achieved.
>
> MARGARET THATCHER, reporting to the House of Commons

CFR (1) Confidential – Final Revise. The pre-publication copies of WHITE PAPERS and other UK government publications (except where market-sensitive), circulated to the LOBBY under EMBARGO to give the media time to report correctly on detailed and complex findings and recommendations. (2) Council on FOREIGN Relations.

CGT *Confédération Générale du Travail*, General Confederation of Labour. France's largest and most militant trade union grouping, allied to the Communist Party; it is strongest in traditional industries, public services and the railways. The trade union movement is fragmented between the CGT, the Catholic CFDT (*Confédération Française du Travail*), and the socialist *Force Ouvrière* (Workers' Force).

chad The fragment discarded from a BALLOT PAPER in which holes are punched, either in voting machines or manually by the VOTER. The word achieved worldwide recognition in the aftermath of the 2000 US Presidential ELECTION where the failure of voters and machines in PALM BEACH COUNTY, Florida to remove the chads cleanly led to weeks of argument over which papers should be allowed, and indeed whether George W. BUSH or Al GORE had won the election. Three types of chad were deemed to be a valid vote: the **hanging door,** attached to the paper by just one corner, the **swinging door**, hanging by two corners, and the **tri**, hanging by three corners. Not accepted were the **dimple chad**, where the paper was indented but not broken, and the **pregnant chad**, bulging, but with all the corners intact.

chair (1) The Chair. In a legislature, the authority represented by the SPEAKER or chairman. It is a convention for members to address the Chair and not each other. (2) A term pioneered in 1980s Britain by POLITICALLY CORRECT and FEMINIST groups to supersede the use of 'chairman', which they deemed discriminatory, and to avoid the alternatives of **chairwoman** or **chairperson**.

behind the chair The space at the rear of the House of Commons CHAMBER where MPs of opposing parties can converse informally without being observed, and where deals are frequently struck.

empty chair (1) The tactic of leaving one's place in a negotiation vacant, either as a protest at a course of action being followed or in an effort to prevent decisions being reached. It has generally proved counter-productive: the Soviet Union's withdrawal from the SECURITY COUNCIL left it unable to VETO UN participation in the KOREAN WAR, and France's refusal to participate in meetings of the EC COUNCIL OF MINISTERS in 1966 failed to produce the endorsement of GAULLIST aims that had been hoped for; instead in produced the LUXEMBOURG COMPROMISE. (2) A means of demonstrating the refusal of one candidate – usually the INCUMBENT – to participate in a live debate with their peers.

by your leave, Mr Speaker, I must borrow your chair a little King Charles I's opening words when he arrived in the HOUSE OF COMMONS on 4 January 1642, accompanied by troops, to have the FIVE MEMBERS arrested. SPEAKER Lenthall made way for the King, who told Members he valued their privileges, but that the five had committed TREASON, and 'I must have them wheresoever I find them.' He then observed: 'I SEE ALL THE BIRDS ARE FLOWN', and with the Speaker refusing to give him any information he left the House. The episode was a landmark on the road to England's CIVIL WAR.

Chairborne Division A WORLD WAR II British Service pejorative for the army of officers and BUREAUCRATS who prosecuted the war from WHITEHALL. It was a none-too-subtle comparison with the combatant *Airborne Division.*

Chairman Mao Mao Tse-Tung (or Mao Zedong, 1893–1976), co-founder in 1921 of China's Communist Party who after 28 years of struggle, including the LONG MARCH, finally overthrew Chiang Kai-Shek's Kuomintang (*see* KMT) government in 1949, then ran China as an autocracy for a quarter of a century. At first friendly with STALIN, Mao broke with Moscow to launch his first experiment in back-to-basics Communism, the GREAT LEAP FORWARD, in 1958. He survived its unpopularity to try again with the extremist CULTURAL REVOLUTION from 1966–69; at its heart was the LITTLE RED BOOK containing Mao's Thoughts (*see below*). Chairman Mao was by now the centre of a PERSONALITY CULT which Stalin would have envied; a memorable feature was his supposed swim across the Yangtse. After the XEONOPHOBIA of the Cultural Revolution he established links with Western leaders to annoy the KREMLIN. Mao remained in apparent total control until his death, though it is claimed that his wife Chiang Ching (Jiang Qing) (*see* GANG OF FOUR) was responsible for some of the most extreme policies.

the Thoughts of Chairman Mao The often banal and mainly negative statements on the merits of revolution set out in the LITTLE RED BOOK, which elevated Mao's personality cult to its highest point. They were memorised and chanted by MAOISTS throughout the world from the late 1960s.

> The best weapon is not the aircraft, heavy artillery, tanks or the atom bomb. It is Mao Tse-Tung thought; the greatest fighting force is the man armed with Mao Tse-Tung thought.
>
> LIN PIAO, speaking to the Army on the eve of the Cultural Revolution, 1965

chamber The hall, generally purpose-built, where a legislature meets. The seats are either set out in rows facing each other, as at WESTMINSTER, reflecting ADVERSARIAL POLITICS, or in a semicircle (*see* HEMICYCLE) as in the US CAPITOL and in Continental legislatures (and the SCOTTISH PARLIAMENT) where the politics of COALITION prevail. The CHAIR is positioned end-on to the rows of seats in the former, and facing the semicircle in the latter.

Chamber of Deputies The formal title of the more powerful House in a number of legislatures, notably France's NATIONAL ASSEMBLY.

> A broken mirror in which the nation cannot recognise its own image.
>
> LEON GAMBETTA, French Prime Minister 1881–82

Old Senate Chamber The original meeting place of the US SENATE, where in 1800 John

ADAMS addressed the first JOINT SESSION of CONGRESS. In 1810 the Chamber was subdivided through the interposing of an extra floor, with the Senate taking the upper portion. After the CAPITOL was burnt by the British in 1814, Benjamin Latrobe rebuilt the Chamber as larger and more ornate; the Senate reoccupied it on 6 December 1819. It was here that Daniel Webster delivered his most memorable speeches, and Preston Brooks launched his near-murderous caning of Charles Sumner (*see* CRIME AGAINST KANSAS). In 1859 the Senate moved to its present chamber and the SUPREME COURT moved upstairs to the Old Senate Chamber, staying three-quarters of a century until its own building was ready. The Old Senate Chamber is now open to the public, restored to its 1850s condition.

second Chamber A general term for the less influential chamber in a BICAMERAL system, at WESTMINSTER the HOUSE OF LORDS. It is also used by UK politicians in debates about what form of Upper House might ultimately supplant the Lords.

Chamberlain, (Arthur) **Neville** (1869–1940), Prime Minister (Conservative) 1937–40. The Premier who led Britain reluctantly into WORLD WAR II but is best remembered as the architect of APPEASEMENT. The son of the charismatic IMPERIALIST Joseph Chamberlain, he went into industry in his native Birmingham, became LORD MAYOR and entered Parliament in 1918. At first he was overshadowed by his half-brother Austen, who warned him portentously: 'Neville, you must remember that you don't know anything about foreign affairs.' He was a successful Minister of Health from 1923 to 1929; offered the Exchequer, he rejected it, writing: 'What a day! Two salmon in the morning, and the offer of the Exchequer in the afternoon.' He took the job in the 1931 NATIONAL GOVERNMENT, establishing himself over the next six years as Stanley BALDWIN's natural successor despite a lack of CHARISMA. Harold Nicolson wrote: 'He has the mind and manner of a clothes brush,' and Aneurin BEVAN described his speaking style as 'like a visit to Woolworth's: everything in its place and nothing over sixpence'. Bevan said of Chamberlain as Chancellor: 'The worst thing I can say about democracy is that it has tolerated him for four and a half years', and when he succeeded Baldwin, Bevan commented:

> In the funeral service of capitalism the honeyed and soothing platitudes of the clergyman are finished and the cortège is now under the sombre and impassive guidance of the undertaker.

Chamberlain became Prime Minister at just the point when HITLER's expansionism and massive military build-up were becoming obvious; according to his critics he sought to co-exist with a threat he never understood, while his supporters assert that he aimed to buy time while Britain too rearmed. In 1938 he flew to Germany to sign the MUNICH AGREEMENT, now viewed as a national disgrace but then hailed as a triumph. The columnist Godfrey Winn wrote: 'Praise be to God and to Mr Chamberlain. I find no sacrilege in coupling those two names'. But Hitler said patronisingly:

> He seemed such a nice old gentleman. I thought I would give him my autograph as a souvenir.

CHURCHILL told him bluntly: 'You were given the choice between war and dishonour. You chose dishonour – you will have war'. Hitler's move into Prague the next March forced Chamberlain to face reality, saying: 'I have decided that I cannot trust the NAZI leaders again'; he gave a GUARANTEE to Poland, but dragged his feet over a defensive pact with the Soviet Union, enabling the Germans to conclude the cynical NAZI-SOVIET PACT. When Hitler invaded Poland in September 1939, Chamberlain declared war (*see* I HAVE TO TELL YOU . . .). He reshaped his government to bring Churchill back from the wilderness (*see* WINSTON IS BACK), but after a period of PHONEY WAR was left woefully exposed by the loss of Norway; his declaration that HITLER HAS MISSED THE BUS did not help. On 7 and 8 May 1940 he came under withering fire from Tory critics (*see* YOU HAVE SAT HERE LONG ENOUGH) in a debate on the conduct of the war; the stubborn and insular Chamberlain said plaintively: 'I have friends in this House', but the Government's majority was slashed from 240 to 81. Chamberlain hung on, Hugh Dalton saying: 'He seems determined to stick to office, like a dirty old piece of chewing gum on the leg of a chair'; Brendan Bracken said that shifting him was 'like trying to get a limpet off a corpse'. But when two days later Hitler launched his BLITZKRIEG against the Low Countries he made way for Churchill. He stayed in the Government, but died of cancer six months later.

> Had he retired or died in 1937, he would have gone down in history as a great social reformer and a great administrator.
>
> HAROLD MACMILLAN

No better than a Mayor of Birmingham, and in a lean year at that. LORD HUGH CECIL

He saw foreign policy through the wrong end of a municipal drainpipe. LLOYD GEORGE

In the depths of that dusty heart there is nothing but surrender. CHURCHILL

champagne socialist *See* LIMOUSINE LIBERAL.

Chanak crisis The crisis in October 1922 that caused the fall of the LLOYD GEORGE COALITION. It was precipitated by the entry of the Turks, aiming to take part of Thrace from Greece, into the British- and French-held neutral zone of Chanak, on the Asiatic side of the Dardanelles. Conservative members of the CABINET felt that L.G. had sided with Greece by reinforcing the British garrison; mistrust of his leadership led to the CARLTON CLUB REVOLT of 19 October, the break-up of the coalition and the formation of the 1922 COMMITTEE. Lloyd George had also called for the DOMINIONS to hold Chanak against the Turks, enraging the Canadian Prime Minister Mackenzie King who refused to 'play the imperial game'.

chancellery. Chancelleries of Europe A phrase, used mainly in the late 19th and early 20th centuries, for the apparently unshakable centres of power in Europe. **Chancellery** (*kanzlerei*) was, and is, the word in German-speaking nations for the offices of the head of government.

spy in the Chancellery The scandal in 1974 that forced the resignation of Willy BRANDT (1913–92) as Chancellor of West Germany. It was discovered that Gunther Guillaume, one of his senior aides, had for many years been spying for the East Germans.

Chancellor (1) In German-speaking countries, the head of government. When Germany was reunified in 1990, the West German Chancellor Helmut Kohl who presided over the process became known as **Chancellor of all the Germans**. (2) Shorthand for **Chancellor of the Exchequer**, a position with mediaeval origins. Since the 18th century the Chancellor has been the senior CABINET member in charge of UK economic and tax policy, and delivers the annual BUDGET.

Can there be a more lamentable figure than a Chancellor of the Exchequer, seated on an empty chest, by the pool of bottomless deficiency, fishing for a budget?
Sir ROBERT PEEL on the WHIGS, 1841

The Chancellor of the Exchequer is a man whose duties make him more or less of a taxing machine. He is trusted with a certain amount of misery which it is his duty to distribute as fairly as he can.
ROBERT LOWE (later Viscount Sherbrooke), House of Commons, 11 April 1870

Chappaquiddick The incident on 28 July 1969 which enveloped Sen. Edward KENNEDY in a lasting fog of scandal and implausibility, and almost certainly prevented him becoming President. Late that night Kennedy was driving 28-year-old Mary Jo Kopechne, who had been one of his brother Robert's campaign team, away from a party on Chappaquiddick Island, off Martha's Vineyard in Massachusetts. Kennedy inexplicably drove away from the ferry, and off a narrow bridge into the water; he escaped but Miss Kopechne did not. The car, with her body, was found before Kennedy was; he had returned to the mainland – swimming, by his own account – but did not report the accident until the next morning, ten hours later. Kennedy later said:

I regard as indefensible the fact that I did not report the accident to the police immediately.

Kennedy STAFFERS realised the damage his conduct could do to his Presidential prospects and to the dynasty, and set in motion a damage limitation exercise that critics termed a COVER-UP (*see* Nobody drowned at WATERGATE); Kennedy himself appealed for public understanding with a dramatic account of how he had dived to try to save Mary Jo. He was given a two-month suspended sentence for failing to report the accident; a closed inquest did not follow up critical questions and exonerated him. Efforts to reopen the case through grand jury hearings proved abortive. But for Chappaquiddick, according to Sen. Edmund Muskie, Kennedy could have had the 1972 nomination 'for the asking'. As it was, Kennedy was confronted with placards reading: 'Swim, don't run in '72'. The scandal was still a powerful issue when he made his unsuccessful run in 1980. And when it was revealed on his marriage to Victoria Reggie in 1992 that he proposed to her while snorkelling, the British humorist Ned Sherrin said:

I don't see how she could hear underwater. Perhaps the car windows were still up.

Q: Would you let Nixon sell you a used car?
A: Yes, but I wouldn't let Teddy drive it.
ANON, Washington, 1969

Senator Kennedy killed that girl the same as if he put a gun to her head and pulled the trigger.
Det.-Lt. GEORGE KILLEN, Massachusetts State Police

chargé d'affaires (Fr. Responsible for business). In diplomatic language, the senior official at an EMBASSY in the absence of an AMBASSADOR, or when no ambassador has been appointed because of poor relations between the countries in question.

charisma The exceptional quality in a political leader that attracts others and enables him or her to influence them, for good or ill. It was originally a religious term, the Greek word for the 'gift of grace' attributed to the early Christian saints. A politician's lack of charisma can give rise to comment; at one UK Conservative conference, a leader said of David Bookbinder, then Labour leader of Derbyshire County Council: 'He thinks charisma is the day after 24 December.' George BUSH senior recognised his own deficiency, telling the 1988 Republican convention in New Orleans: 'I'll try to hold my charisma in check.' He also said during that campaign:

> I think I'm a charismatic son of a gun, but I'm not going to depend entirely on that to win.

Charlemagne Prize The most prestigious international prize recognising an individual's contribution to European unity. It commemorates Charlemagne (Charles the Great), the Frankish king who in the 8th century united Western Europe under his rule to end the Dark Ages and create the Holy Roman Empire. The prize is conferred on Ascension Day each May in the German city of Aachen, which was Charlemagne's imperial capital. Winners since 1945 include CHURCHILL, Sir Edward HEATH and Roy JENKINS.

Charlie's Taj Mahal *See* Taj MaHAUGHEY.

Charlottetown Accord The agreement concluded on 28 August 1992 by the leaders of Canada's provinces in an effort to break the deadlock over the country's constitution. It would have given new powers to Quebec reflecting its **distinct society**, including more seats in the House of Commons than its population warranted, and more say in the Senate for the western provinces. Negotiated for Brian Mulroney's Conservative government by Constitutional Affairs Minister Joe Clark (*see* JOE WHO?), it was put to a REFERENDUM on 26 October 1992 – and rejected.

charter. Charter Movement (1) One of the groups in the US DEMOCRATIC PARTY which was influential in transforming its national organisation c. 1970 and ensuring that its CONVENTION was no longer in the pocket of MACHINE politicians. In the convention that ensued in 1972, blacks and women were properly represented for the first time – but so were radicals from the ANTI-WAR and PROTEST MOVEMENT who pushed through a PLATFORM well to the left even of Presidential nominee George McGovern and helped guarantee his defeat by Richard NIXON. (2) A GINGER GROUP in Britain's CONSERVATIVE PARTY which, especially during the 1980s, agitated for full publication of the party's accounts, a party structure that listened to CONSTITUENCY associations, and the election of the party chairman – traditionally appointed by the Tory leader – by constituency activists. Some of these reforms were implemented.

Charter 77 A group of DISSIDENTS formed in Prague in 1977 (designated 'Year of Rights for Political Prisoners') to monitor abuses of HUMAN RIGHTS by the Czech Communist authorities. Their Charter demanded that the government abide by UN covenants and the HELSINKI ACCORDS. Hundreds from all classes signed it, many subsequently suffering harassment, prison or exile; among those imprisoned was the writer Vaclav Havel, who would be elected President of Czechoslovakia after the collapse of Communism in 1989. Charter 77 was wound up in November 1991.

Charter 88 A UK 'dissident' group set up in 1988 with a title pretentiously linking it to its Czech forebear, and advocating fundamental reforms including a written Constitution, PROPORTIONAL REPRESENTATION and a BILL OF RIGHTS guaranteeing individual freedoms. When the group was founded, Neil KINNOCK dismissed its members as 'wankers, whiners and whingers'; four years later his wife Glenys joined it.

Chartists The mass movement comprising both industrial workers and intellectuals that demanded radical political reforms in early Victorian England; its campaign was most active from 1838 to 1849. It was based in the new but largely unrepresented industrial areas of Birmingham, Clydeside, South Wales, Tyneside and West Yorkshire, a fact that diminished its impact on Parliament. Its objectives were set out in a **People's Charter**, a great PETITION presented at WESTMINSTER on 14 June 1839; they included universal male suffrage, the secret BALLOT, the abolition of property qualifications for the franchise and payment of Members of Parliament. With the exception of a call for annually-elected Parliaments, almost all the Chartist programme was adopted by 1910. The Chartists' effective end came in 1848 when, with Europe aflame with revolution, they staged a mass demonstration at Kennington Common on 10 April; a baker's shop was looted and Wellington mobilised troops to prevent them marching on Westminster. In driving rain they dispersed, and the movement died away.

Chartwell The private country home near Westerham, Kent, of Sir Winston CHURCHILL, now open to the nation. The Churchills moved to Chartwell in 1922, Winston's daughter Sarah describing it as 'wildly overgrown and untidy, containing all the mystery of houses that had not been lived in for many years'. It became in the words of one visitor 'an astonishing combination of private home, Grand Hotel and a Government department'. With the cost of its upkeep imposing considerable financial pressure, Chartwell was the nerve centre of Churchill's campaign against APPEASEMENT and for preparedness for war; in the grounds he perfected his hobby of bricklaying by constructing elegant walls.

Chatham House rules The regime under which politicians, diplomats, academics, strategic experts and journalists meet to pool ideas at Chatham House, the home in St James's Square, London of the Royal Institute of International Affairs. The information is exchanged to ensure that all concerned are better informed, and is thus not supposed to be attributed to a particular source.

Chatila *See* SABRA AND CHATILA.

chattering classes A largely London term for the intermeshing community of left-of-centre and middle-class intellectuals, especially writers, dramatists and political pundits, who believe their views should carry enormous weight and have considerable access to the BBC and much of the media. The term was coined early in Margaret THATCHER's ascendancy to disparage the liberal INTELLIGENTSIA who raged impotently about Thatcherism over the dinner tables of North London. It was popularised in the *Observer* by Alan Watkins, who widened it to include a wider political spectrum; more recently it has started to denote the hard left intellectual opposition to Tony BLAIR, personified by the playwright Harold Pinter.

> The Beatles, James Bond – that's the sort of thing we export to France best, while they send us their ideas. We do not even recognise our ideas merchants over here; we prefer to turn the spotlight on the glitterati, the chattering classes, the *cognoscenti* . . .
>
> *The Independent,* 20 March 1991

chauvinist A person excessively devoted to his or her country or race, and showing unreasoning hostility and disdain for others. The word stemmed from the French soldier Nicholas Chauvin, whose devotion to Napoleon was such that he became a laughing-stock; from 1831 his name was linked to a JINGOIST vaudeville character. The term **white chauvinist** was recorded c. 1930 and **male chauvinist** c. 1950; the derivative **male chauvinist pig** surfaced around 1970.

Che The name by which Ernesto Guevara (1928–67) was known to the generations of leftists and students worldwide who hung his portrait, with his beret bearing a single star, in their rooms. A well-to-do Argentine physician and writer, he became a Marxist, joined Fidel Castro and played a leading role in the Cuban revolution before leaving Cuba secretly in 1965. The next year he appeared in Bolivia, which he considered ripe for revolution, and joined an embryo GUERRILLA movement; he was betrayed, wounded, captured and finally shot on 9 October 1967 by US-trained counter-insurgency forces. His book *Guerrilla Warfare* became required reading for all aspiring revolutionaries.

check. check against delivery The phrase printed on the advance text of almost every political speech in Britain, urging journalists not to file the text to their newspapers until they have checked that the words have actually been uttered.

Checkpoint Charlie The nickname given to the main crossing point for foreigners between East and West Berlin before the demolition of the BERLIN WALL. Standing at the junction of the Friedrichstrasse and Zimmerstrasse, it was a barometer of the level of East-West tension; when this was strained, East German border guards would cause long delays. Checkpoint Charlie has been immortalised in many spy novels and films as one of the places where intelligence agents were supposed to be exchanged. In 1990, at the end of the COLD WAR, Checkpoint Charlie was removed intact to be preserved in a museum. A substitute remains as a reminder; the author had his wallet stolen there in 2001.

checks and balances The principle that dominated the creation of America's system of government by the FOUNDING FATHERS; the notion, particularly associated with John ADAMS, that each arm of government must to a large extent offset the ability of the others to act against the best interests of the people. Americans anxious to advance radical changes or just see things happen have fumed at the way the WHITE HOUSE, HOUSE and SENATE can work against each other, and the restraints arising from the SEPARATION OF POWERS between the EXECUTIVE, JUDICIARY and LEGISLATURE; the historian Richard Hofstadter termed them 'a harmonious system of mutual frustration', but they have survived for over two centuries.

> A majority held in restraint by constitutional checks and balances and always changing easily with deliberate changes of popular opinions and sentiments is the only sovereign of a free people.
>
> ABRAHAM LINCOLN's first INAUGURAL ADDRESS, 4 March 1861

> People . . . prefer divided government. They just don't want one party of scoundrels in there. People believe in checks and balances.
>
> The pollster LOUIS HARRIS

Checkers The dog around whom Richard NIXON crafted a tear-jerking broadcast that kept him on the Republican TICKET in 1952 after disclosures that wealthy backers had given him an $18000 SLUSH FUND. Newspaper editorials urged the Presidential nominee Dwight D. EISENHOWER to drop Nixon as his RUNNING-MATE, and IKE himself was hedging. Then, on 23 September, Nixon went on live television and claimed that the fund was to meet 'necessary expenses' and 'expose Communism'. He denied that his wife Pat had a mink, applauding her for having a REPUBLICAN CLOTH COAT, listed his highly mundane assets and added that he had received another gift:

> A little cocker spaniel dog in a crate [that was] sent all the way from Texas. Black and white spotted. And our little girl Trisha, the 6-year-old one – named it Checkers. And you know, the kids love the dog, and I just want to say about it, we're gonna keep it!

Supportive telegrams poured into Republican headquarters and the nation's radio and TV stations, and the next day Eisenhower embraced Nixon and declared him 'completely vindicated as a man of honour'. WATERGATE lay 20 years ahead.

cheese-eating surrender monkeys *See* MONKEY.

Cheka The original political police agency of the SOVIET UNION, established by LENIN in December 1917. At first known as *Vecheka*, it was intended to investigate sabotage and counter-revolutionary activity, but instead indulged in the arrest, imprisonment and execution of all considered to be enemies of the state. It was disbanded in 1922 and replaced by the GPU, which the following year became the notorious OGPU.

Chequers The official country seat of British Prime Ministers, in Buckinghamshire near Princes Risborough. It was presented to the nation for this purpose by Sir Arthur and Lady Lee (Lord and Lady Lee of Fareham) in 1917, and first officially used by LLOYD GEORGE in 1921. Every Prime Minister plants a tree in the grounds, and on their departure their stained-glass coat of arms is placed in a window of the house's Long Gallery.

> A wonderful place in which to hold a family party, especially as the staff enter into the spirit of the occasion.
>
> JAMES CALLAGHAN

Cheriegate An episode in 2002 – a UK parallel to WHITEWATER – which damaged the standing of Cherie BLAIR, arising from her using Peter Foster, boyfriend of her lifestyle adviser Carole Caplin, as intermediary in securing a £69000 reduction in the price of two flats she was buying in Bristol, one for the Blairs' student son EUAN. The Prime Minister's wife did not appreciate – although everyone in the media was aware – that Foster had served prison sentences in the UK and his native Australia for fraud over the promotion of bogus herbal remedies. When the story broke, she denied through the DOWNING STREET press office that Foster had been her financial adviser and understated the extent of their contact. To the embarrassment of No. 10, further details demonstrated that Mrs Blair, who was that week sitting as a judge, had been in touch with Foster by e-mail for several weeks and had also contacted his solicitors about the status of hearings into his deportation. It was alleged by the Conservatives, and strongly denied by Mrs Blair, that she had tried to influence these proceedings. Mrs Blair largely defused the situation by a tearful apology, though some further uncertainties came to light. Transcripts of mobile phone conversations suggested that Foster had worked to infiltrate himself into the Blairs' confidence by starting a relationship with Ms Caplin, who miscarried their child just as the story broke, but Foster disputed this.

> I have made mistakes, but I was only trying to

> protect my family. . . . I am not Superwoman. The reality of my daily life is that I'm juggling a lot of balls in the air. Sometimes some of the balls get dropped.
>
> CHERIE BLAIR, 10 December 2002

Chernobyl The NUCLEAR disaster in the Ukraine in 1986 – the world's worst at the time – which contaminated much of Europe, revived the public concern over the safety of nuclear power that had first peaked after THREE MILE ISLAND and did much to discredit the Soviet regime with its own people. On 26 April the No. 4 reactor in the Chernobyl power station blew up, killing some 250 people almost immediately, contaminating 2 million people in Belarus and the Ukraine and inflicting slow and painful deaths on many nearby residents and heroes of the clean-up; the fire and escape of radioactive materials were finally ended by entombing the reactor in concrete. The Soviet authorities were at first silent about the disaster; when a sharp increase in radiation was first detected in Sweden a leak nearer at hand was suspected. 135,000 people were evacuated from a 35 km zone around the installation, the area to which the POLITBURO claimed radiation was confined. Farm produce across much of Eastern Europe was destroyed, and radioactive rain over Wales and north-west England left some flocks of sheep unfit for market six years later. The accident was caused by an unauthorised procedure that went wrong, poor design of the building and the slow response of staff to early danger signs. Though Western governments issued reassuring statements about the safety of their own installations, immense damage was done to nuclear energy programmes throughout the world, many being cancelled as a result of public disquiet.

Chevaline The secret project for upgrading and improving the penetration of Britain's POLARIS nuclear missiles so that they could knock out Soviet ABM defences. The project was initiated by the HEATH government in 1971, but the crucial decision was taken later by a group of Labour Ministers without the knowledge of the full CABINET. Chevaline eventually cost the taxpayer £2.25 billion, by which time the Russians had agreed not to extend their ABM system.

Chevening The magnificent 17th-century house near Westerham in Kent which is the official country residence of Britain's FOREIGN SECRETARY, and which played host to the annual strategy meeting of the CHANCELLOR and TREASURY Ministers in the days when he subsequently went into pre-Budget PURDAH. For 250 years Chevening, designed by Inigo Jones, was the home of the Earls of Stanhope. In the early 1970s the last of the line left it to the nation for use by a senior CABINET MINISTER; the original intention was for the LORD CHANCELLOR to have it. In 1988 Sir Geoffrey HOWE was reluctant to give it up when Margaret THATCHER wanted to move him from the Foreign Office; as compensation Chancellor Nigel Lawson was asked to give up DORNEYWOOD while Sir Geoffrey was DEPUTY PRIME MINISTER.

Chicago. Chicago convention The Democratic National CONVENTION in Chicago from 25 to 29 August 1968, at the height of the VIETNAM WAR, which was accompanied by ANTI-WAR protests brutally suppressed by police sent in by Mayor Richard DALEY, who had vowed that 'no one is going to take over the streets'. One clash between police and chanting and brick-throwing protesters ended with what was officially termed a 'police riot' which put 101 demonstrators, 49 police and a number of reporters in hospital. Many of the demonstrators were young idealists who had hoped that, by a miracle, the anti-war Sen. Eugene McCarthy might be nominated over Vice President Hubert Humphrey. The WALKER REPORT blamed the language of the more militant protesters – the words 'Fuck the PIGS' were regularly chanted – for provoking the police. One witness told the committee:

> It seemed to me that only a saint could swallow the rude remarks to the officers. However, they went to extremes in clubbing the YIPPIES. I saw them move into the park, swatting away with clubs at girls and boys in the grass.

The images seen by over 50 million television viewers of the disruption and violence, and the peaceful divisions on the war in the convention, had a serious impact on Humphrey's Presidential campaign, and on the image of the Democrats, and of Mayor Daley, for years after. The Democrats returned peacefully to Chicago in 1996 when Daley's son Richard was mayor.

Chicago Seven The group of ANTI-WAR leaders charged with violating the anti-riot provisions of the 1968 Civil Rights Act during the Chicago Convention. The seven – Abbie Hoffman, Jerry Rubin, Tom Hayden, Rennie Davis, David Dellinger, Lee Weiner and John Froines – were convicted in February 1969 of conspiracy to cross State lines and institute a riot. The BLACK PANTHER leader Bobby Seale, also charged in the case, was bound and gagged with chains after calling the judge a pig; eventually all charges were dropped and convictions reversed on appeal. The label Chicago Seven, used by their supporters and the press, set a trend for the naming of the victims of alleged legal persecution on both sides of the Atlantic (*see* BIRMINGHAM SIX). By the mid-1970s graffiti were appearing in London reading: 'Free the Heinz 57'.

> We were invented. We were chosen by the Government to serve as scapegoats for all they wanted to prevent happening in the 1970s.
>
> TOM HAYDEN

Chicago school The group of economists led by Milton Friedman (1912–), Professor of Economics at the University of Chicago 1948–82, which devised and, where possible, attempted to implement the theory of MONETARISM. Friedman was a powerful influence on the policies of both Margaret THATCHER and Ronald REAGAN.

chicken. chicken Democrats The politest of the Republicans' terms for 51 Democratic members of the Texas state legislature who in May 2003 secretly fled across the state line to Oklahoma to deny the Republican majority a QUORUM and prevent it implementing a REDISTRICTING plan championed by the Congressional Republican leader Rep. Tom DeLay which would have given his party up to seven seats more in CONGRESS. The Democrats were traced to a motel in Ardmore, Oklahoma because while most had hired a bus, one had left Texas in his private plane and had filed a flight plan. The Republicans, left five votes short of a quorum, threatened the Democrats with arrest; Texas Rangers were sent to apprehend them but were reminded by the legislators that they had no power of arrest outside the Lone Star State. The Democrats returned of their own free will a few days later once the time limit for passage of the redistricting and the rest of the Republicans' legislative programme had expired. DeLay's plan went through in the next session.

chicken hawks *See* HAWKS.

chicken tikka massala The measure of British multi-ethnicity controversially chosen in a speech in April 2001 by FOREIGN SECRETARY Robin COOK, in contrast to Norman Tebbit's exclusive CRICKET TEST. He said:

> Chicken Tikka Massala is now Britain's true national dish, not only because it is the most popular, but because it is the perfect illustration of the way Britain absorbs and adapts external influences. Chicken Tikka is an Indian dish. The Massala sauce was added to satisfy the desire of British people to have their meat served with gravy.

Chicken George Originally an amiable, avuncular character in the television blockbuster ROOTS, the name was taken up by the CLINTON campaign in 1992 after George BUSH senior initially refused a televised debate. Derrick Parker, a Clinton supporter in Michigan, put on a CHICKEN SUIT and heckled him at a Republican event, and the idea caught on throughout the country. Bush, unaccountably, began talking to the chickens, ensuring them time on television by seeking them out and telling them 'fish jokes'. Local Republicans fought back, excluding chickens and, in Mississippi, even arresting one. One slipped through in Shreveport, Louisiana by showing Republicans a placard reading 'Poultry Workers for Bush'. Once in, he turned it round to read: 'Chicken George.'

> At first we recruited them, but real soon all the local people wanted to do it.
>
> JAMES CARVILLE

chicken littles A WASHINGTON term for politicians who are reluctant to take or countenance any bold but risky step. In comes from the fairy tale in which Chicken Little was convinced that the sky was falling down.

> We just had too many Chicken Littles in CONGRESS in the last week who seemed to become hysterical over covert aid [to the Nicaraguan CONTRAS].
>
> Unnamed REAGAN administration official, *New York Times*, 15 April 1984

chicken run The phrase used by Labour's Frank Dobson and others in the run-up to the 1997 election to scorn the way a number of prominent Conservatives, expecting defeat in their existing seats, were seeking selection for supposedly safer ones. The scale of Labour's victory, when it came, meant that several who tried this tactic were defeated nevertheless.

chicken suit The wearable version of the RUBBER CHICKEN, and to Americans a source of endless fun. Even before the genesis of CHICKEN GEORGE they were becoming a feature of election campaigns; in 1976 a journalist in a chicken suit greeted Gerald FORD at one airport stop. The practice reached Britain in the 1997 general election when the Conservatives hired a man in a chicken suit to follow Tony BLAIR to highlight his unwillingness to debate with John MAJOR. By the end of the campaign

Blair was also followed by three bears (which tried to kidnap the chicken) and a rhinoceros, while the *Daily Mirror* hired a headless chicken to follow Major.

a chicken in every pot The slogan attributed to Henry IV of France (1553–1610), who is reputed to have said:

> I want there to be no peasant in my kingdom so poor that he is unable to have a chicken in his pot every Sunday.

Herbert HOOVER took it a stage further, promising 'A chicken, two chickens in every pot under Hoover'. John F. KENNEDY commented in the town where he made the promise:

> No Presidential candidate has dared to come back to this community since.

rubber chicken (1) An object much loved by clowns and practical jokers in America, and likely to be produced at an unexpected moment. One day in 1977 the STATE DEPARTMENT spokesman Hodding Carter became so enraged during his morning briefing at provocative questions from the ultra-conservative priest and columnist Lester Kinsolving that, after the question: 'Does the UN have a branch office in northern Philadelphia?' he produced a rubber chicken from under his lectern and threw it at him. In the 1993 New York mayoral race George Marlin, Conservative and RIGHT TO LIFE candidate, produced a rubber chicken as a substitute for the Republican Rudolph Giuliani when he refused to appear. The *New Yorker* declared that 'the rubber chicken won', and Giuliani went on to become one of the city's greatest mayors. (2) Rubber chicken is said by politicians to be the staple menu of FUND-RAISERS and other party dinners. Those who speak frequently at them are said to be on the **rubber chicken circuit**; it is also known in the US as the **mashed potato circuit**.

sick chicken case The case in which the US SUPREME COURT finally imposed Constitutional limits on Franklin D. ROOSEVELT's NEW DEAL. It concerned the powers of the National Recovery Administration (NRA), which critics had increasingly branded as 'HITLERian' and a farcical BUREAUCRACY. In the case of Schechter Poultry Corporation v United States, the NRA was accused of exceeding its powers over interstate commerce by interfering in the trade in kosher fowls in the New York area. As Schechter had offended the NRA by allegedly selling an 'unfit chicken' to a butcher, the proceedings became known as the 'sick chicken case', and on BLACK MONDAY, 27 May 1935, the Court declared the NRA – which had already been reorganised – unconstitutional.

some chicken, some neck The defiant statement on Britain's prospects in WORLD WAR II made by Winston CHURCHILL to the Canadian Parliament on 30 December 1941. He told them:

> When I warned the [the French government] that Britain would fight on alone whatever they did, their Generals [Gen. Weygand] told their Prime Minister and their divided Cabinet: 'In three weeks England will have her neck wrung like a chicken'. Some chicken! Some neck!

Chief. Chief Justice The presiding member of America's SUPREME COURT, appointed by the President on the ADVICE AND CONSENT of the Senate on the same basis as the other eight. The main difference from the other justices, apart from salary, is one of prestige, as a strong Supreme Court will be remembered by the name of the Chief Justice, as in the WARREN COURT.

chief of staff (1) In the WHITE HOUSE, the principal aide of the President, whose task is to run the STAFF and who thus enjoys considerable control over ACCESS to the President, and substantial political influence. This can pit the Chief of Staff against the SECRETARY OF STATE and other senior Cabinet members and officials who feel their own influence is being challenged.

> When I became President I did not want to have a powerful Chief of Staff. Wilson had his Colonel House, EISENHOWER had his Sherman Adams, NIXON his Haldeman, and I was aware of the trouble those top assistants had caused my predecessors. GERALD FORD

(2) The head of one of the armed services, who sits with his counterparts on (in Washington) the JOINT CHIEFS OF STAFF or, (in London) the Defence Staff.

> You may take the most gallant sailor, most intrepid airman, or the most audacious soldier, put them at a table together – what do you get? The sum of all their fears! CHURCHILL

Chief Secretary Not a BUREAUCRAT, but the second CABINET MINISTER at the British TREASURY after the CHANCELLOR OF THE EXCHEQUER. The Chief Secretary's main responsibility is the allocation and control of public spending, through the annual round of negotiations with spending Ministers and the COMPREHENSIVE SPENDING REVIEW.

> The job is like playing poker simultaneously at 18 different tables. JONATHAN AITKEN

chief whip *See* WHIP.

chienlit (Fr. crap-in-the-bed) The barrack-room word with which President DE GAULLE stunned the French public when he used it in a televised appeal for the restoration of order during the ÉVÈNEMENTS of 1968. Trawling back into the vocabulary of the troops from his days as a young officer, the normally staid de Gaulle declared:

Réforme: Oui! Chienlit: Non!

Child Support Agency (CSA) One of the most spectacular failures of recent UK governments: the agency set up with all-party support in 1992 to ensure that absent fathers made a fair financial contribution to the upkeep of their children. It almost instantly became a byword for incompetence, unfeeling BUREAUCRACY, failure to pursue fathers with no intention of contributing, draconian assessments of many of those who were ready to pay and non-payment of what sums were received to needy mothers. Repeated relaunches and reorganisations have removed many of its initial failings, but its performance remains highly controversial.

Chiltern Hundreds The technicality under which a member of the UK HOUSE OF COMMONS resigns his or her seat. Theoretically an MP cannot resign, but can be disqualified by accepting an OFFICE OF PROFIT UNDER THE CROWN. The two sinecures traditionally used are that of steward or bailiff of the three Chiltern Hundreds (local government units from Saxon times) of Stoke, Desborough and Burnham, and that of Steward of the **Manor of Northstead**. Though billed as 'offices of profit', holding them does not generate any income, but when application is made for one of them, a person's membership of the House automatically lapses.

China card The use by America c. 1978 of closer links with China as a means of putting pressure on the Soviet Union to pursue a more moderate foreign policy and make concessions in ARMS CONTROL talks. The gambit at first seemed productive, but was capped by the Soviet invasion of Afghanistan and the subsequent failure of the Senate to ratify the SALT II agreement. *See also* ORANGE CARD, RACE CARD.

China lobby The powerful pressure group that mobilised in WASHINGTON after the defeat of Chiang Kai-Shek's NATIONALIST CHINESE by Mao Tse-Tung's (*see* CHAIRMAN MAO) Communists in 1949 to ensure total US backing for Chiang's claim to be China's lawful ruler, commit America to defend Taiwan (then Formosa) against any Communist attack, and work for the overthrow of the RED CHINESE regime in Peking, as it was then known. Its driving force was Henry Luce, the publisher of *Time*, who had been born in China and idolised the upright but incompetent GENERALISSIMO Chiang. The China lobby, and its slogan of **Who lost China?** with its inference of betrayal, was a great embarrassment to the TRUMAN administration, which was about to take the full force of MCCARTHYISM. Chiang's longevity, and the fervour of his supporters, enabled the China lobby to keep an armlock on US policy for over two decades. Ironically it was Richard NIXON, who as a Senator had shouted: 'Who lost China?', who opened links with Peking (*see* PING-PONG DIPLOMACY).

Chingford skinhead One of the politer nicknames for **Norman** (later Lord) **Tebbit** (1931–) the former airline pilots' union official who sloughed off a reputation as a right-wing BARRACKER in the COMMONS to become a respected Trade and Industry Secretary under Margaret THATCHER before reverting to type. At the height of his powers and influence he was seriously injured in the 1984 BRIGHTON BOMBING which left his wife paralysed. He overcame great pain to fight his way back and become party chairman for the 1987 election. Despite the eventual LANDSLIDE victory the experience was not a happy one; his relations with Mrs Thatcher deteriorated and he retired from the government, re-emerging in 1992 to campaign from the LORDS against the MAASTRICHT TREATY. In later years he spoke controversially on race as well as Europe, setting his own CRICKET TEST to determine whether ethnic communities in Britain were truly British.

Tebbit was the epitome of the social group to whom Mrs Thatcher appealed strongest – hard-working, patriotic, ruthless in their judgements on others – and as he took on the trade unions he became a hero to the upwardly mobile; indeed he used the phrase as the title of his autobiography. Labour politicians hated him, particularly after, as a backbencher, he shouted to the ailing left-wing MP Tom Litterick: 'Why don't you go and have another heart attack?'; Michael FOOT branded him a SEMI-HOUSETRAINED POLECAT. Labour MPs considered his appointment as Employment Secretary a provocation to the unions, Eric Varley saying:

> Putting Norman Tebbit in charge of industrial relations is like putting Dracula in charge of the blood transfusion service.

Yet trade unionists knew where they stood with him, and many came to respect him. At one of his first meetings as a Minister with shipyard shop stewards he floored them by saying: 'The first thing you ought to know is that there's nothing I'd like better than to pin the lot of you to the wall'; productive talks followed.

Tebbit could seldom resist using a tongue which, in the words of one Labour MPs, would have killed him with acid poisoning had he bitten it; he told Dennis Skinner (*see* BEAST OF BOLSOVER): 'Far better to keep your mouth shut and let everyone think you're stupid than open it and leave no doubt', and Neil KINNOCK: 'I'm older than you, sonny, and you can take on men when you grow up.' Chris Patten, his successor as Tory chairman, observed:

> We all try to be as nice as Mr Tebbit.

Yet he regarded himself as a man of honour and humanity, and sued the *Guardian* columnist Hugo Young for suggesting he had declared that no-one with a conscience could vote Conservative.

> *Woman heckler*: Gizza job!
> *Tebbit:* Madam, you're dirty, you're filthy, you're unkempt, you're foul-mouthed and disgusting – why should anyone in their right mind give you a job?

Chips The nickname of **Henry Channon** (1897–1958), the wealthy Conservative backbencher whose diaries are one of the delights of 20th-century British political literature. He became MP for Southend in 1935, and on his death the seat passed to his son Paul, who went on to be one of the most civilised members of the THATCHER Cabinet. The height of Chips' career was a spell as PPS to R.A. (RAB) Butler, but his delight was the backstairs gossip of the COMMONS – which he retailed with a Pepysian eye and a snobbish flourish – and the confidences of the great over dinner at 5 Belgrave Square, where he lived in great style.

Chirac. Jacques René Chirac (1932–), President of France 1995– . The dominant figure in French centre-right politics for two decades who first COHABITED as Prime Minister with the Leftist President MITTERRAND and then sought as his successor to lead France down a more liberal and modernising path while maintaining France's GAULLIST independence in foreign policy, notably in blocking United Nations support for the US-led IRAQ WAR. A Parisian, Chirac flirted with Communism in his youth, then volunteered to fight in Algeria, where he was wounded. He joined the civil service *via* Harvard and the ENA, and at 30 was appointed to head the personal staff of President Pompidou. His ability to get things done earned him the nickname **'Le Bulldozer'** and a caricature as the thrusting young technocrat in *Asterix*. Elected a DEPUTY in 1967, he became within a year State Secretary at the Ministry of Economics, playing a central part in negotiating a truce when the ÉVÈNEMENTS of 1968. In 1972 he became Minister of Agriculture and two years later Minister of the Interior and then Prime Minister under President Giscard, resigning in 1976 to reconstitute the Gaullist UDR – whose secretary-general he became – into a more personal vehicle, the RPR. Mayor of Paris from 1977 to 1995 – with his administration tarnished by a series of party financial scandals – he ran against Giscard for the Presidency in 1981, with Mitterrand coming through to win, and in 1986 became Prime Minister again for the first experiment with *Cohabitation*. Outmanoeuvred by Mitterrand, he took him to a runoff in the 1988 Presidential election but only succeeded to the *Élysee* at the third attempt in 1995, on Mitterrand's retirement. Chirac insisted on resuming French nuclear tests at MURUROA, but in 1996 ended the tests 'once and for all'. Elected on a platform of tax cuts and modest economic reforms, he precipitated National Assembly elections in 1997 to secure a supportive majority but was forced to accept the Socialist Lionel Jospin as Prime Minister in a further *Cohabitation*. The 2002 Presidential election showed Jospin to be even more unpopular than he was, and he won a run-off with the NATIONAL FRONT leader Jean-Marie le Pen with the reluctant support of the Left. With the Socialists in disarray, Chirac seized the moment to convert the PRP into UMP, which remains the governing party. At the 2002 Bastille Day celebrations Chirac survived an assassination attempt by a gunman from the right-wing *UNITÉ RADICALE*. As a moderniser and (by French standards) an economic liberal, Chirac had some things in common with Tony BLAIR, but their relationship soured as Blair tried to accelerate ECONOMIC REFORM within the EU, maintained the pressure for ENLARGEMENT and, above all, sided with George W. BUSH over Iraq. By blocking UN support for the war in the spring of 2003 with support from Russia and China, Chirac appeared, especially when the peace went wrong, to have brought to fulfilment two centuries of French foreign policy. However his stock fell sharply in 2005 when French voters rejected the EUROPEAN CONSTITUTION despite his strong personal support for it; Chirac tried to recoup by launching an attack on the BRITISH REBATE, but suffered a further setback when, despite his personal intervention, the International Olympic Committee unexpectedly chose London over Paris to host the 2012 Olympics. Some of the French media attributed the defeat to comments about British cuisine and MAD COW DISEASE Chirac had made at the KALININGRAD meeting with German and Russian leaders just days before. Chirac did make some progress toward his long-held goal of liberalising elements of the French economy, but was hampered by the inability of his chosen prime ministers, notably Jean-Pierre Raffarin, to push through significant changes without triggering waves of strikes in the public sector.

CHOGM COMMONWEALTH Heads of Government Meeting. The gathering of Prime Ministers or Presidents from all the countries of the Commonwealth, held every two years in a member capital with the leader of the host government in the chair and the Queen, as Head of the Commonwealth, presiding. A regional CHOGM, without the Queen present, is also held by Pacific member states. When CHOGM assembled in Harare, Zimbabwe in 1991, officials asserted that the initials stood for

> Cheap holidays on Government money.

Chowder and Marching Society A fraternity of fifteen Republican CONGRESSMEN which has flourished since 1949, and which is widely seen as grooming those invited to join it for leadership. It was the base for the revolt of YOUNG TURKS that in 1965 ousted Rep. Charles Halleck as MINORITY LEADER and installed Gerald FORD. Founder-members included Ford and the young Richard NIXON.

Christ. Christ and Carrots The nickname, coined by CHURCHILL, for Sir Stafford Cripps (1889–1952), the lawyer who became a fanatical and ascetic Christian Socialist, wartime AMBASSADOR to Moscow and a successful CHANCELLOR in ATTLEE's government. A less flattering alternative was 'Sir Stifford Crapps'. Briefly Solicitor-General under Ramsay MACDONALD, he campaigned during the 1930s for a POPULAR FRONT – getting himself expelled from the LABOUR PARTY – and against APPEASEMENT. CHURCHILL appointed him to Moscow, where STALIN never warmed to 'this man who eats nuts and lectures me on Communism', and in 1942 made him LEADER OF THE HOUSE, and later Minister for Aircraft Production. Attlee made him President of the Board of Trade, and Chancellor in 1948 when Hugh Dalton resigned over the BUDGET LEAK. His self-denying manner echoed the mood of post-war austerity, and he managed to secure the unions' agreement to WAGE RESTRAINT, but ill-health forced his resignation a year after DEVALUING in September 1949. Denis HEALEY rated Cripps, with Ernest BEVIN, the most powerful member of the Labour CABINET, but wrote that in the 1930s he had been 'a political ninny of the most superior quality'. Churchill said of Cripps: 'He has all the virtues I dislike and none of the vices I admire', and also declared: 'There, but for the grace of God, goes God'. CHIPS Channon noted after Cripps dined with him in June 1950, eating 'three scraped carrots, some salad and an orange':

> I felt as if I had breathed the dark, fetid atmosphere of beyond the tomb.

Christian Coalition The ultra-conservative organisation founded by the evangelist Pat Robertson after his defeat in the 1988 US Presidential election, organised by his former campaign director Ralph Reed and based on his mailing list of almost 2 million supporters. 'Issues-centred, not personality-centred', according to Reed, it ran (initially secret) training seminars for candidates for office, and by 1992 exerted influence in 20 State Republican parties. By 1995 it claimed 1.7 million members; its power waned in the CLINTON years after the failure of the Republican right under NEWT Gingrich to radicalise the CONGRESS (*see* CONTRACT WITH AMERICA), but revived during the presidency of George W. BUSH, who broadly sympathised with it. Robertson remained on the fringe of national politics, though always capable of making an impact.

> The political power house of an alternative culture.
>
> SIDNEY BLUMENTHAL, *New Yorker*

Christian Democrats The centre-right and predominantly Roman Catholic parties that are a permanent feature of politics in most Continental European countries except France. They have had the greatest success in Italy, where they had a continuous share in government from the end of WORLD WAR II to the 1990s despite an increasing reputation for jobbery, inertia and corruption, and in Germany (*see* CDU), where they remain one of the nation's two great parties. The European People's Party, usually the second largest grouping in the EUROPEAN PARLIAMENT, is an alliance of Christian Democrats and like-minded secular parties including Britain's CONSERVATIVES.

Christian Socialism *See* SOCIALISM.

Christmas tree In the US CONGRESS, a tax Bill designed to gain a winning coalition support because it contains something for everybody. It is constructed in such a way that if one provision is removed, the rest of the package becomes unworkable.

Christophe The Beverly Hills hairdresser whose $200 haircut for President CLINTON aboard AIR FORCE ONE in May 1993 while the plane was on the runway at Los Angeles reputedly paralysed one of America's busiest airports for over an hour, causing Clinton considerable embarrassment and ridicule.

Church House The administrative headquarters of the Church of England on the far side of Westminster Abbey from the Houses of Parliament. The HOUSE OF LORDS sat in its Convocation Room in 1940–41 and 1944, either when their own House was threatened by bombing or so that the COMMONS, whose own House had been destroyed, could sit in the Lords' chamber.

Churchill, Sir Winston (Leonard Spencer) (1874–1965), the larger-than-life if sometimes wrongheaded figure, and one of the great orchestrators of the English language, who dominated half a century of British politics and came out of the wilderness to lead the nation to victory in WORLD WAR II, being Prime Minister (Conservative) from 1940 to 1945 and from 1951 to 1955. Born at Blenheim Palace, the son of Lord Randolph Churchill (*see* FOURTH PARTY; ULSTER WILL FIGHT) and the glamorous American Jennie Jerome, he fought in the Sudan and was a war correspondent in South Africa, escaping from a Boer prison; the 'Wanted' poster read:

> Englishman, 25 years old, about five feet eight inches tall, indifferent build, walks with a forward stoop, pale appearance, reddish brown hair, small and hardly noticeable moustache, talks through his nose – cannot pronounce his 's's properly.

He entered the COMMONS in 1900 as Tory MP for Oldham, crossing the FLOOR to the Liberals in 1904. He served as Colonial Under-Secretary under CAMPBELL-BANNERMAN, and under ASQUITH as President of the Board of Trade, Home Secretary (*see* SIDNEY STREET SIEGE; TONYPANDY) and First Lord of the Admiralty. A year into WORLD WAR I, he was forced out by the Conservatives because of his support for the disastrous Gallipoli campaign; H.A.L. Fisher wrote to BONAR LAW that Churchill was 'a bigger danger than the Germans by a long way in what is now happening in the Dardanelles'. Churchill's wife 'Clemmie' had begged Asquith to keep him, writing:

> Winston may in your eyes and in those with whom he has to work have faults, but he has the supreme quality which I venture to say very few of your present or future Cabinet possess – the power, the imagination, the deadliness to fight Germany.

He resumed soldiering on the Western front until LLOYD GEORGE recalled him as Minister of Munitions in 1917; from 1919 he was Secretary for War, involved in Britain's intervention against the BOLSHEVIKS in Russia and the Irish crisis of 1919–21, then Colonial Secretary. In 1922 Churchill, who was edging away from the Liberals, lost his seat at Dundee, where he had moved in 1908; he wrote: 'In a twinkling of an eye, I found myself without office, without a seat, without a party and without an appendix.' Two more defeats ensued before he was elected in November 1924 as CONSTITUTIONALIST MP for Epping, becoming CHANCELLOR in BALDWIN's second Government and – on Treasury advice against his own instincts – putting Britain back on the GOLD STANDARD, Sir Oswald MOSLEY declaring:

> Faced with the alternative of saying goodbye to the gold standard, and therefore to his own employment, and goodbye to other people's employment, he characteristically selected the latter course.

Churchill, who rejoined the Conservatives in 1925, published the BRITISH GAZETTE during the 1926 GENERAL STRIKE; Asquith termed him 'a Chimborazo or Everest among the sandhills of the Baldwin Cabinet'. He resigned from the front BENCH in 1931 over Tory support for the granting of DOMINION status to India, and from 1932 spoke out from the back benches with increasing concern against the threat from NAZI Germany – backing this up with numerous newspaper articles written to finance an expensive family lifestyle at CHARTWELL;

F.E. Smith had called him 'a man of simple tastes, always prepared to put up with the best of everything'. Baldwin was tempted to recall him to the Cabinet, but wrote:

> Anything he undertakes he puts his heart and soul into. If there is going to be war, we must keep him fresh to be our war Prime Minister.

In the ABDICATION CRISIS of 1936, Churchill endeavoured to keep King Edward VIII on the throne. By now he was a fervent campaigner against APPEASEMENT, telling critics: 'I decline to be impartial as between the fire brigade and the fire', and in September 1938 narrowly escaped censure by his constituency association for attacking the MUNICH AGREEMENT, but as HITLER renewed his demands, pressure grew for his return to the Government. When war was declared on 3 September 1939, CHAMBERLAIN recalled him as First Lord (*see* WINSTON IS BACK), and his greatest days began. When Hitler's occupation of Norway brought criticism of Chamberlain to a head the following May, Churchill loyally backed Chamberlain (*see* AIR RAID SHELTER), but when Chamberlain fell days later, was the obvious choice to succeed him, Labour refusing to serve under anyone else. Churchill took over a nation on the brink of defeat (*see* BLOOD, SWEAT AND TEARS), but set a bulldog example, steadied the ship through Dunkirk and the Battle of Britain and then as FORMER NAVAL PERSON established a close relationship with President ROOSEVELT prior to PEARL HARBOR in the hope of bringing America into the war; FDR told him: 'It is fun to be in the same decade with you.'

Below WHITEHALL in the CABINET WAR ROOMS, Churchill worked long hours as he presided over the war in a way that led General Wavell to complain: 'Winston is always expecting rabbits to come out of empty hats', and urged on an unprecedented mobilisation of the people. He frequently conducted business in the bath, Lord Boothby recalling:

> At intervals he turned a somersault, exactly like a porpoise, and when his head reappeared at the other end of the bath, he continued precisely where he had left off.

When FDR entered his bathroom, Churchill shouted: 'Come in Mr President. England has nothing to hide from her allies.' He was also partial to brandy, saying: 'I have taken more out of alcohol than alcohol has taken out of me.' Above ground he kept up civilian morale with his hat, cigar and V-SIGN; he said later: I WAS NOT THE LION, BUT I SUPPLIED THE ROAR.

He frequently made long and dangerous flights to meet Roosevelt and other Allied leaders, telling the US CONGRESS on one visit to Washington: 'If my father had been American and my mother British, instead of the other way round, I might have got here on my own.' He also got on well with STALIN; Robert Lewis Taylor wrote:

> The Russians were enormously impressed by Churchill at the table. His appetite for caviar and vodka convinced them they were fighting on the right side.

He managed to keep a grip on the House of Commons save for a brief period in 1943, much helped by the Labour leader Clement ATTLEE, a loyal and capable deputy who once told him: 'I must remind you that a monologue is not a decision', and who complained: 'The trouble with Winston is that he nails his trousers to the mast'.

As US and Soviet military might told, Churchill lost influence in strategic terms, but he emerged from the war a towering world figure. On 8 May 1945 the crowds cheered him to the echo as they celebrated victory over Germany, and Labour's LANDSLIDE win in the election two months later, with Japan still undefeated, was an immense shock. He wrote:

> On the night of the tenth of May [1940], at the outset of this mighty battle, I acquired the chief power in the State, which henceforth I wielded in ever-growing measure for five years and three months of world war, at the end of which time, all our enemies having surrendered unconditionally or being about to do so, I was immediately dismissed by the British electorate from all future conduct of their affairs.

Churchill confided: 'I feel very lonely without a war', but after a spell painting in Morocco and being lionised in formerly Nazi-occupied Europe, he revived the Tory party – which he had never much cared for – in OPPOSITION, ran Labour close in 1950 and became Prime Minister again in 1951 at the age of 77. He also managed, with help from researchers, to complete two formidable literary works: his *History of the Second World War* and *History of the English Speaking Peoples*. 'Winnie' in his last administration was less decisive and interested in detail, being consumed by a desire to end the ARMS RACE before retiring; after Stalin's death in 1953 he believed just one more SUMMIT would do it, but was disappointed. Harold MACMILLAN wrote in 1954:

> He is now quite incapable – mentally as well as

> physically – of remaining Prime Minister. He thinks about one thing all the time – this Russian visit and his chance of saving the world – until it has become an obsession.

He suffered a severe stroke in office with few colleagues realising, and the public – which was lied to – unaware, but eventually bowed to the inevitable and resigned as Prime Minister on 6 April 1955, Macmillan saying of his final Cabinet: 'Now he has really decided to go we are all miserable. Anthony [Eden] made rather a flat speech, then we all shuffled out.'

The Queen – the sixth sovereign under whom he had served in Parliament – paid tribute by coming to DOWNING STREET to dine. Churchill stayed in the Commons until 1964 as FATHER OF THE HOUSE, his contemporaries including the young Margaret THATCHER, but spent most of an honoured retirement reminiscing with friends, notably Lord Beaverbrook, painting on the Côte d'Azur, or resting and building walls at Chartwell with 'Clemmie'. He died at his London home on 24 January 1965; he had said: 'I am ready to meet my maker, but whether my maker is ready for the great ordeal of meeting me is another matter', but his last words were: 'Oh, I am so bored with it all.' Churchill was given the greatest State funeral seen in 20th-century Britain; he is buried at Bladon, near Blenheim.

Above all, Churchill is remembered as an orator, through his wartime speeches in the Commons and the radio broadcasts in which they were repeated, sometimes by the actor Norman Shelley. When the diarist/MP Harold Nicolson congratulated him on being a born orator, Churchill replied: 'Not born in the very least – just hard, hard work.' F.E. Smith asserted that 'Winston has devoted the best years of his life to preparing his impromptu speeches', and Lionel Curtis wrote: 'In private conversation he tries on speeches like a man trying on ties in his bedroom to see how he would look in them.' Aneurin BEVAN, another outstanding Parliamentary orator, declared: 'He never spares himself in conversation. He gives himself so generously that hardly anybody else is permitted to give anything in his presence'; but he also asserted that 'the mediocrity of his thinking is concealed by the majesty of his language'. John F. KENNEDY, quoting Beverly Nichols, put his achievement most concisely:

> He mobilised the English language, and sent it into battle.

Churchill could be caustic about his contemporaries. He said of Joseph Chamberlain: 'Mr Chamberlain loves the working-class man: he loves to see him work'; of Austen Chamberlain: 'He always plays the game – and he always loses it'; of Earl Jellicoe: 'The only man on either side who could lose the war in an afternoon'; of George Bernard Shaw: 'The world has long watched with tolerance and amusement the nimble antics and gyrations of the unique, double-headed chameleon while all the time the creature was anxious to be taken seriously'; of MAHATMA Gandhi: 'a half-naked fakir' who 'should be bound hand and foot and trampled by an enormous elephant ridden by the VICEROY'; of the future Queen Elizabeth II: 'At the age of two she had an authority and reflectiveness astonishing in an infant'; of John Foster Dulles: 'a bull who carries his own china with him'; of Field-Marshal Montgomery: 'in defeat, unbeatable; in victory, unbearable'; and of the Conservative MP Sir Alfred Bossom: 'neither one thing nor the other'. When the flamboyant homosexual Labour MP Tom Driberg married, Churchill observed of his choice of wife: 'Buggers can't be choosers'. He also detested modern art, causing a stir in 1949 in a broadcast Royal Academy speech by asking Sir Alfred Munnings:

> If you met Picasso coming down the street, would you join me in kicking his backside?

When he was presented with a Graham Sutherland portrait by the House of Commons to mark his 80th birthday, he observed: 'It makes me look as if I were straining on a stool'; Lady Churchill quietly destroyed the painting, which Sutherland considered his masterpiece.

At Westminster Churchill is venerated for stories of his REPARTEE, most of them true. He once infuriated Nancy, Lady Astor to the point where she exclaimed: 'If I were married to you, I'd put arsenic in your coffee.' Churchill replied: 'If you were my wife, I'd drink it.' After he rejoined the Conservatives, an indignant lady told him: 'I do not like your new politics, or your moustache'. Churchill responded: 'Madam, pray do not disturb yourself – you are not likely to come into contact with either'. And one night at Westminster he is said to have bumped into the Labour MP Bessie Braddock, who told him: 'Winston, you're drunk, bloody drunk!' Churchill unsteadily fixed his gaze on her and said: 'Bessie, you're ugly – bloody ugly! But I'll be sober in the morning'.

At the end of his Parliamentary career he was in the SMOKING ROOM when a pompous

Tory complained to all and sundry that the policeman outside had not held up the traffic for him. 'Said he didn't know who I was', the MP complained. Churchill roused himself from apparent slumber to inquire: 'All right, then, who *were* you?' Another time, gently reminded that his fly buttons were undone, he reassured his benefactor: 'Dead birds don't fall out of nests.' In the late 1950s, one young Tory MP pointed out Churchill apparently dozing in the corner and said: 'Of course the old man's a bit past it now.' Suddenly a voice boomed out: 'They say he's lost his hearing, too.'

> By his father he is an Englishman, by his mother an American. Behold the perfect man.
>
> MARK TWAIN

> A slippery gentleman, a fraudulent and dishonest politician and no friend of the workers.
>
> G.H. STUART, his Independent opponent at Dundee, 1908

> It's a pity that Winston hasn't a better sense of proportion, and also a larger endowment of loyalty . . . I am really fond of him, but he will never get to the top in English politics, with all his wonderful gifts. ASQUITH, 1915

> Winston has written four volumes about himself and called it *World Crisis.*
>
> ARTHUR BALFOUR

> He would make a drum out of the skin of his mother in order to sound his own praises.
>
> LLOYD GEORGE

> He would go up to the Creator and say that he would like very much to meet his Son, of Whom he had heard a great deal, and, if possible, would like to call on the Holy Ghost.
>
> LLOYD GEORGE

> 50 per cent genius, 50 per cent bloody fool.
>
> ATTLEE

> One layer was certainly 17th century. The 18th century in him is obvious. There was the 19th century and a large slice, of course, of the 20th century; and another, curious layer which may possibly have been the 21st. ATTLEE

> Eating words has never given me indigestion.
>
> CHURCHILL on his changes of tack

> Always in the wrong, always surrounded by crooks, a most unsuccessful father – simply a radio personality who outlived his prime.
>
> EVELYN WAUGH

> Churchill was fundamentally what the English call unstable – by which they mean anybody who has that touch of genius which is inconvenient in normal times. MACMILLAN

> To be alive with him was to have dined at the table of history.
>
> CASSANDRA (William Connor)

Churchill Arch The arch leading from the Members' LOBBY into the CHAMBER of the HOUSE OF COMMONS, which still bears the scars of the bomb that wrecked this part of the Palace of WESTMINSTER in 1941. In the debate in January 1945 on rebuilding the House, Churchill called for the damaged arch to be kept 'as a monument to the ordeal which Westminster has passed through in the great war, and as a reminder to whose who will come centuries afterwards, that they may look back from time to time upon their forebears who "kept the bridge in the brave days of old"'. To the left of the arch is Churchill's statue, its black toecap shined bronze by generations of Conservative MPs touching it for good luck.

Churchill of Asia The term US SECRETARY OF STATE Dean Rusk once unwisely used for South Vietnam's President Ngo Dinh Diem, whose administration became so venal, unpopular and harmful to the war effort that on 1 November 1964 he was killed in a US-backed COUP.

Churchill Room The restaurant adjoining (and below) the riverside TERRACE of the HOUSES OF PARLIAMENT where MPs can entertain guests. Originally named the **Harcourt Room** after Lewis 'Loulou' Harcourt, 1st Viscount and son of the Victorian statesman Sir William, it was rechristened the Churchill Room in 1991 despite protests by over 100 MPs. The room at the time featured a harpist who performed in apparent violation of regulations banning music in the Palace of WESTMINSTER.

> *Peer 1:* We could do with this in the Lords.
> *Peer 2:* Most have got a harp already. We are only waiting for the wings.

churning An opinion POLLSTERS' term for the movement of likely votes between parties during an ELECTION campaign.

CIA Central Intelligence Agency. A department of the US government set up by President TRUMAN under the 1947 National Security Act to conduct intelligence operations abroad; headed at first by Allen Dulles, it was based on the wartime OSS. Much of the work at its McLean, Virginia headquarters consists of analysing information from countries throughout the world, to watch for potential sources of tension that might harm US interests; it was through the CIA that WASHINGTON had prior warning in 1962 of what became the CUBAN MISSILE CRISIS. Its clandestine overseas ventures have mainly been designed to monitor and undermine left-wing regimes, though the WAR ON TERRORISM has prompted a shift in its activities. Its brief in the 1950s and 1960s included the overthrow and even assassination of anti-American leaders. After a series of public relations disasters in the Caribbean, Cuba (*see* Bay of PIGS) and Chile, CONGRESS in the mid-1970s placed the agency on a tight rein. In 1982 the BOLAND AMENDMENT barred the PENTAGON and CIA from training or supplying anyone trying to overthrow the SANDINISTA regime in Nicaragua, but the CIA under the REAGAN appointee William J. Casey went ahead with COVERT OPERATIONS until the subterfuge was detected, Congress retaliating by cutting off all US aid to the CONTRAS. With the end of the COLD WAR the CIA was slow to adjust to new challenges and its morale was undermined by the AMES CASE; after 9/11 it was much criticised for its unpreparedness and its inability to penetrate Islamic fundamentalist groups worldwide. It showed professionalism in its leadership of the IRAQ SURVEY GROUP after the removal of SADDAM HUSSEIN in 2003, but was taxed for failing to discover prior to the conflict that Saddam was not on the point of deploying WEAPONS OF MASS DESTRUCTION, as President BUSH asserted. The CIA's internal counter-intelligence activities are limited, and supposedly operate in conjunction with the FBI; since alleged abuses during WATERGATE they have to be sanctioned by the ATTORNEY-GENERAL, and co-ordination has also now been imposed by the Department of HOMELAND SECURITY.

> No American who works for the CIA is a spy. A spy is a foreign agent who commits treason.
>
> JIM KEEHNER, CIA psychologist, *New Times*, 1976

Cicciolina. La Cicciolina (Ital. the little plump one) Ilona Staller (1955–), the Hungarian-born performer in sex shows and pornographic films who was elected to the Italian parliament in 1987 for the small RADICAL Party on the slogan 'Less NUCLEAR energy, more sexual energy'. She handed the banner on to others after marrying – briefly – the US artist Jeff Koons.

circular firing squad The vivid description of Britain's CONSERVATIVE PARTY during the premiership of John MAJOR, bestowed on it by Jeffrey (Lord) Archer, one of Major's strongest supporters, before his fall from grace. Archer was referring in particular to the bitter infighting over Europe which contributed to the Tories' rout in the 1997 general election. The term was not original, having been used by Rep. Morris Udall of the US DEMOCRATIC PARTY two decades before. *See also* BASTARDS.

CITES The Convention on International Trade in Endangered Species, the agreement under which most countries have banned the trade in elephant ivory, rhinoceros horn and rare animals or products made from them. The Convention was signed at Bern, Switzerland, in November 1976, and the signatories meet every two years to review progress.

Citizen (Fr. *Citoyen*) The form of address decreed to be used by every Frenchman and woman to each other during the FRENCH REVOLUTION. Extreme anti-clerics still use it toward priests as an insult.

Citizen Access A US programme, launched in 1994, which enables individual citizens to send messages to the President by e-mail. Tony BLAIR only went fully on-line in 2003.

Citizen's Charter The initiative pioneered by John MAJOR as his government's BIG IDEA, under which every branch of the public service had to set standards for its dealings with members of the public and compensate them if targets were not met. Unveiled in March 1991 and pursued after the 1992 election, it involved hospitals undertaking to see patients within a certain time of their arriving, officials dealing with the public wearing name tags, compensation for rail passengers whose trains were very late, and government departments replying to letters within a set period. Labour denounced it as a gimmick and no substitute for higher spending on those services, but Major insisted the public was fed up with poor service and deserved better. Labour kept the essentials of the Charter after coming to power in 1997, imposing tougher targets of its own for public service DELIVERY.

second class citizen A member of an ethnic, economic or other group placed at a disadvantage by discriminatory treatment from the State. The phrase reflects the fundamental assumption that all the citizens of any country must have equal rights. Wendell Willkie, in *An American Program* (1944) wrote: 'The CONSTITUTION does not provide for first and second class citizens,' and Dwight D. EISENHOWER, desegregating the US armed forces, declared: 'There must be no second class citizens in this country.'

the humblest citizen of all the land, when clad in the armour of a righteous cause, is stronger than all the hosts of error One of the grandest phrases of

William Jennings Bryan (*see* BOY ORATOR; PRAIRIE AVENGER) during his three POPULIST campaigns for the US Presidency.

the most important office, that of private citizen The dictum of US SUPREME COURT Justice Louis Brandeis (1856–1941) that confirmed the fundamental rights of the individual over the State or any other overweening organisation.

city on the hill One of the most popular images of a better society conjured up by US Presidential candidates. John F. KENNEDY and Walter Mondale (*see* NORWEGIAN WOOD) both used it; Ronald REAGAN first harnessed it in 1976, and relied heavily on it in his 1984 campaign. Mario Cuomo, Democratic Governor of New York, dismissed Reagan's right to talk of a 'shining city on a hill', saying that the President was ignoring the 'despair in the slums' and that America under his leadership was in reality 'a tale of two cities'. The phrase has a long pedigree, having been first used in 1630 by John Winthrop, governor of the Massachusetts Bay Colony; in *A Modell of Christian Discourse*, Winthrop wrote:

> For we must consider that we shall be as a City upon a hill. The eyes of all people are upon us. Soe that if we shall deal falsely with our God in this work we have undertaken, and so cause him to withdraw his present help from us, we shall be made a story and a byword throughout the world.

Needless to say, few if any politicians have dwelt on the retributive part of Winthrop's message.

Civic Forum The Czech DISSIDENT movement that toppled the Communist regime in Czechoslovakia late in 1989; its Slovak counterpart was PUBLIC AGAINST VIOLENCE. A coalition of twelve groups united to form the Forum on 19 November, two days after street protests began; their spokesman was the playwright Vaclav Havel, who had been released from prison that May. They forced the resignation of prime minister Mikloš Jakeš on 24 November, while Alexander Dubček, exiled hero of the PRAGUE SPRING, was addressing a rally of 250,000 people in WENCESLAS SQUARE. The protests continued and on 9 December the hard-line president Gustav Husák finally resigned, with Havel nominated to succeed him and Dubček chairing the Federal Assembly; in elections the following May, Civic Forum and its allies won a convincing majority. Havel was subsequently elected President by popular vote, remaining President of the Czech Republic until 2003.

civil. civil defence The protection of civilians from the consequences of warfare, particularly NUCLEAR, biological and chemical. Civil defence was a political issue throughout the COLD WAR, with governments offering schemes of varying degrees of adequacy to enable at least some of the population to survive a nuclear holocaust, and anti-nuclear campaigners accusing them of fooling the public into imagining that there was any hope of survival. Communist China's precautions have been the most thorough, with entire underground cities excavated in case of a Soviet nuclear attack; the UK government for a long time considered a shallow trench covered by earth and a spare door quite adequate.

civil disobedience Deliberate flouting of the law to make a political point, or to secure a change in the law being broken. The term was first used by David Thoreau in 1849, and the practice was developed most enthusiastically by MAHATMA Gandhi, first in South Africa and later in India. Since WORLD WAR II it has been used by CIVIL RIGHTS protesters in America's Deep South, by generations of NUCLEAR disarmers in Britain (*see* COMMITTEE OF 100), in South Africa against APARTHEID, and in countless other circumstances by groups who believe they are fighting an injustice.

> It has been the teaching of the Church throughout the ages that when government degenerates into tyranny, laws cease to be binding on its subjects.
>
> Bishop TREVOR HUDDLESTON, South Africa, 1952

> I will not pretend to obey a Government that is organising a mass massacre of mankind.
>
> BERTRAND RUSSELL (1872–1970), speaking in Birmingham, 15 April 1961

civil liberties An alternative term for HUMAN RIGHTS, especially in relation to an individual's right to fair treatment by the police and the legal system. The **National Council for Civil Liberties** (now LIBERTY) in Britain and the ACLU in the United States have vigorously defended these rights, even for individuals who were felt by much of society not to deserve them.

Civil List The sum paid annually by the UK Treasury to the Sovereign to finance the performance of her official duties, and those undertaken by certain members of the ROYAL FAMILY. It has been the subject of sporadic political controversy, most recently in 1992 when it was disclosed that a past formula on inflation-proofing had increased it by far more than the cost of living. Such discontent is nothing new; in 1884 Henry Labouchère (*see* LABBY) wrote:

> Nothing has more conduced to shake that decent respect for the living symbol of the State, which goes by the name of Royalty, than the ever-recurring rattle of the money-box.

civil power The non-military apparatus of the state. The term has had a particular application in NORTHERN IRELAND, where the British Army on security duties has been said to be acting 'in support of the civil power', that power being personified by the RUC, or since 2002 the Police Service of Northern Ireland.

civil rights The term given in US politics for a century and a half to the securing for black Americans of the fundamental rights guaranteed to all under the CONSTITUTION, in the face of at times violent opposition from RACISTS and SEGREGATIONISTS. (It has also been used by minorities elsewhere in campaigns to end discrimination against them, notably by Catholics in NORTHERN IRELAND in the late 1960s.) The first **Civil Rights Act**, conferring citizenship and equal rights on black Americans, was passed in 1866, but proved a dead letter after the end of RECONSTRUCTION. For decades the battle for civil rights was fought through the courts by the NAACP and other groups, and in CONGRESS where segregationist Southern Senators (*see* DIXIECRATS) FILIBUSTERED hour after hour against interventionist FEDERAL legislation. The mass Civil Rights movement dates from the 1950s, when blacks and white liberals combined under the leadership of Dr Martin Luther KING and others to demand VOTING RIGHTS, EQUAL OPPORTUNITIES and an end to segregation in housing, education and other facilities. In 1964 the SENATE finally lost patience with obstructionist tactics and ended a filibuster to hand President JOHNSON a radical if over-due Civil Rights Act. Signed on 2 July, it integrated public facilities such as restaurants and hotels, ended job discrimination on grounds of race, sex and religion, and barred racial discrimination in any federally assisted undertaking.

Civil Service In Britain, America and other English-speaking countries, the BUREAUCRACY that actually runs the country, carrying out what it understands to be the decisions of government. Civil servants range from the MANDARINS of WHITEHALL and the career diplomats who staff the STATE DEPARTMENT to thousands of clerks in social security offices. Although Adlai STEVENSON was once moved to remark that 'your public servants serve you right' and Ronald REAGAN had plenty to say about bureaucracy, the greater influence of civil servants in WHITEHALL through the near-absence of POLITICAL APPOINTEES at the highest level has made Britain's Civil Service a particular subject of controversy. Lord Vansittart once remarked that 'the soul of the service is the loyalty with which we execute ordained error', but few politicians are ready to take the blame. Lord Samuel described the Civil Service as 'a difficulty for every solution', R.A. (RAB) Butler as 'a bit like a Rolls-Royce – you know it's the best machine in the world, but you're not quite sure what to do with it', and Shirley Williams (*see* GANG OF FOUR) as 'a beautifully designed and effective braking mechanism'.

> You don't need brains to be Minister of Transport because the civil servants have them.
> ERNEST MARPLES (1907–78)

> A faceless mortal riding like a flea on the back of the dog, Legislation. ANON

> Men who write minutes, make professional assessments, who are never attacked face to face, who dwell in the Sargasso Sea of the civil service and who love the seaweed that conceals them.
> CASSANDRA (William Connor)

civil war The ultimate trauma for a nation: a war between two factions, each intent on governing and each believing in the justice of its cause. Whoever wins, the bloodshed and bitterness leave scars that take generations to heal. England experienced a civil war from 1642 to 1649 when Parliament rose up against the autocratic King Charles I and, after its victory, tried and executed him; Russia after the BOLSHEVIK revolution of 1917 was convulsed by a civil war between REDS and WHITES, which the Reds eventually won; Ireland after PARTITION was riven by a bloody struggle between supporters of the newly-created IRISH FREE STATE and those who would only accept the independence of all 32 COUNTIES. But the most traumatic of all convulsed America from 1861 to 1965.

America's Civil War stemmed from the desire of the CONFEDERATE states to SECEDE from the UNION. The northern position, as the Civil War approached, was put by Rep. David Wilmot of Pennsylvania, who said in 1846:

> I am jealous of the power of the South. The South holds no prerogative under the CONSTITUTION which entitles her to wield forever the sceptre of power in this Republic, to fix by her own arbitrary edict the principles and policy of this government and to build up and tear down at pleasure.

During the conflict Rep. Benjamin Harris of Maryland was censured by CONGRESS for telling supporters of the Union: 'The South asked you to let them live in peace. But no; you said you would bring them into subjection. I hope that you will never subjugate the South.' The war inflicted prodigious casualties on both sides: from FORT SUMTER to APPOMATTOX, 359,000 Union soldiers and 258,000 Confederates died (*see* BLUE AND THE GRAY), and the economy of the South was destroyed. In the process Abraham LINCOLN had EMANCIPATED the slaves of the South, whose continued servitude was one of the causes of the war. Slavery did not return, but after the false dawn of RECONSTRUCTION a new form of repression was inflicted on black Southerners, which did not lift significantly until the mid-20th century.

> In your hands, my dissatisfied fellow-countrymen, and not in mine, is the momentous issue of civil war . . . you can have no conflict without being yourselves the aggressors.
>
> LINCOLN's first INAUGURAL ADDRESS, 4 March 1861

> My paramount object in this struggle is to save the Union, and is not either to save or destroy slavery.
>
> LINCOLN, August 1862

> My opinion is that the Northern states will somehow manage to muddle through.
>
> JOHN BRIGHT (1811–89)

> The Republic needed to be passed through chastening, purifying fires of adversity and suffering; so these came and did their work and the verdure of a new national life springs greenly, luxuriantly from their ashes.
>
> HORACE GREELEY, *Greeley on Lincoln*, 1893

Spanish Civil War *See* SPANISH.

civis Romanus sum (Lat. I am a Roman citizen) Echoing St Paul's appeal to Rome as a citizen of its empire when arrested on his missionary travels, the doctrine used by PALMERSTON to justify Britain's use of naval force against Greece in the case of Don PACIFICO in the HOUSE OF COMMONS on 25 June 1850. He fought off Parliamentary censure by declaring:

> As the Roman, in days of old, held himself free from indignity when he could say: '*civis Romanus sum*', so also a British subject, in whatever land he may be, shall feel confident that the watchful eye and strong arm of England will protect him against injustice and wrong.

> Historically it is an anachronism and a blunder, legally it is an injustice and a wrong, politically it is a folly and a crime.
>
> Sir WILLIAM HARCOURT, 1868

Claim of Right The declaration issued by a wide range of high-profile and non-Conservative Scots in July 1988 which paved the way for the SCOTTISH CONSTITUTIONAL CONVENTION and, ultimately, for DEVOLUTION and a re-established SCOTTISH PARLIAMENT. The Claim countered the attitude of Margaret THATCHER toward the Scots by declaring:

> There is a profound hypocrisy in saying that the Scots should stand on their own two feet while simultaneously denying them management of their own political affairs . . . Scots can stand on their own feet only by refusing to accept the constitution which denies them the power to do so.

claptrap Vacuous rubbish delivered as a political speech. The word dates from the early 19th century, originally describing language intended to win applause (clap-trap).

Claremont picnic The confrontation between Bill CLINTON and NEWT Gingrich at an old folk's picnic on 11 June 1995, at the height of the Republican Congress' campaign to hog-tie the Democratic presidency, arising from a coincidence in scheduling which had both men campaigning in the same New Hampshire neighbourhood. Despite the high political temperature, the event developed into a side-by-side Q&A session.

Clarion, The The newspaper founded by the English Socialist Robert Blatchford, and the Clarion fellowship that stemmed from it, which in the first half of the 20th-century sought to broaden the minds of the people and inspire them to intelligent left-wing ideals. The movement brought many into the LABOUR PARTY through a range of activities from political discussion to rambling, cycling and even a youth hostel; its greatest influence was either side of WORLD WAR I, but the cycling club continues to this day.

Clark diaries The candid journals of the aristocratic, polymathic and lustful Conservative Minister and *bon vivant* Alan Clark (1928–99), which described a number of colleagues in highly unflattering terms. The first volume of Clark's diaries, published in 1994, is a literary masterpiece (a second appeared posthumously). It gives a memorable account of the fall of Margaret THATCHER and Clark's efforts to prevent it, and vivid insights into the workings of WHITEHALL and Clark's own candid political and sexual thoughts. Most headlines were provoked by the revelation that Clark had been having simultaneous extra-marital affairs with Valerie Harkess, the wife of a South African judge, and two of her daughters; he called them **'the coven'**. The Harkess family hit back in the media, leading Clark's wife Jane to observe:

> Quite frankly, if you bed people I call 'below stairs', they go to the papers, don't they?

> The Alan Clark diaries have ruined the market for conventional political memoirs. Who, after peering into the bloody innards of Whitehall through the eyes of Clark, awaits with impatience the recollections of Sir Geoffrey Howe?
>
> MICHAEL DAVIE, *Spectator*

Clark memorandum The declaration by the HOOVER administration in 1930 that America had given up the right to intervene in the internal affairs of Latin American countries through the 'exercise of an international police power'. This clarification of the MONROE DOCTRINE, welcomed in the nations concerned, had been drafted two years earlier by Under-Secretary of State J. Reuben Clark. In 1931 SECRETARY OF STATE Henry Stimson went one step further and renounced President WILSON's policy that new Latin American governments would only be RECOGNISED if they met certain moral criteria.

Clarke-Redwood pact The agreement struck on 18 June 1997 between Kenneth Clarke, the moderate and most experienced candidate for the CONSERVATIVE PARTY leadership, and the right-wing ideologue John Redwood, under which in the event of Clarke defeating William HAGUE, Redwood would serve as his deputy. The deal discredited both men and contributed directly to Hague's victory; one Tory backbencher compared it to the NAZI-SOVIET PACT.

class The basis of MARXIST and COMMUNIST political theory and activity, and in a different sense a preoccupation of most politicians. Social class has long been the basis of politics, as one has usually been dominant and one or more have generally been excluded from power. In an ideal democracy, class would become irrelevant, building on Lord Acton's dictum: 'The danger is not that a particular class is unfit to govern. Every class is unfit to govern.' Traditionally society is said to be divided into haves and have-nots, with the middle class (to which 92% of Americans say they belong) and other more subtle subdivisions conveniently ignored. Yet it was essentially correct for Mirabeau to write:

> Society is composed of two great classes: they who have more dinner than appetite, and they who have more appetite than dinner.

MARX and Engels were not the first political theorists to develop the idea of class, but they were the first to put it at the centre of their ideology. Marx wrote in 1852:

> What I did that was new was to demonstrate: (1) that the existence of classes is merely linked to particular phases in the development of production; (2) that class struggle necessarily leads to the dictatorship of the PROLETARIAT; (3) that this dictatorship itself constitutes the transition to the abolition of all classes and to a classless society.

To some, the existence of social differences is an abomination in itself. William Morris wrote in 1883 that 'the most grinding poverty is a trifling evil compared with the inequality of classes'.

class consciousness The MARXIST notion that a true revolutionary must be aware of the potential of his or her class to change the system, and feel SOLIDARITY with its other members, which will itself inspire action.

class struggle Another basis of Marxism and the movements that sprang from it: the notion that the classes are historically pitted against each other and that in the end the PROLETARIAT shall and must triumph. LENIN wrote that 'the proletariat will inevitably have to wage a class struggle for Socialism against even the most democratic and republican BOURGEOISIE and petty bourgeoisie'. When the BOLSHEVIKS eventually took power in Russia, deputy Prime Minister Vyshinsky, accused of maintaining the Tsarist naval policy of looking for warm-water ports, told his critics:

> The class struggle does not alter geography.

class war (1) Another term for class struggle, with a sharper edge. Stanley BALDWIN once said: 'If there are those who want to fight the class war, we will beat them by the hardness of our heads and the largeness of our hearts.' (2) **Class War** A militant UK ANARCHIST group, centred on Hackney in north-central London, which during the 1980s disrupted upper-crust events like the Henley regatta, and in 1994 staged violent protests against the Conservatives' Criminal Justice Bill which tightened controls on raves and unauthorised demonstrations, during which press photographers were targeted. Class War, and its supporters, were active in a series of violent anti-capitalist MAY DAY demonstrations in the City of London and elsewhere in the capital in subsequent years.

The New Class The book written in 1953 by the Yugoslav Communist Milovan Djilas (1911–95) which argued that Soviet-style COMMUNISM, instead of producing a classless society, had in fact produced a new class system every bit as objectionable as the one it replaced. From a society dominated by ARISTOCRATS and the rich, Communism had moved to one where party officials, the heads of State industries and senior BUREAUCRATS enjoyed a superior standard of living and special privileges, which they defended by using the SECRET POLICE against anyone they perceived as a threat. Djilas, a former minister in TITO's government, was explaining where Marxism had gone wrong, not breaking with it, but his writing earned him several terms in prison.

ruling class A term used by Marxists and many others for the clique of the wealthy and well-born that believes it is naturally entitled to wield authority. Marx and Engels wrote in the COMMUNIST MANIFESTO that 'the ruling ideas of each age have ever been the ideas of its ruling class'. Their English RADICAL contemporary John Bright declared: 'We must oust the dominant class or they will destroy us', and Malcolm Muggeridge, around the time of the PROFUMO AFFAIR, wrote:

> There is nothing on earth so edifying or more ludicrous than the spectacle of the ruling class on the run.

classless society One of the stated aims of COMMUNISM, not necessarily achieved as Djilas (*see above*) pointed out, and of all EGALITARIANS. America is supposed to be a classless society, but is not (*see* ARISTOCRACY, MIDDLE CLASS); in Britain LABOUR leaders, especially Harold WILSON, have made the classless society their aim and John MAJOR, on becoming Prime Minister, did the same, though he soon qualified his initial statement:

> When I have talked of a classless society or an opportunity society, I mean that it just does not matter whether you come from a tiny, scruffy back-to-back in a pretty poor housing area or from one of the best mansions in one of the best parts of town.

classified documents Sensitive papers whose circulation is limited and whose contents it is often an offence to divulge. Depending on how confidential they are, they will be marked in ascending order of sensitivity RESTRICTED, CONFIDENTIAL, Secret, TOP SECRET or EYES ONLY. *See also* OFFICIAL SECRETS ACT.

classified results A UK media term for a complete list of ELECTION results DECLARED by a particular time, given in alphabetical order.

clause A portion of a piece of legislation which deals with a particular aspect of the subject, and covers a specific point or proposal. At WESTMINSTER a BILL is divided into Clauses, and an ACT, once passed, into Sections.

Clause IV The part of the LABOUR PARTY Constitution embracing public ownership as its basic aim, which Tony BLAIR in 1995 persuaded a special conference to replace with a 'statement of aims and values' committing Labour to 'a community in which power, wealth and opportunity are in the hands of the MANY, NOT THE FEW'. Modernisers saw Clause Four, drafted by Sidney Webb in 1918 and revised in 1926, as an ALBATROSS committing the party to wholesale NATIONALISATION, but for the left it was the touchstone of Labour's SOCIALISM. Hugh GAITSKELL's move to scrap it after Labour's defeat in 1959 was thwarted, and no leader risked a confrontation over it until Blair made his sudden move at Labour's 1994 conference. Harold WILSON, asked about Clause Four, said: 'I don't believe God created the world in seven days, but I have no plans to rewrite the Book of Genesis.' But Blair told critics Labout could not win power as a 'preservation society'. Part of the clause's appeal lay in its less-than-specific wording:

> To secure for the workers by hand or by brain the full fruits of their industry and the most equitable distribution thereof that may be possible upon the basis of the common ownership of the means of production, distribution and exchange . . .

Intriguingly, the wording is close to Abraham LINCOLN's in a discussion on the tariff in 1847:

> To [secure] for each labourer the whole product of his labor, or as nearly as possible, is the most worthy object of any good government.

Clause V meeting The meeting of the LABOUR PARTY's (SHADOW) CABINET and National Executive (NEC) which historically took place on the eve of a UK general election campaign to determine 'which items from the party programme shall be included in the manifesto'. At times of strife in the party it was a last opportunity for one faction or the other to grab the initiative. Under the reforms pushed through by Neil KINNOCK and Tony BLAIR its importance has waned.

Clause 28 *See* SECTION 28.

commerce clause The portion of Article 1, section 8 of the US CONSTITUTION that sets limits on the right of the Federal government to regulate interstate trade. Of vital commercial importance, it was tested in the Sick CHICKEN CASE of 1953. Clause 3 states that:

> The Congress shall have power . . . to regulate commerce with foreign nations; and among the several states; and with the Indian tribes.

sweeping clause Also known as the NECESSARY AND PROPER CLAUSE. Clause 18 of the same article of the CONSTITUTION, which states:

> The Congress shall have power . . . to make all laws which shall be necessary and proper for carrying into execution the foregoing powers, and all other powers vested in this Constitution in the Government of the United States, or in any department or office thereof.

Clay Cross councillors The symbol of resistance to the HEATH Government's 1972 Housing Finance Act, which prevented councils from providing subsidised housing at knockdown rents, and a long-running cause for grievance with their own leadership among Labour left-wingers. Labour councillors agreed on a policy of NON-IMPLEMENTATION, but most voted reluctantly to conform. The left-wing council of the Derbyshire mining village of Clay Cross was left facing the music; members who voted not to implement the Act were SURCHARGED by the DISTRICT AUDITOR and barred from office. A campaign by the local MP Dennis Skinner (*see* BEAST OF BOLSOVER) on behalf of the councillors, who included his brother and cousins, failed to earn them a complete remission when Labour returned to power in 1974.

Clayton Antitrust Act The Act of 1914 by which Woodrow WILSON's administration moved against big business, outlawing MONOPOLY practices and establishing a Federal Trade Commission to prevent them recurring. It outlawed anti-competitive pricing in interstate trade, large purchases by corporations of each other's stock, and interlocking directorates in major interstate trading concerns; it also curbed the use of injunctions in labour disputes and permitted peaceful PICKETING.

clean your teeth in the dark The phrase that dogged the career of Patrick (later Lord) Jenkin (1926–) after he exhorted the public to do just that during the THREE-DAY WEEK of early 1974. Jenkin, as newly-appointed Minister for Energy, was exhorting the public to save electricity as a MINERS' STRIKE reduced power supplies to a minimum. He went on to serve under Margaret THATCHER as Secretary for, in turn, Social Services, Industry and the Environment, but his *bon mot* was never entirely forgotten.

clear blue water *See* BLUE.

Clemenceau, Georges (1841–1929), the French STATESMAN and campaigning journalist who as Prime Minister negotiated the 1919 VERSAILLES TREATY imposing draconian and counterproductive peace terms on Germany. A fighter determined to achieve his objectives (his nickname was The TIGER), he was an early campaigner over the DREYFUS CASE, and gained a reputation for destructive use of his newspaper, *La Justice*, to bring down one ministry after another. Prime Minister from 1906 to 1909, he was recalled by President Poincaré as the carnage of WORLD WAR I reached its height, and led France to victory. Clemenceau pursued that aim single-mindedly, telling the NATIONAL ASSEMBLY in March 1918:

> My home policy? I wage war. My foreign policy? I wage war. Always, everywhere, I wage war.

He could be scathing about his generals' performance, remarking of Marshal Joffre: 'The only time he ever put up a fight in his life was when we asked him for his resignation.' He also told CHURCHILL: 'I have no political system and I have abandoned all political principles. I am a man dealing with events as they come in the light of my experience.' Clemenceau emerged from the war a popular hero, but in 1920 DEPUTIES passed over him for the Presidency, and he left politics.

> He had only one illusion: France; and only one disillusion: mankind.
>
> JOHN MAYNARD KEYNES

> Time and time again Monet, who was going blind, wrote that he could do no more. Whereupon Clemenceau would leave his Cabinet room and drive to Monet's studio and bid him take up his brush. Lord CLARK (1903–83)

clenched fist The salute, given with arm raised and where possible by every member of a large crowd, that has long been a feature of COMMUNIST and militant left-wing movements, especially in Continental Europe and Latin America. It is a sign of SOLIDARITY with workers and revolutionaries throughout the world.

clerk. Clerk of the House The officer in charge of recording the transactions of the

HOUSE OF COMMONS at WESTMINSTER and the HOUSE OF REPRESENTATIVES in Washington. In the House of Lords the responsibility rests with the **Clerk of the Parliaments**, and in the US Senate with the **Secretary of the Senate**.

committee clerk The clerk who attends meetings of the committees of an elected body, preparing the AGENDA, taking MINUTES and giving advice on procedure when asked.

Cleveland, Grover (1837–1908). The Democratic lawyer who within four years was elected Mayor of Buffalo, then governor of New York and overcame the Republicans' nickname of the BEAST OF BUFFALO to be elected 22nd President of the United States in 1884; he was also the 24th, coming back in 1892 to oust Benjamin Harrison and serve until 1897. Corpulent and with a walrus moustache, Cleveland exuded firmness, Samuel Tilden stating: 'He has so much backbone that it sticks out in front.' But there was also a skeleton in his cupboard; though he arrived in Washington a bachelor, he had fathered an illegitimate child in Buffalo (*see* MA, MA, WHERE'S MY PA?). In his first term, he married the attractive 21-year-old ward of his former law partner; rumours that he beat her reinforced the 'beast' image. Narrowly elected over James G. Blaine, Cleveland in his first term launched drives to depoliticise the CIVIL SERVICE and end favourable treatment for special interests. Though he was welcomed by the great industrial trusts, the railroad magnate and fraudster Jay Gould telling him: 'I feel that the vast business interests of this country will be safe in your hands', his administration saw the creation of the initially toothless Interstate Commerce Commission. He also VETOED a Bill to distribute $10,000 worth of grain to drought-stricken Texas farmers, declaring:

> Federal aid in such cases encourages the expectation of paternal care on the part of the Government and weakens the sturdiness of our national acharacter.

He ran for re-election in 1888 purely on his record, telling critics: 'What is the use of being elected or re-elected unless you stand for something?' But although Cleveland won the popular vote, Harrison carried the ELECTORAL COLLEGE. Four years later he got his revenge, but his second term was marred by the DEPRESSION of 1893. At its height he had much of his cancerous upper jaw replaced by one of vulcanised rubber, the operation being performed at sea to avoid heightening the economic panic. Cleveland was an industrious President, the WHITE HOUSE usher Ike Hoover saying: 'It was work, work, work all the time.' He also had simple tastes, once confiding:

> I must go to dinner, but I wish it was to eat a pickled herring, a Swiss cheese and a chop at Louis' instead of the French stuff I shall find.

> His huge carcass seemed to be made of iron. There was no give in him, no bounce, no softness. He sailed through American history like a steel ship loaded with monoliths of granite.
>
> H.L. MENCKEN

cliché A hackneyed phrase which nevertheless has a readily-identified meaning; political speakers are much scorned by their peers for using them, especially when they are an alternative to any statement of substance. The classic example of a cliché-ridden speech was reputedly delivered in the Irish Parliament by Sir Boyle Roche (1743–1807); it included the sentence:

> Mr Speaker, I smell a rat; I see him forming in the air and darkening the sky; but I'll nip him in the bud.

Anthony EDEN came in for particular criticism; CHURCHILL is supposed to have once said of his speeches: 'They consist entirely of clichés – clichés old and new – everything from "God is Love" to "Please adjust your dress before leaving"'. Ernest BEVIN was even blunter, describing them as 'clitch, clitch, clitch'. However Eden had some support from Adlai STEVENSON, who voiced the generality that

> One man's cliché can be another man's CONVICTION.

forever poised between a cliché and an indiscretion The silky phrase used by Harold MACMILLAN to describe the eternal dilemma of Britain's FOREIGN SECRETARY. In the COMMONS on 27 July 1953, Macmillan said:

> Nothing he can say can do very much good, and almost anything he may say may do a great deal of harm. Anything he says that is not obvious is dangerous; whatever is not trite is risky. He is forever poised between a cliché and an indiscretion.

clincest The closeness, and extent of intermarriage, between the WASHINGTON press and staff of the CLINTON White House, perceived by right-wing commentators as a reason for the media's failure to probe exhaustively WHITEWATER, ZIPPERGATE and other scandals associated with the Clinton presidency.

Clinton, William Jefferson (1946 –) 42nd President of the United States (Democrat, 1993–2001). The CHARISMATIC former Rhodes scholar and governor of Arkansas who presided over a period of domestic prosperity, secured major foreign policy achievements and remained, out of office, the pre-eminent political figure of his time, but who sullied his own reputation, and the Presidency, by his inability to control his sexual urges which culminated in ZIPPERGATE and his near-successful IMPEACHMENT. Born into an unprivileged family as William Jefferson BLYTHE (he took the surname of his stepfather Roger Clinton) and no ultra-liberal – he had no compunction about imposing the death penalty – Clinton set his sights on the Presidency when still at high school, when he contrived to get his picture taken with John F. KENNEDY at the WHITE HOUSE. At Georgetown University, at Oxford, where he was involved in protests against the VIETNAM WAR and experimented with marijuana (memorably saying later that he 'did not inhale'), at Yale Law School and beyond he single-mindedly put together an index of contacts for future use. As a young lawyer he teamed up with Hillary Rodham, a mid-westerner as academically bright as himself and even more focused, and despite his philandering (*see* BIMBO ERUPTIONS) they built a strong political partnership. In Arkansas he was in turn a law professor, state attorney-general and a practising attorney before being elected governor in 1979. He overcame the trauma of being defeated two years later to return in 1983, earning the nickname the COMEBACK KID and serving until his NOMINATION for the Presidency in 1992.

Clinton was almost sunk before the NEW HAMPSHIRE PRIMARY when Gennifer FLOWERS, a blonde club singer, claimed they had had an eleven-year affair; the charge kept resurfacing but Clinton's response – near-denials coupled with admissions of past 'difficulties' in his marriage – kept him afloat. With all aspects of his past under scrutiny, Mary Matalin, CAMPAIGN director for the Republican incumbent George BUSH – who branded Clinton SLICK WILLIE – observed:

> We have never said to the press that Clinton is a philandering, pot-smoking draft dodger.

Clinton capitalised on his obvious acumen, his Southern charm (*see* BUBBA) and Bush's perceived neglect of the economy. Thanks in part to the intervention of Ross PEROT who polled heavily, Clinton and his running-mate Sen. Al GORE won a clear margin over Bush and Dan QUAYLE in the ELECTORAL COLLEGE and the Democrats hailed their first President since Jimmy CARTER. In office, Clinton's abilities were at once called in question. A move to give homosexuals full rights in the military caused much resentment, and it took months to fill key posts (*see* BAIRD NOMINATION). Clinton had Congressional successes with NAFTA and a crime package combining the BRADY BILL with tough sentencing (*see* THREE STRIKES AND YOU'RE OUT). He presided over a historic handshake between Israeli Prime Minister Yitzhak Rabin and the PLO leader Yasser Arafat as the PEACE PROCESS inched forwards, and sent in US troops to restore democracy in Haiti.

At home, things were stickier. America underwent the trauma of the BRANCH DRAVIDIAN MASSACRE and the OKLAHOMA CITY BOMBING. The complex health reforms he had chosen his wife to spearhead foundered in Congress, and the Clintons' past financial dealings came under scrutiny in the WHITEWATER affair, with key White House aide Vince FOSTER, a close personal friend, driven to suicide and other associates resigning as Congress probed deeper; the TRAVELGATE episode did not help, and neither did the Paula JONES case from his days in Arkansas which came back to haunt him.

Pressure on Clinton increased when the Republicans captured both Houses of Congress in 1994 with the CONTRACT WITH AMERICA; Clinton at first treated most of the package as in tune with his populist agenda, but when the Republicans under Rep. NEWT Gingrich tightened the screws with the 1995 Christmas BUDGET SHUTDOWN, Clinton went onto the offensive and in 1996 comfortably won a second term against the veteran Republican Bob Dole.

Clinton's second term was marked until its closing months by continuing economic strength and by further foreign policy successes, notably the DAYTON AGREEMENT which ended the war in Bosnia, a conflict prolonged by Clinton's hesitation to commit US military might – and therefore NATO – against the Serbs. Other notable features included the eviction of Serb forces from KOSOVO to end ETHNIC CLEANSING of the Albanian majority, the diplomacy of former senator George Mitchell which contributed to the GOOD FRIDAY AGREEMENT in NORTHERN IRELAND and the WYE PLANTATION talks which brought a 'LAND FOR PEACE' agreement that appeared to herald lasting peace in the Middle East. The first stirrings of AL QAEDA were logged by the administration, CRUISE MISSILE attacks were launched in August 1998 aimed at Osama BIN LADEN in Afghanistan and on an alleged germ warfare plant in the Sudan in response to the NAIROBI EMBASSY BOMBING, but the former missed its mark and the latter target turned out to be an innocuous pharmaceutical factory. On the world stage, with some spillover into the domestic politics of both countries, he also developed a strong relationship with Tony BLAIR, which helped Blair return Labour to power in Britain in 1997 (*see* CLINTONISE) but also gave Clinton much-needed support in times of domestic difficulty.

Clinton needed allies, for over fully two years his presidency was dogged by Zippergate, as he did his best to avoid answering the charge that he had had a sexual relationship, even in an ante-room to the OVAL OFFICE, with Monica LEWINSKY, whose semen-stained BLUE DRESS became an electoral totem for the Republicans. Clinton's reluctance to give straight answers (*see* IS) culminated in his impeachment and near-conviction, and although he survived the range of allegations of sexual misconduct against him detracted from what was, politically, a highly successful presidency. Although Clinton had a strong electoral base, notably among the SOCCER MOMS, the damage done by the scandals was enough to prevent Gore winning the presidency in 2000 on his coat-tails, going down instead to the narrowest of defeats when the SUPREME COURT declared George W. BUSH winner of the disputed contest in Florida. The closing stages of Clinton's presidency were marked by the failure of a final bid to secure Palestinian agreement to plans to give them a degree of statehood that Israel could accept, and by controversy over several PARDONS granted by the President to influential but convicted Democrats as he left office. Out of the White House, Clinton, barred from returning to the practice of law in Arkansas, remained highly popular among Democrats and travelled the world as a public speaker as his wife sought, and won, a seat in the Senate. He was prevented from campaigning fully for John KERRY in 2004 by a quadruple heart bypass operation that September, brought on by his gargantuan consumption of fast food.

> Look, we tried this once before, combining the Democratic governor of a very small Southern state with a very liberal vice president and a Democratic congress. America doesn't need CARTER II.
>
> GEORGE BUSH, acceptance speech to the Republican Convention, 20 August 1992

> There was always the sneaking suspicion that Clinton was a bit bored, and that he just needed the thrill of a crisis. JOE KLEIN

> A man of gargantuan appetites and enormous drive, and not only in relation to women.
>
> DAVID BROCK, *American Spectator*

> In my country, first we go to jail and *then* we become President.
>
> NELSON MANDELA to Clinton, 1994

Clinton lite The name, with its resonance from the world of beer, given on CAPITOL Hill to the rival scheme to Bill Clinton's far-reaching health care plan, which was drawn up in 1994 by Rep. Jim Cooper, a Tennessee Democrat, and co-sponsored by Sen. John Breaux of Louisiana. It offered 'universal access' to health care but no caps on insurance premiums or 'employer mandate' as in the Clinton plan. Hillary Clinton, given a key role in shaping health care policy by her husband, attacked it instead of working to modify it, and in the event neither scheme cleared CONGRESS.

Clintonisation The term used by UK LABOUR politicians to cover the adoption by the party in the years prior to the 1997 election of attitudes and policies which were believed to have helped Bill Clinton into the WHITE HOUSE, and were felt likely to do the same for Tony BLAIR. The process of Clintonisation stopped short of Labour embracing the reintroduction of capital punishment.

Cliveden set The clique of APPEASEMENT-minded politicians and journalists who gathered for weekend parties in the late 1930s at Cliveden, the country home of Lord and Lady Astor near Maidenhead, Berkshire. The name first appeared in Claud Cockburn's iconoclastic left-wing journal *The Week*, but the legend may have exaggerated the proven softness toward HITLER among some upper-class right-wingers. A second Cliveden set with rather different priorities emerged in the early 1960s, giving rise to the PROFUMO AFFAIR; it was at Cliveden that John Profumo first met Christine Keeler.

closed. closed rule A resolution by the US HOUSE OF REPRESENTATIVES that it will give immediate consideration to a reported BILL, and will limit or prevent floor AMENDMENTS.

closed shop In industrial relations, the situation in which all employees of a particular company or plant are required to be members of a trade union. Trade unionists argue that the closed shop assists COLLECTIVE BARGAINING and avoids a situation where non-union members can gain preferential treatment and weaken the union's effectiveness. Management sees the closed shop as giving the unions a stranglehold, and the practice was outlawed in Britain by the THATCHER government in the early 1980s (*see* STEP BY STEP).

closure The procedure introduced by Britain's HOUSE OF COMMONS in 1881 to end disruption by PARNELLITE members pressing for Irish HOME RULE. James, later Lord, Bryce wrote:

> It marked the end of the old, dignified, constitutionally regular and gentlemanly House of Commons.

To obtain the closure, the SPONSOR of a BILL (usually the Government) must be able to find 100 members to vote for it; if carried, the proposal under debate is immediately put to the vote. Should the closure on a PRIVATE MEMBER'S BILL fail, it is said to have been TALKED OUT.

kangaroo closure A procedure in the US CONGRESS to enable a whole section of a BILL to be voted on without debate.

cloture The procedure introduced by the US SENATE in 1919 to end the chaos caused by unlimited FILIBUSTERS. The immediate cause was the delaying tactics of a group of Senators known as the 'wilful eleven' who had blocked essential business on the eve of America's entry into WORLD WAR I. Under pressure from Sen. Thomas Walsh of Montana, a provision (Rule 22) was adopted for any sixteen Senators to petition for an end to debate on any 'pending measure'; two days later it would be put to the vote. If passed by a two-thirds majority (later three-fifths), the cloture would take effect and each Senator could then speak for no more than an hour. Cloture was successfully moved on very few occasions – and never between 1927 and 1962 as the rule was whittled away, nor on any CIVIL RIGHTS measure until the landmark Bill of 1964 when Senators' patience with obstruction by Southern conservatives finally ran out. Since then, aided by a liberalisation of the rules in 1975, cloture has frequently been achieved. A further delaying tactic, the post-cloture filibuster, was outlawed in 1979.

cloud cuckoo land The ultimate term of scorn for the fantasy world in which some politicians accuse others of living. Originally the name given by Aristophanes in *The Birds* to a city in the sky built by feathered creatures, it was much used in various contexts by HITLER, using the German *Wolkenkuckucksheim.* More recently, Margaret THATCHER harnessed it to describe closer European union.

CLP Constituency Labour Party. The basic unit of organisation in Britain's LABOUR PARTY. It is made up of WARDS and branches, and sends delegates to the regional party and Labour's annual conference. Its governing bodies are the GMC (General Management Committee) and the smaller executive committee (EC).

Club Med A perjorative term, coined by Northern European politicians, for those member states of the EUROPEAN UNION with a Mediterranean seaboard. Taken from the eponymous chain of exotic holiday resorts, the name reflects those countries' perceived love for and dependence on EU financial support to make their life easier.

CND Campaign for Nuclear Disarmament. The movement that mobilised mass opposition to Britain's independent DETERRENT, and nuclear weapons in general, during the late 1950s and early '60s and again in the early 1980s. Founded in 1958 by a group including the philosopher Bertrand Russell and Canon John Collins, Dean of St Paul's Cathedral, its demonstrations and annual ALDERMASTON MARCHES were a feature of national life for five years or so, fading after the conclusion of the TEST-BAN TREATY. Politically, CND's success and organisation assisted the campaign for UNILATERALISM which in 1960 briefly captured the LABOUR PARTY (*see* FIGHT, FIGHT AND FIGHT AGAIN). In 1961 Russell and other militants who feared CND was losing its edge launched the COMMITTEE OF 100, which carried out a brief campaign of CIVIL DISOBEDIENCE. CND enjoyed a new lease of life two decades later under Monsignor Bruce Kent as controversy grew over America's planned deployment of CRUISE MISSILES in Britain (*see also* GREENHAM WOMEN); a new generation joined in huge demonstrations and Labour once again went unilateralist. It subsided once again with the end of the COLD WAR and the withdrawal of Cruise in return for the destruction of Soviet SS20s; Labour repudiated unilateralism after its 1987 election defeat, but a hard core of activists continued to protest against Britain's maintenance of TRIDENT missiles.

> A load of peanuts who aren't worth a tinker's cuss.
>
> HUGH GAITSKELL, Glasgow May Day parade, 1962

coalition (1) A government comprising members of two or more parties, formed because none has an outright MAJORITY, or to tackle a national emergency. The alternative to coalition is a MINORITY GOVERNMENT or a HUNG PARLIAMENT. A coalition is effectively impossible in the United States; in Britain the two main parties are fundamentally opposed, echoing DISRAELI's statement that 'England does not love coalitions', though Edward HEATH flirted with the idea in 1974; the LIBERAL DEMOCRATS positively advocate them and have governed in coalition with Labour in Scotland and Wales. There have been just two at UK level in peacetime in the past century: under LLOYD GEORGE from 1918 to 1922 in the aftermath of WORLD WAR I, and the NATIONAL GOVERNMENT from 1931 to 1935 to combat the economic crisis. ASQUITH, Lloyd George and CHURCHILL all led wartime coalitions, Asquith observing: 'Nothing is so demoralising to the tone of public life, or so belittling to the stature of public men.' In continental Europe coalitions are far more common, being the basic form of government in Italy, Belgium and the Netherlands and having governed Germany for important periods since WORLD WAR II. (2) The binding together of diverse strands in a political party (*see* BIG TENT, BROAD CHURCH).

> Every political movement, whether conservative or liberal, owes its success to its ability to maintain a coalition between the greedy and the idealistic.
>
> MURRAY KEMPTON

(3) An international grouping in pursuit of a common object, notably the coalition formed under US leadership to carry out UN-authorised military action against Iraq in the GULF WAR, and the narrower group again led by the US which prosecuted the WAR ON IRAQ twelve years later. This latter, comprising essentially the US, the UK, Australia and Poland, was termed the **coalition of the willing** by George W. BUSH.

the Coalition Popular shorthand for the long-standing combination between Australia's LIBERAL and NATIONAL parties, as in 'The coalition needs another defeat' (Paul KEATING, 1995).

Coalition Provisional Authority The US-led organisation that took over the ADMINISTRATION of Iraq after the overthrow of SADDAM HUSSEIN in April 2003. Headed by Paul Bremer, it endeavoured to engineer a return to economic normality and a transition to democratic government, but was hampered by increasing insurgent attacks on US troops and key installations like pipelines. It ceded power to a Provisional GOVERNMENT on 28 June 2004.

Grand Coalition The government formed by West Germany's two main parties, the CDU and SPD, with Kurt Georg Kiesinger (1904–88) as CHANCELLOR, which held office from 1966 to 1969.

Great Coalition The broad government of both GRITS and Bleus (Tories) formed in Canada in 1864 under John Macdonald, at the urging of George Brown, editor of the *Toronto Globe*, to prepare the way for CONFEDERATION.

Rainbow Coalition *See* RAINBOW.

coat-tail effect The means by which an unpopular or unknown CANDIDATE can benefit from the presence on the same TICKET, or even in the same party, of a highly popular and CHARISMATIC figure. The candidate is said to have been elected 'on the coat-tails' of the celebrity, i.e. to have been dragged in by them. The phrase was originated in 1848 by Rep. Alfred Iverson of Georgia and popularised by Abraham LINCOLN, who in the same HOUSE debate noted the success of candidates who had 'taken shelter under General (Zachary) Taylor's military coat tail'.

COBRA Cabinet Office Briefing Room. The suite of offices in WHITEHALL from which all emergencies requiring central co-ordination are handled by UK Government Ministers and officials, and hence the name of the committee convened to deal with such emergencies, for example the FOOT AND MOUTH crisis and anti-terrorist precautions after 9/11.

COCOM Co-Ordinating Committee for Multilateral Export Controls. The Paris-based trading arm of the West in the COLD WAR; set up to prevent advanced technology with military potential falling into Communist hands, it came to be seen by Europeans as a PROTECTIONIST device to maintain US control over trading by firms in other countries. COCOM was disbanded in November 1993.

co-decision A EUROPEAN UNION term for the joint deliberative process of the COMMISSION and the EUROPEAN PARLIAMENT, in which the

Commission remains dominant despite slight shifts in the balance under the MAASTRICHT TREATY and since.

Cod Wars The skirmishes between Icelandic gunboats and British vessels in 1972 after Iceland unilaterally extended its territorial waters from twelve to 50 miles. Britain sent in warships to support trawlers having their nets cut in their traditional fishing grounds but eventually conceded Iceland's right to impose a limit. When the Conservative MP John Watson told a meeting in Yorkshire: 'Things are all right now – we're sending in the Royal Navy', a HECKLER replied: 'And how many bloody fish are they going to catch?' The dispute in March 1995 when Canadian fishery protection vessels arrested and cut the nets of Spanish trawlers for alleged over-fishing, triggering a showdown with the EU and a chorus of approval for Canada from UK EUROSCEPTICS, became known as the **turbot war**.

code. Code Napoléon The comprehensive and neatly organised corpus of laws introduced in France by Napoleon Bonaparte, which forms the basis of French law to this day.

coded message An apparently innocuous remark by a politician that conveys a definite – and usually critical – meaning for those at whom it is aimed. Such messages are frequently used to air dissent without rendering the speaker liable to charges of disloyalty; Peter Walker, who survived for years as a WET in Margaret THATCHER'S CABINET, was a past master of the art.

codification The transformation of a disorganised mass or written and case law into clear and orderly STATUTES. In Britain the process is known as CONSOLIDATION.

CODESA The talks on replacing South Africa's APARTHEID constitution by a multiracial democracy begun in 1991 by President F.W. de Klerk, between nineteen groups including the ANC and INKATHA; the letters stood for *CO*nvention for the constitution of a *DE*mocratic *S*outh *A*frica. The talks survived stalemates on critical issues and BOYCOTTS provoked by political atrocities, notably the BOIPATONG MASSACRE which led the ANC to walk out in June 1992. A POWER-SHARING agreement was reached early in 1993 and a draft constitution that November – in the absence of Inkatha – leading to multiracial elections in April 1994 won by the ANC.

coercion The repressive Irish policy adopted by Britain under DISRAELI from 1874 to 1880 and, briefly, by GLADSTONE before his conversion to HOME RULE. It met the popular upsurge for land reform with measures that one PARNELLITE called 'an open declaration of war on every man in Ireland'. Mass meetings, CIVIL DISOBEDIENCE, rent strikes and violence were countered by special magistrates backed by heavy troop reinforcements. Based, like INTERNMENT a century later, on the belief that resistance would collapse if a few troublemakers were isolated, coercion kept a degree of order at a huge political price. Gladstone's Irish Secretary W. E. FORSTER produced the stiffest measures, passed in 1881 despite Parnellite resistance; the repercussions led to his being dropped from the CABINET. A further Crimes Bill was passed in 1882 after the PHOENIX PARK MURDERS.

Coffeegate One of several scandals over President CLINTON's use of the WHITE HOUSE to raise funds for the Democratic Party. In the eighteen months to August 1996 103 coffee meetings were held there, raising $27 million for campaign funds. There was particular controversy over the presence of the Treasury Secretary, Robert Rubin, and the Comptroller of the Currency, Eugene Ludwig, at one meeting, but each denied knowing it was a party event.

cohabitation In France's FIFTH REPUBLIC, a situation in which a President of one party and a Prime Minister and government of another co-exist in office. The term, with its Gallic sexual inference, originated between 1986 and 1988 when a right-wing government headed by Jacques CHIRAC 'cohabited' with the socialist President François MITTERRAND. Cohabitation came back into vogue from 1993 to 1995 when Mitterrand had to accept a centre-right government under Édouard Balladur, and again from 1997 to 2002 when Chirac, now President, 'cohabited' with the socialist Prime Minister Lionel Jospin.

cohesion The EU term for policies designed to raise the economies of the poorer member states – Greece, Ireland, Spain, Portugal and now several of the ENLARGEMENT countries – towards the level of the rest, mainly through large-scale transfers of funds. The 1992 Edinburgh summit was deadlocked for many hours over Spain's insistence on the largest possible cohesion fund.

COINTELPRO *Co*unter-*Intel*ligence *Pro*gram. The campaign initiated by FBI director J. Edgar Hoover in 1968 against 'Black Nationalist-Hate Groups'; it grew into an operation by 41 of the Bureau's field offices to undermine or discredit any organisation Hoover deemed subversive. The campaign relied heavily on the bugging of prominent black activists, starting with Dr Martin Luther KING, and the 'exposure' of their sexual activities. In the years leading up to COINTELPRO, Hoover told FBI agents he aimed to prevent the coalition of black and CIVIL RIGHTS groups turning into a 'real MAU MAU in America, the beginning of a true black revolution', and 'prevent the rise of a "Messiah" who could unite and electrify the militant black nationalist movement'. Hoover saw Dr King and Malcolm X as potential Messiah figures; by the time COINTELPRO was fully under way, both had been assassinated.

COLAs In America, the annual *C*ost *O*f *L*iving *A*djustments paid to increase social security benefits. After Ronald REAGAN took office in 1981, several Senate Democrats offered him a COLA freeze to reduce the BUDGET deficit by up to $38 billion. Reagan refused, saying he was pledged not to cut social security benefits – only to put forward a benefit-slashing plan of his own two months later. The resulting furore did Reagan considerable political damage. The plan was dropped, and in 1983 a far more modest and BIPARTISAN package was adopted.

cold. Cold War The period of tension between East and West, stopping just short of actual conflict between the SUPERPOWERS, which began within months of YALTA and the end of WORLD WAR II and ended with the breaching of the BERLIN WALL 44 years later. The period – particularly from 1948 to the mid-1960s – was dominated by the fear of NUCLEAR annihilation. The term was first used on 16 April 1947 by Bernard M. Baruch (1870–1965) in a speech to the South Carolina legislature:

> Let us not be deceived – we are today in the midst of a cold war. Our enemies are to be found abroad and at home.

Baruch himself credited the phrase to Herbert Swope, former editor of the *New York World*.

The mood of the Cold War was set in 1946 by Dean Acheson. Though later pilloried as 'soft on Communism', Acheson said:

> We have got to understand that all our lives the danger, the uncertainty, the need for alertness, for effort, for discipline – will be upon us. This is new to us. It will be hard for us.

And in 1949 Harold MACMILLAN wrote:

> With Communists we cannot say it with flowers . . . the Cold War must be fought with as much energy and singlemindedness as the shooting war.

Eventually the ability of America's economy to keep up in the ARMS RACE and the dire economic plight of the Soviet Union, coupled with the rise of Mikhail GORBACHEV and the refusal of eastern Europeans to tolerate repression, brought the Cold War to an end.

> By the grace of God, America won the Cold War.
> GEORGE BUSH Snr, 1992

cold peace The Norwegian diplomat Trygve Lie (1896–1968) who became the first SECRETARY-GENERAL of the UNITED NATIONS, used this term in 1949 to describe the combination of high tension and lack of actual conflict that characterised the early stages of the Cold War.

cold warrior A US/British term for an enthusiastic advocate of belligerent competition with the Soviet Union.

collaborator or **collaborationist** The ultimate insult in countries occupied by NAZI Germany during WORLD WAR II. It described someone who had collaborated willingly with the invaders; many collaborators, or people claimed to be such, paid with their lives – often without trial – once the country had been liberated. *See also* QUISLING, VICHY.

collective. collective bargaining The process under which an employer and a trade union, or groups representing both, negotiate wages and conditions for the workers as a whole. The unions are able to back up their claims with the sanction of industrial ACTION; as the alternative would be for each employee to negotiate his or her conditions of service with little ability to stand up to management, collective bargaining is one of the main reasons for joining a union. Governments may be worried by both the economic impact of the deals arrived at and the power unions wield in unfettered bargaining; attempts to introduce wage and price controls, and legislation to impose checks on union power, are seen by the unions as intrusions into '**free collective bargaining**'.

collective leadership A system in which a nation or party is ruled jointly by several individuals, rather than by a single leader. It does not have an impressive track record; recent examples include federal Yugoslavia prior to its disintegration in 1991–92, and the Liberal-SDP ALLIANCE.

collective responsibility The doctrine, enshrined in Britain's UNWRITTEN CONSTITUTION, under which every member of the CABINET is equally responsible for decisions taken by it, whatever view they expressed at the time. Traditionally any Minister who could not approve a decision had to resign unless there was an AGREEMENT TO DIFFER; in recent times, except for WESTLAND, the tradition has been honoured in the breach.

collective security The principle underlying both the LEAGUE OF NATIONS and the UNITED NATIONS, whereby the nations of the world act together to maintain the peace and to respond to threats to it. The phrase was coined at the League in 1932 by the Czech Foreign Minister Eduard Beneš (1884–1948); a French delegate is said to have protested:

> Impossible; it's not French.

collectivism The theory that a nation's economy, and indeed many aspects of its society, should be operated for the community as a whole, with the individual being subordinated. It appealed especially to COMMUNISTS and FASCISTS, but is echoed in the policies of all but the most conservative parties.

> If the 19th century was the century of individualism, this will be the century of collectivism, and hence the century of the State.
>
> MUSSOLINI (*see* DUCE)

collectivisation The process of forcing peasants and larger farmers (*see* KULAKS) onto state-owned collective farms, pioneered by STALIN in the late 1920s and followed in much of Communist eastern Europe after WORLD WAR II. In Russia especially, it was accompanied by the killing or imprisonment of those who were expropriated. Though Soviet leaders trumpeted the achievements of collective farms for half a century, their productivity was frequently low and the quality of their produce indifferent. However, they lingered on in several countries, notably Hungary, after the end of communism. *See also* BLITZKRIEG.

college. College Green (or **Abingdon Green**) The patch of grass across the road from the HOUSE OF LORDS where television crews line up to interview MPs for news bulletins at busy Parliamentary times. Used since the 1980s, it came into its own as a mecca for RENTAQUOTES during the 1995 Conservative leadership contest. On 15 November 1995 it was the scene of a paint attack on the CONSERVATIVE PARTY chairman Dr Brian Mawhinney.

College of Cardinals In the US CONGRESS, the semi-reverent collective nickname for the chairmen of the House's thirteen APPROPRIATIONS Committees. It reflects the immense power they exercise over the budgetary and legislative process.

Colombey-les-deux-Églises The tiny French village to which General DE GAULLE retired in 1946 after the failure of his efforts to put together and lead a government of national unity, and where he remained until called back in 1958 to be President in the FIFTH REPUBLIC. He retained an immense fondness for Colombey, settling there again on his resignation in 1969 and dying there the following year. Colombey is in the Haute-Marne department of north-eastern France, eight miles east of Bar-sur-Aube.

> What other consolation can be sought when one has faced history?
>
> DE GAULLE, 1969

Colombo Plan An agreement to foster economic development in South and South-East Asia, concluded at Colombo, Ceylon (now Sri Lanka) in 1951. There are annual meetings to discuss economic development plans such as irrigation and hydro-electric schemes, and a permanent office to give technical assistance.

Colonels, the The right-wing military junta led by Georgios Papadopoulos (*see* PAPA DOP) (1919–) which overthrew Greece's constitutional monarchy in 1967 and in the ensuing seven years became a byword for ruthlessness, and a target for world-wide left-wing odium. Costa-Gavras' film *Z*, portraying the murder of the former opposition deputy Gregory Lambrakis, showed the régime's sinister side to the full. Its legacies are the end of the Greek monarchy and – unintendedly – the PARTITION of Cyprus. With King Constantine in exile in Britain, the monarchy was abolished in 1973 and Papadopoulos appointed President, but the army ousted him the same year. The Colonels fell after backing a right-wing coup in Cyprus against the government of Archbishop Makarios, aimed at uniting the country with Greece. The coup, led by Nikos Sampson, was staged after Makarios demanded the removal of Greek officers sent by the Colonels to fan feeling for ENOSIS; it was abortive, but gave Turkey the pretext to occupy the north of the island to protect Turkish Cypriots. The junta collapsed on 23 July 1974 amid riots in Athens, and ex-premier Constantine Karamanlis was called from exile to head a civilian government. The monarchy was formally abolished in a referendum after the return of democracy, and 20 of the Colonels put on trial; Papadopoulos was sentenced to death for treason, soon commuted to life imprisonment.

colonialism The policy of keeping control of a nation's dependent territories for the purpose of exploiting them. Throughout the 1950s and '60s the term was used abusively by MOSCOW-LINE and NON-ALIGNED countries to denounce both the retention of colonies by former imperial powers such as Britain and France, and the foreign policies of the United States.

colony An overseas dependency of a state, especially one to which emigrants have travelled to replicate the home country's economic system and forms of government, while excluding the indigenous people from power. Colonies were first established by the Greeks, Romans and other Mediterranean nations in classical times, but it was Britain that adopted the policy most comprehensively in Africa, Asia, North America, the Caribbean and elsewhere. John Ruskin declared in 1870: 'This is what [England] must do, or she will perish: she must found colonies as fast and as far as she is able, formed of her most energetic and worthiest men.' But the IMPERIALIST Disraeli warned:

> These wretched colonies will all be independent, too, in a few years, and are a millstone round our necks.

self-governing colony The self-defeating constitutional formula under which a colony is permitted to govern itself and embarrass the nation nominally responsible for it. Rhodesia prior to UDI and Gibraltar in blocking contacts with Spain have made Britain pay dearly for this misconceived exercise in DEVOLUTION.

Colossus of Roads The nickname bestowed on Robert Key (1945–), the mountainous Parliamentary Under-Secretary for Transport under John MAJOR, by his fellow minister Steve Norris. It is a pun on the Colossus of Rhodes, the giant statue bestriding the harbour entrance on that Greek island that was one of the seven wonders of the ancient world.

colour bar A term widely used in the 1940s and '50s for racial SEGREGATION, specifically for the exclusion of black people in the United States and South Africa from premises deemed to be for 'Whites only'.

columnist A journalist with editorial space (not always a column in the typographic sense) of his or her own, in America syndicated to papers across the country, comprising comment and analysis (Walter Lippman, Hugo Young), polemics (Lester Kinsolving, Bernard Levin), or exposés (Jack Anderson, Paul Foot). In WASHINGTON, where columnists exert great influence, much revelatory material comes from embittered political or military sources.

combined development TROTSKY's theory explaining why the first successful revolution occurred in a backward agrarian society, not in an advanced capitalist one as MARX had expected.

come. Come home, America *See* AMERICA.

Comeback Kid The nickname adopted by Bill CLINTON as he bounced back from a shaky start in his CAMPAIGN for the 1992 Democratic NOMINATION. It was coined by the Clinton strategist Paul Begala as he won second place in the NEW HAMPSHIRE PRIMARY to stay in the race; Clinton's Republican opponent George BUSH preferred to call him SLICK WILLIE, saying:

> We're not running against the comeback kids, we're running against the Karaoke Kids – they'd sing any tune to get elected.

On the eve of the 2004 election Clinton, now campaigning for John KERRY despite a quadruple heart bypass weeks before, told a Democratic rally:

> I have been called the Comeback Kid – in eight days John Kerry will make America the comeback country.

> I'm a lot like Baby Huey. I'm fat. I'm ugly. But if you push me down, I keep coming back. I just keep coming back. BILL CLINTON

Comecon *Co*uncil for *M*utual *Econ*omic Assistance. The international grouping set up by STALIN in 1949 to promote economic development and trade between the Soviet Union and Communist eastern Europe, except Yugoslavia. Originally a propaganda vehicle to cover Soviet exploitation of its SATELLITE countries, it did come to promote genuine mutual co-operation. In 1989, with Communism collapsing, Comecon announced that it would take account of market forces, but it was soon left meaningless by events.

Comical Ali The nickname given after the defeat of SADDAM HUSSEIN's regime in April 2003 to his information minister Mohammed Said Sahhaf, whose outlandish declarations of imminent victory to the international media as US troops closed in on Baghdad made him an icon in the West.

At one briefing, with the Marines almost within earshot, he declared: 'There are no American infidels in Baghdad. Never.' The nickname was a variant of **Chemical Ali**, applied to the more sinister Gen. Ali Hasan Al-Majid who masterminded the use of chemical weapons against Kurdish civilians in the late 1980s. Chemical Ali was presumed dead in air attacks supporting the British advance on Basra, but was arrested north of Baghdad in August 2003; Sahhaf was rumoured to have hanged himself, but surfaced that June to reject a number of lucrative deals offered him by US and Arabic television.

Cominform *Com*munist *Inform*ation Bureau. A body set up by the Soviet Union in 1947 as a successor to the COMINTERN to encourage world Communist solidarity and co-ordinate party activity and subversion in countries not under its control. Its members were the parties of the Soviet Union, Bulgaria, Czechoslovakia, France, Hungary, Italy, Poland, Romania and Yugoslavia, the last expelled in 1948 for not toeing the MOSCOW LINE. It was dissolved in 1956.

Comintern *Com*munist *Intern*ational. An organisation of world communist parties founded by LENIN in 1919 to hasten the world-wide revolution of the proletariat. Regarded as highly sinister in the West, it was dissolved by STALIN in 1943 as a gesture toward his wartime capitalist allies, re-emerging after the war as COMINFORM.

Anti-Comintern Pact An agreement signed by Germany and Japan on 25 November 1936, and by Italy the following year, ostensibly to counter the activities of the Comintern. The pact reinforced Japan's expansionist plans, hastening the invasion of China in 1937. The agreement, viewed as ominous by the Western democracies and the Soviet Union, foreshadowed the TRIPARTITE PACT between the three AXIS countries.

comity The international custom under which some effect is given to the laws of one state within the territory of another. America has at times – notably under President CARTER's Attorney-General Griffin Bell – invoked the principle with vigour, giving other states the impression that it expects US law to override the domestic legislation and practices of other states.

Command Paper An official UK Government publication, produced 'by command' of the Crown and issued by HM Stationery Office. Command Papers range from WHITE and GREEN papers to the results of consultations, Government replies to the reports of SELECT COMMITTEES and the like.

Commander in chief The supreme position accorded to the PRESIDENT in relation to America's armed forces. The US CONSTITUTION reads:

> The President shall be commander in chief of the Army and Navy of the United States and of the militia of the several states, when called into the actual service of the United States.

Presidential control over the armed forces is not unlimited, CONGRESS having a significant role in the declaration of war. However the President does have the power to send US troops anywhere in the world, and theoretically could take the field in active command, though none has actually done so.

> Any president as commander in chief faces no more solemn decision than whether to send American troops into battle, knowing they will not all return. JOHN F. KENNEDY

commie An abusive term for a supposed or actual COMMUNIST, common in America after WORLD WAR II but which has outlived the age of MCCARTHY. The word, more insulting than 'Communist', has been applied not only to genuine Marxist-Leninists but more loosely to any foreigner, outsider, liberal or person with unconventional views.

commissar Under the early Soviet system, an official with at least as great a responsibility to the Party as to the state. In the RED ARMY, commissars from the Party were attached to each unit to ensure ideological soundness among the troops. Until 1946, Ministers in the Soviet government held the title **People's Commissar**.

Commission, European *See* EUROPEAN COMMISSION.

Commission for Social Justice *See* SOCIAL.

committee A group of individuals, often part or even the whole of a legislature or other elected body, convened to consider a particular matter or range of matters. Committees in their various forms are essential to the workings of government, but can become the weapons of inert BUREAUCRACY. At best a committee can be highly effective in arriving at conclusions, apportioning blame or drafting legislation; at worst it can kill an imaginative proposal, producing a platitudinous report or a clumsy FUDGE.

A cul-de-sac down which ideas are lured and quietly strangled.
Sir BARNETT COCKS, Clerk of the House of Commons (1907–88)

A group that keeps MINUTES and loses hours.
MILTON BERLE

A group of the unwilling, chosen from the unfit, to do the unnecessary. ANON (US)

The best committee is a committee of two, when one is absent. E. V. LUCAS (1868–1938)

A camel is a horse designed by a committee.
ANON

If Moses had been a committee, the Israelites would never have got across the Red Sea.
Salvation Army General WILLIAM BOOTH

In many legislatures, the US CONGRESS in particular, committees provide both the legislative and political engine-room.

A good committee assignment [for a Congressman] can make the difference between a brief and obscure service in the House and the kind of influence that means tenure for decades.
New York Times

When internally unified and buttressed in parliamentary privilege by special rules, they can almost at will dominate the business of the parent chamber. STEPHEN BAILEY

committee clerk *See* CLERK.

Committee Corridor Also known as the WAYS AND MEANS CORRIDOR. The principal business corridor of the Palace of WESTMINSTER, one level up from the CHAMBER and the LOBBIES, which runs the entire length of the building with access to the most prestigious of the Lords' and Commons' COMMITTEE ROOMS, all of them facing the river. Committee members, witnesses and the media mingle in the corridor and many MPs use it as a thoroughfare.

The Skid Row of Westminster.
CHRIS MONCRIEFF, Press Association, speech to 1993 LABOUR PARTY Conference

Committees of Correspondence The bodies formed by discontents in Massachusetts on the eve of the AMERICAN REVOLUTION, which eventually usurped the government of the colony. The first was set up by the Boston TOWN MEETING at the urging of Samuel Adams (1722–1803); by 1774, 300 committees had joined the network. The BOSTON TEA PARTY stemmed from an initiative against Britain's Tea Tax by the Massachusetts correspondence committee.

committee of dukes and earls The nickname given to the grouping of all fifteen Senate committee chairmen pulled together in 1981 by MAJORITY LEADER Sen. Howard Baker to maximise support for the programmes of the newly-elected President REAGAN.

Committee of 100 The militant network forced c. 1961 by members of Britain's Campaign for Nuclear Disarmament (CND) who felt the movement's non-confrontational tactics were doomed to failure. Members took part in mass SIT-DOWNS and other acts of CIVIL DISOBEDIENCE; a number were sent to prison, including the aged philosopher Bertrand Russell (1872–1970).

Committee of the Whole House At WESTMINSTER, a sitting of the HOUSE OF COMMONS, chaired by the Chairman of WAYS AND MEANS rather than the SPEAKER, to hear the CHANCELLOR deliver his BUDGET and to tackle the COMMITTEE STAGES of Bills involving constitutional issues, and key sections of the FINANCE BILL. The US HOUSE OF REPRESENTATIVES can form itself into a **Committee of the Whole** (short for Committee of the Whole House on the State of the Union), with a QUORUM of 100, to consider all measures on the Union CALENDAR – tax and APPROPRIATION Bills – and any other matter on resolution of the House.

Committee of Reasons A five-strong committee of the HOUSE OF COMMONS empanelled to provide reasons for the rejection of LORDS' AMENDMENTS to legislation passed by the Commons. During the November 1993 debates on rail privatisation, the Labour members of the Committee kept it talking until they knew the Lords had given up and gone home.

Committee of the Regions An advisory body of the EUROPEAN UNION established under the MAASTRICHT TREATY, originally with 189 members from regional and local government appointed by twelve member states but now much enlarged; under the Treaty of NICE it will have 350 members in the event of Bulgaria and Romania joining. The EUROPEAN COMMISSION and the COUNCIL OF MINISTERS are obliged to consult the Committee before legislating in areas including COHESION, health, education, culture, training and transport. Representatives of the Committee also took part in the EUROPEAN CONVENTION to devise a constitution for the EU.

Committee on the Present Danger A pro-defence pressure group launched in the early days of the CARTER administration by WASHINGTON insiders, and concerned citizens like the broadcaster Alistair Cooke, who believed America was adopting a dangerously relaxed military posture at a time when the Kremlin under BREZHNEV was posing new threats and challenges, notably deployment of the SS20 missile which CRUISE missiles were developed to counter.

committee room (1) In the US CAPITOL, the Palace of WESTMINSTER and elsewhere, the small rooms to medium-sized halls, depending on the size and prestige of the body, where committees meet to carry out their business.

> Congress, with its committee rooms, is Congress at work. WOODROW WILSON

(2) The basic unit of the electoral machine in Britain: the office in each POLLING DISTRICT which on ELECTION day serves as a party's headquarters and the base from which its workers get out the vote. The NCR or READING pads are put out, street by street, on a table, alongside a heap of leaflets making a last-minute appeal to vote and a list of voters who need transport to the polls. The average committee room is in the living-room of a party supporter sited conveniently close to the POLLING STATION, or sometimes in a vacant shop or office.

Committee Stage At WESTMINSTER, the stage of a BILL between the Second and Third Reading when the measure is considered LINE BY LINE and AMENDMENTS are taken. In the COMMONS, the work is done by a STANDING COMMITTEE except for Constitutional measures and key sections of the FINANCE BILL; protracted debate by the OPPOSITION may lead the Government to seek the GUILLOTINE. In the LORDS, Committee stages are conducted on the FLOOR of the House.

in committee The HOUSE OF COMMONS is said to be in committee when the SPEAKER has left the CHAIR and the MACE is off the table. The discussion of a BILL or other matters by a committee rather than by the whole House is also said to take place in committee.

select committee *See* SELECT.

standing committee *See* STANDING.

common. Common Agricultural Policy *See* CAP.

Common Cause A public-interest lobby founded in the late 1960s which campaigns to keep America a democracy by limiting the scope for outside interests to exert financial influence over politicians. It advocates federal funding for elections, and has long fought to curb the influence of LOBBYISTS and reform the laws on campaign funding; its joint campaign with the People's Lobby in 1974 led to California introducing tough State laws. Common Cause has pressed for stricter observance of existing campaign financing laws, and for an end to the Congressional free-mail privilege which it says enables INCUMBENTS to raise three times as much funding as challengers. It has taken a strong stand against the activities of PACs, reporting in 1985 that many members of the Senate Finance Committee and House WAYS AND MEANS COMMITTEE were receiving campaign funds from PACs eager to win tax breaks for their areas of business. In 1975 Common Cause helped end the rigid SENIORITY system for House chairmanships, sending every member of the Democratic CAUCUS a 'report card' on the record of each committee chairman.

Common European home The phrase used by Mikhail GORBACHEV for the tension-free Europe he hoped could develop following the end of the COLD WAR. Unfortunately for him the Soviet Union, and his own position within it, was abolished before the policy could bear fruit.

Common Market The original Anglophone term for the forerunner of the EUROPEAN UNION; it is now used only by diehard opponents of British membership.

> Neither we nor the Common Market are so affluent that we can long afford to shelter high-cost farms or factories from the winds of foreign competition. JOHN F. KENNEDY

> Given a fair wind, we will negotiate our way into the Common Market, head held high – not crawl in. Negotiations? Yes. Unconditional acceptance of whatever terms we are offered? No.
> HAROLD WILSON, 20 March 1966

common roll In the various constitutions devised by Britain for COLONIES nearing or achieving independence, a common electoral roll was one on which both whites and indigenous people were included on an equal basis. There was normally a further roll giving subjects of the colonial power a guaranteed number of seats; as independence neared, this built-in advantage was eliminated.

Common Sense The revolutionary tract written in Philadelphia by the recent English immigrant Thomas Paine (1737–1809), subsequent author of the AGE OF REASON, and published on 10 January 1776. In it he argued:

> Can we but leave posterity with a settled form of government, an independent constitution of its own, the purchase at any price will be cheap.

Within three months of that momentous

year it had sold 100,000 copies – at a time when there were only 2 million Americans. 500,000 were sold worldwide, but Paine was left out of pocket; he promised the original printer, Robert Bell, that he would subsidise any loss on a first edition of 1000 copies, with any profit divided between Bell and the supply of mittens for the Continental army. Bell insisted he made no profit on the first edition, and refused Paine any payment for the second. George WASHINGTON reckoned the pamphlet 'worked a powerful change in the minds of many men', but in 1819 John ADAMS fumed:

> What a poor, ignorant, malicious, short-sighted crapulous mass is Tom Paine's *Common Sense.*

Common Sense Revolution The initiative launched in September 1999 by William HAGUE to reconnect the CONSERVATIVE PARTY with its traditional support after its overwhelming defeat two years previously. The idea was lifted from the successful 1998 election campaign of the Ontario Progressive Conservative leader Mike Harris, who is credited with coining the phrase. The adoption of 'common sense' did not prevent Hague's party suffering a further LANDSLIDE defeat in 2001.

Common Wealth An idealistic left-wing political party which enjoyed some success in Britain during and shortly after WORLD WAR II. A merger of Sir Richard Acland's **Forward March** and the **1941 Committee**, formed by followers of J. B. Priestley's radio talks, it won seats in wartime by-ELECTIONS where no Labour candidate stood against the defending Tories. It fielded 23 candidates in the 1945 general election but only one was elected alongside Labour's victorious horde. The party did not survive, most of its members being absorbed by Labour.

Commoner, Great *See* GREAT.

Commons, House of *See* HOUSE OF COMMONS.

Commonwealth (1) The (British) Commonwealth. The grouping of 53 nations under the leadership, though not the SOVEREIGNTY, of the British crown, which comprises almost all the nations of Britain's former EMPIRE plus Mozambique, previously a Portuguese colony. The Commonwealth has its own secretariat which assists joint diplomatic and development initiatives, and its Prime Ministers meet every two years in a member capital (*see* CHOGM). The Commonwealth's potency as a trading force was weakened by Britain's attempts from 1962 to join Europe's COMMON MARKET. As a political force, it has been weakened by arguments over SANCTIONS against South Africa, UDI in Rhodesia and more recently the behaviour of President Robert Mugabe in what had become Zimbabwe. At various times Nigeria and Pakistan have been suspended from membership for human rights abuses, and in December 2003 Zimbabwe resigned after CHOGM confirmed its suspension; South Africa was readmitted after the end of APARTHEID. The term 'Commonwealth' was in use long before the Empire formally came to an end with Britain's withdrawal from India:

> There is no need for any nation, however great, leaving the Empire, because the Empire is a Commonwealth of nations.
>
> Lord ROSEBERY

(2) The REPUBLIC established in England, with Oliver Cromwell at its head, following the execution of King Charles I in 1649. It survived until 1660, being governed by the military for the final five years following the disbandment of its increasingly argumentative Parliament (*see* RUMP). (3) The official title of Australia since 1901, and the term used to personify the federal power. (4) The formal status and title of Massachusetts, dating back to colonial times. (5) The status accorded to Puerto Rico by the United States; it falls short of STATEHOOD, support for which is limited by fears on the island that federal aid might be less generous and the people's obligations greater.

Commonwealth of Independent States The grouping set up in late 1991 under Russian leadership in an effort to maintain common services within the former Soviet Union and prevent harmful fragmentation. Its influence soon became shadowy as the Baltic states, Belarus, Georgia and the Ukraine went their own way.

New Commonwealth Member states of Britain's Commonwealth other than the white-ruled DOMINIONS; conversely, all those states ruled by their indigenous peoples. The term was used in the 1970s to categorise the nations of the Caribbean, Africa and the Indian subcontinent whose citizens were migrating in force to Britain, leading both to poor living conditions among many and RACISM from some British people and politicians. *See* POWELLITES, RIVERS OF BLOOD.

White Commonwealth (1) The great DOMINIONS of the former British EMPIRE, in which white people mainly of British origin formed the majority and held power. The governments of the UK, Australia, Canada and New Zealand earned the epithet in the 1960s when at times they and the newly-independent colonies were on opposite sides of the political fence. (2) The LOBBY correspondents of Britain's serious broadsheet press – then *The Times*, the *Daily Telegraph*, the *Guardian* and the *Financial Times* – who on occasion up to the early 1980s were invited to DOWNING STREET for briefings not extended to the popular tabloids.

communautaire A French term meaning 'in the spirit of the European Community', applied to any policy or action which, in the view of the beholder, will further the interests of the EU rather than purely national ends. It is often used in the negative sense by one nationally-motivated politician against another, by the EUROPEAN COMMISSION against anyone trying to inject common sense into its policies, or by the French against anyone challenging their line. **acquis communautaire** *See* ACQUIS.

commune A basic unit of local government, an experiment in collective living (*see* KIBBUTZ) and, specifically, the revolutionary authority set up in Paris in 1870 after France's defeat in the FRANCO-PRUSSIAN WAR. Seen by MARX and others as foreshadowing more permanent revolutions, it was suppressed within months by troops sent in by the government of the embryo THIRD REPUBLIC under Thiers, which was based at VERSAILLES. Participants in the Paris Commune were not Communists but **Communards**.

communiqué The official statement issued at the end of a round of negotiations or a SUMMIT meeting; it is frequently concocted by officials before the talks have even begun, hence the vagueness of the genre.

> Communiqués are like bikinis. What they reveal is alluring, but the essential points remain hidden.
>
> KARL GUNTHER VON HASE (1917–), West German government spokesman, 1967

communism The idea of revolution to overthrow CAPITALISM in the interests of the PROLETARIAT, leading to the withering away of the STATE, which Karl MARX set out with Friedrich Engels in the *Communist Manifesto* of 1848. But also the use (and frequently misuse) of power and the cavalier interpretation of MARXISM-LENINISM by nominally Communist governments from 1917. Either way, it was one of the great forces of 20th-century history, notably through efforts to implement it in Soviet Russia and its SATELLITES, and in China where its political, though not its economic, tenets remain in force. Marx himself termed communism 'the definitive resolution of the antagonism between man and nature'. He and Engels wrote that 'the theory of communism may be summed up in one sentence: Abolish all private property'. Its advocates – some of whom later changed their minds – have had other justifications for it: 'exploitation of the strong by the weak' – Pierre Joseph Proudhon; 'the completion of Socialism' – William Morris; 'the more communism, the more civilisation' – George Bernard Shaw; 'SOVIET power plus electrification of the whole country' – LENIN; 'the logical consequence of Christianity' – Albert Camus.

To some, communism has appeared the lesser of two evils; in 1949 the Labour MP Tom O'Brien declared that Britons 'would rather run the risk of civilising communism than be kicked around by the pot-bellied money magnates of the US'. Others have seen its triumph as inevitable, Nikita Khrushchev telling Sir William Hayter in 1956: 'Every year humanity takes a step towards communism. Maybe not you, but at all events your grandson will be a communist.' Communism has always had a ruthless, disciplinarian backbone which caused many party loyalists to forfeit their lives in pointless and bloody PURGES. Mao Tse-Tung (*see* CHAIRMAN MAO) wrote: 'Communism has nothing to do with love. It is an excellent hammer which we use to destroy our enemy.' And Khrushchev, in his memoirs, wrote:

> We had no use for the teachings of the Gospels, if someone slaps you, turn the other cheek. We had shown that anyone who slapped us on our cheek would get his head kicked off.

The strongest foes of communism have always been its rivals on the left; as early as 1868 the ANARCHIST Bakunin wrote presciently: 'I detest communism because communism concentrates and absorbs all the powers of society into the state.' Political liberals, too, have detested it, partly because they objected to being tarred with the same brush. Communism has been condemned as 'the death of the soul' and 'the corruption of a dream of justice' – Adlai STEVENSON; 'one big phone company' – Lenny Bruce; 'successful FASCISM' – Susan Sontag; and 'a race in which all the competitors come in first with no prizes' – Lord Inchcape. And James Baldwin wrote of America: 'There will never be a communist government in this country, and for this reason. No gospel founded on hate will ever seize the hearts of our people.'

The difference between communism and SOCIALISM has caused many arguments. The left-wing Spanish general José Miaja Menant said: 'The socialists talk first, then act. If the communists talk, they do so after acting.' And numerous writers have described communism as 'socialism in a hurry'. Russian Communism, in its 74 years of power, incurred particularly savage criticism. Half a century before the BOLSHEVIK revolution, Alexander Herzen identified it as 'TSARIST autocracy turned upside down'; at its height Clement ATTLEE termed it 'the illegitimate child of Karl Marx and Catherine the Great'; and in its latter days Alexander Solzhenitsyn wrote: 'For us in Russia communism is a dead dog, while for people in the West it is still a living lion.' Camus wrote: 'Fascism represents the exaltation of the execution by the executioner – Russian communism represents the exaltation of the executioner by the victim.' Stalin's subject peoples in Eastern Europe were even more caustic; Lech Walesa remarked that 'communism has done very much for us – exactly the opposite of what they wanted.'

> Like PROHIBITION – a good idea but it won't work. WILL ROGERS

> A spectre is haunting Europe, the spectre of communism.
> Opening words of the COMMUNIST MANIFESTO

> Those who wait for the USSR to reject communism must wait until a shrimp learns to whistle.
> NIKITA S. KHRUSHCHEV (1894–1971)

> Capitalism is the exploitation of man by man. Communism is the reverse. Polish joke

communism with a human face Often misquoted as 'Socialism with a human face', this was the aim of Alexander Dubček, Czech Communist leader during the PRAGUE SPRING of 1968. It involved freedom of expression and an opening of links with the West, without taking Czechoslovakia out of the Communist bloc; it was not a doctrine the Soviet Union under BREZHNEV would tolerate. The phrase was suggested to Dubček by his colleague Radovan Richta.

goulash communism The somewhat liberalised communism (though still with rigid police surveillance) which operated in Hungary from the late 1970s under Janos Kadar (1912–89), who had taken office as a hardliner after the crushing of the HUNGARIAN UPRISING. With hindsight, it paved the way for the rapid transition to democracy and a market economy that followed Kadar's retirement and death (*see* DEMOCRATIC FORUM), but at the time there was no telling how much relexation the KREMLIN would tolerate. Khrushchev had anticipated the phrase in 1964, saying:

> If we should promise people nothing better than revolution, they would scratch their heads and say: 'Isn't it better to have good goulash?'

Suppression of Communism Act The legislation passed by South Africa's NATIONAL PARTY government in 1950 to hamper resistance to APARTHEID, enabling it to detain, imprison or exile anyone whose views it found uncomfortable under the pretext that he or she was a communist. The legislation, later renamed the **Internal Security Act**, drove the Communist Party underground, some of its leaders joining the ANC.

> Christ in this country would most likely have been arrested under the Suppression of Communism Act.
> Archbishop JOOST DE BLANK, 1963

communist An adherent of communism, the opposite of CAPITALIST, a candidate for preferment (or PURGING) in a MARXIST-LENINIST state and an object of fear and hatred in America. The revolutionary duty of the communist fuelled Western distrust; Khrushchev said that a communist had 'no right to be a mere onlooker', while Mao Tse-Tung (*see* CHAIRMAN MAO) wrote: 'We communists are like seeds and the people are like the soil. Wherever we go we must unite with the people, take root and blossom among them.' CHURCHILL reckoned that 'a communist is like a crocodile; when it opens its mouth you cannot tell whether it is trying to smile or preparing to eat you up', a lesson the Czech democrat Eduard Beneš would have done well to learn; the year before the communist takeover in Prague, he said naïvely: 'If ever we have trouble with the communists in my country, I pick up that telephone and get on to my friend STALIN.' Lyndon B. JOHNSON could see good reason to declare: 'We don't propose to sit here in our rocking chair with our hands folded and let the communists set up any government in the Western hemisphere.' Yet communist intentions and capabilities could both be overestimated: in 1967 Ambassador Edwin O. Reischauer told a Congressional hearing: 'Communists are not supermen at all, but men with feet of clay which extend almost all the way up to their brains.' Ronald REAGAN was even more dismissive, saying: 'A communist is someone who has read the works of MARX and Lenin; a capitalist is someone who understands them.' Adherence to communism, like other left-wing views, is seen by some as a natural phase; CLEMENCEAU reputedly said: 'My son is 22 years old. If he had not become a communist at 22, I would have disowned him. If he is still a communist at 30, I will do it then.' Yet there have always been clear divisions between communists and other left-wingers, the UK Labour leader John Clynes (1869–1949) saying; 'A communist is no more a left-wing member of the LABOUR PARTY than an atheist is a left-wing member of the Christian church.'

> One who has nothing, and wishes to share it with the world.
> ANON

> One cannot be a communist and preserve one iota of one's personal integrity.
> MILOVAN DJILAS

> If I had to do it again I would not even be a communist, and if Lenin were alive today he would say the same.
> Bulgarian ex-President TODOR ZHIVKOV (1911–98)

communist bloc The Soviet Union plus those countries in Eastern Europe which were occupied by its troops after WORLD WAR II and became its SATELLITES. The bloc, so called because it voted uniformly at the UNITED NATIONS, comprised all the signatories of the WARSAW PACT; Yugoslavia was also considered a member at times, despite TITO's disagreements with STALIN. The bloc held together as long as the KREMLIN was ready to use force to maintain it (*see* BREZHNEV DOCTRINE), but it disintegrated within months in 1989 when it became evident Mikhail GORBACHEV was ready to loosen the ties.

Communist Manifesto The 40-page pamphlet written by MARX and Engels, and published in London in 1840, which encapsulated the Marxist analysis of history and set out the case for the 'forcible overthrow of all existing social conditions'. Though the *Manifesto* was not immediately successful, it became the ideological basis of 150 years of communist activity.

Communist Party of Great Britain (CP for short) Formed in 1920 and disowned by the LABOUR PARTY not long after, it was never a mass movement, at most securing two seats in Parliament; it nevertheless exerted considerable influence, notably in the TRADE UNIONS. It suffered a damaging split at the time of the 1939 NAZI-SOVIET PACT; that was soon healed when Russia entered the war, but a second wave of defections in 1956 when Soviet troops crushed the HUNGARIAN UPRISING fatally weakened the party and it disintegrated in the late 1980s. After the party's brief flirtation with EUROCOMMUNISM, hardline elements relaunched it in 1991 as the DEMOCRATIC LEFT.

> Its relationship to democratic institutions is that of the death watch beetle; it is not a party, it is a conspiracy.
> ANEURIN BEVAN

Communist Party of the Soviet Union *See* CPSU.

Communist Party of the United States The party formed legally in 1929 after previous legitimate and clandestine parties had fallen foul of both Moscow and the Federal authorities. A MOSCOW-LINE body which never attracted significant public support, it nevertheless attracted enough FELLOW-TRAVELLERS in the immediate post-war period to pave the way for MCCARTHYISM. Harassment of declared communists culminated in a 1954 Act of Congress which claimed to outlaw the party; this was overthrown by a court decision in 1961, and in 1965 the provisions of the MCCARRAN ACT requiring communists to register were also declared UNCONSTITUTIONAL. The party resumed overt activity in 1966 and has run Presidential candidates, but their support has been negligible.

community. Community Charge *See* POLL TAX.

community politics The basis for the revival of Britain's LIBERAL PARTY from the 1960s, and for the successor LIBERAL DEMOCRATS, through activism at local government level, with councillors winning and holding seats by concentrating on basic problems affecting the voters, gaining a power base for national politics without engaging in national issues. *See* PAVEMENT POLITICS.

Compact of Government The document drawn up by the Pilgrim Fathers aboard the *Mayflower* on 21 November 1620, once it became clear they would make landfall far north of Virginia and outside the jurisdiction of any government. 41 men signed the compact, soon afterward electing Deacon John Carver as governor. The signatories agreed that they

> Solemnly and mutually in the presence of God and one of another, Covenant and Combine ourselves together into a Civil Body Politic . . .

and by virtue hereof to enact, constitute and frame such just and equal laws, as shall be thought meet and convenient for the general good of the Colony.

Company, the The nickname for the CIA long used by its operatives, which entered the public domain during the VIETNAM WAR.

comparability The question of how, and to what extent, pay for workers in the PUBLIC SECTOR should match that in private industry and commerce. Long a thorny question for governments, it culminated in Britain in the Clegg Commission report of 1979, after the WINTER OF DISCONTENT, which recommended 'catching-up' pay rises of over 20%. Margaret THATCHER's Conservatives promised to pay whatever the commission recommended, and stuck to their promise even though it proved highly INFLATIONary. Public sector pay has since been determined by a combination of statutory formulae (the police), advisory review bodies ('top people', the armed forces, doctors and dentists, nurses and teachers) and negotiation limited by strict curbs set on the funds available.

compassion fatigue The phenomenon, complained of by charities and caring politicians, under which the public feels it has exhausted its ability to show sympathy for those in greatest need in the wake of one disaster or humanitarian tragedy after another.

competence creep *See* CREEP.

competition policy A policy designed to remove restrictions on business (including self-imposed ones like cartels) and create a LEVEL PLAYING FIELD between potential competitors so that the MARKET may operate fairly. It can involve the removal of subsidies that give one particular company, or a nation's entire industry, an unfair advantage. Legislation to establish a competition policy was one of the first steps taken, in 1980, by Margaret THATCHER's government. Competition policy is now also a feature of the EU, though the Conservative Commissioner Sir Leon Brittan (1939–) ran into heavy opposition from France and Spain when he introduced it in the early 1990s. For its current application, since the 1998 Competition Act, under the **Competition Commission** *see* MONOPOLIES COMMISSION.

composite A MOTION or resolution formed by reconciling a number of others which make the same point or points in different ways. Composite motions are the life-blood of UK LABOUR PARTY or trade union conferences, the compositing process taking several days before publication of the final AGENDA; in debate on a major policy issue there may be three or four composites setting out different lines of thinking or action, each moved and seconded by the organisations which tabled motions incorporated into that composite.

comprehensive. Comprehensive Spending Review The wholesale review of UK government spending, department by department, introduced by CHANCELLOR Gordon BROWN after Labour's 1997 election victory, which takes place every three years and largely replaces the annual PUBLIC SPENDING REVIEW (*see* PESC). The advantage of the CSR to the rest of WHITEHALL is that departments can plan ahead; the disadvantage is that the TREASURY can more easily resist pressure from departments which find midway through the three-year period that they need to spend more.

Comprehensive Test Ban Treaty *See* TEST BAN TREATY.

comprehensivisation In Britain, the highly controversial process, for a decade from the mid-1960s, under which central government encouraged or acquiesced in the ending of selective education from the age of eleven, with all-ability comprehensive schools replacing grammar schools, technical schools and secondary moderns. Parents fought hard to save the grammar schools, where the brighter children were perceived as receiving a better education; rather fewer took up the cudgels for the secondary moderns. Some grammar schools have survived, as does selection by some education authorities (*see* TOUGH ON HYPOCRISY AND TOUGH ON THE CAUSES OF HYPOCRISY). Though comprehensivisation is claimed by Conservatives as a Labour brainstorm from the 'swinging sixties', Margaret THATCHER when Education Secretary (1970–74) reputedly signed the death warrants of more grammar schools than any Labour minister.

bog-standard comprehensives The dismissive remark about the majority of Britain's state secondary schools from Alastair Campbell, Tony BLAIR's head of communications, that made it plain Labour's 40-year commitment to stereotyped comprehensive schools was over and that in future schools would be encouraged to specialise and diversify. Campbell's comment in February 2001 appalled many teachers, and Education Secretary David Blunkett hastened to say he 'did not recognise' the phrase, but to many parents his admission that the 'one size fits all' model of comprehensive had not been an unqualified success was overdue. The jury is still out on whether the more varied system promoted by NEW LABOUR will have the same effect on raising low standards as its initiatives in primary schooling have had.

compromise The process of finding a single course of action which advocates of two contradictory policies can both accept, ideally by each giving ground. Burke declared that 'all government is founded on compromise and barter', and SPEAKER Joseph Cannon that 'all legislation is the result of compromise'; no wonder Gerald FORD described compromise as 'the oil that makes governments go'. The West German CHANCELLOR Ludwig Erhard described compromise as 'the art of dividing a cake in such a way that everyone believes he has the biggest piece', though G. K. Chesterton observed: 'Compromise used to mean that half a loaf was better than a whole loaf'. To CONVICTION POLITICIANS, compromise is the ultimate sin. LENIN wrote: 'If compromise continues, the revolution disappears', and Golda Meir said of compromise with Arabs pledged to destroy ISRAEL:

> We intend to remain alive. Our neighbours want to see us dead. This is not a question which leaves much room for compromise.

compromise candidate A candidate who has few strong supporters of his or her own, but emerges as acceptable to a majority when backers of two or more candidates of equal strength are deadlocked. When the Democrats chose Franklin Pierce (*see* HANDSOME FRANK) as their Presidential nominee after 48 deadlocked ballots, Sen. Stephen Douglas warned: 'Hereafter no private citizen is safe.'

compromise of 1850 The resolutions put to the US SENATE by the ageing Henry Clay on 29 January 1850 to head off the break-up of the UNION; they were enacted that September. Clay appealed to the North and South to pull back from the 'edge of the precipice', adding to his argument by brandishing fragments of George WASHINGTON's coffin. His plan involved admitting California as a non-slave state, organising New Mexico and Utah as TERRITORIES without settling their slave status, settling the dispute over Texas' boundary with neighbouring states and paying the Texas Republic's debts, ending the slave trade in the DISTRICT OF COLUMBIA and enacting a stricter Fugitive Slave Law. The compromise put off the split for just ten years, creating strains that broke up the WHIG party in 1852, after which American politics rapidly POLARISED.

compromise of 1877 The creation by the US CONGRESS of a fifteen-member commission to adjudicate on the outcome of the 1876 Presidential election, with Democrats agreeing to be a minority in return for a promise that the Republican Rutherford Hayes, if elected, would end RECONSTRUCTION by pulling Federal troops out of the South. The commission 'investigated' alleged vote fraud in three key states, then voted 8 to 7 on straight party lines for Hayes, the apparent loser in the election; he became known as OLD 8 TO 7.

Connecticut compromise *See* CONNECTICUT.

Luxembourg compromise *See* LUXEMBOURG.

Missouri compromise *See* MISSOURI.

comrade The term by which communists and other members of disciplined left-wing organisations have referred to each other; it was also used in some of the more ideological trade unions. In meetings they would refer to each other as 'comrade' and their surname. Right-wingers still scornfully refer to the labour movement, and the left in particular, as 'the comrades'.

Comstock Act The legislation passed by Congress in 1873 which made it illegal to send obscene materials through the mail. Anthony Comstock (1844–1915), a lifelong crusader against drink and pornography, formed the New York Society for the Suppression of Vice to campaign for the measure. Once it was passed, he had himself appointed an agent for the US Post Office, and in his first year claimed to have seized 200,000 pictures and photographs, 100,000 books, over 60,000 condoms, 5,000 decks of playing cards and 30,000 boxes of aphrodisiacs; much of the material was innocuous. Comstock was proud that his campaigning hounded sixteen people to their deaths.

concede To admit defeat in an ELECTION; originally a US term, it is now in general use. A **concession speech** is one in which a CANDIDATE formally tells his or her supporters that their rival has won.

concentration camps Specially-constructed camps in which POLITICAL PRISONERS or members of a victimised ethnic or cultural group are held without (fair) trial, with the chance that they may never be released. The term originated during the BOER WAR, when the British held a large number of Afrikaners in such camps. In Germany, NAZI rule from 1933 brought the establishment of camps to detain socialists and communists, and later Jews, gypsies and homosexuals. This did not deter the ROOSEVELT administration from referring to the RELOCATION CAMPS in which Japanese-Americans were INTERNED after PEARL HARBOR as concentration camps. In WORLD WAR II the Nazi camps at Belsen, Buchenwald, Dachau and Ravensbruck in Germany were augmented by Auschwitz and Treblinka in occupied Poland. The cruelty of the guards, use of slave labour, extreme malnutrition and medical experiments on prisoners made them the most notorious establishments in world history – though in some ways the regime in STALIN's GULAG was as monstrous. The conversion of some into extermination camps in which over 20 million died of disease, starvation and mass murder (including 6 million Jews; *see* FINAL SOLUTION) left an ineradicable stain on the human conscience; the survivors played a major part in building the state of ISRAEL and in both post-war reconciliation and perpetuating the memory of the HOLOCAUST. Some US leaders have found this hard to assimilate; Vice President George BUSH, visiting Auschwitz in September 1987, instead of uttering the customary expressions of remorse, declared:

> Boy, they were big on crematoriums, weren't they!

Ronald REAGAN, anxious to head off criticism of his visit to the German war cemetery at BITBURG by going to a concentration camp, told Cabinet members: 'As horrible as these places were, there were impulses of compassion.' His CHIEF OF STAFF Mike Deaver told colleagues: 'Oh, Christ, don't let this get out. I can see the headlines now: "Reagan says concentration camps are hotbeds of humanity".'

> Camps to turn anti-social members of society into useful members by the most humane means possible. JOSEF GOEBBELS, 1934

> The generation of Buchenwald and the Siberian labour camps cannot talk with the same optimism as its fathers. HENRY KISSINGER

conchies *See* CONSCIENTIOUS OBJECTORS.

concordat A solemn and binding agreement between powerful forces, setting out the boundaries of their influence. The term was first used to describe an agreement between a national government and the Vatican under which the Roman Catholic church was given preferential rights and privileges and the status of Catholic education was assured. The first was concluded in 1801 by Napoleon to establish his relations with the Vatican; another was the LATERAN TREATY between Mussolini (*see* DUCE) and the Church, which secured the Vatican's broad support for the FASCIST regime. James CALLAGHAN described as a concordat the formula devised in the autumn of 1964, after the election of Harold WILSON's first government, to define the responsibilities of the TREASURY under himself and George BROWN's newly-formed Department of Economic Affairs. Under DEVOLUTION, concordats were concluded in 1999 between WHITEHALL Departments and their counterparts in Edinburgh and Cardiff to codify the responsibilities of each.

Condit, Gary *See* Chandra LEVY.

condominium The exercise of SOVEREIGNTY by two nations over a territory; a prime example was the joint colonial authority exercised over the New Hebrides until the mid-1980s by the UK and France.

Conducator (Romanian Leader) The title bestowed upon himself by Nicolae Ceausescu (1918–89), the communist President of Romania until his death. Ostensibly at loggerheads with Moscow, Ceausescu was lionised by Western leaders while pursuing domestic policies of the utmost cruelty and erecting extravagant monuments to his dubious glory. When the anti-communist tide of 1989 reached Romania he was captured despite bitter resistance by the SECURITATE, and with his wife was tried and shot on Christmas Day.

Confederacy The eleven Southern slave states which SECEDED from the United States, starting with South Carolina in December 1860, to form the **Confederate States of America**, and were re-incorporated in the UNION after suffering defeat in the four-year CIVIL WAR. Created on 4 February 1861 and with a Constitution close to that of the US, its President was Jefferson Davis (1808–89), who declared at its INSTITUTION two weeks later:

> All we ask is to be let alone.

Confederation The creation of the Canadian state under the 1867 BRITISH NORTH AMERICA ACT; Ontario, Quebec and the Maritimes were founder members, with other provinces free to join. Dr (later Sir) Charles Tupper, Conservative premier of Nova Scotia, said in 1860 that 'Confederation would give us nationality', and his Ontario counterpart John Macdonald: 'Instead of looking on us as a merely dependent territory, England will have in us a friendly nation.'

> Flora Macdonald [MP for Kingston and later External Affairs Minister] is the finest woman to walk the streets of Kingston since Confederation.
> JOHN DIEFENBAKER

Articles of Confederation The instrument drawn up by the second CONTINENTAL CONGRESS in 1781 for the government of the infant USA, and which applied until the adoption of the CONSTITUTION eight years later. It involved a loose league of independent States, each of which had one vote in a one-house legislature. Despite many shortcomings – Congress could not levy taxes and all thirteen States had to agree to any AMENDMENT – this structure held long enough for final victory to be achieved in the Revolutionary War, and for a more ordered system to be created.

New England Confederation or **Dominion of New England** The union formed in 1643 by the colonies of Massachusetts Bay, Plymouth, Connecticut and New Haven. Its main purpose was to co-ordinate campaigns against the Indians, but it also had authority over boundary disputes, fugitive criminals and slaves. Though not outstandingly successful, it operated until 1684.

conference (1) The process by which the two HOUSES of the US CONGRESS resolve their differences over an item of legislation by setting up a committee of MANAGERS representing interested members of both. The resulting panel of **conferees**, often referred to as the **third House of Congress**, may only narrow the differences until a COMPROMISE is reached; it may not add any new material of its own, or in a tax or spending BILL step outside the range of figures in dispute. Its House and Senate members meet separately, deciding by majority vote, until the panels agree. If they have failed to do so after 20 CALENDAR days, the House may discharge its conferees and appoint new ones.

(2) A gathering of international leaders or representatives convened to discuss a particular problem or range of problems, in many cases with the hope of arriving at a settlement.

> The conference lasted six weeks. It wasted six weeks. It lasted as long as a carnival, and like a carnival it was an affair of masks and mystification. Our Ministers went to it as men in distressed circumstances go to a place of amusement – to while away the time, with a consciousness of impending failure.
> DISRAELI reporting to the HOUSE OF COMMONS, 1864

> We can lick any nation in the world, but we can't come back from a conference in Costa Rica with our shorts on.
> WILL ROGERS

(3) In Britain, the annual gatherings, usually by the seaside or in spa towns and lasting most of a week, held by the various political parties and trade unions. For LABOUR and the LIBERAL DEMOCRATS they are policy-making events at which the leadership can expect a bumpy ride. James CALLAGHAN remarked that at Labour conferences 'policy will be made by those who feel most keenly'; most of the party's great left-right battles were fought out at conference (*see* COMPOSITE; FIGHT, FIGHT AND FIGHT AGAIN), though the leadership has exerted some control since the late 1980s. CONSERVATIVE conferences are customarily STAGE-MANAGED unless an issue of exceptional divisiveness, like Rhodesia or Europe, gets out of hand. Tory leaders prior to Margaret THATCHER only appeared in the hall toward the end of the week; CHURCHILL held court at a hotel some distance away before appearing to make the final speech. Arthur BALFOUR once said that he would no more think of taking advice from the Conservative Party conference than of taking it from his valet; Sir Denis Thatcher, after his wife's resignation, declared in 1991:

> Thank goodness I won't have to go to that bloody thing this year.

conference season The portion of the British political year from the start of September until the second week of October during which all the parties hold their conferences, and when members of the political media are almost continually on the road; for most of this period the HOUSE OF COMMONS goes into recess. It opens with the Trades Union Congress (TUC), followed after a short gap by the LIBERAL DEMOCRATS, the GREENS and the SNP. The LABOUR PARTY has customarily held its conference in Brighton, Blackpool or Bournemouth at the end of September, and the CONSERVATIVES the following week in one of the two resorts that did not play host to Labour. However, Labour broke with tradition by opting to stage its 2006 conference in Manchester.

as I said at the Blackpool conference One of Harold WILSON's favourite phrases when being interviewed, given added currency when repeated by impressionists like Mike Yarwood.

confidence. confidence-building measures Steps to reduce international tension and encourage the confidence of governments in each other's peaceful intentions by such methods as the inspection of military facilities and the installation of HOT LINES. In Europe the CSCE took a leading part in promoting such steps.

no-confidence motion A motion tabled by opponents or critics of a government which, in the WESTMINSTER SYSTEM, will force the resignation of that government if carried. In the UK HOUSE OF COMMONS the traditional wording – echoed by set-piece undergraduate debates at the Oxford and Cambridge Unions – is **'That this House has no confidence in His/Her Majesty's Government'**. Just such a motion, tabled originally by the SNP, was carried by just one vote on 28 March 1979, forcing James CALLAGHAN's Labour government to call an ELECTION, which it lost. But the passage of no-confidence motions is rare; the instance in 1979 was the first of precisely that kind in over a century.

vote of confidence A vote sought by an administration under pressure, or forced on it by a Parliamentary defeat, as in July 1993 after John MAJOR's government was defeated on the SOCIAL CHAPTER of the MAASTRICHT TREATY. If defeated, that administration is obliged to resign or, in Britain, submit to an ELECTION.

Confidential The second step in the ladder of CLASSIFIED documents, RESTRICTED being the lowest.

confidentiality The duty to remain silent about official matters required by both the British and the US governments during the 1980s from present and former employees. Margaret THATCHER applied it specifically and with enthusiasm to ex-members of the security services after Peter Wright's embarrassing revelations about the activities of MI5 in *SPYCATCHER*, so that any further disclosures would be punishable. The REAGAN administration was more concerned about LEAKS by current employees, in 1985 prosecuting a PENTAGON official, Samuel Loring Morrison, for passing CLASSIFIED photographs to *Jane's Defence Weekly*. REAGAN also, in 1983, attempted to make any book, article or speech by 200,000 present or former government employees subject to 'pre-publication review' and make thousands of officials subject to lie-detector tests; after protests in CONGRESS the administration instead made an undertaking to submit to pre-publication review a condition for access to intelligence material.

confirmation The process under which the President's NOMINEE to hold a particular senior political, official, diplomatic or judicial post must be approved by the US SENATE. The ensuing hearings give Senators a chance to expose areas of ignorance, especially among campaign contributors who have been offered ambassadorships, to probe outrageous opinions that may make a candidate unsuitable, or to expose wrongdoing which should disqualify him or her from office. It also gives opponents of the administration an opportunity to weaken the President by rejecting a nominee who may be perfectly well qualified. SENATORIAL COURTESY also requires Senators to block the appointment of anyone to a post in the home STATE of a Senator who objects to the choice. The process of ADVICE AND CONSENT has torpedoed the careers of several nominees for Cabinet posts, such as Bert LANCE, Sen. John TOWER and Zoë BAIRD; it has also led to the rejection of several nominees to the SUPREME COURT (*see* BORK, CARSWELL, HAYNSWORTH) and in 1992 produced the torrid Clarence THOMAS hearings.

> They don't have the guts to say 'This guy is a dud because he doesn't agree with us', so they put him through the ritual of being pecked to death by ducks.
>
> Sen. ALAN SIMPSON on the Senate Judiciary Committee's rejection of William Bradford Reynolds as associate Attorney-General, 1985

confrontational politics or **style** The search by a leader or party for 'enemies' to take on and crush in order to reinforce their own support and political standing, as opposed to a desire to govern without unnecessary conflict. The term was widely used of Margaret THATCHER, who was perceived as regularly needing foes to take on, engage in a gargantuan struggle and then humiliate; the FALKLANDS WAR and the 1984–85 MINERS' STRIKE gave her two such adversaries in President Galtieri and Arthur Scargill (*see* KING ARTHUR), and the rest of Europe and the trade unions generally were always fair game.

Congress (1) The collective term for the two

houses of the LEGISLATURE of the United States: the HOUSE OF REPRESENTATIVES (for which alone the term is sometimes used) and the SENATE. It met in 1789–90 in New York, and from then until 1800 in Philadelphia before moving to WASHINGTON and the first completed portions of the CAPITOL. Congress has played its full part in governing the country, being in Woodrow WILSON's words 'the country in miniature'. Yet, possibly for that reason, it has attracted a rich vein of ridicule both from its own members and from outside observers. Will Rogers cracked: 'Every time they make a joke it's law. And every time they make a law it's a joke.' Harry S TRUMAN reminisced:

> When I came to Washington, for the first six months I wondered how the hell I ever got here. For the next six months I wondered how the hell the rest of them ever got here.

And much more recently Sen. Alan Simpson conceded: 'the reputation of the Congress is lower than quail crap.'

Members of Congress have long asserted the right to say and do exactly what they like. Davy Crockett, arriving in the House, declared:

> I am now here in Congress . . . I am at liberty to vote as my conscience and judgment dictate to be right, without the yoke of any party on me, or the driver at my heels, whip in hand, commanding me to go ge-wo-haw, just at his pleasure.

In the 1970s Rep. William Ford put it another way:

> A person has a constitutional right, when elected to Congress, to be a damn fool and act like one.

But the overriding imperative is to make sure that one's current TERM is followed by at least one more; as Rep. Frank E. Smith put it,

> All members of Congress have a primary interest in being re-elected. Some members have no other interest.

The effects of Congressional decisions on the people are hard to assess, but their impact on the WHITE HOUSE is great and immediate. This was established by the late 19th century when Thaddeus Stevens explained:

> Though the President is COMMANDER-IN-CHIEF, Congress is his commander and, God willing, he shall obey.

In modern times the POLLSTER Louis Harris concluded that 'the more Congress stands up to the President, the more people like it.' Such pressures – always present but the greater when the opposing party to the President controls Congress – led Theodore ROOSEVELT to exclaim:

> Oh, Lord, if only I could be President and Congress for just ten minutes!

President EISENHOWER said in exasperation: 'I simply will not have those monkeys telling us what we can and cannot do', but his predecessor Harry S Truman reckoned the secret lay in how much information they were given:

> If you tell Congress everything about the world situation, they get hysterical. If you tell them nothing, they go fishing.

Ronald REAGAN had a different solution:

> It isn't necessary to make the Congress see the light – make them feel the heat. We can lecture our children about extravagance till we run out of breath. Or we can cure their extravagance by simply reducing their allowance.

Eisenhower's assessment of members' individual quality has been shared by many others. Rep. Sam Steiger admitted 'there are members of Congress you wouldn't hire to wheel a wheelbarrow'. J. Peter Grace of Reagan's cost-cutting panel stated baldly: 'Two thirds of them are clowns.' And Reagan himself once commented:

> If Congress wants to bring the Panamanian economy to its knees, why doesn't it just go down there and run the country?

Plenty has also been said about the probity of members of Congress, who until the late 20th century managed to resist the imposition of firm ethical standards. Mark Twain observed:

> There is no distinctly native American criminal class except Congress.

Rep. Adam Clayton POWELL, condemning his own exclusion, said: 'There is no one here who does not have a skeleton in his closet', while Jack Newfield damningly observed:

> The arrest rate for members of the 95th Congress was higher than the arrest rate among unemployed black males in Detroit.

Those who have watched debates in Congress have been more concerned about their prolixity; Woodrow WILSON defensively explained that 'Congress in session is Congress on public exhibition, while Congress in its committee rooms is Congress at work', and this is by and large true. Boris Marshalov, a Russian visiting the House in the 1930s, observed:

> Congress is so strange. A man gets up to speak

and says nothing. Nobody listens – then everybody disagrees.

Speaker Thomas REED regretted that 'they never open their mouths without subtracting from the sum of human knowledge', and Raymond Clapper commented: 'What you hear in Congress is 99 per cent tripe, ignorance or demagoguery.' However, Speaker Sam RAYBURN maintained:

Too many people mistake the deliberations of the Congress for its decisions.

At the very outset, Thomas JEFFERSON lamented: 'When Congress will rise no mortal can tell, not from the quality but the dilatoriness of its business,' and the reason was apparent, Benjamin Franklin explaining: 'Their nature, by training, is to argue and procrastinate – yet we persist in electing lawyers to Congress.' John ADAMS reputedly observed that 'one man is called a disgrace, two are called a law firm, and three or more become a Congress', and in the mid-20th century Ralph NADER commented:

Almost half the Congress is composed of lawyers, who make up less than one-third of one per cent of the population. Blue-collar workers may get to Congress, but usually as tourists passing through the guided tours.

For the most part illiterate hacks whose fancy vests are spotted with gravy and whose speeches, hypocritical, unctuous and slovenly, are spotted also with the gravy of political patronage.
MARY McCARTHY

WASHINGTON is not the problem; Congress is the problem.
GERALD FORD, acceptance speech, Republican National Convention, 17 August 1976

Usually only scandal, longevity or death distinguishes a member from the pack.
MARY McGRORY

The Congress does not like to take responsibility. And after it has taken an important action, it usually likes to rest. ELIZABETH DREW

The last plantation. Sen. JOHN GLENN

The term 'a Congress' is used for the body that assembles on the 3 January after each biennial election to the House, and sits for the ensuing two years. Each succeeding Congress has borne a number, that elected in 2004 being the 109th Congress.

I've never seen a Congress yet that didn't eventually take the measure of the President it was dealing with. LYNDON B. JOHNSON

(2) A conference, either of an organisation, such as Britain's annual Trades Union Congress (TUC), or of national representatives, for example the 1815 **Congress of Vienna** which determined the shape of Europe after the final defeat of Napoleon, and the 1948 **Congress of Europe** in the Hague, chaired by CHURCHILL, which paved the way for western European union.

(3) **Congress** The movement founded in 1885 which, led by MAHATMA Gandhi and Jawaharlal NEHRU, led former British India to independence in 1947, though with Pakistan splintering away in the process. Its ethos is secular and left-of-centre. Under first Nehru and then his dynasty it became India's dominant party after independence, surviving factional splits to govern as the Congress (I) Party under Nehru's daughter Indira Gandhi and first losing power only in 1979. After years in opposition to the militantly Hindu BJP, it unexpectedly returned to power in April 2004 under Sonia Gandhi, the Italian-born widow of Nehru's grandson Rajiv Gandhi – who then declined to serve as Prime Minister.

Congress Daily A twice-daily newsletter on events, trends, changes and deals on Capitol Hill for those working in the Congress or attempting to influence it, published by the *National Journal*. It is hand-delivered in the Washington area and e-mailed to subscribers further afield.

Congress shall make no law . . . The opening phrase of the FIRST AMENDMENT to the US Constitution which guarantees FREEDOM of religion and OF THE PRESS.

Billion-dollar Congress The 52nd Congress which in 1891–92 appropriated the first-ever peacetime billion-dollar BUDGET, at the urging of President Benjamin Harrison who was promoting development at home with naval and mercantile expansion. When critics used the term derogatorily, Speaker Thomas REED responded: 'This is a billion-dollar country.'

Congress of People's Deputies The popularly-elected body established in the Soviet Union in the late 1980s under the reform programme of Mikhail GORBACHEV, which initially played an important part in the transition to democracy. With a largely ex-communist membership, it briefly survived the end of Communism in 1991 as the assembly of the Russian Republic, but lapsed in late 1993 when the DUMA was elected.

Do-nothing Congress The phrase which President TRUMAN, facing apparent defeat, pinned on his opponents on Capitol Hill in the 1948 election campaign, first using it on 18 September of that year. During his frenetic WHISTLE-STOP tour, GIVE 'EM HELL HARRY told crowds across the country:

> That notorious do-nothing Republican 80th Congress has stuck a pitchfork in the farmer's back . . . These Republican gluttons of privilege want a return of the Wall Street dictatorship. Your typical Republican reactionary is a very shrewd man with a calculating machine where his heart should be.

But George W. BUSH's political adviser David Frum reckoned Truman's target

> the most successful Republican Congress of the modern era. (It) struck decisively when it moved at all. *Weekly Standard,* 1995

Library of Congress The greatest repository of knowledge in WASHINGTON, if not America, it has developed from Congress' own source of reference to a national resource sited since 1897 in its own building a stone's throw from the EAST FRONT of the CAPITOL. Congress in 1800 appropriated $5,000 for 'such books as may be necessary', but they were used for kindling by British troops who burned the Capitol in 1814. The following year JEFFERSON sold to Congress his own library which he said contained 'no branch of science which Congress would wish to exclude from their collections; there is, in fact, no subject to which a Member of Congress may not have occasion to refer.' After the CIVIL WAR the Library expanded rapidly, outstripping its quarters in the Capitol, and in 1886 Congress appropriated funds for a new building.

Radical Congress The Congress elected in 1866 which advocated an aggressive process of RECONSTRUCTION, came within a whisker of IMPEACHing President Andrew Johnson and tried to prosecute CONFEDERATE leaders under the FOURTEENTH AMENDMENT.

Sense of Congress resolution A resolution passed by either or both the Houses of Congress which expresses an opinion or asserts the desirability of a course of action, but is of no legal force because the matter in question requires either detailed legislation or action by the President.

Congressional Accountability Act The ground-breaking first BILL passed by the Republican Congress in 1995 as part of the CONTRACT WITH AMERICA, under which members of the Congress were required to live under the same laws as all other Americans. It was carried with BIPARTISAN support.

Congressional Black Caucus The organisation which since 1967 has brought together black members of the US Congress, to co-ordinate action of matters of common interest, initially CIVIL RIGHTS. It has always been able to punch above its numerical weight.

Congressional Budget Office *See* BUDGET.

Congressional Club The principal fund-raising mechanism that enabled the ultra-conservative Republican Sen. Jesse Helms (1921–) to secure re-ELECTION in North Carolina time after time and to promote candidates and causes he favoured. His 1984 campaign, costing $16.4 million, was at the time the most expensive ever for the Senate; it led Sen. Howard Baker to call Helms 'the Nelson Rockefeller of political fund-raising'. Some felt that Helms and his Senate allies took a needlessly CONFRONTATIONal line on minor issues to keep up the temperature so that funds from supporters would continue to flow into the Club.

Congressional district The area that elects an individual member of the US HOUSE OF REPRESENTATIVES. There are 435 such districts, a few comprising a single State.

Congressional government Woodrow WILSON's expression for the dominance that Congress is able to exercise over the WHITE HOUSE in peacetime, contrasted with the extra power the President can exert in time of war.

Congressional investigations The inquiries set up by committees of Congress into everything from alleged union racketeering and overcharging by defence contractors to the MCCARTHYITE probes after WORLD WAR II into alleged Communist infiltration of the State Department and the motion picture industry. Woodrow WILSON termed the bodies launching such probes 'smelling committees'.

> A legalised atrocity where Congressmen, deprived of their legitimate food for thought, go on a wild and feverish man-hunt, and do not stop at cannibalism. WALTER LIPPMAN

Congressional liaison The efforts made by every WHITE HOUSE to build Congressional support for the President and his policies. Some Presidents, notably Lyndon JOHNSON, have been conspicuously successful; others, notably Jimmy CARTER, have struggled. The Washington observer and liberal Democrat Mark Green termed the procedure 'lobbying by the executive', but it is an essential prerequisite for the smooth functioning of government.

Congressional Medal of Honor The popular term for the medal awarded by the President 'in the name of the Congress of the United States' to Americans who have given outstanding service to the nation. It was authorised by Congress in 1862 for

UNION enlisted men who showed bravery in CIVIL WAR engagements. In 1863 Secretary of War Edwin Stanton approved awards to all 300 men of the 27th Maine Regiment who re-enlisted, but it has since been given more sparingly. Harry S TRUMAN said at a presentation of the medal to 14 service personnel in October 1945:

> I would rather have that medal than be President of the United States.

But when offered it 20 years later, he turned it down, saying he had done nothing to merit it.

Congressional oversight *See* OVERSIGHT.

Congressional Quarterly The prestigious journal, now a weekly, that recounts and analyses the actions and performance of Congress and its members; it can be found in Congressional, government, LOBBYISTS' and media offices throughout WASHINGTON, and much further afield. Founded in 1945 by Henrietta and Nelson Poynter, editor and publisher of the *St Petersburg*, Florida *Times*, it soon became and remains a WASHINGTON fixture, not least because of its success in fighting off rivals. **CQ**, as it is known, comprises a weekly report mailed to subscribers every Saturday, and an annual Almanac covering the legislative year; it is also a publishing house producing books on many fields of politics and public policy.

Congressional Record The official record of proceedings in both Houses of Congress, and of the state of BILLS in progress. First published in 1843 (since 1873 by the FEDERAL government) and a successor to earlier freelance publications, it has a daily circulation of over 30,000 and is also bound annually in hardback. As well as verbatim reports of debates it includes in its back section, which is often two-thirds of the whole, extraneous material of CONSTITUENCY interest – even poetry and recipes – inserted by members; Speaker Champ Clark reckoned that while it was undesirable to have such items appearing in the Record, it was better than having to listen to them. Once **read into the Record**, the text could then be circulated to constituents at the taxpayers' expense. Nowadays anything not actually said by a member is marked by a BULLET. Until 1978 Congressmen could also insert into the Record speeches they had not delivered; under the PRIVILEGE TO REVISE AND EXTEND they can still massage those actually made before they appear in print.

> More a work of fiction than one of fact.
>
> Sen. SAM ERVIN

Congressman A member of the US HOUSE OF REPRESENTATIVES. Although the two Houses are equal in status, Congressmen, being more numerous and less august and required to seek re-election more often, are generally accorded less respect and media interest than Senators. Rep. Clem Miller once said that 'to the congressman, publicity is his lifeblood', but Max Ways was largely correct when he wrote in *Fortune*: 'Journalists who will risk life and limb to find out what the president had for breakfast wouldn't walk around the corner to hear a Congressman give a reasoned explanation of his vote.' When a temporary stenographer asked: 'Is there anything lower [in precedence] than a Congressman?', Rep. Otha Wearin told her: 'If you read my mail long enough you'll find out there probably isn't.' The tone was set long ago; in 1869 a Cabinet officer (probably Interior Secretary Jacob Dolson Cox) told Henry Adams:

> You can't use tact with a Congressman. A Congressman is a hog – you must take a stick and hit him on the snout.

This prompted Adams to ask: 'If a Congressman is a hog, what is a Senator?' Despite the lack of public and media respect, Rep. Otis Pike could assert that 'Congressmen are treated, in Washington at least, like little tin Jesuses'. Will Rogers joked that 'it is not the original investment in the Congressman that counts – it is the upkeep', and plenty of opportunities for GRAFT exist – some being taken. Mark Twain declared that 'to my mind Judas Iscariot was nothing but a low, mean, premature Congressman', and the controversial lobbyist Paula Parkinson said of Congressmen in the mid-1980s: 'Only 15% of them are genuine.' Yet the bulk are honest and conscientious, their performance tempered by the perennial requirement to get re-elected. This long ago produced the observation from Speaker Joe Cannon (*see* FOUL-MOUTHED JOE):

> Some Congressmen keep their ears so close to the ground that they can get both ears on the ground. Only two other animals can do that – a donkey and a jack rabbit.

> I have tried to live my life so that I will never become a Congressman. WILL ROGERS

Congressperson The term for a female member of the US Congress introduced by the feminist Rep. Bella Abzug, a New York Democrat who served from 1970 to 1976. Many women elected since have preferred the title **Congresswoman**.

Congresswallah A local representative or

activist for India's Congress Party, a person with the same influence as a WARD or PRECINCT captain in US politics.

Coningsby Benjamin DISRAELI's most successful novel, which sold 50,000 copies in America alone. First published in 1844, the future Conservative leader wrote it 'to vindicate the just claims of the Tory party to be the popular political confederation of the country', but it was also a satire on PEEL. Apart from the book's hero Henry Coningsby, a model for YOUNG ENGLAND, 'dizzy' introduced Tadpole and Taper, two of his most memorable characters.

Connecticut compromise The compromise accepted by the PHILADELPHIA CONVENTION in July 1787, under which seats in the HOUSE OF REPRESENTATIVES were to be allocated by population, and in the SENATE equally for each State. To placate the larger states, the power to introduce MONEY BILLS was restricted to the House.

conquer. Conquer or die! The general order issued by George WASHINGTON to America's revolutionary army on 2 July 1776, as INDEPENDENCE was declared. He told his troops:

> The time is now near at hand which must probably determine: whether Americans are to be Freemen or Slaves; whether they are to have any property they can call their own; whether their Houses, and Farms, are to be pillaged and destroyed, and they consigned to a State of Wretchedness from which no human efforts will probably deliver them. The fate of unborn Millions now depend, under God, on the Courage and Conduct of this army . . . Our cruel and unrelenting Enemy leaves us no choice but a brave resistance, or the most abject submission; that is all we can expect . . . We have therefore to resolve to conquer or die.

conquered provinces theory The argument advanced during the US CIVIL WAR by leading Republicans including Sen. Benjamin Wade and Rep. Thaddeus Stevens, that by having engaged in the 'crime' of SECESSION, the southern States had placed themselves outside the protection of the CONSTITUTION and must after the war be treated as 'conquered provinces' which CONGRESS had the power to govern. Abraham LINCOLN insisted that as the right to secede did not exist, the Confederate states had never left the UNION. In December 1863 he put forward a plan for RECONSTRUCTION that would have helped all but the most intractable Confederates to resume their place in the Union. However, after Lincoln's assassination the conquered provinces theory reappeared in Congress's own aggressive Reconstruction programme.

conscience The still, small voice for right which speaks within every human and which troubles most politicians, who find decisions confronting them that conflict with their principles. The CBS commentator Elmer Davis once reported:

> Senator H. Alexander Smith of New Jersey spent the day wrestling with his conscience. He won.

conscience clause The provision invoked by Labour MPs at WESTMINSTER when they break with the PARTY LINE on a matter on which they feel strongly, and where they reckon an issue of conscience is involved. It was cited particularly by left-wingers voting against the DEFENCE ESTIMATES because of their opposition to NUCLEAR WEAPONS. The party leadership has long insisted, however, that while the WHIPS are tolerant on genuine issues of conscience, no such clause exists in any party code.

prisoner of conscience A POLITICAL PRISONER detained solely because of his or her opinions, with no suggestion that they have indulged in violent or subversive activity. This has not prevented some convicted TERRORISTS claiming to be prisoners of conscience.

conscientious objector A person who refuses to join their country's armed forces because their conscience prevents them from killing. Both Britain and America behaved harshly toward 'CONCHIES' in WORLD WAR I, until President WILSON in March 1918 recognised the right of men to object to military service on non-religious grounds. He also saved the life of Pvt. Richard Stierheim, sentenced to be shot after deserting three times in France because he refused to kill; Stierheim's sentence was commuted because of his heroism in saving wounded comrades under fire. In WORLD WAR II the Allies took a more sympathetic line, providing alternative forms of war service for those whose objections were considered genuine by a tribunal. The VIETNAM WAR produced both conscientious objectors and DRAFT-DODGING on a massive scale.

> War will exist until that distant day when the conscientious objector enjoys the same reputation and prestige as the warrior does today.
>
> JOHN F. KENNEDY

conscription The compulsory recruitment of individuals for military service, practised by most countries in time of war and by many, for a limited period, in peacetime. The decision by government to conscript, or DRAFT, young men in wartime has frequently provoked political controversy, notably in America during the VIETNAM WAR and in French-speaking Canada both in WORLD WAR I and in 1944 when Mackenzie King ran out of volunteers and was forced to send conscripts to Europe.

> How many French soldiers, or even British soldiers, would they send to America if Canada was attacked by the United States?
>
> HENRY BOURASSA, *Le Devoir*, (Montreal) 1916

consensus Those points of coincident rather than negotiated agreement between parties which a **consensus politician** will work to develop as a basis for action, support and co-operation, and which a CONFRONTATION politician will shy away from. In some European countries consensus politics has been the norm; in the UK it reached its height in BUTSKELLISM but lingered until its repudiation by Margaret THATCHER. *See also* BIPARTISANSHIP.

> A consensus politician is someone who does something he doesn't believe is right because it keeps people quiet.
>
> JOHN MAJOR, 4 January 1991

> When a line of action is said to be supported by 'all responsible men', it is nearly always dangerous or foolish.
>
> HAROLD MACMILLAN

> If you can find something everyone agrees on, it's wrong. Rep. MORRIS UDALL

conservatism The philosophy of conservatives, also a term for fiscal caution. Abraham LINCOLN termed it 'adherence to the old and tried against the new and untried', GLADSTONE 'distrust of the people tempered by fear', Thorstein Veblen 'the maintenance of conventions already in force' and William F. Buckley Jr 'the politics of reality'. Thomas Arnold maintained that 'conservatism destroys what it loves, because it will not mend it', DISRAELI that it 'discards prescription, shrinks from principle, disavows progress, having rejected all respect for antiquity, it offers no redress for the present and makes no preparation for the future'.

> Conservatism, I believe, is mainly due to want of imagination. GRANT ALLEN (1848–99)

> Conservatism goes for comfort, reform for truth.
>
> RALPH WALDO EMERSON

> What brought conservatism into existence was the French Revolution.
>
> Lord HUGH CECIL, *Conservatism*, 1912

conservative A traditionalist who opposes change that he or she sees as destabilising, who disapproves of state intervention in the economy but believes it should set and enforce moral standards. In America the term does not necessarily imply party affiliation; many conservative Democrats are well to the right of liberal Republicans. Franklin D. ROOSEVELT defined a conservative as 'a man with two perfectly good legs who has never learned to walk', Woodrow WILSON as 'a man who just sits and thinks, mostly sits', Elbert Hubbard as 'a man who is too cowardly to fight and too fat to run', Frank Vanderlip as 'a man who thinks nothing new ought to be adopted for the first time', Mort Sahl as 'someone who believes in reform, but not now', William F. Buckley as 'a fellow who is standing athwart history yelling: "Stop!"', and Philadelphia's Mayor Frank Rizzo as 'a LIBERAL who got mugged the night before'.

> When a nation's young men are conservatives, its funeral bell has already rung.
>
> HENRY WARD BEECHER (1813–87)

> Some fellows get credit for being conservatives when they are only stupid.
>
> KIN HUBBARD (1868–1930)

While there have been exceptions, conservatives and radicals are usually considered opposites. Ralph Waldo Emerson wrote:

> Men are conservatives after dinner, or before taking their rest; when they are sick, or aged. In the morning, or when their intellect or their conscience has been aroused; when they hear music, or when they read poetry, they are radicals.

However Woodrow WILSON reckoned that: 'the most conservative persons I have ever met are college undergraduates. The radicals are men past middle life.' The comparison in 20th-century Britain was with socialists. The Australian Prime Minister Robert Menzies (*see* MING) once told Britain's Labour ex-Chancellor Hugh Dalton: 'You are a most extraordinary phenomenon, a Socialist with wit.' Dalton replied: 'You are a more extraordinary phenomenon still, a Conservative with intelligence.'

In Britain, the word has been almost coterminous with the

Conservative Party (1) The party of the traditionalist right in Great Britain (it organised briefly in NORTHERN IRELAND from the late 1980s) which since the 1920s has alternated in government with LABOUR, and prior to that with the LIBERAL PARTY. It stands for the monarchy, law and order and free ENTERPRISE with a minimum of state interference in business. The name was first used in the 1830s by John Wilson Croker (1780–1857); he wrote in the *Quarterly Review*:

> We now are, as we always have been, decidedly and conscientiously attached to what is called the TORY, and which might with more propriety be called the Conservative, party.

Based on the legacy of such Tory statesmen as BURKE, PEEL and DISRAELI, despite his early claim that 'a Conservative government is an organised hypocrisy', it has generally championed evolutionary rather than revolutionary change; reform where necessary, but always within the existing framework of the state and society. Two exceptions were the premierships of Edward HEATH, who took Britain into Europe, and Margaret THATCHER, who pursued a radical and CONFRONTATIONAL agenda. The traditional Conservative stance makes the party attractive not only to those content with the existing order but to those suspicious or afraid of the more radical policies of its opponents. Though primarily a middle-class organisation, the modern Conservative Party has always enjoyed considerable working-class support. Often it has vigorously opposed change, only to accept it once enacted by others, a phenomenon Mrs Thatcher scorned as the RATCHET EFFECT. Examples include the PEOPLE'S BUDGET (1909), the curtailment of the power of the HOUSE OF LORDS (1911), the WELFARE STATE (1945–48) and the independence of India; it took four decades for the Conservatives to reverse Labour's NATIONALISATION of coal, gas, electricity and the railways. The party has always enjoyed the backing of the landowning aristocracy and of successful businessmen, though during the 20th century the balance tipped firmly toward the latter. Since the 1950s its leaders have ceased to be patricians like Harold MACMILLAN and SIR ALEC Douglas-Home, the firmly middle-class Edward Heath, Margaret Thatcher, John MAJOR and William HAGUE reflecting the shift from a party of estate owners to one of estate agents. When Douglas Hurd was criticised for being an Old Etonian during the 1990 leadership contest, he exploded: 'I thought I was running to be leader of the Conservative Party, not some demented Marxist outfit.' Up until 1963 the leader 'emerged' (*see* MAGIC CIRCLE); since then he or she has been elected, first by MPs and since Hague in 1997 by the entire party though Michael Howard in 2005 proposed returning the decision to the MPs. The Party Chairman who controls Conservative CENTRAL OFFICE is appointed by the leader; the heart of the VOLUNTARY PARTY lies in the constituencies.

The rise of Labour after WORLD WAR I could have overwhelmed the Conservatives as well as the Liberals, but for two factors: the enfranchisement of women swelled the Tory vote at a critical time, and frightened Liberal voters who equated Labour with BOLSHEVISM switched to the Conservatives. This shift added the middle-class liberal commitment to personal freedom and equal opportunity to the traditional Tory virtues of maintaining the social system at home and the Empire overseas. An inter-war Tory supremacy emerged from the husk of the NATIONAL GOVERNMENT, under BALDWIN and CHAMBERLAIN, before a return to wartime COALITION government under CHURCHILL, whose relations with the party he had left and rejoined were seldom good. In 1945 the Conservatives were routed in a Labour LANDSLIDE reflecting a desire for social change; in OPPOSITION they regrouped, accepting many of Labour's changes and paving their way for moderate BUTSKELLISM when Churchill returned to power in 1951. Post-war prosperity helped the Tories increase their majority under EDEN in 1955 and, despite the trauma of SUEZ, again under Macmillan in 1959 (*see* YOU'VE NEVER HAD IT SO GOOD). Then the tide turned, working-class voters moving away as the economy faltered, and the PROFUMO AFFAIR making the government look tired after what a revived and reunified LABOUR PARTY branded THIRTEEN WASTED YEARS. Douglas-Home just failed to hold on at the 1964 election, and eighteen months later the party, now under Heath, went down to a heavy defeat. In 1970, however, Heath pulled off a shock win with apparently radical policies in an election Harold WILSON seemed set to win easily. Heath succeeded where Macmillan had failed and took Britain into the COMMON MARKET, but was forced into an economic U-TURN before being brought down by the MINERS' STRIKE of 1974. He lost his majority and the Premiership in February, suffered a narrow but outright defeat by Wilson that October, and early in 1975 Mrs Thatcher ousted him as leader. She shifted the party sharply to the right, and after a nail-biting four years forced an election by defeating Labour in a no-CONFIDENCE vote in March 1979. Two months later Mrs Thatcher was in DOWNING

STREET and the party began eighteen years in office, winning landslide victories over Labour in 1983 and 1987 while the Thatcher government pressed ahead with trade union reform, PRIVATISATION and radical changes to every aspect of society except the constitution, winning the FALKLANDS WAR and crushing the miners in the process. The Thatcher agenda was continued in a minor key by Major, who took over when Tory MPs turned against her in the autumn of 1990 and won a 21-seat majority in 1992 despite a deep RECESSION. Mrs Thatcher's legacy was a deep split over Europe, which caused Major great difficulty over the MAASTRICHT TREATY and eventually led him to take on the right in a leadership contest, beating John Redwood (*see* VULCAN) in July 1995. Disunited and tarnished by SLEAZE, Major's government went down to a landslide defeat by Labour under Tony BLAIR in May 1997; seven CABINET MINISTERS lost their seats. Under Hague and Iain Duncan Smith (*see* IDS), the Conservatives failed to shake off their uncaring and anti-European image (*see* NASTY PARTY); they suffered a further heavy defeat in 2001 and only began to recover their fortunes and confidence after Duncan Smith was ousted in November 2003, the more experienced Michael HOWARD succeeding him.

Howard fought an energetic campaign in 2005, (*see* ARE YOU THINKING WHAT WE'RE THINKING?) but could only cut Labour's majority from 161 to 66; the Conservatives failed to increase their share of the vote, but did regain some ground from the Liberal Democrats. Howard immediately announced that he would go once a new system for electing the Conservative leader was in place.

The Conservatives' opponents have had plenty to say about them. J. S. Mill branded them as 'by the law of their existence the stupidest party'; the left-wing Labour MP Eric Heffer as 'a load of kippers – two-faced with no guts'; and an unsourced car sticker c. 1983 as 'the cream of Britain – thick, rich and full of clots.'

> The trade union for the nation as a whole.
>
> EDWARD HEATH

> Like a bird, it has a right wing and a left wing, but its brains are in the middle.
>
> ANON. Conservative MP

> Conservatives do not worship democracy. For them majority rule is a device.
>
> Sir IAN GILMOUR

> Having committed political suicide, the Conservative Party is now living to regret it.
>
> CHRIS PATTEN, 2003

(2) The traditional name of Canada's PROGRESSIVE CONSERVATIVES, and the name adopted for the party formed in 2003 through the PCs' merger with the CANADIAN ALLIANCE as a single centre-right force to challenge the supremacy of the Liberals in the 2004 federal elections.

> The day the Canadian Pacific busts, the Conservative Party busts the day after.
>
> JOHN HENRY POPE (1824–89)

(3) In New York City and State, a party formed in the 1960s of (mostly) former Republicans tired of Governor Nelson Rockefeller's pseudo-liberalism. One of the party's founders, the writer William F. Buckley Jr, ran for Mayor of New York in 1965, and five years later his brother James F. Buckley was elected to the US SENATE and the Conservatives overtook the tired LIBERAL PARTY to take third place on the ballot in New York state elections. The party has endorsed several moderate Republican Presidential nominees and has been important to the election of several US Senators, notable Alfonse d'Amato (*see* SENATOR POTHOLE).

Conservative Party at prayer A commonly used term for the Church of England with its establishment image, originating in a speech in 1917 by the Congregational minister Agnes Maude Royden (1887–1967) who said:

> The Church should no longer be satisfied only to represent the Conservative Party at prayer.

Conservative Research Department Situated within Conservative CENTRAL OFFICE until the 1990s, the team of researchers which, particularly in opposition, has provided the Conservative Party with fresh and appealing policy ideas. It was at its most fertile in the late 1940s when R. A. Butler (*see* RAB) fostered such creative brains as Enoch POWELL, but while its importance continued into the days of Margaret THATCHER and many of its alumni became successful Tory politicians in their own right, it has at times unnerved the leadership and in 2003 was threatened with disbandment by Iain Duncan Smith (*see* IDS) just before his removal.

Life's better with the Conservatives – Don't let Labour ruin it! The slogan with which Harold MACMILLAN won a landslide victory in the UK's 1959 general election. *See also* SUPERMAC, YOU'VE NEVER HAD IT SO GOOD. At the height of the PROFUMO AFFAIR the cartoonist Trog recast it as 'Life's better under a Conservative'.

neo-conservative *See under* N.

Consolidated Fund Bill At WESTMINSTER, the BILLS introduced three times a year to give statutory confirmation to Parliament's granting of money to the government. The final Consolidated Fund Bill of the year becomes the APPROPRIATION Act. The procedure for such Bills traditionally allowed MPs to stay up all night debating topics of their own choice; until the late 1980s it was possible to prolong debate to wipe out the next day's business.

consolidation (1) The passage of a BILL re-enacting in simpler and coherent form the surviving sections of various long-standing ACTS on one subject, other parts of which have been REPEALed. *See also* CODIFICATION. (2) The underpinning of political gains, instead of moving on to new initiatives. After 1948 Herbert Morrison persuaded ATTLEE's Labour Cabinet to pause after its first burst of NATIONALISATION – the Bank of England, coal, electricity, gas and the railways – instead of pressing ahead with further acquisitions, as left-wing MPs wanted. In 1986 John Biffen angered Margaret THATCHER by calling for 'consolidation' of the social changes pushed through by her government, rather than embarking on a fresh burst of radical measures; she went ahead regardless and the following year dropped Biffen from her Cabinet.

conspiracy theorist Someone who believes that almost any event in politics is the result of a conspiracy by sinister forces, rejecting simpler explanations on offer. Occasionally a conspiracy theory – scores of which are now promoted by their adherents' websites – is true, but the public has no means of telling. The greatest number of such theories have concerned the shooting of President KENNEDY, with the WARREN COMMISSION's conclusion that Lee Harvey Oswald killed him and was the sole assassin still vigorously contested. The death of Princess Diana, and alleged US complicity in 9/11, have also been meat and drink to conspiracy theorists.

constituency (1) The section of the population from which a politician or movement draws support or to which it will appeal. (2) The geographical area whose inhabitants elect a member to a legislature, in particular the UK HOUSE OF COMMONS. *Compare* DISTRICT, RIDING.

constituency day Certain designated Fridays on which the HOUSE OF COMMONS does not sit so as to give MPs time for business in their constituencies. The practice began in 1995 when ten days were thus allocated.

constituents Those who reside in the area represented by a member of a legislature, regardless of whether they voted for him or her – or indeed voted at all. When in the 18th century Alderman Sawbridge of Billingsgate – an area renowned for coarse language – delivered an unusually blunt speech, Lord North declared:

> The Honourable Gentleman speaks not only the sentiments but the language of his constituents.

There was a time when constituents could be dismissed, Sir Henry CAMPBELL-BANNERMAN saying after one speech to his:

> I had nothing to say to my constituents on Friday, and I think I very effectively said it.

When a horde of new Labour MPs arrived at WESTMINSTER after the LANDSLIDE of 1945, one old Tory hand observed:

> Who the hell are these people? They look like a lot of damned constituents.

Exasperation can lead MPs to be forthright with constituents, even today. In the early 1990s the Conservative whip David Lightbown told a woman threatening to throw herself from his office window in Staffordshire in protest at the CHILD SUPPORT AGENCY:

> I can't be doing with people who show such emotion. If you're going to jump out of a window you can jump out of your own at home, not mine.

Members of the US CONGRESS have many more constituents each, and are expected to do more for them (*see* WHAT HAVE YOU DONE FOR ME LATELY?). Rep. Joseph Bryans Jr, a Tennessee Democrat, was unseated in 1940 after saying he 'wouldn't come home to shake hands with the clodhoppers'. 'Clodhopper Clubs' backing an independent opponent sprang up all over the district. Most of the contact is maintained through vast amounts of mail under the FRANKING PRIVILEGE. Rep. John Dowdy made the headlines when a constituent in east Texas who had shotgunned his wife and said he was glad he did it received a condolence card in prison from the Congressman. Rep. William Ayres also used to send condolences to the bereaved in his Akron district, until he got a letter reading:

> I received your letter expressing sympathy concerning the passing of my late husband. If you had known how mean that SOB was to me you would have sent me a letter congratulating me on being rid of the bastard.

Increasing ease of travel has meant that mail is no longer the only contact between members of Congress and constituents, with more and more turning up in Washington. Rep. Morris Udall lamented:

> The jet plane wrecked everything. It used to be when a constituent came in, it was a big deal.

Replies to idiotic constituents have created a rich vein of humour, whether or not the recipients have appreciated the joke. One Congressman received a letter from a man threatening to emigrate to Canada if he voted a particular way; he simply wrote back: 'Bon Voyage!' And just before WORLD WAR II Rep. Stephen McGroarty reputedly blew his top at one constituent impatient for action, writing:

> One of the countless drawbacks of being in Congress is that I am compelled to receive impertinent letters from a jackass like you in which you say I promised to have the Sierra Madre mountains reforested and I have been in Congress two months and haven't done it. Will you please take two running jumps and go to Hell.

When the President of Pakistan presented a thoroughbred horse to Jacqueline Kennedy (*see* JACKIE O) and the US Air Force flew it to her free, Sen. Stephen Young of Ohio got an enraged letter from a constituent demanding a horse for himself, delivered in the same way. He wrote back:

> I am wondering why you should need a horse when there is already a jackass at your address.

There is also an all-purpose reply used on both sides of the Atlantic for 'nut letters', which are frequently written in green ink on both sides of the paper or typed single-space with comments scrawled in the margin:

> I feel I should let you know that a lunatic has stolen your headed notepaper.

The Liberal Democrat MP Paul Tyler had a more elegant suggestion, thanking such correspondents for their interest in the Camelford water poisoning outbreak (a real event).

Back in 1744 the MP Anthony Henley, urged by constituents to oppose the Excise Bill, wrote back:

> May your houses be as open and common to all excise officers, as your wives and daughters were to me when I stood for your rascally Corporation.

Edmund BURKE, standing firm against voters in his Bristol constituency, told them:

> I did not obey your instructions. No. I conformed to the instructions of truth and nature, and maintained your concerns, against your opinions.

In 1906 the humorist and Liberal MP Hilaire Belloc told constituents in Manchester who complained that he was a Catholic:

> If you reject me on account of my religion, I shall thank God that he has spared me the indignity of being your representative.

But sometimes the constituents get the last laugh. One ten-year-old boy asked the Labour MP John Evans:

> Did you used to have a proper job before you came here?

See also HORSEFACE.

constitution The rules under which a country is governed, either written as with the Constitution of the United States or uncodified as with the 'British Constitution', which is based on a combination of legislation, common law and accepted tradition.

The Constitution of the United States, devised at the PHILADELPHIA CONVENTION of 1787 and which took effect on 4 March 1789, is described in its own Article VI as 'the supreme law of the land . . . any thing in the Constitution or laws of any State notwithstanding'. The process of drafting it carried severe risks, John JAY pointing out that

> The Americans are the first people whom Heaven has favoured with the opportunity of deliberating upon, and choosing, the form of government under which they shall live.

Benjamin FRANKLIN left the Convention fearing the document was not perfect:

> I confess that there are several parts of this Constitution which I do not at present approve, but I am not sure I shall ever approve them.

At the same time he professed astonishment that so diverse an assembly should have devised 'this system approaching so near to perfection as it does'. Yet Alexander HAMILTON insisted that 'the system is the best that the present views and circumstances of the country will permit', and George WASHINGTON warned:

> Should the states reject this excellent constitution, the probability is, an opportunity will never again offer to cancel another in peace – the next will be drawn in blood.

James MADISON foresaw that America's constitution had the potential to be a blueprint for others throughout the world. He wrote:

> The free system of government we have established is so congenial with reason, with common

sense, and with a universal feeling, that it must produce an approbation and a desire of imitation.

The Constitution has stood the test of time – which would not have surprised Wendell Phillips who claimed that 'all that is valuable in the United States Constitution is a thousand years old'. Americans' reluctance to tamper with it is explained by Andrew Jackson's assertion that 'perpetuity is stamped upon the Constitution by the blood of our fathers'. Abraham LINCOLN warned against radical changes to it, saying:

> Don't interfere with anything in the Constitution. That must be maintained, for it is the only safeguard of our liberties.

It has in fact been amended just 27 times in well over two centuries – the first ten amendments constituting the BILL OF RIGHTS, ratified on 15 December 1791, and fourteen having been passed since Lincoln's warning. The task of interpreting the Constitution, and whether the actions of the Federal and State governments and courts accord with it, rests with the SUPREME COURT. Thomas JEFFERSON termed the Constitution 'a mere thing of wax in the hands of the judiciary, which they may twist and shape into any form they please', and Charles Evans Hughes, a politician who later became CHIEF JUSTICE, declared:

> The Constitution is what the judges say it is.

> There are very good articles in it, and very bad. I do not know which preponderate.
> THOMAS JEFFERSON

> Every word decides a question between power and liberty. JAMES MADISON

> We have no common oracles but the Constitution. Rep. RUFUS CHOATE, 1833

> A covenant with death, and an agreement with hell.
> WILLIAM LLOYD GARRISON, *The Liberator*, 11 July 1856

> Your Constitution is all sail and no anchor.
> THOMAS BABINGTON MACAULAY, to Henry Randall on US universal male suffrage, 1857

> As the British constitution is the most subtle organism which has proceeded from the womb and the long gestation of progressive history, so the American constitution is, so far as I can see, the most wonderful work struck off at a given time by the brains and purpose of men.
> W. E. GLADSTONE, *North American Review* 1878

> The Constitution was made for the people, and not the people for the Constitution.
> THEODORE ROOSEVELT

> Whenever the Constitution comes between men and the virtue of the white women of South Carolina, I say to hell with the Constitution.
> Governor COLEMAN BLEASE (1868–1942)

> We must remember than any oppression, any injustice, any hatred, is a wedge designed to attack our Constitution.
> FRANKLIN D. ROOSEVELT, to the American Committee for the Protection of the Foreign-Born, January 1940

> The most marvellously elastic compilation of rules of government ever written.
> FRANKLIN D. ROOSEVELT

The English Constitution The classic work of political theory – and practice – published by Walter Bagehot (1826–77) in 1867. In some respects it remains a valuable commentary on the workings of the UK system of government. The most celebrated dictum from it is:

> The SOVEREIGN has, under a constitutional monarchy such as ours, three rights – the right to be consulted, the right to encourage, the right to warn.

European Constitution *See* EUROPEAN.

living Constitution The term used by US jurists and politicians for the total body of law governing the operations of America's system of government, including not just the Constitution as amended but lasting enactments of CONGRESS, major Presidential decisions and landmark decisions by the courts.

unwritten constitution The rules by which a nation is governed, when they have not been codified into a document or series of documents. The classic example is the British Constitution, which is a mixture of statutes, common law and custom and practice.

our constitution is the will of the Führer The philosophy that governed the operation of the NAZI state, as stated by Hans Frank, HITLER's lawyer, who became Governor-General of Poland and was hanged at NUREMBERG.

constitutional An executive act or item of legislation that falls within the Constitution; in America the question of what is constitutional is a matter for the SUPREME COURT. On 6 July 1935 Franklin D. ROOSEVELT wrote to Rep. Samuel Hill of a NEW DEAL measure (probably the WAGNER ACT): 'I hope your committee will not permit doubts as to constitutionality, however reasonable, to block the suggested legislation.' The sentence caused an uproar in the Press, but Roosevelt insisted it had been taken out of context and he had no intention of defying the Court which, on BLACK MONDAY six weeks earlier, had dealt a serious blow to New Deal programmes.

Constitutional Convention (1) *See* PHILADELPHIA CONVENTION. (2) See SCOTTISH CONSTITUTIONAL CONVENTION.

Constitutional Crisis of 1926 *See* CUSTOMS SCANDAL.

constitutional monarchy *See* MONARCHY.

constitutional nationalist The term used in NORTHERN IRELAND for the mainly Roman Catholic Social Democratic and Labour Party (*see* SDLP) and others committed to the reunification of Ireland by peaceful means; it draws a distinction with SINN FEIN which has traditionally seen violence as a legitimate means to the same end.

Constitutionalist The party label on which Winston CHURCHILL stood at Epping in the November 1924 general election, as his journey from the LIBERALS back to the CONSERVATIVE PARTY neared its end. Despite not formally being a Tory, he joined BALDWIN's CABINET as CHANCELLOR, and the following year rejoined the party.

constructive engagement the policy followed toward South Africa by the REAGAN administration, under which US diplomacy aimed at securing the end of APARTHEID by persuasion and involvement rather than SANCTIONS and overt pressure. Liberals claimed that this strategy amounted in practice to tacit acceptance of the Pretoria government's internal policies, and did not contribute to the eventual fall of apartheid.

consul Originally one of the two chief magistrates of Republican Rome; from 1799 until 1804 one of the three heads of the French republic, Napoleon being 'first consul'; now an agent for a government (not necessarily one of its nationals) who assists its citizens and trading interests in a foreign city. A **consulate** is the office from which a consul works; the consular section of an EMBASSY issues visas, and passports to the nationals of its own country living abroad.

> A person who having failed to secure an office from the people is given one by the ADMINISTRATION on condition that he leave the country.
> AMBROSE BIERCE

consultancy An arrangement under which an MP at WESTMINSTER keeps a watching brief for the interests of a company or other organisation in return for payment; such consultancies, which have to be listed in the REGISTER OF INTERESTS, have in a few cases been as lucrative as the Member's Parliamentary salary and there have been occasions when an MP has listed his occupation as 'consultant'. The practice was severely curtailed in the mid-1990s after the explosion of 'SLEAZE' allegations against largely Conservative MPs, culminating in the CASH FOR QUESTIONS scandal.

Consumer Price Index *See* CPI.

Consumption Tax The value added tax (originally known as GST), which Paul KEATING, as Treasurer in Bob HAWKE's Labor government, attempted to introduce to Australia in 1984/85, only to have to retreat in the face of public opposition. Keating and Hawke each blamed each other for the debacle. Keating asserted: 'We were stuck with it because of an undisciplined commitment Bob Hawke gave during the 1984 election', but Hawke claimed Keating 'was obsessed with the GST to an extent that worried many people around him'.

> It was deeply opposed to everything I understood the Labor Party to stand for.
> New South Wales premier NEVILLE WRAN

> It's a bit like Ben-Hur. We've crossed the line with one wheel off.
> PAUL KEATING

Contadora plan The group of Latin American countries that from 1983 worked, with considerable success, for an end to conflicts in Central America, especially Nicaragua and El Salvador. It takes its name from a meeting on Contadora island of representatives of Mexico, Colombia, Panama and Venezuela, backed by a 'support group' of Argentina, Brazil, Peru and Uruguay. The REAGAN administration and Nicaragua's SANDINISTAS both refused to back the draft Contadora agreement, but the **Esquipulas II** peace plan launched in 1987 with Contadora support by President Arias of Costa Rica led to a release of prisoners and direct talks between the Sandinistas and the CONTRAS. These failed, but paved the way for elections in 1990, after the BUSH administration had halted direct military funding for the Contras, in which Violetta Chamorro's National Opposition Union ousted the Sandinistas. Several formulae for ending the GUERRILLA WAR in El Salvador were also advanced, despite US disapproval. The conflict continued to flare sporadically, but the ARENA government elected in 1989 (after elections the FMLN guerrillas boycotted) took firm action against guerrillas and right-wing DEATH SQUADS alike.

containment One of the fundamental aims of US policy during the COLD WAR, the prevention of Soviet expansion by an alliance of encircling states pledged to resist any aggression. The word and the principle were first put forward in 1947 by George Kennan (1904–2005), then head of the State Department's policy planning staff; in an article in *Foreign Affairs* signed 'Mr X', Kennan wrote:

> The Russians look forward to a duel of infinite duration.

The TRUMAN administration speedily adopted the policy, going beyond Kennan's thinking to create challenging military alliances. Containment worked best in Europe, where NATO held a line stretching from Arctic Norway to Turkey; the establishment of the ANZUS, CENTO and SEATO alliances was intended to contain the threat of a Communist advance on all sides, but proved less durable. Though America became even more alarmed at the prospect of a Communist upsurge in Latin America, the traditional political climate of the region (*see* GRINGO FACTOR) ruled out a system of alliances and led to the US taking unilateral action (*see* CUBAN MISSILE CRISIS, IRAN-CONTRA AFFAIR).

contempt. contempt of Congress The offence that either House of Congress may deem to have been committed if an individual refuses to testify before a Congressional committee or does so and commits perjury (the most frequent instance), holds Congress up to ridicule or impedes its activities. Neither House has the power to punish those it holds in contempt; instead it must pass a citation for contempt enforceable by its SERGEANT AT ARMS, or (as more frequently occurs) seek an indictment through the Justice Department and the courts.

contempt of the House The serious charge which the HOUSE OF COMMONS is, by custom, able to bring against anyone alleged to have interfered with its workings – though it very seldom does. The boundaries between contempt and Breach of PRIVILEGE are blurred, but generally a contempt would be committed if an individual or organisation ignored or defied a specific decision. Refusal to appear before a SELECT COMMITTEE when summoned is a contempt of the House. Those judged to have committed a contempt are ordered by the SERJEANT-AT-ARMS to attend the BAR OF THE HOUSE to explain themselves; until 1750 they had to kneel.

Contents The name given to Peers voting for a proposition in the HOUSE OF LORDS. Those voting against are **Not Contents**.

continental. Continental Congress The body representing the 23 American colonies which declared INDEPENDENCE, directed the Revolutionary war and drafted the Articles of CONFEDERATION. The first Congress in Carpenter Hall, Philadelphia in 1774, with Georgia absent, warned of war if Britain tried to subdue Massachusetts, demanded repeal of the Coercive Acts (*see* BOSTON TEA PARTY) and the QUEBEC ACT, imposed a BOYCOTT of British goods, questioned Parliament's authority and urged the Crown to redress grievances. The second made George WASHINGTON commander-in-chief on 23 June 1775, and on 2 July 1776 resolved 'that these United Colonies are, and of right ought to be, free and independent states', New York abstaining. It sat until 1781.

continentalism The question of whether North America has room for two separate nations, the implied answer being 'No'. It has long overshadowed Canadian politics; in the 1840s some US politicians advocated absorbing Canada, Daniel Webster saying:

> A large portion of the people believe that a desire for the conquest and final retention of Canada is the mainspring of public opinion.

contingency reserve The sum included in a BUDGET that is not earmarked for spending on any particular project or service, but is kept in reserve to meet unexpected needs.

continuing resolution In the US CONGRESS, a resolution whose passage keeps the FEDERAL government operating if the House and Senate cannot agree a BUDGET by the fiscal year deadline of 30 September.

Contract with America The ten-point radical right-wing programme on which the Republicans in 1994 took control of both Houses of the US Congress (the 104th) for the first time in 40 years, installing Rep. NEWT Gingrich (its architect) as SPEAKER and Bob Dole as SENATE MAJORITY LEADER. Gingrich pledged to implement it in a HUNDRED DAYS whether or not President CLINTON co-operated, and while failing to meet his deadline had it read out in the House on every one of those days. On the very first, 3 January 1995, the Republican leadership initiated three measures: the SHAYS ACT stating that the Congress was not above the law, the commissioning of a 'Big Six' accounting firm to audit Congress, and a severe cut in Congressional staff and committees. BILLS were introduced for TERM LIMITS, welfare reform, a BALANCED BUDGET Amendment, a line-item VETO to cut out

'PORK', common sense litigation reform, the repeal of liberal elements of Clinton's anti-crime package, an Economic Growth Act cutting capital gains tax and regulation and a 'Pro-Family Bill' to end economic and tax penalties on marriage. Clinton backed the cuts in Congressional power and the line-item veto, and the entire 'Contract' except for term limits passed the House, which also barred American troops from UN PEACE-KEEPING. Gingrich met greater resistance from Republican Senators, who rejected the Balanced Budget Amendment. His radical revolution petered out when the Christmas 1995 BUDGET SHUTDOWN handed the initiative back to Clinton.

Contras (Lat. *Contra*, against). The US-backed GUERRILLA group that fought to overthrow Nicaragua's SANDINISTA government, whose ELECTION in 1984 they disputed. Many Contras had served in the hated Presidential guard of the dictatorial Anastasio Somoza (1925–80), ousted by the Sandinistas in 1978; others were the retainers of expropriated landowners, Based in Miami, Honduras and Costa Rica, they were backed by the REAGAN administration in defiance of CONGRESS (*see* BOLAND AMENDMENT, IRAN-CONTRA AFFAIR). Peace talks brokered by the CONTADORA group and President Arias of Panama led to a prisoner exchange in 1987, then broke down. Direct US funding to the Contras ended when George BUSH senior was elected, and the Sandinistas were defeated at the ballot box in 1990.

> We will not betray you. We will do everything we can to win this great struggle.
>
> RONALD REAGAN

> If you want to squander $440 million be my guest, but not a heritage of honour. Why sacrifice that for this grubby, sleazy little operation?
>
> Sen. LOWELL WEICKER (Rep.), 18 March 1987

control orders *See* HOUSE ARREST.

controlled immigration The Conservative slogan that briefly embarrassed the party at the start of the 2005 election campaign when Ed Matts, its candidate in South Dorset, put out a leaflet showing him with a placard carrying the words, accompanied by former home affairs spokesman Ann Widdecombe. In the original picture, taken at a rally in support of a failed ASYLUM-SEEKER from Malawi, Matts carried a picture of the family and Widdecombe the message: 'Let them stay'. For the election leaflet taking a stance against such immigration, other demonstrators had been eliminated from the picture and the placard of Widdecombe, who knew nothing of the deception, altered to read: 'Nor chaos nor inhumanity'. Matts apologised, then got into further trouble with a leaflet depicting a local Olympic yachting gold medallist who turned out to be a Labour supporter. The controversies did Matts no good. South Dorset was Labour's second most MARGINAL seat, but despite a national swing to the Conservatives the sitting MP, Jim Knight, increased his majority.

convenor A largely Scottish term for the chairman or leader of an organisation, especially a local authority or political grouping. It is used more widely in the trade union movement to denote the leader of a workplace's shop stewards.

convention (1) The most colourful events in the US political calendar, the jamborees at which each party devises its PLATFORM and instals its NOMINEES for the Presidency and Vice Presidency; they are held in the summer of each ELECTION year, the Democrats' several weeks before the Republicans'. No convention has actually decided a candidate since Adlai STEVENSON defeated Estes Kefauver for the Democratic nomination in 1956. But even when a CANDIDATE arrives with enough DELEGATES to be sure of the nomination, the convention can combine high political drama and intrigue with colourful, brassy and supposedly spontaneous **floor demonstrations** by the supporters of each Presidential hopeful and sporadic **balloon drops**, notably after the nominee's ACCEPTANCE SPEECH. Sen. Dale Bumpers, listening to Bill CLINTON's 1992 acceptance speech, said of convention oratory:

> You gotta throw the corn where the hogs can get to it.

Parties hope to avoid disputes over the platform and disturbances outside the building (*see* CHICAGO CONVENTION), and win votes by stage-managing prime-time TV coverage of the acceptance speech; from 1996 the networks dropped their customary GAVEL TO GAVEL coverage and have become increasingly selective. Corporate sponsorship is now a prominent feature and funder of conventions, especially the Republicans'. The first convention was held at Baltimore in 1831 by the Anti-Masonic Party; both parties have held more conventions in Chicago than anywhere else: the Democrats seven and the Republicans nine since 1900.

A chess tournament disguised as a circus.
ALISTAIR COOKE (1908–2004)

The Superbowl of schmooze.
CHARLES LEWIS, Director, Center for Public Integrity

The dirty work at political conventions is always done between midnight and dawn.
RUSSELL BAKER (1925–)

There's a regrettable lack of naughtiness in the Democratic Party. They run around fucking each other.
DOLORES FRENCH, hooker at 1984 and 1988 Democratic Conventions

(2) A TREATY signed by a number of nations, generally to set enforceable standards of conduct, as with the GENEVA CONVENTIONS or the VIENNA CONVENTION.

convention bounce The temporary upsurge in the OPINION POLL rating of a Presidential CANDIDATE after his or her NOMINATION by their party's convention, resulting from saturation media exposure. An increase of 15% is the norm.

brokered convention *See* BROKER.

Constitutional Convention (1) *See* PHILADELPHIA CONVENTION. (2) *See* SCOTTISH CONSTITUTIONAL CONVENTION. (3) *See* EUROPEAN CONVENTION.

National Convention A gathering that can be convened to AMEND the US CONSTITUTION if two-thirds of the States petition the CONGRESS. This has never happened, but in the 1980s the PRO-LIFE movement pressed strongly to pass an amendment outlawing abortion by this means.

conventional warfare *or* **weapons** Warfare that does not involve NUCLEAR WEAPONS, and the weapons with which it is fought. The term dates from the COLD WAR and does not take into account non-nuclear WEAPONS OF MASS DESTRUCTION which may be almost as cataclysmic in their effect. *See also* CFE.

convergence A EUROPEAN UNION term for the ideal scenario in which the economies of the weaker member states 'converge' with those of the soundest, with levels of unemployment, inflation and other INDICATORS drawing closer together. Convergence is seen by supporters of the EURO as both achievable and necessary; sceptics argue that it can never happen and that consequently the SINGLE CURRENCY will fail. To date there are few signs of convergence since the introduction of the euro, though the predicted disaster has also failed to materialise.

Convict #2273 The name adopted by Eugene Debs (1855–1926), socialist candidate in the 1920 US Presidential election, who was serving a ten-year sentence under the Espionage Law for an anti-war speech to his party's Ohio convention two years before (*see* FREEDOM OF SPEECH). Debs' sentence was commuted by President HARDING the following year.

convictions The basic beliefs and ideals that are supposed to motivate a politician; in the 1982 Presidential campaign George BUSH was accused of having fewer convictions that the jailed Mafia boss John Gotti. A **conviction politician** is one who is driven by their beliefs and is loth to compromise. Margaret THATCHER prided herself on being one such, saying:

It must be a conviction government. As Prime Minister I could not waste my time having internal arguments.

Cook. Cook County The subdivision of Illinois which includes Chicago and its immediate suburbs, and which has been governed almost as a whole through the Cook County Democratic Party MACHINE. As the DALEY MACHINE it not only gave Chicago effective government but acquired a reputation for over-enthusiastic delivery of the vote to whichever Presidential candidate Mayor Daley was backing. In 1960 John F. KENNEDY's knife-edge victory over Richard NIXON rested on a few thousand votes in Cook County which swung Illinois, and a similar number in Lyndon B. JOHNSON's Texas, which also aroused suspicions.

Cook resignation The departure from Tony BLAIR's CABINET on 17 March 2003, the eve of military action against Iraq, of Robin Cook (1946–2005), LEADER OF THE HOUSE and former Foreign Secretary, in protest at such action being taken without the support of the UNITED NATIONS. In a powerful PERSONAL STATEMENT, which in breach of Commons tradition was greeted with a round of applause, Cook warned that Britain's determination to act with America despite opposition from France, Germany, Russia and China had turned the UN, NATO and European foreign policy co-operation into 'casualties before the first shot is fired'. His CABINET colleague Clare SHORT, who had publicly threatened to resign, backed down and only quit after the conflict had begun.

cool. cool Britannia The tag which was seized on by NEW LABOUR during the first year of Tony BLAIR's premiership to reflect an upsurge in British cultural life and appeal to the outside world which coincided with

Labour's LANDSLIDE defeat of John MAJOR's tired Conservative government. (*See also* Sofa SUMMIT.) The phrase, coined by the media while Major was still in power, came to haunt the Blairites as cultural icons who had been courted by New Labour turned against the party in government. The phrase, a play on 'RULE, BRITANNIA', was originally the title of a song in the Bonzo Dog Doo-Dah Band's 1967 humorous album *Gorilla*. It began:

> Cool Britannia, Britannia take a trip
> Britons ever, ever, ever shall be hip.

cool, calm and elected The goal set by Margaret THATCHER for the Conservatives' 1983 ELECTION campaign when she addressed Tory MPs and candidates at its start; the phrase was a play on 'cool, calm and collected'. She was successful on all counts; after a campaign with few shaky moments and Labour in disarray, the Conservatives were re-elected with a majority of 144.

cooling-off period In some codes of industrial relations law, notably the US TAFT-HARTLEY ACT, a fixed period during which a union, having given notice of a strike, must suspend action to allow tempers to cool and a settlement to be explored.

Coolidge, Calvin (1872–1933) The monosyllabic (*see* SILENT CAL) 30th President of the United States (Republican, 1923–29). A Governor of Massachusetts who made a national reputation by breaking the BOSTON POLICE STRIKE, Coolidge won the Vice Presidential NOMINATION in 1920 and on 3 August 1923 assumed the Presidency on the death of Warren HARDING. He had avoided association with TEAPOT DOME and other scandals of the Harding administration, and with post-war prosperity apparently assured won re-election in his own right in 1924 by a convincing margin over the Democrat John W. Davis and the Progressives' Robert (BATTLING BOB) La Follette on the slogan **Keep Cool and Keep Coolidge**. Four years later, with America still apparently booming, he decided he had had enough, announcing simply: 'I do not choose to run'; asked why he had not sought a further TERM, he replied: 'No prospect of advancement.' He went home to Massachusetts, dying there four years later. When word of his death reached Dorothy Parker, she asked:

> How could they tell?

Coolidge was a dour and shy man; he once said: 'My hobby is holding office.' Alice Roosevelt Longworth was blunter, observing: 'He looks as if he has been weaned on a pickle.' Even Coolidge's wife, when asked about their early romance, said: 'Have you ever *MET* my husband?' Yet he did have a sense of humour with her; once when she complained of having nothing red to wear to offset the colour of their white dog, he told her: 'If it's contrast you want, why not wear white and paint the dog red?' Mrs Coolidge was very much a FIRST LADY of her time, once observing:

> I am rather proud of the fact that after nearly a quarter of a century of marriage, my husband feels free to take his decisions and act on them without consulting me.

> I always figured the American public wanted a solemn ass for President, so I went along with them.
> COOLIDGE

> An economic fatalist with God-given inertia. He knew nothing and refused to learn.
> WILLIAM ALLEN WHITE

> Distinguished for character rather than for heroic achievement. His great task was to restore the dignity and prestige of the Presidency when it had reached the lowest ebb in our history.
> AL SMITH

> Nobody has worked harder at inactivity with such a force of character, with such unremitting attention to detail, with such conscientious devotion to the task.
> WALTER LIPPMANN, Obituary

> He had no ideas, but was not a nuisance.
> H. L. MENCKEN, Obituary

co-operate. co-operation procedure The process created by the SINGLE EUROPEAN ACT for the approval of EU legislation. It involves a complex network of consultation between the EUROPEAN COMMISSION, which initiates legislation, the EUROPEAN PARLIAMENT and the Council of Ministers, which takes its final decision by QMV.

co-operative An enterprise which is owned and managed jointly by the workers (*see* OWENITES, ROCHDALE PIONEERS). The 1974–79 Labour government, especially early on when Tony BENN was Industry Secretary, backed a series of co-operatives born from the ashes of failed businesses, among them the Meriden motor-cycle works and the *Scottish Daily News*, but none survived.

Co-Operative Party A distinct UK political party, founded in 1917, whose membership is compatible with that of the LABOUR PARTY; it has more than two dozen MPs who sit as **'Labour and Co-Operative'**. Its principal policies, aimed at advancing co-ownership, are set out in *The*

Co-Operative Agenda for Labour and the MANIFESTOS it publishes at each election. The party is closely linked to the Co-Operative retail movement.

co-option The appointment of members of a committee by the committee itself or by other bodies, after directly-elected places have been filled.

Copperheads The minority of northern Democrats who, during the US CIVIL WAR, campaigned for peace and at times verged on TREASON; the name derives from a particularly devious species of American snake. They managed to control the party's platform for the 1864 election – demanding an immediate ARMISTICE and making no mention of SLAVERY – but not the Presidential candidate, Gen. George McLellan rejecting their policies. By the time voting took place the Confederates were on the run, and the Copperhead platform contributed to McLellan's heavy defeat by LINCOLN.

co-presidency The arrangement which Ronald REAGAN considered before choosing a RUNNING-MATE in 1980. It would have applied had he picked former President Gerald FORD; despite the appeal of a dream TICKET, Reagan rejected the idea partly because he was unwilling to give the Vice President a direct stake in the power of the Presidency.

Cordite vote The episode on 21 June 1895 that brought the fall of ROSEBERY's Liberal government; it was defeated 132–125 in a snap HOUSE OF COMMONS vote after the usually sure-footed Sir Henry CAMPBELL-BANNERMAN had botched the Government's defence against charges – never proven – that there was insufficient cordite for the Army.

> A chance blow, but a fatal one.
>
> CAMPBELL-BANNERMAN

> A well-manoeuvred assassination.
>
> AUGUSTINE BIRRELL MP (Lib.)

cordon. Cordon rule The equivalent in the US SENATE of the House's RAMSEYER RULE, setting out the precise form in which a BILL must be REPORTED.

cordon sanitaire (Fr. sterile strip) A strip of territory, or belt of states, seen by a country or countries on one side as protection from those beyond, which they regard as potential aggressors. In February 1946 Harold MACMILLAN suggested that the Soviet Union was preoccupied, defensively, with creating 'a new cordon sanitaire . . . of states made SATELLITE and dependent' between itself and the West.

CORE Congress of Racial Equality. One of the spearheads of America's CIVIL RIGHTS movement from the early 1960s, when black and white activists tested SEGREGATION laws in the Deep South, notably through SIT-INS and the FREEDOM RIDES of 1961. CORE, a previously small organisation founded in Chicago in 1942 and led from 1961 by its co-founder James Farmer, may have owed its name to the old Southern saying:

> White man get the apple, nigger get the core.

COREPER Committee of PERMANENT REPRESENTATIVES. The group comprising the ambassadors to the EUROPEAN UNION of each member state that meets in Brussels every fortnight to conduct business in between formal meetings of the COUNCIL OF MINISTERS.

Corfu Channel incident The naval disaster in October 1946 which intensified the freeze between Britain and Albania at the start of the COLD WAR, 44 sailors being killed and 45 injured when the Royal Navy destroyers *Saumarez* and *Volage* struck mines off the Albanian coast. The channel had been swept clear of mines after WORLD WAR II, and the assumption was that the newly-Communist Albanians had re-mined it. The Soviet Union VETOed a UNITED NATIONS resolution blaming Albania and Britain took the matter to the International Court of Justice. Albania ignored its ruling, and a stand-off continued until 1996 when Britain returned 1.5 tons of gold to Albania on receipt of an apology for the loss of life and compensation of £1.3 million.

Corn Laws The PROTECTIONIST legislation over which PEEL split Britain's old TORY party, and which was widely believed to have exacerbated the IRISH POTATO FAMINE. Introduced by Lord Liverpool's government in 1815 to the accompaniment of riots in London, they banned corn imports when the price sank to £4 a quarter. Serious bread shortages when they were invoked in 1820 led to their amendment eight years later, with the imposition of heavy duties. By 1839 Melbourne was declaring the Corn Laws 'the maddest scheme that had ever entered into the imagination of man to conceive'; in the early 1840s the Anti-Corn Law League began winning Parliamentary seats. When news of the famine reached London, Peel tried and failed to reverse the Tory position by persuading the CABINET to suspend the laws; in January 1846 he formed an alliance with the embryo Liberals to phase out the duties over three years, and by the end of May Parliament had passed the repeal legislation.

corporate. corporate donors Businesses and their top executives who make sizeable donations to party or campaign funds, allegedly in return for preferential treatment when the recipients are in office.

corporate welfare *See* WELFARE.

corporatism A system in which the state works hand in glove with large companies and TRADE UNIONS in pursuit of a single goal. It is disliked both by right-wing politicians who see it as violating the principles of the MARKET and the right of a government to govern, and by the left and union militants who see it as smothering workers' rights. A particular form of corporatism, stemming from the turn-of-the-century theories of Emile Durkheim, lay at the heart of Mussolini's FASCIST state and, even more so, the state and economic structure erected in Spain by the Franco regime (*see* FALANGE).

Corrective Party The UK party started in the late 1980s by the anti-prostitution law campaigner Lindi St Clair (1952–), otherwise known as **Miss Whiplash**, which received an enormous amount of publicity but very few votes. Miss St Clair claimed to have a file on over 100 MPs and peers who had come to her for 'corrective' flagellation; shortly afterward her empty car was found at Beachy Head, a well-known suicide spot. After several days of police inquiries, she was discovered on a cruise liner off Florida.

Corrie Bill The first serious attempt by a BACKBENCHER to tighten David Steel (*see* BOY DAVID)'s liberal Abortion Act of 1967; promoted in 1979 by the Scottish Conservative MP John Corrie (1935–), it gained a SECOND READING but was strangled in Committee the following summer. (*See also* ALTON BILL.)

corrupt. corrupt bargain The name given by angry supporters of the defeated Andrew Jackson (*see* OLD HICKORY) to John Quincy ADAMS' election as President in 1824. Adams had finished behind Jackson, but with no majority in the ELECTORAL COLLEGE the election passed to the HOUSE OF REPRESENTATIVES. Speaker Henry Clay swung two key States, though not quite a majority, to Adams – who then made Clay Secretary of State. The Jacksonians insisted a deal had been struck – a deal, as John Randolph put it, 'between the BLACKLEG and the Puritan' – which probably had not. They had their revenge in 1828 when Jackson brushed Adams aside.

> The Judas of the West has closed the contract and will receive the thirty pieces of silver. His end will be the same. Was there ever such a bare faced corruption in this country before.
>
> JACKSON, letter to W. B. Lewis, 14 February 1825

Federal Corrupt Practices Act The Act passed in 1925 which made a first attempt to control campaign spending and contributions; its aim was limited, and its effect even more so as it did not apply to PRIMARIES. House and Senate candidates were expected to file reports of their spending, but if filed at all these were fragmentary. Donations of $100 or more had to be reported – so gifts of $99.99 became common – but campaign committees only had to name their contributors if they operated in two or more states. In 1972 it was superseded by the **Federal Election Campaign Act**, which was marginally more effective.

> More loophole than laws.
>
> LYNDON B. JOHNSON

corruption A concomitant of politics through the centuries, the remarkable thing being how many men and women without wealth have rejected offers of lucre and done what they believed to be right. The historian Gibbon termed corruption 'the most infallible symptom in constitutional liberty', George WASHINGTON maintained that 'few men have the virtue to withstand the highest bidder', while Mayor Richard DALEY declared: 'You know that if I had ever been corrupted, I wouldn't still be around.' *See also* SLEAZE.

> When I want to buy up any politician I always find the anti-monopolists the most purchasable – they don't come so high.
>
> WILLIAM VANDERBILT (1821–85)

Cortès The two-chamber Parliament of democratic Spain, which in 1977 replaced the single-chamber *Cortès* of Franco's FALANGIST state. It comprises a Congress of Deputies, and a less powerful Senate.

COSLA *C*onfederation *o*f *S*cottish *L*ocal *A*uthorities. The body which has traditionally represented Scotland's councils – the regions and the districts and the single-tier authorities that replaced them in the mid-1990s. Comprising council leaders of all parties, it exerts considerable influence over

Scottish Ministers and the SCOTTISH EXECUTIVE, though its voice was weakened when Glasgow, Clackmannanshire and Falkirk seceded in 2001.

Cosmic Bob The nickname given to Nebraska's Sen. Bob Kerrey (1943–) because of his interest in the ethereal. It haunted him when he made a brief run for the Democratic Presidential NOMINATION in 1992.

coterminosity A situation in which electoral districts for different assemblies share the same boundaries. It became an issue c. 2001 when the Labour government proposed creating constituencies of differing sizes, and consequently different boundaries, for the WESTMINSTER and Scottish Parliaments.

council. Council of Europe *See* EUROPE.

Council of All Ireland *See* SUNNINGDALE.

Council of Ministers The political driving force of the EUROPEAN UNION, at least when members are able to agree. It comprises all the EU's heads of government or their representatives, and provides the EUROPEAN COMMISSION with a working brief. It takes two forms: the Council proper, which holds SUMMIT meetings at least every six months which decide on critical issues, and the monthly meetings of Ministers in specific fields such as finance (ECOFIN), agriculture or transport. *See also* COREPER.

Council of the Federation The upper house of the Russian Parliament or DUMA, inaugurated in December 1993.

Council on Foreign Relations *See* FOREIGN.

council tax The local tax introduced by John MAJOR's government to replace the notorious POLL TAX, which took effect throughout Great Britain in April 1993. Unlike the poll tax or COMMUNITY CHARGE, which was a flat-rate charge on almost all adults, the council tax is property-based, Homes are valued in several bands, and a charge per band is set by each local authority. There is a reduction of 25% for a single householder, and those on social security also pay a lower council tax. One unexpected phenomenon at the start was the number of householders appealing that their home was in too *low* a band because of the stigma they felt was implied. More recently the tax has seemed less benign; in 2003/4 there were widespread protests from pensioners, starting in Devon, at increases far in excess of inflation.

count (1) The tallying of votes once an ELECTION has taken place, conducted in the advanced democracies with safeguards to avoid fraud. In most cases the count begins as soon as ballot papers can be got to central counting points in schools or sports centres; in some remote parts of Britain (plus cities with unimaginative officials) it does not start till the following morning. In the interests of speed, staff from banks or council cashiers are preferred as counters; South Africa for its first multiracial elections went for teachers and counting went on for days. It can also do so in the Irish Republic, because the complicated formula of PROPORTIONAL REPRESENTATION requires candidates to be eliminated one by one. The count has given rise to abuses in many countries; in 1977 the Nicaraguan dictator Anastasio Somoza boasted to his opponents:

> You won the election. But I won the count.

(2) The JOINT SESSION of the US CONGRESS on the 6 January after a Presidential election, to count the votes of the ELECTORAL COLLEGE; if no CANDIDATE has a majority, the House then chooses the President from the three having the largest number of electoral votes, and the Senate the Vice President from the two leading candidates for that office.

counted out At WESTMINSTER, the fate of a sitting of the HOUSE OF COMMONS when not enough MPs are available to 'keep a HOUSE'.

counter-espionage One of the roles of internal security agencies such as America's FBI, Britain's MI5 and Germany's BND: the detection of foreign agents with a view to their arrest or manipulation and the destruction of the organisation behind them.

counter-inflation strategy A term used by politicians either for a PRICES AND INCOMES POLICY or for the curbing of the MONEY SUPPLY.

counter-insurgency The combating of GUERRILLA movements by government forces, a term much used by the Americans to describe the nature of US involvement in VIETNAM in its early stages, but applied more widely.

country. country member In Australia, a Member of the House of Representatives representing an outback constituency. Since 1952 country members have received higher allowances than their urban counterparts.

Country Party The right-wing though originally 'non-political' farmers' movement in Australia which had already won eleven seats in federal elections when it constituted itself as a political party in 1920. In 1923 it went into coalition with the LIBERALS, and remained their junior partner, even though as the **National Party** (the name it adopted in 1982) it became Australia's largest, with 140,000 members. It provided three Prime Ministers, each for less than two months: Earle Page (1939), Arthur Fadden (1941) and John McEwen (1967–68).

a country fit for heroes to live in A phrase popularised by LLOYD GEORGE in a speech on 24 November 1918, a fortnight after the end of WORLD WAR I, in which he set goals for Britain's returning servicemen that proved hard to achieve. What he actually said was:

> What is our task? To make Britain a fit country for heroes to live in.

Lloyd George's sincerity was later questioned by G. K. Chesterton in his verse *A Land Fit for Heroes*, with the ironic subtitle *Refutation of the Only Too Prevalent Slander that Parliamentary Leaders are Indifferent to the Strict Fulfilment of their Promises and the Preservation of their Reputation for Veracity*:

> They said (when they had dined at Ciro's)
> The land would soon be fit for heroes;
> And now they've managed to ensure it,
> For only heroes could endure it.

Ask not what your country can do for you – ask what you can do for your country One of the key phrases of John F. KENNEDY's INAUGURAL ADDRESS on 20 January 1961, which became a text for the NEW FRONTIER and such innovations as the PEACE CORPS. JFK said:

> And so, my fellow Americans, ask not what your country can do for you – ask what you can do for your country. My fellow citizens of the world: ask not what America will do for you, ask what we can do together for the freedom of man.

The words were not entirely original; the funeral oration for John Greenleaf Whittier contained a similar exhortation, Oliver Wendell Holmes made the juxtaposition in a speech in 1884, and after WORLD WAR I, in *The Voice of the Master,* Khalil Ghibran (1883–1931) wrote:

> Are you a politician asking what your country can do for you or a zealous one asking what you can do for your country? If you are the first, then you are a parasite; if the second, then you are an oasis in the desert.

Even the far from eloquent President HARDING said in St Louis in 1923:

> I like people in the cities, in the States and in the nation to ask themselves now and then: 'What can I do for my city?', not 'How much can I get out of my city?'

die for one's country The ultimate sacrifice, urged on young men by their political leaders when war looms. In classical times Horace wrote: 'Sweet and glorious it is to die for one's country', and the sentiment has all too frequently had to be repeated. The American Nathan Hale, facing execution as a spy by the British in 1776, is said to have proudly stated: 'I only regret that I have but one life to give for my country'; sadly for romantics, a witness recalled his actual words as:

> It is the duty of any good officer to obey any orders given him by his commander-in-chief.

The day before Indira GANDHI was assassinated, she said:

> Even if I die in the service of this nation, I would be proud of it. Every drop of my blood, I am sure, will contribute to the growth of this nation and make it strong and dynamic.

And Neil KINNOCK, in a powerful 1987 LABOUR PARTY conference speech, stated in renouncing NUCLEAR WAR:

> I would die for my country, but I would not let my country die for me.

go to the country (1) A traditional UK phrase for the action of a Prime Minister in calling a GENERAL ELECTION. When defeated in a no-CONFIDENCE vote in February 1979, James CALLAGHAN defiantly told the Commons:

> We shall take our case to the country.

(2) In US politics, to report back to the voters with a view to getting re-elected, as in Sen. Orville Platt's comment on the SHERMAN ACT.

I have no country to fight for, my country is the Earth, and I am a citizen of the world The internationalist credo of Eugene Debs (1855–1926), the US socialist presidential candidate and PACIFIST (*see* CONVICT #2273).

I vow to thee, my country The English patriotic verse, ranking with LAND OF HOPE AND GLORY and JERUSALEM, written by Sir Cecil Spring-Rice (1858–1918) and sung to the Jupiter theme from Gustav Holst's *The Planets* suite. The opening couplet runs:

> I vow to thee, my country, – all earthly things above –
> Entire and whole and perfect, the service of my love.

Mother Country, the The term traditionally used to describe England in Australia, and to a lesser extent the other DOMINIONS. It has been heard much less since the 1960s as

Australia asserts its national identity, and more and more of its citizens are non-British in origin.

my country, right or wrong One of the great statements of simple PATRIOTISM, first uttered as a toast in 1816 by the American Stephan Decatur (1779–1820). He proclaimed:

> Our country! In her intercourse with foreign nations, may she always be in the right, but our country, right or wrong!

The argument did not pass unchallenged. In 1872 Sen. Carl Schurz countered:

> The Senator for Wisconsin cannot frighten me by exclaiming: 'My country, right or wrong'. In one sense I say so, too. My country, and my country is the great American republic, my country right or wrong: if right, to be kept right, and if wrong, to be set right.

But G. K. Chesterton (1874–1936) was wholly opposed, saying:

> Our country, right or wrong, is something no patriot would think of saying except in a desperate case. It is like saying: 'My mother, drunk or sober!'

My country, 'tis of thee The US patriotic anthem, known as *America*, written in 1831 by Samuel Francis Smith, a young Boston clergyman, and set by him (unwittingly) to the tune of GOD SAVE THE KING; it stands second in popularity only to the STAR SPANGLED BANNER. The first of four verses runs:

> My country, 'tis of thee
> Sweet land of liberty,
> Of thee I sing:
> Land where my fathers died,
> Land of the pilgrims' pride,
> From every mountainside,
> Let freedom ring.

one country, two systems The formula devised by Teng Hsiao-Ping (1904–97) for the reintegration of capitalist Hong Kong into Communist China, and which was broadly applied after Britain's handover of the colony in 1997. It enabled the CAPITALIST system and a degree of democracy to apply in Hong Kong, in parallel with a more rigidly COMMUNIST system in the rest of the country.

what this country needs is a good 5 cent cigar The classic dictum of Thomas Marshall (1854–1925), Woodrow WILSON's Vice President, delivered from the Chair of the Senate while Sen. Joseph Bristow of Kansas was making an interminable speech on 'What this country needs'.

county (1) In America, the administrative subdivisions into which almost every State is divided. (2) In Britain the traditional large-scale unit of local government; in the 1970s the Scottish counties were replaced by larger regions as the upper tier (themselves now supplanted by UNITARY AUTHORITIES) and the English and Welsh county boundaries were heavily redrawn. **Metropolitan Counties** were created covering six major conurbations outside London, and **Shire Counties** for predominantly rural areas (though often containing one large city); the Metropolitan Counties were abolished some twelve years later, the districts within them becoming unitary authorities.

County Hall The stately building on the South Bank of the Thames, facing the HOUSES OF PARLIAMENT across Westminster Bridge, which from 1933 to 1986 was the headquarters of first the LCC (London County Council) and from 1965 the GLC (Greater London Council). Designed by Ralph Knott and extended in 1963, County Hall symbolised London to many in the capital, but was declared redundant after the GLC's abolition by Margaret THATCHER's government. Moves in 1992 to secure it as a new headquarters for the London School of Economics (LSE) failed, and a Japanese firm reopened most of it as a hotel; some of the annexes became private flats, others remain empty. When Labour set up a Greater London Assembly (GLA) in 2000, County Hall was considered too large for its limited powers, and with the former GLC leader Ken Livingstone (*see* RED KEN) as Mayor it set up shop in the 'FENCING MASK' near Tower Bridge.

coup (d'état) (Fr. blow to the state) The sudden and often violent overthrow of a country's rulers by a faction wanting power for itself. A coup may be mounted by the military, or by civilians.

> Q: What has one wing, is armed to the teeth and produces milk?
> A: A right-wing military coup.
>
> 1960s Scots ANARCHIST riddle

In May 1968 Cecil King, megalomaniac chairman of the *Daily Mirror*, explored the scope for a military coup to oust Harold WILSON's Labour government. On 8 May he invited Earl Mountbatten to form a government of national unity after a successful coup. Sir Solly Zuckerman, the government's chief scientific adviser who was also at the meeting, described the plan as 'rank treachery', adding:

> All this talk of machine guns at street corners is

appalling. I am a public servant and I will have nothing to do with it. Nor should you, Dickie.

Mountbatten then told King his plan was 'simply not on'.

Coupon election The general election held in Britain in December 1918, immediately after victory in WORLD WAR I. The LLOYD GEORGE coalition of Conservatives and much of the LIBERAL PARTY gave a 'coupon' to all candidates pledged to support it, and scored a crushing victory over the orthodox Liberals led by ASQUITH (who lost his seat, denouncing the 'coupon' as a 'wicked fraud'). The coalition won 478 seats, its opponents 229 including 63 Labour, 28 Asquithian Liberals and 73 SINN FEIN. Though L.G. remained as Prime Minister for four years more, the election spelt the end of the Liberal Party as a major force. *See also* HANG THE KAISER; HARD FACED MEN WHO HAVE DONE WELL OUT OF THE WAR.

court. court dress The fancy garb that members of Britain's PRIVY COUNCIL had to wear for its meetings; the practice was relaxed in 1924 when the first Labour government took office, and has since died out.

court-packing The stratagem briefly advocated by Franklin D. ROOSEVELT in reaction to the US SUPREME COURT's invalidation of much of his NEW DEAL legislation in 1935–36 (*see* BLACK MONDAY; Sick CHICKEN CASE). On 5 January 1937 FDR, without consulting Congressional leaders, unveiled a plan to overthrow the nine-man Court's conservative majority by appointing up to six new justices if those aged over 70 did not voluntarily retire. CONGRESS, including many of the President's supporters, was outraged at what it saw as a dictatorial attempt to subvert the CONSTITUTION. Conservative Democrats threatened to withdraw support for the New Deal, and the SENATE rejected the court plan by 70–22. But the Court got the message, and in the summer of 1937 reversed itself to declare the WAGNER ACT constitutional. With the death soon after of several conservative justices and their replacement by liberals, the conflict with the White House subsided, but FDR paid a heavy political price.

cover-up The concealment of their actions by those in authority in order to escape scrutiny, criticism or censure. The most notorious was the WATERGATE cover-up practised by the NIXON White House, but there have been many others; in Britain WESTLAND was widely placed in that category. Ironically Nixon himself had accused President TRUMAN of a cover-up during the 1952 election, saying as MCCARTHYISM hit its stride:

Mr Truman, Dean Acheson and other administration officials for political purposes covered up this Communist conspiracy and attempted to halt its exposure.

covert operations Operations carried out by a security or intelligence agency without the knowledge not only of the populus of the state where they are taking place but of all but a handful of officials of the government for whom they are supposed to be acting. Covert operations by the CIA, including plans to assassinate a number of hostile or inconvenient foreign leaders, led to CONGRESS imposing OVERSIGHT of the agency; however, even specific legislation (*see* BOLAND ANENDMENT) could not prevent the IRAN-CONTRA AFFAIR, described by CIA director William Casey as the 'ultimate covert operation'.

Cowley Street The headquarters of Britain's LIBERAL DEMOCRATS, a red-brick Edwardian building 600 yards west of the PALACE OF WESTMINSTER which was originally taken on by the SDP prior to the 1983 general election and now houses the merged party. Though the newest of the main parties, the LibDems have now been in their headquarters longer than either Labour or the Conservatives.

Coxeyites The army of several hundred jobless men who marched on WASHINGTON in April 1894 as the full effects of the DEPRESSION of 1893 were felt. Led by 'General' Jacob Coxey, a horsebreeder and quarry owner, 20,000 had set off the previous autumn from Massillon, Ohio and other centres to present CONGRESS with a PETITION demanding inflation of the currency and a federal programme of public works. Welcomed and fed by farmers at first, they met a cooler reception in the East and only 600 completed the journey. The protest evaporated after Coxey and two aides were arrested – for walking on the CAPITOL lawn.

CP Universal shorthand for Britain's COMMUNIST PARTY; the party used the abbreviation itself but preferred to be known as the **CPGB**.

CPI Consumer Price Index. The official monthly measure of the rate of INFLATION in both America and the UK, though in the latter it is still often referred to by its previous name as the RPI, Retail Price Index.

CPSU Communist Party of the Soviet Union. The party which ruled the Soviet Union for 74 years following the OCTOBER REVOLUTION, enjoying supreme power, despite regular PURGES, until Boris Yeltsin ordered its dissolution following the KREMLIN COUP of 1991. Party membership was a prerequisite for success, and often survival, in any walk of Soviet life. A successor party exerts considerable influence in Russia's post-Soviet parliament, and components of the old party retain autocratic power in Belarus and some Central Asian republics.

> The party is the rallying point for the best elements of the working class. STALIN

Crabb affair The mysterious episode that overshadowed the successful visit to Britain of the Soviet leaders Bulganin and Khrushchev in May 1956. It hinged on the disappearance of Commander Lionel 'Buster' Crabb, a Royal Navy frogman, while exploring the underside of the Soviet cruiser *Ordjonikidze*, in which B AND K had arrived, in Portsmouth harbour. The UK government insisted he had been working independently and not under orders, but *The Times* discovered that senior detectives had called at Crabb's hotel, removed all record of his stay and ordered staff not to discuss it. The incident was never fully explained; there was speculation that he had DEFECTED to the Soviet Union, drowned by accident or been killed by fellow British agents when it was realised his activities might prove politically embarrassing. But it is most likely he was captured by the Russians while examining the hull, then killed. Anthony EDEN, pressed hard by Labour MPs on the issue, told the COMMONS:

> It would not be in the public interest to disclose the circumstances in which Commander Crabb is presumed to have met his death.

cradle. from the cradle to the grave The ethos of Britain's WELFARE STATE in its ultimate form, as proposed in the BEVERIDGE REPORT and largely created by the 1945 LABOUR GOVERNMENT. (*See also* WOMB TO TOMB.) The phrase, which dates back at least to Edward Bellamy's 1888 novel *Looking Backward*, became an international yardstick for comprehensive social provision by the State, as witness Herbert HOOVER's 1954 statement that

> Even if security from the cradle to the grave could eliminate all the risks of life, it would be a dead hand on the creative spirit of our people.

the hand that rocks the cradle can rock the system The slogan on which the left-wing feminist lawyer Mary Robinson stood for the presidency of the Irish Republic in 1990, pulling off a shock victory over the former FIANNA FAIL TANAISTE Brian Lenihan. It represented her belief that the women of Ireland, traditionally the backbone of the Catholic home, were ready to take a more active political role, and was designed to convince them they could make a difference. She was also helped by the scandal that broke during the campaign over the claim – strongly denied – that Lenihan in 1982 had rung President Hillery at ARAS NA UACHTARAIN to dissuade him from granting a DISSOLUTION to the Fine Gael TAOISEACH Garret FitzGerald.

crash through, or crash The phrase that came to exemplify the increasingly desperate and ultimately doomed efforts of Gough WHITLAM's Labor government to revive Australia's economy, get its policies implemented and remain in office. Whitlam had once told colleagues: 'You must crash through, or crash', and the words became the title of the definitive book on his ministry by Laurie Oakes. Yet Whitlam himself was cautious, and the risks were taken by members of his CABINET, several of whom were sacked for exceeding their brief. *See also* KERR SACKING; LOANS SCANDAL; MOROSI AFFAIR.

Great Crash *See* GREAT.

Crawford The tiny (pop. 631) Texas town eighteen miles west of WACO which achieved worldwide publicity from his election as President in 2000 as the location of George W. BUSH's ranch, being visited thereafter by the travelling media and, occasionally, by visiting world leaders invited to the family home.

> I'm proud of George. He's learned a lot about ranching since those first years when he tried to milk a horse. What's more, it was a male horse.
>
> LAURA BUSH at the WHITE HOUSE Correspondents' dinner, 30 April 2005.

credibility gap The discrepancy between what a politician claims to be the case and those same facts as perceived by the public. The phrase is credited to future President Gerald FORD, who when House MAJORITY LEADER in 1966, contrasted the JOHNSON administration's denial of greater US involvement in the VIETNAM WAR with the evidence available. The following year the veteran COLUMNIST Walter Lippmann wrote:

In order to avoid the embarrassment of calling a spade a spade, newspapers have agreed to talk about the credibility gap. This is a polite euphemism for deception.

credit. Créditistes The allies in Quebec of Canada's SOCIAL CREDIT party, who made a major breakthrough in 1962, winning 26 seats in the House of Commons, ebbed and flowed thereafter and were eliminated in 1980.

Crédit Mobilier affair One of the greatest of the scandals that plagued the GRANT administration, involving Congressional leaders and Vice President Schuyler Colfax, whom Grant dropped from the ticket when it broke in 1872. Rumours of graft involving the *Crédit Mobilier*, the construction company that had built the Union Pacific Railroad, were upheld by a Congressional investigation the next year. It found that Rep. Oakes Ames, a Massachusetts Democrat who owned the company with his brother and had amassed a $10 million fortune through contract-padding, had handed out company stock to legislators (including Colfax, when SPEAKER in 1867–68, and on a small scale to the wife of Henry Wilson, who replaced him as vice presidential nominee) at less than market value to smooth the passage of railroad-friendly legislation. Voters exasperated with all-pervading CORRUPTION took their revenge at the 1874 Congressional elections, overturning the Republican majority. Exposure of the WHISKEY RING and the BELKNAP SCANDAL still lay ahead.

credit squeeze The use of tighter credit to stop the economy OVERHEATING, through controls on lending to businesses and private individuals by banks, finance houses and other financial institutions.

CREEP Committee for Re-Election of the President. The organisation set up to finance the re-election of President NIXON in 1972 which was revealed in the WATERGATE scandal as the conduit for illegal and unethical payments – including to the burglars themselves.

competence creep In the EU, the ability of the COMMISSION to aggregate new powers to itself by involving itself imperceptibly in matters adjacent to, but outside, its defined areas of responsibility.

function creep WHITEHALL-speak for the ability of a department to expand on the specific powers granted to it by a piece of legislation, either deliberately through its drafting or through subsequent opportunism.

grade creep The process by which steadily more lower-grade civil servants are upgraded in order to meet their pressure for higher salaries and status.

In 1955, 8.2 per cent of Federal workers were in the upper middle class of the civil service, grades GS-12 through GS-15. Today the figure is 28.9 per cent. Grade creep means too many chiefs and too few Indians, too many supervisors and too few people to do the work.

CHARLES PETERS, *How Washington Really Works*

mission creep The tendency for forces despatched to one of the world's trouble-spots to remain for longer than was originally planned, generally because the situation is more complex and intractable than those making the commitment had realised or been prepared to admit.

Cresson affair The scandal surrounding the European COMMISSIONER and former French Prime Minister Edith Cresson (*see* LA PARFUMÉE) which in 1999 triggered the resignation of the entire Commission headed by Jacques Santer. It stemmed from the chaotic management of Agenor, an agency for which Mme Cresson was responsible and to which she appointed René Berthelot, an elderly dentist and personal friend. OLAF determined that the Commission had lost all control over the agency, with two further Commissioners also culpable, and after the EUROPEAN PARLIAMENT contemplated exercising its power to remove the Commission, Santer and his colleagues resigned. In June 2004 a Belgian judge dismissed CORRUPTION charges against Mme. Cresson. Unrepentant, her attack on the Parliament that October for launching WITCH-HUNTS against Commissioners, just as Rocco BUTTIGLIONE's nomination was running into trouble, merely helped guarantee a majority at Strasbourg against the entire Commission proposed by José Manuel Barroso.

Crichel Down The scandal in 1954 which brought the ultimate in principled resignations, Sir Thomas Dugdale, Minister of Agriculture, resigning after conduct by his civil servants was criticised. CHURCHILL described his action as 'chivalrous in a high degree', and would not accept the resignations of Dugdale's ministerial team including Lord Carrington who would himself resign as Defence Secretary 28 years later over the invasion of the FALKLANDS. The case stemmed from the compulsory purchase of 725 acres of Dorset farmland in

1938 from three owners for an airfield, and the refusal of the Ministry of Agriculture to let them have it back after the war, insisting it could be farmed more efficiently as a whole. Lt.-Cdr. George Marten, son-in-law of one of the owners, launched a campaign against the decision, backed by his MP and the National Farmers' Union. An inquiry by Sir Andrew Clark QC publicly blamed several civil servants, but Sir Thomas felt it his duty to resign – though he may have gone because he agreed with his officials' decision. A bitter COMMONS debate over Crichel Down on 20 July 1954 established standards for MINISTERIAL RESPONSIBILITY that have not always been honoured since.

cricket test The test of a non-white Briton's national loyalties, raised in 1991 by Norman Tebbit (*see* CHINGFORD SKINHEAD), which aroused accusations of RACISM and briefly reopened the political debate about immigration. Tebbit suggested in a US newspaper interview than many, even in the second generation, would support the visiting cricket team from their country of origin in preference to England.

crime. Crime against Kansas *See* KANSAS.

Crime of '73 The term used by advocates of FREE SILVER in the late 19th century for the **Coinage Act** passed by the US CONGRESS in 1873, which ended the minting of silver dollars and effectively put America back on the GOLD STANDARD. The Act was later blames by advocates of bimetallism for a shortage of coin in circulation, and consequently for falling farm and commodity prices.

tough on crime and tough on the causes of crime *See* TOUGH.

Crimean War The Anglo-French conflict with Russia from 1854 to 1856, fought on the Crimean peninsula in the Black Sea. It arose partly from British fear of Russian influence in Turkey and partly from Russia's suppression of the revolutions of 1848. Best known for the **Charge of the Light Brigade**, its legacies were the routine use of the rifle in warfare, the introduction of competence into the British Army's command structure, and the field nursing pioneered by Florence Nightingale at her hospital at Scutari, Turkey. *See also* EASTERN QUESTION.

> Are we to be the Don Quixotes of Europe, to go about fighting for every cause where we find that someone has been wronged?
>
> RICHARD COBDEN, House of Commons, 22 December 1854

> The Angel of Death has been abroad throughout the land. You may almost hear the beating of his wings.
>
> JOHN BRIGHT, House of Commons, 23 February 1855

crisis. Crisis, what crisis? The highly compromising remark Prime Minister James CALLAGHAN (*see* SUNNY JIM) is supposed to have made about the WINTER OF DISCONTENT on his return to Heathrow from the Guadeloupe economic summit on 10 January 1979. It was, in fact, a headline in the *Sun*, paraphrasing Callaghan's response when asked if he did not agree Britain was in a state of mounting chaos from industrial unrest, but that was enough in a pre-ELECTION atmosphere with the government apparently losing its grip. He actually said:

> I don't think that other people in the world would share the view that there is a mounting crisis.

The *Sun* did the rest.

When written in Chinese, the word 'crisis' is comprised of two characters – one represents danger and the other represents opportunity The comment made by John F. KENNEDY in 1959 which showed his readiness to indulge in BRINKMANSHIP if he thought it would benefit America and the world.

Croke Park The stadium in south-central Dublin of the *Gaelic Athletic Association*, the governing body of hurling which is synonymous with Irish NATIONALISM; GAA facilities in the North remain barred to members of the Northern Ireland Police Service. Croke Park was the scene of the BLOODY SUNDAY MASSACRE by the BLACK AND TANS on 21 November 1920. It remained barred to 'Non-Irish' sports such as rugby and soccer until 2005, when after the abandonment of the BERTIE BOWL project, the GAA voted by a substantial majority to allow international fixtures in these sports to be staged at Croke Park while Lansdowne Road stadium was redeveloped.

cronyism The award of jobs and contracts to close friends, rather than on merit and through fair competition. Harold Ickes, Franklin ROOSEVELT's Interior Secretary and a thorn in the side of corrupt politicians, was an early user of the term when he declared: 'I am against government by crony'. And in 1952 Walter Lippmann wrote:

> The TRUMAN administration appeared to be foundering in a mess of corruption, cronyism, extravagance and so forth.

See also TONY'S CRONIES.

cross. Crossbencher In the HOUSE OF LORDS, a PEER without party affiliation who sits on the Cross Benches, sideways on to the Government and Opposition benches and facing the WOOLSACK. 'Crossbencher' is also the name of a long-running political comment column in the *Sunday Express*. In Australia, the term is used to denote non-partisan members of the SENATE.

cross-border security The efforts of the London and Dublin governments to co-ordinate the actions of their security forces on either side of the border between NORTHERN IRELAND and the Irish Republic. Such co-operation against the IRA and other terrorists has grown steadily closer, but during the TROUBLES embarrassing mis-understandings did occur and there were occasions when British troops or helicopters 'inadvertently' strayed into the Republic. Conclusion of an EXTRADITION agreement between the UK and the Republic and greater political will improved matters, but hard-line UNIONISTS complained until the IRA's ceasefire that security forces were not allowed to cross the border in **hot pursuit**.

Cross of Lorraine The two-barred archiepiscopal cross adopted by General DE GAULLE as the emblem of the FREE FRENCH during WORLD WAR II; it had been the emblem of Joan of Arc, and was also the provincial symbol of Alsace and Lorraine, two departments taken by France from Germany after the FRANCO-PRUSSIAN WAR, and reabsorbed by Germany after its invasion of France in 1940.

> The heaviest cross that I have to bear is the Cross of Lorraine. CHURCHILL, on De Gaulle

cross-voting Almost the political equivalent of cross-dressing, the practice in US elections of registering for one party and then voting in the other party's PRIMARY.

crossing the floor *See* FLOOR.

Crossman diaries The *Diaries of a Cabinet Minister* kept, and eventually published, by the Labour politician Richard Crossman (1907–74). An Oxford don whose *Government and the Governed* was a textbook of how the British CONSTITUTION should perform, Crossman's diaries of life in Harold WILSON's CABINET from 1964 to 1970 was a classic, though not for the reasons intended. They do expose very clearly the workings of government, but also portray their author as obsessed by the need to be part of the 'inner Cabinet' Wilson perennially toyed with setting up, lacking the acute political antennae he believed he possessed, and outflanked by his civil servants. Crossman is best remembered as the LEADER OF THE HOUSE who first tried to introduce daytime sittings in the Commons, and – until frustrated by Michael FOOT and Enoch POWELL – attempted to reform the HOUSE OF LORDS, and also as the Health Secretary who, to Labour's dismay, unwittingly announced increased health charges on the day of the 1969 local elections.

Crown, the The British monarchy personified in the State. The CABINET SECRETARY Sir Robert Armstrong (*see* ECONOMICAL WITH THE TRUTH) advised civil servants that

> The Crown means and is represented by the government of the day.

The fount of power in the British state is the **Crown in Parliament**: the nexus between the legislative and the titular head of the executive.

> The myth of the king in Parliament has lasted for centuries, and it is not quite done yet. It cannot be defended on any grounds except that it happens to be the way the British do things.
> HUGH BROGAN, *Penguin History of America*

Crown Agents The agency of the UK government, supposed to organise bulk purchasing for the smaller COMMONWEALTH countries, which became the subject of a major scandal in 1977. A committee under Mr Justice Fay confirmed rumours that it had lost some £270 million of clients' money through rash involvement with property and fringe banking, without proper monitoring from the Ministry of Overseas Development, the TREASURY or the Bank of England.

Crown Prince In most monarchies, the formal title for the heir to the THRONE; in Britain a male heir is designated PRINCE OF WALES, a female heir receiving no specific title in advance of her accession.

demise of the Crown The formal term for the death of a king or queen, and the constitutional consequences flowing from it. These are strictly limited nowadays, with no requirement since the 19th century for Parliament to be dissolved.

The influence of the Crown has increased, is increasing and ought to be diminished The classic Parliamentary motion tabled on 6 April 1780 by John Dunning, later Baron Ashbourne (1731–83) in protest at what he saw as the increasingly AUTOCRATIC rule of King George III. Its passage is seen as a turning point, ending a period when the HOUSE OF COMMONS had been relatively supine and marking the beginning of its role as a contemporary democratic legislature.

CRS France's national riot police, who are bused into any city when large demonstrations or political unrest are expected, and who have a reputation for meeting force with force (and on occasions getting their retaliation in first). At moments of domestic crisis, such as the ÉVÈNEMENTS of 1968, parts of Paris have become a battleground between rioters hurling paving stones and CRS detachments in riot gear using batons on every cranium within reach and setting off tear gas. The Communist Party c. 1950 staged a riot in the Gare du Nord to provoke the CRS; among the casualties of its restoration of order were three Gaullist DEPUTIES and an archbishop. The CRS's duties are becoming more varied; as well as being sent into the SANGATTE refugee centre to restore order, CRS units also now patrol prestigious beaches on the Riviera to maintain security and reinforce the lifeguards.

cruel. cruel and unusual punishment The phrase in the US CONSTITUTION (the 8th Amendment in the BILL OF RIGHTS) under which the SUPREME COURT in 1972 declared the death penalty to be UNCONSTITUTIONAL. Reached by 5 to 4 after President NIXON had already begun to dilute the liberalism of the WARREN COURT, the ruling was reversed seven years later (*see* GILMORE CASE).

Cruella de Ville The nickname given by fellow Conservative MPs to **Edwina Currie** (1946–), their colourful and outspoken colleague who had a brief and controversial career as junior Health Minister and revealed in 2002 that she had had a four-year affair with John MAJOR in the 1980s. The original was that of the glamorous villainess in the Walt Disney film *101 Dalmatians*. Mrs Currie first attracted attention by brandishing a pair of handcuffs at a Conservative Party conference, and in 1983 was elected MP for South Derbyshire. From that moment she was enveloped in publicity, though in a 1991 libel case she insisted:

> I have not, and never have been, interested in publicity for myself.

Despite her obvious talent, she alienated many colleagues, including Ann Winterton: 'Empty vessels make the most noise', and Andrew Mackay: 'She has done for our party what King Herod did for babysitting'. Others opined: 'I'm sure she has her X-rays retouched', 'She is writing a book. It is called *Famous People Who Have Met Me*', and 'At Christmas I would rather hang her and kiss the mistletoe.' Margaret THATCHER's decision to give her a job was recognition of her ability, and she took it with enthusiasm, telling north-eastern men to lay off the chips because it gave them heart disease, campaigning against heavy smoking (including by her boss, Kenneth Clarke), and saying as the AIDS scare grew:

> My message to the businessmen of this country when they go abroad on business is that there is one thing above all they can take with them to stop them catching AIDS – the wife.

Her most controversial moment came when evidence emerged that a number of people eating eggs were catching *Salmonella*, a severe form of food poisoning. With the public already nervous, Mrs Currie told a television interviewer on 3 December 1988:

> Most of the egg production in this country, sadly, is now infected with *Salmonella*.

Apart from not being true, the statement caused public panic, egg consumption slumping. It enraged the egg industry, Tory MPs with rural constituencies and the Agriculture Minister John MacGregor; a fortnight later Mrs Currie resigned. She resumed her backbench career in slightly muted form, turned down a MINISTER OF STATE's position in Major's government, flirted with a move to Europe and in 1997 lost her seat.

> When she goes to the dentist, he's the one who needs the anaesthetic.
>
> FRANK DOBSON MP (Lab)

cruise missiles The low-flying winged missiles, driven by an air-breathing turbofan, which are one of the most versatile and effective elements of America's NUCLEAR and conventional arsenal; they have a speed of some 885 m.p.h. They are guided by an inertial system which is updated during flight by matching the contours of the land with maps stored in their computer memories. Cruise missiles were a subject of huge political controversy in Western Europe in the early 1980s when America deployed ground-based versions with nuclear warheads, together with PERSHING IIs, to counter the Soviet SS20s; heated campaigns against deployment (*see* GREENHAM WOMEN) failed; they were only withdrawn under the INF agreement of December 1987, which also committed the Soviets to withdraw and destroy its medium-range missiles. The sea-launched *Tomahawk* missile survived some spectacular failures in initial testing to be used with devastating impact in the 1991 GULF WAR, reporters in Baghdad telling enthralled TV audiences that they could be seen following the street pattern and almost stopping at traffic lights. There is also an air-launched version, deployed by the CARTER administration from B52 bombers as an alternative to developing the B1.

crypt (1) At WESTMINSTER, the chapel under ST STEPHEN'S Hall which survived the fire of 1834 and now serves as a place of occasional worship for MPs. Christenings of members' children and the occasional wedding or memorial service are held there, and the Moderator of the General Assembly of the Church of Scotland preaches there each year on his official visit to London. (2) The vault beneath the ROTUNDA of the US CAPITOL, which houses a photographic exhibition of the building's history, the LADIES IN A BATHTUB statue and a huge head of LINCOLN by Gutzon Borglum. In the centre of the floor is a compass stone, marking the point from which all Washington's grid of streets are lettered or numbered. Beneath the crypt lies the tomb that was intended for George WASHINGTON, who was instead interred at MOUNT VERNON; it now contains the bier on which Lincoln's coffin rested in the Rotunda. From 1820 to 1828, in anticipation of Washington's arrival, the floor of the Rotunda lay open for the public to look down into the tomb. The opening was sealed, and the full crypt created, because damp from below was harming the paintings in the Rotunda.

Crypto-Communist or Fascist Someone who is actually a Communist or Fascist, but postures as a member of a less extreme grouping. In an intemperate moment near the end of her Premiership, Margaret THATCHER surprised MPs on both sides of the Commons by calling Neil KINNOCK a 'crypto-Communist'.

CS gas A potent form of tear gas used by France's CRS on rioting students during the ÉVÈNEMENTS of 1968, by the security forces against rioters in NORTHERN IRELAND, especially between 1969 and 1972, by a protester over Ireland who threw a canister into the CHAMBER of the HOUSE OF COMMONS, and by Iranian students who in 1978 rioted on the ELLIPSE against a visit to WASHINGTON by the Shah, gassing the author among others.

CSCE *See* OSCE.

CSU Christian Social Union. The conservative, Catholic party in Bavaria, led for many years by Franz-Josef Strauss (*see* SPIEGEL AFFAIR), which generally operates as an ally of Germany's more moderate CDU.

Cuba. Cuban missile crisis The moment in 1962 when the SUPERPOWERS came closer to war, and the world to NUCLEAR destruction, than at any other point in the COLD WAR. It stemmed from America's discovery from aerial photographs that Soviet experts were building offensive missile bases in FIDEL Castro's Cuba, thus posing a direct threat; US Ambassador Adlai STEVENSON displayed them to great effect at the UNITED NATIONS. On 22 October President KENNEDY ordered a naval QUARANTINE against ships transporting offensive military equipment to Cuba, and demanded the removal of the bases. Two Soviet ships bound for Cuba were stopped by US warships, searched for war materials and allowed to continue when nothing was found. Kennedy and the Soviet leader Nikita Khrushchev were EYEBALL TO EYEBALL, with the risk of war if the Kremlin stood its ground. After days of suspense, Khrushchev blinked first, initially offering to dismantle the bases and pull out the missiles in return for the withdrawal of NATO missiles from Turkey. Kennedy rejected the offer, and Khrushchev eventually settled for a US commitment not to invade Cuba again (*see* BAY OF PIGS). The crisis subsided; the bases were removed to the PENTAGON's satisfaction on 8 November, and the naval blockade was lifted on 20 November. The world breathed an almost audible sigh of relief.

> I guess this is the week I earn my salary.
>
> JFK to his staff

> The Cuban missile crisis enabled the United States to pull defeat out of the jaws of victory.
>
> RICHARD NIXON

> They talk about who won and who lost. Human reason won. Mankind won.
>
> KHRUSHCHEV, November 1962

> We achieved a spectacular success without having to fire a single shot.
>
> KHRUSHCHEV, *Khrushchev Remembers* (1971)

Fair Play for Cuba Committee The pro-Castro organisation which Lee Harvey Oswald, supposed assassin of JFK in DALLAS, joined in New Orleans in 1962. It shared its premises with a CIA-backed group running guns to Castro's opponents.

It is our destiny to have Cuba and it is folly to debate the question The declaration made by Sen. Stephen Douglas in 1858, 37 years before a revolt against Spanish rule gave America the chance its IMPERIALISTS had been waiting for. The ANNEXATION of Cuba had in fact been contemplated in WASHINGTON since the JEFFERSON administration. *See* PLATT AMENDMENT, SPANISH-AMERICAN WAR.

culture. Cultural Revolution The Great Proletarian Cultural Revolution which took place in 1966 under the direction of CHAIRMAN MAO Tse-Tung, arguably doing even more damage than his GREAT LEAP FORWARD. Intended to invigorate revolutionary fervour and avoid stagnation and REVISIONISM, it involved replacing leaders of the old guard, abolishing the formal education system (many universities closed) and mobilising students as RED GUARDS. For almost ten years, until Mao's death, there was social and political turmoil in which foreigners were reviled and millions of urban 'BOURGEOIS reactionaries' were sent to the country to be 're-educated' by manual labour.

> In history it has always been those with little learning who have overthrown those with too much learning. MAO TSE-TUNG

Culture of Contentment The book published in 1992 by the veteran Canadian-born US liberal economist John Kenneth Galbraith (1908–) which argued that the norm for the West was becoming a nation's prosperous two-thirds governing the underprivileged rest. Galbraith maintained that traditionally the prosperous one-third governed, with the rest of the population exerting pressure for reform and greater equality; with prosperity more evenly spread, the pressure on government was less. Government, wrote Galbraith, was now 'accommodated not to reality or common need, but to the beliefs of the contented, who now form the majority of those who vote.'

Cunningham amendment The amendment attached in 1978 to the Labour government's Scotland Bill which provided that a 'Yes' vote in a REFERENDUM on DEVOLUTION would be invalid unless 40% of Scotland's registered voters supported it. Its effects were to bring down James CALLAGHAN's Labour government and put off devolution for two decades. It was the brainchild of the Labour (later SDP) MP George Cunningham, an anti-devolutionist Scot representing a London constituency. There was a narrow 'Yes' majority in the referendum on 1 March 1979 – around 80,000 out of the 2,380,000 who voted – but with a low turnout of 63.8%, only 32.9% of registered votes were in favour. Callaghan accepted that the proposition was lost, and the SNP reacted by putting down a no-CONFIDENCE motion. Margaret THATCHER's Conservatives threw their weight behind the motion and Labour was defeated by one vote; in the ensuing general election an anti-devolution Conservative government was elected and most of the SNP lost their seats (*see* TURKEYS VOTING FOR AN EARLY CHRISTMAS).

Curragh mutiny The threat in March 1914 by British cavalry officers stationed at the Curragh (a training camp in Co. Kildare, west of Dublin) to resign if they were ordered to coerce Ulster into accepting Irish HOME RULE. The threat hardly constituted a mutiny; the greater danger to ASQUITH's government lay with Sir Edward Carson and BONAR LAW, who had pledged to lead the UNIONISTS and Conservatives in armed resistance to ensure that Ulster was not governed from Dublin (*see* ULSTER VOLUNTEERS). Nevertheless the 'mutiny', caused partly by lack of firmness and consistency from the Minister for War Col. J. E. B. Seely (*see* THROW TO THE WOLVES), heightened an already charged atmosphere, and had WORLD WAR I not unexpectedly intervened, the threat could have reasserted itself.

> The Army will hear nothing of politics from me, and I expect to hear nothing of politics from the Army.
> ASQUITH, speaking in his Fife constituency, 6 April 1914

Currie, Edwina *See* CRUELLA DE VILLE.

Customs scandal The scandal that broke in Canada in 1925 over the revelation by a COMMONS committee of extensive CORRUPTION in the Customs Department. Stemming from efforts to evade PROHIBITION in the United States, 'rum-running' across the border and along the coast had developed into wholesale evasion on a range of commodities. The committee reported 'not merely the tacit connivance of a multitude of Customs officials but in many cases their active co-operation in making a wholesale mockery of the Customs laws of Canada'. Faced with the threatened desertion of 24 Progressive MPs to deny him a majority, the Liberal Prime Minister Mackenzie King advised the GOVERNOR-GENERAL, Lord Byng, to dissolve Parliament. As there had been an ELECTION within the past year and King had not been defeated in the Commons, Byng refused. King then resigned and the Conservative Arthur Meighen was asked to form a government, only for it to be defeated within a week. An election did then ensue, and King fought it on his (incorrect) contention that Byng was bound to accept his advice and that the Imperial power was interfering in Canada's internal affairs. (*Compare* the KERR SACKING in Australia.) The Customs Affair thus turned into the **Constitutional Crisis of 1926**, and King was returned with a clear majority.

cut and run To abandon one's duties and pull out of a struggle one is honour-bound to continue; early in his administration President NIXON refused to 'cut and run' by pursuing any policy over the VIETNAM WAR that looked like a US withdrawal. In Britain, where the Prime Minister sets the date of an ELECTION, it is a time-honoured tactic for the OPPOSITION to claim, any time in the last two years of a PARLIAMENT, that the Government is about to 'cut and run' and call an election because it knows the economy is bound to deteriorate. When no election is called, the Opposition then asserts that it has frightened the government out of going to the COUNTRY because it knows it would have lost. Used in US politics as far back as 1764, the phrase has a seafaring origin, meaning to cut the cable and make sail instantly, without waiting to weigh anchor.

cycle of deprivation The theory advanced from the 1970s by Sir Keith Joseph (*see* MAD MONK) and others that poverty is self-perpetuating, even when the conventional methods of the WELFARE STATE are used as an attempted remedy, and that its elimination may be beyond the ability of any government to achieve.

czar An alternative spelling of the Russian TSAR, which is used, especially in WASHINGTON, to describe an all-powerful figure. It became the nickname of House Speaker Thomas REED (1839–1902), reflecting his aggregation of power to himself, and was also applied to his successor Joseph Cannon (*see* FOUL-MOUTHED JOE), who exerted total power by gaining control of the RULES COMMITTEE. It is also used of a powerful industrialist or BUREAUCRAT; during both World Wars it was applied to the heads of key US agencies prosecuting or policing the war effort, and more recently it has been used on both sides of the Atlantic to describe a person given sweeping powers to tackle a particular issue, for instance drugs.

D

D-Notice Defence Notice. The system under which the British media allows itself to be censored in peacetime about sensitive (and supposedly sensitive) security matters. It operates through occasional requests to the media from a special secretariat at the Ministry of Defence not to publish specific items for reasons of security. Two or three D-Notices are usually current at any time, mostly requiring secrecy about a particular training exercise or military project. The system, introduced in 1911 and policed by a committee of editors, has been generally adhered to despite left-wing denunciations of it as a self-policing form of censorship that compromises the Press. The system's advocates say it has avoided a more formal and restrictive regime.

D-Notice affair The episode in 1967 which inflicted terminal damage on Harold WILSON's previously cordial relationship with the political media. It stemmed from a lunch between Chapman Pincher of the *Daily Express* and Col. Sammy Lohan, secretary to the D-Notice committee, at which Pincher gained the impression that he was free to write about the daily shipment of international cables from the offices of Cable & Wireless to the Ministry of Defence for scrutiny. When the *Express* on 21 February splashed the story of this 'BIG BROTHER' invasion of privacy, a furious Wilson told MPs it was a 'clear breach' of two D-Notices; the media joined ranks behind Pincher, and Wilson was obliged to set up a TRIBUNAL under Lord Radcliffe to investigate. When the tribunal reported that Lohan had not made clear to Pincher that the story was covered by a D-Notice, Wilson repudiated its findings, accused Lohan of being too close to journalists and insisted on producing a government report proposing to replace D-Notices by MoD directives. In substance this did not happen, but the episode enhanced Wilson's reputation for paranoia; though it was another nine years before he finally left DOWNING STREET, his relations with the press never recovered.

DA The UK CABINET COMMITTEE responsible for domestic affairs, which is chaired by the DEPUTY PRIME MINISTER.

Dail Eireann (Ir. Assembly of the Irish) The legislature of the Irish Republic, established in 1918 by SINN FEIN members of the UK Parliament who refused to take their seats at WESTMINSTER. On independence from Britain the Dail was legitimised in the Constitution of 1922 as the lower house of the Republic's legislature. It sits, with the SEANAD, in LEINSTER HOUSE.

Daily. Daily Agenda The official term since October 1997 for the House of Commons ORDER PAPER, which was reorganised at that time to make it at least partly comprehensible for outsiders trying to follow Parliamentary business.

Daily Worker The newspapers which served as the official organs of the US and UK COMMUNIST parties respectively. The US version was published in Chicago from 1924 to 1968, and the UK paper in London from 1930 to 1966, when it changed its name to the *Morning Star*, eventually breaking with the Party's EUROCOMMUNIST line and surviving the end of the COLD WAR.

daisy spot An anti-war commercial screened on US television. The term takes its name from a commercial aired just once, on 7 September 1964, by Lyndon B. JOHNSON's Presidential campaign team which did serious damage to the candidacy of his Republican opponent Sen. Barry GOLDWATER. The commercial, devised by the media consultant Tony Schwartz, showed a young girl counting as she plucked petals from a daisy, while a martial voice began a countdown culminating in a NUCLEAR explosion and MUSHROOM CLOUD, with LBJ's voice stating: 'These are the stakes . . .' Furious Republicans secured the commercial's withdrawal, but it succeeded not only in categorising Goldwater as a man who might plunge America into nuclear war, but in demonstrating the power behind a skilfully-crafted negative message.

Daley machine The Democratic organisation and city government in Chicago (COOK COUNTY) ruthlessly but efficiently controlled by Richard J. Daley (1902–76), Mayor from 1955–76 and the last of the big city BOSSES. It was usually able to control Democratic politics in Illinois, and deliver the State to the Presidential nominee of Daley's choice; in 1960 Daley was widely believed to have stolen Illinois for the Democratic ticket, thus ensuring the election of John F. KENNEDY. He responded to this charge, and others, by declaring: 'I resent the insinuendoes.' His son (also Richard) served as Mayor fifteen years after his father's death, but with a much more open and less corrupt political organisation. *See also* CHICAGO CONVENTION; MACHINE POLITICS.

Dallas The Texas city which became on 22 November 1963 the scene of the assassination of President John F. KENNEDY. According to the WARREN COMMISSION Kennedy, who was travelling through the city in a MOTORCADE, was shot by Lee Harvey Oswald from an upper window of the TEXAS SCHOOL BOOK DEPOSITORY (*but see also* GRASSY KNOLL). Jacqueline Kennedy (*see* JACKIE O) was with the President and cradled his head in her arms; so too were Governor John Connally, who was shot and wounded, and Mrs Connally, who a few moments before had told the President:

> You certainly can't say the people of Dallas haven't given you a warm welcome.

DAR Daughters of the AMERICAN REVOLUTION. A patriotic and largely non-partisan (if conservative) group, they acquired notoriety in 1939 when they refused to allow the black singer Marian Anderson to perform in their Constitution Hall. Instead the Interior Department gave her the best stage in WASHINGTON – the steps of the LINCOLN MEMORIAL – and 75,000 people including a host of celebrities turned out on Easter Sunday to hear her sing.

DARPA Defense Advanced Research Projects Agency The secretive and prestigious scientific body set up in the PENTAGON in 1958 in response to the launch of the Soviet Sputnik satellites, to make sure the United States never again lagged behind the technology of its adversaries. The ingenuity of the research it commissions has produced a number of ground-breaking inventions, and it was a driving force behind the development of the internet. Not all the ideas were politically smart; the furore in CONGRESS in 2003 over its FUTURE MAP plan for a futures/spread betting market on likely acts of terrorism forced the abandonment of the programme and the resignation of the agency's director, Admiral John Poindexter, a previous victim of the IRAN-CONTRA AFFAIR.

Das Kapital (Ger. CAPITAL) Karl Marx's definitive work on 'scientific' economics, the first volume of which appeared in 1867, and one of the basic texts of MARXISM. The second and third volumes were completed by Friedrich Engels from Marx's notes, appearing in 1885 and 1894. Many world leaders, among them Harold WILSON, have observed that it is almost unreadable.

> A collection of atrocity stories designed to stimulate martial ardour against the enemy.
>
> BERTRAND RUSSELL

dash for growth The sudden and desperate adoption of REFLATIONARY policies by a government that needs to deliver economic growth, particularly if an ELECTION is looming. In the short term the result is generally an upsurge in economic activity leading to a fall in unemployment and a FEEL-GOOD FACTOR, but before long the economy is OVERHEATING and the brakes have to be applied in the form of higher interest rates or taxation.

date. a date which will live in infamy Franklin D. ROOSEVELT's furious and unforgettable description of Japan's attack on PEARL HARBOR on 7 December 1941. It comes from his speech to a JOINT SESSION of CONGRESS the following day in which he sought a declaration of war – which was granted with just one vote against. FDR's actual words were:

> Yesterday, December 7, 1941 – a date which will live in infamy – the United States of America was suddenly and deliberately attacked by naval and air forces of the Empire of Japan.

Davis, Jefferson (1808–89) President of the CONFEDERATE States of America, 1861–65. A Kentucky-born West Point graduate and cotton planter, Davis was elected to CONGRESS in 1845, fought in the 1846–47 MEXICAN WAR, served as a Senator 1847–50 and Secretary for War 1853–57. As leader of the STATES' RIGHTS Party he urged Congress in 1860 not to outlaw slavery. When the Confederate states seceded, Davis was nominated President for a six-year term; introducing him at Montgomery in 1861 as President-elect, William Yancey declared: 'The man and the hour have met!', yet his Vice President, Alexander Stephens, considered him 'weak and vacillating, timid, petulant, peevish, obstinate but not firm'. His UNION adversaries detected a greater fault, Winfield Scott writing: 'He is not a cheap Judas. I do not think he would have sold the Saviour for thirty shilling; but for the successorship to Pontius Pilate he would have betrayed Christ and the apostles and the whole Christian church.' On the Confederate defeat, Davis was charged with treason by the victorious Union, but released under amnesty in 1868.

> The only American with whose public character Benedict ARNOLD need not fear comparison.
>
> THEODORE ROOSEVELT

Dawes. Dawes Act The measure passed by the US Congress in 1867 which granted 160 acres and US citizenship to heads of Indian families who would abandon their tribal allegiance, with land freed up on reservations being sold to white settlers. Also known as the **Allotment Act**, it benefited the whites more than the Indians, who were to lose 86 million acres of their best land in the next half-century, so fresh incentives were offered in 1906 under the **Burke Act**.

Dawes Plan The American scheme implemented in 1924 to break the deadlock between France and Germany over the non-payment of REPARATIONS. It began the revival of a German economy stricken by inflation and the burden of reparations – and hence that of post-war Europe – but ultimately proved inadequate and was replaced by the YOUNG PLAN. A key element was a massive international loan. It earned its author Brig-Gen. Charles Gates Dawes (1865–1951) the NOBEL PEACE PRIZE (jointly) and NOMINATION as COOLIDGE's Vice President.

day. a day I was meant not to see Margaret THATCHER's reaction to the October 1984 BRIGHTON BOMBING in which she narrowly escaped ASSASSINATION by the IRA. She said that when she was sitting in church three days later, she suddenly realised that 'this was a day I was meant not to see'.

Go ahead, make my day The threat uttered by Clint Eastwood (and backed up with a gun) as Dirty Harry in the 1983 film *Sudden Impact*. Ronald REAGAN took it up in March 1985, telling a business conference when CONGRESS was pressing for tax increases:

> I have my VETO pen drawn and ready for any tax increase that Congress might even think of sending up. And I have only one thing to say to the tax increasers – 'Go ahead, make my day.'

Dayton Agreement The agreement concluded near Dayton, Ohio on 21 November 1995 and signed at Paris the following month which ended four years of war and atrocities in Bosnia. Bosnian, Serb and Croat leaders were put through three weeks of intensive negotiations with US SECRETARY OF STATE Warren Christopher at Wright-Patterson Air Force Base in Ohio; the agreement was reached the day after a deadline set by President CLINTON.

DEs In the sociological and pollsters' scale of social groups from A to E, unskilled and casual workers and their families; for a full explanation see C2S.

de Gaulle, General Charles André Joseph Marie (1890–1970) Leader of the FREE FRENCH during WORLD WAR II, and President of France 1958–69. The inspiration of the GAULLIST movement, with his rigid concept of the destiny of France and his own destiny to lead it. 'When I want to know what France thinks, I ask myself,' he said. He had this certainty even as a young officer when he declared: 'Such as I am, I cannot fail to be, at a given moment, in the centre of the stage.' A 1922 War College report termed him

> intelligent – brilliant – resourceful. He spoils his undoubted talents by his excessive assurance, his contempt for other people's point of view and his attitude of a king in exile.

Having predicted Germany's BLITZKRIEG, the towering de Gaulle escaped to Britain when it happened to lead France's fightback. CHURCHILL found him exasperating, declaring: 'The hardest cross I have to bear is the CROSS OF LORRAINE.' When de Gaulle was proving particularly inflexible, Churchill minuted: 'I have every sympathy with General de Gaulle and his violent tantrums, but let us conquer some of his country before we start squabbling about how it is to be governed.' To Harold MACMILLAN, de Gaulle had 'all the rigidity of a poker without its occasional warmth'. Leaders of the other ANGLO-SAXON peoples for whom de Gaulle developed a life-long resentment felt the same, US Ambassador Robert Murphy calling him a 'Frankenstein monster of which we ought to welcome the opportunity to rid ourselves'. Yet when Germany was defeated, de Gaulle could justifiably claim:

> I was France.

After the LIBERATION, when he walked courageously down a *Champs Élysées* still open to German snipers, he was France's obvious leader, but Communist and other opposition denied him power. He then founded the **RPF** (Rally of the French People), the first Gaullist party, but its support slipped from an initial 40% and in 1953 he gave up the leadership and retired to COLOMBEY-LES-DEUX-ÉGLISES. He was called back in 1958 after successive governments had failed to resolve the Algerian conflict and de Gaulle's supporters in the army were rumoured to be planning a military COUP (*see* THIRTEEN PLOTS OF 13 MAY); as the crisis came to a head he announced:

> Now I shall return to my village and there will remain at the disposition of the nation.

De Gaulle was duly installed as President of the FIFTH REPUBLIC, declaring: 'The national task that has been incumbent on me for 18 years is hereby confirmed.' He then gave Algeria its independence, to the fury of the hard-line officers who had hoped their revolt which hastened his return would reap dividends. The result was the OAS campaign to assassinate him; of one narrow miss he observed:

> They really are bad shots.

He justified his U-turn on Algeria by saying: 'In politics it is necessary either to betray one's country or the electorate. I prefer to betray the electorate.'

In power de Gaulle presided over an upsurge of prosperity and technology, formed a new ENTENTE with West Germany and blocked MACMILLAN's efforts to get Britain into the COMMON MARKET. It was in this period that Franz-Josef Strauss said of de Gaulle: 'He is not a genius, just a political cosmonaut, continually in orbit.' The British revue duo Michael Flanders and Donald Swann were blunter:

> This old man thinks he's St Joan.

De Gaulle survived the ÉVÈNEMENTS of 1968 (*see* CHIENLIT), though only after flying to Germany to ensure French forces there were loyal; at the height of the unrest he was asked for permission to detain Jean-Paul Sartre and replied: 'How do you arrest Voltaire?' But the following year he made a REFERENDUM on regional government a matter of CONFIDENCE, and resigned when defeated.

De Lorean affair The scandal surrounding the collapse of a car plant in mainly Catholic West Belfast founded in 1978 by John Z. de Lorean (1925–2005), with over £80 million in backing from the UK government. De Lorean, a former vice-president of General Motors, planned a revolutionary gull-winged stainless steel car largely for the US market. James CALLAGHAN's Labour government was anxious to back it, as West Belfast was a blackspot for unemployment and IRA terrorism. De Lorean chose NORTHERN IRELAND after an aide told him: 'The worse the area, the more financing they'll give us'; the initial advance alone was £53 million. Margaret THATCHER's government continued to back the project, and the first car was produced in 1981, but there were problems over price and quality, sales were slow and on 19 October 1982 the plant closed with the loss of 2,500 jobs. Only 3,500 cars were built; one achieved fame in the 1985 film *Back to the Future*. The day the receivers moved in, de Lorean was arrested in Los Angeles on a charge of bankrolling a 59lb. cocaine shipment; he was acquitted two years later. He was subsequently charged with defrauding US investors in de Lorean of $4.9 million, and cleared in December 1986. The one proven fraud was committed by Colin Chapman, head of Britain's Lotus Cars, and its finance director Fred Bushell; in 1992 Bushell was jailed for three years in Belfast and fined £2.2 million for defrauding the company, with Chapman, of £10 million. The UK government sued de Lorean to recover its stake, and in August 1992, after selling his New York penthouse, he handed over £5 million. But £30 million in loans from the UK taxpayer had to be written off.

Deacon The US SECRET SERVICE code name for President CARTER.

dead. dead calf One of the best remembered dicta of Margaret THATCHER's husband Denis (*see* ANYONE FOR DENIS?). At the height of her victorious 1979 election campaign Mrs Thatcher, while electioneering in a Cornish cattle market, picked up a calf and held it awkwardly for photographers. Her husband, alive as ever to the potential downside, remarked in the hearing of reporters:

> Unless she's careful, we're going to have a dead calf on our hands.

dead cat's bounce An expected economic recovery that fails to materialise. The phrase, dating from the mid-1980s, draws from the belief that a dead cat thrown from a skyscraper will appear to bounce on hitting the pavement – a movement not to be confused with signs of life.

dead Labour A Cardiff CONSTITUENT's unfortunate description to Speaker George

Thomas (later Viscount Tonypandy) of the political allegiance of her deceased mother, who was laid out in the front room when he called.

dead on arrival (1) There is a tradition/legal fiction that a member of Parliament cannot die in the PALACE OF WESTMINSTER. Any who dies is taken to St Thomas's Hospital (and previously the now-closed Westminster) where it is certified that they are 'dead on arrival'. (2) Any legislation from the WHITE HOUSE which from the outset stands no chance of being accepted by the CONGRESS.

dead parrot (1) The draft constitution for a unified UK LIBERAL and SDP Party which was instantly rejected when put to the parties' MPs early in 1988. It was named after the *Monty Python* sketch in which John Cleese complains to a pet shop owner that the parrot he had just bought was dead. Margaret THATCHER compared the LIBERAL DEMOCRATS, product of the eventual Liberal/SDP merger, with a dead parrot in her 1990 party conference speech; when they won the Eastbourne BY-ELECTION from the Tories shortly after, Conservative Party chairman Kenneth Baker observed:

> The parrot has twitched.

(2) The term memorably applied by the *Sun* on 5 October 1998 to the CONSERVATIVE PARTY under the leadership of William HAGUE, with an evocative front page depicting Hague as a parrot bereft of life.

dead sheep, savaged by a The withering retort from Chancellor Denis HEALEY (*see* GROMYKO OF THE LABOUR PARTY) to his Tory SHADOW, Sir Geoffrey Howe, in a Commons debate on 14 June 1978. Healey said: 'That part of his speech was rather like being savaged by a dead sheep.' He conceded the phrase was not original, noting that CHURCHILL had once dismissed an attack by ATTLEE as 'like being savaged by a pet lamb'. Others attribute its first use to Sir Roy Welensky, describing a hostile book review by Iain Macleod. *Compare* the comment of Paul KEATING on Australia's Liberal leader John Hewson: 'Like being flagellated with a wet lettuce'.

Dear Bill The column in the satirical magazine *PRIVATE EYE* throughout the THATCHER years, and occasionally after, purporting to be a letter from the Prime Minister's husband Denis (*see* ANYONE FOR DENIS?) to his old golfing chum Bill – Lord Deedes, editor of the *Daily Telegraph*. DOWNING STREET insiders felt it gave an alarmingly accurate insight into the workings of that government, the volcanic nature of its leader, and the frank and convivial outlook of its supposed author. Deedes later chose it as the title of his own autobiography.

Dearos The Boston supporters of Boss John 'HONEY FITZ' Fitzgerald (1863–1951), grandfather of John F. KENNEDY. The name came from his description of his power base as 'Dear Old North End'.

death. ***Death of a Princess*** A BBC television drama-documentary, shown on 9 April 1980, built around the alleged execution of a Westernised Saudi princess for an affair with a married man. Its transmission caused a near-rupture in relations between Britain and Saudi Arabia, whose government ordered the British AMBASSADOR home.

Death on the Rock Another UK television programme, this time on the shooting by undercover SAS personnel of three intending IRA bombers – Mairead Farrell, Daniel McCann and Sean Savage – in Gibraltar on 6 March 1988. The documentary, shown on ITV on 28 April despite calls for it to be banned, caused a political storm by disputing the UK government's claim that they had been killed in self-defence; it contended that two of the three had been shot after putting their hands up. A nineteen-day inquest eventually returned a verdict of 'unlawful killing', but continued discrepancies in evidence led the EUROPEAN COMMISSION on HUMAN RIGHTS to conclude in September 1995 by 10 votes to 9 that the killings were unjustified.

death squad A Latin American contribution to global civilisation: members of the military or police under a usually right-wing dictatorship who travel round out of uniform in unmarked cars, liquidating opponents of the regime and anyone else against whom they have a grudge. The concept has spread to parts of Africa, Asia and the Balkans.

deaths in the chamber An occasional feature of any legislature. In the US HOUSE OF REPRESENTATIVES former President John Quincy ADAMS suffered a fatal stroke at his desk in 1848, in 1932 Rep. Edward Eslick, a Tennessee Democrat, dropped dead in mid-speech, and in 1940 Rep. Morris Edelstein, a New York Democrat, died as soon as he had finished denouncing an anti-Semitic speech by Rep. John Rankin of Mississippi. In the late 1940s Rep. Adolphe Sabath, octogenarian chairman of the House RULES

COMMITTEE, pretended to be dying so as to prevent the Georgia Democrat Eugene Cox moving an alteration to the rules. Cox momentarily believed his insistence on his proposal had killed Sabath – then saw the chairman open an eye once the crisis was over.

In the UK HOUSE OF COMMONS, despite the fiction that it cannot happen (*see* DEAD ON ARRIVAL), Michael Roberts, a Welsh Office Minister, collapsed at the DESPATCH BOX in mid-speech on 10 February 1983 and died.

merchants of death A popular term for arms manufacturers and exporters, first heard in 1934 during an investigation of the industry by the United States Senate.

Deaver syndrome The *Washington Post*'s term for the practice of former high US government officials rapidly cashing in on their contacts on leaving office. It gained its name from the scandal surrounding Mike Deaver, who within a year of resigning as President REAGAN's deputy CHIEF OF STAFF in 1985 had lined up six-figure LOBBYING contracts to represent Canada, Mexico, Singapore, Korea, Puerto Rico, CBS, TWA, Philip Morris and Rockwell International. Accused of violating laws barring high office holders from lobbying within a year of leaving their job, he was eventually convicted on three counts of perjury. *See* REVOLVING DOOR, SLEAZE FACTOR.

deBaathification *See* BAATH PARTY.

debate A structured exchange of views in a legislature or other deliberative body, either as part of the passage of a BILL or on a specific question, generally but not always culminating in a vote. Also a similarly-structured exchange between two individuals or bodies of opinion on television or in a debating society.

debate prep A session in which a candidate or other public figure about to face their rival on television is prepared for the event by their own staff and advisers acting as the opposition.

floor debate *See* FLOOR.

Great Debate A national debate on UK educational standards launched in 1978 by James CALLAGHAN and Education Secretary Shirley Williams (*see* GANG OF FOUR).

Lincoln-Douglas debates *See* LINCOLN.

presidential debate A direct confrontation between candidates for the US Presidency on network television; the first was between Richard NIXON and John F. KENNEDY in 1960 (*see* FIVE O'CLOCK SHADOW). President EISENHOWER feared Kennedy would come out on top because 'Nixon was widely known, Kennedy was not', and he did, at least with the TV audience. Nixon scored better in the three debates that followed, largely because a crash course of milkshakes made him look less cadaverous. But fewer voters watched them, the die having been cast. Such debates became a regular feature of campaigns with the FORD-CARTER debates of 1976. In 1980 Raquel Welch termed the Carter-REAGAN debates 'The one with the fat lips v the one with no lips'. And Nixon told Reagan: 'Since I've never won a debate, let me tell you how not to lose one.' In Britain, the format has appealed to numerous Leaders of the OPPOSITION, but incumbent Prime Ministers have always evaded the challenge, bearing in mind Harold MACMILLAN's comment to Bill Deedes (*see* DEAR BILL):

> Never give your political opponent an audience he cannot attract by himself.

Debategate The mystery/scandal in 1980 when briefing papers prepared for President CARTER prior to their television debates fell into the hands of the Reagan campaign team. The Carter camp claimed the loose-leaf folder was stolen; the Reaganites said it had been sent to them anonymously. William J. Casey, Reagan's campaign manager and subsequently head of the CIA, fell under suspicion of having secured the papers, though he denied it.

decapitation In the 2005 UK general election, the LIBERAL DEMOCRATS' strategy of targeting the seats of Conservative leader Michael HOWARD and key members of his SHADOW CABINET. The strategy was an almost total failure, four out of five of those targeted increasing their majorities. The Lib-Dems' only success was in ousting Shadow Education Secretary Tim Collins in Westmorland.

Decent Interval The title of a 1977 book by Frank Snepp, awarded the CIA's Medal of Merit for his work as an analyst in VIETNAM, exposing the chaos and incompetence of the final stages of the American presence. Snepp, who had to resign from the CIA to publish the book, argued that the NIXON administration, and in particular Dr Henry KISSINGER, had cynically abandoned the people of South Vietnam to the Communists under the guise of a lasting peace, and that warnings of the final North Vietnamese offensive in 1975 were systematically ignored. He argued that only the heroism of a few young staff and the ingenuity of the

Defence Attaché had prevented the US Embassy in Saigon falling into Communist hands. The phrase 'decent interval' has come to mean any situation in which a government creates a scenario which after a suitable period can be quietly and cynically unravelled.

decentralisation The practice of moving administrators and departments out of the national capital to provincial centres in order to benefit regional economies, or of DEVOLVING powers previously exercised nationally to the regions.

declaration A portentous announcement, in particular the results of an ELECTION. *See* I BEING THE.

Declaration of Conscience The statement made in the US Senate on 1 June 1950 by Margaret Chase Smith (1897–1995) and six other anti-MCCARTHY Republicans, emphasising the rights of any American to criticise, hold unpopular beliefs, protest or think freely.

(Second) Declaration of Havana FIDEL Castro's violent and revolutionary speech in January 1962 after Cuba's suspension from the OAS in which he appealed to the peoples of Latin America to rise up against IMPERIALISM.

Declaration of Independence *See* INDEPENDENCE.

Declaration of Interdependence John F. KENNEDY's aim, echoing the Declaration of INDEPENDENCE, of a mutually beneficial ATLANTIC partnership 'between the new unions now emerging in Europe and the old American union'. It was an incentive to a strong and unified COMMON MARKET to form close ties with the United States, an aim that has yet fully to be achieved.

declaration of intent Statements made by the leaders of the UK trade union movement to exercise wage restraint in return for pressure to keep down prices. They have generally been made to avoid the imposition of a PRICES AND INCOMES POLICY at times of economic crisis.

declaration of war The formal announcement that a state is opening hostilities against another. The correct terminology is that 'a state of war now exists' between the two nations, the inference being that the state not making the declaration has been the subject of an unprovoked attack.

overnight declaration The announcement of an ELECTION result the day after polling, generally where the count has not begun until that morning.

Universal Declaration of Human Rights *See* HUMAN.

declare an interest *See* INTEREST.

decommissioning The placing out of use by a paramilitary organisation of its weaponry as part of a PEACE PROCESS, and in other circumstances of NUCLEAR power stations, warships and fishing vessels. The sincerity or otherwise of the IRA in decommissioning its arsenal has been a critical factor in NORTHERN IRELAND politics since the GOOD FRIDAY AGREEMENT; the IRA announced a start on 23 October 2001 and some minor 'acts of decommissioning' have taken place, attested to by an independent international commission headed by the former Canadian general John de Chastellain. However, an attempt by the British and Irish governments in December 2004 to get SINN FEIN and the DUP to agree to renewed POWER-SHARING broke down over Dr Ian PAISLEY's demand that there must be photographic evidence of decommissioning, and the IRA's insistence that this would be a 'humiliation' for them. The IRA withdrew from the decommissioning process in February 2005 after being blamed for the £26 million NORTHERN BANK ROBBERY. *See also* ALBERTZHEIMER'S DISEASE.

deep. deep doodoo, in A euphemism for 'in deep shit' – 'in very serious trouble'. It was frequently used by George BUSH senior – and first quoted by the *Wall Street Journal* in 1986; Vice President Bush, asked what would happen to a Chinese official who was too friendly to Americans, said:

> He would have been in deep doodoo.

deep freeze scandal The episode in which Brig.-Gen. Harry Vaughan, President TRUMAN's top military aide, hinted to a Milwaukee deep freeze manufacturer, Harry Hoffman, that he and the President needed new freezers for their homes. Hoffman sent one to Vaughan, one to Truman for his house in Missouri, and also freezers to four key Truman aides. Only Treasury Secretary Fred Vinson sent his back. Acceptance of the freezers was not illegal – only gifts from foreign governments are barred by the Constitution – but Truman's opponents hailed it as a sign of flawed judgement, or worse.

Deep Sproat The nickname bestowed on the Scots Conservative MP Iain Sproat on 8 March 1977 by Robert Hughes, Labour member for a neighbouring Aberdeen seat. Attacking a campaign Sproat had run against social security scroungers, Hughes branded him 'the Linda Lovelace of the

Tory Party, willing to swallow anything he is thrown'. The name stemmed directly from the movie which even more memorably gave rise to

Deep Throat The unnamed source, high in the NIXON administration, who in parking-garage meetings with Bob Woodward gave the *Washington Post* much of the information needed to unravel the WATERGATE story. The name came from the early-1970s pornographic film in which a girl played by Linda Lovelace was supposed to have a clitoris in her throat, and put it to exhaustive use. Nixon's acolytes made frantic efforts to identify the source of such damaging LEAKS, but his identity was only divilged in May 2005 when **Marle Felt**, the by now 91-year-old former deputy director of the FBI, admitted to John O'Connor, a lawyer writing for *Vanity Fair*, that he had been Deep Throat. Woodward (who had first met Felt when he was in the Navy) and Bernstein confirmed this, though Bernstein raised the possibility that Deep Throat had been an amalgam of contacts including Felt.

DEFCON Defence Condition. The stages of alert, devised in the COLD WAR, onto which US forces are placed as war becomes more likely. The lower the number, the greater the state of readiness, hence the PENTAGON phrase **raising the DEFCON**. **DEFCON 5** is the normal peacetime condition; with **DEFCON 4** some Air Force crews are on 12–15 minutes' notice for takeoff; **DEFCON 1** would be declared if hostilities were imminent or already under way.

defeat Many politicians would agree with the US trade union leader Walter Reuther that 'if you're not big enough to lose, you're not big enough to win.' But rejection by the voters still hurts, and is taken in very different ways. CHURCHILL, on his government's surprise defeat in 1945, commented: 'If this is a blessing, it is certainly very well disguised.' And George BROWN, unseated in 1970, was even more philosophical, observing: 'That's how democracy democts.' But the mask often slips, Reginald Maudling (*see* POULSON AFFAIR) saying when Edward HEATH beat him to the Tory leadership: 'What have I to look forward to but to sit here and get pissed?' GLADSTONE, appropriately, took just the opposite view of the Liberals' 1874 election defeat: 'We have been borne down in a torrent of gin and beer.' US politicians have taken defeat just as well, and just as badly. Adlai STEVENSON, after EISENHOWER had beaten him to the presidency, remarked laconically: 'A funny thing happened on the way to the WHITE HOUSE.' But future Speaker Champ Clark, losing his HOUSE seat in 1894, inveighed: 'What was the cause of my defeat? A system of grossest lies, a complex and unlimited use of the boodle of this country, a subsidised press, a lot of conscienceless demagogues that never ought to have even a name, a host of mountebanks and jugglers sent us down.' And Walter Mondale (*see* NORWEGIAN WOOD) chillingly conveyed what it feels like to lose a Presidential election:

> At about 11.30 p.m. on election night, they just push you off the edge of the cliff – and that's it. You might scream on the way down, but you're going to hit the bottom and you're not going to be in office.

Defeat at a CONVENTION has a particular poignancy. In 1980 Edward KENNEDY rallied his troops, declaring: 'For me, a few hours ago, this campaign came to an end. For all those whose cares have been our concern, the work goes on, the cause endures, the hope still lives, and the dream shall never die.' And four years later Gary Hart observed: 'This is one Hart you will not leave in San Francisco.' But Richard NIXON had the last word on electoral setbacks: 'A man is not finished when he is defeated. He is finished when he quits.'

If we win, nobody will care. If we lose, there will be nobody left to care Winston CHURCHILL's sanguine assessment of Britain's prospects in a speech to a SECRET SESSION of the HOUSE OF COMMONS on 25 June 1941, at the height of WORLD WAR II.

snatch defeat from the jaws of victory To throw away an apparently impregnable position; the opposite of the original 'snatch victory from the jaws of defeat'. The term may first have been used by the NEW DEALer Paul Porter about the 1948 Presidential campaign of Thomas DEWEY.

victory has a thousand fathers, but defeat is an orphan *See* VICTORY.

We are not interested in the possibilities of defeat. They do not exist An assertion first made by Queen Victoria about Britain's prospects in the BOER WAR, repeated by Margaret THATCHER over the FALKLANDS. During 'black week' in December 1899, when British forces suffered a number of reverses, Queen Victoria told Foreign Secretary A. J. BALFOUR:

> Please understand that there is no one depressed in this house. We are not interested in the possibilities of defeat. They do not exist.

defector A citizen – frequently an employee or agent – of one state who flees to another, transferring his allegiance, out of repugnance at his own country's policies or regime. The term is also used of individuals who quit one political party for another.

defence (US spelling **defense**) The most basic function of a government. James Wilson declared to the PHILADELPHIA CONVENTION on 11 December 1787: 'A government without the power of defense? That is a solecism.' 188 years later Gerald FORD observed: 'A strong defense is the surest way to peace. Strength makes DÉTENTE attainable, and we cannot rely on the forbearance of others to protect this nation.' Spending on defence has exercised the political community for centuries. The *Kingston Whig* once editorialised: 'An excellent figurehead for battleships would be a formal design of a weeping taxpayer.' And George Jean Nathan (1882–1958) asked: 'What would our government think of a citizen who spent 93 per cent of his income on ammunition?' President EISENHOWER, despite or maybe because of his military background, added a moral dimension: 'Every gun that is fired, every warship launched, every rocket fired signifies a theft from those who hunger and are not fed, from those who are cold and are not clothed. [But] this is the best way of life to be found on the road the world has been taking.' Marshal of the RAF Sir John Slessor countered: 'The most important social service a government can do for its people is to keep them alive and free.' But Monsignor Bruce Kent of CND added a nuclear argument: 'Preparing for suicide is not a very intelligent means of defence.'

Defence Estimates The global budget for Britain's armed forces debated by Parliament every year, which was habitually opposed by Labour left-wingers, especially in the late 1950s when CND first made its impact.

defence review A formal and infrequent reassessment of Britain's military commitments and resources, customarily triggered by pressure to economise but occasionally by geopolitical change.

Defence policy? I didn't know that you had one. I now observe that Labour are all for sanctions imposed by the League of Nations and that you will fully support them; and if this leads to hostilities, you will wage war with bows and arrows The acerbic response of Australia's Robert Menzies (*see* MING) in 1936 to an attempt by Sir Stafford Cripps (*see* CHRIST AND CARROTS) to explain the UK LABOUR PARTY's then NEO-PACIFIST policies to him.

Millions for defence, but not one cent for tribute The anti-French slogan taken up by the American public at the height of the X, Y AND Z FEVER; it was first uttered by Robert Goodloe Harper.

defenestration The beguilingly obscure term for the barbaric practice of throwing one's political opponents out of an upper window. This was the probable cause of death of the Czech Foreign Minister Jan Masaryk, who mysteriously plunged from his office window late in 1948 as Communist pressure on that country's democrats reached its height.

deferred voting. A procedure introduced in the UK HOUSE OF COMMONS in December 2000 under which MPs are supplied in advance with ballot papers for some DIVISIONS and no longer have to be physically present for them.

deficit financing The running of a nation's finances by accepting a BUDGET deficit and bridging the gap between income and expenditure by borrowing.

deflation The opposite of INFLATION, the contraction of the economy through the removal of money from circulation. At times of OVERHEATING, deflationary policies may deliberately be pursued; the difficulty arises if deflation is too severe and a RECESSION or HARD LANDING ensues. Deflation is not the same as DEVALUATION – George W. BUSH caused an upheaval in world currency markets by confusing the two when speaking in Tokyo on 18 February 2002.

Delaney amendment An amendment to America's Food, Drug and Cosmetic Act prohibiting the use of substances that cause cancer. The amendment, promoted in 1970 by Rep. James J. Delaney (1901–87), stated that 'no additive shall be deemed to be safe if it is found, after tests which are appropriate for the evaluation of food additives, to induce cancer in man or animals.' It caused immediate controversy because the Food and Drug Administration interpreted it strictly, irrespective of the dose involved. For instance, in 1970 they banned the use of cyclamates, artificial sweetening agents widely used in the food industry, on evidence that massive doses caused bladder tumours in rats. In 1977, they invoked the amendment again to ban the sweetener saccharine.

delaying power The power of Britain's HOUSE OF LORDS to delay, but not reject, legislation passed by the COMMONS. The PARLIAMENT ACT of 1911 empowered the Lords to delay a BILL for two years before being OVERRIDDEN; the 1949 act reduced the period to a year.

delegate An individual sent by one organisation as its representative to meetings of another. In America, a State's representative at a nominating CONVENTION, often committed to a particular candidate, sometimes not. Also the non-voting members of the HOUSE OF REPRESENTATIVES elected for the District of Columbia, American Samoa, Guam and the Virgin Islands (and, before STATEhood, Hawaii).

delegate count The running tabulation of delegates won by Presidential hopefuls during the PRIMARY season, kept and published by America's main news organisations.

super delegate Additional delegates to a Democratic convention, mainly elected public officials, who have been chosen since 1984 by CONGRESSional CAUCUSES and State conventions to reinforce the voice of the party leadership.

delegation (1) The process of a chief executive or official at any level permitting subordinates to take action on their behalf. Public authorities may well delegate powers to sub-committees or non-elected officials. Not every decision maker finds it easy to delegate; President James Knox Polk (1795–1849) lamented:

> I prefer to supervise the whole operation of the Government myself rather than entrust the public business to subordinates, and this makes my duties very great.

(2) A party representing a government or organisation which travels to meet its counterparts abroad.

delenda est Carthago (Lat. Carthage must be destroyed) The statement with which Cato the Elder (234–149 BC) opened every speech in the Roman Senate. It has become synonymous with any campaign by a lone voice, based on persistent repetition of one simple statement. (*Compare* APRIL FOOL!)

Delhi Pact (1) The agreement between MAHATMA Gandhi, leader of the CONGRESS Party, and Lord Irwin, VICEROY of India, in 1931 which addressed some of the movement's grievances about British rule. It marked a truce in Congress's campaign of CIVIL DISOBEDIENCE and established Congress as the principal conduit of Indian opinion for the ROUND TABLE CONFERENCE. Winston CHURCHILL said of talks in India in early 1931 following the conference:

> It is alarming and odious to see Mr Gandhi, a seditious Middle Temple lawyer, now posing as a fakir of a type well-known in the East, striding half-naked up the steps of the vice-regal palace while he is still conducting a defiant campaign of CIVIL DISOBEDIENCE, to parley on equal terms with the representative of the King-Emperor.

(2) The agreement signed in April 1950 by the Indian Prime Minister Jawaharlal Nehru (*see* PANDIT) and his Pakistani counterpart Liaqat Ali Khan. Prompted by communal RIOTS and massive two-way migration of religious minorities after PARTITION, it ensured the rights of Muslim and Hindu minorities in their respective countries.

delivery The process of providing effective public services in accordance with a MANIFESTO commitment and the expectations of the consumer. The term came into its own during Tony BLAIR's premiership as NEW LABOUR strove to implement its commitments to deliver better health, education and transport services (*see* SCHOOLS AND HOSPITALS FIRST). Frank Dobson, Health Secretary from 1997, promised a '**year of delivery**', a **Delivery Unit** was established in DOWNING STREET, and Gordon BROWN interpreted Labour's re-election in 2001 as an '**instruction to deliver**'.

Delors. Delors report The report, presented to EUROPEAN COMMUNITY heads of government in April 1989, which gave a critical push toward economic and monetary union (EMU). It took its name from Jacques Delors (1925–), President of the EUROPEAN COMMISSION and an ardent advocate of a more centralised community, who sat on the drafting group with a fellow Commissioner, the twelve CENTRAL BANK governors and three outside experts. It proposed three stages toward monetary union: completion of the SINGLE MARKET, creation of an independent 'Eurofed' controlling a proportion of national currency reserves, and the irrevocable locking of exchange rates to create a single currency, managed by the Eurofed (*see* ECB). The strategy was broadly endorsed in the MAASTRICHT TREATY and the subsequent adoption of the EURO.

Delors II The ambitious plan put forward by Delors for substantial increases in the EC budget from 1993 to 1999, financed by an increase in OWN RESOURCES, with special emphasis on COHESION funding for the 'poor four' members and on STRUCTURAL FUNDS for improving the infrastructure. A scaled-down version was adopted at the Edinburgh summit in December 1992, with Delors claiming he had got 80% of what he wanted.

Up Yours, Delors! The ultimate in CHAUVINIST press campaigns, launched by Britain's *Sun* newspaper on 1 November 1990 as the strains between Margaret THATCHER and Delors over moves to closer European union reached their *dénouement* in her overthrow. The campaign was a combined attack on Delors for his perceived vision of a Europe governed by *diktat* from Brussels, and on the French for attempts to sabotage UK farm exports. It began:

> UP YOURS, DELORS!
> At midday tomorrow *Sun* readers are urged to tell the French fool where to stuff his ECU.
> The *Sun* today calls on its patriotic family of readers to tell the feelthy French to FROG OFF. They INSULT us, BURN our lambs, FLOOD our country with dodgy food and PLOT to abolish the dear old pound.
> Now it's your turn to kick THEM in the Gauls.

See also UNION JACQUES.

demagogue A POPULIST who is able to whip up ugly sentiments through obsessive mob oratory. Ambrose Bierce cynically defined a demagogue as 'a political opponent'. In America the word has become a verb: in the late 1970s House MAJORITY LEADER Jim Wright declared: 'Thou shalt not demagogue with thy colleagues', and in 1986 Labor Secretary Bill Brock said: 'The Democrats are making a mistake by demagoguing this issue.'

démarche In diplomacy, an initiative involving an approach by a government to one or more others.

demo 1970s shorthand for a DEMONSTRATION.

democracy (1) A system of government in which SOVEREIGNTY is vested in the people. Over the centuries it has been seen in many lights. 'A government in the hands of men of low birth, no property and unskilled labour' – Aristotle; 'The meanest and worst of all forms of government' – John Winthrop; 'There never was a democracy yet that did not commit suicide' – John ADAMS; 'Were our state a pure democracy, in which all its inhabitants should meet together to transact all their business, there would yet be excluded from its deliberations 1. infants, 2. women, 3. slaves' – Thomas JEFFERSON; a 'government of bullies tempered by editors' – Ralph Waldo Emerson; 'Democracy is only a dream. It should be put in the same category as Arcadia, Santa Claus and Heaven' – H. L. Mencken; 'The art and science of running the circus from the monkey cage' – Mencken; 'The worship of jackals by jackasses' – Mencken; 'The theory that common people know what they want, and deserve to get it good and hard' – Mencken; 'All the ills of democracy can be cured by more democracy' – Al Smith; 'A form of government you have to keep for four years, no matter what it does' – Will Rogers; 'A process by which the people are free to choose the man who will get the blame' – Lawrence J. Peter; 'An institution in which the whole is equal to the scum of the parts' – Keith Preston; 'Information is the currency of democracy' – Ralph Nader; 'Speed of action was never the absolute goal of democracy, because a king is faster than a Congressman on any given day' – Sen. William Cohen; 'A democracy can only exist until the voters discover that they can vote themselves largesse from the public treasury' – Lord Woodhouselee; 'An aristocracy of blackguards' – Lord Byron; 'Democracy will prevail when men believe the vote of Judas as good as that of Jesus Christ' – Thomas Carlyle (*attr.*); 'The bludgeoning of the people by the people, for the people' – Oscar Wilde; 'It substitutes election by the incompetent many for appointment by the corrupt few' – George Bernard Shaw; 'The worst form of government except all those others that have been tried from time to time' – CHURCHILL; 'Democracy is no harlot to be picked up in the street by a man with a tommy gun' – Churchill; 'Democracy means government by discussion, but it is only effective if you can stop people talking' – Clement ATTLEE; 'Democracy means choosing your dictators, after they've told you what it is you want to hear' – Alan Coren; 'A state which recognises the subordination of the minority to the majority' – LENIN; 'The Soviet people want full-blooded and unconditional democracy' – Mikhail GORBACHEV; 'Democracy is a truth in America. In Europe it is a falsehood' – Metternich; 'In a democracy the people elect the leader in whom they have confidence. The elected leader says: "Shut up and obey me"' – Max Weber; 'As long as people are people, democracy, in the full sense of the word, will always be no more than an ideal' – Vaclav Havel.

(2) a democracy. A nation where the conditions of democracy are seen to apply.

arsenal of democracy In a broadcast on 29

December 1941, President Franklin D. ROOSEVELT responded to PEARL HARBOR and Germany's declaration of war on America with a determination to make the United States 'the great arsenal of democracy'. The phrase was not original; in 1928 Josef Goebbels had written: 'We [NAZI deputies] enter Parliament in order to supply ourselves, in the arsenal of democracy, with its own weapons.'

guided democracy The regime which governs the internal workings of Britain's CONSERVATIVE PARTY, notably through the selection of anodyne motions for debate at its annual conference to ensure that criticism of the leadership is kept to a minimum. *See* STAGE-MANAGEMENT.

New Democracy The Greek centre-right party that alternates in power with PASOK. It formed the government from 1989 to 1993 under the premiership of Constantine Mitsotakis (1918–) and returned to power in March 2004 under Kostas Karamanlis.

people's democracy A term used by Communists to describe the system of government in the former Soviet Union and its SATELLITES.

> It's the same difference as between a jacket and a strait jacket. RONALD REAGAN

social democracy *See* SOCIAL.

The world must be made safe for democracy Woodrow WILSON's declaration to a JOINT SESSION of 1 on America's entry into WORLD WAR I, on 2 April 1917. John F. KENNEDY built on the phrase during the COLD WAR, declaring: 'If we cannot now end our differences, at least we can make the world safe for diversity.'

Democrat wars *see* WARS.

democratic centralism Another term used by Communists to justify a political system in which all decisions are taken at the centre, with the party RANK AND FILE expected to fall into line.

democratic deficit The absence of ACCOUNTABILITY, notably within many fields of the EUROPEAN COMMUNITY but now applied more generally. The MAASTRICHT TREATY was designed partly to remedy this by giving the EUROPEAN PARLIAMENT a greater supervisory role over the Commission, which it subsequently exercised (*see* BUTTIGLIONE NOMINATION; CRESSON AFFAIR).

Democratic Forum The centre-right party, led by Joszef Antall (1932–93), which headed the first democratic government in Hungary after the collapse of Janos Kadar's Communist regime in 1989. The Democratic Forum was formed at Lakitelet in September 1987, becoming a political party the following year; it was ousted from power by the socialists in 1994.

Democratic Leadership Council A moderate group within the US party whose 1991 conference effectively launched Bill CLINTON's Presidential candidacy.

Democratic Left (1) The new name adopted in 1991 by the continuing remnants of Britain's COMMUNIST PARTY. (2) The title adopted prior to Ireland's 1992 elections by the WORKERS' PARTY, previously Official SINN FEIN.

Democratic Party One of America's two great political parties, and in the main the more liberal. It has its roots in the vision of Thomas JEFFERSON and the POPULISM of Andrew Jackson (*see* OLD HICKORY), after whose ELECTION in 1828 the party took shape, getting van Buren, Polk, Pierce and Buchanan into the WHITE HOUSE. Yet in 1860 the populist Ignatius Donnelly could declare: 'Like a mule, it has neither pride of ancestry nor hope of posterity.' The New Hampshire anti-slaver Sen. John Hale was more personal, saying: 'I never said that all Democrats were rascals – only that all rascals were Democrats.' The CIVIL WAR split Democrats and left the party seriously weakened; it did not elect another President until CLEVELAND in 1884. The party regained stability as a coalition of the northern urban masses, mid-western populists and southern conservatives, even though Speaker Thomas Reed asserted that 'the Democratic Party is like a man riding in a railroad car; it never sees anything until it has got past it.' The great crusades of William Jennings Bryan (*see* PRAIRIE AVENGER) failed to win majority support, and Woodrow WILSON's election in 1912 was helped by a Republican split. The next year Rep. John Jacob Rogers said:

> The Southern Democrats are in the saddle and the Northern Democrats must tag along as best they may, no matter what ill may betide.

The post-war ISOLATIONIST tide weakened the Democrats, but as the GREAT DEPRESSION bit, Franklin D. ROOSEVELT's INTERVENTIONIST NEW DEAL paved the way for a 20-year Democratic presidency (though not always control of CONGRESS) and the renewal of the mass party as black voters switched to it. The Democrats had always been the white ethnic party, Ray Miller saying in 1948 when running for governor of Ohio:

Canada and Australia have as much opportunity, as many natural resources and as much land, but your mothers and mine came here because this country supports God, and because of the Democratic Party which has always supported God.

The Democrats suffered from the impact of MCCARTHYISM, but John F. KENNEDY proved the coalition's strength in 1960 by becoming the first Catholic president, and in 1964 Lyndon JOHNSON's welfarist GREAT SOCIETY swept the board. The VIETNAM WAR wrecked party unity, producing the spectre of the 1968 CHICAGO CONVENTION and the hijacking of the 1972 platform and candidate selection by ANTI-WAR and other radical groups. Nevertheless the Democrats generally retained control of the Congress – with control slipping away from the southern conservatives from the early 1970s as the SENIORITY system was dented.

Disillusion with Washington after WATERGATE enabled the more conservative Jimmy CARTER to reunite the coalition and win in 1976, only for his ADMINISTRATION's failures and Ronald REAGAN's appeal to BLUE-COLLAR voters to give the Republicans a near-stranglehold in 1980. Jeane Kirkpatrick saw a dilemma for the party in the Reagan years:

The Democrats are in a real bind. They won't get elected unless things get worse, and things won't get worse unless they get elected.

Reagan himself said of the Democrats: 'They have gone so far left, they have left America,' and: 'We need more Democrats in the Senate like Custer needed more arrows.' Even the Democrat Sen. Pat Schroeder confessed: 'Spine transplants are what we really need to take Reagan on.' Yet under Reagan and George BUSH Snr the Democrats rebuilt their strength in Congress, and in 1992 Bill CLINTON regained the Presidency. Though he stopped short of embracing Jesse Jackson's RAINBOW COALITION, Clinton built an electoral base embracing labor, white ethnic, liberal, Jewish, black and Hispanic support, yet reaching out for enough of the middle ground – notably the REAGAN DEMOCRATS and SOCCER MOMS – to win power. The Clinton coalition held in 1996, and despite ZIPPERGATE came within a handful of disputed Florida votes of installing Al GORE (*see* OZONE MAN) in the White House four years later. In 2004 the party came closer under John KERRY to ousting George W. BUSH than had seemed likely.

The nature of the Democrats' support, and until the 1980s the greater ideological content of its programme, made it a more openly fissile party than the Republicans. In 1901 Finley Peter Dunne wrote:

When ye see two men with white neckties go into a street car and set in opposite corners while wan mutters 'thraiter' an' th' other hisses 'miscreant', ye can bet they're two Dimmycratic leaders thryin' to reunite th' gran' ol' party.

Will Rogers insisted: 'I am not a member of any organised political party. I am a Democrat,' and: 'You've got to be an optimist to be a Democrat, and you've got to be a humorist to stay one.' And Speaker Jim Wright described the party as 'a mixture, an amalgam, a mosaic, call it a fruitcake'. At times it can be downright suicidal; Rep. Morris Udall once said: 'When the Democratic Party forms a firing squad, we form a circle.' *Compare* CIRCULAR FIRING SQUAD; *See also* COPPERHEADS, DIXIECRATS.

Democratic-Republican Party The faction formed by Thomas JEFFERSON and his supporters to contest the 1798 Congressional elections and the Presidential election of 1800, which took Jefferson to power.

Democratic Socialism *See* SOCIALISM.

Democratic Study Group (DSG) The powerful informal CAUCUS of liberal Democrats in CONGRESS, founded by Rep. Eugene McCarthy and 79 others after the LANDSLIDE of 1958 to push through the party programme despite the opposition of conservative committee chairmen. The DSG's persistent efforts over more than a decade for greater democracy was a major factor in opening up Congressional committee chairmanships to election and greater ACCOUNTABILITY.

Democratic Unionist Party *See* DUP.

Democrats The centrist party in Australia founded in 1977 by the Liberal MHR Don Chipp. While efforts to merge with other parties were abortive, it has remained in existence with around 5% of the popular vote and has won occasional seats, mainly in Victoria and New South Wales.

demonstration A MARCH or RALLY, with participants carrying their slogans on banners, to protest against a policy or event, or to advocate a cause. The focus is on the mass who turn out to demonstrate, rather than on any speakers who address them.

Quite small and unattended demonstrations can be made to look like the beginnings of a REVOLUTION if the cameraman is in the right place at the right time.

GOUGH WHITLAM

Demos A left-leaning UK THINK TANK founded in 1994, coincidentally the year Tony BLAIR became leader of the LABOUR PARTY, which has heavily influenced government thinking since he came to power in 1997. Geoff Mulgan, founder of Demos, went on to serve in DOWNING STREET for seven years, ultimately as Blair's head of policy.

denationalisation The return of a NATIONALISED industry from public to private ownership. The term was coined by UK Conservatives in their campaigning prior to their return to power in 1951, when they reversed the nationalisation of steel and road haulage. Since the early 1980s the word PRIVATISATION has superseded it.

denazification The filtration process carried out by the victorious Allies from 1945 in what became West Germany. Its aim was to punish NAZI leaders and ensure that party activists were excluded from the country's post-war administration. *Compare* DEBAATHIFICATION.

deniability A US term, current during WATERGATE but not a product of it, for the conduct of a particular issue so that those responsible can subsequently deny all knowledge of it.

One picture is worth a thousand denials The motto of the WHITE HOUSE Photographers' Association, reflecting the snapper's advantage when anything that appears in print can – plausibly or otherwise – be denied by those in power.

Denning Report The report of the inquiry by Lord Denning, Master of the Rolls (1899–1999), in 1963 into the security aspects of the PROFUMO AFFAIR. When published that autumn, the report disappointed the Labour OPPOSITION who hoped it would contain enough compromising material to finish off the Conservative government; however, Harold MACMILLAN retired through ill health shortly after and the Tories narrowly lost power the following year. Denning concluded that the liaison between the former War Minister John Profumo and the call girl Christine Keeler had posed no threat to national security despite Keeler's parallel association with a Soviet naval attaché. He also found no evidence to support rumours about the involvement of other ministers in sexual escapades on the fringe of the scandal. Denning's criticism of security arrangements did lead Macmillan's successor, SIR ALEC Douglas-Home, to establish a standing committee on security.

département One of the administrative units into which Republican France has been divided since 1800. Until 1964 the number was set at 89; it has since risen to 96.

dependency A territory dependent on another for its government, lacking any of its own; as in the former Falkland Islands Dependencies, none of which were permanently inhabited.

dependency culture A phrase first used by sociologists in the late 1970s, and soon after by politicians, for the sector of society which is entirely dependent on welfare benefits and other forms of public assistance, and in time becomes conditioned to having no work nor hope of, or desire for, any earned income.

dependency theory The doctrine, common among radicals in the 1960s and '70s, that the United States and the former colonial powers had not relaxed their control over the THIRD WORLD, and were now using their economic power and those nations' weakness to exert unfair advantage over them in terms of trade. At its extreme, the theory even argues that foreign aid is harmful because it shapes developing economies in a way that ties them even more firmly to the needs of the donors.

de-porking *See* PORK.

deposit The sum which a CANDIDATE in a UK Parliamentary ELECTION has to lodge with the RETURNING OFFICER, to be repaid if he or she obtains a certain share of the poll. Imposed to discourage frivolous candidacies, the deposit was set at £150 until 1985, the threshold for return being 12.5% of votes cast; since then it has been £500, but is only forfeit if the candidate polls less than 5%. A candidate who is within a few votes of saving their deposit will frequently call for a RECOUNT.

depression A very severe and lasting downturn in the economy, the resulting stagnation causing even greater dislocation and hardship than a RECESSION. It usually follows a boom, and brings both high unemployment and weak prices. The GREAT DEPRESSION of the 1930s was the most widespread and severe of recent times.

Deputy (Fr. *député*) A member of France's NATIONAL ASSEMBLY. Also, derivatively, of DAIL ÉIREANN, with the abbreviation TD.

deputy Prime Minister A position seldom made formal in Britain's governmental structure until the late 1980s. RAB Butler did occupy it under Harold MACMILLAN, terming it 'a post I conclude should neither be offered nor accepted'; as he was passed over on Macmillan's retirement, his opinion was understandable. George BROWN held the title of First Secretary of State for a time in the mid-1960s as deputy to Harold WILSON, and from 1979 to 1987 William (late Lord) Whitelaw (*see* WILLIE) was effectively Margaret THATCHER's deputy Prime Minister, though without the title. The position was created for Sir Geoffrey HOWE in 1989–90, and after his resignation triggered Mrs Thatcher's removal John MAJOR gave substance to the title by awarding it, with considerable executive powers, to Michael HESELTINE. After Labour's victory in 1997 Tony BLAIR conferred the title on John Prescott (*see* TWO JAGS), eventually creating an Office of the Deputy Prime Minister (ODPM) to oversee regional and planning matters.

deregulation The policy of removing government controls from a field of commercial activity, for example commercial airlines (*see* OPEN SKIES) or bus transport, in the hope of improving consumer choice or weakening trade union influence.

Dergue The hard-line Marxist government of Ethiopia under Colonel Mengistu Haile Mariam which ruled the country from 1977, three years after officers including Mengistu overthrew Emperor Haile Selaisse (*see* LION OF JUDAH), until 1991, when Mengistu fled the country as a rebel alliance closed in on Addis Ababa. The Dergue's rule was notable for its attempts to impose a Marxist-Leninist economy and political system at a time when much of the country was gripped by desperate famine, and its unsuccessful efforts to defeat SEPARATIST guerrillas in Eritrea and Tigre.

derogation The exemption that a member country of the EU may seek from a piece of community legislation. A derogation will normally only be granted by the EUROPEAN COURT if it would not impact on any other member.

descamisados (Sp. Shirtless ones) The working-class and lower middle-class masses who gave vocal support to Argentina's dictator Juan PERÓN, in return for benign social policies, outright handouts and expropriation of unpopular foreign capitalists. When his popularity seemed threatened, his CHARISMATIC wife Eva (*see* EVITA) would whip up the *descamisados* into a state of frenzy from the balcony of the CASA ROSADA.

desegregation The ending of the provision of separate facilities for people of different races. The breaking down of the COLOUR BAR throughout the United States, and especially in the South, was the immediate aim of the CIVIL RIGHTS movement that reached its heights in the 1970s – and of the KENNEDY/JOHNSON administration. The process was begun with President TRUMAN's desegregation of the armed forces, and hastened by the 1954 SUPREME COURT decision outlawing segregation of public schools in BROWN V TOPEKA BOARD OF EDUCATION.

deselection The removal by a constituency Labour Party (CLP) of a sitting member of Parliament by refusing to reselect them as their candidate for the next general election. The battle over the automatic right of a constituency to deselect deeply divided the party c. 1978–81, and the victory of the CAMPAIGN FOR LABOUR PARTY DEMOCRACY on this issue was one reason for the breakaway of the GANG OF FOUR to found the SDP. The adoption of deselection by the party conference has led to relatively few MPs being ousted – perhaps 20 at the three subsequent elections and a handful since – but forced many others to fight desperately to keep the party nomination, hampering the duties they were elected to fulfil. A number of sitting Conservative MPs have been removed by their constituency associations with just as much acrimony.

desk. desk officer An official who has specific responsibility for a self-contained area of policy, and specifically one in a foreign ministry who looks after relations with and the affairs of a particular country.

banging of desk lids The traditional way in which Conservative BACKBENCHERS at WESTMINSTER show their approval for comments made at the weekly meeting of the 1922 COMMITTEE.

clearing one's desk A euphemism for resigning, being dismissed or expecting to be so, used particularly of government ministers (in America Cabinet Secretaries and senior WHITE HOUSE staffers) whose careers are suddenly terminated. Sometimes the staff of a senior functionary will clear his or her desk in anticipation that they will be replaced; it was rumoured that civil servants in the office of Willie Ross (Lord Ross of Marnock), Secretary of State for Scotland under Harold WILSON, cleared his desk three times when a RESHUFFLE was imminent, only to have to put his papers back hurriedly.

despatch box In the UK HOUSE OF

COMMONS, the brassbound oak boxes on which Ministers and senior Opposition spokesmen may lean when speaking. They contain Bibles and the equivalent for use in swearing in new members.

> The Right Honourable Gentleman's red face looming over the despatch box is a pretty terrifying sight. I was not sure at one stage whether it was indignation, claret or a faulty sun lamp.
>
> PETER SNAPE MP (Lab.) on Cecil (now Lord) Parkinson

> His delivery at the despatch box has all the bite of a rubber duck.
>
> Lady FALKENDER (*see* LADY FORKBENDER) on John (now Lord) Moore

The term is also used, not entirely correctly, for the (usually red) boxes in which Ministers carry official papers (*see* doing the BOXES).

despot, despotism A tyrant, a state governed by a tyrant. Daniel Webster declared: 'Whenever a government is not a government of laws, it is a despotism, let it be called what it may.' Bertrand Russell saw a niche for it, writing: 'Mankind needs government, but in seasons where anarchy has prevailed they will, at first, submit only to despotism.' And Oscar Wilde averred:

> There are three kinds of despot: the despot who tyrannises over the body, the despot who tyrannises over the soul, [and] the despot who tyrannises over the soul and body alike. The first is called the prince. The second is called the Pope. The third is called the People.

In the early days of American independence, Thomas JEFFERSON warned Lafayette: 'We are not to be expected to be transported from despotism to liberty in a feather bed.'

> Despotism and oppression never yet were beaten except by heroic resistance.
>
> LAJOS KOSSUTH, Hungarian revolutionary (1802–94)

> No despot is ever going to give up his throne because you ask him to give it up, or because you beg him to go away. The final word is always an act of war.
>
> MEHDI BAZARGAN, Prime Minister of Iran, 1979

destabilisation Action by one nation or political grouping to undermine the stability of another, for example by promoting dissent or unrest within it.

détente The policy of limited disengagement and PEACEFUL COEXISTENCE between the SUPERPOWERS, though without any reduction in Soviet influence over its SATELLITES, pioneered by Leonid BREZHNEV. He put it forward to rebuild bridges after the crushing of the PRAGUE SPRING in 1968, and to insulate Soviet-US relations from the VIETNAM WAR. President NIXON and Henry KISSINGER responded, and SUMMIT meetings and other contacts produced a THAW. The ARMS RACE continued, but Nixon and Brezhnev did conclude the first SALT agreement; Jimmy CARTER and Brezhnev signed a second, but the SENATE would not RATIFY it. The Soviet invasion of Afghanistan in 1979 finally discredited the process.

deterrence The doctrine that a nation can prevent (specifically NUCLEAR) attacks on itself by possessing overwhelming retaliatory strength. Campaigners for nuclear disarmament have argued that the theory is flawed, but advocates of deterrence point out that the COLD WAR ended after 40 years without any nuclear weapon having been launched. The success of deterrence also depended on a firm and consistent political stance rather than the sending out of confused signals about what actions would provoke retaliation, US Defense Secretary Robert McNamara writing in 1968: 'One cannot fashion a credible deterrent out of an incredible action.'

> Only when our arms are sufficient without doubt can we be certain that they will never be deployed. JOHN F. KENNEDY, 1961

independent deterrent The possession by the UK of NUCLEAR WEAPONS under purely British command, maintained by governments of all parties since the late 1940s, Labour's anti-nuclear phases never coinciding with its periods of office. To nuclear disarmers the possession of such a deterrent by a relatively small nation is a dangerous farce and an invitation to PROLIFERATION, but advocates of the policy argue that Britain's possession of nuclear weapons earns it a place at the top table. *See* NAKED INTO THE CONFERENCE CHAMBER.

> For Honourable Members opposite the deterrent is a phallic symbol. It convinces them that they are men.
>
> GEORGE (later Lord) WIGG (1900–76), speaking from the Labour front bench, March 1964

Deutschland. Deutschland einig Vaterland (Ger. Germany one Fatherland) The popular slogan under which Germany moved toward REUNIFICATION on 3 October 1990, less than eleven months after the breaching of the BERLIN WALL.

Deutschland Über Alles (Ger. Germany above all) The patriotic poem adopted as the

German national anthem after WORLD WAR I, which has remained the ultimate expression of German patriotism, though other less assertive anthems were chosen for the two separate Germanies between 1949 and 1990. The anthem, written in 1841 by Heinrich Hoffmann von Fullersleben (1798–1876) is sung to Haydn's *Imperial Anthem*, the tune being familiar to Anglophones as

> Glorious things of thee are spoken,
> Zion, City of our God.

The verses now sung reflect the culture of the post-war Federal Republic:

> *Einigkeit und Recht und Freiheit*
> *Für das Deutsche Vaterland!*

> (Unity, justice and freedom
> for the German Fatherland.)

Deuxième Bureau (Fr. Second Bureau) The French agency which counters internal subversion, broadly comparable with Britain's MI5 but with a more combative role. External threats are a matter for the SDECE.

Dev The popular nickname for Eamonn de Valera (1882–1975), the New York-born participant in Ireland's EASTER RISING who became a leader of the forces against PARTITION, the founder of FIANNA FAIL, TAOISEACH 1932–48, 1951–54 and 1957–59, and President 1959–73. His American birth having saved him from execution after the Rising, he escaped from Lincoln prison in 1919 and raised $1 million in America for the IRA. A founder member of DAIL EIREANN, he fought in the Civil War of 1922–23, was imprisoned, but renounced violence in 1924. As Prime Minister he repudiated Ireland's allegiance to the British Crown in 1937, kept the Republic neutral during WORLD WAR II, and angered British opinion by sending official condolences on HITLER's death. Highly intelligent and devoutly religious, his premiership covered the period immediately before the emergence of Ireland as not only a sovereign state but a modern one.

> *Lloyd George:* [Negotiating with him is] like picking up mercury with a fork.
> *De Valera:* Why doesn't he use a spoon?

devaluation The unilateral reduction in the value of one country's currency compared with others. Unsuccessful attempts to avoid it have caused British governments considerable anguish, and the economy much pain, in 1948–49, 1964–67 and 1992; the CHANCELLORS forced to devalue were Sir Stafford Cripps (*see* CHRIST AND CARROTS), James CALLAGHAN and Norman Lamont (*see* JE NE REGRETTE RIEN. *See also* POUND IN YOUR POCKET.

> The sky is darkening with the wings of chickens coming home to roost.
>
> Lord CALLAGHAN on BLACK WEDNESDAY, 16 September 1992

deviationism The term used by STALINISTS and other disciplinarian COMMUNISTS for any variation from the PARTY LINE; it was used against both genuine advocates of another course and anyone the leadership wished to get rid of.

devolution The transfer of power from a nation state to one of its constituent parts, or from any central authority to supposedly subordinate bodies, to bring about more localised decision making and ACCOUNTABILITY. The term is used specifically of the handing over of powers and authority by WESTMINSTER to Scotland, Wales and NORTHERN IRELAND, and subsequently to London and, to a lesser extent, the English regions. The argument over HOME RULE stretched back to Victorian times, but devolution became an issue for the UK after the near-breakthrough by the SNP at the first 1974 general election, an outcome that persuaded the incoming Labour government to reverse its previous commitment to centralism. Labour's first attempt to create Scottish and Welsh assemblies passed the COMMONS but perished in two inconclusive REFERENDUMS early in 1979. With the Conservatives under Margaret THATCHER and John MAJOR resolutely opposed, it was eighteen years before Labour's re-election under Tony BLAIR paved the way for action. The SCOTTISH PARLIAMENT and WELSH ASSEMBLY duly took up their powers in 1999, joined sporadically by a NORTHERN IRELAND ASSEMBLY when the behaviour of political parties who had supposedly renounced PARAMILITARY activity permitted. The achievement of devolution has strengthened the political cultures of Edinburgh and Cardiff, but, particularly in Scotland, there has been resentment at both the performance of the country's new political leaders and the retention by the UK government of key powers over the economy. The move to extend devolution to the English regions, championed by John Prescott (*see* TWO JAGS), suffered a severe reverse in November 2004 when residents of the North-East, thought to be the keenest to have it, voted heavily against in a referendum. *See also*

CUNNINGHAM AMENDMENT, GOOD FRIDAY AGREEMENT, SCOTTISH CONSTITUTIONAL CONVENTION.

Power devolved is power retained.
ENOCH POWELL

devolved powers Those powers that have been transferred from Westminster to Edinburgh or Cardiff as a result of devolution; the extent of devolution to Scotland has been greater. RESERVED POWERS are those retained by the UK government.

Devonshire declaration The statement made in 1923 by the Duke of Devonshire, Colonial Secretary in BALDWIN's government, which made it inevitable that white settlers in Kenya and Britain's other East African possessions would eventually find themselves under black rule. Devonshire laid down that the interests of the colony's native peoples had to be 'paramount'; the settlers protested strongly, but the policy stuck. Independence under majority rule was granted 40 years later, after the MAU MAU rising which if anything hastened it. By contrast the whites in Southern Rhodesia were granted self-government at the time of the Devonshire declaration, creating the built-in obstacle to majority rule which enabled Ian Smith to declare UDI in 1965.

DEW line Distant Early Warning line. A network of radar stations, mostly in the Canadian Arctic, established during the COLD WAR and intended to give America early warning of attack by Soviet missiles or aircraft. It was under the control of NORAD.

Dewey. Dewey defeats Truman The notorious headline carried by early editions of the *Chicago Tribune* on 3 November 1948, based on the assumption that Thomas E. Dewey (1902–71) had ousted the incumbent President TRUMAN, as the pollsters had predicted. Truman's GIVE 'EM HELL campaign succeeded to confound the pundits, and the re-elected President did not allow the paper to forget its embarrassing 'scoop', which was emulated by the *Washington Post.* Dewey, the Republican governor of New York, was sincere, but his lack of CHARISMA had been cruelly pointed out even before he ran against ROOSEVELT in 1944, Samuel Grafton asking: 'If a young man is as cold as this at 37, will he reach absolute zero at 50?' David Brinkley wrote of his platform style: 'He spoke so euphoniously that each word emerged polished and glowing like a jewel nestling on its own little velvet pillow,' and Richard Rovere noted: 'He comes out like a man who has been mounted on castors and given a tremendous shove from behind.' Alice Roosevelt Longworth and Grace Flandreau are both credited with saying: 'How can you vote for a candidate who looks like the bridegroom on a wedding cake?', and when Dewey ran against TRUMAN, Mrs Longworth observed: 'You can't make a soufflé rise twice.' Nevertheless post-war malaise and disillusion with the Democrats made him the clear favourite – but he had reckoned without Truman.

Just about the nastiest little man I've ever known. He struts sitting down.
Mrs DYKSTRA

DGSE *Direction Générale de la Securité Extérieure* The French Government agency (under the Ministry of Defence) responsible for military intelligence and external counter-espionage. It has its roots in the intelligence agencies created by the FREE FRENCH during World War II, which were institutionalised by the FOURTH REPUBLIC in 1946 as the SDECE. This organisation was seen by the Communists as too militaristic (one of its missions was to arm the secessionists in BIAFRA to deny Britain supplies of Nigerian oil – and after President MITTERRAND took office with their support, he recast it in 1982 as the DGSE, with an increasingly civilian staff. Since 2003 it has hosted in Paris a joint operations centre with the CIA to co-ordinate the fight against global Islamist terrorism.

d'Hondt formula. One of the most widely supported, if complex and arcane, formulae for PROPORTIONAL REPRESENTATION; it was invented in 1882 by the Professor of Civil Law at Ghent University. In the words of the Conservative MP Desmond Swayne it works in elections for the European Parliament 'by allocating additional seats at each stage to the party with the highest total after dividing the total number of votes they have won across the Euro seat by the total (constituency + list) seats they have plus one.'

DHSS Department of Health and Social Security. The UK government department which was responsible for the NHS and all other aspects of the WELFARE STATE from 1968 until 1988, when it was split into a Department of Health and a separate Department of Social Security (later the Department for Work and Pensions). For almost all its life it was based in the award-winning but monstrous Alexander Fleming House at the Elephant and Castle, two miles south of WESTMINSTER; in its last couple of years its Ministers and key staff operated from the more convenient Richmond Terrace in WHITEHALL. As a single department it was the biggest employer in Europe after the RED ARMY.

> It was in reality Harold WILSON's folly, put together for no greater purpose than satisfying the ministerial ambitions of Dick CROSSMAN.
>
> PETER HENNESSY, *Whitehall*

dial group A panel of voters recruited by a political party to assess changes in the public mood. They are shown a video and asked to register their reaction to it on a dial, turning the knob to the right if they like something or to the left if they do not. With around 25 members, a dial group is larger than a FOCUS GROUP. The technique was pioneered in the United States; it was first used in Britain by the Conservatives after William HAGUE became leader in 1997, to ascertain the strengths and weaknesses of the SHADOW CABINET. An early finding was that Francis Maude's reluctance to wear a jacket played badly with the voters.

dialectical materialism A quasi-MARXIST doctrine (known in Soviet Russia as *DiaMat*) which holds that development and change in societies and economies can only be caused by technical changes in the methods of production. Many leftists use the term more generally for the general process of Marxist thought.

dictator A ruler with absolute power, originally a figure in ancient Rome deliberately entrusted with such powers at times of crisis. Applied particularly to the monolithic leaders of the inter-war period – HITLER, STALIN, Mussolini (*see* DUCE), Franco (*see* CAUDILLO) and others – the term developed sinister and obsessional connotations. Hitler wrote: 'The man who is born to be a dictator is not compelled. He wills it.' Margaret THATCHER, at the time of the FALKLANDS, declared: 'When you stop a dictator there are always risks. But there are greater risks in not stopping a dictator.' And Franklin D. ROOSEVELT warned:

> Dictatorships do not grow out of strong and successful governments, but out of weak and helpless ones.

dictatorship of the proletariat *See* PROLETARIAT.

elective dictatorship The alarmist term used by Lord Hailsham (1907–2001) for the potential of a UK government with a clear majority in the HOUSE OF COMMONS to do whatever it wishes. Hailsham (Quintin Hogg) who sat on the Tory FRONT BENCH in one House or other from 1945 to 1987, was voicing concern about the ability of a Labour government to implement its programme despite the then entrenched Tory majority in the Lords – not the potential for a Conservative administration to be equally ruthless.

die. Fight and die! The chilling order given by STALIN to units of the RED ARMY as German forces closed in on Moscow toward the end of 1941. At that year's commemoration of the OCTOBER REVOLUTION, Soviet troops taking part in the parade through RED SQUARE marched straight on to the front line. Many never returned, but the line was held.

I am as content to die for God's eternal truth on the scaffold as any other way John BROWN's declaration at his trial on 31 October 1859 for treason, criminal conspiracy and murder, having led the raid on HARPER'S FERRY two weeks before. He was hanged on 2 December.

If a man hasn't discovered something he will die for, he isn't fit to live Martin Luther KING's definition of the purpose of life. *See also* die for one's COUNTRY.

It is better to die on your feet than live on your knees The slogan coined by Emilio Zapata during the Mexican Revolution of 1910, and later broadcast by LA PASIONARA on Republican radio during the SPANISH CIVIL WAR.

Diehards The Tory rebels in the HOUSE OF LORDS who, in 1911, rejected the advice of their party leader, A. J. BALFOUR, and pledged to 'die fighting' the Liberals' constitutional changes which became the PARLIAMENT ACT, limiting the Lords' veto over BILLS passed by the COMMONS. Their revolt caused Balfour to resign the Tory leadership in November 1911.

Dief the Chief The nickname coined by Canada's PROGRESSIVE CONSERVATIVES for John **Diefenbaker** (1895–1975), the Saskatchewan lawyer who in the late 1950s revitalised the party as a radical, almost POPULIST force. Leader from 1956 to 1967, he won a narrow majority in the 1957 election and two years later led his party to Canada's greatest LANDSLIDE up to then: 208 Conservative, 49 LIBERAL, 8 CCF. His term of office – ended by defeat by Lester Pearson's Liberals in 1963 – was dominated by a show of independence, coupled with co-operation, in dealings with the United States. Though it was Diefenbaker's government that concluded the NORAD agreement, he frequently irritated WASHINGTON. Diefenbaker once mistakenly thought President KENNEDY had called him a s.o.b., but when the complaint was lodged, JFK said:

> I didn't think he was a son of a bitch. I thought he was a prick.

Dien Bien Phu The village in north Vietnam, surrounded by hills, which was the site of the ignominious defeat of French forces by the Communist VIET MINH in May 1954 which effectively ended colonial rule in Indo-China. After eight years of indecisive conflict that cost 50,000 French lives, General Henri Navarre chose Dien Bien Phu in November 1953 as a land-air base for offensive operations against the rebels; his hope was to tempt them into the open for a decisive battle they would lose. Within a month the Viet Minh commander, General Vo Nguyen Giap (later the architect of America's defeat in the VIETNAM WAR), had surrounded the 15,000-strong garrison with over 40,000 men and heavy artillery in the mountains overlooking the base. The final battle began on 12 March 1954; the French found themselves under bombardment with nothing visible to shoot at, and then the GUERRILLAS closed in for hand-to-hand combat. Dien Bien Phu fell on 7 May, the day before the opening of the international peace conference in GENEVA. President EISENHOWER wisely resisted French appeals for military support, but the lessons of the defeat were ignored by his successors. Dien Bien Phu has become a byword for an untenable position defended with pointless determination; Roy JENKINS described the first WILSON government's defence of the $2.80 sterling rate for three years until a forced DEVALUATION as 'a sort of British Dien Bien Phu'.

Diet Japan's Parliament under its democratic post-war constitution. The **House of Representatives** has 512 members, elected every four years; the upper house (**House of Councillors**) has 252, of which 100 are elected by the party LIST SYSTEM under proportional representation, and 152 from the prefectural districts, half elected every five years.

Dieu et mon Droit (Fr. God and my Right) The motto of the Kings and Queens of England, which appears on the Royal coat of arms.

Diggers The small group of extreme religious and social radicals under Gerrard Winstanley (1609–60) who began digging and planting the common at St George's Hill, Surrey, in 1649, after the overthrow and execution of Charles I, with the aim of giving it back to the people. The Diggers, who formed groups of 20 to 30, were soon suppressed by the Cromwellian army leaders, but Winstanley set out his vision of a true COMMONWEALTH in 1652; in it private family life and ownership were respected, but there would be no money or wages. The Digger philosophy has been invoked by a number of later revolutionary and UTOPIAN movements.

Dikko affair The displomatic incident between Britain and Nigeria prompted by UK Customs officials' discovery of Omaru Dikko, Nigeria's former Transport Minister, drugged and in a crate at Stansted airport on 5 July 1984. With him in other crates were three Israelis, one an anaesthetist, who were charged with kidnapping and administering drugs. The Nigerian authorities had been eager to try Dikko for corruption, and when frustrated by the EXTRADITION process, arranged for him to be kidnapped by the country's National Security Organisation and sent home in the DIPLOMATIC BAG. Britain protested at the violation of its sovereignty, and allowed Dikko to stay. Some weeks later, the Labour MP Peter Snape reduced the COMMONS to laughter by saying of Britain's Transport Secretary Nicholas Ridley (*see* GERMAN RACKET):

> The Nigerians have kidnapped the wrong Minister of Transport.

Dilke case *See* THREE-IN-A-BED.

Dillingham report The 42-volume report published in 1911 which concluded that 'old' Protestant and Nordic immigrants from western and northern Europe were better suited for settlement in America than 'new' Catholic, migrants from Mediterranean countries. The report, from a committee chaired by Sen. William P. Dillingham of Vermont, was commissioned by CONGRESS because of a RACIST upsurge against non-WASPs, fuelled by a spate of pseudo-scientific literature on the 'inferiority' of other races. Dillingham's findings contributed to a series of illiberal laws: the 1917 Immigration Act, passed despite Woodrow Wilson's VETO, the 1921 QUOTA Act and the Johnson-Reed Act of 1921. Their combined effect was to cut immigration from an average 862,514 in pre-war years to a ceiling of 150,000 – with oriental immigration banned outright.

dining clubs The semi-formal and often highly secret gatherings of WESTMINSTER MPs which meet regularly in the private rooms of restaurants and the homes of well-heeled politicians. They may be comprised of the like-minded, or have a particular social cachet; the most raucous members are unlikely to be asked to join one, hence the OTHER CLUB founded by CHURCHILL and F. E. Smith. Dining clubs are particularly influential in Conservative politics, especially when, as happened in 1990, their members form the campaign teams of rival leadership candidates. Fewer Labour MPs form such groups, and those that exist tend to be ideological rather than social (*see* SUPPER CLUB).

diplomacy The art of conducting relations between governments, and the process of resolving disputes through personal contact between emissaries. The Canadian Prime Minister and NOBEL PEACE PRIZE winner Lester Pearson described diplomacy as 'letting someone else have your way'; Henry KISSINGER defined it as 'the art of restraining power', and Isaac Goldberg as 'to do or say/the nastiest things in the nicest way'. STALIN, typically, declared that 'sincere diplomacy is no more possible than dry water or wooden iron'. The purpose of diplomacy is to achieve just settlements while averting war, but at the start of the FALKLANDS WAR the Tory MP Julian Amery memorably accused the FOREIGN OFFICE of failing to distinguish between diplomacy and foreign policy. Yet diplomacy and war are inextricable; Frederick the Great declared that 'diplomacy without armaments is like music without instruments', Chou En-Lai termed diplomacy 'the continuation of war by other means', and Tony BENN argued that 'all war represents a failure of diplomacy.'

> Protocol, alcohol and Geritol.
>
> ADLAI STEVENSON

dollar diplomacy The use of America's economic strength and the power of its business community to promote US interests overseas, especially in Central America. The term, still occasionally used today by critics of US influence in the region, was in use by 1910, being applied to Secretary of State Philander Knox, as the US built its overseas interests through economic muscle. Two years later President TAFT championed the concept, saying:

> The diplomacy of the present administration has sought to respond to modern ideals of commercial intercourse. This policy has been characterised as substituting dollars for bullets. It is one that appeals alike to idealistic humanitarian sentiments, to the dictates of sound policy and strategy, and to legitimate commercial aims.

gunboat diplomacy A show of strength by a COLONIAL or other self-important power against a weak nation to ensure that its aims and view of the world prevail. The name arose from Britain's practice during the 19th century of dispatching a gunboat to any overseas territory where the natives were getting restless, or receptive to overtures from a rival colonial power.

megaphone diplomacy A 1980s term for belligerent and uncompromising statements made by a nation's leaders in the usually vain belief that they will make another country change its policies.

> Megaphone diplomacy leads to a dialogue of the deaf. Sir GEOFFREY (later Lord) HOWE

open diplomacy *See* OPEN.

panda diplomacy Communist China's practice, in CHAIRMAN MAO's last years and subsequently, of cultivating relations with western countries by making their leaders gifts of giant pandas, which were then passed on to zoos. The practice has diminished with the dwindling supply of pandas.

ping-pong diplomacy The means by which the NIXON administration finally opened contacts with Communist China, through the exchange of table-tennis teams. The pandas came later.

shuttle diplomacy The technique, perfected in the Middle East by Henry KISSINGER, by which an intermediary in an international dispute travels repeatedly between the capitals in question in an effort to bridge the gap.

diplomat A representative of one country stationed in another to conduct relations with its government, or based at home to liaise with diplomats from elsewhere. Because diplomacy is a diplomat's stock in trade, the word has come to describe anyone who is able to handle a tricky situation with inexhaustible tact.

> A real diplomat is one who can cut his neighbour's throat without having his neighbour notice it.
>
> UN Secretary-General TRYGGVE LIE (1896–1968)

> One who is disarming, even if his country isn't.
>
> UK Defence, later Foreign Secretary MALCOLM RIFKIND

> A diplomat these days is nothing but a head waiter who's allowed to sit down occasionally.
>
> Sir PETER USTINOV, *Romanoff and Juliet*

diplomatic bag The receptacle, dimensions unspecified, in which documents and larger items are carried between a country's EMBASSY abroad and its home government. Under international conventions, the diplomatic bag is immune from inspection by customs and its confidentiality is respected. However, there have been instances of countries using the diplomatic bag to transport weapons and explosives to revolutionaries abroad, smuggle contraband, or even (*see* DIKKO AFFAIR) to kidnap their citizens and spirit them home.
diplomatic corps The body of overseas diplomats stationed in any one of the world's capitals. The longest-serving is the **doyen**.
diplomatic immunity *See* IMMUNITY.
diplomatic list The list produced by a government containing either the names of its own diplomats or the names and seniority of the DIPLOMATIC CORPS in its capital, in some cases listing their wives as well.
diplomatic relations Formal contact between nations marked by the presence of their diplomats in each other's country; diplomatic relations normally attract attention only when they are strained or broken off. When they are severed, the contacts are kept going by INTERESTS SECTIONS in other countries' embassies. *See also* RECOGNITION.

> The reason for having diplomatic relations is not to confer a compliment, but to secure a convenience.
> CHURCHILL, 1949

diplomatic toothache An 'illness' which a leader is said to be suffering from when he wishes to avoid a particular person or occasion without giving unnecessary offence. Originally the phrase was **diplomatic cold**, stemming from claims by GLADSTONE and the Marquess of Hartington in 1885 that they were suffering from colds when they wished to duck out of a series of speaking engagements; the next day they admitted to being much better. The Soviet leader Nikita Khrushchev invented the diplomatic toothache in the late 1950s when he wanted to avoid pre-arranged meetings with Western leaders visiting Moscow.
activities inconsistent with his/her/their diplomatic status The phrase used by a host government when declaring a foreign diplomat PERSONA NON GRATA for espionage – or alleged espionage in the case of a TIT FOR TAT EXPULSION.

direct. direct mail The technique for large-scale fundraising and mobilisation of opinion pioneered by US conservative and single-ISSUE groups, and pursued with some success in Britain, initially by the Conservatives, from the late 1980s. It has enabled PRESSURE GROUPS in America to build up computer banks of supporters who, at the touch of a button, can be solicited to send in funds or write to a politician urging a vote for or against a particular proposition. As early as the 1950s Marvin Liebman had compiled a list of 1,000,000 names, initially of supporters of NATIONALIST CHINA, and the technique was perfected in the 1970s by Richard Viguerie. It has also enabled parties and campaigns to target and mobilise voters who can be appealed to over particular issues, e.g. Jewish or Italian voters or owners of imported cars. In Britain the reputation of direct mail campaigns has suffered because of the number of appeals sent to well-known politicians on the other side, or to computer-invented persons like 'Mr PhD', 'Mrs OBE' or even 'Mr Deceased', but they have raised considerable sums of money for all the parties, and even more for groups such as GREENPEACE.
direct rule The imposition of central control on a portion of the country where DEVOLVED government is perceived to have broken down. The term is particularly applied to the government of NORTHERN IRELAND since the abolition of STORMONT in 1972, after which a Northern Ireland Office headed by a UK Cabinet Minister – initially WILLIE Whitelaw – was set up to combat terrorism, remove discrimination against Catholics and foster the creation of new democratic structures; the arrangement lasted for over two decades. Despite the eventual conclusion of the GOOD FRIDAY AGREEMENT, the power-sharing executive it gave rise to has itself twice had to be suspended and direct rule reimposed because of breaches of trust by SINN FEIN.
directive A mandate from the EUROPEAN UNION to national governments, requiring them to enact legislation implementing the policy in question by a particular date, usually within two or three years. If a government fails to comply, the COMMISSION may compel it to legislate by taking action through the EUROPEAN COURT OF JUSTICE. Before a directive is issued, a draft will have been debated by ECOSOC and the EUROPEAN PARLIAMENT, and a final decision on enactment taken by the COUNCIL OF MINISTERS.
Directory The Republican government of France established under the CONSTITUTION of 1795, when power was vested in five 'Directors', one of whom retired every year. After a sickly four-year existence, it was

ended by Napoleon's COUP of 18 *Brumaire* (9 November) 1799. *See also* X, Y AND Z FEVER.

dirigisme Rigid control by central government of the economy, and other areas of daily life. The term originated in the centralising policies pursued by Louis XIV and his minister Jean-Baptiste Colbert (1619–83), which are echoed in France to this day; however, the term now has a far wider application.

Dirksen. Dirksen's three laws of politics The principles for a lengthy political career put forward, only half in jest, by Sen. Everett Dirksen (1896–1969). They were:

> 1. Get elected. 2. Get re-elected. 3. Don't get mad, get even.

Dirksen was a respected Illinois Republican who served as Senate MINORITY LEADER from 1959 and whose body lay in state in the ROTUNDA of the CAPITOL after he died in harness; his daughter Joy married Howard Baker, who became Senate MAJORITY LEADER with the REAGAN landslide of 1980. Dirksen's long Congressional career – sixteen years in the House, nineteen in the Senate – included recording a hit single, *Gallant Men*, waging a protracted campaign to have the marigold declared America's national flower, and appearing on television to defend a Congressional pay increase, saying: 'Senators have to eat, too.' His oratorical style earned him the nickname 'the *Wizard of Ooze*'.

Dirksen Building The SENATE office building north-east of the CAPITOL named after Sen. Dirksen; the second such building to be named after a prominent Senator, it was opened in 1958 and named after his death.

dirty bomb A weapon comprising a conventional charge surrounded by NUCLEAR material, which on detonation will scatter radiation over the surrounding area. The use by terrorists of such a weapon has been much feared, especially since 9/11. The term was first used in the 1950s for an ATOMIC BOMB giving off a disproportionately high amount of nuclear fallout.

dirty protest The action taken by convicted IRA prisoners in Northern Ireland's H-BLOCKS in the late 1970s and early '80s in support of their claim for POLITICAL STATUS. They refused to use prison sanitation, smearing excrement over their cell walls until special cleansing squads moved in to spray them clean with disinfectant. The dirty protest, and the parallel BLANKET PROTEST, failed to shift the authorities, so Bobby Sands and other republican hard-liners embarked on a HUNGER STRIKE – also unsuccessful – in a desperate and tragic bid for victory.

disaffiliate To sever an organisation's connection with a political party or other group which it has been supporting. A handful of left-orientated TRADE UNIONS disaffiliated from the LABOUR PARTY from 2001 because they did not feel it was representing their interests, notably the Fire Brigades Union which resented Tony BLAIR's government standing firm when it staged national strikes over pay.

Disappeared, the (Sp. *Desperacidos*) The 7,500 Argentines, many of them political DISSIDENTS or suspected MONTONEROS, who vanished between 1976 and 1982 and are presumed dead at the hands of DEATH SQUADS controlled by the military JUNTA which fell after the FALKLANDS WAR. The fate of the Disappeared is one of the darkest pages in Latin America's HUMAN RIGHTS record; one of the brightest is the bravery of the parents who demonstrated outside the CASA ROSADA for news of those who had vanished, and have since gained some redress in the courts. Tragically the example spread; 40,000 people in Guatemala alone are reckoned to have 'disappeared' for political reasons over 20 years. The term is now also used for those presumed victims of the IRA during the TROUBLES in NORTHERN IRELAND whose bodies have never been found.

disarmament The process of dismantling the armaments of one or every nation, attempted with brief success after WORLD WAR I and with hardly any after WORLD WAR II, but seriously attempted by the SUPERPOWERS after the end of the COLD WAR until other challenges for America appeared. *See also* ARMS CONTROL; CFE; CND; INF; MULTILATERALISM; SALT; START; UNILATERALISM.

> The notion that disarmament can put an end to war is contradicted by the nearest dogfight.
> GEORGE BERNARD SHAW

World Disarmament Conference The conference involving 31 nations held in Geneva between 2 February 1932 and late 1934 to discuss general disarmament. The high point of international efforts to avoid a repetition of WORLD WAR I, it began with brave hopes, but was dogged by the conflicting interests of the participants each trying to strengthen their own hand and, particularly, France's insistence on a guarantee of security from German invasion.

France eventually won a conditional guarantee, but then the NAZIS came to power and on 14 October 1933 the Germans walked out, having refused a British proposal to reduce Europe's armies by nearly 500,000. The conference rejected a number of worthy initiatives, including one from America to ban all offensive weaponry; by the close most nations had concluded that rearmament was their only guarantee of security. A vivid caricature of the national positions was given by the French author Gabriel Chevallier in the opening passage of his comic novel *Clochemerle*.

discharge a committee The procedure under which the full US HOUSE OF REPRESENTATIVES may move to debate a BILL which is stuck in committee for more than a month. When a majority of members sign a motion for discharge, the proposer can seek RECOGNITION on the second or fourth Monday of a month, for a 20-minute debate followed by an immediate vote.

Disco Dick The nickname given by the Canadian press to Richard Hatfield, Conservative premier of New Brunswick from 1970 to 1987, because of his flamboyant lifestyle.

discrimination. positive discrimination The deliberate preferment of candidates for jobs or college places from groups felt to lack the normally-required qualifications because they have been held back through discrimination (*see* AFFIRMATIVE ACTION, BAKKE CASE). Pursued in America from the 1970s to reverse the harm done by racial SEGREGATION and the denial of facilities to black people, it is now practised in a number of countries. Strongly opposed by conservatives, it is known as **reverse discrimination** to those who feel they have been overtaken because they are white or male.

> I am not going to promise a Cabinet post or any other post to any racial or ethnic group. That would be racism in reverse at its worst.
>
> JOHN F. KENNEDY

racial discrimination The act of distinguishing between members of different ethnic groups, usually as a means of giving advantages to whites at the expense of others. In the summer of 1941 pressure from black trade unionists to end the COLOUR BAR that was reserving war jobs for whites compelled Franklin D. ROOSEVELT to issue EXECUTIVE ORDER 8802, which declared that contractors should exercise

> No discrimination on grounds of race, color, creed or national origin.

> Discrimination is a hellhound that gnaws at negroes in every waking moment of their lives, to remind them that the lie of their inferiority is accepted as the truth in the society dominating them.
>
> Dr MARTIN LUTHER KING, Atlanta, 16 August 1967

> That's part of American greatness, is discrimination. Yes, Sir. Inequality, I think, breeds freedom and gives a man opportunity.
>
> LESTER MADDOX, Segregationist Governor of Georgia (1915–2003)

disestablishment The ending of the position of the Church of England as the country's established church, enjoying a privileged position in the life of the nation and with the Sovereign as its SUPREME HEAD. Traditionally the CONSERVATIVE PARTY has strongly supported the maintenance of the estab-lished Church, which became known as the 'CONSERVATIVE PARTY AT PRAYER', and the Liberals opposed it (ASQUITH's Liberal government disestablished the Church in Wales); Labour had no enthusiasm for the status quo, but did not wish to arouse the controversy implicit in changing it. Disestablishment remained a latent issue until 1992, when the separation of the Prince and Princess of Wales led politicians and bishops to question whether the links between Church and State might have to be broken to enable Prince Charles eventually to become King; the issue is now dormant once again.

dish the Whigs *See* WHIGS.

dishonour and disrepute The key words of the resolution condemning Sen. Joseph MCCARTHY's actions as 'unbecoming a member of the United States SENATE', which the Senate (belatedly in the view of many Americans) passed by 69 votes to 22 in December 1954. McCarthy had been exposed as a bully during the ARMY-MCCARTHY HEARINGS that summer, and his hold on the nation's fears and prejudices was broken. Fellow Senators were finally emboldened to distance themselves from him, and the resolution marked the end of the Wisconsin Senator's influence. He died of drink in 1957.

disinformation The deliberate spreading of falsehoods in order to mislead an enemy or rival political force. In 1986 the *Washington Post* revealed that President REAGAN had approved such a strategy against Libya's leader Colonel Gaddafi with the aim of toppling him. A memo to Reagan from his NATIONAL SECURITY ADVISER John

Poindexter (*see* DARPA; IRAN-CONTRA AFFAIR) proposed a plan combining 'real and illusory events – through a disinformation program – with the basic goal of making Gaddafi think there is a high degree of internal opposition to him within Libya, that his key trusted aides are disloyal, that the US is about to move against him militarily.'

Disraeli. Disraeli, Benjamin (1804–81), first Earl of Beaconsfield, twice Prime Minister (February–December 1868, 1874–80), the most romantic politician of the Victorian age who set the tone of the modern CONSERVATIVE PARTY. Disraeli, from a Jewish family that had converted to Anglicanism, entered Parliament in 1837 with a growing reputation as a novelist which did him few favours; when he delivered his MAIDEN SPEECH that December, he struggled to make himself heard and finally shouted: 'Though I sit down now, the time will come when you shall hear me.' Originally he styled himself a Radical, declaring in an unsuccessful bid for Parliament in 1832:

> I am a Conservative to preserve all that is good in our Constitution, a radical to remove all that is bad, I seek to preserve property and to respect order, and I equally decry the appeal to the passions of the many or the prejudices of the few.

Though he flirted with the CHARTISTS, he was elected as a TORY; a string of sycophantic letters to PEEL failed to win him a place in the government that came to power in 1841. Disraeli retaliated by forming YOUNG ENGLAND, and by satirising his leader in CONINGSBY and SIBYL; in this period he declared:

> I am neither Whig nor Tory. My politics are described in one word and the word is England.

Five years later he launched a devastating attack on Peel for betraying his party over the CORN LAWS that sped him into the wilderness and placed Disraeli among the founders of the Conservative Party as the Tories split. He received mixed notices as Chancellor under Lord Derby from 1852 and was succeeded by GLADSTONE, and resigned from Derby's second administration in 1859 because he did not consider it radical enough. The third time he fared better, piloting through as CHANCELLOR the 1867 REFORM BILL that greatly expanded the electorate. He served briefly as Prime Minister in 1868, remarking: 'I have climbed to the top of the greasy pole.' But it was after 1874 that he established the relationship with Queen Victoria that drew her out of her seclusion since the death of Prince Albert and made him her favourite – in sharp contrast with Gladstone. On his appointment he launched a charm offensive, writing of himself to the Queen:

> He can offer only devotion. It will be his delight and duty to render the transaction of affairs as easy to Your Majesty as possible; and in smaller matters he hopes he may succeed in this; but he ventures to trust that, in the great affairs of state, Your Majesty will deign not to withhold from him the benefit of Your Majesty's guidance.

Disraeli bought a half-interest for Britain in the Suez Canal, and with his greatest Imperial flourish had the Queen declared EMPRESS of India. His final diplomatic triumph was the Congress of BERLIN in 1878, which secured PEACE WITH HONOUR in the Balkans, and Cyprus for Britain. But soon afterward the economy turned down, and when Gladstone launched his MIDLOTHIAN CAMPAIGN Beaconsfield's Conservatives went down to a massive defeat. He died the following year.

Disraeli's personality dazzled some, mesmerised many and outraged a few. John Bright said: 'He is a self-made man – and he adores his maker', and Daniel O'Connell launched a series of ANTI-SEMITIC tirades against him, declaring:

> His life is a living lie. He is the most degraded of his species and kind, and England is degraded by having upon the face of her society a miscreant of his abominable, foul and atrocious nature.

O'Connell also said: 'He possesses just the qualities of the impenitent thief who died upon the cross, whose name, I verily believe, was Disraeli.' Yet Disraeli could give as good as he got, describing Lord Liverpool as 'the arch-mediocrity who presided, rather than ruled, over a Cabinet of Mediocrities'; John Wilson Croker: 'A man who possessed, in very remarkable degree, a restless instinct for adroit baseness'; Lord John Russell: 'If a traveller was informed that such a man was LEADER OF THE HOUSE of Commons, he might begin to comprehend how the Egyptians worshipped an insect'; Lord Aberdeen: 'His temper, naturally morose, has become licentiously peevish. Crossed in his Cabinet, he insults the House of Lords and plagues the most eminent of his colleagues with the crabbed malice of a maundering witch'; John Bright: 'That hysterical old spouter'; the diarist Charles Greville: 'The most conceited man I've ever met, though I've read Cicero and known Bulwer-Lytton'; Sir Stafford Northcote: 'A complete Jesuit'; and Joseph Chamberlain: 'He looks and speaks like a cheesemonger.' Gladstone reckoned him 'the greatest master of Parliamentary sarcasm and irony for the past two centuries', and Michael FOOT saw him as 'the greatest comic genius who ever installed himself in DOWNING STREET.' He was also a master of spontaneity: Lord George Hamilton recalled that 'in the middle of a sentence his teeth fell out and he caught them up with extraordinary rapidity . . . turned round apparently to ask a question of his neighbour, put them in and resumed his speech at the exact word where he had left off.'

> Dizzy has the most wonderful courage, but no physical courage. When he has his shower-bath I always have to pull the string.
>
> Disraeli's wife MARY-ANN

> His face was lividly pale, and from beneath two finely arched eyebrows blazed out a pair of intensely black eyes. Over a broad, high forehead were ringlets of coal-black glossy hair. There was a sort of half-smile, half-sneer playing about his beautifully-formed mouth, the lips of which were curved, as we see it in portraits of Byron.
>
> ANON quoted by MONEYPENNY AND BUCKLE, *Life of Disraeli* (1910)

> Disraeli very generously purchased the Panama Canal from the Khalif and presented it to Queen Victoria with a huge bunch of PRIMROSES (his favourite flower) thus becoming Lord Beaconsfield and a romantic Minister.
>
> W. C. SELLAR and R. J. YEATMAN, *1066 and All That* (1930)

dissident The word used from the late 1960s for a critic of the STALINIST rigidity of the Soviet Union and its East European SATELLITES who was ready to risk imprisonment or exile by campaigning for change. The term was first applied to Soviet intellectuals – some of them Jewish REFUSENIKS – who denounced the status quo under BREZHNEV, using the underground press (SAMIZDAT) to argue for greater freedoms. With the formation of CHARTER 77 in Czechoslovakia it gained a wider application.

dissident triangle In WASHINGTON, the informal alliance between critics in the PENTAGON of waste, GOLD-PLATING and the misdirection of spending, members of CONGRESS on the lookout for such issues, and the media which thrives on LEAKS from both. It is pitted against the IRON TRIANGLE of Pentagon brasshats, defence contractors and Congressional supporters of programmes that mean jobs back home.

dissolution In the UK and DOMINIONS and in Ireland, the termination of a Parliament by proclamation so that a GENERAL ELECTION can be held. The Sovereign (or President) would normally grant a request from the Prime Minister for a dissolution, unless an election had only recently been held and the outcome had been conclusive. A **double dissolution** is the process under which the GOVERNOR-GENERAL of Australia may dissolve both the House and the Senate for the simultaneous holding of elections to both.

dissolution honours *See* HONOURS.

distinct society *See* MEECH LAKE.

district The area represented by a US CONGRESSMAN.

district auditor In Britain, the government-appointed accountancy watchdog who supervises spending by local authorities, not only scrutinising their accounts but investigating complaints from taxpayers about the way they spend public money. The district auditor has the power to declare an item of spending *ultra vires* and recommend the imposition of a SURCHARGE on offending councillors. The most spectacular instance of this was the surcharge of over £30 million – recovered in part – imposed on Dame Shirley Porter, former Conservative leader of Westminster Council, over the HOMES FOR VOTES affair.

District of Columbia The administrative title of America's Federal city of WASHINGTON, designated in 1801 on a site selected by George Washington. Originally a ten-mile square was carved out of Maryland and Virginia, but the smaller portion taken from Virginia was later returned. Until the early 1970s the District was governed by CONGRESS; its inhabitants have the right to vote in Presidential elections, elect a non-voting DELEGATE to the House but have only a SHADOW SENATOR. The predominantly African-American city is governed by its mayor and council from the **District Building** at 1350 Pennsylvania Avenue, next to the Department of Commerce. Until WORLD WAR II the vast majority of Washingtonians lived within the **District** line, as the DC boundary is known, but now barely a fifth of the conurbation's 4 million inhabitants do so.

Ditchers *See* HEDGERS AND DITCHERS.

division A WESTMINSTER term for a vote in either HOUSE. In the Commons at the appropriate time the SPEAKER puts the QUESTION, shouts: **'Division! Clear the lobbies!'**, and electric **division bells** are rung throughout the PRECINCTS of the House and in those premises away from it that are ON THE BELL. From the time they start ringing, MPs have ten minutes to get into the Division LOBBIES before the Speaker names the TELLERS and orders the lobby doors locked until the voting figures are declared – generally around thirteen minutes after the Question was put. The Tellers report the outcome to the Speaker (or deputy) who then repeats it. In the HOUSE OF LORDS, peers have one minute less to reach the Division Lobbies. MPs anxious to show their disapproval or delay proceedings have tried many ways of disrupting a division. The most formal and accepted way is to raise a Point of ORDER; until recently a member wishing to do this during a division had to put on a top hat kept specially for the purpose (*see* SEATED AND COVERED). One method that has proved more effective but angers the Chair is to queue to use the lavatory in one of the Division Lobbies, so that the counting of votes is protracted.

division list A list showing how each member of the HOUSE voted, produced by the clerks within minutes of the result of the division being announced and subsequently appearing in HANSARD. The clerks are now issued with special **division pens** for marking the lists of MPs with machine-readable ink, so that a list can be produced more quickly and accurately. Clerks entering the division lobbies show their pens as an extra form of identification.

Dixie The affectionate name of CONFEDERATES for the American South, and the name of the tune its soldiers whistled on the way into battle and which remains the South's unofficial anthem. The origin of the name is disputed; most likely it stems from the MASON-DIXON LINE, which was the boundary between the free and SLAVE STATES before the CIVIL WAR. The name Dixie has also been attributed to the 'dix' or $10 notes issued by a New Orleans bank soon after the LOUISIANA PURCHASE, or to 'Dixie's Land', the name supposedly given to a farm near New York by slaves sent there from Charleston by their master, Johann Dixie. The song was written by Dan Decatur Emmett, a Northerner, in 1859 for a show put on at the Mechanics' Hall on Broadway, New York, by Bryant's black-faced Minstrels; he was paid $300 for it. Its opening lines were:

> I wish I was in the land of cotton,
> Old times there are not forgotten,
> Look away, look away, look away, Dixieland.
> In Dixieland where I was born
> Bright 'n' early on a frosty morn,
> Look away, look away, look away, Dixieland.
>
> I wish I was in Dixie, hooray, hooray,
> In Dixieland I'll take my stand
> To live or die in Dixie.
> Look away, look away, look away, Dixieland.

The song caught on throughout America, but the Confederates claimed it with fervour and a stirring version was played at Jefferson DAVIS's inauguration. Southern sympathisers whistled it to irritate supporters of the Union, but President LINCOLN loved it and, when the Confederates laid down their arms at the end of the Civil War, he startled die-hard Northerners by saying:

> That's a fine-looking band you have there, Colonel. Let's hear it play Dixie!

Dixiecrats The Southern Democrats who fielded the SEGREGATIONIST Governor Strom Thurmond (1902–2003) of South Carolina as a Presidential candidate in 1948, further reducing the chances of President TRUMAN who also faced a left-wing PROGRESSIVE challenge from the former Vice President Henry Wallace. The Dixiecrats walked out of the Democratic Convention after Northern liberals led by Mayor Hubert HUMPHREY of Minneapolis inserted a commitment to CIVIL RIGHTS into the party platform. Thurmond won 1,176,125 votes, carrying Alabama, Mississippi, South Carolina and Louisiana, but could not prevent Truman, with over 24 million, registering a surprise victory (*see* DEWEY). Thurmond went on to mellow, adopting the motto

> The longer you stay, you realise that sometimes you can catch more flies with honey than with vinegar.

Four decades in the SENATE culminated in his becoming the first centenarian Senator, celebrating his 100th birthday in harness in December 2002; he died the following June. His centennial celebration made history in its own right, leading to the resignation of Senate MAJORITY LEADER Trent Lott for apparently endorsing segregation by saying in a tribute: 'When Strom ran for President we voted for him. We're proud of it.'

Dixville Notch The small community in New Hampshire which traditionally casts the first collective vote of the US Presidential ELECTION. Once its electorate of around 20 provided a very crude STRAW POLL as to the likely outcome; it now consistently produces a Republican majority, so receives less attention.

Dizzy The universal nickname for Benjamin DISRAELI, who although he had no rapport with GLADSTONE dazzled Queen Victoria and has won admiration from subsequent generations of politicians, not only ONE NATION Conservatives; Michael FOOT named his dog 'Dizzy' as a tribute.

The soul of Dizzy was a chandelier.
EDWARD CLERIHEW BENTLEY, *A Ballad of Souls*

DLP Democrat Labor Party In Australia, the right-wing and largely Catholic party that split away from LABOR during the split of 1955–57 as GROUPERS left or were expelled from the ALP; it was formally founded in Canberra, with backing from the Catholic hierarchy, in August 1957. At its peak in 1958, the DLP polled over 8% of the federal vote for the House of Representatives, but after 1972 when it still polled 5.2%, it collapsed; its last elected representatives at federal and State level lost their seats in 1974.

DMZ De-militarised Zone. An area between two armies or states in a military confrontation, which it is agreed shall contain no troops or military installations. The DMZ between former North and South Vietnam was an example.

do-nothing Congress *See* CONGRESS.

Do what you have to do. George W. BUSH's response to Al GORE (*see* OZONE MAN) when the Democratic Presidential nominee phoned him on November 8 2000 to withdraw his CONCESSION as it became clear the result depended on the outcome in Florida, which remained too close to call for a further month.

doctor. Doctor Death An unflattering nickname for Dr David OWEN, leader of Britain's SDP, intended to reflect his ruthlessness and political impact rather than his prowess in his previous role as a neurologist. When a LIBERAL DEMOCRAT strategy committee in 1990 was considering if there were votes to be gained by playing up Paddy Ashdown's past with the Special Boat Squadron, one member observed that Ashdown must have killed more people than any other UK politician. But a voice from the back called out:

What about the Doctor?

Doctor's mandate The MANDATE to deal with the financial crisis arising from the onset of the GREAT DEPRESSION, sought by Ramsay MACDONALD's NATIONAL GOVERNMENT in the 1931 UK general election. No comprehensive MANIFESTO was offered, as the partners in the coalition differed on other matters, notably the Conservatives and Liberals over TARIFF REFORM. The Coalition parties – NATIONAL LABOUR, Tories and Liberals – won 554 seats out of 610, and Labour just 53.

Doctors' Plot An alleged conspiracy by a group of leading Soviet doctors to murder prominent political and military figures in STALIN's government. The nine doctors were arrested in January 1953 and charged with poisoning a former Leningrad party leader, Andrei Zhdanov, and acting as US intelligence agents. Stalin's death on 5 March led to the charges being dropped, and some police officers were later executed for fabricating evidence against the doctors. Fears that Stalin had intended the case to be the pretext for an anti-Jewish PURGE, raised because six of the arrested were Jewish, were confirmed by Khrushchev in 1956.

Dod *Dod's Parliamentary Companion*, the squat, blue-bound volume published annually which lists – with photographs – the members of both HOUSES at WESTMINSTER with biographies, election results, details of UK government agencies and the rules of Parliamentary procedure. Until 1960 much of the information about the House of Lords appeared in a separate *Dod's Peerage, Baronetage and Knightage.* In 1990 a parallel *European Companion* covering the EUROPEAN PARLIAMENT, EUROPEAN COMMISSION and member governments was introduced; a *Civil Service Companion* has since also been added. Dod was first published in 1832 by Charles Roger Phipps Dod (1793–1855), son of an Irish clergyman, who headed *The Times* staff in the PRESS GALLERY.

DoD Department of Defense. WASHINGTON shorthand for the PENTAGON.

Dodgy Dossier The name given by political opponents and a hostile media to the dossier published by Tony BLAIR in February 2003 prior to the IRAQ WAR which purported to give the facts on which his Government had concluded that military action to oust SADDAM HUSSEIN (*see* BUTCHER OF BAGHDAD) was justified; it also came to cover a more substantial and authoritative dossier issued the previous September. The document supported the contention that Saddam had WEAPONS OF MASS DESTRUCTION and was in a position to use them against his neighbours and more widely at 45 MINUTES' notice. Blair was careful to say that the information came 'in good measure' from intelligence sources, but it turned out that nineteen pages had been taken verbatim from Ibrahim Al-Marashi, a California Ph.D student who claimed after the war that its use had put his family in Iraq at risk. Foreign Secretary Jack Straw admitted that the February dossier was 'a complete horlicks' and should not have been released. Further claims by the BBC reporter Andrew Gilligan after the war that the September dossier had been **'sexed up'** by Alistair Campbell, Blair's head of communications, led to a stormy hearing of the Foreign Affairs Select Committee at which Campbell flatly denied the charges and demanded an apology from the BBC, which it refused to give. Gilligan's justification of his story and the Government's 'outing' of his source culminated in the David KELLY AFFAIR, when the suicide of Gilligan's informant created a crisis for Blair, the HUTTON INQUIRY which triggered the resignation of the chairman and director-general of the BBC, and the BUTLER INQUIRY which concluded that intelligence in the dossier had been pushed to the 'outer limits but not beyond'.

Dogger Bank incident The tragic and startling attack by ships of the Russian Baltic Fleet on Hull trawlers off the Dogger Bank in the North Sea in October 1904. Two of the British vessels were sunk, with the loss of their skippers. Apparently the Russians, *en route* to fight Japan, mistook the fishing craft for Japanese torpedo boats. After an international inquiry in Paris, Russia agreed to pay Britain £65,000 in compensation.

Dogs The canine world has more to do with politics than one might imagine, quite apart from the dogs owned by politicians (*see* BUDDY; FALA; HIM AND HER; MILLIE; SODA etc.). Lord Avebury (*see* ORPINGTON MAN) decided after his conversion to Buddhism to donate his body to Battersea Dogs' Home, and dogs are even capable of political comment: one guide dog of Labour Home Secretary David Blunkett (*see* OFFA; RUBY; TED) was once violently sick as his colleague Bryan Gould unveiled a policy document at a press conference. Blunkett also remarked, after allegations of vote-rigging at one Labour conference: 'Next time the dog and me will be the SCRUTINEERS.' Having a dog can be a campaign asset: in the 1970s one unmarried US Congressional hopeful went to the trouble of having a fake family photo circulated, including a dog; it is alleged that his subterfuge was rumbled because someone recognised the dog. On the campaign trail, the ULSTER UNIONIST leader James Molyneaux was followed into a constituent's house by a strange dog which wrecked the place while they made conversation. When he got up to leave, the farmer's wife asked: 'Aren't you going to take your dog with you?' Moreover, '**going to the dogs**' is a term frequently used by politicians in opposition to describe the country's fate. A voter once told the Conservative MP Greg Knight that he could not get to the polls because he was going to the dogs (greyhound racing). Knight replied:

> The whole country is going to the dogs, so you'd better come and vote for me.

Not long after WORLD WAR II, the Labour MP Wilfred Paling accused CHURCHILL in the Commons of being a 'dirty dog'. Churchill, with a huge grin, turned to him and said: 'Yes – and you know what dogs do to palings.'

dog licence speech Harold WILSON's outburst against left-wing Labour MPs on 2 March 1967 after they failed to support his government's defence WHITE PAPER. Not normally a man to utter threats against his own party, Wilson cut loose at a meeting of the PLP to threaten disciplinary action if they continued to rebel; whether he could have enforced it is another matter, but his speech angered much of the party. He told them:

> Every dog is allowed one bite, but a different view is taken of a dog that goes on biting all the time. He may not get his licence returned when it falls due.

dog whistle message An originally Australian term for a statement which has one general meaning for the electorate as a whole, and a specific (and often different) one for the group the speaker is targeting, who will be attuned to it. It comes from the way a dog can tell when a whistle comes from the owner.

either way you get the dog back The argument used by the Texas Democrat Lloyd Bentsen in running for the Vice Presidency in 1988 without relinquishing his seat in the SENATE. He told of the Texan vet who set himself up as a taxidermist; when a man called at the surgery with a sick dog and asked why he was following both trades, the vet told him:

> Either way you get the dog back.

Defeated with Michael Dukakis, Bentsen served four more years in the Senate before being appointed President CLINTON's Treasury Secretary.

let sleeping dogs lie The epitome of the doctrine of LAISSEZ-FAIRE, said to be the watchword of Robert WALPOLE, Britain's first PRIME MINISTER to be acknowledged as such.

running dogs Communist, and especially MAOIST, jargon for someone who carries out another's bidding, especially a lackey of CAPITALISM. It is a literal translation of *zou gou*, used by CHAIRMAN MAO when he said:

> People of the world, unite and defeat the US aggressors and their running dogs.

It was taken up, with some of his other picturesque phrases like PAPER TIGER, by devotees of his LITTLE RED BOOK.

Doha round The round of WTO trade negotiations begun by a 142-nation conference in the Gulf state in November 2001 which set a global development agenda. Stalled for two years by disputes over farm subsidies, the availability of pharmaceuticals to the developing world and trade in services, it culminated, after deadlocked summits at SEATTLE and CANCUN, in provisional agreement at Geneva in July 2004. The rich nations agreed to reduce farm subsidies (though no date was set) in return for cuts in TARIFFS by poorer countries.

dollar. Dollar-a-year men The industrialists and corporate lawyers, more than 1,000 in all, brought to WASHINGTON by Franklin D. ROOSEVELT's Office of Production Management (OPM, established in January 1941) to mobilise war production. They got their name because the Federal government paid them just $1 a year, with their peacetime employers meeting the rest of their salary. NEW DEALERS complained that too many were Republicans inimical to the administration, but the OPM's joint head, General Motors president William Knudsen, told FDR:

> There is no Democrat rich enough to take a job at a dollar a year.

dollar diplomacy *See* DIPLOMACY, dollar IMPERIALISM.

constant dollars The budgeting term for the listing of sums as if the value of the dollar were constant, instead of in current dollars which reflect INFLATION.

I was alarmed at my doctor's report. He said I was as sound as the dollar One of Ronald REAGAN's deepest digs at the CARTER administration's economic policies – while at the same time brushing aside concerns about his age and health. The GREAT COMMUNICATOR delivered it in a campaign speech in Jersey City on 1 September 1980.

tax dollars A US term for money paid and collected in taxes.

Dome Secretary The title jocularly accorded to Tony BLAIR's right-hand man Peter Mandelson (*see* BOBBY) when appointed Minister without Portfolio at the Cabinet Office, with special responsibility for the Millennium Dome. At that time (1997) the Dome was widely expected to be the glittering success of the UK's Millennium celebrations; its perceived failure when the time came was an acute embarrassment to NEW LABOUR.

Domingo. Placido Domingo speech Paul KEATING's off-the-record Christmas address to the Canberra press gallery in 1990 which triggered the split in the Labor leadership that put Keating into power. He said in a none-too-veiled reference to Bob HAWKE's premiership:

> Leadership is not about being popular, it's about being right. It's not about going through some shopping centre tripping over TV cords, it's about doing what the country needs.

But the speech got its name from Keating's claim that

> I am the Placido Domingo of Australian politics.

dominion A fully independent member of the British EMPIRE (now COMMONWEALTH) with the British monarch as its HEAD OF STATE, and equal in status with the United Kingdom. The term was first used to describe the newly self-governing Canada in the BRITISH NORTH AMERICA ACT of 1867; it was applied after 1919 to Newfoundland (until its union with Canada), Australia, New Zealand and (until it left the Commonwealth) South Africa. The IRISH FREE STATE, on its formation, was also declared a dominion. The autonomy of the dominions became complete with the 1931 Statute of WESTMINSTER. The term is nowadays seldom used.

Dominion of New England *See* NEW ENGLAND CONFEDERATION.

domino theory A guiding principle of US foreign policy throughout the COLD WAR, and especially during the VIETNAM WAR, on the imperative of containing COMMUNISM. The argument went that if Communism were not resisted in one country, not only would that country be 'lost' but also, before long, its neighbours would fall too. President EISENHOWER explained at a press conference on 7 April 1954:

> You have a row of dominoes set up, you knock over the first one, and what will happen to the last one is that it will go over very quickly.

The domino theory was turned into a moral imperative by the KENNEDY and JOHNSON administrations, justifying involvement in Vietnam to prevent Laos, Cambodia, Thailand and the rest of South East Asia following suit.

donkey The emblem of America's DEMOCRATIC PARTY, a respectable version of the JACKASS.

donkey jacket The garment the Labour leader Michael FOOT (*see also* WURZEL GUMMIDGE) was said by critics, including the Labour MP Walter Johnson, to have worn for the 1981 Remembrance Service at the CENOTAPH. Foot eschewed the conventional dark suit, but he and his wife insisted the coat was perfectly respectable.

donkey vote In Australian elections, a vote cast by simply numbering a House ballot paper straight down and a Senate paper down each group of candidates and across from left to right. The practice was a result of the twin requirements, from 1934, that every elector turn out to vote and that they number every space on the ballot paper; between 1940 and 1984 the law was amended to ensure no party could benefit from this practice, by requiring the position of party groups on each paper to be chosen by lot. *See also* FOUR AS.

Donovan Report The report to Harold WILSON's government in 1968 of the Royal Commission on Trade Unions and Employers' Associations, chaired by the senior judge Lord Donovan. It focused on ways of reducing the number of unofficial strikes in British industry, recommending a move toward agreements negotiated at plant rather than national level. Donovan also advocated an Industrial Relations Commission to investigate problem areas of industry, and Labour Tribunals to examine individuals' grievances against companies or unions. The report was criticised by the Conservatives for rejecting legally enforceable collective agreements and criminal sanctions on unofficial strikes and PICKETING. The Labour CABINET quietly shelved it, then came up with an alternative: IN PLACE OF STRIFE.

don't. don't bind my hands John MAJOR's appeal to EUROSCEPTIC Conservatives on the eve of the 1997 general election as he urged them to let him negotiate terms for Britain's possible entry to the single European currency rather than force him to reject it outright. He said on 16 April 1997:

> Whether you agree with me, disagree with me, like me or loathe me, don't bind my hands while I am negotiating on behalf of the British nation.

His appeal went largely unheard. The feuding continued throughout the election, Major's Conservatives were resoundingly defeated and the incoming Labour government kept out of the EURO.

don't blame me, I voted Conservative (1964), **Republican** (1992) Two bumper stickers which tell their own story, with supporters of a defeated administration (SIR ALEC Douglas-Home's and George BUSH's respectively) highlighting the perceived blunders of its successor (Harold WILSON's first Labour government and the CLINTON administration).

don't get mad, get even *See* DIRKSEN.

don't-knows In OPINION POLLS, those listed as saying they do not know whom they will vote for; some polls omit them and round up the other totals to 100%. The KNOW-NOTHINGS were a US political party.

don't let the buggers grind you down The old military dictum which cost the UK Conservative politician Michael Mates (1934–) his job as a NORTHERN IRELAND Minister under John MAJOR when he had it inscribed on a watch he gave early in 1992 to Asil Nadir, a Conservative party donor and driving force of the Polly Peck group of companies. Nadir's affairs were being vigorously investigated by the Department of Trade and Industry, and after being charged with fraud he jumped bail in May 1993 to Turkish-controlled Northern Cyprus as the company collapsed, to the Tories' embarrassment. Major told the COMMONS that the gift, though foolish, was not a 'hanging matter', but Mates was forced to resign on 24 June, turning his PERSONAL STATEMENT to the House into an attack on the Serious Fraud Office and other agencies for allegedly victimising Nadir and contributing to the collapse of Polly Peck, which earned him a rebuke from the SPEAKER. The dictum is a variant of the well-known 'never let the bastards grind you down', translated into spoof Latin as '*nil illegitimis carborundum*'.

don't mourn – organise! The last words of the US union pioneer Joe Hill before his execution by a Utah firing squad on 18 November 1915. Hill, who had also written most of the WOBBLIES' songs, had been convicted on the flimsiest evidence of murdering a Salt Lake City grocer and ex-policeman; he was executed despite pleas for a REPRIEVE or a retrial from President WILSON and many others. Hill's exact words, in a letter to Bill HAYWOOD, were: 'Don't waste any time mourning – organise!' They became a rallying cry for union activists and the left throughout the world.

don't stop thinking about tomorrow The theme song of Bill CLINTON's successful US Presidential campaign in 1992, a hit for Fleetwood Mac fifteen years before when he was starting his political career. The veteran group had disbanded by the time of the campaign, but they came together to perform at Clinton's Inaugural Ball.

don't tread on me! The motto on the very first flag of the rebel American colonies – and on the first US Navy Jack – which showed a coiled snake ready to strike. The inference was clear: if Britain trod on the rebels it would suffer a poisonous bite.

doomsday. Doomsday clock An image of a clock carried in each issue of the *Bulletin of Atomic Scientists* (founded 1945) that points to the time remaining before the NUCLEAR holocaust. In 1945 the time was set to 11.52, at the height of the COLD WAR it was moved to 11.58, but with the collapse of Communism in Russia and Eastern Europe it was moved back to 11.50. A similar clock at the Worldwatch Institute in WASHINGTON reflects pressures on the planet from population growth.

doomsday scenario The ultimate political nightmare for a nation, a party or individual as considered by political insiders. One example was the concern voiced by some Labour politicians prior to the 1987 and 1992 general elections that if the UK as a whole continued to elect Conservative governments, voters in Scotland where Labour held over two-thirds of the seats would decide their votes were wasted and switch to the pro-independence SNP.

DOP Defence and Overseas Policy. One of the key UK CABINET COMMITTEES. Previously known as ODP, it was given this title under Tony BLAIR.

DORA The popular name for Britain's Defence of the Realm Acts, which imposed many restrictions on individual freedoms for the duration of WORLD WAR I. Their application to munition factories and the drink trade caused particular irritation. The abbreviation passed into common speech after being used in the law courts by Mr Justice Scrutton. In numerous press cartoons Dora was portrayed as a long-nosed, elderly female, personifying crabbed restriction. Yet the legislation did have a purpose; commending it to the COMMONS in 1915, LLOYD GEORGE declared:

> Instead of BUSINESS AS USUAL, we want victory as usual.

Doris Karloff The vivid nickname adopted by the *Daily Mirror* in 1996 for Anne Widdecombe (1947–), the Conservatives' rotund, forceful but not inhumane Home Affairs Minister, comparing her unflatteringly with the late horror movie actor Boris Karloff. The *Mirror* came up with the name, which caused Miss Widdecombe great offence, at the height of a row over women prisoners at Holloway who were allegedly manacled while in labour. In opposition from 1997, Miss Widdecombe (*see also* something of the NIGHT) developed a softer image.

Dorneywood The country house, near Burnham Beeches outside Slough, owned by the National Trust, which is used by a senior British Minister – generally the CHANCELLOR OF THE EXCHEQUER – for entertaining, informal conferences and weekend relaxation. The house, of no great antiquity, was left for this purpose by Lord Courtauld-Thomson. From the 1950s to 1970s it was generally used by the FOREIGN SECRETARY; Sir Geoffrey HOWE used it as Chancellor, but retained it with his successor Nigel Lawson's concurrence in 1989 after becoming DEPUTY PRIME MINISTER. Gordon BROWN, becoming Chancellor in 1997, canvassed other uses for the house, but accepted John Prescott's (*see* TWO JAGS) request to occupy it. In 2004, with Brown now a family man, Prescott offered it back to him.

> A dreary red brick house in flat country. Pictures medium only, but some amusing murals by Rex Whistler.
>
> ALAN CLARK, *Diaries*

double. double-digit inflation *See* INFLATION.

double-dipping A Washington term for the practice of senior military officers and civil servants who retire on a sizeable pension, then find another job (often still in the public service) so that they effectively receive two incomes.

double whammy Two blows which between them constitute a knockout. The phrase entered US politics in the 1980s and the British political vocabulary during the 1992 election. It caught on after being used just before the campaign by the Conservative chairman Chris PATTEN (*see also* GOBSMACKED); Speaker Bernard WEATHERILL commented when pressed: 'I'm not an expert in rhyming slang. I've no idea what a wham is.' On election night Scottish

Secretary Ian Lang, re-elected when he expected to lose both his seat and his job, told jubilant supporters:

> Scotland has rejected SEPARATISM. Britain has rejected socialism. It's a double whammy!

doughnutting The practice, in televised legislatures, of supportive members crowding round a colleague speaking in an otherwise thinly attended chamber, to draw attention to themselves and give the impression that the speaker is highly popular. The area in the view of the camera is the **doughnut**. The words originated in the Canadian Parliament during the 1980s, quickly catching on at WESTMINSTER when televising of proceedings there began at the end of the decade. One notorious 'doughnut' was the phalanx of all-women Labour MPs who sat behind the former Immigration Minister Beverley Hughes for her PERSONAL STATEMENT on resigning in April 2004.

Douglas-Home rules The rules for electing the leader of Britain's CONSERVATIVE PARTY, under which Margaret THATCHER was ousted in 1990. Drawn up by Lord Home (*see* SIR ALEC) as a refinement of the original BERKELEY RULES, they were first tried in 1989 when Sir Anthony Meyer mounted his STALKING-HORSE challenge to Mrs Thatcher. They dictated a two-stage election process, the first effectively being a referendum on the existing leader (who had to win more than half the votes of all Tory MPs and have a clear lead of more than 15% over the nearest challenger). Mrs Thatcher's narrow failure to open up such a lead over Michael HESELTINE was interpreted as a moral defeat, and brought her withdrawal from the more open second stage as her support crumbled. Despite the party establishment's desire to prevent a repetition, little had been changed by the time John Redwood (*see* VULCAN) challenged John MAJOR in 1995; Major's victory was less convincing than his colleagues instantly claimed. William HAGUE when Tory leader, pushed through changes to give party members the final say, but Michael HOWARD after further defeat in 2005 returned the choice to the MPs.

dove The opposite of HAWK, but a word with a far shorter pedigree. The dove of peace became a symbol – widely used, but exploited by the Communists – after Pablo Picasso presented his drawing of one to the World Congress of Intellectuals in Wroclaw, Poland, in 1948. It entered the US political vocabulary during the CUBAN MISSILE CRISIS, Charles Bartlett and Stewart Alsop writing in the *Saturday Evening Post* on 20 December 1962:

> The hawks favored an air strike to eliminate the Cuban missile bases . . . The doves opposed the air strikes and favored a BLOCKADE.

The word really caught on during the VIETNAM WAR, being used particularly by Sen. Robert F. KENNEDY for opponents of US involvement. It was also applied from the mid-1970s to moderate politicians in Israel – mainly from the LABOUR PARTY – who opposed the LIKUD government's policy of provocative confrontation with the Arabs.

Downing Street The cul-de-sac off WHITEHALL, less than 400 yards from PARLIAMENT SQUARE, near the head of which lie NUMBER TEN, the home of Britain's Prime Minister, NUMBER ELEVEN and NUMBER TWELVE. Traditionally crowds gathered there on great political occasions, but in 1979 as the terrorist threat grew it was cordoned off by railings and, in 1989, by heavy gates; these kept out rioters against the POLL TAX but in 1991 could not prevent the IRA firing a mortar at Number Ten from the far side of Whitehall.

Downing Street Declaration The statement agreed at 10 Downing Street on 15 December 1993 by John MAJOR and TAOISEACH Albert Reynolds in the hope of securing an IRA ceasefire and a lasting, agreed settlement in NORTHERN IRELAND. It paved the way for an eventual ceasefire from midnight on 31 August 1994 (though this would be interrupted) and the GOOD FRIDAY AGREEMENT of 10 April 1998. The Declaration stated that Britain had 'no selfish strategic or economic interest in Northern Ireland', but committed the Republic, in an overall settlement, to change its constitution to drop its claim to sovereignty over the North. Contacts between the UK government and SINN FEIN had already begun, and Major promised talks once a ceasefire had lasted three months. Importantly, the Declaration did not provoke the Unionist hostility the ANGLO-IRISH AGREEMENT had aroused.

doyen *See* DIPLOMATIC CORPS.

DPEI Department of Productivity, Energy and Industry. The new and clumsy title allocated to the Department of Trade and Industry after Labour's re-election in 2005. Criticised for ignoring the importance of trade to the UK economy, it lasted only a week before new Secretary of State Alan

Johnson persuaded Tony BLAIR to revert to the original, the two changes in signage costing £30,000. The change had been intended to reflect the priority given by Gordon BROWN to closing the 'productivity gap' between Britain and its competitors.

DPM *See* DEPUTY PRIME MINISTER.

draft (1) The action of the leaders of a US political party, or a CONVENTION, in adopting as a candidate someone not in the race and possibly reluctant to run. Asked if he would accept a draft for the 1980 Democratic nomination – not that one was on offer – Rep. Morris Udall replied:

> Only on three conditions: 1. If a star rose in the East; 2. If three men on camels rode up demanding that I run; 3. If their names are CARTER, Mondale and KENNEDY.

(2) The text of a speech, document or treaty drawn up for consideration and still open to change; as a verb, the process of compiling a text. At the 1989 CHOGM in Kuala Lumpur, Australia's Foreign Minister Gareth Evans brought a frustrating drafting session on SANCTIONS against South Africa to a halt when he remarked in the presence of several Islamic colleagues:

> Geez, we're not trying to draft the fucking Koran!

(3) The form of CONSCRIPTION used in the United States which, in highly selective form, aroused deep controversy during the VIETNAM WAR. Thomas JEFFERSON told James MONROE in 1813: 'We must train and classify the whole of our male citizens, and make military instruction a regular part of collegiate education.' However, Daniel Webster asked the next year: 'Where is it written in the Constitution . . . that you may take children from their parents, and parents from their children, and compel them to fight the battles of any war in which the folly or wickedness of government may engage it?'

> White people sending black people to fight yellow people to protect the country they stole from red people.
>
> GEROME RAGNI and JAMES RADO

> The only way we'll ever get a volunteer army is to draft 'em.
>
> Rep. F. EDWARD HEBERT (1901–79)

The issue of **draft-dodging** goes back at least to the CIVIL WAR, when thousands of men paid others to fight in their place rather than join the Union army. Some opponents of the Vietnam War refused the draft (*see* HELL, NO, WE WON'T GO!), some vanished (often to Canada) and others used connections to ensure they never saw action. President CARTER aroused controversy by declaring a partial AMNESTY, and the issue still raises its head as candidates for office have their efforts to avoid active service revealed. Dan QUAYLE came under fire for having secured a safe berth in the Indiana National Guard, and Republicans were even more critical of Bill CLINTON for having demonstrated against the war while at Oxford.

Drang Nach Osten (Ger. Push to the east) The belief that Germany's destiny requires an eastward extension of its boundaries. It was a powerful element in the policies of the newly created REICH after 1870 and, coupled with Germany's supposed need for LEBENSRAUM, had an echo in HITLER's eastward expansion of the late 1930s.

Dred Scott case *See* SCOTT.

Dreikaiserbund (Ger. League of Three Emperors) The agreement in Berlin in 1872 between the newly proclaimed Kaiser Wilhelm I and the Emperors of Austria and Russia to maintain the *status quo* in Europe, work together over the Balkans as the Ottoman Empire broke up, and promote reform while suppressing socialism. The alliance was renewed every three years, but was dealt a severe blow in 1878 when the Congress of BERLIN passed over Russian ambitions for the region to favour an Anglo-Austrian plan.

Dreyfus case The *fin de siècle* miscarriage of justice, stemming in part from ANTI-SEMITISM, which became a *cause célèbre* reflecting immense discredit on France's military hierarchy. In 1894 Captain Alfred Dreyfus (1859–1935), an artillery staff officer of Jewish peasant origins, was convicted by court martial of betraying military secrets to Germany and sent to Devil's Island. He was convicted on the evidence of a letter, the *bordereau*, signed 'D', which had been retrieved from the German embassy. No-one knew the spy's identity, but to Dreyfus' aristocratic colleagues he was the perfect scapegoat. In 1898 Clemenceau (*see* TIGER) and Emile Zola took up his case, Zola writing his famous open letter J'ACCUSE. In 1899, as a result of the pressure, Dreyfus was retried and again condemned, but was pardoned shortly after. In 1906 the charges were finally quashed, and Dreyfus awarded the LEGION OF HONOUR.

> Military justice is to justice as military music is to music. CLEMENCEAU

> Truth is on the march. Nothing can stop it now.
> ZOLA

Dries (1) In early 20th-century America, the supporters of PROHIBITION. (2) In the CONSERVATIVE PARTY under Margaret THATCHER, the most loyal supporters of her rigorous early economic policies and strongest opponents of the WETS.

drink One of the great perils of political life, with the long, late hours in a legislature, and temptations of being away from home and under pressure making alcohol an attractive comforter. Its effect on many political careers has been tragic; it has also given rise to harmless and hilarious episodes. At WESTMINSTER some of these arise from the fiction that no MP can be drunk if he is in the CHAMBER, and that to suggest otherwise is a CONTEMPT OF THE HOUSE. As the Conservative MP Kenneth Warren put it,

> Members of Parliament are never drunk. They are indisposed.

Some politicians mind more than others when accused of overindulging. In 1957 Aneurin BEVAN, Richard CROSSMAN and Morgan Phillips, general secretary of the LABOUR PARTY, sued the *Spectator* for libel for reporting that they had been drunk at a socialist meeting in Venice. They were awarded £2500 each, but Crossman wrote in his *Diaries* that Phillips, at least, had been 'dead drunk most of the conference'. A senior Labour figure who cared less about his reputation was George BROWN, who once said:

> Many British statesmen have either drunk too much or womanised too much. I never fell into the second category.

Brown's unstable behaviour with the drink taken was legendary (*see* TIRED AND EMOTIONAL). When Foreign Secretary c. 1967, he was at an Embassy reception in Lima when he espied a remarkable creature in flowing red attire, and asked for a dance. The apparition refused, and when Brown asked why, replied:

> First, you are drunk. Second, this is the Peruvian national anthem. And third, I am the Cardinal Archbishop of Lima.

In July 2005 Louise Casey, head of Tony BLAIR's anti-Social behaviour unit, upset Ministers by saying they might do their job better if they came to work drunk, adding:

> Doing things sober is no way to get things done.

Abuse of liquor has long been frowned upon by MIDDLE AMERICA, but from the earliest days it has been a problem in WASHINGTON. Thomas JEFFERSON once confided: 'Were I to commence my ADMINISTRATION again, the first question I would ask respecting a candidate would be: "Does he use ardent spirits?"' Even some Presidents were susceptible; the WHIGS hailed Franklin Pierce (*see* HANDSOME FRANK) as 'the hero of many a well-fought bottle' and Ulysses S. GRANT was a renowned heavy drinker when commander of the Union forces. When politicians complained to Abraham LINCOLN, he reputedly told them: 'Find out what the brand is and I'll give it to my other generals.' CONGRESS has seen its fair share of excess; Sen. Wayne Morse (*see* LONE RANGER) reminisced: 'There has never been one night session of the SENATE in my experience that hasn't witnessed at least one Senator making a fool of himself and disgracing the Senate.' Yet some of the culprits have been able to laugh at themselves; at one Washington party Speaker TIP O'Neill toasted Sen. Thomas Dodd with:

> Here's to the second nastiest drunk in town!

To be sure, I never drank there much meself The reply of the Independent Irish Republican MP Frank Maguire to a HOUSE OF COMMONS policeman in 1974 when told: 'Mr Maguire, had you heard the Duke of Gloucester has gone?' The policeman was referring to the death of that member of the Royal family; Maguire assumed the IRA had blown up another London pub.

Yes – er, no. Unless I was drunk at the time The response, according to PRIVATE EYE, of the Labour MP Michael O'Halloran to party officials who questioned him about alleged irregularities in his selection to fight Islington North prior to the BY-ELECTION in 1968 that took him to WESTMINSTER.

You are drunk. Leave the room at once The message passed to a baffled Chancellor Austen Chamberlain over a dinner for most of BONAR LAW's CABINET given in 1921 by the Tory hostess Mrs Ronnie Greville. The butler had been drinking heavily and was unsteady on his feet; Mrs Greville wrote the note and handed it to him, whereupon he beamed, placed it on a silver salver and delivered it to Chamberlain. *See also* ADULTERY; ASQUITH; CHURCHILL.

dropping the pilot The caption of one of the most celebrated political cartoons carried by the usually humorous magazine *Punch* (1841–1992, revived briefly as a propaganda tool from 1996 by Mohamed Al Fayed, owner of Harrods). Drawn by Sir John

Tenniel in the issue of 28 March 1890, it depicted the aged Bismarck leaving a ship after being 'dropped' by the young Kaiser Wilhelm II. The cartoon summed up precisely the headstrong German ruler's desire to break with the past and make his own way – a course that led to his defeat and exile 28 years later. Nevertheless he and his father's IRON CHANCELLOR were reconciled soon after.

Drudge Report The internet site originated by the investigative reporter Matt Drudge which in January 1998 broke the story of President CLINTON's involvement with Monica LEWINSKY (*see also* ZIPPERGATE). Mainly comprised of Hollywood and media gossip, the site reported that *Newsweek* had the story after negotiations between Kenneth STARR's lawyers and Lewinsky broke down, but that editors were locked in a 'screaming fight' over whether to use it.

Drumcree The greatest flashpoint of NORTHERN IRELAND'S MARCHING SEASON, the church outside Portadown to which Orangemen march each July. The cause of violent clashes most years between the marchers and the police is the Loyalists' determination to march along the Catholic Garvaghy Road, and the refusal of the authorities to let them pass. The worst violence took place in 1996 when, after three days of rioting, the Chief Constable, Sir Hugh Annesley, allowed a group of marchers through to safeguard the lives of his officers. Efforts to defuse the situation in subsequent years through tighter security and inter-communal talks have been partly successful.

DST (Fr. *Direction de la Sécurité du Territoire*, Direction of Territorial Security) France's internal security organisation, the Gallic equivalent of Britain's MI5.

Dublin Castle Under British rule, the seat of government for the VICEROYS of Ireland, and thus a symbol much resented by nationalists. The castle was taken over for purposes of State – including the headquarters of the Revenue Commission – by the Republic of Ireland, the state apartments being lovingly maintained and part of the building turned into a conference suite that has housed several EC/EU SUMMITS and a media centre for the visit of Pope John Paul II in 1979.

Dublin Post Office The focal point of the EASTER RISING in 1916. Bullet-holes from the siege are still visible on the exterior and pillars of the building. The steps of the GPO have become the place where anyone in the Irish Republic with a grievance or a point to make can air it; the right is most frequently exercised by Republicans petitioning for POLITICAL STATUS for the small number of hardliners convicted of terrorist acts after rejecting the GOOD FRIDAY AGREEMENT.

Dubya. The universal nickname for George W. BUSH, stemming from his folksy pronunciation of the middle initial of his name. The W stands for Walker.

Duce, il (Ital. leader) The title chosen for himself by **Benito Mussolini** (1883–1945), first as leader of the FASCIST movement and, from 1924 when the King accepted him as Prime Minister, effective head of the Italian state. An early Fascist slogan was:

> The Duce is always right.

Originally a left-winger, and editor of the Socialist paper AVANTI! until his expulsion from the party for demanding war with Austria, Mussolini progressed from strident nationalism to founding the world's first significant Fascist party. Capitalising on the reservoir of discontent after WORLD WAR I, it pioneered the mixing of uniforms and mildly fatuous ceremonial with policies of nationalism, POPULISM and CORPORATISM; it lacked much of the menace of NAZISM and was only actively ANTI-SEMITIC toward the end, but was rather more corrupt. Elected to Parliament in 1921, Mussolini said in his MAIDEN SPEECH:

> I shall adopt a reactionary line throughout my speech, which will be . . . anti-Socialist and anti-Democratic in substance.

After the Fascists seized the initiative with the MARCH ON ROME in 1922, Mussolini was made Prime Minister to head off conflict between Communists and conservatives, telling Parliament: 'I could have transformed this grey assembly hall into an armed camp for BLACKSHIRTS, a bivouac for corpses. I could have nailed up the doors of Parliament.' He survived an assassination attempt in 1926, telling his followers:

If I advance, follow me. If I retreat, kill me. If I die, avenge me.

Mussolini took total power in 1928, creating a ONE-PARTY STATE. He secured the backing of the Vatican by concluding the LATERAN TREATY, and grandly revived Rome's Imperial ambitions (George Seldes titled his biography of Mussolini *Sawdust Caesar*) by invading Abyssinia in 1935 in contempt of the LEAGUE OF NATIONS. His success led to the formation of the AXIS with Germany and prompted HITLER to embark on his own campaign of conquest; the two leaders also joined forces to back Franco (*see* CAUDILO) in the SPANISH CIVIL WAR. Mussolini's relationship with Hitler was close for one not based on mutual respect. Mussolini said of the Nazis:

> I should be pleased, I suppose, that Hitler has carried out a revolution on our lines. But they are Germans, so they will end by ruining our idea.

As Hitler, unaided, rolled up the map of Europe, Mussolini confided: 'The Italians will laugh at me. Every time he occupies a country, he sends me a message.' In return, the Germans (as later, *see* ITALIAN TANKS) despised Italy's military prowess – Mussolini did not enter the war until 1940, and the Nazi invasion of Russia was fatally delayed when Mussolini had to be rescued from the Balkans. Yet after his opponents on the Fascist Grand Council staged a COUP against him in 1943 following the Allied invasion of Italy to restore constitutional government, Hitler sent crack commandos under Otto Skorzeny to free him from captivity and restore him as *Duce* of the limited SALO REPUBLIC. In the closing days of the war he was captured with his mistress Clara Petacci by Communist PARTISANS; they were shot and their bodies put on display, hanging upside down, in the centre of Milan. The Duce's last words were said to be:

> But, Mr Colonel . . .

> The King presupposes subjects, Il Duce, followers.
> IGNAZIO SILONE, *The School for Dictators*, 1939

> I have a great personal admiration for Mussolini, who has welded a nation out of a collection of touts, blackmailers, ice-cream vendors and gangsters. Letter in the *Saturday Review*.

> This whipped jackal frisking by the side of the German tiger.
> CHURCHILL, House of Commons, April 1941

> The only journalist, so far as I know, to become a dictator.
> JAN MORRIS, *Daily Telegraph*, 1978

> He made the trains run on time. ANON

> Yes, I have a tremendous admiration for Caesar. Still, I belong rather to the class of the Bismarcks.
> MUSSOLINI, in conversation with Emil Ludwig

Uno Duce, una Voce *See* HAUGHEY.

Duchy of Lancaster The ancient Royal estate, almost coterminous with the English county of Lancashire, whose CHANCELLOR still sits in the UK CABINET. The Sovereign, even when a woman, is described in the county as the Duke of Lancaster. The Chancellor accompanies the monarch on visits to Lancashire, but his or her main duties are those of a Minister without PORTFOLIO.

Dudley. a wet evening in Dudley A time and place of no political significance, the phrase being that of then-UK CHANCELLOR Kenneth Clarke. Clarke was asked after the 1992 ELECTION why tax promises made during the campaign had not been kept; his reply was that statements made on 'a wet evening in Dudley' would not automatically be adhered to. Coincidentally or otherwise, the Conservatives lost a Parliamentary BY-ELECTION in the Black Country town in December 1994.

due process clause The clause from the FIFTH AMENDMENT in the US BILL OF RIGHTS which guarantees the due process of law – the right to full and fair legal procedures – to all citizens. More cases have probably been decided by the SUPREME COURT on the basis of this clause than any other part of the CONSTITUTION. It is repeated in the FOURTEENTH AMNENDMENT, ratified in 1868, which binds the States as well as Federal institutions to guarantee due process to all.

Duma (Russ. council) The lower house of the Russian Parliament, with 450 members, which has been the voice of the Republic since it was first elected in December 1993 after the abortive WHITE HOUSE REVOLT against President Yeltsin. The first Duma was the Parliament established after the REVOLUTION OF 1905, which Nicholas II proposed in his OCTOBER MANIFESTO. The TSAR curtailed its powers before it met in May 1906; he could VETO all its decisions and pass laws when it was not sitting, and ministers were ultimately responsible to him, not the Duma. When the first Duma nevertheless proved radical and demanded land reforms, it was dissolved in July 1906. The second Duma, convened in March 1907, lasted only three months. The electoral system was rigged to ensure more conservative third and fourth Dumas (1907–12 and 1912–17), but during WORLD WAR I opposition to the monarchy again swelled in the Duma; after the Tsar was deposed in 1917 a Duma Provisional Committee formed the first Provisional GOVERNMENT.

Dumbarton Oaks The conference held in WASHINGTON from August to October 1944 involving America, the Soviet Union, Britain and China to discuss formation of what became the UNITED NATIONS. It was named after the Georgetown mansion where it was held. There was general agreement over the basic structures, such as the GENERAL ASSEMBLY, SECURITY COUNCIL and secretariat. More contentious were the issues of membership – the Soviet Union wanted seats for all its sixteen republics – and the right of VETO in the Security Council. These questions were reconsidered at YALTA in February 1945, and the SAN FRANCISCO CONFERENCE fixed the UN's final form.

dumping (1) The export of manufactured goods, food or commodities to a country at below cost price in order to undercut other trading nations and that country's domestic suppliers. One reason for the WTO system is to curb dumping by ensuring not only free but fair trade; where the WTO makes no provision, nations retaliate against dumping by imposing stiff tariffs. (2) The removal from the party ticket or nomination of an INCUMBENT who could otherwise have looked forward to re-election.

social dumping A term used by countries with high labour costs or costly social benefits for MULTINATIONALS' practice of switching production to cheaper locations. It was used by French Ministers in 1993 when Hoover switched much of its European production from Dijon to Cambuslang, near Glasgow, on the ground that UK wages and social security costs were far less.

Dunkirk spirit The spirit repeatedly invoked by Harold WILSON in the mid-1960s when urging the British people on to greater sacrifice and effort to pull the economy round. It sought to emulate the country's success at snatching survival, if not victory, from the jaws of defeat in June 1940 when over 300,000 troops were evacuated from the beaches of Dunkirk under the nose of Germany's *Luftwaffe* as NAZI troops advanced through northern France. Wilson's appeals did not spark an upsurge in Britain's economic performance; recovery only began with DEVALUATION, which Wilson had long resisted, in November 1967.

economic Dunkirk The alarming estimate of the prospect facing America given to President REAGAN immediately after his ELECTION in 1980 by David Stockman (*see* MAGIC ASTERISK), who was named BUDGET director soon after, and the conservative Rep. Jack Kemp. Stockman made a deliberately pessimistic pitch at a time when the economy was barely in RECESSION to instil urgency into the new ADMINISTRATION, and prompt Reagan to go for serious cuts in the Budget proposed by the CARTER administration.

DUP Democratic Unionist Party. The party, led by the Rev. Ian Paisley, which has since the early 1970s articulated the mindset of hard-line Ulster LOYALISTS, mainly in working-class East Belfast, the Larne area and other pockets of aggressively fundamentalist Protestantism. By rejecting almost any accommodation with the Irish Republic or the Catholic community, the DUP has kept the official ULSTER UNIONIST party on its toes, and since the GOOD FRIDAY AGREEMENT, in which it reluctantly acquiesced, has made inroads into the Unionists' rural powerbase. In December 2004 the DUP came within a whisker of an agreement with SINN FEIN to share power in a resumed devolved Executive, only for it to break down on the issue of photographic evidence of DECOMMISSIONING of the IRA's weaponry. In the 2005 general election the DUP became the province's largest party, winning nine seats out of seventeen and reducing the Ulster Unionists to one solitary seat.

Durham Report The report to the British government by John Lambton, first Earl of Durham (*see* RADICAL JACK, 1792–1840) which paved the way to responsible GOVERNMENT for the Canadian colonies. Durham was despatched to Canada as GOVERNOR-GENERAL in 1838 after the Mackenzie and Papineau rebellions of the year before. He reported:

> I expected to find a contest between a government and a people; I found two nations warring in the bosom of a single state; I found struggle not of principles but of races.

Durham concluded that Britain was going too far in APPEASING French-Canadians, and that unless a fairer balance was struck, the Anglophone business community would look to the United States. To avert this, he recommended a Union of Upper and Lower Canada (Ontario and Quebec) as a democracy that would be under English-Canadian dominance. This was provided for in an Act of Union in 1840. The Report was deeply unpopular with French Canadians and did much to unite them; Conservatives in Upper Canada were as opposed to democratic rule.

during pleasure The euphemism used in the HOUSE OF LORDS for the period in the evening when PEERS adjourn for dinner.

Occasionally a short debate on a non-controversial subject is staged to avoid giving the impression that 'everything stops for tea'. After the Lords twice adjourned on 3 November 1993 on rail privatisation only to be sent home by an embarrassed government (*see* COMMITTEE OF REASONS), the Lib-Dem Lord Wigoder observed:

> My Lords, is there any limit to the hours of undiluted pleasure which members of Your Lordships' House can enjoy in one evening?

duty. If we believe a thing to be bad, and have a right to prevent it, it is our duty to prevent it and damn the consequences The terms in which Lord Milner (1854–1925) set out the resolve of himself and the other DIEHARDS to oppose the PEOPLE'S BUDGET put forward by LLOYD GEORGE, regardless of the consequences for the HOUSE OF LORDS of doing so. He made the declaration in a speech in Glasgow on 26 November 1909.

Let us therefore brace ourselves to our duty A key phrase of the rallying speech made by CHURCHILL in the HOUSE OF COMMONS on 18 June 1940, after DUNKIRK but with the Battle of Britain ahead and invasion by Germany expected shortly. Churchill said:

> Let us therefore brace ourselves to our duties, and so bear ourselves that if the British Empire and its Commonwealth last for a thousand years, men will still say: 'THIS WAS THEIR FINEST HOUR'.

E

e-government The process under which the workings of government, and the public's access to it, are based on the Internet and other forms of information technology. John MAJOR and Tony BLAIR each appointed an **e-envoy** to urge Whitehall departments to embrace these techniques, but progress has been more limited than was originally hoped.

E Pluribus Unum (Lat. One out of many) The motto on the device forming the Great SEAL of the United States, and the other emblems of the nation; it is written on a scroll held in the beak of an American EAGLE. It is in fact a quote from Virgil, who was referring to the ingredients of a salad.

eagle A traditional symbol of strength, hence of the power of a nation. The emblem of the United States, and before it of Russia, Prussia, Austria-Hungary, Imperial France, Rome, the Kings of Babylon and Persia and the Ptolemies of Egypt. America's national bird is the bald eagle; H. G. Wells wrote:

> Every time Europe looks across the Atlantic to see the American eagle, it observes only the rear end of an ostrich.

The eagle is also a symbol of dominance, CHURCHILL saying after VE DAY: 'The [German] eagle has ceased to scream, but the parrots now will begin to chatter.'

Eagle's lair or nest The Berghof, HITLER's redoubt 1,829m. (6,000ft.) up a mountain near Berchtesgaden in southern Germany, close to the Austrian border. The FÜHRER received many important guests here.

EAPC (previously known as EDP and, before that, E or EA) *e*conomic *a*ffairs, *p*roductivity and *c*ompetitiveness. The principal UK CABINET COMMITTEE dealing with the broad sweep of economic policy, chaired by the CHANCELLOR. Membership is prized, and sometimes demanded, by Ministers keen to influence economy policy.

Earl A senior, hereditary rank in the British PEERAGE (from O.E. *eorl*), but no longer with an automatic seat in the HOUSE OF LORDS. An **earldom** is offered to the most distinguished former Prime Ministers; the last to accept was Harold MACMILLAN (Earl of Stockton).

Early Bird The PENTAGON's confidential daily news sheet, officially called *Current News*, which in sixteen pages distils the overnight news reports of greatest relevance to the department and its followers in the WHITE HOUSE, CONGRESS, the military and the intelligence community. It is now circulated electronically as well as in hard copy.

Early Day Motion *See* EDM.

early voting In US ELECTIONS, the procedure in a number of States under which polling stations open days or even weeks in advance to enable as many registered voters as possible to participate. It was first used on a large scale in the 2004 election, with up to 20% of voters in some States having cast their ballots before the candidates had finished campaigning.

earmarker A particular piece of PORK inserted by a member into a US Congressional spending BILL.

earth. Earth Summits A series of meetings of world leaders – the first in Rio de Janeiro in June 1992 – sponsored by the UNITED NATIONS, to gain agreement on global steps to save the environment. The Rio summit set the pattern through President BUSH's initial refusal to attend and then, once there, to support a Biodiversity Treaty to save endangered species; however, it did establish the principle of SUSTAINABLE DEVELOPMENT. Subsequent Earth Summits have registered limited achievements, but have tended to be overshadowed by accompanying events staged by pressure groups and by anti-GLOBALISATION protests.

earthquake. this is a true earthquake. The justifiable claim made by Jean-Marie Le Pen, leader of France's NATIONAL FRONT, on 22nd April 2002 after he forced the socialist Prime Minister Lionel Jospin into third place in the Presidential election and came within four percentage points of topping the poll, ahead of the incumbent Jacques Chirac. This outcome, caused by concern over immigration and crime, by disillusion that the President and Prime Minister under the system of 'COHABITATION' were running against each other and by Jospin's lacklustre candidacy, ensured a convincing defeat of Le Pen in the RUN-OFF. But it also sent out a wake-up call to an introverted French political class.

east. Eastern Question The overriding foreign policy issue for European states in the second half of the 19th century, stemming from the gradual collapse of the Ottoman Empire and its efforts to retain control in the face of rising Balkan nationalisms, the perceived interests of Austria-Hungary, Britain, France and Germany, and the ambitions of Russia in the region. It came to a head in the CRIMEAN WAR and the Balkan crisis of 1876–78, ending supposedly with the establishment of the modern Turkish state in 1923 but with the warfare in the Balkans in the 1990s demonstrating the continuing instability of the region.

east front The aspect of the US CAPITOL facing the WASHINGTON Monument, and the scene of many Presidential inaugurations. The cornerstone of the Capitol was laid on the east front by George Washington on 18 September 1793; the first portion was completed in 1800. The east front was extended to its present length of 751ft. by 1867, then built out 32½ ft. between 1959 and 1961 to create extra office space.

Easter Rising The uprising in Dublin on Easter Monday 1916 against British rule, which paved the way for the creation of the Irish state. 1,600 volunteers of the IRISH REPUBLICAN BROTHERHOOD ('a minority of a minority' – R. F. Foster) led by Patrick Pearse and James Connolly captured positions in the city, notably Dublin Post Office where Pearse read a 'proclamation of the Republic', and held out for a week. 450 people, including 116 soldiers and 16 police, were killed and 2,614 wounded. Fifteen leaders of the rising were executed, including the wounded Connolly, the revulsion caused greatly strengthening nationalist feeling.

A terrible beauty is born. W. B. YEATS

eat. eat crow To be forced to swallow one's own words. The phrase originated in the 19th-century US joke about a man who claimed he could eat anything; when forced to eat roast crow he declared: 'Yes, I can eat crow! . . . but I'll be darned if I hanker after it.' It was popularised in the 1872 Presidential election when Horace Greeley, who split from the Republican party to run against GRANT, was nicknamed 'boiled crow' by his foes; those who 'ate crow' were ready to swallow their reservations and vote for Greeley. After TRUMAN's shock re-election in 1948, the *Washington Post* advertised a banquet at which political reporters and POLLSTERS would be treated to 'breast of tough old crow, *en glace*'.

Eatanswill The fictitious, corrupt and Rabelaisian BY-ELECTION in Dickens' *Pickwick Papers* which has come to epitomise the squalid, corrupt side of political life in England before the BALLOT ACT.

EC *See* EUROPEAN COMMUNITY.

ECB European Central Bank. The organisation which, since the inception of the EURO at the start of 2002, has set interest rates and otherwise determined central policy for the countries of the EUROZONE. Based in Frankfurt, its Governing Council includes representatives of each member state which has adopted the single currency; non-participants have a say in all ECB decisions not relating to the euro. The ECB and the Eurozone's CENTRAL BANKS between them define and implement monetary policy, conduct foreign exchange operations, hold and manage the zone's foreign currency reserves and promote the smooth operation of payment systems.

ECOFIN The EU's council of Economics and Finance Ministers, which normally meets once a month in Brussels or in the country holding the PRESIDENCY. It supervised development of economic and monetary union (EMU) up to the introduction of the single currency, and still plays an important role in economic co-ordination and in driving policy.

economic reform EU-speak for the process under which Europe's economies could develop greater competitiveness by ending unnecessary regulation, opening up state monopolies to competition and encouraging enterprise and small businesses. The UK has been the most consistent advocate of economic reform, pushing through in 2000 the LISBON AGENDA to which member states remain committed, despite backsliding by France and, to a lesser extent, Germany. The threat of such 'ANGLO-SAXON' economies to the EUROPEAN SOCIAL MODEL was a key factor in the French people's rejection of the EUROPEAN CONSTITUTION in May 2005.

economic Royalists *See* ROYALISTS.

economical with the truth *See* TRUTH.

economics The theoretical study of the production and distribution of wealth, inextricably linked to politics. Thomas Carlyle described it as 'the dismal science'; to George Meany it was 'the one profession where you can gain great eminence without ever being right'. Eugene W. Baer reckoned that 'what's good politics is bad economics'; while Lyndon B. JOHNSON observed:

> Making a speech about economics is a bit like pissing down your leg. It seems hot to you, but it never does to anyone else.

economic advisers A prerequisite for any ruler, but loved by few of them. President TRUMAN begged: 'Give me a one-handed economist. All my economists say "on the one hand . . . on the other".'

> MITTERRAND has a hundred mistresses; one of them has AIDS but he doesn't know which one. BUSH has a hundred bodyguards; one of them is a terrorist, but he doesn't know which one. I have a hundred economic advisers. One is smart, but I don't know which one.
> MIKHAIL S. GORBACHEV

Economic and Monetary Union (EMU). The process of aligning and unifying the economies of EU member states, in advance of the adoption of the EURO.

economic blizzard CHURCHILL's term for the financial crash of 1931, following a series of European bank collapses, which ensured the GREAT DEPRESSION.

economic cycle The cycle in an economy consisting successively of BOOM, RECESSION, DEPRESSION, recovery and boom.

Economic League A UK right-wing organisation with links to the CONSERVATIVE PARTY, which specialises in circulating BLACKLISTS of alleged union troublemakers to employers.

economic miracle (Ger. *Wirtschaftswunder*) West Germany's free-market economic recovery following the devastation of World War II.

Economic Report of the President The annual assessment of the US economy prepared by the President's Council of ECONOMIC ADVISERS.

economic warfare Strategic and financial measures used to back up a military campaign and weaken an enemy's economy, as encapsulated by the UK's WORLD WAR II Ministry of Economic Warfare.

matchstick economics The pursuit of economic policy by the uninitiated using simple logic, from the statement by SIR ALEC Douglas-Home:

> When I read economic documents, I have to have a box of matches and start moving them into position, to illustrate and simplify the points to myself.

voodoo economics George BUSH senior's pejorative for REAGANOMICS during the 1980 Republican primaries. Bush's criticisms, conjuring up images of sleight of hand, mumbo-jumbo and deception, did not prevent Reagan selecting him as his RUNNING-MATE.

> It's the only memorable thing I've ever said, and I've regretted saying it. GEORGE BUSH, Snr

economist (1) A proponent or analyst of economic theory and its application to national economic systems. Ronald REAGAN described an economist as 'the only professional who sees something working in practice and seriously wonders if it works in theory', and said:

> A friend of mine was asked to a costume ball. He slapped some egg on his face and went as a liberal economist.

> There are three kinds of economists: those who can count and those who can't.
> HELEN LIDDELL

(2) In ASQUITH's peacetime CABINET, the faction which argued for economy in spending and, in particular, against an accelerated Dreadnought building programme (*see* WE WANT EIGHT AND WE WON'T WAIT).

economy (1) An economy or the economy: the operation of a nation's finances, wealth creation, production, exchange and employment.

> It is much easier to manage an economy if you can use electrodes on the most sensitive parts of those who refuse to co-operate.
> DENIS HEALEY

> Government's view of the economy can be summed up in a few short phrases. If it moves, tax it. If it keeps moving, regulate it. And if it stops moving, subsidise it. RONALD REAGAN

(2) Prudence in the handling of money, public or otherwise.

> Everyone is always in favour of general economy and particular expenditure.
> ANTHONY EDEN

black economy The portion of the economy operated out of the reach of the tax authorities, largely by the self-employed and benefit recipients.

command economy An economy in which orders are given from the centre and the system is expected to meet set targets, regardless of economic forces. A key feature of Soviet COMMUNISM.

commanding heights of the economy The phrase coined by Aneurin BEVAN for the areas of activity Labour had to NATIONALISE to bring about fundamental change.

mixed economy An economy in which elements of SOCIALISM and CAPITALISM co-exist. The term was particularly used of Britain from the late 1940s, when state controls, the WELFARE STATE and NATIONALISED industries interacted with a classic PRIVATE SECTOR.

permanent war economy An economy permanently distorted by the demands of military spending and procurement, regardless of whether the nation is actually at war.

siege economy An inherently weak economy isolated by a government from external pressures in order to protect and, supposedly, restructure it.

stakeholder economy *see* STAKEHOLDER.

It's the economy, stupid! The sign hung in the WAR ROOM at CLINTON campaign headquarters in LITTLE ROCK during the 1992 Presidential campaign by James Carville (*see* RAGIN' CAJUN). He was anxious to drive home the message to campaign staff that, whatever other issues were raised, the election would be decided on the state of America's economy and the candidates' commitment to tackling it. The full banner read:

> Change vs. more of the same
> The economy, stupid
> Don't forget health care.

ECOSOC (1) The UN Economic and Social Conference. (2) The EU's Economic and Social Committee, a body drawn from all walks of life, which can submit 'opinions' on proposed Community legislation.

ecu European Currency Unit (the *écu* was also a 17th-century French silver coin). The notional currency, based on a 'basket' of ten currencies and with a fluctuating value of approximately $1, which became the basis for the EURO.

hard ecu John MAJOR's proposal when CHANCELLOR for a fixed-value ecu which could gain credibility against national currencies and conceivably supplant then. It was put forward in an unsuccessful effort to head off early moves by other member states toward a common European currency.

Eden, (Robert) **Anthony,** later the Earl of Avon (1897–1977), UK Prime Minister (Conservative) 1955–57. From a landed Co. Durham family, Eden was wounded three times in WORLD WAR I before making an early entry into politics. In 1935 BALDWIN made him Foreign Secretary, the youngest-ever; handsome and dashing, Aneurin BEVAN called him 'the juvenile lead', but Bertrand Russell remarked: 'Not a gentleman. He dresses too well.' To Bonar Thompson he was 'the best advertisement the Fifty Shilling Tailors ever had'. In 1938 he resigned over CHAMBERLAIN's dealings with Fascist Italy, and the – not wholly correct – legend of Eden as the man who stood against the dictators was born. A. J. P. Taylor was to write:

> Eden did not face the dictators; he pulled faces at them.

CHURCHILL brought him back to government in 1940. He again served as Foreign Secretary between 1941–45 and 1951–55, becoming Churchill's heir-apparent and leading him to remark: 'I have been Foreign Secretary for 10 years. Am I not to be trusted?' Harold MACMILLAN wrote: 'Winston thought Anthony would wreck it. That's the reason he held on so long.' When Churchill went, there was some unease, Lord Swinton writing: 'He will be the worst Prime Minister since Lord North', and Macmillan observing: 'It really may be that he has been Prince of Wales too long.'

So it turned out. He started well, increasing the Tory majority in a SNAP ELECTION campaign when, said Macmillan, 'he never put a foot wrong'. Malcolm Muggeridge felt it was all too easy: 'They asked for a leader and were given a public relations officer: here is the news, and this is Anthony Eden reading it.' R. A. Butler (*see* RAB) agreed with a reporter that he was 'the best Prime Minister we have', but privately he described the sensitive Eden as 'half mad baronet, half beautiful woman'; the Labour MP Sir Reginald Paget was as cruel: 'An overripe banana – yellow outside, squashy within.' Yet he could be crushing in the COMMONS. When the notorious homosexual Tom Driberg asked him about his government's 'flirtations with kings', he retorted to gasps:

> 'I do not know how far the Honourable Gentleman is an expert in flirtations, or what kind of flirtations.'

Then came SUEZ, which, said Brendan Bracken, changed Eden from 'charming milksop to blood-lusting monster'. Suez was all Eden's work, with the Prime Minister casting Egypt's Colonel Nasser in the same mould as HITLER. As controversy grew, the military planners vacillated and America turned against the operation, his stock plummeted. Robert Blake was to write: 'He was the last Prime Minister to believe that Britain was a great power; and the first to confront a crisis which proved she was not.' Harold WILSON concluded: 'When he did say boo, it was to the wrong goose and too roughly.' Suez left Eden bitter toward US Secretary of State John Foster Dulles, who had been ambivalent at critical stages; he termed him 'as tortuous as a wounded snake, with much less excuse.' Eden's health began to deteriorate – he had never been well – and early in 1957 he resigned. Lord Carrington concluded that 'Anthony had clearly gone mad', but he lived to a ripe and lucid old age.

EDM Early Day Motion. In the UK HOUSE OF COMMONS, a motion tabled by (usually) BACKBENCH MPs which appears in the later, blue, pages of the full daily ORDER PAPER known as the VOTE. Seldom debated, such motions are mainly tabled to show the strength of support for a particular cause or complaint, the text bearing the number of signatories. Some EDMs are tabled by a single MP to applaud a constituency event; occasionally ones – generally on cruelty to animals – attracts the signatures of more than half the House – a considerable feat as Ministers never sign.

education, education, education The priority set for a NEW LABOUR government by Tony BLAIR in his party conference speech in September 1996.

Education and Information Project The propaganda effort led by James Carville (*see* RAGIN' CAJUN) with President CLINTON's tacit support against Special Prosecutor Kenneth STARR's investigation of WHITEWATER.

EFL External Financing Limit. In Britain, the amount a NATIONALISED industry received in a year in government subsidy, grants and authorised borrowing.

EFTA European FREE TRADE Association. Founded in 1960 with Britain in the lead for western European nations which wanted free trade without the EEC's political and economic union, it became a 'transit lounge' for countries seeking to join the Community – Austria, Denmark, Finland, Portugal, Sweden and the UK have so far done so. Since 1995 its sole members have been Iceland, Liechtenstein and Norway. *See also* EUROPEAN ECONOMIC AREA.

egalitarianism The belief that political systems should be designed to ensure that people became as nearly equal in their social status and economic power as it is practical to achieve. When Tony BLAIR broke with many of Labour's traditional doctrines, Roy Hattersley in particular charged him with ending the party's commitment to egalitarianism.

egg. egghead An INTELLECTUAL preoccupied with erudite matters (supposedly requiring a large, balding head). British slang post-1910, it caught on in the US after WORLD WAR II with Adlai STEVENSON branded as such by his opponents. Stevenson retorted: 'Eggheads of the world unite – you have nothing to lose but your yolks,' and *Via Ovicapitum Dura Est* – 'the way of the egghead is hard'.

eggs As a weapon, found by protesters to be a messy, non-explosive and cheap form of ammunition.

> Those who scream and throw eggs are not the real unemployed. If they were really hard up, they would be eating them.
>
> NORMAN TEBBIT

like playing tennis with a dish of scrambled eggs The vivid description by the Conservative MP Sir Harold Nicolson (1883–1968) of trying to debate in the COMMONS in 1943 with Nancy, Lady Astor, who despite her vigorous style found it hard to keep to the point.

Most of the egg production of this country, sadly, is now infected with salmonella The wildly exaggerated statement made in December 1989 by UK junior Health Minister Edwina Currie (*see* CRUELLA DE VILLE) which sparked a national panic and cost her her job. As the row erputed, the Conservative MP Sir Nicholas Fairbairn reminded her she had been an egg once, adding, 'People on both sides of the House greatly regretted its fertilisation'.

You can't make an omelette without breaking eggs Robespierre's justification for the excesses of the FRENCH REVOLUTION. Anthony EDEN turned it round, saying: 'If you've broken the eggs, you should make the omelette.'

Eichmann trial The trial in Israel of (Karl) Adolf Eichmann (1906–62), one of the architects of Hitler's FINAL SOLUTION for the Jews, in 1961 on WAR CRIMES charges. Eichmann, who had organised the logistics of shipping Jews to death camps and setting up gas chambers, escaped from Allied custody in 1945 and fled to Argentina. Fifteen years later he was abducted by Israeli agents and put on trial in a bulletproof glass booth; he was convicted of the murder of thousands of Austrian Jews, and hanged.

eighteen. 1848, year of revolution The year when urban crowds throughout Europe rose up against despotism, though not all their gains were permanent. They overthrew King Louis-Philippe of France, forced the abdication of the Austrian emperor and the fall of his chief minister Metternich, briefly created republics in Rome (under Garibaldi) and Hungary, and won constitutions from the kings of Prussia and Naples. Only in Spain, where the dictatorship stood firm; Russia, which brutally put down the Hungarian revolt; and Britain, where a massive but peaceful CHARTIST demonstration was the height of pressure, did the *status quo* survive.

18½-minute gap The celebrated gap in one of the most incriminating WATERGATE tapes, found when they were released to CONGRESS. Experts concluded that there had been a deliberate erasure, but Rose Mary Woods (1917–2005), NIXON's secretary for over 25 years, insisted the gap was accidental. In an entertaining Congressional hearing she demonstrated how she could have inadvertently erased the tape by pressing the wrong pedal on her dictating machine, but acknowledged how her action could only have accounted for five minutes of the gap.

Eighteenth Amendment The amendment to the US CONSTITUTION which, in tandem with the VOLSTEAD ACT, introduced PROHIBITION. Ratified on 29 January 1919 (only Connecticut and Rhode Island resisting), it banned the manufacture, sale and transportation of liquor, but not drinking or purchase; the Volstead Act did that. The amendment was repealed by the 21st Amendment, which was proposed on 20 February 1933 and ratified that December.

Ein Volk, Ein Reich, Ein Führer (sometimes *Ein Reich, Ein Volk . . .*) (Ger. One people, one nation, one leader) The slogan of the NAZI party, first used at the September 1934 NUREMBERG RALLY.

Eire The Irish Gaelic name for the island of Ireland, and the Irish nation; from 1937 the official title of the Southern Irish state.

Eisenhower. Dwight David Eisenhower (1890–1969). Supreme Allied Commander Europe in WORLD WAR II and 34th President of the United States (Republican, 1953–61). A career army officer, he told his wife Mamie when they married: 'My country comes first and always will. You come second.' Eisenhower made a world reputation by preparing and commanding the massed force which on 6 June 1944 landed on the Normandy beaches of occupied France, then pressed on to victory. On D-Day he told US troops:

> The eyes of the world are upon us. The hopes and prayers of liberty-loving people everywhere march with you.

The war over, Republicans and Democrats courted him as a Presidential candidate, but Eisenhower had no overweening political ambitions. He once said: 'I can think of nothing more boring for the American people than to have to sit in their living rooms for a whole half hour looking at my face on their television screens', and on another occasion remarked: 'Once in a while I get to the point, with everybody staring at me, where I want to go back indoors and pull down the curtains.' But he eventually accepted the Republican nomination for 1952, against Adlai STEVENSON, who commented: 'If I talk over people's heads, he must be talking under their feet.' Of his ideology, Eisenhower said: 'I'm no reactionary. Christ on the Mountain! I'm as idealistic as hell.' His candidacy amused General Douglas MACARTHUR, who described him as 'the best clerk I ever fired'. Ike hit back: 'I studied dramatics under him for 12 years.'

Eisenhower was a laid-back President, Sen. Robert Kerr terming him 'the only living unknown soldier'. His public image was of a leader who stood back and occupied himself with golf, even putting in the OVAL OFFICE; he had squirrels trapped on the WHITE HOUSE lawn because they interfered with his practice. Emmet John Hughes wrote: 'As an intellectual he bestowed upon the games of golf and bridge all the enthusiasm and perseverance that he withheld from books and ideas.' But David Halberstam had an explanation: 'A subtle man, and no fool. He did not like to be thought of as brilliant; people of brilliance, he thought, were to be distrusted.' Eisenhower himself said:

> At last I've got a job where I stay home nights, and by golly I'm going to stay home.

Eisenhower stood aside from many of the contentious issues of the day. He declined to take on Sen. Joseph MCCARTHY, saying: 'I refuse to get into the gutter with that man'; belatedly the Senate itself saw him off. His first term brought the landmark BROWN case on CIVIL RIGHTS, but it was the SUPREME COURT and not the ADMINISTRATION that acted. Nevertheless he was a man of principle, in George Kennan's words 'the nation's Number One Boy Scout'. He made vigorous efforts to prevent the COLD WAR turning into NUCLEAR conflict, and refused to back the Anglo-French military adventure at SUEZ. On leaving office, he warned of the threat to democracy from the MILITARY-INDUSTRIAL COMPLEX. His tenure was sullied only by the Sherman ADAMS affair. Eisenhower's predecessor Harry S TRUMAN was not impressed with his performance, saying: 'Eisenhower wasn't used to being criticised, and he never did get it through his head that this is what politics is about. He was used to getting his ass kissed.' Yet the overall tone was of prosperous torpor, especially after Eisenhower suffered second-term heart attacks and lowered his profile to the point where one wit cruelly observed:

> Things have never been the same since Ike died.

Eisenhower Commission The commission set up by President EISENHOWER under his brother Milton to investigate the causes and prevention of violence.

Eisenhower Doctrine Eisenhower's promise in January 1957 to commit economic or military aid to Middle Eastern countries under threat from Communist aggression. Though denounced by Egypt and Syria in the wake of SUEZ, it became an integral part of American foreign policy.

Eksund The Panamanian-registered trawler whose interception by French customs off Normandy at the end of October 1987 revealed the extent of GUN-RUNNING between Col. Gaddafi's Libya and the IRA. The vessel, bound for Clogga Beach, Co. Wicklow, was carrying more than two tons of SEMTEX, 1 million rounds of ammunition, 1000 AK-47 assault rifles, 20 SAM-7 anti-aircraft missiles, 12 mortars, 10 heavy machine guns, 430 grenades and 10 rocket-propelled grenade launchers. The shipment was one of five from Libya to the IRA since 1985; the previous four had got through and by 1992 some 300 IRA killings had been attributed to weapons of Libyan origin. Had the Eksund's 150-ton cargo reached Ireland, it would have greatly enhanced the IRA's destructive power; its detection (and apparent betrayal) strengthened the hand of Gerry Adams who was trying to woo the Provisionals toward a political solution.

elastic clause *See* NECESSARY AND PROPER CLAUSE.

elect To choose representatives by a democratic process, or to secure the election of a particular candidate. John F. KENNEDY said at the height of the 1960 Presidential campaign:

> With the money I'm spending I could elect my chauffeur.

electability The quality of fitness for election, and more particularly the suitability of a candidate in the eyes of the voters.

election The actual process of choice, comprising the CAMPAIGN, the BALLOT, the COUNT and the DECLARATION. To the participants and their supporters this is more than a technical process: Edmund BURKE asked: 'What is it we all seek in an election? You must first possess the means of knowing the fitness of your man, and then you must retain some hold upon him by personal obligation or dependence.' And Walt Whitman declared: 'I know nothing grander, better exercise, better digestion, more positive proof of the past, the triumphant result of faith in humankind, than a well-contested American national election.' To Stanley BALDWIN elections were a regrettable necessity: 'I hate elections but you have to have them. They are medicine.' But Baldwin's urbane backbencher Henry 'CHIPS' Channon described an election as 'like a violent love affair'. George Bernard Shaw cynically termed them 'a moral horror, as bad as a battleground except for the blood; a mudbath for every soul concerned with it'. Gerald Lieberman wrote: 'Elections are held to delude the populace into believing that they are participating in government.' And Richard CROSSMAN saw a Royal perspective: 'For the Queen an election simply means that just when she has begun to know us, she has to meet another terrible lot of politicians.'

election address In a UK election, candidate formal communications with the voters, introducing themselves and setting out their policies and claims to be elected, which in a general election the Royal Mail will deliver in the FREE POST.

election court The ultimate guardian of the probity of the British electoral system. Such courts are very seldom convened, but in 2005 one disqualified six Asian Labour councillors from Birmingham who were found in a warehouse with sackfuls of ballot papers during the 2004 municipal elections. (One was reinstated on appeal.) The papers, for POSTAL VOTES, had been allowed as the RETURNING OFFICER had no mechanism for investigating such irregularities short of a police inquiry. The judge, Richard Mawrey QC, observed that the councillors had committed electoral fraud that would 'disgrace a BANANA REPUBLIC'.

Elections are about something more important than choosing between a man with a pipe and a man with a boat Enoch POWELL's view of Britain's general elections of 1966, 1970 and February and October 1974, fought out between Labour under the pipe-smoking Harold WILSON and the Conservative Edward HEATH who was an ocean-going yachtsman (*see* MORNING CLOUD).

direct elections The term used for the 1979 elections to the EUROPEAN PARLIAMENT, when MEPs were for the first time elected directly by the voters instead of being appointed from national legislatures.

free elections The democratic right guaranteed at YALTA for the Soviet-occupied nations of Eastern Europe, but reneged on by STALIN and his successors.

general election In a Parliamentary system, the election of the main house of the legislature, which determines whether the government remains in office or is replaced by a new administration led by a different party. In America, a coincidental Presidential, congressional and local election.

> During a general election, civil servants do what they do the rest of the time: get drunk and have affairs.
>
> KENNETH CLARKE

mid-term election The elections for the US Congress (all the HOUSE OF REPRESENTATIVES, part of the SENATE) that fall midway through a Presidential TERM. The elections of 1934 and 1998 are the only ones in recent times when the party occupying the WHITE HOUSE has registered gains. *See* OFF-YEAR.

snap election *See* SNAP.

special election *See* SPECIAL.

See also COUPON ELECTION, KHAKI ELECTION.

electioneering The process of conducting a partisan election campaign; the production, not necessarily during an election, of arguments and stunts which have more to do with getting elected than with a constructive approach to the problems of government.

elector Someone eligible to vote. Historically, one of the German princelings eligible to vote for the Holy Roman Emperor; George, Elector of Hanover, ascended the British throne in 1714 as King George I.

Electoral College (1) In the US political system, the body comprising delegations from all 50 States (plus the DISTRICT OF COLUMBIA) which meets after the Presidential election actually to select the President. There are 538 votes in the College, 270 being a winning total; if no candidate reaches it, the election is handed to the HOUSE OF REPRESENTATIVES. Each State's delegation is partially weighted according to population, the number of votes being the number of Senators and Congressmen combined. Alaska and Delaware are among several states with three votes; California has 54. Each state casts all its votes for the winning candidate in that state. A nominee piling up votes in key states could thus emerge victorious from the Electoral College despite running second in the popular vote; in 2000 Al GORE (*see* OZONE MAN) not only won the popular vote but came within a few hundred disputed Florida votes of carrying the Electoral College, which could not meet until the SUPREME COURT had considered his challenge to George W. BUSH.

> It affords a moral certainty that the office of President will never fall to the lot of any man who is not in an eminent degree endowed with the requisite qualifications.
>
> ALEXANDER HAMILTON

(2) In Britain, the body representing trade unions (40%), MPs (30%) and constituency parties (30%) set up by the LABOUR PARTY under BENNite pressure in 1981–82 to elect its leaders, instead of the Parliamentary party. Its creation gave impetus to the breakaway SDP; by 1992 when John SMITH was elected leader, the college's preponderance of union BLOCK VOTES was discredited but the college has survived.

Electoral Commission (1) The independent body set up by the UK Parliament in 2000 under the Political Parties, Elections and Referendums Act to supervise the electoral process and encourage public participation. It was proposed by NEW LABOUR as a means of maintaining public confidence in the integrity of the democratic system after the SLEAZE scandals of the 1990s, which had exposed a number of abuses in the funding of candidates. The Commission, initially chaired by Sam Younger, former head of the BBC World Service, is supervised by an all-party committee chaired by the SPEAKER. (2) The body set up by the US CONGRESS in 1877 to resolve the disputed election between Rutherford Hayes and Samuel Tilden; while Tilden won the popular vote, competing sets of returns were submitted by four States which left Tilden one vote short in the ELECTORAL COLLEGE. The Commission divided on straight party lines, giving each state, and the Presidency, to Hayes by an eight-to-seven vote – hence his nickname OLD EIGHT TO SEVEN.

electoral pact A deal between parties under which each stands down some of its candidates in return for support from the other.

electoral reform The umbrella term for moves from a FIRST PAST THE POST SYSTEM toward PROPORTIONAL REPRESENTATION.

Electoral Reform Society The UK body which promotes study of improved voting systems, and also supervises and conducts ballots for a number of trade unions and other organisations.

electoral register *See* REGISTER OF ELECTORS.

electoral truce An agreement by the parties to suspend normal electoral politics at a time of national emergency. In Britain, the Conservatives, Labour and the Liberals operated such a truce during WORLD WAR II. In theory it should have led to the candidate from the party previously holding a seat being returned unopposed at a BY-ELECTION; in practice minor candidates frequently forced a contest and occasionally won.

electorate (1) The number of electors in each electoral district. (2) The Australian term for a CONSTITUENCY. (3) The general body of VOTERS, of which most politicians are very wary, the feeling being mutual. Sen. Henry F. Ashurst wrote: 'The electorate suspects and distrusts men of superb intellect, calmness and serenity'; of the Australian electorate Don Aitkin commented: 'Whatever politicians, activists and manipulators propose, it is the phlegmatic, indifferent, ingrained electorate which disposes.'

> You have to give the electorate a tune they can whistle. ENOCH POWELL

Elegant Arthur The nickname of **Chester Alan Arthur** (1830–86), 21st President of the United States (Republican) from 1881–85. A lawyer and Republican leader in New York State, Arthur was dismissed by President Hayes in 1878 as collector of customs after a patronage scandal; Democrats knew him as a 'spoilsman's spoilsman'. He had never run for office until party bosses nominated him in 1880 as James Garfield's running-mate to appease the New York boss Roscoe Conkling. Arthur himself declared that 'the office of Vice President is a greater honour than I ever dreamed of attaining', but on Garfield's death within months of taking office he found himself in the WHITE HOUSE. One New York associate exclaimed:

> Chet Arthur! President of the United States? Good God!

Arthur came to office regarded, in Woodrow WILSON's words, as 'a nonentity with side-whiskers'. But he proved a success, his failure to win re-election in 1884 ironically stemming from his failure to indulge in CRONYISM. He also kept himself to himself, once telling an inquisitive temperance campaigner: 'Madam, I may be President of the United States, but my private life is nobody's damn business.' When he left the White House, Alexander K. McClure wrote:

> No man entered the Presidency so profoundly and widely distrusted, and no one ever retired more generally respected.

> Nothing like it ever before in the Executive Mansion – liquor, snobbery and worse.
> RUTHERFORD HAYES, 1882

elephant The long-standing emblem of the US REPUBLICAN PARTY, popularised from 1874 by the cartoonist Thomas Nast. Though identified by the Democrats as representing ponderous conservatism, the elephant has understandably been the cause of less satirical comparison than the Democrats' own DONKEY or JACKASS.

> The Republicans are thinking of changing the Republican Party emblem from an elephant to a condom, because it stands for INFLATION, halts production and gives a false sense of security while one is being screwed.
> JOSEPH ROSENBERGER, 1974

elephant on the doorstep The slightly baffling description given by the Labour Welsh Secretary John Morris of the principality's decisive 'No' to DEVOLUTION in the 1979 referendum. He said:

> If you find an elephant on the doorstep, you know what it is.

rogue elephant A politican who bucks party discipline, setting off on campaigns that are frequently destructive of their own side's prospects.

Elf Aquitaine scandal The most spectacular example of graft and corruption in high circles in France under the presidency of François MITTERRAND. The state-owned oil company, under the chairmanship of Loik Le Floch Prigent, paid out bribes and kickbacks on a lavish scale. Between 1989 and 1993, for instance, it paid £6.45 million to Christine Deviers-Joncour, self-styled **'whore of the Republic'** and mistress of the then Foreign Minister Roland Dumas who had found her the sinecure. Dumas was the ultimate recipient of much of the largesse, which the company hoped would, *inter alia,* influence the French government to reverse its policy and sell six frigates built by Thomson, another state-owned company, to Taiwan. Exposure of the payments forced Dumas to resign in 2000 as chairman of France's prestigious Constitutional Council and led to his receiving a prison sentence for receiving bribes. His conviction was reversed on appeal in January 2003, but that November several former Elf executives were jailed.

Elian Elian Gonzalez, a 6-year-old Cuban boy, whose plight split American public opinion in 2000. Elian's divorced mother escaped with him from Cuba in a boat which sank on the coast of Florida, drowning her. He was taken in by relatives in Miami, who demanded that he be allowed to stay in the United States. His father demanded his return and after several months of legal and political argument, the CLINTON administration decided in the face of bitter protests from Cuban exiles in Miami that he should go back. Months later, a few hundred votes in Florida decided the Presidential election against Clinton's Vice President Al GORE.

elder statesman *See* STATESMAN.

élitists Those who believe that a small and carefully-selected group of people should be alone entitled to participate in government or decision-making, and consider themselves among that number.

> A very inbred group of very rich people who go around telling everybody else what to do and how to suffer.
>
> New York Mayor ED KOCH

Ellipse The oval, grassed area due South of the WHITE HOUSE and separated from its gardens by E Street. In 1978 it was the scene of a riot by Iranian students protesting at an official visit by the Shah; teargas emitted in clashes with the police overcame the crowd – including the author – who were attending the WELCOMING CEREMONY on the White House lawn.

Ellis. Ellis Island The gateway to America for millions of immigrants from Europe, and hence a symbol for the welcome they received in the New World. The island in Upper New York Bay was America's main immigration station from 1892 to1943, and was then used until 1954 as a detention centre for illegal aliens. The Statue of Liberty close by with its high-minded motto 'GIVE ME YOUR TIRED, YOUR POOR, YOUR HUDDLED MASSES' contrasted with the impersonal procedures of its at times brutal staff. It is now part of the Statue of Liberty National Monument.

Ruth Ellis case The final instance of a woman being hanged in the UK, the accompanying controversy and revulsion playing a major part in the eventual abolition of the death penalty. Ruth Ellis was sentenced to death for shooting her lover, who was having an affair with another woman; she had recently suffered a miscarriage. The HOME SECRETARY, Gwilym Lloyd George, refused to exercise the ROYAL PREROGATIVE of mercy and reprieve her, despite immense political pressure, and she was hanged at Holloway prison on 13 July 1955. Efforts to have her conviction quashed posthumously failed in December 2003 when the Court of Appeal upheld her conviction.

Élysée. Élysée Palace The official residence and seat of power in the heart of Paris of the President of France.

Élysée Treaty The agreement between President DE GAULLE and the West German Chancellor Konrad Adenauer in 1963 which formalised the close Franco-German co-operation that would steer the European Community for the rest of the century.

emancipation The grant or restoration of CIVIL RIGHTS to groups who have been excluded from a full stake in society, often through some form of servitude. From the Latin *ex*, out of; *manceps*, one who holds property.

emancipation of the serfs The ending of the feudal system in tsarist Russia, though not the plight of its peasantry. Under a ukase of Alexander II published in 1861, 23 million serfs were released from their obligations in March 1863. If this move might appear long overdue, note the date immediately below.

Emancipation Proclamation The proclamation read by President LINCOLN to his Cabinet on 22 July 1862, and signed formally on 1 January 1863, which declared freedom to slaves in all rebel states. He told them:

> I have got you together to hear what I have written down. I do not wish to have your advice about the main matter – that I have determined for myself.

The proclamation freed few slaves – the rights of slaveowners in loyal states were confirmed, and the emancipation of slaves in the South could not be enforced. But it effectively turned the UNION cause into that of ABOLITIONISM, rallying Northern support for the CIVIL WAR, and had an immense international impact, stemming pressure in Europe to recognise the CONFEDERACY. On the advice of Secretary of State William Seward, Lincoln delayed the proclamation until after the battle of Antietam, so that it could appear a sign of strength, not of desperation.

> An arbitrary and despotic measure in the cause of freedom. GIDEON WELLES (1802–78)

Catholic emancipation One of the burning issues of early 19th-century British politics, as tentative steps were taken to end the centuries-old ban on Roman Catholics in English public life and grant basic religious rights to the majority in Ireland. BY-ELECTION victories in Ireland for Catholics who would not take the Anglican oath, and an energetic campaign by Canning, paved the way for reform; the critical legislation was passed in 1829 after Wellington had prevailed on George IV to lift his veto on the CABINET discussing the issue.

> Under a pure despotism a people may be contented, because all are slaves alike; but those who, under a free government, are refused equal participation, must be discontented.
> PALMERSTON

embargo (1) An arrangement under which a public body supplies the media with information, subject to the requirement that it is not published or broadcast before a certain time. (2) A prohibition on trade (or certain types of trade) with a country held to have committed a hostile or repugnant act. Originally a Spanish term for a ban on shipping between two countries, it has come to apply to an officially-imposed restriction on any form of trade. The grain embargoes on the Soviet Union imposed by Presidents FORD and CARTER lost both men critical votes among mid-Western farmers – especially Carter who prior to the Soviet invasion of Afghanistan in 1979 had promised never to take such action.

Great Embargo The embargo on all trade between the United States and Europe, passed by CONGRESS in December 1807. Promoted by JEFFERSON as an alternative to all-out war with Britain, which had been harassing US shipping and press-ganging its sailors, the embargo aimed at starving both Britain and France into respecting America's trading rights. As with later embargoes, however, its main effect was on American grain farmers and merchants. The embargo became a major issue in the 1808 election but MADISON, who backed it, was elected anyway; three days before leaving office, Jefferson repealed the Act.

> Our ships all in motion once whitened the ocean;
> They sailed and returned with a cargo.
> Now doomed to decay they are fallen a prey
> To Jefferson, worms and embargo.
> New Hampshire Federalist song

embassy (1) The working building housing the AMBASSADOR of one country and their staff in the capital of another. The Ambassador generally lives in a separate **residence**. (2) A term from the earlier days of DIPLOMACY for a mission despatched by one government to negotiate with another.

Light up an Embassy A 1960s UK cigarette advertisement, which became a slogan for far-left and revolutionary groups.

emergence The term used up to the 1960s to describe the process by which the leader of Britain's CONSERVATIVE PARTY was chosen. *See* MAGIC CIRCLE.

emergency. Emergency Banking Act One of the first measures pushed through CONGRESS by Franklin D. ROOSEVELT on taking office in 1933. FDR immediately ordered closure of America's banks, and kept them closed for five days while legislation based on plans prepared by the HOOVER administration was enacted. It gave explicit FEDERAL backing to banks found to be solvent, and prevented the weakest from reopening; the federal government took on powers to regulate the entire banking system.

emergency debate A debate in a legislature which takes priority over business on the calendar because of its urgency. In Britain's HOUSE OF COMMONS, an application for such a debate is made to the SPEAKER under Standing Order 24 (formerly Standing Order 20, before that S.O.9); such applications are rarely granted, but they give the member making the application a chance to state the case briefly on the FLOOR of the House.

emergency financing The process used to keep the US government functioning when – as frequently happens in the fall – CONGRESS has failed to pass a BUDGET BILL containing APPROPRIATIONS for the continued payment of federal employees. The process was not robust enough to avert the BUDGET SHUTDOWNS of 1995/96.

emergency powers Powers taken by a government, with the backing of legislation, to keep services running and maintain order during a period of unrest.

Emergency Provisions The regulations under which Britain has conducted DIRECT RULE in NORTHERN IRELAND and the security and legal system created from 1969 to combat TERRORISM. Much of the framework has survived the GOOD FRIDAY AGREEMENT, though many powers are now held in reserve.

state of emergency The condition declared by a government, usually without the need for legislation, to enable it to tackle a natural disaster, damaging industrial dispute or outbreak of violence. Generally it involves drafting in the military to do tasks normally done by civilians, and abridging individual property rights in order to maintain services and public order.

Emily's List A movement begun in the United States to secure the election of more women to political office; the name is an anagram of 'Early Money Is Like Yeast', and one purpose was to provide finance in the early stages of women candidates' campaigns. The British version, of women within the LABOUR PARTY, was founded in 1993; a number of its members won seats at the 1997 general election (*see* BLAIR'S BABES) after the party's candidate selection processes were changed to permit all-women shortlists. Women sponsored by Emily's List receive grants toward the cost of producing a CV, getting training, travelling to and from selection meetings and providing childcare.

Eminent Persons' Group A small group of international statesmen who explore the scope for settlement of an apparently intractable problem. The first such was the seven-strong COMMONWEALTH group, headed by the former Australian Prime Minister Malcolm Fraser and Nigeria's former President Gen. Olusegun Obasanjo, set up to advance political reform in South Africa as pressure for an end to APARTHEID peaked in the 1980s. It was decided on at the Nassau CHOGM in 1985, and visited South Africa the following year. Mainly concerned with the political situation, it gained a cool reception from the country's white government and its report urged a stiffening of SANCTIONS; the 1987 Vancouver CHOGM agreed to these, with Margaret THATCHER dissenting. The group's mission and the policy it represented are given some credit for the subsequent abandonment of apartheid.

emperor or **empress** A sovereign who reigns over a number of diverse nations that are styled an EMPIRE; a king or queen normally reigns over a single nation or ethnic group, though France's Emperors Napoleon I and III held an essentially domestic title. From 1877 until India's independence 70 years later, the British monarch held this style in respect of their sway over the sub-continent.

empire The territory under the rule of an emperor or empress.

Empire Free Trade An unsuccessful campaign (1929–31) to establish FREE TRADE throughout the BRITISH EMPIRE (*see below*). The crusade was launched in their newspapers by the PRESS BARONS Beaverbrook and Rothermere, who founded a (completely unsuccessful) United Empire Party to gain a Parliamentary platform. The campaign foundered on the reluctance of the DOMINIONS to grant free entry to British goods, and collapsed with the onset of the GREAT DEPRESSION.

Empire Loyalists Devotees of the ideals of the British Empire who remained committed to them despite the Empire's transformation into the multicultural COMMONWEALTH. In Britain the League of Empire Loyalists was a right-wing group that launched vitriolic attacks on Conservative governments in the late 1950s for abandoning Britain's COLONIES. In Canada the United Empire Loyalists are a respectable group who uphold the interests of English-speaking Canada and its ties with the Crown.

Austro-Hungarian Empire The empire ruled by the Habsburg dynasty that covered much of middle Europe until Austria's defeat in WORLD WAR I. It covered not just the lands of the Dual MONARCHY but Bohemia, Slovakia, Croatia, Slovenia and parts of present-day Poland and Romania. Lombardy and Venetia were given up in 1859 and 1866, but gains were made in the Balkans as the Ottoman Empire faded; the annexation of Bosnia in 1908 indirectly caused WORLD WAR I (*see* SARAJEVO). The empire was held together from 1848 to 1917 by Emperor Franz Josef, but the following year the defeat of Austria and its German ally paved the way for its dismemberment and its transformation into NATION STATES. The publication of WILSON'S FOURTEEN POINTS was its death-knell; the last emperor, Karl, ABDICATED on 11 November 1918. The dynasty survives: *see* WHO ARE WE PLAYING.

British Empire The empire, arguably the greatest the world has ever seen, which formally came into being on 1 January 1877, when Queen Victoria was proclaimed Empress of India, and gave way to the COMMONWEALTH in December 1958. The title stemmed from Britain's upgraded role in India, a device adopted by DISRAELI to play a supreme compliment to his Queen. CAMPBELL-BANNERMAN objected: 'We cannot add to the lustre and dignity of the Crown of this realm, the most ancient and august in Europe, by tricking it out in a brand new title.' But the ethos of Empire spurred Britain, and its rivals, to consolidate Imperial possessions around the world. Joseph Chamberlain, the high priest of IMPERIALISM, proclaimed in 1904: 'The day of small nations has long passed away. The day of Empire has come.' On another occasion he asked: 'England without an Empire? Can you conceive it?' To Imperialists the Empire was wholly a force for good: a means of mutual security and economic development as well as the supreme expression of British power. Lord Curzon, VICEROY of India (1859–1925), declared: 'There has never been anything so great in the world's history as the British Empire, so great an instrument for the good of humanity.' Canada's Prime Minister Alexander Mackenzie (1822–92) said: 'I am anxious that its glory should be unsullied, that the power should never be abridged and that the English supremacy shall last until the end of time, because it means universal freedom, universal liberty, emancipation from everything degrading.' Australia's Prime Minister William Hughes (1864–1952) reckoned that 'without the Empire we shall be tossed like a cork in the cross-current of world politics. It is at once our sword and our shield.' And in 1927 the future King George VI, opening Australia's first Canberra Parliament, stated:

> The British Empire has advanced to a new conception of autonomy and freedom, to the idea of a system of British nations bound together in unity by allegiance to the Crown, and co-operating in all that concerns the commonweal.

Yet there were always critical voices, and as Britain's power began to ebb they became stronger; Jayaprakash Narayan (1902–79), a founder of India's CONGRESS PARTY, asserted that 'lies are one of the central pillars of the British Empire'.

Apart from the PARTITION of Ireland, the granting of Indian independence in 1947 was the first sign that the Empire would not endure. In 1930 CHURCHILL had claimed:

> The loss of India would mark and consummate the downfall of the British Empire. From such a catastrophe there would be no recovery.

As the break-up accelerated, South Africa's hardline premier Albert Herzog blamed Western decadence, saying: 'The vast British Empire built up over hundreds of years has been reduced to ruins largely through the influence of television.' But as it neared its end, Lord Harlech (1918–85) suggested:

> In the end it may well be that Britain will be honoured by the historians more for the way she disposed of her empire than for the way in which she acquired it.

empire on which the sun never sets, the The archetypal slogan of the late Victorian IMPERIALISTS, which in fact originated before the true days of empire, reflecting the presence of British territories right round the globe. Christopher North (John Wilson, 1785–1854), the Scots poet and essayist, wrote in 1829 in his *Noctes Ambrosianae* of 'His Majesty's dominions, on which the sun never sets'. The expression had been used centuries before of the Spaniards, Captain John Smith writing in 1631: 'Why should the brave Spanish soldier brag the sun never sets in the Spanish dominions?' Its use has outlasted the British Empire, an IRA placard against Prince Charles's 1981 visit to New York reading:

> The sun never sets on the British Empire because God doesn't trust the Brits in the dark.

Empire Strikes Back, The Title of the highly-successful sequel to the 1977 space adventure film *Star Wars,* taken up by *Newsweek* in 1982 as its cover headline when Britain despatched its naval TASK FORCE to recover the FALKLANDS.

evil empire The epithet bestowed upon the SOVIET UNION by Ronald REAGAN in a speech to Evangelical church leaders in March 1983; he also categorised the Soviet state as 'the focus of evil in the modern world' (*compare* George W. BUSH's AXIS OF EVIL). Despite his subsequent 'bomb Russia' gaffe (*see* OPEN MIKE), Reagan reversed his position during his second term in SUMMIT contacts with Mikhail GORBACHEV as the COLD WAR neared its close.

How is the Empire? The supposed last words of King George V as he lay dying in 1936. A more plausible tale is that when the King's doctor told him he would soon be well enough to convalesce at Bognor Regis, he exclaimed: '**Bugger Bognor!**' and died.

lost an empire and not yet found a role

The comment about Britain made on 6 December 1962 by the former US SECRETARY OF STATE Dean Acheson (1893–1971), which enraged Fleet Street and some UK politicians. Acheson, by no means an Anglophobe, made his assertion that Britain was 'just about played out' at the time of that country's greatest uncertainty over where in the world its future lay – and only weeks before DE GAULLE delivered his first NON to Britain's membership of the COMMON MARKET.

empowerment Political action to give the poor and socially excluded a greater say in their own lives and greater individual power within society, a concept now paid lip service to by most political parties. First used in the 1960s by BLACK POWER activists, the term caught on in the late 1980s among conservatives who saw it as enabling the disadvantaged to break out of the straitjacket of public housing and education and dependency on welfare and or public sector jobs; in this respect it is a development of the Victorian doctrine of **self-help**.

empty chair *See* CHAIR.

EMS European Monetary System. The system for stabilising European currencies in the medium term which preceded the introduction of the EURO. Devised by Roy JENKINS when President of the European Commission and adopted at the 1978 Copenhagen summit, the EMS comprised a European Monetary Co-Operation Fund, to which all EC members belonged, and an Exchange Rate Mechanism (ERM) which Britain belatedly joined in October 1990 (*see* MADRID CONDITIONS) only to leave on BLACK WEDNESDAY in September 1992. Countries joining the euro since its inception still have to sign up to a variant of EMS as a transitional measure.

Ems telegram The calculated insult to France with which Bismarck engineered the start of the FRANCO-PRUSSIAN WAR. It arose from the CORTES's choice of the Prussian Prince Leopold of Hohenzollern to fill the vacant Spanish throne. France threatened war unless the candidature was withdrawn and the prince, to Bismarck's disappointment, backed down. Then the French Foreign Minister Gramont sent an emissary, Count Benedetti, to get confirmation of the withdrawal from King William of Prussia at Ems. The King said he understood Prince Leopold had withdrawn, but refused to elaborate; he then telegraphed an account of the meeting to Bismarck. The IRON CHANCELLOR issued the telegram to the Press with a gloss making it appear Benedetti had insulted the King, and had been sharply rebuffed. On 14 July 1870 the telegram was published; the French realised they had been tricked, but with the Parisian crowd chanting 'À Berlin!', had no alternative but to go to war – and a humiliating defeat.

EMU European Monetary Union. One of the two main goals of the MAASTRICHT TREATY, largely achieved at the start of 2002 – five years behind schedule – with the introduction of the euro by all but three of the then fifteen members of the EU. Political union was the other aim; the EUROPEAN CONSTITUTION has been the greatest manifestation of movement in this direction.

ENA (Fr. *École Nationale d'Administration*, National School of Administration) The technocratic forcing-house which produces France's governing CADRE of future ministers and senior civil servants and imbues them with the basics of the self-interested policy pursued by all French governments. It was founded by General DE GAULLE in 1945 to extirpate the spinelessness shown by the VICHY bureaucracy in COLLABORATING with NAZI Germany.

Enabling Act A piece of legislation passed by a democratically-elected legislature which gives those in power the authority to take sweeping action without further, specific, approval. HITLER used this device to seize control of the key organs of the German state after coming to power in the WEIMAR REPUBLIC by more or less democratic means. TROTSKYIST groups in Britain have argued that a Labour government elected on a DEMOCRATIC SOCIALIST platform should pass an Enabling Act to set up a Marxist state.

enabling state The phrase used from the late 1980s to describe a structure in which the state has the power and the duty to help its citizens fulfil their potential, rather than to leave them exposed to market forces or determine everything for them. One of its main exponents was Paddy (now Lord) Ashdown (1941–) (*see* PADDY PANTSDOWN) as leader of the Liberal Democrats.

endorsement A public declaration of support for a CANDIDATE running for office, given by an influential political figure, a labour union or some other interest which believes such support will strengthen the candidate's chances. A **third-party**

endorsement is one solicited by a campaign from a prominent figure who would not necessarily be seen as a supporter, in order to demonstrate the breadth of its appeal.

> I well remember my first campaign. My opponent called me a cream puff. That's what he said. Well, I rushed out and got the bakers' union to endorse me. Sen. CLAIBORNE PELL (1918–)

enemies Every politician has enemies, but their attitudes toward them differ from Abraham LINCOLN's (attributed) 'I am going to destroy them. I am going to make them my friends' to the 19th-century Spanish general Ramon Maria Narvaes, who said on his deathbed: 'I do not have to forgive my enemies. I have had them all shot.' Robert F. KENNEDY's watchword was 'always forgive your enemies – but never forget their names', while Gov. Richard Lamm of Colorado said philosophically: 'I have no permanent enemies – only people I still have to persuade,' and Steve Bell, a Congressional aide, warned: 'When you dig a grave for your enemy, dig two – one for yourself.' Mao Tse-Tung (*see* CHAIRMAN MAO), drawing on his experience of GUERRILLA war, wrote: 'You must despise your enemy strategically, but respect him tactically'; he also declared: 'We should support whatever the enemy opposes and oppose whatever the enemy supports.' Speaker Joe Cannon warned: 'Never attempt to buy the favour of your enemies at the expense of your friends', and the TEAMSTERS' leader Jimmy Hoffa gave as his philosophy: 'You keep your door open to your enemies. You know all about your friends.'

> I have no enemies. Why should I fear?
> President McKINLEY, days before his assassination in 1900

> If you want to make enemies, try to change something. WOODROW WILSON

enemies list A list of President NIXON's perceived adversaries drawn up in 1971, the year before WATERGATE, after WHITE HOUSE counsel John Dean had circulated a memo suggesting ways 'we can use the available Federal machinery to screw our political enemies'. Tactics included harassment of Nixon's critics by the Internal Revenue Service. The list included Carol Channing, Bill Cosby, Jane Fonda, Paul Newman, Tony Randall, CBS correspondent Daniel Schorr and the black Rep. John Conyers of Michigan, against whom was written: 'Has known weakness for white females.'

enemy within, the The phrase used by Margaret THATCHER to charge Arthur Scargill's striking mineworkers (*see* KING ARTHUR, MINERS' STRIKE) with attempting to destroy British society. Speaking at a private meeting with Conservative MPs on 19 July 1984, she said that Argentina's General Galtieri had been the enemy without during the FALKLANDS conflict, and the striking miners and dockers now constituted the enemy within. The phrase had been used by the *Economist* some months before in almost the same context; Mrs Thatcher was accused by Labour MPs of questioning the miners' patriotism.

naked to mine enemies The Shakespearean phrase used during the WATERGATE investigation by Sen. Sam Ervin, when he told Herbert Porter, who eventually served 27 days in jail for lying to the FBI:

> Had I not served God with half the zeal
> I served my King, he would not in mine age
> Have left me naked to mine enemies.

Shakespeare, in *Henry VIII*, put the words into Cardinal Wolsey's mouth, having him say them to his assistant Thomas Cromwell.

our enemies are innovative and resourceful . . . Probably the worst of all the clangers dropped by George W. BUSH, and made at the worst possible time for him. A week after John KERRY's euphoric nomination as Democratic challenger for the WHITE HOUSE, with Republican strategists eager for Bush to recover the initiative on security and terrorism, the President declared at the signing ceremony for a Defense Bill:

> Our enemies are innovative and resourceful, and so are we. They never stop thinking about new ways to harm our country . . . and neither do we.

own worst enemy During Britain's 1945–51 Labour government, an MP in the Commons TEA ROOM is said to have remarked of Aneurin BEVAN: 'NYE's his own worst enemy', only for Ernest BEVIN to break in: 'Not while I'm alive, he ain't.' The retort, if uttered, was not original; Sen. Walter George declared: 'Roosevelt is his own worst enemy'; South Carolina's 'Cotton Ed' Smith replied: 'Not so long as I am alive!'

We love him most for the enemies he has made The slogan coined by General Edward Bragg of Wisconsin when he NOMINATED Grover CLEVELAND for the Presidency at the 1884 Republican CONVENTION; it referred to his independence of TAMMANY HALL, and his readiness to fight corruption. Supporters of Franklin D. ROOSEVELT resurrected it in 1936 to show their contempt for opponents of his NEW DEAL.

Your enemies are behind you *See* ADVERSARY.

enforcer The inelegant term used in the early days of Tony BLAIR's government to describe a senior CABINET Minister who would ensure that commitments were met and problems solved. It was used specifically of Jack Cunningham (1939–), who was appointed to the role in July 1998. Under fire already for his extravagant refurbishment of his office as Minister of Agriculture, he lasted only a year.

England. The kingdom united under Alfred of Wessex in the late 9th century, which became the major and dominant part of the UNITED KINGDOM after conquering Wales in the 13th century, gaining uneasy control over Ireland and uniting with Scotland in 1707. The name is used carelessly by some (though never by Scots) for the entire nation, as in PITT THE YOUNGER's 'England has saved herself by her exertions, and will, as I trust, save Europe by her example' and Napoleon's 'England is a nation of shopkeepers'.

Speak for England! *See* SPEAK.

Young England *See* YOUNG.

English disease The term adopted in Continental Europe in the early 1960s for Britain's unique mixture of poor economic performance and suicidally militant trade unionism. Use of the expression spread worldwide, but subsided in the 1980s as the THATCHER government sorted out the unions and national confidence returned. It had first been used by the French c. 1500 – to describe syphilis.

engrossment In the US CONGRESS, the process of preparing a copy of a BILL in the precise form in which it has been passed by the HOUSE. The task is carried out by the Enrolling Clerk who receives all relevant papers, some of them often in longhand, and prepares a comprehensive version including all the AMENDMENTS carried. The engrossed Bill is printed on blue paper, at which point it becomes an ACT of the House, and a certificate that it has been passed is signed by the Clerk of the House. A reading clerk delivers it to the SENATE, where it is received in a convoluted ceremony in which it is recognised by the PRESIDING OFFICER.

enhanced co-operation. In the EUROPEAN UNION, a procedure for closer joint working by member governments stopping short of bringing the activity in question within the mechanisms of the EU itself.

enlargement The expansion of the EUROPEAN UNION to embrace new members, and the process of bringing it about, involving adjustments to the *modus operandi* of existing members, new members and the institutions of the EU itself. This has been gone through several times since six nations formed the original COMMON MARKET, most notably prior to 1 May 2004 when the then fifteen members of the EU were joined by ten more: Cyprus, the Czech Republic, Estonia, Hungary, Latvia, Lithuania, Malta, Poland, Slovakia and Slovenia. Further candidates are Bulgaria, Croatia, Romania and Turkey.

> It would not be in the interests of the European Community that its enlargement should take place except with the full-hearted consent of the Parliament and people of the new member countries. EDWARD HEATH, 1970

Enoch factor The electoral pull exercised by Enoch POWELL in the February 1974 general election, when he stood down as a Conservative MP and urged his supporters to vote Labour in protest at the HEATH government's taking Britain into Europe. Three days before the poll, Powell told a meeting at Shipley:

> I was born a Tory, am a Tory and shall die a Tory . . . I never heard that it was any part of the faith of a Tory to take the institutions and liberties, the laws and customs which his country has evolved over centuries and merge them with those of eight other nations into a new-made artificial state.

The resulting electoral shift, notably in Powell's native West Midlands, was one factor in the Tories' narrow defeat. That October he stood and was elected as an ULSTER UNIONIST; the Enoch factor, though less pronounced, contributed to Labour achieving a small overall majority.

Enosis (Gr. union) The political union of Cyprus with Greece, the goal of most Greek Cypriots (*see* EOKA) in the 1950s prior to independence from Britain. Archbishop Makarios, later President of Cyprus, was exiled to the Seychelles for supporting Enosis; ironically the 1974 coup backed by the Greek COLONELS which came close to overthrowing him was intended to achieve it.

Enron scandal The collapse of the giant US energy trading corporation at the end of 2001 amid allegations of fraudulent trading and accounting, which brought down with it the global accountancy practice Arthur Andersen, one of whose partners admitted shredding large numbers of documents to prevent their falling into the hands of Federal investigators. Enron had close links to the administration of George W. BUSH, who like the company had his roots in Houston, and Vice President Richard Cheney mounted an abortive rearguard action to prevent his own dealings with Enron from being made public. The scandal's first political casualty was in Britain: Lord Wakeham, who had been Energy Secretary in Margaret THATCHER's government and had served on Enron's remuneration committee and advised the company on public relations. Forced to resign as head of the UK Press Complaints Commission, though he continued to draw his salary for a time, Wakeham and other non-executives were condemned by a Senate committee in July 2002 for lack of diligence. Kenneth Lay, Enron's president, and its CEO, Jeff Skilling, were indicted in 2004 on charges of mail and securities fraud and giving false information.

> Enron robbed the bank. Andersen drove the getaway car. And they say that you were at the wheel.
>
> Rep. JIM GREENWOOD, House Energy Committee, to David Duncan of Arthur Andersen during hearings into the collapse of Enron, March 2002

> Companies come and go. It's part of the genius of capitalism.
>
> US Treasury Secretary PAUL O'BRIEN

entente. Entente Cordiale (Fr. cordial understanding) The agreement between Britain and France, reached in April 1904 and sealed by Edward VII's visit to Paris in 1906, which revolutionised relations between the two neighbours and the diplomacy of Europe. It repaired the damage between them over FASHODA and paved the way for their alliance in WORLD WAR I. It was set up in 1902 by the French Premier Delcasse, who found a willing listener in Colonial Secretary Joseph Chamberlain whose contacts with Germany had broken down. The entente was one of the lasting achievements of BALFOUR's government; though its conclusion was later said by critics to have made war with Germany inevitable, France was at times to doubt Britain's will to turn it into a full-blooded alliance. The term had first been used by King Louis-Philippe in 1845, when he spoke to the French Parliament of

> The sincere friendship which unites me to the Queen of Britain and the cordial understanding which exists between my government and hers.

Franco-German entente The close relationship, through joint leadership of the European Community, which the West German Chancellor Konrad Adenauer (1876–1967) developed with France in the 1950s to heal the wounds of WORLD WAR II. Chancellor from 1949, Adenauer cemented the entente during the five years (1958–63) when he and DE GAULLE led their respective countries (*see* ÉLYSÉE TREATY).

Triple Entente The informal agreement between Britain, France and Russia to seek means of settling their outstanding COLONIAL differences. It was based on the ENTENTE CORDIALE, which had settled Anglo-French differences in Egypt and Africa, and the Anglo-Russian agreement of 1907 over Persia, Tibet and Afghanistan. The Triple Entente became a military pact in 1914, forming the nucleus of the Allied powers in WORLD WAR I.

enterprise A watchword of conservatives and (economic) liberals, the force which they believe will flourish in the free MARKET and which they are equally convinced will be stifled by any form of government intervention. To make the point more forcefully, they often refer to it as FREE ENTERPRISE.

> We must beware of trying to build a society in which nobody counts for anything except a politician or an official, a society where enterprise gains no rewards and thrift no privilege.
>
> CHURCHILL, 1943

> If enterprise is afoot, wealth accumulates whatever may be happening to thrift; and if enterprise is asleep, wealth decays, whatever thrift may be doing.
>
> JOHN MAYNARD KEYNES, *General Theory of Employment*

enterprise culture The society which free-marketeers aim to create, with anyone capable of creating wealth knowing that the climate exists for them to do so. The term caught on in the 1980s as Margaret THATCHER and Ronald REAGAN sought to break free of the COLLECTIVIST attitudes of the previous four decades.

entitlements In US politics, the categories of government spending – some 40% of the whole – which go in social security and other payments to whoever is qualified to receive them. The other categories are defence, interest on the NATIONAL DEBT, and the basic operation of government (stretching out to education, housing, mass transit and the environment).

entrenched provisions or **powers** Functions bestowed, usually on another elected body, by one piece of legislation and which cannot be taken away by another. The granting of entrenched powers is held by critics to violate the doctrine that one Parliament or Congress cannot bind its successors. The argument was foreseen by JEFFERSON in a letter to James MADISON on 6 September 1789:

> The question – whether one generation of men has the right to bind another – seems never to have started either on this (France) or on our own side of the water. I set out on this ground 'that the earth belongs in usufruct to the living, that the dead have neither powers nor rights over it.

It was widely raised during the early arguments over DEVOLUTION, with its opponents objecting to the creation of an elected body with powers that could not be taken away later by WESTMINSTER. Although the repeal of the SCOTLAND ACT and WALES ACT is theoretically possible, it is in practice inconceivable.

entryism The process by which members of a political movement committed to one set of aims instal themselves as members of a larger party devoted to different purposes, and then subvert it. The technique was perfected by the MILITANT TENDENCY, who for two decades from the mid-1960s infiltrated Britain's LABOUR PARTY and through it secured the election of TROTSKYIST councillors and MPs. *See* UNDERHILL REPORT.

environmentalism The political force which has grown most in the West since the late 1960s, giving rise to the GREEN movement, and to greater concern for the need to care for the planet among most other political parties. The issue was recognised on both sides of the Atlantic in 1970 when President NIXON set up the Environmental Protection Agency (EPA), and Edward HEATH a Department of the Environment – though this took little interest in 'green' issues at first. Resistance to concerns over the environment goes back a century to when Speaker Joe Cannon said:

> Not one cent for scenery.

James Watt, Ronald REAGAN's Secretary of the Interior, concurred, once saying:

> America's lands may be ravaged as a result of the actions of the environmentalists.

Rep. Morris Udall retaliated that Watt and EPA administrator Anne Burford had

> Done for the environment what Bonnie and Clyde did for the banks.

See also Friends of the EARTH; GREENPEACE; SIERRA CLUB.

EOKA (Gr. *Ethniki Organisos Kipriakou Agonos,* National Organisation of Cypriot Struggle) The movement founded in 1955 to pursue the political goal of ENOSIS. Led by George Grivas (codename Digenis) and supported up to a point by Archbishop Makarios, it conducted a GUERRILLA campaign against the occupying British forces. It disbanded on independence in 1959, but was re-formed in 1971. Its impact has been minimal since the failure in 1974 of a pro-Enosis coup backed by the Greek COLONELS, but the hanging of EOKA members in 1957 remains a sore point with Greek Cypriots.

EPIC plan End Poverty in California. The campaign for ending the hardship of the GREAT DEPRESSION through widespread state enterprise on which the formerly socialist author Upton Sinclair (1878–1968) sought and won the Democratic nomination for governor in 1934. The radical nature of his campaign, backed by his bestselling book *I, Governor*, and its runaway success galvanised business, the Hearst press and the Republican Party, who spent $10 million to ensure Sinclair's defeat. Despite a hysterical campaign against him, Sinclair polled 37% of the vote, and his running-mate Sheridan Downey was elected to the US SENATE in 1938.

equal. equal opportunity The regime under which a government or other body makes a conscious effort to assist ethnic or other groups it believes need encouragement to catch up. It applies particularly to recruitment policy, with an **equal opportunity employer** making special efforts to attract women, members of ethnic minorities or the disabled to a workforce in which they are under-represented. It is arguable whether such an approach gives a positive edge to applicants from such groups; AFFIRMATIVE ACTION unquestionably does.

> There are many things in life that are not fair, that wealthy people can afford and poor people can't. But I don't believe that the Federal Government should take action to try to make these opportunities exactly equal, particularly when there is a moral factor involved.
>
> President CARTER on the funding of abortions for the poor, 12 July 1977

equal pay The principle under which women receive the same pay as men for doing the same work; established in America for decades and in Britain since Labour's 1975 Equal Pay Act, it is nevertheless widely flouted by employers.

Equal Rights Amendment *See* ERA.

equal time The principle that each side in a political argument should receive equal exposure on radio or television to put their case. It is built into broadcasting standards on both sides of the Atlantic, though less so in America, where the ability of candidates to buy advertising time weakens its effect. In Britain the REPRESENTATION OF THE PEOPLE ACTS impose rigid controls. *See also* FAIRNESS DOCTRINE; Ministerial BROADCAST; PARTY POLITICAL BROADCAST.

All men are created equal One of the axioms of American democracy, set out by JEFFERSON in the second paragraph of the DECLARATION OF INDEPENDENCE. It took the SUPREME COURT well over a century to construe the words as meaning that black Americans were as entitled to the same fundamental rights as whites. The phrase has its variants: the revolutionaries in George Orwell's ANIMAL FARM put forward the slogan '**All animals are equal – but some animals are more equal than others**', and Lord Mancroft (1917–87) wrote:

> All men are born equal, but quite a few get over it.

There will never be complete equality until women themselves help to make laws and elect lawmakers The rallying-cry of the American suffragist Susan B. ANTHONY, written in 1897.

The idea of equality should now be regarded as out of date, since it leads only to confusion and hampers a precise examination of the problem The definitive MARXIST explanation of how 'SCIENTIFIC SOCIALISM' differs from classic LIBERALISM, delivered by Engels in a letter to August Bebel on 28 March 1875.

Equality State The nickname earned by Wyoming because of its pioneering adoption of women's SUFFRAGE. It granted women the vote in 1869, even before being given STATEHOOD, and elected the first woman governor.

equidistance The initial stance of Britain's LIBERAL DEMOCRATS toward Britain's two main parties, positioning themselves midway between the Conservatives and Labour instead of veering toward the left. It was abandoned by 1995, as the unpopularity of John MAJOR's Conservative government made it hard to sustain.

ERA Equal Rights Amendment. The amendment to the US CONSTITUTION, championed most forcefully by the women's movement in the 1970s, which was designed to give women explicit protection from discrimination. It stated:

> Equality of rights under the law shall not be denied or abridged by the United States or by any state on account of sex.

First proposed in 1923, it was passed by CONGRESS in 1972 but lapsed in 1982, having fallen three short of the 38 States needed to RATIFY it. Its opponents, headed by Phyllis Schafly and backed by the religious RIGHT, argued that it ignored the biological differences between the sexes, would harm the institutions of marriage and the family, and was redundant because of protection already offered by the FIFTH and FOURTEENTH AMENDMENTS.

> The Equal Rights Amendment is a must.
>
> BETTY FORD, 1975

> It is about a socialist, anti-family political movement that encourages women to leave their husbands, kill their children, practice witchcraft, destroy capitalism, and become lesbians.
>
> PAT ROBERTSON, 1992

Era of good feelings The name given to James MONROE's two Presidential terms, from 1817 to 1825, partly because of the eclipse of the two-party system; when he ran for re-election in 1820, he did not even need to be nominated and only one vote was cast against him in the ELECTORAL COLLEGE. The phrase was coined early in Monroe's administration when he made a goodwill visit to Boston; his popularity later waned, particularly in New England which fell on hard times, but the memory of 'good feelings' lingered.

ERM Exchange Rate Mechanism. The central structure of the European Monetary System (EMS), in which governments prior to the launch of the EURO or, now, within two years of adopting it have undertaken to keep the value of their currencies within set limits of fluctuation: originally 2.25% from parity (the narrow band) for the most committed states and 6% in a looser broad band, and 15% from 1993 when the system proved impractically tight. If a currency reached the lower or upper limit, other members have had to restrain or support it; if that failed, the country in question had to adjust interest rates. If more drastic action were needed, a member state could agree a REALIGNMENT; the alternative was withdrawal from the ERM for revaluation or DEVALUATION. Britain took the latter course on BLACK WEDNESDAY, 17 September 1992, when the pound crashed through the floor of the ERM despite two rate rises totalling 5%.

Margaret THATCHER's government, with John MAJOR as CHANCELLOR, had joined the ERM in October 1980 despite warnings from her economic adviser Alan Walters that the system was 'half-baked'. Inflation was reduced, but a surge in German interest rates following reUNIFICATION weakened sterling, recriminations broke out with the BUNDESBANK which hastened the slide and forced Chancellor Norman Lamont (*see* JE NE REGRETTE RIEN) to withdraw.

> When Margaret Thatcher is dead and opened, it will be those three words that will be lying in her heart. NICHOLAS RIDLEY

Erskine May The book which has become the ultimate authority on Parliamentary procedure at WESTMINSTER. It takes its name from Thomas Erskine May (1815–86), Clerk of the HOUSE OF COMMONS from 1871–76 who in 1844 published his *Treatise on the Law, Privilege, Proceedings and Usage of Parliament.* Updated and revised by his successors, the 'Bible' of the Commons has passed through 23 editions; the most recent, edited by Sir William McKay and Robert Wilson, appeared in 2004, price £160.

Ervin Committee The popular name for the Senate Select Committee on Presidential Campaign Activities, which between May and August 1973 held televised hearings on the WATERGATE affair. It was chaired by the 76-year-old Democratic Sen. Sam Ervin of North Carolina, who cast off his reputation as an arch-conservative to emerge as an avuncular but no-nonsense defender of the CONSTITUTION. The hearings elicited crucial revelations about the involvement of top WHITE HOUSE aides in Watergate and the COVER-UP, and ultimately of President NIXON himself. It was at one of the Ervin hearings that the existence of the tapes which ultimately destroyed Nixon first came to light.

escalation A dramatic increase in the scale of action or response, a word first used to describe the rapid upgrading of US involvement in VIETNAM by the JOHNSON administration soon after the 1964 Presidential election. Prior to that LBJ had pursued the 'limited' war he had inherited from President KENNEDY; during the election the Democrats savaged Sen. Barry Goldwater for advocating a greatly increased US military involvement – which duly followed.

Essex man A young man of braying coarseness and Neanderthal right-wing opinions, widely supposed to be more easily found in the county of Essex, immediately east of London, than elsewhere. The term was invented in October 1990 by the political columnist Simon Heffer, a native of Essex who shared his creation's view on Europe. Essex man had his say in the 1992 general election when David Amess's Tory win at Basildon, a haunt of the species, pointed the way to an unexpected victory, and in 2001, when Essex alone swung against Tony BLAIR as Labour recorded a second successive LANDSLIDE.

establish. Established Church A branch of the Christian church which has a formal and privileged position in a nation's life. The Roman Catholic church enjoys this position in a number of states through a CONCORDAT; in England the Church of England, with the sovereign as Supreme Governor, is similarly favoured. Indeed the Sovereign is an Anglican in England and a Presbyterian in Scotland, where the Calvinist Church of Scotland enjoys official status. The Anglican church in Wales was DISESTABLISHED in the early 20th century, and there has at times been pressure for the English church to be put on the same footing as all other denominations.

establishment, the The term used since the late 1950s for an influential hierarchy or inner circle, and particularly the informal grouping of academic, government and cultural figures who impose social structure and conformity on the public. The word originated in Britain, and was reflected in the opening in London c. 1961 of a satirical club of that name. Now it is applied throughout the world.

> The establishment is made up of little men, very frightened. Rep. BELLA ABZUG (1920–98)

> We must realise that today's establishment is the new George III. Whether it will continue to adhere to his tactics, we do not know. If it does, the redress, honored in tradition, is also revolution.
> Justice WILLIAM O. DOUGLAS, 1970

> Eastern establishment types, ideological eunuchs whose most comfortable position is straddling the fence.
> Vice President SPIRO AGNEW, speaking in New Orleans, 19 October 1969

establishment clause The first part of the FIRST AMENDMENT to the US CONSTITUTION which is the basis for the separation of church and state, asserting that 'CONGRESS shall make no law respecting an establishment of religion'.

ETA (Basque *Euzkadi ta Azkatasuna*) The militant SEPARATIST movement which since

1975 has conducted a terrorist campaign throughout Spain for an independent state centred on Bilbao. The Spanish government placated some moderate Basques in 1980 by giving the region, know to its people as *Euzkadi*, its own Parliament, but the violence has continued – though to a lesser extent since France began deporting known ETA members operating on its side of the border. The centre-right government of José Maria Aznar lost power in part because of its erroneous claim that the MADRID BOMBINGS on the eve of the 2004 Spanish elections were the work not of AL QAEDA but of ETA.

eternal flame The memorial to President KENNEDY in ARLINGTON NATIONAL CEMETERY, which stands immediately over his grave.

ethics. ethical foreign policy The stance adopted by Robin COOK on his appointment as Tony BLAIR's first Foreign Secretary in 1997. The much-trumpeted policy was founded on a respect for HUMAN RIGHTS and a commitment not to supply armaments to unsavoury regimes or world trouble-spots. Though sincerely meant, the policy achieved little in practice beyond an **Export Control Act** aimed at curbing the sale of arms to objectionable regimes, which as drafted has handicapped the efforts of legitimate UK exporters.

Ethics Committees The bodies formed by both HOUSES of the US CONGRESS in the early 1970s in a partly-successful attempt to force basic standards of probity on their members. Mark Green wrote of the Senate committee:

> The Senate took to its new offspring with all the glee of a father who has found an illegitimate child dropped on his doorstep.

The House Committee got off to an unpromising start, COMMON CAUSE chairman John Gardner calling it 'the worst kind of sham, giving the appearance of serving as a policeman while extending a marvellous protective shield over members of Congress.' One chairman of the committee, Rep. Richardson Preyer, explained: 'It's not much fun sitting in judgment on your colleagues'; his successor Rep. John Flynt set the guideline that 'a member should be in flagrant abuse of his office for the House to act'. Speaker TIP O'Neill stiffened the regime somewhat, telling Rep. David Obey when a code of ethics was mooted: 'If you're going to write one, go all the way. I want a damn good code I can be proud of.'

Ethics in Government Act The legislation passed by CONGRESS in 1978 which, in the wake of WATERGATE, sought to outlaw a range of abuses and conflicts of interest including the practice of former federal officials becoming LOBBYISTS and immediately lobbying their former agencies.

ethnic cleansing The infamous practice adopted by Serb forces in Bosnia in 1992 by which non-Serb inhabitants of an area were expelled, deported to prison camps or killed in cold blood (*see* SREBRENICA); militant forces of other nationalities have practised it since. Ironically the term had earlier been used by Kurt Waldheim, later UN GENERAL SECRETARY and President of Austria, in a report to Goebbels when a staff officer with NAZI forces in Yugoslavia.

ethnic monitoring The practice by which government agencies keep a check on the number and proportion of their staff from various ethnic groups.

ethnic purity An unguarded phrase used by Democratic Presidential nominee Jimmy CARTER during a campaign visit to a Polish area of Cleveland in 1976. Carter used it to praise the cohesiveness of a community that was resisting the influx of other ethnic groups, including blacks; his opponents seized on it as a sign of illiberal Southern attitudes and, at worst, RACISM. Carter, who later withdrew his remarks, said:

> I see nothing wrong with ethnic purity being maintained. I would not force a racial integration of a neighbourhood by government action.

ethnic vote A collective term for the vote from various racial groups that can be mobilised for one party or candidate; it is based on the assumption, not always correct, that most members of a particular minority will vote in a particular way.

Ettrick Bridge coup The replacement of the SDP leader Roy JENKINS by the Liberal leader David Steel (*see* BOY DAVID) as chief campaigner for the ALLIANCE in the middle of Britain's 1983 general election campaign. The change was made at a meeting on 29 May at Steel's home at Ettrick Bridge in the Scottish borders. The Liberals insisted on it, believing the experienced but urbane Jenkins, officially the Alliance's PRIME MINISTER DESIGNATE, was not making a strong enough impact; Jenkins'associates resisted it, detecting unnecessary panic. In the end a statement was issued saying that Steel would take a higher profile in the final ten days of the campaign. Dr David OWEN admired Steel's decisiveness at the time, but later called it a 'ruthless and savage deed.'

Euan test The test set by Tony BLAIR for the acceptability of a policy soon after his election when, with particular reference to the environment, he said he would put it to his son Euan, then 13, and see his reaction. Speaking to a UN environmental conference on 23 June 1997, he said:

> My children complain I am never home. But if there is one summit they want me at, it is this one.

Blair also applied the test that week to the Millennium Dome, indicating that he would cancel the project if it could not be made exciting enough for his children. His statements attracted some derision and he did not repeat them. At an EU summit in October 2002, with war in Iraq looming, President Chirac turned the tables on Blair by referring to his youngest son and asking:

> How will you be able to look Leo in the eye in 20 years' time if you are the leader who helped start a war?

Euratom The European Atomic Energy Community, formed in 1958 by the six founder-members of the European Economic Community (France, Germany, Italy, the BENELUX countries) to promote peaceful uses of atomic energy; it shared the EEC's Parliament and courts. Its functions included joint research projects, safety and health in NUCLEAR installations and creation of a common market in nuclear materials and technology. In 1967 Euratom was merged with the EEC and the EUROPEAN COAL AND STEEL COMMUNITY to form the European Community, forerunner of the EU.

Eureka stockade The skirmish at Ballarat, Victoria on 3 December 1854 between 150 gold prospectors and a force of troopers and police which became Australia's most celebrated rebellion, and a landmark in the securing of popular rights. It was the culmination of diggers' grievances over exorbitant licences for prospecting, police brutality, lack of the vote and a ban on prospecting in Crown lands. Tension rose with the murder of James Scobie, a digger, in October and the acquittal of his alleged killers. On 11 November diggers formed the Ballarat Reform League to petition for redress of grievances; Lieutenant-Governor Charles Hotham responded but on 28 November the arrival of troop reinforcements brought further clashes. The diggers organised into military companies and elected Peter Lalor, a League activist, as commander-in-chief. They built the stockade, and 150 diggers were inside when police surrounded it. They refused to come out, opened fire and were routed in just 15 minutes; 25 diggers and five troopers died. Lalor went into hiding until an AMNESTY was declared; a number of the diggers were accused of treason, but none was convicted. Reforms enacted the following year remedied many of the prospectors' grievances.

Euro. euro The single currency which took effect on 1 January 2002 in twelve EU member states (Austria, Belgium, Finland, France, Germany, Greece, Ireland, Italy, Luxembourg, the Netherlands, Portugal and Spain), and worth roughly $1 at its inception; an original starting date of 1999 had been set by the MAASTRICHT TREATY. The name for the currency, which supplanted such historic units of exchange as the French franc and German mark, was agreed at the Madrid EU summit on 15 December 1995. The UK, Denmark and Sweden stayed out, Tony BLAIR supporting membership in principle but promising a REFERENDUM if the Government made a firm recommendation to go in; Swedes voted against joining in 2003. The ten new member states that joined the EU in 2004 were all initially outside the EUROZONE.

Euro X The committee of eleven EU finance ministers – every participating nation minus Luxembourg, which had no currency of its own – which was formed in 1998 to preside over the launch and stewardship of the single currency. There have been lasting concerns that the UK's absence from the committee's most crucial deliberations would lead to its interests being sidelined.

Eurocommunism The variant of COMMUNISM, not differing greatly from Democratic SOCIALISM, followed by the Communist parties of Italy and Spain from the late 1970s in order to retain their popular support and Parliamentary representation. Their leaderships, to the irritation of the KREMLIN, concluded that both the repressive ethos of Soviet Communism and the failure of Eastern Europe to match the prosperous West required them to follow a different road, with Communism only an ultimate aim. Their example was followed by Communists in some other western countries, though conspicuously not in France, where STALINISM remained alive and well for two further decades.

Eurocrats Shorthand for the BUREAUCRATS who staff the EUROPEAN COMMISSION.

Eurogroup The gatherings of defence ministers from the European member states of NATO (fourteen including France at its inception), instigated in 1968 by UK Defence Secretary Denis HEALEY with the consent of President NIXON. Healey wrote in 1989:

> Differences on strategic policy have prevented it from providing the European pillar inside NATO for which I originally hoped; but it has been of some value in developing common European projects for arms and equipment.

Europe (1) Apart from its correct geographical use, a shorthand used in Britain for the rest of the EU. A constituent told Fred Tuckman MEP while canvassing: 'Europe – but that's abroad!' And Christopher Monckton defined Europe as 'an area geographically to the left of Russia; after MAASTRICHT an area politically to the left of Russia.' The word acquired this sense in the late 1950s when **'going into Europe'** was first contemplated.

> This 'going into Europe' will not turn out to be the thrilling mutual exchange supposed. It is more like middle-aged couples with failing marriages meeting in a darkened bedroom for a group grope.
>
> E. P. THOMPSON, during the 1975 REFERENDUM campaign

Occasionally US officials have used the word in the same sense, to denote the EU. Henry KISSINGER, frustrated by the Community's disunity, once asked:

> If I want to ring Europe, who do I call?

(2) To US politicians, the continent from which they sought to distance themselves by declaring INDEPENDENCE, but which has commanded their attention for much of the past century. At the birth of the nation, WASHINGTON declared: 'Europe has a set of primary interests, which to us have none, or a very remote relation. Hence it must be unwise to implicate ourselves, by artificial ties, in the ordinary vicissitudes of her politics.' JEFFERSON observed: 'It is a maxim with us, and I think a wise one, not to entangle ourselves with the affairs of Europe.' Ralph Waldo Emerson deemed this impossible, saying: 'Europe extends to the Alleghenies; America lies beyond.' ISOLATIONISTS resisted the commitment of US troops in WORLD WAR I and any commitment to preserving peace thereafter; in 1935 Sen. Schall of Minnesota declared: **'To hell with Europe!'** America kept out of WORLD WAR II as long as it was an essentially European conflict, but afterward the COLD WAR and even the KOREAN WAR made such involvement inevitable; Gen. Douglas MACARTHUR declared: 'If we lose the war to Communism in Asia, the fall of Europe is inevitable', and John F. KENNEDY said:

> The United States cannot withdraw from Europe, unless and until Europe should wish us gone.

Europe à la carte Picking and choosing from the treaties governing the EU the elements a member state feels it can live with. A pejorative used by Jacque DELORS and European FEDERALISTS as Denmark attempted to negotiate better terms after its rejection of the MAASTRICHT TREATY in a REFERENDUM.

Europe des Patries (Fr. Europe of the NATION STATES) The original GAULLIST ideal for the EUROPEAN COMMUNITY, of a loose organisation of sovereign states in which France could pursue its national interests, as opposed to a FEDERAL Europe. De Gaulle himself did not originate the phrase; it was first used by Michel Debré on 15 January 1959 on his inauguration as Prime Minister. The doctrine was perfected in the Fouchet Plan of 1961 for closer political co-operation between nation states, and reflected in the European policy of successive French governments into the 1990s, culminating in France's attempt to sabotage the URUGUAY ROUND of world trade negotiations.

Europe of the Regions The notion of the EUROPEAN UNION as a conglomeration of sub-states like Bavaria, Catalonia and Scotland rather than a group of formally-constituted nations.

Concert of Europe The vague post-Napoleonic consensus of the crowned heads of Europe in favour of maintaining the political and diplomatic *status quo*.

Council of Europe The loose grouping of democratic nations established at the Hague in May 1948 which has provided a broad framework for European unity. Many of the ideas eventually institutionalised in the EUROPEAN UNION were first aired at the Council's first assembly in Strasbourg in August 1949, which CHURCHILL dominated – particularly in making sure that WEST GERMANY was asked to join. However, Britain's coolness to closer union ensured that the Council did not itself develop into that union. The Strasbourg-based Council developed instead as a body embracing EEC, EFTA and other free nations, whose activities in such fields as culture and human rights (it is the custodian of the European Convention on HUMAN RIGHTS) supplemented the tighter groupings. After the fall of Communism in 1989 Czechoslovakia, Hungary and Poland were swiftly admitted;

other East European stations have since joined, taking the membership to 43.

> A Council of Europe must inevitably embrace the whole of Europe, and all the main branches of the European family must some day be partners in it.
> CHURCHILL

> A lifeless whale stranded on the banks of the Rhine.
> DE GAULLE

Fortress Europe *See* FORTRESS.
Old Europe *See* OLD.
sick man of Europe The phrase coined by Tsar Nicholas I in 1853, when he said of Turkey in a letter (written in French) to Sir George Seymour:

> We have on our hands a sick man, a very sick man; it will be, I tell you quite frankly, a great misfortune if one of these days he should slip away from us, especially before all necessary arrangements can be made.

At the 1990 LABOUR PARTY conference Glyn Ford, leader of the party's MEPs, branded Britain the **thick man of Europe** because of Tory education policies. Environmental groups have called Britain the **dirty man of Europe** because of what they regard as its poor record on GREEN issues.
the lamps are going out all over Europe The melancholy observation by the Liberal Foreign Secretary Sir Edward Grey (later Viscount Grey of Fallodon, 1862–1933) at dusk on 3 August 1914, the eve of the outbreak of WORLD WAR I. He added: 'We shall not see them lit again in our lifetime', and indeed the Europe Grey knew has never been re-created.
two-speed Europe The hypothetical system, advocated by some FEDERALISTS and feared by poorer and less integrationist nations, under which the keenest advocates of ever-closer union (notably Germany, BENELUX and in some respects France) would press ahead with the creation of a super-state while others liked Britain, Denmark and Greece lagged behind.
united Europe The goal of politicians nobly and otherwise inspired from the days of Julius Caesar and CHARLEMAGNE. Goebbels declared for the NAZIS: 'The aim of our struggle must be to create a united Europe.' The post-war West German Chancellor Konrad Adenauer stated: 'We must free ourselves from thinking in terms of nation states. The countries of western Europe are no longer in a position to protect themselves individually; not one of them is any longer in a position to protect European culture.' And John F. KENNEDY told America's allies: 'Far from resenting the rise of a united Europe, this country welcomes it.'
we are part of the community of Europe – we must do our duty as such One of the most quoted (and wrongly attributed) remarks by a British politician. It was actually made by Lord SALISBURY in a speech at Caernarvon on 11 April 1888; imaginative or slipshod reference-book compilers have also attributed it to GLADSTONE and LLOYD GEORGE – and in one case both.

European (1) A generic term for anyone of Caucasian origin, used especially in Africa and former British possessions generally.

> New Zealand Europeans, and I am not saying this in a bitter way, are peasants. What we have here is aristocratic Maoris and peasant Europeans.
> NZ internal Affairs Minister PETER TAPSELL (a Maori), 1985

(2) Pertaining to Europe. Also one committed to the European ideal and regarding him- or herself as a citizen of the entire continent. To such folk it is a particular compliment to be called a good European. However, John MAJOR, during negotiations on the MAASTRICHT TREATY, observed:

> The good European sometimes says no.

European Central Bank *See* ECB.
European Coal and Steel Community The grouping formed in 1952 by France, WEST GERMANY, Italy and the BENELUX countries, brainchild of the French Foreign Minister Robert SCHUMAN and the driving force for the creation of the European Community; it coexisted with the EEC until 1967 and technically still existed, expanding with the Community, until 23 June 2002. The refusal of ATTLEE's Labour government to join the founders and the concurrence of the Conservatives elected in 1951 lost Britain its best chance to enter a united Europe on even terms.
European Commission The EXECUTIVE BRANCH of the EUROPEAN UNION, comprising 15,000 officials mostly based in Brussels; its seat is the BERLAYMONT. As the sole authority to initiate EU legislation and the body responsible for its enforcement by prosecution in the EUROPEAN COURT, the Commission enjoys immense power but has been widely criticised for lack of accountability, stifling enterprise and an inability to counter graft and fraud (*see* EUROSTAT). Its BUREAUCRACY (*see* JARDIN FRANÇAIS) is divided into 23 Directorates-General (DGs) and a range of auxiliary units, such as for legal and translation services. At its head are **Commissioners** appointed by member

states (originally twelve, two from each state, and now 20), one of whom serves as President; normally fairly senior national politicians, they take an oath to serve the Community rather than their own state. Originally appointed for four years, since the MAASTRICHT TREATY they have served for five; they can only be removed, en bloc, by a vote of the EUROPEAN PARLIAMENT – which has twice been narrowly averted. The threat of such a vote in 1999 over the nepotistic practices of the French commissioner Edith CRESSON triggered the wholesale resignation of the Commission headed by Luxembourg's Jacques Santer, and in 2004 José Maria Barroso withdrew his entire Commission from consideration by the Parliament on the eve of a vote to reject them all because of objections to the appointment as HUMAN RIGHTS Commissioner of Rocco BUTTIGLIONE; the outgoing Commission headed by Romano Prodi had to stay on for over three weeks beyond the 1 November handover date until Barroso could find a reshuffled Commission acceptable to the Parliament.

European Community (EC). The forerunner of the EUROPEAN UNION, the organisation created in 1967 by merging EURATOM, the EUROPEAN COAL AND STEEL COMMUNITY and the EUROPEAN ECONOMIC COMMUNITY, and given its lasting shape by the Treaty of ROME in 1957; since the MAASTRICHT TREATY took effect in 1993, it has survived as the core of the EUROPEAN UNION. The founders were the BENELUX countries, France, Italy and West Germany; the UK (at the third attempt), Denmark and Ireland joined in 1973, Greece in 1981, Spain and Portugal in 1986 and Austria, Finland and Sweden in 1995; Norway twice negotiated membership, only for a referendum to reject it. The Community developed into the world's largest trading bloc (the SINGLE MARKET took effect at the end of 1992) and did much to harmonise commercial laws and product specifications; it also enabled member states to speak on most world issues with a single voice. By contrast the Maastricht Treaty on closer political union, which turned the EC into the EU, was a toughly fought compromise between advocates of a United States of Europe and supporters of national sovereignty.

In Britain, membership has aroused deep emotions: when the Community was first mooted in 1951, when DE GAULLE said: 'NON!' in 1963, when France vetoed Harold WILSON's application in the late 1960s, when Edward HEATH took Britain in in 1973, during the 1975 REFERENDUM campaign, during the debate over Maastricht, whenever closer political or economic union has been under discussion, during the controversies over joining the EURO and the terms of the EUROPEAN CONSTITUTION and whenever some apparently absurd DIRECTIVE was issued from BRUSSELS. CHURCHILL said: 'We will be with Europe, but not of it, and when they ask us why we take that view, we will say we dwell in our own land.' Harold MACMILLAN cautioned that membership would be 'a bracing cold shower, not a relaxing Turkish bath', Hugh GAITSKELL that joining would mean 'the end of a thousand years of history'.

> The EC is about business, not politics.
>
> Professor WALTER HALLSTEIN, President of the Commission 1958–67

> The EC is an economic giant, but still acts like a political pygmy.
>
> DAVID MARTIN MEP (Lab.), report to the European Parliament on closer union

European Constitution The 330-page document designed to consolidate the previous treaties that established in turn the European Economic Community, European Community and EUROPEAN UNION (*see* Treaties of ROME, MAASTRICT, AMSTERDAM, NICE) and in some ways push the process further. It was approved at the Brussels SUMMIT of June 2004, and formally signed by EU leaders in Rome on 29 October that year. It was to take effect once all 25 member states had ratified it, which in several countries including the UK and France entailed a REFERENDUM. This proved its undoing; in May/June 2005 the voters of first France (55%) and then the Netherlands (61%) decisively rejected it, precipitating a crisis over the future governance of the EU. President CHIRAC, severely embarrassed by the defeat responded by launching an attack on the BRITISH REBATE. The rejection did, however, spare Tony BLAIR the need to hold a referendum he had been under no obligation to call and would almost certainly have lost. The Constitution had been drafted by the EUROPEAN CONVENTION (*see below*) but the Convention's text was softened by the Irish PRESIDENCY to ease UK objections to the loss of the national VETO over tax harmonisation and defence policy. While advocates of closer integration had pressed for a formal Constitution for some time, the occasion for it was the admission of ten new member states from May 2004 and the need to change and simplify the internal structure of the EU to reflect this. Another aim was to clarify the EU's external relations, in particular the Common Foreign and Security Policy.

European Convention The assembly set up under the former French President Valéry Giscard d'Estaing to devise a formal constitution for the European Union to make it more accountable and less clumsy after the ENLARGEMENT of the EU in 2004. Set up by the Laeken European SUMMIT in December 1999 and comprising delegates from member and applicant states, it presented in July 2003 its report calling for a new TREATY OF ROME embodying its proposals to be promulgated before the June 2004 European elections.

European Convention on Human Rights *See* HUMAN RIGHTS.

European Council The official term for the SUMMITS of EU heads of government held twice a year in the country holding the PRESIDENCY (or in Brussels), and for special meetings held in between.

European Court of Justice The highest court of the EU, which determines whether its organs have acted within their powers and whether member states are violating European law. The court, comprising up to 25 judges (one for each member state) and six advocates-general, derives its authority from the Treaty of ROME.

> The Court has been responsible for an upheaval in European justice, which has accelerated the shift in power from national to Community institutions. *The European*

European Defence Community The proposal for a single Western European army – including a re-armed WEST GERMANY – under a European Assembly and Defence Council of Ministers, mooted by the French Minister René Pleven in 1950. A parallel to the EUROPEAN COAL AND STEEL COMMUNITY, it gained a general welcome, but Britain soon had reservations and France followed; John Foster Dulles threatened an AGONISING REAPPRAISAL of US policy toward NATO if France did not participate, but the NATIONAL ASSEMBLY blocked the plan, and after discussions on a more 'multilateral' force, it died.

European Economic Area (EEA) An area promoting FREE TRADE and free movement between the EUROPEAN UNION and neighbouring states which enjoy by treaty the benefits of its SINGLE MARKET. States applying to join the EU also apply to join the EEA, which is administered by EFTA. Agreed on at Oporto in May 1993, the EEA came into being at the start of the following year; its current members outside the EU are Iceland, Norway and Liechtenstein.

European Economic Community (EEC) The original name for the EUROPEAN COMMUNITY, underlining its essentially economic nature in the wake of the TREATY OF ROME; it was known colloquially as the COMMON MARKET.

European Free Trade Area *See* EFTA.

European Monetary System *See* EMS.

European Parliament The representative body, proposed by France and Belgium after WORLD WAR II and institutionalised in the Treaty of ROME, which has gradually acquired a role in Community legislation and budgeting and in curbing the EUROPEAN COMMISSION. At first nominated by national legislatures, it has since 1979 been directly elected every five years; its post-ENLARGEMENT size of 732 members was set by the Treaty of NICE. The Parliament meets for a week every month, usually in Strasbourg but once a year in Brussels; its secretariat is based in Luxembourg. It is headed by a President with considerable influence and ceremonial functions, and has a comprehensive committee structure; members sit in trans-national party groups. The MAASTRICHT TREATY slightly increased its powers, and it flexed its muscles during the CRESSON AFFAIR to force the resignation of Jacques Santer's Commission and again in 2004 to block the appointment of the conservative Italian Rocco BUTTIGLIONE to the Commission (an attack on the Parliament by Mme Cresson shortly before it was due to vote merely strengthened MEPs' resolve), but it remains a junior partner of the Commission and national Parliaments.

> When you open the Pandora's box you will find it full of Trojan 'orses.
> ERNEST BEVIN on the original plan

> This place needs a laxative.
> Sir BOB GELDOF, 1985

European People's Party The grouping in the European Parliament comprising CHRISTIAN DEMOCRATS and, since 1992, British CONSERVATIVES, who have at times been uneasy bedfellows. They are the Parliament's second largest group, after the socialists.

European social model A term in wide use among Continental EU members for the structure of social provision in which generous benefits for workers are put ahead of economic competitiveness. France, Germany and some others have resisted attempts by Britain and its allies to water it down in the hope of creating 'real' jobs, partly under pressure from trade unions.

The rejection of the EUROPEAN CONSTITUTION by French and Dutch voters in 2005 was claimed to be a protest at 'Anglo-Saxon' efforts to weaken the model. On assuming the EU Presidency that summer, Tony BLAIR convened a SUMMIT to determine how the model could be made compatible with competitiveness.

European Union The grouping of nations created by the 1991 MAASTRICHT TREATY which, since its inception on 1 November 1993 when it enveloped the EUROPEAN COMMUNITY, has expanded from twelve member states to 25 and become, with over 455 million inhabitants, the world's largest trading bloc. It has also been, except over the IRAQ WAR, an increasingly powerful voice in world affairs. Formed by the MAASTRICHT TREATY of 1991, its essential organs are the EUROPEAN COMMISSION, COUNCIL OF MINISTERS and the EUROPEAN PARLIAMENT. The EU comprises three **pillars**: the continuing EC; intergovernmental co-operation on Foreign and Security Policy; and similar co-operation on Justice and Home Affairs. It has been deepened by the adoption of the EURO by twelve of its members, and by the treaties of AMSTERDAM and NICE, the stillborn EUROPEAN CONSTITUTION was the next step. Since May 2004 its members have been Austria, the BENELUX countries, the Czech Republic, Cyprus, Denmark, Estonia, Finland, France, Germany, Greece, Hungary, Ireland, Italy, Latvia, Lithuania, Malta, Poland, Portugal, Slovakia, Slovenia, Spain, Sweden and the UK.

Europhilia A derogatory term for excessive zeal for European union, coined by critics of the MAASTRICHT TREATY after Denmark rejected it in a REFERENDUM and France came within an ace of doing so. The echoes of 'necrophilia' and 'paedophilia' are intentional, the critics inferring that Europe was dead anyway and that support for closer union was deeply unhealthy.

eurosceptic Someone who regards UK involvement with the institutions of the EUROPEAN UNION with deep scepticism and, in an ideal world, would probably opt to withdraw. The word was coined to cover those in the CONSERVATIVE PARTY, with Margaret THATCHER their spiritual leader, who resisted closer integration before and after the signature of the MAASTRICHT TREATY and caused John MAJOR's government deep discomfiture; their high point came in November 1992 when they came within three votes of blocking RATIFICATION of the Treaty. The word has since come to mean any critic of UK involvement and closer union. *See also* BRUGES GROUP; REFERENDUM PARTY.

> Britain would be greatly diminished if it did not retain its music hall traditions.
>
> CHRIS PATTEN, 2003

Eurostat A financial scandal so great that even the EUROPEAN COMMISSION was belatedly forced to take action, in July 2003, after six years of allegations. Three senior officials of Eurostat, the EU's 730-strong data office based in Luxembourg, including Yves Franchet, its director since 1987, were put on disciplinary charges by Commissioner Neil KINNOCK over revelations that at least 922,000 euros had been looted from the organisation; characteristically, those incriminated continued to draw full pay pending investigation of further claims of dubious accounting, fictitious contracts and kickbacks.

Eurozone The economic entity formed by the twelve national economies that have adopted the EURO.

Evans. Timothy Evans case The miscarriage of justice in England that helped finally persuade Parliament to abolish the death penalty for murder. In 1966 campaigning by the journalist Ludovic Kennedy persuaded Mr Justice Brabin that Timothy Evans, hanged fifteen years before for killing his baby daughter, was 'probably innocent', though Brabin also felt Evans might 'possibly' have been guilty of killing his wife, with which he was not charged. The real murderer was John Christie, who shared 10 Rillington Place in North Kensington with the Evanses, and after Evans' execution was hanged for the murder of six other women whose bodies were found at the house. By the time Brabin reported, the SILVERMAN BILL had been passed and hanging abolished. Doubts about Evans' guilt were voiced as early as 1953 when the bodies were found, but dismissed as unfounded by an inquiry held by Scott Henderson QC.

Évènements (Fr. Events) The understated word by which the French remember the social and political upheavals of May and June 1968, when President DE GAULLE's government came within a whisker of collapsing in the face of militant, often violent protests by students and workers.

The students flooded out of their universities to erect BARRICADES, hurl paving stones at the CRS (who responded in kind) and occupy key buildings like the *Odéon*. The student uprising, ostensibly for a greater say in running their colleges, paralleled widespread industrial unrest, but the student radicals and France's more conventional trade unions only momentarily formed common cause. De Gaulle secretly left Paris to assure himself of the backing of French generals in West Germany, then waited for the uprising to burn itself out (*see also* CHIENLIT). His resignation the following year was over his defeat in a relatively unimportant REFERENDUM.

events, dear boy, events Harold Macmillan's reputed response when asked what any Prime Minister most feared.

everybody will be a millionaire by the end of the century The assertion, containing only a touch of exaggeration, made by Jeffrey (Lord) Archer (*see also* FRAGRANT; STAND AND DELIVER) to a business conference in Bournemouth in October 2004. It reflects the eventual effect of a continuing increase in property prices, which in the UK has already begun to impact on politics not only because of the cost of housing but because large sections of the middle class have been brought into the Inheritance Tax bracket. It is touch and go whether most owner-occupiers will become millionaires first in Britain, where property prices tend to be higher, or in the United States, where the dollar is worth less than the pound.

evil empire *See* EMPIRE.

Evita The nickname by which Maria Eva de Perón (1919–52), wife of the dictator Juan PERÓN, became known to the adoring Argentine masses. A radio actress born in poverty, she married Perón in 1945 and formed a rapport with the poor and needy, revealing great rabble-rousing abilities which were a boon to her husband. After her death from cancer aged 33, he kept her body in a glass coffin at the CASA ROSADA until his overthrow three years later. Her charitable work, perceived beauty and early death all contributed to the myth surrounding her name. Her life became the subject of one of the most successful stage musicals ever – *Evita* by Andrew Lloyd Webber and Tim Rice, which opened in London in 1978 – and a film two decades later starring Madonna and Antonio Bandeiras.

> If a woman like Eva Perón with no ideals can get that far, think how far I can go with all the ideals that I have.
>
> MARGARET THATCHER, 1980.

Ex-Files The scandal that broke in 1996 over the improper scrutiny by the CLINTON administration of confidential FBI files on 408 staff members of the previous Republican administration. It took its name, a pun on 'ex' (departed), from the TV science-fiction series *The X-Files*. The blame was pinned on the inexperience of Craig Livingstone, Clinton's head of WHITE HOUSE Security. Livingstone, a former bar bouncer who had done OPPOSITION RESEARCH for Gary Hart and Al GORE, was forced to quit, and the episode was seized on by Republicans already exercised by TRAVELGATE, WHITEWATER and the suicide of Vince FOSTER (on the White House's response to which Livingstone had also worked), as proof of a lack of political morals at the highest level.

Excalibur The rapid retrieval database, named after King Arthur's legendary sword, which from the late 1990s became essential for any UK political party or campaigning movement, having a crucial role in effective REBUTTAL. It gave instant access to a party's own policy or – more valuably – the past statements of its opponents, and any CANDIDATE could tap into it from their mobile phone. Labour's MILLBANK nerve centre acquired Excalibur first for £300,000, deploying it to deadly effect, and by the 1997 ELECTION the Conservatives had it too.

exchange. exchange controls Restrictions on the amount of a nation's currency that may be taken out for use or investment elsewhere, usually imposed in an attempt to husband scarce reserves or prevent a speculative run on the currency that would force DEVALUATION. Members of the EUROPEAN UNION are supposed to be phasing them out, but Spain, in particular, still limits a wide range of foreign currency transactions.

exchange of letters The ritual gone through when a Minister resigns or is dismissed from the UK government. Traditionally it comprises a letter from the Prime Minister expressing sadness that he or she is leaving, but quite understands why they have to, and a letter from the outgoing Minister saying how sorry they are to be going and how supportive they will continue to be. The letters are closely scrutinised for clues as to what has really happened. When Norman Lamont (*see* JE NE REGRETTE RIEN) was ousted as CHANCELLOR in May 1993, he pointedly sent John MAJOR an impersonal fax.

Exchange Rate Mechanism *See* ERM.

excise duties Taxes levied on certain commodities, notably alcoholic spirits, whose production is kept under close supervision by the State. **Excisemen** – the class so roundly condemned by Robert Burns – were the collectors of such taxes, and also patrolled against smuggling. The UK agency collecting excise duties – now including VAT – has been the **Customs and Excise**; it is now being merged with the **Inland Revenue** which collects direct taxes.

exclusion The action of a legislature in preventing an elected member from taking his or her SEAT. Charles BRADLAUGH was repeatedly barred from the Victorian HOUSE OF COMMONS for refusing to take the OATH; Adam Clayton POWELL was excluded from the HOUSE OF REPRESENTATIVES in 1967 for alleged misuse of Congressional travel funds and being under indictment for contempt of court – the first time the House had taken such action in 46 years. Powell described his exclusion as 'LYNCHING Northern style'; he was readmitted, minus SENIORITY, in 1969 after winning two more elections. *See also* EXPULSION.

Exclusion Order The administrative device under which, for over a decade at the height of the NORTHERN IRELAND emergency, UK Ministers could bar suspected terrorist and their political leaders from travelling to the British mainland. This is probably the only instance of residents of one part of the UNITED KINGDOM being prevented from setting foot in another.

executive. Executive, the One of the three arms of government, coexisting with the JUDICIARY and the LEGISLATURE; it is also known as the **executive branch**. The Executive carries out the business and actions of government. In America it is personified in the PRESIDENT and embraces CABINET SECRETARIES and the rest of the ADMINISTRATION; in Britain it comprises the PRIME MINISTER and CABINET (who are also part of the legislature) and the CIVIL SERVICE. Writing of the Roman Empire, Edward Gibbon wrote:

> The principles of a free constitution are irrecoverably lost when the legislative power is nominated by the executive.

Hence the FOUNDING FATHERS' insistence on a complete SEPARATION OF POWERS in America. Benjamin FRANKLIN justified the system of CHECKS AND BALANCES by stating:

> The executive will always be increasing here, as elsewhere, till it end in MONARCHY.

Yet, as was seen with WATERGATE and as BACKBENCH MPs and civil libertarians in Britain have long asserted, no check will totally prevent the Executive gathering new powers to itself.

> The Constitution supposes, what the History of all Governments demonstrates, that the Executive is the branch of power most interested in war; and most prone to it.
>
> MADISON, letter to JEFFERSON, 1798

> The contest, for ages, has been to rescue liberty from the grasp of executive power.
>
> DANIEL WEBSTER, speaking against Andrew Jackson in the Senate, 27 May 1834

executive agreement An agreement under which the President may enter into undertakings with foreign governments on behalf of the United States without having to submit them afterward to the SENATE. He can act under powers given by CONGRESS, for example, to conclude reciprocal trade agreements, or as chief executive and COMMANDER-IN-CHIEF, as when Franklin D. ROOSEVELT concluded the LEND-LEASE agreement with Britain in 1940.

executive communication In WASHINGTON, a letter from the President, a Cabinet member or the head of an independent agency transmitting the draft of a proposed BILL to the SPEAKER of the House or the President of the Senate. A wave of such letters customarily follows the President's STATE OF THE UNION message.

executive mansion A formal term for the WHITE HOUSE, and also for the Governor's mansion in each of America's 50 States.

Executive Office of the President The resource that provides the President with help and advice in carrying out his principal responsibilities; the Office was created by Franklin D. ROOSEVELT under the Reorganization Act of 1939. *See also* OLD EOB.

Executive Order An order issued by the President dictating a particular way in which the Federal government is to act or be organised. For instance in 1941 Franklin D. ROOSEVELT, following pressure from black trade unionists, issued EXECUTIVE ORDER 8802 requiring all defence contractors to abstain from racial discrimination. Compliance is another matter; during the IRAN-CONTRA scandal it emerged that Col. Oliver North's COVERT OPERATION to support the Nicaraguan Contras lacked the written

Presidential authority required by President REAGAN's own **Executive Order 12333**.

executive privilege The doctrine on which President NIXON relied in his efforts to avoid Congressional investigation of WATERGATE, and to which the SUPREME COURT eventually set strict limits. It was first claimed by JEFFERSON when he refused to answer a subpoena to appear in court and present documents relating to Aaron BURR's trial for treason. When Nixon called for the Senate Judiciary Committee's Watergate hearings to take place *in camera* on grounds of executive privilege, Sen. Sam ERVIN responded:

> That is not executive privilege. That is executive poppycock.

executive session A mainly US term for the SECRET SESSION of a legislature or other deliberative body. In the US SENATE, executive sessions are usually confined to discussion of executive nominations – which used frequently to mean appointments to remote post offices – and treaties.

exhausted volcanoes DISRAELI's withering denunciation of GLADSTONE's first CABINET, delivered in a speech in Manchester on 3 April 1872. It was almost two years before 'DIZZY' was to oust them at a general election. He said:

> As I sat opposite the TREASURY BENCH, the Ministers reminded me of one of those marine landscapes not very unusual on the coasts of South America. You behold a range of exhausted volcanoes. Not a flame flickers on a single pallid chest. But the situation is still very dangerous. There are occasional earthquakes, and ever and anon the dark rumbling of the sea.

exit. exit poll *See* POLL.

exit strategy A well thought-out means of extricating oneself, one's party or one's country from an apparently impossible situation, preferably devised before that situation existed. At the height of GUERRILLA attacks on US and British forces in Iraq in 2004, one year after they had overthrown SADDAM HUSSEIN, the need for President George W. BUSH to develop an exit strategy before that November's election, and for Tony BLAIR to come up with one to save his Premiership, was much discussed.

exocet To destroy a project or a political argument with a sudden deadly move. The term originated in the FALKLANDS WAR when the Argentine air force used the French *Exocet* (flying fish) missile with lethal effect, the most notable casualty being HMS *Sheffield.*

Experience Counts The slogan on which Richard NIXON and Henry Cabot Lodge fought the 1960 Presidential campaign. It was designed to capitalise on Nixon's service for two terms as Vice President to the popular and trusted EISENHOWER, and to imply that, compared with the experienced and responsible Nixon, the youthful John F. KENNEDY was unqualified for the White House. It glossed over the fact that Nixon and Kennedy had both first been elected to CONGRESS in 1946, and that at 47 Nixon was only four years older. Experience is a quality claimed as essential by those already in high office, and dismissed as an irrelevance by challengers who lack it. In Britain's 1987 and 1992 elections, the victorious Conservatives made much of the fact that the Labour leader Neil KINNOCK had never held even the most junior Ministerial office. But when H. Ross PEROT was challenged by George BUSH on his lack of experience during one of the 1992 PRESIDENTIAL DEBATES, he replied:

> They've got a point. I don't have any experience of running up a $4 trillion deficit.

experiment. The country needs, and unless I mistake its temper, the country demands, bold, persistent experiment The philosophy set out by Franklin D. ROOSEVELT as Governor of New York as he mounted his successful campaign for the Presidency in 1932. The words came from FDR's book *Looking Forward*, published after the votes were in.

the Noble Experiment The name given to PROHIBITION by its most ardent and high-minded advocates.

experimental aircraft The expression used by Roy JENKINS for the proposed new party that was later launched as the SDP. He caught headlines with it in a speech to the PRESS GALLERY at WESTMINSTER on 9 June 1980, when he was still President of the EUROPEAN COMMISSION. Jenkins – a former Minister of Aviation – said of creating a new party:

> The likelihood before the start of most adventures is that of failure. The experimental plane may well finish up a few fields from the end of the runway. If that is so, the voluntary occupants will only have inflicted bruises or worse upon themselves. But the reverse could occur and the experimental plane soar into the sky. If that is so, it could go further and more quickly than few now imagine, for it would carry with it great and now untapped reserves of political energy and commitment.

expletive deleted The phrase used in the published transcripts of the WATERGATE tapes to cover for the profanities repeatedly used by Richard NIXON and his aides in plotting the COVER-UP. As the unexpurgated version became available, MIDDLE AMERICA was scandalised at least as much by the sleazy language of the nation's chief executive as by what he and his henchmen had done. From 1974, when the tapes were published and Nixon resigned, 'expletive deleted' came into general use as an alternative to an obscene or blasphemous comment.

expulsion The ultimate disgrace for a legislator: irrevocable ejection from the assembly in which they have sat, on a vote of their fellow members. The expulsion of a member is uncommon in the US CONGRESS and rarer still at WESTMINSTER; when it does occur, it generally follows conviction for a serious criminal offence or some grave breach of discipline or PRIVILEGE. *See also* EXCLUSION.

extra-Parliamentary action Political campaigning based on campaigning, marches and DEMONSTRATIONS in Britain's major cities, rather than through pressure for change in Parliament. In the early 1980s the hard LEFT adopted it as a tactic and as an aim for the LABOUR PARTY, prompting a bitter dispute with its then leader Michael FOOT. In a pivotal moment of his leadership Foot, stung by a challenge from an SDP member, repudiated Peter Tatchell, the party's selected candidate for the 1983 Bermondsey BY-ELECTION, because he had advocated extra-Parliamentary action. Tatchell, a gay Australian Marxist, duly lost the ultra-conservative working-class constituency to the Liberals – a result that firmed up the ALLIANCE's vote prior to that year's general election and contributed to Labour's crushing defeat. Two decades later, the seat was still in Liberal Democrat hands.

extra-territorial jurisdiction The extent to which the writ of a government or a nation's courts runs beyond its boundaries. It has become a matter of international and political controversy, first through sporadic US attempts to enforce the doctrine of COMITY and more recently because governments are anxious to bring to justice TERRORISTS and perpetrators of major frauds and environmental disasters who have harmed their nationals but are based in another jurisdiction.

extradition The legal process under which a suspect for a crime committed in one jurisdiction who has been detained in another is transferred by its courts to stand trial where the offence was committed. When conducted between American states it is known as **interstate rendition**. The extradition of IRA suspects from the Irish Republic to stand trial was a sporadic irritant to relations between London and Dublin into the 1980s; after a string of cases where Irish courts refused to hand over anyone who claimed their offence had been 'political', the Republic changed its law to override such arguments. Further friction was caused when some Irish courts released suspects, claiming that the UK authorities had not complied with all the technicalities; after a further tightening of Irish law the extraditions resumed.

extremism. extremism in defence of liberty is no vice The phrase which haunted Barry Goldwater's 1964 Presidential campaign and contributed to the Republican TICKET's heavy defeat; Goldwater himself attributed it to Cicero when defending Rome against Catiline. Delivered in his ACCEPTANCE SPEECH at the Republicans' San Francisco convention on 16 July 1964, it starkly highlighted Goldwater's LIBERTARIAN beliefs and frightened many liberal Republicans, who detected an echo of the John BIRCH Society's philosophy, into backing Lyndon JOHNSON. Goldwater was unrepentant, telling a protesting ex-President EISENHOWER: 'When you landed your troops in Normandy, it was an exceedingly extreme action taken because you were committed to the defence of freedom.' A grinning Ike replied: 'I never thought of it that way.' Goldwater's actual words were:

> I would remind you that extremism in defence of liberty is no vice. And let me also remind you that moderation in the pursuit of justice is no virtue.

LBJ scornfully countered with:

> Extremism in the pursuit of the Presidency is an unpardonable vice. Moderation in the affairs of the nation is the highest virtue.

extremist One who habitually advocates and pursues an extreme course of action to achieve his or her political ends.

> You show me a black man who isn't an extremist and I'll show you one who needs psychiatric attention. MALCOLM X

> What is objectionable, what is dangerous about extremists is not that they are extreme, but that they are intolerant.
> ROBERT F. KENNEDY

eye. eyeball to eyeball The supreme moment of COLD WAR tension when the leaders of the SUPERPOWERS had each deployed their full strength and were waiting to see whether the other would raise the stakes by initiating nuclear conflict. The phrase originates from the closest shave of all for world peace, the CUBAN MISSILE CRISIS of 1962. When the Soviet leader Nikita S. Khrushchev backed away from an all-out war, US SECRETARY OF STATE Dean Rusk observed:

> We're eyeball to eyeball – and I think that the other fellow just blinked.

eyes only The highest level of CLASSIFIED document, so secret that only the recipient is permitted to read it. The phrase is an American abbreviation for the British **for your eyes only** – hence the title of the eponymous James Bond movie.

when you look in his eyes you see the back of his head The devastating indictment of the 1994 California gubernatorial hopeful Michael Huffington delivered by his fellow Republican Barbara Klinger. A one-term Congressman, Huffington spent $20 million on his campaign but narrowly lost to the Democrat Dianne Feinstein. He had moved from Texas and sold his oil company to build a political career, propelled by his then wife Arianna Stassinopoulos, who at Oxford had earned the cachet 'the Sir Edmund Hillary of social climbing'. Stassinopoulos divorced Huffington after he revealed that he was gay.

F

Fabian Society The principal intellectual grouping within the LABOUR PARTY, which was instrumental in its formation. Founded in 1884, the Society seeks to achieve SOCIALISM by constitutional means; it takes its name from the gradualist tactics of the Roman general Quintus Fabius Maximus. Its influence was greatest up to the 1920s, with Sidney and Beatrice Webb and George Bernard Shaw its leading lights, but it still commands respect.

> For the right moment you must wait, as Fabius did most patiently when warring against Hannibal, though many times censured for his delays, but when the time comes you must strike hard, as Fabius did, or your waiting will be in vain and fruitless.
>
> FRANK PODMORE, the Fabians' co-founder

faction (1) A political grouping, normally informal and by inference involved in dispute or controversy with another. (2) The state of discord between or even within factions.

Fahrenheit 9/11 *See* 9/11.

failed state A nation whose machinery of government has completely broken down, leaving a vacuum which lawlessness and international terrorism can occupy with impunity. The term was most tellingly used of Afghanistan under the Taleban, but applied more appropriately to Somalia, where at the time there was no functioning government at all. It has at times, facetiously, been applied also to Belgium.

failure. all political careers end in death or failure One of the most poignant phrases in the political lexicon, in fact a paraphrase of Enoch POWELL's dictum (in respect of Joseph Chamberlain) that

> All political lives, unless they are cut off in midstream at a happy juncture, end in failure, because that is the nature of politics and of human affairs.

Fair. Fair Deal President TRUMAN's sequel to Franklin D. ROOSEVELT's NEW DEAL. Introduced after his upset 1948 re-election, it comprised national health insurance, help for the elderly, more federal housing, aid to education and an anti-LYNCHING law. Only the housing construction Bills and increases to Social Security and the MINIMUM WAGE got through Congress.

> This programme symbolises for me my assumption of the office of President in my own right.
>
> HARRY S TRUMAN

a fair day's wage for a fair day's work A basic demand of TRADE UNIONS throughout the 19th century, widely seen as fair and responsible.

> 'A fair day's wage for a fair day's work'; it is as just a demand as governed men ever made of governing. It is the everlasting right of man.
>
> THOMAS CARLYLE (1795–1881)

fairness doctrine The principle under which the US Federal Communications Commission curbed partisan broadcasting, requiring airtime to be given to opposing viewpoints. It was abolished by the REAGAN administration in 1987, triggering an expansion of call-in and commentary programmes in which POPULIST radio hosts like Rush Limbaugh and advocates for the RELIGIOUS RIGHT gave vent to their views. At times they impacted on public opinion, notably in 1994 when they were credited with helping the Republicans win a Congressional LANDSLIDE.

Fala President Franklin D. ROOSEVELT's Scots terrier, nicknamed 'the informer' because he insisted on being taken for walks from his train (the FERDINAND MAGELLAN); the sight of the dog and its SECRET SERVICE escort alerted reporters to the VIP traveller's presence. In 1944 Republican allegations that Roosevelt had sent a destroyer to the Aleutians where Fala had supposedly been left behind caused a minor WASHINGTON scandal, FDR remarking:

> His Scotch soul was furious – he has not been the same dog since.

Fala is the first Presidential pet to appear in a statue – in one of the four 'rooms' of the FDR memorial unveiled in Washington in 1997.

Falange (Gr. phalanx, a compact body of troops). The NEO-FASCIST, NATIONALIST movement founded in 1932 by José Antonia Primo de Rivera, son of the Spanish dictator, and later adopted by General Franco (*see* CAUDILLO) as the ruling party of the state forged by his victory in the SPANISH CIVIL WAR; it was disbanded after his death. The **Phalange** is a right-wing Christian party and MILITIA in the Lebanon. The term **Falangist** is a pejorative for any movement dominated by conservative Roman Catholics; Jimmy Reid, then a Communist, used it in 1974 to describe the LABOUR PARTY on Clydeside.

Falklands War The conflict started by the Argentine invasion of the Falkland Islands (*see* MALVINAS), a British COLONY in the South Atlantic, on 2 April 1982, and culminating in the Argentine surrender at Port Stanley on 11 June. It was brought about by UK naval cuts, which left the islands almost undefended, and a perception in Buenos Aires that, in the words of Argentina's military dictator General Galtieri, 'the British won't fight' – a perception the Foreign Office (FCO) had done little to discourage. When Argentine forces landed, the Falklands' governor, Rex Hunt, told their commander: 'It is very uncivilised to invade British territory.' In the electric EMERGENCY DEBATE on the invasion, the Conservative MP Julian Amery declared: 'We have suffered the inevitable consequences of unpreparedness and feeble counsel.' The war embraced a UK political crisis culminating in the resignation of Lord Carrington as Foreign Secretary, the despatch of a naval TASK FORCE by Margaret THATCHER's government, intensive US diplomacy by SECRETARY OF STATE Alexander Haig, the PERUVIAN PEACE PLAN, the sinking of the Argentine cruiser General BELGRANO and the recapture of South Georgia (*see* REJOICE! REJOICE!). After accepting the final Argentine surrender the British commander, Maj.-Gen. Jeremy Moore, sent home the message: 'The Falkland Islands are once more under the government desired by their inhabitants. God Save the Queen!' Argentina's defeat led to the collapse of the Galtieri regime and a return to democracy under President Raul Alfonsin – and Mrs Thatcher's LANDSLIDE victory in the 1983 general election.

> A fight between two bald men over a comb.
> JOSÉ MARIA BORGES

Falklands factor The electoral bonus to Mrs Thatcher's Conservatives prior to and during the 1983 election campaign from Britain's military success.

fall like a ripe fruit The VIET CONG based their protracted GUERRILLA campaign for control of South Vietnam on the belief that they would erode support for the US-backed government to the point where Saigon would 'fall like a ripe fruit' into their hands – as eventually it did.

Falls, the The Falls Road in West Belfast, which runs from the city centre to Andersonstown through the core of the city's Catholic community and of support for SINN FEIN and the Provisional IRA.

Fame is the Spur The British author Howard Spring's 1940 novel in which Hamer Shawcross becomes a pioneer of the LABOUR PARTY as a young Northern idealist, but compromises and eventually joins Ramsay MACDONALD in breaking with the party to form an alliance with the Conservatives (*see* GREAT BETRAYAL).

family. Family Assistance Plan The programme put to CONGRESS by Richard NIXON early in his first term for what was effectively a national welfare system. It would have established a federally guaranteed income, albeit at a maximum $1,600 a year for a family of four with no other means, which would have particularly benefited poor families in the South. Devised by Daniel Patrick MOYNIHAN, the plan passed the HOUSE but was stifled in the SENATE by a coalition of conservative Republicans and Democrats, and liberals who disliked its work requirements. Nixon himself did not fight hard for the plan once it ran into trouble.

Family Compact In Canada, the tightly-knit group of families whose landholdings were granted by successive governors who dominated what was to become Ontario during the first third of the 19th century, pursuing rigidly conservative policies.

family-friendly hours The daytime sessions arranged for the HOUSE OF COMMONS from 2003 arising from pressure by women Labour MPs (BLAIR BABES), and some others, for an end to late-night sittings that impeded normal family life. The main reform was that the House sat on Tuesdays and Wednesdays from 11.30 am to 7 pm instead of from 2.30 pm to 10.30 or later as previously. Within a year traditionalists were rallying to get the old sitting hours – originally set to give MPs a chance to work in the City or at the law before coming to the

Commons – reinstated. MPs from Scotland and the North found themselves with time to kill, but Labour women Cabinet Ministers argued that a reversion would stop them going to the cinema or spending time with their children.

family values One of the watchwords of Republican campaigning in the run-up to the 1992 Presidential ELECTION. The stated message was that the Republicans stood for the nuclear American family; the unstated message that single parenthood was responsible for crime and riots (the Rodney KING riot had recently occurred) and that Bill CLINTON could not be trusted. The issue caught light inadvertently when Vice President Dan QUAYLE, in a speech no-one in the BUSH campaign had bothered to read, enraged liberals by saying of a popular TV show starring Candice Bergen:

> It doesn't help matters when prime time TV has Murphy Brown, a character who supposedly epitomises today's highly paid intelligent professional woman, mocking the importance of fathers by bearing a child alone and calling it just another lifestyle choice.

spend more time with my family The classic reason now given by politicians for resigning from office, originally – and sometimes still – a sincere statement of the pressures of political life; Rep. Gary Myers, announcing that he would not seek re-election in 1978 but return to his old foreman's job at a Pennsylvania steel plant, said:

> The amount of time it takes to do this job is just not compatible with how much time I want to spend with my family. I wanted to know my kids before it was too late.

The phrase came to be code for getting out before being pushed; Nicholas Ridley, not long before he did resign as Trade and Industry Secretary in 1990 (*see* GERMAN RACKET), told Labour MPs who were baiting him:

> I don't want to spend more time with my family.

When Jonathan AITKEN resigned as Chief Secretary to the Treasury in July 1995 to pursue – unsuccessfully – a libel action against the *Guardian* which ultimately led to his imprisonment for perjury, the Labour MP Brian Wilson told the HOUSE:

> He is departing to spend more time with his lawyers.

fanatic An advocate of a cause who loses all sense of proportion and resorts to extreme methods. CHURCHILL's definition was 'one who won't change his mind and won't change the subject'; Franklin P. Jones preferred 'one who sticks to his guns whether they're loaded or not'. Uncannily foreseeing AL QAEDA, Keats versified: 'Fanatics have their dreams, wherein they weave/A paradise for a sect.'

> From fanaticism to barbarism is only one step.
> DENIS DIDEROT (1713–84)

> Without fanaticism, one cannot accomplish anything. EVA PERÓN (1919–52)

Fannie Mae Federal National Mortgage Authority. The best known, and most affectionately regarded, of several mortgage finance agencies set up by the US Government to expand home ownership. Its credibility took a knock in December 2004 when, after being admonished by the Securities and Exchange Commission and facing a restatement of its earnings by up to $9 billion, its chief executive Franklin Raines and chief financial officer Tim Howard resigned. America's other largest mortgage provider, **Freddie Mac**, hit the headlines in June 2003 when its president, David Glenn, was fired after the board raised 'serious questions' about his honesty. The episode hit confidence in the mortgage market, and led to Freddie Mac being regulated by the Securities and Exchange Commission.

FAO The UNITED NATIONS Food and Agriculture Organisation, based in Rome.

faraway. a faraway country of which we know nothing Neville CHAMBERLAIN's notorious reference to Czechoslovakia, in a radio broadcast on 27 September 1938 acquiescing in Germany's annexation of the SUDETENLAND. It was regarded by his critics, then and even more so later, as the ultimate in APPEASEMENT; since WORLD WAR II British Prime Ministers have habitually apologised to the Czechs for betraying them. Chamberlain said:

> How horrible, fantastic, incredible it is that we should be digging trenches and trying on gas-masks here because of a quarrel in a faraway country between people of whom we know nothing.

FARC Revolutionary Armed Forces of Colombia. The hard-line Marxist guerrilla group in Colombia which finances its operations and weaponry through the international drug trade. Founded in 1964 by Manuel 'Sureshot' Marulanda, it came to control 40% of the country, with an estimated $300m annual income from drugs, kidnapping and extortion. The arrest in August 2001 of three members of the IRA, including SINN FEIN's representative in Havana, for allegedly training members of FARC in one of its former safe havens was a serious embarrassment to Gerry Adams and the Irish republican leadership, jeopardising NORTHERN IRELAND's PEACE PROCESS and causing outrage in the United States, putting at risk Sinn Fein's support there. The three were released in April 2004 after being found guilty only of travelling on false passports; eight months later a higher court convicted them in their absence on terrorism charges and sentenced them to lengthy jail terms. In 2003 FARC joined forces with the smaller but equally militant National Liberation Army (ELN) in response to a government crackdown on both group's activities.

farm. Farm Belt The American states radiating out from the mid-West that are largely dependent on agriculture, and on Federal support for farmers. Its people have long been attracted by POPULIST Presidential candidates.

Farmer-Labor *see* LABOR.

Farmers' Platform The programme adopted as the basis for political action by discontented Canadian farmers in WORLD WAR I. Developed by the Canadian Council of Agriculture between 1916 and 1918, it was also known as the New NATIONAL POLICY; it called for reforms including drastic TARIFF cuts and lower freight rates, public ownership of utilities and control of natural resource exploitation, higher taxes on the rich and political changes including REFERENDA and RECALL, PROPORTIONAL REPRESENTATION and votes for women. Only this last was rapidly realised.

buying back the farm In Australia, the WHITLAM government's policy, spearheaded by F. X. Connor, of reclaiming national resources that had been sold overseas.

like a farmer with terminal cancer trying to borrow against next year's crop The devastating description by Hunter S. Thompson in *Rolling Stone* of a flagging Sen. Edmund Muskie campaigning in the 1972 Florida Democratic PRIMARY.

vote yourself a farm The slogan of America's National Reform Association, founded in 1842, which advocated giving 160 acres of land to anyone willing to farm them, a goal largely achieved.

Fascism The right-wing TOTALITARIAN/CORPORATIST ideology and political system devised by MUSSOLINI (*see* DUCE) which was largely adopted by HITLER and Spain's General Franco (*see* CAUDILLO). The name comes from the Latin *fasces*, the bound rods and axes that were the symbol of authority in ancient Rome and in some more recent democracies. Mussolini founded his party in 1919; it took power after the MARCH ON ROME in 1922. Based on a ruthless, uniformed political party, on POPULISM, DEMAGOGY and leader-worship, fascism promoted an intense NATIONALISM (RACIALISM in Hitler's case) which, with territorial claims, was a principal cause of WORLD WAR II. Mussolini declared that 'Fascism is a religion. The twentieth century will be known in history as the century of fascism.' But he also said more candidly:

> Our programme is simple. We wish to govern Italy.

He held that 'for the fascist, everything is the State, and nothing human or spiritual exists, much less has value, outside the State.' And he warned that 'Fascism believes neither in the possibility nor the utility of perpetual peace'. Alfredo Rocco praised it as 'the unconscious awakening of our profound racial instinct', while José Antonio Prima de Rivera, before the outbreak of the SPANISH CIVIL WAR, hailed Fascism as 'a way of knowing everything – history, the state, the achievement of the proletarianisation of public life, a new way of knowing the phenomena of our epoch'. LENIN saw Fascism as 'capitalism in decay', Upton Sinclair as 'capitalism plus murder', and Aneurin BEVAN as 'the future refusing to be born'. John Strachey coined the slogan **Fascism Means War**, while G. D. H. Cole declared: 'Fascism is nonsense, and that is perhaps the gravest indictment of all.' Only in Spain did an entirely Fascist state survive the war, because Franco had shrewdly resisted Hitler's pressure to join the AXIS, but PERONISM in Argentina was closely related. Though small fascist parties and movements survive in many countries, the far right has developed new forms of ugliness and the name is now used mainly as a term of abuse. *See also* COMMUNISM; FALANGE; MOSLEYITES; NAZI.

> Benito Mussolini governed Italy with a new theme of government which, while it claimed to save the Italian people from Communism, raised himself to dictatorial power. As Fascism sprang from Communism, so Nazism developed from Fascism.
>
> WINSTON CHURCHILL, *The Gathering Storm*, ch. i.

> Fascism is not defined by the number of its victims, but by the way it kills them.
>
> JEAN-PAUL SARTRE

If Fascism came to America, it would be on a program of Americanism.
Sen. HUEY (KINGFISH) LONG (1893–1935)

neo-fascist An individual or organisation with similar style or objectives to fascism.
proto-fascist An organisation that is developing fascist tendencies.

Fashoda The crisis in 1898 when Britain and France disputed control of the upper Nile, and therefore of a sizeable part of Africa. It began when French troops under Major Marchand marched from the Congo into the Sudan, halting at Fashoda. British forces under Kitchener confronted them, and after a period of great tension, with the nations on the brink of war, the French withdrew, confirming Britain's supremacy in the region.

fast-track The Trade Promotion Authority, a procedure under which a US President, armed with general Congressional authority, may conduct trade negotiations with other nations without having to gain specific approval each time from the House and Senate and risk having his hands tied. It is hard to obtain; the 'fast-track' granted to George W. BUSH in July 2002 had originally been sought by President CLINTON eight years previously. In order to obtain it, Bush bought off the steel and farmers' lobbies by approving PROTECTIONIST measures favouring those sectors of the US economy.

fat cats (1) Large-scale, and by inference smug and complacent, contributors to political campaigns. The term was coined in the mid-1920s by Frank R. Kent of the *Baltimore Sun*.

I've always wondered why the Democrats call supporters of the Republican party 'fat cats', but their own contributors are called 'public-spirited philanthropists'.
RONALD REAGAN

(2) In the UK, businessmen who derive enormous financial benefits from a minimum of effort, and specifically those who made a killing from PRIVATISATION, either through over-generous salary packages or shareholdings whose value rocketed.

Power corrupts, but electric power corrupts absolutely. GORDON BROWN, 1995

father. Father of his Country A reverential name for George WASHINGTON, first used on a calendar published in Philadelphia in 1778, before the independence of the US had been finally secured and eleven years before he became their first President.

Father of the Constitution The title unofficially bestowed on James MADISON for his part in drafting both the US CONSTITUTION and the BILL OF RIGHTS, and writing the FEDERALIST Papers.

Father of the H-Bomb *See* H-BOMB.

Father of the House The longest continuously-serving member of a legislature. In the UK HOUSE OF COMMONS, the Father of the House takes the CHAIR before members have been sworn in to elect a new SPEAKER.

Fathers 4 Justice The militant UK organisation of men who claim their estranged wives are denying them legally-granted access to their children, two of whose members forced the suspension of the HOUSE OF COMMONS on 19 May 2004 during PRIME MINISTER'S QUESTIONS. They hurled a condom full of purple powder from the Visitors' Gallery, striking Tony BLAIR on the shoulder. They were seated immediately in front of a £600,000 security screen erected weeks before to prevent just such attacks, having won passes for VIP seats signed by the Labour peeress Baroness Golding in a raffle. Lady Golding apologised to the SPEAKER, and an urgent review of security was ordered, not least because had the powder been contaminated, leaving the CHAMBER, as MPs immediately did, would have spread the infection. The security review did not prevent protesting huntsmen storming the Commons chamber four months later (*see* MEN IN TIGHTS); Fathers 4 Justice achieved a further coup on 14 September, the day before that incident, when a member dressed as Batman scaled the fence of BUCKINGHAM PALACE and unfurled a banner for five hours close to its historic royal balcony. Other protests were staged atop the London Eye and on gantries over the main roads into London, paralysing traffic.

Founding Fathers The men who formed the United States and devised its constitution. Improbably, President HARDING was the apparent originator of the phrase. On 22 February 1918 he told a patriotic gathering in Washington: 'It is good to meet and drink at the fountain of wisdom inherited from the founding fathers of the Republic.' And in his INAUGURAL ADDRESS on 4 March 1921, he said:

Standing in this presence, mindful of the solemnity of this occasion, feeling the emotions which no one may know until he senses the great weight of responsibility for himself, I must utter my belief in the divine inspiration of the Founding Fathers.

fatwa The Islamic (Arabic) term for an edict imposed by a religious leader. It became known worldwide in 1989 when the AYATOLLAH Khomeini, spiritual and secular leader of Iran, offered a cash reward to any Muslim who ASSASSINATED Salman Rushdie (1947–), the British author of Indian Muslim origin, for alleged blasphemy in his novel *The Satanic Verses*. The *fatwa* read:

> The author of *The Satanic Verses* book, which is against Islam, the Prophet and the *Koran*, and all those involved in its publication who were aware of its content, are sentenced to death. I ask all Muslims to execute them wherever they find them.

The pronouncement caused a diplomatic and political storm, with fundamentalist Muslims in many countries including the UK rioting and burning Rushdie's books in protest at the publication. Rushdie was forced into hiding, under the protection of the Metropolitan Police, whom the book also ridiculed. *Fatwa*s are regarded by Muslims as the ultimate means of enforcing morality; for instance in the aftermath of the IRAQ WAR when INSURGENT groups were taking and frequently killing foreign hostages, the *ulema*, Iraq's national committee of Sunni Muslim scholars, passed a *fatwa* threatening similar action against anyone who took or failed to release a foreigner.

fault line A geological term which found its way into politics c. 2000, to describe a deep and underlying division in a political movement, or flaw in its programme, which could suddenly come to the surface. A fault in geology is a line on one side of which the strata have slipped, and may slip further.

favour. I should like to do every woman in the United Kingdom a favour The remark which probably aroused greater hilarity in the HOUSE OF COMMONS than any other in recent time. It was made on 21 January 1982 during PRIME MINISTER's QUESTIONS by Geoffrey Dickens (*see* HORSEFACE), the rotund Conservative MP for Littleborough and Saddleworth who had recently been in the headlines because of his colourful personal life. Raising a serious point with Margaret THATCHER about attacks on women, he began his question: 'Mr Speaker, I should like to do every woman in the United Kingdom a favour . . .', then made the mistake of pausing. The House erupted into helpless laughter, with the sole exception of the Prime Minister who saw nothing funny although WILLIE Whitelaw, by her side, was slapping his thigh with mirth. Dickens never finished the question; as the laughter began to die down, Speaker George Thomas observed: 'I am not here to save Hon. Members from themselves.'

No favours, but slightly quicker *See* NO.

favourite son A candidate, often for the US Presidential nomination, put forward by a party BOSS or MACHINE, and stuck to by his home-state delegates regardless of the merits or strengths of the other contenders in the hope of striking a deal. Originally a term of approbation (used of WASHINGTON when he visited Portsmouth, New Hampshire in 1789), it became by the 1820s a term of irony, referring to a beneficiary of nepotism or PATRONAGE.

FBI Federal Bureau of Investigation. The agency of the US Department of Justice founded in 1908 to investigate violations of federal law, becoming under J. Edgar Hoover, Director 1924–72, a force against organised crime in the 1930s, an instrument of MCCARTHYISM in the 1950s and a personal instrument of revenge toward the end of his career (*see* COINTELPRO). It survived the latter years of Hoover's reign to become once again an effective and professional organ of law enforcement, though criticised for lapses prior to 9/11.

FCO Foreign and Commonwealth Office. The nerve centre of British diplomacy, sandwiched in WHITEHALL between DOWNING STREET and the TREASURY. Founded as the FOREIGN OFFICE – the title by which it is still widely known – in 1782, it absorbed in the late 1960s its junior partner, the Commonwealth Relations Office, formerly the Colonial Office.

FDR The popular nickname for Franklin D. ROOSEVELT, the first of three US Presidents to date to be known as much by their initials as by their full names, the others being JFK and LBJ.

fear. let us never negotiate out of fear, but let us never fear to negotiate One of President KENNEDY's most celebrated dicta on COLD WAR diplomacy.

the only thing we have to fear is fear itself The most memorable phrase of Franklin D. ROOSEVELT's INAUGURAL ADDRESS on 4 March 1933. He declared:

> The only thing we have to fear is fear itself – nameless, unreasoning, unjustified terror which paralyses needed efforts to convert retreat into advance.

The phrase was not original. It had first been

used by the Greek philosopher Epictetus, or arguably in *Proverbs* 3:25 ('Be not afraid of sudden fear'). It had been echoed by Montaigne ('The thing of which I have most fear is fear'), Francis Bacon ('Nothing is terrible except fear itself') and Thoreau ('Nothing is so much to be feared as fear').

***Fearless* talks** The talks aboard the British cruiser of that name in October 1968 which marked the second and last attempt by Harold WILSON to persuade Ian Smith to end UDI and return Rhodesia to legality; the TIGER TALKS had been the first.

featherbedding The granting of over-generous subsidies (especially to certain categories of farmer) and wage settlements by governments or public sector bodies.

Fed (1) The Fed. Abbreviation for the US FEDERAL RESERVE system and its governing body. (2) Northern Clubs Federation Bitter, which became an institution in the bars of the HOUSE OF COMMONS after North-Eastern Labour MPs insisted in the 1970s on its being available. Until 2004 the beer was produced by a CO-OPERATIVE of working men's clubs; it is now brewed by Scottish Courage.

federal. Federal Election Commission The body set up by the US Congress in 1974 to oversee new laws on campaign conduct and financing, and administer campaign subsidies (*see* MATCHING FUNDS). Originally it was appointed jointly by the President and CONGRESS, but the SUPREME COURT ruled that as the FEC was executive and not legislative, the President should appoint all its members, subject to the consent of the SENATE.

Federal Government The central government of the United States, based in WASHINGTON and exercising the powers reserved to it, rather than to the STATES, under the US CONSTITUTION. When the Republic was created, Alexander HAMILTON argued for a strong centre, declaring: 'The three great objects of government, agriculture, commerce and revenue, can only be secured by a federal government.' But in recent times Ronald REAGAN said: 'We all need to be reminded that the Federal Government did not create the states – the states created the Federal Government.'

> An American may through a long life never be reminded of the Federal Government, except when he votes in Federal elections, lodges a complaint against the post office, or is required to pay duties of customs and excise.
>
> BRYCE, British Ambassador in Washington 1907–13

Federal Hall The two-storey building in New York, in Wall Street at the head of Broad Street, where the US CONGRESS first met on 4 March 1789. Though heavily modernised by l'Enfant, the planner of WASHINGTON, it was used for only one session before Congress decamped to Philadelphia; it was pulled down in 1816.

Federal period The period from 1781 to 1789 when the Articles of CONFEDERATION served as America's CONSTITUTION, the country being little more than a league of thirteen sovereign states.

Federal Register The daily bulletin, published in Washington, in which the US Government publishes Presidential proclamations, EXECUTIVE ORDERS, and other regulations and notices.

Federal Reserve America's CENTRAL BANKing system created by Woodrow WILSON's Federal Reserve Act, 1913. The nation is divided into twelve Federal Reserve Districts, with a federal reserve bank in each acting as the lender of last resort. Presiding over them is a board of governors (*see* FED) with an independent chairman; they regulate the amount of money in circulation and set the level of interest rates.

The Fed's most powerful and respected chairman in modern times has been Alan Greenspan, who was appointed in 1988 under President REAGAN and in May 2004 at the age of 78 was nominated by George W. BUSH to serve until his TERM LIMIT as a Fed governor expired two years later

Federal Triangle The area of WASHINGTON DC bounded by PENNSYLVANIA AVENUE, Constitution Avenue and 14th Street which was developed from the 1920s as the nerve-centre of the US Federal BUREAUCRACY, but was only completed in 1998 with the opening of the REAGAN BUILDING. It also embraces the Departments of Commerce, Labor, Justice and the Post Office, the DISTRICT BUILDING, the Federal Trade Commission, the Internal Revenue Service and the National Archives. The area was known in the late 19th century as the 'plague spot' of the nation's capital, because brothels and saloons rubbed shoulders with banks and newspaper offices.

Federalism (1) Originally the doctrine advanced by HAMILTON and MADISON for a strong federal government in the United States stopping short of a unitary state, instead of a loose confederation of strong states with a weak centre. When Canada was formed, Lord Acton wrote: 'A great democracy must either sacrifice self-government to unity, or preserve it by federalism. The co-existence of several nations under the same state is the best, as well as the best security of its freedom.' (2) In the EUROPEAN UNION, self-styled Federalists want the whole governed by elected representatives of all the member states and/or their component regions. EUROSCEPTICS take the term to mean direct rule by non-elected bureaucrats from Brussels.

New Federalism, the President REAGAN's unsuccessful initiative in 1982 to transfer major federal programmes and revenues to the States.

Federalist In Europe, 'Federalists' describe themselves as those who aim for a democratic United States of Europe. To opponents of closer union, it is a term of abuse.

> One who wants Britain to be governed by everyone except the British.
>
> CHRISTOPHER MONCKTON.

Federalist (Papers), The The 85 essays in support of ratification of the US CONSTITUTION published in New York newspapers from 1787 to 1788 under the name 'Publius'. The real authors were Alexander HAMILTON, John JAY and James MADISON.

Federalist Party The party formed in the early days of the United States to pursue FEDERALISM against advocates of a weak national government. It was dominant during the administrations of WASHINGTON and John ADAMS, but the party faded after JEFFERSON's election in 1800 and ceased to be a force after 1830.

anti-Federalists The contemporary collective term for those who opposed the adoption of the US CONSTITUTION after its completion in 1787.

federast The ultimate term of abuse for advocates of closer European union by their (mainly British and right-wing) opponents. A corruption of 'pederast'.

feelgood factor The mood of public well-being, generally inspired by the state of the economy, that all leaders, and parties in government, hope to generate in order to ensure their re-election. The term was used early on to describe the mood generated by President REAGAN in his first term after the uncertainties of the CARTER years.

fellow-traveller A pejorative for a person in sympathy with a political party (usually the Communists) but ostensibly not part of it. The term (Russ. *Poputchik*) was coined by TROTSKY, appeared in English in 1936 in an article by Max Lerner (*'Mr Roosevelt and his Fellow-Travelers'*) and became a commonplace early in the COLD WAR amid global concern over covert Communist influence (*see* MCCARTHYISM; UN-AMERICAN ACTIVITIES). By 1957 the lexicographer Eric Partridge was writing: 'It shows signs of being employed so widely and indiscriminately that it becomes mere vogue and probably discredited.'

> He is but one of a reputed short-list of seven fellow-travellers under threat of expulsion.
>
> *Time and Tide*, 1 May 1948, on a Labour Party member facing expulsion

feminism The demand for widespread political and social reform to ensure that women enjoy at least as active and prestigious a place in society as men, and for a recasting of attitudes so that things are seen from an educated woman's perspective, which emerged in late 1960s America and has spread to most of the world. With its roots in earlier movements like the SUFFRAGETTES, the movement has as its basis the demand for political, social and economic rights, and in many countries has achieved significant advances. More militant, often left-wing groups have tried to create an alternative society, rewriting history and even in extreme cases excluding men. In many campaigns, notably that of the GREENHAM WOMEN, feminists have made common cause with anti-NUCLEAR or environmental groups; the universal availability of birth control is also a feminist priority. *See also* NOW; WOMEN'S RIGHTS.

fence-sitting Refusal to take sides in a political argument. LLOYD GEORGE said of Sir John Simon (1873–1954): 'He has sat on the fence for so long that the iron has entered his soul.' Vice President Spiro AGNEW denounced the Eastern ESTABLISHMENT as 'ideological eunuchs, whose most comfortable position is straddling the fence', and the 300-lb Liberal MP Sir Cyril Smith (*see* BIG CYRIL) once declared:

> If a fence is strong enough, I'll sit on it.

mending fences Cultivating a renewed relationship with a political ally or crucial group of supporters whom one has offended, generally out of electoral necessity. Also, to rebuild one's relationship with CONSTITUENTS after a legislative session away from them.

Fencing Mask The popular nickname for London's City Hall, the landmark on the south bank of the Thames between Tower Bridge and London Bridge which since July 2002 has been the seat of the Mayor and the

GREATER LONDON ASSEMBLY. It is an accurate description of the rounded glass building's design: the shape of a human head tilted away from the river, so that a curved expanse on the 'face' offers those working in and visiting the building an impressive riverside view. Also known as 'the headlamp', City Hall was designed by Foster and Partners.

Fenians An Irish Nationalist movement founded in New York in 1857, taking its name from the legendary Irish hero Fionn MacCumhail. It spread rapidly across America, then to Ireland, where it absorbed the Phoenix Society, eventually developing into the IRISH REPUBLICAN BROTHERHOOD, the militant body that paved the way for the EASTER RISING and the IRA. In the late 1860s London was rocked by a chain of Fenian outrages, culminating in the Clerkenwell bombings of 13 December 1867 when a bungled attempt to blast Fenian prisoners free with a barrel of gunpowder caused several deaths. The word 'Fenian' was coined by the 18th-century Irish poetess Charlotte Brooke, ironically a forebear of the 1990s Conservative Northern Ireland Secretary Peter Brooke. It has also become a term of abuse for any Irish Nationalist.

Ferraro, Geraldine Ann (1935–) The first and so far only woman to be run by a major US party on its Presidential ticket, as Vice Presidential running mate to Walter Mondale (*see* NORWEGIAN WOOD) in 1984. A New York lawyer of Italian immigrant stock, she served six years in CONGRESS from 1978, sponsoring legislation to end pension discrimination against women, and earned her place on the 1984 ticket through her work as chief of the Democratic platform committee. She stood up well to the gruelling scrutiny of the campaign trail, despite niggling questions about her realtor husband's finances, but she and Mondale went down to heavy defeat by Ronald REAGAN at the height of his popularity. She stayed in politics, and President CLINTON later appointed her to head the US delegation to the UN HUMAN RIGHTS Commission.

Fianna Eireann The youth movement of SINN FEIN, which bears a superficial resemblance, though no more, to the Boy Scouts and Guides.

Fianna Fail (Ir. Warriors of Ireland) The REPUBLICAN party formed in 1926 by Eamonn de Valera (*see* DEV) to oppose the PARTITION of Ireland which had created the IRISH FREE STATE. Formed of men who had been on the losing side in the Civil War, Fianna Fail first refused to take its seats in the DAIL, but in 1932 it formed a government under de Valera and since then has only been out of power in the periods 1948–51, 1973–77, 1982–87 and 1994–97, alternating with coalitions led by FINE GAEL. The WHELEHAN AFFAIR forced Fianna Fail's Albert Reynolds out of office in December 1994, but within three years Bertie Ahern (*see* ANORAK MAN) ousted a Fine Gael-Labour coalition led by John Bruton, going on to establish his own primacy in Irish politics while the reputations of his predecessors Charles HAUGHEY and Reynolds (*see also* BEEF TRIBUNAL) were tainted by scandal. Fianna Fail has placed a high emphasis on economic self-sufficiency and reviving the Irish language, and while committed in theory to a united Ireland it has enjoyed, under Jack Lynch, Haughey, Reynolds and Ahern generally good relations with British leaders, culminating in the DOWNING STREET DECLARATION and joint stewardship of the GOOD FRIDAY AGREEMENT.

> JOHN BOWMAN of RTE: Surely you are aware that Fianna Fail are on record as saying they will never enter coalition?
> Labour leader FRANK CLUSKEY: Yeagh, but Fianna Fail are also on record as saying they would never enter *Dail Eireann*.
> 1981 election campaign

Fidel. Fidel Castro in a miniskirt The verdict of the ULSTER UNIONIST MP Stratton Mills (1932–) on the electrifying MAIDEN SPEECH in 1969 of Bernadette Devlin (1947–, later McAliskey). The fiery 21-year-old student CIVIL RIGHTS campaigner was elected 'Unity' MP for Mid-Ulster just as years of discrimination against Catholics were starting to produce a BACKLASH, but before the IRA had resumed its terror campaign. She held her seat in 1970 but was not re-elected in 1974; she later joined the Irish Republican Socialist Party and contested elections in Ulster and the Republic as an Independent.

Fidelistas The devoted followers of Fidel Castro (1927–) who from 1956 waged a GUERRILLA campaign from the mountains against the corrupt Batista regime, then joined him in taking power in February 1959. As Castro's regime became rigidly Marxist and pro-Soviet, a number of the original *Fidelistas* were executed or imprisoned, or fled to the United States. *See also* GRANMA.

Fifteenth Amendment The amendment to

the US CONSTITUTION, ratified in March 1870, which guaranteed black Americans the vote, stipulating that Federal or State authorities must not abridge the right 'on account of race, color or previous condition of servitude'. The amendment, too radical even for many Northerners, was a cornerstone of RECONSTRUCTION; when that process was reversed in the late 1870s it ceased to be a guarantee.

Fifth. Fifth Amendment The fifth of ten amendments to the US Constitution in the BILL OF RIGHTS, ratified in December 1791, critically stating: 'nor shall [any person] be compelled in any criminal case to be a witness against himself.' Generations of mobsters called to testify before Congressional committees have 'taken the fifth' to avoid self-incrimination, as did many alleged Communists at the height of MCCARTHYISM; these became known as **Fifth-Amendment Communists**.

Fifth Columnist A member of a community or group with loyalties to a state or body determined to destroy it, who at the appropriate moment will undermine or strike against the order of which he or she appears to be part. The term was originally applied during the SPANISH CIVIL WAR by General Emilio Mola to citizens of Republican Madrid loyal to General Franco (*see* CAUDILLO). When asked in October 1937 which of his four army columns would capture Madrid, he replied: 'The fifth column.'

Fifth Republic The government of France introduced by General DE GAULLE in 1958 to replace the FOURTH REPUBLIC, which had staggered from one crisis to another under a series of unstable COALITIONS since the end of WORLD WAR II. The Fifth Republic remedied this by placing power essentially in the hands of the President, with the Prime Minister operating under the shadow of the ÉLYSÉE. Despite muscle-flexing by Jacques CHIRAC as Premier during the early years of COHABITATION and more recently by Lionel Jospin, this has remained essentially true.

fifty. Fifty-first State The term applied to Britain in the late 1950s and early '60s by left-wingers, and some others, who thought it was too much under US domination and lacked a credible independent foreign and defence policy. Prior to the statehood of Alaska and Hawaii in 1959, Britain was categorised as the **49th State**.

Fifty-four Forty or fight! The slogan on which James Knox Polk (1795–1849) was elected President of the United States in 1844. It staked a claim to all of what was then known as the OREGON territory as far north as Alaska. In 1827 America and Britain has agreed to share the territory after Russia and Spain abandoned claims to it; when it became clear the lands were not worthless as originally thought, America pressed its claim. However, Polk compromised, and on 15 June 1846 the Oregon Treaty was signed, with the US accepting its northern border as the **49th Parallel** – well south of the line Polk's supporters had pressed for.

fight, fight and fight again The most celebrated phrase from the long battle within Britain's LABOUR PARTY over UNILATERALISM. It was spoken by party leader Hugh GAITSKELL during a passionate speech on 5 October 1960 to the party's Scarborough conference after it had voted to commit Labour to scrap Britain's NUCLEAR weapons unconditionally. Brian Walden, the future MP and TV presenter, later claimed credit for the phrase. Gaitskell said:

> It is not in dispute that the vast majority of Labour Members of Parliament are utterly opposed to unilateralism and neutralism. So what do you expect them to do? Change their attitude overnight? There are other people, too, not in Parliament, in the Party, who share our convictions. What sort of people do you think they are? What sort of people do you think we are? Do you think we can simply accept a decision of this kind? Do you think we can become overnight the PACIFISTS, unilateralists and FELLOW TRAVELLERS that other people are? . . . There are some of us, Mr Chairman, who will fight, and fight, and fight again to save the party we love. We will fight and fight and fight again to bring back sanity and honesty and dignity, so that our party, with its great past, may retain its glory and its greatness.

Fighting French *See* FREE FRENCH.

filibuster (Sp. *filibustero*, corruption of the Dut. *vrij buiter*, a freebooter) A speech prolonging debate on a measure to the point where it becomes procedurally impossible for it to progress; a technique honed to perfection in the US SENATE until reform of the rules reduced its capacity to thwart the will of the majority. Filibusters were originally more common in the HOUSE, but in 1841 it passed the ONE-HOUR RULE which limited speeches to that maximum. That same year, the Senate rejected such a change, and the filibuster became part of its workings. No limit at all was imposed until 1917, when filibusters by ISOLATIONIST Senators against WILSON's war preparations led to the CLOTURE being provided for. From 1927 to 1962 the cloture was never achieved and filibusters, normally by Southern conservatives, invariably succeeded. Only after the cloture was invoked in 1964 to pass a CIVIL RIGHTS Bill did matters change; since 1975 filibusters have been rare.

In 1881 Sen. George F. Edmunds justified the filibuster thus: 'It is of greater importance to the public interest that every Bill in your calendar should fail than that any Senator should be cut off from the right of expressing his opinion.' More recently filibusters became as much a matter of pride as of ideology, Sen. Allan Allender saying: 'I held the title of longest filibuster for two or three years, until another idiot [Sen. Wayne Morse] beat my record.' But Rep. Clare Boothe Luce had the last word:

> They say women talk too much. If you have worked in Congress you know that the filibuster was invented by men.

post-cloture filibuster A fresh procedural device which briefly revived the filibuster from 1975 to 1979. Sen. James Allen of Alabama discovered that while speeches were now limited to one hour each after cloture, time-consuming items such as ROLL CALL votes, QUORUM calls and the like did not fall within the limit. After two Democratic senators filed 508 amendments to a gas deregulatrion Bill, keeping the Senate up all night for the first time in thirteen years, MAJORITY LEADER Robert C. Byrd persuaded Vice President Mondale (*see* NORWEGIAN WOOD) to rule such amendments dilatory and out of ORDER.

Final Solution (Ger. *Endlösung*) The chilling euphemism used by the NAZIs for their grotesque policy of exterminating European Jewry. Though implicit in HITLER's MEIN KAMPF, it was 1941 before Goering ordered Heydrich to prepare for 'a total solution of the Jewish question in those territories of Europe which are under German influence'. Schedules were set by Nazi leaders at a conference at Wannsee, Berlin, in 1942; the details were left to Adolf EICHMANN, who almost 20 years later would be executed for GENOCIDE by the Israelis. Most Germans at the time would not have known that the policy involved such a monstrous programme of mass extermination, but once the elaborate apparatus for rounding up and transporting Jews eastward to death camps began to function, the truth about the HOLOCAUST must have dawned on many.

Financial Management Initiative (FMI) A landmark WHITEHALL efficiency exercise set in motion by Sir Derek RAYNER early in the THATCHER administration. A seven-strong team of civil servants and management consultants in May 1982 recommended stimuli for CIVIL SERVICE efficiency comparable to the disciplines of the private sector. Everyone from PERMANENT SECRETARIES downward was expected to define and understand their function, clear responsibilities for spending money were to be set, and managers were expected to have better information about costs, training and access to expert advice. The exercise was based on Michael Heseltine's MINIS, and Mrs Thatcher ordered all her Ministers to implement it, despite protests from Sir Frank Cooper, powerful Permanent Secretary at the Ministry of Defence, that the idea of Ministers as managers was 'nonsense'. FMI was implemented by Rayner's successor Sir Robin Ibbs; the concept of NEXT STEPS AGENCIES was just one of its fruits.

Fine Gael (Ir. Tribe of the Gaels) The party founded by William T. Cosgrave and other members of DAIL EIREANN who supported the Treaty of 1921 that created the IRISH FREE STATE. Considered more conservative and less GREEN than FIANNA FAIL (who have been in power for longer), Fine Gael nevertheless declared a republic and withdrew Ireland from the COMMONWEALTH in 1948 during its coalition with Labour. It was a Fine Gael government, led by Garret FitzGerald, which sought to break the deadlock over NORTHERN IRELAND by negotiating the 1975 ANGLO-IRISH AGREEMENT, though it was Fianna Fail that concluded the DOWNING STREET DECLARATION and GOOD FRIDAY AGREEMENT. Fine Gael most recently held power, in coalition with Labour with John Bruton as TAOISEACH, from 1994 to 1997.

fine-tuning The regulation of an economy by making small changes to taxation, interest rates, money supply, etc., so as to steer a steady middle course between RECESSION and OVERHEATING.

Finland. Finland Station speech The speech made by LENIN on 16 April 1917 at the Finland Station in Petrograd on his return from exile in Switzerland, as the old order in Russia began to collapse; by November of that year his BOLSHEVIKS had taken power. *To The Finland Station*, by Edmund Wilson, is a classic account of the Bolshevik revolution and the forces behind it. In his speech Lenin told supporters:

> Dear comrades, soldiers, sailors and workers! I am happy to hail in you the victorious Russian revolution! I greet you as the advance guard of the world proletarian army. . . The hour is not far off when at the summons of our comrade, Karl Liebknecht, the German people will turn their weapons against their capitalist exploiters. The sun of the world socialist revolution has already risen!

Finlandisation The process of turning the neighbour of a Communist state into a muted semi-client, even if it is politically independent and has a wholly democratic political system. It derives from the position of Finland and the course followed by its government, especially during the four decades after WORLD WAR II. Although Finland was a capitalist democracy, its leaders conducted its affairs in close consultation with, and with acute awareness of, the SUPERPOWER next door. *See also* WINTER WAR.

54 The slip of the tongue made by Stephen Byers (*see also* BURY, FUCKED RAILTRACK), a then rising star of Tony BLAIR's government, when as Schools Minister he was asked in a radio interview in 1998 what 7x8 made. *Compare* POTATOE.

fire. *The Fire Next Time* The best-known work of the black US author James Baldwin (1924–87). Published in 1963, it gave an apocalyptic view of America's future if white attitudes to race remained unchanged. He wrote:

> White people in this country will have quite enough to do in learning how to accept and love themselves and each other, and when they have achieved this – which will not be tomorrow and may very well be never – the Negro problem will no longer exist, for it will no longer be needed.

firebell in the night Thomas JEFFERSON's emotive phrase for the capacity of the issue of SLAVERY to wreck the American union. In a letter to John ADAMS on 22 April 1820 over the MISSOURI COMPROMISE, Jefferson wrote:

> This momentous question, like a firebell in the night, awakened and filled me with terror. I considered it at once as the knell of the Union.

fireside chat A broadcast in which a leader talks easily and intimately to the people. The term was coined in 1933 when Franklin D. ROOSEVELT, eight years after taking office, gave a frank, confiding radio talk about America's problems and his plans for solving them; projecting himself to sound like a family friend, he continued the talks throughout his Presidency and the tradition of the weekly radio address survived into the next century. FDR's successors have sought to emulate his style, Ronald REAGAN coming closest. Some aspirants have conspicuously failed; Mark Russell said of Sen. Henry 'SCOOP' Jackson:

> He gave a fireside speech – and the fire went out.

first. First Amendment The first of ten AMENDMENTS to the US CONSTITUTION ratified in December 1791 which constitute the BILL OF RIGHTS. It guarantees what have become the most sacred freedoms of the American people, reading:

> CONGRESS shall make no law respecting an establishment of religion, or prohibiting the free exercise thereof; or abridging the freedom of speech, or of press; or the right of the people peaceably to assemble, and to petition the government for a redress of grievances.

The SUPREME COURT has customarily given those claiming the right to freedom of speech the benefit of the doubt; the one exception is obscenity. The liberal Justice William O. Douglas maintained: '"Congress shall make no law" does not mean "Congress may make some laws"', but more recently Justice William Brennan wrote: 'Implicit in the history of this amendment is the rejection of obscenity as utterly without redeeming social importance.' The Burger Court ruled in 1973 that states could ban any works that, taken as a whole, appeal to prurient interests, portray sexual conduct in an offensive way, and do not have serious literary, artistic, political or scientific value. Outside the Bible Belt, these constraints have rarely been exercised.

first among equals (Lat. *Primus inter pares*) A term central to the concept of CABINET GOVERNMENT, defining the position of the PRIME MINISTER in relation to other members of the Cabinet. Jeffrey Archer (*see* FRAGRANT), used it in 1983 as the title of a novel chronicling the struggle between four contesting politicians to reach NUMBER TEN. The phrase was probably first used by the Liberal statesman John (later Lord) Morley (1838–1923), who wrote in his 1889 life of WALPOLE:

> Although in Cabinet all its members stand on an equal footing, speak with equal voice, and on the rare occasion when a division is taken, are counted on the fraternal principal of one vote, yet the head of the Cabinet is *primus inter pares*, and occupies a position which, so long as it lasts, is one of exceptional and peculiar authority.

First Bloke One of several nicknames for

Labor Prime Minister Bob HAWKE, reflecting his embodiment of Australian MATESHIP. *See also* SILVER BODGIE.

First Division The highest ranks of Britain's CIVIL SERVICE, numbering some 2,000 officials and including Whitehall's MANDARINS. Its trade union, the **First Division Association,** is a prestigious affiliate of the TUC.

First Dog Most US Presidents have had a pet whose activities have exercised the media – and sometimes the political community (*see especially* BUDDY, FALA), but they held back from using the title 'First Dog' out of deference to the FIRST LADY. The first undisputed holder of the title was George W. BUSH's springer spaniel SPOT (1989–2004).

First Family, The A satirical record album lampooning the KENNEDY family and its life in the WHITE HOUSE which topped America's best-sellers c. 1962.

first in war, first in peace, first in the hearts of his countrymen The tribute paid to George WASHINGTON on his death in a Congressional speech on 26 December 1799 by Henry 'Light Horse Harry' Lee.

First Lady The wife of the President of the United States. The term was known early in the life of the nation, Zachary Taylor (1784–1850) saying of Dolley MADISON: 'She was truly our First Lady for half a century,' but it only came into general use after 1900. Though the First Lady has no Constitutional status, she occupies a niche in the life of the nation and much is expected of her. Grace COOLIDGE subordinated her own identity, saying: 'This was the wife of the President of the United States and she took precedence over me,' and Eleanor Roosevelt (FIRST LADY OF THE WORLD, *see* below) warned the First Ladies who followed her: 'You will feel you are no longer clothing yourself – you are clothing a public monument.' Jacqueline Kennedy (*see* JACKIE O) bridled at first, saying: 'The one thing I do not want to be called is First Lady. It sounds like a saddle horse,' but she relented on the use of the term, at least: 'People have told me 99 things that I have to do as First Lady – and I haven't done one of them yet.' The one First Lady to take an active role in politics, as opposed to social issues, was Hillary CLINTON, who in her husband's first term took charge of an abortive health care initiative and four years after leaving the White House was elected to the Senate. *See also* LAST LADY.

First Lady of the World The title earned by Eleanor Roosevelt (1884–1962), who after the death of her husband Franklin D. ROOSEVELT in 1945 toured the world as an ambassador for peace and the needy. Though she and her husband had been close to divorce before he contracted polio in 1921, she campaigned vigorously for him and on social issues until his death. When FDR was elected in 1932, she told friends: 'Now I'll have no identity,' but soon proved herself wrong. She started by saying: 'If any SECRET SERVICE man shows up and starts following me around, I'll send him right back where he came from.' FDR called her 'my eyes and ears', declaring: 'My missus goes where she wants to, she talks to everybody and does she learn something!' (*see* BONUS ARMY). Despite being, in her husband's words, 'the originator, discoverer and inventor of the Household Economy for Millionnaires', she had a remarkable ability to communicate with the most disadvantaged – and to articulate their hopes where it counted. More liberal than FDR, she even brought her feisty lobbying to the dinner table, her daughter Anna once having to interject: 'Mother, can't you see you're giving Father indigestion.' Eleanor Roosevelt herself said: 'I used to tell my husband that if he could make me understand something, it would be clear to all the other people in the country.' And despite evidence to the contrary, she insisted: 'I never urged on (FDR) a specific course of action, no matter how strongly I felt.' She had none of the glamour of Jacqueline Kennedy, Joe Alsop writing: 'Her hats had the look of having been found under the bed.' But after her wartime tour of the South Pacific theatre, Admiral William F. Halsey reported:

> I marvelled at her hardihood, both physical and mental. She also accomplished more good than any other person, or any group of civilians, who passed through my area.

In her widowhood, she embarked on a new career as a humanitarian on the world stage, remarking: 'When you cease to make a contribution you begin to die.' And as chairwoman of the UN HUMAN RIGHTS Commission, she made a unique contribution.

> No woman has ever so comforted the distressed or distressed the comfortable.
>
> CLARE BOOTHE LUCE (1903–87)

> She would rather light candles than curse the darkness, and her glow has warmed the world.
>
> ADLAI STEVENSON at the United Nations, 9 November 1962

First Mama The CB radio callsign given to

Betty FORD during her husband's tenure of the White House, 1974–77.

First Minister The leader of one of the UK's DEVOLVED administrations. The title was first applied in June 1998 to the NORTHERN IRELAND First Minister David Trimble when he took charge of a POWER SHARING Executive after the GOOD FRIDAY AGREEMENT. The following year Donald Dewar became Scotland's first First Minister after the election of the SCOTTISH PARLIAMENT, and the title has since come into popular use in Wales for the leader of the WELSH ASSEMBLY GOVERNMENT, even though the correct usage is FIRST SECRETARY.

First Minister's Questions *See* FMQS.

first past the post The electoral system in which any number of CANDIDATES compete for a single post, and the one with the highest number of votes is elected even if they have only gained a small proportion of the total. Its most obvious application is in the election of MPs to WESTMINSTER. 'First past the post' is anathema to advocates of PROPORTIONAL REPRESENTATION.

First Reading The initial stage of a BILL's progress through a legislature, generally a formality with no actual proceedings.

First Secretary (1) The title generally, but not always, allocated to Britain's DEPUTY PRIME MINISTER. George BROWN bore the title of **First Secretary of State,** despite also heading a Department; R. A. Butler (*see* RAB) and Michael Heseltime (*see* HEZZA) for part of his tenure were styled **First Secretary**. (2) The initial title of the leader of the devolved administration in Wales, the first holder being Alun Michael in 1999. Before long FIRST MINISTER came to be used in its place, asserting equality of status with the leaders of Scotland and Northern Ireland despite the WELSH ASSEMBLY GOVERNMENT's more limited powers. Members of the Ministerial team are known as Assembly Ministers.

first strike The opening shot in a nuclear war, which the aggressor hopes will destroy the attacked nation's capacity to retaliate. First-strike weapons are usually not protected by missile silos and 'hardened' shelters and are designed, as their name implies, to destroy the enemy's planes, submarines and missiles. Second-strike weapons, to be used in the event of a surprise attack to 'take out' first-strike weapons or if the target nation does manage to retaliate, are heavily protected. *See* NO FIRST USE.

First they came for the Jews, but I didn't protest because I was not a Jew. Then they came for the Communists, but I didn't protest because I was not a Communist. Then they came for the trade unionists, and I didn't protest because I was not a trade unionist. Then they came for me, and there was no one left to protest. The chilling parable of the consequences of failing to stand up to the NAZIS in pre-war Germany, told by Martin Niemöller (1892–1984), the former U-boat commander who became an evangelical pastor and was sent to a CONCENTRATION CAMP in 1937; he survived to become a bishop. Three decades later the black author James Baldwin echoed Niemöller in a message of support to the imprisoned militant Angela Davis, telling her:

> If they take you in the morning, they will come for us at night.

FIS (Fr. Islamic Salvation Front). The political party that was banned by the Algerian military when on the point of winning elections in 1992, and whose military wing thereafter engaged in a bloody armed struggle with government forces. It laid down its arms at the end of the decade, and later sided with the authorities against the even more militant Armed Islamic Groups (**GIA**).

fiscal. fiscal drag The process under which, in a system of progressive TAXATION, an increase in income can take a taxpayer into a higher tax bracket. The effect is to increase revenue without increasing taxes.

fiscal 20xx Washington shorthand for a financial year.

fiscal policy Measures used by governments to influence economic activity, particularly by manipulating the levels and allocation of taxes and spending. They are often used in conjunction with monetary policy to achieve set goals.

> Too often in recent history liberal governments have been wrecked on the rocks of loose fiscal policy. FRANKLIN D. ROOSEVELT, 1933

Fishbait The nickname of William Mosley Miller (1912–87), doorkeeper to the US HOUSE OF REPRESENTATIVES for 28 years. Despite the diminutive stature which earned him the name, the feisty Mississippi-born Miller was no respecter of persons. President TRUMAN warned the future Queen Elizabeth II of this before she visited the CAPITOL; 'Fishbait' greeted her with a cordial: 'Howdy, Ma'am,' then called down from the rostrum to the Duke of Edinburgh's party: 'Hey, pass me up the Prince!' When 'Fishbait' retired, his autobiography under that title cast harsh judgements on many Congressional figures.

Fitz The bulldog hired for a Labour PARTY POLITICAL BROADCAST by Peter Mandelson (*see* BOBBY) prior to the 1997 election. Fitz, whose owner was a Conservative, was intended to underline NEW LABOUR's patriotic and CHURCHILLian credentials to wavering Tory voters. However the choice provoked a backlash from ethnic campaigners who identified it with the BNP and other far-right and racist groups.

five. five economic tests The five criteria which CHANCELLOR Gordon BROWN set for Tony BLAIR's government as a yardstick for deciding whether to recommend to a REFERENDUM that Britain should join the EURO. Set in 1998 when Blair and Brown decided not to join with the first wave of members at the start of 2002, the tests were:

- Has there been substantial convergence between the UK and the euro zone economies?
- Is there sufficient flexibility in the UK economy to respond to shocks if it joined the euro zone?
- What will be the effect of the euro on investment in the UK?
- What will be the effect of the euro on the UK financial services industry?; and
- How will the euro affect UK employment and prosperity?

On 9 June 2003, Brown told the COMMONS that while the government supported membership of the euro in principle, up to that point only the fourth of these criteria had been satisfactorily addressed.

Five Members The five members of the Long Parliament – Pym, Hampden, Haselrig, Strode and Holles – whom Charles I attempted to arrest for treason on 4 January 1642. The King's arrival with troops in the HOUSE OF COMMONS (*see* I SEE THE BIRDS HAVE FLOWN) was a crucial moment on the road to Civil War.

five minute rule The limit imposed by the US HOUSE OF REPRESENTATIVES on questioning of a witness by one member of the APPROPRIATIONS Committee during hearings on the BUDGET. Once all members have asked their questions, further time may be allowed.

five o'clock shadow The stubble on Richard NIXON's chin whose sinister appearance before the cameras was blamed in part for John F. KENNEDY's perceived victory in their first Presidential DEBATE, in Chicago on 26 September 1960. The phrase comes from a 1950s razor blade commercial.

> He looked like a man with shaving and perspirational problems, glumly waiting for the commercial to tell him how not to offend.
>
> ROGER BUTTERFIELD, historian

> I paid too much attention to what I was going to say and too little to how I would look.
>
> RICHARD NIXON

527 A LOBBYING group permitted under US ELECTION law to attack candidates, but not to endorse them. The relationship between 527s and the CANDIDATES who will benefit from their activities is a murky one, as shown by the episode of the SWIFT BOAT VETERANS FOR TRUTH in the 2004 Presidential campaign. The groups take their name from the obscure section of the tax code that permits their activities.

537 The number of votes by which George W. BUSH was finally reckoned to have carried Florida in 2002, and with that State the Presidential election.

Five Year Plan In the Soviet Union and subsequently in some other countries, plans for developing the whole of a nation's economy in a co-ordinated effort over five years. The first Five Year Plan was launched by STALIN in 1928, with the aims of making the Soviet state self-supporting, mechanising agriculture, promoting literacy, etc. Five Year Plans were to be promulgated for the next six decades, but especially after WORLD WAR II there was an increasing divergence between goals set and advances achieved.

flag burning The most controversial form of protest in America, seen by most as highly unpatriotic. It is also long-standing, going back at least to the start of the 20th century. Largely because the gesture was so provocative, anti-VIETNAM WAR militants set fire to the STARS AND STRIPES as an easy way of gaining publicity. A less widespread recurrence in the mid-1980s sparked Congressional efforts to ban such protests, and consequent litigation over whether such legislation – up to and including an AMENDMENT to the Constitution – would violate the FIRST AMENDMENT.

> Flag burning is wrong. Protection of the flag, a unique national symbol, will in no way limit the opportunity nor the breadth of protest available in the exercise of free speech rights. I believe the importance of this issue compels me to call for a constitutional amendment.
>
> GEORGE BUSH Snr, 27 June 1989.

> You flag-burning pigs should not have the right to co-exist with us devout, God-fearing Americans.
>
> Letter to the QUAYLE QUARTERLY from Dominick Swinhart, Olympia, Washington

> If you want a symbolic gesture don't burn the flag – wash it.
>
> NORMAN THOMAS, US socialist leader (1884–1968)

flags and furloughs Democratic nominee Michael Dukakis's characterisation of the successful Republican tactics in the 1988 Presidential ELECTION. It stemmed from George BUSH's call for legislation to outlaw FLAG-BURNING, and his linking of Dukakis with the furlough granted in Massachusetts to the rapist murderer Willie HORTON.

flat. Flat, the The modest living quarters of the PRIME MINISTER on the top floor of NUMBER TEN Downing Street: seven rooms plus four baths, a utility room and kitchen. They were carved out of the building for Clement ATTLEE in 1945; until then family rooms existed cheek-by-jowl with offices. The accommodation in NUMBER ELEVEN next door is actually more spacious; from 1997 the growing BLAIR family lived there while Chancellor Gordon BROWN, eventually with a family of his own, occupied the Flat.

flat tax The 17% across-the-board income tax campaigned for by the colourful Steve Forbes in the 1996 US Republican PRIMARIES.

flatlining In OPINION POLLS, the situation where a party's rating remains stalled at a lower level than it would wish.

flexible response The strategic doctrine that in the event of war a state should have a graduated range of responses to attack open to it, instead of simply the MASSIVE RETALIATION of a full-scale NUCLEAR counterthrust, which was the West's initial stance during the COLD WAR. Its basis is that the option to make a less cataclysmic response may prevent the war ending in global annihilation; as such it requires far more sensitive planning and more careful targeting of weapons. The doctrine was formally adopted by NATO in 1968, with the implicit rider that the West would use nuclear weapons first if its conventional forces were defeated. The term was also applied to the KENNEDY administration's range of options – military, diplomatic and presentational – for countering Soviet ambitions; in July 1961 JFK said:

> We intend to have a wider choice than humiliation or all-out nuclear action.

flier A handbill distributed to voters in support of a CANDIDATE, party or CAMPAIGN – or against them. Originally a US term, it crossed the Atlantic in the 1980s.

flip-flop Repeated reversals of policy or stance which make a leader look capricious, unreliable and not worthy of re-election. The term surfaced during the 1976 Presidential ELECTION in counter-charges between Gerald FORD and Jimmy CARTER; it was frequently used against Carter during his Presidency, and has stayed in the political vocabulary ever since, being revived by George W. BUSH against John KERRY.

FLN (Fr. *Front de Libération Nationale*, National Liberation Front) The Algerian nationalist group that won the war of independence from the French, and has subsequently formed the country's government. Formed in 1954 from three earlier groups, it was the political wing of the ALN (*Arméé de Libération Nationale*) which waged an increasingly successful guerrilla campaign, and set up a Provisional GOVERNMENT in Tunis. In 1962 President DE GAULLE conceded independence after referenda in both France and Algeria, and the FLN under Ben Bella (1916–) became the governing and sole party; multi-party politics was not restored until 1989.

float. floater Originally an American term for voters who sold their support to the highest bidder, and when bought would campaign energetically for them. As **floating voter**, it has been used in Britain since the 1950s for an elector with no firm loyalty to any party, whose change of allegiance could be decisive. As a group, floating voters (*compare* SWING VOTERS) are heavily wooed by all parties.

floating currency A currency whose value fluctuates in response to forces in world markets, instead of being held at or close to a fixed parity as a tenet of national policy.

floor In any legislature, the body of the CHAMBER where members deliver their views and business is transacted in full public view. The word applies particularly to the area, free of seating, between the Government and Opposition in an ADVERSARIAL system.

floor fight A full-scale political battle on the floor of the US HOUSE OF REPRESENTATIVES over a key item of legislation, with the prospect of large-scale defections from their party's position by Republicans, Democrats or both and quite likely of the ADMINISTRATION being defeated on an issue of importance to it. The SPEAKER will generally go to considerable lengths to avoid such showdowns if a compromise would deliver a credible BILL without a public display of opposition.

floor leader A member of a campaign team who marshals DELEGATES supporting a particular candidate on the floor of a US party CONVENTION, and works to maximise their number.

crossing the floor The action of a member of the UK HOUSE OF COMMONS in publicly resigning from his or her own party and joining the party on the opposite side of the Chamber. A rare Parliamentary event, the most recent switcher between the two main parties was Robert Jackson, Conservative MP for Wantage, who joined Labour in January 2005. Paul Marsden was elected Labour MP for Shrewsbury and Atcham in 1997, joined the Liberal Democrats in 2001 but returned to Labour just before the 2005 election which he did not contest. When Sir Hartley Shawcross, ATTORNEY-GENERAL in the 1945–51 Labour government, showed signs of the right-wing views that led him ultimately to quit the party, he was nicknamed **Sir Shortly Floorcross**.

> The Right Honourable and Learned Gentleman has twice crossed the floor of this House, each time leaving behind a trail of slime.
>
> LLOYD GEORGE on Sir John Simon

have the floor To have the leave of the CHAIR to speak, free of interruption.

taken on the floor of the House A WESTMINSTER term for consideration of a measure by the full House, most likely sitting in COMMITTEE, rather than by a separate, far smaller, committee. The WASHINGTON equivalent is a **floor debate**.

yield the floor The action of a legislator who has the floor, but permits another to INTERVENE. The phrase is most frequently used in the US SENATE.

Flower of Scotland *See* SCOTLAND.

Flowers, Gennifer affair The 'BIMBO ERUPTION' at the start of the 1992 Presidential PRIMARIES which looked set to deal a fatal blow to Bill CLINTON's prospects of winning the Democratic nomination. Yet despite Ms Flowers' highly plausible account of a lengthy affair while Clinton was Governor of Arkansas, the alacrity with which Clinton, and even more his wife Hillary, owned up to strains in their marriage that they had overcome enabled him to stay in the race, become President and then become embroiled in ZIPPERGATE.

FLQ (Fr. *Front Libèration du Québec*) A Quebec SEPARATIST terrorist organisation which operated in Montreal and Quebec city from 1963 until its suppression in 1970. It graduated from mail-box bombings in Montreal's Anglophone suburbs to robbery and murder. In October 1970 the FLQ kidnapped Pierre Laporte, a Quebec politician, and British trade commissioner James Cross; when Pierre TRUDEAU and Quebec's Premier Bourassa refused to negotiate, Laporte was murdered. After a massive manhunt producing 400 arrests, Cross was found, Laporte's murderers prosecuted and Cross's kidnappers allowed safe passage to Cuba.

fly. fly-posting The (illegal) practice in Britain of sticking election and other posters to shop windows, bus shelters, walls and trees without permission – sometimes obscuring the other side's propaganda. The political parties are rarely implicated because all their posters have to bear an imprint saying who has published them.

Flying Phil The nickname of Philip Gaglardi (1913–95), Highways Minister in British Columbia's SOCIAL CREDIT government from 1952. Gaglardi embarked on an ambitious highway building programme, and as the quality of the roads improved kept losing his licence for speeding on them. His standard excuse to patrolmen was that he was 'testing the curves', and he complained that any policeman who gave him a ticket was guaranteed promotion. A radio evangelist, he was nevertheless the subject of persistent rumours about GRAFT, and was eventually given a lesser portfolio for taking his daughter-in-law to Dallas in a Highways Department jet. He returned as Welfare Minister, his toughness leading the Opposition to claim that his policy consisted of 'throwing rocks at beggars'. He lost his ministry, and his seat, in 1972 after saying that the Prime Minister was too old and should make way for him.

FMQs First Minister's Questions In the SCOTTISH PARLIAMENT, the 20-minute question-and-answer session held at 3.10 pm each Thursday, in which the FIRST MINISTER is held to account.

Focus The title of the news sheets and associated campaigning through which Britain's LIBERAL DEMOCRAT (previously LIBERAL) party has built its strength at local level since the late 1960s; it has proved effective in winning councils and several Parliamentary seats.

focus group A representative group of voters gathered by a party's POLLSTERS to test their reactions to themes and issues that campaign professionals have thought of highlighting. In 1988 Jim Pinkerton, research director to the BUSH campaign, broke new ground by trying out issues that might destroy Michael Dukakis on a focus group in Paramus, New Jersey. The phrase and practice have their origin in the 'focussed interviews' instigated for research purposes by the US sociologist Robert Merton (1910–2003).

> The focus group may be a perfect symbol of what has happened to democracy in America. Insofar as 'the people' are consulted by political leaders these days, their reactions are of interest not as a guide to policy but simply as a way of exploring the electorate's gut feelings, to see which kind of (usually divisive) message might move them most.
>
> E. J. DIONNE Jr, *Why Americans Hate Politics*

focused A style of government in which those in power succeed in identifying, concentrating on and tackling the key issues. Its wide used by the early 1990s gave rise to the opposite **unfocused**, a person or administration incapable of concentrating on the most urgent priorities.

foetus The highly insulting and damaging description accorded to the Conservative leader William HAGUE by the maverick Labour MP Tony Banks, which he was later persuaded to withdraw. Echoing comments made by the actress Joan Collins, Banks told a TRIBUNE GROUP meeting on 30 September 1997: 'And now, to make matters worse, they have elected a foetus as party leader. I bet there's a lot of Tory MPs who wish they hadn't voted against abortion now.'

Foggy Bottom The nickname of the area in WASHINGTON where the STATE DEPARTMENT was relocated during WORLD WAR II. It stems from the thick, swirling haze that hung over the swamps that stretched from the POTOMAC to the LINCOLN memorial and H Street North-West, but has also come to apply to the impenetrability of the State's bureaucracy and culture. This sense was popularised by James Reston of the *New York Times* in 1947; Richard NIXON exploited it to the full at the height of MCCARTHYISM by attacking

> the 'striped-pants faggots in Foggy Bottom.'

Folletted The colour-co-ordination of women Labour MPs (and some of the men) prior to the 1992 general election by Barbara Follett, wife of the novelist Ken Follett and later MP for Stevenage. Labour's women were decked out in black skirts and red jackets; Robin COOK was told to be 'less autumnal' and wear a dark suit.

follow me if I advance, kill me if I retreat, avenge me if I die A Vietnamese battle cry taken up as a motto by Mary Matalin, political director of George BUSH's unsuccessful 1992 re-election campaign – and future wife of James Carville (*see* RAGIN' CAJUN), her opposite number in the victorious campaign of Bill CLINTON.

Fontainebleau agreement The deal struck between leaders of the European Community on 25 June 1984 at Fontainebleau, near Paris, which established the BRITISH REBATE on the UK's substantial net contribution to the EC budget. It was the conclusion of five years of acrimonious argument between Margaret THATCHER and almost all her fellow leaders at twelve European summits (*see* 'I want my MONEY back').

food chain The term coined by the CLINTON White House, and widely adopted in politics and the media, for the way hostile CONSPIRACY THEORISTS were able to get their theories about supposed scandals like WHITEWATER into the mainstream press by increasing respectable elements in the media picking up an originally dubious story. A 331-page report in January 1997 asserted that the 'chain' ran as follows: right-wing THINK TANKS – Internet websites or the London *Sunday Telegraph* – the *Washington Times*, *New York Post* or *Wall Street Journal* – Congressional calls for an investigation – 'legitimate' stories in the *Washington Post* or *New York Times*.

Foot, Michael (1913–), the left-wing firebrand who mellowed to become leader of Britain's LABOUR PARTY during its most troubled times, from 1980 to 1983, but who could not save it from electoral rout. Chris Patten called him 'a kind of walking obituary for the Labour Party'; the SKETCH WRITER Edward Pearce was kinder: 'He makes up for not believing in God by looking rather like him.' His rumpled appearance earned him the nickname WURZEL GUMMIDGE in later life, and an astounded Norman Mailer wrote:

> To an American it was incredible that this man who looked like an eccentric professor of ornithology could run for Prime Minister.

One of the eminent sons of the West Country Liberal MP Isaac Foot, he fought his first election in 1935 and won his first seat in 1945. He was a fine writer (the biographer of Aneurin BEVAN, whose seat he inherited after losing his own) and an accomplished journalist, briefly editing the wartime *Evening Standard.* He was, above all, the greatest Parliamentary orator of his age. Frank Johnson described him as 'the only man who can get an audience to its feet by exclaiming: "And!"' He complimented Iain Macleod on being 'the most intelligent member of the stupid party', and described Sir Ian Gilmour as 'a philosopher Tory – like military intelligence a contradiction in terms'. When a Conservative MP said of one of his answers as a Minister: 'That's only words!', Foot replied: 'What do you expect? Algebra?' He once made dozens of THATCHERITE backbenchers look foolish by telling them: 'Hands up all those who believe in the Government's economic policies!', then scorning those who had automatically obeyed him.

Foot made his career on the back benches as a Bevanite, then a UNILATERALIST (he was a leading campaigner for CND) and finally a pillar of the TRIBUNE GROUP until agreeing to join Harold WILSON's second government as Employment Secretary, becoming deputy party leader and LEADER OF THE HOUSE in 1976. In November 1980 he unexpectedly defeated Denis HEALEY for the leadership by just 10 votes. His leadership was marked by feuding between BENNITES and those party moderates who had not quit to join the SDP, with Foot himself caught in the crossfire. This feuding produced a deputy leadership contest in which Tony Benn came within a whisker of ousting Healey, and culminated in the chaotic 1983 election (*see* LONGEST SUICIDE NOTE IN HISTORY) which brought Labour its worst defeat in half a century; Foot resigned at once, but adorned the Commons until 1992.

A good man fallen among politicians.

DAILY MIRROR

Michael Foot is leader of the Labour Party The phrase incautiously uttered by Jim Mortimer, general secretary of the Party, at an election press conference on 27 May 1983 which sank any chance Labour might still have had of avoiding a crushing defeat. Mortimer told astonished reporters: 'The unanimous view of the campaign committee is that Michael Foot is Leader of the Labour Party', when no one up to that point had questioned the fact. The campaign committee itself was of dubious use; one member, Jim Innes, reported that so many people turned up for it that on one occasion Foot's Special Branch escorts sat in without anyone realising.

With statements like that one wondered how long either of them would keep his job.

MARGARET THATCHER, *The Downing Street Years*

foot and mouth disease The agricultural disaster that forced the postponement of the 2001 UK general election by a month from May to June and whose mishandling contributed directly to the abolition after the poll of the stand-alone Ministry of Agriculture, Fisheries and Food (MAFF). The outbreak, the first major incidence since 1967, was first detected at an abattoir in Essex, but delays in halting the movement of sheep led to its spreading like wildfire. Over 2,000 farms were infected and 6 million animals were slaughtered in a belated effort to stop the infection spreading, at a cost of £3 billion to the taxpayer and £5 billion to the rural economy, mainly tourism which in places was brought to its knees. The PUBLIC ACCOUNTS COMMITTEE afterward strongly criticised MAFF for having based its planning on a maximum of ten farms being infected, and the Government collectively for hesitating before calling in the Army. The cause has never been established, but illegal meat imports, the feeding to pigs of inadequately cooked swill from restaurants and schools, and sloppy animal husbandry were all blamed. *Compare* MAD COW DISEASE.

Football, the The 30lb. metal briefcase containing the secret codes needed to launch America's nuclear weapons, which aides to the President carry with him wherever he goes, 24 hours a day.

political football An issue with no obvious political connotations which is unfairly seized on and exploited by an individual, party or faction in order to gain political capital.

too much football without a helmet *See* TOO.

footprints in the snow One of the most celebrated of US political TV commercials: the series run by Sen. Bob Dole during the 1988 Republican PRIMARIES questioning the effectiveness of George BUSH Snr in a series of high offices under Presidents FORD and REAGAN. It showed a wintry scene, and as a voiceover listed all Bush's public appointments – head of the CIA, AMBASSADOR to China, VICE PRESIDENT and others – the camera tracked across the snow for footprints; there were none. While the commercial – together with Sen. Edward Kennedy's WHERE WAS GEORGE? speech – did not prevent Bush being elected, its memory may have contributed to his defeat by Bill CLINTON four years later.

force Military or other muscle used by a government to achieve its objectives in the face of defiance or resistance by another country or an element among its own subjects. The term implies violence or something stopping just short of it; the **use of force** in international affairs, which generally requires the endorsement of the UNITED NATIONS to provide it with legitimacy, has inevitably military connotations, being legally equated with WAR.

> The vital principle and immediate parent of despotism.
>
> JEFFERSON. First INAUGURAL ADDRESS, 1801

Force Acts Three Enforcement Acts passed by CONGRESS in 1870–71 to implement RECONSTRUCTION in the face of white Southern resistance. The Act of May 1870 imposed stiff penalties for violation of the FOURTEENTH and FIFTEENTH AMENDMENTS giving black Americans full voting rights and disqualifying former Confederate officials. The Act of February 1871 placed congressional elections under Federal control, and the KU KLUX KLAN Act of April 1871 gave the President military authority to suppress violence in the South – which GRANT used immediately to put down the Klan in South Carolina.

Force de Frappe (Fr. strike force) France's name for its independent nuclear DETERRENT, which it has possessed since the late 1950s; unlike Britain, France has not incorporated its nuclear force into NATO's command structure, or signed the NON-PROLIFERATION TREATY.

force-feeding The method adopted by prison authorities in various countries at various times to keep HUNGER STRIKERS alive. It was most notoriously used in Britain against SUFFRAGETTE prisoners (*see* CAT AND MOUSE ACT).

force majeure (Fr. greater force) The diplomatic and strategic term for the use of single-minded and ruthless force by one power against another. It is often cited as an excuse not to honour one's obligations, the essence of *force majeure* being that its application was so great and unexpected that no precautions could have been taken against it.

Ford, Gerald Rudolf (1913–), 38th President of the United States (Republican, 1974–77). At the start of NIXON's second term, Ford was House MINORITY LEADER; 20 months later he was President after Nixon's resignation over WATERGATE. Less than three years later he was out of office, defeated by Jimmy CARTER in a vote of no confidence in a WASHINGTON Ford had begun to cleanse. Ford's name at birth was Leslie KING; like Bill Clinton (*see* BLYTHE) he later took his stepfather's name. He became a high school football star in Grand Rapids, Michigan – Lyndon JOHNSON later claimed he had played 'TOO MUCH FOOTBALL WITHOUT A HELMET' – going on to study law at Michigan (where he was Most Valuable Player) and Yale before serving in the Navy. In 1948 he was elected to CONGRESS for his home district, and married Betty Bloomer, an intelligent, glamorous home-town divorcee. She later said: 'I wish I'd married a plumber. At least he'd be home by 5 o'clock,' but their marriage was close and happy, despite Betty Ford's troubles with alcohol and pills after leaving the WHITE HOUSE, which she faced with honesty and courage. Ford built a reputation for integrity, and for solidity rather than brilliance (*see* WALK AND CHEW GUM AT THE SAME TIME), and in 1965 Republican YOUNG TURKS in Congress turned to him as their natural leader. Ford was a loyal supporter of Nixon, and when Spiro AGNEW resigned in October after pleading 'no contest' to kickback charges, was an obvious safe choice as Vice President. He was sworn in on 6 December 1973 – and eight months and three days later was President after witnessing the trauma of Nixon's fall at first hand. He said then:

> If you have not chosen me by secret ballot, neither have I gained office by secret promises. I have not campaigned either for the Presidency or the Vice Presidency. I have not subscribed to any partisan platform. I am indebted to no man, and to only one woman – my dear wife – as I begin this very difficult job.

Ford caused an immediate outcry by giving Nixon a PARDON, but the wounds of Watergate began to heal. Another healing process began after final defeat in VIETNAM, which had been quietly written off under Nixon. He had a bruising fight with Ronald REAGAN for the 1976 Republican nomination, and on LABOR DAY was well behind Carter. Yet a robust campaign, based mainly on keeping America 'number one' in defence with the help of the young Donald Rumsfeld (*see* ABU GHRAIB, UNKNOWNS), ate into the gap and Ford went down to a respectably narrow defeat. Carter, in his INAUGURAL speech, paid this tribute:

> For myself and for our nation, I want to thank my predecessor for all he has done to heal our land.

Ford was widely ridiculed for his limitations, and was himself modest and self-deprecating, saying: 'I'm a Ford, not a LINCOLN.' Betty Ford observed: 'Jerry and I are ordinary people who enjoy life and aren't overly impressed with ourselves,' adding in bewilderment: 'People have written to me objecting to the idea of a President of the United States sleeping with his wife.' Ford took pride in being 'the first Eagle Scout Vice President of the United States', and once in the White House observed: 'I guess it just proves that in America anyone can be President.' He also lapsed into his sporting past, saying: 'I only wish I could take the entire United States into the locker room at half time.' Politically he described himself as 'a moderate on domestic issues, a conservative in fiscal affairs and a dyed-in-the-wool internationalist in foreign affairs'; he stood up to the Reaganite right by keeping Henry KISSINGER as SECRETARY OF STATE. His contacts on the HILL were excellent; he once said: 'My motto toward the Congress is communication, conciliation, compromise and co-operation.'

His GAFFES did raise doubts; he was quoted saying 'if Lincoln were alive today he would be spinning in his grave', and he claimed at the height of the 1976 election that Poland was 'not under Soviet domination'. So, too, did his repeated trips and falls, notably when alighting from aircraft. Larry King commented: 'He is so average one almost expects it to be deliberate.' David Frye wrote: 'Gerry Ford looks like the man in the science fiction movie who is the first to see the creature.' And the Rev. Duncan Littlefair of Grand Rapids observed: 'Ford isn't a bad man, but he's dumb. He shouldn't be dumb either – he went to school just like everyone else.' However, Rep. Barber Conable spoke for many when he said: 'Ford has a slow mind, but he has backbone.' And when the Senate was confirming Ford as Vice President, the Democrat Sen. Alan Cranston declared: 'I doubt if there has ever been a time when integrity has so surpassed ideology in the judgement of a man for so high an office in the land.' The public took time to appreciate these qualities; during Ford's Vice Presidency, one anonymous joker wrote:

> A year ago Gerald Ford was unknown throughout America. Now he is unknown throughout the world.

Ford House Office Building The building, half a mile from the CAPITOL on Second and D Streets and originally built for the FBI, which since 1975 has housed Congressional offices. It was named after President Ford in his capacity as former House MINORITY LEADER. The Ford Building was the centre of a national alert on 20 October 2001 when its mailroom tested positive for anthrax; in the wake of 9/11 the packages were thought to be the work of AL QAEDA but are now considered to have been the work of a domestic suspect. The Ford Building was also the centre of claims by Republicans at the height of the drive to IMPEACH Bill CLINTON in 1998 that documents under lock and key there contained testimony from at least one more woman so explosive that it would ensure the President's removal.

Ford to City: Drop Dead The unforgettable front-page headline in the *New York Post* on 30 October 1975, when President Ford rejected the city's application for Federal aid when it was on the verge of bankruptcy. The headline was the creation of the *Post*'s Bill Brink and Mike O'Neill.

Ford's Peace Ship The ship despatched to Europe in December 1916 by the automobile magnate Henry Ford (1863–1947), after PACIFISTS took him up on a pledge to give up half his fortune to shorten the carnage of WORLD WAR I by a single day. The company of pacifists, journalists and Ford's staff feuded on the *Oscar II*'s crossing from Hoboken, New Jersey, to Christiania in Norway; five days after their arrival Ford went home, saying he had seen few signs of peace. A few of the pacifists went on to campaign in Europe, but the episode discredited their cause in America.

Ford's Theatre The theatre on Washington's E Street where Abraham LINCOLN was ASSASSINATED by John Wilkes Booth on 14 April 1865. It survives as a historic exhibit and place of pilgrimage. *See also* PREPARE THREE ENVELOPES.

Fordney-McCumber tariff The TARIFF imposed by CONGRESS under the HARDING administration that put the stiffest duties to date on imported goods – and, within a short time, produced an unprecedented budgetary surplus. By closing US markets to Japan, it also began the economic and political build-up which culminated in PEARL HARBOR. By 1930 even this tight regime – which included the power for a President to vary the tariff on particular goods by 50% either way – was not enough for PROTECTIONISTS in Congress, who imposed the even stiffer SMOOT-HAWLEY TARIFF.

foreign. foreign aid One of the most controversial components of US policy, with many voters and members of Congress seeing it as an unjustified waste of public money that could be spent to better effect at home. Bernard Rosenberg described it as 'taxing poor people in rich countries for the benefit of rich people in poor countries'. **Foreign Aid Bills** have controversial and even irrelevant provisions attached to them on their way through CONGRESS, which may prevent them being signed into law; a popular stratagem is to prevent any funds being used to promote birth control. This troubles the State Department which sees aid as a crucial tool of diplomacy, but delights POPULISTS and ISOLATIONISTS.

Nobody shoots Santa Claus.
AL SMITH, 1936

Is this nation stating it cannot afford to spend an additional $600 million to help the developing nations of the world become strong and free and independent – an amount less than this country's annual outlay for lipstick, face cream and chewing gum?
President KENNEDY, New York, 8 November 1963

The United States is not just an old cow that gives more milk the more it is kicked in the flanks.
Secretary of State DEAN RUSK, testifying to Congress, 4 June 1967

Foreign Office *See* FCO.

Foreign Office view The assessment of international events and how Britain should react to them which is arrived at in the FCO; by inference it differs from the position of the Government as a whole and of NUMBER TEN. Such differences frequently occur, and occasionally prove irreconcilable.

The Ministry of Agriculture looks after farmers. The Foreign Office looks after foreigners.
NORMAN TEBBIT

foreign policy The stance toward the other nations of the world adopted by the government of a particular country. On the outbreak of the FALKLANDS WAR the Conservative MP Julian Amery accused the Foreign Office of being unable to tell the difference between DIPLOMACY and foreign policy. In America, there has been a 200-year argument between CONGRESS and the White House, and between the WHITE HOUSE and the STATE DEPARTMENT, over who should conduct foreign policy and what course should be followed; at the outset Thomas JEFFERSON wrote: 'The transaction of business with foreign nations is executive altogether.'

Just like Canadian foreign policy, all piss and wind. DEAN ACHESON (1893–1971)

English policy is to float largely downstream, occasionally putting out a diplomatic boathook.
LORD SALISBURY *(attr.)*, 1877

Fear is no basis for foreign policy.
MARGARET THATCHER

The purpose of foreign policy is not to provide an outlet for our own sentiments of hope and indignation; it is to shape real events in a real world.
President KENNEDY in Salt Lake City, 26 September 1963

Questioner: How will the REAGAN administration change American foreign policy?
JEANE KIRKPATRICK: We've taken down our 'kick me' signs

Council on Foreign Relations A non-partisan organisation formed in 1921 to improve the understanding of US foreign policy and international affairs, its 3,400 members including nearly all past and present Presidents, Secretaries of State, Defense and Treasury, senior government officials, eminent scholars, and leaders in business, the media and human rights. For this very reason the far right regards the CFR as a subversive organisation dedicated, in league with the TRILATERAL COMMISSION, to destroying America's national sovereignty and undermining reactionary regimes the world over. The CFR's magazine *Foreign Affairs*, first published in 1922, is an international forum for the exchange of ideas on world affairs.

like being in a foreign country The unkind and somewhat racist description of Home Office questions in the COMMONS, c. 1984, which a CABINET member conveyed to Margaret THATCHER. The Home Secretary was then Leon (later Sir Leon) Brittan, and his Labour SHADOW Gerald Kaufman; both were of Baltic Jewish descent and Kaufman's rhetoric in particular had an edge reminiscent of an ancient feud.

forgotten man One of the images with which Franklin D. ROOSEVELT most identified himself with the average victim of the GREAT DEPRESSION and pinned the blame for it on uncaring Republicans. The phrase had first been used by the Yale economics professor William Graham Sumner in 1883, but FDR turned the 'forgotten man' who had been neglected under COOLIDGE and HOOVER but could expect to benefit from the NEW DEAL into a powerful political symbol.

Forkbender. Lady Forkbender The nickname of Lady Falkender (1932–), formerly Marcia Williams, Prime Minister Harold WILSON's long-serving and volatile political secretary and reputed *eminence grise*. Its likely origin is *PRIVATE EYE* (MRS WILSON'S DIARY, 1975): 'So we set off, on a lovely May morning, with Mr Haines at the wheel of his Mini, and myself, Harold and Lady Forkbender in the back.' *See also* LAVENDER LIST.

> Wilson was a weak, bulliable man – Williams was a harridan and a scold. Much might be said for having her ducked in a pond or, better, drowned . . . The entire Williams connection caused the Prime Minister, a man of great gifts, application and decent purpose, to be laughed at.
>
> EDWARD PEARCE, *Macchiavelli's Children*

Former Naval Person The codename adopted by CHURCHILL in his secret correspondence with Franklin D. ROOSEVELT prior to America's entry into WORLD WAR II. It referred to Churchill's previous post (at the start of both World Wars) as First Lord of the Admiralty (*see* WINSTON IS BACK). Roosevelt chose the codename POTUS, short for President of the United States (he was himself a former Naval person, having been Woodrow WILSON'S Undersecretary for the Navy). The talks were kept secret because they involved greater preparedness for war than FDR felt he could reveal during the 1940 ELECTION campaign; a German spy in the US Embassy in London was detected before he could do much damage.

Formula 1. The first major embarrassment for Tony BLAIR'S government, the disclosure that Bernie Eccleston, head of Formula 1 motor racing, had given £1 million to the LABOUR PARTY – as he had also to the Conservatives. Following the donation, the Government came out against an early and complete ban on tobacco advertising, from which Formula 1 earned much of its revenue, and the impression was created that the two events were connected. This was strongly denied, and after damaging hesitation the donation was repaid.

Forster's Education Act The Act passed by GLADSTONE'S Liberal government in 1870 which for the first time gave Britain a school system over and above that provided by churches and charities. It was promoted by William Edward Forster (1818–86), nicknamed 'Buckshot', who was brought up a Quaker and married the daughter of Dr Arnold, headmaster of Rugby. His system of 'board schools' was neither universal nor free, and was criticised by Nonconformists whose taxes were diverted to fund poor pupils in Anglican schools. Yet the Act was one of the great Victorian measures of reform and public provision – and a far cry from Forster's later disasters in Ireland (*see* KILMAINHAM TREATY).

Fort Sumter The engagement in South Carolina which marked the start of America's CIVIL WAR. The fort in Charleston harbour and its garrison of 84 were cut off by land when South Carolina SECEDED from the UNION on 20 December 1863; on 9 January the merchant steamer *Star of the West*, bringing Union reinforcements, was fired on by militia cannon and twice hit. But the war began in earnest at 4.30 a.m. on 12 April, when CONFEDERATE batteries, after a one-hour ULTIMATUM, opened fire from Cummings Point. The bombardment from four sides lasted 34 hours before the fort's commander, Major Anderson, surrendered; 4,000 rounds had been fired but no one was killed until the last gun of a 50-gun victory salute blew up and killed Daniel Hough, who thus became the first casualty of the war. Abraham LINCOLN, inaugurated President on 4 March, was reckoned to have manoeuvred the South into attacking the beleaguered garrison, thus throwing the onus for starting the war onto the Confederacy.

Fortas resignation The first-ever resignation of a justice of the US SUPREME COURT. Abe Fortas, who had been Lyndon B. JOHNSON'S principal legal adviser and was appointed by him to the court in 1965, was forced to quit on 15 May 1969 after allegations that he had accepted money from a foundation that was under investigation, and after the House Judiciary Committee had been requested to inquire into his 'failure of good behaviour'. Fortas' resignation led directly to President NIXON'S notorious HAYNSWORTH NOMINATION.

fortress. Fortress Europe The term used by critics of a closer EUROPEAN UNION for a bloc which, they claim, will become more prosperous by trading within its borders while erecting barriers to commerce with the world outside.

Fortress Falklands A pejorative for Margaret THATCHER'S policy after the FALKLANDS WAR of building up a strong military presence on the islands to deter a fresh Argentine attack. Critics argued that it would prevent any kind of *rapprochement* with Argentina – not that the islanders wanted one. A new airport, under RAF control, was constructed at Mount Pleasant, 25 miles from Port Stanley, and forces of several thousand from all three services – more than twice the civilian population – stationed on the Falklands. Gradually these forces have been reduced, but a strong defensive capability remains. They have not prevented relations being restored with Argentina, though the dispute over the islands is unresolved.

forty. Forty acres and a mule! The slogan of those freed slaves in the former CONFEDERATE States who organised to press the Federal government for ownership of enough land to enable them to support themselves. A certain amount of land was made available from 1886 under the Southern Homestead Act, but it was not very fertile and little was taken up. Increasingly the freedmen drifted back onto the old plantations as sharecroppers.

forty-shilling freeholders Those Englishmen who, prior to the 1832 REFORM ACT, qualified for the vote in certain constituencies because their property had a rental value of £2 a year; the right dated back to 1343. Under the Act a £10 threshold was introduced throughout, but existing forty-shilling freeholders retained the vote.

45-minute claim The assertion by Tony BLAIR prior to the 2003 IRAQ WAR, in the Commons and in the DODGY DOSSIER, that SADDAM HUSSEIN not only had WEAPONS OF MASS DESTRUCTION but that they could be used against Iraq's neighbours at 45 minutes' notice. The claim, based on intelligence, was crucial in persuading many MPs and members of the public of the case for war. However, during the hearings that led to the HUTTON and BUTLER reports the veracity of the intelligence was severely questioned, and in October 2004, after the report of the IRAQ SURVEY GROUP showed that Saddam no longer had WMD, MI6 abandoned the claim, saying that it no longer used that 'line of intelligence'.

> The document discloses that his [Saddam's] military planning allows for some of the WMD to be ready within 45 minutes of an order to use them.
>
> TONY BLAIR in the foreword to the dossier of September 2002

> Shit. (Lord) DENIS HEALEY

49th Parallel The line of latitude that forms the land border between the western United States and Canada. To the north lie British Columbia, Alberta, Saskatchewan and Manitoba; to the south Washington State, Idaho, Montana, North Dakota and western Minnesota. It was accepted in 1818 as the boundary as far west as the Rockies; beyond that the frontier was undefined. By 1844 waves of American settlers arriving on the Oregon Trail were pressing for total US control of the Pacific West, and James Polk was elected president on the slogan FIFTY-FOUR FORTY OR FIGHT. In the event the US and Britain agreed in 1846 on the extension of the 49th parallel to the coast.

49th State *See* FIFTY-FIRST STATE.

Forza Italia! (It. Forward Italy!) The media magnate Silvio Berlusconi's Freedom Alliance, combining the LIGA NORD and neo-Fascist MSI, which came to power after winning elections on 28 March 1994. Berlusconi quit after seven months when his corporation was accused of bribing tax inspectors, but returned to preside over what in the spring of 2004 became the longest-surviving Italian government since the end of WORLD WAR II, a record achieved despite regular brushes with the law.

Foster. Foster suicide Vincent W. Foster Jr, deputy WHITE HOUSE Counsel to President CLINTON, was found shot dead on 20 July 1993 in Fort Marcy Park in suburban Virginia. Critics of the Clinton ADMINISTRATION in CONGRESS and the media linked Foster's death with the WHITEWATER scandal, claiming that Foster had tried to interfere in the probe; claims of a COVER-UP instigated by Hillary Clinton to prevent some darker and possibly sexual secret coming out hinged on the removal of papers from Foster's office by uncleared White House staff after it was supposed to have been locked. Claims that Foster had in fact been murdered, and that he was party to wrongdoing, were rejected first by the Whitewater special counsel Robert B. Fiske and, finally in July 1997, by the Special Prosecutor Kenneth STARR. (*Compare* David KELLY AFFAIR in the UK.)

Foul-mouthed Joe One of many nicknames for **Joseph Cannon** (1836–1926), SPEAKER of the US HOUSE OF REPRESENTATIVES from 1903 to 1911. UNCLE JOE to his supporters (he became Speaker aged 67), he was renowned for his profane language and was said by his opponents to be in the hands of liquor interests. But their real objection was to his tyrannical control of CONGRESS; he appointed himself chairman of the RULES COMMITTEE and blocked any BILL he did not personally support. In 1910 'INSURGENTS' in his own Republican Party ousted him from the committee, thus breaking his power.

foundation hospitals Hospitals within the NHS but able to raise their own finance on the markets, the key to the health reforms promised by Tony BLAIR for New LABOUR's second term but resisted by the health unions and viewed with caution by CHANCELLOR Gordon BROWN. The plan was adopted although 65 Labour MPs rebelled against it in May 2003.

Founding Fathers *See* FATHERS.

four. Four A's The device used by the LABOR PARTY in New South Wales in 1937 to get its candidates into the most advantageous place on the BALLOT paper for elections to the Australian SENATE, which led to a change in the law. A party was entitled to group all its candidates together on the paper, and Labor put forward four candidates whose names began with 'A' – Amour, Armstrong, Arthur and Ashe – to secure the left-hand spot, where voters were most likely to make their mark. All four were elected; three years later the law was changed so that parties drew lots for where their groups would appear on the paper. *See also* DONKEY VOTE.

Four Freedoms *See* ROOSEVELT.

Four Generals, revolt of the The revolt in Algeria in 1961 against President DE GAULLE's policy of granting the territory independence, led by four generals who had backed his rise to power in the belief that he would stick to a policy of ALGÉRIE FRANÇAISE, and now felt betrayed. The four – Edmond Jouhaud, Raoul Salan, Maurice Challe and André Zeller – made their move on 22 April after a period of unrest among Algeria's French community; the bulk of the army stayed loyal and de Gaulle quelled the revolt in a few days.

4-H club The hard core of conservative Republicans in the SENATE who during Ronald REAGAN's Presidency exerted critical influence over legislation and appointments. The four were Jesse Helms of North Carolina, Orrin Hatch of Utah, Gordon Humphrey of New Hampshire and Chic Hecht of Nevada. They formed the nucleus of the Steering Committee of 15–20 Republicans who lunched every Tuesday to set the conservative agenda in the Senate.

Four Horsemen The four powerful Irish-American politicians who in the mid-1970s took charge of the sensitive issue of NORTHERN IRELAND, encouraging the British government to act fairly and positively toward the Catholic minority while reining in pressure from within their own community to support the Provisional IRA. The four were Speaker TIP O'Neill, Sen. Edward KENNEDY, Sen. Daniel Patrick MOYNIHAN and Hugh Carey, Governor of New York.

Four legs good, two legs bad The slogan with which the animals seized control from their human master in George Orwell's *ANIMAL FARM*. *See also* all animals are EQUAL, but some are more equal than others.

four-minute warning Popular shorthand in the 1950s and '60s for the length of time the British public would have to prepare for a Soviet nuclear attack. So brief a warning aroused fears which formed a potent recruiting weapon for CND; it also gave rise to numerous suggestions of how one would spend those four minutes, many of them ribald and some physically impossible.

Four more years! The slogan chanted by supporters of a US President who want him elected for a further TERM. During Margaret THATCHER's ascendancy in Britain, the derivative 'five more years' or even 'ten more years' was heard at election times. The TWENTY-SECOND AMENDMENT which since 1952 has limited a President to two terms means that the chant is only appropriate when an INCUMBENT is completing his first term. When Ronald REAGAN heard it in 1988, he told the crowd: 'Since the CONSTITUTION has something to say about what you've just chanted, I'll assume you're suggesting that I live four more years.'

> *DAN QUAYLE* (September 1992): Four more years!
> *Crowd:* Four more months!

Four Policemen The belief of Franklin D. ROOSEVELT that after WORLD WAR II responsibility for world peace and order would rest with America, the Soviet Union, Britain and China. With France, these nations came after FDR's death to form the PERMANENT FIVE members of the UN SECURITY COUNCIL. Roosevelt believed giving the major powers pre-eminent status would avoid the pitfalls experienced by the LEAGUE OF NATIONS, and make CONGRESS more likely to accept the new order. He even told Molotov that all nations other than the four should be disarmed. YALTA marked the high-point of the policy, before it became blindingly evident that STALIN would act ruthlessly in pursuit of his own interests.

four-power agreement The regime under which military governments from the four victorious powers in WORLD WAR II – America, the Soviet Union, Britain and France – continued to exert a degree of joint control over Berlin after the division of the former German capital between east and west, co-existing with the East and West Berlin civil authorities. Even after the building of the BERLIN WALL, troops from each power were not only responsible for a sector of the city but were able to travel in each other's zone. The Soviet war memorial, for instance, was in West Berlin, and Spandau Prison, where Rudolf HESS was held, remained under four-power control until his death in 1987. The four-power agreement was terminated in 1990 following the reunification of the city; **four plus two talks** involving the former allies and the East and West German authorities dismantled the old regime in the city and prepared the way for total German control.

four score and seven years ago The opening phrase of Abraham Lincoln's GETTYSBURG ADDRESS.

fourteen. fourteen day rule The bar on discussion on radio and television of anything the House of Commons was due to discuss within fourteen days, which stultified BBC coverage of politics until fury over its application during the SUEZ crisis forced first its suspension in December 1956 and subsequently its abolition. The BBC had adopted the rule in 1946 as an offshoot of wartime BIPARTISANSHIP, and the party leaders formalised it in 1955.

fourteen pints The amount of beer that William HAGUE, when UK Conservative leader, claimed to have drunk each day when he was out as a student helping deliver soft drinks from the family firm to pubs in South Yorkshire. The claim, in an interview with *GQ* in August 2000, rebounded on Hague because it was widely disbelieved and left the impression that he was trying to look 'one of the lads'.

Fourteenth Amendment The amendment to the US CONSTITUTION ratified in July 1868, over the objections of President Andrew Johnson, that guaranteed citizenship to black Americans by stipulating that citizenship applied to every person born within the nation's boundaries. The decision in the Dred SCOTT case that they could not be citizens was thus revoked; an accompanying **Civil Rights Act** spelt out that citizen rights were possessed by everyone born in the US, 'of any race and color, without reference to any previous condition of slavery or involuntary servitude'. The situation of Native Americans was then seen as irrelevant.

fourteenth Mr Wilson The riposte of Lord Home (*see* SIR ALEC) on taking office as Prime Minister in October 1963 to charges by Harold WILSON that 'the whole process of democracy has been brought to a halt with a Fourteenth Earl'. Home replied:

> I suppose, if you come to think of it, Mr Wilson is the fourteenth Mr Wilson.

Wilson's Fourteen Points *See* WILSON.

fourth. Fourth Estate A phrase first coined by Edmund BURKE for the influential position of the Press in the British political community; the Estates (*see* THIRD ESTATE) were representatives of the aristocracy, the Church and the Commons in the pre-Revolutionary French national assembly. According to Thomas Carlyle:

> Burke said that there were Three Estates in Parliament; but in the Reporters' GALLERY yonder, there sat a Fourth Estate, more important far than they all.

Fourth International The world body established by TROTSKY in the 1930s in an effort to unite all left-wing parties in an anti-Fascist POPULAR FRONT, which developed into the representative body of world Trotskyism. The original aim failed because Soviet Communism, alarmed at the rise of NAZISM, itself reached out to the Democratic Left through the Third International.

fourth man The suspected fourth Soviet agent involved in the defection of BURGESS AND MACLEAN, and in the espionage that had preceded it. The term came into use after Kim Philby was identified in 1963 as the THIRD MAN; it was another seventeen years before Margaret THATCHER dramatically disclosed that there had indeed been a fourth man – Sit Anthony BLUNT.

Fourth Party The Conservative splinter group headed by Lord Randolph Churchill which from 1880 to 1885 conducted an aggressive and at time humiliating campaign against Sir Stafford Northcote for his lack-lustre leadership of the party in the COMMONS. Churchill, Drummond Wolff, Sir John Gorst and at times the young Arthur BALFOUR conducted their campaign from BELOW THE GANGWAY, being given particular ammunition by Northcote's vacillating handling of the BRADLAUGH CASE; Churchill was adamant that having refused to take the OATH, Bradlaugh had no right to sit in the Commons. The Fourth Party's highly opportunistic campaigning got Churchill into SALISBURY's government, but did not finish Northcote.

Fourth Republic The French Republic established in 1946 in place of the provisional governments that had ruled since the LIBERATION and the collapse of VICHY. Essentially a continuation of the THIRD REPUBLIC (1870–1940), not least in the chaotic instability of its governments, it limped on until DE GAULLE returned in 1958 to establish the more stable FIFTH REPUBLIC.

Fox resignation The resignation of Francis Fox (1939–) as Canada's Solicitor-General in 1978 after a scandal involving his private life. It acquired a historic cachet because Fox's resignation speech to the House of Commons in Ottawa was the first such in a (largely) Anglophone legislature to be delivered live on television. His dignity and frankness earned him respect, and in 1980 Pierre TRUDEAU brought Fox back into the Government as Minister of Communications; he stayed in the Cabinet until the Liberals' defeat in 1984, then returned to private legal practice.

fox-shooting The adoption by one party of a policy or opportunity on which another could logically have been expected to capitalise. In the world of hunting, shooting the fox is the ultimate treason as it deprives the hunt of the thrill of the chase and, probably, the hounds of their prey. In a political sense it goes back at least to November 1947 when, on Hugh Dalton's resignation over the BUDGET LEAK, the Conservative MP Nigel Birch observed:

> My God, they've shot our fox!

fragrant The word that earned Jeffrey (later Lord) Archer (1940–) a second shot at a political career after his resignation as a vice-chairman of the CONSERVATIVE PARTY over allegations in the *Daily Star* that he had paid a prostitute to sleep with him. Archer sued the *Star* for libel, telling the trial in July 1987 that while he had handed over money, he had never had sex with the woman. Archer produced an alibi, but Mr Justice Caulfield placed particular weight on the evidence of his wife Mary; he asked the jury why anyone married to the 'fragrant' Mary Archer would have chosen to indulge in 'insulated' sex with Ms Coughlan. The jury awarded Archer £500,000 damages plus costs, and he re-entered politics (*see* STAND AND DELIVER), being selected in 1999 as the Conservatives' first candidate for Mayor of London. He had to resign prior to the election when it was reported that he had persuaded a friend, Ted Francis, to fake an alibi for him at the trial; in 2001 he was jailed for four years for perjury and perverting the course of justice.

franc. franc fort (Fr. strong franc) The policy of successive French governments prior to the inception of the EURO of maintaining the franc at as high a level as practicable against the world's other main currencies, and especially the German mark. The phrase was deliberately a pun, as **Francfort** is the French word for Frankfurt, the home until monetary union of Germany's BUNDESBANK.

franc-tireurs (Fr. sharp-shooters or snipers) One of the elements in the French RESISTANCE during WORLD WAR II, specifically a Communist grouping known as the *Franc-Tireurs et PARTISANS*. In a political sense a *franc-tireur* is a lone operator who traps his or her opponents with deadly questions or interruptions.

Françaises, Français (Frenchwomen, Frenchmen) The words with which President DE GAULLE prefaced his broadcasts to the French people, and which became his trademark. He usually accompanied them by opening his hands and holding them out, palms upwards.

France The focus of intensive pride among its fractious inhabitants, a beacon of sophistication to the world, a founder of independent foreign policy, and a source of perpetual bafflement to the ANGLO-SAXONS. Despite its intense centralism and DIRIGISME and CHAUVINISM, even an exasperated DE GAULLE once observed:

> No one can simply bring together a country that has 265 kinds of cheese.

Lamartine partly explained the constant ferment when he wrote: 'France is revolutionary or she is nothing at all. The revolution of 1789 is her political religion.' Sir Robert Peel, in a remark that would have seemed topical at almost any time in the century that followed, asserted that 'the modern history of France is the substitution of one crisis for another', and Metternich observed: 'When France has a cold, Europe sneezes.' The British have always regarded the French with a mixture of disbelief, resentment and amusement which transcend the ENTENTE CORDIALE and the French understandably have returned the compliment. CHURCHILL, after one of his many difficulties with de Gaulle, told MPs in 1942: 'The Almighty in his infinite wisdom did not see fit to create Frenchmen in the image of Englishmen.' And when legislation to decriminalise homosexual acts between consenting males was being debated, Viscount Montgomery of Alamein declared:

> This sort of thing may be tolerated by the French, but we are British, thank God.

> When discussing France's international policy, one should not imagine that its object is to react to events or to determine our position in relation to the actions of other powers. It pursues objectives of its own, France's objectives.
>
> President VALÉRY GISCARD D'ESTAING, 1980

France has lost a battle, but she has not lost the war DE GAULLE's assertion in 1940 as he issued his rallying-call from London for loyal Frenchmen to join the FREE FRENCH and fight on.

franchise The right to VOTE in ELECTIONS, which has been steadily extended in most developed countries from a small elite of propertied men to the totality of the adult population of both sexes.

francisation The programme for stamping out the English language in Quebec, embarked on by the province's PQ government after its election victory in November 1976. Its cornerstone was BILL 101 which, among other things, required Anglophone businesses to establish their own francisation programmes, going far beyond such simple but irritating steps as removing English-language signs. Francisation drove some Anglophones out of Quebec, led others – and members of other ethnic groups who had opted to speak English – to use French more actively, but failed to generate a majority for SEPARATISM in a 1980 referendum.

Franco, General Francisco *See* CAUDILLO.

Franco-German motor Eurospeak for the unofficial leadership of the EUROPEAN UNION and its predecessors by France and Germany throughout the life of the Community, stemming initially from the close relationship between DE GAULLE and Konrad Adenauer. It had its foundations in Germany's ECONOMIC MIRACLE and post-NAZI guilt, and France's desire to pursue a foreign policy independent of that of the United States. In Paris such leadership has not only been assumed but has been seen as justification for European union; moves to expand EU membership so as to dilute Francophone influence have been treated by France with suspicion. Assertions of active pro-Europeanism by the UK and Britain's efforts to build alliances within the EU have been seen in Paris as a challenge to the 'motor'; the one time to date that it has stalled was at the 2000 LISBON Summit when Britain and Spain pushed through a radical programme for economic competitiveness which posed a serious threat to France's State-owned monopolies. In the aftermath of French voters' rejection of the EUROPEAN CONSTITUTION in 2005, President CHIRAC immediately formed common cause with Chancellor Gerhard Schroder on using the motor to maintain the initiative.

Franco-Prussian War The brief but decisive conflict in 1870 when Emperor Napoleon III challenged the military machine built up by King Wilhelm I. France declared war (*see* EMS TELEGRAM) but the campaign ended in total Prussian victory, the fall of the THIRD EMPIRE, the convulsion of the PARIS COMMUNE and the creation of a unified German state under Wilhelm, who took the title of Kaiser.

frank. frank exchange of views A polite DIPLOMATIC term for a serious disagreement at a meeting between leaders or emissaries.

to be perfectly frank and honest One of the phrases by which Harold WILSON is best remembered, because of his frequent deployment of it in television interviews and the unwillingness of the public to believe it.

appalling frankness The phrase with which Stanley BALDWIN confessed to the COMMONS on 12 November 1936 that he had not advocated REARMAMENT earlier to meet the threat from NAZI Germany because such talk could have lost the Conservatives the 1935 general election. *See* YEARS THE LOCUSTS HAVE EATEN.

franking privilege The right of members of the US CONGRESS to send out mail to CONSTITUENTS at the public expense. Its use was a scandal as early as 1869, with some Congressmen even posting all their dirty laundry home free of charge, and public opinion forced its abolition in 1873. It was soon re-introduced minus the worst excesses, though well-known politicians have always been accused of abusing it. In 1983 the SUPREME COURT rejected a plea from COMMON CAUSE that the franking privilege was UNCONSTITUTIONAL because it favoured INCUMBENTS. Its use to mail political propaganda and raise funds has snowballed with the advent of DIRECT MAIL, around 4 million items being generated each working day by the 535 voting members of Congress. The annual bill exceeds $100 million; in 1984 one Senator, Pete Wilson, sent $3.8 million worth of free mail. The only limits on its use for ELECTIONEERING are that no mass mailing may be sent within 60 days of an election, and that the world 'I' may not appear more than eight times on a page, which can also contain no more than two personal photos.

> A matter strictly between a member of Congress and his conscience.
>
> US Post Office spokesman, 1966

Franklin The breakaway state created in 1784 by 10,000 frontiersmen in the WATAUGA terriroty as America's migrant population moved westwards. The area had been ceded by North Carolina to the infant Federal government to administer, and its inhabitants banded together to defend and govern themselves. After four years the territory was forcibly reincorporated into North Carolina. It was named after the FOUNDING FATHER.

Benjamin Franklin (1706–90), the printer and inventor who from 1747 was active in the movement that led to INDEPENDENCE. He was sent to England to protest at the taxing of the American colonies without their consent, was a signatory of the Declaration of Independence, secured French support for the new nation and from 1785 to 1787 was America's Minister in Paris, where he was known (mistakenly) as *'Le Bon Quacker'*. He signed the Treaty of peace with Britain, presided over the infant state of Pennsylvania for three terms, and chaired the PHILADELPHIA CONVENTION which drafted the US CONSTITUTION. When he finally retired from politics in 1789, George WASHINGTON wrote to him:

> If to be venerated for benevolence; if to be admired for talents; if to be esteemed for patriotism; if to be beloved for philanthropy, can gratify the human mind, you must have the pleasing consolation that you have not lived in vain.

Franklin once reputedly remarked: 'Where liberty is, there is my country'; the epitaph he wrote for himself read:

> The body of Benjamin Franklin, printer
> Like the cover of an old book
> Its contents worn out
> And stript of its leather and guilding
> Lies here food for the worms!
> Yet the work itself shall not be lost
> For it will, as he believed, appear once more
> In a new and more beautiful edition
> Corrected and amended
> By its Author.

> I succeed him; no-one could replace him.
> JEFFERSON

> Antiquity would have raised altars to this mighty genius who, to the advantage of mankind, compassing in his mind the heavens and earth, was able to restrain alike thunderbolts and tyrants.
> MIRABEAU

> Benjamin Franklin, incarnation of the peddling, tuppeny YANKEE.
> JEFFERSON DAVIS

Franklin D. One of the many nicknames for Franklin D. ROOSEVELT. In the late 1930s a small boy is supposed to have told his father that when he grew up he would like to be President; his father replied: 'What about Franklin D.?'

Franks Report The findings of the inquiry set up under the diplomat and academic Lord Franks (1905–92) by Margaret THATCHER to examine claims that her government had been caught unawares by the Argentine invasion of the FALKLANDS in 1982, and that the ensuing war had been avoidable. Franks and his committee of senior PRIVY COUNCILLORS concluded that though a hardening of Argentina's attitude in the three weeks prior to the invasion had not been recognised in London,

> We would not be justified in attaching any criticism or blame to the present Government for the Argentine JUNTA's decision to commit an act of unprovoked aggression.

The report noted that Lord Carrington, who resigned as Foreign Secretary after the invasion, had repeatedly urged Defence Secretary John Nott in 1981–82 not to withdraw the ice patrol ship *Endurance,* lest the Argentines take it as a sign of weakness; in the COMMONS James CALLAGHAN had urged Mrs Thatcher to countermand the order, which he termed an 'error that could have serious consequences', but she refused, quoting Nott's view that 'other claims on the defence budget should have greater priority'.

> It itemises one unfortunate misjudgement after another, producing a catalogue of errors and missed opportunities which provide the raw material for a formidable indictment. But . . . it was a classic ESTABLISHMENT job. It studiously recoiled from drawing the large conclusions implicit in its detailed findings.
> HUGO YOUNG, *One Of Us*

Fraser Report The report issued in September 2004 by Lord Fraser of Carmyllie, former law officer and Conservative Scottish Office Minister, which pinned the blame for a more than ten-fold cost overrun on the new Scottish Parliament building at HOLYROOD firmly on civil servants. He concluded that Donald Dewar, Scotland's initial FIRST MINISTER, had estimated the cost at £40 million and then increased those estimates only slightly because those were the figures he had been given by officials; the final cost was £431 million. Lord Fraser identified 'management failure of gigantic proportions' in how the project was let and run, though there was some criticism of the Spanish architect Enric Miralles, who like Dewar died when the project was in its early stages, and of the Parliament's PRESIDING OFFICER Sir David Steel (*see* BOY DAVID).

fraternal delegate A DELEGATE who attends the CONFERENCE of one organisation as the representative of another that is friendly to it. *Frater* is Latin for BROTHER; particularly in the Labour, Co-operative and trade union movements, it is customary for leaders of each to appear at the others' gatherings to deliver fraternal greetings. There is an apocryphal story of a trade union official in hospital receiving a letter from his branch extending fraternal wishes for a speedy recovery, and adding:

> The motion was carried by six votes to four, with five ABSTENTIONS.

free. Free at last! Free at last! Thank God almighty – we are free at last! The words from a Negro spiritual with which Dr Martin Luther KING closed his I HAVE A DREAM speech in Washington on 28 August 1963, and which appear as his epitaph in Atlanta's South View Cemetery.

Free Democrats Germany's LIBERAL party, founded after WORLD WAR II, which governed in coalition with, in turn, the CHRISTIAN DEMOCRATS and the SPD. In 1990 it won 79 seats in the first BUNDESTAG of reunited Germany with 11% of the vote and continued in coalition with the CDU, but it has struggled since to retain a presence as the GREENS have proved a powerful alternative third force.

free elections The process promised by STALIN at YALTA for the countries of eastern Europe 'liberated' from NAZI occupation, and which was either prevented by Soviet influence or speedily negated by a Communist takeover. Throughout the 1950s, free elections in Poland and its neighbours were insisted on by the West as prerequisites for a post-war settlement, but none were held until the collapse of Communism.

free enterprise *See* ENTERPRISE.

Free French The movement headed by General DE GAULLE to continue the military struggle against NAZI Germany after the collapse of France in 1940. Later re-christened the **Fighting French**, its troops liberated Paris in 1944, but also found themselves fighting VICHY forces in the Middle East.

free market *See* MARKET.

Free Nelson Mandela *See* GRAFFITI.

free post The facility offered to every CANDIDATE in a UK Parliamentary election, with the Royal Mail making one free delivery to each household. Generally a candidate will send out their ELECTION ADDRESS by these means.

Free Silver The policy on which the POPULIST PARTY was launched to fight America's 1892 elections; it involved INFLATING the currency by the free and unlimited coinage of silver at a ratio of 16 oz. of silver to one ounce of gold. It also formed the basis four years later of the electrifying first campaign for the Presidency of William Jennings Bryan (*see* BOY ORATOR), who in the House in 1893 had advocated it as a panacea. The idea of breaking with the GOLD STANDARD by the coining of plentiful silver captivated the farmers and miners of the West and South, but made little impact on the industrial workers of the East and Midwest.

Free Soilers The faction who seceded from the 1848 Democratic Convention to form their own party to campaign against any westward extension of slavery, which was a forerunner of America's REPUBLICAN PARTY. Their slogan was **Free Soil, Free Speech, Free Labor and Free Men;** what most of them wanted was not an end to slavery but land and opportunities for white pioneers from the Eastern states and the 'oppressed and banished of other lands'. They nominated former President Martin van Buren (*see* OLD KINDERHOOK) as their Presidential candidate, but won only 10% of the vote.

Free Staters In the Irish Civil War (1922–23), supporters of the Provisional GOVERNMENT set up under the Anglo-IRISH TREATY of 1921. Led by Michael Collins (1890–1922), they were opposed by the Republicans under Eamonn de Valera (*see* DEV), who repudiated the treaty because it left NORTHERN IRELAND outside the Irish state and still demanded an OATH OF ALLEGIANCE to the British Crown. Collins died in an ambush in 1922, but the severe measures taken by the Free State government forced the Republicans to abandon the armed struggle in 1923 – though the IRA would resume operations later.

free trade A regime under which nations trade with each other unimpeded by TARIFFS and other barriers. It was traditionally the policy of Britain's LIBERAL PARTY. From 1929 to 1931 the PRESS BARONS Beaverbrook and Rothermere promoted an unsuccessful campaign for EMPIRE FREE TRADE. Free trade within its SINGLE MARKET is a fundamental of the EUROPEAN UNION (*see also* EFTA, EUROPEAN ECONOMIC AREA). It is also the basis of NAFTA and the embryonic CAFTA which aims to parallel the formula in Central America, and in various other regional trading blocs. The WORLD TRADE ORGANISATION exists to make sure that individual nations and groupings like the EU and NAFTA do not simply erect fresh barriers between each other and the developing world.

> The only policy which is technically sound and intellectually right.
>
> JOHN MAYNARD KEYNES

free vote A vote in a legislature where the party WHIPS are off and members are free to vote as they please, or as their conscience dictates. At WESTMINSTER free votes generally apply either to matters where there is no party view, or social or ethical questions such as abortion.

free world A COLD WAR term for the member nations of the ATLANTIC ALLIANCE ranged against the SOVIET UNION and its SATELLITES, and for the pro-Western countries that sided with the allies on world issues.

> The free world is not just a fortress. It is a promised land. ANTHONY EDEN, 1953

freebie A trip, usually overseas and involving a degree of luxury, on which a legislator travels at someone else's expense, generally to encourage him or her to look favourably on the country in question, its government or its policies.

Freedmen's Bureau The Bureau of Refugees, Freedmen and Abandoned Lands created by the US CONGRESS in March 1865 to provide the South's NEWLY-EMANCIPATED former slaves with the basics of life and to protect their CIVIL RIGHTS, and to care for former plantations left abandoned. In February 1866 Congress passed a BILL giving the Bureau an indefinite life as part of its aggressive programme for RECONSTRUCTION. President Andrew Johnson attempted to VETO both this and a further Bill later that year extending the Bureau's powers, which eventually expired in 1872.

freedom The aspiration of enslaved peoples and the stock-in-trade of democratic politicians and revolutionary leaders. Rousseau declared that 'man was born free, and everywhere he is in chains', while Jean-Paul Sartre more gloomily asserted: 'Man is condemned to be free.' Abraham LINCOLN said of slavery: 'Those who deny freedom to others deserve it not for themselves'; the ABOLITIONIST Frederick Douglass that 'he who would be free must strike the first blow'. To John F. KENNEDY 'freedom is indivisible, and when one man is enslaved, all are not free'; Malcolm X militantly asserted: 'Nobody can give you freedom. Nobody can give you equality or justice or anything. You just take it.' Once gained, freedom has to be preserved; as Adlai STEVENSON put it, 'We inherited freedom. We seem unaware that freedom has to be remade and re-earned in each generation of man.' EISENHOWER, who defeated him for the Presidency, asserted that 'only our individual faith in freedom has kept us free'. But General Douglas MACARTHUR warned that 'no man is entitled to the blessings of freedom unless he be vigilant in its preservation', and Kennedy added the caution that 'if the self-discipline of the free cannot match the iron discipline of the mailed fist, the threat to freedom will continue to rise'.

Stevenson asserted that 'a free society is a society where it is safe to be unpopular', and dissent and freedom march hand in hand. MAHATMA Gandhi taught that 'freedom is not worth having if it does not connote freedom to err', Rosa Luxemburg maintained that 'freedom is always and exclusively freedom for the one who thinks differently', and at the other end of the political spectrum, Charles Evans Hughes agreed, saying: 'When we lose the right to be different, we lose the privilege to be free.' With dissent comes tolerance, Richard NIXON cautioning: 'We can maintain a free society only if we recognise that in a free society no one can win all the time.' With freedom also comes law. G. D. H. Cole wrote that 'man in society is not free where there is no law; he is most free where he co-operates best with his equals in the making of laws', and Lord SALISBURY maintained: 'If one man imprisons you, that is tyranny; if two men, or a number of men imprison you, that is freedom.' The law should also prevent violations of freedom; PITT THE YOUNGER warned that 'necessity is the plea for every infringement of human freedom. It is the argument of tyrants; it is the creed of slaves.' Another obstacle to the achievement of freedom is poverty. Stevenson maintained that 'a hungry man is not a free man', Lord Boyd Orr that 'if people have to choose between freedom and sandwiches, then they will take sandwiches'.

> The English people imagine themselves to be free, but they are wrong. It is only during the election of members of Parliament that they are so.
>
> JEAN-JACQUES ROUSSEAU (1712–78), *The SOCIAL CONTRACT*

> If we wish to be free . . . we must fight! I repeat it, Sir, we must fight! An appeal to arms and to the God of Hosts, is all that is left us.
>
> PATRICK HENRY to the Virginia Convention, 23 March 1775

He who dies for freedom dies not for his country alone but for the whole world.
KHRISTO BOTEV, Bulgarian revolutionary (1848–76)

The progress of freedom depends more upon the maintenance of peace, the spread of commerce, and the diffusion of education than upon the labours of Cabinets and Foreign Offices.
RICHARD COBDEN, HOUSE OF COMMONS, 26 June 1850

All the resources of a SUPERPOWER cannot isolate a man who hears the voice of freedom; a voice that I heard from the very chamber of my soul.
NATHAN (Anatoly) SCHARANSKY after his release from the GULAG, 11 May 1986

freedom of assembly The right of individuals to meet and discuss whatever is of interest to them; in America it is guaranteed by the FIRST AMENDMENT.

freedom of association The right of individuals to form organisations, such as political parties and trade unions, to promote their mutual aims.

freedom of conscience or **thought** The right to believe what one chooses, without fear of punishment or persecution by the State. American liberals believe that MCCARTHYISM was a direct challenge to this principle; Adlai STEVENSON declared that 'to strike freedom of the mind with the fist of patriotism is an old and ugly subtlety.'

Without freedom of thought there can be no such thing as wisdom, and no such thing as public liberty without freedom of speech.
BENJAMIN FRANKLIN, 1772

It behoves every man who values liberty of conscience for himself, to resist invasions of it in the case of others.
THOMAS JEFFERSON, 1799

If there is any fixed star in our constitutional constellation, it is that no official, high or petty, can prescribe what shall be orthodox in politics, nationalism, religion or other matters of opinions, or force citizens to confess by word or act their faith therein.
Justice ROBERT H. JACKSON, 1943

Diversity of opinion is the essence of freedom.
LORD DEVLIN, *Report on the Press,* 1967

freedom fighters A term used by fighters for national independence, regarded by themselves as PATRIOTS, by those not involved as GUERRILLAS and by their foes as TERRORISTS.

freedom fries French fries, as renamed in its own eating places by a furious US CONGRESS in March 2003 when France threatened to VETO, and succeeded in blocking, a UN resolution authorising military action by the US and Britain to eliminate the threat supposedly posed by WEAPONS OF MASS DESTRUCTION in Iraq.

Freedom of Information Act (1) The ACT passed by the US CONGRESS in 1974 over President FORD's VETO which gave citizens and the media access to a wide range of information held by the government and documentation on how decisions were reached; an agency is obliged to reply within fourteen days. The Act greatly increased the ACCOUNTABILITY of government and created a better informed public, but most seismic journalism in Washington is still the result of LEAKS. (2) The far less radical measure passed by a reluctant Labour government in 2000, after the original draft had been heavily toned down in WHITEHALL. The Act has established a basic right to know and made government departments aware that their internal workings may be opened up to public scrutiny, but its contribution to a climate of OPEN GOVERNMENT has been relatively modest; individuals stand more change of seeing any files held on them by invoking the Data Protection Act. Whitehall was supposed to yield up its treasure in January 2005, but as well as imposing a hefty inspection fee, civil servants also kept secret 76,000 supposedly sensitive files covering such matters as the armorial device of Queen Salote of Tonga, the membership of the Poole Harbour Commissioners and an application by a hospital to name a ward after a daughter of King George V. A more substantial Freedom of Information Bill promoted by the Liberal MP Clement Freud failed to become law in 1979 when James CALLAGHAN's Labour government fell while the measure was going through the COMMONS.

I question very seriously whether a secret intelligence agency and the Freedom of Information Act can co-exist for very long.
CIA Director WILLIAM J. CASEY, 1982

Information, free from interest or prejudice, free from the vanity of the writer or the influence of the Government, is as necessary to the human mind as pure air and water to the human body.
WILLIAM REES-MOGG, 1970

freedom of the press The right of the media to publish news and comment without fear of suppression or prosecution. This is protected in America by the FIRST AMENDMENT (*see* CONGRESS SHALL MAKE NO LAW); in Britain the laws on libel and contempt have exerted some restraining influence, but governments have declined to implement the 1993 Calcutt Report proposing stiff penalties for invading the privacy of individuals. *See also* POWER WITHOUT RESPONSIBILITY; The PRICE OF PETROL HAS GONE UP BY A PENNY.

Our liberty depends on the freedom of the press, and that cannot be limited without being lost.
THOMAS JEFFERSON

Freedom to publish means freedom for all and not for some.
Justice HUGO BLACK (1886–1971)

Reading about one's failings in the daily papers is one of the privileges of high office in this free country of ours.
Governor NELSON ROCKEFELLER, 29 November 1972

The liberty of the press is the Palladium of all the civil, political and religious rights of an Englishman.
The anonymous pamphleteer JUNIUS (*fl.* 1769–72)

The press is easier squashed than squared.
CHURCHILL

freedom of speech The right of individuals to say what they think without fear of prosecution or victimisation. The right is protected in the FIRST AMENDMENT and in the Common Law of England, but there is perpetual argument over the point at which freedom becomes licence. Oliver Wendell Holmes considered that 'the most stringent protection of free speech would not protect a man in falsely shouting "fire" in a theatre and causing a panic'. To this end most democratic countries have legislation making it an offence to utter blasphemy or obscenities, or to stir up racial hatred. As Adlai STEVENSON put it:

Every man has the right to be heard, but no man has the right to strangle democracy with a single set of vocal chords.

My people and I have come to an agreement that satisfies us both. They are to say what they please, and I am to do what I please.
FREDERICK THE GREAT (1712–86)

Without free speech the search for truth becomes impossible.
CHARLES BRADLAUGH (*attr.*)

I realise that, in speaking to you this afternoon, there are certain limitations placed upon the right of free speech. I must be exceedingly careful, prudent, as to what I say, and even more careful and prudent as to how I say it. I may not be able to say all I think, but I am not going to say anything I do not think.

The anti-war speech delivered by EUGENE DEBS (CONVICT #2273) to the Socialist Party of Ohio on 6 June 1918 which earned him a ten-year prison sentence, commuted by President HARDING in 1921.

Freedom of speech is the greatest safety, because if a man is a fool, the best thing to do is encourage him to advertise the fact by speaking.
WOODROW WILSON, 1919

The right to be heard does not automatically include the right to be taken seriously.
Sen. HUBERT HUMPHREY

Freedom Riders Young members of CORE, black and white, who in 1961–62 travelled by bus through America's Deep South, defying SEGREGATION in bus stations and other public facilities. The first ride, which left WASHINGTON for New Orleans on 4 May 1961, ended in the burning of a bus in Anniston, Alabama, a riot in MONTGOMERY and the riders' arrest in Jackson, Mississippi. Drivers refused to take them further and they finished their journey by plane. Subsequent Freedom Rides led to scores of riders being jailed for alleged breaches of the law; in Montgomery that December, 737 marchers protesting at the prosecution of eleven Freedom Riders were arrested. By then the Interstate Commerce Commission had banned segregation on buses and in terminals.

freedom under the rule of law The basic philosophy of Margaret THATCHER, a lawyer, which she repeatedly articulated as Prime Minister both as an aim for the oppressed peoples of the world, and the main theme of her politics at home.

Four Freedoms *See* ROOSEVELT.

freeloader A politician with a reputation for accepting any form of free hospitality: food, drink or overseas trips. The word apparently originated during WORLD WAR II, so may be of military, rather than political, provenance.

Freemason's apron One of the most intriguing aspects of the PROFUMO AFFAIR was the rumour of an orgy attended by many celebrities at which a man presided, dressed only in a Freemason's apron. The identity of the man was never established beyond a doubt, but one Cabinet Minister had to submit to bodily examination before being cleared of involvement.

freeze. nuclear freeze The idea that both SUPERPOWERS should halt the increase in their nuclear weaponry, first put forward by the Republican Sen. Mark Hatfield as an amendment to the SALT II treaty in 1979. It prompted a mass movement in America that was echoed in Europe; President REAGAN, who opposed a freeze, claimed three years later that the idea's author was Leonid BREZHNEV.

wage or **price freeze** The halting of wage or

price increases, or both, in order to curb INFLATION. Such freezes have occasionally been tried, both in Britain (before Margaret THATCHER came to power) and in America, by the NIXON administration. They have been successful in the short term, but have bottled up inflationary pressures and industrial unrest.

Freikorps A post-WORLD WAR I manifestation of German MILITARISM and right-wing thuggery. First appearing in December 1918, after Germany's defeat, and consisting of ex-soldiers (officers and men), unemployed youths and others, there were soon some 65 groups throughout Germany. The Government used them to beat up left-wing agitators; once they had acquired a taste for such bullying, they chose their targets for plunder and vandalism. Ernst Röhm, a *Freikorps* commander, became head of the BROWNSHIRTS, and many of the groups were later absorbed by the NAZI party. *See also* KAPP PUTSCH.

Frelimo (Port. Front for the Liberation of Mozambique) The MARXIST independence movement and subsequent governing party founded in 1962 by Eduardo Mondlane (1920–69). It fought a ten-year war (1964–74) against Portuguese rule, which succeeded after a leftist military COUP against the right-wing Lisbon government; a counter-coup by whites in Mozambique failed. Portugal's African colonies were granted independence in 1975 and Samora Machel (1930–86), who had become Frelimo's leader when Mondlane was ASSASSINATED, became Mozambique's first President. (After his death his widow Graça married Nelson MANDELA, thus becoming FIRST LADY of a second country.) Frelimo in power gradually modified its Marxist line, eventually taking Mozambique into the COMMONWEALTH, but on the way it was subjected to a violent guerrilla campaign by a new enemy, RENAMO.

French British politicians have always spoken French at their peril; CHURCHILL was aware of this, once warning a delighted audience in Strasbourg's town square:

> *Prenez garde! Je vais parler Français.*
> Beware – I am going to speak French.

Churchill's use of French was picturesque. He once told DE GAULLE: *'Markez mes mots. Si vous me doublecrosserez, je vous liquidaterai.'* And when, intending to tell radio listeners in Occupied France that his past had been divided into two, he reputedly said: *'Mon derrière est divisée en deux parties.'* ['My bottom is divided into two parts.'] Neville CHAMBERLAIN's wife made an equally unfortunate GAFFE. Declining a dinner invitation from the French Ambassador, she said: *'Mon mari est toujours occupé dans le Cabinet avec beaucoup, beaucoup de papier.'* ['My husband is always stuck in the lavatory with lots of paper.'] By comparison, Edward HEATH's French grammar and vocabulary were sound, but his excruciating vowels did the ENTENTE no service. *See also* SIMULTANEOUS TRANSLATION.

French Community An association of former French COLONIES formed in 1958 by the constitution of de Gaulle's FIFTH REPUBLIC. It replaced the former French Union, which was itself the replacement of the French Colonial Empire, and was supposed to maintain cultural and economic uniformity.

French Revolution The turbulent and at times bloody upheavals that began with the Tennis Court OATH and the fall of the BASTILLE in 1789, followed in 1793 by the execution of Louis XVI and Marie Antoinette. PITT THE YOUNGER described the King's execution as 'the foulest and most atrocious deed the world has yet had occasion to attest'; BURKE said of the Queen's:

> I thought ten thousand swords must have leaped from their scabbards to avenge even a look that threatened her with insult. But the age of chivalry is gone.

Robespierre asserted that 'the government of the Revolution is the despotism of liberty against tyranny', and embarked on the Reign of TERROR when the Revolution, in Vergniaud's words, devoured its children. The revolutionary fires subsided in the DIRECTORY, when Napoleon declared himself First Consul and subsequently Emperor. The Revolution aroused terror among England's ruling class and conservatives in Parliament, though Charles James Fox hailed it as 'the most stupendous and glorious edifice of liberty which has been erected on the foundations of human integrity in any time or country', and Wordsworth wrote: '

> Bliss was it in that dawn to be alive
> But to be young was very heaven.

It was seen in America as an echo of that country's own recent and successful struggle for INDEPENDENCE – which had, ironically, been backed by France's *ancien régime*. Its ideals were founded on Thomas Paine's

RIGHTS OF MAN, and while many of its innovations did not survive, little of the old order it destroyed was ever reinstated, giving Napoleon a *tabula rasa* on which to construct new systems of law, weights and measures.

> A clap of thunder for the wicked.
> LOUIS DE SAINT-JUST (1767–94)

> Merely the herald of a far greater and much more solemn revolution, which will be the last . . . The hour has come for the founding of the Republic of Equals – that great refuge open to every man.
> FRANÇOIS-EMILE BABEUF (1760–97)

> It was the best of times, it was the worst of times, it was the age of wisdom, it was the age of foolishness, it was the epoch of belief, it was the epoch of incredulity, it was the season of Light, it was the season of Darkness, it was the spring of hope, it was the winter of despair; we had everything before us, we had nothing before us, we were all going direct to Heaven; we were all going direct the other way . . .
> CHARLES DICKENS, *A Tale of Two Cities*

> The PENDULUM swung furiously to the left because it had been drawn too far to the right.
> THOMAS BABINGTON MACAULAY

the French would veto the telephone book if they had the chance The assertion of the UK Conservative leader Iain Duncan Smith (*see* IDS) on 16 March 2003 after France had warned that it would VETO 'under any circumstances' a UN resolution authorising military action by Britain and America to disarm SADDAM HUSSEIN.

fresh. Fresh Start A right-wing Conservative group whose rudeness to John MAJOR at a meeting on 20 June 1995 reputedly triggered Major's decision to confront his critics by staging a leadership contest (*see* PUT UP AND SHUT UP).

freshman A WASHINGTON term for a newly-elected member of CONGRESS. George WASHINGTON advised newcomers: 'Speak seldom, but to important subjects . . . make yourself perfectly master of the subject. Never exceed a decent warmth, and submit your sentiments with diffidence.' Speaker Champ Clark reckoned that 'a new Congressman must start at the bottom and spell up', and Speaker Sam Rayburn told newcomers:

> Learn your job. Don't even talk until you know what you're talking about. If you want to get along, go along.

fridge mountain. Not for once an EU agricultural surplus, but the mountain of old refrigerators awaiting disposal that developed in the UK in 2002 after Environment Ministers and officials had failed to act on a DIRECTIVE from Brussels requiring them to be broken up in a way that did not release ozone-depleting CFC gases into the atmosphere. The episode damaged the previously charmed career of the Environment Minister Michael Meacher, who against all the odds had performed creditably for five years in Tony BLAIR's government despite being an old-style left-winger; he was sacked the following year, and subsequently urged former colleagues to 'rise up' against the Premier.

Friedmanism The MONETARIST doctrine developed and promoted by the US economist Milton Friedman (*see* CHICAGO SCHOOL) which contradicted KEYNESIANISM and encouraged a free-MARKET economy. Friedmanism was influential in the birth of THATCHERISM, guiding UK government policy in the IRON LADY's early years of power.

friends Often a greater danger to a politician than ENEMIES. The British politician George Canning wrote in the early 19th century: 'Save, oh save me from the candid friend'; GLADSTONE exclaimed: 'Standing up to one's enemies is admirable, but give me the man who can stand up to his friends.' President HARDING confided as the TEAPOT DOME scandal broke: 'My friends – they're the ones that keep me walking the floors at nights', and Alva Johnson said of New York's Mayor La Guardia: 'Anyone who extends to him the right hand of friendship is in danger of losing a couple of fingers.' And in Ireland Charles HAUGHEY's press secretary P. J. Mara reflected that 'sometimes you have to sacrifice your friends to placate your enemies.'

Friends of Bill A WASHINGTON insiders' term, used especially by foes of the President, for the 3,000-strong network of friends and supporters around and behind Bill CLINTON. The term crossed the Atlantic at the time of Tony BLAIR's election to be replicated for the **Friends of Tony**.

Friends of the Earth An environmental pressure group in Britain, uncompromising but less militant than GREENPEACE, which campaigns for recycling and the use of renewable forms of energy, and against pollution and the destruction of the natural habitat.

my good friend In the US SENATE, the customary way of referring to a Senator of the same party.

my honourable friend The way one

member of the HOUSE OF COMMONS refers to another from the same party; a PRIVY COUNCILLOR is referred to as 'my Right Honourable friend', a retired military officer as 'my (Right) Honourable and gallant friend', and a Queen's Counsel (senior barrister) as 'my (Right) Honourable and learned friend'; intriguingly a professor elected to the Commons is not referred to as 'learned'.

fringe. fringe meeting During UK party CONFERENCES, a meeting held close to the conference hall by a faction of the party or outside pressure group. The aim is to attract participants – and often speakers – from the conference, and if possible attention from the media. Many such events attract low-key commercial sponsorship.

lunatic fringe A graphic expression for EXTREMIST members of an otherwise moderate and sane organisation or community who express in outrageous fashion views that are a caricature of those held by the majority. It was coined in 1913 by Theodore ROOSEVELT, who wrote of the PROGRESSIVE PARTY:

> There is apt to be a lunatic fringe among the votaries of any forward movement.

frit The word whose use marked the one time Margaret THATCHER's mask slipped in the COMMONS to reveal her native Lincolnshire dialect; 'frit' means 'frightened'. It came in a taunt to deputy Labour leader Denis HEALEY when he challenged her to call an ELECTION in the spring of 1983; when she did, Labour were routed. Her assertion that 'you're frit' astonished those present, because of her success up to then in smothering her linguistic roots.

Fritz The nickname bestowed by colleagues in the US SENATE on Walter Mondale, who became Vice President under Jimmy CARTER (*see also* GRITS AND FRITZ). Though the name implied a Germanic origin, Mondale's forebears were actually Norwegian, hence his other nickname of NORWEGIAN WOOD.

from each according to his ability, to each according to his needs A slogan that became one of the axioms of SOCIALISM, used by Karl MARX in his *Critique of the Gotha Programme* (1875). He wrote:

> Only in a higher phase of communist society . . . can the narrow horizon of bourgeois right be crossed in its entirety, and society inscribe on its banners: 'From each according to his ability, to each according to his needs!'

Marx did not originate the phrase. Five years before, 47 ANARCHISTS tried at Lyon after the failure of their uprising signed a declaration written by Michael Bakunin (1814–76) which stated:

> We wish, in a word, equality – equality in fact as corollary, or rather, as a primordial condition of liberty. From each according to his faculties, to each according to his needs; that is what we wish sincerely and energetically.

Fronde A political movement that flourished in France c. 1648–53 in opposition to Cardinal Mazarin and his court party, during the minority of Louis XIV. Its supporters were called *Frondeurs* (*fronde*, a sling) because they were compared to urchins who throw stones in the street and run away when anyone in authority appears.

front. front bench *See* BENCH.

front line states The black-ruled states in southern Africa, notably Zambia and Tanzania, whose leaders maintained pressure on Britain from 1965 to 1980 for action to end Rhodesia's UDI. Through the COMMONWEALTH and the OAU, they mobilised international opposition to Ian Smith's regime through the maintenance of SANCTIONS, also backing the GUERRILLA groups whose leaders eventually gained power by democratic means after the LANCASTER HOUSE AGREEMENT.

front-loading In Washington, particularly the PENTAGON, the budgetary tactic of pressing for a large increase in funding for the coming year by promising to take less later. Regardless of whether the promise is kept, the effect of such funds being granted is that capital projects can be begun that often prove impossible to halt.

front organisation A political movement which appears independent but is in fact directed by, and acting on behalf of, another. For instance the WORLD PEACE COUNCIL was not a purely PACIFIST movement, as claimed, but an instrument of Soviet Communism.

front porch campaign A CAMPAIGN in which the CANDIDATE stays at home and selected groups of VOTERS are brought to him, instead of his making extensive travels. The technique was pioneered by 'BOATMAN JIM' Garfield in 1880 and perfected in 1888 by Benjamin Harrison (*see* WHITE HOUSE ICEBERG), who ousted President CLEVELAND by staying home in Indianapolis and receiving thousands of visitors, to whom he made short speeches on the TARIFF; Harrison's campaigning style cannot have been decisive, as Cleveland refused to go on the stump either, sending his 75-year-old RUNNING-MATE Allen Thurman to tour the country instead. MCKINLEY in 1896 and 1900 also won election through a front-porch campaign, but after that the BARNSTORMING of Theodore ROOSEVELT changed the nature of US electioneering for good. *See also* ROSE GARDEN STRATEGY.

front-runner The candidate in an election who is estimated by the OPINION POLLS and political PUNDITS to be ahead at a given moment.

Frost. Frost interviews The first major interviews given by ex-President NIXON after the disgrace of WATERGATE. They were conducted by the UK broadcaster David Frost (*see* THAT WAS THE WEEK THAT WAS) in 1977 at Nixon's SAN CLEMENTE compound in California, and transmitted by Metromedia television. The first, dealing with Watergate, attracted a massive audience; subsequent programmes covering foreign policy and other aspects of the Nixon ADMINISTRATION achieved much lower ratings. *See also* I GAVE THEM A SWORD.

FSB *Federalnaya Sluzhba Bezopasnosti,* Federal Security Service. The quasi-military and more open successor to the KGB which, since 1998, has maintained order within, and on the borders of, the Russian Federation. It is run by a Collegium representing its various components, with the right of appeal to the President in the event of disagreement. President Putin, as a former KGB officer, has taken a close interest in its operations and in August 2003 put in place far-reaching reforms of its organisation and methods.

FTPO For the President Only. The daily intelligence bulletin circulated in Washington containing such sensitive information that fewer than 20 people apart from the President are permitted to see it on a need-to-know basis. Senior ADMINISTRATION officials sometimes have to read through a numbered copy of the four- or five-page document with an armed guard standing by to collect it.

Fuchs case One of the most serious breaches of Western NUCLEAR security prior to and at the start of the COLD WAR. It concerned Klaus Fuchs (1911–88), a German-born British physicist (known by the UK authorities to be a Communist) who worked on the ATOMIC BOMB during WORLD WAR II in both the UK and America – and from 1943 passed details of the research to Soviet agents. In 1950, after the defection of a Soviet cipher clerk in Ottawa exposed him and implicated several other spies, Fuchs, who saw himself as an idealist, was arrested, confessed to espionage and was sentenced to fourteen years' imprisonment. He was released in 1959 and emigrated to East Germany, resuming his research and remaining there until his death. *See also* ROSENBERGS.

fuck The ultimate UNPARLIAMENTARY word, which has nevertheless been heard in debate in both HOUSES at Westminster, though not – as far as the PARLIAMENTARIAN of the HOUSE OF REPRESENTATIVES is aware – in the US CONGRESS. It was apparently first uttered on 15 November 1783 in the HOUSE OF LORDS by the Earl of Sandwich, who mischievously quoted the rhyme

> . . . life can little more supply
> Than just a few good fucks and then we die.

from the *Essay on Woman*, attributed to John WILKES but probably written by his friend Thomas Potter. Though some peers cried: 'Go on! Go on!', the majority were scandalised and the House resolved to prosecute Wilkes for 'a most scandalous, obscene and impious libel'. Sandwich had not forgiven Wilkes for smuggling a baboon dressed as the Devil into a Black Mass celebrated by the Hell Fire Club, where it jumped on the Earl's back, giving him the fright of his life.

The first recorded use of the word in the House of Commons came on 3 February 1982 in a debate on the harmless-sounding Local Government (Miscellaneous Provisions) Bill, when the left-wing Labour MP Reg Race informed members that in a sex shop in his constituency, there was a list of prostitutes with the message:

> Phone them and fuck them!

The Deputy Speaker called Race to order, but passed no comment; the next day Speaker George Thomas (Lord TONYPANDY) said the word would be UNPARLIAMENTARY as long as he was Speaker, adding: 'None of us would use it in our homes.' He also privately rebuked the Editor of HANSARD, who had printed the word as 'f . . . ', for letting even this hint of obscenity appear. Ironically, the only other known use of the word came in 1988, when a radio microphone picked it up in an aside from an exasperated Speaker Bernard WEATHERILL.

Once in the late 1970s, the Canadian Prime Minister Pierre TRUDEAU was accused by furious Tories of uttering the 'F-word' during heated exchanges in the House of Commons. Trudeau insisted he had actually said: 'Fuddle-duddle.'

I agreed it would fuck Gilligan if that (Kelly) was the source An extract from the diary of Tony BLAIR's communications director Alistair Campbell, released in the closing stages of the HUTTON INQUIRY in 2003, which demonstrated DOWNING STREET's belief that the conversation between David KELLY and the BBC journalist Andrew Gilligan which prompted the episode was as damaging for the Corporation as it was for Dr Kelly – not to mention Blair's government. The entry was written before Dr Kelly's suicide; it was prescient as Lord Hutton did conclude, to widespread surprise, that the BBC was more culpable than the Government.

We're all fucked. I'm fucked. You're fucked. The whole Department's fucked. It's the biggest cock-up and we're all completely fucked The reported comment of Sir Richard Mottram, PERMANENT SECRETARY at the Department of Transport, Local Government and the Regions, to officials including the Department's Head of News Martin Sixsmith, in February 2002. It was triggered by Sixsmith's LEAKING to the media of an e-mail accusing Stephen Byers' SPECIAL ADVISER Jo Moore of planning to 'BURY' the announcement of bad news by releasing it on the day of Princess Margaret's funeral. The episode forced the resignation of Moore and the departure of Sixsmith, who dug his heels in after Byers (*see also* RAILTRACK) had told the COMMONS he had agreed to resign. Byers himself resigned that May, saying that his presence in the government had become a 'distraction'. The Department was dismembered in the ensuing reshuffle, Mottram being moved sideways to the Department of Work and Pensions.

fudge An unsatisfactory solution to a problem that in fact solves nothing, cobbled together as an uneasy compromise to avoid facing up to reality. This use of the word is said – implausibly – to originate with a Captain Fudge, who in the 17th century always brought back to England a 'cargo of lies' about the reason for his ship's poor condition. Fudge's existence is proved by a letter dating from 1664, but the rest of the story is not.

fudge and mudge Dr David OWEN's phrase for the inability of the LABOUR PARTY to stand up to the wrecking tactics of its extreme left, frustration with which led the GANG OF FOUR to quit the party early in 1981 and found the SDP. Dr Owen said at the party's Blackpool conference in 1980:

> We are fed up with fudging and mudging, with mush and slush.

fudge factory A derogatory term for the US STATE DEPARTMENT, used by those who consider FOGGY BOTTOM a temple of APPEASEMENT and compromise.

fuel. fuel crisis The desperate shortage of energy in Britain early in 1947 caused by a combination of bitterly cold weather for months on end which immobilised coal stocks, and soaring demand which put strain on a power network debilitated by war and lack of investment. With the need for heat at its greatest, savage power cuts had to be imposed, families shivered in their homes and thousands of workers were laid off as industry ground to a halt; Emmanuel Shinwell (*see* MANNY), Minister of Fuel and Power in the ATTLEE government, was widely criticised. Ministers had known since the previous November that a severe winter might prove disastrous, and Hugh GAITSKELL had voiced the fear that 'as an administrator, Shinwell is hardly a starter'. The Conservatives seized their opportunity with the slogan:

> Starve with Strachey. Shiver with Shinwell.

John Strachey was Minister of Food, and in charge of the equally austere rationing programme.

fuel protest The sudden upsurge of unrest in September 2000 over high fuel prices and duties which halted the distribution of petrol throughout Britain within three days and almost brought the country to a standstill. It was led by small farmers (most of whom did not have to pay the duty anyway) and independent hauliers who were struggling with tight cost margins; their PICKETING of oil refineries and distribution depots proved highly effective. Within days Tony BLAIR's government caved in, Chancellor Gordon BROWN abandoning the 'escalator' brought in by the Conservatives under which fuel duties increased each year by more than the rate of INFLATION to discourage vehicle use and help meet environmental targets. In its later stages the protest also turned into a campaign against Brown's decision, at a time of near-zero inflation, to raise index-linked state pensions by just 75p a week. The protest shook NEW LABOUR, which fell behind in the polls for the only time in its first term, and the oil companies, who discovered they had little hands-on control over their refineries (Shell's Stanlow plant turned out to be being run from Milan) and less over their tanker drivers, who were employed by private contractors.

Führer (Ger. leader) The title – 'Führer of the People' – adopted by Adolf HITLER (1889–1945) on the death of President von Hindenburg in August 1934, when he finally assumed total power and declared the Third REICH. It was also held briefly after Hitler's suicide on 30 April 1945 by Grand Admiral Karl Dönitz, who presided over Germany's final surrender. The title reflected the almost mystical supremacy over the German people that Hitler regarded as his destiny, which galvanised a country that had been shattered by war and internal division and led to its Wagnerian nemesis as the Russians advanced on his BUNKER in a devastated Berlin. Hitler himself had said: 'I go the way that Providence dictates with the assurance of a sleepwalker', 'I am convinced nothing will happen to me, for I know the greatness for which providence has chosen me', and 'I know of no STATESMAN in the world who with greater right than I can say that he is the representative of his people'. *Compare* CAUDILLO; DUCE.

full. full dinner pail One of the slogans which delivered the Presidency to William MCKINLEY, Governor of Ohio, in his 1896 contest with William Jennings Bryan. It emphasised the prosperity that returned to the US economy as the CAMPAIGN unfolded, blunting Bryan's POPULIST challenge. The Republicans used the message: 'McKinley and the full dinner pail!' again in 1900 to secure his re-election. It was revived in the 1928 campaign by Herbert HOOVER, who went a stage further to claim (on the eve of the GREAT CRASH of 1929):

> The slogan of progress is changing from the full dinner pail to the full garage.

full employment A situation in which a job is available for everyone seeking work, which is the ideal for almost all political parties in Western democracies, though only those on the left regard it as achievable. In the 1950s, unemployment reached historic lows throughout the West and it seemed that a political consensus on the maintenance of something close to full employment had been achieved. The situation deteriorated from the 1970s with unemployment eventually exceeding 20 million across Europe, before falling back from the late 1990s. In the late 1970s the US labour movement institutionalised the goal in the HUMPHREY-HAWKINS FULL EMPLOYMENT ACT; in the UK the LABOUR PARTY reasserted full employment as an aim under John SMITH, and in office under Tony BLAIR the jobless total fell to the lowest for a generation, though still with around a million unable or unwilling to work.

full faith and credit clause Article IV, section 1 of the US CONSTITUTION, designed to prevent people 'beating the law' by moving out of a state before a court action can be brought against them, and which also guarantees the validity of a marriage anywhere within the Union. It stipulates that

> Full faith and credit shall be given in each State to the public acts, records and judicial proceedings of every other state.

Fulton report The report of the committee on reforming the culture of WHITEHALL set up by Harold WILSON in February 1966 under Lord Fulton, Vice-Chancellor of Sussex University; its terms of reference were to 'examine the structure, recruitment and management, including training, of the Home CIVIL SERVICE' and make recommendations. Fulton reported in June 1968 that the Civil Service was a 19th-century organisation facing 20th-century problems, in which the cult of the all-rounder or gifted amateur led to specialist experts being ignored. He proposed a Civil Service Department under the Prime Minister, a Civil Service College, greater emphasis on career management, the hiving off of some functions to other bodies and a lessening of secrecy. Many, though not all, of the proposals were implemented; Fulton did not bring about as much of a revolution as intended, but 40 years on the culture (in most if not all departments) had undeniably changed.

Fulton speech The speech made by Winston CHURCHILL at Fulton, Missouri, on 5 March 1946 in which he warned that an IRON CURTAIN was descending across Europe 'from Stettin on the Baltic to Trieste on the Adriatic'. For convenience's sake, many historians have marked this speech, delivered in the presence of President Truman who had read it beforehand, as the start of the COLD WAR.

FUNCINPEC *see* GRUNK.

fund-raiser On both sides of the Atlantic, a person who raises money for a political PARTY, its CANDIDATES and CAMPAIGNS; also in America especially, a dinner or other event staged to raise funds for a political object (*see also* rubber CHICKEN). In parts of the country still controlled by a political MACHINE, municipal office holders are expected to spend hundreds of dollars a plate to attend such functions, in gratitude for the PATRONAGE shown to them. The most expensive fund-raisers can cost thousands of dollars to attend; John F. KENNEDY told one such gathering in Denver in 1960:

> I am grateful to you all. I could say I am deeply touched, but not as deeply touched as you have been in coming to this dinner.

future. Future Map The plan by DARPA to set up a futures/spread betting market on the likelihood of acts of terrorism and regional conflict which caused outrage in the US CONGRESS when its existence was revealed in the summer of 2003, forcing the resignation for the second time of DARPA's head, Admiral John Poindexter, who as President REAGAN's NATIONAL SECURITY ADVISER had been convicted fifteen years previously of complicity in the IRAN-CONTRA AFFAIR.

the future is . . . black The assertion of the black US author James Baldwin (*see* the FIRE NEXT TIME), made in August 1963 on the eve of Dr Martin Luther KING's I HAVE A DREAM speech in WASHINGTON.

I have seen the future, and it works The eventually notorious comment made after a visit to BOLSHEVIK Russia in 1919 by the US journalist and reformer Lincoln Steffens (1866–1936); originally he told the financier Bernard Baruch: 'I have been over into the future, and it works.' William Bullitt, a diplomat who travelled with him, claimed Steffens had been rehearsing the phrase even before he got to Moscow to meet LENIN. Seven decades later, wags at WESTMINSTER adapted it to **I have seen the future and it smirks** to describe the Conservative Education Secretary Kenneth Baker (*see also* GERBIL; SELF-BASTING).

Let us face the future The slogan, presaging a peacetime government of radical achievement, under which Clement ATTLEE led Britain's LABOUR PARTY to a LANDSLIDE victory over CHURCHILL's Conservatives in July 1945.

the only limit to our realisation of tomorrow will be our doubts today The key phrase of the last speech drafted by Franklin D. ROOSEVELT. He wrote it at WARM SPRINGS in early April 1945 for the forthcoming conference to organise the UNITED NATIONS, but died with it undelivered.

Your future in your hands The campaign slogan of Churchill's CONSERVATIVES in Britain's 1950 general election, when they trimmed Labour's majority from 146 to 5, making an early second election and a Tory return to power almost inevitable.

FYROM Former Yugoslav Republic of Macedonia. The nation governed since the mid-1990s from Skopje; its title was carefully crafted to meet the sensibilities of Greece, for whom 'Macedonia' is an internal province, and also of Bulgaria, which has claims of its own.

G

G8 Group of Eight. The West's leading industrial nations – America, the UK, Germany, Japan, France, Canada and Italy – plus Russia, whose leaders meet each year for a largely economic SUMMIT. The Western leaders first met in 1976 as the **G7**, and since 1991, when Mikhail GORBACHEV attended as a guest, Russia's has also taken part, now being a full member. Successive G8s have been confronted with violent anti-GLOBALISATION protests, the 2005 G8 at GLENEAGLES coincided also with the crisis over the EUROPEAN CONSTITUTION, London's unexpected choice over Paris to host the 2012 Olympics, and the LONDON BOMBINGS. The Finance Ministers of the G7 still meet, and in October 2004 broke new ground by inviting China to join them. The **G6** is the G7 minus Italy; these countries concluded the LOUVRE AGREEMENT in 1987.

gadfly A questioner, persistent to the point of irritation; often a maverick politician repeatedly probing on a single issue. The origin is the insect of that name, from the O.E. *gad*: a goad.

Gadsden purchase The agreement of 1853 under which the United States bought a strip of what is now southern Arizona from Mexico for $10 million. It was negotiated by James Gadsden on behalf of President Pierce. The land was required so that a transcontinental railroad serving the southern states could be constructed on US territory throughout.

gaffe An unfortunate statement bringing ridicule on the person making it. Some are harmlessly amusing, others are capable of endangering or even ending a political career. (The origin of the word is French.) There are plenty of celebrated examples, and some that deserve wider exposure. At Westminster, Harold WILSON referred to the then Australian Prime Minister, in his presence, as 'Mr Whit Goughlam'. The veteran Tory MP Dame Irene Ward once asked a Minister who announced that sailors would get new uniforms ahead of female personnel: 'How much longer is he going to hold up the skirts of the Wrens for the convenience of the sailors?' The Conservative MP Geoffrey Dickens, at the height of media exposure of his private life, brought proceedings to a standstill by declaring: 'Mr Speaker, I should like to do every woman in the United Kingdom a FAVOUR.' Another Tory, Tim Janman, celebrated his election by loudspeakering to cows in a field: 'I should like to thank the cows of Bowers Gifford for voting Conservative', unaware that a number of female electors were within earshot. Nicholas Ridley's career as Transport Secretary nearly came to an end when, after the 1987 Zeebrugge ferry disaster, he said of the Environment Minister William Waldegrave: 'He is navigating with his bow doors closed.' Soon after Lord Wakeham, answering questions as LEADER OF THE HOUSE, raised a boffo by saying of Margaret THATCHER:

> The Prime Minister is making herself available to President Gorbachev.

The Conservative Chancellor Kenneth Clarke, touring North-East England in 1995, cited the increased efficiency of the Consett steelworks as proof that Tory policies were working; he had to be told that Consett had closed 15 years previously with the loss of 3,000 jobs. Clarke said he had meant Redcar, which was still open. The same year Transport Minister Steve Norris described commuters as 'dreadful human beings'. And more recently Labour's Schools Minister Stephen Byers demonstrated on a school visit that multiplication was not his strong point (*see* 54).

The best-known gaffe in American politics – at least until the advent of Dan QUAYLE and George W. BUSH – is apocryphal: the out-of-town politician campaigning in New York City who asked: 'Where are the Bronx?' In the 1960 Presidential campaign Richard NIXON appeared to insult his wife by saying in his DEBATE with John F. KENNEDY: 'They can't stand pat.' In 1976 Earl F. Butz, Gerald FORD's Agriculture Secretary, was forced to resign after admitting saying of black Americans: 'All they want is loose shoes, a tight pussy and a warm place to shit.' Ford himself dropped a terminal gaffe debating that year with Jimmy CARTER, when he insisted: 'There is no Soviet domination of eastern Europe – and there never will be under a Ford administration.' And Ford's campaign manager Rogers Morton torpedoed the Republican effort by declaring: 'There is no point in rearranging the furniture on the decks of the *Titanic.*' At the 1980 Democratic Convention it was Carter's turn, delivering a reverent tribute to a great American whom he named 'Hubert Horatio Hornblower.' In 1983 James Watt, Ronald REAGAN's Secretary of the Interior, made his position untenable by confiding that he had formed an advisory group comprising 'a Black, a woman, two Jews and a cripple – and we have talent'. In an inadvertently sexist gaffe the following year Ed Rollins, Reagan campaign chief, described Walter Mondale's selection of Rep. Geraldine FERRARO as his running-mate as 'the biggest political bust of recent years'. And in 1988 George BUSH managed to slight Reagan by saying of Governor George Deukmejian: 'He will go down as *the* great governor of California.' *See also* BLEARS THE BIKE; CLEAN YOUR TEETH IN THE DARK.

> A gaffe is accidental. Mine never are. I like to shock, and I do it deliberately.
>
> ALAN CLARK, *Diaries*

gag rule The rule adopted in 1836 by the US HOUSE OF REPRESENTATIVES which provided that all petitions against slavery 'be laid upon the TABLE', with no action taken; thousands were flooding in and proving highly divisive. Ex-President Rep. John Quincy ADAMS refused to vote on the rule, terming it 'a direct violation of the CONSTITUTION of the United States', and for the next eight years conducted a one-man campaign to evade or repeal it. Eventually, in December 1844, Adams got the rule repealed by 180 votes to 80. In his diary that night, he wrote: 'Blessed, forever blessed, be the name of God!'

Gaitskellites The right-wing pro-American faction in Britain's LABOUR PARTY who rallied behind the party leader **Hugh Todd Naylor Gaitskell** (1906–63), first against Aneurin BEVAN in the mid-1950s, next against Harold WILSON's leadership challenge and finally against the UNILATERALISTS (*see* FIGHT. FIGHT AND FIGHT AGAIN). Gaitskell first made his mark in the FUEL CRISIS of 1947 when he declared: 'Personally, I have never taken a great many baths myself.' He succeeded Sir Stafford Cripps as CHANCELLOR in 1950, being dubbed **Mr Rising Price** by Iain Macleod. Harold MACMILLAN saw him as 'a pupil of Mr [Hugh] Dalton. He has imitated his rather pedantic style, tedious expositions of the obvious, weak gestures and irritating style.' His moderate approach was pursued after 1951 by the Conservative R. A. (RAB) Butler (*see* BUTKSELLISM). But Henry 'CHIPS' Channon reckoned: 'Gaitskell has a Wykehamist voice and manner, and a thirteenth-century face.' He succeeded ATTLEE as Labour leader after the 1955 election, holding the office until his sudden death in 1963, by which time he had taken the party through SUEZ, its internal strife over the Bomb and a heavy defeat in 1959 (*see* YOU'VE NEVER HAD IT SO GOOD) and re-equipped it for power – though he failed to persuade it to ditch its NATIONALISATION policies as set out in CLAUSE FOUR. As Labour leader Bevan described him as a 'desiccated calculating machine' – though he later insisted he was merely setting out the requirements for the job. And Macmillan remarked: 'He is going through all the motions of being in government when he isn't in government. It is bad enough having to behave like a government when one is in government.' Roy JENKINS, a strong supporter, concluded:

> All his struggles illustrated some blemishes as well as exceptional strength. He would not have been a perfect Prime Minister, but he was that very rare phenomenon, a great politician who was also an unusually agreeable man.

> While there's death there's hope.
>
> RICHARD CROSSMAN at the Cambridge Union

gallery The area from where visitors – 'strangers' in the HOUSE OF COMMONS – may observe the proceedings of a legislature.

press gallery The galleries overlooking each HOUSE OF PARLIAMENT, and each chamber in the CAPITOL, and the rooms adjacent, from which journalists report their proceedings. At WESTMINSTER, also the totality of journalists accredited to Parliament (*see also* LOBBY).

Gallipoli The peninsula in the Dardanelles where in 1915 Allied troops made a disastrous attempt to open a second front against Turkey. British, French and ANZAC troops sustained heavy losses – 25,000 dead, 13,000 missing – over ten months after commanders failed to order a rapid advance from the beachheads. The affair sparked national trauma and pride in Australia and New Zealand, and seemed for a time to have finished the career of Winston CHURCHILL, who as First Lord of the Admiralty had championed the expedition.

Gallup poll *See* POLL.

game. the game is over The only official Iraqi comment on the overthrow of SADDAM HUSSEIN as US troops took Baghdad and Saddam and his henchmen vanished, supposedly concluding the war. It was made on 10 April 2003 by Mohammed al-Douri, Iraq's ambassador to the UN. Subsequent events demonstrated that this was far from the case.

Gandhi, Mohandas *See* MAHATMA.

Gandhi, Indira, Sanjay, Rajiv, Sonia *See* NEHRU DYNASTY.

Gang of Four (1) Mao Tse-Tung's (*see* CHAIRMAN MAO) name for the Shanghai-based hard-core radicals of the CULTURAL REVOLUTION, led by Mao's wife (and widow) Jiang Qing. The four – Zhang Chunqiao, Yao Wenyuan, Wang Hongwen and Jiang Qing – attempted to perpetuate Mao's policies after his death, but were arrested and disgraced in 1976. (2) In Britain, the four former senior Labour figures who launched the SDP in 1981: Roy JENKINS, Dr David OWEN, William Rodgers and Shirley Williams.

GAO America's General Accounting Office, the arm of CONGRESS which since 1921 has investigated how effectively public money is spent.

garbagic The term used at LOBBY briefings by Alastair Campbell, Tony BLAIR's high-profile communcations chief from 1997 to 2003, to denote a piece of political reporting which he considered no better than garbage. Unlike BUNKUM AND BALDERDASH, used to similar effect by Margaret THATCHER's press secretary Bernard Ingham, the word was his own invention.

garden. garden girls Elite secretarial staff at NUMBER TEN Downing Street, at least one of whom always travels with the Prime Minister. When LLOYD GEORGE first established the CABINET OFFICE, the girls were housed in a temporary building in the garden of No. 10.

gardening leave A WHITEHALL euphemism, whose use has spread to the world of business, for home leave taken by, or forced upon, an official whose presence in the office has become untenable.

Garfield, James Abram *See* BOATMAN JIM.

garment district The former sweatshop area of New York City, now highly unionised and the base of the International Ladies' Garment Workers' Union, which Democratic presidential nominees traditionally visit for a euphoric reception from the workers. It lies between 20th and 41st Streets and 6th and 8th Avenues.

Garter, Order of the In England and Wales, the highest order of KNIGHTHOOD, in the personal gift of the Crown. Non-hereditary, it was instituted by Edward III c. 1348 and is limited to the Royal Family and 25 Knights, now distinguished (and usually retired) figures from public life. *See* HONI SOIT QUI MAL Y PENSE.

> I could not accept the Order of the Garter from my sovereign, when I have received the Order of the Boot from the people.
>
> WINSTON CHURCHILL to George VI after his defeat in 1945 (he took the Garter in 1953)

Garveyism The doctrine of black self-pride and self-help promoted in America after WORLD WAR I by Marcus Garvey (1887–1940). Garvey, a Jamaican, branded white America corrupt and RACIST, urging blacks to set up their own institutions pending a return to Africa. His Universal Negro Improvement Association raised consciousness and spawned enterprises including a Black Star Steamship Line, but they failed. Garvey was jailed in 1925 for mail fraud and deported on his release; his movement collapsed.

-gate A generic term applied by the headline writers to any budding political scandal, originating with WATERGATE though most have been pale imitations of the revelations that toppled Richard NIXON. Examples on both sides of the Atlantic in the three decades since, some of them better remembered than others, include BETSYGATE; BILLYGATE; CHERIEGATE; COFFEEGATE; DEBATEGATE; KOREAGATE; MULDERGATE; NANNYGATE; OFFICEGATE; TRAVELGATE; THRESHERGATE and, more momentously, ZIPPERGATE which led to the IMPEACHMENT of a second President. Efforts by political foes to cast the IRAN-CONTRA AFFAIR as Irangate were thwarted by newspaper proprietors friendly to President REAGAN, who ordered that the word must not appear.

GATT General Agreement on TARIFFS and Trade. The predecessor of the **WTO**, the Geneva-based world body which from 1948 to 1995 worked to lower trade barriers by eliminating tariffs and quotas. *See* KENNEDY ROUND; MULTI-FIBRE AGREEMENT; TOKYO ROUND.

gauleiter The administrator of a *Gau*, or province, in NAZI Germany and its occupied territories, often appointed directly by the FÜHRER and responsible for all economic and political activities, civil defence and sometimes policing. The word has become a term of abuse for any aggressive figure halfway down the chain of authority.

Gaullism The uniquely French philosophy behind the post-war movement founded by General/President DE GAULLE, which has outlived him healthily. Based on vigorous assertion of the national interest, Gaullism breaks with other right-wing ideologies to advocate state intervention in industry. Its tenets have been adopted even by elements of the French Socialist Party.

> I have myself only become a Gaullist little by little. DE GAULLE

gavel The small, usually wooden, hammer banged by the chairman of a deliberative body to call members to order. The ivory gavel first used by John ADAMS when presiding over the US SENATE broke apart 165 years later in the hand of Richard NIXON. India provided a replica, but the original stays on the Vice President's desk.

gavel-to-gavel Live broadcast coverage from start to finish of a Parliamentary event, conference or CONVENTION.

gay rights The movement for homosexual rights inspired by the impact of the FEMINIST movement in the late 1960s. The **Gay Liberation Front**, founded in New York in 1970, was the forerunner of many homosexual pressure groups of varying brashness, militancy and effectiveness; in the UK **Stonewall** has proved effective though Peter Tatchell's **Outrage!** has captured more headlines. Successes secured by the movement as a whole include the decriminalisation of homosexual acts between consenting adults in private in many jurisdictions where they were still an offence, a lowering of the age of consent for such acts in many countries, the easing of discrimination against gay men and lesbians in employment, housing and financial services, and the granting of rights to homosexual couples through the right to same-sex marriage in a few US jurisdictions, and more widely the registration of Civil Partnerships. *See also* SECTION 28; WOLFENDEN REPORT.

Gaza and Jericho first The formula with which Israel and the PLO broke for a time the deadlock in the Middle East PEACE PROCESS, involving limited self-rule for the Gaza Strip and part of the WEST BANK. It was agreed in September 1993 after the Israeli Prime Minister Yitzhak Rabin and PLO leader Yasser Arafat shook hands at the WHITE HOUSE. The following May the details were settled in Cairo, and the PLO set up headquarters for the PALESTINIAN AUTHORITY in Gaza and brought in its own police force. The period surrounding the handover was marked by Israeli security clampdowns, a massacre at a mosque in Hebron by a Jewish settler and outrages by HAMAS and other Palestinian militants aimed at wrecking the settlement and fuelling conflict with Israel. A decade later the settlement remained incomplete; the assassination of Rabin, the failure of talks at the close of Bill CLINTON's presidency to conclude a more lasting deal on better terms for the Palestinians – Arafat wanted further concessions – the election of the hard-liner Ariel Sharon, a wave of suicide bombings for which Israel blamed Arafat, heavy security crackdowns in Gaza as a prelude to a promised Israeli withdrawal and Israel's construction of a wall separating it from most of the West Bank made peace look further away than ever.

Gaza Strip A belt of land, 26 miles long and 3½–6 miles wide, on the Mediterranean coast between Israel and Egypt, heavily populated by Palestinian refugees. It was ruled by Egypt from 1948, briefly held by Israel in 1956 and seized again in 1967 (*see* SIX DAY WAR) to become one of the OCCUPIED TERRITORIES. A stronghold of the INTIFADA under Israeli rule, the Strip has been under Palestinian administration since 1994, though Israel – despite Ariel Sharon's implementation in 2005 of a pullout and withdrawal of Israeli settlers – has reserved the right to stage raids on alleged militant targets in Gaza.

GCHQ Government Communications Headquarters. The nerve-centre at Cheltenham of SIGINT (Signals Intelligence), the global eavesdropping network that is a key element in British intelligence-gathering, housed since 2003 in a state-of-the-art headquarters next to the M5. Much of the information is shared with the United States, so occasional charges against its staff of espionage (Geoffrey Prime in 1983) or leaking to the media (Katherine GUN in 2004) cause concern in WASHINGTON. So did a trade union campaign of disruption in 1981, which led Margaret THATCHER in

1984 to ban union membership at GCHQ, causing a long-running controversy; the ban was lifted by the incoming Labour government in May 1997.

GDP Gross Domestic Product. The value of all goods and services generated by an economy over a given period, excluding net exports; the most reliable estimate of a nation's economic state and rate of growth.

GDR The former German Democratic Republic, better known as East Germany. It comprised the zone of Germany occupied by the Soviet Union in the wake of HITLER's defeat, with its capital in East Berlin. The Communist state was formally created in 1949 in response to the establishment of a democratic regime (the Federal Republic) covering the British, French and US zones. It survived until 1990.

> Communism fits Germany like a saddle fits a cow. STALIN, 1944

gender balance The securing of an equal number of men and women in a legislature or other organisation. In the context of Labour's efforts to secure gender balance in the first SCOTTISH PARLIAMENT elected in 1999, John MAJOR observed:

> Gender balance, 129 members – God help one of them.

general. General . . . er, General. George W. BUSH's first stab at naming Pakistan's head of state, when questioned about his knowledge of world affairs during a TV interview for a Boston station during his 2000 Presidential campaign. One year later, in the wake of 9/11, Bush was in daily contact with Gen. Pervez Musharraf as a pivotal figure in the ousting of the TALEBAN and the tracing and destruction of AL QAEDA as the WAR AGAINST TERRORISM got under way.

General Accounting Office *See* GAO.

General Assembly The forum of the UNITED NATIONS in which every member state has equal influence by virtue of its single vote (though the former SOVIET UNION had three, two of them nominally for Belorussia and the Ukraine). It sits in New York for three months every year from the third Tuesday in September, elects ten non-permanent members of the SECURITY COUNCIL and can make pronouncements or recommendations – a two-thirds majority is required for important matters. But immediate issues, and key matters of policy, are almost entirely the province of the Security Council.

general election *See* ELECTION.

General Strike A stoppage of work by the entire unionised workforce of a nation or city, in some countries a regular form of protest and display of SOLIDARITY. In Britain, the unique stoppage from 3 to 12 May 1926 when the TUC called out key workers in support of miners resisting a pay cut. It was brought about by a lockout of miners on 30 April, itself the culmination of a long and bitter struggle (*see* NOT A PENNY OFF THE PAY, NOT A MINUTE ON THE DAY). The strike affected the railways, road transport and industries including iron and steel, building, gas, electricity and printing. Stanley BALDWIN's government enacted a STATE OF EMERGENCY and called in troops and civilian volunteers to maintain essential services; the TUC had promised to maintain vital food supplies. Baldwin's object, claimed Sir Oswald MOSLEY, was 'to make working class bees without a sting who were to gather honey for the rich, but to be deprived of the right to defend themselves.' With national newspapers off the streets, the Government produced its own *BRITISH GAZETTE*, belligerently edited by Chancellor Winston CHURCHILL; the TUC countered with its own *British Worker*. Though it had a considerable impact, the strike was not total, and with the TUC losing the political battle it was reluctantly called off. The miners stayed out another six months before being starved back to work on the owners' terms.

> The General Strike has taught the working class more in four days than years of talking would have done. Earl BALFOUR

general will, the The doctrine of Rousseau that 'the body politic, therefore, is also a moral being possessed of a will, and this general will tends always to the preservation and welfare of the whole.' In the FRENCH REVOLUTION, Robespierre declared: 'Our will is the General Will.' And in the 20th century Herbert Marcuse asserted: 'The General Will is always wrong.'

generalissimo The supreme commander, especially of a force drawn from two or more nations or services; also the supreme leader of certain authoritarian regimes. In modern times the title has been applied to Marshal Foch (1851–1929), who commanded the Allied forces in France in 1918; to General Franco (*see* CAUDILLO), who proclaimed himself generalissimo of the Spanish army in 1939; to Joseph STALIN, who was made generalissimo of the Soviet forces in 1943; and to Chiang Kai-Shek (1888–1975), leader of the KMT, who held power in China from 1927 to 1949, and subsequently in NATIONALIST CHINA.

Geneva. Geneva Agreement The settlement signed in Geneva on 21 July 1954 between the warring parties in Indochina, after France's defeat at DIEN BIEN PHU, which was intended to end conflict between French and VIET MINH forces in VIETNAM and ensure the evacuation of Communist troops and GUERRILLAS from Laos and Cambodia. The agreements, signed also by America, the Soviet Union, Britain and China, were signed as a 'midnight or never' deadline set by the French was about to expire – but US Secretary of State John Foster Dulles did so with the worst possible grace out of pique at France's admission of defeat. A CEASEFIRE line was established along the 17TH PARALLEL; although this was not intended as a territorial boundary, Vietnam became divided into the North under Viet Minh control and the South under a US-backed anti-Communist regime. The FREE ELECTIONS envisaged for the whole of Vietnam never took place, and the stage was set for the Vietnam War.

Geneva Conventions Four conventions, the first submitted in 1864 by the International Committee of the Red Cross to a conference of diplomats in Geneva, which govern the conduct of war. The best known covers the humane treatment of prisoners of war, which US personnel at ABU GHRAIB prison were accused of flouting after the overthrow of SADDAM HUSSEIN.

Geneva disarmament conference *See* DISARMANENT.

Geneva Protocol A protocol for the pacific settlement of international disputes, proposed to the LEAGUE OF NATIONS in 1924 by Ramsay MACDONALD and the French Premier, Edouard Herriot. Requiring all disputes to be settled by compulsory ARBITRATION by the Permanent Court of International Justice (*see* WORLD COURT) or other League bodies, it was unanimously endorsed by the League Assembly on 2 October 1924. MacDonald's government fell soon after (*see* ZINOVIEV LETTER), and Stanley BALDWIN's incoming administration disowned the protocol, paving the way for its demise.

Geneva summit (1) The first peacetime SUMMIT conference in the correct meaning of the word, with the leaders of America, Britain, France and the Soviet Union meeting in July 1955 in an effort to reduce world tension in the depths of the COLD WAR; the driving force was CHURCHILL, though he had retired by the time it took place. The leaders rejected war as an instrument of national policy, agreed to set up economic, cultural and economic contacts and had abortive talks on DISARMAMENT and German reUNIFICATION. Though the meeting was largely inconclusive, its good-natured tone did ease the climate for a time. (2) The first meeting, in November 1985, between President REAGAN and Mikhail GORBACHEV. They clashed on Reagan's insistence on America developing STAR WARS, and the meeting was generally unproductive, showing no sign of the two men's future friendship.

genocide The attempted destruction of a national, ethnic or religious group by another, designated a crime under international law by the UN GENERAL ASSEMBLY in 1948. Several Bosnian Serb leaders, plus the former Serb president Slobodan Milosevic, have been put on trial for genocide before a tribunal in the Hague, as have senior Rwandan Hutus accused of organising the massacre of Tutsis. The word, from the Greek *genos*, race, and Latin *caedere*, to kill, was invented by Professor Raphael Lemkin of Duke University, and was used in drafting the official indictment of NAZI war criminals in 1945.

Gens du pays (Fr. People of the land) The romantic nationalist song written by Gilles Vignault which became the anthem of Quebec's SEPARATIST movement from the 1970s. Its first verse and chorus, translated from the French, are:

> The time that it takes to say: 'I love you'
> Is all that is left us at the end of our days.
> The wishes one's made, the flowers one's sown
> Each of them the harvests in oneself
> In the fragrant gardens of passing time.
>
> People of the land, it is your turn
> To be free to talk of love.

gentleman. gentleman's agreement An informal understanding, stopping short of a written contract but still regarded as binding. The term was first applied to the deal struck in 1907 between America and Japan restricting the flow of Japanese emigrants to the US (*see* YELLOW PERIL). It was also used to describe an agreement between Anthony EDEN and the Italian government in 1936 regulating Italian activities in the Mediterranean; Mussolini (*see* DUCE) did not honour his side of the bargain.

Gentlemen, I think we had better start again somewhere else John MAJOR's comment to his CABINET on 2 February 1991 when an IRA mortar bomb fired from the other side of WHITEHALL exploded in the garden only yards away. No-one was hurt by the blast from the bomb – one of three – but it came unnervingly close to its target, and damage to NUMBER TEN was worse than was publicly admitted.

our government of gentlemen Josef Goebbels' wildly inappropriate term for Germany's NAZI rulers. He was speaking in October 1933, soon after HITLER took power.

gentlewomen The term used by colleagues to describe the first women members of the US HOUSE OF REPRESENTATIVES. Rep. Nicholas Longworth, SPEAKER from 1924 to 1930, directed from the Chair that the word be used; it survived a quarter of a century until Congresswomen convinced male colleagues that they found it patronising.

geopolitics The joint application of power politics and geography, pioneered in Germany by F. Ratzel and Karl Haushofer and in Britain by Sir Halford Mackinder (1861–1947). Geopolitics is a respectable science, but geopolitical arguments were used by the NAZIS to back up their demand for LEBENSRAUM.

George The glossy political and style magazine launched by John F. KENNEDY Jr in September 1995; he named it after George WASHINGTON. Though packed with glamorous names and at times an excellent read, *George* failed to secure a profitable niche in the market; it was losing money by the time its founder was killed when the plane he was piloting crashed off Cape Cod in 1999, and closed two years later.

Georgia mafia The coterie of advisers, led by WHITE HOUSE policy chief Hamilton Jordan, whom the newly-elected Jimmy CARTER brought to WASHINGTON in 1977. Most had worked for him during his single term as Governor of Georgia, but despite many qualities had little knowledge of, or feel for, national politics prior to Carter's campaign for the Presidency. They were unfairly lampooned for their down-home manners (*see* TWIN PYRAMIDS OF THE NILE). But their lack of understanding of Washington's ways, and especially of the CONGRESS, caused the Carter ADMINISTRATION great difficulties.

> I treated the Congress as if they were the Georgia state legislature. And they treated me as if I was Governor of Georgia. JIMMY CARTER

Gerbil The Great Education Reform BILL which was the political legacy of Kenneth Baker (1935–, *see* I HAVE SEEN THE FUTURE AND IT SMIRKS; SELF-BASTING), Britain's Education Secretary from 1986 to 1989 and holder of several other CABINET posts. The measure, passed in 1986, was the most significant since the BUTLER ACT, introducing a National Curriculum and paving the way for self-management of schools outside local authority control. The acronym is appropriate – the gerbil is one of the most common primary classroom pets.

German. a German racket The description of closer European union which forced the EUROSCEPTIC **Nicholas** (later Lord) **Ridley** (1929–93) to resign as Margaret THATCHER's Trade and Industry Secretary in the summer of 1990. Ridley, a tetchy but sophisticated aristocrat who was both a talented artist and a trained engineer, made the comments, and others about the Germans, in an interview with the *Spectator*; he later maintained that he thought the interview had finished. He was reluctant to resign and Mrs Thatcher, to whom he was very close, was loth to let him go, but after 48 hours he went. Ridley's apparent arrogance (*see* strut from a SEDENTARY POSITION) and his chain-smoking had been manna to the Labour opposition; Gordon BROWN, accusing him of seeking to dismantle the Department of Trade and Industry, told the Commons:

> Eventually, he will be seated alone at his desk – no in-tray, no out-tray, just an ashtray.

gerrymander To rig electoral boundaries to ensure that one's own party is elected, whatever its level of support. The term originated in Massachusetts in 1812 when the state legislature created a Congressional district that looked on the map like a dragon or salamander. Since Governor Eldridge Gerry (1744–1814) was thought to favour the stratagem, the name stuck. In the UK, the term is most associated with Westminster Council's HOMES FOR VOTES scandal and the action of Home Secretary James CALLAGHAN prior to the 1970 election in getting Labour MPs to vote down a REDISTRIBUTION proposed by the BOUNDARY COMMISSION which he feared would disadvantage the party; Labour lost anyway.

Gershon review The review conducted for Tony BLAIR's Labour government in 2004 by Sir Peter Gershon, former head of the office of Government Commerce, which recommended reductions in the size of some WHITEHALL departments, notably the Department of Trade and Industry, and dispersal of thousands of jobs to the regions.

It was accepted and a start made on 'implementing' it, though some departments tried to include dispersals already in the pipeline. The Conservatives went into the 2005 election with a more radical formula for administrative cuts from the businessman David James, some of it later taken up by the re-elected Labour government.

Gestapo (Ger. *Geheime Staatspolizei*, secret state police) The ruthless and dedicated backbone of the NAZI apparatus of repression, which acquired sinister notoriety throughout Europe. Formed by Hermann Goering, it was later controlled by Heinrich Himmler, under whom it was responsible for terrorising first the German people and then those of occupied territories. It was declared a criminal organisation by the NUREMBERG tribunal in 1946; Himmler had committed suicide as the Allies closed in on Berlin.

In June 1945 CHURCHILL, in an election broadcast, equated Labour with the Gestapo – a remark blamed by some for the scale of his defeat. He said the socialists 'would have to fall back on some kind of Gestapo, no doubt very humanely directed in the first instance'. ATTLEE blamed the PRESS BARON Lord Beaverbrook for this intemperate language, saying:

> The voice was the voice of Churchill, but the mind was the mind of Beaverbrook.

get in (1) In HOUSE OF COMMONS parlance, to get into a debate; to be called by the SPEAKER. (2) To be elected to a legislature. Speaker Bernard (later Lord) WEATHERILL remarked some time after the Tory LANDSLIDE of 1983:

> A number of people got in by mistake at the last election.

get your tanks off my lawn *see* TANKS.

Gettysburg Address The brief speech delivered by Abraham LINCOLN at Gettysburg, Pennsylvania, on 19 November 1863, at the ceremony to dedicate the national cemetery on the battlefield where UNION forces had defeated General Robert E. Lee's CONFEDERATE army the previous July. He delivered the speech, drafted by himself over the previous eleven days, immediately after a 2-hour dedication by Edward Everett, which had left the crowd of 15,000 restless. Lincoln, who was unknowingly nursing smallpox, spoke for barely three minutes, and while he was interrupted three times for applause the true import of a speech that set the parameters for America's second century was not immediately grasped. The *Chicago Times* reputedly (the cutting has not been found) commented:

> The cheek of every American must tingle with shame as he reads the silly, flat and dishwatery utterances of the man who has to be pointed out to intelligent foreigners as the President of the United States.

Ever since, however, the speech has been accepted as a masterpiece in its own right, and a model for the future of the nation; in 1992 David Gates asked: 'How did Lincoln manage to reinvent America in 272 words?', and Margaret THATCHER made a recording of it. The entire speech ran as follows:

> Four score and seven years ago our fathers brought forth on this continent a new nation, conceived in Liberty, and dedicated to the proposition that all men are equal.
>
> Now we are engaged in a great civil war, testing whether that nation, or any nation so conceived and so dedicated, can long endure. We are met on a great battlefield of that war. We have come to dedicate a portion of that field, as a final resting-place of those who here gave their lives that the nation might live. It is altogether fitting and proper that we should do this.
>
> But, in a larger sense, we cannot dedicate, we cannot consecrate, we cannot hallow this ground. The brave men, living and dead, who struggled here, have consecrated it, far above our poor power to add or detract. The world will little note, nor long remember what we say here, but it can never forget what they did here. It is for us, the living, rather to be dedicated here to the unfinished work which they who fought here have thus far so nobly advanced. It is rather for us to be here dedicated to the great task remaining before us, that from these honoured dead we take increased devotion to that cause for which they gave the last full measure of devotion; that we here highly resolve that these dead shall not have died in vain, that this nation, under God, shall have a new birth of freedom; and that government of the people, by the people, and for the people, shall not perish from the earth.

gherao (Hindi *gherna*, to besiege) A form of protest or direct ACTION popular in India, which has been exported to other parts of the world by migrant communities. It consists of gathering outside the home of a politician or employer against whom the crowd has a grievance, serenading them with the maximum amount of cacophonous noise and refusing to leave until the demands of the protesters are met.

ghetto (1) Originally the area, sometimes walled, in a European city where the Jewish community either chose to live or were compelled to live. The name is Italian for foundry; the Venetian ghetto was constructed on the site of a former foundry.

Under the NAZIS, Europe's ghettos became staging posts on the way to the death camps, or a dead end in themselves; in the Warsaw ghetto tens of thousands of Jews were slaughtered. (2) Since the 1960s, the sections of America's INNER CITIES where a largely black UNDERCLASS has grown up, unable to escape either through lack of opportunities or obstacles to grasping them.

ghetto mentality A state of mind which shows an incapacity to break out of a cycle of poverty and deprivation.

ghetto of national sentimentality The stark phrase used by Harold MACMILLAN to describe the mind-set of opponents of his initiative to take Britain into the COMMON MARKET.

GI Bill The legislation under which former US service personnel (GI, Government Issue) receive medical and educational benefits and guaranteed mortgages on returning to civilian life. The Service Readjustment Act, also termed the GI Bill of Rights, was passed by CONGRESS in June 1944 to assure WORLD WAR II combatants a secure future; over a million veterans received a virtually free college education, though some had to live in gymnasiums and even tugboats. Despite fears that the measure would turn America's colleges into a 'hobo jungle', it was immensely successful and remains substantially in force, now costing billions of dollars a year.

Gilmore, Gary The killer whose case triggered in 1977 the resumption of capital punishment in America after almost a decade. Gilmore was executed by firing squad in Utah on 17 January after frenetic appeals by others against his murder conviction and sentence, despite his own determination that it be carried out. The SUPREME COURT, in 1976, had qualified its earlier decision that the death penalty was CRUEL AND UNUSUAL PUNISHMENT. Civil liberties groups and the NAACP (though Gilmore was white) fought the sentence because they feared it would be followed by the execution of 400 other men and women on Death Row, many of them black and some not fairly tried; by 2004 more than 900 Americans would be executed. Gilmore's final words to the squad were:

> Let's do it.

ginger group A small faction within a party or campaign which seeks to 'ginger up' its ideas and level of activity with initiatives of its own, not always appreciated by the leadership.

Ginsburg nomination The controversy in 1987 surrounding President REAGAN's nomination of Judge Douglas Ginsburg to the SUPREME COURT. Ginsburg, Reagan's second choice for the Court after the rejection of Judge Robert BORK, stood down after admitting he had smoked marijuana while a lecturer at Harvard Law School. As Nancy Reagan had recently launched a 'Just Say No' campaign against drugs, the nomination greatly embarrassed the WHITE HOUSE despite Ginsburg's strong legal qualifications.

Giovinezza (Ital. youthfulness) The official anthem of Italy's FASCIST party. Written by Giuseppe Blanc in 1909, it was originally titled *Commiato* (Farewell), and adopted by Turin University. In 1926 Blanc reissued the song with words by Salvatore Gotta, under the title *(la) Giovinezza*. This followed a legal battle to stop a plagiarised version of his original, published in 1918 by Marcello Manni.

Gipper, the One of Ronald REAGAN's nicknames, stemming from his portrayal of the original Gipper – American football star George Gipp (1895–1920) – in the 1940 movie *Knut Rockne – All American*. Gipp played for Rockne's legendary Notre Dame team but died of pneumonia at the height of a brilliant career. On his deathbed Gipp told Rockne:

> Someday, when things look real tough for Notre Dame, ask the boys to go out there and win one for the Gipper.

Reagan repeatedly used the phrase 'win one for the Gipper' until it became his own. And when he arrived at the SENATE as President, SERGEANT AT ARMS Nordy Hoffman, a veteran of the Rockne team, greeted him with: 'Hiya, Gipper!' *See also* BEDTIME FOR BONZO.

girlymen The description of California's state legislators by Gov. Arnold Schwarzenegger (*see* GOVERNATOR) which led them in July 2004 to refuse to approve his Budget, leaving state services unfinanced for 27 days. The package finally approved left the State heading for a sizeable deficit, despite Schwarzenegger refusing to let his fellow Republicans push through a tax break for owners of luxury yachts.

Girondists The moderate republican party during the FRENCH REVOLUTION, so called because its initial leaders were Deputies from the Gironde, the DÉPARTEMENT centred on Bordeaux.

give. Give 'em hell Harry The most picturesque of many nicknames for President Harry S TRUMAN. While it reflected his feisty manner and colourful comments about his opponents, it stemmed directly from his come-from-behind victory in the 1948 Presidential CAMPAIGN. During his WHISTLE-STOP tour, Truman stepped up his rhetoric against Thomas DEWEY, and the crowds shouted: 'Give 'em hell, Harry!' He himself remarked: 'I never give 'em hell; I just tell 'em the truth and they think it's hell.'

give me your tired, your poor, your huddled masses The inscription on the base of the Statue of Liberty which epitomised 19th-century America's role as a refuge for the oppressed of Europe. It came from a sonnet, *The New Colossus*, written specially by Emma Lazarus (1849–1887):

> 'Keep, ancient lands, your storied pomp!' cries she
> With silent lips. 'Give me your tired, you poor,
> Your huddled masses yearning to breathe free,
> The wretched refuse of your teeming shore.
> Send these, the homeless, tempest-tossed to me,
> I lift my lamp beside the golden door.'

Her sentiments were an echo of George WASHINGTON's letter to newly-arrived Irish immigrants in December 1782:

> The bosom of America is open to receive not only the Opulent and respected Stranger; but the oppressed and persecuted of all Nations and Religions; whom we shall welcome to a participation of all our rights and privileges, if by decency and propriety of conduct they appear to merit the enjoyment.

Give us the tools, and we will finish the job CHURCHILL's call to America for assistance in the darkest days of WORLD WAR II, made in a broadcast from London on 9 February 1941. Churchill promised ROOSEVELT: 'We shall not fail or falter; we shall not weaken or tire.'

give way The request made to an MP in mid-speech in the HOUSE OF COMMONS by another who wishes to INTERVENE. By tradition it is up to the member on their feet to decide whether to give way or keep talking, but persistent refusal can cause angry scenes.

GLA Greater London Authority The structure set up by Tony BLAIR's government in 2000 to fill the DEMOCRATIC DEFICIT in the capital left by the abolition of the GLC fourteen years previously, though with more power remaining with the 32 boroughs. A directly elected MAYOR (from the authority's inception Ken Livingstone – *see* RED KEN) has responsibility, with a 25-member **Greater London Assembly** to exercise scrutiny, for fire and emergency services, transport, planning, culture, the environment, public health, economic development and regeneration, and sets the budget for the police. The GLA is based at the 'FENCING MASK' on the South Bank near Tower Bridge.

Gladstone, William Ewart (1809–98), Liberal Prime Minister four times between 1868 and 1894 and a towering figure of the Victorian age, his intense moral rectitude overshadowing the fact that he was far less of a radical than the party he eventually led, being in any event preoccupied far more with religious than secular matters. The son of a Scottish merchant who had prospered in Liverpool, he was elected to Parliament in 1832 as a TORY, first holding ministerial office in 1834 when just 25; Macaulay saw him as 'the rising hope of those stern and unbending Tories'. But he broke with the Tories over the CORN LAWS, and in 1852 became CHANCELLOR in Lord Aberdeen's COALITION; generally successful at managing the economy, he remains the longest-serving Chancellor. By 1865 he was firmly a Liberal, serving as LEADER OF THE HOUSE under Lord John Russell; after two years in opposition he formed his first government in 1868. From then on he alternated first with DISRAELI and then with Salisbury, spending his time in opposition studying theology and the classics, cutting down trees at his HAWARDEN estate, and finding time for an interest in fallen women that may have been ambivalent. His other idiosyncracy was filling his hot water bottle with tea, which he drank cold the next morning. As might be imagined, Disraeli had plenty to say about Gladstone. 'He has not a single redeeming defect'; 'honest in the most odious sense of the word'; 'a sophisticated rhetorician inebriated by the exuberance of his own verbosity.' 'If he fell in the Thames,' Disraeli told the Commons, 'that would be a misfortune. And if anyone pulled him out, that, I suppose, would be a calamity.'

A serious figure in a serious age, Gladstone nevertheless got on badly with Queen Victoria, who met her match in the GRAND OLD MAN and greatly preferred the raffish Disraeli. The Queen objected that 'he speaks to me as if I were a public meeting', and wrote: 'He can persuade himself that everything he takes up is right even though it be calling black white and wrong right.' PARNELL described him as 'like the brass knocker on a coffin', while Lord Derby observed that 'Gladstone's jokes are no laughing matter'. Even Gladstone's wife told him: 'If you weren't such a great man you'd be a terrible bore.' Walter Bagehot was probably close to the truth when he wrote: 'He has the soul of a martyr with the intellect of an advocate.' Gladstone himself wrote:

> Politics would be an utter blank to me were I to make the discovery that we were mistaken in maintaining their association with religion.

His governments lasted from 1868 to 1874, 1880 to 1885, February to August 1886, and 1892 to 1894. Though not an IMPERIALIST, as the disaster at Khartoum showed, he presided over much of Britain's imperial expansion; yet his record bears out the Earl of Kimberley's prediction: 'Foreign affairs are uncongenial to him. He will never shine when they occupy the first place in importance.' The craggy Gladstone is best remembered as a reformer at home. His first government DISESTABLISHed the Church of Ireland, ended religious tests in universities, laid the foundations of a national education system and brought in the secret BALLOT. Gladstone declared: 'All the world over, I will back the masses against the classes'; and T. H. Huxley wrote: 'If working men were today to vote by a majority that two and two make five, Gladstone would believe it, and find them reasons for it that they never dreamed of'; but he was far from being a democrat.

In 1875 Gladstone 'retired', saying: 'At the age of 65, and after 42 years of a laborious public life, I think myself entitled to retire.' But he bounced back five years later with the MIDLOTHIAN CAMPAIGN, in which he showed devastating power as an orator, castigating the Tory government for a weak reaction to Turkey's BULGARIAN ATROCITIES (*see* BAG AND BAGGAGE). He described the resounding Tory defeat that ensued as 'like the vanishing of some vast magnificent castle of Italian romance'. In office again Gladstone, branded by Lord Randolph Churchill as 'an old man in a hurry', extended the FRANCHISE, but he had now resolved that 'my mission is to pacify Ireland' and was increasingly preoccupied with HOME RULE, a policy that wrecked his second and third administrations. When he took office the fourth time the Queen wrote:

> The danger to the country, to Europe, to her vast Empire, which is involved in having all these great interests entrusted to an old, wild, incomprehensible man of 82½, is very great.

Henry Labouchère (*see* LABBY) agreed, calling him 'an aged fetish, thinking of nothing but Home Rule, senilely anxious to retain power, and fancying he can do so by tricking and dodging everyone'. Gladstone finally retired in 1894 at the 'BLUBBERING CABINET'; his biographer Sir Philip Magnus noted: 'He received not one syllable of thanks for all his years of faithful and honourable service, and the Queen's letter was so curt as to be almost insulting.' In her diary the Queen wrote: 'Mr Gladstone has gone out, disappeared all in a moment.' Gladstone remained a powerful voice in the country up to his death, seeing off his successor, ROSEBERY. Asked why he clung to power so long, he said: 'Why, to keep Mr [Joseph] Chamberlain out, of course.' Of his own impact on history, he remarked: 'My name may have buoyancy enough to float upon the sea of time.'

> I do not object to Gladstone always having the ace of trumps up his sleeve, but merely to his belief that God put it there.
>
> LABOUCHÈRE

> Posterity will do justice to that unprincipled maniac Gladstone – extraordinary mixture of envy, vindictiveness, hypocrisy and superstition, and with one commanding characteristic – whether Prime Minister or Leader of the Opposition, whether preaching, praying, speechifying or scribbling – never a gentleman.
>
> DISRAELI

> They told me Mr Gladstone read Homer at school, which I thought served him right.
>
> CHURCHILL

> The W. G. Grace of politics. Earl ATTLEE

glasnost (Russ. openness) One of the key-words of the reform programme introduced by Mikhail GORBACHEV in 1986 after becoming General Secretary of the Soviet Communist Party the previous year. It implied the acceptance of free speech, an end to the persecution of DISSIDENTS and the opening-up of the Communist system of government to criticism. Together with PERESTROIKA (reconstruction), its adoption signalled a final break with STALINISM, a relaxation of nearly seven decades of internal repression, economic reform and, through the lessening of international tension that followed, an end to the COLD WAR. *Glasnost* and *perestroika* also stimulated reform movements and nationalism in the SATELLITE states of eastern Europe. The pace of change ultimately brought the eclipse of Gorbachev through Boris Yeltsin's defeat of the 1991 KREMLIN COUP, and the disintegration of the Soviet Union itself.

glass ceiling The invisible restraint that prevents women from rising beyond a certain point in politics, business and the professions, according to campaigners for greater equality. The phrase was first used in 1987 by Alice Sargent, US author of *The Androgynous Manager*; it has also been used to describe invisible barriers to advancement by members of ethnic minorities. The **sticky floor** is another way of describing such restraints.

Glass-Steagall Act The legislation passed by the US Congress in June 1933 that built on the emergency measures pushed through after Franklin D. ROOSEVELT's inauguration. It separated commercial banking from investment banking, barred banks from dealing in securities, increased the FED's power to curb speculation by member banks, and created the Federal Deposit Insurance Corporation (FDIC) to guarantee bank deposits of up to $5,000 (later raised) in the event of an institution's failure.

GLC Greater London Council. The authority covering the entire capital which formed the upper tier of the local government structure created in 1963, the 32 London boroughs forming the lower. The GLC replaced the London County Council (LCC) but covered a far wider area, reflecting suburban growth. It had largely strategic planning and housing functions, eventually taking control of London Transport. Under the Labour administration of Ken (RED KEN) Livingstone in the early 1980s it pursued radical policies on transport, race, sexuality and NORTHERN IRELAND that brought it into conflict with Margaret THATCHER's government. Despite a vigorous campaign led by the CHARISMATIC Livingstone, the GLC was abolished in 1986 and COUNTY HALL put up for sale.

Gleneagles agreement The undertaking entered into by COMMONWEALTH heads of government in 1977 to ban official sporting links with South Africa until steps were taken to dismantle APARTHEID. The meeting took place at the luxurious Gleneagles Hotel, a golfing resort in Scotland between Stirling and Perth, where Tony BLAIR hosted the G8 summit 28 years later.

globalisation The process under which the economies of the entire world are allegedly being subjected to the whims of giant, mainly US, corporations which deliberately operate against the public interest, stamping out individual and national independence, harming the developing world, polluting the environment and giving the peoples of the planet no alternative but to eat junk food. Protests against globalisation by ANARCHIST groups, on occasion violent, have become a staple of G8 and SUMMIT meetings and world trade talks (*see* SEATTLE), even when those talks are endeavouring to lower trade barriers for the world's poorest countries. The **anti-globalisation** movement has become the most widespread protest movement of the 21st century – ironically being organised on as global a basis as the corporations it is campaigning against. Supporters of globalisation assert that it has brought prosperity to millions – including many of those who oppose it most vociferously.

gloire, la (Fr. glory) The obsession, combining pride, arrogance, self-interest, CHAUVINISM, cynicism and a desire to put noses out of joint, that critics claim has governed France's dealings with the rest of the world, and especially the ANGLO-SAXONS, not least since the ascendancy of DE GAULLE. It is said to manifest itself not only in a ruggedly independent foreign policy (*see* QUAI D'ORSAY) but in a commitment to grandiose architectural projects and advanced home-grown technology, regardless of expense.

Glorious Revolution The upheaval in 1688–89 when the Catholic King James II fled from England as Parliament and the nobility prepared to welcome the Protestant Prince William of ORANGE. The Convention Parliament of 1689 not only confirmed William and his wife Mary, who had the better claim, as joint Sovereigns, but barred Roman Catholics from the succession; it also reasserted the country's traditional liberties. The Revolution was triggered by James's action against Protestant clerics, and the birth of a Catholic male heir. *See also* APPRENTICE BOYS OF DERRY; Battle of the BOYNE.

Gnomes of Zurich Harold WILSON's name for the Continental speculators who he claimed were undermining the pound in the period between Labour's return to power in 1964 and the DEVALUATION of sterling three years later. It originated with George BROWN, Secretary for Economic Affairs, in the sterling crisis of November 1964 and was picked up the Prime Minister, who spoke in the COMMONS of

> All these financiers, all the little gnomes of Zurich and the other financial centres, about whom we keep on hearing.

> What most infuriated George Brown, and Labour MPs such as John Mendelson and Ian MIKardo . . . was that the men they disparaged as the 'gnomes of Zurich' were really giants.
> T. R. FEHRENBACH, *The Gnomes of Zurich*

gobbledygook The term coined as recently as 1944 by the Texas Democrat Rep. Maury Maverick (1895–1954) for the long-winded and virtually unintelligible jargon used by BUREAUCRATS and others instead of plain English. As chairman of the Smaller War Plants Corporation, Maverick was so infuriated by phrases like 'maladjustments co-extensive with problem areas' that he issued a formal order:

> Be short and say what you're talking about . . . No more patterns, effectuating, dynamics. Anyone using the words activation and implementation will be shot.

As the word caught on in WASHINGTON, Maverick explained its origin:

> Perhaps I was thinking of the old bearded turkey gobbler back in Texas who was always gobbledy-gobbling and strutting with ludicrous pomposity. At the end of this gobble there was a sort of gook.

gobsmacked Originally Liverpool slang for being left gaping in disbelief, from *gob*, mouth, this word was made part of Britain's political vocabulary in 1991 by Chris PATTEN, then chairman of the CONSERVATIVE PARTY. His use of the word to describe his reaction to a LABOUR PARTY statement on the Health Service caused much press comment, and Patten was saddled with it in coverage of the following year's election campaign – in which he lost his seat.

God. *God Save the King* or *Queen* The National Anthem of the UNITED KINGDOM since the late 18th century. Attributed by some to Henry Carey (c.1690–1743), it was in print by 1745 and set to a traditional tune (the same as for *My Country, 'Tis of Thee*). Of the three verses, only the first is normally sung.

> God save our Gracious Queen,
> Long live our noble Queen,
> God save the Queen.
> Send her victorious,
> Happy and glorious,
> Long to rein over us,
> God save the Queen!

Goodnight, and God bless John MAJOR's sign-off in his broadcast to the nation and British forces on 24 February 1991 as ground operations in the GULF WAR were begun to drive SADDAM HUSSEIN's occupying force out of Kuwait. When Tony BLAIR was asked by an American journalist on the eve of the 2003 IRAQ WAR whether he intended to invoke the deity in his own broadcast, his communications director Alastair Campbell intervened to say: **'We don't do God'**.

With God on our Side One of the most celebrated PROTEST songs of the early 1960s. Sung by Bob Dylan, it reflected on the patriot's claim always to be acting on the side of right, and how the Germans, against whom Americans had fought with such moral backing, now had God on their side since becoming part of the 'Free West'.

going. going for the Park In Irish politics, running for the Presidency; the Presidential residence (ARAS NA UACHTARAIN) is in PHOENIX PARK on the western edge of Dublin.

going native The process by which politicians or officials despatched to represent their country in a hostile environment take on the views of those they have been sent to tame. The term is used especially by EUROSCEPTICS of those UK European COMMISSIONERS who switch from caution about closer European integration to enthusiastic support within months of arriving in BRUSSELS.

when the going gets tough, the tough get going A slogan said to have been coined, or first used, by Joseph P. KENNEDY, as an exhortation, particularly to his sons, to strive harder in the face of adversity. Used as a publicity slogan for the 1985 movie *Jewel of the Nile*, the next year it was the title of a hit song by Billy Ocean.

Golan Heights A strategically-important hilly area on the Israeli-Syrian border, designated as a buffer zone between the countries in 1949 and bitterly contested in the Arab-Israeli conflicts of 1956, 1967 and 1973. During the 1950s and 1960s Israeli settlements spread eastwards into the area, provoking constant clashes. In the SIX DAY WAR, over 100.000 Syrians fled when the Israeli army stormed the Heights. The Syrians regained some of the territory during the YOM KIPPUR WAR of 1973. The remainder was again designated a buffer zone by the UN, but was annexed by Israel in 1982 in defiance of UN RESOLUTION 242. Together with the WEST BANK and GAZA STRIP, the continued Israeli occupation of the Heights – on the grounds that Syria could shell settlements in Israel from them – remains an obstacle to the PEACE PROCESS. In 1992 Israel told Syria it was ready to discuss concessions, but Damascus rejected these as inadequate.

gold. gold-plating (1) The spending of infinitely more on an item by a government department than it would cost if purchased privately. Though it occurs throughout the world, it has been highlighted most in the PENTAGON through the exposure of excesses in CONGRESS, by WHISTLE-BLOWERS and by Sen. William Proxmire's GOLDEN FLEECE awards. Prize items have included (some of these at 1980s prices) a $640 toilet seat, a $1,118 plastic cap for a stool leg, a nut costing $2,063, a coffee maker modestly priced at $7,622 and a $9,606 wrench. (2) The over-zealous interpretation of legislation, and especially DIRECTIVES from the EUROPEAN COMMISSION, by national governments and implementing agencies so as to impose further restrictions, and force business into more costly remedial measures, than had ever been intended.

gold standard A monetary system based on keeping the currency at the value of a fixed weight of gold. The UK adopted it from 1821, but suspended gold payments in 1914; John Maynard KEYNES in 1924 termed it 'already a barbarous relic' but CHURCHILL, despite strong personal reservations, was persuaded by TREASURY officials to return to it in 1925 ('at far too high a rate' – Nicholas Ridley); the NATIONAL GOVERNMENT's Philip Snowden finally abandoned it in 1931 and from 1997 Gordon BROWN sold off much of Britain's remaining gold reserves. America adopted the gold standard by the Coinage Act of 1873, and abandoned it in 1933 (*see* GREAT DEPRESSION). The strains caused by the Gold Standard prompted William Jennings Bryan's legendary 1896 ACCEPTANCE SPEECH:

> You shall not press down upon the brow of labor this crown of thorns; you shall not crucify mankind upon a cross of gold.

go for gold A phrase with two meanings: to opt for the most lucrative course of action or (from the awarding of gold medals to Olympic winners) to seek the greatest prize. It can be traced back to 1832 when the English radical leader Francis Place (1771–1854) sought to block the formation of a Tory government under the Duke of Wellington with the slogan: 'To stop the Duke, go for Gold.' George Bernard Shaw (1856–1950) wrote at the turn of the last century:

> You have to choose (as a voter) between trusting to the natural stability of gold and the natural stability of the honesty and intelligence of members of the government. As long as the capitalist system lasts – go for gold.

The slogan was taken up by Ronald REAGAN in his re-ELECTION campaign in 1984, the year of the Los Angeles Olympics – and in Britain's 1987 election by the SDP/Liberal ALLIANCE, which had chosen gold as its party colour.

Golden Fleece The award made regularly during his 32-year SENATE career by William Proxmire of Wisconsin (1915–) to highlight Federally funded projects which appeared a waste of taxpayers' money. One instance was the spending of $97,000 on a study on *The Peruvian brothel – a sexual dispensary and social arena*. Much of his campaigning was directed against GOLD-PLATING and cost overruns on defence projects.

golden rule The principle established and followed by Gordon BROWN as CHANCELLOR OF THE EXCHEQUER, that the public finances can only be run into deficit if for investment over the life of a Parliament. He adhered to it for his first six years at the Treasury, but by 2004 commentators were asserting that his return to a sizeable Budget deficit to fund a massive increase in health spending was in breach of the rule.

golden share The critical voting share retained by government in a PRIVATISED industry in order to keep a degree of control, or prevent control of a strategically important company passing overseas. Although keeping a 51% share would have made certain, Margaret THATCHER's government generally settled for less as the whole purpose of privatisation was to remove the dead hand of government.

Goldfine affair *See* Sherman ADAMS.

Goldilocks A somewhat patronising nickname early in his Ministerial career for Michael HESELTINE (*see also* HEZZA; TARZAN).

GOM *See* GRAND OLD MAN.

good. Good Friday Agreement The agreement concluded at STORMONT Castle, Belfast, on 10 April 1998 which formally ended three decades of TROUBLES in NORTHERN IRELAND, though there has been much discord and some bloodshed (notably the OMAGH BOMBING) since. The product of several years of secret and open negotiation, it was concluded by the UK and Irish governments, and all the Northern Ireland parties, from the DUP to SINN FEIN. Under the agreement all parties, including those fronting for PARAMILITARY groups, agreed to renounce violence and participate in the democratic process, with an Assembly headed by a POWER-SHARING Executive taking back powers exercised by UK Ministers since the imposition of DIRECT RULE. Convicted terrorists would be released from prison (though subject to powers of re-arrest which have been seldom used) and steps would be taken toward the DECOMMISSIONING of paramilitary arsenals. The Agreement was a triumph for the UK and Irish Prime Ministers Tony BLAIR and Bertie Ahern (*see* ANORAK MAN), and also for Blair's unorthodox Northern Ireland Secretary Mo Mowlam; it also earned the Unionist leader David Trimble and Sinn Fein's Gerry Adams a joint NOBEL PEACE PRIZE. The Assembly duly came into being, with Sinn Fein and other Ministers taking their places under Trimble as FIRST MINISTER. The level of violence greatly reduced, though there were continuing acts of terrorism by Republican dissidents and outbreaks of strife between LOYALIST groups. The Executive faltered a couple of times because of Republican resistance to demands for decommissioning, then was suspended in October 2002, and direct rule reimposed, when the IRA was found to be running a surveillance operation on potential Unionist targets out of Sinn Fein's office at Stormont. All parties except the DUP insist they remain committed to the Agreement, and the IRA ceasefire has held, though the NORTHERN BANK ROBBERY and the murder of ROBERT MCCARTNEY cast doubts on its totality.

Good Neighbor policy The policy toward Latin America embarked on in 1933 by President Franklin D. ROOSEVELT to allay fears that America was bent on total domination of the continent. Its measures – withdrawal of forces from Haiti, renunciation of the PLATT AMENDMENT and the right to intervene unilaterally anywhere in the hemisphere, removal of trade barriers and a common defence policy – were foreshadowed by FDR in his first INAUGURAL ADDRESS on 4 March 1933:

> In the field of world policy, I would dedicate this nation to the policy of the good neighbor.

Goodman scandal *See* BEEF.

goose. Goose Green A settlement in the FALKLANDS which in May 1982 saw fierce fighting during the British assault on the occupying Argentine forces; outnumbered three to one, the British lost seventeen men dead; 250 Argentine troops were killed – some, it was later claimed, in cold blood – and 1,200 taken prisoner. At the height of the 1983 election Neil KINNOCK caused a furore by saying of Margaret THATCHER's despatch of UK forces in a broadcast interview:

> To prove she has guts, they had to lose theirs at Goose Green.

goose step The style of marching perfected by the NAZI soldiery which sent a sinister message across Europe in the late 1930s. The legs are moved from the hips, the knees being kept rigid and each leg swung as high as possible. In Germany the goose-step (*Stechschritt*) was introduced as a full-dress and processional march in the army of Prussia's Frederick the Great; it was adopted with gusto under the THIRD REICH, and survived in East Germany's army – and some other Soviet bloc forces – until shortly before UNIFICATION in 1990. At the height of the AXIS, the Italian army adopted the goose-step as the *passo Romano*, but it attracted ridicule and was dropped; the British army once tried the step in drilling recruits, but it never caught on.

> It says: 'I am ridiculous, but you dare not laugh at me'. GEORGE ORWELL

GOP Universal shorthand for America's REPUBLICAN Party, standing for **Grand Old Party**. Its use dates from the 1880s. Adlai STEVENSON renamed them 'Grouchy Old Pessimists'.

Gorbachev. Mikhail Sergeyevich Gorbachev (1931–), the CHARISMATIC last leader of the Soviet Union who paved the way for political and economic change with his twin policies of GLASNOST and PERESTROIKA, but was eventually swept aside by a process he could not control. Born in the Crimea, he was elected Communist Party leader in 1985 on the death of Constantin Chernenko, the veteran Andrei GROMYKO telling the POLITBURO: 'This man, comrades, has a nice smile, but he has iron teeth.' Gorbachev received a rapturous welcome (**Gorbymania**) on international visits, especially in West Germany, as he moved to end the COLD WAR; his popularity was fuelled by the Western media. He released Russia's SATELLITE states at the end of 1989 after the fall of the BERLIN WALL. At home he ended Communist rule but his economic reforms ran into the sand; he faced down the KREMLIN COUP of August 1991, but was out of a job four months later when the Soviet state collapsed.

Gorbals Mick A patronising nickname bestowed by newspaper SKETCH-WRITERS on Michael Martin (1945–) the former

Glasgow trade union official who became SPEAKER of the HOUSE OF COMMONS in 2000. It implied that Martin had limited intellectual capacities; in truth he did a conscientious job but suffered by comparison with his predecessor, the flamboyant and highly CHARISMATIC Betty Boothroyd.

Gordon. Gordon Riots The riots in London in 1780, headed by Lord George Gordon, which aimed to force repeal of legislation passed in 1778 to ease discrimination against Roman Catholics. They were the last of the great outbreaks of anti-Catholic violence which convulsed London over two centuries after the Counter-Reformation. Gordon was mentally unstable, and by his death in 1793 had veered from extreme Protestantism to Judaism. Dickens gave a vivid description of the riots in *Barnaby Rudge*.

Gordon Telegram The scathing telegram Queen Victoria despatched to GLADSTONE when news reached London on 5 February 1885 of the fall of Khartoum and the death of Major-General Charles Gordon at the hands of the Mahdi's horde. Gladstone was given the uncoded telegram by an embarrassed stationmaster at Carnforth, Lancs., as he started back to London from Holker Hall (pronounced Hooker), seat of the Marquess of Hartington, Secretary for War. Gordon had been sent to Khartoum to evacuate the Sudan, but stayed and demanded assistance; a relief force under Wolseley was sent, but arrived just too late. Another telegram at the height of the crisis was left unopened for hours in the servants' hall at Holker because Hartington had not given instructions to be woken before noon. The loss of Khartoum caused a wave of public indignation against Gladstone's government; the Queen's was all the greater as she had never cared for the GRAND OLD MAN.

Gore. I am Al Gore, and I used to be the next President of the United States of America The introduction adopted by Al Gore (1948–, *see* OZONE MAN), former Democratic Senator for Tennessee and Vice President to Bill CLINTON, after his defeat by George W. BUSH in the 2000 Presidential election, the closest in modern times; it reflected a brief moment late on election night when it was possible he had actually won, after coming within minutes of conceding defeat. It took a ruling by the SUPREME COURT after weeks of bitter argument for Bush to be declared the winner, by just 537 votes in the pivotal state of Florida. Bush carried the ELECTORAL COLLEGE by the narrowest of margins; Gore actually won the popular vote. After his defeat, Gore retired to academia.

Gosplan *Gos*understvennyy *Plan*ovyy Komitet, the State Planning Committee of the Soviet Union, established in 1921. It was entrusted in 1927 with formulating the first FIVE-YEAR PLAN for Soviet economic development. This was delivered in 1929, after STALIN had PURGED *Gosplan* of its more cautious members to obtain a more optimistic projection. The committee continued to form the apex of the economic planning system, its strictures affecting all reaches of Soviet industry and its decisions being implemented through industry ministries.

govern To direct or regulate the affairs of a nation or state. To the 19th-century French revolutionary Pierre-Joseph Proudhon, 'to be governed is to be watched over, inspected, spied on, directed, legislated at, regulated, docketed, indoctrinated, preached at, controlled, assessed, weighed, censored, ordered about, by men who have neither the right nor the knowledge nor the virtue.' Thomas Paine averred that 'the government is best that governs least', and Thoreau 'that government is best that governs not at all'; DE GAULLE that 'one cannot govern with "buts"', and Pierre Mendès-France that 'to govern is to choose.' Napoleon reckoned that 'the great art of governing consists in not letting men grow old in their jobs', while John JAY reputedly said: 'The people who own the country ought to govern it.'

> Which is the best government? That which teaches us to govern ourselves. GOETHE

> To govern, you need only two things: policemen, and bands playing in the streets. MUSSOLINI

governance An originally political term that has migrated to the corporate world in the wake of the ENRON and other scandals, implying the practice of correct techniques and probity in government. It also reflects the texture of government as a whole, as in Harold WILSON's book *The Governance of Britain*.

Governator, the The nickname instantly bestowed on the Austrian-born Hollywood hardman Arnold Schwarzenegger (*The Terminator*) when he ran as a liberal Republican for governor of California after the success of a conservative-inspired petition for the RECALL of the Democratic Gov. Gray Davis. In a double ballot in October

2003, Californians backed the recall by 55 to 45%, then voted heavily for Schwarzenegger despite allegations of serial sexual harassment that had dogged his brief campaign. Schwarzenegger, a former Mr Universe, was the first member of the KENNEDY clan (through his marriage to JFK's niece Maria Shriver) to seek and win office as a Republican.

government (1) The art or technique of governing. Thomas JEFFERSON wrote that 'the care of human right and happiness, and not their destruction, is the first and only legitimate object of good government'; George WASHINGTON that 'government is not reason, it is not eloquence, it is force, like fire, a troublesome servant and a fearsome master'. Spinoza (1632–77) stated that 'the aim of government is liberty', Jefferson that 'the whole of government is the art of being honest' and 'that government is strongest of which every man feels himself a part' and George Bernard Shaw that 'the art of government is the organisation of idolatry'. Theodore ROOSEVELT concluded that 'the bulk of government is not legislation but administration', Sen. John Sharp Williams that 'most bad government has grown out of too much government', and the US political writer Kenneth Crawford (1902–83) that

> The cocktail glass is one of the most powerful instruments of government.

(2) The institution that administers a country. Henry Ward Beecher termed it 'the worst thing, next to ANARCHY', and Thomas Paine 'even in its best state, a necessary evil . . . like dress, the badge of lost innocence.' But James MADISON pointed out that 'if men were angels, no government would be necessary', and asked: 'What is government itself but the greatest of all reflections on human nature?' LINCOLN said: 'The legitimate object of government is to do for a community of people whatever they need to have done, but can not do at all, or cannot so well do for themselves in their separate, individual capacities.' But he also admitted: 'The first necessity that is upon us is of proving that popular government is not an absurdity.' Walt Whitman cynically observed that 'it is only the novice in political economy who thinks it is the duty of government to make its citizens happy', but Governor William Scranton pointed out: 'The value of government to the people it serves is in direct relationship to the interest citizens themselves display in the affairs of state.' And Stephen Miller noted: 'The more government tampers with the daily lives of its citizens, the less authority it ends up having.' In similar vein, Tom Wicker commented: 'Government expands to absorb resources and then some', and Robert Strauss observed from the inside: 'Everyone in government is like a bunch of ants on a log floating down the river.' Ronald REAGAN, a great foe of BIG GOVERNMENT, had most to say: 'Government is not the solution to the problem – government is the problem'; 'Government is a referee, it shouldn't try to be a player in the game'; and

> Government is like a big baby – an alimentary canal with a big appetite at one end and no sense of responsibility at the other.

The argument in Britain has not always paralleled that in America. Edmund BURKE described government as 'a contrivance of human wisdom to provide for human wants. Men have a right that these wants should be provided for by this wisdom.' Macaulay wrote: 'The business of government is not directly to make the people rich, but to protect them in making themselves rich,' while Lord Melbourne at much the same time declared: 'The whole duty of government is to prevent crime and to preserve contracts.' Lord KEYNES wrote: 'The important thing for government is not to do those things which individuals are doing already and to do them a little better or a little worse, but to do those things which at present are not done at all,' and Lord BEVERIDGE: 'The object of government in peace or war is not the glory of rulers or of races, but the happiness of the common man.' The Canadian Prime Minister Mackenzie King described government as 'organised opinion', and TROTSKY termed it 'an association of men who do violence to the rest of us'.

(3) a government. Any collection of individuals who govern a country at a particular time, usually under the lead of a certain party in office for a set period.

> Every government carries a health warning.
> ANON

> Every country has the government it deserves.
> JOSEPH LE MAISTRE (1753–1821)

William Penn wrote: 'Governments, like clocks, go from the motion men give them, and as governments are made and moved by men, so by them are they ruined too'; a century later Benjamin FRANKLIN declared: 'In free governments the rulers are the servants and the people their superiors and sovereigns,' and George WASHINGTON: 'In a free and republican government you cannot restrain the voice of the multitude.' President CLEVELAND insisted that 'while the people should patriotically and cheerfully support their government, its functions do not include the support of the people'; Garfield that 'all free governments are managed by the combined wisdom and folly of the people'; William Jennings Bryan that 'the chief duty of governments, in so far as they are coercive, is to restrain those who would interfere with the inalienable rights of the individual.' But TAFT pointed out: 'We are all imperfect. We cannot expect a perfect government.' MADISON had put down a marker for the media, writing: 'A popular government, without popular information or the means of acquiring it, is but a Prologue to a Farce or Tragedy – or perhaps both'; almost a century later Wendell Phillips declared: 'We live under a government of men and morning newspapers'; in the 1980s Bernard Ingham (*see* YORKSHIRE RASPUTIN) was to write: 'Confidentiality is the nature of all governments.' H. L. Mencken reckoned that 'the worst government is the most moral', Justice Louis Brandeis that 'if a government is a lawbreaker, it breeds contempt for the law'. Elihu Root pointed out: 'We are apt to forget how little it is possible for any government to do', Harry S Truman that 'Whenever you have an efficient government you have a DICTATORSHIP' (though in Britain LLOYD GEORGE maintained: 'What is a government for except to dictate? If it does not dictate, it is not a government.') John F. KENNEDY warned: 'No government is better than the men who comprise it'; Milton Friedman that 'Governments never learn. Only people learn'; and Ronald Reagan that 'Governments tend not to solve problems – only rearrange them'.

> Lord, the money we do spend on government, and it's not one bit better than the one we got for one third of the money 20 years ago.
>
> WILL ROGERS

> Every government is run by liars, and nothing they say should be believed. I. F. STONE

> A government is the only known vessel that LEAKS from the top. JAMES RESTON

In 18th-century Britain, Dr Johnson wrote that 'any government is ultimately and essentially absolute', and Adam SMITH that 'there is no art which one government sooner learns of another than that of draining money from the pockets of the people'. George Grenville, speaking in 1769 against the expulsion of John WILKES, told the Commons: 'A wise government knows how to enforce with temper, or conciliate with dignity, but a weak one is odious in the former and contemptible in the latter.' A century later, GLADSTONE declared that 'the history of governments is one of the most immoral parts of history', adding: 'It is the duty of the government to make it difficult for people to do wrong, easy to do right.' Lord SALISBURY wrote: 'The best form of government (setting aside the issue of morality) is one where the masses have little power, and seem to have a great deal.' George Bernard Shaw was first to appreciate that 'a government which robs Peter to pay Paul can always depend on the support of Paul', and Lord KEYNES admitted: 'I work for a government I despise for ends I think criminal.' Philip Snowden, shaken by experience, declared: 'It would be desirable if every government, when it came into power, should have all its old speeches burned'; while the author Joyce Cary struck a chord when he wrote:

> The only good government is a bad one in a hell of a fright.

Voltaire laid down that 'governments need to have both shepherds and butchers', while Thoreau maintained: 'The objections which have been brought against a standing army . . . may also . . . be brought against a standing government.' The 1950s British politician Lord Eccles maintained that 'all governments are selfish, and French governments are more selfish than most'; Australia's Frank Crean that

> The man in the street doesn't care who the government is once the election is over. It's just somebody to criticise.

(4) The government. A specific ADMINISTRATION, either the bureaucratic structure or the politicians supposedly in charge of it. Theodore ROOSEVELT told the people: 'The government is us, we are the government, you and I'; and Calvin COOLIDGE: 'The government is not self-existent. It is maintained by the effort of those who believe in it'; but Woodrow WILSON branded the government of the US 'a foster child of special interests'. Will Rogers simply said: 'I don't make jokes. I just watch the government and report the facts.' Sen. Edmund Muskie told the voters: 'You have the God-given right to kick the government around. Don't hesitate to use it'; and Ronald Reagan matched him with: 'Today if you invent a better mousetrap, the government comes

along with a better mouse', and classically

> The ten most frightening words in the English language are: 'Hello, I'm from the Government and I'm here to help.'

(5) Government, compared with ADMINISTRATION. In America 'administration' refers more to a specific political regime than to the practice of government. LINCOLN stated: 'One is perpetual, the other is temporary and changeable. A man may be loyal to his government, and yet may oppose the particular principles and methods of administration.' In Britain, 'administration' applies purely to the practice of government, not to those who conduct it.

government girls The young women who flocked into WASHINGTON from all over America just before and after America's entry into WORLD WAR II, to perform clerical and other duties in the vastly expanded Federal BUREAUCRACY.

Government House In most British COLONIES, the formal residence and/or headquarters of the Governor who headed the colonial administration.

government-in-exile A government set up outside the territory of the nation it aims to represent, either because that territory has been invaded by an outside power or because those forming the regime believe the *de facto* government does not represent the people.

Government of National Unity (GNU) The proposal put forward by Edward HEATH during Britain's October 1974 election to heal the wounds and check growing political POLARISATION by forming a government reaching beyond his CONSERVATIVE PARTY. It was an extraordinary proposal to put forward during an election campaign, and many felt Heath, who had lost power that February over his confrontation with the miners, was not the person to propose it. Yet although Labour had taken the initiative in eight months of minority government, Heath kept their gains to a minimum.

big government *See* BIG.

Cabinet government *See* CABINET.

caretaker government *See* CARETAKER.

central government The institution of government from a nation's capital, as opposed to local or DEVOLVED government.

Congressional government *See* CONGRESSIONAL.

Federal government *See* FEDERAL.

good government The governing of a nation, and the operation of its civil service and public bodies, on a basis of probity, merit, competence and fairness. Long a general principle, it gained a specific application from 1990 as Lynda (later Baroness) Chalker, UK Overseas Development Minister under Margaret THATCHER and John MAJOR, began making aid for THIRD WORLD states conditional on its observance – notably through action to curb corruption and embrace democracy enshrined in the 1991 HARARE DECLARATION. The initiative, continued as part of Labour's ETHICAL FOREIGN POLICY, has had some successes, notably the achievement of democratic changes of government in Kenya (with some slippage since) and Zambia.

Her Majesty's Government The formal name for the UK Government, as in 'This House has no CONFIDENCE in Her Majesty's Government.' It is often abbreviated to **HMG**.

> It is the duty of Her Majesty's Government not to flap or falter. HAROLD MACMILLAN

invitation to form a government The form of words used to describe the Sovereign's contact with the winner of a UK GENERAL ELECTION. The victor drives to Buckingham Palace (after the outgoing Prime Minister has resigned if there is a change of government), and then KISSES HANDS on appointment.

joined-up government A 1990s phrase for government operating as a co-ordinated whole, with departments and agencies working together instead of cutting across each other in order to achieve coherent policy-making and deliver more effective and comprehensible services.

machinery of government The mechanism, particularly at the higher levels of a CIVIL SERVICE, which translates the politicians' decisions into action.

> Lord Hailsham said the other day that the machinery of government is creaking. My Lords, it is not even moving sufficiently to emit a noise of any kind.
>
> VICTOR MONTAGU, Earl of Sandwich, House of Lords, 20 April 1963

National Government *See* NATIONAL.

open government *See* OPEN.

petticoat government A patronising term used until surprisingly recently by men for a government dominated by women. It originally had a more direct and justified meaning, describing the vice-like grip on power exercised in the WHITE HOUSE by Edith Bolling Galt Wilson (1872–1961) (*see* PRESIDENTRESS) for seventeenth months from October 1919, as her husband Woodrow WILSON slowly recovered from a debilitating stroke. Mrs Wilson took total control of access to the President, decided which matters should be brought to his attention, and then emerged to give her account of what he had decided. Vice President Thomas Marshall abetted her by showing no desire to take on Presidential duties, and Mrs Wilson herself always denied having taken on herself the running of the country. But an outraged Sen. Albert Fall declared:

> We have a petticoat government! Mrs Wilson is President!

provisional government A government established after the collapse of a country's political system, or following a REVOLUTION, to administer it until more lasting political structures can be established.

puppet government *See* PUPPET.

Reinventing Government The 1992 book by David Osbourne and Ted Gaebler which impacted heavily on the thinking of the incoming CLINTON administration, and especially Vice President Al Gore, with its emphasis on finding new ways of helping the poor which cannot be impeded by BUREAUCRACY. This process of retargeting government rather than enlarging it was described as a **paradigm shift**.

responsible government The term used in 19th-century Canada, and later in other parts of the BRITISH EMPIRE, for the achievement of a large degree of self-government in place of almost total control from London. It was granted to Canada in the wake of the 1846 DURHAM REPORT. The term was also used by white Rhodesians after UDI to denote their assumption of power, an unflattering comparison being drawn with the MAJORITY RULE favoured by Britain and the international community.

> Give us this truly British privilege, and colonial grievances will soon become a scarce article in the English market.
>
> JOSEPH HOWE, Nova Scotia politician and editor

> It is neither possible nor desirable to carry on the government of any of the British provinces in North America in opposition to the opinion of the inhabitants.
>
> LORD GREY, Colonial Secretary, 1846

government of the people, by the people, for the people The most memorable phrase of Abraham LINCOLN's GETTYSBURG ADDRESS on 19 November 1863, which concluded:

> . . . that government of the people, by the people, and for the people, shall not perish from the earth.

The words that encapsulated the American democratic ideal were not original, Daniel Webster having spoken in 1830 of 'the people's government made for the people, made by the people, and answerable to the people', and Theodore Parker in 1850 of 'government of all the people, by all the people, and for all the people'. They have also spawned numerous variants; Oscar Wilde wrote of 'the bludgeoning of the people by the people for the people', Lincoln Steffens declared that 'city government is government of the people, by the rascals, for the rich', and CHURCHILL described ATTLEE's administration as 'government of the duds, by the duds, for the duds.'

Go back to your constituencies, and prepare for government The rallying-cry of the UK LIBERAL leader David Steel (*see* BOY DAVID) to the party's 1981 Llandudno assembly. In the first flush of enthusiasm for the ALLIANCE with the newly-formed SDP, Steel declared that he was the first Liberal leader for half a century who could make such a claim. His hopes were blunted by infighting over which party should fight which Parliamentary seats, and by the outbreak of the FALKLANDS WAR the following spring.

God reigns, and the government in Washington still lives The key phrase from the dramatic speech made by Rep. (later President) James Garfield (*see* BOATMAN JIM) to calm a panicky New York crowd on 17 April 1865, two days after LINCOLN's assassination.

I'm surprised that a government organisation could do it that quickly President CARTER's comment, during a visit to Egypt, on being told that it took 20 years to build the Great Pyramid.

the negation of God erected into a system of government GLADSTONE's ringing denunciation of the government of Naples, stemming from the persecutions instigated by the BOURBON kings. He made it in 1851 in a letter to Lord Aberdeen.

the smack of firm government The decisive phrase in an article criticising Anthony EDEN's premiership which appeared in the normally-friendly *Daily Telegraph* on 3 January 1956. Written by Donald McLachlan, it accused Eden of indecisiveness and half-measures:

> There is a favourite gesture of the Prime Minister's; to emphasise a point he will clench one fist to smack the open palm of the other hand – but the smack is seldom heard. Most conservatives, and almost certainly some of the wiser trade union leaders, are waiting to feel the smack of firm government.

Eden, angered by this and other charges that he was losing his grip, used a tough line with Egypt over SUEZ as a first chance to prove his critics wrong; it proved his undoing.

governor (1) In America, the elected head of each State government, a title inherited in most of the original States from colonial times. Speaker TIP O'Neill once opined that 'a governor plays in the minor leagues', but the Governor of California, New York State or Texas, for instance, can wield considerable influence nationally while still being locally ACCOUNTABLE. (2) The executive head of a British COLONY or other overseas territory, responsible to the CROWN.

> Unlike my predecessors, I have devoted more of my life to shunting and hooting than to hunting and shooting.
>
> Sir FRED BURROWS (1887–1973), former President of the National Union of Railwaymen, on his appointment as last British Governor of Bengal

Governor Moonbeam One of many nicknames for Gov. Edmund G. 'Jerry' Brown of California (1938–), reflecting his readiness to embrace eccentric policies alongside a genuinely concerned populism. *See also* SPACE CADET.

Governor-General The representative of the Sovereign who acts in place of the HEAD OF STATE in the DOMINIONS of the COMMONWEALTH, notably Australia and Canada. Originally British, the Governor-General is now a native of the country in question, and can trigger bitter controversy, as Australia found with the HOLLINGWORTH RESIGNATION and KERR SACKING.

Well may we say 'God Save the Queen', because nothing will save the Governor-General The comment of Australia's outgoing Labor Prime Minister Gough WHITLAM, on hearing the proclamation dissolving Parliament for the 1975 election following his removal from office by the Governor-General Sir John KERR.

GPU *Gosudarstvennoye Politicheskoye Upravlenye* (Russ. State Political Administration) The Soviet state security organisation, created in 1922 out of the Bolshevik SECRET POLICE, the CHEKA. Its function was to identify 'counter-revolutionaries' and monitor their activities. It was renamed **OGPU** (*Obedinennoye Gosudarstvennoye Politicheskoye Upravlenye:* United State Political Administration) in 1924, and absorbed into the newly formed NKVD in 1934. *See also* KGB.

Gracie Mansion The official residence of the Mayor of New York City (*see* HIZZONER), located at 88 East End Avenue, NY 10028.

Gracious Speech or **Speech from the Throne** The formal title for the QUEEN'S SPEECH, delivered by the Sovereign or her representative at the opening of each SESSION of Parliament at WESTMINSTER and in her DOMINIONS.

grade creep *See* CREEP.

gradualism The variety of SOCIALISM which spurns revolution, maintaining that change achieved through the democratic process can in time bring the major changes sought. It has consistently been advocated by the FABIANS, whose leading light Sidney Webb (later Lord Passfield) told the 1925 LABOUR PARTY conference:

> Let me insist on what our opponents habitually ignore, and indeed what they seem intellectually incapable of understanding, namely the inevitable gradualness of our scheme of change.

graffiti (Ital. scribblings on walls) One of the oldest forms of PROPAGANDA and protest, used in particular by supporters of outlawed movements to get their point across. The Soviet intervention in Czechoslovakia following the 1968 PRAGUE SPRING produced some celebrated examples, among them 'Red Brothers, go back to your reservations', and 'Russian circus in town. Do not feed the animals'. The art of graffiti extends to doctoring slogans already daubed by an opponent. 'No Pope Here!' has been capped by 'Lucky Pope'; 'MOSLEY for Peace' adapted by prefixing it with the word 'Shoot', and 'Free Nelson MANDELA/Astrid Proll' by adding 'with every 4 gallons'.

graft The use of public office for self-enrichment. In US MACHINE POLITICS some practitioners have readily admitted to graft – but insisted it has all been 'honest graft'. The TAMMANY HALL stalwart George Washington Plunkitt (1842–1924) explained 'honest graft' thus:

> I'm tipped off, say, that [my party] are going to lay out a new park at a certain place. I see my opportunity and I take it. I go to that place and I buy up all the land that I can . . . Then the board of this or that makes the plan public, and there is a rush to get my land, which nobody cared for before. Ain't it perfectly honest to charge a good price and make a profit on my investment and foresight?

Gramm-Leach-Bliley Act The Financial Modernization Act passed by the US CONGRESS in 1999 which removed many of the restrictions on America's banks enshrined in the GLASS-STEAGALL ACT; its progenitor, the Texas Democrat-turned-Republican Phil Gramm, was chairman of the Senate Banking, Housing and Urban Affairs Committee. It abolished the legal distinction between commercial banking, investment banking and insurance as well as restrictions on the opening of branches. As such it paved the way for bigger banking conglomerates, but also created scope for massive conflicts of interest as exposed by the ENRON and Worldcom scandals.

Gramm-Rudman Act The Act passed by CONGRESS in 1985 in a desperate effort to check and reverse the growth in the Federal Budget deficit. It was sponsored by Sen. Gramm; Sen. Warren Rudman, a New Hampshire Republican; and the Democratic Sen. Ernest F. Hollings of North Carolina. Democrat leaders ridiculed it as 'government by veg-o-matic', and President REAGAN's disillusioned former budget director David Stockman (*see* MAGIC ASTERISK) termed it 'mindless, destructive gimmickry'. The Act required automatic cuts in Federal programmes if the Budget exceeded certain levels year by year, and ordered annual reductions in the deficit to zero by 1991; Gramm declared: 'We are shooting real bullets', but though the trigger mechanism had some effect the deficit only fell in later years during the subsequent Democratic administration.

> The doomers and gloomers are talking as if it'll close down the entire Federal government. Hmmmmmm. RONALD REAGAN

> Not a model of political responsibility but an exercise in the politics of evasion.
> HEDRICK SMITH, *The Power Game*

Gramm-Stockman Bill The 'budget' drafted in March 1980 by Gramm, then still a Democrat, and Stockman to show how REAGANOMICS could work in practice. It included a 10% cut in individual tax rates and a depreciation-based cut for business, foreshadowed Reagan's massive cuts in welfare, public service jobs and REVENUE-SHARING with States and cities, and also capped spending on a range of other benefits and programmes that Reagan never seriously tackled. The Bill won 140 Republican supporters in the House and 30 Democrats, giving Reagan and Stockman a solid base when they did move.

grand. Grand Coalition *See* COALITION.

Grand Old Man A semi-affectionate nickname for William Ewart GLADSTONE, reflecting his exceptional political longevity; he served as Prime Minister into his 85th year. It was often abbreviated to GOM; the Conservative leader Sir Stafford Northcote reversed it to **MOG** (Murderer of GORDON) after the fall of Khartoum.

Grand Old Party *See* GOP.

We have become a grandmother *See* WE.

Granita The deal supposedly struck between Tony BLAIR and Gordon BROWN at a minimalist Islington restaurant on 31 May 1994 under which Brown agreed not to contest the Labour leadership with Blair following the sudden death of John SMITH, on the understanding that Blair would step aside for him during the second term of a Labour government. Brown's supporters certainly believed there was such a deal, and when by 2003 Blair showed no sign of handing over power, relations at first between the two old friends' supporters and eventually between Blair and Brown themselves became strained. The Granita meeting, the evening after he actually decided not to stand, was difficult for Brown, because until a year previously he was by common consent the senior of the two, but Blair's stock had risen and most of the political village concluded within hours of Smith's death that he was now the obvious successor. For an Australian parallel, *compare* KIRIBILLI.

> The worst mistake Tony Blair ever made.
> ROBERT HARRIS

> [Brown] did not eat much, and was seen later that night in Rodin's restaurant in Westminster enjoying a second dinner.
> JOHN RENTOUL, *Tony Blair*

Granma The 58-foot yacht on which Fidel Castro sailed from Tuxpan, Mexico with 82 followers on 24 November 1956 to begin the Cuban revolution. It was bought for $15,000 the month before from an American couple named Ericson. The expedition was timed to coincide with a rising against President Batista in Santiago de Cuba; that went ahead, but the *Granma* beached on 1 December not at Niquero as planned but the inconvenient Playa de los Colorados. The rebels lost many of their weapons, were betrayed, and dispersed into the Sierra Maestra. Nevertheless the *Granma* expedition was a preliminary to Castro's eventual triumph, and is commemorated in FIDELISTA legend; *Granma* became the name of one of the regime's leading newspapers.

Grantism A late 19th-century term for nepotism, the SPOILS SYSTEM and corruption at the top; it derived from the amount of cronyism and abuse uncovered during the administration of **Ulysses S. Grant** (1822–85), 18th President of the United States (Republican, 1869–77). While the corruption unquestionably existed, the link with Grant was not entirely fair; while he did appoint too many friends and relatives to office, much of the corruption came to light because Grant ordered its exposure.

A regular soldier whose career was hampered by heavy drinking, Grant rose swiftly in the CIVIL WAR to become General-in-Chief of the UNION armies and led them to ultimate victory. Grant said of his success: 'The art of war is simple enough. Find out where your enemy is. Get at him as soon as you can. Strike at him as hard as you can, and keep moving on.' His conduct of the war was nevertheless controversial. Mary Todd Lincoln termed him 'a butcher', and former President John Tyler was even harsher:

> A scientific Goth, resembling Alaric, destroying the country as he goes and delivering people over to starvation. Nor does he bury his dead, but leaves them to rot on the battlefield.

President LINCOLN, under pressure to remove him, explained: 'I cannot spare this man. He fights.' Taxed with Grant's drinking which he had by now largely cured, Lincoln said: 'Find out what the brand is and I'll give it to my other generals.' After the trauma of Lincoln's ASSASSINATION and of Andrew Johnson's brief presidency, Grant was the pre-eminent choice for the 1868 elections, even though William Clafin observed: 'Early in 1869 the cry was for "no politicians", but the country did not mean "no brains".' Grant easily defeated the Democrat Horatio Seymour; newly enfranchised Southern black voters boosted his majority. Political stability returned, with RECONSTRUCTION continuing, though at a more modest pace; Grant dismissed its liberal Republican proponents as 'narrow-headed men, whose eyes are so close together they can look out of the same gimlet hole without winking.' In the WHITE HOUSE Grant sponsored development of the West (*see* GREAT BARBECUE) but did not exude an aura of total control. One visitor detected 'a puzzled pathos, as of a man with a problem before him of which he does not understand the terms', and Joseph Brown declared: 'The people are tired of a man who does not have an idea above a horse or a cigar.' Yet despite growing evidence of corruption, Grant won a LANDSLIDE re-election over Horace Greeley in 1872. After his Presidency, he lost $16 million on Wall Street; his best-selling *Memoirs* were written to help pay off the debt after he had turned down an offer of millions from the showman Phineas T. Barnum. Grant attempted a comeback in 1880, but the Republican convention blocked him; he said: 'Since my name is up, I would rather be nominated. But I will do nothing to further that end.'

> He combined great gifts with great mediocrity.
> WOODROW WILSON

GRAPO The First of October Anti-Fascist Resistance Group, an extreme left-wing terrorist organisation founded in 1975 as the armed wing of the Spanish Communist Party which killed more than 80 people in 25 years, operating in concert with the Basque separatist movement ETA. Committed to the breaking of Spain's ties with the United States, it concentrated on US military targets but also staged armed robberies and murdered Spanish policemen and even a woman doctor in its drive against 'collaborators' with the Madrid 'ESTABLISHMENT'. GRAPO's leader, Fernando Hierro Txomon, was arrested in Paris in 2002.

grass. The grass grows green on the battlefield, but never on the scaffold Winston CHURCHILL's warning after the 1916 EASTER RISING that the execution of its leaders would lead to their martyrdom and prolong Ireland's agony.

grassroots The RANK AND FILE of party ACTIVISTS and supporters in the country, whose views have to be taken into account by those they work to elect and by the party leadership. The phrase dates at least from 1912, when Sen. Albert Beveridge told the BULL MOOSE convention in Chicago:

> This party comes from the grass roots. It has grown from the soil of the people's hard necessities.

grassy knoll The open slope that John F. KENNEDY's limousine was about to pass when he was ASSASSINATED in DALLAS on 22 November 1963. Topped by a wooden fence with trees just behind it, it was claimed, by those who do not believe that Lee Harvey Oswald from the TEXAS SCHOOL BOOK DEPOSITORY was the sole assassin, to be the point from which the fatal shots were fired. Among their arguments is that some of Kennedy's wounds were consistent with a bullet fired from in front, i.e. from the knoll. Two police patrolmen from the Presidential motorcade were so sure it was that they ran up the knoll and saw another 'police officer' behind the fence. They were then called away; the man they saw was later photographed in a uniform, but not a Dallas police uniform. That mystery has never been explained.

gravy train A situation in which one can make financial and other gains for a minimum of effort and at other people's expense. The phrase has been used of a number of governmental systems where the rewards are great and responsibilities and ACCOUNTABILITY limited; the EUROPEAN PARLIAMENT in Strasbourg, where allowances are generous and attendance peaks during the asparagus season, has offered critics plenty of ammunition. At the height of the PROFUMO AFFAIR, Christine Keeler said:

> I'm on the gravy train with a second class ticket.

great. great and the good The virtually closed circle of individuals, few of them known to the general public, who are called upon by successive British governments to advise on how policy or issues should be handled. The phrase, now widely used to describe Britain's apparently effortless governing elite, was originated in 1965 by Anthony Sampson. He wrote:

> A secret tome of The Great and the Good is kept, listing everyone who has the right, safe qualifications of worthiness, soundness and discretion; and from this tome come the stage army of COMMITTEE people.

Such a list is indeed kept in DOWNING STREET, and from it are appointed members of ROYAL COMMISSIONs, heads of inquiries and appointees to QUANGOs. Since the mid-1990s efforts have been made, with some success, to widen the trawl, largely by including more women and members of ethnic minorities.

> Nor ought one exclusively to rely on the CIVIL SERVICE Department's famous 'List of the Great and the Good', all of whose members . . . are aged fifty-three, live in the South-East, have the right accent and belong to the Reform Club.

Great Barbecue The process under which President GRANT offered vast tracts of unsettled land in the West to the railroad companies as an inducement to them to shoulder the immense cost of building lines across the continent.

Great Betrayal The name still used in Britain's LABOUR PARTY for the collapse of Ramsay MACDONALD's Labour Government in 1931 and its immediate replacement by a NATIONAL GOVERNMENT, also under MacDonald, in alliance with the Conservatives, which pursued policies of strict financial orthodoxy and left Labour a shattered rump. MacDonald told his Labour CABINET as the unions resisted planned cuts in unemployment pay: 'If we yield to the TUC now, we shall never be able to call our bodies or souls or intelligence our own.' Some of MacDonald's colleagues thought the National Government was a temporary move rather than a permanent split, Chancellor Philip Snowden bitterly writing later: 'I expected that . . . we should be able to resume our former co-operation in the Labour Party when the emergency legislation had been passed.'

> What would you say of a Salvation Army that took to its heels on the Day of Judgement?
>
> Sir OSWALD MOSLEY

Great Britain The largest of the British Isles, comprising the mainland of England, Scotland and Wales; the official title of the Kingdom from the 1707 Act of Union until the partition of 1921, when it became the UNITED KINGDOM of Great Britain and NORTHERN IRELAND.

Great Commoner A name bestowed on a series of CHARISMATIC political figures who have either had the interests of the people at heart or are seen as having spurned the chance to opt out of representative politics and join the aristocracy. PITT THE ELDER was the first; William Jennings Bryan (*see* PRAIRIE AVENGER) and Sir Winston CHURCHILL are among others to have earned the sobriquet.

Great Communicator The nickname of President Ronald REAGAN, reflecting his uncanny ability to put across a political argument to the American public, albeit often in an oversimplified form, and to make Americans feel better about themselves and their country after the *angst* of the CARTER administration.

Great Crash The collapse of the New York stock market on 24 October 1929 which paved the way for the GREAT DEPRESSION and burst the economic bubble on which President HOOVER had been elected.

Great Debate *See* DEBATE.

Great Depression The world economic crisis of 1929–35, triggered first by the GREAT CRASH on Wall Street, then by economic instability in Europe, and finally in 1931 by the failure of several major banks. It ended the post-war boom of the 1920s, forced the West off the GOLD STANDARD, and plunged America and the other industrialised nations into an era of business failures, mass unemployment, urban and rural poverty and hardship. In Germany it propelled the NAZIS to power and paved the way for WORLD WAR II; in Britain it split the LABOUR PARTY (*see* GREAT BETRAYAL) and brought the formation of the NATIONAL GOVERNMENT; in America it brought Franklin D. ROOSEVELT's NEW DEAL, which while not restoring prosperity gave the country hope and negated the worst effects of the slump. World-wide recovery did not occur until the outbreak of war.

> In the old days we could send out people from the cities to the country. If they went out today they would meet with another army of unemployed coming back from the country to the city.
> J. S. WOODSWORTH, Canadian CCF leader

Great Emancipator One of many nicknames that became attached to Abraham LINCOLN, stemming from his signature of the EMANCIPATION PROCLAMATION and the freeing of the slaves after the UNION's victory in the CIVIL WAR.

Great Engineer The most complimentary nickname awarded to President HOOVER, because of the talents that led him to make a fortune in his profession, then perform administrative miracles as US food administrator in WORLD WAR I and subsequently shine as COOLIDGE's Secretary of Commerce. The magic deserted him once he reached the WHITE HOUSE, but he was to mobilise humanitarian relief again in WORLD WAR II.

Great Leap Forward A radical economic and social reorganisation in China, introduced by CHAIRMAN MAO in 1958, that was intended to transform the country into an industrialised society in the shortest possible time. The policy, which owed much to romantic MAOIST notions of inspiring the peasants and harnessing their latent skills, sought to bypass the lengthy process of developing heavy industry by concentrating on labour-intensive small-scale industries and agriculture. Traditional customs and living patterns gave way to a new system based on communes, but at the cost of major economic disruption compounded by bad harvests and the withdrawal of Soviet technical help. By early 1960 the Great Leap Forward was being modified, with elements of individual incentive and land ownership reintroduced. The Chinese leadership blamed the policy's failure on poor implementation by over-zealous CADRES plus BUREAUCRATIC ineptitude; opponents argued for a more conventional approach to industrialisation.

Great Patriotic War The Soviet name for the theatre of WORLD WAR II in which the USSR was fighting for its life after HITLER's invasion in June 1941. STALIN played down the Communist nature of his regime to stress old-fashioned Russian patriotism, briefly reviving the Orthodox Church to assist him. After 1945 the KREMLIN used the memory of the Great Patriotic War to bind the people to it and justify its own LEGITIMACY; the trauma of the bitter shared experience did much to prolong the Soviet system.

Great Powers A loose term for the four or five nations that at any given moment dominate the world's affairs; HITLER once declared: 'Germany will either be a great power, or no power at all.' Since WORLD WAR II Britain has lost great power status, though she retains considerable influence; Margaret THATCHER said in the 1979 election campaign before reasserting that influence:

> Unless we change our ways and our direction, our greatness as a nation will soon be a footnote in the history books, a distant memory of an offshore island lost in the mist of time like CAMELOT, remembered mainly for its noble past.

In 1987 Paul Kennedy, English-born Dilworth Professor of History at Yale, published *The Rise and Fall of the Great Powers*, which chronicled the predominance in turn of the Habsburgs, the British Empire, the United States and the Soviet Union, and predicted America's eclipse by Japan.

> There never was a nation great until it came to the knowledge that it had nowhere in the world to go to for help.
> CHARLES DUDLEY WARNER (1829–1900)

Great Removal The mass removal westward of Indian peoples from their lands in the 1830s so that whites could settle them. In the most shameful episode of the Jackson (*see* OLD HICKORY) administration, 60,000 members of the 'five civilised tribes', among them the Cherokee and the Choctaw, were ousted under the Indian Removal Act of 1830 from lands guaranteed to them under treaty, suffering hardship and often death before they arrived in the 'Indian territory' of Oklahoma and other less hospitable lands.

Great Rondini Another nickname for President REAGAN, deriving from his ability to shrug off responsibility for any action or situation that looked likely to cause him political damage. *Compare* HOUDINI.

Great Satan The term for the United States used by Iran's AYATOLLAH Khomeini in whipping up Islamic fundamentalist fervour against the West.

Great Society The phrase used by President Lyndon JOHNSON to describe his vision of the caring America he tried to create until the VIETNAM WAR sidetracked him. LBJ first outlined it in a speech at Ann Arbor, Michigan on 22 May 1964:

> In our time we have the opportunity to move not only toward the rich society and the powerful society, but upward to the Great Society. The Great Society rests on abundance and liberty for all. It demands an end to poverty and racial injustice, to which we are totally committed in our time.

Johnson borrowed the phrase from the title of a 1914 book by the economist Graham Wallas. It had also been used by Aneurin BEVAN, who wrote in 1952:

> Personal relations have given way to impersonal ones. The Great Society has arrived and the task of our generation is to bring it under control.

In the 1964 election, the Johnson platform followed up with anti-poverty programmes, and expanded social security schemes and legislation to strengthen voting rights; LBJ won a LANDSLIDE victory, and followed up by getting through CONGRESS the largest volume of welfare legislation in history. However, critics later asserted that the Great Society had brought a huge increase in social security payments, rather than in real opportunities.

> The greatest outpouring of programs since the NEW DEAL.
>
> HEDRICK SMITH, *The Power Game*

> The Great Society lost its greatness in the jungles of Indo-China.
>
> Sen. GEORGE McGOVERN, 1973

Great Unrest The wave of strikes, especially in coal, steel, the railways and the docks, which afflicted Britain between 1911 and 1914, leading Foreign Secretary Edward Grey to observe: 'We are dealing with a condition of civil war.' The strikes took place as the Liberal government was acting to remove some of the irritants that caused them, enacting the PEOPLE'S BUDGET and reversing the TAFF VALE JUDGMENT. They reflected the growing strength of the labour movement, which within a dozen years, and after WORLD WAR I, was to bring both the first LABOUR government and the GENERAL STRIKE.

Great War The original term for WORLD WAR I, used until the outbreak of WORLD WAR II.

Greater East Asian Co-Prosperity Sphere Japan's plan for a new political order in South-East Asia, drawn up in 1941 as the justification for its programme of conquest. It envisaged concentrating industry in Japan, northern China and Manchuria, with other countries in the region supplying raw materials and forming part of the consumer market. By a combination of military conquests and political alliances the plan was embarked on; it collapsed with Japan's defeat in 1945, but did fragment COLONIALISM in the region and fostered aspirations for independence in such nations as Burma, the future Indonesia and Vietnam.

Greater London Assembly *See* GLA.

Greater London Council *See* GLC.

the greatest happiness of the greatest number The definition of the basis for successful government put forward by the English philosopher Jeremy Bentham (1748–1832), who wrote:

> The greatest happiness of the greatest number is the foundation of morals and happiness.

The phrase echoed JEFFERSON'S 'LIFE, LIBERTY AND THE PURSUIT OF HAPPINESS', but was not original. In 1725 the Irish philosopher Francis Hutcheson had written: 'That action is best which procures the greatest happiness for the greatest numbers.'

Greek Island Codename for the spacious COLD WAR bunker constructed from 1959 for the US CONGRESS 250 miles from WASHINGTON beneath the luxurious Greenbrier Hotel near White Sulphur Springs, West Virginia. The bunker, capable of accommodating 1,000 people and sustaining the Congress for 60 days, included two debating chambers, a broadcasting studio, weapons store, decontamination chamber and a crematorium, and was hidden behind a 25-ton blast door. Most members of Congress were unaware of its existence until the press revealed it in 1992; successive hotel managers did not know it was there until one threatened to call in the police over large numbers of staff and supplies which could not be accounted for.

green (1) The colour adopted by the ENVIRONMENTALIST political movement, and the name of the parties representing it, which scored major successes in the 1980s, especially in Germany. (2) The traditional colour of Irish nationalism, the phrase **wearing of the green** going back over two centuries. The extent of an Irish politician's 'greenness' depends on how enthusiastic he or she is for a united Ireland. (3) The sacred colour of Islam, as in the GREEN MARCH.

Green, the *See* COLLEGE GREEN.

Green Book The book setting out the UK TREASURY's annual spending guidelines.

Green Budget *See* BUDGET.

green card (1) At WESTMINSTER, the card that constituents wishing to see their MP complete in the CENTRAL LOBBY; a messenger is then sent with the card to locate the Member. (2) The card issued by the US Immigration and Naturalization Service entitling a person to reside and work in the USA; as such the green card – now actually pink and blue – is highly prized by would-be residents as a guarantee of a better life.

Green March The march into the colony of Spanish Sahara in October 1975 by 350,000 Moroccans armed only with copies of the *Koran* to claim the territory for King Hassan. They penetrated only a few miles, halting when they encountered the Spanish Foreign Legion, but a token party reached the capital of El Aaiun (Layoune). While the march seemed on the ground to have failed, negotiations in Madrid with the post-Franco government led to Spain giving up the territory, the majority passing to Morocco and a portion briefly to Mauritania. The transfer unnerved Algeria and offended a section of the territory's 70,000-odd population, who formed the POLISARIO FRONT to fight for its independence. The march, hundreds of miles from the nearest city and sources of supply, was a logistical masterpiece; just seven participants died, all through drowning when marchers who had never seen the sea walked straight in before military guards could stop them.

Green Party The party that evolved for the UK's Ecology Party in the 1980s, and won several UK seats in the EUROPEAN PARLIAMENT, SCOTTISH PARLIAMENT and GREATER LONDON ASSEMBLY from 1999 with the introduction of PROPORTIONAL REPRESENTATION. Its support has edged up at successive general elections and in 2005 it pulled 22% in Brighton Pavilion.

Green Paper A consultative document issued by the UK government containing proposals for future action. It is the previous stage to a WHITE PAPER, which contains firm proposals for legislation. Proposals still allowing some room for manoeuvre are known as **white with green edges.**

green pound The artificial exchange rate used within the EU's Common Agricultural Policy (CAP) to protect UK farmers from currency fluctuations. Each member nation has its own 'green currency', though most are identical since the inception of the EURO.

green revolution The Western-backed initiative to boost farm production in the THIRD WORLD which from the 1950s produced huge increases in output, but has been blamed for tilting the economic balance in favour of large farmers and encouraging the growth of crops for export rather than domestic use. Supported by the WORLD BANK, the increased use of machinery, fertilizers, pesticides and high-yielding hybrid grains has had a particular impact in India. It has recently been overshadowed by the controversy over the promotion of genetically modified crops by US MULTINATIONALS.

green shoots The phrase used by CHANCELLOR Norman Lamont in October 1991 for the first signs of economic recovery, which boomeranged on John MAJOR's government the following year when the economy turned sharply downwards. John SMITH, on his election as Labour leader on 18 July 1992, said:

> You don't have to be a paid-up member of the Royal Horticultural Society to know that the Chancellor's green shoots and his promised recovery are as far away as ever.

Big Green A radical INITIATIVE for tighter environmental laws which was defeated by California voters in 1992.

Greenback Party The US party advocating the continued use of paper money first circulated during the CIVIL WAR (**greenback** = paper dollar) and opposing the GOLD STANDARD, which flourished among Western farmers before merging into the FREE SILVER movement. Founded in 1875, it won over 1 million votes in the 1878 Congressional elections, taking fourteen seats in the House, but the Gold Standard was reimposed in 1879. The Greenbackers (sometimes as Greenback-Labor) fought four Presidential elections from 1876 to 1888; their nominee in 1880, General James Weaver, would be the candidate of the POPULIST PARTY twelve years later.

greenhouse effect The effect that occurs in the atmosphere which leads to some of the energy of the Sun's radiation being retained by the Earth as heat, causing the temperature of the planet to rise (**global warming**). It is caused by the increasing emission of greenhouse gases, notably carbon dioxide. Coupled with the depletion of the ozone layer (*see* MONTREAL PROTOCOL; OZONE MAN), it is thought by most scientists, though not by the George W. BUSH administration, to pose one of the greatest threats to the future of the Earth and its inhabitants; heavy political pressure for international action from the mid-1980s led eventually to the KYOTO CONVENTION.

Greenpeace The high-profile environmental movement, originating in British Columbia in 1971 and now based in Amsterdam, which aims to persuade governments by DIRECT ACTION to change industrial and other activities that threaten the environment and the Earth's natural heritage. It has gained wide attention by its efforts to protect whales, prevent the killing of baby seals, and thwart NUCLEAR dumping at sea. When Greenpeace acted against French underground nuclear tests in the South Pacific in 1985 their ship, RAINBOW WARRIOR, was sunk by a French saboteur. In June 1995 a Greenpeace campaign forced Shell to drop its plan to dump the obsolete Brent Spar drilling platform in the North Sea, ironically leading to a less environmentally satisfactory form of disposal. *See also* SAVE THE WHALES.

Greenham Common The group of anti-NUCLEAR UK feminists who in September 1981 set up a Peace Camp outside the US Air Force base at Greenham Common, near Newbury, to protest against the planned deployment there of CRUISE MISSILES. The camp became a focus for repeated demonstrations, breaches of the perimeter fencing and harassment of military convoys, but could not prevent the missiles arriving on schedule in 1983. The protesters were hailed by CND activists as the front line in the struggle against nuclear war; their detractors sought to depict them as a bunch of bedraggled lesbians. The cruise missiles were eventually removed in 1988–89, not through the activities of the campers but because of the INF agreement between the SUPERPOWERS. The closure of the camp was announced in 1990, but some protesters remained for several years afterward.

Grenada The invasion of the Caribbean island by US forces on 25 October 1983 to overthrow ultra-leftists led by Bernard Coard who had seized power six days earlier from the NEW JEWEL MOVEMENT, murdering Premier Maurice Bishop and other leaders. President REAGAN feared that the new regime would align itself with Cuba as a base for subversion and revolution in the region, making use of the British-financed airport then under construction; Reagan claimed the airport was being built by Cuban soldiers, but few Cubans were found. The invasions revealed shortcomings in liaison between US forces which led CONGRESS to bang heads together; one Marine commander had to telephone an Air Force base in Georgia with his credit card to direct bombing attacks, because the two services had insisted on developing incompatible radio systems. While the invasion was welcomed on the island, it was condemned by the UNITED NATIONS and also produced one of the few strains between Reagan and Margaret THATCHER. Queen Elizabeth II, Grenada's nominal head of state, had not been consulted and British ministers felt WASHINGTON had lied to them about the decision to attack.

> Notre Dame v. the Little Sisters of St Mary's.
>
> ANON. US officer

grey. Grey Panthers A semi-humorous name (punning on the BLACK PANTHERS) for the US pressure group organised from the 1970s to promote the rights of the retired and elderly.

grey eminence A shadowy figure behind those ostensibly in power, and the author of their policies. The term was originally used of the Italian-born Cardinal Mazarin (1602–61), chief minister to the French King Louis XIV from 1642.

Grey Wolves An extreme right-wing Turkish terrorist group, with Bulgarian Communist connections, which was implicated in the attempted ASSASSINATION of Pope John Paul II in St Peter's Square in May 1981.

Gridiron Club The elite of 60 political writers whose annual dinner at the Capitol Hilton gives 600 Washingtonians the chance to poke fun at one influential figure from each party. Every President since Benjamin Harrison has attended the Gridiron at least once; Ronald REAGAN termed one of his receptions 'the most elegant LYNCHING I have ever seen'. Sheila Tate, press secretary to Nancy Reagan who managed to reverse a previously negative image at one Gridiron dinner, reckoned that 'for an event that has almost no television coverage and almost no press coverage, it is the most influential three or four hours'.

> One of the high tribal rites of Washington insiders . . . a gathering of political celebrities that combines snob appeal with Hollywood glitter.
>
> HEDRICK SMITH, *The Power Game*

> About as much fun as throwing cowshit at the village idiot.
>
> President LYNDON B. JOHNSON

gridlock Washington-speak for a situation in which legislation is making no progress because of conflicts within CONGRESS and between legislators and the ADMINISTRATION.

The word originated in traffic engineering, describing the indefinite traffic jam that could develop because of a blockage at one point in a city's grid system.

Grieve for Solihull! The double-edged slogan on which Sir Percy Grieve QC fought and held the Midlands seat for the Conservatives at six General Elections from 1964 to 1979; his son Dominic, MP for Beaconsfield, has managed without it.

gringo The Latin American pejorative for Americans, reflecting their perceived desire to control their Hispanic neighbours to the south, in use at least since the MEXICAN WAR of 1846–7. The origin is uncertain; one suggestion is that Mexican soldiers heard the YANKEE invaders singing: 'Green grow the rushes, O!' The **gringo factor** denotes the difficulty America has to overcome in dealing with Central American countries because of suspicion of its motives.

Griswold-Lyon brawl The second most dramatic fight in the US CONGRESS, after the beating of Sen. Charles Sumner over the Crime Against KANSAS. In 1798, the FEDERALIST Rep. Roger Griswold of Connecticut accused Vermont's Rep. Mathhew Lyon of cowardice during the Revolutionary War, and Lyon spat in his face. A move to expel Lyon failed, and a fortnight later Griswold attacked him with his cane; Lyon retaliated with a pair of fire tongs and the two rolled across the FLOOR of the House until other members separated them.

Grits The forerunners of Canada's LIBERAL PARTY, the word still being a nickname for the Liberals. They originated in the 1840s as the **Clear Grits** (grit = determination), a radical faction in Upper Canada (Ontario) who wanted a truly democratic constitution. Their slogan of REP. BY POP. alarmed French Canadians and POLARISED national politics into a two-party system (Grits v CONSERVATIVES).

Grits and Fritz A nickname for the 1976 Democratic Presidential ticket of Jimmy CARTER and Walter Mondale (*see* NORWEGIAN WOOD). Carter earned his epithet because of Northerners' belief that Georgians ate nothing but this variant of porridge; FRITZ was Mondale's nickname in the SENATE. Democrats put the two together for the slogan **Grits and Fritz in '76.**

Grocer The nickname attached by the satirical magazine *PRIVATE EYE* to Sir Edward HEATH during his premiership. The epithet stemmed from his classless origins, the white-coated efficiency he sought to promote and the haggling over food prices that accompanied Britain's entry into Europe. When the Portuguese dictator Dr Marcello Caetano visited Heath in Downing Street, he was greeted with a placard reading:

> Grocer meets butcher.

Margaret THATCHER, whom Heath came to loathe, was ironically referred to by some as the **Grocer's Daughter**; this reference by President Giscard d'Estaing to her bourgeois origins (*fille d'épicier*) sparked the anonymous couplet

> She was only a grocer's daughter
> But she showed Sir Geoffrey Howe.

Gromyko of the Labour Party The sobriquet adopted for himself by Denis HEALEY to reflect his longevity in the upper echelons of the UK LABOUR PARTY despite never becoming Prime Minister. He was comparing himself with the durable **Andrei Gromyko** (1909–89), who was at the centre of Soviet foreign policy-making from 1944, attending the YALTA and POTSDAM conferences, until 1985 when he stood down as Foreign Minister, remaining on the POLITBURO until his death. As the old regime in the Kremlin crumbled, Healey said to a Soviet welcoming committee: 'Same old Mafia again, I see!'

Grosvenor Square demonstration The height of the protest campaign in Britain against the VIETNAM WAR, on 27 October 1968. 30,000 demonstrators massed peacefully against the war in Hyde Park, and 5,000, headed by the then revolutionary Tariq Ali, made for the US Embassy in Grosvenor Square. The police held back the mostly good-natured crowd, but the event has since acquired a symbolism for violent protest that was not evident at the time.

ground. Ground Zero The site in Lower Manhattan of the WORLD TRADE CENTER, which in the aftermath of 9/11 became a focus for US and international resolve against terrorism and remembrance for the 2,892 victims of the outrage, and especially for the men of the New York City Fire Department who had perished trying to rescue them. Within days the smoking rubble became a place of pilgrimage, and once it was cleared away the site – in fact seven storeys below ground level – became at first an unofficial shrine to those who had died and, with work starting on 4 July 2004, the growing form of the 1,776ft **Freedom Tower** erected in its place. The third anniversary commemoration of the attacks was the last time Ground Zero could be used for this purpose as the project gathered pace.

Groundnut Scheme The hastily organised and badly-planned scheme by Britain's post-war Labour government to clear large areas of hitherto unproductive land in Tanganyika to grow groundnuts. The venture, started in 1947, was abandoned three years later at a cost to the taxpayer of £30 million. It was an electoral embarrassment to the LABOUR PARTY, and the phrase 'groundnut scheme' came to mean any extravagant enterprise with little or no chance of success.

group In a UK local authority, the collective term for the members of each party; the LEADER of the council will be the leader of the controlling party group.

group Areas Act One of the cornerstones of APARTHEID, the legislation introduced in 1950 by South Africa's ruling NATIONAL PARTY under which residential and business areas were designated exclusively for particular racial groups. It had the effect of expelling Africans, Coloureds and Asians from many suburbs and causing expropriation of their property. For the white minority, the Act served to consolidate their economic and political power. President F. W. de Klerk's promise in 1990 to repeal or radically reform the Act was a critical step in his government's relaxation of apartheid.

Group of Ten *See* PARIS CLUB.

grouper A member of one of the Industrial Groups formed in Australia's LABOR PARTY in the late 1940s, mainly by Catholics, to combat Communist influence in the party and the trade unions. Tension between groupers and the rest of the party culminated in the accusation from the party leader H. V. Evatt that Labor had lost the 1954 Federal elections because of 'the attitude of a small minority of members, located particularly in Victoria, who [have] become increasingly disloyal to the Labor movement and the Labor party.' When Labor split in 1955, many Groupers were expelled, or left to found the DLP. From then on, the battle between left and right rendered the distinction obsolete.

groupthink The adoption by decision-makers of an accepted wisdom instead of analysing properly the evidence before them. Popular for some time among academics studying the decision process in management and politics, the phrase caught light when the Senate Intelligence Committee in July 2004 claimed that use of groupthink had led the INTELLIGENCE COMMUNITY to advise George W. BUSH that SADDAM HUSSEIN was in a position to use WEAPONS OF MASS DESTRUCTION when the evidence fell short of this. Three days later, the BUTLER REPORT delivered a similar verdict on the process in WHITEHALL.

grouse-moor image The phrase describing the upper-class leadership of Britain's CONSERVATIVE PARTY that did it considerable damage in the early 1960s. Built on press photographs of Harold MACMILLAN shooting on the grouse moors and the 'emergence' of the even more aristocratic Lord Home (*see* SIR ALEC) to lead the party when he retired, Harold WILSON seized on it to present himself as a dynamic, unstuffy, classless alternative. The last of the breed, WILLIE Whitelaw, caused a stir in the mid-1980s when he inadvertently shot two beaters; neither was seriously injured.

GRUNK The magnificent initials of the Royal United National Khmer Government – *Gouvernement Royale Unifiée Nationale Khmer* – which ruled parts of Cambodia in the early 1970s under the leadership of Prince Sihanouk (1922–). Sihanouk, who had governed alone from 1941, was overthrown in 1970 by a right-wing coup while abroad, but formed GRUNK in alliance with the KHMER ROUGE. Sihanouk increasingly became a figurehead, and in 1975 the Khmer Rouge overthrew the US-backed government of Lon Nol to begin the return to YEAR ZERO. Sihanouk returned after the Khmer Rouge were driven from power, emerging as King in 1993. In the mid-1990s he formed an even more spectacular regime – **FUNCINPEC** (United Front for an Independent, Neutral and Co-Operative Cambodia) – but later exiled himself to North Korea; he returned, but abdicated in October 2004.

Grunwick The photographic processing factory in north-west London which became an industrial and political battleground in 1976–77 when Asian workers fighting for higher pay were sacked for joining a trade union. They quickly gained widespread union support, and members of James CALLAGHAN's Labour CABINET joined in several peaceful demonstrations. When postal workers blacked delivery of mail to the factory, the right-wing National Association for Freedom (NAFF), of whom Margaret THATCHER was an enthusiastic supporter, won a court ruling that their action breached the Post Office Act. This encouraged the firm's equally hard-line owner, George Ward, who was determined not to give in under any circumstances. In the summer of 1977 the dispute turned violent after Grunwick, backed by NAFF, rejected the conciliation service ACAS' recommendation that the union, APEX, be recognised. Brent Trades Council called a mass picket, and activists from the SOCIALIST WORKERS' PARTY (SWP) moved in to stage a violent attack on the police that horrified television viewers. From then on the Grunwick workers had no chance, and hardliners in the CONSERVATIVE PARTY had the issue they had prayed for to justify tough curbs on the unions; by the 1979 election the WINTER OF DISCONTENT was to give them another.

GS rating Government Service. The grades into which the US CIVIL SERVICE is stratified; they run from GS-1 at the base of the pyramid to GS-14, grades above which have been replaced by the Senior Executive Service, membership of which is much sought by political HOLDOVERS. Most recruits start at grade GS-3. *See also* GRADE CREEP.

GST *See* CONSUMPTION TAX.

Guadalupe Hidalgo, Treaty of The treaty between the United States and Mexico, signed on 2 February 1848, that formally ended the MEXICAN WAR. Under it Mexico gave up the lands that became the states of California, Arizona, Utah, Nevada, New Mexico and part of Colorado, and formally renounced its sovereignty over Texas. The settlement, under which Mexico received just $15 million, left lasting resentment south of the border.

guarantee An undertaking by one country to protect or come to the aid of a second, smaller one if it is attacked, as a deterrent to aggression by another power. Britain's guarantee to Poland against attack by Germany in 1939 failed to deter, but was honoured nevertheless.

gubernatorial (Lat. *gubernator:* governor) Matters relating to the GOVERNOR of an American STATE; for example, an election for governor is known as a **gubernatorial election**.

GUBU The disastrous chain of events for Ireland's FIANNA FAIL party in the autumn of 1982 that led to the heavy defeat of Charles HAUGHEY's government in that November's election; the party was to stay in opposition for five years. GUBU stands for '**grotesque, unbelieveable, bizarre and unprecedented**' – words used by Haughey himself that August when a well-known murder suspect was arrested in the flat of the ATTORNEY-GENERAL, Patrick Connolly. The journalist and diplomat Conor Cruise O'Brien coined the acronym GUBU to refer to Haughey's style of government, and it haunted Fianna Fail to defeat. Haughey's problems also included a backlash against his refusal to support Britain over the FALKLANDS, which ended his relationship with Margaret THATCHER, and a Macchiavellian offer of a EUROPEAN COMMISSIONER's job to a FINE GAEL TD so that Fianna Fail could win his seat at a by-election – which it failed to do.

Gucci Gulch The marble and gilded hallway outside the US SENATE Chamber where Italian-suited LOBBYISTS skulk until the small hours if necessary to pounce on politicians and pursue their corporate interests. The phrase was coined c.1988 by the *Wall Street Journal* reporters Jeffrey Birnbaum and Alan Murray.

Guernica The symbol of the brutality of General Franco's (*see* CAUDILLO) conduct of the SPANISH CIVIL WAR, and a foretaste of what HITLER had in mind for the rest of Europe. Guernica, a historic town near Bilbao which until 1876 housed the Basque Parliament, was flattened on 26 April 1937 by *Luftwaffe* bombers sent by Hitler to assist Franco's forces. The town was bombed indiscriminately, and civilian survivors mercilessly strafed; Goering admitted that the German objective was to test the effectiveness of saturation bombing. The carnage shocked the world, and Pablo Picasso commemorated the event in his pain-racked painting, *Guernica*, completed two months after the attack.

guerrilla warfare (Sp. little war) Irregular warfare carried on by small groups acting independently, especially by INSURGENTS and combatants against a foreign occupier (*see* PARTISANS, RESISTANCE). The word was first used for the Spanish and Portuguese action against the French in the Peninsular War (1808–14). In the 20th century and since, guerrilla warfare has been employed by many movements of national liberation or hoped-for revolution, some successful in achieving power, some able to destroy the economy and spread misery without the popular support to take control, others becoming romantic failures. The VIETNAM

WAR demonstrated the difficulty a large-scale army backed by technology has in combating elusive guerrillas with a degree of popular support. *See also* WAR OF THE FLEA.

> The peaceful population is a sea in which the guerrilla swims like a fish. MAO TSE-TUNG

> The conventional army loses if it does not win. The guerrilla wins if he does not lose.
> HENRY KISSINGER, 1969

urban guerrilla The phrase invented by the Brazilian revolutionary Carlos Marighella (1911–65) which caught on in the 1960s as radical and MAOIST groups began to take their struggle into the teeming cities. Marighella wrote a manual for the urban guerrilla, in which he argued that if terrorists use revolutionary violence, the government will be forced to intensify repression. The notion that authority can be provoked from a political to a military solution was seized on by the BAADER-MEINHOF GANG, and more recently the Provisional IRA. Marighella wrote:

> It is necessary to turn political crisis into armed crisis by performing violent actions that will force those in power to transform the political situation into a military situation. That will alienate the masses who, from then on, will revolt against the army and the police and blame them for this state of things.

Guildhall speech The major speech which Britain's Prime Minister delivers each November as the guest of the LORD MAYOR of London, in which he or she reviews the state of world affairs and elaborates on the Government's foreign policy. *Compare* MANSION HOUSE SPEECH.

guillotine (1) The device which made beheading swift and reliable and gave the FRENCH REVOLUTION its cutting edge. Invented by the French doctor Joseph Ignace Guillotin (1738–1814), it accounted first for King Louis XVI and Queen Marie Antionette and then, during the Reign of TERROR, for hundreds who fell foul of the leaders of the Revolution, and eventually for Robespierre himself. The guillotine as a penalty was not abolished by law in France until 1981, the last execution by it being in 1977. (2) A procedural device for curtailing debate in a legislature. At WESTMINSTER debate on a BILL is recommended for the guillotine if Government BUSINESS MANAGERS consider the OPPOSITION is delaying it unreasonably in STANDING COMMITTEE; a timetable for further debate is put to the whole HOUSE and voted on. Guillotines have become less common since the turn of the century because timetables are often set for major Government Bills at the time of SECOND READING.

guilt. guilt by association A phrase much used in America in the heyday of MCCARTHYISM, reflecting the readiness of campaigners against alleged Communists to assume that anyone who had had any dealings with such people must also be guilty, without their having the chance to clear their name.

Guilty Men The polemic published in London in the summer of 1940 by Gollancz, under the name of *Cato*, which directed withering criticism against those members of CHURCHILL's coalition government who had made war more likely by pursuing APPEASEMENT. The book, which became an immediate best-seller when the newsagents W. H. Smith tried to ban it, was actually written by Frank Owen, editor of the *Evening Standard*, Peter Howard, a *Sunday Express* columnist, and Michael FOOT, who was then the *Standard*'s leader writer.

Gulag The word that the Russian novelist Alexander Solzhenitsyn (1918–) branded on the conscience of the world to represent the nightmare world of forced labour camps to which DISSIDENTS and many loyal members of Soviet society were sent to break their spirit. It entered the English language from Solzhenitsyn's trilogy *The Gulag Archipelago* (1974–78); Solzhenitsyn was expelled from the Soviet Union when the manuscript was discovered. GULAG derives from *Glavnoye Upravlenye Ospravitelno-Trudoyvkh Laverey* (Chief Administration of Corrective Labour Camps), the relevant section of the KGB.

gulf. Gulf Co-Operation Council The grouping of Arab oil-producing states adjoining the Gulf, formed in 1981 primarily to co-ordinate petroleum, investment and customs policies, as well as general economic, social and cultural matters. Its members are Bahrain, Kuwait, Oman, Qatar, Saudi Arabia and the United Arab Emirates.

Gulf of Tonkin Resolution The resolution passed by CONGRESS on 4 August 1964, unanimously by the House and in the SENATE by 88 votes to 2, which granted President Lyndon B. JOHNSON emergency powers to take any action necessary to repel or prevent attacks on US forces in VIETNAM, and to support America's allies on request. The ADMINISTRATION took the resolution as *carte blanche* to wage an undeclared war in South-East Asia without further, more specific reference to Congress. It stemmed from what was erroneously reported as an unprovoked attack by North Vietnamese torpedo boats on the US destroyers *Maddox* and *C. Turner Joy*, to which LBJ retaliated with a 64-bomber raid on military targets in the North; it later emerged that the *Maddox* had been on a spying mission in northern waters, supported by South Vietnamese patrol boats.

The sorriest vote I ever cast was for the Gulf of Tonkin resolution.
Rep. Sam Gibbons (Dem), (1920–)

Gulf War The conflict between Iraq and a US-led COALITION supported by the UNITED NATIONS, precipitated by Iraq's invasion of Kuwait on 2 August 1990. Critically the Soviet Union, a traditional backer of Iraq, raised no objection to the West intervening. SADDAM HUSSEIN refused UN demands to withdraw and placed foreign hostages at potential targets as a HUMAN SHIELD to deter attacks; he also launched Scud missile attacks on ISRAEL. The response was a first foreign policy test for John MAJOR, and the high point of George BUSH Snr's one-term Presidency. On 17 January 1991 Coalition aircraft began attacking Baghdad, and on 24 February ground troops drove into Kuwait and southern Iraq, the Iraqis offering only token resistance but severely damaging the emirate's oil installations. Coalition forces pulled up inside Iraq, as their remit from the UN did not extend to overthrowing Saddam, and a ceasefire was agreed; the Iraqi leader took this opportunity to put down with great brutality risings by Kurds in the north and Shi'ites in the south which America had encouraged. The UN passed the 'MOTHER OF ALL RESOLUTIONS' to maintain SANCTIONS until Iraq had dismantled its NUCLEAR and chemical weapons capability and stopped persecuting its Shi'ites and Kurds; the coalition protected the former from bombing and strafing by Iraqi jets with a NO-FLY ZONE, and the latter by establishing safe havens for the Kurds. Early in 1993 the US, Britain and France launched renewed air strikes in an effort to bring Saddam to heel; his harassment of UN nuclear weapons inspectors continued and the stage was set for an eventual second WAR IN IRAQ in which a much more limited coalition without UN support would topple Saddam.

Saddam Hussein is a man without pity. Whatever his fate may be, I for one will not weep for him.
JOHN MAJOR, February 1991

The coalition will give Saddam Hussein until noon Saturday to do what he must do – begin his immediate and unconditional withdrawal from Kuwait. GEORGE BUSH, 22 February 1991

The last hurrah in the global game.
RAYMOND SEITZ, US Ambassdor to the UK

Gulf War syndrome A range of debilitating ailments suffered on their return by a disproportionately high number of Gulf War combatants, notably from the US and Britain, and blamed on a number of causes including risky injections prior to the conflict and contact with depleted uranium in artillery shells. Repeated attempts by veterans' groups to have a single syndrome for the 100,000 alleged sufferers officially and medically recognised have been only partially successful, the level of recognition being greater in the United States; a US Government study concluded in October 2004 that there was indeed an identifiable condition which could have been caused by certain chemicals used in warfare, by antidotes to them and by pesticides.

gun. Gun case The UK secrets case that caused the BLAIR government great embarrassment in the wake of the 2003 IRAQ WAR. It stemmed from the sacking from GCHQ and subsequent prosecution under the OFFICIAL SECRETS ACT of a young translator, Katherine Gun, for LEAKing to the *Observer* an e-mail from the US National Security Agency requesting UK help in BUGGING key members of the UN SECURITY COUNCIL on the eve of the conflict. Mrs Gun freely admitted leaking the e-mail, saying she had been trying to stop the war, but when the case opened in February 2004, the prosecution offered no evidence, being reluctant to discuss in court intelligence matters or the legal basis for the war. This outcome was embarrassing enough, but Clare SHORT, who had resigned from the CABINET over the war, then stunned the government and the media by declaring that British intelligence had also bugged UN Secretary General Kofi Annan.

gun control One of the keenest-fought issues in the US CONGRESS in the four decades since the assassination of President KENNEDY, with the NRA and other gun owners' groups having successfully lobbied against most significant Federal controls on gun ownership, citing the RIGHT TO KEEP AND BEAR ARMS. Modest restrictions were enacted after the shooting of Sen. Robert Kennedy in 1968; the NRA has pressed for relaxation of these, and through its Congressional supporters was able to delay for thirteen years and then water down the

BRADY BILL stemming from the attempt on the life in 1981 of President REAGAN, who himself opposed the measure. Though a partial ban on assault rifles was passed in 1994, the Republican Congress and George W. BUSH refused to renew it ten years later, calculating that demands for legislation from John KERRY during the Presidential campaign would harm the Democratic ticket.

> What in the name of conscience will it take to pass a truly effective gun control law? Now in this new hour of tragedy, let us spell out our grief in constructive action.
>
> LYNDON B. JOHNSON after the assassination of Robert Kennedy, 6 June 1968

gun-running The illicit supply of weapons to an opposition or guerrilla group, for use in terrorism or an all-out rebellion. The most celebrated gun-running of the 20th century was conducted by the ULSTER VOLUNTEERS, who were organising to stage a military challenge to HOME RULE. It reached its height on 24 April 1914 when 800 volunteers massed at Larne to unload weapons from two steamers, the *Mountjoy* and the *Millswater*. During WORLD WAR I Sir Roger CASEMENT was executed by the British for running guns to the Irish Republicans. In 1970 two Irish Cabinet Ministers, Charles HAUGHEY and Neil Blaney, were acquitted of assisting the running of guns to the IRA, and in the mid-1980s the Provisionals received several shipments of SEMTEX and missiles from Libya before the EKSUND was intercepted by French customs.

Gunpowder Plot The celebrated attempt by Guy Fawkes to blow up the HOUSES OF PARLIAMENT at Westminster on 5 November 1605, the day King James I was due to open a new session. Barrels of gunpowder were found under the HOUSE OF LORDS the night before the ceremony, and Fawkes – a Catholic who aimed to oust the Protestant dynasty imported from Scotland – was put to a grisly death. Justifying the plot, he said:

> A desperate disease requires a desperate remedy.

guns or butter? A common phrase either side of WORLD WAR II for the choice facing a nation between devoting its resources to armaments or the well-being of its people. It became associated with the wartime speeches of HITLER's PROPAGANDA chief Josef Goebbels, but he had used it as early as January 1936, when he said in a speech in Berlin:

> We can do without butter but, despite our love of peace, not without arms. One cannot shoot with butter, but with guns.

Later in the year Goering took up the theme, saying:

> I must speak clearly. There are those in international life who are hard of hearing. They listen only if the guns go off. We have no butter, my good people, but I ask you, would you rather have butter or guns? Should we import lard or metal ores? Let me tell it to you straight: preparedness makes us powerful. Butter merely makes us fat.

Guomindang *See* KMT.

GURN The Government of Unity and National Reconciliation set up in Angola in the late 1990s in one of several sporadic and unsuccessful efforts to end the warfare between the ruling MPLA and Dr Jonas Savimbi's UNITA rebels. It would take the death of Dr Savimbi to halt the bloodshed.

guru (Hindi, venerable) A term borrowed from Hinduism, where a *guru* is a revered teacher, and applied from the early 1970s to the pioneer of an ideology who becomes the focus of reverence by its adherents. Examples are Milton FRIEDMAN and Sir Keith Joseph (*see* MAD MONK) for MONETARISTS, and Ted Grant (*see* MILITANT TENDENCY) and Tony Cliff (*see* SWP) on Britain's far Left. Although he might have disputed it, preferring the title MAHATMA, Gandhi was the *guru* of the non-violent movement.

Gymnich meetings Informal meetings of the EU's General Affairs and External Relations Councils, of which one is held during each six-monthly Presidency. They take their name from Schloss Gymnich, near Euskirchen in North Rhine-Westphalia, where the first took place in April 1974.

Gypsy Moths The liberal north-eastern Republican Congressmen who rebelled against the REAGAN administration's drive in 1981 for large spending cuts, and whom Reagan's budget director David Stockman blamed in part for his failure to balance the books; however, he conceded that the sheer implausibility of REAGANOMICS was the real culprit. The Gypsy Moths pressed with considerable success for the restoration of cuts in funding for Amtrak, MEDICAID, programmes for the poor and unemployed and aid for 'frost belt' industrial plants. They gained their name in part by angering the BOLL WEEVILS (also named after an insect from their region), conservative Southern Democrats who were also essential to a Reagan majority in the HOUSE, by demanding higher taxes on oil. Two dozen also threatened to oppose the budget unless there were significant cuts in defence spending.

H

H. H-Blocks The accommodation blocks at the MAZE PRISON, Long Kesh, near Belfast – named after their layout – in which for a quarter of a century convicted LOYALIST and REPUBLICAN terrorists were held, and which were the scene of the IRA's BLANKET PROTEST and, in 1981, a traumatic series of HUNGER STRIKES. Opened in 1976, the eight single-storey blocks each had 25 cells, a dining room, exercise yard and recreation room. The complex, said at the time to be the most modern in Europe, also included a sports hall, workshops, hospital and two all-weather sports pitches.

H-Bomb The thermonuclear device, first tested by the US at Eniwetok in 1952, which generated far more devastating power than the original A-BOMB. It was based on energy released by the fusion of light atomic nuclei; the A-bomb worked through fission, with heavy nuclei splitting apart. Its development gave a new twist to the ARMS RACE and, through an increased risk of the human race destroying itself, gave birth to the anti-nuclear movement.

> There is an immense gulf between the atomic and the hydrogen bombs. The atomic bomb, with all its horrors, did not carry us outside the hope of human control . . . but [with] the hydrogen bomb the entire foundation of human affairs was revolutionised and mankind placed in a situation both measureless and laden with doom.
>
> CHURCHILL

Father of the H-Bomb Dr Edward Teller (1908–2003), one of three scientists who in 1939 encouraged Einstein to alert Franklin D. ROOSEVELT that the power of nuclear fission could be tapped to create a devastating weapon. Budapest-born Dr Teller worked during WORLD WAR II on the ATOMIC BOMB, then seized on Enrico Fermi's idea that fusion could be even more destructive than fission and in 1949–51 helped produce the US hydrogen bomb, hence his title, which he loathed.

It starts with an H and ends with a Y The most infelicitous statement made in the SCOTTISH PARLIAMENT by Henry McLeish (1948–) while FIRST MINISTER When endeavouring to accuse opponents of hypocrisy during exchanges in February 2001, McLeish taunted them with these words, unaware that he was actually spelling out the first and last letters of his own name. Statements of this kind by McLeish *(see also* OFFICEGATE) became known as **Henryisms**.

Habeas Corpus (Lat. You are to have the body) One of the basic rights enshrined in MAGNA CARTA; confirmed under Charles II in the Habeas Corpus Act and for Americans by Article 1, Section 9 of the CONSTITUTION. The principle is that no one can be detained indefinitely or without charge; anyone held by the State can issue a writ demanding to be brought before a court for reason to be given why they are being held. LINCOLN suspended Habeas Corpus during the CIVIL WAR, but in 1866 the SUPREME COURT ruled that he had had no authority to do so; in England Habeas Corpus has been weakened in practice, especially through anti-terrorist legislation since 9/11. Yet it remains a fundamental of English and American justice, as was shown in June 2004 when the US Supreme Court ruled, in a defeat for President George W. BUSH, that detainees at Guantanamo Bay (*see* CAMP X-RAY) had a right to be heard in US courts.

Haberdasher Harry A nickname for President Harry S TRUMAN; he had opened a haberdasher's store in Kansas City after WORLD WAR I but it failed after two years.

hacienda. go back to your hacienda The bitter response to Sir James Goldsmith, head of the REFERENDUM PARTY, of David Mellor (*see* LAST CHANCE SALOON), who had just lost his seat at Putney to Labour in the 1997 general election. Mellor was provoked into his outburst at the DECLARATION by ill-mannered barracking from Goldsmith (who had polled 1,518 votes, less than the victor's majority) and his supporters. The jibe was a reference to Goldsmith's habitual residence in Mexico, which was not a member of the EUROPEAN UNION, UK membership of which the billionaire was disputing; unbeknown to Mellor, Sir James was suffering from terminal cancer; he died later that year.

Had enough? The Republican slogan in America's 1946 mid-term ELECTIONS – the first since Franklin D. ROOSEVELT's death – which gave the party control of both Houses of CONGRESS for the first time since 1930.

Haddock The surname adopted in September 2002 by Austin Mitchell (1934–), the long-serving and independent-minded Labour MP for Grimsby, in an attempt to get people to eat more fish. 'I thought this would be a fun way of getting more publicity for seafood,' said the new Mr Haddock. 'Fish is the backbone of Grimsby's economy.' He changed his name back several weeks later, admitting failure.

Haganah The force that operated to protect Jewish settlements in Palestine from 1920 until the declaration of the state of ISRAEL in 1948, when it became the basis of the country's armed forces. It avoided the terrorist tactics of the STERN GANG and the IRGUN but was banned under the British mandate, leading to clashes with the British as well as Arabs after WORLD WAR II.

Hague, William Jefferson (1961–) The youthful, bullet-headed and articulate Yorkshire management consultant who took charge of Britain's CONSERVATIVE PARTY after its rout in 1997, democratised it but, despite frequently worsting Tony BLAIR in the Commons, failed to impact on the electorate, losing the 2001 ELECTION by an almost identical margin. Hague had singled himself out for attention at the age of 16, making a powerful and amusing party conference speech (*see* SOME OF YOU . . .) which won him instant comparisons with Labour's Harold WILSON, and rose rapidly after entering the COMMONS in 1988, joining John MAJOR's CABINET as a sure-footed Welsh Secretary. Defeating Kenneth Clarke for the leadership after a dramatic electoral defeat that saw seven Cabinet colleagues lose their seats, he bulldozed through long-overdue reforms to the party's structure but was unable to end Tory infighting over Europe. His efforts to adopt a popular touch (*see* 14 PINTS) did not convince, his popular and attractive wife Ffion doing more for his image than his wearing a baseball cap and appearing at the Notting Hill Carnival. After the further disaster of 2001 – a campaign he tried to turn into a referendum on the single European currency until challenged as to whether he would abide by the result – he handed over the leadership to Iain Duncan SMITH (*see* IDS), but remained active on the back benches.

Hail to the Chief The musical greeting traditionally accorded to the PRESIDENT of the United States. The words are from the *Boat Song* in Sir Walter Scott's *Lady of the Lake*, the tune by James Sanderson. It came into use around 1828, was insisted on by Julia Tyler (FIRST LADY 1844–45), 'retired' by Jimmy CARTER in a bid to end the 'IMPERIAL PRESIDENCY' and reinstated by Ronald REAGAN. During WATERGATE, satirists corrupted it to **Hail to the Thief!**

hair. the wife don't like her hair blown about. The explanation of Deputy Prime Minister John Prescott for his taking two official cars for his wife Pauline – an ex-hairdresser – and himself to cover the 250 yards between the conference hotel and the 1999 LABOUR PARTY conference in Bournemouth. Prescott at the time was the principal advocate of an 'integrated transport policy' for reducing car use; this episode was one reason for Conservative MPs and the media christening him 'TWO JAGS'.

half-breeds The liberal US REPUBLICAN faction who, during Rutherford HAYES's Presidency, rallied round Sen. James G. Blaine of Maine to back Hayes' southern policy and CIVIL SERVICE reforms against the STALWARTS. *See also* OLD 8 TO 7.

Halitosis Hall The derogatory term for Britain's HOUSE OF COMMONS used frequently by the Denis Thatcher character in *Private Eye*'s DEAR BILL letters.

halitosis of the intellect The classic insult delivered to Sen. Huey (KINGFISH) Long in the 1930s by Harold L. Ickes, head of FDR's Public Works Administration. Ickes said:

> The trouble with Sen. Long is that he is suffering from halitosis of the intellect. That's presuming Emperor Long has an intellect.

Hallstein doctrine The policy, adopted by the Federal Republic of Germany in 1955, that recognition of East Germany by another state was a hostile act against the Bonn government. The purpose was to maintain the isolation of the GDR, which Bonn maintained was not a legally constituted state but a barrier to German UNIFICATION. Though named after Dr Walter Hallstein, State Secretary of the West German Foreign Office and later President of the EUROPEAN COMMISSION, the doctrine was actually devised by Wilhelm Grewe, the country's ambassador to the US.

Hamas (Islamic Resistance Movement) A radical Islamic group in Palestine which has repeatedly provoked Israel into suspending the PEACE PROCESS. A REJECTIONIST group committed to the elimination of Israel, it started in Gaza as a branch of the Muslim Brotherhood and was originally backed by Israel as a rival to the PLO. It took its name at the start of the INTIFADA in 1987; Hamas' military wing is the **Qassam Brigade**, named after Sheikh Izzedin al-Qassam, killed by the British in 1935. It was one of the first Palestinian organisations to carry out suicide bombings, from 1992, and established its ruthlessness in 1994 when it torched an Israeli school bus in revenge for the massacre of 30 Muslim worshippers at a mosque in Hebron by a Jewish extremist. Israel rounded up many of Hamas' leaders, but was forced to release them in October 1997 after a MOSSAD operation in Jordan misfired, two agents with Canadian passports being held after trying to kill a Hamas leader there. Hamas was to the forefront in the upsurge of violence in 2002 as Ariel Sharon staged Israeli incursions into areas under Yasser Arafat's control, killing key members of Hamas, culminating in the assassination of its spiritual leader, Sheikh Ahmed Yassin, on 23 March 2004. The political wing led from Qatar by Khaled Meshaal had, by the resumption of the Intifada in 2001, become more popular in Palestine than Arafat's FATAH. Hamas also runs clinics, schools and youth clubs in the OCCUPIED TERRITORIES.

Hamilton, Alexander (1755–1804) George WASHINGTON's wartime aide-de-camp, co-framer of the US CONSTITUTION and principal author of the FEDERALIST (51 of 85 issues). As Secretary of the Treasury from 1789 until he resigned in 1795, Hamilton constructed the financial base of the new Republic.

> He smote the rock of the national resources, and abundant streams of revenue gushed forth. He touched the dead corpse of the Public Credit, and it sprung upon its feet. The fabled birth of Minerva, from the brain of Jove, was hardly more sudden or more perfect than the financial system of the United States as it burst forth from the conceptions of Alexander Hamilton.
>
> DANIEL WEBSTER (1782–1852)

Hamilton, who hailed from the Caribbean island of Nevis, was less successful with his own finances, having paid out well over $1,000 to the blackmailers James and Maria Reynolds, after being seduced into an adulterous relationship with Maria. On a political level his opponents, who knew little of this, declared: 'When a little Alexander dreams himself to be Alexander the Great, he is very apt to fall into miserable intrigues.' His fellow-federalist John ADAMS termed him 'that bastard son of a Scotch pedlar', but to his opponent Thomas JEFFERSON, who recalled that 'Hamilton and myself were daily pitted in the Cabinet like two cocks', Hamilton was 'a colossus . . . he is a host within himself'. Hamilton engineered Adams' defeat in the REVOLUTION OF 1800, but instead of securing the presidency for himself got Jefferson elected. He retired from politics, and in 1804 was killed in the BURR-HAMILTON DUEL.

> The Republic is his monument.
>
> Sen. ARTHUR H. VANDENBERG (1884–1951)

hammer and sickle The twin emblem of world COMMUNISM, as firmly identified with it as the RED STAR. Adopted by the Soviet Union in 1923, they symbolise productive labour in the factory and on the land.

Hampstead set The close friends in the 1950s of the UK Labour leader Hugh GAITSKELL, who like him were mainly Oxford-educated intellectuals living in this fashionable part of north-west London. The group, which included Anthony Crosland, Denis HEALEY, Douglas Jay, Roy JENKINS and Frank Pakenham (later Lord Longford, *see* LORD PORN) were accused by BEVANITES of undue influence over party affairs.

Hancock, John A person's signature, from the bold hand with which John Hancock (1737–93) became the first signer of America's Declaration of INDEPENDENCE, saying:

> There, I guess King George will be able to read that.

hand. handbagging Margaret THATCHER's negotiating tactics, and treatment even of her colleagues. At one CABINET meeting Nicholas Ridley said: 'Why don't we start? The handbag is here.' And US Secretary of State George Shultz presented her with a handbag at his retirement party, telling her:

> You are the only person so far to whom has been awarded the Order of the Handbag.

The term has been ruled UNPARLIAMENTARY in Ireland's DAIL. In 1992 Maire Geoghegan-Quinn, Minister of Transport, was accused of handbagging the board of *Aer Lingus*. She objected that the term was a sexist handover from Thatcherite Britain, and a man acting the same way would have been praised for decisiveness. The SPEAKER agreed.

handbell The 'Victory bell' rung by party chairman Lord Hailsham (Quintin Hogg, 1907–2001) at the Conservatives' 1957 conference during a morale-boosting speech aimed at rallying the party after SUEZ. Ever since, a handbell has been presented to the chairman of the conference. Together with the flat cap he wore as MACMILLAN's Minister for the North-East, it became Hailsham's trademark. He told the conference:

> Let us say to the LABOUR PARTY: 'Send not to ask for whom the bell tolls – it tolls for them!'

Handsome Frank The nickname of **Franklin Pierce** (1804–69), 14th President (Democrat, 1853–57) of the United States. A New Hampshire lawyer with a fine physique, colourful dress and a touch of personal vanity, Pierce was a Congressman at 25 and a Senator at 33, but returned to private practice after one Senate term until the MEXICAN WAR, in which he served as a Brigadier-General. He was nominated in 1852 as a COMPROMISE CANDIDATE after 48 ballots at the Democratic convention had produced deadlock. In the Presidential campaign supporters of the WHIG Winfield Scott termed Pierce, always a hard drinker, 'the hero of many a well-fought bottle' – inferring cowardice in battle; in fact Pierce was thrown from his horse and injured in his only engagement. On his INAUGURATION after defeating Scott, he appealed: 'You have summoned me in my weakness – you must sustain me by your strength.' Stephen Douglas was even blunter, declaring: 'Hereafter, no private citizen is safe,' and his friend Nathaniel Hawthorne told him: 'Frank. I pity you, indeed I do, from the bottom of my heart.' The Pierce ADMINISTRATION brought trade RECIPROCITY with British North America, treaty links with Japan, but the seeds of the CIVIL WAR in the repeal of the MISSOURI COMPROMISE and passage of the KANSAS-NEBRASKA ACT. Pierce himself was a LAME DUCK, his former secretary B. B. French maintaining in 1856: 'Whoever may be elected, we cannot get a poorer cuss than now disgraces the Presidential chair.'

> A small politician, of low capacity and mean surroundings, proud to act as the servile tool of men worse than himself but also stronger and abler. THEODORE ROOSEVELT

> Pierce didn't know what was going on, and even if he had, he wouldn't have known what to do about it. HARRY S TRUMAN

hang. hang me first, and let him speak afterwards The plea of a prisoner about to be hanged in public in 1874 when J. C. S. Blackburn, a CANDIDATE for CONGRESS in Kentucky, offered to speak when the condemned man had no last words.

Hang the Kaiser! A POPULIST slogan in Britain and France at the close of WORLD WAR I, and one of the slogans on which the Lloyd George COALITION won the COUPON ELECTION. It branded Germany's Kaiser (Emperor) Wilhelm II (1859–1941) the principal architect of the war which had brought such slaughter; in the event, he was exiled to Holland.

we must indeed hang together, or most assuredly we shall hang separately Benjamin FRANKLIN's remark to his fellow revolutionary John HANCOCK, at the signing of the Declaration of INDEPENDENCE, 4 July 1776. It reflected the fate that awaited them should America lose the Revolutionary War.

hangers and floggers Shorthand for the powerful lobby for LAW AND ORDER on the right of Britain's CONSERVATIVE PARTY which campaigned in the 1950s for the return of flogging and, from its abolition in 1966, the restoration of capital punishment.

Hangman Foote The mid 19th-century Sen. Henry Foote of Mississippi, who gained his nickname for threatening to hang a New England senator from the tallest tree in his state. In 1850, Foote pulled a loaded revolver in the Senate on Sen. Thomas Hart Benton of Missouri, the only Southern senator to oppose an extension of slavery. Benton cried: 'Let him fire!', but colleagues overpowered Foote.

Hansard The **Official Report** of proceedings in the two HOUSES OF PARLIAMENT at WESTMINSTER. It is named after Thomas Curzon Hansard, son of the government printer Luke Hansard, who produced the first reliable reports of debates from 1803. Previously such reports had been treated as a breach of PRIVILEGE.

> History's ear, already listening.
> Lord SAMUEL, 1949

Happy Nickname of Margaretta Rockefeller, socialite wife of Nelson Rockefeller (*see* ROCKY), Governor of New York and Gerald FORD's Vice President. The name was reputedly given in 1927 by her French nursemaid; bouncing the baby on her knee when she heard that Charles Lindbergh had achieved the first non-stop flight from New York to Paris, the maid saw her respond with happy gurgles and giggles.

Happy days are here again Franklin D. ROOSEVELT's 1932 campaign theme song and the anthem of his NEW DEAL. Written in 1929 by Milton Ager (words) and Jack Yellen (music), it was adopted at the Democratic Convention after FDR's aide Edward Flynn rejected *Anchors Aweigh* as a 'dirge':

> Happy days are here again!
> The skies above are clear again!
> Let's all sing a song of cheer again –
> Happy days are here again!

FDR's choice of the song did not please its writers, who were Republicans.

Happy Warrior Originally the nickname of **Al** (Alfred Emmanuel) **Smith** (1873–1944), Governor of New York and Democratic presidential nominee in 1928. It was accorded him at the 1924 Democratic CONVENTION by Franklin D. ROOSEVELT, who described him in his unsuccessful nominating speech as 'the Happy Warrior of the political battlefield'.

More recently the name has belonged to **Hubert Horatio Humphrey** (1911–78), a lifelong liberal with strong LABOR connections. A Democratic Senator for Minnesota from 1946 to 1964, he served as Vice President to Lyndon B. JOHNSON, then ran for the Presidency himself against Richard NIXON in 1968. His apparently no-hope candidacy for a party hopelessly split over the VIETNAM WAR ran Nixon close after he belatedly distanced himself from Johnson's war policy. Returning to the Senate, he tried for the Democratic nomination again in 1972 and 1976; he died in 1978 after a heroic struggle with cancer.

HHH had a powerful social conscience. He was the architect of the HUMPHREY-HAWKINS FULL EMPLOYMENT ACT which set the elimination of unemployment as a national goal, and in 1966 told a local government convention in New Orleans: 'I'd hate to be in those [slum] conditions, and I'll tell you that if I were in those conditions, you'd have more trouble than you already have because I've got enough spark left in me to lead a mighty good revolt.' But the radical left suspected him, Hunter S. Thompson dismissing him in 1972 as 'a treacherous, gutless old WARD HEELER who should be put in a goddam bottle and sent out with the Japanese current.' Humphrey was a rapid speaker; Barry Goldwater once said: 'He talks so fast that listening to him is like trying to read *Playboy* magazine with your wife turning the pages.' Goldwater also claimed Humphrey had been 'vaccinated with a phonograph needle'. But Humphrey retorted: 'I've never thought my speeches were too long – I've enjoyed them.'

> Above all, Hubert was a man with a good heart. He taught us all how to hope and how to live, how to win and how to lose, he taught us how to live and, finally, he taught us how to die.
>
> Vice President WALTER MONDALE's funeral eulogy, Washington, 15 January 1978

> According to Gandhi, the seven sins are wealth without works, pleasure without conscience, knowledge without character, commerce without morality, science without humanity, worship without sacrifice and politics without principle. Well, Hubert Humphrey may have sinned in the eyes of God, as we all do, but according to those definitions of Gandhi's, it was Hubert Humphrey without sin.
>
> President JIMMY CARTER's funeral eulogy, St Paul, 16 January 1978

Don't worry, be happy The unofficial theme song of George BUSH Snr's successful 1988 campaign for the Presidency. It won a Grammy award for the singer Bobby McFerrin.

Harambee! (Swahili. Let's pull together) The slogan for Kenyan independence and national unity of Jomo Kenyatta (1889–1978), from 1964 the republic's first president, and his KANU party. *See also* MAU MAU; UHURU).

Harare Declaration The declaration committing members of the COMMONWEALTH to GOOD GOVERNMENT free of corruption and human rights abuses, which was agreed at the 1991 CHOGM in Harare, Zimbabwe, at the instigation of John MAJOR. The abuses committed by Robert Mugabe's regime in his declining years still lay ahead. A further **Edinburgh Declaration** on cultural and economic matters followed in 1997.

Harcourt Room *See* CHURCHILL ROOM.

hard. hard cider candidate The US WHIGS' name for their 1840 Presidential candidate William Henry Harrison (1773–1841), whom they contrasted with the 'oriental splendour' of the incumbent Martin van Buren. Harrison won, but caught cold during his INAUGURATION and died 31 days later. *See also* LOG CABIN; TIPPECANOE AND TYLER TOO.

hard faced men who have done well out of the war Stanley BALDWIN's verdict on the businessmen and other prosperous non-combatants who took their seats in the COMMONS after the 1918 COUPON ELECTION to seek vengeance on Germany. His actual words were : 'A lot of hard-faced men who look as if they had done very well out of the war.'

hard-hats The conservative construction workers whose support President NIXON and, even more, Vice President Spiro AGNEW cherished during the closing stages of the VIETNAM WAR. Wearing their safety helmets, they demonstrated for continuing the war and against anti-war protesters. The term later came to describe male working-class Democrats who supported Ronald REAGAN.

hard landing An economically bleak ending to a BOOM cycle, stemming from over-severe measures taken to check it. As Nigel Lawson sought to damp down the UK's boom in 1988, commentators speculated on whether the corrective measures would bring a 'hard landing' or a less painful 'soft landing'. The former were right.

hard left *See* LEFT.

hard-working families The phrase taken up by Tony BLAIR and Gordon BROWN around the time of the 1997 election to identify NEW LABOUR with working people who believed government should reward their industry and let them keep more of their money rather than subsidise the less deserving. The insertion of the word 'hard' gave the phrase a very different political thrust than Labour's commitment in the 1970s to WORKING PEOPLE AND THEIR FAMILIES.

Hardie, Keir *see* QUEER HARDIE.

Harding, Warren Gamaliel (1865–1923), 29th President of the United States (Republican, 1921–23). A low-profile Senator from Ohio chosen in the original SMOKE-FILLED ROOM to break the deadlocked 1920 Republican Convention, Harding defeated James M. Cox in a LANDSLIDE through his appeal for 'NORMALCY' after the WILSON era. Harry Daugherty explained that Harding was nominated because 'he looked like a President', and there could have been few other reasons. Harding himself said: 'I am not fit for this office and never should have been here', and his father once told him:

> If you were a girl, Warren, you'd be in the family way all the time. You can't say 'No'.

Indeed he had a string of extramarital affairs, one producing an illegitimate daughter; a second mistress was sent on a world cruise during the election. His presidency was banal; Harding himself said: 'I am a man of limited talents from a small town. I don't seem to grasp that I am President.' Woodrow Wilson had warned: 'He has a bungalow mind,' and Sen. William McAdoo recorded: 'His speeches leave the impression of an army of pompous phrases moving over the landscape in search of an idea. Sometimes these meandering words would actually capture a straggling thought and bear it triumphantly a prisoner in their midst until it died of servitude and overwork.' H. L. Mencken more tartly observed: 'He writes the worst English I have ever encountered. It is so bad that a sort of grandeur creeps into it.' Mencken's overall verdict on Harding was: 'a tinhorn politician with the manner of a small town doctor and the mien of a ham actor.' Harding died suddenly in San Francisco as the corruption in his administration (*see* TEAPOT DOME) was becoming evident, Samuel Hopkins Adams declaring: 'Few deaths are unmingled tragedies. Harding's was not; he died in time.'

> He was not a bad man. Just a slob.
>
> ALICE ROOSEVELT LONGWORTH

> Pretty raw, some of these Bills. But what can I do? The Organization wants 'em.
>
> HARDING to H. F. Alderfer

harmonisation In the EUROPEAN UNION, the process of bringing member states' taxation systems, industrial specifications, professional qualifications, etc., into line to assist development of the SINGLE MARKET.

Harper's Ferry The most celebrated incident which preceded America's CIVIL WAR. On 16 October 1859 the ABOLITIONIST John Brown and eighteen followers seized the Federal arsenal at Harper's Ferry on the upper POTOMAC and issued a proclamation to the slaves to rise up. US troops under Robert E. Lee forced the raiders to surrender; Brown was taken to Richmond, tried and hanged.

Harrison, Benjamin (1833–1901), 23rd President of the United States (Republican, 1889–93). A CIVIL WAR general and one-term Senator for Indiana, Harrison ousted President CLEVELAND in 1888 despite polling fewer votes. There were also allegations of vote-buying; Pennsylvania's BOSS Matt Quay said: 'He will never know how close a number of men were compelled to approach the penitentiary to make him President.' And Harrison lamented: 'When I came into power, I found that the party managers had taken it all to themselves. I could not name my own CABINET. They had sold every place to pay the election expenses.' Harrison soon became known as the WHITE HOUSE ICEBERG;

Theodore ROOSEVELT described him as 'a cold-blooded, narrow-minded, prejudiced, obstinate, timid old psalm-singing Indianapolis politician'. When Cleveland took his revenge in 1892, Harrison said he felt 'a good deal like the old camp horse that Dickens described: he is so strapped up he can't fall down.'

Harrison, William Henry *See* HARD CIDER CANDIDATE; LOG CABIN; TIPPECANOE AND TYLER TOO.

Hart Building The most opulent, when completed in the early 1980s, of the office buildings sited around the US CAPITOL to provide 1 million sq. ft. of office space and other facilities for the SENATE. With a roof-top dining room, third gymnasium, 16ft. ceilings and a basketball court, it proved so costly (c. $150 million) that the HOUSE suspended APPROPRIATIONS for a time. In October 2001 the building was sealed off for over two months after a letter containing anthrax spores was delivered to the offices there of the Senate MAJORITY LEADER Tom Daschle.

hat in the ring To throw one's hat in the ring is to declare one's availability, or candidacy, for office. It originated with Theodore ROOSEVELT, who said when launching his 1912 BULL MOOSE campaign:

> I am stripped to the buff and my hat is in the ring.

Hatch Act The legislation, enacted in 1939, which barred US civil servants, other than policymaking officers, from participating in party political campaigns. The Act also imposed tentative curbs on campaign financing.

hatchet man A ruthless demolisher of political opponents, by inference acting with the approval of apparently more civilised colleagues. In the 1976 vice presidential DEBATE, Sen. Walter Mondale said Sen. Bob Dole had 'richly earned his reputation as a hatchet man' by asserting that 1.6 million Americans had been killed in 'Democratic wars'. The phrase originated in 19th-century America, describing hired killers from China.

Hatterji The nickname of **Roy Sydney George** (later Lord) Hattersley (1932–), egalitarian, writer, gourmet, Yorkshire nostalgist and from 1983 to 1992 deputy leader of the LABOUR PARTY. The sobriquet, bestowed by *PRIVATE EYE* in the 1960s, did not refer to his Birmingham constituency's high Indian and Pakistani population or a party conference reference by him to 'my Asians' but was an adaptation of 'Chatterji' which appealed to the satirists. The only son of two Sheffield councillors (one a former Catholic priest), Hattersley was a youthful success in local government before being elected an MP. Harold WILSON marked him out for advancement; he became a junior employment minister, a FOREIGN OFFICE Minister in 1974 and joined the CABINET as Prices Secretary in 1976. In OPPOSITION from 1979 he took on the BENNITE left when fellow-moderates were defecting to the SDP. He held his own in Labour's internecine conflicts, as in this 1983 clash with party leader Michael FOOT:

> *Hattersley:* You have betrayed us [by refusing to change the block voting system]. What kind of leadership is that?
> *Foot:* Don't talk to me like that. I'll have the skin off your back.
> *Hattersley:* You couldn't knock the skin off a rice pudding.

Neil KINNOCK defeated him for the leadership in 1983, but Hattersley served as his deputy for nine years in the 'Dream TICKET'. Dr David OWEN saw him as 'the acceptable face of opportunism'; Professor John Vincent asserted that 'there are lies, damned lies and Roy Hattersley', and Norman Tebbit asked: 'Would you want him as your bank manager?' But Hattersley was consistently pro-European, a champion of non-selective education and above all loyal to Labour, though his image of it was moulded in the late 1940s and he found its stance under Tony BLAIR hard to stomach. He was lampooned for his appetite and, unmeritedly by the TV puppet satire *Spitting Image*, for reputedly spraying those around him when he spoke. Ironically the Tory MP Jock Bruce-Gardyne had once said:

> He has a voice like the last splash of a soda siphon.

Hattersley was a robust debater, describing WILLIE Whitelaw as 'one of the last representatives of a dying Tory tradition, possession of land, enthusiasm for shooting small birds and antipathy for reading books.' Yet he got as good as he gave. When he denounced a Tory attack on the CALLAGHAN government as 'an unprecedented example of the triumph of tactics over principle', Norman St John Stevas (later Lord St John) brought the house down by asking: 'Has the Rt Honourable Gentleman ever considered his own career?' And after his retirement the Conservative chairman Sir Norman Fowler described him as

> The only man to move from the Cabinet table to the restaurant table and consider it a promotion.

Hattonistas The MILITANT TENDENCY supporters on Merseyside of Derek Hatton (1948–), deputy leader of Liverpool City Council from 1983 to 1986. The name was an echo of the SANDINISTAS. Through Militant sympathisers in the LABOUR PARTY and local government trade unions, the sharply-dressed and convivial Hatton controlled the council. But his challenges to the THATCHER government in defiance of Labour policy led Neil KINNOCK to denounce him in a dramatic scene at Labour's 1985 conference, scorning

> The grotesque chaos of a Labour council – a Labour council – hiring taxis to scuttle round a city handing out redundancy notices to its own workers.

He was subsequently expelled from the party, disqualified by the courts from serving on the council because of unjustified spending and acquitted on corruption charges before embarking on a new career in broadcasting.

Haughey, Charles (1925–), the CHARISMATIC, larger-than life but ultimately flawed leader of FIANNA FAIL who dominated the Irish political scene for three turbulent decades, arousing intense emotions for and against but only being disgraced after his retirement. The reluctance of middle-class voters in the 1980s to support Fianna Fail as long as Haughey was its leader was formally acknowledged as the **Haughey Factor** and worked into its electoral strategy by its FINE GAEL opponents. Haughey's rise to power was only briefly interrupted by the ARMS CRISIS of 1970, when he was tried but acquitted of GUN-RUNNING to the IRA. Elected a TD in 1957, he was a Cabinet Minister from 1960 to 1970, returned in 1977, and in the same year succeeded Jack Lynch as TAOISEACH. Tougher than expected against terrorism, he enjoyed an initially very warm relationship with Margaret THATCHER, one British official describing their first meeting as 'almost a seduction'; but she turned against him when Ireland blocked EC support for Britain over the FALKLANDS. He headed Fianna Fail governments from 1979 to 1981, February-December 1982 (*see* GUBU), and from 1987 to 1992 (from 1989 in coalition with the PDs), finally being forced out because of the PHONE-TAPPING SCANDAL.

Haughey once said: 'I do not contemplate defeat.' He also asked: 'What would I be doing it I wasn't leading Fianna Fail? It's my life.' It was also his living; under questioning from a government commission in 1997 he admitted to spending £I 300,000 a year beyond his means, and receiving £I 1.2m from the supermarket chief Ben Dunne toward clearing his debts. That August an inquiry under Mr Justice Brian McCracken concluded that he had told eleven lies about his relationship with Dunne, and ruled that it had been 'quite unacceptable' to accept such gifts. Haughey was not alone; the former Fine Gael Minister Michael Lowry had also received payments and evaded tax. But the *Irish Times* editorialised:

> Haughey has brought shame on his country, on himself and on Fianna Fail.

The trail to Haughey began when police were called to a hotel in Orlando, Florida in 1992 where they found Dunne, a woman and 32.5g of cocaine. The involvement of Haughey, who had just retired, came to light because of a row in the Dunne family, who sacked Ben Dunne from the store chain early in 1993. Dunne's sister Margaret Heffernan probed his finances, and the payments to Haughey via his accountant Des Traynor were revealed.

Declan Hibberd wrote that 'his only philosophy appeared to be the retention of power'. To Fianna Fail TD Charlie McCreevy, Haughey was 'only at his best when his back is to the wall'. Conor Cruise O'Brien went further, noting: 'His admirers thought he resembled the Emperor Napoleon, some of whose better-known mannerisms he cultivated.' According to his unofficial biographer Stephen Collins, 'he never wore a watch or carried anything apart from cash in his pockets. If he needed to know the time or wanted anything, he asked a minion who was expected to respond promptly.' To Dublin journalist Tim Pat Coogan, he was 'the epitome of the men in the mohair suits'.

Vincent Browne concluded that 'faced with almost all challenges, except leadership challenges, his instinct has been to back off or fudge'. Yet he could be ruthless. One TD confided: 'Give him enough rope and he'll hang you.' After the WHIP was withdrawn from the future PD leader Desmond O'Malley, Haughey's press secretary P. J. Mara said: '*Uno* DUCE. *Una Voce*. There'll be no more nibbling at my leader's bum.' And Haughey once described his own Cabinet as 'a bunch of gobshites'. His Fine Gael adversary Garret FitzGerald asserted prophetically that Haughey 'comes with a flawed pedigree', yet his stature was immense. New York's Governor Hugh

Carey called him 'the Harry TRUMAN of Irish politics'. To Sen. Edward KENNEDY he was 'a great personal friend'. And many Irish people backed him all the way. Conor Cruise O'Brien wrote: 'They knew perfectly well that he was a rogue, and liked him the better for it.' And when he resigned, a letter in the *Irish Times* termed him

> The only honest gangster ever to run Ireland.

Taj MaHaughey The lavish Prime Minister's Office, also known as **Charlie's Taj Mahal**, which Haughey developed for himself in the Government Buildings on Merrion Street Upper, separated from LEINSTER HOUSE by the Natural History Museum. The complex, shared with some other government departments, is open to the public on Saturdays.

Havana conference A meeting of American states held in 1940 to consider the impact and implications of WORLD WAR II which at that point was largely confined to western and central Europe. The participants agreed to a 'No Transfer' principle under which control over colonies in the Americas could not be transferred between non-American states; this meant they would oppose any move by Germany to take over British, French and Dutch possessions.

Hawarden kite The LEAK in December 1885 by Herbert GLADSTONE of his father's intention to go for Irish HOME RULE: a Dublin Parliament under the Crown and Westminster. The kite thus flown took its name from Gladstone's home at Hawarden, in north Wales just west of Chester. It did considerable political damage to the LIBERAL PARTY, precipitating a split over Ireland.

> It marked the withdrawal from the Liberal Party of the aristocratic element.
> JOHN (later Viscount) MORLEY (1838–1923)

Hawke, Robert (1929–), President of the Australian Council of Trade Unions 1970–80 and Prime Minister (Labor) 1983–91. A son of the manse who once said: 'If I were to be born again, I would want to be a Jew,' Hawke ably made the transition from backroom union technocrat to leader of the movement, to Labor BACKBENCHER, party leader and, one month later, Prime Minister – putting a serious drink problem behind him to become Labor's most successful premier to date, winning four ELECTIONS. Hawke knew he would have to go into politics at the top, saying: 'It would not be sensible for me to put my bum on a backbench seat,' and just before he did enter politics, Peter Blazey wrote:

> He's the most popular politician in Australia without really being one.

Once in the HOUSE OF REPRESENTATIVES, Hawke had a devastating effect on the morale of Malcolm Fraser's Liberal ministry, Lionel Bowen observing: 'It appears that whatever he does in this House, the Government takes fright.' With Bill Hayden underperforming as Labor leader, Hawke was an obvious replacement. Hayden, whom Hawke branded 'a lying cunt with a limited future', complained: 'I can't stand down for a bastard like Bob Hawke', but went just before the 1983 election which Labor duly won. Hawke held power for eight years, Labor's best run for half a century; he won three more elections, playing the environmental card in 1986 and 1990 when the economy was weak, with his brand of right-wing POPULISM displacing the Liberals as the natural party of government. Pursuing deregulatory economic policies that echoed THATCHERISM – floating the dollar, ending exchange controls and curbing the trade unions – he toned down Labor's anti-Americanism and held back the REPUBLICAN tide.

From 1988 he was dogged by the ambition of Paul KEATING to succeed him, and once Keating felt Hawke had broken the KIRIBILLI AGREEMENT to hand over to him, a showdown became a matter of time. Hawke won the first round in June 1991, but as the pressure built again Sen. Gareth Evans (*see* DRAFT; SODA) told him:

> Pull out, Digger. The dogs are pissing on your swag.

Hawke resigned, forced a CAUCUS vote on 19 December in the hope that the party wanted him back, and lost. As he left the LODGE, he observed: 'Eleven years ago I'd have been getting thoroughly drunk.' Hawke tried his hand as a TV interviewer; his debut, interviewing politicians he knew well in Britain's 1992 election, was shaky. He also entered business ventures with rich men he had got to know while in power; he showed lack of judgement in his choice, as several had been imprisoned or censured by the Costigan Commission on organised crime. He published memoirs notable for a series of vitriolic attacks on Keating, and shocked his backers in 1994 by leaving his wife Hazel, who had stuck by him for 38 years, for his biographer Blanche d'Alpuget.

> People, like china ornaments, bewilderingly came apart in his hands.
> BLANCHE D'ALPUGET, 1982

Hawke, who went to school in Perth with Rolf Harris, came to politics with a reputation as a philanderer, gambler and drinker: his feat of drinking a yard of ale in twelve seconds while a Rhodes Scholar at Oxford made it into the *Guinness Book of Records*. Most Australians took to the cricket-loving Hawke (*see also* FIRST BLOKE; SILVER BODGIE) as a 'bloke who will give me a fair shake', but his open style boiled over into tearful appearances on TV, notably in the 1984 election campaign after his daughter Roslyn's heroin addiction became public knowledge, confessing:

> I'd sacrificed my children to a considerable degree in the development of my career. There was a mixture of anguish for her [Roslyn] and guilt for myself.

> A lot of people believed I was weak not to exert greater authority over Keating. BOB HAWKE

> Malcolm Fraser had no small talk of any kind, but Hawke glad-handed everyone, including the Queen. MICHAEL DAVIE, *The Spectator*

> It really began in earnest when Bob stopped drinking in earnest. Then I knew that his ambition to be Prime Minister and the hopes of many people around him could be materialised.
> HAZEL HAWKE

hawks Active supporters of a war policy, and of a belligerent stand on other issues. The term originated with the **war hawks**, Thomas JEFFERSON's term for the party who in 1798 were pressing for conflict with Britain. It was used of Henry Clay, John C. Calhoun and their frontier supporters of the 1812 war with Britain, and of advocates of a military settlement of the 1840s dispute over the US border with Canada. 'Hawk' on its own – and its opposite, DOVE – dates from the VIETNAM WAR; it was popularised by Robert F. KENNEDY. A **chicken hawk** is a public figure who avoided being sent to Vietnam, yet has subsequently taken a hard line on foreign policy issues that could cost the lives of US troops.

Hay-Pauncefote Treaty The treaty signed by America and Britain in 1901 which freed each country from its pledge never to build a canal across Central America on its own or colonise any part of the region. It enabled America to build the PANAMA CANAL, provided all nations could have equal use, and created the CANAL ZONE. The **Hay-Herran Treaty** with Colombia, two years later, gave America a 99-year lease over the Zone. When the Colombian senate refused to RATIFY it, the province of Panama seceded and, with US support, formed a separate Republic which agreed to the creation of the Zone. The treaties with Britain, Colombia and Panama were all concluded by John Hay (1838–1905), Theodore ROOSEVELT's Secretary of State.

Hayes, Rutherford *See* OLD 8 TO 7.

Haymarket riot The outbreak of violence in Chicago on 4 May 1886 arising from a mass meeting of strikers at the McCormick Harvester Company. When police tried to break up the meeting, called to protest against their tactics, a bomb was thrown, killing seven police officers. Both sides opened fire, leaving two strikers dead and a number of police and civilians injured. The bomb-thrower was never found, but eight anarchists were convicted of inciting the crowd and four were hanged. The incident severely damaged the US labour movement, and began the eclipse of the KNIGHTS OF LABOR, even though they were not responsible for it.

Haynsworth nomination The first of President NIXON's defeats by the Senate over nominations to the SUPREME COURT. Federal appeal judge Clement Haynsworth Jr, a Southern Democrat, was Nixon's second nomination after Chief Justice Warren Burger as he moved to reverse the liberal thrust of the WARREN COURT. Nominated to replace the resigning Justice Abe FORTAS, Haynsworth was strongly opposed by CIVIL RIGHTS campaigners and organised labour for his views, but the Senate rejected him in 1969 by 55–45 because he had tried cases involving businesses in which he held small amounts of stock. It was only the second time in the 20th century that such a nomination had been rejected. Nixon fought hard to get Haynsworth confirmed, winning one senator's vote by channelling a $3 million urban grant through his office instead of that of the local Congressman.

Hays, Wayne Hays affair The scandal that erupted in 1976 after the *Washington Post* reported that Rep. Wayne Hays of Ohio, 65-year-old chairman of the House Administration Committee, had been keeping Elizabeth Ray, a former Virginia beauty queen, on the payroll of a subcommittee as a $14,000-a-year clerk in return for sexual favours. Miss Ray, 33, went to the paper after Hays suddenly remarried, telling her: 'You'll be Mistress #1.' She admitted: 'I can't type. I can't file. I can't even answer the phone', and said of Hays:

> He did to me what NIXON did to the country.

Hays was one of the most feared figures on Capitol Hill, but the scandal brought his resignation from CONGRESS. It triggered a rash of disclosures about other legislators, but the New York Congresswoman Bella Abzug was not among them. She said:

> I was never worried about any sex investigation in Washington. All the men on my staff can type.

Haywood case The trial in 1907 of three union leaders for allegedly assassinating former Idaho governor Frank Steuenberg, who was elected as a 'friend of miners' but called in the troops to Coeur d'Alène in 1899 to break a strike. A local man, Harry Orchard, confessed to the bombing and incriminated the 'inner circle' of the World Federation of Miners. Its secretary, Bill Haywood, president, Charles Moyer, and George Pettibone, a BLACKLISTed miner, were extradited to Idaho. The arrests produced a rare unity among US labour and socialist bodies, and a vigorous campaign was launched to save the three; President ROOSEVELT remarkably declared them to be 'undesirable citizens' before the case was heard. After a year on Death Row awaiting trial, they were acquitted following a brilliant eleven-hour defence speech from Clarence Darrow. *See also* DIRECT ACTION; WOBBLIES.

he. He asked to see me again. I think he wants me for my body The comment made by Ken Livingstone (*see* RED KEN), leader of the Greater London Council (GLC), c. 1981 after a meeting with Conservative Transport Secretary Norman Fowler to discuss his revolutionary 'Fares Fair' policy for the London Underground.

He is to the arts what James 'Bonecrusher' Smith is to lepidoptery One of the many derogatory remarks made during the 1980s by the Labour MP Tony Banks against Terry Dicks (1937–), right-wing Tory MP for Hayes and Harlington. Another, anonymous, Member said of Dicks: 'He was born ignorant and has been losing ground ever since.'

He may be a blackguard, but not a dirty blackguard The verdict of Sir Neville Henderson, pre-war British Ambassador in Berlin, on the leading NAZI Hermann Goering. Henderson's remark, in a speech at Sleaford, typified the views of a champion of APPEASEMENT.

He reminds every woman of her first husband A charge levelled against a number of US Presidential hopefuls, starting probably with Thomas DEWEY.

He seen his opportunities and he took 'em The epitaph on George Washington Plunkitt (1842–1924), a one-time butcher's boy of poor Irish stock who rose through mastery of TAMMANY HALL to become a millionaire. In 1870 he was drawing three salaries: as an assemblyman, alderman and police magistrate. His 'office' was an Italian's shoeshine stand in the basement of the old county court office.

He shines and stinks like rotten mackerel at moonlight The stinging insult delivered by John Randolph (1773–1833), Virginian leader of the JEFFERSONians in the HOUSE OF REPRESENTATIVES, against his political foe Edward Livingstone.

He that will not work shall not eate The charge made by Captain John Smith (1580–1631) in 1608 to the Jamestown colony of which he was governor. The phrase became the embodiment of the Protestant WORK ETHIC.

He thinks manual labour is a Spanish peasant The dismissive rebuke directed against an allegedly remote Conservative minister in the 1950s by the left-wing Labour MP Fenner (later Lord) Brockway (1888–1988).

He who is not with us is against us An axiom of STALIN's style of government, lifted from Christ's statement in *Luke* xi, 23 that 'He who is not with me is against me'. Stalin must have remembered it from his days as a seminarian – even if he forgot most of the other basics of Christianity. The Hungarian Communist leader Janos Kadar (1912–89) was also quoting Christ when he reversed the phrase to produce the less confrontational 'He who is not against us is with us'.

He would, wouldn't he The most celebrated saying from the PROFUMO AFFAIR. It was made on 29 June 1963 by the 19-year-old Many Rice-Davis when, during the trial of the osteopath Stephen Ward, she was told that Lord Astor had denied charges she had made.

head. head of Government A generic term covering PRIME MINISTERS in countries where there is a largely ceremonial monarch or President, and Presidents who themselves head the EXECUTIVE, as in the United States.

head of State The formal leader of a country, who may like Britain's sovereign wield only limited, though ultimate, power or who may, as with the French or American President, be in everyday political charge of the nation.

headbanger A UK phrase for a dogmatic left- or right-winger whose views are not only extreme but eccentric. The term originally applied in the 1970s to fans of heavy metal music who shook their heads violently in time to it.

Healey, Denis Winston (later Lord Healey, 1917–), a dominant and at times bruising Labour figure at WESTMINSTER for three decades, Defence Secretary and CHANCELLOR but never party leader. Yorkshire-born of Irish descent and educated at Oxford, Healey had a distinguished war record, serving as a beachmaster at Anzio, and made an impact when he addressed Labour's 1945 victory conference in his major's uniform. He graduated via TRANSPORT HOUSE to Parliament in 1952, and, despite having been a pre-war Communist, settled on the centre-right of the party as a foe of UNILATERALISM. Elected to the SHADOW CABINET in 1959, he served as Defence Secretary throughout the 1964–70 Labour government; PRAVDA branded him the 'atomic maniac', but his critical decisions were to abandon the TSR2 aircraft and Britain's commitments East of SUEZ. In 1974 WILSON made him Chancellor, and he survived a gruelling five years at the TREASURY. He confronted INFLATION nearing 30%, and weathered a party and Cabinet crisis over the spending cuts needed to secure a standby credit from the IMF. The Conservatives ridiculed him for dashing back from Heathrow en route for Manila to speak from the floor at Labour's conference.

With his beetling eyebrows, scorn for his critics as 'silly billies' and love of playing a pub piano on television, Healey became a national celebrity, carefully concealing a formidable intellect and a Milanese's love of opera. Lady Falkender (*see* FORKBENDER) termed him a 'political thug' and Roy JENKINS 'one of the most insensitive know-alls of British politics'; Simon Hoggart wrote: 'One feels that if he were ill, the Parliamentary Labour Party would agree to send a get-well card by 154 votes to 127 with 28 abstentions.' The comedian Bob Monkhouse was even blunter: 'I saw a headline which read: "Denis Healey caught with his pants down". That's a shame – it will make it easier to hear what he's saying.' But Healey was more than a match for his critics; he dismissed Sir Keith Joseph as 'a mixture of Hamlet, Rasputin and Tommy Cooper', and his assertion that he had been 'savaged by a DEAD SHEEP' did lasting damage to Sir Geoffrey HOWE.

By 1979 Healey, now Labour's deputy leader, had overcome the worst of inflation and edged toward MONETARISM, but his pay policy was derailed by the WINTER OF DISCONTENT. James CALLAGHAN told him he would stay on for eighteen months 'to take the shine off the ball for you', but by now the blustering Healey was loathed by the increasingly powerful left, who could not forgive him for the IMF cuts, and in 1980 Michael FOOT unexpectedly defeated him for the leadership. With the secession of Labour moderates to the SDP Healey, his power base weakened, fought back inside the party against unilateralism and the HARD LEFT, surviving by a whisker a 1981 deputy leadership challenge from Tony BENN. At the 1984 Chesterfield by-election when supposedly campaigning for Benn, he said in an ice-skating analogy:

> Healey without Benn would be like Torvill without Dean – I can't get the bugger off my back.

Healey stepped down as deputy leader in 1983, but remained Shadow Foreign Secretary until 1987, going to the LORDS in 1992. He had strong misgivings over the GULF WAR, and a decade later spoke out strongly against Tony BLAIR's commitment of British troops in support of America's IRAQ WAR.

Health Security President CLINTON's flagship health entitlement plan, worked up by his wife Hillary and launched in September 1993. It foundered on opposition in CONGRESS, and a feeling in some quarters that the FIRST LADY should not be involved in the legislative process.

Hear! Hear! The standard expression of agreement with a point made in Parliamentary debate, a gentlemanly alternative to applause. At WESTMINSTER it frequently comes out as a low rumble.

hearing A COMMITTEE session called to take evidence from one or more individuals or organisations, and to question them on it. Hearings are generally part of a process leading either to the CONFIRMATION of an office-holder, the production of a report or the approval of legislation.

heart. A heartbeat away from the Presidency *See* PRESIDENCY.

hearts and minds The securing by a combatant force, usually from another country, of the support of a civilian population. The phrase stemmed from the successful British campaign against Communist GUERRILLAS in Malaya after WORLD WAR II led by Field Marshal Sir Gerald Templar. It became the watchword of America's campaign to win the support of the people of South Vietnam for Western, democratic values and the rejection of Communism. Eventually it was the JOHNSON administration's failure to capture the hearts and minds of many Americans for its Vietnam policy that doomed the war effort. One reason may have been the attitude of the military, one of whom told a visiting journalist:

> Get them by the balls, and their hearts and minds will follow.

In the NIXON WHITE HOUSE, this became the motto of the WATERGATE PLUMBERS. Previously the phrase 'hearts and minds' was linked with President Theodore ROOSEVELT, who told the young Douglas MACARTHUR he had won the leadership of the nation through his ability 'to put into words what is in their hearts and minds but not in their mouths'.

Heath, Sir Edward Richard George (1916–2005), Prime Minister of the United Kingdom (Conservative) from 1970–74 and the leader who took Britain into Europe. Born in Kent and educated at Oxford – once dating Jane Wyman, who became Ronald REAGAN's first wife, on a US debating tour – Heath had a distinguished wartime Army career before becoming editor of the *Church Times*. Elected a Kent suburban MP in 1950, the technocratic Heath was a WHIP within a year, becoming Harold MACMILLAN's Chief Whip, and from 1959 Minister of Labour, LORD PRIVY SEAL and Trade and Industry Secretary. When SIR ALEC Douglas-Home resigned as Conservative leader in 1965, Heath stood in the party's first leadership election (*see* BERKELEY RULES) and won. Defeated convincingly by Harold WILSON in 1966 (*see* ACTION, NOT WORDS), he rebuilt the Tory team and unexpectedly defeated Wilson's bid for a third term in 1970; Wilson had scornfully dismissed him as

> A shiver looking for a spine to run up.

Memorable for his strangulated vowels, his heaving shoulders when amused and his nickname of the GROCER, the essentially liberal Heath came to office committed to an abrasive free-enterprise Toryism (*see* SELSDON MAN), but after two years refusing to support LAME DUCKS was forced to rescue the Rolls-Royce aero engine company by NATIONALising it. This original U-TURN led Norman Tebbit (*see* CHINGFORD SKINHEAD) to observe that 'his government rarely persisted with any of its announced policies once the going got tough – except on Europe', while Enoch POWELL maintained that 'he executed somersaults with the unselfconsciousness of the professional civil servant'. Powell added: 'Ted believes there is an answer to all problems which can be worked out by proper bureaucratic means.'

Heath's great achievement was to take Britain into the EUROPEAN COMMUNITY, the Treaty of ACCESSION taking effect at the start of 1973. He also had to confront the worst of terrorism in NORTHERN IRELAND, abolishing STORMONT and imposing DIRECT RULE by a UK CABINET MINISTER. He also had an almost Gallic commitment to visionary schemes: Concorde, the Channel Tunnel (begun, but cancelled by Labour) and an abortive plan for a London airport at Maplin in the Thames Estuary. Heath set out to reform the trade unions where Labour had failed with IN PLACE OF STRIFE, but his INDUSTRIAL RELATIONS ACT proved over-legalistic and unenforceable (*see* PENTONVILLE FIVE). There was also industrial strife, including a miners' strike in 1972 (*see* SALTLEY) over Heath's efforts to impose a tough PRICES AND INCOMES POLICY. After the U-turn Heath's government decided on a DASH FOR GROWTH, and briefly, during the BARBER BOOM of 1973, prosperity seemed at hand. Then the combination of rising inflation, an Arab oil embargo after the YOM KIPPUR WAR and a further miners' dispute threw the economy into reverse. The pit dispute escalated into a strike; Heath ordered the THREE-DAY WEEK, then, early in 1974, called an election on the theme of WHO GOVERNS BRITAIN? The gamble failed, the Conservatives losing their Commons majority and having to give up power after Heath failed to agree a COALITION with the Liberal leader Jeremy THORPE. That October Wilson went for an overall majority and Heath, advocating a GOVERNMENT OF NATIONAL UNITY, kept Labour's gains to a minimum. In February 1975 Heath submitted himself to re-election by his party's MPs; Margaret THATCHER stood against him while others held back and was elected on the second ballot. Heath had paid the price for his remoteness, Julian Critchley commenting:

> His parsimony when it came to handing out the twice-yearly honours to clapped-out MPs was bitterly resented . . . he was also reluctant to flatter the simple.

The fact and manner of his removal by an ungrateful party soured Heath, and the way Mrs Thatcher moved the party to the right outraged him. Penny Junor commented:

Ted Heath disliked two things above all else: people who disagreed with him, and women. Margaret Thatcher was both.

For fifteen years, until Mrs Thatcher's own overthrow in 1990, Heath glowered at her from the front bench BELOW THE GANGWAY, selectively pouring scorn on her economic policies and her strident attitude to Europe. Mrs Thatcher herself said:

When I look at him, and he looks at me, I don't feel that it is a man looking at a woman. More like a woman looking at another woman.

Heath's attitude aroused bitterness among Thatcherites, Robert Jones MP observing:

Margaret Thatcher and Ted Heath both have a great vision. The difference is that Margaret Thatcher has a dream that Britain will one day be great again, and Ted Heath has a vision that Ted Heath will one day be great again.

Nicholas Fairbairn, even more bluntly, called him 'a little boy sucking his misogynist thumb and blubbing and carping in the corner of the front bench below the gangway.' Heath bore the carping with a mixture of irascibility and humour. HECKLED when he attempted to put his views to the 1981 party conference, he told his audience:

Please don't applaud. It may irritate your neighbour.

Efforts to broker peace between Heath and Thatcher failed, and the stand-off did the party considerable damage. Yet Heath in the early 1980s had few supporters; at times it seemed he was welcome only in Beijing. Mrs Thatcher's keen supporter George Gardiner remarked that 'receiving support from him in a BY-ELECTION is like being measured by an undertaker'. Heath came in from the cold when John MAJOR succeeded Mrs Thatcher, though he raised hackles by visiting SADDAM HUSSEIN to urge the freeing of British hostages just before the GULF WAR. At the 1992 election he became FATHER OF THE HOUSE and a Knight of the GARTER, eventually standing down in 2001 after more than half a century in the Commons.

Heath was not only single-minded but the only single man in modern times to occupy NUMBER TEN; an anonymous wag said that 'every time Ted has a bath he looks down on the unemployed'. Heath himself said: 'PITT THE YOUNGER was a great British Prime Minister. He saved Europe from Napoleon. I don't know whether he could have done it any better or quicker had he been married.' He was also a keen yachtsman (*see* MORNING CLOUD), an accomplished organist and a competent orchestral conductor who recorded Elgar's *Cockaigne* overture. He once said:

Music means everything to me when I'm alone. And it's the best way of getting that bloody man Wilson out of my hair.

That grammar school twit.
ALF GARNETT (Warren Mitchell), *Till Death Us Do Part*, BBC Television, 1966

He became leader before his party was ready for him. JAMES MARGACH, *The Abuse of Power*

If only he had lost his temper in public the way he does in private, he would have become a more commanding and successful national leader.
WILLIAM DAVIS

He had some of the best ideas of any post-war Prime Minister. He was a very radical person.
Dr DAVID OWEN

A political giant. He was the first modern Conservative Leader and we are all in his debt.
MARGARET THATCHER on his death.

Heath: Other countries have far greater problems than we have.
James Wellbeloved MP (Lab.): No, they haven't. We've got you.

heavy manners The slogan adopted by the Jamaican Prime Minister Michael Manley (1923–97) during his unsuccessful RE-ELECTION campaign in 1980; it reflected the stiff austerity needed to pull the island out of economic crisis. Manley, son of Jamaica's independence premier Norman Manley, won power for his National People's Party on a radical socialist programme in 1972, and was re-elected in 1976, blaming rising unemployment on US efforts to DESTABILISE his regime. Defeated in 1980 and 1983 by Edward Seaga's Jamaica Labour Party, he returned on a LANDSLIDE in 1989 to follow more moderate policies, retiring in 1992.

heckling Barbed interruptions at a political meeting designed to throw speakers off their stride. Heckling is a tradition throughout the English-speaking world, but has been dealt a serious blow by the decline in large public meetings as television and tight security have taken over. In 1966 the US film-maker Joseph Strick took a crew to film the heckling at a number of British election meetings, prompting claims that he was encouraging such interruptions; the film he eventually produced was a showcase of politicians triumphing over hecklers and being severely rattled by them. The BBC attempted the same in the 2005 campaign, by which time public meetings were rarer and more orchestrated; the Conservatives made a formal complaint after three hecklers with microphones were detected at one of Michael HOWARD's rallies.

Most of the great recorded exchanges between hecklers and politicians (*see also* RHETORICAL QUESTION; REPARTEE) involve the rout of the heckler; one classic came when Richard NIXON told an interrupter: 'The jawbone of an ass is just as deadly as it was in Samson's time.' Others include:

Heckler: Vote for you? I'd rather vote for the Devil.
John WILKES: And what if your friend is not standing?

Heckler: Speak up! I can't hear you.
DISRAELI: Truth travels slowly, but it will reach you in time.

Heckler: Say Missus, how many toes are there on a pig's foot?
Nancy, Lady ASTOR: Take your boots off, man, and count them yourself.

CHURCHILL (when thrown a cabbage): I asked for the gentleman's ears, not his head.

Heckler: Rubbish!
Harold WILSON: I'll come to your special interest in a minute, Sir.

Heckler: What about VIETNAM?
WILSON: The Government has no plans to increase expenditure in Vietnam.

Heckler: Why are you talking to savages [in Rhodesia]?
WILSON: We don't talk to savages. We just let them come to our meetings.

Heckler: You are two-faced.
GEOFFREY DICKENS MP: Would I bear wearing this face if I had two?

NORMAN TEBBIT to heckler: Calm down, my lad.
Heckler: You're not my dad.
TEBBIT: I would quit while you're ahead, son. It's obvious I'm the only father you'll ever know.

Tory MP: I will have you know that I have asked no fewer than 97 Parliamentary Questions.
Heckler: Ignorant bastard!

MP to heckler: What if everybody was like you and the whole country decided to run away from its problems?
Heckler: At least we'd all be running in the same direction.

Yorkshire Labour candidate: When I am elected, I shall drive prostitution underground.
Heckler: Bloody Labour Party, pampering the miners again!

Heckler: War criminal!
New York Mayor Ed Koch: Fuck off!

Heckler: Pig!
RONALD REAGAN: I'm very proud to be called a pig. It stands for pride, integrity, guts.

Heckler: I wouldn't vote for you if you were St Peter.
Sir ROBERT MENZIES: If I were St Peter you wouldn't be in my CONSTITUENCY.

Heckler: Tell us what you know, Bob. It won't take long.
MENZIES: I'll tell you everything we both know. It won't take any longer.

Heckler: I could swallow you in one bite.
Saskatchewan Premier TOMMY DOUGLAS: If you did, you'd have more brains in your belly than in your head.

hedgers and ditchers The rival groups into which the Conservative majority in the HOUSE OF LORDS split in 1911 over the Liberal government's BILL to curtail the powers of the Upper House. The 'Hedgers' under Lord Lansdowne were prepared to acquiesce rather than risk the mass creation of Liberal peers to ensure the Bill's passage. The 'Ditchers' led by Lord Halsbury were prepared to die in the last ditch rather than yield. The Hedgers, the 'Judas Group', prevailed and the Bill passed by 131 votes to 114, ending the power of the Lords over MONEY BILLS and giving it a DELAYING POWER only over other legislation. *See also* MR BALFOUR'S POODLE; PARLIAMENT ACTS.

hegemony (1) Domination by one nation over others or over a region; Communist China consistently accused Soviet Russia of trying to exercise 'hegemony' over the rest of the socialist world. (2) The theory of the Italian ideologue Antonio Gramsci (1891–1937) that private 'civil society' exercises hegemony, while political society (the State) exercises domination, the effect being that the capitalist CONSENSUS structure is harder to destroy than the 'autocratic' state.

heir apparent The next in line for the THRONE, in the British monarchy the PRINCE OF WALES. In broader politics, the term applies to the apparently obvious successor to a leader.

Hell. Hell, no, we won't go One of the most popular chants against the VIETNAM WAR, especially those facing the DRAFT.

give 'em hell Harry *See* GIVE.

If Hitler invaded Hell . . . *See* HITLER.

I told them to go to Hell Mikhail GORBACHEV's account of what happened when the instigators of the August 1991 KREMLIN COUP came to see him, under house arrest in his Black Sea villa.

The farmers of Kansas must raise less corn and more hell The slogan of the POPULIST movement which arose in America's Midwest during the recession of 1892. It was coined in a speech in 1890 by the Irish-born farmers' leader Mary Ellen Lease, who also said:

> The people are at bay! Let the bloodhounds of money who have dogged us thus far beware!

You may all go to Hell. And I will go to Texas The embittered reaction of the frontiersman Davy Crockett (1786–1836) on losing his seat in CONGRESS. He fared even worse in Texas, perishing at the Alamo.

Helsinki. Helsinki accords or **Final Act** The unexpectedly positive outcome in 1975 of two years of negotiation by 35 nations on a Soviet initiative for a **European Agreement on Security and Co-Operation**, with special reference to confirming post-1945 frontiers. The Final Act included proposals to prevent accidental East-West confrontations, for economic and technical co-operation and reaffirming basic HUMAN RIGHTS. Helsinki backfired on the still repressive Soviet regime, with DISSIDENTS forming a group to monitor its own observance of human rights, and CHARTER 77 in Czechoslovakia following suit. Out of Helsinki grew the OSCE mechanism for confidence-building and averting conflict in Europe, which has outlasted the COLD WAR.

Helsinki summit The SUMMIT in September 1990 between George BUSH and Mikhail GORBACHEV which showed an unprecedented closeness between the SUPERPOWERS. The first to be convened as the result of an international crisis since the end of the COLD WAR, it ended with both leaders pledging themselves to any action, including force, to remove SADDAM HUSSEIN's invading forces from Kuwait; the GULF WAR followed.

hemicycle A semi-circular chamber designed for a Continental-style, NON-ADVERSARIAL legislature. The term is used particularly of the chamber in Strasbourg where the EUROPEAN PARLIAMENT holds most of its plenary sessions; it is also used by the COUNCIL OF EUROPE. There is a further hemicycle in Brussels, where most MEPs would prefer to meet.

Henry VIII clause At WESTMINSTER, a CLAUSE or SECTION of a BILL or ACT that allows parts of itself to be AMENDED or REPEALED by STATUTORY INSTRUMENT rather than by further PRIMARY LEGISLATION, and in some situations without Parliamentary scrutiny. Such clauses take their name from the 1539 Statute of Limitations, which gave Henry VIII power to legislate by proclamation. Pioneered in the 1990 Criminal Justice Bill, which allowed offences to be added or removed by instrument, the process was institutionalised in the Regulatory Reform Act of 2001 – provided the change would not remove necessary protection from the public.

Hepburn Act The legislation passed by the US Congress in 1906 which greatly increased the powers of the Interstate Commerce Commission, giving it the benefit of the doubt in disputes with the railroads and so subjecting the railroads to effective regulation for the first time. It gave the ICC power to reduce unreasonably high and discriminatory rates, subject to JUDICIAL REVIEW, and barred the railroads from transporting goods in whose production they had an interest.

Herbert Divorce Act The 1937 **Matrimonial Causes Act,** a divorce reform measure originating in a Private Member's BILL from the humorist, writer and Independent MP Sir A. P. Herbert (1890–1971). It extended the grounds for divorce to include desertion (for more than three years), insanity (of over five years' duration) and cruelty. It made adultery by a husband as great a cause for divorce as adultery by a wife, and made it possible for a wife to divorce her husband for rape, sodomy or bestiality.

here. Here, borrow these The words of a Birmingham councillor c. 1979, offering his false teeth to a woman who said she could not go to vote because she had lost hers.

here we go again, with both feet planted firmly in the air The scathing comment of Hugh (later Lord) Scanlon (1913–2004), President of Britain's Amalgamated Union of Engineering Workers, in 1973 on his union's attitude to joining the EUROPEAN COMMUNITY. *See also* Get your TANKS off my lawn.

Here we go, here we go, here we go! The song of the Yorkshire MINERS as they spearheaded their union's year-long strike in 1984–85. Set to the tune 'The STARS AND STRIPES Forever', the words were repeated for each line. The chant was taken up by other left-wing demonstrators and by football supporters.

Heritage Foundation A campaigning right-wing THINK TANK and pressure group formed in Washington in the early 1970s by the former Capitol Hill staffers Frank Weyrich and Ed Feulner. Its aim was to achieve rapid political gains by feeding ideas directly to conservative groups and receptive members of CONGRESS. It was one of the most effective elements in the new RIGHT, which capped the election of Ronald REAGAN with a radical agenda. It remained an ideological force throughout the 1980s, and the conservatism of George W. BUSH and those around him is in part its legacy.

Herrenvolk The German word meaning broadly 'master race', which in NAZI usage implied the superiority of the German peoples.

Herri Batasuna *See* BATASUNA.

Heseltine, Michael Ray Dibdin (later Lord; 1933–). The charismatic Swansea-born publishing millionaire on the left of the CONSERVATIVE PARTY who was for a generation the Tories' most effective and shameless campaigner. At various stages of his career he was known as GOLDILOCKS, TARZAN and finally HEZZA. A junior Minister throughout the HEATH government, he held senior posts under Margaret THATCHER until WESTLAND, returning to John MAJOR's CABINET as Environment Secretary, President of the Board of Trade and then DEPUTY PRIME MINISTER after bringing about her downfall. She described the INTERVENTIONIST Heseltine as 'not ONE OF US', but he always insisted: 'I was never a WET in the soft sense'. His high profile as Mrs Thatcher's Environment Secretary trying to revive Merseyside and as Defence Secretary, earned him mixed reviews. The Lebanese Druze militia leader Walid Jumblatt described him to Neil KINNOCK as 'How do you say it? A pryke?' But he turned back the tide against UNILATERALISM before dramatically resigning in January 1986 over WESTLAND. His biographer, the fellow Conservative MP Julian Critchley, wrote:

> The Celt had taken over from the calculator. Samson-like, he kicked out at the columns of the temple, bringing the roof down upon the head of the Prime Minister and burying them both in the rubble.

Heseltine insisted in the autumn of 1989:

> I can foresee no circumstances in which I would allow my name to be put forward for the leadership of the Conservative Party.

But a year later, as controversy grew over Mrs Thatcher's European policies following Sir Geoffrey HOWE's dramatic resignation speech, he announced:

> I am persuaded now that I have a better prospect than Mrs Thatcher of leading the Conservatives to a fourth election victory and preventing the ultimate calamity of a Labour government.

His challenge forced her from office, but did not win him the leadership; he later said: 'He who wields the dagger never wears the crown.' He pledged his loyalty to Major and returned to the Cabinet as Environment Secretary, President of the Board of Trade – in which capacity he promised in 1993 to INTERVENE before breakfast, before tea, before lunch and before dinner', then announced the closure of 31 coal mines – and, after Major saw off a right-wing challenge with his help in 1995, Deputy Prime Minister. He left the Commons in 2001, a heart condition having ruled out a further challenge for the leadership after Major's heavy defeat in 1997.

Heseltine's strength was his mesmeric hold over Conservative Party conferences, which he exercised though his oratory. Simon Hoggart described him as 'rabble-rouser to the gentry', but a Cabinet colleague remarked: 'He may have the looks of Adonis, but he has a mind like Hampstead Garden Suburb.' After he brandished the MACE in 1976 in protest at the NATIONALISATION of aircraft and shipbuilding, Critchley wrote: 'If it is necessary in politics to demonstrate that one has passion and vulgarity, Michael demonstrated that he had both.' Whenever he could, he would escape to cultivate the arboretum at his Northamptonshire home, but landed Tories would point out that inside the house, 'all the furniture is bought.'

> He tends not to be able to see a parapet without ducking below it . . . doing his famous impression of Clint Eastwood playing Mussolini.
>
> JULIAN CRITCHLEY

> He knows where to find the clitoris of the Conservative Party. NOEL PICARDA

> The Kama Sutra of the Conservative Party. He's been in every position except Number Ten.
>
> JOHN PRESCOTT

Hess Mission The bizarre solo flight to Scotland in May 1941 by HITLER's deputy **Rudolf Hess** (1894–1987), apparently to discuss peace terms with the Duke of Hamilton whom he had met at the 1936 Berlin Olympics. Hess was captured and detained in the Tower of London, the last prisoner to be held there; Berlin Radio announced that the Deputy FÜHRER had been suffering from 'hallucinations'. In May 1946 the WAR CRIMES judges at NUREMBERG rejected his plea of insanity, and Hess was sentenced to life imprisonment. He was held in Berlin's Spandau Prison, from 1966 as the sole occupant, until his death, allegedly committing suicide. The last Nazi detainee acquired the nickname **Prisoner of Spandau**, because some CONSPIRACY THEORISTS believed, on the basis of discrepancies in the medical records, that he was not Hess but a 'double' substituted by the Nazis prior to his flight or later by the Allies.

> One of those cases where imagination . . . is baffled by the facts as they present themselves.
>
> CHURCHILL

Hezbollah (Arab. Party of God) The militant Iranian-backed SHI'ITE Muslim militia, formed in 1982 with the aim of setting up an Islamic state in the Lebanon, destroying Israel and reclaiming Jerusalem for Islam. Led by Sheikh Hassan Nasrullah, it spread quickly from South Lebanon, where it harassed occupying Israeli forces, to Beirut where it conducted a campaign of HOSTAGE-taking against Westerners. In 1985 members of Hezbollah hijacked a jet with 104 American passengers aboard after takeoff from Athens, killing a US naval diver; the final 39 hostages were released after seventeen days, in return for the subsequent release of over 700 mostly Shi'ite Lebanese and Palestinian detainees. Hezbollah scaled down its military activities after the Israeli withdrawal from South Lebanon in 2000, but revived in 2002 when Israel began fresh incursions into Palestinian territory.

Hezza The final nickname in a long career (*see also* GOLDILOCKS; TARZAN) of Michael HESELTINE, as the ouster of Margaret THATCHER and DEPUTY PRIME MINISTER to John MAJOR. It is a 1990s corruption of his surname, echoing 'Gazza', universal nickname of the England footballer Paul Gascoigne.

HHS Health and Human Services. The department of the US Federal Government that has overseen all government agencies concerned with the health, social and economic welfare of the people since President CARTER created a separate Department of Education in 1980. Its predecessor, the Department of Health, Education and Welfare (**HEW**) had been founded in 1953.

high. High Commissioner (1) The principal representative of one COMMONWEALTH country in the capital of another, on a par with an AMBASSADOR. (2) The world's pre-eminent figure in the monitoring and assistance of refugees is the UN **High Commissioner for Refugees**.

High Contracting Parties The formal diplomatic term used in TREATIES to describe the nations who have concluded the agreement.

high crimes and misdemeanours One of the grounds for IMPEACHMENT, which has been listed in such proceedings on both sides of the Atlantic since the trial of Warren Hastings in 1788–95.

high ground, to take the To set out the terms of a political debate by taking a morally unimpeachable position.

High Representative The senior functionary given charge of implementing the EUROPEAN UNION's Common Foreign and Security Policy in the wake of the MAASTRICHT TREATY. The first occupant of the post was Javier Solana, the Spanish former SECRETARY GENERAL of NATO. Creation of the post deprived the EU's own Commissioner for External Affairs, then the UK's Chris Patten, of most meaningful aspects of his job. The term is also used for the UNITED NATIONS' custodian of the peace settlement in Bosnia-Herzegovina, since 2002 Lord Ashdown (*see* PADDY PANTSDOWN).

Highgate Cemetery The Victorian cemetery in north-central London where Karl MARX is buried, his grave being a place of pilgrimage for Marxists from throughout the world.

hijacking A common and effective form of political attention-seeking, involving the seizure of an aircraft in flight and the taking hostage of its passengers. In more innocent times the perpetrators aimed for a safe landing, maybe even a welcome, in a country where they would not be punished; since 9/11 there exists the ghastly possibility that the hijackers may use the aircraft as a bomb. The origin of the word is obscure but H. L. Mencken listed it as US criminal slang. It first achieved a political dimension on 1 May 1961 when a National Airlines plane bound for Miami was hijacked to Cuba by an armed passenger. A rash of political misfits and criminals in America began commandeering airliners on internal flights and ordering the pilot at gunpoint to fly to Cuba; that September President KENNEDY made hijacking a Federal crime punishable by death. It has since become the stock-in-trade of Arab terrorists and their European and Japanese associates, and of disturbed people evading lax airport security.

Hill, the (1) Washington shorthand for CAPITOL HILL, and for all the activities of Congress that take place there. As in 'he's worked on the Hill for 15 years', or 'she's been posted to their Washington bureau to cover the Hill'. (2) The Capitol newspaper claiming the largest circulation.

Him and Her The two beagles which President Lyndon JOHNSON picked up by their ears on the WHITE HOUSE lawn in 1964 while entertaining bankers. Self-styled arbiters of Washington taste seized on the episode as proof of LBJ's Texan gaucheness and social unacceptability.

Hinduja passport affair. The apparent scandal that precipitated the resignation of Peter Mandelson (*see* BOBBY) from Tony BLAIR'S CABINET, as NORTHERN IRELAND Secretary on 24 January 2001. Gopichand and Srichand Hinduja were wealthy Indian brothers resident in the UK who had offered to underwrite the £6 million cost of the 'faith zone' of the Millennium Dome when Mandelson was responsible for it (*see* DOME SECRETARY). It was alleged, and never entirely disproved, that Mandelson had intervened with a Home Office Minister to fast-track the Hindujas' applications for UK citizenship. A previous application to the Conservative government had been stalled because of the Hindujas' alleged involvement in India's BOFORS SCANDAL. When the story broke, prompting accusations of Labour 'SLEAZE', Blair asked Mandelson – who had first left the government over the ROBINSON LOAN – to resign again, though he later conceded there may not have been adequate grounds for this. Within four years, Blair had nominated Mandelson to the EUROPEAN COMMISSION.

Hiroshima The Japanese city and military base virtually obliterated on 6 August 1945 by the first ATOMIC BOMB ever dropped in warfare, as America sought to hasten the end of WORLD WAR II. Over 160,000 people, the vast majority civilians, were incinerated or suffered terrible burns, and many more doomed to ultimately fatal radiation sickness. President TRUMAN justified the attack by asserting that 'military objectives and soldiers and sailors are the target, and not women and children'. The flash of the explosion was seen 170 miles away, and a MUSHROOM CLOUD of black smoke rose over where the city had stood to a height of 40,000 feet. Hiroshima – and NAGASAKI, which was also destroyed by a US atomic bomb before Japan surrendered – remains a solemn and humbling warning of the fate confronting mankind in the event of nuclear war, and a powerful symbol for advocates of NUCLEAR DISARMAMENT.

> Sixteen hours ago an American airplane dropped one bomb on Hiroshima . . . It is a harnessing of the basic power of the universe; the force from which the sun draws its powers has been loosened against those who brought the war to the Far East. President TRUMAN, 6 August 1945

> We have resolved to endure the unendurable and suffer what is intolerable.
> Emperor HIROHITO

> The genius of Einstein leads to Hiroshima.
> PABLO PICASSO

his. His Accidency The nickname accorded to Chester Arthur (*see* ELEGANT ARTHUR) by his critics when he succeded to the Presidency in 1881 on the ASSASSINATION of President Garfield. It was applied again 20 years later when Theodore ROOSEVELT became President on McKinley's assassination; 'TEDDY' was upset by such references and resolved to win a Presidential term in his own right which – unlike Arthur – he did.

His chain gang Excellency The title accorded by Harold L. Ickes, Secretary of the Interior throughout Franklin D. ROOSEVELT's presidency, to the UNRECONSTRUCTED Governor Talmadge of Georgia.

His Fraudulency The title bestowed on Rutherford Hayes (*see* OLD 8 TO 7) by opponents who never forgave him or the Republican CONGRESS for depriving Samuel Tilden, who appeared to have beaten him convincingly, of the presidency in 1876. They also called him **Rutherfraud Hayes**.

His Highness the President of the United States, and Protector of their Liberties The original title chosen by the US SENATE for the head of the new nation; they abandoned it when the HOUSE OF REPRESENTATIVES insisted on his simply being called 'President'.

His Rotundity The nickname accorded by Ralph Izard, one of the first US Senators, to Vice President John ADAMS because of his love of pomp and titles; another suggestion was **His Superfluous Excellency**.

His/Her Royal Highness A courtesy form of title for the closest relatives of a monarch, confined in the UK since 1917 to the children of the sovereign, grandchildren in the male line, the wives of sons and male line grandsons and the eldest son of the eldest son of the PRINCE OF WALES. Following the ABDICATION of Edward VIII in 1936, he was denied his wish that Wallis Simpson, the woman for whom he had given up the throne, should be styled 'Her Royal Highness' as well as Duchess of Windsor. Similarly on her divorce from Prince Charles three decades later, Princess Diana retained the title 'Princess of Wales' but without the **'HRH'**.

His Shadowship The nickname gained by the CIVIL RIGHTS campaigner the Rev. Jesse Jackson (1941– , *see also* RAINBOW COALITION) after his election as 'Shadow Senator' for the DISTRICT OF COLUMBIA in 1990. The District has a non-voting DELEGATE to CONGRESS and no representation in the Senate, and Jackson was elected unofficially to keep a watching brief – gaining a new power base in the process.

Hiss case The case in 1948–50 involving alleged espionage by a Communist sympathiser in the State Department, which made Richard NIXON's name and paved the way for MCCARTHYISM. It also led to a series of Congressional investigations into the Department that profoundly embarrassed the TRUMAN ADMINISTRATION and SECRETARY OF STATE Dean Acheson. It stemmed from allegations against **Alger Hiss** (1904–96), a former official at State, by Whittaker Chambers, an ex-Communist and former editor of *Time* magazine, before the House Committee on UN-AMERICAN ACTIVITIES. Nixon, a member of the committee, pursued the allegations with tenacity. Hiss strenuously denied them, and in August 1948 sued Chambers for slander. When challenged for supporting evidence, Chambers produced copies of classified State Department papers he claimed had come from Hiss. Chambers even led investigators to his Maryland farm, where he produced three rolls of microfilm hidden in a pumpkin – the infamous 'pumpkin papers'. Hiss was indicted and appeared before a grand jury on charges of perjury for his denial of passing papers to Chambers. The trial resulted in a hung jury, but at a retrial in January 1950 – the month before McCarthy opened his campaign – Hiss was convicted and jailed for five years; he was released in 1954. Many believed Hiss a victim of the anti-Communist hysteria then sweeping America; Hiss himself would like to have been seen as America's DREYFUS, and won reinstatement to the Massachusetts bar after WATERGATE. But he was probably righly convicted; just before Hiss' death the NATIONAL SECURITY AGENCY declassified cables which concluded post-YALTA that the Soviet agent 'Ales' was 'probably Alger Hiss'.

history. history will absolve me! (Sp. *La historia me absolvera!)* The declaration made by Fidel Castro at his trial in July 1953 for leading an attack on the Moncada barracks in an attempt to overthrow the Bastista regime.

history will never forgive us The keynote of Tony BLAIR's speech to both Houses of the US CONGRESS on 17 July 2003, in which he asserted that even if SADDAM HUSSEIN were found not to have had WEAPONS OF MASS DESTRUCTION, the atrocities he had committed against his own people were ample ground for his removal by US and British forces. Blair received seventeen standing ovations during his speech, which combined support for the American way with an appeal to respect Europe's priorities on such issues as the environment and world trade. Unbeknown to him, David KELLY had already disappeared and the discovery of his body the following day would land Blair in a serious political crisis.

dustheap of history *See* MENSHEVIKS.

I shall not fail before the bar of history, and it is there that I demand to be heard The challenge laid down by President Adolphe Thiers (1797–1877) to the French CHAMBER OF DEPUTIES on 24 May 1873 when facing the CONFIDENCE motion that led to his resignation.

today I am a trillionth part of history The claim made by Arthur Bremer (1950–) after his attempt to assassinate Governor George Wallace of Alabama in a Laurel, Maryland shopping mall on 15 May 1972. Bremer, who had stalked Wallace throughout the Democratic primary campaign, fired several shots at Wallace which left him paralysed; he had to abandon his campaign for the Presidency, but stayed on as Governor.

Hitler, Adolf (1889–1945) The Austrian-born painter who led the NAZI party to power, declared himself FÜHRER of the German people, inaugurated the THIRD REICH, imposed a repressive regime at home and the HOLOCAUST across Europe as he triggered WORLD WAR II and embarked on a programme of conquest that embraced France, the Low Countries, Poland and the Balkans, threatened Britain and brought German troops to the heart of STALINGRAD. Hitler's belief in his destiny developed at the end of WORLD WAR I, in which he won two Iron Crosses with the Bavarian Army and was temporarily blinded in a gas attack. Already steeped in the ANTI-SEMITIC culture of Vienna, he became convinced that Germany had not been militarily defeated but had been betrayed by its leaders, and joined the fiercely anti-Bolshevik German

Workers' Party as its seventh member. In 1921 he ousted the Munich locksmith Martin Dexter as leader of what was now the NATIONAL SOCIALIST German Workers' Party (NSDAP), and began his hypnotic campaign against Marxism and the TREATY OF VERSAILLES. After the failure of the MUNICH BEER HALL PUTSCH in 1923, he was imprisoned for nine months with Rudolf HESS, using the time to dictate the text of MEIN KAMPF, the book that presaged uncannily the policies he would eventually follow. On his release he began cultivating German industrialists, who regarded him as a bulwark against revolution, and in 1926, as the NAZIS' violent confrontations with Communists increased, he formed the SS as his personal force. Hitler's support increased rapidly with the onset of the GREAT DEPRESSION, and with the Nazis close to a majority in the REICHSTAG he mounted a campaign for the Presidency in 1932, polling strongly against Hindenburg. Of his campaigning technique he was to write:

> I learned the use of terror from the Communists, of slogans from the Catholic church, and the use of PROPAGANDA from the democracies.

By now the WEIMAR REPUBLIC was floundering, not least because of Nazi DESTABILISATION, and in January 1933 Hindenburg – who privately referred to Hitler as 'that Bohemian corporal' – finally appointed him CHANCELLOR. The REICHSTAG fire gave him the pretext to suppress all other political parties, and in June 1934 he eliminated his rivals within the movement, including his veteran colleague Ernst Röhm, in the NIGHT OF THE LONG KNIVES.

As *Führer* he set in motion a programme of rapid rearmament and systematic violations of Versailles. When his REMILITARISATION of the Rhineland in 1936 proved to him that Britain and France would not baulk him, he began the systematic persecution of political opponents and Jews, and started an aggressive programme of territorial expansion. This began with the ANSCHLUSS with Austria in March 1938 and the steadily annexation of Czechoslovakia, starting notoriously with the MUNICH AGREEMENT that September. The stop-go nature of Hitler's advance in the face of APPEASEMENT lulled many abroad into a false sense of security; Beverly Nichols wrote:

> Herr Hitler has one of the endearing characteristics of Ferdinand the Bull. Just when the crowd expects him to be most violent, he stops and smells the flowers.

Sir John Simon, after meeting Hitler, concluded:

> If Joan of Arc had been born in Austria and had borne a moustache, she might have conveyed much the same impression.

LLOYD GEORGE, also briefly captivated by him, had declared: 'I don't think Hitler is a fool; he is not going to challenge the British Empire,' but he and others changed their tune as the threat became obvious. Hitler alarmed the West by forming the PACT OF STEEL with Italy, though Alan Bullock was to write: 'He showed surprising loyalty to Mussolini (*see* DUCE), but it never extended to trusting him.' He also provided effective help to the Nationalists in the SPANISH CIVIL WAR, though when he eventually met General Franco (who was to keep out of World War II) he said: 'Rather than go through that again, I would prefer to have three or four of my teeth yanked out.' In August 1939 he concluded the NAZI-SOVIET PACT to pre-empt Russia from joining forces against him with Britain and France, and within ten days invaded Poland. The exiled Kaiser Wilhelm II warned:

> The machine is running away with him as it ran away with me.

His initial successes were devastating: Poland overcome in days, Norway the following spring, and then the BLITZKRIEG that rolled up the Low Countries and France and brought German troops to the English Channel. CHURCHILL, who viewed Hitler as 'that bloodthirsty guttersnipe' and 'Herr SCHICKLGRUBER', became Prime Minister and a personal duel to the death began. Thwarted in his invasion plans by the *Luftwaffe*'s failure to win the Battle of Britain, Hitler resorted to the bombing of British cities, and the following spring turned eastward to take Yugoslavia and Greece after a botched Italian invasion before launching his offensive against Russia. By the end of the year he was at the gates of Moscow and Leningrad, and for the next two years was in sight of toppling STALIN, but the line held and eventually the RED ARMY began moving remorselessly west as German forces took huge casualties. With the turn of the tide, Hitler's insane genius as a gambler turned against him, as did those generals who had never been comfortable with Nazi ideology and the atrocities they knew the regime was committing; up to then they had always been subdued by success and by Hitler's towering rages when anyone ventured to disagree. On 20 July 1944 the STAUFFENBERG PLOT came within an ace of killing him; badly shaken, he reacted with bloody retribution (*see* PEOPLE'S COURTS). Always dependent on drugs, his need increased as defeat drew near, and at the end he gathered his entourage around him in his Berlin BUNKER, married his lover Eva Braun, helped her take poison, and then shot himself; their bodies were burned in the yard of the CHANCELLERY. Instead of a Reich to last a thousand years, Hitler left behind a Germany shattered by war which was to be divided by its conquerors, the Bolsheviks he had fought so passionately rampant in eastern Europe, and the stain of the worst campaign of GENOCIDE the world has ever seen.

> I believe that I am acting in accordance with the will of the Almighty Creator – by defending myself against the Jew, I am fighting for the work of the Lord. HITLER, *Mein Kampf*

> I could not bear it if I ever had to despair of this man. This man has everything needed to be King.
> JOSEF GOEBBELS, *Diaries*

> If Hitler had put his energies into promoting nuclear physics instead of persecuting the Jews, the first atomic bomb could well have exploded over London instead of Hiroshima.
> DAVID IRVING, *The Virus House*

> The people Hitler never understood, and whose actions continued to exasperate him to the end of his life, were the British.
> ALAN BULLOCK, *Hitler: A Study in Tyranny*

Hitler has missed the bus One of the worst recorded examples of political timing: Neville CHAMBERLAIN's complacent speech on 4 April 1940 declaring that Germany had lost the initiative in WORLD WAR II. Five days later Hitler invaded Norway; the BLITZKRIEG followed and by mid-May Chamberlain was out of office. Chamberlain told the Conservative CENTRAL COUNCIL:

> Whatever may be the reason – whether it was that Hitler thought he might get away with what he had got without fighting for it, or whether it was that after all the preparations were not sufficiently complete – however, one thing is certain: he missed the bus.

Hitler Youth (Ger. *Hitler Jugend*) The main boys' organisation of NAZI Germany. Established in 1933 to encompass all the country's existing youth clubs; its equivalent for girls was the League of German Girls (*Bund Deutscher Mädel*). In 1935 Baldur von Schirach was appointed REICH Youth Leader, and the following year all other youth organisations were banned. The Hitler Youth embodied the vehement anti-intellectualism of the FÜHRER, who wanted its members to be 'swift as the greyhound, tough as leather and hard as Krupp steel'. Boys were admitted to the Hitler Youth at fourteen, normally after three or more years in its junior division, the *Deutsches Jungvolk* (German Young People). At eighteen they graduated to the NATIONAL SOCIALIST Party, and so into the adult echelons of Nazism, having been INDOCTRINATED by Hitler's demented philosophy.

If Hitler invaded Hell, I would make at least a favourable reference to the Devil in the House of Commons CHURCHILL's explanation, in his book *The Grand Alliance*, of his readiness to give STALIN his full support after Hitler invaded Russia in June 1941. Echoing the speech he made at the time, he wrote:

> I have only one purpose, the destruction of Hitler, and my life is much simplified thereby.

Hizbollah *See* HEZBOLLAH.

Hizzoner A colloquial name for the Mayor of any major American city, and specifically of New York; it is a corruption of 'His Honour'.

HMG *See* Her Majesty's GOVERNMENT.

Ho Chi Minh. Ho Chi Minh City The name given by the victorious North Vietnamese to Saigon, formerly capital of South Vietnam, after its fall on 30 April 1975 – the final action of the VIETNAM WAR. Ho Chi Minh (1890–1969), a founder-member of the French Communist Party and President of North Vietnam from 1954 to 1969, had led the struggle first against the Japanese, then the VIET MINH against the French and finally the North Vietnamese/VIET CONG campaign to defeat the South and its US allies.

Ho Chi Minh Trail A network of routes running south from North Vietnam, through eastern Laos into Cambodia and South Vietnam, along which the VIET CONG moved GUERRILLAS and military hardware to supply their campaign in the south. The trail, parts of which date back to the late 1940s, comprises a mixture of footpaths, tracks and roads through the mountains and jungles, largely built and maintained by manual labour. Some stretches were suitable for trucks, but most were passable only by bullock cart, by bicycle or on foot. Supplies could take up to six months to pass the full length of the trail. Despite intensive US bombing and efforts by the South Vietnamese army to cut their supply lines, the North Vietnamese and Viet Cong kept the trail open throughout the war; this proved a crucial factor in their ultimate victory.

Ho, Ho, Ho Chi Minh! One of the most provocative chants of America's anti-VIETNAM WAR demonstrators, not only opposing US involvement in the war but actually encouraging the other side.

Hoare-Laval Pact One of the first acts of APPEASEMENT in the years prior to WORLD WAR II: secret proposals for ending the conflict caused by Italy's invasion of Abyssinia (Ethiopia) in 1935, formulated that December by the UK Foreign Secretary Samuel Hoare and his French counterpart Pierre Laval. They granted substantial territorial concessions to Italy, plus a zone of exclusive economic interest; the LEAGUE OF NATIONS would protect Abyssinian sovereignty over remaining areas. The pact was LEAKed to the press on 9 December, causing a storm of protest in Britain. By 18 December the British government had been forced to repudiate the pact, and Hoare resigned, to be succeeded by Anthony EDEN; Laval was executed as a COLLABORATOR by the French after the war. Unhindered and with the League unable to enforce effective SANCTIONS, Mussolini (*see* DUCE) proceeded to complete the conquest of Abyssinia and form the AXIS with Germany.

> No more coals to Newcastle – no more Hoares to Paris.
> KING GEORGE V

holdover An official in the US government who attempts to hang on to his or her job after a change of administration, despite being a POLITICAL APPOINTEE of the outgoing President. Only occasionally are such appointees asked to stay on by the new administration, so during a TRANSITION period there is a rush by those who want to stay put to have themselves reclassified as career civil servants. Few succeed, but it can take the best part of a year to prise out the most determined.

Hollingworth resignation The enforced departure on 25 May 2003 of Peter Hollingworth (1935–), GOVERNOR-GENERAL of Australia, following protracted controversy over his failure when Archbishop of Brisbane to take action over the case of a paedophile priest. His resignation was delayed and the crisis deepened by an unrelated rape allegation from many years before which he strongly denied and which was dismissed by a court, the accuser having just died in a car crash. Dr Hollingworth said that although the allegations against him of covering up for the priest were 'misplaced and unwarranted', the point had been reached where he could not uphold the integrity of his office. *Compare* KERR SACKING.

Hollywood. Hollywood East A derogatory name for WASHINGTON during the REAGAN presidency, with movie stars regular visitors at the WHITE HOUSE and the public face of the presidency orientated strongly toward television (*see* GREAT COMMUNICATOR; Video PRESIDENCY).

Hollywood Ten The group of ten screenwriters, film producers and directors who refused to confirm or deny their affiliation to the US Communist Party during the investigations of the House Un-AMERICAN ACTIVITIES Committee in 1947. They were Alvah Bessie, Herbert Biberman, Lester Cole, Edward Dymytryk, Ring Lardner Jr, John Howard Lawson, Albert Maltz, Sam Ornitz, Adrian Scott and Dalton Trumbo. All were briefly imprisoned for contempt of court in 1950, and on their release were BLACKLISTED and unable to work in Hollywood for several years as MCCARTHYISM thrived; some never returned to the industry.

Holocaust (Gr. *Holos*, whole; *kaustos*, burnt) The extermination of 6 million Jews in CONCENTRATION and death CAMPS by the NAZIS under HITLER between 1940 and 1945, a crime whose enormity has barely been grasped by humanity, yet which has prompted both the existence and HAWKISH policies of the state of ISRAEL, and post-war Germany's reluctance to flex its muscles on the world stage. Holocaust Day is observed in Israel on 27 Nisan (19 or 20 April). The word originally referred to a sacrifice to the Greek gods in which the victim was burned whole. It has now come to mean slaughter, destruction or GENOCIDE on an immense scale, especially by fire, and has also been applied to NUCLEAR WARfare. *See also* EICHMANN TRIAL; FINAL SOLUTION.

> There are many ways of not burdening one's conscience, of shunning responsibility, looking away, keeping silent. When the unspeakable truth of the holocaust became known at the end of the war, all too many of us claimed that they had not known anything about it, or even suspected anything. Whoever refuses to remember the inhumanity is prone to new risks of infection.
> RICHARD VON WEIZÄCKER, President of West Germany, on the 40th anniversary of the end of WORLD WAR II, 1985

Holt drowning The mysterious death of Australia's Liberal prime minister Harold Holt on 17 December 1967, which gave rise to intense speculation over his fate. Holt, a strong swimmer, went into the water off

Cheviot Beach in Victoria, on a coastline hazardous to bathers. The sea 'churned up' around him and he disappeared; no body was ever found. The premier's death caused political turmoil, and speculation about sharks and suicide. The most remarkable theory came fifteen years later, in Anthony Grey's book *The Prime Minister was a Spy*; according to Grey, Holt had swum out to a submarine and been spirited away to Communist China, having completed a nefarious career on behalf of Mao's (*see* CHAIRMAN MAO) regime. The theory was based on Holt's evident desire to accommodate Chinese wishes on various occasions; it also hinted that ASIO knew more about his appearance than was generally supposed. Holt's son ridiculed the theory, saying:

> My father didn't even like Chinese food.

A fresh inquiry into the disappearance was launched in August 2003, after a change in the law to permit an inquest when no body had been found.

Holy. Holy Loch An inlet of the Firth of Clyde west of Glasgow, 2½ miles long, which from 1961 was the British base for US POLARIS submarines. Not far from Dunoon, Holy Loch was from the outset a focus of anti-NUCLEAR protests, both from CND and from militant Scottish nationalists who saw the base as an affront to their country's dignity. Various forms of CIVIL DISOBEDIENCE, including SIT-INS at Ardanadam Pier, continued for a number of years; but when the PENTAGON decided to close the base in 1991 many local people viewed it with regret.

Holyrood. The palace in Edinburgh which for centuries was the official residence of the Kings of Scotland, and subsequently the monarchs of the United Kingdom. Since 1999 also, the colloquial term for the SCOTTISH PARLIAMENT whose permanent home has been constructed at soaring expense close to the palace (*see* FRASER REPORT); it is used in its own right, and as a comparison with the continuing UK Parliament at WESTMINSTER.

home. Home Rule The term originally used by 19th-century campaigners for the restoration of self-government to Ireland, and also sporadically for movements then and since for DEVOLUTION for Scotland and Wales. The phrase was coined by Isaac Butt (1813–70), who began the campaign for Dublin to regain the Parliament it had lost in 1800, though with Ireland remaining part of the British kingdom. Butt mobilised most of Ireland's MPs at Westminster into a Home Rule party, which PARNELL inherited and radicalised. Then, in 1885, GLADSTONE had a 'seismic conversion' to Home Rule (*see* HAWARDEN KITE), his pursuit of which twice caused the fall of Liberal governments. ASQUITH got a Home Rule Bill through Parliament amid growing tension (*see* CURRAGH MUTINY; ULSTER VOLUNTEERS), but the outbreak of WORLD WAR I left it a dead letter and the EASTER RISING paved the way for outright independence of the mainly Catholic South. Though used in the past, the term Home Rule was seldom used in the debates which led to Scotland and Wales achieving devolved government in 1999, save that the Liberal Democrats recalled their historic commitment to **'Home Rule all round'** in what would almost be a FEDERAL United Kingdom.

> Scottish Home Rule involves English Home Rule. Only by local parliaments and local executives in each of the three kingdoms can we settle Home Rule at all.
>
> Sir HENRY CAMPBELL-BANNERMAN

Home Rule is Rome Rule One of the early slogans of the ULSTER UNIONISTS. *See also* ULSTER WILL FIGHT.

Home Secretary The senior UK Cabinet Minister in charge of the Home Office, with responsibility in England and Wales for law and order, the police, prisons, charities and race relations, and throughout the UK for drugs, immigration, extradition and gambling, and also for the Channel Islands and the Isle of Man. In the past the Home Secretary also had responsibility for broadcasting, elections and emergency planning, but even with these transferred struggled to cope. The counterpart of a Continental Minister of the Interior, the Home Secretary formerly held the power of life and death over convicted murderers.

Homelands *See* BANTUSTAN.

homeland security A phrase for securing one's nation against the effects of international terrorism that became current on both sides of the Atlantic after the events of 9/11. George W. BUSH set up a **Department of Homeland Security** under former Pennsylvania Governor Tom Ridge which took responsibility for the relevant activities of 22 existing agencies from the US Customs to the Strategic National Stockpile and the National Disaster Medical System in order to 'anticipate, pre-empt and deter' terrorist threats. The department introduced a five-point, colour-coded Security Advisory

System for the perceived level of risk: Low (green), Guarded (blue), Elevated (yellow), High (orange) and Severe (brown). Up to 16 April 2002, and since 20 May 2003, the threat level has been orange; in between it was reduced to yellow.

homes for votes The scandal over alleged GERRYMANDERING in the 1980s by the Conservatives' 'flagship' Westminster City Council led by Dame Shirley Porter, heiress to the TESCO supermarket fortune. The council sold off houses and flats it owned in MARGINAL wards so that Labour tenants were replaced by Tory owner-occupiers and the Conservative grip on the council was tightened. A seven-year inquiry by the DISTRICT AUDITOR resulted in Dame Shirley and five colleagues being SURCHARGED £31.6 million in 1996. From exile in Israel, Dame Shirley declared her net worth to be just £300,000, but the council identified fourteen individuals or trusts it believed were holding funds on her account and in April 2004 she settled by paying £12.3 million, while still denying any wrongdoing. The episode greatly embarrassed the governments of Margaret THATCHER – of whom Dame Shirley was a strong supporter – and John MAJOR, but the voters of Westminster consistently re-elected the cleaned-up Tory council.

Homestead Act The Act passed by Congress in 1862 that provided 160 acres of land in the West for any current or prospective US citizen who was the head of a family, provided they paid a small fee and lived there for five years. VETOED by President Buchanan in 1860, it was signed by LINCOLN two years later. By 1890, 48 million acres had been distributed – most of it to 375,000 homesteaders, but with millions of acres snapped up fraudulently by developers and railroad companies.

urban homesteading The granting of houses in run-down areas of America's INNER CITIES for a nominal sum to middle-class families prepared to renovate them and rebuild the community. Pioneered in the early 1970s by Baltimore's Mayor William Donald Schaefer, it caught on in many other cities – though in some it ended in failure.

Honest Abe One of Abraham LINCOLN's many nicknames, awarded him by Washingtonians who had been appalled by the graft and scandal surrounding his predecessor James Buchanan.

honey. Honey Fitz The nickname of Mayor **John F. Fitzgerald** of Boston (1863–1951), the Boston-Irish MACHINE politician who was grandfather of the KENNEDY brothers Joe Jr, John (JFK), Robert (RFK) and Edward. A Democratic congressman 1895–1901, he was elected mayor in 1905. Ousted in 1907 by a GOOD GOVERNMENT coalition, he returned in 1909; he would have run again in 1911, had not his young challenger John Michael Curley threatened to expose his relationship with a cigarette girl. The name 'Honey' came both from his charm and the fine voice with which he sang *Sweet Adeline* at party occasions; he sang it again and danced a jig at age 85 when his grandson was elected to Congress. JFK returned the compliment by naming his Presidential yacht the *Honey Fitz.*

> Our present mayor has the distinction of appointing more saloon keepers and bartenders to public office than any previous mayor.
> ANON. Boston clergyman

honeymoon The period following a newcomer's election to high office during which he or she enjoys public goodwill and popularity. It usually ends within a few months when unpopular decisions have to be taken or certain qualities turn out to be lacking; Tony BLAIR, uniquely, enjoyed a honeymoon with the voters lasting a couple of years. Gerald FORD, after assuming the Presidency, told CONGRESS: 'I do not want a honeymoon with you; I want a good marriage.'

> It doesn't matter what kind of majority you come in with. You've got just one year when they treat you right. President LYNDON B. JOHNSON

Honi Soit Qui Mal Y Pense (Fr. evil be to him who evil thinks) The motto of the Order of the GARTER, founded by King Edward III in 1348 or 1349.

honky A term for a white person popularised in the 1960s by militant black Americans; it carries an implication of ignorance or gullibility. Many Americans heard it first on television interviews with the provocative H. 'Rap' Brown.

honour. honor guard The small, smartly uniformed marching party which in America accompanies the STARS AND STRIPES on most ceremonial occasions, even at many sporting events; one will also guard the bier on the death of a great American. A **guard of honour** is the party of troops that a visiting political leader reviews on arriving to meet another head of government or state.

the (Right) Honourable Gentleman or **Lady** or **Member** In the UK HOUSE OF

COMMONS, the way in which a member of one party refers to a member of another; to be Right Honourable, one must be a PRIVY COUNCILLOR. For the gradations of **Honourable and Gallant, Honourable and Learned** etc., *see* My Honourable FRIEND.

Honours List The collection of more than 700 awards made twice yearly by the Sovereign – at New Year and on their 'official birthday' in June – to persons put forward by the Prime Ministers of the UK and certain COMMONWEALTH countries as deserving recognition. They range from senior civil servants and diplomats who receive theirs automatically (*see* CALL ME GOD) through party activists to charity workers, postwomen and telephone engineers. A few nominees reject honours, but generally they mean a lot to those who are offered them. However, the system is widely seen as archaic – not least through the continued granting of Orders of the British EMPIRE, socially stratified and, in the case of awards for political and public service, open to abuse. John MAJOR acknowledged this in 1992 when he suggested reforms to open it up, and it is now a little easier for members of the public to make recommendations. Yet complaints have persisted – under both the Conservatives and Labour – of a correlation between corporate and individual donations to the governing party and the award of honours to those making them. In addition to these twice-yearly honours, there are **Dissolution Honours**, recommended for retiring members of a Parliament, **Resignation Honours**, proposed by an outgoing Prime Minister (*see* LAVENDER LIST), and lists of WORKING PEERS to top up the House of Lords.

> I wonder what you thought of the Honours List. I have never ceased to congratulate myself that I did not figure among the rabble.
>
> NEVILLE CHAMBERLAIN, New Year, 1918

> Just as obituary pages nearly always cause satisfaction – if not *schadenfreude* – so do Honours Lists invariably irritate. Like Parliamentary selections, they always seem to be bestowed on the wrong people. ALAN CLARK, *Diaries*

Honours scandal The controversy that broke in June 1922 over Lloyd George's blatant use of the honours system to reward wealthy contributors to his LLOYD GEORGE FUND, and in particular the unscrupulous South Africa millionaire Sir James Robinson, without regard to their personal reputations or actual philanthropic credentials. Sir James was honoured for 'Imperial and public services', but it emerged that the Colonial Secretary had not been consulted, and that the company he was supposed to be chairing had been liquidated in 1905; he refused the peerage as the agitation grew. A committee of inquiry set up to investigate the alleged sale of honours was told that anyone could buy a barony for £50,000, a baronetcy for £25,000 or a knighthood for £15,000 – payable to 'party funds' which meant Lloyd George's own kitty. As a result of the scandal the Honours (Prevention of Abuses) Act was passed in 1923 – which led to the conviction of Maundy Gregory (1877–1941) ten years later for selling honours at this time – and a Political Honours Scrutiny Committee of senior PRIVY COUNCILLORS, which still weeds out unsuitable nominees, was established. Lloyd George's refusal to yield control of the fund contributed to the downfall of his coalition (*see* CARLTON CLUB REVOLT), even though he gave a share of it to the Conservatives.

Hoover, Herbert (1874–1964), 31st President of the United States (Republican, 1929–33). Hoover came to the Presidency with a reputation as the GREAT ENGINEER, which transcended his ill-fated term in the WHITE HOUSE. As a mining engineer he had built up an international business empire and a personal fortune. In WORLD WAR I he helped the American relief ADMINISTRATION, skilfully co-ordinating aid for starving Europeans. He told critics of food aid for Russia:

> Twenty million people are starving. Whatever their politics, they shall be fed.

After the war he served in the Cabinets of HARDING and Coolidge (*see* SILENT CAL), nominally as Secretary of Commerce but with wider influence, earning the nickname 'assistant Secretary of everything else'. When Coolidge stood down (*see* I do not choose to RUN), the Republicans turned to Hoover with what Elmer Greene called his 'unprecedented reputation for public service as an engineer, administrator and humanitarian', as a potential President, though he had never run for public office. He told them: 'You convey too great a compliment . . . In no other land would a boy from a country village, without inheritance or influential friends, look forward with unbounded hope – I am indebted to my country without any human power to repay.' In the 1928 election Hoover heavily defeated Al Smith (*see* HAPPY WARRIOR) for the Presidency with his declaration that

We in America are nearer to the final triumph over poverty than ever before in the history of any land.

Hopes were high that this was so, but after eight months of OVERHEATING, Wall Street was hit by the GREAT CRASH and the rest of his term was dogged by misfortune. Hoover created a number of weapons that could have eased the Depression, but was reluctant to use them, dismissing INTERVENTION on the ground that 'prosperity cannot be restored by raids upon the public treasury'. He also surprised many in WASHINGTON by his preoccupation with minutiae and an apparent inability to see the big picture. Secretary of State Henry Simson said that 'a private meeting with Hoover is like sitting in a bath of ink', while Bernard Baruch observed: 'Facts to Hoover's brain are as water to a sponge; they are absorbed into every tiny interstice,' and Will Rogers joked:

It's not what he doesn't know that bothers me, it's what he knows for sure just ain't so.

The Presidency took its toll of Hoover, Raymond Moley writing in 1932: 'He seems to me to be close to death. He has the look of being done, but still of going on, driven by some damned duty.' With FDR conducting a positive and energetic campaign, Hoover found the Depression an ALBATROSS and he carried only six of the 48 States. From the White House he went back to business and humanitarian work, and in WORLD WAR II again headed America's relief effort before heading the HOOVER COMMISSIONS; in 1947 the Hoover Dam on the Colorado River at the Nevada-Arizona border, which had been started during his presidency, was named after him.

The greatest engineer in the world. He drained, ditched and damned the United States in three years. — Kansas farmer, 1932

Such a little man could not have made so big an impression. — NORMAN THOMAS

This is not a showman's job. I will not step out of character. — HOOVER

That man has offered me unsolicited advice for six years, all of it bad. — CALVIN COOLIDGE

I think he is a great American, and will some day be so recognized even by the people who have defamed him. — HARRY S TRUMAN, 1948

Hoover Commission The commission set up by CONGRESS in 1947 to reorganise the EXECUTIVE BRANCH of government, which the former President was invited to head. It recommended 36 proposals for change to President TRUMAN, all of which CONGRESS accepted save for a plan to create a single department for health, education and welfare. This was, however, adopted in 1953, the year Hoover was asked by EISENHOWER to head a second commission whose proposals were also implemented.

Hoover Depression The Democrats' name for the GREAT DEPRESSION, pinning the responsibility firmly on President Hoover despite its global causes. The link was exploited by Franklin D. ROOSEVELT in his 1932 campaign for the Presidency. FDR declared:

The present administration has either forgotten or does not want to remember the infantry of our economic army.

Yet the name had already stuck. The homeless of the Depression had named their shanty towns **Hoovervilles**, the newspapers under which they slept became **Hoover blankets**, broken-down motor vehicles hauled by mules **Hoover wagons** and empty pockets turned inside out **Hoover flags**.

Hoover moratorium The concession made by President Hoover in June 1931, allowing European nations to suspend repayment of intergovernmental war debts for one year, to help ease their plight during the GREAT DEPRESSION.

hope. 'Death' of Bob Hope The embarrassing episode when Rep. Bob Strump, an Arizona Republican, announced in the House of Representatives on 5 June 1998 that the veteran comedian Bob Hope had died, and read an erroneous news report into the record. Hope's daughter called in to say he was fine and eating his breakfast. Strump apologised; Hope lived for another five years. This premature eulogy was not unique – *compare* Lawrence WELK.

hopper The receptacle on the side of the Clerk's desk in the Chamber of the HOUSE OF REPRESENTATIVES where any member may at any time place a BILL he or she wishes to introduce. Pending legislation is described as being 'in the hopper'.

horse. horse and buggy A US politicans' term for an outdated way of operation, most notably used by Franklin D. ROOSEVELT after the SUPREME COURT's rejection of the NRA on BLACK MONDAY. FDR said:

Is the United States going to decide, are the people of this country going to decide, that their federal Government shall in the future have no right under any implied power or any court-approved power to enter into a solution of a national economic problem, but that national economic problem may only be solved by the States? We thought we were solving it, and now it has been thrown right straight in our faces. We have been relegated to the horse-and-buggy definition of interstate commerce.

Horseface The name inadvertently given to a constituent c. 1980 by the irrepressible Conservative MP Geoffrey Dickens (*see* BIFFO**;** I should like to do every woman in the United Kingdom a FAVOUR). One weekend as he toured his constituency on the Yorkshire-Lancashire border, he was followed everywhere by a middle-aged woman. A few days later he got a letter from her; she apologised if she had been a nuisance, but had wanted to see her MP in action, was most impressed and would urge her friends to vote for him. She asked if she could have a photograph of Dickens; below her signature was the word 'Horseface'. Dickens signed a photograph: 'To Horseface with very best wishes', bought a frame for it and dropped it in a House of Commons mailbox. Minutes later his secretary came in and said: 'Did you see the letter from that woman? I wrote "Horseface" at the bottom in case you'd forgotten who she was.'

horse-trading Hard bargaining between politicians, with each being ready to make concessions if the other does. The term originates in the tough bargains driven with farmers by horse dealers, and by farmers with each other.

dark horse A candidate with no apparent prospect of victory who comes through to make an unexpectedly strong showing. The term was first used of James Polk (1795–1849), whose election to the WHITE HOUSE in 1844 was engineered by ex-President Andrew Jackson. Though he had made a bid for the Vice Presidency in 1840, Polk was one of the least-known candidates in the field, but defeated Henry Clay to become America's 11th President. Polk (*see* FIFTY-FOUR FORTY OR FIGHT!) was exhausted by a single term, dying four months after leaving office, but he achieved some of the expansionist policy objectives he set for himself.

stalking horse *See* STALKING.

don't swap horses while crossing a stream The phrase with which Abraham LINCOLN argued during the 1864 election campaign against a change of President with the CIVIL WAR not won. In a speech on 9 June, he spoke of:

An old Dutch farmer, who remarked to a companion once that it was best not to swap horses in mid-stream.

In the 1920s F. E. Smith reacted to calls for a change in Britain's Conservative leadership by declaring:

We must not swap donkeys crossing the stream.

it's the horse that comes in first at the finish that counts One of the many homespun ways in which President TRUMAN dismissed OPINION POLLS during the 1948 election campaign which put his Republican challenger Thomas DEWEY ahead by a wide margin. Truman won.

Horton. Willie Hortonism The use of RACISM as a subliminal weapon in election propaganda. The phrase stems from the issue which gave George BUSH Sen. his comfortable margin over his Democratic challenger Michael Dukakis in the 1988 Presidential election, but also heightened concerns about negative and misleading campaigning that were to rebound on Bush four years later. At the height of the campaign, the Republicans aired advertisements claiming that Dukakis, as Governor of Massachusetts, was directly responsible for the fact that a black convict named Willie Horton raped a white woman in Marylands while on furlough from a Massachusetts prison. The commercial attracted furious Democratic complaints of racism and of being grossly misleading, as Dukakis had had no direct involvement with the case. But it succeeded in making Dukakis, against whom Bush was using 'LIBERAL' as a term of abuse, look weak on crime; the Governor made matters worse by giving a feeble answer when asked what he would do if a man broke into his house and attacked his wife.

You can't find a stronger metaphor, intended or not, for racial hatred in this country than a black man raping a white woman. And that's what the Willie Horton story was.

SUSAN ESTRICH, Dukakis campaign manager

Why should you let a guy like that, who had no chance for parole, out for a weekend with no supervision?

LEE ATWATER, Bush campaign manager

hostage. hostage crisis The humiliation of America which (together with INFLATION) brought down the CARTER administration. It arose from the seizure of the US Embassy in Tehran on 4 November 1979 by student supporters of the AYATOLLAH Khomeini, who detained 52 diplomats and other staff in protest at the overthrown Shah's presence in America for medical treatment. The plight of the hostages, and America's shame, increased when an effort to rescue the hostages by helicopter in April 1980 broke down in the desert 200 miles short of its goal; the Naval chopper had not been proofed for desert conditions. Secretary of State Cyrus Vance, who had opposed the mission, resigned. President Carter had pledged himself not to campaign for re-election until the hostages were freed, but eventually entered the contest when Sen. Edward KENNEDY mounted a strong challenge. The hostage crisis eventually hurt Kennedy as the Iranians hailed him as an 'American prophet', prompting the *New York Times* headline: 'Teddy is the toast of Tehran.' By now the Ayatollah and his fanatical supporters saw the crisis as a trial of strength, and were determined not to let Carter off the hook, though he never gave up negotiating. The deal was almost in place as Carter prepared to leave the WHITE HOUSE, and despite the pain he kept his sense of humour. After President REAGAN called on him for a briefing, Carter told his right-hand man Hamilton Jordan: 'I briefed him on what was happening to the hostages, but when I finished he said: "What hostages?"' They were finally released through Algerian MEDIATION immediately after Reagan was sworn in, Carter flying to Germany to welcome them. *See also* OCTOBER SURPRISE.

> The hostages became a concrete metaphor for the nation's sense of impotence.
>
> HEDRICK SMITH, *The Power Game*

Beirut hostages The action of Iranian-backed Shi'ite Muslim extremists in taking hostage Americans, Britons and other westerners who had stayed on in Beirut despite the complete breakdown of law and order in the early 1980s. At one time over 26 were held in darkened rooms in and around the city. Though some were detained as alleged spies, there seemed no logic to their seizure, and their captors appeared to have no idea what to do with them. Three were killed, and the rest eventually released after anything up to six years in captivity. The detention of the hostages led to Syria sending troops into Beirut to restore order and impose its influence, and also created the backdrop for the IRAN-CONTRA AFFAIR with its sub-plot of ARMS FOR HOSTAGES, in which the subsequent British hostage, the Archbishop of Canterbury's envoy Terry Waite, was allegedly implicated. By 1992 all but two of the hostages, Germans held by a splinter group, had been released; they followed soon after.

> Freeing the hostages is like putting up a stage set – which you do with the captors, agreeing on each piece as you slowly put it together. Then you leave an exit through which both the captor and the captive can walk with sincerity and dignity.
>
> TERRY WAITE, 3 November 1986 (before his own captivity)

hot line The direct link between the WHITE HOUSE and the KREMLIN which, since 30 August 1963, has provided a means of instant communication to avert 'accidental' NUCLEAR war; the contact is generally between senior members of the US and Russian national security staffs. Initially a telex circuit, it has been steadily upgraded over the years. Communication has not been continuous; in the late 1960s it was interrupted when a mechanical digger in Finland sliced through the line.

Hotel Cecil The name given by its Liberal opponents to Lord SALISBURY's second government (1886–92), because of the number of his relatives who served in it. Among them was the future Prime Minister Arthur BALFOUR, who went to Ireland as Chief Secretary; Balfour was 'Bob' Salisbury's nephew and his appointment is said to have spawned the phrase **Bob's your uncle** for an action that suddenly solves a problem.

Hotel Matignon The elegant official residence and headquarters, on Paris' Left Bank, of the French Prime Minister; it is renowned for the imposing façade that can be seen through the arch from the street, with its balcony with lion motifs, and its courtyard with low ranges of buildings on either side. Commissioned by the Prince de Tigny in 1722 and completed by the Comte de Matignon when he ran out of funds, the Hotel Matignon was an aristocratic residence – its occupants included Talleyrand, the Princes of Monaco and the pretender to the French throne – until it became the Austro-Hungarian Embassy in the late 1880s. Requisitioned by the French Government as 'enemy property' after WORLD WAR I, it became the headquarters of the President of the Council from 1935 when Pierre Flandrin moved in. It was seized by the Resistance when Paris was liberated in 1944; General DE GAULLE proclaimed the provisional government there, and did so again in 1958 when, in establishing the FIFTH REPUBLIC, he designated it as the home of the Prime Minister.

Hotel 1600 The damning term coined for

the Clinton WHITE HOUSE during the 2000 New York senatorial race by Rep. Rick Lazio, who ran unsuccessfully against Hillary Clinton. It referred to the way wealthy Democratic donors had been allowed to stay as paying guests in the LINCOLN ROOM and others. After the 1996 election it was revealed that 938 party donors had slept at the White House; a memo from the President to an aide who asked how to react to an offer of $100,000 to sleep in the Lincoln Room read: 'Ready to start overnights right away.'

Houdini A politician who develops an ability to escape unscathed from seemingly impossible situations. The original great Houdini (Erik Weiz, 1874–1926) was the world's most celebrated escapologist, who even managed to escape from the condemned cell in WASHINGTON jail. The term has been applied to many leaders, including Franklin D. ROOSEVELT and – up to WATERGATE – Richard NIXON. Ronald REAGAN, who deserved the title even more until the IRAN-CONTRA affair, was known as the GREAT RONDINI.

house. the House At WESTMINSTER, shorthand for the HOUSE OF COMMONS though essentially applied to the premises; in WASHINGTON, for the HOUSE OF REPRESENTATIVES.

house arrest The method used by repressive regimes from South Africa under APARTHEID to Burma under SLORC to curb their political opponents and which, as a last resort, was adopted by Tony BLAIR's government to deal with ten foreign terrorist suspects who could not be brought to trial because of the sensitive nature of the evidence but could not be deported because their home countries could not guarantee their safety. Arrested in the wake of 9/11, they were held in Belmarsh prison, south-east London under anti-terrorist legislation until the Lord of Appeal ruled that it violated the EUROPEAN CONVENTION ON HUMAN RIGHTS. Ministers decided on house arrest as the least unsatisfactory alternative, but the BILL to authorise it only scraped through the COMMONS and suffered a series of defeats in the LORDS on the eve of the deadline for releasing the prisoners. It only received the ROYAL ASSENT after three rounds of overnight PING-PONG between the Lords and the Commons, when Blair conceded that a judge, not the Home Secretary, must be the arbiter of each **control order** and offered a renewal within twelve months which he insisted was not the SUNSET CLAUSE demanded by the OPPOSITION.

House Bank scandal An episode in 1992 which brought considerable discredit on the HOUSE OF REPRESENTATIVES. It stemmed from the disclosure that a number of members had used the House bank run by the SERGEANT AT ARMS to run up overdrafts that would have been denied them anywhere else. The bank was closed after sustaining sizeable losses, but there was widespread criticism that its practices would have been illegal in the outside world. Three Democratic members who had abused the bank were unseated that November. The worst offender, Rep. Tommy F. Robinson of Arkansas who wrote himself 996 overdrafts, had already retired and was never proceeded against.

house divided speech The courageous – some feared suicidal – speech on the future of the UNION delivered by Abraham LINCOLN on 16 June 1858 at the close of the Republican CONVENTION in Springfield, Illinois, which nominated him to run for the US SENATE against Stephen Douglas. The key words are a paraphrase of *Mark* 3:25. Lincoln said:

> A house divided against itself cannot stand. I believe this government cannot endure, permanently half slave and half free. I do not expect the Union to be dissolved – I do not expect the house to fall – but I do expect it will cease to be divided. It will become all one thing, or all the other.

House Magazine The weekly journal that chronicles events and personalities at WESTMINSTER for members of both Houses when they are sitting. It is privately produced under the supervision of an all-party board of MPs and peers. It is instantly recognisable by the cartoon of a member which usually adorns its neutrally green cover.

House of Assembly *See* LEGISLATIVE ASSEMBLY.

House of Commons The principal, elected house of the WESTMINSTER Parliament (and also of the Parliament of Canada), traditionally held out as a model for democratic assemblies throughout much of the English-speaking world. Its origins date back to 1258, when Simon de Montfort, leading the barons against King Henry III, summoned representatives of the towns together. Kings, too, convened such Parliaments, with PEERS sitting with representatives of the boroughs and the counties. During the 1350s the LORDS and Commons began to sit separately, and later that century the Commons settled at Westminster, using ST STEPHEN'S CHAPEL from 1549/50. They had a SPEAKER from at least 1376, and by 1458 it was accepted that for a BILL to become law, the consent of the Crown, Lords and Commons was necessary. In 1642 Parliament went to war against Charles I, defeating, trying, and in 1649, executing him. Though the Monarchy was restored in 1660, Parliament had gained the right to tax and spend, and thus held ultimate power. The Commons were decisive in ousting James II in the GLORIOUS REVOLUTION of 1688–89, and in 1707 the ACT OF UNION brought in representatives of Scotland; Irish members followed in 1801. With the birth of a democratic America, the FRENCH REVOLUTION and the Industrial Revolution, the Commons came to look (and be) increasingly unrepresentative, and the 1832 REFORM ACT gave the new cities their first voice, abolishing the worst ROTTEN BOROUGHS. In 1834 the Palace of Westminster was razed to the ground, and in the late 1840s the Commons moved into the Chamber they occupy today – though completely rebuilt since, after taking a direct hit from a German bomb in 1941. Though the electorate was steadily extended, universal adult suffrage was only achieved with the 'Flapper VOTE' in 1928.

The House of Commons, elected at most every five years and currently with 646 members, sits from (generally) November to November, with a two-months' RECESS from mid-July to mid-September, a brief break after the party CONFERENCES and others at Christmas, Easter and Whitsun; until 2002 MPs had a three-month late summer recess but this became steadily harder to justify. Under this same process of MODERNISATION the traditional five-day week with a 2.30 p.m. start except on Fridays when the House met at 9.30 a.m. was changed to allow more FAMILY-FRIENDLY sittings and more Mondays and Fridays for MPs in their constituencies. Though critics doubt that it can effectively control the EXECUTIVE, the process of QUESTION TIME and the establishment in 1979/80 of departmental SELECT COMMITTEES have kept it a powerful instrument, even though many of its procedures remain arcane and its work is increasingly done away from the CHAMBER. Recent Speakers, starting with Bernard WEATHERILL from 1993, have gone out of their way to confirm that in the Chamber Ministers enjoy no advantages over BACKBENCHERS.

Members of the House, and those watching from the galleries, have had no shortage of views on it: 'better than a play' – King Charles II; 'a parcel of younger brothers' – PITT THE YOUNGER; 'four-fifths composed of country squires and great fools' – Richard Brinsley Sheridan; 'a parcel of button-makers, pin-makers, horse jockeys, gamesters, pensioners, pimps and whore-masters' – James Otis; 'I never saw so many shocking bad hats in all my life' – the Duke of Wellington (*see* IRON DUKE); 'an elaborate conspiracy to prevent the real clash of opinion which exists outside from finding an appropriate echo within its walls' – Aneurin BEVAN; 'hours and hours of exquisite boredom' – Bevan; 'a palace of illogicalities' – George BROWN.

Party combat is not all, and away from the clash of debate and committee work the Commons has a culture of its own. LLOYD GEORGE remarked that 'to anyone with politics in his blood, this place is like a pub to a drunkard', and Henry 'CHIPS' Channon noted: 'I love the House of Commons so much that if I were to be offered a peerage, I should be tempted to refuse it. Only tempted, of course.' But Shirley Williams (*see* GANG OF FOUR) disliked it as 'not so much a gentlemen's club as a boys' boarding school'.

In the Commons, modest backbenchers rub shoulders with the mighty. DISRAELI declared that 'we come here for fame!' but Beverly Baxter noted: 'A great many persons are able to become members of this House without losing their insignificance.' ASQUITH maintained that 'the first duty, if not the only duty, of a private member of the House of Commons is to speak as little and vote as often as he can', and Augustine Birrell, who served in his CABINET, wrote: 'I know of no place where the great truth that no man is necessary is brought home to the mind so remorselessly, and yet so refreshingly.' In the same vein Palmerston (*see* PAM) concluded:

> The House of Commons allows itself to be led, but does not like to be driven, and is apt to turn against those who attempt to drive it.

See also HALITOSIS HALL.

> When in that House MPs divide,
> If they've a brain and cerebellum too.
> They have to leave their brains outside
> And vote just as their leaders tell 'em to.
>
> W. S. GILBERT, *Iolanthe*

> Today for the first time I really liked it; boredom passed and a glow of pleasure filtered through me. But I wish I understood what I was voting for. HENRY CHANNON, 1936

> A writer of crook stories ought never to stop seeking new material.
>
> EDGAR WALLACE, standing for election

When you stand up to speak, the bench in front of you seems to catch you just below the knee and gives you the impression that you are about to fall headlong over. HAROLD MACMILLAN

House of Keys The 24-strong directly elected lower house of TYNWALD, the Isle of Man parliament; eight of its members also serve on the appointed LEGISLATIVE COUNCIL.

House of Lords The dazzlingly ornate gilded chamber at the south end of the Palace of Westminster, and the Upper House of Parliament that meets there. Essentially a REVISING CHAMBER, the Lords, despite reforms enacted in 1999, and the erosion of the inbuilt Conservative majority, remain idiosyncratic rather than august, being distinguished from the Commons by its members' high average age and the fact that not one of them has been elected by the public at large. The membership is fluid, depending on the number of Life PEERS that successive governments persuade the Sovereign to appoint, but is generally around 670. It was twice the size (though attendance was not) until 1999 when all but 92 of the hereditary peers who had traditionally formed its backbone – and, apart from bishops and senior judges, had until 1958 been its entire membership – were deprived of the right to sit and vote (*see* WEATHERILL AMENDMENT). A series of formulae for having a proportion of the House of Lords directly elected were all defeated in the Commons in February 2003 (a proposal to have 80% elected fell by just eight votes). The Lords have traditionally been presided over by a LORD CHANCELLOR who is also the head of the judiciary and a political member of the CABINET; Tony BLAIR in his June 2003 RESHUFFLE determined to split the three functions, with Lord Irvine of Lairg (Blair's former Head of Chambers, *see* MASTER OF THE ROLLS) stepping aside as the last Lord Chancellor in the full sense of the word and Lord Falconer of Thoroton (his former flatmate) becoming the first Secretary of State for Constitutional Affairs. Blair's intention to establish a separate SUPREME COURT, stripping the Lords of its function as England's highest court of appeal, and let the Lords elect a conventional SPEAKER met stiff resistance from judges and peers alike, and Lord Falconer found himself having to don the Lord Chancellor's robes and sit on the WOOLSACK.

Even with its composition partly reformed, the House of Lords still appears an anachronism; the deliberate good manners and relaxed nature of the proceedings, coupled with the age of many peers attending and the fact that no member will have to seek re-election, make a mellow contrast with the Commons. The experience of the many former Ministers who are moved up to the Lords, and the presence of eminent scientists and other experts, also gives the Lords an authoritative edge the Commons may lack; the party conflict is muted, though the House's former inbuilt Tory majority had few hesitations about amending, if not rejecting, Labour legislation (*see* SALISBURY COMPROMISE) and can be equally difficult with Conservative measures it disapproves of. The powers of the Lords have been reduced under the PARLIAMENT ACTS, so that it cannot prevent the BUDGET taking effect and can only delay legislation passed by the Commons for a year; the 1991 WAR CRIMES ACT was passed after the Commons voted to OVERRIDE the Lords and the upper house was also unable to prevent legislation in 2004, to outlaw hunting with dogs. *See also* MR BALFOUR'S POODLE; Working PEERS.

Most comments made about the Lords emphasise the unrepresentativeness, age and political impotence of its members. To the 18th-century Earl of Chesterfield it was 'that hospital of incurables'; to CAMPBELL-BANNERMAN 'a mere annexe of the Unionist party'; to LLOYD GEORGE '500 men, ordinary men, chosen accidentally from among the unemployed'; to Clement ATTLEE 'a glass of champagne that has stood for five days'; to the Methodist preacher Lord Soper 'good evidence of life after death'; to Tony BENN 'the British Outer Mongolia for retired politicians'; and to Frank Field 'a model of how to care for the elderly'. When the Earl of Arran (1910–83) was asked why the House had been packed for a Bill reforming the law on homosexuality but half-empty for one to protect badgers, he replied:

There are no badgers in the House of Lords.

I am dead – dead but in the Elysian Fields.
DISRAELI on his elevation as Earl of Beaconsfield

A severe though not unfriendly critic of our institutions once said that the cure for admiring the House of Lords was to go and look at it.
WALTER BAGEHOT (1826–77)

The House of Peers, throughout the war
Did nothing in particular,
And did it very well. W. S. Gilbert, *Iolanthe*

There are no credentials. They do not even need a medical certificate. They need not be sound in either body or mind. They only require a certificate of birth – just to prove that they were the first of the litter. You would not choose a spaniel on those principles.

LLOYD GEORGE delivering his PEOPLE'S BUDGET, 1909

If like me you are over 90, frail, on two sticks, half dead and half blind, you stick out like a sore thumb in most places, but not in the House of Lords. Besides, they seem to have a bar and a loo within 30 yards in any direction.

The Earl of Stockton (HAROLD MACMILLAN)

House of Representatives The larger house of the US CONGRESS, though co-equal in power with the SENATE (also the lower and more powerful house of Australia's Federal parliament); it has greater power over finance, but none over treaties and Presidential appointments. Comprising Representatives elected every two years by Congressional DISTRICTS of roughly equal population, it has had 435 voting members since 1912; there are also a non-voting DELEGATE from the District of Columbia, and similar members with a watching brief for America's overseas TERRITORIES. A member must be 25 years old, have been a US citizen for seven years and live in the State for which he or she was elected. The most powerful member is the SPEAKER, who not only presides over the House but is its political head, overshadowing the MAJORITY LEADER. The House has met in its present Chamber – in which Members may sit where they like – since 16 December 1857; before then it met for half a century in what is now the STATUARY HALL along the corridor. The House does much valuable work, especially in committee, but the requirement to seek re-election every two years creates an atmosphere of permanent ELECTIONEERING, which accentuates the contrast with the more measured pace of the Senate. Vice President Alben Barkley made another comparison with the Senate:

When I was in the House I was told that the difference between the House Foreign Affairs Committee and the Senate Foreign Relations Committee was that senators were too old to have affairs – they only had relations.

It is tempting to see the House as a stepping stone to the Senate and even the Presidency, but many legislators choose to spend a lifetime as Congressmen or –women, serving their constituents.

Until the Republicans under Rep. NEWT Gingrich seized control at the 1994 mid-term elections with their CONTRACT WITH AMERICA, the House for four decades had a Democratic majority, leading Hedrick Smith to term it 'the Gibraltar of the Democratic party'. It has had for far longer a not entirely unjustified reputation as a haven for eccentricity and SLEAZE; Walter Winchell called it 'the House of Reprehensibles', and one anonymous observer christened it 'a large body of egos surrounded on all sides by LOBBYISTS'. Speaker Thomas Reed was convinced that 'the House has more sense than anyone in it', though he also believed it was 'no longer a deliberative body'. Members have frequently complained, as in most legislatures, about the difficulty of getting anything done or having their own views taken seriously. Congresswoman Bella Abzug complained during the VIETNAM WAR: 'I'm tired of listening to a bunch of old men who are long beyond the DRAFT age standing there and talking about sending our young men to be killed in an illegal and immoral war', and Rep. Dante Fascell said more measuredly: 'Being in the House is sometimes like trying to push a wheelbarrow up a hill with ropes and handles.'

Composed of very good men, not shining but honest and reasonably well-informed, and in time they will be found to improve, and not to be much inferior in eloquence, science and dignity to the British Commons.

FISHER AMES, 1789

I have accepted a seat in the House of Representatives, and thereby have consented to my own ruin, to your ruin, and to the ruin of our children. JOHN ADAMS to his wife Abigail.

I find speaking here and elsewhere almost the same thing. I was about as badly scared, and no more than when I speak in court.

ABRAHAM LINCOLN after his MAIDEN SPEECH

There is something peculiar in the temper of the House. A clear strong statement of a case, if made too soon or late, fails. If well made at the right time it is effective. It is a nice point to study the right time.

Rep. (later President) JAMES GARFIELD, 1874

To be quite blunt about it, I'm not impressed with the overall calibre of members of the House.

Vice President DAN QUAYLE.

House-Senate conference *See* CONFERENCE.

Journal of the House* or *Senate The official record of the proceedings of each House, published at the end of each session under the direction of the Clerk of the House and the Secretary of the Senate.

keeping a House At WESTMINSTER, the ability to keep enough members in and around the CHAMBER to prevent the COMMONS being COUNTED OUT and enable business to continue.

losing the House Making a speech in the CHAMBER that loses the attention of other members; the term is used particularly of Ministers and Leaders of the OPPOSITION at WESTMINSTER who have the opportunity to make an impact in a crucial debate, but throw it away with a tedious or off-key speech.

Houses of Parliament The new Palace of WESTMINSTER erected on the site of the jumble of mainly medieval Parliamentary buildings destroyed in the fire of 1834. The idea of moving to a more salubrious location was considered, but Wellington (*see* IRON DUKE) insisted:

> You must build your House of Parliament upon the river, so that the populace cannot exact their demands by sitting down round you.

Tsar Nicholas I described the completed building as 'a dream in stone'; when it was rebuilt almost in replica after severe damage in WORLD WAR II, Clement ATTLEE observed:

> The British have the distinction above all nations of being able to put new wine into old bottles without bursting them.

Hoverthorpe The nickname bestowed by the UK media on the Liberal leader Jeremy THORPE (1929–) when in the late summer of 1974 with a general election imminent he campaigned by landing on seaside beaches in Devon from a hovercraft to win the holidaymakers' vote.

Howard, Michael (1941–) The leader of Britain's CONSERVATIVE PARTY from 2003, after the ousting of Iain Duncan Smith (IDS) who pulled back some ground from Labour in the 2005 General Election, then divided his party by announcing his intention to quit, but only months later after a new system had been decided on for electing his successor. Howard, an accomplished Welsh barrister of Rumanian-Jewish origin, rose rapidly in Margaret THATCHER's government before serving in John MAJOR's Cabinet as Environment Secretary and finally as a purportedly hard-line Home Secretary. After the Conservatives' crushing defeat in 1997 his hopes of the leadership were torpedoed by his former deputy Anne Widdecombe's description of him as exuding 'something of the NIGHT'; satirists frequently made the comparison with Transylvania's most celebrated inhabitant, Count Dracula. Right-of-centre though not extreme and hard-line in opposition on law and order and asylum (areas on which his record in government had been weaker than his rhetoric) he delivered for his successor a larger and more vigorous Parliamentary party than pre-election polls had suggested, having not only won seats from Labour but blunted the DECAPITATION strategy of the Liberal Democrats who had targeted Howard and several of his front bench.

Howe resignation The event that triggered the overthrow of Margaret THATCHER: the resignation on 1 November 1990 of Sir Geoffrey (later Lord) Howe (1926–). Howe (*see* DEAD SHEEP; MOGADON MAN) had become increasingly disenchanted with the IRON LADY since, having loyally supported her for a decade, she demoted him from FOREIGN SECRETARY to LEADER OF THE HOUSE and, in name only, DEPUTY PRIME MINISTER. His discontent grew as she took a steadily harder line against the moves toward closer European union that would culminate in the MAASTRICHT TREATY, and dug in her heels against eventual membership of the ERM until Howe and Chancellor Nigel Lawson threatened to resign. His resignation was provoked by Mrs Thatcher's statement to the Commons after the Rome EC summit (*see* NO!, NO!, NO!) in which she departed from her text to attack not only closer union but the 'Hard ECU' plan of Chancellor John MAJOR. Sir Geoffrey's resignation alone Mrs Thatcher might have survived, but on 13 November he stunned the COMMONS with a PERSONAL STATEMENT amounting to a devastating indictment of her style of government. On Europe, he said:

> If some of my former colleagues are to be believed, I must be the first Minister in history to resign because he was in full agreement with Government policy.

He described Mrs Thatcher's attitude to her Ministers' efforts to negotiate in Europe, as

> like sending your opening batsmen to the crease only for them to find, the moment the first balls are bowled, that their bats have been broken by the team captain.

The trauma inflicted on the CONSERVATIVE PARTY by Sir Geoffrey's speech led Michael Heseltine (*see* HEZZA) to declare himself a candidate in a leadership election which, coincidentally, was imminent. Just over two weeks later, Mrs Thatcher left NUMBER TEN – to be replaced by Major.

> This final act of bile and treachery.
>
> MARGARET THATCHER

Huang affair The scandal that broke in WASHINGTON during the 1996 Presidential ELECTION over the fund-raising activities for the Democratic National Committee of John

Huang, the party's Chinese-born chief link to Asian American donors and a man much praised by President CLINTON, whom he had met in Hong Kong in the 1980s and whom he visited weekly in the WHITE HOUSE. Through his extensive business contacts in Asia and the US, Huang secured sizeable donations, some from foreign corporations that should not legally have contributed and some from individuals who apparently lacked the means – notably monks at a Buddhist temple in Hacienda Heights, California, who despite living on $40 a month donated $140,000 when Vice President Gore (*see* OZONE MAN) paid a visit. The scandal heavily implicated the Indonesia-based Lippo Group and its controlling family, the Riadys, and Paul Berry, a former room-mate of Clinton who had become a Washington LOBBYIST. *See also* SOFT MONEY.

HUD The US Department of Housing and Urban Development, established by CONGRESS in 1965 at the prompting of President Lyndon JOHNSON. To demonstrate his commitment to CIVIL RIGHTS, LBJ appointed as its first head Robert Weaver, who thus became the first black CABINET SECRETARY. The name is always pronounced 'Hud', as in the film.

Hughes Loan The $200,000 secret loan from the billionaire Howard Hughes to Richard NIXON's brother Donald, which became an issue in the Republican's campaign for Governor of California in 1962. When Nixon visited Chinatown in San Francisco, he was handed a fortune cookie, opened it – and found the motto 'What about the Hughes loan?' Nixon was furious at the stunt, staged by the prankster Dick Tuck. He lost the election to the Democrat 'Pat' Brown, then announced his retirement from politics (*see* LAST PRESS CONFERENCE).

> I have made mistakes, but I am an honest man.
> NIXON, press conference 1 October 1962

Hughligans The group of Conservative MPs led by Lord Hugh Cecil (hence their name) and F. E. Smith who staged bitter protests in the COMMONS in 1911 as the ASQUITH government pushed through the PARLIAMENT ACT to curb the powers of the HOUSE OF LORDS. For half an hour they barracked the Prime Minister at the DESPATCH BOX with cries of: 'Traitor!' Of Lord Hugh, Asquith's daughter Lady Violet Bonham Carter wrote half a century later:

> [He] screamed: 'The King is in duress!', and in his frenzied writhings seemed like one possessed. His transformation, and that of many other personal friends, was terrifying. They behaved, and looked, like mad baboons.

human rights The basic freedoms of human beings to live, express themselves and hold opinions without fear of persecution by the state or from any other quarter. These rights are constantly under threat from TOTALITARIAN regimes, and occasionally from democracies as well. The concept dates back to antiquity, but was championed by thinkers in the 18th century including America's founding fathers who upheld the rights to 'LIFE, LIBERTY AND THE PURSUIT OF HAPPINESS'. Alexander HAMILTON, in *The Farmer Refuted*, wrote:

> The sacred rights of mankind are not to be rummaged for among old parchments or musty records; they are written, as with a sunbeam, in the whole volume of human nature, by the hand of the divinity itself; and cannot be erased or obscured by any mortal power.

Even in the age of Empire, the rights of those being conquered had their champions. At the height of his MIDLOTHIAN CAMPAIGN, GLADSTONE told an audience:

> Remember the rights of the savage, as we call him. Remember the happiness of his humble home, remember that the sanctity of life in the hill villages of Afghanistan, among the winter snows, is as inviolable in the eye of Almighty God as can be your own.

Theodore ROOSEVELT took up the banner of human rights in his opposition to America's PLUTOCRATS; in 1910 he said in Paris: 'Human rights must have the upper hand, for property belongs to man and not man to property.' Human rights also began at home for Eleanor Roosevelt; on 27 March 1958 the FIRST LADY OF THE WORLD told the UN Commission on Human Rights:

> Where, after all, do universal human rights begin? In small places, close to home – so close and small that they cannot be seen on any map of the world.

The phrase came into its own after the election of Jimmy CARTER as President in 1976. Carter made the promotion of human rights throughout the world a principal aim of his ADMINISTRATION, declaring them 'the soul of our foreign policy'. Many conservatives objected that he was interfering in the affairs of other countries and harming America's influence abroad, but his campaign struck a positive chord in much of the THIRD WORLD and behind the IRON CURTAIN. However, the black Congresswoman Barbara Jordan found it necessary to remind him:

> Human rights apply equally to Soviet DISSIDENTS, Chilean peasants and American women.

The worldwide drive for human rights had already produced the HELSINKI ACCORDS of 1975 which, while not immediately honoured by the Soviet Union and its SATELLITES, set a yardstick against which their conduct was measured, and against which democratic governments were judged after the collapse of Communism. Human rights were also the driving force behind the ETHICAL FOREIGN POLICY pursued by Robin COOK as Foreign Secretary during the first term of the 1997 UK Labour government. Some governments have been shamed into improving the treatment of their citizens, yet sadly it remains true that if a regime is unconcerned enough about world opinion and can resist pressure from the UN and major world powers, it can violate the rights of its people with relative impunity.

Human Rights Act The legislation passed in 2000 which incorporated the EUROPEAN CONVENTION ON HUMAN RIGHTS into UK law, thus increasing the protection and remedies available to citizens who believed their rights had been abused. It prompted a rash of court challenges to existing legislation, minor elements of which had to be changed.

European Convention on Human Rights The document drawn up by the Council of EUROPE in 1950, and signed by all member states, which commits them to protect and develop human rights; it was extended in 1989 to cover torture and loss of liberty. Most countries have now incorporated it into their national laws; the UK did so belatedly with the HUMAN RIGHTS ACT. The Council also formed a **European Commission on Human Rights** to investigate complaints by governments, organisations or groups that their rights have been abused; cases that cannot be resolved are passed to the EUROPEAN COURT OF JUSTICE for a decision.

Universal Declaration of Human Rights The text adopted by the UNITED NATIONS General Assembly in 1948 setting out fundamental rights and freedoms to which all are entitled. They include the right to life, liberty, freedom from servitude, fair trial, marriage, ownership of property, freedom of thought and conscience, and freedom of expression. They also include the rights to vote, to work and to be educated. Article 1 reads:

> All human beings are both free and equal in dignity and rights.

human shield The detention and location of hostages from one country by the leadership of another at potential military targets in the hope that the country whose nationals are held will be deterred from attacking them. The tactic was first employed during the GULF WAR of 1990–91 by SADDAM HUSSEIN (*see* Butcher of BAGHDAD), who had 700 US, British, French, German and Japanese nationals (and captured aircrew) sent to installations that were most liable to attack. In the event none were killed, but Saddam's readiness to use civilians in this way in violation of the GENEVA CONVENTIONS confirmed the international view of him as a ruthless psychopath.

Humphrey The stray black and white cat adopted by staff at NO. 10 Downing Street soon after John MAJOR became Prime Minister and named after SIR HUMPHREY, the fictitious CABINET SECRETARY in the TV series YES, MINISTER. Humphrey's time at NUMBER TEN was eventful and closely monitored by the media; in 1994 he was suspected of killing four robins which vanished from their nesting box at the Cabinet Office, he had to be put on a special diet for kidney problems caused by eating too many biscuits, and in 1996 he went missing and was given up for dead, only for it to be discovered that he had got in a Post Office man and gone to the Royal Army Medical College half a mile away for a three-month sabbatical. When Tony BLAIR succeeded Major, his wife Cherie found she was allergic to Humphrey and he was 'pensioned off' to a family in the suburbs; photographs of Humphrey in retirement had to be produced to quell rumours that the Blairs had had him put down.

Humphrey, Hubert *see* HAPPY WARRIOR.

Humphrey-Hawkins Full Employment Act The measure promoted in the late 1970s by Sen. Hubert Humphrey and Rep. Gus Hawkins of California, which put the US Government under moral pressure to stimulate the economy and combat widespread unemployment. Widely seen at the time as the work of Democratic members of CONGRESS paying their dues to Big LABOR, it was largely a dead letter. The Act imposed a number of duties on the Federal government, and requires the chairman of the FED to report twice yearly to Congress on the state of the economy.

hundred. Hundred Days A term used by many political leaders who have wished to appear dynamic for an initial dramatic burst of executive action to put the nation right. *Compare* HONEYMOON.

The original 'hundred days' was Napoleon's brief return to power between his escape from Elba and his final defeat at Waterloo (1815); the phrase was coined by the Comte de Chambord to contrast that time with the length of King Louis XVIII's exile. It was first invoked in its present sense by Mussolini (*see* DUCE), with Franklin D. ROOSEVELT, John F. KENNEDY and Harold WILSON among incoming leaders to follow suit. Wilson said in a 1964 campaign speech:

> We are going to need something like that which President Kennedy had after years of stagnation – a programme of a hundred days of dynamic action.

After 100 days in the WHITE HOUSE, President CLINTON reflected:

> At this point in his administration, William Henry Harrison had been dead 68 days.

FDR's 'hundred days of dynamic action' from 9 March to 16 June 1933 was the most dramatic and successful, with an unprecedented torrent of legislation aimed at averting economic collapse, checking the GREAT DEPRESSION and laying the ground for the NEW DEAL. He began it by calling Congress into emergency session, closing the banks and giving the first of his FIRESIDE CHATS. Roosevelt launched a 'second hundred days' of New Deal legislation after BLACK MONDAY, 27 May 1935, when the SUPREME COURT declared the NRA unconstitutional; this time a Social Security Act was at its heart.

Hundred Flowers policy The short-lived policy of liberalisation in China instituted by CHAIRMAN MAO Tse-Tung in 1957. Mao set it out in a speech in Beijing on 17 February:

> A policy of letting a hundred flowers blossom and a hundred schools of thought contend is the policy for promoting the flourishing of the arts and the progress of science.

Mindful of the recent HUNGARIAN UPRISING and Khrushchev's denunciation of STALIN, Mao was trying to 'resolve the contradictions' becoming increasingly apparent within the Chinese Communist state. Critics of the regime saw the speech as a green light, and a barrage of complaint was directed at the regime, especially from liberals and anti-Communists. Party bosses became alarmed and on 8 June a policy change was signalled by the publication of Mao's speech in amended form. This was followed in July by a crackdown on the most outspoken critics.

See also CULTURAL REVOLUTION.

hung Parliament A newly-elected Parliament in which no party has an overall MAJORITY, and in which the largest party has to decide whether to govern on its own or do a deal with smaller groups. A hung Parliament was the aim of the Liberal/SDP ALLIANCE, outside its moments of greatest euphoria, and remains the LIBERAL DEMOCRATS' best hope of power, but whenever one has seemed likely the voters have shied away from it. When the Liberal Democrat leader Paddy Ashdown's past affair with his secretary came to light prior to the 1992 election (*see* PADDY PANTSDOWN) it was suggested the party was aiming for a 'well-hung Parliament') The last hung Parliament was elected in February 1974; after abortive negotiations between the outgoing Tory Prime Minister Edward HEATH and the Liberal leader Jeremy THORPE, Labour under Harold WILSON formed a minority government; it won an election outright that October but lost its majority at BY-ELECTIONS and bought time through the LIB-LAB PACT. John MAJOR's government also lost its majority toward the end of the 1992–97 Parliament, but struggled on alone, assisted by a few ULSTER UNIONISTS.

Hungarian uprising The popular revolt against Soviet control of Hungary that cost over 30,000 lives in the autumn of 1956. It started on 23 October – now Hungary's most sacred national day – when police tried to break up a student demonstration in Budapest for the reinstatement of Imre Nagy, the reformist leader ousted in April 1955 by the hard-line Matyas Rakosi. Rakosi's policy of limited liberalisation while strengthening ties with Moscow became untenable in the face of mounting pressure for radical change, intensified by deSTALINisation in the Soviet Union and the Poznan revolt in Poland on 28 June; on 18 July he was forced to resign. MOSCOW-LINE Communists struggled to contain the situation under the equally repressive Erno Gero, but the students set off widespread anti-Soviet riots. In Budapest, Soviet flags were burned and Stalin's statue destroyed.

Hungary's own police and army backed the uprising, while members of the notorious SECRET POLICE (AVO) were hunted down. Nagy was installed as Prime Minister on 24 October and promised the withdrawal of Soviet troops. But fighting was intense, especially in east Hungary, and by 30 October some 10,000 lives had been lost.

Nagy announced that Hungary had quit the WARSAW PACT and was now NEUTRAL. He appealed for UNITED NATIONS intervention; deep splits between Western nations over the SUEZ operation were given as an excuse for allowing the KREMLIN a free hand, but America had privately indicated after the rising in Poland that it would not intervene militarily in such cases.

The Soviet counterstrike began on 4 November with the bombing and military takeover of Budapest; the troops were invited in by Nagy's co-leader Janos Kadar (1912–89), who had fled to the east as the tension rose. An estimated 190,000 Hungarians had fled to Austria by the end of 1956. On 18 November Nagy was tricked into leaving his refuge in the Yugoslav embassy, taken to Romania and shot. The Kadar government imposed its authority on the country and the uprising was extinguished everywhere, except in the hearts of the Hungarian people. Kadar eventually loosened the reins, and in the month of his death, July 1989, Nagy was reinterred for a moving State funeral. By the turn of the year, Hungary was a democracy.

Hunger March *See* JARROW CRUSADE.

hunger strike *See* STRIKE.

Hurricane Karen Karen Hughes, George W. BUSH's most trusted political confidante during his successful 2000 campaign for the Presidency, and for his first two years in the WHITE HOUSE until stepping down as 'Counsellor to the President' to put her son through school in Texas. Mrs Hughes shaped Bush's message through two campaigns for governor and the primary and general elections of 2000, during which her bruising manner earned the nickname. In the White House she fell foul, as a moderate, of hard-line NEO-CONSERVATIVES who despised the 'compassionate conservatism' she staked out as Bush's territory, but returned for Bush's successful 2004 re-election campaign.

Hurry Upkins The nickname given by Londoners to **Harry Hopkins** (1890–1946), President ROOSEVELT's emissary to London in the months before America entered WORLD WAR II (*see* FORMER NAVAL PERSON; LEND-LEASE). It reflected both the break-neck pace of his missions and also Britons' desire for America to 'hurry up' and join in the war. In March 1941 Hopkins reported to FDR that the UK's two main needs were food and refrigerated cargo vessels, and that German bombing of gas mains had created a demand for food that did not need cooking. He was back in August – when he also made a three-day secret visit to Moscow for talks with STALIN on supplying US war *matériel* to help combat Germany's invasion of the Soviet Union.

hustings, the Any place from which an ELECTION speech is made, but more specifically a platform from which all the CANDIDATES in an election address the VOTERS; formerly a booth where votes were counted.

Hutton inquiry The inquiry into the circumstances that led to the death of the Ministry of Defence scientist Dr David KELLY which sat in public in London during the summer of 2003, producing unprecedented insights into the workings of Tony BLAIR's government, the nexus between the intelligence services and the purveyors of SPIN in the run-up to the IRAQ WAR, and the BBC's handling of a news story which, Blair told the inquiry, would 'if true, have merited my resignation'. Set up by Blair after Kelly's apparent suicide, the inquiry, conducted by Lord Hutton (1931–), former Lord Chief Justice of NORTHERN IRELAND, was a model of speed, conciseness and economy. Hutton's conclusion, published in January 2004, was that Blair and his staff had done nothing wrong and that responsibility rested with the BBC for inaccurate journalism by the radio reporter Andrew Gilligan, poor editorial control and failure to check the veracity of Gilligan's story before manning the trenches against NUMBER TEN in the face of demands for an apology from Blair's communications director Alastair Campbell. These findings, greeted with consternation by politicians and journalists who at least had expected the forced resignation of Defence Secretary Geoff Hoon, instead triggered the resignation of the BBC chairman Gavyn Davies, its director-general Greg Dyke (under protest) and finally of Gilligan, who attacked Hutton's conclusions as 'unbalanced'. *See also* the subsequent BUTLER INQUIRY; DODGY DOSSIER; 45-MINUTE CLAIM.

Hyannis Port The compound of white clapboard cottages in an exclusive and otherwise quiet resort on Massachsetts' Cape Cod coast that served as JFK's summer WHITE HOUSE, and both the vacation home and the tribal centre of the KENNEDY DYNASTY. Kennedy's father Joseph would divide his time between there and Palm Beach, Florida. At times of decision or of crisis, notably in the wake of CHAPPA-

QUIDDICK and after the death on the way to a family wedding there of John F. Kennedy Jr, the Kennedy clan and their advisers would mass in the Hyannis compound to recover their strength and consider the next move, while the world's media massed at police barriers nearby.

Hybrid Bill At WESTMINSTER, a BILL combining general questions of policy with specific references to particular commercial undertakings that has to be dealt with by special and complicated Parliamentary procedures; one such was the Act passed in 1987 for the construction of the Channel Tunnel.

Hybridity Hyslop The nickname earned by the Conservative MP (Sir) **Robin Maxwell-Hyslop** (1931–), who in 1976 delayed Labour's legislation to NATIONALISE Britain's aircraft and shipbuilding industries for a year by pointing out that the Government had inadvertently promoted a Hybrid Bill. The SPEAKER's ruling in favour of Maxwell-Hyslop was a blow to Labour, which was nursing a COMMONS majority of 3, and a tonic for Margaret THATCHER's Conservatives, but the Bill eventually went through.

Hyde Park The 187-acre estate and birthplace of Franklin D. ROOSEVELT, in New York state four miles north of Poughkeepsie; it is now a historic landmark. It took its name from its builder Edward Hyde, Lord Cornbury, the eccentric cross-dresser who governed New York from 1702 to 1708. In 1939, before he bowed to pressure to run for a third term, FDR wrote:

> I want to go back to Hyde Park. I want to take care of the trees. I want to make the farm pay. I want to finish my little house on the hill.

FDR did indeed go back; he is buried at Hyde Park, which is preserved as he left it. In October 1995, Bill CLINTON met the Russian President Boris Yeltsin at Hyde Park, using the same chairs as FDR and CHURCHILL had more than 50 years before.

Hymietown The word that did lasting damage to the Presidential ambitions of the Rev. Jesse JACKSON, alienating many Jewish voters and New Yorkers. On 13 February 1984 the *Washington Post* revealed that when talking to black reporters, Jackson referred to Jews as 'Hymies' who only wanted to talk about Israel, and to New York City as 'Hymietown'. Jackson hedged for two weeks before admitting he had been accurately quoted; he insisted he had not been ANTI-SEMITIC but was merely using language that was common in Chicago when he was young. Then Louis Farrakhan, leader of the 'Nation of Islam', weighed in by denouncing the reporter who had broken the story as a traitor worthy of death. Jackson managed to mend a number of fences in time for a more serious challenge in 1988; in the long run his closeness to Farrakhan probably did him more damage with white voters than his 'Hymie' comments.

hyperinflation *See* INFLATION.

hypocrite Someone who pretends to be what they are not, or whose speeches run counter to their actions. Abraham LINCOLN typified a hypocrite as 'the man who murdered his parents, [then] pleaded for mercy on the grounds that he was an orphan'; Adlai STEVENSON as 'the kind of politician who would cut down a redwood tree, then mount the stump and make a speech for conservation'. The word 'hypocrite' is UNPARLIAMENTARY; 'hypocrisy' is not.

hypothecation The levying of a tax, the receipts from which are earmarked for a particular purpose. In Britain, hypothecation has long been resisted by the TREASURY, partly because it inhibits WHITEHALL's freedom to spend incoming revenues as it wishes, but also because anti-war groups and individuals with ethical objections to aspects of government spending could seek to withhold the specific portion of their taxes earmarked for activities of which they disapproved.

I

I accuse *See* J'ACCUSE.

I address you neither with rancor nor bitterness in the fading twilight of my life, with but one purpose in mind. To save my country General Douglas MACARTHUR's opening words to a JOINT SESSION of CONGRESS on 19 April 1951, eight days after President TRUMAN dismissed him from command of US forces in KOREA. His audience hailed the speech as one of the most memorable in Congress, but Truman dismissed it as 'nothing but a bunch of damn bullshit'. *See also* OLD SOLDIERS NEVER DIE.

I am a novel principle – here to be endured The Conservative MP Nancy, Lady Astor, the first woman to take her seat in the HOUSE OF COMMONS, making her MAIDEN SPEECH in 1919. Countess Markievicz (SINN FEIN, Sligo) had been elected in 1918, but stayed away in accordance with her party's policy of BOYCOTTING Westminster.

I am not a crook Richard NIXON's declaration on 17 November 1973 as the WATERGATE affair gathered pace. He said:

> I made my mistakes, but in all my years of public life I have never profited, *never* profited from public service. I have earned every cent. And in all my years of public life I have never obstructed justice . . . I welcome this kind of examination because people have got to know whether or not their President is a crook. Well, I am not a crook.

I am the man, the very fat man, who waters the workers' beer The chorus of a comic song, popular from the 1930s, parodying but also sympathetic with left-wing denunciations of CAPITALIST exploitation.

I, being the (acting) returning officer for the – constituency, hereby give notice that the number of votes cast for each candidate is as follows The formal DECLARATION of the result of a UK Parliamentary ELECTION.

I disapprove of what you say, but will defend to the death your right to say it The most celebrated statement attributed to Voltaire (1694–1778). The closest he is known to have come to it is when he wrote to Abbé le Riche in 1770:

> I detest what you write, but I would give my life to make it possible for you to continue to write.

I do solemnly swear (or **affirm**) **that I will faithfully execute the office of President of the United States, and will to the best of my ability preserve, protect and defend the Constitution of the United States** The OATH of office required of the President under Article II, clause 7 of the US Constitution.

I gave them a sword Richard NIXON's view of WATERGATE and his resignation as President in the 1977 FROST INTERVIEWS. It encapsulated both his own acceptance that he had been the architect of his downfall, and his continuing belief that the liberal and media ESTABLISHMENT was against him. Nixon told his interviewer:

> I gave them a sword. And they stuck it in and they twisted it with relish. And I guess if I'd been in their position I'd have done the same thing.

I have a dream The culmination of Dr Martin Luther KING's address from the LINCOLN MEMORIAL to a crowd of over 200,000 at the close of the 'MARCH ON WASHINGTON FOR JOBS AND FREEDOM' on 28 August 1963. His powerful oratory was interspersed with cries of 'Dream some more!' from the crowd. The occasion forced the KENNEDY administration to take a more active stance in support of CIVIL RIGHTS. Dr King said:

> Now is the time to rise from the dark and desolate valley of segregation to the sunlit path of racial justice . . . There will be neither rest nor tranquillity in America until the Negro is granted his citizenship rights . . . No, we are not satisfied and we will not be satisfied until justice rolls down like water and righteousness like a mighty stream . . . I say to you today, even though we face the difficulties of today and tomorrow, I still have a dream. It is a dream that is deeply rooted in the American dream. I have a dream that one day this nation will rise up, live out the true meaning of its creed: We hold these truths to be self-evident, that all men are created equal. I have a dream that

> one day on the red hills of Georgia the sons of former slaves and the sons of former slave-owners will be able to sit down together at the table of brotherhood. I have a dream that my four little children will one day live in a nation where they will not be judged by the color of their skin but by the content of their character. I have a dream today . . . I have a dream that one day every valley shall be exalted, every hill and mountain shall be laid low. The rough places will be made plain and the crooked places will be made straight . . . Free at last, free at last, thank God almighty, free at last.

The final phrases form his epitaph.

I have been to the mountain top Dr King's speech to striking Memphis sanitation workers on 3 April 1968, the eve of his assassination. In it he compared himself to Moses, who had been shown the Promised Land even though he might not enter it.

> I don't know what will happen now. We've got some difficult days ahead. It really doesn't matter with me now, because I've been on the mountain top. I won't mind. Like anybody, I would like to lead a long life. Longevity has its place. But I'm not concerned about that now. I just want to do God's will. And he's allowed me to go up to the mountain. And I've looked over, and I've seen the promised land. I may not get there with you, but I want you to know tonight that we as a people will get to the promised land. Well, I'm happy tonight. I'm not worried about anything. I'm not fearing any man. Mine eyes have seen the glory of the coming of the Lord!

I have neither eyes to see, nor tongue to speak here, but as the House is pleased to direct me The definitive statement of the freedom of the HOUSE OF COMMONS from outside interference, delivered by Speaker William Lenthall (1591–1662) on 4 January 1642 when King Charles I demanded to know where the FIVE MEMBERS could be found. *See also* I SEE ALL THE BIRDS ARE FLOWN.

I have to tell you that no such undertaking has been received The words with which Neville CHAMBERLAIN told Britain that WORLD WAR II had begun. In a radio broadcast from NO. 10 Downing Street on 3 September 1939, he said:

> This morning, the British ambassador in Berlin handed the German Government a final note stating that, unless we heard from them by 11 o'clock that they were prepared at once to withdraw their troops from Poland, a state of war would exist between us . . . I have to tell you that no such undertaking has been received, and that consequently this country is at war with Germany.

I have too great a soul to die like a criminal The claim of John Wilkes Booth, assassin of Abraham LINCOLN. The words were not his last; those were 'Useless, useless', as he was dragged by Federal troops, mortally wounded, from a burning farmhouse where he had been cornered. Booth was treated by a Dr Mudd, who was ostracised thereafter – hence the saying: **'His name is Mud.'**

I hereby resign the office of President of the United States The full text of the letter which Richard NIXON wrote to Secretary of State Henry KISSINGER on 8 August 1974, when IMPEACHMENT as a result of his role in WATERGATE had become inevitable.

I, John Brown, am now quite certain that the crimes of this guilty land will never be purged away but with blood The final statement of the leader of the ABOLITIONIST raid on HARPER'S FERRY before being hanged at Richmond, Virginia on 2 December 1859.

I may have signed my death warrant The prophetic remark of the Irish patriot Michael Collins (1890–1922) as he signed the Treaty with Britain in December 1921 establishing the IRISH FREE STATE. When the document was signed, the Lord Chancellor, Lord Birkenhead (the former F. E. Smith, 1872–1930), said: 'I may have signed my political death warrant tonight.' Collins, commander-in-chief of the government forces in Ireland's CIVIL WAR and a reluctant participant in the Treaty talks, replied: 'I may have signed my death warrant.' He was killed by Republicans in an ambush in Co. Cork on 22 August 1922.

I offer neither pay, nor quarters, nor provisions; I offer hunger, thirst, forced marches, battles and death. Let him who loves his country in his heart, and not with his lips only, follow me The rallying call of the Italian patriot Giuseppe Garibaldi (1807–82) in his struggle to unite his country under liberal rule (*see* RISORGIMENTO). He delivered it in a speech to his surrounded Legion in Rome on 2 July 1849.

I refer the honourable Member to the reply I gave some moments ago At WESTMINSTER, the standard reply given by the Prime Minister in the HOUSE to each OPEN QUESTION asking him or her their engagements for the day, once the initial answer has been given. Since the MODERNISATION of Prime Minister's Questions after the 1997 ELECTION, this formality has generally been dispensed with.

I paid for that microphone Ronald REAGAN'S COMMENT IN THE 1980 REPUBLICAN PRIMARIES when staffers for his rival George BUSH tried to prevent him appearing on the same platform as their CANDIDATE. The phrase echoed throughout America, particularly among movie buffs who remembered a 1948 Spencer Tracy – Katherine Hepburn film *State of the Union*, from which Reagan's memory lifted it. Despite the tussle, Bush became Reagan's running-mate.

I see all the birds are flown King Charles I's comment on 4 January 1642 after arriving in the HOUSE OF COMMONS to arrest the FIVE MEMBERS against whom he had issued writs for high TREASON. When rumours of the action against the five reached WESTMINSTER, the House asked them to leave, lest soldiers be sent to remove them forcibly. No sooner had they left than the King arrived. He took the SPEAKER's CHAIR, surveyed the House and then apologised for 'this occasion of coming unto you', asserting that 'I must have them wheresoever I find them' and asking the House to hand them over when they returned. 'I never did intend any Force but shall proceed against them in a legal and fair way, for I never meant any other,' he said. He then asked Speaker Lenthall where the five were, and Lenthall refused to answer unless the House so directed. The King then left, with the House in disorder, and the CIVIL WAR had come a step nearer.

I see the river Tiber foaming with much blood *See* RIVERS OF BLOOD.

I shall not seek, and I will not accept . . . Lyndon B. JOHNSON's announcement in March 1968 that he would be stepping down from the Presidency. LBJ decided not to run again because of the divisions opening up in the Democratic Party over his VIETNAM WAR policy; the anti-war Sen. Eugene McCarthy had run strongly against him in the early PRIMARIES. His surprise announcement came at the end of a broadcast on Vietnam. Johnson said:

> It is true that a HOUSE DIVIDED against itself cannot stand. There is a division in the American house now, and believing as I do, I have concluded that I should not permit the presidency to become involved in the partisan divisions that are developing in this political year. Accordingly, I shall not seek, and I will not accept, the nomination of my party for another term as your President.

Other political figures have been as categorical as LBJ, but some have changed their minds. The former SNP leader Alex Salmond repeatedly ruled out a comeback in similar language before announcing on John Swinney's resignation in 2004 that he was indeed ready to run.

I stand here with a deep sense of the improbability of this moment The reaction of Spiro T. AGNEW (1918–), when Richard NIXON nominated him for the Vice Presidency at the 1968 Republican CONVENTION. Liberals were quick to assert that Agnew was right and the prospect of his being a HEARTBEAT AWAY FROM THE PRESIDENCY was preposterous. It seemed even more so in 1973, when Agnew resigned under a cloud.

I, too, was a carpenter A remark attributed to the Labour left-winger Eric Heffer (1922–91), the comparison with Christ reflecting both his high self-opinion and his deep religious faith. Heffer, one of the most popular members of the HOUSE OF COMMONS though a disruptive force when Labour was in government, represented Liverpool Walton for 27 years until his death from cancer; on one of his last appearances in the CHAMBER, John MAJOR, newly installed as Prime Minister, earned the rare compliment of a round of applause by crossing the FLOOR of the House to shake his hand.

I wanted to dance, but couldn't find any nice ladies to dance with The despairing account by the UNITED NATIONS secretary-general Javier Perez de Cuellar (1920–) of his final visit to Baghdad in January 1991, undertaken in an effort to avert the GULF WAR.

I warn you not to be ordinary . . . Neil KINNOCK's apocalyptic warning at the close of the 1983 ELECTION campaign of the impact of THATCHERISM on all but the most privileged members of society. Despite Labour's heavy defeat, the speech had a great effect and contributed to his choice as party leader after the poll. Speaking at Bridgend on 7 June 1983, Kinnock declared:

> If Margaret Thatcher wins on Thursday, she will be more a leader than a Prime Minister. That power produces arrogance and when it is toughened by Tebbitry and flattered and fawned upon by spineless sycophants, the boot-licking tabloid Knights of Fleet Street and placemen in the QUANGOS, the arrogance corrupts absolutely.
>
> If Margaret Thatcher wins on Thursday –
> I warn you not to be ordinary.
> I warn you not to be young.
> I warn you not to fall ill.
> I warn you not to get old.

ICBM Inter-Continental Ballistic Missile. Those missiles with a range in excess of 5,500km, i.e. capable of reaching the former Soviet Union when fired from the US or vice versa. *See* ABM TREATY; FIRST STRIKE; MIRV; NUCLEAR WAR; SALT; START AGREEMENTS.

ice axe The ultimate symbol of betrayal and brutal removal of one's opponents, from the murder of TROTSKY in Mexico in 1940 on the orders of STALIN. Trotsky was killed with an ice-axe by Ramon Mercader, a Spaniard whose mother was the mistress of an NKVD general. The murder was savage even by Stalin's standard, and gave a new lease of life to Trotskyists' hatred of Soviet Communism.

Ich. Ich bin ein Berliner (Ger. I am a Berliner) President KENNEDY's defiant identification with the people of West Berlin when he spoke in the free enclave on 26 June 1963 at the height of COLD WAR tension. It did much to raise the morale of the 2 million Germans surrounded the previous year by the BERLIN WALL, and emphasise to the KREMLIN that America would stand as firm over Berlin as it had over Cuba. JFK said:

> Two thousand years ago the proudest boast was *civis Romanus sum*. Today, in the world of freedom, the proudest boast is *Ich bin ein Berliner* . . . All free men, wherever they may live, are citizens of Berlin, and, therefore, as a free man, I take pride in the words *Ich bin ein Berliner*.

The phrase is not strictly correct, grammatically or factually: mischievous Germans point out that a *Berliner* is actually a doughnut. When Jimmy CARTER was to visit Germany in 1978, his adviser Gerald Rafshoon jokingly suggested he go to Frankfurt and make a similar pronouncement.

Ich Dien (Ger. I serve) The motto of the PRINCE OF WALES.

idealism The aim for total perfection or the most ethical outcome, often a refusal to compromise with reality. Aldous Huxley dismissed it as 'the noble toga that political gentlemen drape over their will to power', Woodrow WILSON asserted that 'America is the only idealistic nation in the world', but Speaker Joe Cannon (*see* FOUL-MOUTHED JOE) said: 'You can't make a silk purse out of a sow's ear, and you can't change human nature from intelligent self-interest into pure idealism – not in this life, and if you could, what would be left for paradise?'

> I have never been an idealist. That implies that you aren't going to achieve something.
>
> ARTHUR SCARGILL

ideology The driving philosophy behind a political or social movement, generally of an abstract or dogmatic nature. A formulator or proponent of an ideology is an **ideologue**.

> As a citizen I would hesitate, or not like to see, any political party outlawed on the basis of its ideology. We have spent 170 years in this country on the basis that democracy is strong enough to stand up and fight against the inroads of any ideology.
>
> RONALD REAGAN, for the Screen Actors' Guild, answering Rep. Richard NIXON in 1947

ideological warfare The battle of rival ideologies, specifically between left and right, or totalitarianism and democracy.

IDS Not a software company, but **Iain Duncan Smith** (1954–), leader of the UK CONSERVATIVE PARTY from 2001–03. A former regular army officer who became a protégé of Norman Tebbit (*see* CHINGFORD SKINHEAD), whose north-east London seat he inherited in 1992, Duncan Smith was one of the EUROSCEPTIC rebels who dogged the premiership of John MAJOR. Under William HAGUE he showed promise as Social Security and then Defence spokesman, and when Hague resigned after the Conservatives' second LANDSLIDE defeat Duncan Smith defeated the pro-European and more liberal Kenneth Clarke for the leadership in the first ballot of the party's entire membership. His brief tenure was punctuated by infighting which reduced CENTRAL OFFICE to a virtual standstill and prompted unfounded allegations of SLEAZE (*see* BETSYGATE), and policy arguments which prompted him to appeal to the party to UNITE OR DIE. Styling himself a determined if QUIET MAN, he made little impact on Tony BLAIR, whose decision to join the IRAQ WAR he firmly supported. Discontent with his leadership led to his losing a CONFIDENCE vote of Conservative MPs on 23 October 2003 by 90–75; Michael HOWARD was elected his successor by acclamation.

> You can imagine the sign hanging outside Conservative Central Office: 'Shop closed – out to lunch'.
>
> MICHAEL HESELTINE, 23 August 2001

> Like watching the leader of the Morecambe Amateur Dramatic Society trying to do Hamlet
>
> Sir MAX HASTINGS.

> At least with Iain Duncan Smith we were all united in trying to get rid of him.
>
> ANON. Conservative MP, *The Daily Telegraph*, 4 October 2004

if. If it ain't broke, don't fix it A dictum of Henry FORD, picked up by Margaret

THATCHER as an argument against unnecessary Government intervention.

If it's not hurting, it isn't working Chancellor John MAJOR's defence in October 1990 of high interest rates as a means of bringing down inflation, which earned him much adverse comment at the time. With the economy reviving early in 1996, the Conservatives put out a poster reading: 'Yes it hurt. Yes it worked.'

If pressed further . . . The phrase sometimes placed in documents used by WHITEHALL officials to brief the media, indicating more information that may be given under persistent questioning.

If you can't beat or **lick 'em, join 'em** A favourite saying of Sen. James E. Watson (1864–1948), taken up by Sen. Everett DIRKSEN. The reverse, 'if you can't join them, beat them', was said by the Danish Foreign Minister Uffe Elleman-Jensen in May 1992 when, after Denmark's rejection of the MAASTRICHT TREATY, the Danish football team was co-opted into the European football championship at the last minute in place of war-torn Yugoslavia – and beat Germany to win the competition.

If you can't convince them, confuse them A favourite saying of President TRUMAN.

If you can't stand the heat, get out of the kitchen Another Trumanism, directed at those politicians without the nerve to take tough decisions – and at himself on deciding not to seek re-election in 1952. Truman himself attributed it to Maj. Gen. Harry Vaughan. It was frequently quoted by Harold WILSON.

If you don't constantly sharpen your knife, it will rust A justification of continued REVOLUTIONARY violence from CHAIRMAN MAO Tse-Tung.

IGs Inter-departmental groups that meet to co-ordinate US government policy, especially those in the field of foreign affairs which are generally under the chairmanship of STATE.

IGC Inter-governmental council/conference. In the EUROPEAN UNION, a series of meetings involving officials, Ministers or even Heads of Government to consider and agree on changes to its Treaties, generally in pursuit of greater effectiveness for the EU and closer economic or political union. The first such was set up at the Rome summit in December 1990 to draft what became the MAASTRICHT TREATY.

Ike The universal nickname for President Dwight D. EISENHOWER, confirmed in the slogan **'I Like Ike'** on which the Republicans fought and won the 1952 and 1956 Presidential elections.

> I like Ike. I like Ike so well I'd send him back to the Army if I had a chance.
>
> HARRY S TRUMAN, 12 October 1952.

illegals Illegal immigrants to the United States who have evaded all controls and found jobs, their vulnerability to detection creating a subculture. At first the term applied mainly to illicit arrivals from central America; later other groups, notably the Irish, adopted it.

Illinois baboon or **gorilla** Just two of the many nicknames for Abraham LINCOLN, stemming from his height, stark hirsute face and long arms.

ILO International Labour Organisation. The body, originally established in 1919 as an organ of the LEAGUE OF NATIONS, which regulates employment practices throughout the world, with government, employer and union representatives from each country. One of the last survivals of the Treaty of VERSAILLES, the ILO is now an agency of the UNITED NATIONS.

> It cannot enforce decisions, but it can publicly humiliate disobedient members.
>
> BLANCHE D'ALPUGET.

ILO unemployment The less rigorous of the two measures used by the UK government to assess the number of people out of work. Generally giving a reading around 600,000 more than the **claimant count**, which records only those claiming unemployment benefits from the State, it has been the preferred measure of the post-1997 Labour government.

ILP Independent Labour Party. The party founded in 1893 by Keir Hardie and others, as a forerunner to Britain's LABOUR PARTY. An ILP of sorts, with a left-wing slant, continued to exist after Labour's formation, with five rebel MPs claiming allegiance to it in 1929. It remained AFFILIATED to Labour until 1932; when forced to choose, the bulk of its adherents went to Labour, but a dwindling rump continued for over half a century.

I'm. I'm all right, Jack The phrase which characterised industrial relations in 1950s Britain, and the title of a film in which Peter Sellers played a Communist shop steward. The film made a considerable impact, but such was the strength of the trade unions that it was over 30 years before workable legislation was passed to curb wildcat strikes. The phrase dates back to 1910, when Sir David Bone (1874–1959) had a character in his seafaring novel *The Brassbounder* say: 'It's "Damn you, Jack – I'm all right" with you chaps.'

I'm so pleased to be here in . . . The standard opening to one of the most frequent political GAFFES, especially during frantic ELECTION campaigning. The speaker proudly announces that they are glad to be in one town (or country) and has to be reminded that they are in fact somewhere else. SIR ALEC Douglas-Home had a tendency to do this; his wife got round the problem by whispering: 'Peking, Alec, Peking', or whatever the correct venue might be. Examples are legion. In the 1940 Presidential campaign Wendell Wilkie began a speech with the words: 'Now we are in Chicago', to be told by a HECKLER: 'No, you're in Cicero.' Wilkie made matters worse (with Chicago voters) by replying: 'Well, all right, this is Cicero. To hell with Chicago!' In 1980 Jimmy CARTER told a crowd in Gerald FORD's home town of Grand Rapids that he was pleased to be in Cedar Rapids; Ford capped him in the gaffe stakes by saying Carter didn't know Michigan was one of the 48 states (there had been 50 for quite some time). Ronald REAGAN once welcomed Premier Lee Kuan Yew of Singapore to the WHITE HOUSE with the words: 'Welcome to Singapore!' while at a White House dinner in 1996 Irish President Mary Robinson referred to Bill CLINTON as 'President Kennedy'. In the 1984 campaign George BUSH Snr told a crowd in Green Bay, Wisconsin how much he liked the Minnesota Vikings. Margaret THATCHER once praised the delights of Malaysia while visiting Indonesia, and during Britain's 1992 campaign the Liberal Democrat leader Paddy Ashdown (*see* Paddy PANTSDOWN) arrived in Cornwall with the words: 'It's nice to be in Devon again.'

IMF International Monetary Fund. A specialised agency of the UNITED NATIONS established by the 1944 BRETTON WOODS conference to promote international trade by easing liquidity problems and stabilising exchange rates. With the WORLD BANK, it has come to be criticised in the THIRD WORLD for imposing economic policies which impede development and ignore the local situation. Based in WASHINGTON, the IMF makes funds available to countries experiencing short-term BALANCE OF PAYMENTS difficulties, and also supervises economic reform and restructuring in countries moving away from a command ECONOMY. Deposits of gold or domestic currency are made by member states, who can then borrow automatically up to the limit of their reserve. In 1970 SPECIAL DRAWING RIGHTS (SDRs) were introduced to allow members to borrow in convertible currencies from each other, and became the IMF's unit of account. In Britain, the IMF was at the heart of a political crisis in 1976 when the Labour government was split over swingeing spending cuts demanded before it would authorise a £2.3 billion standby credit to stabilise sterling; Prime Minister James CALLAGHAN asked a hostile meeting of Labour MPs: 'Do you want us to go on?' The IMF, egged on by the US Treasury, got £2 billion of cuts; it later turned out that the available data were faulty and they had probably not been necessary. The exercise alienated Chancellor Denis HEALEY from the left (probably costing him the leadership in 1980) and gave the Tories a stick with which they beat Labour relentlessly until their own economic crisis sixteen years later.

immobilisme A French term for the paralysis in decision-making resulting from unstable COALITIONS and frequent changes in government. It related particularly to the politics of the THIRD (1870–1940) and FOURTH (1946–58) REPUBLICS, which left France without a stable EXECUTIVE, with all power vested in the NATIONAL ASSEMBLY, from which governments were formed. It was handicapped by a multi-party system reflecting the complex structure of French society, and a form of PROPORTIONAL REPRESENTATION which encouraged unstable coalitions.

> Neddy, I've been talking to one of the French governments . . .
>
> PETER SELLERS as Gritpype Thynne in *The Goon Show*, BBC radio, c. 1957

immunities The exemption from civil legal action for the consequences of industrial disputes, which Britain's trade unions enjoyed from the remedying of the TAFF VALE JUDGMENT by the Liberals in 1906 until Margaret THATCHER's government removed it through STEP BY STEP legislation in the early 1980s.

Congressional immunity The immunity of members of both HOUSES from lawsuits resulting from what they say on the FLOOR. This right, which does not extend to what legislators say elsewhere, is enshrined in

Article I, Section 6 of the US CONSTITUTION, which also exempts them from arrest for 'treason, felony or breach of the peace.'

diplomatic immunity The privilege accorded to DIPLOMATS under which they and their households are exempt from taxes, customs duties and prosecution for all but serious criminal offences when serving in another country. The right is guaranteed by the VIENNA CONVENTION.

impeachment The trial by the LEGISLATURE of an office-holder, even a HEAD OF STATE, and his or her removal from office if members so vote. Impeachment was a valued weapon of the WESTMINSTER Parliament as it sought to prevent abuses of power. In 1769 John Hatsell wrote: 'Impeachments are the groans of the people, and carry with them a greater supposition of guilt than any other accusation.' The most celebrated came in 1788, when the enemies of Warren Hastings, former Governor-General of India, had him brought before the HOUSE OF LORDS; he was acquitted after a seven-year trial, but reduced to poverty. Edmund BURKE, leading the charge, declared:

> I impeach him in the name of the people of India, whose rights he has trodden under foot, and whose country he has turned into a desert. Lastly, in the name of human nature itself, in the name of both sexes, in the name of every age, in the name of every rank. I impeach the common enemy and oppressor of all!

In September 2004, fourteen MPs headed by the Welsh Nationalist Adam Price tried to initiate impeachment proceedings against Tony BLAIR for having gone to war in Iraq.

America's FOUNDING FATHERS included impeachment in the CONSTITUTION as a sanction against 'Treason, Bribery, or other HIGH CRIMES AND MISDEMEANOURS'. Benjamin FRANKLIN argued that without such a process against an alleged wrongdoer, 'recourse was had to assassinations, in which he was not only deprived of his life but of the opportunity of vindicating his character.' And in 1970 – just two years before WATERGATE – Rep. Gerald FORD stated: 'An impeachable offense is whatever the HOUSE OF REPRESENTATIVES considers [it] to be at a given moment in history; conviction results from whatever offense or offenses two-thirds of the other body considers to be sufficiently serious to require removal of the accused from office.'

The procedure is for the HOUSE OF REPRESENTATIVES to draw up a Resolution of Impeachment and, if it is passed, for the SENATE to conduct the trial; a two-thirds vote is required for conviction. Over two centuries the House has instituted more than 50 impeachments, though only a dozen have reached the Senate. There have only been five convictions, all of Federal judges – such as Harry Claiborne for tax evasion.

Three Presidents have faced impeachment – the first for political reasons, the second for judicial, the third because of sex. Andrew Johnson was impeached in 1868 by supporters of RECONSTRUCTION, which he strongly opposed. Joseph Medill noted: 'Like an aching tooth, everyone is impatient to have the old villain out,' and Rep. Thaddeus Stevens declaimed: 'He is surrounded, hampered, tangled on the meshes of his old wickedness. Unfortunate, unhappy man, behold your doom!' Johnson faced his critics head on, saying: 'Let them impeach and be damned!' The House voted a resolution of impeachment by 126 to 47 – but the vote in the Senate fell one short and Johnson served out the term to which LINCOLN had been elected. Benjamin Wade, PRESIDENT PRO TEM of the Senate, had been so certain of a vote to impeach that he had even named his own Cabinet. Sen. Edmund Ross, who tipped the vote against conviction and paid the price with the voters, warned prophetically:

> Conditions may arise some day when the exercise of the power to impeach and remove the President may be quite as essential to the preservation of our political system as it threatened to become in this instance destructive of that system.

So it proved in 1974, when the WATERGATE plot and COVER-UP were traced back to Richard NIXON despite his denials. On 27 July the House Judiciary Committee voted 27 to 11 to recommend impeachment, and Nixon resigned the following week to avoid the embarrassment of a trial. As the revelations of wrongdoing gathered pace late in 1973, Sen. George Aitken said: 'May I now pass on to this Congress advice which I received recently from a fellow Vermonter – either impeach him or get off his back.'

The impeachment of Bill CLINTON over ZIPPERGATE, including the Paula JONES case, was not an edifying process on either side. The President had indisputably tarnished his office, but the zeal with which Republican majority in the House went after him led some Americans to complain about the filth they were being exposed to in news bulletins. The House Judiciary Committee voted on 5 October 1998 to open an impeachment inquiry, and on 12 December Clinton was impeached on two counts of perjury and obstruction of justice. In February 1999 the Senate cleared him by margins ranging from 55–45 to 50–50; he restored some momentum to his presidency, but the episode had undermined Vice President Al GORE's campaign to succeed him, and in 2000 George W. BUSH just scraped home.

One recent successful impeachment took place in 1992, when the Brazilian Congress removed President Fernando Collor on charges of massive corruption.

imperial. Imperial Conferences The conferences held in London between the Prime Ministers of the DOMINIONS of the BRITISH EMPIRE between 1907 and 1946. They had their origins in the Colonial Conference held in 1887 on the occasion of Queen Victoria's Golden Jubilee. Since 1948, Commonwealth conferences (*see* CHOGM) have replaced them.

Imperial Preference A system for encouraging trade between the countries of the British Empire, and particularly between them and Britain, by applying preferential TARIFFS, or none at all. The issue was live as early as 1903, when Joseph Chamberlain said: 'If you are to give a preference to the colonies, you must put a tax on food.' The system was finally negotiated at the 1932 Imperial Economic Conference in Ottawa; after 1948 it applied to the Commonwealth. It was gradually dismantled as a result of the anti-PROTECTIONIST conditions imposed by GATT from 1947 and by Britain's desire to join the COMMON MARKET. Commonwealth preference was finally abandoned in 1977.

Imperial Presidency *See* PRESIDENCY.

imperialism The upsurge of feeling for overseas expansion and the seizure of colonial possessions that swept the great nations of western Europe, and America, at the end of the 19th century. Originally the word for supporting an emperor, imperialism took on a new meaning in Britain after DISRAELI had Queen Victoria proclaimed Empress of India, with Africa its main focus and Joseph Chamberlain (1836–1914) its most enthusiastic advocate; similar aims were pursued by France (*see* FASHODA), Germany and to a lesser extent Belgium and Italy. US Imperialism reached its crescendo in the SPANISH-AMERICAN WAR and the election of MCKINLEY; Sen. Mark Hanna was its driving force. Lord Rosebery, the founder of Liberal Imperialism in Britain, argued that 'imperialism – sane imperialism – is nothing but a larger patriotism.'

The eclipse of the great empires (except the British) in WORLD WAR I, Mussolini's brief attempt to rebuild Rome's imperial grandeur in Africa and the rise of COMMUNISM turned imperialism and colonialism into terms of abuse; LENIN compared them to 'the monopoly stage of capitalism'. And as imperialism retreated, its detractors grew shriller. In 1958 Nelson MANDELA declared: 'The Communist bogey is an American stunt to distract the peoples of Africa from the real issue facing them, namely American imperialism'; Egypt's President Nasser dismissed Israel as 'nothing more than one of the consequences of imperialism'. But it took the end of the COLD WAR for the last empire to be sustained by force – the Soviet Union's SATELLITES in eastern Europe – to collapse.

> The struggles waged by the different peoples against US imperialism reinforce each other and merge into a torrential worldwide tide of opposition to US imperialism . . . Since World War II, US imperialism has stepped into the shoes of German, Japanese and Italian fascism and has been trying to build a great American empire by dominating and enslaving the whole world.
>
> LIN PIAO (1908–71), Chinese Minister of Defence

In its time (1898) the ultimate argument of the imperialist was spelt out by Hilaire Belloc (1870–1953) when he wrote:

> Whatever happens, we have got
> The Maxim gun, and they have not.

dollar imperialism The term used by Communist and NON-ALIGNED leaders during the COLD WAR to denounce what they saw as economic exploitation of the developing world by US interests.

impoundment Withholding by a US President of funds APPROPRIATED by CONGRESS for programmes of which he does not approve, pending a BILL from the ADMINISTRATION setting different BUDGET priorities. The limited power presidents had traditionally exercised to balance the books was turned by Richard NIXON into an instrument of policy, directed mainly against social programmes, and was severely restricted by Congress in 1974.

imprint The statement that under UK electual law has to appear at the foot of any poster or leaflet issued by a party or candidate. It must give the name and address of the printer and publication of the material, the publisher usually being the candidate's AGENT.

in. In God We Trust The motto stamped on US coins since the 1950s, reflecting an upsurge in religious feeling and a belief that the words did not violate the FIRST AMENDMENT's stipulation that 'Congress shall make no law respecting an establishment of religion.'

In Place of Fear The title of Aneurin BEVAN's 1952 book setting out the case for radical disarmament, which became part of the credo of the Labour left.

In Place of Strife The WHITE PAPER proposing controls over the trade unions which Harold WILSON's Employment Secretary Barbara Castle produced in January 1969. She was assisted by a small drafting group including Tony BENN, later a vehement opponent of curbs on the unions, and Peter Shore. Its central proposal, to outlaw unofficial strikes with the Government itself taking unions and strikers to court, infuriated the unions and split the CABINET, which had had little chance to discuss it. Home Secretary James CALLAGHAN led the opponents; he described Mrs Castle, who wanted legislation that summer, as 'galloping ahead with all the reckless gallantry of the Light Brigade at Balaclava'. Cabinet resistance grew, and when the TUC agreed to police unofficial disputes itself, Wilson dropped the plan to legislate.

> The unions were blameworthy for failing, despite Barbara Castle's warning, to make their own programme for reforms effective . . . This, coupled with the excesses of some activists in the 1970s, led inexorably to . . . legislation and the intervention by the courts in their affairs.
>
> JAMES CALLAGHAN

In your heart you know he's right The slogan on which Arizona's Republican Sen. Barry Goldwater (1909–98) fought an ultra-conservative campaign for the Presidency in 1964, going down to a LANDSLIDE defeat by Lyndon B. JOHNSON. The Democrats parodied the slogan as: **In your guts you know he's nuts**, and Hubert HUMPHREY said: 'He'd have been a great success in the movies – working for 18th-Century Fox.' Goldwater had sought the Presidency despite active discouragement from John F. KENNEDY, whom he would have faced but for DALLAS; when Goldwater took JFK's photograph and sent him a copy, the President signed it: 'For Barry Goldwater, whom I urge to follow the career for which he has shown so much talent – photography.' Goldwater was philosophical about his origins, saying: 'I told Paradise Valley I was half-Jewish – could I play the back nine?' But I. F. STONE commented: 'It was hard to listen to him and realise that a man could he half Jewish and yet appear twice as dense as the average Gentile.' Goldwater also crossed swords with the veteran columnist Walter Lippmann; when he complained: 'I won't say the papers misquote me, but I sometimes wonder where Christianity would be today if some of those reporters had been Matthew, Mark, Luke and John', Lippmann shot back: 'The Senator might remember that the Evangelists had a more inspiring subject.' Conservatism made a return with Ronald REAGAN, and Goldwater survived his defeat to serve as a distinguished Senator until 1986; he exercised great influence over WATERGATE, defending Richard NIXON until the die was cast against him and then telling the President the game was up.

inauguration The ceremony at which the PRESIDENT of the United States is sworn in by the CHIEF JUSTICE of the SUPREME COURT at the start of his four-year term. Until 1932 the President was inaugurated in March, four months after being elected; since the start of Franklin D. ROOSEVELT's second term the inauguration has taken place on 20 January, unless that day falls on a Sunday. The ceremony itself is usually held in the open air on either the EAST or WEST FRONT of the CAPITOL. After taking the OATH OF OFFICE, the President delivers the **Inaugural Address**; this is followed by a parade down Pennsylvania Avenue to the WHITE HOUSE – President CARTER and his wife got out and walked, mingling with the crowd – and in the evening there is the Inaugural Ball. There are in fact several such balls, with contributors to the victor's campaign having the best chance of a ticket.

incomes policy An element of economic policy designed to keep wages under control, either by securing voluntary agreement between employers and unions, or by legislation. It has a better chance of success when parallel action is taken to restrain prices, creating a PRICES AND INCOMES POLICY. Governments on both sides of the Atlantic operated such policies in the late 1960s and well into the '70s, but they lost favour with the election of Margaret THATCHER and Ronald REAGAN.

incumbent A current holder of an elective office who is seeking, or intends to seek, RE-ELECTION. An incumbent, unless personally unpopular, generally enjoys an advantage over challengers known as the **power of the**

incumbency. While an incumbent Prime Minister in most countries has the advantage of being able to choose the date of an election, the benefits are even stronger in America where an incumbent President can allocate funds to SWING DISTRICTS and States, and a Senator or Congressman can use their FRANKING PRIVILEGE to deluge electors during their term with mail carefully pitched to secure votes. These and other advantages are reckoned to be worth $500,000 in campaign funds to each incumbent; the effect is that at most Congressional elections only a handful of members are unseated. There are exceptions; in the 1994 MID-TERM elections, even the Democratic Speaker Thomas Foley was defeated.

independence The state of being a nation with SOVEREIGNTY resting in itself; the goal of COLONIAL peoples throughout the ages and notably of a growing proportion of America's population during the 18th century.

> The country shall be independent, and we are all satisfied with nothing short of it.
>
> SAMUEL ADAMS, 1774

Independence, Missouri The town, now an eastern suburb of Kansas City, which for more than 70 years was the home of President Harry S TRUMAN, and to which he and his wife Bess retired on leaving the WHITE HOUSE in 1953. Truman is buried in the courtyard of the library named after him in Independence, which also contains a replica of the OVAL OFFICE.

Independence Day The anniversary of the date on which a nation achieved its independence, in America's case 4 July 1776 when the last draft of the Declaration of Independence was reported to the CONTINENTAL CONGRESS and voted on. Though 4 July soon became the nation's greatest secular holiday, John ADAMS put the historic date two days before when a resolution for independence was carried, writing:

> The second day of July, 1776, will be the most memorable epoch in the history of America. It ought to be commemorated, as the Day of deliverance by solemn acts of devotion to God Almighty. It ought to be solemnized with pomp and Parade, with Shews, Games, Sports, Guns, Bells, Bonfires, Illuminations from one end of this Continent to the other from this Time forward forever more.

Declaration of Independence The document on which America's nationhood and freedoms are founded. It proclaimed the secession of Britain's thirteen American colonies, blaming the break on the 'injuries and usurpations' of King George III which were designed to bring about an 'absolute tyranny'. The Declaration, which received only brief mention in the London papers, was suggested by Thomas Paine and drafted by Benjamin FRANKLIN, John ADAMS, Roger Sherman, Robert Livingston and Thomas JEFFERSON, whose language shines through it. No one actually signed it on 4 July; most of the 56 signers did so over the next two months, but six added their names some time later, Thomas McKean in 1781, while Livingston never signed. *See* John HANCOCK; LIFE, LIBERTY AND THE PURSUIT OF HAPPINESS; We Hold These TRUTHS TO BE SELF-EVIDENT; WHEN, IN THE COURSE OF HUMAN EVENTS.

> It gave liberty not only to the people of this country, but hope to all the world.
>
> ABRAHAM LINCOLN

> In 1776, the Americans laid before Europe that noble Declaration, which ought to be hung up in the nursery of every king, and blazoned on the porch of every royal palace.
>
> HENRY THOMAS BUCKLE, 1861

> The rights of man, through MAGNA CARTA, the Bill of Rights, the HABEAS CORPUS, trial by jury and the English common law find their most famous expression in the American Declaration of Independence.
>
> WINSTON CHURCHILL at FULTON, Missouri, 1946

Independent (1) **registered Independent** In America, a voter who wishes to specify that they are neither a Republican nor a Democrat, though at times they may vote for either party's candidates. As many as one-third of Americans may put themselves in this category.

> The guy who wants to take politics out of politics.
>
> ADLAI STEVENSON.

(2) In Britain, a local councillor who has been elected as an individual candidate and not under a party label, though in some cases they may belong to a party (usually the Conservatives). Some local authorities, especially in rural areas, are still controlled by Independents, though their number has fallen steadily since WORLD WAR II. Rarely, an independent candidate is elected to Parliament: in 1997 Martin Bell (*see* MAN IN A WHITE SUIT), in 2001 and 2005 the Kidderminster health services campaigned Dr Richard Taylor, and in 2005 the Labour independent Peter Law in Blaenau Gwent. The **independent network** was formed by Bell, Dr Taylor and others prior to the 2005

election to resource non-party candidates.

> You need a good cause, a well-known candidate and a vulnerable incumbent.
>
> MARTIN BELL

index-linking A system by which increases in pay, social security benefits and the like are determined by the increase in the cost of living. In Britain during the rapid INFLATION of the 1970s, the index-linking of CIVIL SERVICE pensions were claimed by some to be a reward for failure to devise a workable policy to keep prices under control.

Indian. Indian Mutiny The uprising in 1857 by native sepoys under British command, which was sparked by an order that troops use the new Enfield rifle, which had cartridges greased by pig or cow fat that had to be bitten off before loading. This offended Muslims and Hindus alike, most troops issued with the rifle refused to use it and some were jailed in Meerut. Their comrades mutinied, freed them and then carried out mass atrocities against Britons, including women and children, in Cawnpore, Delhi and Lucknow. The public at home was outraged both by the slaughter and by the measured way the Governor, Lord Canning, tried to restore order without unnecessary bloodshed. Once the Mutiny had been crushed, the post of Governor was abolished and those portions of India under British rule made the responsibility of a Secretary of State in the CABINET.

Indian Reorganisation Act The law put through CONGRESS in 1934 by Secretary for the Interior Harold Ickes (1874–1952) which finally turned the tide for what was left of the native American peoples. It undid much of the damage done by the well-meaning DAWES ACT, halted the pillage of Indian lands by commercial interests and white settlers, allocated funds for land acquisition, recognised tribal authority while encouraging modernisation of tribal government, and supported Indian education.

The only good Indian is a dead Indian The regrettably immortal comment of General Philip Sheridan (1831–88) at Fort Cobb in January 1869, when told he would be meeting a good Indian chief.

indicator A statistic – for instance the level of production in an industry like housebuilding – which is taken, along with others, to show the current level of economic activity and point to trends for the near future. In America a specific index of **key indicators** is published regularly by the Federal government.

lagging indicator Data – such as unemployment figures – which reflect past trends in the economy rather than pointing to how it is developing at present, or will develop in the future.

indoctrination The instilling in someone of a political IDEOLOGY, implicitly by continuous repetition, by duress or by subliminal means.

Industrial Relations Act The legislation introduced by Edward HEATH's government in 1971 in an effort to curb the excesses of Britain's trade unions. Though introduced by the liberal Employment Secretary Robert Carr, it was heavily influenced by Sir Geoffrey HOWE and other Tory lawyers. Based on the TAFT-HARTLEY ACT, it involved a more rigid and legalistic approach than Labour's abortive IN PLACE OF STRIFE; its centrepiece was a National Industrial Relations Court (NIRC). Unions lost all IMMUNITIES against legal action unless they agreed to register, and were held responsible in law for the activities of their members. The unions and the LABOUR PARTY strongly resisted passage of the legislation, and once it took effect the NIRC found its authority repeatedly flouted. The Act finally lost credibility when the Official Solicitor had to intervene to get the PENTONVILLE FIVE released from prison; they had defied the court's order for them to end secondary PICKETING, but their imprisonment led to a wave of sympathy strikes and the threat of public disorder.

Industry Act forecasts The predictions of economic growth, unemployment and the rate of inflation which a CHANCELLOR OF THE EXCHEQUER delivers to Parliament each Autumn in his PRE-BUDGET REPORT. They were first required by the 1975 Industry Act, which also established the TREASURY MODEL to make the predictions.

INF Treaty Intermediate Nuclear Forces Treaty. The first accord to provide for comprehensive ARMS CONTROL, signed by Presidents REAGAN and GORBACHEV in WASHINGTON in December 1987. It ended the round of the ARMS RACE in which the Soviet Union had deployed SS20 medium-range nuclear missiles throughout eastern Europe from the mid-1970s, and America had matched them – to the fury of anti-NUCLEAR campaigners – with CRUISE and PERSHING missiles. The US undertook to destroy 358 missiles and the Soviets 573; as some of the Soviet missiles carried three warheads, the advantage to the West was even greater than the numbers suggest.

infantile leftists The pejorative used by LENINIST leaders for self-styled Communists who lacked the discipline and restraint to toe the party line, but rushed into indiscriminate revolutionary action without considering the long-term interests of the movement.

inflation The rate of increase in the level of prices, reflecting an increase in the MONEY SUPPLY not accompanied by economic growth. Save for the GREAT DEPRESSION when prices actually fell, inflation was latent throughout the 20th century and at times – in Germany in the 1920s when a suitcase of notes was needed to buy a loaf, Britain in the 1970s and Latin America most of the time – became a rampant and destabilising force. High inflation for any length of time attacks the value of savings, **double-digit inflation** of over 10% per annum starts to disrupt an economy and impose strains on society, while **hyperinflation**, of 50% or more each month, renders the conduct of a money-based economy almost impossible. Milton FRIEDMAN, whose views greatly influenced Margaret THATCHER, argued that inflation was

> The one form of taxation that can be imposed without legislation.

The only cure, he wrote, was 'a slower rate of increase in the quantity of money'.

> Inflation in the Sixties was a nuisance to be endured, like varicose veins or French foreign policy. BERNARD LEVIN

> Having a little inflation is like being a little pregnant.
> LEON HENDERSON (1895–1986)

influence peddling WASHINGTON-speak for what anywhere else would be called bribery and corruption. In terms of the US CONGRESS, it involves the gaining of influence by LOBBYISTS and others through the distribution of favours in the hope – or expectation – that they will be reciprocated. A classic example was KOREAGATE, but there have been many others despite efforts by the Congressional leadership to impose ethical standards.

infomercial On US television, a paid-for political message or slot. Although TV advertising has been a staple of the American political process for decades, the idea of the infomercial was created and the name given by Ross PEROT in 1992.

informal, an A meeting of an EU Ministerial council held without a formal agenda, generally to discuss a particular theme or issue without needing to arrive at a detailed conclusion. Informals are frequently held over a weekend in the relaxed atmosphere of a resort, away from large number of officials and the media.

Information Scandal The scandal in South Africa in 1978–79 which first brought down the Minister of Information, Mr Connie Mulder, then forced the resignation of B. J. Vorster first as Prime Minister (in September 1978, on grounds of ill health) and then as State President on 4 June 1979. It revolved around covert government funding for pro-APARTHEID media, approved by Mulder – who said Vorster had known all about it. Dr Eschel Rhoodie, former Secretary for Information, fled abroad and gave interviews defending his use and control of the secret funds, which financed a failed takeover bid for the anti-NATIONAL PARTY SAAN newspaper group, and then set up the pro-government *Citizen*; property was also purchased in South Africa, France and Miami. Supreme Court Justice Mostert tabled charges of corruption, and these were investigated by a commission under Mr Justice Erasmus. The **Erasmus Commission** severely criticised Vorster's judgement, saying he shared responsibility with Mulder for the department's ineptitude; he immediately resigned as President. Unusually for a scandal which provided South African liberals with political capital, **Muldergate** inflicted lasting damage on the Afrikaner political establishment.

informed source *See* SOURCES.

Ingham, Bernard *See* YORKSHIRE RASPUTIN.

inhale 'I smoked marijuana, but I didn't inhale' – the classic FUDGE from Bill CLINTON at the start of his drive for the Presidency, getting round the issue of whether he had taken drugs as a student at Oxford and was therefore unfit for the WHITE HOUSE in the eyes of more staid Americans. He had similar explanations ready to explain why he had not served in VIETNAM, the extent to which he had joined in anti-War protests while a Rhodes Scholar at Oxford, and above all whether he had had a sexual relationship with Monica LEWINSKY. *See also* IS.

> We spent enormous amounts of time trying to teach him to inhale. He absolutely could not.
> Oxford contemporary MARTIN WALKER

initiative A procedure by which electors can directly bring about a change in the law, used at various times by 22 American States, starting with South Dakota in 1898; there is no provision for it at federal level. In some states the initiative process can also trigger the RECALL of a Governor or other State official. The combination of initiative and public REFERENDUM, pioneered by Oregon in 1902, was seen as a means of circumventing MACHINE POLITICS. Usually the signatures of 10% of voters are required for a proposal to be submitted to either the state legislature or the people for approval. Even if an initiative is defeated by popular ballot, the campaign for it can bring about a change in legislators' attitudes.

Inkatha (Freedom Party) *Inkatha Yenkululeko Yesizwe*, National Cultural Liberation Movement. (*Inkatha* is the grass coil Zulu women use to carry loads on their heads; its strength depends on the waving together of many strands.) The political movement, led by Chief Mangosuthu Gatsha Buthelezi (1928–), which has spearheaded in more senses than one the claims of tribalist Zulus for a special position in post-APARTHEID South Africa. Founded in 1928 as a mainly cultural organisation, it was revived by Buthelezi in the 1970s as a political force. While opposing apartheid, Inkatha pursued a less radical approach than the ANC, opposing SANCTIONS and foreign disinvestment and preferring some form of POWER-SHARING to black majority rule; it was thus promoted by the NATIONAL PARTY government as a potential electoral ally and counterweight to the ANC. Recruiting heavily among hostel-dwelling migrant workers in the Rand and championing their right to carry clubs and spears as 'cultural symbols', Inkatha combined assertions of Zulu strength with sporadic murderous attacks on ANC supporters (*see* BOIPATONG MASSACRE) in the run-up to the 1994 multiracial elections, which it only joined at the last minute. Nelson MANDELA invited Buthelezi to join his Cabinet; after the 2004 elections when Inkatha was beaten in its heartland of KwaZulu-Natal, Mandela's successor Thabo Mbeki sacked him.

INLA Irish National Liberation Army. A small but ultra-radical Irish Republican terrorist group, best known for its assassination in 1979 of Margaret THATCHER's NORTHERN IRELAND spokesman and close confidant Airey NEAVE. INLA stayed outside the PEACE PROCESS, but wound down its operations after the GOOD FRIDAY AGREEMENT and declared a ceasefire on 22 August 1998 after the OMAGH BOMBING. Its political wing has been the **Irish Republican Socialist Party**, whose Belfast estate stronghold was known as the '**planet of the IRSPs**'.

inner cities The densely populated and increasingly run-down central areas of cities throughout the West where bad housing, deteriorating public services, poverty, deprivation and a concentration of ethnic minorities can produce an UNDERCLASS and serious social tension. In America from the 1960s, and Britain from the early 1980s, frustration heightened by tension with the police has spilled over into sporadic riots. Heavy concentration of government money and effort has impacted on some of these communities' problems, but by no means all.

> When you've seen one inner-city slum, you've seen them all.
>
> Vice President SPIRO AGNEW, campaign speech in Detroit, 18 October 1968

> We've got a big job to do in some of those inner cities.
>
> MARGARET THATCHER at Conservative CENTRAL OFFICE after her 1987 election victory

inoperative The immortal word used during WATERGATE by Richard NIXON's press secretary Ron Ziegler (1939–2003) to categorise a statement he was now admitting to have been untrue; the word was actually put to him during a WHITE HOUSE briefing by R. W. Apple of the *New York Times,* and he rose to the bait. On 17 April 1973 as the conspiracy and White House involvement broke surface, Nixon said that 'serious' charges had come to light and his staff would not be immune from prosecution. Ziegler, who had always denied there was anything in Watergate, was relentlessly grilled at the daily briefing until, asked for the 18th time if all his statements had been untrue, he replied:

> This is the operative statement. The others are inoperative.

inside the Beltway The phrase used by WASHINGTON insiders for the culture of government and the political village surrounding it. The Beltway is the 64-mile Interstate 495, which circles the capital ten miles from its heart; most of Washington's government, political and media activity takes place within it, and most people involved – though the proportion is declining – also live inside it. Outside the

Beltway, beyond a few miles of suburbs and shopping malls, lies real America.

Institutional Revolutionary Party (PRI) The once-radical party that governed Mexico from 1929 to 2000, keeping power regardless of its popularity and despite a fully democratic constitution. The **National Revolutionary Party** was founded in 1929 by **Jefe Maximo** Plutarco Calles. In 1938 Lazaro Cardenas renamed it the **Party of Mexican Revolution**, with four CORPORATIST sectors, one of them military. It took its present name in 1946 when the military sector was abolished; Miguel Aleman, an economic reformer, became leader and after that it alternated between outward-looking policies and economic nationalism. By the 1980s the PRI was losing its grip; President Carlos Salinas de Gortari met protests over his election in 1988 by loosening the reins and allowing the PRI to lose some provincial elections. The party tightened its grip again in 1994 after the shock of the **Zapatista** uprising, making sure Ernesto Zedillo won that year's Presidential election. He proved a more credible reformer, allowing the arrest in February 1995 of Salinas' brother Raul in connection with the murder of the party's original candidate, Luis Donaldo Colosio, and planning the murder of PRI secretary-general José Francisco Ruiz Massieu; the charges – which eventually failed – forced Carlos Salinas to pull out of running for nomination to head the WTO. Zedillo, elected in Ruiz' place, tried to reform the party but it lost the lower house of Congress after 68 years in 1997, and finally the presidency in 2000 with the election of Vicente Fox.

insular cases The series of SUPREME COURT judgments between 1901 and 1903 settling the status of the various island TERRITORIES – COLONIES in all but name – that America had acquired. They established the principle that the CONSTITUTION need not apply in full to residents of US possessions, freeing Congress to administer each virtually as it chose.

insurgency *See* COUNTER-INSURGENCY.

Insurgents (1) The independent-minded liberal Republicans elected to CONGRESS in the early 1900s free of, and sometimes in opposition to, local party MACHINES. Spurning the Congressional leadership as a tool of big business, they pressed a radical agenda including TARIFF reforms, and when Speaker Joe Cannon (*see* FOUL-MOUTHED JOE) blocked them, they combined with the Democrats to strip him of his near-absolute power. Their leaders included Sen. Robert La Follette of Wisconsin and Reps. George Norris of Nebraska and Jonathan Dolliver of Iowa. (2) The GUERRILLA forces which prevented a return to normality in Baghdad and other major cities after the IRAQ WAR, pinning down US and, to a lesser extent, British forces while insisting that they left. They comprised three main elements: remnants of the former Iraqi army loyal to SADDAM HUSSEIN and the BAATH PARTY, who were strongest in the SUNNI TRIANGLE; Shi'ite militias supporting the radical cleric Moqtada al-Sada who dropped their campaign after a few months; and Arab fighters from outside Iraq, some of them connected to AL QAEDA.

insurrection A popular and apparently spontaneous uprising against the established government.

> When a government violates the people's rights insurrection is for the people, and each part of the people, the most sacred of rights and the most indispensible of duties.
>
> LAFAYETTE to the French National Assembly, 20 February 1790

> Insurrection, by means of guerrilla bands, is the true method of warfare for all nations desirous of emancipating themselves from a foreign yoke.
>
> GIUSEPPE MAZZINI (1805–72)

> Insurrection is an art, and like all arts it has its laws. LEON TROTSKY (1879–1940)

integrationist One who believes that different races should be encouraged to live side by side in a single society; integration is the opposite of SEGREGATION. Americans of all races have debated the extent of integration desirable and how to achieve it (*see* BUSING) since the 1950s. James Baldwin asked: 'Who needs to be integrated into a burning house?' Sen. Barry Goldwater declared: 'Forced integration is just as wrong as forced segregation', but the Georgia CIVIL RIGHTS campaigner Julian Bond explained:

> What we mean by integration is not to be with [Whites] but to have what they have.

intellectuals A respected political vanguard in continental Europe, a key constituent of the revolutionary Communist movement ('**workers, peasants and intellectuals**') and a term of abuse in England: Hugh Dalton dismissed them as 'semi-crooks, diabetics and under-sized Semites'. Intellectuals have not had a much better press in America (*see* EGGHEADS).

intelligence Information gathered about another country, usually an actual or potential enemy, or a group considered subversive, by a process of espionage, BUGGING, contact with informants or deduction. Many politicians are suspicious of this twilight world; US Secretary of State Henry Stimson, who closed his department's code-breaking Black Chamber in 1929, justified his action by saying: 'Gentlemen do not read each other's mail.'

intelligence community An especially American term for all those engaged in intelligence-gathering for a particular government. It refers specifically to the CIA and the NATIONAL SECURITY AGENCY, based on opposite sides of WASHINGTON; the FBI, which monitors subversion at home, is regarded by them as a lesser being. The community is reckoned both by itself and those who fantasise about it to have a culture and attitudes entirely of its own. 9/11 also demonstrated that America's gatherers of intelligence – and one suspects other nations' as well – would do anything rather than share their information with each other.

intelligentsia An originally Russian term for the intellectual or cultured classes, who were supposed to be in the vanguard of political liberalism and reform.

Interahamwe (Kinyarwanda*:* Those who kill together) The pro-Government Hutu militias in Rwanda who in 1994 slaughtered up to 1 million Tutsi, rendering large numbers homeless as the fighting spreading into the adjoining Democratic Republic of Congo. The UNITED NATIONS sent a force which, lacking direction because of infighting in the SECURITY COUNCIL, largely stood by and watched the carnage. In June 2004 Sylvestre Gacumbitsi, former Mayor of Rusomo, was jailed for 30 years by a United Nations tribunal in Tanzania for ordering the murder of 20,000 people and personally leading murder and rape squads.

interdependence The way in which each of the world's nations is dependent on the others for a balanced economy and continuing peace. *See* DECLARATION OF INTERDEPENDENCE.

interest. interest groups Sections of society which may be concerned about a particular area of policy and will band together to make their views known; for instance all those affected by the likelihood of a cut in subsidy to dairy farmers, or higher taxes on a particular sphere of commerce.

interests Matters which a nation considers to be its business, and in which it reserves a right to intervene. Palmerston said of Victorian Britain: 'The sun never sets on the interests of this country.' He is also reputed to have said: 'A nation has no friends, only interests', but he actually told the Commons on 1 March 1848:

> We have no eternal allies, and we have no eternal enemies. Our interests are eternal and perpetual, and those interests it is our duty to follow.

interests section The section of a country's EMBASSY in a foreign capital that represents the interests of a third nation, usually because that nation and the host country have broken off diplomatic relations.

conflict of interest A situation where elected representatives have commercial or other interests which could prevent them forming an impartial view on a matter that has to be decided. Anyone in this position is supposed to **declare an interest**; in Britain it is a criminal offence for a local councillor not to do so, and an MP not making such a declaration would now be severely dealt with.

outside interests Business or other activities by an elected representative which bring in remuneration and impose demands on his or her time, but do not necessarily constitute a conflict of interest.

register of interests A list kept by most legislatures in which each member is supposed to record his or her business connections and outside sources of income. Some are more fully observed than others; for years completion of the register in the HOUSE OF COMMONS was voluntary, because Enoch POWELL refused to sign it on principle.

special interests Commercial and other groups which are anxious to secure reliable support from politicians, paying for it if necessary. The ANTI-TRUST LAWS were an early attempt to weaken the power of such interests; Bill CLINTON's attempts to limit PAC contributions are a recent example.

> When I have to choose between voting for the people or the special interests, I always stick to the special interests. The people forget.
>
> Sen. HENRY F. ASHURST (1874–1962)

vested interests Those entrenched personal, class or corporate interests, usually but not necessarily financial, which act within a social and political system to prevent change that might have implications for them.

Interior. Department/Secretary of the Interior The department of the US Government, and its political head, which are charged with the administration of federal lands, mainly in the West, and which therefore have a powerful voice in oil exploration, Indian affairs and wildlife conservation. Founded in 1849, the Department has a chequered history of corruption, failure to protect native Americans and inertia on GREEN issues, though its record under most recent ADMINISTRATIONS has improved.

Minister of the Interior In France and many other Continental countries, the Cabinet member responsible for the maintenance of public order and security. In the UK, the task falls to the HOME SECRETARY.

intern A young person, often fresh out of university, who takes a job for minimal wages with a member of the US CONGRESS, in an arm of the Federal government or, if they are very lucky, in the WHITE HOUSE in order to gain experience and contacts for a career in administration or politics. The most celebrated intern, and not a typical one, was Monica LEWINSKY.

internal settlement The formula put forward in 1978 and implemented by Ian Smith (1919–) for a multi-racial Rhodesia achieved with safeguards for the whites and without ending UDI; his hope was that Britain and other countries would concede that MAJORITY RULE had been achieved, and restore RECOGNITION to the country. It involved renaming the country **Zimbabwe-Rhodesia**, and holding elections from which ZANU-PF would be excluded to produce a non-militant black government; one was duly elected in 1979 under Bishop Abel Muzorewa. Even the incoming Margaret THATCHER was not persuaded a RETURN TO LEGALITY had been achieved, and UDI was eventually ended and majority rule achieved by the 1980 LANCASTER HOUSE AGREEMENT. In the ensuing elections, Muzorewa's party won only three seats.

Internal Security Act *See* SUPPRESSION OF COMMUNISM Act.

international. International Brigades The foreign volunteers who fought for the Republicans against General Franco (*see* CAUDILLO) in the SPANISH CIVIL WAR (1936–39). There were seven brigades, divided by nationality; most came from Europe – many from Britain, including the novelist George Orwell and the poet W. H. Auden – but there was also an Abraham LINCOLN Brigade of Americans. Recruitment was largely organised by the Communist Party (though not all volunteers were Communists); the Brigades included intellectuals and writers, adventurers, the unemployed and ordinary workers. They took part in the defence of Madrid in November 1936, and reinforced Republican forces to defend the Jarama Valley and Guadalajara the following spring. In 1938 the brigades suffered heavy losses in the Ebro Valley, and as defeat loomed for the Republican Government, they departed with honour.

International Court of Justice *See* WORLD COURT.

International Criminal Court. The tribunal established by the 1998 Statute of Rome to try individual acts of GENOCIDE, crimes against humanity, WAR CRIMES and the so far undefined crime of aggression. It came into being in July 2002 and its eighteen judges were sworn in in March 2003, by which time 89 countries had ratified the Statute – but not the United States, which briefly VETOED the continuance of UNITED NATIONS peacekeeping in Bosnia lest its own troops run the risk of prosecution. The US's case was critically weakened by the ABU GHRAIB affair, which gravely damaged the global reputation of its armed forces and their discipline.

International Development Agency *See* WORLD BANK.

International Labour Organisation *See* ILO.

International Monetary Fund *See* IMF.

Internationale, the The international socialist anthem, first heard during the PARIS COMMUNE of 1871, which was the Soviet national anthem from 1917 to 1944. It is still played in China whenever there is a pretext. The words were written by Eugene Pottier, a French transport worker, and the tune by Pierre Degeyter.

C'est la lutte finale
Groupons-nous, et, demain
L'Internationale
Sera le genre humain.

Or

This is the final conflict
Let us form up, and, tomorrow
The Internationale
Will be [or unites] the human race.

internationalism The belief that no nation can develop and exist alone, and either that all nations have common interests or that they should take joint action. An **internationalist** is (1) someone who has such an outlook, or (2) one who accepts the policies of one of the Internationals that have concerted World Marxism.

We deny your [Socialist] internationalism because it is a luxury which only the upper class can afford; the working people are hopelessly bound to their native shores. MUSSOLINI

internment The detention of members of a political movement or ethnic group by a government unable or unwilling to deprive them of their liberty through the judicial process. 'Internment camps' were used by the North in America's CIVIL WAR, thousands of 'enemy aliens' were interned by the UK government during WORLD WAR II, while the US government even interned Japanese-Americans in RELOCATION CAMPS. The most controversial – and counter-productive – use of internment in peacetime was in Ireland; the UK and Irish governments both used it to end an IRA terrorist campaign in the 1950s, and on 9 August 1971 the UK authorities, against Army advice, had 342 IRA suspects in Ulster rounded up in a bid to curb an upsurge in terrorism. Many of the wrong people were detained, and 23 people died in the ensuing riots. The number of internees swelled, and with it the protests, culminating in BLOODY SUNDAY the following January. Internment was ended in 1976, but marches against it continued for two decades.

interregnum (Lat. between reigns) The period between the termination of one government or form of government and the inauguration of another. The word originally applied to the gap between the death or departure of a monarch and the installation of the next, when some doubt had arisen about the succession.

interruption The word that appears (bracketed) in HANSARD when there is a disturbance in the House of Commons, or when some comment brings proceedings to a standstill. It also applies to interjections designed to interrupt a speech, which have not been recognised by the Chair as a formal INTERVENTION. The Conservative MP Oliver Stanley (1896–1950) once said of a tiresome interrupter:

> I wish the Honourable Gentleman's interruptions were as inaudible as they are unintelligible.

intervene. intervene before breakfast, before lunch, before tea and before dinner The celebrated boast of Michael HESELTINE to the 1992 CONSERVATIVE PARTY conference, proving his credentials as an INTERVENTIONIST President of the Board of Trade after years of THATCHERITE non-involvement. He said:

> If I have to intervene to help British companies – like the French government helps French companies, or the German government helps German companies, or the Japanese government helps Japanese companies – then I tell you, Mr Chairman, I'll intervene – before breakfast, before lunch, before tea and before dinner. And I'll get up the next morning and I'll start all over again.

Heseltine's credibility was undermined the following week when he announced the closure of 31 coal mines without consultation – a decision that aroused a political storm, was ruled illegal by the High Court, but was eventually implemented.

intervention (1) In the HOUSE OF COMMONS and other assemblies, a contribution – often a challenge or a question – from one member in the middle of a speech made by another, made after the person speaking has agreed to GIVE WAY. (2) The action of a CENTRAL BANK in buying, or less frequently selling, its own currency in order to halt a slide in exchange rates. (3) In the EU's Common Agricultural Policy (CAP), the purchase by member states of farm produce, in order to keep market prices up to pre-set minima.

> Purchase by Eurocrats of local farm produce which no one else wants at prices no one else will pay, for storage in conditions no one else would accept and eventual subsidised export to countries no one else would dream of subsidising.
> CHRISTOPHER MONCKTON

interventionism (1) In America, a social policy which actively assists one disadvantaged (often ethnic) group in preference to others. Ronald REAGAN was elected Governor of California in 1966 after accusing the Democrat 'Pat' Brown of excessive interventionism to assist the state's black population. (2) An activist industrial policy under which a national government supports its industries, intervening in management decisions, giving assistance or incentives and even investing in particular companies. Anathema to THATCHERITES, it was tried briefly for Labour by Tony BENN and has been pursued by most French governments.

Intifada (Arab. uprising) The campaign of CIVIL DISOBEDIENCE and riots staged by the PALESTINIAN inhabitants of the OCCUPIED TERRITORIES from December 1987 in protest at Israel's failure to grant them autonomy. Shops closed for long periods, and bands of men and boys threw stones at Israeli troops, who retaliated by opening fire, killing over 300 Palestinians in the first year alone while themselves suffering a dozen casualties. The protest petered out when GAZA and Jericho came under PLO control in 1994, with

HAMAS providing a more extreme and deadly opposition to Israel. As the PEACE PROCESS stalled, a **Second Intifada** began in 2000, this time overshadowed by suicide bombings. Following the death of Yasser Arafat, Israel and Palestine agreed a ceasefire on 8 Feburary 2005; it was largely respected at first even by militant Palestian groups.

introduction (1) In the HOUSE OF COMMONS, the procedure by which a newly elected member takes their seat. Waiting at the BAR OF THE HOUSE until called by the SPEAKER, the new member steps up to the CHAIR to take the OATH OF ALLEGIANCE or affirm, signs the register and shakes the Speaker's hand. (2) The start of a BILL's passage through the US CONGRESS, either being sent formally to each house by the ADMINISTRATION or placed in the HOPPER beside the Clerk's table in the HOUSE OF REPRESENTATIVES.

Invergordon mutiny The mutiny in the Royal Navy's Atlantic fleet at its base north of Inverness on 15 November 1931. Ratings led by Able Seaman Len Wincott refused to prepare ships for sea in protest at pay cuts ordered by the NATIONAL GOVERNMENT, which they first heard about over the radio. The Board of Admiralty agreed to keep the cuts below 10%, but the mutiny accelerated the financial crisis.

invisibles 'Invisible earnings' from tourism, shipping and insurance taken into account in calculating a nation's BALANCE OF PAYMENTS. In Britain's case they have traditionally made an alarming deficit look slightly more palatable.

Iowa caucuses The effective start of a US Presidential CAMPAIGN, the small gatherings of registered voters at the close of the year before the election at which Iowa's DELEGATE selection process for the Democratic National Convention the following summer is begun. They attracted little attention until Jimmy CARTER won headlines and invaluable momentum there in 1975, stealing a march on rivals who had been waiting for the NEW HAMPSHIRE PRIMARY. His initiative effectively extended the campaign by two to three months.

IPPR Institute for Public Policy Research. The UK's leading progressive THINK TANK, with strong links to the LABOUR PARTY but an independent cast of mind. Launched in 1988 by the media magnate Lord Hollick and Neil KINNOCK's economic adviser John Eatwell, it played an important role in Labour's preparations for power, notably through the Commission on SOCIAL JUSTICE set up by John SMITH and has retained its influence with Labour in office.

IRA Irish Republican Army (also, confusingly, IRA stands in America for Individual Retirement Account). The body that, with varying degrees of moral legitimacy, has conducted a violent campaign for the independence of all Ireland's 32 counties, regarding itself as the true government of the Irish Republic, but which since the 1998 GOOD FRIDAY AGREEMENT has professedly committed itself to the democratic process through SINN FEIN. Its slogan is ***Tiocfaidh ar La*** ('Our day will come'). The IRA was formed in 1919 as a GUERRILLA force by Michael Collins from veterans of the EASTER RISING and the former Irish Volunteers, confronting the Royal Irish Constabulary and the BLACK AND TANS until PARTITION. Collins joined the Free State government, but a faction of the IRA carried on the fight; Collins died in an ambush soon after. The IRA went underground after the short and bloody civil war, and Dublin banned it in 1936 as sporadic attacks continued. The outbreak of WORLD WAR II halted a campaign of bombings in London and Coventry, and in the 1950s there were sporadic but largely bloodless raids on British Army barracks and bombings of telephone boxes. When civil unrest broke out in NORTHERN IRELAND in 1969 the IRA did not immediately mobilise, British troops being welcomed as deliverers by the Catholic population. But heavy-handedness by STORMONT, the violence of the B-SPECIALS and misjudgements by the SECURITY FORCES culminating in BLOODY SUNDAY gave the IRA a fertile recruiting ground and a grievance on which to fight. It split into the **Officials**, or **'Stickies'**, who opposed all-out violence, eventually renouncing it to become the WORKERS' PARTY in the Republic, and the PROVISIONALS, who stepped up the struggle with indiscriminate bombings and shootings aimed at cowing the people of Ulster and terrorising Britain into withdrawal; what would happen then was never clear, as LOYALIST extremists in the North showed readiness to hit back ruthlessly. The IRA's ACTIVE SERVICE UNITS, operating with increasing discipline and sophistication, had killed over 2,000 people by the time it called a ceasefire on 31 August 1994 for talks between the British government and Sinn Fein. Though that ceasefire ended in February 1996 with the Canary Wharf bombing, contacts continued and the

Good Friday Agreement ensued. Since then the Provisionals have not resumed their armed struggle, though they have been slow to DECOMMISSION their arsenals, have continued with punishment beatings and shootings in their own community, and have continued with targeting and intelligence gathering; one such operation at Stormont brought the collapse of the power-sharing executive. A few dissidents have broken away to continue the struggle as the REAL IRA and Continuity IRA.

The IRA's most notorious actions over a quarter of a century included the 1974 BIRMINGHAM pub bombings which killed 21 people, the murder of Earl Mountbatten off the coast of Co. Sligo in 1979, the attempted assassination of Margaret THATCHER and her Cabinet in the 1984 BRIGHTON BOMBING, the Remembrance Day bombing in Enniskillen (1987), attacks on British bases in Germany and England, a nearly successful mortar bomb attack on John MAJOR's Cabinet in NUMBER TEN Downing Street in 1991 and the bombing of a fish shop in Belfast's SHANKILL ROAD in 1993 that killed ten people including one IRA man and heightened pressure for peace. In 1992 the IRA turned its mainland campaign to weakening the UK economy, starting with a bombing in the City of London just after the general election that killed three people and panicked insurers by causing millions of pounds of damage. The IRA has enjoyed considerable support from Irish-descended Americans (*see* NORAID), Canadians and Scots, but its political wing Sinn Fein had limited success in Northern Ireland and less in the South until it engaged in the peace process. By the end of 2004 the IRA professed itself ready to renounce its weaponry so that Sinn Fein could share power with its old enemy the DUP, but the deal broke down over the DUP's insistence on seeing photographic evidence of decommissioning. The IRA withdrew its offer to decommission in February 2005 after being blamed for the £26 million NORTHERN BANK ROBBERY. Forced further onto the defensive by the discovery of a £2–3 million money-laundering operation in Co. Cork and the murder of Robert MCCARTNEY, the IRA was challenged by Sinn Fein president Gerry Adams that April to choose the peaceful path. On 28 July 2005 the IRA called an end to the armed struggle from 1600 that day, ordered all its units to dump their arms and committed itself to pursue its objectives through 'exclusively peaceful means'. *See also* DOWNING STREET DECLARATION; FALLS; FARC; INLA; INTERNMENT; NO GO AREA; OWN GOAL; PARAMILITARY; REPUBLICAN; SECTARIANISM; SEMTEX; SHOOT TO KILL; STALKER REPORT; WE ONLY HAVE TO BE LUCKY ONCE.)

Real IRA A splinter group from the IRA, opposed to the GOOD FRIDAY AGREEMENT, which continued a sporadic campaign of terrorism in Ireland and on the British mainland; its most notorious exploit was the 1999 OMAGH BOMBING, after which it was shamed into a brief ceasefire by the enormity of what it had done. The Real IRA is backed politically by the 32-COUNTY SOLIDARITY COMMITTEE; its leader Michael McKevitt, brother-in-law of Bobby SANDS and the Provisionals' former quartermaster, was jailed in Dublin for 20 years in August 2003 for 'directing terrorism'. In May 2004 a Belfast judge caused consternation by ruling that the Real IRA had never been specifically outlawed.

Iran-Contra affair The scandal in 1986–87 that tarnished Ronald REAGAN's second term as President, creating serious doubts over both his credibility and his control over key members of his ADMINISTRATION. Also known as **Irangate**, it concerned a plan devised by Marine Lieut.-Col. Oliver North, on the staff of NATIONAL SECURITY ADVISER Adml. John Poindexter (*see also* DARPA), to supply Israeli arms to the AYATOLLAH's regime in Iran, with which America had not had relations since the captivity of the Teheran HOSTAGES, and use the proceeds to ship arms to the right-wing CONTRAS in Nicaragua, in defiance of CONGRESSional resolutions to give them no assistance. The deal also aimed to enlist the violently anti-American regime in Teheran to press for the release of seven hostages held by Shi'ite extremists in Beirut. Exposure of the deal in a Lebanese magazine in November 1986 brought the firing of North and the resignations of Poindexter and White House CHIEF OF STAFF Donald Regan who, echoing Harry S TRUMAN, said: 'The buck doesn't even pause here'; former National Security Adviser Robert McFarlane, who had gone to Teheran bearing a cake from the President, attempted suicide. An unrepentant North declared: 'I thought that using the Ayatollah's money to support the Nicaraguan resistance was a good idea', but Secretary of State George Shultz fumed: 'We are signalling to Iran that they can kidnap people for profit.' The bizarre nature of the dealings baffled many Americans, but

North explained: 'We were always stuck with intermediaries who really couldn't be trusted.' North, who insisted that 'throughout I believed that the President had approved such activity', became a hero of the militant right, as did his glamorous, loyal secretary Fawn Hall, who asserted: 'Sometimes you have to go above the written law, I believe', but the episode did lasting damage to Reagan. The President at first denied everything, then said he had known nothing about it, then justified what had been done and finally ordered the arms trading to stop. When Reagan announced seven years later that he had contracted Alzheimer's disease, some wondered whether these had been early symptoms.

The TOWER COMMISSION reported in March 1987 that Reagan has failed to supervise his staff properly, and that the administration's policies toward both Iran and the Contras were underpinned by deception and a disregard for Federal laws. Former Secretary of State Ed Muskie said:

> We were appalled by the absence of the kind of alertness and vigilance to his job and to these policies that one expects of a president.

A Senate committee chaired by Sen. Daniel Inouye was less charitable; it disbelieved claims by North and Poindexter that they had kept Reagan in the dark, and held that if the President did not know about questionable and illegal acts by his staff in such a sensitive area, he should have done. Inouye described the case as

> A chilling story, a story of deceit and duplicity and the arrogant disregard of the rule of law. It is a story of withholding vital information from the American people, from the Congress, from the Secretary of State, from the Secretary of Defense, and according to Admiral Poindexter, from the President himself.

Poindexter had said:

> I made a very deliberate decision not to ask the President, so I could insulate him from the decision and provide some future deniability for him even if it leaked out.

North had told senators: 'I don't think that there's another person in America that wants to tell this story as much as I do', but took the FIFTH AMENDMENT. Charges were brought against several of the conspirators including North, who was convicted in 1988 of obstructing a Congressional investigation, falsifying documents and accepting an illegal gift; he was sentenced to 120 hours' community service and a $150,000 fine, but on appeal won a retrial which proved abortive. Poindexter was sentenced to, but did not serve, six months in prison. George BUSH Snr, then Vice President, may also have been closely implicated; one of his last acts in the White House was to PARDON former Defense Secretary Caspar Weinberger (*see* CAP THE KNIFE) on the eve of his trial on perjury charges. It was widely believed that Weinberger might have been forced under oath to confirm that Bush had been involved, despite his denials. In 1994 SPECIAL PROSECUTOR Laurence Walsh concluded that Reagan had 'broken no laws' but had set the stage for wrongdoing. Walsh added that Bush 'would always have to answer for his part'.

> The ultimate irony, the ultimate COVERT OPERATION
>
> CIA director WILLIAM CASEY

> The most stunning case of the surreptitious accumulation of STAFF power in recent presidencies.
>
> HEDRICK SMITH, *The Power Game*

> I have never carried out a single act, not one, in which I did not have authority from my superiors.
>
> OLIVER NORTH

> A few months ago I told the American people I did not trade arms for hostages. My heart and my best intentions still tell me that is true, but the facts and the evidence tell me that it is not.
>
> RONALD REAGAN, 1987

> This is going to make a great movie one day.
>
> RONALD REAGAN

Iran-Iraq War The conflict that began with Iraq's invasion of western Iran in 1980 and ended without benefit to either side in 1988. A conventional war fought on a heroically destructive scale, it brought the deaths of hundreds of thousands of combatants, toxic gas attacks by Iraq, and Iranian rocket attacks on Iraqi cities. The suffering caused did not deter Saddam Hussein from further adventures; within months of the conflict ending, he sent in his forces to gas recalcitrant Kurds, and within two years staged the invasion of Kuwait that triggered the GULF WAR and sowed the seeds for his own overthrow by a US-led COALITION in 2003.

> It couldn't have happened to two nicer guys.
>
> HENRY KISSINGER

Iraq Survey Group The team of 1200 US and other inspectors who in the months after the IRAQ WAR scoured the country for evidence that SADDAM HUSSEIN had indeed had and was able to deploy WEAPONS OF MASS DESTRUCTION, the threat of which had been one of the main justifications for war cited by George W. BUSH and Tony BLAIR (*see* DODGY DOSSIER). It reported in October 2003 – and confirmed a year later after further study – that while Saddam had wanted to develop WMD, and had used them on his own people in the past, there was no evidence that he possessed them when the US and Britain moved to overthrow him.

> We in Congress would not have authorised that war by 75 votes if we had known what we know now.
>
> Sen. JAY ROCKEFELLER, Vice-chairman, Senate Intelligence Committee, 9 July 2004

Iraq War The three-week campaign during March/April 2003 when US forces led a COALITION which also included the UK, Australia and small contingents from other countries including Poland in invading Iraq and overthrowing the regime of SADDAM HUSSEIN. The term has also come to embrace the disorder, with far greater coalition casualties, that followed the overthrow of Saddam, with BAATH PARTY loyalists, members of Saddam's disbanded army, Shi'ite militias and foreign Arab fighters loosely linked to AL QAEDA mounting resistance from towns where the coalition's writ did not run and staging car-bombings and ambushes in Baghdad and other cities. The 2003 attack was mounted despite the refusal of a majority of the United Nations SECURITY COUNCIL to endorse action against Saddam for repeatedly flouting UN resolutions over arms inspection, and in the face of bitter opposition at home, especially in Britain. Fears that Saddam's much-vaunted WEAPONS OF MASS DESTRUCTION would be used against coalition forces proved unfounded – indeed they were never found – and while troops met stiff resistance in places the outskirts of Baghdad were reached in a few days. Securing the capital proved tougher – Saddam was still visible there at first and his spokesman COMICAL ALI continued to predict the annihilation of the invaders. But eventually Saddam's crack units evaporated – many of them to reappear a year later as heavily-armed insurgents – and Saddam's statue in central Baghdad was torn down by jubilant Iraqis. Law and order immediately broke down, more so in Baghdad than in British-controlled Basra, and an edgy military occupation began.

Ireland. Ireland would not be a difficult country to govern – were it not that all the people were intractable and all the problems insoluble The conclusion reached by the Liberal politician John (later Viscount) MORLEY (1838–1923) after several spells as Chief Secretary for Ireland. His bafflement was typical of the English attitude in the years between the fall of PARNELL and the EASTER RISING. Morley's contemporary Viscount Esher declared that 'if the Irish were Mahommedans or Hindus, we should have no difficulty with them', and Lord SALISBURY asked: 'Is it not just conceivable that there is no remedy that we can apply for the Irish hatred of ourselves?' Even in the 1980s Charles HAUGHEY could say: 'It seems that the historic inability in Britain to comprehend Irish feelings and sensibilities still remains.' The following reputed exchange shows the gulf in attitudes:

> *CHURCHILL*: The situation in the United Kingdom is serious, but not hopeless.
> *TAOISEACH:* The situation in my country is hopeless, but not serious.

England's difficulty is Ireland's opportunity An early 20th-century Irish nationalist slogan revived in the late 1980s by leaders of Provisional SINN FEIN.

New Ireland Forum The multi-party body set up by Garret FitzGerald's FINE GAEL-LABOUR coalition in 1983 to devise a future form of government for NORTHERN IRELAND that all democratic parties in the island (i.e. not SINN FEIN) could agree on and which could be put to the UK government as a means of breaking the constitutional deadlock. Its report, in May 1984, showed a preference for a unitary Irish state, but also a readiness to consider a federal solution, or joint authority with Britain over the SIX COUNTIES. Charles HAUGHEY upstaged the launch by playing up the report's references to a united Ireland; Margaret THATCHER was unenthusiastic. Yet the Republic's readiness to be constructive paved the way for the ANGLO-IRISH AGREEMENT the following year.

uncrowned King of Ireland The title bestowed on Charles Stuart PARNELL (1846–91) when, at the height of his powers, his imprisonment for the militancy of his campaign for reduced Irish land reform caused unprecedented civil unrest. It was accorded him by a speaker at a Ladies' Land League meeting in Dublin on 2 January 1882, and the name stuck with Parnell after his release under the KILMAINHAM TREATY.

Young Ireland *See* YOUNG.

Irish Free State The TWENTY-SIX COUNTIES of Southern Ireland that were granted DOMINION status under the IRISH TREATY of 6 December 1921. Its first premier, W. T. Cosgrave (1880–1965), was replaced in 1932 by Eamonn de Valera (*see* DEV), founder of FIANNA FAIL, who had fought for total independence. In 1937 the

Free State was renamed **Eire**; it stayed NEUTRAL during WORLD WAR II, but remained a member of the COMMONWEALTH until 1949 when it became the **Republic of Ireland**.

Irish National Caucus A group formed in WASHINGTON in 1977 by Fr Sean McManus, a priest from 'one of the English-occupied counties of Ireland', to lobby for a united Ireland. It gained the support of up to 100 members of CONGRESS with its campaigning for Ireland to be 'one nation, indivisible under God' regardless of the views of the majority in the North. The Caucus early on was effective in discouraging US investment through rigid application of the MCBRIDE RULES. It stopped short of supporting the IRA, but helped create fertile ground in America for militant Republicanism. The British government saw it then as a dangerous purveyor of half-truths; the Caucus accused London of spending millions to counteract its influence and perpetuate discrimination against Catholics in Ulster. However, even prior to the GOOD FRIDAY AGREEMENT, its emphasis was shifting to representing the sensibilities of Irish-Americans; in 1983 it persuaded ESPN to pull a promotional clip jesting about the IRISH POTATO FAMINE.

Irish National Liberation Army *See* INLA.

Irish National Volunteers An irregular force raised by the IRISH REPUBLICAN BROTHERHOOD in November 1913 to counteract the ULSTER VOLUNTEERS. It had attracted over 150,000 recruits by June 1914, but then split, the majority, the National Volunteers, following the moderate nationalist leadership of John Redmond, and the minority Irish Volunteers under the radical Eion MacNeil. The outbreak of WORLD WAR I gave this latter group the initiative as it campaigned against the war and CONSCRIPTION, and by 1919 the Irish Volunteers had evolved into the IRA.

Irish potato famine The disaster from 1845 caused by the collapse of the potato crop on which western Ireland had become totally dependent. Caused by blight, it left thousands starving, prompted mass emigration by embittered survivors whose descendants are among the IRA's strongest supporters, and fed resentment among those who stayed against the London government and absentee landlords for failing to alleviate it. It also hastened the repeal of the CORN LAWS. In 1998 Tony BLAIR apologised to the Irish people for the British government's failure to avert or remedy the famine, saying:

> Those who governed in London at the time failed their people through standing by while a crop failure turned into a massive human tragedy. That one million people should have died in what was then part of the richest and most powerful nation in the world is something that still causes pain as we reflect on it today.

Irish Question The problem that dogged British politicians from 1844, when DISRAELI defined it, until PARTITION in 1921 – and survives today in another form. Disraeli told the COMMONS on 16 February 1844:

> Consider Ireland. One says that it is a physical question; another a spiritual. Now it is the absence of the aristocracy, now the absence of railways. It is the Pope one day and potatoes the next. Thus you have a starving population, an absentee aristocracy, and an alien Church, and in addition the weakest executive in the world. That is the Irish Question.

Having defined the question, solving it was another matter. In *1066 and All That* (1930), W. C. Sellar and J. S. Yeatman wrote:

> GLADSTONE spent his declining years trying to guess the answer to the Irish Question. Unfortunately whenever he was getting warm, the Irish secretly changed the question.

And in 1919 Keith Fraser MP told the House of Commons:

> I have never met anyone in Ireland who understood the Irish Question, except one Englishman who had been there only a week.

Irish Republican Army *See* IRA.

Irish Republican Brotherhood The pledge-bound secret organisation founded in 1858 that became known as the FENIANS. Its aim was war with England, and it originally hoped that Irish-American soldiers demobilised after the CIVIL WAR would fight for Ireland's freedom; in fact its offshoot *Clan na Gael* rallied US opinion and raised money. By 1873 it had abandoned secrecy and switched to militant political campaigning, joining forces with PARNELL and advocates of HOME RULE. However, it retained its Military Council, and with the outbreak of WORLD WAR I its 1660 members in Ireland prepared again for the fight, playing a large part in the EASTER RISING of 1916.

Irish Republican Socialist Party *See* INLA.

Irish Treaty The agreement concluded on 6 December 1921 by LLOYD GEORGE and the leaders of SINN FEIN, ending English rule over the 26 southern counties of Ireland. It granted DOMINION status to what became known as the IRISH FREE STATE. Hard-line nationalists rejected the treaty and waged a bloody civil war which claimed the life of many including Michael Collins, a signatory of the treaty who took a key role in the new nation's government (*see* I MAY HAVE SIGNED MY DEATH WARRANT).

The Irish was born to rule One of the basics of MACHINE POLITICS in America's cities, as set out by the TAMMANY HALL grafter George Washington Plunkitt (1842–1924). Though Irish-Americans did not invent the political machine or the corruption that it bred, they made the system their own, creating many municipal advances along with its sleazier features.

Irgun *Irgun Zvai Leumi* (Heb. National Military Society) A Jewish terrorist organisation founded in 1931; it was active in Palestine from 1946 to 1948. Its most notorious act was the KING DAVID HOTEL BOMBING of 22 July 1946. It claimed responsibility for over 200 acts of terrorism against the British and Arabs before being disbanded in 1948, when members took an oath of loyalty to the newly founded Israeli state.

Iron. Iron Butterfly The nickname given to **Imelda Marcos**, wide of the Philippines' president Ferdinand Marcos (1917–89), who revelled in power, built up the world's largest collection of unworn shoes (3000 pairs), went into exile with her husband when ousted by PEOPLE POWER in 1986, and after his death returned in 1992 in an unsuccessful bid for the presidency. A beauty and a singer in her youth, her vanity was only matched by her desire for power and riches; until their downfall, she and her husband would croon to each other adoringly on election platforms. After they fled, crowds flocked to the Presidential mansion to view Imelda's collection of gowns, corsets and shoes; when she appeared in a New York court charged (unsuccessfully) with looting the Philippine treasury, her counsel termed her a **'world class shopper'**. The nickname 'Iron Butterfly' had originally been used of the US singer and film star Jeannette Macdonald (1901–65).

Iron Chancellor The nickname bestowed (by his supporters) on Gordon BROWN in recognition of the tough line on public expenditure which he took during the first two years of Tony BLAIR's government (1997–99) in order to stabilise the UK economy, balance the books and build up a war chest for heavily increased spending, especially on health, toward the end of Labour's first term and throughout its second. It was originally, and lastingly, applied to **Prince Otto von Bismarck** (1815–98), the mastermind of the rise of Prussia and the creation of the German state. From 1862 he increased the influence of his master King Wilhelm I, bringing the SCHLESWIG-HOLSTEIN QUESTION to a head, fomenting a brief and victorious war with Austria and provoking the FRANCO-PRUSSIAN WAR through the EMS TELEGRAM. With Wilhelm installed as Kaiser, Bismarck became Chancellor of the Second REICH and set out to create a modern industrial state with universal suffrage and even welfare benefits. The only person in Europe to match Bismarck's influence was Queen Victoria; she called him 'the most mischievous and dangerous person alive'; after an audience with her, Bismarck exclaimed: 'What a woman!' He presided over the 1878 Congress of BERLIN and survived two assassination attempts, but broke with the young Kaiser Wilhelm II in 1890 (*see* DROPPING THE PILOT); they were reconciled in 1894. Bismarck's last words were:

> I do not want a lying official epitaph. Write on my tomb that I was the faithful servant of my master, the Emperor William, King of Prussia.

> He lied with consistency and enjoyment, although unlike LENIN he did not actually prefer lying to telling the truth.
>
> EDWARD CRANKSHAW

> He had been as ruthless and unscrupulous as any other politician. What distinguished him was his moderation. A.J.P. TAYLOR

Iron Curtain The fortified line between the free and Communist states of Europe imposed by the Soviet Union after WORLD WAR II. It blocked the movement of people and ideas between East and West for over 40 years until the breaching of the BERLIN WALL in 1989 signalled the collapse of Communism. The phrase was popularised by CHURCHILL in his FULTON SPEECH (5 March 1946):

> From Stettin on the Baltic to Trieste on the Adriatic, an iron curtain has descended across Europe.

Hitler's PROPAGANDA chief Josef Goebbels had used almost the same words on 23 February 1945. The phrase goes back at least to 1817, when it appears in the Duke of Munster's journal. Queen Elizabeth of the Belgians in 1914 spoke of a 'bloody iron curtain' between her and the Germans, Ethel Snowden used it in 1920 with reference to BOLSHEVIK Russia, and Lord d'Abernon in 1925 with regard to the proposed LOCARNO pacts.

Iron Duke The affectionate nickname for **Arthur Wellesley, 1st Duke of Wellington** (1769–1852), who led Britain's armies to victory in eight years of campaigning culminating with the battle of Waterloo (1815), which he termed 'a damned close run thing'. Of the eve of battle the diarist Creevey noted: 'Lord W. was at the Ball tonight, as composed as ever.' First elected an MP in 1807, he was rewarded after Waterloo with a dukedom and was Prime Minister 1827–30 and briefly in 1834, also being Minister without Portfolio under PEEL 1841–46; of this last spell he said: 'I have no small talk and Peel has no manners.' In office the Irish-born Duke strongly opposed the REFORM BILL but supported Catholic EMANCIPATION; he said of his policies:

> I have invariably objected to all violent and extreme measures, which is not exactly the mode of acquiring influence in a political party in England, particularly one in opposition to government.

Wellington was a peppery character. When threatened with the publication of letters about a love affair, he told his blackmailer: 'PUBLISH AND BE DAMNED.' When a man mistook him for the painter George Jones, he replied: 'Sir, if you believe that, you will believe anything.' And when in his old age Queen Victoria asked him what would clear sparrows from the glasshouses of the Great Exhibition, he told her: 'Try sparrowhawks, Ma'am.' He had far less respect for the Prince Regent, of whom he said: 'He speaks and swears so like Falstaff that, damn me, if I wasn't ashamed to walk into a room with him.'

> It is incredible what popularity environs him in his latter days. He is followed like a show everywhere he goes and the feeling of the people for him seems to be the liveliest of all popular sentiments, yet he does nothing to excite it, and scarcely seems to notice it.
>
> CHARLES GREVILLE, 1847

> The Duke, getting on for 80, wrote Baroness Burdett Coutts 850 letters, but was distinctly rattled when she proposed marriage. The Duke retreated in disorder.
>
> DIANA ORTON, *A Biography of Angela Burdett Coutts*

> The Duke of Wellington has exhausted nature and has exhausted glory. His career was one long unclouded day.
>
> *The Times* obituary, 16 September 1852

Iron Guard The Romanian FASCIST party founded in 1927 by Cornelieu Zelca Codreanu, which carried out a number of terrorist atrocities in the 1930s. By 1938, when King Carol tried to suppress it, the Iron Guard, which was never fully backed by NAZI Germany, was backed by 17% of voters.

Iron Lady The name bestowed on Margaret THATCHER in her early days as Conservative leader by a Soviet Defence Ministry newspaper. Responding to a Commons speech from her on the Soviet threat to the West, *Red Star* on 24 January 1976 accused her of trying to revive the COLD WAR in the face of the 'peace-loving policy of the Soviet Union'. The attack backfired, making it appear that the KREMLIN saw Mrs Thatcher as a formidable threat. A week later she struck back, telling a dinner in London:

> I stand before you in my green chiffon evening gown, my face softly made up, my hair gently waved. The Iron Lady of the Western world. Me? A Cold War warrior? Well, yes, if that is how they wish to interpret my defence of values and freedoms fundamental to our way of life.

The British press were quick to retranslate the phrase as the **Iron Maiden**, a medieval instrument of torture; Clive James wrote:

> She deserves credit for her iron guts, even if you think her brains are made of the same stuff.

Iron Triangle A Washington term for the interlocking network of the military services, defence contractors and members of CONGRESS whose home districts benefit from military spending. The relevance of a project to the security of the nation is not their highest priority.

cast-iron man The nickname of John C. Calhoun (1772–1850), who was Andrew Jackson's Vice President and ran for the Presidency against John Quincy ADAMS in 1824. It was given him by the English economic writer Harriet Martineau:

> The cast-iron man, who looks as if he had never been born, and could never be extinguished.

irredentism A movement for areas outside a nation state's borders but sharing the same language and culture to be joined to that state. The term comes from *Italia irredenta*, 'Unredeemed Italy', the patriotic movement formed after the union of Italy in 1866 to incorporate Italian-speaking lands still outside, notably the South Tyrol and the northern Adriatic coast. Italy's determination to win these lands from the Austro-Hungarian empire brought it into WORLD WAR I in 1915; the VERSAILLES conference granted Italy most of the territory, though not Rijeka (Fiume). which Gabriele d'Annunzio seized in 1919.

is Probably the shortest word ever to have become the subject of political controversy and derisive comment. During the questioning of Bill CLINTON over his relationship with Monica LEWINSKY as House Republicans moved to IMPEACH him, 'is' was one of the words over whose precise meaning Clinton argued with investigators. *See also* INHALE; ZIPPERGATE.

Iskra (Russ. spark) The revolutionary newspaper edited by LENIN in London in the early 1900s, and the group that sprang from it, devoted to 'the preservation of orthodox Marxism'.

Islamic Jihad One of the longest-standing of the many fanatical Islamic groups in the Middle East, believed to have close links with AL QAEDA. Until overtaken in the mid-1990s by HAMAS, it was the most influential REJECTIONIST organisation. Founded by Fathi Shiqaqi who was assassinated in Malta by MOSSAD in 1995, Islamic Jihad was active first in Egypt, carrying out the assassination of President Anwar Al-Sadat in 1981; later it was run from Damascus by Ramadan Shallah, a former Florida State University professor. Bankrolled by Iran, Islamic Jihad aims to eliminate Israel and set up a strict Islamic state covering the whole of former Palestine, within which it enjoys limited popular support.

Islamist An umbrella term for the numerous and loosely linked extreme Islamic groups that since the late 1990s have radicalised young Muslims through the world and promoted intolerance, JIHAD and campaigns of terror against all – including fellow Muslims – who do not share their mindset. AL QAEDA is but one element in this movement.

island. an island of coal surrounded by fish The shorthand term for Britain coined by Aneurin BEVAN. At Labour's victory conference in Blackpool on 18 May 1945, Bevan said:

> This island is almost made of coal and surrounded by fish. Only an organising genius could produce a shortage of coal and fish at the same time.

isolationism The belief that America should not involve itself in the affairs of Europe, which became a potent political force prior to the US entry into WORLD WAR I, after it when the Senate rejected the LEAGUE OF NATIONS, and from the late 1930s as WORLD WAR II became inevitable. Franklin D. ROOSEVELT reckoned that this last retreat into isolationism 'was started not by a direct attack against international co-operation, but against the alleged imperfections of the peace'; he warned that if isolationists had their way, Americans could become 'a people lodged in prison, handcuffed, hungry and fed through the bars from day to day by the contemptuous unpitying masters of other continents'. However, the isolationist Sen. Robert Taft (*see* MR. REPUBLICAN) said: 'The President confuses the defence of Britain with the defence of the United States.'

> We do not want the racial antipathies or national antagonisms of the Old World transformed to this continent – as they will, should we become a part of European politics.
>
> Sen. WILLIAM BORAH, 1936

> It is not possible for this nation to be politically internationalist and economically isolationist. This is just as insane as asking one Siamese twin to high dive while the other plays the piano.
>
> ADLAI STEVENSON

splendid isolation Britain's position in relation to Europe in the late 19th century, which some EUROSCEPTICS a century later would have liked to re-create. The phrase is commonly credited to the Liberal Unionist George (later Viscount) Goschen (1831–1907), who said on 26 February 1896:

> We have stood alone in what is called isolation – our splendid isolation, as one of our colonial friends was good enough to call it.

And, indeed, the previous month Sir George Foster (1847–1931) had spoken in the Canadian House of Commons of

> the days when the great Mother Empire stands splendidly isolated in Europe . . .

Israel the Jewish state, created in 1948, in the aftermath of the HOLOCAUST, for a people that had suffered and been divided for centuries, building on the BALFOUR DECLARATION of 31 years before. Its foundation and entire history are set against a backdrop of tension with the country's Arab neighbours, lightning wars generally won by Israel, Palestinian terrorism, the INTIFADA and suicide bombings, Israeli resistance to international pressure to give LAND FOR PEACE, and almost automatic support from America. The relationship with America was summed up by Gen. Moshe Dayan's comment to Secretary of State Cyrus VANCE: 'Whenever you accept our views, we shall be in full agreement with you.' US loyalty was stretched to the limit as successive LIKUD governments took what was seen in WASHINGTON as a dangerously aggressive line, to the point where Secretary of State James Baker declared:

> Mr (Yitzhak) Shamir wants to talk peace: our telephone number is area code 202–456–1414.

How far Israel is justified or wise in taking military or repressive action in the WEST BANK or GAZA STRIP to maintain its own security remains a matter of fierce controversy, and will doubtless continue to be so. Israeli politicians argue that when they have put real concessions on the table, the Palestinian leadership has always found an excuse for rejecting them.

> The Jews and the Arabs should sit down and settle their differences like good Christians.
> WARREN R. AUSTIN (1877–1962), *attr.*

> It took the Jewish people 2000 years to found a state, then along comes a lunatic like [Menachem] Begin and puts everything at risk.
> German Chancellor HELMUT SCHMIDT, 1981

> An outlaw state.
> Rev. JESSE JACKSON

> *Christopher Mayhew MP* (Lab.): The Arabs never said they would drive the Jews into the sea. I will give £5000 to anyone who can ever prove that such a statement was made.
> *Jewish Tory MP:* If I hear six, perhaps we could do business

issues The particular matters of controversy that attract or polarise the voters, especially during an election campaign.

> Issues are like snakes. They just refuse to die. They keep coming back, time after time.
> Sen. HOWARD BAKER (1925–)

> Voters do not decide issues. They decide who will decide issues. GEORGE F. WILL (1941–)

issues-orientated campaign A campaign in which party leaders address specific problems facing the nation, instead of concentrating on personalities or indulging in airy rhetoric.

bread and butter issues A British term for basic issues of direct relevance to the general public, largely but not necessarily economic.

pocket-book issues The US version, but with a purely economic thrust.

single-issue campaign A campaign or organisation that seeks to influence public opinion on one specific theme, for instance abortion or gay rights.

it It's morning again in America *See* AMERICA.

It's Scotland's oil The slogan launched by the Scottish National Party (SNP) in September 1972 which drove home to discontented Scots that the wealth of North Sea oil was not reaching them. The SNP registered strong gains in the two 1974 elections, panicking the incoming Labour government into committing itself to DEVOLUTION.

It's shapely, it wiggles and its name is Ainsley Gotto The phrase that came to haunt Australia's Liberal Prime Minister John Gorton and contributed to his replacement on 10 March 1971. Miss Gotto, his English-born private secretary, known as 'the shape', was felt by members of his ministry to wield excessive influence. Picked from the typing pool at just 21 to be Gorton's secretary, she was soon seen as the power behind the throne; the key phrase was coined by Dudley Erwin when, sacked as Air Minister in 1969, he was asked why Gorton had got rid of him.

It's the hinge that squeaks that gets the grease The justification put forward by Malcolm X for revolutionary, rather than peaceful, action by black Americans to secure their rights.

It's Time! One of the shortest-ever election slogans, and one of the most successful. It was aired in Australia's 1972 election campaign by Gough WHITLAM's Labor Party, as it strove to end thirteen years of Liberal/Country Party rule. The slogan was just part of a promotional package put together by the ALP's Federal secretary, Mick Young, with help from marketing and advertising executives. It gained the ALP eight seats – and won the election.

It's time for me to go The refrain from Al Gore's CONCESSION speech after the SUPREME COURT ruling on 12 December 2000 which effectively awarded the Presidency to George W. BUSH. It echoed the slogan of **It's time for them to go** – referring to Bush's father and Vice President Dan QUAYLE – adopted by Gore and Bill CLINTON at the 1992 Democratic CONVENTION.

Italy. Italy is a geographical expression The assertion made by the Austrian statesman Prince Metternich (1773–1859) after the revolutions of 1848 had failed to ignite the politically fragmented country. Within thirteen years, Italian national unity had been proclaimed, at Austria's expense, but by the 1990s the LOMBARD LEAGUES and subsequently the LIGA NORD were arguing that Metternich was right.

Italian tanks The story told by West German Chancellor Helmut Schmidt (1918–) at a military college passing-out ceremony that brought a formal protest from the Italian government. The story, which

Schmidt had first heard as a young conscript in the *Luftwaffe*, went something like this:

> I hear that our Italian allies have just ordered a new generation of tank, specifically designed for their needs. It is fitted with four reverse gears . . . and one forward, in case the enemy attack from behind.

ITT scandal A series of interlocking revelations in the early 1970s of the involvement of the corporate giant ITT (International Telephone and Telegraph) in both US and overseas politics. In 1972 the *Washington Post* columnist Jack Anderson published a memo written by Dita Beard, an ITT LOBBYIST, indicating that the corporation had agreed to underwrite the cost of that year's Republican CONVENTION to the tune of $400,000 in return for the settling of ANTI-TRUST suits by the NIXON administration. ITT also channelled funds through the CIA to support the right-wing opposition to Chile's President Salvador Allende because he was committed to NATIONALISING ITT's 70% stake in the Chilean telephone company *Chitelco*. After the stake was expropriated, ITT drew up an 18-point plan to create disorder in Chile, culminating in a COUP against Allende which was adopted by the Nixon administration. Allende was overthrown by right-wing officers on 11 September 1973 and committed suicide.

Iveagh House The elegant former home of the Iveagh (Guinness) family on St Stephen's Green, Dublin, which now houses Ireland's Foreign Ministry. Charles HAUGHEY once referred to its occupants as 'dog handlers'.

Izvestiya The official national newspaper of the Soviet government from 1917, when it was established in Petrograd as an organ of the revolution, to 1991, when the state disintegrated and the Communist Party, for a time, was outlawed. Transferred to Moscow in 1918, its circulation had grown to 1.5 million by 1932, and in the decades after WORLD WAR II it was considerably higher; it was reckoned to make better cigarette paper than *PRAVDA*. It represented the government's views, especially on foreign policy and international relations, reproduced official documents at length and was intended to educate and inform the public in the light of official policy. Izvestiya has outlasted Communism to be one of the leading newspapers in post-Soviet Russia.

J

J'accuse (Fr. I accuse) The title of the first of two open letters from Émile Zola to the President of France demanding justice in the DREYFUS CASE. Each paragraph of the letter, published in *L'Aurore* on 13 January 1898, began with the phrase. Georges Clemenceau (*see* TIGER) later claimed to have coined the phrase.

Jack the Zipper. *See* ZIPPER.

Jackal, the or **Carlos. Illich Ramirez Sanchez** (1949–), the Cuban-trained son of a wealthy Venezuelan lawyer who worked for terrorist groups in the Middle East, Europe and Asia until his eventual capture. The name comes from Frederick Forsyth's classic 1970 thriller *The Day of the Jackal*, in which the OAS hires an assassin codenamed 'The Jackal' to kill DE GAULLE. Sanchez joined the Popular Front for the Liberation of Palestine in the late 1960s, masterminding the 1972 Lod Airport massacre at Tel Aviv when 25 people were killed, and the kidnapping of eleven OPEC oil ministers in Vienna in 1975; he introduced himself as 'the famous Carlos'. He operated from Iraq, South Yemen, Hungary and Yugoslavia, and after the COLD WAR lived in Syria with his wife Magdalena Kopp, formerly of the BAADER-MEINHOF GANG. In August 1994 he dropped his guard and was arrested by the French, who had several charges outstanding against him; within weeks he tried to charm a female lawyer into finding how well armed his guards were. In December 1997 he was sentenced to life imprisonment for the murder of three policemen in Paris 22 years before; since then he has continued to unnerve his captors.

jackass (1) A term for a stupid or ignorant person, applied in America by 1820 when Rep. John Randolph of Virginia told Rep. Tristam Burgess (Rhode Island), who had spoken of his alleged impotence: 'You pride yourself upon an animal faculty, in respect of which the slave is your equal and the jackass infinitely your superior.' Opponents branded Sen. William Borah of Utah (1865–1940) 'Son of the Wild Jackass'; the CONGRESS to its critics is 'the great American jackass'. (2) The precursor (derogatorily) of the DONKEY as the symbol of the DEMOCRATIC PARTY, in a Thomas Nast cartoon of 1870. To Republicans the two coincide, as in Richard NIXON's 'if the economy may be turning down . . . the Democrats could nominate a jackass and probably win.'

jackboot, under the Originally a term for NAZI control of a nation, now used for any authoritarian domination. Jackboots, large leather boots extending over the knee, were first worn by 17th-century cavalry troopers, gaining notoriety as part of the Nazi stormtrooper's uniform (*see also* GOOSE-STEP).

Jackie O The nickname in later years of **Jacqueline Kennedy Onassis** (1929–94), the stylish widow of President John F. KENNEDY who in 1968 married the Greek shipping magnate Aristotle Onassis (1906–75), denting for many Americans the legend of CAMELOT. Even in her husband's lifetime President DE GAULLE predicted: 'I can see her in 10 years on the yacht of a Greek petrol millionaire'; Kennedy's secretary Evelyn Lincoln believed Jackie began an affair with Onassis on his yacht while recovering from the death of her baby Patrick, weeks before JFK's assassination. In WASHINGTON she set the tone for the glittering Kennedy years; her bearing after JFK was shot in DALLAS on 22 November 1963 earned the nation's respect and made her the world's most celebrated widow. On Onassis' death – the two had been close to divorce over her extravagance – she began a publishing career in New York, which she quietly adorned until her death from cancer.

> *SIR ALEC Douglas-Home:* I wonder what would have happened if it had been Khrushchev, and not Kennedy, who had been assassinated.
> *CHAIRMAN MAO:* I do not think that Aristotle Onassis would have married Mrs Khrushchev.

Jackson, Andrew *See* OLD HICKORY.

Jackson, Jesse (1941–) The Baptist

minister and former aide to the Rev. Martin Luther KING who in the 1984 and 1988 Democratic PRIMARIES became the first serious black challenger for the US Presidency. In his first campaign he told black voters in New York: 'I cast my bread on the waters long ago. Now it is time for you to send it back to me – toasted, and buttered on both sides.' His electoral weapon was the RAINBOW COALITION; he told the 1984 Democratic Convention: 'My constituency is the desperate, the damned, the disinherited, the disrespected and the despised.' His campaign transcended the races, but earned him the distrust of many Jews (*see* HYMIETOWN); New York Mayor Ed Koch said of him:

> As a person, there is much to admire in him. As a potential President of the United States, there is much to fear.

Jackson had earned widespread respect after King's assassination for his promotion of black self-empowerment, telling Chicago school students: 'It's not the dope in your veins – it's the hope in your brains.' After his runs for the Presidency, he settled for a role as 'Shadow Senator' for Washington DC (*see* HIS SHADOWSHIP) and was a leading campaigner against the IRAQ WAR.

Jackson-Vanik amendment The amendment to President NIXON's 1973 Trade Bill by Sen. Henry Jackson (*see* SCOOP) and Rep. Charles Vanik, which linked Most Favoured NATION status for the Soviet Union to the level of Jewish emigration. President FORD signed the Act in 1975; the KREMLIN responded by ignoring the initiative and reducing the flow of emigrants still further. *See also* REFUSENIKS.

Jacobins in the FRENCH REVOLUTION, the revolutionary party led until his execution by Robespierre who between November 1789 and November 1794 fought for a national parliament as the sole sovereign power. It was at the time, and remains, a general term for democratic radicals, but in France specifically refers to the advocates of rigid centralisation.

jam. jam tomorrow Promises of better things to come which never arrive; from the saying: 'Jam yesterday, jam tomorrow, but never jam today'.

jamming Electronic procedures by which authoritarian governments prevent their people receiving radio broadcasts from overseas. In the early 1980s the Soviet Union was spending $1 billion a year on a network of stations jamming foreign broadcasts. Jamming has lost much of its force since the advent of the Internet.

Jameson Raid The incursion into independent Transvaal at the turn of 1895–96 by a detachment of police from what is now Zimbabwe, led by Dr Leander Starr Jameson (1853–1917), which stoked IMPERIALIST feeling in Britain prior to the BOER WAR. The intruders, who were supposed to link with a revolt of 'Uitlander' mineworkers and overthrow President Kruger (*see* OOM PAUL), were captured by the Boers and repatriated. The episode caused a major crisis for Lord SALISBURY's Conservative government, though the complicity of the Colonial Secretary, Joseph Chamberlain (*see* LYING IN STATE), was not proved until after his death. Jameson was tried in London and imprisoned for fifteen months. *See also* KRUGER TELEGRAM.

Janata The right-of-centre government of India under Morarji Desai which took power from Indira Gandhi's (*see* NEHRU DYNASTY) CONGRESS party in 1977, and whose components included a forerunner of the more abrasively Hindu nationalist BJP. Mr Desai was an ascetically observant Hindu; at a reception on a visit to London journalists casually demolished a bowl of nuts, only to be told: 'That was the Prime Minister's lunch.'

Janjaweed ('Demons on horseback') The ethnic Arab militia in the Darfur province of south-west Sudan which in 2004–05 drove 2 million Africans (mostly Muslims like themselves) from their homes with great brutality in a form of ETHINC CLEANSING; many died, and hundreds of thousands ended in refugee camps in Chad. The Sudanese government connived at the violence, and was widely thought to have encouraged it; as the scale of the humanitarian disaster grew, Sudan promised UN Secretary-General Kofi Annan that it would act against the militias but failed to do so, beyond arresting a handful who had perpetrated the worst atrocities and issuing others with police uniforms. On 31 July 2004 the SECURITY COUNCIL lost patience and threatened 'measures' against Khartoum if the *Janjaweed* were not withdrawn within 30 days, a timescale thought too generous by aid workers who feared mass starvation; Sudan replied that it would act within a 90-day schedule it claimed had been agreed by Annan, but the harassment continued.

jardin à la Française BRUSSELS-speak for

the system that allowed France for the first half-century of the EUROPEAN COMMISSION to treat it as an extension of its own bureaucracy. Successive waves of EU expansion did little to dilute French influence, but on the signature in April 2003 of a treaty to admit ten new members, Neil KINNOCK observed:

> Nobody has dug up the French lilacs, but it does mean there are some other plants growing as well.

Jarrow Crusade The October 1936 'Hunger March' by workers from Jarrow, on the Tyne, to London in protest at the closure of Palmer's shipyard, which left two-thirds of the town's workers unemployed. The march was organised by Jarrow council and led by the town's Labour MP, Ellen ('Red Ellen') Wilkinson. After 26 days on the road, she presented a petition in the COMMONS for government aid to ease unemployment in depressed regions. Now a central part of Labour's mythology, the march was at the time shunned by the party establishment for its alleged Communist connections – though enthusiastically supported by many of the general public.

jaw To talk, often to excess. HOUSE OF REPRESENTATIVES Speaker Thomas Reed (1839–1902) described the dandyish Westerner J. Hamilton Lewis as 'a thing of beauty and a jaw forever'; Lewis had pointed out a newspaper headline calling Reed 'a thing of beauty and a joy forever'.

jaw, jaw is better than war, war The peacemaking phrase widely attributed to CHURCHILL, but in fact a *New York Times* headline refining his comment at the WHITE HOUSE in 1954 that 'talking jaw to jaw is better than going to war'.

jawboning Tough talk by a political leader to bring powerful interests into line with his policies. It was notably used of JFK's success in bringing steel industry leaders to heel and rescinding an announced price increase.

Jay's Treaty A treaty between the US and Britain negotiated in 1795 by Chief Justice **John Jay**. Inspired by Alexander HAMILTON, it aimed to resolve problems caused by Britain's abuse of US neutrality during its war with revolutionary France. It secured British withdrawal from Detroit and other north-western forts, but was attacked by WASHINGTON's opponents as a sell-out because it ignored British violations of US neutrality at sea and the impressment of American sailors into the Royal Navy; the Treaty only scraped through CONGRESS.

je ne regrette rien (Fr. I have no regrets) The title of the song by Edith Piaf which Chancellor Norman Lamont used on 23 April 1993, during the Newbury BY-ELECTION, to justify his heavily-criticised stewardship of the economy. The Conservatives lost the seat, and on 27 May Lamont was sacked by John MAJOR (*see* EXCHANGE OF LETTERS).

Jefferson, Thomas (1743–1826) Third President of the United States (1801–09). A Virginia lawyer and plantation owner, he was the author at 33 of the Declaration of INDEPENDENCE, Governor of Virginia 1779–81, Minister to France, and Secretary of State from 1789. Defeated for the Presidency in 1796 by John ADAMS, he served as his Vice President, then was elected President as a Republican (i.e. ANTI-FEDERALIST) in the REVOLUTION OF 1800. An ardent Francophile and the ultimate all-rounder, his inventions included an automatic door, the dumb waiter, the thumbtack and a machine that duplicated his letters as he wrote them; he said: 'Science is my passion, politics my duty.' James Parton described him as 'a gentleman who could calculate an eclipse, survey an estate, tie an artery, plan an edifice, try a cause, break a horse, dance a minuet and play the violin'. And President KENNEDY told a gathering of Nobel laureates:

> I think this is the most extraordinary collection of talent, of human knowledge, that has ever been gathered at the WHITE HOUSE – with the possible exception of when Thomas Jefferson dined alone.

Jefferson was not always seen in such a light; on his election, the *Connecticut Courant* editorialised:

> Murder, robbery, rape, adultery and incest will be openly taught and practised. The air will be rent with the cries of distress, the soil soaked in blood and the nation black with crimes. Where is the heart that can contemplate such a scene without shivering with horror?

Martha Washington is said to have called him 'one of the most detestable of mankind, the greatest misfortune our country has ever experienced', while Alexander HAMILTON wrote: 'The moral character of Jefferson was repulsive. Continually puling about liberty, equality and the degrading curse of slavery, he brought his own children to the hammer, and made money of his debaucheries'; this was a reference to Jefferson's rumoured liaison after the death of his wife with his mulatto slave Sally Hemings.

Jefferson has gone down in history as a

noble figure, committed to liberty. He himself said: 'I have sworn upon the altar of God, eternal hostility against every form of tyranny over the mind of man', and again: 'That peace, safety and concord may be the portion of our native land, and be long enjoyed by our fellow-citizens, is the most ardent wish of my heart, and if I can be instrumental in procuring or preserving them, I shall think that I have not lived in vain.' Nor was he wedded to politics. He once remarked that 'the happiest moments of my life have been the few which I have past at home in the bosom of my family . . . Public employment contributes neither to advantage nor happiness. It is an honourable exile from his family and affairs.' And toward the end of his life he remarked: 'I have sometimes asked myself whether my country is the better for my having lived at all.' *See also* MONTICELLO.

> The principles of Jefferson are the definitions and axioms of a free society.
>
> ABRAHAM LINCOLN

Jefferson-Jackson Day The annual commemoration by America's DEMOCRATIC PARTY of the two Presidents it regards as its founders – Jefferson and Andrew Jackson (*see* OLD HICKORY). It is usually celebrated on or around 15 March (Jackson's birthday in 1767) or 13 April (Jefferson's in 1743). In some states, such as Virginia, it can also be marked on WASHINGTON's birthday, 22 February.

> The Democratic Party's annual political rain dance.
>
> DAVID BRINKLEY

Jefferson Memorial The memorial to Jefferson among the Japanese flowering cherry trees beside WASHINGTON's Tidal Basin which was authorised by CONGRESS in 1934 and dedicated in 1943. Of classical design and based, like MONTICELLO, on the Pantheon in Rome, its circular chamber is dominated by a large statue of Jefferson by Rudolph Evans; above the entrance is a sculpture commemorating Jefferson's role in creating the Declaration of INDEPENDENCE.

Jefferson's decalogue of canons Ten rules for 'observation in personal life' written by Jefferson in 1825. The first is: 'Never put off till tomorrow what you can do today.'

Jeffersonian democracy Jefferson's ideal, born of its pre-industrial time, for a limited government for an agrarian society, with a natural aristocracy, strong state and weaker federal governments, guaranteed freedom of religion, speech and the press, and a LAISSEZ-FAIRE economy. It was superseded by **Jacksonian democracy**, from the days of Andrew Jackson's presidency, in which the notion of an aristocracy gave way to rule in accordance with the desires of the people.

Jenin. The Palestinian town on the WEST BANK which in April 2002 was the scene of an alleged massacre when troops sent in by Prime Minister Ariel Sharon to avenge suicide bombings in Israel devastated a refugee camp previously occupied by some 15,000 people in what was claimed to be a careful operation to weed out known Palestinian terrorists. The failure of the Israelis to allow in relief supplies and medical help for thirteen days caused an international outcry and led the UNITED NATIONS to send in a fact-finding mission, but Sharon was unrepentant, as he had been after the massacres at SABRA and CHATILA. The eventual confirmed death toll was 53, not the hundreds which even Israeli military sources had originally claimed.

Jenkins, Roy Harris, later Lord Jenkins of Hillhead (1920–2003), possibly the greatest British political liberal of the second half of the 20th century, the sponsor as a Labour backbencher and then HOME SECRETARY of significant social reforms – with the Conservatives and even some of his own side later accusing him of having created the PERMISSIVE SOCIETY – deputy leader of the Labour Party, President of the EUROPEAN COMMISSION, a member of the GANG OF FOUR who founded the SDP and the party's first leader, Chancellor of Oxford University and the author of acclaimed biographies of Dilke (*see* THREE-IN-A-BED), ASQUITH, GLADSTONE and CHURCHILL. He left unfinished a biography of Franklin D. ROOSEVELT, which was completed by Professor Richard Neustadt, husband of Shirley Williams, who also died before publication. The son of a Welsh miners' MP, Jenkins went from grammar school to Oxford and via the Army into banking and politics, becoming an MP in 1948. In opposition he promoted the landmark Obscene Publications Act, and as Home Secretary in 1965–67 and 1974–76 oversaw further reforms including the abolition of the death penalty and the legalisation of abortion. He was Minister of Aviation in Harold WILSON's first government, Chancellor from 1967 to 1970 (turning in a BUDGET surplus) and deputy Labour leader 1970–72, standing down because Wilson did not then share his enthusiasm for Europe. From 1977 to 1981 he was President of the European

Commission, in which he was known, in a play on his name, as *Le Roi Jean Quinze*; the European Monetary System (EMS) was his principal achievement.

Even before his return Jenkins was loth to rejoin a Labour Party that was heading leftwards, and after floating the idea of a new party in his 1980 EXPERIMENTAL AIRCRAFT speech he joined the Gang to found the SDP the following spring. Jenkins (*see also* WOY) developed a misleadingly grand manner, once remarking of Speaker Bernard WEATHERILL: 'Never cared much for the fellow. He made me a terrible suit once.' This style, and his love of good wines, led to the new party being burdened with jokes about its fondness for claret. Becoming SDP leader, he fought and nearly won a BY-ELECTION at Warrington before triumphing at Glasgow Hillhead in March 1982. In the 1983 election he was the ALLIANCE's PRIME MINISTER DESIGNATE, though his role was reduced before polling in the ETTRICK BRIDGE COUP. He resigned the leadership after the party's poor showing, making way for David OWEN, of whom Jenkins said: 'I was more of a Garibaldi – he was more of a TITO.' After losing his seat in 1987 he became the LIBERAL DEMOCRATS' leader in the HOUSE OF LORDS.

> The only thing Roy ever fought for was a table for two at the Mirabelle. Former Labour colleague

Jenkins Committee The committee, chaired by Lord Jenkins, which was set up by Tony BLAIR, in consultation with the Liberal Democrats, after the 1997 ELECTION to advise on the most viable system of PROPORTIONAL REPRESENTATION for electing the HOUSE OF COMMONS. Its recommendations, published in October 1998, were ignored, ending the close relationship between the parties at WESTMINSTER which had nearly brought Liberal Democrats into Blair's CABINET.

Jenkins Hill The original name for the HILL on which the US CAPITOL was built.

War of Jenkins' Ear *See* WAR.

Jerusalem The anthem of the Christian and non-Marxist elements of English SOCIALISM, as well as of generally non-political bodies like the WOMEN'S INSTITUTE, setting the goal of re-creating the holy city of Jerusalem in the soul of England. The Scottish MEP Janey Buchan termed it 'a call to action'. It was written by William Blake (1757–1827), and later set to music by Thomas Parry:

> And did those feet in ancient time
> Walk upon England's mountains green?
> And was the holy Lamb of God
> On England's pleasant pastures seen?
> And did the countenance divine
> Shine forth upon our clouded hills?
> And was Jerusalem builded here
> Among these dark Satanic mills?
>
> Bring me my bow of burning gold!
> Bring me my arrows of desire!
> Bring me my spear! O clouds, unfold!
> Bring me my chariot of fire!
> I shall not cease from mental fight,
> Nor shall my sword sleep in my hand,
> Till we have built Jerusalem
> In England's green and pleasant land.

New Jerusalem The ideal – exemplified by the hymn – to which 19th-century socialists, and many since, have aspired. During a party conference debate on GAY RIGHTS in 1986, one delegate said: 'I joined the LABOUR PARTY to build Jerusalem, not Sodom and Gomorrah.' And Margaret THATCHER in 1992 asked: 'When will they [Labour] learn that you cannot build Jerusalem in BRUSSELS?'

Jewish Agency Set up in 1929 by Chaim Weizmann to encourage Jewish settlement in Israel. In its early days it took a conciliatory stance, raising funds for the national home (*see* BALFOUR DECLARATION), overseeing immigration and helping ease resulting tension with Palestinian Arabs, establishing the Youth Aliyah programme to resettle Jewish orphans fleeing the NAZIS, and representing Jewish interests at the LEAGUE OF NATIONS. From 1935 under David Ben Gurion it gradually abandoned its ancillary roles to become an uncompromising instrument of militant ZIONISM. In 1948 it became officially identified with the World Zionist Organisation.

Jewish Defence League A militant VIGILANTE group, formed in New York City in the late 1970s by Rabbi Meir Kahane, to defend Jews against RACIST attack and to cow potential attackers into keeping well clear. The aggressive conduct of the JDL caused controversy among American Jews as well as in the community at large. Kahane moved to Israel in the mid-1980s and adopted a provocative anti-Arab line that embarrassed even the hard-line LIKUD government; eventually Kahane was murdered by an Arab.

JFK The initials of **John Fitzgerald Kennedy**, by which the President was widely known. Their use was encouraged, as it drew comparison with his Democratic predecessor FDR. Since December 1963, after Kennedy's assassination, the initials have also applied to New York's main airport, formerly Idlewild. By coincidence, JFK are also the initials of John KERRY, another Massachusetts Senator who contested the Presidency 38 years after Kennedy. Kerry, like Kennedy, was brought up a Catholic, but his roots were in part Jewish.

Jihad In Islam, a Holy War against the unbeliever. The Jihad is frequently invoked by militant Muslim leaders in both religious and secular causes; some (*see* ISLAMISTS) consider it a duty, and this state of mind has been encouraged and capitalised on by AL QAEDA.

Islamic Jihad *See* ISLAMIC.

Jim. Jim Crow laws Legislation, especially in America's southern states, depriving black people of CIVIL RIGHTS. The term probably originated in the 1828 minstrel song *Jim Crow* by Thomas D. Rice; it came to stand for segregation, as in the **Jim Crow car** (a railroad car for blacks only) and even as a reference to black people as such.

Jim is very, very sorry Margaret THATCHER's comment in 1980 about her Employment Secretary James Prior, one of the most effective of the Cabinet WETS. Prior had criticised British Steel's handling of a lengthy strike to journalists, and when word of the briefing leaked out Mrs Thatcher was asked by an interviewer if she would sack him. She replied: 'We all make mistakes now and then. It think it was a mistake and Jim Prior was very, very sorry indeed for it, and very apologetic. But you don't just sack a chap for one mistake.' Prior, who had not apologised, was furious.

Boatman Jim *See* BOATMAN.

Sunny Jim *See* CALLAGHAN; SUNNY.

Jingoism Extravagant, populist IMPERIALIST feeling, notably in late 19th-century Britain. It was summed up by, and possibly stemmed from, the 1878 music hall song by G. W. Hunt:

> We don't want do fight, but, by Jingo if we do,
> We've got the ships, we've got the men, we've got the money too.
> We've fought the Bear before, and while Britons shall be true,
> The Russians shall not have Constantinople.

Practitioners of Jingoism, on both sides of the Atlantic, were known as **Jingoes**.

Jix The nickname of William Joynson-Hicks, the 1st Viscount Brentford (1865–1932), Home Secretary in BALDWIN's 1924–29 Conservative government. A noted puritan, he was prominent in Parliament's blocking the adoption by the Church of England of its revised Prayer Book in 1928.

> Regarded by most as a preposterous figure.
> ROBERT RHODES JAMES

job. Job Corps The Federal programme set up by the Comprehensive Employment and Training Act (**CETA**) of 1973, providing training or work experience for disadvantaged youths for up to two years, though six to twelve months has been more usual. Uniquely the Job Corps has offered accommodation for most participants.

jobs for the boys The exercise of CRONYISM, appointing one's friends and associates to key or lucrative positions on taking office. The phrase dates back at least to the 1930s.

get a job at Tesco *see* TESCO.

Saddam Hussein still has a job. Do you? A bumper sticker from the Democrats' 1992 Presidential campaign contrasting George BUSH's failure to oust the Iraqi tyrant with the domestic recession.

Joe Who? Nickname for Charles Joseph **Clark** (1939–), the Conservative who defeated Pierre TRUDEAU in 1979 to become Canada's youngest Prime Minister, but lost power a year later. As PC leader he acquired a bad press on the CAMPAIGN trail: he was said to carry a turkey with him 'in case he needs spare parts'. In 1983 he lost the leadership to Brian Mulroney, who the following year appointed him External Affairs Minister. In 1992, as Constitutional Affairs Minister, he attempted through the CHARLOTTETOWN ACCORD to end the deadlock over how to amend the Constitution that had begun with PATRIATION and remained unsolved by MEECH LAKE.

> No shirt is too young to be stuffed. ANON

Foul-mouthed Joe *See* FOUL.

Uncle Joe *See* UNCLE.

Johnson, Lyndon Baines (1908–73), 36th President of the United States (Democrat, 1963–69). A self-made Texan of questionable business and electoral propriety (*see* LANDSLIDE LYNDON) who became the ultimate political technician, he was elected Senate MAJORITY LEADER at 44 in his first term, drove himself to a heart attack at 47 but won the Vice Presidential nomination five years later. His techniques were not always subtle; he once remarked: 'I never trust a man unless I have his pecker in my pocket.' But they were effective. 'Not since James F. Byrnes had CONGRESS seen a man so skilled in modifying a measure to enlist the widest possible support, so adept at the arts of wheedling, trading and arm twisting, so persistent and so persuasive,' wrote Arthur Schlesinger.

A larger-than-life and elemental figure who picked up his dogs by their ears (*see* HIM AND HER), he was ridiculed as gauche and naïve by WASHINGTON society. But he had the last laugh on them after being pitchforked into the presidency on the assassination of John F. KENNEDY. Addressing Congress for the first time, he said: 'All I have, I would gladly have given not to be standing here today.' But he added:

> I am going to build the kind of nation that President ROOSEVELT hoped for, President TRUMAN worked for and President Kennedy died for.

LBJ manoeuvred Kennedy's stalled NEW FRONTIER programme through Congress and took a tougher stance on CIVIL RIGHTS than any previous President. Ralph Ellison termed him 'the greatest American President for the poor and for the Negroes'. Schlesinger simply stated: 'Kennedy promised, Johnson delivered.' Johnson won a landslide victory in his own right over Barry Goldwater in 1964, piling up a record majority of 15 million. He saw this as a mandate for the GREAT SOCIETY, but his domestic achievements were overshadowed by the torture of the VIETNAM WAR. LBJ steadily ESCALATED Kennedy's limited US involvement in Vietnam in the face of lack of results on the ground, declaring: 'I am not going to lose Vietnam. I am not going to be the President who saw South-east Asia go the way China went.' And to US troops he said: 'I salute you. Come home with that coonskin on the wall.' But Johnson developed a persecution complex: 'I wake up at 5 a.m. some mornings and hear the planes coming in at National Airport and I think they are bombing me,' he told one aide. And adverse press coverage provoked him to say: 'If one morning I walked on the water across the Potomac, the headlines that afternoon would read: "President can't swim".' He once asked the veteran diplomat Dean Acheson why he was unpopular; Acheson replied:

> Let's face it, Mr President, you're not a very likeable man.

Against this background, the ridicule resumed. Hugh Sidey saw LBJ as 'a great raw man of immense girth, wandering as a stranger in the Pepsi generation. Coarse, earthy – a brutal intrusion into the misty Kennedy renaissance that still stuck to the land.' His close aide Jack Valenti said: 'He doesn't like cold intellectuals around him. He wants people who will cry when an old lady falls down in the street.' But his approach is best summed up by an episode when a young Marine officer directed him to his helicopter. 'Son,' LBJ told him, 'these are *all* my helicopters.'

Johnson's home life was basically happy, despite his habit of turning up in the rooms of female house guests and saying: 'Move over – this is your President.' He once said: 'I'm the luckiest man alive. None of my girls drinks or smokes or takes dope and they both married fine men.' He and his wife LADY BIRD made a good team, she explaining: 'Lyndon stretches you. He always expects more of you than you're mentally or physically capable of putting out. Somehow that makes you try a little more.'

With Johnson preparing to run again in 1968, the shock of the Viet Cong's TET OFFENSIVE split the Democratic Party, and when the anti-war Sen. Eugene McCarthy defeated him in early primaries, he withdrew (*see* I SHALL NOT SEEK). He secured a BOMBING HALT just before the November election, but it was too late to save his Vice President Hubert HUMPHREY from defeat. He handed over the WHITE HOUSE to Richard NIXON early in 1969 and went home to Texas.

> I knew he would be bitterly disappointed by the ingratitude of those he tried to help.
>
> RICHARD NIXON, *Memoirs*

Join the Army, see the world, meet interesting people and kill them A 1960s PACIFIST variant of the WORLD WAR II recruiting slogan 'Join the Army and see the world'.

joined-up government. *See* GOVERNMENT.

joint. Joint Chiefs (of Staff) The principal military advisers to the President as COMMANDER-IN-CHIEF, in the structure created by the National Security Act of 1947. The chairman is America's highest-ranking military officer; the other chiefs, appointed for four-year terms, are the Army chief of staff, the Director of Naval Operations, the chief of staff of the Air Force and, on matters concerning his service, the commandant of the Marine Corps. It is not a unified command, and until 1986 the Chairman represented the views of all the service chiefs; now he outranks them and gives his own view. Two years earlier the then Chairman, Gen. John W. Vessey, said his role was 'to give the President and the Secretary of Defense military advice before they know they need it'.

A façade of jointness.
Joint Chiefs of Staff Chairman, General DAVID JONES

joint session A meeting of the two houses of the US CONGRESS, generally to hear an address by the President or a distinguished foreign visitor. The first, in 1800, was addressed by John ADAMS. Until 1976, when the House rebelled, every visiting head of government was accorded this privilege.

joint sitting In Australia, a combined sitting of the two Houses of Parliament which under certain circumstances may pass legislation rejected by the SENATE, thus overriding the upper house's VETO. A joint sitting in 1974 to pass six of the Labor government's measures the Senate had blocked was the first sitting of the Canberra Parliament to be televised. In Britain, the term is used for the occasional functions in the Royal Gallery of the House of Lords when MPs and peers are addressed by a visiting foreign dignitary; they do not amount to a formal session.

Joint tax On CAPITOL HILL, the Joint Committee on Taxation, a non-partisan committee which services both the Senate Finance Committee and the House WAYS AND MEANS Committee. Its highly skilled members assist legislators in putting together workable tax packages for submission to their respective committees.

Jones. Paula Jones case. The sexual harassment case which formed the background to ZIPPERGATE and culminated in President CLINTON in 1998 settling $850,000 on the claimant, paying $25,000 in fines and accepting a five-year suspension from legal practice in his home state of Arkansas. The Jones case, the most celebrated 'BIMBO ERUPTION' dating from his time as Governor of Arkansas, stemmed from the accusation that Clinton sexually harassed the then Paula Corbin, an Arkansas state employee, in a Little Rock hotel room in May 1991, and defamed her from the WHITE HOUSE when she complained. Ms Jones went public with the allegations early in 1994 after they had surfaced in the press, but the White House stalled a prosecution for three years; it only went ahead after the SUPREME COURT unanimously rejected the claim that Clinton could not be prosecuted while President for a private act committed beforehand. The Jones case was not only significant in adding to the background of sexual SLEAZE surrounding the Clinton presidency – her evidence published in 1998 included four depositions by other women accusing Clinton of molesting them, and testimony from his former police bodyguards in Arkansas that he used them to solicit women – but because Monica LEWINSKY first featured as a witness subpoenaed by Ms Jones.

Joseph, Sir Keith *See* MAD MONK.

Journal, the (1) The official record of each House of the US CONGRESS, the Senate having four such. Each gives a sketchy account of the business done, in contrast to the voluminous CONGRESSIONAL RECORD. In the Senate, reports of House-Senate CONFERENCE committees cannot be presented while the Journal is being read. (2) The nearest thing Britain has to a STATUTE BOOK, listing the BILLS passed in each SESSION; it has been checked by the CLERK TO THE PARLIAMENTS ever since the 1880s, when the clerk compiling it slipped in a divorce for himself.

Judaea and Samaria The name given by militant ZIONISTS, and at times the LIKUD party, to the WEST BANK. They claim Biblical authority for its incorporation into the state of ISRAEL and the creation of Jewish settlements there on previously Arab land.

Juden raus! (Ger. Jews, get out!) One of the most offensive throwbacks to the days of NAZI persecution of the Jews, when the slogan was daubed by officially-inspired ANTI-SEMITES on the fronts of Jewish homes, shops and synagogues. Its use, regrettably, persists to this day.

judicial review (1) In America, the power of the courts to rule on whether legislation is CONSTITUTIONAL, and to refuse to enforce legislation that in their view fails that test. No provision was made for it in the Constitution, but Alexander HAMILTON argued for it in the *FEDERALIST* and in 1803 it was established by Chief Justice John Marshall in the case of Marbury v MADISON; he ruled that as special guardians of the Constitution, the courts must prefer it to any other law wherever there was a conflict. (2) In England and Wales, judicial review of decisions by Ministers and public authorities, to determine whether they have operated within the law, has become increasingly common since the 1970s.

judicial supremacy The power of America's courts, and ultimately the

SUPREME COURT, to be the final interpreters of the CONSTITUTION. The court adopted this power in the light of the constitution's position as America's supreme law.

> The maxim that the Constitution is what the Supreme Court says it is.
>
> HUGH BROGAN

> There is hardly a political question in the United States that does not sooner or later turn into a judicial one.
>
> ALEXIS DE TOCQUEVILLE (1805–59)

Judiciary, the A nation's courts, one of the three components of government with the EXECUTIVE and the LEGISLATURE. In America the Judiciary is supreme (*see above*); in Britain it will rule on whether the actions of the Executive accord with the law, will interpret the wishes of Parliament in Statute, will make rulings on grey areas or in the light of the Common Law, but will not go against the stated decisions of Parliament.

> The subtle corps of sappers and miners constantly working under ground to undermine the foundations of our confederated fabric.
>
> THOMAS JEFFERSON, 1820

> For heaven's sake discard the monstrous wig which makes the English judges look like rats peeping through branches of oakum.
>
> JEFFERSON

July Measures The steps taken on 20 July 1966 by Harold WILSON's Labour government to support STERLING as estimates of the year's BALANCE OF PAYMENTS deficit rose from £100 to £350 million. They included tighter hire purchase controls, higher drink, tobacco, petrol duties and Purchase TAX, a 10% surcharge on military and civil spending overseas – and a six-month FREEZE on prices and wages. Despite these measures, the pound had to be DEVALUED sixteen months later.

Junior Tuesday *See* SUPER TUESDAY.

junket An excursion or lavish meal for politicians which has only the thinnest pretence of being connected with their duties, but which costs either the taxpayer or their benefactor a great deal. In America a regular recipient of such hospitality is a **junketeer**. *See also* BOONDOGGLE; FREEBIE.

junta A government formed by a small group, frequently of military men, after a COUP D'ÉTAT.

> I will be perfectly calm when I personally command the firing squad that shoots those junta bastards.
>
> Gen. KONSTANTIN KOBETS, Russian Defence Minister, after the failed KREMLIN COUP of August 1991

The name is Spanish for a council of state (in Turkish it fittingly begins with a 'c'), but also has origins in the **Junto**, who from 1672 to 1710 exercised critical influence in Britain's HOUSE OF COMMONS and for a time held office. It was made up of WHIGS desperate for power, among them Charles Montagu, later Earl of Halifax; Admiral Edward Russell, Earl of Orford; Sir John (later Baron) Somers; and Thomas Wharton. The Junto was eventually broken by Robert Harley (1661–1724), the nearest to a PRIME MINISTER prior to Walpole, and Sarah Churchill, Duchess of Marlborough (1660–1744), lost her influence with Queen Anne.

juste retour (Fr. fair returns) The argument which Britain long pursued over the European Community Budget: that the amount a nation pays in should be reflected in what it gets back. The principle was hotly resisted by France, which gained heavily from the Common Agricultural Policy (CAP) that took up 70% of that budget. Successive British Prime Ministers pressed for a formula limiting Britain's liability for the CAP, and Margaret THATCHER, after lengthy and acrimonious negotiations, eventually secured a BRITISH REBATE at FONTAINEBLEAU in 1984 which has survived for two decades. *See also* I want my MONEY back.

K

K Shorthand for a KNIGHTOOD, used by British civil servants and especially Conservative politicians. As in 'I hope he gets a K'.

K Street Strategy The strategy masterminded by House MAJORITY LEADER Tom DeLay in 2004–05 to give Washington LOBBYISTS an unprecedented role in writing legislation in turn for donations to Republican causes and undertakings to hire only Republicans.

Kalashnikov The Soviet-made (and much copied) AK47 automatic or semi-automatic assault rifle that has become the hallmark of liberation, GUERRILLA and terrorist movements throughout the world. Capable of firing 600 rounds a minute, it was devised by Mikhail Kalashnikov (1919–) in a Siberian woodshed after he was invalided out of the Red Army in 1941; it went into production in 1947 (over 80 million have been made) and initially was carried in a special case so that enemies could not see its design. Kalashnikov was installed in a factory in the Urals and not allowed even to tell his wife what he was doing, but in 1994 received a public visit of thanks from President Yeltsin. In 1990 he was invited to the United States to compare notes by Eugene Stoner, multi-millionnaire designer of the ARMALITE.

> It's a dreadfully simple gun to use. You just pour torrents of fire from it. It requires very little effort, you don't need the hands to hold it, or the ability to aim properly. You can't shoot at any range, but the great thing is it never jams.
>
> CHRISTOPHER BEESE, deputy head of the UN monitoring mission in Bosnia, 1993

> The only brand-name of global significance (other than the lethal cocktail named after Mr Molotov) to have come out of the Soviet Union.
>
> *THE GUARDIAN*

> My life has not been easy. I wanted my invention to serve peace. MIKHAIL KALASHNIKOV

kaleidoscope. the kaleidoscope has been shaken The pivotal words from perhaps Tony BLAIR's most celebrated speech, to the LABOUR PARTY Conference in Brighton on 2 October 2001, less than a month after 9/11. The burden of his speech was sympathy with the American people after the outrages – 'We were with you at the first. We will stay with you till the last' – a plea for better understanding between moderate Muslims and Western opinion, adherence to the 'inalienable rights' set out in the US CONSTITUTION and a determination to bring AL QAEDA and its backers to account. The complete passage, from his PERORATION, was:

> This is a moment to seize. The kaleidoscope has been shaken. The pieces are in flux. Soon they will settle again. Before they do, let us re-order this world around us.

Kaliningrad meeting The meeting on 3 July 2005 between Presidents Putin and CHIRAC and Chancellor Gerhard Schröder to mark the 750th anniversary of Kaliningrad, formerly Königsberg. The former capital of East Prussia and its environs were seized by STALIN in 1945, and after the collapse of the SOVIET UNION formed a Russian enclave on the Baltic bordered by Poland and Lithuania. Intended to concept the Russian, French and German positions before the G8 summit at GLENEAGLES, it also gave rise to Chirac's comments on British cuisine and MAD COW DISEASE which sections of the French media blamed for Paris' surprise defeat by London days later for the right to host the 2012 Olympics.

kamikaze tactics Reckless political action bordering on the self-destructive, after the Japanese *kamikaze* ('divine wind') suicide pilots of WORLD WAR II.

kangaroo closure *See* CLOSURE.

Kangaroo Group A cross-party grouping in the EUROPEAN PARLIAMENT which has long campaigned for the removal of frontier barriers and other obstacles to individual movement and trade within the EU.

kangaroo ticket A pair of candidates, for President and Vice President or Governor and LIEUTENANT GOVERNOR, on which the one seeking the lesser post is the stronger. The kangaroo comparison stems from the marsupial's strong hind and weak front legs.

Kansas. Kansas Coolidge or **Kansas Sunflower** Nicknames for **Alf** (Alfred Mossman) **Landon** (1887–1987), Governor of Kansas 1933–37 and the Republican Presidential nominee routed by Franklin D. ROOSEVELT in 1936; he carried only Maine and Vermont, but as a consolation lived to be 100. Democrats presciently declared in a campaign bumper sticker: 'Sunflowers wilt in November.'

Kansas-Nebraska Act The measure, devised by Sen. Stephen Douglas and signed by President Pierce in 1854, which helped draw the battle-lines for the CIVIL WAR. Ostensibly designed to facilitate a northern transcontinental railroad, it carved two jurisdictions out of the Nebraska territory, nominally opening the region to slavery but in practice – because of its population of Northerners – excluding it. To appease the South, the Act also repealed the MISSOURI COMPROMISE, causing bitter Northern protests, splitting the WHIGS and leading directly to the foundation of the REPUBLICAN PARTY.

> Part and parcel of an atrocious plot to exclude from a vast unoccupied region immigrants from the Old World and free laborers from our own States, and convert it into a dreary region of despotism, inhabited by masters and slaves.
>
> Sen. SALMON P. CHASE (1808–73)

Bleeding Kansas The minor CIVIL WAR that broke out in Kansas following the election of 1856 in which thousands of slave-owning 'ruffians' crossed from Missouri to vote to make the territory a slave state. An army of Northern ABOLITIONISTS, John BROWN among them, moved in to contest the fraudulent vote, and before long the two factions were capturing towns and taking prisoners. The pro-slavery government of Kansas remained in office, but was effectively neutered. Excesses of propaganda by both sides did much to raise the temperature in advance of the Civil War; it emerged later that while President Buchanan had been elected because of his neutrality on 'bleeding Kansas', some of his appointees had paid out heavy bribes to ensure it became a slave state.

crime against Kansas The speech that sparked one of the most shameful acts of violence in the history of the US CONGRESS. It was delivered on 20 May 1856 by the ABOLITIONIST Sen. Charles Sumner of Massachusetts, and consisted of two hours of vituperation and sexual allusion. Sumner's speech caused a furore, splitting the SENATE down the middle. He described supporters of slavery as 'hirelings picked from the drunken spew and vomit of civilisation', and abused Sen. Andrew Pickens Butler of South Carolina as 'one of the maddest zealots' who had chosen a black mistress who 'though polluted in the eyes of the world, is chaste in his sight – I mean the harlot Slavery'. Butler was not in the Senate Chamber to hear the attack, but three days later his nephew Rep. Preston Brooks strode in and beat Sumner almost to death with his cane. Messages of sympathy to Sumner poured in from the North, while Brooks was inundated with new canes from well-wishing Southerners inscribed 'Hit him again!' Lengthy House hearings established the severity of the attack, and with expulsion on the cards Brooks resigned and won re-election – only to die of drink five months later. It was two years before Sumner could walk, read or write again; his empty chair became a potent symbol to the anti-slavery campaign.

KANU Kenya African National Union. The ruling (and for most of the time the only) political party in almost four decades of Kenyan independence, until resoundingly defeated in December 2002. Founded in 1960 by Jomo Kenyatta (1891–1978) as a pan-tribal independence movement, it was successor to the Kenya African Union (established by Kenyatta in 1944) and, prior to that, the Kikuyu Central Association, founded in 1908 but banned by the British in 1940. KANU won the pre-independence elections in 1963, Kenyatta becoming Prime Minister; after independence Kenyatta became President and turned the country into a one-party state. COMMONWEALTH pressure for GOOD GOVERNMENT eventually forced Kenyatta's successor, Daniel arap Moi, to allow OPPOSITION parties. Obliged by the CONSTITUTION to stand down after 24 years, Moi fielded Kenyatta's uncharismatic son UHURU as his successor. The **National Rainbow Coalition** of Mwai Kibaki took its place, promising less venal government, an undertaking kept in part.

Kapital *See* DAS KAPITAL.

Kapp putsch An armed rising in 1919 by the Erhardt FREIKORPS Brigade, which marched into Berlin in protest at the German government's acceptance of the Treaty of VERSAILLES, which required the Brigade's dissolution. The WEIMAR REPUBLIC was declared overthrown and a right-wing journalist, Wolfgang Kapp (1888–1922) declared Chancellor. The putsch collapsed after five days in the face of a GENERAL STRIKE by Berlin workers and the regular Army's refusal to back the Freikorps. Kapp fled to Sweden.

Katie Graham's going to get her fat tit caught in the wringer One of the most celebrated sayings of WATERGATE. The comment, accompanied by a number of threats against the *Washington Post*, was made by former Attorney-General John Mitchell (1913–88) to Carl Bernstein of the *Post*, when the reporter woke him for reaction to the first Watergate story that directly incriminated him; Mitchell's target was Mrs Katharine Graham, the paper's publisher. The quote appeared in the next day's paper minus the words 'her tit', the *Post*'s editor Ben Bradlee explaining: 'We are a family newspaper.' Mitchell subsequently served nineteen months for conspiracy, obstruction of justice and perjury.

Katyn massacre The mass execution of 5000 Polish officers in April-May 1940 by Soviet secret service officers in a wood near Smolensk. The Poles belonged to a force of 15,000 captured and imprisoned by the Soviets after their occupation of eastern Poland under the 1939 NAZI-SOVIET PACT. The Germans discovered the graves in 1943 and the KREMLIN refused to co-operate in a Red Cross investigation, blaming the atrocity on the Nazis. The dispute caused the Polish government-in-exile to break off relations with its Soviet 'ally'. The Soviet Union finally admitted responsibility in 1989, but the whereabouts of the remaining 10,000 Poles is still a mystery.

Keating Five The five US SENATORS questioned by the Ethics Committee over their receipt of over $1.3 million in campaign contributions from Charles Keating, Arizona property developer and owner of the Lincoln Thrift of Irvine, California, which collapsed owing the taxpayer $2 billion. Keating had sought the senators' help in 1986 when sued by the Federal government for fraud and racketeering. The five were Sens. Alan Cranston, John Glenn, Donald Riegle, Dennis deConcini and John McCain; the committee found a case only against Cranston, saying there was 'substantial credible evidence' of improper conduct. He was formally reprimanded by the Senate in 1991.

> The few courageous regulators were intimidated by powerful Senators who, if they had not actually been bought off by Charles Keating, the wealthy chairman of Lincoln Savings & Loan, behaved as if they had.
>
> CHARLES PETERS, *How Washington Really Works*

Keating, Paul (1944–) Prime Minister of Australia (Labor) from 1991 to 1996 who ran a successful administration after ousting Bob HAWKE but was frustrated in his desire to break the link with the British monarchy. He made his reputation in eight years as Federal Treasurer under Hawke, FLOATING the dollar, ending exchange controls and letting in foreign banks. The battle over the CONSUMPTION TAX turned him against Hawke, whose consensual style he came to despise. He killed the Liberals' 1987 campaign by finding a $540 million mistake in their tax package that had taken two years to draw up – and received no public thanks from Hawke. In 1988 Keating reported Australia's biggest ever BUDGET surplus, 'the one that brings home the bacon – pulls the whole thing together'. Hawke went on television and said he could manage without Keating, but Keating told him: 'This government's got two leaders in it and I'm the other one'. Keating demanded an agreement that he would succeed to the leadership after the 1990 election (*see* KIRIBILLI), and when Hawke stayed he made his move (*see* Placido DOMINGO SPEECH).

Keating's challenge in June 1991, the first ever to a serving Prime Minister, failed. He moved to the BACK BENCHES, denouncing the Budget he had planned for. Six months later Hawke called a second ballot and lost 56–51.

In office Keating, with strong Irish roots (*see* LIZARD OF OZ), raised eyebrows with his Republicanism (he was also criticised for being over-familiar with the Queen) and his UNPARLIAMENTARY language; in 1992 the Senate censured him for 'references to individuals as scumbags, scum, suckers, thugs, dimwits, swill, a pigsty, fools and incompetents, perfumed gigolos and stupid foul-mouthed grubs'. Keating, a cultured man who collected antique clocks and was able to deliver a university lecture on the history of art, described the censure as the 'act of pansies'.

Keating pushed through the work of modernising Australia's society, economy and working practices that Hawke had begun, including forced mergers of trade unions with buyoffs to break the power of the most corrupt. In March 1993 he led Labor to a decisive election victory over the Liberals under John Hewson. In June 1995 he paved the way for a referendum on making Australia a republic, but by the time the proposition was narrowly defeated he had lost a further election in March 1996 heavily to a COALITION headed by John Howard.

His greatest fault is the flip side of his brilliance as an advocate. He passionately believes in what he is saying, no matter what it is.
Sen. PETER WALSH

I found Mr Keating refreshingly orthodox on finance – a far cry from the British Labour Party.
MARGARET THATCHER, *The Downing Street Years*

I was never able to master the trick of looking confident when I wasn't. When I'm confident, you know it.
PAUL KEATING

kebab To confront a politician suddenly with a hostile question on an unexpected subject during a supposedly friendly interview. The term was coined by Neil KINNOCK in 1987 when interviewed by James Naughtie on BBC radio's *The World at One*. When Naughtie raised an unexpected issue, Kinnock told him: 'I'm not going to be bloody kebabbed.' The exchange was not broadcast, but a tape of it reached the newspapers. Some time later Naughtie and his wife took the Kinnocks to a Lebanese restaurant to put the episode behind them, and the speciality of the house turned out to be – an enormous kebab.

keep. Keep Left *See* LEFT.

Keep the faith, baby A slogan adopted in 1960s America by black activists, urging on the struggle for CIVIL RIGHTS regardless of setbacks. It had been popularised by Rep. Adam Clayton POWELL when he was expelled from CONGRESS.

Keep Sunday Special The campaign backed by English and Welsh evangelical churches and the shopworkers' union USDAW which brought the defeat in 1987 of government legislation to repeal laws against Sunday trading. It held the line until December 1993, when limited opening was approved by 75 votes; the supermarkets had started opening anyway from late 1991, John MAJOR's government infuriating Keep Sunday Special by not intervening. Sunday trading had always been legal in Scotland.

Kefauver hearings The first televised US Congressional hearings, in May 1950, which held the nation spellbound. Sen. Estes Kefauver (1903–63) was chairing a special senate committee to investigate 'Organised Crime in Interstate Commerce'. The advertising agency Young and Rubicam took out press adverts saying the hearings had shown 'a broader picture of the sordid intermingling of crime and politics, of dishonor in public life'.

Kellogg pact The high-water mark of the international community's desire to avoid a repetition of WORLD WAR I, signed in Paris in 1928 by every eventual major participant in the next war except the Soviet Union and eventually by 48 nations. Popularly named after US Secretary of State Frank B. Kellogg (1856–1937), it renounced conflict without enabling ISOLATIONISTS to claim that America was entering any alliance. After some minor successes in Latin America, it proved unable to halt the Japanese invasion of Manchuria in 1931 and the expansionism of Mussolini (*see* DUCE) and HITLER. It was also known as the **Kellogg-Briand pact** (after the French Prime Minister Aristide Briand) and the **Pact of Paris**.

An international kiss. FRANK B. KELLOGG

Kelly. David Kelly affair The political crisis in Britain caused by the suicide on 18 July 2003 of the Ministry of Defence microbiologist David Kelly, who had been the source for the BBC reporter Andrew Gilligan's controversial story that May that Alistair Campbell, Tony BLAIR's director of communications, had 'sexed up' the September 2002 dossier (*see* DODGY DOSSIER) alleging that SADDAM HUSSEIN was poised to use WEAPONS OF MASS DESTRUCTION in order to gain support for military action against Iraq. Kelly was given a torrid time by the Foreign Affairs Select Committee after his identity had been revealed by the MoD; while admitting having met Gilligan, Kelly denied having been the source of the charges against Campbell. After his death three days later the BBC admitted that he had, though suggestions remained that Gilligan's line of questioning had been prompted by Clare SHORT. Kelly's death, discovered just after Blair had been given a triumphal reception by both HOUSES of the US CONGRESS, rocked the Labour government and put the future of Defence Secretary Geoff Hoon in jeopardy. A judicial inquiry was immediately instigated under Lord HUTTON, but allegations of government SPIN against Kelly continued (*see* PMOS). The Hutton inquiry criticised the MoD for not warning Kelly that his identity as Gilligan's source would be released to the media, but otherwise put the blame squarely on the BBC for allowing Gilligan to broadcast a highly exaggerated version of what Kelly had told him. *Compare* Vince FOSTER AFFAIR in Washington.

> All we ever wanted was an incorrect story corrected.
> TONY BLAIR, press conference, 30 July 2003

> The wages of spin is death.
> Editorial, *THE DAILY TELEGRAPH*, 19 July 2003

Ken and Eddie show The monthly meetings in the mid-1990s between Chancellor Kenneth Clarke and Eddie George, Governor of the Bank of England, at which Britain's base interest rate was set. They ended in 1997 when Labour was elected and Gordon BROWN immediately gave the Bank its independence to set interest rates, which it now does through the MONETARY POLICY COMMITTEE.

Kennebunkport The seaside vacation home in Maine of President George BUSH Snr, on Ocean Avenue at Walker's Point, 90 miles north of Boston. When Bush had an announcement to make or a VIP visitor to greet, he would be filmed in front of the wooden porch to a small cottage. His actual home was 100 yards behind the cottage; when the cameras beckoned, he would drive to the back door of the cottage in a golf cart and come out of his modest LOG CABIN to greet the WHITE HOUSE media.

Kennedy dynasty The CHARISMATIC but tragic political family descended from and motivated by **Joseph Kennedy** (1888–1969), Boston-Irish stock market speculator, Securities and Exchange Commission chairman and US ambassador to Britain. Their glamour and torment have captivated America and the world for four decades. Kennedy, described by Harry S TRUMAN as 'as big a crook as we've got anywhere in this country', was ambitious for his sons. The eldest, **Joe Jr**, was blown up in WORLD WAR II by tons of high explosive he had volunteered to fly despite being ordered home on furlough; the mantle then fell on **John Fitzgerald Kennedy** (1917–63). JFK had, according to his mother, been 'rocked to political lullabies'. Joseph Kennedy said: 'I told him Joe was dead and it was his responsibility to run for CONGRESS. He didn't want to. But I told him he had to.' A wartime torpedo boat commander (*see* PT-109), he was elected to the House as a Democrat in 1947 and the Senate in 1952, and won a Pulitzer Prize for his 1956 book PROFILES IN COURAGE. In Hedrick Smith's words he was 'no great shakes as a Congressman or Senator, but he won a mass following'. In 1960, to the amusement of party regulars, he sought the Presidential nomination; Lyndon B. JOHNSON remarked: 'Have you heard the news? Jack's paediatricians have given him a clean bill of health', but he ended as Vice Presidential candidate on the Kennedy ticket. The party welcomed the boyish but assertive JFK as 'a TRUMAN with a Harvard accent'; one Southern Senator observed:

> He seems to combine the best qualities of Elvis Presley and Franklin D. ROOSEVELT.

Pitted against Richard NIXON in a campaign which included the first televised Presidential DEBATES, Kennedy scraped home (*see* COOK COUNTY) to become the 35th (and youngest) President – and the first Roman Catholic in the WHITE HOUSE. He had defused this issue by declaring: 'I am not the Catholic candidate for the Presidency. I am the Democratic Party's candidate for President who happens to be Catholic. I do not speak for my church on public matters – and the church does not speak for me.' Pope John XXIII joked to reporters: 'Do not expect me to run a country with a language as difficult as yours'.

Kennedy struck a visionary and dynamic note, contrasting with the torpor of the EISENHOWER years. After his election he declared: 'Courage, judgment, integrity, dedication – these are the historic qualities which, with God's help, will characterise our Government's conduct in the four stormy years that lie ahead.' And his inaugural address in January 1961 set a challenge for the NEW FRONTIER, with its enjoinder: 'Ask not what your COUNTRY can do for you – ask what you can do for your country.' Quoting George Bernard Shaw, he said: 'Some men see things as they are and say: "Why?" I see things that never were and say: "Why not?"'

Kennedy took America into the space age, setting the goal of putting a man on the Moon by 1970. The notion that a new era had dawned was also felt on a social and cultural level, as a dour Executive Mansion was transformed into CAMELOT. Kennedy opened the White House to the greatest names in the arts, leading John Steinbeck to write: 'What a joy that literacy is no longer prima facie evidence of treason, that syntax is no longer subversive at the White House.' And the visiting Harold MACMILLAN observed: 'There is something very 18th-century about this young man. He is always on his toes during our discussion. But in the evening there will be music and wine and pretty women.' And one pretty woman in particular, Kennedy's chic wife Jacqueline (*see* JACKIE O). She had proved a great asset in the 1960 campaign, Kennedy remarking:

'As usual, Jackie's drawing more people than we are.' As FIRST LADY, Jackie Kennedy not only exuded style in the White House but charmed the world. JFK described himself as 'the man who accompanied Jackie Kennedy to Paris', and the visit was worth it, President DE GAULLE hailing Kennedy as 'a European'. Their marriage was not easy. The couple suffered personal tragedy, a baby son dying weeks before Kennedy's own assassination. Jackie was extravagant; Kennedy in his will left her income 'to enable her to maintain the standard of living to which she has been accustomed'. JFK himself had a prodigious reputation, carefully concealed by a loyal press, as a womaniser; Marilyn Monroe, Marlene Dietrich and Judith Campbell, girlfriend of the Chicago mobster Sam Giancana, were among his conquests. When he took office, one aide gleefully remarked: 'This administration is going to do for sex what the last one did for golf', and it did. Once Jackie, finding a female undergarment under a pillow, told her husband: 'They're not even my size.' Theodore H. White concluded: 'Kennedy loved his wife, but Kennedy the politician exuded that musk odor which acts as an aphrodisiac to many women.'

JFK's optimism was soon dented by the BAY OF PIGS fiasco, and tested by a series of COLD WAR confrontations including the construction of the BERLIN WALL (*see* ICH BIN EIN BERLINER) and, finally, the CUBAN MISSILE CRISIS. Kennedy had prepared himself for this ultimate exercise in BRINKMANSHIP: 'In the long history of the world, only a few generations have been granted the role of defending freedom in its hour of maximum danger. I do not shrink from this responsibility – I welcome it.' His demeanour when the superpowers went EYEBALL TO EYEBALL alarmed some. Robert Ruark saw him as 'practically cold all the way, with a hard blue eye on Valhalla', and Norman Mailer wrote: 'It is true that we have a President with a face. And it is the face of a potential hero. But he embodies nothing, he personifies nothing, he is power, rather a quizzical power, without light or principle.' Yet Khrushchev, the Soviet leader, appreciated his firmness, saying: 'I had no cause for regret once Kennedy became President.' And Nixon later wrote: 'Contrary to myth, Kennedy did not relish confrontation. Prudence was one of his favourite words.' In private Kennedy could be caustic. When steel bosses went against his wishes to impose a price hike (*see* JAWBONING), he observed: 'My father always told me that all businessmen were sons of bitches, but I never believed it until now.' Later he added: 'They are a bunch of bastards – and I'm saying this on my own now, not because my father told it to me.' (*See also* DIEF THE CHIEF.)

Kennedy's domestic record was mixed. Early on he remarked: 'When we got into office, the thing that surprised me most was that things were just as bad as we had been saying they were', and before long he was saying bemusedly: 'The worse I do, the more popular I get.' His initiatives made little headway in Congress, Sen. Everett DIRKSEN saying they had 'about as much impact as a snowflake on the bosom of the POTOMAC'. He was also slow to embrace CIVIL RIGHTS until Martin Luther KING delivered a movement he could not ignore (*see* I HAVE A DREAM). And in the autumn of 1963 James Reston wrote: 'There is a vague feeling of doubt and disappointment in the country about President Kennedy's first term.'

JFK prepared a vigorous re-election campaign – but it ended at DALLAS on 22 November 1963 when he was assassinated, in all probability by Lee Harvey Oswald. Before his election Kennedy had told staff: 'I'm 43 years old and I'm the healthiest candidate for the Presidency of the United States. You have travelled with me enough to know that I'm not going to die in office.' But in office he became fatalistic, remarking just before Dallas: 'If someone is going to kill me, they will kill me.'

> I should have known that he was magic all along . . . I should have guessed that it would be too much to ask to grow old with him and see our children grow up together . . . Now he is a legend when he would have preferred to be a man.
>
> JACQUELINE KENNEDY

> Since 1963 the world has seemed a bleaker place, and for me and I suspect millions of my contemporaries he remains the lost leader – NEVER GLAD CONFIDENT MORNING AGAIN.
>
> Lord HARLECH

The Presidency passed to Johnson, and the Kennedy torch to JFK's younger brother, **Bobby** (Robert Fitzgerald) **Kennedy** (1925–68). **RFK** had, against Jack's advice, worked as an investigator for Sen. Joseph MCCARTHY; he later made his mark prosecuting union racketeers. He ran his brother's Presidential campaign, then was controversially appointed ATTORNEY-GENERAL, JFK remarking: 'I can't see that it's wrong to give him a little legal experience before he goes out to practice law.' Bobby Kennedy made an impact with a vigorous line on civil rights, but also made enemies; according to Henry Brandon, 'people feared his quick temper and his adherence to one of the less attractive Kennedy traits: "If you are not for us, you are against us."' In 1968, after breaking with LBJ over VIETNAM, Bobby, now a Senator for New York, reignited the Kennedy magic by entering the Presidential race. But his candidacy was not a return to Camelot; when Jackie Kennedy remarked: 'Won't it be wonderful when we get back into the White House again?', Bobby's wife Ethel tartly replied: 'What do you mean, we?' Then tragedy struck again; Bobby Kennedy's campaign looked in sight of success when, straight after winning the California primary, he was shot at a Los Angeles hotel by the Jordanian-born Sirhan Sirhan.

> My thanks to you all. And now it's on to Chicago . . . and let's win there!
>
> RFK's last public remark

On Bobby's death, the youngest brother, **Teddy** (Edward Moore) **Kennedy** (1932–) became head of the clan (save for the matriarch, Rose Kennedy, who would live on until 1995 aged 104). Teddy Kennedy said:

> Like my three brothers before me, I pick up a fallen standard and sustained by the memory of our priceless years together, I shall try to carry forward that special commitment to justice, to excellence, to courage that distinguished their lives.

Teddy Kennedy had succeeded to JFK's Senate seat in 1962, his opponent dismissively saying: 'If his name wasn't Kennedy he wouldn't be in the race', and in 1969 became the youngest-ever majority WHIP; he went on to serve in the Senate for over four decades. As uncle of numerous orphaned children, he was reluctant to tempt fate; his cousin and longtime associate Joe Gargan said: 'You can pick up the standard without picking up the Presidency. The standard is the cause – the work, the poor, the Blacks.'

CHAPPAQUIDDICK left him tainted despite an outstanding record as a legislator, and persistent tussles with sex and alcohol maintained the image. Yet he knew, as Sen. Edmund Muskie put it, that 'power is constantly enhanced when people perceive that you could be President someday'; and to George F. Will he was 'the Democrats' heavy hitter'. He also remained in Hedrick Smith's words 'the 1970s cult figure of the left', and in 1980 he went for the Democratic nomination against President Jimmy CARTER. He lost, but fatally weakened Carter's bid for re-election against Ronald REAGAN. Teddy Kennedy summed up his ambitions when he said:

> I don't mind not being President. I just mind that somebody else is.

The **Kennedy curse** did not end with Teddy Kennedy. Drug problems, accidents and traumatic illnesses have plagued the next generation, overshadowing those eager to take up the standard in their turn. A couple of members of the Kennedy clan have managed the odd term in Congress, but to date the most successful has been a Republican, the movie hunk **Arnold Schwarzenegger**, husband of JFK's niece Maria Shriver, who was elected Governor of California in 2003 (*see* GOVERNATOR). Much was expected from **John F. Kennedy Jr**, who had moved all America as a toddler when he saluted his father's coffin; he founded the glossy political/celebrity magazine GEORGE, and a political career seemed in prospect when, on 16 July 1999, he piloted his own plane to a family wedding at HYANNIS PORT with his wife Carolyn and sister-in-law Lauren Bessette, and crashed into the sea at night on the approach to Martha's Vineyard.

Kennedy Airport Generally known as JFK, New York City's international airport, formerly known as Idlewild and renamed after the President's assassination.

Kennedy Center The John F. Kennedy Center for the Performing Arts, erected in his memory in Washington beside the Potomac.

> A national tragedy – a cross between a concrete candy box and a marble sarcophagus in which the art of architecture lies buried.
>
> ADA LOUISE HUXTABLE

Kennedy Round The round of GATT talks from 1964 to 1967, intended to lower world trade barriers and instigated by Kennedy through his US Trade Expansion Act. It secured average TARIFF cuts of 35%.

Cape Kennedy The space launch centre at Cape Canaveral, Florida, which was renamed Cape Kennedy in the assassinated President's memory, but has since reverted to its original title.

Senator, you're no Jack Kennedy The most crushing put-down to date from any of the televised DEBATES between candidates on a national ticket, from the Vice Presidential debate of 1988.When Dan QUAYLE defended himself against charges of inexperience by saying: 'I have as much experience in the Congress as Jack Kennedy did when he sought the Presidency', the veteran Texas Sen. Lloyd Bentsen told him magisterially:

> Senator, I worked with Jack Kennedy. I knew Jack Kennedy. Jack Kennedy was a friend of mine. Senator, you're no Jack Kennedy.

Kent State The fatal shooting by Ohio national guardsmen of four protesting students – nine more were wounded – at Kent State University on 4 May 1970 at the height of protests against the VIETNAM WAR. The guardsmen were provoked by coeds calling them 'shit-heels, motherfuckers and half-ass pigs'. The deaths brought to a head campus opposition to US involvement in Indo-China, and caused widespread revulsion among America's parents.

kerbstone politics *See* PAVEMENT POLITICS.

Kerensky A moderate politician whose accession to power is the prelude to a takeover by extremists whom he proves unable to control or resist. **Alexander Kerensky** (1881–1970) was the moderate socialist who headed the second Provisional GOVERNMENT of Russia from July to November 1917. After a series of disastrous setbacks in the war with Germany and a wave of revolutionary agitation, the BOLSHEVIKS under LENIN forced him from power.

kernel of evil The description given to Saudi Arabia, hitherto considered a loyal ally, in respect of its support for (or at best ambivalence over) anti-US Islamic extremism by Laurent Maurawiec, an analyst for the RAND CORPORATION in a report submitted to the PENTAGON in August 2002. The report was disclaimed by the BUSH administration, but nevertheless reflected a growing belief that many of America's global difficulties were being made worse by the stance of the Saudis and that over-dependency on Saudi oil was no longer in America's best interests. *Compare* AXIS OF EVIL.

Kerner Commission The BIPARTISAN Advisory Commission set up by President JOHNSON under former Illinois governor Otto Kerner to investigate the causes of INNER CITY riots. The panel's unanimous report, issued in 1968, blamed the intolerable economic, social and psychological conditions of urban blacks, stating: 'White racism is essentially responsible for the explosive mixture.' Republican Presidential nominee Richard NIXON accused the commission of blaming 'everyone except the perpetrators of the riots' and demanded retaliation against them.

Kerr sacking The most controversial episode in Australia's political history, revolving around the dismissal of the Labor Prime Minister Gough WHITLAM on 11 November 1975 by the GOVERNOR-GENERAL, Sir John Kerr (1914–91). Whitlam's ministry had been in increasing difficulties through the refusal of the OPPOSITION majority in the SENATE to vote SUPPLY, but refused to contemplate an ELECTION. Kerr was worried about the government's plans to borrow the money instead; he came to feel he was being treated like a RUBBER STAMP and had 'no wish for the vice-regal position to be diminished'. As tension rose, Whitlam joked to Kerr: 'It would be a question of whether I got to the Queen first for your recall, or you got in first with my dismissal', but Whitlam never imagined he would be removed. On the day, Kerr summoned Whitlam to YARRALUMLA and, without informing the Queen, sacked him. Kerr wrote:

> On 11 November 1975, time having in practical terms run out, I acted to end the deadlock. In exercise of the Governor General's reserve powers I withdrew the commission of the Prime Minister of Australia, Mr Whitlam, and his colleagues, appointed the leader of the opposition, Mr [Malcolm] Fraser, as Prime Minister, and swore in a CARETAKER GOVERNMENT. I obtained immediate passage through the senate of the blocked Supply Bills, and dissolved the House of Representatives and the Senate.

Whitlam was outraged. He felt Kerr should have discussed the options with him first, and believed (correctly) that the Governor-General had handed the initiative to Fraser's Liberals, who won the ensuing election. Kerr ignored a NO-CONFIDENCE motion in Fraser from the House of Representatives, and had the proclamation read which dissolved both Houses. It ended with the words 'GOD SAVE THE QUEEN', whereupon Whitlam commented:

> Well may we say God Save the Queen, because nothing will save the Governor-General.

To the end, Kerr defended his decision as right and proper, but Labor's outrage was unabated and Kerr was frequently booed in public. The episode did much to stir up REPUBLICAN feeling within the ALP.

Kerry. I'm John Kerry and I'm reporting for duty The pay-off line of the ACCEPTANCE speech delivered to the 2004 Democratic National CONVENTION by Sen. John F. Kerry (1943–) of Massachusetts (*see* *also* JFK), the party's Presidential NOMINEE. It was designed to recall Kerry's service in Vietnam, and thus to counter claims by supporters of George W. BUSH that Kerry was too liberal and too indecisive to be President. The details of Kerry's record were to be disputed (*see* SWIFT BOAT VETERANS FOR TRUTH) and conservatives also pointed out that Kerry had come back from Vietnam at 27 to testify to CONGRESS against the handling of the war. Yet Kerry came out ahead in the Presidential DEBATES and gave Bush a contest right down to the wire, the outcome of the election hinging on Ohio, where despite a close result and with 125,000 Provisional BALLOTS uncounted, Kerry decided to CONCEDE rather than stage a challenge to the counting process less justified than in 2000.

key. key indicator *See* INDICATOR.

Key Biscayne President NIXON's vacation retreat, on the Florida Keys 20 miles south of Miami.

keynote address The main political speech at a Republican or Democratic nominating CONVENTION, at which a prominent party figure – other than the NOMINEE – sets the tone for the CAMPAIGN ahead. It has customarily given the party its best opportunity to capture the public's imagination in PRIME TIME – though the networks nowadays feel under no obligation to carry it live. A **keynote speech**, more generally, is the speech setting the tone for any political conference and subsequent campaign, generally delivered at or near the start.

Keynesianism The economic doctrine of **John Maynard Keynes**, 1st Baron Keynes (1883–1946), that a stagnant economy can be revived, and unemployment reduced, by the injection of funds raised by the State for public investment projects – in short, to 'spend their way back to prosperity'. Keynes' *A Treatise on Money* (1930) and *General Theory of Employment, Interest and Money* (1936) countered the orthodox view that unemployment was unavoidable, and were influential in formulating the NEW DEAL. THATCHERISM and REAGANOMICS were to take precisely the opposite view.

KGB (Russ. *Komitet Gosudarstvennoi Bezopasnosti*, Security Committee) The agency in the Soviet Union, and in some of its successor states, responsible for internal security, intelligence gathering, foreign operations and border control. Set up in 1954, it developed into the largest and most powerful secret service in the world, with a highly sinister reputation. At its height it employed an estimated 90,000 officers supported by 150,000 technicians and clerical staff, with 250,000 border guards and 25,000 agents abroad. Its budget was estimated at $6–12 billion. It was disbanded by President Yeltsin in December 1993 after some officers of the Interior Ministry backed the attack on Parliament in the WHITE HOUSE SIEGE. Its successor in Russia is the FSB.

Khaki election The UK general election of 1900, fought against the background of the BOER WAR. It took its name from the olive-green colour of the new uniforms worn by troops in South Africa. Public enthusiasm for the war was running high, with the opposition LIBERAL PARTY split on the issue. Lord SALISBURY's Conservatives won only a slight increase in seats despite claiming that 'a vote for the Liberals is a vote for the Boers'. Lord ROSEBERY, a Liberal supporter of the war, termed it a 'wanton election'. The term has come to be used for any election fought in an atmosphere of euphoria over war or victory.

Khmer Rouge (Fr. Red Cambodians) The Chinese-backed Communist political and military movement led by Pol Pot which in the late 1970s won global notoriety for GENOCIDE in Cambodia, allegedly killing more than 3 million people in its drive to stamp out urban and all other forms of civilisation (*see* KILLING FIELDS; YEAR ZERO). The Khmer Rouge took power in 1974 after a lengthy GUERRILLA campaign, but were ousted after five years by the Vietnamese, who condemned Pol Pot to death *in absentia*. After Vietnam agreed to withdraw in 1988 the Khmer Rouge became active again, but when its leaders arrived in 1991 to join a UN-sponsored COALITION, angry crowds forced them to flee to the forests, where Pol Pot died and several other leaders surrendered.

kibbutz (plural **kibbutzim** Heb. *qibbutz*, a gathering) The collective agricultural (or sometimes industrial) settlements that became the ideological backbone of the Israeli state and of the Labour Party which ruled the new nation for almost 30 years. The pioneer settlements were established by the Jewish Colonisation Association, formed by Edmond de Rothschild and Maurice de Hirsch in 1899. The kibbutzim, in which children are collectively reared, prospered despite violent opposition from Palestinian Arabs, and after Israel was born in 1948 played a key role in its defence. More recently many young kibbutzniks have given up the austere rural life for the cities.

kick upstairs To promote a politician to an apparently senior but less influential post – in Britain generally by giving them a seat in the HOUSE OF LORDS. The phrase was coined by George Savile, Marquis of Halifax (1633–95), who said: 'I had known many kicked downstairs, but I never knew any kicked upstairs before.' In 1900 BOSS PLATT of New York decided to 'kick upstairs' Theodore ROOSEVELT, who had uncomfortably turned out to be a reforming Governor, to be the Republican Vice Presidential NOMINEE. The move backfired; within a year Roosevelt had succeeded the assassinated MCKINLEY as President.

kill. killer rabbit One of a series of mishaps that afflicted Jimmy CARTER during 1979 and injected ridicule into media coverage of his Presidency. Shortly after he collapsed while taking part in a 'fun run', he suffered minor injuries when bitten by a rabbit near his home in PLAINS, Georgia. After his press secretary Jody Powell had briefed on the incident, the media, intrigued by its sheer improbability, depicted the offending creature as a 'killer rabbit'.

killer spot A key element of negative campaigning in US elections; the brief television commercial by one candidate intended to wreck a rival's chances.

killing fields The sinister countryside around Phnom Penh, dotted with the mass graves of Cambodians killed by the KHMER ROUGE between 1974 and 1979. After taking power the Khmer Rouge proclaimed YEAR ZERO, forced the entire population into agricultural labour camps and embarked on a horrifying social experiment including the extermination of all professionals and INTELLECTUALS. In four years over a quarter of the population died through starvation, disease, overwork or execution. These brutal and genocidal events were harrowingly told in *The Killing Fields* (1984), a film based on the true story of one man's struggle to survive this monstrous regime.

Kilmainham Treaty The agreement reached between GLADSTONE's government and Charles Stewart PARNELL to defuse the agitation for Irish land reform and against COERCION by releasing him from prison on 2 May 1882. Parnell had been imprisoned the previous October on a warrant accusing him and others of intimidating people from paying just rents. It was while Parnell was in prison that he was christened the UNCROWNED KING OF IRELAND; the outcry was such that the government had to negotiate through Captain O'Shea, husband of Parnell's mistress, for him to come out. FORSTER, the architect of COERCION, resigned from the Cabinet and there was a flicker of hope for peace. But four days later the PHOENIX PARK MURDERS revived the tension.

Kincora A boys' home in Belfast whose inmates were subjected to sexual assaults for eight years from the 1970s by men including at least one leading LOYALIST. Colin Wallace, a former Ministry of Defence press officer in NORTHERN IRELAND sacked for LEAKS and later jailed for a manslaughter he always denied, alleged that the intelligence organisation MI5 had covered up the abuses. Ministers consistently denied this, but Wallace pressed on; he did win an admission of his related charge that elements in the security waged a black PROPAGANDA campaign in the 1970s against politicians on both sides of the SECTARIAN divide.

Kinder, Kirche, Küche (Ger. children, church, kitchen) The motto of conservative German nationalists, embraced by the NAZIs, which allocated a purely domestic role to women in order to maintain traditional values. It was partly responsible for Germany's defeat in WORLD WAR II, as HITLER flatly refused to permit the conscription of women for even civilian duties. In Britain, by contrast, almost the entire female population was mobilised for the war effort.

king. King and Country debate The debate at the Oxford University Union on 9 February 1933 on the motion 'This House will under no circumstances fight for King and Country'. It was carried by 275 votes to 153; though most of the students gave it little further thought, it was widely reported and its passage was later widely blamed for NAZI Germany's mistaken belief as WORLD WAR II approached that Britain would not fight.

> We have all seen with a sense of nausea the abject, squalid, shameless avowal made in the Oxford Union . . . one can almost feel the curl of contempt upon the lips of the manhood of Germany, Italy and France when they read the message sent out by the Oxford Union in the name of Young England.
> CHURCHILL

King Andrew the First The nickname accorded President Andrew Jackson (*see* OLD HICKORY) by his enemies as they formed the WHIG party. It was intended to equate Jackson's allegedly dictatorial style –

particularly in VETOing the Bill chartering the Second Bank of the United States – with the high-handedness of King George III.

King Arthur The not entirely sympathetic nickname bestowed on **Arthur Scargill** (1938–), the militant President of Britain's National Union of Mineworkers from 1981, who sought confrontation with successive Conservative governments, culminating in the MINERS' STRIKE of 1984–85 which came close to wrecking the industry but failed to shift his greatest adversary, Margaret THATCHER. Scargill stayed on, with a lucrative package from the union, as the industry, and the NUM's membership, went into sharp decline.

King Billy The reverently affectionate name by which ORANGEMEN and Ulster LOYALISTS refer to William of ORANGE (1650–1702), who defeated the ousted King James II at the Battle of the BOYNE to secure the Protestant succession and the Protestant ascendancy in northern Ireland. William, a Dutch prince whose claim to the English throne lay mainly through his wife Mary, was summoned by Parliament once James, a Catholic, had begotten a male heir, and reigned as William III from 1689 to 1702. His portrait on horseback can be seen on many a gable-end in Protestant areas of Belfast.

King David Hotel bombing The greatest atrocity by the Jewish terrorist organisation IRGUN ZVAI LEUMI against British rule in Palestine. On 22 July 1946 an Irgun gang led by Yeisrael Levy (1926–90) planted a bomb at the hotel in Jerusalem, headquarters of the British administration, which claimed 91 lives. In the short term the bombing delayed the foundation of the state of Israel, heightening the ATTLEE government's reluctance to pull out and leave Jews and Arabs to fight a CIVIL WAR. But within two years Israel was born.

King Dick The nickname given to Richard John Seddon, Liberal Prime Minister of New Zealand 1893–1906, by critics who felt his style despotic.

Kingfish The populist **Huey Pierce Long** (1893–1935) earned this nickname as his demagogic style ('always be sincere, even if you don't mean it') earned him near-total control over the state of Louisiana as well as a seat in the US SENATE. The social and economic reforms Long championed as State Governor (1928–31) and Senator from 1931, with a NOMINEE running the state, echoed the CORPORATISM of Mussolini (*see* DUCE) and outstripped the NEW DEAL, which he scorned as feeble; taxes on large corporations financed spending to relieve unemployment and improve health and education standards. Long built a powerful political MACHINE, aimed at winning the presidency with a 'Share Our Wealth' programme. But on 8 September 1935 he was assassinated at the state Capitol in Baton Rouge by Dr Carl Austin Weiss, who nursed a family grudge. Long's last words were:

> I wonder why he shot me.

An investigation in 1992 rejected the Weiss family's claim that Long had been shot by a bodyguard's bullet. *See also* HALITOSIS OF THE INTELLECT.

kingmaker A power-broker who can make or break a candidate; from Warwick the Kingmaker, an all-powerful English baron in the late Middle Ages.

King of Ulster *See* ULSTER.

King over the water Originally the term used by JACOBITES for their pretender to the English crown, in exile on the Continent of Europe. Now any politician out of favour or power whose followers hope can make a comeback, usually by ousting the present party leader.

King Street Shorthand for the leadership of Britain's COMMUNIST PARTY, from the address of its London headquarters from its founding in 1920 until the 1980s. The building on the fringe of Covent Garden was ironically within a stone's throw of Moss Bros, London's grandest formal dress-hire shop.

King, Leslie The name at birth (Leslie Lynch King Jr) of Gerald FORD, 38th President of the United States. When he was two his parents divorced; his mother soon after married a paint salesman named Gerald Rudolph Ford, who adopted the young boy. The facts about his birth and adoption were kept from young Gerald (known as Junior) until he was sixteen, and he only saw his father twice; both meetings were unfriendly and Ford ruled out further contacts.

Dr Martin Luther King Jr (1929–68) Black America's pre-eminent campaigner for CIVIL RIGHTS, who as a young Baptist minister began campaigns of CIVIL DISOBEDIENCE that eventually shamed the political establishment into action. A follower of Gandhi's (*see* MAHATMA) doctrine of NON-VIOLENCE, King was at the height of his influence in the early 1960s when his activities in BIRMINGHAM and SELMA, his campaign to make Chicago an 'open city' (he said: 'I have never seen such hate as in Chicago'), his massive MARCH ON

WASHINGTON and his oratory (*see* I HAVE A DREAM) spurred the KENNEDY and JOHNSON administrations to outlaw SEGREGATION and racial discrimination. Throughout his campaigns he suffered imprisonment, threats and actual violence (his house was dynamited), false allegations of graft and tax evasion, and harassment by FBI director J. Edgar Hoover (*see* COINTELPRO). Hoover was convinced King was a Communist and was also intrigued by his sexual adventures, repeatedly bugging his bedroom; Hoover branded him 'the most notorious liar in the country'. By 1967 King was being outflanked by militant advocates of violence and BLACK POWER, but before he could lose control of mass black opinion he was assassinated in a Memphis motel (*see* I HAVE BEEN TO THE TOP OF THE MOUNTAIN) by James Earl Ray, a white drifter.

> What has violence ever accomplished? What has it ever created? No martyr's cause has ever been stilled by his assassin's bullet. No wrongs have ever been righted by riots and civil disorders. A sniper is only a coward, not a hero. And an uncontrollable mob is only the voice of madness and not the voice of the people . . . What we need in the United States is not division. What we need in the United States is not hatred. What we need in the United States is not violence or lawlessness, but love and wisdom and compassion toward one another, and a feeling of justice toward those who still suffer in our country whether they be white or they be black. Let us dedicate ourselves . . . to tame the savageness of man and make gentle the life of this world. Let us dedicate ourselves to that and say a prayer for our country and our people.
>
> ROBERT F. KENNEDY on King's assassination, shortly before his own

Rodney King riots The anarchy that broke out in southern Los Angeles on 28 April 1992, leaving 58 people dead and 2000 hurt, and causing $1 billion in damage, much of it to Korean-owned stores. The riots, California's worst, followed the acquittal by an all-white jury in suburban Simi Valley of four Los Angeles police officers who had beaten senseless Rodney King, a young black man whom they had ordered from his car. Video film of the incident shamed the nation when shown on television, but did not impress the jury. Such was the public outcry that President George BUSH Snr, facing re-election, ordered a Federal investigation, saying:

> None of this is what we wish to think of as American. It is as if we were looking in a mirror that distorted our better selves and turned us ugly.

In 1994 Rodney King was awarded $3.8 million damages against the Los Angeles Police Department.

uncrowned King of Ireland *See* IRELAND.

Kinnock, Neil Gordon (later Lord Kinnock, 1942–) The working class grammar-school boy from South Wales who transformed Labour's fortunes during nine years as party leader, but fell just short of regaining power at the 1992 general election and went on to serve for even longer as a member of the EUROPEAN COMMISSION. Elected to Parliament in 1970 as a red-haired firebrand who modelled himself on Aneurin BEVAN, he took over the leadership when the party was on the point of disintegration after the founding of the SDP and Labour's near-annihilation in the 1983 election. Just two years before, he had said: 'As for being leader, I can't see it happening and I'm not particularly keen on it happening.' Denis HEALEY felt that 'he is politically intelligent, has character and courage, but has never been a Minister, lacks experience and people know it'. Yet Kinnock proved himself a leader of unprecedented organisational rigour, able to drive dissident groups out of the party (*see* MILITANT TENDENCY), abandon unpopular policies he himself had espoused such as UNILATERALISM, modernise the party machine and make it ELECTABLE. He was blessed in his wife Glenys with a highly intelligent, supportive and effective partner. And above all he had ambition, Edward Pearce writing: 'To get to DOWNING STREET he'd boil his granny down for glue.'

Kinnock had an infectious sense of humour, but also a withering tongue. He once said of the Conservatives: 'You cannot fashion a wit out of two half-wits.' When the Tory MP Robert Adley asked: 'Can you name one thing on which you haven't changed your mind?' Kinnock replied: 'You and I came into the HOUSE on the same day. I formed the opinion that you were a jerk, and I haven't changed my mind.' Of the THATCHER Cabinet he observed: 'Norman Fowler looks as if he were suffering from famine, and Nigel Lawson looks as though he caused it,' and when Sir Geoffrey HOWE, then Chancellor, lost his trousers on a train he remarked: 'I never knew until now what the Tories meant when they said inflation was bottomless.' He described Norman Tebbit (*see* CHINGFORD SKINHEAD) as 'a boil on a verucca' and Sir Keith Joseph (*see* MAD MONK) as 'a mind without any visible means of support'. But he was sometimes hard to pin down. New York's Mayor Ed Koch once told him: 'Sure, we all want peace in Ireland. But what's your position?' and the electricians' leader Frank Chapple said: 'He reminds me of those beauty queen competitors who always smile and say they want to work with children and travel a lot.' Kinnock was an emotional and effective campaigner, though one commentator wrote in 1987 that 'he looks like a tortoise having an orgasm'. But at critical moments at WESTMINSTER such as the WESTLAND crisis he proved unable to press home Labour's advantage, and two election defeats (one by Margaret THATCHER, one against the odds by John MAJOR) were enough for him. He gave up the leadership at 50, the age at which twelve years earlier he had said he would like to retire to play 'cricket in the summer and geriatric football in the winter'. Later in 1992 his successor John SMITH proposed Kinnock as a European Commissioner; Major bowed to Tory objections then but appointed him two years later when Tony BLAIR nominated him. He went to Brussels as Transport Commissioner at the start of 1995, joining his wife who had just been elected to the EUROPEAN PARLIAMENT, and stayed for ten years, surviving the mass resignation of the Commission over the CRESSON AFFAIR to take on the internal reform portfolio. He had limited success in making the Commission more effective, more transparent, less bureaucratic and less corrupt (*see* EUROSTAT), but disproved the claims from his years leading the OPPOSITION that he lacked executive ability.

> In all his years as Opposition leader, he never let me down. Right to the end, he struck the wrong note.
>
> MARGARET THATCHER, *The Downing Street Years*

Kinnock – the movie The campaign film – shown twice on all British TV channels – which created a devastating impact at the start of the 1987 election campaign by putting Neil Kinnock firmly on the map. The video, which showed Kinnock the family man, Kinnock the visionary campaigner and Kinnock the ruthless cleanser of his own party, was directed by Hugh Hudson, who had made the Oscar-winning *Chariots of Fire* and whom Labour had just recruited back from the SDP. It had an even greater effect across the Atlantic: Sen. Joseph Biden pirated part of Kinnock's text in a TV spot of his own for the 1988 Presidential race, and dropped out when the plagiarism was spotted by a Labour activist working for a rival campaign.

Kiribilli agreement The deal struck between Bob HAWKE and Federal Treasurer Paul KEATING at Kiribilli House, the Prime Minister's Sydney residence, on 25 November 1988 under which Keating expected Hawke to hand over to him after the 1990 election. When Hawke stayed put, a furious Keating began his campaign to dislodge him. *Compare* GRANITA.

> At no point was there any undertaking that two terms was it and then I'd hand over to him.
>
> BOB HAWKE.

kiss. kissing babies The archetypal way CANDIDATES supposedly demean themselves in the quest for VOTES. The tradition goes back a long way: in 1832 Andrew Jackson (*see* OLD HICKORY), confronted with a filthy baby, praised it as 'a beautiful specimen of American childhood', then got his friend John Eaton to kiss it. In 1960 John F. KENNEDY refused to pose with one for a campaign photo, saying: 'Kissing babies gives me asthma.'

kissing hands The formality with which a new British Prime Minister takes office, receiving the SEALS OF OFFICE from the Sovereign. No actual kiss takes place.

Give us a kiss, love Three WESTMINSTER MPs found themselves c. 1979 in a small New Zealand hotel. The two Conservatives shared a room, leaving the only single to Walter Harrison, a bluff Yorkshire Labour WHIP. One Tory complained that his colleague's snoring kept him awake, so Harrison took his place. The next day Harrison came down to breakfast looking fresh, and the offending Tory with bags under his eyes. 'What did you do?' asked the now-rested first Tory. 'I turned out the light and said: "Give us a kiss, love!" said Harrison. 'He didn't sleep a wink.'

You can kiss my ass Senator George McGovern's exasperated remark to an airport HECKLER at Battle Creek, Michigan, on 2 November 1972, just before his LANDSLIDE defeat by Richard NIXON. McGovern apologised profusely, but 'KMA' badges started to appear at his rallies and Sen. James Eastland of Mississippi, at the other extreme of the Democratic party, told him:

> That was the best line of the campaign!

Kissinger, Henry Alfred (1923–) The German-born Harvard professor who became President NIXON's NATIONAL SECURITY ADVISER, outgunning Secretary of State William Rogers who termed him 'MACCHIAVELLIAN, deceitful, egotistical, arrogant and insulting'. His negotiations to end the VIETNAM WAR brought him the 1973 NOBEL PEACE PRIZE (one South Vietnamese said his joint award with Le Duc Tho was 'like nominating a whore as honorary chairman of the PTA') and his Middle East SHUTTLE DIPLOMACY eased tension after the YOM KIPPUR WAR, but the right loathed his backing of DÉTENTE. Hugh Brogan rated him 'the most remarkable diplomat to emerge in America since 1945'. Kissinger traded on his image, once saying: 'There cannot be a crisis next week. My diary is already full.' He claimed that power was 'the ultimate aphrodisiac', but Barbara Howar observed: 'Henry's idea of sex is to slow down to 30 miles an hour when he drops you off at the door.' Kissinger once remarked: 'The nice thing about being a celebrity is that when you bore people, they think it's their fault.' Eventually Secretary of State to Presidents Nixon and FORD, he held no public office after 1977 but remained a figure of great influence.

kitchen cabinet *See* CABINET.

kitchen debate The impromptu debate on the merits of Communism and capitalism between Vice President NIXON and the Soviet leader Nikita S. Khrushchev in the model kitchen of a US exhibition in Moscow on 3 August 1959. Nixon only gained State Department clearance for a purely 'ceremonial' visit, but in the kitchen, in front of the cameras, he cut loose. Voices were raised, but Khrushchev was at his most expansive, throwing his arms around a Soviet worker and asking: 'Does this man look like a slave labourer?' Reporters present scored it a Nixon victory.

kite-flying The unofficial floating of an idea before it has become established policy to see how the electorate or the political community will react, or its premature release so as to condition opinion for the inevitable. *See* HAWARDEN KITE.

kith and kin The rallying cry of supporters in Britain of Ian Smith's regime in Rhodesia following UDI in 1965. They argued that Britain could not act against a people who were essentially its own – the 5% of whites who controlled the country and were out to head off MAJORITY RULE. Left-wingers ridiculed the notion with their own slogan:

> Kith my arse!

kleptocracy Government by thieves, from the Greek *kleptes*, thief. The term was first applied to Zaire under President Mobutu Sese Seko Kuku Ngbendu Wa Za Banga (1930–), who with his officials looted the country of billions of dollars for three decades from 1965 as its economy and infrastructure reverted to jungle.

KMT Kuomintang/Guomindang. China's National People's Party, founded by Sun Yat-Sen (1866–1925) in 1905; it took power in a revolution in 1911 but was persecuted by President Gen. Yuan Shikai, who had forced the abdication of the last emperor. Sun, acknowledged founder of modern China, went into exile after leading a failed coup, returning in 1923 as President of the Canton-based Southern Republic. Only in 1926 was China united under KMT rule; the party subsequently passed under the control of GENERALISSIMO Chiang Kai-Shek (1877–1975). Before long the KMT was having to vie for power with Mao Tse-Tung's (*see* CHAIRMAN MAO) Communists and Japanese forces of occupation, who each seized Chinese territory. Chiang saw off the Japanese, but in 1949 was driven out by the victorious Communists. The Kuomintang has governed Taiwan, claiming with ever-decreasing conviction to be the true government of China, for most of the last half-century, but is now in opposition. In April 2005 Lien Chan, leader of the KMT, was feted in Beijing on the first visit by a party official for over half a century. The warmth of Communist China's welcome – sealed with the offer of two pandas, which the Taipei ADMINISTRATION rejected – was intended to undercut Taiwan's pro-independence stance which had led Beijing to pass legislative authority action to coerce the island if it broke away. However the KMT was still narrowly defeated in Taiwanese elections shortly after.

knee. kneecapping The classic punishment administered from the early 1970s by extremist PARAMILITARY groups in NORTHERN IRELAND to alleged petty criminals, troublemakers and informers. It consists of boring through the miscreant's kneecap with a Black & Decker electric drill, or blasting it with a shotgun. Victims of kneecapping generally recover, but usually refuse to tell the police who gave them their injuries or why. The term has come more generally to signify a severe punishment meted out by one's peers.

knee-jerk A reflex reaction to an opinion or event; one that is automatic and requires no thought. It is derived from the patellar reflex, the involuntary jerk of the leg caused by tapping just below the knee. The term became popular in 1970s America, often in combination, e.g. a knee-jerk liberal is one whose liberal response to any situation is automatic rather than considered.

Kneel! One of the oldest apocryphal stories at WESTMINSTER, describing how in the Central LOBBY one MP calls out: 'Neil!' to another and an overawed tourist falls to his knees, imagining a general command has been given. The story has been told of a fellow-member greeting Neil KINNOCK, before him of the Conservative Minister Neil Marten, and before him of Niall MacDermot QC (1916–96), a Labour MP 1957–59 and 1962–70 and a Minister in the first Wilson government. No doubt it goes back even further.

Knesset (Heb. Assembly) The Israeli parliament, a single CHAMBER consisting of 120 members elected every four years by PROPORTIONAL REPRESENTATION. The first Knesset opened in Jerusalem on 16 February 1949, electing Chaim Weizmann (1874–1952) as the country's first President.

knight. Knights of Labour A pioneering US labour union, founded in 1869 by Uriah S. Stephens, a Philadelphia tailor. In 1878 Terence V. Powderly became Grand Master of this Noble Order and turned it from a secret society into a mass union, which at its peak reported over 700,000 members in 5892 chapters. The Knights, politically and industrially moderate, called for one single union for all workers, black and white, EQUAL PAY for women, abolition of child and foreign contract labour, industrial safety, the encouragement of CO-OPERATIVES, and government ownership of railroads and telegraph lines. The union's fame spread when it wrung concessions from the hated railroad magnate Jay Gould in 1885, but decline set in after a series of unsuccessful strikes in 1886. A mistaken public belief after an anarchist riot in Chicago that the Knights advocated violence, and the alienation of skilled workers, hastened its end. The craft union dissidents were instrumental in founding the American Federation of Labor (*see* AFL-CIO).

knights of the shires The long-serving farming and landowning MPs of generally right-wing views, coupled with sound common sense about the politically possible, who formed the bedrock of the CONSERVATIVE PARTY at WESTMINSTER until well into the 1970s.

Plumed Knight The accolade given Rep. James G. Blaine, popular favourite for the 1876 Republican Presidential nomination, by Robert G. Ingersoll (1833–99) in his nominating speech. Ingersoll orated:

> Like an armed warrior, like a plumed knight, James G. Blaine marched down the halls of the American CONGRESS and threw his shining lance full and fair against the brazen forehead of every traitor to his country and every maligner of his fair reputation.

Mud thrown at Blaine over the favouritism he had shown certain railroads when SPEAKER of the House had stuck, and the Republicans nominated Rutherford Hayes instead. But Ingersoll's speech is still rated a classic.

knighthood The award, short of a PEERAGE, bestowed by the sovereign each year on several dozen distinguished Britons, some of them politicians. In the political world a knighthood, which carries the prefix 'Sir' and enables a wife to style herself 'Lady', usually goes to a BACKBENCH Conservative MP after some 20 years' service. Occasionally it goes to an ex-Minister who is staying in the COMMONS rather than take a peerage. Knights are non-hereditary, except for the now rarely-created **Baronets** whose title is handed down from father to son. The only baronet created in recent times was Sir Denis THATCHER on his wife's departure from DOWNING STREET; on his death it passed to their son Mark.

knocking-up The term used by party activists in Britain for getting out the vote on polling day, and particularly in the evening when time starts to run out. It involves calling at the homes of known supporters who have not voted and offering, where necessary, to give them a lift to the polls. In America the word has a very different meaning. *See also* NCR; READING SYSTEM.

know. Know-how Fund The fund established by the THATCHER government in 1990, and expanded under John MAJOR, to finance training for key personnel in the former Communist countries of eastern Europe. Under it, professional people such as bankers, broadcasters and lawyers either travelled to Britain to gain experience of Western ways or received training on the spot.

Know-Nothings The popular name for the **American Party,** formed in 1845 on an anti-Catholic, anti-immigrant platform after its founders had polled strongly at state level. It gained its name because members were bound by an oath to say they knew nothing if questioned on its policies, which were agreed at secret grand councils; how they managed to campaign or attract votes is a mystery. In 1851 they nominated Daniel Webster for President, but he did not take up the offer. The party's influence peaked in 1854 as the pre-CIVIL WAR tide of immigration reached its height, and horrified former WHIGS deserted to it; there were 'Know-Nothing riots' in Washington and Know-Nothing governors or legislatures were elected in four New England states, Maryland, Kentucky and California. The party tried to ignore the slavery issue, but split as its leaders were forced to take positions on the KANSAS-NEBRASKA ACT. Northern Know-Nothings adopted an anti-slavery platform and were at once eclipsed by the newly-formed Republican Party. The American Party's LAST HURRAH was the 1856 Presidential campaign of former President Millard Fillmore (1800–74); by 1859 it was confined to the border states.

> Where is the true-hearted American whose cheek does not tingle with shame to see our highest and most courted foreign missions filled by men of foreign birth to the exclusion of the native-born?
> MILLARD FILLMORE, 1856

> As a nation, we began by declaring that 'all men are created equal'. We now practically read it 'All men are created equal, except Negroes.' When the Know-Nothings get control, it will read: 'All men are created equal, except Negroes, and foreigners, and Catholics.'
> ABRAHAM LINCOLN

Komsomol The youth wing of the Soviet COMMUNIST PARTY, formerly known as the All-Union Leninist Young Communist league. It was formed in 1918 as a BOLSHEVIK youth organisation for agitation and propaganda, and membership became essential for anyone wishing to make their mark in Soviet life. Its offshoots included the daily newspaper *Komsomolskaya Pravda*.

Königswinter (1) The castle on the Rhine, 20 miles south-east of Cologne, which since the end of WORLD WAR II has had an influential role as a conference centre, both for Germany's CHRISTIAN DEMOCRATS and for bringing together Germans in key positions in politics, business and the media and their counterparts from other European countries and beyond. Such meetings played an important part in re-integrating post-war Germany into the democratic world. (2) Specifically, the Anglo-German meetings which have become the world's longest-established bilateral forum. Founded in 1950, Königswinter meets in alternate years at the castle and in Cambridge, with 80 prestigious delegates on each side from all walks of life. There is also a junior Königswinter for promising younger people.

Korea. Korea, Communism and Corruption The keywords of the 1952 Republican Presidential campaign, decrying the Truman administration for its handling of the Korean War, its alleged infiltration by Communists and the INFLUENCE-PEDDLING that tarnished its final years; the campaign contained more than an echo of MCCARTHYISM.

Koreagate The scandal that broke in WASHINGTON in 1977 over INFLUENCE-PEDDLING by Tongsun Park, a South Korean rice broker who claimed over nine years to have spent $850,000 in gifts and cash to 31 Democratic Congressmen. In 1978 a grand jury indicted him on 36 counts of conspiracy, bribery, mail fraud, racketeering, failure to register as a foreign agent and making illegal campaign contributions. Washington sat back for a juicy trial, especially as a glamorous political *demi-mondaine*, Tandy Dickenson, was at the heart of the case. But all charges against Park were dropped in return for his testimony. California Rep. Richard T. Hanna served a year in jail for conspiracy to defraud the government; he had attended a meeting in Seoul in 1968 with Park and the former director of South Korea's CIA which had agreed to have Park made Korea's exclusive rice purchasing agent. Part of the $9 million due to him in commission was spent to influence Congressmen, notably by inviting them to Korea on 'goodwill trips' and giving their wives envelopes stuffed with cash. But Speaker TIP O'Neill was cleared by the HOUSE of wrongdoing in attending a birthday party Park staged for him, and only three Congressmen were reprimanded. The most serious charge proven by the House was that Rep. John McFall had failed to report a $4000 contribution and had spent the money on himself. Three decades later Park re-emerged as a shadowy figure in the OIL FOR FOOD scandal at the UNITED NATIONS.

> Lobbying is built into the American system. Teachers and labor unions do it. Why shouldn't foreign countries? TONGSUN PARK

Korean War The bitter and ultimately inconclusive three-year conflict precipitated by Communist North Korea's surprise attack on the democratic South on 25 June 1950. At the end of WORLD WAR II Korea had been temporarily divided by the allies at the 38TH PARALLEL; attempts by the UNITED NATIONS to reunite the country had failed. The UN – with the Soviet Union critically leaving an empty CHAIR – raised an international force to combat the invasion, dominated by the US contingent and led by General Douglas MACARTHUR. President TRUMAN declared:

> The attack upon Korea makes it plain beyond all doubt that Communism has passed beyond the use of subversion to conquer independent nations, and will now use armed invasion and war.

He told Secretary of State Dean Acheson: 'Dean, we've got to stop those sons of bitches, no matter what.' MacArthur masterminded the Inchon landings in September 1950 which cut the Communists' supply line, then drove them back to the Yalu River, the boundary between North Korea and China. China entered the war that November, pushing the UN forces back beyond the 38th parallel and capturing Seoul, the southern capital. The UN forces turned the tide and Seoul was recaptured in April 1951. In the same month Truman fired MacArthur for publicly advocating taking the war into China after being told he would not be given such orders and gave the command to General Matthew Ridgway. Of MacArthur's plan, Gen. Omar Bradley said it would create 'the wrong war, in the wrong place, at the wrong time, with the wrong enemy'. Negotiations began on a Soviet initiative in July 1951, but the fighting dragged on until an ARMISTICE was signed at PANMUNJOM on 27 July 1953; intermittent border incidents continued for almost four decades, and can still flare up though tension has now switched to North Korea's NUCLEAR programme. The war left 55,000 US personnel dead, and 12,000 other UN troops (including British), compared with 260,000 South Korean and 1.5 million Communist fighters.

I shall go to Korea The dramatic pledge that clinched the Presidency for Dwight D. EISENHOWER. Speaking in Detroit on 24 October 1952, he described the war as 'never inevitable – always inescapable', and announced that he would go to Korea to end it. 'I shall make that trip,' he promised. 'Only in that way could I learn how best to serve the American people in the cause of peace.' His opponent Adlai STEVENSON had considered such a move, but to his regret rejected it; the headline 'I shall go to Korea' made a huge impact on public opinion.

Kosovo campaign. The first military action ever undertaken by NATO, in which allied forces between March and June 1999 bombed the Yugoslav province of Kosovo, and targets in Serbia, in an attempt to end the ETHNIC CLEANSING of its Albanian majority by the controlling Serbs. The Serbs withdrew just as Britain and the US were debating sending in ground forces, and multinational forces including a Russian contingent occupied Kosovo to restore order.

Kraft durch Freude (Ger. Strength through joy) A popular NAZI scheme for cheap package holidays, which allowed thousands of Germans to visit remote areas of the country, or travel abroad, during the 1930s. Based on the Italian FASCIST organisation *Dopo Lavoro*, it was initially funded from confiscated trade union funds but later became big business, generating considerable income for the Nazis. KdF also organised sports and artistic activities such as subsidised theatre visits and travelling cabaret shows. The scheme, which proved a valuable PROPAGANDA vehicle, was given its name by Robert Ley (1890–1945), head of the Nazis' Labour Front.

Kremlin (1) The 12th-century citadel at the heart of Moscow whose name epitomised the ruthless power of TSARIST and Soviet Russia, and which remains the Presidential seat. Looking out over the River Moskva and with a frontage on RED SQUARE, the Kremlin's walls contain the former Imperial palace, three cathedrals and a number of government offices.

> Like a baby, it has an appetite at one end and no sense of responsibility at the other.
>
> RONALD REAGAN

(2) The STRANGERS' Bar in the basement of the HOUSE OF COMMONS, close to the TERRACE. It gets its name from its forbidding demeanour – equalled for years by that of its barman, Ted, who once refused to serve the chairman of the 1922 COMMITTEE – and the serried ranks of elderly trade union Labour MPs who used to occupy it. Only MPs and their guests are permitted to use it, and only MPs may order drinks.

Kremlin coup The attempt in August 1991 by Communist hard-liners led by Deputy President Gennady Yenayev to oust Mikhail GORBACHEV and turn back the tide of reform. On 19 August the plotters put Gorbachev under house arrest at his Crimean holiday home, and announced:

Fellow Countrymen! Citizens of the Soviet Union! In a dark and critical hour for the destiny of our country and of our peoples we address you! A mortal danger hangs over our homeland!

The plotters failed to arrest the Russian President Boris Yeltsin, who went to the WHITE HOUSE and organised resistance as the tanks moved in. Yeltsin rallied Western support and key military commanders refused to obey orders; after three days Gorbachev was invited back. He had known from foreign radio broadcasts that the plotters had not met with the success they claimed. Gorbachev said:

The lads rigged up an aerial and we were able to catch some broadcasts and find out what was happening. We got the BBC best of all.

The coup, in which three demonstrators were killed, proved disastrously counter-productive; Yeltsin's resistance gave him the initiative, and by the end of the year the coup leaders were in jail, the Soviet Union had collapsed and Gorbachev had gone into retirement.

The democratic genie is out of the bottle in the Soviet Union, and I don't believe they are going to be able to get it back in again.

JOHN MAJOR

Now is the time for Bolshevism's NUREMBERG [TRIALS].

VYTAUTIS LANDSBERGIS, President of Lithuania

Kremlinology The science of ascertaining what the Soviet regime was doing and intended to do; nowadays the process of discovering what is going on in any secretive system. As practised by governments, academics and the media, it consisted of monitoring the Soviet media and reading between the lines, and building up personal and professional contacts. Kremlinology, unlike espionage, was an entirely reputable business.

Kristallnacht (Ger. Night of glass) The night of 9–10 November 1938 when mobs led by NAZI BROWNSHIRTS roamed towns and cities across Germany and Austria, smashing the windows of shops and houses belonging to Jews (hence the name). The looting of their property and the burning of synagogues were for many Jews the last straw in the humiliating persecution they had suffered at the hands of HITLER, his Nazi Party and many ordinary citizens who supported him. Those who were able to fled to Britain, America or anywhere else that would accept them; among this exodus were many of the physicists who were to be key figures in the creation of the ATOMIC BOMB.

I could scarcely believe that such things could happen in a 20th-century civilisation.

FRANKLIN D. ROOSEVELT.

Krokodil (Russ. crocodile) The humorous magazine which for most of the lifetime of the SOVIET UNION provided the only officially-tolerated satire on the regime and life under Communism. The paper, published by *PRAVDA*, normally went for 'safe' targets, but nevertheless had an enthusiastic readership.

Kronstadt mutiny The highly significant revolt against BOLSHEVIK rule in March 1921 by elite sailors at the Soviet naval base in the Gulf of Finland. The privations of the CIVIL WAR, including inadequate food distribution and harsh labour regulations, created widespread discontent with the new regime, manifested in a series of strikes in the cities. The Kronstadt sailors formed a provisional revolutionary Committee in support of the strikers and demanded an end to the COMMUNIST PARTY dictatorship, full 'power to the SOVIETS', the release of non-Bolshevik prisoners and greater political freedoms. Although the mutiny was crushed by TROTSKY and Marshal Tukachevsky, it prompted LENIN to implement the milder NEW ECONOMIC POLICY soon afterwards.

Kruger telegram The telegram from Kaiser Wilhelm I to President Kruger of the Transvaal (*see* OOM PAUL) congratulating him on tackling the JAMESON RAID. Its publication in London took considerable heat off Lord SALISBURY's government in the winter of 1885–86 when it was under heavy political fire for alleged complicity in the raid.

Ku Klux Klan The RACIST secret society, mainly active in America's deep South, whose initials KKK, 'night riders' in hooded white robes, LYNCHINGS and cross-burnings have struck terror into black people ever since it was founded in the aftermath of the CIVIL WAR. The name is a corruption of the Greek *kuklos*, a drinking-bowl; 'Klan' reflected the Scotch-Irish roots of its native Pulaski, Tennessee. Founded in 1866 as a social club for ex-CONFEDERATES with a fanciful ritual, it soon developed into a vehicle for intimidating blacks emancipated by RECONSTRUCTION; there were also numerous imitators. The Klan's terrorist activities led to laws being passed against it in 1870–71; despite its disbandment by the Grand Wizard in 1869, local activity continued for some time.

In 1915 a new organisation, The Invisible Empire, Knights of the Ku Klux Klan was founded in Atlanta by an itinerant preacher, William Simmonds. He adopted much of the original ritual, adding further puerile ceremonial, titles, nomenclature, etc., turning the Klan against Jews, Catholics and foreigners as well as blacks. Klansmen held Klonvocations and their local Klaverns were ruled by an Exalted Cyklops, a Klaliff, etc. Advocating supremacy for native-born Protestant whites, support for PROHIBITION and opposition to the theory of evolution, it grew rapidly after WORLD WAR I, first among poor whites in the South and then sweeping the Mid-West; at its peak it claimed 20 million supporters. It gained real political influence by unsavoury methods, dominating politics in a dozen states with numerous Congressmen among its members; at the 1924 Democratic CONVENTION a resolution denouncing the Klan – which had secured a stake in the nominating process – was defeated. But after a series of scandals it shrank back by 1930 to a hard core of support which exuded FASCIST sympathies as WORLD WAR II approached. In 1944 it was again disbanded, but continued locally; in 1965 a Congressional committee was set up to investigate it after a resurgence of Klan activity against enforcement of CIVIL RIGHTS legislation, and the murder by four Klansmen of a white woman driving a black man near Montgomery, Alabama. There was a further minor re-emergence in the economic downturn of the early 1990s.

> The Negro is not a menace to Americanism in the sense that the Jew or Roman Catholic is a menace. He is not actually hostile to it. He is simply racially incapable of understanding, sharing or contributing to Americanism.
>
> Imperial Wizard HIRAM W. EVANS, 1924

kulaks (Russ. fists) Prosperous Russian peasants who owned land and livestock, and were capable of employing labour and leasing land. They were a key element in the economic, social and administrative structure of pre-revolutionary Russian agriculture. Under LENIN, the kulaks' position was gradually undermined, though their economic and political value was exploited to maintain production along quasi-capitalist lines. The policy of rapid COLLECTIVISATION pursued by STALIN after 1919 aimed at the destruction of the kulaks as a class; by 1934 most had been arrested, deported to remote areas or executed, and their property confiscated.

Kuomintang *See* KMT.

Kyoto Convention The landmark international treaty concluded in 1997 under the auspices of the UNITED NATIONS to combat global warming by restricting 'greenhouse' emissions from industry. 160 nations endorsed the convention, but it was stymied by America's initial hesitation (under the CLINTON administration), and subsequent outright refusal (by George W. BUSH in March 2001), to ratify it on the ground that it would damage the US economy. It took effect on 16 February 2005 after Russia reversed its previous position and agreed to ratify it, but the US, Australia and other important polluters remain outside it.

L

La Guardia New York City's domestic airport, named after Fiorello Henry La Guardia (1882–1947), US Congressman and three times Mayor of New York (1933–45) who campaigned for the airport's construction. A political PROGRESSIVE and habitual dissenter, he is remembered as the most honest and best loved occupant of GRACIE MANSION. *See also* HIZONNER.

laager mentality The inward-looking mind-set of the Afrikaner political community as it imposed APARTHEID on South Africa and then maintained it in defiance of world opinion. In Afrikaans a *laager* is a compound fortified against an outside threat, the equivalent of a circle of wagons in the old American West. The term has come to denote the attitude of any group which adopts increasingly extreme attitudes because it considers itself under ideological or actual threat.

Labby The nickname of **Henry Labouchère** (1831–1912), radical British Liberal MP and owner/editor of the weekly *Truth.* Queen Victoria refused to allow him in GLADSTONE's CABINET because of his republican views.

Labo(u)r. Labor Day The first Monday in September, in America a public holiday and, in ELECTION years, the start (or restart) of campaigning after the summer break.

labor law reform The US unions' campaign to relax the RIGHT TO WORK laws, defeated by employer interests in 1978.

Labor Party Australia's oldest political party, dating from the FEDERATION of the colonies in 1901. It formed its first Federal government under John Christian Watson from April to August 1904, since when ten Labor administrations have held power for some 30 years. The present ALP came into existence when William Melbourne Hughes split the informal Labor group; it split again in 1931 over policies for the GREAT DEPRESSION, but returned to power in 1941, guiding Australia from the darkest point of WORLD WAR II to the post-war period. Periodic splits between predominantly Catholic and extreme left elements kept it out of power from 1949 to 1972; Liberal Prime Minister Sir Robert Menzies (*see* MING) asked: 'If Labor cannot govern itself, how could they govern Australia?' By 1972 leading academics were opining that 'if denied office any longer, the Labor Party is in danger of disintegrating as a force in political life.' Gough WHITLAM brought Labor back to power, but his pioneering ministry was ousted in 1975 (*see* KERR SACKING) amid bitter controversy and financial scandal. Prior to Labor's 1983 return to power under Robert HAWKE, Malcolm Fraser said: 'If Labor win it'll be safer to put your money under the bed.' Yet this time Labor governed more soberly, despite the inevitable rows, liberalising the economy and even curbing the power of the unions. Paul KEATING continued the process after ousting Hawke, but also gave Labor a REPUBLICAN tinge before losing to a coalition under John Howard in March 1996.

> In my experience of the Labor Party, the fact that someone is a bastard has never been a disqualification from leadership.
>
> Sen. JOHN BUTTON

Big Labor A pejorative for the influence of America's major unions, with the inference that the interests of the individual member are lost sight of. It reflects an almost corporate stance, akin to Big Oil.

Farmer-Labor For much of the 20th century, the main radical force in the State of Minnesota.

organised labour Collective term for the trade union movement, personified in America by the AFL-CIO and in Britain by the TUC. The Labour politician Arthur Henderson, leaving ASQUITH's coalition, said that 'in consequence of the decision of organised labour to oppose the Military Service Bill, I have no alternative but to tender you my resignation.'

> Capital organises, and therefore labor must organise.
>
> THEODORE ROOSEVELT

Labour Party (1) The democratic socialist,

predominantly working-class party, found in 1906, which has provided Britain with its government or opposition continually since 1924 when Ramsay MACDONALD became the first of (to date) just five Labour Prime Ministers; it has held power in January-November 1924, 1929–31, 1945–51, 1964–70, 1974–79 and since 1997. Keir Hardie (1856–1915), one of its founders, declared: 'The demand of the Labour Party is for economic freedom. It is the natural outcome of political enfranchisement.' When it first took office, King George V wrote: 'Today, 23 years ago, dear Grandmama [Queen Victoria] died. I wonder what she would have thought of a Labour government?' In the wilderness from 1931 (*see* GREAT BETRAYAL), Labour bounced back at the close of WORLD WAR II to win a LANDSLIDE victory under Clement ATTLEE. At that election Aneurin BEVAN said:

> We have been the dreamers. We have been the sufferers. Now we are the builders. We want the complete political extinction of the Tory Party – and 25 years of Labour government, for we cannot do in five years what requires to be done.

Labour promised a 'Socialist Commonwealth of Great Britain', and by its defeat in 1951 had created the WELFARE STATE, with the NHS its crowning achievement, and NATIONALISED the public utilities. Labour's roots in religious nonconformism led Harold WILSON, who led it back to power in 1964, to state on its re-election in 1966

> This party is a moral crusade, or it is nothing.

As a left-wing party, Labour has always been beset with ideological feuds and splits. Wilson said it was

> . . . like a stage coach. If you rattle along at great speed everybody inside is too exhilarated or too seasick to cause any trouble. But if you stop, everybody gets out and argues about where to go next.

Disputes over defence policy, with the PACIFIST, later the UNILATERALIST, wing occasionally capturing the party (*see* FIGHT, FIGHT AND FIGHT AGAIN) and over how far Labour should remain committed to public ownership (*see* CLAUSE FOUR) have helped render Labour unelectable for long periods. Hugh GAITSKELL reminded activists when leader in the 1950s that 'we can never go farther than we can persuade at least half of the people to go'; Richard CROSSMAN said in the 1950s: 'The two most important emotions in the Labour Party are a doctrinaire faith in nationalisation, without knowing what it means, and a doctrinaire faith in pacifism, without facing the consequences', and this held good until at least the '80s. The columnist Cassandra (Sir William Connor) wrote: 'What a genius the Labour Party has for cutting itself in half and letting the two parts writhe in public.' And Edward HEATH observed: 'I don't often attack the Labour Party – they do it so well themselves.' The difference between the party factions has at times been hard to judge; Nigel Lawson suggested that 'the difference between their moderates and their extremists is that the extremists want to abolish private education now, while the moderates want to wait until their own children have finished school.' And Sir Norman Fowler, CONSERVATIVE PARTY chairman, said in 1992:

> Those whom the gods wish to destroy they first make leader of the Labour Party.

Labour's history has been accompanied by prophecies of doom. Austin Mitchell (*see* HADDOCK) termed it: 'The Red *Titanic* on a ski-slope to disaster.' CHURCHILL pronounced it 'not fit to govern' in 1920, and in 1945 'not fit to manage a whelk stall', and in 1992 the Scottish Secretary Malcolm Rifkind said: 'Scotland needs Labour like Sicily needs the Mafia.' Yet Labour has remained one of Britain's two great parties despite, until the 1990s, chronic shortage of funds and what Wilson termed a 'penny-farthing organisation'. Indeed one voter told Mitchell: 'I don't belong to any organised party – I'm Labour.'

Wilson brought Labour back to power in 1974, and from 1976 James CALLAGHAN governed without a majority (*see* LIB-LAB PACT) till defeated by Margaret THATCHER in 1979. In OPPOSITION, the party turned in on itself with Tony BENN forcing it leftwards and nearly 30 moderate MPs breaking away in 1981 to form the SDP. Benn's almost successful deputy leadership challenge to Denis HEALEY left the party's fortunes at their nadir; in 1983 a far-left manifesto (*see* LONGEST SUICIDE NOTE IN HISTORY) brought Labour its heaviest defeat in half a century under Michael FOOT; Healey blamed the result on 'disunity, extremism, crankiness and a general unfitness to govern'. It was to be a long haul back. Labour bottomed-out and revived under Neil KINNOCK, who defeated the Bennites, banished the MILITANT TENDENCY, pushed through more moderate policies, reorganised the party and tried to broaden its appeal, saying:

> The idea that there is a model Labour voter, a blue-collar council house tenant who belongs to a union and has 2.4 children, a five-year-old car

and a holiday in Blackpool, is patronising and politically immature.

Not everyone was impressed: Dr David OWEN scorned 'the party of verbal Elastoplast' and Norman Tebbit declared: 'The voters are not daft. They can smell a rat, whether it is wrapped in a red flag or covered with roses.' Kinnock clawed back a little ground in 1987 and conspicuously more in 1992, but voters stayed suspicious of Labour's fitness to govern and its tax policies. Following the 1992 defeat, John SMITH kept up the pace of reform by forcing through One Member, One VOTE against strong union resistance, and after Smith's sudden death in 1994 Tony BLAIR, under the mantle of NEW LABOUR, removed what he saw as the final barrier to power by having Clause Four rewritten.

Labour swept to power in May 1997 with a majority almost as large as in 1945 and embarked on an ambitious programme of constitutional reform: DEVOLUTION, PROPORTIONAL REPRESENTATION for some elections (though not for WESTMINSTER) and reform of the HOUSE OF LORDS; there was even a joint CABINET committee for a time with the LIBERAL DEMOCRATS. The emphasis switched prior to the 2001 election to improving the public services (*see* SCHOOLS AND HOSPITALS FIRST), though Blair's determination to link higher spending – generated by Gordon BROWN's stewardship of the economy – to reform unnerved the unions and what remained of the left. Re-elected with another huge majority, Blair was confronted by 9/11 and gave whole-hearted support to George W. BUSH in the WAR ON TERRORISM; his decision also to back Bush in invading Iraq in search of WEAPONS OF MASS DESTRUCTION split the party and weakened it in the run-up to a 2005 election in which Labour won a record third term but with its majority more than halved.

The party has had some memorable slogans. **Let's Go With Labour**, with its thumbs-up symbol, accompanied its resurgence under Wilson prior to the 1964 election. It was re-elected in 1966 with **You Know Labour Government Works**. The most scurrilous anti-Labour slogan was **If you want a nigger for your neighbour, vote Labour**, used by some Conservative canvassers in the West Midlands in 1964. The most effective was **Labour Isn't Working**, a poster campaign on unemployment by the advertising agency Saatchi and Saatchi that made a big impact prior to the Conservatives' 1979 victory; **Labour's Tax Bombshell** made a smaller but still decisive impression in 1992.

(2) In Israel the **Labour Party** (originally *Mapai*) was one of the guiding forces of the new state from its birth, and represented the political ESTABLISHMENT until 1977, when the right-wing LIKUD forced it into opposition. It returned to power in 1995 as the dominant partner in a coalition led by Yitzhak Rabin, but lost to Likud again in 1996 after Rabin's assassination. Labour briefly regained power under Ehud Barak, but after Palestinian stalling on a last-minute peace deal which Bill CLINTON attempted to broker, Barak was defeated in 2001 by the ultra-hard line Likud leader Ariel Sharon (*see* SABRA AND CHATILA). When faced with defections over his plan to withdraw from Gaza, Sharon in 2004 formed a new coalition with Labour.

(3) Ireland's **Labour Party** has been the Republic's political third force for decades, joining a coalition with FINE GAEL in the 1980s and, in 1993, under Dick Spring forming a COALITION with FIANNA FAIL. It has lost ground since as Ireland's party structure has fragmented.

(4) New Zealand's **Labour Party**, founded in 1916, has held power sporadically since 1935.

Labour and Co-Operative Labour MPs at WESTMINSTER who are also sponsored by the CO-OPERATIVE PARTY.

Labour Research Department A left-wing body financed by trade unions – and not connected with the party – which provides authoritative data on political and employment issues, including (until these had to be made public) a tally of corporate donations to the CONSERVATIVE PARTY and bodies connected to it.

National Labour The Labour MPs who followed Ramsay MACDONALD into supporting the 1931 NATIONAL GOVERNMENT.

New Labour *See* NEW.

Labourism The sometimes ruthless pursuit of cautious policies beneficial to right-wing trade union leaders and other vested interests in the party.

Lacey Act The pioneering US law on wildlife conservation. Promoted by Rep. John Fletcher Lacey (1841–1913) and passed in 1913, it forbade the interstate transportation of illegally killed game.

lady/ladies. Ladies and gentlemen, we got him The words with which Paul Bremer, US civil administrator in Iraq, announced on 14 December 2003 the capture by US forces of SADDAM HUSSEIN to a euphoric press conference.

Ladies in a Bathtub Nickname for the eight-ton marble memorial in the crypt beneath the Rotunda of the US CAPITOL, presented by women's organisations in 1921 to honour the pioneer SUFFRAGISTS Susan B. Anthony, Lucretia Mott and Elizabeth Cody Stanton.

Lady Bird The usual name for President Lyndon JOHNSON's wife Claudia, giving her, too, the initials LBJ. It was given her not by her husband but by her childhood nurse who thought her 'purty as a ladybird'.

Lady Bird Act The 1965 Highway Beautification Act which curbed billboards on highways, passed by CONGRESS at Lady Bird's urging.

Lady Forkbender *See* FORKBENDER.

the Lady's not for turning Margaret THATCHER's strident assertion to the 1980 CONSERVATIVE PARTY conference, rejecting any suggestion of a U-TURN. Her statement: 'U-turn if you want to. The lady's not for turning' was an adaptation by her speechwriter Sir Ronald Millar of Christopher Fry's 1948 play title, *The Lady's Not For Burning.*

Lafayette Square The open park in WASHINGTON DC across Pennsylvania Avenue from the WHITE HOUSE. It was named after Marie Joseph, Marquis de Lafayette (1757–1834), French soldier, reformer and diplomat and one of the greatest friends of the American Revolution. Customarily the scene of DEMONSTRATIONS, and at times of depression the home of down-and-outs demonstrating their plight, it has since 9/11 been separated from the Executive Mansion by security barriers as well as the pre-existing iron fence.

Laffer curve The tabulation of the economic theory that under certain conditions cutting tax rates can increase government revenues by increasing the incentive to work. Devised by Arthur Laffer of the University of Southern California, the curve became a fundamental of SUPPLY-SIDE economics. It showed that if taxes were set either at 0% or 100%, the government would receive nothing, and that somewhere between these two points lay the optimal tax rate.

> Less a breakthrough in economic thought than a public relations miracle.
>
> E. J. DIONNE Jr, *Why Americans Hate Politics*

lagging indicator An economic statistic – unemployment figures are a case in point – which reflects events that have already taken place in the economy, rather than forecasting future trends. A **leading indicator,** such as new factory orders for consumer goods, gives a clue as to the future health of the economy.

laissez-faire Non-intervention in economic matters by the state, with the MARKET left totally free to operate. Its origin lies either in the mediaeval French jousting phrase *laissez faire – laissez passer* ('leave alone, let pass) or with finance minister Colbert in 1751 (as *laissez faire*, 'let us get on with it'). First described as such by François Quesnoy in 1765, *laissez-faire* became the byword for classic LIBERALISM.

> We have passed beyond the times of the laissez-faire school which believes that the Government ought to do nothing but run a police force.
>
> PRESIDENT TAFT, Milwaukee, 1909

Lake nomination The nomination by President CLINTON of Anthony Lake (1939–), director of his National Security Council, as director of the CIA, which was withdrawn in March 1997 after Senate Republicans had blocked it alleging lapses of judgement. Lake had originally been on Henry KISSINGER's staff during the NIXON administration, resigning in protest at US intervention in Cambodia and incurring Republicans' lasting enmity.

Lambeg drum An outsize bass drum whose booming rhythm drives the fife bands that are an essential of ORANGE and LOYALIST parades in Northern Ireland, especially during the MARCHING SEASON. It is named after the village of Lambeg, on Lough Neagh west of Belfast.

Lambton affair The scandal in Britain in 1973 when Lord Lambton (1922–) was forced to resign as Under-Secretary for the RAF after photos of him with Hanora (Norma) Levy, an Irish prostitute, were offered to the Press. 'I have behaved with credulous stupidity,' he said, resigning his COMMONS seat for exile in Italy. When Edward HEATH asked his Ministers if any more of them had something to hide, Trade Minister Earl Jellicoe also resigned, citing 'casual affairs' with call-girls.

lame duck (1) A mainly US term for an INCUMBENT President, other elected official or ADMINISTRATION in its final term, barred from re-election and enjoying waning power and influence. It applies especially to a President serving out his final weeks of office after his successor has already been elected. A **lame duck appointment** is one made by

a President under these circumstances. The phrase has its origin in an 18th-century London stock market term for jobbers who defaulted on their obligations, went bankrupt and limped out of Exchange Alley with much quacking. The **Lame Duck Amendment** is the 20th Amendment to the US Constitution, ratified in 1933, which ended the situation in which members of an outgoing CONGRESS returned to WASHINGTON for a three-month 'lame duck' session after the next Congress had been elected, but before it could take office.
(2) Edward HEATH's term for UK businesses which had come to rely on State subsidies because of their inability to 'stand on their own two feet'. His government began withdrawing such aid, but after its U-TURN it increased aid to industry and actually NATIONALISED the troubled Rolls-Royce aero engine company.

Lancaster House The UK government's official hospitality centre, midway between Buckingham Palace and WHITEHALL, which has housed European and G7 SUMMIT meetings. The house was built for the 'grand old' Duke of York, eldest brother of George IV, in the 1820s by Benjamin Wyatt; when the Duke died in 1827 it was sold almost complete for £72,000 to the Marquess of Stafford and became known as Stafford House. In 1911 its lease was bought by Lord Leverhulme, who presented it to the nation as a home for the London Museum – since moved to the Barbican – and a centre for government hospitality; it then took on its present name. Plain and Corinthian outside, it has an ornate interior.
Lancaster House agreement The agreement on the future of Zimbabwe/Rhodesia brokered by UK Foreign Secretary Lord Carrington in December 1979 after months of tense talks with former premier Ian Smith, then-premier Bishop Abel Muzorewa and the GUERRILLA movements led by Robert Mugabe (*see* ZANU-PF) and Joshua Nkomo. Under it the country ended fourteen years of illegal independence (*see* UDI) and RETURNED TO LEGALITY under the Crown as a prelude to independence. The agreement stuck for two decades before Mugabe began expropriating white farmers and terrorising the political opposition (*see* MDC).

Lance. Bert Lance affair The controversy that broke out in WASHINGTON in 1977 when President CARTER nominated Thomas Bertram Lance (1931–), chairman of the Calhoun First National Bank in his home state of Georgia, to head the Office of Management and Budget (OMB). Senators raised doubts over his nomination after alleged irregularities in his past banking practice were reported, and after long and gruelling hearings Lance resigned. He was tried in 1980 on 33 counts ranging from conspiracy to falsifying statements and misapplying bank funds; fourteen were dismissed and the jury acquitted Lance and three associates on a further thirteen; a retrial on the remaining six charges was averted when Lance agreed in 1986 to pay a $50,000 fine and was barred from involvement with any Federally-insured bank. In the meantime Walter Mondale (*see* NORWEGIAN WOOD) hurriedly withdrew an invitation to Lance to chair his 1984 Presidential CAMPAIGN after adverse public reaction.

land. land fit for heroes to live in, a *See* COUNTRY.

land for peace The concept that peace between ISRAEL, the PALESTINIANS and neighbouring Arab states can be achieved by Israel giving up some of the OCCUPIED TERRITORIES. Since its emergence in 1992, 'land for peace' has been seen as the way forward by the LABOUR PARTY but espoused only intermittently under American pressure by LIKUD, which has been in power for most of this time.

Land of Hope and Glory The patriotic hymn written by A. C. Benson (1862–1925) at the height of IMPERIALIST fervour to the tune of Elgar's *Pomp and Circumstance March No. 1.* First sung by Dame Clara Butt in 1902 and traditionally sung at the last night of the Proms, it became an unofficial English national anthem – and also of the CONSERVATIVE PARTY. Its sentiments and Tory associations make it anathema to those who do not share them.

> Land of hope and glory, Mother of the Free,
> How shall we extol thee, who are born of thee?
> Wider still and wider shall thy bounds be set;
> God who made thee mighty, make thee mightier yet!

Land of My Fathers The national anthem of Wales, written by Evan James, a weaver from Pontypridd, in 1866 – his son James based the tune on an old harp melody – and accepted since the National Eisteddfod of 1874 as being the song that most expresses national sentiment. Titled in Welsh *Hen Wlad fy Nhadau*, it is sung at sporting events and political rallies, one notable occasion being when John Redwood (*see* VULCAN) as

Welsh Secretary in John MAJOR's government proved unable to join in. An English translation reads:

The land of my fathers is dear to me,
A land of poets and minstrels, famed men.
Her brave warriors, patriots much blessed,
It was for freedom that they lost their blood.

Homeland! I am devoted to my country;
So long as the sea is a wall
to this fair beautiful land,
May the ancient language remain.

Länder The semi-autonomous provinces into which modern Germany is divided, each being called a *Land*.

landslide An overwhelming ELECTION victory in which the losing side is virtually swept away; its corollary was the CANADIAN MELTDOWN of 1993, in which the governing PROGRESSIVE CONSERVATIVES were annihilated. CAMPBELL-BANNERMAN's LIBERALS in 1906 won 400 seats (512 with their allies), the largest working majority in the COMMONS since the 1832 REFORM ACT; F. E. Smith said that they 'came floating into Parliament like corks on top of a dirty wave'. Other noted landslides are the NATIONAL GOVERNMENT's one-sided victory in 1931, Labour's in 1945 and 1997, and the Conservatives' in 1983. US Presidents to have been elected by a landslide include Franklin D. ROOSEVELT in 1936, Lyndon B. JOHNSON in 1964, Richard NIXON in 1972 and Ronald REAGAN in 1984. In 1983 Margaret THATCHER dropped Francis Pym from her CABINET for suggesting during the campaign that 'landslides on the whole don't produce successful governments'. In America, said the scholar James Sundquist, 'the system only works really well right after a landslide election', but Bryce Harlow wrote: 'The President who wins real big will blow himself up.' Joseph Tumulty declared that Warren HARDING's Presidential victory in 1920 'wasn't a landslide – it was an earthquake'. And during his 1952 Senate election, John F. KENNEDY joked of receiving a note from his wealthy father saying:

Dear Jack, Don't buy a single vote more than necessary. I'm damned if I'm going to pay for a landslide.

Landslide Lyndon Not a reference to Lyndon JOHNSON's swamping of Barry Goldwater in 1964, but to his narrow victory in the 1948 Senate race in Texas. His enemies claimed Johnson supporters had stuffed the ballot boxes. The story was told of a little Mexican boy found sobbing for his father in a San Antonio street. When reminded his father was long dead, the boy blubbed: 'But he came back to vote for Lyndon Johnson and he didn't come to see me.'

Lansdowne letter A letter sent by the Irish peer Henry Charles Petty-Fitzmaurice (1845–1927), fifth Marquess of Lansdowne, to the *Daily Telegraph* on 29 November 1917. It advocated a compromise peace with Germany to end WORLD WAR I – including guarantees of Germany's continuance as a political, commercial and territorial power. Despite evidence that many MPs and even some members of LLOYD GEORGE's COALITION shared his views, the letter was violently repudiated by the government and the press as an act of disloyalty that weakened the Allied resolve to fight. As a result Lansdowne was expelled from the CONSERVATIVE PARTY.

last. Last Call speech President Franklin D. ROOSEVELT's speech on 27 May 1941 appealing to nations throughout the Americas to join in a common defence of democracy as the danger grew of war with the AXIS powers. The phrase means a final opportunity, as in 'last call for dinner'.

Last Chance Saloon In 1989 the then Home Office Minister David Mellor (1949–) warned Britain's tabloid press that repeated breaches of individuals' privacy had left it 'drinking in the Last Chance Saloon'; one more abuse, and there might have to be legal curbs. When, in July 1992, Mellor was found by one of those tabloids to have been carrying on an extra-marital affair with out-of-work actress Antonia de Sancha, the *Sun* editorialised:

It was certainly rich of Mellor to warn the press it was drinking in the Last Chance Saloon, while all the time he was playing the piano in the bordello next door.

last hurrah A politican's final moment of glory, often in a brave but unsuccessful re-election CAMPAIGN. Edwin O'Connor coined the phrase, *The Last Hurrah* being the title of his 1956 novel, loosely based on the life of Boston's Mayor James Curley, about a New England POL undertaking the last campaign of his life; Spencer Tracy played the lead when it was made into a film two years later.

Last Lady Rep. Adam Clayton POWELL's derogatory nickname for Bess Truman (1885–1982), wife of President Harry S TRUMAN, contrasting Mrs Truman's low profile with the hyperactivity of her predecessor Eleanor Roosevelt (*see* FIRST LADY OF

THE WORLD). Mrs Truman had the last laugh; she went on to become the longest-lived FIRST LADY, while Powell was ousted from CONGRESS.

Lateran Treaty The CONCORDAT concluded between the Holy See and the Kingdom of Italy in 1929, with Italy confirming the SOVEREIGNTY of the 109-acre Vatican City and Pope Pius XI graciously recognising the existence of the Italian state. It ended the **Roman Question**, dating from 1870 when Italian reunification (*see* RISORGIMENTO) finally abrogated the wider temporal power of the Papacy and Rome became the national capital, but with the Holy See refusing to accept the outcome.

laundering A term popularised in the political *demi-monde*, and which has now spread to the general world of crime, of the circulation of money between numerous concealed accounts to disguise its true origin. Though in use by the 1930s to describe the way criminals made their ill-gotten assets respectable, it caught on as a result of WATERGATE, being used in the 1973 CONGRESSional hearings to describe the processing for use by the NIXON campaign of over $200,000 illegally brought in from Mexico.

laundry list (1) An over-long and probably not sincere list of pledges in a (by definition boring) ELECTION speech, or a comprehensive list of grievançes, such as the charges levelled at King George III in the US Declaration of INDEPENDENCE. (2) A 'laundry-list candidate', in US parlance, is one so popular his party TICKET could be a list for the laundry rather than a slate of other vote-winning candidates.

Laura Norder *See* LAW AND ORDER.

Lausanne. Treaty of Lausanne The peace settlement signed on 24 July 1923 which ended the conflict between Greece and Turkey after WORLD WAR I, but could not end the bitterness. It replaced the **Treaty of Sèvres**, imposed on the Turks in 1920 by the Allies after the defeat of the pro-German Ottoman Empire. The Turks agreed to surrender non-Turkish sections of the former Empire, Greece returned Smyrna (Izmir) to Turkey, which also regained Thrace, Adrianople and the Dodecanese, and the Bosphorus and Dardanelles were demilitarised and opened to international shipping. The Treaty also provided for a forced exchange of national minorities between Greece and Turkey which has left powerful resentments, especially among Greeks.

Lavender List The controversial resignation HONOURS LIST drawn up by Harold WILSON in 1976 to reward prominent supporters of himself and the LABOUR PARTY, which earned him lasting discredit. It included worthy and popular choices, but the number of financiers in it surprised the party, and a couple were subsequently disgraced – one, Lord Kagan, manufacturer of the Gannex raincoat which was Wilson's trademark, being imprisoned for evading excise duties, and another, Eric Miller, committing suicide on the eve of a scandalous bankruptcy. Remarkably, the list also included Jimmy Goldsmith (*see* HACIENDA). The list, rumoured to have been even more controversial in first draft, got its name because it was drafted on lavender-coloured paper by Wilson's political secretary Marcia Williams (*see* Lady FORKBENDER). Mrs Williams, herself a beneficiary, was seen by Wilson's enemies as his *eminence grise* and they alleged that the choice of names was hers rather than the Prime Minister's.

> Wilson was made to look, yet again, naïve, weak and bossed about, not impressions which . . . any statesman should end with.
>
> EDWARD PEARCE, *Macchiavelli's Children*

Law, Andrew Bonar *See* BONAR LAW.

law and order A key domestic issue, which at times of fear over rising crime can be whipped into an ELECTION issue by populists and DEMAGOGUES. Gore Vidal concluded that: 'to the right wing law and order is often just a code phrase, meaning "get the niggers". To the left wing it often means political oppression.' Central to it is the assertion that more visible or aggressive policing and tougher sentencing will make the community safer; as J. Edgar Hoover pointed out, 'justice is incidental to law and order'. In the 1968 Presidential election all three candidates – Richard NIXON, George Wallace and Hubert HUMPHREY – played the law-and-order card, leading San Francisco's Mayor Joseph Alioto to comment:

> None of the candidates is running for President. They're all running for sheriff.

Though the issue strikes a chord with every social class, Herbert Marcuse observed that 'law and order are everywhere the law and order which protects the established hierarchy'. Uganda's tyrant Idi Amin took this argument to the extreme, saying:

> I have to keep law and order, and it means that I have to kill my enemies before they kill me.

Humorists in the late 1970s even converted

the issue into a person, **Laura Norder** (*compare* SOLOMON BINDING).

Law Commission A body established in 1965 by the Labour LORD CHANCELLOR Lord Gardiner to monitor the law of England on a continuing basis with a view to its systematic development and reform. It has a permanent staff headed by five Commissioners – two academics, two lawyers and a judge – and considers the need for CODIFICATION of the law, the elimination of anomalies, the repeal of obsolete measures, and general simplification and modernisation. Its reports are often accompanied by draft legislation for the government to introduce into Parliament, which it usually does in due course.

slip law The first official publication of a statute enacted by the US CONGRESS and the President (or passed without his agreement). Published as an unbound pamphlet but having full legal force, it outlines the history of the measure and gives the President's view, if he has one. Copies of slip laws are delivered to the document rooms of both HOUSES, where they become available to officials and the public; they can be purchased from the Government Printing Office.

sunshine laws Laws which become a vogue in 1970s America, requiring CONGRESS and the Federal and state BUREAUCRACIES to carry out more of their functions in the public eye instead of behind closed doors.

If the government becomes a law-breaker, it breeds contempt for the law The dictum of Justice Louis Brandeis, dissenting, in the 1928 SUPREME COURT ruling on *Olmstead et al. v The United States,* which became a central principle of journalists, lawyers and politicians combating the WATERGATE cover-up. When applied to the President, the Supreme Court had long held that 'No man is so high that he is above the law'. In England Lord DENNING enunciated a similar principle – '**No man, be he ever so high**' – in the Court of Appeal in the late 1970s in striking down a series of decisions by the Labour government which he held to conflict with individual freedom.

Sometimes you have to go above the written law The argument advanced in defence of wrongdoing in the IRAN-CONTRA AFFAIR by Fawn Hall, secretary to Colonel Oliver North.

The best way to get a bad law repealed is to enforce it strictly Abraham LINCOLN's dictum which was amply proved in America during PROHIBITION when the EIGHTEENTH AMENDMENT and the VOLSTEAD ACT eventually alienated most voters, and in England and Wales over Sunday trading in the years prior to reform in 1993.

The less people know about how laws and sausages are made, the better they will sleep at night The comment attributed to Bismarck which both reflects the unscientific nature of the legislative process and the IRON CHANCELLOR's contempt for democratic institutions.

Lawrence. Stephen Lawrence case The scandal which finally forced London's Metropolitan Police to tackle the '**institutional racism**' in its culture. Stephen Lawrence, a law-abiding eighteen-year-old black architecture student, was murdered on 22 April 1993 at a bus stop in Eltham by a gang of white thugs, and the police's reaction to the crime scandalised not only the black community but the public at large. The police ignored the obvious suspects and endeavoured to incriminate Lawrence's (black) friend who had been waiting with him. The Crown Prosecution Service dropped a murder case against two suspects because of 'insufficient evidence'; a private prosecution against three others also failed. In 1997 the *Daily Mail* labelled the five 'murderers' and challenged them to sue for libel; they did not. Two internal police inquiries found no cause for concern, but in 1997 the new Home Secretary, Jack Straw, ordered an independent inquiry under Mr Justice MACPHERSON. This exposed incompetence and worse – officers arriving at the scene did not give first aid, leads were not followed up, suspects were not arrested and senior officers showed a failure of leadership. The Macpherson Report demanded action to combat 'institutional racism' in the police, other public services, the legal system and the machinery of government, and many of its recommendations were implemented.

LBJ The initials, and nickname, of President Lyndon JOHNSON; his wife LADY BIRD and two daughters shared the initials also.

All the way with LBJ The Democrats' slogan in his triumphant 1964 Presidential CAMPAIGN.

Hey, hey, LBJ, how many kids did you kill today? Perhaps the cruellest slogan of the ANTI-WAR movement as it campaigned against Johnson's enthusiastic support, after initial reservations, for the US commitment in Vietnam.

LCC (1) **London County Council** The elected body, led by such giants as John Burns and Herbert Morrison, which made the government of what is now inner London a model between its foundation under the 1888 London Government Act and 1965, when it was replaced by the GLC, covering a larger geographical area to reflect suburban growth. It inherited the powers of the Metropolitan Board of Works, founded in 1855, and from 1903 ran the capital's schools; until 1933 it also operated most of London's tramways. Its most visible symbol was its headquarters, COUNTY HALL. (2) **Labour Co-Ordinating Committee** A hard LEFT group and an irritant to the Labour leadership when founded in 1979, it became a decade later a moderate but active force for non-ideological party reform and revival.

LDCs Less-Developed Countries. A term widely used by politicians discussing the THIRD WORLD to avoid describing the poorest nations as 'underdeveloped'. See also ACP; LOMÉ CONVENTION.

LEA Local Education Authority. Those local authorities in England and Wales – county councils and Metropolitan districts – which were responsible for all state schools until the advent of OPTING OUT. Since then the LEAs have retained control over the vast majority, but with council reorganisation they now also include UNITARY AUTHORITIES. Formed in 1902 to replace the previous School Boards, their number was reduced and their duties clarified by the 1944 BUTLER EDUCATION ACT. LEAs have been responsible for providing local primary and secondary education, further education (now transferred to a separate Funding Council) and employing teachers.

lead. I lead my party – you follow yours Tony BLAIR's devastating put-down of John MAJOR in the COMMONS on 25 April 1995 after Major restored the WHIP to nine Tory MPs who had rebelled over Europe without seeking assurances as to their future conduct. When Major reminded Blair that Labour had its share of dissidents, he hit back:

> There is a very big difference. I lead my party – he follows his.

The Labour benches erupted, and Blair continued:

> He's caved in, the party is still split and the white flag flies over Downing Street.

Blair's one-liner upturned the cynical comment: **I must follow them. Am I not their leader?** Attributed to figures from DISRAELI to GANDHI, its probable originator was Alexandre Ledru-Rollin (1807–74), a leader of the FRENCH REVOLUTION of February 1848.

Leader of the Council In Britain, the political leader of a local authority, being leader of the governing party group. Except for a few authorities (including London) where since 2002 the MAYOR has been popularly elected to lead the council, that office is purely ceremonial.

Leader of the House At WESTMINSTER, the Minister responsible for the BUSINESS of the COMMONS, and for answering Business QUESTIONS. While getting the government's legislation through is the Leader's top priority, he or she traditionally has a responsibility to members of all parties.

Leaderene, the A nickname for Margaret THATCHER coined by Tory WETS early in her premiership. It connected the idea of the all-powerful leader with the Biblical Gadarene swine, who rushed into the sea after Christ instilled in them an evil spirit he had cast out of a man.

leadership contest The election of a leader of one of Britain's political parties. The Conservatives, whose leader traditionally EMERGED, now ballot their MPs after briefly giving the final say to the entire membership. Labour in the early 1980s moved on from a ballot of MPs to an ELECTORAL COLLEGE of MPs, trade unions and constituency parties, and the Liberal Democrats switched to a ballot of all party members at just the point when they finally had enough MPs to hold a meaningful election.

leading indicator *See* LAGGING INDICATOR.

League of Nations The world organisation created by the Treaty of VERSAILLES to ensure WORLD WAR I was never repeated, and to police Woodrow WILSON's new order of NATION STATES. He had proposed

> an organisation of peace which shall make it certain that the continued power of free nations will check every invasion of right and serve to make peace and justice more secure by affording a definite tribunal of opinion to which all must submit.

The League, based in Geneva, was formed on 10 January 1920, but the US SENATE inflicted a crippling blow by rejecting it. The ISOLATIONIST Sen. Henry Cabot Lodge (1850–1924) denounced 'the evil thing with a holy name', saying: 'I have loved but one flag and I cannot share that devotion and give affection for the mongrel banner invented for a League.' Franklin D. ROOSEVELT, running for Vice President in

1920, said: 'It may not end war, but the nations demand the experiment.' By the time he took office in 1933 he termed it 'nothing more than a debating society, and a poor one at that'. Yet despite America's absence and the exclusion of the Soviet Union, the League for over a decade offered the nations of the world – 60 at its peak – a useful platform and vehicle for co-operation. As late as 1929 Ramsay MACDONALD could assert: 'The League of Nations grows in moral courage. Its frown will soon be even more dreaded than a nation's arms, and when that happens, you and I shall have security and peace.' But NAZI Germany's withdrawal in 1933 and Italy's invasion of Abyssinia, when the League failed to impose SANCTIONS, sealed its fate. It lingered on into WORLD WAR II, finally meeting on 18 April 1946 by which time the UNITED NATIONS had supplanted it.

> What was everybody's business in the end turned out to be nobody's business. Each one looked to the other to take the lead, but the aggressors got away with it.
>
> JAN CHRISTIAN SMUTS, 1943

League of Women Voters The respected non-partisan group best known in US politics for its role in organising televised DEBATES between presidential candidates. The League was founded by the SUFFRAGIST Carrie Chapman Catt in 1920, just before the 19TH AMENDMENT giving women the right to vote was ratified. It has concentrated on encouraging public participation in the political process, educating the voters about their political rights and the issues of the day, promoting HUMAN RIGHTS and campaigning for clean and ACCOUNTABLE government. It has been prepared to take sides on social issues, successfully campaigning in 1983 against a PRO-LIFE amendment to the CONSTITUTION.

leak The unauthorised disclosure of (usually) embarrassing information from within government, particularly to the Press. The term goes back at least to Lord Chancellor Francis Bacon, Viscount St Albans (1561–1616), who wrote:

> As for Cabinet Councils, it may be their motto, *'plenus rimarum sum'* [I am full of leaks]. One futile person, that maketh it his glory to tell, will do more hurt than many that know it their duty to conceal.

There were leaks galore in the early days of the United States. HAMILTON's aides leaked to JEFFERSON's associates that the Treasury Secretary was going to put the new nation under British hegemony, and Jefferson himself was to write: 'The abuse of confidence by publishing my letters has caused me more than all other pains.' But it was with the explosion of the Washington media from WORLD WAR II that leaks came into their own. Even in an era of FREEDOM OF INFORMATION, they have provided the best news stories. President TRUMAN fumed that '95 per cent of our secret information has been leaked in newspapers and slick magazines.' Lyndon JOHNSON complained: 'This goddam town leaks like a worn-out boot'. Richard NIXON, at the height of WATERGATE, stormed: 'I don't give a damn how it's done. Do whatever has to be done to stop these leaks.' And Jimmy CARTER said in exasperation: 'If there is another outbreak of misinformation, distortion or self-serving leaks, I will direct the Secretary of State to discharge the officials responsible . . . even if some innocent people might be punished.' Ronald REAGAN had two views on leaks. On the one hand he complained that 'sometimes I read memos in the paper I haven't even gotten yet', and declared: 'I've had it up to my keister with leaks'. But former Secretary of State Alexander Haig noted:

> In the Reagan ADMINISTRATION, leaks were not a problem – they were a way of life. Leaks constituted policy, they were the authentic voice of government.

In Britain, the historic climate of official secrecy and the relative lack of contact between journalists and officials – though not with Ministers, who have always been a rich source – has made leaks rarer and more appreciated by the media, though they have become more prevalent in recent time. In 1873 Sir Ralph Lingren wrote: 'The unauthorised use of official information is the worst fault a civil servant can commit. It is on the same footing as cowardice by a soldier.' And Sir Robert Armstrong, CABINET SECRETARY for most of the THATCHER years, commented ironically of a letter he wrote to Whitehall MANDARINS against leaks: 'I was very sad it took as long as six weeks to leak.'

There are numerous reasons for leaking. Richard Darman, Reagan's budget director, said: 'Winners leak out of pride in what they have won. Losers leak to try and change policies.' And PENTAGON spokesman Henry Catto declared: 'We object to the expression of minority opinions via leaks to the news media designed to influence the course of events.' Four generic kinds of leak have been identified: the

grudge leak when an official whose advice has been rejected, who has been passed over for promotion or feels hard done by in some other way goes public. Such leaks are the staple of many Washington COLUMNISTS; the **pre-emptive leak** designed to expose a course of action prematurely so that public opinion will stop it; the **trial-balloon leak,** a form of KITE-FLYING to test whether the public or political community will wear some policy or action; and the **whistle-blower leak** carried out to expose some activity the leaker considers disgraceful.

> There is nothing so incontinent as a British Cabinet Minister.
>
> SIR BERNARD INGHAM

> The more you worry, the more there are.
>
> JAMES CARVILLE (*see* YORKSHIRE RASPUTIN)

leak inquiry The investigation customarily carried out within any bureaucracy once a leak with major implications has taken place. In WHITEHALL it is axiomatic that the inquiry will fail; sometimes, as with WESTLAND, ensuring that the culprit is not identified requires considerable skill. In WASHINGTON under the REAGAN ADMINISTRATION, lie-detector tests were introduced to track down leakers.

leap-frogging The process by which a nation that sees a competitor gaining more devastating armaments than it possesses will equip itself with an even more formidable arsenal, after which the other nation may in turn acquire yet greater weaponry. Neil KINNOCK's use of the phrase in a 1984 discussion with French socialists caused a brief misunderstanding, when Lionel Jospin, Secretary of the French party, only caught the word 'frog'. Jospin was eventually persuaded that the Labour leader had not uttered an insult.

lease-lend *See* LEND-LEASE.

Lebensraum (Ger. room for living) Territory coveted by a state for expansion, to meet economic and population pressures or simply for national aggrandisement. HITLER seized on the concept to justify NAZI Germany's designs on a swathe of territory in central and eastern Europe, and beyond. The Nazi interpretation of the word included the forcible removal or murder of the existing non-German inhabitants (a forerunner of ETHNIC CLEANSING), a policy that underlaid some of the worst atrocities of the period prior to and during WORLD WAR II.

left, or **left-wing** The umbrella term for egalitarian, SOCIALIST or MARXIST political tendencies of every kind. It originated just before the FRENCH REVOLUTION in the Estates-General, where supporters of the *status quo* sat on the right and opponents of the King's policies on the left. Within left-wing movements themselves, the term is used to define the most radical elements; Richard CROSSMAN described the left in Britain's LABOUR PARTY as 'a group of people who will never be happy unless they can convince themselves that they are about to be betrayed by their leaders'. To those on the right, the term has sinister connotations; Michael HESELTINE once brought a Conservative conference to its feet by exclaiming: 'I hear the trade unions tramping towards us – Left; Left; Left, Left, Left!' Being on the left involves a political philosophy (or rather, one of many) as well as organisation; George Orwell wrote that 'so much left-wing thought is . . . playing with fire by people who don't even know that fire is hot.'

Left Book Club The imprint founded by the publisher Victor Gollancz in the late 1930s which, through such books as GUILTY MEN, did much to rally the British non-Communist left prior to and during WORLD WAR II, and contributed to the election, programme and ethos of the 1945 Labour government.

broad left The (usually non-Communist) coalition of left-wing elements which exerted considerable influence in Britain's trade and student unions during the 1980s.

hard left In Britain, a range of groups spearheaded by the CAMPAIGN FOR LABOUR PARTY DEMOCRACY which came within a hair's breadth of securing Tony BENN's election as Labour's deputy leader in 1981. It was instrumental in securing the RESELECTION of Labour MPs and the ELECTORAL COLLEGE to choose the party leader, previously elected by Labour MPs. It exerted great influence in local government, particularly in London, in the early 1980s, and gave rise to the CAMPAIGN GROUP of Labour MPs, but went into decline after Neil KINNOCK became party leader.

Keep Left A group of left-wing Labour MPs critical of the 'COLD WAR' policy toward Soviet Russia of Foreign Secretary Ernest BEVIN. Launched in November 1946, the group produced a pamphlet with the same title in April 1947, written by Richard CROSSMAN, Michael FOOT and Ian MIKARDO, and signed by twelve other Labour MPs; the name was taken from Britain's most ubiquitous traffic sign. The group, which met regularly at the COMMONS, advocated a 'third force', a European socialist alliance based on the UK and France, to hold the middle ground between the US and the Soviet Union, heal the widening breach between East and West and lessen Britain's dependence on America.

loony left A derogatory 1980s term for the more extreme elements of Labour's hard left, particularly in London. It encompassed militant feminism, support for gay rights, positive DISCRIMINATION for ethnic minorities, frantic support for the single issue of the moment, and above all POLITICAL CORRECTNESS. The former Labour, by then Tory, Minister Lord Marsh (1926–) categorised the loony left as 'one-legged black Lambeth lesbians against fox-hunting'. By the mid-1990s the term had also taken hold in America.

New Left *See* NEW.

soft left A term produced as the hard left reached its greatest influence to describe the traditional democratic left in the LABOUR PARTY, focused on the TRIBUNE GROUP of MPs. The division became institutionalised after the 1981 deputy leadership contest, when the soft left refused to vote for Tony BENN; the following year the Tribune Group split, with a minority of its members forming a hard left CAMPAIGN GROUP.

left can speak to left The argument used for the wartime CHURCHILL coalition's despatch of the far left Sir Stafford Cripps as British ambassador to Moscow. STALIN was less impressed, scorning the faddish Cripps as 'CHRIST AND CARROTS'. The phrase also epitomised the initial hopes of Ernest BEVIN that as a Socialist Foreign Secretary he could deal with the Russians when America was hitting a brick wall; he very soon changed his mind.

We're going to have to move left and right at the same time The strategy offered by former California governor Edmund G. 'Jerry' Brown (1938–) in his 1992 campaign to develop a 'new politics' in America. *See also* SPACE CADET.

Legion of Honour The sole mark of distinction awarded in Republican France, first instituted by Napoleon in 1802. Members can be identified by a tiny red flash worn in their lapel.

legislation (1) Laws as enacted by the LEGISLATURE and approved, if necessary, by the EXECUTIVE.

> Foolish legislation is a rope of sand which perishes in the twisting.
>
> RALPH WALDO EMERSON (1803–82)

> The quality of legislation passed to deal with a problem is inversely proportional to the volume of media clamor that brought it on.
>
> G. RAY FUNKHOUSER, US researcher

(2) The process of enacting laws, embodying the decision that the measure is necessary along with consideration of its detail.

> In legislation we all do a lot of 'swapping tobacco across the lines'.
>
> Speaker JOSEPH CANNON (1836–1926)

portmanteau legislation A BILL or ACT which incorporates a range of unrelated items instead of concentrating on addressing a particular problem. The name is a Victorian reference to a sizeable suitcase into which almost anything would fit.

primary legislation At WESTMINSTER, a full-blooded BILL rather than an ORDER or STATUTORY INSTRUMENT, which will need to go through the entire legislative process and will thus require scarce Parliamentary time. However desirable a measure, it will always have to compete with others for a slot in the government's legislative programme. Frequently Ministers can be heard to say: 'We could do that, but it would require primary legislation.'

Legislative Assembly The lower house of legislature in New South Wales, Victoria and Western Australia and the sole chamber in the CAPITAL TERRITORY, Northern Territory and Queensland. In South Australia and Tasmania it is known as the **House of Assembly**.

legislative assistant In the US CONGRESS, an aide to a SENATOR or Congressman who researches and writes BILLS, drafts speeches and sits in on committees relevant to the legislator's interests. Any member of Congress will have among their staff a legislative assistant and an **administrative assistant**.

legislative branch The term used in America to refer to CONGRESS by comparison with the EXECUTIVE BRANCH of government (the WHITE HOUSE) and the JUDICIARY. James Madison wrote in the FEDERALIST: 'In republican government the legislative authority necessarily predominates', and this is broadly true despite the dignity of the Presidency and the ability of the SUPREME COURT to determine what is and what is not CONSTITUTIONAL.

Legislative Calendar *See* CALENDAR.

legislative call system The system of lights and bells or buzzers in the US CAPITOL and its satellite buildings that alerts Members to votes and other occurrences – with a special combination of the two for the onset of NUCLEAR war.

Legislative Council (1) The upper house of legislature in every Australian state except for the CAPITAL TERRITORY, Northern Territory and Queensland, which have a UNICAMERAL system. (2) *See* HOUSE OF KEYS.

legislative day The period from when the US SENATE adjourns to when it next adjourns. Because the Senate frequently RECESSes rather than adjourns at the end of a working day, a legislative day can last weeks or even months. Only at the beginning of a legislative day is the CALENDAR called for consideration.

legislative hold In the US SENATE, a courtesy under which consideration of a Presidential appointment is delayed if a single member has personal objections. Most use it rarely, for instance if they want to meet the nominee prior to CONFIRMATION, but a handful of mavericks, notably Sen. Jesse Helms of South Carolina, have used it frequently to stress a political point.

legislator A member of a LEGISLATURE, whose principal interest need not be legislation.

> The best legislator is the one who votes for all APPROPRIATIONS and against all taxes.
> Rep. WALTER F. BROWNLOW (1851–1910), *attr.*

> Legislators represent people, not trees or acres. Legislators are elected by voters, not farms or cities or economic interests.
> Chief Justice EARL WARREN (1891–1974)

legislature The body in a democracy which is elected (with the notable exception of the HOUSE OF LORDS) to enact laws and provide a check on the EXECUTIVE. The term also covers America's state legislatures and all other sub-national elected bodies with the power to legislate.

> The great virtue of a strong legislature is not what it can do but what it can prevent.
> Sen. J. WILLIAM FULBRIGHT (1905–95)

the legislature A formal description for the US CONGRESS.

> The tyranny of the legislature is really the danger most to be feared. THOMAS JEFFERSON.

> No man's life, liberty or property are safe while the legislature is in session.
> GIDEON J. TUCKER (1826–99)

> The legislature, like the executive, has ceased to be even the creature of the people; it is the creature of pressure groups and most of them, it must be manifest, are of dubious wisdom and even more dubious honesty.
> H. L. MENCKEN, 1930

legitimacy The status of a government that has been lawfully and democratically elected.

> A government isn't legitimate just because it exists. JEANE KIRKPATRICK (1926–)

> Of course the Government has no legitimacy – they're a bunch of bastards.
> GEORGE GALLOWAY MP (1954–)

Leinster House The building in central Dublin, between the National History Museum and National Gallery of Ireland, where DAIL EIREANN and the SEANAD meet. Designed by Richard Cassels, it was built between 1745 and 1748 at the east end of Molesworth Street by the Earl of Kildare, and known as Kildare House until he was granted the earldom of Leinster. The Dail chamber was originally the lecture theatre of the Royal Dublin Society. Prior to the Act of Union, Ireland's Parliament met in the recent Bank of Ireland building on College Green.

Lemonade Lucy The nickname earned by Lucy Webb Hayes (1831–89), the highly religious wife of President Rutherford Hayes, because of her ban on alcoholic beverages in the WHITE HOUSE.

Lend-lease (sometimes known as **Lease-lend**) The critical assistance given to Britain and her allies by President Franklin D. ROOSEVELT prior to America's entry into WORLD WAR II. Based on a precedent set in 1892, it involved 'lending' guns, ships and other equipment to 'any country whose defense the president deems vital to the defense of the United States' on the understanding that they would be 'returned in kind' after the war. FDR promised this to overcome opposition in CONGRESS to his **Lend-Lease Act**, passed in March 1941, while making clear to Britain it would not be saddled with crippling post-war debt if victorious. The policy began with 50 superannuated destroyers sent to Britain in return for the US being granted bases in Britain and its Empire. By the end of the war America had received back less than one-sixth of the $50 billion worth of *matériel* it had 'lent', though a heavier price was eventually exacted. 60% went to COMMONWEALTH countries, but 35 other nations including Soviet Russia also benefited.

> Suppose my neighbor's house catches on fire, and I have a length of garden hose four or five hundred feet away. If he can take my garden hose and connect it up with his hydrant, I may help him to put out his fire. Now what do I do? I don't say to him before that operation: 'Neighbor, my

> garden hose cost me fifteen dollars. You have to pay me fifteen dollars for it.' . . . I don't want fifteen dollars. I want my hose back after the fire is over.
>
> FRANKLIN D. ROOSEVELT, 17 December 1940

Lenin The adopted name of **Vladimir Ilyich Ulyanov** (1870–1924), Russian REVOLUTIONARY and founder of the SOVIET UNION; the word has no obvious meaning in Russian. Lenin was deeply scarred by the execution of his elder brother, Alexander, by police in 1887, after he had attempted to assassinate the TSAR; after being expelled from two universities (the second time being exiled to Siberia for three years) he became a professional revolutionary. In 1900 he joined other MARXISTS in exile in Europe, waiting and preparing for the ideal moment to launch the revolution in Russia; he also mixed with democratic socialists, describing one, George Bernard Shaw, as 'a good man fallen among FABIANS'. In his 1902 book *What Is to be Done?* he placed his faith in the idea of the party as the engine of revolutionary CLASS CONSCIOUSNESS and the 'vanguard of the PROLETARIAT'. Maxim Gorky wrote: 'The working class is for Lenin what ore is for a metal worker.' At a conference of the Russian Social Democratic Workers' Party in London in 1903, the majority (BOLSHEVIKS) supported Lenin's proposals for the organisation and revolutionary role of the party. After the collapse of the Tsarist government in March 1917, Lenin returned to Russia in a SEALED TRAIN with the connivance of Germany (*see* FINLAND STATION).

> The Germans turned upon Russia the most grisly of all weapons. They transported Lenin in a sealed truck, like a plague bacillus, from Switzerland into Russia.
>
> WINSTON CHURCHILL, 1929

With the aid of the Bolshevik-organised Red Guard, Lenin overthrew the provisional government in the OCTOBER REVOLUTION, seizing power in the name of the people. For five years he wrestled to transform Russia's society and economy, while fighting a CIVIL WAR exacerbated by Western intervention. He suffered a stroke in 1922, by which time he had moderated his initially ruthless economic policies (*see* NEW ECONOMIC POLICY), and died on 21 January 1924, leaving in his writings a legacy of applied Marxism (LENINISM) and a final *Testament*, warning colleagues against choosing STALIN as his successor and urging his removal as General Secretary of the party. The party CENTRAL COMMITTEE failed to act on the Testament and Stalin suppressed it; in 1956 Khrushchev caused a sensation by reading it to the 20th Party Congress. Lenin's body was embalmed and installed in a black and red granite MAUSOLEUM in RED SQUARE, which became a place of pilgrimage for millions of Russians, newly-weds frequently calling there to pay their respects and receive his 'blessing'. Stalin's body too was displayed there from 1953 to 1961. The mausoleum survived the fall of Communism, though it now only opens for a limited time on four days a week and Lenin, in a jacket and polka-dot tie instead of the military uniform he wore until the 1950s, is showing signs of age despite regular attention from a special team of scientists.

> The Russian people's worst misfortune was his birth, their next worst . . . his death.
>
> CHURCHILL

> The dominant streak in his character and political practice was a ruthless will to coerce, dictate and subjugate. Stalin's terror and Stalin's tyranny are unmistakably foreshadowed by Leninism.
>
> MILOVAN DJILAS (1911–95)

Lenin Prize An award granted for outstanding scientific, technical and cultural achievements, awarded under the SOVIET UNION from 1950 as a counterpart to the NOBEL prizes, the winner being announced on May Day each year.

Order of Lenin The highest decoration in the former Soviet Union, established by the Presidium of the Supreme Soviet in 1930. It was conferred for outstanding service in fields including medicine, science and technology, defence, agriculture, education, fine arts, music, film, theatre and literature. The recipient was presented with a gold medal and enjoyed income-tax exemption, pension rights, transport privileges and a monthly honorarium.

Leningrad The name given in 1924 after Lenin's death to Petrograd which, until 1914, was known as **St Petersburg**; it reverted to this title in 1991 after a referendum. The former Tsarist capital founded by Peter the Great in 1703, it was best known as Leningrad for its heroic resistance to a two-year German siege in WORLD WAR II.

Leningrad purge *See* PURGE.

Leninism Lenin's elaboration of MARXIST political and economic thought, adapting it to contemporary conditions of industrially underdeveloped and mainly agricultural societies, such as Russia in the early 20th century. In *What is to be Done?* he stressed the indispensable role of a disciplined professional Communist party:

> Lenin's method leads to this; the party organisation at first substitutes itself for the party as a whole, then one central committee substitutes itself for the party organisation, and finally a single dictator substitutes himself for the central committee. TROTSKY

In *Imperialism – The Highest Stage of Capitalism* (1916) Lenin differed from Marx in stressing the revolutionary potential of pre-capitalist societies and the importance of a worker-peasant alliance in achieving revolution. *Left-wing Communism* (1920), written with experience of power, emphasised the importance of flexibility and PRAGMATISM in achieving revolutions and then sustaining Communist authority. This last book marked a clear divergence from the economic and historical determination of orthodox Marxism.

> A combination of two things which Europeans have kept for some centuries in different compartments of the soul – religion and business. JOHN MAYNARD KEYNES

> Leninism is Marxism of the era of imperialism and the proletarian revolution. STALIN, 1917

let. let freedom ring *See* LIBERTY BELL.

Let Harold and Bob finish the job The slogan on which Robert Maxwell (1923–91), the larger-than-life and ultimately crooked Czech-born socialist tycoon, stood for re-election as Labour MP for Buckingham in 1966. Maxwell, first elected in 1964, held the seat until 1970; the Harold with whom he modestly associated himself was Harold WILSON.

Let our children grow tall, and some taller than others if they have it in them to do so The statement with which Margaret THATCHER established herself with American conservatives, made on her first US tour as Tory leader in 1975.

Let sleeping dogs lie *See* DOGS.

Let the word go forth from this time and place, to friend and foe alike, that the torch has been passed to a new generation of Americans – born in this country, tempered by war, disciplined by a hard and bitter peace The central message of President John F. KENNEDY's INAUGURAL address, delivered on 20 January 1961.

Let them eat cake (Fr. *Qu'ils mangent de la brioche*) Reputedly the comment of Queen Marie-Antoinette (1755–93) when told that the mob were protesting that they had no bread during the shortage of 1789. It was cited to justify the FRENCH REVOLUTION and the execution of Louis XVI and his queen. If fact the saying is much older, dating back at least to Queen Marie-Thérèse (1638–83), wife of Louis XIV, who asked: 'Why don't they eat pastry?'

Let us go forward together and put these grave matters to the proof The challenge which Winston CHURCHILL, as a member of ASQUITH's Liberal government, threw down to militant ULSTER UNIONISTS on 14 March 1914 as they threatened to use force to obstruct HOME RULE. Churchill said:

> If Ulster is to become a tool in party calculations, if the civil and parliamentary systems under which we have dwelt for so long, and our fathers before us, are to be brought to the rude challenge of force; if the Government and Parliament of this country and greater Empire are to be exposed to menace and brutality; if all the loose, wanton and reckless chatter we have had to listen to these many months is, in the end, to disclose a sinister and revolutionary purpose, then I can only say to you: 'Let us go forward and put these matters to the proof.'

Let's call for a hatchet Richard NIXON's blast during the 1952 Presidential campaign against alleged Communism in the TRUMAN administration. He declared:

> If the dry rot of corruption and Communism, which has eaten deep into our body politic during the past seven years, can only be chopped out with a hatchet – then let's call for a hatchet.

Let's do it The last words of Gary GILMORE prior to his execution by a Utah firing squad on 17 January 1977, resuming America's implementation of the death penalty.

Letelier assassination The murder in Washington on 21 September 1976 of Orlando Letelier (1932–76), former Chilean ambassador to the United States, who had been Foreign Minister and Defence Minister in the left-wing government of Salvador Allende. He was killed with his American assistant Ronni Moffitt in a car-bomb explosion by agents of the Chilean intelligence agency DINA, as part of a campaign against supporters of the former regime which included the assassination of Allende's army Chief of Staff, Gen. Carlos Prats, in Argentina. Michael Townley, an American prosecuted along with Chilean agents for his role in Letelier's murder, implicated President PINOCHET; involvement of the CIA in both Allende's overthrow and the killing of Letelier has also been alleged. Political assassinations in WASHINGTON's diplomatic quarter are almost unheard of, and the episode confirmed US liberals' worst suspicions about the Pinochet regime.

level. Levellers An ultra-republican group of Puritans active only for a few years during the English CIVIL WAR, but whose views were to form one of the bases of radical and socialist demands two centuries later. Led by John Swinburne (1614–57), the Levellers, mainly comprised of soldiers in the Parliamentary army, were an influential force between 1647 and 1649; their demands, including universal male suffrage and an end to all class distinctions, ultimately proved too much for Oliver Cromwell and his Parliamentary/military governing group.

level playing field A situation in which all proponents of differing arguments, or all contenders for a contract, enjoy an equal chance of success, instead of the odds being stacked in favour of one of them. Successive UK governments have come under fire for their determination to create such a regime in competition between British and European firms when other EU members are felt to give preference to their own, in practice handicapping domestic industry. The phrase originated in financial services to describe equality of regulation, and was picked up by President REAGAN in 1986.

Leviathan The landmark work of political theory written by Thomas Hobbes (1588–1679) and published in 1651 in the early years of the English COMMONWEALTH. Hobbes maintained that humankind advanced from the state of nature to the political state by way of a contract, giving up the right to act as individuals to a 'sovereign', which could be an individual or an assembly. By transferring those rights the people became part of a great commonwealth or 'Leviathan' (a biblical name for a great sea creature). Hobbes argued that rebellion against a sovereign was never justified, but that if one succeeded, this proved the sovereign incapable of ruling. Absolute obedience to the sovereign was essential, for

> How could a state be governed . . . if every individual remained free to obey or not to obey the law according to his private opinion?

Levy. Chandra Levy affair The scandal that in 2001 destroyed the career of Rep. Gary Condit, who three years earlier had scorned Bill CLINTON's conduct and advised him to come clean about his affair with Monica Lewinsky. Ms Levy was a 24-year-old Congressional INTERN who fell in love with the California Democrat, then vanished, triggering an inconclusive police inquiry until her body was found a year later in the WASHINGTON park where she jogged. Condit, who had already earned the nicknames of **Condom Condit**, **Mr Blowdry** and the **Hunk on the Hill**, at first denied having had an affair with Levy, but eventually admitted it. Widely regarded as the prime suspect in her disappearance, he brazened out the scandal but went down to a heavy primary defeat when he sought re-election.

Lewinsky. I did not have a sexual relationship with that woman . . . Monica Lewinsky Bill CLINTON's most public denial of the carnal relationship with a White House INTERN that almost cost him the Presidency. He made the assertion, repeated elsewhere under oath, at a televised press conference on 26 January 1998, in the face of disclosures to the contrary that led to the IMPEACHMENT proceedings against him over the ZIPPERGATE affair. Monica Lewinsky (1974–) went to work at the OLD EXECUTIVE OFFICE BUILDING in the summer of 1995, after graduating from college in Oregon. Making full use of her access to the White House, she began a relationship with Clinton that November, and the following month joined the full-time staff of the Presidential Legislative Affairs Office. Lewinsky and the President stopped just short of penetrative sex; her prize trophy was a BLUE DRESS stained with his semen. Moved to the PENTAGON in 1996 because her superiors thought she spent too much time hanging round the ROSE GARDEN, she confided in a new work friend, Linda Tripp, about the relationship. Word leaked out to lawyers for Paula JONES, who were trying to prove a pattern of sexual harassment by the President, and the special prosecutor Kenneth STARR also got wind of the affair. At this point, with Lewinsky in touch with senior Presidential advisers about what she should say to the investigators following her initial denials on oath that she had had a sexual relationship with Clinton, the story broke in the media (*see* DRUDGE REPORT). Lewinsky, who had been negotiating a job at Revlon in New York through Clinton's personal advisor Vernon Jordan, had little choice but to embark on a new career as a semi-celebrity.

L.G. The most neutral and dignified nickname for David LLOYD GEORGE; he remains the only British Prime Minister, other than the successful but less CHARISMATIC C-B

(Campbell-Bannerman), to be identified by his initials.

Liaison Committee The panel comprising all 35 chairs of SELECT COMMITTEES which wields considerable power within the HOUSE OF COMMONS. On July 16 2002 Tony BLAIR was questioned by it, the first time a Prime Minister had appeared before a Select Committee since Neville CHAMBERLAIN in 1938; such sessions have since become a twice-yearly occurrence, and occasionally a forum for major announcements.

liar A term which is UNPARLIAMENTARY in any legislature, but is nevertheless uttered both in debate and outside. The 18th-century playwright Richard Brinsley Sheridan tried to get round the prohibition with this apology:

> Mr Speaker, I said the honourable gentleman was a liar it is true and I am sorry for it. The honourable member may place the punctuation where he pleases.

In the US SENATE on 14 March 1925 Sen. Richard Ernst tried another tack, saying: 'I wish to know if there be any way under the rules of the Senate whereby I can, without breaking those rules and without offending the senators around me, call a fellow member a wilful, malicious, wicked liar?' But Sen. Kenneth McKellar slipped the leash to describe the COLUMNIST Drew Pearson as

> An infamous liar, a revolting liar, a pusillanimous liar, a lying ass, a natural born liar, a liar by profession, a liar of living, a liar in the daytime, a liar in the night time, a dishonest, ignorant, corrupt and grovelling crook.

Big Bill Thompson (1869–1944), Mayor of Chicago, had the ultimate answer to accusations of this kind. He once advised:

> If your opponent calls you a liar, call him a thief.

See also LIES.

Those who know me best know that I am not a liar The parting words of Stephen Byers on resigning as Tony BLAIR's Transport Secretary on 28 May 2002. Byers' department had been devastated for months by arguments over SPIN between his SPECIAL ADVISER Jo Moore (*see* BURY) and Head of News Martin Sixsmith, to the point where the PERMANENT SECRETARY Richard Mottram declared that they were all 'FUCKED' and Byers resigned, stating that his continued presence in the government had become a 'distraction'.

Lib-Dems The normally-used abbreviation for Britain's LIBERAL DEMOCRATS.

Lib-Lab Pact (1) A secret arrangement reached in 1903 by Herbert Gladstone for the LIBERALS and Ramsay MACDONALD, for the infant Labour Representation Committee, to give LABOUR candidates a clear run in a limited number of seats provided the Liberals faced no Labour representation in a far larger number. (2) The arrangement in 1977–78 under which James CALLAGHAN's Labour government, which had lost its majority, remained in power through the support of David Steel's (*see* BOY DAVID) Liberals, who were consulted on major issues. Labour hung on for several months after the Liberals terminated the pact, before being defeated in a no-CONFIDENCE vote.

Lib-Labs Labour representatives elected to Parliament on a Liberal platform before the foundation of the LABOUR PARTY in 1906. The Lib-Labs were dominant in working-class politics between 1860 and 1880, but economic instability and unemployment, the enfranchisement of manual workers in 1867 and 1884 and the failure of the Liberals to meet workers' aspirations led to the formation of the Labour Representation Committee in February 1900. This officially became the Labour Party after the 1906 election; the last Lib-Lab MPs, together with the Miners' Federation which sponsored them, joined the Labour Party in 1909.

liberal (1) A person to the LEFT of centre who takes a benign, tolerant view on moral and social issues; also a pejorative for someone with a sentimental, charitable view of human nature, and even, as when used by George BUSH Snr against Michael Dukakis in the 1988 Presidential CAMPAIGN, a term of abuse. Ronald REAGAN called liberalism the 'L-word', and his Interior Secretary James Watt declared: 'I never use the words Republican and Democrat. It's liberals and Americans.' Definitions of a liberal include: 'a man too broadminded to take his own side in a quarrel' – Robert Frost; 'a man who is constantly being kicked in the teeth by the Commies and in the pants by the National Association of Manufacturers' – Anon.; 'a conservative who's been mugged by reality' – Anon.; 'a man who will give away everything he doesn't own' – Frank Dane.

> What the liberal really wants to bring about is change which will not in any way endanger his own position.
>
> STOKELY CARMICHAEL (1941–)

> It is Hamlet-like torture to be truly liberal.
>
> LEONARD BERNSTEIN (1918–92)

Liberals think that goats are just sheep from broken homes.
MALCOLM BRADBURY and CHRISTOPHER BIGSBY

If God had been a liberal there would have been ten suggestions. *Ditto*

If optimism were a disease, they'd be immune for life. RONALD REAGAN

A liberal is a person who believes that water can be made to run uphill. A conservative is someone who believes everybody should pay for his water.
THEODORE H. WHITE

(2) Traditionally, a supporter of LAISSEZ-FAIRE, Free MARKET economic policies, now paradoxically on the right of politics and generally opposed to social liberals.

liberal consensus The humane, tolerant and permissive climate of opinion in the 1960s which has subsequently been blamed, initially by conservatives and then, in July 2004, by Tony BLAIR for the perceived subsequent decline in family values and civilised behaviour.

liberal democracy The combination of representative democracy and the observance of fundamental human and civil rights which most Western nations would reckon to practise.

Liberal Democratic Party The party that has ruled Japan almost continuously, and presided over its economic success, since the country's political reconstruction after WORLD WAR II, except for brief periods when the electorate has tired of its corruption. It is an essentially conservative party, enmeshed with the business community and divided between factions in which powerful bosses exercise PATRONAGE. *See also* LOCKHEED SCANDAL; RECRUIT SCANDAL.

Liberal Democrats In Britain the party formed from the merger in 1988 of most of the LIBERAL PARTY and the bulk of the SDP, and initially known as the **Social and Liberal Democrats** (SLD or SALADS). Under Paddy Ashdown (*see* Paddy PANTSDOWN) it recovered from abject poll ratings and humiliation by the GREEN party in the 1989 Euro-elections to take 20 Westminster seats in 1992, 46 in 1997 and (under Charles Kennedy) 52 in 2001. After Labour's LANDSLIDE victory in 1997 Tony BLAIR invited the Liberal Democrats into a joint CABINET committee to promote constitutional and other reform, and came close to offering Ashdown a place in the Cabinet itself. But NEW LABOUR's enthusiasm for PROPORTIONAL REPRESENTATION waned (*see* JENKINS COMMITTEE), and under Kennedy the LibDems took a more independent line, strongly opposing the IRAQ WAR and making gains from Labour in the 2005 election to achieve 62 seats, the best showing by a third force for 80 years despite the failure of the DECAPITATION strategy to oust leading Tories. From 1999 the party shared power in Scotland in coalition with Labour, Liberal Democrat Jim Wallace (and later Nicol Stephen) being Deputy First Minister. *See also* LITERAL DEMOCRAT.

Electoral support for them would be impressive only if it were measured on the Richter scale.
NICHOLAS BENNETT MP (Con.)

Labour is the music of dire straits. The Tories are the music of simple minds. But we are the new kids on the block.
CHARLES KENNEDY, 1991

Liberal Imperialists The Liberal MPs who in the late 19th century supported Britain's imperial expansion, without going so far as Joseph Chamberlain and realigning themselves with the Conservatives. ASQUITH, Edward Grey and R. B. Haldane were prominent in the late 1880s, but the most consistent Liberal Imperialist was Lord ROSEBERY, whose enthusiasm strained the party for over a decade after he resigned the leadership in 1896.

Liberal International The body representing Liberal parties from Britain, continental Europe, Canada and other nations where political liberalism is an organised force.

Liberal Party (1) The left-of-centre party which for almost a century from 1835 formed either Britain's government or the principal OPPOSITION. The party was born from the declining WHIGS and non-aligned MPs from a (successful) campaign to oust Manners Sutton, Tory SPEAKER of the COMMONS; the following year Liberal candidates made heavy gains in the first council elections since the reform of local government. The division of loyalties into Liberal and CONSERVATIVE only came about after PEEL split the Tory party in 1846, triggering a wholesale REALIGNMENT which took until 1859 to complete. Melbourne, Lord John (later Earl) Russell, Palmerston (*see* PAM) and Rosebery led the party before its great days under GLADSTONE, who served four times as Prime Minister between 1868 and 1894. DISRAELI's Conservatives often outflanked the Liberals as reformers, and the party became best known for Gladstone's enthusiasm for HOME RULE and its embodiment of the NONCONFORMIST CONSCIENCE. However, after Lord Rosebery's failure as Prime Minister and the Liberals' split over IMPERIALISM, Ulster and the BOER WAR, the party, repositioned to the left, returned to power in 1905 under CAMPBELL-BANNERMAN to begin a burst of reform unprecedented until ATTLEE's government of 1945. Although ASQUITH, Prime Minister from 1908, stood firm against VOTES FOR WOMEN, he led the struggle to curb the powers of the HOUSE OF LORDS, while LLOYD GEORGE laid the foundations of the WELFARE STATE. Asquith continued with a makeshift COALITION for the first two years of WORLD WAR I before Tory discontent with the conduct of the war installed LLOYD GEORGE in DOWNING STREET – though Asquith remained leader of the party. The struggle between the two weakened the Liberals before the break-up of the coalition in 1922, and with Labour breaking through to form a minority government in 1924 the Liberals slumped to third place – a position from which they never recovered. The Liberals were reduced to just five seats in 1951, with the party rumoured to hold its meetings in a telephone kiosk; Sir Gerald Nabarro (*see* NAB) called them 'the shadow of a splinter'. Revivals in the early 1960s (*see* ORPINGTON MAN), the early 1970s and (in conjunction with the SDP) early 1980s gave fleeting hopes of a return to power; indeed in 1977–78 the Liberals did have a stake in it through the LIB-LAB PACT. After the collapse of the ALLIANCE in 1987 David Steel (*see* BOY DAVID) forced through the merger of the party with the SDP – leading to desertions from both and a slump in support before the LIBERAL DEMOCRATS emerged as a serious third force.

> Every boy and every girl,
> That's born into this world alive
> Is either a little Liberal
> Or else a little Conservative.
>
> W. S. GILBERT, *Iolanthe*

> Liberalism has ever been a devotee of Mammon.
>
> KEIR HARDIE

> There is nothing to be got by being a Liberal today. It is not a profitable or a remunerative career.
>
> ASQUITH, 1920

> I am an English Liberal – I hate the Tory party – their words, their men and their methods.
>
> WINSTON CHURCHILL, c. 1910

> So few and so futile.
>
> CHURCHILL, c. 1950

> The popularity of the Liberal Party is so low that they are considering employing Jacques Cousteau to see if anything can be done to resuscitate it.
>
> AUSTIN MITCHELL MP (Lab.), 1976

> Dr Barnardo's home for orphan voters.
>
> GERRY NEALE MP (Con.)

Liberal Party (2) Australia's principal centre-right party, formed in 1944 by Sir Robert Menzies (*see* MING) and the direct successor of the Liberal Party (1909–17), the Nationalist Party (1917–31) and the United Australia Party (1931–44). For more than half its life it has been led by three men: Menzies (until 1966), Malcolm Fraser (1975–83) and John Howard (since 1996). The Liberals have held power at COMMONWEALTH level in 1949–67 (Menzies and Harold HOLT), 1968–72 (John Gorton and William MacMahon), 1975–83 (Fraser) and since 1996 (Howard), as well as frequently in the states; at federal level they have often governed and campaigned in coalition with the COUNTRY PARTY, now the NATIONAL PARTY. The Liberal Party's Federal President Jim Forbes called it 'a loose confederation of autonomous divisions'; Paul KEATING was characteristically blunter, terming the Liberals 'perfumed gigolos' and saying:

> They wouldn't know a fiscal policy if it got up and bit them on the arse.

Liberal Party (3) One of Canada's two great parties, slightly left of centre though at times more radical. It began to emerge c. 1849 as GRITS, ROUGES and Reformers coalesced into one movement, Alexander Mackenzie leading it to power from 1873 to 1878. (Sir) Wilfrid Laurier led a Liberal government from 1896–1911, being defeated over RECIPROCITY with the United States. After his death in 1919 William Mackenzie King took charge, serving three times as Prime Minister between 1927 and 1948; the Statute of WESTMINSTER shaping the COMMONWEALTH was largely his work, and his contact with President ROOSEVELT proved crucial to the Allied war effort. Louis St Laurent succeeded him, governing until the Liberals' defeat in 1957. The diplomat Lester Pearson took office (1963–68) without a majority as Quebec SEPARATISM began to stir, and the status and restlessness of French Canada dogged Pierre TRUDEAU, the Liberals' most CHARISMATIC leader, throughout his premiership from 1968–79; he held out for 'One Canada' and faced down the separatists. Trudeau resigned after his defeat, but came back to oust the Tories in 1980 after a few months; he finally retired in 1984, after which the party under John Turner lost power. Brian Mulroney's Conservative ascendancy kept the Liberals in opposition until 1993, when the CANADIAN MELTDOWN gave them an overwhelming mandate; under Jean Chrétien they governed with stability for a decade, retaining power under Paul Martin in 2004 despite losing their clear majority.

The flying saucers of politics. No one can make head or tail of them and they are never twice seen in the same place. JOHN DIEFENBAKER

The Liberals talk about a stable government, but we don't know how bad the stable is going to smell.
NDP leader TOMMY DOUGLAS, 1965

Liberal Party (4) In New York City and state, a grouping which normally sides with the Democrats but occasionally endorses liberal Republican candidates, giving a critical boost if the contest is tight.

Liberal Party (5) A small splinter group of Britain's Liberal Party which refused to merge with the SDP in 1988 and has returned to field occasional candidates at elections.

Liberal Unionists The 93 Liberal MPs at WESTMINSTER who, led by Joseph Chamberlain, voted against GLADSTONE's first HOME RULE Bill in June 1886, confirming the split in the party over Ireland. Many eventually crossed the FLOOR to sit with the Conservatives, who have been known ever since as the Conservative and UNIONIST Party.

limousine liberal A derogatory US term for a person with liberal leanings and an opulent lifestyle, the implication being that it is easy to have soft, humane views when one is being chauffeured in comfort. The phrase was invented by Mario Proccacino, the conservative Democrat defeated in 1969 by New York's liberal Republican Mayor John Lindsay. Its UK counterpart is **champagne socialist**.

National Liberals *See* NATIONAL.

white liberal In America and South Africa, a white person who has strongly opposed racial discrimination – sometimes also lamenting that cheap black domestic help is hard to find. The term is often used as a pejorative, both by right-wingers who feel many white liberals can afford to take such a stance because they live in comfortable all-white neighbourhoods, and by black militants who doubt their commitment and sincerity.

A man who tosses worms into the river – all the fish who take him for a friend, and think the worm's got no hooks in it, usually end up in the frying pan. MALCOLM X

The Strange Death of Liberal England The book by George Dangerfield (1923) which examined how the party that provided a reforming government with a large Parliamentary majority up to 1910 could within thirteen years be in terminal decline. The phrase has stuck in the vocabulary of British politics; Roy JENKINS reminded Liberals and Social Democrats of it during the euphoric days of their ALLIANCE.

Liberalism A term variously used for the philosophy of both political and economic liberals, and of the various Liberal parties. GLADSTONE described it as 'trust of the people tempered by prudence', the poet Stephen Spender as 'politics without IDEOLOGY', and Harry Roskolenko as 'the first refuge of political indifference and the last refuge of leftists'.

Ultraliberalism today translates into a whimpering isolationism in foreign policy, a mulish obstructionism in domestic policy, and a pusillanimous pussyfooting on the crucial issue of law and order.
Vice President SPIRO T. AGNEW

New Liberalism The reforming, CORPORATIST and WELFARIST creed adopted by leading British Liberals, especially LLOYD GEORGE, during the party's final period of governing alone, from 1905 to 1914.

liberation The freeing of any country or people from enemy occupation, and specifically the ousting of German forces from occupied France by the Allies (including the FREE FRENCH) in 1944.

liberation theology The religious teaching of radical Catholic clergy in Latin America, with its emphasis on social reform through Christ's commitment to liberate the oppressed. It is seen by right-wing military regimes as synonymous with support for MARXIST guerrillas; the idea that the way they are governing is morally indefensible either does not occur to them or does not trouble them.

Liberator, The The newspaper published by William Lloyd Garrison in Boston from 1831 which gave a powerful voice to the campaign for the abolition of slavery. Garrison's message, welcomed enthusiastically by his largely black readership, was that only extirpation of the sin of slavery would be acceptable to God. His insistence on campaigning for every kind of reform and his refusal to compromise caused friction with many who could have advanced his cause.

libertarian. Libertarian Party The most successful US political party in terms of Presidential voting since 1976, apart from the REFORM PARTY which developed from the personal candidacy of H. Ross PEROT. Founded in 1972, its philosophy is that one should be able to live as one pleases without government interference through 'confiscatory' taxation, gun control and the like.

libertarianism Classic LIBERALISM, whose proponents – notably the philosopher Ayn Rand (1905–82) – have argued that the state should have no role in individuals' lives or the economy, confining itself solely to maintaining order and defending the nation. Though firmly on the right of the spectrum, it thus differs only in degree from ANARCHISM, save that anarchism is based on a concept of social responsibility and libertarians place less emphasis on self-restraint. Libertarianism was an influential force in the 1980s, especially on the REAGAN administration which was open to radical right ideas; Margaret THATCHER's strong opposition to moral freedoms limited its impact within her CONSERVATIVE PARTY, though a small element did press for decriminalisation of most drugs.

Liberty The principal campaigning body in the UK for CIVIL LIBERTIES, having been formed in 1934 as the National Council for Civil Liberties, adopting its present name in 1989. Set up originally to oppose the use of AGENTS PROVOCATEURS by the police during political demonstrations, it has built a reputation – and made enemies – campaigning against legislation (and its application) by all governments which it regards as oppressive; on the way it has survived internal arguments over whether to advise members of the NATIONAL FRONT and whether it should take sides over the CLOSED SHOP. Liberty achieved one of its goals when Tony BLAIR's Labour government enshrined the EUROPEAN CONVENTION ON HUMAN RIGHTS into UK law, but later strongly opposed its legislation for a national identity card scheme.

Liberty and Livelihood The theme of the massive COUNTRYSIDE ALLIANCE march through central London on 22 September 2002, protesting mainly against the Labour government's readiness to allow through a BILL to ban foxhunting but also at the decline in community services from schools to banks and shops in rural areas and to the perceived urban bias of Parliament as a whole. While most DEMONSTRATIONS attract wild estimates of the number of participants, 407,791 supporters, who had marched from three different directions, were electronically counted through; the total did not include those who had applauded the march but not joined it.

Liberty AND union, now and forever, one and inseparable! The PERORATION of the speech by Daniel Webster (1782–1852) to the US SENATE on 26 January 1830, endeavouring to defuse the permanent conflict between advocates of a strong UNION and campaigners for STATES' RIGHTS. It was delivered over two days as the climax to debate on a proposal from Samuel Foote of Massachusetts to keep Western lands vacant until those nearer the East Coast had been fully occupied. This was seen as a YANKEE centralist ploy against the independence of the States. Robert Y. Hayne denounced Foote, with the slogan **Liberty first and Union afterwards**. But Webster's speech hitting back was immediately recognised as a classic.

Liberty! Equality! Fraternity! (Fr. *Liberté! Égalité! Fraternité!*) The motto of the FRENCH REVOLUTION and subsequently of France's Republican state. It goes back at least to a resolution passed by the *Club des Cordeliers* on 30 June 1793, which concluded; 'Unity, the indivisibility of the Republic, Liberty, Equality, Fraternity or death!' The words 'or death' were dropped in 1795.

> At its birth the Republic gave voice to three words: Liberty! Equality! Fraternity! If Europe is wise and just, each of these words signifies peace.
> ALPHONSE DE LAMARTINE (1790–1869)

Liberty Bell The bell commissioned by Pennsylvania to mark the 50th anniversary in 1751 of William Penn's Charter of Privileges, which became the fundamental law of the colony until Independence. It was rung on 8 July 1776, along with many others, to announce the Declaration of INDEPENDENCE, and has been known as the Liberty Bell since about 1839. The name comes from the Biblical inscription it carries: **'Proclaim liberty throughout the land unto all the inhabitants thereof'** (Leviticus XXV, 10). The bell, now with a sizable crack in one side, is housed in a pavilion close to Independence Hall. When Queen Elizabeth II paid her Bicentennial visit to the cradle of American Independence, the greatest talking point was whether or not she actually touched the bell; the author was present as one of the press POOL and did not see. The Queen also presented a replica bell whose inscription 'Let freedom ring' – from '*My* COUNTRY, *'tis of Thee*' – drew complaints from fundamentalists who claimed the Bible was being slighted.

Liberty Bill The name given by supporters to William Lemke, a Republican Congressman from North Dakota who ran for the

Presidency in 1932 for the right-wing agrarian populist Union Party. The play on words was unfortunate; critics pointed out that the Liberty Bell was also cracked. Upstaged ON THE STUMP by the RADIO PRIEST Fr. Gerald E. Coughlin and the Louisiana populist Rev. Gerald L. K. Smith, Lemke still polled 882,479 votes.

Liberty Lobby One of the most vocal and influential ultra-conservative pressure groups in Washington, founded by Curtis B. Dall in 1955. It has campaigned against higher taxes, CIVIL RIGHTS legislation, public housing, farm subsidies, FOREIGN AID, US participation in the UNITED NATIONS, and for cancellation of ARMS CONTROL agreements.

Liberty's in every blow/Let us do or die The stirring call to arms penned by Robert Burns (1759–96) in his verse *Scots, Wha Hae* (formally titled *Robert Bruce's March to Bannockburn*). Though that battle was fought by the Scots against the invading English, Burns' slogan has come to represent his passionate belief in the dignity and equality of mankind.

Eternal vigilance is the price of liberty These exact words were uttered by Wendell Phillips in 1852 and have been attributed to Thomas JEFFERSON. But in 1790 the Irish politician John Philpot Curran told the PRIVY COUNCIL:

> The condition upon which God hath given liberty to man is eternal vigilance.

Give me liberty or give me death! The phrase with which Patrick Henry (1736–99) is said to have ended his speech to the Virginia Convention in Richmond on 23 March 1775. Urging Virginians to reject compromise and take up arms in the revolutionary war, Henry supposedly said:

> Why stand we here idle? What is it that gentlemen wish? What would they have? Is life so dear, or peace so sweet, as to be purchased at the price of chains and slavery? Forbid it, Almighty God! – I know not what course others may take, but as for me, give me liberty, or give me death!

No note of the speech was taken, and the text as now quoted was reconstructed 42 years after the event by Henry's biographer William Wirt. Henry's speech was certainly dramatic but, tellingly, 'Give me liberty or give me death!' did not become a household phrase until after Wirt's book appeared in 1817.

Let every nation know, whether it wishes us well or ill, that we shall pay any price, bear any burden, meet any hardship, support any friend, oppose any foe to assure the survival and success of liberty One of the key phrases from the INAUGURAL address of President KENNEDY, on 20 January 1961, and one of the seven inscriptions carved on the walls by his grave in ARLINGTON NATIONAL CEMETERY.

life, liberty and the pursuit of happiness The 'inalienable rights' of human beings spelt out in America's Declaration of INDEPENDENCE by Thomas JEFFERSON and others.

Oh Liberty! Oh Liberty! What crimes are committed in thy name! (Fr. *O Liberté! O Liberté! Que de crimes on commet en ton nom!*) The last words of the French revolutionary Mme Marie Roland (1754–93) as she mounted the steps to the GUILLOTINE for her own execution during the Reign of TERROR.

The tree of liberty must be refreshed from time to time with the blood of patriots and tyrants. It is natural manure An unexpectedly bloodthirsty declaration from Thomas JEFFERSON, in a letter to W. S. Smith on 13 November 1787.

Sons of Liberty The society formed by Massachusetts tradesmen which led the protests throughout Britain's American colonies against the STAMP ACT of 1764, and became one of the moving forces behind the AMERICAN REVOLUTION. As well as encouraging political action, the Sons of Liberty egged on the mob partly to forestall smuggling charges faced by some of the 'Loyal Nine' who founded the movement.

> They are of the opinion that no-one is entitled to riot but themselves.
>
> ANON. British officer, c. 1766

The movement spread from colony to colony until it held sway in eleven out of thirteen, but with Massachusetts under Samuel ADAMS firmly in the lead. Once independence was declared, the name became synonymous with the patriotic movement as a whole; the Sons of Liberty were later cited as the inspiration for America's WHIG party.

Library of Congress *See* CONGRESS.

Libyan bombing The raid on 14 April 1986 by US aircraft against the Libyan capital of Tripoli, in reprisal for alleged Libyan involvement in the bombing of a West Berlin disco used by American troops. The raid, carried out by planes from Upper Heyford, Oxfordshire, caused widespread damage and killed a number of people including one of President Gaddafi's children; President REAGAN denied Gaddafi himself was the target but US officials privately insisted he was. The planes flew from Britain by a circuitous route because other Western countries, notably France, refused to allow their facilities or air space to be used; the attack provoked a political storm in London – where it was seen as Margaret THATCHER's 'thank you' to Reagan for help during the FALKLANDS WAR – as well as in WASHINGTON. When the culprit for the 1988 LOCKERBIE bombing was first being sought, revenge for the Tripoli attack was seen as the motive for Libyan involvement.

lid The WHITE HOUSE press corps' term for the time in the evening beyond which they have been told by the Presidential press office to expect no further news.

lie(s) As with LIAR above, the term is UNPARLIAMENTARY. In 1867 Rep. John Hunter was censured by the HOUSE OF REPRESENTATIVES for saying of another's comments: 'So far as I am concerned, it is a base lie.' Winston CHURCHILL was more clever, getting away in the COMMONS with a rejoinder to one of Aneurin BEVAN's speeches that 'I should think it hardly possible to state the opposite of the truth with more precision'. *See also* TERMINOLOGICAL INEXACTITUDES.

A lie can be halfway round the world before the truth has got its boots on A phrase widely credited to James CALLAGHAN after he used it in a speech on 1 November 1976, but in fact originated by the 19th-century Baptist preacher the Rev. C. K. Spurgeon.

Big Lie The basis, on his own admission, of the appeal of HITLER and his NAZI party to large sections of the German public. In MEIN KAMPF he wrote:

> In the big lie, there is always a certain force of credibility. In the primitive simplicity of their minds, the great mass of people will more easily fall victim to a big lie than a small one.

bodyguard of lies CHURCHILL's justification of the use of BLACK PROPAGANDA in wartime. He told STALIN at the 1943 TEHRAN CONFERENCE:

> In time of war truth is so precious, it must be attended by a bodyguard of lies.

I'll never tell a lie The promise made to the American people by the born-again Baptist Jimmy CARTER during his 1976 campaign for the presidency. Though his single term was widely rated a failure at the time, it was a promise he came close to keeping.

If they stop telling lies about me, I'll stop telling the truth about them Perhaps the best one-liner in politics, it stems from a statement by Sen. Chauncey Depew (1834–1928):

> If you will refrain from telling any lies about the Republican Party, I'll promise not to tell the truth about the Democrats.

It was refined by the Democratic Presidential nominee Adlai STEVENSON, who said in Fresno, California, on 10 September 1952:

> I offer my opponents a bargain. If they will stop telling falsehoods about us, I will stop telling the truth about them.

The rulers of states are the only ones who should have the privilege of lying, either at home or abroad; they may be allowed to lie for the good of the state Plato's assertion, in Book II of *The Republic*, of what is now termed the RIGHT TO LIE.

Lieutenant Governor (1) In America, the deputy to the GOVERNOR of a State. A handful of states manage without a lieutenant governor; of the majority with one, some elect them separately from the governor so they need not be of the same party. If a governor is unable to complete his term of office, the lieutenant will generally take over, though not in the case of RECALL. The post generally carries little political or administrative clout. (2) With a hyphen, in Canada the appointed representative of the Federal government in each PROVINCE.

life. life, liberty and the pursuit of happiness *See* LIBERTY; the GREATEST HAPPINESS OF THE GREATEST NUMBER.

life wasn't meant to be easy A cliché widely heard in the late 1970s after its use by the Australian Prime Minister Malcolm Fraser, in reference to his government's situation. What Fraser actually told his LIBERAL PARTY in 1977 was:

> It occurred to me that there are times when life is a little easier than it's meant to be.

Life's better with the Conservatives *See* CONSERVATIVES.

Lifted The 1996 song by the Newcastle-based duo the Lighthouse Family which Labour adopted as its theme tune in the 2001 general election campaign. The party chose it from a shortlist because it reflected Labour's 'lifting Britain up and taking it to a better future'; the left-winger Billy Bragg (*see* RED WEDGE) could not help noting a reference to a 'bright blue space up above the clouds' which had 'connotations of watered down conservatism'.

The chorus runs:

> . . . 'Cos we could be Lifted, Lifted, Lifted
> We could be Lifted
> From the shadow, Lifted
> Oh we could be lifted up today
> Lifted all the way, you and I forever
> Baby, lifted, lifted, lifted, hey ey ey.

Liga Nord The semi-SEPARATIST and right-wing Italian party formerly known as the LOMBARD LEAGUE. Led by Umberto Bossi, the Liga broke through in the 1993 elections as Christian Democrat and socialist votes collapsed; the following year they formed part of Silvio Berlusconi's briefly victorious FORZA ITALIA! In September 1996 Liga Nord declared an independent state of **Padania**, prompting massive fascist and right-wing demonstrations in support, 350,000 people turning out in Milan. The declaration lost the Liga wider support and its Mayor of Milan was defeated in 1997, but it has remained an element in Silvio Berlusconi's governing COALITION.

light. light at the end of the tunnel A widely-used phrase in the early 1980s for the first indications of economic recovery (*see also* GREEN SHOOTS). By the end of the decade cynics were pointing out that the light might, instead of daylight, turn out to be an oncoming train.

light on the hill The oft-quoted objective of the Australian LABOR PARTY, introduced in a speech by J. B. Chifley in 1949. It is synonymous with 'light at the end of the tunnel' but also echoes Ronald REAGAN's subsequent CITY ON THE HILL and Blake's JERUSALEM. It acquired a particular relevance to Australian socialists, and became a standard phrase in the repertory of the movement's leaders. It represents the ideal that no person should be deprived of the hope of improving their lot.

Likud The right-wing and aggressively nationalist party which from 1977 eclipsed LABOUR's ascendancy and governed Israel under a series of hard-line leaders: Menachem Begin, Yitzhak Shamir, Benjamin Netanyahu and most recently Ariel Sharon. Begin, to the surprise of many, concluded the CAMP DAVID AGREEMENT restoring relations between Israel and Egypt, but his successors increasingly combined token support for the PEACE PROCESS with increasingly assertive handling of the Palestinians, culminating in Sharon's construction of a barrier separating most Palestinian territory from Israel with the stated purpose of deterring suicide bombers. Likud governed outright from 1977 to 1984, but has subsequently had to form COALITIONS; even Sharon found his policy of closing down Jewish settlements in the GAZA STRIP while entrenching others on the WEST BANK unacceptable to much of his own party, let alone coalition partners even further to the right.

Limehouse Declaration The statement of aims issued on 15 January 1981 by the GANG OF FOUR who were soon to form Britain's SDP, after a meeting at Dr David OWEN's home in Limehouse, on the north bank of the Thames in London's Docklands. It said:

> The calamitous outcome of the LABOUR PARTY's Wembley conference [entrusting the choice of the party leader to an electoral college] demands a new start in British politics . . . We propose to set up a Council for Social Democracy . . . We believe that the need for a realignment of British politics must now be faced . . .

Limehousing A once-common term for violent abuse of one's political opponents; from a speech by LLOYD GEORGE at Limehouse on 30 July 1909 when he poured scorn and abuse on dukes, landlords, financial magnates, etc.

limousine liberal *See* LIBERAL.

Lincoln, Abraham (1809–65), 16th President of the United States (Republican, 1861–65). Perhaps America's greatest President, who led the UNION through the CIVIL WAR to victory over the CONFEDERACY, EMANCIPATING the slaves, but was ASSASSINated before he could settle the peace. Born in Kentucky of poor frontier stock (*see* LOG CABIN TO WHITE HOUSE; RAIL-SPLITTER) he was raised in Illinois; his cousin Dennis Hanks said: 'If you heard him fellin' trees in a clearing you would say there was three men at work by the way the trees fell.' As a young man he combined practising law with politics, starting his very first CAMPAIGN speech: 'Fellow-citizens, I believe you all know who I am.' His law partner William Herndon recalled: 'Politics were his life, newspapers his food and great ambition his motive power.' He became a WHIG Congressman in 1846, opposing the MEXICAN WAR; returning all but 75¢ of $200 given by his party for the campaign, he said:

> I did not need the money. I made the canvass on my own horse, my entertainment being at the houses of friends cost me nothing, and my only outlay was 75¢ for a barrel of cider, which some farmhands insisted I should TREAT them to.

Lincoln quit after one term when his ambitions were thwarted, but returned to politics as an opponent of slavery and the

KANSAS-NEBRASKA ACT; he lost narrowly in an 1855 SENATE race, and again in 1858 when he challenged Sen. Stephen Douglas, author of the Act. Lincoln characterised Douglas as 'as thin as the homeopathic soup that was made by boiling the shadow of a pigeon that had been starved to death'. Despite his defeat, his craggy looks and the drama of his debates with Douglas up and down the state made him a national figure. Lincoln said:

> Nobody ever expected me to be President. In my poor, lean, lank face nobody has ever seen any cabbages sprouting.

And after his ELECTION the future President James Garfield would note:

> He has been raising a respectable pair of dark-brown whiskers, which decidedly improve his looks, but no appendage can ever render him remarkable for beauty.

Indeed he was christened the ILLINOIS BABOON, and the Republicans who nominated him in 1860 said: 'We know old Abe does not look very handsome, but if all the ugly men in the US vote for him, he will surely be elected.' He was also taciturn, his campaign manager David Davis reckoning him 'the most reticent, secretive man I ever saw or expect to see'. But he already had the command of words he would show in the GETTYSBURG ADDRESS, saying:

> I know there is a God, and he hates injustice and slavery. I see the storm coming, and I know that his hand is in it. If he has a place and work for me – and I think he has – I am ready.

In the campaign, dominated by Southern threats to secede from the Union, Lincoln carried all Northern states to be elected with just under 40% of the vote; his old foe Douglas was well behind. He told his hometown voters:

> My friends, I now leave, not knowing when, or whether, I may return, with a task before me greater than that which rested upon WASHINGTON. Without the assistance of that Divine Being, who ever attended him, I cannot succeed. With its assistance, I cannot fail.

As soon as Lincoln was confirmed by the ELECTORAL COLLEGE, South Carolina seceded and the Civil War began. The new President declared: 'I believe in the providence of the most men, the largest purse and the longest cannon.' Lincoln manoeuvred the South into firing the first shot at FORT SUMTER, then welded together a credible war machine while leaving options open for reconciliation in the future. His slowness in acting against slavery upset many ABOLITIONISTS, Frederick Douglass branding him 'the slow coach to Washington'. To Wendell Phillips he was 'a huckster in politics – a first-rate second-rate man', while Richard Henry Dana noted: 'In Washington, the most striking thing is the absence of personal loyalty to the President. It does not exist. He has no admirers, no enthusiastic supporters, none to bet on his head.' And Maryland's Sen. Willard Salusbury declared:

> I never did see or discourse with so weak and imbecile a man as Abraham Lincoln, President of the United States.

The war was a long haul and the combination of reverses and heavy casualties – and his wife Mary's extravagance – brought Lincoln plenty of criticism; the *New York Herald* called him 'a joke incarnate'. He admitted to setbacks, saying: 'It is my ambition and desire to so administer the affairs of the government while I remain President that if at the end I have lost every other friend on earth, I shall have at least one friend remaining and that one shall be down inside me.' But he also confessed: 'All my life I have been a fatalist.'

By the time he sought re-election in 1864 the war was nearing its end, but war fatigue in the North prompted a COPPERHEAD campaign from the Democrats, who fielded General George McLellan, to whom Lincoln had once written: 'If you don't want to use the army, I should like to borrow it for a while.' He won as Union forces moved in for the kill, and six weeks after Lincoln's second INAUGURATION the war was over. In his last speech, on 11 April 1865 after Lee's surrender, he said: 'We meet this evening not in sorrow, but in gladness of heart'. Three days later he was shot at FORD'S THEATRE in Washington, where he had gone to celebrate the end of the war. His assassin, John Wilkes Booth, declared:

> Our country owes all her troubles to him, and God simply made me the instrument of His punishment.

Lincoln's assassination stunned the world. Thomas d'Arcy McGee declared: 'Never yet did the assassin's knife reach the core of a cause or the heart of a principle,' while George P. A. Healey noted of its political consequences: 'With his death the possibility of peace with magnanimity died.' In the 1950s the sick question was posed: 'Apart from that, Mrs Lincoln, how did you enjoy the play?'

If it is (God's) will that I must die at the hand of an assassin, I must be resigned. I must do my duty as I see it, and leave the rest with God.
LINCOLN, 1864

Now he belongs to the ages.
Secretary of War EDWIN STANTON at Lincoln's bedside

He was the greatest character since Christ.
Lincoln's personal secretary JOHN HAY

Not so often in the story of mankind does a man arrive on earth who is both steel and velvet, as hard as rock and soft as drifting fog, who holds in his heart and mind the paradox of terrible storm and peace unspeakable and perfect.
CARL SANDBURG (1878–1967)

The cruellest thing to happen to Lincoln since being shot has been to fall into the hands of Carl Sandburg. EDMUND WILSON

Here we have the overall philosophy of Lincoln: in all things which deal with people, be liberal, be human. In all those things which deal with the people's money or their economy, be conservative – and don't be afraid to use the word.
DWIGHT D. EISENHOWER, 1954

In this temple
As in the hearts of the people
For whom he saved the Union
The memory of Abraham Lincoln
Is enshrined forever.
ROYAL CORTISSOZ (1869–1948), inscription above the statue on the Lincoln Memorial Washington D.C.

Lincoln bedroom The former Cabinet Room on the second floor of the WHITE HOUSE which President TRUMAN fitted out with bedroom furniture from Lincoln's time. The imposing rosewood bed was bought by Mrs Lincoln in 1861. The room is now used as a guest room for VIPs and friends of the President's family; Sir Winston CHURCHILL and Queen Juliana of the Netherlands both reckoned to have seen Lincoln's ghost while staying there. There was a furore in 1996 after press revelations that Democratic Party contributors had paid to spent the night there. *See* HOTEL 1600 PENNSYLANIA AVENUE: OVERNIGHTS.

Lincoln-Douglas debates The great debates between Lincoln and Sen. Stephen Douglas (*see* LITTLE GIANT) in 1858 when they were contending for Douglas' Illinois seat in the Senate. They met seven times throughout the state, speaking to crowds of up to 15,000 and attracting national publicity; Douglas won the vote, but Lincoln made the lasting impact.

Lincoln Memorial The first of the memorials to America's great Presidents – JEFFERSON, Franklin D. ROOSEVELT and WASHINGTON are the others – erected on or close to the MALL in the heart of Washington during the 20th century. Constructed between 1911 and 1922, when President HARDING attended the dedication, the rectangular building with 36 tall columns – one for each state at the time of Lincoln's assassination – would be majestic enough even without the commanding seated statue of Lincoln himself, by Daniel Chester French. The memorial also bears an inscription commemorating Dr Martin Luther KING's 'I HAVE A DREAM' speech, delivered from its steps in August 1963.

Lincoln's ten points A list of rules for living attributed to Lincoln but not traced back before the 1940s. The first is: 'You cannot bring about prosperity by discouraging thrift'.

line. line by line The WESTMINSTER term for the consideration a Bill receives during its COMMITTEE STAGE, with detailed, exhaustive and sometimes excessive discussion of the text.

line of route The course followed by parties shown round the PALACE OF WESTMINSTER by official guides.

linkage A compromise in which progress in solving one problem is made dependent on comparable progress over another. It was much relied on by Henry KISSINGER during his negotiations in the 1970s. A subsequent example is SADDAM HUSSEIN's effort during the GULF WAR to make his withdrawal from Kuwait conditional on the establishment of an independent Palestinian state.

The two countries [America and the Soviet Union] also offered to work together for peace between Arabs and Israelis after the war ends. Mr Bessmertnykh [Soviet foreign minister] denied that there was 'linkage' between the two issues.
The Times, 30 January 1991

lion. Lion of Judah The title of Haile Selaisse (1892–1975), emperor of Ethiopia from 1930 to 1974 except for the years of the Italian occupation (1936–41) when he lived in exile in Britain. In 1974 he was deposed by a military coup and Ethiopia was declared a socialist republic (*see* DERGUE). Rastafarians regard him as the Messiah, the incarnation of God; the name 'Rastafarian' comes from his real name, *Ras Tafari Mokonnen.* He assumed the title *Haile Selaisse*, meaning 'Might of the Trinity', on becoming emperor. The lion is the emblem of the tribe of Judah, Christ sometimes being referred to as 'the lion of the tribe of Judah'.

Lion of the British Parliament The

accolade accorded George Galloway (*see* RESPECT) by the CBS television network after his bravura appearance before the Senate Permanent Sub-Committee on Investigations on 17 May 2005. Galloway had demanded to be heard after the Committee concluded from documentary evidence and interviews with former colleagues of Saddam Hussein that Galloway, the former French interior minister Charles Pasqua and a number of Russian opinion-formers had been given allocations of Iraqi oil to sell under the UN's OIL FOR FOOD programme. Denouncing the documents as forged and the charges against him as 'the mother of all smokescreens', Galloway, with an oratory seldom seen on Capitol Hill, tore into the committee and the Bush administration for accusing him of illegality when the war itself had illegally caused the death of 100,000 people. When challenged over how often he had met Saddam, Galloway replied:

> I have had two meetings with Saddam Hussein . . . In fact I've met with Saddam Hussein exactly the same number of times as [US Defense Secretary] Donald Rumsfeld met him. The difference is, Donald Rumsfeld met him to sell him guns and to give him maps to better target those guns. I met him to try to bring an end to sanctions, suffering and war.

> It appears that Galloway used a children's cancer foundation to conceal his oil transaction.
> MARK GREENBLATT, the committee's chief investigator, at the hearing

> You have nothing on me except my name on lists from Iraq – drawn up after the installation of your puppet administration.
> GEORGE GALLOWAY, to the committee

I was not the lion. But I supplied the roar CHURCHILL's characterisation of his role in rallying the British people in WORLD WAR II. His actual words, from his speech at WESTMINSTER on his 80th birthday (30 November 1954), were:

> It was the nation and the race dwelling all round the globe that had the lion's heart. I had the luck to be called on to give the roar.

Lipsius building The glass and marble skyscraper in the rue de la Loi in central Brussels, completed in 1996, which is the headquarters of the EU's COUNCIL OF MINISTERS and, during the rebuilding of the BERLAYMONT across the road from 1991 to 2004, doubled as the seat of the EUROPEAN COMMISSION. It is named after Justus Lipsius (Joest Lips, 1547–1606), the Belgian Renaissance scholar who attempted to revive ancient Stoicism in a form compatible with Christianity and published *Six Books on Politics and Civil Doctrine*.

liquidation A euphemism used by Communist and other TOTALITARIAN regimes for the execution or murder of their political opponents – frequently members of the governing party who are considered a threat.

liquorice allsorts Clement ATTLEE's nickname for Conservatives and Liberals who joined forces, standing down for each other in certain constituencies, in 1950 to keep Labour out. In both Bolton and Huddersfield, the arrangement led to one Liberal and one Tory MP being elected; the Liberals repudiated it before the 1964 ELECTION and lost both seats.

Lisbon agenda The agenda for European ECONOMIC REFORM championed by Tony BLAIR at the 2000 EU summit in Lisbon and pushed through in alliance with Spain, in particular, to the consternation of the French. The agenda committed the EU to less regulation, support for small business, removal of remaining barriers to competitiveness and support for new technologies, with the twin aims of creating 18 million high quality jobs and making Europe the world's leading competitor in the knowledge-based economy by 2010. The agenda has led to some opening of markets and some streamlining of regulations, but the reluctance of the French to open up their state-owned energy monopolies to competition and Franco-German opposition to a SINGLE MARKET in services, has limited its effectiveness.

list. list MSP A member of the SCOTTISH PARLIAMENT elected under the regional LIST SYSTEM and not for a specific CONSTITUENCY. List MSPs from the SNP, in particular, have come under fire for opening an office in a constituency they hope to represent in future and campaigning against the sitting Labour member.

list system Under PROPORTIONAL REPRESENTATION, a system where the voters are presented with lists of candidates by the respective parties and cast one vote for the entire SLATE. Seats are then allocated from the top downwards on each list according to the share of the votes received. List systems are now used for elections to the EUROPEAN PARLIAMENT, SCOTTISH PARLIAMENT and WELSH ASSEMBLY, in the latter cases alongside FIRST PAST THE POST for individual constituencies.

closed list A list with only parties on the

ballot paper, between whose individual candidates the voter may not choose. The HOUSE OF LORDS in 1998 three times rejected such a system for elections to the EUROPEAN PARLIAMENT, but were overridden by the COMMONS.

listen. I have listened and I have learned The comment of an apparently chastened Tony BLAIR as he returned to DOWNING STREET on 6 May 2005 to start an unprecedented THIRD TERM of Labour government, but with a majority cut by 100 because of discontent over the IRAQ WAR and his leadership. Gordon BROWN had set the tone the night before in his victory speech, saying:

> We will isten and learn, so that we can serve our country and our communities even better in the years to come.

Literal Democrat The misleading party tag chosen in the mid-1990s by a Mr Richard Huggett, which cost the LIBERAL DEMOCRATS one seat and almost a second before the electoral law was changed. Mr Huggett, who insisted he was not a 'spoiler', polled enough votes to prevent a LibDem victory at Devon and East Plymouth in the 1994 European elections, then at Winchester in 1997 polled 680 votes, with the Liberal Democrat Mark Oaten capturing the seat with a majority of just two. The defeated Conservative Gerry Malone had the result overturned on a technicality – but lost the ensuing by-election by a mile. RETURNING OFFICERS now have the power to keep off the ballot paper party descriptions they regard as deliberately misleading.

litmus test An issue to which a candidate's attitude will give an indication as to their wider outlook. For instance, the attitude of eminent US judges toward abortion has been a litmus test of the stance they might adopt on broader issues if promoted to the SUPREME COURT. The phrase comes from chemistry, a litmus paper turning blue in alkaline solutions or red in acid.

little. Little Ben One of the nicknames of Benjamin Harrison (1833–1901), 23rd President of the United States (Republican, 1889–93). The cigar-chewing, deeply religious former CIVIL WAR general stood only 5ft. 6ins. (*See also* WHITE HOUSE ICEBERG).

Little Black Banda The derogatory nickname for Dr Hastings Banda (1898–1997), Prime Minister of Malawi from 1963 and President from 1966, bestowed by David FROST in THAT WAS THE WEEK THAT WAS. It was patterned on *Little Black Sambo*, a character in a children's story now considered racially offensive.

Little Englanders Originally those late Victorian Liberals opposed to the IMPERIALISM of Lord ROSEBERY, the term has come to apply to anyone who considers that Britain has no international role or interests. Margaret THATCHER was thus labelled by Tories and others who resented her lack of enthusiasm for Europe.

Little Entente The political alliance formed between Czechoslovakia, Yugoslavia and Romania in 1920–22 to prevent the restoration of Habsburg power, which later became broader in scope.

Little Giant The nickname of Sen. Stephen Douglas (1813–61), author of the KANSAS-NEBRASKA ACT, who in 1858 defeated Abraham LINCOLN to retain his Illinois seat in the Senate after the epic series of LINCOLN-DOUGLAS DEBATES; Lincoln in fact polled a larger popular vote. Two years later Douglas ran against Lincoln for the Presidency, but pro-slavery Southern Democrats ensured his defeat by nominating Vice President John C. Breckinridge to split the anti-Republican vote.

> Douglas can never be president, Sir. His legs are too short, Sir. His coat, like a cow's tail, hangs too near the ground, Sir.
>
> Sen. THOMAS HART BENTON (1782–1851)

little local difficulty The phrase used by Harold MACMILLAN on 7 January 1958 to describe the resignation of the entire team of TREASURY Ministers – Peter Thorneycroft, CHANCELLOR OF THE EXCHEQUER, Enoch POWELL and Nigel Birch – in protest against increases in public spending they considered imprudent; it is often cited as an instance of SUPERMAC's unflappability. The Ministers resigned as Macmillan was about to start a six-week Commonwealth tour; instead of cancelling to restore his government's equilibrium, he went ahead with the trip, saying at Heathrow Airport:

> I thought the best thing to do was to settle up these little local difficulties and then turn to the wider vision of the Commonwealth.

Little Magician One of many nicknames for President Martin van Buren (*see* OLD KINDERHOOK). He earned it with his skill in organising the **Albany Regency** – one of the earliest political MACHINES and a forerunner of the DEMOCRATIC PARTY – in New York State during the 1820s and '30s.

Little Neddies *See* NEDDY.

Little Red Book The quotations of CHAIR-

MAN MAO, a red plastic-bound pocketbook produced in 1964 for the INDOCTRINATION of China's PEOPLE'S LIBERATION ARMY. It contained political quotations, homilies and aphorisms from Mao's writings, designed to stimulate revolutionary awareness. During the CULTURAL REVOLUTION zealous RED GUARDS and workers brandished the book as they heeded Mao's call to purge REVISIONISTS from the governing elite. It also enjoyed a vogue among student radicals in Europe and America. *See* POWER GROWS FROM THE BARREL OF A GUN.

Little Rock The state capital of Arkansas, scene in September 1957 of a confrontation between 500 US paratroops and the SEGREGATIONIST Governor Orval Faubus, who had used the NATIONAL GUARD to prevent nine black students from attending the previously all-white central High School. A court ordered the Guard to withdraw, but taunting whites kept the children out until President EISENHOWER reluctantly ordered in the troops. They guarded the eight students who continued to attend for the entire academic year; then the school was closed. The incident was decisive in speeding school segregation in the Deep South and changing white attitudes; 35 years later another Governor of Arkansas, Bill CLINTON, became President, supported by most black voters.

Live 8 The chain of global rock concerts organised for 2 July 2005 by Bob Geldof, who had triggered *Live Aid* twenty years before, to pressure the G8 meeting at GLENEAGLES to take serious action to ease poverty in Africa. Geldof incurred criticism by urging the London audience to march on Edinburgh, but Gordon BROWN gave his support and the G8 did make some progress, with Germany – not the US – as expected – the most reluctant.

Lizard of Oz The nickname, a play on the film title *Wizard of Oz*, bestowed by the London *Sun* on Australian Prime Minister Paul KEATING in February 1992 after he attacked the country's British connections. Ironically the *Sun*'s Australian proprietor Rupert Murdoch shared Keating's republican views. Keating, of rebel Irish stock, had told Parliamentary opponents:

> I learned about self-respect and self-regard for Australia, not about some cultural cringe to a country which decided not to defend the Malayan peninsula, not to give us our troops back to keep us free from Japanese domination. This was the country that you wedded yourselves to. Even as they walked out on you and joined the COMMON MARKET, you were looking for your MBEs and your knighthoods.

Lloyd George, David (later Earl, 1863–1945), Britain's Prime Minister (Liberal as leader of a COALITION, 1916–23). A Celtic spellbinder whose nicknames ranged from the prosaic 'L.G.' to 'the Goat' and 'the WELSH WIZARD', Lloyd George was inspirational as 'the man who won the war' and one of the founders of the WELFARE STATE through his PEOPLE'S BUDGET and other social measures. He was a compelling orator; Arnold Bennett cynically reported: 'Mr Lloyd George spoke for a hundred and seventeen minutes, in which period he was detected only once in the use of an argument,' and Harold MACMILLAN recalled:

> I can see, above all, the beautiful hands, an actor's or an artist's hands, by the smallest movement of which he could make you see the picture he was trying to paint.

Regardless of these gifts, he was regarded as PRAGMATIC to the point of duplicity. CHURCHILL termed him 'the vehement, contriving, resourceful, nimble-leaping Lloyd George', and A. J. P. Taylor saw him as 'a master of improvised speech and improvised policies'. F. S. Oliver wrote: 'He is without malice of any kind, without prejudices, without morals. He has many enemies and no friends. He does not understand what friendship means . . . and yet he is the best man we have got.' And Stanley BALDWIN said: 'He spent his whole life plastering together the true and the false, and therefrom manufacturing the implausible.' Lloyd George himself confessed: 'BONAR [LAW] can't bear being called a liar; now I don't mind.' He was a confirmed womaniser, and also led a double life with his secretary Frances Stevenson for 30 years before marrying her on the death of his wife. Miss Stevenson said of him:

> He is incapable of achieving anything without reducing all around him to nervous wrecks.

Lloyd George's power of invective was considerable, Margot Asquith saying: 'He could not see a belt without hitting below it.' Of the defeated Tories in 1906, he observed: 'They died with their drawn salaries in their hands'; Lord Derby was 'a harpooned walrus', and of Sir Herbert Samuel he remarked: 'When they circumcised him, they threw away the wrong bit.' Once when he called on Lord Beaverbrook and was told he was out walking, he replied to the butler: 'Ah, on the water, I suppose.'

Elected MP for Caernarvon in 1890, he

represented the seat for almost 55 years. He made his name leading the left wing of the LIBERAL PARTY against the BOER WAR, was appointed President of the Board of Trade by CAMPBELL-BANNERMAN in 1906 and CHANCELLOR OF THE EXCHEQUER by ASQUITH in 1908. He introduced pensions and National Insurance, and his 1909 People's Budget prompted a constitutional clash with the HOUSE OF LORDS which led to curbs on its powers under the 1911 PARLIAMENT ACT. When war broke out, Lloyd George overcame his pacifist leanings, and in 1915 became Minister for Munitions and the next year Minister for War. His intrigues with the Conservatives at the close of that year brought the ousting of Asquith and a coalition led by Lloyd George himself. This prosecuted the war with greater vigour but only ended it, with American help, after almost two more years of slaughter. Lloyd George played a major role in the peace talks at VERSAILLES and at home won the COUPON ELECTION, but the Liberals lost ground and from now on he was dependent on Tory votes to stay in office. Then, with the CARLTON CLUB REVOLT of 1922, the Conservatives left the coalition and won the ensuing election; the Liberals never held power again. Lloyd George, still feuding with Asquith and under a shadow from the HONOURS SCANDAL, made several efforts to reunite and revive the party, most notably with the YELLOW BOOK of 1929. But like Churchill he became a voice in the wilderness; Harold Nicolson depicted him as 'an old Rolls-Royce, backfiring and spluttering'. At first receptive to HITLER's wiles, he later came out strongly against APPEASEMENT and gave Churchill critical support in the worst days of WORLD WAR II.

> Of the three parties I find Labour least painful. My objection to the Tories is temperamental, and my objection to the Liberals is Lloyd George.
>
> BERTRAND RUSSELL

> Lloyd George was greater than Churchill, and the greatest tribute to Churchill is that he recognised it.
>
> Sir WALTER ELLIOTT

> He did not care in which direction the car was travelling, as long as he remained in the driver's seat.
>
> Lord BEAVERBROOK

> He would have had a better rating in English mythology if he had shared the fate of Abraham LINCOLN.
>
> JOHN GRIGG (Lord Altrincham)

Lloyd George Fund The fund established and controlled by Lloyd George to finance a LIBERAL PARTY organisation loyal to him after his split with ASQUITH, who remained party leader. His blatant use of the honours system to reward contributors provoked the HONOURS SCANDAL of 1922. A commission was set up to investigate Lloyd George's administration of the fund; his refusal to relinquish control hastened the fall of his coalition government.

Lloyd George knew my father Every Welshman's facetious claim to fame, and an Englishman's self-deprecating hint at a murky past; also one of the best known (and cleanest) rugby songs. The reputed originator of the saying was Tommy Rhys Roberts QC (1910–75), whose father, Arthur Rhys Roberts, set up a solicitor's practice with L. G. in London in 1897. He sang the lines 'Lloyd George knew my father, father knew Lloyd George' to the hymn tune *Onward Christian Soldiers* at circuit dinners, and Welsh rugby clubs and Liberal assemblies took it up. The phrase also became the title of a play by William Douglas Home, first performed in London in 1972.

Loans scandal The political storm surrounding Gough WHITLAM's Australian government in 1975 which gave the OPPOSITION a pretext to block SUPPLY and bring it down. It concerned two attempts to borrow in the Middle East to bolster Australia's fragile economic position. The first loan, for up to US$4 billion, was to have been negotiated by the Minerals and Energy Minister Francis X. Connor; TREASURY officials objected and it apparently was not proceeded with. Then on 6 March 1975 the Executive Council authorised Jim Cairns, the Federal treasurer, to borrow US$500 million overseas; Cairns gave George Harris, a Melbourne businessman, power to act as an intermediary in return for a commission. Cairns denied to Parliament that a letter in these terms existed, and when Whitlam found that it did, he sacked Cairns. It then emerged that Connor, three days after his authority to negotiate had been revoked, had received and responded to a telex from Tirath Khemlani, a 'fixer' with Mafia connections in the US, on progress with arranging the original loan. Amid devastating press coverage, Hawke concluded that Connor had also misled Parliament by stating that the negotiations were at an end, and asked him too to resign. Within a month Whitlam himself had gone, with the KERR SACKING.

> Inspired by the purest and most benevolent motives, but executed secretly, deviously and with astonishing incompetence.
>
> BLANCHE D'ALPUGET

lobby (1) The entrance-hall through which members of a LEGISLATURE must pass to enter the CHAMBER. (2) A pressure group for a particular policy, tax break or course of action, for example the China Lobby or the LIBERTY LOBBY. To lobby means to press one's case with legislators by whatever means one can; when the evangelist Billy Graham set up an office in WASHINGTON, he declared: 'I just want to lobby for God'. *See also* LOBBYIST below.

> The most effective lobbies on CAPITOL Hill have always been the ones that played most skilfully to the Congressmen's egos.
>
> WILLIAM GREIDER

(3) **The Lobby** The informal and once semi-secret organisation of journalists at WESTMINSTER – now some 150 strong – which since 1884 has held regular meetings with DOWNING STREET spokesmen, Ministers and OPPOSITION leaders at which they are given information on a non-attributable basis. The group's name is taken from the Members' Lobby, where its members are permitted to stand except when a DIVISION is in progress to talk with politicians – on the understanding that nothing said is used for quotation. Criticised by some as a means of NEWS MANAGEMENT, its success has hinged on a combination of mutual trust and a readiness by members to ask tough questions and get them answered. At one point in Harold WILSON's last premiership NUMBER TEN halted the briefings, claiming the Lobby could not be trusted; its members had in fact seen through a deliberate attempt to mislead them. In the late 1980s the *Guardian,* the *Independent* and the *Scotsman* boycotted lobby meetings for a time in protest at only being permitted to quote 'Downing Street sources'. Over the following decade government's formal dealings with the lobby became more open; from February 2000 the text of the morning briefing of the Lobby by the PMOS (Prime Minister's Official Spokesman) was posted on the No. 10 website. There is also a less formal meeting on Fridays with the Sunday press, who were traditionally given a cup of tea. Originally the morning meeting took place in the Press Secretary's office at No. 10, but the room became too small and a briefing room in the basement, accessible from the side of the building rather than its world-famous front door, was fitted out early in Tony BLAIR's premiership. From October 2002 this meeting was opened up to specialist and foreign journalists and the cameras, and moved from Downing Street to the Foreign Press Association in Carlton Gardens. In January 2004 Robert Phillis, chief executive of Guardian Media, reported to Ministers that confidence between government, media and the public had broken down and recommended the end of briefings purely for the Lobby, with the cameras there as of right.

> An extremely secret organisation that everyone at Westminster knows about.
>
> Sir GERALD KAUFMAN

> Representatives of the Press accredited by the SPEAKER to patrol the corridors of power.
>
> STEPHEN KOSS

> The golden thread in Britain's Parliamentary democracy.
>
> HAROLD WILSON

lobby fodder A derogatory term for legislators who show no individualism, and can be relied on to vote with their party no matter how misguided its policy.

Lobby Room The room, in a turret atop the PALACE OF WESTMINSTER, where the Lobby meets daily – 4pm Monday to Thursday, 11am on Friday – with the PMOS when Parliament is sitting to run through the day's political schedule and ascertain new twists in government policy and thinking. There is also a weekly meeting with the LEADER OF THE HOUSE; the Leader of the OPPOSITION also used to brief in the room, but now generally meets the Lobby in his office.

Central Lobby The *Rialto* of the PALACE OF WESTMINSTER, the crossroads midway between the COMMONS' and LORDS' chambers where members of the public gather, and wait to meet their MPs. On one side of the ornately-decorated hall is a post office; on another the entrance to the STRANGERS' GALLERY.

Clear the lobbies! In the HOUSE OF COMMONS, the cry of the SPEAKER on calling a DIVISION.

division lobbies The corridors on either side of each CHAMBER at Westminster, and in many other legislatures, through which members have to pass during a DIVISION to have their votes recorded by the TELLERS and the clerks attending them. In the HOUSE OF COMMONS each lobby used to have two desks at which votes are recorded; a third in each was added by Speaker Betty Boothroyd in June 1997 to speed voting after Labour's LANDSLIDE election victory produced a large imbalance in numbers.

Liberty Lobby *See* LIBERTY.

mass lobby At WESTMINSTER, an organised visit by hundreds or even thousands of people exercising their democratic right to see their MP as a means of pressing a particular case – for instance for THIRD WORLD development. The mass lobby has evolved as a campaigning weapon because it provides contact with individual MPs – and because demonstrations as such are banned from the PRECINCTS OF THE HOUSE.

Members' Lobby The lobby at the entrance to the HOUSE OF COMMONS CHAMBER at WESTMINSTER; the CHURCHILL ARCH links the two. It is dominated by life-size bronze statues of Churchill, LLOYD GEORGE and ATTLEE, MPs of their respective parties touching their toe-caps for luck, Churchill's being the shiniest. Doors from it lead to all three WHIPS' OFFICES, and the VOTE OFFICE is next to the arch. The lobby, to which only MPs, Lobby journalists and officers of the House are admitted, is guarded by two police officers at the 'public' end and two BADGE MESSENGERS beneath the arch. The lobby is at its most animated just after a DIVISION, when MPs who have come in for the vote catch up with one another, or buttonhole Ministers they have been trying to reach.

> Benign and yet menacing, she would stalk through the lobby, one arm weighted with the heavy satchel which contained the papers on family allowances, another arm dragging the even heavier satchel in which were stored the more recent papers about refugees. Recalcitrant ministers would quail before the fire of her magnificent eyes.
>
> HAROLD NICOLSON on the Independent MP Eleanor Rathbone, the *Spectator,* 1946

on Lobby terms A conversation conducted under the rules of the lobby; most lunches between political journalists and senior WESTMINSTER figures take place on this basis, with information freely imparted provided the source is not divulged.

lobbyist A person who, often quite properly, attempts to influence legislators to pursue courses of action more favourable to either a single business or interest, or a range of clients. The term originated in New York state politics, when men eager to extract favours from legislators waited for them in the lobby of the State Capitol as they were not allowed on the Floor. As early as 1819 Dennis Lynch could write:

> Corruption has erected her court on the heights of the Hudson, in the avenues of Albany, in the lobbies of the legislature . . . Her throne was the lobby.

Lobbyists were evident in the US Capitol by 1832, and throughout the 19th century were seen by those not in receipt of their favours as the vanguard of corruption. Isaac Bassett, first a Senate PAGE and then assistant doorkeeper from 1831 to 1895, wrote: 'Most of them are blackmailers. They are so crafty and treacherous that public men, men of reputation and means, are always on the alert against them.' President Buchanan denounced 'the host of contractors, speculators, stock-jobbers and lobby members who haunt the halls of Congress all desirous . . . on any and every pretext to get their arms into the public treasury, and sufficient to alarm every friend of the country'. As the Federal government and regulation grew, so did the scope and number of lobbyists. Sen. James Reed of Mississippi was moved to declare: 'A lobbyist is anyone who opposes legislation I want', and Harry S TRUMAN said: 'The President is the only lobbyist 150 million Americans have. The other 20 million are able to employ people to represent them.' The practice of lobbying, and with it lobbying firms great and small, has spread to all the world's major LEGISLATURES. Since 1946 all lobbyists in WASHINGTON have been required to register; that has not eliminated blatant INFLUENCE-PEDDLING, but it has enabled reputable lobbyists to maintain professional ethics. They had a friend in John F. KENNEDY, who wrote in 1956:

> Lobbyists are in many cases expert technicians and capable of explaining complex and difficult subjects in a clear, understandable fashion. Because our congressional representation is based on geographical boundaries, the lobbyists who speak for the various economic, commercial and other factional interests of the country serve a very useful purpose and have assumed an important role in the legislative process.

These technical skills make it hard for members of CONGRESS to out-argue them. Rep. Allard Lowenstein said: 'They have people who are able to spend out their time collating data on why pollution is good for River X. What Congressman can match that?'

> Lobbyists are men of revolutionary background – they are careful to see that no one who is taxed is unrepresented. Sen. EUGENE McCARTHY

> They protect a Congressman with small favours, while the rest of the world beats him up.
>
> WILLIAM GREIDER

Locarno Pacts A series of NON-AGGRESSION PACTS formulated at Locarno, Switzerland on 16 October 1925 and signed in London on 1 December. They guaranteed the post-VERSAILLES TREATY frontiers between

Germany and France, and Germany and Belgium. This settlement of Franco-German differences and the implied British and Italian guarantee of French territory appeared to herald a new era of peace and security (the Locarno spirit), and Germany was admitted to the LEAGUE OF NATIONS soon after (September 1926); ten years later, in March 1936, Germany renounced Locarno and remilitarised the Rhineland.

Loch Fyne summit The impromptu meeting on 9 May 2004 at which Gordon BROWN and John Prescott (*see* TWO JAGS) reputedly discussed a 'peaceful succession' for the Chancellor on the departure of Tony BLAIR. Press reports of the encounter, and the comment of Prescott, Blair's deputy, that the 'tectonic plates' in the party were shifting, were the first acknowledgment from within the Labour Cabinet that Blair's initially-charmed tenure might be coming to an end, rendered electorally weak by his association with George W. BUSH's policies and the conduct of US forces in Iraq (*see* ABU GHRAIB). Brown and Prescott were said to have conversed in the car park of the Loch Fyne Oyster Bar at Cairndow, Argyll, on their way back to the airport from a ceremony on Iona to mark the 10th anniversary of the death of John SMITH, at which Blair had not been present. The main weakness in the story was that the two men had spent three hours together in an official car with a security-cleared chauffeur, and had no need to stop to meet anywhere.

lock A hold exercised by a party on a particular organ of government. The term was invented by the US political commentator Horace Busby, who concluded that the Republicans had between the 1968 and 1984 elections secured a 'lock' on the Presidency, winning 77% of ELECTORAL COLLEGE votes. Correspondingly, the Democrats had a 'lock' on the HOUSE OF REPRESENTATIVES from 1954 to 1994, even in years of a Republican LANDSLIDE in elections to the WHITE HOUSE and SENATE.

lock-in In WHITEHALL, the terms under which journalists working against a deadline, and spokesmen for OPPOSITION parties, are allowed access to extremely sensitive documents shortly in advance of publication on condition that they do not leave the room until the document is either in the public domain, or so close to it that they are unable to LEAK the contents. The procedure was first used in 1996 for the release of the SCOTT REPORT and has since been used with increasing frequency; less sensitive documents continue to be circulated to the media beforehand as CFRs with an EMBARGO on publication.

lock-out The exclusion from their workplace of workers taking or threatening INDUSTRIAL ACTION by their employers in order to pressure them into abandoning their action, negotiating or having terms forced upon them. A **lock-in** is a form of action that originated in America in the late 1960s, where workers occupy their workplace to win concessions from management or attempt to prevent its closure.

Lockerbie The UK's worst air disaster, caused by an act of terrorism that compounded and prolonged the international community's ostracism of Colonel Gaddafi's Libya. On 21 December 1988 a bomb made of SEMTEX exploded in the hold of a Pan American Boeing 747 en route from Frankfurt and London to New York, over the small southern Scottish town of Lockerbie. All 259 passengers, and eleven people on the ground, were killed. Pre-flight airport checks had been inadequate, despite warnings of terrorist attack received by the authorities weeks before. There were also claims that the CIA had been forewarned, as a number of US government personnel cancelled seats on the pre-Christmas flight. Two Libyan security agents were eventually named as complicit in the bombing, and after years of diplomatic standoff Gaddafi handed them over in 1999 for trial by a Scottish court in the Netherlands (*see* CAMP ZEIST). In January 2001 Amin Khalifa Fhimah was acquitted, but Abdelbasset el Meghrai was found guilty of murder and sentenced to a minimum 20 years; he was moved to Barlinnie prison, Glasgow, in March 2002 after his appeal was dismissed. Megrahi admitted being a Libyan agent, but denied involvement with the bombing. Some relatives of the victims continued to press for a public inquiry, disputing that Libya was the culprit; other alleged suspects included ABU NIDAL. Yet Gaddafi admitted responsibility to the UNITED NATIONS in August 2003, offering compensation to the families on a sliding scale depending on whether the UN agreed to lift SANCTIONS imposed in 1992. Diplomatic and commercial relations began to be restored later that year, first by Britain and later by America.

Lockheed scandal The furore arising from the discovery in 1976 that America's Lockheed Aircraft Corporation, in its eagerness to win overseas orders, had paid out $24.5 million in bribes. The former Japanese Prime Minister Kakuei Tanaka was arrested for receiving 500 million yen to ensure that All Nippon Airways bought Lockheed aircraft, though the charges never resulted in a conviction, and Prince Bernhard of the Netherlands, the consort of Queen Juliana, was disgraced for receiving $1.1 million; she abdicated soon after. In Italy eight arrests were made and two former defence ministers implicated over the purchase of Lockheed planes for the Air Force. The episode led CONGRESS to push through the Foreign Corrupt Practices Act against overseas bribery by US corporations, with some success.

locofocos The New York-based branch of the DEMOCRATIC PARTY in the mid to late 1830s, which opposed banks, paper money and all monopolies, and demanded equal rights for all men. They got their name, which was not intended as a compliment, because the conservatives who controlled TAMMANY HALL found themselves outnumbered at a meeting on 29 October 1835 and tried to end it by turning out the gas lights. The radicals lit candles, using the newly-invented 'loco-foco' friction matches, and continued the session. The next day the *New York Courier and Enquirer* christened them 'Locofocos', and the name stuck.

locomotive for growth A country whose economic strength is such that, if it chose, it could REFLATE its economy and drag the rest of the industrialised world out of RECESSION. The term has most frequently been used of Germany, in the late 1970s when Britain and America each urged Bonn in vain to adopt a more expansionist policy, and again in 1992 when Britain and other European states pressed for the BUNDESBANK to reduce its cripplingly high interest rates.

Lodge, the The official residence in Canberra of the Prime Minister of Australia.
Lodge Reservations The fourteen objections to the VERSAILLES TREATY proposed in September 1919 by the US Senate's Committee on Foreign Relations, aimed at limiting the scope of the LEAGUE OF NATIONS and America's involvement in it. They were named after the committee's chairman, Sen. Henry Cabot Lodge Snr President WILSON asserted that the reservations nullified the Treaty and urged his supporters to oppose the Treaty itself if they were added to it. In the event the Senate rejected the Treaty – with or without the reservations.

log. log cabin and hard cider A WHIG slogan in America's 1840 Presidential election, praising the supposedly simple ways of General William Harrison (*see* TIPPECANOE AND TYLER TOO) compared with the foppish extravagances of President van Buren (*see* OLD KINDERHOOK). In fact Harrison was anything but a cider-swilling frontiersman, his lavish lifestyle putting him heavily in debt until he found two lucrative sinecures. The origin of the slogan was a comment by one of Henry Clay's friends at the nominating convention in 1839:

> Give him a barrel of hard cider and a pension of two thousand a year and, my word for it, he will sit the remainder of his days in a log cabin, by the side of a sea-coal fire and study moral philosophy.

The phrase caught on so much that Daniel Webster felt he had to apologise for not having been brought up in a log cabin.
Log Cabin Bill An early 1840s forerunner of America's HOMESTEAD ACT, signed by President Tyler, under which settlers moving westward could claim 160 acres of land before it was put on sale, later paying $1.25 an acre.
Log Cabin to White House An essential of the American Dream, the rise of a humble backwoods boy to become President. The phrase, striking echoes of 'LOG CABIN AND HARD CIDER', was the title of the 1881 biography of President Garfield (*see* BOATMAN JIM) by W. M. Thayer, but became linked with Abraham LINCOLN (*see* RAIL-SPLITTER). For his 91st birthday in 1959, John Nance Garner (*see* CACTUS JACK), Vice President to Franklin D. ROOSEVELT, was presented with a cake in the form of the log cabin he had been born in.

> It is harder for a leader to be born in a palace than in a log cabin.
> WOODROW WILSON, campaigning in Denver, 7 October 1912

logrolling In the US CONGRESS, dealings enabling members to get their BILLS through, from the phrase: 'Help me roll my log, and I'll roll yours.' For instance, in the 1930s urban legislators backed farm Bills, so those from farm states voted for urban reforms. The term also covers concessions a President will make to get his programmes enacted.

> A game of trading favors, in which the President gives Congressmen bonbons and pastries to make them give away steak and potatoes.
> MARK GREEN, *Who Runs Congress?*

Loi Toubon Legislation promoted in 1994 by Edouard Balladur's Culture Minister

Jacques Toubon outlawing English words in many aspects of French life. France's Constitutional Court ruled that it was too sweeping and Toubon had to amend it, but it still made a considerable impact. *Compare* BILL 101 in Quebec.

Lok Sabha (Hindi. House of the People) The directly elected lower house of India's Parliament in New Delhi, whose majority governs the world's largest democracy under a CONSTITUTION approved in 1950. The upper house, elected from state LEGISLATURES, is the Council of States (*Rajya Sabha*).

Lollards A group of Tory WETS founded in the mid-1970s to counter the influence of the THATCHERite right. It took its name – with its Medieval connotations of heresy – from the location of its first meeting, in the Lollards' Tower of Lambeth Palace where one member had a flat. During John MAJOR's premiership the Lollards worked with the 'Marsham' group, founded in 1993, to oust the hard right from key positions in the 1922 COMMITTEE.

Lombard League The ground-breaking movement, centred on Milan, that mushroomed in northern Italy from the late 1980s, transforming itself into LIGA NORD. Its twin targets were the drag of the crime- and poverty-stricken South on Italy's economy and government corruption; it was scarred by indictments against some of its own leaders.

Lomé Convention The agreements between the EUROPEAN COMMUNITY and 68 developing countries in Africa, the Caribbean and the Pacific (*see* ACP COUNTRIES) that authorise development aid and trade preference for some, but not all, of the world's poorest countries. The original agreement, signed in the capital of Togo, benefited 46 countries, mainly former French colonies; it was renewed in 1979, 1985, 1995 and 2000 (until 2007). The latest update angered some campaigning groups because it not only proffered aid but mandated the repatriation of citizens of signatory nations illegally present in the EU; in practice this has been little enforced.

London. London Bombings The UK's worst encounter with terrorism today (except for LOCKERBIE), the simultaneous explosions caused – by British-born Islamist SUICIDE BOMBERS – on three London underground trains at the height of the morning rush hour on 7 July 2005 and one on a bus an hour later that killed at least 56 people and injured 700 more. The worst of the casualties were on a Piccadilly Line train between Kings Cross and Russell Square, in a tight tunnel with rescue workers taking days to work through the front coach that had been most severely damaged. The atrocities took place the morning after London had been chosen over Paris to host the 2012 Olympics and while the G8 was in session at GLENEAGLES.

> We are all Londoners today.
>
> BERTRAND DELANOË, Mayor of Paris

> An atrocity like this redoubles everyone's determination not to be beaten by the bastards who did this.
>
> Health Secretary PATRICIA HEWITT

London Conference The conference in August 1992 where John MAJOR, as president of the EC COUNCIL OF MINISTERS, tried to open a PEACE PROCESS in Bosnia to end the war between the largely Muslim government, insurgent Serbs, and Croats. It generated an ineffective NO-FLY ZONE and a Geneva peace conference, with Dr David OWEN and former US Secretary of State Cyrus Vance engaged to bring the factions together. It would take military action against the Serbs and the belated engagement of the CLINTON administration to bring about a settlement at DAYTON.

London effect The damage done to the LABOUR PARTY in London and its environs in the 1987 general election by the antics of the 'Loony LEFT' in the party and local councils in the capital. While Labour registered modest gains elsewhere, it lost seats in and around London.

London Gazette The official daily publication in which the UK government issues public announcements. Few members of the public ever see it.

London Naval Conference A meeting between the UK, America, France, Italy and Japan between 21 January and 22 April 1930, which strengthened the WASHINGTON NAVAL TREATY, agreed on the regulation of submarine warfare and a five-year moratorium on capital ship construction, and limited US, British and Japanese battle-ship tonnage to a ratio of 10:10:7.

Declaration of London The international agreement of 1909 codifying the wartime rights of belligerents and NEUTRALS. Its interpretation brought difficulties between Britain and America early in WORLD WAR I over the Royal Navy intercepting US merchant ships to seize cargos bound for neutral ports. The dispute was soon overshadowed by Germany's warning in February 1915 that its submarines would sink any neutral (including American) ship trading with Britain, and that citizens of neutral countries should stay off Allied ships.

Secret Treaty of London A secret alliance concluded with Italy on 26 April 1915 by the Triple ENTENTE of Britain, France and Russia. It agreed terms for Italy's entry into WORLD WAR I against Germany and Austria, which had also been courting her since war broke out. Italy committed her forces to the Entente in return for promises of territory: South Tyrol, Trentino, Trieste and portions of Dalmatia. The Allies also promised to recognise Italian sovereignty over the Dodecanese and let Italy expand her holdings in Libya, Somalia and Eritrea. The text of the treaty was LEAKED by the Bolsheviks in 1917 and published in a Swedish newspaper, causing embarrassment at the 1919 Paris peace conference where Woodrow WILSON was pledged to stamp out secret diplomacy.

Lone Ranger The nickname bestowed by US Senators on their Democratic colleague **Wayne Morse** (1900–74) of Oregon, because he was so frequently left voting in a minority. The original Lone Ranger was the fictitious sole survivor of six Texas Rangers ambushed by the 'Hole-in-the-Wall' Butch Cavendish gang, who became a masked crusader against injustice in the West with his trusty Indian companion Tonto. He was created in 1933 by the radio scriptwriter Fran Striker and producer George W. Trendle; the first Lone Ranger film was made in 1938, starring Lee Powell and Chief Thundercloud; the TV series of over 200 episodes, starring Clayton Moore and Jay Silverheels, ran from 1949 to 1957.

long. long hot summer The climate in which INNER CITY tensions boil over into riots. Originally used of the sticky summer climate in the GHETTO areas of America's big cities, the term has crossed the Atlantic to cover violence on summer nights in Britain's inner cities and run-down housing estates – and the travails of a government faced with successive crises at this time of year. The phrase emerged during July/August 1964, when looters ran riot in the ghettos of New York, Rochester, Philadelphia, Chicago and three New Jersey cities. The wave of violence began on 18 July when an off-duty New York policeman shot a black youth; in the ensuing riot one person was killed, 114 injured, 185 arrests were made and 112 businesses attacked. The WATTS riots the next year, and the three summers' widespread disorder that followed, gave the phrase universal currency, though such unrest has become much less frequent.

Long March The epic migration in 1934–35 of 100,000 Chinese Communists from Kiangsi Soviet in south-east China to a new base at Yenan in the north-west. The KMT army under Chiang Kai-Shek had launched a series of offensives against Kiangsi after 1931; in October 1934 CHAIRMAN MAO led a breakout through Nationalist lines and marched north. They arrived in October 1935, but after a trek of 6,000 miles through rugged terrain, subject to near starvation, freezing cold and Nationalist attacks, only 30,000 of the Red Army survived. In Yenan, Mao consolidated his leadership of the Communist Party and prepared the military, economic and political foundations for the eventual Communist victory in 1949.

Long Tom A contemporary nickname for Thomas JEFFERSON, who stood 6ft. 2½in. tall.

longest suicide note in history The damning verdict passed on the LABOUR PARTY's 1983 election manifesto, 'PEACE, JOBS, FREEDOM', on which the party went down to its worst defeat since 1935, by Gerald Kaufman (1930–), who as a moderate member of the SHADOW CABINET was poles apart from its trenchantly left-wing content.

Longworth Building The second of the huge office buildings erected on and around CAPITOL HILL since 1908 to accommodate CONGRESSmen's offices, committee rooms and other facilities; being less lavish than more recent additions, its rooms are allocated to junior members of the HOUSE. It is named after Nicholas Longworth (1869–1931), Speaker of the House 1924–30. Longworth had a reputation as a womaniser. Once a Congressman rashly ran his hand over Longworth's bald pate and said: 'It feels just like my wife's backside.' Longworth felt it himself and replied: 'So it does.'

loony left *see* LEFT.

loop, the An originally WASHINGTON term for the tight circle within which important decisions are taken and sensitive information circulated. Those '**in the loop**' in and close to the WHITE HOUSE receive essential digests of information, including the FTPO, have their own secure telephone network and have ACCESS to the President. Those '**out of**

the loop' are not part of the apparatus of power. The term is now in general use for any person or group involved in a particular decision-making process.

loose cannon An uncontrollable ally, someone who although determinedly on one's side is prone to counterproductive actions and comments. Used by WASHINGTON officials and journalists since the 1980s – during the IRAN-CONTRA revelations, Lt.-Col Oliver North was referred to as a loose cannon in the REAGAN ADMINISTRATION – the term now has global application. The expression dates from the days of sail, when a cannon not properly secured to a warship's deck was a danger to the crew when the ship pitched and rolled.

Lord The blanket colloquial title for any British PEER save for a DUKE. The custom is to refer to Viscount, Earl or Lord X on the first occasion and Lord X thereafter, but frequently 'Lord' is used throughout.

Lord Advocate The head of Scotland's legal system. The Lord Advocate used to be a member of the UK government, generally with a PEERAGE, but with DEVOLUTION the post lost its semi-political status. The post in any event has generally gone to a distinguished lawyer who supported the party in power, rather than to an active politician.

Lord Chancellor The senior UK CABINET member who has traditionally been both head of the English legal system and SPEAKER of the HOUSE OF LORDS. At the State Opening of Parliament, the Lord Chancellor has to present the Sovereign with the text of the GRACIOUS SPEECH, then walk backwards down the steps of the Throne to avoid turning his back on the monarch. Queen Elizabeth II eventually granted an exemption to the octogenarian Lord Hailsham because he had an arthritic knee. Tony BLAIR marked the post, which dates back to the Middle Ages, for abolition in his RESHUFFLE of June 2003 on the departure of Lord Irvine (*see* MASTER OF THE ROLLS), who had hoped to be its final occupant. But having appointed his former flatmate Lord Falconer to the new position of Secretary for Constitutional Affairs and declared his intention to replace the Lords' judicial functions with a SUPREME COURT, Blair discovered that legislation was needed for this. Falconer was obliged to take the title of Lord Chancellor, put on the wig and gown that went with the job and sit on the WOOLSACK. However, unlike his predecessors, Falconer, though amply qualified, did not sit as a judge. Senior judges and Conservative peers fought a rearguard action against Blair's plan, but when the 2005 Constitutional Reform Act, was eventually passed, the Lord Chancellor now does not need to be either a peer or a lawyer.

Lord Cupid The nickname bestowed on Viscount Palmerston (*see* PAM) in the 1830s by *The Times*. It referred to his devastating reputation with women.

Lord Haw-Haw Possibly the best-known nickname to come from WORLD WAR II, that of **William Joyce** (1906–46), who broadcast NAZI PROPAGANDA to the British people from Germany. The name, coined by Jonah Barrington, radio correspondent of the *Daily Express*, reflected his drawling, exaggerated Oxbridge accent. Joyce's broadcasts, intended to threaten and demoralise, made him a figure of derision and loathing in Britain, but their tone and remarkably well-informed material attracted hundreds of thousands of listeners. This worried the government, even though the broadcasts probably stiffened British determination rather than weakening it. Joyce was hanged for TREASON after the war, despite being of Irish descent and insisting he was not a British subject.

Lord High Everything Else An all-purpose politician, generally invaluable to his or her leader or loyal to the point of subservience, who may be appointed or volunteer to take on almost any task. The title originally belonged to POOH-BAH, in Gilbert and Sullivan's *The Mikado*.

Lord Lieutenant The title of the Queen's official representative in each UK county or region; the position is largely ceremonial and has no political significance, but conveys considerable prestige.

Lord Love-a-duck of Limehouse The title which the Labour Prime Minister Clement ATTLEE once said he would choose if forced to accept a PEERAGE, 'Lord love-a-duck' being a Cockney expression for 'come off it'. In old age he relented, accepting an EARLDOM.

Lord Mayor *See* MAYOR.

Lord Porn The tabloids' nickname for Frank Pakenham, 7th Earl of Longford (1905–2001), a champion of moral causes, who in 1972 held an unofficial inquiry into pornography in Britain and on the Continent, and the state of the nation's morality. He campaigned for a ban on school sex education without parental consent, stiffer penalties for breaches of the obscenity laws, and a higher moral tone for films, television and the Press. He earned his nickname leading a fact-finding mission to the sex parlours of Scandinavia, accompanied by a throng of Fleet Street journalists who couldn't believe their luck. Longford, a convert to Catholicism, had previously been an Allied representative in post-war Germany, capturing hearts by insisting on kissing the ring of a German cardinal who called at his office; he served in two Labour governments, resigning as LORD PRIVY SEAL in 1968 in protest at Harold WILSON's deferment of an increase in the school leaving age. Wilson described him to the *Daily Mirror* publisher Cecil King as

> Quite hopeless. Frank has a mental age of twelve.

Lord President of the Council The member of the UK CABINET who heads the PRIVY COUNCIL in its meetings with the Sovereign. The post is often combined with that of Leader of the COMMONS or the LORDS.

Lord Privy Seal Traditionally the title of the keeper of the Great SEAL of England, and now of a member of the CABINET, sometimes a second Minister in a department (such as the Foreign Office), sometimes a Minister without PORTFOLIO. Confusingly, the Lord Privy Seal is usually not a member of the HOUSE OF LORDS.

> Neither a lord, nor a privy, nor a seal.
> S. D. BAILEY, *British Parliamentary Democracy*

Lord Suit The nickname bestowed by *Private Eye* on Lord Young of Graffham (1932–), the close associate of Margaret THATCHER who was brought in from the private sector in 1982 to chair the Manpower Services Commission, was appointed to the CABINET in 1984 and went on to serve as Employment Secretary and Trade and Industry Secretary. He was eager to become CONSERVATIVE PARTY chairman after the 1987 ELECTION, but was blocked by Tory grandees headed by Viscount Whitelaw (*see* WILLIE). Lord Young earned the sobriquet because he epitomised the MEN IN SUITS with successful business careers who lionised Mrs Thatcher and were rewarded with high positions. His tenure at the DTI is chiefly memorable for large payments to advertising agencies and a botched reorganisation of Britain's pubs; he later became chairman of the PRIVATISED telecoms company Cable and Wireless.

> Other Ministers bring me problems; David brings me solutions. MARGARET THATCHER

Lords, House of *See* HOUSE.

Lords and Commons The title of a number of sports teams comprising, MPs, peers and their friends which play friendly matches against club sides, mainly in the London area. The cricket XI is a particular institution; a sample eleven c. 1980 included Peter Brooke (*see* MY DARLING CLEMENTINE), Michael Morris, later Deputy Speaker, the future NORTHERN IRELAND Minister and MEP Robert Atkins, two Tory backbenchers, a recent Oxford blue and the author.

loser. The winner of this Presidential election may never be known, but the identity of the loser is perfectly clear. The observation of Justice John Paul Stevens on 12 December 2000 in the case of BUSH V GORE which finally determined the outcome of the Presidential election. The official final margin of Bush's hotly disputed victory over Gore in the decisive state of Florida was just over 500 votes.

Louisiana purchase America's acquisition from France in 1803 of the 828,000 sq. miles (2,144,000 sq. km.) of territory between the Mississippi and the Rockies, which doubled the young country's size. Though they included New Orleans, the lands involved stretched well north and west of Louisiana. They were unexpectedly offered by Napoleon, who had just recovered them from Spain, for a bargain $11.5 million, plus $3.75 million to settle claims against France by US citizens. Talleyrand told emissaries from President JEFFERSON who signed the transfer on 30 April without the prior authority of CONGRESS:

> I suppose you will make the most of it.

Louvre accord An agreement between the G6 countries, reached in Paris in February 1987, to halt the slide of the dollar on world currency markets and establish a better balance of trade, and encourage NON-INFLATIONARY world economic growth. It stabilised the dollar in the short term by boosting confidence in the US currency and attracting funds to New York, but has been blamed by some for the stock market crash on BLACK MONDAY that October.

Love Story The tear-jerking 1970s film of a Harvard student and his girlfriend who dies of cancer, for which Vice President Al GORE claimed in 1997 to be the inspiration. Gore maintained that the story was 'loosely based' on himself and his wife Tipper; the couple had known *Love Story*'s author Eric Segal at university. The story was half true: Segal had in fact based the character of the preppy hockey player Oliver Barrett IV partly on Gore and partly on his college roommate, the actor Tommy Lee Jones.

loyal. Loyal Address The formal reply sent by the HOUSE OF COMMONS to the GRACIOUS SPEECH (QUEEN'S SPEECH), which provides the peg for four or five days of debate that take place immediately after the Sovereign has delivered it.

Loyalists (1) The supporters during the AMERICAN REVOLUTION of continued links with the British crown, tens of thousands of whom sailed for Canada when the cause was lost. *See also* EMPIRE LOYALISTS. (2) In NORTHERN IRELAND, the vociferous, sometimes violent, usually working-class, supporters of an enduring UNION with Britain. The term came into its own in the early 1970s with the formation of Loyalist PARAMILITARY groups, and the GENERAL STRIKE by Loyalist workers in 1974 which brought down the first POWER-SHARING Executive.

loyalty boards The panels set up by President TRUMAN under an EXECUTIVE ORDER of 22 March 1947 to investigate the loyalty (freedom from Communist links) of over 3 million Federal employees. Two thousand resigned, 212 were fired as SECURITY RISKS and just one, Judith Coplon, was twice convicted of spying, but freed because of illegal FBI BUGGING. Truman's initiative fuelled the climate of anti-Communist hysteria that enabled MCCARTHYISM to flourish, but did not prevent the Republicans branding him 'soft on Communism'.

LP The UK CABINET COMMITTEE which puts together and supervises the legislative programme embodied in the QUEEN'S SPEECH. It is chaired by the LEADER OF THE HOUSE.

LSE London School of Economics (and Political Science). The unspectacular complex of buildings in Houghton Street, off the Aldwych, which since 1895 has turned out many of the English-speaking world's political leaders and thinkers. Most but by no means all have been on the left, influenced by such mentors as the School's founder Sidney Webb (1858–1947), the controversial LABOUR PARTY chairman Harold Laski (1893–1950, *see* THANK YOU FOR YOUR LETTER) and Professor Anthony Giddens, progenitor of the THIRD WAY. LSE, part of London University since 1900, was the scene of bitter student unrest in 1968. In 1991 a proposal for it to move to then-vacant COUNTY HALL attracted widespread support, but the School was outbid by a Japanese hotel chain.

Lublin committee Polish Committee of National Liberation. A group of left-wing Poles sponsored by the Soviets during WORLD WAR II as a pliant alternative to the Polish government-in-exile in London. After the RED ARMY's liberation of east Poland in July 1944, and after the Germans had been cynically left to put down the WARSAW UPRISING, the committee was installed in Lublin and recognised by Moscow as the legitimate authority. It was recognised by Britain and America on 5 July 1945, two months after the end of the war in Europe.

Lubyanka One of Moscow's most notorious prisons under Soviet rule, reserved for political prisoners only. Thousands of NKVD victims were imprisoned, interrogated, tortured and executed there. The Lubyanka, in Dzerzhinsky Square, was originally the headquarters of an insurance company; it was taken over by the CHEKA in the 1920s. The NKVD offices occupied the outer section and the prison cells were located within an inner courtyard in a nine-storey building once used by the insurance company as a boarding house. Around 110 cells held up to 200 prisoners; executions were carried out in the basement.

Lucy (1) The name given by the Labour Cabinet Minister Barbara (later Baroness) Castle (1910–2002) to the vivid red wig that superseded the equally fiery locks of her youth. In her *Diaries*, she recorded how when visiting an old people's home near Nottingham destroyed by fire in 1974, 'Lucy' was caught by a wire trailing from the ceiling. The TV cameras were on Mrs Castle, then Social Services Secretary, and she 'froze in embarrassment'. Fortunately for her, no one present noticed – including the author. (2) The guide dog who accompanied David Blunkett prior to Labour's victory in 1997, and then when he was Education Secretary and, for a while, Home Secretary. Lucy, a cross between a Labrador and a curly coat retriever, took over from OFFA in 1994 and retired in January 2003, succeeded by her half-sister SADIE. Lucy made her mark in politics by vomiting on the floor of the COMMONS Chamber in 1999. After William HAGUE asked his final questions as Conservative leader in 2001, she got up and left the Chamber.

Luddite An intransigent, irrational opponent

of industrial progress; a term much used of UK TRADE UNIONS in the 1960s and '70s, and applied in America to any stubbornly backward-looking person.

I voted for Mario Cuomo for Governor of New York in 1982 because I liked what he was saying and because I thought his opponent, Lewis E. Lehrman, was a social Luddite and a moral troglodyte.
WILLIAM E. KENNEDY, *New York Times Book* Review, 13 May 1984

The original Luddites were workmen discontented by mechanisation who, from 1811 to 1816, toured factories (especially in the Nottingham area) breaking the new machines they believed were putting men out of work. They were named after Ned Ludd, a simple boy from Leicestershire, who chased boys who were baiting him into a house and broke two stocking-frames there; the fictitious leader of the protesters was called General Ludd.

Lukens case The scandal surrounding Rep. Donald (Buzz) Lukens, an Ohio Republican, who was jailed for 30 days in 1989 for a sexual act with a minor, a CAPITOL lift operator. Lukens was defeated in the 1990 elections while appealing against his conviction.

lunatic fringe *See* FRINGE.

lust in my heart The key phrase of an extraordinary interview Jimmy CARTER gave to *Playboy* magazine at the height of the 1976 Presidential CAMPAIGN which staggered Americans with its frankness, even naïveté, and disconcerted some of his fellow 'born again' Christians. At the end of the interview with Robert Scheer, Carter made one last attempt to show that he was not a narrow-minded fundamentalist; his remarks about sex certainly did that when *Playboy* appeared on 20 September, to headlines like 'Carter on Sin and Lust . . . I'm Human, I'm Tempted'. Referring to Christ's teaching that 'anyone who looks on a woman with lust in his heart has already committed ADULTERY', Carter said:

I've looked on a lot of women with lust. I've committed adultery in my heart many times. This is something that God recognises I will do – and I have done it – and God forgives me for it. But that doesn't mean that I condemn someone who not only looks on a woman with lust but leaves his wife and shacks up with somebody out of wedlock . . . Christ says, Don't consider yourself better than someone else because one guy screws a whole bunch of women while the other guy is loyal to his wife. The guy who's loyal to his wife ought not to be condescending or proud because of the relative degree of sinfulness.

Carter offered up a politically embarrassing hostage to fortune in the same interview, bracketing LBJ with Richard NIXON for 'lying, cheating and distorting the truth'; he backtracked on this, but LADY BIRD Johnson made clear her frosty disapproval.

Jimmy talks too much, but at least people know he's honest and doesn't mind answering questions. ROSALYNN CARTER

Luxembourg compromise The informal arrangement within the EU's COUNCIL OF MINISTERS under which a member state can claim the right to VETO a decision if its 'very important interests' are at stake, instead of the issue being decided by a qualified MAJORITY. The Compromise, which has no legal status, stems from a statement by France when ending a six-month boycott of the Council (*see* empty CHAIR) in Luxembourg in 1966. The other five members at the time accepted it, and it has been invoked from time to time since, mainly over farm legislation; Britain tried and failed to do so in a bid to block the Community's SOCIAL CHAPTER. It has fallen into disuse, despite the occasional threat, since the MAASTRICH TREATY took effect.

lying in state (1) A people's penultimate tribute to an exceptional leader or national figure, when the coffin containing their body stands, prior to a State funeral, in a revered public place so that the public may pass by it. In Britain, WESTMINSTER has seen the lying-in-state of kings and queens, and statesmen from GLADSTONE to CHURCHILL. In WASHINGTON, the coffins of 27 Americans – some Presidents (four of them assassinated), distinguished Senators and the Unknown Serviceman from the VIETNAM WAR – have lain in the ROTUNDA of the CAPITOL. (2) The sobriquet bestowed by cynics on the evidence given by the Colonial Secretary Joseph Chamberlain to the Parliamentary inquiry at WESTMINSTER into the JAMESON RAID, in which he insisted that he had not been involved in planning the attack on the Transvaal and had no foreknowledge of it; only after his death did evidence come to light confirming that he had indeed lied to the inquiry.

lynching The ugliest feature of American life in the near past (though it has occurred elsewhere): the 'execution' by a mob of a person believed to have escaped punishment, or simply of the 'wrong' colour, which became common in the Deep South after the CIVIL WAR, though not confined to that region. Up to 5000 Americans have been lynched since records were first kept in 1885; most were black, though Jews, Catholics and Italians were also killed. Leaders of lynch mobs, often members of the KU KLUX KLAN, were seldom punished locally, and in 1900 a black North Carolina Congressman, G. H. White, brought in a BILL to make lynching a Federal crime. In that year 105 black Americans were lynched; the number declined as economic revival made Southern whites less interested in finding scapegoats, but revived during WORLD WAR I to a point where President WILSON compared the mobs with the German enemy. Between 1918 and 1927 454 people were lynched, 416 of them black; 42 were burned to death. President TRUMAN proposed an anti-lynching law as part of his FAIR DEAL, but Southern conservatives in Congress stifled it. Occasional lynchings continued into the 1950s, but they virtually ended with the advance of the CIVIL RIGHTS movement.

The word originates with Capt. William Lynch (1742–1820), a Virginia magistrate who on 22 September 1780 formed a band to clear Pittsylvania County of 'unlawful and abandoned wretches' by such means; the 'lynch-men' were sworn to secrecy. The diary of the surveyor Andrew Ellicott records that under Lynch's system of justice

> the person who it was supposed ought to suffer death was placed on a horse with his hands tied behind him and a rope about his neck which was fastened to the limb of a tree over his head. In this situation the person was left, and when the horse in pursuit of food or any other cause moved from his position the unfortunate person was left suspended by the neck – this was called 'aiding the civil authority'.

> It may be true that the law cannot make a man love me, but it can keep him from lynching me, and I think that's pretty important.
>
> MARTIN LUTHER KING Jr

lynching Northern-style *See* Adam Clayton POWELL.

judicial lynching *See* Clarence THOMAS CASE.

Lynskey Tribunal The tribunal set up by Clement ATTLEE in 1948 under Mr.Justice Lynskey to investigate allegations in the Board of Trade that Ministers and officials had been taking bribes. The key witness was Sydney Stanley, a Polish-born confidence trickster who had made money by trading on his supposed links with people in power. Stanley was exposed as a liar, but some Ministers had been slow to see through him. No successful bribery on any scale was detected, but misjudgements and unwise acceptance of gifts were; John Belcher, a junior trade minister, was forced out of politics, and George Gibson, a trade union-nominated director of the Bank of England, reprimanded. The affair also damaged Hugh Dalton (*see* BUDGET LEAK), who had been offered a directorship by Stanley while out of office (he had just returned as Chancellor of the DUCHY OF LANCASTER) and had written him a 'Dear Stan' letter.

Lysenkoism The bogus science, based on the maverick ideas of the Soviet geneticist **Trofim Denisovich Lysenko** (1898–1976) and the horticulturist I. V. Michurin (1855–1935), that caused an ideological and political upheaval in Soviet academic circles from the 1930s and convinced Western scientists of the lunacy of STALINISM. Lysenko claimed to have proof that environmentally-induced changes in cereal seed to improve germination could be inherited by successive generations of plant. This contradicted prevailing scientific orthodoxy, notably the genetic theories of Mendel and others. Stalin, untroubled by lack of corroboration, threw his weight behind the young Lysenko, and Soviet IDEOLOGUES entwined his ideas with orthodox MARXISM to denounce the conventional wisdom as BOURGEOIS. Nicolai Vavilov, a notable critic of Lysenko, was in 1938 replaced by him as president of the V. I. Lenin All-Union Academy of Agricultural Sciences; Vavilov was exiled to Siberia with other respected geneticists, dying in 1943. Lysenko became director of the Genetic Institute of the Soviet Union in 1940, and in 1948 reached the peak of his influence with a report – backed by the CENTRAL COMMITTEE of the Communist Party – entitled *The Position in Biological Science*; all textbooks were rewritten to accommodate his theories. Lysenkoism kept its influence under Khrushchev; only after his fall in 1964 was it exposed as a fraud that had made Soviet genetics a laughing-stock for over three decades.

M

M0 One of seven definitions of MONEY SUPPLY used by economists and at various times from 1979 by successive Conservative CHANCELLORS OF THE EXCHEQUER – though much less by Gordon BROWN – choosing the measure or measures they considered most accurate and/or politically advantageous. M0 covers notes and coins in circulation plus banks' till money and balances with the Bank of England. **M1** is money in circulation plus private sector current accounts and transferable deposit accounts. **M2** was the FED's measure of growth in the money supply till disowned by Alan Greenspan in 1993, when he told CONGRESS in his HUMPHREY-HAWKINS message that US money supply was no longer SHADOWING M2.
M3 (formerly Sterling M3) is M1 plus all other private sector bank deposits plus certificates of deposit. When Nigel Lawson embraced M3, Labour MPs branded him the '**M3 rapist**' after a criminal of the day. **M4**, adopted by Norman Lamont after the DEVALUATION of 1992, is notes and coins in circulation plus private sector current accounts and most private sector bank deposits, plus holdings of money-market instruments.

Ma, Ma, Where's my pa? A Republican chant at the expense of the 1884 Democratic Presidential NOMINEE Grover CLEVELAND (*see* BEAST OF BUFFALO), who had improbably fathered a child out of wedlock by a 36-year-old Buffalo widow, Maria Halpin. Cleveland took the issue on the chin, telling aides: 'Above all, tell the truth.' With the Republicans attacking Cleveland as a 'moral leper' and the Democrats denouncing his rival James G. Blaine as a liar, Lord Bryce wrote that the contest seemed over 'the copulative habits of one and the prevaricative habits of the other'. The Democrats had the last laugh: when Cleveland was elected, they completed the couplet:

> Gone to the WHITE HOUSE, Ha! Ha! Ha!

Maastricht Treaty The treaty agreed by EUROPEAN COMMUNITY leaders at Maastricht in southern Holland in December 1991, which created the EUROPEAN UNION. Europe's greatest milestone since the Treaty of ROME provided for tighter political and economic union, the exercise of more SOVEREIGNTY by the Community itself, closer inter-governmental co-operation on foreign policy and justice, and a SINGLE CURRENCY. Britain initially opted out of the Treaty's SOCIAL CHAPTER and has so far failed to sign up to the single currency. The ratification process was long and painful, the treaty taking effect only on 1 November 1993. Denmark's 'No' vote in a referendum on 2 June 1992 and France's approval by just 2% put the treaty in jeopardy, critics led by Margaret THATCHER creating strong pressure in Britain's CONSERVATIVE PARTY for John MAJOR to renounce it. Major saw off rebels led by Norman Tebbit (*see* CHINGFORD SKINHEAD) at the party conference, but only scrambled a 3-vote majority with Liberal Democrat support in the PAVING DEBATE to start what turned into a marathon COMMITTEE STAGE of the Treaty Bill, despite a huge SECOND READING majority some months before. The UK ratified the Treaty on 2 August 1993, but only after a late government defeat on the Social Chapter, with a Vote of CONFIDENCE needed to override it.

MacArthur sacking President TRUMAN's dismissal of General Douglas MacArthur (1880–1964), US commander in the KOREAN WAR, for campaigning to extend the war by bombing and invading China against Truman's express orders. MacArthur's removal on 11 April 1951 caused a sensation, the young Sen. Richard NIXON saying:

> The happiest people in this country will be the Communists and their stooges.

The hero of America's Pacific victory and architect of post-war Japan was given ticker-tape welcomes in great cities and hailed by a JOINT SESSION of CONGRESS (*see* OLD SOLDIERS NEVER DIE). Commentators claimed his speech as one of the most memorable heard in the CAPITOL; Truman dismissed it as 'a bunch of bullshit'. MacArthur's political impact tailed off, leaving Truman largely vindicated. He reminisced:

> I fired MacArthur because he wouldn't respect the authority of the President. I didn't fire him because he was a dumb son of a bitch, although he was, but that's not against the law for generals. If it was, half to three-quarters of them would be in jail.

MacBird A satirical play staged in California in 1968 in protest at the VIETNAM WAR, and widely published as a pamphlet and pocket book. Based on Shakespeare's *Macbeth*, it equated President Lyndon B. JOHNSON with the murderous Lady Macbeth. Its author was Barbara Garson, who in 1992 would be the Socialist Party Vice Presidential candidate though declaring herself a 'proud, but inactive' member of the group.

MacBride principles The agenda for AFFIRMATIVE ACTION to secure jobs for the Catholic minority in NORTHERN IRELAND devised in 1976 by Dr Sean MacBride (1904–88), the former IRA chief of staff who renounced violence to become a distinguished international jurist. Its main thrust was the need for US companies to threaten to disinvest in the province to get more Catholics into skilled and managerial jobs. Supporters of the principles argued that Fair Employment legislation outlawing discrimination against Catholics had not broken the Protestant grip on what was left of the province's heavy industry. In America, the principles were used prior to the GOOD FRIDAY AGREEMENT to discourage corporate investment in Ulster and as a stick to beat the UK government. Few US corporations signed up to them, and SINN FEIN was the only Northern Ireland political party to endorse them.

McCarran Act The Internal Security Act passed by CONGRESS in September 1950, over President TRUMAN's VETO. It set up a Subversive Activities Control Board to register members of 'Communist-action or Communist-FRONT groups', made compassing the establishment of a TOTALITARIAN state a criminal conspiracy, and allowed for the establishment of 'emergency' CONCENTRATION CAMPS. The Act paved the way for MCCARTHYISM; Dean Acheson described its sponsor, Sen. Pat McCarran (1876–1954), as 'not a man who in the 18th century would have been considered a man of sensibility'. A second measure, the 1952 **McCarran-Walter Act**, again passed over Truman's veto, codified the immigration law, retaining the quota system but cutting numbers from eastern Europe while allowing a trickle from Pacific nations including Japan, which was allowed 185 migrants a year. The Act also gave the ATTORNEY-GENERAL power to deport any 'subversive' and any Communist or member of a Communist front group.

McCarthyism The anti-Communist WITCH-HUNT conducted in America between 1950 and 1954 by Sen. Joseph McCarthy (1909–57). McCarthy pilloried prominent people from film stars to senior officials of the TRUMAN administration as traitors, Communists and FELLOW-TRAVELLERS. His campaign cost many citizens their livelihoods, sent ten Hollywood scriptwriters to jail, ended several careers and led one senator to commit suicide; he even accused General George MARSHALL and Secretary of State Dean Acheson of treason. Communists were indeed active in America, but McCarthy's central charge was never proved. McCarthy, a Wisconsin Democrat, took his seat in 1946 despite a SUPREME COURT ruling against him after fabricating a heroic war career, running on the slogan '**Congress needs a tail-gunner**'. He was facing defeat for re-ELECTION when the FBI leaked highly suspect documents to him; at that point, said his assistant Roy Cohn, he 'bought Communism in much the same way as other people purchase a new automobile'. On 9 February 1950, in a speech at Wheeling, West Virginia, McCarthy claimed to have a list of 205 Communists 'known to the Secretary of State' working in the State Department; the next day the number was down to 57. The Republican establishment embraced him, Sen. Robert Taft telling him: 'If one case doesn't work, try another.' Richard NIXON was one of McCarthy's most vocal supporters, asserting that

> 96 per cent of 6,926 Communists, fellow travellers, sex perverts, people with criminal records, dope addicts, drunks and other security risks removed under the EISENHOWER security programme were hired by the Truman administration. Mr.TRUMAN, Dean Acheson and other administration officials covered up this Communist conspiracy and attempted to halt its exposure.

The campaign, promoted by McCarthy as **Americanism with its sleeves rolled up**, continued relentlessly with the Republican Eisenhower in office; he found it distasteful but shied away from confrontation. But in 1954 McCarthy overreached himself in the Army-McCarthy hearings (*see below*), was accused of taking bribes, hit back with an attack on Eisenhower that finally alienated his party and was 'condemned' by the SENATE; he died of drink three years later.

To the right, McCarthy was a patriot unveiling a dastardly plot, to liberals he was an obsessive who threatened them personally. Joseph Alsop termed him 'the only major politician in the country who can be labelled "liar" without the fear of libel'. General Marshall said McCarthy would 'sell his grandmother for any advantage'. The veteran WASHINGTON hostess Alice Roosevelt Longworth cut him dead: 'The policeman and trashman may call me Alice. You may not.' And Truman fumed: 'When even one American who has done no wrong is forced by fear to shut his mouth, then all Americans are in trouble. It is the job of us all to rise up and put a stop to this terrible business.'

> As squalid an episode as any in American history.
> HUGH BROGAN

Army-McCarthy hearings The episode that killed McCarthyism. On 22 April 1954 Senate hearings began into McCarthy's charge that the Secretary of the Army was thwarting the investigation of 'spying' at the Fort Monmouth, New Jersey signal facility; the Army claimed McCarthy had launched the probe because it refused one of his aides preferential treatment. Thirty-six days of testimony destroyed McCarthy's credibility. Under skilful cross-examination from army counsel Joseph B. Welch, the Senator was exposed as a bully. At the critical moment before 20 million viewers, Welch told him:

> Until this moment, Senator, I think I never really gauged your cruelty or your ruthlessness. Let us not assassinate this lad further. Senator, have you no sense of decency, sir, at long last? Have you left no sense of decency?

McCartney. Robert McCartney murder The episode which, together with the NORTHERN BANK ROBBERY, demonstrated at the start of 2005 that after ten years of the Northern Ireland PEACE PROCESS, the IRA and SINN FEIN had not fully accepted the rule of law. Robert McCartney from a strongly Republican family, was stabbed outside a Belfast bar by known IRA men on 30 January. Sinn Fein activists helped clean up afterwards. His five sisters appealed for justice, to the point, where the IRA expelled three of its members, Sinn Fein suspended seven activists and its president Gerry Adams indirectly (but unprecedentedly) handed the names of suspects to the police OMBUDSMAN. The IRA then offered the family to shoot the culprits itself – a proposal that further damaged Sinn Fein's hopes of re-entering devolved government. Adams now urged witnesses (who feared victimisation) to go to the police, which the movement had previously refused to recognise. None did; on St Patrick's Day the McCartney sisters were welcomed at the WHITE HOUSE, while Adams was denied an invitation. Later several arrests were made.

MacDonald, J. Ramsay (1866–1937), the first, and most controversial, British Labour Prime Minister and progenitor of the NATIONAL GOVERNMENT. A founding activist in the LABOUR PARTY, he led it from 1911 to 1914, resigning over its support for WORLD WAR I, and in 1922–31. He led Labour to power at the start of 1924, only to lose it at the close of the year after the ZINOVIEV LETTER affair. As party leader during the GENERAL STRIKE, he advised caution, saying:

> With the discussion of general strikes and Bolshevism and all that kind of thing, I have nothing to do at all. I respect the Constitution.

Labour returned to power in 1929, again as a minority government, but two years later economic crisis split the MacDonald Cabinet and 'RAMSAY MAC' and a minority of Labour Ministers and MPs formed the National Government in alliance with BALDWIN's Conservatives and a few Liberals. MacDonald's action became known to the majority who stayed with Labour as the GREAT BETRAYAL. But he felt he had to do it, writing: 'I commit suicide to save the crisis. If there is no other way I shall do it as cheerfully as an ancient Jap.' But breaking with his origins as the illegitimate son of a Scots servant girl had its attractions. As he made the break, he said: 'Tomorrow every duchess in London will be wanting to kiss me.' And MacDonald once observed: 'If God were to come to me and say: "Ramsay, would you rather be a country gentleman or Prime Minister?" I should say: "Please, God, a country gentleman."' But Henry Channon (*see* CHIPS) commented cruelly: 'Fatuous old snob, he is hated by all parties.' MacDonald's political somersaults led CHURCHILL to call him the BONELESS WONDER. LLOYD GEORGE declared that 'he has sufficient conscience to bother him, but not enough to keep him straight', while to Beatrice Webb he was 'a super-autocrat'.

Philip Snowden, who as CHANCELLOR had seen the National Government as a temporary expedient, warned: 'He will be used by the Tories for the same purpose as the reformed drunkard is used at the temperance meeting.' And as the Tory grip over his government increased, ATTLEE described him as

> a melancholy traveller on the Conservative ship.

MacDonald handed over to Baldwin prior to the 1935 election, in which he was unseated by Emmanuel (MANNY) Shinwell. He found another seat and stayed in the CABINET, but was in decline. He had never been good with words, Churchill once remarking: 'He has, more than any other man, the gift of compressing the largest amount of words into the smallest amount of thought.' But by the end he was telling the COMMONS: 'Society goes on and on and on. It is much the same with ideas.' During one of his last speeches the Labour MP James Maxton cried out: 'Sit down, man. You're a bloody tragedy.' He died on an ocean cruise, leading an anonymous obituarist to write:

> He dies as he lived, at sea.

mace (1) Throughout the English-speaking world, the visible symbol of the LEGISLATURE in session, removed when the SPEAKER vacates the CHAIR. At WESTMINSTER, a silver-gilt ornamental club carried by the SERJEANT-AT-ARMS to attend the Speaker (the LORD CHANCELLOR in the Lords). A mace has been used since at least 1415; the present one, with a head in the form of a closed crown, dates from 1660. Oliver Cromwell removed a previous mace to terminate the RUMP with the words: 'What shall we do with this bauble? Here, take it away.' Michael HESELTINE seized the mace and brandished it in 1976 in protest at the passage of legislation to nationalise aircraft and shipbuilding. And in 1989 Labour's Ron Brown (*see* AFGHAN RON) was suspended for removing the mace and dropping it, causing minor damage. In WASHINGTON, the first HOUSE mace was destroyed when the British burned the CAPITOL. The present one is a silver and ebony copy of the original, made in 1841. Slim, elegant and 46 inches long, it comprises an eagle on a globe surmounting bound rods representing the first thirteen States. (2) A form of riot gas, causing a burning sensation in the eyes, nose and throat and temporarily incapacitating the recipient. It was used by police in America in the late 1960s and early '70s, particularly against anti-VIETNAM WAR demonstrators. The name is probably taken from the spice obtained from nutmeg.

Machiavellian Referring to the ruthless and cynical exercise of power for self-seeking purposes, so that the end justifies the means. From the doctrines of the Florentine diplomat and political theorist Niccolò Machiavelli (1469–1527), whose best-known work is *The Prince*. Machiavelli, Edward Pearce points out, was 'a rather unsuccessful politician who suffered torture and imprisonment', but his advice has left a lasting impact. Some examples are benign, such as that 'a man who is made prince by the people should work to retain their friendship'. But he also wrote:

> A man who wishes to act virtuously necessarily comes to grief among so many who are not virtuous. Therefore if a prince wishes to maintain his rule he must learn how not to be virtuous.

> If an injury has to be done to a man, it should be so severe that his vengeance need not be feared.

> A wise prince sees to it that never, in order to attack someone, does he become the ally of a prince more powerful than himself. If you win, you are the powerful king's prisoner.

One of the most ringing denunciations of *The Prince* came from John Wesley (1703–91), the founder of Methodism, who wrote:

> If all the other doctrines of devils which have been committed to writing since letters were in the world were collected together in one volume, it would fall short of this; and that, should a Prince form himself by this book, so calmly recommending hypocrisy, treachery, lying, robbery, oppression, adultery, whoredom and murder of all kinds, Domitian or Nero would be an angel of light compared to that man.

machine politics In America, the interweaving of patronage and political organisation to create a self-perpetuating, normally Democratic, city or state government under powerful BOSSes, dedicated to serving its own, but on occasionally fulfilling genuine public, needs. Strongly rooted by the 1820s in East Coast Irish communities, it spread westward and across ethnic divides. New York (TAMMANY HALL), Chicago (the DALEY MACHINE) and Boston have been prime examples. Rep. John Kluczynski explained to President TRUMAN that in Chicago 'the Poles get the votes and the Irish get the jobs'. Since the 1960s this style of government has virtually disappeared, largely because of WHITE FLIGHT to the suburbs.

> Machine politics and the SPOILS SYSTEM are as much an enemy of a proper government system

of civil service as the boll weevil is of the cotton crop.

WILLIAM H. TAFT, *The President and His Powers*, 1916

Macho Man – moi? The semi-indignant response of Tony BLAIR's deputy John Prescott (*see* TWO JAGS) after he was accused by the French Environment Minister Dominique Voynet of male chauvinism. She levelled the charge after Prescott accused the French of torpedoing a possible deal between the EU nations and the United States over global warming at a conference in the Hague in November 2000.

McKinley, William (1843–1901), 25th President of the United States (Republican, 1897–1901), a lawyer, a six-term Congressman and a former Governor of Ohio. When the Republicans were seeking a nominee in 1896, Speaker Thomas Reed, asked about his own chances, said: 'They might do worse, and they probably will'; when McKinley won on the first ballot, Reed commented:

He has about as much backbone as a chocolate éclair.

Short, stout, always wearing a red carnation and devoted to his invalid wife, McKinley overcame William Jennings Bryan's first POPULIST campaign. In office he became the symbol of US IMPERIALISM; when the Philippines were captured he confessed: 'I could not have told where those damned islands were within 2,000 miles'. The anti-war party denounced him as 'a white-livered cur', but popular feeling for expansionism helped McKinley defeat Bryan more decisively in 1900; his slogan was **Stand pat with McKinley**. His running-mate was Theodore ROOSEVELT, whom the Republican establishment deeply distrusted; on his re-election McKinley's campaign manager Mark Hanna told him: 'Your duty to the country is to live four years from next March.' But only months into his second term he was shot in Buffalo by a young anarchist, Leon Czolgosz. As he fell, McKinley saw security guards beating his assailant and told them: 'Be easy with him, boys.' Then he added: 'My wife – be careful about her – she's sleeping, break the news gently to her.'

That kind, fatherly way of McKinley's made all comers feel that he was their friend, but left doubt in all minds as to the substantial result they had come to accomplish.

WHITE HOUSE usher IKE HOOVER

He would never consent to be photographed in a negligent pose and always took the most meticulous care about every detail of his appearance and his posture. He embalmed himself, so far as posterity is concerned.

C. W. THOMSON, *Presidents I Have Known*

McKinley tariff The PROTECTIONIST tariff imposed by the US CONGRESS in 1890 which raised import duties to their highest level, averaging 50%; the President was authorised to impose duties on those items still untaxed. Its author, the future President, described himself as 'a tariff man on a tariff platform'.

Macmillan, Harold (Earl of Stockton, 1894–1986), Prime Minister (Conservative, 1957–63). The liberal Tory under whom Britain experienced a forerunner of the FEELGOOD FACTOR (*see* SUPERMAC) before scandal and economic forebodings brought an end to thirteen years of Conservative rule.

An active member of the Macmillan publishing family who made much of being the grandson of a Scottish crofter, he was wounded three times in WORLD WAR I, then served as ADC to the GOVERNOR-GENERAL of Canada. He was MP for the north-east town of Stockton 1924–29 and 1931–45, identifying strongly with its misery during the GREAT DEPRESSION; he wrote: 'The memory of massive unemployment began to haunt me then and for many years to come.' As he pioneered the social doctrine of the MIDDLE WAY, he was at serious odds with the Tories over social policy when WORLD WAR II broke out; his biographer Alistair Horne wrote:

It is difficult to believe that he could have stood as an orthodox Conservative candidate if a general election had been held in 1939 or 1940.

CHURCHILL made him a junior Minister, then in 1942 sent him to North Africa as Resident Minister at Allied HQ where, according to his private secretary John Wyndham, he became 'VICEROY of the Mediterranean by stealth'; in 1944 he correctly estimated: 'If I do become Prime Minister, it will be in about 12 years.'

From 1945 as MP for Bromley, he helped mould the party's BUTSKELLITE post-war line in opposition. In 1951 he returned as Minister of Housing, setting an apparently unattainable target of 300,000 homes a year and reaching it; Churchill told him on his appointment:

It is a gamble – make or mar your political career. But every humble home will bless your name if you succeed.

Macmillan was briefly Defence Minister and then Foreign Secretary, but for most of the brief EDEN government he was CHANCELLOR; though a strong supporter of intervention at SUEZ, it was he whom the MAGIC CIRCLE wanted to succeed Eden (*see* WAB OR HAWOLD?). Of Suez Macmillan was soon saying: 'I was all for going in, but I know now I should never have agreed.' As the operation collapsed, Brendan Bracken cruelly observed:

> Until about a week ago Macmillan, whose bellicosity was beyond description, was wanting to tear Nasser's scalp off with his own fingernails. Today he might be described as the leader of the bolters.

Harold WILSON branded him as 'first in, last out', and even more cuttingly remarked:

> He had an expensive education – Eton and Suez.

Taking office in January 1957, Macmillan restored Tory morale, presided over unprecedented prosperity (*see* YOU'VE NEVER HAD IT SO GOOD) and won a LANDSLIDE victory over Labour in October 1959. In transatlantic affairs, where he acted as 'wise uncle' to John F. KENNEDY during the CUBAN MISSILE CRISIS and concluded the TEST BAN TREATY, his winning streak continued; the outgoing Eisenhower told JFK Macmillan was 'a good friend whose counsel you should listen to'. In Africa he hastened the end of EMPIRE while warning white South Africans of a 'WIND OF CHANGE'. But at home things went sour: the economy began slipping (*see* PAY PAUSE), his urbanity slipped with the NIGHT OF THE LONG KNIVES in 1962 when he sacked seven Ministers, DE GAULLE vetoed his attempt to take Britain into the COMMON MARKET (*see* NON!), and the PROFUMO AFFAIR left his government teetering. Before he had a chance to weather Profumo, Macmillan had prostate trouble diagnosed in October 1963, and believing it worse than it was, he resigned, declaring:

> I will not be able to carry the physical burden of leading the Party into the next General Election. I hope it will soon be possible for the customary processes of consultation to be carried on within the party about its future leadership.

Of the scene when the Queen came to accept his resignation, he wrote:

> The bed covers were down, and concealed underneath the bed was a pail, with a tube full of bile coming out of me. I made my resignation to the Queen of England for an hour, in great discomfort.

His immediate legacy was dynamite: the choice of Lord Home (*see* SIR ALEC) to succeed him rather than the more obvious RAB Butler or Quinton Hogg (Lord Hailsham). Macmillan left the Commons in 1964 for the literary world – only to make a devastating return to politics in 1984 when Margaret THATCHER, no friend of what he stood for, gave him an EARLDOM. Until his death two years later, he pilloried her policies from the House of Lords (*see* SELLING OFF THE FAMILY SILVER). Roy JENKINS observed: 'His brief Parliamentary resurrection as Earl of Stockton was theatre with high box-office appeal', but Frank Johnson opined: 'One can never escape the suspicion that all his life was a preparation for elder statesmanship'.

With his Edwardian manner, lugubrious voice, drooping moustache and ability to conjure up tears, Macmillan was varyingly praised as a political actor and condemned as a fraud. Lord WOOLTON once complained:

> A public man has to be something of an actor. I wonder whether it is really necessary for him to be a showman as well.

and Bernard Levin wrote: 'It was almost impossible to believe he was anything but a down-at-heel actor resting between engagements.' There was a widespread view that one seldom saw the real Macmillan. Pamela, Lady Egremont said: 'One moment you had a salmon in your hand, the next it was a horse.' The Labour MP David Marquand once asked: 'What is he trying to hide? The obvious answer is, himself.' But to Malcolm Muggeridge he was simply 'a parody of a Conservative politician in a novel by Trollope.'

Quintin Hogg rightly called him 'unflappable'; to Henry (CHIPS) Channon he was 'that very nice ass'; to the Young Conservative Harry Phibbs, who in Macmillan's final year accused him of betraying fleeing Cossacks in 1945, he was 'a war criminal'. His concern for the jobless earned him a mixed press from Labour. ATTLEE reckoned him 'by far the most radical man I've met in politics', MANNY Shinwell as 'not a true Socialist, but compassionate'; however Maurice Edelman wrote:

> His sympathy was undoubted; his manner was all wrong. His forays were like those of a public school missionary to the East End.

Michael FOOT thought him 'unctuous and grandiloquent' and Aneurin BEVAN declared: 'He and all his middle-of-the-roaders are the parasites of politics.' Macmillan also epitomised the GROUSE-MOOR IMAGE, his supposed humble beginning betrayed by the fact that his wife, Lady Dorothy, was a daughter of the

Duke of Devonshire. Lady Dorothy had a long-running affair with Macmillan's Parliamentary colleague Lord Boothby, the actual father of one of 'his' children. Macmillan's son Maurice observed:

> What he minded most was being dishonoured.

> In dignity, voice, manners, dress and personality almost the American popular image of an English gentleman. Ambassador ROBERT MURPHY

> He has inherited the streak of charlatanry in DISRAELI without his vision, and the self-righteousness of GLADSTONE without his dedication to principle. HAROLD WILSON

> He held his party together by not allowing his left wing to see what his right wing was doing. Lady VIOLET BONHAM-CARTER

> He seems, in his very person, to embody the national decay he supposed himself to be confuting. He exuded a flavour of mothballs. MALCOLM MUGGERIDGE

> The eyes were hooded, they seemed to hover always on the verge of a wink at his fantastic good fortune at being set down in the country of the blind, where none could see through him. BERNARD LEVIN

Macpherson Report The report from Mr Justice Macpherson, published in 1998, into the Stephen LAWRENCE case which concluded that '**institutional racism**' was rife in London's Metropolitan Police and called for a revolution in officers' attitudes. It concluded that officers investigating the murder of the eighteen-year-old black architecture student had done everything possible to avoid bringing the obvious suspects to justice. The Home Secretary Jack Straw came in for criticism after a list of witnesses who had given evidence to the inquiry in confidence was inadvertently attached to an advance copy of the report, forcing several families to leave home for their own safety.

McSharry plan The plan for reform of the EC's Common Agricultural Policy (CAP) put forward in 1990 by Agriculture Commissioner Ray McSharry (1938–). The aim of the former Irish TANAISTE was to check the Community's soaring farm budget and head off retaliation by America that threatened the URUGUAY ROUND of GATT talks. McSharry proposed cutting subsidies by up to 30% – less that half of what WASHINGTON was pressing for, but twice the amount the EC's COUNCIL OF MINISTERS eventually agreed to – spread over several years.

MAD *See* MUTUALLY ASSURED DESTRUCTION.

mad cow disease The brain disorder among cattle, correctly Bovine Spongiform Encelopathy, whose appearance in the UK severely embarrassed Margaret THATCHER and John MAJOR, both domestically and in their dealings with Europe. The disorder, caused by sloppy and mercenary animal feed and husbandry practices, resulted from livestock being fed with offal, their own processed waste and other non-natural feeds. Its appearance led the EC to ban the import of British beef by member states, triggering a series of rows between the UK and its partners. Facing a slump in demand for beef and with farmers already livid over the way Edwina Currie (*see* CRUELLA DE VIL) had fuelled a salmonella scare, Ministers struggled to restore confidence, Agriculture Minister John Gummer famously being pictured giving his daughter a beefburger at a fete. The controversy also hurt Tony BLAIR's government in its early months, Agriculture Minister Jack Cunningham earning unpopularity by banning the sale of beef on the bone because of fresh concerns that BSE might cause a new variant of Creuzfeld-Jacob Disease in humans. Labour's greater difficulties over FOOT AND MOUTH DISEASE lay ahead. President CHIRAC returned to the issue at the July 2005 KALININGRAD meeting, observing to Vladimir Putin and Gerhard Schröder in terms which some French media blamed for Paris' loss of the 2012 Olympics to London days later.

> The only thing [the British] have brought to European agriculture is Mad Cow Disease. You can't have confidence in people who have such a dreadful cuisine. After Finland, it's the country where one easts worst.

Mad Monk Originally used to describe **Rasputin** (1871–1916), the sinister cleric at the court of Tsar Nicholas II; more recently the nickname of the intellectually self-torturing **Lord** (Sir **Keith**) **Joseph** (1918–94), Margaret THATCHER's free-market GURU and a member of the HEATH and Thatcher CABINETS. His most notable public pronouncement was a speech in Birmingham in 1974 implying that the birth-rate of the improvident should be reduced; typically he was clarifying and apologising for the speech even before it was delivered.

madam. Madam Speaker The form of address chosen by **Betty Boothroyd** (1929–) following her ELECTION in 1992 as the first woman SPEAKER of the HOUSE OF COMMONS. Yorkshire-born Miss Boothroyd, once a high-kicking Tiller Girl, served a long political apprenticeship, entering Parliament (for West Bromwich in 1973) at the fifth attempt. She was a CHARISMATIC Speaker, occupying the CHAIR for eight years until moving up to the LORDS.

Madame Écosse (Fr. Mrs Scotland) Nickname at the EUROPEAN PARLIAMENT for the Scottish Nationalist MEP Mrs **Winifred Ewing** (1929–), the former Westminster MP who in 1979 became the SNP's first member at Strasbourg and who in 1999 would be the first member to speak in the reconstituted SCOTTISH PARLIAMENT.

Madison, James (1751–1836), 4th President of the United States (1809–17). Too frail for the Continental Army, he was a leading drafter of the US CONSTITUTION, co-author of the *FEDERALIST*, architect of the BILL OF RIGHTS and JEFFERSON's Secretary of State. Rep. Fisher Ames hailed him as 'a man of sense, reading, address and integrity. He is our first man.' But Madison, 'a withered little apple-John' as Washington Irving described him, did not exude power. John C. Calhoun commented: 'Our President, though a man of amiable manners and great talents, has not I fear those commanding talents which are necessary to control those about him.' Indeed **'Jemmy'** was probably less popular than his lively wife Dolley; Charles C. Pinckney, whom Madison defeated in 1808, said: 'I was beaten by Mr and Mrs Madison. I might have had a better chance had I faced Mr Madison alone.' Dolley Madison went on to distinguish herself by her calm disdain when the British sacked WASHINGTON in 1814 after her husband had gone to war. Madison justified his action thus: 'I flung forward the flag of the country, sure that the people would press onward and defend it.' But it revived the Federalist opposition, and Madison only narrowly won a second term.

Madison Group A powerful group of conservative Senate STAFFERS, allied to Sen. Jesse Helms, which was instrumental in keeping up right-wing pressure on President REAGAN.

Marbury v Madison The case from 1803 in which the US SUPREME COURT established its power of JUDICIAL REVIEW. Chief Justice John Marshall held that it was the duty of the judiciary to say what the law was, and to strike down any law that conflicted with the CONSTITUTION.

Madrid. Madrid bombings The terrorist attacks on 11 March 2004 on four Madrid commuter trains by a Moroccan-based ally of AL QAEDA which killed 191 people and injured 1600. The worst peacetime atrocity in contemporary western Europe up to that point, LOCKERBIE apart, it was blamed on Spain's participation in the IRAQ WAR the previous year and its stationing of forces in that country. It prompted demonstrations against terrorism by 12 million Spaniards and an unexpected defeat in the general election three days later of the centre-right government of José Maria Aznar, with Tony BLAIR the principal supporter of George W. BUSH's WAR AGAINST TERRORISM. Aznar's Ministers had initially blamed the Basque separatist group ETA, and were held to have done so in the face of evidence to the contrary for party political reasons. The suspected leader of the bombers, Serhane Ben Abdelmajid Farkhet, blew himself up with four colleagues when police stormed their flat near Madrid three weeks later.

Madrid conditions The terms set by Margaret THATCHER at the Madrid EC summit in 1988 for UK participation in the exchange rate mechanism (ERM). They were that Britain would join (1) when it had reduced inflation to close to the EC average; (2) when the European SINGLE MARKET was close to completion; and (3) when all EC countries had abolished exchange controls and freed capital movements. She set the conditions when Chancellor Nigel Lawson and Foreign Secretary Sir Geoffrey HOWE threatened to resign unless she made a commitment to join. John MAJOR, as Chancellor, eventually secured Mrs Thatcher's agreement to join the ERM in October 1990, with the conditions not fully met; UK membership ended with the disaster of BLACK WEDNESDAY. *Compare* FIVE ECONOMIC TESTS.

Mae West factor Pollsters' term for the tendency of some uncommitted voters to opt for the challenger on the ground that he or she could not be worse than the incumbent. From the Hollywood star's attributed claim:

> Whenever I'm caught between two evils, I take the one I've never tried.

MAFF Initials of the UK Ministry of Agriculture, Fisheries and Food, wound up after its disastrous handling of the 2001 FOOT AND MOUTH DISEASE outbreak; coincidentally it rhymed with 'naff'.

mafficking Extravagant and boisterous celebration of a national sporting or military triumph. From the uproarious scenes and unrestrained exultation in central London on the night of 18 May 1900, when news arrived that the South African town of Mafeking had been relieved after a 217-day siege by the BOERS. The town had been defended by Col. Robert Baden-Powell, who subsequently founded the Boy Scouts.

Magellan, Ferdinand President Franklin D. ROOSEVELT's private railway carriage. Built by the Association of American Railroads and sold to the WHITE HOUSE for $1, it was equipped with two lifts to get FDR's wheelchair on and off, an office, a lounge, a bedroom and a galley. The floor was of foot-thick steel-lined concrete to guard against explosions on the track. There were three underwater escape hatches from Navy submarines in case the train toppled into a river. Engine drivers said the carriage was so heavy that pulling it was like pulling a fishing line with a lead sinker at the end.

Maggie, Maggie, Maggie – Out! Out! Out! The standard cry of anti-Tory demonstrators throughout the years of Margaret THATCHER's government. With the exception of the 'IRON LADY', 'Maggie' was one of the very few nicknames used by her supporters rather than her opponents; Mrs Thatcher herself both appreciated and used it.

magic. magic asterisk The accounting device invented early in the REAGAN administration by David Stockman's budget team to make it appear that targets would be met. Stockman admitted:

> We invented the magic asterisk. If we couldn't find the savings in time – and we couldn't – we would issue an IOU. We would call it 'Future savings to be identified'. It was marvellously creative. A magic asterisk item would cost negative $30 billion . . . $40 billion . . . whatever it took to get a balanced budget.

magic circle In British politics, the term coined by Iain Macleod in 1963 for the milieu in which a new Tory leader 'emerged', prior to the adoption in 1965 of a system of election. It was used specifically to describe the senior party figures who, on Harold MACMILLAN's resignation, ensured that Lord Home (*see* SIR ALEC) was chosen ahead of RAB Butler and Lord Hailsham. Macleod wrote:

> It is some measure of the tightness of the magic circle on this occasion that neither the Chancellor of the Exchequer nor the Leader of the House of Commons had any inkling of what was happening.

Announcing his resignation, Macmillan had said: 'I hope that it will soon be possible for the customary processes of consultation to be carried out within the party about its future leadership.' The thinking behind the 'emergence' of the Tory leader was summed up in 1921:

> Great leaders of parties are not elected, they are evolved. It will be a bad day for this or any party to have solemnly to meet to elect a leader. The leader is there, and we all know it when he is there. ERNEST PRETYMAN (1860–1931)

Maginot Line The 195-mile defensive barrier built by France along its eastern border from Alsace to Switzerland after WORLD WAR I to prevent Germany ever again invading. Named after its promoter, Minister of Defence André Maginot (1877–1932), the Line lulled France into a false sense of security, proving useless when, in 1940, German forces turned the Line's northern flank and invaded France through Belgium. A **Maginot mentality** is consequently a false sense of security in politics, based on outdated views and tactics.

Magna Carta The charter of rights forced on King John by his barons in 1215 which became one of the basics of English common law, and of the liberties of America and other English-speaking nations. The charter, agreed at Runnymede near Windsor, was intended to reinforce the barons' position rather than enshrine general HUMAN RIGHTS. But such provisions as that requiring no one to be tried except by their equals paved the way for trial by jury, due process of law and no taxation without representation.

> An insult to the Holy See, a serious weakening of the royal power, a disgrace to the English nation, a danger to all Christendom.
>
> Pope INNOCENT III (1160/1–1218)

Mahatma The title (Sanskrit. great soul) accorded by his followers to **Mohandas Karamchand Gandhi** (1869–1948), the champion of the poor whose CIVIL DISOBEDIENCE and NON-VIOLENCE hastened Indian independence, earning him worldwide respect. A former lawyer who had experienced the worst of racial prejudice in South Africa, Gandhi's stature grew each time he was imprisoned by the British, who could not cope with his authority or his twinkling humour; asked his view of Western civilisation, Gandhi replied: 'I think it would be a very good idea.' He was assassinated by Hindu fanatics who resented his fasting to get Hindus and Muslims to halt their strife after independence.

> I do not know how to tell you and how to say it. Our beloved leader is no more.
>
> JAWAHARLAL NEHRU, announcing Gandhi's death

maiden speech A member's first speech in a legislature. In Britain's HOUSE OF COMMONS it customarily includes a non-political tribute to the previous member; the next speaker is supposed to offer congratulations. Making a maiden speech is an ordeal, and so can be hearing one; in Australia, wrote Blanche d'Alpuget, 'listening to maiden speeches is one of the tiresome duties of a new Parliament, from which members usually excuse themselves.' Few are classics; DISRAELI had such a rough ride that he blustered: 'The time will come when you shall hear me!' He glossed over this when writing of 'an MP so inaudible that it was doubtful whether, after all, the young orator really did lose his virginity'. The 18th-century Joseph Addison was so nervous that he paused three times on 'I conceive' before giving up; the next speaker cruelly commented that he had 'conceived three times and brought forth nothing'. But occasional maiden gems stand out (*see* FIDEL CASTRO IN A MINISKIRT). The editor J. L. Garvin wrote of that by F. E. Smith (later Lord Birkenhead) on 12 May 1906:

> He spoke for an hour, and put the House in his pocket.

mail-in election An election conducted entirely by post. Isolated local elections in America have been conducted by mail since the early 1980s, but the first for a seat in CONGRESS took place in February 1996 when Rep. Ron Wyden, a Democrat, defeated Gordon Smith, Republican president of the State Senate, for a vacant US SENATE seat in Oregon. The UK was slow to follow suit, the first all-postal local election taking place in 2000. Entire regions voted by post in the 2004 EUROPEAN PARLIAMENT elections, but while the percentage poll was up sharply there were problems over the Royal Mail's failure to deliver ballot papers in some areas and blatant interference and vote-rigging by councillors in some Asian neighbourhoods. (*See* ELECTION COURT.)

major. Major, Sir John (1943–), UK Prime Minister (Conservative) 1990–97. The dark-horse successor to Margaret THATCHER who, despite a deep recession, won a record fourth Conservative victory against the odds in 1992, then struggled with Mrs Thatcher's unhelpful legacy over Europe and frequent allegations of SLEAZE against members of his government before going down to a crushing defeat at the hands of Tony BLAIR. Born in south London to elderly parents (his father had once been a trapeze artist), he left school early to support his family making garden gnomes, was turned down for a job as a bus conductor, spent some time unemployed, then joined a bank, where the loss of a kneecap in a road accident in Nigeria ended a promising cricket career. Major got his first political experience chairing Lambeth Housing Committee; 'RED' KEN Livingstone, who sat opposite, said: 'All Tories are monsters. John Major is charming. Therefore John Major isn't a Tory.'

Elected MP for Huntingdon in 1979, his great charm and acute political skills earned him rapid advancement, entering the CABINET in 1987 as Chief Secretary to the Treasury. Mrs Thatcher admired his ability, loyalty and readiness to stand up to her, promoting him for an uncomfortable two months as Foreign Secretary in 1989 before making him Chancellor on Nigel Lawson's resignation. When Michael HESELTINE toppled her, Major became her favoured successor; 'He is another ONE OF US', she told her supporters. The fervent Thatcherite Alan CLARK wrote in his diary on 17 November 1990:

> John Major . . . being calm and sensible, is infinitely preferable to that dreadful charlatan H[eseltine]. But John is virtually unknown, too vulnerable to the subtle charge of 'not yet ready for it'.

The charge was to stick as Major humoured his right wing by giving ground on Europe in public while condemning them in private as 'BASTARDS', and developed a cutting edge in his clashes with John SMITH, Neil KINNOCK and Blair, which did not ring true with his personal warmth.

Major was genuinely surprised to become Prime Minister. His wife Norma had said: 'Things like that don't happen to people like us.' Major himself told his first Cabinet meeting: 'Well, who would have thought it?' One Minister described that Cabinet, after Mrs Thatcher's, as 'like the released slaves' chorus from *Fidelio*'. Major was immediately confronted with the GULF WAR, leading the nation through the brief conflict to free Kuwait and sharing George BUSH Snr's reluctance to finish off SADDAM HUSSEIN. At home he was dogged by the twin problems of recession and Thatcher-inspired rebellions over Europe before and after he concluded the MAASTRICHT TREATY; his Cabinet was also disrupted by a nearly-successful IRA mortar attack on 2 February 1991 (*see* GENTLEMEN, I THINK WE HAD BETTER START

AGAIN SOMEWHERE ELSE). He repealed the POLL TAX, then called at the last possible moment an ELECTION he looked sure to lose, but on 9 April 1992 pulled off a shock victory over Kinnock with a majority of 21. He was now premier in his own right, but Lady Thatcher remarked: 'I don't accept that all of a sudden Major is his own man', and when the Danes rejected Maastricht and the French almost followed suit, the CONSERVATIVE PARTY was at war again. On BLACK WEDNESDAY that September, the UK was forced by a run on sterling to leave the ERM and DEVALUE; Major's authority was further dented by a furore over the planned closure of more than half Britain's remaining coal mines, the MATRIX-CHURCHILL affair and a wave of scandals involving Conservative Ministers and MPs (*see* especially CASH FOR QUESTIONS). The economy was now starting to recover, but to balance the books Norman Lamont put VAT on domestic fuel, a decision Labour branded a classic broken election promise and, with help from Tory rebels, was able to mitigate. Mishandling of the Maastricht debate led to a knife-edge COMMITTEE STAGE lasting over six months and culminating in a defeat on the SOCIAL CHAPTER, which took a Vote of CONFIDENCE to reverse. Frustratingly, economic recovery did not generate a FEEL-GOOD FACTOR, while the IRA ceasefire in August 1994 following the DOWNING STREET DECLARATION earned Major respect, rather than votes, as Labour under Blair grew rampant. Growing friction with the right led Major to force a leadership contest in July 1995 (*see* PUT UP OR SHUT UP); he defeated John Redwood (*see* VULCAN) by a just credible 218–89, then attempted to relaunch his premiership. However, the effective loss of his Parliamentary majority, rows with Europe over MAD COW DISEASE and continuing sleaze allegations kept him on the back foot, and on 1 May 1997 the Conservatives went down to their biggest electoral defeat for almost a century. Major remained in the Commons until 1997, speaking out particularly against NEW LABOUR's policies for DEVOLUTION and constitutional change. He was seen in a new light from 2002 when Edwina Currie (*see* CRUELLA DE VILLE) revealed that she and Major had had a four-year affair in the 1980s. In 2005 he was made a Knight of the GARTER.

Major's banking background and vocabulary led commentators to brand him 'grey'. When also accused of arrogance, he complained: 'I can't be grey *and* arrogant.' Edward Pearce termed him 'the man who ran away from the circus to become an accountant'; Jackie Mason won easy laughs by saying: 'He makes George Bush look like a personality', and John Smith branded him 'the man with the non-Midas touch'. But William Waldegrave remarked: 'No man ever double crosses John twice', and one Irish official praised him as 'one of the very few British politicians I have ever met who is in no way patronising in his dealings with us'. He also had to rein in his wit. As a young MP he heard Teddy Taylor (a former Glasgow MP who had moved to Southend, then heard there was a vacancy in Glasgow) say: 'I've had hundreds of letters asking me to stand.' Major riposted: 'How many were from Southend, Teddy?' But he could also be on the receiving end: when candidate for St Pancras in 1974, he reputedly had this exchange:

> *Voice:* Who is it?
> *Major:* I am John Major, your Conservative candidate.
> *Voice:* Who is it?
> *Major:* I am John Major, your Conservative candidate.
> *Voice:* Who is it?
> Major opens the letter-box and sees . . . a parrot.

Major League asshole The biggest of several *faux pas* in George W. BUSH's 2000 Presidential CAMPAIGN: an aside about Adam Clymer, a *Wall Street Journal* reporter covering the ELECTION, which he made to his running-mate Richard Cheyney during an appearance at Naperville, Illinois on 5 September which was relayed to the audience via an OPEN MIKE.

majority. majority leader The head of the larger party in the US SENATE, and in the House the most powerful figure after the SPEAKER. Sen. Howard Baker said: 'There are two roles for a majority leader in the Senate. One is the President's spear carrier, the other is an independent force. I chose to be a spear carrier.' In the House, said Rep. Jim Wright, the majority leader has 'a hunting licence to persuade.'

majority rule 1960s code for African, rather than white minority, rule in British COLONIES approaching independence. At the height of the UDI controversy, Ian Smith declared:

> I don't believe in black majority rule ever in Rhodesia – not in a thousand years.

absolute majority More than 50% of the seats available or votes cast, giving a party or candidate more support than all the others put together.

Moral Majority A US right-wing evangelical movement, founded by the Rev. Jerry Falwell, which claims the authority to impose its views in such areas as prayer in schools, in parallel with the campaign against abortion. The Religious RIGHT and the more focused CHRISTIAN COALITION followed from it.

overall majority In a legislature where one party has the numbers for it to govern alone, the difference between the number of seats held by it and by all other parties combined.

qualified majority The weighted formula for voting in the EU COUNCIL OF MINISTERS to settle issues not requiring unanimity under the LUXEMBOURG COMPROMISE, a mechanism enabling three of the Community's largest members, or two large ones with allies, to block a majority decision. The formula was renegotiated after MAASTRICHT, and again for the EUROPEAN CONSTITUTION with the accession of ten new members in 2004; approval of the Constitution was delayed several months as Spain and Poland tried to hold existing members to an earlier compromise that would have given them voting strengths close to big-country status. Qualified majority voting is usually abbreviated to **QMV**.

silent majority The term popularised by President NIXON for the uncounted millions who can be counted on to support a conservative regime, undetected by opinion-formers. Liberals categorised the silent majority as 'unyoung, unpoor and unblack'. Nixon took up the phrase, not his own, on 3 November 1969 in a speech rallying support for the VIETNAM WAR, saying:

> And so tonight, to you – the great silent majority of my fellow Americans – I ask for your support.

working majority A majority of more than a handful, large enough for a ruling party in a legislature to govern without the continual risk of defeat.

a majority can do anything The attributed doctrine of Joe Cannon (1836–1926), SPEAKER of the HOUSE OF REPRESENTATIVES (*see* FOUL-MOUTHED JOE). CHURCHILL agreed, reckoning that 'one is enough'. But at the birth of American democracy, Thomas JEFFERSON advised: 'Great innovations should not be forced on slender majorities.' When elected President in 1960 John F. KENNEDY commented: 'The majority is narrow, but the responsibility is clear. There may be difficulties with the CONGRESS, but **a majority of one is still a majority**.' However, Speaker Sam RAYBURN cautioned at the other end of the scale: 'When you get too big a majority, you're immediately in trouble.'

one man with courage makes a majority A saying of President Andrew Jackson, much modified by US politicians and commentators. Wendell Phillips (1811–84) wrote that 'one on God's side is a majority'; House Speaker Thomas Reed (1839–1902) in turn qualified this with: 'One, with God, is always a majority, but many a martyr has been burned at the stake.' And Calvin Coolidge, accepting the Republican Vice Presidential nomination in 1920, said that 'one, with the law, is a majority'.

putting a majority together is like a one-armed man wrapping cranberries The verdict of Sen. Bob Dole, himself with only one arm, on the difficulties of forming a winning COALITION for a BILL in the US CONGRESS.

the majority are always wrong It has often been claimed that CONSENSUS politics produces disastrous results, and the American socialist Eugene Debs (1855–1926) observed:

> When great changes occur in history, when great principles are concerned, as a rule the majority are wrong.

See also PLURALITY.

malice. with malice toward none, with charity for all The keynote of Abraham LINCOLN's second INAUGURAL ADDRESS on 4 March 1865, marking the start of what he hoped would be four years of reconciliation between North and South following the CIVIL WAR. Exactly two months later, Lincoln's hopes having been dashed with his assassination, the same words were read over his grave. Lincoln had said:

> With malice toward none; with charity for all; with firmness in the right, as God gives us to see the right, let us strive on to finish the work we are in; to bind up the nation's wounds; to care for him who shall have borne the battle, and for his widow, and his orphan – to do all which may achieve and cherish a just, and a lasting peace, among ourselves, and with all nations.

Mall, the In WASHINGTON DC, the flat expanse, nearly a mile long, overlooked by the WEST FRONT of the CAPITOL and stretching to the WASHINGTON MONUMENT. Originally bounded by Constitution Avenue to the north and Independence Avenue to the south, the National Gallery, Air and Space Museum and other public buildings have encroached on it.

Malthusianism The doctrine of Thomas Malthus (1766–1834), historian and economist, that 'population, when unchecked, increases in a geometric ratio' while food supplies increase only arithmetically. He aimed to solve 'the perpetual struggle for room and food' by postponing marriage and requiring strict continence.

Malvinas, las Islas The Argentine name for the FALKLANDS, from the French *Les Malouines* (the people of St Malo, an apparent reference to the first settlers). It is also used by those UK politicians who accept Argentina's claim to SOVEREIGNTY over the islands.

man. Man from Missouri One of many nicknames for President Harry S TRUMAN.

man in a white suit The former BBC television foreign correspondent Martin Bell (1938–), who at the height of the controversy over SLEAZE stood as an Independent in the 1997 general election against the former Conservative Minister Neil Hamilton (*see* CASH FOR QUESTIONS) in the normally safe Tory constituency of Tatton, Cheshire, and roundly defeated him, helped by the withdrawal of the Labour and Liberal Democrat candidates. Bell, whose trademark on television and in the COMMONS was his white suit, proved an effective MP and champion of Parliamentary ethics. Having promised at the outset not to seek a second term he passed up in 2001 the chance of probable victory at Tatton to contest Brentwood & Ongar, where some local Tories were concerned about links between the party locally and a fundamentalist church, but while polling strongly failed to capture the seat. In 2005 he supported other candidates in the INDEPENDENT NETWORK, notably Reg Keys, who stood against Tony BLAIR after losing his son in Iraq.

Man of Steel The English rendering of the Russian name STALIN, adopted by the Soviet dictator Joseph Vissarionovich Dzugashvili. The name coincidentally reflected both his hardline political beliefs and the ruthlessness with which he dealt with his enemies.

Man on Horseback A larger-than-life, capable and by inference authoritarian figure who will appear from outside the political world and solve a nation's problems; equally, a military personage who aspires to political power. The term was applied to Napoleon, to General Ulysses S. GRANT as he sought the Presidency and to other ambitious men since, but it is linked most with General Georges Boulanger (1837–91), who briefly saw himself as a potential dictator of France and, when a widely-expected COUP failed to materialise, was accused of treason. He shot himself at his mistress's grave. In 1961 John F. KENNEDY, attacking the last vestiges of MCCARTHYISM, denounced 'those who call for a 'man on horseback' because they do not trust the people'. And former California Governor Edmund G. 'Jerry' Brown (*see* SPACE CADET) said:

> Politics is a jungle and it's getting worse. People want a dictator these days, a man on a white horse, to ride in and tell them what to do.

man on the Clapham omnibus The average member of the public, whose views such a person might represent. The phrase became popular in 19th-century Britain, and has stuck.

Man on the Wedding Cake An unflattering nickname for Thomas E. DEWEY which was partly held responsible for his unexpected defeat by Harry S TRUMAN in the 1948 Presidential ELECTION. The phrase, with its overtones of ridicule, stiffness and lack of character, was bestowed by Grace Hodgson Flandreau, and given maximum circulation in WASHINGTON by Alice Roosevelt Long-worth.

manage. management of decline The phrase summing up the defeatist atmosphere in WHITEHALL during the 1970s, with Britain seen as inevitably on the slide. It was used by William Armstrong, Head of the CIVIL SERVICE, to appalled members of Edward HEATH's Cabinet in 1973; he told them the business of his administrative corps was 'the orderly [some members recall 'peaceful'] management of decline'.

manager The combined chief executive and principal administrative officer of an American city, appointed as an alternative to a political MAYOR who exercises a leadership role. The manager is appointed by, and responsible to, the elected council. The first municipality to adopt the system was Sumter, South Carolina, in 1912; about one-third of communities with over 5,000 population now operate the system.

managers The appointees of both HOUSES of the US CONGRESS who take part in a House-Senate CONFERENCE on a disputed BILL. The name is also reserved for the House appointees who prosecute an accused President in an IMPEACHMENT trial before the Senate.

Manchester school The grouping of Liberal MPs and their followers in the booming northern city, headed by Richard Cobden (1804–65) and John Bright (1811–89), who from the early 1840s championed the cause of the working man, of wider democracy and – above all – of FREE TRADE. As a movement their impact on WESTMINSTER lasted barely a decade, but the name – invented by DISRAELI, who did not intend it as a compliment – has stuck.

mandarins The occupants of the highest level – the FIRST DIVISION – of Britain's CIVIL SERVICE: PERMANENT SECRETARIES and the policy officials immediately beneath them. The term reflects the widespread belief among politicians and political journalists that WHITEHALL retains an inscrutably aristocratic culture of its own, whose leaders are able to manipulate the workings of government while using language of suave opacity but deadly effect. This image was devastatingly, but accurately, conveyed in the BBC comedy series YES, MINISTER.

mandate (1) The legitimacy given to a government or individual and their policies by having won an ELECTION. In 1984 after Ronald REAGAN's 49-state victory, James Baker said:

> We're going to play down the mandate. We need to be gracious winners.

(2) The authority under which the LEAGUE OF NATIONS delegated the administration of certain territories after WORLD WAR I to member governments. The most controversial was Britain's mandate over Palestine, the longest-running South Africa's over South West Africa, which it refused to relinquish until Namibian independence in 1990. In 1945 mandates were formally superseded by the UN's TRUSTEESHIP system.

doctor's mandate *See* DOCTOR.

dual mandate The situation of someone elected simultaneously to two legislatures at different levels, e.g. the HOUSE OF COMMONS and the EUROPEAN PARLIAMENT, or the House of Commons and the SCOTTISH PARLIAMENT or WELSH ASSEMBLY. Although such duplication occurred when the assemblies at Strasbourg, Holyrood and Cardiff Bay were set up, dual mandates are now rare.

mandating In US government, the practice of one level of government requiring another to finance a particular programme or function.

Mandela, Nelson Rolihlahla (1918–), President of South Africa (ANC) 1994–99, winner of the 1993 NOBEL PEACE PRIZE and arguably the politician with the greatest moral authority in the 20th century after MAHATMA Gandhi, despite having spent 27 years in prison. Born in the Transkei, the son of a Tembu chief, he gained a law degree, joined the ANC in 1944 and, as the NATIONAL PARTY imposed APARTHEID from 1948, took part in active resistance. He went on trial for treason in 1956–61 but was acquitted. After the banning of the ANC in 1960, Mandela gained the movement's acquiescence in the formation of a military wing, UMKHONTO WA SIZWE. Mandela was arrested in 1962 and jailed for five years, but the following year was also put before the RIVONIA TRIAL and on 12 June 1964 was sentenced to life imprisonment. For the first eighteen years he was incarcerated on ROBBEN ISLAND, and for nearly eight years more in Pollsmoor Prison, in the Cape, until President F. W. de Klerk ordered his release as a step toward the dismantling of apartheid. De Klerk and others feared unrest at home and opprobrium worldwide should Mandela die in jail despite the global campaign for his release. Released on 18 February 1990, Mandela managed in four years to achieve a peaceful transition to multiracial rule. He was elected President of the ANC in 1991, and helped establish through the CODESA process a constitution acceptable (if only just) to every political group save the most extreme Afrikaners. In April 1994 the ANC triumphed in South Africa's first universal elections, and when Parliament met Mandela took office as President. He set out to deliver jobs, housing, water and electricity to poor black South Africans, but also to heal the nation's wounds through a TRUTH AND RECONCILIATION COMMISSION and his personal support for South Africa's hosting of the Rugby World Cup. After five years, by now 81, he handed over the presidency to Thabo Mbeki, but remained an active ambassador for the new South Africa and a trenchant critic of what he saw as wrongdoing on the world stage, notably the WAR ON IRAQ. In 2004, after securing the 2010 soccer World Cup for South Africa, he 'retired' again, though continuing to campaign for the relief of suffering in Africa, always with a twinkle in his eye. Mandela suffered much pain when his second wife Winnie, who had stood by him for most of his years in prison and had her own powerbase in the ANC, was accused of corruption, involvement with murderous young gangs and personal infidelity. But after divorcing her he found new contentment with Graça Machel, widow of the former President of Mozambique.

Mandy *See* BOBBY.

Manhattan Project The codename given to the US project which resulted in the development of the ATOMIC BOMB. Franklin D. ROOSEVELT ordered action after PEARL HARBOR, having resisted a proposal from Einstein as early as 1938 for a fission bomb of unparalleled destructive power. Great secrecy and haste were required to construct such a bomb before the Germans, who were thought to be working on a similar project. It began at Columbia University, New York, in 1942, and the next year an international team of scientists under the physicist J. Robert Oppenheimer was brought together at Los Alamos, New Mexico, to develop the bomb; as early as February 1944 some were concerned that it would bring post-war tension between the SUPERPOWERS. Uranium-235 was produced at Oak Ridge, Tennessee, and plutonium at Hanford, Washington State. The Manhattan Project culminated in the testing of the first atomic bomb on 16 July 1945, and its first use in war at HIROSHIMA on 6 August. Total expenditure on the project was around $2 billion.

We knew the world would not be the same.
J. ROBERT OPPENHEIMER, 1945

Manifest Destiny The doctrine that America should put westward expansion at the top of its priorities, and that it had a historic mission to stretch to the Pacific and occupy all and more of its present coastline – and much of Canada. First advanced under other names in the late 18th century, it became a political catchphrase just prior to the MEXICAN WAR when America was absorbing Texas. The phrase was coined in 1845 by the Democratic journalist John L. O'Sullivan; he argued that it was America's 'manifest destiny to overspread the continent allotted by providence for the free development of our yearly multiplying millions'. *See also* FIFTY-FOUR FORTY OR FIGHT.

manifesto A document issued by a political party at or in advance of an ELECTION setting out its programme for government, and making pledges that will be held against it if it does not keep them.

Manifesto Group A centre-right grouping of Labour MPs, counterbalancing the TRIBUNE GROUP, which enjoyed considerable support in the late 1970s. The name reflected a desire to defend Labour's 1974 manifesto against the left's calls for even more radical policies. The defection of a number of members to the SDP in 1981 marked the end of the group's effectiveness.

Road to the Manifesto Labour's key policy document in the run-up to the 1997 election. Published in July 1996, 'NEW LABOUR: New Life for New Britain' avoided specific commitments but nevertheless set the stage for a total break with the Labour past and Conservative present. Much of the document was written by Tony BLAIR himself, and John Prescott (*see* TWO JAGS) campaigned energetically for it in the country. The maverick Labour MP Austin Mitchell (*see* HADDOCK) described himself as 'a squashed hedgehog on the road to the manifesto' after publicly criticising its lack of content. *See also* THINGS CAN ONLY GET BETTER.

Tamworth Manifesto *See* TAMWORTH.

Manila Pact The treaty signed in Manila on 8 September 1954 on the creation of SEATO; the signatories were America, Australia, Britain, France, New Zealand, Pakistan, the Philippines and Thailand. It came into force on 19 February 1955 and was formally ended in 1977.

Mann Act The Act passed by the US CONGRESS in 1910 to curb prostitution and 'white slavery'. It made it an offence to transport women across State lines, or bring them into the country, for immoral purposes. The act closed red light districts in 30 American cities, but New Orleans survived it.

Mann-Elkins Act Also passed in 1910, this measure finally made government regulation of America's railroads effective by empowering the Interstate Commerce Commission to suspend freight rates it felt excessive without first having to argue the case in the courts.

Manny The nickname of **Emmanuel** (later Lord) **Shinwell** (1884–1986), who began as a Glasgow street boxer and ended as Britain's longest-lived peer. Jailed in 1921 for inciting a workers' riot, he became an MP in 1923 and the next year served in Ramsay MACDONALD's first Labour government; in 1935 he unseated MacDonald, now Prime Minister of the NATIONAL GOVERNMENT, at Seaham. Shinwell helped ATTLEE draft the manifesto for Labour's LANDSLIDE victory in 1945, and as Minister for Fuel and Power NATIONALISED the coal industry. The FUEL CRISIS of 1947 dented his reputation, and despite impressing as Minister of Defence he never held higher office. After serving in the 1960s as chairman of the PLP, he retired from the COMMONS in 1970 with a LIFE PEERAGE. In his old age Shinwell, who in his day had threatened to punch opponents on the nose, gained new repute as an avuncular raconteur.

Manor of Northstead *See* CHILTERN HUNDREDS.

Mansfield judgment The ruling in 1722 by Lord Mansfield (1705–93), Lord Chief Justice, which established that slavery was illegal in England and Wales. Ruling on a claim by the owner of James Somersett, a runaway slave, to recover him, Mansfield said:

> The exercise of the power of a master over his slave must be supported by the laws of particular countries; but no foreigner in England can claim such a right over a man; such a claim is not known to the laws of England.

Mansion House speech The speech made each year, in June or October, by Britain's CHANCELLOR OF THE EXCHEQUER at the Mansion House, headquarters of the City of London and its LORD MAYOR, in which he sets out his view of the domestic and world economy. LLOYD GEORGE's speech in 1910 attracted particular attention, as he departed from the habitual subject to warn Germany that Britain would support France in any conflict that arose from the AGADIR CRISIS. The rigid formality of the occasion was eased from 1997 by Gordon BROWN's insistence on wearing a lounge suit instead of the customary white tie.

(the) many, not the few The key phrase in the reworked wording of CLAUSE FOUR of the LABOUR PARTY's CONSTITUTION pushed through by Tony BLAIR in 1994/95 after his ELECTION as party leader, as a prerequisite for electoral victory after eighteen years in the wilderness. The wording, which replaced a concrete commitment to 'common ownership of the means of production, distribution and exchange', had a lengthy pedigree, going back at least as far as the 17th-century poet Alexander Pope who, in the opposite sense to Blair, described political parties as 'the madness of many, for the gains of the few'. Clause Four now reads:

> The Labour Party is a democratic socialist party. It believes that by the strength of our common endeavour we achieve more than we achieve alone, so as to create for each of us the means to realise our true potential and for all of us a community in which power, wealth and opportunity are in the hands of the many, not the few. Where the rights we enjoy reflect the duties we owe. And where we live together, freely, in a spirit of solidarity, tolerance and respect.

Maoists Adherents of the highly disciplined, revolutionary brand of Communism advocated by CHAIRMAN MAO Tse-Tung. Maoist elements appeared in a number of Communist Parties after the rift between Moscow and Beijing in the early 1960s; the SHINING PATH movement in Peru achieved its greatest strength two decades after Mao's death, and it took even longer for Maoist rebels to gain critical mass in Nepal.

Maquis A name for the French RESISTANCE in WORLD WAR II, taken from the thick scrubland of the Mediterranean coast to which bandits formerly retreated to avoid capture.

march A form of DEMONSTRATION in which those making their point parade with banners between two points, usually with a RALLY at the start and/or one at the end. *See* ALDERMASTON; LIBERTY AND LIVELIHOOD; SELMA.

march my troops toward the sound of gunfire The rallying call issued to the conference of Britain's LIBERAL PARTY on 15 September 1963 by its leader, Jo (later Lord) Grimond (1913–93). With the 1964 ELECTION in prospect and hopes of a revival high, Grimond told his party:

> In bygone days, commanders were taught that, when in doubt, they should march their troops towards the sound of gunfire. I intend to march my troops towards the sound of gunfire.

March on Rome The descent on Rome of Mussolini (*see* DUCE) and thousands of his BLACKSHIRTS on 28 October 1922, shortly before his establishment of a FASCIST state in Italy. They travelled there by various means – largely by rail – and entered the city with little or no opposition from military or civil authorities. The head of the Cabinet resigned and King Victor Emmanuel III invited Mussolini to form a new government.

March on Washington for Jobs and Freedom The largest demonstration in WASHINGTON up to that time, staged in August 1963 to support President KENNEDY's landmark CIVIL RIGHTS Bill, then being debated by CONGRESS. Marchers who had reached the capital on foot from the South were joined on the final leg from the WASHINGTON MONUMENT to the LINCOLN MEMORIAL by 200,000 people, some 60,000 of them white. They were addressed from the Memorial by black and white civil rights leaders, the high point being Dr Martin Luther KING's historic I HAVE A DREAM oration.

hunger march *See* JARROW CRUSADE.

Million Man March The demonstration staged in WASHINGTON in October 1995 to give African-American men a new sense of purpose, organised by the Nation of Islam and led by Louis Farrakhan, whose inflammatory statements about Jews on other occasions limited his credibility with whites. Police estimated the participants at 400,000 – twice the number who had turned out for Dr King but still less than an anti-VIETNAM WAR protest in 1969.

marching season The period during the summer when the ORANGE Lodges and other LOYALIST groups in NORTHERN IRELAND take to the streets with drum-and-flute bands to commemorate William of Orange's victory at the Battle of the BOYNE in 1689, the resistance of the APPRENTICE BOYS OF DERRY and other past triumphs over the Catholics. The marches are occasionally routed through Catholic areas in order to provoke the inhabitants (*see* DRUMCREE), and a **Parades Commission** now adjudicates on the routes to be followed. In 1980 the then Northern Ireland Secretary Humphrey Atkins (later Lord Colnbrook) asked an RUC inspector the difference between the Temperance Lodges and the Total Abstinence Lodges who had joined one parade. The policeman replied:

> It's simple. By the end of the day the Temperance will be well away, and the total abstainers will be fucking paralytic.

However, regular marchers insist they never touch alcohol until the parades are over.

Marconi affair A financial scandal with tarnished LLOYD GEORGE when CHANCELLOR OF THE EXCHEQUER, but did not halt his rise. In 1912 he bought shares worth £2000 in the US Marconi company, at a preferential rate through its managing director Godfrey Isaacs, brother of Attorney-General Rufus Isaacs (later Lord Reading). Meanwhile British Marconi shares rose rapidly as the result of a government contract to build radio stations. While the two companies were separate, there were inevitably rumours of corruption. The SELECT COMMITTEE set up to investigate the matter cleared Lloyd George and Isaacs of corruption, though describing the transaction as imprudent; when pressed in the HOUSE on their Marconi holdings, neither had volunteered having speculated in the US company's stock. Lloyd George, who at one stage showed a paper profit but eventually made a loss on the deal, offered to resign; ASQUITH stood by him but wrote:

> I think the idol's wings are clipped.

margin. margin of error The term used by POLLSTERS for the allowance for SAMPLING ERROR that should be left in interpreting their results. For example a margin of error of 3% would mean that a POLL putting Party A on 51% and Party B on 49% could reflect a 54–46% lead for Party A or a 52–48% lead for Party B, or any result in between.

marginal seat In British politics, a Parliamentary seat held by one party with a narrow majority over another and always likely to change hands between them, the equivalent of a SWING DISTRICT. In US parlance, any electoral unit where the INCUMBENT was elected with 55% or less of the total vote.

key marginal A party organisers' phrase for a seat the capture of which is essential to take power in a closely-fought election.

three-way marginal A seat where three parties all finished close together at the previous ELECTION, and where each has a strong hope of victory next time. There are even a handful of *four-way marginals*. Conservative, Labour, LibDem and Nationalist or GREEN.

marginalisation The tactic of manoeuvring a party or grouping into a position where it loses influence and support and becomes irrelevant. The word originated in America, but has been widely used in Britain since the late 1980s.

Marine One The first-choice helicopter of the President of the United States (*see* Lyndon JOHNSON: 'Son, these are all my helicopters'). It is a reminder to the American people, and the other armed forces, that of all the services with helicopters, the Marine Corps has been chosen to supply the Presidential chopper. Marine One is based at Oswego, NY. At the end of 2004 the BUSH administration prompted a storm in CONGRESS by opting for the US101, a variant of the Anglo-Italian EH101, as the new generation of Marine One instead of an all-American Sikorski.

market, the A situation in which economic and other forces compete freely, without being distorted for good or ill by outside agencies.

> The best test of truth is the power of the thought to get itself accepted in the competition of the market.
>
> Justice OLIVER WENDELL HOLMES (1841–1935)

> You cannot buck the market.
>
> MARGARET THATCHER

market economy An economy which operates subject to the disciplines of market forces of supply and demand, without any interference from or regulation by government. It is also known as the **free market**.

When REAGANOMICS proved a less than runaway success, President REAGAN said:

> The system has never failed us once. But we have failed the system every time we lose faith in the magic of the marketplace.

> The trouble about a free market economy is that it requires so many policemen to make it work.
> NEAL ASCHERSON, *The Observer*, 1985

market testing The process of establishing which functions carried out by a public body or government department could be opened up to commercial disciplines.

Single Market *See* SINGLE.

social market An economic policy concept combining development of a relatively free market with a high level of social provision. It originated in Germany (Ger. *Soziale Marktwirtschaft*), and was taken up in the mid-1970s by Sir Keith Joseph (*see* MAD MONK) en route to the greater austerity of THATCHERISM, and in the early 1980s by Dr David OWEN and the muscular wing of the SDP (*see* CARING BUT DARING); it is now reflected in some NEW LABOUR thinking, and is advanced by the non-party **Social Market** Foundation. To left-wingers it is 'Thatcherism with a human face'; right-wingers like Nicholas (later Lord) Ridley have scorned it, inferring that 'the main point of the free market is to provide the resources for the social services, and lavish provision for all is the main purpose of political life'.

markup session In the US CONGRESS, the often-private sessions at which the draft of a proposed BILL is reviewed by the relevant committee.

> It is here that outside interests can slip in a loophole with the help of a committee staffer.
> MARK GREEN, *Who Runs Congress?*

Marples Must Go *See* BALFOUR MUST GO.

Marseillaise, la The stirring battle-song of the FRENCH REVOLUTION which became the national anthem of Republican France. It was written in April 1792 by Claude Joseph Rouget de Lisle (1760–1836), a captain in the French garrison at Strasbourg and ironically a Royalist, for the mayor who wanted a marching song. He entitled it '*War Song for the Rhône Army*', but it was renamed after revolutionary soldiers from Marseille sang it on their march to the Tulieries that 10 August. The opening lines of the *Marseillaise*, which ends with a call for citizens to take up arms, are:

> Allons, enfants de la patrie,
> Le jour de gloire est arrivé.
> (Let's go, children of our country,
> The day of glory has arrived.)

Marshall Aid or **Plan** The popular name for the programme devised by US Secretary of State General George C. Marshall (1880–1959) and announced by him in a speech at Harvard on 5 June 1947, to bring economic aid to stricken Europe after WORLD WAR II. The plan, fleshed out at a conference with potential recipients in Paris, was intended both to end Europe's suffering and act as a bulwark against Communism; the Soviet Union refused to participate, and her SATELLITES were ordered not to, easing President TRUMAN's task in getting the plan through CONGRESS. $13 billion in aid – food, raw materials and machinery – was gratefully accepted between 1948 and 1951 by sixteen non-Communist European countries, including Britain.

> General, I want the plan to go down in history with your name on it. And don't give me any arguments – I'm your Commander-in-Chief.
> President TRUMAN

> The most unsordid act in history. CHURCHILL

martial law The imposition of arbitrary power under military discipline by a government threatened by war or internal unrest. The most notorious instances in recent time have been the martial law imposed in Poland by General Jaruzelski to halt the spread of the SOLIDARITY trade union, and that imposed by the SLORC junta in Burma to thwart the people's choice of a civilian government.

Marxism The ideology formulated by Karl Marx (1818–83) as the basis of COMMUNISM, which has three main strands: that economic forces control political and social conditions; that private property must be abolished to ensure equality and an end to exploitation; and that Communism can only come about through the PROLETARIAT or its leaders gaining power. CHAIRMAN MAO Tse-Tung asserted: 'There may be thousands of principles of Marxism, but . . . they can all be summed up in one sentence: Rebellion is justified'. Fidel Castro testified that for him 'discovering Marxism was like finding a map in a forest'. George Bernard Shaw, a FABIAN, wrote off Marxism as 'not only useless, but disastrous as a guide to the practice of government'. But Harold MACMILLAN is said to have observed in the 1950s: 'We are all Marxists now'.

Marx himself was the father of Communism. He fled to Brussels when his activities in Germany put him at risk, and in exile teamed up with Friedrich Engels (1820–95) to write the basic texts of the movement, the COMMUNIST MANIFESTO (1848) and DAS KAPITAL (1867–94). Marx moved to London, where he worked in the British Museum reading room, spent a quiet but seldom dull life dogged by real or imagined ill-health, and was buried in Highgate Cemetery.

> All I know is I am not a Marxist. MARX

> Karl Marx wasn't a Marxist all the time. He got drunk in Tottenham Court Road.
> MICHAEL FOOT

> Marx sought to replace national antagonisms by class antagonisms. H. G. WELLS

> The world would not be in such a snarl
> Had Marx been Groucho instead of Karl.
> IRVING BERLIN

Marxism-Leninism LENIN's elaboration of Marxist political and economic thought, and the stated credo of all disciplined Communists from the mid-1920s to the mid-1980s. Communist regimes who were at each other's throats (e.g. Moscow and Beijing) each stressed their own Marxist-Leninist credentials, and their position as custodians of the true faith. In this respect Marxism-Leninism certainly did take the place of religion for true believers.

Mason-Dixon Line The boundary between Pennsylvania and Maryland drawn in 1767 to end half a century of argument and litigation. Its significance is that it marked the border between the SLAVE STATES and those where slavery was illegal, and consequently the fault-line in the UNION.

mass. mass meeting A meeting of all a trade union's members at a plant, called usually in the open, to vote on the outcome of negotiations with management and whether to take strike or other action. Voting was done on a show of hands, and abuses of the process were one factor behind the THATCHER government's imposition of strike and other BALLOTS on trade unions in the early 1980s. Such meetings are now a rarity, used purely for imparting information.

Mass Observation The social monitoring organisation whose surveys throughout WORLD WAR II gave the British government an unprecedented, and at times unwelcome, insight into the state of public morale and opinion.

mass party A political party that aims to maximise its membership among the voters, by contrast with those, notably the former Communist parties, whose strategy involved recruiting only a chosen élite.

Massachusetts miracle The technology-based boom in Massachusetts which the state's Democratic governor Michael Dukakis (1933–) made much of in his unsuccessful 1988 Presidential CAMPAIGN. The 'miracle' collapsed not long after the inauguration of his Republican rival George BUSH Snr.

massive retaliation The words of US Secretary of State John Foster Dulles in 1953 which were meant to signal a slight but important variation to the policy of immediate and devastating response to any NUCLEAR attack which dominated Western thinking, and the policy of DETERRENCE, early in the COLD WAR. Dulles spoke of 'massive retaliation at a time and place of our own choosing', but only his first two words attracted attention and were taken as reinforcing previous policy. Even the policy Dulles meant to outline was a far cry from the doctrine of FLEXIBLE RESPONSE with which NATO replaced it in 1968.

Master of the Rolls The nickname given by the media to Lord Irvine of Lairg (1940–), LORD CHANCELLOR 1997–2002, because of the lavish and costly wallpaper with which he insisted on his official apartments in the Palace of WESTMINSTER being redecorated soon after he took office. It is a legal pun; the Master of the Rolls is in fact another of England's senior judges. Irvine, a tiler's son from Paisley who became inexorably grand in office, had recruited both Tony and Cherie BLAIR to his legal chambers when he left university, and was thus also known as **Cupid, QC**.

masterly inactivity A now common phrase first used, of France's THIRD ESTATE when it convened in 1789, by the Scottish lawyer and politician James Mackintosh (1765–1832). He wrote:

> The commons, faithful to their system, remained in a wise and masterly inactivity.

It has often been used since in UK and American politics, most notably by Vice President John C. Calhoun in the NULLIFICATION crisis, telling the South Carolina LEGISLATURE in 1831:

> If the Government should be taught thereby, that the highest wisdom of a State is a 'wise and masterly inactivity', an invaluable blessing will be conferred.

matching funds (1) The Federal subsidy for Presidential campaigns, introduced by the Election Campaign Act of 1974 in response to the abuses thrown up by WATERGATE. The funds are offered to Presidential candidates (including candidates in the PRIMARY process), provided they have reached certain fund-raising thresholds themselves and conform to strict rules on where they accept private contributions from. The Act also imposed spending limits on all candidates taking up the subsidy, and tightened reporting requirements on candidates' fund-raising. (2) Funding provided by central government for a local government or privately-undertaken project, provided a similar amount is being contributed by the other party.

Mateship A blokish expression for camaraderie, egalitanianism and a sense of community which was included in the proposed republican constitution for Australia. Inheriting the constitution from Labor, John Howard was forced to drop the reference to 'mateship' by the Democrats, before the Constitution was narrowly rejected in a REFERENDUM, to Howard's relief, in 1999.

Matignon *See* HOTEL MATIGNON.

Matricides The term used by diehard THATCHERITES for those Conservative Ministers and MPs who they believe plotted her removal in November 1990 (*see also* CATHERINE PLACE MEETING). It stems from their own description of the then Prime Minister as MOTHER.

Matrix-Churchill affair The scandal that broke at WESTMINSTER in November 1992 after the collapse of the trial of three executives of the Coventry machine tool firm Matrix-Churchill on charges of illegally trading with Iraq prior to the GULF WAR. It emerged that the three – one an agent for British intelligence – had been acting with the encouragement of Ministers, who had loosened the arms embargo on Iraq imposed during the IRAN-IRAQ WAR without telling Parliament. The trial was halted after former Trade and Defence Minister Alan CLARK retracted evidence he had given to the Customs and Excise, and the judge found that four documents ruled confidential by Ministers proved the defendants had government backing. MPs were incensed that Ministers had been conniving in the arming of SADDAM HUSSEIN just before he invaded Kuwait, and had apparently been ready both to deceive them about this change of policy and let three men go to prison rather than reveal it. A judicial inquiry under Lord Justice SCOTT stopped just short of condemning Ministers, but John MAJOR continued to pay the price for misconduct by members of his predecessor's administration.

Matteotti murder The assassination by the FASCISTS of the Italian socialist politician Giacomo Matteotti (1885–1924). On 30 May 1924 Matteotti spoke out against the Fascists in the Chamber of Deputies; several days later he was abducted and murdered by six assassins allegedly hired by Fascist Party officials. The discovery of Matteotti's body on 16 August was a damaging blow for Mussolini's (*see* DUCE) government. The assassins were brought to trial; three were acquitted and the others given light sentences which were later remitted. A retrial in 1947 resulted in sentence of 30 years' penal servitude for the three previously found guilty.

Mau Mau The secret political society among Kenya's Kikuyu people which sponsored a violent rebellion in the early 1950s against white settlers, and Africans who refused to join. Formed in the 1940s as a breakaway from the Kenya African Union, Mau Mau's main aim was to drive the Europeans out of Africa by terrorism (the word *mau* means 'Get out!'); its members were bound by oaths and dire threats if they were broken. It remained secret until 1952 when the rebellion against the British colonial government broke out with a series of atrocities, each member of a Mau Mau band sharing in every killing. Between 1952 and 1956 Mau Mau killed over 100 Europeans and 200 Africans, but suffered 11,000 losses in conflict with British and African troops. In 1953 Jomo Kenyatta, later the first post-Independence President of Kenya, was jailed for seven years as a suspected leader of Mau Mau; tough security subdued the rebellion, but it lingered on until 1959. For a time, 'to mau-mau' became US slang for to harass or bully.

Maurice letter The episode that did more than any other to wreck Britain's LIBERAL PARTY, making irreparable the split between ASQUITH and LLOYD GEORGE just as LABOUR was preparing its decisive challenge. The letter was sent to the press in May 1918 by Maj-Gen. Sir Frederick Maurice, who had just been removed as Director of Military Operations at the War Office, contradicting Lloyd George's claim that the British army in France was 'considerably stronger' at the start of the year than twelve months before. Maurice admitted it was a breach of military discipline, but Lloyd George also detected a plot against him by the Prime Minister he had ousted; Asquith was a friend of Maurice, but only heard about the letter when the papers did. Asquith moved for a SELECT COMMITTEE into the facts of the case in an uncertain speech, Lloyd George made a barnstorming appeal for instant vindication. Asquith divided the House and Lloyd George won, with the Liberals split: 100 for Asquith's motion, 71 for Lloyd George.

> *Asquith:* What is the alternative to a Select Committee?
> *Charles Stanton MP (Lab.):* Get on with the war.

mausoleum A building which houses the revered remains of a leader. The most celebrated of recent times is LENIN's in RED SQUARE, once visited by all Communist newlyweds, which has survived the collapse of the Soviet system.

maverick An unpredictable, independent-minded loner who cannot be relied upon to follow the party line. The name originated in Texas where the rancher Samuel A. Maverick (1803–70) neglected to brand many of his calves; before long any beast running free was known as a maverick and by the 1880s the term was current in US politics. In October 2004, in an extreme example of POLITICAL CORRECTNESS, staff of the Welsh Development Agency were ordered not to use the word as it referred to cattle and might thus cause offence to Hindus.

maximum. max out In US politics, to donate the maximum amount that can legally be contributed to a candidate. Sen. Alan Cranston once explained why politicians go after the large donors: 'It's not worth my time to raise it in $100 amounts. I have to concentrate on the people who can max out.'

maximalist A person or party that insists on all their demands being met and all their goals achieved in full, rejecting all thought of COMPROMISE.

Maximum John The nickname of US District Judge John Sirica (1904–92), who in 1973 blew open the WATERGATE scandal. He did so by imposing punitive sentences of up to 40 years on the burglars, on the correct assumption that they would break their silence about who was behind the raid, and by ruling that the court, not the President, would decide whether the Watergate Tapes were evidence. Sirica earned his reputation as a tough sentencer well before Watergate, but the crisis gave him comparable status as a jurist; all his rulings were upheld by the SUPREME COURT.

Maxwell-Fyfe rules The archetypal guidance on whether a Minister should take responsibility for actions by their civil servants and resign, as laid down by the Home Secretary Sir David Maxwell-Fyfe (later Lord Kilmuir) in 1954 after the CRICHEL DOWN affair.

> There is nothing more like death in life
> Than Sir David Maxwell-Fyfe.
> Qouted by DENIS HEALEY in the COMMONS, 22 November 1990

May Day The public holiday observed in many countries, on 1 May or the first Monday in the month, to celebrate international workers' SOLIDARITY; in many cases it is a festival of SOCIALISM. In Moscow May Day traditionally saw a massive military parade through RED SQUARE, with the Soviet leadership reviewing its might from the rostrum on the KREMLIN wall above Lenin's MAUSOLEUM. There was much speculation among KREMLINOLOGISTS in Communist days as to who would appear on the rostrum, and in what order. Disciplined May Day parades survive in the remaining Communist countries; elsewhere the celebrations are less forced and more festive.

Mayaguez A US container ship seized by Cambodia in the Gulf of Siam on 12 May 1975. She was released after President FORD, anxious not to appear weak after America's retreat from VIETNAM, ordered air strikes against KHMER ROUGE gunboats and the bombing of mainland Cambodia. On 14 May, US Marines landed on the Tang Islands, claimed by the Khmers, and boarded the deserted ship. Thirty-nine crew members of the *Mayaguez* were freed – at a cost of 38 US lives.

Mayflower The yacht based on the POTOMAC which was used by US Presidents from MCKINLEY to COOLIDGE. It was named, of course, after the ship in which the Pilgrim Fathers sailed.

Mayor The civic head of a town or city. In America, France and some other countries the Mayor heads the city government and wields considerable power; in England and Wales the position until recently was invariably ceremonial, though the Mayor did hold the CASTING VOTE during his or her year of office. Since 2002, however, elected Mayors have taken office in a number of English towns (*see* H'Angus the MONKEY, RED KEN). English and Welsh cities usually have a **Lord Mayor** – the title is bestowed by Royal Charter, usually on communities with over 250,000 inhabitants.

Maze Prison The high-security prison opened just south-west of Belfast in the early 1970s to hold suspected or convicted terrorists. Though it closed in the wake of the GOOD FRIDAY AGREEMENT, it still holds a powerful symbolism, with REPUBLICANS in Ulster referring to it by its original name of **Long Kesh** or simply 'the Kesh'. Both LOYALIST and Republican prisoners were held there, at first housed in Nissen huts; after a Republican hunger strike in 1972 for prisoner of war status, convicted prisoners were granted 'special status'. This decision was reversed in 1976, when new inmates – segregated on SECTARIAN lines – were housed in the newly-constructed H-BLOCKS; Republican prisoners began a campaign for reinstatement of their special status, refusing to wear prison uniform and from 1978 staging first a BLANKET PROTEST, then a DIRTY PROTEST and finally, in 1981, a HUNGER STRIKE in which Bobby Sands, elected to Parliament while in the Maze, starved himself to death on 5 May. The British Government refused to concede, despite a wave of rioting in the province; after nine further deaths the Republicans abandoned their campaign. The authorities suffered further embarrassment on 25 September 1983, when 38 IRA men staged a mass breakout, stabbing a warder to death. The escape brought a highly critical report from Sir James Hennessy, Chief Inspector of Prisons; the prison governor resigned but NORTHERN IRELAND Ministers refused to follow suit. Nineteen prisoners were still at large six months later and went on to play a major part in IRA campaigns; most were later arrested on the Continent and in America, though two were still free when the Good Friday Agreement was concluded. The prison, and particularly the H-blocks, remained a potent propaganda symbol for SINN FEIN and militant Loyalists throughout the 1980s and beyond.

MDC Movement for Democratic Change The democratic OPPOSITION to ZANU-PF in Zimbabwe, formed in 1999, which attracted strong enough support to be seen as a threat by President Robert Mugabe, who has used a combination of strong-arm tactics and constitutional change to prevent its leader, Morgan Tsangvirai – who has faced a series of treason charges – having the chance to win power at a fair ELECTION. In July 2004 the MDC 'suspended' participation in elections, saying it would be a waste of time to contest the 2005 national elections without 'real' electoral reforms. It did contest them, was heavily defeated and complained that they had been rigged.

me-tooism The practice for a political party or candidate of trying to win votes by offering policies very similar to those of their opponents. The term, used by those who believe elections can best be won by offering the voters a real choice, has been common in US politics since the late 1940s.

means test The principle that evidence of need must be proven to qualify for support from public funds, e.g. a test of one's means. Such tests were introduced by the UK's NATIONAL GOVERNMENT in 1931 for those whose unemployment benefit was exhausted, and the resulting inquisition was much resented – leading the LABOUR PARTY to adopt a rigid opposition to means-testing that lasted half a century. The test involved listing any earnings by members of the household and all monetary assets, and penalised the provident. The regulations governing public assistance were modified after WORLD WAR II, but some non-contributory benefits have remained means-tested, to be joined under Gordon BROWN's Chancellorship by Pensioner's Credit and Family Credit, both of which are extra payments dependent on a less demeaning proof of means. In America the principle has been established for some welfare payments for several decades, and was tightened under the REAGAN administration.

Mebyon Kernow (Cornish. Sons of Cornwall) The society of Cornish nationalists, established in 1951, which has contested a number of Parliamentary ELECTIONS with minimal success. It advocates cultivation of the once-extinct but revived Cornish language, and a degree of self-government in concert with other Celtic peoples such as the Bretons, the Welsh, the Irish and Gaelic-speaking Scots. Their flag is the emblem of St Piran, a 5th- or 6th-century saint who reputedly discovered tin in Cornwall. It consists of a white cross, symbolising the mineral, on a black field for the ground rock from which it is extracted.

meddle and muddle The colourful phrase first used by the Earl of Derby (1799–1869) to describe the foreign policy of the Liberal leader Earl (formerly Lord John) Russell. Derby told the House of Lords on 4 February 1864:

> The foreign policy of the noble Earl may be

summed up in two short, homely but expressive words: 'Meddle and muddle.'

media The press, radio and television (**electronic media**), a powerful force (*see* FOURTH ESTATE) capable of exposing scandals like WATERGATE, or hounding or misrepresenting a party or its leaders; consequently a whipping-horse for every politician who dislikes criticism. Enoch POWELL remarked philosophically that 'politicians who complain about the media are like ships' captains who complain about the sea', but Ronald REAGAN, who had a better press than Powell, complained:

> People in the media say they must look at the President through a microscope. But boy, when they use a proctoscope, that's going too far.

John F. KENNEDY, for whom the media covered up again and again, was moved to tell the press: 'I have always said that when we don't have to go through you bastards, we can really get our story over to the American people', while 'RED' KEN Livingstone, a target of Fleet Street in the early 1980s, observed; 'If I blew my nose they would say I was trying to spread germ warfare.'

> To hell with them. When history is written they will be the sons of bitches, not I.
>
> HARRY S TRUMAN

media event An event of no real political significance, arranged by public relations personnel specifically to attract media coverage; it generally includes a PHOTO OPPORTUNITY.

mediation The role of a third nation or independent figure in bringing together two parties to an international, political or industrial dispute in an effort to generate agreement between them.

Medicaid The US public-health programme to provide hospital and medical care for those who cannot afford it. It was established by CONGRESS in 1965 as a joint plan in which the Federal government funded 50–80% of a state's costs, depending on its citizens' average income. Each state must meet Federal standards, but may choose the services it wishes to provide. Any indigent person qualifies for Medicaid, and some states stretch this to the 'medically indigent', who cannot meet medical bills incompatible with their earnings.

Medicare The insurance programme to provide hospital and medical care to Americans aged 65 or over, and some disabled persons. First proposed by President KENNEDY and approved by CONGRESS in 1965, it is funded by a tax added to social security contributions. It covers treatment in hospitals, in nursing homes and at home (after a deductible sum of over $500 is paid each year), and meets 80% of physician and medical costs not covered by the hospital insurance. In 1988 Congress passed the Medicare Catastrophic Coverage act to expand its reach, but so many elderly Americans objected to the surtax to fund its cost (more than $32 billion over five years) that it was repealed the next year. In 2003 the BUSH administration pushed through Congress a Medicare 'drug benefit plan' aimed at providing affordable generic drugs for retirees, but which incurred heavy criticism for paying pharmaceutical companies $40 billion a year to make the drugs available. (*See* Corporate WELFARE).

medium term financial strategy (MTFS) The name adopted by Margaret THATCHER, and her first Chancellor Sir Geoffrey HOWE, at the suggestion of Nigel Lawson, for the MONETARIST strategy they adopted from 1979, with monetary targets published several years ahead. Known to sceptics as **'Mrs Thatcher's Final Solution'**, the MTFS was adhered to seriously for a couple of years, but the name and the targets lived on for several more.

> I would not bow to demands to reflate; it was this which turned the MTFS from an ambitious aspiration into the cornerstone of a successful policy.
>
> MARGARET THATCHER, *The Downing Street Years*

> Intended to set a reliable framework of government policy within which the markets could form 'rational expectations', it simply demonstrated that no one should take seriously anything a Conservative Chancellor said.
>
> DENIS HEALEY

Meech Lake The agreement negotiated between the Canadian provinces in 1987 by Brian Mulroney which attempted to resolve the deadlock over amending the Federal constitution by granting Quebec **distinct society** status. The accord was always fragile, and collapsed in 1990 when Manitoba and Newfoundland failed to ratify it. A constitutional crisis ensued, which the equally-abortive CHARLOTTETOWN ACCORD of 1992 was designed to resolve.

Meet the challenge. Make the change The slogan with which the LABOUR PARTY under Neil KINNOCK relaunched itself after its

POLICY REVIEW, and went into the 1992 ELECTION campaign with high hopes – only to suffer its fourth successive defeat. Labour's updated image and its jettisoning of controversial policies like UNILATERALISM enabled it to slash the Tory majority, but left the voters uneasy as to what 'the change' would actually be.

Mein Kampf (Ger. My Struggle) The book in which HITLER set out his political and racial theories and misreadings of history; the combination of autobiography, anti-Semitic rantings and an alarmingly accurate prediction of how he would transform central Europe became the NAZI 'Bible'. It was published in two parts in 1925 and 1927; the first was written in prison after the abortive MUNICH BEER HALL PUTSCH of 1923. The original title was *Four and a Half Years of Struggle against Lies, Stupidity and Cowardice*, but the author was persuaded to think of something snappier. The outbreak of WORLD WAR II and the revelation of the HOLOCAUST left many educated people in Germany and beyond claiming to be surprised, but anyone who read *Mein Kampf* and took it literally would have known what to expect.

Mellon fiscal policy The policies pursued at the US Treasury from 1921 to 1932 by the oil and commodities magnate Andrew Mellon (1855–1937). Reckoned the second richest man in America, Mellon served three Presidents – HARDING, COOLIDGE and HOOVER – and was allowed ever greater latitude until the GREAT DEPRESSION struck. He set up the Bureau of the Budget in 1921, and pressed for lower taxes on corporations and the wealthy, meeting resistance in CONGRESS until prosperity became widespread after 1924. Hailed by Republicans as the greatest Treasury Secretary since HAMILTON, he was an unashamed supporter of the business community and the MARKET. Though he conspicuously failed to foresee the GREAT CRASH, few of his peers did, either.

melt. meltdown The sudden, spectacular collapse of a political CAMPAIGN which has appeared to be going well. The term is taken from the NUCLEAR industry, meltdown being the point at which the rise in a reactor's temperature becomes irreversible, making disaster inevitable (*see* CHERNOBYL).

melting pot The image of America as a society capable of absorbing members of disparate races and cultures and rendering them into a single and unified whole with opportunities for all, relied on heavily by those who oppose limits on immigration. The phrase was the title of a popular play by the English Jew Israel Zangwill (1864–1926), staged in New York in 1909. In its first scene a character says:

> America is God's Crucible, the great Melting Pot where all the races of Europe are melting and re-forming.

Within two years the concept was rebutted by the DILLINGHAM REPORT which paved the way for tight controls on immigration, but by 1915 Woodrow WILSON was declaring:

> There is here a great melting pot in which we must compound a precious metal. That metal is the metal of nationality.

While a rainbow of ethnic groups continues to swell America's population, many groups would agree with the Rev. Jesse JACKSON:

> I hear that melting pot stuff a lot, and all I can say is that we haven't melted.

Some commentators have suggested America's ethnic mix is more of a tossed salad, with each legume remaining identifiable. But native American singer Buffy Ste Marie put it more starkly:

> Here the melting pot stands open – if you're ready to get bleached first.

men. Men Behind the Wire, the Irish Republicans' appreciative shorthand for the IRA men convicted or INTERNED in NORTHERN IRELAND, the wire being the perimeter fencing of the MAZE (*see also* H-BLOCKS) or another of the province's prisons. *The Men Behind the Wire* was also a popular Republican song of solidarity with the detainees at the height of the TROUBLES.

men in grey suits The silent power brokers of Britain's CONSERVATIVE PARTY, who at the critical moment will call on its leader and indicate that he or she no longer enjoys the confidence of the party and should resign. **men in suits** was a dismissive term for the clone-like and slightly flashy middle-aged businessmen who surrounded Margaret THATCHER and were frequently appointed by her to responsible jobs (*see* LORD SUIT; PARKINSON AFFAIR).

men in tights The dismissive sobriquet for the SERJEANT AT ARMS and other traditional officials of the PALACE OF WESTMINSTER, bestowed by MPs who regard their functions and dress as anachronistic. It was applied by Labour MPs, in particular, in 2004 when the House authorities failed to prevent first the throwing at Tony BLAIR of a condom full of purple powder from the STRANGERS'

GALLERY by protesters from FATHERS 4 JUSTICE, and then the invasion of the CHAMBER by five huntsmen demonstrating against the vote on 15 September to outlaw foxhunting with dogs. In this latter incident the assistant Serjeant at Arms, sword at his side, had to wrestle one of the demonstrators to the floor. The incidents, and a further security breach when protesters from GREENPEACE scaled Big Ben, led MPs on both sides to insist that the police and security services be given primacy in keeping Parliament secure.

men in white coats An old Americanism for the male nurses who would lead away those of unsound mind to detention in a mental institution. In politics anyone felt by colleagues to be uttering suitably eccentric views is said to be liable to a visit from them.

men or measures The argument over whether the composition or policies of a government is more important, and whether a party offering one rather than the other is the more worthy of ELECTION. Though it has never subsided, it was at its height in England in the late 18th and early 19th centuries.

> The cant of 'men, not measures', a sort of charm by which many people get loose from every honourable engagement.
>
> EDMUND BURKE, *Thoughts on the Cause of the Present Discontent, 1770*

> If the comparison must be made . . . men are everything, measures comparatively nothing.
>
> GEORGE CANNING, House of Commons, 9 December 1802

mending fences *See* FENCES.

Mensheviks (Russ. Minority) The moderate wing of the Russian SOCIAL DEMOCRATIC Workers' Party which initially worked alongside the BOLSHEVIKS to overthrow the Tsarist political system, then opposed the OCTOBER REVOLUTION of 1917. They believed that gradual reform would lead to a socialist state and the primacy of the working class, and were deeply divided over co-operating with the Bolsheviks and KERENSKY's provisional government after the February 1917 revolution. As the Bolsheviks seized power, TROTSKY told their former allies:

> You are miserable isolated individuals. You are bankrupt. You have played out your role. Go where you belong – to the dustheap of history.

The Mensheviks tried to continue as a legitimate opposition party, but by 1922 their leaders had been killed by the Bolsheviks or had fled into exile.

Menzies, Sir Robert *See* MING.

MEOW *See* MORAL EQUIVALENT OF WAR.

MEP Member of the EUROPEAN PARLIAMENT. The official abbreviation and designation for members of the Strasbourg-Brussels assembly.

Mercosur (Sp. Market of the South). The FREE TRADE area and customs union comprising Argentina, Brazil, Paraguay and Uruguay which was ordained by the **Treaties of Asuncion** in 1991 and **Ouro Preto** three years later and came into being at the start of 1995, with 2006 set as the target for completion of the market. With more than 200 million inhabitants and a combined annual gross product at the time of $800 billion, it was then rated the world's fourth largest market after NAFTA, the European SINGLE MARKET and Japan. Association agreements were signed with Chile and Bolivia in 1996; two years later a common mechanism for political consultation was launched for all six countries, and in 2003 a heavyweight Committee of Permanent Representatives and a Dispute Settlement Court were established.

merger The issue that destroyed the SDP/Liberal ALLIANCE following the 1987 UK general election. Less than 48 hours after the two parties' poor showing (22 seats between them) the LIBERAL leader David Steel (*see* BOY DAVID) called for immediate moves for them to merge. Many SDP members had anticipated a merger and were ready to negotiate, but others including the party leader Dr David OWEN felt Steel was 'bouncing' them; Owen resigned that August, and Robert Maclennan took his place. The first attempt that winter to produce a blueprint for a merged party pleased no one (*see* DEAD PARROT), but eventually a deal was struck and on 3 March 1988 the parties merged; in July Paddy Ashdown (*see* Paddy PANTSDOWN) defeated Alan Beith for the leadership of what were at first known as the Social and Liberal Democrats (SALADS). Dr Owen persevered with a continuing SDP with three MPs, coming close to winning a by-election at Richmond, Yorkshire in February 1989, but as the LIBERAL DEMOCRATS picked up speed the SDP faded away.

merit system The system for CIVIL SERVICE recruitment and promotion which largely replaced PATRONAGE in Britain and America in the third quarter of the 19th century. In WHITEHALL the principle of recruitment by competitive examination was established after bitter resistance through the NORTHCOTE-TREVELYAN REFORMS; in WASHINGTON Rep. Thomas Jenckes introduced a BILL for similar reforms in 1865, and President Hayes (*see* OLD 8 TO 7) struck several blows against patronage, but it took the assassination of President Garfield (*see* BOATMAN JIM) to introduce merit selection for all but the highest posts, which remain open to POLITICAL APPOINTEES.

meritocracy Rule by those of superior intellect and talents. The term was popularised by the educationalist Michael Young (later Lord Young of Dartington) in his 1958 book *The Rise of the Meritocracy*, in which he argued that educational achievements had replaced noble birth and inherited wealth as the route to power in society.

Messina conference The conference held in Sicily in June 1955 which began serious planning for the creation two years later of the EUROPEAN ECONOMIC COMMUNITY, by the Treaty of ROME. Anthony EDEN turned down an invitation for Britain to participate, and the six nations whose foreign ministers and technical experts attended went on to found the Community in their own image and pave the way for the creation of the European COMMON MARKET, the EEC and EURATOM.

Mexican stand-off Ronald REAGAN's comparison of SUPERPOWER tension with a confrontation between two gunslingers, America and the Soviet Union, each with NUCLEAR pistols drawn 'and if one man's finger flinches, you're going to get your brains blown out'.

Mexican War The war between the United States and Mexico provoked by the admission of Texas to the UNION at the end of 1845. It resulted in total American victory, but lasted almost two years and has hardened Mexican attitudes ever since. Mexico refused to recognise the Rio Grande boundary of its former province of Texas, and after several months of manoeuvring its troops crossed the river on 30 April 1846. The battle of Palo Alto followed, after which CONGRESS declared war on 13 May. The following February, General Zachary Taylor with 5500 troopers took on and defeated a Mexican force almost four times as large at Monterey. Battles followed at Resaca de la Palma and Buena Vista, and General Winfield Scott captured Mexico City. The war ended on 2 February 1848 with the Treaty of GUADALUPE HIDALGO, under which Mexico conceded California and what are now the states of Arizona, Colorado, Nevada, New Mexico and Utah.

> I do not think there was ever a more wicked war. I thought so at the time, when I was a youngster, only I had not moral courage enough to resign.
>
> ULYSSES S. GRANT, *Memoirs*

MHR Member of the House of Representatives. The abbreviation used to describe a member of the lower and more powerful house of Australia's Federal parliament.

MIAs The more than 2400 American service personnel still Missing In Action when the final US forces withdrew from South-East Asia in 1975. The families of many refused to believe they were dead, as the North Vietnamese and other former enemies claimed and as WASHINGTON seemed to want to believe. Several freelance expeditions were mounted with support from ultra-conservative groups to bring back men who had reputedly been seen alive, but none succeeded. Public eagerness to locate and REPATRIATE any MIAs who had survived became an issue in several election campaigns, and also triggered a series of inconclusive Congressional investigations. As relations improved, a number of bodies were returned, but into the 1990s stories were still coming to light of men held in remote areas beyond the end of the war, who might still be there.

MI5 The popular name for Britain's **Security Service**, which is charged with the detection and surveillance of those known or thought to be engaged in espionage, or subversion, in the UK. In 1992 MI5, which is answerable first to the HOME SECRETARY and then to the Prime Minister, was made responsible for thwarting IRA terrorism on the mainland, as the police struggled to cope; it had previously had a largely COLD WAR focus. The same year it gained its first woman director, Mrs Stella Rimington; her appointment was the first to be publicly announced, following legislation by John MAJOR's government to bring MI5 out of the shadows and put it on a statutory basis. Since 9/11 its range has been widened and its manpower increased to keep tabs on Islamic extremists in the UK. MI5 (Military Intelligence, section five) was the agency's original title when established in 1916. Its headquarters are at Thames House on MILLBANK.

MI6 Again a title long since dropped but still a household phrase, this time for the **Secret Intelligence Service** (SIS), Britain's equivalent of the CIA. In government and security circles it is often referred to just as 'Six'. Headed by 'C', its members are engaged on espionage and other intelligence activities abroad, using British agents and disaffected nationals of the countries in which they operate; its focus, like that of MI5, has changed markedly since the end of the COLD WAR and even more since 9/11. The SIS was formed as MI6 (Military Intelligence, section six) in 1921; it is responsible to the FOREIGN SECRETARY, and ultimately to the Prime Minister.

mid-term elections *See* ELECTIONS.

Middle America A social and geographical term for the 'Silent MAJORITY' of Americans, who believe in traditional values and reject extreme views or tastes. They believe their views are ignored by the MEDIA based largely on the East and West Coasts, hence their concentration in America's heartlands. The term was coined in 1968 by the WASHINGTON commentator Joseph Kraft, with reference to the people to whom Richard NIXON pitched his electoral appeal. Though essentially conservative, Middle America is not universally HAWKISH; prior to both the GULF WAR and the IRAQ WAR many of its mothers protested against the likely involvement of their sons.

middle class A term for the social grouping which takes pride in having differentiated itself from the WORKING CLASS 'beneath' it, and on having more refined if narrower attitudes. Traditionally the smooth operation of democracy is supposed to be dependent on a strong middle class – or on not annoying it. A survey in America during the 1992 election showed that 92% of the population regarded themselves as middle-class. In Britain this group in the 1960s and '70s felt itself unfairly squeezed by taxation (according to the *Daily Mail* it still does); Margaret THATCHER saw herself as the embodiment of middle-class values. This was a mixed blessing; as her government went down to a crushing defeat in the HOUSE OF LORDS c. 1980 on a plan to charge rural and Roman Catholic parents for their children's use of school buses, an Earl from the BACKWOODS turned to the hereditary Labour peer Lord Ponsonby in the DIVISION LOBBY and observed:

> Trouble with the middle classes – never did understand the people!

Labour voters in this grouping have customarily felt a touch of guilt and social obligation. Hugh GAITSKELL remarked: 'Middle-class Socialists have got to have a profound humility', and Tony BLAIR said when campaigning for the leadership: 'I wasn't born into this party; I chose it.'

> The British people, being subject to fogs and possessing a powerful middle class, require grave statesmen. DISRAELI

Middle England The core of the British electorate, in numerical terms and in the mind of political strategists, and the supreme target of NEW LABOUR prior to and since the party's LANDSLIDE return to power in 1997. Tony BLAIR and his colleagues were convinced that the party could only be elected if it reached out beyond its traditional support to the cautious and moderately conservative mass of the English middle class, and tailored Labour's appeal accordingly while endeavouring not to lose too much of its working-class support. 'Middle England' also has geographical connotations, being located outside the major conurbations in precisely the semi-rural constituencies where Labour made its most dramatic gains in 1997 and held them four years later.

middle ground The body of voters in the political CENTRE, who can be captured by a party ready to renounce extremism and offer moderate and attractive policies. This group is generally considered vital to electoral victory, though Margaret THATCHER'S LANDSLIDE wins in 1983 and 1987 resulted as much from an equally divided opposition as from the readiness of voters in the middle ground to support her brand of radicalism.

middle of the road A voter or politician who stays obdurately in the centre, resisting the blandishments of the right or the left. Dwight D. EISENHOWER, the ultimate middle-of-the-roader having been wooed for the Presidency by both main US parties, commended it as 'all the usable surface. The extremes, right and left, are the gutters.' But Aneurin BEVAN said in 1953:

> We all know what happens to people who stay in the middle of the road. They get run over.

Middle Way, The The book published by Harold MACMILLAN in 1938 which set out in full the KEYNESIAN philosophy he had been developing over the previous six years, out of conviction that LAISSEZ-FAIRE and a deliberate avoidance of planning could not solve the problems of the GREAT DEPRESSION. Among his most radical proposals were the replacement of the Stock Exchange by a National Investment Board and the introduction of a MINIMUM WAGE – something Labour would only advocate half a century later. He saw these views, first aired in 1932 in his pamphlet *The Next Step*, as a middle course between hands-off capitalism and egalitarian socialism (*compare* Tony BLAIR's THIRD WAY). *The Middle Way* was not liked by the Tory leadership, and Macmillan's old nanny said of it:

> Mr Harold is a dangerous pink.

But it was welcomed by Labour thinkers, and by liberal Tories at Oxford including Edward HEATH and Hugh Fraser. At various times after, notably as the WETS regrouped in the early days of THATCHERISM, the phrase 'The Middle Way' would become a rallying-cry for the left of the party.

Midlothian campaign The barnstorming radical campaign with which the supposedly retired GLADSTONE returned to politics at the start of 1880, aged 71. Adopted as Liberal candidate for Midlothian, the area of Scotland south-west of Edinburgh, Gladstone embarked on an aggressive 'stump' CAMPAIGN, peppered with public meetings at which the GRAND OLD MAN poured scorn on DISRAELI's foreign policies, which he said had failed from the Balkans to South Africa. It set the tone for a vigorous election campaign that saw the Liberals returned to power that April with a paper majority of 176 – though heavily dependent on the CELTIC FRINGE and the Irish nationalists.

MiGs The family of jet fighters with which Soviet Russia, and its customers in China, eastern Europe and the non-aligned world, achieved primacy in the air in the decades after WORLD WAR II. The planes were named after their designers, Mikoyan and Gurevich. The early MiGs had advanced jet engines, the technology for which was obligingly supplied by Rolls-Royce with the approval of the British government – to the incredulity of STALIN. In the KOREAN WAR MiG 15s with such engines shot down a number of British fighters.

> Wogs have MiGs.
> JULIAN AMERY MP (Con.)

Mik The Westminster nickname for **Ian Mikardo** (1908–93), the Labour MP for READING (1945–59) and for Poplar (1964–87) who was a leading BEVANITE in the 1950s, a pillar of the TRIBUNE GROUP and a key left-wing member of Labour's national executive (NEC). The beetling Mikardo hit the headlines in 1975 when, at Tribune's party conference FRINGE MEETING, he launched an attack on the WILSON government's PRICES AND INCOMES POLICY which provoked the Transport Union leader Jack Jones to storm off the platform, grab the microphone from Mikardo and shout: 'I detest these attacks on the trade union movement.' Yet Mikardo was voted off the NEC in 1978 for his greatest service to the party: the **Mikardo compromise** to resolve the conflict between hard LEFT advocates of mandatory RESELECTION of MPs and the leadership who wanted the *status quo*. The compromise scraped through, and Mikardo's supporters ditched him, claiming betrayal. The subsequent abandonment of the compromise triggered the warfare that led to the formation of the SDP, Labour's disastrous performance in the 1983 ELECTION, long years in OPPOSITION and the ultimate eclipse of the left.

> Not as nice as he looks. CHURCHILL

milch-cow Any easily tappable source of funds, especially for Congressmen seeking PORK BARREL projects. Originally a word for a cow kept for milking, this essentially American term incidentally reflects the role of the Federal government as provider for the FARM BELT.

militancy The pursuit of political aims by vigorous, almost obsessive, argument, campaigning and action; because of the energy with which the views are promoted, the assumption will be that they are extreme. The term is an old one, a reference to the 'Church militant' stemming from 1413. In 1905 the SUFFRAGETTES officially adopted 'Militancy' as their watchword – its first manifestation was the breaking up by Christabel Pankhurst and Annie Kenney of a meeting in Manchester addressed by the Liberal statesman Sir Edward Grey, ironically a strong supporter of VOTES FOR WOMEN.

Militant Tendency The TROTSKYIST movement in the UK founded by the South African-born ideologue Ted Grant, whose ENTRYIST tactics reduced parts of the LABOUR PARTY to near-paralysis in the early 1980s, until Neil KINNOCK took decisive (though slow-working) action against it. Originally the Revolutionary Socialist League, it began burrowing into the Labour Party in 1964, when its weekly newspaper *Militant* was founded under the editorship of Peter Taaffe. Though its prophecies of the imminent collapse of capitalism and its call for 'NATIONALISATION of the 250 major monopolies, the banks and insurance companies under WORKERS' CONTROL' remained unchanged for almost three decades, its sellers varied their appeal. Bob Edwards, a member of Militant's Central Committee, once sold the paper to homeward-bound commuters with the slogan:

> All the winners! All the winners! Marx! Lenin! Engels! Trotsky!

Organising a PARTY WITHIN A PARTY, it built a national organisation while recruiting Labour Party members in the constituencies. Its influence grew, despite repeated warnings to Labour's National Executive (NEC), culminating in the UNDERHILL REPORT; at its height *Militant*'s annual rally filled the Royal Albert Hall and there was talk of making the paper a daily. By late 1982 even the left-dominated NEC had run out of patience as tales of mayhem poured in from the constituencies; *Militant* was declared ineligible for affiliation to the party and expulsion proceedings began against the paper's five-strong editorial board; it took months of court challenges before they were ousted. In 1983 two Militant supporters, Terry Fields and Dave Nellist, were elected as Labour MPs, and Militant captured the Labour group on Liverpool City Council, and thus the council itself. Militant had always avoided confrontation with the Labour leadership, but the activities of the council's deputy leader Derek Hatton in defying the government in breach of party policy, coupled with rumours of thuggery and corruption, provoked Kinnock into a searing attack at Labour's 1985 conference. An inquiry led to organisational changes and around a dozen expulsions from the party, and a National Constitutional Committee was set up solely to deal with expulsions, to prevent the NEC hearing demanded by each Militant turning into a media circus. Militant's march was checked despite the election of two more MPs in 1967, but expulsions went at a snail's pace and it took another provocation in Liverpool to break it. When the veteran Labour MP Eric Heffer (*see* I, TOO, WAS A CARPENTER) died in 1990, Militant opposed Labour at the ensuing by-election, suffering a humiliating defeat and opening its campaigners to expulsion from the party. Militant split between advocates of entryism and proponents of a separate party; its influence in England collapsed, but key members regrouped in Scotland, at first as Militant Labour but then to great effect as the SCOTTISH SOCIALIST PARTY (SSP).

militarism A national stance based on pressures for war and domination by an army or military class. The term was particularly used of Prussia's aggressive mindset, both before and after its creation of the German state in 1870.

> A fever for conquest, with peace as a shield, using music and brass buttons to dazzle and divert the populace. ELBERT HUBBARD

> We want to get rid of the militarist not simply because he hurts and kills, but because he is an intolerable thick-voiced blockhead who stands hectoring and blustering in our way to achievement. H. G. WELLS, 1920

> The day that militarism is undermined, capitalism will fall.
> HELEN KELLER, *My Life*

military-industrial complex The network of defence contractors, PENTAGON officials and generals who, to their critics, have a vested interest in arming America beyond its needs and, ultimately, in war. Intriguingly, the phrase was coined by President EISENHOWER; IKE said on 17 January 1961 in his farewell address:

> In the councils of government, we must guard against the acquisition of unwarranted influence, whether sought or unsought, by the military-industrial complex. The potential for the disastrous rise of misplaced powers exists and will persist . . . Only an alert and knowledgeable citizenry can compel the proper meshing of the huge industrial and political machinery of defence with our peaceful methods and goals, so that security and liberty may prosper together.

Sen. Barry Goldwater later remarked: 'Thank heaven for the military-industrial complex. Its ultimate aim is peace in our time.'

military wing *See* POLITICAL WING.

militia A citizen force kept in reserve to combat any threat or emergency. The RIGHT TO KEEP AND BEAR ARMS in the US CONSTITUTION specifies the need for a militia, hence the NATIONAL GUARD. In VICHY France the *Milice* were the COLLABORATIONIST reserve police. In Lebanon in the 1980s each Christian and Muslim faction had a 'militia' supposed to protect its community; they ranged from rival warlords' private armies to pro-Iranian terrorist groups.

> The citizens of America from 18 to 50 Years of Age should be borne on the Militia Rolls, provided with uniform arms, and so far accustomed to the use of them that the Total strength of the country might be called forth at Short Notice on any very interesting emergency.
> GEORGE WASHINGTON to Alexander Hamilton, 2 May 1783

Michigan Militia The 12,000-strong far-right organisation with neo-NAZI connections linked to the 1995 OKLAHOMA CITY BOMBING through its convicted perpetrators, Timothy McVeigh and Terry Nicholls. The Militia was one of a chain of PARAMILITARY groups set up by far-right and almost exclusively white Americans to protect individual rights, notably that to bear arms, from Federal interference.

milk. milk-snatcher Margaret THATCHER's first nickname, and one of the most hostile. It stemmed from her action as Education Secretary in Edward HEATH's government in cutting off funds for the provision of free daily milk for schoolchildren. Up to that time every child in Britain received one-third of a pint during the morning break.

Milk Street Mafia The CABAL of influential Tories who met at the height of the leadership contest in January 1975 and concluded that Edward HEATH was finished. The meeting was convened by Edward du Cann, chairman of the 1922 COMMITTEE, who had himself considered standing, in the flat over his City of London offices in Milk Street. When the oleaginous du Cann, renowned at WESTMINSTER as a plotter, was asked later if he was still loyal to Heath, he replied:

> I think I'm the only one who is.

Millbank (1) The broadcasting complex at 4 Millbank, across the road and 200 yards along from the PALACE OF WESTMINSTER, from which all electronic news organisations now operate. Originally an adjunct to news-gathering within the Palace and around it, Millbank became from the mid-1990s a gathering point for LOBBY correspondents as key politicians made increasing use of its studios. (2) The headquarters of the LABOUR PARTY from 1996 to 2002 on the lower floors of the contemporary Millbank Tower, between Lambeth Bridge and Tate Britain, which became a byword for SPIN and centralised control of the party message under the influence of Peter Mandelson (*see* BOBBY) in the run-up to Labour's 1997 LANDSLIDE victory. David Triesman, Labour's general secretary from 2001 to 2003, complained that the party's slogan for the month was even displayed in the toilets, and hailed the move to OLD QUEEN STREET as reflecting a new, more open style of campaigning. Labour had used the building's 230-seat conference suite for party events for several years before the full move from WALWORTH ROAD.

Millie The dog who provided the lighter moments of George BUSH Snr's presidency. In May 1991 she was suspected of having passed an auto-immune disease to her master and mistress, and in a campaign speech on 29 October 1992 Bush said of his Democratic challengers Bill CLINTON and Al Gore:

> My dog Millie knows more about foreign policy than those two bozos.

Million Man March *See* MARCH.

minder An experienced political operator, usually an MP, who is drafted into a UK BY-ELECTION campaign to keep a close eye on a party's candidate and guide them through potentially embarrassing moments. The parties began to appoint minders in the mid-1980s after a series of catastrophic performances by inexperienced candidates at the hands of a probing and hostile media. The term comes from Fleet Street where tabloids that had 'bought up' members of the public at the heart of sensitive stories would give them a rugged companion to keep them out of the clutches of the competition; *Minder* was also a hugely successful TV series as the parties first deployed such handlers.

Mine eyes have seen the glory of the coming of the Lord The opening line of the Battle Hymn of the Republic, the most stirring of America's patriotic anthems. It was written at the height of the CIVIL WAR by the feminist and peace worker Julia Ward Howe (1819–1910) after seeing President LINCOLN review over 50,000 UNION troops at Bailey's Crossroads outside Washington on 20 November 1861. She felt they should have something more suitable to sing than JOHN BROWN'S BODY and composed these words to the tune; they were published in the *Atlantic Monthly* the next February. When Lincoln heard the song, he asked to hear it again and gave it his personal endorsement.

miners' strike The term used at the time for a series of confrontations between Britain's National Union of Mineworkers and Conservative governments, in 1972 and 1974 over pay and 1984–85 over pit closures; the miners won the first two, winning pay increases and in the second bringing down Edward HEATH's government. The phrase is now used solely for the third and bitterest strike, when the NUM President Arthur Scargill (*see* KING ARTHUR) took on Margaret THATCHER over pit closures he claimed were imminent. There was widespread support in the union for a strike, but Scargill refused to allow a BALLOT and Nottinghamshire miners, joined by an increasing number of others, defied flying PICKETS to stay at work. The strike lasted over a year, with strikers and their families suffering great hardship, before the combination of large coal stocks at power stations, the output of the WORKING MINERS and the impact of Tory union legislation outlawing secondary action broke the dispute. The strike harmed the LABOUR PARTY, which traditionally supported the miners but was split over Scargill's tactics. Neil KINNOCK, who was endeavouring to shed Labour's extremist image, did his best to distance himself from Scargill while sympathising with the miners' personal plight. But it did even greater damage to the NUM, as the working miners split away to form the Union of Democratic Mineworkers and the collapse of the strike was followed by a closure programme at least as severe as Scargill had predicted in more prosperous times (*see* ENEMY WITHIN; Battle of ORGREAVE).

The miners, united, will never be defeated The chant, to a Marxist-originated Latin American rhythm, of supporters of the National Union of Mineworkers in the strike of 1984–85 (*see also* HERE WE GO, HERE WE GO, HERE WE GO).

Ming The nickname of Australia's Liberal Prime Minister Sir Robert Menzies (1894–1978), based on the Scottish pronounciation of his name ('Mingis'). It was coined also by analogy with Ming the Merciless, a character in the Flash Gordon cartoon strip series. The long period of Menzies' premiership (1939–41 and 1949–66) inevitably came to be known as the **'Ming dynasty'**. At WESTMINSTER the name was later given to the deputy Liberal Democrat leader and former Olympic athlete Menzies Campbell QC (1941–), MP for North East Fife from 1987.

Miniature for Sport The nickname given at WESTMINSTER to the diminutive Conservative MP Colin Moynihan (1955–) in 1987 when he became Margaret THATCHER's Minister for Sport. Moynihan, who in 1980 won an Olympic silver medal as cox to the UK rowing eight, subsequently served as an energy minister under John MAJOR before losing his seat in 1992.

mini-budget *See* BUDGET.

minimum lending rate (MLR) From 1971 to 1981, the rate at which the Bank of England would lend to discount houses, and thus the determinant of the rates charged and paid by banks and building societies throughout the economy. Before 1971 this was known as the **Bank Rate**; since 1981 as the **Base Rate.** When the government suspended the MLR as a measure of policy in 1981, it reserved the right to reintroduce it at any time if needed; it did so for one day in January 1985. Since 1997 the government has left the setting of interest rates to the Bank.

minimum wage A long-standing feature of US economic life (since 1938), but in the UK an aspiration only of the far left and militant trade unionists until the mid-1980s when it became official Labour policy, being enacted by Tony BLAIR's government after the party's LANDSLIDE victory in 1997. Conservative claims that it would wipe out jobs and force up INFLATION have not, thus far, been borne out, and while some employers ignore the legislation, it has led to real improvements in the lot of the lowest-paid. The level of the minimum wage – as in the US the lowest hourly rate that can legally be paid – is set annually by the Trade and Industry Secretary on the advice of the Low Pay Commission.

> The Republicans favour a minimum wage – the smaller the minimum, the better.
>
> HARRY S TRUMAN

MINIS The management information system pioneered at the UK Department of the Environment in 1980 by its Secretary of State Michael HESELTINE, which became a model – after initial resistance by CABINET colleagues and civil service MANDARINS who dismissed it as 'nonsense' – for similar techniques elsewhere in WHITEHALL. Designed to instil what Heseltine called a 'private sector management ethos', it involved asking the heads of the DoE's 66 directorates to define their tasks, explain the reason for doing them, and state the cost. Heseltine concluded that nine of them were unnecessary; a restructuring was carried out, which was claimed to have saved a considerable amount of money, and a series of charts were drawn up setting out the department's new management and functional structure.

Minister (1) A term used widely (except in the United States) for a member of a government or CABINET. It should not technically be used of the most senior UK Ministers, as the entire Cabinet except for the Ministers without PORTFOLIO and the CHIEF SECRETARY have the rank of SECRETARY OF STATE. The rank of **Minister of State**, the sub-Cabinet deputy to each Departmental Minister (some have two), dates back only to the 1940s, when the burden of work became too much for a Secretary of State and Parliamentary Under-Secretaries alone to handle. The term **junior minister** should correctly only apply to Parliamentary Secretaries and Under-Secretaries.

> Very shining Ministers, like the sun, are apt to scorch when they shine their brightest; in our constitution I prefer the milder light of a less glaring Minister.
>
> EARL OF CHESTERFIELD, writing to his son, 1754

> God help the Minister that meddles with art.
>
> VISCOUNT MELBOURNE (1779–1848)

> The first concern of a Minister should be the health of the people.
>
> DISRAELI, speech in Manchester, 3 April 1872

> Ministers exist to tell the civil servant what the public will not stand.
>
> Sir WILLIAM HARCOURT (1827–1904)

> If you are not careful as a Minister, you find yourself the titular head of a bureaucratic structure.
>
> MICHAEL HESELTINE

Also, (2) traditionally, the title of a senior diplomatic representative, for instance the British Minister in St Petersburg. Henry Clay, in his 'EMANCIPATION of South America' speech in the HOUSE OF REPRESENTATIVES on 28 March 1818, said:

> Yes, Sir, from Constantinople, or from the Brazils; from Turk or Christian; from black or white; from the Dey of Algiers or the Bey of Tunis; from the devil himself, if he wore a crown, we should receive a Minister.

Minister of Fun The title unofficially given to David Mellor (1949–) on his appointment by John MAJOR in 1992 as Britain's first Secretary of State for National Heritage, with responsibilities including sport and the arts. Mellor took the title a little too literally; that summer the tabloids (*see* LAST CHANCE SALOON) revealed that he had had a toe-sucking affair with Antonia de Sancha, a small-time actress, and when it also transpired that September that he had accepted a family holiday from Mona Bauwens, daughter of a senior figure in the PLO, he reluctantly resigned. The hand of Israel was detected in this latter revelation; while on a visit to the OCCUPIED TERRITORIES Mellor had had a confrontation with Israeli security officers.

> Like most people I couldn't care who he goes to bed with, as long as it isn't me.
>
> KEN LIVINGSTONE

Ministerial broadcast *See* BROADCAST.

Ministerial Code The rules for proper conduct by members of a UK government, set out by the CABINET SECRETARY, circulated to all Ministers and updated periodically to give more specific guidance on areas where doubt or controversy has arisen. They succeeded QUESTIONS OF PROCEDURE FOR MINISTERS, whose contents until 1992 were confidential. A revision of the code was ordered in November 2004 after publicity over steps taken by the Home Secretary, David Blunkett, to assist his former lover Kimberley Fortier/Quinn which included his checking of her application form for a visa for her nanny and his giving her two travel vouchers intended for members' spouses; he repaid the £180 cost of this latter as pressure grew on him to widen the inquiry he had set up into whether he had acted improperly over the nanny's visa.

Ministerial responsibility The doctrine that Ministers in charge of WHITEHALL departments take absolute responsibility for errors or wrongdoing (other than in personal matters) by their officials, and that if a sufficiently grave injustice comes to light, they should resign. It was most strictly observed in the CRICHEL DOWN affair, when the Minister of Agriculture resigned over actions of which he had no knowledge, but in recent years it has been honoured in the breach. The spinning off of many departmental functions into free-standing agencies has also reduced the area within which strict Ministerial responsibility can apply.

Ministry (1) A UK government department headed by a member of the CABINET. Most have now been upgraded to a Department, the notable exception being one of the most important, the Ministry of Defence. (2) In Australia, the government of the day, as in 'the Howard Ministry'. The term was formerly used in Britain, as when Walter Bagehot wrote in *The English Constitution*: '*The Times* has made many ministries.'

Ministry of All the Talents The name given, a touch ironically, to William Grenville's COALITION government of 1806–07, because followers of both PITT THE YOUNGER and Charles James Fox agreed to serve in it. Its contemporary equivalent would be the DREAM TICKET.

Ministry of Truth The all-pervading organ of State PROPAGANDA in George Orwell's novel *1984*. *See also* BIG BROTHER.

minority (1) Any element of the population

which by race, religion, culture, sexual orientation or political opinion, is outnumbered by those of a different background or persuasion. Many political ESTABLISHMENTS see articulate minorities as a threat, no matter how small their numbers. Justice Oliver Wendell Holmes once said of America: 'If a man is in a minority of one, we lock him up', and Al Smith (*see* HAPPY WARRIOR) observed: 'The thing we have to fear in this country is the influence of organised minorities'; the Norwegian dramatist Henrik Ibsen showed the reason for such concern when he asserted: 'The minority is always right.'

> So long as a minority conforms to the majority, it is not even a minority. They must throw their whole weight in the opposite direction.
>
> MAHATMA GANDHI, 1907

> The white race is in the minority, the free-enterprise system is in the minority, and the majority are looking at us harder and longer than they ever looked before.
>
> JOHN F. KENNEDY

(2) In the US CONGRESS, the formal term for the party with the smaller number of members in either HOUSE. Speaker Thomas Reed declared:

> The right of the Minority is to draw its salaries, and its function is to make a QUORUM.

minority government A government that lacks an overall majority in the legislature from which it is drawn, e.g. Harold WILSON's Labour government of March-October 1974. During that HUNG PARLIAMENT, the Liberal leader Jeremy THORPE observed:

> Looking around the House, one realises that we are all minorities now – indeed, some more than others.

minorities Specifically, ethnic groups who form less than 50% of a nation's population. Shortly after the OCTOBER REVOLUTION when the BOLSHEVIKS briefly granted a degree of autonomy to non-Russian communities, LENIN assumed the post of Commissar for Minorities.

Minority Leader The leader of the party with the smaller number of seats in the US SENATE or HOUSE OF REPRESENTATIVES. *See also* RANKING MEMBER.

minority mentality The mind-set that comes from being in a permanent minority; in the mid-1980s Rep. NEWT Gingrich claimed that the House Republican leadership had 'as a culture, a defeatist, minority mentality'.

minority President A President of the United States elected with less than 50% of the popular vote; examples include Presidents George W. BUSH (2000), CLINTON (1992), NIXON (1968), KENNEDY, EISENHOWER (1956), TRUMAN, WILSON (twice) and LINCOLN.

minority report A separate report issued by one or more members of a committee who cannot agree findings or recommendations with the rest.

minute A WHITEHALL term for a memorandum from a Minister or senior official; also used as a verb, e.g. 'The Home Secretary minuted the Prime Minister that xxxx was a threat to national security.' Also a communication by a Government Department to Parliament, as in a **Treasury Minute.**

minutes The record of decisions taken at a meeting, which is written down contemporaneously and generally put to the next meeting of the same body for approval. One of the strongest criticisms of Tony BLAIR's government in the BUTLER REPORT was that informal meetings were held in the run-up to the IRAQ WAR of which no minutes were kept. In UK local government, the monthly meeting of a council consists largely in going through the Minutes of its previous meeting and those of all its committees, with the opportunity for questions, amendments and observations before going on to deal with other business.

Minutemen (1) A small, armed and ultra-right-wing US organisation formed during the COLD WAR to conduct GUERRILLA warfare in the event of a Communist invasion. The original Minutemen were militiamen who, at the onset of the War of Independence, promised to take arms at a minute's notice; the war began when 75 Minutemen intercepted 700 British troops at Lexington, Massachusetts, on 18 April 1775 (*see* THE BRITISH ARE COMING!). (2) The name of a US ICBM. (3) The self-appointed border patrol mounted by retirees in Arizona in 2005 in an effort to patrol and plug gaps in immigration control along the border with Mexico and stem the tide of ILLEGALS.

Miranda decision The landmark decision of the US SUPREME COURT in 1966 that requires police to explain, when arresting a suspect, that they have the right to remain silent during questioning and be represented by a lawyer, and that anything they do or say may be used against them. This protection is found in the FIFTH and SIXTH amendments to the CONSTITUTION, but until then it did not have to be spelt out to anyone being arrested. The Court laid down the rule in reversing an Arizona court's conviction of Ernesto A. Miranda, who had confessed to kidnapping and rape but had not been advised of his rights. Miranda was killed in a bar fight in 1976, and his killer was read his rights in accordance with the Miranda decision.

MIRV Multiple Independently Targeted Re-entry Vehicles. The multiple warheads fitted from 1968 to US (and later Soviet) strategic missiles, so that warheads from one rocket could hit a number of different targets. The deployment of such weapons first destabilised the ARMS RACE in America's favour, then accelerated it as the Soviet Union caught up, with SS-18s each carrying ten warheads. The MIRV warheads were highly accurate and designed to knock out enemy missile silos; Sen. Al Gore and others believed this greatly increased the risk of a FIRST STRIKE. MIRVs were outlawed by the START II agreement between the US and Russia at the close of 1992.

MISC 'Miscellaneous'. A UK CABINET COMMITTEE set up to tackle a specific challenge. Examples are **MISC 13** to consider action against animal rights extremists, **MISC 19** to monitor the implementation of universal banking, and **MISC 26** preparing for the 2012 London Olympics.

misery index The yardstick, combining the rates of INFLATION and unemployment, developed by Jimmy CARTER's 1976 Presidential CAMPAIGN to demonstrate how the FORD administration had failed the American worker. Carter successfully exploited the index's reading of 15.3 – but it boomeranged on him in 1980 when Ronald REAGAN pointed out that under Carter it had shot up to 21.3.

mislead the House A WESTMINSTER phrase for something that is very nearly a LIE. A member accusing another of misleading the House will generally be asked to WITHDRAW, but will have got the point across. ASQUITH pointed up the inference of trickery when he took the War Office to task for producing three sets of figures,

> . . . one to mislead the public, one to mislead the Cabinet and the third to mislead itself.

misquote Legislators who make comments and then come in for criticism when they are reported in the MEDIA frequently claim to have been misquoted: that what was printed was not what they said. At times their complaints are justified, but at others the tactic is a means of evading responsibility (*see also* DENIABILITY). Labour's Sir Gerald Kaufman once achieved a crushing put-down of a speech from former Chancellor Nigel Lawson by saying:

> Not only has the Right Honourable Gentleman made an idiot of himself, but he has achieved the remarkable feat of misquoting himself.

missile. missile gap The issue raised by John F. KENNEDY during the 1960 US Presidential election, with Kennedy claiming that the EISENHOWER/NIXON administration had allowed the Soviet Union to build up a more powerful strategic nuclear arsenal. When the Democrats came to power, they found that America was in fact considerably stronger.

unguided missile A more deadly version of a LOOSE CANNON, a politician who not only may go off in any direction but may do so with thermonuclear force. The term was most notably used of Dr Jeane Kirkpatrick, Ronald REAGAN's hard-line ambassador to the UN, by the liberal Republican Sen. Charles Percy. Earlier, in the mid-1960s, Dr Martin Luther KING had said:

> We have guided missiles and misguided men.

mission creep *See* CREEP.

Missouri Compromise (1) The series of ACTS passed by the US CONGRESS in 1820 to resolve the dilemma over whether to admit Missouri to the Union as a SLAVE STATE. The compromise, engineered by Henry Clay, prohibited slavery from all parts of the LOUISIANA PURCHASE north of latitude 36°30′ except in Missouri; Maine was admitted simultaneously as a free state. It kept the peace for a time, but at the price of exacerbating feeling for and against slavery in the longer term; Thomas JEFFERSON regarded it as a FIREBELL IN THE NIGHT. The Compromise was effectively repealed in 1854; three years later the SUPREME COURT, in the Dred SCOTT case, declared it UNCONSTITUTIONAL, enraging Northerners and stoking up the fires for the CIVIL WAR. (2) The process under which Sen. Harry S TRUMAN of Missouri emerged as Franklin D. ROOSEVELT's Vice Presidential choice at the 1944 Democratic CONVENTION. FDR wanted Henry Wallace, but party regulars deemed him too liberal; his second choice, James F. Byrnes, was unacceptable to liberals because of his views on race and labour unions. Truman trailed Wallace on the first ballot, but was nominated on the second – and was President within a year.

Missy LeHand The willowy private secretary to Franklin D. ROOSEVELT who from the early 1920s (after he had been struck by polio) until her retirement through illness in 1940 was FDR's mistress, apparently with Eleanor Roosevelt's tacit consent. The public knew nothing of the affair until FDR's son Elliott detailed it in a book of reminiscences. Margaret LeHand, whom Roosevelt met in the 1920 election campaign, was not his only lover; the most serious was Lucy Mercer (later Rutherford), then Eleanor's social secretary, whom FDR fell for in 1918. He might have divorced Eleanor for her, had not his mother threatened to cut off his inheritance. After Missy's death in 1943, Roosevelt resumed contact with Lucy, travelling to her New Jersey home; she was with him at WARM SPRINGS when he died.

> Missy LeHand had her own suite in the WHITE HOUSE consisting of a living room, a bedroom and bath. It was not uncommon to see Missy in the President's suite at night in a nightgown, or in the OVAL OFFICE on his lap. The extent of Missy's discretion . . . was in not remaining in the President's bedroom when his breakfast tray was served.
>
> SHELLEY ROSS, *Fall from Grace*

mistake. A man who believes the 20th century is a mistake The verdict of the Westminster SKETCH WRITER Frank Johnson on Sir John Stokes (1917–), the UNRECONSTRUCTED Conservative who represented Halesowen from 1970 to 1992.

I beseech you in the bowels of Christ, think it possible you may be mistaken Oliver Cromwell's despairing plea to the General Assembly of the Church of Scotland, in a letter sent in 1650 as his exasperation with inflexible Puritan divines was reaching its height.

Most mistakes in politics arise from flat and inexcusable disregard for the plain maxim that it is not possible for the same thing to be and not to be The conclusion reached, at the end of a long political career, by the British Liberal statesman John (later Viscount) Morley (1828–1923).

The politician who didn't make a mistake is never a politician; and the politician who admitted them to you wouldn't be a politician John MAJOR's standard reply to reporters when asked if a particular government policy had proved a mistake.

We made our mistake when we sent him to college where he learned to read The comment made by Frances McCoy McGee, the Republican mother of Gale McGee (1915–), on his election as a Democratic Senator for Wyoming.

When I make a mistake, it's a beaut One of the candid sayings of New York's Mayor Fiorello LA GUARDIA.

mister. Mr Chamberlain's pocket handkerchief LLOYD GEORGE's description of a UNION JACK waved by a HECKLER at a Liberal meeting during the KHAKI ELECTION of 1900. His reference to the UNIONIST Colonial Secretary Joseph Chamberlain (*see* JAMESON RAID) was seized on by the Tories as confirmation that Lloyd George was PRO-BOER. When the heckler shouted and waved the flag, L.G. said:

> I didn't realise it had become Mr Chamberlain's pocket handkerchief.

Mr Clean (1) Anyone in politics who has a reputation for being incorruptible. (2) A compliment from ENVIRONMENTALISTS to a politician who has promoted anti-pollution legislation; an early recipient was Sen. Edmund Muskie.

Mr Cube The sugar lump in human form devised by the sugar refiners Tate & Lyle in 1950 to fight the threat of NATIONALISATION by Clement ATTLEE's Labour government. Prior to the ELECTION at the end of the year, the company plastered hoardings with pictures of Mr Cube and the slogan **Tate, not State**; Labour won the election, but with a majority too small to press ahead with much more nationalisation. Mr Cube stayed on the sugar packets for years after the original reason for him had been forgotten.

Mr President The way in which the PRESIDENT of the United States is formally addressed.

Mr Republican The nickname for the conservative **Sen. Robert Taft**, son of America's 26th President and Senate MAJORITY LEADER. An ISOLATIONIST in foreign policy, he was co-promoter of the TAFT-HARTLEY ACT and an initial supporter of sen. Joseph MCCARTHY, telling him of his drive against supposed Communists in high places: 'If one case doesn't work, try another.' Taft fought Dwight D. EISENHOWER for the 1952 Presidential NOMINATION, and died of cancer the following year. He fought to the end; weeks before he died he was seen in the Senate chamber filling in an order for a new refrigerator.

Mr Sam The affectionate nickname in the US House of Representatives for Sam Taliaferro Rayburn (1882–1961), the Texan who served as SPEAKER with four Presidents from FDR to KENNEDY.

Mr Speaker The title of every male SPEAKER of the House of Commons, and the form of address used by Members when speaking; all their comments must be addressed to the CHAIR and not to other members.

Mrs Wilson's Diary The column that appeared in *PRIVATE EYE* throughout Harold WILSON's two spells of government (1964–70, 1974–76), giving a plausible caricature of life in NUMBER TEN. Purporting to be the diary of Wilson's wife Mary, who was known not to enjoy the political life, it brought to life vividly the world of Wilson, Lady FORKBENDER and Boris the handyman, who had a peculiar foreign accent and knew a surprising amount about electronics.

Mrs Wilson's Stewardship The period from October 1919 until well into the following year during which Edith Galt Wilson, second wife of President Woodrow WILSON, effectively ran the United States while her husband was recovering from a stroke; some historians believe she retained control until he left office in March 1921. *See also* Petticoat GOVERNMENT; PRESIDENTRESS.

Mitchell Commission The three-man commission headed by former US Senator George Mitchell, set up in November 1995 to facilitate DECOMMISSIONING of terrorist weapons in NORTHERN IRELAND. The following January it produced a six-point plan based on the realisation that the IRA would not give up any weapons in advance of a peace agreement. Mitchell's fellow commissioners were the former Finnish prime minister Harri Holkeri and the Canadian defence chief John de Chastelain, who after the GOOD FRIDAY AGREEMENT headed a further commission to facilitate, supervise and verify decommissioning.

MITI Japan's Ministry for International Trade and Industry, the organ of government which from the end of WORLD WAR II spearheaded the country's development into an industrial superpower by assisting new industries and technology, while facilitating an orderly run-down of outdated industries. In 1969 it took the critical decision to lift restrictions on Japanese investment overseas.

Mittal affair An episode which prompted early accusations of SLEAZE against Tony BLAIR. Lakshmi Mittal, an Indian industrialist with a home in London but just 80 of his company's 125,000 staff in the UK, donated £125,000 to the Labour Party in 2001 two months before Blair wrote to the Romanian Prime Minister in support of Mittal's efforts to purchase a steelworks there. The charges were pursued most keenly by PLAID CYMRU, which argued that Blair was promoting the interests of a magnate whose commercial activities and lobbying (notably in the United States) were costing steel jobs in the UK, and in Wales in particular.

Mitterrand, François (1916–1996), the longest-serving President (1981–95) of Republican France. The first President to be elected twice by a popular vote, Mitterrand was nominally a socialist but as head of state adopted the tone of a philosopher-king. He presided over a period of general prosperity and promoted grand projects to be remembered by: the arch of *La Defense*, the glass pyramid in the courtyard of the Louvre and the Channel Tunnel – a collaborative project with Britain that offset his primary aim of a strong alliance with Germany to take the lead in Europe, a commitment that resulted in the MAASTRICHT TREATY. Yet he wanted limits to Germany's power, and disliked (though less publicly than Margaret THATCHER) the reunification of Germany. He was also less anti-American than DE GAULLE or his own successor Jacques Chirac, almost unequivocally supporting the 1991 GULF WAR.

A right-winger in his youth, Mitterrand served the VICHY government until it was clear the Germans were losing the war, then switched to the RESISTANCE, in which he became known as 'Capitaine Morland'. When de Gaulle spotted Mitterrand in the reception committee when Paris was liberated, he declared cuttingly: *'Ah, Mitterand! Encore vous'*. In 1946 he was elected a left-wing DEPUTY, first serving as a Minister the following year; as a supporter of ALGÉRIE FRANÇAISE, it was Mitterrand who as Justice Minister in 1955–56 authorised the use of torture against FLN rebels. Mitterrand challenged de Gaulle for the Presidency in 1965, running him close in the second ballot with 44.8% of the vote, and during the ÉVÈNEMENTS of 1968 offered to head a provisional government that would pacify the rebelling workers and students; de Gaulle hung on and Mitterrand's career suffered. In 1971 he engineered his election as First Secretary of the Socialist Party, to which, remarkably, he had never previously belonged. He masterminded an alliance with the Communists in 1972, came within a whisker of defeating Valéry Giscard d'Estaing for the Presidency in 1974, defeated Giscard five years later, secured a massive socialist majority in the NATIONAL ASSEMBLY, marginalised the Communists and for a time ruled unchallenged. With Chirac winning a Parliamentary majority in 1986, he developed a doctrine of CO-HABITATION by which a socialist President could retain primacy over, yet work with, a right-wing Premier with a Parliamentary majority; in practice cohabitation enabled him to jettison socialist policies to which he felt no personal commitment. He also adopted PROPORTIONAL REPRESENTATION to force Chirac out by giving the extreme right NATIONAL FRONT representation in the Assembly, but when he changed the rules back again this factor and the brief but disastrous premiership of Edith CRESSON, later to be disgraced as a EUROPEAN COMMISSIONER, produced a socialist rout in 1993 and another period of cohabitation with Edouard Balladur as Premier. Mitterrand was diagnosed in 1992 with prostate cancer and did not survive long out of office; for his final meal he reputedly asked to be served a dish of ortolans, an endangered species of bird whose consumption is illegal. Grand projects apart, his legacy was a daughter, Mazarine, conceived with one of the numerous mistresses he pursued despite a happy marriage to Danielle Gouze, whom he had met in the Resistance. *See also* TONTON.

Miz Lillian The family nickname for Lillian Carter (1898–1983), mother of President Jimmy CARTER, whom he sent on a number of international goodwill and charitable missions. A tough Southern lady who lent unspoken support to her son, she did much to underpin his ADMINISTRATION's humanitarian credentials. The President's brother was another matter (*see* BILLYGATE). Miz Lillian was quoted in 1977 as saying:

> Sometimes when I look at my children I say to myself: 'Lillian, you should have stayed a virgin.'

MLA Member of the Legislative Assembly. (1) A member of NORTHERN IRELAND's at times power-sharing assembly set up in the wake of the 1998 GOOD FRIDAY AGREEMENT. (2) A member of the legislative house of that name (the lower or the only one) in each Australian state except South Australia and Tasmania.

MLC Member of the Legislative Council. A member of the upper house of the LEGISLATURE in every Australian state with a BICAMERAL system.

MLF Multilateral Force. The proposal emanating from the 1962 Nassau meeting between President KENNEDY and Harold MACMILLAN for a force to which all NATO members would contribute, with Britain including its POLARIS submarines. France opposed the idea on principle, Germany only supported it to make its *rapprochement* with France acceptable to WASHINGTON, and the force was stillborn although it took the JOHNSON administration until the end of 1964 to admit it.

> A Heath Robinson contraption whose only purpose was political; it was designed to control the British and French strategic NUCLEAR WEAPONS and to give the non-nuclear Europeans the impression that somehow they would share in the decision to use America's nuclear deterrent.
>
> DENIS HEALEY

M'Lords The formal term used by members of the HOUSE OF LORDS in the CHAMBER to address those present, instead of addressing the CHAIR as in the COMMONS.

MLR *See* MINIMUM LENDING RATE.

moaning Minnies Margaret THATCHER's dismissive term for critics of her economic policies, which caused considerable offence when she uttered it on a visit to Tyneside, where several unemployment blackspots remained even in the boom of 1988.

mob, the In political terms, not the Mafia but the mass of the urban population who at critical moments can take to the streets and change the course of history. JEFFERSON wrote: 'The mobs of great cities add just so much to the support of pure government as sores do to the strength of the human body.' And Calvin COOLIDGE noted that 'the only difference between a mob and a trained army is organisation'.

moderate One who avoids extremes in politics, and takes a more cautious line than other members of a party. Moderation is frequently interpreted as weakness, and the term is also misapplied; the *Daily Telegraph* once carried a report about 'bomb-throwing moderates' in the Lebanon. Thomas Paine took the view that 'moderation in temper is always a virtue, but moderation in principle is always a vice', and Metternich cautioned: 'Any plan conceived in moderation must fail when the circumstances are set in extremes.' More passionately, William Lloyd Garrison wrote of slavery: 'Tell a man whose house is on fire to give a moderate alarm; tell him to moderately rescue his wife from the hands of the ravisher; tell the mother to gradually extricate her babe from the fire into which it has fallen; but urge me not to use moderation in a case like the present.'

> The hardest job today is to have the courage to be a moderate. HUBERT HUMPHREY

I stand astounded at my own moderation The response of Lord Clive (1725–1774) during Parliamentary cross-examination in 1773 on his conduct in India, which had given rise to allegations of corruption and self-enrichment.

moderator An impartial person appointed to chair a partisan debate or discussion; the Moderator of the General Assembly, a member of the clergy elected for a year, is the leading figure in the Church of Scotland.

modern. modern movements The collective euphemism used by Sir Oswald MOSLEY in the 1930s to praise the FASCIST parties that had taken control in Italy and Germany, and his own BLACKSHIRT movement, with the inference that the DUCE and the FÜHRER presented a vision of the future and that the established political institutions were on their way out.

modernisers In Britain's LABOUR PARTY in the 1990s, under the leadership of John SMITH and Tony BLAIR, the element that wished to press ahead with change to the party and its ethos in order to guarantee a return to power; those wedded to the *status quo*, and in particular the retention of CLAUSE FOUR, were the TRADITIONALISTS.

modified, limited hangout One of the stratagems prepared in the NIXON White House for surviving WATERGATE. Revealed when the Watergate tapes were made public, it involved forming a defensive position behind a highly limited and selective disclosure of the facts.

Mogadon Man An uncomplimentary nickname bestowed by the media on Sir Geoffrey (later Lord) HOWE (1926–), Chancellor, Foreign Secretary and DEPUTY PRIME MINISTER to Margaret THATCHER between 1979 and 1990. It reflected his sleep-inducing speaking style (*see* DEAD SHEEP), Mogadon being a tranquiliser; this widely-held view made his dramatic resignation speech, which set in motion Mrs Thatcher's fall from power, all the more devastating.

mole A word popularised by the novels of John le Carré for a spy or traitor who obtains a position of trust, especially in a government or intelligence organisation, and uses it to feed information to his or her true masters; it reflects the hidden undermining activities of such agents. The word became current in the early 1980s just after the ultimate mole was exposed: Sir Anthony BLUNT, who had spied for Russia when a wartime member of MI5 and went on to become Surveyor of the Queen's Pictures – a post he was allowed to keep even after his treachery was proven.

Molotov cocktail A home-made anti-tank grenade, invented and first used by the Finns against the Russians in 1940 and adopted in the UK as one of the weapons of the Home Guard. It consisted of a bottle filled with petrol or other inflammable liquid, with a slow match or cloth protruding from the top. When it was lit and thrown at a tank the bottle burst, the liquid igniting, spreading over the plating of the tank and (with luck) setting fire to it. It was named after the Soviet Prime Minister and Foreign Affairs COMMISSAR Vyacheslav Molotov (*see* NIET!), real name Skriabin, either because the Finns saw his hand in the Soviet invasion or because such bombs became a weapon of pro-Communist GUERRILLAS and rioters the world over.

moment of madness The incident on Clapham Common in October 1998 that led to the resignation of Ron Davies (1946–) as Welsh Secretary in Tony BLAIR's government, also disqualifying him from standing as Wales' inaugural FIRST MINISTER. When it emerged that he had had his car, mobile phone, wallet and COMMONS pass stolen on the Common at 9.30pm on an October evening, Davies first claimed he had been mugged while taking a walk, then admitted he was robbed at knifepoint by a Rastafarian he had picked up on the Common. Explaining that he was bisexual and had been seeking 'high risk situations', Davies resigned from the CABINET and as leader of Welsh Labour and gave up his safe Parliamentary seat. He divorced his second wife, remarried and made a new start in the Welsh Assembly he had hoped to lead, but in March 2003 quit politics after the *Sun* caught him in the act with a 48-year-old builder in woods by the roadside near Bath.

> Labour stands for the common man, and Ron Davies has been out on Clapham Common looking for him. JASPER CARROTT

monarchy A system of government where the ultimate SOVEREIGNTY is vested in a King or Queen, almost always hereditary rather than elective, and supported to varying degrees by an ARISTOCRACY. The poet Shelley denounced monarchy as 'the string which ties the robbers' bundle'.

> A monarchy is a ship which sails well but will sometimes strike a rock and go to the bottom; a republic is a raft which will never sink, but then your feet are always in the water.
> Rep. FISHER AMES (1758–1808)

> The best reason why a monarchy is a strong government is that it is an intelligible government. The mass of mankind understand it, and they hardly anywhere in the world understand any other. WALTER BAGEHOT (1826–77)

A **constitutional monarchy** operates in a largely ceremonial capacity with a democratically elected legislature enjoying comprehensive powers, as in Britain, Scandinavia, Spain and the BENELUX countries. Harold WILSON described the contemporary British monarchy, surrounded by an extended Royal family, as 'a labour-intensive industry'.

> When a monarchy gradually transforms itself into a republic, the executive power there preserves titles, honours, respect and even money long after it has lost the reality of power.
> ALEXIS DE TOCQUEVILLE (1805–59)

absolute monarchy *See* ABSOLUTISM.

Dual Monarchy The twin crowns of Austria and Hungary between 1867, when the Hungarian kingdom was given a separate existence within the Austrian Empire, though with the same monarch, and 1919 when that empire collapsed.

Fifth Monarchy Men A fanatical Puritan sect, aligned to the LEVELLERS, who maintained during the English CIVIL WAR that Christ was about to return and establish the fifth universal monarchy. The four preceding monarchies had been the Assyrian, the Persian, the Macedonian and the Roman. As with other such sects, their existence and assurance that they alone were right hampered Oliver Cromwell's efforts to establish a stable and enlightened Republican government.

monarchist In countries where the rival claims of a republic and a monarchy are debated, the faction that supports the maintenance of royal rule. The term is also used for US conservatives who attach almost royal respect to the presidency.

Monday Club A stridently right-wing group of UK Conservatives, founded in 1961 by the Marquess of Salisbury, Julian Amery and others. It originally met on a Monday, which was also the day Harold MACMILLAN returned from making his WIND OF CHANGE speech in South Africa, to which the Club's founders took strong exception. In its early years the Monday Club championed white South Africa and Rhodesia's UDI, and endorsed POWELLITE views on race and Europe; it subsequently took a strongly pro-UNIONIST line on NORTHERN IRELAND. In the 1970s and early '80s it was shunned by mainstream Conservatives, but its activities became less strident and controversial and senior party figures became readier to speak at its meetings.

Monday morning quarterback A US phrase for a political observer gifted with 20/20 hindsight. It was originally, and remains, a sporting term, for the 'expert' who arrives for work at the start of a new week able to explain how his football team could have won at the weekend.

monetarism The economic doctrine that sees the MONEY SUPPLY as the centre of macroeconomic policy and the determinant of economic forces. First formulated by David Hume (1711–76), it was revived from the mid-1970s, especially by Enoch POWELL, Sir Keith Joseph (*see* MAD MONK) and Margaret THATCHER under the influence of Milton FRIEDMAN, as the panacea for breaking with KEYNESIANISM. They argued that an expansion of the money supply would create INFLATION rather than jobs, and from 1979 until c. 1985 Chancellors Geoffrey HOWE and Nigel Lawson stuck rigidly to the policy, creating the foundations for a BOOM which subsequent relaxation of the money supply sent out of control.

punk monetarism The condemnatory phrase of Denis HEALEY for the more ruthless and ideological varieties of economic policy pursued in the mid-1980s by some of Mrs THATCHER's most committed Ministers.

Monetary Policy Committee The seven-strong committee of economists empanelled by the BANK OF ENGLAND which meets monthly to set the UK's interest rates. Rates were set by the CHANCELLOR OF THE EXCHEQUER (*see* KEN AND EDDIE SHOW) until 1997, when Gordon BROWN gave the Bank its independence in this field.

money. Money Bill At WESTMINSTER, legislation of a fiscal nature which, since the 1911 PARLIAMENT ACT, cannot be blocked by the HOUSE OF LORDS. In the US CONGRESS, Money Bills can under the CONSTITUTION only be introduced in the HOUSE OF REPRESENTATIVES.

money resolution A resolution put to the

HOUSE OF COMMONS immediately after the SECOND READING of a BILL, authorising money to be spent in connection with it; for major measures there is an opportunity for further debate.

money supply The amount of money available to the economy of a nation. Since the mid-1970s most Western nations have accepted the central tenet of MONETARISM, that an increase in the money supply leads to INFLATION. There are at least seven different ways of defining the money supply (*see* M0), with M1 the tightest, covering only cash in circulation and bank deposits.

a billion here, a billion there, and pretty soon you're talking about real money A dictum of Sen. Everett DIRKSEN, said OFF THE CUFF while campaigning in Illinois, according to his confidant John Kriegsman.

I want my money back Margaret THATCHER's blunt statement to fellow EC heads of government when pressing for Britain to be given a rebate on its payments to the Community budget, to reflect its position as the largest net contributor after Germany. She first made the demand at the 1979 Dublin summit, and reiterated it at all further meetings until the BRITISH REBATE was conceded at FONTAINEBLEAU five years later.

politics has got so expensive, it takes a lot of money even to get beat with One of the most celebrated sayings of the comedian Will Rogers, who up to his death in a plane crash in 1935 was both unofficial court jester to the US CONGRESS and a highly respected visitor to CAPITOL HILL. Here Rogers was taking a dig at the spiralling cost of getting elected – without venturing too far into what the money was spent on.

monkey. Monkey Business The yacht that in 1987 sank the Presidential ambitions of the Democratic front-runner Gary Hart. With Hart on its cruise to Bimini were Donna Rice, the 29-year-old from Miami with whom he was having an affair, her friend Lynn Armadt and Hart fundraiser William Broadhurst; Hart and Broadhurst claimed they had been on a separate boat to the girls, but Armadt told the *National Enquirer* that Hart and Rice shared the master bedroom. After intense media scrutiny of Hart's private life, which he at first encouraged (*see* ADULTERY), the *Miami Herald* on 3 May broke the news of Hart's affair with Rice, and then the *Enquirer* told of the cruise just as Hart and his wife were pulling out of the Presidential race; he tried a comeback in the winter of 1987–88, but flopped. Hart's womanising was notorious; Rice's other amours allegedly included Prince Albert of Monaco, the Saudi arms dealer Adnan Kashoggi and a convicted drugs dealer, James Bradley Parks.

cheese eating surrender monkeys The label pinned on the French in 2003 by furious right-wing US commentators following their opposition attitude at the UNITED NATIONS to military action against Iraq (*See also* FREEDOM FRIES). One joke going the rounds of WASHINGTON was:

> *Q:* Why are there shade trees along the Champs Elysées?
> *A:* So the Germans don't get sunstroke when they invade.

H'Angus the Monkey The victor of the first election for a MAYOR of Hartlepool, north-east England, in May 2002: Stuart Drummond, a 28-year-old call centre worker better known as H'Angus the Monkey, the mascot of Hartlepool FC. Drummond, who campaigned in his monkey suit on a platform of free bananas for schoolchildren, comfortably defeated the Labour nominee, but promised to be 'serious' in administering his budget of over £100 million. H'Angus took his name from the incident at the start of the 19th century when a Napoleonic warship was wrecked off Hartlepool leaving just one survivor: the ship's monkey whom the townspeople promptly hanged as a French spy. John Prescott, (*see* TWO JAGS), who hated the town's MP Peter Mandelson (*see* BOBBY), declared:

> Hartlepool is the only town in Britain represented by two monkeys.

Drummond was re-elected in 2005 with an increased majority.

organ-grinder and monkey *See* ORGAN-GRINDER.

Monopolies Commission A commission established by the UK government in 1948 as the Monopolies and Restrictive Practices Commission; it became the Monopolies and Mergers Commission in 1973 and though its title changed again in 1999 to the **Competition Commission**, the name has stuck. It conducts in-depth inquiries into mergers, markets and the regulation of the major regulated industries, mergers requiring investigation under the 1973 Fair Trading Act, and any uncompetitive or restrictive practices uncovered by the COMPETITION ACTS of 1980 and 1998.

> Why is there only one Monopolies Commission?
> OFFICIAL MONSTER RAVING LOONY PARTY Manifesto, 1987

Monroe doctrine America's resolution not to countenance any further acquisitions in the Western hemisphere by Europe's colonial powers, and in return not to interfere in purely European affairs, or in existing colonies. It was adumbrated by James Monroe (1758–1831), 5th President of the United States (1817–25), who said in his annual message to CONGRESS on 2 December 1823:

> The American continents . . . are henceforth not to be considered as subjects for future colonisation by any European powers.

Monroe, the third successive Virginian President after JEFFERSON and Madison, presided over the ERA OF GOOD FEELINGS when party politics ceased to exist; he was re-elected in 1820 with only one vote against in the ELECTORAL COLLEGE. Jefferson praised him as 'a man whose soul might be turned wrong side outwards without discovering a blemish to the world'; his biographer Arthur Styron wrote:

> His virtue was not in flying high but in walking orderly, his talents were exercised not in grandeur but in mediocrity.

The doctrine, only named after Monroe 30 years later, was actually created by Secretary of State John Quincy ADAMS in response to a suggestion from Foreign Secretary George Canning that Britain and the US jointly warn the Holy Alliance of Russia, Austria, Spain and France against a restoration of Spanish rule in the newly independent republics of Latin America. The most serious challenge to the Monroe Doctrine came in 1864 when Emperor Napoleon III attempted to instal Archduke Maximilian of Austria on the Mexican throne; France ignored US protests and war seemed imminent, but trouble in Europe forced withdrawal of the French troops supporting Maximilian and he was executed by his 'subjects'.

> The Government of the United States is not entitled to affirm as a universal proposition that its interests are necessarily concerned in whatever may befall . . . states simply because they are in the Western hemisphere.
>
> LORD SALISBURY on the boundary dispute over Venezuela, 26 November 1895

> In the Western hemisphere, adherence . . . to the Monroe Doctrine may force the United States, however reluctantly, in flagrant cases of wrong-doing or impotence, to the exercise of an international police power.
>
> THEODORE ROOSEVELT, message to Congress, 6 December 1904

> Nations should with one accord adopt the doctrine of President Monroe as the doctrine of the world: that every people should be left free to determine its own policy, its own way of development, unhindered, unthreatened, unafraid – the little along with the great and powerful.
>
> WOODROW WILSON, speech to the Senate, 22 January 1917

Montgomery bus boycott A peaceful BOYCOTT of bus services in Montgomery, Alabama, from December 1955 by black protesters against racial SEGREGATION. Organised by Dr Martin Luther KING, it was reputedly sparked by a white bus driver's offensive treatment of Mrs Rosa Parks, who refused to sit at the back of the bus where blacks were supposed to travel. After an eleven-month boycott the SUPREME COURT gave victory to the protesters by declaring racially segregated seating in local transportation UNCONSTITUTIONAL. The protest achieved more than the desegregation of Montgomery's buses; it brought the CIVIL RIGHTS movement to the attention of the nation and encouraged Dr King to take his place at its head.

Monticello The graceful and sophisticated home atop a 500ft. hill near Charlottesville, Virginia, which Thomas JEFFERSON designed for himself and built in the 1770s. Owing much to the influence of the Italian architect Palladio, it is modest in size by Virginia planters' standards, but includes many of Jefferson's inventions, in marked contrast to WASHINGTON's strictly traditional home at MOUNT VERNON. Jefferson retired to Monticello and died there; in 1926 the ladies of Virginia purchased it as a national shrine, which it remains.

> Mr Jefferson is the first American who has consulted the Fine Arts to know how he should shelter himself from the weather.
>
> Marquis de CHASTELLUX, 1780

Montoneros The militant wing of the PERONIST youth movement which waged a terrorist campaign against the military JUNTA under, in turn, Generals Videla and Galtieri, that ruled Argentina after the overthrow of Isabel Perón in 1975 until the armed forces' humiliation in the FALKLANDS WAR. The military acted against all actual or suspected Montoneros with total ruthlessness, many joining the DISAPPEARED.

Montreal protocol The international agreement in 1988 to protect the ozone layer by phasing out damaging **CFCs** (chlorofluorocarbons), then widely used in aerosol sprays and refrigeration, by 2000. The first worldwide initiative to halt destruction of the layer, it proved a total success, a further meeting in Copenhagen in 1992 having tightened the deadline.

moral. moral equivalent of war The phrase popularised by President CARTER in 1977 to describe America's energy dilemmas, abbreviated by his critics to **MEOW**. Its originator was William James (1842–1910), who in an essay the year he died criticised 'anti-militarists' for having found 'no substitute for war's disciplinary function, no moral equivalent of war'. On 18 April 1977, Carter said in a broadcast to the nation:

> Our decision about energy will test the character of the American people and the ability of the President and the CONGRESS to govern this nation. This difficult effort will be the 'moral equivalent of war', except that we will be uniting our efforts to built and not to destroy.

Moral Majority *See* MAJORITY.

Moral Rearmament *See* REARMAMENT.

moral values One of the main reasons given by the 59 million Americans who turned out to vote for George W. BUSH rather than John KERRY in the 2004 US Presidential election. It was shorthand for Bush's embracing of the Religious RIGHT in his campaigning, for his opposition to same-sex marriages and inferences that the Democrats would permit them (though Kerry opposed them too) and, to a lesser extent, his opposition to stem-cell research, strongly objected to by PRO-LIFE campaigners.

we know of no spectacle so ridiculous as the British public in one of its periodic fits of morality A truism attributed to many, in particular Oscar Wilde, but actually coined by Thomas Babington (Lord) Macaulay in his *Moore's Life of Byron*, published in 1830.

morganatic marriage A marriage contracted by a crowned head or heir to the throne, generally with a commoner, in which his wife does not become queen and the children are excluded from the succession. The most celebrated morganatic marriage was that between Archduke Franz Ferdinand, whose assassination at SARAJEVO triggered WORLD WAR I, and Sophie Chotek. Such a marriage was suggested at the time of Britain's ABDICATION CRISIS as a means of enabling Edward VIII to keep his throne, yet still marry Mrs Wallis Simpson, and more recently to permit Prince Charles marrying Camilla Parker-Bowles without alienating public opinion after the death of Diana, Princess of Wales.

Morgenthau Plan A project for the 'pastoralisation' of Germany after WORLD WAR II, drawn up by US Treasury Secretary Henry Morgenthau (1891–1967) and Secretary for War Henry Stimson and presented to ROOSEVELT and CHURCHILL at the 1944 QUEBEC CONFERENCE. It proposed 'eliminating the war-making industries in the Ruhr and the Saar', and 'converting Germany into a country primarily agricultural and pastoral in character'. Churchill reluctantly accepted the proposal, but Roosevelt and TRUMAN did not pursue it.

Morley-Minto reforms The administrative and representative reforms to the British Raj pursued between 1905 and 1910 by the VICEROY the Earl of Minto (1845–1914) in consultation with John (Viscount) Morley (1838–1923), Secretary for India, which gave a voice to the Indian people. An Indian was appointed to the Viceroy's executive council for the first time, and others brought into the legislative and consultative organs of government. Born of the confidence given the CAMPBELL-BANNERMAN/ASQUITH government by its large majority, the reforms were pursued even when civil disorder broke out and Lord and Lady Minto narrowly escaped assassination.

morning. *Morning Cloud* The name given by Sir Edward HEATH to each in turn of his five ocean-going yachts, most of which he skippered in the Admirals' Cup and other major races. With music, yacht racing was Heath's main way of releasing the tensions of politics. The third *Morning Cloud* came to a tragic end, being wrecked off Sussex in September 1974 with the loss of two crewmen who were ferrying her between berths; the most recent was launched in 1977.

morning hour The time set aside at the start of business in the US SENATE – and very occasionally in the HOUSE – for the consideration of routine business, such as a message from the President, messages from the other House, presentation of petitions, reports from committees and the introduction of BILLS and resolutions. The first part of a session following an ADJOURNMENT, the morning hour need not be in the morning and can last up to two hours.

Morning Star The name given in 1966 by the Communist Party of Great Britain to the relaunched *Daily Worker*; the aim was to produce a tabloid daily that would broaden the appeal of contemporary Communism. In fact the paper became more hard-line, sticking to the MOSCOW LINE in the late

1980s as the party flirted with EURO-COMMUNISM, and with the collapse of Soviet Communism in 1991 it lost the guaranteed overseas market that had provided most of its 30,000 sales. Though chronically short of money, it has struggled on, outliving the party and remaining on the hard left.

it's morning again in America *See* AMERICA.

never glad confident morning again *See* NEVER.

Moro kidnapping The abduction and murder after 54 days' captivity in May 1978 by Italy's RED BRIGADES of the leading CHRISTIAN DEMOCRAT Aldo Moro (1916–78). Four times Prime Minister between 1963 and 1976, Moro was party president when, on 16 March 1978, he was kidnapped in Rome on his way to a special session of Parliament; the Red Brigades threatened to 'try and execute' him unless thirteen of their comrades on trial in Turin were released. Moro in government had opposed deals with terrorists, but in letters from captivity he urged negotiation; the government initially stood firm, but with the Red Brigades assassinating a string of key security officials, splits were beginning to open when Moro's body was found in a car in Rome on 9 May. The last of his kidnappers were sentenced in 1983.

Morosi affair The furore in Australia over the appointment in 1974 by Dr Jim Cairns, deputy LABOR Prime Minister and Federal Treasurer, of the glamorous 41-year-old Juni Morosi to run his private office. The OPPOSITION claimed Mrs Morosi had been allocated a government apartment out of turn, and that she and her husband were involved in shady business deals; their company was bankrupt, but the couple were cleared of illegality. Once Prime Minister Gough WHITLAM was satisfied there was no financial impropriety, he treated the appointment as a matter for Cairns. But some Labor parliamentarians thought the presence of Morosi, described as 'a stunning cross between Jacqueline Kennedy, Elizabeth Taylor and Brigitte Bardot', was harming the party, and persuaded her to resign. Then, on 29 December 1974, Cairns reappointed her. The following February, during the ALP's conference at Terrigal, they gave an interview that knocked the conference out of the news; the *Sydney Sun* headlined its story 'My Love for Juni'. Tensions grew between Cairns and the rest of his staff, which proved damaging when the LOANS SCANDAL broke, forcing his resignation as Treasurer that June. The Morosi affair also indirectly facilitated the KERR SACKING that November. The publicity led Whitlam to delay appointing Sen. Lionel Murphy to a vacancy in the High Court; by the time he did, the political climate in New South Wales had changed and Murphy was replaced by an Independent, not a Labor, Senator, depriving Whitlam of a crucial vote to break the deadlock over SUPPLY.

> Either Cairns was extraordinarily naïve or he enjoyed his notoriety. Whatever it was said little for his political acumen.
>
> LAURIE OAKES, *Crash Through or Crash*

> When everything has been said on the Morosi controversy the inescapable conclusion remains: in the final analysis, it was sexist. She was that most disturbing thing – a woman with influence.
>
> GRAHAM FREUDENBERG, *A Certain Grandeur*

Moscow. Moscow conference A meeting between CHURCHILL, STALIN and the US ambassador Averell Harriman in Moscow from 9 to 20 October 1944 to discuss the partition of South-East Europe at the end of WORLD WAR II. The Soviet Union was given a controlling interest in Romania, Bulgaria and Hungary, and Britain in Greece; Yugoslavia was to be a zone of counter-balanced Soviet and British influence. The last of these decisions proved academic with the rise of TITO.

Moscow line The line of policy set by the KREMLIN and dictated to Communist parties throughout the world, who were expected to follow it unquestioningly. In those parties and movements where there was genuine debate over tactics and policy, the **Moscow-liners** were those who advocated the Soviet position.

Moscow theatre siege Until the BESLAN SIEGE, also a Chechen attack on Russia, probably the largest ever hostage-taking, and almost certainly the one terminated with greatest loss of life. A 50-strong Chechen suicide squad who had strapped explosives to themselves seized the Russian capital's Nord Auditorium and an audience of over 800 during a performance on 24 October 2002. Special forces stormed the theatre after 54 hours, having overpowered the Chechens – who were shot in their seats – with an anaesthetic opiate gas which also killed 118 of the hostages and left 45 more in intensive care. President Putin apologised for the loss of life before its full extent became known; the hospital was unable to give the casualties an antidote because the Russian military refused to say what the gas was.

Mosleyites The FASCIST supporters of **Sir Oswald Mosley** (1896–1980) after his break with the LABOUR PARTY in 1930 following its refusal to accept his NEW DEAL-type plan for tackling mass unemployment. Mosley, originally elected a Conservative MP in 1918, CROSSED THE FLOOR to Labour in 1924, served in Ramsay MACDONALD'S Cabinet, broke with him and founded first the NEW PARTY and then, in 1932, the British Union of Fascists. The BUF, or BLACKSHIRTS, staged mass rallies at which Mosley styled himself after HITLER (*see* MODERN MOVEMENTS), and ANTI-SEMITIC demonstrations in the East End of London which inevitably led to violence (*see* Battle of CABLE STREET). The 1936 Public Order Act restricted the activities of the Mosleyites, who are reckoned to have been 20,000 strong. The BUF was banned in 1940, and Mosley was INTERNED from 1940 to 1943 with his second wife, the former Diana Mitford whose sister Unity was besotted with Hitler.

> I am not, and never have been, a man of the right. My position was on the left and is now in the centre of politics.
>
> Sir OSWALD MOSLEY, 1968

> He stinks of money and insincerity.
>
> HUGH DALTON

Mossad Israel's ruthless secret intelligence service, which has become a byword for harassment of the country's opponents overseas and for the cloak-and-dagger murder or abduction of individuals whose existence or public comments are inconvenient to Jerusalem. Its law-breaking in foreign countries has compromised Israel's relations with friendly nations from Canada, whose citizens Mossad agents impersonated to murder a target in Jordan, to New Zealand, where they were caught in 2004 trying to obtain a passport in the name of a man confined to his wheelchair. Yet most Israelis consider its activities necessary for the preservation of their state. The Committee for Illegal Immigration – *Mossad le Aliyeh Beth* – was formed in 1937 as part of the Jewish defence force, HAGANAH, to arrange the smuggling of Jews into Palestine from around the world, but especially NAZI-threatened central and eastern Europe. It was revived after WORLD WAR II to organise – through a network of agents directed from Paris – the illicit migration of Jews displaced by the horrors of the HOLOCAUST, first to Allied refugee camps and thence to Palestine, where they were landed secretly in defiance of the British authorities. By 1948 Mossad members were engaged in GUN-RUNNING and other covert activities; with the foundation of the Israeli state the agency formed the basis of the new nation's intelligence service. Institutionalised in 1951, it has played a crucial role in the conflict with surrounding Arab states, and above all in Israel's struggle first against the PLO and its offshoot GUERRILLA groups, and more recently with HEZBOLLAH, HAMAS and other Islamist threats to national security.

mossback A US term for a REACTIONARY. Southerners who fled to the woods and swamps to avoid conscription to the Confederate army were known as 'mossy-backs', and the term reappeared in the 1860s to describe western farmers in general, and conservative Ohio Democrats in particular.

most favoured nation The status bestowed on those countries to which CONGRESS grants open access to US markets. The term is British in origin, dating back at least to 1905, but it was taken up by America in the 1920s and was developed first into a basis of US trading policy and eventually into one of the bases for the world system of freer trade embodied in GATT and the WTO. There is no such thing as a 'less favoured nation', though under the JACKSON-VANIK AMENDMENT most favoured nation status was denied to 'non-market economy' countries that refused to allow their Jews to emigrate, e.g. the Soviet Union.

Mother One of the many nicknames for Margaret THATCHER, this one originated and mainly used by reasonably-devoted supporters. *See also* MATRICIDES.

Mother Country *See* COUNTRY.

mother test A simple rule-of-thumb for determining whether the public will understand a piece of legislation or government initiative. When Hillary CLINTON appeared before the House WAYS AND MEANS Committee on 28 September 1993, she was asked by a member how she could explain her HEALTH SECURITY plan to his mother. The FIRST LADY replied: 'If we can't pass the mother test, we aren't going to succeed, are we?' *Compare* EUAN TEST.

motherhood and apple pie Vacuous utterances by politicians combining sentimental patriotism with appeals to traditional values, coupled with a total absence of positive or original content. Though the phrase originated in America where such speeches trip lightly from the tongue and find willing audiences, its use, and relevance, have crossed the Atlantic.

mother of all resolutions The resolution (no. 687) passed by the UN SECURITY COUNCIL in March 1991 which governed the ceasefire in the GULF WAR, and maintained tough SANCTIONS against SADDAM HUSSEIN's regime. It echoes Saddam's defiant warning that any move by the UN-backed COALITION to retake Kuwait after his invasion the previous August would trigger the 'mother of all battles'.

Mother of Parliaments A now-hackneyed term for Britain's HOUSE OF COMMONS, and its ethos which has been replicated in LEGISLATURES across the English-speaking world - – even if some have failed to take root. The phrase was first used by the English radical John Bright (1811–89) when, in a speech at Birmingham on 18 January 1865, he declared:

> England is the mother of Parliaments.

motion A proposal formally put forward to be debated and voted on, and often capable of AMENDMENT.

Early Day Motion *See* EDM.

motor. Motor-Voter Act America's 1993 National Voter Registration Act, which obliges the States to register voters on forms used for drivers' licence applications and welfare claims; it replaced or supplemented POSTCARD REGISTRATION. A record 11.2 million Americans registered to vote in the year after it took effect, half of them while getting drivers' or vehicle licences. Intended to increase registration of underprivileged (and largely Democratic) voters, it may have helped the party in the 1996 elections but did nothing long-term to arrest the decline in TURNOUT.

motorcade A procession of cars in support of, or escorting, a visiting politician or candidate for office; in the case of a dignitary in office or a Presidential candidate, it will be accompanied by motorcycle outriders. The most celebrated motorcade was that taking President KENNEDY through DALLAS at the moment of his assassination.

Motorman The codename of the security operation in NORTHERN IRELAND in July 1972 when the British army moved in strength into NO-GO AREAS which had been established by the Provisional IRA. Motorman re-established control by the SECURITY FORCES, especially over west Belfast and parts of Derry, and for a time blunted the terrorist campaign, but at the price of heightened resentment by Republican supporters.

motormouth A politician who is unable to stop talking. Before the internal combustion engine caught on, the phrase was 'automatic mouth'. In the 1890s Rep. Marriott Brosius of Pennsylvania told a fellow Congressman who kept interrupting him:

> You love your automatic mouth;
> You love its giddy whirl;
> You love its fluent flow;
> You love to wind your mouth up;
> You love to hear it go!

Mount Rushmore A mountain in the Black Hills of Dakota, the side of which bears the epic sculpture by Gutzon Borglum (1876–1941) of the heads of four Presidents: WASHINGTON, JEFFERSON, Theodore ROOSEVELT and LINCOLN, each measuring 60ft. from the chin to the top of the forehead. Borglum began the work in the 1920s; when finished, it soon became one of America's most popular tourist attractions. It was also the scene of the memorable final confrontation of Cary Grant and Eva Marie Saint with the villainous James Mason in Alfred Hitchcock's 1959 thriller *North by Northwest.* Borglum began another massive carving – of General Robert E. Lee, Stonewall Jackson, Jefferson DAVIS and 1200 Confederate soldiers – on Stone Mountain, but the project was plagued by disagreements and Borglum died with it uncompleted.

Mount Vernon The genteel but not lavish Virginia plantation home of George WASHINGTON, beside the POTOMAC just south of the city named after him, which is preserved in its 18th-century condition as a national memorial to the leader of the Revolutionary Army and the United States' first President. Visitors find the separate slave quarters of particular interest.

mountain. beef mountain, butter mountain Derogatory terms for the surpluses of farm produce run up by Europe's Common Agricultural Policy (CAP), especially during the late 1970s and early '80s. At times there were a million tons of beef in cold stores, which could not be sold within the community without lowering prices (which was supposed in BRUSSELS to be a bad thing). Much of the butter mountain (there was also a WINE LAKE) was sold at knockdown prices to the Soviet Union, though some – and a little beef – was made available to Europe's needy old folk.

I have been to the top of the mountain *See* I.

move. We shall not be moved One of the

best known PROTEST SONGS of the 1960s – and also one of the fastest – first heard in a political context at the civil rights SIT-INs a decade earlier when demonstrators refused to budge. It was originally a Negro spiritual

> We shall not, we shall not be moved.
> We shall not, we shall not be moved.
> Just like the tree that's standing by the waterside.
> We shall not be moved.

Football spectators in Britain will have heard the same verse sung with the third line rendered as 'Just like the team that's going to win the F. A. Cup'.

modern movements *See* MODERN.

this great movement of ours *See* THIGMOO.

mover The person who leads the sponsors of a MOTION or RESOLUTION, and opens the debate on it.

movers and shakers Those in the political milieu who believe themselves able to influence public opinion and bring about change in high places. The 19th-century British poet Arthur O'Shaughnessy wrote:

> We are the music-makers
> And we are the dreamers of dreams . . .
> Yet we are the movers and shakers
> Of the world, forever, it seems.

moving the goalposts Sneakily changing the terms of debate midway through, so that a person arguing a point finds it dismissed as irrelevant. The phrase is often used by contractors who have tendered for a project only to find the specifications have changed. The term comes from informal games of soccer or hockey where the goalposts at either end are portable, and a player who thought he was shooting for goal finds he has been tricked into missing the target.

Let's get America moving again The slogan used by John F. KENNEDY in his successful 1960 campaign for the Presidency; it harnessed his youth and vigour to the notion, not now accepted, that the US economy had stagnated under EISENHOWER. It has since been used, in suitably amended form, by challengers to the INCUMBENT government in many countries.

Moynihan Report An internal paper written for the JOHNSON administration in 1965 by **Daniel Patrick Moynihan** (1927–), then Assistant Secretary for Labor and later a prominent if MAVERICK Democratic senator, which drew attention to the emergence of a black UNDERCLASS, though the word did not yet exist. It argued that while middle- and working-class blacks were making progress, a lower group frequently composed of single-parent families was falling behind; borrowing a phrase from the black sociologist Kenneth Clark, Moynihan maintained that 'At the centre of the tangle of pathology is the weakness of the Negro family'. He argued that white America had broken the will of black American families through slavery, and that forcing black men to take submissive jobs 'worked against the emergence of a strong father figure'. Moynihan was immediately accused of RACISM, and of diverting attention from the need for government to act against poverty, and it was many years before the plight of the underclass was addressed again.

MP Member of Parliament. The universally-used abbreviation for members of the HOUSE OF COMMONS at WESTMINSTER, and of its Canadian cousin in Ottawa.

MSI Italian Social Movement. The NEO-FASCIST party which after 48 years of keeping the flame alive eventually gained a share of power in 1994 as a member of Silvio Berlusconi's FORZA ITALIA! coalition. The Milan-based party was founded in 1946 and was led until just before his death in 1988 by Giorgio Almirante, who had been a junior Minister under Mussolini (*see* DUCE). Renamed the MSI-National Right in 1973, the party polled around 6% in national elections under Italy's fragmented party system until the formation of the LOMBARD LEAGUE/LIGA NORD widened and diluted its appeal. At EU level the MSI has operated in partnership with France's NATIONAL FRONT.

MSP Member of the Scottish Parliament. The formal abbreviation for members of the HOLYROOD legislature.

muck-rakers The name bestowed by Theodore ROOSEVELT in 1906 on investigative journalists, whom he branded as sensationalist and 'irresponsible'. Sensationalism was indeed used to boost circulation, notably by William Randolph Hearst's papers whose IMPERIALISM had catapulted 'TEDDY' to fame and office. But many reforms were brought about through articles in magazines such as *Collier's* and *McClure's*, and in newspapers led by Hearst's *New York Journal* and Joseph Pulitzer's *New York World*. Two effective muckrakers were Ida M. Tarbell (1857–1944), whose 1904 exposé of Standard Oil encouraged new ANTI-TRUST legislation, and Lincoln Steffens (1866–1936, *see also* I have seen the FUTURE), who the same year exposed municipal corruption. Upton Sinclair's book *The Jungle* (1906), exposing insanitary practices in the meat industry, led directly to the Food and Drugs Act that same year. Roosevelt coined the word when he laid the stone of the first House office building on 14 April 1906; quoting from John Bunyan's *Pilgrim's Progress*, he compared them to

> the Man with the Muckrake . . . who when offered the Celestial crown could look no way but downward [and continue] to rake the filth on the floor.

He added:

> The men with the muck-rakes are often indispensable to the well-being of society; but only if they know when to stop raking the muck.

muddle. a muddle, not a fiddle *See* OFFICEGATE.

mudslinging Attempting to secure political advantage or win an ELECTION by revealing (or inventing) unsavoury facts about one's opponent and broadcasting them as widely as possible in the hope that some of the mud will stick. By the 1990s its practitioners were terming it NEGATIVE RESEARCH (*see also* NERD SQUAD).

> He who slings mud usually loses ground.
>
> ADLAI STEVENSON

mugwump A US term for a political INDEPENDENT, or more specifically a REPUBLICAN who will not support the party's TICKET or, even worse, has gone over to the Democrats. It also covers active Republicans or Democrats who remain officially 'unaffiliated', often because their employment prevents them 'going public'. The word, originally the Algonquin for 'chief' and later applied to the self-important, was being used for Independents by 1872; in the 1884 Presidential election it was applied by their opponents to idealistic, liberal Republicans who switched from the party's nominee James G. Blaine to the more attractive Grover CLEVELAND.

> A mugwump always has his mug on one side of the political fence and his wump on the other.
>
> *Attr.* Both to HAROLD WILLIS DODDS, President of Princeton University 1933–37, and the jurist ALBERT J. ENGEL (1904–)

mujaheddin (Arab. fighters) Originally the loose coalition of US-backed rebel groups in Afghanistan who after ten years of GUERRILLA warfare drove out the Soviet occupiers in 1989, the hardest-line of whom, to America's dismay, later became the core of the TALEBAN and AL QAEDA. Comprising a wide range of political and ethnic factions including Sunni and Shi'ite Muslims, Islamic traditionalists and fundamentalists and led mainly from across the border in Pakistan, they were armed by China, Iran, Saudi Arabia and Egypt as well as the West, also relying heavily on captured Soviet weaponry. When in 1992 the government of Najibullah Ahmadzi fell, the *mujaheddin*, who had formed a provisional government in exile, took over, only for fighting to break out immediately between rival groups, paving the way for the eventual Taleban takeover. The name has come to apply to anti-Western Islamist fighters generally; prior to the IRAQ WAR, SADDAM HUSSEIN formed a *mujaheddin* of fanatical BAATH PARTY loyalists to protect him – while they failed, they managed with foreign Arab fighters to cause severe disruption and heavy casualties once the Americans had taken over.

Muldergate *See* INFORMATION SCANDAL.

multi-. multiculturalism The educational, social and political view that has gained ground in Western countries since the 1970s, that it is wrong to impose a stereotyped national culture on those arriving from foreign lands. It has sparked keen public argument over whether, for example, children should be taught in their mother tongue or the language of their new country, and whether the former will lead to 'cultural ghettoes' and make it harder for second-generation immigrants to integrate.

Multi-Fibre agreement (MFA) An agreement concluded in 1973 by more than 50 countries that provided for two decades a framework for international trade in products made of wool, cotton or man-made fibres, retaining a degree of PROTECTIONISM for the older industrialised nations. By establishing a QUOTA system it enabled THIRD WORLD countries to export to the developed world without fear of prohibitive TARIFFS, yet without killing established textile industries. After the creation of the WTO, it was replaced from the end of 2004 by a completely open market, prompting complaints from the poorest exporters like Bangladesh that they would lose business to better-organised industries in China and India.

multilateralist (1) Someone who believes that America should work in concert with other nations instead of pursuing a UNILATERALIST foreign policy based entirely on self-interest; the term has caught on in response to the agenda of the George W. BUSH administration and its neo-conservative backers. (2) An advocate of nations disarming step by step with each other, unlike a UNILATERALIST who believes that for moral reasons their own country should abandon NUCLEAR WEAPONS without any prior commitment from others to do so.

multinational force A long-sought-for goal of military planners and diplomatists, now coming to fruition in the EU's development of shared military capabilities between its non-NEUTRAL members and specifically in a combined Franco-German brigade. Historically it applied to a force in which troops drawn from several nations served alongside each other without this degree of integration. The term was used particularly of US, UK, French and other troops who made a vain attempt to keep the peace in the Lebanon in the early 1980s (*see* BEIRUT AIRPORT BOMBING).

multinationals Large global corporations with more power than many governments, who have the ability to boost or wreck the economy of a country or region by establishing a plant or closing it. Their perceived arrogance, and for some even their existence, was a spur to the rise of the anti-GLOBALISATION movement.

Munich agreement The agreement concluded by HITLER, Neville CHAMBERLAIN and the French premier Edouard Daladier (with the Italians also present) in Munich on 29 September 1938 for the transfer of the SUDETENLAND to NAZI Germany in return for assurances that the rest of Czechoslovakia would not be touched. The high point of Chamberlain's policy of APPEASEMENT was widely hailed in Britain as bringing PEACE IN OUR TIME and PEACE WITH HONOUR, and its critics were in a small minority. On arrival at Heston Airport next day, Chamberlain told the crowd:

> This morning I had another talk with the German Chancellor, Herr Hitler, and here is the paper that bears his name upon it as well as mine. We regard the agreement signed last night and the Anglo-German naval agreement as symptomatic of the desire of our two nations never to go to war with one another again.

He appeared on the balcony of Buckingham Palace and was cheered in the COMMONS by Tory MPs; Harold MACMILLAN recalled:

> I saw one man silent and seated – his head sunk on his shoulders, his whole demeanour depicting something between anger and despair. It was CHURCHILL.

Churchill branded Munich 'a defeat without a war', and Christopher Mayhew '*reculer pour mieux reculer*'; Clement ATTLEE declared:

> We have today seen a gallant, democratic and civilised people betrayed and handed over to a ruthless despotism.

One Minister, the First Lord of the Admiralty Duff Cooper, resigned, saying he could not have stayed in the government with his head erect. The pro-appeasement editor of *The Times*, Geoffrey Dawson, inserted into his LOBBY correspondent's account of Cooper's speech the words 'damp squib'; the reporter, Antony Winn, also resigned.

The agreement was discredited six months later when Hitler invaded Bohemia and Moravia; by the outbreak of WORLD WAR II less than a year after Munich, it was seen as a shameful act and the **Men of Munich** were vilified. Chamberlain's supporters argue that it was essential to give Britain a year to prepare for war; his critics that it merely encouraged Hitler, who was re-arming faster, to grab more territory. The word 'Munich' is now shorthand for betrayal, and when Margaret THATCHER visited Prague in 1990 she made a public apology to the Czechoslovak Parliament.

Munich beer hall putsch The abortive attempt by Adolf HITLER on 12 November 1923 to take control of Bavaria. It took place in Munich's largest beer hall, the *Bürgerbraukeller*, where Gustav von Kahr, the state commissioner, was speaking. Hitler and his BROWNSHIRTS burst in and took the floor, claiming the support of the war hero Field Marshal von Ludendorff (1865–1937). Hitler, Ludendorff and others including Rudolf HESS were arrested, Hitler being sent to prison, where he wrote MEIN KAMPF.

Murchison letter A Republican hoax in the 1888 US Presidential election CAMPAIGN that damaged Grover CLEVELAND's chances of re-election and gravely embarrassed the British government. Charles Osgoodby, a California Republican, wrote to Sir Lionel Sackville-West, the British Minister in WASHINGTON, claiming to be an American of English origin who favoured Cleveland over Benjamin Harrison, a high-TARIFF man who was 'a believer in the American side in all questions' and 'an enemy to British interests', and asking how he should vote. Sir Lionel was stupid enough to tell him, saying that the Democrats were 'still desirable of maintaining friendly relations with Great Britain' and that Cleveland would 'manifest a spirit of reconciliation'.

Osgoodby released his letter and the reply to the press, and waited for the bang. Faced with a barrage of embarrassing headlines, Cleveland asked the British government to recall Sackville-West and when they refused, rejected his credentials. But the dirt stuck, and although Cleveland finished narrowly ahead in the popular vote, he was handsomely beaten in the ELECTORAL COLLEGE.

Murder, Inc. President REAGAN's name for Iran under the AYATOLLAH, bestowed because of Tehran's involvement in terrorist activity against US citizens and interests. It made the involvement of senior subordinates in the IRAN-CONTRA affair all the harder for Americans to credit.

Murphy Brown *See* FAMILY VALUES.

Mururoa The French Polynesian atoll 60km in perimeter, situated at 21° 52′S, 138° 55′W, which with its smaller neighbour Fangataufa was the site of French NUCLEAR tests between 1960 and 1996, to the fury of GREENPEACE which tried to halt them (*see* RAINBOW WARRIOR), and the governments of New Zealand and other South Pacific islands. Altogether 41 underground tests (up to 1975) and 134 in boreholes were carried out; the final eight, after a moratorium, were ordered by Jacques Chirac after his election as President in 1995, prior to the conclusion of the **Rarotonga Treaty** making the region nuclear-free. The islands were declared a part of Metropolitan France for the duration of the testing programme, which was controlled from Hao, 450km to the north-west.

mushroom cloud The terrifying trademark of NUCLEAR WAR, from the characteristic shape of a nuclear explosion, especially one near ground level. The massive energy release of the explosion creates a shock wave and fireball which render the air luminous. Such a cloud was first witnessed by scientists of the MANHATTAN PROJECT who detonated a prototype ATOMIC BOMB at the Almogordo test site, New Mexico, on 16 July 1945. The physicist Enrico Fermi described it:

> After a few seconds the rising flames lost their brightness and appeared as a huge pillar of smoke with an expanded head like a gigantic mushroom that rose rapidly beyond the clouds, probably to a height of the order of 30,000 feet.

The next month America exploded nuclear weapons over HIROSHIMA and NAGASAKI, and the mushroom cloud claimed its first victims.

Mussolini, Benito *See* DUCE.

mutual aid The practice within Britain's CONSERVATIVE PARTY under which safe constituencies are linked to those the party might win (or avoid losing) with enough help, party workers being ferried there at election times.

mutually assured destruction Appropriately abbreviated to **MAD**. The ultimate form of nuclear DETERRENCE, the likelihood that if NUCLEAR WAR broke out both SUPERPOWERS would be obliterated because of the sheer size of their nuclear arsenals. Pursued by America and the Soviet Union from the 1960s, MAD maintained the BALANCE OF TERROR through the knowledge that enough of the nuclear firepower of each would survive a FIRST STRIKE to set off devastating retaliation.

MVD (Russ. *Ministerstvo Vnutrennikh Del*, Ministry of Internal Affairs) The Soviet police organisation that replaced the NKVD in 1946. The official duties of its uniformed members included general police work, the control of labour camps, the supervision of border troops, the issue of passports and visas, etc. The MVD is also believed to have been involved in the secret trial and punishment of STALIN's opponents. It was replaced in 1960 by the KVD, but has been renamed as the border police of post-Soviet Russia.

MX Missile Experimental (Missile X). A sophisticated 'silo-busting' ICBM developed during the 1970s as part of a drive to modernise the ageing US arsenal of Titan and MINUTEMAN III missiles. The MX was designed to carry ten MIRVed warheads and deliver them with pinpoint accuracy, using the latest inertial guidance technology. It was also planned for delivery from mobile launchers to survive a FIRST STRIKE, but a successful and cost-effective method of concealing and moving the missiles underground could not be found. In 1983 CONGRESS refused further funding for mobile launch (**Racetrack**) development; Defense Secretary Caspar Weinberger (*see* CAP THE KNIFE) briefly suggested the alternative of **Densepack**, under which the MXs would be based so close together that Soviet missiles targeted at them would blow each other up as they approached. Development proceeded on the understanding that a limited number would be deployed in old Minuteman silos. But the START II agreement on MIRVs limited MX to a single warhead.

my. my distinguished colleague The way

in which US SENATORS refer to colleagues from their own party.

My fellow Americans The phrase with which the President customarily greets the people at the start of a nationwide broadcast, especially at a time of crisis or difficulty. It dates back to the early days of broadcasting, and its institutional status was acknowledged in the 1996 movie comedy of the same name in which Jack Lemmon and James Garner played two former Presidents from opposite ends of the political spectrum.

my honourable friend *See* FRIEND.

My Lai massacre For many Americans, including firm supporters of US intervention, the most shameful episode of the VIETNAM WAR: the machine-gunning of over 300 old men, women and children by US soldiers at the village of My Lai (also known as Song My) in Quang Ngai province; some of the women were also raped. The massacre was carried out on 16 March 1968 by Charlie Company of 1st Battalion 20th Infantry, led by Lieutenant William Calley; they had been led to expect a head-on battle with a VIET CONG battalion. Army officers conspired to conceal the truth, but a year later Ronald Ridenhour, a soldier serving in Vietnam who had heard of the incident, wrote an open letter to the Army Department and members of CONGRESS demanding an investigation. Later in 1969 photographs of the massacred villagers, taken by Army photographer Ron Haeberle, appeared in a newspaper alongside Haeberle's eye-witness account. In November 1970 Calley and 24 other men went on trial for murder at Fort Benning, Georgia, Four months later all but Calley, who at one point said of the massacre 'It was no big deal, Sir', were acquitted. Calley was dismissed the service and sentenced to life imprisonment, but President NIXON ordered a review and he was paroled after three years. Calley's defence rested on the claim that he was 'following orders' and that the guilt lay with his superiors, and ultimately the US people. For many Americans the episode confirmed their worst fears; others regarded Calley as the dupe of an incompetent and undisciplined command structure – or even a martyr. *Compare* ABU GHRAIB.

my last appeal to reason HITLER's speech to the REICHSTAG on 19 July 1940, following the fall of France and with the invasion of Britain imminent, at which the FÜHRER held out a final offer of peace. Hitler – still perhaps influenced by CHAMBERLAIN's APPEASEMENT – imagined the British people had no desire to fight, but were being led by the nose by the warlike CHURCHILL. He appealed to them directly, and several days later the *Luftwaffe* dropped copies of the speech over southern England; a cinema newsreel showing a copy being cut up and hung on a lavatory wall won huge applause. Hitler was greatly annoyed when the Foreign Secretary, Lord Halifax, rejected the overture.

my lips are sealed The gist of Stanley BALDWIN's comments to the COMMONS on 10 December 1935, when his government was under attack at the height of the crisis over Italy's invasion of Abyssinia. Attempting to convince Tory backbenchers that he could not give a full explanation because promising initiatives were under way, he told them:

> I shall be but a short time tonight. I have seldom spoken with greater regret, for my lips are not as yet unsealed. Were these troubles over I would make a case, and I guarantee that not a man would go into the lobby against us.

What was under way was the conclusion of the ignominious HOARE-LAVAL PACT, which eight days later forced Samuel Hoare to resign as Foreign Secretary after details were LEAKed in Paris; the 38-year-old Anthony EDEN succeeded him.

N

NAACP National Association for the Advancement of Colored People. America's most respected organisation combating racial DISCRIMINATION, regarded by successive ADMINISTRATIONS as the voice of black Americans. Founded in 1908 at the National Negro Congress in New York by W. E. B. DuBois, Jane Addams, William Dean Howells and others as a bi-racial group demanding civil, constitutional and educational rights, much of its early work was against LYNCHING. Its legal challenges to discrimination brought gains as early as the 1920s and particularly in post-war years, but by the 1940s it was also using SIT-IN tactics to force DESEGREGATION. It supported the 1955 MONTGOMERY BUS BOYCOTT led by Dr Martin Luther KING and his 1963 MARCH ON WASHINGTON. By then, despite wise leadership from Roy Wilkins, the NAACP was losing the initiative to black radicals who scorned its relative conservatism, and the emergence of a strong black middle class also lessened its impact. But it retains its credibility, especially as a vehicle for promoting the rights of black Americans through the courts.

Nab Nickname for **Sir Gerald Nabarro** (1913–73), flamboyant and eccentric Conservative MP, first for Kidderminster and then South Worcestershire. He campaigned against anomalies in the Purchase Tax which preceded VAT, asking: 'Why is there this invidious distinction between doorknocking nutcrackers and nutcracking doorknockers?' He named his autobiography *NAB 1* after the registration number of his favourite Rolls-Royce; he had six cars altogether, registered NAB 1 to 6. In 1972 he secured, and won, a retrial after being convicted of driving NAB 1 the wrong way round a roundabout; he claimed his secretary had been at the wheel.

nabobs All-powerful figures in the US CONGRESS, and the political and media establishment outside. The origin of the word is the Hindi *nawab*, a wealthy provincial administrator of the Moghul empire. The phrase 'rich as a nawab', corrupted to 'nabob', was applied to British merchants who became wealthy in India and returned home; the word crossed the Atlantic to apply to Southern plantation owners, and later to persons of power and influence generally.

> In the United States today, we have more than our share of nattering nabobs of negativism.
>
> Vice President SPIRO T. AGNEW

Nader's raiders The team of consumer affairs lobbying researchers built up in Washington by **Ralph Nader** (1934–) after the success of his book UNSAFE AT ANY SPEED. From the mid-1960s they pressed CONGRESS for tighter legislation on consumer protection, pollution and FREEDOM OF INFORMATION. Nader's organisation Public Citizen Inc. has kept up the campaigning on a more formal basis. Nader later engaged in elective politics, his independent Presidential candidacy in 2000 tipping the balance against Al Gore.

NAFTA North American Free Trade Area. The common market comprising 360 million inhabitants of the United States, Canada and Mexico which is planned to eliminate all TARIFFS between the three countries over fifteen years from 1994, create international haulage routes across America, enable US financial institutions to open up in Mexico, and prevent European and Far Eastern firms using Mexico to penetrate US markets. Agreed in August 1992, the passage of NAFTA threatened to derail the CLINTON administration, with Ross PEROT and labour unions claiming it would cost America hundreds of thousands of jobs. But Vice President GORE turned the tables on Perot in a televised debate, and the HOUSE approved it in 17 Nov 1993 by 234–200 after generous injections of PORK. While the outsourcing of American jobs had become a reality by 2004, most were not going to Mexico. *Compare* CAFTA.

Nagasaki The port city in West Kyushu,

Japan, largely destroyed on 9 August 1945 by the dropping of the second ATOMIC BOMB. Damage was less severe than at HIROSHIMA, but 75,000 people were killed or wounded, hastening Japan's surrender and the end of WORLD WAR II. The city was speedily rebuilt, but its destruction continues to serve as an awful warning to the world.

Nairobi bombing The attack by constituents of AL QAEDA on 7 August 1998 on the US Embassy in the Kenyan capital which left more than 220 people dead, thirteen of them Americans; a simultaneous attack in Dar Es Salaam caused a further ten deaths. The bombings triggered CRUISE MISSILE attacks on Osama BIN LADEN's bases in Afghanistan and on a Sudanese plant wrongly suspected of making weapons for Al Qaeda.

naked into the conference chamber Aneurin BEVAN's warning to fellow Labour left-wingers at the 1957 party conference that he could not embrace UNILATERAL nuclear disarmament. Many former Bevanites could not understand what they saw as a SELL-OUT, pleading with him: 'Come back NYE, unilaterally.' But Bevan told them:

> If you carry this resolution and follow out all its implications, you will send a Foreign Secretary . . . whoever he may be, naked into the conference chamber. You call that statesmanship – I call it emotional spasm.

naked to mine enemies *See* ENEMIES.

name recognition One of the first things a candidate has to achieve to stand any chance of election, or a local politician to achieve national office. One of the basics of opinion polling is questions to the voters on which politicians and aspirants they have heard of; high name recognition is usually a pointer to success with the voters.

naming The action taken by the SPEAKER against a member of the HOUSE OF COMMONS for grossly disorderly conduct, disregarding the authority of the CHAIR or persistently disrupting business. The Speaker first names the member, and a motion for suspension is then put. If this is carried, the offender must leave the CHAMBER at once and remain outside the PRECINCTS OF THE HOUSE for five sitting days for a first offence, twenty for a second.

Nannygate The episode that forced the resignation of David Blunkett (1947–) as Home Secretary on 15 December 2004, just as he was preparing to take through the COMMONS the tougher anti-crime and anti-terrorism legislation on which Tony BLAIR planned to fight a general ELECTION the following spring. Blunkett, the first blind person (*see* OFFA, RUBY, SADIE, TED) to serve in the British CABINET and a divorced man, had been in a three-year relationship with Kimberley Fortier, publisher of the SPECTATOR, which began just after her marriage to her fellow American Stephen Quinn. Blunkett wanted to make it public, Ms Fortier broke it off and weeks later, as Blunkett sought paternal rights over Ms Fortier's son who he believed to be his, newspaper stories alleged that he had improperly fast-tracked an application for a visa for her Filipino nanny, Leoncia Casalme. Blunkett, confident of vindication, set up an inquiry into his conduct under the former senior civil servant Sir Alan Budd, but before it could report he was informed of the discovery of a compromising e-mail sent by one of his officials and resigned (*see* NO FAVOURS, BUT SLIGHTLY QUICKER). Blunkett's position had been weakened by candid comments he had made, for the record, about Cabinet colleagues to a biographer, who published them at the height of the furore; his successor, Charles Clarke, was among those he had criticised. The week after Blunkett resigned, Budd reported that while there was a 'chain of events' linking him to the processing of the visa in half the normal time, there was no direct evidence that he had sought preferential treatment for Miss Casalme. It also emerged that Ms Fortier/Quinn had been having a relationship with the political commentator Simon Hoggart, the *Spectator*'s wine correspondent, prior to, and after, her marriage to Quinn and the commencement of her affair with Blunkett who returned after the 2005 election as Work and Pensions Secretary.

> In time, people will come to understand what I have been prepared to sacrifice for that little boy.
> DAVID BLUNKETT, 15 December 2004

napalm An explosive jelly formed from a petroleum compound – *na*pthenic acid and *palm*itic acid – which causes severe burns. Used in bombs and flame-throwers in WORLD WAR II and KOREA, it became to anti-war groups one of the most abhorrent of weapons because of its indiscriminate use, causing horrific injuries to civilians. The sight on US television of napalm casualties in VIETNAM intensified demands for withdrawal.

NASA National Aeronautics and Space Administration. The body which, since

1958, has co-ordinated America's space programme, excluding military projects. Since landing the first man on the Moon in 1969, the agency has struggled to maintain its initial impetus, not helped by CONGRESSional pressure to curb funding. After the *Challenger* disaster on 28 January 1986, the agency was completely reshaped to counter charges of bureaucratic atrophy and inadequate safety checks. Sadly, after the *Columbia* shuttle disintegrated over Texas on 1 February 2003, with the loss of a further seven astronauts, a board of inquiry blamed exactly the same cultural weaknesses that had led to the *Challenger* disaster. A leaner and more commercially-minded NASA is now responding to the challenge set by George W. BUSH in 2004 to get back to the Moon as a prelude to a manned mission to Mars, with Congress still trying to slash its budget. It was little noticed that the president's father had set the same challenge thirteen years previously.

NASCAR dads The middle- and upper-working-class fathers who voted narrowly for Bill CLINTON but switched en masse to George W. BUSH, and whom John KERRY needed to recapture to have a chance in 2004. NASCAR is America's most popular car-racing network. *Compare* SOCCER MOMS.

Nassau Conference The meeting in the Bahamas in 1962 between President John F. KENNEDY and Prime Minister Harold MACMILLAN. Macmillan's decision during the conference to opt for the US POLARIS missile system rather than an Anglo-French alternative greatly angered President DE GAULLE and fuelled his determination to keep Britain out of a united Europe (*see* NON!).

Nasty Party The description of Britain's CONSERVATIVE PARTY used by its own chairman, Theresa May, at its 2002 Bournemouth conference to drive home to the grassroots how it was widely perceived. Her speech was much praised in the media, but upset the party's aggressive right, and especially Lord Tebbit (*see* CHINGFORD SKINHEAD) who considered it an attack on himself and the values he represented. Mrs May said:

> There's a lot we need to do in this Party of ours. Our base is too narrow and so, occasionally, are our sympathies. You know what some people call us: the Nasty Party . . . Twice we went to the country unchanged, unrepentant, just plain unattractive. And twice we got slaughtered.

nation. nation of shopkeepers A pejorative term for Britain reflecting its inhabitants' perceived small-mindedness, popularly attributed to Napoleon but first used in 1770 by Josiah Tucker, Dean of Gloucester. Samuel ADAMS used it in describing British reaction to the Declaration of INDEPENDENCE – and Adam Smith in his WEALTH OF NATIONS wrote:

> To found a great empire for the sole purpose of raising up a people of customers . . . is extremely fit for a nation governed by shopkeepers.

Nation shall speak peace unto nation The motto of the BBC, devised by a schoolmaster, Montague John Rendall (1862–1950), in 1927 as the winning entry in a competition.

nation state An independent nation with a clear ethnic or cultural entity or with distinctive boundaries, contrasted with loose empires or city-states. It was the basis, at Woodrow WILSON's insistence, of the post-1918 world order.

> The nation state system that enables one or two men to decide life or death for the planet is the common enemy – not Russians, not Americans, capitalists or Communists. I.F. STONE

most favoured nation *See* MOST.

One Nation *See* ONE.

Two Nations The situation in England that DISRAELI exposed and was eager to remedy. In his *Sybil, or the Two Nations* (1845), Egremont said: 'I was told that an impossible gulf divided the Rich from the Poor; I was told that the Privileged and the people formed two Nations, governed by different laws, influenced by different manners, with no thoughts or sympathies in common; with an innate inability of mutual comprehension.'

national. National Assembly The LEGISLATURE of the French Republic, comprising the CHAMBER OF DEPUTIES and the SENATE. Its origins date back to the TENNIS COURT OATH of 1789.

National Committees The bodies that represent and administer America's two great political parties on a permanent basis. Formed of one man and one woman from each of the 50 states, plus state party chairs and other key officials, its main task is to make arrangements for the party's national CONVENTION in a Presidential ELECTION year, but it remains in being throughout the electoral cycle. The chairman of a national committee is often the choice of the President or Presidential NOMINEE.

> We made no progress at all, and we didn't intend to. That is the function of a National Committee. RONALD REAGAN

national debt The debt that a state has built up through borrowing to finance its activities, most frequently war, the development of the economy and unfundable public spending. JEFFERSON was 'for a government vigorously frugal and simple, applying all the possible savings of the public revenue to the discharge of the national debt'. And Alexander HAMILTON said: 'A national debt, if it is not excessive, will be to us a national blessing'; but MADISON was convinced that 'a public debt is a public curse, and in a republican government a greater than any other'. This was a reversal of PITT THE YOUNGER's declaration that 'a public debt is a public blessing'. The radical William Cobbett (1762–1835) took a more THATCHERITE view: 'Nothing is so calculated to produce a death-like torpor in a country as an extended system of taxation and a great national debt.' But Franklin D. ROOSEVELT, elected to balance the budget, soon reversed his position to say: 'Our national debt is after all an internal debt owed not only by the nation but to the nation. If our children have to pay interest on it, they will pay that interest to themselves.' Nevertheless, as Gordon BROWN demonstrated, the generation of a budget surplus to pay off some of the debt immediately reduces the national expenditure in interest payments, improving the finances further.

A crazy aunt we keep down in the basement.
H. ROSS PEROT, 1992

National Front (1) A far-right UK RACIST party that attracted some working-class support in the mid-1970s. It never made an electoral breakthrough, but did prompt the formation of anti-racist groups like the ANTI-NAZI LEAGUE and assist the recruitment of far-left organisations like the SWP. (2) The extreme right-wing anti-immigrant party led for three decades by Jean-Marie Le Pen (1928–), an ex-paratrooper and former POUJADIST deputy who in April 2002 caused an 'EARTHQUAKE' in France by beating the socialist Prime Minister Lionel Jospin into third place in the Presidential election; the next month Le Pen was crushingly defeated by the incumbent Jacques CHIRAC, but still polled 5.5 million votes. That June the party failed to win a single seat in the NATIONAL ASSEMBLY.

National Government The UK administration formed with largely Conservative support by Ramsay MACDONALD in 1931 when his minority Labour government split over an economy package (*see* GREAT BETRAYAL). Chancellor Philip Snowden expected the grouping to be purely temporary, saying later: 'The Tories have got the power, and they mean to use it.' It remained nominally in existence after MacDonald's retirement under the Conservatives BALDWIN and CHAMBERLAIN until the outbreak of WORLD WAR II.

National Guard America's citizen soldiery, part-time and organised on a state-by-state basis, which can be mobilised by a GOVERNOR in support of the civil power at times of turbulence or emergency, or activated in wartime to reinforce the regular US armed forces.

National Health Service *See* NHS.

National Intelligence Director The CABINET-level post recommended by the 9/11 COMMISSION and established after the briefest hesitation by George W. BUSH, to co-ordinate America's disconnected intelligence services in the struggle against terrorism. Bush acted in August 2004 as Democratic Presidential nominee John KERRY made plain that security would be a key plank of his campaign, but stopped short of fully integrating the CIA, which would continue to have a separate director. Setting in motion an overhaul of the 1947 National Security Act, Bush also stressed that the Commission wanted CONGRESS to reform the way it handled intelligence and security matters; HOMELAND SECURITY Secretary Tom Ridge had had to testify almost 140 times before different Congressional panels.

national interest, the The cause in which political leaders claim to be acting when pursuing a policy unpopular with the electorate or with other states – or especially pursuing their own interests. It is also common for information to be withheld from the people most affected by it 'in the national interest'.

National Labour Those Labour MPs who supported the NATIONAL GOVERNMENT in 1931 while the bulk went into OPPOSITION. Twenty made the break – including Philip Snowden, Sir John Sankey and J. H. Thomas – and thirteen survived that autumn's general election. Ramsay MACDONALD had hoped they would form the core of a new movement, but they became a rump in an overwhelmingly Tory administration.

National Liberals The 25 LIBERAL MPs led by Sir John Simon (1873–1954) who broke with their party over FREE TRADE in what they saw as an emergency requiring PROTECTIONIST measures and backed the

NATIONAL GOVERNMENT, thus weakening the already divided Liberals still further. They outlasted their NATIONAL LABOUR colleagues; their Liberal National group survived until 1948, being renamed the National Liberal Party but steadily integrated with the Conservatives. Its last four MPs joined the CONSERVATIVE PARTY in 1966.

National Military Establishment The forerunner of America's unified Department of Defense (DOD), set up in 1947 under the National Security Act. Until then each service had its entirely separate bureaucracy.

National Origins Plan The regulations introduced by the US government in 1929 under the QUOTA ACT of 1924, which set the number of immigrants from outside the Western Hemisphere at approximately 150,000 a year. Each country was given a quota based on the proportion of that 'national origin' in the total US population for 1920. Each European country was allowed at least 100 people a year, but all immigration from Asia was prohibited. The quota system lasted until 1965. *See also* DILLINGHAM REPORT.

National Party (1) The centre-right party in Australia (changing its name from the National COUNTRY PARTY in 1982) which shares power in government with the LIBERALS, most recently under John Howard. (2) The leading centre-right party in New Zealand. (3) In South Africa the largely Afrikaner party founded in 1914, which pioneered APARTHEID, governing continuously from 1948 to the end of the system under F. W. de Klerk and the victory of the ANC in the country's first multi-racial elections in 1994. It struggled to find a role in post-apartheid South Africa and its leaders merged into the ANC and its successor party the **New National Pary** wound itself up in 2005 after a disastrous showing in elections the previous year.

National Plan The blueprint for five years' economic development and revival in the UK issued in 1965 by the newly-established Department of Economic Affairs headed by George BROWN. Aiming for a 25% increase in national output by 1970, it was the first and only attempt by Harold WILSON's first government to assert control over the entire economy and significantly not from the TREASURY. It was 'blown off course' in Wilson's words by periodic BALANCE OF PAYMENTS difficulties culminating in the JULY MEASURES of 1966.

National Policy The programme on which Sir John Macdonald's Conservatives swept the country in the 1878 Canadian election: PROTECTIONISM; completion of the Pacific railway; a new drive for immigrants to populate the prairies and incentives for investors.

National Policy Forum The body set up under Tony BLAIR's reforms of the LABOUR PARTY to take detailed policymaking out of the hands of the annual party conference, involve the party GRASSROOTS in policy-making at an earlier stage, weaken the influence of trade union BLOCK VOTES and reduce the scope for confrontational and electorally counterproductive conference debates on divisive issues. The Forum refines policy proposals into a document presented to Conference in time for its inclusion in the MANIFESTO for an upcoming ELECTION; the first Forum was elected in 1998 and met the following year. The change has not prevented conference showdowns on issues of the day, or impeded the capacity of the leadership to make policy on the hoof, for instance over student top-up fees or FOUNDATION HOSPITALS.

national question, the Shorthand in the Irish Republic for the argument over the continued existence of NORTHERN IRELAND as a separate entity and the claim formerly asserted in the Irish Constitution to sovereignty over all 32 states. The debate has continued in a minor key since the conclusion of the 1998 GOOD FRIDAY AGREEMENT.

National Recovery Administration *See* NRA.

National Review The magazine founded by William F. Buckley Jr in 1955 whose right-wing RADICALISM paved the way for the revival of CONSERVATISM in US politics, for the unsuccessful Goldwater campaign in 1964 and eventually for the triumph of Ronald REAGAN.

National Rifle Association *See* NRA.

national security A largely US term for the protection of the state against external, and sometimes internal, threat, and the regime acquired to achieve this.

National Security Adviser The President's principal adviser on foreign policy and related matters, sometimes, as with Henry KISSINGER, overshadowing the SECRETARY OF STATE.

National Security Agency The organisation co-ordinating the US government's communications and eavesdropping systems. Established under the Defense Department in 1952, it embraces the communications, code-breaking and electronic intelligence-gathering operations of the armed services, CIA, FBI and other agencies. Its activities, notably its signals monitoring arm at Fort Meade, Maryland (*compare* GCHQ), and worldwide installations including several in the UK, are even more secret than those of the CIA.

National Socialism The ideology behind Germany's NAZI party, based on HITLER's MEIN KAMPF. Its essentials were the superiority of the German race and its expansionist destiny, and hatred of the Jews. CHURCHILL branded it a 'perverted science', but Hermann Goering (1893–1946) revelled in it:

> Our movement took a grip on cowardly Marxism, and from it extracted the meaning of socialism. It also took from the cowardly, middle-class parties their nationalism. Throwing both into the cauldron of our national way of life there emerged, as clear as crystal, the synthesis – National Socialism.

National Union Until its abolition in 1998 under William HAGUE's reforms, the voluntary organisational wing of Britain's CONSERVATIVE PARTY. Its executive committee was the party's governing body, though with, in theory, no say over policy. The National Union's annual meeting was the Conservative CENTRAL COUNCIL each March.

National Unity The banner under which the former Republican Rep. John Anderson of Illinois (with former Democratic Gov. Patrick Lucey of Wisconsin) sought the Presidency in 1980. Their platform was fiscally conservative but liberal on social issues. Anderson finished third to Ronald REAGAN, with 5,719,000 votes but none in the ELECTORAL COLLEGE.

National Urban League Formed in 1910 as a bi-racial group to help black migrants from the rural South adjust to city life, it has been, along with the NAACP, a leading voice in America's black communities. In the 1960s it developed a programme of vigorous but NON-VIOLENT community action under A. Whitney Young, taking a firm stand against BLACK POWER.

nationalisation The transfer of sectors of industry and commerce from the PRIVATE SECTOR to state ownership, with or without compensation. In the UK, the traditional keystone of LABOUR's economic and social policies, implemented from 1945 (the Bank of England) to 1977 (aircraft and shipbuilding) (*see* CLAUSE FOUR). The Conservatives strongly contested most instances of nationalisation, reversing them where they were not too firmly entrenched (steel was nationalised and denationalised twice), though Edward HEATH's government did nationalise Rolls Royce to prevent the company collapsing. The reverse process became known under Margaret THATCHER as PRIVATISATION. NEW LABOUR, far from reversing Thatcherite privatisations, has continued them in a minor key while restoring the railways to a degree of state control, but specifically not ownership (*see* RAILTRACK). CHURCHILL is reputed to have taunted ATTLEE in the 'Gents' of the HOUSE OF COMMONS: 'Anything that's large and successful, you want to nationalise it.' Hugh Dalton (1887–1962) once dreamed he was chairing a Labour Party conference where a proposal to nationalise the Solar System was going through smoothly until an AMENDMENT was moved with the words: 'and the Milky Way'. In Egypt, the nationalisation of the Suez Canal by President Nasser precipitated the SUEZ CRISIS.

Morrisonian nationalisation The formula followed by Herbert Morrison (Later Lord Morrison of Lambeth, 1888–1965), the ATTLEE government's nationalisation supremo, of a rigidly centralised hierarchy for newly acquired industries and no role for worker representation or participation.

nationalism Devotion to the cause of a nation and its independence. Nationalism has come to be regarded as a disruptive force in international relations; Albert Einstein (1879–1955) termed it 'an infantile disease; the measles of mankind'.

> Patriotism is when love for your own people comes first; nationalism, when hate for people other than your own comes first.
>
> DE GAULLE

New Nationalism The policy of radical economic regulation and intervention set out by Theodore ROOSEVELT in 1910, with the explanation: 'The citizens of the United States must effectively control her mighty commercial forces which they have themselves called into being.' A feature of his BULL MOOSE campaign against President TAFT two years later, it accepted the reality of large concentrations of power in business, provided they were regulated.

nationalist (1) A practitioner of nationalism generally. (2) In the early days of American independence, the opposite of a FEDERALIST, advocating a more unitary state. (3) An advocate, peaceful or otherwise, of the reunion of NORTHERN IRELAND with the Irish Republic (formerly, of HOME RULE).

Nationalist China The state established on Taiwan by Chiang Kai-Shek (*see* GENERALISSIMO) following the Communist capture of power on the mainland, which has survived in increasing prosperity for half a century despite friction over its claim to speak for China and China's insistence that it is a breakaway province. *See* CHINA CARD; CHINA LOBBY; KMT; QUEMOY AND MATSU; WHO LOST CHINA?

nationalities question The issue of how the many diverse peoples of the SOVIET UNION could be controlled from the Kremlin, and how much power, if any, should be devolved to them. Initially they enjoyed some autonomy, under LENIN's supervision as COMMISSAR for the Nationalities, but STALIN subjected them to rigid control. He even had the Chechens deported en masse from their homeland to Siberia for having allegedly COLLABORATED with the Germans; the post-Communist Russian leadership must have wished they had stayed there when separatist violence in Chechnya from the early 1990s was accompanied by terrorism, crime and banditry in adjoining Republics and even in Moscow (*see* BESLAN, MOSCOW THEATRE SIEGE).

NATO North Atlantic Treaty Organisation. The ATLANTIC ALLIANCE of twelve nations that grew to sixteen during the COLD WAR and now comprises 26 countries including several former Soviet republics and SATELLITES. It was formed by the signature of the North Atlantic Treaty on 4 April 1949 as a conventional and nuclear DETERRENT to Soviet aggression against any member; its Communist counterpart was the WARSAW PACT. NATO's headquarters, SHAPE, is at Chièvres, Belgium, and its first supreme commander was General Dwight D. EISENHOWER; customarily the US provides the commander and a European member the Secretary-General. Its political arm is the NORTH ATLANTIC COUNCIL and its military decision-making body the **Defence Planning Group**. Lord Ismay (1887–1965) confessed that NATO had been set up 'to keep the Russians out, the Americans in and the Germans down'. A secondary aim was to enrol the Greeks and the Turks to prevent them fighting each other. Since the end of the COLD WAR, it has become a less battle-ready partnership, anxious to stress that it is not targeting a democratic Russia; its purpose lacks clarity, however, and its principal military action has been to intervene in KOSOVO.

President KENNEDY stressed the partnership role early on: 'I want two strong towers in NATO, one American and one European.' But France withdrew in 1966 because President DE GAULLE saw the alliance as unacceptably dominated by the Americans. She has partially re-engaged, but the Defence Planning Group, which France has boycotted, was revived in 2003 specifically to sidestep her opposition to supporting Turkey in the event of war in Iraq. Harold MACMILLAN dismissed the notion of American dominance, saying: 'There might be one finger on the trigger, but there are 15 fingers on the catch.' Its nuclear deterrent role was played down by Supreme Allied Commander Gen. Bernard Rogers, who said: 'The last thing we want to do is make Europe safe for a conventional war.' Pierre TRUDEAU was dismissive of its political dimension: 'NATO heads of state and governments meet only to go through the tedious motions of reading speeches drafted by others, with the principal objective of not rocking the boat.' And Ken Livingstone (*see* RED KEN) said of Gerald Kaufman, Shadow Foreign Secretary during Labour's 1980s' strife over UNILATERALISM:

> He has crawled so far up the backside of NATO, you can't even see the soles of his feet.

Natural Law Party The movement, based on Oriental mysticism and the benefits of 'yogic flying', which lost hundreds of DEPOSITS in Britain's 1992 general election, but generated a good deal of mirth. It fielded CANDIDATES in a number of other countries, but soon subsided.

naturellement The word used four times more often by Jacques CHIRAC than the average Frenchman, according to a study published in 2005 by the researcher Damon Mayaffre, who had analysed 2348 of the President's public pronouncements. Mayaffre concluded that Chirac used the word to greatest effect as a means of justifying the indefensible.

Naught for your Comfort One of the classic texts against APARTHEID, written in South Africa in 1956 by the Anglican priest Fr. Trevor Huddleston (1913–98), later an Archbishop and a founder and president of Britain's Anti-Apartheid Movement.

naval. naval estimates crisis The cause of the fall of GLADSTONE's last government. All his Ministers became convinced during

1893 of the need for higher naval spending; Gladstone accused them of falling for a 'monstrous conspiracy' by the admirals. The crisis came to a head in early 1894; Gladstone finally retired at the 'blubbering CABINET' of 1 March.

naval holiday The ten-year pause in the construction of warships over 10,000 tons agreed at the WASHINGTON CONFERENCE in February 1922 by America, Britain, Japan, France and Italy; Germany, having been forcibly disarmed after WORLD WAR I, was not thought to pose a threat.

Naval Observatory The official WASHINGTON home of the VICE PRESIDENT, within the Observatory Circle between Massachusetts and Wisconsin Avenues, NW.

Navigation Acts The 17th-century British mercantilist legislation which confined many cargoes to specifically British ships. It thus barred Britain's colonies, notably in America, from trading with other powers, so was a major factor in provoking American Independence. Subsequently an irritant also to Canada, the Acts were finally repealed in 1849.

Nazi The German abbreviation for HITLER's NATIONAL SOCIALIST German Workers' Party (*Nationalsozialistische Deutscher Arbeiterpartei*), which became worldwide shorthand not just for the party but its adherents and its warped ideology.

Nazi-Soviet Pact The NON-AGGRESSION PACT concluded by Germany and the Soviet Union on 23 August 1939 which freed HITLER's hands to attack Poland, thus starting WORLD WAR II. Also known as the **Ribbentrop-Molotov Pact**, it was signed in Moscow by Germany's foreign minister Joachim von Ribbentrop and the Soviet foreign affairs commissar Vyacheslav Molotov (*see* NIET!). The two countries agreed not to support any third party that launched an attack on the other, and to consult on matters of mutual interest. Even more significant was a secret PROTOCOL that effectively partitioned Europe into German and Soviet spheres, enabling STALIN to acquire eastern Poland as a strategic buffer when Germany made its move the following week. The readiness of the two arch-enemies to conclude such a deal stunned the world, and wrongfooted Britain, which had been making desultory contacts with Moscow with a view to concluding a similar treaty. When the pact was announced, a FOREIGN OFFICE spokesman in London opined:

> Isms have become wasms.

Anti-Nazi League *See* ANTI.

NCR No carbon required. The Conservative equivalent of Labour's READING SYSTEM for monitoring TURNOUT of the party's supporters on POLLING DAY; though somewhat eclipsed by technology and a shortage of volunteers, it remains a useful tool. Supporters who have voted are crossed off the uppermost sheet of the pad at regular intervals, thanks to reports of numbers taken by the TELLERS, with the impression of the crossings-out being reproduced on sheets underneath. KNOCKERS-UP are sent out with these sheets at intervals to persuade those yet to vote to do so.

NDP New Democratic Party. Canada's democratic socialist party, founded in 1961 by the CCF in consultation with the Canadian Labour Congress. It has formed several provincial governments, but has yet to gain power nationally. Indeed between 1993 and 1997 it lost official party status at Ottawa, having just nine seats against the twelve required; it recovered to 21 in 1997 but exerted greater influence with slightly fewer seats from 1994 because Jean Chrétien's Liberal government had lost its majority.

Neanderthal A stone-age CONSERVATIVE, from the hominid remains found near Dusseldorf in 1856. The term was probably first used by Judge Samuel Rosenman in a 1948 memo to President TRUMAN: 'The Neanderthal men of the Republican Party.'

Neave assassination The murder by an INLA car bomb on 30 March 1979 of Airey Neave (1916–79), the former Army intelligence officer and Colditz escaper who masterminded Margaret THATCHER's election as Tory leader in 1975, was her hard-line Shadow NORTHERN IRELAND Secretary and would have given her crucial support and advice in government. He died the day after the defeat of the Labour government on a no-CONFIDENCE motion made an election certain and a Tory victory probable. Neave was the first of several MPs to be killed in the TROUBLES, others being Ian Gow, another confidant of Mrs Thatcher, and Anthony Berry, killed in the BRIGHTON BOMBING. He was also the first in over 150 years to be murdered in the PRECINCTS OF THE HOUSE. He was targeted because of his tough line on Ulster and his closeness to Mrs Thatcher; the bomb was attached to his car outside his flat, and went off on the ramp down to the Commons' underground car park.

NEC The National Executive Committee of Britain's LABOUR PARTY, its guiding body and the heart of its policymaking – whatever its leader might think – until emasculated by Neil KINNOCK in the 1980s.

necessary and proper clause Also known as the **elastic clause**, the provision in the US CONSTITUTION (Section 8, clause 18) empowering CONGRESS to 'make all laws which shall be necessary and proper' for carrying out the functions vested in it. It does not give Congress *carte blanche* to enact whatever laws it wishes.

necessity knows no law The words used by the German Chancellor Bethmann-Hollweg in the REICHSTAG on 4 August 1914 as justification for the infringement of Belgian NEUTRALITY. He said:

> Gentlemen, we are now in a state of necessity, and necessity knows no law. Our troops have occupied Luxembourg and perhaps have already entered Belgian territory.

necklace killings The particularly vicious method used by extremists in South Africa's black townships in the dying days of APARTHEID to 'execute' their political opponents: fixing a rubber tyre round their neck, filling it with petrol, then setting fire to it. When Nelson MANDELA announced that he and his militant wife Winnie were separating, a columnist in the *Scotsman* wrote: 'Nelson's getting the Mercedes and Winnie will keep the tyres.' In Haiti the petrol-filled tyre was known as 'Père Lebrun', after a local tyre dealer.

Neddy Britain's National Economic Development Council, set up by Harold MACMILLAN in 1962 as a forum for communication and economic assessment involving all sides of industry; it fell into virtual disuse under Margaret THATCHER, who saw it as CORPORATIST, and it was wound up by Norman Lamont in 1992. **Little Neddies** were the mini-versions of Neddy which concentrated on particular sectors of the economy. **NEDO** was the National Economic Development Office, whose staff submitted forecasts and economic assessments to Neddy.

negative income tax A form of UNIFIED TAX AND BENEFIT SYSTEM under which a person whose income does not merit taxation receives social benefits through the same system of assessment.

negative research A polite term, rife since the 1992 US Presidential CAMPAIGN, for the unearthing of sleazy facts or rumours about the opposing candidate and their planting on the media. *See also* NERD SQUAD.

Nehru dynasty The domination of Indian politics for over half a century by the family of the statesman **Jawaharlal Nehru** (1889–1964). Educated at Harrow and Cambridge, Nehru became a disciple of MAHATMA Gandhi, and as president of the Indian National CONGRESS Party from 1929 was imprisoned nine times for his opposition to British rule. He became Prime Minister of independent India in 1947 and remained in the post until his death, providing much-needed political stability.

He groomed his daughter **Indira Gandhi** (1917–84) as his successor. Although no relation to the Mahatma and at times ruthless in pursuit of her chosen policies, the name reinforced her claim to power and helped her become Prime Minister from 1966 to 1977 and again from 1980 to 1984. She in turn prepared her son **Sanjay Gandhi** (1946–80) to succeed her, and when he was killed in a plane crash she brought her more agreeable elder son **Rajiv** (1942–91), previously an airline pilot, into the political limelight.

When Indira Gandhi's suppression of Sikh unrest led to her assassination by Sikh members of her bodyguard, Rajiv replaced her as Prime Minister. As leader of the Congress (I) Party, he continued Nehru's balancing act between differing political and religious traditions, but lost office in 1989. In a third tragedy to strike the family, Rajiv was killed during the 1991 election campaign by a terrorist bomb. Congress remained in opposition to the Hindu nationalist BJP until 2004 when Rajiv's Italian-born widow **Sonia Gandhi**, with a campaign stressing the need to fight poverty, led Congress to an unexpected victory despite defections by senior Congress figures who objected to having a foreign-born leader. She then declined to serve as Prime Minister when the Bombay stock market crashed amid concerns over her left-wing programme, saying she was obeying the voice of her 'inner self'. She restored stability by choosing the economist Manmohan Singh as Prime Minister, but kept the party leadership.

Nenni telegram The telegram sent by 37 British Labour MPs to the pro-Communist Italian socialist Pietro Nenni and his supporters during the 1948 Italian general election, in defiance of the Labour leadership which backed the more independent Italian Socialist Party. Two of the MPs, John

Platts-Mills and Konni Zilliacus, were EXPELLED from the party as a result, though Zilliacus was later readmitted.

neo-. neo-colonialism The exercise of influence by a nation over a former colony in such a way as to perpetuate its dependency. **neo-Communism/Fascism/Nazism** A philosophy, programme or movement which apes the original but fails to be identical, lacking its momentum and discipline. For instance most neo-Nazi groups, especially in Germany, are so scruffy that HITLER would instantly have had them imprisoned.

neo-conservatives The ideological driver behind the presidency of George W. BUSH. The term was invented by the socialist democrat Rep. Michael Harrington for Democrats who took a harder line against liberal positions than many Republicans. The ideological core of early neo-conservatism was the magazine *The Public Interest*, founded in 1965; in their later years Henry 'SCOOP' Jackson and Daniel Patrick MOYNIHAN, both liberals at the outset, were regarded as neo-conservatives in the fields of defence and welfare respectively. But the tendency came of age in the late 1990s when radical ideologues such as Irving Kristol and Karl Rove heightened their impact just as the Bush CAMPAIGN was being put together. Neo-conservatism has had especial influence on foreign policy, both through its UNILATERALIST readiness for America to wage war despite the opposition of some of its allies, and its alliance with the RELIGIOUS RIGHT in shifting the Republicans to a more pro-Israeli position just as the leadership of the Jewish state has become more belligerent.

NEP *See* NEW ECONOMIC POLICY.

nerd squad A 'dirty tricks' unit of Republicans in the 1992 Presidential campaign who planted derogatory tales about potential Democratic candidates – notably Bill CLINTON – with the media (though eclipsed by the stories that broke subsequently, *see* Paula JONES; WHITEWATER). Similar Democratic units engaging in NEGATIVE RESEARCH about President George BUSH Snr were known as **propeller-heads**. Not to be outdone, H. Ross PEROT traded charges with the Bush campaign that each had been planting BLACK PROPAGANDA about the other.

nervous Nellies President Lyndon JOHNSON's term for opponents of the VIETNAM WAR as Congressional criticism grew in May 1966. He was particularly outraged by a charge from Sen. William Fulbright (1905–95) that America was 'succumbing to the arrogance of power'. *Compare* MOANING MINNIES.

neutrality The status of a nation which chooses not to take sides in any conflict between others, rendering it supposedly free from attack; notable examples are the Irish Republic, Laos, Sweden and Switzerland. A neutral country must not help the warlike purposes of any of the combatants, but in other respects may continue trading with them. George WASHINGTON issued a Proclamation of Neutrality in April 1793, just after commencing his second term. On the outbreak of WORLD WAR I President WILSON said that America 'must be neutral in fact as well as in name during these days that are to try men's souls. We must be impartial in thought as well as in action.' Seen by its adherents either as a noble moral position or a way of avoiding suicidal entanglements (*see* ISOLATIONISM), it has been criticised as a token of weakness or a means of evading responsibilities; nor did it prevent Belgium twice being invaded or America being sucked into two World Wars. At the height of the COLD WAR, John Foster Dulles described neutrality as 'an obsolete conception, and except under very exceptional circumstances an immoral and short-sighted conception'. President KENNEDY quoted Dante (1265–1321) as saying that 'the hottest places in Hell are reserved for those who in a period of moral crisis maintain their neutrality', and Richard NIXON in 1965 came close to agreeing, saying: 'Neutrality where the Communists are concerned means three things: we get out, they stay in, they take over.' The Hungarian patriot Kossuth (1802–94) declared that 'neutrality as a lasting principle is an evidence of weakness', and Mussolini (*see* DUCE) said: 'Neutrals have never dominated events. They have always gone under.' And the radical Indian foreign minister Krishna Menon declared: 'Positive neutrality is a contradiction in terms. There can no more be positive neutrality than there can be a vegetarian tiger.' Even politicians can have difficulty grasping the concept. Eamonn de Valera (*see* DEV) was once asked in the DAIL:

> Who are we neutral against?

Neutrality Acts The Acts passed by the ISOLATIONIST majority in CONGRESS between 1935 and 1937 to assume foreign policy powers in an attempt to thwart any attempt by Franklin D. ROOSEVELT to involve America in the coming World War. Their provisions, notably a requirement on the President to ban the export of war materials to belligerents, severely tied FDR's hands, but Congress eased them slightly after the outbreak of war in 1939 and he was able to sidestep those remaining through such provisions as LEND-LEASE until PEARL HARBOR changed the mood in Congress overnight.

armed neutrality A position designed to stay out of conflict through strength, pioneered by Russia's 18th-century Empress Catherine the Great in response to Britain's high-handedness during the Seven Years' War. Declaring war on Germany in April 1917, President WILSON stated sadly:

> Armed neutrality, it now appears, is impracticable.

neutron bomb A type of tactical NUCLEAR WEAPON developed by America and publicised in the mid-1970s. Hailed as a 'clean' bomb that destroyed people and not buildings, President CARTER urged its deployment by NATO forces in Europe as a deterrent to Soviet tank attacks. Vocal public opposition in Europe – though not from the British and German governments – led Carter to drop the plan. Delivered by missiles or artillery shells, the bomb created a blast over only a few hundred yards but threw off intense neutron and gamma-ray radiation over a large area. This could penetrate defences including tank armour, killing attacking troops outright or causing their death in a few days.

never. Never again! The slogan used by advocates of lasting global peace after WORLD WAR I, the horrific war that was supposed to end all wars. In the 1960s the JEWISH DEFENSE LEAGUE revived it to recall the HOLOCAUST and justify militant action against Arabs.

never complain, never explain DISRAELI's advice to fellow politicians under fire, cited by Lord BALDWIN in 1943 at the height of the press campaign against him for allegedly having not only brought about WORLD WAR II by hesitating to rearm (*see* APPALLING FRANKNESS) but then refusing to hand over the wrought iron gates of his house for the war effort.

never forget, rarely forgive The pungent political motto of Edward Koch (1924–), Democratic Mayor of New York City from 1978 to 1989.

never glad confident morning again The payoff line from Robert Browning's poem *The Lost Leader*, in which he complained that Wordsworth had lost the revolutionary zeal of his youth. It was employed to deadly effect in the HOUSE OF COMMONS on 17 June 1963, at the height of the PROFUMO AFFAIR, against Harold MACMILLAN and his government by the former Conservative Minister Nigel Birch. He told Macmillan: 'I myself feel the time will come very soon when my Rt Hon. Friend ought to make way for a much younger colleague . . . I certainly will not quote at him the savage words of Cromwell (*see* YOU HAVE SAT HERE LONG ENOUGH), but perhaps some words of Browning might be appropriate in his poem on *The Lost Leader*:

> Let him never come back to us!
> There would be doubt, hesitation and pain.
> Forced praise on our part – the glimmer of twilight,
> Never glad confident morning again!'

Barely three months later, Macmillan resigned through ill health.

never in the field of human conflict was so much owed by so many to so few Winston CHURCHILL's tribute at the height of the Battle of Britain to the fighter pilots of the Royal Air Force, in a HOUSE OF COMMONS speech on 20 August 1940. The format has since been copied; for instance John MAJOR said of press inquiries about his school examination results:

> Never has so much been written about so little.

never lose your temper with the Press or public The SUFFRAGETTE Christabel Pankhurst (1880–1958) considered this a 'magical rule of political life'. She did not extend her magic rule to relations with the police; she was once arrested for assaulting an officer who had removed her from an election meeting.

never murder a man who is committing suicide Woodrow WILSON's reason for not countering the attacks on his administration from his Republican opponent Charles Evans Hughes during his 1916 campaign for re-election.

never take advice from experts, pigs or Members of Parliament The dictum of Kermit the Frog, debating at the Oxford Union on 28 October 1994, at the height of the CASH FOR QUESTIONS scandal.

never trust a man whose eyes are too close to his nose One of the more printable homespun dicta of Lyndon B. JOHNSON during his career in WASHINGTON.

New Class, The *See* CLASS.

New Covenant The programme put forward

by Bill CLINTON in 1992 which helped secure him the Presidency. It embodied improved incentives for enterprise, guaranteed health care, skills training for young people not bound for college and a drive to cure the problems of the INNER CITIES.

New Deal (1) President Franklin D. ROOSEVELT's policy of KEYNESIAN economic reconstruction, announced on 2 July 1932 at the start of his campaign for the Presidency, which set America's political divisions until PEARL HARBOR. The announcement came in typically dramatic fashion: FDR broke with tradition by flying to Chicago to accept the Democratic nomination in person, and declared:

> I pledge you, I pledge myself, to a new deal for the American people.

The phrase was not his own; LLOYD GEORGE had used it in 1919 and others before him, but it stemmed immediately from a book by Stuart Chase, published that same year. FDR's programme of action to end America's economic tailspin after the GREAT CRASH of 1929, which was throwing millions into poverty, contrasted starkly with the self-imposed near-paralysis of the HOOVER administration. When a friend told him: 'If the New Deal is a success, you will be remembered as the greatest American president,' FDR replied:

> If I fail, I will be remembered as the last one.

On taking office (*see* HUNDRED DAYS), Roosevelt immediately closed the banks while plans were drawn up to regulate them, underpinned farm prices and stimulated industrial recovery to curb mass unemployment, over time creating a large number of agencies such as the NRA to administer New Deal programmes. He explained: 'These unhappy times call for plans that build from the bottom up, not from the top down, that put their faith once more in the forgotten man at the bottom of the economic pyramid.' Richard Hofstadter wrote that the essence of the New Deal was 'Roosevelt's confidence that even when he was operating in unfamiliar territory he could do no wrong, commit no serious mistakes'. It also led to accusations against him of socialism and FASCISM; Sen. Daniel Hastings said the New Deal gave the President 'more power than any good man should want, and more power than any other kind of man ought to have.' Eventually the SUPREME COURT came to the same conclusion (*see* SICK CHICKEN CASE).

The New Deal had three phases: a First New Deal from March 1933 which concentrated on economic relief and recovery from the depths of the GREAT DEPRESSION through public works, a Second New Deal concerned with social reform – collective bargaining, unemployment benefits, old-age pensions – from 1935, and a Third New Deal in 1938 to maintain the momentum as the economy again faltered. It was the onset of war that finally put America fully back to work.

(2) Gordon BROWN's package of measures after Labour came to power in 1997 to reduce and where possible eliminate long-term unemployment among the young, older workers, single mothers and the disabled in the UK, by making training, further education or community programmes available to them all and stopping the benefits of those who passed up the chance. Youth unemployment, in particular, was greatly reduced, though the Conservatives argued that each job created cost the taxpayer dear and – through clenched teeth – that the fall in unemployment was largely the result of a strong economy.

New Dealer A supporter of or participant in ROOSEVELT's New Deal programmes, and subsequently any Democratic politician who continued to advocate INTERVENTIONIST, Keynseian prescriptions for poverty and a sluggish economy.

New Democracy *See* DEMOCRACY.

New Democrats 1) Canada's democratic socialist party (*see* NDP).

(2) The post-liberal element in America's political community whom Bill CLINTON embraced when running for President in 1992 and after the Democrats' defeat in the 1994 MID-TERM elections. The most radical proposal taken up by Clinton, though not entirely followed through, was to raid CORPORATE WELFARE for funding for education and break the power of the teachers' unions.

New Economic Policy (NEP) A series of economic reforms introduced by LENIN in March 1921 to quell widespread discontent with the BOLSHEVIK regime. The policy was announced at the Tenth Party Congress in the wake of urban riots, strikes and the KRONSTADT MUTINY. It amounted to a complete reversal of the previous economic strategy; rigid centralised planning was replaced by a mixed economy. Heavy industry and banking remained in state ownership, but agriculture and the production of consumer goods returned to the private sector, cash wages were reinstated for industrial workers and the profit motive encouraged to promote growth. The NEP was successful in reviving the economy and restoring popular support for the regime; its early years (1921–28) also brought a flowering of Soviet art and culture. But STALIN's seizure of power after Lenin's death in 1924 signalled the end of the NEP. In 1928 he announced the FIVE-YEAR PLAN, which enforced a return to centralised planning, outlawed private enterprise and began the COLLECTIVISATION of agriculture.

New Frontier President KENNEDY's vision of a more challenging and outward-looking agenda for America after the torpor of the EISENHOWER years. Accepting the Democratic Presidential nomination on 15 July 1960, the youthful JFK said:

> We stand today on the edge of a new frontier. But the new frontier of which I speak is not a set of promises. It is a set of challenges. It sums up not what I intend to offer the American people, but what I intend to ask of them. It appeals to their pride, not their pocketbook – it holds out the prospect of more sacrifice instead of more security.

The phrase went back to the 1930s, when the future Democratic Vice President Henry Wallace had used it in a book and FDR's 1936 Republican opponent used in ON THE STUMP, but Kennedy made it his own. In terms of social reform, the New Frontier was not a great success; the narrowness of Kennedy's majority and lack of a Congressional MANDATE stalled a legislative programme that was never over-adventurous. But in terms of the SPACE RACE, America's relationship with the developing world and, above all, the intellectual ferment of the BEST AND THE BRIGHTEST, the Kennedy WHITE HOUSE gave an impression of dynamic change.

New Hampshire primary Traditionally the first major event of a US Presidential election year (the IOWA CAUCUSES excepted), the chance to establish the BIG MO and a graveyard for many hopes. Held in late winter, this opening PRIMARY in a small state attracts saturation coverage from Presidential hopefuls and the media alike; one woman questioned by a reporter said of a candidate: 'Oh, no, I couldn't possibly vote for him, I've only met him four times.' An early exploiter of the New Hampshire primary as a way to get onto the national TICKET was Sen. Estes KEFAUVER, whose unexpectedly strong showing in 1956 won him the Democratic Vice Presidential nomination. For decades the primary was overshadowed by the viciously right-wing campaigning of William Loeb, publisher of the *Manchester Union-Leader*; his obituary recalled that 'he called President EISENHOWER a dope and Senator Eugene McCarthy a skunk'. McCarthy's moral defeat of President Lyndon JOHNSON in New Hampshire in 1968 led LBJ to quit the race; four years later Loeb's promotion of the CANUCK LETTER caused Sen. Edmund Muskie to self-destruct. In 1992 President George BUSH Snr was given a fright by the ultra-conservative Pat Buchanan; Bush campaigner Bill Bennett said:

> New Hampshire wasn't a wake-up call. It was BIG BEN falling on your head.

New Imperialism *See* IMPERIALISM.

New Jewel Movement The radical, but democratic, movement led by Maurice Bishop which governed GRENADA until overthrown in October 1983 with great violence by ultra-leftists. The coup triggered the controversial US invasion six days later.

New Labour The rebranding under which Tony BLAIR led Britain's LABOUR PARTY to power in 1997 after eighteen years in the wilderness, the title implying a break with unpopular and outdated policies and a new harmony with the aspirations of the voters. To Blair and his intimates, New Labour was the embodiment of the PROJECT they had set themselves and of a shift in ideology from traditional socialism to the THIRD WAY; to cynics, it was a means to an end, manifesting itself once the party had won a LANDSLIDE victory in a culture of SPIN (*see also* COOL BRITANNIA). Blair took up the theme soon after being elected leader in 1994, making the slogan for that year's party conference 'New Labour: New Life for New Britain' and ramming home the culture change by springing the abolition of CLAUSE FOUR on the startled faithful. In the run-up to the 1997 election the party campaigned as 'New Labour' in every respect bar changing its official name; for years afterwards the party's website address remained www.labour.org.uk. And on arriving in DOWNING STREET on 2 May 1997, Blair told the crowd carefully assembled by Peter Mandelson (*see* BOBBY): 'We were elected as New Labour and we shall govern as New Labour.' After two terms, neither its supporters nor its critics could dispute that the Blair government had broken markedly with the party's traditional policies, not least in renouncing NATIONALISATION and going to war in Iraq.

> The perfect marriage between ambition and compassion.
>
> TONY BLAIR to party donors, September 1997

> In the end New Labour may be little more than a humane rhetorical mirage that technocrats like Tony Blair have created to prove to themselves that they haven't become middle-aged conservatives.
>
> JOE KLEIN, *The New Yorker*, April 1997

New Left In America, the grouping which emerged from the PROTEST movement of the 1960s to challenge traditional liberalism. Its stated aim was to win for individuals power over the decisions that affected their own lives. The New Left gained its impetus from opposition to the VIETNAM WAR; though largely anti-Communist, this led to its being widely perceived as UN-AMERICAN. New Left activism overlapped into the DEMOCRATIC PARTY, having a considerable say in the platform on which Sen. George McGovern lost heavily in 1972.

new localism The formula for a Conservative recovery put forward in the spring of 2005 after the party's third successive election defeat by a group of young MPs, candidates and advisers. It stems from the belief that voters have become disillusioned with the political process largely because it has become too centralised and unresponsive to local concerns, but big government having restricted personal freedom and responsibility to such an extent that local democracy had been all but extinguished.

New Nationalism *See* NATIONALISM.

New Order The reshaping of Europe under the domination of Germany as envisaged by HITLER. In Berlin on 30 January 1941, the FÜHRER said:

> I am convinced that 1941 will be the crucial year of a great New Order in Europe. The world will open up for everyone.

After the collapse of Communism in eastern Europe and the Soviet Union, George BUSH Snr spoke of a NEW WORLD ORDER in which the former SUPERPOWERS would generate an atmosphere of co-operation. His hopes reached their height when the KREMLIN in 1991 acquiesced in US-led military action under the auspices of the UNITED NATIONS to oust Iraqi forces from Kuwait, but as democratic Russia weakened and the threat from Islamist terrorism grew, it appeared that one threat had merely been replaced by another which was harder to quantify and respond to.

New Palace Yard At WESTMINSTER, the courtyard facing PARLIAMENT SQUARE through whose gates Ministers and MPs arrive at the HOUSE OF COMMONS. It is lined with catalpa trees and adorned by a fountain. Below ground is a four-level car park, in whose entrance ramp the Conservative NORTHERN IRELAND spokesman Airey NEAVE was assassinated by an INLA bomb in 1979.

New Party The party formed by Sir Oswald MOSLEY when he resigned from the Labour government after the 1930 party conference spurned his KEYNESIAN programme to tackle the economic crisis and unemployment. Seventeen Labour MPs signed Mosley's December memorandum expanding these policies, and in February 1931 six of them joined him in founding the New Party. It won no seats in the general election, only Mosley of its MPs saving his DEPOSIT, and in 1932 was renamed the British Union of FASCISTS.

new realism In the British trade unions, the readiness in the late 1980s to embrace the climate created by THATCHERISM, with worker share ownership and a common interest in wealth creation replacing conflict. Class warriors accused its advocates, mainly in the electrical and engineering unions, of selling out to the employers.

New Republic The weekly forum for America's liberals since Herbert David Croly founded it in 1914, backed financially by Standard Oil heiress Dorothy Whitney Straight. Croly envisaged it 'starting little insurrections', but the magazine's tone soon moderated; it backed Woodrow WILSON, opposed the Treaty of VERSAILLES and the RED SCARE, opposed Franklin D. ROOSEVELT but rallied to his NEW DEAL. Former Vice President Henry Wallace, made editor in 1946, moved it so far left that Michael Straight forced him out. Today the *New Republic* reflects a range of views, being seen overall as neo-liberal.

New Statesman The traditionally moderate but not complacent socialist weekly which for almost a century has nurtured the FABIAN end of Britain's LABOUR PARTY, save for a disastrous venture into AGITPROP in the 1980s. Founded in 1913 by Sidney and Beatrice Webb, its golden age was between 1930 and 1960 under the editorship of Kingsley Martin (1897–1969). Its relaunch in 1993 under Steve Platt was marred by libel writs from John MAJOR and Clare Latimer, a London caterer, after the magazine accused them of having an affair. By the start of 1996 the *Statesman* was 'hopelessly insolvent'; it was rescued by the millionaire future Treasury minister Geoffrey Robinson, and aroused controversy with Peter Wilby as editor by sniping at BLAIR's leadership, especially over the IRAQ WAR, from what it saw as the intellectual high ground.

Newcastle programme The first comprehensive PLATFORM adopted by a British political party, following on from the UNAUTHORISED PROGRAMME of 1885. Drafted by the National LIBERAL Federation in 1891, it committed the party under GLADSTONE to Irish HOME RULE, DISESTABLISHMENT of the Scottish and Welsh churches, employers' liability to compensate workers injured in accidents, local options on selling liquor, payment for MPs, universal male suffrage and three-year Parliaments.

> It held everything and nothing like a bottomless net; almost no one believed in all these things.
> MICHAEL BENTLEY, *Politics Without Democracy*

Newman assassination Australia's first ever political ASSASSINATION, the shooting on 5 September 1994 outside his home in Cabramatta, Sydney, of John Newman, a Labor member of the New South Wales state assembly, who had been campaigning against Chinese and South Asian gangs who were terrorising the community. Newman was shot as he sat in his car with his Chinese fiancée Xiao Jing (Lucy) Wang; a fortnight later she disappeared.

news management The presentation of events in the best possible light for a government, politician or party, with its converse that disagreeable news received little attention (*see* BURY). Timing is critical, with news scheduled for times when bigger stories do not dominate the news. Harold WILSON in Britain, and the REAGAN White House, were supreme practitioners of the art. So too was Alastair Campbell, Tony BLAIR's head of communications from 1997 to 2003; however, by then the media were alive to SPIN and every action or utterance in NUMBER TEN came to be viewed with suspicion.

Newt The obvious shorthand for Newt Gingrich (**Newton Leroy Gingrich**, 1943–), author of the CONTRACT WITH AMERICA, the right-wing Republican who took WASHINGTON by storm after the party captured both HOUSES in the 1994 Congressional elections; his supporters were known as **Newtoids**. Speaker Gingrich, a pugnacious Georgian who had made his name by taking on TIP O'Neill from the floor of the House, swept aside 40 years of Democratic control and for a time virtually sidelined President CLINTON, making an unprecedented broadcast to report on the first 100 days of the '**Newt Deal**'. Gingrich pushed through much-needed legislation to reform the House, then went on to force a BUDGET SHUTDOWN of Federal government at the end of 1995; this was blamed on Gingrich's pique at having to take a back seat in AIR FORCE ONE on the flight home from Yitzhak Rabin's funeral in Israel. Democrats ridiculed him as a 'cry baby' and newspaper headlines spoke of 'Newt's Tantrum'; the WHITE HOUSE said Gingrich had been treated with the 'utmost courtesy'. A less confident Gingrich was narrowly re-elected Speaker after the 1996 elections, but in January 1997 was fined $300,000 and reprimanded for use of tax-exempt funds and misinforming the Ethics Committee, the first time such action had been taken against a Speaker. All but one of 90 charges against him were dismissed, but he left politics after defeat in 1998 but has been reportedly considering a run for the Presidency in 2008. *See also* NUCK FEWT.

> I will do almost anything to win a Republican majority in the Congress.
> Rep. NEWT GINGRICH, *Los Angeles Times*, 25 August 1991

Next Steps agencies Sections of the UK CIVIL SERVICE that have been converted into free-standing agencies, headed by chief executives through whom they are responsible to Ministers. Sir Robin Ibbs, head of Margaret THATCHER's Downing Street efficiency unit, proposed them before the 1987 election; early examples included the Driver and Vehicle Licensing Directorate and the Civil Service College. The agencies have stood the test of time, but MPs often complain that the agencies' separation from the WHITEHALL machine reduces their ACCOUNTABILITY.

NGOs Non-Governmental Organisations. A term that surfaced in the 1980s for charities and other private sector groups providing THIRD WORLD development aid. It has since come to refer to any organisation outside government in any country that interacts with it or performs parallel functions.

NHS National Health Service. Founded by Aneurin (NYE) BEVAN in 1948, Britain's free medical service for all was the centrepiece of the WELFARE STATE and the 'jewel in the crown' of Labour's immediate post-war achievements. Resisted fiercely by the medical profession, it pulled a patchwork of private, local authority and charitable hospitals and practices into a single organisation, still Europe's largest employer after the Russian army. Bevan said soon after its foundation:

> The NHS and the Welfare State have come to be

used as interchangeable terms, and in the mouths of some people as a reproach.

His fellow Labour Minister Douglas Houghton declared: 'The NHS has emancipated the sick.' Bevan imagined the NHS would reduce demands for health care, but the opposite has happened; within a year the service came under pressure to economise, and Bevan, Harold WILSON and John Freeman resigned from the CABINET in 1951 when charges for spectacles and false teeth were imposed to help pay for the KOREAN WAR. Bevan said:

> The Government's abandonment of the principle of a free and comprehensive health service would be a shock to our supporters in the country and a grave disappointment to socialist opinion throughout the world.

The NHS has gone through countless reorganisations and purists deplore the elements of private financing and competition between hospitals that have been introduced. Margaret THATCHER's assurance that **the NHS is safe in our hands** was not accepted by the public as her government opened the NHS to some of the disciplines of the MARKET, and the NHS has remained a trump card for Labour (*see* WAR OF JENNIFER'S EAR; SCHOOLS AND HOSPITALS FIRST) despite the dilution of its public-sector purity, to which the trade unions strongly object (*see* FOUNDATION HOSPITALS).

NIBMAR No Independence Before Majority African Rule. The principle urged by African leaders on Harold WILSON's government as it sought during 1964 and 1965 to prevent Ian Smith's white ADMINISTRATION in Southern Rhodesia declaring UDI.

Nice. Treaty of Nice The agreement reached by EUROPEAN UNION member states at Nice in December 2000 which paved the way for the admission of ten new members, achieved in May 2004, and the adaptation of the EU's institutions to cope with this expansion. Pending the deliberations of the EUROPEAN CONVENTION in drafting a EUROPEAN CONSTITUTION, it took a number of interim decisions, for instance on the number of votes each member should have in the COUNCIL OF MINISTERS when a QUALIFIED MAJORITY was in prospect, and the number of seats each state in an expanded EU should have in the EUROPEAN PARLIAMENT. The former of these was not adhered to when the Constitution was finally agreed, to the anger of Poland and Spain. With the ratification process for the Constitution stalled, the Treaty has had an unexpected longevity.

Niet! (Russ. No!) The trademark of Vyacheslav Mikhailovich MOLOTOV (1890–1986), Soviet ambassador to the United Nations from 1945 to 1953, the most critical years of the COLD WAR. Molotov's regular use of the Soviet VETO paralysed the world organisation and earned him notoriety throughout the West. He had already attracted odium in 1939 as the joint signatory with Ribbentrop of the NAZI-SOVIET PACT.

night. Night of the Long Knives (1) In Germany, the night of 30 June 1934 when the leaders of the BROWNSHIRTS (SA), homosexuals occupying key positions in the NAZI party and some Catholic leaders, were murdered by the GESTAPO on Hitler's orders. The shootings, mainly in Munich and Berlin, actually began on the Friday night of 29 June and continued on the Sunday; between 60 and 400 people were killed in a PURGE whose main aim was to break the influence of the SA and its chief of staff Ernst Röhm. Himmler presented the assassins with daggers of honour inscribed with their names. (2) The sacking of seven Cabinet Ministers by Harold MACMILLAN on 12 July 1962, which earned him the nickname '**Mac the Knife**'. The principal casualty was Chancellor Selwyn Lloyd. Macmillan acted to remodel his government as its popularity slumped, but worse lay ahead in the shape of the PROFUMO AFFAIR.

> Greater love hath no man than he who lays down his friends for his life. JEREMY THORPE

something of the night The devastating phrase with which the former Home Office Minister Ann Widdecombe destroyed the chances of her former boss, Michael HOWARD, succeeding John MAJOR as Conservative leader after the party's crushing defeat in the 1997 general election. Asked by a reporter how she felt about having Howard as leader, she replied: 'I have always felt there was something of the night about him.' This reference to the former Home Secretary's Transylvanian origins (he is of Romanian Jewish descent) was Widdecombe's payback for a series of semi-public disagreements in government, especially on prison policy. Her putdown left the way clear for William HAGUE to defeat Kenneth Clarke (*see* KEN AND EDDIE SHOW) and lead the party to a further heavy defeat in 2001; when Howard eventually became leader by acclamation on the resignation of Iain Duncan Smith (*see* IDS) in 2003, Widdecombe had little to say.

nightmare scenario A combination or sequence of events too ghastly to contemplate, but which nevertheless could well become reality. A classic example was the scenario prior to the GULF WAR in which the UN-backed COALITION won the conflict while leaving SADDAM HUSSEIN's war machine largely intact – as eventually happened, with devastating consequences for the West in the form of a second IRAQ WAR to remove Saddam and anarchy in the country afterwards.

our long national nightmare is over Gerald FORD's remarks which closed the door on WATERGATE, made when he took the oath of office on 9 August 1974. Despite the controversy over his subsequent PARDON of Richard NIXON, Ford proved right. He said:

> My fellow Americans, our long national nightmare is over. Our Constitution works; our great Republic is a government of laws and not of men. Here the people rule. But there is a higher Power, by whatever name we honour Him, who ordains not only righteousness but love, not only justice but mercy.

nihilism (Lat. *nihil*, nothing) The ultimate in negative political philosophies, which enjoyed a vogue in Tsarist Russia in the late 19th century. From it grew a TERRORIST movement that aimed to wipe out all existing institutions of society in order to start anew.

Nimbyism An acronym for Not In My Back Yard, first noted in America in 1980, to describe people who are vociferously in favour of progress, and especially new construction, unless it directly affects them. Initially it referred to supporters of NUCLEAR power or the storage of nuclear waste, whose attitude suddenly changed in the face of a proposal to site such activities locally. Nicholas Ridley, when UK Environment Secretary, was accused of Nimbyism when he objected to plans for new homes in his village after overriding objections to new rural housing projects elsewhere.

9/11 The most apocalyptic date in US history after PEARL HARBOR, and a signal to the Western world that the threat from ISLAMIST terrorism would have to be resisted, when on 11 September 2001 airliners hijacked by AL QAEDA were crashed without warning by their suicide pilots into each tower of the WORLD TRADE CENTER, the PENTAGON, and farmland in Pennsylvania (with the passengers on this plane struggling to retake control), killing everyone on board and over 3000 people in the targeted buildings. President George W. BUSH was told of the unfolding horror while on a televised visit to a school in Florida; his return to WASHINGTON by AIR FORCE ONE was circuitous because of the risk of further attacks. The events of that day sparked the WAR ON TERRORISM, initially against Al Qaeda and the TALEBAN who were harbouring them in Afghanistan, then spread wider as the network stepped up its atrocities against civilians from BALI to MADRID. '9/11' is the US abbreviation of 11 September; in most other countries the abbreviation would signify 9 November, but it has nevertheless gained currency as an appalling collective term for a series of attacks that were almost beyond the capacity of the Western mind to imagine. The composer Karlheinz Stockhausen was censured by his fellow musicians for observing:

> People rehearse like mad for 10 years – totally, fanatically – for a concert and then die. That's the greatest work of art there is in the entire cosmos.

9/11 Commission The body set up by CONGRESS after the events of 9/11 to probe widespread circumstantial evidence that the US authorities had enough hints and information about impending terrorist activity to have prevented the attacks on the PENTAGON and WORLD TRADE CENTER, given competence and political will. Its 567-page report, issued in July 2004, catalogued 'failures of imagination, policy, capabilities and management' by organs of the US government, criticised a lack of attention to the danger from AL QAEDA from the CLINTON and pre-9/11 BUSH administrations, and called for a unified intelligence command in the fight against Islamist terrorism. Evidence during the hearings that the CIA and FBI had failed to communicate, that known terrorist suspects had been able to enter the country and that the FBI had failed to investigate tip-offs that young Arabs were learning how to fly planes but not to land them, triggered the early retirement of CIA director George Tenet. The commission concluded that Al Qaeda had originally planned ten hijackings, targeting the WHITE HOUSE, the CIA and FBI headquarters in Washington, nuclear power stations and the tallest buildings in California and Washington State. It also embarrassed Bush by detecting no evidence that SADDAM HUSSEIN had been implicated in the 9/11 attacks, although Al Qaeda had explored the possibility; it did however implicate Iran in allowing some of the hijackers safe passage. The high point of its hearings came on 8 April 2004 when Condoleezza Rice, George W. Bush's

NATIONAL SECURITY ADVISOR whom the White House had originally tried to shield, rebutted claims that the President and those around him had ignored clear indications that Al Qaeda was about to attack because of his obsession with Iraq. The Commission also took evidence in private from the President and Vice President Dick Cheney.

Fahrenheit 9/11 The documentary film by Michael Moore, winner of the *Palme d'Or* at the 2004 Cannes film festival, which not only pilloried George W. BUSH for prosecuting the WAR ON IRAQ and chronicled the lack of evidence linking SADDAM HUSSEIN with Al Qaeda, but also alleged that Bush might have been in some way responsible for the events of 9/11 through his family's links with the BIN LADEN clan and the way relatives of Bin Laden were allowed to leave America immediately after the outrages. Not intended to be objective, the movie played to packed houses of opponents of the war on both sides of the Atlantic.

Ninepence for fourpence The slogan with which LLOYD GEORGE launched Britain's first National Insurance scheme in 1911. By requiring a contribution from employers as well as employees, he was able to offer a sickness insurance scheme where workers who had paid 4*d.* a week into the scheme would receive 9*d.* when unable to work. Many Liberals, including ASQUITH, questioned whether the proposal was attractive enough and feared it would be an electoral ALBATROSS; however WORLD WAR I prevented an ELECTION being held until 1918, by which time other issues predominated.

nineteen. Nineteenth Amendment The amendment to the US CONSTITUTION, otherwise known as the **Anthony Amendment** after the suffragist Susan B. Anthony, which gave all American women the vote. It read:

> The right of citizens of the United States to vote shall not be denied or abridged by the United States or by any state on account of sex.

It was passed by the HOUSE on 10 January 1918, but the conservative SENATE held out for eighteen months; it was eventually ratified by the states on 18 August 1920.

1922 Committee The group embracing all BACKBENCH Conservative MPs at WESTMINSTER, which meets weekly when Parliament is in session. Formed by Sir Gervais Rentoul after the 1922 general election, it takes its name from the CARLTON CLUB REVOLT earlier that year when Tory MPs forced the break-up of the LLOYD GEORGE coalition. The '22, through its meetings, its chairman and its executive, enjoys immense influence over the party leadership; any initiative or policy that falls foul of it will be hastily withdrawn. Applause in the meeting is signified by the banging of desks.

> The first three people to speak at the 1922 Committee on any subject are invariably mad.
>
> DAVID WALDER MP (Con., 1928–78)

> Too frequent attendance can result in what religious people call 'doubts'.
>
> JULIAN CRITCHLEY MP (Con., 1930–99)

Nineteen Eighty-Four The nightmarish vision of a TOTALITARIAN future, conjured up by George Orwell (Eric Arthur Blair, 1903–50) in his final novel of that name. Published in 1949, it depicted a state in which history had been destroyed, and truth replaced by PROPAGANDA, while surveillance on behalf of BIG BROTHER was all-pervasive. The novel, based partly on Orwell's experiences in Britain's wartime Ministry of Information, was a warning against authoritarian tendencies present in Communist and Western societies after WORLD WAR II. Orwell chose the date by transposing the final digits of 1948, the year he wrote the book; until the actual year was reached, 1984 was a 'doomsday' date. *See also* ANIMAL FARM.

1992 The year in which Europe's SINGLE MARKET was due for completion, and thus shorthand in advance of that date for the achievement of an important phase of European unity. In fact the package of 265 (originally 301) legislative changes in member states took effect over a period, not being completed until 1993.

1997 The date set by Britain and China for the reversion of Hong Kong to Chinese SOVEREIGNTY, and thus shorthand for the point at which the colony would become a capitalist enclave within a Communist state. The New Territories were to revert to China in 1997 under a treaty of 1898; Britain had concluded in the early 1980s that it would be impractical for the far smaller Crown COLONY of Hong Kong, with its teeming population and limited water supplies, to survive beyond then as a separate entity. The handover took place amid emotional scenes at midnight on 30 June 1997, with the Prince of Wales overseeing the lowering of the Union Jack and departing on the royal yacht *Britannia* with the colony's last governor, Chris PATTEN. During his four-year tenure Patten had tried to introduce an element of democracy; China resented this and in 2004 took steps to reverse it, in the face of big demonstrations.

92 Group A right-wing pressure group of Conservative MPs which had considerable impact in the late 1980s in maintaining the radical thrust of Margaret THATCHER's government, and was later an irritant to John MAJOR. It grew out of a dining club of the same name which until the early '80s did not admit women. The group took its name from 92 Cheyne Walk, one of the locations where its members dined, and not, as was widely supposed, from the claimed size of its membership.

> One of the earlier, less hidebound, utterly snob-free groups. NORMAN TEBBIT

> It personifies in extreme form the characteristics found in the majority of MPs – stupidity and egomania. ALAN CLARK, *Diaries*

Ninety-two Resolutions The document in which Louis-Joseph Papineau in 1834 listed the political grievances of the French-speaking majority in British-ruled Quebec. Papineau, speaker of the House of Assembly, put forward a radical programme for autonomy which the British government rejected; in 1837 his supporters rebelled and Papineau fled to the United States.

Ninety-eight, the The disjointed rebellion against British rule in Ireland that broke out around Dublin in late May 1798 and ended with the defeat of the patriot Wolfe Tone and a French force that November. There were in fact three serial uprisings. The first brought sporadic fighting from Wexford to Sligo, and ended in the Wexford rebels' defeat at Vinegar Hill on 21 June. Two months later a French force landed at Killala in the hope of broadening the struggle; after defeating government troops on 27 August at the 'Races of Castlebar', it surrendered at Ballinamuck on 8 September. Tone, returning from exile, landed on Lough Swilly with a further French force on 3 November; he was captured and committed suicide in prison on 19 November. The '98 was followed by the abolition of the Irish Parliament and by greatly heightened sectarian feeling; it came to take pride of place in Irish NATIONALIST mythology.

Nixon, Richard Milhous (1913–94), 37th President of the United States (Republican, 1969–74), the only President ever to have been forced to resign in the face of almost certain IMPEACHMENT, one of the ablest holders of the office but doomed by his personal flaws. An embittered and insecure man even at the height of his powers, Nixon scrapped his way to the WHITE HOUSE without ever earning the affection of the American people. Denis HEALEY described him as 'more lacking in self-confidence than any other leading politician I have known'; his successor Gerald FORD observed: 'He seemed to prefer dealing with paperwork to dealing with people', and Nixon himself once said:

> If ever the time comes when the Republican Party are looking for an outwardly warm, easygoing, gregarious type, then they will not want the sort of man I am.

But for WATERGATE, Nixon might have been remembered as an outstanding President for his achievements in foreign affairs – but his record made it more than likely he would overreach himself. From a poor farming family, the hard-working and obsessive Nixon battled his way to law school and the California Bar, serving in the Navy during WORLD WAR II despite being exempt as a Quaker. In 1946 he answered an advertisement from local Republicans for a CONGRESSional candidate, was nominated as the best of an unpromising bunch, and defeated the INCUMBENT Jerry Voorhis by branding him a 'friend of the Communists' despite his active work on the House UN-AMERICAN ACTIVITIES Committee – to which Nixon was promptly appointed. In Washington Nixon immediately made a name for himself by pursuing the HISS CASE, and in 1948 he won re-election with the backing of local Democrats as well as Republicans, Two years later, aged 38, he beat Mrs Helen Gahagan Douglas after a scurrilous campaign (*see* PINK LADY) to enter the SENATE; he was helped by the right-wing columnist Gerald L. K. Smith who wrote:

> The man who uncovered Alger Hiss is in California to do the same housecleaning here. Help Richard Nixon get rid of the Jew-Communists.

Back in Congress he championed General Douglas MACARTHUR against President TRUMAN, and formed a close working alliance with Sen. Joseph MCCARTHY. As the 1952 Presidential election neared, he ingratiated himself with Dwight D. EISENHOWER by undermining the candidacies of Sen. Robert Taft (*see* MR. REPUBLICAN) and his fellow Californian Earl WARREN. Eisenhower picked Nixon as his RUNNING-MATE, one Republican pol recalling: 'We took Dick Nixon not because he was right-wing or left-wing, but because he came from California and we were tired.' The campaign went well until the CHECKERS affair broke, IKE being poised to drop him from the ticket until Nixon turned the situation round. At one point Nixon told the Presidential nominee: 'General, there comes a point when you have to piss or get off the pot.' The signs of menace were also evident on the campaign trail: at one stop Nixon told a HECKLER:

> When we're elected we'll take care of people like you.

As Vice President, Nixon at first took a low profile and, with McCarthy broke Eisenhower would have dropped him in 1956 but for conservative pressure; asked what decisions his VEEP had participated in, he told reporters: 'If you give me a week, I might think of one.' In his second term he was more active, braving anti-American demonstrators in Latin America and conducting his celebrated KITCHEN DEBATE with the Soviet leader Nikita Khrushchev. In 1960 he was well placed for a first run at the Presidency, but was wrong-footed after the inert Eisenhower years by the 'youth' challenge of Sen. John F. KENNEDY, who in reality was little younger than Nixon. The Republican nominee fought a workmanlike campaign and 'won' the DEBATES with Kennedy on radio – but his FIVE O'CLOCK SHADOW contributed to his 'losing' them on television and he went down to a very narrow defeat; indeed the outcome was questionable (*see* COOK COUNTY), but Nixon creditably declined to mount a challenge in the courts.

Two years later he took on 'Pat' Brown for the governorship of California (*see* HUGHES LOAN), and on losing announced his retirement, telling reporters: 'You won't have NIXON TO KICK AROUND ANY MORE'.

For the next six years Nixon quietly and conscientiously built a network of support in the Republican Party, and in 1968 was the pre-eminent candidate to recapture the White House from the split and demoralised Democrats. Nominating at the Republican National CONVENTION, Spiro AGNEW proclaimed:

> When a nation is in crisis and history speaks firmly to that nation, it needs a man to catch the time. You don't create such a man; you don't discover such a man – you recognise such a man.

And Nixon, in his ACCEPTANCE SPEECH, declared: 'Let us begin by committing ourselves to the truth.' With Agnew, he went on to defeat Vice President Hubert HUMPHREY, though not by as much as expected.

In office Nixon assumed the trappings of the IMPERIAL PRESIDENCY, attracting some ridicule, but he set in place a capable ADMINISTRATION which initially pursued radical domestic policies before lapsing into BENIGN NEGLECT. On the world stage he was greatly helped by his National Security Adviser Henry KISSINGER as he first prosecuted and then wound down the VIETNAM WAR, established DÉTENTE with the Soviet Union, wielded unprecedented influence in the Middle East and then – reversing his own deep commitments of two decades before – paved the way for normal relations with Communist China.With the Democrats in 1972 committed to a suicidally radical PLATFORM, Nixon massively won re-election over Sen. George McGovern, but sowed the seeds of his disgrace in the process. Kissinger was later to observe:

> Nixon had three goals: to win by the biggest electoral LANDSLIDE in history; to be remembered as a peacemaker; and to be accepted by the ESTABLISHMENT as an equal. He achieved all these objectives – and he lost them all two months later.

The Watergate burglary never caught on as an election issue, but in the ensuing months the COVER-UP and related lawbreaking were traced ever closer to the White House, and the administration was not helped by Agnew's enforced resignation as Vice President for accepting kickbacks when governor of Maryland. Nixon pursued his foreign policy agenda faster and faster while fighting an increasingly desperate battle to persuade Congress and the American people that Watergate was not his problem, and becoming ever more embattled, telling close aides: 'Nobody is a friend of ours, let's face it.'

The disclosure of the Watergate tapes did Nixon incalculable damage; his statement on releasing them: 'I am placing my trust in the American people' was not reciprocated. Of this period Dan Rather commented:

> There were days when the entire White House seemed to be in the grip of a morbid obsession, not unlike the mood aboard the *Pequod* when Ahab was at the helm.

Kissinger, more prosaically but just as alarmingly, observed: 'Sometimes I get worried. The President is like a madman.' With the House of Representatives moving to IMPEACH him, he resigned the Presidency on 8 August 1974. Echoing his Checkers broadcast, he declared:

> I have never been a quitter. To leave office before my term is completed is abhorrent to every instinct in my body.

Nixon – PARDONed almost immediately by Ford – flew in disgrace to his compound at SAN CLEMENTE with his loyal wife Pat. He said of her demeanour over Watergate: 'She has always conducted herself with masterful poise and dignity. But, God, how she could have gone through what she does, I simply don't know.' Nixon suffered a serious illness (phlebitis) before beginning a gradual political rehabilitation. His FROST INTERVIEWS in 1977 were marked by self-justification and an unwillingness to concede the full scale of his wrongdoing, but he did admit:

> I let down my friends, I let down my country, I let down our system of government.

They also reminded Americans of his considerable abilities, and Nixon's subsequent autobiography, *RN*, further demonstrated the strengths that had made him in many ways a highly accomplished President. Disbarred in New York in 1976, he made a first political reappearance in Kentucky in 1978, and in 1981 returned to centre stage at a FUND-RAISER in Ohio. In his old age he remained a figure of controversy, but no longer the pariah he had been after his resignation.

> He has no taste. JOHN F. KENNEDY

> Wandering limply and wetly about the American heartland begging votes on the excuse that he had been too poor to have a pony when he was a boy.
> MURRAY KEMPTON, 1960

> Nixon is a shifty-eyed goddam liar end everyone knows it. He is one of the few men in the history of this country to run for high office talking out of both sides of his mouth at the same time and lying out of both sides.
> HARRY S TRUMAN, *Plain Speaking*

> He had the morals of a private detective.
> WILLIAM S. BURROUGHS

> His motto was, if two wrongs don't make a right, try three. NORMAN COUSINS

> I happen to believe very strongly that Dick Nixon was one of the finest, if not the finest, foreign policy presidents of this century.
> GERALD FORD

> To have striven so hard, to have moulded a public personality out of so amorphous an identity, to have sustained that superhuman effort only to end with every weakness disclosed and every error compounded: that was a fate of Biblical proportions. HENRY KISSINGER

> I would have made a good Pope. NIXON

See also I AM NOT A CROOK; Last PRESS CONFERENCE; TRICKY DICK; WOULD YOU BUY A USED CAR FROM THIS MAN?

Nixon doctrine The policy enunciated by President Nixon in July 1969 that America would in future expect her allies to provide for their own defence, so that conflicts like the VIETNAM WAR could be avoided. The statement, made informally to reporters on Guam, was intended to clarify his policy of VIETNAMISATION, but the WHITE HOUSE subsequently elevated it into a general doctrine of US foreign policy.

Nixon 2000 – he's not as stiff as Gore A classic Republican bumper sticker from the 2000 Presidential election campaign, in which the wooden style of the Democratic nominee Al GORE was widely lampooned. Richard Nixon was, of course, dead by then.

Nixon's the one The slogan on which Richard Nixon campaigned in the 1968 Republican PRIMARIES and on into the Presidential election. This time the Democrats had the last laugh: a prankster persuaded a heavily pregnant black woman to picket Nixon's hotel at the Republican CONVENTION carrying a 'Nixon's the one!' placard.

Mundt-Nixon Bill Richard Nixon's first legislative attempt, after his election to CONGRESS in 1946, to crack down on 'subversives'. Even fellow-Republicans considered the measure excessive, Thomas DEWEY denouncing it as a move 'to beat down ideas with clubs', and Congress refused to pass it.

New Nixon The media's categorisation of the Richard Nixon who campaigned for the Presidency in 1968, showing a mellow statesmanship instead of the grudging partisanship with which he had 'retired' from politics six years before.

US v Nixon The 1974 SUPREME COURT case whose outcome effectively ensured Richard Nixon's resignation as President. It was connected with WATERGATE, or more specifically the Watergate tapes and whether the President had the right under EXECUTIVE PRIVILEGE not to respond to a subpoena. The Court decided that 'neither the doctrine of SEPARATION OF POWERS, nor the need for confidentiality of high-level communications, without more, can sustain an absolute, unqualified Presidential immunity from judicial process under all circumstance.'

You won't have Nixon to kick around any more Nixon's farewell remarks in November 1962 after failing to win the governorship of California. When told the press wanted a statement from him, Nixon responded: 'Screw them', then, looking nervous and dishevelled before the cameras, launched into this tirade which has gone down in political history:

> Now that all the members of the press are so delighted that I have lost . . . I have no hard feelings against anybody, against any opponent and least of all the people of California . . . And as I leave the press, all I can say is this. For 16 years, ever since the HISS CASE, you've had a lot of fun – a lot of fun – that you've had an opportunity to attack me . . . Just think about how much you're going to be missing. You won't have Nixon to kick around any more because, gentlemen, this is my LAST PRESS CONFERENCE.

Nixonland The scathing description devised by the Democratic nominee Adlai STEVENSON (1900–65) during the 1956 Presidential campaign for the twilight world of MCCARTHYISM and Vice President Nixon's links to it. Stevenson said:

> Our nation stands at a fork in the political road. In one direction lies a land of slander and scare; the land of sly innuendo, the poison pen, the anonymous phone call and hustling, pushing, shoving; the land of smash and grab and anything to win. This is Nixonland. But I say to you that it is not America.

NIXXON *Mad* magazine's comment when the Esso petroleum company changed its name to EXXON. (It had earlier opted for 'Enco' before discovering that this was Japanese for a broken-down car.) *Mad* carried a cartoon of the Nixon WHITE HOUSE flying a flag bearing the word 'Nixxon'; the caption read: 'It's the same old gas.'

Nkosi Sikelele Afrika (God Bless Africa) The unofficial anthem of the ANC and many other movements campaigning for freedom and equal rights in southern Africa, which was adopted on 1 April 1994 as joint national anthem, with the Afrikaner *Die* STEM VAN SUID-AFRIKA, of post-APARTHEID South Africa; under *apartheid*, singing it could earn a prison term. Composed by Enoch Sontonga in 1897, the first verse reads:

> Nkosi Sikelele Afrika
> Maluphakamisu phondo lwayo
> Yizwa imithandazo yethu
> Nkosi sikelela
> Thina lusapho lwayo.

NKVD (Russ. *Narodniy Kommissariat Vnutrennykh Dyel*, People's Commissariat for Internal Affairs) The Soviet agency responsible for state security from 1934 to 1943. Succeeding the OGPU (*see* GPU), it was notorious for carrying out STALIN's PURGES. In 1943 its state security function was taken over by another agency, the NKGB, but it continued to manage internal affairs, becoming a Ministry – the MVD – in 1946.

no. No, No, No! Margaret THATCHER's ringing denunciation of Jacques DELORS' vision of European union in the HOUSE OF COMMONS on 30 October 1990, which sowed the seeds of her downfall. The strength of her language when she departed from a carefully crafted statement on the Rome EC SUMMIT was one factor behind Sir Geoffrey HOWE's resignation as Deputy Prime Minister, which in turn contributed to her removal from the Conservative leadership one month later. Answering MPs' questions, she said:

> The President of the Commission, Mr Delors, said at a press conference the other day that he wanted the EUROPEAN PARLIAMENT to be the democratic body of the Community. He wanted the Commission to be the EXECUTIVE, and wanted the COUNCIL OF MINISTERS to be the Senate. No, no, no!

no, not a sixpence! The terms in which Charles Cotesworth Pinckney, US Minister to France, reported on 27 October 1797 his country's response to a French request for a bribe before it would discuss the release of captured American ships. He gave this verdict on the X, Y AND Z AFFAIR in a letter to Timothy Pickering.

No Child Left Behind Act The centrepiece of George W. BUSH's educational reforms, the Elementary and Secondary Education Act of 2001 which Bush signed on 8 January 2002. The Act greatly expanded Federal involvement in education by providing sizeable additional funds, potentially for every public school in America, targeted on mathematics and reading and the improvement of test results in those subjects. While some liberal teachers complained that its focus was too narrow and others objected to being told what to do by WASHINGTON, even many of Bush's opponents regarded it as an important step forward.

No favours, but slightly quicker The five words in a Home Office e-mail that precipitated the resignation of David Blunkett (1947–) as Home Secretary on 15 December 2004 (*see* NANNYGATE). The following week an inquiry under the former senior civil servant Sir Alan Budd concluded that while there was a 'chain of events' linking Blunkett to the speeding up of a visa application for the nanny of his former lover, Kimberly Quinn, there was no detectable evidence that Blunkett had sought special help from his officials.

no first use One of the formulae put forward by peace campaigners and others in the 1980s to ease tension between the SUPERPOWERS. Had it been adopted, both America and the Soviet Union would have agreed not to unleash any of their nuclear weapons unless the other had already gone for a FIRST STRIKE.

no-fly zone An area from which all flights by a country's military aircraft are barred by other nations – under threat of being shot down – on the ground that they would lead to hostilities or attacks by those aircraft on civilians. The first such zone, south of the 32nd parallel, was agreed in August 1992 by the GULF WAR coalition plus Russia in response to Iraq's bombing, strafing and NAPALMing of Shi'ites in its southern marshlands in violation of US resolutions; a smaller zone north of the 36th parallel was later imposed in the north to protect Iraq's Kurds. Largely but not totally honoured, these zones were still in force when the IRAQ WAR broke out in 2003. Later in August 1992 the LONDON CONFERENCE on former Yugoslavia proposed a no-fly zone barring Serbian military aircraft from the skies over Bosnia; this remained more or less in force until the DAYTON peace settlement.

no-go area Originally an area barred to unauthorised persons for security reasons, the term achieved notoriety when PARA-MILITARY groups in NORTHERN IRELAND sealed off parts of Belfast and (London) Derry to prevent troops and police patrolling them. Certain deprived and crime-ridden INNER-CITY areas are also described as no-go areas, implying that the police, and indeed other members of the public, enter at their own risk.

no man, be he ever so high *See* IF THE GOVERNMENT BECOMES A LAWBREAKER . . .

no more Mr Nice Guy A picturesque way for politicians to say that the gloves are off, and that whatever scruples (if any) they previously possessed will now be abandoned. In 1972 aides of Sen. Edmund Muskie (see CANUCK LETTER) said it as their candidate tried to shed his virtuous image. In the mid-1950s a joke surfaced that HITLER had decided on a comeback – 'but this time, no more Mr Nice Guy'.

no overall control In UK local government, another term for a HUNG COUNCIL where no one party has an outright MAJORITY.

No Popery! The slogan against Roman Catholic influence in British (and particularly Northern Irish) political life which dates back at least to the 18th century, when it sparked the GORDON RIOTS. It is still the regular cry of the PAISLEYITES.

no such thing as society *See* SOCIETY.

No Surrender! (1) The rallying cry of generations of Ulster LOYALISTS in the face of any Nationalist or Catholic challenge to the Protestant supremacy, or any moves toward a united Ireland. (2) The Bruce Springsteen song which was John KERRY's campaign theme in the 2004 US Presidential election.

No taxation without representation! The slogan widely believed to have triggered the AMERICAN REVOLUTION, stemming from the imposition of the STAMP ACT on Britain's American colonies, which had no voice in the Parliament that took the decision. It stemmed from the declaration of James Otis (1725–83) that 'taxation without representation is tyranny'. In 1947 the historian Arnold Toynbee, pressing for greater UK representation at the UNITED NATIONS, devised the slogan: **'No annihilation without representation!'**

No Turning Back The most die-hard group of THATCHERITE MPs, mainly from the 1983 intake, who remain firmly wedded to her radical free-MARKET policies. On the night of 21 November 1990, leaders of the group made a dramatic appeal to Mrs Thatcher not to stand down as Prime Minister and party leader after being forced to a second leadership ballot by Michael HESELTINE. Its influence has faded with the Conservatives' heavy defeats in 1997 and 2001; two of its heavyweight members, Michael Portillo and Francis Maude, resigned from the group in 2000, but John Redwood (*see* VULCAN) continued as chairman.

No Surrender! *See* SURRENDER.

Nobel Peace Prize One of the six international awards established under the will of Alfred Nobel (1833–96), the Swedish chemist who invented dynamite. Winners have included Dr Albert Schweitzer (1875–1965), Chief Albert Luthuli (1899–1967), Dr Martin Luther KING, the NORTHERN IRELAND adversaries Gerry Adams and David Trimble, and most controversially Le Duc Tho (1911–90) and Dr Henry KISSINGER for supposedly bringing peace to Vietnam; two of the prize committee resigned in protest. First made in 1901, it is awarded by the Norwegian Parliament (Sweden and Norway were then united) and presented in Stockholm.

nodding through The procedure at WESTMINSTER under which an MP who is well enough to get to the HOUSE OF COMMONS but not to pass through the DIVISION LOBBIES can have their vote recorded; in the last months of the 1945–51 and 1974–79 Labour government and John MAJOR's Conservative administration when every vote was critical, MPs were brought to the House in ambulances, some even being nodded through in oxygen tents. Labour forfeited power in the no-CONFIDENCE vote of 28 March 1979 because Ministers and whips refused to summon Dr Alfred Broughton to vote, knowing he was dying; had he voted the result would have been a tie, and the government would have staggered on.

Nolan Committee The ten-member panel headed by Lord Nolan, a senior appeal court judge, which in 1995 recommended the first independent checks on the behaviour of MPs and Ministers in the 730-year history of Parliament. The committee was set up by John MAJOR after a tidal wave of SLEAZE allegations against Ministers and backbenchers, mostly for lapses in conduct committed before he became Prime Minister. Nolan recommended a ban on MPs working for LOBBYING companies, full disclosure of MPs' earnings and contracts for providing Parliamentary services, CABINET MINISTERS to need permission to take private sector jobs within two years of leaving office, a Parliamentary Commissioner for Standards to deal with rule breaches and complaints, and a Public Appointments Commission to control membership of QUANGOS. The COMMONS accepted the recommendations and the Nolan machinery was made permanent, though Sir Edward HEATH, who had refused to co-operate with Nolan, continued to withhold details of his involvement with the Lloyd's insurance market.

nomenklatura In the Soviet Union and across the Communist world, those selected by the PARTY and its leadership for advancement and privileges and to perform key tasks; often they did not know they had been singled out in this way.

nomination The process by which a CANDIDATE is entered for an ELECTION. In most forms of election, nomination is achieved by the lodging of papers with the relevant authorities bearing the signature of the candidate and a certain number of supporters. In a US Presidential election the placing of the **nominee**'s name on the BALLOT is overshadowed by the CONVENTION at which the decision to nominate is taken. Margaret Taylor, wife of the future President Zachary Taylor, described his nomination by the WHIGS in 1848 as 'a plot to deprive me of his society, and shorten his life by unnecessary care and responsibility'; it turned out to be just that. Gen. William Tecumseh Sherman (1820–91) is said to have told Republicans who wanted to nominate him: 'I will not accept if nominated, and will not serve if elected.' And in 1980 the former Democratic Presidential hopeful Rep. Morris Udall joked: 'If nominated I will run to Mexico. If elected I will fight for extradition.'

nominating speech The CONVENTION speech which formally proposes a candidate for nomination; if no candidate has established a clear lead, several such speeches are made. The making of a dramatic enough nomination speech, such as Franklin D. ROOSEVELT's for Al Smith in 1924, can be the first step in a subsequent Presidential campaign on the nominator's own behalf.

Non! UK media and political shorthand for President DE GAULLE's effective veto on British membership of the COMMON MARKET, delivered at an ÉLYSÉE press conference on 14 January 1963. It took France another two weeks to persuade the other five member states to reject the application. Harold WILSON said of the snub, administered to Edward HEATH who had headed the negotiating team:

> No British Minister must ever again be put in the position of waiting outside in the cold while others decide our fate.

> What knocked the stuffing out of MACMILLAN's government – and Macmillan himself – was de Gaulle's veto on our joining the EEC, which fell like a death sentence on 14 January. It left the Government without an objective; Macmillan said on 28 January: 'All our policies at home and abroad are in ruins. We have lost everything except our courage and determination.'
>
> LORD DEEDES, *The Daily Telegraph*, 1 January 1994

non-aggression pact A TREATY under which two countries agree not to attack each other. It can form the basis of friendship or improved relations – but equally, as with the NAZI-SOVIET PACT of 1939, be the prelude to grand betrayal by a stronger power mired in cynicism.

non-aligned movement The 'third force' of states linked to neither SUPERPOWER, which was founded at the BANDUNG CONFERENCE in 1955; its prime movers included Jawaharlal NEHRU of India and Yugoslavia's President TITO. Britain, and even more so America, harboured doubts about the movement's genuine independence because of its denunciation of COLONIALISM. Though its influence has diminished over the decades, it has offered for the most part a genuinely independent, if inconvenient, voice.

Nonconformist conscience One of the driving forces of 19th-century LIBERAL politics in Britain, and to a lesser extent of the developing LABOUR PARTY. The phrase originated c. 1870 to describe the POLITICISATION of many Methodists, Congregationalists, Baptists and others in opposition to the FORSTER EDUCATION ACT and relaxation of the liquor licensing laws, and in favour of DISESTABLISHMENT. Nonconformists had been barred from Parliament until the early 19th century, but by 1880 they comprised a quarter of all Liberal MPs and their influence because disproportionate to their numbers. The 'Nonconformist conscience' probably exerted its greatest impact in the 1906 election, when the BALFOUR government was rejected partly because it had permitted the import of indentured Chinese labourers to the Transvaal, a process CAMPBELL-BANNERMAN castigated as 'slavery'.

non-cooperation The tactics pursued by John MAJOR's government in its dealings with the EUROPEAN UNION in the spring of 1996 in protest at its ban on imports of British beef because of the risk of MAD COW DISEASE. Major dropped the tactic at the Florence summit that June in return for a partial lifting of the ban, only for Germany to refuse to enforce it.

non-implementation The stand taken against the HEATH government's 1972 Housing Finance Act by CLAY CROSS and other left-wing Labour councils which felt they were being compelled to make a profit from their tenants instead of providing housing as a social service. Several major councils, among them Sheffield, initially backed the campaign but reversed their position as the consequences of illegality became clear.

Non-Intervention Committee An international committee formed in 1936 to prevent other countries becoming involved in the SPANISH CIVIL WAR. As Germany and Italy stepped up their participation in the conflict, the committee and its proceedings became increasingly irrelevant; Britain interpreted non-intervention as doing nothing to assist Spain's Republican government, even in non-military matters.

non-person The status to which anyone who fell foul of the COMMUNIST hierarchy in the Soviet Union or one of its eastern European SATELLITES could be reduced. It involved the deletion of any reference to their past achievements, or even their existence, from the country's history or media.

Non-Proliferation Treaty The treaty signed in 1968 by America, Britain and the Soviet Union undertaking not to provide the technology for making NUCLEAR WEAPONS to countries that had not already acquired it; France and China refused to sign, but have subsequently done so. The treaty, under which almost 200 countries have since renounced nuclear weaponry, was based on the belief that with the SUPERPOWERS in nuclear deadlock, the greatest threat to world peace would be the development of nuclear weapons by some unstable and fanatical regime outside their control. Cuba, Israel, India and Pakistan remain outside the NPT and the treaty has not prevented North Korea, and allegedly Iran, from pursuing nuclear weapons programmes. But several other countries, including Brazil and South Africa, wound down their nuclear weapons potential before ratifying the Treaty, and it has been a moral force against even greater PROLIFERATION.

non-violence The principle of winning political arguments by moral force which was pioneered by MAHATMA Gandhi and developed by Dr Martin Luther KING. Gandhi, who organised non-violent protests in South Africa and then India, wrote: 'Non-violence is the first article of my faith. It is also the last article of my creed.' He also said: 'Non-violence is the law of our species as violence is the law of the brute.' Dr King first advocated non-violence in 1955 when he led the year-long MONTGOMERY BUS BOYCOTT, declaring: 'The negro all over the South must come to the point where he can say to his white brother: "We will soon wear you down by our sheer capacity to suffer."' He said of his philosophy: 'The ultimate weakness of violence is that it is a descending spiral, begetting the very thing it seeks to destroy.' By the mid-1960s black militants were challenging the notion that non-violence could bring real change, George Jackson (*see* SOLEDAD BROTHERS) saying: 'In a non-violent movement there must be a latent threat of eruption, a dormant possibility of sudden and violent action, if concessions are to be won.'

> Organised love. JOAN BAEZ (1941–)

none of the above The phrase sometimes

written on BALLOT papers by voters who are dissatisfied with the choice offered to them, or as a protest against the entire political system.

noose. a halo only has to slip nine inches to become a noose A telling summary of the suddenness with which a promising political career can be ended by scandal; the nine inches may have a phallic significance or represent the distance from the top of a man's head to his Adam's apple. The phrase is said to have been coined by Iain Macleod, the Conservatives' most devastating wordsmith in OPPOSITION from 1964 to 1970.

no noose is bad noose Ostensibly an argument for the return or retention of hanging, the slogan – an adaptation of 'no news is good news' – probably originated with anti-hangers. **No** NUKES **is bad nukes** is a variant, making the same statement about NUCLEAR WEAPONS.

NORAD North American Air Defence. The joint command protecting the United States and Canada from Soviet air attack from the Arctic, set up in 1957; until 1981 it covered only aircraft because of Canadian sensibilities over linkage with US ballistic missile systems. To America NORAD secures the northern flank and is sound common sense. Canada's LIBERALS objected to the agreement when the Diefenbaker government signed it, but later broadened its scope; the NDP has gone into some elections pledged to withdraw if elected.

Noraid Irish Northern Aid. The Irish Republican fund-raising organisation in the United States (and to some extent in Canada) which channelled millions of dollars to the IRA between the early 1970s and the run-up to the GOOD FRIDAY AGREEMENT. Its officials always insisted the money, much of it collected openly at charity events in New York and other cities, was for the welfare of prisoners' families and other non-military purposes, but the British and US authorities have always doubted this.

Norder, Laura *See* LAW AND ORDER.

normalcy The reassuring offer made to the American people by Warren G. HARDING in the 1920 Presidential CAMPAIGN. Before his NOMINATION, Harding declared:

> America's present need is not heroics, but healing; not nostrums, but normalcy; not revolution, but restoration; not agitation, but adjustment; not surgery, but serenity; not the dramatic, but the dispassionate; not experiment, but equipoise; not submergence in internationality, but sustainment in triumphant nationality . . .

He returned to the theme of 'normalcy' throughout the campaign, but once he was in the WHITE HOUSE the word turned out to be shorthand for an unprecedented orgy of graft and corruption (*see* TEAPOT DOME).

normalisation The process of re-establishing relations with a country with whom there have been no formal contacts. The term was used by Richard NIXON and the Chinese leaders CHAIRMAN MAO Tse-Tung and Chou En-Lai in 1972 to describe the process of establishing contacts, broken 23 years before when the Communists finally defeated the NATIONALIST CHINESE. The process began at a low level with an exchange of table tennis teams (*see* Ping-Pong DIPLOMACY), contacts were gradually developed and formalised, and full diplomatic relations were restored by the CARTER administration in 1979.

north. North Atlantic Council The political arm of NATO, in which France remained when she withdrew from its defence planning organisation. Never as pre-cooked in its deliberations as the UNITED NATIONS, the Council showed a very public split in February 2003 when France, Germany and Belgium blocked a move by Britain and America to plan for assistance to Turkey in the event of an Iraqi invasion triggered by the launch of US and British military operations against SADDAM HUSSEIN.

North Briton The paper in which the radical John WILKES (1725–97) ridiculed Lord Bute, Prime Minister 1762–63, to such an extent that, coupled with blistering polemics from Wilkes in the HOUSE OF COMMONS, it brought about Bute's downfall. The title was a reference to Bute's Scottish origins; the *Dictionary of National Biography* says of him:

> The details of his ADMINISTRATION are peculiarly disgraceful, and for corruption and financial incapacity it is not likely to be surpassed.

In Issue 45 of the *North Briton*, Wilkes turned his guns on King George III, charging that Ministers had put lies in his mouth in the King's Speech at the opening of Parliament; his vitriolic attack landed him in the Tower of London, but he was acquitted of libel on the grounds of Parliamentary PRIVILEGE. Exiled to France, he returned in 1768 to serve a two-year sentence for obscenity for his *Essay on Woman*; a mob of his supporters demonstrating outside the prison was dispersed with heavy loss of life. The number 45 was daubed on doors throughout England, and the French ambassador was dragged from his carriage and had the number chalked on the soles of his feet.

north of Watford The phrase used in English politics to explain and condemn the parochiality of the southern English and the WESTMINSTER/WHITEHALL Establishment, who are felt to regard all events as centred on London and everything beyond the capital's northern fringe as an irrelevance. Watford typifies the edge of the conurbation: the last of the contiguous built-up area before leaving London heading north-west, and the first large town outside the Greater London boundary.

North-South debate Shorthand for the problems of the developing world (the South) and the interest the prosperous industrialised nations (the North) have in finding a solution for them. It stems from *North-South: A Programme for Survival*, the title of the BRANDT COMMISSION's first report published in 1980. The term came to apply to any dialogue between the two blocs, and indeed the timebomb which the lack of THIRD WORLD development threatened for more prosperous states.

North-South divide The apparently unclosable gap between the largely prosperous South of England and the generally depressed North. Diversion of industry and cash grants have had some impact, but only in the RECESSION of 1991–92 did the gap narrow, through the South de-industrialising faster. The most recent manifestation is the proposal by John Prescott (see TWO JAGS) to demolish housing developments in parts of the North where the residents have voted with their feet, while pressure for new housing in the South-East continues to increase.

> There is a growing division in our comparatively prosperous society between the South and the North and Midlands, which are ailing, that cannot be allowed to continue.
>
> Maiden speech of the Earl of Stockton (HAROLD MACMILLAN), House of Lords, 15 November 1984

Northcote-Trevelyan reforms The radical changes to Britain's CIVIL SERVICE instigated by Sir Charles Trevelyan (1807–86) and Sir Stafford Northcote (later the Earl of Iddesleigh, 1818–87). This WHITEHALL high-flier and civil servant turned politician outraged Ministers by proposing competitive examinations to fill administrative posts. It took exposures after the CRIMEAN WAR of inept officials appointed by PATRONAGE to bring action; a Civil Service Commission was set up in 1855, and Trevelyan and Northcote finally got their way in 1970.

> In future the Board of Examiners will be in place of our Queen. Our institutions will become as harshly republican as possible, and the new spirit of public offices will not be loyalty, but republicanism.
>
> Lord JOHN RUSSELL to GLADSTONE

Northern Bank robbery The £26 million robbery in Belfast in December 2004 which was blamed by the British and Irish security services on the IRA. Achieved through a brutal hostage-taking, it was suspected almost from the outset of being the work of the Provisionals despite their ceasefire; SINN FEIN strongly denied this, and claims that the party itself had known of plans for the raid during almost-successful talks that autumn about a return to POWER-SHARING, and at the start of February 2005 the IRA, exuding righteous indignation, pulled out of the DECOMMISSIONING process.

Northern Ireland The portion of Ireland left in the United Kingdom after PARTITION in 1921, a political entity in its own right whose history, particularly from 1969 to 1994, is dominated by TERRORISM. Consisting of the SIX COUNTIES of the province of ULSTER, it was governed from STORMONT by the UNIONIST majority until DIRECT RULE was imposed in 1972 as 300-year-old SECTARIAN conflicts reopened; WILLIE Whitelaw, the first Northern Ireland Secretary, said on arriving; 'I do not intend to prejudge the past'. From then until the IRA ceasefire, the province was convulsed by sporadic outbreaks of terrorist savagery by REPUBLICANS and LOYALISTS alike, with British troops, RUC and prison officers and members of rival factions the stated targets and hapless civilians often the victims. Nearly 20,000 troops and 7500 police officers were deployed as political initiatives foundered, including, in 1974, a POWER-SHARING Executive and Assembly. The 1985 ANGLO-IRISH AGREEMENT gave Dublin an advisory role in the North, provoking Loyalist outrage without stemming Republican violence. As the death toll topped 2300, Britain, the Irish Republic and all Northern Ireland parties except SINN FEIN opened talks in 1991. The DOWNING STREET DECLARATION of December 1993 followed; pessimism within the IRA and contacts between SDLP leader John Hume and Sinn Fein's Gerry Adams helped bring the ceasefire and talks between Sinn Fein and the British government. It took until April 1998 for all factions to be brought together to negotiate the GOOD FRIDAY AGREEMENT, which set up a further devolved power structure, with Sinn Fein and Loyalist paramilitaries both within the system. Prisoner releases followed, and in the period since the province has been generally at peace despite outrages by dissident Republicans, notably the OMAGH BOMBING, and murderous feuds between Loyalists. Sinn Fein took its place in a new power-sharing Executive under the Unionist David Trimble, but this has three times been suspended. Nevertheless the peace had broadly held, thousands of troops have been withdrawn, the RUC has been reformed and normality has returned to all but the most hard-line areas.

> Britain stands towards peace in Northern Ireland today where America stood in South-East Asia during the early 1960s.
>
> Sen. EDWARD KENNEDY, 1971

Northern Ireland Assembly The 108-member elected body set up under the GOOD FRIDAY AGREEMENT which is the basis for the POWER-SHARING Executive that has governed the province sporadically since DEVOLUTION took effect on 2 December 1999. SINN FEIN and representatives of some LOYALIST paramilitary groups have played a full part in its workings, with Sinn Fein and the DUP both holding Ministerial portfolios. The Assembly has been suspended three times by the British Government, twice because of IRA foot-dragging over DECOMMISSIONING its weaponry and the third time, on 14 October 2002, when the IRA was found to be using Sinn Fein's office at Stormont to monitor potential targets. Further elections were held in November 2003, in the hope that the Assembly could be reconvened once UK and Irish Ministers have completed a review of the Good Friday Agreement.

Northwest Ordinance The decision by America's new government in 1787 that at most five states could be carved from the area between the Appalachians and the Mississippi, north of the Ohio River. It outlined a system of transitional governments, provided that when 60,000 people (native Americans excluded) had settled in each embryo state, it could join the Union 'on an equal footing with the original states'. It was promised that the new states would guarantee civil and religious rights and prohibit slavery.

Norwegian Wood The nickname former Democratic Vice President Walter Mondale (1928–) attracted during his Presidential campaign against Ronald REAGAN in 1984. He earned his tag, from a song by the Beatles, through his Scandinavian descent and deadpan delivery. A campaign aide said after one television apprarance:

> The speech was typed better than it was read.

Mondale came out of retirement for the 2002 Senate election in Minnesota on the death of the incumbent Paul Wellstone in a plane crash the week before polling. He was hot favourite to win, but went down to defeat as the pro-BUSH tide captured the SENATE for Republicans; Mondale's age (74) told mildly against him, but a bigger negative was a memorial service for Wellstone which turned into an election rally, with Gov. Jesse (THE BODY) Ventura walking out. *See also* FRITZ.

Not a penny off the pay, not a minute on the day The slogan of Britain's miners, led by A. J. Cook, in the dispute over wage cuts and longer hours that culminated in the 1926 GENERAL STRIKE.

Not Contents In the HOUSE OF LORDS, the voters against a proposition; those voting for are described as CONTENTS.

not for attribution In political, especially LOBBY, journalism, information divulged by a SOURCE on condition that he or she is not named.

Not in my name The rallying call of groups opposed to British and American military action against Iraq in the spring of 2003, prior to and during hostilities. While the attack aroused much anger in the Arab world, the largest demonstrations against it were in London beforehand, and in San Francisco when it began.

not invented here The insistence of one armed service on developing its own costly and incompatible equipment rather than demean itself by purchasing an item working perfectly well for a rival. It applies to everything from aircraft worth billions to the tiniest of widgets; the consequence, in theatres of war from GRENADA to IRAQ, has been that, for instance, members of a forces have had to communicate with each other by credit card phone or their own mobile phones, often via headquarters in the home country, because the services' battlefield communications could not speak to each other.

note-taker A relatively senior official, often a diplomat, who sits in on BILATERAL and even TÊTE À TÊTE meetings between HEADS OF GOVERNMENT to keep a record and remind the participants of what was discussed and agreed.

nothing for nothing The stark warning that 'there is nothing for nothing any longer' quoted by President CARTER in his 1980 State of the UNION message. It was originally given by the columnist Walter Lippmann on 18 June 1940 to the 30th reunion of the Harvard class of 1910. Lippmann told them:

> You have lived the easy way, henceforth you will have the hard way . . . You came into a great heritage made by the insight and the sweat and the blood of inspired and devoted and courageous men; thoughtlessly and in utmost self-indulgence you have all but squandered this inheritance. Now only by the heroic virtues which made this inheritance can you restore it again . . . You took the good things for granted. Now you must earn them again. For every right that you cherish, you have a duty which you must fulfil. For every hope that you entertain, you have a task that you must perform. For every good that you wish to preserve, you must sacrifice your comfort and your ease. There is nothing for nothing any longer.

The phrase also has a resonance outside US politics; Mussolini (*see* DUCE), at the height of his power, declared: 'My foreign policy is "nothing for nothing".'

Notting Hill set *See* BED-BLOCKERS.

November 17th A left-wing and anti-American terrorist group in Greece which between 1995 and 2002 murdered 23 people, including the CIA station chief in Athens and the British defence attaché Stephen Saunders. The group, headed by Alexandros Giotopoulos, a veteran of the Paris ÉVÈNEMENTS of 1968, took its name from the date of a crackdown by the Greek COLONELS on student protesters; it operated with impunity until one of its members severely injured himself in July 2002 while carrying a bomb, and its arsenal was located. In December 2003 over a dozen members of November 17th were convicted of terrorist offences; Giotopoulos and its hit-man Dimitris Koufodinas were jailed for life.

Novus Ordo Seculorum (Lat. The new order of the ages) The motto of the United States of America. One of several Masonic phrases adopted by the newly-formed nation, it appears on the Great SEAL, and has become a fixture on the reverse of the dollar bill.

NOW National Organization of Women. The largest and most influential organisation behind the women's movement in America, which since 1966 has taken legal and political action to end sex discrimination. Founded largely on the initiative of Betty Friedan, author of *The Feminine Mystique*, it played a leading role in getting the Equal Rights Amendment (ERA) through CONGRESS, but just failed to secure RATIFICATION.

NRA (1) National Recovery Administration. One of the lead agencies of Franklin D. ROOSEVELT's NEW DEAL, set up during the first HUNDRED DAYS of his Presidency. Its initial role was as a confidence-booster; its first head, General Hugh Johnson (who had served in WILSON's wartime administration), chose a blue eagle as its motif and staged huge parades of NRA participants, the largest of which brought almost 2 million people onto the streets of New York on 13 September 1933. But its purpose was to promote industrial recovery through a series of regulatory codes to limit unfair competition, improve working conditions, establish a MINIMUM WAGE and guarantee the right to collective bargaining. Employers subscribing to the codes (eventually there were 357 basic and 208 supplementary codes) were allowed to display a Blue Eagle emblem. Despite its bureaucracy, it did register successes including an end to child labour in US cotton mills, but although it created 2 million jobs it became a scapegoat for disillusion with the New Deal, and was widely criticised for giving large firms advantages over small businesses. It was declared UNCONSTITUTIONAL by the SUPREME COURT on 27 May 1935 (BLACK MONDAY), but many of its provisions were incorporated into later legislation. Sen. Huey 'KINGFISH' Long branded the NRA the 'National Racketeers' Arrangement', 'Nuts Running America', and 'Never Roosevelt Again'.

> For two dizzy years, America had a fling at NATIONAL SOCIALISM.
>
> ALISTAIR COOKE

(2) National Rifle Association. One of the most formidable LOBBIES in US politics, through its ability to mobilise millions of hunters and persuade them that any move toward GUN CONTROL to curb inner-city crime would be a violation of their constitutional RIGHT TO KEEP AND BEAR ARMS. With 3.4 million members at its peak in the early 1990s and a 250-strong staff in Washington, it was long successful in blocking the BRADY BILL and other measures to restrict the sale, ownership and use of firearms. The NRA bitterly opposed Bill CLINTON's 1994 Crime Bill (*see* THREE STRIKES AND YOU'RE OUT) because it banned nineteen kinds of assault rifle including the KALASHNIKOV; it also launched a crusade

against authoritarian government with the veteran movie star Charlton Heston as its spokesman, but membership slumped after the OKLAHOMA CITY BOMBING.

Nuck Fewt The spoonerism which enabled Democratic car drivers to voice their disapproval of Rep. Speaker NEWT Gingrich in his triumphal period (1994–96) in a bumper sticker without quite falling foul of the laws against public obscenity.

nuclear. nuclear freeze *See* FREEZE.

nuclear-free zone A territory or community from which all NUCLEAR WEAPONS are banned, and often all nuclear activity including reactors for peaceful uses and the transport of nuclear waste. The concept attracted some world leaders who saw the exclusion of nuclear weapons from, say, continental Europe as a way of limiting the spread of a war between the SUPERPOWERS. It was taken up by nuclear disarmers in various countries, and in particular left-wing Labour councils in the UK who designated communities under their control as 'nuclear free'. Conservatives denounced the concept as fatuous in the extreme. The author once lived in a block of flats through which ran the boundary between a nuclear-free council and one that was not; in the event of nuclear war the residents agreed they would shelter in one of the 'nuclear-free' apartments.

nuclear proliferation The process under which the ownership and potential for use of nuclear weapons spreads from a handful of major powers to smaller or more unstable governments and even terrorist groups, making atomic warfare more likely and the task of its prevention more difficult. The NON-PROLIFERATION TREATY has done much to curb it.

nuclear sword of Damocles John F. KENNEDY's vivid characterisation of the threat of nuclear annihilation which hung over the world throughout the COLD WAR. In ancient mythology, the tyrant Damocles awoke to find a sword suspended over his head by a thread.

nuclear umbrella The role of America's nuclear arsenal in protecting the non-nuclear nations of the democratic West against the threat of invasion or extermination by the Soviet Union. Americans charged that the umbrella sheltered states with much-publicised moral quirks about possessing nuclear weapons themselves.

> We are not bent on conquest or on threatening others. But we do have a nuclear umbrella that can protect others, above all the states to which we are allied or in which we have a great national interest.
>
> President NIXON, *New York Times* interview, 8 March 1971

nuclear war The most devastating conflict mankind has yet devised, and if it ever breaks out, probably its last. Nikita S. Khrushchev is reputed to have said that if such a war did break out, 'the survivors would envy the dead', and few would disagree. One who did was Sen. Richard Russell, a supporter of strong US nuclear defences, who told the SENATE on 2 October 1968: 'If we are to start again with another Adam and Eve, then I want them to be Americans and not Russians, and I want them on this continent and not in Europe.' Seven years before, General Douglas MACARTHUR told the Congress of the Philippines that nuclear war was 'a Frankenstein to destroy both sides', adding: 'This very thought of scientific annihilation has destroyed the possibility of war being a medium for the practical settlement of international differences.' And another veteran of WORLD WAR II, General Omar Bradley, said bluntly:

> The way to stop an atomic war is to make sure it never starts.

nuclear weapons Types of weapon in which an explosion is produced by a nuclear reaction, rather than a chemical reaction as in so-called CONVENTIONAL devices. Their vastly increased destructive power, first witnessed at HIROSHIMA, has transformed world politics and the exercise of power as well as placing the human race at risk of annihilation. Nuclear weapons are of two types: fission weapons such as the original ATOMIC BOMB, and fusion weapons like the later and even more destructive H-BOMB.

> It's like having a cobra in the nursery with your grandchildren. You get rid of the cobra or you won't have any grandchildren.
>
> THEODORE M. HESBURGH, President, Notre Dame University 1952–87

> If the third world war is fought with nuclear weapons, the fourth will be fought with bows and arrows.
>
> Earl MOUNTBATTEN of Burma (1900–79)

nuclear winter *See* WINTER.

nukes Slang for nuclear weapons, also, as a verb, for using them. An Americanism from the 1970s, its use has spread throughout the English-speaking world. The nuclear disarmers' slogan **'No nukes is good nukes'** (*compare* NOOSE) is an example of its first application; the cry of **'Nuke the bastards!'** an example of the second.

nullification The strategy devised by Andrew Jackson's Vice President John C. Calhoun (1782–1850) as an alternative to the secession of the Southern states from the Union. It came to a head when South Carolina flexed its sovereignty by 'nullifying' a heavy TARIFF imposed by CONGRESS in 1828 on English imports which Calhoun feared would bring British retaliation that would endanger cotton production, and the system of slavery that it sustained. Jackson denounced as TREASONable South Carolina's refusal to let US customs officials enforce the tariff and, with no other state following suit, prepared forces to march on Charleston; meanwhile Henry Clay persuaded Congress to accept a less draconian tariff. The narrowness by which conflict had been avoided killed nullification, and Calhoun's hopes of the Presidency.

number. Number Ten 10 DOWNING STREET, the office and generally the home of PRIME MINISTERS since WALPOLE and nerve-centre of the British government; also shorthand for the power of the Prime Minister. It is a modest and much-extended 17th-century town house halfway up Downing Street on the right, facing the rear of the FOREIGN OFFICE; at one time the crowds could gather freely outside and small boys, including the young Harold WILSON, could be photographed outside its famous front door. Access has been restricted since the assassination of Earl Mountbatten in 1979, but in February 1991 the IRA came close to wiping out John MAJOR's CABINET in a mortar attack on No.10 from the other side of WHITEHALL, causing some damage to the building. No.10 itself – it was renumbered from No.5 in 1778 – has 60 rooms, ranging from the ground-floor CABINET ROOM and ceremonial and meeting rooms to the offices of the GARDEN GIRLS and the Prime Ministerial FLAT, occupied most recently by Chancellor Gordon BROWN and his family. 130 people work in Number Ten, which is linked to NUMBER ELEVEN next door and the CABINET OFFICE. It has been heavily restored since CAMPBELL-BANNERMAN, who died there, branded it 'this rotten old barracks of a house' and Margot ASQUITH termed it 'an inconvenient house with three poor staircases'. Several premiers, including James CALLAGHAN, have only slept there when business required.

> More of a monastery than a power house.
>
> MARCIA WILLIAMS (*see* Lady FORKBENDER)

> From the street outside it is a classic example of British understatement. Today it harbours only Britain's crises, but once it was the eye of the storms that shook the world.
>
> JOE HAINES, Harold WILSON's press secretary

beer and sandwiches at Number Ten *See* BEER.

measuring the curtains for Number Ten The interest shown by the wife of a prospective Prime Minister in the prospect of her spouse's early arrival in Downing Street.

Number Eleven The official residence in Downing Street, next door to NUMBER TEN, of the CHANCELLOR OF THE EXCHEQUER. It is more of a home (Tony BLAIR lived there from 1997 because the FLAT in No.10 was too small for his young family), and there is less office space. The front halls of the two houses are connected by a corridor, so that the Chancellor can visit the Prime Minister without their consultations becoming public knowledge.

Number 11 bus *See* BUS.

Number Twelve 12 Downing Street, the house at the head of the street facing WHITEHALL which until 2001 was the office of the Government CHIEF WHIP and now houses the Number Ten press office, Strategic Communications Unit and Research & Information Unit. .

Nuremberg defence The argument by a functionary accused of wrongdoing that they are blameworthy because they were following orders from a superior. It was established at the NUREMBERG TRIALS that this is no defence in international law, but that has not stopped miscreants adopting it since. It was advanced by Lieutenant Richard Calley over the MY LAI MASSACRE, and by Private Lyndee England during her 2004 court martial for physical abuse and sexual humiliation of Iraqi detainees at ABU GHRAIB.

Nuremberg laws The NAZI decrees announced by HITLER at the close of the 1935 NUREMBERG RALLY, and unanimously ratified by the REICHSTAG, which made all Jews second-class citizens, closed the professions to them and forbade marriage or sexual relations between Jews and ARYANS; this last was said to be for 'the protection of German blood and honour'.

Nuremberg rallies The mass gatherings and parades organised by the NAZI party for PROPAGANDA purposes, first held in January and August 1923 and then annually from 1926, first in July and then in September, until 1938. Organised by Goebbels to generate nationalistic hysteria and intimidate the Nazis' opponents, they took an increasingly elaborate form, with massed torchlight parades and the use of anti-aircraft searchlights to surround the assembly with vertical columns of light, always culminating in a speech from the FÜHRER. The 1934 rally lasted a full week and was the subject of Leni Riefenstahl's *The Triumph of the Will*, perhaps the most powerful propaganda film ever made. The same year Hitler's architect Albert SPEER was commissioned to design a massive permanent auditorium for the rallies; its grandiose structure was never completed and it remains a bleak memorial to the evil of the THIRD REICH. The term 'Nuremberg rally' has come to be used derogatorily for any STAGE-MANAGED event involving unthinking adulation for a political leader; it was frequently applied by critics to the closing speeches Margaret THATCHER delivered at CONSERVATIVE PARTY conferences.

Nuremberg trials Primarily the trial for WAR CRIMES and GENOCIDE of 23 surviving NAZI leaders conducted at Nuremberg from September 1945 to May 1946 by an International Military tribunal of eight US, British, French and Soviet judges. Goering, Ribbentrop and nine others were sentenced to death, three were acquitted and the rest sentenced to terms of imprisonment. Goering and GAULEITER Robert Ley committed suicide before they could be executed; Rudolf HESS remained in Spandau Prison until his death in 1987. The Nuremberg tribunal established in international law (*see* NUREMBERG DEFENCE, above) that it is no defence for the accused to say simply that they were following orders. In the full series of Nuremberg trials of 177 Germans and Austrians over two years, 25 were sentenced to death, 117 imprisoned (20 for life) and 35 acquitted.

Nye The usually affectionate nickname for Aneurin BEVAN; 'Nye' is a corruption of his Welsh Christian name. In 1955, at the height of the strife between the left-wing Bevanites and the party leadership, ATTLEE told Labour's National executive in a Biblical pun:

> If thy Nye offend thee, pluck it out.

And in the 1959 election, Labour supporters in Northampton hoisted a placard reading:

> Repent, for the kingdom of Bevan is Nye!

O

O. O God, this sea is so great, and my boat is so small An old Breton prayer which President KENNEDY kept on his desk. It was given by Admiral Hyman Rickover to each NUCLEAR submarine commander.

O my darling Clementine The song, sung on a late-night Dublin television show by NORTHERN IRELAND Secretary Peter (later Lord) Brooke (1934–) in 1991, nearly ending his political career. Brooke was coaxed into song by the chat-show host Gay Byrne, unaware of the strength of reaction to the terrorist shooting of seven construction workers near the border earlier that evening. There was an outcry from Northern Ireland politicians; Brooke dramatically told the HOUSE OF COMMONS he was ready to resign, but John MAJOR insisted he stay on.

OAS (1) Secret Army Organisation (*Organisation de l'Armée Secrète*) The far-right French terrorist organisation, based in the military, which conducted a bombing campaign and plotted the assassination of President DE GAULLE because of his 'betrayal' of Algeria (*see* ALGÉRIE FRANÇAISE). The incident in which it came closest to success, in September 1961, prompted Frederick Forsyth's novel *The Day of the Jackal*. The OAS collapsed in 1962 after the arrest and trial for TREASON of its leader General Raoul Salan (1899–1984). (2) Organisation of American States. Founded in 1948 but based on earlier pan-American groups, the OAS was designed to bring together free governments for a common purpose. Canada has never joined, Cuba was expelled at WASHINGTON's insistence in 1962. With headquarters in Washington, the OAS has tended to side with the US on crucial issues, making it vulnerable to left-wing and nationalist criticism in Latin America. It has also been weakened over time by dictatorship and internal conflict in member states.

> They couldn't pour piss out of a shoe if the instructions were printed on the heel.
>
> LYNDON B. JOHNSON

oath. oath of allegiance At WESTMINSTER, the oath a newly-elected or re-elected MP (and peers at the start of each PARLIAMENT) must swear or affirm before he or she can sit and vote:

> I swear by Almighty God that I will be faithful and bear true allegiance to Her Majesty Queen Elizabeth, her heirs and successors according to law, so help me God.

SINN FEIN MPs have consistently refused to take the oath, and prior to the GOOD FRIDAY AGREEMENT were accorded none of the rights of membership. They are now allowed to take offices at Westminster and draw their salaries and allowances, but still cannot sit unless they take the oath. Not all MPs from mainland Britain take it seriously; in 1997 the republican Tony Banks pointedly crossed his fingers while it was administered.

oath of office In America, the oath all elected and appointed officials below the rank of President must take:

> I, AB, do solemnly swear [or affirm] that I will support and defend the Constitution of the United States against all enemies, foreign and domestic; that I will bear true faith and allegiance to the same; that I take this obligation freely, without any mental reservation or purpose of evasion; and that I will well and faithfully discharge the duties of the office on which I am about to enter. So help me God.

Presidential oath *See* I DO SOLEMNLY SWEAR.

Tennis Court oath The oath sworn in 1789 on a tennis court at VERSAILLES by representatives of the locked-out THIRD ESTATE. They declared themselves a NATIONAL ASSEMBLY, and vowed not to disband until a constitution was established for France. They got rather more than they bargained for in the form of the FRENCH REVOLUTION.

OAU Organisation of African Unity The original name of the AFRICAN UNION, which it officially became in 2002.

Object! At WESTMINSTER, when uttered by one (usually government) WHIP or backbencher, this word is usually enough to block a Private Member's BILL by preventing it being passed ON THE NOD in the Commons. In the US HOUSE OF REPRESENTATIVES, this cry from any member while the Clerk is reading the Consent CALENDAR will result in the relevant Bill being carried over until the Calendar is next called. If three or more members object, the Bill is stricken from the Calendar for the rest of that session.

Occupied Territories A collective term for the GAZA STRIP, GOLAN HEIGHTS and WEST BANK, captured by Israel from Egypt, Syria and Jordan respectively in the war of 1967. Control over them has been a stumbling block to hopes for peace in the Middle East ever since. *See* INTIFADA; LAND FOR PEACE; PEACE PROCESS.

October. October Manifesto The proclamation by TSAR Nicholas II, following the abortive REVOLUTION of 1905, that he would allow the establishment of an elected DUMA.

October Revolution The BOLSHEVIK revolution in October 1917 (November in the western calendar) in which LENIN came to power, overthrowing KERENSKY and the MENSHEVIKS. It ushered in 74 years of Communist rule.

October surprise A last-minute occurrence which wrong-foots one contender or other toward the close of a US Presidential election. Most recently the videotape issued by Osama BIN LADEN the weekend prior to the 2004 election was seen by pundits as potentially clinching a hitherto tight race for George W. BUSH. The original October surprise was the coup the Republicans feared during the closing stages of the 1980 campaign, in the form of a last-minute breakthrough that would have enabled the CARTER administration to take credit for the release of the Tehran HOSTAGES. In the event, Iran only agreed to free them on the last full day of Carter's presidency – and then held back until Ronald REAGAN had taken office. The term boomeranged on the first BUSH administration in 1991 when Gary Sick published a book alleging that during the 1980 campaign George Bush Snr, as Republican Vice Presidential nominee, and future CIA director William J. Casey collaborated with the hostages' captors to ensure they were not released until the Reagan/Bush ticket had defeated Carter. Bush strongly denied the charge, and a Congressional investigation cleared him.

Octobrists A constitutional CENTRE party in Russia supported by landlords and wealthy property interests, which was prominent in the DUMA between 1907 and 1914. It took its name from the OCTOBER MANIFESTO.

Ode to Joy The hymn to freedom by the German poet Schiller which Beethoven set to music as the final movement of his *Ninth (Choral) Symphony*. With its message that 'all peoples will be brothers' (*alle Menschen warden Brüder*), it has become the anthem of the EUROPEAN UNION.

Oder-Neisse line The German-Polish border imposed under Soviet pressure after WORLD WAR II which follows the rivers Oder and Neisse, leaving a large slice of pre-war Germany in Poland; in a parallel action, STALIN incorporated a similar belt of Polish territory into the Soviet Union (now Belarus). Poland and East Germany recognised it in 1950, but Western powers did not. In West Germany right-wingers and exiles from the lost territories pressed for their recovery, but after reUNIFICATION in 1990 Helmut Kohl's government formally accepted the border.

> A frontier of peace.
>
> NIKITA S. KHRUSHCHEV

ODPM Office of the Deputy Prime Minister. The UK government department created in 2002 for Deputy Prime Minister John Prescott (*see* TWO JAGS), with responsibility for planning, housing, local government and regional policy. Tony BLAIR set it up both to perpetuate Prescott's departmental power base in his chosen field of regional policy and English DEVOLUTION, but also out of necessity on the implosion of Stephen Byers' Department of Transport, Local Government and the Regions (*see* FUCKED).

OECD Organisation for Economic Co-Operation and Development. An international body to expand world trade, encourage growth and promote best practice in economic governance. Originally founded by Western European nations after WORLD WAR II as the Organisation for European Economic Co-operation, it was relaunched as OECD in 1960. Based in Paris, its 30 members include 22 EU and EFTA countries, the US, Canada, Mexico, Japan, South Korea, Australia, New Zealand and Turkey.

off. off-message *See* ON-MESSAGE.

off the cuff Extempore or impromptu comments, originally from the practice of waiters taking down orders by jotting them on their shirt cuffs. President NIXON once said that 'no television performance takes such careful preparation as an off the cuff attack'. Sometimes confused with:

off the record Comments made and information given to a reporter to give background, but not for specific use and certainly NOT FOR ATTRIBUTION to the source providing them. Those which may be quoted and sourced are said to be **on the record**.

off-year In US politics, any year in which there is not a Presidential ELECTION, including those even-numbered years when there is a MID-TERM election for CONGRESS.

Offa The guide dog, a German shepherd/golden retriever cross, who accompanied David Blunkett through eight years of UK Opposition politics after succeeding TED in 1988. His first public engagement was BBC television's *Question Time*, his sole political statement when he was sick during a 1992 press conference by Blunkett's colleague Bryan Gould. He retired aged eight in 1994, going to the Bristol veterinarian who had saved his life when he went down with stomach torsions during the 1992 election campaign.

office The state of holding a post of responsibility to the electors or to the state, also that post itself.

> It requires great patience and self-command to repress the loathing I feel towards a hungry crowd of unworthy office-seekers who often crowd my office.
>
> President JAMES K. POLK, *Diary*, 6 April 1848

office of honor or profit in the civil or uniformed services A position requiring the holder to take the US OATH OF OFFICE. Under the Constitution 'no person holding any office under the United States' can be a member of either House of CONGRESS.

office of profit under the Crown A UK CIVIL SERVICE or other PUBLIC SECTOR position whose holder is consequently disqualified from sitting in Parliament.

outer office The office which controls ACCESS to a head of government or senior member of an administration. Sir Les Patterson (the comedian Barry Humphreys) said of Australia's WHITLAM ministry:

> You can pick up your money from the Arab in the outer office.

in office, but not in power The withering jibe against John MAJOR's style of government delivered by Norman (now Lord) Lamont (1942–) in his PERSONAL STATEMENT to the COMMONS in June 1993 after his removal as CHANCELLOR OF THE EXCHEQUER.

private office In the UK and other COMMONWEALTH countries, a Minister's personal CIVIL SERVICE nerve-centre, which handles their diary and correspondence. The PERMANENT SECRETARY in each WHITEHALL department also has one.

seals of office *See* SEALS.

Tenure of Office Act *See* TENURE.

Officegate The scandal which forced the resignation in November 2001 of Scotland's FIRST MINISTER Henry McLeish (1948–). It arose from McLeish's failure, while a Labour MP at WESTMINSTER prior to DEVOLUTION, to declare to Parliamentary authorities the subletting of parts of his constituency office for which he was paid an allowance by the COMMONS. Though he derived no financial benefit from the arrangement, describing it as **'a muddle, not a fiddle'**, McLeish's hesitant and partial confirmation of the facts as they emerged eroded confidence in him and, in the face of continuing pressure from Conservative MSPs and the media, he resigned. Although the Procurator Fiscal ruled out a prosecution, McLeish also stood down in 2003 as MSP for Central Fife.

official. Official IRA *See* IRA.

Official Monster Raving Loony Party In Britain, a deliberately facetious party which contested BY-ELECTIONS and other high-profile elections as a joke from the early 1980s. Its main candidate was the top-hatted former rock singer Screaming Lord Sutch, who fought dozens of by-elections and in the 1987 general election opposed Margaret THATCHER. Over his career he polled some 13,000 votes in dozens of contests, and delivered the knockout blow to the SDP by outpolling it in the Bootle by-election of 1990.

> We will introduce a 99p coin to save change.
>
> OFFICIAL MONSTER RAVING LOONY PARTY manifesto, 2005

Official Report At WESTMINSTER, the formal name for HANSARD.

Official Secrets Act The legislation that enabled Britain to be governed with almost total secrecy for most of the 20th century. An Official Secrets Act was first passed in 1889, but the most notorious was enacted in a single afternoon in 1911 to counter a Germany spy scare. It not only imposed sanctions on the passing of information to a potential enemy, but through its CATCH-ALL Section 2 enforced an almost total blackout on the publication of any facts concerned with the functions of government. After a series of controversial trials of civil servants for LEAKing information to MPs and the media brought the Act into disrepute and the SPYCATCHER affair showed its limitations, it was relaxed in 1989, notably through the repeal of Section 2.

> The acme of clumsy and illibertarian legislation conceived in panic and passed in haste.
> PETER HENNESSEY

Official Unionists *See* UNIONIST.

official visit A visit to another country with full honours by a HEAD OF GOVERNMENT who is not the HEAD OF STATE.

officialdom The culture of government and BUREAUCRACY.

officialese A pejorative for the jargon of civil servants.

offset *See* TWO-WAY STREET.

OGPU *See* GPU.

Ohio Gang The friends and cronies of President Warren G. HARDING whose corruption, most spectacularly through the TEAPOT DOME affair, cast a cloud over his presidency; growing worry as he discovered the extent of their wrongdoing may have contributed to his death. Charles R. Forbes milked the Veterans Bureau for nearly $250 million for friendly contractors and suppliers. Colonel Thomas W. Miller as Alien Property Custodian allowed his office to distribute captured industrial patents at bargain prices. The Department of Justice under Harry Daugherty distributed liquor permits and pardons to criminals for hard cash, and Interior Secretary Albert B. Fall became the first Cabinet officer to be sent to jail for his role in Teapot Dome.

Ohio idea A keystone of the unsuccessful 1868 Democratic election campaign, headed by Presidential nominee Horatio Seymour. The brainchild of Congressman George H. Pendleton, it involved easing the post-CIVIL WAR financial burden, especially on farmers, by paying off the NATIONAL DEBT in GREENBACKS.

OH(B)MS On Her (Britannic) Majesty's Service. The initials on every envelope of government mail in Britain and some Commonwealth countries, and on official bags.

oil-for-food The UNITED NATIONS programme which between the 1991 GULF WAR and the overthrow of SADDAM HUSSEIN twelve years later allowed his regime, despite UN SANCTIONS, to sell some oil in return for food and medical supplies. Designed to save the population from starvation and disease, it in fact became a vehicle for Saddam and his henchmen to skim off billions of dollars. They used much of the money to bribe UN officials and key opinion formers (worldwide but especially in France and Russia) to lobby against continued sanctions, while nominal and substandard relief supplies were distributed. Investigations after the fall of Saddam revealed a fraudulent exercise involving one senior UN official and several international fixers including Tongsun Park of KOREAGATE fame. UN Secretary General Kofi Annan was embarrassed by connections to his son Kojo. In May 2005 a US Senate committee named the newly-elected RESPECT MP George Galloway as a recipient of oil vouchers from Saddam; Galloway, who had won libel damages from *The Daily Telegraph* for alleging on the basis of different documents that he had been an agent for Saddam, fiercely denied the charge (*see* LION OF THE BRITISH PARLIAMENT).

Oireachtas The official, Irish-language name for the Parliament of the Irish Republic (*see* DAIL EIREANN; LEINSTER HOUSE; SEANAD).

Oklahoma City bombing The most devastating act of terrorism in the United States prior to 9/11, the bomb which destroyed the Alfred Murrah Federal Building in Oklahoma City on 19 April 1995, killing 168 people. The blast was initially blamed on Middle Eastern terrorists, causing a BACKLASH against Arab-Americans, but within 48 hours charges were brought against Timothy McVeigh, a 27-year-old ex-soldier linked to the extreme right-wing MICHIGAN MILITIA. McVeigh was convicted of all charges on 2 June 1997, sentenced to death and executed by lethal injection more than six years later. A remorseful Terry Nicholls, believed to have planned the operation and McVeigh's getaway, was sentenced in August 2004 to life without parole on 161 murder charges; he was already serving life on federal charges of conspiracy and involuntary manslaughter of eight federal officers who died in the blast.

OLAF Not a Viking, but the **Office de Lutte AntiFraude**, the EUROPEAN COMMISSION's anti-fraud watchdog. While it has not been able to stem the tide of fraud against the EU's institutions, its investigations were instrumental in forcing the resignation of Jacques Santer's Commission in 1999 over the CRESSON AFFAIR and precipitating action over irregularities at EUROSTAT four years later.

Old. Old Bullion The nickname of **Thomas Hart Benton** (1782–1858), one of the first US Senators for Missouri who, after seeing the misery caused by the crash of the Second Bank of the United States in 1819, campaigned throughout his political life against an all-powerful national bank and for 'hard money'.

Old 8 to 7 One of many derogatory nicknames accorded **Rutherford Hayes** (1822–93), 19th President of the United States (Democrat, 1877–81), because of the circumstances in which he took office. In the 1876 ELECTION he lost in the popular vote to Samuel Tilden, who seemed certain of victory with 184 votes in the ELECTORAL COLLEGE to Hayes' 165. Twenty votes (in Florida, Louisiana and South Carolina, plus one in Oregon) were disputed, and just one would give Tilden victory. The Republican NATIONAL COMMITTEE, and subsequently the party's majority in CONGRESS, colluded with massive fraud to hand the results in all states to Hayes. The crowning event was the 8–7 vote by an ELECTORAL COMMISSION of both Houses of Congress, on straight party lines in favour of Hayes. Tilden retired from politics, saying: 'I shall receive from posterity the credit for having been elected to the highest position in the gift of the people, without any of the cares and responsibilities of the office.' Prior to his election, Hayes had a reputation as a man of duty. While serving in the Army he had refused to campaign for his House seat, saying: 'An officer fit for duty who at this crisis would abandon his post to electioneer ought to be scalped.' In office he proved, according to Sen. John Sherman, 'a very modest man, but a very able one', and Hayes felt he had done well, saying: 'No one ever left the Presidency with less regret, less disappointment, fewer heartburnings, or general content with the result of his term (in his own heart, I mean)'. But the popular verdict was inevitably harsh:

> Mr Hayes came in by a majority of one, and goes out by unanimous consent. ANON.

Old EOB The Old Executive Office Building next to the WHITE HOUSE in WASHINGTON, which originally housed the STATE DEPARTMENT. An office there is not as prestigious as one in the WEST WING of the White House; Mike Deaver said that people would work in closets in the White House rather than be banished to 'Death Row' in the Old EOB where there was no ACCESS to the President. Francis X. Clines called the EOB 'a mass of Victorian tiles and granite that resembles a battleship in the rain and a wedding cake in the sun'; President TRUMAN simply termed it 'the greatest monstrosity in America'.

Old Europe The notion that carries for American politicians the same resonances that 'ANGLO-SAXONS' does for the French: the idea that unlike young, vibrant America the nations of Europe are effete and wedded to diplomacy rather than resolute action, and are incapable of responding to the challenges of modern times. It is usually thought rather than articulated out loud, hence the furore when the expression was used by George W. BUSH's Defense Secretary Donald Rumsfeld (*see* UNKNOWNS) on the eve of the 2003 IRAQ WAR to describe the attitudes of France and Germany, who were working (successfully) to block US and British efforts to gain UNITED NATIONS approval for the use of force. Rumsfeld's comment did not just infuriate its targets; Spain's Prime Minister José Maria Aznar, a staunch supporter of the US-led COALITION, urged Bush to gag Rumsfeld lest he make matters even worse. Intriguingly the words that caused such offence had first been used by Thomas JEFFERSON, who wrote in 1816:

> Old Europe will have to lean on our shoulders, and to hobble along by our side, under the monkish trammels of priests and kings, as best she can. What a colossus we shall be.

Old Glory Affectionate term for the STARS AND STRIPES, devised in 1831 by the Salem, New England seaman William Driver. Saluting the flag as it was unfurled at the start of a voyage to Asia, he said: 'I name thee Old Glory.' The phrase caught on among troops in the UNION army during the CIVIL WAR.

old guard (1) The most committed and determined, and often the most reactionary, stalwarts of a political movement or culture. The name stems from Napoleon's Old Guard, who at Waterloo mounted one last despairing charge in an attempt to reverse the fortunes of their Emperor's final battle; when urged to surrender, they responded: 'The Guard dies, but it does not surrender.' (2) In Australia, the 25,000-man right-wing organisation of armed volunteers, mainly ex-service small farmers, which formed up in the New South Wales countryside to confront the inter-war Labor premier Jack Lang. In 1932 one of its most dashing figures, Captain Francis de Groot, galloped ahead of Lang to slice the tape and open the Sydney Harbour Bridge.

Old Hall of the House *See* STATUARY HALL.

Old Hickory The affectionate nickname of

Andrew Jackson (1767–1845), 7th President of the United States (Democrat, 1829–37). A frontier lawyer born in poverty and a Revolutionary volunteer at fourteen, he won national fame as the hero of a campaign against the Creek Indians and as victorious general of the Battle of New Orleans. His troops named him after hickory, the toughest wood they knew. In 1827 Thomas D. Arnold, an anti-Jackson Congressional candidate, said of him: 'He spent the prime of his life in gambling, in cock-fighting, in horse-racing, and to cap it all tore from a husband the wife of his bosom.' Jackson was combatively loyal to his pipe-smoking wife Rachel, whom he had rescued from a previous unhappy marriage, wedding her when he mistakenly believed her divorce was through. He once killed a man in a duel for casting a slur on her. When any man referred to her, Jackson would exclaim: 'Great God! Do you mention *her* sacred name?' And Sen. Thomas Hart Benton (OLD BULLION) reminisced:

> Yes, I had a fight with Jackson. A fellow was hardly in the fashion who hadn't. But mine was different from his other fights – it wasn't about Rachel.

Jackson was thus a far cry from the gentlemen who preceded him in the WHITE HOUSE, but rose through the HOUSE and the SENATE and a narrow defeat by John Quincy ADAMS in 1824 (*see* CORRUPT BARGAIN) to gain his revenge in 1828 and become the first President to be the 'people's choice' of the new nation. In 1824 he said of himself: 'I can command a body of men in a rough way, but I am not fit to be President.' And JEFFERSON warned: 'I feel much alarmed at the thought of seeing General Jackson President. He is one of the most unfit men I know for such a place.' His fears seemed borne out when frontiersmen flooded into Washington to celebrate Jackson's INAUGURATION in hillbilly fashion, an event the capital has still not forgotten. Daniel Webster noted: 'I never saw such a crowd here before. Persons have come 500 miles to see General Jackson, and they really seem to think that the country is rescued from some dreadful danger.' Jackson's presidency, though his methods were rough and ready, was a success. It was marred by his wife's death soon after he entered the White House, an assassination attempt (the first on a President) in 1835 and ferocious clashes with the backers of the second Bank of the United States, whose monopoly he tried to break. 'The bank is trying to kill me, but I will try to kill it,' Jackson exclaimed. He declared war on the Senate after it rejected his nomination of Martin van Buren (*see below*) as Minister to Britain, exclaiming: 'By the Eternal, I'll smash them.' Nor was he afraid of the SUPREME COURT. When Chief Justice Marshall urged him to secure the release, ordered by the Court, of two missionaries imprisoned in Georgia for living among the Cherokee, Jackson stood firm, saying: 'John Marshall has made his decision. Now let *him* enforce it!' On leaving office, Jackson declared: 'I have only two regrets – that I have not shot Henry Clay or hanged John C. Calhoun.' *See also* the PEOPLE'S PRESIDENT.

> A barbarian who cannot write a sentence of grammar and can hardly spell his own name.
>
> JOHN QUINCY ADAMS, 1833

> Haughty and sterile intellectualism opposed him. Musty reaction disapproved of him. Hollow and outworn traditionalism shook a trembling finger at him – all but the people of the United States.
>
> FRANKLIN D. ROOSEVELT

Old Kinderhook The nickname of **Martin van Buren** (1782–1862), 8th President of the United States (Democrat, 1837–41), taken from his home in New York state. The first President born under the Stars and Stripes, van Buren was a lawyer and, as organiser of the 'Albany regency', one of the earliest MACHINE politicians. He served in the SENATE, as Governor of New York, Secretary of State and Jackson's (*see previous entry*) Vice President before defeating four different Whig opponents in 1836 for the Presidency – the last Vice President to move up to the WHITE HOUSE by election until George BUSH Snr Jackson hailed him as 'a true man with no guile', but his subdued style was in marked contrast to his rumbustious predecessor. John Randolph wrote that van Buren 'rowed to his object with muffled oars', while John C. Calhoun declared: 'He is not of the race of the lion or the tiger; he belongs to the lower order – the fox.' In the early stages of his presidency he was known as 'Matty Van' and 'the LITTLE MAGICIAN', but as the DEPRESSION of 1837 took hold the Whigs branded him 'Martin van Ruin' and 'Van, Van, the used-up man'. Van Buren was said to live in 'oriental splendour' – which gave an easy target to the LOG CABIN AND HARD CIDER campaign of William Henry Harrison and John Tyler which swept van Buren from office in 1840. Unusually, he made two attempts at a comeback, seeking the Vice Presidential nomination in 1844 and standing as FREE SOIL candidate in 1848.

The Old Man, the Old Flag and the Old Policy The slogan on which the Canadian Premier John Macdonald's Conservatives fought his last election, in 1891; Macdonald's majority was sharply reduced and he died, exhausted, within months.

Old Man Eloquent The nickname won by John Quincy ADAMS during his lengthy (1830–48) career as a Congressman after losing the Presidency. He was a greater success in the HOUSE than as President, and himself said: 'No election or appointment conferred on me ever gave me so much pleasure.' He earned the sobriquet during his nine-year campaign to repeal the GAG RULE against the discussion of anti-slavery petitions. When the House finally backed him, in 1844, he exclaimed: 'Blessed, forever blessed, be the name of God!' He died in the CAPITOL in 1848.

Old Oil-Jug The nickname of Felix Walker, an 1820s Congressman from North Carolina, earned for his flowing speeches in praise of his native Buncombe County (*see* BUNKUM).

Old Queen Street The headquarters, close to the HOUSES OF PARLIAMENT, into which the LABOUR PARTY moved in August 2002 on leaving MILLBANK. The move was largely made on grounds of cost, but it also gave the party the opportunity to break with the culture of SPIN with which Millbank was indelibly associated. The title of the building stemmed from its address, 16 Old Queen Street, not from anyone's sexual orientation.

Old Red Socks A derogatory term for the Pope among hard-line Protestants in ULSTER.

Old Rough and Ready The nickname of **Zachary Taylor** (1784–1850), 12th President of the United States (Whig, 1849–50). An Indian fighter who became a national hero as a Brigadier-General in the MEXICAN WAR, he was thus named by his soldiers for his sloppy uniform, his cursing and his tobacco-chewing. Daniel Webster described him as 'an illiterate frontier colonel'; Taylor himself had never voted in a Presidential election until nominated in 1848. He classed himself 'a Whig, but not an ultra-Whig', and once said: 'The idea that I should become President seems too visionary to require serious answer. It has never entered my head, nor is it likely to enter the head of any sane person.' His wife Margaret regretted his nomination as 'a plot to deprive me of his society and to shorten his life by unnecessary care and responsibility.' Taylor was elected to the WHITE HOUSE after the rival Democrats split, and began robustly. When asked how he would treat SECESSIONists, he replied: 'Persons taken in rebellion against the Union I would hang, with less reluctance than I hanged deserters and spies in Mexico.' But he died after fifteen months in office, through eating too much in blazing heat during the Fourth of July celebrations.

Old soldiers never die; they just fade away The most quoted phrase from Gen. Douglas MACARTHUR's address to a JOINT SESSION of the US CONGRESS on 19 April 1951 after his dismissal by President TRUMAN. MacArthur probably heard it first at West Point, from which he graduated in 1903; it is a soldiers' parody of a 19th-century gospel hymn '*Kind words can never die*'.

Old Squiffy *see* ASQUITH.

Old Veto The title conferred by his Democrat opponents on **John Tyler** (1790–1862), 10th President of the United States (Whig, 1841–45). A lawyer who served in both HOUSES OF CONGRESS and as Governor of Virginia, Tyler was elected Vice President in 1840 as junior partner in the TIPPECANOE AND TYLER TOO ticket. The first Vice President to assume the Presidency, when Harrison died (some argued he was not actually President), he earned his nickname by VETOing a then-record nine BILLS in less than four days of office; he survived the first serious attempt to IMPEACH a President, for 'gross usurpation of powers', on a resolution from ex-President John Quincy ADAMS after the Whig Party expelled him and all but one of his Cabinet resigned. Yet despite his differences with the Congress over STATES' RIGHTS, where he sided with the South, he initiated landmark legislation including the LOG CABIN BILL. Charles Dickens commented that he 'looked somewhat worn and anxious, and well he might be, being at war with everybody'. Widowed in the WHITE HOUSE, Tyler caused a sensation by marrying 23-year-old Julia Gardner, a Washington beauty 29 years younger than himself; she bore him seven children.

Ole Miss An affectionate nickname for the University of Mississippi, scene in 1962 of an episode that gained worldwide notoriety. When James Meredith became the first black student to qualify for admission, the university refused him and the SEGREGATIONIST Governor Ross Barnett intervened to bar him, despite Meredith obtaining a court order. Four times Meredith failed to register, blocked by Barnett personally (the last time with State troopers and a crowd of 2500 whites). The fifth time Meredith, now escorted by US marshals, succeeded – but the ensuing riot by white students left two people dead and 375 injured, including 166 marshals. It took 3000 Federal troops and National Guardsmen to restore order. Meredith was shot and wounded in 1966 while leading a march encouraging blacks in Mississippi to register to vote; the university was soon fully integrated.

oligarchy In Greek, government by the few. In common usage, a clique that keeps power in its own hands, regarding others as incapable of exercising it or as a threat. The **oligarchs** are the handful of entrepreneurs who seized, by fair means or foul, the opportunities presented by the collapse of Communism in Russia to seize the commanding heights of the economy and generate enormous wealth for themselves. Allowed a free hand by Boris Yeltsin, they were forced onto the defensive by his successor Vladimir Putin, who forced some into exile and had others arrested, breaking up the media empire of Boris Berezovsky and virtually bankrupting the oil conglomerate Yukos, with seismic effects on world oil prices. While there was little doubt the oligarchs had committed excesses and appropriated funds lent or donated by the West to rescue the Russian economy, there were plausible complaints that the crackdown was an attempt by supporters of the old regime to stifle a genuine capitalism that was emerging.

Olive Tree coalition The centre-left grouping in Italy that was elected in April 1996, the first left-wing ADMINISTRATION in half a century. Comprising GREENS, Communists and former Communists, it was led by Professor Romano Prodi, later President of the EUROPEAN COMMISSION.

Olympia rallies The mass rallies of BLACKSHIRTS in the mid-1930s at Olympia, the West London exhibition centre, at which Sir Oswald MOSLEY attempted to emulate HITLER's feats of mesmerism and demagogy. The British public found them partly threatening, partly ridiculous.

Omagh bombing The worst terrorist atrocity in NORTHERN IRELAND, committed on 14 August 1998 by dissident Republicans after the worst of the TROUBLES were over and the peace process was well under way. This attack on the GOOD FRIDAY AGREEMENT killed 28 Saturday-afternoon shoppers and injured 330; the Real IRA claimed it was directed against a 'commercial target'. Public revulsion triggered a ceasefire by INLA, which had stayed outside the peace process, and a government/Republican crackdown on terrorism. Colm Murphy was jailed for fourteen years in Dublin in 2002 for being part of the conspiracy (the conviction was overturned and a retrial ordered in 2005); Sean Gerárd Hoey was charged with the murders themselves in May 2005. The UK government has funded a civil action by the victims against suspects against whom there was not enough admissible evidence for a criminal trial, most of the proof coming from intercepts of mobile-phone conversations.

OMB The US Office of Management and Budget, which prepares the BUDGET and controls the ADMINISTRATION's legislative agenda. For any BILL with financial implications put forward by the EXECUTIVE BRANCH, OMB's endorsement is essential, and its director normally wields great influence in the WHITE HOUSE. The Bureau was established by President HARDING in 1921 as the Bureau of the Budget, and given its present name in 1970. It is known in WASHINGTON as **'TOMB'** because of the near impossibility of getting anything out of it.

> The real switchboard of the Executive Branch.
> DAVID STOCKMAN

ombudsman (Swed. proxy) An impartial official who takes up complaints from the public to protect the rights of the individual against infringement by the state. The post originated in Sweden, which has had an ombudsman since 1809; Denmark followed in 1955, Norway and New Zealand in 1962 and the UK in 1967 (official title: the **Parliamentary Commissioner for Administration**); the British Ombudsman can only act on complaints fed to him through a Member of Parliament. Ombudsmen have since been appointed in Britain for local government and the National Health Service. Many other western countries and several American States have followed suit, though not the US federal government, largely because members of CONGRESS see it as a threat.

OMOV The abbreviation for 'one member, one VOTE' used by activists in Britain's LABOUR PARTY and trade union movement as pressure for the balloting of individual members in leadership elections and on policy issues grew from the mid-1980s.

OMOV is the basis of reforms in the party that transferred power from trade union BLOCK VOTES and constituency activists to individual members. Before the process began, Neil KINNOCK joked:

> There is one man, one vote in this party, and I am the man.

John SMITH took up OMOV after becoming leader in 1992, clashing with union bosses who were accused of being the tail wagging the dog; however, John MAJOR told the COMMONS:

> The unions are the dog, and Labour are the lamp-post.

OMOV scraped through Labour's 1993 conference in the teeth of strong resistance from the giant T&G and GMB unions. Smith's victory took much private arm-twisting to win over union votes, a private threat from him to resign and a devastating speech from John Prescott (*see* TWO JAGS) whose fractured nature made it almost unreportable. Matthew Parris wrote of Prescott's speech in *The Times*:

> He went twelve rounds with the English language and left it slumped, bleeding, over the ropes.

The vote appeared to pave the way for a modernised party under Smith's leadership. However, Smith died the following May, and at the special conference in April 1995 over Tony BLAIR's plan to rewrite CLAUSE FOUR it became clear that several unions intended to ignore the OMOV decision where their role in Labour's decision-making was concerned. In the subsequent decade, both they and Blair ignored the OMOV rule when it suited them.

on. on his bike The remark for which Norman Tebbit (*see* CHINGFORD SKINHEAD) will best be remembered. At the 1982 CONSERVATIVE PARTY conference Tebbit, then Employment Secretary, responded to public unrest over high unemployment by saying:

> My father did not wait around. He didn't riot. He got on his bike and looked for work, and he kept looking until he found it.

This angered trade union leaders, the left and militant youth groups, but many voters felt it logical and justified.

on message Being completely in tune with, and able to regurgitate, one's party leadership's current position on any issue. The term originated in the 1992 US Presidential campaign with James Carville (*see* RAGIN' CAJUN), and was taken up by NEW LABOUR; anyone regarded as OFF MESSAGE instantly lost the trust of Tony BLAIR's inner circle. When in 1999 police and immigration officers raiding a Thai massage parlour in Northampton apprehended the Labour MP Joe Ashton, the *Sun* suggested he had thought the party wanted him to be 'on massage.'

on the bell A house, flat, office or restaurant within DIVISION BELL range of the PALACE OF WESTMINSTER, i.e. where a division bell is fitted and from which, when it rings, an MP can be sure of getting to the COMMONS in time to vote. In practice this means just under twelve minutes' walk. MPs with money often look for a home 'on the bell' – a factor which inflates property prices in Westminster.

on the knocker A British, mainly Labour, term for door-to-door campaigning, covering both CANVASSING and KNOCKING-UP. It harks back to the time when every door had a knocker but few had a bell.

on the nod The passage of an item of legislation without either discussion or a vote. At WESTMINSTER the nod in question is one of approval from the SPEAKER, as a Private Member's BILL makes progress without debate at the close of business on a Friday in the absence of a cry of 'OBJECT!' from a Government WHIP or any backbencher.

on the record *See* OFF THE RECORD.

oncer The political equivalent of a one-hit wonder, a mainly Australian term for an elected representative who wins a seat he or she is unlikely to retain and who, from the moment of election, looks incapable of winning a second term.

one. 1–800 The format of a broadcast public discussion between a US Presidential candidate and individual voters who can CALL IN on a toll-free (1–800) telephone line. First used by former California Governor Jerry Brown (*see* SPACE CADET) during his abortive quest for the 1992 Democratic NOMINATION, it was used that summer to great effect by H. Ross PEROT when campaigning as an UNDECLARED CANDIDATE.

one-club golfer The implementer of an economic policy which relies entirely on one element of control, ignoring all others. The phrase was coined by Sir Edward HEATH c. 1985 to describe Chancellor Nigel Lawson's total reliance on interest rate policy.

one-hour rule The rule passed in 1841 by the US HOUSE OF REPRESENTATIVES to end FILIBUSTERS by imposing a one-hour limit on members' speeches. It was criticised for hastening the end of true oratory in the

House, Sen. Thomas Hart Benton terming it 'an eminent instance of permanent injury done to free institutions'.

one-house Bill *See* BILL.

one-house veto *See* VETO.

one-liner (1) A jocular throw-away line in a politician's speech that is designed to elicit immediate laughter and then stick in the public memory. (2) At WESTMINSTER, a one-line WHIP, in practice an indication to legislators by the BUSINESS MANAGERS that they need not be present.

one man's wage increase is another man's price increase Harold WILSON's dictum on the inflationary effect of wage increases, uttered in January 1970 when his Labour government was trying to curb pay claims after a period of WAGE RESTRAINT.

one member, one vote *See* OMOV.

one-minute speeches Speeches on any subject that members of the US HOUSE OF REPRESENTATIVES are permitted to make at the start of a legislative day, provided they last no more than 60 seconds.

One Nation (1) A liberal Toryism that believes in perpetuating DISRAELI's paternalist approach. Under Margaret THATCHER it was seen as code for WETness, though her successor John MAJOR was proud to use the label. In January 1996 she caused consternation by declaring of One-Nation Tories that 'because of their views on European federalism they would be better described as "no-nation conservatives"'. (2) A group of Conservative MPs formed in 1950 to press for a greater commitment by the party to the social services. Its pamphlet, *One Nation*, was published that October; after the Conservatives under CHURCHILL returned to power a year later, it strongly influenced government social policy. *Compare* MIDDLE WAY. (3) In Australia, the RACIST party led by Pauline Hanson, a former chip shop owner, which polled 24% of the vote in Queensland in June 1998 and made an impact at national level. It lost its Parliamentary representation at the Federal election later that year despite polling almost 1 million votes, and faded as the Howard ministry took an increasingly strong line against admitting ASYLUM SEEKERS. Mrs Hanson was sentenced to three years' jail in August 2003 for dishonestly obtaining almost £200,000 in election funding by misrepresenting supporters as paid-up party members, but was freed three months later on appeal.

one of us Margaret THATCHER's ultimate term of approval for a colleague or subordinate, denoting a fellow true believer in her own free-MARKET economic theories. Hugo Young chose it as the title of his acclaimed Thatcher biography, first published in 1989. Mrs Thatcher's use of the term in its rigidly exclusive sense may have been new, but the phrase itself was not; when the BEVERIDGE REPORT was published in 1943, Labour's Hugh Dalton wrote that Beveridge, a Liberal, had produced a 'fine, stimulating document', even though 'he is not one of us'.

one-party state *See* PARTY.

one settler, one bullet The motto of the military arm of South Africa's PAC; after the party polled less than 2% of the vote in multiracial elections in 1994, it was changed to 'one child, one education'.

one-term President *See* PRESIDENT.

Oom Paul The Afrikaner nickname for Stephanus Johannes **Paulus Kruger** (1825–1904), who led the revolt against Britain's annexation of the Transvaal in 1877, and as the territory's President in 1883 resisted the incursion of *Uitlander* gold prospectors and settlers. His rout of the JAMESON RAID in 1896 and the KRUGER TELEGRAM in which Kaiser Wilhelm II congratulated him stoked IMPERIALIST feeling in Britain, paving the way for the BOER WAR. When war broke out, Kruger was eclipsed and moved to Switzerland.

OPEC Organisation of Petroleum Exporting Countries. An international cartel of (mainly Middle Eastern) oil producers formed in 1960 to combat exploitation by Western companies, largely through NATIONALISING member states' production and regulating output. Based in Vienna, it sets process and production levels for roughly 30% of the world's supply. OPEC became a household word in 1973 when, after acquiescing for years in low producer prices, it quadrupled them, triggering world INFLATION and economic slowdown. OPEC's pricing policy has caused a significant transfer of wealth from industrialised nations to developing countries with oil deposits, though in the present decade it has influenced prices indirectly by setting production levels for its members. OPEC's members include Algeria, Ecuador, Gabon, Indonesia, Iraq, Iran, Kuwait, Nigeria, Qatar, Saudi Arabia, the United Arab Emirates and Venezuela. The US, Russia, other former Soviet republics and Britain have never belonged.

open. open convention In US politics, a party's nominating CONVENTION at which all

DELEGATES are released from the CANDIDATES they were sent to support so that they can make an independent choice. In 1980 Sen. Edward KENNEDY sought to frustrate Jimmy CARTER's renomination by calling for an open Democratic convention; when he was voted down he withdrew from the race, but Carter had to make concessions on the PLATFORM.

open diplomacy The demand made by Woodrow WILSON in the first of his Fourteen Points for a peace settlement and new order in Europe at the end of WORLD WAR I : **'Open covenants of peace openly arrived at**, after which there shall be no private international understandings of any kind.' It was an attempt to stamp out the practice of secret treaties, under which nations agreed to carve up third parties' territory or give each other a free hand to make territorial gains. Yet the VERSAILLES Treaty itself, though its terms were made public, was negotiated in secret, mainly by Wilson, CLEMENCEAU and LLOYD GEORGE. With the rise of the dictators and the onset of WORLD WAR II, Wilson's first point, like most of the other thirteen, proved a dead letter.

Open Door policy The China policy devised in 1899 by US Secretary of State John Hay, and reluctantly agreed to – though only after the shock of the BOXER REBELLION – by Britain, Germany, Russia, France, Italy and Japan. Its essence was that none of these nations claiming a sphere of influence in China should interfere with the trade of others, thus ensuring American traders equal access. The Open Door policy checked the scramble for Chinese trade and territory, largely because of generous payments to the countries concerned, including America, from the Chinese Treasury.

open government The doctrine and practice of the workings of government being conducted in the public eye, rather than behind a cloak of secrecy. In WASHINGTON, the FREEDOM OF INFORMATION Act has for three decades given an insight into decision-making – though not the whole picture, most major scandals still being revealed through LEAKS to the press. In Britain the THATCHER government embarked on a limited 'open government' initiative in the early 1980s, but WHITEHALL retained its climate of obsessive secrecy even after the repeal of Section 2 of the OFFICIAL SECRETS ACT, John MAJOR's publication of QUESTIONS OF PROCEDURE FOR MINISTERS and Labour's subsequent enactment of more modest Freedom of Information legislation than America's.

> The Government being the people's business, it necessarily follows that its operations should be at all times open to the public view. Publicity is therefore as essential to honest ADMINISTRATION as freedom of speech is to representative government.
>
> WILLIAM JENNINGS BRYAN, US Secretary of State, 1915

open housing The popular US term for the ending of racial discrimination in housing, notably against black Americans. The SENATE's blocking in 1966 of a BILL for open housing was one of the few reverses for President JOHNSON's CIVIL RIGHTS programme. But a similar law was passed two years later, forbidding discrimination in the rental or sale of housing on the basis of race, colour, religion or ethnic origin. LBJ's last great legislative victory brought an end to major abuses, but discrimination continues in subtle forms.

open letter Ostensibly a letter sent by a politician to another person (in Britain, frequently by a Minister or MP to his or her constituency chairman, or by a group of eminent people to the Prime Minister), but in practice purely a device for its contents to be released to the media.

open mike One of the greatest pitfalls of modern politics: the radio microphone or public address system left switched on which catches a politician's unguarded comments. Ronald REAGAN's 'Bomb Russia' GAFFE is a prime example, as was his statement during a sound test heard by reporters in November 1982:

> My fellow Americans, I've talked to you on a number of occasions about the economic problems and opportunities our nation faces. And I'm prepared to tell you, it's a hell of a mess . . . we're not connected to the press now yet, are we?

In 1991 George BUSH Snr, in conversation with Arnold Schwarzenegger (*see* GOVERNATOR), said of microphones generally:

> These, they're dangerous. They trap you, especially those furry ones [the roving mikes used by TV news crews] . . . it's the furry guys that get you into real trouble.

Bush's son ignored his advice, dropping his own clanger when he referred on an open mike to the *Wall Street Journal* reporter Adam Clymer as a 'MAJOR LEAGUE ASSHOLE'.

open selection A bone of contention during the brief lifetime of the Liberal-SDP ALLIANCE. One faction wanted a central decision on which party's candidate should fight each constituency; the other, which eventually prevailed, wanted the choice made locally through 'open selection' by members of both parties.

open skies Initially, the policy of airline DEREGULATION initiated in America by the CARTER administration, with no-frills airlines competing with, and in some cases driving out of business, the established carriers. In the 1990s 'open skies' became code for the right of US airlines to operate unlimited services to and from any airport in Europe, with America retaining as many as possible of its limits on foreign carriers; it also implied constraints on foreign ownership of US domestic airlines and the **'Fly America'** rule which bars US officials on government business from using foreign airlines if the route is served by an American carrier. The EU has been keen to conclude an 'open skies' agreement with WASHINGTON covering all member states, but the UK has persevered with its efforts to negotiate a bilateral successor to BERMUDA 2.

an open mind is like an open sewer A typical dictum of Ernest BEVIN, the blunt former trade union leader who from 1945 to 1951 was one of Britain's most respected Foreign Secretaries.

opening to the left or right A move by a party or leader onto the territory of another, either by shifting their own ground or through some kind of arrangement with the other party. It embodies an element of outflanking, or of STEALING AN OPPONENT'S CLOTHES.

opera. The opera ain't over till the fat lady sings The phrase coined by the San Antonio sportswriter Dan Cook c. 1976 to emphasise the importance of playing on till the very last moment; it echoed an old Texas saying 'The rodeo ain't over till the bull riders ride'. Washington Bullets' basketball coach Dick Motta took it up as his motto in the 1978 NBA playoffs; it was taken up by politicians, and especially Presidential contenders, to stress that no candidate is home and dry (or defeated) until the final vote has been cast and counted.

Operation Candour The campaign conducted by President NIXON to clear himself of allegations of complicity in the WATERGATE burglary and cover-up. During the second half of 1973 he professed to be open and frank, particularly about the zeal with which he claimed to be trying to ascertain the truth, while concealing his true involvement.

Operation Push The drive to wean INNER-CITY black children away from drugs and toward a future of achievement, spearheaded in Chicago in the mid-1970s by the Rev. Jesse JACKSON. His slogan was:

> It's not the dope in your veins – it's the hope in your brains.

opinion. opinion-formers The editors, columnists, television pundits, academics, members of THINK TANKS and others who can shape public opinion and thus need to be cultivated. *See also* QUOTE SLUTS.

opinion polls (*see also under* POLL) The surveys of national and local voting intentions, and of public attitudes on key issues, which have come to dominate political life, especially during election campaigns. The first such polling, on a sociological basis, was carried out by George S. Gallup in America just before WORLD WAR II. Australia's first polls were conducted in 1941 by the Roy Morgan Research Centre; they were first used in a British election in 1945, though Mass Observation surveys had given the wartime government valuable insight into public attitudes and the state of morale. Rosalynn CARTER gave the definitive politician's attitude to polls during her husband's presidency, saying: 'Don't worry about polls – but if you do, don't admit it.' *France-Soir* once editorialised that 'there is as much difference between an opinion poll and an election as between shooting blank cartridges and live ones', and Margaret THATCHER declared: 'If you are guided by opinion polls, you are not practising leadership – you are practising followship.'

Opium Wars The 19th-century conflicts during which Britain established influence over much of China. The first was fought over the right of British merchants to sell opium to the Chinese; it ended in the 1842 Treaty of Nanking which ceded Hong Kong to Britain (*see* 1997).

> A war more unjust in its origins, a war more calculated to cover this country with permanent disgrace, I do not know, and I have not read of.
>
> GLADSTONE

A second war broke out after the CRIMEAN WAR; Britain's influence was confirmed in 1858 with the Treaty of Tientsin, but the fighting continued for several years.

opportunist A politician who seizes chances for political gains, easy popularity and self-advancement (*see also* CAREERIST) rather than following the course of principle. The word originated in 19th-century French politics and was adopted with enthusiasm by Communists, eager to denigrate opponents especially within their own ranks. Around

1900 LENIN wrote: 'Axelrod and Martov have dropped into the opportunist wing of our Party . . . They have to repeat opportunist phrases to seek some kind of justification for their position.' The word is now in everyday use among politicians and their critics generally.

opposition The task of opposing the government of the day within the confines of democracy, a position institutionalised in the WESTMINSTER system into **His** or **Her Majesty's Loyal Opposition**. The phrase, minus the 'loyal', was first applied to the principal opposition party in 1826 by the English radical politician John Cam (later Baron) Hobhouse (1786–1869); it is usually shortened to **The Opposition**. It is said that **'the duty of the Opposition is to oppose'**, or more fully, as put by an early 19th-century English Whig named Tierney: 'The duty of an opposition is very simple: to oppose everything and propose nothing'. Lord Hailsham in the mid-20th century took the same view, saying of a Labour measure: 'The Conservatives do not believe it necessary, and even if it were necessary we would oppose it.' Yet in practice the Parliamentary system hinges on the Opposition allowing the elected Government to get its BUSINESS through, provided that Government behaves reasonably. CAMPBELL-BANNERMAN struck that balance when he said: 'The duty of an opposition, if it has no ambition to be permanently on the left-hand side of the SPEAKER, is not just to oppose for opposition's sake, but to oppose selectively.' GLADSTONE went a stage further, arguing: 'It is, when strictly judged, an act of public immorality to lead an opposition on a certain plea, to succeed, and then in office to abandon it.' The concept of a loyal opposition is far from universal; STALIN once opined: 'My real opposition is myself.' But the notion of a COALITION of political forces essentially opposing the ADMINISTRATION, yet not contemplating its overthrow is a given in US politics. As long ago as 1865 Thaddeus Stevens told Charles Sumner: 'While we hardly approve of all the acts of government, we must try to keep out of the ranks of the opposition.'

Opposition days The WESTMINSTER term for days when the Opposition can choose the subject for debate. Until the late 1980s they were known as **Supply days**.

opposition research A polite US term – sometimes abbreviated to **'oppo'** – for dirty tricks and black propaganda on the campaign trail; *see also* NERD SQUAD.

in opposition The situation of the principal party which is out of power. Anthony Trollope (1815–82) reckoned that 'the delight of political life is altogether in opposition – the very inaccuracy which is permitted to opposition is in itself a charm'. But Margaret THATCHER, with her eye on radical change, took the contrary view: 'When you are in government, five years is a very short time. When you are in opposition, it is a hell of a long time.' And one of her advisers, Sir Adam Ridley, warned that 'parties come to power with silly, irresponsible policies because they have spent their whole period in opposition destroying the lessons they learned in government.'

> There is only one thing worse than the first term in opposition, and that's the second.
>
> JOHN HOWARD

Leader of the Opposition The formal position allocated in Britain's unwritten CONSTITUTION to the leader of the principal opposition party. He or she receives a Ministerial salary, has the right to grill the Prime Minister at QUESTION TIME and is briefed on sensitive matters on PRIVY COUNCIL TERMS. The Leader of the Opposition holds the post at the pleasure of their party. Despite the status, the position does not appeal to outgoing Prime Ministers. In 1945 CHURCHILL heard that a Yugoslav woman had written in alarm of his election defeat: 'That poor Mr Churchill. I suppose he will now be shot.' Churchill observed: 'They have reserved a far worse fate for me than that.' When Sir William Harcourt resigned as Liberal leader in 1898 after being pilloried for his handling of the FASHODA crisis, he wrote:

> The leader of opposition who finds his whips speaking and voting against him cannot maintain that respect which is due to his position, still less when he finds the organisation of his party working against him in the country.

oppositionism A state of mind in which members of a party are not only used to being in opposition but prefer it, because they would have to show responsibility and be positive were they to find themselves in power.

opting out The doctrine first advanced by Margaret THATCHER's Conservatives in their 1987 election MANIFESTO, under which individual undertakings in the PUBLIC SECTOR could become self-governing. It was tried first with schools, which could opt out of local authority control if parents voted for **grant-maintained status**; several hundred did so. More controversially, hospitals were from 1992 encouraged to detach themselves from the NHS bureaucracy and turn themselves into free-standing trusts, competing for business within the Health Service. Labour opposed both forms of opting-out, but in government from 1997 allowed it to continue in most respects, refining the principle from 2004 by establishing FOUNDATION HOSPITALS in the teeth of opposition from the health unions.

Options for Change The strategy for drastic reductions in the size of Britain's armed forces following the end of the COLD WAR and the conclusion of INF and other ARMS CONTROL agreements, set out by Tom King, Defence Secretary under Margaret THATCHER, and developed by his successor Malcolm Rifkind. Central to it was the halving of British forces in Germany and the disbanding and amalgamation of historic regiments and RAF squadrons. While the process of refocusing and retrenchment continued under Labour, the conceived wisdom ten years later was than in some respects Options for Change had gone too far.

Orange The Royal House of the Netherlands, which assumed the British crown in 1689 when the Protestant **William of Orange** (King William III or KING BILLY) and his wife Mary were invited by Parliament to take the throne jointly. The concurrent defeat at the Battle of the BOYNE of Catholic forces loyal to the ousted King James II ensured the Protestant succession and the Protestant ascendancy in Ireland; the **Orange Order**, founded in 1795, champions that ascendancy in Ulster to this day (*see* MARCHING SEASON).

Orange Book The policy tract published prior to the UK LIBERAL DEMOCRATS' 2004 conference which sought to move the party on from some of its more EGALITARIAN policies, while at the same time stressing a continuity with the philosophy of the old LIBERAL PARTY. Subtitled 'Reclaiming Liberalism', the *Orange Book* was edited by Paul Marshall and David Laws MP; its title was a deliberate echo of the Liberals' radical YELLOW BOOK of 1929.

Orange card, playing the The whipping-up of LOYALIST sentiment in Ulster in order to frustrate first HOME RULE and, since the PARTITION of Ireland, any accommodation between London and Dublin or the imposition of POWER-SHARING in the province. The term dates back at least to Lord Randolph Churchill (1849–94), who wrote of GLADSTONE c. 1886:

> I decided some time ago that if the G. O. M. went for Home Rule the Orange Card would be the one to play. Please God it may turn out to be the ace of trumps and not the two.

Orange Revolution The popular upheaval in the Ukraine in November/December 2004 following the narrow and apparently-rigged ELECTION victory in Presidential elections of the pro-Moscow Prime Minister Viktor Yanukovich over the pro-Western Viktor Yuschenko. Thousands took to the streets of Kiev as the result was declared in protest at the alleged stuffing of ballot boxes after the polls had closed, and stayed there in a tense but non-violent atmosphere for days in freezing temperatures until the Supreme Court ruled the contest invalid and ordered a re-run. Similar large demonstrations in Donetsk, in the Russian-speaking east of the country, took place in support of Yanukovich, who had been strongly backed by Russia's President Putin. On 26 December Yuschenko, who in the meantime had been diagnosed with dioxin poisoning, was elected by a clear majority – 7% compared with 3% to Yanukovich before – and was inaugurated the following month.

oratory The art of delivering not just a political speech but a *tour de force*, which has been pronounced dead at regular intervals since the mid-19th century. The American socialist Norman Thomas declared it 'the harlot of the arts, so subject is it to abuse and degradation', and the Italian statesman Vittorio Emanuele Orlando conceded this, saying: 'Oratory is like prostitution – you must have little tricks'. In the late 18th century Benjamin FRANKLIN scathingly observed: 'Here comes the orator, with his flood of words and his drop of reason'; by the mid-19th such criticism had struck home with Wendell Phillips declaring: 'If you want to be an orator, first find your great CAUSE'. Memorable oratory has been most common among POPULISTS of the right and firebrands of the left; the greatest at WESTMINSTER in the 20th century, CHURCHILL apart, were probably LLOYD GEORGE, Aneurin BEVAN, Michael FOOT, Iain Macleod and Enoch POWELL.

> Oratory has rarely been a Tory failing.
>
> JULIAN CRITCHLEY

Boy Orator of the Platte *See* BOY.

order. Order! Order! The words with which the SPEAKER calls the HOUSE OF COMMONS into session and prefaces new items of business. When radio broadcasting of the Commons began in the late 1970s, Speaker George Thomas (Viscount Tonypandy, 1909–97) became an instant national celebrity for his rich Welsh delivery of the phrase. The single word **Order!** is shouted from the CHAIR if the conduct of the House is becoming unruly.

Order Paper The paper produced each day by each House at WESTMINSTER which lists the business for that day. The Commons Order Papers lists, in turn, Private BILLS to be considered, oral QUESTIONS, TEN-MINUTE RULE BILLS, the remaining ORDERS OF THE DAY (*see below*), Committees sitting that day, written questions, and important matters pending. The name persists despite its having been retitled the *DAILY AGENDA* in October 1997. *See also* The VOTE.

Order in Council In Britain, measures subordinate to primary LEGISLATION, which are enacted in the name of the SOVEREIGN by a committee of the PRIVY COUNCIL acting with the authority of the CABINET.

Order of Merit The award made personally by the SOVEREIGN to individuals who have excelled in the arts, public life or other fields, when a KNIGHTHOOD is not considered an adequate distinction. It was instituted in 1902 by King Edward VII, and limited to 24 members; there is a military and a civil class.

Orders of the Day The business down for discussion in the HOUSE OF COMMONS on a particular day, once QUESTION TIME has been completed and any STATEMENTS, Urgent QUESTIONS or requests for EMERGENCY DEBATES have been dealt with.

call to order The formal opening by the CHAIR of the proceedings in a LEGISLATURE. In both Houses of the US CONGRESS, the call to order is usually at 12 noon.

out of order Conduct or statements when a LEGISLATURE is in session that violate its STANDING ORDERS or Rules of Order. In Britain, 'out of order' has become general slang for any conduct that is socially unacceptable.

point of order The pretext under which a member of an elected body can interrupt business, a speech by another member or even a DIVISION, to argue that its rules have just been violated. It is often used as a device for raising a political point before the CHAIR has the chance to rule that a point of order is bogus.

special orders In the US HOUSE OF REPRESENTATIVES, the point around 7 p.m. when the regular order of business is completed and members can make long speeches about points of interest to them or their constituents. Since the advent of C-SPAN this part of the legislative day has taken on new importance as up to 250,000 Americans may be watching, unaware that the CHAMBER is almost empty.

Oregon question The long-unresolved dispute between Britain and America over the western border between the US and Canada, and the status of the Oregon Territory which stretched from California to Russian Alaska. It caused severe tension in the early 1840s before the adoption of the 49TH PARALLEL as the dividing line. *See* FIFTY-FOUR FORTY OR FIGHT.

oreo A black American considered by others to act like a white one. The term, in use since at least 1968, comes from the cookie of that name which is black on the outside with a white filling. Mike Steele, successful 2002 black Republican candidate for LIEUTENANT GOVERNOR of Maryland, was pelted with oreos by black activists when he spoke at a rally in Baltimore.

organ grinder and monkey One of the most devastating put-downs in the 20th-century HOUSE OF COMMONS, uttered by Aneurin BEVAN in the wake of the SUEZ crisis. It recalls the days when the man playing a barrel-organ in the street kept a monkey on a chain to amuse the crowd and collect the money. When Selwyn Lloyd, the Foreign Secretary, rose to answer him instead of Prime Minister Harold MACMILLAN, Bevan said:

> I am not going to spend any time whatsoever attacking the Foreign Secretary. Quite honestly, I am beginning to feel extremely sorry for him. If we complain about the tune, there is no reason to attack the monkey when the organ grinder is present.

William Safire suggests it may have originated with CHURCHILL, when the British Ambassador in Rome was offered an audience with Mussolini's foreign minister Count Ciano instead of Il DUCE himself. The author is not convinced.

organic change Gradual and natural, yet still fundamental change to a political movement or system; the opposite is change imposed by legislation or some other concrete act. Roy HATTERSLEY, in a slip of the tongue, once told the author that

> The LABOUR PARTY is going through a period of orgasmic change.

Orgreave, battle of One of the pivotal confrontations of the 1984–85 MINERS' STRIKE, when a mass PICKET of several thousand of Arthur Scargill's (*see* KING ARTHUR) Yorkshire miners tried to shut down British Steel's coking plant outside Sheffield; there were in fact several confrontations, on 29 and 30 May, 1 and 18 June 1984. A pitched battle between miners and mounted police ended with a number of arrests, and miners complaining that undue force had been used against them. A year later the charges against fourteen miners accused of riot and unlawful assembly were dropped.

original intent The issue, of vital importance to the courts and CONGRESS, of what precisely the framers of the US CONSTITUTION meant. It tends to be used by conservatives as a code word in seeking to reverse or roll back SUPREME COURT decisions on social and individual rights issues.

Orpington Man The generic term coined, after the stunning Liberal victory in the 1962 Orpington BY-ELECTION, for a disenchanted Tory commuter in south-east England who kicks over the traces. Eric Lubbock (later Lord Avebury, 1928–), who won the seat from the Conservatives, triggering a brief Liberal revival, and held it until 1970, was himself a commuter from Orpington, on London's Kentish fringe. He later shrugged off his connection with the average man by announcing that he would leave his body to the inmates of Battersea Dogs' Home.

Osborne judgment The HOUSE OF LORDS ruling in 1909 outlawing the POLITICAL LEVY which Britain's trade unions raised from members for their own campaigning and to finance the infant LABOUR PARTY. W. V. Osborne, a member of the Amalgamated Society of Railway servants (later NUR, now RMT), contended that the union had no right to use its own funds to support the party or to impose a levy. The legality of the political levy, provided members were allowed to contract out of it, was restored in the 1913 Trade Union Act. The Osborne judgment also hastened the introduction in 1911 of salaries for MPs, Labour members usually having no other source of income. In 2003 the RMT disAFFILIATED from Labour.

OSCE Organisation for Security and Co-Operation in Europe. The security framework established under the 1975 HELSINKI ACCORDS, which has grown to involve 55 countries including the US and Canada and was until 1995 entitled **CSCE** – the Conference on Security and Co-Operation in Europe. At conferences in Belgrade (1977), Madrid (1980) and Vienna (1986–89) progress was made on CONFIDENCE-BUILDING measures, and with the sudden end of the COLD WAR, to which the process had contributed, CSCE emerged with the potential to provide security and stability for NATO and former WARSAW PACT countries alike. It spawned the European Bank for Reconstruction and Development and the CHARTER OF PARIS, but proved powerless to check the civil war in former Yugoslavia though it has been active in post-war reconstruction in Bosnia/Herzegovina.

O'Shea case A landmark case in Australian trade unionism, stemming from the refusal of Clarrie O'Shea, Communist secretary of the Victorian Tramways Employees' Union, to yield up the union's books to allow the recovery of fines imposed on it. Justice John KERR of the Commonwealth Industrial Court jailed O'Shea for contempt on 15 May 1969, and half a million workers went on strike. It took the intervention of an anonymous citizen who had won $200,000 in a lottery to get O'Shea out of jail after five days and end the strike. The penal provisions that Kerr had exercised were never used again. The judge went on to become Sir John and GOVERNOR-GENERAL of Australia, and cause the country's biggest-ever political furore by sacking Prime Minister Gough WHITLAM in 1975.

Oslo process The process which for a decade appeared to offer the best opportunity yet to secure lasting peace between Israel and its neighbours, but which ultimately foundered on the intransigence of Israeli and Palestinian leaders who feared being outflanked by their own extremists. Secret contacts between Israel and the PLO from 1991 culminated in the initialling of a joint Declaration of Principles on 19 August 1993, and an agreement signed in WASHINGTON by the Israeli Prime Minister Yitzhak Rabin and the Palestinian leader Yasser Arafat on 13 September 1993. The declaration created a framework for areas of negotiation and the rapid handover of GAZA AND JERICHO to Palestinian control. The other most contentious issues, such as Jerusalem, the future of Israeli settlements in occupied territory and the status of Palestinian refugees, would be dealt with in 'permanent status talks'. The **Oslo II** agreement on 28 September 1995 settled points of detail on a handover to the Palestinians, after which Israeli troops withdrew from six major West Bank cities and hundreds of Arab villages. Despite Rabin's assassination by a right-wing extremist, his successor Shimon Peres pressed ahead with Oslo II; in January 1996 Arafat was elected chairman of the PALESTINIAN AUTHORITY and the permanent status talks opened that May. The return of a LIKUD government and a gradual upsurge of terrorism by HAMAS and other groups slowed progress, but hopes lingered until the failure of talks on a comprehensive peace settlement at CAMP DAVID just before President CLINTON left office, with Arafat turning down a deal which came to look improbably generous to the Palestinians.

OSS Office for Strategic Services. The US espionage and sabotage organisation which was the forerunner of the CIA and the equivalent of Britain's wartime SOE (Special Operations Executive). It was established by President ROOSEVELT in June 1942 and put under the direction of his intelligence adviser General 'Wild Bill' Donovan (1883–1959). Its role combined information-gathering and analysis with covert operations including GUERRILLA warfare, the rescue of Allied servicemen, and support for underground resistance movements.

Ossewa-Brandwag (Afrik. Ox wagon sentinel) A South African pro-Nazi PARAMILITARY organisation that emerged in 1938 after the symbolic re-enactment of the Great Trek, achieving popular support following German victories early in WORLD WAR II. An elite inner unit, the *Stormjaers* (stormtroopers), was dedicated to sabotaging South Africa's war effort. Led by Hans van Renseberg, the OB included numerous prominent Afrikaners such as John Vorster, later Prime Minister (1966–78), and Hendrik van den Bergh, who became head of BOSS. With the defeat of Germany the OB disintegrated; its remnants were incorporated in the NATIONAL PARTY as it came in sight of power.

Ossi The nickname given to residents of former East Germany when the country was reUNIFIED in 1990. A Westerner became known as a **Wessi**.

Ostpolitik (Ger. Eastern policy) The dramatic West German policy shift to NORMALISE relations with East Germany and other east European Communist countries, embarked on by Willy BRANDT, the country's SPD Chancellor from 1969 to 1974. Previous West German foreign policy had been constrained by the HALLSTEIN DOCTRINE, prohibiting diplomatic relations with any country that recognised East Germany; Brandt's initiative did much to ease the tension over BERLIN and hasten the end of the COLD WAR. The term OSTPOLITIK was also used before the collapse of Communism in 1989 to signify any conciliatory policy by a Western nation toward the East.

other. the other body The way in which members of each House of the US CONGRESS refer to members of the other in debate.

other place, the or **another place** The similar courtesy which members of the HOUSE OF LORDS and HOUSE OF COMMONS extend to each other, and to the Houses in which they sit; a debate in the Lords will be said by MPs to have been 'in another place'. Soon after losing his Commons seat in 1970 and accepting a PEERAGE, Lord George-BROWN told an interrupter in the Lords who objected to his abrasive style:

> I could never be shouted down in the other place, and I am not going to be shouted down here.

Other Club, the A dining club founded in 1911 by Winston CHURCHILL and F. E. Smith (later Lord Birkenhead). It was said to be so named because the two rumbustious politicians were not wanted at an existing fraternity known as The Club. The Other Club is still discreetly in existence.

Ottawa agreements The PROTECTIONIST measures agreed at the Imperial Economic Conference in the Canadian capital from 21 July to 20 August 1932, at the depth of the GREAT DEPRESSION. They were a series of bilateral agreements establishing a system of IMPERIAL PREFERENCE, by which Britain and her colonies and DOMINIONS exchanged TARIFF preferences to promote trade within the Empire and exclude certain classes of goods from outside it.

our. Our Country Cousin The play which Abraham LINCOLN and his wife were watching at Ford's Theatre, Washington on 14 April 1865 when John Wilkes Booth opened the door of the Presidential box and shot him. The play, first staged in England in 1851, starred Laura Keene.

Our language, our institutions, our laws The motto of the newspaper *Le Canadien*, founded at the end of the 18th century by radicals in Quebec, which became the first focus of French-Canadian nationalism and was suppressed by Sir James Craig, Governor of Lower Canada 1807–11. Its owners were sent to prison, but the political movement it had fostered lived on.

out. out of area capability The ability of a nation or alliance – notably NATO – to take military or PEACEKEEPING action outside its accepted geographical sphere of operations.

out of the loop *See* LOOP.

Outer Seven The original members of the European Free Trade Association (EFTA) on its formation in 1959: Austria, Denmark, Norway, Portugal, Sweden, Switzerland and the UK. 'Uuter' was a contrast with the 'inner' six founder-members of the European Community: France, Germany, Italy and the BENELUX countries.

outing A public declaration by militant homosexuals that a prominent person whose sexual orientation has not been a matter of record is in fact gay. It originates from 'out of the closet', the phrase describing the open acknowledgement by an individual that they are homosexual. Militant gays, such as the UK group Out-Rage, reckon that those who conceal their homosexuality are perpetuating the climate of shame that traditionally put everyone thus oriented at a disadvantage.

outseg Short for 'outSEGREGATE': to adopt an even more RACIST stance than one's opponent in order to attract white votes. This term, inevitably from America's Deep South, replaced the more blatantly offensive **outnigger**, as in 'I'm not going to let myself be outniggered by George Wallace'.

Oval Office The WHITE HOUSE office of the President of the United States and as such the heart of the government of America, sited since 1934 in the south-east corner of the WEST WING overlooking the Rose Garden; the name only came into general use under President NIXON. Built for President Theodore ROOSEVELT and then moved from the centre of the building, its elliptic design was copied from the White House's Blue Room. Its bullet-proof windows have a purplish tinge. The Oval Office, where successive Presidents have been photographed deep in thought, or conferring with their advisers or visiting dignitaries, holds a sanctity for the American people and most, at least, of their Presidents. Ronald REAGAN never took off his jacket out of respect for his surroundings, and George BUSH Snr invoked this ethos when pressed by a reporter during the 1992 campaign about an alleged extra-marital affair:

> I'm not going to take any SLEAZE questions. You're perpetuating the sleaze by asking the question, to say nothing of asking it in the Oval Office.

Yet within four years, Bill CLINTON was disporting himself with Monica LEWINSKY in an ante-room to the Oval Office, possibly the aspect of ZIPPERGATE that most demeaned him.

The Oval Office is also the presidency personified. When Chief of Staff James Baker rebuked Budget Director David Stockman for giving a damagingly frank interview about REAGANOMICS, he told him: 'When you go through the Oval Office door, I want to see that sorry ass of yours dragging on the carpet.'

> You know, every day, important papers come across the desk in that marvellous Oval Office, and very few items remain there for long. Got to keep that paper moving or you get inundated. Your snorkel will fill up and there will be no justice. GEORGE BUSH Snr

over. overflow meeting A gathering in an adjacent hall or in the open comprising members of the public unable to get into a political meeting because the hall is full; a common feature of political life up to the mid-20th century but much rarer nowadays. Sometimes the speaker at the main meeting will give a further, impromptu address to those outside; more often, the proceedings will be relayed to the overflow crowd. The most embarrassing thing for a political organiser is to lay on facilities for an overflow meeting and then find that there is no demand for it.

overheating The situation in an economy which has expanded too fast, so that too much money chases too little capacity and prices and borrowing rise sharply. Demand and interest rates have to be managed to cool the economy down; corrective measures have to be firm enough to have the required effect, but if too severe can precipitate a HARD LANDING or RECESSION.

overkill Originally this was a term from the nightmare vocabulary of NUCLEAR WARfare, popularised during the KENNEDY administration, reflecting the ability of the SUPERPOWERS' nuclear arsenals to wipe out the population of the world several times over.

> Why make the rubble bounce? CHURCHILL

> There is a limit. How many times do you have to hit the target with nuclear weapons? JOHN F. KENNEDY

It has since come to apply to an excessive response or over-reaction of any kind.

override The ability of the US CONGRESS to force through legislation despite the imposition of a Presidential VETO. It can do this on a vote of two-thirds of both the Senate and the House; the question put is: 'Shall the BILL pass, the objections of the President to the contrary notwithstanding?'

oversight The role of CONGRESS in supervising the operations of the US government to ensure that agencies are faithfully executing the law. This was first recognised in legislation as recently as 1946, and it is only since the 1970s that Congress has taken its powers of oversight as seriously as its power to enact new laws. Cynics argue that the word is fortuitously ambiguous, reflecting both the responsibility incumbent on Congress and its frequent 'oversights' in omitting to exercise the requisite degree of control.

overstretch A situation in which a country's armed forces, specifically Britain's, are barely able to undertake the commitments required of them by their political masters. The term came into use after the manpower and capability cuts made under OPTIONS FOR CHANGE, as the post-COLD WAR situation required a military presence and operations in unforeseen new theatres, notably former Yugoslavia.

Ovra The Italian FASCIST secret police established in 1927 by Arturo Bocchini, Mussolini's chief of security from 1926 to 1940. The origin of the word is a mystery; it may have been coined by Il DUCE as a vaguely sinister term to frighten his opponents. Ovra was used to spy on anti-FASCISTS and supporters of the movement alike. Though it used torture on its victims, its activities were never on the same scale as those of the GESTAPO; at most it employed under 1000 informers.

Owenites (1) The followers of **Robert Owen** (1771–1858), the Welsh-born pioneer of socialism and the CO-OPERATIVE movement, who in *A New View of Society* (1813) maintained that an individual's character is moulded by their social environment. Humbly born, Owen became the manager of a cotton mill at nineteen and bought his own at 29, soon becoming a millionaire. He offered model conditions to workers at his mill at New Lanark, Scotland, including a co-operative shop, day nursery, infant school and adult education classes in the village attached to it. An attempt to promote similar ideals in the US, through a manufacturing community in Indiana, lost him most of his fortune; New Lanark was restored to much of its former glory in the 1970s. (2) The followers of the former Labour Foreign Secretary and GANG OF FOUR member **Dr David** (now Lord) **Owen** (1938–), who in 1987 as leader of the SDP rejected the Liberal leader David Steel's (*see* BOY DAVID) post-election call for a MERGER of the two parties. With most Social Democrats going to join the merged LIBERAL DEMOCRATS, Owen kept a separate SDP going with two fellow-MPs, John Cartwright and Rosie Barnes, and in February 1989 nearly won a by-election at Richmond, Yorkshire. But the party failed to establish itself, and Owen wound it up the following summer after it was outpolled at Bootle by the OFFICIAL MONSTER RAVING LOONY PARTY.

Dr Owen was seen by his supporters as a man of principle, by his allies as infuriating. Steel said:

> I am reminded of Dame Sybil Thorndike's comment on her long marriage. She considered divorce never, murder frequently. With Dr Owen it is murder, occasionally.

Labour simply regarded him as a traitor. Neil KINNOCK accused him of having 'an ego fat on arrogance and drunk on ambition', or being 'orthopaedically arrogant in every corpuscle' and of 'purveying retread THATCHERism'; Dennis Skinner (*see* BEAST OF BOLSOVER) termed him more simple 'a pompous git' (when the Speaker protested, he withdrew the word 'pompous').

See also VANCE-OWEN PLAN.

own. own goal A terrorist attack, usually a bombing, in which the would-be perpetrator fails to eliminate their target but is killed by their own weapon. The term comes from soccer, where an own goal is one scored by a player against their own team. It acquired its political connotation in the British Army in NORTHERN IRELAND in the 1970s for the at first numerous occasions when IRA bombers inadvertently blew themselves up.

own resources An EU term for the amount the COMMISSION can budget to spend each year, which has been received from member states as a fixed share of their GDP. Historically it was 1.2%, but after JACQUES DELORS lobbied hard for a more ambitious budget, the 1992 Edinburgh summit agreed a phased increase to 1.27% by 1999. With ENLARGEMENT this ceiling is again under pressure.

Oxford by-election The notorious electoral test of the MUNICH agreement in the autumn of 1938, when A. D. Lindsay, Master of Balliol, stood as an ANTI-APPEASEMENT candidate against the official Conservative nominee, Quintin Hogg (later Lord Hailsham), in a contest that POLARISED the city, the University and the country. Harold

MACMILLAN, who had resigned the Tory whip, and the young Edward HEATH campaigned for Lindsay, but Hogg ran out the winner to begin a Parliamentary career that included 42 years on the Front BENCH and the dramatic renunciation of his title in a vain bid for the Tory leadership.

Oxford group *See* Moral REARMAMENT.

oxygen of publicity Respectability or glamour conferred on an organisation or activity that is illegal, dangerous or unacceptable as a result of undue attention from the media. Margaret THATCHER gave currency to the phrase when she protested against the publicity, especially on television, given to terrorists and the IRA in particular. The phrase was actually coined by Britain's Chief Rabbi Lord Jakobovits; Mrs Thatcher told the American Bar Association's London meeting on 15 July 1985:

> Democracies must try to find the way to starve the terrorist and the hijackers of the oxygen of publicity on which they depend.

For this reason, her government in 1988 imposed a broadcasting ban on SINN FEIN; the words of the party's leading lights had to be spoken by actors. It was lifted in 1994 having itself contributed to the mystique of violent Republicanism.

ozone man George BUSH Snr's scornful nickname for Sen. Al GORE, conferred in the closing days of the 1992 Presidential campaign, which swung a few votes to the Republican ticket but reinforced Gore's credentials with most Democrats. Bush intended to link the Vice Presidential nominee with cranky environmentalists by playing up the fact that he had written a book, *Earth in the Balance*, highlighting the threat to the ozone layer (*see* MONTREAL PROTOCOL) and the risks of global warming. Gore and Bill CLINTON went on to win the election, but their ADMINISTRATION failed to endorse the KYOTO CONVENTION and the Bush clan had the last laugh when the former President's son defeated Gore in the 2000 election on the strength of a few hundred disputed votes in Florida.

P

P2 The Masonic lodge headed by the shadowy, ruthless and corrupt Licio Gelli (1919–), which in the late 1970s gained a stranglehold on Italy's political ESTABLISHMENT, bringing down the CHRISTIAN DEMOCRAT government when its activities were exposed in 1981. In its prime the lodge, said to have links with the Naples-based *Camorra* crime syndicates, had four Cabinet Ministers, 38 Parliamentary deputies and 195 military officers as members. Gelli, a former FASCIST who once gave Pope Paul VI a gold-plated bed as an attempted bribe, became head of the lodge in 1976, the year it was expelled from organised freemasonry. His contacts included the media magnate and future prime minister Silvio Berlusconi, and he was tried for complicity in a string of right-wing terrorist outrages, and convicted of acting as paymaster to the bombers who killed 86 people at Bologna station. Gelli fled to Switzerland, but was EXTRADITED in 1987 to face further, minor charges; in 1992 he was reported to be rebuilding its influence as its former sixteen-strong 'board of directors', including generals and five high-ranking secret service officers, went on trial on charges up to plotting to overthrow the constitution. P2, and Gelli, have also been linked with the supposed suicide of Roberto Calvi, the Milan banker jailed after the collapse of the Vatican-linked Banco Ambrosiano, who was found hanged under Blackfriars Bridge in London; in July 2003 prosecutors in Rome reported that in their view Calvi had been murdered by the Mafia; in April 2005 four people were charged.

PAC (1) Pan Africanist Congress. The only rival to (though much smaller than) the ANC as a black freedom movement in South Africa. More militant and with a MAOIST slant, it claimed 125,000 members under APARTHEID; its military wing, the AZANIA People's Liberation Army, supposedly had an elite of 750 GUERRILLA fighters trained in Libya, and in Tanzania by the Chinese. The PAC was founded in 1959 with Robert Sobukwe as its president after a split with MOSCOW-LINERS in the ANC. Sobukwe explained:

> To us the struggle is a national struggle; to the ANC it is a class struggle. We claim Africa for the Africans; the ANC claims South Africa for all.

Like the ANC, the PAC was banned in 1960; though the ban was lifted in 1990 the PAC refused to join the CODESA talks on a democratic constitution unless ELECTIONS were held first. When those elections did take place, it secured a humiliating five seats; it responded by abandoning its slogan of ONE SETTLER, ONE BULLET! but has remained on the fringe.
(2) Political Action Committee. In the US, a body set up by business, labour or single-interest groups (pro-Israel, pro-LIFE *etc.*) to lobby CONGRESS and raise CAMPAIGN funds for candidates who support the cause or can be won over, or to defeat its opponents; candidates themselves have been able to set up PACs as a way round the rules. They have their genesis in the early 1970s when Congress imposed curbs on funding presidential, but not congressional, campaigns, and several thousand PACs now dispense twice as much money as the parties themselves; Bill CLINTON was elected President on a pledge to curb their spending. They have the advantage of being relatively impervious to political criticism, NCPAC (National Conservative PAC) chairman John T. Dolan observing:

> A group like ours could lie through its teeth and the candidate it helps stays clean.

The benefits offered by support from a PAC are not lost on the politicians. Business and Industry PAC manager Bernadette Budde confessed: 'I called this place the doctor's office because we had [politicians] line up waiting to come in.' Those seeing the impact of lobbying by PACs on the governmental process question their place in a democratic system.

> One step away from bribery.
> LLOYD CUTLER, Carter White House counsel

(3) Public Accounts Committee. At WESTMINSTER, the most influential SELECT COMMITTEE of the COMMONS, with an effective record as a watchdog of public spending and the application of funds; it works closely with the National Audit Office, which provides much of its ammunition.

Pacific Rim Collective term for the economically powerful nations of East Asia, notably Japan and South Korea, and their strategically important non-Communist neighbours. It was increasingly used under the REAGAN administration, with its roots in California, to embrace both those Asian powers and America's western states, and as shorthand for a Pacific-orientated range of policies. It has lost a little of its meaning with China's emergence as an economically-capitalist force.

Pacific scandal The Canadian scandal which brought about the fall of Sir John Macdonald's Conservative government in 1873. Macdonald had won re-election in 1872 on funds secretly solicited from Sir Hugh Allan's consortium for building a trans-Canadian railway, in return for Macdonald awarding him the contract.

> By the base betrayal of private communications, the names of certain members of the Government, including myself, were mixed up in the obtaining of these subscriptions.
>
> SIR JOHN MACDONALD

> The Thermopylae of Canadian virtue.
>
> *TORONTO GLOBE*

pacification The process, usually military, of subduing or eliminating enemy or terrorist activity by rendering the affected area inhospitable or unusable. It was tried particularly during the VIETNAM WAR by US forces in an effort to deprive the VIET CONG of support in rural areas. Unlike PEACE-KEEPING, it is carried out during hostilities to win peace, typically by securing the co-operation of the local population (*see* HEARTS AND MINDS) or removing them from the area. Buildings, food supplies, crops, animals and ground cover that could offer support or protection to the enemy may be destroyed.

Pacifico, Don David Pacifico, a Spanish Jew born in Gibraltar and thus claiming to be a British subject despite having been naturalised by the Portuguese. At Easter 1846, an anti-Semitic mob burst into Pacifico's house in Athens, manhandled his wife and child, stole jewellery and set fire to the building. The authorities refused to compensate Pacifico, who had been the Portuguese consul, and he appealed to Britain. In 1847 Lord Palmerston (*see* PAM) threatened force if Pacifico were not compensated and also given £27,000 he claimed to be owed by the Portuguese government (*see* CIVIS ROMANUS SUM). Two years later British ships blockaded Piraeus in pursuit of this and several other grievances, Palmerston declaring:

> It is our long forbearance, and not our precipitation, that deserves remark.

Greece paid Pacifico £8500; his claim against Portugal was found by arbitrators to be essentially fraudulent and he was awarded just £150. Palmerston treated the episode as the height of British influence for good; the truth was somewhat murkier.

pacifism The belief that the use of violence under any circumstances is immoral; the basis for all specifically anti-war movements. With strong roots in the Society of Friends (Quakers), pacifism became an organised political force in the early 1930s, especially in the UK through the PEACE PLEDGE UNION, as a public horrified by WORLD WAR I sought to avert a second conflict. Since 1945 pacifism has given rise to a loosely-organised 'peace movement', has been a major influence on the anti-nuclear movement (*see* CND) and has been a factor in the opposition to conflicts from VIETNAM to the IRAQ WAR.

> My pacifism is not based on any intellectual theory but on deep antipathy to every form of cruelty and hatred.
>
> ALBERT EINSTEIN, on the outbreak of World War I

pack To infiltrate supporters of a faction, candidate or point of view into a meeting, televised debate or political CONVENTION to distort any debate and create the impression of one-sidedness. An overcrowded meeting is often (wrongly) described as a **packed meeting;** the term is intended for one hijacked by an element in this way. **Packing the galleries** is a stratagem used at a US party's nominating convention to stampede uncommitted delegates and those of rival candidates into supporting the one that seems to have the momentum.

Packwood resignation The departure from his chairmanship, the US Senate and political life in 1995 of the Oregon Republican Sen. Bob Packwood (1932–), chairman of the Senate Finance Committee. He was forced to quit after the Senate Ethics Committee (unanimously) and leaders of both parties demanded his expulsion for sexually harassing at least 29 women over a

21-year period; ironically he had a political track record as a defender of women's rights. Packwood, who had used legal action to stall a *Washington Post* exposé until after his narrow re-election in 1992, hoped to cling on by confronting his accusers at public hearings of the Ethics Committee, but his determination to do this wrecked a compromise that would have allowed him to keep his seat but not his chairmanship. Packwood's sexual harassment of his staff and constituents was chronicled in his diaries, which he refused to hand over to the Ethics Committee until ordered to by a court, despite a 94–6 vote from the Senate to back the subpoena. Packwood was pursued around Oregon by demonstrators challenging him to justify himself and chanting: **'Hit the Road, Pack!'** Packwood blamed his habitual misbehaviour on a drink problem.

> Like (Richard) NIXON, Packwood remained in office long after his reputation was destroyed, and resigned only when his last remaining supporters abandoned him.
>
> ALAN BRINKLEY, *The New Yorker*

pact. Pact of Steel The formal ALLIANCE between Germany and Italy, concluded in March 1939, which cemented the AXIS by committing Italy to support Germany in the event of war. Mussolini (*see* DUCE) coined the term after wisely abandoning his first choice, 'Pact of Blood'.
Lib-Lab Pact *See* LIB-LAB.
Nazi-Soviet Pact *See* NAZI.
non-aggression pact *See* NON-AGGRESSION.

Paddy Pantsdown The nickname bestowed by the *Sun* on Paddy (Jeremy John Dunham, later Lord) Ashdown (1941–), leader of Britain's LIBERAL DEMOCRATS from 1988 to 1999, when on the eve of the 1992 election he disclosed a five-year-old affair with a former secretary. The publicity did Ashdown little harm after the immediate trauma to himself, his family and his ex-mistress; his party's poll rating rose by one-half to 18%, and the Lib-Dems went on to register gains at the next four elections.

pages In the US CAPITOL, the corps of young people, chosen by the legislators themselves, who run errands for them. Used in the HOUSE since at least 1800 and the SENATE since 1829, they keep members' desks – and the Senate snuffboxes – filled and sit on the steps of the Senate rostrum and on benches in the House in case they are needed. Visitors frequently ask them for advice; one new page, asked why the bells kept ringing for a QUORUM, said:

> I don't know. But I think maybe one of them has escaped.

There are 66 pages aged sixteen to eighteen in the House, and 30 aged fourteen to sixteen in the Senate; until 1971 all were boys, but pages of both sexes have on occasion been sexually harassed by Congressmen. Before reporting for work they attend high school in the LIBRARY OF CONGRESS.

pair The arrangement under which a legislator may arrange to miss all but the most important votes if another from the other side of the house does the same. At WESTMINSTER, pairs are made on a lasting basis, and registered with the party WHIPS. The opponent with whom a member regularly makes such arrangements is known as his or her pair. When the governing party has a narrow majority, the OPPOSITION may step up pressure by refusing to make pairing arrangements. (*See also* BISQUE). In the US CONGRESS, pairing was operating by the 1820s; pairs are announced by the CLERK OF THE HOUSE and listed in the CONGRESSIONAL RECORD after the names of members not voting.
breaking a pair The ultimate in Parliamentary sharp practice, turning up to vote when a pair has been made for you.
general pair In CONGRESS, an arrangement to cover several votes on differing subjects over a period of days.
live pair A US legislator who is able to vote despite being paired, so withdraws his vote and simply declares himself 'present' to protect the other member.
pairing whip *See* WHIP.
unpaired A member who lacks a pair on the other side, and is thus unable to get away.

Paisleyite A supporter of the Rev. Ian Paisley (1926–), MP, MEP, Free Presbyterian minister and leader of NORTHERN IRELAND's militantly LOYALIST and predominantly working-class DUP. From the 1960s into the 21st century he led the opposition to all efforts to introduce POWER-SHARING between the Protestant majority and the Catholic minority, and to any links with the Irish Republic, notably the ANGLO-IRISH AGREEMENT, but acquiesced reluctantly in the GOOD FRIDAY AGREEMENT.

Pakis The highly offensive (in the UK, at least) racial term for Pakistanis used inadvertently by George W. BUSH in an address on 8 January 2002. Bush, who had persuaded the government of Pakistan to side with America in the WAR AGAINST TERRORISM, said with reference to the ongoing dispute over Kashmir:

> I am working hard to convince the Indians and the Pakis that there is a better way than going to war.

See also GENERAL.

Palace, the Westminster shorthand for BUCKINGHAM PALACE, official London residence of the SOVEREIGN, and for the political locus and influence of the monarch and the royal advisers, e.g. 'The Palace are very upset about this.'

palace guard WASHINGTON-speak for the inner core of WHITE HOUSE aides who control ACCESS to the President. The term, with echoes of the IMPERIAL PRESIDENCY, was first used of H. R. Haldeman and John Ehrlichman who, critics claimed, sealed off Richard NIXON.

Palace of Westminster *See* WESTMINSTER.

palace revolution A revolution within the clique or élite governing a country, power changing hands without the people being in any way involved. The term is said to date from an occasion in a Latin American republic when the ruling general was woken by a fellow-member of the JUNTA to be told that he was no longer President. The usurper went downstairs to announce that he had taken power, only to be ousted by the head of the palace guard. The phrase has come to mean any upheaval within a self-contained organisation.

Palestine Liberation Organisation *See* PLO.

Palestinian Any Arab who lived in, or is descended from residents of, the area between the River Jordan and the Mediterranean; more specifically, any Arab inhabitant of, or refugee from, the WEST BANK or GAZA STRIP, occupied by Israel following the SIX-DAY WAR of 1967. The word dates back at least to 1875. Though the West Bank was previously part of Jordan and Gaza – which housed many refugees displaced by the foundation of Israel – had been administered by Egypt, the Palestinians under Israeli rule developed a strong aspiration for their own state, an outcome eventually favoured by the United States, moved toward in the OSLO agreements but denied so far by repeated failures of the PEACE PROCESS.

Palestinian Authority The body set up to govern a Palestinian state if and when it comes into existence, which in the meantime controls civil functions in those parts of the OCCUPIED TERRITORIES over which Israel is prepared to relax its grip. The PLO leader Yasser Arafat was elected chairman of the Authority in elections held in January 1996 after conclusion of the OSLO II agreement. Negotiations since then aimed at extending the power and reach of the Authority in return for greater security for Israel have repeatedly broken down; Arafat was blamed by Israel for failing to check the upsurge in suicide bombings (*see* HAMAS), and by militants in his own community for inertia, nepotism and corruption which prevented the communities under the Authority's control realising their economic potential. After Arafat's death, Mahmoud Abbas was elected president in January 2005 and moved to instal a cleaner and more vigorous government.

Palm Beach County The Florida county where the 2000 US Presidential election was decided – or rather not decided. Disputes here over the number of votes cast for George W. BUSH or Al Gore in turn affected the outcome in Florida, which overall was a virtual dead heat, and of the election nationally as Florida was the decisive state. The uncertainty, which led to weeks of argument and the eventual resolution of the election by the SUPREME COURT, stemmed from the antiquated voting machines used by the county's 460,000 electors, which did not cleanly stamp out the CHADS from the ballot papers and led to arguments over which ballots were valid. The confusion was not entirely confined to Palm Beach; in a neighbouring county, several hundred elderly Jewish voters were found to have supported the staunchly anti-Israeli Pat Buchanan because they had misread a confusingly-designed BUTTERFLY BALLOT paper.

Pam The universal nickname for **Henry John Temple, Viscount Palmerston** (1784–1865), who was twice British Prime Minister (1855–58; 1859–65). A WHIG who flirted with Toryism, Palmerston held office for 48 years altogether, and as Foreign Secretary and Prime Minister during the CRIMEAN WAR and the US CIVIL WAR was the embodiment of British world power (*see* CIVIS ROMANUS SUM). Metternich saw this coming; when Palmerston was denied the Foreign Office in 1845 the Austrian observed: 'We can sleep easier in our beds'. Queen Victoria was not amused by his robust line toward other European rulers, most of them her relatives. Though his sheer efficiency made his eventual choice as Prime Minister inevitable – though he was just as responsible as other Ministers for failure in the Crimea – the Queen reckoned that 'he will be a source of mischief to this country as long as he lives'. On his death she wrote:

> We had, God knows, terrible trouble with him about foreign affairs. Still, as Prime Minister, he managed affairs at home well, and behaved to me well, but I never liked him.

His relations with the Queen were not helped by his reputation – justified – as a roué. After Palmerston, at the age of 69, had displayed 'temerity' in the bedroom of a female guest at WINDSOR, the diarist Charles Greville recorded: 'The Queen has not forgotten and will never forgive it.' Of the same incident involving a Mrs Brand, Prince Albert noted: 'He had barricaded the door and would have consummated his fiendish scheme by violence had not the miraculous efforts of his victim and such assistance accompanied by her screams saved her.' Lady Stanley complained of the way he courted married women into his 80s: 'Ha! Ha! I see it all – beautiful woman neglected by her husband, allow me, etc . . .' Urged to capitalise on Palmerston's sexual indiscretions in his old age, DISRAELI declined, lest his opponent sweep the country.

Palmerston was famed for his temperament and unpredictability. According to Princess Lieven, 'Europe depended on which leg – left or right – he put out of bed first'. Lord Lytton wrote: 'Palmerston is Mama England's spoilt child and the more mischief he does, the more she admires him. "What spirit he has!" cries Mama – and smash goes the crockery.' And Greville observed: 'His great fault is want of punctuality, and never keeping an engagement if it did not suit him, keeping everybody waiting for hours on his pleasure or caprice.' Indeed it was a standard saying in London society that 'Palmerston always misses the soup'. His free-wheeling attitude earned him the hostility of the rising Disraeli, who sharply observed: 'He will not give trouble about principles.' On a personal level he was even more scathing, describing him as 'at best ginger beer, not champagne', and 'that great Apollo of aspiring understrappers, menacing Russia with a perfumed cane'. Palmerston's last words were reputedly: 'Die, my dear Doctor? That's the last thing I shall do.'

> If the Devil has a son
> It is surely Palmerston. ANON.

Pan-Africanist Congress *See* PAC.

Pan-Serbism The feeling for a greater Serbia, and for the rights of Serbs in neighbouring republics to be governed by Serbs, traditionally with the sympathy of Russia. The depth with which this sentiment is held sparked off WORLD WAR I through the assassination of Archduke Franz Ferdinand in SARAJEVO in 1914 by a Bosnian Serb, Gavrilo Princip; it also contributed to the bloodshed following Croatia's secession from Yugoslavia in 1991, and in Bosnia from the following year, and the ETHNIC CLEANSING in Bosnia and later in Kosovo which brought military intervention from NATO.

Panama Canal treaties The treaties under which America undertook to hand control of the Panama Canal to Panama by 2000 – and did so – in return for its NEUTRALISATION and permanent rights of passage for US warships, and return the CANAL ZONE to Panama immediately. Concluded by the CARTER administration, they were ratified by the SENATE in 1978 by the narrowest of margins after a conservative rearguard action.

> We built it, we paid for it, and we're going to keep it. RONALD REAGAN

> The culmination of that pattern of surrender and APPEASEMENT that has cost us so much all over the world. Sen. ORRIN HATCH

Panama intervention The US action in December 1989 to overthrow Panama's strongman Manuel Noriega after disputed elections, and to secure his prosecution in America for drug-running. Indicted in the US, Noriega announced that Panama was at war with the United States. US troops swiftly broke resistance from the Panamanian military and Guillermo Endora, apparent winner of the elections, was sworn in as president. Noriega held out for eleven days, eventually emerging from the Vatican embassy to give himself up. President George BUSH Snr was criticised in Latin America for sending in the troops, but his action came to be seen as justified. Noriega claimed he had been put into the drugs trade by the CIA and that Bush must have known this; nevertheless a Florida court in July 1992 sentenced him to 40 years in jail.

> An act of hemispheric hygiene. GEORGE F. WILL

Panama scandal The financial and political scandal in France which broke in 1892 over the discovery that corrupt means had been used to keep public and private investment flowing into the Panama Canal Company, with three governments falling as a result. Ferdinand de Lesseps, who had been lionised for successfully constructing the Suez Canal, had got into deep water in his efforts to construct a Panama Canal without locks and with a heavy death toll for his workers. From 1888 he paid newspapers to report that the project was going well to maintain investor confidence, and bribed Deputies to vote for new bonds to allow the canal to be finished; nevertheless the Panama Canal Company went bankrupt in 1889, with 800,000 investors losing their stakes. Three years later disclosure of the corruption in right-wing papers discredited most of the ruling Radical Party, who were heavily implicated, including Clemenceau (*see* TIGER), and triggered a wave of anti-Semitism and anti-Protestantism because of the number of Jews and anti-clericals involved in the project. It thus created the climate for the DREYFUS CASE.

Pandit (Hindi a wise and learned man) The courtesy title accorded in India to Jawaharlal NEHRU (1889–1964), who led the nation to independence and was its first Prime Minister. *See also* PUNDIT.

panel (1) In the UK, a list of qualified persons compiled by a political party, from which CANDIDATES for local or Parliamentary ELECTION may be chosen. (2) In OPINION POLLing, a group of individual voters who are repeatedly questioned during a CAMPAIGN to detect shifts in opinion.

Panmunjom The village just south of the 38TH PARALLEL where the truce ending the KOREAN WAR was negotiated; signature on 27 July 1953 was not actually at Panmunjom but at nearby villages in the North and South where the respective commanders appended their signatures. The village of Panmunjom was destroyed in the fighting, but on its site is a Joint Security Area (JSA), 800 metres wide, which bisects the Military Demarcation Line separating the two Koreas; at its centre is a conference room containing a green felt-covered table where the two former combatants – the UNITED NATIONS and the Korean People's Army and Chinese People's Volunteers – meet to discuss the operation of the truce. The JSA is visited by 100,000 people a year, 90% of them tourists from the South. Tourists are warned not to wave at the North Koreans, lest they appear in a Pyongyang newspaper saluting the glories of STALINISM.

Papa Doc Nickname for **François Duvalier** (1907–71), President-for-life of Haiti, who was sustained in office by a reign of terror conducted by the TONTONS MACOUTE. His son Jean-Claude Duvalier (1951–), who succeeded him and ruled for fifteen years before being overthrown, was known as **Baby Doc**.

Papa Dop The unflattering nickname bestowed by left-wingers on Georgios Papadopoulos (1919–99), leader of the dictatorship imposed by the Greek COLONELS in 1967. The comparison with the Haitian leader was intentional, signifying the brutality with which the Colonels treated their opponents.

papabile Suitable for the highest office, from the Ital. *papabile* (fit to be Pope).

paper candidate *See* CANDIDATE.

paper tiger An apparent threat posing no actual danger. The term originated in 19th-century China (in Chinese *tsuh lao fu*) and was popularised by CHAIRMAN MAO Tse-Tung.

> The atomic bomb is a paper tiger which the US reactionaries use to scare people. It looks terrible, but in fact it isn't. All reactionaries are paper tigers.
> MAO TSE-TUNG, 1946

Papists A hostile term for Roman Catholics, reflecting their allegiance to the Pope. It was first used in 16th-century England and subsequently by anti-Catholic political groups into Victorian times (and more recently in NORTHERN IRELAND). *See also* GORDON RIOTS.

para-. paramilitary (1) A semi-official or secret political organisation which takes on the trappings of a military force, frequently also having an outright terrorist wing to press home its aims; also an individual member of such a body. A typical paramilitary group is the Ulster Defence Association, whose members drill and wear uniforms, yet which operated within the law for over 20 years; its murkier activities are carried on by nominally-separate groups. A well-known though less brutal US example was the BLACK PANTHERS. *See also* DEATH SQUADS. (2) Uniformed and armed civil forces or organisations that legitimately support military forces.

parastatal Especially in Africa, a state-owned concern engaged in commercial activity, frequently on a monopoly basis.

pardon The exemption of an individual from the rigours of the law for an action which either threatens them with criminal charges or had already led to a conviction. The most controversial has been President FORD's pardon of Richard NIXON for his role in

WATERGATE. Just one month after Nixon's resignation in August 1974, Ford caused a political storm by announcing a 'full, complete and absolute pardon' for his predecessor. This act freed Nixon from any threat of prosecution, though many of those involved in the conspiracy subsequently went to jail. Had Nixon been IMPEACHED, Ford would have been barred by the CONSTITUTION from pardoning him. Ford justified his action thus:

> I do believe that the buck stops here, that I cannot rely upon public opinion polls to tell me what is right. I do believe . . . that I, not as President but as a humble servant of God, will receive justice without mercy if I fail to show mercy.

The furore died down, and Ford's action – if premature – is now widely seen as having helped the healing process.

Presidents have since incurred odium for granting pardons just before their departure from office. At Christmas 1992 George BUSH Snr pardoned President REAGAN's Defence Secretary Caspar Weinberger (*see* CAP THE KNIFE), who was about to stand trial on charges of lying to CONGRESS over the IRAN-CONTRA AFFAIR. Leaked testimony from Weinberger indicated not only that he had known more than he admitted, but that Bush, despite his denials, was also in the LOOP. Weinberger claimed the charges against him were a political stunt; Democrats that Bush had pardoned him to avoid himself having to testify under oath.

Eight years later President CLINTON was heavily criticised for pardoning 200 convicted or indicted criminals prior to leaving office, including a number of his political supporters and his brother Roger, who had pleaded guilty to distributing cocaine. The most controversial pardon went to the financier Marc Rich, who had fled the country in 1983 rather than face trial on charges of racketeering, conspiracy, tax evasion, mail fraud, wire fraud and trading with the enemy (Iran, during the hostage crisis). His former wife, Denise Rich, raised over $500,000 for the Democrats, contributed to Clinton's legal defence fund over ZIPPERGATE, then lobbied successfully for a pardon for Rich, who by then was living in Switzerland.

Parfumée, la (Fr. the perfumed one) The nickname of Edith CRESSON (1934–), the French socialist politician who was briefly President MITTERRAND's highly controversial Prime Minister during 1991 and 1992, and whose recklessness in awarding jobs and contracts as a EUROPEAN COMMISSIONER brought down Jacques Santer's Commission in 1999.

Paris. Paris Club Also known as the **Group of Ten**, an informal forum under the auspices of the French Treasury that provides a channel between western officials in overseeing government-to-government loans, especially to assist the THIRD WORLD. The nations first met in Paris in 1962, agreeing to lend money to the International Monetary Fund (IMF) and inaugurated the concept of SPECIAL DRAWING RIGHTS as a standard unit of account. There are now actually eleven members: Belgium, Canada, France, Germany, Italy, Japan, the Netherlands, Sweden, Switzerland, the UK and United States. Governors of their CENTRAL BANKS meet bi-monthly at the BANK OF INTERNATIONAL SETTLEMENTS.

Paris Commune The working-class revolution in Paris in 1871 after France's defeat in the FRANCO-PRUSSIAN WAR. The Commune, backed by the National Guard, abolished CONSCRIPTION, separated Church and State, reduced officials' salaries to those of skilled workmen, brought women into government and planned to transfer empty factories to workers' control. On 21 May, the regular army of the new VERSAILLES-based French Republic under Thiers entered Paris, executed 20,000 COMMUNARDS, arrested 36,000 citizens and jailed or deported 15,000. Engels hailed the Commune as 'the dictatorship of the proletariat'; Marx more realistically called it 'a heroic self-holocaust'.

Paris peace talks The long-running talks aimed at ending the VIETNAM WAR which opened in May 1968, finally producing an agreement in January 1973 that America would end direct military aid to its southern ally. The final talks, between a US delegation headed by Henry KISSINGER and North Vietnamese officials led by Le Duc Tho, earned both men the NOBEL PEACE PRIZE, but the American withdrawal led to a North Vietnamese takeover (*see* DECENT INTERVAL).

Paris summit A pioneering SUMMIT meeting between President EISENHOWER, Nikita S. Khrushchev, Harold MACMILLAN and President DE GAULLE, which was scheduled for 16 May 1960. All four leaders arrived in Paris, but the summit was abandoned at the last minute when Eisenhower refused Khrushchev's demand that he apologise for the U-2 incident.

Charter of Paris The agreement reached by the CSCE countries in Paris in November 1990 to monitor threats to peace throughout

Europe and endeavour to prevent conflicts breaking out in and between the countries experiencing their first freedom after the collapse of Communism. CSCE proved impotent when war broke out in former Yugoslavia the following year; the meeting was most memorable as Margaret THATCHER's final appearance on the international stage, the crucial vote denying her re-election as Conservative leader on the first ballot taking place while she was in Paris.

Treaty of Paris (1) The treaty concluded on 3 September 1783 that ended the American WAR OF INDEPENDENCE. Britain recognised American independence and made peace, and the new republic gained generous boundaries and the right to fish in Canadian waters. (2) The treaty of 30 March 1856 that embodied the settlement of the CRIMEAN WAR, an ARMISTICE having been agreed in Paris a month before. The key point was the demilitarisation of the Black Sea, a major gain for Britain and a setback for Russia. (3) The treaty signed on 10 December 1898 which disposed of Spain's empire after its defeat in the SPANISH-AMERICAN WAR. The treaty gave Cuba its independence, ceded the Philippines to the US for $20 million and also gave America Guam and Puerto Rico. (4) The treaty of 27 May 1952 between France, West Germany, Italy and the BENELUX countries that set up a European Defence Community. The community was still-born because the French National Assembly refused to ratify the treaty, seeing it as a back-door means of German rearmament. However, the Western European Union (WEU), serving many of the same purposes, was agreed on soon after.

parish (1) In rural England, the smallest unit of local government, based on the area originally served by a village's parish church. The **parish council** or **parish meeting** is the governing body. (2) In Louisiana, the unit of government corresponding to a COUNTY in the rest of the United States.

parity (1) The situation in an elected body, especially at local level, when two parties enjoy an equal level of representation. At election times parity is gained by the party making ground, lost by the party falling back. (2) In employment, the far-off point where AFFIRMATIVE ACTION programmes and other measures have given women, ethnic minorities and other groups the share of the employment market that they are proportionately entitled to. (3) In COLD WAR nuclear strategy, the point at which the two SUPERPOWERS would have arsenals of equivalent strength.

Parkinson affair The scandal which curtailed, and seemed for a time to have ruined, the political career of **Cecil** (later Lord) **Parkinson** (1932–), one of Margaret THATCHER's favourite Ministers. In May 1983 Parkinson, who had just chaired the CONSERVATIVE PARTY to a LANDSLIDE victory, told Mrs Thatcher that his former secretary Sara Keays, with whom he had had a long affair, was expecting his baby. Parkinson decided to stay with his wife and daughters. That October, the week before the Tory party conference, *The Times*, briefed by Miss Keays' father, broke the story and other papers gave it banner headlines. The LABOUR PARTY conference was in session, one delegate exclaiming from the rostrum:

> Is there nothing the Tories won't do to keep us off the front page?

Parkinson, by now Trade and Industry Secretary, stood his ground, with DOWNING STREET declaring:

> The question of Cecil Parkinson's resignation does not, and will not, arise.

The embattled Minister won a warm but not euphoric reception when he appeared with his wife at the Tories' Blackpool gathering. But after further revelations from Miss Keays he resigned on the final night. The spurned Miss Keays duly had a daughter, and an embittered Parkinson went into the wilderness. He came back in 1987 as Energy Secretary and later Transport Secretary, but when Mrs Thatcher was ousted in 1990 he was out of the succession, and left the government.

> Had Cecil been a Minister of the THIRD REPUBLIC, the Parkinson Affair would have made him President.
>
> JULIAN CRITCHLEY MP (Con.)

> *Q:* Why is Cecil Parkinson like MFI?
> *A:* One loose screw, and the whole Cabinet falls apart. ANON.

Parliament (Fr. *parlement*, a meeting to exchange views) (1) In Britain and COMMONWEALTH countries, the Houses that make up the LEGISLATURE and (as the HOUSE OF LORDS tends to be overlooked) the embodiment of democracy. Cromwell's victory in the English Civil War created an image of Parliament as all-powerful; in 1648 the Earl of Pembroke declared:

A Parliament can do anything but make a man a woman, and a woman a man.

Edmund BURKE told the electors of Bristol that: 'Parliament is a deliberative assembly of one nation. You choose a Member indeed, but when you have chosen him, he is not the Member for Bristol, but he is a Member of Parliament.' And Anthony Trollope, just as loftily, wrote: 'I have often thought that to sit in the British Parliament should be the highest ambition of every educated Englishman.'

Parliament does not always inspire such noble thoughts. Prior to the UNION of 1707, a popular Scottish prayer was: 'God bless the Houses of Parliament, and overrule their deliberations to the benefit of the common people.' Thomas Carlyle advised that 'Parliament will train you to talk; and above all things to hear, with patience, unlimited quantities of foolish talk'. He also argued that: 'A Parliament with newspaper reporters firmly established in it is an entity which by its very nature cannot do work, but talk only.' And the Russian jurist Konstantin Podednostsev (1827–1907) maintained that

Parliaments are the great lie of our time.

Charles II described Parliament, despite what it had done to his father, as 'better than a play'. In Victorian times Robert Louis Stevenson observed: 'We all know what Parliament is – and we are all ashamed of it.' Sir Cyril Smith (*see* BIG CYRIL) termed it 'the longest-running farce in the West End', and former Beatle George Harrison, backing the NATURAL LAW PARTY in the 1992 election, told an Albert Hall rally:

All we need now is to get rid of those stiffs in Parliament and we'd be laughing.

(2) A Parliament. The duration of a Parliamentary term, in Britain a maximum of five years but frequently less. Radicals have traditionally advocated shorter, fixed-term Parliaments – in the CHARTISTS' case with ELECTIONS every year to increase ACCOUNTABILITY. Henry Labouchère (*see* LABBY) wrote at the turn of the 19th/20th century: 'Long Parliaments are as fatal to sound business as long credits are to sound trade.'

Parliament Acts The legislation passed in 1911 and 1949 under which the HOUSE OF LORDS lost its right to kill BILLS passed by the Commons (it retains a DELAYING POWER, reduced from two years to one in 1949), and any say in the passage of the Budget and other MONEY BILLS. The first Act, which also reduced the maximum life of a Parliament from seven years to five, was pushed through by ASQUITH's Liberal government, after two general elections in 1910 had given it a MANDATE, following the Lords' rejection of the PEOPLE'S BUDGET. Only the threat to create hundreds of Liberal peers broke the Lords' resistance; they approved it finally on 10 August 1911 (*see* HEDGERS AND DITCHERS) by just 131 votes to 114, with George V writing: 'I am spared any further humiliation.' The second stemmed from the Lords' rejection of the ATTLEE government's plans for steel NATIONALISATION. It is now up to the Government to decide whether to override the Lords by invoking the Parliament Acts if it defeats a Bill; in 1991 the WAR CRIMES BILL was pushed through by the MAJOR government despite being defeated in the upper house; in 2005 the COUNTRYSIDE ALLIANCE unsuccessfully challenged in the courts the validity of the 1949 Parliament Act under which Tony BLAIR's government had overcome peers' resistance to the Hunting Bill.

Parliament House The new A$1 billion building in Canberra opened for Australia's Parliament on the nation's bicentenary, 25 August 1988. The first substantive item of business was Paul KEATING's Budget statement.

Parliament Square The square at the heart of Britain's government quarter, whose nondescript grassy centre is graced by CHURCHILL's statue. The TREASURY abuts part of its north side, which faces up Parliament Street to WHITEHALL and the CENOTAPH. To the east lie Bridge Street and Westminster Bridge, NEW PALACE YARD and WESTMINSTER HALL, to the south St Margaret's Church, Parliament's own, and to the west Victoria Street and the Middlesex Guildhall. Political demonstrations in Parliament Square are supposed to be banned under the SESSIONAL ORDERS, but from June 2001 a permanent display of scruffy banners has faced the Carriage Gates of New Palace Yard; most are from supporters of foxhunting and opponents of the IRAQ WAR, notably Brian Haw, a former carpenter, who conducted a three-year vigil. From August 2005 a half-mile exclusion zone was being imposed around Parliament. This had the effect of empowering the police to remove Mr Haw and his banners, and also to ban loud-hailers in the square during daylight hours; MPs of all parties had complained of Mr Haw haranguing them.

High Court of Parliament One of the

British Parliament's official titles, reflecting both its function as the ultimate arbiter on behalf of the people and, more specifically, the continuing judicial functions of the HOUSE OF LORDS (pending the establishment of a SUPREME COURT) as the ultimate court of appeal.

hung Parliament *See* HUNG.

Imperial Parliament A term popular in the early 20th century for WESTMINSTER's predominance among the Parliaments of the British Empire, and also for its role as the legislature for the entire United Kingdom.

Parliamentarian (1) At WESTMINSTER, a politician who demonstrates outstanding commitment to, and grasp of, the ways of the HOUSE OF COMMONS. Such a figure frequently infuriates his own party and makes common cause with rebels on the other side of the House who feel their rights are being threatened. Three outstanding Parliamentarians of recent times have been Tony BENN, Michael FOOT and Enoch POWELL. (2) In the US CONGRESS, the senior official of the HOUSE OF REPRESENTATIVES who advises the SPEAKER on procedure and on what is or is not permitted.

Parliamentary agents The specialised law firms operating in the WESTMINSTER area who will present Private BILLS to Parliament or lodge objections to them.

Parliamentary Commissioner for Administration In Britain, the official title for the OMBUDSMAN.

Parliamentary draftsmen The legal technicians in WHITEHALL who draft government legislation and make sure that amendments and Private Members' BILLS are worded in watertight fashion.

Parliamentary leper Harold WILSON's electrifying description when Parliament opened on 5 November 1964 of Peter Griffiths (1928–), who had won Smethwick from Labour the previous month with a campaign widely perceived as RACIST. This CAMPAIGN, though not Griffiths himself, was said to have spawned the slogan: 'If you want a nigger for neighbour, vote Labour'. Wilson told the Commons:

> Smethwick Conservatives can have the satisfaction of having topped the poll, of having sent a Member who, until another election returns him to oblivion, will serve his time here as a Parliamentary leper.

Griffiths lost his seat in 1966, but in 1979 made a non-controversial return as MP for Portsmouth North, serving until 1997.

Parliamentary occasion An event at WESTMINSTER considered memorable by those present, for instance the Saturday emergency debate on 3 April 1982 that followed Argentina's invasion of the FALKLANDS.

Parliamentary Private Secretary (PPS) At Westminster, MPs probably bound for Ministerial office who served as the unsalaried 'eyes and ears' of Ministers, sitting behind them when they are speaking or answering questions. PPSs are part of the PAYROLL VOTE, and are expected to resign if they fail to vote with the government on a controversial matter. The LEADER OF THE OPPOSITION also has a PPS to keep in touch with the backbenchers; Iain Duncan Smith (*see* IDS) and Michael HOWARD have each had two, one for each wing of the CONSERVATIVE PARTY.

Parliamentary Secretary or **Under-Secretary** The most junior Ministerial rank in the British government. Most departments have two or more, carrying out duties delegated to them by the more senior members of the team.

Parliamentary system The system in which the HEAD OF GOVERNMENT is based in the LEGISLATURE, as opposed to the PRESIDENTIAL system, as in France or the United States, where the political leader of the nation is elected separately and doubles as the HEAD OF STATE.

Manual of Parliamentary Practice The document drawn up by Thomas JEFFERSON in 1800 which set out the first rules of ORDER and procedure for the US CONGRESS. They still form part of the rules of the HOUSE OF REPRESENTATIVES, which Jefferson reckoned needed them more than the SENATE.

Parnellites The supporters of **Charles Stewart Parnell** (1846–91), the 'UNCROWNED KING OF IRELAND', who during the 1880s led a militant campaign at WESTMINSTER for HOME RULE. From a Protestant landowning family in Co. Wicklow, Parnell entered the COMMONS in 1875 and was soon manipulating Parliamentary procedure to obstruct government business. This attribute, and his presidency of the Irish National Land League which raised £70,000 in America to revive agriculture after the IRISH POTATO FAMINE, led Irish MPs to elect him their chairman in 1880. Parnell's advocacy of BOYCOTTS against absentee landowners led to violence and his imprisonment with 34 other Irish MPs. He was freed under the KILMAINHAM TREATY after undertaking to denounce Nationalist excesses in return for a government promise to soft-pedal on rent arrears.

In 1885 the 86 Parnellite MPs threw their weight behind GLADSTONE's first Home Rule Bill. They brought down Lord SALISBURY's government, but the Bill failed because of defections by Liberal MPs. When the Unionists won the ensuing election Parnell, described by T. P. O'Connor as 'a madman of genius', was thrown into an alliance with Gladstone. This was only a convenience for Parnell, the Liberal G. W. E. Russell observing:

> He hated England, he condemned the House of Commons, he despised the Liberals much more profoundly than the Tories, and he regarded his followers as merely voters, or at best fit for work too dirty for a gentleman to undertake.

In 1889 Parnell was cleared by a Commission of Enquiry of complicity in the PHOENIX PARK and other outrages, in which he had been implicated by a forged letter reproduced in *The Times*. Richard Piggott, the forger, fled to Madrid and shot himself. But his character was only briefly rehabilitated; the following year Captain O'Shea, husband of Parnell's mistress Kitty, cited him in the divorce court and costs were awarded against the Irish leader. The Irish party first re-elected him, then rescinded their decision under pressure from Gladstone; CAMPBELL-BANNERMAN declared: 'He has shown by his acts that he is unfit to be the leader of a political party.' The following year Parnell died suddenly in Brighton, five months after his marriage to Mrs O'Shea, and in the 1892 election all but nine of his party lost their seats.

> The fall of Parnell left Ireland with a dead god instead of a leader. G. M. YOUNG

> As a Protestant he was probably the only man who might eventually have conciliated Ulster.
> CHURCHILL

partisan (1) A participant in the political process who puts his or her party or faction above all other considerations. (2) The adjective to describe such a person or attitude, the opposite of bipartisan.

> In the hour of danger there is no partisanship. In that hour we shall all stand as one people in support of America.
> House Minority Leader JOSEPH W. MARTIN, after PEARL HARBOR

> We cannot have any great issue of the day decided on the basis of partisanship.
> BILL CLINTON, Charleston, West Virginia, 10 August 1993

(3) A Communist GUERRILLA fighter, notably a member of TITO's units in NAZI-occupied Yugoslavia though partisans also operated behind German lines in the Soviet Union, and elsewhere. The title reflects the role of the underground Communist Party in organising resistance.

partition The division of a territory, usually along ethnic or religious lines, in an effort to create homogenous communities, or to dilute the threat posed by a single entity. Notable 20th-century examples were Ireland (by treaty between Britain and the newly-formed IRISH FREE STATE), India (by Britain in creating independent states of India and Pakistan, after Muslim leaders refused to accept a single Hindu-majority state), Germany (through the creation of separate western and Communist states in the great powers' respective zones), Vietnam (under the GENEVA AGREEMENT following the French defeat at DIEN BIEN PHU) and Cyprus (after Turkey's occupation of northern Cyprus in 1974). None has entirely solved the problem it was set up to remedy, and it has become fashionable to blame Britain for seeing partition as a panacea. But only Vietnam and Germany have been reunited.

Partnership for Peace The agreement for interim association between NATO and eastern European members of the former WARSAW PACT, which was concluded in Brussels in 1994. It stopped just short of membership of NATO for the former Communist signatories, reflecting the concerns of Russia, which was also party to the agreement, that the alliance still posed a threat to it. Most of the non-Russian participants eventually joined NATO.

Partnership in Power Labour's policy-making framework in government, pushed through by Tony BLAIR after the party's 1997 victory to avoid public rows between the government, the unions and the 'old Labour' rank and file by limiting the scope for confrontations at party conference. It worked better than some elements of the party would have liked, UNISON in 2003 demanding a fresh look at the agreement because the government had ignored its opposition to the IRAQ WAR, PPPs and FOUNDATION HOSPITALS.

party The basis of political organisation in a democracy, bringing together people of supposedly like mind to secure the ELECTION of their representatives in government. The American scholar James Sundquist defines party as 'the tie that binds, the glue that fastens, the bridge that unites the disparate institutions that make up the government'. It was not always so. In the 17th and 18th centuries parties were regarded as inherently harmful to the process, Alexander Pope describing them as 'the madness of many, for the gains of the few', and George Savile, Earl of Halifax, asserting: 'The best party is but a kind of conspiracy against the nation. Ignorance maketh most men go into a party, and shame keepeth them from getting out of it.'

The FOUNDING FATHERS of the United States were deeply divided over whether there should be political parties. George WASHINGTON, in his Farewell Address, said: 'Let me . . . warn you in the most solemn manner against the baneful effects of the spirit of party generally'. John ADAMS confessed: 'There is nothing I dread so much as the division of the Republic into two great parties.' But James MADISON argued that 'No free country has ever been without parties, which are a natural offspring of freedom', and eventually his view prevailed.

The mood changed in England, too. In the 1790s Edmund Burke could commend a party as 'a body of men united for promoting by their joint endeavours the national interest, upon some particular principle in which they are all agreed'. Parties, he said, 'must ever exist in a free country'. And by DISRAELI's time the argument was almost over. Applauding the party system as 'organised opinion', he said: 'You cannot choose between party government and Parliamentary government. I say you can have no Parliamentary government if you have no party government.' And he reminded the statesmen of the day: 'It is not becoming in any minister to decry party who has risen by party. If we were not PARTISANS we should not be Ministers.' Yet in more cynical mood, Disraeli once exclaimed:

> Damn your principles! Stick to your party!

Nevertheless the uniformity imposed by the party system continued to cause amusement and concern. Ralph Waldo Emerson described party as 'an elegant incognito designed to save a man from the vexation of thinking'. And in *HMS Pinafore*, W. S. Gilbert had Sir Joseph Porter, First Lord of the Admiralty, declare:

> I always voted at my party's call
> And I never thought of voting for myself at all.

Abraham LINCOLN once said that 'the party lash and the fear of ridicule will overrule justice and liberty'. But later Presidents disagreed. Rutherford Hayes observed: 'He serves his party best who serves his country best.' James Garfield asserted that 'all free governments are party governments'. And Calvin COOLIDGE later insisted: 'It is necessary to have party organisation if we are to have effective and efficient government.'

Lord SALISBURY, one of the last great reactionaries, felt that 'parties are formed more with reference to controversies that are gone by than to the controversies which these parties actually have to decide'. And Woodrow WILSON also reckoned they could be hollow vessels, saying: ''The success of a party means little unless it is being used by the nation for a great purpose.' The inter-war FASCIST movements took the argument further, the Portuguese dictator Antonio Salazar asserting:

> We have arrived at a stage in which a political party founded upon the individual rights of citizens or electors has no longer the right to exist.

In America the party system underwent a friendlier onslaught from Will Rogers, who at various timed declared: 'I am for the party which is out of power, no matter which one it is'; 'No party is as bad as its leaders'; and 'The more you read about politics, you've got to admit that each party is worse than the other.' Stanley BALDWIN echoed this last remark, declaring: 'No party is on the whole better than another.' But A.P. Herbert, a rare Independent MP, defended the system as 'right and necessary', saying: 'All cannot be fly-halves – there must be a scrum.'

But is it a case of 'my party, right or wrong'? The Canadian poet John Bengough asserted that 'you cannot influence a political party to do right if you stick to it when it does wrong'. John F. KENNEDY once declared that 'sometimes party loyalty asks too much'. But Harold WILSON believed that 'no one should be in a political party unless he believes that party represents his own highest religious and moral ideas'.

Party, the The term used by COMMUNISTS to describe the all-embracing control, the unique and totalitarian nature of their own party.

> The Party in the last instance is always right, because it is the single historic instrument which the working class possesses for the solution of its historic problems. TROTSKY

party line Again originally a Communist term, the position set out by a party's leadership or decision-making body to which members are expected to adhere. The Yugoslav Communist dissident Milovan Djilas once observed of TITO's rule: 'The Party Line is that there is no Party Line.'

party managers The shadowy figures who manipulate power behind the scenes, frequently ACCOUNTABLE to no one.

> When I came into power, I found that the party managers had taken it all to themselves. I could not even name my own Cabinet. They had sold out every place to pay the election expenses.
>
> President BENJAMIN HARRISON

party political broadcast In Britain, a statement from a political party, carried free of charge on BBC television, ITV and Channel 4, and BBC radio, with time allocated in ratio to the votes polled by each party at the last ELECTION and (during a CAMPAIGN) the number of CANDIDATES it is fielding. Often treated by the voters as an opportunity to put the kettle on, occasional broadcasts like the 1987 KINNOCK video or the Labour broadcast in 1992 that sparked the WAR OF JENNIFER'S EAR have made an impact.

party room An Australian term for a Parliamentary CAUCUS meeting.

party within a party The Labour leadership's characterisation of the MILITANT TENDENCY at the height of its influence; also the constitutional grounds for the expulsion of Militant's adherents from the party as belonging to an organisation with its own separate and identifiable programme and membership.

multi-party system A democratic society in which the voters have a choice between three or more serious parties.

Now is the time for all good men to come to the aid of the party The sentence devised to test the speed of the first typewriter in Milwaukee in 1867. Charles E. Weller, historian of the machine, may have been the author; he did not himself claim credit, merely saying that the sentence was appropriate because the machine was tested 'during a political campaign'.

one-party state Pioneered by FASCISTS and COMMUNISTS and perpetuated largely by megalomaniacs, a state in which only one party is permitted. It is both a means of enforcing uniformity, and of governing a country with limited reserves of talent without half of it being 'wasted' in OPPOSITION. This last pretext was used by many rulers in post-colonial Africa for imposing an effective dictatorship; the idealistic Julius Nyerere tried it in Tanzania, Robert Mugabe in Zimbabwe has been edging towards it, but Kenya and Zambia have backed away.

post office parties *See* POST.

the party's over The warning, in the words of an old song, to Britain's local authorities from the Labour Environment Secretary Anthony Crosland (1918–77) that they could not carry on with spending plans seen by WHITEHALL as lavish, at a time when the economy was in crisis.

third party US shorthand for a movement which in any Presidential election gains the momentum to pose a threat to the Republicans or Democrats, more often by slicing into the vote of one of them than by threatening to carry the ELECTORAL COLLEGE. Examples include Theodore ROOSEVELT's BULL MOOSE ticket, the DIXIECRATS of 1948 and Ross PEROT's Reform Party candidacy of 1992. Under campaign funding legislation, a third party can receive Federal funds in one election if its Presidential candidate four years previously received between 5 and 25 per cent of the votes cast.

third party endorsements The practice, beloved by SPIN DOCTORS, of lining up prior to any significant announcement statements of support from people of consequence who are perceived as relatively independent, and whose views will therefore carry weight with the voters. *See also* QUOTE SLUTS.

two-party system A system in which the electors regularly have a choice between just two parties, whose policy stances are supposed to fluctuate to reflect changing times and mores. The Unites States since 1928, and Britain from 1931 to 1974, have been two-party systems. In 1858 Sen. Stephen Douglas asserted: 'There can be but two great political parties in this country', and in England his contemporary John Stuart Mill wrote: 'A party of order and stability, and a party of progress and reform, are both necessary elements of a healthy state of political life.' More cynically Ralph Waldo Emerson observed: 'The two parties which divide the State, the party of Conservatism and that of innovation, are very old, and have disputed the possession of the world ever since it was made.' And in 1891 Charlie Glyde, leader of a strike in Bradford that helped create the LABOUR PARTY, said:

> We have had two parties in the past; the can't and the won't; and it's time we had a party that will.

In America, Speaker Tom REED once said: 'The best system is to have one party govern and the other party watch.' But the Russian revolutionary Nikolai Bukhanin took the idea one stage further: 'We might have a two-party system, but one of the two parties would be in office and the other in prison.'

Pasionaria, La (Sp. the passionate one) The Communist Dolores Ibarruri (1895–1989), who as an inspirational leader during the SPANISH CIVIL WAR with her cries of ¡*No pasaran*! (*see* THEY SHALL NOT PASS *below*) and 'It is better to die on your feet than live on your knees!' Revered in exile during the Franco (*see* CAUDILLO) years, she returned when democracy was restored and was re-elected a Communist member of the CORTÈS.

> The only person with whom I felt La Pasionaria could be compared was the woman I had always regarded as the greatest actress I had seen, Eleonora Duse. She had Duse's wonderful grace and voice, but she was much more beautiful, with rich colouring, large dark eyes, and black wavy hair. She swept into the room like a queen, yet she was a miner's daughter married to a miner – a woman who had had the sorrow of losing six out of eight children.
>
> KATHERINE, DUCHESS OF ATHOLL (*see* RED DUCHESS)

PASOK The Pan-Hellenic Socialist Party, founded by Andreas Papandreou (1919–96) in 1974 as the regime of the Greek COLONELS collapsed. Shrilly left-wing and anti-American in opposition, it won power in 1981 and governed in more pragmatic vein. Pasok was forced from office in 1989; Papandreou had suffered a heart attack and divorced his wife to marry an air hostess, and Pasok was tarnished by the looting of the Bank of Crete, which ministers were later cleared of assisting. In October 1993 the voters ousted NEW DEMOCRACY; Papandreou returned but resigned in January 1996 after two months semi-conscious with kidney and lung failure and died that June. Costas Simitis became Prime Minister, moving Pasok toward the centre; on his resignation in January 2004 Papandreou's son George attempted to galvanise the party but was defeated by New Democracy that March.

pass. Pass Laws The laws regulating the movement of black labour which were a hated keystone of APARTHEID in South Africa. Introduced in 1948, they barred rural Africans from visiting towns for longer than 72 hours without a special permit, on pain of arrest or deportation. Such measures had been sporadically applied in some Afrikaner areas since the 18th century, but the all-embracing nature of the laws and their clear political thrust provoked deep resentment, and protest campaigns from the ANC and later the PAC. Arrests for violating the Pass Laws peaked at 381,858 in 1976. In 1986 the NATIONAL PARTY government announced the scrapping of the laws as it moved toward dismantling *apartheid*.

They shall not pass! *See* THEY.

Passkey The US SECRET SERVICE code word for President Gerald FORD.

passive resistance A form of protest combining NON-VIOLENCE with CIVIL DISOBEDIENCE, in which those staging the protest refuse to co-operate with the authorities but commit no positive acts of obstruction. It was pioneered by MAHATMA Gandhi, who said: 'The sword of passive resistance does not require a scabbard and one cannot be forcibly dispossessed of it.' Gandhi confessed: 'I do not like the term. Still, I adopt the phrase because it is well known and easily understood.' Zambia's President Kenneth Kaunda (1924–) did not consider passive resistance an effective political weapon; he dismissed it as 'a sport for gentlemen . . . or ladies.'

PATCO Professional Association of (American) Air Traffic Controllers. The trade union who enabled Ronald REAGAN to demonstrate early in his ADMINISTRATION that he would not tolerate disruption in the public services. In August 1981 Reagan fired 11,400 members of PATCO who had joined a strike, which was illegal as they were Federal employees; they had imagined they were safe because of the specialised and safety-critical nature of their work, but the planes kept flying with military controllers and civilian recruits. The dismissals became a *cause célèbre* for organised labour, but also cowed the unions. The ban on PATCO was lifted by President CLINTON in 1993, but by then there was little scope for the sacked strikers to get their jobs back.

paternalism (Lat. *pater,* father) The provision of welfare and other services in a way that implies that the mass of the people are unable to decide for themselves and need government to resolve basic issues for them. The intention is often honourable, but there is an element of self-interest – paternalism was at the heart of British TORYism in the first half of the 19th century, and of DISRAELI's social reforms which aimed to benefit the working class while keeping it out of the political process. In America the word is often used as a pejorative, especially by organised labour which detects in paternalism by employers not a desire to benefit the workforce but an attempt to deny the unions a recruiting ground.

patriality The concept introduced into UK law by James CALLAGHAN's controversially restrictive 1968 Immigration Act. It confined the basic right to enter and settle in Britain to 'patrials' – those intending immigrants who could claim a parent (or in some cases a grandparent) born in the country.

patriation The term used in Canada for the transfer of the country's CONSTITUTION from British to Canadian law. For over a century Canada was governed under the BRITISH NORTH AMERICA ACT passed at WESTMINSTER in 1867; efforts to patriate the constitution from the mid-1970s were held up by political and legal wrangles over what degree of consent between the provinces short of unanimity would enable its subsequent amendment. Finally, in 1982, the UK Parliament passed the **Canada Act** which handed all responsibility for the Constitution to Ottawa and the provinces.

patriotism One of the most basic forces in politics the world over, stemming from the conviction, in George Bernard Shaw's words, that 'this country is superior to all other countries because you were born in it'. Calvin COOLIDGE injected a further note of self-interest, declaring that 'patriotism means looking out for yourself by looking out for your country'. Lord ROSEBERY reckoned: 'There is no word so prostituted as patriotism. Every government fails in it, and every opposition glows with it.' But many statesmen have echoed the words of the British author Tobias Smollett (1721–71) that 'true patriotism is of no party'.

Patriotism, and its exploitation by politicians, has always aroused cynicism. William Randolph Hearst asserted that 'a politician will do anything to keep his job – even become a patriot'. Dr Samuel Johnson memorably wrote that 'patriotism is the last refuge of a scoundrel', and Bertrand Russell observed that 'patriots always talk of dying for their country, and never of killing for their country'. Moreover August Bebel, co-founder of Germany's SPD, declared in 1870: 'In time of war the loudest patriots are the greatest profiteers.'

The American nation was founded on an open and assertive patriotism. Benjamin FRANKLIN claimed at the outset that the English 'believe that threepence in the pound of tea is sufficient to overcome the patriotism of an American'. And in his farewell message, George WASHINGTON told the people: 'Citizens by birth or choice, of a common country, that country has a right to concentrate your affections. The name of American, which belongs to you, in your national capacity, must always exalt the just pride of Patriotism, more than any appellation derived from local discriminations.' The founders of the Soviet Union looked for something less noble, TROTSKY declaring: 'Patriotism to the Soviet state is a revolutionary duty; whereas patriotism to a bourgeois state is treachery.'

Patriot Act *see* USA PATRIOT ACT.

Patriotism is not enough The final words of Edith Cavell (1865–1915) before being shot by a German firing squad in Brussels on 12 October 1915. Nurse Cavell, who had tended wounded Britons and was alleged to have spied on the Germans, told the chaplain who attended her:

> Standing, as I do, in the view of God and eternity, I realise that patriotism is not enough. I must have no hatred or bitterness towards anyone.

The shooting of Edith Cavell caused outrage in Britain and did much to sustain support for the prosecution of WORLD WAR I.

No money – no patriotism The blunt assessment of the English 'Friends of Liberty' made by the statesman and diplomat Charles Maurice de Talleyrand (1754–1838) at the height of the FRENCH REVOLUTION. The 'Friends' had angered him by seeking French support while offering the Revolution no financial help.

patronage The use of political power to allocate jobs to supporters and relatives, frequently in return for political loyalty or hard cash. Practised over the centuries, patronage reached its height in England during the ministry of WALPOLE, who once declared, 'There is enough pasture for all the sheep', and is wrongly alleged to have said: 'Every man has his price', and in America in the era of MACHINE POLITICS. In the early days of the new nation, Thomas JEFFERSON wrote: 'We are endeavouring to reduce the government to the practice of a rigorous economy, to avoid burdening the people and arming the magistrate with a patronage of money which might be used to corrupt and undermine the principles of our government.' And at the height of the CIVIL WAR, Secretary for War Edwin Stanton wrote to Mary Todd LINCOLN explaining his refusal to appoint a man she had put forward:

> If I should make such appointments, I should strike at the very root of all confidence of the people in the government, in your husband and you and me.

Patronage in Whitehall was effectively ended by the NORTHCOTE-TREVELYAN REFORMS; the PENDLETON ACT greatly reduced patronage in US Federal employment, though pockets have remained.

Patronage Secretary At WESTMINSTER, one of the semi-official titles of the Government CHIEF WHIP.

> No one knows better than a former patronage secretary the limitations of the human mind and the human spirit. Sir EDWARD HEATH

Patten Report The report of the Independent Commission on Policing chaired by the former CONSERVATIVE PARTY chairman and Hong Kong governor Chris (later Lord) Patten (1944–), which recommended in 1999 a completely new ethos for the police in NORTHERN IRELAND in the wake of the GOOD FRIDAY AGREEMENT. Patten's proposals were highly controversial: its 175 recommendations included the renaming of the RUC, abolition of its 'militaristic' ethos and structure, new recruits to be drawn from a 50–50 pool of Protestants and Catholics, a reduction in force size from 13,500 to 7500, abolition of the force's harp and crown badge, HUMAN RIGHTS training for police officers and a new policing board to replace the existing police authority. Ulster LOYALISTS bitterly resented the change of name, the abolition of the cap badge, reform of its much-criticised Special Branch and disbandment of its full-time reserve; Republicans concentrated on claiming that the government would break the spirit of the Agreement by not implementing the most important recommendations. In the event, most have been implemented; the Police Service of Northern Ireland replaced the RUC in November 2001 and has done its best to be what Tony BLAIR termed a 'normal police force' given the efforts of PARAMILITARIES on both sides to prevent it from doing its job, and a campaign of murder by dissident Republicans against Catholic members of police boards.

pavement politics (or **kerbstone politics**) The building of a power-base, especially at local level, by concentrating on small issues of immediate importance to voters, such as broken paving stones, rather than national issues or matters of high principle. *See also* COMMUNITY POLITICS.

Paving Bill *See* BILL.

Pax Americana (Lat. American Peace) The notion of a world order imposed by the United States, canvassed by non-ISOLATIONISTS at various junctures, particularly at the close of WORLD WAR II before it was clear there would be a lasting challenge from the Soviet Union, and after the COLD WAR (*see* NEW WORLD ORDER) before the threat from AL QAEDA became evident. It is derived from **Pax Britannica** (British Peace), the phrase coined in Palmerston's (*see* PAM) day to give a benevolent edge to Britain's world role, which Joseph Chamberlain later used to categorise British authority in India. *See also* WORLD POLICEMAN.

pay. pay freeze *See* FREEZE.

pay pause The initiative to restrain UK wage increases taken in 1961 by Chancellor (later Lord) Selwyn Lloyd (1904–78) as prosperity under the MACMILLAN government began to wane. Lloyd's drive for voluntary WAGE RESTRAINT and general economic belt-tightening after a period of near-boom led Labour to coin the term STOP-GO for Tory policies.

payroll padding Filling non-existent vacancies in a public agency as a form of PATRONAGE for supporters of oneself or one's party.

payroll vote The term used at WESTMINSTER for the support a government can mobilise in a critical DIVISION, comprising both Ministers and unsalaried PARLIAMENTARY PRIVATE SECRETARIES who are expected to toe the line; any PPS who cannot support the government is expected to resign. The use of this patronage to defeat Private Members' BILLS which the government finds inconvenient has been a source of controversy.

PC (1) The formal abbreviation for PRIVY COUNCILLOR. (2) Popular shorthand for POLITICAL CORRECTNESS. (3) PCs. Canada's PROGRESSIVE CONSERVATIVES.

PDs The Progressive Democrats, the new-look, liberal Irish party launched on 21 December 1985 by the former FIANNA FAIL Minister Desmond O'Malley (1939–). A parallel 'mould-BREAKer' to Britain's SDP, the PDs – intended to end Ireland's domination by parties rooted in the Civil War of the 1920s – showed greater staying power. Though their strength in the DAIL has fluctuated and not matched that of the main parties, the PDs have participated three times in government, as junior COALITION partners with Fianna Fail from 1989–92 and again from 1997–2002 and from June 2002 with Bertie Ahern (*see* ANORAK MAN) as Taoiseach and the PDs' leader Mary Harney as TANAISTE. The first of these coalitions broke up when the Fianna Fail Taoiseach Albert Reynolds accused O'Malley, then

Minister for Industry and Commerce, of giving dishonest evidence to the Commission into the BEEF SCANDAL.

peace. peace at any price The slogan on which the KNOW-NOTHINGS fought the 1856 US Presidential election. The full wording, 'Peace at any price; peace and union', referred to the party's readiness to live with slavery if that would avoid a CIVIL WAR. The phrase was used earlier in the 19th century by the French foreign minister Alphonse de Lamartine, but has been traced back to the Earl of Clarendon's *History of the Rebellion*, written in 1647.

Peace Ballot The national ballot organised in Britain for 17 June 1935 by the National Declaration Committee, chaired by Lord David Cecil and closely linked to the LEAGUE OF NATIONS Union. Over 11.5 million votes were cast in favour of adherence to the League and its policy of COLLECTIVE SECURITY, and over 10 million for a reduction in armaments. The ballot discouraged the NATIONAL GOVERNMENT under Stanley BALDWIN from rearming (*see* APPALLING FRANKNESS) and was interpreted by the AXIS powers as a sign of British weakness.

Peace Corps The organisation founded by President KENNEDY to assist THIRD WORLD and other countries by supplying young volunteers to perform skilled tasks 'at the same level as the citizens of the countries they are sent to'. Kennedy also hoped the arrival of idealistic Americans sharing the burdens of others would break down suspicion of the West in developing countries. The Corps was announced by Kennedy in March 1961 and ratified by CONGRESS in the Peace Corps Act that September; it is operated by the STATE DEPARTMENT. The first project was for engineers to help build roads in Tanganyika (now Tanzania). Peace Corps volunteers work for subsistence wages, usually for a two-year tour with a brief training session beforehand. About half are teachers; the rest include agricultural experts, engineers and health workers and community development workers. For the most part, the Peace Corps has proved a success.

peace dividend The boost to the economies of the West that was supposed to follow the end of the COLD WAR, through the relaxation of tension and the reduction in forces and weaponry – and military spending – that could follow. The GULF WAR, the conflict in former Yugoslavia and the weakness of the former Soviet economies meant that the full forecast benefit was not felt.

peace in our time The highly unfortunate phrase attributed to Prime Minister Neville CHAMBERLAIN at the high point of his APPEASEMENT policy, after flying back on 30 September 1938 from meeting HITLER in MUNICH. The optimism was misplaced; in less than a year Hitler had gone back on his assurances and Britain and Germany were at war. The words come from a versicle in Church of England morning prayer: 'Give peace in our time, O Lord.' What Chamberlain actually said to the cheering crowd in DOWNING STREET was: 'My good friends, this is the second time in our history when there has come back from Germany PEACE WITH HONOUR. I believe that it is *peace for our time*. Go home and have a nice, quiet sleep.' Lord Home (*see* SIR ALEC), who as Lord Dunglass was Chamberlain's PPS, said 40 years later:

> Chamberlain regretted those words the moment he had spoken them.

peace is indivisible The phrase coined by Maxim Litvinov (1876–1951), Soviet COMMISSAR for Foreign Affairs, in a speech in February 1920. It means that nations cannot claim peace exists in one theatre when they are engaged in conflict elsewhere – a rebuke to Britain and other WORLD WAR I allies who were using force against the Soviet regime while claiming to have negotiated a post-war peace.

Peace, Jobs, (and) Freedom (1) The slogan on which Britain's LABOUR PARTY fought, and went down to a humiliating defeat in, the 1983 general election. It was the title of the party's encyclopaedic campaign document (*see* LONGEST SUICIDE NOTE IN HISTORY). (2) With the 'and', the slogan of Nelson MANDELA and the ANC in South Africa's first multiracial elections in 1994, which swept the movement to power.

peace offensive An active and co-ordinated programme of DIPLOMACY designed to secure peace. Winston CHURCHILL, in his book *The Gathering Storm*, attributed the phrase to Neville CHAMBERLAIN; it has been frequently used since by political leaders.

Peace People The movement founded in 1976 by Mairead Corrigan and Betty Williams to campaign for an end to SECTARIAN violence in NORTHERN IRELAND. Mrs Corrigan's sister had seen her three children killed when a car ran out of control after the gunman at the wheel was shot by a British Army patrol. There were mass demonstrations against all terrorism, REPUBLICAN and LOYALIST alike, and in 1977 the Peace People won the NOBEL PEACE

PRIZE. Then the movement faded away amid much-publicised splits, and denigration from the IRA.

Peace Pledge Union Britain's leading PACIFIST organisation, founded in 1936 by Canon Dick Sheppard of St Martin-in-the-Fields. Its influence was greatest prior to WORLD WAR II; since the late 1950s it has been overshadowed by CND.

peace process Originally the US-sponsored search for peace between Israel, its Arab neighbours and the Palestinians, now any patient and long drawn-out process of bringing intractable parties together to achieve a lasting settlement; the NORTHERN IRELAND peace process is the other prime example, though there are and no doubt will be others. The Middle East peace process was begun by Henry KISSINGER – though the name came later – and has continued, sporadically, to test ever since the claims of the participants to want peace; the CAMP DAVID AGREEMENT is its most durable product. The Northern Ireland peace process was born of contacts in the late 1980s between the UK government and the IRA, and between the SDLP leader John Hume and SINN FEIN's Gerry Adams. The GOOD FRIDAY AGREEMENT is its crowning achievement to date, though the process is far from over.

Peace, Retrenchment and Reform The personal platform of the MANCHESTER SCHOOL Liberal John Bright (1811–89), and a slogan of the embryonic Liberals a generation before. On 28 April 1859 Bright told a meeting in Birmingham:

> I am for 'Peace, Retrenchment and Reform', the watchword of the great Liberal Party 30 years ago.

Peace Ship *See* FORD.

peace through strength Ronald REAGAN's words for the stated aim of almost every US President, starting with George WASHINGTON, who said in his first address to CONGRESS in 1790:

> To be prepared for war is one of the most effectual means of preserving peace.

peace with honour The phrase used by DISRAELI after the Congress of BERLIN in 1878, which Neville CHAMBERLAIN unfortunately revived 60 years later (*see* PEACE IN OUR TIME). In the HOUSE OF LORDS on 16 July 1878 after signing the Berlin Treaty, Disraeli said:

> Lord SALISBURY and myself have brought you back peace – but a peace, I hope, with honour!

The words originated with Lord John (Earl) Russell (1792–1878), who said at Greenock on 19 September 1853 of the growing crisis in the CRIMEA:

> If peace cannot be maintained with honour, it is no longer peace.

And Salisbury himself had written in 1864:

> Peace without honour is not only a disgrace, but, except as a temporary respite, it is a chimera.

peace without victory A formula for ending WORLD WAR I which President WILSON put to the combatants in an address to the SENATE in January 1917. His initiative was ignored, and within three months America had been sucked into the conflict.

All we are saying is give peace a chance The first line of the song written by John Lennon and recorded by his *Plastic Ono Band* which in 1969 became almost the mantra of the movement against the VIETNAM WAR, and since then of peace campaigners generally.

(an) extra mile for peace The phrase conjured up by George BUSH Snr after Iraq's invasion of Kuwait in August 1990 to indicate his desire to go as far as was necessary to secure SADDAM HUSSEIN's peaceful settlement and avert the GULF WAR which his intransigence prompted the following year.

every night, whisper 'peace' in your husband's ear The appeal of Soviet Foreign Minister Andrei GROMYKO to Nancy REAGAN at a WHITE HOUSE reception in 1984. It was almost the last throw of the old-timers at the KREMLIN before the advent of Mikhail GORBACHEV and the end of the COLD WAR.

(a) just and lasting peace The theme of Abraham LINCOLN's second INAUGURAL ADDRESS on 4 March 1865, which also pledged 'malice toward none, and charity for all'. The end of the CIVIL WAR was just six weeks away – as was Lincoln's assassination.

land for peace *See* LAND.

open covenants of peace, openly arrived at *See* OPEN.

Since wars begin in the minds of men, it is in the minds of men that the defences of peace must be constructed The preamble to the constitution of UNESCO, adopted in London on 16 November 1945. It has been attributed to Prime Minister Clement ATTLEE and, more recently, to Archibald MacLeish, chairman of the US delegation to the London conference.

Uniting for Peace resolution The motion carried by the United Nations GENERAL ASSEMBLY late in 1950 at the urging of America, providing that if the SECURITY

COUNCIL failed to act on 'important questions', the Assembly itself would recommend to members collective action to preserve world peace. It was under this resolution that the UN interposed an Emergency Force between Israel and Egypt at the end of the SUEZ crisis.

We are going to have peace, even if we have to fight for it A comment attributed to President EISENHOWER, who on other occasions, despite his military pedigree, spoke of the overwhelming desire of the peoples of the world for peace. He must have been speaking at the height of the COLD WAR, when I. F. STONE condemned US policy as:

> We Smiths want peace so bad we're prepared to kill every one of the Joneses to get it.

We prepare for war like ferocious giants, and for peace like retarded pygmies A scathing comment from the era of COLD WAR tension and sabre-rattling by Canada's Liberal Prime Minister Lester Pearson (1897–1972).

Where the peace has been broken anywhere, the peace of all countries everywhere is in danger Franklin D. ROOSEVELT's warning to the American people on 3 September 1939, as WORLD WAR II broke out in Europe.

winning the peace Many politicians have used this phrase, but the French Prime Minister Georges Clemenceau (*see* TIGER) may have been the first. He is reputed to have said at the close of WORLD WAR I:

> We have won the war. Now we have to win the peace – and that may be very difficult.

For Clemenceau 'winning the peace' involved rendering Germany powerless through REPARATIONS and other means, a strategy that proved counterproductive. After WORLD WAR II, 'winning the peace' had two meanings: the securing of the territories liberated from NAZI rule for democracy, and the pursuit of domestic policies to bring lasting prosperity and avoid a repeat of the GREAT DEPRESSION.

peaceful coexistence The doctrine adumbrated after STALIN's death in 1953 by Georgi Malenkov, who had won the first of a series of power struggles in the KREMLIN. Responding to the Republicans' 'New Look' in foreign policy, he talked of 'peaceful coexistence' with capitalist countries and a switch at home from defence equipment to consumer goods, and began releasing political prisoners. The policy collapsed when East Germans, encouraged by his message, rose up against their Stalinist rulers and were brutally suppressed by Soviet troops. But Khrushchev, the ultimate winner of the struggle to succeed Stalin, frequently used the term himself.

peacekeeping The use of military forces to preserve a truce, or police or separate two or more hostile armies or communities, generally within a country. It has become the most visible function, disaster relief excepted, of the UNITED NATIONS.

peaceniks A term of abuse for America's ANTI-WAR campaigners, and others who objected to US policy during the COLD WAR. Much loved by the political right, it bore overtones of PEACE AT ANY PRICE and of fanatical detachment from reality; the 'nik' conveyed undertones of scruffiness, and of pro-Sovietism.

peak too soon For a party or candidate to achieve its highest level of popularity well before election day, the inference being that it will slip back. When Labour's opinion-poll rating reached the mid-30s at the start of Britain's 1983 election, party wags warned their leader Michael FOOT that he was in danger of 'peaking too soon'; Labour finished on 27%, its worst showing since 1935.

Pearce Commission The commission headed by Lord Pearce, a retired Lord of Appeal, that was set up in November 1971 by SIR ALEC Douglas-Home, Foreign Secretary in Edward HEATH's government, to determine whether proposals for a settlement of Rhodesia's UDI were acceptable to the people as a whole. Opponents of UDI saw it as a WHITEWASH until it reported on 23 May 1972 that the African majority strongly opposed the scheme agreed by Sir Alec and Rhodesia's breakaway premier Ian Smith. This involved a steadily increasing African stake in the colony's parliament as they achieved the same qualifications as whites. The commission arrived in Salisbury (now Harare) on 11 January to demonstrations for MAJORITY RULE, with some violence. A week later the Smith regime arrested Garfield Todd, a former premier of Southern Rhodesia, and his daughter Judith for campaigning against UDI; Pearce took evidence from the Todds in jail.

Pearl Harbor The surprise Japanese attack on the Hawaiian base of the US Pacific fleet on 7 December 1941 that brought America into WORLD WAR II; President Franklin D. ROOSEVELT declared war on Japan on 9 December, and on Germany and Italy two days later. When told of the attack, FDR exclaimed: 'This means war!' and CHURCHILL: 'So we have won after all!' For almost two hours 350 Japanese carrier-borne aircraft strafed, bombed and torpedoed the fleet at anchor; eight battleships and sixteen other vessels were sunk or seriously damaged, and 175 aircraft destroyed on the ground. The attack cost 2335 American lives and left a further 1178 wounded. Its impact would have been even greater in terms of casualties and US capacity to mount a counter-attack had not the aircraft carriers based at Pearl sailed shortly before. On the same day the Japanese also attacked the Philippines, Guam, Hong Kong and the Malay peninsula. Japan had intended to present an ULTIMATUM in WASHINGTON immediately before the attack, but this was delayed, so there was no warning. The failure of the Pearl Harbor command to act on intelligence of Japanese movements was severely criticised by a government inquiry; some sceptics wondered if FDR had allowed the attack to happen, as it unified all but the most ISOLATIONIST politicians behind a war which the President had been preparing for against strong domestic opposition. Indeed, Sen. Gerald Nye of North Dakota complained:

> This is just what Great Britain planned for us. We have been manoeuvred into this by the President.

Pearl Harbor, a base constructed on Oahu under an 1887 treaty with then-independent Hawaii, became a byword for unpreparedness and the ruthless deviousness of an enemy, Roosevelt instantly proclaiming a DATE THAT WILL LIVE IN INFAMY. This did not stop George BUSH Snr telling an American Legion convention on *7 September* 1988: 'Today you remember – I wonder how many Americans remember – today is Pearl Harbor Day.' Nor did it prevent his son, on a Presidential visit to Tokyo on 18 February 2002, declaring: 'For a century and a half now, America and Japan have formed one of the great and enduring alliances of modern times.'

> I fear all we have done is awaken a sleeping giant and fill him with a terrible resolve.
>
> Admiral ISOKURU YAMAMOTO (1884–1943), *attr.*

Peasants' Revolt The name given by the Conservative MP Julian Critchley to the BACKBENCH upsurge that installed Margaret THATCHER as leader in February 1975, with echoes of the insurrection under Wat Tyler in 1381. Edward HEATH believed the former Education Secretary with increasingly right-wing views and little obvious support had no chance of toppling him, and told her as much. But discontent with Heath was greater than he realised, and Mrs Thatcher won votes because she had the courage to stand when more obvious challengers held back; her campaign was shrewdly organised by the one-time Colditz escaper Airey NEAVE. In the first ballot on 4 February she polled 130 votes, against 119 for Heath and 16 for Hugh Fraser. Heath dropped out and contestants previously loyal to him came forward, headed by WILLIE Whitelaw. But in the second ballot a week later Mrs Thatcher won outright with 146, against 79 for Whitelaw, 19 for Sir Geoffrey HOWE, 19 for James Prior and 11 for John Peyton. It was fifteen years before she was herself ousted in a similar revolt.

Pecora Committee The Congressional committee, named after its special attorney Ferdinand Pecora (1885–1971), which at the time of Franklin D. ROOSEVELT's INAUGURATION in 1933 was investigating corruption in the world of high finance. The probe was conducted with such insight and ruthlessness that it unnerved America's bankers more than FDR's closure of the banks to restore stability. The Pecora probe gave Roosevelt the ammunition he needed to introduce a BILL making the issue of a misleading company prospectus a crime. Pecora himself was one of the first members of the Securities and Exchange Commission (SEC) until becoming a New York SUPREME COURT justice; he served fifteen years until resigning to make an unsuccessful run for Mayor of New York.

Peel, Sir Robert (1788–1850), Prime Minister 1834–35 and 1841–46, best known for founding the Metropolitan Police in 1829 and splitting the Tory party by repealing the CORN LAWS, is one of the great enigmas of British politics. He was groomed for power, his father, himself an MP, telling him:

> Bob, you dog, if you are not Prime Minister one day I shall disinherit you.

Elected an MP in 1809, he was a junior Minister at 24, but had to resign in 1818 because of his strong opposition to Catholic EMANCIPATION; the same issue led him to quit as Home Secretary in 1827, but he reluctantly reversed his stand in 1829. His inability to toe a party line was already evident; in 1830 he told a friend: 'I feel a want of many essential qualifications which are requisite in party leaders.' Peel would have become Prime Minister in July 1834, but was in Rome, and the job went to Wellington who was easier to reach; he finally got it that December, surviving only four months. The BEDCHAMBER CRISIS over the young Queen Victoria's refusal to part with her Whig ladies in waiting when the government fell prevented Peel's Tories taking power in 1839, but he took office again in 1841 after a convincing win at the polls. He told the HOUSE:

> No considerations of mere political support should induce me to hold such an office as that which I fill by a servile tenure, which would compel me to be the instrument of carrying other men's opinions into effect.

In his second ministry, Peel blocked Whig moves for FREE TRADE and countered dissent in Ireland, having Daniel O'Connell (1775–1847) tried for sedition. But the IRISH POTATO FAMINE convinced him 'cheap corn' was essential; hearing the radical Richard Cobden speaking out against the Corn Laws, he turned to Sidney Herbert and said: 'You must answer this, for I cannot.' Resigning from the government on 29 June 1846, he told the House:

> In relinquishing power I shall leave a name severely censured, I fear, by many who on public grounds deeply regret the severance of party ties . . . but it may be that I shall leave a name sometimes remembered with expressions of goodwill in the abodes of those whose lot it is to labour.

He then destroyed the old Tory party by leading the PEELITES out of it, leaving the embittered DISRAELI to remark:

> He is so vain that he wants to figure in history as the settler of all the great questions, but . . . things must be done by parties, not by persons using parties as tools.

Four years later he was killed in a riding accident.

As a man, Peel aroused mixed feelings. Walter Bagehot ascribed to him 'common opinions and uncommon abilities', adding: 'No man has come so near to our definition of a constitutional STATESMAN: the powers of a first-rate man and the creed of a second-rate man.' O'Connell memorably described Peel's smile as 'like the silver plate on a coffin', and Disraeli underlined the impression of a cold fish, saying: 'He is reminiscent of a poker. The only difference is that a poker occasionally gives off signs of warmth.' Disraeli wrote later: 'When he attempted to touch the tender passions it was painful. His face became distorted, like that of a woman who wants to cry but cannot succeed.'

Harold MACMILLAN commended Peel as 'the first of the modern Conservatives', but BALFOUR sourly observed:

> He smashed his party, and no man has the right to destroy the property of which he is a trustee.

Lord ROSEBERY wrote of his reversals on Catholic emancipation and the Corn Laws: 'Granted that he was right in the first transition, he should not have repeated it; the character of public men cannot stand such shocks.' But the most eloquent verdict came from an anonymous Tory who compared Peel with

> The Turkish admiral who steered his fleet into the enemy's port.

Peelites The 110 Tory MPs, headed by Sir Robert Peel, who up to then had been Prime Minister, who broke away in 1846 over FREE TRADE after Peel has split the party by repealing the CORN LAWS. Peel's secession, taking with him most of the CABINET and the organs of the Tory party, marks the effective start of the CONSERVATIVE PARTY from the ranks of Tory MPs who were left behind by their leader and had to start a new movement from scratch. Initially the Peelites held the BALANCE OF POWER; after the 1847 election which gave the WHIG Lord John Russell a paper majority over the Tories among whom DISRAELI was the strongest force, they still numbered over 70 but were handicapped by the uninterest of their nominal leader, who wrote:

> I will take care not again to burn my fingers by organising a party.

A leading Peelite and future Liberal, Edward Cardwell (1813–86), complained:

> Sir Robert Peel's party saved England from confusion and has been rewarded by its own annihilation.

The Peelites survived their leader's death in 1850, and in 1852, still 52 strong, joined forces with the Whigs under Peel's former Foreign Secretary, the Earl of Aberdeen. GLADSTONE, himself a Peelite, brought down that government in 1857; in the subsequent election only 26 Peelites kept their seats. After the deaths of several senior Peelites in 1860–61, the rump of the group joined the Whigs in the new LIBERAL PARTY.

peer. hereditary peer A member of Britain's aristocracy, until 1999 entitled to sit in the HOUSE OF LORDS: a Duke, EARL, Countess, Marquess, VISCOUNT, BARON or Baroness. Up to that time peers, whose titles and privileges are traditionally passed down from father to son (very few women succeed to peerages in their own right), could vote in the Upper House but not in Parliamentary elections – in common with 'lunatics and convicted felons'. Since 1999 only LIFE PEERS have retained automatic membership of the House of Lords, just 92 of the hereditaries, chosen by a ballot of their colleagues, retaining their seats, the rest having forfeited their locus in the political system. The ban on peers sitting in the House of Commons, resisted so vigorously by Tony BENN, was also lifted, and at the 2001 general election Lord (John) Thurso became the first to be elected an MP.

> The layer of blubber which encases an English peer, the sediment of permanent adulation.
>
> CYRIL CONNOLLY (1903–74)

> I don't have a vote because I'm a peer. If I did, I'd vote Labour. But I think my butler's a Conservative.
>
> Earl MOUNTBATTEN OF BURMA (1900–79), *attr.*

> I have not sought, and do not seek, a hereditary peerage.
>
> MARGARET THATCHER, 1991 (she was created a life peer the following year)

life peer A member of the HOUSE OF LORDS appointed to serve for the remainder of their life, without their heirs having any claim on a seat. The idea was first mooted by Lord SALISBURY in 1888, but it was 1958 before Harold MACMILLAN recommended the first life peers to Queen Elizabeth II. At first a small minority, life peers now dominate the membership of the House; in the 35 years before the bulk of the hereditaries were excluded, just three new hereditary peerages had been created, only the Earl of Stockton (Macmillan himself) having male heirs who would perpetuate the title.

spiritual peers The two archbishops of the Church of England and 24 senior diocesan bishops (including London, Durham and Winchester) who are eligible to sit in the HOUSE OF LORDS as long as they remain in post.

temporal peers All the peers who are not bishops.

working peers Life peers well below retirement age, created on the nomination of the political parties to strengthen their teams of spokesmen in the UPPER HOUSE. LABOUR relies heavily on such creations even after the exclusion of most of the hereditary peers, as the Conservatives still enjoy a large majority both among hereditaries and among life peers created by previous Tory governments, and has had until recently to draw on slim resources of ageing retired politicians in the Lords to staff its FRONT BENCH.

(the) peers against the people LLOYD GEORGE's slogan as he rallied the public behind his 1909 PEOPLE'S BUDGET and against the efforts of the HOUSE OF LORDS to defeat it. For the first time in 250 years, the Lords threw out the Budget, but in two general elections in 1910 the Liberals won a renewed MANDATE after campaigning on the slogan. The Lords passed the Budget a year late, and after a threat by ASQUITH to create hundreds of Liberal peers to force the government's legislation through, the Lords (*see* HEDGERS AND DITCHERS) accepted limitation of their powers under the 1911 PARLIAMENT ACT.

peerage The rank or dignity of a peer, as conferred on those newly created. Not everyone regards the offer of a peerage as a compliment. The newspaper magnate who eventually became Lord Northcliffe reputedly said: 'When I want a peerage, I shall buy one like an honest man.' And when Clement ATTLEE offered R. H. TAWNEY a peerage, the political scientist wrote back:

> Thank you for your letter. What harm have I ever done the LABOUR PARTY?

Attlee himself initially considered the idea of taking a peerage ludicrous, suggesting the title 'LORD LOVE-A-DUCK OF LIMEHOUSE'.

disclaim a peerage For a hereditary peer, to give up the right to one's title and to one's seat in the LORDS, without affecting one's heirs. The practice has been rendered almost pointless by the exclusion of most hereditaries in 1999 and the granting to them of full political rights, including the right to stand for the HOUSE OF COMMONS. Peerages were disclaimed because (1) someone succeeding to a peerage would prefer to stand for/stay in the House of Commons, (2) the son of an eminent peer felt his father had made the title unique, (3) the inheritor was well known in his own right and did not wish to change his name, or (4) the inheritor did not believe in the House of Lords or hereditary titles. Winston CHURCHILL first suggested to ASQUITH in 1911 that peers be permitted to disclaim, but it was only after Tony BENN had twice been elected an MP and denied his seat after inheriting his father's title of Lord Stansgate that the law was changed in 1963. Fortuitously, the change took place just in time for Lords Home and Hailsham to promise to disclaim their titles and compete for the Tory leadership that autumn, with Home (*see* SIR ALEC) emerging the winner and Hailsham hamstrung by his pledge to return to the Commons.

elevation to the peerage The creation of a peer, comprising the SOVEREIGN's declaration, normally announced from DOWNING STREET but sometimes from Buckingham Palace, that the honour is being bestowed, and the new peers' subsequent introduction to the HOUSE OF LORDS once they have chosen the title by which they wish to be known.

Pendleton Act The legislation passed by the US CONGRESS in 1883 that freed much of the CIVIL SERVICE from political PATRONAGE. Sponsored by Sen. George H. Pendleton, it stemmed from public outrage at the corruption revealed at the trial of President GARFIELD's assassin, himself denied a civil service post. Backed by President Arthur (*see* ELEGANT ARTHUR), the Act set up a three-member commission to draft and administer competitive examinations to establish applicants' merit, banned the collection of campaign funds from federal officeholders and established a list of positions (10% at first) to be filled by merit. Ironically Arthur had been removed as Collector of Customs for the port of New York by President Hayes (*see* OLD 8 TO 7) because his efforts to establish a MERIT SYSTEM there had not been vigorous enough.

pendulum The apparently inevitable swing of support in a two-PARTY system from one to another and back again. When the social and economic system continues to develop in a set direction despite such swings a RATCHET EFFECT is said to apply. The argument that '**the pendulum will swing back**' put forward by Speaker Joe Cannon (*see* FOUL-MOUTHED JOE), emphasised that ideas out of fashion one day may become accepted wisdom again the next.

pendulum arbitration *See* ARBITRATION.

Pennsylvania Avenue The main street of WASHINGTON DC, commencing at the foot of CAPITOL HILL and running north-westward between government buildings to 15th Street before forming a dog-leg around the US Treasury Department and the front of the WHITE HOUSE; it then heads toward fashionable Georgetown, terminating at the junction with M Street. The section of Pennsylvania Avenue outside the White House, with LAFAYETTE SQUARE to its north, was blocked to traffic in May 1995 following the OKLAHOMA CITY BOMBING. The street's actual title is Pennsylvania Avenue NW; Pennsylvania Avenue SE, which continues south-eastward from the Library of CONGRESS and over the John Philip Sousa Bridge to the District Line, where it becomes the dual-track Maryland State Highway 4 (still named Pennsylvania Avenue), seems to have attracted less attention.

Pentagon The massive headquarters of the US Department of Defense (DOD) across the Potomac from Washington; the concrete building, with three times the office space of the Empire State Building, takes its name from its five-sided shape. The term 'Pentagon' has also come to personify America's military BUREAUCRACY and US defence policies; one Russian commentator observed: 'The Pentagon has five sides on every issue.' The Pentagon was planned in 1941 when 41,000 civilian employees of the military were spilling out of 23 buildings across the capital. CONGRESS jibbed at the $35 million cost (it eventually rose to $87 million) and questioned its necessity, Sen. Everett DIRKSEN saying: 'We may not need all that space when the war comes to an end.' President ROOSEVELT was unhappy with the site close to ARLINGTON NATIONAL CEMETERY and the windowless design; he was still objecting when the War Department sent in the contractors, who finished the job in under a year. When they finished, 40,000 administrators moved in – but it was already too small.

> That immense monument to modern man's subservience to the desk.
>
> British Ambassador OLIVER (later Lord) FRANKS, 1952

> A place where costs are rounded to the nearest tenth of a billion dollars.
>
> C. MERTON TYRRELL, 1970

> Bombing can end the war – bomb the Pentagon now!
>
> Anti-VIETNAM WAR slogan

On 9/11, in Washington's worst ever terrorist atrocity, the Pentagon suffered severe damage to its west side and the loss of 189 lives – with dozens more seriously injured – when at 9.37 a.m. AL QAEDA hijackers flew American Airlines Flight 77, with 64 people aboard, into the building just after the attacks on the WORLD TRADE CENTER. President George W. BUSH ordered that the Boeing 757, which had turned off its identification transponders over Kentucky 50 minutes before, be shot down, but as a result of delays and lapses of procedure at NORAD and the Federal Aviation Administration identified by the 9/11 COMMISSION, the hijackers went unchallenged. The fire started by the fuel from the plane burned until the following day.

Pentagon Papers An official, secret and brutally frank history of US involvement in VIETNAM which was LEAKed to the *New York Times* in 1971 by Daniel Ellsberg, a former Pentagon employee who had become convinced the war was immoral. It revealed that the American public had been systematically lied to, and told of miscalculations, unauthorised offensives and policy clashes at the heart of the JOHNSON administration. When the first instalment hit the news stands the NIXON administration tried to halt publication, but the SUPREME COURT ruled by 6 to 3 that such a ban would violate the FIRST AMENDMENT. The leak gravely embarrassed Nixon and the shapers of US policy in Indo-China and infuriated supporters of the war. An outraged President set up the PLUMBERS' unit to get even with Ellsberg and combat what he saw as a campaign of subversion; WATERGATE, and Nixon's own fall, were the result.

> The greatest representative democracy the world has known, the nation of JEFFERSON and LINCOLN, has let its nose be rubbed in the swamp by petty war lords, jealous Vietnamese generals and grand-scale dope pushers.
>
> Sen. MIKE GRAVEL on the message of the *Papers*

Pentagonese A style of language characterised by euphemisms, circumlocutions and vagueness, frequently attributed to US military bureaucrats, especially in their dealings with CONGRESS.

Pentonville Five The five dockers sent to Pentonville Prison for contempt of court in July 1972 for picketing an East London cold store in defiance of an order from the National Industrial Relations Court. The episode finally discredited the HEATH government's INDUSTRIAL RELATIONS ACT, introduced not long before, and through the subsequent absence of any legislation against secondary PICKETING paved the way for the WINTER OF DISCONTENT seven years later. The jailing of the men brought widespread sympathy action, the withdrawal of the TUC from talks with ministers on the economy, and the threat of the first GENERAL STRIKE since 1926. With constant mass demonstrations outside the prison, the government was rescued by a HOUSE OF LORDS decision in another case that enabled the NIRC to release the men without their purging their contempt. As the dockers were led away to prison, one had shouted:

> How can they arrest me? The UNION JACK grows out of my bloody head.

people. people bath In US politics, a welcoming crowd on the CAMPAIGN trail that swamps a CANDIDATE. The term sounds contemporary, but was first used by Abraham LINCOLN.

people power The NON-VIOLENT popular SOLIDARITY that brought Mrs Corazon Aquino (1933–), widow of the murdered opposition politician Benigno Aquino, to power as President of the Philippines in 1986 after the incumbent President Ferdinand Marcos rigged the outcome of elections she had clearly won. When the Church, the Army and (belatedly) the REAGAN administration withdrew their support after massive demonstrations, Marcos was forced to concede defeat and flee the country. *See also* POWER TO THE PEOPLE.

People's Budget The Budget introduced in April 1909 by David LLOYD GEORGE, so-called because it proposed to raise money for old age pensions (and rearmament) by increasing the tax burden on the landed classes. Death duties were doubled, taxes on land and unearned income were raised to unprecedented levels, and a new supertax levied on all income over £5000 p.a. The Budget provoked a violent outcry from Tory landowners, who denounced it as legalised robbery. Until then the Budget had been purely an exercise in balancing the books; now for the first time it was used as a direct instrument of social policy. So radical did it seem to the aristocracy that the HOUSE OF LORDS refused to pass it (*see* PEERS AGAINST THE PEOPLE) until threatened with the loss of their powers.

> We are placing the burdens on the broadest shoulders. I made up my mind that in forming my Budget, no cupboard should be barer, no lot should be harder to bear.
>
> LLOYD GEORGE, 30 July 1909

people's courts The infamous tribunals that tried political offences in NAZI Germany, and most notoriously the conspirators against HITLER in the STAUFFENBERG PLOT. Altogether some 7000 people were brought before the 'people's courts' during the THIRD REICH and some 2000 sentenced to death; no evidence for the defence was permitted. On Hitler's orders, several of the 20 July conspirators were sentenced to be hanged 'like carcasses of meat', suspended by nooses of piano wire from meathooks at the Plotzensee barracks; the FÜHRER had home movies shot of this revolting scene.

people's democracies The self-justifying and blatantly false description of their regimes adopted by the Communist leaders of the Soviet Union's eastern European SATELLITES after WORLD WAR II.

The people's flag is deepest red The first line of *The* RED FLAG.

People's Liberation Army The official title of the army of Communist China, often carelessly described as the RED ARMY, which was the military of the former Soviet Union.

the People's President One of the nicknames accorded Andrew Jackson (*see* OLD HICKORY) during his successful campaign for the Presidency in 1828; it reflected his undoubted popularity with the mass of the American people and their desire to reverse the CORRUPT BARGAIN with which John Quincy ADAMS was reckoned to have captured the WHITE HOUSE four years previously.

the people's princess Tony BLAIR's tribute to Diana, Princess of Wales in his first reaction to her death in a car crash in Paris with her boyfriend Dodi Fayed in the small hours of 31 August 1997. His words caught the mood of the British public, a mood spectacularly not caught by the Queen and other leading members of the Royal Family, whom Blair had to press hard to show some empathy with a grieving people. The tragedy helped prolong Blair's electoral HONEYMOON, which lasted well into the following year, if not longer.

People's Republic The title chosen by Mao Tse-Tung (*see* CHAIRMAN MAO) for the Communist state established in mainland China after Chiang Kai-Shek's Nationalists were finally driven out in 1949.

the People's War The name bestowed by Woodrow WILSON on WORLD WAR I on 14 June 1917, not long after he had belatedly declared war on Germany. In his Flag Day address, Wilson anticipated his Fourteen Points when he said:

> This is the People's War, a war for freedom and justice and self-government amongst all the nations of the world, a war to make the world safer for the peoples who live upon it . . . the German peoples themselves included.

The American people are slow to wrath, but when their wrath is once kindled, it burns like a consuming flame Franklin D. ROOSEVELT's description of the outraged response of American opinion to PEARL HARBOR, quoted by Ronald REAGAN in 1981 in a televised warning to CONGRESS that public patience was running out with its failure to tackle the crisis facing the economy.

The American people have spoken; it will take some time to work out what they have said. President CLINTON's first comment on the outcome of the election of his successor in November 2000, the result of which took several weeks to decide because of confusion over whether George W. BUSH or Al Gore had taken the decisive state of Florida.

God gave the land to the people The stirring anthem of radicals in Britain's LIBERAL PARTY, led by LLOYD GEORGE, in the years prior to World War I. It was sung to the tune of *Marching Through Georgia.*

I do not know a method of drawing up an indictment against a whole people The warning of Edmund BURKE to his Bristol constituents in 1777 on the futility of Britain's efforts to retain its American colonies by force.

My plan cannot fail if the people are with us, and we ought not to succeed unless we do have the people with us The words with which the POPULIST William Jennings Bryan in 1899 rejected the steel magnate Andrew Carnegie's appeal to him to join him in working to defeat the peace treaty concluded at the end of the SPANISH-AMERICAN WAR; he was anxious not to compromise the purity of his own campaign. Bryan told him:

> I cannot wish you success in your effort to reject the treaty because while it may win the fight it may destroy our cause.

No-one ever went broke underestimating the intelligence of the American people The ultimate cynical view of the inhabitants of the United States, taken by H. L. Mencken.

One fifth of the people are against everything all the time A remark made by Robert F. KENNEDY in 1964 which is borne out by study of the way public opinion behaves. RFK was arguing that no politician should let predictable opposition from a small and easily-defined section of the electorate prevent the adoption of policies that would be supported by the rest.

One third of the people of the world are asleep at any given moment, the other two-thirds are awake and probably stirring up trouble somewhere US Secretary of State Dean Rusk voicing the deepest thoughts of all in high office, 1966.

People of the same trade seldom meet together, even for merriment and diversion, but the conversation ends in a conspiracy against the public, or in some contrivance to raise prices The cynical but regrettably often true axiom on the proliferation of cartels which Adam Smith (1723–90) put forward in his *WEALTH OF NATIONS*.

Religion is the opium of the people The best-known saying of Karl MARX, who wrote in his *Critique of the Hegelian Philosophy of Right*: 'Religion is the sigh of the oppressed creature, the heart of a heartless world, and the soul of soulless conditions. It is the opium of the people.'

Set the people free The title of the MANIFESTO on which Winston CHURCHILL and his Conservatives fought and won Britain's 1951 general election.

There is no cause half so sacred as the cause of the people Woodrow WILSON's declaration to a campaign rally of over 12,000 people at Madison Square Garden on 31 October 1912. The future President was so overwhelmed at the hour-long ovation he received that he forgot his prepared speech and delivered these lines instead, saying also: 'There is no idea so uplifting as the idea of the service of humanity.' Not all great Americans have regarded the people in this light; Alexander HAMILTON once told JEFFERSON:

> Your people, Sir, is nothing but a great beast.

To make a people great, it is necessary to send them to battle, even if you have to kick them in the pants A typical dictum of Mussolini (*see* DUCE), speaking volumes both about the philosophy of the founder of FASCISM and his view of the Italian people he led.

Trust the people The axiom of TORY DEMOCRACY credited by CHURCHILL to his father Lord Randolph Churchill (1849–95). He said: 'I was brought up in my father's house to believe in democracy. Trust the people: that was his message.' The phrase was taken up in 1956 by the Democratic Presidential nominee Adlai STEVENSON, who said: 'If I was to attempt to put my political philosophy into a single phrase, it would be this: Trust the people.'

We the people The opening words of the United States CONSTITUTION. The first paragraph reads:

> We the people of the United States, in order to form a more perfect union, establish justice, ensure domestic tranquillity, provide for the common defence, promote the general welfare, and secure the blessings of liberty to ourselves and our posterity, do ordain and establish this Constitution for the United States of America.

Would it not be easier for the government to dissolve the people and elect another? The savagely ironic comment of Bertolt Brecht (1898–1956) after the Communist government of East Germany had called in Soviet troops to put down the popular uprising of 17 June 1953. Brecht also remarked that

> The people had lost the confidence of the government and could only win it back by renewed efforts.

You may fool all the people some of the time; you can even fool some of the people all the time. But you can't fool all the people all the time A saying attributed to Abraham LINCOLN, who is supposed to have uttered it in a speech at Clinton, Illinois on 2 September 1858. However, there is no evidence that he ever said it, and it has been attributed with equal conviction to the showman Phineas T. Barnum.

Peoria To presidents and presidential hopefuls, the heart of MIDDLE AMERICA and the embodiment of the electorate their policies must satisfy. Peoria is a town in Illinois with a population of around 130,000; its name comes from an Indian word meaning 'place of fat beasts'. It has been a cultural yardstick at least since the end of the 19th century when Ambrose Bierce noted in the 'Dullard' entry for his *Devil's Dictionary* that 'the intellectual center of the race is somewhere about Peoria, Illinois'. The term was bandied about for decades before becoming a catchword in the NIXON White House, where the test of anything planned was **Will it play in Peoria?** John D. Ehrlichman, who made it his own, explained to William Safire:

> Onomatopeia was the only reason for Peoria, I suppose. And it personified – exemplified – a place, remote from the media centers on the coasts, where the national verdict is cast, according to the Nixon doctrine.

percentage poll *See* TURNOUT.

perestroika (Russ. restructuring) The policy, linked with GLASNOST, with which Mikhail GORBACHEV set out to transform the SOVIET UNION by introducing economic and political reform and allowing greater freedom of expression. Gorbachev, Communist Party leader from 1985 and President from 1988, saw *perestroika* as a means of renewing the Soviet state, but instead it hastened its collapse. His reform programme met with stiff resistance inside the POLITBURO, but he nevertheless said in May 1988: 'Every member of our leadership is deeply committed to the cause of *perestroika*.'

> If the Russian word *perestroika* has easily entered the international lexicon, it is due to more than

just interest in what is going on in the Soviet Union. Now the whole world needs restructuring; that is, progressive development, fundamental change.

GORBACHEV, in his book, *Perestroika*

Perestroika has transformed and reformed society – but it is not the Soviet Union that is falling apart but the system – and Gorbachev started the process.

Russian President BORIS YELTSIN addressing MEPs in Strasbourg, 15 April 1991

Perfidious Albion (Fr. *L'Albion perfide*) The phrase which embodies one strand of French attitudes toward England: the conviction that, deep down, it can never be trusted. It is revived by the media in one country or the other whenever the two are at loggerheads, which happens frequently despite (or because of) their mutual membership of the EUROPEAN UNION. Differences over the IRAQ WAR apart, the two most spectacular ruptures in recent times have been DE GAULLE's 'NON' to Britain's first application to join the Common Market, and Britain's unilateral cancellation of the Channel Tunnel project in 1975. It is no coincidence that both decisions were later reversed. The phrase originated with the cleric Jacques-Bénigne Bossuet (1627–1704) who wrote:

England, ah, faithless England, which the rampart of the seas made inaccessible to the Romans, the faith of the Saviour spread even there.

It was refined into its popular form by the poet Augustin, Marquis of Ximénez (1726–1817), who in a revolutionary poem written in 1793 included the phrase:

Let us attack in her own waters
Perfidious Albion!

Pergau Dam The scandal that broke at the end of 1993 when it emerged that £234 million of UK aid for the Pergau Dam project in Malaysia – which officials had advised was not a sensible programme – had been given in return for a £16 billion arms order. The deal was negotiated by Defence Secretary George Younger in 1988 and supported by Margaret THATCHER; her successor John MAJOR and Foreign Secretary Douglas Hurd stuck by it despite protests from the head of the Overseas Development Administration. The resulting political storm triggered allegations of SLEAZE and of political corruption in Malaysia which prompted the country's Prime Minister, Mahathir Mohammed, to impose a trade embargo on British goods.

permanent. permanent members Also known as the **permanent five**. The five victorious WORLD WAR II allies who sit on the United Nations SECURITY COUNCIL as of right and alone possess the power of VETO. They are the US, UK, Russia, China and France. Pressure has been growing since the 1980s for Germany, Japan and maybe India to have permanent status instead of taking one of the less prestigious seats filled in strict rotation.

permanent representative In BRUSSELS, a diplomat of AMBASSADORial rank who heads a member state's mission to the EUROPEAN UNION, in Britain's case UKREP. The permanent representatives shadow the COUNCIL OF MINISTERS through their regular meetings as COREPER.

permanent revolution The doctrine promulgated by TROTSKY that the BOLSHEVIK revolution, once begun, would spread to engulf the entire world. He set it out most fully in his 1930 book *The Permanent Revolution*, refuting STALIN's programme for SOCIALISM IN ONE COUNTRY:

The democratic revolution grows directly into the socialist revolution and thereby becomes a permanent revolution . . . The completion of the socialist revolution within national limits is unthinkable . . . The socialist revolution begins in the national arena, it unfolds in the international arena, and is completed in the world arena.

Permanent Secretary The Whitehall MANDARIN occupying the highest CIVIL SERVICE position in each UK government department; occasionally a department such as the Treasury will have a Second Permanent Secretary to reflect its status, workload or breadth of responsibilities.

The first Permanent Secretary I ever met told me he always judged a Secretary of State by whether he brought home the groceries.

KENNETH CLARKE

Peronism The nationalist, largely working-class movement in Argentina which **Juan Perón** (1895–1974) used as the mass base for his two spells as dictator, from 1946 to 1955 and 1973 until his death. Perón wooed Argentina's powerful unions through his fixing of a minimum wage as a member of the military JUNTA that ruled from 1943, and his charismatic wife Eva (*see* EVITA) secured the fanatical backing of the DESCAMISADOS of the lower classes. He did not take kindly to opposition, declaring: 'The order of the day for every Peronist is to answer a violent action with a still more violent action.' Perón's fellow officers jailed him in 1945 as his influence soared, but were forced to release him, and the next year he was elected

President. He set out to establish a CORPORATIST dictatorship, but while his expropriation of British-owned firms was popular, the increasing brutality and incompetence of his regime were not; even the cult of Evita which he promoted after her death in 1952 could not save him, and he was exiled to Spain in 1955. His party continued, and when the military eventually allowed a free Presidential election the victorious candidate stood down for him and he returned in triumph with his new wife Isabel, a Madrid nightclub singer. Isabelita, as the Peronists called her, succeeded Perón on his death, but showed little flair for government and was ousted by the military in 1976. When General Galtieri's junta was overthrown after the humiliation of defeat in the FALKLANDS, the Peronist *Partido Justicialista* re-emerged as a force and has supplied several subsequent leaders including President Nestor Kirchner, elected in 2003.

> If I had not been Perón, I would have liked to be Perón. JUAN PERÓN, 1960

> Without me there will be chaos.
> ISABEL PERÓN

peroration The final portion of a political speech, in which the speaker tries to rouse his or her audience to a climax of enthusiasm for the message being put across, frequently employing repetition or flowery phrases that would sound overblown in the main body of the speech, and setting the stage (hopefully) for an ovation.

Perotnistas The supporters of H. Ross PEROT, the refreshingly MAVERICK Texas billionaire who won 19% of the popular vote in the 1992 Presidential election, despite pulling out of the race from July to September, probably taking more votes from the incumbent George BUSH Snr than from his successful challenger Bill CLINTON. The word, a play on 'Peronistas', was invented by the novelist Peter Tauber. Bush's speechwriter Peggy Noonan described Perot as resembling 'a hand grenade with a bad haircut', but millions warmed to his message that America could do better without the politicians despite his amateurish and bizarre campaigning style based on INFOMERCIALS, and persistent media suggestions that he had a persecution complex and had put his own staff and his opponents under surveillance. Perot spent $65 million on his 1992 campaign; when he ran again in 1996 under the REFORM PARTY banner he applied for Federal funding which limited his own input to $55,000. This time round he pledged to abolish NAFTA, clean up politics and establish a national health system; he finished a bad third with 7% of the vote.

perquisites The side benefits of being a US CONGRESSMAN, over and above the official salary. They include cheap meals and haircuts on the premises, free plants from the botanical garden, a free photography service, free ice, 33 free trips to their home district each year, and free travel abroad if an official pretext can be found. However, by contrast with UK Members of Parliament who can earn what they like outside unless they hold Ministerial office, and who enjoy similar privileges, members of Congress are only supposed to earn 15% on top of their salaries.

Pershing missile A US intermediate-range ballistic missile which became a subject of controversy in the early 1980s when deployed in Western Europe alongside CRUISE missiles to counter the threat from the Soviet medium-ranged SS20, which had already been based throughout Eastern Europe. Pershing first became operational in 1962; Pershing II, developed in the late 1970s, had a range of 425 miles and was ten times more accurate than its predecessor. Together with Cruise, the Pershing IIs were removed from Europe under the INF TREATY of December 1987, and for the most part destroyed. They were named after General John J. Pershing (1860–1948), who commanded US forces in WORLD WAR I.

persona non grata The Latin term used in the world of diplomacy and foreign affairs for an official of one country who is no longer welcome in another, usually because of espionage or some personal lapse. Sometimes country A orders the expulsion of diplomats from country B, whose conduct has been faultless, as a 'tit for tat' reprisal for the action of country B in justifiably expelling country A's representatives.

personal capacity The words that often appear in advance notice of a meeting in support of a controversial campaign, after the name of one or more of the speakers. It indicates that although that individual holds office in a political party or a trade union, they are not representing that organisation at the meeting but speaking purely in their own right.

personal statement At WESTMINSTER, the statement a Minister who has resigned or an MP facing a personal crisis is entitled to make to the HOUSE OF COMMONS on application to the SPEAKER. By convention such statements cannot be interrupted or questioned. John PROFUMO owed his downfall to lying to the House in a personal statement in which he denied any sexual relationship with Christine Keeler; the most celebrated personal statement in recent years was that of Sir Geoffrey HOWE in October 1990 which triggered the fall of Margaret THATCHER.

personality cult The raising of the leader of a TOTALITARIAN regime to an almost God-like pre-eminence, completely subordinating both the ideology of the regime and other members of the government. It came into use in the early 1950s as a codeword for STALINISM, which had raised such excesses to an art form; it was taken up by the supporters of CHAIRMAN MAO, and more recently it has been taken to the point of absurdity in North Korea.

> The cult of the individual acquired such monstrous size because Stalin himself, using all conceivable methods, supported the glorification of his own person. Comrades! We must abolish the cult of the individual decisively, once and for all.
>
> NIKITA S. KHRUSHCHEV to the Secret session of the 10th Party Congress, 25 February 1956

personation Under UK ELECTION law, the act of an individual in gaining an extra vote by claiming to be someone else. Traditionally a regular feature of NORTHERN IRELAND elections until identity rules were tightened c. 2000, it is a growing problem in Asian communities, especially with the introduction of universal postal voting.

Peruvian peace plan A proposal for settling the dispute over the FALKLANDS, put forward by President Belaunde of Peru at approximately the time the Royal Navy sank the BELGRANO. While Britain showed interest in the plan, Argentina flatly rejected it in the wake of the sinking. Opponents of the war and CONSPIRACY THEORISTS have claimed ever since that Margaret THATCHER ordered the sinking specifically to frustrate the peace plan and ensure that Britain could fight a victorious war to recapture the islands. The plan, like several others carried between London and Buenos Aires by US Secretary of State Alexander Haig, involved Argentine withdrawal, the halting of the approaching British task force, joint UK/Argentine control of the islands under US supervision, and negotiations over SOVEREIGNTY which would have protected the islanders' position for a period.

> Those of us who took the decision at Chequers [to attack the Belgrano] did not at that time know anything about the Peruvian proposals.
>
> MARGARET THATCHER, *The Downing Street Years*

PESC Public Expenditure Scrutiny. The annual method of fixing UK public spending, department by department, from the 1980s until Gordon BROWN perfected the COMPREHENSIVE SPENDING REVIEW. The exercise involved the CHIEF SECRETARY to the TREASURY determining the level of spending for the financial year starting the following April in time for the CHANCELLOR to announce in his AUTUMN STATEMENT. It included BILATERALS with all spending Ministers at which their pet schemes would come under scrutiny as their 'bids' were squeezed down to the overall spending level set by the CABINET. Up till 1991 the final say lay with a 'STAR CHAMBER' to which individual Ministers could appeal. Some elements of the PESC system survive under the CSR, but it is left to Ministers to allocate the pain, or the expansion, within their own programmes.

PEST *See* TORY REFORM GROUP.

Peter the Painter *See* SIDNEY STREET SIEGE.

Peterloo The bloody scene in Manchester on 16 August 1819 when cavalry attacked a peaceful crowd of 60,000 that had assembled in St Peter's Fields to hear 'Orator' Hunt speak on Parliamentary reform. Eleven people were killed, 140 others run through with sabres and a further 400 injured. The atrocity caused public anger and increased the pressure for reform, but made little impression on Lord Liverpool's government. The name was an ironic comparison with the British Army's triumph at Waterloo just four years before under Wellington, who had since entered the CABINET. But much of the opprobrium fell on Foreign Secretary Castlereagh, who had certainly not been privy to a decision taken by local magistrates.

> I met murder on the way –
> He had a mask like Castlereagh.
>
> SHELLEY, *The Mask of Anarchy*, 1819

petition A request to a government or legislature for action, or redress of grievances, made directly by members of the public who gather signatures of supporters. In the HOUSE OF COMMONS petitions ranging from a prisoner's request for parole to a call for legislation to protect hedgehogs can be introduced by individual MPs after the main business of the day; there are similar procedures in both houses of the US CONGRESS.

Petrov case The espionage case in 1954 which raised suspicions of links between FELLOW-TRAVELLERS in Australia and Soviet agents, further weakening the already divided LABOR PARTY. On 13 April, the Liberal Prime Minister Sir Robert Menzies (*see* MING) announced that Vladimir Petrov, a junior diplomat at the Soviet embassy in Canberra and an organiser of the MVD's espionage service, had sought and been granted POLITICAL ASYLUM. Petrov's wife was recalled to Moscow, but after her escort was disarmed at Darwin she spoke to Petrov and was also granted asylum. It also emerged that ASIO had been working on Petrov, who was paid £!5,000 when he handed over papers. The Russians alleged Petrov had broken Soviet law and that his wife had been forcibly detained, and on 23 April broke off relations with Australia. A ROYAL COMMISSION into the security implications of the case was immediately set up, and the parties agreed not to make it an issue in the pending Federal elections. The Labor leader, Dr H. V. Evatt, twice appeared before the commission to defend two of his staff mentioned as possible sources for an Australian Communist journalist; Evatt claimed the affair was a plot to discredit Labor, alleging that some party documents had been forged for the purpose. Labor failed to regain power in the elections, and split while the commission was sitting, seven anti-Communist MHRs and one Senator breaking away. In 1955 the commission confirmed that the Soviet embassy had been used as cover for espionage, but that no Australian had committed an offence. However, a further election in December 1955 strengthened Menzies' grip, the Labor split fragmenting the anti-Liberal vote.

PFI Private Finance Initiative The policy, launched by John MAJOR and continued under Tony BLAIR, whereby capital projects in the PUBLIC SECTOR are financed by private capital to reduce their immediate cost to the TREASURY. Launched in November 1992 and fiercely resisted by public service unions and some academics, it has enabled larger hospital and school building programmes to go ahead than would have been the case had the borrowing had to appear in the public accounts from the outset, but at higher rates of interest and with allegations of corner-cutting, for example fewer beds in new hospitals than the ones they replaced. *Compare* PPP.

PFLP Popular Front for the Liberation of Palestine. One of the most militant and active Palestinian terror groups prior to the INTIFADA, led by Ahmed Jibril. It was responsible for a number of spectacular atrocities, including the 1972 Lod Airport massacre when 25 people were machine-gunned to death. *See also* JACKAL.

Phalange A right-wing Christian MILITIA in the Lebanon, based on Spain's FALANGIST movement and founded by Pierre Gemayel in 1936, the same year General Franco (*see* CAUDILLO) started the SPANISH CIVIL WAR.

PHARE The European Community's major economic aid programme for central and eastern Europe after the collapse of Communism, which played a part in preparing the recipients for EU membership in 2004. The acronym stood for Poland Hungary Assistance Reconstruction Economy, and replicates the French *phare*, lighthouse. It was quickly extended to East Germany, the Czech Republic, Slovakia and the Baltic states. Much of the aid went to the Black Triangle, an area of high unemployment and environmental devastation from lignite mining and air pollution centred on Görlitz in Saxony, and spilling over into Poland and Bohemia.

Philadelphia Convention The gathering in Philadelphia from May to September 1787, presided over by George WASHINGTON, at which the US CONSTITUTION was framed. Convened to amend the Articles of CONFEDERATION, it went considerably further. All thirteen states bar Rhode Island were represented, and most of the Revolutionary leadership; Thomas JEFFERSON was away in Paris, and Tom Paine refused to go, saying: 'I smell a rat.' The structure of the new nation was agreed on the basis of the VIRGINIA PLAN, and the balance between large and small states at Federal level by the CONNECTICUT COMPROMISE; arguments over slavery were pushed to one side, with their fissile potential recognised. By ten votes to none, delegates also voted against adding a BILL OF RIGHTS – a decision reversed within four years. The Constitution itself, which they termed 'the supreme law of the land', was approved with sixteen delegates dissenting and put to the states for ratification. As the convention broke up, a woman asked the ageing Benjamin FRANKLIN: 'Well, doctor, what have we got?

A republic or a monarchy?' Franklin replied: 'A republic, if you can keep it.'

> An assembly of demi-gods.
>
> THOMAS JEFFERSON

phone bank A highly organised telephone CANVASSING operation mounted from a central point. A regular feature of US political and election campaigning by 1992, it was first tried on a sizeable scale in British politics by Labour from MILLBANK in 1997 and is now a powerful complement to traditional doorstep canvassing. It could only become so when almost every elector could be reached by telephone.

phone-in A radio (or less frequently, television) programme where a political leader or candidate is exposed to telephone questioning from the public. It is known in America as a call-in (*see also* 1–800). The callers are sometimes more effective at drawing blood than highly-paid professional interviewers: one example was Mrs Diana Gould's effective and damaging questioning of Margaret THATCHER in the 1983 election campaign over the sinking of the BELGRANO.

phone-tapping scandal The episode in early 1992 that finally ended Charles HAUGHEY's dominance of Irish politics. It stemmed from the commitment by his FIANNA FAIL/PD government to bring in a BILL to regulate phone tapping. This outraged Sean Doherty, speaker of the SEANAD, whose own career had been seriously damaged in 1982 when he carried the can for the BUGGING of political reporters. On 21 January 1992 Doherty called a press conference at a Dublin hotel at which he said:

> I am confirming tonight that the TAOISEACH, Mr Haughey, was fully aware in 1982 that two journalists' phones were being tapped, and that he at no stage expressed a reservation about this action.

Within two days, Haughey had resigned as *Taoiseach* and as leader of Fianna Fail.

Phoney War The period in WORLD WAR II between Germany's invasion of Poland at the start of September 1939 and Britain's declaration of war, and the sudden NAZI push into Norway, Denmark and the Low Countries the following spring, during which there was little activity on the Western front, prompting Neville CHAMBERLAIN to claim injudiciously: 'HITLER HAS MISSED THE BUS'. There were doubts throughout the world during this period over Britain's resolve to fight.

photo opportunity A MEDIA EVENT where a politician is made available for photographs but not for questioning by reporters. The aim is to secure favourable coverage by shutting off the supply of words and providing an upbeat picture, but the ploy is not always successful. In 1982 the WHITE HOUSE barred television networks from sending reporters with camera crews to such occasions because ABC's stentorian Sam Donaldson had made a practice of shouting questions to President REAGAN – who had insisted on answering them.

picketing The practice of stationing supporters of or participants in an industrial dispute outside a workplace that may or may not be related to it to encourage, persuade or – illegally – intimidate those employed there to stop work or otherwise show sympathy. Its origins lie in the military practice of posting pickets or sentries. Seen by TRADE UNIONS as essential to the prosecution of an effective STRIKE, the right to picket and the laws governing the practice were the subject of reversal and political strife throughout the 20th century in most democratic countries.

picket line The point where workers arriving at a plant or hauliers delivering goods to it are met by pickets. Refusal to cross a picket line has traditionally been a fundamental of working-class SOLIDARITY, crossing one the ultimate betrayal.

don't picket, it'll bleed A flippant parody from the late 1970s labour movement of politicians' condemnation of industrial militancy. From the old parental advice to children to leave their spots alone: 'Don't pick it; it'll bleed.'

flying picket A group of pickets who travel from one plant to another attempting to halt operations, with surprise an important factor. The tactic was pioneered in Britain during the miners' strikes of 1972 and 1973/4 by Arthur Scargill (*see* KING ARTHUR).

mass picket A concentration of pickets so great as to hamper the operation of a plant through sheer weight of numbers, even if the workers show no interest in joining the dispute. Pioneered again by Scargill (*see* SALTLEY), it was harnessed at GRUNWICK by a combination of trade union, left-wing and ethnic groups and reached its peak in violent clashes with the police at ORGREAVE, during the MINERS' STRIKE. Even before then, a government code of practice supported in theory by the TUC had set a limit of six pickets per plant.

secondary picketing The practice, at the heart of the PENTONVILLE FIVE affair and during the WINTER OF DISCONTENT, of picketing a plant with little or no connection with a dispute in order to bring its employees out on strike or halt its operations, increasing disruption and pressure for a settlement.

Pierce, Franklin *See* HANDSOME FRANK.

pigeonholing The shelving of a BILL in either HOUSE of the US CONGRESS when a committee refuses to vote on whether to allow it to go to the full House or SENATE for consideration. More than 90 per cent of all Bills suffer such a fate.

pigs The derogatory term for the police that became the hallmark of the PROTEST MOVEMENT during the VIETNAM WAR. Its origins go back to 1800, but it came into its own when used against the police by demonstrators at the 1968 CHICAGO CONVENTION and thereafter. Faced with student protesters the year before, the conservative California academic (and later Senator) S. I. Hayakawa said:

> When you've got a problem with swine, you have to call in the pigs.

Pigs, Bay of The abortive invasion of Cuba by CIA-backed *émigrés* which was the first military adventure, and the greatest catastrophe, of the KENNEDY presidency. Kennedy reluctantly approved plans inherited from the EISENHOWER administration for the CIA to equip and train secretly 1400 Cuban refugees to land on the island and start a popular rising to overthrow Fidel Castro. On 17 April 1961 they landed at the *Bahia de Cochinos* (Bay of Pigs) on Cuba's southern coast. Without air support and with minimal US reinforcements, they were routed and the 1100 survivors soon rounded up; they were later 'ransomed' for $53 million of aid to the MARXIST regime. The adventure was denounced throughout Latin America, and its approval and failure harmed Kennedy's standing at home. He recovered ground by taking full responsibility and promising to learn the lessons of the affair.

> All my life I've known better than to depend on the experts. How could I have been so stupid, to let them go ahead?
> JFK

living proof that a pig's bladder on a stick can be elected as a member of Parliament One of a string of insults in the HOUSE OF COMMONS directed against Terry Dicks (1937–), Conservative MP for Hayes and Harlington in the 1980s, by Tony Banks (1943–), former Labour chairman of the GLC Arts Committee and a subsequent Sports Minister. The taunts were provoked by Dicks' opposition to what he deemed frivolous and unnecessary spending on arts projects.

pillars *See* EUROPEAN UNION.

ping-pong WESTMINSTER-speech for the batting to and fro of contentious legislation between the HOUSE OF COMMONS and HOUSE OF LORDS until arguments over detail are resolved; it applied notably to the 32 hours of debate on 10–11 March 2005 before the BLAIR government's plans were ultimately accepted with one major modification – to introduce HOUSE ARREST for terrorist suspects who could neither be brought to trail nor deported.

pink A pejorative used by both the left and the right for mildly left-wing people, the colour being a watered-down version of the red associated with socialism and Communism. Most fashionable at the height of the COLD WAR, it dates back at least to 1837 when Thomas de Quincy wrote:

> Amusing it is to look upon any political work of Mr Shepherd's . . . and to know that the pale pink of his Radicalism was then accounted deep, deep scarlet.

Behind its use by right-wingers was the inference that 'pinks' might be dupes of Communism. A more insulting derivative of 'pink' is **pinko**, used against liberals and other 'UN-AMERICAN' types from the late 1960s by Vice President Spiro AGNEW and other US conservatives.

Pink Lady Richard NIXON's denunciatory name for Rep. Helen Gahagan Douglas, the liberal former film actress whom he defeated in 1950 to become Senator for California at the age of 38. In a 'pink sheet' circulated throughout the state, Nixon claimed that on 354 occasions she had voted the same way as a 'notorious Communist-line congressman'. It failed to mention that Mrs Douglas, whom he described as 'pink down to her underwear', had frequently voted against that Congressman, or that on 112 occasions Nixon had voted with him. Despite the accusations against her, Ronald REAGAN, then president of the Screen Actors' Guild, campaigned for Mrs Douglas, but he was so impressed by Nixon that he never supported a Democrat again.

pink triangle The symbol that the NAZIS required homosexuals to wear in the CONCENTRATION CAMPS, singling them out for attention and for ridicule by implying effeminacy.

parlour pink The predecessor of RADICAL

CHIC, a derogatory term from COLD WAR America for affluent and stay-at-home supporters of world workers' solidarity, CIVIL RIGHTS and other liberal causes.

Pinochet case The standoff between Britain, Chile and Spain resulting from the arrest in London on 16 October 1998 on an EXTRADITION warrant from a Spanish court of the former Chilean strongman Gen. **Augusto Pinochet** (1915–) on 94 counts of having Spanish nationals tortured after his right-wing JUNTA overthrew President Salvador Allende in 1973. The regime Pinochet led from then until 1990 – during which time 3197 Chileans died at its hands or disappeared – was regarded with distaste throughout the world, but Margaret THATCHER valued his support during the FALKLANDS WAR and he remained a regular visitor to Britain after yielding up his office, though not his power. On a 1998 visit for medical treatment he was arrested on a warrant issued by the Spanish judge Baltazar Garzon; he remained in Britain under house arrest for seventeen months during extradition proceedings, while a political row raged over his future. Home Secretary Jack Straw, who as a left-wing student had worked in Chile before Pinochet's emergence, was at its centre, with Conservatives accusing him of bias and demanding that he intervene to cancel the proceedings, the Chilean government demanding Pinochet's return and the Spanish prosecutor insistent on justice. The HOUSE OF LORDS agreed to his extradition, then decided to re-hear the case after complaints that one of the original judges was a member of AMNESTY INTERNATIONAL, which had campaigned against torture in Chile. The extradition proceedings were then overtaken by legal arguments about Pinochet's health, which resulted in Straw deciding on 2 March 2000 to return him to Chile. Attempts to prosecute him there were hampered by Pinochet having declared himself a senator for life, with consequent IMMUNITY, which Chile's Supreme Court eventually lifted in August 2004. Repeated efforts have since been made to bring him to trial first for human rights abuses and for money-laundering following disclosures about his dealings with Riggs Bank in Washington, and for complicity in the 1974 murder by a car bomb in Buenos Aires of Carlos Prats, Allende's army chief of staff. *See also* LETELIER ASSASSINATION.

Pioneers The youth movement of the Soviet Communist Party, emulated throughout Eastern Europe and modelled on the Boy Scouts, LENIN replacing God as their object of reverence. Lucky members of the Russian Pioneers could even operate their own scaled-down railway system.

PIRA *See* PROVISIONALS.

Pitchfork Ben The nickname of South Carolina's Sen. Benjamin Tillman (1847–1918), a wealthy plantation owner and former state governor. He gained it during the 1894 campaign that won him his seat by saying of Grover CLEVELAND:

> If I go to the Senate I promise that I will use a pitchfork in the President's fat old ribs.

Tillman was re-elected three times despite being censured for manhandling his fellow South Carolina senator in the chamber. President Theodore ROOSEVELT was so affronted by Tillman's behaviour that he withdrew an invitation for him to meet Prince Henry of Germany at the WHITE HOUSE. Tillman was also an unashamed WHITE SUPREMACIST. The Indiana Republican Rep. James Watson assured his own re-election by paying Tillman $250 a time to address open meetings in his district; black voters who attended were so enraged by Tillman that they rallied to the Republican ticket.

Pitt the Elder The posthumous nickname of **William Pitt**, 1st Earl of Chatham (1708–78), thrice Prime Minister and the most forceful critic of Britain's treatment of its American colonies. Entering Parliament in 1735 as an opponent of WALPOLE, he quickly made his mark as a forceful speaker; Walpole declared: 'We must muzzle this terrible cornet of horse,' but Pitt was unrepentant, telling the COMMONS: 'The atrocious crime of being a young man . . . I shall neither attempt to palliate nor deny.' As war loomed with France in 1756 he declared: 'I know that I can save the country and that no one else can.' That December he became Prime Minister, but George II dismissed him after four months. The King had to reinstate him 11 weeks later, nominally under Newcastle. Pitt's mastery of the Commons was complete, largely because of his opposition to the growth of party. George III plotted with Bute against him; he resigned in October 1761, refusing the governorship of Canada. He told the CABINET:

> I was called by my Sovereign and the Voice of the People to assist the State when others had abdicated the service of it. That being so, no one can be surprised that I will go on no longer since my advice is not taken.

He returned to power in July 1766, taking the title Earl of Chatham. The GREAT COMMONER's elevation was unpopular with the people, Lord Chesterfield noting: 'The joke here is that he had a fall upstairs.' In 1767 he was struck by mental illness, resigning in October 1768; David Hume commented: 'He is not mad – that is, no madder than usual.' Gout soon relieved the disorder, and in 1774 Pitt began his campaign for 'a more gentle way of governing America'. He spoke brilliantly in the crisis years of 1776–77, warning: 'You may ravage, but you cannot conquer.'

Pitt the Younger. **William Pitt** (1759–1806), second son of Pitt the Elder. Britain's youngest Prime Minister (1784–1800, 1804–06), with the most meteoric career of any holder of the office. He gained early advantage from his father's reputation, but before long Edmund BURKE was hailing him as 'not merely a chip off the old block, but the old block itself'. Entering Parliament when barely 22 as a member of Lord North's opposition, he became Chancellor of the Exchequer and Leader of the Commons at 23, declining the Premiership when Lord Shelburne resigned. In 1784, aged only 24, he became Prime Minister. Though ridiculed for his inexperience by Charles James Fox, he stayed in office seventeen years through one of the most turbulent periods in Britain's history. He healed wounds opened by the loss of the American colonies, reduced the NATIONAL DEBT, ended public hangings at Tyburn and allowed Roman Catholics into the army and the legal profession. But his greatest success was in insulating Britain from the FRENCH REVOLUTION; Ralph Creyke wrote:

> I shall ever revere his memory for standing between the dead and the living, and staying the plague which in the French Revolution had infected the continent, and might have spread and desolated this island.

Georgiana, Duchess of Devonshire, detected one reason for his survival: 'His eloquence was so great that he could explain every disaster into almost the contrary.' And Samuel Rogers wrote: 'Pitt's voice sounded as if he had worsted in his mouth.'

In 1800 Pitt, by now a declining 41 and scorned by William Cobbett as 'the great snorting bawler', resigned in protest at George III's opposition to Catholic EMANCIPATION and his merging of Ireland's government with that of Britain. Pitt returned to meet the threat of Napoleon, but was broken by his victory at Austerlitz; he died at 46 shortly after hearing of Nelson's victory at Trafalgar. His last words were: 'I think that I could eat one of Bellamy's veal pies.' His death brought a moving epitaph from Sir Walter Scott:

> Now is the stately column broke,
> The beacon-light is quench'd in smoke;
> The trumpet's silver sound is still,
> The warden silent on the hill.

Byron was more cynical:

> With death doomed to grapple
> Beneath this cold slab, he
> Who lied in the Chapel
> Now lies in the Abbey.

(The Chapel is St Stephen's Chapel where the Commons then met.)

place. place in the sun Germany's demand for COLONIES, on a par with Britain, France and the other European nations. Realising that the newly-united state had been left behind in the Scramble for AFRICA and other IMPERIALIST adventures, the future Chancellor Bernhard von Bülow told the REICHSTAG on 6 December 1897:

> In a word, we desire to throw no one into the shade [in East Asia], but we also demand our own place in the sun.

Less than four years later, after the AGADIR CRISIS and German muscle-flexing in China, Kaiser Wilhelm II remarked: 'We have fought for our place in the sun and won it. Our future is on the water.'

placeman Someone who owes his office purely to PATRONAGE, generally having paid the patron or entered into some other corrupt commitment to obtain it.

> Patriot: a candidate for place. Politics: the art of getting one.
>
> HENRY FIELDING (1707–54)

Placido Domingo speech. *See* DOMINGO.

Plaid The Welsh term for any political party, also shorthand for **Plaid Cymru** (Party of Wales), the Nationalist party set up in 1925. Plaid won its first Parliamentary seat in 1966, survived an overwhelming 'No' vote in the 1979 DEVOLUTION referendum, had four MPs elected in 1992, campaigned with Labour to secure a narrow 'Yes' in a second referendum, and since 1999 has been the second party in the WELSH ASSEMBLY. Traditionally its support has been in the Welsh-speaking North and West, but it has become the main opposition to Labour in some former mining valleys in the South; however, it lost ground in the 2005 general election.

Plains The tiny home town, near Americus in southwest Georgia, of President Jimmy CARTER. It became the focus of media attention during Carter's CAMPAIGN for the Presidency and term of office; for a brief period the Carter peanut farm and the town depot where brother Billy (*see* BILLYGATE) held court became household names.

Plame leak The episode from the run-up to the IRAQ WAR that came to haunt George W. BUSH almost as the David KELLY AFFAIR dogged Tony BLAIR. Valerie Plame, a CIA officer, had her identity revealed to the press – a criminal offence – by unnamed officials furious at her husband, former ambassador Joe Wilson, for undermining the President's pre-war claim that Saddam Hussein was trying to acquire uranium from Niger. Suspicion centred on Bush's political advisor Karl Rove (*see* TURDBLOSSOM), with whom Democrats had long sought to get even; by the summer of 2005 the issue was in the hands of a Grand Jury.

plan. Five-year plan *See* FIVE.

National Plan *See* NATIONAL.

planning agreements The concept arrived at by the LABOUR PARTY in 1972–73 and championed by Tony BENN for agreements between government and individual companies on their future production and development. They were a key feature of Labour's economic programme in the two 1974 general elections, but the WILSON and CALLAGHAN governments never put them into practice, except where firms were forced to go to the State for financial assistance.

planning blight The dead hand that falls over a property or neighbourhood which is the subject of a proposed new development, such as a road, especially when the exact location has yet to be decided. Blight makes homes and other property unsaleable and leads to the deterioration of the area; in Britain compensation has increasingly been offered to relieve the problem.

Plant Commission The group set up by Britain's LABOUR PARTY in 1991 under Raymond Plant, Professor of Politics at Southampton University, to consider the case for PROPORTIONAL REPRESENTATION. Neil KINNOCK hoped it would resolve divisions in the party between those, such as Robin COOK and Arthur Scargill (*see* KING ARTHUR), who were keen to see PR adopted, and trenchant advocates of FIRST PAST THE POST like Roy Hattersley (*see* HATTERJI). Its interim report suggested PR for European elections and elections to a SCOTTISH PARLIAMENT, but not for the HOUSE OF COMMONS; this is precisely what happened when Labour eventually took office under Tony BLAIR, despite the appointment of a further commission under Lord JENKINS to assess the case for PR for Westminster elections.

planted question *See* QUESTION.

platform (1) The programme on which a party fights an election. In America, a party's platform is hammered out in drafting sessions by a **platform committee** immediately before its nominating CONVENTION, by which the draft must be endorsed.

> A political platform is just a breach of promise.
> ARNOLD GLASGOW

(2) A mainly UK term for the dignitaries who sit behind a party leader or other keynote speaker at conferences or mass meetings.

Platt amendment The notorious measure which gave America the right to intervene at will in Cuba. It was forced through CONGRESS in 1901 as a RIDER to an APPROPRIATIONS Bill by Sen. Orville H. Platt of Connecticut, as a condition for withdrawing US forces. The amendment stipulated that Cuba would sign no treaty affecting its SOVEREIGNTY without US permission, that the US could intervene to protect its independence or political stability, and that Cuba would give it land for naval bases; one was established at Guantanamo. Cuba was prevented from incurring international debt, and obliged to include the terms of the amendment in its constitution. Franklin D. ROOSEVELT had it repealed in 1934 under his GOOD NEIGHBOR policy toward Latin America; the naval base survives (*see* CAMP DELTA).

Plaza Agreement An agreement reached in New York in September 1985 by the Group of Five – America, Britain, France, Japan and West Germany – to maintain world currency stability by lowering the value of the US dollar. Finance ministers agreed to use 'co-ordinated intervention' in the markets to bring this about, and did so well into 1986.

> In retrospect, I believe this was a mistake. The Plaza Agreement gave Finance Ministers – Nigel [Lawson] above all perhaps – the mistaken idea that they could defy the markets indefinitely. This was to have serious consequences for all of us.
> MARGARET THATCHER, *The Downing Street Years*

Please accept, (your) Excellency, the assurances of my highest consideration

The standard sign-off for a formal letter between high-ranking diplomats of different countries.

plebiscite A REFERENDUM by an entire people of a nation or region to determine by whom it should in future be administered. The most frequent use of plebiscites was in the wake of WORLD WAR I in communities over which two countries had a claim, notably Germany and Poland and Germany and Belgium. The name comes from ancient Rome, being a vote taken by the *plebs*, the common people.

Pledge of allegiance Now a cornerstone of American life, the Pledge of allegiance to the flag is not steeped in antiquity but was first published in the *Youth's Companion* of 8 September 1892 and recited at the dedication of the Chicago World's Fair grounds that 21 October. Its author is believed to have been Frank Bellamy, chairman of the executive committee for the first Columbus Day celebrations. The full text is:

> I pledge allegiance to the Flag of the United States of America, and to the Republic for which it stands, one Nation under God, indivisible, with liberty and justice for all.

The words 'under God' were added in the 1950s and there has been pressure in recent years for their removal. The Pledge became an issue in the 1988 Presidential election when the Bush camp accused Michael Dukakis of having 'vetoed the Pledge'. What the Democratic nominee had in fact done was to vote for a Bill that would not force the children of Jehovah's Witnesses to recite the pledge in school.

PLO Palestine Liberation Organisation. A politico-military organisation founded in 1964 to represent PALESTINIAN Arab refugees and re-establish a Palestinian state; after four decades it has achieved a PALESTINIAN AUTHORITY with limited territory and powers. Its aims have pitted it against ISRAEL, as the Palestinians lay claim to most of the OCCUPIED TERRITORIES, but it has also crossed swords with Jordan (*see* BLACK SEPTEMBER) and hastened civil war in the Lebanon. Since 1967 the PLO has been dominated by the ALFATAH group headed until his death by Yasser Arafat (1929–2004); it has been recognised since 1974 by the UNITED NATIONS and by Israel since 1993 under the GAZA AND JERICHO FIRST agreement, though from 2003 the Israeli government refused to deal with Arafat. The PLO has been plagued by splits; in 1983 Arafat and 5000 supporters were forced to quit the Lebanon for Tunis. The PLO initially conducted terrorist campaigns itself against Israel, including the murder of eleven Israeli athletes at the 1972 Munich Olympics. But in 1988 the leadership declared the existence of a Palestinian state, renounced terrorism and recognised Israel's right to exist within secure borders. Under Arafat it continued to encourage the INTIFADA, and has failed to check terrorist activity by some of its more militant offshoots; Arafat was also accused of nepotism and incompetence in running the Palestinian Authority, and in rejecting peace settlements which gave the Palestinians most of what they wanted.

> A humanitarian organisation, entirely devoted to helping elderly, disabled Americans off the decks of cruise liners. *PRIVATE EYE*

> The PLO never pass up an opportunity to pass up an opportunity. ABBA EBAN (1915–2002)

PLP Parliamentary Labour Party. The body comprising all Labour MPs at WESTMINSTER, which until 1981 elected the party leader. It meets twice weekly: on Wednesdays to discuss policy and party matters, and briefly on Thursdays to consider the following week's BUSINESS.

plum book The book listing the 7000-odd jobs in WASHINGTON that are filled by POLITICAL APPOINTEES and change hands with a new President. It is the 'Bible' of an incoming ADMINISTRATION's TRANSITION team. Titled *Policy and Supporting Positions* and produced after each election by the House Committee on the Post Office and Civil Service, it was first published in 1960.

Plumbers The 'dirty tricks department' of the NIXON White House, which was embarrassingly exposed as the WATERGATE scandal broke. Its true name was the 'special investigations unit', and Nixon formed it in June 1971 to 'stop security leaks and investigate other sensitive matters'. On 3 September that year the Plumbers, led by ex-CIA agent Howard Hunt, broke into the office of Lewis J. Fielding, the psychiatrist counselling Daniel Ellsberg, who had confessed to leaking the PENTAGON PAPERS. For this operation, intended to recover incriminating information, the CIA lent Hunt a red wig, a special camera and a 'speech-altering device'. The Plumbers got away undetected, but came to grief a year later when they were caught red-handed in the Watergate building.

> *John Dean*: These people are going to cost $1 million over the next two years.

Richard Nixon: You could get a million dollars. You could get it in cash. I know where it could be gotten. *Watergate Tapes*, 21 March 1973

pluralism A political system which accommodates different views and traditions, and thus provides for competing parties and ideologies. US political theorists have developed the concept into a culture in which power shifts between competing groups, with the political process in the hands of an elite.

plurality The MAJORITY of a winner over their nearest challenger; in America the word 'majority' applies to the winner's absolute majority over all others combined. In order to secure a majority, a RUN-OFF election may be needed.

plutocracy A democracy dominated by wealth; a **plutocrat** is one who has power because of their riches. The word comes from *Plutus*, the Greek god of wealth.

PM The abbreviation for PRIME MINISTER that frequently occurs in WHITEHALL conversation; as in 'He's been asked to go in and brief the PM.'

PMC In Australia's Federal government, the Department of Prime Minister and Cabinet.

It sets public servant against public servant.
Liberal leader ANDREW PEACOCK (1939–)

PMOS Prime Minister's Official Spokesman The title originally created in November 1997 for Tony BLAIR's communications chief Alastair Campbell, for the person to whom statements made on the Prime Minister's behalf at LOBBY briefings could be attributed by the media. From 2001 Campbell (*see* GARBAGIC) withdrew from regular briefing and the post devolved to the career civil servant who took his place, initially Godric Smith and later also Tom Kelly. Hopes of keeping it low-profile were shattered when at the height of the David KELLY affair in 2003, Tom Kelly (no relation) described the deceased government scientist in an off-the-record conversation with a journalist as a 'Walter Mitty'. The remark gave the impression that, despite a pledge of silence pending the HUTTON INQUIRY, NUMBER TEN was conducting a campaign of SPIN against Kelly beyond the grave. Tom Kelly apologised after being reprimanded by John Prescott (*see* TWO JAGS) in Blair's absence on holiday.

PMQs *See* QUESTIONS.

PNQ *See* Urgent Notice QUESTION.

Pocatello 'You can't go back to Pocatello' has come to signify the reluctance or inability of some home-town politicians to make their way back from WASHINGTON once their Congressional career is over. The inference that the attraction of home – Pocatello, Idaho for example – palls when compared to the fleshpots of the capital is similar to

How you gonna keep 'em down on the farm
After they've seen Paree?

The phrase was coined in 1943–44 by Richard Neuberger, later a Senator for Oregon (it is not recorded if he went back there) and Jonathan Daniels, an aide in the ROOSEVELT White House.

pocket veto *See* VETO.

pocketbook issues A US term for the issues which register with the voter because they affect their personal economic state – their income, the taxes they pay, the level of their mortgage or pension, and their job.

pogrom (Russ. destruction or riot) A drive to massacre or terrorise an ethnic minority, specifically the Jewish rural population of Russian-governed eastern Europe in the decades prior to WORLD WAR I. Pogroms were for a time an unofficial arm of Tsarist policy, particularly in Poland, the Ukraine and western Russia; they prompted mass emigration to the United States, and the start of the movement of Jews back to Palestine.

point. Point Four programme The foreign policy initiative President TRUMAN announced in his INAUGURAL address in January 1949 after his surprise victory over Thomas DEWEY. Its aim was to counter Soviet influence in what is now the THIRD WORLD by offering practical assistance to its people. Over the next three years America spent nearly $40 million on medical and technological aid, despite Congressional objections that 'charity begins at home' and elements in some recipient countries who denounced it as 'IMPERIALISM'.

point man A person appointed to spearhead a US political CAMPAIGN, either for a party or CANDIDATE or against a policy pursued by others. The term grew out of its WORLD WAR II usage for the front soldier in a military patrol, the man most likely to be hit. It was popularised with President CARTER's use of his black UN ambassador Andrew Young as point man on key issues. When President REAGAN needed support in 1986 for his STAR WARS policy, he sent Vice President George BUSH Snr to Europe as point man to allay the growing doubts.

point of order *See* ORDER.

pointy-heads A term for intellectuals in use in America since WORLD WAR II, the inference being that their heads would fit neatly into dunces' pointed caps. It was popularised by Gov. George Wallace of Alabama during his campaigns for the Presidency; he applied it particularly to eastern LIBERALS and opponents of the VIETNAM WAR.

> As an aide to Gov. Wallace and his national campaign director in 1970–71, I helped the Gov'nuh blame it all on those 'integrating, scallywagging, race-mixing, pointy headed liberals who can't even park their bicycles straight'.
>
> TOM TURNIPSEED, *New York Times*, 30 August 1984

pol An American abbreviation, the equivalent of 'cop' for policeman but less complimentary; it refers not so much to a politician as to one of the fatted patrons of MACHINE POLITICS. Hugh Rawson, in his *Dictionary of Invective*, notes:

> The short form reeks of SMOKE-FILLED ROOMS and is almost always used pejoratively.

Polaris The submarine-launched ballistic missile that formed one leg of the US nuclear TRIAD from the 1960s, and provided Britain's sole naval nuclear deterrent throughout the 1970s and 1980s. It was developed by America in the late 1950s to help bridge the perceived MISSILE GAP between the SUPERPOWERS. The first Polaris-equipped nuclear submarine, USS *George Washington*, was launched on 15 November 1960. In 1962 President KENNEDY offered Polaris technology to Britain (*see* SKYBOLT); the first UK Polaris submarine, HMS *Renown*, was completed in 1968. The US Navy replaced its Polaris with Poseidon missiles from 1969, but Britain updated its missiles with MIRV warheads under the CHEVALINE programme, completed in 1982; these weapons were in turn replaced from the early 1990s by TRIDENT, which has a far greater THROW-WEIGHT but is again dependent on US facilities.

polarisation A situation in which each party in a two-PARTY system adopts a steadily more extreme position, with the gulf between them steadily increasing and the voters being offered an ever starker choice. Such a process, as witnessed in Britain in the early 1980s, increases social tension and unrest and can also lead to a stampede by voters towards a moderate third party until the established parties veer back toward the MIDDLE GROUND.

policy The course of action a government intends and endeavours to pursue, overall or in respect of a particular subject or issue. Politicians have long argued over whether policy is dictated by events or can be used to determine them. The 19th-century Austrian statesman Metternich declared that 'policy is like a play in so many acts, which unfolds inevitably once the curtain is raised. [For] intelligent people the problem lies in the decision whether the curtain is to be raised at all.' Lord SALISBURY reckoned there could be 'no such thing as a fixed policy, because policy, like all organic entities, is always in the making'; and MAHATMA Gandhi described a policy as 'a temporary creed liable to be changed, but while it holds good it has got to be pursued with apostolic zeal'.

policy review The wholesale reassessment of its policies conducted by the LABOUR PARTY after sustaining its third successive election defeat in 1987. The principal casualties of the review were Labour's commitments to NATIONALISATION and UNILATERALISM; when Labour narrowly lost a further election in 1992, the review was seen as having helped narrow the gap with the Conservatives – but also as having weakened the party's ideological base.

> A sort of BOSTON TEA PARTY with Labour jettisoning electoral liabilities wherever they are discovered.
>
> ANON. Conservative MP.

Policy Unit The dozen or more civil servants and SPECIAL ADVISERS, based in NUMBER TEN, who advise Britain's Prime Minister on the merits of policies that might be adopted and assess those being implemented. Its power is considerable; after John Prescott (*see* TWO JAGS) announced his Integrated Transport Policy in 1998, Policy Unit members killed key elements of it which they considered anti-motorist and thus politically risky.

policy wonk Someone with an interest, bordering on an obsession, in the policy options open to government; THINK TANKS are heavily populated with them. Originally a Harvard term, it was given a wider currency when Bill CLINTON self-deprecatingly used it to describe himself.

Centre for Policy Studies The pioneer THATCHERITE think tank, founded in 1974 by Sir Keith Joseph (*see* MAD MONK), which under Alfred Sherman eclipsed the official Conservative Research Department and originated many of the radical economic and social policies implemented by the 1979–97 Conservative government. It was set up with Edward HEATH's permission on condition that it did not compete for funds with the party's traditional backers; the promise was not kept, and Heath regarded the funding of the CPS as one element of the 'treachery' that installed Mrs THATCHER in his place.

My policy is to have no policy A semi-serious statement made by Abraham LINCOLN, but not original; in 1826 Metternich had written: 'The only good policy is to pursue no policy.'

Polisario Front (*PO*pular front for the *LI*beration of *SA*guira hamra and *RIO* de oro) The movement of Saharwi tribesmen which has been fighting for the independence of the Western Sahara since the withdrawal of the Spanish colonial authorities after Morocco's GREEN MARCH in 1975. Backed by Algeria, Polisario formed a government-in-exile, the Saharwi Arab Democratic Republic (**SADR**), in 1976. Some 70 countries now recognise it, and in 1989 it was accepted at the OAU. Morocco and Mauritania inbitially divided the territory between them, and when Mauritania dropped its claim in 1979 Morocco tried to annex the whole territory, which at the time was claimed to have fewer than 80,000 inhabitants. Twenty thousand Polisario guerrillas armed by and operating from Algeria drove King Hassan's troops back, since when Morocco has controlled part of the territory, with rich phosphate deposits, from behind a defensive wall and minefields. The UN has voted Western Sahara the right of SELF-DETERMINATION, but repeated efforts to stage a PLEBISCITE in the territory have broken down over who is eligible to vote.

Polish corridor The strip of former German territory given to Poland by the 1919 VERSAILLES Treaty to ensure the new state access to the Baltic. The corridor, roughly along the line of the river Vistula, broke through to the sea west of Danzig (Gdansk), which became a free city, cutting East Prussia off from the rest of Germany. Loss of the corridor, inhabited largely by Germans, was a cause of friction between Germany and Poland from the outset and gave Hitler an additional pretext for invading Poland in 1939, the offensive which finally triggered WORLD WAR II.

Politburo The chief policy-making body of the COMMUNIST PARTY of the Soviet Union, first formed in 1917. The five-member committee reviewed decisions to be taken before they were submitted to the government. The Politburo has been replicated in Communist regimes throughout eastern Europe and Asia; in 1952 it was superseded in the Soviet Union by the Presidium of the Communist Party's CENTRAL COMMITTEE, but that body was renamed the Politburo in 1966. 'Politburo' became a derogatory term in the West for any group of decision-makers who displayed arrogance and lacked ACCOUNTABILITY. President REAGAN's budget director David Stockman once referred to the House Democratic committee chairmen as 'the Politburo of the WELFARE STATE'.

political. political animal Someone with an instinctive interest in or flair for politics. Aristotle reckoned that 'man is by nature a political animal', but he meant by this that participation in society is a natural human activity.

political appointee Someone appointed to a post, not necessarily one with any political connotations, by virtue of their political allegiance or the PATRONAGE of a politician or party. Such appointments are much more widespread in America than in most other democracies, including all the most senior positions in Federal departments and agencies.

political asylum The right of a person persecuted for their political beliefs or activity in their own country to seek refuge in another. The granting of asylum to those under threat, with criteria set by the UNITED NATIONS, has been a hallmark of Western democracy. But ever since the end of the COLD WAR triggered a wave of immigration to Germany from eastern Europe, to Italy from Albania and subsequently to Britain from war-torn areas from Kosovo to Somalia and Afghanistan, the right has come under pressure from governments hard pressed to determine which ASYLUM SEEKERS are genuinely at risk and which are economic migrants. *See also* SANGATTE.

political clearance In WASHINGTON, the process under which qualified applicants for jobs under PATRONAGE secure the necessary partisan political backing; such backing is also sometimes sought for appointments under the merit system, though this is illegal.

political co-operation The EUROPEAN UNION term for agreement by member states to pursue joint foreign policy initiatives; it has largely been superseded by the emergence of a Common Foreign and Security Policy.

political correctness The doctrine widely held and enforced by radical US academics that the only acceptable terminology is that which accords with their beliefs; it is most rigidly applied in cases of race, gender and disability. Its rationale, entirely laudable, is a desire to avoid causing offence to particular groups, but in practice it has escalated from insisting that 'black' people be referred to as 'African-Americans' to demanding, at the extreme, that the dead be described as 'terminally-challenged', and rewriting history texts to assert as fact that most celebrated people in world history were in fact black (or female) or that Dr Livingstone created slavery. Advocates of political correctness regard it as an assertion of human dignity; critics condemn its most extreme manifestations as a form of academic FASCISM. Some US newspapers employ a computer check to make sure their language is politically correct, but the programs have their limitations; the financial page of one California paper reported that a previously loss-making corporation had now 'moved into the African-American'.

political engineering Constructing political support for a project so that its adoption is guaranteed. A US-originated term stemming from defence contractors' endeavours to ensure that work on a proposed aircraft or system is spread among so many Congressional districts that cancellation becomes impossible. The tactic was first used with the B1 BOMBER.

political football An issue which is seized on and exploited by one or more political factions for their own ends, with disregard for the real interests of those affected.

political levy The levy raised from their members by Britain's TRADE UNIONS, primarily to support and finance the LABOUR PARTY. It was established after the OSBORNE JUDGMENT barred the unions from contributing to the party from their general funds; the debate has continued ever since over whether the onus should be on members who do not want to pay to contract out, or on active Labour supporters to contract in. Under legislation passed by the THATCHER government, contracting-out continues, provided a ballot of union members agrees.

political prisoner Someone detained purely or primarily because of their political beliefs, not having committed any crime under the civil law. Notorious regimes the world over have always imprisoned their opponents rather than submit to rational argument and the judgement of the people. The political inmates of HITLER's CONCENTRATION CAMPS and the occupants of the Soviet GULAG were among the many 20th-century victims, and SLORC's detention of Aung San Suu Kyi after her party won a democratic election has spanned two centuries. AMNESTY INTERNATIONAL has campaigned steadfastly for the release of political prisoners the world over. For the **Unknown political prisoner,** *see* UNKNOWN.

> Nothing can be more abhorrent to democracy than to imprison a person or keep him in prison because he is unpopular. That is the real test of civilisation.
>
> CHURCHILL, 21 November 1943

political science The science or study of government, and the interaction of political forces, with reference to its principles, aims, methods and conduct.

political status The special status accorded to suspected terrorists INTERNED in NORTHERN IRELAND in the early 1970s, which convicted Republican and LOYALIST prisoners subsequently sought for themselves. The demand for political status was pursued in the H-BLOCKS through the BLANKET and DIRTY PROTESTs, and ultimately through a traumatic HUNGER STRIKE in which Bobby Sands and nine other IRA prisoners died before the goal was abandoned.

political union One of the twin aims of the MAASTRICHT TREATY, the binding together more closely of the member states of what the treaty rechristened the EUROPEAN UNION and the development of common political institutions; this process has been taken further in the Treaties of AMSTERDAM and NICE and the EUROPEAN CONSTITUTION, but to the dismay of FEDERALISTS progress has not been as fast as toward economic union.

political wing In a PARAMILITARY organisation, the part which acts as a legitimate party or movement, as opposed to the MILITARY WING which engages in terrorism. For example, the political wing of the Provisional IRA is SINN FEIN.

politician A practitioner of the art of POLITICS, essential to the working of human society but frequently despised by those outside the political arena; indeed the word is sometimes a term of abuse. In ancient Greece Aristophanes wrote that 'under every stone lurks a politician', Shakespeare 2000 years later wrote in *King Lear*:

> Get thee glass eyes
> And like a scurvy politician, seem
> To see things thou dost not.

Every humorist, and many non-humorists, have put forward their own definition of a politician: 'Like the bones in a horse's shoulder. Not a straight one in sight' – Wendell Phillips; 'An eel in the fundamental mud upon which the structure of organised society is reared. When he wiggles, he mistakes the agitation of his tail for the trembling of the edifice. As compared with the STATESMAN, he suffers the disadvantage of being alive' – Ambrose Bierce; 'an animal who can sit on the fence and yet keep both ears to the ground' – H. L. Mencken; 'an arse upon which everyone has sat except a man' – e. e. cummings; 'a statesman who approaches every question with an open mouth' – Adlai STEVENSON; 'that insidious and crafty animal whose councils are directed by momentary fluctuations of affairs' – Adam Smith; 'little tin gods on wheels' – Rudyard Kipling; 'a number of anxious dwarfs trying to grill a whale' – J. B. Priestley; 'dangerous lunatics to be avoided when possible, and carefully humoured; people, above all, to whom we must never tell the truth' – W. H. Auden; 'An acrobat. He keeps his balance by saying the opposite of what he does' – Maurice Barrès; 'someone who divides his time between running for office and running for cover' – Anon.

Shakespeare's *doppelganger* Francis Bacon observed: 'It is as hard and severe a thing to be a true politician as it is to be truly moral.' Mencken reckoned that 'a good politician is quite as unthinkable as an honest burglar'; Walter Lippmann stated that 'successful democratic politicians are insecure and intimidated men. They advance politically only as they can placate, appease, bribe, seduce, bamboozle or otherwise manage to manipulate the demanding and threatening elements in their constituencies'; Simon Cameron said more sharply: 'An honest politician is one who, when he is bought, stays bought'. Frank Kent declared: 'The only way a reporter should look at a politician is down'; Sam Shaffer that 'the effectiveness of a politician varies in inverse proportion to his commitment to principle', while Brendan Francis noted: 'Politicians, like prostitutes, are held in contempt. But what man does not run to them when he needs their services?' Lucille Ball announced: 'Just say the word "politician" and I think of chicanery', while the veteran election-watcher Theodore H. White confided: 'The best time to listen to a politician is when he is on a street corner, in the rain, late at night, when he's exhausted. Then he doesn't lie.'

The politician's stock in trade is words. Theodore ROOSEVELT reckoned that 'the most successful politician is he who says what everyone is thinking, more often in the loudest voice'; Enoch POWELL went a stage further, saying: 'A politician crystallises what most people mean – even if they don't know it.' Paul Harwitz wrote: 'The reason politicians make strange bedfellows is because they all use the same bunk', but Clare Boothe Luce drew comfort from her belief that 'sooner or later all politicians die of swallowing their own words'. Sen. Henry F. Ashurst asserted that 'the politician must always tell the people what they want to hear', Ed Murrow that 'the politician is trained in the art of inexactitude'. G. K. Chesterton noted tartly that 'every politician is emphatically a promising politician', the ICI chairman Sir Paul Chambers that 'exhortation of other people to do something is the last resort of politicians who are at a loss to know what to do themselves', and Iain Macleod that 'a politician's pronouncements have a news value in direct proportion to his prospects of power'. DE GAULLE cynically observed that 'since a politician never believes what he says, he is surprised when others believe him', and Khrushchev that 'politicians are the same all over. They promise to build a bridge even when there is no river.'

There have been some equally picturesque views of the characteristics required of a politician: 'A horrible voice, bad breath and a vulgar manner' – Aristophanes; 'the ability to foretell what is going to happen tomorrow, next week, next month and next year – and the ability afterwards to explain why it didn't happen' – CHURCHILL; 'One has to be a low-brow, a bit of a murderer; ready and willing to see people sacrificed, slaughtered for the sake of an idea – whether a good one or a bad one' – Henry Miller; 'three hats: one for throwing in the ring, one for talking through, and one for pulling rabbits out of if elected' – Carl Sandburg. Sen. Mike Mansfield once observed that 'even a politician is human', but many people are not so sure. John F. KENNEDY confessed: 'Mothers all want their sons to grow up to be President, but they don't want them to be politicians in the process', the *New Orleans Times* editorialised: 'It is no wonder politicians get hard-boiled. They're always in hot water', and Richard Harris reckoned 'selective cowardice' was an attribute of most. Edward HEATH said: 'If politicians lived on praise and thanks, they'd be forced into some other line of business', so Australia's Stanley Melbourne Bruce was at an advantage when he asserted: 'My chief advantage as a politician is that I did not give a damn.' Field-Marshal Montgomery reminisced: 'I have spent most of my life fighting the Germans and fighting the politicians. It is much easier to fight the Germans.' Harold MACMILLAN warned idealists: 'If people want a sense of purpose they should get it from an archbishop. They should certainly not get it from their politicians', while Harold WILSON concluded that 'the practised performance of latter-day politicians is the game of musical daggers – never be left holding the dagger when the music stops.'

> I wish politicians would go out and get another sensible job and spend less time telling us all what to do and how to live. JEREMY IRONS

> Render any politician down and there's enough fat to fry an egg. SPIKE MILLIGAN

> Your politicians will always be there when they need you. CARTER campaign T-shirt, 1980

> We are not politicians. We made our revolution to get the politicians out.
> FIDEL CASTRO, 1961

> It has been the great fault of our own politicians that they have all wanted to do something.
> ANTHONY TROLLOPE

politicisation (1) The arousal of political consciousness and activism among a previously apathetic section of the population, either by positive campaigning from a motivated group or (more often) by some blunder or act of malice on the part of the authorities. (2) The injection of a political dimension into some aspect of life which has hitherto been free from it.

Politico's WESTMINSTER's pioneering political bookshop and, subsequently, publishing house, and incidentally the publishers of this dictionary. Politico's was founded by Iain Dale in 1997 and the shop in Artillery Row became not only a comprehensive stockist of political literature and generator of new titles, but a centre for political thought, gossip and intrigue, notably at its regular book launches. With Dale embarking on a political career himself, the Politico's imprint was sold to Methuen in April 2003 and the shop was taken over by them the following year; Dale narrowly failed to regain Norfolk North for the Conservatives in 2005. Politico's unique contribution to London's political village continues.

politics The conduct of government at all levels, and the interaction of political parties and movements within a social system, and of men and women within those movements. Also the views held by an individual, as in 'What are her politics?' and the political dimension of an issue, as in 'What are the politics of it?' There is no shortage of definitions: 'Nothing more than a means of rising in the world' – Dr Johnson; 'the gizzard of society, full of guts and gravel' – Thoreau; 'an ordeal path among red hot ploughshares' – John ADAMS; 'the systematic organisation of hatreds' – Henry Adams; 'not a science, but an art' – Bismarck; 'a deleterious profession, like some poisonous handicrafts' – Ralph Waldo Emerson; 'the conduct of public affairs for private advantage; a means of livelihood affected by the more degraded portion of our criminal classes' – Ambrose Bierce; 'the art of looking for trouble, finding whether it exists or not, diagnosing it incorrectly and applying the wrong remedy' – Sir Ernest Benn; 'a dog's life without the dog's decencies' – Rudyard Kipling; 'the art of preventing people from busying themselves with their own business' – Paul Valéry; 'all politics is apple sauce' – Will Rogers; 'the gentle art of getting votes from the poor and campaign funds from the rich, by promising to protect each from the other' – Oscar Ameringer; 'the science of who gets what, when and why' – Sidney Hillman; 'war without bloodshed' – CHAIRMAN MAO; 'the art of government' – Harry S TRUMAN; 'a blood sport' – Aneurin BEVAN; 'the division of trivial men who, when they succeed in it, become important in the eyes of even more trivial men' – George Jean Nathan; 'the skilled use of blunt objects' – Lester Pearson; 'too serious a matter to be left to the politicians' – DE GAULLE; 'politics is property' – Murray Kempton; 'a form of astrology, and money is its sign' – John Leonard; 'yesterday's answers to today's problems' – Marshall McLuhan; 'a thing that only the unsophisticated go for' – Kingsley Amis; 'like Brahma's horns – a point here, a point there and a lot of bull in between' – Ruth Fountain; 'like sex in a hula hoop' – Richard Reeves; 'showbiz for ugly people' – Paul Begala; 'the art of acquiring, holding and wielding power' – Indira Gandhi.

> All politics is local. TIP O'NEILL

Above all, politics is a rough and tumble. CHURCHILL wrote: 'Politics are as exciting as war, and quite as dangerous. In war you can be killed only once, but in politics many times', and LLOYD GEORGE said: 'Piracy, broadsides, blood on the decks – you'll find them all in politics.' Konrad Adenauer reckoned that 'the art of politics consists in knowing precisely when it is necessary to hit an opponent slightly below the belt', Kenneth Clarke that 'the more caring the subject, the rougher the debate', while the Australian Fred Daley ruefully noted: 'Politics is a funny game. One day you're a rooster, the next a feather duster.' Yet James Reston identified the magic of politics when he described it as 'like booze and women: dangerous but incomparably exciting'. And Lord Hailsham warned: 'The moment politics becomes dull, democracy is in danger.'

> Until you've been in politics
> You've never really been alive
> It's rough and sometimes it's
> Dirty and it's always hard
> Work and tedious details
> But, it's the only sport for grownups – all other
> Games are for kids.
>
> Quotation from *Henlein* in Sen. John Culver's private office

The idea of politics as a game has produced numerous sporting comparisons. Sen. Eugene McCarthy asserted: 'Being in politics is like being a football coach. You need to be smart enough to understand the game – and dumb enough to think it is important'; John F. KENNEDY reckoned that 'politics is like football – if you see daylight, go for the hole', and Art Buchwald mischievously commented: 'I always wanted to get into politics, but was never light enough top make the team'. Sen. Henry Ashurst felt politics was more like roller skating: 'You go partly where you want to go, and partly where the damn things take you.' Julian Bond noted 'a thin line between politics and theatricals', and Professor C. Northcote Parkinson observed of the British: 'If they cannot be playing golf or tennis, they can at least pretend that politics is a game with very similar rules.'

Opinions have differed on the personal qualities required for politics. Robert Louis Stevenson considered it 'perhaps the only profession for which no preparation or thought is necessary', and George Bernard Shaw wrote: 'He knows nothing and thinks he knows everything. That points clearly to a political career.' Napoleon declared that 'in politics, absurdity is not a hardship', Thiers that 'One must take nothing tragically and everything seriously', and Lord Carrington that 'If you take yourself seriously in politics, you've had it.' Barbara Castle was convinced that 'In politics, guts is all', Henry Adams that 'practical politics consists in ignoring facts', while James C. Wright lamented:

> A rhinoceros is an animal with a hide two feet thick, and no apparent interest in politics. What a waste.

Lyndon B. JOHNSON put the case for intuition, saying: 'If you're in politics and you can't tell when you walk into a room who's for you and who's against you, you're in the wrong line of work.' Woodrow WILSON ruled out tolerance as 'an admirable intellectual gift, but of little use in politics. Politics is a war of causes, a joust of principles.' John Kenneth Galbraith reckoned that 'nothing is so admirable in politics as a short memory', echoing de Tocqueville's observation: 'I have often noticed in politics how men are ruined by having too good a memory', and Chris PATTEN quickly discovered that 'it rarely pays in politics to be wise before the event'. As to what politics does to its practitioners, Ronald REAGAN asserted: 'The only experience you get in politics is how to be political', and Josef Goebbels revealingly stated: 'Politics ruin the character. They develop the worst and meanest qualities.'

> I am not made for politics because I am incapable of wishing for or accepting the death of my adversary. ALBERT CAMUS (1913–60)

> Men enter local politics largely as a result of being unhappily married.
>
> Professor C. NORTHCOTE PARKINSON (1919–93)

The morality of politics has been in question since Plato branded it 'nothing but corruption', though Aneurin BEVAN maintained: 'I have never regarded politics as the arena of morals. It is the arena of interests.' MACCHIAVELLI, not surprisingly, reckoned that 'politics have no relation to morals'; Rousseau that 'those people who treat politics and morality separately will never understand either'; DISRAELI that 'in politics there is no honour'; Lord ROSEBERY that 'a gentleman may blithely do in politics what he would kick a man downstairs for doing in ordinary life', and LENIN that 'there are no morals in politics, only expedience'. Lord Bryce asserted that 'a political career brings out the basest qualities in human nature', and FDR's aide Louis Howe that 'you cannot adopt politics as a profession and remain honest.' Russell Long concluded that 'the first rule of politics is not to lie to somebody unless it is absolutely necessary', while Ronald REAGAN quipped: 'I used to say that politics is the second oldest profession, and I have come to know that it bears a gross similarity to the first.'

Politics, it seems to me, for years, or all too long
Has been concerned with right and left instead of
right and wrong. RICHARD ARMOUR

The cardinal rule of politics: never get caught in bed with a live man or a dead woman.
Larry Hagman as J. R. EWING in CBS Television's *Dallas*

Politics and money are inextricably connected; indeed Jesse Unruh termed money 'the mother's milk of politics'. This is even truer in America than in Britain, Will Rogers observing: 'Over there politics is an obligation; here it's a business.' Harry S TRUMAN remarked: 'The difficulty with businessmen entering politics, after they've had a successful business career, is that they want to go straight to the top.' Politicians reckon they handle businessmen on their own terms; Unruh explained: 'If you can't drink their booze, take their money, fool with their women and then vote against them, you don't deserve to be in politics.' And Donald Rumsfeld, with one eye on the farm lobby, warned: 'When anyone with a rural accent says: "I don't know anything about politics", zip up your pocket.'

The venal side of politics generates revulsion both within and outside the political community. President TAFT opined that 'politics, when I am in it, makes me sick', and the Royalist French Minister Chamfort declared: 'One would be disgusted if one saw politics, justice and one's dinner in the making.' Yet the ultimate comment came from the anonymous American who wrote:

Nothing can be said about our politics that hasn't already been said about haemorrhoids.

The nexus between politics and morality also embraces religion. Edmund BURKE argued that 'politics and the pulpit are terms that have little agreement. The case of civil liberty and civil government gains as little as that of religion by [the] confusion of duties.' Lord Hailsham reckoned that 'the introduction of religious passion into politics is an end to honest politics, and the introduction of politics into religion is a prostitution of true religion', and declared: 'The man who put politics first is not fit to be called a civilised being, let alone a Christian'. The Beirut hostage Terry Waite stated with devastating simplicity:

Politics come from man. Mercy, compassion and justice come from God.

And the theologian Reinhold Niebuhr conceded: 'The sad duty of politics is to establish justice in a sinful world.'

Where does the ordinary citizen fit in? Truman reckoned that 'a man who is not interested in politics is not doing his patriotic duty towards maintaining the Constitution of the United States', and Dwight D. EISENHOWER that 'politics ought to be the part-time profession of every citizen who would protect the rights and privileges of free people and who would preserve what is good and fruitful in our national heritage.' Yet H. L. Mencken considered that 'the whole aim of practical politics is to keep the populace alarmed (and hence clamorous to be led to safety) by menacing it with an endless series of hobgoblins, all of them imaginary', and James Reston concluded that 'all politics are based on the indifference of the majority'. Dolley Madison saw politics as 'the business of men', but Hermione Gingold observed: 'There are too many men in politics, and not enough elsewhere.'

Everything you need to know about politics you learned when you learned to drive. If you want to go forward you put it in D. If you want to go backward you put it in R. Just remember that and you'll be fine.
Senate MAJORITY LEADER TOM DASCHLE, 2002

What makes good television makes bad politics.
RICHARD NIXON

The end move in politics is always to pick up a gun.
R. BUCKMINSTER FULLER (1895–1987)

There is life after politics.
BOB HAWKE, on his resignation, 1991

community politics *See* COMMUNITY.

gesture politics The cultivation of electoral support by associating oneself dramatically with a cause or the resolution of a crisis in a way that achieves little practical good.

kerbstone politics *See* PAVEMENT.

machine politics *See* MACHINE.

pavement politics *See* PAVEMENT.

porcupine politics A US term for the achievement of power and results, especially in CONGRESS, by prickly MAVERICKS who can make life awkward or painful for the majority.

wholesale politics The politics of mass communication, selling the big picture of oneself or one's party to a national television audience. Retail politics, by contrast, is dealing in small-scale issues, in direct contact with individual voters.

politics is the art of the possible The ultimate statement of PRAGMATISM identified with R. A. Butler (*see* RAB), but originally used by Bismarck in 1867 in a conversation with Meyer von Waldeck. John Kenneth Galbraith has since ventured to disagree, writing: 'Politics is not the art of the possible. It consists in choosing between the disastrous and the unpalatable.'

politics of envy A term used mainly by right-of-centre politicians for those political movements and policies among the have-nots which they regard as motivated by a resentment of the wealthy and a desire to expropriate them.

> Envy is capable of . . . making the rich moderate their habits for fear of arousing it. It is because of the existence of envy that one does not drive Rolls-Royces through the slums of Naples.
>
> Sir KEITH (later Lord) JOSEPH (1918–94)

politics of fear A phrase much heard on both sides of the Atlantic in 2004, first as George W. BUSH narrowly won re-ELECTION in a CAMPAIGN which played on Americans' fear of terrorism after 9/11, and then as Tony BLAIR and his Home Secretary David Blunkett brought forward a pre-election legislative programme dominated by tougher measures against terrorism and crime.

politics ooze from his every orifice The vivid description of the attributes of the Scottish Labour MP and Minister George FOULKES (later Lord) (1942–) given to the Glasgow *Herald* by his Liberal Democrat friend and contemporary Sir Archy Kirkwood.

a week is a long time in politics The most celebrated dictum of Harold WILSON, taken by critics as a sign of the deepest pragmato-cynicism. Wilson probably said it first at a meeting with LOBBY correspondents during a sterling crisis soon after Labour took office in 1964; he repeated it a number of times in 1965 and 1966. There was a precedent; in 1886 Joseph Chamberlain said to BALFOUR: 'In politics there is no use looking beyond the next fortnight.' However, Chamberlain was making a point about the impossibility of foreseeing the future; Wilson was also conveying the message that in politics almost anything may be forgotten in a short time.

confound their politics An example of 'politics' being used in a derogatory sense; a controversial phrase from the seldom-sung second verse of GOD SAVE THE QUEEN. It forms part of an appeal to the Almighty to scatter the Sovereign's enemies, and all who intrigue against the throne.

The Triumph of Politics The controversially frank account by David Stockman, President REAGAN's first budget director, of the illusory and almost fraudulent nature of REAGANOMICS, which caused the ADMINISTRATION considerable embarrassment when published in 1986.

poll (1) An ELECTION, as in 'the only poll that counts is the one on the day'. It has its origin in *polle*, the old Teutonic for head; in olden days the heads of voters would be counted by someone standing on high ground. (2) A test of public attitudes or voting intentions, an OPINION POLL.

poll of polls A device much loved by newspapers and television stations that lack the resources to conduct opinion polls of their own. Instead, the expressions of opinion from all the polls conducted in the previous few days are grossed up and averaged out to provide a single and supposedly more reliable forecast of voting intentions.

poll tax (1) The mediaeval tax on the King of England's subjects which provoked the PEASANTS' REVOLT of 1381 and other upheavals. (2) The tax imposed in America's Deep South on those registering to vote, which in the 19th and early 20th centuries disenfranchised many blacks and poor whites. Ten states adopted a poll tax between 1889 and 1902; as late as 1937 the SUPREME COURT ruled Georgia's constitutional. Poll taxes for Federal elections, still in force in five states, were finally outlawed in 1964 by the 24th Amendment. Such taxes pre-dated the CIVIL WAR; in 1846 Henry David Thoreau refused to pay his $1 Massachusetts poll tax as a protest against slavery and was jailed until his aunt paid the next morning. (3) The controversial flat-rate local tax, officially termed the COMMUNITY CHARGE, brought in by Margaret THATCHER's government to replace the RATES. Introduced in Scotland in 1989 and England and Wales in 1990, it proved so unpopular (with riots in the streets of London) that John MAJOR moved to abolish it as soon as she left office. It was hated because the less well-off paid as much per head as the wealthy, because some Labour councils pushed up the tax to make the government unpopular, and because the 25% of the people who had never paid local taxes disliked having to do so. When the COUNCIL TAX replaced it in 1993, it was denounced as unfair by many householders who had paid less under the poll tax; twelve years later some councils were still trying to collect arrears of poll tax from non-payers.

> The proposal would be completely unworkable and politically catastrophic.
>
> NIGEL LAWSON, 1985

> One of the greatest acts of political folly in the history of British democracy.
>
> PETER SHORE

eve of poll The night before voting takes

place in a UK ELECTION, when each Parliamentary CANDIDATE traditionally suspended CANVASSING to hold an **eve-of-poll meeting** or rally in their constituency. The practice is fast dying out as public meetings go out of vogue.

exit poll A survey of how electors have voted, taken as they leave the polling stations, and made public the moment voting has finished. If an exit poll is truthful, it should give an accurate PROJECTION of the result well before it is officially declared; in the UK elections of 1987 and 1992 a reluctance of voters to admit they had supported the Conservatives led to exit polls suggesting Labour had done far better than was actually the case, but in 1997, 2001 and 2005 the exit polls were close to the mark. The exit pollsters called the 2000 Presidential election badly wrong, handing it to Al Gore on the basis of partial results in Florida; in 2004 the networks held back from using the exit polls, to their relief as once again they understated support for George W. BUSH.

Gallup poll Traditionally the best known of the OPINION POLLS, instituted in 1935 by Dr George Gallup (1901–84) of the American Institute of Public Opinion. Gallup set the pattern for over six decades of polling by numerous other organisations, notably **Harris**, **MORI** and **NOP**, with trained interviewers interrogating a carefully selected but small (usually around 1000) cross-section of the population. For the British election of 1945, 1809 out of 25 million voters were interviewed and the forecast was within 1% of the outcome; however, in the 1948 US Presidential election the Gallup forecast – like everyone else's – was wrong. Gallup remained in the forefront of such research on both sides of the Atlantic, though in 2003 the *Daily Telegraph* abandoned it for the Internet-based YOUGOV.

> Polling is merely an instrument for gauging public opinion. When a president or other leader pays attention to polling results, he is in effect paying attention to the views of the people. Any other interpretation is nonsense.
>
> GEORGE GALLUP

percentage poll *See* TURNOUT.

private polls The polls conducted for a political party to give it instant and confidential information on how its campaign is going and what issues are gaining and losing it votes.

rogue poll An opinion poll way out of line with others taken at the time, and thus assumed to be wrong. On rare occasions the poll denounced as a 'rogue' has turned out to be the only one accurately pointing to the result of an election.

straw poll An informal test of opinion, such as a reporter arriving in a town may conduct among the first few people he or she meets.

> A straw vote shows only which way the hot air is blowing. O. HENRY

tracking poll One of a series of polls conducted for a party, candidate or news organisation which shows underlying and longer-term trends, rather than giving a snap verdict.

polling booth In UK elections, the wooden cubicle to which the voter takes his or her BALLOT paper and where they mark their X with a pencil before folding the paper and putting it into the BALLOT BOX.

polling day The day on which voting takes place in an election.

polling district In UK politics, the area whose electors use a single POLLING STATION; it is usually a subdivision of a local government WARD, with anything from half a dozen to 4000 voters on the electoral register.

polling station The premises where electors turn out to vote; it may be anything from a school or church hall to a caravan or even the front room of a house. Staffed by local government officials who check voters' names against the ELECTORAL REGISTER and hand out BALLOT PAPERS, it contains POLLING BOOTHS and one or more BALLOT BOXES, depending on the number of elections taking place. Outside there are usually TELLERS from the political parties to check on how many of their supporters have voted, and periodically a policeman.

pollster A colloquialism for the political scientists who initiate and conduct opinion polls, then interpret them to the public. Every presidential campaign has had its own pollster; the pioneers in the 1970s were Robert Teeter for the Republicans and Patrick Caddell for the Democrats.

Pollard (Jonathan) case The issue which came closer to causing a rupture between the United States and Israel than any other event since SUEZ, arising from the imprisonment in 1986 of Jonathan Pollard, a PENTAGON employee, on charges of passing naval secrets to Israel. Pollard is regarded as a martyr by hard-line Israelis and a traitor by many Americans. Repeated efforts by Israel to secure his release have been unsuccessful; at the close of the WYE PLANTATION summit in 1998 Prime Minister Benjamin Netanyahu tried to bounce President CLINTON into freeing him by claiming that the agreement reached had been contingent on his release.

pollute. polluter pays The principle under which the cost of remedying damage to the environment is met by the industry (or nation) responsible. Initially a feature of environmentalist campaigning, it was taken up by some American states and has worked its way through into a number of national and international policies.

> It actually means the customers of the polluter.
> NICHOLAS RIDLEY

Eighty per cent of pollution comes from plants and trees Ronald REAGAN's remark alleged by his critics to show a breathtaking incomprehension of the crisis facing the environment. What he actually said, toward the close of the 1980 Presidential campaign, was: 'Approximately 80% of our air pollution stems from hydrocarbons released by vegetation, so let's not go overboard in setting and enforcing tough emission standards from man-made sources.' When attacked by Sen. Edward KENNEDY, he retorted: 'I didn't say 80%, I said 92%, 93%, pardon me. And I didn't say air pollution, I said oxides of nitrogen. And I am right. Growing and decaying vegetation in this land are responsible for 93% of the oxides of nitrogen.'

> Put the President of the SIERRA CLUB in a sealed garage with a tree. Put Ronald Reagan in a sealed garage with a running automobile, and wait to see which of them yells to get out first.
> *San José Mercury-News*

PONC Person of No Consequence. A US government official or journalist obliged, through their lower status and lack of ACCESS, to fly in the plane in front of AIR FORCE ONE rather than in the same aircraft as the President.

poncho. Thanks for the poncho President CLINTON's GAFFE when visiting Romania in July 1997, when thanking his hosts for presenting him with what was in fact their national flag with the Communist emblem in the centre cut out.

Ponting affair The case which finally destroyed the credibility of the CATCH-ALL Section 2 of Britain's 1911 OFFICIAL SECRETS ACT, severely embarrassing Margaret THATCHER's government. Clive Ponting, a senior official in the Ministry of Defence, was acquitted by an Old Bailey jury in March 1985 of breaching the Act after LEAKing the previous summer classified information suggesting the Ministers had lied to the COMMONS for two years over the circumstances of the sinking of the General BELGRANO in 1982. Ponting acted when Defence Secretary Michael HESELTINE and his officials decided to stick to the previous line that the *Belgrano* had been sunk because it posed an immediate threat to the British fleet. Ponting passed the papers to the Labour MP Tam Dalyell, in the hope that Parliament would learn the true facts. His acquittal torpedoed the doctrine advanced by the prosecution, that the interests of the state are identical with those of the government of the day.

Pooh-Bahs Highly influential and slightly stuffy politicians whose writ extends over a number of varying fields of legislation and PATRONAGE. A term often used on CAPITOL HILL, it arises from the characterisation of Pooh Bah, the 'Lord High Everything Else' in W. S. Gilbert and Sir Arthur Sullivan's 1885 comic opera *The Mikado.*

pool reporter One of a small group of journalists representing and reporting for the media as a whole, who will be chosen to accompany or interview a political leader when there is either insufficient space for the entire media pack, or when such reporting would be preferable to a PRESS CONFERENCE or a series of individual interviews. The pool will be selected to include, for instance, a news agency representative, a national newspaper journalist, a reporter from one of the television networks, a photographer and so forth. The author was one of the pool who accompanied Queen Elizabeth II when she inspected the LIBERTY BELL in its confined surroundings in Philadelphia; he (and others) neglected to see whether she actually touched it, which was what their non-pool colleagues all wanted to know afterwards.

Poor Bastards' Bill *See* BASTARDS.

Poor Law The laws governing the support, management or confinement of the poor in England from 1601 until the BEVERIDGE REPORT. Originally the system was based on PARISH relief, to assist the aged and settled sick and prevent the poor moving from one parish to another. After 1834 a system of workhouses was set up, to house the poor and give them tasks – often including labour on a treadmill; from 1890 the system was humanised, toys, books and tobacco being allowed to the inmates. The Poor Law system broke up after further reforms in 1919–20 reduced the number of authorities by three quarters, and the post-war DEPRESSION was the final straw, the Poplar guardians being SURCHARGED in 1922 for paying higher benefits than the government would approve.

The poorest he that is in England hath a life to live, as the greatest he The argument for democracy put forward by Colonel Rainborough, in disputation with Oliver Cromwell, at the PUTNEY DEBATES of 1647. Cromwell retorted that there was not sufficient ground to argue that 'by a man's being born here, he shall have a share in that power that shall dispose of the lands here'.

Pope. The Pope, how many divisions has he got? STALIN's dismissive response to the French Foreign Minister Pierre Laval, who urged him on 13 May 1935 to encourage Catholicism in Russia so as to placate the Pope.

No Popery! *See* NO.

Popish Plot The alleged Jesuit conspiracy to murder King Charles II and enthrone his Catholic brother the Duke of York (later James II), which was 'exposed' by WHIGS in 1679, largely on the perjured evidence of Titus Oates (1649–1705). What the Whigs really feared, but could not allege, was a joint conspiracy by the King and his brother against the Protestant religion. The unveiling of the 'plot' created public hysteria in London, followed by the execution of 35 innocent Catholics, including the Primate of Ireland, after blatantly rigged trials. When James came to the throne in 1685, Oates was pilloried, whipped and imprisoned.

poppycock Another word for nonsense, deriving from the Dutch *pappekak*, soft dung. Its use in a political context dates back at least to 1865 when Charles Faffar Browne wrote: 'You won't be able to find another pack of poppycock gabblers as this present CONGRESS of the United States.' In February 1973 when Sen. Sam ERVIN, confronted with the NIXON administration's insistence that senior officials testify to the Senate WATERGATE committee in secret on grounds of EXECUTIVE PRIVILEGE, responded: 'Executive poppycock!'

Popular Front An alliance of left-wing parties (Communists, socialists, Liberals, radicals, etc.) against a reactionary government or the threat from right-wing DICTATORS abroad. Anti-FASCIST Popular Fronts were proposed by the Communist International in 1935; such a government was set up in Madrid that year, but was unable to avert the SPANISH CIVIL WAR. France had a Popular Front government from 1936 to 1938 under Léon Blum, but apart from enabling the French Communist Party to strengthen its power base it could not achieve long-term unity on the left or pose an effective counterweight to fascism or NAZIsm in neighbouring states.

populism A political philosophy or movement appealing to voters' visceral feelings, with a touch of DEMAGOGY from its leaders. Frequently populism manifests itself in a SINGLE-ISSUE campaign: against abortion, against high – or any – taxes (*see* POUJADISTS), against a particular ethnic group (*see* RACISM). In America it has had a special meaning, representing the successive Populist or PROGRESSIVE movements based in the FARM BELT that have combined religious fundamentalism with demands for a fairer economic deal (or preferential treatment) from WASHINGTON.

Populist Party The party formed in 1892 by discontented Mid-Western and Southern farmers under the slogan 'We do not ask for sympathy or pity: We ask for justice'. It advocated FREE SILVER, tax cuts, government ownership of the railroads and help with farm marketing and, as a pitch to industrial workers, an end to the use of the Pinkerton agency to break strikes and a curb on immigration. The Populists nominated James Baird Weaver, a former Union general and GREENBACK Presidential candidate, for President, and James C. Field, a former Confederate general, for Vice President; this ultimate balanced TICKET polled over a million votes. The Populists managed to elect four State governors (Colorado, Kansas, North Dakota, Wyoming), two Senators, eleven Congressmen and 354 State legislators, and held their ground in the 1894 elections. The party joined with the Democrats in 1896 to nominate the BOY ORATOR William Jennings Bryan, but a ferocious counter-attack by Republican big business saw McKINLEY ELECTED.

> A taste for charming and cultivated friends, and a tendency to bathe frequently, causes in them the deepest suspicion.
>
> THEODORE ROOSEVELT

pork barrel One of the greatest American political institutions, despite the efforts of successive Presidents to curb its excesses; the practice of members of CONGRESS of obtaining large-scale funding for marginally useful or completely pointless projects at home for electoral purposes. The building of canals and waterways, the siting of military bases and the awarding of military aircraft contracts in order to shore up politicians' power bases have all been subjects of controversy. The phrase dates from old plantation days, when slaves assembled at the pork barrel to receive their allowance of meat. **'Pork'** has come to be shorthand for the Federal contracts won by the champion pork barrelers.

> During the AMERICAN REVOLUTION, George WASHINGTON used to call for 'beef, beef, beef'; but the Continental Congress called out for 'pork, pork, pork'.
>
> ANON., quoted by Rep. CLARENCE CANNON (1879–1964)

> Pork Barrel spelt backwards is infrastructure.
>
> Rep. JAMES HOWARD (1928–88)

de-porking The removal of 'pork barrel' expenditure from a BILL it has been attached to. The term generally applies to Presidential efforts to remove such items, but was particularly applied to the gutting of Bill CLINTON's 1994 Crime Bill by Bob Dole and Senate Republicans, who removed $3.2bn in supposedly 'anti-crime' spending before it squeezed through.

King of Pork The nickname of Sen. Quentin Burdick (1908–92), a Republican-turned-Democrat who during 32 years as a Senator lived by the motto 'I'll get everything North Dakota is entitled to – now.' He finally overreached himself in 1990 when he persuaded CONGRESS to appropriate millions of dollars for a museum to honour the band-leader Lawrence Welk. With the Federal budget careering out of control, Burdick's plan attracted ridicule as the ultimate in pork-barrelling, and the following year Congress cancelled the appropriation.

> I'm all for Lawrence Welk. Lawrence Welk is a wonderful man. He used to be, or what, or . . . wherever he is now, God bless him.
>
> GEORGE BUSH Snr in the NEW HAMPSHIRE PRIMARY, 16 February 1992

Port Huron statement The definitive policy statement of America's NEW LEFT prior to the VIETNAM WAR, drawn up at Port Huron, Michigan in 1962 by the leaders of Students for a Democratic Society (SDS); it was largely written by Tom Hayden. It demanded a share for every individual in decisions affecting their lives, and the organisation of society to encourage personal independence and participation.

Portcullis House The futuristic £250 million Parliamentary building across the road from BIG BEN, constructed above Westminster Underground station which, when opened in 2000, finally provided most MPs with an office. Much criticised for its topping which resembles a row of blast furnaces, for the expenditure of £120,000 on fig trees imported from Florida for its atrium, for its leaking roof and its complete absence of clocks, it has nevertheless greatly improved working conditions for 200 MPs and 400 support staff, and provided valuable catering, committee and meeting facilities.

portfolio The area and weight of responsibilities allocated to a CABINET member, Minister or European COMMISSIONER. A **Minister without Portfolio** is one with no specific departmental responsibilities, who is able to take on special projects and chair committees as the need arises. When William Deedes (*see* DEAR BILL) was Minister without Portfolio in the MACMILLAN government with the remit of presenting its case, David FROST commented:

> The reason that he is without portfolio is because the Government has got no case.

porthole to porthole WASHINGTON-speak for the way senior ADMINISTRATION officials are always chauffeured by limousine from building to building, air-conditioned all the way and with no contact with the general public. Such a service is provided for CABINET SECRETARIES, the JOINT CHIEFS OF STAFF and half a dozen other key figures.

position The stance adopted by a politician on any particular issue; a CANDIDATE running for office will have a **position paper** on every conceivable subject, prepared by a STAFFER. Adlai STEVENSON maintained that 'all progress has resulted from people who took unpopular positions', but Robert Foss wrote:

> When a politician changes his position, it's sometimes hard to tell whether he's seen the light or felt the heat.

consider your position The phrase intended to make the person it is delivered to sit down and write out their letter of resignation forthwith. In UK politics, it will be delivered by the Prime Minister to a member of the Government who has committed an act or omission that makes it impossible, in the PM's judgement, for them to remain in office; similarly, it is used by Ministers to an appointee they feel should resign. For instance the Conservative Transport Secretary Paul Channon told the chairmen of London Transport and London Underground, Sir Keith Bright and Dr Tony Ridley, to consider their positions after the Kings Cross disaster; Sir Keith did instantly, Dr Ridley after hesitating.

positioning The art of aligning oneself so as to capitalise on a wave of public interest or concern over a particular issue, for instance an upsurge in crime. Shrewd positioning, combined with luck, can enable a party to appear ahead of the game or make its opponents look curmudgeonly or over-reactive, while in an election campaign it can prevent an opponent carving out the space to present distinctive policies of their own.

positive discrimination *See* DISCRIMINATION.

positive vetting The method of screening those in line for sensitive jobs in the UK CIVIL SERVICE, to weed out SECURITY RISKS. The system, under which all candidates have to complete a questionnaire and answer questions truthfully, no matter how great the embarrassment, is designed to bring out disloyalty or the potential for blackmail; however, a man or woman admitting to an affair, for example, would not lose marks for having the affair, but for denying it if the security services already knew about it. In the case of applicants to work at GCHQ, the questionnaire covers the previous ten years. Positive vetting was introduced by the MACMILLAN government; when Macmillan's own private secretary John Wyndham was required to answer the question: 'Are you in debt?', he replied truthfully: 'Yes, about £1 million.'

post-Fordism The idea promulgated by liberal Marxists in the 1980s that industrial society had advanced from the mass production methods of Henry FORD, dependent on vast workforces which became heavily unionised, to smaller units within which workers had greater freedom. The implicit message was that left-wing parties could no longer claim to represent the workforce without offering them something in return.

post neo-classical endogenous growth theory Possibly the one phrase that Gordon BROWN regrets having delivered in public. Included in a speech on Labour's economic policy written by his lieutenant Ed Balls, then 27, and delivered to a conference in London on 27 September 1994, it earned a special award for gobbledygook from the Plain English Campaign. Brown said:

> Ideas which stress the growing importance of international co-operation and new theories of economic sovereignty across a wide range of areas: macroeconomics, trade, the environment, the growth of post neo-classical endogenous growth theory and the symbiotic relationship between growth and investment in people and infrastructure, a new understanding of how labour markets really work and the rich and controversial debate over the meaning and importance of competitiveness at the level of individuals, the firm or the nation and the role of government in fashioning modern industrial policies which focus on maintaining competitiveness.

James Bartholomew in the *Daily Mail* translated this as 'We have been reading some books and we still want to intervene'; Michael HESELTINE could not resist telling the CONSERVATIVE PARTY conference a fortnight later:

> So there you have it. The final proof, Labour's bold new shining modernists' economic dream. It's not Brown's – it's Balls.

post office parties Political party organisations in certain American states which conducted no serious campaigning, existing largely to perceive PATRONAGE – such as appointments to postmasterships – when that party held power in WASHINGTON. The term was applied particularly to the Republican Party in the South during the first half of the 20th century. In 1952 backers of Dwight D. EISENHOWER successfully challenged the right of delegates from 'post office parties' in Texas, Louisiana, Florida and Georgia who were pledged to his rival Sen. Robert Taft to vote at the Republican CONVENTION. The exclusion sparked a revival of genuine Republican organisation in the South, followed by a recovery in the GOP's electoral fortunes.

postal vote *See* VOTE.

potatoe The last great GAFFE of Dan QUAYLE's Vice Presidency, when on 15 June 1992 he looked into a classroom in Trenton, New Jersey, and saw twelve-year-old William Figueroa write the word 'potato' on the blackboard. Quayle immediately told the boy he had spelt the word wrong – and added a final 'e'. Figueroa was subsequently paid $4000 by a California computer company to endorse its new spelling game. Prior to the Vice Presidential campaign DEBATE, Quayle asked if his Democratic challenger, Sen. Al Gore, minded his bringing a copy of Gore's book, *Earth in the Balance* (*see* OZONE MAN); Gore said he had no objection, provided Quayle let him bring a potato.

Potemkin village A situation created to mislead voters into believing things are much better than they are. The term originates from Catherine the Great's minister and former lover Count Grigory Potemkin (1735–91), who had plywood villages erected along the Volga in 1787 to give Catherine the illusion that peasants in her newly acquired southern dominions were well cared for.

Potomac WASHINGTON's broad river, running between the DISTRICT OF COLUMBIA and the Virginia suburbs where the PENTAGON, the CIA and ARLINGTON NATIONAL CEMETERY are situated. Abraham LINCOLN once declared in desperation:

> I could as easily bail out the Potomac river with a teaspoon as attend to all the details of the Army.

Potomac fever The addiction to political power and inside information that comes from working in WASHINGTON as a member of CONGRESS or the ADMINISTRATION, a LOBBYIST or political journalist. It is also used specifically for a politician's determination to become President, regardless of the odds.

> [Sen. George] McGovern did not become a peace advocate until 1968 when he contracted Potomac fever. And he is still infected.
>
> RONALD REAGAN, 1972

Potsdam conference The last Allied wartime conference, held from 17 July to 2 August 1945 at the old Prussian imperial capital of Potsdam, just west of Berlin. It was attended by STALIN, TRUMAN, CHURCHILL and ATTLEE (who took over from Churchill as Prime Minister in mid-conference). In a declaration on 26 July they demanded the unconditional SURRENDER of Japan; from Potsdam Truman ordered the preparations for dropping the atomic bomb on HIROSHIMA, but did not tell Stalin. The conference went on to agree the basis of the post-war settlement in Germany, with the country and Berlin divided into four zones administered by the occupying powers: the Soviet Union, America, Britain and France. The Soviet delegation gave the first signs that it would be less co-operative with the war in Europe over, and the subsequent imposition of Communism on East Germany made many of the Potsdam agreements unenforceable, hastening the COLD WAR.

POTUS The SECRET SERVICE's code for the President of the United States. When George BUSH Snr was sick over the Japanese Prime Minister at an official dinner in Tokyo, the message sent to WHITE HOUSE press staff by his security detail read: '**Potus barfed**'. Franklin D. ROOSEVELT used the code himself in his secret correspondence and conversations with CHURCHILL in 1940–41, before America entered WORLD WAR II (*see* FORMER NAVAL PERSON). **Potus phones** are direct telephone lines to the President, the ultimate status symbol for senior White House officials.

Poujadists The French political party – the *Union de la Défense des Commerçants et Artisans* (Union for the Defence of Merchants and Craftsmen) – founded in 1953 by the right-wing stationer-demagogue Pierre Poujade (1920–2003) and led by him with diminishing success for 30 years. It was born out of a tax revolt, led by Poujade, of small shopkeepers and farmers in the Lot, who also felt threatened by the end of food rationing and the post-war growth of big retail chains. Poujade's vitriolic attacks on the tax inspectorate and parliamentary government, his support for ALGÉRIE FRANÇAISE, and the quixotic demand for the recall of the Estates General to represent the voice of the little man briefly attracted mass support. In France's 1956 elections the Poujadists won 2.5 million votes, a surprising 11.6% of the poll, and 50 seats in the NATIONAL ASSEMBLY. Amongst its DEPUTIES was Jean-Marie le Pen, future leader of France's NATIONAL FRONT, whom Poujade disowned just before his death.

Poulson affair The corruption scandal that shook British politics, CIVIL SERVICE and local government at the same time as WATERGATE. Brought to light in 1972 during bankruptcy hearings over the Yorkshire architect John Poulson, it involved the large-scale bribery of national and local politicians and officials over a 22-year period in the hope of securing design contracts and other favours. Poulson, who eventually went to prison, brought down with him the Conservative Home Secretary Reginald Maudling, who resigned over gifts from Poulson to a theatre supported by Mrs Maudling; T. Dan Smith, the Labour former city boss of Newcastle, who went to prison; George Pottinger, Secretary of the Scottish Department of Agriculture, convicted of corruption; senior councillors and officials of councils, British Rail and health authorities; and the Conservative MP John Cordle, who resigned from the HOUSE OF COMMONS in 1977 when facing expulsion. The deputy Labour leader Ted Short (later Lord Glenamara) found himself explaining the receipt of a £250 consultancy fee twelve years before.

> Over the years Mr Poulson had succeeded in corruptly penetrating high levels of the civil service, the National Health Service, two nationalised industries and a number of local authorities.
>
> *Royal Commission on Standards of Conduct in Public Life, 1976*

pound. the pound in your pocket The phrase used by Harold WILSON in his broadcast on 19 November 1967 to explain the DEVALUATION of the pound which, in the words of his biographer Ben Pimlott, 'ricocheted through the rest of his career' as an instance of his supposed deviousness. Wilson aimed to avoid a repetition of the 1949 devaluation when the public thronged the banks fearing that for every pound invested, they would only get seventeen shillings back. But the words he used were turned against him, the accusation being that he kidded the public into believing that devaluation would have no effect at all. Wilson said:

> From now on the pound abroad is worth 14 per cent or so less in terms of other currencies. It does not mean, of course, that the pound here in Britain in your pocket or in your purse or in your bank has been devalued.

green pound *See* GREEN.

run on the pound A situation in the currency markets when dealers sell sterling on a large scale, forcing down the value of the currency.

poverty line The level of income below which a family or individual is officially classified as poor, and thus 'below the poverty line'. In America it is arrived at by taking the sum that the Department of Agriculture estimates a household needs for a minimally adequate diet and multiplying it by three.

poverty trap The invidious situation in which low earners who manage to increase their income find themselves worse off through the loss of welfare benefits or the need to start paying income tax, and which thus deters those on benefit from seeking work. Ending the trap is the aim of many politicians, but the only foolproof solution is a UNIFIED TAX AND BENEFIT SYSTEM.

Powell. Adam Clayton Powell case The repeated scandals surrounding the hedonistic black Harlem Congressman Adam Clayton Powell, who remained a hero to his constituents despite (or perhaps because of) his flagrant disregard for the mores the HOUSE tried to impose on him. He was known as the **Congressman from Bimini** or the **Harlem globetrotter** because of his frequent vacations, often with attractive women and always at government expense. His one achievement was to end racial SEGREGATION in the CAPITOL. He put his wife on the Congressional payroll although she was living in Puerto Rico, and in 1958 was indicted for tax evasion, but by 1961 he had enough SENIORITY (22 years) to become chairman of the Education and Labour Committee, a job he treated as a sinecure. By 1966 he could not return to his district because of the threat of arrest, and in January 1967 the Democratic CAUCUS stripped him of his chairmanship and the House voted 365–65 to deprive him of his seat – the first time a member had been excluded for 46 years. With the Justice Department threatening an indictment for falsifying expense claims, the seat was declared vacant and a SPECIAL ELECTION held; Powell was re-elected and won a declaration from the SUPREME COURT that he should never have been excluded, but in 1970 was defeated in the Democratic primary.

> You are looking at the first black man who has ever been lynched by Congress.
>
> ADAM CLAYTON POWELL, 1967

Powell, J. Enoch (1912–98), the MAVERICK UK politician who attracted mass support from the late 1960s because of his views on race and immigration, and from the early 1970s through his opposition to membership of the European Community; he was also an early advocate of MONETARISM and a foe of the ANGLO-IRISH AGREEMENT. Powell, a Black Countryman, became a Cambridge don and was Professor of Greek at Sydney University when WORLD WAR II broke out, returning to become the British army's youngest brigadier. After the war his relentless application of logic caught the attention of CHURCHILL, who wrote to R. A. (RAB) Butler:

> I have had a letter from a man called Powell who says we could reconquer India with four divisions. Is he all right?

Elected to Parliament in 1950, he served as a junior Minister under EDEN and MACMILLAN, resigning in 1957 over the relaxation of spending curbs (*see* LITTLE LOCAL DIFFICULTY). Macmillan brought him back as Minister of Health; when Macmillan retired, he urged Butler to press for the Tory leadership and when SIR ALEC Douglas-Home emerged as Prime Minister, Powell refused to serve under him. He never held office again. He served in Edward HEATH's Shadow CABINET, but was sacked after his RIVERS OF BLOOD speech in April 1968, his subsequent campaign for the REPATRIATION of immigrants earning him enthusiastic racist support. *The Times* commented:

> In dismissing Mr Powell, Mr Heath takes the known risk of having Mr Powell as an enemy; that fortunately is less grave than the risk of having Mr Powell as a colleague.

Despite his dismissal, Powell's views probably helped the Tories win the 1970 election; Tony BENN caused a furore by saying:

> The flag of racialism which has been hoisted in Wolverhampton is beginning to look like the one which fluttered 25 years ago over Dachau and Belsen.

When Heath took Britain into Europe, Powell bitterly opposed him, and in February 1974 gave up his seat, urging his supporters to vote Labour as the only way of keeping Britain out (*see* ENOCH FACTOR). That autumn he came back as an ULSTER UNIONIST MP, and until his defeat in 1987 opposed any accommodation with the Irish Republic. Margaret THATCHER admired his economic views and referred to him early on as 'that golden-hearted Enoch', and he supported her over the FALKLANDS, but they drifted apart, particularly after his bitter attacks on the Anglo-Irish Agreement.

> A populist is a politician who says things because he believes them to be popular. I have never been that. My worst enemies wouldn't say that.
> ENOCH POWELL, 1981

> He suffers from an excess of logic.
> IAIN MACLEOD

Disembowel Enoch Powell! One of the favourite slogans of left-wing and anti-RACIST groups in the early 1970s, who linked Powell's views on immigration to APARTHEID in South Africa – a system which Powell never publicly supported.

power The elusive, elemental force of politics and government, described as 'a dangerous thing to leave lying about' – Edmund BURKE; 'the simple indestructible will of the people' – Fidel Castro; 'the ultimate aphrodisiac' – Henry KISSINGER; 'like a seafront: when you achieve it, there's nothing there' – Harold MACMILLAN; 'merely the organised power of one class for oppressing another' – Marx and Engels; 'like a woman you want to stay in bed with forever' – Patrick Anderson; 'the ability to make something happen and keep it happening' – Hedrick Smith. So where does power lie? Bismarck said that 'he who has his thumb on the purse has the power'; Theodore H. White that 'power in America today is control of the means of communication'. Jimmy Breslin doubted it exists at all, writing: 'All political power is illusion: mirrors and blue smoke'; Sen. Wyche Fowler that 'people have power when other people think they have power'. Tacitus declared that 'the lust for power, for dominating others, influences the heart more than any other passion'; BOSS TWEED that 'the way to have power is to take it.' Once achieved, Burke wrote, 'the greater the power, the more dangerous the abuse', but Aneurin BEVAN believed that 'the purpose of getting power is to be able to give it away.'

> An honest man can feel no pleasure in the exercise of power over his fellow citizens.
> THOMAS JEFFERSON

> Men of power have no time to read, yet the men who do not read are unfit for power.
> MICHAEL FOOT

> Being powerful is like being a lady. If you have to tell people you are, you ain't. JESSE CARR

power base The geographical area, community or group of fellow politicians that provides a political figure with their fundamental support.

power broker *See* BROKER.

power corrupts; absolute power corrupts absolutely One of the classic dicta about politics which was never said in precisely those words. What Lord Acton (1834–1902) actually said in a letter to Bishop Mandell Creighton in April 1887 was:

> Power tends to corrupt, and absolute power corrupts absolutely.

Nor was the remark entirely original, PITT THE ELDER having said: 'Unlimited power is apt to corrupt the minds of those who possess it.' Adlai STEVENSON had a different view, declaring:

> Power corrupts – but lack of power corrupts absolutely.

power dance US black slang for resistance to oppression, as expressed in riots and looting.

power-sharing A system in which a community's ethnic or political minority has an institutionalised stake in power. The creation of a system of power-sharing in NORTHERN IRELAND has been the aim of UK governments since the abolition of STORMONT in 1972, and has twice apparently been achieved. In 1973 the Northern Ireland Secretary WILLIE Whitelaw announced that Protestant and Catholic leaders had agreed to serve together in an assembly responsible for all domestic matters, except security; the SUNNINGDALE AGREEMENT confirmed this. The Assembly opened in January 1974 under the leadership of a power-sharing Executive headed by the moderate Unionist Brian Faulkner (1921–77). From the start it faced organised disruption from Protestant extremists led by the Rev. Ian PAISLEY, and that May it was toppled by a GENERAL STRIKE of LOYALIST workers, backed by widespread intimidation. DIRECT RULE was reimposed, lasting – despite several abortive attempts at DEVOLUTION – until the GOOD FRIDAY AGREEMENT permitted the election in 1999 of an assembly including SINN FEIN and some of the loyalist PARAMILITARIES. A fresh Executive took power under the Unionist David Trimble, with Sinn Fein and DUP Ministers working side by side if not together. However, after being suspended once because of IRA foot-dragging over the DECOMMISSIONING of its weapons, it was put into cold storage in October 2002 when the Provisionals were found to be running a targeting operation from Sinn Fein's offices at Stormont.

power to the people The slogan of the BLACK PANTHERS c. 1969, turned into a best-selling single by John Lennon and Yoko Ono.

Power to the Soviets! *See* SOVIET.

power without responsibility, the prerogative of the harlot throughout the ages The devastating phrase with which Stanley BALDWIN torpedoed the campaign of the PRESS BARONS for EMPIRE FREE TRADE in a BY-ELECTION speech at the Queen's Hall, London on 17 March 1931. Baldwin's cousin Rudyard Kipling had supplied him with it; the Conservative leader's actual words were:

> The papers conducted by Lord Rothermere and Lord Beaverbrook are not newspapers in the ordinary acceptance of the term. They are engines of PROPAGANDA for the constantly changing policies, desires, personal wishes, personal dislikes of two men. What are their methods? Their methods are direct falsehood, misrepresentation, half-truths, the alteration of the speaker's meaning by publishing a sentence apart from the context . . . What the proprietorship of these papers is aiming at is power, and power without responsibility – the prerogative of the harlot throughout the ages.

Lady Diana Cooper, who was in the audience, wrote: 'I saw blasé reporters, scribbling semi-consciously, jump out of their skins to a man.' And the Duke of Devonshire turned to his son-in-law Harold MACMILLAN and observed:

> Good God, that's done it. He's lost us the tarts' vote.

balance of power *See* BALANCE.

concentration of power A situation in which all effective power in a nation or community has gravitated into the hands of few, generally unACCOUNTABLE, people. Woodrow WILSON described it as 'what always precedes the destruction of human initiative, and therefore of human energy'.

corridors of power The heart of WHITEHALL where Britain is effectively governed by a class anonymous to the outside world. The phrase was coined by C. P. Snow (1905–80) in the book *Homecomings* (1956), where he wrote:

> The official world, the corridors of power, the dilemmas of conscience and egotism – she disliked them all.

It immediately caught on among political commentators – Sir Douglas Corridor being invented as the ultimate Whitehall MANDARIN – and Snow used the phrase again as the title of a further, highly successful novel in 1964.

in power Holding political OFFICE and exercising power, by contrast with the impotence of being out of it. In his 1931 novel *Maid In Waiting*, John Galsworthy (1867–1933) had a character advise:

> Don't say in power what you say in opposition. If you do, you only have to carry out what the other fellows have found impossible.

political power grows from the barrel of a gun One of the most celebrated sayings of CHAIRMAN MAO, extolling the virtues of GUERRILLA war. He first used it in *Problems of War and Strategy*, published in November 1938.

protecting power The nation whose EMBASSY protects the interests of another's nationals in a foreign capital after DIPLOMATIC RELATIONS have been broken off.

transfer of power The process under which a COLONY ceases to be dependent on the power that has controlled it, and becomes INDEPENDENT.

concurrent powers One of many types of authority derived from the US CONSTITUTION, being one which the Federal and State governments can exercise at the same time, e.g. through levying taxes. **Enumerated powers** are those specifically set out; **exclusive powers** are those possessed entirely by the Federal government (only CONGRESS can declare war); **expressed powers** are those covered by the NECESSARY AND PROPER CLAUSE; **implied powers** are given without being spelt out (the power to incorporate the FED stemming from the power to issue coinage); **national police powers** are those covering public safety, health and morality; **reserved powers** (1) are the principle embodied in the TENTH AMENDMENT that gives the states, or the people, any power not specifically reserved to the Federal government; **resulting powers** are those possessed by the Federal government which stem from a combination of expressed powers in the Constitution, such as the powers to wage war, make treaties or acquire territory.

reserve powers The phrase which caused Australia's greatest political controversy, the KERR SACKING of 11 November 1975. The GOVERNOR-GENERAL, Sir John Kerr, considered that he possessed reserve powers under the constitution to dismiss a Prime Minister despite his having a majority in the HOUSE OF REPRESENTATIVES; the ousted Labor government fervently disagreed.

reserved powers (2) The opposite of DEVOLVED POWERS: those powers retained by WESTMINSTER and the UK GOVERNMENT after an act of devolution. They are greatest with Wales and less extensive with Scotland.

PPB In Britain, the political village's abbreviation for PARTY POLITICAL BROADCAST.

ppc A prospective parliamentary CANDIDATE, selected but not yet ADOPTED. This abbreviation is used by all UK political parties, and always in lower case.

PPP Public-Private Partnership. A means of financing capital investment projects without their appearing as a liability in the public accounts, devised by Gordon BROWN and John Prescott (*see* TWO JAGS) prior to Labour's 1997 election victory. It was designed for larger and more complex issues than straightforward construction projects, already catered for under PFI. In office Labour applied PPP to a number of schemes, most controversially the modernisation of the London Underground. The Mayor of London Ken Livingstone (*see* RED KEN) argued with some justification that PPP was unnecessarily costly because of the expense of negotiating the agreements and the rates of return guaranteed to the private firms taking part, but there was no other way of conforming to the TREASURY's theology.

PPS At Westminster, shorthand for PARLIAMENTARY PRIVATE SECRETARY.

PQ (1) In Canada, abbreviation for *Parti Québecois*, the Quebec SEPARATIST party. Since the 1970s the PQ has periodically been elected to power on a commitment to divorce the province from the rest of Canada, via a referendum. However, each such referendum has resulted narrowly in a 'No' vote, most recently that held in October 1995 where the margin was 50.6% to 49.4%. Despite the defeat, the PQ retained power in Quebec under Jacques Parizeau and Lucien Bouchard until 2003 before losing to the Liberals. At Ottawa the PQ is partnered by the BLOC QUÉBECOIS. (2) WESTMINSTER shorthand for a Parliamentary QUESTION, as in 'put down a PQ'.

PR The universal abbreviation for PROPORTIONAL REPRESENTATION.

pragmatism Government on the merits of each issue (or the needs of the moment) rather than by ideology. Harold WILSON made a virtue of being a pragmatist; his critics used it against him. More recently Chris PATTEN said of Margaret THATCHER's ADMINISTRATION:

> The government has a heroic commitment to hard-nosed pragmatism.

Despite its apparent origins in classical Greek, the word was only invented in 1878, by the US logician Charles Sanders Preece; he disowned it in 1905, saying its use had been 'corrupted'.

Prague Spring The blossoming of cultural freedom in Czechoslovakia during 1968 under the leadership of Alexande Dubček (1921–92), who advocated 'COMMUNISM WITH A HUMAN FACE'. The Spring extended into August, when it was snuffed out by a Soviet invasion in pursuit of the BREZHNEV DOCTRINE. It would be 21 years before many of the same idealists, by now in late middle age, would take part in the VELVET REVOLUTION.

Prairie Avenger The nickname of **William Jennings Bryan** (1860–1925, *see also* BOY ORATOR), the POPULIST Nebraska lawyer and former Congressman who three times contested the Presidency for the Democrats, being defeated by MCKINLEY in 1896 and 1900, and TAFT in 1908. Bryan's impact in 1896 was devastating, rousing the Democratic convention with a speech for FREE SILVER that concluded:

> You shall not press down upon the brow of

labour this crown of thorns, you shall not crucify mankind upon a cross of gold!

Handsome and with a riveting oratorical style, Bryan conjured up in Western farm states what one observer described as 'the fanaticism of the crusades', but a powerful Republican counter-attack based on the FULL DINNER PAIL ensured his defeat. In 1900 he fought on the issue of McKinley's EXPANSIONIST policy after the SPANISH-AMERICAN WAR, but lost by a wider margin. Not all the eloquence was on one side, McKinley's Secretary of State John Hay describing Bryan as 'a half-baked glib little briefless jackleg lawyer . . . grasping with anxiety to collar that $50,000 salary, promising the millennium to everybody with a hole in his pants and destruction to everybody with a clean shirt'. Theodore ROOSEVELT observed sourly that Bryan 'represents only that type of farmer whose gate hangs on a hinge, whose hat supplies the place of the missing window pane, and who is more likely to be found out at the crossroads grocery store than behind the plow'. In 1908 Bryan, mellowing but still evangelistic, failed to rouse America against Taft with his slogan 'Shall the people rule?', polling fewer votes than in 1896. Bryan's LAST HURRAH came in the final year of his life when he successfully led the prosecution in the infamous SCOPES CASE – a hollow victory for the forces of religious fundamentalism.

His mind was like a soup dish, wide and shallow; it could hold a small amount of nearly everything, but the slightest jarring spilt the soup into somebody's lap. IRVING STONE

Pravda (Russ. Truth) The mass-circulation daily paper which was the mouthpiece of the SOVIET state for over 70 years. Founded underground in St Petersburg by LENIN and others in 1912, it moved to Moscow with the BOLSHEVIK revolution; its editors included STALIN, MOLOTOV and Beria. With GLASNOST in the late 1980s *Pravda*'s hard line softened; with the banning of the Communist Party in 1991 it struck out as an independent paper. President Yeltsin suspended it for one month after the WHITE HOUSE REVOLUTION of September 1993; it was bought by Greek businessmen who shut it down in July 1996 after a dispute with the editor. It reappeared, and can now be read on the Internet, but remains on the fringe of Russia's mass media.

prawn cocktail offensive Shadow Chancellor John SMITH's heavy programme of lunches in the City of London prior to the 1992 general election to convince the financial community that Labour's policies would be good for the economy. They improved Labour's credibility, but not enough to swing the outcome.

Never have so many crustaceans died in vain.
MICHAEL HESELTINE

prayer At WESTMINSTER, a motion tabled against the passage of an ORDER IN COUNCIL, to ensure that it is debated in the COMMONS.

prayer card The cards available to MPs during Prayers with which they can reserve their place in the CHAMBER for that day. Taking a prayer card signifies to the House authorities that an MP is in attendance.

prayer groups In both HOUSES of the US CONGRESS, informal pressure groups of like-minded Democrats or Republicans. Some are *ad hoc*, others have a continuing existence.

prayer room A room in the US CAPITOL set aside for prayer. A stained glass window bears the motto: 'Preserve me, O God, for in thee do I put my trust.'

Prayers Said as the prelude to the day's proceedings in most LEGISLATURES. In the HOUSE OF COMMONS, press and public are excluded from the galleries while they are said, the few MPs present turning to face the wall. In the LORDS they are said by a bishop. In the US CONGRESS, the rules of the House prevent a member raising 'no QUORUM' during the daily prayer. Under George W. BUSH, Cabinet meetings have also opened with a prayer.

preamble The text at the start of a BILL which sets out its purpose or the ill it is designed to redress.

precedence The order in which the mighty of the nation should appear at a state event. In America the President, Vice President and Speaker of the House take the first three places. In Britain, the Royal family headed by the Sovereign, the Archbishop of Canterbury and the Lord Chancellor head any procession.

precedent An event, decision or action which becomes a guideline for future conduct; in particular, previous judicial decisions bind the courts. 'The precedent, Mr Prime Minister, is an accomplished fact', Henri Bourassa said to Sir Wilfrid Laurier on Canada's participation in the BOER WAR.

precedents In the US CONGRESS, the customs of the HOUSE and the SENATE, based on previous practice and decisions of the CHAIR and running into many volumes. **Hinds' precedents** are the 7346 House precedents put together and published in 1907 by Asher Hinds (1863–1919), clerk at the Speaker's table and subsequently a member of the House, and added to since. It is augmented by **Cannon's precedents**, to 1935, and **Deschler's precedents**, from 1936.

precept In UK local government, a set amount creamed off from local taxes by a body other than that which immediately collected the money, e.g. a police or transport authority.

precinct In America, the subdivision which organises the basic unit of voting and political organisation. A **precinct captain** is a local party organiser who is expected to deliver the vote. President COOLIDGE said:

> If you can't carry your own precinct, you're in trouble.

precincts of the House At WESTMINSTER, the area including and immediately adjoining the HOUSES OF PARLIAMENT, over which the Commons exercises a degree of authority, for instance through a ban on demonstrations (though since the mid-1990s this has not been rigidly enforced).

prefect Originally a Roman commander or magistrate, now the administrative head of a French DÉPARTEMENT, a province of Italy, and jurisdictions in some other countries. In France, the post was created by Napoleon in 1800 as an important element in his centralised state, and it retains this function.

premier From the French *Premier Ministre*, First Minister, a colloquialism for a national Prime Minister but also, correctly, the head of government in a Canadian PROVINCE or an Australian STATE. In Australia John Carrick, Malcolm Fraser's Federal Affairs Minister, observed:

> The Premiers don't believe in federalism; they believe in STATES' RIGHTS.

Prendergast machine The corrupt Democratic political organisation in Kansas City built up by 'Big Tom' Prendergast in the early 20th century. Its one conspicuously honest member, whom Prendergast in consequence only reluctantly promoted, was Jackson County judge – and later President – Harry S TRUMAN. Prendergast's backing was crucial in Truman's unexpected 1934 Senate victory.

prepare three envelopes President Jimmy CARTER's story of the advice left him by his predecessor, Gerald FORD. Carter joked that on stepping down as President, Ford handed him three envelopes, to be opened when times got tough. After a year, with his administration in trouble, Carter opened the first, to find the message: 'Blame your predecessor.' He made a speech attacking Ford and his fortunes for a time improved. A year later and in trouble again, he opened the second and found the message: 'Blame the Congress'; he did, and won a further remission. A year later and in even deeper trouble, he opened the third envelope, to find the message:

> Prepare three envelopes.

A similar, but stranger story was told c. 2005 in respect of Sen. Hillary CLINTON's Presidential ambitions. On her first night in the WHITE HOUSE the ghost of George WASHINGTON appeared. She asked him: 'How best can I serve my country?' and he responded: 'Never tell a lie,' 'I don't know about that,' she told Washington, 'I have told so many.' On the second night Thomas JEFFERSON appeared to her. Mrs Clinton asked him the same question; he replied: 'Listen to the people', and she said: 'I don't really want to do that.' On the third night, she was awakened by the ghost of Abraham LINCOLN. 'How better can I serve my country?' she asked him. Lincoln smiled quietly and told her: 'Relax . . . Take the night off . . . Go to the theatre.' (*see* FORD's THEATRE).

prerogative The scope a ruler or government has to take decisions and make appointments without reference to the LEGISLATURE and free of challenge from the courts. In Britain, the government of the day enjoys wide powers under the ROYAL PREROGATIVE, starting with the Prime Minister's right to appoint their CABINET. Governments throughout the world can also exercise a prerogative of mercy to reprieve or free those sentenced to death or imprisonment.

Prescott, John *See* TWO JAGS.

preselection In Australia, the process by which a CONSTITUENCY party chooses its CANDIDATE to contest an ELECTION.

presidency (1) The office of President of the United States. According to Hedrick Smith, it 'combines the functions of chief of state and Prime Minister'; Anthony Burgess saw it as 'a Tudor monarchy plus telephones'. Theodore ROOSEVELT used it as a 'BULLY PULPIT' and Franklin D. ROOSEVELT as 'a position of moral leadership'. But the presidency is not all-powerful. Harry S

TRUMAN said: 'People think I sit here and push buttons and get things done. Well, I spent today kissing behinds.' He also warned: 'When you get to be President, there are the honours, the 21-gun salute, all those things. You have to remember it isn't for you – it's for the Presidency.' And when making way for his successor, he cautioned: 'He will sit there and he'll say: "Do this", "Do that". And nothing will happen. Poor IKE – it won't be a bit like the Army. He'll find it very frustrating.'

Some incumbents have revelled in the office, notably the Roosevelts and Ronald REAGAN; others have hated it. George WASHINGTON, the first occupant, was the first to have forebodings, saying: 'My movements to the chair of government will be accompanied by feelings not unlike those of a culprit who is going to the place of execution.' His successor John ADAMS declared that 'no one who has ever held the office of President would congratulate a friend on obtaining it'. Thomas JEFFERSON warned that 'no one will ever bring out of the presidency the reputation he carries into it'. He also called it 'a splendid misery', compared with which the office of VICE PRESIDENT was 'honourable and easy'. Martin van Buren (*see* OLD KINDERHOOK) declared: 'The two happiest days of my life were those of entrance upon the office and my surrender of it.' Garfield, prophetically, exclaimed: 'My god! What is there in this place that a man should ever want to get into it?' And John F. KENNEDY was blunter:

> What a lousy, fucked-up job this turned out to be.

Seekers for the presidency are distrusted. Wendell Phillips wrote: 'You can always get the truth from an American statesman after he had turned seventy or given up hope of the presidency', and Sen. Eugene McCarthy said: 'You really must be careful of politicians who say they have no further ambitions: they may run for the presidency.' David Broder was even more cynical: 'Anybody that wants the presidency so much that he will spend two years organising and campaigning for it is not to be trusted with the office.'

> Like the glory of a morning sunrise, it can only be experienced. It cannot be told.
>
> CALVIN COOLIDGE, *Autobiography*

> The office of the President is generally esteemed a very high and dignified position, but . . . the public would not so regard it if they could . . . observe the kind of people by whom I am often annoyed.
>
> President POLK, *Diaries,* 19 October 1848

> Everyone who has lived in the White House and served in the presidency feels a stab when a member of that fraternity dies.
>
> LADY BIRD JOHNSON

(2) In the EUROPEAN UNION, the institution under which member states take it in turn to preside for six-month periods over the COUNCIL OF MINISTERS and hence over the political workings of the Community, e.g. 'the Luxembourg Presidency'. Under the EUROPEAN CONSTITUTION it would be replaced by a permanent presidency.

Imperial Presidency The criticism, prior to WATERGATE, that the NIXON presidency was taking on more trappings of pomp than befitted the leader of a democracy; Ruritanian uniforms for the WHITE HOUSE honour guard were a particular cause for ridicule. The charge was not new: at the PHILADELPHIA CONVENTION Edmund Jennings Randolph denounced the proposed office of President as 'the foetus of monarchy'. Yet in 1980 Gerald FORD was declaring: 'We have not an imperial presidency but an imperilled presidency.'

storybook presidency Hedrick Smith's term for the image created by President REAGAN's video managers, 'using the pageantry of presidential travel to hook the networks and capture the popular imagination . . . The more Reagan wrapped himself in the flag, the harder it became for mere mortal politicians to challenge him.' Smith also coined the phrase **video presidency** for the priority given by Reagan's WHITE HOUSE staff to playing to the requirements and appetite of the television networks to get their message across. *See* PHOTO OPPORTUNITY; SOUND BITE; VIDEO FEED.

a cancer within, close to the presidency John Dean's warning to Richard NIXON on 21 March 1973 as the WATERGATE scandal began to grow. In a taped conversation, he said:

> We have a cancer within, close to the Presidency, that is growing. It is growing daily. It's compounded, growing geometrically now, because it compounds itself.

a heartbeat away from the Presidency Since the 1950s, shorthand for the position of the VICE PRESIDENT, who at any moment might have to take over the reins of power. After George BUSH Snr was elected with Dan QUAYLE as his Vice President, the story went round WASHINGTON that Quayle was accompanied everywhere by two armed CIA men – with orders to shoot Quayle if anything happened to Bush.

President The HEAD OF STATE in a Republic, either largely ceremonial as in Germany or highly political as in France, or the United States where the President is also the HEAD OF GOVERNMENT and COMMANDER-IN-CHIEF. Under the US CONSTITUTION, 'the Executive power shall be vested in a President of the United States of America.' He or she must be a natural-born US citizen, at least 35 years old, and have resided in the country for at least fourteen years. Americans often refuse to believe their system throws up the best candidate. Ambrose Bierce defined the President as 'the leading figure in a small group of men of whom – and of whom only – it is positively known that immense numbers of their countrymen did not want any of them for president.' The view goes back some way; in 1840 John Stuart Mill wrote: 'He is now always an unknown mediocrity, or a person whose reputation has been acquired in some field other than politics.' Such sentiments led Treasury Secretary Salmon Chase to say: 'I would rather that people should wonder why I wasn't President than why I am.' Henry Clay declared: 'I had rather be right than president', but the socialist Norman Thomas was more flexible:

> While I'd rather be right than President, at any time I'm ready to be both.

Becoming President is the ultimate American dream. Clarence Darrow wrote: 'When I was a boy I was told anybody could become President; I'm starting to believe it.' Adlai STEVENSON was as cynical: 'In America, any boy may become President. I suppose that's just one of the risks he takes.' Sen. Barry Goldwater sadly noted after his 1964 defeat: 'It's a great country where anyone can grow up to be President – except me.' And Averell Harriman doubted if the effort was worthwhile, saying: 'Anyone who wants to be President should have his head examined.' Or, as Gore Vidal put it,

> Any American who is prepared to run for President should automatically be disqualified from ever doing so.

The President is not just a partisan figure but, in Edwin Corwin's words, 'the American people's one authentic trumpet'. Harry S TRUMAN put it differently: 'All the President is is a glorified public relations man who spends his time flattering, kissing and kicking people to do what they are supposed to do anyway.' He also said: 'Being President is like riding a tiger. A man has to keep on riding, or be swallowed.' Ronald REAGAN's philosophy of government was more relaxed: 'Surround yourself with the best people you can find, delegate authority and don't interfere.'

The President, under the Constitution, does not govern alone. Abraham LINCOLN, when in Congress, asked: 'He is the representative of the people . . . elected by them, as well as Congress is. But can he, in the nature [of] things, know the hearts of the people as well as 300 other men, coming from all the various localities of the nation? If so, what is the propriety of having a Congress?' It is a question many Americans have asked since. Yet a President does have awesome power and responsibilities. Woodrow WILSON felt that 'no one but the President seems to be expected to look out for the general interests of the country', adding: 'Let him rightly interpret the national thought and he is irresistible.' According to COOLIDGE, 'the first lesson a President has to learn is that every word he says weighs a ton'. And EISENHOWER told the incoming KENNEDY: 'There are no easy matters that will come to you as President. If they are easy they will be settled at a lower level.' NIXON put it another way: 'I have always felt that the country can more or less take care of itself. A President's first job is dealing with peace and war.' Kennedy himself came to feel that a President 'must wield extraordinary powers under ordinary limitations'. He might have cited TAFT's opinion that 'the President can exercise no power which cannot fairly and reasonably be traced to some specific grant of power . . . in the Federal Constitution or an Act of Congress . . . There is no undefined residuum of power which he can exercise because it seems to him to be in the public interest.' But Nixon stood the argument on its head when he declared:

> When the President does it, that means it is not illegal.

Being President can encourage remoteness and self-importance. John Eisenhower reckoned that 'the longer a President is in office, the more headstrong he becomes'. And Truman said: 'The President has a hundred voices telling him he's the greatest man in the world. He must listen carefully indeed to hear the one voice that tells him he is not.' Such advice may come from world-weary confidants like Henry KISSINGER, who once said: 'When you've seen one President, you've seen them all.' Yet George Reedy cautioned:

> Nobody is strong-minded around a President. It is always 'Yes, Sir', 'No, Sir'. The 'No, Sir' comes when he asks whether you're dissatisfied.

Eisenhower found one compensation in being President. 'There is one thing about being President. Nobody can tell you when to sit down.' And to the outsider David Frye, 'being President is never having to say you're sorry.'

> The major part of the work of a President is to increase the gate receipts of expositions and fairs and bring tourists into the town.
> WILLIAM HOWARD TAFT

> Presidents, whether good or bad, get the blame. I understand that. GEORGE W. BUSH

> Even a President has feelings.
> THEODORE ROOSEVELT, letter, 1904

> A Prime Minister must keep himself in favour of the majority. A President need only keep alive.
> WOODROW WILSON, 1885

> Presidents don't have power. Their job is to draw attention away from it.
> FORD PREFECT, *Hitch Hiker's Guide to the Galaxy*

President Bartlet One of the best-known Presidents, but a fictitious character: Josiah Edward 'Jed' Bartlet (1942–), President of the United States (Democrat, 1998–), the central figure in NBC Television's *The* WEST WING. Played by Martin Sheen, Bartlet is a NOBEL PRIZE-winning economist who was a three-term New Hampshire Congressman and two-term Governor; while President, he has been diagnosed with multiple sclerosis and been wounded in an attempted assassination. Married to Abigail, he claims that an ancestor signed the Declaration of INDEPENDENCE on behalf of New Hampshire. He originally intended to become a priest, and remains deeply religious; he also says: 'I am not comfortable with violence. I know this country has enemies but I don't feel violent towards any of them.'

> The President likes to hear from smart people who disagree with him. JOSH LYMAN

> I don't think much of blind loyalty, but I think a lot less of blind betrayal.
> President BARTLET

President-elect A President whose election has been confirmed by the ELECTORAL COLLEGE but who has yet to be inaugurated.

President of the European Commission The head of the BRUSSELS administration of the EU, and usually a powerful political figure in his own right. He is chosen every four years by the COUNCIL OF MINISTERS, usually after a bitter dispute between the UK and FEDERALIST Continental governments who want a President who will make rapid progress to even closer union.

President of the Senate In the US CONGRESS, the post held in the first instance by the VICE PRESIDENT, or in his absence by a **President pro tem,** short for *pro tempore* (Lat. for the time being). The President pro tem is generally the most senior Senator, from 1996 until his retirement as a centenarian Sen. Strom Thurmond (*see* DIXIECRATS). His main duty is to open each day's proceedings.

President's Commission A body set up by the President and reporting to him, generally concerning some controversial event (*see* WALKER COMMISSION into the CHICAGO CONVENTION riots), national calamity (the WARREN COMMISSION into the assassination of President KENNEDY) or a disquieting social trend. There is a close comparison with the ROYAL COMMISSIONS set up from time to time by UK and Commonwealth governments.

acting President Under the 25th Amendment, ratified in 1967, the President may in the event of his incapacity hand over his powers to the VICE PRESIDENT, who becomes 'acting President'. If the President is incapable of taking this step or will not do so, the Vice President and CABINET can take it for him. Until 1967 there was no machinery to cover a President being in office but incapacitated; when Woodrow WILSON was unfit to govern, his wife simply took care of matters.

All the President's Men Bob Woodward and Carl Bernstein's best-selling book on their role in uncovering the WATERGATE scandal and the subsequent film starring Robert Redford and Dustin Hoffman. The phrase, symbolising unquestioning loyalty to the President, originated with Henry KISSINGER who had said when discussing the NIXON administration's policy on Cambodia in 1970: 'We are all the President's men.'

accidental President A President who comes to office other than by election. In American so far five VICE PRESIDENTS have come to power owing to an assassination, three through natural death and one through resignation. That last, Gerald FORD, had not been elected to the Vice Presidency either; he was appointed on the resignation of Spiro AGNEW.

assistant president The sobriquet bestowed on former Senator and Supreme Court Justice James Byrnes, who as head of Franklin D. ROOSEVELT's Office of War

Mobilisation wielded immense power in WASHINGTON.

former president The official position of anyone still living who has held the office; generally there are four or five. Henry Watterson, for 50 years editor of the *Louisville Courier-Journal*, has a simple answer to the problem of finding a role for them:

> Take them out and shoot them.

Making of the President, The The classic series of books on successive Presidential election campaigns throughout the 1960s and '70s by Theodore H. White (1915–86); the first, closely analysing KENNEDY's win over NIXON in superb narrative style, revolutionised the way campaigns are covered. 'Everything was sitting around waiting to be reported', said White. The books spawned imitations and so did the title, notably *The Selling of the President*, in which Joe McGinniss catalogued the role of advertising men in getting NIXON elected in 1968, and *The Breaking of the President*, a 1969 *Washington Post* column in which David Broder condemned anti-VIETNAM WAR activists for their attacks on the Nixon ADMINISTRATION.

one-day president The unique position of Sen. David Rice Aitchison, who took office for a day in March 1849 between the expiry of President Polk's term and the INAUGURATION of Zachary Taylor. Aitchison, PRESIDENT PRO TEM of the Senate, took over because Taylor would not take the Presidential OATH on a Sunday. Aitchison later claimed to have slept right through his term.

one-term president A President who serves only one of the permitted two TERMS in the WHITE HOUSE. It applies especially to one, like Jimmy CARTER or George BUSH Snr, who sought a second term and was defeated. The voters' refusal to re-elect them is taken as proof that their presidency has been a failure; the verdict of history comes later.

State President The executive HEAD OF STATE in South Africa – both prior to and since the end of APARTHEID – since the separate office of Prime Minister was abolished by P. W. Botha.

Tell him he's no longer President The comment made to the butler of Charles Evans Hughes, who went to bed thinking he had defeated Woodrow WILSON in 1916 and woke up to find he had lost.

The President is dead, but the Government lives and God omnipotent reigns The moving statement of then-Congressman James Garfield (*see* BOATMAN JIM) on the assassination of LINCOLN; Garfield was to meet the same fate sixteen years later.

presidential action The action a President must take within ten days, to sign or VETO any piece of legislation sent to him by CONGRESS.

Presidential debates *See* DEBATE.

Presidential Medal of Freedom The highest award an American civilian can receive in peacetime. Instituted by President KENNEDY in 1963, it is given for achievement in a wide range of fields, including the arts.

Presidential-style campaign In UK politics, an ELECTION campaign which concentrates on the personality of a party's leader, to the exclusion of its other leading figures and of its policies. The term has been used in a derogatory sense of many leaders, starting with LLOYD GEORGE.

Presidential succession Prior to 1947 there was no provision for governing the United States if both the President and the Vice President were dead or incapacitated. In that year an ACT was passed under which the SPEAKER of the HOUSE OF REPRESENTATIVES would take over as President in such circumstances.

Presidential system The system under which a country like the US, France or South Africa is governed by a strong chief executive, with or without a subordinate Prime Minister. George BUSH Snr said in 1991:

> I count my blessings that we have a Presidential system and not a Parliamentary system.

Presidentress The nickname bestowed on the formidable Edith Bolling WILSON (1872–1961) who for up to seventeen months from September 1919 effectively ran the Federal government in place of her ailing husband Woodrow, even decoding secret telegrams. Mrs Wilson insisted:

> I myself never made a single decision regarding the disposition of public affairs.

Presidents' Day The US public holiday on the third Monday of February that commemorates the birthdays around that time of WASHINGTON and LINCOLN. It was signed into law by President NIXON in 1971 after lobbying from the resort industry.

presiding officer (1) The VICE PRESIDENT of the United States in his role of presiding over the SENATE or, when he cannot attend, the Senator who performs the task (*see* PRESIDENT PRO TEM).

I have seen a Presiding Officer of the US Senate amusing himself, while a Senator was speaking, catching flies on the Vice President's desk.
Assistant Doorkeeper ISAAC BASSETT (1819–95)

(2) In the SCOTTISH PARLIAMENT or WELSH ASSEMBLY, the Member elected when the body first convenes to CHAIR its deliberations. (3) In UK elections, the local authority official in charge at each POLLING STATION.

press. press barons Newspaper proprietors in Britain who have been raised to the PEERAGE, either out of gratitude from a government they helped to elect or in the misguided hope that they will become less critical. In many cases (*see* POWER WITHOUT RESPONSIBILITY) they have used the media they own to promote eccentric or POPULIST opinions of their own. Rupert Murdoch, the most recent owner with such influence, has not received a peerage (1) because he is a republican and (2) because he has been first an Australian and subsequently a US citizen. Conrad Black, proprietor of the *Telegraph* group from 1986 to 2004, renounced his Canadian citizenship to become Lord Black of Crossharbour; he was subsequently accused of looting $400 million from the papers' parent company.

press conference A formal occasion at which a politician responds to questions put to him by journalists who have gathered for the purpose, rather than a carefully selected group. Presidents of the United States – the first was MCKINLEY – and of the French republic regularly stage such events; in Britain, until the advent of Tony BLAIR only Edward HEATH had done so, except when overseas. Herbert HOOVER refused to hold them at all, saying: 'The President of the United States will not stand and be questioned like a chicken thief by men whose names he doesn't even know'; subsequent Presidents with an eye on re-election have made a point of getting to know them. Since WORLD WAR II regular press conferences by the chief executive have been a constant of WASHINGTON life, and from 2003 they have been a fixture at WESTMINSTER.

last press conference The occasion on 7 November 1962, thus christened by Richard NIXON, when the defeated Republican candidate for governor of California announced his retirement from public life. As well as announcing that 'YOU DON'T HAVE NIXON TO KICK AROUND ANY MORE', he declared:

The media have a right and a responsibility, if they're against a candidate – give him the shaft, but also recognise, if they give him the shaft, put one lonely reporter on the campaign who will report what the candidate says now and then.

press corps The accredited pack of journalists who cover the activities, both ceremonial and political, of the President of the United States from their base in the Press Room of the WHITE HOUSE. When the President travels, the entire operation travels with him. Richard NIXON earned particular popularity from the press corps (who steered clear of WATERGATE) by ferrying reporters' girl friends and spouses to his holiday homes in Florida and California for as little as $25 when there was room on the plane. One reporter dumped his girl friend at one such destination – only to encounter her as a hotel clerk when the Nixon entourage hit Rome a few months later. He was not given one of the best rooms.

Press Gallery (1) At WESTMINSTER, the balcony overhanging the SPEAKER's chair in the HOUSE OF COMMONS where reporters from the media and HANSARD take notes of Parliamentary debates; a gallery reporter is one who produces news items based solely on speeches and events in the CHAMBER, ignoring the LOBBY. The self-styled elite of SKETCH WRITERS also have seats in the Gallery. The Press Gallery is also the complex of facilities behind that balcony where the Parliamentary media operate: the **Lower Gallery** where press releases are distributed and instant briefings held, a smaller **Upper Gallery**, now only used on major occasions, for the foreign press, over a dozen offices shared by various written media, a library, a television room, a bar, a restaurant and a café. The HOUSE OF LORDS has a small reporters' gallery and a single workroom. (2) The organisation to which all reporters at Westminster are accredited, its total membership (including the overseas press) exceeding 300. Charles Dickens was an early member. (3) In the US CAPITOL each HOUSE has a reporters' gallery; the Senate's is the more spacious of the two, but other Congressional facilities for the media are concentrated in the House. Overall they are far less spacious and comprehensive than those at Westminster.

pressing the flesh The ritual of endless hand-shaking by any candidate running for office or hoping for re-election. The phrase was first heard c. 1910, and in America soon acquired a political connotation.

pressure group A group that tries to exert pressure on legislators, government officials, the media and public opinion to implement its own agenda: sometimes a single interest, sometimes on behalf of an industry or sector of the economy. Such groups' campaigns – conducted through letter-writing, DEMONSTRATIONS, LOBBYING or advertising – are often aimed at promoting, killing or amending new legislation.

pretzel The harmless (to anyone else) object that came close to ending George W. BUSH's presidency when he choked on one while watching television on 14 January 2002. Once recovered, he observed:

> My mother always said: 'Chew before you swallow.'

Prezza One of several nicknames for John Prescott (*see* TWO JAGS); it reflected both his presidential role over large areas of government as Tony BLAIR's DEPUTY PRIME MINISTER, and also the fact that the job had previously been held under the Conservatives by Michael HESELTINE, whose nickname was HEZZA.

PRI *See* INSTITUTIONAL REVOLUTIONARY PARTY.

price. prices and incomes policy A government policy that attempts to restrict rises in both the price of goods and services and individual earnings in order to control INFLATION. It can be based either on voluntary restraint, negotiated with unions and employers, or statutory controls. In Britain, the embryo of such a policy was Selwyn Lloyd's PAY PAUSE, but Harold WILSON in the late 1960s was the first to restrict both prices and incomes, with a degree of short-term success. Both main parties tried it in the '70s, but since the advent of THATCHERISM the whole idea of government interference with market forces – save for the MONEY SUPPLY and the determination of pay levels for government employees – has fallen from favour.

a price worth paying Chancellor Norman Lamont's comment on unemployment which became a millstone around the neck of John MAJOR's government in the run-up to the 1992 general election. In the COMMONS on 16 May 1991, Lamont said:

> Rising unemployment and the recession have been the price we have had to pay to get inflation down. That price is well worth paying.

The price of petrol has gone up by a penny The wartime *Daily Mirror* cartoon by Zec which so enraged CHURCHILL that he tried to have the paper closed down. It showed a sailor from a torpedoed oil tanker adrift on a raft in mid-Atlantic, and was intended to show the sacrifices being made to keep ungrateful motorists supplied, but Churchill took it differently. On 19 March 1942 Sir John Anderson, Home Secretary, told the COMMONS that the *Mirror* had been warned that it if published anything else 'calculated to foster opposition to the successful prosecution of the war', it would be closed down.

primary A BALLOT held in an American state in the opening months of a Presidential election year to choose delegates to the parties' nominating CONVENTIONS, and therefore to establish support for rival contenders. In most recent elections, a candidate has emerged from the primaries with enough delegates, or enough momentum, to make sure of their party's presidential NOMINATION. Not all states hold primaries, but they have become steadily more widespread (*see also* SUPER TUESDAY). The first primary was held by Democrats in Crawford County, Pennsylvania in 1842; the first state to require them was Wisconsin in 1903.

> Primary fights are a lot more emotional, corrosive and painful than general elections. It's easy to hate Democrats, but brother-against-brother in the Primaries gets really ugly. It's like the CIVIL WAR.
> MARY MATALIN, *All's Fair*

Primary Colors The novel giving a Rabelaisian and alarmingly accurate picture of Bill CLINTON's campaign for the Presidency which fascinated WASHINGTON when published early in 1996, largely because its 'Anonymous' author had uncanny insights into what made Clinton tick. After six months of intense speculation, 'Anonymous' was revealed as the CBS and Newsweek commentator Joe Klein. The book was later made into a successful film.

closed primary A primary in which only party members may participate; this applies to the majority of such contests.

New Hampshire primary *See* NEW.

white primary Primaries held in the Deep South in which only white voters could participate. Because the DEMOCRATIC PARTY was a voluntary organisation, it was able to operate such primaries legally until the SUPREME COURT outlawed them in 1944, in the Smith v Allwright case brought by the NAACP.

Prime Minister The HEAD OF GOVERNMENT in Britain and most other countries, either the effective source of power under a CONSTITUTIONAL MONARCH or ceremonial PRESIDENT, or as in France firmly subordinate to the President. The name originated as a term of abuse in 17th-century Britain, and was being used in government circles by 1710 when the WHIG White Kennett was asking:

> Who is, or ought to be, prime minister, the Earl of Rochester or Mr Harley [Robert Harley, later Earl of Oxford]?

At first the term was applied to the Minister most in the monarch's favour, but under the supremacy of Robert WALPOLE from 1721 to 1742, the term acquired its present meaning – not least through Walpole's spectacular use of PATRONAGE. Officially, however, the head of government was known as First Lord of the TREASURY (the title on the front door of NUMBER TEN) or LEADER OF THE HOUSE; the first Prime Minister actually to bear the title was CAMPBELL-BANNERMAN on his appointment in 1905. The post of Prime Minister is, as DISRAELI put it, 'the top of the greasy pole'. Yet Enoch POWELL rightly remarked that 'on the evidence of history, more than any other position of eminence, that of Prime Minister is filled by fluke'. On the same evidence James CALLAGHAN concluded: 'Prime Ministers tend either to be bookmakers or bishops, and they take it in turn.' Stanley BALDWIN said in a gloomy moment that 'the work of a Prime Minister is the loneliest job in the world'. And Harold MACMILLAN elaborated:

> On the whole nobody comes to see you when you are Prime Minister. The nice people don't come because they don't want to be thought courtiers, and the tiresome people – you don't want to see *them*.

Under the doctrine of CABINET GOVERNMENT the Prime Minister is supposed to be FIRST AMONG EQUALS. ROSEBERY, a sound observer if a signal failure at Number Ten, wrote that 'a First Minister has only the influence with the Cabinet which is given him by his personal argument, his personal qualities, his personal weight.' Callaghan claimed that being Prime Minister was 'the easiest job in the world. Everybody else has an instrument to play – you just stand there and conduct.' And Harold WILSON reckoned that 'the main essentials of a Prime Minister are sleep and a sense of history'. The potential power a Prime Minister can exercise is awesome; according to Tony BENN 'no mediaeval monarch in the whole of British history ever had such power as every modern British Prime Minister has in his or her hands. Nor does any American president have power approaching this.' Yet the Australian writer Patrick Weller was correct to observe: 'Prime Ministers need help. They cannot do everything.' And CHURCHILL woefully reminisced: 'Headmasters have powers at their discretion with which Prime Ministers have never yet been invested.' A secretary could persuade Melbourne to take the job by arguing that it was 'a position no Roman or Greek could ever aspire to'. And GLADSTONE could console Lord Aberdeen when he lost office: 'You have now been Prime Minister of England. You are one of a lofty line.' Moreover the post continues to reflect Britain's influence in the world, during good times and lean; in the mid-1970s at the trough of national self-confidence Bernard Levin wrote:

> Once when a British Prime Minister sneezed, men half a world away would blow their noses. Now when a British Prime Minister sneezes, nobody else will even say 'bless you'.

Prime Minister designate The somewhat clumsy title accorded to Roy JENKINS when he headed the ALLIANCE's campaign in Britain's 1983 general election. It was designed to quell any confusion among voters over who would lead a LIBERAL/SDP government if the parties between them won a Parliamentary majority. The arrangement barely held until POLLING DAY, David Steel (*see* BOY DAVID) and other key Liberals reducing Jenkins' authority in the ETTRICK BRIDGE coup.

Prime Minister, think again Harold WILSON's broadcast appeal to the Southern Rhodesian premier Ian Smith in November 1965, on the eve of Smith's declaration of UDI.

Prime Minister's Office A uniquely Canadian institution, giving the Prime Minister a department of his own with far-reaching influence. It reached its greatest power under Pierre TRUDEAU. Australia's PMC has to date carried less clout.

Prime Minister's Questions *See* QUESTIONS.

The best Prime Minister we have The remark quoted most often as a sign of R. A. (RAB) Butler's deviousness. It was in fact a reporter who asked Butler when he landed at Heathrow in 1955: 'Mr Butler, would you say that he [EDEN] is the best Prime Minister we have?' All Butler did was reply: 'Yes'.

next Prime Minister but three A semi-serious term for a political prodigy, maybe with a hint that he or she will fall by the wayside. In his *Cautionary Tales*, Hilaire Belloc (1870–1953) has the youthful Lord

Lundy told after some harmless peccadillo:

We had intended you to be
The next Prime Minister but three:
The stocks were sold; the Press was squared;
The Middle Class was quite prepared;
But as it is! . . . My language fails!
Go out and govern New South Wales!

prime time The peak viewing hours for television – generally from 7 to 11 p.m. – which command the highest advertising rates. Politicians naturally wish to command the largest audience for positive messages about themselves and negative propaganda about their opponents. In the eyes of the American public and political community, the most damning sign of the amateurism of the 1972 Democratic CONVENTION was that George McGovern delivered his ACCEPTANCE speech (*see* COME HOME, AMERICA) well after prime time, when few viewers were still at their sets.

Primrose League The primrose was DISRAELI's favourite flower, and the League survives as a Conservative organisation loyal to his memory. Tim Renton, later Tory CHIEF WHIP and arts minister, found a different view of the flower when CANVASSING a Sheffield steelworker in 1970:

Renton: Did you know primroses were Disraeli's favourite flower?
Steelworker: Is that so? I'll dig the buggers up tomorrow.

Prince, the *See* MACCHIAVELLIAN.

Prince of Darkness The nickname accorded to **Richard Perle** (1941–), Ronald REAGAN's hard-line Assistant Secretary for Defense for International Security and a Washington HAWK for three decades. As former assistant to Sen. Henry 'SCOOP' Jackson, one of the most influential Congressional figures in this area, Perle was an inveterate foe of ARMS CONTROL negotiations with the Soviet Union. Under George W. BUSH he headed the PENTAGON's Defense Policy Board until forced to resign over a CONFLICT OF INTEREST eight days into the 2003 conflict with Iraq. The phrase, from Shakespeare's *King Lear*, has also been applied to Peter Mandelson (*see* BOBBY) because of his proficiency in the dark art of SPIN.

Prince of Piffle One of many derogatory nicknames earned by Sen. Huey 'KINGFISH' Long.

Prince of Wales The principal title of the heir to the throne of the UNITED KINGDOM, when that heir is the monarch's first-born son.

principles Fundamental moral beliefs, which for a politician are often challenged by opportunities to earn popularity. The Australian Labor leader Arthur Calwell put the noble view: 'It is better to be defeated on principle than to win on lies,' and America's Sen. Henry F. Ashurst the cynical: 'You must learn that there are times when a man in public life is compelled to rise above his principles.' The British union leader Ron Todd commented: 'You don't have power if you surrender all your principles – you have OFFICE,' but Lord Melbourne noted long before: 'Nobody did anything very foolish except from some strong principle.' Some politicians feel they have no choice; Eric Williams, premier of Trinidad, confessed:

A small country like hours has only principles.

in principle A phrase accepting that it is right for something to be done, with the implication that there are obstacles to doing it at present. Bismarck brazenly admitted:

When you say that you agree to something in principle, you mean that you have not the slightest intention of carrying it out in practice.

man of principle One of the highest accolades a politician (often an unsuccessful one) can achieve. Sen. Everett DIRKSEN self-deprecatingly sought to have it both ways, declaring: 'I am a man of firm and unbending principle, the first of which is to be flexible at all times.'

Damn your principles! Stick to your party! *See* PARTY.

private. private enterprise The system on which CAPITALISM and MARKET economics is based, in which business enterprise by individual entrepreneurs and companies creates economic activity, jobs and wealth.

The sole function of government is to bring about a condition of affairs favourable to the beneficial development of private enterprise.
HERBERT HOOVER

Private Eye The satirical fortnightly magazine, founded in October 1961 by Richard Ingrams, Christopher Booker, William Rushton and Peter Cook, which has been an irritant to UK governments of all parties ever since. In its early days its satirical impact was reinforced by the parallel television programme THAT WAS THE WEEK THAT WAS. As well as providing a diet of gossip, some of it true, it has exposed humbug and scandal in government from the PROFUMO and POULSON affairs to the Iraqi SUPERGUN. *Private Eye*, whose future has frequently been jeopardised by massive libel damages awarded against it, has been edited since 1988 by Ian Hislop.

Private John The nickname of Congressman **John M. Allen** of Mississippi, born at an 1884 election meeting he shared with his opponent, former Confederate General Tucker. Tucker recalled how 'after a hard fought battle on yonder hill, I bivouacked under yonder clump of trees.' Allen followed him to the podium and said: 'I was a vedette picket and stood guard over the general while he slept. Now then, fellow citizens, all of you who were generals vote for General Tucker, and all of you who were privates and stood guard over the generals while they slept, vote for Private John Allen!' Allen, who always signed himself 'Private John Allen, Tupelo, USA', won the election.

Private Member's Bills *See* BILLS.

Private Notice Question *See* Urgent Notice QUESTION.

private office The team of civil servants, usually including a private secretary, an assistant private secretary, a diary secretary and a correspondence clerk, who in WHITEHALL departments service a CABINET or junior Minister, or the PERMANENT SECRETARY. In Australia Prime Ministers, starting with Gough WHITLAM, have used their private office as a political powerhouse.

private sector The sector of the economy actuated by private enterprise, consisting of companies owned by their shareholders and by small businesses. In a MIXED ECONOMY, it coexists with the PUBLIC SECTOR.

private visit A visit to another country by a HEAD OF STATE or government or other senior figure which includes no formal, official or public engagements.

private opulence and public squalor The emotive phrase coined by Professor John Kenneth Galbraith (1908–) to describe the situation in some Western countries where individual wealth coexists with ill-financed and inadequate public services for the masses.

privatisation The process of transferring state-owned industries to the PRIVATE SECTOR by selling shares in them to the public. Margaret THATCHER was not the first British Prime Minister to sell off NATIONALISED INDUSTRIES, but it was her supporters who coined the term; previously the process was known as DENATIONALISATION. Privatisation was bitterly opposed by the trade unions and the LABOUR PARTY as threatening the services provided by utilities like gas, electricity, telephones and the railways and for creating FAT CATS, and questioned by some Conservatives (*see* SELLING OFF THE FAMILY SILVER). But it was emulated all over the world, particularly behind the former IRON CURTAIN. In 1991 the Soviet Prime Minister Valentin Pavlov declared:

> Privatisation must come from the liberalisation of prices.

privilege The special rights enjoyed by a LEGISLATURE and its members in terms of freedom from arrest except on a criminal charge, and freedom to speak one's mind in debate without fear of legal action.

privilege to revise and extend *See* REVISE.

breach of privilege The offence with which the HOUSE OF COMMONS, advised by its **Select Committee on Standards and Privileges**, may charge whoever tries to impede its work. Such charges have been brought against editors of newspapers that have indulged in malicious criticism of Parliament, and trade unions which have sought to compel their SPONSORED MPs to act in a particular way. An alleged offender may be called to the BAR OF THE HOUSE to be admonished; in theory they could, as in times past, be imprisoned on the premises.

executive privilege *See* EXECUTIVE.

motion of the highest privilege In the US HOUSE OF REPRESENTATIVES, a procedural motion of the utmost importance. One occasion for such a motion is when, after 20 calendar days, House-Senate CONFEREES have failed to report agreement.

personal privilege motion Again in the US CONGRESS, a motion enabling a member to raise a controversial matter relating to his or her own personal affairs.

under the cloak of privilege The WESTMINSTER term for comments made in the COMMONS chamber by an MP which would have been actionable for libel had they been said outside. The procedure is used from time to time to unmask some wrongdoing; sometimes a private citizen who feels they have been unjustly attacked in the Commons will challenge the member to repeat the allegations outside.

Privy Council The pool of UK and COMMONWEALTH statesmen, judges and others who have been admitted to the councils of the SOVEREIGN; membership is for life. In practice the Council, which advises the monarch and transacts some official business, especially at times of emergency, comprises a handful of current UK Ministers, with the Sovereign (or designated representative) and the LORD PRESIDENT OF

THE COUNCIL always present. Proceedings are brief and to the point, though Clare SHORT did once breach the formality when her mobile phone rang; the Queen told her: 'You'd better answer it. It might be someone important.' The Privy Council as an institution is said to have its roots in a council instituted by King Alfred in 895. Its Judicial Committee is the final court of appeal for a diminishing number of Commonwealth countries.

privy council terms The basis of total confidentiality on which a Prime Minister briefs and consults OPPOSITION leaders at WESTMINSTER. To enable this to take place, the leaders of the Labour and Liberal Democrat parties, and exceptionally special Prime Ministerial envoys such as Ann Clwyd, Tony BLAIR's human rights monitor in Iraq, are admitted to the Privy Council, membership of which carries with it a strict oath of secrecy.

pro-. pro-Boer The name given to opponents and critics of the BOER WAR and its conduct by Britain's IMPERIALISTS, during the war itself and in the KHAKI ELECTION campaign.

pro-choice The label assumed in the mid-1980s by advocates of more liberal abortion laws, especially in America. It was devised as a counter to

pro-life The highly effective name chosen in the 1970s by American opponents of abortion, and taken up by their allies throughout the West. Supporters of the RIGHT TO LIFE regard the destruction of any unborn foetus as murder, and thus seek to outlaw abortion and ban experiments on embryos. In 1989 George BUSH Snr supported pro-life marches prior to a SUPREME COURT decision that put new restraints on abortion, limiting the landmark ROE V WADE ruling. His son took a stronger pro-life line, urging the UNITED NATIONS to impose a global ban on stem cell research.

pro-Marketeers Supporters of UK membership of the COMMON MARKET and its successors. The term had a particular force in the 1960s and early '70s when it was an open question whether Britain would join or stay in.

procurement The commissioning or purchase of items needed by a government department or agency, especially the process of developing and obtaining military hardware of all kinds from the defence industries and endeavouring to get it into service on time and to budget.

Prod In NORTHERN IRELAND, a mildly offensive term for a Protestant. It is considerably less abusive than TAIG, used by some Protestants of Catholics.

Profiles in Courage The best-selling book, published in 1956, for which then-Senator John F. KENNEDY won a Pulitzer Prize. It described senators who had stood bravely against public opinion, and established the link between 'Kennedy' and 'courage' in the public mind. Kennedy wrote the book while recovering from a second spinal operation to ease the pain from his war wounds (*see* PT-109). His recovery kept him away from the Senate during the crucial debates on whether to censure Sen. Joseph MCCARTHY; Kennedy's eagerness to be associated with courage did not prompt him to voice an opinion on the matter.

Profumo affair The sex-and-security scandal which riveted the British public for months in 1963, forced the resignation of a CABINET MINISTER and contributed to the end of the Conservative government first elected in 1951. **John Profumo** (1915–), Secretary for War in Harold MACMILLAN's government, resigned in June 1963 after admitting lying to the HOUSE when he denied having a liaison with the call-girl Christine Keeler (1942–). She had also been sleeping with Lt-Cdr Yevgeny Ivanov, an assistant Soviet naval attaché, suspected of being a spy, who had pumped her for information. Profumo first met Keeler in July 1961, naked in a swimming pool at CLIVEDEN, the country estate of Lord Astor; also at the party was Dr Stephen Ward, with whom Keeler lived. Ward, an artist/osteopath with famous patients to whom he occasionally supplied 'popsies', had already introduced Keeler to Ivanov. MI5 learned of Profumo's association with Keeler through Ward, who was also informing them on Ivanov's activities. Warned by a colleague of MI5's concern at the implications of having a Secretary for War sharing a mistress with a Soviet agent, Profumo broke off the relationship. But after a shooting incident at Ward's flat in December 1962 aimed at her even younger friend Mandy Rice-Davis, the press latched on to Keeler's activities and rumours of Profumo's relationship with her became rife; they were hinted at in PRIVATE EYE and the BBC's newly-launched satirical programme THAT WAS THE WEEK THAT WAS. On 22 March 1963 Profumo told MPs in a PERSONAL STATEMENT:

> There was no impropriety whatsoever in my

> acquaintance with Miss Keeler . . . I shall not hesitate to issue writs for libel and slander if scandalous allegations are made or repeated outside the House.

Though subsequent pressure from the OPPOSITION on the security angle forced his resignation, it was his lie to the Commons, soon revealed as such, that lost him his own party's support; he even lied to Cabinet colleagues when they pressed him. Macmillan had been kept in ignorance by MI5, and his apparent unworldliness led a Tory ex-Minister, Nigel Birch, to ask: 'What does the Prime Minister think whores are for?' *The Times* summed up the ESTABLISHMENT's feeling of grubbiness and betrayal with a leader headed: 'It *is* a moral issue', and the new Labour leader Harold WILSON moved in for the kill, declaring:

> There is something nauseous about a system of society which pays a harlot 25 times as much as a Prime Minister, 250 times as much as it pays its Members of Parliament and 500 times as much as it pays its ministers of religion.

Michael FOOT said in scorn: 'The members of our secret service have apparently spent so much time looking under the bed for Communists that they haven't had time to look *in* the bed.' MI5 and Macmillan both declared themselves satisfied that there had been no breach of security, and the subsequent DENNING REPORT broadly agreed. Yet the political furore at times made the government seem on the verge of collapse, though Macmillan said afterwards:

> I was determined that no British Government should be brought down by the action of two tarts.

This echoed Lord Hailsham's words that 'a great party is not to be brought down by a scandal involving a woman of easy virtue and a proven liar'. Hailsham's moralising earned from the fox-hunting Labour MP Sir Reginald Paget one of the most stinging denunciations heard in the Commons:

> From Lord Hailsham we have had a virtuoso performance in the art of kicking a fallen friend in the guts . . . When self-indulgence has reduced a man to the shape of the Right Honourable and Noble Gentleman, sexual continence requires no more than a sense of the ridiculous.

Stephen Ward was tried in July 1963 on charges ranging from running a brothel to arranging then-illegal abortions. The trial turned into a farrago of two-way mirrors, whips and a masked man in a FREEMASON'S APRON whose identity was too sensitive to be revealed. When Lord Astor repudiated the evidence of Mandy Rice-Davis, who was Ward's mistress, she replied: 'HE WOULD, WOULDN'T HE'. Ward killed himself on 3 August with an overdose of Nembutal. Profumo devoted himself to charity work at Toynbee Hall in London's East End, and in 1975 was REHABILITATED with the award of a CBE. Keeler achieved lifelong notoriety and was jailed for nine months for perjury; the *News of the World* paid £23,000 for her story but the scandal brought her neither wealth nor happiness. Mandy Rice-Davis declared: 'I am notorious. I may go down in history as another Lady Hamilton', and became prosperous and respectable. Ivanov was recalled to Moscow as the scandal broke and spent some time in a mental institution. Macmillan resigned that autumn while in hospital for prostate surgery; his government, now headed by SIR ALEC Douglas-Home, narrowly lost the 1964 general election.

> The Tory party ran screaming from side to side of the sinking ship before tossing Harold Macmillan over the side in an act of propitiation.
>
> JULIAN CRITCHLEY

> 'What have you done?' cried Christine.
> 'You've wrecked the whole party machine!
> To lie in the nude
> May be quite rude
> But to lie in the House is obscene.' ANON.

progressive In general term, a person or movement advocating progress or reform. Hugh Brogan has called it 'a curiously empty word', but from time to time a party (usually a POPULIST one) has taken the word for its title. America has had three Progressive Parties. The first was founded in a rebellion in 1910 by Congressional Republicans against the Speakership of Rep. Joe Cannon (*see* FOUL-MOUTHED JOE; UNCLE JOE). In 1911 Sen. Robert La Follette of Wisconsin (1855–1925) founded the **National Progressive Republican League**, and ex-President Theodore ROOSEVELT stepped forward to head it; the Progressives backed his 1912 BULL MOOSE candidacy before fading away. A second **Progressive Party** was launched in 1924 by malcontents in Wisconsin and other farm states, with La Follette as its Presidential nominee. It proposed a 'housecleaning' in WASHINGTON, public control of natural resources, public ownership of railroads and tax cuts. La Follette polled nearly 5 million votes, but carried only his home state. Finally, in 1947, former Vice President Henry Wallace launched a leftist **Progressive Party** to protest at the TRUMAN administration's deteriorating relations with Soviet Russia, and demand an end to the MARSHALL PLAN. Truman loyalists feared Wallace's intervention might ensure a Republican win, but the ticket polled a disappointing 1,156,103 votes and won no electoral seats.

In Canada a farmer-backed **Progressive Party** took power in Ontario in 1919, and in the 1921 general election won 65 Parliamentary seats, mainly in the west and 15 more than the Conservatives. Mackenzie King manoeuvred the Progressives under T. A. Crerar into backing his minority government; they were reduced to 24 MPs in the 1925 election and in a further poll following the 1926 CONSTITUTIONAL CRISIS they were wiped out. But they turned Canada into a multi-party democracy, which it has remained for most of the time since.

In Britain the term has had less significance, though in the early 20th century the non-Labour group on the London County Council (LCC) termed themselves **Progressives**.

Progressive Conservatives The centre-right party, which adopted this name in 1942 to underline its commitment to reform and social provision, and has alternated with the LIBERALS as Canada's governing party from the early days of CONFEDERATION – apart from the decade after the CANADIAN MELTDOWN of 1993. The party of MacDonald, Borden, Bennett and DIEFenbaker, it traditionally supported the COMMONWEALTH, a favourable climate for business and close ties with America including FREE TRADE (*see also* NAFTA). The Progressive Conservatives held power most recently from 1984 when Brian Mulroney (1939–) ousted Pierre TRUDEAU's Liberals, until its shattering defeat under the abrasive Kim Campbell (*see* 'Don't mess with me – I got TANKS') who succeeded Mulroney earlier in 1993. The Progressive Conservatives made a slow and partial recovery, getting back up to 20 seats in 1997, before merging with the CANADIAN ALLIANCE in 2003 to form a united right-of-centre party. In the 2004 election it won 99 seats, just enough to deprive Jean Chrétien's Liberals of their overall majority.

> As leader of the Progressive Conservatives I thought (Brian Mulroney) put too much emphasis on the adjective as opposed to the noun.
>
> MARGARET THATCHER, *The Downing Street Years*

progressive taxation *See* TAX.

Prohibition The ban on the sale or consumption of intoxicating liquor introduced in America in 1920 following the passage of the VOLSTEAD ACT and ratification in 1919 of the 18th AMENDMENT. Introduction of the 'Noble EXPERIMENT' was the result of decades of pressure from temperance and church groups, and especially the Anti-Saloon League, formed in 1893. Combining opposition to liquor with evangelical Protestantism, it had by late 1917 persuaded more than half of the states, with two-thirds of the US population, to ban the liquor traffic; that December CONGRESS passed the Amendment. Maine had banned alcohol as long ago as 1856, a PROHIBITION PARTY was formed, and Prohibition was a key element of the PROGRESSIVE platform. By 1906, eighteen states had introduced some form of restriction or ban on the sale of alcohol, and many counties and cities were also DRY by virtue of a 'local option' offered by state legislatures; when grain ran short during WORLD WAR I and drinking by servicemen was seen as a problem, the pressure intensified. Prohibition, however, proved unenforceable; the supply of illicit liquor to a thirsty population by bootleggers spawned organised crime and widespread corruption among police and politicians. It was repealed in December 1933, though eight states remained 'dry' and some jurisdictions, mainly in the South, do to this day.

> There is as much chance of repealing the 18th amendment as there is for a humming bird to fly to the planet Mars with the WASHINGTON MONUMENT tied to its tail. This country is for temperance and prohibition, and it is going to continue to elect members to Congress who believe in that.
>
> Sen. MORRIS SHEPPARD (1875–1941), 24 September 1930

Prohibition Party The US political party set up with that objective in 1869, which has contested Presidential elections ever since. During the 2004 campaign the party split, a more militant faction in Colorado claiming that Earl Dodge, the party's candidate since 1984, was too interested in promoting campaign buttons and that a new nominee was needed to improve on the 208 votes Dodge polled in 2000.

Project, the The name given by Tony BLAIR and his closest advisers, notably Peter Mandelson (*see* BOBBY) and the former Social Democrat Roger Liddle, from the mid-1990s to their ambition of creating a centre-left force capable of governing for a generation and reducing the Conservatives to irrelevance. Crucial to the Project were the abandonment of Labour's left-wing BAGGAGE so as to appeal to MIDDLE ENGLAND, and co-ordination of electoral tactics – and some fields of policy – with the LIBERAL DEMOCRATS, up to and including seats for the LibDems in a Blair CABINET. The Project was devastatingly successful in sweeping Labour to power in 1997 and securing its re-election in 2001, though by this time relations with the LibDems had frayed over Labour's failure to introduce PROPORTIONAL REPRESENTATION for Parliamentary elections.

projection A computerised estimate of the outcome of an election, based on the analysis of the first few results, which is then updated as further results come in.

proletariat The poorest labouring class; the ancient Roman word for those so poor that they could only breed children for military service, taken up by MARXISTS to represent the elements in society who should rightfully capture power. Marx and Engels wrote in the COMMUNIST MANIFESTO of 1848: 'The proletariat alone is a truly revolutionary class', and LENIN in *One Step Forward, Two Steps Back* declared:

> In the struggle for power the proletariat has no other weapon but organisation.

dictatorship of the proletariat The penultimate stage in social progress as envisaged by MARX and his spiritual heirs. In the COMMUNIST MANIFESTO Marx stated: 'The class struggle necessarily leads to the dictatorship of the proletariat, and that dictatorship itself only constitutes the transition to the abolition of all classes and to a CLASSLESS SOCIETY.'

lumpenproletariat Marx's term, coined in 1850, for the very poorest of the working class. The word combines the Ger. *lump*, ragamuffin, and *proletariat*. Though not intended as a term of denigration, it widely became such.

prompt cards Cards for a politician to carry to remind him- or herself of key phrases or SOUNDBITES to utter before an audience or the cameras. Much use was made of them by Ronald REAGAN's advisers, in an effort to keep up the flow of apparently spontaneous ONE-LINERS and to offset his ability to forget or alter basic facts.

propaganda (Lat. to be spread) The insistent spreading of information favourable to the regime or organisation disseminating it, often with little regard to its veracity. Originally a term from the 17th-century Roman Catholic church, it was taken over and perfected by the COMMUNIST and FASCIST regimes of the inter-war period and their spiritual successors; HITLER's Propaganda Minister Josef Goebbels, a supreme practitioner, claimed: 'we have made the Reich by propaganda.' Powerful groups in the democracies are also skilled in its use; President TRUMAN once observed that 'the US Marine Corps have a propaganda machine that is almost equal to STALIN's.'

black propaganda is information circulated in the knowledge that it is false, in order to discredit an enemy or opponent.

> The art of persuading others of what one does not believe oneself.
>
> Israeli Foreign Minister ABBA EBAN (1915–2002)

> The propagandist's purpose is to make sure one set of people forget that certain other sets of people are human.
>
> ALDOUS HUXLEY (1894–1963)

propeller-heads *See* NERD SQUAD.

property. property-owning democracy The principle and the appeal of Britain's CONSERVATIVE PARTY from the 1950s, based on the belief that home ownership would give individuals a greater stake in society – and make them more likely to vote Conservative; the latter argument was crudely encapsulated in the HOMES FOR VOTES scandal. As Labour resisted the RIGHT TO BUY, it was equally claimed by Conservatives that Labour wished to 'imprison' its supporters on council estates to prevent them realising their economic potential and thinking for themselves politically. The phrase, much used by generations of senior Tories, was coined by the Scottish Conservative MP Noel Skelton (1880–1935), whose promising Ministerial career was cut short by his early death.

Property is theft One of the classic slogans of COMMUNISM and ANARCHISM, devised in 1840 by Pierre-Joseph Proudhon (1809–65).

Government has no other end but the preservation of property A typically minimalist statement from the English philosopher John Locke (1632–1704), made in his *Second Treatise on Government* (1690).

Next to the right of liberty, the right of property is the most important individual right guaranteed by the Constitution and the one which . . . has contributed more to the growth of civilisation than any other. The philosophy of President TAFT, set out in his book *Popular Government* (1913).

Our civilisation is built up on private property, and can only be defended by private property Winston CHURCHILL's rejoinder in 1947 to proposals by the ATTLEE government to take sweeping 'transitional powers', including the right to direct labour, to hasten post-war reconstruction and the rebuilding of the economy. Churchill saw the plan as TOTALITARIAN and a threat to basic human rights; it was not fully implemented.

There is something that governments care for far more than human life, and that is the security of property The rationale set out by Emmeline Pankhurst (1858–1928) for SUFFRAGETTES to take MILITANT and destructive action. In a speech at London's Royal Albert Hall on 17 October 1912, she continued:

> So it is through property that we shall strike the enemy . . . Be militant each in your own way . . . I incite this meeting to rebellion.

proportional representation A system of electing a LEGISLATURE or other body which attempts directly to reflect the overall vote cast for each party; the opposite is FIRST PAST THE POST, under which the winner in each constituency is elected whether or not they have a majority of the votes case. A system of PR was recommended for Britain by a SPEAKER'S CONFERENCE after WORLD WAR I but never implemented; the same fate befell the report issued by the JENKINS COMMITTEE in 1998. However, Tony BLAIR's government did introduce PR for elections to the EUROPEAN PARLIAMENT (*see* D'HONDT FORMULA), SCOTTISH PARLIAMENT and WELSH ASSEMBLY, initially giving a boost to Labour's opponents. Traditionally the third-party Liberals/LIBERAL DEMOCRATS have been the greatest advocates of PR, but Labour switched from the mid-1980s from total opposition to wary interest (*see* PLANT COMMISSION). Opponents of PR argue that, as no party ever gains 50% of the total vote, their own party would never achieve an outright Parliamentary majority; its advocates see it as a way of preventing other parties exercising total power with 40% or less of the vote. Critics also point to the chronic instability of governments in some countries with PR, notably Italy, and argue that the system gives small parties excessive power. There are numerous forms of PR including the ADDITIONAL MEMBER, Alternative VOTE and Single Transferable VOTE.

NORTHERN IRELAND has had PR for all but Parliamentary elections since the 1920s. After the anti-H-BLOCK candidate Owen Carron won the Fermanagh and South Tyrone BY-ELECTION in 1981, the Liberal MP Stephen (later Lord) Ross asked Margaret THATCHER if the result did not prove the case for PR. 'As there were only two candidates, I don't see what difference it would have made', she replied.

> PR is fundamentally undemocratic.
> NEIL KINNOCK, 1983

Proposition 13 The revolutionary INITIATIVE approved by California voters in 1978 which slashed property taxes in half. The taxes, pegged to soaring real estate values, had been rising far more sharply than incomes, and home owners led by the conservative businessman Howard Jarvis rebelled. It took Jarvis years to get the proposition onto the ballot, but it was carried by a 2–1 majority. Dire warnings of the collapse of government if tax revenues were pegged were not borne out, and Proposition 13 became a precedent for the application of REAGANOMICS three years later.

> The WATTS RIOT of the white middle class.
> Letter to the *Los Angeles Herald-Examiner*

Proposition 187 A proposition passed in 1994 which barred illegal migrants and their children from education and welfare benefits, and obliged citizens to report them. In that year's US Senate campaign, California's Democrat Dianne Feinstein and Republican Michael Huffington each accused the other of employing 'ILLEGALS'.

Proposition 209 A third landmark initiative from California, this one approved in 1996. It compelled every public service institution in the state to abandon AFFIRMATIVE ACTION.

prorogation The act of terminating a PARLIAMENT so that elections for a new one may be held. Prorogation is ordered by the SOVEREIGN, and takes the form of a brief ceremony in each HOUSE to **prorogue** it.

prospective candidate *See* CANDIDATE; PPC.

protectionism The policy of protecting a nation's industries by erecting a TARIFF or other barrier to make imports and rival services uncompetitive, thereby risking retaliation against one's own products. In America the tradition runs deep, as witness the number of occasions when tariffs imposed by the second BUSH administration have been ruled illegal by the WTO. Thomas JEFFERSON, in a letter in 1815, wrote:

> I have come to a resolution myself, as I hope any good citizen will, never again to purchase any article of foreign manufacture which can be had

of American make, be the difference of price what it may.

Protectionism reached its height in late 19th-century America, with senators imposing rigorous tariffs even when the WHITE HOUSE wanted cuts. In a campaign speech in 1923, Herbert HOOVER warned:

> The grass will grow in the streets of a hundred cities, a thousand towns; the weeds will overrun the fields of millions of farms if [protection] is taken away.

Protectionism has been less of a force in Britain, though IMPERIAL PREFERENCE was as much a form of co-ordinated protectionism by a number of countries as a move toward FREE TRADE; some would argue the same of the European SINGLE MARKET. When Joseph Chamberlain began his campaign for Imperial Preference in 1903, Margot Asquith wrote:

> This caught on like wildfire with the semi-clever, moderately educated, the Imperialists, Dukes, journalists and Fighting Forces.

Protectorate (1) The formal title of the COMMONWEALTH, the republican form of government in England over which Oliver Cromwell (1599–1658) presided as Lord Protector from 1653 until his death. (2) A territory in the British Empire administered by Britain without ANNEXATION and without its inhabitants being granted British citizenship; Bechuanaland (Botswana) was one example.

protest. Protest and survive The slogan launched by CND in the early 1980s in response to a UK government civil defence leaflet entitled *Protect and Survive*, which suggested that elementary precautions could enable a considerable number of people to survive a NUCLEAR war.

protest movement The initially student movement which from c. 1967 staged frequent outrageous protests against the basics of American society, with SIT-INS and take-overs in many universities. It was given a moral edge by the depth and sincerity of opposition to the escalating VIETNAM WAR, while some of its adherents flirted with MARXISM. The movement, which emphasised peace and NON-VIOLENCE, despite some excesses caught the imagination of many young people as the cultures of rock music, drugs and Flower Power shattered many taboos. It invigorated the NEW LEFT, and enraged conservatives typified by the NIXON administration. Vice President Spiro T. AGNEW waged a counter-offensive against extremists in the movement who were silencing all opposition, and in 1969 set out Ten Commandments of Protest:

> Thou shalt not allow thy opponent to speak.
> Thou shalt not set forward a program of thy own.
> Thou shalt not trust anybody over 30.
> Thou shalt not honour thy father or mother.
> Thou shalt not heed the lessons of history.
> Thou shalt not write anything longer than a slogan.
> Thou shalt not present a negotiable demand.
> Thou shalt not accept any ESTABLISHMENT idea.
> Thou shalt not revere any but TOTALITARIAN heroes.
> Thou shalt not ask forgiveness for thy transgressions, rather thou shalt demand AMNESTY for them.

protest songs The canon of popular songs against war, poverty and injustice and the policies that cause them, pioneered by Bob Dylan in the early 1960s (*Blowin' in the Wind*; *The Times They are a-Changin'*) and taken up by Joan Baez and many other singers and songwriters.

protest vote *See* VOTE.

protocol (1) The draft of a TREATY, or an agreement appended to a treaty, or an international agreement of less moment than a treaty. A protocol may sometimes become a treaty when enough nations have RATIFIED it. (2) In diplomacy, the body of etiquette which determines both the conduct of relations between states and their representatives and, specifically, the ceremonial involved in STATE and OFFICIAL VISITS.

province In Canada, the ten units that make up the Confederation (plus the Yukon and North-West Territories and autonomous Inuit jurisdictions within them). The provinces have jealously guarded their rights in respect of the Federal government in Ottawa and each other; efforts to put them on an agreed and durable basis have consistently broken down because of disagreements between Quebec and the western provinces (*see* CHARLOTTETOWN ACCORD; MEECH LAKE).

provisional ballot *See* BALLOT.

Provisional IRA (also **Provos** and – to the British military – **PIRA**) The force, formed in 1969 when the Irish Republican Army (IRA) split into the OFFICIAL IRA (*see also* STICKIES), who preferred mainly political action to secure a united Ireland, and the belligerently high-profile Provisionals and their political wing, SINN FEIN. From then until the negotiation of the 1998 GOOD FRIDAY AGREEMENT, the Provisionals carried on a terrorist campaign against British rule in NORTHERN IRELAND which left over 3000 people dead, two-thirds killed by the Provisionals. They also killed over 50 in attacks on the British mainland (the worst being the 1974 Birmingham pub bombings, *see* BIRMINGHAM SIX), and a number of UK service personnel in continental Europe. The movement remains on standby should the PEACE PROCESS collapse; a ceasefire has been largely honoured, but punishment attacks within the Catholic community have continued, there has been only marginal DECOMMISSIONING of the Provisionals' arsenal, and the targeting of potential targets from Sinn Fein's office at Stormont led to the suspension of POWER-SHARING in October 2002. The Provisionals have also been implicated in the murder of Robert MCCARTNEY and the NORTHERN BANK ROBBERY. Some hard-liners have moved to the REAL IRA (responsible for the OMAGH BOMBING) and Continuity IRA, but the movement as a whole has backed the peace process with varying degrees of enthusiasm, Gerry Adams and Martin McGuinness becoming key figures in electoral politics, and almost all the convicted terrorists freed under the Agreement have remained out of trouble. During its terrorist campaign, and probably since, the Provisionals were financed through robberies, protection rackets, fund-raising from well-wishers at home and Irish romantics abroad (notably through NORAID in America), and apparently legitimate businesses; their fighters were trained in Communist eastern Europe and the Middle East, and much of their arsenal, including large supplies of SEMTEX, came from Libya. After three decades of struggle which posed severe strains on the UK and the Irish Republic, the Provisionals' ACTIVE SERVICE UNITS could still call on a pool of up to 300 dedicated fighters.

Provost In Scottish local government, the ceremonial head of a municipality, the equivalent of a non-executive MAYOR in England. In the great cities of Scotland, he or she takes the title of **Lord Provost**.

proximity talks In delicate international or industrial negotiations, talks in which the conflicting parties are in adjacent rooms and mediators shuttle between them.

proxy. proxy bomb A bomb delivered under duress by someone other than the terrorists who intend it to explode. A car, taxi or truck is HIJACKED, a bomb placed on board, and the driver ordered at gunpoint to take it to a sensitive security target. The PROVISIONAL IRA has used this technique both in NORTHERN IRELAND and in London.

proxy vote A vote legitimately cast by one person on behalf of another who is unable to be present, for reason of illness, business or removal, and has given their authority.

proxy war A war fought not directly between major powers but between client states in another theatre; an example was the 1978 conflict between Cambodia and Vietnam, which was seen as reflecting tensions between China and the Soviet Union.

PSBR PUBLIC SECTOR Borrowing Requirement. The amount the UK government has to borrow in any financial year when there is not a budget surplus, to cover the gap between receipts (from taxes, PRIVATISATION proceeds, etc.) and total government expenditure.

psephology The study of electoral behaviour as reflected in elections and opinion polls. The word was invented in 1948 by the Cambridge classical scholar Frank Hardie, but did not cross the Atlantic until c. 1970. It comes from the Greek *psephos*, a pebble; Classical Athenians voted by putting pebbles in one of two jars.

PSOE (Sp. *Partido Socialista Obrero Español,* Spanish Socialist Workers' Party) The Democratic SOCIALIST party that emerged after the death of General Franco (*see* CAUDILLO) as the principal force on the left. It is the successor of the Socialist Party founded by Pablo Iglesias in the late 19th century, which was part of the POPULAR FRONT government against which Franco launched the SPANISH CIVIL WAR. Under the leadership of Felipe Gonzalez, the PSOE governed from 1982 to 1996, during which time Spain joined both the European Community and NATO. It returned to power under José Luis Rodriguez Zapatero in March 2004 in the wake of the MADRID BOMBINGS, which the Popular Party government of José Maria Aznar had inadvisedly blamed on the Basque terrorist group ETA. Almost its first action was to fulfil a MANIFESTO commitment to pull Spanish troops out of Iraq.

PSX The UK CABINET COMMITTEE, chaired by the Chancellor, that presides over public services and expenditure. From 1997 to 2005 it was known as **PX**, before that **EDX**.

PT-109 The torpedo boat which John F. KENNEDY commanded in the Pacific during WORLD WAR II, and the title of a 1962 film about his naval exploits starring Cliff Robertson. In 1943 the boat was rammed and sunk by a Japanese destroyer; Kennedy was thrown against the cockpit bulkhead, aggravating an old back injury, but rounded up the ten survivors and swam with them to a nearby island, holding with his teeth for several hours the life preserver of one too badly wounded to swim. He won the Navy Medal and a Purple Heart, but his back was to trouble him for the rest of his life; when Kennedy embarked on a political career, his father went to great pains to publicise and amplify his heroism.

Public Against Violence The Slovak counterpart to the Czech lands' CIVIC FORUM; between them they took power from the Communists in the VELVET REVOLUTION of 1989. The former liberal Communist hero Alexander Dubček, banished to obscurity after the PRAGUE SPRING, was among its leaders.

public diplomacy The promotion of a government's foreign policies by the harnessing of public relations skills instead of purely through the diplomatic process. Britain's FOREIGN AND COMMONWEALTH OFFICE gained under Robin COOK a public diplomacy unit staffed by career diplomats with a remit of explaining general policies and particular initiatives to the public at home and abroad, especially over Europe.

Public Energy Number One One of the many nicknames of Eleanor Roosevelt (*see* FIRST LADY OF THE WORLD); she gained it for her boundless energy on her own account and as her husband's ambassador during his presidency. It is a play on the FBI's 'Public Enemy Number One.'

public inquiry In UK environmental politics, a hearing held before a government inspector to determine whether a new building scheme – residential, commercial or an infrastructure project – should go ahead. The inspector submits a report to the relevant Secretary of State, who is not obliged to accept its findings but otherwise runs the risk of JUDICIAL REVIEW.

public interest, the A phrase which means very different things to different people. To campaigners for greater openness and ACCOUNTABILITY, it implies the interest of the people as a whole; to those in power it too often means the interest of the governing clique, to which excessive public exposure is anathema.

public interest groups A phrase from the US political lexicon with two overlapping meanings: either quasi-governmental voluntary associations like the Council of State Governments and the US Conference of Mayors, or more partisan but nevertheless respectable pressure groups like COMMON CAUSE or the LEAGUE OF WOMEN VOTERS.

Public Interest Immunity Certificates Documents which a UK Minister may sign preventing certain material from being disclosed to a court on grounds of national security. The use of such certificates has been curbed after their abuse during the MATRIX-CHURCHILL AFFAIR.

public opinion The view of the community as a whole, and a voice which many politicians aim to reflect and to which all must ultimately listen. Abraham LINCOLN declared: 'Public opinion in this country is everything,' Bulwer Lytton that 'when people have no other tyrant, then public opinion becomes one', and Franklin D. ROOSEVELT observed: 'A government can be no better than the public opinion which sustains it.' John C. Calhoun described public opinion as 'nothing more than the opinion or voice of the strongest interest or combination of interests'; Sir Robert PEEL as 'a compound of folly, weakness, prejudice, wrong feeling, right feeling, obstinacy and newspaper paragraphs'; Clarence Darrow as 'the greatest enemy that ever confronted man'; Mark Bonham-Carter as 'the last refuge of the politician without any opinion'.

> No Minister ever stood, or could stand, against public opinion.
>
> JOHN WILSON CROKER, 1835

Public Order Act *See* CABLE STREET.

public ownership Another word for NATIONALISATION, though lacking the overtone of rigid centralised control associated with that term.

> It is inconceivable that we could transform this country without a major extension of public ownership. NEIL KINNOCK, 1983

public sector The portion of a nation's economic activity conducted and financed by organs of central and local government, and their agencies. With the PRIVATE SECTOR, it makes up the totality of the economy.

Public Sector Borrowing Requirement *See* PSBR.

public speaking The art of making SPEECHES, often but not always in a political context. The phrase 'unaccustomed as I am to public speaking' has become a caricature of how not to begin a speech.

> The human brain starts working the moment you are born, and never stops until you stand up to speak in public. GEORGE JESSEL

public spending was described by the early US Congressman John Randolph as 'the most delicious of all privileges: spending other people's money'; but Thomas JEFFERSON put a more responsible view: 'The same prudence which in public life would forbid our paying our own money for unexplained projects, forbids it in the dispensation of the public moneys.' COOLIDGE was equally firm, stating: 'The appropriation of public money always is perfectly lovely until someone is asked to pay the bill', and the subsequent big spender Franklin D. ROOSEVELT, before his election in 1932, said in a broadcast:

> Any government, like any family, can for a year spend a little more than it earns. But you and I know that continuation of the habit means the poorhouse.

publicist A mildly derogatory term for a person who conducts a vigorous campaign, often by writing articles and leaflets, in support of a particular party, campaign or course of action. In Hollywood, but not yet in politics, it also refers to a celebrity's or studio's public relations promoter.

Publish and be damned! The classic response to a blackmailer, delivered by the Duke of Wellington to Joseph Stockdale who was threatening to publish the memoirs of the IRON DUKE's former mistress Harriette Wilson. Stockdale had written to Wellington: 'I have stopped the Press for the moment; but as the publication will take place next week, little delay can necessarily take place.' Wellington wrote his response across the letter and posted it back.

Publius The anonymous author of the FEDERALIST Papers, the pamphlets putting the case for RATIFICATION of the US CONSTITUTION, which were produced in New York between October 1787 and the following August. They were in fact written by Alexander HAMILTON, James MADISON and, to a lesser extent, John JAY.

Pugin room A sedate tea-room and bar in the Palace of WESTMINSTER, above the riverside TERRACE, where MPs may entertain their guests. It was named in the early 1980s after Augustus Welby Pugin (1814–52), the workaholic prodigy who was responsible for the richly Gothic style of the new Palace's internal decoration.

Pugwash A series of annual conferences held to promote the constructive and peaceful uses of scientific knowledge; Pugwash and its founder Professor Joseph Rotblat were awarded the NOBEL PEACE PRIZE for 1995. The first was held in 1957 at the home of the Canadian philanthropist Cyrus Eaton in Pugwash, Nova Scotia. It was inspired by the Einstein-Russell memorandum, which catalogued the appalling consequences for humanity of NUCLEAR conflict and called for a conference of scientists from both sides of the IRON CURTAIN. Subsequent meetings have been held in many countries; subjects have included nuclear disarmament, environmental issues and the problems of the developing world. The Pugwash movement, organised by an International Co-ordinating Committee, has produced several reports on ARMS CONTROL, contributing to the course of disarmament since the 1970s. The name Pugwash brings a smile to British faces, as Captain Pugwash was a faintly ridiculous pirate in a BBC children's cartoon.

pump priming The direction of relatively small amounts of state investment or tax revenue to stimulating promising sectors of the economy whose expansion could speed a general economic recovery and hasten overall growth.

pundit Hindi for a person learned in the Sanskrit disciplines, and hence in English someone who is an eminent authority on a particular subject. Pundits can be seen, for example, on television giving their expert ideas on such subjects as the political or economic situation or the best strategy to be followed in wartime. The more subjects a person is seen to speak on, the less likely they are to be referred to as a pundit. *See also* PANDIT.

puppet government A regime with no true independence, having been installed or being maintained in office by a foreign power to do its bidding, the inference being that someone else is pulling its strings. Examples have been the QUISLING regime in NAZI-occupied Norway and the Communist regimes in post-war eastern and central Europe, kept in power by Soviet might regardless of their lack of public support. The politicians and technocrats attempting to govern in Baghdad since the IRAQ WAR found it hard to live down the charge of being American puppets. The term can also apply to a nominal civilian government in a state controlled by the military.

purdah The isolation into which the British governmental MACHINE retreats during and immediately prior to a GENERAL ELECTION, not processing any announcements which might sway the electorate – for, say, a new hospital – after a set deadline. Purdah also applies to the activities of central government during a local election campaign. The CHANCELLOR OF THE EXCHEQUER traditionally retreated into purdah for two months before his BUDGET, to make quite certain he did not let slip any clues about the package he was preparing. He would answer questions in the HOUSE, and receive deputations pressing him to take one course of action or another, but would not comment on what was to come. The practice was abolished by Kenneth Clarke when he became Chancellor in 1993; Clarke remained just as opaque about what he was planning, but his Labour successor Gordon BROWN made the Budget-making process more open. The word is the Urdu and Persian term for the curtain that separates the women's quarters in a Muslim household, and thus describes the state of seclusion in which strict Islamic men maintain that women should live.

purge The removal from office, disgrace and often execution by a TOTALITARIAN leader of apparently loyal colleagues. While HITLER and other extreme rightists indulged in purges (*see* NIGHT OF THE LONG KNIVES), they were turned into a grotesque art form by STALIN in the 1930s, and later by his post-war PUPPETS in eastern Europe. The first and greatest Communist purge was the orgy of arrests, SHOW TRIALS and executions between 1934 and 1938 by which an increasingly paranoid Stalin eliminated the BOLSHEVIK old guard, most of the command of the RED ARMY, and thousands of Communist Party members and ordinary Soviet citizens. The era of purges was triggered by the Law of 1 December 1934 issued on Stalin's orders after the murder of his aide Sergei Kirov by a deranged gunman; they were resumed after the GREAT PATRIOTIC WAR when unity against a common enemy was no longer instinctive. One of the grisliest post-war purges was carried out in the Leningrad party organisation after the death of the city's party boss Andrei Zhdanov in 1948. Conducted by Abukamov, the ruthless wartime head of SMERSH, it was probably initiated by Georgy Malenkov and Paul Beria to eliminate supporters of Zhdanov, who had been Malenkov's chief rival for Stalin's favour. Over 2000 party functionaries who had survived appalling wartime privations were executed, including A. A. Kuznetsov, a CENTRAL COMMITTEE member, and Nikolai Voznesensky, a member of the POLITBURO.

Put up or shut up The challenge issued on 22 May 1995 by an exasperated John MAJOR to right-wing Conservative MPs (*see* BASTARDS) who had been conducting a running battle against his government, mainly over Europe, at a time when BY-ELECTION losses and defections had almost eliminated its majority in the COMMONS. The challenge was taken up by John Redwood (*see* VULCAN), who resigned as Welsh Secretary to challenge Major for the leadership; Major defeated him but not overwhelmingly, his position strengthening for a time largely because of the skilful SPIN with which his margin over Redwood was portrayed by Cabinet colleagues as a knock-out.

Putney debates The debates in Putney church, south-west London, in 1647 in which LEVELLERS and other radical elements in the Cromwellian army argued with their leaders for the establishment of a genuinely democratic and tolerant society. They were held to argue out the principles under which England should be governed after the CIVIL WAR; the outcome was inconclusive and no new or democratic framework was ever established. *See also* the POOREST HE THAT IS IN ENGLAND.

putsch The sudden or violent overthrow of a government or political system, from the Swiss German word for a revolution. *See also* KAPP PUTSCH; MUNICH BEER HALL PUTSCH.

PX The committee of the UK CABINET which resolves questions of public expenditure, overall and between departments. Prior to 1997, it was known as **EDX.**

Q

QMV, qualified majority voting *See* MAJORITY.

Questors *See* BUREAU.

quadriad The four bodies – the COUNCIL OF ECONOMIC ADVISERS, the FED, OMB and the TREASURY DEPARTMENT – which dominate US economic policy and keep it under review.

Quai d'Orsay The home beside the Seine in Paris of the French foreign ministry, and of a ruggedly independent foreign policy pursued by governments regardless of political shade. Intriguingly, its occupants include British diplomats on secondment.

quango Quasi-Autonomous National (or Non-) Government Organisation. A body independent from the department that created it, save for the appointment of its members from the ranks of the GREAT AND THE GOOD, and nominally under the control of its Minister, though not fully ACCOUNTABLE to the legislature. The proliferation of quangos in Britain became a political issue in the late 1970s, but the initial THATCHERITE drive to 'cull' unnecessary quangos has not been sustained, though sporadic efforts have been made by Labour and Conservative governments alike to scrap those that have outlived their usefulness.

quarantine Action, preferably international, to isolate an offending nation both economically and politically. In 1937 Franklin D. ROOSEVELT, in a speech that enraged ISOLATIONISTS, called on the world to 'quarantine the aggressors'. He said:

> It seems to be unfortunately true that the epidemic of world lawlessness is spreading. When an epidemic of physical disease is about to spread, the community approves and joins in a quarantine of the patients in order to protect the health of the community against the spread of the disease.

President KENNEDY, citing the charter of the OAS, imposed a naval quarantine on ships carrying military hardware for CUBA during the missile crisis of 1962.

quartet The four founders, and custodians from 2003, of the ROAD MAP for Middle East peace, the United States, the UNITED NATIONS, the EUROPEAN UNION and Russia. After the death of Yasser Arafat and the election of Mahmoud Abbas to succeed him as head of the PALESTINIAN AUTHORITY, they secured through a special summit in London on 1 March 2005 – which Israel refused to attend – agreement on the framework for a Palestinian state.

quasi-judicial The role, especially but not exclusively in British government, of a Minister, official or agency charged with making decisions from which an appeal might be made to the courts, and which consequently inhibits them from comment during the decision-making process.

Quayle, J. Danforth (Dan) Quayle (1947–), VICE PRESIDENT (Republican) 1989–93 and the most lampooned US politician of modern times, entirely as a result of his own utterances. There was even a *Quayle Quarterly*, an ostensibly learned magazine chronicling his performance and dicta, whose closure was announced the moment the BUSH/Quayle ticket was defeated in 1992. Quayle's nomination after serving as a Congressman and Senator for Indiana brought questioning of his ability, and criticism of the man who chose him. William Watson of Morton Grove, Illinois, observed: 'The real proof that George Bush might be a dangerous person is the fact that he selected this privileged airhead as his RUNNING-MATE.' Quayle's ultra-conservatism also sat oddly with his record of having joined the National Guard rather than serve in Vietnam. 'Vietnam', he said, 'is a jungle . . . Kuwait, Iraq, Saudi Arabia you have sand.' He was also criticised for not releasing his school grades, and having entered college on a disadvantaged students' programme despite his family's wealth. But Democrat efforts to embroil him in a sex scandal failed, his wife Marilyn saying: 'Anyone who knows Dan Quayle knows he would rather play golf than have sex any day.'

In the 1988 campaign (*see* Senator, you're no Jack KENNEDY) one television critic wrote that he performed 'like Bambi on ice', and *Time* observed: 'Quayle, who often seems as lost as an actor missing half the pages of his script, struggled to overcome his own THROTTLEBOTTOM image – and lost.' Art Buchwald reckoned: 'Viewers like watching Quayle for the same reason they enjoy watching a train wreck.' And Maureen Dowd commented: 'He treats language like a Lego set, taking a phrase, repeating and building on it, often without regard to meaningful content.' At the close the *Buffalo News* editorialised:

> Dan Quayle is still justly regarded as unfit for presidential duty by a large majority of Americans.

In office, Quayle kept his infelicity with words, with unfortunate results. He termed the HOLOCAUST 'an obscene period in our nation's history', said that America expected El Salvador to 'work toward the elimination of human rights', and said of Alexander Dubček, hero of the PRAGUE SPRING, 'Who would have predicted that Dubček, who brought in the tanks in 1968, is now being proclaimed a hero in Czechoslovakia?' Quayle told Western Samoans: 'You all look like happy campers to me. Happy campers you are, happy campers you have been, and as far as I am concerned, happy campers you always will be.' Of the rise of the former KU KLUX KLAN leader David Duke, he observed: 'Unfortunately, the people of Louisiana are not racists.' And he told one interviewer that 'Republicans understand the importance of bondage between parent and child.' Passing mourners at a funeral, he urged them to 'Have a nice day.' He told one Republican meeting: 'My friends, we can and we will never, never, never surrender to what is right.' On TERM LIMITATION, Quayle declared: 'I support efforts to limit the terms of members of Congress, especially members of the House and members of the Senate.' Seeing the effects of the Oakland freeway earthquake, he observed: 'Well, it looks as if the top part fell on the bottom part.' And to him the GULF WAR was 'a stirring victory for the forces of aggression against lawlessness.' *See also* POTATOE.

Some of Quayle's utterances were downright incomprehensible. He baffled the United Negro College Fund by converting its slogan 'A mind is a terrible thing to waste' into 'What a waste it is to lose one's mind, or not to have a mind is being very wasteful'. He once observed: 'Every once in a while, you let a word or phrase out and you want to catch it and bring it back. You can't do that – it's gone forever.' And trying to explain his remark on the Holocaust, he said: 'We all lived in this century – I didn't live in this century.'

Some opponents underrated him. Sen. Birch Bayh of Indiana, whom Quayle ousted, told his handlers prior to the contest: 'The boy's retarded.' And Quayle also had self-confidence, Roger Simon noting that 'the inability to see your own inadequacies can be a tremendous plus in politics.' Halfway through his term Adam Myerson was reporting: 'In conservative circles there is a feeling that Dan Quayle has been an outstanding vice president.' And Kevin Phillips wrote: 'On the CHICKEN-dinner circuit he has a very strong core of support. Among grassroots conservatives he is more popular than Bush.' Yet there was widespread disquiet that Quayle was 'A heartbeat away from the PRESIDENCY'. The *Chicago Tribune* editorialised that 'a heart flutters, a nation shudders', while Washingtonians joked: 'The six words the world fears most are: 'Dan, I don't feel very well.' Arsenio Hall said dismissively that Quayle had 'the IQ of lunch meat'.

Quayle attracted a plethora of jokes. A writer to the *Los Angeles Times* said of his 'overlord' role in the space programme: 'NASA got where it is by putting monkeys in high places.' One story was that 'he was asked to become a Jehovah's Witness, but said he hadn't seen the accident'. One anonymous gagster said: 'Quizzed about the SOVIET BLOC, Dan said it wasn't as good as Lego.' In California, *Mother Jones* magazine organised a 'pin the tail on Dan Quayle' competition.

He was aware of his reputation, saying frankly: 'I stand by all the misstatements that I've made.' He told reporters: 'I'm my own handler. There's not going to be any more handler stories because I'm the handler . . . I'm Doctor SPIN.' Yet a handler was still needed. Campaigning in a shopping mall in 1992 he said to a woman: 'I'm Dan Quayle. Who are you?' She replied: 'I'm your SECRET SERVICE agent.'

Quebec Act One of the measures passed by the WESTMINSTER Parliament that precipitated American independence. Enacted in 1774 at the urging of Governor Sir Guy Carleton, it strengthened the hand of the French-Canadian upper class, restored

Catholic liberties – thus upsetting Protestant New England – and, more explosively, extended Quebec's boundaries to include the region between the Ohio and the Mississippi. Though Montreal fur traders were still the dominant economic force in this region, its assignment to Quebec was seen as a provocation and a long-term threat to westward expansion by the thirteen American colonies, four of whom already had claims in the area.

Quebec conference The conference, code-named **Quadrant**, held at the Citadel in Quebec from 11–24 August 1943 between ROOSEVELT, CHURCHILL and other allied leaders. Its aim was to discuss preparations for the Allied invasion of Europe, and to review strategy and command.

Quebec resolutions The 72 resolutions agreed at Quebec in 1864 by provincial leaders, which formed the basis of the BRITISH NORTH AMERICA ACT and paved the way for CONFEDERATION.

Vive le Québec libre! (Fr. Long live free Quebec!) *Québec Libre* was the slogan of the SEPARATIST movement seeking independence for French-speaking Quebec from Canada (*see* FLQ; PQ). It was notoriously recited by President DE GAULLE in a speech in Montreal in 1967; the ensuing furore led to the cancellation of the rest of his Canadian tour. De Gaulle explained his outburst as 'an opportunity to make up for France's cowardice' during WORLD WAR II.

Queen. Queen Lil Liliuokalani, the last native ruler of Hawaii, who came to the throne in 1891 but was overthrown two years later by a committee of American businessmen headed by Sanford B. Dole when she insisted on 'Hawaii for the Hawaiians'. President CLEVELAND demanded her restoration and refused to submit a Treaty of ANNEXATION drafted by Dole to the Senate, but Dole proclaimed himself President of Hawaii in 1894. America annexed Hawaii in 1898; it achieved STATEHOOD in 1959.

Queen's or **King's commission** The invitation from the SOVEREIGN to the victor of a UK GENERAL ELECTION, or the chosen successor to an outgoing PRIME MINISTER, to form a government.

Queen's or **King's speech** In the WESTMINSTER and many COMMONWEALTH Parliaments, the address delivered at the opening of a new session detailing the government's legislative programme. It is written for the SOVEREIGN by Ministers. When the Sovereign cannot be present, it is delivered by a representative: at Westminster a senior member of the Royal family, and by the GOVERNOR-GENERAL in Commonwealth countries where the Sovereign is HEAD OF STATE. *See* the CROWN IN PARLIAMENT; GRACIOUS SPEECH.

Queensland strategy. An attempt by a party way behind in the polls to win an election by harping on the likelihood of its opponents winning by a LANDSLIDE, thus reducing the motivation to vote of supporters of the party in front. The tactic was applied successfully by Queensland's NATIONAL PARTY in the 1995 State elections against a LABOR administration that appeared certain of re-election. In the 2001 UK general election, William HAGUE's Conservatives were accused of doing the same; if so, it was spectacularly unsuccessful as Labour was returned with only a fractionally reduced majority. Four years later the Conservative campaign, now overseen by the Australian Lynton Crosby, faced the same accusation, this time in the context of allegedly making disenchanted Labour voters feel it safe to switch to the LIBERAL DEMOCRATS. In the event Labour lost several seats to the LibDems, though the IRAQ WAR, as much as any Tory manoeuvring, was the cause.

Queer Hardie Nickname for the British Labour pioneer (James) **Keir Hardie** (1856–1915). It refers to his eccentricity; on his first day in Parliament in 1900 he arrived in the cloth cap that became his trademark. A former Scots miner and trade unionist, he was a co-founder and chairman of the Independent Labour Party (ILP) and the Labour Representation Committee, which became the LABOUR PARTY in 1906; for the last fifteen years of his life he was MP for Merthyr Tydfil. An ardent pacifist, he died disillusioned with Labour's support for WORLD WAR I.

Quemoy and Matsu Two islets off the Chinese coast which remained in NATIONALIST hands after the Communist victory on the mainland in 1949. They became a flash point in the COLD WAR when in 1954 the Communist Chinese premier, Chou En Lai, pledged himself to oust the Nationalists, and from that September they were shelled repeatedly. Despite a renewed bombardment of Quemoy in 1958 the Communists never attempted to invade; indeed the Nationalist build-up prompted US objections and finally brought an end to America's commitment to the FREE WORLD 'recovering' China. As symbols of Communist ambition, Quemoy and Matsu played a major part in the 1960 DEBATES between KENNEDY and NIXON.

> Those damned little islands. Sometimes I wish they'd sink.
>
> EISENHOWER to Republican leaders, 1956

question A central feature of British Parliamentary life, both in writing and, more theatrically, to Ministers at **Question Time** on the floor of the COMMONS, and now also in Edinburgh (*see* FMQs) and Cardiff. Question Time is allocated an hour each day that the Commons are sitting, except Fridays, with the ritual of PRIME MINISTER's QUESTIONS scheduled for 30 minutes from noon on Wednesdays. The Conservative MP Michael Fallon described Question Time as 'like setting pet mice to work on a toy treadmill'. Question Time (**Question Period** in Ottawa) is also a feature of many COMMONWEALTH Parliaments and, in a limited way, the EUROPEAN PARLIAMENT.

Question! Shouted to a questioner by unsympathetic legislators or members of an audience, to encourage him or her to get to the point.

Questions of Procedure for Ministers The forerunner of the MINISTERIAL CODE, the 44-page 'Bible' on the conduct of government which the CABINET SECRETARY traditionally circulated to all newly-appointed Ministers in WHITEHALL. Until John MAJOR made the contents public in 1992, it was treated as confidential. Unlike the code which puts Ministerial ethics in a wider context, it left the distinct impression that Ministers were there for the benefit of the Civil Service MANDARINS.

Business Questions The session every Thursday when the LEADER OF THE HOUSE takes questions on the following week's business, allowing MPs to raise almost any matter of their choice.

cash for questions *See* CASH.

first order questions On days when more than one Department's questions are to be answered orally, those questions addressed to the first Ministerial team to come to the Despatch Box.

open question The standard backbenchers' question asking the Prime Minister to list his or her engagements for the day, as a prelude for raising the issue on their mind; until 1998 the question was asked and responded to in full; now this exchange is taken as read and the Member rises to make their point immediately.

oral question A question asked and responded to in the House of Commons CHAMBER; those listed on the order paper and not reached are answered in writing.

planted question A question which Ministers arrange to have asked so that they can place a particular item of information on the record, make an announcement or score a political point. Originally tabled with a degree of subterfuge, they earned respectability from 2003 when they were recast as **Written Ministerial Statements**.

Prime Minister's Questions The highlight of the week at WESTMINSTER, when the Prime Minister and LEADER OF THE OPPOSITION cross swords, their two sets of exchanges interspersed with hostile, sycophantic and straightforward questions from BACKBENCH MPs and one round of sparring with the leader of the LIBERAL DEMOCRATS. Until 1997 PMQs were allocated fifteen minutes every Tuesday and Thursday afternoon; since 21 May 1997 there has been one 30-minute session, at noon on Wednesdays. PMQs, broadcast live on radio since the 1970s and on television since 1990, are at their best high political theatre, with PUNDITS assessing which of the three party leaders has come out on top. William HAGUE observed of his jousts with Tony BLAIR: 'It's a bit like when you are driving along a country lane and you see a rabbit caught in the headlights. If it's a rabbit, of course, you stop.' After watching PMQs on C-SPAN, George BUSH Snr said: 'I count my blessings for the fact that I don't have to go into that pit that John MAJOR stands in, nose-to-nose with the Opposition, all yelling at each other.' However, the Tennessee Congressman Jim Cooper asked: 'Why can't *we* do this?'

Private Notice Question *See* Urgent Notice QUESTION.

putting the question The action of the CHAIR in calling a vote.

rhetorical question *See* RHETORICAL.

Roman Question *See* LATERAN TREATY.

supplementary question *See* SUPPLEMENTARY.

the question is . . . At WESTMINSTER, the way the SPEAKER puts a MOTION to the VOTE. Having set out its terms, he adds: '**As many as are of that opinion say "Aye".**'

Urgent Notice Question At WESTMINSTER, a question on a matter of urgency tabled either by an OPPOSITION frontbencher or by a member on either side of the House with a direct interest, e.g. by a member whose constituents have been lost in a fishing disaster. If the SPEAKER grants the application, the member rises after QUESTION TIME to elicit a reply from the Minister responsible, who makes a statement on the matter in hand. A period of questioning from MPs on both sides follows. Until the procedural modernisation during the 1997 Parliament, such a question was known as a **Private Notice Question**, or **PNQ**. Older members still speak of '**having a PNQ running**', when the application for an urgent question has been lodged and it is not yet known whether the Speaker will accept it.

written question Unglamorous, but a staple of Parliamentary and political life, the scores, often hundreds, of questions put on the ORDER PAPER each day by MPs (and a few peers) to elicit information, garner material for speeches or political campaigning or to secure ammunition. Most are answered a few days later, with a **holding reply** sent if the facts cannot immediately be ascertained; since 2003 it has been possible to table questions and receive replies to them during a Parliamentary RECESS. The wording of all questions has to be cleared with the TABLE OFFICE.

See also IRISH QUESTION, SCHLESWIG-HOLSTEIN QUESTION, WEST LOTHIAN QUESTION.

quiet. Quiet, calm deliberation/ Disentangles every knot The couplet from a song by W. S. Gilbert which Harold MACMILLAN hung as a motto in his private office.

quiet man The description of himself that Iain Duncan Smith (*see* IDS) used in his party conference speech at Bournemouth on 11 October 2002 to underline his strength of conviction and determination for the Conservatives to succeed. It was designed to evoke memories of the quiet strength of John Wayne in the 1952 Oscar-winning film of the same title; little over a year later he was ousted. Duncan Smith said:

> Those who do not know me yet will come to understand this: when I say a thing, I mean it. When I set myself a task, I do it. When I settle on a course, I stick to it. Do not underestimate the determination of a quiet man.

Quiet Revolution The transformation wrought in Quebec from 1960 by the provincial LIBERAL government of Jean Lesage, which both curbed Anglophone cultural domination and tackled the corruption and archaism of traditional Francophone politics and society. The party held office until 1966, when it was ousted by the Union Nationale; after its defeat René Levesque, having failed to move it to a more nationalist position, resigned and founded the PQ.

Quinquennial Act The popular term for the provision of the 1911 PARLIAMENT ACT that reduced the life of a Parliament (the TERM of a government) at WESTMINSTER from a maximum of seven years to five.

quisling A traitor or puppet COLLABORATOR, named after **Vidkun Quisling** (1887–1945), the former Norwegian Defence Minister who founded a tiny NAZI party and declared himself Prime Minister when the Germans invaded. Berlin recognised him and he sent over 1000 Jews to CONCENTRATION CAMPS. He was shot for treason, theft and murder after liberated Norway specially reinstituted the death penalty. The term became current within days of Quisling seizing power, Ed Murrow saying on CBS radio: 'I don't think there were many quislings in the Norwegian Army or Navy.' In December 1941 CHURCHILL spoke of 'a vile race of quislings – to use the new word which will carry the scorn of mankind down the centuries'.

quorum The number of members of a LEGISLATURE or committee who must be present for its proceedings to be valid. At WESTMINSTER, the quorum for the HOUSE OF COMMONS is 40 – but 100 are needed for the CLOSURE if a vote is to be taken. In the US SENATE or HOUSE OF REPRESENTATIVES, a quorum is a majority of the membership; for the COMMITTEE OF THE WHOLE, it is 100. In the SUPREME COURT, six justices constitute a quorum.

quorum call In the US CONGRESS, the summons to legislators – by bell – to raise a quorum or ascertain if one is present.

> *Guest*: I thought I heard a quorum call.
> *Anon. Senator*: No doubt you did. This is their mating season.

quorum count In the US CONGRESS, the process of confirming whether a quorum is present.

disappearing quorum A delaying tactic used by Congressmen from the 1860s; though present, they would avoid voting. The practice was stamped out by the newly-elected Speaker Thomas REED in 1890.

quota A numerical or proportional limit imposed in trade, immigration, employment, etc. to prevent a particular competing nation or ethnic group strengthening its position or becoming over-represented (*see* POSITIVE DISCRIMINATION). Also, the shares subscribed by individual member nations to the IMF.

quote slut A delightfully frank US political insiders' term for an expert who, if primed in advance, will be ready to give an apparently independent endorsement of a government, party or politician's views or actions should anyone from the media happen to call them.

If you are about to stage a major event, there's nothing that can help you more than to anticipate who the media is going to call to comment on it, and get there first. You call a guy and say: 'Look, I just wanted to let you know what's coming down the pike. We're going to do this today. This is the reason for doing it.' That person is flattered. They are a group of people we call Quote Sluts.

JAMES CARVILLE, *All's Fair*

R

R In Britain and in COMMONWEALTH countries acknowledging the monarchy, the signature of the SOVEREIGN, an abbreviation of the Latin *Rex* (King) or *Regina* (Queen), as in 'Elizabeth R'. Also, the monarch's legal person as representing the civil power; *R v Smith* is the equivalent of *The People v John Doe.*

R-word The polite word for RECESSION, used ironically by politicians in both Britain and America in the late 1980s when the economy was heading into recession and neither the BUSH administration nor the THATCHER government was prepared to admit it.

Rab The nickname of the British Conservative politician **R**(ichard) **A**(usten) **Butler** (1902–82), later Lord Butler of Saffron Walden, formed from his initials. Harold WILSON is said to have regarded him as 'the best Prime Minister we never had'. He served before and into WORLD WAR II as a Foreign Office minister; Harold MACMILLAN branded him 'the most clinging of the MUNICHites'. He masterminded the BUTLER EDUCATION ACT, then after the Tory rout of 1945 brought together **Rab's Boys**, bright young Tories who reshaped Conservative social and economic policy. They were mostly, like Iain Macleod, Reginald Maudling and Enoch POWELL, members of the Conservative research department or the party's industrial policy committee; Butler headed both. They are credited with changing Tory attitudes to the WELFARE STATE, NATIONALISATION and unemployment, and of instituting the CONSENSUS POLITICS which lasted until Margaret THATCHER became leader. In 1962 David FROST said of Butler:

> Let us never forget that after the last war it was Mr Butler who transformed the Conservative Party into the fresh, liberal, lively, progressive, radical force it was after the last war.

As Chancellor from 1951, Butler pursued the middle way known as BUTSKELLISM; he went on to hold a wide range of senior posts until 1963, from CHURCHILL's retirement in 1955 being seen as heir to the leadership. Yet he fell short, lacking the killer touch when first EDEN (*see* WAB OR HAWOLD) and then Macmillan retired. When Macmillan succeeded Eden, Butler said: 'I couldn't understand why, when I had done a most wonderful job picking up the pieces after SUEZ, they then chose Harold.' Nigel Nicolson felt Butler had lost out by having no clear view on Suez, and Alistair Horne wrote: 'As the absent Eden's deputy he was in the unhappy position of having to answer, officially, to all the accumulated anger in the party in the aftermath of Suez.' Butler consoled himself with the thought that 'it's not every man who nearly becomes Prime Minister of England', and that

> If you're not made Pope, you can still be a perfectly good Cardinal Archbishop of Milan.

When Macmillan was taken ill in 1963 Butler was again wrong-footed, with the MAGIC CIRCLE choosing Lord Home (*see* SIR ALEC); Butler left politics to become Master of Trinity College, Cambridge. His Cabinet colleague Anthony Head remarked: 'If Rab had been more forceful he could have been Prime Minister, but there was an ambivalence in him all the way.' And Macmillan observed: 'He had the ambition but not the will, like saying it would be nice to be Archbishop of Canterbury.'

> He lacked the dash, the vulgarity, the smoking-room popularity . . . Like oysters and gulls' eggs, he was an acquired taste. CHRIS PATTEN

> I think the Prime Minister has to be a butcher, and know the joints. That is perhaps where I have not been quite competent, in knowing the ways you can cut up a carcass. R. A. BUTLER

Rab's law Butler's one consistent rule was 'Never resign'. He had seen too many Ministers do it as a mark of protest in the hope of winning their point, then sink without trace.

race (1) Colloquial, mainly US, term for an electoral contest, e.g. 'the race for the White House', 'the gubernatorial race'. (2) The biological, tribal or (to a lesser extent) national groups into which humankind is divided, thus the most obvious determinant between people, a cause of prejudice and an explosive issue in politics.

> I am in favour of the race to which I belong having the superior position.
>
> ABRAHAM LINCOLN

> All those who are not racially pure are mere chaff.
>
> ADOLF HITLER

race categories The ethnic categories used by the US Equal Employment Opportunity Commission for reporting purposes: **white, not of Hispanic** origin; **black, not of Hispanic** origin; **Hispanic**; **American Indian or Alaskan** native; or **Asian or Pacific** islander. The SUPREME COURT has also specified that Jews and Americans of Arab origin may bring charges of racial discrimination.

race relations industry A pejorative for the network of committees, QUANGOS and agencies set up to assure ethnic minorities of their rights, which critics see as provocative, wasteful and self-perpetuating and having little relevance to those actually being discriminated against.

race track *See* MX.

playing the race card Injecting race as an issue into an ELECTION, often by subliminal or indirect means.

racialism A mainly British term, dating from the early 20th century, for the support for, or practice of, DISCRIMINATION and SEGREGATION between the races, instigated by the dominant group as a matter of policy. It is not quite the same as, though it has largely been supplanted by

racism Belief in the genetic superiority of a particular race (invariably one's own), and the display and exercise of prejudice against another, or all other, racial groups. Although that prejudice has always existed, it was elevated in the 19th century into a pseudo-science, based on the writings of the Comte de Gobineau, whose *Essay on the Inequality of the Human Races* was published in 1853. Racism was a driving force of the NAZIS, then in the 1950s and '60s became an issue in US politics. **Anti-racism** has become a rallying-point not just for the hard LEFT but for a broad spread of political groups. *See* ANTI-SEMITISM; ANTI-NAZI LEAGUE; APARTHEID; BLACK; COLOUR BAR; KU KLUX KLAN; LYNCHING; POWELL; RIVERS OF BLOOD.

institutional racism *See* MACPHERSON REPORT.

Rachmanism Bullying and extortionate behaviour toward tenants by a private landlord. From the activities of Peter Rachman (1920–62), a Polish immigrant to Britain whose undesirable activities in the Paddington area came to light during the PROFUMO AFFAIR and prompted political pressure for new safeguards for private tenants. Despite these, some landlords continue to prosper by terrorising those who rent from them.

radical, radicalism An adherent of, or the pursuit of, bold and fundamental policies for change within the democratic system, with the inference that nothing is sacrosanct. From the Latin *radix*, root. It originated in Britain with the late 18th-century reform movement within the WHIG party, before long becoming a pejorative; in 1819 Sir Walter Scott wrote: 'Radicalism is a word in very bad odour here, being used to denote a set of blackguards.' One group in America who gained the name were those Republicans who opposed President Andrew Johnson over Reconstruction. The term was traditionally applied to the LEFT ('a person whose left hand doesn't know what their other left hand is doing' – Bernard Rosenberg), and to UNAMERICANISM ('There is a foreign atmosphere about him, the stamp of an alien radical, a strong resemblance to the type ANARCHIST as portrayed, bomb in hand, in newspaper cartoons' – Eugene O'Neill). Radicals were seen by critics as woolly-minded ('a radical is a man with both feet planted firmly in the air' – FDR) and fractious ('two deputies, one of whom is a Radical, have more in common than two Radicals, one of whom is a DEPUTY', Robert de Jouvenel wrote of Radicals in France). Since the mid-1970s radicalism has been largely the province of the RIGHT as THATCHERISM, REAGANOMICS and, most recently in America, NEO-CONSERVATISM have taken hold, with the term radical right denoting a range of free-MARKET, LIBERTARIAN philosophies.

> Only radicals have accomplished anything in a great crisis.
>
> JAMES GARFIELD, *Diary*, 16 December 1876

radicalise To encourage or provoke a body of people into adopting a radical set of policies or course of action that would otherwise not have occurred to them.

radical chic Trendiness in adoption of good causes, literature and fashion dictated by (left-wing) radicalism (*see also* POLITICAL CORRECTNESS). The expression was coined by the US journalist and writer Tom Wolfe (1931–) to describe the late 1960s fad among members of high society for Marxism and sympathy with revolutionaries.

Radical Jack The nickname of John Lambton, first Earl of Durham (1792–1840), who played a leading part in the passage of the 1832 REFORM ACT and subsequently produced the DURHAM REPORT on the future of Canada.

Radio Doctor Dr Charles Hill, later Lord Hill of Luton (1904–89), who in WORLD WAR II became a celebrity in Britain by broadcasting as the BBC's 'Radio Doctor'. His common touch gave him an audience of over 14 million, making him 'the doctor with the greatest number of patients in the world'. He was secretary of the British Medical Association from 1944 to 1950, spanning the introduction of the NHS, which it opposed, and then a key figure in the Conservatives' near-successful 1950 campaign. He later became Minister of Health, and chairman successively of the Independent Television Authority and the BBC.

Radio Priest Fr Charles E. Coughlin, a broadcast sermoniser from Michigan who originally supported the NEW DEAL but broke with FDR to become a virulent opponent of his 'communistic' ADMINISTRATION and of Wall Street. In 1936 his Society for Social Justice backed the Union Party challenge of the Republican Rep. William Lemke (*see* LIBERTY BILL). In a speech in Cleveland that July, Coughlin ripped off his clerical collar and denounced 'Franklin Double-Crossing Roosevelt' as a liar and a 'betrayer'. The Union Party polled fewer than 900,000 votes as Roosevelt won by a LANDSLIDE.

Ragged Trousered Philanthropists, The The novel by Robert Tressell, written c. 1906, which became one of the basic texts of Britain's LABOUR and trade union movement. It described evocatively the hard lives of a group of tradesmen renovating a house for its absentee owner; three years before its publication in 1914 Tressell, an Anglo-Irish house painter, died in Liverpool from tuberculosis aged 40.

Ragin' Cajun The nickname of James Carville, Bill CLINTON's chief strategist in his successful Presidential CAMPAIGNs of 1992 and 1996, reflecting both his bombastic nature and his Louisiana origins. Remarkably he married Mary Matalin, his near-counterpart in the 1992 campaign of George BUSH Snr, whom Clinton ousted from the WHITE HOUSE. He said of that victory: 'We didn't find the key to the electoral lock. We just picked it.' *See also* BOILER ROOM; It's the ECONOMY, STUPID.

If your opponent is drowning, throw the SoB an anvil. JAMES CARVILLE

CLINTON (when criticised for offering his wife a government job): Heck, if I wasn't married to Hillary she'd be first in line for any of these appointments.
CARVILLE: Heck, if you weren't married to Hillary you wouldn't be making any of these appointments.

rail-splitter The ultimate accolade for a US politician as a homespun outdoor type, originating in Abraham LINCOLN's successful campaign for the 1860 Republican nomination. His cousin John Hanks brought to a meeting in Illinois 'two [fencing] rails from a lot made by Abraham Lincoln and John Hanks in the Sangamon Bottom in the year 1830.' Lincoln said he could not remember splitting those rails, but he was sure he had split rails every bit as good. Soon his son Tad would say: 'Everyone in this world knows Pa used to split rails.' Lincoln's opponent Stephen Douglas argued that 'we want a statesman, not a rail-splitter, for president', but battalions of rail-splitters were marching for Lincoln. Candidates ever since have been pictured with an axe and timber to make the connection (*see* LOG CABIN TO WHITE HOUSE), but EISENHOWER said of his Democratic opponent Adlai STEVENSON: 'He's no rail-splitter – just a hair-splitter'.

Railtrack The flagship of the PRIVATISATION of Britain's railways by John MAJOR's Conservative government, the company set up to maintain and upgrade the railway infrastructure which was floated on the Stock Exchange in 1995 only to implode six years later. After an initially profitable start which saw the share price soar, a series of high-profile train crashes caused by poor maintenance and managerial inertia generated public alarm and political controversy. The company incurred heavy cost overruns on modernising the West Coast Main Line and began to withdraw from other projects on financial grounds. In October 2001, to the fury of investors, Transport Secretary Stephen Byers invoked a provision of the 1993 Railways Act and put it in administrators pending the formation of a not-for-profit body to take over Railtrack's functions. This body, known as **Network Rail**, took over in October 2002, but only after Byers had first had to retract his initial statement that the government would pay no compensation to the shareholders and then been forced to resign after it emerged that he had told safety campaigners some weeks beforehand that Railtrack's days were numbered. As this book went to press a lawsuit by some Railtrack shareholders accusing Byers of 'malfeasance in public office' and engineering the collapse of Railtrack was before the High Court. Byers told it:

> I did not abuse my position. I did not act unlawfully. I put the public interest first throughout.

However Byers also admitted he had not told the truth to a Commons committee about how long administration had been under consideration.

rainbow. Rainbow Coalition The coalition of ethnic and liberal forces and the socially disadvantaged, put together by the Rev. Jesse JACKSON in pursuit of his CAMPAIGN for the Democratic presidential nomination in 1984 and 1988.

> Our flag is red, white and blue, but our nation is a rainbow – red, yellow, brown, black and white – and we are all precious in God's sight . . . America is not like a blanket – one piece of unbroken cloth, the same colour, the same texture, the same size. America is more like a quilt – many patches, many pieces, many colours, many sizes; all woven and held together by a common thread.
>
> JESSE JACKSON

Rainbow Nation The ethos of multiracial South Africa as it has evolved since the end of APARTHEID and the election of Nelson MANDELA as STATE PRESIDENT in 1994. It is reflected in South Africa's new, multi-coloured flag, devised by Thabo Mbeki, Mandela's successor as President, at the birth of the post-apartheid state.

Rainbow Warrior The flagship of GREENPEACE, sailed by activists to impede whalers and marine dumpers, and into NUCLEAR test zones – or more correctly a series of such vessels. One *Rainbow Warrior* became the subject of a diplomatic incident and worldwide protests in 1985 when French agents sank it in Auckland harbour, with the loss of one life, to prevent Greenpeace protesting against French (underground) nuclear tests at MUROROA ATOLL in the South Pacific. The agents, Alain Mafart and Dominique Prieur, were imprisoned in New Zealand but soon handed over to the French authorities after pressure from Paris; an undertaking that they would be kept in detention was not adhered to. On the tenth anniversary of the sinking, 10 July 1995, French commandos stormed the successor craft off Muroroa.

National Rainbow Coalition *See* KANU.

rainmaker Political fixer – lawyer, PR person or LOBBYIST – who can make things happen for their clients. The term originates with the Native Americans who would call in a rainmaker to perform the rituals that would break a drought. Its political use dates back to 1968 when David Hoffman of the *Washington Post* used it for the former JOHNSON administration aides who had helped their clients secure lucrative trans-Pacific air routes.

> Rain-making is a situation where an individual who is trying to obtain a favour for a client does things that for the record never happened.
>
> Former Attorney-General JOHN MITCHELL during his first WATERGATE trial, 1974

raison d'état (Fr. reason of state) The justification for any action, no matter how unethical, on the grounds that the interests (and maybe the survival) of the state require it.

rally A large set-piece political meeting to which the like-minded are brought from a distance to hail their leaders or demonstrate support for a particular cause. The word has a positive cast, in contrast to DEMONSTRATION, which implies opposition to something.

Ramsay Mac The nickname for J. Ramsay MACDONALD, Britain's first LABOUR Prime Minister. When he formed the NATIONAL GOVERNMENT (*see* GREAT BETRAYAL) in 1931, Labour loyalists sang:

> We'll hang Ramsay Mac on a sour apple tree,
> We'll hang Snowden and Thomas to keep him company,
> For that's the place where traitors ought to be.

Ramseyer rule In the US CONGRESS, the requirement that a Committee of the House REPORTing a BILL must list all changes it would require in the existing law, and the text of laws being repealed. The SENATE equivalent is the CORDON RULE.

RAND Corporation The first scientific THINK-TANK which, though mainly composed of economists, became the leading source of advice on COLD WAR strategy and has maintained its reputation since. It was formed at the end of WORLD WAR II as the US Air Force's PROPAGANDA agency under the guise of a scientific institute, initially as an adjunct to the Douglas Aircraft Company in

Santa Monica, California. The name was a composite of 'R and D' (Research and Development). Its ability to THINK THE UNTHINKABLE, a role which has partly gravitated to DARPA, generated such chilling concepts as MUTUALLY ASSURED DESTRUCTION. RAND specialised in computerised war games; when asked in 1968 when America would win in Vietnam, the computer answered: 1964.

rank and file The ordinary membership of a movement or organisation, as opposed to its leaders. Leaders of minority groups within an organisation usually claim to represent it.

ranking member The senior member of a Congressional committee from the minority party. The word 'ranking' dates back at least to the CIVIL WAR, when it was used for the most senior member of a military unit.

Rapacki plan A proposal put forward in 1957 by Adam Rapacki, Poland's Communist foreign minister, for NUCLEAR disengagement in central Europe and cuts in conventional forces by both NATO and the WARSAW PACT.

Rapallo treaties Two treaties signed after WORLD WAR I at Rapallo, a coastal resort in north-west Italy. Under the first, in November 1920, Italy renounced its claim to Dalmatia, the independence of Fiume (Rijeka) was acknowledged, and the rights of Italians and Yugoslavs in each other's territories were established. The second, signed on 16 August 1922 by the German and Soviet foreign ministers, brought the immediate resumption of DIPLOMATIC RELATIONS between the two countries and enabled Germany to develop secretly on Soviet territory weapons banned under the Treaty of VERSAILLES.

rapid. rapid deployment force A small, lightly serviced and easily-transportable force capable of being sent into action in any theatre at short notice should the situation require it. The prototype was the one designed for emergencies in the Middle East which America developed after the failed attempt to rescue the HOSTAGES from Tehran in 1980.

rapid reaction force The force created by European members of NATO after the end of the COLD WAR to deal primarily with OUT-OF-AREA threats.

rapporteur In committees of the EUROPEAN PARLIAMENT, the member chosen to analyse the proposal under discussion and prepare a draft report on it for the committee to consider. If approved, the draft becomes a public document and the *rapporteur* joins in negotiations within the Parliament on its ultimate adoption.

rat As an insult: US Interior Secretary Harold Ickes described Governor Eugene Talmadge of Georgia (*see* HIS CHAIN-GANG EXCELLENCY) as looking 'more like a rat than any other human being I know; [with] all the mean, poisonous and treacherous characteristics of that rodent.'

to rat To desert one's party or cause, like a rat leaving a sinking ship; one **rats on** one's colleagues. First used in 1792 by the Earl of Malmesbury, it is recorded in America in 1800. CHURCHILL, who left the Conservatives for the Liberals, then rejoined the Tories, said on making his second move: 'Anyone can rat, but it takes a certain amount of ingenuity to re-rat.' This did not deter him from saying when a war hero joined the Liberals in 1948 to contest a seat for them: 'It's the first time I heard of a rat swimming out to join a sinking ship.'

ratfucking Distasteful stunts to sabotage an opponent's campaign, such as bugging offices, forging and stealing correspondence, cancelling or disrupting rallies, or ordering delivery of vast quantities of unwanted food, ready-mixed concrete or manure. Popularised in the late 1950s as a student prank in California, it became a household word as WATERGATE unfolded. Donald H. Segretti, a University of California graduate, had used these tactics from the WHITE HOUSE to organise the collapse of Democratic challengers' CAMPAIGNs prior to the 1972 election so that Richard NIXON would face the least electable Democrat, George McGovern. His actions ranged from sending unordered pizzas to Muskie headquarters to circulating letters falsely asserting that Sen. Henry (SCOOP) Jackson was a homosexual and that Sen. Hubert HUMPHREY had been involved with a call girl.

ratchet effect The gradual but relentless shifting of political and economic assumptions from left to right, or *vice versa*, despite successive changes of government. The phrase is often conjured up to highlight the inadequacies of the opposition in resisting such a process.

> Britain is no longer in the politics of the pendulum, but of the ratchet.
>
> MARGARET THATCHER, 1977

rates The form of local taxation in Britain, based on notional rental values for property, which aroused widespread discontent among householders and businessmen until replaced by the POLL TAX. Each local authority fixed its own rate at so much in the pound. The even greater controversy aroused by the poll tax led Labour to promise a return to a system of 'fair rates' if it won the 1992 election, but in government from 1997 it stuck with the COUNCIL TAX, though holding a fresh review of the options in 2004 when that tax too became unpopular. Business continued to pay a modified but standardised version of the rates, the **Uniform Business Rate**.

ratepayers Those liable for payment of rates – less than half the electorate – who, particularly under LABOUR councils, considered they were subsidising extravagance toward voters who made no contribution. In some towns and cities they organised to contest local elections and serve on the council, usually as an alternative to or in alliance with the Conservatives.

Rate Support Grant The block grant paid by central government toward the cost of local services, to keep down the level of domestic rates. With the end of the rates it was renamed the **Revenue Support Grant**.

ratification The process under which the LEGISLATURE or ELECTORATE of a state endorses the action of its government in concluding a TREATY with another power or powers. In America, treaties negotiated by the President require a two-thirds majority of the SENATE; the PANAMA CANAL TREATIES just overcame the hurdle, the Treaty of VERSAILLES and the SALT II treaty did not. The term also applies to the role of the STATES in approving AMENDMENTS to the CONSTITUTION; three-quarters have to ratify an amendment for it to take effect. In Britain, treaties are confirmed by Act of Parliament, as with the MAASTRICHT TREATY, or by ORDER. In the Irish Republic, the nation itself ratifies treaties affecting the Constitution in a REFERENDUM.

rattlesnake A common term of US political abuse, with undertones of guile and readiness to strike back. In 1975 the Missouri Democrat Rep. Richard Bolling said of the 81-year-old Texas Democrat Wright Patman:

> The old man has always been a rattlesnake, and now he's senile.

Ravenscraig The steelworks at Motherwell, south of Glasgow, the forlorn fight against closure of which became a rallying-point for advocates of a self-contained Scottish economy and opponents of the rundown of its heavy industries. Steelmaking at the plant finally ceased in June 1992 after a battle lasting more than six years. British Steel chairman Sir Robert 'Black Bob' Scholey and the Conservative government were cast as the villains of the piece; Ministers were privately dismayed with the way the company brought the closure about, but argued that with the evaporation of the markets Ravenscraig had been built with grants from the MACMILLAN government to serve, its retention could not be justified despite record productivity.

Rawhide The codename allocated by the US SECRET SERVICE to President REAGAN, reflecting his career in films and his desire to be seen as a latter-day Wild West figure.

Rayburn Building The second office block to be built for the US HOUSE OF REPRESENTATIVES as space in the CAPITOL was exhausted. Opened in 1965, it commemorated **Samuel Taliaferro Rayburn** (1882–1961; *see* MR. SAM), longest serving SPEAKER of the House (21 years). Costing $122 million even at 1960s prices and built in a style known as 'Mussolini Modern' or 'Texas Penitentiary', it measures 720ft by 450. It contains 25 elevators, 23 escalators, garage space for 1600 cars, a swimming pool, a gymnasium and several overnight rooms.

> A national disaster. Its defects range from profligate waste of 50 acres of space to elephantine aesthetic brutality at record costs. It is quite possible that this is the worst building for the most money in the history of the construction art. It stuns by sheer mass and boring bulk.
>
> ADA LOUISE HUXTABLE

Rayner scrutiny The detailed efficiency reviews conducted on selected programmes throughout WHITEHALL by Sir Derek (later Lord) Rayner, Margaret THATCHER's efficiency adviser from 1979 to 1983. Rayner, a senior executive at Marks & Spencer who had worked on defence procurement for Edward HEATH, was a committed Thatcherite who aimed to 'travel light and dig deep' in searching for economies. He told his scrutineers to 'look for bad news only' and come up with a solution within 90 days. By the time he left, five waves of scrutinies involving 155 agencies, programmes and tasks had identified potential savings of £421 million a year – about half of which were made. The reviews tailed off after Rayner returned to Marks, but he left a legacy in the FINANCIAL MANAGEMENT INITIATIVE and, eventually, the NEXT STEPS agencies.

razor gang An originally Australian term for a group of senior members of a government who get together to detect and ruthlessly enforce savings in expenditure. It was first used of a group of ministers in Malcolm Fraser's government, headed by John Howard.

reactionary A CONSERVATIVE who not only opposes progress but longs for, and is anxious to return to, the ways of the past. The word is also an adjective; TITO wrote:

> Any movement in history which attempts to perpetuate itself becomes reactionary.

read. read into the record In the US CONGRESS, to seek to have written into the CONGRESSIONAL RECORD a speech, article or other text of which a member strongly approves, or whose publication will boost their prospects of re-election.

Read my lips. No new taxes The phrase used by George BUSH Snr in his ACCEPTANCE speech to the Republican CONVENTION on 19 August 1988 which played a major part in his defeat of Michael Dukakis, but came back to haunt him two years later when taxes were indeed raised. Promising to resist Congressional pressure to raise taxes, Bush said:

> I'll say no, and they'll push and I'll say no, and they'll push again, and I'll say to them: 'Read my lips. No new taxes.'

The expression 'Read my lips' dates back at least to 1978, when the British rock artist Tim Curry used it as an album title. It carries the inference that the speaker thinks the listener to be stupid, and unable to grasp the meaning of simple words. Bush amended it to 'read my hips' when asked major political questions while out jogging.

reading The name given to each stage of the progress of a BILL through a LEGISLATURE. At WESTMINSTER the FIRST READING is a formality when a Bill is presented; the SECOND READING debate is on the principle of the measure, the THIRD READING gives approval for the Bill as amended in committee and at REPORT STAGE. In the US CONGRESS, the procedure is essentially the same; the First Reading is deemed to have taken place once it has been introduced and printed in the CONGRESSIONAL RECORD.

Reading system The basis for the KNOCKING-UP system used by Britain's LABOUR PARTY, its name taken from the Berkshire constituency of Ian Mikardo (*see* MIK) where it was pioneered in the early 1950s. Now somewhat overtaken by more technological methods, it involves a pad of lined sheets on which party supporters in a street are listed, similar to the Conservatives' NCR system except that carbon paper was initially used; the Liberal Democrats' pads are known as **Shuttleworths**. As each team of helpers is sent out on election night, it is given a sheet from the pad, with the names of those already recorded by the TELLERS as having voted crossed out.

Reagan, Ronald Wilson (1911–2004) The rangy, personable former B-movie actor who became Governor of California and at the age of 69 was elected 40th President of the United States; his two terms in the WHITE HOUSE (1981–89) were marked by radical CONSERVATISM and FEELGOOD politics, and are looked back on by Republicans as a golden age. From a poor Irish family in Illinois, Reagan became a radio sportscaster after graduating from college, and in 1937 signed with Warner Brothers, going on to make 54 films (*see* the GIPPER). Initially a liberal Democrat and supporter of the NEW DEAL, Reagan was president of the Screen Actors' Guild from 1947 to 1952, standing out against the worst excesses of MCCARTHYISM. J. K. Galbraith recalled: 'I once started a trade union with Ronald Reagan. He was quite a lot to the left of me then. A real firebrand.' But he began to shift after marrying his second wife Nancy (his first was his fellow film star Jane Wyman); as his career branched into television, he declared himself a Republican in 1962, worked for the party's 1964 campaign, and was elected Governor of California two years later. At the start of the campaign Jack L. Warner said incredulously: 'No, Jimmy Stewart for Governor, Reagan for best friend.' Though both he and his opponents later depicted his tenure of the statehouse as rigidly conservative, it was in fact relatively mild. He flirted with a challenge for the Presidency in 1968, then built support on the conservative wing of the Republican Party which in 1976 enabled him to run President FORD close for the nomination. Four years later he was an obvious choice, and after defeating George BUSH Snr for the nomination, he routed Jimmy CARTER, whose campaign was dogged by the HOSTAGE CRISIS and high INFLATION.

At his INAUGURATION, Reagan pledged to 'restore the great, confident roar of American progress and growth and optimism.' He hit the ground running with a dramatic programme of REAGANOMICS: tax and spending cuts, coupled with a military build-up; these and other initiatives were backed initially by a majority of both HOUSES of CONGRESS. Reagan's combination of tough talk towards America's enemies, his inference that everything was now under control but anything wrong in WASHINGTON was nothing to do with him, and his canny ability to touch the public mood – even over a disaster like the BEIRUT AIRPORT BOMBING – made him immensely popular. That popularity touched a record high after the attempt on his life in Washington on 30 March 1981. Seriously wounded, he told the surgeons: 'Please assure me that you are all Republicans', and said to Nancy: 'Honey, I forgot to duck.' When his aide Lyn Nofziger told him: 'Everything in Washington is working normally,' Reagan replied: 'What makes you think I'd be happy about that?' Reagan's greatest attribute was to make the Presidency look easy, instead of the treadmill it had been for his predecessor. Simon Hoggart described him as 'the first man for 20 years to make the Presidency a part-time job, a means of filling up a few of the otherwise blank days of retirement.' He himself said: 'They say hard work never hurt anybody, but I figure why take the chance?' and observed: 'Over there in the White House there's a fellow that puts a piece of paper on my desk every day that tells me what I'm going to be doing every 15 minutes. He's the most powerful man in the world.' And well into his second term he quipped: 'The last few weeks have been really hectic, what with Libya, Nicaragua, the Budget and taxes. I've really been burning the midday oil.' And after one crisis he joked: 'I've laid down the law to everyone from now on about everything that happens no matter what time it is, wake me – even if it's in the middle of a Cabinet.' The Reagans restored the pomp of the WHITE HOUSE which had been banished by the Carters, adding a touch of showbiz glitter. Hedrick Smith wrote: 'He rekindled the ceremonial magic of the presidency,' but Gore Vidal remarked: 'There's a lot to be said for being *nouveau riche*, and the Reagans mean to say it all.' Nancy was credited with considerable influence, but Reagan said: 'The idea that she's involved in government decisions . . . and being some kind of dragon lady, there is nothing to that.' Yet she could freeze out a White House staffer she disliked; when she and CHIEF OF STAFF Don Regan were at loggerheads, Reagan joked: 'Nancy and Don tried to patch things up. They met privately over lunch, just the two of them and their food tasters.' Intellectuals resented his popular touch, bemoaning his lack of interest in culture; Jonathan Hunt joked: 'In a disastrous fire in President Reagan's library both books were destroyed. And the real tragedy was that he hadn't finished colouring one.' Political observers were more worried by an imprecision which would cost him dear in the IRAN-CONTRA scandal. James David Barber called him 'the first modern President whose contempt for the facts is treated as a charming idiosyncrasy', while House Majority Leader Jim Wright observed:

> It pains me to have to correct inaccuracies uttered by the President about meetings which I attended and he did not. Maybe it's not an intentional lie. If not, it's amnesia.

The liberal cartoonist Herblock noted: 'It didn't matter whether the words were factual – it only mattered that they were presented well and sounded good.' And David Stockman, his budget director in the golden days of Reaganomics, remarked: 'If he didn't understand the big picture, how could he take the right decisions?' His ability to mis-speak himself was legendary. In 1976 he told a Republican women's rally that 'Simpson slew the Philippines with the jawbone of an ass'; he said to Denis HEALEY: 'Nice to meet you, Mr Ambassador,' and called Princess Diana 'Princess David'. More seriously, he sidestepped questions about the SLEAZE that blighted his administration by professing ignorance of all such matters.

Reagan's stock peaked when America intervened in GRENADA in 1983, and with the economy finally showing signs of an upturn, he was re-elected in 1984 by a large majority over Walter Mondale (*see* NORWEGIAN WOOD), who belaboured his handling of the economy, saying: 'Let's tell the truth. Mr Reagan will raise taxes and so will I. He won't tell you. I just did.' Reagan's age (73) could have told against him, but he turned it into a joke, telling college students: 'When I was attending college – now I know many of you probably think that was back when there were dinosaurs roaming the earth – actually there weren't, it was about the time Moses was parting the Red Sea.' He also declared: 'Just to show you how youthful I am, I intend to campaign in all thirteen states.' He was well-nigh unbeatable, TIP O'Neill confiding:

> Reagan is the most popular figure in the history of the US. No candidate we put up would have been able to beat Reagan this year.

To O'Neill Reagan was an enigma. He found him 'warm and congenial, but his policies hurt people', and termed him 'President HOOVER with a smile', but conceded that 'every time you compromise with him, he gets 80 per cent of what he wants.' When O'Neill pressed him hard over one measure, the President told him: 'You can get me to crap a pineapple, but you can't get me to crap a cactus.'

Reagan had promised of his second term: 'I learned a lesson in my former profession. We're saving the best stuff for the last act.' But this was not the case. He lost his way with Congress, adopted softer but costlier economic policies as Reaganomics stalled, and dropped his talk of the Soviet Union being an Evil EMPIRE, holding four SUMMIT conferences with Mikhail GORBACHEV; at REYKJAVIK he stunned his advisers by briefly agreeing to work for total nuclear disarmament, but eventually the two SUPERPOWER leaders did conclude an INF agreement. Reagan, strongly supported by Margaret THATCHER with whom he developed a close friendship, turned up the heat on Russia to abandon its confrontation with the West, memorably appealing in Berlin: 'Mr Gorbachev, tear down this wall!' and having his call answered within a year of leaving the White House. But he also kept up America's macho image, ordering air strikes against LIBYA in retaliation for its alleged role in the bombing of a disco in Berlin used by US troops; he said of Colonel Gaddafi: 'He's not only a barbarian but he's flaky.' He also stood by the CONTRAS in Nicaragua despite Congressional votes to cut off funding, but the efforts of underlings to finance it led to the Iran-Contra affair of 1986–87 which seriously dented his reputation for competence and questioned his veracity. He insisted: 'I'm not smart enough to lie', but his various explanations were inconsistent. Reagan managed to dissociate himself from the worst of the wrong-doing, but never again exuded the total aura of power.

At the same time the economy was thriving – even if it meant the first ever 3 trillion dollar budget. And while he handed over to BUSH at the 1988 election, he would almost certainly have been re-elected despite his age, had the Constitution permitted it, despite having had two operations for cancer. He quipped: 'Since I got to the White House, I got two hearing aids, a colon operation, and was shot. I've never felt better in my life.' He even paved the way for Reagan nostalgia, saying: 'Do you remember when I said that bombing would begin in five minutes? When I fell asleep during an audience with the Pope? Those were the good old days.' In retirement he remained popular, though eyebrows were raised in some quarters at the size of lecture fees he was paid in Japan; he got a rousing welcome when he joined Bush's unsuccessful re-election campaign in 1992. One of the catch-phrases of Iran-Contra had been 'What did the President forget, and when did he forget it?', so it was doubly tragic that a forgetfulness which had seemed an endearing affectation should give way in retirement to the ravages of Alzheimer's disease. Reagan announced that he was suffering from Alzheimer's the weekend before the 1994 mid-term elections, in which the Republicans swept to control of both Houses, and bore his affliction with great dignity for almost ten years until his death at 93, nursed to the end by Nancy. *See also* GREAT COMMUNICATOR; GREAT RONDINI.

> He has never been a good manager or strategist. His great political talent is as a visionary leader, painting themes and values broadbrush and in bold colours and thereby capturing the public imagination.
>
> HEDRICK SMITH, *The Power Game*

> Reagan may be remembered less as the engine of late 20th century conservatism than as its jaunty, if somewhat wayward, caboose.
>
> KEVIN PHILLIPS

> This nice, amiable King Victoria.
>
> Rep. NEWT GINGRICH

> Ronald Reagan must love poor people. He's creating so many more of them.
>
> Sen. EDWARD KENNEDY

> Q: What do the USA and McDonald's have in common?
> A: Both are run by a clown named Ronald.
>
> Letter to the *Los Angeles Times*

> Ronald Reagan had a higher claim than any other leader to have won the Cold War for liberty, and he did it without a shot being fired.
>
> MARGARET THATCHER

Reagan Building The Ronald Reagan Building and International Trade Center, the first federal building in WASHINGTON DC designed to house both governmental and private sector organisations. Located at 1300 PENNSYLVANIA AVENUE, it also has frontages on Constitutional Avenue and 14th Street, from which its main entrance lies through a domed rotunda. Opened in October 1998, it completed the FEDERAL TRIANGLE after its site had been used for half a century as a parking lot. Designed by Pei, Cobb, Freed and Partners, the building –

whose main feature is a cone-shaped horizontal glass skylight over a central atrium – covers seven acres and houses nearly 7000 federal employees as well as global trade organisations and the DC Visitor Information Centre. CONGRESS authorised its construction in 1987 to realise President KENNEDY's vision of revitalising Pennsylvania Avenue; in 1995 Congress unanimously decided to name it after President Reagan, who had signed the BILL but would be too unwell to attend its dedication in May 1998.

Reagan Democrats Traditional Democratic voters (mainly BLUE-COLLAR) who switched to the Republican ticket out of conservatism in 1980 to elect Ronald Reagan, stayed with him in 1984 and gave George BUSH Snr their support in 1988; in 1992 many swung back to the Democrats to elect Bill CLINTON.

Reagan doctrine President Reagan's policy of supporting GUERRILLA movements against Communist-backed governments in THIRD WORLD countries, such as the MUJAHEDDIN in Afghanistan, UNITA in Angola, and the CONTRAS in Nicaragua. WHITE HOUSE communications director Pat Buchanan categorised the doctrine as rejecting the notion that nations that had gone into the Communist camp must remain there for ever, saying: 'America reserves the right – and may even have the duty – to support these people.' The IRAN-CONTRA AFFAIR was a direct result; so, indirectly, was the rise of the TALEBAN and AL QAEDA.

Reagan National Airport The Ronald Reagan Washington National Airport, the domestic airport for WASHINGTON DC, over the POTOMAC four miles south of the city centre in Arlington County, Virginia but with a flight path directly over the WHITE HOUSE; the 'Washington' in the title also commemorates George WASHINGTON. Opened in 1941, it was known as National Airport until 1998. After the hijackings and terrorist attacks of 9/11 on the PENTAGON and WORLD TRADE CENTER, with other national targets at risk, the airport was closed for several weeks, and stringent security procedures remain in force.

Reaganauts The devoted right-wing coterie who set the agenda for Reagan on his election to the Presidency in 1980 and throughout his first term. It stems from the Argonauts of classical Greece; Margaret THATCHER's attempt to depict her followers as Argonauts came unstuck in the COMMONS when Robin COOK pointed out the catalogue of disasters that befell them as a result of their leader Jason's pig-headedness.

Reaganomics The policy which Reagan claimed would balance the federal budget through a combination of massive tax cuts, cuts in WELFARE programmes and a huge increase in defence spending. The term is credited to Speaker TIP O'Neill. Reaganomics were denounced by Democrats and sceptical Republicans ('VOODOO ECONOMICS' – George BUSH Snr; 'a riverboat gamble' – Sen. Howard Baker; 'the only way you can do that is with mirrors' – Rep. John Anderson), but Reagan pursued it in office. He secured most of the tax cuts, using the SUPPLY-SIDE argument that resulting economic growth would boost federal revenues. But the spending cuts proved hard to achieve (*see* MAGIC ASTERISK), and the budget deficit soared. The days of Reaganomics were numbered when one of its progenitors, budget director David Stockman, confessed in a December 1981 *Atlantic Monthly* interview with William Greider:

> None of us really understands what's going on with all these numbers.

In his book *The Triumph of Politics*, Stockman later confessed:

> We insisted that we had found the economic Rosetta Stone. But our Rosetta Stone was a fake.

real. Real IRA *See* IRA.

Real Lives A BBC television documentary on the life of Republican and LOYALIST activists in NORTHERN IRELAND which was pulled from the schedule in August 1985 at the urging of the Home Secretary, Leon Brittan. It included interviews with Martin McGuinness, a leading spokesman for the PROVISIONAL IRA, and a high-ranking member of the UDA. Brittan's intervention, apparently anticipating anger from Margaret THATCHER if a programme 'advocating terrorism' were transmitted, provoked a strike by BBC staff who felt management had been spineless in the face of government interference. Brittan was widely felt to have acted heavy-handedly; he was moved to the Department of Trade and Industry soon after. When the programme was eventually screened, few objections were raised.

real wages The level of wages after allowance has been made for INFLATION.

realpolitik A term forever associated with Bismarck (*see* IRON CHANCELLOR), having been brought to prominence in 1853 by the German writer Ludwig von Rochau. The word means 'practical politics', but generally construed as involving a streak of ruthlessness and the triumph of PRAGMATISM over principle, the end justifying the means.

realignment A fundamental change in the party structure of a country, with the balance changing between competing parties on either the left or the right, maybe with parties merging or splitting. In Britain, the term has long been used for a scenario in which LABOUR and the Liberals (now LIBERAL DEMOCRATS) join forces, possibly with the Labour left forming a new, firmly socialist party. The first of these aims, at least, lay at the heart of Tony BLAIR's PROJECT. In America, the last successful realignment occurred when the Republicans attracted Southern voters from the Democrats in the 1960s and early '70s, paving the way for the GOP to occupy the WHITE HOUSE for 20 years out of 24.

reapportionment A US term for the revision of electoral boundaries within a jurisdiction so as to allocate elected representatives on a fairer basis. *See* REDISTRICTING.

rearmament The process of halting the rundown of a nation's armed forces after one war and re-equipping them so as to lessen the chances of another, or to fight if it becomes unavoidable. The question of whether or not to rearm was the dominant issue in British politics in the mid-1930s.

> I do not hold that we should rearm in order to fight. I hold that we should rearm in order to parley.
>
> CHURCHILL, 8 October 1951

German rearmament The issue which caused divisions in most West European countries in the early 1950s, when Britain, America and other NATO members decided to end the post-WORLD WAR II prohibition on West Germany having significant armed forces, so that it could take a front-line (but non-nuclear) role in defending the West against Communist attack from behind the IRON CURTAIN.

Moral Rearmament A movement founded in Oxford in 1938 by Frank Buchman (1878–1961) to promote Christian values in every walk of life. It grew out of the **Oxford Group**, as Buchman's followers in the 1920s called themselves. Its influence spread to a number of countries, and after WORLD WAR II it played an important part in right-wing resistance to Communism in several major trade unions. The 21st-century politician who has most closely echoed its attitudes is Tony BLAIR.

rebellion Originally an armed uprising against a government, the term has come to embrace resistance by dissident BACK-BENCHERS to their own party leadership, and acts of dissent by rugged individuals. Benjamin FRANKLIN, at the time of the AMERICAN REVOLUTION, declared that 'rebellion against tyrants is obedience to God'; after the new nation had been founded, Thomas JEFFERSON confessed that 'a little rebellion now and then is a medicine necessary for the sound health of government.'

rebuttal The forceful, rapid and co-ordinated denial of media reports or other allegations that could prove damaging to a party or a government. The object, where possible, is not just to crush the negatives but to turn the situation to one's advantage. Rebuttal was very much a creation of 1990s UK politics; it is seen as a concomitant to SPIN, having been pioneered by the LABOUR PARTY; prior to the 1997 election Labour set up a Rebuttal Unit at MILLBANK (*see* EXCALIBUR) under the command of Peter Mandelson (*see* BOBBY) and Brian Wilson. Before long it was a recognised technique throughout the political and commercial world.

recall (1) The process, adopted by many states in the USA and local communities within them, under which elected officials may be deprived of office by a majority in a ballot if enough voters petition for one. The idea was borrowed from Switzerland by US POPULISTS; Los Angeles in 1903 was the first city to adopt it and other mainly Western jurisdictions followed, with state governors the prime target, though in Arizona judges are also liable to recall. The existence of recall has acted as a check on bad government and as a safety valve. In 1921 North Dakota's governor, attorney-general and agriculture commissioner were all ousted. Successful recalls after that were rare until, in October 2003, California's Democratic Gov. Gray Davis was ousted in a recall ballot only a year after being re-elected as dissatisfaction arose over an economic downturn and energy crisis; Californians elected the movie star Arnold Schwarzenegger (*see* GOVERNATOR), a Republican, to succeed him. (2) At WESTMINSTER, the reconvening of Parliament during a RECESS to debate some matter of urgency that has arisen. The SPEAKER will generally recall Parliament if the Prime Minister agrees to a request from the Leader of the Opposition.

recess (pronounced RE-cess in WASHINGTON, re-CESS at WESTMINSTER). A period when a legislature is not in session. At Westminster it applies solely to the holidays taken in the summer and the early autumn, at Christmas, Easter and Whitsun. In the US CONGRESS it covers any time when a recess is called from the Chair; when on 1 March 1954 Puerto Rican nationalists shot five Congressmen from the House gallery, Rep. Joe Martin, presiding, shouted: 'The House stands recessed', then ran for his life.

recess appointment A Presidential appointment that will require CONFIRMATION by the SENATE, made when CONGRESS is not in session. Such appointees may start work at once, but the President must submit their NOMINATION when the Senate reconvenes and the appointment will lapse if the nominee has not been confirmed by the end of the next session.

recession A cyclical downturn in the economy, which officially comes into existence when national product (GDP) has declined for two or more successive quarters. In times of economic difficulty, those in power go to enormous lengths to argue that a recession is not on the way or has not arrived (*see* R-WORD). Harry S TRUMAN once said: 'It's a recession when your neighbour loses his job, it's a DEPRESSION when you lose your own'; Ronald REAGAN in 1980 expanded this to:

> It's a recession when your neighbour loses his job, it's a depression when you lose your own – and it's a recovery when Jimmy CARTER loses his!

Two weeks before the 1992 Presidential election George BUSH Snr, in a telling slip of the tongue, thanked Republican workers in New Jersey for 'your lovely recession'.

Reciprocity Treaty The US-Canadian treaty of 1854 which lifted TARIFFS from non-manufactured goods traded between the two countries, and authorised reciprocal use of Atlantic fisheries and the St Lawrence-Great Lakes waterways. The Canadian negotiators 'floated through it on a sea of champagne', allied with Southern legislators who saw it as a first step toward Canada being absorbed by the United States. America refused to renew the treaty in 1866 because of irritation over Canada's alleged lack of support for the North in the CIVIL WAR. Canada continued to seek FREE TRADE with its southern neighbour; 'Unrestricted Reciprocity' was a Liberal slogan in the 1891 election. But it was almost a century later before a comprehensive free trade agreement was concluded, in NAFTA.

recognition (1) In the US CONGRESS, the act of the CHAIR in calling a member who wishes to speak. A member hoping to be called – or with the right to be called under rule – is said to be seeking recognition. (2) Refusal to recognise Britain's criminal courts by entering a plea has at times been the practice of IRA men accused of terrorist offences. (3) The act of one nation in agreeing to open diplomatic contacts with another. Recognition can be *de facto*, where it is accepted that a regime is in control, or *de jure*, where a government takes power by constitutional means.

> If you recognise anyone, it does not mean that you like him. We all, for instance, recognise the Rt Hon. Member for Ebbw Vale [Aneurin BEVAN].
>
> Winston CHURCHILL on UK recognition of Communist China, 1952

recommit To send a BILL back to a committee that has considered it at an earlier stage. The term is particularly used in the US HOUSE OF REPRESENTATIVES after the previous QUESTION has been ordered on the passage of a Bill or joint resolution.

reconciliation In the US CONGRESS, the procedure under which APPROPRIATIONS, TAX-WRITING and other committees are directed to determine and recommend changes in laws and BILLS to bring about the tax and spending levels set by a BUDGET resolution. The committees are instructed what total amounts must be changed, but are free to decide how and in what areas the adjustments should be made. Reconciliation is normally resorted to only if the committees have twice failed to recommend the necessary changes without targets being set for them.

Reconstruction The process of bringing the defeated South back into the political system of the United States after the CIVIL WAR. Some Northerners saw it as an opportunity for vengeance and self-enrichment, but the 1867 Military Reconstruction Act also brought for a time widespread black suffrage and some representation. The Act divided the ten UNRECONSTRUCTED states into five military districts; for each to be restored to the Union a constitutional convention of blacks and loyal whites had to pass a state constitution guaranteeing suffrage for all, qualified voters were to elect a state legislature to ratify the FOURTEENTH AMENDMENT and, after ratification, the state could apply for representation in CONGRESS. The political argument over how to restore the South began before LINCOLN's assassination and intensified as Andrew Johnson took a moderate line. Sen. Charles Sumner accused Johnson of 'throwing away the fruits of the victory of the Union Army', and in December 1865 Congress set up a joint committee which wrested control of Reconstruction from the President and produced an aggressive programme of its own. Tales of a reign of terror against freed slaves based on the BLACK CODES whipped up public support; the future Interior Secretary Carl Schurz (1829–1906), named **Carl Squirt** by Southerners, reported:

> The lash and murder is resorted to to intimidate those whom fear for an awful death alone causes to remain, while patrols, negro dogs, and spies disguised as Yankees, keep constant guard over those unfortunate people.

Johnson's continued opposition to Reconstruction even after the Act was passed led to the almost-successful move to IMPEACH him in 1868. The effective period of Reconstruction lasted until 1877, the period during which Federal troops were stationed in the former CONFEDERATE states. By then, Northern profiteers had pocketed hundreds of millions in fixed assets and funds for post-war development, WHITE SUPREMACISTS had regained control of the South, and Congress had largely lost interest.

> We have the right to treat them as we would any other province that we might conquer.
> Rep. THADDEUS STEVENS, 1863

recount The counting of votes a second or further time because of claims that a mistake has been made or because of the narrowness of the result. In America the criteria and procedures vary between jurisdictions; the most celebrated recount was the one in Florida (especially PALM BEACH COUNTY) on which hung the result of the 2000 Presidential election, eventually resolved by the SUPREME COURT. In UK Parliamentary elections a recount can normally be sought by the losing party if the margin is less than 1,000 votes, sometimes a little more; one may also be sought by candidates who have narrowly lost their DEPOSITS.

Recruit scandal The scandal concerning the Recruit Cosmos real estate company that brought down the Japanese government of Noburu Takeshita. In November 1988 some sixteen politicians were accused of insider trading in the company's shares and one, the socialist Takumi Veda, resigned from the DIET. Five days later an official of the company was arrested on charges of trying to bribe investigators. In December the Justice and Finance Ministers were forced to resign because of their involvement – and the next year the scandal reached the Prime Minister.

red. red(s) (1) A derogatory term for COMMUNISTS, revolutionary leftists and socialists in general. The colour red has been associated with revolution since at least 1848, when the workers of Paris manned the BARRICADES under red banners (but *see* RED FLAG *below*). 'Reds' became a general journalistic term for Communists with the Russian Civil War of 1918–22, in which TROTSKY's RED ARMY ultimately triumphed over the WHITES. Its use was especially prevalent during the MCCARTHYITE era in America, when it was applied to alleged subversives of every kind. (2) The colour of Britain's LABOUR PARTY, used throughout its activities and not simply as a means of distinguishing it from the Conservatives' BLUE at elections. (3) The campaign colour of America's REPUBLICAN PARTY.

red and blue states A political shorthand that gained wider usage during the 2004 Presidential election campaign as the TV networks classified states as 'red' or 'blue' according to the likelihood of George W. BUSH winning them for the Republicans or John KERRY for the Democrats.

Red Army The highly disciplined and immense army of the SOVIET UNION, originating in the forces organised by TROTSKY to defend the infant BOLSHEVIK regime. Eventually victorious in the 1918–22 civil war against the conservative WHITES, the Red Army was weakened in the late 1930s by a series of PURGES that stripped it of most of its commanders, leaving it weakened and prone when HITLER invaded in 1941. It took four years of the most bitter fighting the world has known, at times in atrocious weather, for the invaders to be repelled and crushed; Stalingrad lives on as its greatest triumph. With the collapse of Communism and the break-up of the Soviet Union, its successor armies are of varying degrees of quality, training, competence, equipment and preparedness.

> The hopes of civilisation rest on the worthy banners of the courageous Red Army.
> General DOUGLAS MACARTHUR, 1942

Red Army Faction (RAF; Ger. *Rote Armee Faktion*) The preferred name of West Germany's BAADER-MEINHOF GANG, normally used for the terrorist splinter group that survived its founders and continued with sporadic acts of violence into the 1980s.

By 1985 it was down to an estimated 20 hardcore activists, 200 militants willing to help in guerrilla attacks, and about 2000 supporters who would protect other members if required. Its slogan was:

> Don't argue – destroy.

red-baiting The practice of tarring one's opponent as a Communist in order to turn the voters against them. It was carried out to perfection by Richard NIXON in his 1950 Senate race against Rep. Helen Gahagan Douglas; though there was not a shred of evidence against her, Nixon branded her the 'PINK LADY' and went on to defeat her.

Red Book The annual Financial Statement and BUDGET report, published by HM TREASURY on Budget Day the moment the CHANCELLOR OF THE EXCHEQUER has finished his statement to the COMMONS.

> The unread book. WILLIAM HAGUE

Red Brigades (Ital. *Brigade Rosse*) The Italian left-wing terrorist group that was responsible for the kidnap and murder in 1978 of Aldo MORO, ex-prime minister and president of the Christian Democratic Party, and an estimated 414 other killings. It was formed in 1969 with the aim of attacking the heads of large corporations, such as Fiat and Pirelli, who were regarded as 'enemies of the working class'. It subsequently conducted a campaign of kidnappings, bombings and murders of police chiefs, judges and government officials as well as business leaders with the aim of undermining the Italian state and initiating a MARXIST revolution. The Brigades were linked to other terrorist groups including the RED ARMY FACTION. In January 1982 the Italian police scored a major success in freeing the US Brigadier-General James Dozier, a deputy NATO commander, who had been abducted in Verona in December 1981. Leading Brigades ideologues, such as Renato Curcio (1948–) and Alberto Frascechini, as well as those responsible for the Moro and Dozier kidnappings, were captured, tried and convicted. During the 1980s the authorities had increasing success in penetrating and neutralising the Brigades' CELLS throughout the country, but the murders continued up to 1999 and a further trial of thirteen suspects was held in 2004.

Red China The colloquial term used in America for the PEOPLE'S DEMOCRACY established in Beijing by CHAIRMAN MAO Tse-Tung in 1949 following the final Communist victory over Chiang Kai-Shek's NATIONALISTS.

Red Clydeside Shorthand for the upsurge of revolutionary socialism and civil unrest in and around Glasgow at and just after the close of WORLD WAR I. During the war several left-wingers who called on workers to strike were imprisoned, including the pacifist John Maxton (1885–1946). In January 1919 the CABINET sent in English troops to quell what the Lord PROVOST feared was an imminent Bolshevik rising; Scots troops were confined to barracks, and tanks, machine gunners and artillery were put into position – but no uprising came. The wartime agitation was led by the schoolmaster John Maclean, who to Tory alarm had been elected an honorary president of the First All-Russian Congress of SOVIETS; from 1922 Red Clydeside had a democratic voice with the election of a strong Labour/ILP contingent to WESTMINSTER, led by Maxton. The bulk of the ILP eventually merged with Labour, but Maxton left the party in 1932, claiming it had betrayed socialism. Some historians argue that Labour's breakthrough in the West of Scotland in fact came because the PARTITION of Ireland enabled Catholic voters to switch from Irish Nationalist to Labour.

> No government is going to take from me my right to speak, my right to protest against wrong, my right to do everything that is for the benefit of mankind. I am not here, then, as the accused; I am here as the accuser of capitalism dripping with blood from head to foot.
>
> JOHN MACLEAN addressing a Glasgow court, 1918

> If I had to live in conditions like that, I would be a revolutionary myself.
>
> KING GEORGE V to John Wheatley

Red Dean The nickname of Dr Hewlett Johnson (1874–1966), Anglican Dean of Canterbury from 1931 and former Dean of Manchester. He attracted controversy for his assertions, in the face of all the evidence, that STALIN's SOVIET UNION was a model for the practical application of Christian ethics.

Red Duchess The scarcely-deserved nickname given by members of her own party to Katherine Stewart-Murray, Duchess of Atholl, who in 1923 became the first Scottish woman MP. Elected as a Conservative, she was a junior Minister under BALDWIN, and after losing office in 1929 campaigned against oppression in the Soviet Union. She also spoke out against Italy's invasion of Abyssinia and her government's tolerance of General Franco (*see* CAUDILLO) during the SPANISH CIVIL WAR, having witnessed *Luftwaffe* air raids on civilian targets (*see* La PASIONARA). Her support for the INTERNATIONAL BRIGADE and her attacks on HITLER led to her party withdrawing the WHIP. In 1938 she resigned her seat at Kinross and West Perthshire to force a by-election over APPEASEMENT, but lost to an official Conservative candidate by 1313 votes. After WORLD WAR II she campaigned against Soviet domination of Poland, Czechoslovakia and Hungary.

Said the Duchess of Atholl to me:
'Young man, do you fart when you pee?'
Replied I with much wit:
'Do you belch when you shit?'
And I thought that was one up to me.
Rhodesian army limerick, World War II

red flag The red flag which became the standard of British SOCIALISM was devised by Richard Lewis, a South Wales ironworker hanged in Cardiff gaol for his part in the Merthyr uprising of 1831 when hundreds rampaged through the town demanding the right to vote. They ambushed the militia and held the town for five days, under a flag dipped in calves' blood, until troops regained control. One soldier was killed, and Lewis was regarded as the ringleader.

Red Flag, The The anthem of Britain's LABOUR PARTY and of democratic SOCIALISTS throughout the English-speaking world. It is sung to the German tune of *O Tannenbaum* ('O Christmas Tree'). Labour MPs sang it in the House of Commons CHAMBER when they took their seats after their 1945 LANDSLIDE; Tories present were horrified. It is also sung at the close of Labour's annual CONFERENCE. The words were written in 1889 by James Connell (1852–1929):

The people's [workers'] flag is deepest red;
It shrouded oft our martyred dead,
And ere their limbs grew stiff and cold
Their heart's blood dyed its every fold.
So raise the scarlet standard high!
Beneath its shade we'll live or die.
Tho' cowards flinch and traitor sneer,
We'll keep the red flag flying here.

In 1939 the Labour leader Clement ATTLEE, eager to discourage talk of a POPULAR FRONT or any alliance with other parties, had this verse anonymously printed in the *Daily Herald*:

The people's flag is deepest pink,
It is not red blood but only ink.
It is supported now by [the FABIAN] Douglas Cole,
Who plays each year a different role.
Now raise our Palace standard high,
Wash out each trace of purple dye,
Let Liberals join and Tories too,
And Socialists of any hue.

A more irreverent version, lampooning working-class SOLIDARITY and definitely not written by Attlee, begins:

The working class can kiss my arse,
I've got the foreman's job at last.
And now that he is on the dole,
You can stuff the red flag up your hole.

Red Guards The young, fanatical supporters of CHAIRMAN MAO during China's CULTURAL REVOLUTION, first mobilised at a rally in Beijing's TIENANMEN SQUARE on 18 August 1966. These unruly mobs consisted chiefly of students from secondary schools, colleges and universities; their task was to rampage through the streets and countryside, harassing and attacking Mao's supposed enemies and opponents, and destroying private and public property – anything that represented 'old' ideas, culture, customs or habits. They wore red armbands and carried copies of Mao's LITTLE RED BOOK.

Red hunt The anti-Communist crusade begun on New Year's Day 1920 by the 'fighting Quaker', US Attorney-General A. Mitchell Palmer. In an act of OVERKILL even for the height of the RED SCARE and despite President WILSON's appeals for caution, he ordered simultaneous raids on every alleged BOLSHEVIK cell in the country. In a week over 6000 people were arrested, their property confiscated, their friends detained for aiding revolutionaries; the raids on these supposed insurgents yielded just three pistols. Palmer was actuated partly by an attempt on his own life, but more by Presidential ambitions.

Palmer, do not let this country see red.
WOODROW WILSON

Red Ken The popular nickname for **Ken Livingstone** (1947–), a former cancer lab technician and quixotic left-winger who led the Greater London Council (GLC) from 1981 until its abolition in 1986, was a more moderate than the name suggests though unpredictable Labour MP for Brent East 1987–2001, and in 2000 was elected London's first MAYOR. The putsch against group leader Andrew Mackintosh the day after the 1981 GLC elections that gave him power, and his outspoken views, especially on NORTHERN IRELAND, at first made him a bogeyman of the right-wing tabloids, one of which termed him 'The Most Odious Man In Britain'. But Livingstone countered this onslaught by presenting himself as a self-deprecating type whose great love was his tank of newts and salamanders. His policies at COUNTY HALL, ranging from support for highly unpopular fringe groups to a popular farecutting programme for London transport, were increasingly seen as a provocation by Margaret THATCHER. Her decision in October 1983 to abolish the GLC, and Livingstone's vigorous and ingenious campaign for its survival, turned Red Ken into a folk hero for many Londoners who had previously detested him. His switch to WESTMINSTER did not give him equal status in national politics, and the BLAIR government's decision to devolve some power to the capital suited him perfectly. Livingstone was elected mayor as an Independent after the Labour selection was rigged to secure the nomination of former Health Secretary Frank Dobson (a process Dobson deplored), and embarked on a bruising and costly struggle with Deputy Prime Minister John Prescott (*see* TWO JAGS) over the London Underground PPP. Livingstone lost that battle but was still set to defeat an official Labour candidate in 2004, so Tony BLAIR invited him back into the party despite their many differences.

> The Minister has asked to see me again. I think he wants me for my body.
>
> KEN LIVINGSTONE after a meeting with Transport Secretary Norman Fowler, c. 1981

Red Letter *See* ZINOVIEV LETTER.

Red Robbo The media nickname for Derek Robinson (1937–), the militant shop stewards' convenor at British Leyland's Longbridge, Birmingham plant who was sacked by the company chairman Sir Michael Edwardes in 1976. Edwards claimed that unofficial strikes and other disputes fomented by Robinson had cost the plant £200 million. Robinson's union, the AUEW, concluded that he had been unfairly dismissed and gave notice that its entire membership would strike; the threat was lifted after Edwardes threatened to sack them all. The plant survived a further 29 years, MG Rover finally collapsing just before the 2005 general election.

red rose The emblem of Britain's LABOUR PARTY at every election since 1987, and of Continental socialists, especially in France and Spain. Labour's rose, selected by Peter Mandelson (*see* BOBBY), stands alone; its Spanish counterpart is held in a clenched fist.

> The voters are not daft. They can smell a rat, even when it is wrapped in a red flag or covered with roses. NORMAN TEBBIT

Red Scare The phobia about an imminent Communist takeover that swept America following the RUSSIAN REVOLUTION. As revolution spread in Europe, the conviction grew that aliens and subversives were plotting the overthrow of the US government and its institutions; the foundation of the US COMMUNIST PARTY in 1919 and that year's BOSTON POLICE STRIKE added to the alarm. At the end of 1919 almost 250 foreigners whose views were regarded as dangerously radical were deported to the Soviet Union. Attorney-General A. Mitchell Palmer's RED HUNT was given a tragic boost when, on 16 November 1920, a bomb exploded on Wall Street killing 38 people; Palmer declared that the Reds were ready to 'destroy the government at one fell swoop'. It was in this climate that the Italian anarchists SACCO AND VANZETTI were sentenced to death in 1921 for a murder they insisted they did not commit. The Red Scare triggered a revival of the KU KLUX KLAN, but the anti-Communist hysteria subsided as it became clear that the world revolution was not materialising.

Red Square The square at the heart of Moscow beside the KREMLIN, which contains LENIN's mausoleum. Throughout the Soviet era it witnessed massive and choreographed demonstrations of military power and popular enthusiasm on MAY DAY and the anniversary of the OCTOBER REVOLUTION, overseen by members of the POLITBURO; in 1941 the troops marched straight off the square into the front line. The word 'red' has nothing to do with Communism here, and predates Lenin by several centuries; the Russian word also means 'beautiful'.

red star Like the HAMMER AND SICKLE, a symbol of international Communism; it also appears as a gold star on a plain red banner.

Red Wedge A collective of rock musicians, headed by Billy Bragg, who before and after the 1987 UK general election campaigned and staged concerts to woo young voters to Labour. Bragg kept up his involvement, but considered the 1997 Labour government disappointingly un-radical.

red, white and blue The patriotic and national colours of numerous countries, including Britain, the United States, France, Russia and the Netherlands.

> White is for purity, red for valour, blue for justice.
>
> Sen. CHARLES SUMNER (1811–74)

> The politicians were talking themselves red, white and blue.
>
> CLARE BOOTHE LUCE (1903–87)

reds under the bed An excessive preoccupation with Communists and a belief that they are behind anything one disapproves of. The phrase dates from the

MCCARTHYITE WITCH-HUNT, when supposed Communists were said to have been found lurking in the most unlikely and dangerous places, hence 'reds under the bed'. *See also* PROFUMO AFFAIR.

better dead than red or **better red than dead** The double-sided phrases that summed up the extreme positions of COLD WARRIORS and NUCLEAR disarmers respectively. One would rather perish in nuclear war than see Communism prevail, the other opposed such conflict even if the price was subservience to Moscow. It is arguable which came first. *Time* magazine in 1961 claimed (wrongly) that the 'better red' version had been taken up by CND as its slogan; however, Bertrand Russell (*see* COMMITTEE OF 100) did write:

> If no alternative remains except Communist domination or extinction of the human race, the former alternative is the less of two evils.

clear red water *See* clear BLUE water.

Danny the Red Nickname for Daniel Cohn-Bendit (1945–), a French student born of German-Jewish refugee parents who led a student revolt at Paris' Nanterre campus during the ÉVÈNEMENTS of 1968. He was later deported to West Germany, where as a GREEN politician he became deputy mayor of Frankfurt in the late 1980s.

The East is Red One of the great anthems of MAOIST rule in China; its simple message included an implied dig at the Khrushchev regime in Moscow for alleged backsliding from true Communist principles.

redlining In America, the practice of systematically denying loans, mortgages and insurance to property owners and prospective buyers in the poorest sections of a city. Although financial institutions argue that redlining is used purely to minimise financial risk, there is considerable evidence that it has been used to practise racial discrimination because the areas in question frequently have large black, Hispanic or other minority populations. Redlining originated in the late 1960s as America's INNER CITY problems first surfaced; it takes its name from the supposed practice of outlining such areas in red on a map.

redneck A patronising US term for a country person who is poorly educated, narrow-minded and boorishly right-wing. Traced back to 1830, it originally described white Southern farmers (the backs of their necks red from working in the fields under hot sun), but its use spread in the late 1960s to describe anyone with uneducated right-wing views – not just a rural Southerner with a baseball cap and a pickup truck. The phrase spread to Britain in the 1980s.

Redshirts (1) The volunteer force of Italian patriots (*see* THOUSAND) raised by Giuseppe Garibaldi in 1860 to overthrow the Bourbon monarchy in southern Italy as a step to reuniting the country under a single crown (*see* RISORGIMENTO). (2) The private army formed in South Carolina in the 1870s by former CONFEDERATE General Wade Hampton against the Republican state government elected under RECONSTRUCTION. It was formed consciously in the image of Garibaldi's movement.

Redeemers The Southerners who organised in the dying days of RECONSTRUCTION to redeem the states of the former CONFEDERACY for self-rule under the Democratic Party. They campaigned with skill and vigour, making promises they often intended to keep to give freed slaves a better deal than they had received from swindling Yankee CARPETBAGGERS. They increased their influence by forming an alliance with liberal Republicans in an unsuccessful challenge to the corruption in the GRANT administration. The Redeemers took over in the state Capitols of the South after President Hayes withdrew Federal troops in 1877, but were soon outflanked by arch-conservative WHITE SUPREMACISTS.

redistribution (1) The use of taxation and other measures to transfer wealth from the richest to the poorest members of society, and sometimes *vice versa*. Redistributive policies are those consciously designed to bring about such a shift.

> It is less important to redistribute wealth than to redistribute opportunity.
>
> Sen. ARTHUR H. VANDENBERG (1884–1951)

(2) In the UK, the redrawing of boundaries for Parliamentary CONSTITUENCIES to keep their ELECTORATES of approximately equal size. Such redistributions are carried out by the independent BOUNDARY COMMISSION roughly every fifteen years; they generally involve a reduction of seats in INNER-CITY areas and an increase in representation for commuter areas further out. The process has traditionally tended to benefit the Conservatives at the expense of Labour, though the redistribution that took effect at the 1997 election favoured Labour. In 1969 Home Secretary James CALLAGHAN presented ORDERS for a redistribution as required by law, then got Labour MPs to vote them down so that the 1970 election could be

fought on less adverse boundaries; Labour lost the election anyway.

redistricting The reallocation of US Congressional DISTRICTS within a State, with the ostensible purpose of creating more even representation. However, because the process is overseen by State LEGISLATURES, there have been frequent allegations of GERRYMANDERING: the party in control aims to give itself as many districts as possible, and confine its opponents to a minimum number where their support is solid.

Reed rules The rules for the conduct of the US HOUSE OF REPRESENTATIVES pushed through in 1890 by the Republican SPEAKER Thomas Reed (1839–1902; *see* CZAR), and still in force today. Strongly resisted by the minority Democrats, they greatly reduced the scope for FILIBUSTERS and other forms of obstruction, and marked the emergence of the Speaker as a dominant force in the legislature. When the rules were safely through, Reed raid:

> Thank God1 The House is no longer the greatest deliberative body in the world.

reference back A decision by a legislative or executive body to refer a recommendation about which it is unhappy back to a COMMITTEE for further consideration. **Moving reference back** is a standard ploy from the floor to thwart passage of a motion without opposing it outright.

referendum (Lat. something that must be referred) A BALLOT in which the voters of a nation or region give a binding decision on a particular aspect of policy which their government feels unable to determine itself, or which under law it must refer to the people (*compare* PLEBISCITE) In some countries (Switzerland, Denmark, France, the Irish Republic) referendums are a regular feature of national life. In Britain there was strong resistance to them by traditionalists who saw there was as a weakening of Parliamentary SOVEREIGNTY, until in the 1990s they realised they could be used as a brake on Britain's involvement with Europe. In 1945 ATTLEE told CHURCHILL:

> I could not consent to the introduction into our national life of a device so alien to our traditions as the referendum, which has only too often been the instrument of NAZISM and FASCISM.

To date there have been five referenda on constitutional issues in the UK: in 1975 on continued membership of the European Community, and in 1979 and 1997 over DEVOLUTION for Scotland and Wales. There have also been a number in NORTHERN IRELAND. John MAJOR's government resisted pressure for a referendum on the MAASTRICHT TREATY despite Margaret THATCHER's call to 'let the people speak'; Tony BLAIR promised a referendum in the event of his government recommending that the UK adopt the EURO; initially he rejected calls for a referendum on the EUROPEAN CONSTITUTION, but in a U-TURN in the spring of 2004 he agreed to it. The left-wing journalist James Cameron described the 1975 referendum on Europe, which resulted in a resounding 'Yes', as

> Like asking a patient: 'Would you like your appendix back?'

Referendum Party The UK party founded by the Anglo-French financier Sir James Goldsmith (1933–97) in November 1994 to campaign for a referendum on the MAASTRICHT TREATY. It fielded 547 candidates at the 1997 general election (including Sir James at Putney – *see* HACIENDA), polling 810,778 votes though all but 25 lost their DEPOSIT. Its intervention cost the Conservatives an estimated fourteen seats. When Sir James died soon after the election, the former Conservative Party chairman Lord McAlpine took over as leader. With further moves to closer European integration replacing Maastricht as the big issue for EUROSCEPTICS, the party turned itself into the Referendum Movement, and UKIP became the main anti-European party.

reflation Stimulation of an economy that has had demand taken out of it to the point where it has become deflated and RECESSION looms; too great a reflation will fuel INFLATION.

reform The achievement of substantial change in the political and social system while preserving its essentials, brought about through the process itself. REVOLUTIONARIES both scorn reformers and feel threatened by them. TROTSKY wrote: 'A reformist party considers unshakeable the foundations of that which it intends to reform.'

> Cautious, careful people, always casting about to preserve their reputation and social standing, can never bring about a reform.
>
> SUSAN B. ANTHONY (1820–1906)

> A reformer is a guy who rides through a sewer in a glass bottomed boat.
>
> New York Mayor JAMES J. WALKER, 1928

> We have not got democratic government today. We have never had it and I venture to suggest . . . that we never shall have it. What we have done in

all the process of reform and revolution is to broaden the base of the oligarchy.

ANTHONY EDEN

Reform Acts The landmark legislation from 1832 that converted Britain's HOUSE OF COMMONS from being (largely) a body of PLACEMEN representing tiny or even non-existent electorates to a legislature democratically elected by limited male SUFFRAGE. The original battle was by far the fiercest, as the unreformed House of Commons was elected on boundaries and a franchise that had been barely democratic three centuries before, and change was resisted both by reactionaries in the HOUSE OF LORDS, and those MPs who felt it would destroy the COMMONS. There was vast support for the 1831–32 Bill from the urban working and middle class, even though it did nothing for them; it merely ended the Rotten BOROUGHS and the worst of the other anomalies and gave a few seats to the new industrial cities. As tensions rose, Lord Brougham campaigned in the 1831 election for 'The Bill, the whole Bill and nothing but the Bill', and Macaulay declared: 'The voice of great events is proclaiming to us: "Reform, that you may preserve."' However, the Duke of Wellington (*see* IRON DUKE), a leader of the diehards, insisted that 'beginning reform is beginning revolution', and as the Bill finally went through Lord Melbourne commented:

If it was not absolutely necessary, it was the foolishest thing ever done.

Reform Party (1) In Canada, a moderate predecessor of the LIBERAL PARTY, formed in the 1840s by the Quebec lawyer Louis H. Lafontaine, the Toronto lawyer Robert Baldwin and the editor and banker Francis Hincks. The Reformers did much after the DURHAM REPORT to develop the case for responsible GOVERNMENT. (2) Again in Canada, the right-wing, POPULIST and predominantly Western party led by Preston Manning which broke through in the October 1993 'CANADIAN MELTDOWN' to take 52 seats at Ottawa and almost annihilate the PROGRESSIVE CONSERVATIVES. Its programme, echoing Ross PEROT, opposed immigration and POLITICAL CORRECTNESS, took a tough line on Quebec, and demanded elimination of the Budget deficit in three years. In 1997 it gained seats to become the official OPPOSITION, but still with no seats east of Manitoba. In 2000 it changed its name to the CANADIAN ALLIANCE, which merged prior to the 2004 election with the somewhat revived Progressive Conservatives. (3) The POPULIST party that emerged from, and outlasted, Ross PEROT's attempts on the US Presidency in 1992 and 1996; its main achievement has been the election of Jesse Ventura (*see* the BODY) as governor of Minnesota in 1998.

To hell with reform! Perhaps the best known slogan of TAMMANY HALL, reflecting the desire of its leaders to keep their SNOUTS IN THE TROUGH.

refusenik A citizen of the SOVIET UNION who was refused an exit visa, mostly Jews wishing to emigrate to America or Israel. Under Soviet law emigration was a state-granted privilege, though the 1975 HELSINKI ACCORD, which the USSR signed, made is a basic HUMAN RIGHT. During the 1970s many Jews were allowed out, partly through pressure from the West (*see* JACKSON-VANIK amendment), but other applicants were branded as DISSIDENTS and persecuted by the authorities. One of the most prominent was Anatoly (later Nathan) Scharansky, imprisoned in 1978 for treason but allowed to settle in Israel in 1986, where he founded and led an extreme right-wing party. Under Mikhail GORBACHEV's policy of GLASNOST restrictions on emigration were gradually removed; 72,500 Jews left in 1989 and some 200,000 in 1990. But wholesale abolition of exit visas, dreaded by some Western countries which feared an unwanted influx of economic migrants, took Boris Yeltsin's Russian government some years to process.

regency A situation in which a MONARCH, through youth, insanity or other incapacity, cannot govern or is not allowed to, and an individual or council governs on their behalf. Sometimes, as with Admiral Horthy in Hungary between the wars, a regent may rule when the monarchy has effectively been abolished, using the title to conceal his personal power. The term also has connotations of grandeur, deriving from the upsurge in culture and foppishness which accompanied the regency of the future King George IV in early 19th-century Britain. America's **Albany Regency**, Martin van Buren's political organisation in New York State during the 1820s and '30s, may have owed its title to this trait.

regime The persons and ideology governing a country, the word implying a degree of AUTHORITARIANISM and a lack of LEGITIMACY; as in 'the PINOCHET regime in Chile', 'Rhodesia's illegal Smith regime' or 'the oppressive regime in Pyongyang'.

In judging a regime it is very important to know what it finds amusing.
PALMIRO TOGLIATTI (1893–1964), founder of the Italian Communist Party, 1924

regime change Intervention in the affairs of a country in order to bring about a change of regime. This phrase first gained currency immediately prior to the IRAQ WAR of 2003 as the second BUSH administration, and even more Tony BLAIR's UK government, sought to allay concerns that military action was conceived by NEO-CONSERVATIVES in Washington as a means of ousting Saddam Hussein because he had outwitted the President's father. It was this factor that led Blair, especially, to stress the threat posed by Iraq's WEAPONS OF MASS DESTRUCTION, failure to find which would lead after the war to the David KELLY AFFAIR.

register of electors The list of all those in the United Kingdom entitled to vote, compiled by local authorities from forms which every household is required to complete each October and from door-to-door CANVASSING. The list, carried over from year to year, is printed in slim white editions which each cover a POLLING DISTRICT; it is supposed to be comprehensive but, especially in INNER CITY areas with a transitory population, it may be only 75% accurate. Introduction of the POLL TAX led some voters to remove themselves from the register in an effort to avoid payment.

Register of Interests *See* INTERESTS.

new register An important factor in the timing of UK elections, especially Parliamentary elections. The new electoral register takes effect each year in mid-February; the old register will by then be 18 months out of date and a party believing it will gain or lose advantage will either stage the election at the last moment possible under the old register or delay it so that the new one is in effect.

registration In America, the process involved in registering one's eligibility to vote; in some states its complexity – for instance a need to drive 50 miles to register – has deterred many of those entitled to vote from doing so. The hurdles were erected mainly to prevent blacks and poor whites from voting. But some survive as a general inhibitor. In the mid-1970s liberal groups pressed hard for **postcard registration**, under which anyone could obtain the vote simply by writing in, but there was resistance from the more conservative states; the Motor-VOTER Act is designed to overcome this. Registration usually involves not only gaining the qualification to vote, but declaring oneself a REPUBLICAN or DEMOCRAT to gain the right to vote in the PRIMARIES, or (in a few states) an INDEPENDENT.

regulation The moderation by government of the trading policies of commercial concerns in the PRIVATE SECTOR, and the imposition of good working practices such as health and safety. 'Excessive regulation' is a cry frequently raised by business on both sides of the Atlantic; sometimes it is justified.

It is hardly lack of due process for the government to regulate that which it subsidises.
Justice ROBERT H. JACKSON, US SUPREME COURT, 1943

Regulation 18b A provision of Britain's Emergency Powers (Defence) Acts of 1939, amended by Parliament in 1940 to give the HOME SECRETARY the power to detain without trial any members of any organisation sympathetic to an enemy power. Defence Regulation 18b(1A) was specifically targeted at the British Union of FASCISTS and its leader, the former Labour minister Sir Oswald MOSLEY, who was arrested and imprisoned in Brixton from 23 May 1940 until November 1943, when he was released for health reasons. Altogether 763 BUF members were rounded up, including Mosley's wife Diana, who was sent to Holloway; 1769 British subjects suspected of AXIS sympathies were INTERNED during the war, most of them in Peel Camp on the Isle of Man.

regulator, the (1) The power available to a CHANCELLOR OF THE EXCHEQUER to vary rates of INDIRECT TAX without requiring a separate BUDGET and FINANCE BILL. (2) In the early days of PRIVATISATION, the arbiter appointed by the UK government to regulate a specific sector of industry, normally one in which a former State-owned concern, like British Telecom, is dominant or where an essential service is provided, as with energy. Over a period individual regulators were replaced by boards, the last sole regulator, the railways' Tom Winsor, stepping down in July 2004.

regulatory agencies The plethora of agencies of the US government that perform regulatory functions over industry and commerce. In some cases they involve a greater BUREAUCRACY than if the federal government actually owned the industry in question.

There are a thousand agencies that can regulate, restrain or control [the great corporations], but

there is a corporation we may all well dread. That corporation is the Federal Government.
Sen. BENJAMIN H. HILL, US Senate, 27 March 1878

rehabilitation The reinstatement in official esteem of a previously-disgraced public figure. A frequent practice in COMMUNIST countries, especially after the death of STALIN, rehabilitation would occasionally mean the return to a position of responsibility of someone previously denounced as a traitor or a REVISIONIST; more often it involved the withdrawal of unfavourable obituaries and the reinterment of the body in a more prominent plot.

Reich (Ger. empire or realm) *Deutsches Reich* was the official title of the German state from its creation in 1871 to the surrender of the NAZI leadership in 1945, including the period of the WEIMAR REPUBLIC. The **First Reich** was the mediaeval Holy Roman Empire, which lapsed in 1806; the **Second Reich** the unified state established in 1871 when Wilhelm I was proclaimed Kaiser, which ended with the abdication of Wilhelm II in 1918 (*see* HANG THE KAISER!), and the **Third Reich** the regime established by HITLER in January 1933, which he claimed would last a thousand years but which perished in flames just twelve years later.

Reichstag The Parliament, first of the loose German confederation, then of Imperial Germany, finally of the WEIMAR REPUBLIC, which lost its power under the NAZIs. Its building in central Berlin, completed in 1894, was restored after being fought over in the final days of WORLD WAR II as a shrine to democracy. It housed the first meeting of the Bundestag after REUNIFICATION in 1990 and became its seat when Germany's capital moved back from Bonn. HITLER described the election of Nazi deputies to the *Reichstag* as 'a means to an end', and in 1933 proved his point when on 27 February the building was gutted. The

Reichstag fire was almost certainly started by the Nazis. It was critical to Hitler's seizure of absolute power, enabling him to blame the Communists, who with the rest of the left had blocked total Nazi supremacy. A 24-year-old Dutchman, Marius van der Lubbe, was identified as the Communist who had started the blaze, tried and executed on 10 January 1934; in the four days after the fire, 5000 Communists were rounded up. During the post-war NUREMBERG TRIALS, the German Chief of General Staff recalled hearing Goering boast: 'The only one who really knows about the *Reichstag* is me, because I set it on fire.' Sefton Delmer, Berlin correspondent of the *Daily Express*, was telephoned by Goering with the news before the fire was public knowledge; he filed an exclusive story, only to be told that the paper could not use it unless he could say how many fire engines attended the blaze.

rejectionists Militant PALESTINIANS and other Arabs who reject any Middle East peace settlement and advocate the total destruction of ISRAEL.

Rejoice! Rejoice! Margaret THATCHER's euphoric pronouncement on the steps of 10 DOWNING STREET after British forces recaptured South Georgia from its Argentine occupiers on 25 April 1982. It was the first good news for Britain since Argentina's capture of the Falklands three weeks earlier; Mrs Thatcher's injunction to the nation showed her at her most buoyant and, her critics said, her most militaristic. She said:

> Just rejoice at that news and congratulate our forces and the marines . . . Rejoice!

South Georgia had been a pretext for the FALKLANDS WAR; Argentine scrap dealers arrived in the British dependency without permission on 19 March to remove material from an old whaling station at Grytviken, and less than two weeks later Argentine forces evicted a tiny Royal Marine garrison – but not before the lieutenant in charge had holed their ship with an anti-tank missile.

Mrs Thatcher's words were echoed by Tony BLAIR a generation later when, in the highly-charged COMMONS debate on the BUTLER REPORT after the Iraq War on 20 July 2004, he told anti-war MPs: 'Whatever mistakes have been made let us rejoice, let us be pleased Iraq has been liberated.'

religious Right *see* RIGHT.

relocation camps The camps in Wyoming, Arkansas, Colorado and the California desert where over 100,000 Japanese-Americans were INTERNED by federal authorities following PEARL HARBOR in a reaction now seen as almost as infamous as the Japanese surprise attack itself. President Franklin D. ROOSEVELT championed the plan, even referring to the camps as CONCENTRATION CAMPS, despite being warned by the Attorney-General that it was both objectionable and UNCONSTITUTIONAL; the SUPREME COURT took until 1944 to strike it down. It was the 1980s before CONGRESS passed legislation to compensate survivors of the anti-Japanese hysteria who had been branded potential traitors and torn away from their homes and jobs, some for almost five years.

Relugas compact The abortive attempt by senior LIBERAL IMPERIALISTS to reduce the party's leader, Sir Henry CAMPBELL-BANNERMAN, to a cipher after its LANDSLIDE election victory in 1905. Sir Edward Grey, Herbert ASQUITH and R. B. Haldane, the instigator, met that September at Grey's fishing lodge in north-east Scotland and decided that they would not join Campbell-Bannerman's government unless he agreed to go to the HOUSE OF LORDS, with Asquith effectively leading the government as CHANCELLOR OF THE EXCHEQUER. Edward VII sounded Campbell-Bannerman out about a PEERAGE, but he dug in his heels; once in office three months later, C-B according to his own account called in the plotters and told them:

> Now look here, I have been playing up till now . . . But now let me just say – that it is I who am the head of this Government; it is I who have the King's Command; I am on horseback, and you will all be pleased to understand that I will not go to the House of Lords; that I will not have any condition of the kind imposed on me.

All three took senior posts in Campbell-Bannerman's government, and worked harmoniously until his death early in 1908, when Asquith succeeded him.

Remember the Maine! The cry of the Hearst newspapers which precipitated the SPANISH-AMERICAN WAR. The battleship USS *Maine* blew up on 15 February 1898 in Havana harbour with the loss of 260 lives while on a goodwill visit to Spanish-ruled Cuba. The cause of the explosion was never traced but IMPERIALISTS led by William Randolph Hearst pointed the finger at Spain – which had no reason to stage such a provocation – and with Congressional elections due, the unwarlike President MCKINLEY bowed to pressure and declared war two months later. The phrase is thought first to have appeared under a front-page cartoon by Clifford Berryman in the *Washington Post* of 3 April; the caption read:

> Stout hearts, my ladies! If the row comes, *remember the Maine*, and show the world how American sailors can fight.

remilitarisation The reintroduction of armed forces into a region from which they have been removed under a peace agreement or other international accord, by the nation that had been required to withdraw them. The word is most often used of HITLER's despatch of German troops to the Rhineland in March 1936 in breach of the LOCARNO PACTS. Hitler had feared Britain and France would call his bluff and order him to remove them; their acquiescence encouraged him in the view – justified during the era of APPEASEMENT, but ultimately mistaken – that he could expand Germany's borders at will.

remit (1) With the emphasis on the first syllable, the terms of reference for a committee or inquiry, within which it has *carte blanche* but beyond which it is not supposed to investigate. (2) With the second syllable emphasised, the action taken by a LABOUR PARTY conference in REFERRING BACK to the NEC a proposal about which it has doubts, when it is unwilling to embarrass the platform by inflicting an outright defeat. The platform will often ask the MOVERs of a critical resolution to remit it rather than force a vote; if they feel strongly enough, they will insist that it be put to the conference.

Renamo National Resistance of Mozambique. The movement, led by Alfonso Dhaklama, that for sixteen years fought a ruthless GUERRILLA campaign against Mozambique's Marxist FRELIMO government, from shortly after independence from Portugal in 1975 to a ceasefire in 1992. Backed by Bavarian and exiled Portuguese businessmen and with some help from South Africa, it developed – ironically as Frelimo moderated – into a force ready to cause mass starvation through civil war. The presidents of Kenya and Zimbabwe brought Dhaklama and President Joaquin Chissano together in December 1989; peace talks in Rome eventually ended the violence. Renamo finally 'buried the axe of war' in August 1994, while denying ever having committed atrocities. In elections that November 1994, it was defeated 129–112 by Frelimo.

rentacrowd A crowd specially organised or paid to swell the numbers or show appropriate emotions at a political event. Such a group may be organised by a candidate's campaign manager to mob him or her to convince television viewers that the candidate has a real chance. The word was coined in 1962 by the *Daily Telegraph* columnist Peter Simple (Michael Wharton) who wrote of

> Rentacrowd Ltd – the enterprising firm that supplies crowds for all occasions, and has done so much to keep progressive causes in the public eye.

rentamob A term that has taken over the original meaning of RENTACROWD, as a travelling collection of extremists who can be turned out to demonstrate for or against almost anything.

rentaquote Those UK politicians – mainly BACKBENCH MPs with no serious prospects – whose views have since the early 1970s been splashed all over the media, especially on quiet weekends and during Parliamentary recesses. For some unfathomable reason, most, though by no means all, are Conservatives. They gained their fame through the diligence of Chris Moncrieff, long-serving political correspondent of the *Press Association* news agency, who has the ability to tempt MPs into uttering crass statements that will generate headlines, not that some require much encouragement. During one recess, two Cabinet Ministers asked a LOBBY correspondent why, after a week, no-one had demanded the RECALL of Parliament. 'Moncrieff's on holiday', they were told.

Rep. The formal abbreviation for REPRESENTATIVE, the name by which a US CONGRESSMAN is known.

Rep by Pop Representation by Population, the slogan of the GRITS in the mid-1850s in what was soon to become Ontario; they wanted seats in Canada's LEGISLATURE to be allocated by population instead of the main provinces being equally represented. This would have put Quebec and other French-speaking regions at a disadvantage; it led to many French Canadians breaking with the Reform Alliance and siding with the Conservatives, who thus became the second national party after the Grits/Liberals.

reparations The transfer of money, industrial machinery, ships, railway equipment and other goods essential to a productive economy from the loser of a war to the victors, as compensation for the loser's perceived responsibility for damage done during the conflict. Reparations on a massive scale were prised from Germany by France under the Treaty of VERSAILLES; the DAWES PLAN and YOUNG PLAN scaled them down because of Germany's inability to pay in full, but large sums were still owing when HITLER repudiated them in 1935.

repartee One of the joys of politics, the swift and devastating capping of one well-turned phrase with another. Examples of repartee are scattered throughout this dictionary (*see*, particularly, HECKLING; RHETORICAL QUESTION), but a selection is given here. Two involve Horatio Bottomley (1860–1933), the larger-than-life UK Liberal MP who ended in prison for fraud. When Bottomley heard that F. E. Smith had been appointed Lord Chancellor, he told him: 'I shouldn't have been surprised to hear you'd also been made Archbishop of Canterbury.' 'If I had', said Smith, 'I should have asked you to my installation. I would have needed a crook.' While Bottomley was in jail, a visitor found him sewing mailbags. 'Ah, Bottomley, sewing?' asked the visitor. 'No, reaping,' he replied.

The actor-Labour MP Andrew Faulds, easily angered by Tory laughter, once said: 'This is a serious matter, even for the Girl Guides opposite.' When a woman Conservative replied: 'There's nothing wrong with Girl Guides,' Faulds hit back: 'Perhaps I have known more Girl Guides than the Honourable Lady.' In the mid-1980s Labour's John Maxton was asking if vasectomy operations at a Scottish hospital were at risk, when the Conservative Jerry Hayes broke in: 'I didn't know they went in for micro-surgery.'

When, after the release of Nelson MANDELA from prison, the Labour front-bencher Dr Jack Cunningham asked Sir Geoffrey HOWE to ensure 'proper accommodation for Mr Mandela to address members when he comes here next week', the boisterous Tory Nicholas Soames interjected: 'How about the rifle range?' Soames was on the receiving end when, as Food Minister, he declaimed that 'the British countryside is not set in aspic.' The Labour MP Tony Banks interjected: 'You'd eat it if it was.' And when Tristan Garel-Jones, the Old Etonian deputy Tory chief whip and Euro-Minister, once told the Yorkshire miners' MP Mick Welsh: 'We public schoolboys and you miners have one thing in common. We're both used to communal showers', Welsh replied: 'Aye, lad. But we didn't have to watch out when we bent down for the soap.'

Politicians can also be on the receiving end of withering put-downs from civilians. One of the best came from a cowman working for the Labour minister Richard CROSSMAN, who had patronisingly invited the cockney chief whip Bob Mellish to his farm for a glimpse of country life. When Mellish asked why a cow was lying in a particular posture, Crossman told him: 'They often do that', only for the cowman to interrupt: 'That one be dead, zur.' The Labour MP Dr Edith Summerskill was floored when she went on television to argue the case against boxing with the British and Commonwealth heavyweight champion Henry Cooper. Getting nowhere, she turned to the boxer and asked: 'Mr Cooper, have you ever looked in the mirror and seen the state of your nose?' Cooper counterpunched: 'Madam, have you ever looked in the mirror and seen the state of your nose? I done it boxing – what's your excuse?'

> Labour MP: I can't vote tonight. I'm supposed to be in Crete.
> Whip WALTER HARRISON: If you're not here at 10 tonight you'll be in concrete.

The US CONGRESS has always offered a rich vein in repartee. In the early 19th century John Randolph of Roanoake met Henry Clay in a narrow alley, and told him: 'I never GIVE WAY for a scoundrel.' Clay gallantly stepped aside, saying: 'I always do.' Clay also had the last word when Alexander Smith, during a lengthy speech, grandly told him: 'You, sir, speak for the present generation, but I speak for posterity.' Clay retorted to Smith: 'Yes, and you seem resolved to speak until the arrival of your audience.' A few decades later, a Congressman said to Georgia's Alexander Hamilton Stephens: 'You little shrimp! Why, I could swallow you whole.' Stephens replied: 'If you did, you'd have more brains in your belly than ever you had in your head.' Sen. Chauncey Depew (1834–1928) once said of Joseph Choate: 'All you need to get a speech out of Mr Choate is to open his mouth, drop in a dinner and up comes a speech.' Choate retorted: 'If you open your mouth and drop in one of Mr Depew's speeches, up will come your dinner.'

More recently, Rep. William Jenner, an Indiana Republican, brought the House to a standstill during a wordy and sentimental speech from Idaho's Rep. Glen Taylor. When Taylor told how 'my father was an itinerant Baptist preacher. He baptised 15,000 people in the great West. Why, he baptised me five times', Jenner shouted: 'Son-of-a-gun's waterlogged!' One day in a Senate elevator, Sen. Edward KENNEDY told Sen. Tom Eagleton: 'I've got a new Polish joke.' When the Polish-descended Sen. Ed Muskie pointed out: 'I'm in this elevator too, Ted', Kennedy told him: 'All right, Ed, I'll tell it slowly.' Adlai STEVENSON was a master of the art, but was sometimes content not to have the last word. He once met a woman who gushed: 'Oh, Mr Stevenson, your speech was superfluous!' Stevenson, deadpan, replied: 'Thank you, Madam, I'm thinking of having it published posthumously.' The woman came back: 'Won't that be nice. The sooner the better!'

Tony BENN tells of a reputed meeting between Nikita Khrushchev and Chou En-Lai when China's Communist rulers were starting to chafe at the Kremlin's HEGEMONY. Khrushchev said: 'Isn't it remarkable that you, a member of the middle class, and I, from the working class, should control the two greatest socialist nations that ever existed?' 'Yes,' replied Chou, 'and more remarkable still, each of us has betrayed the class from which he came.'

repatriation The return to their country of origin of prisoners of war, illegal immigrants or convicted criminals. Enoch POWELL opened bitter divisions in Britain from the time of his RIVERS OF BLOOD speech in 1969 by advocating the repatriation of legal Commonwealth immigrants; this became a rallying-call for the extreme right throughout the 1970s. In the late 1980s America objected strongly to Britain repatriating Vietnamese BOAT PEOPLE who had fled to Hong Kong but were held not to be genuine refugees. More recently some ASYLUM-SEEKERS arriving in Britain have destroyed their documents to conceal their country of origin, in the hope that this will prevent them being sent home.

repeal The abolition by a LEGISLATURE of a measure previously passed, because it is reckoned inappropriate, unnecessary or obsolete. This may be done by promoting a new BILL to repeal a particular law, or including the repeal in a broader measure; most new laws involve the repeal of at least parts of some previous Acts, but there are also non-controversial Bills specifically to abolish laws that have become archaic. Celebrated repeals include that of the CORN LAWS in 1846, which split the old TORY party, and the repeal of PROHIBITION through the 21st AMENDMENT to the US Constitution, ratified in December 1933.

report. Report Stage In either HOUSE at WESTMINSTER, the step in the legislative process between COMMITTEE STAGE and THIRD READING. After LINE-BY-LINE consideration by a STANDING COMMITTEE, a BILL comes back to the FLOOR of the House for the principal AMENDMENTS (including those from the OPPOSITION that have been rejected in Committee) to be fully debated and voted on. Except for the most wide-ranging and controversial of Bills, the Report Stage takes less than a day of Parliamentary time before the formal debate and vote on Third Reading.

reporting a Bill In the US CONGRESS, the action of a committee in approving a Bill for further consideration. One of the members of the committee is designated to write a report stating the purposes and scope of the measure and the reasons for approving it. Under the RAMSEYER RULE, the report must set out all changes the Bill would make to existing law, and the text of all laws being repealed. Committee amendments must be set out, and explained, and executive communications regarding the Bill be quoted in full. The committee report, after which the Bill is reprinted with its report number – different ones for the House and Senate committee reports, which are respectively encoded '**H. Rept.**' and '**S. Rept.**' – is of particular use to the courts and executive departments in explaining the purpose and meaning of a law once passed.

representation (1) The role of a legislator or other person elected to a public body in acting on behalf of the people in whose name they hold office. The Libyan leader Colonel Gaddafi declared that 'representation is fraud'; the British Labour MP Bill Stones went to the other extreme when he said: 'There's a lot of bleeding idiots in this country, and they deserve some representation'. For a similar American comment *see* Sen. Roman Hruska on the CARSWELL NOMINATION. (2) When one is attempting to gain a favour or concession, especially from an unsympathetic foreign government, one is said to be '**making representations**' to it.

Representation of the People Acts The body of legislation passed during the 20th century under which UK Parliamentary ELECTIONS are held and regulated, and seats in the HOUSE OF COMMONS distributed.

no taxation without representation *See* NO TAX.

proportional representation *See* PROPORTIONAL.

representative (1) An individual elected to represent a community or a number of people. Daniel Webster declaimed in 1834: 'We have been taught to regard a representative of the people as a sentinel on the watch tower of liberty', but Alphonse de Lamartine, confronted with the shambles of mid-19th century French politics, confessed:

> The more I see the representatives of the people, the more I admire my dogs.

A strict distinction is drawn between a representative who acts as he or she thinks best on behalf of those represented, and a DELEGATE who is under instruction to vote in a particular way. In 1774 Edmund BURKE told the electors of Bristol:

> Your representative owes you, not his industry only, but also his judgement.

(2) The official title of a US CONGRESSMAN. A Representative must be at least 25 years old, have been a US citizen for at least seven years, and reside in the State for one of whose districts they have been elected to Congress. (3) A participant in a British CONSERVATIVE PARTY conference attending on behalf of constituency ASSOCIATIONS; they are never known as delegates.

representative democracy or **government** Those systems of government in which decisions are taken by elected representatives, on behalf of the population as a whole.

reprieve The suspension of a legal penalty, specifically the death penalty, and substitution of a lesser punishment. In America the decision generally rests with the GOVERNOR of a State (or with the President for Federal offences); in Britain it has been a matter for the HOME SECRETARY. The difference between a reprieve and a PARDON is that a person pardoned is absolved of all penalties, while one reprieved still has a sentence to serve.

reprimand One of the disciplinary actions against erring members that is available to both HOUSES of the US CONGRESS. Under it, a member is rebuked for their conduct in terms less severe than a CENSURE, and continues to serve. The KOREAGATE scandal led to the House voting to reprimand three members; a more recent reprimand was administered to Rep. Barney Frank (1940–) of Massachusetts in 1990. Frank, a gifted legislator and openly gay, had allegedly allowed a former assistant/male friend to use his apartment for prostitution. The House Ethics Committee did not accept this, but recommended a reprimand because of a letter Frank had written to the man's probation officer and his fixing of 33 parking tickets. The reprimand was voted by 408–18.

republic (Lat. *res publica*, the public concern) A state in which the supreme power is not vested in a MONARCH; its HEAD OF STATE, or PRESIDENT, will often be HEAD OF GOVERNMENT as well. A republic should be a DEMOCRACY, but in practice it is often not. Thomas JEFFERSON reckoned it 'the only form of government which is not eternally at war with the rights of mankind', but Palmerston (*see* PAM) asserted that 'large republics seem to be incessantly and inherently aggressive'.

> The republican form of government is the highest form of government, but because of this it requires the highest type of human nature – a type nowhere at present existing.
> ROBERT SPENCER (1820–1903), *The Americans*

> The republic is a dream;
> Nothing happens unless it is first a dream.
> CARL SANDBURG, *Washington Monument by Night*

> *Lady*: Well, doctor, what have we got? A republic or a monarchy?
> *Benjamin Franklin* (leaving the PHILADELPHIA CONVENTION, 1787): A republic, if you can keep it.

Battle Hymn of the Republic *See* MINE EYES HAVE SEEN THE GLORY OF THE COMING OF THE LORD.

Plato's *Republic* The blueprint for an ideal state set forward c. 370 BC by the Greek philosopher Plato (427?–347 BC). He set its population at 5040, the most he felt could be addressed by an orator, and divided the citizenry into guardians (rulers), auxiliaries (warriors), farmers and artisans, and slaves. The top two tiers were to hold property, meals and children in common, with only the 'best' permitted to breed.

Republican (1) An advocate of a republican form of government in place of a monarchy, notably in Britain or Australia. (2) In newly-independent America, the supporters of Thomas JEFFERSON and James MADISON who by 1792 were accusing George WASHINGTON and Alexander HAMILTON of being 'monarchists', both because of the first President's love of pomp and his Treasury Secretary's ambitious tax schemes. From them is descended the DEMOCRATIC PARTY. (3) In Ireland, an advocate of revolutionary action to reunite the island as a 32-country republic.

Republican cloth coat The phrase used by Richard NIXON about his wife Pat in his 1952 CHECKERS speech, which convinced most viewers that he had not enriched himself from a $18,000 secret fund set up by supporters. His assertion that his wife wore such a plain garment was a dig at INFLUENCE-PEDDLING under the TRUMAN administration; E. Merl Young, a former examiner for the Reconstruction Finance Corporation, had accepted a mink coat for his wife, a WHITE HOUSE secretary, from a lawyer who had applied for an RFC loan. Nixon declared:

> It isn't very much, but Pat and I have the satisfaction that every dime we've got is honestly ours. I should say this – Pat doesn't have a mink coat. But she does have a respectable Republican cloth coat. And I always tell her that she'd look good in anything.

Republican Party The party of Abraham LINCOLN and Ronald REAGAN, which has occupied the WHITE HOUSE for almost 90 years since its foundation in 1854, but has controlled either House of CONGRESS for far less a period. Originally a radical party in the old sense, it moved to the right in the late 19th century but retains a liberal element, though this has been in eclipse since the 1980s and the NEO-CONSERVATIVES have been in the ascendant. Harry S TRUMAN remarked that 'the Republican Party either corrupts its liberals or expels them', Adlai STEVENSON that 'every four years the Republican programme is interrupted by the liberal hour', while Sen. Eugene McCarthy declared: 'The function of liberal Republicans is to shoot the wounded after the battle.' The party's emblem is an ELEPHANT, which Stevenson considered appropriate:

> The elephant has a thick skin, a head full of ivory and proceeds best by grasping the tail of its predecessor.

The party was formed by Democrats who broke away after Sen. Stephen Douglas introduced the KANSAS-NEBRASKA ACT in January 1854. The name Republican was proposed by Alan Bovay, an attorney from RIPON, Wisconsin, and adopted by a meeting at Jackson, Michigan on 6 July 1854. Appealing to national rather than sectional interests, it absorbed the remaining WHIGS and KNOW-NOTHINGS, and won control of the House in elections that November. Its first national CONVENTION was held in Philadelphia on 17 June 1856, John C. Fremont being nominated for President. Four years later the Republicans nominated Lincoln, a former WHIG Congressman, and he carried the election. Lincoln said that the Republicans were

> For both the man and the dollar, but in case of conflict the man before the dollar.

The CIVIL WAR installed the Republicans as the party of the UNION and of ABOLITIONISM, Frederick Douglas (*see* LIBERATOR) declaring:

> I recognise the Republican Party as the sheet anchor of the coloured man's political hopes and the ark of his safety.

With Lincoln's assassination at the close of the war, triumphant northern Republicans adopted an aggressive programme of RECONSTRUCTION. For the rest of the 19th century, save for the presidencies of Grover CLEVELAND, they were the dominant power in federal politics, becoming steadily more identified with big business and correspondingly more conservative. The TARIFF, the GOLD STANDARD and IMPERIALISM gave them a new lease of life under Theodore ROOSEVELT and TAFT; but the BULL MOOSE split of 1912 let in Woodrow WILSON. Post-war prosperity and ISOLATIONISM brought the election of HARDING, COOLIDGE and HOOVER, after which the GREAT DEPRESSION put them in the wilderness even though Will Rogers insisted:

> I don't want to blame the Republicans for the depression. They aren't smart enough.

For a generation the Republicans were seen as WASPS with *pince-nez*, but they fought back to win control of Congress just after WORLD WAR II, and captured the White House with EISENHOWER in 1952. The prosperous inertia of his ADMINISTRATION gave John F. KENNEDY a strong suit to defeat Richard NIXON in 1960 – though only just – and a flirtation with Barry Goldwater's ultra-conservatism brought a heavy defeat in 1964. However, a 'new Nixon' won in 1968, partly because the Democrats were in disarray over VIETNAM but also because the Republicans were making inroads in the conservative South. The coalition held in 1972, and the Republicans overcame the trauma of WATERGATE for Gerald FORD to come close in 1976. Then came the Reagan years, when a revival of conservatism plus the FEELGOOD FACTOR gave the Republicans three terms in the White House, the last under George BUSH Snr; yet only for the first years could Reagan put together a majority in Congress, and even then he was dependent on conservative Democrats in the House. It took the election of Bill CLINTON for the Republicans at last to capture both Houses with the CONTRACT WITH AMERICA; although NEWT Gingrich's brand of Republicanism did not prove durable and many voters blamed the Republicans as much as Clinton for ZIPPERGATE, conservatism – and right-wing radicalism – was a strong enough force to see George W. BUSH into the White House in 2000 by the closest margin in history. Concern over terrorism in the wake of 9/11 merely strengthened the Republican hegemony.

> The Republicans have their splits right after an election – Democrats have theirs just before.
>
> WILL ROGERS

> They've been peddling eyewash about themselves and hogwash about the Democrats. What they need is a good mouthwash.
>
> LYNDON B. JOHNSON

> We're the party that wants to see an America in which people can still get rich.
>
> RONALD REAGAN, 1982

> The one thing we're able to do is raise money.
>
> DAN QUAYLE

Mr Republican *See* MISTER.

resale price maintenance (RPM) The issue which caused the governments of Harold MACMILLAN and SIR ALEC Douglas-Home the greatest difficulty with their own supporters: legislation finally pushed through by Edward HEATH as Trade and Industry Secretary just before the 1964 election – which the Conservatives narrowly lost – to outlaw the fixing of retail prices for goods by their manufacturers. The only major items exempted were books (until 1997) and medicines (until 2001). The abolition of RPM was bitterly resisted by small shopkeepers who feared that having to cut prices would drive them out of business; such a threat did eventually arise, but only with the dominance of the supermarkets, of which there were then only a handful.

rescission The power of a President to notify CONGRESS that he will not spend certain funds that have been APPROPRIATED. Until 1974 the President could act unilaterally; in that year the law was changed to make rescission subject to a majority in both Houses. *See also* IMPOUNDMENT.

research assistant At WESTMINSTER, the only member of staff an MP is likely to have apart from a secretary. Advertisements for research assistants usually stress the low pay offered, and many individuals just out of university do the job for almost nothing as a first step on the ladder.

reselection The process by which a constituency Labour Party (CLP) with a sitting MP determines whether he or she should continue as its candidate. Until 1980 the reselection of a member wishing to stand again was almost automatic, but then the party gave way to BENNITE pressure for '**mandatory reselection**'. This obliged each constituency to hold a full candidate selection process prior to every election regardless of whether there was a sitting member. Some parties tried to get round this by approving a SHORT-LIST of one, so that the MP was unopposed at the final selection stage. The hard LEFT saw reselection as a means of ousting right-wingers and installing hard-liners through manipulation of the electoral process, where the decision rested with the constituency management committee and not with all party members. In the event no more than half a dozen sitting members were ousted prior to the 1983 and 1987 elections, but a number of others gave up in exasperation and at least one who fought off a challenge was harried to an early grave. The sting has since gone out of mandatory reselection, with party members as a whole choosing the candidate, but a handful of MPs before each election still fall by the wayside.

reserve. reserve currency An internationally-traded currency that CENTRAL BANKS will keep as part of their reserves, along with gold, and will use when necessary to meet their foreign commitments. The US dollar holds price of place, with the EURO, the yen and the pound some way behind.

reserved powers *See* POWERS.

reshuffle A periodic feature of UK politics, a Prime Minister's reconstruction of the Cabinet, with Ministers being moved between jobs and usually some new faces to replace Ministers who have retired, resigned or been sacked. Anthony EDEN confided that 'the worst of being sacked is that you can never find your car'; the public sector trade union leader Rodney Bickerstaffe described the impact of one of Margaret THATCHER's reshuffles as 'like being cured of diarrhoea and then finding that you have dysentery', while Reginald Maudling, dropped from her SHADOW CABINET, remarked bitterly: 'There comes a moment in every man's life when he must make way for an older man.'

> It does no harm to throw the occasional man overboard, but it does not do much good if you are steering full speed ahead for the rocks.
>
> Sir IAN GILMOUR (1926–), after being sacked by Mrs Thatcher

Resident Commissioner The title given to Puerto Rico's elected delegate to the US HOUSE OF REPRESENTATIVES. In common with the DELEGATES from the District of Columbia and America's island territories, he or she has most of the privileges of a Congressman, including the right to speak, but may not vote. The Delegates are elected for two years, the Resident Commissioner for four.

Resignation Honours *See* HONOURS LIST.

resilience A word that has entered the vocabulary of government since 9/11: the ability of the vital systems of government, commerce and society to withstand terrorist attack and continue operating if a disaster has impacted on other parts of the national infrastructure.

Resistance The underground organisation in German-occupied and VICHY France during WORLD WAR II that continued the struggle after the country's leaders surrendered. It sabotaged enemy operations, passed information about troop movements to the Allies by clandestine radio, hid members of the Allied forces (escaping prisoners of war and airmen who had been shot down) and helped them get home. From May 1943 the various Resistance groups – including former army officers, Communists and supporters of DE GAULLE (*see* FREE FRENCH) – were co-ordinated in the *Conseil National de la Résistance*, led by Jean Moulin (and after his arrest in June 1943 by Georges Bidault). In February 1944 the MAQUIS, provincial guerrilla groups operating in the countryside, became part of the newly formed *Forces Françaises de l'Intérieur* (FFI), which played a vital role in the LIBERATION. During World War II there were also active resistance groups in Belgium, Holland, Denmark, Norway, Poland, Yugoslavia (*see* PARTISANS), Greece, Italy and the occupied Soviet territories.

Resolute desk The desk used by Presidents of the United States in the OVAL OFFICE of the WHITE HOUSE. It is made of timbers from HMS *Resolute*, a Royal Navy ship sent to the Arctic in the vain search for Sir John Franklin's expedition and salvaged by American whalers after being abandoned by her crew; the ship was returned by the US Navy to its embarrassed owners in pristine condition. Presented by Queen Victoria to President Hayes, the desk has been variously sited in the Yellow Oval Room, where Presidents Benjamin Harrison, CLEVELAND, Franklin D. ROOSEVELT and TRUMAN used it, and more recently in the Oval Office; it was heightened for President REAGAN.

resolution. Resolution 242 Perhaps the most famous UN SECURITY COUNCIL resolution, the one which has governed peacemaking efforts in the Middle East since shortly after the SIX DAY WAR. Approved on 22 November 1967, it states that conquest is inadmissible; a just and lasting peace must be established, belligerency ended and demilitarised zones established; Israeli troops should withdraw from occupied territories; refugee problems should be solved; and acknowledgment made of the sovereignty and territorial integrity of all states in the region and their right to live in peace within secure and recognised boundaries.

affirmative resolution In the UK legislative process, the specific approval required from the COMMONS (in some cases both Houses) before an ORDER can take effect.

Budget resolutions *See* BUDGET.

concurrent resolution Resolutions put to both Houses of the US CONGRESS, not necessarily simultaneously, concerning their operations. They are not legislative in nature, do not require a Presidential signature when passed and cover such issues as the time when the Congress should adjourn.

joint resolution In the US CONGRESS, a piece of legislation virtually indistinguishable from a BILL, used for specific matters like a single APPROPRIATION but also the sole instrument for proposing an AMENDMENT to the CONSTITUTION. Despite its name, a joint resolution does not have to be considered simultaneously by the House and Senate.

money resolution *See* MONEY.

mother of all resolutions *See* MOTHER.

simple resolution A resolution concerning the operation of one House only of the US CONGRESS, which is considered by it alone, without reference to any other authority.

RESPECT Respect, Equality, Socialism, Peace, Environment, Community, Trade Unionism. The far-left coalition, motivated by opposition to the WAR IN IRAQ, which George Galloway (*see* OIL FOR FOOD) founded early in 2005 after his expulsion from the LABOUR PARTY, and under whose banner he won Bethnal Green and Bow for Labour in the 2005 general election (*see* MR BLAIR, THIS IS FOR IRAQ). The party also finished second in three other seats with strong Muslim populations, and Galloway promised an ongoing campaign to finish off NEW LABOUR.

respect. culture of respect The key phrase from the QUEEN'S SPEECH launching Tony BLAIR's third term of government, coincidentally delivered on 17 May 2005, the day Galloway launched his onslaught on the IRAQ WAR in testimony on Capitol Hill (*see* LION OF THE BRITISH PARLIAMENT). It summed up Labour's plans to restore politeness to society and crack down on unruly and anti-social behaviour by what one police chief described as 'feral youths', Blair saying:

> Bringing a proper sense of respect and responsibility cannot be the job of Parliament alone. Parents, local communities, local people have to join with law makers and law enforcers to make a difference. It is time to reclaim the streets for the decent majority.

Restricted One of the lowest levels of sensitivity of official documents which a government or military service wishes to keep secret. Although care is taken to limit a restricted document's circulation, it is less vital to security than one marked CONFIDENTIAL, and far less sensitive than one marked TOP SECRET.

retreads A WESTMINSTER term for MPs who come back to the COMMONS to resume a political career interrupted by the loss of their original seat. *Compare* VIRGINS. The term originates in the motor trade, retreads being tyres reconditioned for use after being worn out.

return. return to legality The phrase used throughout the fourteen-year Rhodesian crisis for the process of ending UDI by the Smith regime and the setting up of an internationally recognised government. A return to legality was said by successive British governments to be a prerequisite for the lifting of SANCTIONS.

Returning Officer In UK Parliamentary elections, the official of the relevant local authority in charge of conducting the election in a given CONSTITUENCY, ensuring that the law is observed, conducting the COUNT and announcing the result.

duplicate return The document listing the outcome of any US Congressional election which is sent direct to the relevant House of CONGRESS by the authorities of the State where it was held.

unopposed return (1) The outcome of an election where only one candidate is put forward to fill a vacancy, and the result can be notified without the need to conduct a poll. (2) The procedure under which a report or other document is lodged with Parliament with no provision for it to be debated.

reunification The dream of West German politicians for four decades after the division of their country into zones by the victorious WORLD WAR II allies, and no doubt the private aspiration of many East Germans, even if some hoped to see the reunited nation under Communist control. As long as the COLD WAR persisted, Moscow viewed talk of a reunified Germany as a PROVOCATION, especially as its likely capital, Berlin, lay in the heart of the Soviet zone. It took the fall of the BERLIN WALL in November 1989 to make reunification a real possibility, and at the time no-one expected the process to be completed in little over a year, driven through by Chancellor Helmut KOHL and facilitated by the TWO PLUS FOUR TALKS. Indeed on the day the wall fell, a German professor emotionally told a seminar at the BROOKINGS INSTITUTION attended by the author that he now believed his country might be reunified within fifteen years. Reunification – which the German political establishment at the time insisted on calling **unification** – removed an artificial political division, but there has been a price to pay. Growth in the previously-booming West was slowed as huge sums were diverted to renew the East's crumbling infrastructure, and more recently the stagnation of the economy as a whole and high levels of unemployment in the East have left some hankering for the bad old days – not of a divided Germany but of Communism.

revaluation (1) The opposite of DEVALUATION, and thus a word of which the British have no direct experience. It involves a country's CENTRAL BANK unilaterally increasing the value of its currency against others, because pressures in the currency markets make it impossible to hold it down. At a number of points since the collapse of the BRETTON WOODS system in 1971, there has been pressure from other countries for either the now-abolished German mark or the Japanese yen to be revalued. (2) The process within the system of UK property taxes under which the value of a property is reassessed by the Inland Revenue to take into account the passage of time and fluctuations in price. It was a revaluation which triggered the opposition to the RATES that led to the POLL TAX; the outcome of revaluations under the present system of COUNCIL TAX and business rates will not be much more popular.

revanchism The stirring-up of a population to regain its national territory, taken away by war or a treaty signed under duress. After each of the two World Wars, the defeated nations, especially Germany, were shorn of what they regarded as integral parts of their country. It has taken the end of the COLD WAR and the ENLARGEMENT of the European Union to the east to end the territorial claims, but friction continues over financial claims, notably between Poland and Germany.

revenue. revenue-neutral A budgetary package constructed so as neither to raise nor to lower the overall level of taxation that will have to be imposed, extra spending in one area being offset by cuts in others, and minor tax adjustments cancelling each other out.

revenue-sharing The scheme devised by the Republican RIPON SOCIETY and implemented by the NIXON administration, under which a proportion of federal tax revenues is passed back to state, city and county governments. The original aim was both to decentralise spending and decision-making and to lower property taxes; revenue-sharing also gave a powerful boost to social programmes at state and local level. The REAGAN administration, immediately after taking office in 1981, sought to scrap it as a way of saving billions of tax dollars; an alliance of CONGRESS and the US Conference of Mayors defeated that proposal, but revenue-sharing was cut back later in the decade.

reverse. reverse discrimination *See* DISCRIMINATION.

I have no reverse gear Tony BLAIR's challenging statement to the LABOUR PARTY conference in Bournemouth on 1 October 2003, when facing left-wing and union demands for the abandonment of public service reforms and censure over the WAR ON IRAQ. Refusing to back down or alter course, he told delegates:

> I can only go one way. I've not got a reverse gear.

Blair's assertion prompted instant comparisons with Margaret THATCHER's assertion over two decades before that 'the LADY'S NOT FOR TURNING'.

revise. privilege to revise and extend The latitude accorded by the CONGRESSIONAL RECORD for members of Congress to edit or clarify their spoken remarks before they appear in print. Without it, one Congressman has said, the *Record* would be 'really sad reading next day – the best comic you ever saw'. The danger in the procedure is that it could make it harder for courts subsequently to ascertain the true intent of Congress in passing a particular item of legislation.

revising chamber A subordinate chamber in a LEGISLATURE which lacks the power to determine policy, but performs a valuable role in ensuring that measures passed by or to be submitted to the more powerful house are sound in detail, watertight and workable. The term is frequently used to justify the HOUSE OF LORDS.

revisionism An abusive Communist term for any sign of original thought, and of deviation from the Party's set ideological path into dangerous heresies. At times Communists have used it about each other, notably the Chinese leadership after their break with Moscow. Revisionism was originally a moderate, non-revolutionary form of socialism first advocated in Germany in 1899 by Eduard Bernstein, who felt the socialist movement should include all classes and not be restricted to workers.

> There is only one answer to revisionism: smash its face in. LENIN, 1904

revisit A euphemism for the discarding by a victorious CANDIDATE of a promise or commitment made during the election campaign. Shortly before his INAUGURATION in January 1992, Bill CLINTON said that after studying BUDGET projections, he would have to 'revisit' his promise to cut taxes on the middle class.

Revolt of 1910 The coup mounted in the US HOUSE OF REPRESENTATIVES by Republican INSURGENTS to oust Speaker Joe Cannon (*see* FOUL-MOUTHED JOE) from the RULES COMMITTEE and thus break his near-total influence. Cannon, by selecting the committee and sitting on it himself, had been able to halt the progress of any BILL of which he disapproved. Exasperated by what they saw as his dictatorial conduct, a minority of Republicans led by George W. Norris of Nebraska joined with Democrats in March 1910 to force through a rule change depriving the SPEAKER of the power to appoint members to the Rules Committee or serve on it himself. The Democrats, after winning the 1910 elections, went on the following year to bar the Speaker from appointing members of STANDING COMMITTEES.

revolution A sudden and complete change in a country's system of government brought about by radical opponents of the previous regime; Napoleon termed revolution 'an opinion backed by bayonets', Germaine Greer 'the festival of the oppressed', Ambrose Bierce more dubiously 'an abrupt change in the form of misgovernment'.

Some revolutions take place within the ESTABLISHMENT (*see* PALACE REVOLUTION). PLATO wrote: 'In any form of government, revolution always starts from an outbreak of dissension in the ruling class.' Others involve the overthrow of democracies: Richard CROSSMAN considered that 'a revolutionary party is a contradiction in terms'; G. K. Chesterton that 'You can never have a revolution in order to establish a democracy. You must have democracy in order to have a revolution.' Aristotle identified a more general factor: 'Revolutions are not about trifles, but they spring from trifles.' Some are planned for years by highly motivated groups determined on change; LENIN maintained an element of patience and surprise, saying: 'It is impossible to predict the time and progress of revolution. It is governed by its own more or less mysterious laws'; TROTSKY's view was that 'the revolution does not choose its paths. It made its first steps toward victory under the belly of a Cossack's horse.' Those committed to revolution generally feel there is no other course open to them. Pierre Joseph Proudhon asserted: 'There is no middle way between REACTION and revolution,' Alexander Herzen that it is 'better to perish with the revolution than to seek refuge in the almshouse of reaction', but Heinrich Heine was realistic enough to argue that 'a revolution is a misfortune – but an unsuccessful revolution is an even greater misfortune'. However, CHE Guevara proclaimed that 'in a revolution one wins or dies', and CHAIRMAN MAO Tse-Tung that 'to die for the reactionary is as light as a feather, but to die for the revolution is heavier than Mount Tai.'

The Italian patriot Mazzini proudly asserted that 'great revolutions are the work rather of principles than of bayonets', but the bayonets come in useful, particularly when the revolution is spearheaded by a minority of zealots; indeed Robespierre, just before the Reign of TERROR, asked: 'Citizens, do you want a revolution without revolution?' Lenin insisted: 'The substitution of the proletarian for the bourgeois state is impossible without a violent revolution.' Mao Tse-Tung wrote: 'A revolution is not the same thing as inviting people to dinner, or writing an essay, or painting a picture . . . A revolution is an insurrection, an act of violence by which one class overthrows another'; and Malcolm X told black Americans: 'Revolutions are never waged singing: "We shall overcome". Revolutions are based on bloodshed.'

The ruthlessness – and the revolution – may continue once the revolutionaries have taken power. STALIN in 1917 declared: 'The revolution is incapable either of regretting or of burying its dead,' and the Algerian revolutionary leader Ahmed Ben Bella: 'It is an illusion to think that you can have a revolution without prisons.' What revolutions achieve for the people is a matter of opinion. Many are born of idealism, and Abraham LINCOLN said in apparent approval that 'revolutions do not go backward'; but Shirley Williams lamented: 'The saddest illusion of revolutionary socialists is that revolution itself will change the nature of human beings.' The Czech statesman Jan Masaryk (*see* DEFENESTRATION) considered that 'revolution or dictatorship can sometimes abolish bad things, but they can never create good or lasting ones'; George Bernard Shaw that 'revolutions have never lightened the burden of tyranny; they have only shifted it to another shoulder'. Metternich wrote that 'in revolutions those who want everything always get the better of those who only want a certain amount'; Che Guevara that 'a revolution that does not continue to grow deeper is a revolution that is retreating'; and on a lighter note Indonesia's President Sukarno declared: 'We must be on guard lest our revolution die out. Therefore give it romanticism.'

> Revolution is the pod
> Systems rattle from
> When the Winds of Will are stirred.
>
> EMILY DICKINSON (1830–66)

> One revolution is just like one cocktail; it just gets you organised for the next. WILL ROGERS

> The word 'revolution' is a word for which you kill, for which you die, for which you send the labouring classes to their death, but which does not possess any content.
>
> SIMONE WEIL (1909–43), *Oppression and Liberty*

> If you want to know the taste of a pear, you must taste the pear by eating it yourself. If you want to know the theory and methods of revolution, you must take part in revolution.
>
> MAO TSE-TUNG, 1937

See also AMERICAN REVOLUTION; FRENCH REVOLUTION; GLORIOUS REVOLUTION; OCTOBER REVOLUTION; ORANGE REVOLUTION; PERMANENT REVOLUTION; QUIET REVOLUTION; RUSSIAN REVOLUTION; VELVET REVOLUTION.

Revolution of 1800 Thomas JEFFERSON's own words for his election as President and the changes in American government that followed. With Jefferson and Aaron BURR tied on 75 electoral votes each, and John ADAMS and Charles Pinckney just behind, the election went to the HOUSE OF REPRESENTATIVES, and after six deadlocked ballots Jefferson was elected with ten states to Burr's four. Some ultra-FEDERALISTS threatened a new election or even a military COUP, but Jefferson was sworn in and the TWELFTH AMENDMENT was passed to require separate voting in future for the President and Vice President; the role of parties was thus acknowledged in the CONSTITUTION. Jefferson's Republicans also regarded the federalist-appointed Supreme and Federal Courts with suspicion; they repealed the 1801 Judiciary Act under which the outgoing John Adams had manned an expanded court system with federalist appointees, and sought unsuccessfully to IMPEACH Chief Justice Samuel Chase.

> As real a revolution in the principles of our government as that of 1776 was in its form.
>
> Chief Justice OLIVER ELLSWORTH

Revolution of 1905 The combination of a successful GENERAL STRIKE by urban workers and rural uprisings by various ethnic minorities that led Tsar Nicholas II to concede modest reforms, including the reconvening of an elected DUMA. Russia's recent humiliating defeat by Japan, and the impact of atrocities against demonstrators by Tsarist troops, weakened Nicholas' hand.

revolution of rising expectations The phrase coined in 1953 by Adlai STEVENSON for the upsurge of political awareness and desire for prosperity in the developing world, transcending the COLD WAR, that has since profoundly changed the horizons of Western politicians. Stevenson wrote in *Look* magazine of 22 September 1953:

> Many of the world's troubles are not just due to Russia or communism. They would be with us in any event because we live in an era of revolution – the revolution of rising expectations. In Asia, the masses now count for something. Tomorrow, they will count for more. And, for better or worse, the future belongs to those who understand the hopes and fears of masses in ferment. The new nations want independence, including the inalienable right to make their own mistakes. The people want respect – and something to eat every day. And they want something better for their children.

revolutionary A person who makes their career of revolution, or puts their commitment to revolution above everything else. Fidel Castro stated the obvious, that 'the duty of every revolutionary is to make a revolution', but disciplined MARXISTS are divided from others over whether the revolution should be planned for. Castro, with the benefit of experience, declared that 'it does not matter how small you are as long as you have faith and a plan of action', and Daniel Cohn-Bendit (*see* Danny the RED) argued anarchistically that 'the moment you have a plan you cease to be a revolutionary'. The revolutionary needs an indomitable spirit, the BLACK PANTHER Bobby Seale saying: 'You can jail a revolutionary, but you cannot jail the revolution', but his YIPPIE contemporary Abbie Hoffman said more realistically: 'The first duty of a revolutionary is to get away with it.' Albert Camus declared sourly that 'every revolutionary ends by becoming either an oppressor or a heretic', but Castro disagreed: 'A man who does not believe in human beings is not a revolutionary'.

> If today I stand here as a revolutionary, it is as a revolutionary against the revolution.
>
> HITLER at his trial after the MUNICH BEER HALL PUTSCH, 1924

> The revolutionary wants to change the world; the rebel is careful to preserve the abuses from which he suffers so that he can go on rebelling against them.
>
> JEAN-PAUL SARTRE (1905–80), *Baudelaire*

> Revolution allows the revolutionary to sublimate his sado-masochistic, neurotic, anal tendencies into a concern for the working class.
>
> ANON. *graffiti*

revolving door WASHINGTON-speak for the situation in which government officials leave their jobs and immediately start work for a corporation with which they have been dealing or which they have been regulating. At the highest level, immediate moves are ruled out by the Ethics In Government Act, but concern is frequently voiced about the traffic between the PENTAGON and defence contractors; a scandal in 2003 when Darleen Druyun, the DoD official negotiating a multi-billion air tanker contract with Boeing, was offered and agreed to take a job with the corporation before the deal was signed, forced the resignation of Boeing's president and chief financial officer and led to criminal charges. The revolving door is also found in WHITEHALL, with Ministry of Defence officials the most frequent leavers for companies with which they have been dealing.

He wouldn't go two rounds with a revolving door The memorable description of Billy Snedden, leader of Australia's LIBERAL party 1972–75, by the DLP Senator Vince Gair.

Rexists A Belgian Catholic party advocating FASCIST methods, formed by Léon Degrelle in 1936. Markedly COLLABORATIONIST during the German occupation, it was suppressed when the occupying forces were driven out in 1944. The name is an adaptation of *Christus Rex*, Christ the King, the watchword of the Catholic Young People's Action Society founded in 1925.

Reyjkavik summit The meeting between Ronald REAGAN and Mikhail GORBACHEV in the Icelandic capital in October 1986, at which the Soviet leader offered to reduce his nation's stockpile of medium-range and strategic nuclear missiles if Reagan agreed to a ten-year moratorium on aspects of the STAR WARS programme. Reagan refused, and the summit came to a sudden end. However, the next time they met, in WASHINGTON in December 1987, they signed the INF treaty.

> President Reagan's refusal to trade away SDI for the apparent near-fulfilment of his dream of a nuclear-free world was crucial to the victory over Communism.
>
> MARGARET THATCHER, *The Downing Street Years*

Reyne. La Reyne le veult (Norman Fr. the Queen wishes it) The phrase uttered by the Queen or her representative which constitutes the ROYAL ASSENT for legislation passed by the UK Parliament. **Le Roi le veult** would be the equivalent under a king.

Reynolds v Sims The 1964 SUPREME COURT ruling which finally established that electoral districts for America's state legislatures must be devised on a basis of equal population, and not on any other grounds. In determining that LEGISLATURES should represent 'people, not trees or acres', the Court rejected the argument that a state could follow the example of CONGRESS in having one HOUSE with its seats strictly allocated on the basis of population, and the other on the basis of territory, thus advantaging rural voters.

RFK The initials of Robert Fitzgerald ('Bobby') KENNEDY, almost as often used as those of his brother JFK; they became the title of WASHINGTON's football stadium.

rhetoric The showy and hectoring over-use of language in political speeches, from the Greek *rhetor*, a professional orator. At a WHITE HOUSE meeting on combating hunger on 17 March 1969, Richard NIXON told members of his ADMINISTRATION:

> Use all the rhetoric – as long as it doesn't cost money.

rhetorical question A question asked by a political speaker to make a point, rather than because they wish to hear the answer. It poses the hazard that as the speaker pauses for effect before continuing, someone in the audience may give a highly inappropriate answer. At a feminist FRINGE MEETING at the 1983 LABOUR PARTY conference, a speaker asked: 'What do women in the Labour Party really want?' Before she could continue, a voice shouted: 'Cut Neil KINNOCK's balls off.' But perhaps the most celebrated befell the normally astute Harold WILSON during the 1964 election campaign. At a critical moment in his speech he declaimed: 'And why do I place such emphasis on the Royal Navy?' Back came the unscripted response:

> Because you're in Chatham!

rich. Don't make the rich poorer, make the poor richer A quotation from Abraham LINCOLN that Margaret THATCHER, not surprisingly, carried in her HANDBAG. Lincoln also said: 'I don't believe in a law to prevent a man getting rich; it would do more harm than good', and 'That some should be rich shows that others may become rich, and hence is just encouragement to industry and enterprise.'

eat the rich! A slogan used in the 1980s by militant ANARCHISTS.

soak the rich! An aim imputed to the LABOUR PARTY by its Conservative opponents when it was committed to a WEALTH TAX; it was not, however, a slogan the party ever used, though many left-wingers would have applauded it.

squeeze the rich until the pips squeak *See* SQUEEZE.

riddle wrapped inside a mystery inside an enigma, a CHURCHILL's words on the ambiguities of Soviet policy in the early weeks of WORLD WAR II, delivered in a radio broadcast on 1 October 1939. They were prompted by the Soviet occupation of eastern Poland on 18 September, in league with the Germans. At the time Britain had no idea whether the NAZI-SOVIET PACT would stick, or whether STALIN realised that HITLER would inevitably turn against him and was simply being opportunistic. Churchill's phrase has often been used out of historical context, as if it were a general reflection on the Russian character. He said:

> I cannot forecast to you the action of Russia. It is a riddle wrapped in a mystery inside an enigma.

rider In the US SENATE, an unrelated proposal tacked onto an APPROPRIATION Bill; in the House AMENDMENTs to a Bill must be germane to its purpose. In 1943 Senators tacked a rider withholding the salaries of three federal officials; President ROOSEVELT was opposed to this but let the Bill go through unsigned because it authorised essential funds for the operation of government. A rider may only be attached if a day's written notice is given and there is a two-thirds vote for it to be considered.

riding The Canadian term for a member of Parliament's CONSTITUENCY.

right (1) The right wing, a political tendency that is almost invariably NATIONALIST and usually CONSERVATIVE, and may also now be RADICAL. Its adherents usually want a lean but strong government that does not interfere with them. The term derives from France's pre-revolutionary Estates-General, in which those who were neither aristocratic nor clerical, and were thus more likely to favour progress, sat on the left and the others on the right. THATCHERISM marked the triumph of the right wing of Britain's CONSERVATIVE PARTY, challenging Harold MACMILLAN's judgement that

> A successful party of the right must continue to recruit from the centre and even from the left centre. Once it begins to shrink itself into a snail, it will be doomed.

America's REPUBLICAN PARTY also moved firmly to the right at much the same time under Ronald REAGAN, though its continuance in that course has brought it more success than the Tories. (2) Virtue and justice in politics, and particularly in international relations. Woodrow WILSON judged that 'right is more precious than peace', Theodore ROOSEVELT maintained that 'aggressive fighting for the right is the noblest sport the world affords', but HITLER went one further, saying:

> There is only one right in the world, and that is one's own strength.

The word is also used in connection with the morality of politicians in office. Harry S TRUMAN used to quote Mark Twain's adage: 'Always do right. This will gratify some people, and astonish the rest', and Daniel O'Connell is reputed to have said: 'Nothing is politically right which is morally wrong.' Abraham LINCOLN acknowledged that the right course was not always obvious, saying:

> I know that the Lord is always on the side of right. But it is my constant anxiety and prayer that I and this nation should always be on the Lord's side.

Lyndon B. JOHNSON put it his own way: 'Doing what's right isn't the problem. It's knowing what's right.'

> The best way I know to win an argument is to start by being in the right.
>
> LORD HAILSHAM

> There are times in politics when you must be on the right side and lose.
>
> Professor JOHN KENNETH GALBRAITH, 1968

The Right Approach The first of two policy documents that started to develop the THATCHERITE bent of Britain's CONSER-

VATIVE PARTY. It appeared in 1976, the year after Mrs Thatcher's election as leader. The following year a more detailed paper, *The Right Approach to the Economy*, was produced; put together by Sir Keith Joseph (*see* MAD MONK), Sir Geoffrey HOWE, David Howell and the Heathite James Prior, it advocated control of the money supply, lower direct taxation and 'firm management of government expenditure'. Some right-wingers thought it too timid, particularly toward the unions, and more forceful policies were subsequently adopted. But it discarded much of the Heath legacy, including any thought of an INCOMES POLICY.

Right Honourable Gentleman *See* HONOURABLE GENTLEMAN; Honourable FRIEND.

The Right Road for Britain The first comprehensive policy statement from the CONSERVATIVE PARTY after WORLD WAR II and its defeat in the 1945 election, drafted by R. A. (RAB) Butler and launched by CHURCHILL on 23 July 1949; marking a clear break from the negativism of pre-war years, it sold 2.2 million copies in the first three months. Its proposals foreshadowed the BUTSKELLITE line taken in government from 1951; it advocated the reform and modification of the WELFARE STATE created by Labour, and added a commitment – not implemented – to EQUAL PAY.

The Right Stuff The 1930s US Army slang phrase adopted by the author Tom Wolfe (1931–) to describe the special quality of steadiness and courage, going beyond routine bravery and excluding all those without it, required by America's fraternity of test pilots. Wolfe chose it as the title for his book (1979) on the trials and tribulations of the first US astronauts. It later attached itself to John Glenn, one of the astronauts, who had become US Senator for Ohio and challenged for the Democratic presidential nomination in 1984, just after the film of *The Right Stuff* went on general release. It soon emerged that Glenn lacked the right stuff to become President, but astoundingly he went back into space in 1998 as a guinea-pig for research on the elderly. Wolfe wrote:

> The idea was to prove at every foot of the way up . . . that you were one of the elected and anointed ones who had the right stuff and could move higher and higher and even – ultimately, God willing, one day – that you might be able to join that special few at the very top, that elite who had the capacity to bring tears to men's eyes, the very Brotherhood of the Right Stuff itself.

the right to be consulted, the right to encourage and the right to warn The three powers attributed to the SOVEREIGN in a Constitutional MONARCHY by Walter Bagehot in *The English Constitution* (1867).

Right to Buy The trump card of the MANIFESTO on which Margaret THATCHER's Conservatives fought and won Britain's 1979 general election: the granting to millions of families renting houses or flats from local authorities the right to buy them on easy terms. Many Labour councils resisted 'Right to Buy', but it caught the imagination of over 2 million council tenants who not only bought their homes but, in many cases, switched their votes to the Tories for the next three elections.

right to choose The 'BIG IDEA' for both Labour and the Conservatives in the run-up to the 2005 general election: greater freedom for the citizen to choose the hospital they would be treated in or the school their children could go to. For Labour it meant greater choice within the state system; for the Conservatives the chance to use – and thus build up – the PRIVATE SECTOR.

right to keep and bear arms The right campaigned for by the NRA and other US gun-owners' groups whenever GUN CONTROL legislation is before CONGRESS. It stems from the Second Amendment to the CONSTITUTION, contained in the BILL OF RIGHTS:

> A well regulated militia being necessary to the security of a free state, the right of the people to keep and bear arms shall not be infringed.

The NRA has long argued that the Amendment does not simply refer to the maintenance of the NATIONAL GUARD, but to a right to keep guns for any purpose. However, Congress was able in 1934 to pass an anti-gangsterism law regulating the sale and distribution of shotguns less than 18 inches long without its being ruled UNCONSTITUTIONAL.

right to kidnap The term used by critics for the 1992 SUPREME COURT decision authorising US agents to kidnap suspects abroad and bring them back for trial in the absence of a bilateral EXTRADITION treaty. The case arose from a 1990 kidnapping in Mexico, and was denounced by three dissenting justices and most Latin American leaders as a 'judicial monstrosity'.

> When we wake one day to learn that the director of the Federal Bureau of Investigation languishes in some Tehran prison after being abducted from his Washington home, we shall know that our SUPREME COURT, the custodian of our law-based state, has brought this outlaw code upon our heads.
>
> Sen. DANIEL PATRICK MOYNIHAN

right to lie The notion, advanced by Assistant Secretary for Defence Arthur Sylvester after the CUBAN MISSILE CRISIS, that a government has a 'right to lie' in moments of national emergency. Sylvester's assertion that 'the inherent right of the Government to lie to save itself when faced with nuclear disaster is basic' carried some weight despite the furore it caused, but gave later generations of political leaders (not just in America) a cast-iron excuse for telling falsehoods to the people. *Compare* Bodyguard of LIES.

right to life The demand of PRO-LIFE groups for the tightest possible restrictions on abortion, and if possible its total prohibition. The phrase dates back at least to the formation of the US National Right to Life Committee in 1970, and was soon in use on both sides of the Atlantic. In Britain the lobby has had limited success, partly because David Steel's (*see* BOY DAVID) Bill broadly legalising abortion was passed in the late 1960s before it had fully mobilised, and partly because it refused to compromise when legislation such as the ALTON BILL and CORRIE BILL were promoted to tighten it. The lobby has, however, impeded moves to permit stem-cell research. In America the pro-life campaign has been far more bitter, with picketing and even fire-bombing of birth control and abortion clinics and the murder of at least one doctor conducting abortions. It has encouraged both BUSH administrations to boycott or hamper a range of international programmes for development aid, either because they involved birth control drives or because there was no guarantee funds would not be spent on abortions. In this more conservative climate the SUPREME COURT in 1992 tightened its ROE V WADE decision; George Bush Snr signed more restrictive regulations just before leaving office only for Bill CLINTON to revoke them, and the second Bush administration backed Bills to outlaw late-term abortion.

right to work The laws passed by many Southern US states to limit the ability of labour unions to organise, and thus to encourage corporations to move their plants to the SUNBELT from more unionised states. They had considerable success, especially during the 1970s and '80s, but with the advent of NAFTA corporations began moving jobs straight to Mexico and as world trade has liberalised, they have since transferred production further afield from the RUSTBELT.

New Right The highly motivated combination of religious fundamentalists and LIBERTARIAN right-wingers who were galvanised into political action from the 1970s by such apparent liberal triumphs as the Supreme Court decision on abortion in ROE V WADE and the PANAMA CANAL TREATIES, gave crucial support to Ronald REAGAN's presidency, and formed the core of the NEO-CONSERVATISM that drove especially the second of the BUSH administrations.

religious Right Overlapping the above, the often fundamentalist and Creationist evangelical Protestant groupings, concentrated in the South and Midwest, whose opinions and priorities have heavily influenced the REPUBLICAN PARTY particularly during the presidency of George W. BUSH, in whose re-election they were a powerful force, Bush securing 80% of the vote among church-going males. Embracing the CHRISTIAN COALITION and the Moral MAJORITY, they owe much of their original impetus to the fundamentalist right-wing television preachers whose influence spilled into politics in reaction to the election as President in 1976 of Jimmy CARTER, a born-again Christian but a Democrat. Several conservative televangelists threw their weight behind Ronald REAGAN's 1980 campaign and the moral thrust of his presidency. In 1988 Pat Robertson, head of the Christian Broadcasting Network, made a bid for the WHITE HOUSE himself, running a strong third in the Republican primaries to George Bush Snr and Sen. Bob Dole. The religious Right gathered further momentum in the BACKLASH against the moral laxity of Bill CLINTON, and came into their own on the election of George W. Bush. They have had an especially strong impact on policy on education, abortion and stem-cell research, and the Middle East; in a generation the Republicans moved from being cooler toward ISRAEL than the Democrats to coming close to supporting the position of the Israeli right that the Biblical foundation of the Jewish state justified its claims to JUDAEA AND SAMARIA and any degree of repression against the PALESTINIANS. This in turn had profound repercussions for America's standing in the region, especially when WASHINGTON showed only half-hearted support for its own ROAD MAP for a Middle East settlement after the IRAQ WAR.

to the right of Genghis Khan A largely British phrase used from the 1980s for anyone with alarmingly extreme right-wing views; it was initially applied to the more fanatical THATCHERITES.

rights Those inalienable essentials to which humanity is supposedly entitled; the US Declaration of INDEPENDENCE lists them as 'Life, LIBERTY and the pursuit of happiness'. Harry Weinberger, in a letter to the *New York Post* after America's declaration of war in 1917, asserted that 'the greatest right in the world is the right to be wrong'; the liberal former US Attorney-General Ramsey Clark explained in 1977 that 'a right is not what someone gives you; it's what no one can take from you.'

> The public good is in nothing more essentially interested, than in the protection of every individual's private rights.
>
> Sir WILLIAM BLACKSTONE, *Commentaries on the Laws of England* (1783)

> I am not interested in picking up crumbs of compassion thrown from the table of someone who considers himself to be my master. I want the full menu of rights.
>
> Archbishop DESMOND TUTU, 1985

Rights of Man, The Thomas Paine's treatise on government that started as an inflammatory reply to Edmund BURKE, forced him to flee from England in 1792 when facing prosecution for treason, and earned him an honoured place as one of the theoreticians of the FRENCH REVOLUTION, despite his difficult nature. Paine's ideas struck a chord in Britain, where his demand for a WELFARE STATE caused a sensation, in France where his defence of the Revolution is commemorated to this day, and in America where his COMMON SENSE had been a runaway best seller.

Bill of Rights *See* BILL.

civil rights *See* CIVIL.

human rights *See* HUMAN.

women's rights *See* WOMEN.

ring-fencing In the budgetary process, the allocation of money to a particular programme with a safeguard that it cannot be diverted to any other purpose, and that if the project is cancelled the cash must be returned.

Rinka The name of the dog belonging to the male model Norman Scott that was shot on Exmoor by Andrew Gino Newton in October 1975 to frighten Scott out of publicising his past affair with the UK LIBERAL leader Jeremy THORPE. The attempt failed, and Thorpe was eventually disgraced, though acquitted of a charge of conspiring to murder Scott, who had been blackmailing him.

Riom trials The trials of a number of French politicians and military men, held from February 1942 before a supreme court set up by the VICHY government at Riom, just north of Clermont-Ferrand. Opponents of the COLLABORATIONIST regime of Marshal Pétain, including Edouard Daladier, Léon Blum, Paul Reynaud and Maurice Gamelin, were blamed for the fall of France in 1940. The trials were suspended indefinitely after two months and the accused spent the rest of WORLD WAR II in prisons and CONCENTRATION CAMPS.

riot An act of mass violence against symbols of authority that either has begun as a political protest or has from the start been an expression of frustration. Martin Luther KING, urging the redressing of injustices before the patience of black Americans finally ran out, said: 'A riot is at bottom the language of the unheard.'

> Black people have never rioted. A riot is what white people think blacks are involved in when they burn down stores.
>
> JULIUS LESTER (1939–)

> A rioter with a MOLOTOV COCKTAIL in his hand is no more fighting for CIVIL RIGHTS than a Klansman with a sheet on his back and a mask over his face.
>
> President LYNDON B. JOHNSON, speech in Washington, 20 August 1965

Riot Act The Act of 1714 which gave magistrates in Britain the power to order rioters to disperse in the SOVEREIGN's name, on pain of life imprisonment (originally death) if they persisted. The magistrate's action, which could not take place until after twelve or more people had been rioting for an hour, was known as **'reading the Riot Act'**. The Act was repealed as an archaism early in the 1980s – but might well have been invoked during the 1984–85 MINERS' STRIKE or the 1990 riots against the POLL TAX had it still been in force; it had last been invoked during the Liverpool police strike of 1919.

communal riots Mass violence in the cities of the Indian sub-continent by Hindus against Muslims, or *vice versa*.

Gordon Riots *See* GORDON.

Rodney King riots *See* KING.

It took a riot The title of a MINUTE prepared for Margaret THATCHER in the late summer of 1981 by the then Environment Secretary Michael HESELTINE, which called for major investment in Britain's INNER CITIES and the giving of responsibility for one city each to Cabinet colleagues. It stemmed from the riots in Brixton (south London), Toxteth (Liverpool) and elsewhere that June. Officials were impressed, but Mrs Thatcher believed spending extra on the inner cities would make it look as though rioting paid off, and stacked the decisive Cabinet committee against Heseltine. He was, however, allowed to develop a modest programme for Merseyside.

Ripon Society A liberal, intellectual grouping in the US REPUBLICAN PARTY, founded in 1962 and modelled on Britain's BOW GROUP. Named after the home city in Wisconsin of the group's founder, Alan Bovay, the society had strong Harvard connections. It put forward a number of radical policy ideas, including REVENUE-SHARING (which was adopted), an all-volunteer army and a NEGATIVE INCOME TAX, but lacked the persuasive power to prevent the party moving to the right, Barry Goldwater's abortive 1964 Presidential campaign providing a pointer to the GOP's post-NIXON stance.

Ripper Act Legislation passed by the US Congress to abolish posts held by members or supporters of the opposition party, where they are too entrenched to be dismissed after a change of ADMINISTRATION.

rise In the US HOUSE OF REPRESENTATIVES, the COMMITTEE OF THE WHOLE 'rises' to report a BILL to the House with amendments that have been adopted; the House itself comes back into session, with the SPEAKER replacing the chairman of the relevant committee in the CHAIR.

Rise and Fall of the Great Powers See GREAT.

Rise of the House A WESTMINSTER term for the point at which either House ADJOURNS. The House is said to be UP.

rise to the occasion The classic double-entendre delivered in the HOUSE OF COMMONS in 1990 by the Armed Forces Minister Archie Hamilton (1941–). When asked how hitherto all-male crews of Royal Navy ships would react to the presence of servicewomen (Wrens) on board, he replied:

> I am sure they will rise to the occasion.

Risorgimento (Ital. rebirth, awakening) Italy's great national revival of the mid-19th century when Garibaldi and other patriots, and the diplomacy of Foreign Minister Cavour of Piedmont, reunited the country under a single crown. It involved the expulsion (with help from France) of the Habsburgs from Lombardy and Venetia, the overthrow of the BOURBON kingdom of Naples and Sicily, and the eclipse of the temporal power of the Vatican.

river. river companies Shadowy commercial organisations, named after the rivers of England, through which the CONSERVATIVE PARTY has channelled much of its income from business and other sources for more than three decades. Their existence was unknown even to many in the party until the *Independent* tracked them down in 1989.

rivers of blood The most notorious political speech in modern British history, the attack on coloured immigration and claims about its consequences delivered by Enoch POWELL in Birmingham on 20 April 1968. It led Edward HEATH to sack him from the SHADOW CABINET for exacerbating social tensions, but made Powell the hero (unwitting or otherwise) of Britain's RACISTS, receiving 100,000 letters of support. Some would see the riots in Bradford and Burnley in 2001, outbreaks of gun crime in Jamaican communities and the fact that by the turn of the century the indigenous white population of some London boroughs was in a minority, as proving elements of Powell's case, if not excusing the language in which he raised it. Powell said:

> Those whom the gods wish to destroy, they first make mad. We must be mad, literally mad, as a nation to be permitting the annual inflow of some 50,000 dependants, who are for the most part the material of the future growth of the immigrant-descended population. It is like watching a nation busily engaged in heaping up its own funeral pyre . . . As I look ahead, I am filled with foreboding. Like the Roman, I seem to see the 'River Tiber flowing with much blood'.

Powell, a former professor of classics, was quoting from Virgil, who in Book VI of the *Aeneid* had the Sybil prophesy to Aeneas of his return to Italy:

> I see wars, horrible wars, and the Tiber foaming with much blood.

He later said that he had been evoking a prophecy of doom and not forecasting a bloodbath, but by then the damage was done. CHURCHILL had used a similar phrase in 1948 when, speaking in a less inflammatory context on European unity, he said:

> We are asking the nations of Europe between whom rivers of blood have flowed to forget the feuds of a thousand years.

Rivonia trial The year-long trial on 'sabotage' charges of ANC activists in South Africa which culminated in Nelson MANDELA and seven others being sentenced to life imprisonment on 12 June 1964. Mandela (who had been on the run for seventeen months) and four others admitted sabotage, but argued that they had been driven to it because all legitimate forms of protest were barred to them. As the trial neared its close the UN SECURITY COUNCIL urged its abandonment, but Prime Minister Henrik Verwoerd said South Africa would not give in to pressure even if the death penalty were imposed.

road map A sketch of the way ahead in a PEACE PROCESS to be put to the parties involved for negotiation. Essentially applied to the situation between Israel and the Palestinians, it was first used by the United States in 2002 and specifically, under pressure from Britain and in co-ordination with the QUARTET, during the IRAQ WAR the following spring. The 'map' lost credibility in mid-2004 when America accepted Ariel Sharon's plan for almost complete withdrawal from GAZA offset by the construction of fresh Jewish settlements in the WEST BANK, and was repudiated by Sharon that September.

Robben Island The island fortress in Table Bay, ten miles from Cape Town, which once housed a mental hospital and leper colony and became a secure prison for opponents of South Africa's APARTHEID regime. Nelson MANDELA was incarcerated there from 1964 to 1982; his cell is now a national shrine.

Robinson loan The transaction that triggered the resignations on Christmas Eve, 1998 of two high-profile members of Tony BLAIR's government and effectively ended the political career of one of them: the loan of £373,000 by Geoffrey Robinson (1938–), the millionaire PAYMASTER-GENERAL, to Peter Mandelson, Trade and Industry Secretary (*see* BOBBY) to purchase a house in London. Robinson had made many enemies by using Labour's eighteen years in opposition to make money and then lavishing hospitality on Blair when he became leader, and Mandelson was equally unpopular because of his mastery of SPIN; each, however, had proved a highly competent Minister and Robinson was close to Chancellor Gordon BROWN. What made the loan controversial was its secrecy, the fact that Mandelson had obtained a mortgage on the same property without declaring that Robinson had a charge on it, and that neither MP had declared it in the Register of INTERESTS. Mandelson would twice make a comeback, as Northern Ireland Secretary until the HINDUJA PASSPORT AFFAIR, and later as a EUROPEAN COMMISSIONER; Robinson would not, though he retained loyal friends in government.

> Everyone has a CONFLICT OF INTEREST in the Treasury; most people have a mortgage, all of them have cars and use petrol.
>
> GEOFFREY ROBINSON

> He never has any change in his pocket smaller than a £50 note. *The Independent*

Rochdale pioneers The founders of Britain's CO-OPERATIVE movement, who in 1844 opened their first shop in Toad Lane in the Lancashire mill town of Rochdale. Their basic principles were: membership open to all; democratic control with one member, one vote; limited interest on capital invested; and the distribution of the trading surplus in proportion to the amount spent. The Rochdale experiment was widely copied, and in 1869 the Co-Operative Union was formed.

Rock around the Clock The 96-hour final swing of the Republican Presidential candidate Bob Dole through fifteen States in the 1996 election. It was partly designed to counter Democratic claims that Dole was too old to serve – he was 73 at the time, later attributing his energy to Viagra – and proved successful in narrowing the gap with Bill CLINTON and keeping the CONGRESS Republican. Dole took the name from the 1956 hit record by Bill Haley and the Comets, and the subsequent film, which launched rock'n'roll around the world.

Rock the Vote A campaign tried successfully in the US, and subsequently in Britain, to get 18–24-year-olds to register to vote. The UK version was launched by the comedian Eddie Izzard in April 1996; it had the blessing of John MAJOR's government, but if successful was always likely to benefit Labour. John Preston, chairman of the British Phonographic Institute, was one of the prime movers. *Compare* the openly pro-Labour RED WEDGE of the previous decade.

Rocky The nickname of **Nelson Rockefeller** (1908–79), four-term Governor of New York (Republican, 1966–73) and VICE PRESIDENT from 1974 to 1977; he was nominated by Gerald FORD on his own succession to the Presidency in place of Richard NIXON after WATERGATE. Rockefeller, a liberal who for years had formed a close team with his second wife HAPPY, died suddenly of a heart attack while working on an art book with his 25-year-old special assistant Megan Marshak; his press secretary unfortunately stated that the former VEEP was 'having a ball' at the time.

Roe v Wade The landmark judgment of the US SUPREME COURT on 23 January 1973 that struck down State laws imposing a total ban on abortion and, in the eyes of its critics, virtually permitted abortion on demand; it made the option of abortion a Constitutional right during the first three months of pregnancy and a limited right up to the sixth month. (The Roe in the case was a fictitious 'Jane Roe' whose real name was Norma McCorvey.) The decision enraged and galvanised the PRO-LIFE movement, which has campaigned ever since for tighter abortion laws and even a Constitutional ban on the practice, gaining the support of Presidents REAGAN and George BUSH Snr In 1989 a more conservative Court voted 5–4 to uphold a Missouri law that restricted a woman's access to an abortion, and in 1992, in *Planned Parenthood v* Casey, further tightened the regime, though nothing like enough for hard-line anti-abortionists.

roll. roll, to WASHINGTON slang for putting together a COALITION to outvote someone who appears to have a majority, e.g. a Republican President pushing a programme through the House against the wishes of a Democratic Speaker.

roll call (1) In the US CONGRESS, a vote where each member has to answer by name; in the House, with 435 voting members, the process can take 25 minutes. In the Senate asking for a roll call is a means of delaying business, but a Senator making the request loses the FLOOR. In the 1890s one Senator whose mind was on other things is supposed to have called out: 'Not guilty!' when the clerk read out his name. A roll call is also taken to determine whether a QUORUM is present for formal business to be conducted. (2) The twice-weekly newspaper of Congress, which keeps inhabitants of the CAPITOL HILL village, legislators and staff alike, in touch with events of common interest.

rolling programme A programme of spending on capital projects which lasts for a number of years, new schemes being budgeted for as others finish.

Roll up the map; it will not be wanted these ten years The exclamation made by PITT THE YOUNGER in December 1805 on hearing the news of Napoleon's victory at Austerlitz. He was correct almost to the month; Bonaparte's sway over the continent ended in 1815.

Rome. Treaty of Rome The basic legal text governing the establishment, structure, powers and development of what has become the EUROPEAN UNION. It was in fact concluded in Brussels on 17 April 1957, and signed by the six founder members: France, West Germany, Italy and the BENELUX countries. The Treaty has been substantially amended since, notably by the SINGLE EUROPEAN ACT and the MAASTRICHT TREATY, and stands to be in part superseded by the EUROPEAN CONSTITUTION.

Roman Question *See* LATERAN TREATY.

Rooker-Wise amendment The UK legislation under which the annual BUDGET and FINANCE BILL provide for the automatic indexation of tax allowance thresholds in line with inflation unless the COMMONS specifically decides otherwise. It was the brainchild of the Labour MPs Jeff (now Lord) Rooker (1941–) and Audrey Wise (1935–2000), who in June 1977 pushed through their amendment with Conservative support, against the wishes of the Labour government which desperately needed the £40 million it cost in tax revenue. Rooker-Wise remains in force, but has on occasion been overruled.

> It has created a great panic and it looks as if the Government is falling apart at the seams.
>
> TONY BENN, *Diaries,* 14 June 1977

Roosevelt, Franklin Delano (1882–1945), author of the NEW DEAL, America's WORLD WAR II leader and its 32nd and longest-serving President (1933–45). A patrician and fifth cousin of Theodore Roosevelt (who did not rate him), he joined a smart New York law firm, married his fourth cousin Eleanor and at 28 won a spectacular State senate CAMPAIGN. At 30 he was picked by Woodrow WILSON, who called him 'the handsomest young giant I have ever seen', as Assistant Secretary of the Navy. His wartime performance won him the Democratic Vice Presidential nomination in 1920; he boosted his reputation despite the ticket's heavy defeat. Then, in August 1921, he was paralysed by polio while vacationing at CAMPOBELLO. Crippled from the waist down, he fought his way back to fitness, boasting: 'Maybe my legs aren't so good – but look at those shoulders!' In 1924 he came back with a stirring speech to nominate Al Smith (*see* HAPPY WARRIOR) for the Presidency, and four years later was elected Governor of New York. In 1932 he ran for the WHITE HOUSE, his wife saying: 'If the polio didn't kill him, the Presidency won't.' FDR himself confided: 'If you have spent two years in bed trying to wiggle your big toe, then anything else seems easy.' Paul Conklin wrote:

> Polio made the aristocratic Roosevelt into an underdog. For him it replaced the LOG CABIN.

Roosevelt won the Democratic nomination on the fourth ballot and, despite being scorned by HOOVER as 'a chameleon on plaid', swept to power, carrying all but six States. Many PUNDITS were convinced he was not up to the job; Walter Lippman wrote: 'He is a pleasant man who, without any important qualifications for the office, would like to be President. Here is a man who has made a good governor, who might be a good cabinet officer, but who simply does not measure up to the tremendous demands of the office of President'; and Murray Kempton: 'I have always found Roosevelt an amusing fellow, but I would not employ him, except for reasons of personal friendship, as a geek in a common carnival.' FDR set his sights low, saying: 'I have no expectation of making a hit every time I come to bat. What I seek is the highest possible batting average.'

Roosevelt was elected on a promise to balance the BUDGET, but with the GREAT DEPRESSION crushing the US economy, he declared in a ringing inaugural speech: 'The only thing we have to FEAR is fear itself'; 400,000 Americans wrote him letters of appreciation. He closed the banks, promised a HUNDRED DAYS of decisive action and pushed legislation through CONGRESS for numerous federal agencies to get the country working again. The powers he took spawned the Washington BUREAUCRACY and led H. L. Mencken to write: 'I am advocating making him King in order that we may behead him if he goes too far beyond the limits of the endurable. A president, it appears, cannot be beheaded, but kings have been subject to the operation since ancient times.' His first term appalled Republicans, but he pressed on, confident, as Richard Hofstadter put it, 'that even when he was operating in unknown territory he could do no wrong, commit no serious mistakes.'

In 1936, having made some impact on the Depression, FDR was re-elected by an even greater margin. Republicans denounced his programmes as 'Socialism', but the women of New York's GARMENT DISTRICT caught the mood in a poster reading: 'We love him most for the ENEMIES HE HAS MADE'. FDR said:

> I should like to have it said of my first administration that in it the forces of selfishness and lust for power met their match. I should like to have it said of my second administration that in it those forces met their master.

But he found his second term tougher. Unemployment crept up and the SUPREME COURT declared key New Deal legislation UNCONSTITUTIONAL (*see* BLACK MONDAY, sick CHICKEN CASE). Roosevelt threatened COURT-PACKING legislation, but backed off when Congress baulked. He kept on creating new agencies to kick-start the economy, Earl Goldman writing: 'Restless and mercurial in his thinking, a connoisseur of theories but impatient with people who took theories seriously, he trusted no system except the system of endless experimentation.' FDR attracted some trenchant critics: Georgia's Governor Eugene Talmadge, who called him 'that cripple in the White House', Hugh Johnson: 'the man who started more creations since Genesis – and finished none', Alice Roosevelt Longworth: 'Franklin is two-thirds mush and one-third Eleanor', and the ISOLATIONIST Sen. Burton Wheeler – 'a warmonger'. Anthony EDEN saw him in those years as 'a conjuror skilfully juggling with balls of dynamite', but H. L. Mencken commented: 'If he became convinced tomorrow that cannibalism would get him the votes he so sorely needs, he would begin fattening a missionary in the White House backyard come Tuesday'. It was the outbreak of war in Europe that finally got America back to work, turning it into the great 'Arsenal of DEMOCRACY'.

Roosevelt was re-elected in 1940 by a slimmer margin, promising not to take America into another war but quietly doing what he could to help Britain. After PEARL HARBOR (*see* a DATE THAT WILL LIVE IN INFAMY) he galvanised America into an unprecedented military and industrial effort. Isolationist opposition almost ceased, but FDR had to set up new agencies to get American industry to deliver the goods at a fair price. He also alienated labour leaders by his determination to get results; the United Mineworkers' leader John L. Lewis said: 'It ill-behoves one who has been supped at labour's table and who has been sheltered in labour's house to curse with equal fervour and fine impartiality both labour and its adversaries when they become locked in deadly embrace.'

From his inauguration, FDR cast a spell over most of the American people through his dynamism and his FIRESIDE CHATS, and his magnetism increased in wartime. Hugh Brogan wrote that 'he was better able to respond to people in numbers, at a distance, than to the needs of his intimates', and his relationship with Eleanor (*see* FIRST LADY OF THE WORLD) had been purely political since before his paralysis; each genuinely supported the other's campaigning, but he met his sexual needs elsewhere. Yet to those meeting him he exuded dynamism. He once told Orson Welles: 'There are only two great actors in America. You are the other one,' and Winston CHURCHILL felt that 'meeting him is like opening a bottle of champagne.' When Madame Chiang Kai-Shek asked him not to stand up when she entered the room, he chuckled: 'My dear child, I couldn't stand up if I had to.' He would tell inattentive White House guests: 'I murdered my grandmother this morning,' and say to bores: 'The ablest man I ever met is the man you think you are.' He also had powerful lungs; Harry S Truman remarked: 'With Roosevelt you didn't need a phone. All you had to do was raise the window and you could hear him.' FDR won and held an adoring following among white and black Americans alike, though he did little to advance the cause of CIVIL RIGHTS. Harold MACMILLAN recalled: 'Apparently unconscious of conditions either in Harlem or the Deep South, he expressed concern about the low standard of living in many of the West Indian islands.'

During the war Roosevelt cemented a solid relationship with Churchill, and believed he could handle STALIN. But by YALTA, after winning a record fourth term with a further-reduced majority, his powers were failing. On his return he made his only public reference to his disability, telling Congress: 'I hope you will pardon me for the unusual posture of sitting down. It makes it a lot easier for me not having to carry about 10 lbs. of steel around on the bottom of my legs.' And within weeks he was dead, suffering a cerebral haemorrhage at WARM SPRINGS while sitting for a portrait. After a train journey back to Washington along a track lined with grieving sharecroppers, FDR was buried in his garden at HYDE PARK. His death dumbfounded America, and momentarily raised NAZI hopes of deliverance, Goebbels writing: 'This was the Angel of History! We felt its wings flutter through the room. Was this not the future we awaited so anxiously?'

> Franklin, I hope you never become President.
> GROVER CLEVELAND to FDR as a boy

> The only man we ever had in the White House who could understand that my boss is an s.o.b.
> ANON. American worker, 1945

> He saved the capitalist system by simply forgetting to balance the books.
> ALISTAIR COOKE (1908–2004)

> The greatest American we have ever known and the greatest champion of freedom who has ever brought aid and comfort from the New World to the Old.
> CHURCHILL

Roosevelt, Theodore (TEDDY) 1858–1919, 26th President of the United States (Republican, 1901–09). A law graduate and professional author from a wealthy old Dutch family, who became a cowboy to get over the death of his first wife, the rumbustious, toothy, fiercely patriotic and populist Roosevelt won his first election (in New York state) at 23; he resigned as assistant Secretary of the Navy when the SPANISH-AMERICAN WAR broke out, and became a national hero organising the ROUGH RIDERS. Elected Governor of New York on his return in 1900, his reforming zeal unnerved BOSS PLATT who arranged to KICK HIM UPSTAIRS by nominating him as MCKINLEY's Vice President. Within months, McKinley was dead and Roosevelt was rampant in the WHITE HOUSE. The Republican kingmaker Mark Hanna declared:

> I told McKinley that it was a mistake to nominate that man as Vice President. Now that damned cowboy is President of the United States.

A 'hands-on' President, Roosevelt said: 'I did not usurp power, but I did greatly broaden the use of executive power.' His techniques were not subtle, George Bernard Shaw maintaining: 'His idea of getting hold of the right end of the stick is to snatch it from the hands of someone who is using it effectively and hit him over the head with it.' His vigorous foreign policy, including the creation of the CANAL ZONE, and his attacks on monopolies, won him easy re-election in 1904, enabling him to say: 'I am no longer a political accident'. Four years later he stood down after a happy presidency in favour of TAFT, but his successor's lack of charisma so appalled him that he made a comeback with the BULL MOOSE campaign of 1912, forcing Taft into third place but handing the Presidency to Woodrow WILSON. A big-game hunter and conservationist who was also the first White House jogger, Roosevelt remained immensely popular, and up to his sudden death was still a Presidential contender.

Roosevelt, in the words of Henry Adams, was 'pure act'. A relative said: 'When Theodore attends a wedding he wants to be the bride and when he attends a funeral he wants to be the corpse.' He insisted: 'I am only an average man, but, by God, I work harder at it than an average man.' And he revelled in challenges, declaring:

> I wish to preach not the doctrine of ignoble ease, but the doctrine of the strenuous life. For us is the life of action, of strenuous performance of duty; let us live in the harness, striving mightily; let us rather run the risk of wearing out than rusting out.

His opinions of others were pungent. He branded the revolutionary Thomas Paine 'that dirty little atheist'; President Marroquin of Colombia 'a pithecanthropoid'; President Castro of Venezuela 'an unspeakably villainous little monkey'; Sen. William Alfred Peffer 'a well-meaning, pinheaded, anarchistic crank, of hirsute and slabsided aspect'; the writer Henry James 'a very despicable creature, no matter how well equipped with the minor virtues and graces, literary, artistic and social – a miserable little snob'; and Charles Evans Hughes, the 1916 Republican nominee, 'the bearded iceberg'. As he ended an age of corruption, Roosevelt also set a high moral tone. He once fired a ranch hand who had branded one of his neighbour's cattle, telling him: 'A man who will steal for me will steal from me.'

Alistair Cooke wrote: 'T. R. is affectionately remembered as a half-heroic, half-comic figure, a bespectacled barrel of a man, choking with teeth and happiness.' But Hugh Brogan described him, beneath the bluster, as 'the ablest man to sit in the White House since LINCOLN, the most vigorous since Jackson, the most bookish since John Quincy ADAMS.' And Cooke noted that despite his love of the outdoors 'he was the first influcntial man of his time to see clearly that the United States was no longer a rural nation but an industrial giant running amok.'

In his later years Roosevelt could justly claim: 'No man has had a happier life than I have led; a happier life in every way.'

> While President, I have BEEN President emphatically.
>
> THEODORE ROOSEVELT after leaving office

Roosevelt corollary The expansion of the MONROE DOCTRINE by President Theodore Roosevelt to provide for active US intervention in unstable central American states. In his State of the UNION message to CONGRESS in December 1901, Roosevelt announced:

> Chronic wrongdoing or an impotence which results in a general loosening of the ties of civilised society, may [compel the United States] to the exercise of an international police power.

His initiative was spurred by threats of force from France, Italy and Belgium against the Dominican Republic for non-payment of its debts. Roosevelt and subsequent Presidents went on to intervene in the Dominican Republic, Haiti and Nicaragua.

Roosevelt Memorial The memorial to Franklin D. Roosevelt, on a 7.5-acre site beside WASHINGTON's Tidal Basin next to the JEFFERSON MEMORIAL, which was dedicated by President CLINTON in 1997. Walled in red granite, the memorial is divided into four rooms, one for each of FDR's Presidential terms. There was controversy over the cost – $48 million – when Roosevelt had wanted a simple memorial, and even more so over the omission from the sculptures within of his cigarette or his wheelchair; disruption of the dedication ceremony by disabled lobbyists was averted by a last-minute Senate vote to install a wheelchaired Roosevelt among the secondary sculptures.

Roosevelt's four freedoms The vision and parameters for the future of a secure world (implicitly after the defeat of NAZI Germany) set out by Franklin D. Roosevelt in his State of the UNION message on 6 January 1941, eleven months before America entered WORLD WAR II. FDR said:

> In future days, which we seek to make secure, we look forward to a world founded upon four essential freedoms. The first is FREEDOM OF SPEECH and expression – everywhere in the world. The second is the freedom of every person to worship God in his own way – everywhere in the world. The third is freedom from want – which translated into world terms, means economic understandings which will secure to every nation a healthy peacetime life for its inhabitants – everywhere in the world. The fourth is freedom from fear – which translated into world terms, means a world-wide reduction of armaments to such a point and in such a thorough fashion that no nation will be in a position to commit an act of physical aggression against any neighbour – anywhere in the world.

Rose Garden At the WHITE HOUSE, the garden outside the French doors of the OVAL OFFICE where the President traditionally receives foreign dignitaries and recipients of the CONGRESSIONAL MEDAL OF HONOR. Occasionally it is used for Press conferences or State dinners. The first roses were planted by President WILSON's first wife Ellen in 1913; the garden was redesigned in 1962 by Mrs Paul Mellon at John F. KENNEDY's request. In 1976 Gerald FORD updated the FRONT PORCH CAMPAIGN by adopting what became known as a **Rose Garden strategy**: spending much of the PRIMARY campaign firmly rooted in the White House appearing Presidential. He abandoned it when it was clear Ronald REAGAN was mounting a serious challenge for the Republican nomination; Reagan described Ford's campaigning style as 'a sure winner if all you want is the horticultural vote'. In 1981, at the height of controversy about Interior Secretary James Watt, Reagan told a dinner in New York:

> He would be here, but he's working on a lease for strip-mining the Rose Garden.

Rosebery, Archibald Philip Primrose, 5th Earl of (1847–1929). The IMPERIALIST Liberal aristocrat who was GLADSTONE's successor as Prime Minister for a brief but disastrous spell. Twice Foreign Secretary – managing to combine the post with the chair of the LCC – he appeared the obvious heir to the GRAND OLD MAN and succeeded him in 1894 after the 'Blubbering CABINET'. He had always shown a marked lack of enthusiasm for high office, saying: 'So be it' to Gladstone when first offered the Foreign Office, and once confiding:

> The secret of my life, which seems to me sufficiently obvious, is that I have always detested politics.

And when Gladstone retired, Sir William Harcourt told Rosebery: 'Without you the government would have been ridiculous. With you, it is only impossible.' As Prime Minister he showed from the start the languor and lack of consistent interest that was to mark the rest of his political life, ASQUITH soon writing: 'The leadership of the Liberal party, so far as I am concerned, is vacant.' The next year his government was mercifully defeated in the CORDITE VOTE and lost the ensuing election, Rosebery characteristically commenting:

> There are two pleasures in life. One is ideal, the other real. The ideal is when a man receives the SEALS of office from his SOVEREIGN. The real pleasure comes when he hands them back.

Rosebery remained, uneasily, as party leader until 1896, when he roused himself from his inertia and resigned – Harcourt accusing him of 'funking the future he saw before him' – and then began a decade of sporadic activity which raised repeated and tantalising suspicions of a comeback. This was heightened by his active support for the BOER WAR. On 19 July 1901 Rosebery said in London:

> For the present, at any rate . . . I must plough my own furrow alone. This is my fate, agreeable or the reverse. But before I get to the end of that furrow, it is possible that I may find myself not alone.

Asquith, near the end of his patience, accused him of 'ploughing the sands'. Rosebery's political interest continued to splutter throughout the Edwardian era. But he concentrated increasingly on writing political biographies, and on his real love – horse racing; he owned three Derby winners.

> He sought the palm without the dust.
>
> Rosebery's tutor at Eton

> When he tries to roar like a lion, he only brays like an ass. General Sir GARNET WOLSELEY

> He never missed an occasion to let slip an opportunity.
>
> GEORGE BERNARD SHAW (*compare* PLO)

> By marrying a young Rothschild, becoming Prime Minister and winning the Derby he demonstrated that it was possible to improve one's financial status and run the Empire without neglecting the study of form.
>
> CLAUD COCKBURN

Rosenbergs, the The case of the US couple Julius (1918–53) and Ethel (1915–53) Rosenberg, who were arrested in 1950 on suspicion of supplying the Soviet Union with atom bomb secrets and were executed three years later. The episode, at the height of the COLD WAR and MCCARTHYISM, was an uncanny echo of the SACCO AND VANZETTI case during the RED SCARE after WORLD WAR I. The case was based largely on the evidence of Harry Gold, a Soviet agent, and David Greenglass, Ethel Rosenberg's brother, who worked at the Los Alamos research base (*see* MANHATTAN PROJECT); both had been exposed by the arrest of Klaus FUCHS. Greenglass – one of three others convicted – claimed that his own spying, which he admitted in return for leniency, was instigated by the Rosenbergs, both of whom protested their innocence throughout. The main physical evidence was two halves of a *Jell-o* carton said to have been used by the spies to identify each other. The political climate of the time and the outbreak of the KOREAN WAR – for which the trial judge blamed them – gave the Rosenbergs little chance. They were sentenced to death in March 1951, but a series of appeals and stays of execution (coupled with world-wide pleas for mercy and demonstrations) prolonged the agony until 19 June 1953, when they were electrocuted in Sing Sing prison. The Rosenbergs would have been REPRIEVED had they confessed, but they steadfastly refused. The question of their guilt or innocence may never be resolved; research has suggested that Julius Rosenberg was indeed guilty, but that his wife was framed by the FBI in a vain attempt to pressure her husband into revealing his full espionage activities.

> I can only say, that by immensely increasing the chance of an atomic war, the Rosenbergs may have condemned to death millions of innocent people all over the world.
>
> President EISENHOWER

> Ethel wants it made known that we are the first victims of American FASCISM.
>
> JULIUS ROSENBERG, on the day of their execution

rostrum (Lat. a beak) A platform for an individual public speaker; the original *rostra* in the forum of ancient Rome were adorned with the prows, or beaks, of captured ships.

Rosty The nickname on CAPITOL HILL of Rep. Dan Rostenkowski (1928–), the seventeen-term Democratic Congressman from Illinois who built an enviable power base during thirteen years as chairman of the House WAYS AND MEANS COMMITTEE, securing in 1983 legislation to keep the social security system solvent and in 1986 playing a major role in the passage of a new federal tax code. In 1994 he was indicted by a federal grand jury on seventeen counts of misappropriating over $500,000, and tampering with a witness; he pled guilty to two charges of mail fraud in return for a fine and a seventeen-month jail sentence. After striking the deal he told reporters: 'I do not believe I am any different from the vast majority of members of Congress.' With his trial pending, he was unexpectedly defeated in the 1994 Congressional election. He served his time, and at Christmas 2000 was PARDONED by President CLINTON.

rosy scenario The name given by WHITE HOUSE aides and economists to the forecasts for the impact of REAGANOMICS prepared in 1981 by Budget director David Stockman. Their author had realised at the time that the predictions, including a balanced Budget by 1984, were wildly out of line. *See also* MAGIC ASTERISK; the Triumph of POLITICS.

rotten borough *See* BOROUGH.

rottweiler A UK term for a ruthless political fighter who verbally savages his or her opponents. It became current in the late 1980s when the rottweiler became first a popular pet and guard dog, and then – if neglected – notorious for savaging young children.

Rotunda The 180ft-high circular hall at the centre of the US CAPITOL, beneath the Dome, where 26 of the most famous Americans including Presidents LINCOLN, Garfield, MCKINLEY, KENNEDY and REAGAN and the Unknown Soldiers have lain in state. One cynic remarked that it was 'built so the statesmen will find it easier to run round in circles'. Completed in 1824 in time to welcome the visiting LAFAYETTE, its walls are adorned with oil paintings, four by John Trumbull depicting scenes from the AMERICAN REVOLUTION, and four depicting colonial events; one by John Chapman on *The Baptism of Pocahontas* includes a six-toed Indian. The Rotunda's fresco, started by Constantino Brumidi, also shows scenes from early America; the bronze doors by Randolph Rogers, depicting events in the life of Columbus, were cast in Germany and hung in 1871. The Rotunda was the scene of the first attempted assassination of a President, Andrew Jackson (*see* OLD HICKORY) in 1835, and in 1852 Henry Clay was the first politician to lie in state there. It was converted into a 1500-bed military hospital during the CIVIL WAR, and in 1985 staged President Reagan's second INAUGURATION because of severe weather.

Rouges (Fr. reds) The Radicals in 19th-century QUEBEC who were a powerful force in the formation of Canada's LIBERAL PARTY.

Rough Riders The 1st regiment of the US Cavalry Volunteers in the SPANISH-AMERICAN WAR, which was organised by Theodore ROOSEVELT and gave critical impetus to his political career; it got its nickname from the cowboys of Buffalo Bill's Wild West show. Roosevelt was not in fact their commander – that task fell to Leonard Wood, who had military experience – and the Rough Riders actually fought on foot in Cuba, having left their horses in Florida. Roosevelt feared after the chaotic engagement of San Juan Hill on 1 July 1898 in which the victorious but inexpert Americans lost one-tenth of their men that they would in the end be defeated, but the Spanish defenders proved even more inept and he returned a hero.

round. round robin Originally a joint letter of mildly subversive nature with all the signatures in a circle so that none would appear the ringleader; now any proposal collectively signed by several people and sent to higher authority or otherwise circulated.

Round Table conference A conference between nations or disputing parties at which a point is made of giving all the participants equal status, with none obviously at the head of the table or monopolising the CHAIR. The idea comes from the legendary Round Table of CAMELOT round which all of King Arthur's knights were seated to make sure that none predominated. One significant Round Table conference was that initiated by Ramsay MACDONALD's Labour government in 1930 on the future of India, to which all interested parties including MAHATMA Gandhi were invited.

round-tabling A WASHINGTON term for submitting a proposal by all the members of the CABINET or other responsible body before a final decision is taken on it.

Who is Mr Round and why does he object? *See* WHO.

royal. Royal Assent The point at which an ACT of Parliament in any of the countries in which the British SOVEREIGN is HEAD OF STATE becomes law. It is signified at WESTMINSTER by a brief ceremony in the HOUSE OF LORDS after the monarch has given their assent. *See also* La REYNE LE VEULT.

Royal Brute of England The abusive nickname for King George III popularised during the AMERICAN REVOLUTION by the radical English migrant Thomas Paine (*see* COMMON SENSE; RIGHTS OF MAN).

Royal Commission In Britain, a vehicle for conducting the most thorough investigation into some area of public policy where a new direction is needed. Normally composed of the GREAT AND THE GOOD, such commissions take a couple of years to report, and the government is not bound to accept their conclusions. Margaret THATCHER refused to set up any, preferring to put her theories into practice in the certainty that they would work; John MAJOR reactivated the process in 1991 by setting up a Royal Commission on Criminal Justice, but there have been few since, though a standing Royal Commission on Environmental Pollution continues its work. In Australia Royal Commissions are more frequently set up, often to enquire into a specific matter like the deaths of Aboriginal suspects in police custody.

> A broody hen sitting on a china egg.
>
> MICHAEL FOOT

> They take MINUTES and waste years.
>
> HAROLD WILSON

Royal family or **Royals** The collective term for the House of WINDSOR; the SOVEREIGN and his or her immediate family, and those less closely related who nevertheless carry out official engagements and whose activities can give rise to embarrassing headlines in the tabloids. The Royal family, like the institution of MONARCHY, has gone through phases of public reverence, indifference and hostility. In 1894 Keir Hardie (*see* QUEER HARDIE) wrote in the *Labour Leader*:

> The life of one Welsh miner is of greater commercial and moral value to the British people than the whole Royal crowd put together, from the Royal great-grandmama down to the puling Royal great-grandchild [the future King Edward VIII].

Royal prerogative The provision under Britain's unwritten CONSTITUTION enabling the government of the day to act without reference to Parliament. In February 1993 a heated but largely academic row broke out over whether John MAJOR's government could sign the MAASTRICHT TREATY under the Royal prerogative if Parliament failed to RATIFY it. The general view was that it might technically be free to do so, but that such a course of action would be politically suicidal.

Royal Ulster Constabulary *See* RUC.

Royal we The use by a reigning monarch of the plural when talking about themselves, as in 'We are not amused', Queen Victoria's reaction to an off-colour joke. Margaret THATCHER incurred public ridicule when she declared of a new addition to her family: 'WE HAVE BECOME A GRANDMOTHER'.

Royalists The faction in any state, usually one where the monarchy has been ousted from power but hopes to return, who make the need for such a form of government the principal plank of their platform.

economic Royalists Franklin D. ROOSEVELT's tag early in his second term for big business and its Republican backers in CONGRESS, whom he blamed for a revival of unemployment. He used the phrase to push further NEW DEAL legislation through Congress – though without the same impact on the economy as his initial measures.

> The Royalists of the economic order have conceded that political freedom was the business of government, but they have maintained that economic slavery was nobody's business.
>
> FDR's acceptance speech to the Democratic National Convention, 1936

RPA The shorthand for the REPRESENTATION OF THE PEOPLE ACT used by UK campaign strategists and broadcasters, especially in the context of its provisions for fairness and EQUAL TIME between the parties on television and radio.

RPI *See* CPI.

RPM *See* RESALE PRICE MAINTENANCE.

RSG (1) Regional Seats of Government. The

subterranean headquarters built during the COLD WAR so that each region of Britain would have its own government in the event of NUCLEAR WAR. A CND offshoot, **Spies for Peace**, published the locations of the RSGs early in 1963, and embarrassed the government even more by revealing which bureaucrats would be whisked to safety when the FOUR-MINUTE WARNING sounded. (2) RATE/REVENUE Support Grant, the principal instrument by which central government in Britain channels funds to local authorities to supplement taxes raised locally.

rubber. rubber bullets *See* BULLET.

rubber chicken *See* CHICKEN.

rubber stamp A LEGISLATURE which has been so denuded of real power that it merely confirms the actions of the EXECUTIVE.

> The Senate is not meant to be a rubber stamp and is not going to be a rubber stamp.
> Majority Leader Sen. ROBERT BYRD, 1976

Ruby The first guide dog owned by David Blunkett (1947–), who overcame blindness to become Education Secretary and HOME SECRETARY in Tony BLAIR's Labour government. Ruby was the first guide dog allowed into the PALACE OF WESTMINSTER, when Blunkett visited the COMMONS in 1971; she was succeeded by TED.

RUC Royal Ulster Constabulary. The force which attempted to undertake the civilian policing of NORTHERN IRELAND, between the PARTITION of Ireland and its supercession by the Police Service of Northern Ireland in November 2001 under the PATTEN REPORT. Though for the most part highly professional and largely impartial, the RUC was seen by Irish REPUBLICANS as anti-Catholic; this was in part due to the small number of Catholics joining, in turn a result of intimidation. The main body of the force, usually armed and in distinctive green uniforms, was in other respects little different from the force on the mainland, but its Special Branch, which sought to avert and investigate political offences, its notorious B-SPECIALS who were disbanded under the HEATH government, and (less controversially) its full-time reserve which was largely disbanded under Patten, set it apart. The courage of its officers was unquestioned; between 1969 and 2001, 302 were killed and almost 9000 injured in terrorist attacks – many staged by LOYALISTS – and civil disorder. In 2000 the Queen presented the RUC with the George Cross for gallantry, an honour only previously bestowed collectively on the wartime population of Malta. *See also* SHOOT TO KILL.

ruffles and flourishes The brief musical introduction, akin to a fanfare, played just before the PRESIDENT of the United States makes his appearance at many official engagements. The ruffles were customarily drumbeats, the flourishes the tune picked out by the brass.

rule (1) To govern a nation. Louis de St Just, advocating the trial of Louis XVI in the French NATIONAL ASSEMBLY on 13 November 1792, put forward the ANARCHIST argument that 'no one can rule guiltlessly'. The leftist James Connolly, one of the leaders of Ireland's EASTER RISING, was convinced that 'those who rule industrially will rule politically', and H. L. Mencken cautioned:

> The urge to save humanity is almost always a false face for the urge to rule it.

(2) A regulation: in the US CONGRESS the rules (the equivalent of STANDING ORDERS at WESTMINSTER) govern the conduct of business. Speaker Thomas Reed (*see* CZAR; REED RULES) once asserted:

> The only way to do business inside the rules is to suspend the rules.

Rule, Britannia The boisterously defiant national song originating in Britain's maritime tradition, which is sung irreverently at the Last Night of the Proms but still has a patriotic expression. It was woundingly sung by a number of Tory BACKBENCHERS when CHAMBERLAIN fell in May 1940 (*see* YOU HAVE SAT HERE LONG ENOUGH). *Rule, Britannia* was written just 200 years before by the Scottish poet James Thomson (1700–48) as part of the libretto for Thomas Arne's masque *Alfred*; the first stanza runs:

> When Britain first, at heaven's command
> Arose from out the azure main,
> Arose, arose, arose from out the azure main,
> This was the charter, the charter of the land
> And guardian angels sang this strain:
> 'Rule, Britannia! Britannia, rule the waves!
> Britons, never, never, never will be slaves!'

rule of law The vital concept behind a truly democratic state: that principles of justice, fairness and due process are applied automatically and indiscriminately to all by every organ of the State and the legal and judicial system.

> If you are a murderer or a rapist you will still have the protection of the rule of law. But if you are a political danger to rulers, you will have none.
> ALAN PATON, on South Africa, 1976

Rules Committee The fulcrum of the HOUSE OF REPRESENTATIVES, which through its power to set the agenda for debate can accelerate or block the progress of any BILL. Its history has thus been marked by struggles between its members and the House as a whole. Speaker Joe Cannon (*see* FOUL-MOUTHED JOE) made himself chairman of the Rules Committee in 1903 and appointed every member, thus gaining a personal VETO on all legislation; Republican INSURGENTS removed him from the committee in 1910, making it responsible to the House. From the 1930s to the early '60s it was dominated by a coalition of southern Democrats and conservative Republicans who frustrated progressive legislation; a reforming move in 1949 to force any Bill out of the committee within 21 days was reversed two years later. The Committee even refused to send on an EISENHOWER administration Bill authorising federal funding for school construction to a House-Senate CONFERENCE after both Houses had passed it. This dictatorial regime was broken in 1961 when the House expanded the committee to ensure that its chairman, Rep. 'Judge' Howard Smith of Virginia, could be outvoted. It still flexes its muscles occasionally; when in 1974 it blocked legislation that would have safeguarded North Carolina farmers and wildlife against a new dam, the columnist Colman McCarthy branded it

> A government within a government, a mediaeval court of magnificos and viziers that holds terrifying power over people's lives and uses that power without fear of accountability.

> The Rules Committee has an almost complete power to determine in important issues whether the rest of us can vote at all.
>
> Rep. MORRIS UDALL

> Counted on to keep off the FLOOR bills that would embarrass too many members.
>
> TOM WICKER

rules of engagement The parameters set for those ordered to carry out a military operation by their political masters. In the case of the FALKLANDS they aroused particular interest because of the controversy over whether the torpedoing of the *General* BELGRANO fell within them.

ruling class *See* CLASS.

Manual of Rules The 'Bible' that determines how the US SENATE conducts its business.

rum. Rum, Romanism and Rebellion The anti-Catholic crack that probably cost James G. Blaine the Presidency in 1884. It was uttered on 29 October by the Rev. Samuel Burchard as he welcomed the Republican nominee to a meeting of supportive Protestant clergy in New York. Burchard, quoting a remark made about the Democrats by Garfield in 1876, ended:

> We are Republicans, and don't propose to leave our party and identify ourselves with the party whose antecedents have been Rum, Romanism and Rebellion.

Blaine and most of the audience missed the punchline, but a reporter contacted the Democrats, who were stunned that he had not disowned it; the CLEVELAND campaign immediately flooded Irish-American neighbourhoods with FLIERS carrying the remark. The day got even worse for Blaine; he went on to a banquet at Delmonico's with some of America's wealthiest men, which lowered his credibility still further. He went on to lose New York state by 1149 votes – and with it the election.

rum, sodomy and the lash Winston CHURCHILL's devastating response when an admiral objected that an operation the then FIRST LORD OF THE ADMIRALTY was supporting ran against the traditions of the Royal Navy. Churchill responded:

> Don't talk to me about naval tradition! After all, what is it? Rum, sodomy and the lash!

The phrase was popularised in the mid-1980s as the title of an album by the Irish folk-rock group the Pogues.

rumour factory A tightly-knit, almost incestuous community where the atmosphere creates unlikely rumours that are often taken seriously. WASHINGTON, with its various political and bureaucratic forcing houses, is regarded as such, but it is not in the same league as the financial centre of the City of London, where political rumours have an effect on the market in inverse proportion to their plausibility.

Rump The remnant of England's Long Parliament which was finally ejected by Oliver Cromwell in April 1653 (*see* YOU HAVE SAT HERE LONG ENOUGH); also the later remnant of that same Parliament that was restored in May 1659 after Cromwell's death, and dissolved by General Monk the following February prior to the Restoration of King Charles II, which its members strongly opposed.

run The US word for contesting an ELECTION, other than as the INCUMBENT, the UK equivalent being to STAND. The British historian Hugh Brogan explained:

> In England, of course, we stand for election; in more dynamic America, they run.

Colorado state Senator Martin Hatcher (1927–) tried to put running for office into context: 'Running for the third Congressional district is my second priority. My first is swimming naked through a pool of piranhas.'

I do not choose to run for President in 1928 The deadpan words, despatched by telegram, with which Calvin COOLIDGE opted out of seeking a second full Presidential term.

You can run, but you can't hide A phrase associated with the US world heavyweight champion Joe Louis (1914–81); he used it before his victory over Billy Conn in 1946, but probably did not invent it. President REAGAN used it in 1985 as a warning to all international terrorists after the hijacking by Palestinian extremists of a TWA airliner to Beirut; Neil KINNOCK taunted John MAJOR with it in 1991 when the Tories decided against calling a general election they might well have lost.

run-off A decisive electoral contest between two candidates after a first poll involving a large number, none of whom has obtained a clear majority.

running against Washington *See* WASHINGTON.

running-dogs *See* DOGS.

running-mate The candidate for VICE PRESIDENT running on the same ticket as a particular Presidential nominee; it is also used, less often, of the Presidential candidate as partnering the Vice Presidential. A running-mate is a racehorse used to pace another; the term was first used politically by Woodrow WILSON at the 1912 Democratic convention in introducing Thomas Marshall as his choice to share the ticket.

rural proofing The examination by a government of its policies to ensure that they do not have an adverse effect on rural life and communities that their city-dwelling framers had not anticipated. Tony BLAIR's government introduced rural-proofing c. 2003 in response to criticism by the COUNTRYSIDE ALLIANCE, but though championed by the farm and rural ministry DEFRA, it has been studiously ignored by some other departments, notably the Home Office.

Russell Building The first, and most easterly, of the three huge office buildings erected for the US SENATE on CAPITOL HILL. Named in 1972 after Sen. Richard B. Russell of Georgia (1897–1971), it was authorised in 1904 and opened in 1909; its main features are its three-storey rotunda, and the CAUCUS Rooms which have witnessed some of the Senate's most dramatic investigations: into the sinking of the Titanic, the TEAPOT DOME scandal, the Army-MCCARTHY hearings and WATERGATE. Extended in 1933, it stands at the corner of Constitution and Delaware Avenues, and is the terminal of the SENATE SUBWAY.

Russia. Russia has two generals on whom she can rely – Generals Janvier and Février (Fr. Generals January and February). The axiom of Tsar Nicholas I (1897–1855), reflecting the role of the terrible winter of 1812 in driving Napoleon from Moscow but whose reality was borne home even more horribly to the invading Germans as they froze on the Russian front from 1941 to 1944.

Nothing has changed Russia's policy. Her methods, her tactics, her manoeuvres may change, but the pole star – world domination – is immutable Not an overly-frank admission by one of Soviet Russia's Communist leaders or even an expansionist TSAR, but the assessment of Karl MARX, in a speech in London on 22 January 1867.

Russian revolution The process of ferment and, eventually, violence beginning with the overthrow of TSAR Nicholas II early in March 1917, the establishment of a provisional government under KERENSKY, the mobilisation of Lenin's BOLSHEVIKS to seize power in the OCTOBER REVOLUTION, the introduction of COMMUNISM and the ruthless crushing of all opposition, and eventual victory for the RED ARMY in a bitter CIVIL WAR. CHURCHILL, as a member of a government which had had to finish the war against Germany without support from Russia, said in April 1919:

> Every British and French soldier killed last year was really done to death by Lenin and TROTSKY – not in fair war, but by the treacherous desertion of an ally without parallel in the history of the world.

Sixty years later, before the collapse of the Soviet state was widely foreseen, the DISSIDENT Roy Medvedev declared:

> The Russian people have moved forward, not by way of religious uplift but through revolution, and despite all their disappointments . . . they will leave our descendants not a religious heritage but socialism and democracy.

Russo-Japanese War The conflict in 1904–05 in which the Japanese inflicted a crushing defeat on the Russians, establishing themselves on the world stage with shattering force. The Japanese were determined to crush all Russian power in Korea and Manchuria and to establish their own HEGEMONY in the region. In February 1904 they launched a pre-emptive strike against Port Arthur on the tip of Manchuria's Liaotung Peninsula, which inflicted serious damage on the Russian fleet at anchor there. Port Arthur was then besieged by Japanese land forces, surrendering in January 1905. The conflict between the opposing armies in central Manchuria was less decisive. However, in May 1905, in the Battle of Tsushima, the Japanese fleet under Admiral Togo inflicted severe losses which brought Russia to the conference table. By the **Treaty of Portsmouth** in September 1905, the Russians surrendered Port Arthur and half of Sakhalin to Japan as well as evacuating Manchuria. Japan's victory torpedoed the myth of the superiority of white Europeans over Orientals, and its effect on Russia was immediate and traumatic: loss of confidence in the TSARIST system, leading within months to the REVOLUTION OF 1905, and a switch of interest by the KREMLIN from Asia to expansion in Europe, stoking the fires in the Balkans that generated WORLD WAR I. *See also* DOGGER BANK INCIDENT.

Rustbelt The opposite of SUNBELT, the traditional 'smokestack' industrial areas of the north-eastern United States, from which production and jobs have been shifted first to the less unionised and lower-cost South, and more recently abroad.

S

S The complete middle name of Harry S TRUMAN. It was a compromise by his parents who could not decide between Shippe (his paternal grandfather's middle name) and Solomon (his maternal grandmother's Christian name).

S&L scandal The crisis that broke in 1989, at the start of the first BUSH administration, with the collapse of a number of savings and loan institutions, which had taken advantage of lack of regulation in the REAGAN years and made excessive payments to their own executives and imprudent loans and investments. In 1982 the Democratic CONGRESS, most of whose members had received campaign contributions from S&Ls, had passed legislation removing the restriction limiting their investment activity to home mortgages. The ensuing bonanza led to 15% out of over 3000 S&Ls becoming insolvent or close to it; of the hundreds taken over by the federal government at an initial cost to the taxpayer of $166 billion, 60% were riddled with fraud. The ramifications of the scandal reached the US SENATE (*see* KEATING FIVE).

> The Reagan administration opened the door to the vault, the Congress laid out the 'Welcome' mat, the rest of the country looked the other way and the scoundrels walked right in.
>
> JOHN WEST, President/CEO, First National Bank of Livingstone, Texas

Sabra and Chatila Two Palestinian refugee camps in Beirut which were the scene in 1982 of massacres of civilians by Israeli-sponsored Lebanese militia, which were widely blamed on the then Israeli Defence Minister Ariel Sharon. The events at Sabra and Chatila prompted an unsuccessful attempt to have him prosecuted in Belgium for WAR CRIMES; they were replicated on a much lesser scale 20 years later when Sharon, by now Prime Minister, sent Israeli troops into the refugee camp at JENIN on the West Bank.

Sacco and Vanzetti The electrocution of the Italian ANARCHIST immigrants Nicola Sacco and Bartolomeo Vanzetti on 23 August 1927 for killing two men in a payroll robbery at a South Braintree, Mass., shoe factory became a *cause célèbre*. Their trial and conviction in a Massachusetts court in July 1921 passed largely unnoticed by the US public, but the news of the case aroused radical indignation abroad, provoking demonstrations and attacks against US property in Europe and South America. Publicity about these events divided American opinion between those who believed they had been convicted because of their political beliefs and those who felt those beliefs compounded their guilt. Evidence that the two were victims of mistaken identity was strengthened by the dignified demeanour of the defendants themselves, but an independent commission appointed by the state governor upheld their conviction. They were refused clemency and executed, prompting a silent demonstration by 250,000 in Boston, bomb explosions in New York and Philadelphia and protests throughout the world.

> Never in our full life could we hope to do such work for tolerance, for justice, for man's understanding of man as we do now by accident.
>
> VANZETTI's last letter

SACEUR Supreme Allied Commander Europe, the Brussels-based head of all NATO forces in Europe. His headquarters are at SHAPE.

sachem An office-holder of TAMMANY HALL, the term coming from a native American word for leader.

sacred cow A programme or institution that cannot be interfered with or criticised because of popular sentiment. From the Hindu reverence for the cow and its consequent immunity from slaughter in India.

SADC Southern Africa Development Community. The organisation established by the **Windhoek Treaty** of 17 August 1992, which promotes economic development and stability in the region and of which South Africa is by far the most powerful member. With headquarters in Gaborone, Botswana, it has fourteen members: Angola, Botswana,

Democratic Republic of the Congo, Lesotho, Malawi, Mauritius, Mozambique, Namibia, Seychelles, South Africa, Swaziland, Tanzania, Zambia and Zimbabwe. Its core activities are in trade, industry and economic development; agriculture; infrastructure; and social and human development. It has also set up a unit to preserve the rhinoceros; its efforts to foster democracy in the region have met with more mixed results.

Saddam Hussein *See* BUTCHER OF BAGHDAD.

Sadie The fifth of David Blunkett's guide dogs, who replaced her half-sister LUCY in January 2003, during her master's tenure as HOME SECRETARY, and was with him when he resigned late the following year (*see* NO FAVOURS, BUT SLIGHTLY QUICKER). A black curly-coated Labrador/retriever cross, she was two years old when she took over.

safe. safe haven A concept implemented in dangerous countries by the UNITED NATIONS, primarily at British instigation. It involves guaranteeing UN protection to a community which is under threat, provided its citizens remain within a set area. It was tried with some success in Kurdish areas of Iraq after the GULF WAR, backed up by a NO-FLY ZONE, but failed totally when applied to Muslims in Bosnia because the desire of the Serbs to exterminate them (*see* SREBRENICA) was far greater than the will of the UN to protect them.

safe pair of hands A fairly high accolade for a politician: that they can be trusted to deal with any situation they are confronted with without making a mess of it; there is, however, just an undertone that the price to be paid for such safety is a lack of inspiration. The term has its origin in rugby football, at least as early as the 1920s.

safe seat A seat which an MP or Congressman, once elected to it, should have no difficulty in holding because of the strength of their party's support. In America, where STRAIGHT FIGHTS are the order of the day, having 60% of the vote is considered to make one's seat safe.

Safety First The slogan of Stanley BALDWIN's governing Conservatives in Britain's 1929 general election. Taken from a road safety campaign, it implied a risk in voting for radical Labour or Liberal policies; a minority Labour government under Ramsay MACDONALD was elected, only to collapse two years later.

> My unhappy constituents did not want 'safety'. That meant the dole. They wanted work. So they very properly voted me out.
>
> HAROLD MACMILLAN

safety net Limited social provision by the state, concentrating on protecting those suffering greatest hardship or disadvantage, as opposed to a comprehensive WELFARE STATE. In his successful 1992 campaign for the Presidency, Bill CLINTON argued instead for a 'springboard', to provide the disadvantaged with opportunities. The term – which originates in the net placed under the high wire at a circus in case the performers lose their footing – was much used by the REAGAN administration and then crossed the Atlantic; it is credited to Rep. Jack Kemp who wrote in 1980:

> Americans have two complementary desires . . . They want an open, promising ladder of opportunity. And they want a safety net of social services to catch and comfort those less fortunate than themselves.

Sailing the seas depends on the helmsman One of the great propaganda anthems of Communist China in the 1960s, dedicated to CHAIRMAN MAO Tse-Tung.

St Stephen's entrance The public entrance to the Palace of WESTMINSTER, halfway along the building on its landward side. It leads up through security checks to an ante-chamber on the site of **St Stephen's Chapel**, where the COMMONS sat from 1547 until the fire of 1834, and up again to the Central LOBBY.

Salads A pejorative for Britain's Social and Liberal Democrats (abbreviated to SLD), formed in 1988 by the merger of most of the LIBERAL PARTY and a majority of the SOCIAL DEMOCRATS. The name was refined the next year to 'LIBERAL DEMOCRATS', but the original and its abbreviation – with its connotations of wetness and lack of substance – remained in use.

salami tactics The post-war Hungarian Communist leader Matyas Rakosi's term for his successful operation in repeatedly slicing off the most moderate sections of the non-Communist left until a hard-line rump remained which could be merged with the Communist Party. It came to mean any strategy based on persistence where a little more ground was gained each time. In May 2004 Germany's Foreign Minister Joschka Fischer accused UK Foreign Secretary Jack Straw of 'salami tactics' in attempting to firm up the UK's negotiating position on the EUROPEAN CONSTITUTION.

salary grab The 50% pay increase, retroactive for two years, which US Senators and

Congressmen voted themselves – along with the President (whose salary was doubled) and the judiciary – in 1873. The millionaire Massachusetts Congressman Ben Butler thought less affluent members needed the money – and said any legislator not worth it should resign. Public anger was such that Congress was forced to repeal the rises the following year, though a Constitutional technicality meant that SUPREME COURT justices kept their back pay. Butler lost his seat.

Salisbury, Robert Arthur Talbot Gascoyne-Cecil, 3rd Marquess of (1830–1903). Leader of the CONSERVATIVE PARTY 1881–1902 (jointly with Sir Stafford Northcote until 1885) and three times Prime Minister (1885–86, 1886–92, 1895–1902). The last great Victorian political leader, and probably the most REACTIONARY since Wellington. He took an Olympian but low-key view of affairs, though haunted by the fear of social revolution. Joseph Chamberlain told a meeting that Salisbury 'constitutes himself the spokesman of a class, of the class to which he himself belongs, who "toil not, neither do they spin"'. And Lord Curzon termed him 'that strange, powerful, inscrutable and brilliant constructive deadweight at the top'. Yet he could be a forceful speaker; DISRAELI described him as 'a great master of jibes and sneers', and G. W. E. Russell wrote: 'The combination of such genuine amiability in private with such calculated brutality in public utterance is a psychological phenomenon.' Lord Randolph Churchill was a particular target; asked after Churchill's resignation as Chancellor whether he would have him back, Salisbury replied: 'Have you ever heard of a man who, having had a boil on his neck, wanted another?' He had earlier observed: 'I have four departments: the Prime Minister's, the Foreign Office, the Queen and Randolph Churchill; the burden of them increases in that order.' Of Sir Michael Hicks Beach, he observed: 'He would make a very good Home Secretary, and hang everybody.' Salisbury said of himself: 'I rank no higher in the scheme of things than a policeman, whose utility would disappear if there were no criminals.' Though his foreign policy was consistent and he presided over peace in Europe and expansion of the EMPIRE, Bismarck described him as 'lath painted to look like iron.'

Salisbury convention The doctrine formulated by the 6th Marquess (*see* BOBBETY) as Leader of the Opposition in the HOUSE OF LORDS to ATTLEE's Labour government. It lays down that the Tory peers may use their inbuilt majority to amend, but not defeat, legislation for which the electorate has clearly voted. Successive leaders of Tory opposition peers have had to strike a balance between avoiding a constitutional crisis and mounting an effective attack on legislation the party sees as damaging and misguided. The convention has come under strain since the passage of the WEATHERILL AMENDMENT under which a limited number of overwhelmingly Conservative hereditary peers remain, chosen by their own number, as those elected consider they have a MANDATE to block government legislation.

Salo Republic The puppet FASCIST government established by Mussolini on Lake Garda in October 1943 after German paratroops under Otto Skorzeny had rescued him from Allied custody. Firmly under HITLER's thumb, the Salo Republic nominally controlled the portion of Italy still under NAZI occupation until early 1945, when the DUCE tried to flee the country and was captured and shot by Communist PARTISANS.

SALT Strategic Arms Limitation Talks. The SUPERPOWER negotiations on reducing ballistic missiles (ICBMS), begun by Presidents JOHNSON and BREZHNEV in 1969, which led to a **SALT I** treaty signed by President NIXON and Brezhnev in 1972 and **SALT II** concluded by President CARTER and Brezhnev in 1979. SALT I was RATIFIED by the Senate and took full effect, technically expiring in 1977 but continuing to be observed. SALT II was never ratified because the Soviet invasion of Afghanistan intervened, but was observed by the US until 1986.

Salon des Refusés The clique of superannuated and bitter politicians, overlooked for or discarded from office, which is the bane of any government – not least because once in a while they can prove to be right. The phrase originates in a rift in the Parisian art world between the *Académie des Beaux-Arts* and the numerous competent *avant-garde* artists who believed they were being unfairly excluded from its annual *Salon.* Tempers became so inflamed that in 1863 Emperor Napoleon III commanded that a *Salon des Refusés* be staged to give these painters a chance. The exhibition incurred ridicule because of the low standard of much of the work, but it did include the odd gem such as Manet's *Le Déjeuner sur l'herbe* which, astonishingly to a 21st-century audience, had been excluded on grounds of taste.

Saltire The cross of St Andrew, diagonal white on dark blue, the national flag of Scotland. In 832, at Athelstaneford, East Lothian, King Angus McFergus saw the cross in the sky when confronted by an English army. He routed it, then adopted the flag.

Saltley, 'battle of' The mass picket at a Birmingham coke depot in support of the 1972 MINERS' STRIKE which established its leader, Arthur Scargill (*see* KING ARTHUR), as a national figure and virtually settled the dispute in the National Union of Mineworkers' favour.

samizdat Unauthorised, and therefore 'underground', literature published and circulated by DISSIDENTS in Soviet Russia – some directly political, much simply out of step with the cultural tone permitted by the regime. An abbreviation of the Russian *samizdatelstvo*, self-publishing house, it entered the English language in the mid-1960s.

sample In opinion polling, a group selected as representative of the electorate as a whole.
sampling error Faulty selection of a sample which produces a rogue POLL.

Samuel Commission The commission under Sir Herbert Samuel set up early in 1926 to settle a coal strike caused by mine-owners cutting wages and extending working hours. Its report did not achieve its purpose; the TUC subsequently called the GENERAL STRIKE in an unsuccessful effort to win the dispute for the miners.

San Clemente The compound on the California coast, midway between Los Angeles and San Diego, to which Richard NIXON retired and where he spent his final two decades after his resignation over WATERGATE in 1974.
San Francisco Conference The meeting of 46 nations which settled the UNITED NATIONS Charter, signed on 25 June 1945, and created the structure for the world organisation. Though a momentous occasion, it was overshadowed by President ROOSEVELT's death shortly before, CHURCHILL's absence as he sought (and failed to win) re-election, and STALIN's refusal until the last minute to let Foreign Minister MOLOTOV attend.

sanctions Steps taken by one nation, or a concert of nations, against a state that has transgressed against international law or basic morality – or is claimed to have done so. They were first used as a form of law-enforcement by the LEAGUE OF NATIONS against Italy in the 1930s over its invasion of Abyssinia – also setting the precedent that sanctions are seldom effective. When America was advocating them against Japan before WORLD WAR II, Anthony EDEN observed: 'There are two kinds of sanctions, effective and ineffective. To apply the latter was provocative and useless. If we were to apply the former, we ran the risk of war.' Sanctions were imposed against Rhodesia after UDI; when future President Robert Mugabe wanted them tightened, Margaret THATCHER told him: 'If you want to cut your throat, don't come to me for a bandage.' There was also a long-running campaign, partly successful, for international sanctions against South Africa in protest against APARTHEID. The UNITED NATIONS imposed sanctions against Iraq following SADDAM HUSSEIN's invasion of Kuwait; these were retained after the GULF WAR and were used by Saddam as a PROPAGANDA weapon, claiming they were impoverishing his people while skimming immense sums from the UN's OIL-FOR-FOOD programme. Sanctions were also imposed on Libya after LOCKERBIE, being lifted fifteen years later when Colonel Gaddafi finally took responsibility for the bombing and offered compensation to the victims' families.
sanctions-busting The use of subterfuge or sheer brazenness to evade sanctions, by the nation being isolated and by its suppliers. *See* BINGHAM REPORT.

Sandinistas The leftish Sandinist National Liberation Front, which took power in Nicaragua after the overthrow of the dictatorial President Anastasio Somoza-Debayle and ruled for thirteen years until defeated in elections in 1990. Named after August Cesar Sandino, an insurgent leader executed in 1934, the movement was founded in 1962 as an anti-Somoza guerrilla group, finally ousting him seventeen years later in an offensive launched from Costa Rica and Honduras. Ironically Somoza had come to power on the defeat of the original Sandinistas after a six-year guerrilla war in which 136 US Marines were killed; Somoza personally executed Sandino. Once in power under President Daniel Ortega Saavedra, the latter-day Sandinistas came under attack from the CONTRAS, guerrillas who included right-wing Somoza loyalists but also attracted some disillusioned Sandinistas. WASHINGTON saw the Sandinistas as Communists and a threat to regional peace; the backing the Contras received from the REAGAN administration gave rise to the IRAN-CONTRA affair. Ceasefire talks in 1988 led to free elections, which the Sandinistas and their supporters around the world expected them to win. In conceding defeat to the National Opposition Union's Violetta Barrios de Chamorro, Ortega declared:

> We, the Sandinistas, have given Nicaragua this democracy and peace.

See also CONTADORA PLAN.

Sangatte The Red Cross refugee centre close to the Channel Tunnel entrance near Calais from which thousands of ASYLUM-SEEKERS and illegal migrants attempted in 2000–02 to gain entry to Britain, forcing the suspension of traffic at times as they broke into the Tunnel and the adjoining freight yard. A number of the migrants were killed falling from freight trains they had boarded, and the CRS riot police were called in to deal with fighting at the centre between rival ethnic groups. The failure of the socialist government of Lionel Jospin to check the traffic, which they regarded as a British problem, seriously strained Anglo-French relations, and it was only after the election of a centre-right government under Jean-Pierre Raffarin in June 2002 that action was taken. Sangatte was closed that December, with Britain agreeing to take 1000 Iraqi Kurds and 200 Afghans from the centre; the remaining 3600 occupants were offered asylum in France or money to return home.

SANROC The South African Non-Racial Olympic Committee, one of the bodies that led the sporting boycott of South Africa in protest against APARTHEID which was almost totally effective for a quarter of a century.

sans-culottes (Fr. without breeches) An originally derisive term for a radical or REVOLUTIONARY, dating back to the FRENCH REVOLUTION. The poor people of Paris wore trousers *(pantalons)* instead of the knee-breeches or *culottes* worn by the upper classes. In cartoons lampooning the revolutionaries, the sans-culottes were depicted as completely unclothed below the waist. The word has come to represent the lowest class in any revolutionary or anarchic movement.

Sarajevo The capital of Bosnia and flash-point of 20th-century Europe, from the assassination that started WORLD WAR I to the bloody siege of 1992–93 as Serb forces tried to oust Croats and Muslims through ETHNIC CLEANSING. Sarajevo first gained infamy on 28 June 1914 when the Archduke Franz Ferdinand, heir to the Habsburg throne, was shot by 19-year-old Gavrilo Princip, a Bosnian Serb and a member of the violently nationalist BLACK HAND GANG. The shots fired in the name of Serb independence from Austria reverberated round the world. Austria despatched a humiliating ULTIMATUM to Serbia, which was only partly accepted; Austrian then declared war on Serbia on 28 July. This prompted Russia to mobilise in solidarity with Serbia, which provoked Germany to declare war on Russia (1 August) and France (3 August). Germany then invaded Belgium in accordance with the SCHLIEFFEN PLAN, prompting Britain to declare war on Germany (4 August) in defence of Belgian NEUTRALITY. The spot where Princip fired the fatal shot is marked by two footprints in the pavement. The football manager Brian Clough, shown them when in Sarajevo with his Derby County team, observed:

> If I'd just shot an archduke I wouldn't stand around with my feet in wet cement.

Sarajevo returned to the headlines in 1992 when, after Croatia's secession from Yugoslavia, Bosnia declared itself independent and a three-way battle for territory broke out between Muslims, Serbs and Croats, with the Serbs the best armed. Sarajevo was the greatest prize and the city took a battering from the Serbs who held some of the suburbs; a UNITED NATIONS operation to fly in relief supplies was only possible after France's President MITTERRAND braved the threat of artillery and snipers' bullets to visit the city, much of it reduced to rubble.

Sarbanes-Oxley Act The legislation hastily passed by the US CONGRESS and signed by President George W. BUSH in 2002 in the wake of the ENRON, WorldCom and other scandals. which obliged chief executives of major corporations to sign a sworn statement as to the veracity of their accounts. The key reporting clause – 404 – came into effect in stages, for large US corporations in 2004, for smaller ones in July 2005 and for foreign-based firms listed on US stock markets a year later after the CBI and other foreign business groups persuaded the Securities and Exchange Commission that they needed more leeway.

Satanic Verses, The *See* FATWA.

satellite countries Small countries adjacent

to and firmly under the control of a larger one – specifically the Communist nations of central and Eastern Europe, under rigid Soviet control during the COLD WAR. The implication, from the satellite's inability to break out of orbit, is that the satellites have no will of their own. The expression was first been used in a political sense in 1776 by Thomas Paine, in denying such a connection between America and Britain, and thus predated by 180 years the launch of Russia's first *Sputnik.*

Saturday Night massacre One of the pivotal events of the WATERGATE crisis, which led directly to the HOUSE OF REPRESENTATIVES empowering its Judiciary Committee to consider IMPEACHMENT proceedings against President NIXON. On 20 October 1973 Nixon ordered Attorney-General Elliot Richardson to fire the Watergate SPECIAL PROSECUTOR Archibald Cox, because Cox was seeking key tapes of Nixon's conversations in the WHITE HOUSE. Richardson refused, and resigned. Deputy Attorney-General William Ruckelshaus also refused, and was fired. Nixon then promoted Robert Bork, Solicitor-General, to acting Attorney-General; he fired Cox and abolished the office of special prosecutor. All the resignations were announced by the White House that Saturday night. The Congressional and public reaction was so hostile that three days later Nixon offered to release the tapes Cox had sought, and to re-establish the special prosecutor's office. But he never recovered his position.

sausage. custodians of the national sausage Harold WILSON's scornful description of the HEATH government for its failure to keep INFLATION under control. It came in a speech during the February 1974 election in which Wilson reeled off a series of price increases in staple foods, culminating with the rise in the price of sausages.

threat to the British sausage The phrase used by EUROSCEPTICS to characterise the propensity of BRUSSELS to interfere in everyday aspects of British life. There has indeed been an effort by the European Commission to determine what sausages in member states must contain. But it was a case of life imitating art, as the words were first used in an episode of YES, MINISTER when the fictional Minister Jim Hacker was able to redeem his reputation by detecting a plot in Brussels to 'standardise' the British sausage out of existence.

SAVAK The notorious secret police of the Shah's regime in Iran, prior to his overthrow in 1979. With over 60,000 agents, SAVAK was active in monitoring and curbing dissent in Iranian communities throughout the world as well as at home.

save. Save the Argylls! The slogan of the successful campaign waged in the 1960s for the exemption of the Argyll and Sutherland Highlanders from merger with another regiment of the British army under the Labour government's defence cuts.

Save the Whales! The most emotive, and best-known, slogan of ecological campaigners from the mid-1970s. It became a global watchword not only for the battle to keep traditional whaling nations like Japan and Norway from resuming the slaughter, but generally GREEN campaigning. When John SMITH launched his PRAWN COCKTAIL OFFENSIVE to woo the City of London for Labour, Michael HESELTINE made an impassioned plea in the Commons to **'save the prawns!'** Equally, US opponents of environmental campaigning and liberal causes generally produced a bumper sticker reading: **'Feed Jane Fonda to the whales!'**

Say it out loud, I'm black (gay) and I'm proud Originally the title of a song by James Brown, the phrase was taken up as a slogan of self-belief in the late 1960s by black activists in America. Before long, GAY RIGHTS activists were chanting their own version.

scab The greatest insult in Britain's labour and trade union movement, directed (and frequently chanted) against workers brought in to break a strike *See* BLACKLEG.

scapegoating The practice of singling out an individual or group and blaming them for the failure of a policy or a situation of acute political or economic difficulty.

> The (1990) elections raised the prospect that one of the most dismal traditions of American political life might be revived: that of scapegoating racial minorities in times of trouble.
>
> E. J. DIONNE Jr, *Why Americans Hate Politics*

schedule An appendix to a BILL or an ACT of Parliament, listing specific matters to which the measure applies.

Schengenland The area of the EUROPEAN UNION within which border controls for EU nationals have been totally abolished under the **Schengen Agreement** of 14 June 1985 and the subsequent **Schengen Convention** of 1990. Stemming from an agreement between France and Germany the previous year to work toward elimination of their common border controls, Schengen extended to Austria, the BENELUX countries, Italy, Portugal and Spain by the time of ENLARGEMENT in 2004. Switzerland voted to join in June 2005. There are now separate streams at airports for those exempt from checks, but the tide of ASYLUM SEEKERS and illegal migrants began to strain the system in the late 1990s and since 9/11, in particular, many informal checks have been reimposed because of doubts over the true identity of the bearers of EU passports.

Schicklgruber The original surname of Adolf HITLER's father: Alois Schicklgruber (1837–1903), an official in the Austrian Imperial customs, whose mother, Maria Anna Schicklgruber, conceived him by Johann Georg Heidler, whom she married in 1842. Alois kept his mother's surname until he was nearly 40, when he adopted the name Hitler, based on a local priest's misspelling. The FÜHRER went to considerable lengths to conceal his ancestry, though details were dredged up by opponents of the NAZIs in the early 1930s. When CHURCHILL wanted to make his contempt for Hitler most evident, he would describe him as 'Herr Schicklgruber'. No firm evidence has ever substantiated Hans Frank's claim at the NUREMBERG TRIALS that Hitler's father was the child of a Jew from Graz, named Frankenberger, in whose household Maria Anna became pregnant while working as a maid.

> HEIL SCHICKLGRUBER!
>
> Headline in an Austrian newspaper during the July 1931 German elections

Schleswig-Holstein Question The dispute between Denmark and Prussia, which flared sporadically between 1848 and 1866, over two duchies lying between them; they were eventually incorporated into Prussia.

> There are only three men who have ever understood it; one was Prince Albert, and he is dead; the second was a German professor who became mad; I am the third and I have forgotten all about it.
>
> PALMERSTON

Schlieffen Plan The plan on which Germany eventually fought WORLD WAR I, devised by Count von Schlieffen (1833–1913), Chief of Staff 1890–1906. It envisaged a war on two fronts, against France to the west and Russia to the east. Schlieffen's strategy for a quick victory was to hold off Russia with minimal forces, then overwhelm the French armies with a massive flanking movement through neutral Belgium, thus avoiding the formidable barriers along France's eastern border. Germany's main forces would then be free to confront the Russians who, it was assumed, would be slow to mobilise. The plan was initially successful when implemented in August 1914 by Schlieffen's successor, Helmuth von Moltke. But Moltke had modified the blueprint by weakening the crucial right wing of the German advance from 90% to 60% of the total forces. At the Battle of the Marne in September, the Allies halted the advance of the German First Army under General Alexander von Kluck. The subsequent trench warfare marked the failure of the modified strategy, and on 14 September Moltke was replaced by the German Minister of War, Erich von Falkenhayn.

> When you march into France, let the last man on the right brush the Channel with his sleeve.
>
> Count von SCHLIEFFEN

schools and hospitals first The slogan which Tony BLAIR's LABOUR PARTY took up during the 2001 UK general election as it sought to fight the campaign on its plans for investment and reform in the public services, and especially the NHS, while the Conservatives tried to turn the election into a referendum on the EURO. Labour's re-election with a majority of 165 was a vindication of the strategy.

schools you can walk to A phrase used by candidates in US elections as shorthand for 'no blacks', usually when competing for blue-collar ethnic votes. It stems from the advent of BUSING, when some school districts began transporting white children to schools in overwhelmingly black areas to create a racial mix. To promise 'schools you can walk to' – a phrase also used by realtors to imply a purchaser would have few black neighbours – quickly became code for a commitment to fight busing of white children out, and of black children in to previously all-white schools. Even liberal candidates would use the phrase, as it looked harmless out of context and could be essential to their chances of getting elected.

Schuman Plan The plan put forward in 1950 by the French Prime Minister Robert Schuman (1886–1963) which was the genesis of first the EUROPEAN COAL AND STEEL COMMUNITY and eventually of the EUROPEAN UNION. Ostensibly a proposal to pool French and German coal and steel production, it was designed to go much further and tie the two countries so closely together that another war between them would be impossible. Britain's Labour government refused to join in, a decision Dean Acheson termed 'the greatest mistake of the post-war period'. And while CHURCHILL praised it from OPPOSITION, he stayed out on his return to power the following year.

> Not just a piece of convenient machinery. It is a revolutionary, and almost mystical conception.
> HAROLD MACMILLAN, Strasbourg, 15 August 1950

SCLC Southern Christian Leadership Conference. The organisation headed by Dr Martin Luther KING which assumed the leadership of America's CIVIL RIGHTS movement in the late 1950s. It brought about many of the gains of the following decade, and outlived its founder. Formed in Atlanta in January 1957, the SCLC was from the start committed to non-violent Direct ACTION to back up the campaigning of the NAACP which was falling foul of racist violence; its initial title 'The Southern Christian Leaders' Conference on Transportation and Integration' reflected the bus boycotts (*see* MONTGOMERY) being waged at the time. The SCLC's Crusade for Citizenship began with 22 simultaneous mass meetings across the South on 12 February 1958; from 1961 it attacked the literacy problem with 'citizenship schools'. The Student Non-Violent Co-Ordinating Committee (SNCC) was an offshoot of the SCLC.

> There has been nothing in the annals of American social struggle to equal this phenomenon, and there probably never will be again.
> BAYARD RUSTIN (1912–87)

Scoop The nickname of Sen. Henry Jackson (1912–87), the heavyweight Democrat who combined strong liberal domestic policies with a HAWKISH line toward defence and the Soviet Union. Co-author of the JACKSON-VANIK AMENDMENT and a strong opponent of the SALT agreements, he made an unsuccessful bid for the Presidency in 1976. The nickname was given him at the age of four by his sister; as a young man he was known as **Soda Pop Jackson** because of his crusade as a moralistic district attorney against prostitution and bootlegging. A Washington state Congressman from 1940 and Senator after 1952, he was responsible for the pioneering National Environmental Policy Act.

Scopes case The trial in July 1925 of a Dayton, Tennessee schoolmaster for teaching the theory of evolution to his high school biology class. John Scopes had challenged a newly-passed state law prohibiting the teaching in its schools of 'any theory that denies the story of the divine creation as taught in the Bible . . . and that man has descended from a lower order of animals'. The case, headlined as the **'monkey trial'**, turned into a *cause célèbre*; Clarence Darrow led for the defence, while William Jennings Bryan (*see* PRAIRIE AVENGER), making his final contribution to American history, was one of the prosecutors. Scopes was found guilty and fined $100, but the Fundamentalist case attracted world-wide ridicule and it was six decades before Creationism, as it is now known, regained serious political adherents.

> There is no more reason to believe that man has descended from some inferior animal than there is to believe that a stately mansion has descended from a small cottage.
> WILLIAM JENNINGS BRYAN

Scorecard The US SECRET SERVICE's codename for Vice President Dan QUAYLE.

Scotland. Scotland Act (1) The Act promoted by Tony BLAIR's Labour government, and passed by the WESTMINSTER Parliament in 1998, following a REFERENDUM, which established DEVOLUTION for Scotland, with a SCOTTISH PARLIAMENT and Ministers to be accountable for all matters which were specifically not RESERVED. The Act also gave the Parliament the power to vary income tax by up to 3p in the £ – a power it has not yet used. (2) The measure promoted by James CALLAGHAN's Labour government, and passed in 1978, which offered devolution to Scotland, subject to a referendum. The Bill only passed after anti-devolutionist Labour MPs had hitched on the CUNNINGHAM AMENDMENT, which contained the seeds of the proposal's defeat.

Scotland Free in '93 The slogan on which the Scottish National Party (SNP) fought the 1992 general election, substantially increasing its vote but emerging with just three seats, the same as in 1987. The SNP leader Alex Salmond had the slogan sprung on him, and would have preferred something more cautious.

Scotland Office The UK government department which took responsibility for Scotland where reserved matters were concerned after devolution took effect in 1999; initially with its own Secretary of State, it was rolled into the new Department of Constitutional Affairs in June 2003, with a Scottish member of the Cabinet speaking for it. It is based in Dover House, Lord Melbourne's former residence in Whitehall which had been the London headquarters prior to devolution of the all-powerful **Scottish Office**.

Flower of Scotland Scotland's unofficial national anthem, adopted first by Scottish boxing supporters in the 1970s and later by the Scottish Rugby Union. It commemorates the Scots' victory over the English at Bannockburn in 1314, but is of no great age itself, having been written in 1966 by the late Roy Williamson of the folk group the Corries.

> Oh flower of Scotland when will we see your like again
> That fought and died for yon wee bit hill and glen
> And stood against him proud Edward's army
> And sent him homeward tae think again.
>
> The hills are bare now
> And autumn leaves lie thick and still
> O'er land which is lost now
> Which those so dearly held
>
> Those days are past now
> And in the past must remain
> But we can still rise now
> And be the nation again

Scott. Dred Scott case The explosive US SUPREME COURT decision in March 1857 which ruled the MISSOURI COMPROMISE unconstitutional and made the CIVIL WAR almost inevitable. It concerned an illiterate slave, originally from Virginia, who had drifted away from his owner and was freed in Missouri by the son of his first master. The proceedings to give Scott that freedom ended with first the Missouri Supreme Court and then the Supreme Court ruling that he was still a slave. By seven to two, the justices ruled that slaves could not become US citizens, and so could not sue in the nation's courts – and that slavery was valid in Missouri despite the painful compromise reached by CONGRESS 37 years before. The case – *Dred Scott v Sandford* – was only the second (MARBURY V MADISON in 1803 being the first) when the Supreme Court ruled an act of Congress to be unconstitutional. It was overturned by the THIRTEENTH and FOURTEENTH AMENDMENTS.

Scott Report The damning indictment of the conduct of Conservative Ministers delivered in February 1996 by Sir Richard Scott, the senior judge who had spent three years investigating how the THATCHER and MAJOR governments changed their policy on arms sales to Iraq without informing Parliament and allowed the MATRIX-CHURCHILL trial to take place. Though Sir Richard cleared Ministers of a 'duplicitous intention' and of conspiring to deny the Matrix-Churchill defendants a fair trial, he determined that government statements on exports to Iraq had 'consistently failed' to comply with recognised standards, that the trial 'ought never to have commenced', that William Waldegrave had deliberately failed to inform Parliament of the change of policy when a Foreign Office Minister and that Sir Nicholas Lyell, Attorney-General, had shown 'unsound judgement' and 'a serious misunderstanding of the role and duty of a minister' in his approach to the trial and the granting of PUBLIC INTEREST IMMUNITY CERTIFICATES. Remarkably, no heads rolled. Ian Lang, Trade and Industry Secretary, pre-empted an attack by Shadow Foreign Secretary Robin COOK by accusing Labour of defaming Tory ministers before the report's publication and claiming that they had been exonerated. In the ensuing COMMONS division, Waldegrave and Lyell survived demands for their resignation by one vote.

Scottish Constitutional Convention The forum representing most of civic Scotland – the trade unions, the churches, the Labour and Liberal Democratic parties – which in 1989–90 drew up a blueprint for devolution in the face of the determination of John MAJOR's Conservative government to retain power at WESTMINSTER . In essence, this was the plan implemented by Tony BLAIR's government in the 1998 SCOTLAND ACT, following overwhelming support in a REFERENDUM. *See also* CLAIM OF RIGHT.

Scottish Executive The body of Ministers, and the administrative entity, based in Edinburgh at **St Andrew's** House, that since DEVOLUTION from WESTMINSTER in 1999 has controlled the bulk of Scotland's domestic affairs.

Scottish National Party *See* SNP.

Scottish Parliament The 129-member assembly elected under the 1998 **Scotland Act**, which first convened the following year; 73 of its members are elected for four-year terms on a constituency basis, and the rest by PROPORTIONAL REPRESENTATION under a regional LIST SYSTEM. The Ministers of the Scottish Executive are drawn from the Parliament, which elects its own PRESIDING OFFICER. The Parliament sat initially in the Church of Scotland General Assembly Building on the Mound, until its futuristic building at HOLYROOD at the other end of the Royal Mile was ready. Initially budgeted at £40 million, the structure finally cost £431 million. The brainchild of the initial FIRST MINISTER Donald Dewar and the Catalan architect Enric Miralles, neither of whom lived to see it taking shape, it hosted its first Parliamentary session on 7 September 2004; the following week the FRASER REPORT largely exonerated Ministers over the scandal of the cost, but severely criticised civil servants. On 9 October the building was formally inaugurated by the Queen.

> There shall be a Scottish Parliament.
> WHITE PAPER '*Scotland's Parliament*', 1997

> I like that.
> DONALD DEWAR, introducing it

Scottish Raj The pejorative term, recalling Britain's imperial rule of India, used by the BBC interviewer Jeremy Paxman on 13 March 2005 to describe the preponderance of Scots in Tony BLAIR's government, Gordon BROWN and John Reid being the most prominent. He used it in a *Sunday Times* article after bruising exchanges with Reid on *Newsnight* which culminated in Paxman calling the Health Secretary 'an attack dog' and Reid retaliating in kind. Underlying Paxman's phrase was the fact that health in Scotland was DEVOLVED; Reid as a Scottish MP had no say in health matters north of the Border, but could still be Minister responsible for the NHS in England.

Scottish Socialist Party The TROTSKYIST party led until 2005 by the charismatic Tommy Sheridan (1964– ; *see* SUNBED SOCIALIST) which rose from the ashes of the MILITANT TENDENCY to become a vocal, populist hard left force in Scottish politics, benefiting from PROPORTIONAL REPRESENTATION to win one seat in the Scottish Parliament in 1999 and six in 2003. The SSP's roots were in the faction of Militant which, when the Tendency split in the late 1980s, abandoned ENTRYISM to campaign and organise in its true colours as a party separate from Labour. Standing as Militant Labour, it won several Scottish council seats in 1992, lost all but Sheridan's in Glasgow in 1995, but gained momentum after NEW LABOUR came to power two years later and DEVOLUTION gave it new opportunities.

scramble. scramble for Africa *See* AFRICA.

scrambler A telephone used by senior government and military figures and others in sensitive positions. Calls to and from it are 'scrambled' electronically, so that anyone tapping the line will not be able to decipher what is being said.

scrap of paper The description of the 1839 Treaty of LONDON made on 4 August 1914 by the German Chancellor Theobald von Bethmann-Hollweg (1856–1921). Under the Treaty Britain was committed to defending Belgian NEUTRALITY, which was violated by Germany's invasion (in accordance with the SCHLIEFFEN PLAN) on 4 August, following its declaration of war on France and Russia. On 3 August Britain informed Germany that it would stand by the Treaty, prompting Bethmann-Hollweg's contemptuous reply to the British ambassador Sir Edward Goschen:

> Just for a word – 'neutrality', a word which in wartime has so often been disregarded – just for a scrap of paper, Great Britain is going to make war on a kindred nation which desires nothing better than to be friends with her.

screening The process under which a country's security authorities check the background of present or potential public servants to ascertain their 'trustworthiness, patriotism and integrity' (*see also* POSITIVE VETTING). In WASHINGTON the word also covers lie-detector tests on federal officials in sensitive posts. In 1983 President REAGAN sought to make such tests compulsory for thousands of bureaucrats; he dropped the plan after a furore in CONGRESS, but in 1985 4863 non-intelligence officials in the PENTAGON alone took lie-detector tests. Secretary of State George Shultz said of the move to introduce the tests:

> The moment in this government I am told I am not trusted is the day I leave.

scrutineers In many forms of BALLOT, particularly in political parties and trade unions, the invigilators who supervise the voting process and announce the result. In the LABOUR PARTY their role was critical until the adoption of a computerised recorded VOTE in the mid-1980s, with union leaders and others regularly claiming – often for tactical reasons – that their votes at the party CONFERENCE had been miscounted. After one such dispute David Blunkett made a joke of his blindness by declaring:

> Next time the scrutineers will be me and my dog.

scuttle The withdrawal of a colonial power from its overseas possessions with indecent haste, without any warning or the creation of a governmental structure to take over. The most notable example was Belgium's departure from the Congo which gave rise to a decade of anarchy. On 20 December 1946 Winston CHURCHILL told the COMMONS on negotiations for the independence of Burma:

The British Empire seems to be running out almost as fast as the American loan. The steady and remorseless process of divesting ourselves of what has been gained by so many generations of toil, administration and sacrifice continues . . . This haste is appalling. 'Scuttle' is the only word that can be applied.

SDECE *See* DGSE.

SDI Strategic Defence Initiative. *See* STAR WARS.

SDLP Social Democratic and Labour Party. The mainly Roman Catholic party in NORTHERN IRELAND which takes a moderate and democratic NATIONALIST position, favouring POWER-SHARING and closer links with the Irish Republic. Founded in 1973, it has competed from the start for Catholic votes with SINN FEIN, which advocated all-out support for the IRA and its campaign of terrorism. Up to the GOOD FRIDAY AGREEMENT, which its then leader John Hume had done much to bring about, it could count on a majority of Catholic votes, but by 2003 it had been overtaken by Sinn Fein, just as the official Unionists were overtaken by the more extreme DUP.

SDP Social Democratic Party. The party launched on 16 March 1981 by the GANG OF FOUR defectors from the LABOUR PARTY, which for brief moments in the early to mid-1980s looked as if it might achieve its aim of BREAKING THE MOULD of British politics. The SDP gained its impetus from the strife in the Labour Party as the BENNITE left came close to taking control, and from widespread initial support from voters alarmed at the POLARISATION of politics who had never previously taken an active interest; Roy JENKINS had anticipated it in his EXPERIMENTAL AIRCRAFT speech the previous year. It soon attracted 30 MPs – 29 from Labour, one from the Conservatives – and briefly topped 50% in the opinion polls; under Jenkins it began negotiating an ALLIANCE with David Steel's (*see* BOY DAVID) LIBERAL PARTY. The SDP's middle-class image and moderate policies, which led to them being known as 'soggy Dems', attracted ridicule from Labour and Tories alike. Roy HATTERSLEY accused them of 'trying to build a land fit for credit card holders', Norman Tebbit described them as 'like a bunch of bananas – green round the edges, soft in the middle and not quite straight', while the political journalist Walter Terry simply termed them 'the bland leading the bland'. Many of the jokes revolved around Jenkins' love of fine claret; the Conservative Party chairman Lord Thorneycroft remarked:

I had rather thought of joining myself. After all it isn't a party, it hasn't a programme and I'm told the claret is good.

Francis Pym, the Conservative Defence Secretary, dismissed their policies as 'stale claret in new bottles – a confidence trick not to be mistaken for the elixir of life.'

The SDP won spectacular BY-ELECTION victories at Crosby (Shirley Williams) and Glasgow Hillhead (Jenkins) but was squeezed hard by the FALKLANDS FACTOR and won only six seats at the 1983 election. Under Dr David OWEN it developed a sharper touch with such slogans as 'CARING BUT DARING' and 'Tough but Tender', but tension with the Liberals over defence weakened its appeal and despite a further breakthrough at Greenwich it lost ground at the 1987 election. The party then split over Steel's efforts to force a merger with the Liberals, a majority under Robert Maclennan eventually merging to form the LIBERAL DEMOCRATS and a rump SDP under Dr Owen continuing until 1990, when it collapsed after finishing behind the OFFICIAL MONSTER RAVING LOONY PARTY in the Bootle by-election.

A social democratic party without deep roots in the working-class movement would quickly fade into an unrepresentative intellectual sect.

ROY JENKINS, 1972

The heterosexual wing of the Liberal Party.

SHIRLEY WILLIAMS

Speaker at the 1986 SDP conference: What have the Liberals got that we haven't?
Voice: MPs.

SDS Students for a Democratic Society. One of the seminal groups of America's NEW LEFT, founded in 1959 at the University of Michigan by Al Haber and Tom Hayden. By 1962 it was protesting on campus against research which might embroil America in a VIETNAM WAR, against the chemical firm producing NAPALM and against the presence of the ROTC (Reserve Officers' Training Corps). It set out a range of liberal and idealistic principles in the 1962 PORT HURON STATEMENT, but was gradually hijacked by extremist militants set on violence and was eclipsed as the ANTI-WAR movement got under way; nevertheless a number of its activists matured into the mainstream of a DEMOCRATIC PARTY which had itself become more radical.

seal The ultimate symbol of endorsement by

the SOVEREIGN POWER, dating back at least 1200 years: a wax seal applied to a document bearing the emblem of that power (in the UK the monarch, and in America the President), the seal generally being kept by the LORD CHANCELLOR.

seals of office The emblems of authority granted by the CROWN to SECRETARIES OF STATE, and surrendered by them on their resignation or dismissal.

sealed train The train in which the German authorities despatched LENIN and his closest associates from exile in Switzerland to Russia in 1917, lighting the fuse for the RUSSIAN REVOLUTION. The train was locked to prevent the revolutionaries contaminating the people with their ideology as it passed through German-held territory.

Seanad (Ir. Senate) The upper house of the Parliament of the Irish Republic; it does not have the power of VETO over decisions taken by the DAIL.

search and destroy politics The quest by the media and OPPOSITION politicians for skeletons in the cupboard of anyone nominated for or seeking public office. The term – originating in military operations to flush out GUERRILLAS in VIETNAM – was first used in this context by Linda Chavez, George W. BUSH's nominee for Secretary of Labor, after she was forced to withdraw in January 2001 when it was found she had employed an illegal Guatemalan immigrant. However, as early as 1981 Margaret THATCHER was said by an anonymous colleague to have carried out a 'search and destroy mission in the tea room' after an outbreak of dissent among Conservative MPs.

Searchlight (1) The US SECRET SERVICE codename for President NIXON. (2) In Britain, a trenchantly anti-FASCIST paper produced by the campaigning journalist Gerry Gable, which for over a generation has exposed extreme right-wing groups and highlighted what he sees as instances of their infiltration into mainstream British life.

seasonally adjusted The adjustment of economic statistics, published monthly or quarterly, to eliminate seasonal fluctuations, caused for instance by fine summer weather boosting tourism, winter snows shutting down the construction industry, or the pre-Christmas shopping boom.

> With seasonally unadjusted temperatures you could abolish weather in Canada.
>
> ROBERT STANFIELD (1914–2003), Progressive Conservative leader

seat The place a legislator occupies in the CHAMBER, and thus the thing he or she acquires by being elected. The relative strength of parties in any LEGISLATURE is tallied in terms of seats, not individuals.

> Timid and interested politicians think much more about the security of their seats than about the security of their country.
>
> THOMAS BABINGTON MACAULAY (1800–59)

seat of government The building, complex of buildings or city from which a government exercises its authority.

marginal seat *See* MARGINAL.

open seat In US elections, a seat where there is no INCUMBENT running for re-election.

safe seat *See* SAFE.

target seat *See* TARGET.

seated and covered In the HOUSE OF COMMONS, the anachronistic procedure which survived until 1998 under which a member wishing to make a Point of ORDER during a DIVISION could send from his seat for one of two top hats kept specially for the purpose and put it on. It was replaced by a requirement for any MP with a point of order to make to sit close to the CHAIR.

SEATO South East Asia Treaty Organisation. An organisation for mutual defence against 'Communist aggression' and for economic co-operation, formed on the model of NATO. The treaty was concluded in Manila on 8 September 1954 by the US, Australia, the UK, France, New Zealand, Pakistan, the Philippines and Thailand, in the wake of the French defeat at DIEN BIEN PHU and the Communist takeover of North Vietnam; Laos, Cambodia and South Vietnam were given 'protection'. China saw it as a threat and immediately began shelling QUEMOY AND MATSU; India, Burma, Ceylon and Indonesia felt it a provocation and refused to join. SEATO proved toothless, and after 1964 the UK, France and Pakistan reduced their commitment to avoid becoming involved in the VIETNAM WAR. In 1975, with Indo-China effectively under Communist control, the treaty was ended, the remaining non-Communist Asian nations forming ASEAN for mutual economic aid.

Seattle summit The WORLD TRADE ORGANISATION meeting in December 1999 which gave rise both to total deadlock between participating nations and to the first serious ANTI-GLOBALISATION riots. Two more rounds of talks were needed, at CANCUN in September 2003, and in Geneva the following July, for outline agreement to be reached.

secession The term used in the years preceding America's CIVIL WAR for the threatened withdrawal of certain slave states from the UNION. It recalled the secession of the plebs in ancient Rome, when the representatives of the lower orders of the free citizenry pulled out of the Republic's government. After Abraham LINCOLN's election in 1860 South Carolina led the first states out of the Union; by his inauguration in March 1861 seven states had gone and war was inevitable.

> The constitution of the United States forms a government, not a league . . . secession does not break a league, but destroys the unity of a nation.
> ANDREW JACKSON, NULLIFICATION proclamation, 1832

On 7 January 1861 Sen. Robert Tombs said of the secessionists:

> They appealed to the Constitution, they appealed to justice, they appealed to fraternity, until the Constitution, justice and fraternity were no longer listened to in the legislative halls of their country, and they then prepared for the arbitrament of the sword; and now you see the glittering bayonet, and hear the tramp of armed men from your capital to the Rio Grande.

Second Amendment The amendment to the US CONSTITUTION, ratified in the BILL OF RIGHTS, which gives the American people the RIGHT TO BEAR ARMS in order to maintain a citizen militia, and which is relied on by opponents of GUN CONTROL. The NRA and others see it as giving anyone the right to carry firearms, but in 1988 former SUPREME COURT Justice Lewis Powell, speaking of handguns, said:

> It is not easy to understand why the Second Amendment, or the notion of liberty, should be viewed as creating a right to own and carry a weapon that contributes so directly to the shocking number of murders.

Second Front Now! The slogan pushed by the UK and (after PEARL HARBOR) the US Communist Parties between the NAZI invasion of the Soviet Union in 1941 and the D-Day landings three years later. Its purpose was to pressure Britain, the US and their allies to invade occupied France at the earliest possible moment so as to divert Axis forces from the Russian Front. Establishing a Second Front was a matter of urgency for STALIN, who feared his Western allies would let the Soviet Union and Germany fight each other to extinction. In May 1942 MOLOTOV, the Soviet Foreign Minister, was promised in WASHINGTON that a Second Front would open soon to relieve the pressure; the next month CHURCHILL told ROOSEVELT that US plans to invade France in 1942 were unrealistic, and in August he explained this to Stalin. However, in October 1942 Allied landings (Operation Torch) did take place in North Africa. Churchill was determined there should be no invasion until success was assured and sufficient forces were available; at CASABLANCA in January 1943 it was again postponed, and a British plan to invade Sicily adopted. With domestic political pressure growing, Churchill agreed at the QUEBEC Conference of August 1943 that France should be invaded on 1 May 1944. **D-Day** eventually took place on 6 June. Though German forces mounted stiff resistance, they were by now retreating in the east; the time taken to open the Second Front meant that instead of the West rescuing Stalin, the Soviet leader was able to dictate the post-war shape of central Europe.

> There is no doubt that the absence of a second front in Europe considerably relieves the position of the German Army, nor can there be any doubt that the appearance of a second front on the Continent of Europe – and this undoubtedly will appear in the near future – will essentially relieve the position of our armies to the detriment of the German Army.
> STALIN, radio broadcast, 6 November 1941

Second Reading Despite its title, the first consideration of a BILL by either HOUSE at WESTMINSTER. The First Reading is a formality; the Second generally involves a full day's debate on the principle of the measure (sometimes less, occasionally two days), culminating in a DIVISION; if passed, the Bill goes to a STANDING COMMITTEE for line-by-line consideration. The Second Reading may be accompanied by a MONEY RESOLUTION, or sometimes by a REASONED AMENDMENT from the OPPOSITION explaining why, although they support the principle of the Bill, they have major objections to aspects of it. In the US HOUSE OF REPRESENTATIVES, the Second Reading applies to the procedure in the COMMITTEE OF THE WHOLE where the Bill is read section by section, with members having the right to offer amendments to each section in turn, and speak on them for up to five minutes.

seconder Where two sponsors are required for a MOTION or an AMENDMENT in any political forum, the proposer must find a seconder to give public support to the proposal before it can be put to the vote.

secondary action *See* PICKETING.

secret. Secret Intelligence Service *See* MI6.

secret police In all TOTALITARIAN states and some others, a shadowy body whose purposes are to gather intelligence about opponents of the regime, arrest them or worse (*see* DEATH SQUADS) and instil fear into the population, ensuring that they appreciate that resistance is useless. Some secret police forces, like HITLER's GESTAPO or the Soviet KGB, had a high profile on occasions and a clearly-known structure; others like East Germany's STASI concentrated on undercover work, often clandestinely inducing members of suspected DISSIDENT families to inform on each other.

Secret Service The body, operating under the auspices of the US TREASURY, which affords protection to the President and other public figures who might be at risk – alongside its original role of protecting the currency. The Secret Service were purely Treasury investigators until 1901, when agents were drafted in to protect President Theodore ROOSEVELT in the wake of MCKINLEY's assassination; the VICE PRESIDENT has only been protected since 1951, and the Presidential family, President elect and former Presidents more recently still. Members of the Secret Service detail accompanying the President are clearly recognisable, as they are continuously scrutinising the crowds. Out of the spotlight their duties remain the protection of the person they guard from attack. When the secret serviceman assigned to protect President Ford's daughter Susan was asked what he would do if one of her dates became over-amorous, he replied:

> I'm here to protect her from other people, not from herself.

secret session A session of a LEGISLATURE from which the Press and public are excluded, generally on grounds of national security. The HOUSE OF COMMONS regularly met in secret session during WORLD WAR II, with only one significant LEAK of information (in 1942) ever coming out. *See also* EXECUTIVE SESSION.

secret treaty or **protocol** An agreement concluded between countries who desire all or part of it to remain confidential; it may involve plans to attack or dismember another state, or might prove fatal in terms of domestic politics. The renunciation of such treaties was one of WILSON's FOURTEEN POINTS.

> All there is to do is publish the secret treaties, then close the shop.
>
> TROTSKY, after becoming Soviet COMMISSAR for Foreign Relations in 1917

Official Secrets Act *See* OFFICIAL.

Top Secret Government information about which the greatest secrecy is required; 'EYES ONLY' is the only higher level of classification. 'Top Secret' is for a very few, 'Secret' may be shared a little more widely, and 'CONFIDENTIAL' to a less limited number.

secretary. Secretary-General The chief executive officer of a number of international bodies, including the UNITED NATIONS and NATO. While the decisions are taken by member states, the Secretary-General has an important diplomatic role both in securing agreement and in making sure the decisions are implemented, as well as in administration.

Secretary of State (1) The prestigious Presidential appointee who conducts America's FOREIGN POLICY; as well as being head of the STATE DEPARTMENT and thus of the foreign service, the Secretary of State is the senior member of the CABINET and the principal member of the ADMINISTRATION after the President. The most dramatic confirmation of this was the addressing to Secretary of State Henry KISSINGER of Richard NIXON's letter resigning the Presidency. President KENNEDY observed that 'everybody wants to be Secretary of State', and the post is indeed sought after for the influence and ACCESS that it generally commands; however, in the early Nixon years and again under George W. BUSH the NATIONAL SECURITY ADVISER has wielded greater power. (2) The title accorded to the most senior members of a UK government apart from the Prime Minister and CHANCELLOR, and to most but not quite all the members of the CABINET; a Secretary of State presides over a Department, a Minister over a Ministry. Since the abolition of MAFF in 2001, the only non-Secretaries of State in the Cabinet, with the lower SENIORITY that entails, are the CHIEF SECRETARY to the Treasury and Ministers without PORTFOLIO. (3) The official who in each of America's STATES – and elected in 36 of them – is responsible for the official paperwork of government, administering elections, motor vehicle registration and similar tasks.

sectarianism (1) In NORTHERN IRELAND and anywhere else where religion is a determining factor in politics, the pursuit of policies supposedly designed to further one religious faction at the expense of another. (2) In especially left-wing politics, the fragmentation of a movement as proponents of slightly varying ideologies or strategies pursue them with quasi-religious zeal and intolerance.

Section 28 Otherwise known as CLAUSE 28, the provision inserted into the THATCHER government's 1988 Local Government Bill (originally as its Clause 27) by backbench Tories which outlawed the propagation of homosexuality in schools, and which became for GAY RIGHTS campaigners over fifteen years the totem of a homophobic state. Its proponents claimed it was necessary because some LOONY LEFT local councils were encouraging gay teachers to tell their classes that homosexuality was not only normal but desirable; no prosecutions were ever brought under it. Section 28 was repealed at WESTMINSTER in September 2003, and earlier by the SCOTTISH PARLIAMENT, after bitter public debate and a heavy 'No' vote to repeal in an unofficial referendum run by the Stagecoach transport magnate Brian Souter.

Section 301 The section of successive US Foreign Trade Acts that allows the ADMINISTRATION to take unilateral action against unfair trading practices by other countries. **Super 301** is an EXECUTIVE ORDER showing the President's intention to take such action; President CLINTON signed one on 3 March 1994 to heighten pressure on Japan to open its markets to US goods.

Securitate The hated SECRET POLICE of the Romanian dictator Nicolae Ceausescu (1918–89). They remained loyal to the Communist autocrat after his capture, trial and execution in December 1989, fighting running battles with the army (who had joined in the popular uprising) and firing at random into crowded streets. They were supposedly eliminated after a week of fighting believed to have left more dead than any other European conflict to that time since WORLD WAR II; a number secretly regrouped after the advent of democracy and for a time continued campaigns of terror against ethnic Hungarians, gypsies and advocates of a break with the past.

security The degree of protection afforded to a nation by a combination of a sound defence, often in alliance with others, and an unambiguous foreign policy, which is considered adequate to remove the threat of attack. Also, the maintenance of the integrity of the state and its government against internal threats.

> There is no security on this earth; there is only opportunity.
>
> General DOUGLAS MACARTHUR (*attr.*)

> If all that Americans want is security, they can go to prison.
>
> DWIGHT D. EISENHOWER, Speech at Galveston, 8 December 1949

> The difference between defence and security is much the same as the difference between sex and love. ALAIN LAMASSOURE, MEP, 1981

security clearance The confirmation required from a security or intelligence agency that a person is loyal and trustworthy enough to handle sensitive information. *See also* POSITIVE VETTING.

Security Council The main executive organ of the UNITED NATIONS, with primary responsibility for the maintenance of international peace and security. The UK, America, France, Russia and China sit on it as of right (*see* PERMANENT MEMBERS), and ten other nations (originally six) serve for two years in rotation. The Council has proved more effective than the LEAGUE OF NATIONS in maintaining COLLECTIVE SECURITY because of its range of military, economic and diplomatic sanctions for use against member states, yet these powers have been only intermittently successful. During the COLD WAR effective action was often blocked by the VETO from either SUPERPOWER to prevent action against its own interests. The UN intervention in the KOREAN WAR, for instance, was only possible because of the Soviet Union's absence from the Security Council. The Council passed the first test of its effectiveness after the Cold War by mobilising forces to expel SADDAM HUSSEIN from Kuwait in 1991 (*see* GULF WAR), but the strife after the disintegration of Yugoslavia proved a tougher nut to crack and efforts to arrive at an agreed position before the 2003 IRAQ WAR ended in disarray.

> If I were redoing the Security Council, I'd have one permanent member – the United States.
>
> Under-Secretary of State JOHN BOLTON, 2004

security forces A frequently used umbrella term for the forces of law and order in a society afflicted by terrorism, embracing the police, the military and sometimes more sinister organs of the state.

security risk A person of doubtful loyalty, whose background and associations make their employment in state service inadvisable, especially in posts with access to confidential information likely to be useful to a hostile government. Officialdom's idea of a security risk has not always accorded with the facts; throughout the COLD WAR innocuous individuals suffered through unjustified suspicions, while Communist agents sometimes operated with impunity for years.

homeland security *See* HOMELAND.

SED (Ger. *Sozialistiche Einheitspartei Deutschlands,* German Socialist Unity Party) The party that ruled East Germany throughout the state's existence, under a series of mainly colourless and always unprepossessing leaders subservient to the KREMLIN. It was formed prior to the creation of the German Democratic Republic through a forced absorption of social democrats in the Soviet zone of occupation into the Communist Party. Many members of the SPD refused to co-operate, and either fled to the West or were forced out of politics.

sedentary position The term used in the HOUSE OF COMMONS to describe the situation of a member in their seat, especially when they interrupt without trying to catch the SPEAKER's eye. Gwyneth Dunwoody claimed that only Mrs THATCHER's CABINET favourite Nicholas Ridley was able to 'strut from a sedentary position'; the same had earlier been said in America of Thomas DEWEY.

sedition Any action alleged to be directed at the undermining of the state but which falls short of TREASON. The criminal charge of **seditious libel** was once regularly brought against the authors and publishers of provocative or inflammatory articles.

segregation The separation of the races, notably as practised in the American South and beyond until the 1960s as a means of DISCRIMINATING against the black population. Well-meaning white politicians long accepted segregation as legitimate, even Woodrow WILSON telling black leaders in 1913 that it was 'not a humiliation but a benefit', and EISENHOWER saying in 1948: 'If we attempt to force someone to like someone else, we are fast going to get into trouble.' **Segregationists** were those Southerners who held out for RACIST policies and practices as CIVIL RIGHTS legislation began to bite, under George Wallace's slogan of 'Segregation now, segregation tomorrow and segregation forever'. Martin Luther KING condemned the practice as

> The offspring of an illicit intercourse between injustice and immorality.

Sejm The UNICAMERAL Parliament of Poland, both under Communist rule and under democracy.

Select Committee A body set up by a legislature to investigate or monitor a particular topic or range of activities. In the US CONGRESS the system has long been developed; at WESTMINSTER, apart from the PAC, Select Committees enjoyed limited power and prestige until specific committees were directly linked in 1979/80 with the work of government departments. Brought about by the then Leader of the House Norman St John-Stevas (later Lord St John of Fawsley), this system was patchily effective at first, but has shown its mettle during the WESTLAND, SUPERGUN and David KELLY affairs.

selection conference Under the system used by Britain's LABOUR PARTY until the mid-1980s for selecting Parliamentary candidates, a meeting of the constituency party's general management committee before which SHORT-LISTed applicants would appear and which would select the prospective CANDIDATE by ballot. Such meetings were criticised by advocates of OMOV because party members as a whole had no direct say, and such a committee could be hijacked by an ENTRYIST group to DESELECT the sitting member in a Labour-held seat.

selectman/woman The annually-elected administrators, whose origins date back to the 17th century, who provide local government in some New England townships,

self. self-basting The devastating adjective, normally applied to oven-ready turkeys, which the columnist Edward Pearce directed against Kenneth (later Lord) Baker, Education Secretary and CONSERVATIVE PARTY Chairman under Margaret THATCHER, and John MAJOR's first Home Secretary. One Conservative MP elaborated: 'I don't think he has his hair cut – just an oil change.'

Self-Defence Forces The official name for Japan's armed forces in the period since WORLD WAR II, when the country's constitution has specifically ruled out their use for aggressive purposes. It was not until 1992 that they served overseas, Japanese troops taking part in UN PEACEKEEPING operations in Cambodia.

self-determination The right of a people to decide whether it should have the independence and attributes of a NATION STATE, or form part of the nation of its choice. At

Woodrow WILSON's insistence, self-determination for the peoples of Europe – especially of the former Austro-Hungarian Empire – became a key feature of the peace settlement after WORLD WAR I. Wilson declared:

> Self-determination is not a mere phrase. It is an imperative principle of action, which statesmen will henceforth ignore at their peril.

self-government The right of a people or community to govern itself, either as a separate nation or within a national framework. After Spain's colonies in South America won their independence, Thomas JEFFERSON wrote:

> The qualities of self-government in society are not innate. They are the result of habit and long training, and for these they will require time and much suffering.

self-immolation The grisly but highly effective protest against the authorities of the day perfected by Buddhist monks in South Vietnam in the early 1960s; it involved soaking themselves in petrol, assuming a prayerful posture and then being set on fire. Images of the monks meeting their death were flashed around the world and did much to undermine support for the US-backed Diem regime; they also inspired the Czech student Jan Palach to carry out a similar act in WENCESLAS SQUARE in 1969 in protest at the Soviet occupation of his country. Palach's funeral became a national day of mourning for the PRAGUE SPRING, and the square to this day contains an informal shrine to his sacrifice.

self-regulation The notion that financial institutions and the professions can be most effectively cleansed of abuses, irregularities and even corruption by policing themselves, rather than through an outside investigative and disciplinary body. Long the practice in the City of London, self-regulation reached its apotheosis in the 1986 Financial Services Act, under which UK financial institutions, following the Big Bang, were placed under the supervision of five self-regulatory organisations answerable to a Securities and Investment Board (SIB). The system was effective up to a point, but when Gordon BROWN decided in 1997 to remove banking supervision from the Bank of England, the stage was set for the creation of a Financial Services Authority (FSA), which now regulates all aspects of the industry.

sell. sell-out One of the most wounding accusations in politics, that a politician has betrayed the principles on which he or she was elected. Specifically it involves abandoning a principled course of action for a cosier one, letting down in the process the people the politician was supposed to be representing; there is an inference of material gain.

selling off the family silver The withering denunciation of PRIVATISATION delivered at the end of his political career by Harold MACMILLAN, after his ennoblement as Earl of Stockton. He told a meeting of the TORY REFORM GROUP in 1984:

> First of all the Georgian silver goes, then all that nice furniture that used to be in the salon. Then the Canalettos go.

Sellafield The NUCLEAR installation on the Cumbrian coast of north-west England, which has been a source of lasting political and diplomatic controversy since an accident at the site (then known as Windscale) in 1957 released radioactive substances into the air and contaminated milk over 500 sq. km. Plutonium has been manufactured there since 1942 and nuclear fuel reprocessed since 1952; in 1956 the world's first nuclear power station at Calder Hall came on stream within the complex. The level of radioactive discharge into the Irish Sea, greatly reduced since the early 1970s, has aroused persistent protests from GREENPEACE, increasingly the Irish government and most recently the EUROPEAN COMMISSION. There have also been repeated claims that the plant has induced a cluster of leukaemia cases in the local community. The State-owned British Nuclear Fuels Ltd. (BNFL) insists that after a period when safety standards were not strict enough, it is now operating one of the safest plants in the world. But it was not helped when, in 2000, Japan sent back a cargo of reprocessed nuclear fuel after it was revealed that staff at Sellafield had falsified some (non safety-critical) readings. In 2005 a leak undetected for several months forced a lengthy closure of Sellafield's costly THORP plant.

Selma The seat of Dallas county, Alabama, which in 1965 became the focus of the battle over CIVIL RIGHTS when Dr Martin Luther KING chose it to dramatise the bars to black voting in many Southern states; only 335 of Selma's voting-aged blacks were registered to vote, despite the passage of the 1964 Civil Rights Act. The peaceful protest – begun on 18 January after four years of court orders had proved fruitless – was bitterly resisted by local whites; two protesters were killed and 2000 arrested. On 7 March, 200 state police attacked the demonstrators with TEAR GAS, whips and nightsticks; Governor George Wallace refused to protect a second march from Selma to Montgomery, and President JOHNSON mobilised the NATIONAL GUARD. He went on to introduce the VOTING RIGHTS ACT, enforcing the FIFTEENTH AMENDMENT to guarantee the vote to all US citizens.

Selsdon Man The name, with primitive anthropological echoes, with which Harold WILSON branded Edward HEATH's Conservatives as ruthless and unfeeling in the run-up to the 1970 general election. It stemmed from a meeting Heath convened with his SHADOW CABINET on 31 January 1970 at the Selsdon Park Hotel, near Croydon, to review party strategy. Publicity accompanying the meeting gave the impression that Heath was adopting harder-line, more right-wing policies. Except in the field of industrial policy (*see* LAME DUCKS) this was not borne out once he had won the election, but Wilson seized on it, telling a meeting in Birmingham on 21 February:

> Selsdon Man is not just a lurch to the Right, it is an atavistic desire to reverse the course of 25 years of social revolution. What they are planning is a wanton, calculated and deliberate return to greater inequality. Selsdon Man is designing a system of society for the ruthless and the pushing, the uncaring. His message to the British people would be simple and brutal. It would be: 'You're out on your own.'

semi-. semi-detached The phrase used by Margaret THATCHER's press secretary Bernard Ingham (*see* YORKSHIRE RASPUTIN) to describe John Biffen at a meeting with LOBBY journalists c. 1986. Biffen, then LEADER OF THE HOUSE, had been a loyal THATCHERITE but had started to campaign for CONSOLIDATION of gains already made instead of embarking on fresh radical initiatives. Ingham's description of Biffen as a 'semi-detached member of the CABINET' was assumed to have Mrs Thatcher's approval, and was thus seen as a way of undermining him. Once the Conservatives had won the following year's election, Biffen was duly sacked.

semi-housetrained polecat Probably the rudest thing ever said by one member of the HOUSE OF COMMONS about another without being ruled UNPARLIAMENTARY. The description was used c. 1977 by the then Employment Secretary Michael FOOT about Norman Tebbit (*see* CHINGFORD SKINHEAD) after Tebbit had provoked him by asking: 'Does Mr Foot know he is a FASCIST?'

Semtex The devastating, nitrogen-based plastic explosive manufactured in Czechoslovakia which became a favourite of terrorists in the early 1980s because it is also odourless and thus very hard to detect. Large quantities were supplied to Libya, which passed it on to militant Palestinian groups and the IRA, to whom it was shipped with conventional arms on the motor vessel *Eksund*, until French customs seized the ship. The Provisionals used Semtex to deadly effect on the British mainland, and at the start of DECOMMISSIONING were believed to have enough for 150 years of operations. When the playwright Vaclav Havel became Czech president in 1990, he curbed exports of Semtex but reported to Western governments enough was already in the hands of terrorists around the world to last them into the 22nd century. Bohumil Sol, the 'father of Semtex', blew himself up with the explosive in May 1997, wrecking the sanatorium in Moravia where he was a patient; it took more that 24 hours to recover his remains.

Senate The Upper House of the LEGISLATURE in most of the world's democracies (*see also* SEANAD). The name – meaning a group of old men – is taken from the governing body of ancient Rome, the motto on whose legions' standards was *Senatus PopulusQue Romanus*, The Senate and People of Rome. Specifically (1) the senior house of the US CONGRESS, presided over by the VICE PRESIDENT when he is available, or the PRESIDENT PRO TEM, and comprising two members from every state of the Union, popularly elected every six years; since 1959 there have been 100 members, each of whom is assigned their own desk. Until the ratification of the SEVENTEENTH AMENDMENT in 1913, Senators were elected by state legislatures; if a vacancy occurs, the appropriate state legislature is still empowered to nominate a replacement to serve until an election can be held.

The Senate was designed as a restraint on both the HOUSE and the President; when Thomas JEFFERSON asked why it was necessary, George WASHINGTON replied:

> Why do I pour coffee in a cup? To cool it.

James MADISON put it less obliquely, writing: 'The ends to be served by it: first, to protect the people against their rulers, secondly to protect the people against the transient impressions into which they might be led.' The Senate was also supposed to be an elite; Gouverneur Morris declared: 'It must have great personal property; it must have the aristocratic spirit; it must love to lord it through pride', and John ADAMS stated: 'The rich, the well-born and the able acquire an influence among the people that will be too much for the simple honesty of a House of Representatives. The most illustrious must be separated from the mass and placed by themselves in a Senate.' It took time for the Senate to acquire augustness; in 1826 Anne Royall noted: 'I attended a few times to hear the debate but was unable to hear, owing to the noise made in the galleries, lobbies and that made by the slamming of the doors. I was greatly surprised that so little order was maintained,' and Charles Dickens wrote in 1842:

> The state to which the carpets are reduced by universal disregard of the spittoon do not admit of being described.

The Senate has traditionally been more conservative than the HOUSE, though this has become less marked as the SENIORITY system has eased. It is generally what Woodrow WILSON termed 'a body of individual critics' rather than an assembly divided by party. It was long the home of special INTERESTS, Theodore ROOSEVELT observing:

> When they call the roll, senators do not know whether to answer 'present' or 'not guilty'.

In the early 1970s Sen. Robert Kerr said: 'If everyone ABSTAINED on grounds of personal interest, I doubt if you could get a QUORUM on any subject.' And in 1990 Rep. Pat Schroeder, a former Senator, declared: 'It's a never-never land, a genteel millionaires' club.'

The Senate is also the home of the FILIBUSTER, the great weapon used by conservative Southern senators to resist what they see as harmful progress. As late as the mid-1980s Sen. Tim Wirth of Colorado could say: 'In the House you learn how to get something done by putting together a coalition. But in the Senate, people's power arises from their ability to say no, their power to block anything.' Vice President Dan QUAYLE, a former Indiana senator, made a different distinction:

> In the House you get a bunch of guys and go down to the gym and play basketball. You can't do that in the Senate.

GLADSTONE hailed the Senate as 'the most remarkable of all the inventions of modern politics'. Yet Sen. John Spooner (1843–1919) felt moved to remind those making such claims that the Senate was 'not the greatest legislative body in the world; [but] one of the branches of perhaps the greatest legislative body in the world'. And its members have differed sharply over whether the prestige is merited. John F. Gladstone scorned it as 'the iron lung of politics', South Dakota's Sen. James Abourezk, retiring early, said: 'I can't wait to get out of this chickenshit outfit', and Sen. John Sharp Williams declared after the Senate's rejection of the LEAGUE OF NATIONS: 'I'd rather be a hound dog and bay at the moon from my Mississippi plantation than remain in the United States Senate.' As for what the Senate actually does, Sen. J. William Fulbright said: 'We have the power to do any damn fool thing', and KENNEDY, once President, opined: 'I never realised how powerful the Senate is until I left it and came up to this end of PENNSYLVANIA AVENUE.' Yet Sen. Bob Dole once confessed: 'We spend a lot of time doing very little, and that may be an understatement.' Sen. David Pryor of Arkansas declared in a moment of frustration that 'being in the Senate is like getting stuck in an airport and having all your flights cancelled', and Sen. Philip Hart of Michigan admitted: 'There's a terrible tendency here to think that everything we do or say, or omit to do, is of world consequence. But you know full well that you go across the street and the bus driver couldn't care less.' Most of the Senate's real work takes place in committee, and as for its status as a debating forum, Sen. William Proxmire claimed: 'The so-called greatest deliberative body in the world hasn't even had a third-class debate in years. And even if we had it no-one would be on the FLOOR to hear it.' Eventually the MAJORITY LEADER Sen. Mike Mansfield had to remind colleagues: 'None of us was DRAFTED for this job. With the position goes a duty to attendance on the floor of the Senate.'

> I will receive no message from those damned scoundrels.
>
> ANDREW JACKSON, 5 March 1835

> A club of prima donnas intensely self-orientated – 99 kings and one queen dedicated to their own personal accommodation.
>
> Sen. MARGARET CHASE SMITH (1898–1995)

> A place filled with goodwill and good intentions, and if the road to hell is paved with them, the Senate is a pretty good detour.
>
> Sen. HUBERT HUMPHREY, 1998

> *Lost visitor*: How do I get out of the Senate?
> *Sen. Harry New of Indiana (just defeated)*: Madam, I advise you to run in an Indiana primary.

> The windows need washing.
>
> Arkansas Sen. HATTIE CARRAWAY, arriving to take her seat, 1931

(2) The less powerful upper house of many other legislatures, including most in the COMMONWEALTH. In Australia the Senate, with 76 members elected by PROPORTIONAL REPRESENTATION and with the influence of the smaller states weighted, has no powers over the ADMINISTRATION or foreign affairs, but as in 1975 can bring a MINISTRY to its knees by failing to vote SUPPLY. Canada's Senate is nominated and has few powers, constitutional amendments to add to its powers having fallen because of continued deadlock over the status of QUEBEC. Kenneth McNaught described the Canadian Senate as 'even less successful than the HOUSE OF LORDS in opposing the full development of democratic politics centred in the Commons'.

half-Senate election In Australia, an election for half the seats in the Senate which may be called by the Ministry to break a deadlock between the two Houses by ensuring it – if victorious – a majority in both.

Senator A member of the United States SENATE (and, indeed, of all other Senates). To qualify for the Senate, you must be at least 30 years old, have been a US citizen for at least nine years, and reside in the state you represent. In 1886 Sen. George Hearst declared that Senators are 'the survivors of the fittest', and in terms of the political process they are, having overcome every hurdle except those of a Presidential campaign. Henry Adams wrote in 1906: 'No man, however strong, can serve ten years as a schoolmaster, priest or senator and remain fit for anything else', but most have taken to the life and served far more, the voters permitting. As for their duties, Sen. Henry Ashurst admitted: 'I am not in WASHINGTON as a STATESMAN. I am there as a very well paid message boy doing your errands. My chief occupation is going round with a forked stick picking up little fragments of PATRONAGE for my constituents.' Keeping an eye on the ADMINISTRATION takes other forms: Dean Acheson as SECRETARY OF STATE found that 'Senators are a prolific source of advice and most of it is bad.'

> I look at the Senators and pray for the country.
> Senate chaplain EDWARD EVERETT HALE (1822–1909)

> If we introduced the Lord's Prayer here, senators would propose a large number of amendments to it.
> Sen. HENRY WILSON (1812–75)

> Senators prey on women as if they were groupies.
> HARRIET WOODS, National Women's Political Caucus

Senator, you're no Jack Kennedy *See* KENNEDY.

Senator Pothole The nickname accorded to Alphonse d'Amato, Republican Senator for New York state from 1980–98, for his assiduous championing of local issues.

the distinguished Senator from – A courtesy by which members of the US Senate refer to their colleagues. Sen. Alben Barkley warned FRESHMEN that

> If he refers to you as 'the able and distinguished Senator from Ohio', be on your guard, for the knife is going in sharper. If he refers to you as 'the able and distinguished Senator from Ohio and my good friend', then duck fast because he's trying to see if the jugular vein is exposed. And should he refer to you as 'my very good friend, the able, distinguished and outstanding Senator', run for your life.

junior Senator The Senator from a particular state who has most recently been elected; the longer-serving of the two is correspondingly referred to as 'the senior Senator from . . . '

shadow Senator The individual elected by the DISTRICT OF COLUMBIA, which is unrepresented in the Senate, to represent its interests as if he or she were a Senator. *See* HIS SHADOWSHIP.

Senatorial courtesy The custom under which a Senator may object to a federal appointment proposed for their State. The rest of the Senate will go along with the objection by refusing to approve the appointment.

send. send for papers The technicality on which a member of the HOUSE OF LORDS raises a subject in debate; when a peer once asked for the papers, no one knew what they actually were, and a bundle had hastily to be put together and tied with red ribbon.

Send them a message! The slogan on which Governor George Wallace campaigned for the Presidency in 1972, the inference being that the Washington ESTABLISHMENT had no idea what ordinary Americans were thinking. In 1976 Jimmy CARTER, tapping the same vein though with vastly different views on race, said:

> Don't send them a message. Send them a President.

send to Coventry The action of ostracising someone by refusing to speak to them. The practice was frequently used by UK trade unionists in the 1950s against workmates they felt had been over-co-operative with management, but its origins lie in the English Civil War. Coventry was a

Parliamentary stronghold and Royalists captured in Birmingham were sent there to be guarded by the townspeople, who refused to speak to them. In his speech of 19 September 1880 that began Ireland's BOYCOTTing campaign, Charles Stewart PARNELL said:

> When a man takes a farm from which another has been evicted, you must show him . . . by outing him into a moral Coventry, by isolating him from his kind as if he were a leper of old. You must show him your detestation of the crimes he has committed.

seniority The US Congressional term for years of service beyond the first two, and from c. 1910 until the early 1970s the sole factor in determining the allocation of committee chairmanships. Described by Jack Anderson as the 'Senility System', it ensured that most chairmanships were in the hands of elderly members of the majority party, who tended to be conservative Southern Democrats. More important, it enshrined enormous power in the hands of a self-selected group. Newly-elected Democrats broke the system in 1975 by rebelling and ousting four committee chairmen, since when such posts have been filled by election. In the Senate the seniority system has largely survived, but committee chairmen have become more responsive to the public mood.

> The committee member who has served 30 years is not just 5 per cent more powerful than the member who has served just 19 years. If he is chairman he is 1,000 per cent more powerful.
>
> Rep. MORRIS UDALL

separate. separate but equal The guiding principle for racial SEGREGATION in America's South, set by the SUPREME COURT in 1896 in the case of *Plessy v Ferguson*, which endured for over half a century. The ruling – one of the court's most invidious and taken with only one dissenting opinion – justified separate carriages for black passengers on Louisiana's railroads, and volunteered that 'separate but equal' schools could be lawful. Only in 1938 did the Court rule that for separate facilities to be CONSTITUTIONAL, they had to be truly equal – not inferior as was almost always the case. Not until the landmark case of BROWN v TOPEKA BOARD OF EDUCATION was the principle overthrown, paving the way for true CIVIL RIGHTS for black Americans. However, in 1968 the KERNER COMMISSION on riots in America's INNER CITIES warned that urban blacks were becoming 'separate and unequal'.

separate development One of several euphemisms for APARTHEID used by South Africa's NATIONAL PARTY government, notably after it began to coerce the black population into taking the citizenship of nominally-independent BANTUSTANS to prevent them acquiring rights in white urban society.

separation of Church and State One of the fundamentals of the US CONSTITUTION, the FIRST AMENDMENT specifying that 'Congress shall make no law respecting an establishment of religion'. In recent years it has generated fierce controversy over the continued references to God on coins, banknotes, stamps and in the PLEDGE OF ALLEGIANCE. Those who advocate a similar division in England are said to favour DISESTABLISHMENT of the Anglican church. When John F. KENNEDY was seeking the Presidency, extreme Protestants claimed that he would be under the influence of the Catholic church, and that the separation would not be observed. But Kennedy told them:

> I believe in an America where the separation of church and state is absolute, where no Catholic prelate should tell the President (should he be a Catholic) how to act.

separation of powers An even more critical basic of the American state, and of many other democracies: the complete separation of the EXECUTIVE, the LEGISLATURE and the JUDICIARY, with none of the three – the PRESIDENT, the CONGRESS or the SUPREME COURT – able to exercise supreme authority. Explaining it, James MADISON said: 'Ambition must be made to counter ambition', and John ADAMS stated:

> The judicial power ought to be distinct from both the legislature and the executive, and independent of both, so that it may be a check upon both, as both should be checks upon that.

In PARLIAMENTARY systems the separation is not total; the Prime Minister and CABINET are drawn from the legislature. Moreover in Britain the LORD CHANCELLOR has traditionally had a foot in all three camps, as a judge, a Cabinet Minister and 'Speaker' of the House of Lords; Tony BLAIR moved to change this in 2003, only to come under fire from the Lords and some senior judges who felt their position would be weakened.

separatism A movement for the separation of a region or community from the state of which it forms part. The term, the opposite of IRREDENTISM, has been most frequently used of the Quebec separatists (*see* PQ), but also applies to a number of other movements throughout the world, notably in islands of Indonesia and the Philippines. The Canadian Prime Minister Brian Mulroney, himself a Quebecker, once told a separatist HECKLER:

> To hell with you! You can't be a part-time Canadian.

September 11th *See* 9/11

September 11 Commission *See* 9/11 COMMISSION.

Sequoia The Presidential yacht used on the Potomac by Presidents JOHNSON, NIXON and FORD before being pensioned off by Jimmy CARTER as an extravagant hangover from the Imperial PRESIDENCY. At the time it was costing nearly $800,000 a year to run. Nixon used to hold dinners on the *Sequoia*, ostentatiously having the waiter serve him with the finest Margaux, his guests receiving cheap wine with the waiter's napkin obscuring the label.

Seretse Khama affair The joint action in 1949 by Britain's Labour government and South Africa's newly-elected SEGREGATIONIST National Party to exile the Bamangwato tribal leader Seretse Khama (1921–80) from the British protectorate of Bechuanaland (now Botswana) for marrying a white Englishwoman. Seretse, chief-designate of the tribe, took his new wife, Ruth Williams, a 24-year-old typist, home after qualifying as a barrister in London. The marriage outraged the South Africans, who wanted to ANNEX Bechuanaland, perturbed the British and flouted the wishes of Seretse's uncle and REGENT, Tshekedi Khama. Despite support for Seretse from the tribe generally, it was decided that he should be exiled for six years; he returned in 1956 after renouncing the chieftainship. In 1965 he was elected head of government, and on Botswana's independence in 1966 he became its first president; the same year the Queen made up for his past treatment by KNIGHTing him. Sir Seretse ruled over Botswana until his death fourteen years later.

Sergeant at Arms The official in each HOUSE of the US CONGRESS who carries out a range of ceremonial and practical functions, and generally ensures the smooth and safe running of the LEGISLATURE. Sergeant at Arms in the House, for instance, carries the MACE, used to round up members for a QUORUM and, until abuses by members forced its closure in 1992, operated a HOUSE BANK for members in his office. It was the Senate Sergeant at Arms of the day who delivered the IMPEACHMENT summons to President Andrew Johnson. In happier times, he greets the President when he arrives to deliver the State of the UNION Message; Nordy Hoffman, the Sergeant at Arms who greeted Ronald REAGAN (*see* GIPPER), said of his charges:

> We've got more egos up there on the HILL than we've got any place else in the world. And if you can handle those, you can handle anybody.

Serjeant-at-Arms The functionary, ACCOUNTABLE only to the Royal Household though always ready to accommodate the SPEAKER, who exercises supreme power through a large staff over the ceremonial, administration and good order of the HOUSE OF COMMONS. (There is also a Serjeant-at-Arms in the Lords, but his powers are limited, the real authority resting with BLACK ROD.) The Serjeant-at-Arms is supposed also to be in charge of security, MPs as a body having resisted until recently the idea of the police or MI5 having ultimate control as the threat of terrorism has grown. However, a series of security breaches in 2004 culminating in the invasion of the CHAMBER by supporters of foxhunting brought to a head concerns on the Labour side, at least, that the time had come for a professional approach (*see* MEN IN TIGHTS). Over the years the House has gained some control over its own affairs, but the Serjeant-at-Arms, usually a retired military officer, has ultimate control over who enters the Commons' end of the Palace of Westminster and its surrounding office buildings and what they can do there; he even has the power, occasionally exercised, to have MPs' cars towed away if they are parked in the wrong space. The office dates back to the days of King Richard II; its holder has a uniform of cocked hat (seldom worn), cutaway coat, lace ruffle at the throat, knee breeches, black silk stockings and silver-buckled shoes.

Sermon on the Mound Margaret THATCHER's address to the General Assembly of the Church of Scotland on 21 May 1988 which was intended to prove to Scots Calvinists that Thatcherism was in line with their thinking; the Mound is where the Assembly convenes, as opposed to the Mount where Christ delivered his sermon. Mrs Thatcher's words in fact convinced most Scots that she was from another planet; one of the clergy present described it as 'a disgraceful travesty of the Gospel'. Her theme was that the creation of wealth was not unChristian:

> How could we invest for the future or support the wonderful artists and craftsmen whose work also glorifies God, unless we had first worked hard and used our talents to create the necessary wealth?

SERPS State Earnings Related Pension Scheme. A UK government scheme pioneered by the Labour Social Services Secretary Barbara Castle and introduced in 1978, which aimed to provide every employed person with an earnings-related pension in addition to the basic flat-rate pension. Contributions came from earners' National Insurance payments; the pension, initially payable at 65 for men and 60 for women, was calculated using a formula based on their earnings. When the cost of SERPS was found to be spiralling in the late 1980s, Margaret THATCHER's government began offering contributors incentives to contract out and join a personal or occupational pension scheme instead, and millions have done so.

session The cycle of SITTINGS by a LEGISLATURE, lasting approximately a year. The US CONGRESS is required by the CONSTITUTION to convene on 3 January each year unless an exception is made; it generally sits until late the same year. Each Congress is made up of two sessions. In Britain, the Parliamentary session begins with the STATE OPENING, usually in November. It lasts just under a year except when a general election intervenes; if so, the session will be truncated and the first session of a new Parliament may last as much as eighteen months, e.g. from May or June until late October the following year, as in 1992–93, 1997–98 and 2001–02.

closed session A session of a legislature or other body that is closed to press and public (*see* SECRET SESSION). British party conferences, and especially LABOUR's. occasionally go into closed session to discuss organisational matters. In 1953 the Labour conference at Margate did so to debate a proposal to expel Aneurin BEVAN; however, no one had thought to switch off the public address system on the roof of the hall, and reporters simply gathered round the loudspeaker to report the proceedings.

joint session *See* JOINT.

Sessional Orders. The resolutions formally passed by the HOUSE OF COMMONS at the start of each annual session, to reassert its rights and privileges and govern the ability of Parliament to carry out its business. They include the outlawing of double election returns, forbidding bribery at elections and authorising the publication of the House's proceedings. The best-known Sessional Order requires MPs to have unobstructed access to the building at all times, and prohibits demonstrations in PARLIAMENT SQUARE; failure to enforce this last in recent years, notably during votes on reducing the age of homosexual consent and banning hunting with dogs, has led to violent incidents and breaches of security. In 2005 this aspect of the Orders was superseded by controls imposed under the Serious and Organised Crime Act.

set-aside The payment of farmers to set aside arable land for uses other than the production of crops, in order to reduce the EU's agricultural surpluses.

set asides The provision in certain US government contracts for a proportion of the value of the work to be done by minority-owned businesses.

settled will The conclusions of the Scottish CONSTITUTIONAL CONVENTION were described by participants, and by John SMITH and Donald Dewar, as the 'settled will' of the Scottish people. As such it formed the basis of the devolved structures proposed by the incoming Labour government in 1997, endorsed in a REFERENDUM and enshrined in the SCOTLAND ACT of 1998.

Seventh of March speech The speech delivered in the US Senate on 7 March 1850 by Daniel Webster (1782–1852) which proved crucial to the COMPROMISE OF 1850. By repudiating his FREE SOIL followers and also compromising his previous opposition to any extension of slavery, it also cost him his last chance of the Presidency.

Seventeen. Seventeenth Amendment The amendment to the US CONSTITUTION, RATIFIED on 31 May 1913, that provides for the popular election of SENATORS. Up to then, they had been elected by state legislatures, a system that denied the voters a choice and was open to abuse. The change reduced the power of the states, and increased popular control over CONGRESS.

Seventeenth Parallel The CEASEFIRE line dividing North and South Vietnam, set up by the GENEVA AGREEMENT signed by France and the VIET MINH on 21 July 1954. The agreements stressed that it 'should not in any way be interpreted as constituting a political boundary', but should be a temporary division pending FREE ELECTIONS in

July 1956. It separated the North, under Viet Minh control, from the South, under the French-supported Emperor Bao Dai. America, which has not signed the Agreement, staged rigged elections in the South in which its client Ngo Dinh Diem heavily defeated Bao Dai and created a non-Communist state south of the Seventeenth Parallel. This paved the way for an eventual recurrence of hostilities between HO CHI MINH's Communist régime in the North and the US-backed South that became the VIETNAM WAR.

Sèvres. Sèvres meeting The secret meeting between French and Israeli leaders on 22–24 October 1956 at Sèvres, ten miles south-west of Paris, which agreed that an Israeli invasion should give Britain and France the pretext to intervene in SUEZ and overthrow Egypt's President Nasser. Those present were the French Prime Minister Guy Mollet, with Christian Pineau and Maurice Bourges-Manoury, and the Israeli premier David Ben Gurion with Shimon Peres, Moshe Dayan and Mordechai Bar-On. Under the plan drawn up by General Maurice Challe, Israel would attack Egypt, Britain and France would issue an ULTIMATUM to both to withdraw, and when Egypt refused they would attack. Ben Gurion was unenthusiastic, the more so after a brief visit from British Foreign Secretary Selwyn Lloyd who seemed equally luke-warm toward a plan enthusiastically backed by Anthony EDEN, but Dayan talked him round and on 24 October the agreement was signed, Britain being represented by officials. When Eden heard that a written agreement existed, he sent the officials back to Paris to urge its destruction; the request was refused but Britain's copy, which was sent to Eden, has disappeared. Anthony Nutting, who resigned as a Foreign Office minister shortly afterward over Suez, described Sèvres as 'a sordid conspiracy'. On 29 October Israel attacked, and the Suez fiasco began.

Treaty of Sèvres *See* Treaty of LAUSANNE.

Seward's folly The contemporary reaction to America's purchase of Alaska in 1867 for $7.2 million, or just under two cents an acre. The deal was negotiated in the small hours of 30 March by Secretary of State William H. Seward and the Russian Minister Baron de Stoeckl, who had called on him at home, interrupting a game of whist. The Senate RATIFIED the treaty of cession in June, but the House did not APPROPRIATE the money until 27 July because funds were tight after the CIVIL WAR. In 1959 Alaska achieved STATEHOOD. The 49th State was, as now, the largest by area and the smallest by population; its oil reserves were still undetected.

Sewel motion In the SCOTTISH PARLIAMENT, a motion authorising Parliament at WESTMINSTER to legislate on an issue devolved to Holyrood under the SCOTLAND ACT. Such a motion is most often put forward when the UK government is planning to legislate for the rest of the United Kingdom in a way that would make sense for Scotland, to avoid purely Scottish legislation containing exactly the same provisions. The procedure takes its name from Lord Sewel (1946–), the Scottish Office Minister who guided the part of the Scotland Bill dealing with the competencies of the two Parliaments through the LORDS.

sex. a conversation about sex and travel On the margins of a COMMONS committee debating charges for dental examinations in the late 1980s, the government whip David Lightbown had two short, sharp words for the Tory backbencher Jerry Hayes for pointing out that Margaret THATCHER had committed the party not to introduce them. Asked what the words were, Hayes said:

> We had a conversation about sex and travel.

sexed up *See* DODGY DOSSIER.

sexism The practice of DISCRIMINATION on grounds of sex, generally against women. The word is thought to have been coined by Pauline M. Leet, director of special programmes at Franklin and Marshall College, Lancaster, Pennsylvania, in a talk she gave on 18 November 1956 on '*Women and the Undergraduate*'. The word, and its derivative **sexist**, were given currency in the late 1960s by the feminist author Caroline Bird:

> Sex prejudice is so ingrained in our society that many who practise it are simply unaware that they are hurting women. It is the last socially acceptable prejudice.

sexual politics The role of gender in political, business and social institutions. Traditionally women have been discriminated against in most churches (not to mention Islam), the armed forces, law, medicine and banking in relation to advancement, and often even to employment. The US feminist Kate Millett introduced the phrase in her book *Sexual Politics* (1970); the women's movement maintains that the socio-cultural role of gender differs from the biological gap of sex, and that sexual equality will change political and social structures for the better. *See also* WOMEN'S RIGHTS.

shadow. Shadow Cabinet At WESTMINSTER, the chief spokesmen of the principal OPPOSITION party who 'shadow' the activities of government. Headed by the Leader of the Opposition, it includes the Shadow Chancellor and a team of senior front BENCHers responsible for areas of policy broadly matching those of their opposite numbers, on whom they lead the attack at each departmental QUESTION TIME. A Conservative Shadow Cabinet is appointed by the leader; the bulk of a Labour Shadow Cabinet is elected by Labour MPs as their **Parliamentary Committee**.

shadow Senator *See* SENATOR.

shadowing The policy of keeping the value of a nation's currency in line with that of another. It applied particularly with the pound in 1987–88 when Chancellor Nigel (later Lord) Lawson was **shadowing the Deutschmark**, producing increasing disagreements between himself and Margaret THATCHER. The effect of Lawson's strategy was the same as if Britain had joined the ERM; when the UK economy headed into RECESSION at the end of the decade, this management of sterling was felt by many to have contributed to it.

> I only learnt that Nigel had been shadowing the Deutschmark when I was interviewed by journalists from the *Financial Times* . . . [He] had pursued a personal economic policy without reference to the rest of the Government. How could I possibly trust him again?
>
> MARGARET THATCHER, *The Downing Street Years*

Shakes The nickname of William Shepherd Morrison (later Lord Dunrossil, 1883–1961), who was a wartime Minister, then SPEAKER of the HOUSE OF COMMONS from 1951 to 1959, earning tributes for his handling of the House at the time of SUEZ. He served as GOVERNOR-GENERAL of Australia from 1960 until his death.

Shankill Road The heart of Ulster LOYALISM, a street of terrace houses that runs due west from the centre of Belfast, just north of and almost parallel to the equally strongly Nationalist FALLS. Locally it is known just as 'The Shankill'. The **Shankill bomb** was the highly counterproductive IRA atrocity in the Shankill Road on 23 October 1993, revulsion against which gave momentum toward the DOWNING STREET DECLARATION and subsequent Republican ceasefire. Ten people were killed, including the bomber, in an attack on a crowded fish shop.

SHAPE Supreme Headquarters of the Allied Powers, Europe; the military headquarters of NATO at Chièvres, Belgium.

Share-our-Wealth movement The rival to Franklin D. ROOSEVELT'S NEW DEAL put forward by Sen. Huey (KINGFISH) Long of Louisiana. Long wanted the federal government to guarantee every American family a homestead worth $5000 and a minimum annual income of $2000. The appeal of this and other simplistic and extremist plans to counter the GREAT DEPRESSION heightened FDR's sense of urgency in pressing ahead with practical measures of his own.

Sharpeville The mass shooting on 21 March 1960 of demonstrators against South Africa's PASS LAWS in the black TOWNSHIP of Sharpeville, 40 miles south of Johannesburg. Sixty-nine were killed (many shot in the back) and 180 injured after Transvaal police panicked when 20,000 protesters without passes offered themselves for arrest at the police station. The killings provoked worldwide condemnation, and anger in South Africa led the government to declare a STATE OF EMERGENCY. In the aftermath of the massacre both the PAC, which had called the demonstration, and the ANC were banned. Eighteen thousand people were arrested and draconian powers introduced to suppress dissent, effectively transforming the country into a police STATE. Sharpeville precipitated South Africa's expulsion from the COMMONWEALTH and the campaign for global SANCTIONS to force an end to APARTHEID.

Shaw. Norman Shaw Building The two Victorian buildings at WESTMINSTER, formerly New Scotland Yard, headquarters of the Metropolitan Police, which the HOUSE OF COMMONS took over as members' offices when the police moved to St James's Park in the 1970s. Facing the Thames embankment just north of PORTCULLIS HOUSE, they are known after their architect as Norman Shaw North and Norman Shaw South.

Shays Act The linchpin of the CONTRACT WITH AMERICA, passed as the first act of the Republican-controlled CONGRESS in 1995. It required that all laws applying to the rest of the country should apply equally to the Congress and its members.

She didn't say yes, she didn't say no The old song which Harold MACMILLAN memorably quoted to the CONSERVATIVE PARTY conference in Llandudno in October 1962, scorning Labour's stance on his government's efforts to enter the COMMON MARKET. Macmillan said:

> What did the Socialists do? . . . They solemnly asked Parliament not to approve or disapprove, but to TAKE NOTE of our decision. Perhaps some of the older ones among you will remember that popular song:
>
> She didn't say yes, she didn't say no,
> She didn't say stay, she didn't say go.
> She wanted to climb, but dreaded to fall,
> She bided her time and clung to the wall.

The song was written by Jerome Kern and Otto Harbach for the 1931 musical *The Cat and the Fiddle*; Macmillan did not sing the words, but PRIVATE EYE came to his 'assistance' by issuing the speech as a record with musical backing. *Compare* THERE I WAS, WAITING AT THE CHURCH.

sheep in sheep's clothing Someone who is totally weak, by contrast with a wolf in sheep's clothing who looks malleable but is not. CHURCHILL is said to have used the phrase about first Ramsay MACDONALD and later Clement ATTLEE; however, Churchill never underestimated Attlee, whom he trusted totally as his wartime deputy and whose victory in 1945 he at least respected. The phrase is known to have a much older origin: the British writer and critic Edmund Gosse (1849–1928) used it of his contemporary T. Sturge Moore.

savaged by a dead sheep *See* DEAD.

Sheffield rally The extravaganza staged by Britain's LABOUR PARTY a week before the 1992 general election, whose triumphalist tone was widely blamed for the party's shock defeat. Almost the entire SHADOW CABINET gathered under a montage of rippling flags before 12,000 party faithful bused in from all over northern England and beyond, to demonstrate that Labour was confident of victory and ready to govern. With one opinion poll putting Labour 7 points ahead that evening, the atmosphere was euphoric and Neil KINNOCK jarringly fervent. Those present rated the event a success, but the juxtaposition on television of Kinnock shouting: 'Well . . . all right!' and Labour's growing lead frightened many floating voters into switching from Labour or the LIBERAL DEMOCRATS to John MAJOR's Conservatives.

> A mixture of *Götterdämmerung* and the Eurovision song contest.
>
> NORMAN LAMONT

> You don't belch till you've had the meal.
>
> DEREK FULLICK, head of the train drivers' union ASLEF

shenanigan A good Irish word for any kind of devious and dishonest behaviour aimed at preventing the obvious from happening; in politics its applications are numerous.

Sherman Act The pioneer ANTI-TRUST legislation passed by the US CONGRESS in 1890 in the face of widespread anger at the strength and ruthless defiance of the public interest of the great trusts, controlling the supply of essentials like steel and oil. Although the Act is linked in history with the Republican Sen. John Sherman of Ohio, the Bill was proposed by President Benjamin Harrison; Sherman agreed to introduce it in the SENATE. Its aims were 'to protect trade and commerce against unlawful restraints and monopolies' by outlawing 'every contract, combination in the form of trust or otherwise, or conspiracy, in restraint of trade and commerce among the several States, or with foreign nations'. Although more effective than the Interstate Commerce Act passed three years before had been in curbing the excesses of the railroads, its impact on the trusts was limited; indeed, until 1902 when President Theodore ROOSEVELT used it against a deal negotiated by the banker J. P. Morgan to end competition between north-western railroad magnates, it was only invoked to restrain labour unions. One of the Act's framers, Sen. Orville Platt of Connecticut, admitted when President Harrison signed it:

> The conduct of the Senate . . . has not been in the line of honest preparations for a Bill to prohibit and punish trusts. It has been in the line of getting some Bill with that title that we might go to the country with.

sherpas The senior officials, one from each participating country, who prepare the ground for SUMMIT meetings, especially the annual gatherings of the G8 heads of government, and fill in the details of agreements reached there for the final COMMUNIQUÉ. The original Sherpas are the Nepalese mountain guides who accompany climbers attempting Everest and other great Himalayan peaks.

shield laws Laws passed by many American STATES to enable reporters to protect the confidentiality of their SOURCES. Journalists have no right under federal law to refuse to disclose their sources, the SUPREME COURT having ruled that the FIRST AMENDMENT does not stretch that far. The term also applies to legislation protecting witnesses, especially children, and victims of crime from being questioned oppressively in open court.

Shin Bet The internal security arm of the Israeli state, MOSSAD handling external security. Its name is taken from its Hebrew initials, which stand for General Security Services. Shin Bet is an investigative agency with a special interest in potential sabotage – and, in recent times, suicide bombings – terrorism generally, and security matters with a political flavour.

Shining Path (Sp. *Sendero Luminoso*) The MAOIST guerrilla group led by Abimael Guzman (1935–) which between 1980 and his arrest in 1992 killed 23,000 people in an attempt to destroy Peru's political fabric. By 2000 it was estimated that 69,270 people had died in the conflict, 54% (37,400) of them killed by the guerrillas and 37% by the police according to Peru's TRUTH AND RECONCILIATION COMMISSION. The name originated in the doctrine of José Carlos Mariátegui, a Peruvian leftist of the 1920s, who advocated a 'shining path' return to the co-operative agricultural system of the Incas. Guzman, a former philosophy professor, split the Peruvian Communist Party to found Shining Path c. 1970; it went underground in 1979 and on 17 May 1980 declared war on the Peruvian state. Shining Path has been noted for its Messianic PERSONALITY CULT (Guzman was praised as Chairman Gonzalo) and the fanatical barbarism of its campaign; at onc point its cadres hanged dogs from traffic lights in Lima, their mouths stuffed with dynamite and placards round their necks denouncing the Chinese leader Deng Xiao-Ping. They cut off Lima's electricity during a Papal visit, then illuminated the capital with HAMMER-AND-SICKLE bonfires. Guzman was arrested in Lima in September 1992 amid surprise that the security forces had been able, and had wanted, to take him alive; the next month he was jailed for life, but the violence went on.

shock and awe The military tactics promoted by US Defense Secretary Donald Rumsfeld in the early 2000s which preferred the use of special forces, air power, high technology and the movement of troops by air rather than by sea to the deployment of large, slow-moving ground forces. Put to the test in the IRAQ WAR of March/April 2003, the tactics took their name from Harlan Ullman's 1996 book *Shock and Awe: Achieving Rapid Dominance,* which emphasised the need to open any military campaign with a shattering display of aerial force.

shoo-in An Americanism for a candidate considered a certainty to be elected.

shoot to kill The alleged policy pursued by the security forces in NORTHERN IRELAND toward IRA suspects, which led to the controversy over the STALKER REPORT. Critics of the Army and, especially, the RUC claimed that suspects were being shot in cold blood at roadblocks and ambushes without any effort being made to challenge or detain them. The charges were strongly disputed, but the evidence suggested that some breaches of procedure, in one case involving innocent civilians, did occur. LOYALIST politicians countered that the IRA had always followed a 'shoot to kill' policy, never giving its victims a chance.

short. short-list The list from which the final choice of a party's electoral CANDIDATE, or an appointed official, is made after less promising applicants have been eliminated.

Short money The financial assistance given by the State for the functioning of OPPOSITION parties at WESTMINSTER. It is named after the Labour Leader of the House Edward Short (later Lord Glenamara, 1912–), who first agreed to it in 1975. The money, intended for paying staff in the party leaders' offices, is paid according to the number of MPs a party has and the number of votes it received at the previous election.

Short resignation The dramatic if belated departure from Tony BLAIR's government on 12 May 2003 of Clare Short (1946–), International Development Secretary since 1997, largely in protest at the IRAQ WAR and the lack of UN involvement in post-war reconstruction. Ms Short, a left-winger from Irish Nationalist stock, had twice resigned from Labour's front bench in opposition. Two months earlier, on 16 March, she branded Blair three times in a radio interview as 'reckless' and said she would resign if he went to war without UN approval. Her criticism was unparalleled for a Minister who was not resigning at that point; Blair, who was trying to hold the LABOUR PARTY together in advance of the decision to invade, did not sack her, and when Robin COOK resigned on the eve of conflict, Ms Short decided to stay on, saying resignation would be 'cowardly'. But after the war she missed crucial COMMONS votes and a CABINET meeting before resigning, claiming that Blair had broken undertakings to her to fully involve the UN in reconstruction. In a scathing PERSONAL STATEMENT to the Commons, she accused Blair of acting without accountability and centralising power 'into the hands of a small number of advisers who make decisions in private without proper discussion'. She subsequently called for Blair to quit, and after the GUN CASE declared that British intelligence had been bugging the UN SECRETARY-GENERAL Kofi Annan.

short, sharp shock The tough regime introduced at some young offenders' institutions from 1979 by the Conservative Home Secretary WILLIE Whitelaw in response to pressure from party hard-liners on LAW AND ORDER. Whitelaw himself used the phrase in a party conference speech on 10 October that year. The regime involved near-military drill, discipline, haircuts and dress, and an emphasis on obeying orders. It was not a conspicuous success, one London magistrate observing:

> At least now when they re-offend they stand straight up in the dock and call me 'Sir'.

short-termism A preference for finding instant answers to problems rather than more productive and durable long-term solutions. The term is used particularly of financial institutions which demand immediate high rates of return from a business rather than allowing it to secure its long-term future through investment.

Shortly-Floorcross, Sir *See* CROSSING THE FLOOR.

show of hands A vote in which participants show their assent or disapproval by raising one hand to be counted. Democratic in small groups, the system has been widely abused when larger number are voting, especially at union MASS MEETINGS; indeed such votes in Britain were outlawed by the THATCHER government after evidence that workers opposed to the line being taken by their local leadership were being intimidated, and that majorities against strike action were being ignored by leaders bent on confrontation.

show trial One of the most potent weapons of STALIN and other ruthless TOTALITARIAN leaders: the trial of former members of the regime for alleged TREASON against it. A key feature was a grovelling apology by the defendants for crimes they had almost certainly not committed, accompanied by a glorification of the man who was sending them to almost certain death. Such trials were a feature of the great PURGES in the Soviet Union just before WORLD WAR II, and of Soviet SATELLITE states in Europe in the years after it. Occasionally the offence had genuinely been committed, sometimes there had been a policy difference with the losing faction playing the price; more often personality clashes or simply the egotism and insecurity of the great leader were responsible.

shroud-waving In UK politics, the practice of campaigning for greater government spending on the National Health Service (NHS) by claiming that patients are suffering or even dying through underfunding. The word was first used c. 1980 to describe hospital consultants who were using such tactics to demand more money for their own specialities; it was taken up by John MAJOR in the 1992 election to denounce the tenor of Labour's campaigning over the NHS, culminating in the WAR OF JENNIFER'S EAR. *Compare also* WAVING THE BLOODY SHIRT.

Shrub The nickname given to George W. BUSH when he was unexpectedly elected Governor of Texas in 1994, defeating the Democratic incumbent Anne Richards. The name reflected his public image as a minor-key version of his father, who had left the WHITE HOUSE the previous year. DUBYA's younger brother Jeb was defeated for the governorship of Florida at the same time, but was successful next time round.

shuffle The random process at WESTMINSTER by which oral QUESTIONS that have been tabled are placed in numerical order on the ORDER PAPER. Until 1989 the SPEAKER presided over a draw conducted by his staff; since then the shuffle has been conducted by computer.

shuttle diplomacy *See* DIPLOMACY.

Shuttleworths *See* READING SYSTEM.

Siberian pipeline The greatest irritant to US-European relations in the early 1980s: the efforts of the REAGAN administration to kill plans for a pipeline to supply Siberian natural gas to West Germany. WASHINGTON argued that completing the pipeline would boost the Soviet economy and amount to endorsement of BREZHNEV's invasion of Afghanistan. European nations, including Britain, argued that the pipeline meant much needed work for their construction and petrochemical companies, and that without it Europe would face damaging energy shortages. More bluntly they asserted that the project, from which US firms had been barred by their own government, was none of America's business. On 13 November 1982 President Reagan announced that the

EMBARGO was being lifted after the 'industrialised democracies reached substantial agreement'; Britain and France both insisted there had been a climbdown by Washington.

> A lesson in how not to conduct Alliance business.
> MARGARET THATCHER, *The Downing Street Years*

Sic semper tyrannis! (Lat. Thus always to tyrants!) The motto of the State of Virginia, but also the cry of John Wilkes Booth after he shot Abraham LINCOLN at FORD'S THEATRE in Washington on 14 April 1865. Lincoln's bodyguard was so entranced by the play, *Our Country Cousin*, that he left his post and Booth stepped into the President's box. After shooting him, Booth jumped down to the stage, but one of the spurs he was inexplicably wearing caught in a drape of bunting and he fell, breaking his left leg. He managed to stand up and shout: '*Sic simper tryannnis* – the South is avenged!' before escaping through the wings.

sick chicken case *See* CHICKEN.

Sidney Street siege The dramatic siege by the police, Scots Guards and Horse Artillery of a house (100 Sidney Street) at Stepney, in London's East End, on 3 January 1911. It was witnessed by Winston CHURCHILL, Home Secretary in ASQUITH's government, who had sent in the troops to flush out the 'Houndsditch Gang', three Latvian ANARCHISTS led by **Peter the Painter**, a signwriter from Riga. They had killed three policemen three weeks before following an abortive raid on a jeweller's shop in Houndsditch. Two of the anarchists died when the troops stormed the house; Peter the Painter escaped.

Sierra Club One of America's most active and prestigious ENVIRONMENTALIST pressure groups, based in San Francisco and taking its name from California's High Sierras, whose preservation is one of its highest priorities. Founded in 1892, it has over 700,000 members across the United States and Canada and campaigns across the range of environmental issues, including global warming, world population growth and rainforest preservation.

signing ceremony The event at which the PRESIDENT of the United States signs into law a BILL which has his particular support, which thus becomes an ACT. Such a ceremony is usually held in the WHITE HOUSE, but on occasion will be stage-managed somewhere else to create a MEDIA EVENT – at the PENTAGON, for example, if national defence is the issue. The President will be flanked by the Senators and Congressmen who took the Bill through both Houses, by the relevant CABINET SECRETARY and maybe by other officials or celebrities whose presence will impress the public.

Silent Cal The nickname of **Calvin Coolidge** (1872–1933), 30th President of the United States (Republican, 1923–29). Coolidge's economy with words was legendary. One Washington hostess declared: 'He is so silent he is always worth listening to', and another, 'every time he opens his mouth, a moth flies out.' He revelled in his reputation; once at a dinner, a young girl told him: 'I've made a bet with a friend that I can get you to say at least three words this evening,' Coolidge replied: 'You lose', then sat silent for the rest of the evening. Another time, he was asked on leaving church what the sermon had been about. Coolidge said: 'Sin', and when asked what the preacher had actually said, added: 'He said he was against it.' He said of himself: 'I have never been hurt by anything I didn't say.' And he explained: 'Many times I say "Yes" or "No" to people. Even that is too much; it winds them up for 20 minutes more.' To Will Rogers this put him at an advantage over his contemporaries; after the SCOPES CASE Rogers proclaimed Coolidge

> A better example of evolution than either Bryan or Darrow, for he knows when not to talk, which is the biggest asset the monkey possesses over the human.

In truth, Coolidge's reluctance to speak was born of shyness. He once said:

> It's hard for me to play this game. In politics one must meet people, and that's not easy for me.

silent majority *See* MAJORITY.

Silent Spring, The The book written by Rachel Carson and published in America in 1962 which did as much as any to create the ENVIRONMENTALIST movement, by arousing public concern over the destruction of wildlife and danger to the food chain caused by the use of dangerous pesticides.

A period of silence on your part would be welcome *See* THANK YOU FOR YOUR LETTER . . .

Silver Bodgie The nickname of Australia's Labor Prime Minister Bob HAWKE, a reference by his critics to the way he had his mane of silver hair styled when he joined the governing ESTABLISHMENT; 'bodgie' is Australian for a 1950s teddy boy.

From underneath his cockatoo hairdo, the platitudes he has got by heart.

PATRICK WHITE

free silver *See* FREE.

Silverman Bill The Private Member's BILL to abolish the death penalty in Britain, sponsored by the left-wing Labour MP Sidney Silverman, which the COMMONS first passed in 1955 after the Ruth ELLIS case but the LORDS rejected. The EDEN government, after a counterproductive delay, brought in a Homicide Bill limiting hanging to specific forms of murder. Silverman who first got a suspension of hanging through the Commons in 1948, kept up his campaign, eventually succeeding in 1965.

Simonstown agreement The long-standing arrangement under which the Royal Navy used Simonstown naval base near Cape Town, greatly assisting its operations in the South Atlantic and Indian oceans. The deal, involving manoeuvres with South Africa, was bitterly criticised by the left in Britain as APARTHEID became more repressive, and was terminated by the Labour government in the late 1970s, a decade too late for most of the party. As late as 1974 Harold WILSON rebuked Tony BENN for attacking the agreement in Labour's NEC.

simultaneous translation A burgeoning feature of international political life since the mid-20th century, with the growth of international organisations whose proceedings need to be instantly translated from a myriad of languages into as many others. A translator's work is difficult and thankless; they must cope with regional accents, poor syntax and sheer waffle. The EUROPEAN PARLIAMENT has provided some spectacular mistranslations. One Frenchman congratulating his colleague's *prudence Normande* was baffled by laughter from British MEPs who had heard him compared with Norman Wisdom, a professional idiot, and a UK member speaking about inseminating cattle with frozen semen met a similar French reaction when this was translated as *matelots congelés* (frozen seamen). The author heard an excellent translator in the Reichstag speak of an 'Anglo-Dutch amphibian force', while Sir Geoffrrey HOWE, on a mission to the KREMLIN, was intrigued to hear his comment: 'The spirit is willing, but the flesh is weak' translated as 'The vodka's OK but the meat is underdone.' The most prominent victim of mistranslation was President CARTER; the impact of his arrival in Warsaw was destroyed when the translator hired by the State Department converted his protestation of respect for the Poles into the shattering news that he desired them carnally.

sing from the same hymnsheet A phrase that has come into common use since the 1980s, reflecting the need for every member of a government, party or any collective leadership to stick to the same lines in public. It has its origin in church services where the hymns are on a sheet distributed to the congregation, rather than in a book; sometimes inadvertently a few sheets for a different service are handed out.

single. Single European Act The amendment to the Treaty of ROME in 1987 that paved the way for the SINGLE MARKET, and substituted qualified MAJORITY voting, in most cases, for the previous requirement that decisions of the COUNCIL OF MINISTERS, must be unanimous.

single currency *See* EURO.

Single Market The wide range of measures to complete FREE TRADE, in goods at least, within the EU that took effect early in 1993; the target date had been 1992, but a handful of the 301 ddirectives involved, notably on eliminating border controls, took longer to implement. The success of the Single Market, advocated in the CECCHINI REPORT, depended on the initiative of individual businesses and the readiness of governments to eliminate red tape; Britain's Customs & Excise responded to the final removal of barriers by demanding a 650-page report in quadruplicate each month from companies engaged in external trade. Since 1993 the Single Market has expanded geographically, even prior to the ENLARGEMENT of the EU in 2004, and has also been extended to areas of the service sector, though some barriers in fields such as insurance remain.

Sinn Fein (Ir. Ourselves Alone) The Irish nationalist movement founded by Arthur Griffith in 1907, which in its present incarnation is the POLITICAL WING of the Provisional IRA and has come in from the cold with the GOOD FRIDAY AGREEMENT to be the larger if more extreme of NORTHERN IRELAND's Catholic parties, with a foothold also in the Republic. After the EASTER RISING, Sinn Fein organised as the party of independence, winning a string of BY-ELECTIONS, starting with Count Plunket's victory at Roscommon in February 1917. In the 1918 COUPON ELECTION it almost swept the board under de Valera (*see* DEV), winning 73 seats whose holders (including Countess Markiewicz, the first woman elected to the

Commons) stayed away to form the first DAIL EIREANN. The party split in 1922, the pro-IRISH TREATY faction winning a large majority in the Dail; opponents of PARTITION joined or were marginalised by FIANNA FAIL but retained some support on either side of the Border; in 1957 they got four TDs elected.

When the TROUBLES flared again in 1969, Sinn Fein gained an influx of support but split again. The Marxist Officials (or STICKIES) evolved first into the WORKERS' PARTY and then the DEMOCRATIC LEFT; Provisional Sinn Fein backed the Republican terror campaign against British rule. Sinn Fein, through a combination of COMMUNITY POLITICS and intimidation, benefited from the HUNGER STRIKES of 1981, winning council seats in many Nationalist areas of Ulster. In 1983 its articulate leader Gerry Adams was elected MP for West Belfast; he BOYCOTTed the Commons both up to his defeat in 1992 and again after his re-election in 1997. During the terrorist campaign Sinn Fein prevented the SDLP, then with much greater support, from speaking for the entire Nationalist community; it also gave LOYALIST paramilitaries an excuse to organise. The UK and Irish governments both gagged Sinn Fein for a time by preventing its spokesmen being heard on radio and TV except during elections (*see* OXYGEN OF PUBLICITY). Secret contacts with the UK government opened in 1993, assisted ironically by the SDLP leader John Hume, intensified after the DOWNING STREET DECLARATION, and after the IRA ceasefire developed into talks with Ministers. The contacts were dogged by the question of whether the IRA should DECOMMISSION its arsenal as part of the peace process; Adams stalled as long as possible, and during this time was given a warm reception by the CLINTON White House, to the fury of John MAJOR. With the Good Friday Agreement Sinn Fein claimed full democratic credentials, and two of its senior figures took up Ministerial posts in the executive under the UNIONIST John Trimble. The party made steady electoral gains to overtake the SDLP, but the discovery that the IRA had been tracking potential targets from its offices at STORMONT led to the suspension of POWER-SHARING in October 2002. Sinn Fein also increased its support in the Republic, and in 2001 had three MPs returned to WESTMINSTER; they refused as before to take the OATH OF ALLEGIANCE, but were for a time nevertheless allocated offices in the Palace of Westminster. Sinn Fein came close to agreeing a new deal on power sharing with the DUP late in 2004, but the NORTHERN BANK ROBBERY and the murder of ROBERT MCCARTNEY in which its activists were implicated barred its way back into government

> A vote for Sinn Fein is a vote for peace.
> GERRY ADAMS

Sir The prefix to the name of anyone in Britain, and a handful of its overseas possessions, who has been awarded a KNIGHTHOOD, in place of Mr, Dr or whatever. A male recipient becomes *Sir* Paul, a woman thus honoured *Dame* Pauline.

Sir Alec The affectionate nickname earned by the former and future **Lord Home** (1903–95) during his seven years in the Commons (1963–70), first as Prime Minister (October 1963–October 1964), then as Tory leader and finally as Shadow Foreign Secretary. (A less flattering sobriquet was BAILLIE VASS.) A Scottish landowner of immense tact and charm, Home overcame Harold WILSON's depiction of him as a chinless and probably brainless aristocrat to be a competent Premier, a successful Foreign Secretary before and after his premiership, and a revered Tory elder statesman. His childhood was sheltered, his nurse Florence Hill recalling: 'I had to see that master Alec didn't talk to the servants and that he didn't leave our part of the house.' Illness left him with almost skeletal looks; one Tory MP commented: 'I have seen better-looking faces on a pirate flag.' When a TV make-up girl told him: 'You have a head like a skull,' Home replied: 'Doesn't everybody?'

As Lord Dunglass, he was a Conservative MP from 1931 to 1951, and PPS to Neville CHAMBERLAIN at MUNICH. In 1951 he succeeded his father as 14th Earl of Home (pronounced Hume), and as a PEER served as Commonwealth Secretary and Leader of the Lords. In 1960 MACMILLAN made him Foreign Secretary; when SUPERMAC resigned through ill-health in October 1963 Lord Hailsham renounced his peerage to challenge RAB Butler for the succession, but Home was Macmillan's choice, to the astonishment of many politicians and the incredulity of the media. Wilson could not believe his luck, trumpeting:

> After half a century of democratic advance, the process has ground to a halt with a 14th Earl.

Home retorted that he imagined his rival must be the FOURTEENTH MR WILSON, but even the pro-Tory *Sunday Express* commented:

> The only real and distinctive achievement of a 14th earl was to have been heir of the 13th.

Home became Prime Minister, noting laconically: 'The doctor unfortunately said I was fit.' He RENOUNCED his title to become plain Sir Alec Douglas-Home (he was a KNIGHT of the Thistle in his own right). A seat was found for him at Kinross and West Perthshire and he won a BY-ELECTION to re-enter the Commons. Home had once said he would never become Prime Minister 'because I do my sums with matchsticks', but despite his matchstick ECONOMICS he was successful. He had less than a year at NUMBER TEN before going down to electoral defeat, but restored shattered Tory morale and came close to denying Labour a majority. In opposition he harried the first Wilson government for a year before standing down as leader, Edward HEATH succeeding him. He remained in the Shadow Cabinet and from 1970 to 1974 was again Foreign Secretary before returning to the Lords as a LIFE PEER.

> There are two problems in my life. The political ones are insoluble and the economic ones are incomprehensible.
>
> SIR ALEC when Prime Minister

> He is used to dealing with estate workers. I cannot see how anyone can say he is out of touch.
>
> Daughter-in-law Lady CAROLINE DOUGLAS-HOME

> In the 18th Century he would have been Prime Minister before he was thirty; as it is he appeared honourably ineligible for the struggle of life.
>
> CYRIL CONNOLLY, *Enemies of Promise* (1938)

> Alec Douglas-Home, floating on the lethargic sea of his own simplicity, could not for a moment compare with Wilson. BERNARD LEVIN

Sir Humphrey A personification of the Whitehall MANDARIN, stemming from the silken and duplicitous CABINET SECRETARY Sir Humphrey Appleby (played by Nigel Hawthorne) in the 1980s BBC television comedy series YES, MINISTER.

SIS Secret Intelligence Service. The formal name for the UK's external intelligence agency better known as MI6.

sisters The term used by FEMINISTS in politics to refer to each other, in much the same way as left-wingers used to refer to each other as COMRADES. However, the term is essentially collective rather than individual. Anti-feminists use it as a term of contempt.

sit At WESTMINSTER, each MP is said to sit for the CONSTITUENCY they represent, and each House is said to be sitting when it is in session.

sit-down A widely-practised form of protest, frequently involving CIVIL DISOBEDIENCE, when demonstrators for or against a particular policy or practice sit down in a place where they will attract maximum attention or cause the most disruption, and refuse to move until their demands are met.

> I want every American free to stand up for his rights, even if he has to sit down for them.
>
> JOHN F. KENNEDY

sit-in The US refinement of the sit-down which became a highly effective part of the CIVIL RIGHTS campaign and was taken up by student protesters against the VIETNAM WAR and other perceived wrongs. It was born on 1 February 1960 when four black students from the Agricultural and Technical College of North Carolina occupied a 'Whites only' lunch counter at Woolworth's in Charlotte and refused to leave unless served. The idea, which accorded perfectly with the NON-VIOLENT teaching of Dr Martin Luther KING, caught on like wildfire; the first victory was won in San Antonio on 21 March, and by the end of 1961 eating facilities in 108 cities across the South had been DESEGREGATED, after sit-ins involving an estimated 75,000 young people – 3600 of whom had been arrested and 245 expelled from their colleges. Their success prompted kneel-ins to desegregate churches, read-ins to integrate libraries, and wade-ins to end 'Whites-only' beaches.

Sit Room *See* SITUATION ROOM.

sitting At WESTMINSTER, the daily cycle of business in either House from PRAYERS until the House is ADJOURNED. An all-night sitting, if it goes on long enough, can lead to the next day's BUSINESS being lost; while this happened occasionally up to the mid-1980s, it is very rare now, partly because of rule changes and partly because far fewer late-night and all-night debates are scheduled.

sittings motion The first item considered by a STANDING COMMITTEE of the House of Commons that is handling the COMMITTEE STAGE of a BILL. The motion sets out how often each week, and at what times, the committee shall sit. Occasionally, when the government wishes to make indecent haste or members feel the Bill should not be immediately considered, this becomes a matter of controversy. Debate on the sittings motion will also be prolonged if the

OPPOSITION wishes to FILIBUSTER against a Bill it particularly objects to.

Situation Room The small room in the basement of the WHITE HOUSE where NATIONAL SECURITY COUNCIL staff and others handle (mainly international) crises, with the President in attendance at critical stages; generally the crisis management team is chaired by the Vice President. The room gained the name – often abbreviated to **Sit Room** – under the KENNEDY administration, having been used for that purpose since the reconstruction of the White House under President TRUMAN. President MCKINLEY had a small **War Room** established on the second floor during the SPANISH-AMERICAN WAR; Winston CHURCHILL on an early wartime visit had a **Map Room** installed on the first floor and Franklin D. ROOSEVELT liked it so much that he had it moved to the ground floor afterwards so that it would be more accessible; it still bears the name.

The situation has not developed entirely to our advantage The explanation of the state of WORLD WAR II given by Emperor Hirohito to the Japanese people, most of whom had never previously heard his voice, after the destruction of HIROSHIMA by the first ATOMIC BOMB.

Six, the The six nations – France, West Germany, Italy and the BENELUX countries – who were the original participants in the three constituent parts of the European Community: the EUROPEAN COAL AND STEEL COMMUNITY (1951), the European Economic Community (1957) and EURATOM.

Six Counties The counties – Armagh, Antrim, (London)Derry, Down, Fermanagh and Tyrone – which, at the PARTITION of Ireland in 1921, became part of NORTHERN IRELAND instead of being included in the IRISH FREE STATE. The term came to be shorthand, particularly in the South and among Northern Catholics, for the British enclave in the North.

> The Six Counties have, towards the rest of Ireland, a status and a relationship which no Act of Parliament can change. They are part of Ireland. They always have been part of Ireland, and their people, Catholic and Protestant, are our people.
>
> DE VALERA (*see* DEV) to CHURCHILL, 26 May 1941

Six Day War The short but bloody conflict between Israel and its Arab neighbours in 1967 in which Israel conquered East Jerusalem and the WEST BANK from Jordan, the GAZA STRIP from Egypt and the GOLAN HEIGHTS from Syria, giving the country defensible borders, inflicting a shattering blow to Arab morale and creating the plight of the PALESTINIANS. The suddenness of Israel's assault, which pre-empted an expected Arab attack, led *Time* to term it 'the **Blintzkrieg**'. In May, Egypt's President Nasser secured the removal of UN PEACE-KEEPING troops from his border with Israel, closed the Gulf of Aqaba to Israeli shipping and signed a security pact with King Hussein of Jordan. On 5 June Israel struck against Egypt, destroying over 400 jets on the ground, then poured tanks into Sinai, reaching the SUEZ CANAL in four days. Meanwhile, Israeli forces repulsed an attack by Jordan, occupying the old city of Jerusalem and the West Bank; they also defeated Syrian attacks to secure the Golan Heights. A UN-arranged ceasefire came into effect on 11 June. Almost four decades later, diplomatic deadlock remained over the scope for the Palestinians in the lands captured then (*see* OCCUPIED TERRITORIES) to govern themselves. *See* INTIFADA; LAND FOR PEACE.

> If we lose this war, I'll start another in my wife's name. General MOSHE DAYAN (*attr.*)

600-ship navy The goal set by the REAGAN administration in its early months, reflecting its determination to boost America's naval strength after a period of decline. Reagan inherited 479 ships (50 of them started under the CARTER administration); Navy Secretary John Lehman made an increase to 600 his top priority and did his best to further it by persuading Secretary of Defense Caspar Weinberger (*see* CAP THE KNIFE) to authorise not one, but two new aircraft carriers – which meant two new carrier groups. The impetus toward such a large fleet had dissipated by the end of the COLD WAR in 1989.

Sixteenth Amendment The amendment to the US CONSTITUTION, proposed in February 1909 and RATIFIED four years later, which specifically authorised the CONGRESS to levy a federal income tax. Such a tax was imposed during the CIVIL WAR, but when it was revived in 1894 the SUPREME COURT ruled it a DIRECT TAX and therefore UNCONSTITUTIONAL. The importance of allowing Congress to imose an income to meet extraordinary expenses, as in wartime, was widely acknowledged, but the amendment was only approved after heated debate.

1600 Pennsylvania Avenue The postal address of the WHITE HOUSE; the zip code is Washington, DC 20004.

size matters The interview with Tony and Cherie BLAIR, on the eve of the 2005 election, with which the *Sun* called on its readers to give Labour the largest possible majority. Crammed with doubles entendres, the article was widely seen in party and media circles as demeaning.

sketch-writers The select band of journalists at WESTMINSTER who, since the 1930s, have reported the proceedings of the COMMONS (and occasionally the LORDS) in the form of a theatrical review rather than a news report. The format enables the wordsmith to be exceptionally rude about a politician supported by the paper employing them, or to compliment one whose politics their paper's leader columns detest. Norman Shrapnel of the then *Manchester Guardian* was a pioneer of the art-form; other gifted sketch-writers have included Colin Welch of the *Daily Mail*, Frank Johnson of the *Daily Telegraph*, Andrew Rawnsley of the *Guardian* and Matthew Parris of *The Times*, a former Conservative MP.

Skinner, Dennis *See* BEAST OF BOLSOVER.

skunk A classic North American term of political abuse, from the stripy creature that squirts evil-smelling liquid over anyone or anything that annoys it. An insult by 1840, it was considered so offensive by politicians that in this historic clash on 19 May 1856 between Senators Charles SUMNER and Stephen Douglas (*see* STEAM ENGINE IN BRITCHES) the animal could not be named:

> *Sumner:* No person with the upright form of a man can be allowed, without violation of all human decency, to switch out from his tongue the perpetual stench of offensive personality . . . The noisome, squat and nameless animal to which I now refer is not a proper model for an American senator. Will the Senator from Illinois take notice?
> *Douglas:* I will, and therefore will not imitate you, Sir.
> *Sumner*: Mr President, again the Senator has switched his tongue, and again he fills the Senate with an offensive odour.
> *Douglas*: . . . I will only say that a man who has been branded by me in the Senate, and convicted by the Senate of falsehood, cannot use language requiring reply, and therefore I have nothing to say.

Later generations were less bashful. In the 1968 NEW HAMPSHIRE PRIMARY William Loeb, publisher of the *Manchester Union-Leader*, castigated Sen. Eugene McCarthy as 'a skunk's skunk's skunk'. And in the early 1970s an anonymous Congressman said of Rep. Wayne HAYS:

> Getting into a debate with him is like wrestling with a skunk. The skunk doesn't care – he likes the smell.

Skybolt The air-delivered missile with which America agreed to supply Britain in 1960 when the UK abandoned its own BLUE STREAK ground-launched system; it was to be delivered from RAF V-bombers. Two years later the KENNEDY administration cancelled the project without consulting Britain, but at Nassau in December 1962 Harold MACMILLAN persuaded Kennedy to supply POLARIS instead.

slagheap affair One of a series of supposed scandals with which Harold WILSON's opponents, backed by much of Britain's press, attempted to smear him between the two 1974 general elections when Labour was governing without a majority. It involved property deals by Tony Field, brother of Wilson's political secretary Marcia Williams (*see* LADY FORKBENDER), and a letter on HOUSE OF COMMONS notepaper to Ronald Milhench, a Wolverhampton insurance broker who had discussed with Field the sale of a slagheap and quarry at Ince-in-Makerfield, Lancashire. The letter bore Wilson's signature, which Milhench was later convicted of forging. Field bought the land in 1967 and made Mrs Williams co-director of the quarry company; it lost money, but property prices took off and Field – who had by now been working in Wilson's private office – sold it at a profit of nearly £200,000. Field became involved in a further deal with Milhench, which fell through when the issue became public. Wilson was in no way involved and Field had done nothing illegal, but Wilson, who had known about the deals, defended them with counter-productive stridency. The Conservatives and the press made much of the way Wilson, who had always condemned speculation, defended it when it could be called 'reclamation'.

> If you buy land on which there is a slagheap 120ft. high and it costs £100,000 to remove it, that is not land speculation in the sense we condemned it, but reclamation.
>
> HAROLD WILSON, House of Commons, 4 April 1974

slate A list of candidates for a range of offices from President downwards in the same election, or for a multi-member body (often the executive of a political party or a trade union) put forward either by a party or semi-formally by a particular faction. A **slate card** in US political life is a list of such candidates handed to electors by a party before they cast their vote.

slavery The institution under which one group of human beings keeps others in servitude, exerting total and generally brutal control over every aspect of their lives and treating them as chattels to be bought, sold and exploited. The MANSFIELD JUDGMENT of 1772 confirmed that slavery was illegal in England, but it thrived in the Caribbean and American colonies as slave-owners shipped in half-dead Africans to till the plantations. In America's South it became the staple of the economy, and revolutionaries such as George WASHINGTON (*see* MOUNT VERNON) and Thomas JEFFERSON saw no inconsistency between their belief in equality and the ownership of slaves; however, some in the new nation were affronted by the practice, Dr Benjamin Rush saying in 1773:

> The plant of liberty is of so tender a nature that it cannot thrive long in the neighborhood of slavery.

Britain abolished the slave trade to its remaining colonies in 1809, and the institution of slavery in 1833, three days before the death of the ABOLITIONIST William Wilberforce who said:

> Thank God, that I should have lived to witness a day in which England is willing to give twenty millions sterling for the abolition of slavery.

From the MISSOURI COMPROMISE of 1820 (*see* FIREBELL IN THE NIGHT) through the KANSAS-NEBRASKA ACT, slavery became an ever more divisive issue for the expanding America, with abolitionist fervour growing in the North and the South opposing any attempt to limit the number of **slave states,** let alone any move to emancipate slaves. President Buchanan warned:

> There are portions of the Union where if you emancipate your slaves they will become your masters. Is there any man who would for a moment indulge the horrible idea of abolishing slavery by the massacre of the chivalrous race of men in the south?

Abraham LINCOLN did not come to the Presidency intent on abolishing slavery. He had told Stephen DOUGLAS in one of their DEBATES in 1856: 'I have no purpose, either directly or indirectly, to interfere with the institution of slavery in the states where it exists.' He believed it could be strangled, saying:

> Let us draw a cordon around the slave states and the hateful institution, like a reptile poisoning itself, will perish by its own infamy.

Then came the CIVIL WAR; though it was strictly fought over the right of the CONFEDERATE states to SECEDE from the Union, it was slavery that drew the moral battle-lines and moved Lincoln to sign the EMANCIPATION PROCLAMATION. Lincoln now declared: 'If slavery is not wrong, nothing is wrong,' and maintained:

> I can clearly foresee nothing but the rooting out of slavery can perpetuate the existence of our union by consolidating it in a common bond of principle.

He confessed: 'Whenever I hear anyone arguing for slavery, I feel a strong impulse to see it tried on him personally.' And to those who claimed that he was advocating forcible integration of the races, Lincoln replied:

> I protest, now and forever, against the counterfeit logic which presumes that because I do not want a negro woman for a slave I do necessarily want her for a wife. My understanding is that I do not have to have her for either.

Slavery duly ended with the defeat of the Confederacy, though it was a century before black Southerners began to be truly free. The institution lives on in some Middle Eastern countries and parts of Africa and India, where the revulsion of the rest of the world makes no impression.

half slave, half free *See* HOUSE DIVIDED.

SLD Social and Liberal Democrats. The original name (*see* SALADS) of the party created in 1988 by the MERGER of Britain's LIBERAL PARTY and the SDP; next year they took the shortened title of LIBERAL DEMOCRATS.

sleaze A phrase borrowed from showbiz and originally used politically in Washington c. 1984 to categorise financial and other misconduct by politicians. Initially it was used to describe the large number of members of the REAGAN administration accused of breaches of ethics or the criminal law – 225 when the House Civil Service Sub-Committee last counted. It crossed the Atlantic with a vengeance in the early 1990s to describe the tidal wave of financial, sexual and other misdemeanours which forced the resignation of several Ministers from the THATCHER and MAJOR governments, the disgrace of several, the death of one MP from a bizarre sex game and the imprisonment of former Chief Secretary Jonathan Aitken for perjury, and was a factor in the Conservatives' rout in the 1997 election. Though the elements of each example of misconduct were different, they came to a head in the CASH FOR QUESTIONS affair, which led to the appointment of the NOLAN COMMITTEE and the belated establishment of an ethics code and watchdog for MPs. While it is fair to say that most breaches of ethics come to light several years after the event, Conservative efforts to portray Tony BLAIR's government as equally 'mired in sleaze' lacked credibility, despite such episodes as FORMULA ONE and the ROBINSON LOAN. The word 'sleaze' (from the original 'sleazy') apparently stems from the products of Silesia, on the Polish-German border, which were regarded in the 17th century as inferior; it conveys a whiff not only of corruption but of tackiness.

> White House pollster Richard Wirthlin said Wednesday the resignation of Attorney-General Edward Meese III doesn't erase the 'sleaze factor' for Vice President George Bush in the fall presidential campaign, but makes it easier for him to deal with.
>
> *Associated Press* report, 7 June 1988

> Our administration has been the victim of individuals who haven't had the judgment or integrity to put the public's interest above their own selfish interest.
>
> Vice President GEORGE BUSH Snr

> Every so often John [Major] and I will be sitting in Number Ten talking about how things are going, and a private secretary comes in and says: 'Prime Minister, there's something else we think you ought to know.' We know what's coming, and it's got to the point where we just look at each other and burst out laughing.
>
> Chancellor KENNETH CLARKE, private conversation with the author, c.1994

sleep A commodity in short supply for persons in public life who frequently work long and unsocial hours and have exhausting travel schedules; British Foreign Secretaries have a particular track record of falling asleep when back on home turf. It is also a political trap for politicians who are unable to stay awake. UK Defence Secretary Fred Mulley (1918–) attracted front-page headlines in 1977 when he fell asleep next to the Queen at an air display; the US media were more tolerant of President REAGAN who frequently nodded off in Cabinet meetings and once quipped: 'Remember when I fell asleep during my audience with the Pope?' Margaret THATCHER deplored such tendencies, saying of her husband Denis: 'I can trust him not to fall asleep on a public platform and he usually claps in the right places.' But Ernest Brown (*see* TELEPHONE), a member of Stanley BALDWIN's government, stated bluntly:

> I like a nap. A man who cannot sleep ought not to be in the Cabinet.

Much depends on the kind of sleep. Henry (CHIPS) Channon experienced the right kind, writing:

> I slept for five hours this afternoon in the library of the HOUSE OF COMMONS. A deep House of Commons sleep. There is no sleep to compare with it – rich, deep and guilty.

Norman Willis, general secretary of the TUC, was less fortunate:

> I've no problems. I sleep like a baby, one hour sleeping and one hour crying.

Sleep can be a blessed release when someone else is making a bad speech. A fellow-peer once said to Lord North during an interminable speech: 'My Lord, I fear you have been asleep'; North replied: 'I wish I had.'

> He had only one really valuable talent. He slept more than any other President whether by day or by night. Nero fiddled – but Coolidge only snored.
>
> H. L. MENCKEN on Calvin Coolidge

sleeper (1) A terrorist who 'goes to ground' as an apparently normal member of the community for years, waiting for eventual instructions to start shooting or bombing. (2) In WASHINGTON, a BILL whose full import is not appreciated until after it has been enacted, usually because of an amendment quietly tabled which has a far-reaching and unpublicised impact.

sleepwalking into a nightmare The final, despairing appeal to British voters just three days before the 1997 general election from Michael HESELTINE to stick with John MAJOR's Conservatives and not be seduced by Tony BLAIR and NEW LABOUR, who seemed to be – and were – heading for a LANDSLIDE victory. On 29 April 1997, Heseltine pleaded:

> The best way to avoid sleepwalking into a nightmare is to wake up.

Slick Willie The nickname given to Bill CLINTON by George BUSH Snr during the 1992 Presidential campaign which was designed to cast doubts on the Democratic nominee's trustworthiness. The sobriquet, originally a Southern term for anyone who is hard to pin down, entered the popular vocabulary, but did not prevent Clinton winning. The original political Slick Willie was Willie Brown, elected Mayor of San Francisco in 1896.

> The appearance of the phrase 'Slick Willie' was not particularly noted by me or anyone on our staff. Shows how wrong you can be.
>
> JAMES CARVILLE, *All's Fair*

slip, to A term used by WHIPS in the HOUSE OF

COMMONS: a member can be slipped by them from being present to vote if they have pressing business elsewhere, and likewise a Minister can be slipped from CABINET.

slogan Originally the war cry of a Scottish clan, a slogan has become the brief phrase which sets the key for a political campaign or (closer to its origins) a chant raised during a DEMONSTRATION. **Sloganising** is the conduct of politics through the exchange of such phrases, rather than through a meaningful dialogue.

> If you feed the people with revolutionary slogans they will listen today, they will listen tomorrow, they will listen the day after tomorrow, but on the fourth day they will say: 'To Hell with you!'
>
> NIKITA KHRUSHCHEV

SLORC State Law and Order Restoration Committee The junta which seized power in Burma (now Myanmar) in 1988 under Sung Maung and has governed with brutality ever since, despite being defeated in the only elections ever held in the country by the party led by Aung Sung Suu Ky (*see* TITANIUM ORCHID). SLORC's violations of human rights attracted worldwide protests, but most other Asian nations and some Western investors have chosen to overlook them. To improve its image, the junta renamed itself the State Peace and Development Council – but did not moderate its policies.

slump Another word for a DEPRESSION, involving a nosedive in all forms of economic activity.

slush fund An undisclosed fund used by well-heeled supporters of a politician to give them some invisible means of support; such a fund may well consist of corrupt or illegal payments and be used for same. The term was well established when Richard NIXON went on television in 1952 to make his CHECKERS speech after the disclosure of such a fund; it was Nixon again whose career was ruined by the uses to which CREEP's secret fund was put prior to and after the WATERGATE break-in. Slush was the money sailors made from selling waste fat from the ship's galley (*slusk*: Norwegian for slops).

Small is Beautiful The book (1973) by the German-born UK economist E. F. Schumacher (1911–77) whose title became the slogan of opposition to huge conglomerates and centralised government. Schumacher wanted to call it *The Homecoming*; the eventual title came from his publishers Anthony Blond and Desmond Briggs. One devotee was Edmund G. (Jerry) Brown (*see* SPACE CADET), former governor of California and a Presidential contender in 1976 and 1992.

SMERSH (Russ. *Smert' Spionem*, Death to Spies) The KGB section notorious (after the Russians stopped using the name) for eliminating enemies abroad and Western agents; SMERSH teams murdered TROTSKY on STALIN's orders and found HITLER's body, but had less success with the fictional British agent James Bond, whose creator Ian Fleming popularised the word.

Smith. Smith Act The Aliens Registration Act, promoted by Rep. Howard W. Smith of Virginia and passed by CONGRESS on 28 June 1940 as war in Europe heightened fears of Communist and fascist subversion. Requiring all aliens to register and be fingerprinted and outlawing organisations advocating the overthrow of the US government, it was used in 1949 against the US COMMUNIST PARTY as MCCARTHYISM took hold; the SUPREME COURT ruled this UNCONSTITUTIONAL in 1951.

Smith-Connally Act Pushed through CONGRESS by conservatives after John L. Lewis called a miners' strike in 1943 in defiance of President ROOSEVELT, this first of several attempted curbs on strikes authorised the federal government to operate strike-hit plants and outlawed disruption in them.

Smith, John (1938–94), leader of Britain's LABOUR PARTY from July 1992 until his sudden death on 12 May 1994, who would, had he lived, almost certainly have become Prime Minister in 1997, rather than Tony BLAIR. Son of an Argyll headmaster, a committed Christian and a strong family man, the stocky, bespectacled Smith graduated from Glasgow University to a successful legal career. Elected MP in 1970 for Lanarkshire North (later Monklands East), he was an energy and DEVOLUTION minister in the WILSON/CALLAGHAN government, and Trade Secretary for its final months. In OPPOSITION he rallied party moderates against the BENNITE left, encouraging them to fight back rather than defect to the SDP. He then gained authority as trade and industry spokesman and Shadow Chancellor. He recovered from a first heart attack in October 1988 with a vigorous regime 'bagging' Munros, Scotland's peaks over 3000ft. Before the 1992 election he launched the PRAWN COCKTAIL OFFENSIVE, and a 'Shadow Budget' proposing tax increases, which the Conservatives seized on to great effect. When Neil KINNOCK resigned on Labour's defeat, Smith beat Bryan Gould for the leadership, then continued Kinnock's modernisation by securing OMOV in party decision-making, narrowly defeating the left and major unions at the 1993 Brighton conference after privately threatening to resign. By May 1994 the forceful, gregarious Smith had put a united party in a commanding position, but the week after large local election gains he had a second heart attack at his London flat and died. There was an outpouring of grief in Parliament, the party and the country; after an emotional funeral in Edinburgh he was buried on the isle of Iona.

> He could start a party in an empty room, and often did.
>
> DONALD DEWAR MP, Funeral address 20 May 1994

> The opportunity to serve our country is all we ask.
>
> JOHN SMITH's final words to a fund-raising dinner the night before his death

Smith, Sir Cyril *See* BIG CYRIL.

Smith Square The quiet square, 600 yards west of the Palace of WESTMINSTER with St John's Church in its centre, which for half a century was the nerve centre of British politics, housing the headquarters of both major political parties: TRANSPORT HOUSE, Labour headquarters from 1928 to 1982, and facing it Conservative CENTRAL OFFICE, where the Tories remained until moving to Victoria Street in 2004.

Adam Smith Institute A radical, right-wing THINK TANK, named after Adam Smith (*see* WEALTH OF NATIONS) which was set up under Margaret THATCHER's patronage to reflect and stimulate the thinking of her government, urging even more adventurous policies. Originally under the direction of Dr Madsen Pirie, it has remained a seedbed for new ideas, and has been given a respectful hearing by NEW LABOUR.

John Smith House The WALWORTH ROAD headquarters of the LABOUR PARTY, renamed in 1994 in honour of its lost leader; the title lapsed when Labour moved to MILLBANK, but was bestowed in 2000 on the party's Scottish headquarters in West Regent Street, Glasgow.

smoke and mirrors A telling metaphor for the ethereal nature of political power, and the way its substance can sometimes dissipate to reveal a void. The phrase was coined by the US columnist Jimmy Breslin, who wrote in 1975 of political power as an illusion:

> Mirrors and blue smoke, beautiful blue smoke rolling over the surface of highly polished mirrors, first a thin veil of blue smoke, then a thick cloud that suddenly dissolves into wisps of blue smoke, the mirrors catching it all, bouncing it back and forth. If somebody tells you how to look, there can be seen in the smoke great, magnificent shapes, castles and kingdoms, and maybe they can be yours.

The phrase soon entered the political vocabulary, and has also become associated with SPIN. *Compare* POTEMKIN VILLAGE.

smoke-filled room The selection of a candidate or adoption of a policy by a group of shadowy but powerful figures striking a deal away from the public gaze and in their own interests. The CAUCUS CLUB that ran colonial Boston in the 18th century has been called the original smoke-filled room, but the title was first bestowed in 1920 by the Ohio politician Harry Daugherty on the process that led to Warren HARDING receiving the Republican nomination:

> The convention will be deadlocked, and after the other candidates have gone the limit, some 12 or 15 men, worn out and bleary-eyed for lack of sleep, will sit down about 2 o'clock in the morning in a smoke-filled room in some hotel and decide the nomination. When that time comes, Harding will be selected.

The room in question was Suite 404–6 on the 13th floor of the Blackstone Hotel in Chicago, where Harding was summoned by fifteen Republican power brokers and asked to swear that there were no skeletons in his cupboard. After retiring for ten minutes to ring one or both of his mistresses, Harding returned to assure them there were not, and was handed the nomination. There followed the most corrupt ADMINISTRATION in American history.

smoking bimbo An attractive and probably air-headed young girl who is waiting for a critical moment in an election campaign to 'kiss and tell' about an affair – real or alleged – with one of the candidates. The phrase, coined after the exposure of Gary Hart in 1988 (*see* MONKEY BUSINESS), gained wider currency after the charges levelled by Gennifer Flowers against Bill CLINTON at the start of the 1992 campaign (*compare* BIMBO ERUPTION). It was a derivation of:

smoking gun One of many graphic phrases given to the political vocabulary by WATERGATE, which has entered the political vocabulary to signify any piece of evidence, previously unknown, that may come to light to provide incontrovertible evidence of guilt that may end a career. The original smoking gun was a tape of a conversation with his CHIEF OF STAFF H. R. Haldeman which proved that NIXON had ordered the Watergate COVER-UP six days after the break-in. It took a unanimous ruling by the SUPREME COURT before the WHITE HOUSE would hand over the tapes; within hours of the transcript's release, previously pro-Nixon members of the House Judiciary Committee threw their weight behind a first article of IMPEACHMENT.

Smoking Room The inner sanctum close to the CHAMBER of the HOUSE OF COMMONS, beyond the TEA ROOM, where MPs – customarily mainly Conservatives – may relax away from the pressures imposed by staff, visiting constituents and the press.

> The toffs' bar.
>
> RICHARD NEEDHAM MP (Con.)

Smoot-Hawley tariff The PROTECTIONIST measure passed by the US CONGRESS in 1930 that raised TARIFFS to their highest levels ever – the average duty rising from the already high FORDNEY-MCCUMBER levels to 60% – and was widely blamed for the severity of the GREAT DEPRESSION. The world economy was already tottering, not least because of the GREAT CRASH on Wall Street, but Smoot-Hawley was seen as the final shove. A thousand economists petitioned President HOOVER to VETO the BILL, but he ignored their warnings. By the end of the year, 33 countries had taken retaliatory action and world trade was spiralling into SLUMP. Sen. Reed Smoot, the Bill's co-sponsor, was the first Mormon senator when he took his seat in 1903 (*see* ADULTERY).

> It gave protectionism, with which Congress had been preoccupied for almost a century, a bad name and dethroned the tariff as a dominant issue in American politics.
>
> JAMES H. HUTSON, *To Make All Laws*

snail darter *See* SPOTTED OWL.

snake check WASHINGTON-speak for the last check through a political speech before it is delivered to make sure nothing counter-productive is lurking in it. The term comes from the night-time check in a camp to make sure the tents are clear of poisonous snakes.

snake in the tunnel The forerunner of the Exchange Rate Mechanism (ERM) of the European Monetary System (and nothing to do with the one-eyed trouser snake of the Australian entertainer Barry Humphries). The 'snake' applied to a graph of how the values of Europe's currencies had to perform against each other. If a currency rose above or below the 'tunnel' of permitted relative values, that member state would either have to take remedial economic measures, or make a formal DEVALUATION or REVALUATION. Edward HEATH's government joined it in 1972 as a preliminary to entering the European Community, but left after six weeks with sterling under strain.

snake oil salesman A political trickster, trading false promises for votes. The term originated in 19th-century America, where hucksters offered bogus cures and medicines (snake oil being one of them) at country fairs.

snap election In a system (like Britain's and those of many COMMONWEALTH countries) where the HEAD OF GOVERNMENT is free to determine when an election can be held, the sudden announcement of an election at a time when the political community is not expecting it. Such elections are usually called well before the last appointed date, at a moment when a government, usually one with a slim majority, believes it can capture the initiative and tighten its grip on power.

SNCC Student Non-Violent Co-Ordinating Committee. A CIVIL RIGHTS organisation founded by black and white student activists in Raleigh, North Carolina, in April 1960. In the early 1960s the SNCC joined other groups, such as CORE and Dr Martin Luther King's SCLC, to organise SIT-INS to desegregate lunch counters and other facilities in the South; it also campaigned to encourage black voter registration. The SNCC originally espoused King's non-violent philosophy, hence its title, but by 1966, under Stokely Carmichael, it had abandoned this for the militancy of BLACK POWER, supporting the revolutionary tactics of the BLACK PANTHERS, whose emblem it had adopted in 1965. It collapsed in 1969 when Carmichael's successor, Hubert 'Rap' Brown, was convicted of armed robbery.

> The only position for women in the SNCC is prone. STOKELY CARMICHAEL, 1965

snouts in the trough The graphic phrase for trade unions' determination to get at least their share of the economy – though with the unions now weaker it has come to apply to anyone, including politicians, who sees an opportunity to enrich themselves at others' expense. It was popularised in the late 1970s by Sid (later Lord) Weighell (1922–), general secretary of the National Union of Railwaymen. He told the LABOUR PARTY conference on 6 October 1978:

> If you want it to go out . . . that you now believe in the philosophy of the pig trough – that those with the biggest snouts get the largest share – then I reject it.

But during the election campaign the following April, Weighell said:

> I don't see how we can talk with Mrs THATCHER . . . I will say to the lads: 'Come on, get your snouts in the trough.'

SNP Scottish National Party. The party that since 1928 has campaigned for independence for Scotland as a sovereign nation, and since DEVOLUTION in 1999, which it supported as a halfway house, has been the principal OPPOSITION party in the SCOTTISH PARLIAMENT; it has the support of over a quarter of the country's voters. It was founded as the National Party of Scotland by a combination of disaffected ILP members, journalists, intellectuals and nationalist activists, and retains both the intellectual and the propaganda high ground. The party, which merged with others in 1934 to take its present form, won its first Parliamentary seat (briefly) at Motherwell in 1945, but had to wait until the late 1960s for lasting success. Disenchantment with the established UK parties, the decline of the Scottish economy and the discovery of North Sea oil gave the SNP a head of steam, and in 1967 Winifred Ewing (*see* MADAME ÉCOSSE) won the Hamilton BY-ELECTION from Labour. In 1970 the SNP doubled their vote at any previous election and took one seat (Mrs Ewing losing hers). In February 1974 they captured seven seats and that October won 30% of the vote, taking eleven seats and panicking Labour into embracing DEVOLUTION. When Labour held a REFERENDUM in March 1979, the SNP pressed for a 'Yes' vote while hinting that rejection of devolution would mean a general election and the end of the CALLAGHAN government. This duly happened, but the SNP, who tabled the crucial no-CONFIDENCE motion, were as heavy losers (*see* TURKEYS VOTING FOR AN EARLY CHRISTMAS). From 1979 the SNP slipped back as Labour, now in opposition, reasserted itself as Scotland's dominant party. It suffered strains and splits between its left wing and those anxious for gains outside the central belt (*see* Tartan TORIES). The party's fortunes revived toward the close of Margaret THATCHER's government, and the aggressive leadership of Alex Salmond and a sudden upsurge of media support for independence helped rebuild its support in the 1992 election, though still with only three seats. Labour's LANDSLIDE win in 1997 brought an immediate second referendum on devolution, with Salmond joining the campaign for a 'YES, YES' vote, and in the first elections for the SCOTTISH PARLIAMENT two years later the SNP polled strongly enough to force Labour into a COALITION with the LIBERAL DEMOCRATS. Salmond gave up his seat at Holyrood and John Swinney took over as leader, but the party's failure to break through in the 2001 general election or the 2003 Holyrood poll brought Salmond back in August 2004, leading the party from WESTMINSTER with the feisty Nicola Sturgeon his deputy in Edinburgh. At the 2005 general election the SNP recovered slightly to six seats.

> They dream of the politics of *Brigadoon*.
>
> DONALD DEWAR, Scotland's initial FIRST MINISTER

> The day the SNP's problems began was the day it took on its second member.
>
> FERGUS EWING MSP (SNP)

> Political maggots.
>
> DENNIS CANAVAN MP (Lab, later Ind. Lab)

so little done, so much to do The last words of Cecil Rhodes (1853–1902), financier, Prime Minister of Cape Colony 1890–96 and founder of Rhodesia (*see* CAPE TO CAIRO). His words have often been misquoted as 'So much to do, so little time.' Rhodes looked in his will to the 'ultimate recovery [by Britain] of the United States of America'. Some sources claim his actual last words were

> Turn me over, Jack.

S.O.24 Standing Order 24. The rule of the HOUSE OF COMMONS under which MPs may seek an EMERGENCY DEBATE. It entitles any member, at the end of QUESTION TIME, to apply to the SPEAKER for the suspension of STANDING ORDERS for a debate on a matter or urgency. It is for the Chair to decide whether the issue is so important that it should be given precedence over scheduled business. On the rare occasions that such a request is granted, the debate takes place that afternoon/evening or the following day. Confusingly, the number of this rule keeps changing; until the mid-1980s it was S.O.9, then S.O.20 and briefly S.O.23 before settling down as S.O.24.

Soames. l'affaire Soames The furore in 1969 caused by the LEAKing of uncomplimentary remarks about President DE GAULLE by Sir Christopher (later Lord) Soames (1920–87), British Ambassador in Paris and Sir Winston CHURCHILL's son-in-law. Soames went on to become Leader of the Lords under Margaret THATCHER and the Governor of Rhodesia who presided over the RETURN TO LEGALITY after the 1979 LANCASTER HOUSE AGREEMENT.

soapbox campaign An election campaign featuring informal street-corner speeches, delivered standing on a wooden box. Though the exception for many decades, it has remained a strand of British politics into the 21st century, Jack Straw speaking regularly from a soapbox in his Blackburn constituency. John MAJOR, who began his political career making such speeches in Brixton, took it up to great effect during his come-from-behind election campaign in 1992. Many Tory voters who turned out for his early WALKABOUTS complained that he did not speak; when the soapbox was produced from his campaign bus, all that changed. Neil KINNOCK observed scornfully: 'What's at issue in this election is not soap boxes that Prime Ministers stand on. It's cardboard boxes that people live in.' Major had the last laugh by winning that election, but in 1997 even the soapbox could not save him.

SOCA Serious and Organised Crime Agency. The nearest equivalent in Britain to the FBI, established in 2005. It was pulled together from elements of the police and the Customs and EXCISE to tackle drug-related crime, people-trafficking, money laundering and other major offences, though not terrorism. Its establishment followed a series of botched prosecutions by the Customs and Excise, and the realisation by Ministers that the separate agencies were struggling to keep up with these kinds of crime.

soccer moms The mothers of school-age children, so named because they made contact at soccer games to which they ferried their charges, who swung heavily to Bill CLINTON in 1992 and 1996 and back to the Republicans in 2000, putting George W. BUSH (by a hair's breadth) into the WHITE HOUSE. (*Compare* NASCAR DADS).

Social. Social Chapter The section of the MAASTRICHT TREATY which advanced Europe's social dimension and the functions and competency of the EU in social affairs; it was only to apply to eleven of the twelve signatories as Britain insisted on being exempted. In July 1993 a vote on the Chapter came within a whisker of bringing down John MAJOR's government; it only survived after demanding a vote of CONFIDENCE. Labour moved to ratify the Chapter within three days of winning the 1997 election.

> There can be no Europe without a social dimension. JACQUES DELORS

Social Charter The package of social measures devised and largely implemented by the EC in advance of MAASTRICHT. It dealt with such areas as maternity leave, night work and maximum hours. Margaret THATCHER refused to accept it, but UK Ministers then opted back into two-thirds of its provisions.

Social Contract or **Social Compact** Originally the blueprint for DEMOCRACY advocated in 1762 by the French philosopher Jean-Jacques Rousseau. It was based on the concept of the GENERAL WILL. Rousseau wrote:

> In order that the social compact may not be an empty formula, it tacitly includes the undertaking . . . that whoever refuses to obey the general will shall be compelled to do so by the whole body. This means nothing less than he will be forced to be free.

The idea terrified generations of conservatives, Metternich writing to Tsar Alexander I: 'You only have to mention a social contract and the revolution is made.'

In 1973 Harold WILSON adopted 'Social Contract' as the title for the agreement reached between the LABOUR PARTY and the TUC: Labour agreed to pursue economic and social policies that would benefit trade union members, and in return the unions promised to hold down wage claims. But Labour was elected the following year with the economy deteriorating, and in autumn 1975 the unions were obliged to accept a voluntary PRICES AND INCOMES POLICY. Later pacts between Labour and the unions were known as the 'Social Compact'.

> You might as well try to control a rutting elephant with a pea-shooter. LORD HAILSHAM

Social Credit An economic doctrine based on the ideas of an English engineer, Clifford Douglas (1879–1952), which spawned a political movement in Canada after 1930. Douglas believed that money, or 'social credit', should be distributed to give people access to the goods and services produced by a capitalist economy, and that lack of that credit provoked economic instability. During the GREAT DEPRESSION a Social Credit party came to power in Alberta in 1935 under the radio evangelist William Aberhart (1878–1943); backed by hard-pressed ranchers with heavy mortgages, it won nine successive elections, staying in power until 1971 while becoming increasingly conservative. British Columbia elected a Social Credit government in 1952. The federal party held seats at Ottawa until 1980; the Alberta party disbanded before Social Credit's final eclipse by the REFORM PARTY. *See also* CRÉDITISTES.

social democracy In the late 20th century a term for a socially-concerned and left-of-centre political stance, firmly anti-Communist, but originally a term commensurate with MARXISM. The term **Social Democrat** was adopted by Wilhelm Liebknecht and August Bebel when they founded Germany's Social Democratic and Labour Party in 1869. Britain's first Marxist party was the Social Democratic Federation, founded by H. M. Hyndman in 1881; it amalgamated with other groups to create the British Socialist Party in 1911 and the COMMUNIST PARTY of Great Britain in 1920. The rump of the SDF was dissolved in 1958.

> The main characteristics of the tactics of social democracy are not 'invented' but are the result of a continuous series of great creative acts of the elementary class struggle.
>
> ROSA LUXEMBURG (1871–1919)

As social democracy moved toward the centre, STALIN denounced it as 'the moderate wing of fascism'. In Britain, it reached its apotheosis with the SDP, or maybe with NEW LABOUR.

social exclusion The effective exclusion of the underprivileged from the most fruitful and satisfying elements of society by virtue of poverty, poor education, housing or health. Very much a 1990s concept though with deep roots in both SOCIALIST and PATERNALIST traditions, the tackling of social exclusion and the raising-up of the UNDERCLASS were key commitments of Tony BLAIR's Labour government. Though child poverty, fuel poverty among the elderly, deprived communities and long-term structural unemployment were all targeted to some effect, it was unclear whether this was due to the specific policies like the NEW DEAL or the strong state of the economy under Gordon BROWN.

Social Fund The fund devised by Margaret THATCHER's government, and implemented by John MAJOR as social security minister, to make loans – instead of the previous grants – to the needy poor. The payments were made whenever there was proven need; the Social Fund is CASH-LIMITED.

social justice Another 1990s concept from left of centre, though maybe a case of old wine in new bottles: the notion that economic and other imbalances in society had to be tackled as a moral imperative. The theme was taken up vigorously by John SMITH as Labour leader; he set up a **Commission on Social Justice** which in its report, after his death in 1994, set out challenges for a Labour government in tackling inequalities and fighting family and child poverty. Ten years on, the IPPR which had produced the original report said that while NEW LABOUR had taken large numbers of children out of poverty, the gap between rich and poor had widened overall.

social market *See* MARKET.

social ownership Ownership of industries or enterprises by the community. The term embraces NATIONALISATION, but covers a number of other ways in which the public can be STAKEHOLDERS.

social security The system of payments made by modern states to cushion the effects of poverty, unemployment, disability and other forms of disadvantage on members of the community. In America the 1935 Social Security Act was a central feature of the NEW DEAL; but the decision initially to finance the scheme totally from employees' contributions slowed the economy. Social security has expanded over the decades from a small number of private sector workers to almost all employees; MEDICARE was added in 1965 and COLAs in 1972. The British system, pioneered by LLOYD GEORGE and made comprehensive in Attlee's WELFARE STATE, has always required contributions from employee *and* employer and is thus disliked by business as a STEALTH TAX. The cost of social security in every industrialised country is expected to become increasingly hard to support during the 21st century as retirees become a steadily larger proportion of the population compared with those in work.

socialised medicine A generally unfriendly American term for any system of health care which is administered or financed by the state instead of through the MARKET. Efforts by successive Democratic administrations to broaden such care out from MEDICARE and MEDICAID has met fierce resistance from the medical and business ESTABLISHMENT, to which schemes such as Britain's NHS and those operating in parts of Canada are anathema.

socialism The most durable and broadly-based of the political doctrines to have emerged from the Industrial Revolution. Its essence is common provision for those with less by those with more, with common ownership of the economy (or elements of it) and an ultimate goal of equality. One of its early champions, Keir Hardie, declared: 'Defeat is not in the Socialist dictionary' – a theme taken up by *The* RED FLAG. It has also traditionally had a strong visionary and romantic element (*see* JERUSALEM). COMMUNISTS have seen socialism as an ultimate objective, but have been unwilling or unable to achieve it. Indeed LENIN wrote:

> We cannot outline socialism. What socialism will look like when it takes on its final form we do not know and cannot say.

Despite its intellectual adherents, socialism has inherently been a mass movement. First advocated in coherent form in France by Louis Blanc (1811–82) at much the same time as MARX and Engels were developing Communism, it developed differently country by country, with varying degrees of militancy. In Britain it became the ideology of the LABOUR PARTY; it drew inspiration from Marxism, OWENISM, religious nonconformism and trade unionism, and its heart was CLAUSE FOUR. Socialism in the US has never been able to shrug off connotations of UN-AMERICANISM. Earl WARREN captured the American mindset when he observed: 'Many people consider the things government does for them to be social progress, but they consider the things government does for others as socialism.' Nevertheless Eugene Debs (*see* CONVICT 2273) and Norman Thomas of the SOCIALIST LABOUR PARTY polled up to 2 million votes as Presidential candidates, and one socialist was elected to CONGRESS in 1990.

The deepest division between socialists has been over how far to go in achieving their aims. Georges Sorel (1847–92) maintained that 'socialism would not continue to exist without an apology for violence', and Rosa Luxembourg declared: 'The victory of socialism will not descend like rain from heaven.' The American trade unionist William HAYWOOD insisted that 'no socialist can be a law-abiding citizen'. But Claude-Frédéric Bastiat (1801–50) argued: 'You would oppose law to socialism. But it is the law that socialism invokes. It aspires to legal, not extralegal plunder.' To George Bernard Shaw socialism meant 'equality of income or nothing', to H. G. Wells it was 'no more or less than a criticism of the idea of property in the light of public good', while the more prosaic Herbert Morrison asserted:

> Socialism is what a Labour government does.

In the ATTLEE years 'equality of opportunity' was the watchword, while Harold WILSON asserted: 'If there is one word I would use to identify modern socialism, it is "science".'

Socialism has had its fair share of critics. John Maynard KEYNES, in the 1920s, termed it 'a dusty survival of a plan to meet the problems of 50 years ago, based on a misunderstanding of what someone said 100 years ago'; the *Detroit Journal* tagged it 'Bolshevism with a shave'. To CHURCHILL socialism was 'the philosophy of failure, the creed of ignorance and the gospel of envy'; the rumbustious Tory Lord Hailsham saw it as 'an excellent way of sharing misery, but not a good way of creating abundance', and Sir Gilbert Longden argued that 'since excellence is the first casualty of equality, socialism is the standard-bearer of the second-rate'. More recently Norman Tebbit declared socialism 'not dead but brain-dead', and numerous Tories have claimed the line: 'Socialism is workable only in heaven, where it isn't needed, and hell, where they've got it.' Margaret THATCHER denounced socialism as 'an alien creed', and Frank Dobson told a Labour SELECTION CONFERENCE: 'The two greatest obstacles to socialism are Margaret Thatcher and Camden housing department;' he gave the credit for the one-liner to his colleague Jack Straw.

As to socialists themselves, George Orwell, after his bitter experiences in Spain, declared: 'As with the Christian religion, the worst advertisement for socialism is its adherents.' And the playwright Tom Stoppard wrote: '"Socialists treat their servants with respect and then wonder why they vote Conservative.' Britain's CONSERVATIVE PARTY for decades insisted on referring to Labour as 'the Socialists', and Tory-controlled newspapers followed suit, making the study of election results mildly confusing.

socialism by the back door Margaret THATCHER's characterisation of the plans of Jacques DELORS for a more comprehensive EUROPEAN COMMUNITY, especially in the social field.

socialism in one country The doctrine that the SOVIET UNION should develop as a Communist state on a national, rather than an international, basis; it was at first scorned by LENIN and STALIN, but was subsequently adopted by Stalin in opposition to TROTSKY's doctrine of PERMANENT REVOLUTION.

Socialism In Our Time The policy statement issued by Britain's Independent

Labour Party (ILP) in 1927. Its main proposal, based on the views of the KEYNESIAN economist J. A. Hobson, was that a future Labour government should introduce a 'living wage' to keep up demand and maintain full employment. For two years Ramsay MACDONALD was pressed to adopt this policy, but he opted for a less radical approach.

socialism is the language of priorities A watchword for realistic socialist progress sounded by Aneurin BEVAN, speaking for ATTLEE's government, at Labour's 1950 party conference. His actual words were:

> The language of priorities is the language of socialism.

Within months, Bevan had resigned over the CABINET's decision to impose charges for NHS false teeth and spectacles.

socialism with a human face *See* COMMUNISM.

African Socialism The doctrine and style of government evolved in post-colonial Africa by Julius Nyerere (1922–), president of Tanzania for a quarter of a century from 1962, and others. To its supporters it is a vigorous and appropriate means of caring for the people, to many Westerners a byword for stagnation and decline; its one undisputed success has been to reduce tribalism as a disruptive force.

Arab Socialism The combination of Arab nationalism and State direction of the economy pioneered from the 1950s by Egypt's Gamel Abdul Nasser and taken up by other leaders ranging from the idealistic (Tunisia's Habib Bourgiba) to the psychopathic (SADDAM HUSSEIN). The title was as much a nod in the direction of the Soviet Union in the hope of attracting patronage as a reflection of any deep sympathy for MARXIST ideals.

Christian Socialism The catch-all name for a variety of movements and tendencies that have promoted socialism as the Kingdom of God on Earth, or regarded it as identical with the social teachings of Christ. MARX and Engels scorned it as 'the holy water with which the priest consecrates the heart-burnings of the aristocrat', and Pope Pius IX scathingly dismissed it as 'a contradiction in terms'. It has had considerable influence in Britain through its advocates in the LABOUR PARTY, most recently John SMITH and Tony BLAIR.

creeping socialism President EISENHOWER's categorisation of the NEW DEAL policies of Franklin D. ROOSEVELT and Harry S TRUMAN. Opposing continued expansion of the TVA, EISENHOWER said on 11 June 1953:

> I believe that for the past 20 years there has been a creeping socialism spreading in the United States.

democratic socialism The ethos of Britain's LABOUR PARTY for most of its history, and of most western European socialist parties since 1945. The term emphasises a contrast with the centralist nature of Communism, and with SOCIAL DEMOCRACY which lacks the cutting edge of a concrete ideology. Yet according to the Australian Russell Prowse, 'the term "Democratic Socialism" makes as much sense as "pregnant virginity".'

designer socialism Not quite the same as RADICAL CHIC, designer socialism is a term current from the 1980s suggesting a watered-down ideology composed of trendy off-the-peg notions with superficial, glitzy appeal.

Future of Socialism, The The seminal book, published in 1956 by the British Labour politician Anthony Crosland (1918–77), which argued that socialist parties would increasingly have to veer away from ideology to concentrate on provision for the disadvantaged. It was attacked from the left as a GAITSKELLITE heresy, but since the mid-1980s Labour has adopted a very similar stance.

gas and water socialism In Britain, the powerful strain in the LABOUR PARTY before and after WORLD WAR II involved in the provision of ever-improving public services through municipal socialism (*see below*) or state ownership. The powerful base Labour established between the wars in the government of London and other major cities heightened this emphasis on the community as provider, through its elected representatives. After Labour took office in 1945 most of the municipal services were transferred to the state (*see* Morrisonian NATIONALISATION) with an immediate loss of ACCOUNTABILITY, though with scope for national provision and economies of scale.

guild socialism A movement, prominent in early 20th-century Britain, that sought to reorganise each industry under workers' guilds, creating a form of WORKERS' CONTROL and with close similarities to CO-OPERATIVES. Its ideological impetus came from J. A. Penty's *The Restoration of the Guild System* (1906) which proposed reviving the medieval craft guilds; this argument was taken up by A. R. Orage and S. G. Hobson, who developed a comprehensive blueprint for modern guilds based on existing trade unions, with a strongly SYNDICALIST tinge. Orage and Hobson maintained that the guild system would avoid the BUREAUCRACY inherent in a centralised socialist state. The National Guilds League, founded in 1915, promoted the idea within the unions and at first made a considerable impact. But its influence waned as the unions became firmly politicised at the end of WORLD WAR I. A National Building Guild enjoyed some success building low-cost houses, but petered out when its government contract ended.

municipal socialism The doctrine and practice under which elected local authorities create as much of a CRADLE TO GRAVE support system for their people as central government will permit. Some Labour councils in Britain have diversified beyond transport systems and comprehensive social services to back – and even attempt to own – local industries.

Save America from Socialism The Republicans' campaign slogan in 1936 when they put forward Alf Landon (*see* KANSAS COOLIDGE) to challenge Franklin D. ROOSEVELT and his NEW DEAL.

scientific socialism The term used for COMMUNISM by the founders of the movement, and made much of in the 1970s and '80s by the Soviet leadership and leaders of Communist regimes in eastern Europe.

> These two great discoveries, the materialistic conception of history and the revelation of the secret of capitalistic production through surplus-value, we owe to Marx. With these discoveries, socialism becomes a science.
>
> FRIEDRICH ENGELS (1820–95)

Socialist International The body, initially comprising mainly Western European parties, which brings together the world's principal democratic socialist movements. Its affiliates in central and eastern Europe have for the most part struggled to make an impact since the collapse of Communism.

Socialist Organiser A far-left group, based like MILITANT on a magazine, which in the 1980s caused the leadership of Britain's LABOUR PARTY considerable embarrassment, resulting in a number of its activists being expelled from the party; it was strongest in London.

Socialist Labour Party The left-wing splinter party founded in 1996 by Arthur Scargill (*see* KING ARTHUR), who accused Labour under Tony BLAIR of embracing the 'devil of capitalism'. It attracted a few hard left trade unionists who used it as a base for industrial militancy, but made no electoral impact.

Socialist Party of America Founded in 1901 after a split in the less successful **Socialist Labor Party**, the only major US left-wing party to flourish for a significant period in the 20th century. It was the party of Victor Berger, Eugene Debs and Norman Thomas.

socialist realism The approved – and only permitted – method of artistic expression in the SOVIET UNION from the 1930s, devoted to building and glorifying the socialist achievement. Though it produced some interesting results at first, e.g. in the work of Andrei Goncharov, the style degenerated into formulaic representations of the alleged heroic successes of the Soviet economy and society, devoid of artistic and literary merit. Its mirror-image was a rigid censorship of the arts.

Socialist Workers' Party (SWP) Britain's most active party to the left of Labour from the mid-1970s, steadily eclipsing its rival the WORKERS' REVOLUTIONARY PARTY. It grew from International Socialism, a sect originally within the LABOUR PARTY founded by Tony Cliff c. 1960. It places particular emphasis on ANTI-RACISM and opposition to curbs on ASYLUM and immigration, but makes sure its posters are prominent at any left-wing demonstration; it builds on this impression of strength by not contesting elections.

> We don't pretend we believe in the Parliamentary system. We bloody well don't believe in it.
>
> SWP spokesman DUNCAN HALLAS, 1982

> The SWP are the worst kind of racists – liberal racists. They are the ones who believe they have to help blacks. They don't believe blacks can help themselves. LINTON KWEZI JOHNSON

We are all socialists nowadays A remark attributed both to King Edward VII when PRINCE OF WALES, and to Sir William Harcourt (1827–1904), Liberal Chancellor of the Exchequer. It was made in 1895, when many in the political community felt – and some regretted – that a lasting and progressive CONSENSUS had been achieved on social and economic issues.

socialised medicine A generally hostile US term for a system of free medical care financed by the state, with doctors paid by the agency running the system rather than by their patients. Used habitually to denigrate such systems in Britain and Canada, it is also turned by conservatives against any scheme to improve health care for America's less fortunate – starting with the nevertheless costly MEDICAID and MEDICARE.

society The totality of a nation's population, encompassing the way in which its members interact with each other. Politicians and sociologists during the 20th century gave labels to a number of the social climates in which they believed their own society to be operating: the **affluent society** of the late 1950s and '60s (primarily a British term), the CLASSLESS SOCIETY as the regimentation of heavy industry declined, the GREAT SOCIETY aspired to by Lyndon B. JOHNSON, the **permissive society** with its sexually liberal attitudes said by conservatives to have been created by reforms and cultural changes of the 1960s.

there is no such thing as society The remark made by Margaret THATCHER early in her premiership which, to her critics, encapsulated her view that everyone should be left to fend for themselves and that the community should take no responsibility for the weakest; they saw it as the benchmark of an ideology which caused severe strains within a social structure whose existence she would not acknowledge. Mrs Thatcher claimed that her comment, in a women's magazine interview, had not been fully understood; her argument was that 'It's our duty to look after ourselves and then look after our neighbour', and that as economic wealth grew people would take more responsibility for those around them. In short,

> Society for me was not an excuse, it was a source of obligation.

Socks The black and white cat who moved into the WHITE HOUSE with the CLINTON family in January 1993, and on their departure eight years later went to live with the former President's loyal secretary Betty Currie. Chelsea Clinton's parents had bought Socks in 1990 to help her over the death of her dog Zeke. The close media attention Socks attracted after her master's election led to pet psychiatrists offering to help her adjust to the high profile she would have in WASHINGTON after the tranquillity of Little Rock. Within months of Socks' arrival, the ROSE GARDEN corridor smelt of cat; during Bill Clinton's second term, she had to coexist with BUDDY.

Soda One of the family terriers (the other was Whisky) of Chris PATTEN, the final Governor of Hong Kong until 1997, which went missing in November 1992, soon after arriving. Australia's Foreign Minister Gareth Evans (*see* DRAFT), who was visiting the colony, suggested Soda might have been served up as a delicacy by the Hong Kong Chinese; he was swiftly forced to apologise, and the dog turned up safe and sound. Whisky hit the headlines in May 1994 when he bit a Chinese repairman at the Governor's mansion.

sofa style The informal style of decision-making followed by Tony BLAIR and his inner circle in the run-up to the 2003 IRAQ WAR, and roundly condemned in the BUTLER REPORT into how unreliable intelligence on WEAPONS OF MASS DESTRUCTION was over-estimated as a pretext for war. Lord Butler, as a former CABINET SECRETARY, was particularly concerned that decisions were apparently reached at informal meetings at which no MINUTES were kept. Blair acknowledged this failing, and undertook that in any future conflict he would set up a proper WAR CABINET.

sofa summit *See* SUMMIT.

soft A party's electoral support if less than enthusiastic, being less likely to turn out in an election. As in 'the Tory vote in Yorkshire is looking soft'. Jody Powell, Jimmy CARTER's press secretary, defined the soft vote as 'those who don't care enough to come vote for you in the rain'.

soft landing The term coined by political and economic commentators c. 1989 for the hoped-for stabilisation of the UK economy after the BOOM of the previous two years and the raising of interest rates by Chancellor Nigel Lawson (1932–) when it was evident the economy was dangerously OVERHEATING. John MAJOR, who succeeded Lawson when he resigned in October 1989, confided to the author that he wondered if there would be a landing at all, as the record 15% interest rate took time to bite. But by the time he became Prime Minister late in 1990 it was clear there would be a very HARD LANDING.

soft left A pejorative comparison first made in the early 1980s between Britain's committed, BENNITE, HARD LEFT and the more moderate, TRIBUNITE, left of the Labour Party, notably Neil KINNOCK, who instinctively backed Michael FOOT. The term lost its sting as the hard left, which at WESTMINSTER coalesced into the CAMPAIGN GROUP, lost its influence under Kinnock's leadership of the party.

soft money US campaign contributions that circumvent the 1974 Federal Election Campaign Act, which limits candidates to direct contributions from individuals of

$1500, or $5000 from corporations, labour unions or PACs. Soft money is channelled through political parties, which can put out advertisements attacking the beneficiary's opponent or diffuse the money for local operations such as voter registration.

Soldier's Song, A (Irish *Amhran na bhFiann*) The national anthem since 1926 of the IRISH REPUBLIC. It was written in English and Irish in 1907 by Patrick Kearney, the music jointly with Patrick Heeney. Until the mid-1980s it was an offence to play the tune in NORTHERN IRELAND lest it inflame SECTARIAN feeling. The first stanza is:

> Soldiers are we, whose lives are pledged to Ireland,
> Some have come from a land beyond the wave.
> Sworn to be free, no more our ancient sireland,
> Shall shelter the despot or the slave.
> Tonight we man the *bearna bhoil* (gap of danger);
> In Erin's cause, come well or weal;
> 'Mid cannon's roar and rifle's peal,
> We'll chant a soldier's song.'

Soledad brothers A *cause célèbre* for US liberals and black revolutionaries, arising from the shooting of the BLACK POWER activist George Jackson on 28 August 1971 as he tried to escape from San Quentin prison in California. The belief persisted in the radical community that Jackson had been encouraged to escape to give a pretext for the shooting. Jackson had become a hero to opponents of Martin Luther KING's creed of NON-VIOLENCE through his book *Soledad Brother*, written in the prison of that name 25 miles south of San Francisco. His parents were less understanding, Jackson writing to his mother on 26 March 1967:

> You don't want us to resist and defeat our enemies. What is wrong with you, Mama?

solid South *See* SOUTH.

solidarity (1) The principle of 'one for all and all for one', particularly among trade unionists and between left-wing international movements. (2) In EUROPEAN UNION jargon, the assurance by nations or the EU itself of the means to provide each family with its basic needs. (3) The free, strongly Catholic trade union movement in Poland, which challenged the Communist system and survived persecution to take power. Solidarity (Pol. *Solidarnośc*) was born of the 1979 Gdansk shipyard strike over the sacking of the workers' leader Lech Walesa (1943–) from his job as an electrician. In 1980 he was re-employed, and that August founded Solidarity. In November 1980 Solidarity forced the authorities to register it as a trade union, with rights of free association and COLLECTIVE BARGAINING. But its rising popularity (it soon gained 10 million members) and the effectiveness of the strikes it organised for better conditions alarmed the government of General Jaruzelski, and in 1981 it was banned and martial law declared. Walesa was imprisoned, but released the next year, though Communist efforts to smear his reputation continued. With the Kremlin in retreat under Mikhail GORBACHEV, Solidarity stood its ground and in 1989 took a stake in Eastern Europe's first non-Communist government for four decades. In 1990 Walesa was elected President in Poland's first free elections for 45 years; however, neither his power nor the all-conquering strength of Solidarity endured long in the post-Communist era. Walesa finally broke with Solidarity in 2005.

> He who once became aware of the power of Solidarity and who breathed the air of freedom will not be crushed.
>
> LECH WALESA

Solomon Binding As with LAURA NORDER, not a person but a political idea: the 'solemn and binding' agreement the trade unions offered Harold WILSON's government in 1969 in return for the abandonment of the reforms advocated in IN PLACE OF STRIFE. There was widespread scepticism, which proved justified, over the unions' ability or readiness to put their house in order, and before long the phrase had turned into this fictitious individual, scornfully created by Denis HEALEY.

some of you may not be here in 30 to 40 years, but I will be and I want to be free The dramatic words to the 1977 CONSERVATIVE PARTY conference of the 16-year-old Yorkshire schoolboy William HAGUE, which delighted Margaret THATCHER despite the media's comparison of Hague with the young Harold WILSON. Twenty years later, Hague would in turn become leader of the party, only to lead it to an overwhelming defeat by Labour in 2001.

something must be done The verdict of King Edward VIII (1894–1972) on the GREAT DEPRESSION, given on a visit to a closed-down steelworks in South Wales during his brief reign in 1936. His remarks embarrassed the BALDWIN government, but gave him lasting popularity in the Welsh valleys. The King said:

> These works brought all these people here. Something must be done to find them work.

something of the night *See* NIGHT.

Sonnenfeldt doctrine America's acceptance during the FORD administration that encouraging resistance to Communism by citizens of Europe's Soviet SATELLITES would bring a brutal crackdown, not freedom. The doctrine was proposed in 1976 by Helmut Sonnenfeldt, a senior member of the NATIONAL SECURITY COUNCIL. After the brutal Soviet suppression of the 1956 HUNGARIAN UPRISING with the loss of 7000 lives, Congressional hearings blamed the US-sponsored Radio Free Europe for inciting the people to rebel. The intervention by WARSAW PACT countries to end the PRAGUE SPRING of 1968 reinforced the West's impotence in face of the BREZHNEV DOCTRINE. The Sonnenfeldt doctrine also reflected the NIXON/Ford ADMINISTRATION's belief that a less hawkish line toward Communism would aid DÉTENTE; the CARTER administration abandoned it in reaction to the Soviet invasion of Afghanistan at the end of 1978.

sound. sound bite A term first used by American TV and radio journalists c. 1968, and seized on by political managers, for a brief quote making the maximum political impact. The proliferation of the sound bite stems from research showing that most viewers and listeners can absorb information for at most 30 seconds. In 1968 a Presidential candidate could speak uninterrupted during the average interview for 43 seconds; by 1988 it was down to 9 seconds. Aware of this, SPIN DOCTORS began crafting phrases of just a few words encapsulating a candidate's core message which they were schooled to get into any interview as early as possible, and then repeat. In 1992 some networks refused to let sound bites set the agenda and insisted that any statement broadcast must last 20 seconds; the experiment failed and even shorter attention spans are now being catered for.

> When NIXON went out to make a statement in the WHITE HOUSE briefing room, he insisted that he be given one hundred words – and we had to count 'em.
>
> DAVID GERGEN (1942–), later Communications Director in the REAGAN and CLINTON White Houses

sound on A mainly British term for a legislator's reliability on a particular issue, e.g. 'he's sound on Europe'.

> Most MPs are not clever – it is just enough that they are sound.
>
> JULIAN CRITCHLEY MP (Con.)

source The lifeblood of political journalism, a person supposedly or actually 'in the LOOP' who will tell a reporter what they know, generally under the cloak of anonymity.

> We will give immunity to a very good source as long as the information he offers is better than what we have on him
>
> WASHINGTON columnist DREW PEARSON

sources close to the Prime Minister The phrase traditionally used by WESTMINSTER journalists to describe the DOWNING STREET press secretary, who under LOBBY convention could not be named unless he chose to speak 'on the record'. There has been little need for it since Alastair Campbell, Tony BLAIR's initial spokesman, allowed remarks made at the twice-daily Lobby briefings to be sourced to the Prime Minister's official spokesman (*see* PMOS) and had the text circulated on the Internet. When the phrase does surface these days, it normally denotes some other senior personage in NUMBER TEN.

informed source The phrase used in political journalism for an insider who provides information but does not wish to be named; the writer will naturally wish to convey the impression that the provider is exceptionally well-placed.

> Nobody believes the official spokesman, but everybody trusts an unidentified source.
>
> Gerald FORD's press secretary RON NESSEN

South, the The area covered by the states of the CONFEDERACY, who were on the losing side in America's CIVIL WAR, and that part of the United States which had embraced and perpetuated slavery. Distrusted by Northerners for a century after the conflict, the South came of age politically through the election of Presidents Lyndon B. JOHNSON, a Texan who pushed through CIVIL RIGHTS, Jimmy CARTER and Bill CLINTON, former Governors of Georgia and Arkansas respectively. The distinctive culture of the South has survived and been enriched by the belated ending of racial SEGREGATION.

South Lawn The expanse of grass beneath the south portico of the WHITE HOUSE, facing toward the ELLIPSE, on which WELCOMING CEREMONIES are held when world leaders arrive to meet the President.

> Someone asked why we didn't put a stop to Sam [Donaldson] shouting out questions at us when we're out on the South Lawn. We can't. If we did, the starlings would come back.
>
> RONALD REAGAN

South Sea Bubble The first, and still the most spectacular, scandal in the City of

London despite having taken place as long ago as 1720, and one that had profound political consequences. The collapse of the South Sea Company, founded under Royal charter in 1711, after it first took on the government's entire war debt and then used its capital reserves to inflate its stock price caused widespread ruin, implicated George I, his mistresses and his Ministers, and paved the way for the WHIG supremacy from 1721 to 1942, during which Robert Walpole, who had devised a scheme to extract Britain from the mess, established himself as the first undisputed PRIME MINISTER. In an uncanny foreshadowing of the dot.com bubble of the late 1990s, share promoters at the height of the South Sea Bubble were able to raise capital from speculators for projects of total vagueness and improbability.

Solid South The power base of conservative Democrats in the century following the CIVIL WAR, with the Republicans discredited among white voters as the party of blacks, CARPETBAGGERS and RECONSTRUCTION. Between 1876 and 1920, the Republicans failed to carry a single Southern state in a Presidential election. The almost automatic re-election of INCUMBENTS, combined with the SENIORITY system, gave its representatives a stranglehold on Congressional committee chairmanships until the 1970s, when the posts were opened to election. The term became current in the 1880 election, when after the withdrawal of federal troops southern whites were free to 'vote as they shot' in the Civil War, and Republicans warned that the old Confederacy, with a few Northern allies, could win control of the federal government.

Southern strategy The strategy followed by REPUBLICAN Presidential candidates from Barry Goldwater onwards, to capture the WHITE HOUSE with a conservative platform that would win key Southern states from the Democrats, and critical votes in the ELECTORAL COLLEGE. At the heart of the strategy initially were an emphasis on STATES' RIGHTS and a reluctance to expand CIVIL RIGHTS legislation. Under the REAGAN and BUSH presidencies this has moved to embracing the agenda of the RELIGIOUS RIGHT and opposing GUN CONTROL.

sovereign A supreme ruler or head; specifically, the monarch of the United Kingdom and those COMMONWEALTH countries which acknowledge the CROWN. King Charles I held that 'a subject and a sovereign are clear different things', and paid for his belief with his head.

> Obedience to the laws and to the Sovereign is obedience to a higher Power, divinely instituted for the good of the people, not of the Sovereign, who has equal duties and obligations.
>
> Queen VICTORIA

sovereignty The 'absolute and perpetual' power of a nation to control its own affairs. In the United Kingdom that power is customarily vested in the CROWN IN PARLIAMENT, though some of that sovereignty has since 1973 been 'pooled' within what is now the EUROPEAN UNION. CHURCHILL anticipated this development, saying in 1950: 'National sovereignty is not inviolable, and it may be resolutely diminished for the sake of all the men in all lands finding their way home together.' Soon after, Anthony EDEN observed: 'Every successive scientific discovery makes greater nonsense of the old-time conceptions of sovereignty.' Margaret THATCHER, especially in her anti-MAASTRICHT mood after losing office, did not agree. In America the concept of sovereignty relates both to federal and (arguably) to state jurisdictions. Henry Clay declared in 1850: 'I owe allegiance to two sovereignties; one is to the sovereignty of this Union and the other is to the sovereignty of the state of Kentucky.' However Abraham LINCOLN, with the CIVIL WAR looming, asserted: 'Much has been said about the "sovereignty" of the states, but the word even is not in the National Constitution nor, it is believed, in any of the state Constitutions.'

sovereignty association The formula for a looser relationship between Quebec and Canada, amounting to political but not economic independence, which the separatist PQ premier René Levesque put to a REFERENDUM on 20 May 1980. After a strong campaign against the proposal by federal Prime Minister Pierre TRUDEAU, 59.2% of electors voted 'Non', including 52% of French speakers.

popular sovereignty The theory, embodied in the US CONSTITUTION, that sovereignty rests in the people and not in a crowned head. In 1795 George III removed Charles James Fox from the PRIVY COUNCIL for giving the toast: 'Our sovereign, the people!' The Austrian statesman Metternich later dismissed the concept because 'the sovereignty of the people must be delegated by them to an authority other than the sovereign'.

Soviet A local council or workplace body elected by workers, peasants or soldiers, and a fundamental of the BOLSHEVIK state established by LENIN in Russia from 1917. The system came to cover the entire Union of Soviet Socialist Republics (SOVIET UNION), with the higher tiers containing representatives of those below.

Soviet bloc The term which gained currency after WORLD WAR II for the voting bloc of Communist states in the UNITED NATIONS headed by, and dictated to by, the Soviet Union, and the geographical entity they comprised. The term lapsed in the 1970s with Communist China's admission to the UN.

Soviet Union (Russ. *Sovietski Soyuz:* Union of Soviet Socialist Republics). The state founded formally by LENIN in December 1922 in the wake of the RUSSIAN REVOLUTION, which was presided over with varying degrees of brutality by STALIN, Khrushchev and BREZHNEV, emerging like the United States as a SUPERPOWER after being tested in WORLD WAR II. Its NUCLEAR capability, its immense conventional military power, its stranglehold over its SATELLITES and its appeal to the developing world made it America's equal for two decades, even acquiring an edge in space with the launch of the first *Sputnik* in 1957, but its political and especially its economic structures atrophied and it collapsed in the autumn of 1991. As the Soviet Union ossified but remained threatening under Brezhnev, President Carter's NATIONAL SECURITY ADVISER Dr Zbigniew Brzezinski termed it 'the only nation entirely surrounded by hostile Communist countries', and Denis HEALEY as 'Upper Volta with rockets'. After the brief interregna of Yuri Andropov and Konstantin Chernenko, Mikhail GORBACHEV from 1985 abandoned key aspects of Soviet policy and ideology, bringing an end to the COLD WAR. His inability to reform the economy prompted the reactionary KREMLIN COUP of 19 August 1991, but while Gorbachev defeated it, power now passed to the Soviet Union's successor republics.

> Judged by every standard which history has applied to governments, the Soviet government of Russia is one of the most tyrannical that has ever existed in the world. It accords no political rights. It rules by terror. It punishes political opinions. It suppresses free speech. It tolerates no newspaper but its own. It persecutes Christianity with a zeal and a cunning unmatched since the times of the Roman emperors. It is engaged at this moment in trampling down the peoples of Georgia and exterminating their leaders by hundreds.
> CHURCHILL, 1924

> Under Lenin the Soviet Union was like a religious revival, under Stalin like a prison, under Khrushchev like a circus and under Brezhnev like the US Post Office.
> Dr ZBIGNIEW BRZEZINSKI to the US Cabinet, 7 November 1977

Supreme Soviet The ultimate executive authority of the Soviet Union, the peak of the pyramid of the system of Soviets.

All power to the Soviets! A slogan adopted by BOLSHEVIK forces during the OCTOBER REVOLUTION of 1917, and taken up officially by the new Soviet state.

Sox Act Corporate America's nickname for the SARBANES-OXLEY ACT.

space. Space Cadet The nickname accorded to Jerry (Edmund G.) Brown (1938–) as he developed from an environmentally-sensitive Governor of California who as the spiritual heir of Robert F. KENNEDY made a strong pitch for the Presidency in 1976, into a long-shot candidate in 1992 with an almost New Age philosophy and a yen for direct public ACCOUNTABILITY (*see* 1–800).

> Edward G. (Jerry) Brown Jr, the former Governor of California who has been alternately labelled a visionary and a 'space cadet', was elected chairman of the state Democratic Party late Sunday.
> *New York Times*, 13 February 1989

space race The defence-related rivalry between the COLD WAR'S SUPERPOWERS to get a man into space, a man to the Moon and then onward to interplanetary travel. The launch of the first Soviet *Sputnik* in 1957 began the race, and John F. KENNEDY accelerated it when he told a JOINT SESSION of CONGRESS on 25 May 1961:

> I believe that this nation should commit itself to achieving the goal, before this decade is out, of landing a man on the Moon and returning him safely to earth.

On 20 July 1969, when America won the race to the Moon, Richard NIXON declared:

> For years politicians have promised the moon. I'm the first one to be able to deliver it.

Spaceship Earth The concept of our planet as a spacecraft that carries its inhabitants as passengers. The implication is that we are travelling through space alone, with our survival depending on a fragile ecology with limited natural resources and threatened by a polluted environment. The idea dates back at least to 1965 when Adlai STEVENSON, in his last speech to UNESCO, said:

> We travel together, passengers on a little space ship, dependent on its vulnerable reserves of air and soil.

It was popularised by the *Operating Manual for Spaceship Earth* (1969), by R. Buckminster Fuller, the US architect who developed the geodesic dome, and was influential in creating the GREEN movement.

> The most important thing about Spaceship Earth: an instruction book didn't come with it.
> R. BUCKMINSTER FULLER

> There are no passengers on Spaceship Earth. Only crew.
> MARSHALL McLUHAN (1911–81)

SPAD WHITEHALL shorthand for SPECIAL ADVISER, as in 'I've just been in to see the Health SPADs'.

Spanish. Spanish-American War The five-month conflict in 1898, triggered by sensationalist reports of Spanish 'atrocities' in Cuba, which resulted in America gaining the Philippines, Guam and Puerto Rico as colonies under the Treaty of PARIS, and Cuba securing nominal independence. President MCKINLEY declared America's first foreign war for 50 years under pressure from the Hearst newspapers after the USS *Maine* blew up in Havana harbour on 15 February 1898 (*see* REMEMBER THE MAINE!). It brought Theodore ROOSEVELT to prominence through the feats of his ROUGH RIDERS, gave McKinley the popular support he needed to defeat William Jennings Bryan (*see* PRAIRIE AVENGER) a second time in 1900, and gave the US interests in the Pacific that were eventually to bring it into conflict with Japan.

> The most absolutely righteous foreign war.
> THEODORE ROOSEVELT

Spanish Civil War The bitter conflict (1936–39) between Spain's Republican government and Nationalist insurgents, which for contemporaries represented a classic struggle between good and evil, though they were divided over which was which, and drew ideological battle lines for WORLD WAR II. The democratically elected POPULAR FRONT government supported by urban workers, farm labourers, ANARCHISTS, Communists and much of the INTELLIGENTSIA was challenged by a reactionary coalition of the Army, the Catholic church, monarchists, industrialists and landowners. Support for the rebels from HITLER and Mussolini (*see* DUCE), and more limited backing for the Republicans from the Soviet Union, and left-wing volunteers from Europe and America in the INTERNATIONAL BRIGADES, broadened the struggle into a foretaste of the world conflict to come. Up to a million people were killed, many in massacres committed by both sides.

A military coup in July 1936, led by Generals Franco and Mola, gave the rebels control of much of the south and north-west, but Barcelona and Madrid – where Soviet aid and the International Brigades proved crucial – were saved for the government by workers' militias. There followed a war of attrition, in which the Republican forces succumbed over three years to the Nationalists' superior economic and military resources. The Republicans were starved of support from the European democracies by the Anglo-French formation of a NON-INTERVENTION COMMITTEE. Openly contemptuous, Hitler sent the fighters and bombers of the Condor Legion, and Mussolini 100,000 Italian troops, to fight for Franco; both dictators used Spain as a testing ground for their latest weaponry. By 1937 Bilbao and the Basque country had been bombed into submission (*see* GUERNICA); the Nationalists then drove eastward to the Mediterranean, splitting the republic in two in April 1938. Catalonia was overrun by 7 February 1939; fighting then erupted in Madrid between rival Communist factions, and on 28 March the city surrendered to the Nationalists. The war established Franco as unchallenged CAUDILLO of Spain for 36 years (*see also* FALANGE).

Spartacists An extreme socialist group in Germany that flourished between 1916 and 1919. It was founded by Karl Liebknecht who, with Rosa Luxemburg, led the attempted GERMAN REVOLUTION of January 1919; it was crushed by the government of Karl Ebert, with both being killed. The movement took its name from the Thracian gladiator Spartacus, who in 73 BC led a slave rebellion against Rome.

Spartist A professionally leftist agitator with comically infantile and KNEE-JERK views. The term was coined in Britain c. 1970 by PRIVATE EYE, which carried a column of militant but incoherent ramblings from the bearded 'Dave Spart', which satirised the pitch made by many in the PROTEST MOVEMENT. Dave Spart was joined in the late 1970s by Deirdre Spart, a FEMINIST with equally predictable and ludicrous opinions; the pair figured regularly in lampoons of the hard LEFT.

SPD (Ger. *Socialdemokratische Partei Deutschlands*, German Social Democratic Party) The party which for almost a century and a half has been the principal left-of-centre force in democratic Germany, for most of that time in opposition, and which since 1998 has held power under Gerhard Schröder, in coalition with the GREENS. Founded in Leipzig by Ferdinand Lasalle as the All-German Workers' Party in 1863, before the unification of the state, it merged in 1875 with August Bebel's Social Democratic Workers' Party to form the SPD. Three years later Bismarck used two attempts on the Kaiser's life (not by Social Democrats) to ban the party. Legitimised again, it emerged from elections in 1890 as the largest party in the Reich, with 19.7% of the vote; by 1912 its share of the vote was 34.8%. On the Kaiser's abdication after Germany's defeat in WORLD WAR I, the SPD's Friedrich Ebert was elected first president of the WEIMAR REPUBLIC. When HITLER came to power in 1933, the SPD was the only party in the REICHSTAG to vote against the NAZIS' ENABLING ACT; many party activists were sent to CONCENTRATION CAMPS and others fled the country or continued to organise secretly. The division of the country after Germany's further defeat in 1945 split the party; in the Soviet-occupied East the SPD was forcibly merged into the ruling SED, with 5000 dissidents being arrested, but in the West the party rebuilt its organisation and formed a 'constructive opposition' in the first BUNDESTAG. The SPD was still bound by its essentially socialist **Erfurt Programme,** agreed in 1891, but as the COLD WAR and the ECONOMIC MIRACLE took hold the party recognised that this stance made it unelectable and in 1959 it adopted the BAD GODESBERG DECLARATION which embraced the MARKET ECONOMY. In 1969 Willy Brandt, one of the architects of the SPD's new look, was elected Chancellor. Five years later, after the Spy in the CHANCELLERY affair, he handed over to Helmut Schmidt, who held power until 1983 when the SPD's FREE DEMOCRAT coalition partners switched to support the CHRISTIAN DEMOCRATS. REUNIFICATION enabled the SPD to organise once again throughout Germany, eventually returning to power under Schröder.

speak. Speak for England! The resounding cry of the anguished Conservative backbencher Leo Amery (1873–1955) at Neville CHAMBERLAIN's failure to give a lead on the eve of WORLD WAR II. At 7.30 p.m. on 2 September 1939, Chamberlain disappointed the COMMONS by stating that further negotiations were under way to persuade HITLER to withdraw his troops from Poland. What both sides of the House wanted was an ULTIMATUM. As Chamberlain sat down to a dismayed silence, Arthur Greenwood, the acting Labour leader (ATTLEE was ill) rose to speak and Amery called out: 'Speak for England!' Greenwood's declaration that 'every minute's delay now means the loss of life, imperilling our national interests . . . imperilling the very foundations of our national honour' was probably the push Chamberlain needed to send the ultimatum next morning. The absence of a German reply (*see* I HAVE TO TELL YOU THAT NO SUCH UNDERTAKING HAS BEEN RECEIVED) led Britain and France to declare war on Germany on 3 September.

Speak softly and carry a big stick One of the most celebrated sayings of Theodore ROOSEVELT; in a speech at the Minnesota State Fair on 2 September 1901, he said:

> There is a homely old adage which runs: 'Speak softly and carry a big stick; you will go far.' If the American nation will speak softly, and yet build and keep at a pitch of the highest training a thoroughly efficient navy, the MONROE DOCTRINE will go far.

> Jimmy Carter wants to speak loudly and carry a fly swatter.
>
> GERALD FORD, campaign speech 19 October 1976

Speaker (1) A person who engages in public speaking, or who is delivering a speech at a particular time.

> A speaker who doesn't strike oil in ten minutes should stop boring.
>
> LORD MANCROFT (1917–87)

(2) The officer who since 1376 has presided over Britain's HOUSE OF COMMONS and defended its liberties and privileges, notably against King Charles I. The Speaker is elected from among MPs to represent the House to the LORDS and the Crown, and to chair it in an impartial fashion; it is customary for a newly elected Speaker to put up a show of resistance before taking the CHAIR. The Chair is normally the last stopping-place in a political career, though the Speaker need not be elderly; Lord ROSEBERY wrote: 'I hate to see a man of real ability embedded in that pompous tomb.' In 1992 Betty Boothroyd was elected the 186th Speaker, and the first woman (*see* MADAM SPEAKER). Her predecessor, Bernard (later Lord) WEATHERILL, was the first speaker to be regularly televised at work. The Speaker has a distinctive uniform of wig, gown and breeches; this was adapted for Miss

Boothroyd and the wig is not now always worn.

The Speaker is their mouth, and trusted by them, and so necessary as the House of Commons cannot sit without him.

Sir EDWARD COKE (1552–1634)

There is much exaggeration about the attainments required of a Speaker. All Speakers are highly successful, all Speakers are deeply regretted, and are generally announced to be irreplaceable. But a Speaker is soon found, and found, almost invariably, from among the mediocrities of the House.

LORD ROSEBERY to Queen Victoria

One of the jobs that, if you want it, you will never get it – and if you're seen to want it, you will certainly never get it.

BERNARD WEATHERILL

I am not here to save Hon. Members from themselves.

Speaker GEORGE THOMAS (Viscount Tonypandy, 1909–97)

(3) The member presiding over the principal HOUSE of almost every LEGISLATURE in the COMMONWEALTH; also the member elected to chair the NORTHERN IRELAND ASSEMBLY. (4) The most powerful figure in the US HOUSE OF REPRESENTATIVES, combining the roles of Chairman, intermediary with the President, administrative head and leader of the House, outranking the MAJORITY LEADER. This role was not spelt out in the CONSTITUTION, which merely stipulates that there shall be a Speaker, but built up by Henry Clay (1777 and 1852) between 1812 and 1825. Clay not only enforced order; he also ensured that committees were dominated by his supporters, that legislation he favoured made progress and that the President took his views into account. The prestige – as opposed to the power – of the Speaker has fluctuated, but revived during the 21-year tenure of Sam RAYBURN (1882–1961), and was more recently maintained by TIP O'Neill.

As Speaker, a constitutional officer of this House, I must be more charitable and responsible toward my colleagues than they sometimes are towards me.

TIP O'NEILL

Speaker in the Chair! The cry that goes out from attendants in the Members' LOBBY and elsewhere the moment the Speaker has taken their seat for the start of business in the HOUSE OF COMMONS.

Speaker's Conference At WESTMINSTER, an all-party discussion convened under the Speaker to consider potential reforms to the structure of the HOUSE or the electoral system. In the late 1970s such a conference was convened to determine how many MPs NORTHERN IRELAND should have; it agreed to raise the number from an arbitrary twelve to the seventeen the province's population would require.

Speakers' Corner A paved area of London's Hyde Park, close to Marble Arch, where any citizen may exercise their right of FREEDOM OF SPEECH and try to catch the attention of passers-by. The makeshift rostrums used by some of the speakers have also earned it the name of SOAPBOX Corner.

Speaker's House The portion of the Palace of WESTMINSTER, facing the river, which forms the official residence of the Speaker.

Speaker's Lobby The panelled corridor behind the Speaker's chair, with anterooms through arched doorways, which is an informal meeting place for members of the US HOUSE OF REPRESENTATIVES. It is lined with portraits of former Speakers.

Speaker's procession The ritual which precedes the start of a day's business in the HOUSE OF COMMONS, when the Speaker processes with mace-bearer, chaplain and attendants from the SPEAKER'S HOUSE through the Central and Members' LOBBIES to the CHAMBER.

catching the Speaker's eye The WESTMINSTER phrase for being called to speak or ask a question, reflecting the way MPs bob up and down in the hope of catching the attention of the CHAIR. Stanley BALDWIN, reflecting the frustration of generations of MPs at not being called as often as they felt they might, described the Speaker's eye as

That most elusive organ that nature has ever yet created.

Madam Speaker *See* MADAM.

Mr Speaker *See* MISTER.

special adviser A person appointed by UK CABINET MINISTERS to work closely with them, advising on the politics of decisions being taken, providing political input into those decisions, helping civil servants understand what the Minister is trying to achieve, liaising with the governing party and its MPs, and keeping the media informed and on-side. Labour and Conservative Ministers (and now the Liberal Democrat leader in the SCOTTISH EXECUTIVE) have appointed SPADS since at least the 1970s; a Cabinet Minister is now entitled to two – generally one dealing with policy and sometimes purely technical issues and the other being a point of contact for the media – and a Minister outside the Cabinet but entitled to attend it may have one. A couple of dozen political appointees and technical advisers in NUMBER TEN also have special adviser status, enabling them to work alongside civil servants on tasks it would be inappropriate for a career official to undertake. Under Tony BLAIR this brought the total number of SPADs to just over 80. Most special advisers are in their early 30s, having graduated from the party's research department or campaigning groups (and in Labour's case the trade unions) and many will have ambitions for a SEAT, possibly with a lucrative spell in LOBBYING en route. SPADs, who have temporary civil servant status, are resented by some career civil servants and dismissed by some newspapers as SPIN DOCTORS paid by the taxpayer who brief against other Ministers, but their principal detractors are OPPOSITION MPs who were themselves special advisers before securing a seat. Moves are now afoot to cap the number of SPADs at fewer than 80, and to clarify the rules for their interaction with civil servants after concern that Alistair Campbell, Blair's first press secretary, was actually tasked with giving instructions to career officials.

special district In US local government, a unit performing a single function which overlaps city, county and even state boundaries. It has responsibility for some function that transcends those boundaries or can best be performed on a less fragmented scale, such as transportation or sewerage.

Special Drawing Rights An international unit of reserve currency created by the IMF in 1969; from 1981 it comprised a 'basket' of the most-traded currencies: the US dollar, the deutschmark, the French franc, sterling and the yen. Even before the advent of the EURO, it had become overshadowed by the ECU which was traded to a greater extent.

special election In America, an election to fill a vacancy in CONGRESS or a state LEGISLATURE caused by death or resignation. The governor of a state is empowered to set in motion a special election for the HOUSE or the SENATE, except where the state legislature has provided for the vacancy to be filled by a nominee of the governor.

special interests *See* INTEREST.

special prosecutor In particularly sensitive cases of alleged wrongdoing in high places in America, a lawyer with the highest credentials may be appointed special prosecutor in order to ascertain what criminal charges, if any, should be brought. The most celebrated use of a special prosecutor was over WATERGATE; the IRAN-CONTRA AFFAIR and WHITEWATER/ZIPPERGATE (*see* STARR REPORT) are just some of many other episodes that one has been appointed to investigate.

special relationship The relationship that is supposed to exist between Britain and America, to Britain's political advantage, by virtue of their common language and historical ties. The phrase predates WORLD WAR II, but it was CHURCHILL who promoted it as he sought to draw America into the war, then build the ATLANTIC ALLIANCE. While Churchill clearly enjoyed a 'special relationship' with Franklin D. ROOSEVELT, he wanted the concept to last; in the COMMONS on 7 November 1945 he said:

> We should not abandon our special relationship with the United States and Canada about the atomic bomb.

And in his 1946 FULTON SPEECH, he asked:

> Would a special relationship between the United States and the British Commonwealth be inconsistent with our overriding loyalties to the World Organisation [UN]?

The special relationship has been strained by a number of crises, starting with SUEZ, when one of the parties took unilateral action. It has also been warped by America's ever-greater relative strength and US reluctance to make any exceptions from PROTECTIONIST trading policies. It has tended to look strongest when Britain had a strong leader. The closeness between President REAGAN and Margaret THATCHER and the extent of US aid for Britain during the FALKLANDS conflict made it look artificially strong, and the incoming Bill CLINTON in 1993 made clear his personal commitment, having lived in Britain. The controversial IRAQ WAR partnership between George W. BUSH and Tony BLAIR in some ways reinforced the relationship, but at a time of many differences on other issues.

> The dependence of London on WASHINGTON for the supply of our so-called independent NUCLEAR WEAPONS is all that remains of the 'special relationship'. It is really a ball and chain limiting our capacity to play a more positive role in the world. TONY BENN

Spectator, The The weekly magazine published in London since 1828 which has built a reputation for political comment, thought and good writing which informed the CONSERVATIVE PARTY's policy-making process. Its editors have included such Tory heavyweights as Iain Macleod and Nigel Lawson. Owned throughout the 1990s by the Telegraph Group, it has interchanged staff and columnists with the *Daily* and

Sunday Telegraph. It made the headlines for less august reasons in the second half of 2004 when its editor, Boris Johnson MP, was sacked as Conservative arts spokesman by Michael HOWARD for not owning up to having had an adulterous affair with the *Spectator* staffer Petronella Wyatt, when revelations about the relationship between Home Secretary David Blunkett and its publisher Kimberly Fortier/Quinn led to Blunkett's resignation (*see* NO FAVOURS, BUT RATHER QUICKER), and finally when it emerged that she had simultaneously been conducting an extra-marital relationship with the magazine's wine columnist (and *Guardian* writer) Simon Hoggart.

speech (1) The process and art of public speaking; HITLER wrote: 'The broad mass of the people will only be moved by the power of speech.' (2) An address to an audience or legislature, scripted or otherwise but comprising more than a question or interjection. CHURCHILL described speech-making as 'the art of making deep sounds from the stomach sound like important messages from the brain'. Gerald FORD stated the obvious when he said: 'When a man is asked to make a speech, the first thing he has to decide is what to say,' but the English statesman John Morley reckoned otherwise: 'Three things matter in a speech – who says it, how he says it and what he says – and of the three, the last matters the least.' And Sen. Henry Ashurst maintained that 'a speech is entertaining only when serenely detached from all information'. Perhaps the crispest advice to would-be speakers has come from the Duke of Wellington ('Don't quote Latin. Say what you have to say. Then sit down'), Franklin D. ROOSEVELT ('Be sincere, be brief, be seated') and the Scottish Labour MP John Maxton ('Dinna put too much meat in your pie').

To legislators and members of the public alike, lengthy speeches have always been a trial. Samuel Pepys wrote in 1668 after speaking in the HOUSE OF COMMONS: 'We were in hopes to have a vote this day in our favour, and so the generality of the House was; but my speech being so long, many had gone out to dinner and come in again half-drunk.' Thomas JEFFERSON observed that 'speeches measured by the hour die within the hour', and DISRAELI is reputed to have said: 'It is better, when a member resumes his seat after he has made a speech, for the House to have the feeling that they wish he had gone on longer instead of wondering why he did not stop sooner.' Lord Brabazon of Tara advised that 'if you cannot say what you have to say in 20 minutes, you should go away and write a book about it', and Lord Mancroft noted: 'A speech is like a love affair. Any fool can start it, but to end it requires considerable skill.' A 1984 House of Commons motion advocating time limits stated: 'This House recognises that for a speech to be immortal it does not have to be eternal.' Making a brief speech requires particular skill; Woodrow WILSON once said: 'If I am to speak ten minutes, I need a week for preparation; if fifteen minutes, three days; if half an hour, two days; if an hour, I am ready now.' Sometimes speeches are prolonged because the speaker inadvertently reads part of it twice; when WILLIE Whitelaw had this pointed out to him by gleeful Labour MPs, he told them: 'Don't you realise that this is the most important page of my speech?' Some speeches are tedious and others downright dreadful; in 1974 Michael FOOT said of one by the Tory frontbencher John Davies: 'I have been in this House for 30 years. I thought that when I heard the Right Honourable member for Mitcham [Robert Carr] I had heard the worst speech ever delivered in the Commons. I was to be proved wrong.' When Will Rogers addressed Congressmen in 1933, he told them: 'You should stay awake tonight. This is one speech you haven't heard a dozen times.' And CHURCHILL once told a woman who congratulated him on the turnout for one of his speeches: 'If instead of making a speech I was being hanged, the crowd would be twice as big.'

Perhaps the most extraordinary (and tasteless) speech ever heard in an English-speaking legislature was delivered by Davy Crockett (1786–1836), who alongside his other achievements served three terms in Congress. He once rose and said:

> Who-Who-Whoop-Bow-Bow-Wow-Yough! I say, Mr Speaker, I've had a speech on soak this six months, and it has swelled me like a drowned horse; if I don't deliver it I shall burst and smash the windows . . . I'm a screamer, and have got the roughest racking horse, the prettiest sister, the surest rifle and the ugliest dog in the district . . . My father can whip any man in Kentucky, and I can lick my father. I can outspeak any man on this floor, and give him two hours' start. I can run faster, dive deeper, stay longer under, and come out dryer, than any chap this side the big swamp. I can outlook a panther and outstare a flash of lightning, tote a steamboat on my back and play at rough and tumble with a lion, and an occasional kick from a zebra. To sum it all up in one word, I'm a horse. Goliath was a pretty hard colt, but I could choke him . . . I can walk like an ox, run like

a fox, swim like an eel, yell like an Indian, spout like an earthquake, make love like a mad bull, and swallow a nigger whole without choking if you butter his head and pull his ears back.

Speech! The cry that goes up when a celebrity is not due to speak, and those present want to hear him (or her). Sometimes the shout is ironically delivered at the close of a particularly poor speech.

The Speech The standard address that a CANDIDATE delivers throughout an election campaign, varied according to where he or she is speaking, the interests of the audience and any topical developments in the campaign. The candidate and travelling election aides will be able to recite The Speech from memory by the end of the campaign, as will journalists who have been covering the campaign and know when to put down their pencils because they have heard (and reported) it before.

speechwriter A professional who either drafts speeches for a senior politician or business leader or embellishes a DRAFT prepared by civil servants or the speaker themselves into a polished final article. While politicians have always had help with their speeches, the first to appoint one full time was President HARDING, who recruited Judson Welliver as his 'literary clerk'. Presidents and Prime Ministers now have several people on their staff who are able to turn out a speech; for the most important ones like a State of the UNION message or a keynote party CONFERENCE speech, they will all work as a team, with outside contributors also brought in. UK CABINET MINISTERS rely on their officials for non-political speeches and on their SPECIAL ADVISERS for those with partisan content.

Speer? The question mark that saved the life of Albert Speer (1905–81), the architect who, after designing some of HITLER's grandest projects, became his Armaments Minister, after the failure of the STAUFFENBERG PLOT on 20 July 1944. The conspirators had drawn up a post-Hitler Cabinet, but had left a query against Speer's name as they could not reach him to find if he would serve. Speer survived the war and was imprisoned at NUREMBERG as a war criminal because his success at keeping the NAZI war machine supplied was based on slave labour. In 1966, after his release, he wrote *Inside the Third Reich*, a revealing account of the functioning of the Nazi system in which he maintained he had done his best to mitigate its most evil effects.

spend more time with my family *See* FAMILY.

SPGB Socialist Party of Great Britain. A small, dedicated and purist but not militantly left-wing party that operated on the margins of British politics throughout most of the 20th century. Though it occasionally contested elections, its adherents generally wrote the word 'Socialism' on the ballot paper, thus SPOILing it.

sphere of influence A state, combination of states or region which one nation considers vital to its interests, and consequently under its HEGEMONY. Attempts by any other power to assert its influence in such a sphere will give rise to tension and, if persisted in, war.

***Spiegel* affair** The scandal in October 1962 which forced the resignation of the West German defence minister Franz Josef Strauss (1915–88), and was probably decisive in denying him the CHANCELLORSHIP. The editors of the news weekly *Der Spiegel* (The Mirror) were arrested and office files seized on suspicion of treason for publishing details of a NATO exercise. The ensuing furore forced Strauss, ultra-conservative leader of Bavaria's CSU, to resign from the Cabinet; he returned in 1966 but his reputation was permanently damaged.

Spies for Peace *See* RSG.

spillover The period each year, usually for three weeks or so from mid-October, when Parliament reconvenes at WESTMINSTER after the summer or conference RECESS to clear up outstanding business before the SESSION is concluded. Frequently it involves the LORDS returning for longer than the COMMONS, as most legislation completes its progress in the Upper House and it thus has the greater backlog.

spin The line put to the media in an orchestrated way on behalf of a party or candidate, whether credible or not, to make events look more favourable or less disastrous than they are. The word, relating to the spin given to a ball in flight to fool the recipient, and spin as an identifiable technique, first came to prominence in the 1984 US Presidential election campaign. By 1992 Nancy Nord, the executive director of Lawyers for BUSH-QUAYLE Leadership, could fax to members the message: 'If we can get people to call the show today, it will help with spin.' The first Presidential election fought out publicly with spin on both sides was that year, with James Carville (*see* RAGIN'

CAJUN) spinning Bill CLINTON to victory and his opposite number in the BUSH campaign, Mary Matalin, so much his equal that they subsequently married. The word 'spin', and the institutionalisation of techniques which have been used for centuries, soon crossed the Atlantic. The Conservatives made successful early use of it, notably in portraying John MAJOR's 1995 defeat of John Redwood (*see* VULCAN) as decisive, but it was NEW LABOUR who became acknowledged past masters of spin (and allegedly of its excesses) either side of their 1997 election LANDSLIDE, under the auspices of Peter Mandelson (*see* BOBBY) and Tony BLAIR's chief spokesman and press secretary, Alastair Campbell. Blair's first term was punctuated by rows – often started by former Conservative SPIN DOCTORS who were now MPs – over ministerial aides apparently spinning against each other, an alleged concentration on spin over substance and the repeated re-announcement of the same initiatives and allocations of funds. The controversy reached its height in the wake of 9/11 over Jo Moore's controversial suggestion that the opportunity be taken to BURY bad news. Campbell's departure in August 2003 was claimed in some circles as 'the end of spin' in the wake of the David KELLY affair, but all parties and governments are bound to make use of it, while hopefully holding back from its worst excesses. The most extreme critics of spin ignore the fact that most political journalists are not gullible; in the author's experience they are resistant to spin and quite a few will not be persuaded even of established fact. *See also* PUBLIC DIPLOMACY; QUOTE SLUTS; THIRD PARTY ENDORSEMENTS.

> Spin, or presentation, bought us the time and the space to change the underlying reality.
>
> PETER MANDELSON

spin doctor A campaign official, public relations expert or media aide attached to a party or politician whose task is to channel facts to the media in a way that puts the best possible construction on them. By 1998 the US media had adopted **spinmeister** for a particularly accomplished practitioner; the UK press preferred **sultan of spin**, a pun on the Dire Straits CD *Sultans of Swing*. Female spin doctors are known – not in their hearing – as **spin nurses**.

> You just have to be economical with the truth. You should never lie, but it's very difficult. They [the media] understand. They will certainly understand tomorrow and forgive me.
>
> CHARLIE WHELAN, then Gordon BROWN's SPECIAL ADVISER, September 1997

Spitting Image The satirical puppet programme broadcast from 1986 by Britain's Central TV which made its name by Rabelaisian lampoons on the CABINETs of Margaret THATCHER and John MAJOR, OPPOSITION figures of the day and the ROYAL FAMILY. It was devised by the cartoonists Luck and Flaw.

splinter group A small group that breaks away from a party or movement, leaving the parent body relatively unaffected and sometimes relieved. If the group is large enough, the splintering turns into a

split A division within a party, movement or Cabinet over an issue or series of issues that weakens it in the eyes of the voters and can, on rare occasions, develop into a permanent break. Splits are much sought by political journalists, and are most frequently found in ideologically-based parties, often of the left.

> The Republicans have their splits right after the election, and Democrats have theirs just before an election. WILL ROGERS (1879–1935)

splitting the anti-X vote The accusation levelled by the second-placed candidate in an election against a third who has intervened and weakened the challenge to the front-runner, e.g. in Britain a Labour candidate trying to oust a Conservative may accused an intervening Liberal Democrat of 'splitting the anti-Tory vote'.

splitting the ticket *See* TICKET.

spoil. spoiled paper A BALLOT PAPER rejected by officials conducting the COUNT because it contains marks or comments other than the simple 'X' or other symbol required by law.

spoiler A candidate who intervenes in an election with no interest in victory, but purely to weaken the chances of another or maybe compel them to increase their spending. They may have a similar name to the candidate they wish to harm, adopt a confusingly similar party label (see LITERAL DEMOCRAT) or campaign on a very similar programme.

spoils system The system of patronage, originating in the Albany regency of the 1820s and '30s, which became the basis of US MACHINE POLITICS and even, for a time, of the Presidency. Under it, a change of political control at federal, state or local level brought the dismissal of all office-holders assumed to belong to the defeated faction, and their replacement by supporters of the new administration at even the humblest levels; inevitably this was a recipe for graft and corruption. The scramble for the trough every four years was a feature of WASHINGTON life for much of the 19th century, and slackened only when the shooting of President Garfield in 1881 by a disappointed office-seeker brought the extent of corruption to light. At national level the system survives only in the uppermost reaches of government (*see* HOLDOVER; TRANSITION), but it is alive and well in some cities.

> If you have a job in your department that can't be done by a Democrat, then abolish the job.
>
> President ANDREW JACKSON

to the victor, the spoils The principle behind the spoils system, again stemming from the Albany regency. Sen. William Learned Marcy told the Senate on 25 January 1832:

> It may be, Sir, that the politicians of New York are not so fastidious as some gentlemen are, as to disclosing the principles on which they act. They boldly preach what they practise. When they are contending for victory, they avow their intentions of enjoying the fruits of it. If they are defeated, they expect to retire from office. If they are successful, they claim, as a matter of right, the advantages of success. They see nothing wrong in the rule that to the victor belong the spoils of the enemy.

spokesman (1) A legislator nominated by their party to put across its policies, and question and challenge opposing parties on theirs. In the WESTMINSTER system where the Opposition SHADOWs the government, spokesmen not in the Shadow Cabinet have a formal place. (2) A person who, officially and 'on the record' (*see* OFF), represents the policies and activities of a government or other organisation to the media.

> *David FROST*: You are a spokesman?
>
> *William Rushton*: Yes, I've just been promoted from being an informed SOURCE.
>
> *THAT WAS THE WEEK THAT WAS*, BBC television, 1962

sponsor A legislator who places his or her name on a BILL at the start of its progress. In the US CONGRESS any member may sponsor almost any category of Bill; at WESTMINSTER Ministers alone sponsor government Bills and backbenchers only Private Members' BILLS.

sponsored candidate/member In Britain, a Parliamentary candidate or MP who receives ENDORSEMENT and a degree of funding from a body other than their own party; the practice applies primarily to trade unions sponsoring Labour candidates and MPs who belong to their organisation.

Spot George W. BUSH's long-lived English springer spaniel, who had a double claim to be America's FIRST DOG, having been born in the WHITE HOUSE in March 1989 during Bush's father's presidency and lived to return with his master. Spot was one of only two witnesses of the PRETZEL incident in January 2002 which nearly terminated the second Bush presidency; he was put down in February 2004 after a stroke.

daisy spot *See* DAISY.

spotted owl The species whose plight in the face of threatened wide-scale logging in Oregon became a rallying-point for conservationists, triggering listing in 1992 of the spotted owl under the Endangered Species Act to restrict felling, at the cost of thousands of jobs. An equivalent dispute over the equally rare **snail darter**, a small riverine fish, had dominated earlier Congressional discussion of a dam project for Tennessee. In 1994 four Republican Congressmen from California retaliated by trying to get *homo sapiens* listed under the ESA.

> Wood and pulp products in short supply – wipe your ass with a spotted owl.
>
> Sign in gas station at Elsie, Oregon, August 1993

Spycatcher The political storm in Britain between 1985 and 1988 caused by the attempts of the former MI5 operative Peter Wright (1917–95) to publish his eponymous autobiography. It purported to expose a catalogue of abuses by the agency, which Wright said had 'BUGGED and burgled our way across London'; his principal charge was that there had been a conspiracy within MI5 to undermine and overthrow Harold WILSON in the mid-1970s. Although books saying much the same had already appeared, Margaret THATCHER decided *Spycatcher* had to be stopped, and a series of legal actions to prevent publication were started throughout the world. The critical action was fought out in Australia, where Wright now lived. The CABINET SECRETARY, Sir Robert Armstrong, was despatched to defend the decision in the Supreme Court of New South Wales, arguing that publication would breach security and the national interest. Armstrong received a gruelling cross-examination, at one point rashly conceding that he had been 'economical with the TRUTH'. Efforts to ban it in Britain continued for some years, ending in defeat for the government; at this point Mrs Thatcher promoted legislation imposing an 'obligation of confidentiality' on retired members of the security services.

square deal The ambitious, pioneering programme of social and political reform followed from 1901 to 1909 by Theodore ROOSEVELT on behalf of the poorer sections of American society. It involved an attack on the power of MONOPOLIES, conservation of America's natural resources, and a new relationship with labour unions that brought improved working conditions.

> When I say I believe in a square deal, I do not mean . . . it's possible to give every man the best hand. If the cards do not come to any man, or if they do come, and he has not the power to play them, that is his affair. All I mean is that there shall not be any crookedness in the dealing.
>
> THEODORE ROOSEVELT, speaking in Dallas, 5 April 1906

squeaker A mainly US term for a desperately close election victory; the winning candidate is said to have 'squeaked in'.

squeeze The pressure exerted on a party during an election campaign as the voters perceive that its candidates have little chance of election and POLARISE between those perceived as having a better chance, or being more likely to defeat the government. In Britain the squeeze always threatens to damage the LIBERAL DEMOCRATS during a GENERAL ELECTION, but at BY-ELECTIONS Labour or the Conservatives may have their vote squeezed if a LibDem BANDWAGON gets going.

squeeze question A term from the new century: a question put in CANVASSING on the telephone or the doorstep, the reply to which will tell the activist asking it whether the voter being spoken to is likely to be a supporter or not.

squeeze until the pips squeak The threat made by successive generations of POPULISTS against supposedly privileged, undeserving or discredited groups. It was used first by LLOYD GEORGE against property speculators, then most notoriously by Sir Eric Geddes (1875–1937) against the Germans on post-World War I REPARATIONS. On 10 December 1918 Geddes told an election meeting in Cambridge:

> The Germans, if this Government is re-elected, are going to pay every penny; they are going to be squeezed – as a lemon is squeezed – until the pips squeak. My only doubt is not whether we can squeeze hard enough, but whether there is enough juice.

In the highly-charged political atmosphere of the 1970s, Denis HEALEY came under fire for levelling the same threat against the rich as he contemplated the taxes an incoming Labour government could levy on the rich. The Labour Chancellor insisted he never said it, though he had quoted his Cabinet colleague Anthony Crosland as repeating it. However, Healey did say at Labour's 1973 conference:

> But before you cheer too loudly, let me warn you that a lot of you will pay extra taxes, too. That will go for every member of Parliament in this hall, including me . . . There are going to be howls of anguish from the 80,000 people who are rich enough to pay over 75% on their last slice of income. But how much do we hear from them today of the 85,000 families at the bottom of the earnings scale who have to pay over 75% on the last slice of *their* income?

Squiffites The ASQUITHian Liberals, who followed their leader into opposition after his overthrow by LLOYD GEORGE in December 1916, and remained a separate faction under the party's titular leader for the next decade. They were called after Asquith's nickname of '**Old Squiffy**'; the great man's heavy drinking explains why 'squiffy' remains a synonym for 'tipsy'. Asquith and many of his supporters refused to serve under Lloyd George in the reshaped COALITION government; while they stopped short of condemning the handling of the war, L.G. was convinced they were plotting against him, and the breach became irreparable with the MAURICE LETTER debate in May 1918. In the 1918 COUPON ELECTION the Squiffites won 26 seats against 136 for the Lloyd George faction, with Asquith himself unseated. He returned at a BY-ELECTION, and with the party nominally reunited after the Tories' CARLTON CLUB REVOLT of 1922 his faction coexisted uneasily with Asquith's dominant force until Asquith belatedly stood down as party leader in October 1926.

Srebrenica The town in Bosnia that in July 1995 was the scene of the worst massacre in Europe since the end of WORLD WAR II, when Bosnian Serb forces slaughtered over 7,000 Muslim men and boys. Srebrenica was supposed to be a UNITED NATIONS 'safe haven', but the UN had given its unarmed Dutch troops an inadequate mandate and they stood by while Serb forces broke their promise not to harm the population. In April 2002 the official report on the massacre from a panel of Dutch historians precipitated the resignation of the coalition government led by Wim Kok.

SSP *See* SCOTTISH SOCIALIST PARTY.

stab in the back The legend that Germany had not been on the point of military collapse in November 1918 when its new

Republican leaders ordered its troops to surrender, and that a military capable of fighting on had been betrayed by unpatriotic and treacherous politicians. Spread with vigour both by arch-conservative generals such as Ludendorff and by political nationalists including the recently demobilised Adolf HITLER, the 'stab in the back' became a cornerstone of NAZI doctrine and motivation. The fervour with which the belief was held was one reason for the Allies' demand for unconditional SURRENDER in WORLD WAR II; they could not risk again a resurgent Germany which asserted that it had not suffered military defeat.

stability and growth pact The agreement supposed to keep the economies of the EUROZONE countries in line, which was brought under strain from its early days by the insistence of any member state in breach of it that its transgression should be ignored. In October 2002 Romano Prodi, president of the Commission, denounced it as 'stupid', and in November 2003, after France and Germany defied the Commission to register excessive Budget deficits, the sanctions provided for under the pact were waived to avert a confrontation, to the dismay of smaller and fiscally orthodox member states. In July 2004, the EUROPEAN COURT ruled that while member states could formally amend the pact, they could not ignore it, but that December, after Greece's deficit figures were found to have been overstated in order to qualify the country for the EURO, the Commission abandoned its attempts to penalise France and Germany. The terms of the pact were relaxed in March 2005 at the insistence of Germany, which claimed the structural costs of UNIFICATION made the targets impossible for it to meet.

staff. Chief of Staff *See* CHIEF.

staffers In WASHINGTON, the backroom technicians who make the wheels of power go round and do the detailed work for politicians, both in the WHITE HOUSE and on the HILL. Some staffers, especially for Congressional committees, exercise more influence than the elected members; according to Ralph NADER:

> Special interests long ago learned that gifts, free trips, cash and women lavished on key committee or other Congressional staffers can result in the desired behaviour by the boss without much risk of exposure.

Ken McLean, staff director of the Senate Banking, Housing and Urban Affairs Committee, took a less sinister view: 'To be a politician you have to go out and shake a lot of hands. It's much more fun to be a staffer', while Sen. Eugene McCarthy said of his staff: 'You need them for protection, to go to lunch for you.' Of White House staffers, John Eisenhower noted:

> The staffer sometimes takes the President more seriously than the great man himself.

staffing In WASHINGTON, the process of sending out the text of a proposed Presidential speech or statement for checking and comment by staff in any federal agency that might be affected; for a comprehensive policy speech, some 50 officials may be consulted. It does not follow that the President will automatically take up the suggestions.

stage-management The art of turning a potentially unwieldy political gathering which may give off negatives into a vehicle for presenting the most favourable aspects of the party or candidate. The term has been used with the greatest justice for the NUREMBERG RALLIES, for rallies of Soviet citizenry and forces in RED SQUARE, and of the Communist hierarchy in the KREMLIN, of the annual conferences of Britain's CONSERVATIVE PARTY and of recent US political CONVENTIONS. The Soviets proved marginally the most successful in ensuring prolonged ovations for the leadership, and in preventing any criticism from the rostrum; to this day resolutions selected for debate at the Conservative conference are almost totally anodyne, a situation the Labour leadership has done its best to echo. A senior Soviet diplomat observing the 1982 Tory conference in Brighton told the author:

> It's very similar. We don't invite 6000 people to the Kremlin to find out what they think.

Conservative stage-management reached a high point under Margaret THATCHER, through techniques introduced by Harvey Thomas, who had also worked on Billy Graham's evangelistic crusades; at the same time Peter Mandelson (*see* BOBBY) was reorganising the set for Labour's conferences to end the downbeat and negative message put across by frowning left-wingers on the platform.

stagflation An economic situation in which INFLATION coincides with stagnant output, making future prospects look grim. The word was coined by the Conservative frontbencher Iain Macleod (1913–70) in November 1965, when he told the COMMONS:

> We now have the worst of both worlds – not just

inflation on one side or stagnation on the other, but both of them together. We have a sort of stagflation situation.

stakeholder A term much loved by NEW LABOUR – that has come into use since the 1990s – for the role of the individual in the economy and political society, and a crucial element in Tony BLAIR's THIRD WAY. Blair unveiled the idea of a '**stakeholder economy**' in a speech in Singapore on 8 January 1996; in government its main manifestation has been **stakeholder pensions**, but the word has come into common use, notably for those people or groups to be consulted when a decision affecting them is to be taken.

Mine's a sirloin.
DENNIS SKINNER MP, House of Commons, 1996

Stakhanovite A fanatically hard worker, originally a follower of the Soviet system of encouraging higher productivity among all workers by making heroes of those with spectacular achievements. The name comes from Alexander Stakhanov (1906–77), a Donetz coal miner who was credited with an astonishing daily output. In 1935 STALIN held a conference of Stakhanovites in which he extolled the working man.

Stalin (Russ. Man of steel) The name chosen by Joseph Vissarionovich Dzugashvili (1879–1953), the Communist who for almost 30 years governed the SOVIET UNION with the utmost ruthlessness. Originally a candidate for the priesthood in his native Georgia, he became a BOLSHEVIK in 1903, and was frequently imprisoned and exiled prior to the OCTOBER REVOLUTION of 1917. By 1922 he was general secretary of the COMMUNIST PARTY under LENIN, who did not trust him and left a Testament urging the party not to make him its leader; Lenin said: 'This cook will give us nothing but spicy dishes.' Stalin seized control anyway after Lenin's death in 1924, breaking with TROTSKY, who observed: 'It was the supreme expression of the mediocrity of the apparatus that Stalin rose to his position,' and eventually having him murdered. By 1929 he wielded absolute power and embarked both on the FIVE-YEAR PLANS and a reign of terror that made his assumed name synonymous with brutality and repression. Enforced COLLECTIVISATION cost the lives of 10 million peasants, who starved to death or were executed, and mass PURGES and SHOW TRIALS not only stripped the Soviet hierarchy of all potential rivals but left the RED ARMY almost leaderless when HITLER launched his surprise attack. Before then Stalin had shown a cynicism matching his paranoia by concluding the 1939 NAZI-SOVIET PACT which divided Poland with Germany and left Hitler free to launch his BLITZKRIEG on the West; in 1941 he refused to heed Western warnings that a Nazi attack on the Soviet Union was imminent. Stalin, despite bouts of alcoholic depression, remained in the KREMLIN as the Germans advanced to within twelve miles of Moscow, and achieved a new status as a national leader fighting a GREAT PATRIOTIC WAR. Yet he himself said of the Russian people: 'We are under no illusion that they are fighting for us. They are fighting for Mother Russia.'

His western allies kept him supplied and did their best to show loyal support, ROOSEVELT declaring: 'UNCLE JOE is my man.' Yet he showed by allowing the non-Communist Warsaw Uprising to fail that he would be as ruthless as ever once the war was over. And in the late 1940s he presided over yet greater repression at home, and after YALTA took and kept an iron grip over central and eastern Europe. Even with the IRON CURTAIN descending, President TRUMAN said: 'I like old Joe Stalin. He's a good fellow but he's a prisoner of the POLITBURO.' Before long he revised that opinion to 'a lying son of a bitch'. ATTLEE, more circumspect, foreshadowed Margaret THATCHER's view of Mikhail GORBACHEV when he termed Stalin 'a man you could do business with; he was obviously the man who could take decisions, and he was obviously going to be difficult'. Stalin died in 1953, suspecting his intimates to the last and not hesitating to have them shot.

Stalin, that great lover of peace, a man of giant stature who moulded, as few others have done, the destinies of his age.
PANDIT NEHRU, obituary speech, 9 March 1953

I, like everyone else, called him 'the Boss'; in the same way the Jews of the past never pronounced the name of God.
ILYA EHRENBURG (1891–1967)

Every great leader is a reflection of the nation he leads and Stalin, in this sense, was Russia.
I. F. STONE

Stalin was a bureaucrat, an office politician, a man who would have risen irresistibly within the BBC or IBM or the Hanson organisation. He lacked style and force in public speech; his addresses on film sound like any bored Minister of State reading a brief, and quite lack the zing of John Gummer.
EDWARD PEARCE, *Macchiavelli's Children*

> My father died a difficult and terrible death. God grants an easy death only to the just.
> SVETLANA ALLILUYEVA, Stalin's daughter, *Twenty Letters to a Friend*

Stalin's granny The nickname among Labour right-wingers for Joan Maynard (1921–98), the formidable hard-left champion of the North Yorkshire agricultural workers over four decades who was one of Tony BENN's strongest supporters on Labour's national executive for fifteen years from 1972, chaired the CAMPAIGN GROUP and from 1974 to 1987 was MP for Sheffield Brightside. The name has also been applied, less credibly, to other senior Labour women.

Stalinism The ruthless personalised form of MARXISM-LENINISM forced on the Soviet peoples by Stalin, which outlived him both in the USSR and throughout eastern Europe and survives even now in North Korea. It involved unthinking obedience to a centralised party that might change its position at any moment, a PERSONALITY CULT for frequently uncharismatic and often sinister leaders, ruthless control from the KREMLIN of SATELLITE states through PUPPET governments, suppression of dissidents and rivals in PURGES, and general political terror centred on a system of GULAG forced labour camps.

> He turned Marxism on its head by making it fit his own theories. GEORGE LUKACS

destalinisation The debunking of the Stalin myth following his death in 1953. A campaign to discredit Stalin's memory was begun by his successor, Nikita S. Khrushchev (1894–1971) in a bitter speech at a Closed SESSION of the 20th Party Congress in March 1956. He denounced Stalin as a despot and brutal mass murderer interested only in 'the glorification of his own person'. It has been said that Khrushchev's speech was interrupted by a shout from the audience of: 'Why didn't you stop him?' Khrushchev glared at the delegates and shouted: 'Who said that?' Nobody spoke, and Khrushchev continued: 'Now you know why!' Khrushchev also told the Congress:

> What could we do? There was a reign of terror. You just had to look at him wrongly and the next day you lost your head.

Stalin's body was removed from Lenin's MAUSOLEUM the following year, but destalinisation was not a smooth or irreversible process; the suppression of the HUNGARIAN UPRISING in 1956 and the PRAGUE SPRING of 1968, the continued persecution of DISSIDENTS and the brutal maintenance of the BERLIN WALL all showed that Stalinism was alive and well into the dying days of the Soviet Union.

> Many people thought we had changed cars at the 20th Congress. Quite wrong: we threw out some luggage, but we are still travelling in the same car.
> ALEXANDER SURKOV, First Secretary of the Soviet Writers' Union 1953–60

Stalker report The interim report completed in 1985 by John Stalker, deputy chief constable of Greater Manchester, on his investigation of an alleged SHOOT TO KILL policy against suspected IRA terrorists by members of the Royal Ulster Constabulary. The circumstances surrounding delays by the RUC in forwarding it to Ulster's Director of Public Prosecutions gave CONSPIRACY THEORISTS a field day. Stalker was convinced that five men, four of them IRA suspects, had been unlawfully killed, and was believed to have uncovered irregularities implicating senior officers. He had compiled the report despite resistance within the RUC, which had refused him access to a tape of the shooting of one victim. In May 1986, while still pursuing his inquiries, Stalker was accused of misconduct in dealing with Kevin Taylor, a suspected criminal in Manchester. His investigation in Ulster was completed by Colin Sampson, chief constable of West Yorkshire, who also led inquiries into Stalker's own conduct; Sampson was handed the vital tape within days. Stalker was exonerated, but resigned from the force; Taylor was cleared of all charges. The Sampson report, when published in 1988, was dismissed by some as a WHITEWASH; it resulted in disciplinary action against 20 junior RUC officers.

stalking horse A candidate who enters an election with little hope of victory, in order to establish support for a challenge by a more serious contender. The term was particularly used of the backbench Tory WET Sir Anthony Meyer, who in 1989 challenged Margaret THATCHER for the party leadership. It was widely perceived that Meyer, who polled just 31 votes, was testing the water for Michael HESELTINE, whose challenge the following year ousted the IRON LADY without winning him the Premiership. A stalking horse was one trained to conceal a hunter stalking wild fowl, but as early as 1612 it had come to mean a person acting as a decoy, John Webster in his play *The White Devil* writing:

> You . . . were made his engine and his stalking horse to undo my sister.

stalwarts Conservative Republicans during the Hayes ADMINISTRATION who had supported President GRANT and looked to Sen. Roscoe Conkling of New York as their leader. The Stalwarts, who included Senators Benjamin Butler and John Logan and ex-senator Zachariah Chandler, were ranged against the HALF-BREEDS, led by Sen. James G. Blaine, who backed Hayes' Southern policy and civil service reform. When in 1881 Charles Guiteau shot President Garfield – a half-breed – he was heard to shout:

> I am a Stalwart, and Arthur is President now!

Stamp Act The Act passed at WESTMINSTER in 1765 which taxed documents and newspapers in the American colonies to help pay for their defence. It sparked non-compliance and bitter opposition from educated men who were fast becoming revolutionaries. It was a light tax, but in Americans' eyes broke new ground by taxing them without their consent, provoking the cry of 'NO TAXATION WITHOUT REPRESENTATION'. That October representatives of nine colonies met in New York for a Stamp Act Congress, which set out moderate statements of the American case. When word of resistance reached London, PITT THE ELDER, who wanted justice for the colonies, not their independence, declared:

> I rejoice that America has resisted. Three millions of people so dead to all the feelings of liberty as voluntarily to submit to be slaves, would have been fitting instruments to make slaves of the rest.

stand To put oneself forward for election; a UK term whose US equivalent is RUN. One speaks both of standing for office, the council, Parliament etc., and of a candidate standing at Barnsley, Torquay or wherever.

stand and deliver! The classic highwayman's order to his victims to hand over their riches, updated by Jeffrey (Lord) Archer at the 1993 CONSERVATIVE PARTY conference as an enjoinder to Home Secretary Michael HOWARD to deliver the effective policies on law and order that the Tory grassroots yearn for. Archer's dramatic message, tumultuously applauded by the audience, had an equally theatrical sequel: in 2001 he would be imprisoned for persuading a friend to give him a fictitious alibi in his 1987 libel action (*see* FRAGRANT) against the *Daily Star* for exposing his dealings with the prostitute Monica Coughlan. Archer told the conference on 6 October 1993:

> I say to this Conference: Back this man. Back the Home Secretary so that everyone realises when the next election comes that it's the Conservatives who are the party of law and order. Michael, the time has come for you to stand and deliver!

stand part In the COMMITTEE STAGE of a BILL in the HOUSE OF COMMONS, a motion that a clause 'stand part' of the Bill is tabled when consideration of all amendments to that clause has been completed.

stander Conservative *argot* for a STANDING OVATION at one of the party's annual conferences.

Standing committee (1) In the US CONGRESS, the 38 committees of the HOUSE and the SENATE which each oversee a particular area of government and which write, amend and consider and review the functioning of legislation relevant to them. (2) At WESTMINSTER, the eight or so committees of the HOUSE OF COMMONS empanelled each session to conduct the COMMITTEE STAGES of BILLS (other than purely private legislation) that have received a SECOND READING. One standing committee customarily handles most Private Members' BILLS, one or two each deal purely with Scottish legislation or Europe, and the rest, known by letter as 'standing Committee A' and so on, deal in turn with government legislation.

standing orders The basic rules for the conduct of meetings of a UK elected body or political party. The US equivalent is RULES OF ORDER.

standing ovation An enthusiastic display of support for a politician shown by standing to applaud, usually at the end of a major speech, occasionally at the beginning and, exceptionally, in mid-speech. When Tony BLAIR addressed both HOUSES of the US CONGRESS on 17 July 2003 (the night before David KELLY's body was found), he received seventeen. SPIN DOCTORS and STAGE-MANAGERS try to ensure such displays when there is particular media attention, notably when the leader of the CONSERVATIVE PARTY delivers their keynote CONFERENCE speech; as a result, journalists time the ovation with stop-watches and look for signs of flagging and lack of spontaneity.

Standards, Battle of the The popular name for the US election campaign of 1896, when the Republicans under McKINLEY championed the GOLD STANDARD and William Jennings Bryan (*see* BOY ORATOR; PRAIRIE AVENGER) led a coalition of Democrats, POPULISTS and breakaway Republicans to press for FREE SILVER.

star. Star Chamber The CABINET committee established by Margaret THATCHER as the ultimate arbiter of disputes between the TREASURY and spending ministers during the annual public spending negotiations (PESC). Initially chaired by Mrs Thatcher's deputy WILLIE Whitelaw, it was seldom convened as Ministers were anxious to resolve such arguments without having judgement passed on them by colleagues. The system was scrapped in 1992 when John MAJOR's Cabinet began to set global targets for departments, within which each had to set its own priorities. The original Star Chamber was a civil and criminal court, abolished in 1641, which met without a jury and was empowered to use torture. The term, derived from the blue ceiling of the old Council chamber at WESTMINSTER where it met, came to stand for any organ of the state which denied those at its mercy a fair hearing.

Star Spangled Banner The patriotic song written in 1814 by Francis Scott Key (1779–1843) during the British bombardment of Fort McHenry to commemorate the resolution shown by the young nation's troops. It was formally adopted as America's national anthem by EXECUTIVE ORDER in 1916 and by Act of CONGRESS in 1931; the tune is taken from an English drinking song by J. S. Smith, *Anacreon in Heaven.* The first verse is:

> O say! Can you see by the dawn's early light
> What so proudly we hailed at the twilight's last gleaming,
> Whose broad stripes and bright stars through the perilous fight
> O'er the ramparts we watched were so gallantly streaming?
> And the rockets' red glare, the bombs bursting in air
> Gave proof through the night that our flag was still there.
> O say, does that star spangled banner yet wave
> O'er the land of the free and the home of the brave?

Star Wars The Strategic Defence Initiative (SDI), the system backed by President REAGAN from 1983 for defending America against NUCLEAR attack by using laser-beam weapons orbiting in space to shoot down Soviet missiles with nuclear-generated blasts. His support was given to a general concept, and the reliability, cost and technical details were still being researched and argued over when the COLD WAR ended. President CLINTON effectively cancelled the project in May 1993, though George W. BUSH has canvassed its revival. The nickname came from the 1977 movie blockbuster *Star Wars*, reflecting the surreal, sci-fi aspect of the project.

> The great PORK BARREL in the sky.
>
> PAUL WARNKE

> The notion of a defence that will protect American cities is one that will not be achieved, but it is that goal that supplies the political magic in the President's vision.
>
> Former Defence Secretary JAMES SCHLESINGER, 1987

Stars and Bars The flag of the eleven CONFEDERATE States that seceded from the United States in 1861 at the start of the CIVIL WAR. It consisted at first of two horizontal red bars with a narrow white bar between them; in the top left was a blue square bearing eleven white stars in a circle. The term is more popularly applied to the later Confederate flag of a thirteen-starred blue diagonal cross with white fringe on a red background; the two extra stars represented Kentucky and Missouri, who were claimed for the Confederacy but were not part of it.

Stars and Stripes The familiar name for the flag of the United States, which has flown – with the addition of extra stars for newly-admitted States – since 1777. This name for OLD GLORY gained world-wide currency with John Philip Sousa's march, *Stars and Stripes Forever* (1897); it was also the name of the US Army newspaper in both World Wars. Originally there was one stripe per State, and the stars (again one per State) formed a circle on a blue ground until squared up in 1818; while the number of stars equals the number of States, no star represents a particular State. The number of stripes at first increased with the number of States, but in 1815 they were reduced to thirteen. The Stars and Stripes in its present form, with 50 stars, was first flown in 1960, after the admission of Alaska and Hawaii to the Union.

stark raving bonkers The denunciatory phrase popularised in the late 1950s by the pugnacious CONSERVATIVE PARTY chairman Lord Hailsham (1907–2001), when he said of Labour's programme: 'If the British public falls for this it'll be stark raving bonkers.' The term – which caused a stir at that comparatively genteel time – has nothing to do with the later slang word 'bonk' (to have sexual relations); it was originally 1920s slang for being tipsy or light-headed, and came to mean downright crazy. In 1983 Sen. Gaylord Nelson said of Interior Secretary James Watt: 'The Secretary has gone bonkers. It's time the white-coat people took him away.'

Starr. Blaze Starr affair The 1950s political scandal arising from the relationship between Louisiana's Governor Earl Long and Blaze Starr, a New Orleans stripper. Gov. Long, who served 1948–52 and 1956–60, inherited the Louisiana MACHINE from his brother, Sen. Huey (KINGFISH) Long, and ran it for 25 years. In his second term his increasingly erratic behaviour, including his public dalliance with Ms Starr, led to his committal to a mental hospital. According to Ms Starr, who wrote a book on their affair that was later turned into a film, *Blaze*, the governor had a penchant for sex with his boots on. Long won election to CONGRESS in 1960, but died before he could take his seat.

Starr Report The report by the SPECIAL PROSECUTOR Kenneth Starr into the ZIPPERGATE affair, issued in September 1998, which concluded that President CLINTON's handling of his relationship with Monica LEWINSKY had given rise to eleven offences meriting his IMPEACHMENT. In particular Starr concluded that Clinton had lied in the Paula JONES case and before a WASHINGTON grand jury about his relationship with Ms Lewinsky. Starr did not, however, uphold claims that the Clintons had acted illegally in the WHITEWATER affair or that the death of the assistant WHITE HOUSE counsel Vince FOSTER in 1993 had been other than suicide.

START agreements Strategic Arms Reduction Talks. The two ARMS CONTROL agreements between the SUPERPOWERS, concluded respectively by America with the Soviet Union in 1991 and Russia at the close of 1992, which brought the ARMS RACE to an end and for the first time imposed major cuts in strategic NUCLEAR arsenals. The first START agreement, signed by George BUSH Snr and Mikhail GORBACHEV in Moscow on 31 July 1991 after nine years of talks, called for 30% cuts in strategic nuclear missiles, with America retaining its slight edge. The second, signed by Bush and Boris Yeltsin in Moscow on 3 January 1993, involved a two-thirds reduction in strategic nuclear delivery systems over ten years, with an end to ground-launched MIRVed missiles. START II was not ratified by the Russian DUMA until April 2000.

Stasi The (un)popular name for East Germany's hated and pervasive State Security Police (*Staatssicherheitsdienst*). Responsible for espionage, counter-espionage and the suppression of political dissent, they were notorious for their minute surveillance of every citizen's life – often by suborning other family members. The *Stasi* were disbanded in December 1989, a few weeks after the breaching of the BERLIN WALL. A number of prominent Germans – East and West – were later accused of having been *Stasi* informers, several having to quit politics regardless of the veracity of the charges.

Stassen candidacy A quest that starts off as real and becomes increasingly forlorn. From the pursuit of the US Presidency by Harold Stassen (1907–2001), who became Minnesota's youngest-ever Senator at 31 and then two-term State Governor, and at the 1948 Republican CONVENTION forced Thomas DEWEY and Sen. Robert Taft to a third ballot. Stassen holds the record for the number of Presidential attempts (nine), in 1948, 1952, 1964, 1968, 1976 (the last time he obtained a delegate), 1980, 1984, 1988 and 1992. He also ran for governor of Minnesota four times (filing papers for a fifth attempt from his nursing home shortly before his death), governor of Pennsylvania twice, the Senate twice and mayor of Philadelphia once. He did make it to the WHITE HOUSE, under EISENHOWER from 1953 to 1958, first as Mutual Security Director (foreign aid), then Special Presidential Assistant for disarmament. He survived despite making a notable attempt to dump Richard NIXON as Vice President in 1956. Stassen's lasting achievement was as one of the principal drafters of the Charter of the UNITED NATIONS; he was also president of the University of Pennsylvania for five years.

state (1) The state, the body politic and core of a nation, and its power personified. To INTERVENTIONISTS and WELFARISTS it is a weapon for good, to DEMAGOGUES and TOTALITARIANS a means of power to be captured, to THATCHERITES and opponents of BIG GOVERNMENT a BUREAUCRACY to be slimmed, to MARXISTS something that will wither away once they have power, to ANARCHISTS something that is unnecessary and to REVOLUTIONARIES in general anathema – until they control it. Hegel termed the state 'the divine idea as it exists on earth'; Bakunin saw it as 'the most flagrant negation, the most complete and cynical negation of humanity', Engels as 'an instrument of oppression of one class by another – no less so in a democratic republic than in a monarchy'. Kroptokin declared that 'the word "state" is identical with the word "war",' and LENIN that 'so long as the State exists there is no freedom. When there is freedom there will be no State,' but Goebbels cynically reckoned: 'Whoever can conquer the street can one day conquer the State.' Edmund BURKE wrote: 'A state without the means of some change is without the means of its conservation,' and Paul Valéry observed: 'If the State is strong, it crushes us. If it is weak, we perish.' Lord BEVERIDGE maintained: 'The State is, or can be, master of money. But in a free society it is master of little else.'

Of the relationship between the state and the individual, Montesquieu wrote: 'The state owes to every citizen an assured subsistence, proper nourishment, suitable clothing and a mode of life not incompatible with health.' Macaulay tartly observed that 'no particular man is necessary to the state', and J. S. Mill considered that 'the worth of a state, in the long run, is the worth of the individuals comprising it.'

> The State exists for the sake of society, not society for the sake of the State.
>
> WOODROW WILSON

> The State has no business in the bedrooms of the nation. PIERRE TRUDEAU, 1967

> A state cannot be expected to move with the celerity of a private businessman; it is enough if it proceeds, in the language of the English Chancery, with all deliberate speed.
>
> Justice OLIVER WENDELL HOLMES, 1911

(2) A SOVEREIGN national entity whose existence and borders are recognised by others, often referred to as a NATION STATE. Almost all such entities – and almost no others – are members of the UNITED NATIONS. Bakunin argued that 'every state must conquer or be conquered', Treitschke that 'no state can pledge its future to another'. (3) One of the 50 component and in many ways sovereign jurisdictions of the United States. Friction between the states and the federal power goes back to the earliest days of the UNION, when George WASHINGTON wrote: 'The primary cause of all our disorder lies in the different state governments, and in the tenacity of that power which pervades the whole of their system.' Yet in 1819 Chief Justice John Marshall declared: 'No political dreamer was ever wild enough to think of breaking down the lines which separate the states, and of compounding the American people into one common mass.'

> I do not think the United States would come to an end if we lost our power to declare an Act of Congress void. I do think that the Union would be imperilled if we could not make that declaration as to the laws of the several states.
>
> Justice OLIVER WENDELL HOLMES, 1913

> It is one of the happiest incidents of the federal system that a single courageous state may, if its citizens choose, serve as a laboratory; and try novel social and economic experiments without risk to the rest of the country.
>
> Justice LOUIS BRANDEIS, dissenting in *New State Ice Co. v Liebmann*, 1932

(4) The six British colonies which came together in 1901 to form the Commonwealth of Australia; there are now seven plus the CAPITAL TERRITORY. (5) WASHINGTON and diplomatic shorthand for the STATE DEPARTMENT.

state capitalism A phrase coined by LENIN and briefly used by him to describe BOLSHEVIK economic policy between the OCTOBER REVOLUTION and the launching of the NEW ECONOMIC POLICY. He meant that Russia had not yet experienced the complete transformation from feudalism to capitalism; moderate leftists argued that, if so, progress to socialism should wait until bourgeois capitalism broke down, but Lenin responded that the state could hasten the process by developing a full infrastructure under PROLETARIAN control. The phrase was subsequently used by TROTSKYISTS and others to scorn the undemocratic and unimaginative nature of Soviet Communism.

State Department The section of the US government which has since 1789 conducted its relations with other countries and been in charge – at times nominally – of America's FOREIGN POLICY. Located since WORLD WAR II at FOGGY BOTTOM and headed by the SECRETARY OF STATE, it has, despite the professionalism of its diplomats, been the subject of even more scathing criticism from right-wing politicians than the FOREIGN OFFICE in London.

> Full of weaklings, sissies and people with mush for brains.
>
> Sen. GORDON HUMPHREY, 1982

state funeral The funeral, with all the pomp of a state occasion and accompanying military honours, accorded to a pre-eminent STATESMAN by a grateful nation. Often, as with CHURCHILL's spectacular obsequies in 1965, details have been arranged by the departing figure well in advance. Harry S TRUMAN planned 'a damn fine show – I just hate that I'm not going to be around to see it', but when he died in 1972 his widow Bess ignored the plans and ordered the simplest of ceremonies instead. WASHINGTON's most moving in living memory was that of John F. KENNEDY after his assassination in Dallas in November 1963. A state funeral will generally be preceded by a LYING IN STATE, though as with President REAGAN the coffin may simply be removed from the Capitol ROTUNDA for a quiet ceremony elsewhere.

state of emergency The suspension of normal constitutional procedures, declared by a government to enable it to take speedy action to tackle a civil emergency, keep services moving despite a disruptive industrial dispute, or maintain order at a time of war or civil unrest.

state of the parties In UK politics, the tabulation of the number of SEATS held by the respective parties in the HOUSE OF COMMONS; it covers the up-to-the-minute tally of results as the votes are counted after a GENERAL ELECTION and also a snapshot of the composition of the House at any point during a Parliament. The SPEAKER, and sometimes a handful of non-voting deputies, are excluded from the calculation.

State of the Union *See* UNION.

state of war A phrase used in a Declaration of WAR, asserting that 'a state of war now exists' between the two countries in question.

State opening The glittering annual occasion at which the SOVEREIGN opens a new SESSION of Parliament at WESTMINSTER, travelling in pomp from Buckingham Palace with available members of the ROYAL FAMILY in a procession of horse-drawn carriages and donning the Crown to deliver the GRACIOUS SPEECH from the THRONE in the HOUSE OF LORDS. When the Sovereign cannot attend – sometimes because she is in a Commonwealth country where she may be opening Parliament with rather less splendour – a senior member of the Royal family takes her place and delivers the Speech, which is in any case written by Ministers. The State opening generally takes place in November, unless a general election has produced a break in the Parliamentary timetable at another time of year.

state terrorism A phrase used predominantly by left-wingers for the use by governments of security methods which, if carried out by anyone else, would be categorised as terrorism. It has applied to the activities of government-sponsored DEATH SQUADS in Latin America and Africa, but more specifically to Israel's attacks on Palestinian militants and their homes, especially in GAZA.

State visit A visit made by a HEAD OF STATE to another country, where their counterpart receives them with full honours. Customarily the streets of the host capital are decked with the flag of the visitor, and host and guest hold lavish official banquets for each other. Most state visitors to Britain used to arrive at Victoria Station from Gatwick Airport, be greeted there by the Queen and then driven in procession the few hundred yards to Buckingham Palace; this procedure was largely abandoned in the late 1980s because of its paralysing effect on London's traffic.

State We're In, The The book published in 1995 by the UK economic commentator Will Hutton which became a core text for the THIRD WAY espoused in office by Tony BLAIR. Hutton argued that the UK financial sector was preoccupied with speculation rather than enabling industry to invest; looking to the German model, he argued for STAKEHOLDERS to take a more active role in the economy and in communities.

enabling state The phrase used by the LIBERAL DEMOCRAT leader Paddy Ashdown (*see* PADDY PANTSDOWN) in the run-up to the 1992 UK general election, to describe a society in which citizens are encouraged and assisted to maximise their potential.

nanny state The derogatory term devised by THATCHERITES in the 1980s for a central government which indulged in what they saw as unnecessary and even harmful supervision of the public at large, protecting them from the normal risks of life. The term has now passed into universal use.

nation state *See* NATION.

Offences Against the State Act The legislation that has formed the backbone of the Irish Republic's legal machinery in dealing with the IRA, and other REPUBLICAN terrorist groups whose aims encompass not only the freeing of NORTHERN IRELAND from British rule but the replacement of the Dublin government by a Marxist state. A key element is the provision that a person may be imprisoned if a senior police officer testifies that, in their belief, that person is a member of an illegal organisation. First passed in 1939, the Act has been strengthened several times since, most recently in 1985 when provision was made for the confiscation of terrorists' assets.

police state A political and social system in which the SECRET POLICE detect and crush any opposition to those in power.

welfare state *See* WELFARE.

withering away of the state In the eyes of MARXIST revolutionaries, the ultimate achievement of COMMUNISM, the point at which central authority becomes unnecessary. The concept was advanced in 1787 by Friedrich Engels (1820–95), who wrote in his ANTI-DÜHRING:

> The first act by which the state really constitutes itself the representative of the whole of society – the taking possession of the means of production in the name of society – is at the same time its last independent act of the state. The state is not abolished; it withers away.

statecraft The art of conducting government and managing state affairs.

statehood In America, the achievement by a TERRITORY of full membership of the United States; Alaska and Hawaii in 1959 were proclaimed the 49th and 50th States of the Union. The people of Puerto Rico, now a COMMONWEALTH, have long been divided over whether statehood would benefit them; a STATEHOOD PARTY enjoys considerable, but not majority, support.

States of . . . The LEGISLATUREs that govern the Channel Islands of Jersey and Guernsey (including Alderney), which though under British sovereignty are not fully part of the United Kingdom, being unrepresented at WESTMINSTER and outside the EUROPEAN UNION.

States' Rights The doctrine, dating back to the foundation of the United States, that the individual states should have more freedom to act, compared with the federal government. The argument over states' rights became embroiled with that over slavery, Abraham LINCOLN declaring: 'Each community, as a state, has a right to do exactly as it pleases with all the concerns within that state that interfere with no other state, and the general government, upon principle, has no right to interfere with anything other than that general class of things that does concern the whole.' After the CIVIL WAR States' Rights increasingly became shorthand for the ability of the SEGREGATIONIST South to defy federal CIVIL RIGHTS legislation. In 1948 the DIXIECRAT Strom Thurmond ran for the Presidency under the banner of a **States' Rights Party**.

> I say the time has come to walk out of the shadow of states' rights and into the sunlight of HUMAN RIGHTS.
>
> HUBERT HUMPHREY to the 1948 Democratic Convention

statement At WESTMINSTER, a formal announcement made to either HOUSE by a Minister. He or she delivers the statement, the appropriate OPPOSITION statesman gives a speech dressed up as a lengthy and comprehensive question which is responded to, and questions are then taken from each side of the House in turn until the SPEAKER ends the exchanges. The Speaker gives permission for the statement to be made, but the scheduling is a matter for the Minister and for BUSINESS MANAGERS. Occasionally a Minister blunders. On 9 May 1969 Richard CROSSMAN, Secretary for Health and Social Security, announced an increase in NHS charges on the day of local elections; he was widely blamed for Labour's disastrous showing. Crossman, who prided himself on his mastery of government, wrote laconically in his diary:

> When I got to the office I found waiting for me a statement on teeth and spectacles. I knew this was a bit unpleasant.

Autumn Statement The name given from the early 1980s until 1992 to the Pre-BUDGET Report delivered by the CHANCELLOR OF THE EXCHEQUER to the HOUSE OF COMMONS every November. It was instituted by Sir Geoffrey HOWE, who added substance to what had previously been little more than a recital of the INDUSTRY ACT FORECASTS. Howe told the author that the Autumn Statement would never supplant the Budget, but in 1993 and for the four years following, the Budget and the Autumn Statement were merged.

business statement *See* BUSINESS.

personal statement *See* PERSONAL.

statesman A complimentary term for a politician, implying wisdom, vision, dignity and a lifetime of experience. Once in common use, the word has acquired *gravitas* to the point where it is used of relatively few senior figures. Originally the word had connotations of cunning, Davy Crockett saying in 1833:

> Statesmen are gamesters, and the people are the cards they play with . . . the way they cut and shuffle is a surprise to all young beginners.

Before long the term became a positive one, the 19th-century French premier Gustave Thiers remarking:

> A statesman should be possessed of good sense, a primary political quality; and its fortunate possessor needs a second quality: the courage to show that he has it.

Next a hint of stuffiness crept in. The British Liberal G. W. E. Russell wrote in 1912:

> The perfection of parliamentary style is to utter platitudes with a grave and informing air; and if a little pomposity may be superadded, the House will recognise the speaker as a statesman.

Dean Acheson took the process one stage further, saying: 'The first requirement of a statesman is that he be dull. This is not always easy to achieve.' However, DE GAULLE restored the balance by declaring that 'the true statesman is the one who is willing to take risks'; Henry KISSINGER added that 'the statesman's duty is to bridge the gap between his nation's experience and his vision'.

The comparison between a statesman and a politician has produced many definitions. DISRAELI declared that 'the world is weary of statesmen whom democracy has degraded into politicians', LLOYD GEORGE that 'when you're abroad you're a statesman; when you're at home you're a politician'; he also said: 'A politician is a person with whose policies you do not agree. If you agree with him, he's a statesman.' The US humorist Austin O'Malley reckoned that 'the statesman shears sheep – the politician skins 'em'; Harry S TRUMAN that 'a statesman is a politician who's been dead 10 to 15 years'; Adlai STEVENSON that 'a politician is a statesman who approaches every question with an open mouth'; and Governor John Connally that 'when you're out of office you can be a statesman'. Sen. Margaret Chase Smith put it the other way round: 'Before you can become a statesman you have to get elected. And to get elected you have to be a politician, pledging support for what the voters want.' President Georges Pompidou declared that 'a statesman is a politician who places himself at the head of the nation. A politician is a statesman who places the nation at his service'; Richard CROSSMAN that 'a statesman imposes his will and his ideas on his environment; a politician adapts himself to it'.

> My father was a statesman. I am a political woman. My father was a saint. I am not.
>
> INDIRA GANDHI on PANDIT Nehru

elder statesman A political figure who is in retirement after a lifetime of valued service and whose advice and support are valued. When a reporter once referred to Harry S TRUMAN as an elder statesman, he replied:

> I'm not an elder statesman. I hate elder statesmen. I'm a Democrat and a politician and I'm proud of it.

New Statesman *See* NEW.

act of statesmanship A step – generally an unpopular one – which requires wisdom and apparent sacrifice to achieve an outcome benefiting the community as a whole.

statism Control by the state of social and economic affairs, and the belief that such control should be exercised.

> We are going down the road to statism . . . If some of the new programs seriously proposed should be adopted, there is the danger that the individual – whether farmer, worker, manufacturer, lawyer or doctor – will soon be an economic slave pulling on an oar in the galley of the state.
>
> JAMES F. BYRNES, former head of FDR's Office of War Mobilisation, speech at Lexington, Virginia, 18 June 1949

Statuary Hall or **Old Hall of the House** The semi-circular chamber with deep rose hangings in which the US HOUSE OF REPRESENTATIVES met from 1806 to 1957; gutted by the British in 1814, it was rebuilt for the 16th CONGRESS, partly rectifying what a Congressional committee had termed 'its only defect – difficulty of hearing and speaking in it'. It was the scene of six Presidential INAUGURATIONS, and also witnessed John Quincy ADAMS' fatal stroke in 1848. In 1864 Congress invited each state to place in the now empty hall the statues of two distinguished citizens; to date 95 have been donated, ranging from Ethan Allen, the hero of Ticonderoga, to Dr John Gorrie, the Floridan who invented the first ice machine, and Jeannette Rankin, the Montana Congresswoman who voted alone against the declaration of WORLD WAR I – and 25 years later against the declaration of WORLD WAR II. The Hall cannot accommodate them all or bear their weight, so many now line corridors elsewhere in the CAPITOL.

> Handsome, and fit for anything except the use intended.
>
> Rep. JOHN RANDOLPH (1773–1833)

Statute of Westminster *See* WESTMINSTER.

Statutes at Large The totality of the laws passed by the US CONGRESS; after each SESSION a new volume is published containing the measures enacted during it.

on the statute book A UK term for a law currently in force; Parliament's passing of an ACT is known as putting it onto the statute book. No one such book exists; all new Acts are bound into volumes, SESSION by session.

statutory instruments At WESTMINSTER, regulations, ORDERS and other items of secondary legislation made by Ministers which may or may not be subject to approval by Parliament. A special committee of MPs determines whether or not such approval is necessary.

statutory woman A pre-feminist term for the frequent appointment of a sole woman to UK public bodies, because convention required it rather than out of any interest in hearing her views.

Stauffenberg plot The unsuccessful attempt by idealistic members of the German officer corps to assassinate HITLER with a bomb on 20 July 1944. A briefcase containing the bomb was left by Colonel Claus von Stauffenberg under the conference table at the FÜHRER's headquarters (Wolf's Lair) at Rastenberg, East Prussia. In a parallel plan, known as 'Operation Valkyrie', the conspirators were supposed to seize key government installations in Berlin after Hitler's death, and a few officers went ahead and arrested leading NAZIS. However, Hitler, shielded by the heavy oak table, escaped with only shock and minor injuries, commenting:

> Who says I am not under the special protection of God?

He was well enough to meet Mussolini (*see* DUCE) two hours later. Not unexpectedly, revenge was instant and savage. Stauffenberg and three others were immediately shot, Rommel was forced to take poison and 7000 other suspects were arrested and in many cases tortured and tried by PEOPLE'S COURTS; 4000 were executed. A number were hanged with piano wire, Hitler then watching a film of their agony. *See also* SPEER?

Stavisky affair The financial scandal surrounding the affairs of Serge Alexandre Stavisky (c. 1886–1934), a Russian-born French swindler, which came to a head in 1933–34, threatening the survival of the THIRD REPUBLIC. Stavisky, an adept at establishing fraudulent businesses, led an extravagant lifestyle, mixing with influential society in Cannes and Deauville until in December 1933 he was exposed in a Fr. 500 million bond swindle involving the Bayonne municipal pawnshop. He fled to the resort of Chamonix, where he was found dead the next month, supposedly by his own hand; many suspected he had been killed by the police to protect his influential patrons in government, the judiciary and the *Sûreté* itself. In February 1934 widespread suspicion of government corruption prompted violent demonstrations in Paris led by the right-wing ACTION FRANÇAISE and *Croix de Feu*, which brought down the government and momentarily threatened Parliamentary democracy.

steady as she goes! The nautical phrase with which Chancellor James CALLAGHAN (*see also* STOKER JIM) characterised his 1967 BUDGET. He ended his speech by saying:

> I sum up the prospects for 1967 in three short sentences. We are back on course [after the JULY MEASURES of 1966]. The ship is picking up speed. The economy is moving ahead. Every seaman knows the command at such a moment: 'Steady as she goes!'

Callaghan's hopes were not borne out. Three months later the SIX DAY WAR produced a run on the POUND, and the blockage of the Suez Canal damaged Britain's BALANCE OF PAYMENTS. That November, Callaghan DEVALUED and left the Treasury. He wrote of his Budget phrase:

> This was a hostage to fortune which rapidly returned to haunt me. But I feel no remorse, for I know of no one who foretold . . . that by November both sterling and I would be shipwrecked.

It described a condition of being all at sea.
EDWARD PEARCE, *Macchiavelli's Children*

stealing an opponent's clothes The adoption by one party of another's distinctive policies, leaving them without a worthwhile programme to campaign on. The phrase was coined by DISRAELI when on 28 February 1845 he said of PEEL:

> The Rt Honourable Gentleman caught the WHIGS bathing, and walked away with their clothes.

stealth Anything that exists undetected, the term having its origin in America's B2 **Stealth bomber**, developed in the late 1980s, which is configured and made of such materials that it can be almost invisible to enemy radar.

Stealth Building The WASHINGTON headquarters of the National Reconnaissance Office, which operates all US spy satellites for the PENTAGON and the CIA, which was disguised as a corporate centre for Rockwell International and which CONGRESS unwittingly paid $310 million in 1990 to finance. The four-building complex housing 3000 NRO staff on a 68-acre site at Chantilly, Virginia, 30 miles outside Washington, was 'outed' by President CLINTON in 1994 after Senators complained that they had been duped.

stealth campaign A vigorous campaign by a party to maximise its support at election times, conducted without its opponents realising the scale of the activity. Up to the 1992 UK general election which John MAJOR's Conservatives were reckoned to have won by such methods, such a strategy was known as a **subterranean campaign**. Major's unexpected victory stemmed from the holding of key MARGINAL SEATS through intensive telephone CANVASSING of past Conservative supporters, rather than trying to win converts and alerting the other parties.

stealth candidate A phrase first heard in the 1992 Congressional campaign: a candidate dialling for dollars behind closed doors instead of getting out to meet the voters.

stealth issue An issue that suddenly emerges as crucial, having been nurtured by one candidate or party without their opponents or even the media seeing it coming.

stealth taxes This one has a largely UK application: taxes which impact on the finances of ordinary people without their being aware of it. The charge of levying stealth taxes was levelled by the Conservatives at Chancellor Gordon BROWN when, while keeping rates of income tax low, he increased NATIONAL INSURANCE contributions, taxed the pension funds and pocketed a steep rise in proceeds from inheritance tax as rising property prices caught more family homes when their occupants died. *See also* EVERYBODY WILL BE A MILLIONNAIRE BY THE END OF THE CENTURY.

steam engine in britches The nickname accorded the US Statesman Sen. Daniel Webster (1782–1852) by the English writer, cleric and philosopher Sydney Smith (1771–1845). He wrote of the great orator: 'Daniel Webster struck me much like a steam engine in trousers', and Americans took up the phrase. It was also applied to Sen. Stephen Douglas (*see* LITTLE GIANT), who narrowly defeated Abraham LINCOLN in Illinois in 1858 after a memorable series of DEBATES, but lost the Presidency to him two years later.

Steel, David *See* BOY DAVID.

Steel Magnolia Washington's nickname for Rosalynn Carter, wife and close collaborator of President Jimmy CARTER; it reflected both her determined temperament (steel) and her Southern origins (magnolia).

Steiger amendment The reduction in capital taxes brought about in 1978 when a rebellion led by Rep. William Steiger, a Wisconsin Republican, overturned a key element of President CARTER's tax programme. Together with the defeat of a BILL to allow common site PICKETING the year before, it demonstrated to business how shrewd LOBBYING could bring it results even in a Democratic CONGRESS – and was followed by a massive influx of trade associations and lobbying firms anxious to press their own agendas.

Stem van Suid-Afrika (Afrik. The Voice of South Africa) The national anthem of white-ruled South Africa, introduced in 1936 and replacing GOD SAVE THE QUEEN in 1957. To non-Afrikaners of all colours, *Die Stem* was the symbol of Boer supremacy and APARTHEID; when it was played at a rugby international in Johannesburg in 1992, the ANC threatened to reactivate the world sporting boycott of South Africa. Remarkably, it has coexisted in the multiracial South Africa with the ANC anthem *NKOSI SIKELELE AFRIKA*, with some nerve-ends in both camps starting to heal.

step by step The description given by James (later Lord) Prior (1927–), Margaret THATCHER's first Employment Secretary from 1979 to 1981, to his gradualist approach to the introduction of laws curbing the power of Britain's trade unions. In OPPOSITION and then in government, Prior resisted strong right-wing pressure (not least from Mrs Thatcher, *see* JIM IS VERY, VERY SORRY) for instant and draconian measures in favour of a series of BILLS outlawing one set of abuses at a time. His successors, including his critic Norman Tebbit (*see* CHINGFORD SKINHEAD), continued the approach.

Stepford Wives The phrase employed by the left-wing Labour MP Brian Sedgemore on February 1998 for newly-elected and studiously loyal female Labour MPs (*see* BLAIR BABES): 'female, NEW LABOUR MPs who've had a chip inserted in their brains to keep them ON MESSAGE.' It was taken from the eponymous US novel and subsequent film about husbands who kill their wives and replace them with automata. On his retirement from the COMMONS seven years later, Sedgemore defected to the Liberal Democrats.

sterling The British pound, whose erratic performance on world currency markets in the 1960s and '70s became what Enoch POWELL, with tongue in cheek, once called 'an index of our national turpitude'. At the height of the 1966 election campaign Harold WILSON told a BBC interviewer:

> I hope no-one is going to bring sterling into this election. Sterling should be above politics.

It was a pious hope. That summer a sterling crisis led to the JULY MEASURES to maintain the parity of the pound at $2.80, and in November 1967 Wilson's government was forced to DEVALUE. Wilson had barely retired from politics when a further sterling crisis in the autumn of 1976 obliged

Chancellor Denis HEALEY to obtain a standby credit from the IMF.

sterling area An association (also called the sterling bloc, or scheduled territories) formed after Britain left the GOLD STANDARD in 1931, when a large number of countries agreed to stabilise their currencies in terms of the pound and hold **sterling balances** as part of their reserves. It included the then independent members of the COMMONWEALTH (except Canada), Eire, Jordan, Iraq, Libya, Burma and Iceland. The sterling area declined in importance after 1949, as the progressive devaluation of sterling made it less attractive as a reserve currency, and the need to maintain the value of the sterling balances became a millstone around the neck of successive UK governments in the 1960s and '70s. Few countries, except for some members of the Commonwealth, now hold sterling on a large scale, preferring more stable currencies like the euro and the yen.

Stern Gang A small Jewish terrorist organisation, founded in Palestine in 1940, which concentrated on assassinating British personnel. It was named after an early leader, Abraham Stern (1907–42), who was killed in a gunfight with British police. On 6 November 1944 the gang murdered Lord Moyne, Minister of State for Middle East Affairs, in Cairo. From 1945 it collaborated with two other groups, the IRGUN ZVA LEUMI and HAGANAH, in a GUERRILLA campaign to force the establishment of a Jewish state in Palestine. Although denounced by the official ZIONIST leadership, the activities of the Stern Gang and others were effective in helping to secure British withdrawal, which eventually led to the founding of ISRAEL in May 1948. A former leading member of the Stern Gang, Yitzhak Shamir, served as the LIKUD Prime Minister of Israel (1983–4 and 1986–92).

Stevenson. Adlai Stevenson moment A dramatic disclosure which pulls the rug from under one's opponents, as at the height of the CUBAN MISSILE CRISIS when Adlai Stevenson (1900–65), US Ambassador to the UNITED NATIONS, confronted his Soviet opposite number with photographic proof that the Kremlin had been installing missile sites in Cuba. The phrase was heavily used early in 2003 as America and Britain prepared for military action against SADDAM HUSSEIN, the argument being that widespread global and domestic opposition might be defused if President BUSH were dramatically to publicise evidence obtained by US intelligence agencies that Saddam was indeed developing WEAPONS OF MASS DESTRUCTION in breach of UN resolutions. In the event, the evidence turned out to be exaggerated and the IRAQ SURVEY GROUP found no trace of WMD after the war. Stevenson, a successful Governor of Illinois, twice ran against EISENHOWER for the Presidency; he made his first run in 1952 after President TRUMAN told him: 'Adlai, if a knucklehead like me can be President and not do too badly, think what a really educated smart guy like you could do with the job.' Stevenson took up the challenge reluctantly, saying: 'Nobody needs to save the Republic from IKE, and couldn't if they tried.'

Stockholm appeal A petition to ban the ATOMIC BOMB, allegedly signed by 500 million people in 70 countries, which was launched at the Communist-organised World Peace Congress in Stockholm in March 1950. The Congress was to have been held in Sheffield, but Britain's Labour government refused visas to a number of participants.

Stoker Jim One of several nicknames for the Labour Prime Minister James CALLAGHAN (*see also* SUNNY JIM), reflecting his wartime service in the Royal Navy. He was not, in fact, a stoker but a Sub-Lieutenant who served in home waters and the Far East, also writing the Naval Manual on Japan.

stone. Stone of Destiny Also known as the **Stone of Scone**, the coronation stone of the kings of Scotland which was positioned beneath the THRONE in Westminster Abbey from the 14th century, when it was seized by Edward I, 'Hammer of the Scots', until 1996, apart from a brief interlude in 1950 when it was 'repatriated' by four nationalist students from Glasgow University, turning up four months later at Arbroath Abbey. The stone was reputed to be the 'pillow' on which Jacob rested his head at Bethel; Kenneth MacAlpin, who united the Picts and the Scots, is believed to have been the first king crowned on it at Scone, Perthshire, in 839. In July 1996 John MAJOR and his Scottish Secretary Michael Forsyth staged its return to Scotland, escorted by pipers and Scottish troops, in an abortive bid to quell nationalist and devolutionist feeling. It was unveiled at Edinburgh Castle on St Andrew's Day, 1996.

I. F. Stone's Weekly The one-man newsletter circulated from Washington by the liberal journalist Isidore F. Stone (1907–82). Stone published this irritant to the government and military ESTABLISHMENT from 1952 to 1971, achieving influence well beyond its 74,000 subscribers.

Stonehouse affair The bizarre circumstances surrounding the disappearance of the former Labour Cabinet Minister John Stonehouse in November 1974 when his clothes were found on a beach in Florida, and his discovery in Melbourne not long after. An early supporter of Harold WILSON, Stonehouse had been a rising star in the 1964–70 government as Postmaster-General and Minister of Aviation, but MI5 marked his card as a SECURITY RISK – something apparently confirmed in 1971 by a Czech DEFECTOR – and colleagues increasingly saw him as a shallow OPPORTUNIST; when Labour returned to power in 1974 Stonehouse, who now had interests in property and banking but was not a wealthy man, stayed a BACKBENCH MP. He aimed to fake his death to convince his wife and family and, with a false passport obtained in the name of a dead CONSTITUENT in Walsall, start a new life with his Commons secretary Sheila Buckley. He left behind large queries about his activities as chairman of a Bangladeshi bank, and was eventually EXTRADITED from Australia. He continued to attend the Commons as an Independent, ostracised by former colleagues, while insisting he was the victim of a plot. On 5 August 1976 Stonehouse, who had conducted his own defence, was convicted on eighteen out of nineteen charges of theft, fraud, forgery and conspiracy, and imprisoned for seven years. Ms Buckley was found guilty on five counts out of six, receiving a two-year suspended sentence. Later that month Stonehouse applied for the CHILTERN HUNDREDS; Labour's defeat in the subsequent BY-ELECTION eventually contributed to the fall, by one vote, of the CALLAGHAN government. Released after three years, he married Ms Buckley and started a business, but died in 1989.

Stonewall *See* GAY RIGHTS.

stop. stop-go A pejorative coined c. 1960 for government economic policies that seek to REFLATE the economy when there is high unemployment, then slam on the brakes at the first signs of OVERHEATING. It implies that a government, incapable of long-term thinking, can only control the economy by short-term reflexes. In 1963 the new Labour leader Harold WILSON ridiculed Harold MACMILLAN and his Chancellor Selwyn Lloyd as **'Stop-go and Son'** – a play on the then-new BBC television sitcom *Steptoe and Son*. *Compare* BOOM AND BUST.

Stop the '70 tour! The slogan under which opponents of APARTHEID in Britain prevented the 1970 cricket tour by an official South Africa team from taking place. Cricket in South Africa was then SEGREGATED, and in 1968 Pretoria had refused to accept an MCC team because the coloured South African player Basil d'Oliveira was included. With civil disorder looming and security costs rising even for a truncated tour, the Cricket Council on 19 May 1970 ruled that there would be no further tours to England until South Africa selected its team on a non-racial basis.

> Blackmail has become respectable.
>
> Sir ROBERT MENZIES

Stop the War Coalition The umbrella group which on the eve of the IRAQ WAR in March 2003 brought almost 1 million protesters out peacefully onto the streets of London to protest against UK/US military intervention, the city's largest DEMONSTRATION. Although its supporters came from all points of the political spectrum, the nucleus of the coalition lay on the far left.

stopping the clock The technique used in EUROPEAN UNION Ministerial meetings to avoid a breakdown of negotiations when a deadline for agreement expires, under which a decision is made to 'stop the clock' just before the deadline but keep talking.

storm. the gathering storm The phrase about the imminence of WORLD WAR II that Anthony EDEN used in November 1938 in a speech to the National Association of Manufacturers in New York. It was later taken up by CHURCHILL for the title of one of his own books of reminiscence, and in 2003 was the title of an acclaimed BBC docu-drama about Churchill's opposition to APPEASEMENT.

Stormont The seat of the DEVOLVED government under which NORTHERN IRELAND was administered, and the UNIONIST supremacy that prevailed; also since the 1998 GOOD FRIDAY AGREEMENT the home of the POWER-SHARING executive that has sporadically exercised power. The centrepiece of the 300 acres of parkland six miles east of Belfast is the Parliament House, designed in 'Official Classical' style by Sir Arnold Thornley and opened in 1932 by King George V. Nearby stands Stormont Castle, formerly the official residence of Viscount Craigavon, Northern

Ireland's first Prime Minister; since 1972 it has housed the offices of the Secretary of State and other Northern Ireland ministers. The other main administrative building is Dundonald House, designed by Gibson and Taylor and opened in 1963. The last entirely Unionist Stormont government resigned in 1972 in protest at the British government's assumption of responsibility for law and order, after which the province was governed by DIRECT RULE from Westminster except during experiments in power-sharing.

straight fight In UK politics, an election fought out between just two candidates.

Strangelove A COLD WAR term for a fanatical or insane MILITARIST who advocates large-scale pre-emptive nuclear strikes; more generally, a WASHINGTON term for anyone in the PENTAGON who THINKS THE UNTHINKABLE. The name comes from Stanley Kubrick's 1963 black comedy, *Dr Strangelove, or How I Learned to Stop Worrying and Love the Bomb*, in which the title role and two other parts were played by Peter Sellers. An insane USAF general, played by George C. Scott, comments:

> I don't say we wouldn't get our hair mussed, but I do say no more than 10 to 20 million people killed.

strangers At WESTMINSTER, the HOUSE OF COMMONS expression for members of the public for four centuries until October 2004, when MPs voted by 242–167 to replace it with something less hostile. The word was applied to the **Strangers' Gallery** (now the Public Gallery) from which citizens can watch proceedings in the Chamber, and the **Strangers' Bar** (*see* KREMLIN). **Strangers withdraw**, a procedural motion aimed at delaying or disrupting Commons BUSINESS when the mover would call out: **'I see strangers'**, has been replaced by the motion **'that this House do now sit in private'**, first moved on 5 December 2001 by the Liberal Democrat Paul Tyler. Once the motion has been proposed, a DIVISION has to be held on the technicality of whether the public and press should be ejected from the galleries, using up fifteen minutes of time.

Strength through joy *See* KRAFT DURCH FREUDE.

Stresa Front An agreement signed in April 1935 by Britain, France and Italy at Stresa in Italian Piedmont, in response to German REARMAMENT which HITLER had declared the month before. They agreed to uphold the status quo imposed by the Treaty of VERSAILLES and other post-WORLD WAR I settlements, and defend Austria's independence from the threat of a forced ANSCHLUSS with Germany. The Front presented no serious threat to German ambitions in Europe and collapsed within six months when Mussolini (*see* DUCE) invaded Abyssinia.

strike (1) In industrial relations, the organised withdrawal of labour by workers in pursuit of improved pay or conditions or to force redress of a grievance. In many countries it has also been a political weapon, but has seldom been used as such in America, and never in Britain save for the GENERAL STRIKE of 1926. The right to strike is much prized by organised labour and, subject to some curbs on its abuse, notably in Britain by Margaret THATCHER's government (*see* STEP BY STEP), is a hallmark of a free society; indeed Abraham LINCOLN remarked:

> I am glad to know that there is a system of labour where the labourer can strike if he wants to! I would to God that such a system prevailed all over the world.

Other Presidents were less charitable. Grover CLEVELAND, ordering in troops to break a rail strike in Chicago, said:

> If it takes the entire army and navy of the United States to deliver a postcard in Chicago, that card will be delivered.

And during the BOSTON POLICE STRIKE Calvin COOLIDGE stated as trenchantly:

> There is no right to strike against the public safety by anybody, anywhere, any time.

The right to strike has also been seen by generations of revolutionaries as a means to an end. Engels wrote:

> If trade unionists failed to register their protest by striking, their silence would be regarded as an admission that they acquiesced in the pre-eminence of economic forces over human welfare.

And Rosa Luxemburg declared:

> Mass strikes appear as the natural method to mobilise the broadest proletarian layers into action, to revolutionise and organise them.

See also Industrial ACTION; PICKETING.

(2) A form of extortion practised by Senators and Congressmen in late 19th-century WASHINGTON; it involved promoting legislation aimed at inconveniencing big business, in the expectation that the interests involved would offer handsome bribes to withdraw it.

first strike *See* FIRST.

hunger strike A time-honoured and potentially fatal form of political protest by the most committed and self-sacrificing adherents of a cause, generally when imprisoned. It was practised prior to WORLD WAR I by Britain's SUFFRAGETTES (*see* CAT AND MOUSE ACT), and after it by Terence McSwiney, Lord Mayor of Cork, who perished after 74 days in 1920 in an effort to precipitate Irish independence. The Welsh Nationalist MP Gwynfor Evans threatened a hunger strike c. 1980 to bring about a Welsh language television channel, only to be told by his Tory counterpart Delwyn Williams:

> You realise you can only do this once.

The most concentrated, and deadly, use of the hunger strike as a weapon was in 1981 by convicted Provisional IRA prisoners in the H-BLOCKS, in support of their campaign for 'political status' which had already included BLANKET and DIRTY PROTESTS. They hoped to force concessions from Margaret THATCHER by confronting her with horrendous deaths, sparking civil unrest in Ulster and world-wide pressure to capitulate. Yet the hunger-strikers had met their match. Mrs Thatcher stood firm when the first, Bobby Sands, died on 5 May after fasting for 66 days, telling the COMMONS:

> Mr Sands was a convicted criminal. He chose to take his own life. It was a choice that his organisation did not allow to many of its victims.

Nine more hunger strikers died that summer before the Provisionals abandoned their campaign.

miners' strike *See* MINERS.

three strikes and you're out *See* THREE.

stroke. at a stroke The phrase that haunted Edward HEATH as INFLATION began to take hold during his ADMINISTRATION, earning him many taunts from Harold WILSON and other opponents. During the 1970 election campaign Heath was supposed to have said: 'We will reduce the rise in prices at a stroke.' The words were not actually said by Heath, but a handout distributed at one of his election press conferences read:

> This [tax cuts and a freeze on nationalised industry prices] would, at a stroke, reduce the rise in prices, increase productivity and reduce unemployment.

at the stroke of a pen The flourish with which John F. KENNEDY promised as a Presidential candidate in 1960 to end racial discrimination in federal housing. CIVIL RIGHTS groups lamented that it took him almost two years to carry out his pledge, not picking up the pen until November 1962.

strong man A euphemism for a DICTATOR, usually claiming to be pro-Western and generally with a military power base. The term is most often used in a Latin American contest, sometimes describing an officer who wields the real power in a state while not being the titular head; an example was Gen. Omar Torrijos of Panama. It was also used to describe General PINOCHET during and after his presidency of Chile, Ngo Dinh Diem, South Vietnam's Prime Minister in the early stages of the VIETNAM WAR, and certain rulers of Thailand and South Korea.

structural funds Special funds allocated by the EUROPEAN UNION for projects in member states, especially those whose economies are less advanced and are eager for assistance to help them catch up (*see* COHESION). Spain has been a particular beneficiary of structural funds, despite not being among the EU's poorest members, ever since the 1992 Edinburgh summit agreed a substantial increase in the funds and Spain's Prime Minister Felipe González held out for the lion's share.

STUC Scottish Trades Union Congress. Scotland's autonomous equivalent of the TUC, with more status and political muscle reflecting the more concentrated and pervasive nature of trade unionism north of the Border. Andrew Marr, in *The Battle for Scotland*, wrote that for many years the STUC could almost be regarded as 'the political wing of the LABOUR PARTY in Scotland'.

stuff and tell Not a raunchier version of 'kiss and tell', but the twin chores of electioneering in Britain which have customarily been carried out by (especially Conservative) women, putting leaflets in envelopes for delivery and telling at polling stations. *Compare* WOMEN MAKE POLICY AS WELL AS TEA.

stuffing A largely US term for the rigging of an ELECTION, with supporters of a CANDIDATE or party organising the casting of large numbers of illicit votes, and thus stuffing the BALLOT BOX. The introduction of voting machines was designed to put an end to such practices. Unless officials supervising the actual casting of the votes are corrupt – as was sometimes the case – the actual stuffing of a ballot box is impossible to achieve.

stump. on the stump A mainly US term for the form of campaigning in which a CANDIDATE gets out and makes often-impromptu **stump speeches**, instead of concentrating on set-piece appearances. The phrase dates back to the early 19th or even 18th century, when candidates campaigning in the backwoods of the West harangued crowds from the stumps of newly-felled trees. The phrase **stumping the country** has the same origin.

STV Single Transferable Vote. One of the most popular forms of PROPORTIONAL REPRESENTATION. Under it each elector lists the candidates in order of preference; if their first choice finishes bottom of the poll, the second preferences for that candidate are distributed among the others, and so on until one candidate has over 50% of the total.

style versus substance The late 20th-century counterpart of MEN OR MEASURES, the comparison between a candidate or leader with strong personal CHARISMA and one with greater governmental skills or intellectual weight.

sub-committee A formally- or informally-constituted body composed of members of a COMMITTEE, and reporting to it; generally it deals with a portion of the full committee's remit, or matters deemed too routine for the entire panel to consider in detail. In Britain, sub-committees are primarily found in local government. In the US CONGRESS, they came into their own in 1974 when the HOUSE OF REPRESENTATIVES devolved much of the power of its 22 STANDING COMMITTEES to 172 sub-committees. At a stroke, this broke the power of the BARONS who had controlled the main committees through their SENIORITY, and catapulted relatively junior members into positions of some influence.

sub judice (Lat. under a judge) The convention that matters that are currently the subject of legal proceedings may not be commented on in Parliamentary debate, lest anything said prove prejudicial. There is some flexibility over cases already decided by a jury that are the subject of an appeal, on the ground that the judges hearing the appeal are above being influenced in the same way as jurors.

Subcomandante Marcos *See* ZAPATISTAS.

Sublime Porte (Fr. Lofty Gate) The central government in Istanbul of the Ottoman Empire, which was eclipsed during WORLD WAR I. It took its name from a building near one of the city's twelve gates called *Bab-i-Humajun*, which itself had a tall gate. It was both the official residence of the vizier, and the offices of all chief ministers of state from which Imperial edicts were issued.

subliminal influence The influencing of voters without their being aware of it, for instance by the repeated transmission of a slogan on television for too brief an instant for viewers to realise that they have seen it. Subliminal techniques first appeared in the world of advertising in 1957, when James Vicary demonstrated a 'tachistocope' which would flash a message lasting 0.03 of a second onto a cinema screen every five seconds. The political applications of such a technique are obvious and it has been tried, but although subliminal PROPAGANDA is widely seen as unethical, few concrete steps have been taken to prevent it.

subsidiarity The doctrine in EUROPEAN UNION affairs, contested vigorously by FEDERALISTS, that BRUSSELS should only undertake those functions that national governments cannot perform as effectively, and that whatever member states can handle best should be left to them. It was advanced by John MAJOR in the debate across Europe on the MAASTRICHT TREATY, as a brake on greater centralisation of power in the hands of the COMMISSION, but was seen by some Continental leaders as at best meaningless and at worst an attempt to hamper the functioning of the community. Nevertheless the 1992 Birmingham and Edinburgh SUMMITS agreed that subsidiarity – together with TRANSPARENCY – should be applied to the EU's activities, and the doctrine has continued to carry some weight.

subsidy junkies Individuals, communities, sectors of the population and public bodies who have lost the wish and the capability to handle their own finances because they have become dependent on subsidies from the state. The phrase, not a compliment, was coined at the turn of the century by conservatives on both sides of the Atlantic as they put forward proposals to end such dependency which, as the phrase implies, they considered a form of addiction.

subterranean campaign *See* STEALTH CAMPAIGN.

subversion The undermining of a state from within, without the public as a whole being aware of the existence or nature of the threat (*see also* DESTABILISATION; FIFTH COLUMNIST). The process of unmasking alleged **subversives** can be just as damaging to the social fabric; in the days of MCCARTHYISM, the belief that every aspect of life was at risk from them led to the BLACKLISTING of many law-abiding Americans. In 1981 the newspaper publisher Jacobo Timerman (1923–), arguing against the unlawful methods (*see* DISAPPEARED) used by Argentina's military dictatorship to combat subversion, wrote:

> The political defeat of subversion is as important as military defeat. Applying legal methods to repression eliminates one of the major elements exploited by subversion: the illegal nature of repression.

succession The chain of individuals who, in turn, would stand to fill a particular post if the occupant should die or otherwise leave it. In Britain the line of succession to the throne is established on a basis laid down by law, the **Act of Succession**; it passes first to the SOVEREIGN's eldest son, if there is one, and to first his sons and then his daughters. Next in line come the Sovereign's other sons and their heirs, or the daughters of the monarch and their families if there are no sons. Roman Catholics are excluded, a situation which has led to protests in the SCOTTISH PARLIAMENT. The line of succession to the US PRESIDENCY starts with the VICE PRESIDENT, but the question of how to proceed if neither President nor Vice President is able to serve has posed problems. Under an Act of 1886 the succession passed to members of the CABINET in order of precedence, starting with the SECRETARY OF STATE. In 1947 this was modified to put the SPEAKER of the HOUSE OF REPRESENTATIVES and the PRESIDENT PRO TEM of the Senate ahead of the Cabinet members. Neither of these provisions was ever invoked, and in 1967 the TWENTY-FIFTH AMENDMENT provided for the President to nominate a new Vice President, subject to Congressional approval. Under this amendment Richard NIXON appointed Gerald FORD after Spiro AGNEW's resignation, and Ford in turn appointed Nelson Rockefeller (*see* ROCKY) after his own elevation to the Presidency on NIXON's disgrace.

Sudeten crisis The war scare provoked by HITLER's claim to the German-speaking Sudetenland in Czechoslovakia, which was eventually conceded by British, French and Italian leaders at MUNICH in September 1938. The Sudeten Germans, formerly subjects of the Habsburg emperors, had been placed in Czechoslovakia in 1919 by the Treaty of St Germain. In the 1930s, the NAZIS fomented agitation for regional autonomy and the redress of economic grievances; the demands were met by the Czech government in April 1938 but the agitation continued. Hitler seized his opportunity, and at Munich the Prague government was ordered to cede the Sudetenland to Germany by 10 October 1938; within months Hitler was in Prague, and within a year Europe was at war. When peace returned in 1945, the Sudetenland was restored to Czechoslovakia, which expelled most of its German population.

> Before us stands the last problem which must be solved, and will be solved. It is the last territorial claim I have to make in Europe, but it is the claim from which I will not recede and which, God willing, I will make good. With regard to the problem of the Sudeten Germans, my patience is now at an end.
>
> HITLER, speech at the Berlin *Sportpalast*, 26 September 1938

Sudeten Scots The scathing term for Conservative MPs unseated in Scotland who returned to WESTMINSTER representing English constituencies, coined in the late 1960s by the Labour Scottish Secretary William Ross (later Lord Ross of Marnock). As the Conservatives lost ground north of the border over three decades, several of those unseated moved south, the most notable being Sir Teddy Taylor, Michael Ancram and finally Sir Malcolm Rifkind.

Suez. Suez Canal purchase Benjamin DISRAELI's purchase for the British government in 1875 of 177,000 shares in the Suez Canal – 44% of the ordinary shares – from the near-bankrupt Khedive Ismail of Egypt, just five years after the canal's completion. The price he paid was £4 million, borrowed from the banker Lionel de Rothschild until Parliamentary approval could be secured. The deal gave Britain a degree of control over the waterway for which it provided 80% of the traffic, and which was becoming the umbilical cord between Britain and its new Indian empire.

Suez crisis The botched military adventure by Britain and France in 1956 to retake the Suez Canal after its NATIONALISATION by the Egyptian leader Colonel Gamel Abdul Nasser. It finally destroyed British illusions of Empire, strained the US-UK SPECIAL RELATIONSHIP almost to breaking point, gravely damaged British influence in the Arab world and made Nasser an instant hero, enabled Russia to crush the HUNGARIAN UPRISING unchallenged by the West, and ended the political career of

Anthony EDEN. Nasser nationalised the canal on 26 July in the wake of America's refusal – brought about by ever closer links between Cairo and Moscow – to finance the ASWAN HIGH DAM as previously promised. This incensed the British and French, who had been the canal's main owners and feared for the security of their oil supplies. While making overt diplomatic moves to resolve the crisis, they prepared secret plans for the conquest of the canal zone and the overthrow of Nasser, whom Eden perceived as a latter-day HITLER. Eden was backed by most of his own party; he was egged on particularly by his Chancellor, Harold MACMILLAN, who said:

> If Nasser gets away with it, we are done for.

But Walter Monckton, who was about to retire as Minister for War, enquired: 'How do we actually start this war?' and Dick White, director of MI6, described the invasion plan as 'a pretty tall order'. The Labour leadership was initially supportive, Hugh GAITSKELL saying on 2 August:

> It is all very familiar. It is exactly the same that we encountered from Mussolini and Hitler.

But the Labour Party, spurred by GRASS-ROOTS opinion, soon turned against a military adventure, and a small but vocal group of Tory rebels, including the Foreign Office Minister Anthony Nutting who resigned in protest at 'this sordid conspiracy', also warned that the exercise would end in tears. When it did, the party turned against them, one, Nigel Nicolson, being rejected by his constituency.

An agreement was reached at SÈVRES under which ISRAEL, threatened by Egypt since its foundation in 1948, invaded on 29 October and Anglo-French forces landed at Port Said and Port Fuad on the pretext of enforcing a call from the UNITED NATIONS to separate the combatants. Macmillan had told Eden: 'IKE's not going to make any real trouble if we have to do anything drastic', but the duplicity of this action enraged President EISENHOWER, who was facing a re-election ballot within days, and Secretary of State John Foster Dulles told him: 'The British and the French are deliberately keeping us in the dark'. Eisenhower, and Dulles who had been ambivalent over whether US support would be forthcoming, threatened to back a call from the UN GENERAL ASSEMBLY for economic SANCTIONS against Britain and France. In the process America triggered a run on the POUND and the franc that forced the invaders to withdraw: the British and French on 22 December, the Israelis the following March. By then Eden had resigned through ill-health. *See also* ARMED CONFLICT.

> I want Nasser destroyed – not removed, destroyed.
> EDEN

> God damn it, we're going to apply sanctions, we're going to the United Nations, we're going to do everything that there is so we can stop this thing.
> EISENHOWER to Dulles, 29 October 1956

> During the past few weeks I felt sometimes that the Suez Canal was flowing through my room.
> Eden's wife LADY CLARISSA EDEN, November 1956

> Like going through the preliminaries without having an orgasm.
> ANTHONY HEAD, Monckton's successor as Minister for War

Suez Group The hard core of right-wing Conservative MPs who gave enthusiastic support for the Suez venture, but despaired of Eden's handling of it. Led by Julian Amery and Hugh Fraser, they pressed for the military operation to continue in the face of US and UN objections until the Canal was under Anglo-French control.

East of Suez The world, rather than regional, role for Britain's armed forces, and specifically their commitment to Singapore and the Gulf. The maintenance of a presence east of Suez was an emotive political issue in the late 1960s, with Harold WILSON's Labour government reluctantly taking the decision to pull out and Edward HEATH's Conservatives completing its implementation. The phrase originated with Rudyard Kipling (1865–1936), who wrote in his poem *Mandalay:*

> Ship me somewheres east of Suez, where the best is like the worst,
> Where there aren't no Ten Commandments, an' a man can raise a thirst:
> For the temple bells are callin', an' it's there that I would be –
> By the old Moulmein Pagoda, looking lazy at the sea.

suffrage. universal [manhood] **suffrage** The possession of the right to vote by all. At first it implied only votes for all adult men; VOTES FOR WOMEN came later, though in America a convention at Seneca Falls, New York, demanded votes for all as early as 1848.

> Universal suffrage exists in the United States, without producing any very frightful consequences.
> THOMAS BABINGTON MACAULAY, in the HOUSE OF COMMONS, 2 March 1831

Universal suffrage is counter-revolution.
PIERRE-JOSEPH PROUDHON (1809–65)

women's suffrage *See* WOMEN.

Suffragettes Members of the Women's Social and Political Union, founded in 1903 by Emmeline Pankhurst (1858–1928), who conducted a campaign of increasing MILITANCY in Edwardian Britain to secure the vote. Some sought VOTES FOR WOMEN on the same property qualifications as then applied to men; others wanted universal adult suffrage. The militants, led by Mrs Pankhurst and her daughter Christabel (1880–1958), chained themselves to railings, attacked property, refused to pay taxes, staged DEMONSTRATIONS and disrupted meetings addressed by male politicians. Thwarted in their aims by the attitude of ASQUITH, their tactics also alienated many of his CABINET, LLOYD GEORGE saying when one group interrupted him:

I see some rats have got in; let them squeal, it doesn't matter.

The suffragettes were repeatedly imprisoned (*see* CAT AND MOUSE ACT), and endangered their lives by hunger STRIKES which the authorities tried to break with brutal FORCE-FEEDING. On the outbreak of WORLD WAR I the suffragettes suspended their campaign and supported the war effort; in 1918 Lloyd George recognised the important role played by women in achieving victory by granting the vote to women over 30, subject to property qualifications. In 1928 these last restrictions were removed and the vote extended to all women over 21 (*see* Flapper VOTE).

We have taken this action, because as women . . . it is our duty even to break the law in order to call attention to the reasons why we do so . . . we are here, not because we are law-breakers, we are here in our efforts to become law-makers.
EMMELINE PANKHURST, speaking in court, 21 October 1908

Sullivan principles The weapon against APARTHEID wielded effectively, through US business, by black Americans from the late 1970s. Devised by the Rev. Leon Sullivan, a black Philadelphia minister appointed at the time to the board of General Motors, the principles laid down that US public bodies and other organisations would BOYCOTT any firm that failed to disinvest in South Africa. They were largely effective, most US businesses only re-establishing an obvious presence in the early 1990s as apartheid crumbled.

summit Originally a meeting between the most influential of world leaders, but now any gathering of two or more national leaders, or even the leaders of a particular industry or those across the spectrum concerned with solving a particular problem. The word has been much devalued since CHURCHILL used it in the early 1950s for his ambition of a 'parley at the summit' between President EISENHOWER, himself and the successors of STALIN to ease the ARMS RACE and the COLD WAR. True summit meetings should really cover few more than the periodic meetings between the Presidents of the United States and Russia (*see also* GENEVA; HELSINKI; PARIS; REYKJAVIK), but even before Russia's loss of SUPERPOWER status the term was being stretched a little to cover the annual 'economic summit' of the leaders of the G7 countries, and further to include the six-monthly meetings of the leaders of the EUROPEAN COMMUNITY. It is now also applied to meetings between the French President and German Chancellor, and any regularly-scheduled meetings between HEADS OF GOVERNMENT. The practice and art of conducting summit meetings are known as summitry. *See also* SHERPAS.

The conventional way to handle a meeting like this is to have meetings for several days . . . have discussions and discover differences . . . and then put out a WEASEL-worded COMMUNIQUÉ covering up the problems.
RICHARD NIXON to Chou-en-Lai, 1972

The only summit meeting that can succeed is one that does not take place.
Sen. BARRY GOLDWATER

seasick summit US officials' name for the meeting between George BUSH Snr and Mikhail GORBACHEV off Malta in December 1989, the month after the breaching of the BERLIN WALL and with Communism collapsing throughout central and eastern Europe. The meeting gained its name from the appalling seas in which the leaders were ferried between warships belonging to their respective navies.

shamrock summit The meeting of President REAGAN and Candian Prime Minister Brian Mulroney in QUEBEC City on 17 March 1985. It gained its name from the capital both leaders made of their common Irish origin, culminating in them joining in a chorus of *When Irish Eyes are Smiling*. On a more serious note, the meeting paved the way for talks on RECIPROCITY in trade, which in turn led ultimately to NAFTA.

sofa summit The epitome of COOL

BRITANNIA in NEW LABOUR's earliest days, the meeting between Tony BLAIR and France's President CHIRAC and Prime Minister Lionel Jospin on 7 November 1997 in a suite designed by Terence Conran on the 38th floor of London's Canary Wharf tower.

suicide bomber An alarming and effective weapon of ISLAMIST terrorist groups, the operative who is ready, or even eager, to lose their own life in taking the lives of others. Until the 1980s almost all bombers killed by their own devices were victims of OWN GOALS. However, suicide bombing was taken up as a weapon by extreme Palestinian groups and subsequently by AL QAEDA, for which it formed the basis of the attacks on 9/11. Despite its inherent grisliness, suicide bombing is actually a recruiter for the groups that practise it – perpetrators are convinced they will be rewarded with virgins in Heaven, and their families are treated with reverence by those in the community who share this warped interpretation of Islam. UK intelligence chiefs have toyed with the idea of starting a rumour amid these extremist groups that in consequence of the number of suicide bombings, the supply of virgins in Heaven has run out.

sun. it's the *Sun* wot won it The slogan modestly taken up after the 1992 UK general election by the best-selling tabloid the *Sun*, which under Rupert Murdoch's ownership had helped deliver an unlikely victory for John MAJOR. On polling day the paper's front page carried a picture of Labour leader Neil KINNOCK, with a call for the last *Sun* reader leaving Britain if Labour was elected to turn out the lights. Five years later the *Sun*, sensing the change in public mood, switched to Labour despite its more pro-European policies after Tony BLAIR had courted Murdoch. This time the result was so one-sided that the paper could not claim to have been decisive, though its stance certainly contributed to Blair's LANDSLIDE.

place in the sun *See* PLACE.

Sunbed Socialist The tag pinned on Tommy Sheridan (1964–), first leader of the SCOTTISH SOCIALIST PARTY, in the early days of DEVOLUTION by his Labour opponents and parts of the Scottish media. It referred to the glowing suntan which Sheridan always sported, despite not having been far outside Glasgow where hot sun is a rarity.

Sunbelt strategy In US politics, a strategy for winning the presidency (or control of CONGRESS) by picking up votes in what has since the late 1960s been known as the Sunbelt: the chain of states running west from Florida, which with their RIGHT TO WORK laws attracted jobs and prosperity from the 'rustbelt' of the North-East until they began to move overseas. The term was first used to describe Richard NIXON's breakthrough in traditionally Democratic southern states in 1972, and again for Ronald REAGAN's defeat of Jimmy CARTER on his home ground in 1980.

Sunny Jim The most widely used nickname for Prime Minister James CALLAGHAN (STOKER JIM was the other). The original Sunny Jim was the character used to advertise Force breakfast cereal, invented *c.* 1902 by Minny Maud Hanff and Edward Ellsworth.

sunset legislation Legislation to which a term is set, so that the programme, agency or powers created under it automatically lapse after that period unless there is a specific vote to continue it. Such laws were pioneered by US state governments in the mid-1970s – starting with Colorado – in a bid to curb BUREAUCRACY and spending. The anti-terrorism legislation enacted for the UK after 9/11 contains **sunset clauses** which require regular renewal by Parliament, as an assurance against unnecessary restrictions on HUMAN RIGHTS.

sunshine legislation Laws to make sure the public is kept informed about the process of government, guaranteeing admission to meetings, and the availability of documents and other information. *See also* FREEDOM OF INFORMATION ACT; TRANSPARENCY. **Sunshine rules** are the rules passed by the US HOUSE OF REPRESENTATIVES in 1973 and the SENATE in 1975 requiring committee meetings to be open to the public unless a majority of members vote to go into CLOSED SESSION.

Sunni Triangle The triangle of towns 30 miles to the north and west of Baghdad which are a stronghold of Sunni Muslims and the home turf of SADDAM HUSSEIN, who hailed from Tikrit, and thus the power base of the BAATH PARTY. During the insurgency that followed the 2003 IRAQ WAR, the Triangle was a centre of resistance to, and attacks on, US and even Iraqi forces by diehard supporters of the old regime and foreign Arab fighters.

Sunningdale agreement The high point of early hopes for POWER-SHARING in Ulster: the agreement brokered in the summer of

1973 by Edward HEATH at Sunningdale, Berkshire, to reinforce the newly-elected Assembly at STORMONT with a **Council of all Ireland**, drawing members from both the Assembly and the DAIL; there was also to be an **All-Ireland Court**. It was agreed by Heath, his NORTHERN IRELAND Secretary Francis Pym, Liam Cosgrave, TAOISEACH of a FINE GAEL-Labour coalition, and members of the Executive that was due to take power in Ulster. However, the deal meant different things to each of the participants, and soon fell apart. First the ULSTER UNIONISTS rejected it, then the Irish government temporised when challenged in the courts by Kevin Boland (*see* ARMS CRISIS) over Sunningdale's legality. Then Heath called a general election for February 1974; in Britain it was a referendum on the MINERS' STRIKE, in Ulster it was a referendum on Sunningdale. Pro-executive candidates were routed by the hard-line slogan **'Dublin is only a Sunningdale away'**, and when a minority Labour government took office it was forced by a GENERAL STRIKE of Loyalist workers to scrap the entire power-sharing experiment.

> It was typical of Ted Heath that he thought he achieved something at Sunningdale by dragooning people into accepting something they not only didn't mean, but which those upon whom they depended, the electors upon whom they depended, couldn't possibly mean.
>
> ENOCH POWELL

super. supergun The scandal that broke in early 1991 about the supply of components by UK firms to the regime of SADDAM HUSSEIN for a massive artillery piece, capable of firing projectiles against ISRAEL or beyond. It came to light in hearings of the COMMONS Trade and Industry Committee that organs of the British government had circumvented their own EMBARGO on the export of military hardware to combatants in the IRAN-IRAQ WAR. The guilty parties contrived to muddy the waters, only for the issue to resurface more damningly in the MATRIX-CHURCHILL AFFAIR late in 1992, leading to the SCOTT REPORT.

Super 301 *See* SECTION 301.

Super Tuesday A Tuesday in the early spring of a Presidential election year when the largest number of State PRIMARIES are held, their combined results having a heavy and often decisive effect on the nominating process. The phrase, which first stuck during the 1976 campaign since when the number of primaries has increased, was borrowed from American football. **Junior Tuesday** is a more recent phenomenon: the first Tuesday in March on which, by 2004, eight primaries were being staged.

Supermac The nickname that stuck to Harold MACMILLAN at the sunny height of his premiership, after the *Evening Standard* cartoonist Vicky (Victor Weisz, 1913–66) depicted him on 6 November 1958 as the US comic strip hero Superman. Macmillan said of his public image: 'I am MacWonder one moment, and Macblunder the next.'

superpowers The term used during the later part of the COLD WAR for the United States and the Soviet Union, as they confronted each other with their massive NUCLEAR arsenals. Since the collapse of the Soviet Union, the term has been applied to America alone. Its origin was a 1944 book of the same name by the US strategic expert William Fox, which forecast much of the post-war pattern in world affairs. Such a pattern – without the name – had actually been predicted in the late 1830s by Alexis de Tocqueville, who in his *Democracy in America* wrote:

> There are now two great nations in the world which, starting from different points, seem to be advancing toward the same great goal: the Russians and the Anglo-Americans.

> The Superpowers often behave like two heavily-armed blind men feeling their way around a room, each believing himself in mortal peril from the other whom he assumes to have perfect vision.
>
> HENRY KISSINGER

Supper Club A secret DINING CLUB of left-wing and other Labour MPs dissatisfied with the thrust of policy under Neil KINNOCK whose existence embarrassingly came to light at the height of the GULF WAR, which they opposed. The group, including several Shadow Ministers, was rash enough to circulate an AGENDA for its discussions, and a copy left in a COMMONS photocopier swiftly found its way to the media.

supplementary At QUESTION TIME in the HOUSE OF COMMONS, the follow-up to an initial question set out on the ORDER PAPER. When the Minister has given a response, the member comes back with a supplementary, again in question form, to seek further information or respond to what has been said. The term also applies to subsequent questions asked by other MPs on the same point before the SPEAKER moves on to the next one.

supplementary estimates In WHITEHALL and UK local government, extra APPROPRIATIONS for spending over and above the sums originally voted for the year. They have to be put to Parliament or the council for approval.

supply The financial life-blood that has to be voted by a Parliament for the operations of government to continue. The clash between the HOUSE OF LORDS and ASQUITH's government over the PEOPLE'S BUDGET amounted to a refusal to vote supply. In WASHINGTON, where the term is seldom used, the equivalent was the BUDGET SHUTDOWN imposed on the CLINTON administration by radical Congressional Republicans. In Australia both Jack Lang's New South Wales government in 1932, and Gough WHITLAM's Labor ministry in 1975, were removed from office because they could not guarantee supply.

supply days *See* OPPOSITION DAYS.

supply side economics The approach to macro-economics popular on the right of politics from the late 1970s and now more widely accepted; it was pioneered by the US economist Jude Wanniski in *The Way The World Works*, a tract based on the theories of the 18th-century French economist Jean-Baptiste Say. Wanniski argued that the KEYNESIAN idea of fighting recession by boosting demand had merely created INFLATION, and that a better way would be to boost production and supply, with demand bound to rise as the MARKET came into play. A key element in supply side economics, and one on which REAGANOMICS and the economic aspects of THATCHERISM were based, was the doctrine that cutting taxes would stimulate the economy and thus more than offset the initial loss in revenues. *See also* LAFFER CURVE.

> On the side of the people who are well supplied.
> HERBLOCK

> The good news is that a busload of supply-side economists has plunged over a cliff. The bad news is that three seats were unoccupied at the time.
> Rep. MORRIS UDALL

Supreme. Supreme Court (1) In America, the nine justices, appointed in most cases by previous Presidents, who are the ultimate arbiters of whether the actions of the ADMINISTRATION, the CONGRESS, the STATES, public agencies, corporations and individuals accord with the CONSTITUTION. At times (*see* BLACK MONDAY) it has been a conservative brake on a reforming President; at others (*see* WARREN COURT) a liberal irritant to an administration wedded to the *status quo*. The resulting strains date back at least to the days of Abraham LINCOLN, who cautioned:

> If the policy of the government upon vital issues affecting the whole people is to be increasingly fixed by decisions of the Supreme Court, the people will have ceased to be their own rulers.

Franklin D. ROOSEVELT attempted to limit the justices' power by COURT-PACKING, but was thwarted by Congress; since then it has been accepted that only through filling CASUAL VACANCIES will the balance of the court be changed. As Sen. George W. Norris (1861–1944) put it, 'the people can change Congress, but only God can change the Supreme Court'.

> An institution of political judgment masquerading as a council of priests.
> THEODORE H. WHITE

> The Constitution is not a panacea for any blot upon the general welfare, nor should this Court, ordained as a judicial body, be thought of as a general haven for reform movements.
> Justice JOHN M. HARLAN (dissenting), 1964

> However the court may interpret the provisions of the Constitution, it is still the Constitution which is the law and not the decision of the court.
> CHARLES WARREN (1868–1954)

> The Supreme Court follows th'illiction returns.
> Mr Dooley (FINLEY PETER DUNNE) (1867–1936)

(2) The body proposed by Tony BLAIR in June 2003 as a free-standing inheritor of the judicial functions of the HOUSE OF LORDS, and the ultimate court of appeal in the English legal system. This profound constitutional change was announced through a Cabinet RESHUFFLE in which Lord Irvine of Lairg (*see* MASTER OF THE ROLLS) was retired as LORD CHANCELLOR, together supposedly with the title, and replaced by another of Blair's legal intimates, Lord Falconer of Thoroton, with the title of Secretary of State for Constitutional Affairs. A Department of Constitutional Affairs was established, taking over much of the Lord Chancellors Department, the SCOTLAND OFFICE and the Wales Office. Legislation was tabled to move the most senior judges out of the House of Lords, both physically and in terms of the SEPARATION OF POWERS; the situation in which the Lord Chancellor was head of the judicial system, a member of the Cabinet and SPEAKER of the House of Lords was to end. The announcement caused bitter controversy and in the short term turned out to be impractical, Lord Falconer being obliged to assume the office and activities of the Lord Chancellor. Peers campaigned unsuccessfully to retain a Lord Chancellor on the WOOLSACK, and senior judges objected both

to their loss of a stake in Parliament and to the premises first proposed for them, the Middlesex Guildhall in PARLIAMENT SQUARE.

Supreme Head of the Church The title borne by the kings and queens of England since Elizabeth I, reflecting their status as temporal head of the Church of England – a role which explains (though does not excuse) the exclusion of Roman Catholics from the SUCCESSION. Crossing into Scotland, SOVEREIGNS become Presbyterians through their status in the Church of Scotland.

Supreme Soviet *See* SOVIET.

surcharge A sum which members of a UK local authority may be ordered to pay if the DISTRICT AUDITOR concludes that they have improperly authorised expenditure by the authority. The most notable examples have been the case of the CLAY CROSS COUNCILLORS and the Westminster Council HOMES FOR VOTES scandal.

Surgeon General The head of the US public health service, who wears an admiral's uniform; the holder of the office is best known for determining the warning to be carried on cigarette packets. It is virtually impossible to get any nominee for Surgeon General confirmed, as almost any view on or experience of abortion will alienate some influential senators. In 1994 Jocelyn Elders, having overcome that hurdle, was forced to resign for suggesting that masturbation be taught in schools.

> Only God and the Pope could be confirmed as Surgeon General. And I wonder about the Pope.
>
> JOCELYN ELDERS

surgery The word used by MPs for the advice bureaux they conduct in their CONSTITUENCIES. Most hold a surgery every weekend or at least once a fortnight; MPs with urban seats may always hold them in the same place, those representing rural constituencies will rotate between a number of locations: party or local council offices, public libraries, village halls and the like. Most MPs enjoy helping solve constituents' problems, but some are tedious or persistent and others worse: in 2000 Nigel Jones, Liberal Democrat MP for Cheltenham, was wounded and his constituency assistant killed when a complainant armed with a sword burst into the surgery and attacked them.

surrender. No surrender! *See* NO.

unconditional surrender The war aim agreed by CHURCHILL and ROOSEVELT at CASABLANCA in January 1943, requiring that the conflict against all the Allies' enemies be pressed home until they laid down their arms. Some critics believed that the commitment stiffened German resistance, but it did something to ease STALIN's paranoia that the Atlantic allies might conclude a separate peace. At POTSDAM on 27 July 1945 the war leaders sent Japan a warning of 'utter devastation' unless they surrendered; it was ignored, and the holocaust of HIROSHIMA followed. The phrase had been used at least as early as 1862, when General Ulysses GRANT told Simon Bolivar Buckner, CONFEDERATE commander at Fort Donelson:

> No terms except unconditional and immediate surrender can be accepted. I propose to move immediately against your works.

we shall never surrender *See* WE SHALL FIGHT.

we surrender The message, in Russian, recorded on a telephone answering machine that the MAVERICK Danish politician Mogens Glistrup proposed in the late 1970s should replace the country's armed forces. It won his party, which also opposed taxes, a substantial number of Parliamentary seats.

suspend (1) To compel a legislator to stay away for a period following a breach of discipline. (2) The action of the CHAIR in halting proceedings for a time because of disorder or some other emergency. (3) suspension of STANDING ORDERS, in a UK body, or of the RULES, in America, to enable urgent business to be dealt with. In the HOUSE OF REPRESENTATIVES a motion to suspend the rules may be put any Monday or Tuesday in the last six days of a SESSION for an individual member to put forward a BILL or resolution.

Sussex Drive The official residence in Ottawa – at No. 24 – of Canada's PRIME MINISTER.

Sussex pledge Germany's promise to America in March 1916 that its submarines would not sink merchant vessels 'without warning and without saving lives'. It followed the sinking of the French steamer *Sussex* in the English Channel, in which two Americans were among the injured. President WILSON gave Germany an ULTIMATUM that America would break off diplomatic relations unless it ended indiscriminate submarine warfare; the threat worked until 31 January 1917 when Germany announced that it was resuming. The following month America did break off relations with Germany, and began arming merchant ships.

sustainable development An increasingly prominent theme of international politics since the 1988 BRUNDTLAND REPORT, of which it was the central theme: the doctrine that economic growth, particularly in the developing world, should be encouraged as far as is consistent with maintaining the environment. It aims to strike a constructive balance between poor countries who argue that they have to develop their economies regardless of the environmental cost, and wealthy ones who insist that the environment of the THIRD WORLD remain inviolate, even if the price is continuing poverty. Increasingly the argument has extended from the developing to the developed world, as most industrialised countries except the United States have accepted the need to balance the needs of business and the economy against the damage caused by continuing emissions of greenhouse gases (*see* KYOTO ACCORD).

swamping The phrase used about immigration to Britain by Margaret THATCHER in January 1978, which led non-white Britons to fear that the Conservatives in power would indulge in RACISM. Though offensive to many Tories, it did have the effect of neutralising such truly racist parties as the NATIONAL FRONT or BNP for a considerable time, the far right believing that Mrs Thatcher was 'one of them'. What she said in a television interview, having not consulted colleagues on the subject, was that there was a legitimate fear among white Britons of being 'swamped by people with a different culture'. There would be 4 million black people in Britain by the end of the century, and 'we are not in politics to ignore people's worries, but to deal with them'. Under pressure from her Home Affairs spokesman WILLIE Whitelaw, she never repeated her remarks, but they had in her view served their purpose. The Tories did not pursue racist policies in office, and ironically it was the Labour Home Secretary David Blunkett who in April 2002 resurrected the term, and the controversy, when warning that local schools could be 'swamped' by the children of ASYLUM SEEKERS.

Swampy The figurehead of the environmentalist protest movement against new roads in England in the late 1990s. Daniel Hooper, then 23, became a household name early in 1997 by leading protesters who took refuge in tunnels and up trees to prevent the Newbury bypass, Manchester Airport second runway and other schemes being built. They caused considerable delay and frustration, but ultimately failed.

> He should be buried in concrete.
>
> Conservative Transport Minister JOHN WATTS

swastika The symbol of HITLER's NAZI movement and of the evil state it created. It was the reverse of a cross-shaped design with arms, known also as the *gammadion* or *fylfot*, which had long been used in India and the Near East as a charm to ward off evil and bring good luck (the word is derived from the Sanskrit *svasti*, good fortune). It was adopted by Hitler around 1920, probably from the German Baltic Corps, who wore it on their helmets after service in Finland, on whose aircraft it was a distinguishing mark. Described by CHURCHILL as the 'crooked cross', it was to become feared throughout Europe.

swear in To induct an elected head of state or office-holder, or an appointee, to office through the administration of an OATH.

sweetbreads Franklin D. ROOSEVELT's least favourite food, which was repeatedly served to him at the WHITE HOUSE until he told his wife Eleanor (*see* FIRST LADY OF THE WORLD):

> I am getting to the point where my stomach rebels, and this does not help my relations with foreign powers. I bit two of them today.

Compare BROCCOLI.

Swift Boat Veterans for Truth The lobbying group (*see* 527) who aired TV commercials in the summer of 2004 disputing Sen. John KERRY's claims about his VIETNAM WAR record, in an attempt to undermine his credibility. In the commercials, veterans who had served near, but not with, Kerry, claimed he had lied about having rescued a comrade from the water under fire, and about having seen action in Cambodia. Kerry strongly disputed the charges, as did men who had served with him including the officer he rescued. The BUSH campaign first insisted it had no connection with the group, then backed down when it turned out that a member of the President's veterans' advisory committee had appeared in the commercial and that Benjamin Ginsberg, a senior counsel to the Bush campaign, had been advising the group. Ginsberg resigned, and Bush publicly attested to Kerry's exemplary war record, but the whispering continued.

swing (1) The statistical measure by which the switch of voters from one party to another on a national or constituency basis can be judged. It is calculated by adding the rise in one party's percentage vote to the fall of the other, and dividing by two. Thus if the vote of party A rises between elections or opinion polls by 3% and that of party B falls by 2%, there is a 2.5% swing from party B to party A. The calculation of swing becomes more complex, and ultimately meaningless, in a multi-party system, though it can still work on a local basis if comparisons are needed. (2) A US term for a burst of activity by a politician, usually a candidate, involving a series of appearances in rapid succession in a chain of cities, each within easy reach of the next; in a Presidential campaign such a swing will take the candidate to three or four states. The term dates back at least to September 1866 when President Andrew Johnson tried to rally the people behind him with a **swing round the circle** through Northern and Western states. The tour proved disastrous; Johnson was shouted down in city after city and trailed back to Washington, having lost the initiative and with a narrow escape from IMPEACHMENT ahead of him.

swing district In US politics, a Congressional district held by one party that is seen as potentially winnable by the other, and is likely to be TARGETED for extra effort by both prior to the two-yearly elections.

swing voters The US equivalent of Britain's FLOATING VOTERS: the critical groups in the electorate whose loyalties are not set in concrete and who might be persuaded to change party allegiance, determining the fate of key seats.

swingometer The device that has formed the centrepiece of BBC television coverage of UK GENERAL ELECTIONS since its invention by the Oxford PSEPHOLOGIST David Butler in 1955. In its crude form, it consisted of a cardboard arrow, pointing downward, against a sundial-like background showing the number of seats that would fall to a swing to either party of 1%, 2%, etc., with a particular reference to the swing needed for a change of government. Though gradually refined, it remained essentially the same up to 1979. The swingometer was retired for the elections of 1983 and 1987, when a three-way split in the electorate reduced the relevance of a straightforward calculation of swing between the Conservatives and Labour, but was resurrected in high-tech form for the 1992 election by the presenter Peter Snow and has retained its appeal, despite the fragmentation of the two main parties' votes.

variable swing The degree to which the swing between parties may differ from one region or electoral district to another.

SWP *See* SOCIALIST WORKERS' PARTY.

Sybil The novel completed by Benjamin DISRAELI in 1845 in which he set out the condition of the TWO NATIONS; indeed, that was its alternative title. While *Sybil*, like CONINGSBY, was a satire on PEEL, it also dwelt on the condition of the poor in early Victorian England. Disraeli, in his preface, had to warn genteel readers:

> So little do we know of the state of our own country, that the air of improbability which the whole truth would inevitably throw over these pages, might deter some from their perusal.

Sykes-Picot agreement A secret pact, negotiated by Sir Mark Sykes for Britain and François Georges-Picot for France, for dividing up the Ottoman Empire after WORLD WAR I. France was given control of coastal Syria, the Lebanon and Mosul, while Britain would control southern Mesopotamia, including Baghdad, and the ports of Haifa and Aqaba. Palestine was to be placed under international control, and a number of independent Arab states were to be created. The agreement was conditional on the agreement of Russia, which was given in May 1916 in return for control over Turkish Armenia; the Italians, also promised Ottoman territory by the Treaty of LONDON, assented in August 1917 in return for portions of Anatolia. The treaty was made public by Russia's BOLSHEVIK government after the OCTOBER REVOLUTION, causing the allies considerable embarrassment as it contradicted the BALFOUR DECLARATION of 2 November 1917 which had just promised the Jews a national home in Palestine, and made pledges to Hussein, the Sherif of Mecca.

sympathetic action *See* ACTION.

syndicalism (Fr. *syndicalisme,* trade unionism) The overthrow of the political and industrial system by STRIKES and other forms of industrial ACTION, with the aim of securing a takeover of the means of production by the TRADE UNIONS and the installation of a government comprising a federation of union bodies. The concept originated c. 1890 in France, where it was known as *syndicalisme révolutionnaire*, and gained currency through Georges Sorel's

Réflexions Sur La Violence (1906). Syndicalism played an important part in the GREAT UNREST in Britain just before WORLD WAR I and in the development of the WOBBLIES in America; the syndicalists were also a prominent faction in the SPANISH CIVIL WAR. *See also* ANARCHO-SYNDICALISM; WORKERS' CONTROL.

T

table (1) The point for settling disputes, a place at the table being the status inherent in being allowed to participate.

> If we can't be at the table, we'll saw the fucking legs off. JAMES FORMAN at SELMA

(2) To lodge a formal proposal for discussion. In Britain, specifically to put down an AMENDMENT to a BILL or motion. In America, confusingly, also to shelve a proposal that has been under discussion but lacks the support to make further progress.

shape of the table The cause of bitter arguments before international conferences aimed at resolving intractable disputes. 'Arguing about the shape of the table' has become shorthand for the reluctance of participants in talks to get down to the issues. The problem is nothing new; in the legend of King Arthur, his knights had to be given a round table as they disputed who was the greatest among them with the right to sit at the head of the table.

Table Office In the HOUSE OF COMMONS, the office which receives questions, etc., from Members for insertion in the ORDER PAPER and has the right of veto over permitted forms of wording and subject matter.

tactical voting The casting of votes by electors for a party other than that which they normally support in an effort to defeat the one they most dislike. It works most effectively in a three- or even four-party system; in Britain the LIBERAL DEMOCRATS hope to benefit from tactical voting by Labour supporters in seats where they have a better chance of ousting the Conservatives, and from Tories where they are in with a chance of defeating Labour.

tactical weapons Nuclear weapons of smaller (but still awe-inspiring) power than those designed to eliminate cities, fired on projectiles with a reach of tens or hundreds of miles rather than thousands, which might be used on the battlefield to halt an enemy advance. In COLD WAR planning, such weapons would be used to halt an overwhelming Soviet advance westward from East Germany, which NATO lacked the manpower and conventional armour to withstand.

Taff Vale judgment The HOUSE OF LORDS ruling in July 1901 that a TRADE UNION is liable in law for the acts of its agents, which severely limited the unions' ability to take industrial ACTION and precipitated the formation of the LABOUR PARTY. It arose from a suit by the Taff Vale Railway against the Amalgamated Society of Railway Servants (now RMT) for breach of contract under the Conspiracy and Protection of Property Act, 1875 by picketing its Cardiff station. The ruling was followed in December 1902 by an award of £23,000 against the union. The decision, backed by the Conservative government, convinced trade unionists that direct Parliamentary representation for their members was essential; union affiliation to the embryo Labour Party rose dramatically, and it increased its MPs from two in 1900 to 29 in 1906. The unions' IMMUNITY against legal action for prosecuting a dispute was reinstated by the Liberals' 1906 Trade Disputes Act, but partly removed again by the THATCHER government in the 1980s.

> Trade unionism is being assailed, not by what the law says of it, but by what judges think the law ought to say of it. That being so, it becomes necessary for the unions to place men in the House of Commons, to challenge the decisions which I have no doubt will follow.
>
> RAMSAY MACDONALD

taffia A derogatory term (a combination of 'Taffy' and 'mafia') for the interlocking group of non-elected appointees who run the traditionally powerful QUANGOS in Wales. Although the word was coined in the 1980s to describe the cosy relationship between some Welsh businessmen and Conservative ministers, it has applied just as much to Wales's Labour ESTABLISHMENT. In 2004 FIRST MINISTER Rhodri Morgan announced that the functions of Wales' largest quangos, covering industrial development, housing and education, were being taken back in-house by the WELSH ASSEMBLY GOVERNMENT, with Ministers at CARDIFF BAY directly ACCOUNTABLE.

Taft, William Howard (1857–1930), 27th President of the United States (Republican, 1909–13). The son of a US Attorney-General, he was a career lawyer whose ambition of becoming CHIEF JUSTICE was derailed for a time by his wife's insistence that he seek the Presidency. His own view was that 'politics, when I am in it, makes me sick'. When Theodore ROOSEVELT first offered Taft a justiceship when he was Governor of the Philippines, he declined. Roosevelt telegraphed him:

> Taft, Manila. All right stay where you are. I shall appoint someone else to the Supreme Court. Roosevelt.

Taft went on to serve as Roosevelt's Secretary for War, and was elected President in 1908 as his hand-picked successor; his supporters' slogan was:

> Roosevelt has cut enough hay. Taft is the man to put it into the barn.

In the WHITE HOUSE Taft gained a reputation for aloofness, Ring Lardner Jr once writing: 'He looks at me as if I was a side dish he had ordered.' But he had a sense of humour, as shown by this exchange with Sen. Chauncey Depew about the size of Depew's pregnant-looking stomach:

> *Depew:* I hope if it is a girl, Mr Taft will name it for his charming wife.
> *Taft:* If, as I suspect, it is only a bag of wind, I shall name it Chauncey Depew.

Taft described his ADMINISTRATION as 'very humdrum', but Roosevelt despaired, saying: 'Taft meant well, but he meant well feebly.' Taft's frostiness and conservatism led Roosevelt to mount a comeback, splitting the REPUBLICAN PARTY with his 1912 BULL MOOSE campaign which pushed Taft into third place. Taft commented: 'No candidate was ever elected ex-President by such a large majority,' and in later years he insisted: 'I don't remember that I ever was President.' He went on to be Professor of Law at Yale, and eventually was appointed Chief Justice in 1921, serving until 1930.

> It's very difficult to understand how a man who is so good a Chief Justice could have been so bad a President.
>
> Justice LOUIS BRANDEIS (1856–1941)

Taft-Hartley Act Landmark legislation, promoted by Sen. Robert Taft (*see* MR REPUBLICAN) and Rep. Fred Hartley, and passed by the Republican-controlled US CONGRESS in 1947 which limited the trade unions' ability to pursue industrial disputes. It outlawed STRIKES by government employees, banned the CLOSED SHOP, made unions liable for breach of contract, barred them from financing political campaigns and gave the President power to impose a 60-day COOLING-OFF PERIOD. Union leaders also had to swear they were not Communists before they could approach the National Labor Relations Board. President TRUMAN termed the Act 'a slave labour law', but Congress overrode his VETO. In recent years it has seldom been invoked; President CARTER did so early in 1978 when faced with a miners' strike, and George W. BUSH used it in October 2002 to get West Coast longshoremen back to work.

Taig A derogatory term for a Roman Catholic used by working-class Protestants in NORTHERN IRELAND, especially Belfast. It originated in the Irish Christian name *Tadhg* and its 17th-century corruption *Teague*, an Irishman. It is more abusive than PROD, which is used in the other direction.

take. take down In the US HOUSE OF REPRESENTATIVES, a call from an objecting member for the clerk to 'take down' what has been said by a colleague requires the member in question to repeat the words, with the PARLIAMENTARIAN deciding whether the House rule forbidding personal attacks and insults has been violated.

take note In the HOUSE OF COMMONS, a 'take note' resolution records the passing of an event or the publication of a document without forming a view on it. This can avoid an embarrassing DIVISION for one side or the other.

take-up A percentage figure indicating what proportion of the people eligible to receive a particular welfare benefit have applied for it.

Taleban The fundamentalist and highly reactionary Islamic movement, led by Mullah Omar and backed by elements in Pakistani military intelligence, which seized control of the bulk of Afghanistan in the mid-1990s in a series of bitter and destructive battles and imposed a Stone-Age authoritarianism, forcing women to wear the *burqa* and denying them all rights and education, banning music and other forms of entertainment and dynamiting the gigantic Buddha at a UN World Heritage Site. The Taleban sowed the seeds of its own destruction by giving Osama BIN LADEN carte blanche to operate in the

80% of Afghanistan it controlled, running training camps for AL QAEDA and planning terrorist operations including the bombings in September 2001 of the WORLD TRADE CENTER and the PENTAGON. In revenge for 9/11, the US joined with its allies and with Afghan warlords to overthrow the Taleban and hunt down Omar, bin Laden and their supporters. The Taleban was driven from Kabul into lawless and inaccessible terrain on the Pakistani frontier, from where it continued to menace the forces of the US-backed government and Western aid workers, but was unable to prevent a reasonably free Presidential election taking place in October 2004.

talk out In the HOUSE OF COMMONS, to continue debate on a BILL when its SPONSORS need to force an immediate vote or see it run out of time. It normally applies to the tactics used against Private Members' BILLS. *See also* FILIBUSTER.

talk up The action of a party or a politician in boosting the fortunes of an opponent to suit their own purposes. In the 1983 UK general election Margaret THATCHER, concerned lest the complete collapse of Labour hand the initiative to the SDP/Liberal ALLIANCE, declared: 'The LABOUR PARTY will never die'. In the 2004 Presidential election campaign, Republicans gave the campaign of Ralph NADER a clear wind in states where the Democrats were trying to challenge it, in the hope that Nader would pick up crucial votes from John KERRY as he had from Al Gore in 2000.

talks about talks Tentative exploration of the scope for negotiations, ascertaining whether there is a chance of progress or if the talks would break down, making matters worse.

tall poppy syndrome An Australian term for the national characteristic of cutting the rich, prominent or self-important down to size. It has been current since 1931, when Jack Lang (1876–1975), LABOR premier of New South Wales, described his EGALITARIAN policies as 'cutting the heads off the tall poppies'. It derives from the legend that Tarquin, king of Rome, showed his intentions for the captured city of the *Gabii* by decapitating the tallest poppies in his garden; accordingly, the leading citizens were executed. Margaret THATCHER may not have known this when, before becoming Prime Minister, she defined her philosophy to a US audience by saying: '**Let your poppies grow tall**.'

Tallaght strategy The initiative taken in September 1987 by Ireland's FINE GAEL leader Alan Dukes which wrongfooted Charles HAUGHEY's minority government by pledging to support it, provided it followed 'responsible' economic policies. The decision was taken at a meeting in Tallaght, a south-western suburb of Dublin.

tallyman In Irish politics, a person who counts the voters as they arrive at the poll, and can tell a candidate who has voted for them and whether they will win. *Compare* TELLER.

Tamil Tigers Liberation Tigers of Tamil Eelam. The SEPARATIST movement which has waged a bloody civil war in Sri Lanka for a quarter of a century, mirrored by the determination of some politicians in Colombo not to pursue a political solution when one seemed achievable. Velupillai Prabhakaran founded the Tamil New Tigers in 1972 when just 18, and the LTTE in June 1976, with the ultimate goal of an independent state in Tamil-dominated areas in the north of the country. The Tigers grew into a formidable and ruthless GUERRILLA force with up to 15,000 fighters, capable of defeating the Sri Lankan army in the field, and for five years ran a de facto state in north-western Sri Lanka based on Jaffna City. The conflict ebbed and flowed, with heavy loss of life, before a ceasefire took effect in 2003 despite the Tigers pulling out of peace talks that February. In April 2004 a splinter group led by Col. Kaurana rose up against the Tiger leadership, who put it down ruthlessly. The reluctance of the Sri Lanka government to channel aid to Tamil areas after that December's tsumani imposed fresh strains, but not a resumption of conflict.

Tammany Hall A derogatory term for MACHINE POLITICS and political graft, from the Democratic organisation in New York city and state, which throughout the 19th century and into the 20th was a byword for corruption, PATRONAGE and manipulation of voters, especially recent immigrants. Founded in 1786 as a social and patriotic body, the 'Society of St Tammany' took its name from the Delaware chief Tamanend who reputedly welcomed William Penn to America in 1682 and became the unofficial patron saint of the revolutionary army. Tammany's corruption was evident by 1807, but it reached its greatest notoriety under BOSS TWEED later in the century.

Look at the bosses of Tammany Hall in the last

20 years. What magnificent men! To them New York owes pretty much all it is today. John Kelly, Richard Croker and Charles F. Murphy – what names in American history compared with them, except WASHINGTON and LINCOLN?

Of course, we aren't all bookworms and professors. If we were, Tammany might win an election once in 4000 years.

GEORGE WASHINGTON PLUNKITT (1842–1924), interviewed in 1905

Tamworth Manifesto Sir Robert PEEL's election address to his constituents in 1834, regarded as one of the foundations of pragmatic TORYism. It committed the Tories to accepting the 1832 REFORM ACT and to a 'careful review of institutions' without further widening the franchise. DISRAELI called it 'an attempt to construct a party without principles'.

Tanaiste (Ir. Heir-apparent) The official title of the deputy Prime Minister of the Irish Republic.

Tanaka memorial A Japanese blueprint for aggressive expansion in China, said to have been presented to the Emperor in 1927 by the Prime Minister, General Tanaka Gilchi (1864–1929). The memorial, widely circulated in China in the late 1920s, supposedly stemmed from a conference of top military officials called by Tanaka on taking office. Its authenticity has not been proved, but subsequent Japanese aggression in China followed a strategy similar to that reported.

tankies A 1980s term for hard-line STALINISTS who believed the Soviet Union was entitled to maintain its control over central and eastern Europe by sending in the tanks.

don't mess with me. I got tanks The warning issued to a CABINET rival by Kim Campbell (1947–) when Canadian Defence Minister. In 1993 the combative, twice-divorced Mrs Campbell succeeded Brian Mulroney as PROGRESSIVE CONSERVATIVE leader and that October led the party to the CANADIAN MELTDOWN, almost eliminating it as a political force. She was previously best known for being photographed apparently (but not) naked, apart from the legal trappings of her appointment, when Attorney-General.

get your tanks off my lawn The archetypal rebuff from a Labour Prime Minister to trade union leaders seeking to coerce the government into following their agenda, the parallel drawn being the Soviet crushing of the 1968 PRAGUE SPRING. It was delivered by Harold WILSON to the engineers' leader Hugh (later Lord) Scanlon during the controversy the following year over the trade union reform White Paper IN PLACE OF STRIFE. When Scanlon accused Wilson of becoming a Ramsay MACDONALD Wilson told him:

I have no intention of being a MacDonald. Nor do I intend to be another Dubček. Get your tanks off my lawn, Hughie!

Italian tanks *See* ITALIAN.

Tante Yvonne (Fr. Aunt Yvonne) The nickname of Yvonne Charlotte Anne Marie, *née* Vendroux, wife of President DE GAULLE, who was renowned for her preference for domesticity and her prudishness. Ironically she is best remembered in Britain for an apparently risqué answer she gave an interviewer during the de Gaulles' STATE VISIT to London in 1959. Asked what she would most like in life, her audience thought she said 'a penis'. Her husband hurriedly intervened to correct her pronunciation to ''appiness'.

Taoiseach (Ir. chieftain, pronounced *tee-shuk*) The official title of the Prime Minister of the Irish Republic.

target seats Seats held by one party on which another concentrates its greatest effort, reckoning them to be the ones needed to bring about a change of government or political control. While all MARGINAL SEATS are keenly fought, special effort is made in some, and occasionally seats that look safe on paper fall to well-planned targeting.

targeting (1) The concentration of campaigning activity in an election on those seats that look the most winnable, instead of spreading effort indiscriminately, or concentrating on those voters who can make the greatest difference, and whose allegiance can most easily be won. (2) Ensuring that the neediest groups receive social security payments.

tariff A PROTECTIONIST tax on imports which shields domestic producers while depressing world trade and inviting retaliation. The issue of whether to impose tariffs, to protect home industry and agriculture while forcing up prices to the consumer, was a burning issue throughout the English-speaking world for much of the 19th and 20th centuries, splitting parties and bringing down governments. There are still powerful voices in the US CONGRESS for equally naked forms of protectionism. *See also* FORDNEY-MCCUMBER; FREE TRADE; GATT; IMPERIAL PREFERENCE; MCKINLEY; SMOOT-HAWLEY; UNDERWOOD.

No more than a means of casting feudal interests in capitalist form.
ROSA LUXEMBURG (1871–1919)

Tariff Reform The campaign launched in Britain by Joseph Chamberlain (1836–1914) which tore apart BALFOUR's Unionist COALITION and paved the way for the LANDSLIDE Liberal victory of 1905. Chamberlain unilaterally launched the campaign, aimed at strengthening the bonds of the British Empire through IMPERIAL PREFERENCE, on 15 May 1903 in a speech in Birmingham, alienating FREE TRADE supporters of the government. It was 1932, after further disasters over the issue for the CONSERVATIVE PARTY, before PROTECTION was re-introduced.

a tariff man on a tariff platform The slogan on which William MCKINLEY won the US Presidency in 1896.

non-tariff barriers Obstructionist measures to discourage imports without recourse to a tariff; excessive paperwork, changes in specification and delays at frontiers all fall into this category. In the early 1980s France sought to check imports of Japanese video recorders by insisting that all be checked through a tiny customs post at Poitiers. France's attitude to Japanese imports generally became known as the 'spirit of Poitiers'.

Tartan Tax The phrase popularised by John MAJOR's final Scottish Secretary Michael Forsyth for Labour's proposal to allow a devolved SCOTTISH PARLIAMENT to vary the standard rate of income tax north of the Border by 3p in the £, presumably upward. Despite Forsyth's appeal to Scots' canniness, every Conservative MP in Scotland including himself was unseated at the 1997 general election and a twin referendum that September (*see* YES, YES) endorsed the principle of the tax by almost as large a majority as devolution itself. To date, however, no party at HOLYROOD has dared implement the provision.

tartan Tories *See* TORY.

Tarzan The nickname during the middle part of his political career for Michael HESELTINE. He earned the comparison with Edgar Rice Burroughs' leopard-skin-clad aristocrat swinging from tree to tree through high-profile acts of political daring (rashness, his critics would say) and his flowing mane. *See also* GOLDILOCKS; HEZZA.

task force (1) A naval flotilla comprising complementary types of ship dispatched to perform a specific task, ranging from recovery of the FALKLANDS to a visit to far-off parts to 'show the flag'. (2) A group of experts, advisors and/or officials set to work to sort out a particularly difficult area of policy; while a regular feature of WHITEHALL, task forces blossomed in the early years of NEW LABOUR.

TASS *Telegrafnoe Agentstvo Sovetskoyo Soyuza*, the official news agency of Soviet Russia from 1925 when it replaced the original Bolshevik agency, *Rosta*, until the collapse of the state and its eclipse in post-Communist Russia – though TASS remained in existence – by *Interfax*. TASS was the main source of news for Soviet national newspapers, television and radio, its pronouncements reflecting the MOSCOW LINE on domestic and world affairs. With bureaux in over 100 countries – some a cover for espionage – it provided bulletins in a variety of languages for clients overseas.

It's always a compliment to be denounced by TASS. New York City Mayor ED KOCH

tax and spend To raise taxes to boost public spending on vote-catching projects for a party's client groups, while ignoring the resistance of the rest of the population to having the state use their money. Originally a denunciation by US conservatives of north-eastern and liberal Democrats with their penchant for expensive social programmes, it entered UK politics in the mid-1990s. The phrase may originate from a 1938 statement attributed to Harry Hopkins (*see* HURRY UPKINS): 'We shall tax and tax, and spend and spend, and elect and elect.'

tax base The element of the economy on which taxes are levied: individual incomes, real estate, sales of particular goods etc.

tax loophole A lacuna in the system of taxation, sometimes unintended, occasionally deliberate, which leaves specific goods or services untaxed when others like them are liable. In the American system loopholes are sometimes deliberately created at the urging of LOBBYISTS.

tax reform In WASHINGTON, the process of reconstructing the tax structure so as to make it simpler, fairer and more effective, supposedly without altering its thrust. Efforts to achieve it are generally frustrated by the determination of individual Congressmen and interest groups to preserve specific tax breaks which have lost their relevance to general policy. House WAYS AND MEANS Committee chairman Rep. Dan Rostenkowski (*see* ROSTY) reckoned that 'passing a tax reform bill is like walking through an eggfield'. And Sen. Russell Long summed up the principle behind it as:

> Don't tax you, don't tax me, tax the fellow behind that tree.

tax writing The art of compiling a tax BILL for the US CONGRESS, as practised by the House WAYS AND MEANS Committee, the Senate Finance Committee, their staffs and JOINT TAX.
purchase tax The predecessor in Britain to VAT, levied on a far narrower range of goods and not at all on services. It was targeted heavily on luxury goods – or what were then perceived as such – whose tax level actually fell when VAT was introduced in 1973 after Britain joined the EUROPEAN COMMUNITY.
stealth taxes *See* STEALTH.
tartan tax *See* TARTAN.
wealth tax The tax on the total assets of better-off Britons which the LABOUR PARTY was pledged to introduce in the mid-1970s – but lacked the clear Parliamentary majority to push through. It was based on a similar tax, believed to have been widely evaded, in France.
the power to tax is the power to destroy This much-quoted phrase, delivered in 1819 by Chief Justice John Marshall in the case of *McCulloch v Maryland,* was a variant of Daniel Webster's words in the case: 'An unlimited power to tax involves, necessarily, a power to destroy.'
to tax and to please, no more than to love and be wise, is not given to men One of the best-known dicta of Edmund BURKE.
direct taxation Taxes imposed directly on a person's means; income tax is the prime example.
double taxation The imposition of taxes on the same income or assets of an individual or company by two or more nations. A US/UK Double Taxation Treaty generally prevents this happening to individuals from these two countries with a foot in both economies, though occasionally US state governments try to overstep the mark.
indirect taxation Taxes like VAT or sales taxes, levied on a person's purchases or consumption rather than directly on their income or assets. Indirect taxation is increasingly favoured as a means of side-stepping tax evasion caused by non-declaration of income; however, VAT itself is widely evaded in the black ECONOMY.
progressive taxation Taxes which bite most heavily on the best off, with the least impact (if any) on the poor. Direct taxes, and especially income tax, normally work this way.
regressive taxation The opposite: taxes which impact disproportionately on the worst off, or at the very least hit them as hard as those with more ability to pay.
unitary taxation The system, insisted on by the state of California for many years despite world-wide protests, under which a multinational company based in another state or country was taxed in California on its global, rather than local, activities.
no taxation without representation *See* NO.
the art of taxation consists in so plucking the goose as to obtain the maximum amount of feathers with the smallest possible amount of hissing A dictum of the French finance minister Jean-Baptiste Colbert (1619–83), echoed by Chancellor Norman Lamont in his 1991 BUDGET speech.
nothing is certain in this life except death and taxes A statement that was to become a proverb, but was in fact originated by Benjamin FRANKLIN. His actual words were: 'In this world nothing can be certain except death and taxes.'
taxpayer 'Someone who works for the Federal government but doesn't have to take a civil service examination' – a dictionary definition coined by Ronald REAGAN.

Taylor, Zachary *See* OLD ROUGH AND READY.

TB The amicable if respectful nickname for Tony BLAIR used by his closer associates. At the height of the David KELLY affair Blair's head of communications Alastair Campbell noted in his diary that the latest developments were 'bad for TB, bad for me'.

TD (Ir. *Teachta Daila,* Member of the Dail) The Irish Republic's equivalent of an MP; the alternative is 'DEPUTY'.

tea. tea room In the HOUSE OF COMMONS the tea room, together with the SMOKING ROOM, constitutes the inner sanctum where MPs may relax and converse without any intrusion. The various groups – factional or regional within each party – have tables and clusters of chairs of their own. Anyone holding or seeking high office is well advised to mingle with BACKBENCHERS in the tea room to show themselves 'in touch'. After one particularly bad day in the Commons, Margaret THATCHER was said by shell-shocked Tory rebels to have conducted a 'search and destroy mission in the tea room'.
Boston tea party *See* BOSTON.
cold tea The beverage served on request to members of the US CONGRESS during PROHIBITION, and at other times when

CONSTITUENTS opposed to hard liquor were present. Despite the genteel cup and saucer it was not, in fact, tea.

Teapot Dome One of the greatest scandals in American political history, and one of a series that made the HARDING administration a byword for corruption. It stemmed from the discovery that Albert B. Fall, Secretary of the Interior, had secretly leased government oil fields, part of the Teapot Dome naval oil reserves in Wyoming, to a private company. Fall then negotiated drilling rights with Harry F. Sinclair of the Monmouth Oil Company and granted similar rights in reserves at Elk Hills and Buena Vista Hills, California, to an old friend, Edward F. Doheny. Fall quit the Cabinet in March 1923 as a Senate investigation found blatant evidence of corruption – his family had received $200,000 in bonds from an 'unknown source'. The inquiry led to a series of civil and criminal court actions, which kept the affair in the headlines for years and made 'Teapot Dome' synonymous with political corruption. Reading news reports of the case, the eleven-year-old Richard NIXON told his mother:

> When I get big, I'll be a lawyer who can't be bribed.

In November 1929 Fall was finally convicted of receiving at least $404,000 in bribes and sentenced to a year in prison – becoming the first US Cabinet Secretary jailed for crimes committed in office.

Teapot Dome was the tip of the iceberg. Charlie Forbes, head of the Veterans' Administration, was caught bootlegging hospital drugs to narcotics dealers and profiteering on war surplus goods. Thomas Miller, the alien property custodian, was found to have looted the assets in his care. And Attorney-General Harry Daugherty, Harding's campaign manager, had taken kickbacks from violators of the PROHIBITION laws – and failed to prosecute Forbes despite clear evidence against him. Two years after being fired by President COOLIDGE, Daugherty was tried for conspiracy to defraud the government, and acquitted.

Harding died in office in August 1923, before the full extent of his appointees' crimes was known. He had some clue that things were amiss, once asking Herbert HOOVER: 'If you knew of a great scandal in your administration, would you for the good of the country and the party expose it publicly, or would you bury it?' But he had also declared in April 1922:

> If Albert Fall isn't an honest man, I'm not fit to be President of the United States.

It was left to his successor to clear up the mess; as the full extent of the scandal broke, Coolidge stated:

> If there has been any crime, it must be prosecuted. If there has been any property of the United States illegally transferred or leased, it must be recovered . . . Every law will be enforced. And the right of the people and the Government will be protected.

Teamsters America's giant labour union – the International Brotherhood of Teamsters, Chauffeurs, Warehousemen and Helpers of America – which for two decades from the 1950s was a byword for racketeering and corruption, and has struggled to shake off its past. The union – a teamster is the handler of a team of horses or mules – was founded in 1899, and by 1940 had become America's biggest with over a million members. Persistent allegations of racketeering led to its expulsion from the AFL-CIO in 1957. That year Jimmy Hoffa was elected President of the Teamsters; under his leadership the union became synonymous with gangsterism and organised crime. Hoffa allowed his criminal friends to use the Teamsters as a front for their activities, and in return he and the union acquired great wealth, much of which they used to bribe politicians. Eventually, as a result of an investigation led by Attorney-General Robert KENNEDY, Hoffa was imprisoned in 1967; the feud between Hoffa and Kennedy was a powerful sub-plot to mid-1960s politics, and there are even claims that the death of Marilyn Monroe was connected to Teamster efforts to blackmail RFK. Hoffa was paroled by President NIXON in 1971 and in 1975 disappeared, presumably murdered by fellow-gangsters. Two of Hoffa's three immediate successors as union president also fell foul of the law, in 1986 the PRESIDENT'S COMMISSION on organised crime dubbed the Teamsters America's 'most corrupt' union, and in 1988 the Justice Department indicted its entire eighteen-man executive and over 20 suspected gangsters for racketeering; 246 Congressmen protested. Federal appointees took over the running of the union, and in 1991 Ron Carey was elected general president on a 'get the bums out' platform. Taking office in 1992, he took speedy action to clean up the union and halt a slide in membership from its peak of 2 million. Carey fought off a challenge from James Hoffa Jr in 1996, but was expelled from the Teamsters two years later because of massive corruption in his re-election campaign.

tear gas A worldwide instrument of RIOT control, and often of repression. When disorder breaks out, police or troops fire a gas (or dispersed liquid or powder) from gun-like canisters which reduces the rioters to tears, temporarily disables and generally breaks up the protest. Tear gas is a blanket term for various chemical compounds which in recent decades have included CS GAS and MACE. Sometimes the boot is on the other foot; when the Shah of Iran visited President CARTER early in 1978, protesting Iranian students fired tear gas at police on the ELLIPSE and the wind blew it straight at the WELCOMING CEREMONY, gassing the official party on the WHITE HOUSE lawn. As the choking cloud enveloped the attendant media, including the author, a photographer exclaimed:

> I was in the 'Nam, man, and you gotta be ready,

and slapped on a gas mask he had brought as a precaution.

Tebbit, Norman *See* CHINGFORD SKINHEAD.

technocracy A system of government by technical experts (**technocrats**). A radical US movement advocating the control of society by engineers and scientists adopted this name in the 1930s; it took its ideology from Thorstein Veblen's *The Engineers and the Price System* (1921), which sought to replace the irrationality of the free MARKET by a PLANNED ECONOMY. The movement lost impetus with the improvement in social and economic conditions brought about by the NEW DEAL.

Ted(dy) The blind UK Labour politician David Blunkett's second guide dog and successor to RUBY, a labrador and curly coat retriever cross. Ted was the first guide dog allowed into the Gallery of the COMMONS, in 1986, and onto the floor of the CHAMBER the following year when his master was first elected MP for Sheffield Brightside. He retired in 1988, to be replaced by OFFA.

Teddy The affectionate nickname for President Theodore ROOSEVELT, reflecting his larger-than-life and perceivedly cuddly nature. The teddy bear was christened after him, following a bear hunt in 1903 whose organisers stunned a young bear and tied it to a tree to make sure the President made a kill.

teenage scribblers The dismissive term for Britain's financial press coined by Nigel (later Lord) Lawson (1932–) during his initially successful period as Margaret THATCHER'S CHANCELLOR OF THE EXCHEQUER. The hubristic Lawson, himself a former financial journalist, built after 1983 on foundations laid by Sir Geoffrey HOWE to create a runaway boom, but resigned in 1989 after a clash with the Prime Minister over the activities of her economic adviser Sir Alan Walters, with the economy heading for a HARD LANDING and RECESSION. The 'scribblers' ensured him a bad press in the years that followed.

Teflon Presidency The ability of the REAGAN presidency to dissociate itself from misdeeds, SLEAZE and incompetence by those close to the seat of power. Teflon is the non-stick substance which by the 1980s was lining pans in every Western kitchen.

> He has achieved a breakthrough in political technology – the Teflon Presidency. He sees that nothing sticks to him.
>
> Rep. PAT SCHROEDER (1940–)

Tehran Conference The meeting of the 'Big Three' WORLD WAR II leaders in the Persian capital from 28 November to 1 December 1943; CHURCHILL and ROOSEVELT's first meeting with STALIN. The main decision was to launch a SECOND FRONT by invading France in May 1944, instead of staging the main offensive in the Mediterranean theatre as Churchill preferred. Stalin, who had pressed hard for a Second Front, promised a strong Soviet offensive to coincide. He also gained Roosevelt's agreement to Soviet expansion into eastern Poland and Poland's acquisition of Danzig and East Prussia. There were inconclusive talks on the zoning of post-war Germany and the form the UNITED NATIONS should take, and commitments to Persia's post-war independence and greater aid for TITO's PARTISANS in Yugoslavia. Their closing declaration said:

> We leave here friends in fact, in spirit and in purpose.

telegram. the telegrams The term used by Britain's FOREIGN OFFICE for the daily communications to or from embassies and High Commissions throughout the world. Signed always with the surname of the Ambassador or High Commissioner or the Foreign Secretary, they are seen by Ministers and senior officials across WHITEHALL, and the Queen.

Ems telegram *See* EMS.

Kruger telegram *See* KRUGER.

telephone. telephone box The reputed meeting place of Britain's LIBERAL MPs in the early 1950s, when they were reduced to just five seats in the HOUSE OF COMMONS.

Why doesn't he use the telephone? The exasperated comment of Stanley BALDWIN at the noisy conversation of Ernest Brown, his Minister of Labour. Hearing Brown bellowing (down the telephone) in an adjoining room, he asked what was going on and was told: 'Mr Brown is talking to Birmingham.' Baldwin replied: 'Why doesn't he use the telephone?' There was a sequel in WASHINGTON; when the HOUSE was considering installing a public address system, Franklin D. ROOSEVELT said from the WHITE HOUSE: 'Why? I can hear Florence Kahn's voice without it.' The booming-voiced California Republican lost her seat after just one term in 1936, when her CONSTITUENTS decided they had heard enough.

teleprompter The device used by television presenters to read a script; the text is scrolled down on a screen built into the camera. A variant, involving a transparent reflective lectern attached to the ROSTRUM, was pioneered for major speeches by Ronald REAGAN and Margaret THATCHER; it is now in general use.

teller vote *See* VOTE.

tellers (1) The individuals deputed to supervise the recording or counting of votes in a LEGISLATURE or conference. At WESTMINSTER the tellers do not vote, and a teller from the winning side announce the result of each DIVISION. (2) Party representatives who take up position outside a POLLING STATION to keep track of which of their supporters have voted as the day progresses, so that the others can be called on and persuaded to turn out.

Temple Mount The site of the AL-AQSA mosque in Jerusalem, holy alike to Muslims and Jews. A visit there by Ariel Sharon in September 2000 effectively ended the OSLO peace process and triggered a renewed INTIFADA. Far-right Jewish groups regarded Israel's subsequent ban of non-Muslims from the site as a 'blasphemy'.

ten. *Ten Days that Shook the World* The title of the epic book on the RUSSIAN REVOLUTION written in 1919 by the American socialist John Reed (1887–1920), whose experiences were the basis for the film *Reds*.

10 Downing Street *See* NUMBER TEN.

Ten Minute Rule Bill *See* BILL.

Ten per cent plan Abraham LINCOLN's plan for RECONSTRUCTION, proclaimed in December 1863 for Arkansas, Louisiana, Tennessee and Virginia. It pardoned all Southerners who would swear allegiance to the United States and accept anti-slavery legislation, except high CONFEDERATE officials and those who had deserted federal posts. It also authorised the establishment of new governments, represented at national level, in any state where one-tenth of its qualified voters took the oath. It amounted to an invitation to southerners to rebuild the South's political structures without delay, then re-enter national life. It was bitterly resented by many in CONGRESS, which retaliated with the WADE-DAVIS BILL, and was one of the first casualties after Lincoln's assassination.

Ten words The mini-programme that the UK Conservative leader Michael HOWARD gave his party to remember at its October 2004 conference, with an election expected the following spring. He urged them to memorise and campaign on:

> School discipline; more police; cleaner hospitals; lower taxes; controlled immigration. Ten words to address the problems that are worrying people today. Remember those words, and remember one more: ACCOUNTABILITY.

Tenth amendment The last of the Constitutional amendments in the US BILL OF RIGHTS ratified in December 1791. It specifically leaves to the STATES all powers not granted by the CONSTITUTION to the federal government.

Tenure of Office Act An Act passed in 1867 by the Republican-controlled CONGRESS in an attempt to prevent President Andrew Johnson dismissing Secretary for War Edwin Stanton, who was secretly reporting Johnson's plans to Republican radicals. Making any dismissal by the President subject to Senate approval, it was eventually ruled UNCONSTITUTIONAL. Johnson fired Stanton anyway, triggering IMPEACHMENT proceedings which almost succeeded.

term The length of time a representative of the people is elected to serve. A US Presidential term is four years, against six for a Senator and two for a Congressman. In Britain the maximum Parliamentary term is five years.

term limitation The principle that no one should be allowed to serve indefinitely even if the voters are ready to re-elect them. Republican distaste at Franklin D. ROOSEVELT's unprecedented fourth term (*see* *below*) led to the TWENTY-SECOND AMENDMENT, limiting any President to two terms. Ironically, the President most likely since that time to have been re-elected for a third term, Ronald REAGAN, was a Republican. In 1992 fourteen states approved legislation limiting their Senators to two terms, and Congressmen to from three to six terms. Action by Congress itself to set a limit on terms served was a key element of the CONTRACT WITH AMERICA, but when a vote was taken in March 1995 support from those whose terms were to be limited fell well short of the two-thirds required for a Constitutional amendment.

> The United States ought to be able to choose for its President anybody that it wants, regardless of the number of terms he has served.
> PRESIDENT EISENHOWER, 1956

one-term President *See* PRESIDENT.

second term The term, commencing with a President's second and INAUGURATION, during which, since the passage of the TWENTY-SECOND AMENDMENT, he has become a LAME DUCK. Yet election for a second term is also proof that the first victory was no fluke.

> Anyone can be elected by accident. Beginning with a second term, it's worth paying attention.
> ABRAHAM LINCOLN

third term Margaret THATCHER introduced the phrase and the concept (the Conservatives' 1959 victory was won by their third leader in eight years) with her third successive general election triumph in 1987. Tony BLAIR repeated the achievement for Labour in 2005. In America, there was a tradition that no President would seek a consecutive third term until Franklin D. ROOSEVELT ran in 1940. When Republicans backing Wendell Willkie cried 'foul', the Democrats replied:

> Better a third-termer than a third-rater.

fourth term FDR's decision to seek a fourth term aroused less controversy than his third, although the result of the 1944 election was closer. The lack of protest was primarily due to America being immersed in WORLD WAR II, and to a perceived need for continuity in leadership. Margaret Thatcher failed in her ambition to win a fourth or even a fifth term, but the CONSERVATIVE PARTY did secure a fourth term on 9 April 1992 under John MAJOR's leadership.

terminological inexactitudes The classic euphemism for a lie, attributed to Winston CHURCHILL since he said in the House of Commons on 22 February 1906:

> It cannot in the opinion of His Majesty's Government be classified as slavery in the extreme acceptance of the word without some risk of terminological inexactitude.

It is UNPARLIAMENTARY for one MP to accuse another of being a LIAR, or accuse them of telling a lie. Churchill's phrase is acceptable as a substitute and so is 'economical with the TRUTH' since Sir Robert Armstrong's unfortunate use of the phrase (*see* SPYCATCHER). However, Churchill's son Randolph insisted that his father never intended 'terminological inexactitude' to mean an outright lie.

terra nullius The legal doctrine devised in Australia to assert that the country had been vacant before the first colonists arrived and hence that the Aborigines had no land rights. Australia's High Court did not overthrow it until June 1992, and in December 1993 the Senate and House passed a **Native Rights Act** which restored land rights and allowed Aborigines and Torres Strait Islanders to press claims for some 10% of the continent, while respecting mining, ranching and other leases. Opposition leader John Hewson accused Paul KEATING of 'selling out the interests of all Australians', but Keating said the Bill solved 'the longest continuing problem that Australia has faced for 200 years – recognising that indigenous people . . . had a right to their own soil.'

Terrace The paved terrace overlooking the River Thames which runs along almost the entire south-east frontage of the Palace of WESTMINSTER; it faces across the river to St Thomas's Hospital. On summer evenings, the terrace and its marquee containing a bar and reception rooms are crowded with MPs, their families, researchers and acquaintances, and staff of the House; the festive scene gets a mixed reception from trippers passing on riverboats. Members of the LOBBY were barred from the terrace without a specific invitation in the early 1990s; ironically the only misbehaviour recorded there is of two Labour MPs who a decade earlier had dangled a kissogram girl upside down over the parapet. Since the terrace was constructed in the 1850s, its level has had to be raised to prevent flood tides spilling over the parapet and inundating lower floors of the building; the Thames Barrier downstream at Woolwich has now removed for a few decades that threat, which led to the Connaught Rooms, a Masonic suite in Holborn, being designated as an emergency

Parliament building. Before the barrier stabilised the flow of the river, MPs on the terrace could at times observe the flow of used contraceptives flushed from London's drainage system.

Territorial Army The force of part-time and mainly ex-regular soldiers which supplements the British Army at times of conflict and OVERSTRETCH; its full title is the Territorial Army and Volunteer Reserve. Its naval and airborne equivalents are the **Royal Navy Volunteer Reserve** and the **Royal Air Force Volunteer Reserve**. Specialists in the TAVR, especially medics and communications experts, have been called up regularly to serve in Iraq.

territorial departments The UK government departments responsible for all the affairs of Scotland and Wales until DEVOLUTION, and for RESERVED matters and liaison since. Prior to 1999 the Scottish Office and Welsh Office, each with the bulk of their staff on the ground and a small presence in WHITEHALL, were sizeable forces; the NORTHERN IRELAND Office had a narrower role because the BUREAUCRACY of devolved government had existed since the province was run from STORMONT. With devolution in 1999 the SCOTLAND OFFICE and Wales Office opened up in Whitehall with far more limited powers and only a residual presence in their home countries. Four years later, both were merged into the new Department for Constitutional Affairs, keeping their identities but losing their separate SECRETARY OF STATE; the functions of each were given to a CABINET MINISTER with other responsibilities.

incorporated territories Areas lacking full statehood which are integral parts of the United States. Only the DISTRICT OF COLUMBIA now fits that category. **Unincorporated territories** enjoy basic Constitutional rights without being fully part of the nation. Guam, Samoa, the Virgin Islands and the Pacific Trust areas fall into this category.

Occupied Territories The territory captured by Israel during the SIX DAY WAR of 1967 and retained by it ever since, despite the concession of a limited amount of Palestinian self-government. East Jerusalem and the WEST BANK were seized from Jordan, the GAZA STRIP from Egypt and the GOLAN HEIGHTS from Syria. Israel's determination to retain these territories for defensive purposes (and under LIKUD, reasons of Biblical precedent), its denial for a quarter of a century of any rights to the Palestinians and the creation of Jewish settlements in the territories have been a major obstacle to the PEACE PROCESS. Since 1992 Israel has accepted the case for some Palestinian self-government, but partial withdrawals from the West Bank and Gaza have been followed by punitive Israeli raids when those areas became bases for terrorists who opposed any compromise.

territory An area of land lacking full self-government, and specifically the component parts of the United States before they achieved STATEHOOD.

terror. Great Terror STALIN's grotesque and ruthless PURGES of the 1930s, when at least 10 million people were executed or deported to labour camps on the flimsiest of pretexts to ease the Soviet leader's pathological insecurity. The persecution of supposed DISSIDENTS and opponents of the regime began in 1935, and from 1936 to 1938 its chief instigator was Nikolai Ivanovich Yezhov (1884–1940), head of the NKVD. Yezhov, a brutal man of low intelligence and barely five feet tall, was described by one contemporary as 'a bloodthirsty dwarf'. He began by purging the NKVD itself, cut a swathe through the RED ARMY's high command, and then staged SHOW TRIALS of Stalin's old comrades in the BOLSHEVIK leadership. Although these purges were orchestrated by Stalin, Yezhov became synonymous with the Great Terror, but in December 1938 he too was arrested, and replaced as head of the NKVD by Beria. He was probably shot two years later, a convenient scapegoat for a campaign of state murder that exceeded even the HOLOCAUST, and which left the Soviet Union critically weak after HITLER invaded.

Reign of Terror The bloody 420 days during which the FRENCH REVOLUTION devoured its own children, and the GUILLOTINE reigned supreme in the hands of the JACOBINS. It began with the fall of the GIRONDISTS on 31 May 1793, four months after the execution of Louis XVI and Marie Antoinette, and ended with the overthrow of Robespierre on 27 July 1794. The perpetrators of the Terror revelled in the title, Bernard Barère de Vieuzac, who outlived it, telling the National Convention: 'Let us make terror the order of the day.' Robespierre proclaimed in February 1794:

> Terror is nothing but justice: prompt, secure and inflexible.

But he would soon face the guillotine himself and find out just how inflexible it was.

terrorism The use of violence or intimidation to secure political ends, usually involving the shooting or bombing of innocent civilians in cold blood. Terrorism is in the eye of the beholder, its perpetrators being hailed as freedom fighters or would-be martyrs for a worthy case by whoever supports them, regardless of the extent of their atrocities. Walter Laqueur termed terrorism 'PROPAGANDA by deed', and Richard E. Rubinstein 'the violence of the intelligentsia'. Most governments are pledged to resist it, but a few (including some Communist countries, Libya, Iran and Syria) have fomented and encouraged it against other governments, or have created STATE TERRORISM. Terrorism has evolved from the individual would-be assassin, through anti-imperialist movements like MAU MAU, to radical leftist groups such as the BAADER-MEINHOF GANG, nationalist guerrillas such as ETA, the IRA and militant Palestinian groups to the Islamist suicide terrorists of AL QAEDA. All terrorists nurse the conviction that even if they personally fail, ultimately their cause will prevail and bring down the regime they consider oppressive or win freedom for a people they believe downtrodden. Their belief is strengthened by a number of instances in which one day's so-called terrorist has become a respected hero of liberation.

> We are not going to tolerate these attacks from outlaw states, run by the strangest collection of misfits, looney tunes and squalid criminals since the advent of the Third Reich.
>
> RONALD REAGAN

> All terrorists at the invitation of the Government end up with drinks at the Dorchester.
>
> HUGH GAITSKELL

Prevention of Terrorism Act The legislation first passed after the 1974 BIRMINGHAM pub bombings under which the authorities could bar anyone they considered a terrorist suspect from entering mainland Britain from NORTHERN IRELAND, and terrorist suspects in Britain could be held for questioning for longer than the standard 48 hours. With its key provisions renewed year by year, it remained in force for a quarter of a century until the GOOD FRIDAY AGREEMENT changed the climate. Elements of the Act survive in current anti-terrorist legislation, which was reinforced after 9/11 with its emphasis switched from Irish to international terrorism.

Tesco Retail Broadwater Park – now open 24 hours The slogan that Sir Malcolm Rifkind, to his mortification, formally unveiled in Edinburgh on 5 May 2001 to launch the Scottish Conservatives' general election campaign. The van supplied by their advertising agency bore not the wording chosen by the party but a puff for a supermarket in Hertfordshire, and was not checked beforehand.

get a job at Tesco The highly damaging remark made by Margaret Hodge, Work and Pensions Minister, on a visit to Birmingham on 16 June 2005 in the wake of the closure of the MG-Rover plant at Longbridge with the loss of 6000 jobs. Ms Hodge said at the opening of a new Tesco store:

> I am saying that some of the jobs are in Tesco, and they will meet the needs of some of the unemployed and people looking for work in the district. There are also jobs arising out of other new industrial developments.

Trade union leaders and Conservative MPs accused Ms Hodge of insulting highly skilled workers laid off in the closure by suggesting they take a job in a supermarket, and of suggesting the Labour government had given up on manufacturing industry. Ms Hodge insisted she had been talking about opportunities for the unemployed in general. Ironically her comments came weeks after a general election in which Labour fared better in the West Midlands than nationally, despite the Longbridge closure.

test. Test Act The Act passed in 1673 that barred Roman Catholics and Protestant dissenters from holding national or local office in England and Wales. It required anyone elected to take a 'test' of loyalty to the sacraments of the Church of England. It was not repealed until 1829, and then only after a bitter struggle between supporters of Catholic EMANCIPATION and upholders of the status quo, who included King George IV.

Test Ban Treaty (1) The treaty concluded by America, the Soviet Union and Britain in July 1963 which ended atmospheric – but not underground – testing of atomic weapons by the then NUCLEAR powers. It was the first SUPERPOWER agreement after the CUBAN MISSILE CRISIS, and a historic step in getting the ARMS RACE under control, but was as much a victory for environmentalists as for disarmers, given growing concern about the level of nuclear fall-out. Eventually more than 110 nations have endorsed the treaty, France being the principal exception. Britain's governing Conservatives, facing defeat in an imminent general election, put out an advertisement showing an anti-nuclear campaigner with a CND placard, captioned: 'Meanwhile the Conservatives have signed the Test Ban Treaty.'

> A journey of a thousand miles must begin with a single step.
>
> President KENNEDY, quoting a Chinese proverb

(2) The **Comprehensive Test Ban Treaty**, outlawing all nuclear tests, which was approved by the UNITED NATIONS General Assembly on 10 September 1996 by 158 votes to 3, with 5 abstentions. To date it has been ratified by 119 nations, most of them non-nuclear – the CLINTON administration pressed hard for the Senate to vote on ratification but failed – but only India and Pakistan (neither of which have signed the treaty) have pressed ahead with testing.

Tet offensive The co-ordinated surprise attack by the VIET CONG on more than 100 towns and cities, launched on 31 January 1968, which traumatically called in question America's ability to win the VIETNAM WAR. The month-long onslaught by 70,000 troops backed by North Vietnamese jets and gunships which broke the Tet (lunar New Year) truce came as a total shock to the US public; for the first time in the war they saw their troops fighting the Viet Cong not deep in the countryside but for their own bases at Da Nang and Khe Sanh, in the streets of Hué and Saigon – and even in the US Embassy. Ever since ground troops were first committed in 1965, the military had assured politicians, the media and the people that the Communists were on the verge of collapse; even though the Tet offensive was beaten back with very heavy Communist losses, it suggested the opposite and was thus an important psychological victory for the Viet Cong. The following month Walter Cronkite, the 'most trusted face' on network TV, reported from Saigon: 'It now seems more certain than ever that the bloody experience of Vietnam is to end in a stale mate.' President JOHNSON, watching, commented that if he lost Cronkite he had lost America, and indeed the Tet offensive was the final nail in his presidency. Public support for the war, already starting to slip, fell more rapidly and with even his own staff starting to urge US disengagement, Johnson announced in March that he would not seek re-election and ordered a BOMBING HALT.

tête à tête (Fr. head to head) The most pivotal discussions between world leaders, when they sit down one-on-one, except for the presence of a translator and/or NOTE TAKER, to share their real thoughts and concerns or to make an effort to resolve a pressing problem that a larger meeting would struggle with.

Texas School Book Depository The building in DALLAS from whose sixth floor window Lee Harvey Oswald (1939–63) is supposed to have fired the shots that killed President KENNEDY. Oswald, a former US Marine who had married the daughter of a KGB colonel and lived for a time in Russia, had started work in the Depository a month before the shooting. A witness to the WARREN COMMISSION testified that the shots were fired from the fifth floor; those who believe someone else shot Kennedy reckon they came from the GRASSY KNOLL nearby.

Texas v Wade The case on which the US SUPREME COURT ruled in 1869 that the UNION was constitutionally indestructible, and that the defeated South had thus never left it. *See also* HELL.

Thank you for your letter, contents of which have been noted The crushing response of Clement ATTLEE in May 1945 to a letter from Professor Harold Laski, chairman of the LABOUR PARTY, telling him that 'the continuance of your leadership is a grave handicap to our hopes of victory in the coming election', and urging him to resign. Laski did not take the hint, even after Attlee had led Labour to its greatest victory, with a majority of 180 over CHURCHILL's Conservatives; this time he told Attlee that he could not consider himself leader unless endorsed by the newly-elected Parliamentary party. At this point the monosyllabic Attlee came as close as he ever did to snapping, writing back on 20 August: '**A period of silence on your part would be welcome**'. The episode speaks volumes about Laski's lack of political judgement (*see also* Even if it means VIOLENCE).

that. That these United Colonies are, and of right ought to be, free and independent States, that they are absolved from all allegiance to the British crown, and that all political connection between them and the State of Great Britain is, and ought to be totally dissolved The first of three resolutions passed by the CONTINENTAL CONGRESS on 2 July 1776 which paved the way for the Declaration of INDEPENDENCE. They were drawn up in advance, and presented, by Richard Henry Lee on behalf of Virginia.

That this House has no confidence in Her Majesty's Government The standard wording of a no-CONFIDENCE motion in the HOUSE OF COMMONS, defeat on which leads by custom to the resignation of the government or the holding of an election.

That this House will in no circumstances fight for King and Country The motion whose passage by the Oxford Union in its KING AND COUNTRY debate on 9 February 1933 fostered the impression that Britain would not stand up to the DICTATORS.

That the noble Lord be no longer heard The motion that exasperated PEERS will put as a last resort in the HOUSE OF LORDS if one of their number refuses to sit down in the face of repeated requests from the CHAIR for them to stop talking and resume their seat.

That Was The Week That Was The pioneering satirical programme, transmitted live by BBC television from 24 November 1962, which shot David FROST to stardom and critically undermined Harold MACMILLAN's government, notably through its savage treatment of the PROFUMO AFFAIR. Produced by Ned Sherrin, it could also be serious; its spontaneous and moving tribute to President KENNEDY on his assassination earned it a transatlantic reputation. **TW3**, which ran intermittently for just over a year, was taken off as a looming general election made the BBC hierarchy nervous; Millicent Martin, William Rushton, Roy Kinnear and Lance Percival were among others to make their names in it.

Thatcher, Margaret Hilda (later Baroness) **Thatcher** (1925–), Prime Minister 1979–90 and leader of the CONSERVATIVE PARTY from 1975. Britain's first woman Prime Minister, whose right-wing firmness revived Britain's standing in the world and transformed both the economy and social attitudes – though not always in a way that those on the receiving end appreciated. Born Margaret Hilda Roberts in the monochrome Lincolnshire town of Grantham, she showed the temperament that would make her a world force at the age of nine, when on winning her first school prize, she said: 'I wasn't lucky. I deserved it.' She gained an Oxford science degree; Dame Janet Vaughan described her as 'a perfectly good second-class chemist'. She went into industry, a 1948 ICI personnel report terming her 'headstrong, obstinate and dangerously self-opinionated'. She fought her first seat at Dartford in 1950 and 1951, meeting her businessman husband Denis at the selection meeting, she qualified as a barrister, brought up twins and in 1959 was elected MP for Finchley. She made an immediate impact and in 1961 became a junior minister in Harold MACMILLAN's government. In OPPOSITION from 1964 she climbed the political ladder through hard work, and in 1970 Edward HEATH made her Education Secretary (*see* MILK-SNATCHER). After Heath lost the February 1974 election, she began her obvious move to the right under the influence of Sir Keith Joseph (*see* MAD MONK). Early the next year she stood against Heath for the party leadership when others held back, and was elected. In four years as Leader of the Opposition, with the collapse of the Labour government always possible, she moved the party rightwards – but did not easily establish command in the House. After Labour's defeat in a NO-CONFIDENCE vote, she fought a spirited election campaign and on 4 May 1979 the Tories were returned to power with a majority of 43.

She offered a healing administration (*see* WHERE THERE IS DISCORD), and in office coupled a MONETARIST economic policy and a determination to move rightwards on LAW AND ORDER with an unexpectedly open mind on Rhodesia, refusing to endorse Ian Smith's INTERNAL SETTLEMENT. The unions she froze out, almost from the start:

> *Syd Bidwell MP* (Lab.): Are you aware that Mr Len Murray, general secretary of the TUC, insists that when he sees you, it is like having a dialogue with the deaf?
> *Mrs Thatcher:* I had no idea that Mr Murray was deaf.

Scorning past Tory feebleness, she ground down the Cabinet WETS and surrounded herself with loyalists; when the economy seemed to be running into trouble, she insisted: 'THE LADY'S NOT FOR TURNING.' She adopted a bulldog attitude toward the EUROPEAN COMMUNITY, whose fellow-leaders she lectured relentlessly (*see* I want my MONEY back); Sir Ian Gilmour, one of the first wets to go, said:

> She will insist on treating other heads of government as if they were members of her Cabinet.

She was hostile to the Soviet Union, of whose evil she was convinced (*see* IRON LADY), and formed a very close working relationship with President REAGAN. As the Conservatives moved right and Labour moved left the SDP was formed, making inroads into the moderate Tory vote; defeat at the next election looked possible when the FALKLANDS WAR, and her determination on victory, transformed the political landscape. In June 1983, with her opponents evenly split, Mrs Thatcher won re-election with a LANDSLIDE majority of 144. Her second term was marked by a campaign of PRIVATISATION, a turnround in the economy, Mrs Thatcher's recognition that in Mikhail GORBACHEV the Soviet Union had a leader who would end the COLD WAR, and the ANGLO-IRISH AGREEMENT. But it also brought the BRIGHTON BOMBING of October 1984 in which she narrowly escaped death, the year-long MINERS' STRIKE in which she crushed the National Union of Mineworkers led by Arthur Scargill (*see* KING ARTHUR), and the WESTLAND affair, which nearly brought her downfall and left lasting doubts about the ethics of her inner circle. The business activities of her son Mark magnified these doubts. In June 1987 Mrs Thatcher led the Conservatives to a record third term, with a reduced but still large majority of 102. With the economy booming until late 1988, she now seemed untouchable; the dismantling of the PUBLIC SECTOR accelerated and she set a triumphalist tone in home policy – epitomised by her advocacy of the POLL TAX – and foreign affairs. Standing out at a Commonwealth conference against tighter sanctions on South Africa, she said:

> If it is 48 against one, I feel sorry for the 48.

And when her daughter-in-law had a baby, she incurred ridicule by proclaiming 'WE HAVE BECOME A GRANDMOTHER'. Fissures opened between Mrs Thatcher and Chancellor Nigel Lawson on the economy, and with Sir Geoffrey HOWE, her most senior Minister, on Europe, and while her BRUGES speech did not split the party her refusal to contemplate closer union did (*see* NO!, NO!, NO!). A STALKING-HORSE challenge to her leadership in 1989 by Sir Anthony Meyer sounded a warning she ignored; Sir Geoffrey's resignation over Europe triggered a challenge from Michael HESELTINE in November 1990. She fell four votes short of the margin she needed, and after defiantly declaring: 'I fight on, I fight to win', she resigned on 28 November, to be succeeded by John MAJOR. She said of her defeat: 'It's a funny old world', and of him:

> He won't falter and I won't falter. It's just that I shan't be pulling the levers there. But I can be a very good back seat driver.

She left DOWNING STREET in tears and found retirement hard to take, saying wistfully: 'Home is where you go when you have nothing else to do.' She gathered a coterie of hard-line devotees, and they fired off criticism of Major's policies on Europe and the economy that made his job all the harder. Edwina Currie (*see* CRUELLA DE VIL), who later owned up to an affair with Major, declared:

> She is in danger of becoming the Tony BENN of the Tory party – old and mad and silly and wrong.

She left the Commons at the 1992 election and took a Life PEERAGE, remaining active in speaking out against the MAASTRICHT TREATY; her most poignant appearances in later years were at her husband's funeral and that of President Reagan, for whom she had prepared a taped address as her doctors had advised her some time previously not to speak in public.

Margaret Thatcher aroused very strong feelings: 'A man with tits' – the feminist Labour MP Maureen Colquhoun; 'the plutonium blonde' – Arthur Scargill; 'a brilliant tyrant surrounded by mediocrities' – Harold MACMILLAN; 'she thinks Sinai is the plural of sinus' – Jonathan Aitken; 'a cross between Isadora Duncan and Lawrence of Arabia' – *Daily Telegraph*; 'a heady mixture of whisky and perfume' – Dr David OWEN; 'David Owen in drag' – the *Rhodesia Herald*; 'that bloody woman' – Edward Heath; 'she who must be obeyed' – Julian Critchley; 'clearly the best man among them' – Barbara CASTLE; 'crocodile tears with crocodile teeth' – Neil KINNOCK; 'the Enid Blyton of economics' – Richard Holme; 'the eyes of Caligula and the lips of Marilyn Monroe' – François MITTERRAND; 'the GROCER'S DAUGHTER' – Valéry Giscard d'Estaing; 'she is of such charming brutality' – Helmut Kohl; 'she is trying to wear the trousers of Winston CHURCHILL' – Leonid BREZHNEV. Denis HEALEY was the rudest of all, calling her 'the lady with the blowlamp', 'Pétain with petticoats', 'Miss Floggie', 'Rhoda the Rhino' and 'the Castro of the Western world, an embarrassment to all her friends. All she lacks is the beard', and saying: 'The Prime Minister tells us that she gave the French president a piece of her mind – not a gift I would receive with alacrity,' and 'Mrs Thatcher is doing for monetarism what the Boston Strangler did for door-to-door salesmen.'

MAGGIE was adored in the constituencies, Critchley writing: 'She seemed to share the views so often expressed by party workers and, worse, to articulate them.' But the liberal CHATTERING CLASSES loathed her.

Keith Waterhouse declared: 'I cannot bring myself to vote for a woman who has been voice-trained to speak to me as though my dog has just died.' She won the votes of the C2S, but was detested in Scotland (*see* SERMON ON THE MOUND). She was susceptible to flattery from flashy, middle-aged men; the party ESTABLISHMENT had backed her believing they could control her, but she turned away from them and encouraged not just an ENTERPRISE CULTURE but, at the height of the boom, a Philistine get-rich-quick element, some of whom ended in prison when the recession bit. Harold Macmillan observed:

> She has taken our party from the Etonians and given it to the Estonians.

Nor did she do women any favours; saying: 'I owe nothing to WOMEN'S LIB', she believed other women could succeed on their own as she had. Feminists said:

> She may be a woman but she isn't a sister.

Her relationship with the one woman she had to defer to was reputedly fraught, Anthony Sampson writing: 'The weekly meetings between the Queen and Mrs Thatcher – both of the same age – are dreaded by at least one of them.' She had expected not to become Prime Minister because of male resistance; in 1969 she said: 'No woman in my time will be Prime Minister or Chancellor or Foreign Secretary – not the top jobs. Anyway, I would not want to be Prime Minister; you have to give yourself 100 per cent'; and in 1972:

> I don't think it will come for many, many years. I don't think it will come in my lifetime.

Mrs Thatcher's firm anti-Communism and her support for DISSIDENTS in Eastern Europe earned her warm support behind the former IRON CURTAIN. Robin Oakley wrote: 'She may have lost Scotland and Wales for the Tories, but she could have had Eastern Europe any time she wanted'; Alexander Dubček simply called her 'the kind lady'.

Her husband Denis (*see* ANYONE FOR DENIS?) gave her financial security and moral support; he was also an unreconstructed right-winger (*see* DEAR BILL) who advocated resuming sporting links with South Africa and who, after hearing Reagan speak to a London business event in 1969, put her in touch with him. US Secretary of State George Shultz said: 'If I were married to her, I'd be sure to have the dinner ready when I got home'; Denis, when asked who wore the trousers in the house, said: 'I do. I also wash and iron them.' Yet when Education Secretary, Mrs Thatcher would break away from meetings to buy bacon for his breakfast.

Mrs Thatcher's overriding attribute was her determination. While she lacked an obvious sense of humour, she could win laughs with her strident REPARTEE. When she took office James CALLAGHAN said: 'May I congratulate you on being the only man in your team?' She struck back: 'That's one more than you've got in yours.' Yet she insisted: 'I'm not hard – I'm frightfully soft. But I will not be hounded.' And she said:

> I am extraordinarily patient – provided I get my own way in the end.

At the same time she wanted to be stood up to, saying: 'I love argument. I love debate. I don't expect anyone just to sit there and agree with me. That's not their job.' And of her critics she said: 'I always cheer up immediately when an attack is particularly wounding because that means they have not got a single political argument left.'

> She sounded like the *Book of Revelation* being read out over a railway public address system by a headmistress of certain age wearing calico knickers.
> CLIVE JAMES

> The nanny seemed to be extinct until 1975 when, like the coelacanth, she suddenly and unexpectedly reappeared in the shape of Margaret Thatcher.
> SIMON HOGGART, *The Observer*

> She addressed me as though I was the NUREMBERG RALLY.
> New Zealand Prime Minister DAVID LANGE

> She's democratic enough to talk down to anyone.
> AUSTIN MITCHELL MP (Lab)

> Margaret Thatcher plays, I suspect, to an unseen gallery of headmistresses, economists and the Madame Tussaud version of Winston Churchill.
> KATHARINE WHITEHORN, *The Observer*

> She has turned the British bulldog into President Reagan's poodle.
> DAVID STEEL

> Trying to tell her anything is like making an important phone call and getting an answering machine.
> DAVID STEEL

> If you want to change her mind, you don't use argument – you look for a transplant surgeon.
> GMB union leader JOHN EDMONDS

> Bawling out trade unionists, the unemployed, foreigners and other miscreants has been part of her enduring appeal to the British public.
> JULIAN BARNES

> When the undertakers come to lay her out, they will find a colonel's uniform on underneath.
> RENEE SHORT MP (Lab)

I hope she will go on until the end of the century looking like Queen Victoria.
NORMAN TEBBIT

I wish the old cow would resign.
NORTHERN IRELAND Minister RICHARD NEEDHAM, November 1990

She was constitutionally always right. Power never corrupted her. NICHOLAS RIDLEY

A towering Prime Minister who left her country in a far better position than she found it.
JOHN MAJOR

Paddy Ashdown is the first trained killer to be a party leader . . . Mrs Thatcher being self-taught.
GILBERT ARCHER, President of Edinburgh Chamber of Commerce, 1992

See also A DAY I WAS MEANT NOT TO SEE; I WARN YOU NOT TO BE ORDINARY; JIM IS VERY, VERY SORRY; REJOICE! REJOICE!; THERE IS NO ALTERNATIVE; TINA.

Thatcherism The rigorous economic and political ideology, and the personal style of leadership, associated with Margaret Thatcher; though the word came into general use when she was in power from 1979, it was used by Tony BENN as early as December 1976. Thatcherism embodied an ENTERPRISE CULTURE: the unhindered operation of the free MARKET, cuts in direct taxation and the regulation of business, the PRIVATISATION of public utilities, the encouragement of share ownership and the sale of council houses. MONETARISM replaced KEYNESIANISM, the individual ousted SOCIETY, and the power of the TRADE UNIONS was curtailed. Thatcherism is now remembered not only for its considerable achievements but for the stridency and divisiveness of its tone, and a belief by those at the bottom of the heap that it was designed to make their lot worse.

No obligation to the community, no sense of solidarity, no neighbourhood, no number other than one, no time other than now, no such thing as society – just me! And now!
NEIL KINNOCK

thaw The term used throughout the COLD WAR for any period when the hostility between East and West eased somewhat.

theoretician In an ideologically-based party, state or movement, a person who develops the theory behind the practice of government or the programme to be followed.

there. There are no gains without pains An axiom of politics coined by the Democratic nominee Adlai STEVENSON in a Presidential campaign speech in Chicago on 26 July 1952. What he actually said was:

Let's talk sense to the American people. Let's tell them the truth, that there are no gains without pains.

Its linking of progress with sacrifice puts it in a long line of dicta from Walter Lippmann's NOTHING FOR NOTHING to John MAJOR's IF IT'S NOT HURTING, IT'S NOT WORKING.

There are three groups that one should never provoke: The Vatican, the Treasury and the miners A rule of thumb for British politics frequently attributed to Stanley BALDWIN, and much quoted during the MINERS' STRIKES of 1972, 1974 and 1984–85. Arthur BALFOUR and, more plausibly, Harold MACMILLAN have also been credited with it, the Macmillan version being: 'There are three bodies no sensible man directly challenges: the Roman Catholic Church, the Brigade of Guards and the National Union of Mineworkers'.

There is no alternative The assertion that formed the basis of THATCHERISM, which was uttered by the IRON LADY herself at the Conservative women's conference on 21 May 1980. Justifying the harsh economic measures taken in her first year of office, she said:

There is no easy popularity in that, but I believe people accept there is no alternative.

The phrase was seized on by both Mrs Thatcher's supporters and critics as exemplifying her approach; Young Conservatives soon abbreviated it to **TINA**.

There is no Democratic or Republican way of cleaning the streets The argument put forward by New York City's Mayor Fiorello LA GUARDIA to justify the adoption of good city government rather than the pursuit of old-style MACHINE POLITICS.

There is no free lunch A fundamental of the American Dream, variously attributed (by Alistair Cooke) to an Italian immigrant asked what 40 years of life in America had taught him, and by others to the economist Milton Friedman (*see* MONETARISM) in a lecture in 1973.

There I was, waiting at the church The old music hall song quoted by James CALLAGHAN in his speech to the TUC on 5 September 1978, as he teased the Tory opposition over when he would call an election. The rhyme told of a woman left waiting at the church to marry a man who eventually sent a note reading:

Can't get away to marry you today.
My wife won't let me.

Union delegates loved it, but Callaghan's levity had a sting in its tail. Two days later,

Callaghan enraged Margaret THATCHER and staggered his own party by going on television to announce that he saw no point in having an election and that his minority government would carry on. He eventually called an election (which Labour lost) the following spring after being defeated by one vote on a no-CONFIDENCE motion. *Compare* SHE DIDN'T SAY YES, SHE DIDN'T SAY NO.

There you go again Ronald REAGAN's dismissive comment to Jimmy CARTER in their PRESIDENTIAL DEBATE in Cleveland on 28 October 1980. Delivered when the President was pressing him on points of detail, the phrase implied that Reagan was in command of the evening; coupled with his question to voters, ARE YOU BETTER OFF THAN YOU WERE FOUR YEARS AGO?, it gave him the edge.

they. They have asked for my trousers, and I have given them; for my coat, I have given that also; now they want my life, and that I cannot give The defiant message toward the British of President Paulus KRUGER (*see also* OOM PAUL) on 7 September 1899 as the BOER WAR reached its height.

They may be sons of bitches, but they're our sons of bitches Franklin D. ROOSEVELT's retort to reformist Democrats who asked him how he could do deals with big city BOSSES and SEGREGATIONIST Southern senators. In the 1992 Presidential campaign one Indiana voter said of Vice President Dan QUAYLE:

> He may be an idiot but he's our idiot.

They now ring their bells, but they will soon wring their hands The apocalyptic warning of Britain's first recognised PRIME MINISTER, Robert WALPOLE, as public enthusiasm greeted the outbreak of the WAR OF JENKINS' EAR. The war with Spain, and broader conflicts that ensued, not only led to the setbacks that Walpole feared but also brought the end of his 21 years in office.

They shall not pass! (Fr. *Ils ne passeront pas!*) The rallying cry associated with Marshal Pétain during the fighting between the French and German armies at Verdun in WORLD WAR I. In fact, it was uttered by his subordinate General Robert Georges Nivelle (1856–1924) in an order of the day in June 1916. As ¡*No pasaran*! the cry was taken up by the Communist leader LA PASIONARA (Dolores Ibarruri) in the SPANISH CIVIL WAR.

THIGMOO This Great Movement of Ours. An affectionate but ironic shorthand term for Britain's TRADE UNION movement, popular from the early 1970s.

Things Can Only Get Better The theme tune of LABOUR's 1997 election campaign which resulted in a LANDSLIDE victory for Tony BLAIR; the 1994 record by D'Ream and its lead singer Peter Cunnah. The tune was first used for the party by the film maker John Deery in Labour's 1996 *Road to the* MANIFESTO video, featuring John Prescott (*see* TWO JAGS). The Conservatives tried to get it banned from Radio 1 when it was re-released for the election; Labour sympathisers slipped it into *Eastenders,* but it was cut from the repeat after Tory protests.

think pod The corner for quiet reflection provided for the office of every MSP in the Scottish Parliament building at HOLYROOD, with a panoramic window providing views of the historic Old Town.

think tank A group of people with specialised knowledge and intellectual gifts, brought together to study particular problems (usually social, political and technological) and to provide possible solutions and new directions. America's RAND CORPORATION was among the first; in WASHINGTON the BROOKINGS INSTITUTION was a pioneer. Edward HEATH in 1970 set up a think tank within 10 DOWNING STREET, titled the **Central Policy Review Staff**. Headed by Lord Rothschild (1910–90), its function was to provide the CABINET and individual Ministers with advice on strategy. It survived until 1983 when Margaret THATCHER, who had used it to torpedo policy initiatives she disliked, wound it up and handed its vestigial functions to the No. 10 POLICY UNIT. In both US and British politics, there has since the 1970s been a burgeoning of think tanks rooted on each wing of the political spectrum. In Washington Brookings was the first on the centre-left, the HERITAGE FOUNDATION to the right; Mrs Thatcher herself was involved in the 1974 launch of the Centre for POLICY Studies and later of the Adam SMITH Institute; Tony BLAIR has relied heavily on DEMOS and the IPPR.

thinking the unthinkable The process, indulged in especially in WASHINGTON during the COLD WAR, of considering the details and merits of particular types of NUCLEAR WAR, rationally but without thought for the consequences for the planet. Those involved in such discussions argued that they had to take place if a credible defence policy were to evolve; nuclear disarmers regarded them with horror. *See also* STRANGELOVE.

Third Estate (Fr. *Tiers État*) The commoners in France's pre-Revolutionary parliament; the aristocracy and the bishops formed the first two estates. It was the Third Estate who met to demand reform and basic HUMAN RIGHTS at the onset of the Revolution. *See* Tennis Court OATH.

> What was the Third Estate? Everything. What has it hitherto been in the political order? Nothing. What does it ask? To be something. Who will dare deny that the Third Estate contains within itself all that is needed to constitute a nation?
>
> Abbé EMMANUEL SIEYÈS (1748–1836), 1789

Third Man The third Soviet agent suspected of being involved in the defection of the British diplomats BURGESS AND MACLEAN in 1951; there was widespread press speculation, and ironically he turned out to be a journalist, H. A. R. 'Kim' Philby of the *Observer.* As early as 1955 Harold MACMILLAN, then Foreign Secretary, was asked point blank by the Labour MP Marcus Lipton if Philby was a spy; as there was no conclusive proof, Macmillan was obliged to clear him. In 1963 Philby, then working in Beirut, also defected to Moscow and the whole story came out. The name came from the 1949 Graham Greene and Carol Reed film *The Third Man,* a tale of intrigue in post-war Vienna.

Third Party *See* PARTY.

third party endorsement A handy concomitant to SPIN, the practice of securing for an announcement, a party or a candidate the support or approval of experts or celebrities not perceived as involved in politics, so as to make the public more comfortable. The practice has come into its own since the late 1990s, but existed beforehand though without the label. *Compare* QUOTE SLUTS.

Third Reading At WESTMINSTER, the penultimate stage through which a BILL passes in one HOUSE before going to the other (the final one being consideration of any amendments made by the other House). On major Bills it involves a full day after the completion of the REPORT STAGE; on less controversial measures it follows on immediately and may only take a couple of hours. In the US CONGRESS the Third Reading is a vote taken after debate on a Bill reported from the COMMITTEE OF THE WHOLE.

Third Reich *See* REICH.

Third Republic The regime under which France was governed from the defeat of the Second Empire by Prussia in 1870 to the fall of France to NAZI Germany in 1940 (*see* VICHY). The Third Republic was noted for its political instability, especially after 1918 when governments came and went with great rapidity before the advent of the POPULAR FRONT. The Republic was punctuated by a series of crises that threatened the Parliamentary system itself; these included the machinations of General Boulanger (*see* MAN ON HORSEBACK), the DREYFUS CASE and the STAVISKY SCANDAL. Yet the Third Republic came through WORLD WAR I, produced an outstanding statesman in CLEMENCEAU and proved the most durable system of governing France since the Revolution.

Third Way The doctrine adumbrated by Tony BLAIR in the wake of NEW LABOUR's 1997 election victory, that the community could be better served by a caring market-orientated political approach than by old-style democratic socialism or the harsh approach of THATCHERISM. Formulated largely by Professor Anthony Giddens of the LSE, the Third Way was endorsed early on by Bill CLINTON and Germany's Chancellor Gerhard Schröder, but did not become a deep-rooted philosophy.

Third World The underdeveloped and developing countries of Africa, Asia and Latin America, which are heavily dependent on subsistence agriculture, and thus cannot develop industries and infrastructure of their own and a competitive economy without help from other, wealthier nations. Prone to famine and population pressures and too often to civil strife, they are weighed down by heavy debt to Western banks and governments (*see* TRINIDAD TERMS); recognising the resentments and the potential for conflict posed by their poverty, many Western politicians – urged on by campaigning NGOs – have sought to relieve Third World debt and mobilise help (*see* BRANDT COMMISSION; NORTH-SOUTH). The Third World was named by the French writer Georges Balandier in comparison with the capitalist Western nations (First World) and the states of the then Communist bloc (Second World); it is an echo of the pre-Revolutionary THIRD ESTATE.

thirteen. Thirteen plots of 13 May The dramatic and secretive plotting and counter-plotting that returned General DE GAULLE to power in France in May 1958 after twelve years in the political wilderness, and which ended the FOURTH REPUBLIC. A powerful body of Gaullists had been intriguing to secure his return: malcontents in the Army and among French settlers (*pieds-noirs*) in

Algeria, angered by what they saw as inadequate backing from Paris, plus right-wing opponents of the government in metropolitan France. On 13 May, as a new Prime Minister, Pierre Pfimlin, was about to be appointed, a large crowd took over the government office in Algiers, establishing a Committee for Public Safety. The army generals supported the Committee's call for de Gaulle's return, and on 15 May he dramatically announced that he was ready to assume power if invited. The Algerian rebellion escalated; on 24 May Algerian-based troops occupied Corsica and there were rumours that the generals planned to occupy Paris on 27 May. Against this background of political crisis, heightened by fears of an imminent military coup and the threat of civil war, Pfimlin agreed to step down in favour of de Gaulle. On 1 June the NATIONAL ASSEMBLY confirmed de Gaulle's appointment as premier, gave him full power for six months and left him to draw up a new constitution. De Gaulle was certainly aware of the plots to secure his return, but wisely refused to commit himself until the collapse of the Fourth Republic was certain; he could then assume power on his own terms.

thirteen wasted years The emotive, and effective, theme of LABOUR's campaigning in the run-up to the 1964 UK general election, and during the election itself. Harold WILSON and colleagues took every opportunity to depict SIR ALEC Douglas-Home's Conservative government, first elected under CHURCHILL in 1951, as worn out and bankrupt of ideas. In the event the Tories pegged Labour back to a majority of six – well short of the LANDSLIDE Wilson had hoped for, and for which he had to wait a further eighteen months.

Thirteenth Amendment The amendment to the US CONSTITUTION, ratified on 16 December 1865, that finally outlawed slavery. The last state to ratify it was Mississippi, in March 1995.

thirty year rule The cornerstone of secrecy in WHITEHALL, the provision that the contents of no government document not intended for publication shall be made public for 30 years, if then. Despite the passage of the FREEDOM OF INFORMATION ACT, the rule continues to cover many government papers. Slightly relaxed by John MAJOR in 1992, the procedure has been for all papers to be sent to the Public Record Office; all but the most sensitive are released to researchers and the press at year's end 30 years on. In 1993 it was discovered that the Foreign Office had yet to declassify files from 1782 relating to the WHIG politician Charles James Fox.

32-County Solidarity Committee The political backers of the Real IRA, headed by Bernadette Sands McKevitt, sister of the HUNGER STRIKER Bobby Sands. Her husband Michael was jailed in the Irish Republic in 2003 on charges of directing terrorism, arising from the OMAGH Bombing.

Thirty-six faceless men The newspaper caption seized on by Robert Menzies' ruling Liberals which did Australia's LABOR Party immense damage in the 1963 Federal elections. The faceless men were the 36 delegates to Labor's policy-making federal conference; the photo showed the ALP leader Arthur Calwell and his deputy Gough WHITLAM standing under a lamp-post outside the meeting waiting to be given the PARTY LINE. The inference that Labor's leaders were puppets in the hands of anonymous and maybe sinister forces contributed to the party's heavy defeat.

38th Parallel The dividing line between North and South Korea, agreed by America and the Soviet Union in 1945 as a temporary device for accepting the surrender of Japanese forces in the region; it was hastily suggested by the US as Soviet forces moved into northern Korea in the final days of the war. Stalin surprisingly agreed, though the absence of US forces would have enabled him to push father south. The division left America in control of the capital, Seoul, two-thirds of the population and the main agricultural region, while the Soviets controlled the industrial North. COLD WAR tensions turned the 38th Parallel into a rigid border between East and West; after the outbreak of the KOREAN WAR US troops crossed it on 7 October 1950 in their first advance. When the fighting was halted, the 38th Parallel was once again the border between North and South Korean (*see* PANMUNJOM). When President EISENHOWER made a particularly banal remark at a WHITE HOUSE press conference, one commentator remarked:

> Ike's just crossed the 38th platitude.

this was their finest hour Winston CHURCHILL's defiant speech to the HOUSE OF COMMONS on 18 June 1940 after the collapse of France, when a German invasion seemed imminent. It was indeed prevented only by the Royal Air Force's defeat of the *Luftwaffe* in the Battle of Britain later that summer. Churchill said:

> What General Weygand called the Battle of France is over. I expect that the Battle of Britain is about to begin. Upon this battle depends the survival of Christian civilisation. Upon it depends our own British life, and the long continuity of our institutions and our Empire. The whole fury and might of the enemy must very soon be turned on us. HITLER knows that he will have to break us in this island or lose the war. If we can stand up to him, all Europe may be free and the life of the world may move forward into broad, sunlit uplands. But if we fail, then the whole world, including the United States, including all that we have known and cared for, will sink into the abyss of a new Dark Age made more sinister, and perhaps more protracted, by the lights of perverted science. Let us therefore brace ourselves to our duties, and so bear ourselves that, if the British Empire and its Commonwealth last for a thousand years, men will still say: 'This was their finest hour'.

After his Democratic CONVENTION speech in 1988 went down badly, Bill CLINTON said:

> It wasn't my finest hour. It wasn't even my finest hour and a half.

Thomas. Clarence Thomas case The Senate hearings in 1992 over George BUSH Snr's nomination of the black Judge Clarence Thomas to the SUPREME COURT, which turned into a televised trial of claims of sexual harassment by him from a former colleague, Professor Anita Hill. Both Judge Thomas and Professor Hill, who insisted 'I am not given to fantasy', fought their corners with passion and total conviction. Senators pitched in with sharp questioning, leading Sen. John Danforth to declare: 'This is not ADVICE AND CONSENT. This is slash and burn.' And his fellow-Republican Sen. Arlen Specter, Professor Hill's sharpest questioner, said: 'The senate is on trial.' The hearings aroused intense feeling, especially among feminists who felt the Senate's eventual approval of Judge Thomas was an insult to women. The judge called his ordeal 'a high-tech LYNCHING for uppity blacks', protesting:

> This is not America. It is Kafkaesque. It has got to stop. It must stop for the benefit of future nominees and our country. Enough is enough. No job is worth what I've been through.

> I would have preferred an assassin's bullet than this kind of living hell they have put me and my family through. Justice THOMAS

> I know of no system of government where when you add the kerosene of sex, the heated flame of race and the incendiary nature of television lights, you're not going to have an explosion. Sen. JOSEPH BIDEN

Thorpe case The astonishing farrago of homosexual intrigue, dog-shooting and murder plots that racked Britain's LIBERAL PARTY in the late 1970s. It revolved around the debonair Jeremy Thorpe (1929–), party leader from 1967 to 1976. That March Andrew Gino Newton, an airline pilot, was jailed for two years for shooting Norman Scott's dog RINKA on Exmoor. During the trial Scott, a male model, claimed to be in fear of his life because he was writing a book about a homosexual relationship between himself and Thorpe; Newton said he shot the dog because Thorpe was blackmailing him. Thorpe denied the whole story, but over a period a highly incriminating correspondence, interspersed with tales of teeth marks in Thorpe's COMMONS desk, hit the media; he was forced to resign that summer as party leader. In 1978 he and three other men were charged with conspiracy to murder Scott, but were acquitted after a lengthy trial; by then he had lost his North Devon seat in the 1979 election after a campaign in which the columnist Auberon Waugh intervened as a Dog Lovers' candidate. All the time the scandal was emerging, Thorpe kept up his political activity; on one appearance in the Commons in 1976 his colleague Cyril Smith (*see* BIG CYRIL) called out:

> Shot any good dogs lately?

those damned dots Lord Randolph Churchill's denunciation of decimal points, recorded by his son Winston; from a CHANCELLOR OF THE EXCHEQUER (briefly in 1886), Lord Randolph's confession that 'I could never make out what those damned dots meant' was mildly unnerving.

those folks George W. BUSH's first, bathetic, description of the AL QAEDA hijackers who provoked the WAR ON TERRORISM on 9/11 by flying aircraft into the WORLD TRADE CENTER and the PENTAGON with the loss of over 3000 lives. Informed of the outrages while visiting a school in Sarasota, Florida, Bush made no immediate comment on the advice of his press secretary Ari Fleischer. Flown on AIR FORCE ONE from Sarasota to Barksdale Air Force Base in Louisiana, the official transcript of his statement on arrival reads: 'The United States will hunt down and punish those responsible for these cowardly acts.' However, reporters quoted him as pledging himself to

> conduct a full-scale investigation to hunt down and find those folks who committed these cowardly acts.

thousand. Thousand, the The irregular

force of REDSHIRTS who in 1860 precipitated the unification of Italy under the crown of Piedmont by overthrowing the Bourbon monarchy of the Two Sicilies. Capitalising on an abortive revolt in Palermo that April, Garibaldi, impatient with diplomatic initiatives to secure a united Italy, sailed with his ill-prepared volunteers from Genoa, landed at Marsala on 11 May and in less than three months overcame a force 20 times as strong to conquer the whole of Sicily. Garibaldi on 14 May took possession of the island in the name of King Victor Emmanuel. The Bourbon King Francis II belatedly granted a constitution, but the Thousand crossed to the mainland and on 7 September Garibaldi made a triumphant entry into Naples. Francis fled, and his army was finally defeated at the battle of the Volturno on 1 October. On October 26 Garibaldi greeted Victor Emmanuel on Neapolitan soil, and after overwhelming support for unification in PLEBISCITES in the territory, the Kingdom of Italy was declared in Turin on 17 March 1861; Rome, however, remained under Papal control. *See also* RISORGIMENTO.

Thousand Days Arthur Schlesinger Jr's characterisation of the dynamic, dazzling ADMINISTRATION of John F. KENNEDY (*see* CAMELOT). From Kennedy's INAUGURATION on 20 January 1961 until his assassination on 23 November 1963 was in fact 1036 days.

1000 per cent support The phrase that haunted George McGovern's 1972 campaign for the Presidency. McGovern used it when standing by his original vice presidential choice, Sen. Tom Eagleton of Missouri, when it emerged that he had been treated several times for severe mental depression. Party and media pressure soon forced McGovern to ditch Eagleton and replace him with former PEACE CORPS director Sargent Shriver; despite Shriver's popularity, competence and KENNEDY connections, the Eagleton episode told heavily against the Democratic ticket as Richard NIXON won a second term by a LANDSLIDE.

a thousand points of light The inspirational phrase from George BUSH Snr's ACCEPTANCE SPEECH at the 1988 Republican convention, conjured up by the REAGAN/Bush speechwriter Peggy Noonan (*see* TOUCH THE FACE OF GOD); it was supposed to symbolise individual endeavour and charitable effort. On Bush's INAUGURATION the following January, 40,000 people in Washington were issued with torches to switch on and dramatise the point. Bush frequently garbled the phrase; once when he called it '1000 points of life' the *Washington Post* cartoonist Herblock drew a drunk pledging his vote to Bush because he had promised '1000 pints of Lite'. What Bush originally said was:

> I will keep America moving forward, always forward – for a better America, for an endless enduring dream and a thousand points of light.

Thousand year Reich *See* REICH

three. three acres and a cow The slogan of the English radical Jesse Collings (1831–1920) for his land reform scheme which was part of the Liberals' UNAUTHORISED PROGRAMME, championed by Joseph Chamberlain prior to the 1885 general election. On 27 January 1886 Collings moved the proposal as an amendment to the LOYAL ADDRESS after the opening of the new Parliament; sixteen Liberals voted with the Conservatives against it, SALISBURY's government fell over Ireland soon after and the moment never returned. John Stuart Mill (1806–73) originated the phrase, writing in his *Principles of Political Economy* (1848):

> When the land is cultivated entirely by the spade and no horses are kept, a cow can be kept for every three acres of land.

three-cornered fight An electoral contest that takes place between three candidates or parties, compared with a STRAIGHT FIGHT between two.

three-day week The tight regime for British industry ordered by the HEATH government on 13 December 1973 to counter the Arab oil boycott and the National Union of Mineworkers' overtime ban, which later developed into an all-out STRIKE. The three-day week, which took effect from 31 December, was viewed at the time as devastating to the economy, but statistics later showed that production actually increased. However, the strike achieved its political objective; after a period of increasing privations (*see* CLEAN YOUR TEETH IN THE DARK), Heath called an election on the question of WHO GOVERNS BRITAIN? – and lost.

Three-in-a-bed The nickname of Sir Charles Dilke (1843–1911), the radical Liberal lawyer/politician whose alleged sexual antics scandalised English society, and Queen Victoria in particular. Appointed GLADSTONE's Local Government Minister in 1882, he lost his seat in 1886 after being cited as co-respondent in a divorce case.

Dilke's young sister-in-law Mrs Donald Crawford accused him of seducing her, teaching her 'every French vice' and persuading her to share a bed with Fanny, his servant girl. Even before the case came to trial, Gladstone had marked Dilke as 'unavailable' for his new government. At the first hearing the case was dismissed, but Crawford was granted a decree *nisi*. Dilke had the case reopened, and in the second trial Mrs Crawford added the 'odious details'. Dilke was publicly branded a perjurer and an adulterer, his credibility weakened by having cut holes from several pages of his diary. Dilke returned to the COMMONS in 1892 and served until his death, but lived under a permanent shadow.

> The victim of a conspiracy, the main lines of which are shrouded in mystery.
>
> ROY JENKINS

three I's Ireland, Italy and ISRAEL, the three ethnic and foreign-policy interests US presidential hopefuls (especially Democrats) have traditionally taken up at election times to gain vital community support.

Three Mile Island The site near Harrisburg, Pennsylvania, of America's most serous nuclear reactor accident, which gave an impetus to the anti-nuclear campaign and effectively brought the construction of US NUCLEAR power stations to a halt. On 29 March 1979, due to human and technical failure, the fissile core, normally immersed in water, became exposed to the air and began to melt, releasing radioactive gases into the air. Complete MELTDOWN of the core was avoided, but the public realised it had had a narrow escape. President CARTER visited Three Mile Island; when Vice President Walter Mondale (*see* FRITZ; NORWEGIAN WOOD) was asked if the plant was safe once again, he replied:

> If it wasn't safe, they'd have sent the Vice President.

three strikes and you're out President CLINTON's evocative phrase – taken from baseball – for the legislation passed by Congress in 1994 which imposed an automatic life sentence on anyone convicted of a third violent crime. The measure was already in prospect when Clinton used the words in his State of the UNION message on 25 January 1994, but his terminology enabled him to take ownership of a Crime Bill which also included wider use of the death penalty for federal offences and, despite fierce opposition from the NRA, a ban on nineteen kinds of assault rifle which continued until George W. BUSH refused to extend it just before the 2004 election.

300 Group The group which since the late 1970s has campaigned for more women in Britain's HOUSE OF COMMONS. Led by the former Liberal candidate Lesley Abdela, it set 300 women members as its target. The group was well short of its target until the 1997 general election when 121 women MPs out of 659 were elected and came closer in 2005 with 127 out of 646.

Threshergate The bizarre episode in November 1992 when Norman Lamont, CHANCELLOR OF THE EXCHEQUER, took umbrage at a press report that he had bought a bottle of Bricout champagne and 20 Raffles cigarettes for £17.47 at Thresher's off-licence in Praed Street, Paddington. Two of the shop's staff confirmed to reporters that Lamont had been the customer. However, the Treasury vehemently denied the story, insisting that Lamont had bought three bottles of wine at another branch of Thresher's the previous night; the staff first stuck to their story, then changed it when the chain's head office took an interest. The Chancellor's denials were fully accepted and a till receipt for the three bottles of wine eventually produced. The episode built on the bad press Lamont had received for not resigning after BLACK WEDNESDAY, breaching his credit card limit 22 times in eight years, and allowing the Treasury and an anonymous party fund-raiser to meet legal expenses for evicting a 'sex therapist' from a house he owned.

threshold agreements Pay agreements negotiated through COLLECTIVE BARGAINING under which workers receive a fixed increase, plus further automatic rises if the rate of INFLATION exceeds a set figure. Pioneered by the HEATH government in the early 1970s, they proved counterproductive by ensuring that when prices were rising fastest, they automatically triggered pay increases which forced up the rate of inflation still further, triggering further increases . . .

throne The ceremonial seat on which a MONARCH sits, and hence a word that personifies the monarchy itself, as in **heir to the throne**. King Charles X of France, who reigned from 1824 until forced into exile six years later, told Talleyrand: 'There is no middle course between the throne and the scaffold'; Talleyrand replied presciently:

> You are forgetting the postchaise.

steps of the throne The edge of the podium in the HOUSE OF LORDS on which stands the throne from which the sovereign delivers the GRACIOUS SPEECH, otherwise known as the **speech from the throne**. Sons of PEERS, and members of the HOUSE OF COMMONS, are permitted to squat on the steps of the throne to hear debates in the Upper House.

throttlebottom A US term for a bumbling, incompetent politician; it originated in the 1931 musical *Of Thee I Sing*, in which Vice President Alexander Throttlebottom was such a nonentity that WHITE HOUSE guards did not recognise him and refused to let him in. By chance the stars of the show included the song-and-dance man George Murphy, who later became a Republican senator. Politicians against whom the epithet has been used include Harry S TRUMAN and Dan QUAYLE.

throw. throw-weight The amount of destructive force delivered by a NUCLEAR missile. It is normally given in megatons: the equivalent of a million tons of TNT. However, this measure takes no account of the radiation and nuclear fall-out generated.

throw money at To try to eradicate an area of deprivation or solve some other policy conundrum by large-scale spending, rather than detailed appraisal of what might work. As long ago as 1834, Sir Robert PEEL told the HOUSE OF COMMONS:

> Of all the vulgar acts of government, that of solving every difficulty which might arise by thrusting the hand into the public purse is the most delusory and contemptible.

throw to the wolves To sacrifice an unpopular politician to his or her critics to prevent that unpopularity attaching to the entire party or government to which he or she belongs. When J. E. B. Seely offered to resign as Britain's Minister for War in March 1914 after his misjudgements had precipitated the tensions in the Army that led to the CURRAH MUTINY, BONAR LAW told the COMMONS:

> We have heard of people being thrown to the wolves, but never before have we heard of a man being thrown to the wolves with a bargain on behalf of the wolves that they would not eat him.

thundering disgrace The comments by Ireland's Defence Minister Paddy Donegan in 1976 about President Cearbhall O'Dalaigh (1911–78) that prompted O'Dalaigh to resign, complaining that his office had been insulted. Donegan was angered by the President using his powers to delay legislation designed to thwart IRA terrorism; O'Dalaigh, a former Chief Justice of the Supreme Court, considered the measure UNCONSTITUTIONAL. Though Donegan, who was speaking to military personnel, was quoted by the reporter present as calling O'Dalaigh a 'thundering disgrace', it was known that the Minister's actual words were 'a fucking disgrace'. O'Dalaigh was never an easy man; when he visited the EUROPEAN PARLIAMENT in Strasbourg he insisted on addressing Irish journalists in Irish, which not all of them understood; they had to wait until he spoke to the British press, and hide behind pillars to listen.

Tienanmen Square The immense paved open space next to Beijing's Forbidden City which forms the heart of China, but which was also the centre of the massacre in June 1989 of 2000 unarmed civilians by the PEOPLE'S LIBERATION ARMY during pro-democracy demonstrations headed by university students. The protests started in late April during the funeral of Hu Yaobang, a deposed former general secretary of the Chinese Communist Party; by mid-May more than a million demonstrators, including some government officials, were staging the largest protest in Communist China's history. They were encouraged by Hu's fellow liberal, the party chief Zhao Ziyang, who aimed to 'enhance democracy, expose corruption and expand openness', and took heart from a visit by the reforming Soviet leader Mikhail GORBACHEV, who on 16 May interrupted his schedule to lay a wreath in the square. The students turned the protest into a permanent occupation and erected a Statue of Liberty. Then, on 20 May, Communist hard-liners loyal to the veteran Deng Hsiao-Ping rallied and imposed martial law, and on 3 June some 10,000 troops entered the city; the next day tanks and armoured personnel carriers went in to kill the retreating students, one of whom had stood defiantly before them. The massacre, and the ensuing arrests and executions, provoked worldwide condemnation and trade reprisals. For the regime, however, they served their purpose, as while China has since experienced a near-capitalist boom, political controls remain tight and few dare to voice dissent.

ticket The combination of CANDIDATES put forward by a party for ELECTION to different offices; in America it will be headed (if there is a contest for those positions that year) by the Presidential and Vice Presidential candidates, candidates for the SENATE and the HOUSE, for governor and other state offices, for the state LEGISLATURE and then for local offices. The term originated in America prior to the universal adoption of the Australian BALLOT in 1884; in those states where voting was by ballot, the parties prepared their own ballots and handed them out near voting stations. Such papers were known as the parties' tickets.

ticket-splitting To vote for some candidates on one party's ticket and some from the other; e.g. a Republican for President and a Democrat for the Senate.

balanced ticket A range of candidates representing contrasting opinions and cultures within a party. Usually a US Presidential nominee chooses a RUNNING-MATE from another part of the country and often from a different tradition in the party; the belief is that this will bring in votes the nominee alone could not attract, or provide reassurance. In the 1987 UK election, John Biffen (*see* SEMI-DETACHED) called on Margaret THATCHER to put forward a balanced ticket by giving a high profile to party moderates eager for CONSOLIDATION, as well as hard-line radicals in her own image. Mrs Thatcher campaigned at full throttle to win a large majority, then dropped Biffen from her CABINET.

dream ticket A combination of candidates of such obvious charm, appeal and ability to work together that their election is supposedly assured. The term was used in 1980 by Republicans who hoped Ronald REAGAN would name former President Gerald FORD as his running-mate. Neil KINNOCK and Roy Hattersley (*see* HATTERJI) were given this accolade by Labour SPIN DOCTORS in 1983; their election as party leader and deputy was seen as ending Labour's nightmare of internal strike and electoral disaster. However, it took a further fourteen years and a different leadership to take Labour back to power; in the meantime Jeffrey Archer told the 1983 Conservative conference:

> It really doesn't matter, because *we* have the return ticket.

kangaroo ticket *See* KANGAROO.

run ahead of the ticket To get more votes running as a candidate for CONGRESS than the party's Presidential candidate secures in the district or state. To do so is a sign either that the candidate is personally very popular, or that their supporters detect good reasons for not voting the party's national ticket.

voting the ticket The action, almost automatic for some, of voting for every one of a party's nominees without seriously considering any others.

tiger. Tiger, the The nickname of the French statesman and journalist Georges CLEMENCEAU, earned by his fire and tenacity first as a campaigner and then as France's inspirational leader in WORLD WAR I.

> There the old Tiger would be sitting, in his grey gloves and grey skull-cap, usually wearing grey slippers, looking like a grey cat.
>
> BERNARD BARUCH (1870–1965)

***Tiger* talks** The first of two negotiations aboard Royal Navy cruisers (the second were on HMS FEARLESS) at which Harold WILSON urged the Rhodesian leader Ian Smith to end UDI and RETURN TO LEGALITY. In the *Tiger* talks, off Gibraltar in December 1966, Wilson offered Smith concessions to secure an agreement, and believed one had been reached; when the deal was rejected by hard-liners in Salisbury (Harare), he made his negotiating hand public, creating astonishment over how far he had been prepared to go. The former Rhodesian Prime Minister Sir Edgar Whitehead said the agreement would have postponed 'the possible date of African MAJORITY RULE almost certainly beyond the end of the century.'

tightly knit group of politically motivated men The phrase rashly used by Harold WILSON to denounce the prime movers of the 1966 SEAMEN'S STRIKE; it hinted at deliberate Communist wrecking tactics without saying so outright. Speaking in the COMMONS on 20 June 1966, Wilson said that 'a few individuals' had pressured the executive of the National Union of Seamen to prolong the dispute over pay and hours by refusing to negotiate; those responsible were 'a tightly knit group of politically motivated men who, as the last General Election showed, utterly failed to gain acceptance of their views by the British electorate' and were now determined to endanger the security of the industry and the welfare of the nation. Wilson held back from naming names because at the last minute he saw John Prescott (*see* TWO JAGS), who was one of the strike leaders, in the Gallery and remembered he had been a Labour candidate in the election. Yet even with this lone element of caution Wilson's biographer Ben Pimlott reckoned that 'everything was wrong with this statement', which was based on innuendo from the security services. It told trade unionists their phones were being tapped, and exaggerated the Communists' power to sway a group of obvious individualists. Wilson's conspiracy theory was regarded by some colleagues as 'completely bonkers', and did long-term damage to his relations with trade union leaders.

See also BEER AND SANDWICHES AT NUMBER TEN; JULY MEASURES.

time The critical commodity in a Parliamentary system, its allocation determining whether a government can get its BUSINESS through. The one power an OPPOSITION has is to restrict the time available; a government thus has to avoid causing needless irritation to parties which cannot defeat it but can frustrate its legislative intentions.

time agreement In the US SENATE, a 'unanimous consent agreement' to bring forward a measure on the CALENDAR for consideration, generally with a time limit set for debate and a list of amendments to be considered. By tradition it is for the MAJORITY LEADER to propose such an agreement.

Time for a change The official slogan of the Republicans in the 1944, 1948 and – finally and successfully – 1952 US Presidential elections, reflecting their and their supporters' frustration at the Democrats' 20-year tenure of the WHITE HOUSE under ROOSEVELT and TRUMAN. More generally, it has been the thrust of every campaign by a party that has been out of office for a long time and hopes the public is ready for change. In 1992 Bill CLINTON told George BUSH Snr: 'It's time for you to go.'

It's time! *See* IT'S.

Timetable for Action The pre-election package of commitments launched by Britain's CONSERVATIVE PARTY at its October 2004 conference. What was notable about the programme under which Michael HOWARD led the party into the polls was not so much the specific pledges, as his setting deadlines for them to be honoured. He also made service in a Conservative Cabinet less attractive by promising that any Minister who failed to reach their target would be sacked. *See also* TEN WORDS.

TINA A nickname for Margaret THATCHER, being an abbreviation of her message that 'THERE IS NO ALTERNATIVE' to her tough economic policies of 1980–81.

tinhorn An Americanism for a pretentious, shabby and worthless politician; it originates in the British 'tinpot', current by the late 19th century, and the US 'tinhorn gambler'. The word was probably first applied to a politician by William Allen White in an editorial in the *Emporia* (Kansas) *Gazette* on 25 October 1901.

Tip The everyday name of Thomas P. O'Neill (1912–94), SPEAKER of the US HOUSE OF REPRESENTATIVES 1977–86, formed from compressing his first two initials. An affable but tough Massachusetts-Irish POL, who termed himself an 'old-hat FDR liberal Democrat', he presided over the Democrat-controlled House under Jimmy CARTER and for most of the REAGAN presidency, once declaring of the latter: 'I am the Opposition.' He demanded absolute party loyalty, once locking out a MAVERICK Democrat to prevent him abstaining on a key vote. O'Neill took over John F. KENNEDY's Congressional seat, and guided the novice President Carter; though he was known as 'Jimmy Carter's best friend in WASHINGTON', Carter's distrust of CONGRESS made the relationship difficult. As O'Neill could make or break the President's legislative programme, his influence was immense. When Reagan took office, the Speaker told him: 'I'll give you your right but, Jesus, don't push me'; but once, angered by what he saw as White House meddling, he stormed: 'Did you ever hear of the SEPARATION OF POWERS?' In the House O'Neill, one of the FOUR HORSEMEN, commanded respect as a strong Speaker, declaring: 'I set the agenda.' But he shrugged off his native tradition of MACHINE POLITICS to become a considerable reformer.

> Everyone knew Tip O'Neill was an old shoe – a friendly, clubbable backroom man. But he became a modern politician who changed the ways of the House.
>
> HEDRICK SMITH, *The Power Game*

Tippecanoe and Tyler too The slogan on which the WHIG ticket of General William Henry Harrison (1773–1841) and John Tyler (1790–1862) were elected President and Vice President respectively in 1840. Harrison was **Old Tippecanoe**, after the victory to which he led his troops in the Indian Wars. Harrison was a nationalist and Tyler an advocate of STATES' RIGHTS; the New York Whig Philip Hone considered the ticket a mismatch, with 'rhyme, but no reason'.

Harrison had gone on from fighting the Indians and the British to serve in the HOUSE and the SENATE, serving as Minister to Colombia and a court clerk to pay off debts run up by high living. Despite this he portrayed himself as the LOG CABIN AND HARD CIDER candidate, in contrast with the 'oriental splendour' of Martin van Buren (*see* OLD KINDERHOOK), whom he defeated to become America's 9th President; privately he described himself as 'a clerk and a clodhopper'. He served for just 31 days before dying of a cold caught while delivering his INAUGURAL ADDRESS. Tyler (*see* OLD VETO) was the first Vice President to take up the reins of office, and was only confirmed as having legally been President in 1967 (*see* TWENTY-FIFTH AMENDMENT). Theodore ROOSEVELT reckoned him 'a politician of monumental littleness'.

> Harrison comes in upon a hurricane; God grant he may not go out upon a wreck!
>
> JOHN QUINCY ADAMS

> (An) active but shallow mind, a political adventurer not without talents but self-sufficient, vain and indiscreet.
>
> JOHN QUINCY ADAMS

tired and emotional A euphemism for 'drunk' that has proved useful to the UK media, which has to be mindful of the libel laws. The expression was first used by a BBC press officer in November 1963 to explain the overwrought condition in which George BROWN, then deputy leader of the LABOUR PARTY, had appeared on the night of President KENNEDY's assassination. It was immediately taken up by PRIVATE EYE to refer to anyone in a similar condition, and before long the phrase had general application – though it was frequently used of Brown throughout his colourful CABINET career. *See also* DRINK.

tit for tat expulsions The expulsion of one or more of a country's DIPLOMATS by a foreign country, in return for a similar number of explusions by the other. Failure to respond in this way creates a presumption that the diplomats expelled in the first place were guilty of whatever they were accused of: usually espionage. Consequently the majority of expulsions are followed by tit-for-tat action, regardless of whether they are justified.

Titanium Lady Madeleine Albright (1937–), America's first woman SECRETARY OF STATE, serving in the CLINTON administration from 2001 having previously been AMBASSADOR to the UNITED NATIONS. She was given the nickname c. 1997 by the Russians for her toughness (*compare* IRON LADY), and her enthusiasm for the expansion of NATO, which they then saw as a threat. The charismatic Ms Albright, a divorcee with three daughters, came from Czech refugee stock; she was brought up a Catholic in the US, but discovered while at the State Department that she was of Jewish origin.

Titanium Orchid The Burmese pro-democracy leader Aung San Suu Kyi (1945–), the nation's most popular political figure who for that reason was kept under house arrest (and at times in prison) by her country's military rulers (*see* SLORC); she was unable to visit her dying husband in England for fear of being forced into permanent exile. Leader from 1989 of the National League for Democracy, which she led to an election victory that the military refused to recognise, she was awarded the NOBEL PEACE PRIZE in 1991.

Titoism The pragmatic communism implemented in Yugoslavia after 1945 by Josip Broz Tito (1892–1980), the Croat former Austro-Hungarian soldier who joined the RED ARMY and helped found the Yugoslav Communist Party. Tito welded the wartime PARTISANS into a formidable and victorious force, then rejected the Soviet model of social and economic development imposed by STALIN on Russia's SATELLITES, believing instead in 'separate roads to Socialism'. His policies included decentralised profit-sharing workers' councils and a NON-ALIGNED stance in world affairs. Alone among eastern Europe's communist parties and governments, Tito stood up to Stalin, though Tito carried out a less publicised but almost as deadly PURGE of Stalinists in his own party. The partisans' war record probably persuaded Stalin not to try crushing Tito's reformist movement, as the KREMLIN later did in East Germany, Hungary and Czechoslovakia. Tito's regime became stagnant in his old age, but his triumph in holding the country together only became evident in the early 1990s when it disintegrated in a bloody civil war.

toecutter In Australia, a particularly ruthless or unscrupulous politician who will stop at nothing to get his or her own way. Originally a toecutter was a gangster who would cut off someone's toes with boltcutters to prise information out of them.

tokenism The practice of some companies, schools, sports teams – even political parties – of conforming to pressure for EQUAL OPPORTUNITIES by accepting or promoting a token number of women or ethnic minority candidates. This early-1960s Americanism crossed the Atlantic in the following decade (*see* STATUTORY WOMAN). **Showcase nigger** is black slang for a token black person given high visibility in a company's front office, when few if any others are employed in responsible jobs.

Tokyo Round The round of GATT world trade negotiations between 1974 to 1979 which built on the TARIFF reductions achieved by the KENNEDY ROUND, the resulting agreements being further built on by the URUGUAY ROUND, begun seven years later.

Tolpuddle Martyrs The six Dorset farm labourers sentenced at Dorchester Assizes in 1834 to transportation to Tasmania for seven years for setting up their own TRADE UNION, who are hailed as pioneers of British organised labour. They were charged with administering 'illegal oaths' – declarations of loyalty to the ideals of organised labour – to members of their 'friendly society'. Public outrage at the sentence led to their being PARDONed two years later, but it was another two years before they were brought home. One of the six, George Loveless (1805–40), told the court:

> If we have violated any law it was not done intentionally. We have injured no man's reputation, character, person or property. We were meeting together to preserve ourselves, our wives and our children from utter degradation anjd starvation.

Tonton The universal nickname of France's President François MITTERRAND, until in his latter years it was superseded by **Dieu** (God). Tonton is nursery French for 'Uncle'; it was originally the ÉLYSÉE bodyguards' name for him.

Tontons Macoute (Creole. Uncle Knapsack, a bogeyman who hunts naughty children and puts them in his sack) The fearsome private MILITIA and SECRET POLICE created in Haiti by President François (PAPA DOC) Duvalier (1907–71) who ruled the country from 1957. They were Duvalier loyalists (and often voodoo practitioners) who, in return for weapons and occasionally money, were licenced to terrorise, torture and murder those perceived as enemies of the regime. Many of the recruits (known after 1960 as the VSN – Volunteers for National Security) were ex-soldiers, many were criminals; all could be easily identified by their unofficial uniform – smart suit, dark glasses and bulging hip holsters. When Duvalier died the Tontons transferred their loyalty to the new president, his son Jean Claude 'BABY DOC' Duvalier; when he was toppled by a revolution in 1986, they remained in existence to terrorise the voters during election campaigns and overthrow the governments that were elected; despite US intervention, the country has remained in anarchy ever since.

Tony's cronies The phrase coined in June 1998 by the Conservative historian Lord Blake to denote the circle around Tony BLAIR, and seized on by opponents of NEW LABOUR to indicate a relationship based on SLEAZE. While BLAIR had habit of acting on the advice of friends informally proffered, the phrase held an inference that a Prime Minister should only seek advice from people he did not know and appoint nobody he was acquainted with to public bodies.

Tonypandy The myth that Winston CHURCHILL, when Liberal HOME SECRETARY in 1910, authorised troops to fire on striking South Wales miners, killing a number of them; in fact no miners died and Churchill was largely responsible for preventing bloodshed. The episode created a distrust of Churchill from the labour and trade union movement that outlived him, despite his COALITION with Labour in WORLD WAR II. On 10 November 1910 the Chief Constable of Glamorgan requested the local military authorities to curb violent riots at Tonypandy, in the Rhondda Valley. When Churchill heard that a small force of troops was on its way, he insisted that it be held in reserve and that extra unarmed police be sent instead; they managed to restrain the rioters without causing serious injury. The issue caused a flare-up in the COMMONS during the 1978–79 WINTER OF DISCONTENT, Prime Minister James CALLAGHAN referring to Churchill's alleged use of troops against the strikers and his grandson, the Conservative MP Winston Churchill, furiously demanding that he WITHDRAW. The temperature was dramatically lowered by Speaker George Thomas (later Viscount Tonypandy), a babe in arms at the time of the riots, who told the House:

> I never imagined a former pupil of Tonypandy Grammar School would have the last word on this.

too. too bad all the people who know how to run the country are busy driving cabs and cutting hair One of the classic complaints of politicians frustrated by repeated lectures from know-all taxi drivers and barbers, and heard in all cultures. Its origin seems to have been a non-politician, the centenarian comedian George Burns (1896–1996).

too much football without a helmet Lyndon B. JOHNSON's withering verdict on the cause of Gerald FORD's supposed intellectual limitations, delivered when he was House MINORITY LEADER. LBJ, who did not live to see Ford enter the WHITE HOUSE, was referring to his past as a star college footballer in Michigan.

toomorrow The mis-spelt word used three times by Tony BLAIR in a letter of support to Chris Mole, Labour candidate in the November 2001 Ipswich BY-ELECTION. It attracted far more national publicity than the by-election itself, and may have increased both the TURNOUT and the margin of Mr Mole's victory. (*Compare* POTATOE.)

top six WESTMINSTER-speak for the tabler and first signatories of an Early Day Motion (EDM). The promoter of such a motion seeking the widest possible support will enlist half a dozen highly respected BACKBENCHERS from all parties to be the top six, as an encouragement to other MPs to sign. If only a single MP is tabling the motion, they run the risk that the other five will be strange political bedfellows.

top-up fees The new system of student funding, put forward by Tony BLAIR and Education Secretary Charles Clarke, which split the Parliamentary LABOUR PARTY at the start of 2004 and which only scraped through the COMMONS by five votes despite Labour's massive majority. Opponents argued that requiring graduates to pay more for their education would discourage working-class students from aiming for the best universities; the real difficulty was that a target of getting 50% of young people to university, originally set by the Conservatives, had lowered standards in higher education while making the system very difficult to finance.

Tortilla Curtain The fences along the US-Mexican border that are meant, but largely fail, to keep illegal immigrants from Central America (*see* WETBACKS) out of the United States. An echo of the IRON CURTAIN, the phrase refers to the cornmeal pancake that is a staple of the Mexican diet.

Tory (1) At the time of the AMERICAN REVOLUTION, a supporter of the colonies remaining under the British crown; thousands of Tories sailed for Nova Scotia when WASHINGTON's forces emerged victorious. (2) A colloquialism for a supporter of Britain's CONSERVATIVE PARTY, the two names being interchangeable. The word is of 16th-century Irish origin; a corruption of *toraidhe* (pursuer), it was first used as an abusive term for Catholic outlaws who attacked English soldiers and settlers. The original political Tories emerged as a force under Charles II, opposed the GLORIOUS REVOLUTION of 1688–89, became a governing force by 1710, and were tarred with being JACOBITES during the 18th century, the WHIG Horace Walpole writing:

> All the sensible Tories that I ever knew, were either Jacobites or became Whigs; those that remained Tories remained fools.

Despite a highly conservative CV, elements of the Tory party were often more radical than the Whigs, who in the 18th century were founded on a corrupt political ESTABLISHMENT sustained by PATRONAGE. Yet they were terrified by the FRENCH REVOLUTION (*see also* BURKE), and as consistent backers of lost causes opposed the REFORM BILL. When their government fell in 1831 as a result, Macaulay wrote:

> Dark and terrible beyond any season within my remembrance of political affairs was the day of their flight. Far darker and more terrible will be the day of their return.

That return was short-lived, the party splitting fatally in the 1840s over the repeal of the CORN LAWS, being rebuilt as the Conservative Party by PEEL and DISRAELI, who declared in 1872:

> The Tory party, unless it is a national party, is nothing.

The Tories' opponents have always had plenty to say about them. John Bright declared: ''They have always been wrong, they will always be wrong; and when they cease to be wrong, they will cease to be the Tory party'; Sir William Harcourt that 'it is not the *métier* of a Tory to have a policy, any more than it is that of a king to be a democrat'; LLOYD GEORGE: 'a tired nation is a Tory nation'; the Canadian Premier Sir Wilfrid Laurier: 'Toryism like the serpent sheds its skin, but ever remains the same reptile'; and the 1960s Boilermakers' Union leader Ted Hill: 'I wouldn't trust the Tories any farther than I can throw them. And I'm an old man, and I can't throw very far.' Prior to the 1997 general election, the far younger Gordon BROWN ended every one of his attacks on the Conservatives' record and promises with: **'You can never trust the Tories.'**

> No amount of cajolery, and no attempts at ethical and social seduction, can eradicate from my heart a deep burning hatred for the Tory Party . . . So far as I am concerned they are lower than vermin.
> ANEURIN BEVAN, speaking in Manchester, 4 July 1948

> The Tories never panic, except at times of crisis.
> Sir JOHN HOSKYNS, first head of Margaret THATCHER's POLICY UNIT

> The Tories have ceased to be gentlemen without becoming democrats.
> WILLIAM REES-MOGG, 1963

Tory democracy The aggressive Toryism that Lord Randolph Churchill (1849–95) attempted to promote from 1885 as a counter to Joseph Chamberlain's UNAUTHORISED PROGRAMME, each causing considerable embarrassment to their parties' official leaders. Churchill seized on the BRADLAUGH CASE to build a popular base among Anglicans, also scorning the Toryism of the country squires. Lord Randolph told a meeting in Manchester on 6 November 1885:

> What is the Tory democracy that the Whigs should deride it and hold it up to the execration of the people? It has been called a contradiction in terms; it has been described as a nonsensical appellation. I believe it to be the most simple and most easily understood political denomination ever assumed. The Tory democracy is a democracy which has embraced the principles of the Tory Party.

Tory men and Tory measures The classic formula for government put forward by Taper in DISRAELI's CONINGSBY:

> 'A sound Conservative government', said Taper, musingly. 'I understand: Tory men and Tory measures.'

See also MEN OR MEASURES.

Tory party at prayer *See* CONSERVATIVE.

Tory Reform Group (TRG) A pressure group for moderate Conservatism, seen by Margaret THATCHER as a nest of WETS. For a member of her CABINET to speak at its meetings was an act of rebellion, though Peter Walker, an acknowledged wet, managed to combine being the TRG's patron with sitting at her Cabinet table for a decade; John MAJOR's appearance at a TRG reception within days of becoming Prime Minister was seen as evidence of a clean break with his predecessor. The group had its origins in the Tory Reform Committee, formed during WORLD WAR II with members including Quintin Hogg (Lord Hailsham), and PEST (Pressure for Economic and Social Toryism), formed in the mid-1960s by Michael Spicer, later a MAASTRICHT rebel.

High Toryism The strongly PATERNALISTIC Toryism that thrived c. 1820–40, closely linked to the Anglican ESTABLISHMENT and backed by the great landowners; its adherents regarded PEEL as their greatest foe.

tartan Tories The pejorative for the Scottish National Party (SNP) coined in the late 1960s by William Ross (later Lord Ross of Marnock), Labour's strongly anti-separatist Secretary of State for Scotland.

totalitarianism A system of government in which the rulers not only control every aspect of political life, but deny the individual the right to make decisions in every other sphere of activity. The test of whether a DICTATORSHIP or AUTHORITARIAN government is totalitarian is not just the power it possesses, but how it uses it.

> This ADMINISTRATION expects to be running some sort of totalitarian government either before or after the end of the war and is prudently getting ready for same.
> The *New York Daily News* on the proliferation of wartime agencies under the ROOSEVELT administration

touch the face of God Ronald REAGAN's memorable remarks on 28 January 1986 (written by his SPEECHWRITER Peggy Noonan) in a TV broadcast after NASA's *Challenger* disaster. He was quoting *High Flight*, a poem by the Royal Canadian Air Force pilot John Gillespie Magee, who was killed aged nineteen on 11 December 1941 on a Spitfire training flight from RAF Scopwick, Lincolnshire. His poem, which was circulated to all RCAF bases and became the sign-off for a WASHINGTON TV station, included the lines:

> Oh! I have slipped the surly bonds of earth
> And, while with silent lifting mind I've trod
> The high, untrespassed sanctity of space,
> Put out my hand and touched the face of God.

tough on crime and tough on the causes of crime The phrase used by Tony BLAIR – though actually coined for him by Gordon BROWN – that did more to win over MIDDLE ENGLAND than anything else prior to the 1997 general election. He first said in a BBC interview on 10 January 1993, while Shadow Home Secretary during the leadership of John SMITH, and his twin message of law and order policies that worked coupled with support for families and communities became a key theme of Blair's next four years of campaigning. In government, it proved a difficult pledge to live up to; though overall crime rates did fall under Labour, this was not the public perception (*see* ASBOs). It also lent itself to imitation, not always supportive. When the Labour frontbencher Harriet Harman was found to be sending her son to a selective grammar school (*see* COMPREHENSIVISATION), John MAJOR declared himself 'tough on hypocrisy and tough on the causes of hypocrisy'. And when Blair moved to abolish CLAUSE FOUR, the cartoonist Steve Bell described him as 'tough on four and tough on the clauses of four'.

Tower Commission The three-member special review board into the IRAN-CONTRA AFFAIR set up by President REAGAN in 1986, which was headed by former Senator John Tower of Texas. Its report, published in February 1987, attacked members of the President's staff for undertaking actions that CONGRESS had expressly forbidden, and criticised Reagan for 'lax management' and for a 'disengagement' that left him unaware of the WHITE HOUSE foreign policy process. It described the ADMINISTRATION's policies toward Iran and the Contras as being underpinned by deception and disregard for the law of the nation, but argued that the exercise had been an 'aberration'. The report triggered the resignation of Donald Regan as White House CHIEF OF STAFF and his replacement by former Senator Howard Baker.

town meeting The traditional form of community government in New England, with all the inhabitants who wish to attend deciding on actions to be taken. Its influence has spread further; the township form of government can be found as far west as Nebraska. Presidents and candidates now hold 'town meetings' in selected communities to keep in touch with public opinion; Bill CLINTON caused some resentment in the WASHINGTON press corps by opting after his INAUGURATION to hold televised 'town meetings' with the public in preference to press conferences. Sen. Bill Bradley of New Jersey built up a reputation for holding **walking town meetings**, engaging the voters on the beaches of his State.

township A settlement in South Africa where black or coloured people who worked in the cities had to live because APARTHEID prevented them living in areas near their work; most still have to live in the townships for economic reasons. The government provided the basics of a road grid and concrete sites for small houses with a water pipe, but the community was left to provide its own facilities; where they are still absent despite the ANC's efforts to provide them, frustration and political tension can spill over into violence. The townships were traditionally strongholds of the ANC, with INKATHA drawing most of its strength from migrant hostel-dwellers; the largest townships, like Soweto outside Johannesburg, are larger than many European capital cities.

T. R. The initials of President Theodore ROOSEVELT, commonly used in place of a nickname.

trade. Trade Expansion Act The legislation, signed by President KENNEDY in 1962, that eased the TARIFF system to facilitate flexible dealings with the EUROPEAN COMMUNITY. It freed the MARKET by permitting the President to lower tariff duties by as much as 50% over five years, and to abolish tariffs on certain goods produced both by America and the SIX founder members of the EC. The Act was one of a range of US measures to stimulate world trade, the KENNEDY ROUND of trade negotiations being another. Kennedy said:

> We must either trade or fade.

trade gap The difference between the value of what a nation imports and what it exports; the term implies that imports are the larger. The difference between a trade gap and a BALANCE OF PAYMENTS deficit is that the latter makes allowances for INVISIBLES such as shipping and insurance premiums.

trade union An organisation of workers with similar employment and skills who combine to improve their conditions through COLLECTIVE BARGAINING backed by the sanction of industrial ACTION, and to secure their employment. The former TUC General Secretary Len (later Lord) Murray declared:

> Trade unions are about individuals, and the right of a man to answer back to his boss.

The term has largely fallen out of use in America, 'labor union' (*see* AFL-CIO; TEAMSTERS) being preferred; however, the US union pioneer Samuel Gompers (1850–1924) did say:

> We will stand by our friends . . . to secure the election of intelligent, honest, earnest trade unionists, with clear, unblemished, paid-up union cards in their possession.

H. L. Mencken saw the unions as essentially a reactionary and negative force, writing:

> Unionism seldom if ever uses such power as it has to ensure better work; almost always it devotes a large part of that power to safeguard bad work.

And when the Teamsters – for decades out of the mainstream of American unionism though now trying to return – were repeatedly in the headlines for their leaders' links with organised crime, Robert Orben declared:

> Unions are getting such a bad name, it's no wonder they're called Brother Hoods.

At the peak of their influence in the 1970s, British trade unions could claim almost 10 million members, proportionately a far greater degree of unionisation than has ever been achieved in the United States. With its roots in the 1830s (*see* TOLPUDDLE MARTYRS), the movement developed throughout the 19th century, the Trades Union Congress (TUC) being formed in 1868; the first trade union members of Parliament were elected (as Liberals) the same year, and in the 1870s suppressive laws against unions were repealed. The unions were instrumental in forming the LABOUR PARTY in 1906 and funding it (*see* OSBORNE JUDGMENT), and most have remained closely linked to it – a fact that has benefited both on occasions but also fuelled public suspicion as to who is running whom (*see* BEER AND SANDWICHES AT NUMBER TEN; Get your TANKS OFF MY LAWN; Block VOTE). In 1947 Emmanuel ('MANNY') Shinwell told the electricians' union:

> We know that you, the organised workers of this country, are our friends. As for the rest, they do not matter a tinker's cuss.

The unions' link with Labour survived disagreements over OMOV and the rewriting of CLAUSE FOUR, but with the Conservatives for the time being not a threat, some left-wing unions, notably the railwaymen and the firefighters, have severed their links with NEW LABOUR for not pursuing what they see as the interests of the working class.

Britain's trade unions have a culture of their own, based on rigid adherence to their own procedures and rule books. Ernest BEVIN reckoned that 'the most conservative man in the world is the British trade unionist when you want to change him', but Aneurin BEVAN, well to his left, termed the unions 'islands of anarchy in a sea of chaos'.

The unions – in Britain, America, Australia and elsewhere – have always been targeted by leftist groups, most notably the highly-disciplined COMMUNIST PARTY, either to build a vanguard of working-class support or to DESTABILISE the established order. LENIN wrote shortly before his death in 1924:

> It is necessary to be able, if need be, to resort to all sorts of stratagems, manoeuvres and illegal methods, to evasion and subterfuge in order to penetrate trade unions, to remain in them and carry out communist work in them at all costs.

Some unions withstood such infiltration; others, in the UK notably the electricians (*see* BALLOT-RIGGING) and in Australia several, succumbed to it. In France, and some other Continental countries, there was historically a separate Communist trade union movement (*see* CGT). But the threat of a Communist takeover, though real, was often exaggerated by the political opponents of labour.

The most cathartic moment in the British unions' history was in 1926 when they called a GENERAL STRIKE to support miners resisting a wage cut, and lost. John Maynard KEYNES wrote then of

> The trade unionists, once the oppressed, now the tyrants, whose selfish, sectional pretensions need to be bravely opposed.

While individual unions have indulged in extremism and militancy, they have never again taken such concerted action. The movement has achieved many of its aims, though in the 1980s and '90s FULL EMPLOYMENT seemed as far away as ever. But its perpetuation of outdated demarcation lines and working practices after WORLD WAR II, the inability of its leaders to check unofficial strikes, the abuse of PICKETING and the final straw of the WINTER OF DISCONTENT gave the THATCHER government broad public support for putting them on a tight rein. Previous efforts – Labour's IN PLACE OF STRIFE and the Conservatives' INDUSTRIAL RELATIONS ACT – had ended in failure. Mrs Thatcher succeeded in ending trade unions' IMMUNITIES and making them ACCOUNTABLE to their members, and while the BLAIR government has restored the right to union recognition and some others, their wings remain firmly clipped; however, it is recognised on all sides that if workers have a genuine grievance, it will take more than the law to contain them.

> The trade union movement has become, with the hereditary peerage, an avenue to political power through which stupid untrained persons may pass up to the highest office.
>
> BEATRICE WEBB, 1917

> As a trade unionist, people often ask me why I vote Conservative. The answer is, because I am a stupid cunt.
>
> PRIVATE EYE election record, 1964

Trades Union Congress *See* TUC.

Board of Trade The permanent committee of the PRIVY COUNCIL established by King William III in 1696 (stemming from one first founded in 1621) that was the direct ancestor of the UK's present Department of

Trade and Industry. Reformed in 1786 to become a conventional government department, it was in the thick of many Victorian reforms – notably the repeal of the CORN LAWS – and became the guinea-pig for the NORTHCOTE-TREVELYAN REFORMS. Until the formation of a separate Ministry of Labour it also collected employment statistics and INTERVENED to resolve industrial disputes. It became the DTI in 1970, but reverted to its previous title from 1992 for a while under Michael HESELTINE.

traditionalists The element in Britain's LABOUR PARTY who opposed the drive by Tony BLAIR to break with its traditional totems, such as CLAUSE FOUR, and to operate and campaign as if the need for a working class-based party were obsolete. Supporters of the Blair PROJECT were known as MODERNISERS.

Trafalgar Square The customary venue for great DEMONSTRATIONS in London, being the nearest point to the Palace of WESTMINSTER where it is legally permissible to hold a public meeting. It was the scene of BLOODY SUNDAY in 1887, the start and then the finish of the ALDERMASTON MARCHES, and the scene of the riots against the POLL TAX in 1990.

Traficant affair The expulsion from the US CONGRESS in July 2002 and subsequent imprisonment for eight years of Rep. James Traficant (Republican, Ohio) for having used his Congressional office as a racketeering enterprise. Traficant was only the second member to be expelled in the history of the HOUSE OF REPRESENTATIVES. He ran again for Congress from his prison cell that November and received 15% of the vote.

Train of Shame The title given by travelling media and party officials to the train that the infant SDP used to ferry its leaders between Perth, Bradford and London for its 'rolling conference' in September 1981. The experiment – which gave rise to its own songbook – was repeated the following year, then dropped because of the length of time the leadership was marooned in the Fens when the train broke down *en route* to Great Yarmouth.

transition The ten to eleven weeks (though less in the disputed 2000 contest) between the ELECTION that decides who the new President of the United States will be, and the day when that President is INAUGURATED. If there is a change of party as in 1976–77, 1980–81, 1992–93 or 2000–01, a new ADMINISTRATION has to be formed from scratch, to take over the running of the country from 20 January. A victorious CANDIDATE will normally have been too busy campaigning to think much about whom they want, and a frantic search for a Cabinet balanced politically, geographically and in terms of gender and race then ensues. The process is slowed because of the need for the transition team to screen all the POLITICAL APPOINTEES who will require CONFIRMATION by the SENATE; the 1993 BAIRD NOMINATION highlighted the pitfalls. No matter how energetically the President's special **transition team** works, it will be months before all 3000 jobs in the PLUM BOOK are filled and would-be HOLDOVERS weeded out.

translation *See* SIMULTANEOUS.

I'd like that translated if I may The reaction of Harold MACMILLAN at the UNITED NATIONS in 1960 when the Soviet leader Nikita Khrushchev showed his anger at the U-2 AFFAIR, and alleged 'colonialism' by the West, by taking off his shoe and banging it on his desk.

transparency The need for the operation and decision-making of governments to be as open to public sight and scrutiny as is practicable, in order to prevent the people being misled or devious deals being struck. A word that is now universally applied as pressure to end secrecy has grown, one of its earliest uses was in the early 1990s when efforts were made to bring EUROPEAN COMMUNITY decision-making into the open. Transparency, along with SUBSIDIARITY, was pressed for by John MAJOR and other leaders after the signature of the MAASTRICHT TREATY, and the 1992 Edinburgh Summit agreed that more information should be made available. In practice, however, the EUROPEAN COMMISSION remains as secretive as ever.

Transport House The headquarters in SMITH SQUARE, Westminster, of Britain's Transport and General Workers' Union (T&GWU), which from 1928 to 1980 also housed the LABOUR PARTY. The building, the brainchild of Ernest BEVIN, also housed the TUC until 1958. To RANK AND FILE members of the Labour Party, 'Transport House' came to symbolise the solidly right-wing party machine, which until well into the 1960s took a firm line against rebellion and dissent by even the humblest party member.

Travail, Famille (Patrie) (Fr. Work, Family [Country]) The motto of the VICHY government which ruled the portion of

France not occupied by the Germans from 1941 to 1944. The traditional republican slogan of LIBERTY! EQUALITY! FRATERNITY! was considered too explosive by Marshal Pétain's COLLABORATIONIST government, most of them arch-conservatives.

Travelgate The firing of staff in the WHITE HOUSE travel office in 1993 by aides of Bill CLINTON including the President's cousin Catherine Cornelius. Billy R. Dale, ousted director of the office, was charged with embezzlement, but political opponents claimed the firings were a pretext for the appointment of cronies of Hillary Clinton and the diversion of business to a Little Rock travel agency with ties to the First Family. Linda Tripp, a travel office staffer later to feature in ZIPPERGATE as the confidante of Monica LEWINSKY, testified to Congressional committees about the affair but was urged by her lawyers – picked by the White House – not to volunteer information about the role of Mrs Clinton, who was shown by documents to be at the heart of it.

TRB The anonymous column in the NEW REPUBLIC written from 1943 to 1983 by Richard L. Strout (1898–1990), which was required reading for anyone involved in US politics. The signature was the initials of the Brooklyn Rapid Transit in reverse, dating from when the *New Republic* was produced in New York and the then editor, Bruce Blevin, had to carry copy by subway. Strout, a New Yorker who began his journalistic career in England on the *Sheffield Independent*, joined the *Christian Science Monitor* in 1921 and in 1923 moved to WASHINGTON, going on to observe every President from HARDING to REAGAN. He took on the already-running TRB in 1943, turning it into a revered institution; he wrote of EISENHOWER's new ADMINISTRATION:

> He has picked a Cabinet of eight millionaires and a plumber.

In his final column, Strout noted:

> You can measure the passage of time by counting the things we knew wouldn't happen.

treason The compassing of the overthrow of the STATE (and in Britain, of the SOVEREIGN). In the UK, treason was one of the very few offences for which one could be executed, though no charges have been brought since the aftermath of WORLD WAR II. By definition, an act of treason is one that fails; Sir John Harrington wrote in 1618:

> Treason doth never prosper, what's the reason?
> For if it prosper, none dare call it treason.

Talleyrand had a similar view, declaring:

> Treason is a matter of dates.

In 1765 Patrick Henry (1736–99), warned that his speeches against Britain's treatment of its American colonies were verging on the treasonable, told the Virginia Convention:

> Caesar had his Brutus – Charles the First his Cromwell – and George III ['Treason!' cried the Speaker] . . . may profit by their example. If this be treason, make the most of it.

When the US CONSTITUTION was framed, treason was the only crime defined in it; Article III, Section 3 states that treason 'shall consist only in levying war against [the United States] or in adhering to their enemies, giving them aid and comfort'. As a safeguard against the malicious use of treason charges, it requires that two witnesses are needed to testify to the same overt act.

Treason trial The four-year trial in Pretoria from 1957 to 1961 in which the South African government tried, and failed, to break resistance to APARTHEID. 156 anti-government activists were arrested in December 1956, and the following year 91 were committed for trial by a special three-judge court in a former synagogue. The indictment was quashed by a higher court, but 30 of the accused, including Nelson MANDELA, were subjected to a new trial. Eventually 28 were acquitted; one died and one absconded. The trial provided opponents of apartheid with a world-wide cause to rally round and raise funds for; the NATIONAL PARTY government responded to its failure with new forms of repression as internal resistance, particularly from the African National Congress (ANC), increased.

Treasury The government department that in Britain (and Australia) exerts an unrelenting brake on public spending (and especially on investment), and which controls much of the agenda in government; with a powerful CHANCELLOR, notably Gordon BROWN, the Treasury's influence becomes all-pervasive. It is small enough to be democratic, with staff at all levels expected to chip in with their views, but the Treasury view is nearly always cautious, something the Chancellor and CHIEF SECRETARY have always to be aware of. Descended from the Medieval Exchequer whose name the Chancellor still carries, it gained control over the rest of WHITEHALL in the late 17th century, and was also responsible for the CIVIL SERVICE until the late 1960s. Harold WILSON tried to break the Treasury's grip over economic policy in 1964 by forming a separate **Department of Economic Affairs**, but the experiment failed. Justifying the attempt, Wilson wrote:

> I had spent 20 years in Whitehall and Westminster watching, and whenever possible countering, the wily and dominating ways of the Treasury. I was determined that this department should be cut down to size.

In 1993 after the Public Accounts Committee (PAC) unveiled massive irregularities in the Treasury-run Forward civil service catering organisation, the Labour MP Terry Davis commented:

> A taxpayer would wonder why we think the Treasury could manage the British economy when they cannot run a tea shop.

> The Crown is, according to the saying, the 'fountain of honour', but the Treasury is the spring of business.
> WALTER BAGEHOT, *The English Constitution* (1867)

> Like inverted Micawbers, waiting for something to turn down.
> WINSTON CHURCHILL

> A bunch of bank clerks who think they are mandarins.
> LORD BELOFF (1913–99)

> The engine room of government.
> BRUCE ANDERSON, *John Major*

> The Treasury never sleeps.
> MICHAEL HESELTINE

In WASHINGTON the Treasury department, founded in 1789, originally had as extensive powers, but the foundation of the Bureau of the Budget (now OMB) in 1921 greatly reduced its scope. The Secretary of the Treasury remains the financial advisor to the President, and the Treasury administers the collection of most federal taxes, the manufacture of the coinage, and law enforcement agencies such as the SECRET SERVICE and ATF.

Treasury bench *See* BENCH.

Treasury-driven In UK politics, a project or policy, usually involving the counter-productive saving of money, which is assumed to be the work not of the sponsoring department but of the Treasury.

Treasury model The computerised matrix for forecasting the UK economy which the Treasury was required to maintain under the 1975 INDUSTRY ACT, into which the impact of various future policies can be fed.

First Lord of the Treasury The official title of Britain's PRIME MINISTER; although the title of Prime Minister gained legal recognition in 1905, the brass plate on the door of NUMBER TEN still reads 'First Lord of the Treasury'.

treating The provision of liquor, food or other hospitality by a CANDIDATE for the voters. George WASHINGTON won a seat in the Virginia House of Burgesses in 1758 after providing 160 gallons of drink for just 391 electors, and even HONEST ABE Lincoln admitted to spending 75 cents on a barrel of cider for supporting farmhands. In Britain, treating was an accepted feature of elections to the unreformed HOUSE OF COMMONS, but has long been outlawed. This rule is scrupulously observed at election times and any MP found to have broken it would lose their seat; the rule was fractionally relaxed before the 2005 election to permit the innocent purchase of a cup of tea by a candidate for someone who happens to be a constituent.

treaty A solemn agreement between two or more sovereign states to conclude or guarantee peace, to resolve differences, to establish or further peaceful mutual goals, to take forward some common project or to come to each other's help if attacked. Treaties concluded by the UK government require the approval of Parliament; those negotiated by the US ADMINISTRATION need a majority of two thirds of the Senators present for RATIFICATION.

> The first object of a treaty of peace should be to make future war impossible.
> LORD SALISBURY

> Treaties are like roses and young girls: they last while they last. CHARLES DE GAULLE

Treaty Room The room in the WHITE HOUSE where the US CABINET met from 1865 to 1902, when it became a sitting room. President KENNEDY renamed it after restoration in 1961 in the Victorian style of the GRANT administration. Since then it has served as a meeting room and the setting for the signature of important documents, such as the TEST BAN TREATY on 7 October 1963 and the ABM TREATY on 30 September 1972. The President uses it as an office when he is in the East (residential) Wing.

Trendinistas One of several pejoratives for wealthy Americans who take up fashionable left-wing causes, a combination of 'trendy' and 'nistas' from SANDINISTAS. Trendinistas are slightly more militant than LIMOUSINE LIBERALS.

Trevi group The grouping of Interior Ministers from EUROPEAN UNION countries that meets regularly to co-ordinate national action against terrorism, drug trafficking and illegal immigration. It is being rendered obsolescent by the EU's own increasing competence over these areas, which were previously dealt with as a free-standing PILLAR.

TRG *See* TORY REFORM GROUP.

triad A PENTAGON term for the three legs of America's nuclear DETERRENT: land-based missiles (*see* CRUISE; ICBM; MINUTEMAN; MX), submarine-launched missiles (*see* POLARIS; TRIDENT) and air-launched missiles and bombs.

trial balloon The deliberate LEAKing of a policy or initiative under consideration to test what the public reaction would be if it were adopted. The phrase comes from meteorology, and the practice of sending balloons carrying instruments into the upper atmosphere.

triangulation The strategy put forward by the former Republican strategist Dick Morris for Bill CLINTON's 1996 re-election CAMPAIGN. It involved what Morris called a 'move to the center' to capture the MIDDLE GROUND – a move that proved successful given the conservative line adopted by the Republican challenger Bob Dole.

Trianon Treaty The Treaty concluded at VERSAILLES in 1920 which set new national boundaries in central Europe following the collapse of the Austro-Hungarian Empire. Its most notable and traumatic feature was the dismemberment of Hungary, large numbers of whose nationals found themselves as members of sizeable minorities in surrounding states. The *Grand Trianon* and *Petit Trianon* are ornate pavilions in the grounds of the Palace of Versailles.

Tribunal of Inquiry The most powerful instrument of investigation available to a British government, but one that is seldom used. It comprises a panel chaired by a senior judge which has the power to compel witnesses to attend and to answer questions. Tribunals have been convened by the government of the day to inquire into alleged corruption in high places (*see* LYNSKEY TRIBUNAL) and security leaks (*see* VASSALL TRIBUNAL), but Ministers and senior civil servants consider them too weighty and majestic for most inquiries. There is concern that the setting up of a tribunal may impede the operation of the criminal law – and also on occasion a fear that something embarrassing that has not yet come to light may surface.

Tribune The independent and perpetually financially strapped weekly newspaper that since 1936 has given the left wing of Britain's LABOUR PARTY an articulate and often thoughtful voice. Most closely associated with its founder Aneurin BEVAN and its long-term editor Michael FOOT, it has harassed both Conservative governments and Labour leaderships. Ironically, it was during Foot's leadership in the early 1980s that *Tribune*, under Chris Mullin who in turn would become a Labour Minister, briefly went BENNITE; the relationship hit a low point when Mullin went to interview Foot and was asked to leave after accusing him of selling out the left. Following a bitter struggle for control of the paper, it settled down again as the at times prickly voice of Labour's non-extremist left.

Tribune Group The group of Labour MPs, originally organised around the newspaper, who formed the heart of the BEVANITE opposition to Hugh GAITSKELL in the early 1950s. The Parliamentary party voted for its disbandment in 1952, but it was soon reconstituted and until the breakaway of the harder-line CAMPAIGN GROUP in 1982 was the only organised forum for the Labour left at WESTMINSTER; it remains an important element in the Parliamentary party. It has always enjoyed strong support within the constituency parties, reflected – until the system of election was changed – in the domination of the constituency section of the National Executive Committee (NEC) by T**ribunites**.

trickle-down The theory advanced by some conservative politicians and economists that the greater the prosperity of the better-off, the more chance there is of some of it filtering down to improve the lot of the UNDERCLASS. Its proponents use it to justify tax cuts and incentives for the wealthy, as opposed to higher spending TARGETED on the neediest. The term is widely assumed to be a product of the NIXON administration, but it was actually invented by the humorist Will Rogers (1879–1935) with regard to the policies of Herbert HOOVER. Very similar language was used as far back as 1896 by Wiliam Jennings Bryan (*see* PRAIRIE AVENGER) when he told the Democratic National CONVENTION:

> There are those who believe that if you will only legislate to make the well-to-do prosperous, their prosperity will leak through on those below. The Democratic idea, however, has been that if you make the masses prosperous, their prosperity will

find its way up through every class which rests upon them.

Tricky Dick The nickname that haunted Richard NIXON throughout his political career, save for an accomplished first term as President before the disgrace of WATERGATE revived it with full force. He was first given the name in 1950 by California's *Independent Review* as he fought Rep. Helen Gahagan Douglas – who took it up with alacrity – in a campaign marked by innuendo about her supposed (and non-existent) Communist sympathies (*see* PINK LADY). It stuck to him throughout the controversies over his CHECKERS speech, the HUGHES LOAN and other politico-financial dealings that tarnished him. In 1968, during his second bid for the Presidency, Nixon told his staff:

> All right. They still call me 'Tricky Dick'. It's a brutal thing to fight. The carefully cultivated impression is that Nixon is devious. I can overcome this impression in one way only: by absolute candor.

The rest is history. *See also* WOULD YOU BUY A USED CAR FROM THIS MAN?

tricolour Any national flag made up of equal bands of three colours. In the case of the French and the Irish flags the combination has had revolutionary connotations; indeed until the mid-1980s it was an offence to fly the Irish flag in NORTHERN IRELAND in some circumstances.

Trident (1) The codename of the US-British conference held in WASHINGTON from 12–25 May 1943. At it Franklin D. ROOSEVELT pressed for a British commitment to open a SECOND FRONT by the cross-Channel invasion of France; CHURCHILL argued for a landing on Sicily followed by an invasion of Italy. A compromise was reached, with FDR agreeing to preparations to invade Italy and Churchill committed to landings in France on 1 May 1944; prior to these, there would be a combined bombing offensive to destroy German military, industrial and economic capacity. The US Pacific strategy was approved – and it was secretly agreed that the MANHATTAN PROJECT to develop the ATOMIC BOMB should be a joint enterprise. (2) The US submarine-launched ballistic missile (SLBM) system developed as a replacement for Poseidon, which Britain acquired as an infinitely deadlier successor to POLARIS. Deployed by America from the early 1980s, each submarine can carry twelve missiles armed with up to 96 100-kiloton MIRV warheads with a range of up to 6900 miles (11,000km). Trident II, with greater accuracy and more powerful warheads, was developed for deployment by both America and Britain from the early 1990s, but with the end of the COLD WAR the number of warheads actually carried on each submarine has been greatly reduced. The political storm in Britain over Trident was less intense than over cruise missiles, though a hard core of demonstrators continue to target the submarines' base at Faslane, north-west of Glasgow. However, government now confronts the need to decide on whether to commission a successor to Trident, and what form it should take.

Trilateral Commission A group of 325 highly influential current and retired political figures from Western industrial nations who meet regularly to discuss world problems and offer possible solutions. Founded in 1973 with funding from Rockefeller interests, and with an unlisted number in New York City, the Commission is seen by some CONSPIRACY THEORISTS in America as a vehicle for bypassing and subverting elected governments in pursuit of an unstated grand design against the true interests of mankind; the truth is almost certainly far more prosaic and innocuous.

trimmer A PRAGMATIST who trims his or her sails to catch the prevailing political wind, changing tack instead of remaining true to fixed principles (*see* VICAR OF BRAY). The term dates from the 1680s, when George Savile, 1st Marquess of Halifax (1633–95) gained the nickname 'Halifax the Trimmer' because of his uncommitted position between WHIGS and TORIES and his willingness to compromise and shift his ground. Halifax treated it as a compliment, saying:

> True virtue hath ever been thought a Trimmer, and to have its dwelling in the middle of two extremes.

Trinidad terms A formula for forgiving the debts of the world's poorest countries proposed by John MAJOR when CHANCELLOR OF THE EXCHEQUER, agreed by Commonwealth finance ministers in Port of Spain, Trinidad in September 1990, and subsequently largely accepted by the PARIS CLUB and the main creditor nations. By early 1993 $3.5 billion in debt had been rescheduled or forgiven. Gordon BROWN took the process forward to have debt forgiven on an even greater scale.

Tripartite Pact The extension of the Rome-Berlin AXIS on 27 September 1940 to include Japan; it committed the signatories to a ten-year military alliance. Japan had initially refused HITLER's invitation to join the Axis in 1939 but reversed its decision after the outbreak of war, when German successes against France and its pressure on Britain left their Far Eastern colonies vulnerable to Japanese attack. Japan hoped that support from Germany and Italy would deter the Soviet Union and America from opposing her plans for southward expansion. In the event, there was no attempt to co-ordinate German and Japanese strategy after 1940, though in 1941 Hitler unwisely promised to support Japan if she attacked America. After PEARL HARBOR Germany duly declared war on America, effectively guaranteeing her own defeat. The Axis was later joined by Hungary, Bulgaria, Romania, Slovakia and Croatia.

Triple Alliance The pact between unions representing Britain's miners, dockers and railwaymen to threaten a national strike for improved conditions in the autumn of 1914. It built on the success of a wave of strikes two years before, but was rendered abortive by the outbreak of WORLD WAR I. The miners tried to revive the alliance in 1921, but only found concerted support during the brief GENERAL STRIKE of 1926.

troika The Russian word for a carriage drawn by three horses, which has a number of political and diplomatic applications. It is used for any three representatives of different governments working to achieve a particular end. Specifically it applies to the three EU foreign ministers who conduct diplomacy together to ensure continuity; they represent the state now holding the PRESIDENCY, the previous presiding nation and the one that will take over at the end of the current half-year. In WASHINGTON the term is applied to the combination of the Treasury, the Office of Management and Budget (OMB) and Council of Economic Advisers when they stage a joint review of the economy.

Troika plan The demand, first made by Nikita S. Khrushchev on 23 September 1962, for the replacement of the Secretary-General of the UNITED NATIONS by a three-man troika of one Western representative, one from the Soviet bloc and one from the NON-ALIGNED countries. Throughout the 1950s the Soviet Union regarded the UN as a tool of the capitalist West and its Secretary-General, Dag Hammarskjold, as a NATO puppet. Khrushchev's attempt after Hammarskjold's death to replace the post was rejected as an assault on the world body's independence and capacity to act, and a ploy to extend Soviet influence.

trot UK shorthand for a **Trotskyist**, a supporter of the ideology of PERMANENT REVOLUTION promulgated by Leon TROTSKY. The term has been applied not only to the MILITANT TENDENCY, who prided themselves on being Trotskyists, and its successors in the SCOTTISH SOCIALIST PARTY, but loosely, incorrectly and as a term of abuse to the entire non-Communist revolutionary left.

Trotsky, Leon (Lev Davidovich Bronstein, 1879–1940), the driving force with LENIN of the BOLSHEVIK takeover of Russia, the creator of the RED ARMY which ensured the survival of the Revolution, and the man STALIN identified as the greatest threat to his mastery of the Soviet Union. A Jew born in the Ukraine, Bronstein was exiled to Siberia for revolutionary activities but escaped in 1902 to join LENIN in London. He returned to Russia in 1905 after that year's abortive revolution to head the first SOVIET in St Petersburg, but again went through the cycle of arrest, exile and escape. Expelled from Paris in 1916 for PACIFIST propaganda, he returned to Russia with Lenin the next year (*see* SEALED TRAIN) to organise the OCTOBER REVOLUTION. As COMMISSAR for Foreign Affairs from 1917 to 1925, he negotiated the peace of Brest-Litovsk with Germany, but is better remembered for forming the Red Army, a force of 5 million men, to defend the Revolution. In Trotsky's view, that revolution could only survive if there were continual and parallel revolutions in the West, but as the prospect of this receded, so did his chances of succeeding Lenin. On Lenin's death in 1924 Stalin manoeuvred himself into power; when Trotsky organised factions of his own, Stalin had him expelled from the party in 1927 and exiled two years later. From this point, Trotsky became a traitor in the eyes of MOSCOW-LINE Communists, and 'Trotskyist' a term of abuse. After a time fomenting revolution in Turkey, Trotsky mobilised his supporters to fight in the SPANISH CIVIL WAR, then in 1937 settled in Mexico – where three years later he was murdered with an ICE-AXE by a Stalinist agent, Ramon Mercader.

> Our standard is, clearly, political, imperative and intolerant.
>
> TROTSKY, *Literature and Revolution* (1924)

> In a serious struggle there is no worse cruelty than to be magnanimous at an inopportune time.
>
> TROTSKY, *History of the Russian Revolution* (1933)

> The end may justify the means, as long as there is something that justifies the end.
>
> TROTSKY, *An Introduction to His Thought*

Troubles, the The term originally applied to the vicious civil war in Ireland between January 1919, when the newly-formed IRA took up arms to drive out the British, and April 1923 when rival forces in the newly independent IRISH FREE STATE laid down their arms. The initial conflict was bloody enough, especially after Britain introduced the BLACK AND TANS to coerce the population. But the civil strife south of the Border imposed in 1921 was more bitter still, with forces for and against the IRISH TREATY indulging in an orgy of terrorism and murder, which a few extreme Republicans continued after the majority accepted PARTITION in 1922. The word is nowadays used also to describe the civil and sectarian strife between 1969, when Britain sent in regular troops to protect urban Catholics against harassment, and the IRA's ceasefires of the mid-1990s. During that period over 3000 people were killed as the Army became the target of a renewed terrorist campaign by the Provisional IRA, with LOYALIST gunmen responding in kind and both sides indulging in racketeering and extortion.

Truck Acts The Acts passed at WESTMINSTER in 1831, 1887 and 1896 to end the system under which some companies refused to pay their workers in cash, instead allowing them credit at a company store. The practice was not confined to Britain; Tennessee Ernie Ford, in his 1956 hit *16 Tons*, sang of having 'pledged my soul to the company store'. The Acts were repealed in 1985 as an anomaly preventing firms paying staff wages straight into their bank accounts.

Trudeau, Pierre-Elliot (1919–2000), Prime Minister of Canada (Liberal) from 1968 to 1984 (apart from a short break in 1980–81). Canada's most CHARISMATIC leader, and a world figure in his own right. A radical Francophone Montreal law professor and propagandist who had originally backed the NDP, he joined the Liberals and in 1966 was elected to the Commons, where he made an immediate impact. The next year he became Minister of Justice and Attorney-General, taking an uncompromising line with Quebec SEPARATISTS who quickly came to loathe him, and in 1968 succeeded Lester Pearson as Prime Minister. Trudeau, an open man with a trendy streak just right for young voters at the end of the 'swinging sixties', immediately called and won an election – and was to be re-elected in 1974 and 1979. At home the integrity of the nation was his greatest headache as the separatist FLQ stepped up its campaign and he met force with toughness (*see* BLEEDING-HEARTS; WAR MEASURES ACT). After the violence subsided, the Parti Québecois (PQ) won power in the province but failed to win a REFERENDUM to win approval for its SOVEREIGNTY-ASSOCIATION form of separatism. Trudeau commented of his handling of the situation:

> My driving forces were twofold. One was to make sure that Quebec would not leave Canada through separatism and the other was to make sure that Canada wouldn't shove Quebec out through narrow-mindedness.

Trudeau adopted an independent line toward the United States, renouncing NUCLEAR WEAPONS in 1977, but behind the scenes he was quietly co-operative. Trudeau gave Canada a strong voice in the COMMONWEALTH, and also made the country respected in the THIRD WORLD. His public image always stirred interest; his marriage to the young 'flower child' student Margaret Sinclair attracted comment, but nothing like as much as when she deserted him and their three young sons for a series of flings with celebrities – once leaving Trudeau to host alone a dinner for James CALLAGHAN – before finally walking out on him. At least one of Trudeau's election victories was attributed in part to his appearance on the STUMP as a lone parent with the boys alongside. Yet Trudeau himself also had a deserved reputation as a *bon vivant*. In the House he could be mordant, saying of one critic: 'The Honourable Gentleman disagrees. I hear him shaking his head.' And when he was criticised for installing a new swimming pool at SUSSEX GARDENS, he told them: 'You may come over any time to practise your diving – preferably before the water is in.' Discontent over the economy, among other things, brought him defeat in 1980 at the hands of Joe Clark (*see* JOE WHO?), but he was back the following year and served until 1984 before finally stepping down. The main achievement of his final term was the PATRIATION of Canada's constitution, but he was unable to follow this up with agreement among the provinces on how to amend it.

> In Pierre-Elliott Trudeau, Canada at last has a political leader worthy of assassination.
>
> IRVING LAYTON (1912–), *The Whole Bloody Bird* (1969)

For Socialists, getting into bed with him is like having oral sex with a shark.

LARRY ZOFF (1934–)

Trudeau pilgrimage The mildly derogatory name given by Canadian Conservatives to the 'peace mission' undertaken by Trudeau in the autumn of 1983. With East-West tension rising, Trudeau visited world leaders to propose a combined effort to cool US and Soviet tempers over nuclear arms, Nicaragua, Poland and other issues. Trudeau got a warm welcome in most COMMONWEALTH countries, but his mission upset the REAGAN administration, one Under-Secretary of State comparing him with a leftist high on marijuana. Trudeau replied:

The kind of third-rate, third-level pipsqueaks who say I'm not allowed to participate in the peace process because we don't contribute enough to NATO – that's baloney.

Truman. Harry S Truman (1884–1972), 33rd President of the United States (Democrat, 1945–53). The earthy Vice President from Missouri who found himself catapulted, on the death of Franklin D. ROOSEVELT, into leadership of the WORLD WAR II alliance a month prior to the defeat of NAZI Germany and with the decision looming on whether to use the ATOMIC BOMB – of which he had known nothing – against Japan. Truman went on to serve as helmsman of the West at the advent of the COLD WAR, but throughout his Presidency he had to endure criticism that his ADMINISTRATION was soft on Communism. At home he supervised a successful transformation from a wartime to peacetime economy, though his administration did little to advance the cause of CIVIL RIGHTS beyond desegregating the armed forces. His first term proved more successful than his second, won after a remarkable upset victory over Thomas DEWEY achieved through his feisty campaigning (*see* GIVE 'EM HELL HARRY); graft within his administration and setbacks in the KOREAN WAR presaged an end to Democratic tenure of the WHITE HOUSE after two decades and in 1952 he did not seek re-election.

The son of a prosperous farmer, John Anderson 'Peanuts' Truman, his main childhood interest was piano playing. He was also bookish, saying in his retirement: 'Without my glasses I was blind as a bat and, to tell the truth, I was a bit of a sissy. If there was any danger of getting into a fight, I always ran. I guess that's why I'm here today.' A slump in family fortunes ruled out a college education, and until the age of 33 he marked time, helping with the farm and taking on white-collar jobs. Then came WORLD WAR I. He volunteered for the Army, won officer status and came home from France a much-commended Captain. Armed with a new confidence, Truman went into business (*see* HABERDASHER HARRY), but it failed. He turned to politics, and with the aid of the PRENDERGAST MACHINE was elected a judge, and in 1934, despite having built a reputation for honesty, was elected to the US SENATE. By 1940 Tom Prendergast was in jail for tax evasion and Roosevelt was backing a rival candidate, but Truman stumped the state, driving his own car, to win a narrow re-election. His second Senate term put him on the map; after an angry speech from him complaining about wartime waste and graft, the Senate set up the TRUMAN COMMITTEE. Its work kept him in the headlines, and by 1944 WASHINGTON reporters were putting him second only to FDR in promoting the war effort. With Roosevelt seeking a fourth term, Truman was offered the Vice Presidency but replied: 'Tell him to go to hell. I'm for Jimmy Byrnes.' Democratic National Committee chairman Bob Hannegan told the President that Truman was 'the contrariest Missouri mule I've ever dealt with', and he only agreed to join the ticket when FDR said:

If he wants to break up the Democratic Party in the middle of a war, that's his responsibility.

Truman's three months as Vice President were no preparation for the White House, despite Roosevelt's failing health. Martha G. Kempton wrote that he 'scarcely saw President Roosevelt, and received no briefing on the development of the atomic bomb or the unfolding difficulties with Soviet Russia'. On 12 April 1945 he was called from the CAPITOL to be told by Eleanor Roosevelt that her husband was dead. Truman said to White House reporters: 'Boys, if ever you pray, pray for me now. I don't know whether you fellows ever had a load of hay fall on you, but when they told me what had happened, I felt like the moon, the stars and the planets had fallen on me.'

There were many to say he would fail. The union leader Al Whitney declared: 'You can't make a President out of a ribbon clerk.' Admiral Ernest King wrote him off as 'a pipsqueak haberdasher', and the TVA chairman David Lilienthal wrote: 'The country and the world don't deserve to be left this way, with that THROTTLEBOTTOM Truman at the head of the country at such a time.' But he imposed his authority, steered

America through the last months of war and authorised the dropping of atomic bombs on HIROSHIMA and NAGASAKI. Averell Harriman said: 'I had talked with Mr Truman for only a few minutes when I began to realise that the man had a real grasp of the situation. What a surprise and a relief that was!' And CHURCHILL told him: 'I must confess, Sir, I loathed your taking the place of President Roosevelt. I misjudged you badly. Since that time you, more than any man, have saved Western civilisation.' The problems of peace proved great, even though the economy continued to thrive. The start of the Cold War, the nuclear issue and the formation of the state of ISRAEL, which led Ernest BEVIN to comment: 'He would lick any Jewish arse that promised him a hundred votes', were some of his preoccupations. He was also careless in his appointments, leading to allegations of graft and drift. The Republicans controlled Congress, and Washington COLUMNISTS were scathing. Walter Lippmann wrote in 1946: 'Mr Truman is not performing, and gives no evidence of his ability to perform, the function of COMMANDER-IN-CHIEF. At the very centre of the Truman administration there is a vacuum of responsibility and authority.' And two years later Arthur Krock commented: 'The president's influence is weaker than any president's has been in modern history.' Truman replied: 'Whenever the press quits abusing me I know I'm in the wrong pew.' But he also remarked: 'Why in hell does anyone want to be a head of state? Damned if I know.' And on a surprise after-lunch visit to the Senate when he took his old seat, he confessed: 'Right here is where I've always wanted to be, and the only place I've ever wanted to be. The Senate – that's just my speed and style.' He knew his strengths, saying: 'I'm proud that I'm a politician. A politician understands government, and it takes a politician to run a government.' And he said of his presence in the White House: 'Sure it's a big joke, but I don't know anyone who can do it better than I can.'

Truman started the 1948 campaign well behind; even the Democratic Convention was lukewarm; one banner read: **'We're just mild about Harry'**. Sen. Robert Taft (MR REPUBLICAN), set his party's tone when he declared: 'It defies all common sense to send that roughneck ward politician back to the White House.' But Truman stumped the country relentlessly, beat Dewey convincingly despite the intervention of the left-wing former Vice President Henry Wallace and the conservative DIXIECRAT Strom Thurmond and a press who assumed he would lose (*see* DEWEY DEFEATS TRUMAN), and enjoyed a lavish INAUGURATION budgeted by Republicans who had expected their man to win – and who still took both houses of Congress. Yet his second term was less happy. His administration was dogged with charges of INFLUENCE-PEDDLING, and by the HISS CASE and other controversies that gave rise to MCCARTHYISM (*see also* WHO LOST CHINA?). When Secretary of State Dean Acheson, hounded as a 'COMMIE-LOVER', offered to resign for standing by Hiss, Truman told him: 'Dean, always be shot in front – never behind.' The KOREAN WAR set fresh challenges, culminating in Truman's electrifying decision to fire General MACARTHUR (*see* OLD SOLDIERS NEVER DIE).

In retirement, he campaigned for Democratic candidates and kept up a stream of comment – mainly directed against Richard NIXON. In 1971 he refused the CONGRESSIONAL MEDAL OF HONOR, saying: 'I do not consider that I have done anything which should be the reason for any reward, Congressional or otherwise.' Of all presidents, Truman was one of the most unspoiled, once saying:

> Three things can ruin a man: money, power and women. I never had any money, I never wanted power and the only woman in my life is up at the house right now.

He never pulled his punches. His most famous onslaught was against Paul Hume, the *Washington Post* music critic who in 1950 panned a song recital by his daughter Margaret. The President wrote to him:

> I have just read your lousy review buried in the back pages of the paper. You sound like a frustrated old man who never made a success, an eight-ulcer man on a four-ulcer job, and all four ulcers working. I have never met you, but if I do you'll need a new nose and plenty of beefsteak and perhaps a supporter below . . . Westbrook Pegler, a guttersnipe, is a gentleman compared to you. You can take that more as an insult than a reflection of your ancestry.

His greatest target was Nixon. In the 1960 campaign Truman said on the STUMP that 'anyone who voted for Nixon and Lodge ought to go to hell' and that 'Nixon never told the truth in his life'. Under pressure, he denied the first statement but said: 'They can't challenge the second.' In his old age, he told Merle Miller: 'Nixon's a shifty-eyed goddam liar and everyone knows it.'

Truman reminisced: 'My choice early in life was either to be a piano player in a whorehouse or a politician. And to tell the truth there's hardly any difference.' Asked for his secret of success, he replied: 'Never kick a fresh turd on a hot day', and when a friend complained to his wife Bess that Truman was indelicately using the word 'manure', she replied: 'It's taken me 25 years to get him to say "manure".'

> I did my damnedest and that's all there is to it.
> TRUMAN

> He ended up one of the greatest presidents of this century. CHARLES KRAUTHAMMER

> The last authentic American, with all the characteristic faults and virtues of his breed, to occupy the White House.
> MALCOLM MUGGERIDGE

> One of the most extraordinary human beings who ever lived. DEAN ACHESON

> A lot of people admired the old bastard for standing by people who were as guilty as hell and, damn it, I am that kind of person.
> RICHARD NIXON, April 1973

Truman Committee The committee investigating graft and incompetence in America's military and war industries which made Harry S Truman's national reputation, and saved the taxpayer an estimated $15 billion from its formation in 1941. Truman heard of waste and corruption at first hand in Missouri during his 1940 re-election CAMPAIGN, and on his return made such a fuss that the SENATE set up a special panel and put him in charge of it. Its effectiveness in unearthing scandals turned Truman from someone hardly known outside his home state into FDR's choice as his Vice President in 1944.

Truman Doctrine The strategy set out by President Truman in March 1947 for the CONTAINMENT of the Soviet Union by granting US economic and military aid to the peoples of Europe to resist Soviet aggression and encroachment. It was a response to Soviet pressure on Greece and Turkey, and the inability of Britain, out of money and paralysed by the FUEL CRISIS, to help them resist. Truman went before a JOINT SESSION of CONGRESS to ask for $350 million in assistance for the two countries and was granted it; but the principle was general and set the tone for US policy throughout the COLD WAR. Truman told Congress:

> It must be the policy of the United States to support free peoples who are resisting attempted subjugation by armed minorities or by outside pressures.

To err is Truman One of the slogans from Thomas E. DEWEY's 1948 Presidential campaign, which appeared victorious until the last votes were counted. It was a play on the old saying 'to err is human'.

trust. anti-trust legislation *See* ANTI.

blind trust A ring-fenced entity into which politicians taking salaried public office may put their personal assets in order to avoid a conflict of INTEREST. The critical feature of the trust should be that it is administered without the involvement of the beneficiary. Blind trusts have long been a feature of US politics. They surfaced in the UK in the mid-1990s, firstly as a way for donors to finance the private offices of members of the Labour OPPOSITION without any suggestion that the beneficiary was pocketing the money, and later through CHERIEGATE, when the distance between Tony BLAIR and his wife and the blind trust comprised of the proceeds from the sale of their Islington house came under close media scrutiny.

don't trust anybody over 30 One of the basic mottoes of late-1960s student radicals, coined in 1965 by the Free Speech Movement at Berkeley University, California.

when a man assumes a public trust, he becomes public property Thomas JEFFERSON's dictum about the need for probity and TRANSPARENCY among public servants, said to Baron Humboldt in 1807. On other occasions Jefferson voiced resentment at the loss of privacy he had suffered through public interest in his personal affairs.

You can never trust the Tories *See* TORY.

trusteeship The procedure under which certain COLONIAL territories being prepared for independence were assigned by the UNITED NATIONS to a member state for ADMINISTRATION. The lands in question were previously mandated to member states of the LEAGUE OF NATIONS, or were colonies taken from the defeated powers at the end of WORLD WAR II. The last such land to receive independence was Namibia, a former mandated territory retained by South Africa until the end of APARTHEID in defiance of the UN.

truth A less controversial commodity in politics than LIES, though cynics would say that is because there is less of it around. It can also meet with greater suspicion: DISRAELI remarked that 'something unpleasant is coming when men are anxious to speak the truth'; Bismarck that 'when you want to fool the world, tell the truth', and

Adlai STEVENSON that 'the truth is often unpopular. We Americans are suckers for good news.' Thomas JEFFERSON took the purist view that 'It is error alone that needs the support of government. Truth can stand by itself.' And Gerald FORD, after WATERGATE, asserted: 'Truth is the glue that holds governments together'. Yet Arthur BALFOUR insisted: 'It has always been possible to tell the truth, but seldom possible (if ever necessary) to tell the whole truth,' and Speaker Sam RAYBURN warned colleagues: 'You'll get mixed up if you simply tell the truth. Then you don't have to remember what you have said, and you never forget what you said.' Will Rogers put it even more bluntly:

> If you ever injected truth into politics, you would have no politics.

Truth and Reconciliation Commission The non-partisan body set up in 1995 by the post-APARTHEID government of South Africa in a bid to defuse the anger and bitterness caused by four decades of RACIST abuses of human rights, and the violence, excesses and humiliation that accompanied them. The Commission, chaired by Archbishop Desmond Tutu, spent eight years hearing ordinary South Africans, most of them black or coloured, tell of their sufferings and, on occasion, of atrocities they themselves had committed. Some white police officers and vigilantes came forward too with confessions, though in his final report Archbishop Tutu voiced regret that more whites had not admitted their guilt for abuses in which they participated. Nevertheless the Commission is reckoned to have done much to lower the temperature, enable some wounds to heal, and help the people of multiracial South Africa to move on.

> Quite improbably, we as South Africans have become a beacon of hope to others locked in deadly conflict that peace, that a just resolution, is possible. If it could happen in South Africa, then it can certainly happen anywhere else. Such is the exquisite divine sense of humour.
>
> ARCHBISHOP TUTU, Report

The idea of a Truth and Reconciliation Commission has indeed been tried elsewhere, starting in Peru in an effort to put the carnage of the SHINING PATH guerrilla war behind it.

truth is the first casualty The warning about the propensity of governments to tell lies to justify their conduct of a war, first given in that form either by Sen. Hiram Johnson (1866–1945) in a speech to the US Senate when America was entering WORLD WAR I, or in Britain by Arthur Ponsonby at much the same time. Johnson said:

> The first casualty when war comes is truth.

And Ponsonby: 'When war is declared, truth is the first casualty.' The sentiment was not original, however; in 1758 Dr Samuel Johnson wrote in *The Idler*:

> Among the calamities of war, may be justly numbered the diminution of the love of truth, by the falsehood which interest dictates, as credulity encourages.

More recently Speaker TIP O'Neill broadened the saying's application, declaring with equal justification:

> Truth is the first casualty in the heat of a political campaign.

truth squad A group from an opposing party who follow a candidate round correcting their public statements; the technique predates REBUTTAL by a couple of decades.

economical with the truth The words for which the SPYCATCHER affair is best remembered, and which demonstrated the cultural gulf between the Whitehall MANDARIN and the rest of humanity – particularly in Australia. They were uttered in the Supreme Court of New South Wales in November 1986 by the UK CABINET SECRETARY Sir Robert Armstrong (1927–), who was testifying in support of Margaret THATCHER's determination to prevent Peter Wright's book on wrongdoing in MI5 being published in Australia. The critical exchange ran:

> *Malcolm Turnbull* (counsel for Wright): What's a misleading impression? A kind of bent untruth?
> *Armstrong*: As one person said, it is perhaps being economical with the truth.

Armstrong was intending to deliver a silken *bon mot* about the use of language, but appeared to his down-to-earth observers to be trying to admit telling a lie without actually doing so; not surprisingly the UK government lost the case. The trip was a harrowing one for Armstrong, who on leaving Heathrow had taken an out-of-character swing at a press photographer. The words were not in fact a devious invention; the cultured Armstrong was repeating a phrase previously used by (among others) Samuel Pepys, Edmund BURKE, Mark Twain and Arnold Bennett. But it has since entered the political vocabulary as a euphemism for a lie, the meaning being underlined when Alan CLARK during the MATRIX-CHURCHILL trial confessed to having been **'economical with the vérité'**.

pricking the bladder of falsehood with the poignard of truth One of the most elegant phrases used in Parliament by Aneurin BEVAN, in an exchange with Winston CHURCHILL over the DEVALUATION of the pound. When Churchill complained that he was being accused of telling lies, the SPEAKER replied: 'Oh, I thought that was a quotation'. MPs present marvelled, as on many other occasions, at Bevan's ability to bring to life with colourful language what others would have delivered as a routine and impactless insult.

We hold these truths to be self-evident: That all men are created equal, that they are endowed by their Creator with certain inalienable rights, that among these are life, liberty and the pursuit of happiness The majestic opening sentence to the second paragraph of the preamble to the Declaration of INDEPENDENCE, as finally drafted by Thomas JEFFERSON. It forms part of a longer extract inscribed on the Jefferson memorial in Washington DC. Jefferson had not wanted to write the Declaration, but John ADAMS, another of the five-strong drafting team, told him: 'You write ten times better than I do.' Jefferson's original draft in June 1776 began:

> We hold these truths to be sacred and undeniable: that all men are created equal and independent, that from that equal creation they derive rights inherent and inalienable, among which are the preservation of life, and liberty, and the pursuit of happiness.

Tsar The title of the former Emperors of Russia, the autocratic and frequently brutal system which they headed being known as the **Tsarist** state. The word is, like *Kaiser*, a corruption of the Latin *Caesar*. *See also* CZAR.

TSR2 The strike-reconnaissance aircraft cancelled by Britain's Labour government in April 1965 after hundreds of millions of pounds had been spent on its development. The aerospace lobby dates the end of Britain as a major aircraft-building power from this date, but Defence Secretary Denis HEALEY argued that the total cost of the programme, which had tripled to £750 million since 1960 with the first production plane still two years away, could not be justified when the cheaper US F-111 could be bought 'off the shelf'. Three years later, the F-111 purchase was cancelled. Healey reckoned that a British solution could have been found at the outset by a variant of the Royal Navy's Buccaneer strike aircraft – but the RAF would not accept a Navy product.

Tube Alloys The codename of the committee set up in October 1941 to supervise Britain's wartime research into NUCLEAR fission. It was formed as a division of the Department of Scientific and Industrial Research under Sir John Anderson, Lord President of the Council. The Tube Alloys committee itself was headed by Wallace Akers, research director of ICI, and his assistant Michael Perrin. At the TRIDENT conference in May 1943 it was secretly agreed that developing an ATOMIC BOMB should be a joint effort between Tube Alloys and America's MANHATTAN PROJECT.

TUC Trades Union Congress. The body founded in 1868 which represents and co-ordinates the activities of most of Britain's TRADE UNIONS, and was memorably compared with a CARTHORSE by the left-wing cartoonist Low; its executive body is the General Council. The TUC Congress at the start of each September is not only the annual showcase for the views of organised labour, but the start of the CONFERENCE SEASON. With an affiliated membership that has at times exceeded 8 million, the TUC in theory has enormous strength, but has seldom exercised it. Its most critical moment on the politico-economic stage came in 1926 when it orchestrated the GENERAL STRIKE in support of the miners; in the early 1980s it staged a series of markedly unsuccessful 'Days of ACTION' against trade union laws planned by the THATCHER government (*see* STEP BY STEP). For most of its history individual unions and their leaders have either been in the forefront, or have been so divided by personalities or ideology as to blunt the movement's effectiveness. Few of the TUC's general secretaries have been heavyweights; exceptions have included Walter (later Lord) Citrine who, with Ernest BEVIN, chairman of the General Council, handled the General Strike and afterward developed a less confrontational stance that led CHURCHILL to include Bevin in his wartime government, with conspicuous success. The TUC has a close relationship with the LABOUR PARTY, but the membership and interests of the two are not identical; several 'non-political' unions are not affiliated to the party, and in recent time the railwaymen and the firefighters have been active in the TUC but left the party. The TUC is able to influence Labour governments, and vice versa (*see* SOCIAL CONTRACT), but the relationship has traditionally frayed if Labour tries to control wages or STRIKES without first wooing the unions. Traditionally the TUC and Tory governments have attacked each other in public but talked quietly behind the scenes, but Margaret THATCHER broke with this by ignoring both the TUC and the unions as a whole; the last tie was broken in 1992 with the abolition of NEDDY. The refusal of some unions to accept the NEW REALISM of the 1980s led the electricians to withdraw for a time, but the TUC under John Monks went into the new century trying to rebuild union membership after two decades of decline and with militancy confined to a handful of unions. Monks opened a dialogue with the LIBERAL DEMOCRATS as NEW LABOUR attempted to retain its funding from the unions while insisting they no longer had a central role in shaping party policy.

If the TUC entered a javelin-throwing contest, they would elect to receive.
NORMAN WILLIS, TUC General Secretary 1984–93

The TUC left Planet Zog 20-odd years ago. But a few union leaders go back for the occasional day trip.
Employment Minister ALAN JOHNSON (Lab.), 16 April 2003

Tupac Amaru Revolutionary Movement (MRTA) The Cuban-inspired Peruvian GUERRILLA group, far smaller than the SHINING PATH but just as ruthless, who took c. 360 VIPs hostage at a Japanese Embassy reception in Lima in December 1996, demanding the release of jailed comrades. The guerrillas took their name from Tupac Amaru, the last great Inca leader to hold out against the Spaniards. The siege ended the MRTA as a credible force; after a lengthy stand-off Peruvian troops stormed the embassy to free the hostages, and the 20 guerrillas they killed, led by Nestor Cerpa Cartolini, included most of the movement's leadership. Since then the MRTA has carried out only isolated atrocities.

Tupamaros (MLN – *Movemiento de Liberacion Nacional*) Another terrorist group named after Tupac Amaru, this time in Uruguay. The Tupamaros were urban GUERRILLAS, mostly professional men and women, who in the early 1970s reduced the country to near-chaos with kidnappings, bank robberies and daring escapes from prison – one in 1972 involving a breakout by fourteen detainees through a 200ft tunnel. Well armed and equipped, they had not only a network of safe houses but laboratories capable of forging almost any document and a chain of emergency clinics. The Tupamaros were formed c. 1963 out of a militant socialist faction in a sugar workers' union. From 1973 they were ruthlessly suppressed by the military under President Juan Maria Bordaberry.

Everybody dances, or nobody dances.
Tupamaro slogan

Turdblossom The nickname bestowed by George W. BUSH during his 1994 Texas gubernational campaign on Karl Rove, the right-wing strategist who in the White House came to be known as Bush's 'brain'. The two first met in 1973, and by Bush's run for the Presidency in 2000 were so close that aides said they could 'finish each other's sentences'. However in Bush's second term Rove's position was jeopardised by his alleged involvement in the PLAME LEAK.

turf war A dispute between two politicians, officials or government agencies in which each claims responsibility for a certain programme, area of policy or set of staff. Turf wars surface repeatedly even in the most supposedly sophisticated of governments, partly through human ambition and partly because many issues can inevitably be claimed as their own by more than one group of policymakers.

turkeys voting for an early Christmas The memorable phrase used by James CALLAGHAN in the HOUSE OF COMMONS on 28 March 1979 to describe Scottish National Party (SNP) MPs who had tabled a no-CONFIDENCE motion in the government and stood to lose their seats if the vote forced a GENERAL ELECTION. He was also making the point that while the SNP might consider Labour over-cautious about DEVOLUTION, they had no chance of achieving it if Margaret THATCHER's Conservatives came to power. Callaghan's forecast was accurate: Labour lost that night by one vote (311–310), the SNP lost nine of their eleven seats and Mrs Thatcher went on to become the most unpopular Prime Minister in Scotland in living memory. It took 20 more years, and the return of another Labour government, for devolution to be secured.

turncoat Someone who deserts a political cause and goes over to its opponents. The word was reputedly first used of a Duke of Saxony whose coat was white (for France) on one side, and blue (for Spain) on the other; its use in a political sense dates back to 1557, but after four and a half centuries it is as cutting a term of abuse as ever.

turnout The percentage of registered voters who cast their ballots in an election, a figure ranging from 10% or less in some UK council by-elections to over 100% in a few areas where PERSONATION is rife. Turnout in US Presidential elections has customarily been lower than in Britain, but in 2004 it surged to 60%, compared with the UK's all-time low of 59% registered in the 2001 general election. In Australia where voting is compulsory, the figure is nearer 95%, deaths and unavoidable absences making up most of the difference. The term **percentage poll** is used as an alternative. In its 1989 Euro-election results coverage, the *Guardian* programmed the word 'poll' to appear as 'turnout' throughout. This was unfortunate for the victorious Labour candidate Anita Pollack, whose name appeared both in the paper and a subsequent attempted correction as 'Anita Turnoutack'.

TV affair The farcical scandal that broke in Australia in April 1982, costing two Ministers their jobs and weakening the grip on power of Malcolm Fraser's LIBERAL government, over an alleged COVER-UP of the import of a television set the previous October by the Health Minister, Michael Mackellar. Mackellar's customs declaration card, signed by one of his staff, had 'No' written against the question of whether he had a TV set with him, even though he was carrying it under his arm. Colour sets were liable to duty, black-and-white sets not, and Mackellar and the customs officer who challenged him had different recollections of which he said it was; it was in fact colour. Customs Minister John Moore rang Mackellar to voice concern and told officials he wanted no more inaccurate statements; the matter was then regarded as closed. Mackellar then wrote offering to pay any duty and received no reply, despite a 1976 circular stressing that Ministers must not receive preferential Customs treatment. When the story broke, Fraser demanded that Mackellar and Moore produce a statement of what had happened, and when they could not agree the wording, he and the media pressed them to resign, which they did. When told by other colleagues that he was setting excessively high standards, Fraser replied:

> Some of my colleagues would find it difficult to understand the distinction which a prime minister has to maintain between loyalty to values and loyalty to people . . . If he is not loyal to the values that are important, who else is going to be?

TVA (1) Tennessee Valley Authority. The federal corporation created by Franklin D. ROOSEVELT in 1933 as one of the first elements in his NEW DEAL, to develop the basin of the Tennessee River, mostly to build dams for flood control and to provide cheap electric power. Its central feature was the Wilson Dam and accompanying electric plants and factories at Muscle Shoals, begun as a munitions complex in WORLD WAR I but never completed owing to conservative opposition in CONGRESS. The agency set up by FDR to supervise this and further tasks was 'clothed with the power of government but possessed of the flexibility and initiative of private enterprise'. Critics assailed this measure to combat the effects of the GREAT DEPRESSION in an already impoverished area as 'creeping Socialism', and the TVA's existence remained a source of political controversy for years, with private electric companies fuelling the opposition. However, the TVA is now highly regarded; it has turned a once-backward area into a prosperous farming and industrial centre. Its 39 dams and about 160 non-profit-making power distributors provide electricity at one-third less than the US average cost to consumers in an 80,000 sq. mile area. The river, which once flooded regularly, has been converted into a series of lakes. (2) In France, the abbreviation for VAT (*Taxe de Valeur Additionelle*).

Tweed ring *See* BOSS TWEED.

Twelfth amendment The amendment to the US CONSTITUTION, proposed in December 1803 and RATIFIED the following September, which prevented anyone from seeking the offices of both President and Vice President, and thus established the principle of PARTY and the TICKET. Until then the runner-up in the Presidential contest automatically became Vice President, regardless of whether the two held compatible opinions or even wanted to work together. It stemmed from the outcome of the REVOLUTION OF 1800 when Thomas JEFFERSON and Aaron BURR, whose names were on the same ballot even though Burr was known to be Jefferson's choice as his deputy, tied and it took 36 ballots in the HOUSE OF REPRESENTATIVES to decide between them.

Twenty-two, the The colloquial name among Conservative MPs at WESTMINSTER for the 1922 COMMITTEE.

Twenty-second amendment The amendment to the US CONSTITUTION forced through by Republicans during the TRUMAN administration to check the Democratic ascendancy by ensuring that no President ever again served more than two TERMS, as Franklin D. ROOSEVELT had done. It was to rebound on them, as two of the three Presidents since then who might have sought, and won, a third term – Dwight D. EISENHOWER and Ronald REAGAN – have been Republicans. Under the amendment, proposed in 1947 and ratified in March 1951, no President who has completed two terms, or who has completed two or more years of another President's term and then served a term of their own, can run again. The maximum a President could thus serve would be ten years minus one day; Truman was exempt from this provision, but decided not to run again in 1952.

Twenty-fifth amendment The further amendment to the US CONSTITUTION, proposed in 1965 and ratified in February 1967, which sought after John F. KENNEDY's assassination to end confusion over the PRESIDENTIAL SUCCESSION. It established for the first time that a VICE PRESIDENT taking over the office of President actually became President, thus validating the position of John Tyler (*see* TIPPECANOE AND TYLER TOO) who on William Harrison's death in 1841 had to establish that he was President in name and fact. It also provided for the President to nominate a new Vice President if a vacancy arose, subject to confirmation by a majority of both Houses of CONGRESS; this provision was exercised twice in 1973–74, with Gerald FORD, the first nominee on Spiro AGNEW's resignation, becoming President within months when Richard NIXON also resigned over WATERGATE. The amendment also empowered the President to designate the Vice President as acting President in the event of his own incapacity, and the Vice President and Cabinet to do so if the President becomes 'unable to discharge the powers and duties of his office'. A two-thirds majority in each House of Congress would be necessary for such a Vice Presidential declaration to take effect.

Twenty-Six Counties The term used by Irish Republicans for the IRISH FREE STATE and the fully sovereign republic that succeeded it. There are 32 Irish counties, and reference to the Republic in this way is a statement of support for a united Ireland and the ending of PARTITION. By the same token, Nationalists refer to NORTHERN IRELAND as the SIX COUNTIES. (*See also* THIRTY-TWO COUNTY SOVEREIGNTY COMMITTEE).

26th July movement The political group formed in Cuba by Fidel Castro at a meeting with close colleagues on 19 July 1955 to further his revolutionary goals, and support the trained GUERRILLA group he hoped to form in Mexico (*see* GRANMA) to overthrow President Fulgencio Batista; it evolved into a guerrilla group itself. Many members were to be prominent in the Marxist government Castro eventually formed after toppling Batista in 1959. The movement's name was adopted in the weeks after its formation; it apparently refers to an inaugural meeting of the members who stayed behind when Castro left for Mexico.

twin. twin pyramids of the Nile The alleged remark by President CARTER's CHIEF OF STAFF Hamilton Jordan at a WASHINGTON dinner in 1977 that delighted prurient gossip columnists in the capital, and enabled them to build on the myth that Carter's entourage even at the highest level were gauche Georgia REDNECKS. Jordan, the astute political strategist who had played a large part in propelling the virtually unknown Carter into the WHITE HOUSE, was supposed to have used the phrase while staring down the cleavage of Mme Ghorbal, wife of the Egyptian ambassador.

twin-track strategy Any policy combining two separate but parallel courses of action. It was heavily used by Western politicians to characterise NATO's dual policy on CRUISE MISSILES of deploying them to meet the threat from Soviet SS20s in eastern Europe while negotiating for the removal of both. And at his first WHITE HOUSE meeting with President CLINTON in February 1993, John MAJOR used it to describe the relief programme for Bosnia, combining distribution of food by land by UK and other forces, and US plans to air-drop supplies to Muslim communities behind Serb lines that ground forces could not reach.

Twinkle The codename allocated by the US SECRET SERVICE to President George W. BUSH's effervescent twin daughter Jenna.

Two Brains The nickname given by Michael White of the *Guardian* to David Willetts (1956–), the progenitor of many of the social policies embraced by the Conservatives under John MAJOR and during their subsequent years in opposition. Willetts, who served in Margaret THATCHER's POLICY UNIT and the CENTRE FOR POLICY STUDIES before entering Parliament in 1992, pioneered in particular the Conservatives' NHS reforms, and proposals to raise the pensionable age to 67. The sobriquet is used with a touch of irony, for although Willetts is not only an intellectual but an effective politician he has had to learn the hard way; in 1996 he had to resign as PAYMASTER-GENERAL for having tried, when a WHIP, to influence the supposedly-independent Select Committee into Members' Interests into blocking an inquiry into Neil Hamilton's involvement with CASH FOR QUESTIONS.

Two Camps doctrine The doctrine, first advanced by LENIN, that the Communist and capitalist worlds are condemned to a struggle that must end in victory for one side or the other; many would argue that he has been proved right, if not in the way he had hoped. Communists long expected the climactic event to be a war resorted to by the capitalists because they could not succeed in peaceful competition. As the doctrine developed under STALIN, there could be no such thing as a single world society, and thus no impartial and all-embracing role for a world body like the UNITED NATIONS. *See also* TROIKA PLAN.

two-door system A way round the statute dating from 1863 which prohibits members of the US CONGRESS who are lawyers from representing clients with claims against the federal government. A Congressman's name will appear on his law firm's front door, through which the bulk of his clients enter; next to it is another door minus the legislator's name, through which those with cases in the restricted category are ushered. New York's Rep. Emmanuel Celler, who served almost 50 years in the House, came under media criticism for the practice, Robert Sherrill terming it 'one of the longest-standing and most notorious embarrassments to Congress'. Celler replied:

> Your constituents are the final arbiter of any conflicts [of interest], and I'm always re-elected.

Shortly afterward, in 1972, Celler was unseated in a Democratic PRIMARY by Elizabeth Holtzman.

Two Jags The nickname applied by the Conservatives and much of the media to John Prescott (1938–), DEPUTY PRIME MINISTER in Tony BLAIR's Labour government from 1997, reflecting his fondness for classic cars and the contrast between this and his 'integrated transport policy' which aimed to get people out of their cars and onto public transport – especially when he used his official car to travel 250 yards at a party conference (*see* The wife don't like her HAIR BLOWN ABOUT). A former steward on Cunard liners and seamen's union activist (*see* TIGHTLY KNIT GROUP OF POLITICALLY MOTIVATED MEN), the colourful and sometimes explosive Prescott came ashore to become MP for Hull West in 1970, led the Labour delegation to the EUROPEAN PARLIAMENT in the late 1970s, and served as a front-bench spokesman through eighteen years of OPPOSITION. He secured his place in Labour's succession at the party's 1993 conference with a passionate speech in support of John SMITH (*see* OMOV), and when Smith died the following year Prescott contested the leadership with Blair (*see* BAMBI AND THUMPER) but was happy to serve as his deputy. In government from 1997, he at first headed a mega-Department of the Environment, Transport and the Regions (DETR) as well as chairing key Cabinet committees and deputising for Blair; from 2001 he settled for a smaller Office of the Deputy Prime Minister only to take back responsibility for local government and planning when Stephen Byers' Department of Transport, Local Government and the Regions imploded (*see* FUCKED). The integrated transport policy ran out of steam, and Prescott's other crusade, for elected regional assemblies was halted by an adverse REFERENDUM vote in the North-East in 2004. Prescott made his greatest electoral impact in more ways than one during the 2001 campaign when, attacked by a pro-hunting demonstrator in North Wales, he got in a couple of left jabs that brought the campaign to life. There were brief fears in the Labour hierarchy that Prescott might have to resign, but Blair stood by him; the Labour MP Lewis Moonie after campaigning in a former Fife mining village the following day, reported:

> 60% said John had done the right thing, and the other 40% said he should have hit him harder.

Prescott's abilities as a campaigning orator were not matched by an adherence to grammar and syntax. On 13 July 2004 he reduced the COMMONS to turmoil by announcing: 'The Government intend to reduce – and probably eliminate – the homeless by 2008', adding: 'I am sorry, but the House knows that I have problems with English.' Another classic is:

> This was released I think in February and so it is a great deal of fuss being made. It hasn't in fact been given public release, it was released in February.

two plus four talks The talks which hammered out the legal and constitutional small print of German REUNIFICATION in 1990, and the end of the four-power status under which Berlin was still nominally under the control of the WORLD WAR II allies: the US, Soviet Union, Britain and France. They involved representatives from West and East Germany and the four 'occupying' powers, but in practice it was the Germans who took the decisions, the others (despite misgivings from Margaret THATCHER) having no wish or ability to prevent the Germans reuniting.

two-way street A phrase often heard, but seldom honoured, in speeches about transatlantic defence procurement. It stems from repeated attempts by Britain and other European countries to ensure that in return for their agreeing to purchase costly items of American hardware, the PENTAGON will either purchase a corresponding amount of equipment from them or **offset** the cost by arranging for some of the manufacture to be carried out in the purchasing country. Promises have frequently been made, especially in the 1970s, but even if the opportunity were there for large-scale US purchases from its allies, CONGRESS would almost certainly complain about a loss of American jobs. Indeed just before the 2004 Congressional elections the Pentagon had to persuade PROTECTIONISTS in the House to drop a plan to make offset illegal on the ground that it would torpedo US defence exports. Shortly before, the UK Defence Secretary Geoff Hoon had told his US opposite number Donald Rumsfeld that Britain would have to reconsider large-scale procurements from US suppliers if it were not allowed into the American market. A US decision to opt for an Anglo-Italian helicopter as the next MARINE ONE followed.

Tydings-McDuffie Act The Act passed by the US CONGRESS in 1934, and unanimously ratified by the Philippine legislature, that established the then US COLONY as a COMMONWEALTH, to become fully independent in 1946. Manuel Quezon became the Philippines' first President and prepared the way for independence, which came on schedule despite the Japanese occupation of the islands from 1941 to 1945.

Tyler, John *See* OLD VETO; TIPPECANOE AND TYLER TOO.

Tynwald The Parliament of the Isle of Man, whose principal House is the HOUSE OF KEYS. Until 1992 the PRESS GALLERY of WESTMINSTER boasted a display of photographs and prints of *Parliament Houses of the Empire*, Tynwald being depicted by an open-sided marquee beside which its ceremonial opening was conducted.

tyranny The ruthless, absolute and by inference illegal exercise of power, the ruler – if it be a single person – being a **tyrant**. John Locke (1632–1704) asserted that 'wherever law ends, tyranny begins'; William Penn (1644–1718) is reputed to have said: 'Men must be governed by God or they will be ruled by tyrants', and Thomas JEFFERSON declared that 'resistance to tyrants is obedience to God'. Jefferson's contemporary Thomas Paine, though a supposed atheist, also stressed the need for resistance, writing: 'Tyranny, like hell, is not easily conquered . . . yet the harder the conflict, the more glorious the triumph.' MAHATMA Gandhi took the high ground to argue: 'The willing sacrifice of the innocents is the most powerful retort to insolent tyranny that has yet been conceived by God or man.' Definitions of tyranny are highly subjective. De Tocqueville spoke of the 'tyranny of the majority'; Dostoevsky asserted that 'tyranny is a habit. It may develop, and does develop at last, into a disease'; Pierre Joseph Proudhon that 'whoever puts his hand on me to govern me is a usurper and a tyrant; I declare him my enemy'; Louis de St Just that 'hc who makes jokes as the head of a government has a tendency to tyranny.' But James MADISON was the most comprehensive, writing:

> The accumulation of all power, legislative, executive and judiciary, in the same hands, whether of one, a few, or many, and whether hereditary, self-appointed or elective, may justly be pronounced the very definition of tyranny.

> The only tyranny I accept in this world is the still voice within.
> GANDHI

> Tyranny is the normal pattern of government. It is only by intense thought, by great effort, by burning idealism and unlimited sacrifice that freedom has prevailed.
> ADLAI STEVENSON

U

U-turn A fundamental reversal of policy by a political leader, generally following repeated pledges that the previous course of action was unchangeable; the term is familiar to any motorist. It was first used to describe the HEATH government's decision in December 1971 to abandon its previous reliance on MARKET forces to curb inflation and revive the economy (*see* LAME DUCKS), and embark on an INTERVENTIONIST industrial strategy with wage and price controls. In October 1980 Margaret THATCHER scorned assertions by Tory WETS that she would be forced into a similar capitulation when she told the CONSERVATIVE PARTY conference:

> U-turn if you want to. The LADY'S NOT FOR TURNING.

More recently, Tony BLAIR came under fire for an ideological U-turn when he announced in April 2004 that a REFERENDUM would be held on the new EUROPEAN CONSTITUTION, having consistently rejected the idea.

The term can also be used in a non-ideological sense. When Mrs Thatcher's LEADER OF THE HOUSE John Biffen (*see* SEMI-DETACHED) married well into middle age, the Labour front-bencher Denzil Davies said in the Commons:

> I congratulate the Rt Hon. Gentleman on his own personal U-turn.

U-2 affair The incident that torpedoed the much-heralded 1960 PARIS SUMMIT, intensifying and prolonging the COLD WAR. On 1 May 1960, a fortnight before the Soviet leader Nikita S. Khrushchev was due to meet his three Western counterparts, an American U-2 high-level reconnaissance aircraft was shot down over Soviet territory; its pilot, Francis Gary Powers, was captured and confessed to spying. This was the first intimation of US spy missions over the Soviet Union, which President EISENHOWER admitted had been under way for four years. Eisenhower did halt the flights, but refused to apologise, calling them a 'distasteful but vital necessity' brought about by the Soviets' 'fetish of secrecy and concealment'; Khrushchev cancelled the conference and Eisenhower's planned visit to the Soviet Union. In 1962 the Russians returned Powers in exchange for Colonel Rudolf Abel, a Soviet spy held in America; he became a helicopter pilot for a TV station in Los Angeles and was subsequently killed in a crash.

UDA Ulster Defence Association. The principal LOYALIST group of PARAMILITARIES in NORTHERN IRELAND from 1971 until the end of the TROUBLES, when it began to fragment. It operated within the law at first with the **Ulster Freedom Fighters (UFF)** acting as its terrorist wing, but in August 1992 was banned in Ulster – though not in mainland Britain. After the GOOD FRIDAY AGREEMENT it became locked in a feud with the **LVF** (Loyalist Volunteer Force) in which at least three people died before it was ended in November 2002. After a further bloody power struggle within the UDA, the organisation declared a ceasefire on 21 February 2003, apologising for having trafficked in drugs and pressing the need for a lasting settlement in the province. However, in January 2005 it asked the government for £70 million to wean its 1000-plus members off drug dealing and extortion. The UDA is strongest in East Belfast, but has enjoyed considerable support in western Scotland and even in Canada.

UDI Unilateral Declaration of Independence, specifically that of Southern Rhodesia (now Zimbabwe) on 11 November 1965 (*see* PRIME MINISTER, THINK AGAIN). Southern Rhodesia was a self-governing British COLONY, and the government of Ian Smith (1919–), elected by white voters, made the break, which had no legal validity, rather than accept black MAJORITY RULE. Harold WILSON imposed SANCTIONS and predicted that UDI would crumble in WEEKS, RATHER THAN MONTHS. But aided to an extent by SANCTIONS-BUSTING and the APARTHEID government of South Africa, Smith was able to outwit successive British governments and fight off the nationalist guerrillas of what became ZANU-PF for fourteen years, though toward the close he had conceded an INTERNAL SETTLEMENT that was leading toward moderate black rule. UDI was ended by the 1979 LANCASTER HOUSE AGREEMENT, with British rule re-established prior to free elections and legitimate independence. *See also* FEARLESS TALKS; NIBMAR; RETURN TO LEGALITY; TIGER TALKS.

> We have struck a blow for the preservation of justice, civilisation and Christianity; and in the spirit of this belief we have this day assumed our sovereign independence.
>
> IAN SMITH, 11 November 1965

UDR Ulster Defence Regiment. The combined regular and part-time volunteer military force raised in NORTHERN IRELAND to support British forces and the RUC during the TROUBLES. It was formed in 1970, following disbandment of the B SPECIALS, as a more professional and non-sectarian force; but partly because of threats against Catholic members from the IRA it became overwhelmingly Protestant, and some personnel were convicted of acts of LOYALIST terrorism. The UDR had a strength of just over 6000; more than 200 serving personnel plus a number of former members were killed by the IRA. Under OPTIONS FOR CHANGE in the early 1990s, the UDR was amalgamated with the Royal Irish Rangers, and thus absorbed into the mainstream British Army.

Uhuru (Swahili. Freedom) The slogan of many African independence movements of the 1950s and '60s, but specifically that of KANU and of independent Kenya under Jomo Kenyatta. Kenyatta named his son Uhuru, and in October 2002 President Daniel arap Moi named Uhuru Kenyatta, who had not been active in politics, as his successor. The choice was strongly opposed within KANU and among the opposition as a means of Moi retaining power through a puppet. That December Uhuru, and KANU, were resoundingly defeated.

UK rebate *See* BRITISH REBATE.

UKIP United Kingdom Independence Party. The party committed to withdrawal from the EUROPEAN UNION which gained a toehold in the 1999 European Parliament elections, the first held under PROPORTIONAL REPRESENTATION, then in 2004 captured twelve seats out of 78, taking more votes from the Conservatives than from Labour and pushing the Liberal Democrats into fourth place. That campaign was fronted by Robert Kilroy-Silk, the former Labour MP who was sacked as a BBC chat show host months before for writing an article in the *Sunday Express* attacking Arabs. UKIP's other high-profile recruits in the 2004 election campaign were the actress Joan Collins and a clutch of Conservative peers. UKIP's success with a general election imminent alarmed the Conservatives; Michael HOWARD stiffened their line on Europe and prominent donors switched their cash to the Tories. At this point Kilroy-Silk made a bid to oust UKIP's leader, the former Conservative MP Roger Knapman; when it failed, the party's MEPs withdrew the WHIP from him and Kilroy-Silk resigned to form his own party, VERITAS. Neither made an appreciable impact in the 2005 general election, though in seventeen constituencies UKIP's vote was larger than Labour's majority over the Conservatives.

UKREP The United Kingdom Permanent Representation (in effect Embassy) to the European Union, in Brussels. It is headed by the PERMANENT REPRESENTATIVE, a senior member of the Diplomatic Service.

Ulster Historically the province comprising the nine northern counties of Ireland; since PARTITION the SIX COUNTIES of NORTHERN IRELAND (Ulster less Cavan, Donegal and Monaghan). To LOYALISTS Ulster is the Protestant heartland which owes loyalty to the CROWN and defies attempts to subordinate it to Dublin.

> Ulster will never agree to send representatives to an Irish Parliament in Dublin, no matter what safeguards and guarantees you may provide.
>
> GEORGE V to ASQUITH

Ulster Covenant The pledge by Protestant ULSTER UNIONISTS led by the lawyer/politician Sir Edward Carson (1854–1935) to resist the imposition of all-Ireland Home Rule, signed in Belfast City Hall on 28 September 1912. The 'solemn covenant' echoed the anti-PAPIST Solemn League and Covenant signed by Scottish Presbyterians in the early 17th century. The queue waiting to sign stretched for three-quarters of a mile, and the covenant eventually carried 471,474 signatures, many inscribed in the signers' own blood.

Ulster Freedom Fighters *See* UDA.

Ulster Unionists The main body of Protestant voting strength in NORTHERN IRELAND, which opposed HOME RULE, provided the backbone of the STORMONT Parliament, and maintains Ulster's commitment to the UNION with the rest of the

UNITED KINGDOM. Until 1972 its MPs at WESTMINSTER took the Conservative whip. The Unionist tradition split around that time into the **Official Unionists**, the ESTABLISHMENT party led by James Molyneux and subsequently David Trimble, and the more militant Democratic Unionists or DUP under the Rev. Ian PAISLEY. The Official Unionists originally had far more support, but the balance has gradually shifted, especially after the GOOD FRIDAY AGREEMENT which Trimble negotiated did not bring rapid DECOMMISSIONING of the IRA's weaponry, and in the 2003 Assembly elections the DUP outpolled the traditional party and in 2005 the DUP secured nine Westminster MPs to the DUP's one, with Trimble losing his seat.

> We must be prepared, the morning Home Rule is passed, ourselves to become responsible for the government of the Protestant province of Ireland.
> Sir EDWARD CARSON

Ulster says No The rallying call of the LOYALIST protest campaign against the 1985 ANGLO-IRISH AGREEMENT. 'No' is the word most often heard on the lips of Loyalist politicians.

Ulster Volunteers A private army founded by Carson (*see above*) in 1913 to resist HOME RULE. Within months the Ulster Volunteer Force had up to 100,000 members drilling publicly – a sight which, coupled with Carson's threats, the Volunteers' GUN-RUNNING and the CURRAGH MUTINY, convinced ASQUITH's government that special provision would have to be made for the Protestant North. The outbreak of war in 1914 led to the whole question being shelved. The present-day Ulster Volunteer Force (UVF) is a Protestant terrorist organisation, outlawed since 1966.

Ulster will fight, and Ulster will be right Lord Randolph Churchill's emotive slogan against GLADSTONE's HOME RULE initiatives of the 1880s, which did much to create militant Unionism.

King of Ulster Nickname from the early 1980s for the Rev. Ian PAISLEY, bestowed by critics of his highly personal style and of alleged British ambitions at the time to instal him as leader of a devolved administration at STORMONT.

ultimatum A challenge issued by one government to another, requiring it to take certain action by a specified time or face the consequences – as in Britain's ultimatum to Germany at the start of September 1939 to withdraw its invading forces from Poland. *See* I HAVE TO TELL YOU THAT NO SUCH UNDERTAKING HAS BEEN RECEIVED.

umbrella group A body comprising adherents of various political parties brought together for a specific campaign, notably the 'Yes' and 'No' campaigns in Britain's 1975 REFERENDUM on membership of the EUROPEAN COMMUNITY. Also a group of disparate organisations brought together to LOBBY on a particular issue, e.g. the relief of THIRD WORLD debt.

nuclear umbrella *See* NUCLEAR.

Umkhonto we Sizwe (Zulu. Spear of the Nation) In the years of APARTHEID, the military wing of the African National Congress. It was founded in 1961 by Nelson MANDELA, who had urged the ANC to form such a grouping itself and was told by its executive that members who resorted to violence would not be stopped. The authorities tried to break Umkhonto by arresting Mandela and several of its other leaders and securing stiff sentences for them at the RIVONIA TRIAL, but ANC military activity continued, mainly through training camps in FRONT-LINE STATES to the north.

UMP (*Union pour un Mouvement Populaire*) The party which since the 1970s has been the leading centre-right force in France, and which provided Jacques Chirac with the vehicle to become in turn Mayor of Paris, Prime Minister and eventually President. Claiming the support of GAULLISTS, CHRISTIAN DEMOCRATS, LIBERALS and RADICALS, the UMP has provided a series of Prime Ministers, most recently Jean-Pierre Raffarin, and since November 2004 has been led by Nicolas Sarkozy, the former Interior and Finance Minister.

UN Initials of, and the universal abbreviation for, the UNITED NATIONS.

unacceptable face of capitalism *See* CAPITALISM.

un-American activities The holding and propagation of views seen by MIDDLE AMERICA as subversive. To LIBERALS, the essence of MCCARTHYISM. Specifically, the activities probed from 1938 to 1975 by the House Committee to Investigate Un-American Activities, set up at the instigation of the New York Republican Rep. Hamilton Fish and the American Federation of Labour to investigate NEO-FASCISTS, but turned against COMMUNISTS by Rep. Martin Dies of Texas. In 1947 alone the committee collected files on over a million known or suspected Communists, FELLOW-TRAVELLERS, 'dupes' and 'BLEEDING-HEART liberals'. The investigations petered out after the fall of McCarthy. President TRUMAN called the committee 'the most un-American activity in the whole Government', and its activities 'simply a red herring'. When committee members investigate Hollywood, Humphrey Bogart declared: 'They will nail anyone who ever scratched his ass during the National Anthem.' And Lillian Hellman told them: 'I cannot and will not tailor my conscience to this year's fashions.' The historian Hugh Brogan described the process as 'a cause of shame for Americans ever since'. *See also* FIFTH AMENDMENT; WITCH-HUNT.

unanimous consent In US politics, a legislator may seek the 'unanimous consent' of colleagues to allow a non-controversial matter through, rather than go through the formalities of a vote. It is customary in the SENATE, for example, for a Senator to seek and be given unanimous consent for an item to be inserted in the CONGRESSIONAL RECORD.

unassailable The British equivalent of 1000 PER CENT, a declaration of confidence that turns out to be anything but. The word was used by Margaret THATCHER in the autumn of 1989 about her Chancellor Nigel Lawson, and the myth grew that she had described him as unassailable at the time her economic adviser Professor Alan Walters was being allowed to undermine him, with Lawson eventually resigning. On this basis, any Conservative Minister in trouble was greeted with OPPOSITION shouts of 'Unassailable'. In fact, Mrs Thatcher made her comment only after Lawson quit. On television on 30 October 1989 she said: 'Nigel's position is unassailable. He was a very strong Chancellor.' Neil KINNOCK took this up and used it to ridicule Lawson, and history was quietly rewritten.

Unauthorised Programme The POPULIST programme put forward by Joseph Chamberlain and Jesse Collings (*see* THREE ACRES AND A COW) in Britain's 1885 election campaign without the consent of the Liberal leadership. It pulled in enough votes to leave the Conservative government on the point of collapse, but was an embarrassment to GLADSTONE and was quietly ignored when he returned to power.

uncle. Uncle Joe (1) The nickname in the West during WORLD WAR II for STALIN, widely if naïvely seen as a benign figure by his allies. (2) One of several names in WASHINGTON for Rep. Joe Cannon (1836–1926), SPEAKER of the HOUSE from 1903 to 1911, known also known as 'the hayseed member from Illinois' and 'FOUL-MOUTHED JOE'. President TAFT warned Alice Roosevelt Longworth never to get between Cannon and his spittoon; at one poker evening where none was provided, Cannon said the umbrella stand would do just fine.

Uncle Sam The affectionate personification of the United States, and its government. It is said to be based on Sam Wilson (1766–1854), an Army meat inspector in New York State during the war of 1812, who stamped 'U.S.' on barrels of salt pork and beef for the troops. The term was certainly in use by 1813, often by New Englanders disenchanted with the ADMINISTRATION's handling of the war, and in 1816 *The Adventures of Uncle Sam* was published. He first appeared as a cartoon character in 1830, wearing a toga. He acquired his tall hat, goatee beard and swallowtail coat in LINCOLN'S time, reaching his apotheosis in the cartoons of Thomas Nast. His costume was based on that of the comic YANKEE character Maj. Jack Downing, created by the humorist Seba Smith. The WORLD WAR I 'I Want You' recruiting poster confirmed him as a national institution; CONGRESS recognised him as the national symbol in 1961.

Uncle Tom A black American too ready to accept the limitations set by white prejudice and domination. The name was taken from Harriet Beecher Stowe's 1852 novel *Uncle Tom's Cabin*, which provoked a wave of hatred against slavery; when Abraham LINCOLN met the author at the height of the CIVIL WAR, he greeted her with:

> So this is the little lady who made this big war!

uncommitted delegates Delegates sent to a US political party's nominating CONVENTION from a PRIMARY or a CAUCUS who are not committed to support any particular candidate, and in a tight vote can sway the outcome.

unconstitutional Not in accordance with the spirit of the US CONSTITUTION. The grounds on which the SUPREME COURT will hold that an action or an item of legislation cannot be permitted.

> The illegal we do immediately. The unconstitutional takes a little longer.
>
> HENRY KISSINGER

uncrowned King of Ireland *See* IRELAND.

undead The term coined in August 1994 by *US News and World Report*'s columnist John

Leo for disgraced politicians who seek rehabilitation; he cited the comeback attempt of former Washington DC Mayor Marion Barry, and attempts by WATERGATE's Gordon Liddy, the IRAN-CONTRA affair's Oliver North, the strategist Mike DEAVER and even Richard NIXON to regain respectability or even relaunch their careers. The term originated with Bram Stoker's DRACULA, the vampire who had not fully succumbed to death.

> Nixon had five Presidents at his funeral. If Nixon can do it, Himmler should be able to do it.
>
> JOHN LEO

undeclared candidate A politician campaigning hard for a particular office without actually admitting that he or she is in the race. A classic example was the US Presidential campaign of the billionaire H. Ross PEROT in the spring of 1992, before his sudden withdrawal; when he relaunched his campaign in September, it was as a declared candidate for the Presidency.

under. underclass Those individuals and families at the bottom of the social pile: poor, jobless, often in bad housing, lacking education and often from ethnic minorities, whose lot continues to worsen whatever welfare provision is made. They are ALIENATED from the established political order, and thus perceived as a threat to it.

underdog A candidate in an apparently losing position who gains popular sympathy, support and sometimes as a result even the votes needed to win.

Underground Railroad The escape routes set up from the 1790s to enable slaves from America's South to escape to the Northern states and on to Canada. Secrecy was essential, as any escaped slave who was recaptured was shipped back to his master without recourse to law. Fourteen Northern states were involved in the operation, which at its height c. 1840 was helping 500 to 1000 escapers each year. The term predated by at least two decades the first actual underground railway, which opened in London in 1863.

Underhill Report The document that first informed Labour's national executive in 1979 of the full extent of ENTRYISM being carried out by the MILITANT TENDENCY. It was prepared by Reg (later Lord) Underhill (1914–93), the party's national agent, and was pigeonholed by the NEC in February 1980. The report was eventually LEAKed to the press, but although Michael FOOT, leader from 1980 to 1983, described Militant as a 'pestilential nuisance', it was 1985 before the party, under Neil KINNOCK who had himself at first opposed action, dealt with the tendency head-on.

Underwood tariff One of the main accomplishments of Woodrow WILSON's first ADMINISTRATION, the first TARIFF passed by CONGRESS since the CIVIL WAR to lower appreciably the barriers erected to protect US manufacturers against foreign competition. Named after the conservative Rep. Oscar W. Underwood of Alabama, the tariff also imposed a graduated income tax to offset the anticipated loss of revenue.

UNESCO United Nations Educational, Scientific and Cultural Organisation. An autonomous agency of the UNITED NATIONS, based in Paris, with the remit of promoting learning worldwide, preserving the global heritage, and the exchange of ideas and information between nations. UNESCO owes its origins to the founding assembly of the UN in 1945, and began operating the next year with Julian Huxley as its director-general. It now has some 160 member states, though America and Britain both pulled out for a time from the mid-1980s in protest at what they saw as nepotism, bureaucracy and anti-Western propaganda.

ungovernable A nation, society or community whose organs of government have lost control, but which cannot yet be branded a FAILED STATE. Commentators used the term of both Britain and New York City in the 1970s, when successive ADMINISTRATIONS appeared powerless to confront problems of economic decline, squalor and failing public services, and in the UK trade union militancy and growing political extremism.

unicameral system A political structure in which the LEGISLATURE comprises a single House rather than two. From the Latin *unus*, one; *camera*, chamber.

unification *See* REUNIFICATION.

unified tax and benefit system A system in which individuals' liability to pay income tax and eligibility for welfare benefits are assessed in the same process and a single demand or payment is issued. It is supposed to be less bureaucratic than separate tax and benefit systems, with some people paying taxes and getting the money back from other agencies. Proposals to introduce it in Britain have been strongly resisted by civil servants; Gordon BROWN's system of tax credits for families and the elderly is a step toward it, though a separate MEANS TEST is still required.

unilateralism (1) The doctrine of the complete renunciation by Britain of all NUCLEAR WEAPONS, championed from the mid-1950s by the Campaign for Nuclear Disarmament (CND), most of the left of the LABOUR PARTY and more recently by the GREENS. It was adopted as official Labour policy briefly in 1960, against the wishes of the leadership (*see* FIGHT, FIGHT AND FIGHT AGAIN), and again in the early 1980s under the leadership of Michael FOOT, a founder of CND. After Labour's 1987 defeat Neil KINNOCK, himself a unilateralist, concluded that the policy was keeping Labour from power and won its abandonment. (2) The conviction that America must remain a free agent, outside the entanglement of foreign alliances, and has the right to take military action in pursuit of its foreign policy objectives whatever the views of its allies or the UNITED NATIONS (and its predecessor the LEAGUE OF NATIONS which the US refused to join). A cornerstone of ISOLATIONISM during the 1930s, it relied on the absence of such links since the infant state ended its treaty with France during the Revolutionary War. The doctrine was little heard of during the COLD WAR when America built up a global chain of anti-Communist alliances, but resurfaced with a vengeance as an article of NEO-CONSERVATIVE faith during the presidency of George W. BUSH. The term was most notably applied to Bush's determination to overthrow SADDAM HUSSEIN's regime in Iraq despite the failure of the UN to give its approval.

unincorporated area In US local administration, an urban area that has not become a municipality in its own right and therefore is run purely as part of a COUNTY.

Union, the (1) The states forming the United States of America, from the time of its inception. As the PHILADELPHIA CONVENTION struggled with the shape of the new nation, Benjamin FRANKLIN observed:

> That a Union is necessary, all are agreed. But when it comes to the form and nature of such a Union, their weak noddles are perfectly distracted.

Alexander HAMILTON described the original thirteen states as 'bound together in a strict and indissoluble union'. But the division between believers in a single nation and advocates of STATES' RIGHTS was there from the outset. It came into the open at a WHITE HOUSE banquet in 1830, when President Jackson gave the toast: 'Our Union – it must be preserved', and a shocked Vice President John C. Calhoun responded:

> The Union, next to our liberty, most dear. May we all remember that it can only be preserved by respecting the rights of the States and by distributing equally the benefits and burdens of the Union.

It was to defuse such tension that Daniel Webster delivered his celebrated LIBERTY AND UNION speech.

When the CONFEDERATE States SECEDED, it was natural that the North should fight the ensuing CIVIL WAR in the name of the Union, which Abraham LINCOLN declared 'the last, best hope of Earth'. In 1862 Lincoln wrote to Horace Greeley: 'My paramount object in this struggle is to save the Union . . . If I could save the Union without freeing any slave, I would do it; and if I could save it by freeing some and leaving others alone, I would also do that.' But Robert E. Lee retorted:

> A union that can only be maintained by swords and bayonets, and in which strife and civil war are to take the place of brotherly love and kindness, has no charm for me.

(2) The formal joining together of two nations to be governed as one. One example is the Union between Great Britain and NORTHERN IRELAND which survived the PARTITION of Ireland in 1921, and which is regarded as sacrosanct by the ULSTER UNIONISTS, the ORANGE movement and LOYALIST groups. Another is the Union between England and Scotland, enshrined in the 1707 ACT OF UNION. In contemporary politics only the SNP is opposed to continuance of the Union, but the CONSERVATIVE PARTY has positioned itself as being the most Unionist of the other parties, and thus the least supportive of DEVOLUTION. A further example is the union between Britain and France, offered by CHURCHILL in 1940 as German armies overran France; Marshal Pétain said of it:

> To make a union with Great Britain would be fusion with a corpse.

Union Jack Technically the Union Flag is the flag of the United Kingdom, and the Jack is the post from which it is flown. The flag comprises the cross of St George (for England), red on white; the cross of St Andrew (Scotland), white on blue (diagonal) (*see* SALTIRE); and the cross of St Patrick (Ireland), red on white (also diagonal), the crosses superimposed on each other. There is no cross to represent Wales, which at the time of the Unions of England with Scotland and Ireland was assumed to be synonymous with England. The same device appears as part of the flags of a number of nations including Australia and New Zealand, three Canadian provinces and the state of Hawaii. The flag in its present form dates from the 1801 Act of Union when the Irish Parliament was abolished and that land governed from WESTMINSTER; from 1606 until then the old 'Union Flag' bearing simply the crosses of St George and St Andrew had been flown. Only a trained observer can tell when the flag is being flown upside-down (the diagonal white stripes are a different width), but flag-waving politicians, notably the Rev. Ian PAISLEY, sometimes make the claim to embarrass the authorities. The flag of the EUROPEAN UNION, a circle of twelve gold stars on a dark blue background, is known as the ***Union Jacques***, after Jacques DELORS, who formally adopted it in 1986 when President of the Commission; the flag, the number of whose stars has not increased as the EU has expanded, was first used in 1955 by the COUNCIL OF EUROPE.

Union Nationale The conservative Francophone party which governed Quebec for most of the middle third of the 20th century. Founded by Maurice Duplessis from the remnants of the province's old Conservative party and reforming Liberals, it overthrew the corrupt Taschereau regime in 1936 but in office developed some of the same habits. Ousted when war broke out, the *Union Nationale* returned to power in 1946 and ruled for fourteen years, all but one of them under Duplessis. It won a third spell in office in 1966 when Daniel Johnson was elected on a virtually SEPARATIST programme; this moderated after Johnson died in 1968, but the party lost to the Liberals two years later.

Union Treaty The framework for the survival of the SOVIET UNION as a loose confederation, which Mikhail GORBACHEV was endeavouring to persuade the constituent republics to accept at the time of the coup against him in August 1991 and the collapse of the Union that autumn.

one big union for all the workers The slogan of the American Railroad Union, formed in 1894 by Eugene Debs (*see* CONVICT #2273). The union was immediately plunged into a strike in support of Pullman workers, and when 260,000 railroad workers stopped work federal troops were sent to Chicago, the strike's main centre. The strike degenerated into violence, with 34 strikers killed and troops called out in several states. Debs, who had opposed moves to promote a GENERAL STRIKE, was jailed for conspiracy and the men drifted back to work. One reason for the strike's failure was that despite its slogan, the union did not admit black workers; it was thus easy to recruit them as strikebreakers.

State of the Union The message which the PRESIDENT of the United States delivers to the CONGRESS at the start of each year. It is now a high point of the political calendar, but only since Woodrow WILSON has the President delivered it in person. George W. BUSH's 2003 message caused lasting controversy by citing British intelligence reports that SADDAM HUSSEIN was obtaining uranium from Niger in support of his assertion that military action against Iraq was needed because Saddam possessed and might use WEAPONS OF MASS DESTRUCTION. When Tony BLAIR came under fire after the IRAQ WAR for having made similar claims about WMD (*see* DODGY DOSSIER), the CIA disowned that passage of the speech, saying that the evidence of uranium shipments from Niger was suspect (*see also* PLAME LEAK). Blair stuck by the intelligence, and was backed by MI6 who had received it.

Union of Democratic Control (UDC) An *ad hoc* coalition of socialists, radicals and PACIFISTS formed in Britain in September 1914, just after the outbreak of WORLD WAR I. Its main aims were parliamentary control over foreign policy, a negotiated peace on reasonable terms to all, and more open diplomacy to break with the secret alliances and covenants that were widely blamed for the war. The UDC, whose founders included Ramsay MACDONALD, Bertrand Russell and Joseph Rowntree, were widely regarded as traitors and their meetings broken up by soldiers on leave. E. D. Morel, its secretary, was imprisoned and Russell fined for a pamphlet alleged to discourage recruiting. Much of the UDC platform was adopted by the LABOUR PARTY from 1917; it remained active until WORLD WAR II.

Unionist The full title of Britain's CONSERVATIVE PARTY has historically been the Conservative and Unionist Party. This reflects mainly the merger between Tories and Liberal supporters of the Union with Ireland in the late 19th century, but the Union with Scotland has since become a factor. (2) During America's CIVIL WAR, supporters of the North were known as Unionists.

UNITA (Port. National Union for the Total Independence of Angola). A GUERRILLA organisation headed by Dr Jonas Savimbi

(1934–2002) that was in the forefront of the struggle against colonial rule but, after Portugal's withdrawal in 1975, fought a civil war for a quarter of a century against the Marxist MPLA, which took power the following year. UNITA's initial support from the West and acceptance of South African backing discredited it in the eyes of many Africans, but Savimbi exuded personal CHARISMA and enjoyed strong regional support. UNITA refused to accept an agreement devised in Geneva in 1988 to end the conflict, but talks with the MPLA did bring an uneasy truce and elections in 1992. When the MPLA were declared the winners, UNITA having polled less than 40%, Savimbi refused to accept the result, and the war restarted with greater popular suffering than ever. The flouting of a ceasefire agreed in 1994 led the UNITED NATIONS to impose sanctions on UNITA in 1998, but the carnage continued until Savimbi was killed in battle in February 2002. On 4 April that year UNITA and the MPLA government signed an agreement under which the rebels re-formed themselves as a political party, with UNITA personnel eligible to join the Angolan army and police.

unitary authority In UK local government, an authority in which all powers not exercised over an area by central government are in the hands of a single elected body, e.g. not divided between a county and a district council. Examples include Scotland's single-tier system of authorities, and in England the metropolitan districts, plus unitary authorities such as Nottingham which have been re-created, reversing Peter Walker's wholesale reforms of 1973/4.

unite or die The challenge thrown down to a feuding CONSERVATIVE PARTY by its leader, Iain Duncan Smith (*see* IDS; QUIET MAN) at a press conference on 5 November 2002. Intended to quell speculation about his leadership after eight senior Tories defied a three-line WHIP and supported plans to allow gay and unmarried couples to adopt children, the event was widely seen as demonstrating Duncan Smith's lack of judgement and highlighting the rifts in the party. He told the WESTMINSTER media, and through them his party:

> My message is simple: unite or die.

When the party did unite a year later, it was to remove him.

Unité Radicale The far-right group banned by the French government in August 2002 after one of its members, Maxim Brunevic, tried to assassinate President CHIRAC at the BASTILLE Day parade in Paris.

united. United Kingdom The nation that took shape as the CROWN of England gained sway over Wales, Scotland and Ireland. It acquired its present form after the PARTITION of Ireland in 1922, now comprising England and Wales, Scotland (between them the island of GREAT BRITAIN) and NORTHERN IRELAND.

United Nations The world organisation founded at the close of WORLD WAR II, as the successor to the failed LEAGUE OF NATIONS, to prevent another world conflict and maintain peace, and to promote collective international action for the common good. It has its origins in the ATLANTIC CHARTER agreed by Franklin D. ROOSEVELT and CHURCHILL in 1941; the name 'United Nations' was coined by Roosevelt to cement the wartime alliance without the need to refer a treaty to CONGRESS. The organisation itself sprang from the 1944 DUMBARTON OAKS conference between America, Britain and the Soviet Union; its charter was drawn up at the SAN FRANCISCO CONFERENCE of May-June 1945, President TRUMAN declaring:

> We did much more than draft an international agreement among 50 nations. We set down on paper the only principles that will enable civilised human life to continue to survive on this globe.

The UN was inaugurated on 21 October 1945 with 51 founder-members; more than three times as many states now belong. It held its first formal session in London in January 1946; at its close SECRETARY-GENERAL Paul Henri Spaak (1899–1972) said: 'Our agenda is now exhausted. The Secretary-General is exhausted. All of you are exhausted. I find it comforting that, beginning with our very first day, we find ourselves in such complete agreement.' Temporarily housed at Lake Success, New York state, the UN moved into its skyscraper HQ in New York City in 1952. There have been frequent complaints from civic leaders about the anti-Americanism of many delegations, the activities of some of the diplomats attached to it, displays of opulence by representatives of supposedly destitute countries and the traffic gridlock caused by visiting VIPs, Mayer Ed Koch terming the UN 'a cesspool'. But it has stayed there ever since.

John F. KENNEDY termed the UN 'the protector of the small and weak, and a safety valve for the strong'. US Ambassador Henry

Cabot Lodge was blunter: 'This organisation is created to prevent you from going to hell. It is not going to take you to heaven.' And Dag Hammarskjold (1905–61), its greatest Secretary-General (though not liked by the Soviets, *see* TROIKA PLAN), wrote: 'It is not the Soviet Union or indeed any other big powers who need the United Nations for their protection. It is all the others.' The most controversial Secretary-General (though not during his tenure) was Austria's Kurt Waldheim, who after becoming his country's president turned out to have been a member of the NAZIS' elite *Waffen SS* (*see* ETHNIC CLEANSING).

The UN has had a stormy career. During the COLD WAR its efforts to create a civilised world were hampered by frequent Soviet use of the VETO. With the break-up of the British and other empires, it also became a cockpit for anti-Western and anti-colonialist propaganda by Communist countries and their clients in the developing world. This led Enoch POWELL to describe it as 'the very capital and the New Jerusalem of humbug', and South Africa's Prime Minister Henrik Verwoerd to declare: 'The grand adventure of nations has become a sordid scramble for the microphone – the new toy for the exhibitionist and agitator.' The cost of the organisation and the nepotism practised by some member governments prompted the Australian R. J. D. Turnbull to denounce it as 'a temple to Parkinson's Law, where inefficiency and extravagance worship at its shrine and hypocrisy at its altars'. Yet the US Ambassador Warren R. Austen had an answer to claims that the UN was just a talking-shop: 'It is better that aged diplomats get bored than for young men to die.'

The UN's efforts to enforce SANCTIONS during a number of conflicts and diplomatic standoffs have seldom had much success (*see* OIL FOR FOOD). But it developed from its early days a technique of PEACEKEEPING which has quietly prevented conflict in numerous flashpoints, though failure to give adequate orders could not prevent massacres in SREBRENICA and Rwanda despite the presence of UN troops. Through its numerous agencies it has also carried out important humanitarian work, for children (through UNICEF), for refugees through successive UN HIGH COMMISSIONERS FOR REFUGEES, and for the starving. The UN Secretary-General has become a moral authority, and a respected figure in efforts to resolve world crises. And, first in KOREA (after a Soviet walkout from the Security Council prevented the KREMLIN exercising its veto) and more recently in the 1991 GULF WAR, the authority of the UN has been carried onto the battlefield. However, the failure in 2003 of America and Britain to obtain similar backing in advance for the WAR ON IRAQ, largely because of French opposition, even though it was ostensibly a punitive action against SADDAM HUSSEIN for defying UN resolutions, has left lasting tensions. The UN's GENERAL ASSEMBLY, in which every member country has a seat and an equal voice, holds a highly publicised plenary session every autumn. Matters of urgency are dealt with by a 15-member SECURITY COUNCIL, five of whose seats are held by PERMANENT MEMBERS – America, Britain, China, France and Russia.

> Our strength and hope is the United Nations, and I see little merit in the impatience of those who would abandon this imperfect world instrument because they dislike our imperfect world.
>
> JOHN F. KENNEDY, State of the Union message, 29 January 1961

United States Code The entire body of law enacted by the US CONGRESS, minus repetitive language in Acts of amendment, published under 50 title headings in largely alphabetical order. Prepared by the Law Revision Counsel of the House of Representatives, new editions are published every six years, the most recent in January 2001. So far 23 of the titles have been revised and re-enacted.

United States of America The title given to Britain's rebelling colonies by the CONTINENTAL CONGRESS of 1775; it came into use on 7 June that year. The name was devised by Thomas Paine (1737–1809; *see* COMMON SENSE; RIGHTS OF MAN). The nation grew to be the world's most powerful, CHURCHILL stating: 'The United States is like a gigantic boiler. Once the fire is lighted under it, there is no limit to the power it can generate.' And Pierre TRUDEAU remarked: 'Living next to it is like sleeping with an elephant. No matter how friendly and even-tempered is the beast, one is affected by every twitch and grunt.' Yet American leaders have seen limits to it. John F. KENNEDY said in 1961: 'We must face the fact that the United States is neither omnipotent nor omniscient – that we are only 6 per cent of the population, that we cannot impose our will upon the other 94 per cent of mankind – that we cannot right every wrong or reverse every adversity – and that therefore there cannot be an American solution to every problem.' Jimmy CARTER shared that view, but some other presidents from Theodore ROOSEVELT to George W. BUSH might have disagreed. Yet whatever the limits to its power, George Bush Snr struck a chord when he described his country as

> The best and fairest and most decent nation on the face of the earth.

United We Stand The political movement arising from Ross PEROT's third-force challenge for the Presidency in 1992, which he hoped would perpetuate the fresh approach that brought him 19% of the popular vote. It did not fulfil all Perot's hopes, but did develop into the REFORM PARTY.

United we stand, divided we fall A much-used motto, taken from *The Liberty Song* (1768):

> Then join hand in hand, brave Americans all –
> By uniting we stand, by dividing we fall.
> JOHN DICKINSON (1732–1808)

unity is strength An even older expression of common purpose, much loved by trade unionists. It originated in Aesop's classical fable, *The Bundle of Sticks*; Aesop's words have been literally translated from the Greek as 'In Union there is strength', and 'Union gives strength'.

Uniting for Peace Resolution *See* PEACE.

Unknown Political Prisoner The subject of a UNITED NATIONS-backed competition after WORLD WAR II for a sculpture to commemorate all those imprisoned for their beliefs; it was won by the UK sculptor Reg Butler.

Unknown Prime Minister The epitaph bestowed by ASQUITH on Andrew BONAR LAW. At Law's funeral in Westminster Abbey after his death from cancer in 1923, Asquith observed: 'It is fitting that we should have buried the Unknown Prime Minister by the side of the Unknown Warrior' – the 'unknown soldier' from the dead of Flanders who had been 'buried among the Kings' three years before.

unknowns Factors of which decision-makers are unaware that can exercise a crucial influence on events. The concept was exploited to, and beyond, the full by the US Defence Secretary Donald Rumsfeld (*see also* ABU GHRAIB) during the WAR ON IRAQ in March/April 2003, his comments at one PENTAGON press briefing being turned into a poem by the author Hart Seely:

> As we know,
> There are known unknowns.
> There are things we know we know.
> We also know
> There are known unknowns.
> That is to say
> We know there are some things
> We do not know.
> But there are also unknown unknowns,
> The ones we don't know
> We don't know.

Unlock! The cry of police and attendants at the HOUSE OF COMMONS as they unlock the LOBBIES after a DIVISION.

unpaired A member of a legislature who does not possess a PAIR on the opposing side, and consequently cannot miss a vote without affecting the outcome.

unparliamentary A word or expression which is regarded as too profane, obscene, derogatory or uncouth to be uttered in a legislature. The use of such words will prompt the CHAIR to intervene, and refusal to WITHDRAW could lead to a member being ordered from the CHAMBER. At WESTMINSTER words regarded as unparliamentary include **blackguard**, **cad**, **corrupt**, **coward**, **criminal**, **hypocrite**, **jackass**, **murderer**, **rat** and **traitor**. The Labour MP Tam Dalyell, at the height of his campaign over the BELGRANO and WESTLAND, memorably tacked most of them together to brand Margaret THATCHER 'a **bounder**, a LIAR, a **deceiver**, a **cheat** and a **crook**'. In the Australian Federal Parliament almost anything goes; in the US Congress better conduct is generally observed (*see* FUCK), but Speaker Sam RAYBURN once observed:

> If they're from the Bible they're not unparliamentary.

unreconstructed Originally those Southern states who emerged from RECONSTRUCTION under the same conservative, racist rule that the exercise had been intended to abolish. Now a term for anyone, not necessarily a right-winger, whose views on an issue have remained unchanged despite the passage of time, the course of events, or the facts.

Unsafe At Any Speed The celebrated (and to Detroit notorious) book by Ralph NADER about the poor safety record of General Motors' Corvair and the company's indifference to it, which caused a sensation when published in 1965 and is widely credited with the birth of effective consumerism in America. GM reacted to the book by denying the charges and putting private investigators onto Nader, a young lawyer, and 50 of his friends and neighbours. This attempt to 'dig up dirt' backfired during Congressional hearings; GM was subsequently ordered to pay Nader $300,000 damages for harassment.

Up At WESTMINSTER, each HOUSE was traditionally said to be 'Up' when it adjourned for the night. Since c. 1998 the COMMONS has stopped using the word; its ANNUNICATOR now says: 'House adjourned'; but the LORDS' system still describes their House as 'Up'.

upper house The term used world-wide for the more senior, though not necessarily the more powerful, chamber of a BICAMERAL legislature: SENATEs throught the world, and the HOUSE OF LORDS. Traditionally, and still vestigially in Britain today, the upper house had aristocratic connotations. Upper houses tend to be less representative, the House of Lords being a mixture of hereditary and nominated members and some Senates like Canada's not being directly elected.

upset A surprise defeat for an INCUMBENT legislator or government that had appeared certain of re-election. The word is used in its sense of reversal rather than disappointment.

upstairs. taken upstairs The term used in the HOUSE OF COMMONS for consideration of a BILL in a STANDING COMMITTEE, rather than on the FLOOR of the House. Most such committees meet either in the large committee rooms off the COMMITTEE CORRIDOR on the first floor, or in smaller committee rooms on the second; occasionally nowadays they meet in PORTCULLIS HOUSE.

urban guerrilla *See* GUERRILLA.

urban renewal The programme begun in America as far back as 1949 to revitalise decaying inner city areas, generally by large-scale redevelopment. It has injected new life into many locations, though often – at least in its early days – at the cost of fragmenting strong black and other ethnic communities. Alternatives such as urban HOMESTEADING have been designed to achieve more at less cost through a more subtle approach, and the emphasis has increasingly moved to **regeneration** of neighbourhoods, wherever possible through the efforts of the community itself, backed by public funding.

Urgent Question *See* QUESTION.

Uruguay Round The round of global negotiations, begun at Punta del Este, Uruguay, in 1986, which concluded after much diplomatic BRINKMANSHIP in the agreement signed at Marrakesh on 12 April 1994 establishing a World Trade Organisation (WTO) to replace GATT. The greatest difficulty was over farm subsidies; America refused to sign until Europe slashed them by more than envisaged in the MCSHARRY PLAN, while stepping up its own support to the FARM BELT, and the CAIRNS GROUP pressed for fairer competition from the US and EC alike. EC and US negotiators finally settled their differences over oilseed production – at BLAIR HOUSE in December 1992 despite frenetic attempts by France and EU president Jacques DELORS to derail the process.

US(A) *See* UNITED STATES OF AMERICA.

US Code *See* UNITED STATES CODE.

US v Curtiss-Wright The SUPREME COURT ruling, handed down in 1936, that defines the President's constitutional position in foreign affairs. The case stemmed from a proclamation banning arms sales to some South American nations, issued by Franklin D. ROOSEVELT under an Act passed by CONGRESS in 1934. The Curtiss-Wright Corporation contended that the President had no constitutional authority to interfere in its business, but the Court ruled that in the international sphere, the President must enjoy 'a degree of discretion and freedom from statutory restriction which would not be admissible were domestic affairs alone involved'.

US v Nixon *See* NIXON.

USA Patriot Act The measure rushed through by the US CONGRESS in 46 days after the terrorist attacks of 9/11, which gave domestic law enforcement agencies unprecedented powers of investigation and surveillance, especially over foreigners. The name is an acronym of its full title: the Uniting and Strengthening America by Providing Appropriate Tools Required to Intercept and Obstruct Terrorism Act.

Ustase The Croatian nationalist movement which conducted a terrorist campaign against Austro-Hungarian rule in the 19th century, revived it against Serb domination of Yugoslavia in the 1920s, produced a NEO-FASCIST, PUPPET regime during WORLD WAR II and revived briefly but bloodily on the break-up of Yugoslavia from 1990. It was implicated in the murder of King Alexander I in 1934, and under the COLLABORATIONIST regime of Ante Pavelic from 1941 was accused of widespread atrocities by Serbs, PARTISANS and others. The Ustase conducted a sporadic terrorist campaign against TITO's unified Communist state in the 1960s and '70s, and was seen by Serbs as a sinister influence behind the breakaway Croatian regime of Franjo Tudjman, established in 1991 with German diplomatic support.

usual channels At WESTMINSTER, the means of communication between government and opposition BUSINESS MANAGERS and WHIPS, either directly or through staff of their respective offices. It is these contacts that defuse procedural emergencies, and determine the agenda for debate, the amount of TIME given to particular measures and the size and composition of committees.

> The most polluted of waterways.
>
> TONY BENN

Utopia (Gr. Nowhere) The name of the ideal and imaginary state devised by Sir Thomas More (1478–1535) to set out his theories of government, and now applied to any concept of a perfect or better world, with the inference that it is unachievable. In his book *Utopia* written in 1516, More described a crescent-shaped island including 54 cities of roughly 100,000 people each, sited at least 24 miles apart. The (patriarchal) family was to be the basic political and industrial unit, with an elected hierarchy of magistrates topped by a prince, chosen yearly from four names submitted by the people. Everyone would have to do two years of agricultural labour before taking up a trade passed down in the family; there would be no private property. A high premium would be placed on cultivation of the mind.

> A map of the world that does not include Utopia is not even worth glancing at.
>
> OSCAR WILDE

> The Socialist dream is no longer Utopia, but Queuetopia.
>
> WINSTON CHURCHILL on the post-war Labour government

> For other nations, Utopia is a blessed past never to be recovered; for Americans it is just beyond the horizon.
>
> HENRY KISSINGER

Utrecht, Treaty of The basis for Britain's continuing rule of Gibraltar, which continues to generate sporadic action by Spain. Under the Treaty, concluded in 1713, Britain and France acknowledged Spain's sovereignty over its territories in the New World in return for her surrender of Gibraltar, Naples and Sicily, Milan and her final influence in the Netherlands. In Spain's view the treaty was one-sided and exacted under duress.

UVF *See* ULSTER VOLUNTEERS.

V

V The symbol of victory to the WORLD WAR II Allies (especially to Britain and western European countries under German occupation). It was based on the Morse code letter V (. . . -), the opening bar of Beethoven's *Eroica* symphony), the French *'victoire'* and the Flemish *'vrijheid'* (freedom). The letter as a sign of defiance was originated by Victor de Laveleye in a BBC broadcast to Belgium on 14 January 1941, the four taps by 'Colonel Britton' (Douglas Ritchie) on 31 July 1941. As a sign of defiance in occupied territory, it was painted on walls and stuck as a paper cut-out on German soldiers' backs. It was popularised by CHURCHILL as a sign made by the third and index fingers of the right hand, the other two and thumb crossed over a palm facing outwards. The same sign used in reverse with an upward movement of the hand is a gesture of obscene contempt first used by English archers at Agincourt in 1415.

> The PM will give the V sign with two fingers in spite of the representations repeatedly made to him that this gesture has quite another significance.
>
> Sir JOHN COLVILLE, Churchill's private secretary, 1941

The symbol was subsequently taken over by the 1960s Peace Movement as its own, and known as the 'peace sign'.

Vacher's *Vacher's Quarterly* (until 2004 *Vacher's Political Companion*), a slim blue paperback published at WESTMINSTER which gives a complete list of MPs, PEERS, Parliamentary and senior government officials and members of the LOBBY. It now shares a publisher with the fatter but less frequently updated *Dod*. In recent years Vacher's has faced competition, notably from the pocket-edition ***Parliamentary Companion***.

value If you value it, vote for it. (*See* BRITAIN FORWARD, NOT BACK)

values The moral instincts that define a politician, party, programme, society or voter.

> It is not our affluence, or our plumbing, or our clogged freeways, that grip the imagination of others. Rather, it is the values upon which our system was built.
>
> Sen. WILLIAM FULBRIGHT (1905–95)

core values The essential ethics of a party's philosophy and programme.

Victorian values The term applied by Margaret THATCHER in 1982 to the virtues of thrift, industry, self-reliance, provision for the family and personal charity which she saw her government as embodying – 'the values when our country became great'.

van Buren, Martin *See* OLD KINDERHOOK.

Vance-Owen plan The constructive but doomed plan for peace in Bosnia prepared in 1993 by the former US Secretary of State Cyrus Vance (1917–2002) and former UK Foreign Secretary Dr David OWEN, as co-chairmen of the Geneva peace talks convened the year before as a result of the LONDON CONFERENCE on the crisis in former Yugoslavia. It was the fruit of extensive SHUTTLE DIPLOMACY and frequent visits to the war zone.

variable geometry The attribute of an organisation, specifically a grouping of nations, whose members would opt into or out of particular functions, e.g. political but not economic, participation or non-participation in joint defence or a single currency. The term originated in the 1960s to describe 'swing-wing' aircraft.

Vassall Tribunal The Commission of Inquiry under Lord Radcliffe set up in 1962 by Harold MACMILLAN's government after William Vassall, a homosexual Admiralty clerk, was found to have been passing secrets to Moscow for seven years. Two journalists, Reginald Foster and Brendan Mulholland, were jailed for refusing to disclose their sources to the Tribunal. It cleared Ministers – one, T. G. D. Galbraith, had resigned – of any impropriety. But the scandal left the government vulnerable when the PROFUMO AFFAIR broke the following year.

VAT Value Added Tax. An INDIRECT tax on most goods and services levied at differing rates (currently 17.5% in the UK – 5% for domestic energy) by all member states of the EU, largely replacing national sales taxes (PURCHASE TAX in Britain's case). Each trader has to remit the tax to the revenue authorities after deducting the amount of VAT they have themselves paid out; the tax is thus borne by consumers but collected by business. A percentage of receipts pass as a PRECEPT to Brussels to finance the Community budget (*see* OWN RESOURCES).

Veep Shorthand for the VICE PRESIDENT of the United States, especially in newspaper headlines. It was first applied to Alben Barkley, Vice President to Harry S TRUMAN from 1948–52.

vegetables A no doubt apocryphal story which is widely told about Margaret THATCHER, reflecting her domination of her CABINET. One day they were eating together when Mrs Thatcher was asked by the *maître h'hotel* what she would like. 'A steak, please,' she replied. 'And what about the vegetables?', Mrs Thatcher was asked. 'Oh, they'll all have steaks too.' When Mrs Thatcher was taxed about whether this was true by an American radio interviewer, she replied that she could not understand what was supposed to be funny about it.

velcroid A person at a political function who attaches themselves to the principal guest and can only be prised off with difficulty. This Americanism makes the comparison with Velcro, the fabric that will bond with whatever material it is pressed against it.

Velvet Revolution The peaceful uprising in Czechoslovakia at the close of 1989 that overthrew the hard-line Communist regime of Gustav Husák and installed a democracy under the presidency of Václav Havel, previously imprisoned as a DISSIDENT. It was triggered by a brutal police attack on protesting students – said to have been ordered by the KGB to prompt Husák's overthrow and let in more moderate Communists. Led by intellectuals, it was marked by mass rallies in Prague's WENCESLAS SQUARE at which the former Communist leader Alexander Dubček (*see* PRAGUE SPRING) re-emerged to adulation after 20 years as a NON-PERSON.

Venceremos! (Sp. We shall conquer!) A slogan of the defeated Republican forces in the SPANISH CIVIL WAR.

Venezuela boundary case The dispute which, since America's CIVIL WAR, brought the US and Britain closest to conflict. The disputed boundary between Venezuela and British Guiana (now Guyana) became an explosive issue when gold was discovered there in the 1800s. America volunteered in 1886, 1890 and 1894 to act as MEDIATOR, but both countries rejected the offer. Then, in 1895, Secretary of State Richard Olney sent London a series of blunt notes asserting America's interest under the MONROE DOCTRINE and arguing that only ARBITRATION could settle the issue. When the Foreign Secretary, Lord SALISBURY, rejected these arguments, President CLEVELAND sought Congressional approval to set up a commission to draw a boundary which the US would defend against Britain. This sparked an outbreak of war fever in America, but tempers on both sides of the Atlantic soon subsided; in 1897 Britain and Venezuela signed under US auspices a treaty providing for an international board of arbitration. It reported in 1899, upholding Britain's claim.

Vereeniging Treaty The treaty that ended the second BOER WAR, agreed at Vereeniging and signed in Pretoria on 31 May 1902. The South African republic and Orange Free State were placed under British military administration, but promised eventual self-government. A general AMNESTY was declared. The civil population disarmed and £3 million allocated for payment of war debts and to provide for economic reconstruction of the Transvaal. The issue of native voting rights was left until after the granting of self-government, which helped smooth the creation of a united South Africa in 1910 but opened the way for black and coloured South Africans to be eventually stripped of their rights through APARTHEID.

verification The process under which nations bound by ARMS CONTROL agreements determine whether their co-signatories are observing them. The extent to which agreements might be verifiable was long a sticking point in negotiations on arms limitation.

Veritas (Lat. Truth) The political party founded in February 2005 by the former Labour MP and TV chat show host Robert Kilroy-Silk after his resignation from UKIP. It proved a damp squib in that year's general election, Kelroy-Silk finishing fourth in the Erewash constituency with just 2957 votes. One of his former UKIP colleagues christened the party 'Vanitas' in reference to its leader's ego.

verkrampte (Afrik. inflexible) The hard-line faction in South Africa's NATIONAL PARTY that opposed any erosion of APARTHEID; many broke away in the early 1980s to join the *Herstigte National Partei* and in the late 1980s to form the fractionally less extreme Conservatives, The opposite of verkrampte is verligte (enlightened), a term used for the more liberal Afrikaners, a few of whom exist and have had less difficulty coming to terms with the end of white rule.

Versailles The splendid palace just to the west of Paris of the former kings of France, from Louis XIV onward, and briefly the nation's capital. It played host to the 1919 Peace Conference at which the 'Big Four' – President WILSON, Prime Ministers CLEMENCEAU and LLOYD GEORGE and the Italian Prime Minister, Orlando, imposed a crippling post-WORLD WAR I settlement on Germany at French insistence. The four took control of the conference after nine weeks of shambolic deadlock in Paris; Lloyd George wanted to HANG THE KAISER; Clemenceau wanted territory as well as REPARATIONS. The **Treaty of Versailles**, agreed on 28 July 1919 with no German representatives present and imposed under threat of resuming the war, was one of a series of separate treaties with each of the former adversaries. It included the Covenant of the LEAGUE OF NATIONS, but also draconian peace terms. Germany lost one-eighth of its European territory, including Alsace-Lorraine, the Rhineland (to be occupied by Allied troops) and the Saar, placed under League of Nations control for fifteen years pending a PLEBISCITE. Germany also lost Eupen and Malmédy to Belgium and North Schleswig to Denmark. Poland was given access to the Baltic along a POLISH CORRIDOR, at the head of which was Danzig (now Gdansk), declared a free city under League control. Austrian independence was guaranteed following the dismemberment of the Austro-Hungarian Empire, and Germany forfeited all her colonies, which became MANDATES of the League. The military terms were also harsh. Germany was to disarm, abolish military service, maintain an army of not more than 100,000 and reduce the size of her navy. In Article 231, the famous War Guilt clause, Germany had to accept responsibility for the war and pay reparations for damage caused to Allied nations. The treaty gave rise to German disaffection throughout the WEIMAR REPUBLIC, and was thus a major factor in the rise of HITLER and the NAZIS and – although Germany systematically violated it in the 1930s – in the eventual outbreak of WORLD WAR II. The refusal of the US SENATE to RATIFY the treaty because it would commit America to the LEAGUE OF NATIONS did not prevent it taking effect, but it did reflect an ISOLATIONISM that dominated US politics until PEARL HARBOR; Wilson's illness had prevented him completing his campaign for its adoption.

> Dare we reject it, and break the heart of the world? WOODROW WILSON

vesting day In Britain, during the process of NATIONALISATION, the date on which ownership of an industry formally passed from the private shareholders to the state. Conversely, during PRIVATISATION, it is the date on which a formerly state-owned undertaking becomes a commercial entity.

veto (Lat. I forbid) A vote which will, when cast, prevent a majority decision taking effect. (1) Exercised by the President of the United States in dealings with CONGRESS or by a state governor. A President can veto any BILL or joint resolution of Congress, except one to amend the CONSTITUTION. When Congress is in session, the President has ten days, excluding Sundays, to veto a Bill, or it becomes law without his signature. When a President vetoes a Bill, it is returned to the HOUSE where it originated, with reasons for the veto, in what is known as a **message veto**. Franklin D. ROOSEVELT, determined that Congress should not be 'uppity', vetoed a record 635 Bills; he was only OVERRIDDEN on nine. When President CLINTON vetoed the Budget Bill passed by the Republican Congress on 9 December 1995, he ostentatiously took out the pen with which Lyndon B. JOHNSON had signed the MEDICARE health programme 30 years previously, only to discover that it would not write until dipped repeatedly in a bottle of ink. (2) At the UNITED NATIONS, the last resort available to any of the five PERMANENT MEMBERS of the SECURITY COUNCIL; originally pressed for by America, vetoes were most frequently cast by the outnumbered Soviet Union during the COLD WAR, though America has used them regularly to block resolutions critical of ISRAEL and France was ready to use her veto in 2003 had the Security Council looked like approving US/British military action in Iraq. While regular Soviet use of the veto blocked decisive action by the UN and weakened it, the veto did also prevent one SUPERPOWER attacking the other with UN backing. (3) In the EU the veto can be exercised, in an ever-decreasing range of circumstances, by a member state in the European Council (*see* LUXEMBOURG COMPROMISE; Qualified MAJORITY).

Cat Bill veto *See* CAT.

double veto In the US CONGRESS, the ability of either HOUSE to frustrate the President's legislative plans.

legislative veto A device first adopted by CONGRESS in 1932 to give it control over REGULATORY AGENCIES without infringing the SEPARATION OF POWERS. This is achieved by writing into legislation establishing or empowering such agencies the right of Congress to pass resolutions forbidding them from following policies opposed by the LEGISLATURE; such resolutions are not subject to Presidential veto. Despite a SUPREME COURT ruling in 1983 (*INS v* Chadha) that once Congress delegates authority to an agency it cannot interfere in its actions, legislation containing such provisions continues to be passed. The tactic is also known as a **one-house veto**, as the provision can be inserted into a Bill by either the House or the Senate.

line-item veto The ability to veto individual items in a Bill or BUDGET, enjoyed by most state governors but historically denied to the President (though key staffers of the Congressional Budget office exercise it unofficially). President REAGAN repeatedly requested such authority in order to eliminate PORK without rejecting the entire Budget; President CLINTON finally obtained it in a Bill he signed in April 1996, in reaction to the previous winter's BUDGET SHUTDOWN, but in June 1998 the SUPREME COURT, by a 6–3 margin, ruled it UNCONSTITUTIONAL.

loyalist veto The term traditionally applied by Irish nationalists, and at times the Dublin government, for the capacity of the nearly two-thirds Protestant majority in NORTHERN IRELAND to thwart through the UK political system demands within the Roman Catholic community for an equal say and political links with the Republic. Since the GOOD FRIDAY AGREEMENT, it has been used by SINN FEIN to characterise the ability of hard-line Loyalist politicians to prevent devolved government operating in protest at the IRA's continuing failure to disarm and disband.

Old Veto *See* OLD.

pocket veto The procedure under which the President can prevent a BILL becoming law once CONGRESS has passed it by failing to sign it before Congress ADJOURNS.

scorched earth veto strategy The term used by Donald Regan, President REAGAN's CHIEF OF STAFF, for regaining the political initiative early in his second term by confronting CONGRESS on every issue.

vicar A representative, usually of God or the Church but also used in a political sense. Secretary of State Alexander Haig described himself as President REAGAN's vicar on foreign policy.

Vicar of Bray A politician skilled at adapting to sudden shifts in the prevailing ideology (*see* TRIMMER). The origin of the phrase is the anonymous 18th-century English rhyme with the chorus:

> And this is law that I'll maintain
> Until my dying day, Sir.
> That whatsoever King may reign
> Still I'll be the Vicar of Bray, Sir.

vicar on Earth A pejorative, taking the analogy of the Pope as Vicar of Christ, for the more accessible acolyte of a remote or lofty political figure, without strong views of their own. While Tony BENN was out of the COMMONS after losing his seat in the 1983 general election, Neil KINNOCK damaged the prospects of his left-wing stand-in Michael Meacher by describing him as 'Benn's vicar on Earth'.

Vice President Elected on the same TICKET as the PRESIDENT of the United States to serve as his deputy and succeed as chief executive in the event of his death or resignation; he also acts as PRESIDING OFFICER of the SENATE. His office is normally in the Old Executive Office Building (OLD EOB), though some Vice Presidents have worked from the WHITE HOUSE; since the 1970s the Naval Observatory off Massachusetts Avenue has been his official residence.

The vice presidency has come in for criticism ever since its inception. John ADAMS termed it 'the most insignificant office that ever the invention of man contrived', and said of his own tenure: 'I am vice president; in this I am nothing, but I am everything.' Theodore ROOSEVELT, who briefly held the office before being rescued by a Presidential assassination, scorned it as 'a stepping-stone to oblivion'. On becoming vice president, he observed: 'I have taken the veil.' Thomas R. Marshall (1854–1925), vice president to Woodrow WILSON, concluded that 'the vice president of the United States is like a man in a cataleptic state: he cannot speak; he cannot move; he suffers no pain; and yet he is perfectly conscious of everything that is going on around him'; ironically when Wilson was in precisely such a condition, Marshall was unable to act on his behalf because Wilson's wife Edith (*see* PRESIDENTRESS) pre-empted him. John Nance Garner (*see* CACTUS JACK) saw himself as 'the spare tire of the Constitution', but once declared: 'It's not worth a pitcher of warm piss; it doesn't amount to a hill of beans.' To Harry S TRUMAN the vice presidency was 'about as useful as a cow's fifth teat', and Lyndon B. JOHNSON remarked: 'All Hubert [Humphrey] needs over there is a girl to answer the phone and a pencil with an eraser in it'; Humphrey, under fire because of Johnson's VIETNAM policy, said; 'The President has not made me his slave and I am not his humble servant.' Ronald REAGAN never was vice president; not surprisingly as he once said: 'There is no circumstance whatsoever under which I would accept that spot. Even if they tied and gagged me, I would find a way to signal by wiggling my ears.' But Dan QUAYLE inevitably saw it in a better light: 'I used to be a Batman fan until I had this job. Now all of a sudden Robin looks good.'

Commentators and political scientists have had a more sober view of a job whose holder is 'a heartbeat away from the PRESIDENCY'. A 20th Century Fund report described the vice president as 'the presumptive front-runner for his party's nomination', though no vice president between Martin van Buren (*see* OLD KINDERHOOK) and George BUSH Snr succeeded to the WHITE HOUSE except by a presidential death or resignation. Bill Vaughan said the office was 'the last cookie in the plate. Everyone insists he won't take it, but somebody always does', while Sol Barzman observed:

> It was the cynical attitude of the politicians, and not the office itself, that gave us the near-disasters we have stoically endured in the vice presidential chair.

viceroy A ruler, 'vice-king', acting with royal authority in a territory overseas. Under the British EMPIRE, ultimate power in India was vested in a viceroy responsible to the CROWN; Ireland for a time also had a viceroy, but his role was more limited. The GOVERNOR-GENERAL of a DOMINION is technically a viceroy.

Vichy (France) The half of the country not occupied by AXIS forces after the fall of France in 1940, and the regime that governed it from the spa town of Vichy, in the central DÉPARTEMENT of Allier, under the COLLABORATIONIST Marshal Pétain. The Vichy regime was later vilified for co-operation with NAZI atrocities and its key public figures – **Men of Vichy** – were put on trial. But at the time it enjoyed broad public support, and its colonial troops put up strong resistance to the FREE FRENCH. *See also* TRAVAIL, FAMILLE, PATRIE.

Vichy mentality Over-keenness by an organ of a state or a political party to accept defeat. It was used of the UK Foreign Office by the Labour MP Brian Sedgemore in his 1977 MINORITY REPORT to the Select Committee on the CIVIL SERVICE.

Victoria Tower The crowning glory of Sir Charles Barry's Palace of WESTMINSTER, at 336ft taller than the clock tower of BIG BEN and topped by a 76ft flagpole with a UNION JACK the size of a tennis court. Constructed over a ceremonial arch ready for Queen Victoria to pass through in 1852, its interior was left incomplete because of the weight of the structure. From 1959 it was completely reconstructed after being found in imminent danger of collapse; it now houses historic documents.

victory Political success depends on winning struggles as well as elections; Richard NIXON observed in *Six Crises* (1962) that 'in politics, victory is never total'. However, electoral victories are the most obvious and public, and the winners have at times had surprising comments to make. Guy Barnett, on unexpectedly winning the South Dorset BY-ELECTION for Labour in 1963, declared: 'Frankly, I'm amazed.' And the Liberal Bill Pitt, victor at Croydon North-West in 1981, exclaimed: 'Mind my suit!' when sprayed with champagne.

> Having lost a close one eight years ago and having won a close one this year, I can say this – winning's a lot more fun.
>
> RICHARD NIXON, New York City, 1968

victory at all costs Winston CHURCHILL's first speech in the HOUSE OF COMMONS as Prime Minister, on 13 May 1940, included the passage:

> You ask: 'What is our aim?' I answer in one word: 'Victory.' Victory at all costs, victory in spite of all terror, victory no matter how hard or long the road may be: for without victory there is no survival.

victory has a thousand fathers, but defeat is an orphan John F. KENNEDY's rueful comment after the fiasco of the BAY OF

PIGS, for which he shouldered responsibility. It was not original, having been used with 'a hundred fathers' by Mussolini's Foreign Minister Count Galeazzo Ciano in 1942.

victory of the cradle The French-Canadian nationalist dream up to the late 19th century of taking control of the country through a higher birthrate than that of Anglophones.

Victory Special The campaign train of Thomas E. DEWEY in the 1948 US Presidential election.

to the victor the spoils *See* SPOILS SYSTEM.

video feed In the US CONGRESS from the 1980s, a means used by members of both parties to maximise their exposure to the voters by recording their own reactions to major events and beaming them direct to hometown and state television stations, bypassing the networks.

Vienna Convention The international agreement concluded in 1961 under which nations undertake to respect the rights, privileges and IMMUNITIES of each other's diplomats and embassies.

Viet Cong (Short for *Viet Nam Cong Sam*, Vietnamese Communists) The Communist GUERRILLA force in South Vietnam which fought government, US, Australian and other forces from 1957 to 1975, ultimately bringing about union with the North. The Viet Cong was formed from some 10,000 VIET MINH insurgents who stayed behind after the GENEVA AGREEMENT of 1954 under which the French withdrew and the country was partitioned. Its political wing was the National Liberation front, formed in 1960.

Viet Minh The Communist and nationalist GUERRILLA movement under Ho Chi Minh, formed in 1941, which resisted Japanese occupation of Indochina during WORLD WAR II and forced the French to leave after several years of insurgency – masterminded, like the VIETNAM WAR, by General Vo Nguyen Giap – culminated in victory at DIEN BIEN PHU. It became the government of North Vietnam, and three years later began military support for the VIET CONG.

Vietnam War America's most traumatic conflict since the CIVIL WAR, with repercussions that linger to this day. US troops were deployed in South Vietnam from 1961 to 1974, first as 'advisers' and then in combat strength of up to 544,000 (1969) in an ultimately vain attempt to prevent the VIET CONG and North Vietnamese forces taking control of South Vietnam. Over 58,000 US personnel were killed in combat and 365,000 wounded. The losses were borne with none of the stoicism shown by the North Vietnamese, whose losses were far heavier. The war, though backed by the Silent MAJORITY, prompted widespread and passionate opposition at home (*see* ANTI-WAR MOVEMENT), led to world-wide student riots and crystallised in Sen. Eugene McCarthy's challenge for the Democratic Presidential nomination in 1968 and Lyndon B. JOHNSON's decision not to seek re-election (*see* I SHALL NOT SEEK, AND I WILL NOT ACCEPT). The war spilled over into Laos, Cambodia and North Vietnam and was supposedly ended by the PARIS PEACE AGREEMENT of 1973, but South Vietnam had always been a frail political entity and in 1975, after US troops had been withdrawn, Saigon finally fell to Viet Cong and North Vietnamese forces.

The US build-up was almost indiscernible, with Presidents insisting America was not fighting the war for its client. John F. KENNEDY said: 'We can help them, we can give them equipment, we can send our men out there as advisers, but they have to win it, the people of Vietnam, against the Communists.' And President Johnson declared: 'We are not about to send American boys nine or ten thousand miles away from home to do what Asian boys ought to be doing for themselves.' But when the crunch came, Johnson declared: 'Just like the Alamo, somebody damn well needed to go to their aid. Well, by God, I'm going to Vietnam's aid.' His argument was that 'if America's commitment is dishonoured in Vietnam, it is dishonoured in 40 other alliances we have made', and that 'if we quit Vietnam, tomorrow we'll be fighting in Hawaii, and next week we'll have to fight in San Francisco' (*see* DOMINO THEORY). Johnson was not only criticised by the DOVES; in 1965 Ronald REAGAN said: 'We should declare war on North Vietnam. We should pave the whole country, put parking stripes on it and still be home for Christmas.' When it was over, Reagan said US forces had been 'denied permission to win'. Former President EISENHOWER also felt fatal half-measures were being undertaken: 'I believe when you get in a war [you] get everything you need and win it.' Later in the build-up, IKE said: 'With 450,000 troops now in Vietnam, it is time that Congress decided whether or not . . . a state of war now exists with North Vietnam'.

Johnson was not alone, however, in his confidence that American might and values would prevail. Arthur Goldberg said: 'We are confident that we can get the enemy to mend his ways,' and before his election to the Presidency Richard NIXON insisted: 'There is no substitute for victory in South Vietnam.' During his 1968 campaign he declared: 'Never has so much military, economic and diplomatic power been used as ineffectively as in Vietnam.' Once elected he told US troops in the field: 'Out here in this dreary, difficult war, I think history will record that this may have been one of America's finest hours, because we took on a difficult task and we succeeded.' And in 1970 he said: 'I would rather be a one-term President and do what is right, than a two-term President at the cost of seeing America become a second-rate power and see this nation accept the first defeat in its proud 190-year history.' But by the next year Nixon was ruminating: 'I seriously doubt if we will ever have another war. This is probably the very last one.' With the war almost over, in 1975, Gerald FORD declared: 'The Communist leaders in Moscow, Peking or Hanoi must fully understand that the United States considers the freedom of South Vietnam vital to our interests.' But Australia's Prime Minister John Gorton was more realistic: 'I don't think we will have achieved our objectives, but it was fair enough for us to have attempted them.' Throughout the war American leaders realised they were vulnerable on the home front. Nixon declared: 'North Vietnam cannot defeat or humiliate the United States. Only Americans can do that.' Dean Rusk, Johnson's Secretary of State, once asked reporters: 'Which side are you on?' And Vice President Spiro AGNEW characteristically observed: 'A spirit of national masochism prevails, encouraged by an effete corps of impudent snobs who characterise themselves as intellectuals.' The opponents used moral, legal and political arguments against the war. To Dean Acheson it was 'worse than immoral – a mistake'. Sen. William Fulbright asserted that 'the United States is succumbing to the arrogance of power'. And one of the leading anti-war campaigners, the child psychologist Dr Benjamin Spock, maintained: 'To win in Vietnam we have to exterminate a nation.' An emotional Sen. George McGovern told the Senate: 'It doesn't take any courage at all for a Congressman or a Senator or a President to wrap himself in our flag and say we're staying in Vietnam. Because it isn't our blood that's being shed.' At the World Council of Churches, Eugene Carson Blake insisted: 'We cannot remain silent on Vietnam. We should remember that whatever victory there may be possible, it will have a racial stigma . . . it will always be the case of a predominantly white power killing an Asian nation.' And Lieut. John F. KERRY, spokesman for Vietnam Vets Against the War, termed it 'the war the soldiers tried to stop'. *See* CHICAGO CONVENTION; DRAFT DODGING; GROSVENOR SQUARE DEMONSTRATION; GULF OF TONKIN RESOLUTION; KENT STATE; MY LAI MASSACRE; PENTAGON PAPERS; TET OFFENSIVE.

> Vietnam was lost in the living rooms of America, not on the battlefields of Vietnam.
>
> MARSHALL McLUHAN on the impact of television coverage

> The last crusade. CHESTER COOPER

Vietnamisation The policy adopted by President JOHNSON in 1968, and followed by his successor, of gradually removing US forces from Vietnam and transferring responsibility for prosecuting the war to the South Vietnamese.

Vietnam syndrome The impact of the loss of Vietnam on the US political community, reflected in the short term in a lack of confidence about America's role in the world and a reluctance to engage in risky foreign commitments which continued until 9/11.

> By God, we've kicked the Vietnam syndrome once and for all. GEORGE BUSH Snr

Vietnam Vets A vocal, largely unorganised lobby of disillusioned and often disabled men who had served in Vietnam and either took exception to the way the war was being conducted – like John KERRY – or found America ungrateful and eager to forget them. They were partly assuaged by Ronald REAGAN's dedication in 1982 of the **Vietnam Memorial** in Washington DC, a sombre wall designed by 21-year-old Maya Wing Lin bearing the names of the dead which has become a focal point for national grieving.

vigil A silent and static DEMONSTRATION with an implied note of anguish and prayer as well as protest, often continuing overnight or for several days. Religious in origin, and often directed against an impending execution or the detention of a hostage whose life is in danger (or in the past a NUCLEAR test or APARTHEID), a vigil will be held either in a church, a city centre or a location selected to embarrass those demonstrated against.

violence A frequently inevitable adjunct of politics, regarded by some of the most committed as an acceptable or even desirable means to an end, and by a few extremist groups as an end in itself (*see* GUERRILLA; INSURGENT; REVOLUTION). To the BLACK POWER activist H. 'Rap' Brown, 'Violence is as American as cherry pie'. The former Zambian President Kenneth Kaunda observed that 'the power which establishes a state is violence, the power which maintains it is violence, the power which eventually overthrows it is violence'; Kaunda ironically became one of the very few giants of post-independence Africa to accept defeat in a democratic election. As America's PROTEST MOVEMENT reached its height in 1970 and the threat of INNER CITY riots lingered, the liberal Justice William O. Douglas wrote:

> Violence has no constitutional sanction, and every government from the beginning has moved against it. But where grievances pile high and most of the elected spokesmen represent the Establishment, violence may be the only effective response.

But at Drogheda in 1979 Pope John Paul II appealed to the IRA and other TERRORISTS in NORTHERN IRELAND:

> Violence is a lie, for it goes against the truth of our faith, the truth of humanity. Violence is against humanity, for it destroys the very fabric of society. On my knees I beg you to turn away from the paths of violence.

even if it means violence The phrase used by Professor Harold Laski (1893–1950), chairman of Britain's LABOUR PARTY, which brought about his eclipse as a political force. Laski uttered the words in an election speech at Newark in 1945; it was in the context of the party's determination to introduce socialism. The *Daily Express* printed a scathing editorial and Laski sued for libel; after an erratic performance in the witness box, Laski lost his case and had to pay the *Express* £13,000 in costs. *See also* A period of SILENCE ON YOUR PART WOULD BE WELCOME; THANK YOU FOR YOUR LETTER.

Virginia Plan The blueprint for the US CONSTITUTION reflecting the ideas of James MADISON, which Governor Edmund Randolph of Virginia presented to the PHILADELPHIA CONVENTION in 1787.

virgins A WESTMINSTER term for incoming MPs who have never served in Parliament before. *Compare* RETREADS.

Viscount In the British system of nobility, a hereditary PEER, senior to a BARON but junior to an EARL. While very few hereditary peerages have been created since the 1960s, Margaret THATCHER did recommend them for Speaker George Thomas (Viscount TONYPANDY), and WILLIE Whitelaw; neither had male heirs, so the title died with them.

Visegrad Four The group comprising the Czech Republic, Hungary, Poland and Slovakia which after the fall of Communism promoted the development of jointly-shared values and contact with their Western European neighbours as a step toward their entry into the EUROPEAN UNION. It has its origins in a meeting in Visegrad, northern Hungary, on 15 February 1991 between József Antall, President of Hungary, Lech Walesa, President of Poland, and Václav Havel, President of Czechoslovakia, at which the three signed a declaration of close co-operation toward European integration. The original **Visegrad Three** became four when the Czech Republic and Slovakia separated in 1993; they achieved their goal when all four countries joined the EU on 1 May 2004.

vision. the vision thing George BUSH Snr's description of his world view, when challenged in May 1988 by journalists who claimed he did not have one. Bush attempted – with limited success given his command of the English language – to articulate this vision during the otherwise successful Presidential campaign that followed.

Vlaams Blok (Flemish. Flemish bloc) The most successful in recent times of the RACIST parties that draw a degree of support from Belgium's Flemish community; this one's career was cut short in November 2004 when the High Court in Brussels banned it. The *Blok*'s 19% share of the vote in northern Belgium in national elections in May 2003 had alarmed the political ESTABLISHMENT and CIVIL LIBERTIES groups. After the ban, it immediately re-formed as **Vlaams Belang** (Flemish interest).

volatility The readiness of sections of the electorate repeatedly to switch from one party to another instead of showing consistency. Volatility shows a contrast with traditional voting patterns, based on party loyalty with a fairly small number of SWING VOTERS.

Volcker Commission The National Commission on the Public Service chaired by Paul Volcker (1927–), former Chairman of the US FEDERAL RESERVE, which in 1989 issued a report deploring the low calibre, poor pay and low morale of federal employees. In 2004 Volcker chaired a further commission into abuses of the United Nations' OIL FOR FOOD programme with Iraq.

Völkischer Beobachter (Ger. Observer of the Race) The official daily newspaper of the NAZI party, published in Berlin prior to and throughout the THIRD REICH.

Volstead Act The Act passed by the US Congress in 1919 over the VETO of President WILSON which introduced PROHIBITION by implementing the 18th Amendment to the Constitution, prohibiting the manufacture, transportation and sale of all alcoholic beverages. Unlike the amendment, it also banned their purchase and consumption, and defined an alcoholic drink as containing more than 0.5% of alcohol by volume. Its promoter was Rep. Andrew Volstead (1860–1947) of Minnesota. Prohibition was abolished by the 21st Amendment in 1933, but Franklin D. ROOSEVELT amended the Act after his INAUGURATION two years earlier to allow production of beer and light wine.

voluntary party The term used by British Conservatives for the party in the country, specifically the volunteers in the constituencies who raise money, get supporters to the polls and, since 1997, elect the party leader.

vote, to To reach a decision by voting, or to cast one's vote when a decision is taken or a choice made.

the vote (1) The point of decision. (2) The instrument available to each person in a democracy for choosing their rulers or taking collective decisions, or the right to exercise that choice by participating in elections.

> The right of voting for representatives is the primary right by which other rights are protected. To take away this right is to reduce a man to slavery. THOMAS PAINE

> The vote is the most powerful instrument ever devised by man for breaking down injustice and destroying the terrible walls that imprison men because they are different from other men. LYNDON B. JOHNSON

Thoreau reckoned that 'all voting is a sort of gaming, like checkers or backgammon, with a slight moral tinge to it'; H. L. Mencken that 'voting is simply a way of determining which side is the stronger without putting it to the test of fighting.' Richard NIXON took the high ground with critics of the system, saying: 'One vote is worth a hundred obscene slogans.' But Ronald REAGAN was more down to earth: 'I had an uncle who was a Democrat in Chicago. He received a silver cup from the party for never having missed voting in 15 elections. He'd been dead for 14 of them.' On voting in the US Congress, John F. KENNEDY said: ''You can milk a cow the wrong way and still be a farmer, but vote the wrong way on a water tower and you're in trouble.' In Britain, G. D. H. Cole reckoned: 'Voting is merely a handy device; it is not to be confused with democracy, which is a mental and moral relation of man to man.' And the playwright Tom Stoppard claimed: 'It's not the voting that's democracy, it's the counting' – a refrain taken up by US Democrats after the 2000 election and their 537-vote defeat in Florida. (3) At WESTMINSTER, the bundle of blue and white papers circulated to MPs each morning listing the proceedings of the previous day, giving the ORDER PAPER for the day ahead and questions, motions and debates pending beyond that.

Vote early and vote often A slogan attributed to Irish ward activists in their home country and – by 1858 – in American MACHINE POLITICS. It was first quoted by Sen. William P. Miles.

Vote for me – get one free A tongue-in-cheek slogan taken up by Bill CLINTON in his successful 1992 campaign for the Presidency, capitalising on the political strengths of his wife Hillary who he intended should be more than a conventional FIRST LADY. Though her drive to get HEALTH SECURITY through the CONGRESS was to fail and efforts by opponents to smear her over the Vince FOSTER SUICIDE, TRAVELGATE and WHITEWATER had some success, her dignity during ZIPPERGATE earned her respect and she would be elected to the SENATE in 2002. Clinton's slogan was also a way of stressing the enduring nature of his marriage in the face of persistent BIMBO ERUPTIONS.

vote of confidence Not quite the same as a NO-CONFIDENCE motion: a vote of support sought by an ADMINISTRATION at a time of crisis, generally after a defeat on a particular policy or item of legislation. If defeated, that administration is obliged to resign or, in Britain, submit to an election.

Vote Office At WESTMINSTER, the office at the HOUSE OF COMMONS from which members obtain the VOTE, HANSARD and other Parliamentary papers. When the House is sitting the documents are issued from a window onto the Members' LOBBY, at other times from a basement room two floors below.

vote of thanks At the end of a meeting or dinner of a political (or non-political) group, a motion put by a member of the audience to show appreciation of the guest speaker.
Vote, Vote, Vote for Nigel Barton A humorous 1960s BBC television drama by Denis Potter which laid bare the workings of Britain's constituency party oprganisations.
Votes for Women The slogan of the SUFFRAGETTES.
alternative vote The system of PROPORTIONAL REPRESENTATION in which electors cast a second vote (and sometimes more) which comes into play if their preferred candidate finishes at the bottom of the poll; the second-preference votes are then distributed among other candidates who are eliminated until there is a winner.
block vote In Britain, the system under which trade unions dominate decision-making in the LABOUR PARTY by casting millions of votes which may or may not reflect the view of their members; its impact has been reduced, but not eliminated, by OMOV.
bullet vote *See* BULLET.
card vote In many political and trade union organisations, a BALLOT that is held on request from the floor if a SHOW OF HANDS is too close to call or the issue is important enough to require a recorded tally.
cemetery vote *See* CEMETERY.
crossover vote In US Presidential PRIMARIES, a vote cast by a registered supporter of one party for a candidate for the other party's nomination. Such votes are sometimes cast by the genuinely enthused, and sometimes in an effort to make sure the other party's weakest candidate is nominated.
cuckoo vote Finding someone registered to vote at an address who does not live there, as with the cuckoo laying its eggs in another bird's nest. The practice came to the media's attention in the late 1990s when used by some over-enthusiastic Asian members of Britain's LABOUR PARTY to recruit bogus party members to back a particular candidate in party elections.
deferred vote In the US HOUSE OF REPRESENTATIVES, votes held back to the end of the day, or a two-day period, by the SPEAKER to be decided in a batch before further business is begun.
Don't vote – it only encourages them A 1960s ANARCHIST and PROTEST slogan.
flapper vote The electoral impact in Britain of women aged 21–29, enfranchised under the Equal Franchise Act in time for the 1929 general election, and known as 'flappers' from the hairstyle of the day – a pigtail that 'flapped' against a girl's back.
informal vote In Australia, a vote on a ballot paper disallowed because it does not follow the instructions for preferential voting.
payroll vote *See* PAYROLL.
one man, one vote The basis of democracy ('man' being taken to include 'woman). In 1780 John Cartwright wrote: 'One man shall have one vote'. It has since 1964 been the US SUPREME COURT's basis for REAPPORTIONMENT of Congressional seats, and was also the key British demand which Ian Smith refused to countenance in Rhodesia before and after UDI.
one member, one vote *See* OMOV.
personal vote The extra support a candidate (usually an INCUMBENT) receives from voters who do not share their politics but support them as an individual because of their principles or, more usually, their record of service to the community.
popular vote The tally of votes that each candidate receives in a US Presidential election, by contrast with the votes delivered by the ELECTORAL COLLEGE. As in 'Al Gore got the larger popular vote in 2000, but George W. BUSH carried the Electoral College'.
postal vote A ballot cast by post in advance of the election, traditionally available to the chronically sick and those away on business but now more freely available in many countries. As an experiment, several local and European elections and regional referenda in England were conducted entirely by post in 2003/04; they boosted TURNOUT but there were widespread allegations of malpractice, particularly in some Asian communities where local councillors obtained handfuls of ballot papers from voters to fill in. The worst of these abuses were eventually punished by an ELECTION COURT, and after the 2005 general election there were moves to limit the scope for abuse.
Present vote A vote cast in the US HOUSE OF REPRESENTATIVES to register an ABSTENTION.
protest vote Votes cast individually or collectively for one candidate or party as a protest against another. In Britain, they have frequently been blamed by ousted parties for BY-ELECTION upsets, traditionally by the LIBERALS; in recent times SINGLE-ISSUE candidates, notably on local health issues, have benefited. In US elections, the protest votes for Ralph NADER and Ross PEROT have helped swing the outcome, without the protest candidate benefiting.
reconsider a vote In the US CONGRESS, a

device for suspending action on an issue which has just been voted on; reconsideration cannot be called for by a member who was on the losing side in the original vote. Reconsideration is often moved as a matter of course, and then TABLED.

recorded vote A vote in which the choice made by those being balloted is formally noted for the public record. The US CONSTITUTION requires a recorded vote if CONGRESS decides to OVERRIDE a Presidential VETO.

roll-call vote In the US CONGRESS, a vote in which every member must answer 'Yea', 'Nay', or 'PRESENT'. In the House of Representatives, a roll-call vote must be taken if one-fifth of those present rise to demand it.

Service vote (1) The element in the electorate made up of serving military personnel; specifically the overwhelmingly pro-Labour vote cast by British servicemen in 1945 which sealed Clement ATTLEE's landslide victory. (2) The vote available to a man or woman serving in the armed forces, which may be cast in their home electoral district. In Britain such voters were marked with an 'S' on the electoral register until the mid-1980s, when the mark was removed lest it make them targets for terrorists.

single transferable vote A form of PROPORTIONAL REPRESENTATION involving multi-member constituencies with the voter listing candidates in order of preference. Candidates receiving a set 'quota' are automatically elected, and any votes above this transferred to the voter's second choice.

standing vote A form of voting used in both HOUSES of the US CONGRESS, where members for and against a proposition stand and are counted, but the individual votes are not recorded.

supplementary vote A variant of PROPORTIONAL REPRESENTATION, tentatively recommended by the PLANT COMMISSION, under which voters take part in an essentially FIRST PAST THE POST election but list second preferences which are taken into account only if no candidate gains an outright majority.

sympathy vote Votes cast for a candidate out of sympathy rather than through party or personal support, e.g. because of the death of a popular predecessor or some tragedy involving themselves.

teller vote The unrecorded VOICE VOTES, especially on amendments, which were taken in the HOUSE OF REPRESENTATIVES until 1970; reformers believe their replacement by recorded votes has discouraged PORK BARREL projects because Congressmen can no longer support them anonymously.

Twilight Zone vote A vote at a US party CONVENTION that could fall just short enough of a target to enable a candidacy to be derailed by procedural challenges to delegates. It originated in the vote between George McGovern and Hubert HUMPHREY at the 1972 Democratic convention.

voice vote A WASHINGTON term for a vote in which the Yeas and Nays each shout out their vote in chorus, with the Chair determining which were the more vocal. The same occurs in the HOUSE OF COMMONS, but no name is given to it.

voter An actual or potential participant in the elective process. The defeated Rep. Morris Udall declared: 'The voters have spoken – the bastards!' Bernard Epton, a Chicago mayoral candidate, said: 'They are just slime.' With the cynicism of office, Richard NIXON observed: 'Voters quickly forget what a man says'; also saying: 'It doesn't matter whether they knock down the wall when they vote for you or hold their noses. It all counts just the same.' But Hedrick Smith had the last word: 'The voters do not want their leader to appear too much smarter than they are.' Generally they succeed.

voter ID NEW LABOUR-speak for CANVASSING, covering contact by telephone to identify supporters as well as the traditional method of knocking on doors.

absent voter A qualified voter who cannot be present to vote and is permitted to do so by post or by PROXY.

first-time voter A UK term for a young person eligible to vote for the first time after reaching the age of eighteen. Parties make direct appeals to them at election times, sometimes juxtaposing a first-time voter with a person in their 90s who has always supported the party and will vote for it again; media cynics refer to the latter as 'last-time voters'.

floating voter *See* FLOAT.

League of Women Voters *See* LEAGUE.

Motor-Voter Act *See* MOTOR.

voting. voting intentions The basic information collected by OPINION POLLS, recording which party or candidate an interviewee would support if an election were held that day.

voting machine A device used in many American jurisdictions, particularly in elections with lengthy party TICKETS or large numbers of INITIATIVES on the ballot. Some – such as those whose failure to punch out CHADS cleanly caused such havoc in Florida during the 2000 Presidential election – use punch cards; increasingly computerised systems and the use of touch-screens are taking over.

voting record A tabulation of elected representatives' voting performance on key issues, often kept by pressure groups (*see* ADA RATING).

Voting Rights Act 1965 One of a series of such Acts, the cornerstone of the CIVIL RIGHTS programme championed by Lyndon B. JOHNSON, who said it would 'strike away the last major shackle' of the Negro's 'ancient bonds'. Its main provision was a ban on POLL TAXES.

bloc voting In a legislature, when groups from different parties with a common interest join together to push through programmes or legislation that they support, regardless of the stance of their leaders. George Wallace won re-election as Governor of Alabama in 1970 by campaigning against its use in the state legislature, slurring his words so that RACIST white voters thought he was promising to end the 'black vote'.

compulsory voting The obligation to vote or pay a fine, imposed in a number of countries, notably Australia (since 1925 for the House, 1934 for the Senate).

early voting *See* EARLY.

electronic voting In the US HOUSE OF REPRESENTATIVES, the process by which recorded and roll-call VOTES (*see above*) and QUORUM CALLS are usually taken; each member has a vote-ID card which can be swiped at vote stations throughout the Chamber, marked 'yea', 'nay', 'present' or 'open'.

ghost voting In the US CONGRESS, a trick, in violation of the rules, by which Congressmen can get their votes recorded while away from the CAPITOL.

If voting changed anything, they'd make it illegal An ANARCHIST graffito from Britain's 1979 general election.

plural voting The ability of an elector to cast their vote in more than one electoral district, if REGISTERED there. It is illegal to do this in national elections; the legal position over voting in two different municipalities on the same day is open to question.

preferential voting Under PROPORTIONAL REPRESENTATION as in Australia, a system where an elector expresses a preference (usually in numerical order) for several candidates on the ballot paper instead of making a single cross.

tactical voting *See* TACTICAL.

voucher scheme An important element since the late 1970s of the RADICAL right's proposals for giving citizens choice in their use of public services. It has most frequently been advocated in the context of education, with parents allocated vouchers to be used at the school of their choice – including private schools, according to some. So far it has seldom been put into practice for mainstream schooling, though John MAJOR did introduce it for nursery education.

Vox populi, vox Dei The dictum of the 8th-century English philosopher Alcuin that 'the voice of the people is the voice of God'. General William Tecumseh Sherman corrupted it to **Vox populi, vox humbug**, and Abraham LINCOLN earned the nickname **Fox populi**. The phrase gave rise to **vox pop**, interviews conducted at random in the street by TV and radio reporters to ascertain the public mood.

Vredeling directive In the EUROPEAN COMMUNITY, measures for greater worker participation in industrial decision-making approved by the COMMISSION in 1989, requiring companies to share basic information with their workers and consultation on issues such as plant closures. It took its name from Henk Vredeling, the Dutch Social Affairs Commissioner who developed the proposals.

Vulcan, the The unflattering nickname widely applied to the UK Conservative politician John Redwood (1951–) on account of his far-fetched (to some) right-wing formulae for curing the nation's ills and his supposed facial resemblance to Mr Spock in *Star Trek*. Originally a member of Margaret THATCHER's policy unit and chairman of the NO TURNING BACK group, Redwood became Welsh Secretary under John MAJOR, famously proving unable to sing LAND OF MY FATHERS with the cameras on him, and challenged Major for the leadership in 1995 when the Prime Minister threw down a challenge to his critics on Europe to PUT UP OR SHUT UP. A member of William HAGUE's team in OPPOSITION, he proved an effective shadow to John Prescott (*see* TWO JAGS), but was dropped, only returning to Michael HOWARD's Shadow Cabinet prior to the 2005 election.

W

W The middle initial (DUBYA) of George W. BUSH. Departing members of President CLINTON's WHITE HOUSE staff greeted the incoming Republican team in January 2001 by removing the letter from most computer keyboards in the building.

Wab or Hawold? (Rab or Harold?) The question put to each member of Anthony EDEN's CABINET by Lord Salisbury (*see* BOBBETTY), Leader of the House of Lords, in the first week of 1957 to ascertain whether R. A. Butler (*see* RAB) or Harold MACMILLAN should succeed him as Prime Minister. Salisbury reported their almost unanimous preference for Macmillan to the Queen, who appointed him. *See also* MAGIC CIRCLE.

Waco siege *See* BRANCH DRAVIDIANS.

Wade-Davis Bill A measure for radical RECONSTRUCTION of the South after America's CIVIL WAR, passed by CONGRESS on 4 July 1864 but pocket-VETOed by President LINCOLN. The Bill, fiercely supported by Horace Greeley, would have required a majority of white male citizens in each CONFEDERATE state to take an oath of past as well as future loyalty to the Union, and barred former Confederate office-holders and military volunteers from voting. Promoted by Sen. Benjamin Wade and Rep. H. Winter Davis, its purpose was to prevent Lincoln 'letting the South off too easily'.

wage restraint A phrase from the 1960s and '70s: a climate in which trade unions, at the urging of government, deliberately press for lower pay increases than they could secure by all-out COLLECTIVE BARGAINING and industrial ACTION. Union leaders are loth to embark on such a course, which is unpopular with the RANK AND FILE especially at a time of high INFLATION, but may agree to it as part of a SOCIAL CONTRACT, under which the government takes parallel action to keep down price increases.

Wagner Act The National Labor Relations Act, promoted by Sen. Robert F. Wagner and enacted in 1935 with the backing of President ROOSEVELT, that guaranteed American trade unions' right to organise and engage in COLLECTIVE BARGAINING following decades of 'union-busting'. Also known as the **Wagner-Connery Act**, it established the National Labor Relations Board to supervise bargaining and union elections. After its constitutionality was upheld by the SUPREME COURT in 1937, a number of states passed 'Wagner Acts' of their own; with the TAFT-HARTLEY ACT, it remains a cornerstone of US industrial relations.

> The United Auto Workers and the CIO have paid cash on the barrel for every piece of legislation that we have gotten. The Wagner Act cost us many dollars in contributions to the Roosevelt ADMINISTRATION with the explicit understanding of a *quid pro quo*.
>
> JOHN L. LEWIS (1880–1969)

wait and see The remark which became ASQUITH's catch phrase. Originally said to Lord Helmsley on 3 March 1910, 'We had better wait and see' became his habitual response to questioners, initially over whether hundreds of Liberal PEERS would have to be created to push LLOYD GEORGE's Budget through the House of Lords. Before long, Tory backbenchers would chant: 'Wait and see' whenever Asquith answered questions in the COMMONS. His opponents turned the phrase against him over his alleged lack of urgency in prosecuting WORLD WAR I.

walk. walk and chew gum at the same time Lyndon B. JOHNSON's celebrated jibe at Gerald FORD's clumsiness in the days before circumstances catapulted him into the Presidency. The full phrase as published was 'Jerry Ford is so dumb he can't walk and chew gum at the same time', but Johnson actually said 'fart', not 'walk'. *See also* TOO MUCH FOOTBALL WITHOUT A HELMET.

walk in the woods The occasion in 1982 of a potential breakthrough in US-Soviet ARMS CONTROL talks, when their respective negotiators at Geneva, Paul Nitze and Yuri Kvitsinsky, broke away from formal talks to reach an understanding on limiting intermediate-range missiles in Europe. The understanding was sabotaged by the PENTAGON, enabling KREMLIN hardliners also to disown it.

walkabout An occasion when a politician stops his or her car and mingles with the crowd, without delivering a speech or making any meaningful remarks. A walkabout was originally an Australian term for when an Aborigine sets off to roam the country for months on end. First used in the 1960s of Queen Elizabeth II, the walkabout has become a fixture in many politicians' schedules. *See also* PHOTO OPPORTUNITY.

walking-around money In US politics, money paid out at local level on behalf of a candidate to supporters for knocking on doors, which sometimes ends up being used for more nefarious purposes. The practice dates back to the days of the great MACHINES, but is alive and well. After the 1993 New Jersey gubernatorial election, the winner Christine Todd Whitman's experienced campaign director Ed Rollins told reporters he had given out $500,000 in walking-around money to keep mainly black Democrats at home, bribing black Ministers to tell voters that Gov. Jim Florio should not be re-elected. Investigators found no evidence; Rollins confessed to 'bravado and fantasy', but it seriously damaged his reputation.

Walker Report The report of the President's Commission on the Causes and Prevention of Violence, set up after the riots at the 1968 CHICAGO Democratic CONVENTION. It blamed much of the violence on the provocative use of obscene language by the demonstrators, but termed the occasion 'a police riot'; because Chairman Daniel Walker insisted on listing the words used by the rioters, the Government Printing Office refused to print the report. *See also* DALEY MACHINE; YIPPIES.

wall poster The standard method of political expression in China during the CULTURAL REVOLUTION. Supporters and opponents of CHAIRMAN MAO published their views through this medium, but it proved a particularly effective way for the radical elements in the regime to undermine officials not considered fervent enough. When Defense Secretary Les Aspin was under fire in the PENTAGON in 1993, he was said to be going through a 'wall poster phase'.

Wallenberg hearing An international hearing convened in Stockholm in January 1980 to hear evidence suggesting that the Swedish banker and diplomat Raoul Wallenberg (1912–?) had not died in a Soviet prison in 1947 as claimed by Moscow but had remained alive in the GULAG. Wallenberg has earned the gratitude of humanity for his brazen success in snatching some 25,000 Hungarian Jews from imminent transportation to NAZI death camps by claiming they had Swedish citizenship. But when the Russians entered Budapest in 1945 Wallenberg was arrested, purportedly for espionage, and taken to Moscow. In 1991 the dying Soviet state handed Wallenberg's personal belongings to his family, but insisted he died in 1947. Although reasonably firm evidence of sightings was reported well into the 1960s, the truth will probably never be known. Many countries have paid tribute to Wallenberg: in Israel he has a place at Yad Veshem, the memorial to the HOLOCAUST, as the most outstanding of the righteous Gentiles; Budapest now boasts a fine memorial to him, and the United States declared him an honorary citizen in 1981, when there were hopes he might yet be alive.

Walpole, Sir Robert, later Earl of Orford (1676–1745). Generally reckoned Britain's first PRIME MINISTER (WHIG), and the longest-serving (1721–42). Appointed First Lord of the TREASURY and CHANCELLOR OF THE EXCHEQUER to King George I in 1715, he was from 1721 head of an inner circle of Ministers. He held office for so long by adroit use of PATRONAGE; Jonathan Swift declared:

> The whole system of his ministry was corruption, and he never gave bribe or pension without telling the receivers frankly what he expected of them, and threatening them to put an end to his bounty if they failed to comply in every circumstance.

But Walpole said in his own defence:

> I have lived long enough in the world to know that the safety of a Minister lies in his having the approbation of this House. Former Ministers neglected that and therefore they fell. I have always made it my first study to obtain it, and therefore I hope to stand.

The doctrine that 'every man has his price' has been attributed to him, but Walpole was actually speaking of his opponents when he said: 'All those men have their price.' Walpole was a country gentleman of his time, G. M. Trevelyan writing: 'Even as Prime Minister, he was said to open his gamekeeper's letters the first of the bunch.' He was essentially concerned with maintaining the *status quo* rather than with the excitement of change; 'LET SLEEPING DOGS LIE' was reputedly his motto. He was finally brought down by his handling of the Spanish-Austrian War of Succession, saying of his fall: 'I have led a life of business for so long, I have lost my taste for reading. And now what shall I do?'

> The cur-dog of Britain, and spaniel of Spain.
> Dean SWIFT

Walworth Road The headquarters of the LABOUR PARTY for fifteen eventful years from 1981, when it moved from TRANSPORT HOUSE, until its move to MILLBANK; the building was paid for by the trade unions. The term came to be used for the party bureaucracy generally, even in the final couple of years after it was renamed John SMITH HOUSE.

war. War Against Terrorism George W. BUSH's description of the global engagement against AL QAEDA and other Islamist groups compassing violence against Western interests, in the wake of 9/11. Though the words were Bush's, the idea predated his presidency; President CLINTON's Secretary of State Madeleine Albright (*see* TITANIUM LADY) had spoken of the **War of the Future** in the context of the 1998 CRUISE MISSILE attacks on Osama BIN LADEN's bases in Afghanistan and an alleged germ warfare plant in the Sudan in retaliation for the NAIROBI and Dar es Salaam embassy bombings.

> We will win the war and there will be costs.
> GEORGE W. BUSH, 17 September 2001

war aims The objectives of a state engaged in conflict, sometimes published, sometimes not. WILSON'S FOURTEEN POINTS are a prime, though unusually virtuous, example.

War between the States A Southern term for America's CIVIL WAR.

War Book (1) A preparedness plan kept by the military, for activation if war becomes imminent. (2) The file kept by the chairman of Britain's CONSERVATIVE PARTY for the conduct of a general election campaign, and handed down by one holder of the office to the next.

War Cabinet *See* CABINET.

war crimes The actions of political leaders in wartime in demanding or authorising atrocities, generally against civilians and amounting at their worst to GENOCIDE. The first prosecution of **war criminals** was at NUREMBERG in 1946 when 22 NAZI leaders were tried for torture, deportations, persecution, murder and mass extermination. Twelve were sentenced to death. In the US zone of Germany alone, 500,000 ex-Nazis were convicted of less serious offences. In Japan an international tribunal in Tokyo tried 25 civil and military leaders for planning an aggressive war and committing crimes against humanity; seven, including ex-Prime Minister Hideki Tojo, were hanged. The bestiality of the war in former Yugoslavia in the early 1990s (*see* SREBRENICA) has led to a series of war crimes trials in the Hague, mainly of Bosnian Serbs but with some Croats and a few Muslims also indicted. After further alleged ETHNIC CLEANSING in Kosovo, the former Serbian President Slobodan Milosevic was also put on trial. Further trials for war crimes have been held under UNITED NATIONS auspices in Tanzania, as alleged perpetrators of genocide in Rwanda have been brought to book.

War Crimes Act The UK legislation passed in 1991, despite resistance from the HOUSE OF LORDS, for natives of Continental countries now resident in Britain to be tried for crimes allegedly committed by them in NAZI-occupied territory. Though several intensive police investigations were held and a handful of charges brought, none has resulted in a conviction.

War Game, The A TV drama-documentary on the devastating effect of NUCLEAR WAR, withdrawn by the BBC in 1963 despite strenuous efforts by CND to have it shown.

war games Theoretical exercises, often highly detailed, in which military planners test out possible scenarios for war.

War Hawks *See* HAWKS.

war is Hell General William Tecumseh Sherman's celebrated observation dispelling the romance of war, based on his personal experiences in America's CIVIL WAR. Speaking in Columbus, Ohio, in 1880, Sherman said:

> There is many a boy here today who looks upon war as all glory, but, boys, war is hell.

As complications multiplied after WORLD WAR II, President TRUMAN observed: 'Sherman was wrong. Peace is hell.'

War is Peace. Freedom is Slavery. Ignorance is Strength The motto of the MINISTRY OF TRUTH in George Orwell's 1984.

War Measures Act Canada's 1914 wartime internal security legislation, first invoked in peacetime by Pierre TRUDEAU in 1970 to combat terrorism by Quebec SEPARATISTS. Trudeau justified the action by saying: 'The Government is acting to make clear to kidnappers that in this country laws are made and changed by the elected representatives of all Canadians, and not by a handful of self-styled dictators.' But the NDP leader T. C. Douglas described it as 'using a sledgehammer to crack a peanut'.

War of Independence *See* AMERICAN REVOLUTION.

War of Jenkins' Ear The war between Britain and Spain which began in 1739 after the 'war party' at WESTMINSTER had brought a Captain Jenkins to testify to the COMMONS that the ear he carried in a little box had been cut off by privateers protecting the Spanish Main. It is more likely the ear had actually been cut off by a common hangman, but the event propelled a reluctant WALPOLE into declaring war. His action was greeted with public rejoicing, but Walpole observed:

> They now ring the bells, but they will soon wring their hands.

His words were prophetic; the war went badly for Britain and within three years Walpole was out of office.

War of Jennifer's Ear The most contentious episode of the 1992 UK general election. Labour screened a broadcast based on seven-year-old Jennifer Bennett's lengthy wait for an NHS ear operation. The Conservatives branded it inaccurate, Jennifer's parents took different sides. Neil KINNOCK's press secretary Julie Hall emotionally denied LEAKing it to the press, then Health Secretary William Waldegrave admitted the Conservatives had put the doctor in the case in touch with the *Daily Express* after another paper had got onto the story. There was a sequel thirteen years later prior to the 2005 general election: the **Battle of Margaret's Shoulder**. Michael HOWARD raised in Question Time the case of 69-year-old Mrs Margaret Dixon, who had had a major shoulder operation at a Warrington hospital cancelled on allegedly seven occasions. Howard blamed Labour's stewardship of the NHS; Tony BLAIR and Health Secretary John Reid hit back hard, Reid refusing to meet Mrs Dixon at her house because he believed 'minders' from Conservative CENTRAL OFFICE were there. The episode effectively launched the election campaign, but enabled Labour to stress overall improvements in the NHS.

War of the Flea Robert Taber's definitive book on GUERRILLA war. He wrote:

> The guerrilla fights the war of the flea, and his military enemy suffers the dog's advantages: too much to defend; too small, too ubiquitous and agile an enemy to come to grips with.

War on Iraq *See* IRAQ WAR.

war on poverty The theme of Lyndon B. JOHNSON's first State of the UNION message in January 1964; it provided close to $1 billion for a range of community action projects for better health and housing, and a Job Corps to train young people, under an Office of Economic Opportunity. Johnson said:

> This ADMINISTRATION today, here and now, declares unconditional war on poverty in America. I urge this CONGRESS and all Americans to join with me in that effort.

Despite massive spending to secure the GREAT SOCIETY, poverty in America remained. And 20 years later Ronald REAGAN declared:

> In the war on poverty, poverty won.

War Powers Act or **Resolution** The crucial measure, passed by CONGRESS in 1973 over President NIXON's veto, which curbed the Executive's ability to commit US forces abroad in the wake of the VIETNAM WAR. Congressional approval is required for forces to be committed to a combat zone for more than 90 days unless war is declared. Sen. John Warner said any attempt by Congress to invoke it would put US forces in 'a Byzantine thicket of quicksand', and even for the GULF WAR it was not invoked.

War room The two-storey building in Little Rock, Arkansas from which Bill CLINTON's campaign team fought and won the 1992 Presidential election; it was given the name by Hillary Clinton. The room in the WHITE HOUSE from which wartime operations are overseen is the SITUATION ROOM.

war to end wars A popular contemporary term to justify WORLD WAR I, or to explain its horrors. The origin of the phrase was H. G. Wells' 1914 book *The War that Will End War*. It was adapted as 'the war to end war' by Woodrow WILSON, who said: 'The war we have just been through, though it was shot through with terror, is not to be compared with the war we would have to face next time.' More cynically, and perceptively, LLOYD GEORGE observed: 'This war, like the next war, is a war to end war.'

declaration of war The notification that one nation going to war against another is required by international law to serve on its opponent. Most international conflicts take place without war being declared; WORLD WAR II was the last where the formalities were observed. Neville CHAMBERLAIN made a radio broadcast stating that as Germany had not responded to Britain's ULTIMATUM, served by her AMBASSADOR in Berlin, to withdraw its troops from Poland, 'a state of war now exists' between the two countries (*see* I HAVE TO TELL YOU THAT NO SUCH UNDERTAKING HAS BEEN RECEIVED). Franklin D. ROOSEVELT responded to PEARL HARBOR by going before CONGRESS to request that it 'declare that since the unprovoked and dastardly attack on Sunday December 7th, 1941 (*see* A DATE THAT WILL LIVE IN INFAMY) a state of war has existed between the United States and the Japanese empire'. Hostilities since have been variously described as a 'police action' – Dwight D. EISENHOWER on KOREA; 'ARMED CONFLICT' – EDEN on SUEZ; or unashamedly as wars, some, like the GULF WAR, fought with the support of the UNITED NATIONS, others, like the IRAQ WAR, not.

Democrat Wars The long-standing belief among more conservative and ISOLATIONIST Republicans that the inevitable product of Democratic Presidents' interest in the rest of the world is the involvement of the United States in avoidable wars outside the hemisphere. This view, deeply and sincerely held, was exploited by Bob Dole in his 1996 campaign against Bill CLINTON for the Presidency, with the charge (and reminder), that Democrat Presidents had embroiled America in WORLD WAR II and VIETNAM. Republicans of an older generation would have added WORLD WAR I.

Dirty War The campaign of terror against left-wing elements pursued by the Argentine military under the dictatorship of generals Viola, Videla and Galtieri in the late 1970s and early '80s. *See* DISAPPEARED; MONTONEROS.

He kept us out of war Woodrow WILSON's re-election slogan in 1916 – months before he took the US into WORLD WAR I.

I have told you once and I tell you again: your boys will not be sent into foreign wars Franklin D. ROOSEVELT's promise in his 1940 re-election campaign, nullified by PEARL HARBOR.

I want to stand by my country, but I cannot vote for war The Montana Congresswoman Jeannette Rankin voting against declaring war on Germany in 1917. She was the sole Congressional opponent of going to war then, and again in 1941 after PEARL HARBOR.

In war, resolution. In defeat, defiance. In victory, magnanimity. In peace, goodwill A dictum attributed to CHURCHILL during WORLD WAR II, but first said by his aide Sir Edward Marsh (1872–1953).

Just War The doctrine of St Thomas Aquinas (c. 1225–74) setting out the circumstances in which war is permissible in the eye of God:

> In order for a war to be just, three things are necessary. First, the authority of the sovereign . . . Secondly, a just cause . . . Thirdly, a rightful intention.

limited war The notion that war can be levied against a particular enemy without the conflict escalating to involve other countries or more deadly forms of weaponry.

Make love, not war A slogan from the hippie end of the PEACE MOVEMENT from the late 1960s.

> It didn't look to me as if they were capable of either. RONALD REAGAN

moral equivalent of war *See* MORAL.

phoney war *See* PHONEY

there ain't gone be no war Anthony EDEN's comment on returning to London from the 1955 four-power East-West SUMMIT in Geneva. It came from the c. 1910 musical *Pelissier's Follies:*

> There ain't going to be no war
> As long as we've a king like good King Edward.

There will be no war Woodrow WILSON's forecast in January 1917, three months before America finally entered WORLD WAR I.

There will be no war this year, or next year either Lord Beaverbrook's uncompromisingly optimistic slogan on the masthead of his *Daily Express*, placed there after he wrote in a signed editorial on 28 May 1938: 'Britain will not be involved in war. There will be no major war in Europe this year or next year. The Germans will not seize Czechoslovakia. So go about your business with confidence in the future and fear not.' The slogan remained on the front page throughout the SUDETEN CRISIS and after MUNICH, and was quietly removed the following year after HITLER rolled up the rest of Czechoslovakia.

total war Goebbels' term for war fought with total devastation, enunciated as the tide of WORLD WAR II began to turn against Germany. It became universal currency, but the doctrine predated the NAZIS, Matthias Erzberger having said in 1914:

> If a way was found of entirely wiping out the whole of London it would be more humane to employ it than to allow the blood of a single German soldier to be shed on the battlefield.

trench warfare Originally the static but

bloody conflict in Flanders in WORLD WAR I; later political debate between two sides sniping from entrenched positions with no intention of shifting their battle-lines; also industrial struggles of a similar nature. When in 1978 the management of the nationalised British Leyland motor company was arguing with the Labour government over the release of public funds to it, Industry Secretary Eric Varley accused them of indulging in **tranche warfare**.

warmonger A COLD WAR expression used by STALIN and subsequent Soviet leaders for Western leaders who had the temerity to arm against them.

ward The basic electoral unit, especially in local politics. In Britain, the area a councillor represents.

ward heeler A pejorative in US politics for one of the cogs in a MACHINE, who delivers favours for the voters on behalf of his prestigious patron. The term is reminiscent of a dog at the heel of its master. *See also* HAPPY WARRIOR.

Warm Springs The Georgia retreat where Franklin D. ROOSEVELT went for relaxation, and where he died on 12 April 1945 of a cerebral haemorrhage while recovering from the YALTA conference. FDR's former lover Lucy Mercer Rutherford was with him when he died – she left hurriedly before Eleanor Roosevelt could get there.

Warren Commission The seven-member Commission under Chief Justice Earl Warren (*see below*) set up by Lyndon B. JOHNSON to investigate the circumstances of President KENNEDY's assassination, particularly claims that Lee Harvey Oswald had not been the sole assassin or indeed the assassin at all. The commission took 26 volumes of testimony from over 500 people. In an 888-page report published in 1964, it concluded that Oswald had acted alone in shooting Kennedy, and that the night club owner Jack Ruby had also acted on his own in shooting Oswald while the alleged assassin was in police custody. Yet the speculation has continued: in 1979 the House Select Committee on Assassinations concluded that JFK was 'probably' killed as the result of a conspiracy.

Warren Court The liberal and judicially active SUPREME COURT presided over from 1953 to 1969 by Earl Warren (1891–1974), former Democratic Governor of California. It opened the way for the promotion of CIVIL RIGHTS with the landmark BROWN decision of 1954 outlawing segregated public schools, and in 1964 struck down laws that rigged state legislatures in favour of rural voters. President EISENHOWER described his appointment of Warren as 'the biggest damfool mistake I ever made'.

Warsaw Pact The treaty of friendship, co-operation and mutual assistance concluded in 1955 between the Soviet Union and its central and east European SATELLITES – Albania (until 1968), Bulgaria, Poland, Czechoslovakia, East Germany, Hungary, Poland and Romania – as a counter to NATO, which West Germany had joined. The only European Communist country not to join was Yugoslavia. It gave the Soviet Union the right to station troops in signatory states, and the pretext to stamp out reform movements (Hungary 1956, Czechoslovakia 1968). The pact was scrapped in April 1991.

Warsaw uprising (1) The revolt in the Warsaw GHETTO on 19 April 1943 of its remaining Jews in a desperate bid to halt their transportation to NAZI death camps. The 1500 Jewish guerrillas managed to kill several hundred Germans before resistance was ended on 16 May. (2) The attempt by the Polish underground to liberate Warsaw from the Germans as the RED ARMY approached from the east. The rising, on 1 August 1944 by the 50,000-strong Home Army and armed civilians, was not directed against the Russians – but the Soviet command, within striking distance of the capital, called a halt while the Nazis brutally suppressed the uprising. STALIN even vetoed the dropping of supplies by the Western allies until the rebels were certain of defeat. After a battle in which 15,000 Poles died, the last resisters surrendered on 27 September, after which the Germans killed 200,000 civilians in reprisal. Only when he was sure the non-Communist Home Army had been eliminated did Stalin let the 'liberation' of Warsaw proceed.

washing machines in Dusseldorf Harold WILSON's disparaging comment about the merits of membership of Europe's COMMON MARKET as Shadow Foreign Secretary when responding in the COMMONS on 3 August 1961 to Harold MACMILLAN's first proposal that Britain should join. In a speech that was otherwise far from hostile, Wilson said when speaking of Britain's links with the COMMONWEALTH:

> We are not entitled to sell our friends and kinsmen down the river for a problematical and marginal advantage in selling washing machines in Dusseldorf.

Washington, George (1732–99) Supreme commander (from 1775) and outstanding general of the American revolutionary army, and first President of the United States (1789–97). A Virginia gentleman and a senior officer in the colony's militia, he emerged as a natural leader as tension with Britain rose; when appointed commander-in-chief, he wrote:

> I am embarked on a wide ocean, boundless in its prospect and in which, perhaps, no safe harbour is to be found. I can answer for but three things: a firm belief in the justice of our cause, close attention in the prosecution of it, and the strictest integrity.

That reputation for integrity went back to his boyhood, when he allegedly told his father when asked if he had cut down a cherry tree: 'I cannot tell a lie, Pa; you know I can't tell a lie. I did cut it with my hatchet.' And as commander-in-chief he wrote:

> I beg leave to assure the Congress that as no pecuniary consideration could have tempted me to accept this arduous employment at the expense of my domestic ease and happiness I do not wish to make any profit from it.

Nevertheless he was to observe in old age:

> I long ago despaired of any other reward for my services than the satisfaction arising from a consciousness of doing my duty, and the esteem of my friends.

Throughout the revolutionary struggle, he maintained the spirits of his army and the movement it served. After the loss of Ticonderoga, he said: 'Under a full persuasion of the justice of our cause, I cannot entertain an idea that it will finally sink, though it may remain for some time under a cloud.' At times he professed to revel in the military life, saying: 'I have heard the bullets whistle and, believe me, there is something charming in the sound.' But he also declared:

> From the day I entered upon the command of the American armies, I date my fall, and the ruin of my reputation. £50,000 should not induce me to do again what I have done.

Although the office of PRESIDENT was created for him, Washington took it with reluctance, saying: 'My movement to the chair of government will be accompanied by feelings not unlike those of a culprit who is going to the place of his execution.' He seriously considered retiring after one term, and in 1796 was adamant that eight years as President was enough.

Washington had his sycophants, but he also had his critics, notably Thomas Paine, who wrote:

> As to you, sir, treacherous to private friendship (for so you have been to me, and that in the day of danger) and a hypocrite in public life, the world will be puzzled to decide whether you are an apostate or an impostor, whether you have abandoned good principles or whether you ever had any.

Sen. William Maclay considered him overbearing as President: 'He wishes to tread on the necks of the Senate . . . to bear down our deliberations with his personal authority and presence.' And Benjamin Bache declared: 'If ever a nation was debauched by a man, the American nation has been debauched by Washington.'

Washington made a great impression on most who met him. Lafayette exclaimed: 'Never before had I beheld so superb a man.' According to Abigail Adams, 'he has a dignity which forbids familiarity, mixed with an easy affability which creates love and reverence'. To JEFFERSON,

> his mind was slow in operation but sure in conclusion. On the whole his character was, in its mass, perfect, in nothing bad, in a few points indifferent; and it may truly be said that never did nature and fortune combine more perfectly to make a man great.

John ADAMS observed that 'dignity with ease and complacency, the gentleman and the soldier, look agreeably blended in him. Modesty marks every line and feature of his face.' But Adams did once remark: 'He is too illiterate, unread, unlearned for his station and reputation.' Gilbert Stuart noted those same characteristics: 'All his features were indicative of the most ungovernable passions, and had he been born in the forests, it is my opinion that he would have been the fiercest man among the savage tribes.' To Samuel Eliot Morison, Washington was 'the last person you would ever suspect of having been a young man'. And Nathaniel Hawthorne was to remark: 'He had no nakedness, but was born with clothes on, and his hair powdered, and made a stately bow on his 1st appearance in the world.'

On his death, Henry 'Light Horse Harry' Lee set the tone with a eulogy describing Washington as 'FIRST IN WAR, FIRST IN PEACE, AND FIRST IN THE HEARTS OF HIS COUNTRYMEN'. Byron hailed him as 'next only to the divinity', writing:

> Washington
> Whose every battlefield is holy ground
> Which breathes of battles saved, not worlds undone.

To GLADSTONE, he was 'the purest figure in

history'; Thackeray wrote of 'a life without a stain; a fame without a flaw'; and Thomas A. Bailey reckoned him 'the only man in the history of the presidency bigger than the government itself'. Daniel Webster orated that 'the character of Washington is among the most cherished contemplations of my life. It is a fixed star in the firmament of great names, shining without twinkling or obscuration, with clear, steady, beneficent light.' LINCOLN declared:

> Washington is the mightiest name on earth – long since mightiest in the cause of civil liberty, still mightiest in moral reformation. On that name no eulogy is expected. It cannot be. To add brightness to the sun or glory to the name of Washington is alike impossible. Let none attempt it. In solemn awe pronounce the name and in its naked deathless splendour leave it shining on.

But by the late 19th century Robert Ingersoll could write: 'Washington is now only a steel engraving. About the real man who lived and loved and hated and schemed, we know but little.'

Washington's farewell address The message to the nation, largely drafted by Alexander HAMILTON, which the retiring President Washington published in the newspapers on 7 September 1796. He voiced satisfaction with his achievements on the home front, but regretted the onset of the party strife which was already shaping the divisions that led to the CIVIL WAR. On foreign affairs, he did not warn against all 'entangling alliances' (the phrase was JEFFERSON's). But he did say: 'Taking care always to keep ourselves . . . on a respectable defensive posture, we may safely trust to temporary alliances for extraordinary emergencies.'

Washington DC (DISTRICT OF COLUMBIA) America's federal capital, named after George Washington and established on a ten-mile square site taken from Virginia (later returned) and Maryland during his presidency. The Washington conurbation now has a population exceeding 4 million, but at the outset it barely possessed the basic amenities, leading Sen. Gouverneur Morris to complain: '[We need only] houses, cellars, kitchens, well informed men, amiable women, and other little trifles of this kind to make our city perfect.' Habits were basic too, Charles Dickens naming Washington 'the headquarters of tobacco-tinctured saliva'. The climate did not help, President Buchanan declaring it 'no place for a civilised man to spend the summer'. Things were slow to improve, Horace Greeley branding it 'not a place to live in. The rents are high, the food is bad, the dust is disgusting and the morals are deplorable.' President Garfield (*see* BOATMAN JIM) once exclaimed: 'My God! What is there in this place that a man should ever want to get into it?' And as late as the 1960s, President KENNEDY could mock Washington as

> a city of Northern charm and Southern efficiency.

Washington has developed from what Henry Adams termed 'a mere political camp' into the ultimate company town – and, through its urban problems, one of America's murder hotspots. To many politicians it has held a special magic, President TAFT once exclaiming: '[This] is a Federal City, and it tingles down to the feet of any man, whether he comes from Washington state, or Los Angeles, or Texas, when he comes and walks these city streets.' John Mason Brown drew a different moral: 'The more I observed Washington, the more I understood how prophetic L'Enfant was when he laid it out as a city that goes round in circles.' And as the modern Washington mushroomed, Ada Louise Huxtable branded it 'an endless series of mock palaces clearly built for clerks'. Washington has a large migrant political population. EISENHOWER observed that 'everyone has been too long away from home', and Sen. Claiborne Pell that 'people only leave Washington by way of the box – ballot or coffin'. Fanny Dixwell Holmes noted that 'Washington is full of famous men and the women they married when they were young', while one commentator termed it 'a city where half the people want to be discovered and the other half are afraid they'll be found out'. To Elliott Richardson it was 'a city of cocker spaniels – people who are more interested in being petted and admired, loved, than rendering the exercise of power'. President TRUMAN tartly observed: 'If you want a friend in Washington, buy a dog', Speaker Sam RAYBURN reckoned it 'a sour-bellied place', while President CLINTON's White House counsel Vince FOSTER lamented in his suicide note:

> Here, ruining people is considered sport.

Political Washington has been called 'the hubbub of the Universe', and 'the only place where sound travels faster than light'. To Douglas Cater it was 'a crazy quilt of people who have each other by the vulnerable parts'. George E. Allen trustingly reckoned: 'People who think the mighty in Washington can be persuaded, or corrupted, if you will, by anything less than votes just don't understand what it's all about and never will. They don't know what Washington juice is made of.' Sen. Strom Thurmond reckoned that 'The longer you stay, you realise that sometimes you can catch more flies with honey than with vinegar'. Tim McNamar observed: 'When you ask what time it is you get different answers from Democrats and Republicans; 435 answers from the House of Representatives; a 500-page report from some consultants on how to tell the time; no answer from your lawyer and a bill for $1000.' And George Shultz admitted: 'Nothing ever gets settled in this town. People never give up, including me.' Washington's remoteness from typical America is legendary: Sen. Huey Long said: 'The heart of America is felt less here than at any place I have ever been', and Jimmy CARTER found the capital 'isolated from the mainstream of our nation's life'. One wit branded the city '69.2 square miles surrounded by reality'.

Americans reckon a streak of lunacy runs through their capital and its proceedings. Mark Twain termed it it 'a stud farm for every jackass in the country'. Irwin S. Conn declared: 'If I wanted to go crazy I would do it in Washington because it would not be noticed.' Ronald REAGAN reckoned that 'common sense is about as common in Washington as a Fourth of July blizzard in Columbia, S.C.', and Anne Burford, head of the Environmental Protection Agency, deemed it 'too small to be a State, but too large to be an asylum for the mentally deranged'. Politicians know this, Norman Ornstein saying:

> If you are a member of Congress, the last thing you want is to be compared with all those creeps in Washington.

'Washington' has become a collective term for the US government, the administrative community, its lifestyle and state of mind. At the outset JEFFERSON wrote: 'Were we directed from Washington when to sow and when to reap, we should soon want bread.' And during his 1964 Presidential campaign, Sen. Barry Goldwater remarked: 'I fear Washington and centralised government more than I fear Moscow.'

Washington Conference The first Allied conference of WORLD WAR II, codenamed *Arcadia*, between Franklin D. ROOSEVELT and Winston CHURCHILL, from 22 December 1941 to 12 January 1942. Hurriedly convened after PEARL HARBOR, it established long-term Allied strategy. Churchill secured a US commitment to the defeat of Germany in the Atlantic and European theatres before concentrating on Japan. A joint declaration, formally announcing an alliance to defeat the AXIS powers, was signed by 26 countries including China and the Soviet Union.

Washington Monument The 555ft obelisk on the MALL in America's federal capital which is the nation's monument to its first President. Designed by Robert Mills as the world's tallest free-standing masonry tower, it took decades to build, being completed in 1885. 90,000 tons of stone were used to construct the Monument, whose interior stairway has 897 stone steps and 50 landings; the stairs have been closed since the 1970s, and all 800,000 visitors a year now use an elevator to the observation area at the top. The monument was closed from September 2004 to the spring of 2005 to undergo 'security enhancements'; it overlooks the WHITE HOUSE and many federal buildings, and is close to the flight path for REAGAN NATIONAL AIRPORT.

Washington Naval Treaty The 1922 agreement, masterminded by Secretary of State Charles Evans Hughes (1862–1948), which ended for a decade the naval race between the great powers, the US, Britain and Japan each agreeing to scrap large parts of their navies and respect each other's holdings in the Pacific. This was the only effective measure of disarmament achieved between the wars.

Washington State The most north-westerly state of America barring Alaska, which has a silhouette of George Washington as its emblem. Acquired from Britain in 1846, it achieved STATEHOOD in 1889.

Mr Smith Goes to Washington Frank Capra's 1939 film, starring James Stewart as an idealistic young Wisconsin senator who sets out to cleanse the capital's Augean stables of corruption.

running against Washington Campaigning for office by depicting oneself as an outsider fighting an inert and all-embracing system of government; both Jimmy CARTER and Ronald REAGAN used this tactic to good effect.

Treaty of Washington The 1871 agreement between the US and a British/Canadian delegation which settled the boundary between Vancouver Island and Washington State, admitted Canadian fish to America free of duty, gave America ten-year access to Canadian fisheries, and determined navigation rights on the Great

Lakes and St Lawrence River. It also referred the ALABAMA incident to an international tribunal.

WASPs White Anglo-Saxon Protestants. A derogatory term for America's traditionally dominant ethnic group, and especially the North-eastern upper class.

Watauga Association America's first free civil government, set up in 1772 by settlers in the North Carolina and Tennessee mountains, between the Ohio and Tennessee rivers. As the settlers lived outside the colonies, Britain allowed them to band together; they secured the land in 1768 by agreement with the Indian 'Six Nations', and drew up the 'Articles of the Watauga Association' under which an elected thirteen-member assembly chose a ruling committee of five. *See also* FRANKLIN.

watching for googlies The cricketing analogy used by UK party managers for eternal vigilance against potentially damaging events, issues and remarks. It was coined by Angus (later Lord) Maude (1912–93), the Minister in Margaret THATCHER's original CABINET responsible for presenting government policy. A googly is an off-break delivered by a bowler with a leg-break action; the term originated in Australia in 1903–04 when the MCC tourist B. J. T. Bosanquet used the delivery to great effect.

water. like trying to nail a drop of water to the wall The verdict of Rep. George Danielson on the House Judiciary Committee's efforts to question former Attorney-General John Mitchell (*see* KATIE GRAHAM'S GOING TO GET . . .) on his involvement in WATERGATE, 10 July 1974. *Compare also* JFK's remarks on BUREAUCRACY.

Watergate The greatest peacetime crisis in America's political history, culminating in the resignation in disgrace of President Richard NIXON on 8 August 1974. It took its name from the modernistic complex of apartments and offices in WASHINGTON beside the Potomac, where on 17 June 1972 a security guard named Frank Wills caught five men breaking into the headquarters of the Democratic NATIONAL COMMITTEE. With the Democrats facing heavy defeat in the coming election, Washington insiders felt the burglary was 'like breaking into the Ford HQ to steal the plans for the Edsel'. Partly as a result of investigative reporting by Carl Bernstein and Bob Woodward of the *Washington Post*, the five – and two accomplices – were found to have links with the WHITE HOUSE. Gradually over the succeeding months a trail of 'LAUNDERED' money was identified leading back from the five to Nixon's campaign committee (CREEP). Nixon denied any involvement, and the issue failed to take off during the 1972 Presidential campaign, largely because of fierce denunciations of the Press from Vice President Spiro AGNEW, who was soon afterwards disgraced over a completely separate matter. But after the election, first through ferocious sentencing of the five by Judge John Sirica (*see* MAXIMUM JOHN) which led the burglars to talk, a chain of misdeeds and corruption came to light involving almost all Nixon's closest associates except Dr Henry KISSINGER; by 1977, many would be in jail. Both Houses of CONGRESS began hearings which brought damaging evidence to light; Nixon alleged that 'the fine hand of the KENNEDYs' was behind the Senate's 70–0 vote to investigate. When White House staff were subpœnaed to testify, Nixon said publicly: 'I condemn any effort to COVER UP this case', but he told them:

> I don't give a shit what happens. I want you to stonewall . . . plead the FIFTH AMENDMENT, cover up, or anything else. If that will save it, save the plan.

Nixon fought back by concentrating on 'business as usual', saying: 'Let others wallow in Watergate. We are going to do our job.'

The case achieved critical mass in mid-1973. First, White House counsel John Dean, ignoring Nixon's advice, told the Senate's ERVIN COMMITTEE that former Attorney-General John Mitchell (*see previous column*) had consented to the burglary, that Nixon's CHIEF OF STAFF H. R. Haldeman and domestic affairs adviser John Ehrlichman were aware of it – and that Nixon had approved the cover-up. Then in July White House aide Alexander Butterfield revealed the existence of the WHITE HOUSE TAPES: tapes Nixon had kept of all his conversations in the OVAL OFFICE. Nixon at first resisted pressure to release the tapes, claiming EXECUTIVE PRIVILEGE. And when his own appointees demanded that he comply, he carried out the SATURDAY NIGHT MASSACRE to remove them. When the transcripts were finally released on 30 April 1974 with Nixon insisting: 'The President has nothing to hide', they became a best-seller; the coarseness of Nixon's language and the depth of his involvement scandalised the nation. Vice President FORD made a virtue of this, saying: 'I cannot imagine any other country in the world where the opposition would seek – and the Chief Executive would allow – the dissemination of his most private and personal conversations with his staff – which, to be honest, do not exactly confer sainthood on anyone concerned.' The tapes brought to the forefront the central question of Watergate: WHAT DID THE PRESIDENT KNOW AND WHEN DID HE KNOW IT?

In July 1974 the SUPREME COURT voted 'eight-zip' that Nixon must hand over all tapes to the SPECIAL PROSECUTOR, and the House Judiciary Committee voted 27–11 to recommend Nixon's IMPEACHMENT. Nixon began to lose heart, telling his new Chief of Staff Gen. Alexander Haig: 'Well, there goes the Presidency.' He also told Haig: 'In your business you have a way of handling problems like this. Someone leaves a pistol in the drawer. I don't have a pistol.' With almost all his former supporters deserting him, an emotional Nixon admitted on 5 August that he had approved the cover-up and impeded FBI investigations; with impeachment now certain, he quit on 8 August to facilitate 'the process of healing which is so desperately needed in America', and flew off to exile at SAN CLEMENTE; Gerald Ford was sworn in, PARDONing Nixon soon after. Ford said: 'I assume the presidency under extraordinary circumstances. This is an hour of history that troubles our minds and hurts our hearts.' And he concluded:

> Never again must America allow an arrogant, elite guard of political adolescents to bypass the regular party organisation and dictate the terms of a national election.

Twenty-five of those 'political adolescents', though not Nixon, ended in jail. *See also* DEEP THROAT; FROST INTERVIEWS; I AM NOT A CROOK; I HEREBY RESIGN THE PRESIDENCY OF THE UNITED STATES; INOPERATIVE; KATIE GRAHAM'S GOING TO GET . . .; MODIFIED, LIMITED HANGOUT; PLUMBERS; RATFUCKING; SMOKING GUN; WHITEWASH.

> Nixon essentially impeached himself. He had done everything possible to show how guilty he was. Rep. JOHN CONYERS (Dem.)

> Worse than a crime – it was a blunder.
> NIXON

> I brought myself down. I gave them a sword and they stuck it in and they twisted it with relish. And I guess that if I'd been in the same position, I'd have done the same thing.
> NIXON to David Frost

nobody drowned at Watergate The comparison made with CHAPPAQUIDDICK by Republican partisans eager to make the point that Democrats could act even more outrageously than Richard Nixon and get away with it. It was voiced publicly by Agriculture Secretary Earl Butz, who less than two years after Watergate was forced to resign from Gerald FORD's Cabinet for offensive remarks about black Americans.

watershed A political event, generally but not always an election, which is seen as marking a break with the past and the opening of a new era. Watersheds are frequently identified by politicians and commentators at the time, but often seem less obvious in the light of history. A watershed is a geographical term for the elevated ridge of land from either side of which streams feed into different river systems.

Watts The scene, from 11–16 August 1965, of the worst INNER-CITY riots in Los Angeles prior to the Rodney KING riot of 1992. Ten thousand black rioters burned and looted an area of 500 blocks, and 15,000 police and National Guardsmen were brought in to restore order. The riot was sparked on a hot, smoggy day when a police patrolman drew his gun on a young black motorist; it left 34 people dead – 28 of them black; over 3900 people were arrested and over 200 businesses destroyed. The *Los Angeles Times* angered city officials by blaming the riots on poor contact between themselves and the black community, and demanding anti-poverty measures to combat 30% local unemployment.

waving the bloody shirt Rabble-rousing methods to perpetuate Northern hostility toward the South after America's CIVIL WAR. In March 1868 A. P. Huggins, a tax collector and superintendent who had come to Mississippi from Ohio, was wakened by Klansmen, stripped, given 75 lashes and ordered on pain of death to leave the state in ten days. Huggins reported the incident to the military, and an officer took his blood-stained nightshirt to Washington and gave it to the radical Massachusetts Congressman Ben Butler. When Butler proposed a Bill enabling President Johnson to use the army to enforce federal laws in the South, he waved Huggins' gory shirt in the House Chamber. For the rest of the 19th century Republican orators would 'wave the bloody shirt' against the Democrats at election time. The term became used for any political campaigning designed to reopen old enmities.

After Dr Martin Luther KING was shot in

April 1968, the Rev. Jesse JACKSON actually put on the bloody shirt. Though a storey away from King when he was gunned down in a Memphis motel, the next day Jackson appeared before the cameras in a turtleneck covered with blood.

Ways and Means (1) In the US HOUSE OF REPRESENTATIVES, the powerful committee that writes tax legislation. Its 37 members handle every aspect of the raising of revenues – including taxes, tariffs and social security levies – and debt policy. (2) At WESTMINSTER, the blanket term for the provision of public revenue; BUDGET proposals are set out in **Ways and Means Resolutions** on which the FINANCE BILL is based. The deputy SPEAKER of the Commons is officially known as the **Chairman of Ways and Means**, after a committee first established in 1644; he or she presides over the Budget statement. The COMMITTEE CORRIDOR which runs the length of the Palace of Westminster is known also as the **Ways and Means Corridor**.

we. We are the masters now The assertion by Attorney-General Hartley (later Lord) Shawcross (1902–2002) which summed up for Opposition Tories the quasi-revolutionary nature of the 1945 ATTLEE government. Speaking in the COMMONS on 2 April 1946, Sir Hartley (*see* Sir Shortly FLOORcross) said:

> We are the masters at the moment, and not only at the moment, but for a very long time to come.

When Labour was next returned to power by a LANDSLIDE, Tony BLAIR told Labour MPs on 7 May 1997:

> The people are the masters. We are the servants of the people. We will never forget that and, if we ever do, the people will very soon show that what the electorate gives the electorate can take away.

We don't do God *See* GOD.

We got clobbered Press Secretary Bill Hagerty's verdict on the violent reception accorded Vice President and Mrs NIXON when they arrived in Caracas, Venezuela, in May 1958. For twelve miles from the airport the crowd pelted their motorcade with garbage, spat and attacked the cars with baseball bats.

We grammar school boys must stick together The celebrated put-down administered by Leader of the House John Biffen (*see* SEMI-DETACHED) to Dennis Skinner (*see* BEAST OF BOLSOVER) in 1987 when the Labour left-winger was in full flight condemning Tory-sponsored inequality.

We have become a grandmother The joyful remark made by Margaret THATCHER on 3 March 1989 to celebrate the birth of her son Mark's first child, which provoked a degree of ridicule because of her apparent use of the ROYAL WE instead of describing herself in the first person. It came to be seen as the point when her awareness of the place she had earned in history got the better of her.

We only have to be lucky once The IRA's chilling message to Margaret THATCHER after it had narrowly failed to assassinate her in the BRIGHTON BOMBING of October 1984 (*see* A DAY I WAS MEANT NOT TO SEE).

We're just mild about Harry *See* TRUMAN.

We shall fight on the beaches, we shall fight on the landing grounds, we shall fight in the fields and in the streets, we shall fight in the hills, we shall never surrender CHURCHILL's speech in the HOUSE OF COMMONS on 4 June 1940 after the successful evacuation of over 350,000 British and Allied troops from Dunkirk, but with the threat of German invasion looming. This section of the speech, also delivered on radio, began: 'We shall go on to the end, we shall fight in France, we shall fight on the seas and oceans, we shall fight with growing confidence and growing strength in the air, we shall defend our island whatever the cost may be', and ended:

> And even if, which I do not for a moment believe, this island or a huge part of it were subjugated and starving, then our Empire beyond the seas, armed and guarded by the British Fleet, would carry on the struggle, until, in God's good time, the New World, with all its power and might, steps forth to the rescue and the liberation of the old.

We shall overcome The opening line of one of the anthems of America's CIVIL RIGHTS movement in the 1960s. Written by Zilphia Horton and added to by Pete Seeger and others, it began:

> We shall overcome,
> We shall overcome,
> We shall overcome some day.
> And it's deep in my heart
> I do believe
> That we shall overcome some day.

> Revolutions are never waged singing '*We Shall Overcome*'. Revolutions are based upon bloodshed.
> MALCOLM X, 1964

We want eight and we won't wait The slogan taken up by advocates of a strong Royal Navy in 1909 in an effort to pressure Britain's Liberal government into boosting the building programme for Dreadnoughts (battle cruisers) to match Germany's buildup. The Admiralty proposed building six; LLOYD GEORGE and CHURCHILL considered four enough. ASQUITH satisfied all parties with a compromise under which four ships were laid down immediately, with a further four as and when the need was proved; within a few months all eight were under construction.

We will bury you The alarming threat to the West, with its inference of nuclear war, delivered by the Soviet leader Nikita S. Khrushchev (1894–1971) at a Polish embassy reception in Moscow in November 1956; coming at the time of the HUNGARIAN UPRISING, it was no doubt also a reminder to the Poles to stay in line. Three years later Khrushchev explained in WASHINGTON that he had been referring to the inevitable triumph of the Communist economic system over capitalism.

Wealth of Nations, The One of the great works of political economys, published in 1776 by the Scottish economist Adam Smith (1723–90). It became one of the basics of liberal and free-market economics, and was one of the Bibles of THATCHERISM (*see* Adam SMITH INSTITUTE). Smith was robust in arguing the harmful effect of cartels, writing:

> People of the same trade seldom meet together but the conversation ends in a conspiracy against the public, or in some diversion to raise prices.

And this argument on taxation found powerful adherents in the 1980s:

> There is no art which one government sooner learns of another than that of draining money from the pockets of the people.

weapons of mass destruction The weapons SADDAM HUSSEIN's supposed possession of which were the pretext for the 2003 IRAQ WAR, and which in the wake of the COLD WAR and the rise of AL QAEDA are deemed to embrace chemical and biological as well as NUCLEAR WEAPONS. While the former SUPERPOWERS eventually agreed to limit their nuclear arsenals and to run down their chemical and biological capabilities, aggressive rogue states are bound by no such scruples regardless of which international agreements they have or have not signed. The break-up of the Soviet Union led to the scattering of skills and materials throughout Asia and beyond, and Saddam certainly did have WMD programmes, even though it now appears he had wound these up before being overthrown (*see* IRAQ SURVEY GROUP). Nuclear capability remains a headache with North Korea and Iran, while a range of largely ISLAMIST terrorist groups are thought to have access to and the skills to propagate not only a simple atomic bomb but deadly chemicals such as sarin – now blamed for GULF WAR SYNDROME – and viruses like anthrax, the mailing of which (probably by a disaffected American) wrought havoc on CAPITOL HILL in the wake of 9/11. *See also* DODGY DOSSIER; HUTTON REPORT; David KELLY AFFAIR; PLAME LEAK.

> We got it all wrong.
>
> DAVID KAY, former CIA chief weapons inspector, to the Senate Armed Services Committee

weasel words Words of convenient ambiguity, or consummate evasiveness. The phrase dates back to a story by Stewart Chaplin in the *Century Magazine* of 1900:

> Why, weasel words are words that suck the life out of the words next to them, just as a weasel sucks the egg and leaves the shell.

Theodore ROOSEVELT popularised the term when he said in 1916 of a speech by Woodrow WILSON:

> You can have universal training, or you can have voluntary training, but when you use the word voluntary to qualify universal, you are using a weasel word; it has sucked all the meaning out of universal. The two words flatly contradict one another.

Prior to the 1992 general election, John MAJOR said of an evasion by Labour's employment spokesman Tony BLAIR over whether a minimum wage would push up unemployment: 'It would make a weasel blush.'

Weatherill amendment The compromise amendment to the BLAIR government's plans for reform of the HOUSE OF LORDS which enabled hereditary peers to elect 98 of their number to continue sitting in the upper house for an unspecified transitional period. The brokering of this compromise in 1999 by Lord Weatherill, former SPEAKER of the Commons, defused outright opposition by Conservative peers to the removal of the bulk of the hereditaries, the survivors henceforward claiming to have been 'elected' and thus enjoying a MANDATE. The failure of the Commons early in 2003 to agree on what proportion, if any, of a reformed upper house should be elected has given the amendment a longer currency than had originally been envisaged.

Weathermen Members of the **Weather Underground**, a US revolutionary terrorist group that operated during the VIETNAM WAR as the violent fringe of the NEW LEFT.

The youthful militants were responsible for a series of bombings; three of them died when a town-house bomb factory on New York City's West Eleventh Street exploded in 1970. Some of the group later turned to crime in protest against the capitalist system; three Weathermen, including their leader Kathy Boudin, were arrested in 1982 after two police officers and a security guard were killed in an attempted robbery of a Brinks armoured truck.

> The Weathermen were not the conscience of their generation, but more like its id.
>
> TOM HAYDEN (1940–)

Webster-Ashburton Treaty The agreement between Britain and America in 1842 that fixed the US-Canadian border around the state of Maine, giving more than half the land in dispute to America. It was negotiated by Secretary of State Daniel Webster (1782–1852) and Lord Ashburton, head of the Baring banking house and a former Tory MP, whose wife was American.

> Most disgraceful and disadvantageous.
>
> Lord PALMERSTON

wedge issue An issue that can split an ethnic or socio-economic grouping so that some can be won over to the party or candidate doing the splitting. The term came into use in late 1980s US politics and was popularised by Stu Eizenstat, a former adviser to President CARTER, to describe the way aides to George BUSH Snr were trying to use the relationship between AFFIRMATIVE ACTION and racial QUOTAS to split the predominantly Democratic BLUE-COLLAR vote. James Carville (*see* RAGIN' CAJUN) picked up on it in planning Bill CLINTON's successful 1992 campaign for the Presidency, saying that Republicans had gone to wedge issues on the basis that 'We can't lead the country, so maybe we can divide it.'

Red Wedge *See* RED.

Wedgie A nickname passed down from father to son. Originally that of William Wedgwood Benn (1877–1960), first Viscount Stansgate, a Liberal MP who switched to Labour and became Secretary of State for India and Secretary of State for Air. It passed to his son Tony BENN as he discarded the 'Wedgwood' and his patrician origins after refusing to accept the PEERAGE he inherited. The transformation from patrician to left-wing POPULIST took place in the 1970s, during which time Benn junior excised from his *Who's Who* entry the fact that he had been educated at the prestigious Westminster School.

Wednesday Club In the US HOUSE OF REPRESENTATIVES, an informal moderate Republican CAUCUS – the most prestigious of such groupings, outranking even the CHOWDER AND MARCHING SOCIETY – which has its own staff and offices; in the SENATE, an even less formal informational gathering.

Wedtech affair The scandal that resulted in Lyn Nofziger, President REAGAN's former political director, being fined $30,000 and being sentenced to 90 days in jail for violating federal ethics laws. It stemmed from Nofziger's opening a LOBBYING firm in 1982, eight months after leaving the WHITE HOUSE, with the military contractor Wedtech as a client. Nofziger solicited the help of deputy Attorney-General James Jenkins in securing a $32 million Army contract for Wedtech, which misrepresented itself as minority-owned and had been barred from competing because of poor performance. Wedtech hired Jenkins as a consultant and gave Nofziger's firm stock worth almost $1 million. The ensuing scandal resulted in four Wedtech executives pleading guilty to stealing $2 million from the corporation and bribing federal, state and local officials, the conviction of two Maryland politicians for accepting bribes to obstruct a Congressional investigation and the indictment of a New York Congressman for racketeering.

week. a week is a long time in politics A comment made by Harold WILSON to LOBBY correspondents on his election in October 1964 , which has almost become his political epitaph. It was seized on by his detractors as representing a uniquely cynical approach, inferring that any action, no matter how unpopular, will be forgiven or forgotten by the voters. Wilson's intent was to stress that politics should be seen on a longer time-scale and not judged by day-to-day concerns.

weeks, not months Wilson's over-optimistic forecast for the early collapse of Ian Smith's UDI regime in Rhodesia in the face of economic sanctions. It was made at the Commonwealth Prime Ministers' meeting in Lagos on 12 January 1966; Rhodesia's RETURN TO LEGALITY took until 1980 to achieve, and Wilson came to be accused of complacency and glibness for his prediction, which he had made with reluctance in order to save a meeting that was heading for failure. He said:

> The cumulative effects of the economic and financial sanctions might well bring the rebellion to an end within a matter of weeks rather than months.

Weimar Republic The German federal republic established under the Constitution of 1919 after the forced ABDICATION of the Kaiser, which lasted until it was overthrown in 1933 by HITLER, the last Chancellor to be elected under it. It took its name from the Thuringian town of Weimar, otherwise known for its association with Goethe, where the Constitution was adopted by a National Assembly.

welcoming ceremony The ceremonial greeting staged on the SOUTH LAWN of the WHITE HOUSE for foreign HEADS OF STATE and of government. The visitor, plus spouse and principal aides, is driven to the lawn, where a band and HONOR GUARD are on hand for the Presidential greeting. White House personnel along with staff and families from the visitor's embassy look on as President and guest stand on a ROSTRUM to exchange pleasantries, and occasionally comments of substance.

welfare The US term for social security and anti-poverty schemes, and the payments received by the needy. MIDDLE AMERUCA increasingly sees 'welfare people' as INNER-CITY and usually black one-parent families, and thus nothing to do with them or even with SOCIETY (*see* ALIENATION; UNDERCLASS). Welfare and foreign aid are the only fields of public spending where American voters consistently demand cuts.

> Hated by those who administer it; mistrusted by those who pay for it; and held in contempt by those who receive it.
>
> PETER GOLDMARK (1937–), JOHNSON administration Budget Director

welfare queens The emotive phrase taken up by Ronald REAGAN to describe women – by inference single and with large and prosperous-looking families – who were using food stamps and other means-tested benefits to buy luxuries, presenting him with further pretexts for taking a hatchet to the welfare system. (*Compare* BLUDGERS). Its use was bitterly resented; Sen. Charles Grassley told Reagan:

> You've got to realise that there are welfare queens in the PENTAGON, too. They're the big contractors.

welfare state The system of comprehensive social security and services provision in Britain advocated by the BEVERIDGE REPORT and introduced by ATTLEE's Labour government. Providing for sickness, unemployment, retirement, want and other needs, its cornerstones were the 1946 National Insurance Act and the National Health Service (NHS). The British welfare system was much admired in Europe and beyond during the 1950s, but has since grown in cost rather than effectiveness. The left argues that it has been starved of funds and commitment, with the elderly in particular losing out, the right that it has spawned a DEPENDENCY CULTURE; in US politics the phrase is generally used in a negative context. Its use predates Beveridge, being credited to William Temple (1881–1944), Archbishop of Canterbury, who wrote in 1941:

> In place of the conception of the Power State, we are led to that of the Welfare State.

welfare to work The rationale behind the NEW DEAL introduced by Tony BLAIR's Labour government from 1997, to assist those with the potential to work to find training and jobs instead of relaying on state handouts. While the process had some success, by the end of Blair's second term a hard core of young and long-term jobless which had managed to avoid work by getting onto incapacity benefits was again forming, to the frustration of Ministers.

corporate welfare The charge levelled by Democrats against the two BUSH administrations: that government spending programmes were designed to reward corporate America for its support for the Republican administration rather than deliver benefits for the people. Payments to pharmaceutical companies under MEDICARE came in for particular criticism.

welfarism A mildly derogatory term for the social policies characteristic of a welfare state, and the attitudes that sustain them.

well, the The small space in the CHAMBER of the US HOUSE OF REPRESENTATIVES between the podium and the front row of seats, in which members mingle during and after a vote.

> Bills are won and lost in the well. If you see a guy who has voted for you in the well, he is going to switch. Rep. PHILIP BURTON (1926–83)

Wellington, Arthur Wellesley, 1st Duke of *See* IRON DUKE.

Welsh Assembly Government The title unilaterally adopted for itself in 2001 by the devolved administration of Wales led by FIRST MINISTER Rhodri Morgan. Of the UK's three devolved administrations, that of Wales is the only one to style itself a government, despite enjoying fewer powers than either the SCOTTISH EXECUTIVE or

NORTHERN IRELAND EXECUTIVE, when that body is functioning.

Welsh windbag The unflattering nickname for Neil KINNOCK, reflecting the over-lengthy and repetitive nature of some of his speeches, his prolixity when interviewed and his protracted contributions in party meetings. It does not reflect his parallel ability to electrify an audience with oratory almost comparable to that of Aneurin BEVAN.

Welsh wizard The popular nickname for David LLOYD GEORGE. It derived from his inspiring oratorical style, his ability to pull off political surprises – and in critics' eyes his deviousness.

> This siren, this goat-footed bard, this half-human visitor to our age from the hag-ridden and enchanted woods of Celtic antiquity. One catches in his company that flavour of final purposelessness, inner irresponsibility, existence outside or away from our Saxon good or evil, mixed with cunning, remorselessness, love of power . . .
>
> JOHN MAYNARD KEYNES (1883–1946)

Weltanschauung (Ger. world view) The political outlook or IDEOLOGY of a person, movement or party. The word sets that ideology in the context of an overall perception of the world or society, and the working of political, social and economic systems.

Wenceslas Square The broad, sloping street in the heart of Prague where Czechs have customarily massed at times of crisis to demonstrate the strength of their feelings. In 1968 it was the scene of resistance to the Soviet tanks that moved in to crush the PRAGUE SPRING, and subsequently of the SELF-IMMOLATION of the student Jan Palach, whose memorial there became a shrine during the period of hard-line rule that followed. The almost continuous demonstrations that filled the Square in late November 1989, and the readiness of the Czech and Slovak media to televise them, were a major factor in the VELVET REVOLUTION that ended Communist rule; the most poignant moment was the heroes' reception accorded the DISSIDENT playwright Václav Havel and Alexander Dubček (*see* COMMUNISM WITH A HUMAN FACE), a NON-PERSON for the previous two decades.

Wessel. Horst Wessel Song The stirring official marching song of Germany's NAZI party, which came to send a chill through the hearts of HITLER's opponents and victims. It was written by Horst Wessel, a student and Nazi stormtrooper, and adopted by the movement as Wessel was elevated to the status of a martyr by Josef Goebbels after his murder in a street brawl in 1930, supposedly by Communists. The tune was taken from an old fishermen's song; the lyrics incorporate many odious sentiments dear to the Nazis. The first verse translates as:

> Hold high the banner! Close the hard ranks serried!
> The SA marches on with sturdy pride.
> Comrades, by Red Front and reaction killed, are buried,
> But march with us in image at our side.

Wessi The name given by former East Germans at the time of the nation's REUNIFICATION in 1990 to their opposite numbers from the West. The eastern counterpart was OSSI.

West, the The collective term for the United States and its NATO allies during the COLD WAR, also used more generally to describe the advanced democracies of industrialised North America and Western Europe. Use of the term, and talk of 'Western values', conveyed a sense of moral superiority – though not always to the listener.

West Bank The territory between the River Jordan and the eastern frontier of ISRAEL. Formerly part of Palestine, it became part of Jordan after the ceasefire of 1949 but was occupied by Israel after the SIX DAY WAR of 1967. As the largest of the OCCUPIED TERRITORIES, with over 1 million Arab inhabitants in towns, villages and refugee camps against some 60,000 Jews, it has been the focus of pressure for the creation of a Palestinian state. Successive LIKUD governments saw the West Bank, under the name JUDAEA AND SAMARIA, as part of Israel's Biblical birthright; 60% of the land is Jewish-owned, some 180 Jewish settlements have been built there since 1967, and in recent years large numbers of Soviet Jews have been encouraged to settle there. Israel has granted a degree of autonomy to the Palestinians and at times has been prepared to cede territory (*see* GAZA AND JERICHO FIRST; WYE PLANTATION), but since the breakdown of negotiations on a radical peace plan in 2002 Israel has shored up its position in the West Bank while stating its intention to pull out of Gaza. The construction of a bitterly-opposed security barrier to seal off much of the West Bank from Israel, ostensibly to deter suicide bombers but incidentally dividing Palestinians from some of their lands and livelihoods, has heightened tensions further. Despite its continuing role in world affairs, the West Bank has not registered with everyone; Enzo Scotti, Italian Foreign Minister for 25 days in July 1992, asked his officials if it was a publicly- or privately-owned US institution of credit.

West Front The elevation of the US CAPITOL atop JENKINS HILL, overlooking the MALL and facing the LINCOLN MEMORIAL and its Reflecting Pool. This is the aspect seen from the WHITE HOUSE and the heart of the government district. Benjamin Latrobe's original design of 1810 was heavily modified between 1817 and 1829 by Charles Bulfinch. The crumbling sandstone of its central section was restored between 1983 and 1987; CONGRESS rejected the option of expanding the building outward to a new frontage. The West Front witnessed its first Presidential INAUGURATION when Ronald REAGAN was sworn in in 1981.

West Germany The everyday name for the German Federal Republic formed in 1948 from the zones of Germany under US, British and French occupation, plus West Berlin. A sovereign democracy, it soon became a member of NATO. The term became obsolete on 3 October 1990 when Germany was reunified.

West Lothian question The question, asked repeatedly by Tam Dalyell, Labour MP for West Lothian, in 1977 in debates on the Scotland Bill, which exposed a central flaw in proposals for DEVOLUTION. It revolved around whether, once a Scottish Parliament had been set up, a full quota of Scottish representatives at WESTMINSTER could justifiably cast their votes on purely English matters. Faced with similar proposals in 1914, Arthur BALFOUR had asked:

> Are you going to leave the whole of these 72 Scottish members here to manage English education?

The answer, when devolution eventually took effect in 1999, turned out to be 'Yes', though at the 2005 election the number of Scottish MPs was reduced by thirteen to lessen a previous over-representation. The persistence with which Dalyell (*see* BELGRANO, CAMPAIGN GROUP) pursued the point 63 years later led Enoch POWELL to name it after his constituency. When the daughter of Malta's prime minister Dom Mintoff threw a bagful of horse manure from the GALLERY and some landed on Dalyell, John SMITH told him:

> That's the answer to the West Lothian question.

West Wing (1) The wing of the WHITE HOUSE which since 1902 has housed the offices of the President and his most valued staff; it replaced greenhouses built on the site of JEFFERSON's west pavilion. Bounded by the portico where visitors are greeted on one side and the ROSE GARDEN on the other, it includes the OVAL OFFICE, Cabinet Room, Roosevelt Room and Reception Room, and also houses the Press Room; the two-storey building is deceptively small as there is working space below ground. Though doubled in size in 1909, further enlarged in 1927 and 1934 and remodelled in 1969, it is still too small for all but the most essential functions of government; many aides have to make do with an office in the OLD EOB next door and consequently lack ACCESS to the President.

> People will kill to get an office in the West Wing.
> MIKE DEAVER

(2) The popular and realistic TV series aired by NBC since 1999 concerning the high-level workings of the White House under the fictional PRESIDENT BARTLET.

Western White House The name given by President REAGAN's staff and the White House media to the President's ranch home north-west of Santa Barbara, California, where he had lived before taking office, returned to during his presidency, and to which he retired in 1989 and went though his long ordeal with Alzheimer's disease.

Westland affair The explosive chain of events in December 1985 and January 1986 that brought Margaret THATCHER's government to its knees and triggered the resignations of two CABINET Ministers. It stemmed from a move by the US helicopter company Sikorski to take a substantial stake in Westland, its smaller British counterpart. Leon Brittan, Trade and Industry Secretary, backed Westland's directors in supporting the bid; Defence Secretary Michael HESELTINE vehemently opposed it, championing a European consortium against a Cabinet majority. In a bitter propaganda war, Ministers briefed against each other as their own meetings became more acrimonious. On 6 January a letter from the Solicitor-General accusing Heseltine of 'material inaccuracies' was fed to the press by Colette Bowe, head of information at the Department of Trade and Industry; Brittan had given his approval, and although a LEAK INQUIRY later fell just short of implicating DOWNING STREET, hostility from the 1922 COMMITTEE forced his resignation on 24 January. By then Heseltine had already staged the most dramatic resignation in generations. Three days after the leak, he found himself faced in Cabinet with an ultimatum from Mrs Thatcher and colleagues; he said: 'I cannot accept that decision' and walked out of the building – only returning after toppling Mrs Thatcher five years later. When these events, which cast great doubt on the government's integrity, were debated in the COMMONS, Mrs Thatcher reputedly told a colleague: 'This may be my last day as Prime Minister,' but an unimpressive speech from Neil KINNOCK let her off the hook. Yet Kinnock did utter the memorable phrase that Britain was experiencing 'government not only rotten to the core, but rotten from the core'. Ironically, Westland has since 2004 been under wholly Italian ownership, under the name of Agusta Westland (*see* MARINE ONE).

> Two men overboard and the captain confined to her cabin. JULIAN CRITCHLEY

Westminster The location of Britain's HOUSES OF PARLIAMENT, and shorthand for the inward-looking and self-sustaining world that exists there (WHITEHALL is the comparable term for the world of administration). Parliament is housed in the **Palace of Westminster**, the inconvenient Gothic spectacle designed by Sir Charles Barry (1795–1860) after the sprawling mediaeval palace on land reclaimed from the Thames was razed to the ground in 1834. The building, which has slowly yielded up large under-used areas held back by officers under royal patronage, now accommodates some 3000 MPs, secretaries, research assistants, committee staff, security, maintenance and catering staff and a sizeable press corps, though as with the US CAPITOL new office space has had to be created elsewhere, notably in PORTCULLIS HOUSE. The House of Commons uses the north end of the building and the Lords the south, with ST STEPHEN'S ENTRANCE and the CENTRAL LOBBY at the midway point and the TERRACE (externally) and COMMITTEE CORRIDOR (internally) running its entire length. The whole is presided over by the clock tower of BIG BEN and the even taller VICTORIA TOWER. Adolf HITLER, in *Mein Kampf*, described it as

> Barry's masterpiece, its thousand windows reflected in the waters of the River Thames.

When this phrase appeared (unattributed) in the Palace's post-war official guide with the bombed-out Commons chamber still under reconstruction, the young James CALLAGHAN complained and a piece of paper was stuck over it.

Westminster Hall (1) The only part of the medieval palace to survive the fire. Built in 1099, the 238ft long, 67ft wide stone-built Hall with its fine wooden hammer-beam roof (dating from 1394) housed for centuries many activities of Parliament, plus the Law Courts until 1882 and even some shops. It was the scene of the trials of Guy Fawkes and King Charles I, the IMPEACHMENT of Warren Hastings and the LYING IN STATE of GLADSTONE, CHURCHILL and a host of kings and queens, most recently Queen Elizabeth the Queen Mother in 2002. The Hall was nearly lost on 10 May 1941 when a dozen German bombs reduced the adjoining Commons chamber to rubble and severely damaged other parts of the Palace. The Conservative MP Walter Elliott broke down the Hall's oak door with an axe, shouting:

> Let the pseudo-Gothic go. We must save the Hall!

The historic roof and the Hall itself were saved – though Elliott could simply have opened the side door kept unlocked for emergencies. (2) The room up a flight of stairs from Westminster Hall – previously known as the Grand Committee Room – where since the turn of the new century MPs have been able to hold ADJOURNMENT DEBATES, four or five in a single morning, and where larger set-piece debates, for example on the work of SELECT COMMITTEES, are held. This opportunity to engage with Ministers has given BACKBENCHERS far more scope for bringing government to account than under the previous dispensation where they were limited to a single adjournment debate per day, often late at night. It has, correspondingly, increased the workload of junior Ministers who have to respond.

Westminster system The system of Parliamentary democracy exported by Britain, in some cases only briefly, to its former overseas possessions. At its heart are a sovereign elected chamber where a SPEAKER maintains good order, a government formed from the majority with a PRIME MINISTER answerable to the House, and a loyal OPPOSITION.

Statute of Westminster The legislation enacted by the British Parliament in 1931 which gave complete autonomy (barring a handful of residual powers mostly reserved to the PRIVY COUNCIL) to within what became the COMMONWEALTH, Australia, Canada, New Zealand, South Africa, Eire and Newfoundland. The Statute, which stemmed from pressure exerted by these states at Imperial Conferences in 1926 and

1930, recognised the right of each to control its own foreign as well as domestic affairs, to establish a diplomatic corps and to be represented at the LEAGUE OF NATIONS.

Wet (1) An opponent of PROHIBITION in the United States; the Wets emerged as a force during the COOLIDGE presidency as it became evident the 'noble experiment' was having social effects at least as disastrous as those it was supposed to cure. (2) An opponent at the start of her premiership of the hard-line MONETARIST policies pursued by Margaret THATCHER, and a supporter of generous social provision by the state. The term was applied condescendingly by Conservative right-wingers to the remaining supporters of Edward HEATH, but even more to the originally large element in Mrs Thatcher's CABINET who opposed her policies but seldom united to check her.

> Wet is, I think, a schoolboy word to describe some wretched boy who doesn't dare do anything either athletic or naughty. The zenith of wetness is when somebody is described as 'so wet you could shoot snipe off him'.
>
> NICHOLAS RIDLEY

wetback An illegal Mexican immigrant to the United States, the word implying that he or she had to swim the Rio Grande to evade border controls. The use of 'wet' to describe livestock smuggled from Mexico dates back to frontier times; it has applied to humans since visa requirements were imposed in 1924. The word has also been used for party activists from one state who travel to another to whip up support for their FAVOURITE SON; in 1983 Sen. Ernest F. Hollings of South Carolina had to apologise for claiming 'wetbacks' from California had boosted that state's Sen. Alan Cranston at his expense in the IOWA CAUCUSES.

wet concrete A serious hazard to CANVASSERS, and others involved in door-step electioneering, as stepping in it can bring instant unpopularity from the voter who laid it, not to mention the mess. The Leeds Labour MP Stan Cohen (1927–2004) once saw he had trodden a newly-concreted path to deliver a party leaflet – so he rescued it from the letter box and put a Conservative one in instead. For another hazard of wet concrete, *see* SARAJEVO.

slippery when wet The wording of one of America's most common highway signs, picked up by George BUSH Snr to describe his Democratic rival Bill CLINTON in his ACCEPTANCE SPEECH at the Republicans' Houston convention in August 1992.

WEU Western European Union. The Paris-based grouping formed in 1955 to harmonise defence and security among its founding member states: France, Germany, Italy, the BENELUX countries, Portugal, Spain and Britain. Virtually dormant for 35 years, it was reactivated in 1990 to provide a European defence organisation which in Britain's view would supplement NATO – as it has up to a point – or in France's supersede it – which it has not, as former Communist countries have queued to join the Atlantic alliance.

what. What is that man for? The unnerving question a little girl is supposed to have asked her mother on seeing Charles James Fox (1749–1806), the English liberal politician who was groomed for the premiership but spent almost all his career in OPPOSITION (*see* MINISTRY OF ALL THE TALENTS). Many politicians in a different time and place would have found such a question hard to answer.

What did the President know and when did he know it? The central question of WATERGATE, as put by Richard NIXON's ally Sen. Howard Baker, which was largely answered when the tapes of the President's conversations were made public at the end of April 1974. The question encapsulated the issue of how deeply implicated Nixon was in the COVER-UP of WHITE HOUSE involvement in the original burglary and in subsequent efforts to frustrate enquiries by the FBI and by CONGRESS. The answer, it transpired, was that Nixon not only knew about the cover-up but had orchestrated it. Barely a decade later, the question was being asked in a new form: **What did the President forget, and when did he forget it?**, as Ronald REAGAN played absent-minded in a largely successful effort to avoid being saddled with responsibility for the IRAN-CONTRA AFFAIR.

What people listening at home want to know is . . . The standard retort used by Tony BENN to divert a broadcast interview from the subject the interviewer wished to question him about to the issue Benn was anxious to discuss. It has also proved a masterful way of catching the audience's attention and getting them to identify with him.

What's good for General Motors is good for the country A paraphrase of testimony by Charles E. Wilson, president of General Motors, to the Senate Armed Services Committee in January 1953. Wilson had been nominated as President EISENHOWER's

Secretary of Defense, and did not wish to sell his GM stock as required by law. He told the committee:

> For many years I thought that what was good for our country was good for General Motors, and vice versa.

What have you done for me lately? The punchline of a story told by the Kentucky Democrat Sen. Alben Barkley, later US Vice President, during his 1938 re-election campaign. Barkley recalled meeting a CONSTITUENT for whom he had done favours as prosecuting attorney, county judge, Congressman and Senator, yet who was still thinking of voting for his opponent. Barkley reminded the man how he had got an access road built to his farm, visited him in hospital in France when wounded in WORLD WAR I, fixed him veterans' benefits and farm credit and got him a disaster loan when floods destroyed his home, and asked: 'Surely you remember all these things I have done for you?' 'Yeah, I remember,' said the farmer. 'But what have you done for me lately?'

Whelehan affair The scandal that forced Albert Reynolds (*see* ALBERTZHEIMER'S DISEASE) to resign as TAOISEACH on 17 November 1994. It stemmed from his nomination of Harry Whelehan, an old FIANNA FAIL associate, to be President of the High Court, the Republic's second most senior judicial office. Mr Whelehan was forced to resign later that day over his mishandling as attorney-general of a child sex abuse case involving a priest in the Republic, the processing of warrants for Fr Brendan Smyth's extradition to Northern Ireland having been stalled for seven months. Whelehan had also come under fire as attorney-general for preventing a 14-year-old rape victim travelling to Britain for an abortion. When the CABINET demanded an explanation for the handling of the Smyth case, Whelehan said (truthfully) that he had never handled it himself, but was accused by Dick Spring, Labour leader and TANAISTE, of 'a serious breach of public responsibility'. Labour left the coalition and the government fell. Reynolds would later be tarnished also by the report of the BEEF COMMISSION, but he left office amid plaudits for his efforts for peace in NORTHERN IRELAND.

> It's amazing. You cross the big hurdles, and when you get to the small ones you get tripped.
>
> ALBERT REYNOLDS, resignation speech to the DAIL

when. When Adam delved and Eve span, who was then the gentleman? The slogan of the PEASANTS' REVOLT of 1381, taken from a sermon by John Ball, the priest who was among its leaders. He was executed after the collapse of the rebellion.

When in the course of human events . . . The opening words of the Preamble to the Declaration of INDEPENDENCE, written (and heavily revised) by Thomas JEFFERSON. The first sentence, containing four changes from Jefferson's draft, reads:

> When, in the course of human events, it becomes necessary for one people to dissolve the political bands which have connected them to another, and to assume, among the powers of the Earth, the separate and equal station to which the laws of nature and of nature's God entitle them, a decent respect to the opinions of mankind required that they should declare the causes which impel them to the separation.

When you have to kill a man, it costs nothing to be polite CHURCHILL's comment when insisting that the declaration of war against Japan on 8 December 1941 (*see* a DATE THAT WILL LIVE IN INFAMY) should follow the correct ceremonial wording.

where. Where's the beef? Walter Mondale's challenge to his fellow Democratic challenger at a DEBATE in Atlanta in April 1984, which became a catch-phrase of that Presidential campaign. The words came from a little old lady in a TV commercial for Wendy's hamburgers; at the suggestion of his campaign manager Robert Beckel, Mondale (*see* NORWEGIAN WOOD) used them to disparage Hart's much-vaunted 'new ideas' and suggest there was nothing to them.

Where's the Rest of Me? The title of a 1965 autobiography by Ronald REAGAN, taken from his own line in the film *King's Row* when the character he played had just had his leg amputated.

Where there is discord, may we bring harmony. Where there is error, may we bring truth. Where there is doubt, may we bring faith. Where there is despair, may we bring hope A variant of the prayer of St Francis of Assisi, quoted by Margaret THATCHER on the steps of 10 DOWNING STREET on 4 May 1979 as she arrived to form her government after the first of her three election victories.

Where was George? The scornful question asked repeatedly by Sen. Edward KENNEDY about George BUSH Snr's part in the REAGAN administration at the 1988 Democratic CONVENTION. The speech, reckoned one of Kennedy's finest, echoed criticism about

Bush's alleged lack of achievement in a series of high offices levelled by Sen. Bob Dole in commercials (*see* FOOTPRINTS IN THE SNOW) during the Republican PRIMARIES.

whiff of grapeshot The use of troops to disperse demonstrators or rioters by firing either at or over them. The phrase was first used by Thomas Carlyle (1795–1881) in his *History of the French Revolution* to describe how Napoleon, as a young officer, quelled a minor riot in Paris.

Whigs (1) In Britain, the party born in the late 17th century to champion the Protestant succession, and which became broadly the predecessor of the LIBERAL PARTY, plus an important landed element. Its title was a nickname given by supporters of the Catholic King James II to the Parliamentary faction led by Shaftesbury which between 1679 and 1682 tried to exclude him from the succession; it probably stems from an acronym of the Covenanters' motto 'We Hope In God'. The Whigs became the dominant faction in English politics from 1685 as opposition to James grew; when he was ousted in the GLORIOUS REVOLUTION of 1688 they took control, the rival TORIES being tarred with their support for the exiled Catholic house of Stuart. The Whigs gradually shifted from being a party of patronage and complacency to one of enlightenment, social reform and curbs on the power of the throne. Their ascendancy was consolidated under WALPOLE from 1721 to 1742, and though in opposition for most of the late 18th and early 19th century, they held power intermittently until the Liberal Party became established; most of the Whig aristocracy gradually shifted to the Conservatives.

> Nought's permanent among the human race
> Except the Whigs not getting into place.
>
> Lord BYRON (1788–1824), *Don Juan*

> False, designing hypocrites, with liberty on their lips and tyranny in their hearts.
>
> WILLIAM COBBETT (1762–1835)

> An unnatural party standing between the people and the Tory aristocracy, chiefly for the pecuniary value of offices and the vanity of power. Their hearse is ordered.
>
> JOSEPH PARKES (1796–1865), 1836

(2) In America, the original Whigs supported the Revolution, blaming the ills of the colonies on George III; the TORIES had been loyal to the Crown, opposing independence. At the height of the Revolutionary War the American Gen. Nathaniel Greene wrote from South Carolina:

> The animosity between the Whigs and the Tories renders their situation truly deplorable. The Whigs seem determined to extirpate the Tories, and the Tories the Whigs . . . If a stop cannot soon be put to these massacres, the country will be depopulated in a few months more.

The Whig Party grew out of the National Republican Party, being founded in 1836 by opponents of Andrew Jackson. It secured the election of the Harrison/Tyler ticket (*see* TIPPECANOE AND TYLER TOO) in 1840 and Taylor/Fillmore in 1848, but disintegrated over the issue of slavery in the early 1850s, most of its adherents joining the embryo REPUBLICAN PARTY; Abraham LINCOLN was originally a Whig.

dish the Whigs To wrong-foot one's opponents by opportunistically adopting their policies, as in STEALING AN OPPONENT'S CLOTHES. It originated in the passage by the Conservatives under Lord Derby of the 1867 REFORM BILL, increasing the franchise by 2 million, as the Whigs had aimed to do. Support from DISRAELI was crucial. Asked why his ADMINISTRATION has passed such a radical measure, Derby beamed: 'Don't you see we have dished the Whigs?' The phrase has remained in use ever since.

Last of the Whigs The nickname of Millard Fillmore (1800–74), who became 13th President of the United States on 9 July 1850 after the death of Zachary Taylor. Elected on the Whig ticket, he could see the party breaking up during his term; the Whig nominee General Winfield Scott was routed in 1852, and Fillmore ran as a KNOW-NOTHING when he tried a comeback in 1856.

Whine on, harvest moon George BUSH's put-down of his Vice Presidential opponent Rep. Geraldine Ferraro's electioneering style in the 1984 campaign. It was a play on the old song title *Shine on, Harvest Moon*. Normally a chivalrous man, Bush's attitude to this DEBATE was shown in his subsequent remark:

> We kicked a little ass last night.

whip (1) A parliamentary BUSINESS MANAGER responsible for maintaining discipline, ensuring the maximum attendance for any vote, reporting the mood of the party to its leadership and keeping an eye on members' personal problems. The word comes from 'whipper-in', the huntsman who keeps the pack of dogs together. Whips operate in most legislatures, but the system is most highly developed in the UK HOUSE OF COMMONS, where the two main parties operate a rigid disciplinary system under a

Chief Whip; and the Liberal Democrats and minor parties mirror the system as far as their numbers require. Sir Robert PEEL felt that the post of Chief Whip 'combines all the qualities of a gentleman, but unfortunately no gentleman would ever accept it'. Beneath the Chief Whip, officially a TREASURY Minister, are a deputy and up to ten junior whips who each have responsibility for a region of the country and an area of policy. Many of these pass through the **Whips' Office**, the engine room of the system, to become Ministers; Chris PATTEN termed it 'that amalgam of officers' mess and political cell'; Robert Atkins, another member of the THATCHER and MAJOR governments, once declared:

> Parliament without a whips' office is like a city without sewage.

In the US CONGRESS the system is less developed and less disciplinarian; though the majority and minority whips in the HOUSE OF REPRESENTATIVES are politicians of substance, being deputies to their party leader, they have been known not only to tolerate dissent but to kick over the traces and lead rebellions, the initial debates on NAFTA in 1993 being a prime example. Junior whips maintain liaison between the leadership and Congressmen from America's various regions.

(2) The summons to vote for one's party on a particular matter; the fiction of delicacy is maintained by requesting attendance rather than crudely demanding a vote, but the threat is implicit. At WESTMINSTER the number of times the request is underlined indicates the strength of the summons; a **three-line whip** means that attendance is obligatory. (3) **The Whip**, at Westminster, is also the sheet of paper sent weekly to its members by each party outlining events they may wish to attend; there is also an all-party whip setting out a calendar of non-partisan occasions. (4) The term 'whip' is also synonymous with membership of one's party. An MP who becomes disenchanted will, as a last resort short of joining another party, **resign the whip**, placing him- or herself outside the party's reach. A party which becomes correspondingly disenchanted with a legislator who will not toe the line may **withdraw the whip**; the Member will sit as an independent alongside former colleagues until they either clamber back on board or go down to defeat by an official party candidate.

whipless nine The nine hard-line anti-European MPs who had the party whip withdrawn in November 1994 for persistently attacking John MAJOR and formed the nucleus of the CAMPAIGN team when John Redwood (*see* VULCAN) ran against him for the party leadership the following summer. The nine, whose loss of the whip lost the government its overall MAJORITY, were Nicholas Budgen, Michael Carttiss, Christopher Gill, Teresa Gorman, Tony Marlow, Richard Shepherd, Sir Teddy Taylor, John Wilkinson and Sir Richard Body, who actually resigned. All eventually returned to the fold.

Whiskey Rebellion The revolt by western Pennsylvania farmers against George WASHINGTON'S ADMINISTRATION in 1794, in protest at the levying of federal taxes on whiskey, which they used as a means of exchange. Alexander HAMILTON, who had imposed the tax in 1791, persuaded WASHINGTON to call out 15,000 militiamen to put the rebellion down; the rebels stayed home and the reputation of Hamilton, who accompanied the troops, suffered greatly.

Whiskey Ring A secret association of distillers and federal officials whose frauds on the government became a major scandal for the GRANT administration in 1875. It was headed by General John McDonald, supervisor of the Internal Revenue Bureau in St Louis; his agents, in partnership with distillers, falsified production figures to lessen tax liability and used the proceeds to bribe other officials. The President knew McDonald well; when Treasury Secretary Benjamin Bristow began uncovering the scandal, Grant told him: 'There is at least one honest man in St Louis on whom we can rely – John McDonald.' When Grant's private secretary General Orville Babcock was also implicated, the President belatedly ordered Bristow:

> Let no guilty man escape if it can be avoided. Be specially vigilant – or instruct those engaged in the prosecution of fraud to be – against all who insinuate that they have high influence to protect – or to protect them. No personal consideration should stand in the way of performing a high public duty.

McDonald was sent to jail and Babcock acquitted of corruption; the affair, together with the subsequent CRÉDIT MOBILIER scandal, tarnished Grant's reputation even though there is no evidence he himself was involved.

whistle. whistleblower An official, or other well-placed person, who comes into the open to expose GRAFT, malpractice or a COVER-UP to the media. The word derives from the phrase 'to **blow the whistle on**', meaning to stop a corrupt practice in the same way a football referee blows his whistle to stop play after a foul. Whistle-blowing is endemic to administrative and corporate cultures where the emphasis is not on doing things right but in covering one's tracks; the EUROPEAN COMMISSION has proved a rich vein in this respect, with the whistleblowers facing near-certain dismissal despite the accuracy of their claims that the taxpayer is being defrauded and the EU's supposed commitment to human rights. WASHINGTON's most celebrated whistleblower was A. Ernest Fitzgerald, fired from the PENTAGON in 1969 by President NIXON after telling CONGRESS of cost overruns on the C-5A cargo plane. It took him 13 years to win reinstatement through the courts, but in 1984 the Air Force barred him from testifying to Congress on his work on financial management. The SENATE subcommittee subpœnaed him, and he told them that a 'blue curtain' had been drawn around him, so that he could not advise on current overcharging by contractors. WHITEHALL's best-known whistleblower, apart from deliberate violators of the OFFICIAL SECRETS ACT such as Clive PONTING, Sarah Tisdall (jailed for leaking secret information about CRUISE MISSILE deployment to the *Guardian*) and Katherine GUN – was Leslie Chapman, a former Property Services Agency official who wrote a book titled *Your Disobedient Servant*, and became an adviser to Margaret THATCHER.

whistle-stop tour A campaign SWING in which a candidate travels on a train, making brief appearances at each town en route. Though tours of this kind had been a regular feature of US politics since at least the days of Theodore ROOSEVELT, the name only stuck when Harry S TRUMAN took to the train in his 1948 UNDERDOG campaign against Thomas DEWEY (who had his own VICTORY SPECIAL). Presidential candidates no longer travel by train throughout, but still make occasional trips on a train with an open platform at the rear to provide PHOTO OPPORTUNITIES and whip up a sense of nostalgia about small-town America. The phrase originates in railway practice, a whistle-stop being a town where trains only halt if signalled to do so.

white (1) A member of the Caucasian race.

> Whites must be made to realise that they are only human, not superior. Same with blacks. They must be made to realise that they are also human, not inferior.
>
> STEVE BIKO (1946–77) (*see* BLACK CONSCIOUSNESS)

> Be nice to whites. They need you to rediscover their humanity.
>
> Archbishop DESMOND TUTU (1931–)

(2) The Whites – as opposed to the REDS – were the conservatives who sought to reverse the RUSSIAN REVOLUTION by defeating the BOLSHEVIKS; their White Army fought an ultimately unsuccessful CIVIL WAR against TROTSKY's RED ARMY. The term **White Russian** came to apply to the aristocratic and middle-class *émigrés* who fled Russia for Paris and other centres as the Bolsheviks took control, remaining in exile in genteal poverty for decades.

White Army The secret army of 30,000 men formed between the wars by conservative small farmers in the Australian state of Victoria which backed up a campaign of militant agitation. Its title echoed that of the anti-Communist Russian Whites.

White Australia policy The policy embodied in the 1901 Australian Immigration Restriction Bill which barred immigrants from 'non-White' countries, especially Japan and China. The fear of the economic and cultural impact of such immigration on Australia was a powerful impetus toward federation in 1900; it echoed concern in America about the YELLOW PERIL which led to the US-Japanese GENTLEMAN'S AGREEMENT. In the first COMMONWEALTH Parliament of 1901, all parties agreed on the need to keep Australian society predominantly European and the Bill was enacted. It excluded Asians by the simple device of a dictation test in a European language, which all immigrants were required to pass. Determination to preserve Australia for whites remained a feature of government policy even after the dictation test was abolished in 1958; only in the mid-1960s did the *Bulletin*, a national newspaper, drop the motto **Australia for the White Man** from its masthead and the measures against Asian immigration were officially relaxed.

> Two Wongs don't make a White.
>
> ARTHUR CALWELL, Labor Party leader 1960–67

White Citizens' Councils The bodies which used intimidation to resist the CIVIL RIGHTS campaign in America's Deep South during the 1950s and '60s. Known as 'country club Klans', they aimed to unite middle-class professionals in maintaining SEGREGATION, to terrorise blacks into letting slip their rights, and to hound out of public life white legislators who favoured change. The White Citizens' Council at LITTLE

ROCK, Arkansas, took a particularly high profile in combating school desegregation.

white flight The process, most notable in America, of white middle-class and blue-collar voters moving out of the INNER CITIES into more prosperous, safer and less highly-taxed suburbs. In the process they reduce the prosperity and the tax base of the area they have left, leaving it to struggle to maintain public services. Under way since at least the 1950s, it carries an inference of trying to escape from increasing concentrations of black and other ethnic groups perceived as hostile.

white heat of technology The most celebrated phrase coined by Harold WILSON during his eighteen months as leader of Britain's LABOUR PARTY before taking power in October 1964. It was seen as committing Labour to creating a modern, technologically-based Britain, in contrast to the GROUSE-MOOR IMAGE exuded by the Conservative government; Wilson also intended it as a signal that Labour was breaking with LUDDITE trade unionism. Addressing the party conference at Scarborough on 1 October 1963, Wilson said:

> We are redefining and we are restating our socialism in terms of the scientific revolution . . . The Britain that is going to be forged in the white heat of this revolution will be no place for restrictive practices or outdated methods on both sides of industry.

White House (1) The official Washington residence of the PRESIDENT of the United States, and the heart of the US government. Designed by Dublin-born James Hoban, the grey sandstone 'President's Palace' was built at 1600 PENNSYLVANIA AVENUE, a boggy site selected by George WASHINGTON. The cornerstone was laid at a Masonic ceremony on 13 October 1792, and its first rooms were just habitable for John and Abigail ADAMS to move in on 2 November 1800; water had to be brought from five blocks away and washing hung in the East Room, but Mrs Adams said: 'This home is built for ages to come' and her husband, on their second day wrote:

> I pray Heaven to bestow the best of blessing on this house, and on all that shall hereafter inhabit it. May none but honest and wise men ever rule under this roof!

The British burned the house when they captured Washington on 28 August 1814. It took three years to rebuild and was now painted white, hence its title. Extended and modified countless times, it now has 132 rooms, including 34 bathrooms and eleven bedrooms; portable anti-aircraft missiles were rumoured to be deployed on the roof even before 9/11.

Over the years the White House has aroused strong feelings among those required to live in it, Harry S TRUMAN branding it 'the finest prison in the world' and John Quincy Adams' wife Louisa writing:

> There is something in the great unsocial house which depresses my spirit beyond expression and makes it impossible for me to feel at home or to fancy that I have a home anywhere.

And Jacqueline KENNEDY (*see* JACKIE O) complained:

> It looks like it's been furnished by discount stores. There is no trace of the past.

It was a deficiency she quickly managed to rectify, giving the Executive mansion a style it has retained over four decades.

The White House's claustrophobic nature has deterred many from seeking to become President. General Tecumseh Sherman declared:

> Having to choose between the White House and the penitentiary, I'd choose the penitentiary.

And the film actress Debra Winger, asked in 1992 if she would be FIRST LADY to Sen. Bob Kerrey (*see* COSMIC BOB) who was making a run for the Presidency, said:

> If I wanted to live in an aquarium, I'd buy an aquarium and live in it.

The White House, like 10 DOWNING STREET, is both home and office combined. To Ronald REAGAN this was second nature:

> When I was a very small boy in a small town in Illinois, we lived above the store where my father worked. I have something of the same arrangement here.

Benjamin HARRISON, having served one term, was less impressed, writing in 1897:

> There is only one door – that is never locked – between the President's office and what are not very accurately called his private apartments. For everyone else in the public service there is an unroofed space between the bedroom and the desk.

As well as denoting the building, the phrase 'the White House' personifies the Presidency, denotes the headquarters of the EXECUTIVE BRANCH of government, is said to speak through official utterances and briefings, and is used as shorthand for a complex that also includes the OLD and New EXECUTIVE OFFICE BUILDINGS and BLAIR

HOUSE. Reagan's CABINET SECRETARY Al Kingon termed the White House 'the most defensive operation in government. You're constantly under barrage.' Alexander Haig, Richard NIXON's Chief of Staff and Reagan's Secretary of State, considered that 'there are three main levers of power in the White House: the flow of paper, the President's schedule and the press.'

> The President never really leaves the White House. He takes most of it with him.
>
> HEDRICK SMITH, *The Power Game*

(2) The concrete and glass building nearly a mile from the KREMLIN which houses the Parliamentary offices of the Russian republic. The **House of the Duma** is the actual Parliament building. It was the scene of the siege in 1991 after the KREMLIN COUP when Boris Yeltsin and his supporters defied Soviet tanks to remain at their posts until Mikhail GORBACHEV was freed from house arrest in the Crimea and flown back to Moscow. Two years later, ironically, Yeltsin sent in the troops, leaving 150 people dead, when the Parliament became the centre of resistance to his rule by refusing to accept its dissolution.

White House Iceberg The nickname of President Benjamin HARRISON, reflecting his aloofness. One anonymous Senator said of him: 'It's like talking to a hitching-post.'

White House tapes The tapes of his private conversations in the OVAL OFFICE, kept as a matter of routine by President NIXON, which proved his downfall when CONGRESS found out about them after WATERGATE. The bulk of the tapes were released with great reluctance by the White House on 30 April 1974, ten months after their existence had been confirmed; they became an instant best-seller, not least because of the language Nixon had used (*see* EXPLETIVE DELETED) and an 18½-MINUTE GAP fuelled suspicions of a further COVER-UP. The release of these tapes set the central question of Watergate: WHAT DID THE PRESIDENT KNOW AND WHEN DID HE KNOW IT? The 'White House tapes' came more specifically to be a further batch withheld by Nixon, which were only handed over to the SPECIAL PROSECUTOR in July 1974 at the insistence of the SUPREME COURT; these proved Nixon's guilt beyond a doubt and within days the House Judiciary Committee voted to recommend Nixon's IMPEACHMENT. Asked at a press lunch in 1986 what he considered the greatest lesson of Watergate, Nixon replied:

> Just destroy all the tapes.

As of now, I am in control here in the White House, pending the return of the Vice President The statement issued by Secretary of State Alexander Haig on 30 March 1981 shortly after John Hinckley's attempt to assassinate President REAGAN. With George BUSH Snr flying back to Washington from Texas, it was intended to demonstrate that the situation was under control despite the serious injuries the President had suffered, and that there was no excuse for panic. However, Haig exceeded his constitutional powers, and the statement was seen by other senior members of the ADMINISTRATION as a grab for power. They praised Haig for his prompt action, then sidelined him.

coffee and Danish at the White House Washington code for breakfast meetings at which the President tries to sell his legislative agenda to Congressional leaders and others. The phrase originated during the CARTER administration; to the uninitiated 'Danish' are Danish pastries. *Compare* BEER AND SANDWICHES AT NUMBER TEN.

white man's burden The late 19th-century IMPERIALIST view of the responsibility the colonial powers owed to the people of the territories they had taken over. The phrase was probably originated by Rudyard Kipling (1865–1936) who wrote:

> Take up the White Man's Burden –
> Send forth the best ye breed –
> Go, bind your sons to exile
> To serve your captives' need;
> To wait in heavy harness
> On fluttered folk and wild –
> Your new-caught, sullen peoples,
> Half-devil and half-child.

White March The protest march through Brussels in October 1996 by 325,000 people carrying white roses, lilies and balloons to protest against corruption in public life, triggered by the murder of four young girls by a paedophile ring led by Marc Dutroux. The demonstration, one of the biggest in the country's history, stemmed from the public conviction that Dutroux could have been caught earlier, and some of the murders avoided, but for police incompetence and a COVER-UP involving people in high places. The years it took eventually to convict him heightened these suspicions.

White Paper A document published by a government setting out the policy it has decided to follow on a particular matter, or giving authoritative information. In Britain publication of a White Paper generally amounts to a commitment to legislate; if there is any flexibility the paper is said to have **green edges**. In America a White Paper contains facts the ADMINISTRATION wants to get across; one of the most celebrated was prepared for the KENNEDY administration by Arthur Schlesinger to demonstrate prior to the Bay of PIGS that Fidel Castro had betrayed his own Cuban revolution by turning it over to the Communists. White Papers are also prepared by the EUROPEAN COMMISSION to indicate the next step it believes should be taken toward closer or deeper union.

white supremacist The attitude of the (predominantly Democratic) political community that ran and represented the Deep South from the end of RECONSTRUCTION until the establishment of CIVIL RIGHTS for black Americans from the early 1960s. The term is both a noun and an adjective.

Whitehall The broad thoroughfare in London linking Trafalgar Square with Parliament Square (its southernmost section is actually called Parliament Street). DOWNING STREET runs into it, and it is mainly lined by government departments. 'Whitehall' has become shorthand for the upper reaches of the government BUREAUCRACY, a collective term juxtaposed with WESTMINSTER, which refers to the politicians. In the 1960s the veteran political journalist James Margach branded it 'a conspiracy of secrecy'.

the gentleman in Whitehall knows best The statement in 1947 by the junior Labour Minister Douglas Jay (later Lord Jay, 1907–96) which summed up both the high-minded intentions of the ATTLEE government and what the Conservatives saw as a nightmare of BUREAUCRACY and centralised controls. In his book *The Socialist Case*, Jay wrote:

> In the case of nutrition and health, just as in the case of education, the gentleman in Whitehall really does know better what is good for people, than the people know themselves.

Whitelaw, William (Viscount) *See* WILLIE.

whitewash An attempt to make a misdeed by those in office, or an ugly episode or policy, look harmless. In the early days of MCCARTHYISM, Congressional Republicans claimed that the TRUMAN administration's investigations of federal employees' loyalty were only a whitewash. And in December 1973, as the WATERGATE scandal started to assume ominous proportions for Richard NIXON, the President promised the most thorough investigation, pledging:

> There can be no whitewash at the White House.

Whitewater The scandal surrounding an investment by Bill and Hillary CLINTON, years before entering the WHITE HOUSE, in a retirement community in north Arkansas. Seized on by the political right and sections of the media – notably the *Wall Street Journal* – as a serious case of corruption, it was merged by them with the FOSTER SUICIDE (Vince Foster had files on the case in his office and was claimed to be part of a COVER-UP inspired by Hillary Clinton), TRAVELGATE and other episodes culminating in ZIPPERGATE as proof of Clinton's unfitness to govern. Corruption there had been – in May 1996 a LITTLE ROCK jury handed down 24 guilty verdicts out of 30 counts of conspiracy, wire fraud and false bookkeeping against Gov. Jim Guy Tucker and Susan McDougal, a former business partner of the Clintons – but the central contention that the Clintons had profited from illegal dealings through their connections in the state, or at all, was never proven. In 1978 Bill Clinton, then state Attorney-General, his wife, McDougal and her then husband Jim bought 203 acres in the Ozark Mountains for the venture. Four years later the McDougals set up the Madison Guaranty savings and loan bank, and in 1985 Susan McDougal secured a $300,000 loan and illegally channelled part of it into Whitewater; whether the Clintons were aware of this is not known. There were also claims that Clinton had used a $30,000 payment from Madison to pay off past election expenses. In 1989 Madison collapsed, costing the taxpayer $65 million, and at the end of 1992, prior to being sworn in as President, Clinton handed back his loss-making stake in Whitewater to Jim McDougal. When the Clintons were named by the US Treasury in 1993 as 'potential beneficiaries' of illegal activity at the bank, a political storm led to the appointment of a SPECIAL COUNSEL, Robert Fiske, and, then, in August 1994, a SPECIAL PROSECUTOR, Kenneth STARR. The Republicans hoped that Starr would find enough evidence to charge Hillary Clinton with perjury. Highly partisan Senate hearings were held in 1995 after the Republicans took control of Congress, but no SMOKING GUN was found. In January 1996 Hillary Clinton was subpoenaed to appear before a grand jury on Whitewater, the first FIRST LADY ever put under such a sanction. The issue subsided, Starr's 1998 report concentrating on Clinton's failure to tell the truth about his dalliance with Monica LEWINSKY. But it did claim a number of victims apart from the McDougals and Vince Foster: Roger Altman, deputy Treasury Secretary, who resigned after being accused of misleading Congress with his testimony about White House contacts with the Treasury over a probe into Madison; Jean Hanson, the Treasury's top lawyer, who ran into similar problems; Bernard Nussbaum, White House counsel; and Webster Hubbell, a former law partner of Hillary Clinton who was imprisoned for billing irregularities after resigning as associate Attorney General.

> Whitewater never seemed real, because it wasn't.
> HILLARY CLINTON

Whitlam, Gough (1916–) The LABOR Prime Minister of Australia (1972–75) controversially sacked by the GOVERNOR-GENERAL, Sir John KERR, as his ministry got into difficulties. An intellectual but robust lawyer, he entered the New South Wales Parliament in 1952 and in 1955 made his name with a bid to oust the party leadership; his colleague Fred Daly said: 'Any one of us could have put up a solid fight, but Gough wanted three at a time.' Elected to the House of Representatives in 1956, he became party leader in 1967. Labor lost the 1969 federal election, but in 1972 he led it back to power (*see* IT'S TIME!) after twelve years in the wilderness. A non-sectarian radical, his ADMINISTRATION was progressive but not extreme, and he and his tall, literary wife Margaret occupied the LODGE with dignity. He saw himself as a reformer, saying: 'From the time when John Curtin was Prime Minister in 1944 I was determined to do all I could to reform the Australian constitution.' The political writer Patrick Weller called him 'a brilliant parliamentarian, witty, articulate, capable of wounding with vicious shafts of ridicule', and if necessary he could act tough with his fractious party (*see* BASTARDS).

Labor's grip on power weakened in the 1974 elections, and its supporters' high hopes were dashed as the economy deteriorated and a series of Ministers became involved in financial scandals. Those at the heart of the controversy objected to Whitlam's style, Federal Treasurer Dr Jim Cairns (*see* MOROSI AFFAIR) asking: 'Whose party is this, ours or his?' But Whitlam's speechwriter Graham Freudenberg wrote: 'He could not accept that economic expertise was a necessary qualification for political leadership.' With Parliament in deadlock over SUPPLY, Kerr abruptly called in Whitlam on 11 November 1975 and dismissed him; Labor was outraged, but lost the subsequent general election. When the party finally returned to power under Bob HAWKE in 1983, Whitlam was appointed ambassador to UNESCO, serving until 1986. Looking back on his career and its controversial climax, he said:

> My place in history will bring no discredit.

Whitley Council The negotiating body, comprising representatives of staff, management and the Department of Health, that determines pay and conditions for many workers in the UK's National Health Service (NHS). Doctors and nurses have their own pay review bodies.

who. Who am I? Why am I here? The revealingly frank question asked by Admiral James Stockdale, Ross PEROT's running-mate, when caught in crossfire between Dan QUAYLE and Al GORE in the televised vice presidential debate in Atlanta on 13 October 1992.

Who are we playing? The response reputedly given by the West German MEP Otto von Habsburg (1912–), son of the last Austro-Hungarian emperor and theoretical heir to the throne, when asked if he would be watching an Austria-Hungary football match. Crown Prince at the age of four and pretender to the throne, Franz Josef Otto Robert Maria Anton Karl Max Heinrich Sixtus Xavier Felix René Ludwig Gaetano Pius Ignazius von Habsburg opposed the ANSCHLUSS, spent WORLD WAR II in America, renounced his claim to the throne in 1961 and was allowed back to Austria five years later, though he continued to live in Germany. He served as a CSU member of the EUROPEAN PARLIAMENT from 1979 to 1999.

Who goes home? At WESTMINSTER, the traditional call from police officers in the LOBBIES of the HOUSE OF COMMONS when it rises for the night.

Who governs Britain? The theme of the general election of February 1974, and the unofficial slogan of Edward HEATH's governing Conservatives. Heath fought the election at the height of a miners' strike, with the country on a THREE-DAY WEEK; he aimed to win a new MANDATE by rallying the voters on the side of authority against the unions. The Tory MP Jock (later Lord) Bruce-Gardyne knew the strategy was doomed when he used the slogan at a public meeting and a constituent told him: 'If you have to ask that question, you shouldn't be running the country.' The election resulted in a HUNG PARLIAMENT, Labour took power and a year later Heath was replaced by Margaret THATCHER.

Who is Mr Round and why does he object? Winston CHURCHILL's baffled marginal note on receiving a proposal at the end of which an official had written 'Round objects'. The official, who regarded the proposal as idiotic, had wanted to write 'Balls!' but did not feel he should use such language in a MINUTE to the Prime Minister.

Who lost China? *See* CHINA LOBBY.

Who? Who? Ministry The derisive name given by its critics to the Earl of Derby's first TORY government, formed in July 1852. It originated in the shouts of 'Who? Who?' from the aged Duke of Wellington as the names of its members were read to him; they were little better known to the public, and the government did not survive an election five months later.

Whore of the Republic *See* ELF AQUITAINE.

Whose finger on the trigger? A paraphrase of the front-page headline carried by Britain's *Daily Mirror* the day before the October 1951 general election. In full it read: 'Whose finger do you want on the trigger when the world's situation is so delicate?', the message being that with the COLD WAR and KOREAN WAR at their height, the cautious Clement ATTLEE would be safer for world peace than the Tories' war leader Winston CHURCHILL. The headline reflected a campaign Labour had been running since that May when Hugh Dalton had warned: 'If we get Churchill and the Tory party back at the next election we shall be at war with Russia within twelve months.' Churchill sued the *Mirror* for libel, and Labour lost the election.

why. *Why England Slept* The best-seller written by the young John F. KENNEDY, telling of Britain's complacency on the eve of WORLD WAR II. Based on his senior political science thesis at Harvard which won him a *magna cum laude*, it drew on insights and contacts he gained through his father's position as US ambassador in London.

Why not the best? The slogan of the outsider Jimmy CARTER's 1976 campaign for the Presidency, and the title of the book he wrote to accompany and explain his challenge.

Why, Sir? The two words which, used as a SUPPLEMENTARY, can floor a Minister at QUESTION TIME in the HOUSE OF COMMONS. They take effect when the Minister responding has been given a highly technical brief by his civil servants and has no personal knowledge of the subject. The most devastating instance was in the early 1980s when Peter (later Lord) Walker, then Minister of Agriculture, had the question sprung on him by the Labour MP Tam Dalyell, and was unable to respond.

wig. If I had a wig, would I have bought one with a hole in it? The response of George (later Lord) Robertson, UK Defence Secretary and later Secretary-General of NATO, to a constituent who had accused him of wearing a hairpiece. *See also* LUCY.

wiggle room An expressive US term for the space an experienced politician will leave themselves to alter their position in the light of experience or criticism.

Wild Thing A spoof of the No. 1 hit single by the UK group the Troggs, recorded in America in 1967 by 'Senator Bobby', who purported to be Robert F. KENNEDY. A parody of efforts by politicians in general to be trendy as much as of RFK himself, it had the 'Senator' delivering such lyrics as 'wild thing . . . you move me' in a deadpan monotone, with voices off urging him to inject more feeling.

Wilkes and Liberty! The slogan with which the London mob embraced the radical and libertine John Wilkes (1727–97) after his imprisonment and exclusion from Parliament for publishing the NORTH BRITON and his *Essay on Woman*, which was peppered with four-letter words. Wilkes was a member of the Hell Fire Club, which staged exhausting and notorious orgies, until he entered politics; it took bribery to get elected, including paying a sea captain to deliver to Norway a boatload of voters shipped in by a rival candidate. But he became a popular hero for his opposition to Lord Bute and his advocacy of the rights of the people, and he was honoured in America for his sympathies with the colonists in their eventual move for independence. He overcame the political ESTABLISHMENT to become Sheriff of Middlesex and Lord MAYOR of London and returned triumphantly to the Commons in 1774, but the mob deserted him when he spoke out against the GORDON RIOTS of 1780.

Williams v Mississippi The US SUPREME COURT ruling in April 1898 which endorsed the suffrage clauses of the Southern states' new constitutions, under which the white supremacist BOURBONS had effectively disfranchised almost all black voters, and many poor whites. The Court held that they did not strictly discriminate between races, and were thus 'within the field of permissive action under the limitations imposed by the Federal Constitution'. The decision paved the way for further rulings upholding JIM CROW laws.

Willie The affectionate nickname of William Stephen Ian (later Viscount) Whitelaw (1918–99), the old-school Tory, bluff landowner and former Scots Guards officer who from 1979 to 1988 served Margaret THATCHER as a loyal, trusted and much-liked deputy, causing her to observe innocently: **'every Prime Minister needs a Willie'**. Elected to Parliament in 1955, he was a junior Minister under MACMILLAN and SIR ALEC Douglas-Home, was Leader of the Commons, NORTHERN IRELAND Secretary (the first) and Energy Secretary under Edward HEATH, and showed his loyalty by only standing for the Tory leadership in 1975 once Mrs Thatcher had knocked Heath out of the running; had he challenged at the outset, he might have won. Mrs Thatcher immediately appointed him her deputy, and in 1979 he kept that position when he became Home Secretary. At the Home Office Whitelaw had a bumpy ride, notably over the 1981 Brixton riots and the entry of an intruder into the Queen's bedroom. His imposition of the SHORT, SHARP SHOCK regime for young offenders was not enough to head off Tory demands for the return of hanging; he was furious when Mrs Thatcher applauded these critics during his 1981 conference speech, telling her:

> I have been loyal to you through thick and thin, and I expect as much in return.

Whitelaw acted as Prime Minister in her absence, chairing key CABINET committees and telling the COMMONS at the depth of the RECESSION of the early 1980s that he did not understand her economic policies but was sure they were splendid. She placed great faith in his ability to detect political BANANA SKINS, and in 1983 sent him to the Lords as its Leader, with a hereditary Viscountcy. Whitelaw pushed through a mountain of legislation, but in 1987 suffered a stroke at the Parliamentary carol service and, though making a full recovery, decided to retire.

Slick Willie *See* SLICK.

Wilson, (James) **Harold,** later Lord Rievaulx (1916–95), the Yorkshire-born academic prodigy who led Britain's LABOUR PARTY from 1963 to 1976 and was Prime Minister 1964–70 and 1974–76, winning four of the five elections into which he led the party. Best known for his pipe and Gannex raincoat, his homespun accent and manner, mordant wit, a dominant speaking style, a touch of paranoia and a MACCHIAVELLIAN sense of intrigue, he held his party together and presided over a period of social and economic change which he was never quite able to control. He grew up near Huddersfield where 'more than half the children in my class never had any boots or shoes to their feet. They wore clogs, because they lasted longer than shoes of comparable price.' The Conservative MP Ivor Bulmer-Thomas commented: 'If Harold Wilson ever went to school without boots, it was merely because he was too big for them.' An Oxford don at 21 and a wartime Whitehall economist under CHURCHILL, he was elected to Parliament in the 1945 Labour LANDSLIDE and at 31 was PRESIDENT OF THE BOARD OF TRADE in ATTLEE's Cabinet; of one early visit to Moscow when he took part in an impromptu cricket match, he recalled: 'I must be the only Minister to have been dropped at silly mid-on by a member of the NKVD.' In 1951 Wilson resigned with Aneurin BEVAN in protest at the imposition of NHS charges to help finance REARMAMENT, thus gaining credentials as a left-winger. Yet Wilson was not that close to Bevan, hence this reported exchange:

> *Bevan*: Where did you say you were born, boy?
> *Wilson*: Yorkshiremen are not born – they are forged.
> *Bevan*: I always knew there was something counterfeit about you.

Wilson showed flair in OPPOSITION, saying in 1957: 'Every time that Mr MACMILLAN comes home from abroad, Mr Butler (*see* RAB) grips him firmly by the throat.' And though never fully a Bevanite, he had the left's backing in a challenge to Hugh GAITSKELL's leadership in 1960. Three years later when Gaitskell died, he won the leadership over George BROWN and James CALLAGHAN. Amid near-euphoria, he showed a new CHARISMA in parliamentary duels with Macmillan, united the party with talk of the WHITE HEAT OF TECHNOLOGY, and in the wake of the PROFUMO AFFAIR led Labour to a tight election victory in 1964. Adverse trade figures and a refusal to DEVALUE the pound boxed in the new government's hopes for economic expansion through a NATIONAL PLAN, and a six-vote majority prevented it carrying out its full programme of NATIONALISATION. In early

1966 Wilson called a SNAP ELECTION, and Labour won a majority of almost 100. Again the party's hopes were frustrated by further economic squalls, leading to the JULY MEASURES and, in November 1967, eventual devaluation (*see* The POUND IN YOUR POCKET). However, Wilson presided over a wide range of social reforms, and managed to keep British troops out of VIETNAM without wrecking Anglo-US relations, though left-wingers vilified him for subservience to WASHINGTON. Challenged by them at a party conference, he said: 'I am nobody's gigolo.' Wilson described himself as a PRAGMATIST, saying: 'I'm not a Kennedy. I'm a Johnson. I fly by the seat of my pants.' David FROST put it another way: 'You knew where you were with Macchiavelli.' He held his party together despite frequent flare-ups with the colourful Brown, who eventually resigned from the Cabinet but remained deputy leader. But he was quick to detect 'plots' against him by Cabinet colleagues, READ THE RIOT ACT to rebellious MPs in the DOG LICENCE SPEECH and told party activists in 1968:

> I know what is going on. I am going on.

His kitchen CABINET, and particularly the influence of his political secretary Marcia Williams (*see* Lady FORKBENDER) attracted controversy, as did his relationship with the press which deteriorated sharply in the late 1960s. Being in Wilson's governments could be unnerving; Roy JENKINS wrote: 'His style of leadership was so much more like that of the acrobat skilfully riding a bicycle on the tightrope than of the ringmaster imperiously cracking the whip that a fall seemed constantly possible.' In the spring of 1970, with the economy recovering under Jenkins, Wilson went to the country early; halfway through the campaign Labour was 13% ahead, but unexpectedly lost to Edward HEATH's Tories. Wilson was blamed for a vacuous campaign, but survived as leader though the party was moving uncomfortably to the left. Early in 1974, frustrated by a crippling miners' strike, Heath called an election on the theme of WHO GOVERNS BRITAIN?, and lost. Wilson returned as head of a minority government, and that October won a narrow majority. For two years he presided over an economy dominated by inflation that peaked at 27%, and industrial decline. His main achievement was the renegotiation of Britain's EC membership, confirmed in a REFERENDUM in 1975 that settled an issue on which the Labour Cabinet was firmly divided without weakening the government. In April 1976 Wilson suddenly resigned; conspiracy theorists believed some dark secret was about to emerge, but the truth was that after thirteen years he had had enough. He has also detected the rise of the MILITANT TENDENCY and other far left groups, telling Labour's 1975 conference: 'I have no wish to lead a party of political zombies.' His retirement was followed by controversy over the LAVENDER LIST of impresarios and property developers he nominated for honours. Wilson took a life peerage in 1983, but his retirement was dogged by ill-health; early on he told a former colleague that he was busier than ever, only to be told: 'You may be busy, but are you actually doing anything?'

Wilson's common touch applied to the point of philistinism attracted ridicule; he once said: 'If I had the choice between smoked salmon and tinned salmon, I'd have it tinned. With vinegar.' His wife Mary, who preferred poetry to politics, confided: 'If Harold has a fault it is that he will smother everything with HP sauce.' Colleagues were wary of him from the start; Bevan scorned him as 'all bloody facts, no bloody vision', Hugh Dalton as 'NYE's little dog.' Nor was he widely trusted. One MP said: 'You can always tell when he's lying. His lips move'; Iain Macleod declared: 'Double-talk is his mother tongue'; William F. Buckley Jr called him 'the world's most unbelievable politician', and Rebecca West wrote: 'He always looks as if he were on the verge of being found out.' He could be savage in his judgements, calling Robert Maxwell (prophetically) 'the bouncing Czech' and saying of a political journalist: 'She missed the last LOBBY briefing. At the vet's with hard pad, no doubt.' He was devastating with HECKLERS, once telling an errant leaflet thrower: 'Your aim is as good as your material.'

> A petit-bourgeois, he will remain so in spirit even if made a viscount. NEIL KINNOCK

> He was essentially a weak leader of a broad party. To become a ruthless leader of a narrow party was not his style. ROY JENKINS

> One of the world's most adroit politicians, but with a touch of paranoia about him.
> US Ambassador DAVID BRUCE

Wilson, Woodrow (1856–1924), 28th President of the United States (Democrat, 1913–21). A Southern educationalist who entered politics with a burning moral commitment, Wilson was forced into WORLD

WAR I against his beliefs, sought to dictate a moralistic peace settlement, and after a stroke in September 1919 governed through his second wife Edith (*see* PRESIDENTRESS). A Virginia lawyer who became a 'reformed character' as President of Princeton, Wilson became Governor of New Jersey in 1910 and in 1912 was elected President when the BULL MOOSE ticket of Theodore ROOSEVELT, who scorned him as a 'Byzantine logothete', split the Republicans. Wilson, who termed himself a 'progressive with the brakes on', took office with high hopes of improving the American tone of life, even bringing in sheep to control the WHITE HOUSE lawn. He once wrote:

> Why has Jesus Christ so far not succeeded in inducing the world to follow his teachings? I am proposing a practical scheme to carry out his aims.

He also said: 'Sometimes people call me an idealist. Well, that is the only way I know I am an American.' He pushed himself relentlessly, saying: 'It is only by working with an energy which is almost superhuman and looks to uninterested spectators like insanity that we can accomplish anything worth the achievement.' Yet he confessed ominously: 'It would be the irony of fate if my ADMINISTRATION had chiefly to deal with foreign affairs.' Indeed, had world peace held, he would probably be best remembered as the President who VETOed PROHIBITION. When war broke out in Europe, he resolved to keep America clear, saying: 'There is such a thing as a man being too proud to fight.' He won re-election in 1916 as 'peace President', to the frustration of LLOYD GEORGE who said: 'He has no international conscience. He thinks of nothing but the ticket.' But two months after his INAUGURATION, U-boat atrocities and the ZIMMERMAN NOTE forced him into war.

America's intervention ensured eventual defeat for Germany, and Wilson set about drafting a peace settlement (WILSON'S FOURTEEN POINTS) that would free the peoples of Europe and prevent America ever again having to fight. George Slocombe wrote: 'He was the Messiah of the new age, and his crucifixion was yet to come.' He was foiled at VERSAILLES, where CLEMENCEAU asked: 'How can I talk to a fellow who thinks himself the first person in two thousand years to know anything about peace on earth?', and on his return isolationists in CONGRESS objected to the LEAGUE OF NATIONS, which he had promoted. He stumped the country to rally support; in Pueblo, Colorado on 25 September 1919 he said:

> My clients are the children, my clients are the next generation. They do not know what promises and bonds I undertook when I ordered the armies of the United States to the soil of France, and I intend to redeem my pledges to the children; they shall not be sent on a similar errand.

That night he collapsed; back at the White House he suffered a stroke and the battle for the League was lost.

Wilson had been devoted to his first wife, who died in 1914, and was as close to his second whom he married the next year. Edith once confided: 'When he proposed to me, I fell out of bed', and when the British Ambassador Lord Grey repeated this the President refused to receive him for nine months. Once he had suffered his stroke, Edith Galt Wilson told the President's subordinates what decisions he had 'taken' (*see* Petticoat GOVERNMENT). His physician, Dr Francis Dercum, told her: 'For Mr Wilson to resign would have a bad effect on the country, and a serious effect on our patient.' When the isolationist Sen. Albert Fall visited the recuperating Wilson and said: 'Well, Mr President, we have all been praying for you', Wilson asked him: 'Which way, Senator?'

> The greatest president of this century – and the best-educated. RICHARD NIXON

> The President spent much of the evening entering Mrs Galt.
> *Washington Post* misprint, 1915

> The air currents of the world never ventilated his mind. WALTER HINES PAGE

> There was something about the stiff white cuffs, the gleaming collar, the sparkling pince-nez, the beautifully pressed trousers, that he had dressed in a disinfected room with the assistance of a highly efficient valet, who had put on the clothes with pincers. He was like a dentist or a distinguished surgeon.
> BEVERLEY NICHOLS

Wilson's Fourteen Points The 'only possible program' for a new world order after WORLD WAR I, put forward by President Wilson in an address to CONGRESS on 8 January 1918. The 'points' were drafted by the COLUMNIST Walter Lippmann after criticism from overseas of Wilson's long-winded speeches. The first point was 'OPEN COVENANTS OF PEACE, OPENLY ARRIVED AT'. Wilson also proposed freedom of the seas, FREE TRADE, DISARMAMENT, impartial settlement of colonial claims, SELF-

DETERMINATION for the peoples of Europe and a LEAGUE OF NATIONS. Though welcomed by America's allies for their high moral tone as war aims, they ran into resistance at VERSAILLES once the war was over, and the League fell foul of ISOLATIONISTS in Congress, who kept America out. Wilson contributed to this by not including a senior Republican in the US delegation to the peace talks.

> Fourteen? The good Lord only has ten.
>
> CLEMENCEAU

wimp factor One of the electoral minuses that George BUSH Snr overcame to become President, based on his privileged background and a belief that, despite a courageous war record, he was not a man who enjoyed facing challenges or taking decisive steps. The term had been used of previous candidates, such as Walter Mondale (*see* NORWEGIAN WOOD).

Mush from the Wimp The headline anonymously inserted into the *Boston Globe* on 15 October 1980 over a report of President CARTER's anti-inflation programme. Earlier editions had borne the authorised headline: 'All must share the burden.'

wind. wind of change The phrase used dramatically by Harold MACMILLAN in a speech to the South African Parliament on 3 February 1960 to point up the inevitability of black rule in Africa and the futility of APARTHEID. He said:

> The most striking of all the impressions I have formed since I left London a month ago is the strength of this African national consciousness . . . The wind of change is blowing throughout this continent, and, whether we like it or not, this growth of national consciousness is a political fact.

The phrase in this context was not original; on 4 December 1934 Stanley BALDWIN told a meeting in London:

> There is a wind of nationalism and freedom blowing round the world, and blowing as strongly in Asia as elsewhere.

wind-up At WESTMINSTER, the final speeches from OPPOSITION and government in a major debate, leading up to a DIVISION, and often accompanied by increasing noise and disruption as members return to the CHAMBER prior to the vote.

windbag Someone who speaks at great length, without necessarily saying a great deal or knowing much. John F. KENNEDY kept his INAUGURAL address short because 'I don't want people to think I am a windbag'. Neil KINNOCK was known to his critics as the WELSH WINDBAG.

window of opportunity A limited amount of time when a particular action can be taken before unfavourable factors come into play. It is used particularly in UK politics when discussing the best moment for a Prime Minister to call an ELECTION; in international affairs it often refers to a moment when there is a better chance than usual of making progress, for instance in the Middle East PEACE PROCESS.

Windsor (House of) The official name of the British ROYAL FAMILY, adopted in 1917, in deference to anti-German sentiment, to replace the previous name of Saxe-Coburg-Gotha, derived from Queen Victoria's consort Prince Albert. It was changed in 1960 to Mountbatten-Windsor for the descendants of Queen Elizabeth II, other than those entitled to the style of Royal Highness, Prince or Princess. After his ABDICATION on 11 December 1936, King Edward VIII was created Duke of Windsor. The name comes from **Windsor Castle**, the mediaeval fortress 20 miles west of London which is one of the Queen's official homes and where the Prime Minster dines and stays each spring. Parts of the castle were severely damaged by fire in November 1992, after which a political storm broke over the government's announcement that it would foot the bill for repairs; John MAJOR dampened the controversy by disclosing that the Queen had agreed to pay income tax, from which the SOVEREIGN had been exempt since 1937.

wine lake The vast surplus of virtually undrinkable red wine produced from Mediterranean wines which became an embarrassment for the EUROPEAN COMMUNITY in the late 1970s and early '80s. It was caused by a combination of high subsidies from BRUSSELS and parallel restrictions on price-cutting to reduce demand. *See also* MOUNTAIN.

Winnie The nickname which attached to Winston CHURCHILL in the latter part of his political career. During his final year as Prime Minister, one Fleet Street cartoonist depicted him as **Winnehaha** in a pastiche of *Hiawatha*, with President EISENHOWER in the title role.

Winston is back The memorable signal telegraphed to all the ships of the Royal Navy by the Board of Admiralty on 3

September 1939, after Britain's declaration of war on Germany, when CHURCHILL was recalled from the political wilderness to be First Lord of the Admiralty in CHAMBERLAIN's CABINET. He had been a highly popular First Lord 25 years before at the start of WORLD WAR I, until forced to resign in May 1915 over the Dardanelles offensive which he had championed, but which had been shambolically executed. This time he would leave the Admiralty to become Prime Minister.

winter. Winter of Discontent The period of bitter industrial strife in Britain early in 1979 which discredited the Labour government of James CALLAGHAN and probably guaranteed Margaret THATCHER's election victory that May. After three years of government-imposed WAGE RESTRAINT, the frustration of PUBLIC SECTOR workers boiled over into strikes by dustmen, hospital porters, road haulage and oil tanker drivers and – most emotively – gravediggers in Liverpool who refused to bury the dead. The phrase, taken from the opening couplet of Shakespeare's *Richard III*:

> Now is the winter of our discontent
> Made glorious summer by this sun of York.

was used by Larry Lamb, editor of the *Sun*, to describe the industrial climate; it was taken up by the rest of the media, then by the political community. *See also* CRISIS, WHAT CRISIS?

Winter War The Russo-Finnish War, fought from 30 November 1939 to 13 March 1940, which encouraged HITLER to believe the RED ARMY, PURGED by STALIN, could easily be defeated. When Finland resisted Soviet overtures for a mutual defence pact to protect its north-west flank, Stalin launched an air attack on Helsinki and poured nearly a million troops into Finland. They were held at the **Mannerheim Line** across the Karelian isthmus by 300,000 more mobile and better organised Finns, mostly reservists, under the veteran Marshal Baron Carl Mannerheim. Britain and France prepared an expeditionary force to aid the Finns, but Norway and Sweden refused it passage. By March a massive Soviet assault in the north-west, coupled with incessant attacks on the Mannerheim Line, forced a breakthrough and the Finns sued for peace. The war cost the Soviet Union 200,000 men, 700 planes and 1600 tanks, against Finnish losses of 25,000, and prompted a radical reorganisation of the Red Army.

nuclear winter A period of darkness and intense cold after a thermonuclear war, threatening much of the surviving life on earth. The term was coined in 1983 by a group of US scientists who had studied the possible after-effects of large-scale NUCLEAR WAR. They suggested that use of NUCLEAR WEAPONS on a global scale would cause uncontrolled firestorms; the smoke, particularly from plastics and other petroleum products in burning cities and factories, would eventually cover much of the northern hemisphere, blotting out the sun for several weeks. Low temperatures and lack of light would kill off much animal and plant life, and add to the human death toll from nuclear blasts and radioactive fall-out. Some scientists suggest the results would be less extreme – more of a nuclear autumn.

Wirtschaftswunder *See* ECONOMIC MIRACLE.

Wisconsin idea The revolution in state government brought about by Robert La Follette (*see* BATTLING BOB) after his INAUGURATION as Republican governor of Wisconsin in 1901. Intended as a PROGRESSIVE model for other states, it provided for tax reform, a state railroad commission, direct PRIMARIES and other measures to weaken political BOSSES.

witch-hunt A ruthless and over-zealous search within a nation, community or party for those lacking loyalty or total commitment, with those under suspicion facing ostracism or punishment unless they can prove their innocence. The term, originating in the hysteria against alleged witches in 17th-century New England, was invoked by American liberals as MCCARTHYISM reached its height, and by supporters of the MILITANT TENDENCY when the drive to PURGE them from Britain's LABOUR PARTY began in the mid-1980s.

withdraw (1) To leave the CHAMBER of a LEGISLATURE, specifically when requested to do so by the CHAIR as an alternative to being ordered to leave. (2) To pull out of an electoral contest. When Marilyn QUAYLE asked Louisiana governor Edwin Edwards in the middle of the 1992 BUSH/Quayle re-election campaign if there was 'anything we can do to help you all' after Hurricane Andrew, Edwards said: 'You could withdraw from the race.' (3) To retract a term deemed UNPARLIAMENTARY at the request of the Chair. In the HOUSE OF COMMONS the Labour MP George Foulkes was once rebuked by the SPEAKER for calling a Tory member an 'arrogant little shit'; he replied:

> Which word do you want me to withdraw: 'Arrogant', 'little' or 'shit'?

The word is often shouted by members who feel a remark is out of ORDER. When the Labour MP Willie Hamilton criticised Harold WILSON's U-TURNS on Europe as 'the politics of *coitus interruptus*', several members were quick to shout: 'Withdraw!'

Wizard of Ooze *See* DIRKSEN; compare LIZARD OF OZ.

WMD Shorthand for WEAPONS OF MASS DESTRUCTION, widely used in US and the political and military circles in the aftermath of the 2003 IRAQ WAR when SADDAM HUSSEIN's possession of such weapons was the pretext for the conflict but none were found.

Wobblies The nickname of the International Workers of the World (IWW), a radical labour movement founded in Chicago on 7 July 1905 in response to the formation of the conservative AFL, which excluded unskilled and non-white workers. The firmly socialist IWW was plagued from its inception by divisions between SYNDICALISTS such as the miners' leader William D. (Big Bill) HAYWOOD, who wanted a campaign of strikes and sabotage, and those who favoured more conventional political methods. At the height of its popularity, 1912–17, the movement had over 100,000 members, mainly among migratory workers in western farms, lumber camps and mines. But violence by activists alienated popular support and allowed the federal and state governments to arrest IWW members and, by the mid-1920s, hound the organisation out of existence. The radical vision of the IWW lives on in popular folk songs, such as *Joe Hill* (*see* DON'T MOURN, ORGANISE); the phrase 'pie in the sky' derives from another song adapted for use by the Wobblies. Immigrants who joined the IWW c. 1908 sang the more basic 'Hallelujah, I'm a bum!'

wobbly Thursday The day, a week before polling in the 1987 UK election campaign, when it looked for a moment as if Labour, who had started strongly (*see* KINNOCK – THE MOVIE) might overtake a CONSERVATIVE PARTY which had made a lacklustre and accident-prone start. There was a bad attack of jitters in Conservative CENTRAL OFFICE as Labour made up ground in the polls, after which a sense of proportion returned and the Tories, with Lord Young (*see* LORD SUIT) and advertising guru Tim Bell drafted in to help chairman Norman Tebbit (*see* CHINGFORD SKINHEAD), cruised to a LANDSLIDE victory.

> Wracked by an abscess on her tooth and suffering from an attack of nerves, Mrs THATCHER blamed Central Office and Norman Tebbit. Voices were raised, but best faces put forward.
>
> JULIAN CRITCHLEY, *Heseltine*

> Since we did not wobble but the news looked black I prefer . . . 'black Thursday'. I had talked to David Young the previous night about my worries about the campaign, which seemed to me unfocused . . . The following day, Norman Tebbit and I had a ding-dong row. This cleared the air. The press conference that day was a disaster, and I was held to blame.
>
> MARGARET THATCHER, *The Downing Street Years*

wog An unpleasant term for a foreigner, specifically from the Middle East or the Indian subcontinent; it is a common British expression that ultra-nationalists believe **Wogs begin at Calais.** The word originated in the 1920s; it is believed to stand for 'Westernised Oriental Gentleman', but champions of political correctness have convinced the public that the word stems from 'golliwog', resulting in these harmless dolls being banned. At the height of the SUEZ adventure in 1956 the Conservative MP Julian Amery, warning of the danger from Egyptian air power, told the Commons: '**Wogs have Migs**'. (MIGS were the main type of Russian jet fighter for four decades). Ironically it was an Egyptian, Boutros Boutros-Ghali, who responded in 1992 to UK press criticism of his performance as UNITED NATIONS General Secretary by saying: 'Perhaps it's because I'm a wog.'

Wolfenden Report The report of the Home Office's Departmental Committee on Homosexual Offences and Prostitution, chaired by the academic Sir John (later Lord) Wolfenden, which in 1957 recommended the decriminalisation in Britain of homosexual acts between consenting male adults; lesbian acts had never been a criminal offence because Queen Victoria did not believe them possible. The immediate fruit of the committee's work was the Street Offences Act, which made soliciting for prostitution in a public place an offence and for a time drove prostitutes off the streets. It was ten years – Home Office officials had predicted fourteen – before Parliament liberalised the law on homosexuality. Wolfenden was invited to chair the committee in 1954 by the then Home

Secretary Sir David MAXWELL-FYFE on a night sleeper from Liverpool to London. In his memoirs he wrote that as an expert on neither homosexuality nor prostitution he was baffled to be chosen, but

> iI a government wants somebody to examine as objectively and dispassionately as possible some area which is likely to be controversial, it is not a bad thing to look to the universities to provide him.

womb to tomb One of the catchy phrases coined to describe the all-embracing nature of Britain's WELFARE STATE. 'From the CRADLE TO THE GRAVE' is another.

women. Woman make policy as well as tea The slogan of women in Britain's LABOUR PARTY in the mid- to late 1980s; although they had always been prominent in party affairs, many had become irritated at the readiness of middle-aged male trade union officials to get each other selected as Parliamentary candidates, while women were still expected to make the tea in COMMITTEE ROOMS when the election came round. Such attitudes were not confined to Britain; in 1976 the Louisiana politician Moon Landrieu told *Esquire* magazine of women's role in electioneering:

> Women do the lickin' and the stickin'.

Women's Institute speech One of the more disastrous episodes of Tony BLAIR's premiership, when on 6 June 2000 a supposedly non-controversial speech to an audience firmly rooted in MIDDLE ENGLAND was greeted with HECKLING and a slow handclap. Blair intended to use the speech on his return to work after the birth of his son Leo to stress his commitment to traditional values to the WI's Wembley conference. But vocal elements in the audience were upset that sections of the speech had been trailed with the media in advance and given a pro-Labour SPIN, despite the fact that its contents were not partisan.

Women's issues are people's issues The response of the Colorado Congresswoman and Senator Pat Schroeder (1940–) to criticism that feminists were concentrating too much on 'women's issues' such as abortion, child care and job opportunities.

Women's Lib The high-profile feminist movement aimed at freeing women from the domination of a male-ordered society that emerged in the late 1960s. It grabbed the headlines through protests such as bra-burning, but helped pave the way for the spread of new social attitudes that eventually gave women a greater role in politics and a greater stake in the political agenda. The name caught on on both sides of the Atlantic (*see* NOW); in Britain it is linked to the formation of the Women's Liberation Workshop in London in 1969.

women's rights The umbrella term for the campaign to secure for women the same CIVIL RIGHTS as men, including (but not confined to) the vote. Susan B. ANTHONY, in her book *The Revolution*, gave the rallying-call: 'The True Republic: Men their rights and nothing more; Women their rights and nothing less.' Such slogans and the response of many women to them horrified Queen Victoria, who wrote on 29 May 1870:

> The Queen is most anxious to enlist everyone who can speak or write to join in checking this mad, wicked folly of women's rights, with all its attendant horrors, on which her poor feeble sex is bent, forgetting every sense of womanly feeling and propriety. Lady Amberley ought to get a good whipping.

The struggle did not end with the winning of the vote, or even with EQUAL PAY. LADY BIRD Johnson would regularly ask her husband: 'What did you do for women today?', and Gloria Steinem told fellow-feminists:

> We already know how to lose, thank you very much. Now we want to know how to win.

Margaret THATCHER enraged such people in 1982 when she insisted, on the basis of her own experience, that

> The battle for women's rights has been largely won.

women's suffrage The securing of the VOTE for women on the same basis as for men, achieved throughout the United States with the ratification of the NINETEENTH AMENDMENT in February 1921 and in Britain in 1928 with the enfranchisement of women from 21 to 30 (*see* Flapper VOTE). In America Wyoming granted women the vote as early as 1869, and by 1918 male voters in fifteen states had given them equal suffrage; the rise of POPULISM and the campaigning of Susan B. ANTHONY and Carrie Catt played a crucial part, though the SENATE resisted until the last moment. In Britain the serious campaign started later, with the SUFFRAGETTES both mobilising and alienating public opinion from the turn of the century; the main obstacle, however, was ASQUITH, whose biographer Roy JENKINS wrote:

> There were only two effective obstacles to female enfranchisement before 1914. The first was the excesses of MILITANCY; and the second was the

person of the Prime Minister in opposition to a majority of his own Cabinet.

Even more than in America, the role of women in Britain's war effort broke down resistance, and women over 30 were granted the vote in 1918. That year Countess Markievicz became the first woman elected to Parliament, but as a member of SINN FEIN she never took her seat; that distinction went soon after to the American-born Nancy, Lady Astor. The first woman elected to the US Congress was the Montana Republican Jeannette Rankin in 1916; she earned a place in history, and the STATUARY HALL, by voting alone against America's entry into both world wars.

> Serious and responsible women do not want to vote. GROVER CLEVELAND, 1905

> The exclusion of women from the franchise is neither expedient, justifiable nor politically right.
> SIR HENRY CAMPBELL-BANNERMAN

> As women we realise that the condition of our sex is so deplorable that it is our duty even to break the law in order to call attention to the reasons why we do so.
> EMMELINE PANKHURST, speech in court, April 1913

Women's Suffrage Amendment The contemporary name for the NINETEENTH AMENDMENT (or ANTHONY AMENDMENT) which gave all American women the vote. The deciding vote was cast in the Tennessee House of Representatives on 18 August 1920 by its youngest member, 24-year-old Harry Burns. His mother had written to him:

> Don't forget to be a good boy and help Mrs Catt put 'rat' in 'ratification'.

If you can't get a fighting man, get a fighting woman The slogan under which Nancy, Lady Astor fought when Labour put up the PACIFIST W. T. Gay against her in an election at Devonport.

If you want anything said, ask a man. If you want anything done, ask a woman One of the most often-repeated dicta of Margaret THATCHER, when asked how she controlled the decision-making process as Britain's first woman Prime Minister.

Woolsack The cushion stuffed with COMMONWEALTH wool on which the LORD CHANCELLOR sits to chair the HOUSE OF LORDS. The use of a woolsack instead of a chair dates back to the 14th century, when it was introduced to underline the importance of wool to the English economy. It has been said of several of the less impressive occupants that

> you couldn't tell where the Woolsack ended and the Lord Chancellor began.

Woolton pie A pie making use of leftovers and vegetables which was recommended to the British public during WORLD WAR II as a means of making rationed food stretch as far as possible. It was one of the recipes publicised under the aegis of Frederick Marquis, 1st Earl of Woolton (1883–1964), Minister of Food from 1940 to 1943. Though not a politician by origin, Woolton showed his organising genius after the war as a highly successful chairman of the CONSERVATIVE PARTY (1946–55).

work. work ethic or **Protestant work ethic** The mind-set attributed specifically to northern Europeans (apart from the Catholic Irish) and their descendants in America who believe in hard work as the principal cause of self-respect and economic and social advancement. The term is, understandably, used most frequently by members of those groups and is regarded as a RACIST slur by some of those excluded from it.

work to rule A common form of Industrial ACTION stopping short of an all-out STRIKE, in which workers carry out their tasks to the letter, thus taking an inordinate time over them and causing loss and disruption to their employers. The tactic was frequently adopted by UK PUBLIC SECTOR workers in the 1960s or '70s, usually inconveniencing railway passengers, hospital patients and the like rather than the employing bureaucracies.

right to work *See* RIGHT.

Daily Worker *See* DAILY.

workers' bomb The term first used by STALINISTS to justify the Soviet nuclear arsenal, which was taken up by some extreme leftist groups in the 1950s to press for the international working class movement to have the capacity to threaten monopoly capital with nuclear annihilation if it did not mend its ways. How such a bomb, if used, would leave workers unscathed was never explained.

workers' control The doctrine, central both to the CO-OPERATIVE movement and to TROTSKYISM, that the workers in an industry or other undertaking should be in charge of it. Critics of Soviet Communism and MORRISONIAN NATIONALISATION alike pointed out that each form of public ownership left the workers subordinate, as before, with BUREAUCRATS, and even in some cases former bosses replacing the previous capitalist owners.

Workers of the world, unite! You have nothing to lose but your chains The slogan of working-class SOLIDARITY based on the closing words of the COMMUNIST MANIFESTO. What Marx and Engels actually wrote in 1848 was;

> Let the ruling classes tremble at a communist revolution.
> The PROLETARIANS have nothing to lose but their chains.
> They have a world to win. Working men of all countries, unite!

Workers' Party The left-wing democratic party in both parts of Ireland that evolved from Official SINN FEIN in the 1980s, before transforming itself into the DEMOCRATIC LEFT.

workers, peasants and intellectuals The three social classes identified by LENIN as critical for the success and continued forward thrust of the BOLSHEVIK revolution.

Workers' Revolutionary Party A far-left UK fringe group from the 1970s and '80s containing more revolutionaries than workers, and best know for its active support of PALESTINIAN terrorist groups at the height of tension in the Middle East. Though it possessed some rank-and-file members, its best known activists were actors, notably Vanessa Redgrave and some of her family.

What about the workers? The archetypal left-wing HECKLER's comment at a Conservative meeting in Britain in the second quarter of the 20th century and a little beyond – archetypal, at least, to those who seldom attended such meetings. Real-life interruptions from the floor were generally more original and to the point.

workfare A system pioneered in several US states ('work/welfare') under which the receipt of social security payments by the unemployed is conditional on their taking work if offered it – generally on environmental schemes and public works. In the UK an experimental scheme was authorised for the Norfolk constituency of Ralph Howell, workfare's strongest advocate in the Commons; the NEW DEAL subsequently brought in by Labour includes traces of workfare.

working class A collective term for those engaged on manual and industrial labour and their families, used mainly by members of political parties and trade unions who see themselves as entitled to their support. The potential of the working class was grasped to the full by the pioneers of COMMUNISM; Engels declared: 'In England a real democratic party is impossible unless it be a working man's party', Marx that 'the emancipation of the working classes must be achieved by the working classes themselves', and LENIN, a touch disillusioned, that 'the history of all countries shows that the working class, exclusively by its own effort, is able to develop only trade union consciousness.' The patrician Lord ROSEBERY was equally dubious about the working class's capacity for self-advancement:

> I believe that the labour of those who would ameliorate the conditions of the working class is slower and more imperceptible than that of the insect which raises the coral reef from the bed of the ocean.

> I never knew the working classes had such white skins.
>
> Lord CURZON after a rare visit to an industrial city

> The advantage of a working-class background is that I do not make the mistake of thinking every worker is a revolutionary.
>
> JANOS KADAR, last Communist ruler of Hungary

working class movement An umbrella term for the left and the more politically conscious trade unions, used more often by Communists than by democratic socialists.

the working class can kiss my arse *See* The RED FLAG.

The working men of Scotland have not a representative to urge their claims. It is in order to remedy this admitted grievance that I now claim your support The appeal of Keir Hardie (*see* QUEER HARDIE) to the voters of Mid-Lanark, when standing as the first ever LABOUR candidate in 1888. Hardie soon became philosophical about how long the workers would elect their own, saying:

> It will take the working man 20 years to elect his equals to represent him. And then it will take another 20 years not to elect his equals.

working miners The pitmen who kept working during Britain's MINERS' STRIKE of 1984–85, insisting they were not BLACKLEGS but were entitled to stay at work as Arthur Scargill (*see* KING ARTHUR), president of the National Union of Mineworkers, had refused to call a national ballot. This refusal not only led to enough men continuing to work to prevent the strike succeeding; it also triggered a split in the NUM and the formation of the breakaway Union of Democratic Mineworkers.

an irreversible transfer of wealth and power to working people and their

families The key phrase – for left-wingers – of the policy document approved by Britain's LABOUR PARTY in 1972–73, which formed the heart of its February 1974 election MANIFESTO. The adoption of the document by the party CONFERENCE enabled Tony BENN and his supporters to make it the central theme of their policy campaigning well into the 1980s.

working the fence/crowd/room The enthusiastic seizing of hands by a candidate out on the STUMP, or any capable politician faced with a group of people on whom he or she wishes to leave an impression, systematically making contact with as many as possible. The fence is the barrier behind which supporters – often rounded up by an advance team of campaign workers – are penned at an airport through which the candidate is passing.

workshop of the world *See* WORLD.

world. World Bank The International Bank for Reconstruction and Development, established in accordance with the 1944 BRETTON WOODS agreements; the 'twin' of the IMF. It began operations in 1947, providing economic aid to member countries, initially to finance the construction of war-torn Europe; since 1949 its efforts have been largely directed to funding projects in developing countries, though it also raises money on international capital markets. It operates strictly as a commercial entity, lending at commercial rates of interest to governments, or to private concerns with the government as guarantor, and only to countries capable of servicing and repaying debt. An affiliate agency, the **International Development Agency**, was established in 1960 to provide low-interest loans to the poorest countries.

world class shopper *See* IRON BUTTERFLY.

World Court The popular name – insofar as the public are aware of its existence – for the **International Court of Justice** in the Hague. The Court, which has borne this name since 1945 as an adjunct of the UNITED NATIONS, began its life as the International Court of Arbitration, founded as a result of conferences in 1899 and 1907 convened by the Scottish-born US steel magnate and philanthropist Andrew Carnegie. When the LEAGUE OF NATIONS was formed, it became a World Court; the US SENATE refused to ratify membership even though an apparently sound formula was twice negotiated, but the Court did appoint two Americans as judges. The Court now comprises fifteen jurists elected for nine-year terms by the GENERAL ASSEMBLY and SECURITY COUNCIL. Nations have made sparing use of the court, largely because they do not want the stigma of a ruling against them, but it has set a standard for international morality which most would accept.

World Criminal Court *See* INTERNATIONAL CRIMINAL COURT.

World Peace Council An organisation that flourished in the early years of the COLD WAR; it claimed to campaign for an end to war, but in fact championed the ends of international Communism while attracting support from the occasional gullible idealist.

world policeman The role that America spent most of the 20th century trying to avoid, then took up at critical moments. President Benjamin HARRISON declared in 1888: 'We Americans have no commission from God to police the world', and Robert McNamara, Lyndon JOHNSON's Defense Secretary, said much the same 78 years later:

> Neither conscience nor security suggests that the United States is, or should be, the global gendarme.

world power An alternative term for a GREAT POWER, emphasising a global rather than a regional or hemispheric influence; in his GUILDHALL speech on 16 November 1964, Harold WILSON said of Britain:

> We are a world power, and a world influence, or we are nothing.

World Service The external broadcasting arm of the BBC which, since 1932, has built up a reputation for objective reporting of world events, free of influence by the UK government. This point was underlined in 1985 when staff at its Bush House headquarters in London went on strike in protest at the cancellation of the REAL LIVES television documentary at the request of Home Secretary Leon Brittan. The World Service, financed by a grant from the Foreign Office, broadcasts radio and television services of news, current affairs, cultural items and entertainment; Bush House also transmits vernacular programmes in over 30 languages, its authority virtually unimpaired by a series of damaging reorganisations imposed by successive BBC directors-general.

World Trade Center The scene of the worst terrorist atrocity in recorded history, the 110-storey twin towers near the foot of Manhattan – at 1368ft and 1362ft the tallest buildings in New York City – into which two of four airliners hijacked by AL QAEDA were crashed on 9/11 (11 September 2001). At least 2752 lives (67 of them UK citizens) were lost: passengers on the aircraft, those killed in the explosions when the planes impacted, those trapped above the fires who jumped from the uppermost storeys rather than be burned alive, those who were crushed when the towers collapsed before they could escape, firefighters and police who were endeavouring to combat the blaze or evacuate the buildings, and the hijackers themselves. Perhaps 15,000 other people who were in the towers at the moment of impact were led to safety. The Center, opened in 1973, was the subject of a previous Islamist attack on 26 February 1993 when terrorists bombed an underground garage in the north tower, blasting through four sub-levels of concrete, killing six people and injuring over 1000 others. The six men convicted of that bombing in 1997 and 1998 were still appealing their convictions when the Al Qaeda terrorists struck. The catastrophic loss of the World Trade Center not only transformed the New York skyline but galvanised the city's inhabitants, led by Mayor Rudolph Guiliani who, though on the point of retirement, took charge in a way that earned him respect around the world. The Center is being rebuilt as the 1776ft Freedom Tower and the Memory Foundations complex of buildings. *See also* GROUND ZERO; PENTAGON; THOSE FOLKS.

World Trade Organisation *See* WTO.

World Turned Upside Down, The The popular tune of the day – originally a DIGGER song – which was reputedly played at YORKTOWN on 17 October 1781 by regimental bands as British troops stacked their arms following General Cornwallis's surrender which ended America's Revolutionary War.

World War I The bloody conflict between 1914 and 1918, the 'WAR TO END WARS', which engulfed the whole of Europe and eventually brought in the United States, spreading to the Middle East, the Atlantic and (on a small scale) southern Africa. It was started by the shooting of the Habsburg Archduke Franz Ferdinand in SARAJEVO, after which Austria issued an ULTIMATUM to Serbia, causing Russia to mobilise. Russia's Foreign Minister Serge Witte asserted:

> The world is in flames today for a cause that interests Russia first and foremost; a cause that is essentially the cause of the Slavs, and which is of no concern to France and England.

ASQUITH's first reaction to the gathering storm was similar: 'Happily there seems no reason why we should be anything more than spectators', and as the risk of British involvement grew, Queen Mary confided:

> To have to go to war on account of tiresome Serbia beggars belief.

However, Germany mobilised and France responded, and when Germany moved against Belgium, brushing its NEUTRALITY aside, Britain and its empire entered the war on 4 August 1914. Lord Kitchener declared: 'I do not believe any nation ever entered into a great controversy with a clearer conscience', and the Kaiser said much the same: 'We draw the sword with a clean conscience and clean hands.' Sir Edward Grey (*see* 'The lamps are going out all over EUROPE') declared percipiently that 'if there is war, there will be Labour governments in every country – and quite right too!'

Millions died in sterile trench WARFARE in Flanders on the western front, and the conflict spawned air warfare, nerve gas, submarines, Zeppelins and tanks. Italy and Turkey (*see* GALLIPOLI) also became involved. In 1916 Asquith's still largely Liberal government became a casualty, with LLOYD GEORGE forming a more vigorous COALITION. Woodrow WILSON, who had done all he could to keep America out of the war, relented in February 1917 after Germany's ZIMMERMAN NOTE seeking to entrap Mexico into an alliance with offers of US territory, and threats of unrestricted submarine warfare. Wilson told Congress:

> It is a fearful thing to lead this great peaceful people into war, into the most terrible and disastrous of all wars, civilisation itself seeming to be in the balance. But the right is more precious than peace.

America's intervention ultimately broke the stalemate in the summer of 1918, and on 11 November, with Germany on the point of collapse but not defeated in the field, an ARMISTICE was called. By then the war had triggered the RUSSIAN REVOLUTION, and the die was cast for the collapse of the Austro-Hungarian and Ottoman empires, the exile of the Kaiser and the instability in Germany that gave rise to HITLER. The Treaty of VERSAILLES both closed the book on 19th-century Europe and made WORLD WAR II inevitable.

> We shall never sheathe the sword, which we have not lightly drawn, until Belgium receives in full measure all and more than all that she has sacrificed; until France is adequately secured against the menace of aggression; until the rights

of the smaller nationalities of Europe are placed upon an unassailable foundation; and until the military domination of Prussia is wholly and finally destroyed. ASQUITH

The program of the world's peace is our program. WOODROW WILSON

A war of no tactics, no strategy, no mind. Just slaughter. PAUL FUSSELL

A war of plugging shellholes with live soldiers. SANCHE DE GRAMONT

World War II The truly global conflict which began with Germany's ANNEXATION of Poland in September 1939 and ended with Japan's surrender in August 1945. At the outset and during the PHONEY WAR Britain and France were pitted against Germany, a strongly ISOLATIONIST America being determined not to be sucked into a European conflict as in 1917; Sen. Burton K. Wheeler echoed the mood when he argued:

By setting the United States on fire we will not help put out the fire in Europe.

1940 brought Germany's BLITZKRIEG into Norway, the Low Countries and France and CHURCHILL's emergence to lead Britain after the failure of APPEASEMENT (*see* YOU HAVE SAT HERE LONG ENOUGH). Then came HITLER's invasion of Russia and Japan's unprovoked attack on PEARL HARBOR, sealing the great ATLANTIC ALLIANCE that was formed between CHURCHILL and Franklin D. ROOSEVELT and which endures to this day. America, Britain and its empire, the Soviet Union under STALIN and the FREE FRENCH under DE GAULLE were now ranged against Germany (which was perpetrating the HOLOCAUST), Japan and Italy. The main theatres of war were Western Europe, the Atlantic and the Mediterranean, the German-Russian Eastern Front, and the Pacific. The turning points were the aerial Battle of Britain in 1940, the defeat of Germany's *Afrika Korps* at El Alamein in 1942, the air-sea battle of Midway the same year and, above all, the Soviet victory after a bitter siege at Stalingrad early the following year. The war ended, after YALTA and the death of Roosevelt, in the destruction of the NAZI state and the partition of Germany between Western democracy and Communism, the Soviet HEGEMONY in eastern Europe, the dropping of the ATOMIC BOMB at HIROSHIMA, the UNITED NATIONS, the COLD WAR, the eclipse of Britain as a global force and the rise of the SUPERPOWERS.

World War III An apocalyptic term frequently used by politicians and peace campaigners in the 1950s and '60s for the NUCLEAR conflict between East and West which many then feared to be inevitable. It was also hyperbole for any violent argument that erupted during that period.

the world's best hope JEFFERSON's description of the young American republic from his INAUGURAL ADDRESS of 4 March 1801, much repeated since by others. He identified the strength of the new nation as its unified love of justice and of nationhood.

We have it in our power to begin the world all over again The closing words of Thomas Paine's COMMON SENSE, quoted by Ronald REAGAN in his Presidential DEBATE with Walter Mondale (*see* NORWEGIAN WOOD) on 7 October 1984. Paine had also said: 'The world is my country, all mankind are my brethren and to do good is my religion.'

workshop of the world A description of Victorian Britain taken from a speech by DISRAELI in the HOUSE OF COMMONS on 15 March 1838. It does not tell the whole story; what DIZZY presciently said was:

The Continent will not suffer England to be the workshop of the world.

Would you buy a used car from this man? The most damaging remark ever made about Richard NIXON, eerily catching his ingratiating yet insecure manner and recalling his early nickname of TRICKY DICK. It was reputedly made by the comedian Mort Sahl (1927–), and stuck to Nixon like a second skin for most of the 1960s and beyond.

Wounded Knee One of the most shameful episodes in America's treatment of its native population: the massacre by the US 7th Cavalry on 29 December 1890 at Wounded Knee Creek, South Dakota, of 350 half-starved survivors of the Sioux people (230 of them women and children) after a hidden rifle was discovered. The Sioux had been taken prisoner after they were interrupted at their Ghost Dance, which the federal government had barred them from celebrating six years before. 51 wounded Indians survived; 24 troopers died, mainly shot by their comrades. Some historians see in Wounded Knee the end of the Frontier and the birth of IMPERIALISM, as from then on America had to expand outward. In February 1973 the trading post and church at Wounded Knee were occupied by members of the American Indian Movement to highlight continuing grievances.

wowser An Australian term for a puritanical person or killjoy, originally in the 1890s a fervent advocate of PROHIBITION. In 1983 Pierre TRUDEAU, on a visit to Australia, declared:

You have wowserism – we have Toronto.

Woy The nickname of Roy (later Lord) JENKINS, playing on his inability to pronounce the letter R. A celebrated instance occurred in 1976 when he was leaving WESTMINSTER for Brussels, and taking his Parliamentary colleague David Marquand to join his CABINET. When Jenkins told a farewell meeting with Labour MPs: 'I am leaving without bitterness or wancour', a voice at the back shouted: 'I thought you were taking Marquand with you.'

WPA Works Progress Administration. A NEW DEAL agency established by the ROOSEVELT administration in 1934 to provide employment for some of the many creative Americans unable to find work during the GREAT DEPRESSION. Five thousand artists worked on projects including the decoration of public buildings with enormous murals; writers produced histories of the states and playwrights took theatre to the most depressed parts of the Union. The artistic projects were closed down in 1939.

writ. writ of summons The documents sent at the direction of the LORD CHANCELLOR at the start of each new PARLIAMENT to all PEERS eligible to sit in the HOUSE OF LORDS; similar writs are sent to all those hereditaries elected by their peers to sit in the Lords or to peers created during a Parliament.

moving the writ The procedure that has to be gone through in the HOUSE OF COMMONS before a BY-ELECTION can be held. Customarily it is a formality, undertaken by a WHIP from the party that has previously held the seat, which allows that party to determine the timing of the poll; however, if other parties feel the delay is excessive, unauthorised attempts by other MPs to move the writ are sometimes made. Exceptionally, the SPEAKER may move the writ during a Parliamentary RECESS at the whips' request.

write-in The addition to the BALLOT by an individual voter of the name of a person not listed as a CANDIDATE. In US elections, especially PRIMARIES, it is not uncommon for a write-in campaign to be waged on behalf of an UNDECLARED CANDIDATE, with or without their permission; indeed there have been numerous occasions where a write-in candidate has won, notably in Mayoral elections.

written answer At WESTMINSTER, the reply given by a Minister, and published in HANSARD, to a written QUESTION tabled a few days previously. MPs can ask several hundred such questions a day, peers a couple of dozen. Traditionally such answers could only be given when Parliament was sitting, but since the turn of the century it has been permissible for them to be given throughout a RECESS.

written Ministerial statement *See* Planted QUESTION.

WTO World Trade Organisation. The Geneva-based global body set up in 1995 as a result of the URUGUAY ROUND of world trade negotiations to replace GATT as the arbiter of trade disputes and an engine toward freer trade, though with an enhanced role. The WTO has become a target for anti-GLOBALISATION protesters (*see* SEATTLE), but has successfully completed the DOHA ROUND of trade liberalisation measures.

Wurzel Gummidge The nickname accorded by PRIVATE EYE and TV crews to Michael FOOT during his leadership of the LABOUR PARTY from 1980 to 1983. It was an unflattering comparison with the scarecrow hero of a popular children's book and television series, a point hammered home in 1982 when opponents accused him of attending the CENOTAPH in a DONKEY JACKET.

Wye Plantation The conference centre in Maryland, 70 miles from Washington, which hosted the nine-day negotiations in October 1998 between President CLINTON, the Israeli Prime Minister Benjamin Netanyahu and the Palestinian leader Yasser Arafat, which produced a LAND FOR PEACE agreement that broke for a time the deadlock in the Middle East PEACE PROCESS. Israel increased from 3% to 14.2% the amount of the WEST BANK where the Palestinians would enjoy full autonomy, and the Palestinians pledged to stem terrorism by Islamic militants and abolish the provisions in their charter demanding the abolition of the Jewish state. There were misgivings from the outset over whether it would stick; Netanyahu had threatened to walk out, and Israel claimed as the agreement was signed that it was contingent on the US releasing the convicted Israeli spy Jonathan POLLARD from prison.

X

X The mark placed by a voter on a BALLOT paper to denote their choice of candidate in a FIRST PAST THE POST election.

X factor The magic factor that makes a candidate or party appeal to the voter; a play on X as above and on an intangible (mystery) ingredient.

X, Y and Z fever JEFFERSON's term for the clamour for America to go to war with France over the refusal in 1798 of Talleyrand, the French Foreign Minister, and the DIRECTORY to negotiate on calling off sea raiders and resuming commercial relations unless paid a $250,000 bribe. President John ADAMS reported the insult to Congress and the Senate printed the correspondence, referring to the offending Frenchmen only as X, Y and Z. *See* NO, NOT A SIXPENCE.

Malcolm X The assumed name of Malcolm Little (1925–65), a US black militant leader and an influential figure in the struggle for racial equality. The son of a Baptist minister, he was converted to the faith of the BLACK MUSLIMS in prison in 1952. He changed his name to Malcolm X – he considered his surname a relic of slavery – and became actively involved in the sect on his release the following year. In 1963 he left the Black Muslims after a disagreement and founded the rival organisation of Afro-American Unity, which endorsed the use of violence in the pursuit of racial justice. He said at the time:

> The Negro revolution is controlled by foxy white liberals, by the Government itself. But the black revolution is controlled only by God.

He subsequently converted to orthodox Islam, taking the name Malik El-Shabazz. The rivalry and hatred between the Black Muslims and Malcolm X's group culminated in his assassination at a rally in New York's Audubon Ballroom on 21 February 1965. Three Black Muslims were convicted of the killing, though some doubts remain as to the true culprits. A few weeks before, Malcolm X, hitherto a strict SEGREGATIONIST, had opened contacts with Dr Martin Luther KING and others on creating a broader front for racial equality.

xenophobia Fear of foreigners verging on paranoia (Gr. *xenos,* foreigner; *phobos,* fear). Often harnessed by POPULISTS and TOTALITARIAN regimes to stir up hatred; also a factor in RACISM, as recognised in the EUROPEAN PARLIAMENT's committee on racism and xenophobia. *See also* CHAUVINISM.

Y

yahoos Noisy, uncouth, ill-informed and vicious elements, a word mainly used in US politics. The original Yahoos were found by Gulliver as slaves to the horse-like Houyhnhnms while on his *Travels* (1726). His creator Jonathan Swift described them as brutes in human form with vicious propensities.

Yalta The conference in the Crimea from 4 to 11 February 1945 at which STALIN, ROOSEVELT and CHURCHILL met for the second and final time. To many in the West, Yalta became a symbol of betrayal of the countries left behind the IRON CURTAIN, with a dying FDR and a tired Churchill bullied by a militarily strong Stalin into conceding a post-war Soviet takeover of central and eastern Europe. This came about because Stalin promised to accept a broad-based democratic government in Poland, and FREE ELECTIONS in other countries under RED ARMY occupation, but then went back on his word. The leaders endorsed the ATLANTIC CHARTER, convened the SAN FRANCISCO CONFERENCE to draw up the UNITED NATIONS charter, agreed to divide Germany into four post-war ZONES and established the post-war German-Polish border on the ODER-NEISSE LINE; Roosevelt also gained Stalin's commitment to enter the Japanese war three months after the end of the European conflict, which he did. Roosevelt complained of the timetable, but Churchill told him:

> I do not see any other way of realising our hopes about world organisation in five or six days. Even the Almighty took seven.

Roosevelt returned home to hail the outcome as 'the end of the system of UNILATERAL action and exclusive alliances and SPHERES OF INFLUENCE AND BALANCE OF POWER and all the other expedients that have been tried for centuries – and failed'.

Yank This derivative of 'YANKEE' was originally used by US forces in WORLD WAR I ('the Yanks are coming'), but was turned against them during and after WORLD WAR II, especially in the UK.

Yanks go home A common slogan of post-war UK Communists and peace activists, who objected to the presence of US forces in Europe. Anti-litter stickers were doctored to read:

> Keep Britain tidy – kick out the Yanks.

Yankee An American, specifically from New England or the Northern states, or on the UNION side in the CIVIL WAR. Often a term of abuse, first by LOYALISTS, then by CONFEDERATES and more recently Latin American POPULISTS (*see* GRINGO). The word was devised in 1713 from an Indian corruption of the word 'English' by Jonathan Hastings of Cambridge, New York, to describe anything of superior or American make or origin.

Yankee Doodle The nonsense rhyme concluding:

> Yankee Doodle went to town
> Riding on a pony
> Stuck a feather in his cap
> And called it Macaroni.

It became a revolutionary air, being updated c. 1755 from a rhyme referring to Oliver Cromwell, by Dr Richard Shuckburgh, a British Army surgeon in upper New York. First played by the British as an insult to the colonials, it was turned against them by WASHINGTON's forces, most memorably at Saratoga.

Damned Yankee Originally used in the Revolutionary War against Northern 'provincials' by 'Yorkers' in General Schuyler's army, this became an abusive term for all North-easterners, especially since the CIVIL WAR.

Yarralumla (Aboriginal: echo) The official residence in Canberra of the GOVERNOR-GENERAL of Australia, which became notorious as the scene of the KERR SACKING in 1975. It is a modest and rambling edifice on the site of an 1830s farmhouse; when in 1953 Field Marshal Sir William Slim planned to mark his arrival as Governor-General with a dance for 600 guests there, he had to be told it was too small. The house has long been said to be haunted, and in the 1960s the Governor-General's secretary Sir Murray Tyrrell, encountered the ghost; a guard dog which was summoned retreated from the apparition, baring its teeth.

sprint for Yarralumla A decision to call a snap ELECTION, so termed because of the need for Australia's Prime Minister to secure a DISSOLUTION from the Governor-General.

years the locusts have eaten Stanley BALDWIN's term for the late 1920s and early '30s when Britain's military capacity was eroded while Germany was rearming. It was taken from the Bible, Joel II:25 reading: 'And I will restore to you the years that the locust hath eaten.' On 12 November 1936 Baldwin told the COMMONS:

> I want to say a word about the years the locusts have eaten . . . I put before the House my views with appalling FRANKNESS . . . You will remember the election at Fulham in the autumn of 1933 when a seat . . . was lost about no issue but the pacifist . . . Supposing I had gone to the country and said that Germany was rearming and we must rearm . . . I cannot think of anything that would have made the loss of the [1935] election more certain.

The speech was turned against Baldwin as the world crisis deepened and war approached, G. M. Thomson writing that its echoes 'pursued him to his dying day'. More recently the term was used of the late 1960s, when Harold WILSON's first Labour government lost its momentum amid a chain of economic crises.

year zero The devastation inflicted on Cambodia by the KHMER ROUGE after their capture of power in 1975, eradicating as many traces of civilisation as possible and killing an estimated 1.2 million people (*see* KILLING FIELDS).

year zero jinx The tragic historical coincidence that only one US President elected since 1840 in a year ending in a zero has yet left the WHITE HOUSE alive, the exception being Ronald REAGAN (1980). William Henry Harrison (*see* TIPPECANOE AND TYLER TOO) died of pneumonia a month after his INAUGURATION; LINCOLN (1860) was assassinated, as were Garfield (*see* BOATMAN JIM – 1880) and MCKINLEY (1900). HARDING (1920) died after a seizure three years later; Franklin D. ROOSEVELT, re-elected for a third term in 1940, died in office soon after commencing his fourth, and KENNEDY (1960) was assassinated. George W. BUSH, elected in 2000, has yet to complete his second term.

yeas and nays The way the votes are declared and counted in the US CONGRESS (*compare* AYES AND NOES at Westminster).

yellow. Yellow Book '*We can conquer unemployment*', the ambitious programme which in many ways foreshadowed Roosevelt's NEW DEAL, with which LLOYD GEORGE's Liberals hoped to re-emerge as a serious force at the 1929 UK general election. They gained nineteen seats, but with only 59 finished a poor third.

yellow dog Democrats In the American South, someone who will vote for whoever the party nominates, 'even a yellow dog'. It originated in 1928 when many Democrats refused to support the party's nominee Alfred E. Smith because of his Catholicism, but others stuck by him as the party's choice despite their reservations. Since the 1960s, automatic loyalty by Southern whites to the Democratic Party has evaporated.

yellow peril A term used, especially in America and Australia, to dramatise the 'threat' posed by potential immigration from China, Japan and the Far East. First coined in Germany in the 1890s (*die gelbe Gefahr*), the expression was taken up in 1905 by the Hearst newspaper chain in an emotive campaign against Asian immigrants. The ensuing controversy led San Francisco to SEGREGATE 100 Japanese children in a separate school, a decision Theodore ROOSEVELT denounced as 'worse than criminal stupidity'. But Roosevelt was obliged to negotiate the GENTLEMAN'S AGREEMENT with Japan to halt further immigration before public anxiety subsided.

yellow star The cloth badge which Jews were ordered to wear in NAZI Germany and the lands its armies occupied. It enabled them to be identified for victimisation by ANTI-SEMITIC members of the public, for brutality by Nazi thugs, and eventually for deportation and probable death in CONCENTRATION CAMPS.

yes. *Yes, Minister* The highly popular early 1980s BBC comedy series which depicted Ministers as vain, credulous and totally under the control of suave Whitehall MANDARINS given to subterfuge and double-speak. The programme, written by two former civil servants, Jonathan Lynn and Anthony Jay, was one of Margaret THATCHER's favourites. It starred Paul Eddington as Jim Hacker, the bumbling Minister and eventual Prime Minister, and Nigel Hawthorne as the PERMANENT SECRETARY, later CABINET SECRETARY, SIR

HUMPHREY Appleby. The words 'Yes, Minister' were normally uttered at the end of the episode by Sir Humphrey when he had manoeuvred Hacker into doing precisely the opposite of what he wanted, while letting Hacker believe he had scored a great personal success. The title probably originated from this passage in the CROSSMAN DIARIES:

> My Minister's room is like a padded cell, and in certain ways I am like a person who is suddenly certified a lunatic and put safely into this great, vast room, cut off from real life. Of course they don't behave quite like nurses, because the Civil Service is profoundly deferential. 'Yes, Minister!', 'No, Minister!', 'If you wish it, Minister!'

Yes, Yes The slogan of the PRO-DEVOLUTION campaign in the second, September 1997, REFERENDUM on re-establishing a SCOTTISH PARLIAMENT. The two 'Yes'es referred to the two questions on the BALLOT PAPER: whether to set up a Parliament with powers devolved from WESTMINSTER, and whether to grant it the power to vary the standard rate of income tax by 3p in the £ (*see* TARTAN TAX). Both propositions were carried overwhelmingly.

She didn't say Yes, she didn't say No *See* SHE.

won't take yes for an answer The rebuke administered to the BREZHNEV regime by Sir Geoffrey HOWE during a visit to Moscow c. 1985. The accusation stemmed from the KREMLIN's refusal to accept an ARMS CONTROL package offered by the West, which was very similar to one they had previously been urging. The phrase was actually coined by Malcolm Rifkind, then Howe's deputy at the Foreign Office.

Yesterday's Men A slogan used by Labour's advertising campaign prior to the 1970 election which wrote off plasticine models of Edward HEATH and other leading Tories as has-beens, which was turned back on Harold WILSON and his senior colleagues by the BBC with devastating effect after their unexpected defeat. The *24 Hours* programme fronted by David Dimbleby was broadcast in June 1971 only after what Anthony Smith, its editor, described as 'the biggest and most furious row that a television programme in the English language has ever provoked', with several interviewees threatening to withdraw their contributions and the governors of the BBC ordering several cuts. The programme sought to show how former senior Ministers were faring in OPPOSITION, and the row centred on Dimbleby's questioning Wilson about the money he had made from his book about the 1964–70 Labour government; Wilson replied: 'Why don't you ask Heath where he got the money for his yacht?' The programme went out with a comment from Dimbleby that 'Only Harold Wilson became richer in opposition; using his privileged access to government papers he wrote 300,000 words in six months about Labour's time in office.' Wilson considered this an accusation that he had abused his position for financial gain and sued for libel; he won an apology, but not damages.

yield (1) The action of a member of a LEGISLATURE who is speaking in GIVING WAY, or yielding the FLOOR, to another who wishes to INTERVENE. (2) The energy produced by a nuclear explosion, usually measured in tons or megatons of TNT (*see also* THROW-WEIGHT).

Yippies US slang for a politically-active hippie, from the initials of the Youth International Party, one of the noisiest and most anarchic (though outrageous rather than violent) elements of America's PROTEST MOVEMENT. Founded by Abbie Hoffman (1938–94) and Jerry Rubin, it put up a pig as a Presidential candidate at the CHICAGO CONVENTION, but achieved little else apart from scandalising MIDDLE AMERICA.

YMCA A progressive group of Conservative MPs at Westminster founded c. 1927 by Harold MACMILLAN, Robert (later Lord) Boothby, Oliver Stanley and John Loder. The name, copied from the Young Men's Christian Association, was bestowed on the group by critics in the party.

yogic flying *See* NATURAL LAW PARTY.

Yom Kippur War The three-week Middle East war in October 1973 begun by Egypt and Syria attacking ISRAEL, but ending in the rout of Arab forces and Israel's conquest of the Sinai peninsula. The attack was timed for Yom Kippur, the holiest day in the Jewish calendar, to heighten the element of surprise. Israel's Prime Minister Golda Meir knew the attack was coming, but held back from pre-emptive action because Israel would then have been branded the aggressor. The war was Egypt's final attempt to wipe out the Jewish state; five years later the CAMP DAVID AGREEMENT established an uneasy peace and returned Sinai to Egypt.

Yorkshire Rasputin The nickname of Sir Bernard Ingham, the bluff former journalist, ex-Labour candidate and senior civil servant who served as Margaret THATCHER's press secretary from shortly after her election in 1979 until her overthrow eleven years later, in latter years as head of the Government Information Service. It stems from his strong Yorkshire roots and the belief of the liberal media that he was able to manipulate both the press and the government itself on Mrs Thatcher's behalf. For the Rasputin comparison *see* MAD MONK.

> A menace to the Constitution.
> Sir EDWARD HEATH

> The sewer, not the sewage. JOHN BIFFEN

Yorktown The battle on the Virginia coast which resulted in the final surrender on 19 October 1781 of Lord Cornwallis' forces, and thus the end of America's Revolutionary War. Cornwallis had been waiting for the British fleet to assist him, but French ships kept them away and Yorktown fell after a siege of 24 days. Cornwallis reputedly surrendered to the tune 'the WORLD TURNED UPSIDE DOWN'; General O'Hara, acting for him, wanted to turn over his sword to the French Count de Rochambeau who commanded three-quarters of the force, but he insisted the honour belonged to George WASHINGTON.

> Oh God! It is all over.
> LORD NORTH (1732–92)

you. You ain't seen nothing yet Ronald REAGAN's promise for the coming four years on his re-election in 1984. The words were originally uttered by Al Jolson at the start of the first talking picture, *The Jazz Singer.*

You can't hold a man down without staying with him The judgement of the pioneer black educationalist Booker T. Washington (1856–1915) on (specifically RACIST) oppression and what it does to the oppressor.

You have sat there long enough for any good you have been doing. Depart, I say, and let us have done with you. In the name of God, go Oliver Cromwell's dismissal of the RUMP Parliament on 20 April 1653. It was used against Neville CHAMBERLAIN's government with deadly effect from the Conservative benches by Leo Amery in the debate on 7 May 1940 which brought the fall of Chamberlain and CHURCHILL's appointment as Prime Minister. In WASHINGTON, it was later used by Sen. James McClure in frustration at slow Senate business.

You may say that, but I couldn't possibly comment The catchphrase of political journalism articulated by the villainous CHIEF WHIP Francis Urquhart (played by Ian Richardson) to the LOBBY correspondent Mattie Storin in the 1990 BBC television adaptation of Michael Dobbs' *House of Cards.* Politicians, imitating art, began to use the phrase in their conversations with reporters at WESTMINSTER. Dobbs was well placed to observe such intrigues, as an advertising man who had gone into Conservative CENTRAL OFFICE as a deputy chairman of the party to improve its media image.

You shall not press down upon the brow of labor this crown of thorns; you shall not crucify mankind upon a cross of gold The electrifying PERORATION of William Jennings Bryan's ACCEPTANCE SPEECH at the 1896 Democratic convention, denouncing President CLEVELAND's commitment to the GOLD STANDARD. Bryan (*see* BOY ORATOR; PRAIRIE AVENGER) went on to fight a rousing POPULIST campaign, but was defeated by economic recovery.

> The importance of this speech, with its declaration of holy war against the rich and mighty, and its invocation of the sacred names of Jefferson and Jackson, was that, together with Bryan's subsequent campaign, it re-committed the Democratic Party to its original principles.
> HUGH BROGAN

you're frit *See* FRIT.

You've never had it so good The slogan coined by the retiring President TRUMAN to counter Republican assertions in the 1952 election campaign that it was 'time for a change'. In Britain, the public mood which Harold MACMILLAN captured in 1959 to lead the Conservatives to re-election with a 100-plus COMMONS majority. On 20 July 1957, Macmillan had told a meeting in Bedford:

> Let's be frank about it; most of our people have never had it so good.

One Parliament later, as Macmillan's government floundered in the wake of the PROFUMO AFFAIR, cartoonists adapted the slogan to 'You've never had it so often'.

You were quite right; I forgot Goschen The gloomy reaction of Lord Randolph Churchill (1849–95) in December 1886 on realising that he had lost his power struggle with Lord Salisbury. Churchill had resigned as CHANCELLOR in an effort to impose his terms, not realising that the Prime Minister had been itching to be rid of him. Instead of surrendering to Churchill and inviting him back, Salisbury simply sent for the former Liberal Minister and financial expert George Goschen and made him Chancellor,

Churchill never again held office, dying of syphilis nine years later.

YouGov The Internet-based polling organisation, founded in 2000 by Peter Kellner, Nadhim Zahawi and Stephan Shakespeare which from 2003 supplanted GALLUP as *The Daily Telegraph*'s choice to conduct its OPINION POLLS. In the face of doubts from conventional PSEPHOLOGISTS over the soundness of polls conducted online, Professor Anthony King argued for the *Telegraph* that random sampling by telephone as carried out by Gallup and other polling organisations had consistently overestimated Labour's vote since 1997, and that 'the internet method is quicker and cheaper and allows more detailed questions to be asked'. YouGov, he stated, had accurately predicted election results in Britain and Australia, and had also correctly forecast that Will Young would win *Pop Idol.* YouGov was vindicated at the 2005 general election when it, almost alone among polls, did not over-estimate Labour's lead over the Conservatives.

Young. Young England An idealistic and patriotic, if ineffective, group of young Tory MPs active between 1837 to 1847, with DISRAELI among its members. They tried to form an alliance between the aristocracy and the working class to achieve social reforms, and thus outflank the middle-class LIBERALISM promoted by the Tories' opponents. But they never progressed beyond effete Lakeland reading parties.

Young Fogeys In Britain, a group of middle-class young men, mainly journalists, who from the mid-1980s adopted a tweedy, middle-aged style of dress dating back to the turn of the century, and anachronistic right-wing opinions to match. The best known were A. N. Wilson, Charles Moore and Simon Heffer; their main outlets at first were the *Spectator* and the opinion pages of the *Sunday Telegraph* whose Canadian proprietor, Conrad Black, felt a nostalgia for the England they seemed to invoke. Most Young Fogeys were ardent supporters of Margaret THATCHER and especially her opinions on Europe; they mourned her overthrow and, through their opposition to the MAASTRICHT TREATY and their hostility toward his policies, were an irritant to John MAJOR. Moore went on to edit the *Daily Telegraph* and become Lady Thatcher's official biographer.

Young Ireland An organisation of young intellectuals under William Smith O'Brien (1803–64), who promoted violent opposition to British rule as the only means of ending deportations resulting from the IRISH POTATO FAMINE. Its members' outspokenness prompted the arrest in 1848 of Smith O'Brien and other leaders before any uprising had been organised.

Young Plan An agreement negotiated in The Hague during 1929–30 under which the Allied powers reduced the burden of REPARATIONS on Germany imposed by the Treaty of VERSAILLES. The plan, which came into operation on 17 May 1930, was named after Owen D. Young (1874–1962), a US banker and chairman of the Allied Committee, offering Germany greater relief than its predecessor the DAWES PLAN. It cut penalties by 75%, with the balance of 89 billion Reichsmarks to be paid in annuities into a Bank for International Settlements until 1988. Allied control of German finances was removed, German securities taken into Allied hands were returned, Germany was allowed responsibility for converting reparation payments into foreign currency, the Reparations Commission was abolished and the Allies gave up the right to impose SANCTIONS if Germany defaulted. The plan was fiercely attacked by the NAZIs and German conservatives, and payments were in any case suspended the following year when the GREAT DEPRESSION struck; HITLER formally repudiated reparations in 1935.

Young Turks Young men in a political organisation who see themselves as having a future and are impatient to take over leadership from an older generation they see as staid and tired. The term originates from the reforming party of that name which transformed the decadent Ottoman Empire into a modern European state. Founded in Geneva in 1891, the Young Turks – officers who included Kemal Ataturk – overthrew Sultan Abdul Hamid and replaced him with his reforming brother Mohammed V. The Young Turks remained a force until the end of WORLD WAR I. The term has frequently been used of factions among Conservative MPs at WESTMINSTER and both parties in the US CONGRESS. In 1965 one such group of Republican Congressmen, demanding more energetic leadership, ousted Charles Halleck as House MINORITY LEADER and installed future President Gerald FORD.

Yuppie factor The impact on the electoral politics and representation of a run-down and traditionally working-class area caused by an influx of the prosperous and upwardly-mobile young. The word Yuppie (Young

Upwardly-mobile Professional Person) dates from the 1980s. In America this factor has tended to benefit the Republicans at the expense of the Democrats; in Britain the Conservatives at the expense of Labour, though the national swing to Labour in the 1997 and 2001 elections rendered it irrelevant for the time being.

Z

Zanu-PF Zimbabwe African National Union – Popular Front. The governing party in Zimbabwe since its victory in the 1980 elections which followed the end of UDI in the former Southern Rhodesia and the RETURN TO LEGALITY under temporary British colonial rule. Led by Robert Mugabe, the party was based on the most effective of the GUERRILLA forces combating the regime of Ian Smith, who had already handed over the premiership to the black Bishop Abel Muzorewa. Zanu-PF took power as a Marxist party, but governed with moderation for more than a decade before Mugabe embarked on a policy of confiscating the land of white farmers and giving it to 'war veterans' who were his political supporters in a situation which sparked sporadic violence; from 1999 its primacy came under threat from the MDC, but Mugabe retained power through a combination of intimidation and allegedly-rigged elections as the country's economy disintegrated.

Zapatistas Zapatista Army of National Liberation. A militant leftist peasant movement in Mexico's southern Chiapas province which came from nowhere to launch a revolt against the PRI government on 1 January 1994, the day NAFTA came into force. It took its name from Emilio Zapata, leader of the great Mexican revolution of 1910. 3000 strong and led by the shadowy **Subcomandante Marcos**, the 37-year-old former academic Rafael Guillen Vicente, Marxist son of a businessman, the Zapatistas killed 145 people in their first surprise offensive; controversy over the government's repressive reaction led President Salinas to offer the rebels an amnesty. The Zapatistas continued as a militant force, setting up a temporary 'capital' in Chiapas during the 1994 presidential election with renewed threats of violence causing the crash of the peso that December. A ceasefire was agreed in April 1995, by which time 2000 estates had been taken over by the peasants. In August 1996 Franco-Mexican relations were strained when Danielle Mitterrand, wife of the French President, and the Marxist Régis Debray attended the Zapatistas' congress. Despite the subsequent ousting of the PRI as Mexico's federal government, the Zapatistas remain a potent force and in 2003 joined anti-GLOBALISATION protesters lobbying world trade talks at Cancun. In June 2005 the Zapatistas renounced the armed struggle.

Zapruder film The most important item of evidence on the assassination of President KENNEDY in DALLAS to those who disputed the conclusion of the WARREN COMMISSION that there had been only one gunman, Lee Harvey Oswald. Abraham Zapruder was the only cameraman whose film showed the President's car almost throughout the incident. In it, Kennedy's head jerked backwards as if he had been shot from the GRASSY KNOLL ahead of him, and not only by Oswald, behind and above the President in the TEXAS SCHOOL BOOK DEPOSITORY. In 1999 the film was acquired for the nation for $16 million.

zero. zero-based budgeting The accounting practice pioneered by Jimmy CARTER as Governor of Georgia and in his campaign for the Presidency, under which every government programme has to be justified anew for each year, instead of growth automatically being built in. Its partial adoption did not have the impact Carter had hoped, largely because he introduced it at a time when resources were scarce and growth was thus being reined in anyway. Abandoned at federal level under the REAGAN administration, it remains a useful tool in US state and local government.

zero deficit The aim set for budgeting by most US Presidents, and since 1985 by Congress. *See* GRAMM-RUDMAN ACT.

zero option The proposal put forward in the mid-1980s by President REAGAN, and previously by some European SOCIAL DEMOCRATS, that the Soviet Union withdraw its SS20 missiles from eastern Europe in return for non-deployment in the West of

America's CRUISE and PERSHING II systems. The KREMLIN under BREZHNEV and Andropov did not respond, and the US missiles were deployed. Both sides' systems were eventually scrapped under the INF TREATY.

zero sum game A political battle from which there is no face-saving way out and victory for one side or the other is total, yet the outcome of which is entirely unpredictable. A classic example of a zero sum game was the estimated political fall-out of Osama BIN LADEN's threat of further attacks on the US on the eve of the 2004 Presidential election. One the one hand it reminded Americans that George W. BUSH had failed to locate the leader of AL QAEDA and deal with him, on the other that the world remained a dangerous place and that Bush had a stronger line against terror than his challenger John KERRY.

zero tolerance The elimination of serious crime in the community by stamping out minor wrongdoing, a strategy pioneered with great success in the late 1990s by Rudolph Guiliani, the Republican Mayor of New York City. Attempts to replicate it in Britain have brought controversy rather than success.

Ground Zero *See* GROUND.

year zero *See* YEAR.

Zil The limousine specially built for the highest-ranking COMMUNIST PARTY officials in the final years of the SOVIET UNION and its SATELLITES. Production was halted in February 2003 through lack of demand.

Zimmerman Note The message from Alfred Zimmerman, German Under Foreign Secretary, to his ambassador in Mexico which finally provoked Woodrow WILSON into abandoning US NEUTRALITY and entering WORLD WAR I. Published by the Associated Press on 1 March 1917, it said that unrestricted submarine warfare was about to begin and that, while Germany wanted America to stay neutral, it would offer Mexico an alliance and the incentive of recovering Texas, New Mexico and Arizona. Wilson was given the text by British intelligence, but Zimmerman admitted its authenticity.

Zinoviev Letter A key factor in the defeat of Ramsay MACDONALD's first Labour government in the 1924 general election. The letter, purportedly from Grigoriy Zinoviev (1883–1936), president of the COMINTERN, to Britain's Communists, incited them to violent revolution and enabled the Conservatives to scorn Labour's policy of better relations with Russia. Conservative CENTRAL OFFICE paid handsomely for the document, which was published on 25 October, four days before the election. Labour leaders believed it a fake, its authenticity was denied by the Soviet Union, and in 1966 the *Sunday Times* published a letter establishing that the letter was indeed a forgery, perpetrated by a group of WHITE Russian émigrés and suggesting that certain individuals at Central Office – though not the Tory party at large – knew it to be a fake.

Zionism The movement arising from the belief that the Jews should have a national home where they can be free from persecution, and that that home should be the Biblical land that is now ISRAEL. It was founded by Theodore Herzl in 1897 at the First World Zionist Congress in Basel. Zionism bore fruit in the BALFOUR DECLARATION which asserted the right to a Jewish national home, and in 1948 in the founding of the state of Israel. Through subsequent Arab-Israeli conflict and Israel's settlement of the OCCUPIED TERRITORIES which hard-line Zionists call JUDAEA AND SAMARIA, Zionism has, to its critics, come to typify opposition to Palestinian rights; for a time, the UNITED NATIONS officially equated it with RACISM.

> Put three Zionists in a room and they will form four political parties.
>
> Prime Minister LEVI ESHKOL (1895–1967)

Zippergate The most embarrassing sex scandal to tarnish an incumbent US President, stemming from President CLINTON's liaision with the White House INTERN Monica LEWINSKY and his protracted efforts to evade questioning on whether they had performed sexual acts in an ante-room to the OVAL OFFICE; a semen-stained BLUE DRESS kept by Miss Lewinsky proved conclusive. Zippergate also embraced the Paula JONES affair, Clinton's pre-White House liaison with Gennifer FLOWERS and a series of other 'BIMBO ERUPTIONS' including sexual advances toward Kathleen Willey, a former White House staffer well connected in the DEMOCRATIC PARTY. From the start of 1998 when the Lewinsky affair became public (*see* DRUDGE REPORT) Clinton, who had almost managed to weather the WHITEWATER affair, was under siege for the rest of his presidency over his sexual conduct. Motivated by revulsion – and opportunism – in the Republican-controlled HOUSE OF REPRESENTATIVES at Clinton's behaviour, the House Judiciary Committee voted on 5 October 1998 to open an IMPEACHMENT inquiry into his conduct, and legal manoeuvring, over Miss Lewinsky and other women, including Paula Jones. On 12 December he was impeached on two counts of perjury and obstruction of justice, but the Senate cleared him in February 1999 by margins ranging from 55–45 to 50–50. Just before leaving office, Clinton and the SPECIAL PROSECUTOR originally appointed to investigate Whitewater struck a deal under which he admitted lying under oath and agreed to meet his own legal costs in return for an agreement not to prosecute him. (*See also* IS).

> I tried to walk a fine line between acting lawfully and testifying falsely, but I now recognize that I did not fully accomplish this goal and that certain of my responses to questions about Ms Lewinsky were false. BILL CLINTON, 19 January 2001

> Presidents have been laid low by assassins, dragged down by war and dissent, disgraced by their own corruption. But no one, up until now, had ever been laid low by a young girl desperate for attention. *Newsweek,* 2 February 1998

Jack the Zipper A play on 'Jack the Ripper', the nickname adopted by the Edinburgh *Evening News* in November 2001 for Jack McConnell, Scotland's FIRST MINISTER-elect, after he called a press conference to admit to a liaison seven years previously with an employee of the Scottish Labour Party, of which he had then been General Secretary.

Zircon The codename for a satellite surveillance system developed by Britain's Ministry of Defence, a television programme about which caused a political storm in 1987. The BBC's Director-General, Alasdair Milne, barred transmission of a documentary revealing the existence of the project, to develop a satellite to 'eavesdrop' on civilian and military communications. The NEW STATESMAN then printed an article describing Zircon, and a tape of the programme was shown to MPs by its originator, Duncan Campbell (*see* ABC TRIAL). The SPEAKER barred a repetition and a row over Parliamentary PRIVILEGE ensued; when new rules to codify this ruling were put to the COMMONS, Tony BENN persuaded MPs through a MANUSCRIPT AMENDMENT that their rights were threatened and the rules were rejected. On 31 January the police Special Branch raided BBC studios in Glasgow, seizing tapes of the programme and the series of which it was part. In August *The Times* reported that Zircon – named after a gemstone with a very high refractive index – had been abandoned after £70 million had been spent on it because it would be obsolete by the time it entered service.

Zollverein (Ger. customs union) The FREE TRADE area between German states which operated before the unification of most of them in 1871 under the Prussian crown.

zones The four portions into which Germany was divided by the victorious Allies – America, the Soviet Union, Britain and France – at the close of WORLD WAR II; Berlin was also divided, into **sectors**. The nation in charge of each zone was responsible for maintaining military control, each of the occupiers (France to a much lesser extent) setting up bases for its own forces. In 1948 the zones occupied by the three Western allies combined to form WEST GERMANY; the Soviet Zone became the German Democratic Republic or GDR. However, in terms of the military occupation – though it ceased to be described as such and Allied troops were said to be the front line of defence against a Soviet drive westwards – the zonal divisions persisted until the REUNIFICATION of Germany in 1990. Even now, many of the US and British troops remain.

zoning The designation of particular areas of a local government district for particular forms of use and development: industrial, housing, recreation, commercial and the like. An American word, it denotes a practice undertaken by local jurisdictions since the 1920s.

Demilitarised Zone *See* DMZ.

zoo plane The aircraft in which television technicians and non-regular members of the travelling media accompany a US Presidential CANDIDATE during the CAMPAIGN. The atmosphere is much more free-wheeling than on the plane occupied by the 'serious' press. Reporters whom a candidate or his handlers cannot stand, or who have filed stories they dislike, are also banished to the 'zoo'.

> The kinkier members of the press tended to gravitate on to the Zoo Plane. The atmosphere was much more comfortable. There were tremendous amounts of cocaine, for instance.
> TIMOTHY CROUSE, *The Boys on the Bus* (1973)